W0391221

THE PENGUIN ENGLISH DICTIONARY

Consultant Editor
Robert Allen

PENGUIN BOOKS

PENGUIN BOOKS

Published by the Penguin Group
Penguin Books Ltd, 80 Strand, London WC2R 0RL, England
Penguin Putnam Inc., 375 Hudson Street, New York, New York 10014, USA
Penguin Books Australia Ltd, Ringwood, Victoria, Australia
Penguin Books Canada Ltd, 10 Alcorn Avenue, Toronto, Ontario, Canada M4V 3B2
Penguin Books India (P) Ltd, 11, Community Centre, Panchsheel Park, New Delhi – 110 017, India
Penguin Books (NZ) Ltd, Private Bag 102902, NSMC, Auckland, New Zealand
Penguin Books (South Africa) (Pty) Ltd, 5 Watkins Street, Denver Ext 4, Johannesburg 2094, South Africa

Penguin Books Ltd, Registered Offices: 80 Strand, London WC2R 0RL, England

First published as *The New Penguin Compact English Dictionary* 2001
Reprinted in this edition, without supplementary material, as
The Penguin English Dictionary 2002
2

Original material copyright © Merriam-Webster Inc. and Longman Group Ltd, 1986
Revisions, updating, and new material copyright © Penguin Books, 2000, 2001
All rights reserved

Typeset in ITC Stone
Printed in England by Clays Ltd, St Ives plc

Except in the United States of America, this book is sold subject
to the condition that it shall not, by way of trade or otherwise, be lent,
re-sold, hired out, or otherwise circulated without the publisher's
prior consent in any form of binding or cover other than that in
which it is published and without a similar condition including this
condition being imposed on the subsequent purchaser

Contents

Guide to the Dictionary

The display below shows the main features of a dictionary entry, and this is followed by notes on special points of interest and an explanation of the pronunciation system.

headword

cross-reference

earthenware *n* ceramic ware made of slightly porous opaque clay fired at a low temperature: compare STONEWARE.

earthling *n* an inhabitant of the earth, *esp* in science fiction.

part of speech

earthly *adj* **1a** characteristic of or belonging to the earth. **b** relating to human life on earth; worldly. **2** (*in negative or interrogative contexts*) possible: *There is no earthly reason for such behaviour.* ➤➤ **earthliness** *n.*

earth mother *n* **1** the female principle of fertility. **b** a woman who embodies the earth mother, *esp* in being generously proportioned and maternal.

definition

earthquake *n* a sudden violent earth tremor caused by volcanic action or processes within the earth's crust.

earth science *n* any or all of the sciences, such as geology, that deal with physical aspects of the earth.

earthshattering *adj* having tremendous importance or a widespread often violent effect. ➤➤ **earthshatteringly** *adv.*

earthwork *n* (*also in pl*) an embankment, fortification, etc made of earth.

earthworm *n* a widely distributed hermaphroditic worm that lives in the soil.

inflected forms

earthy *adj* (**-ier**, **-iest**) **1** consisting of or resembling earth or soil. **2** crude or coarse. ➤➤ **earthily** *adv*, **earthiness** *n.*

earwax *n* the yellow waxy secretion from the glands of the outer ear.

earwig[1] *n* a small insect with slender antennae and a pair of appendages resembling forceps.

word history

Word history

Old English *ēarwicga,* from *ēare* ear[1] + *wicga* insect. Earwigs were once thought to crawl into people's ears.

earwig[2] *v* (earwigged, earwigging) *informal* to eavesdrop.

ease[1] *n* **1a** freedom from pain or anxiety. **b** freedom from embarrassment or constraint; naturalness. **c** rest or relaxation. **2** facility or effortlessness. **3** easing or being eased. ✻ **at ease 1** free from pain or discomfort. **2** (*also* **at one's ease**) free from restraint or formality; relaxed. **3** used as a military command: standing with the feet apart and the hands behind the body. ➤➤ **easeful** *adj*, **easefully** *adv.*

ease[2] *v* **1a** to make (pain, suffering, etc) less severe or intense. **b** to free from something that causes pain or anxiety. **2** to make less difficult. **3** to manoeuvre gently or carefully in a specified way.

4 (*often* + off/up) to decrease in activity, intensity, severity, etc.

grammatical information

east[1] *n* **1** the direction 90° clockwise from north that is the general direction of sunrise. **2a** regions or countries lying to the east. **b** (*usu* **the East**) regions lying to the east of Europe. **c** (**the East**) formerly, the bloc of communist countries in eastern Europe. ⋙ **eastbound** *adj and adv.*

east[2] *adj and adv* **1** at, towards, or coming from the east. **2** of the wind: blowing from the east. ✻ **east by north/south** in a position or direction between east and east-northeast (or east-southeast).

Easter *n* a Christian feast commemorating Christ's resurrection, observed on a Sunday between 21 March and 25 April.

easterly[1] *adj and adv* **1** in an eastern position or direction. **2** of a wind: blowing from the east.

easterly[2] *n* (*pl* **-ies**) an easterly wind.

eastern *adj* **1** in or towards the east; inhabiting the east. **2** (*often* **Eastern**) of or stemming from Oriental traditions, in contrast with those of Europe or America. ⋙ **easternmost** *adj.*

Eastern Church *n* **1** (*also* **Eastern Orthodox Church**) a Christian Church originating in the Eastern Roman Empire and forming the main Christian Churches in Greece, Russia, Serbia, etc. **2** (*also* **Eastern church**) a Christian Church of North Africa and the Middle East.

alternative spelling

Eastertide *n* the period of time around Easter.

easting *n* **1** distance due east in longitude from the preceding point of measurement. **2** easterly progress.

east-northeast *n* the direction midway between east and northeast. ⋙ **east-northeast** *adj and adv.*

east-southeast *n* the direction midway between east and southeast. ⋙ **east-southeast** *adj and adv.*

eastward *adj and adv* towards the east; in a direction going east. ⋙ **eastwards** *adv.*

derived word with meaning deducible from headword

easy[1] *adj* (**-ier**, **-iest**) **1** causing or involving little difficulty. **2a** marked by peace, comfort, or freedom from constraint. **b** not hurried or strenuous. **c** free from pain, annoyance, or anxiety. **3** *informal* readily persuaded to have sexual relations. **4** *chiefly Brit, informal* not having strong preferences on a particular issue. ✻ **be easy on** to be lenient with (somebody). **easy on the eye** *informal* attractive. **easy on the ear** *informal* pleasant to listen to. ⋙ **easiness** *n.*

usage label

idioms and phrases

easy[2] *adv* **1** easily. **2** slowly or cautiously. ✻ **go easy on** to deal leniently with (somebody). **take it easy 1** to relax or rest. **2** to remain calm.

easygoing *adj* **1a** taking life easily. **b** placid and tolerant. **2** unhurried, relaxed, or comfortable.

easy meat *n chiefly Brit* somebody who is easily duped, imposed upon, or mastered.

regional label

easy street *n informal* a position of affluence.

eat *v* (*past tense* **ate**, *past part.* **eaten**) **1** to put (food) in the mouth and swallow it, usu after chewing it. **2a** (+ away/into/through) to destroy, erode, or corrode gradually. **b** (+ into) to use a great deal of (a limited resource). **3** *informal* to worry or annoy (somebody): *What's eating them?* ✻ **eat one's heart out** to grieve bitterly, *esp* for something desired but unobtainable. **eat one's words** to retract what one has said, *esp* in an ignominious way. **eat out of somebody's hand** to do everything somebody asks. ⋙ **eater** *n.*

illustrative example showing word in use

eatable *adj* suitable for eating.

Usage note

eatable or **edible**? Both *eatable* and *edible* mean 'reasonably pleasant to eat', but the primary meaning of *edible* is 'nonpoisonous': Are these berries *edible*?

usage note on points of grammar and language sensitivity

eatables *pl n* food.

Alternative spellings

Some words in English can be correctly spelt in more than one way. In these cases the alternative forms are given after the headword or at an appropriate place in the entry if they apply to a particular meaning:

bandolier *or* **bandoleer** *n* a belt worn over the shoulder and across the chest with pockets or loops for cartridges.

Spellings that are used in American English are shown with the label *NAm*:

colour[1] (*NAm* **color**) *n* **1a** the visual sensation, e.g. of redness, blueness, etc, caused by the wavelength of perceived light that enables one to differentiate otherwise identical objects …

Spellings labelled as American are sometimes also found in British English and in other varieties of English, while British spellings are also sometimes found in American English and in other varieties.

Inflections

Inflections, or changes in the endings of words (mainly nouns, verbs, and adjectives), are given when they are irregular or, though regular, cause users difficulty.

The following inflections are regarded as regular and are not routinely given:

- third person singular present tenses of verbs formed by adding *-s* to the stem, or *-es* to stems ending in *-s, -x, -z, -sh,* or soft *-ch,* e.g. **look, looks; stare, stares; mash, mashes; crunch, crunches.**
- past tense and past participles of verbs formed by adding *-ed* to the stem, verbs ending in a silent *-e* dropping this *e*: e.g. **look, looked; stare, stared.**
- present participles of verbs formed by adding *-ing* to the stem, verbs ending in a silent *-e* dropping this *e*: e.g. **look, looking; stare, staring.**
- plurals of nouns formed by adding *-s* to the stem, or *-es* to stems ending in *-s, -x, -z, -sh,* or soft *-ch*: **bat, bats; fox, foxes; sash, sashes; church, churches.**

Other types of inflection are shown after the headword:

brag[1] *v* (**bragged, bragging**) to talk boastfully.
➤➤ **bragger** *n.*

query *v* (**-ies, -ied**) **1** to question the accuracy of (e.g. a statement) …

go[1] *v* (*past tense* **went,** *past part.* **gone**) **1a** to proceed on a course; to travel …

hero *n* (*pl* **-oes**) **1** a person, *esp* a man, admired for special courage, nobility, or great achievements …

Comparative and superlative forms of adjectives and adverbs are shown when these involve modification of the stem, principally doubling of a final consonant or changing a final *y* to *i*:

hot[1] *adj* (**hotter, hottest**) **1a** having a relatively high temperature …

bulky *adj* (**-ier, -iest**) having too much bulk, *esp* unwieldy or cumbersome.

Grammar

The traditional names are used to identify wordclasses or parts of speech. These are *n* (= noun), *v* (= verb), *adj* (= adjective), *adv* (= adverb), *pronoun, conj* (= conjunction), *prep* (= preposition), and *interj* (= interjection or exclamation).

The words used to link words (especially verbs) to other words in sentences, known as collocations, are shown in round brackets:

bargain² *v* (*often* + with) to negotiate over the terms of a purchase, agreement, or contract ...

Typical objects of transitive verbs are shown by means of round brackets:

combine¹ *v* **1a** to bring (people or things) into such close relationship as to obscure individual characters; to merge. **b** to unite or cause (substances) to unite into a chemical compound ...

Other labels used to show grammatical information are:

verbs

in passive: shows that the verb is used in the passive voice in the meaning being given:

distribute *v* **1** to divide or apportion among a number of recipients. **2** (*usu in passive*) to disperse or scatter (something) over an area ...

nouns

in pl: shows that the noun is used in the plural form in the meaning being given:

ablution *n* **1** (*usu in pl*) the washing of one's body or part of it ...

used as sing.: shows that the noun is used in the plural but takes a singular form of verb:

bellows *pl n* (*used as sing.*) **1** a device with handles and pleated expandable sides used to create a current of air, *esp* to fan a fire ...

Idioms and phrases

These are put in a single alphabetical sequence at the end of the entry:

die¹ *v* (**dies, died, dying**) **1** to stop living; to undergo the ending of physical life. **2a** to pass out of existence, to cease. **b** to be forgotten. **3** (*also* + for) to long keenly or desperately. **4** (+ of) to be almost overwhelmed with (e.g. boredom). ❋ **die hard** of habits or attitudes: to take a long time to change or disappear. **never say die** *informal* never give up. **to die for** *informal* excellent or desirable.

Multi-word items that are noun-equivalents (such as **man of God**) and invariable are usually entered as main entries in their own right.

Phrasal verbs consisting of a verb and an adverb (e.g. **come off, take in**) are entered as main entries.

Usage labels and notes

Levels of formality with which words are associated are shown by the following labels:

formal	shows that the word is normally confined to written and printed documents
literary	shows that the word is normally found in literature
archaic	shows that the word is mainly found in older usage and has a dated or old-fashioned effect in modern contexts
non-standard	shows that the word is not regarded as standard (e.g. *ain't*) either in writing or in speech
dated	shows that the word is no longer in general use but is occasionally heard or seen in print
rare	shows that the word is only occasionally found

humorous	shows that the word is normally intended to sound amusing or witty
dialect	shows that the word is not part of standard English but is used locally in parts of the English-speaking world
informal	shows that the word is normally confined to conversation and informal writing
slang	shows that the word is highly informal and is mainly used by particular groups (e.g. young people)
coarse slang	used for slang words that are regarded as vulgar or offensive
derog (= derogatory)	shows that the word is normally used in a depreciatory or disapproving way
offensive	shows that the word normally causes offence
taboo	shows that the word is normally regarded as socially unacceptable
euphem (= euphemistic)	shows that the word is normally used as a euphemism, i.e. as a more pleasant-sounding alternative for an unpleasant word or concept

Special notes are given at some entries to alert the user to usage that is controversial or disputed:

deceitful *adj* having a tendency or disposition to deceive; dishonest: *a deceitful child.* ➤➤ **deceitfully** *adv,* **deceitfulness** *n.*

Usage note

deceitful or **deceptive**? Generally speaking, only people can be described as *deceitful. Deceptive* is applied to things.

Regional labels

Words and meanings that are chiefly used in certain regional varieties of English are marked accordingly:

bagman *n* (*pl* **bagmen**) **1** *chiefly Brit, dated* a sales representative; a travelling salesman. **2** *chiefly NAm* a person who collects or distributes dishonestly or illegally gained money on behalf of another.

Many uses identified as North American or as British are also used in other parts of the English-speaking world, such as Australia and New Zealand, and uses identified as Australian may also have filtered into North American use and even into occasional British use.

Cross-references

References to other entries in the dictionary are shown in small capital letters:

botanic *adj* = BOTANICAL.

da capo /dah akahpoh/ *adj and adv* used as a direction in music: repeat or repeated from the beginning: compare DAL SEGNO.

Word histories

Historical accounts of the origins of words and phrases are shown at the end of some entries:

cabal *n* a clandestine or unofficial faction, *esp* in political intrigue.

Word history

The word *cabal* orig meant 'secret', soon extended to 'secret meeting' and 'clandestine group'. The latter was particularly applied to a committee of the privy council, which in 1670 had five members whose initials spelt the word *cabal*: Clifford, Arlington, Buckingham, Ashley, and Lauderdale.

Pronunciation

Pronunciations are shown within slashes / / after headwords or other word forms. Pronunciations vary within the British Isles and throughout the English-speaking world. The system followed here is the so-called 'Received Pronunciation' characteristic of educated speech in south-east England and conventionally used as a model in the teaching of English.

The following characters are used to represent sounds in English:

consonants

b, d, f, h, k, l, m, n, p, r, s, t, v, w, and z have their normal values.

ch	stands for the sound as in	**ch**eer
dh	stands for the sound as in	**th**ey
g	stands for the sound as in	**g**et
j	stands for the sound as in	**j**ump
kh	stands for the sound as in	lo**ch**
ng	stands for the sound as in	si**ng**
nh	stands for the sound as in	restaur**ant**
sh	stands for the sound as in	**sh**ip
th	stands for the sound as in	**th**ing
y	stands for the sound as in	**y**ell
z	stands for the sound as in	**z**ero

vowels

short vowels:

a	stands for the sound as in	h**a**t
e	stands for the sound as in	b**e**d
i	stands for the sound as in	s**i**t, happ**y**
o	stands for the sound as in	p**o**t, c**ou**gh
u	stands for the sound as in	m**u**d, t**ou**gh
ə	stands for the sound as in	**a**like, port**er**

The symbol (ə), with round brackets, indicates that the following consonant (normally l, m, or n) has a syllabic value, as in *garden*.

long vowels:

ah	stands for the sound as in	f**a**ther
aw	stands for the sound as in	h**o**rn, **aw**ful
ee	stands for the sound as in	sh**ee**p, t**ea**m
ie	stands for the sound as in	b**i**te, f**igh**t
oh	stands for the sound as in	b**o**ne, l**oa**n
oo	stands for the sound as in	b**oo**k, p**u**t
ooh	stands for the sound as in	b**oo**t, l**u**te
uh	stands for the sound as in	b**ir**d, abs**ur**d

A vowel sound is called 'strong' when the syllable is pronounced with special emphasis, as in *I'll* ***be*** (= /bee/) *there* as distinct from *I'll be* (= /bi/) ***there***.

diphthongs (vowels made up of two sounds) and triphthongs (vowels made up of three sounds):

ay	stands for the sound as in	d**ay**
eə	stands for the sound as in	h**air**, th**ere**
ie·ə	stands for the sound as in	f**ire**
iə	stands for the sound as in	b**eer**, h**ere**
ooə	stands for the sound as in	c**ure**, j**ur**y
ow	stands for the sound as in	n**ow**, r**ou**t
owə	stands for the sound as in	s**our**, p**ower**
oy	stands for the sound as in	b**oy**, l**oi**ter

The main stress in a word, i.e. the syllable that receives the main emphasis, is shown by the raised symbol ', as in

dilettante /dili'tanti/

A secondary stress, if any, is shown by the inferior symbol ˌ, as in

femme fatale /ˌfam fəˈtahl/

List of Abbreviations

Abbreviations in general use (such as AD and i.e.) are given in the main text.

Special abbreviations are as follows:

abbr	abbreviation	*d.*	died	*orig*	originally
adj	adjective	*derog*	derogatory	*part.*	participle
adv	adverb	*dimin.*	diminutive	*pers*	person
attrib	attributive(ly)	*esp*	especially	*pl*	plural
Aus	Australian	*euphem*	euphemistic	*prep*	preposition
aux	auxiliary (verb)	*fem*	feminine	*prob*	probably
b.	born	*fl*	floruit	*SAfr*	South Africa(n)
Brit	British	*interj*	interjection	*Scot*	Scottish
c.	circa	*intrans*	intransitive	*sing.*	singular
Can	Canadian	*irreg*	irregular(ly)	*specif*	specifically
cent.	century	*masc*	masculine	*superl*	superlative
cents	centuries	*n*	noun	*trans*	transitive
comb. form	combining form	*NAm*	North American	*usu*	usually
compar	comparative	*N Eng*	Northern English	*v*	verb
conj	conjunction	*NZ*	New Zealand	*v aux*	auxiliary verb

A a

A^1 *or* **a** *n* (*pl* **A's** *or* **As** *or* **a's**) **1** the first letter of the English alphabet. **2** a mark or grade rating a student's work as excellent. **3** in music, the sixth note of the diatonic scale of C major. **4** in the ABO system of human blood classification, a type containing the A antigen. ✻ **from A to Z** from beginning to end.

A^2 *abbr* **1** ampere. **2** answer.

Å *symbol* angstrom.

a^1 *or* **an** *indefinite article* **1** used before a singular noun to denote a person or thing not previously specified. **2a** one single: *a third.* **b** one particular: *Glucose is a simple sugar.* **c** any: *An aeroplane has wings.* **3** used before a proper name to denote: **a** membership of a family or class. **b** resemblance. **c** a person named but not otherwise known. **4** every; per.

Usage note

a *or* an? *An* should be used instead of *a* in front of all words beginning with *a* or *i*, most beginning with *e*, *o*, and *u*, and a few beginning with *h*: *an ace; an interesting evening*. The exceptions are as follows: when *u* is pronounced *yoo*, it is preceded by *a*: *a unit*; words beginning with *eu* (also pronounced *yoo*) take *a*: *a eucalyptus tree*; *one* and words beginning with the same sound take *a*: *a one-off*. Words spelt with an unpronounced initial *h* take *an*: *an hour*. Other words beginning with *h* should be preceded by *a*: *a historian, a hotel*.

a^2 *abbr* **1** acceleration. **2** are (unit of area). **3** arrives (used in timetables). **4** *Brit* away (used of sports fixtures).

a-^{1} *prefix* **1** on; in; at; to: *abed; ajar.* **2** in the specified state or condition: *ablaze.* **3** in the specified manner: *aloud.* **4** in the specified act or process: *gone a-hunting; atingle.*

a-^{2} *or* **an-** *prefix* not; without: *asexual; anaesthetic.*

a-^{3} *prefix* see AD-.

A1 *adj informal* of the finest quality; first-rate.

A3 *n* a size of paper 297 × 420mm (about 11 × 16in.).

A4 *n* a size of paper 297 × 210mm (about 11 × 8in.).

A5 *n* a size of paper 210 × 148mm (about 8 × 5in.).

AA *abbr* **1** Alcoholics Anonymous. **2** anti-aircraft. **3** Automobile Association.

A and E *abbr* accident and emergency (hospital department).

aardvark *n* a large burrowing African mammal with an extendable tongue, large ears, and a heavy tail that feeds on ants and termites.

Aaron's rod *n* a plant of the foxglove family with tall stems and spikes of yellow flowers.

AB^1 *n* in the ABO system of human blood classification, a type containing both A and B antigens.

AB^2 *abbr* **1** able seaman. **2** Alberta (Canadian postal abbreviation).

ab- *prefix* from, away, or off: *aberrant.*

abaci *n* pl of ABACUS.

aback *adv* of a sail: in a position to catch the wind on what is normally the leeward side. ✻ **taken aback** surprised or shocked.

abacus *n* (*pl* **abaci** *or* **abacuses**) an instrument for performing calculations by sliding beads as counters along rods or in grooves.

abaft^1 *adv* towards or at the stern of a ship.

abaft^2 *prep* in a ship, nearer the stern than (a given position).

abalone *n* an edible rock-clinging invertebrate, related to the snails and limpets, with a flattened ear-shaped shell lined with a type of mother-of-pearl.

abandon^1 *v* (**abandoned, abandoning**) **1** to give (something) up completely. **2** to leave or desert (somebody or something), often in the face of danger, or in spite of an allegiance, duty, or responsibility. **3** to give (oneself) over unrestrainedly to (a feeling or emotion). ➤➤ **abandonment** *n.*

abandon^2 *n* freedom from constraint or inhibitions.

abandoned *adj* **1** forsaken or deserted. **2** wholly free from restraint.

abase *v* to bring down in rank, office, prestige, or esteem. ➤➤ **abasement** *n.*

abash *v* (*usu in passive*) to destroy the self-possession or self-confidence of; to disconcert. ➤➤ **abashment** *n.*

abate *v* **1** to decrease, or to reduce (something), in amount, intensity, or degree. **2** in law, to put an end to or abolish (a nuisance). ➤➤ **abatement** *n.*

abattoir *n* = SLAUGHTERHOUSE.

abbacy *n* (*pl* **abbacies**) the office, jurisdiction, or tenure of an abbot or abbess.

abbatial *adj* of an abbey, abbess, or abbot.

abbé *n* a member of the French secular clergy in major or minor orders.

abbess *n* the superior of an abbey of nuns.

abbey *n* (*pl* **abbeys**) the buildings, *esp* the church, of a monastery or a former monastery.

abbot *n* the superior of a community of monks.

abbreviate *v* to make briefer, *esp* to reduce (a written word or phrase) to a shorter form.

abbreviation *n* a shortened form of a written word or phrase, e.g. *dept* for *department*.

Usage note

In abbreviations made up of the initial letters of a number of words the usual modern practice is to omit full stops: *BBC, UN, USA*. In British, but not in American English, it is also becoming increasingly common to omit the full stop after an abbreviation containing the first and last letters of a word (*Dr, Ltd, St*).

ABC[1] *n* (*pl* **ABC's** *or* **ABCs**) **1** the alphabet. **2** the rudiments of a subject. **3** an alphabetical guide or manual.

ABC[2] *abbr* **1** American Broadcasting Company. **2** Australian Broadcasting Corporation.

abdicate *v* **1** of a monarch: to renounce the throne. **2** to relinquish (sovereign power). **3** to renounce (a responsibility or right). » **abdication** *n,* **abdicator** *n.*

abdomen *n* **1** the part of the body between the thorax and the pelvis containing the liver, gut, etc. **2** in an insect or arthropod, the rear part of the body behind the thorax. » **abdominal** *adj.*

abduct *v* to carry (somebody) off secretly or by force. » **abduction** *n,* **abductor** *n.*

abeam *adv and adj* at right angles to the length of a ship or aircraft.

abed *adv and adj archaic* in bed.

Aberdeen Angus *n* an animal of a breed of black hornless beef cattle, originating in Scotland.

Aberdonian *n* a native or inhabitant of Aberdeen, in NE Scotland. » **Aberdonian** *adj.*

aberrant *adj* deviating from what is right, usual, or natural. » **aberrance** *n,* **aberrancy** *n.*

aberration *n* **1** a departure from a normal state or moral standard. **2** an unsoundness or disorder of the mind. **3** the failure of a mirror, lens, etc to produce an exact correspondence between an object and its image. » **aberrational** *adj.*

abet *v* (**abetted, abetting**) to give active encouragement or approval to. » **abetment** *n,* **abetter** *n,* **abettor** *n.*

abeyance *n* a period or state of temporary inactivity, suspension, or being without a legal owner or claimant.

ABH *abbr* actual bodily harm.

abhor *v* (**abhorred, abhorring**) to regard with extreme repugnance; to loathe. » **abhorrer** *n.*

abhorrent *adj* **1** causing horror; repugnant. **2** opposed or contrary to (something). » **abhorrence** *n.*

abide *v* (**abided** *or* **abode, abiding**) **1** (*usu* **cannot abide** *or* **could not abide**) to bear (somebody or something) patiently. **2** to remain stable or fixed. **3** *archaic* to dwell. ✱ **abide by 1** to comply with (a rule or law). **2** to remain true to (one's word or a decision). » **abidance** *n,* **abider** *n.*

abiding *adj* enduring for a long time. » **abidingly** *adv.*

ability *n* (*pl* **abilities**) **1a** the physical, mental, or legal power to do something. **b** natural or acquired competence in doing something; skill. **2** (*usu in pl*) a natural talent; aptitude.

ab initio *adv* from the beginning.

abiotic *adj* not involving or produced by living organisms.

abject *adj* **1** in the worst degree; wretched; miserable; degraded. **2** very humble, *esp* to the point of self-abasement or servility. » **abjection** *n,* **abjectly** *adv,* **abjectness** *n.*

abjure *v* to renounce on oath, solemnly, or formally. » **abjuration** *n,* **abjurer** *n.*

ablation *n* **1** the wearing away of something by abrasion, erosion, melting, or vaporization. **2** the surgical removal of a body part or tissue. » **ablate** *v.*

ablative *adj* denoting a grammatical case typically expressing separation, source, cause, or instrument. » **ablative** *n.*

ablaze *adj and adv* **1** on fire. **2** radiant with light or bright colour. **3** showing strong emotion.

able *adj* (**abler, ablest**) **1** having sufficient power, skill, resources, or qualifications to (do something). **2** marked by intelligence, knowledge, skill, or competence. » **ably** *adv.*

-able *or* **-ible** *suffix* **1** forming adjectives from verbs, with the meaning: able, liable, or worthy to act or be acted on in the specified way: *breakable; reliable.* **2** forming adjectives from nouns, with the meaning: marked by, providing, or possessing the quality or attribute specified: *knowledgeable; comfortable.* » **-ably** *suffix.*

able-bodied *adj* physically strong and healthy; fit.

ableism *n* discrimination against disabled people. » **ableist** *adj.*

able seaman *n* a seaman ranking above ordinary seaman and below leading seaman in the Royal Navy.

ablution *n* **1** (*usu in pl*) the washing of one's body or part of it. **2** the washing of hands, sacred vessels, etc in ritual purification. **3** *informal* (*in pl*) a place with washing and toilet facilities. » **ablutionary** *adj.*

ABM *abbr* antiballistic missile.

abnegate *v* to surrender, relinquish, or renounce, *esp* as an act of self-denial. » **abnegation** *n,* **abnegator** *n.*

abnormal *adj* deviating from the normal or average, *esp* markedly and disturbingly irregular. » **abnormality** *n,* **abnormally** *adv.*

Abo *n* (*pl* **Abos**) *Aus, usu derog* an Australian Aborigine. » **Abo** *adj.*

aboard *prep and adv* on, onto, or within (a ship, aircraft, train, or road vehicle).

abode[1] *n formal* a home or residence.

abode[2] *v* past tense of ABIDE.

abolish *v* to do away with wholly; to annul. » **abolishable** *adj,* **abolisher** *n,* **abolishment** *n,* **abolition** *n,* **abolitionary** *adj.*

abolitionism *n* principles or measures fostering the abolishing of something, e.g. of slavery in the 19th cent. » **abolitionist** *n and adj.*

A-bomb *n* = ATOM BOMB.

abominable *adj* **1** causing disgust or hatred; detestable. **2** *informal* very disagreeable or unpleasant. » **abominably** *adv.*

abominable snowman *n* (*often* **Abominable Snowman**) a large manlike animal reported as existing high in the Himalayas. Also called YETI.

abominate *v* to hate or loathe intensely and unremittingly; to abhor. » **abominator** *n.*

abomination *n* **1** something or somebody abominable; *esp* a detestable or shameful action. **2** extreme disgust and hatred.

aboriginal[1] *adj* **1** growing or living in a particular place from the earliest times. **2** (**Aboriginal**) of Australian Aborigines. » **aboriginally** *adv.*

aboriginal[2] *n* **1** an aboriginal person, animal, or plant. **2** (**Aboriginal**) = ABORIGINE (2).

Usage note

Aboriginal *or* Aborigine? It is correct to refer to the indigenous people of Australia either as *Aborigines* or as *Aboriginals*.

aborigine *n* **1** an indigenous inhabitant, *esp* as contrasted with an invading or colonizing people. **2** (**Aborigine**) **a** a member of the indigenous people of Australia. Also called ABORIGINAL[2]. **b** any of the languages of this people. Also called ABORIGINAL[2]. **3** (*in pl*) the original fauna and flora of an area.

Usage note

Aborigine *or* Aboriginal? See note at ABORIGINAL[2].

abort *v* **1a** to induce the abortion of (a foetus). **b** to expel a premature nonviable foetus. **2** to end prematurely. **3** to fail to develop completely; to shrink away.

abortifacient[1] *adj* inducing abortion.

abortifacient[2] *n* a drug or other agent that induces abortion.

abortion *n* **1a** the induced expulsion of a foetus in order to terminate a pregnancy. **b** the spontaneous expulsion of a foetus before it is able to survive independently. **2** the failure or abandonment of an enterprise. **3** *informal* a monstrosity. ⋙ **abortionist** *n.*

abortive *adj* **1** fruitless; unsuccessful. **2** of an organ or organism: imperfectly formed or developed. ⋙ **abortively** *adv.*

ABO system *n* the system of classifying human blood into four blood groups, A, B, AB, or O, on the basis of the presence or absence of either or both of two antigens.

abound *v* **1** to be present in large numbers or in great quantity. **2** (+ in, with) to be amply supplied, crowded, or infested with.

about[1] *adv* **1a** on or to all sides; round. **b** here and there. **2** in succession or rotation. **3** approximately. **4** almost. **5** in the vicinity. ✱ **about to 1** on the verge of. **2** used in the negative to express intention or determination.

about[2] *prep* **1** with regard to or concerning. **2a** on or near the person of (somebody). **b** in the makeup of (somebody). **3** engaged in or concerned with. **4** surrounding. **5** in different parts of.

about-turn[1] (*NAm* **about-face**) *n* **1** a 180° turn to the right, *esp* as a military drill movement. **2** a reversal of direction, policy, or opinion.

about-turn[2] (*NAm* **about-face**) *v* to make an about-turn.

above[1] *adv* **1a** in or to a higher place. **b** higher on the same or an earlier page. **2a** in the sky overhead. **b** in or to heaven. **3** in or to a higher rank or number.

above[2] *prep* **1** higher than the level of. **2** more than. **3** beyond or transcending. **4a** superior to, e.g. in rank. **b** too proud or honourable to stoop to. **5** upstream from. ✱ **get above oneself** to become excessively self-confident.

above all *adv* before every other consideration; especially.

aboveboard *or* **above board** *adj and adv* free from deceit or dishonesty.

abracadabra *interj* used to accompany conjuring tricks.

abrade *v* to roughen, irritate, or wear away by friction. ⋙ **abrader** *n.*

abrasion *n* **1** a process of wearing, grinding, or rubbing away by friction. **2** an abraded area, *esp* of the skin.

abrasive[1] *adj* **1** having a rough surface used for grinding away, smoothing, cleaning, or polishing. **2** causing irritation; rude or unpleasant.

abrasive[2] *n* an abrasive substance, e.g. emery.

abreaction *n* in psychoanalysis, the release of tension due to a repressed emotion by reliving the situation in which it first occurred.

abreast *adj and adv* **1** side by side and facing in the same direction. **2** (+ of) up-to-date with (trends, developments, news, etc).

abridge *v* **1** to shorten (a book or other piece of writing) by omission of words without loss of sense. **2** to reduce (something) in scope. ⋙ **abridgeable** *adj,* **abridgement** *n,* **abridger** *n,* **abridgment** *n.*

abroad *adv and adj* **1** beyond the boundaries of one's country. **2** over a wide area; widely. **3** in wide circulation; about. **4** *dated* away from one's home; out of doors.

abrogate *v* to abolish (a law or agreement) by authoritative action; to annul or repeal (it). ⋙ **abrogation** *n.*

abrupt *adj* **1a** occurring without warning; unexpected. **b** unceremoniously curt. **2** rising or dropping sharply; steep. ⋙ **abruptly** *adv,* **abruptness** *n.*

ABS *abbr* anti-lock braking system.

abscess *n* an accumulation of pus surrounded by inflamed tissue. ⋙ **abscessed** *adj.*

abscissa *n* (*pl* **abscissas** *or* **abscissae**) in mathematics, the coordinate of a point obtained by measuring the distance from the y-axis parallel to the x-axis: compare ORDINATE.

abscission *n* the natural separation of flowers, leaves, etc from plants.

abscond *v* to depart secretly, *esp* so as to evade retribution. ⋙ **absconder** *n.*

abseil *v* to descend a vertical surface by sliding down a rope secured from above and wound round the body.

absence *n* **1** the state of being absent. **2** the period of time that somebody or something is absent. **3** (+ of) a lack of (something).

absent[1] *adj* **1** not present or attending; missing. **2** not existing; lacking. **3** not paying attention; preoccupied. ⋙ **absently** *adv.*

absent[2] *v* to take or keep (oneself) away.

absentee *n* **1** somebody who is absent. **2** (*used before a noun*) absent from one's family or from a place.

absenteeism *n* persistent and deliberate absence from work, school, duty, etc.

absentminded *adj* **1** unaware of one's surroundings or actions. **2** forgetful, *esp* habitually. ⋙ **absentmindedly** *adv,* **absentmindedness** *n.*

absinthe *or* **absinth** *n* **1** = WORMWOOD (1). **2** a green liqueur flavoured with wormwood or a substitute, and aniseed.

absolute[1] *adj* **1** complete; perfect: *absolute bliss.* **2a** having no restriction or qualification. **b** completely free from constitutional or other restraint. **3** not relative, independent of external references or comparisons. **4** in grammar, standing apart from a usual syntactic relation with other words or sentence elements. ⋙ **absoluteness** *n.*

absolute[2] *n* **1** something that is absolute, *esp* something independent of human perception or valuation. **2** (*usu* **Absolute**) the transcendent or underlying unity of spirit and matter.

absolutely *adv* **1** often used alone to express emphatic agreement: totally, completely. **2** in an absolute manner.

absolute majority *n* a number of votes greater than half the total cast or exceeding the total of votes for all other candidates.

absolute pitch *n* **1** the pitch of a note determined by its rate of vibration. **2** the ability to sing a note asked for or name a note heard.

absolute temperature *n* temperature measured on a scale that has absolute zero as its lower reference point.

absolute zero *n* the lowest temperature theoretically possible, equivalent to about -273.15°C or 0°K.

absolution *n* the act of absolving; *specif* a declaration of forgiveness of sins pronounced by a priest.

absolutism *n* government by an absolute ruler or authority, or the theory favouring this. ⯮ **absolutist** *n and adj.*

absolve *v* **1** (*often* + of/from) to set free from an obligation or the consequences of guilt. **2a** to declare (somebody) forgiven for a sin. **b** to declare (a sin) forgiven. ⯮ **absolver** *n.*

absorb *v* **1a** to take up (a liquid or other substance). **b** to take in (e.g. information). **2** to make part of an existing whole; to incorporate. **3** to engage or occupy wholly. **4** to receive and transform (sound, radiant energy, etc) without reflecting or transmitting it. ⯮ **absorbability** *n,* **absorbable** *adj,* **absorber** *n,* **absorption** *n.*

absorbent *adj* able to absorb a liquid, gas, etc. ⯮ **absorbency** *n,* **absorbent** *n.*

absorbing *adj* engaging one's full attention; engrossing. ⯮ **absorbingly** *adv.*

abstain *v* **1** to refrain from something deliberately, and often with an effort of self-denial. **2** to refrain from casting a vote. ⯮ **abstainer** *n.*

abstemious *adj* sparing, *esp* in eating or drinking. ⯮ **abstemiously** *adv,* **abstemiousness** *n.*

abstention *n* **1** abstaining. **2** an instance of withholding a vote.

abstinence *n* voluntary forbearance, *esp* from drinking alcohol. ⯮ **abstinent** *adj,* **abstinently** *adv.*

abstract[1] *adj* **1** theoretical rather than practical. **2** of art: having little or no element of pictorial representation. **3** said of a noun: naming a quality, state, or action rather than a thing; not concrete. ⯮ **abstractly** *adv,* **abstractness** *n.*

abstract[2] *n* **1** a summary of the main points, e.g. of a piece of writing. **2** an abstract concept or state. **3** an abstract composition or creation. ✱ **in the abstract** in general; without being specific.

abstract[3] *v* **1** to remove, separate, or extract. **2** to consider in the abstract. **3** to make an abstract of (a piece of writing). **4** *euphem* to steal or purloin. ⯮ **abstractor** *n.*

abstracted *adj* preoccupied or absentminded. ⯮ **abstractedly** *adv.*

abstract expressionism *n* art in which the artist attempts to express attitudes and emotions spontaneously through non-representational means.

abstraction *n* **1a** an abstract idea or term. **b** the act or process of abstracting something. **c** the quality of being abstract. **2** preoccupation or absentmindedness. **3** an abstract composition or creation. ⯮ **abstractive** *adj.*

abstruse *adj* difficult to understand; recondite. ⯮ **abstrusely** *adv,* **abstruseness** *n.*

absurd *adj* **1** blatantly or ridiculously unreasonable or incongruous; silly. **2** lacking order or value; meaningless. ⯮ **absurdity** *n,* **absurdly** *adv,* **absurdness** *n.*

absurdism *n* the belief that human beings exist in an irrational and meaningless universe. ⯮ **absurdist** *n and adj.*

ABTA *abbr* Association of British Travel Agents.

abundance *n* **1** a very large quantity; a profusion. **2** the relative plentifulness of a living organism, substance, etc in an area or sample. **3** affluence or wealth.

abundant *adj* **1** occurring in large quantities. **2** (+ in) amply supplied with. ⯮ **abundantly** *adv.*

abuse[1] *v* **1** to put to a wrong or improper use. **2** to attack in words; to revile. **3** to harm or injure by wrong or cruel treatment. ⯮ **abuser** *n.*

Usage note

abuse *or* **misuse**? *Abuse* usually suggests morally improper treatment, often involving a breach of trust: *to abuse somebody's hospitality; child abuse. Misuse* may refer simply to incorrect use (*to misuse a word*), though it often has suggestions of moral disapproval as well: *a misuse of taxpayers' money.*

abuse[2] *n* **1** improper use or treatment. **2** vehemently expressed condemnation or disapproval. **3** physical maltreatment, *esp* sexual assault. **4** a corrupt practice or custom.

abusive *adj* **1a** using or consisting of verbal abuse. **b** involving physical abuse. **2** characterized by wrong or improper action; corrupt. ⯮ **abusively** *adv,* **abusiveness** *n.*

abut *v* (**abutted, abutting**) **1** (+ on/upon) of an area: to touch (another area) along a boundary. **2a** (+ on/against) to terminate at a point of contact with. **b** (+ on/upon) to lean on for support. ⯮ **abutter** *n.*

abutment *n* **1** the place at which two things abut on each other. **2** the part of a structure that directly receives thrust or pressure, e.g. from an arch.

abuzz *adj* said of a place: filled with excitement, conversation, or activity.

abysmal *adj* **1** deplorably bad. **2** *chiefly literary* immense or unfathomable, *esp* immeasurably deep. ⯮ **abysmally** *adv.*

abyss *n* **1** an immeasurably deep chasm or void. **2** an irrecoverably bad state or situation.

abyssal *adj* at or of the bottom or deepest part of the ocean.

Abyssinian *n* **1** in former times, a native or inhabitant of Abyssinia. **2** (*also* **Abyssinian cat**) a small slender cat with short brownish hair. ⯮ **Abyssinian** *adj.*

AC *abbr* **1** air conditioning. **2** aircraftman. **3** alternating current. **4** appellation contrôlée. **5** athletic club.

Ac *abbr* the chemical symbol for actinium.

a/c *abbr* **1** account. **2** air conditioning.

ac- *prefix* see AD-.

acacia *n* a tree or shrub of the pea family, of warm regions, with white or yellow flowers.

academia *or* **academe** *n* the academic environment, *esp* of colleges and universities, or an academic community.

academic[1] *adj* **1** relating to formal study or education; scholarly. **2a** theoretical with no practical or useful bearing. **b** very learned and unconcerned with or inexperienced in practical matters. **3** conventional; formal. ⯮ **academically** *adv.*

academic[2] *n* a member of the teaching staff or a research student at an institution of higher learning.

academician *n* a member of an academy for the advancement of the arts or sciences.

academicism *n* purely speculative thought and attitudes.

academy *n* (*pl* **academies**) **1a** a college in which special subjects or skills are taught. **b** used in names: a secondary school, *esp* a private high school. **2** a society of learned people organized to promote the arts or sciences.

Word history

Latin *academia* from Greek *Akadēmeia,* name of the gymnasium where Plato taught, from *Akadēmos* Attic mythological hero; largely via French *académie* university. Plato's gymnasium was on land formerly dedicated to Akadēmos.

Academy Award *n* = OSCAR.

Acadian *n* **1** an inhabitant of Acadia, a former French colony on the NE seaboard of N America. **2** a French-speaking descendant of the early Acadians. ➤➤ **Acadian** *adj.*

acanthus *n* (*pl* **acanthuses** *or* **acanthi**) **1** a large prickly plant or shrub, *esp* of the Mediterranean region, with spiny leaves and white or purple flower spikes. **2** an ornamental device representing the leaves of the acanthus, e.g. on a Corinthian column.

a cappella *or* **a capella** *adj and adv* of music: performed without instrumental accompaniment.

acaricide *n* a substance, e.g. a dust or spray, used to control or kill mites, ticks, etc.

ACAS *abbr* Advisory, Conciliation, and Arbitration Service.

accede *v* (*usu* + to) **1** to give consent to. **2** to take up (an office or position, *esp* the throne). **3** to become a party to (e.g. a treaty).

accelerando *adj and adv* of a piece of music: to be performed with increasing speed.

accelerant *n* = ACCELERATOR (2).

accelerate *v* **1a** to move faster; to gain speed. **b** to increase the speed of (something). **2** to happen, or to cause (something) to happen. ➤➤ **acceleration** *n,* **accelerative** *adj.*

accelerator *n* **1** a pedal in a motor vehicle that controls the speed of the engine. **2** a substance that speeds up a chemical reaction. Also called ACCELERANT. **3** in physics, an apparatus for giving high velocities to charged particles, e.g. electrons.

accelerometer *n* an instrument for measuring acceleration.

accent[1] *n* **1** a distinctive pattern of pronunciation and intonation that is characteristic of a geographical area or social class. **2a** prominence given to one syllable over others by stress or a change in pitch. **b** greater stress given to one musical note. **c** rhythmically significant stress on certain syllables of a verse. **3a** a mark added to a letter, e.g. in *à, ñ, ç,* to indicate how it should be pronounced. **b** a symbol used to indicate musical stress. **4** special concern or attention; emphasis. ➤➤ **accentual** *adj.*

accent[2] *v* **1a** to stress (a vowel, syllable, or word). **b** to mark (a word or letter) with a written or printed accent. **2** to make (something) more prominent; to emphasize (it).

accented *adj* spoken or pronounced with an accent, *esp* a regional or foreign accent.

accentuate *v* to accent or emphasize (something). ➤➤ **accentuation** *n.*

accept *v* **1a** to agree to receive. **b** to agree to. **c** to be able or be designed to take or hold. **2** to give admittance or approval to. **3a** to endure without protest. **b** to regard as proper, normal, or inevitable. **c** to recognize as true, factual, or adequate. **4** to undertake the responsibility of. ➤➤ **acceptance** *n,* **acceptor** *n.*

acceptable *adj* **1** capable or worthy of being accepted; satisfactory. **2** welcome or pleasing to the receiver. **3** tolerable. ➤➤ **acceptability** *n,* **acceptably** *adv.*

accepted *adj* generally approved or used; customary.

access[1] *n* **1a** freedom to approach or reach somebody or something. **b** a means of access, e.g. a doorway or channel. **2a** the ability to look at or make use of something. **b** in computing, the ability to retrieve data from. **3** (+ of) a fit of tense feeling; an outburst.

access[2] *v* to get at (something, *esp* data); to gain access to.

accessary[1] *n* see ACCESSORY[1].

accessary[2] *adj* see ACCESSORY[2].

accessible *adj* **1** of a place: capable of being reached. **2** (*often* + to) of or in a form that can be readily grasped intellectually. **3** (+ to) able to be influenced by. ➤➤ **accessibility** *n,* **accessibly** *adv.*

accession *n* **1** the act of entering on a high office. **2** something acquired or added; *specif* a book added to a library. **3** the act by which a nation becomes party to an agreement already in force. ➤➤ **accessional** *adj.*

accessorize *or* **accessorise** *v* to furnish (e.g. an outfit or a room) with accessories.

accessory[1] *or* **accessary** *n* (*pl* **accessories** *or* **accessaries**) **1** an inessential object that adds to the beauty, convenience, or effectiveness of something else. **2** a person involved in or privy to a crime, but not present when it is committed. ➤➤ **accessorial** *adj.*

accessory[2] *or* **accessary** *adj* **1** contributing in a secondary way; supplementary. **2** involved in a crime, but not present when it is committed.

access time *n* the time lag between the request for and delivery of stored information, e.g. in a computer.

accident *n* **1a** an event occurring by chance. **b** lack of intention or necessity; chance. **2** an unexpected happening causing loss or injury. **3** a non-essential property or condition of something. **4** an irregularity of a surface, e.g. of the moon.

accidental[1] *adj* **1a** occurring unexpectedly or by chance. **b** happening without intent or through carelessness and often with unfortunate results. **2** arising incidentally; non-essential. ➤➤ **accidentally** *adv.*

accidental[2] *n* in music, a sharp, flat, or natural sign placed before a note that is not in the key indicated by a key signature.

accident-prone *adj* tending to have more accidents than is usual.

accidie /'aksidi/ *n* a condition of hopeless listlessness; spiritual apathy.

acclaim[1] *v* to applaud or praise. ➤➤ **acclaimer** *n.*

acclaim[2] *n* = ACCLAMATION (1).

acclamation *n* **1** a loud expression of praise, goodwill, or assent. **2** an overwhelming affirmative vote by cheers or applause rather than by ballot.

acclimate *v NAm* to acclimatize. ➤➤ **acclimation** *n.*

acclimatize *or* **-ise** *v* to adapt to a new climate or situation. ➤➤ **acclimatization** *n.*

acclivity *n* (*pl* **-ies**) an ascending slope. ➤➤ **acclivitous** *adj.*

accolade *n* **1a** a mark of acknowledgment or honour; an award. **b** an expression of strong praise. **2** a ceremony marking the conferral of knighthood, in which each of the candidate's shoulders is touched with a sword.

accommodate *v* **1a** to have or make adequate room for. **b** to provide with lodgings. **2** (+ to) to make fit or appropriate. **3** to give help or consideration to.

accommodating *adj* helpful or obliging. ➤➤ **accommodatingly** *adv.*

accommodation *n* **1a** lodging or housing. **b** pace or premises. **2a** an adaptation or adjustment. **b** a settlement or agreement. **c** the automatic adjustment of the eye for seeing at different distances.

accommodation address *n* an address to which letters may be sent to somebody who does not have a permanent address.

accompaniment *n* **1** a subordinate instrumental or vocal part supporting a principal voice or instrument. **2** an addition intended to complete something; a complement.

accompanist *n* a player of a musical accompaniment, e.g. on a piano.

accompany *v* (**-ies, -ied**) **1** to go with (somebody) as an escort or companion. **2** to perform an accompaniment for a singer or musician. **3a** to supplement (something) with (something). **b** to happen, exist, or be found with (something).

accomplice *n* somebody who collaborates with another, *esp* in wrongdoing.

accomplish *v* **1** to bring to a successful conclusion. **2** to manage to do.

accomplished *adj* **1** fully effected; completed. **2a** skilled or proficient. **b** having many social accomplishments.

accomplishment *n* **1** completion; fulfilment. **2** an achievement. **3** an acquired ability or social skill.

accord[1] *v* **1** to grant or concede. **2** to give or award. **3** to be consistent with something.

accord[2] *n* **1a** agreement; conformity. **b** a formal treaty of agreement. **2** balanced interrelationship, e.g. of colours or sounds; harmony. ✱ **of one's own accord** on one's own initiative; voluntarily. **with one accord** with the consent or agreement of all.

accordance *n* agreement or conformity.

accordant *adj* in agreement or conformity.

according ✱ **according as** depending on how or whether. **according to 1** in conformity with. **2** as declared by. **3** depending on. **4** in proportion to.

accordingly *adv* **1** as suggested; appropriately. **2** consequently.

accordion *n* a portable musical instrument in which wind is forced past free steel reeds by means of a hand-operated bellows and notes are produced by pressing keys or buttons. ➤➤ **accordionist** *n.*

accost *v* **1** to approach and speak to (*esp* a stranger), usu boldly or challengingly. **2** of a prostitute: to solicit (a prospective client).

account[1] *n* **1** a statement of the facts or events; a relation. **2** a record of debits and credits relating to a particular item, person, or business. **3a** a business arrangement allowing money to be deposited in and withdrawn from a bank or other financial institution. **b** a facility allowing customers to purchase goods on credit. **c** a statement listing purchases made on such an account. **d** a commission to carry out a particular business operation, e.g. an advertising campaign, given by one company to another. **4** value or importance. **5** profit or advantage. **6** careful thought; consideration. ✱ **give a good account of (oneself)** to acquit (oneself) well. **on account of** due to; because of. **on no account/not on any account** under no circumstances. **on one's own account 1** on one's own behalf. **2** at one's own risk. **on somebody's account** for somebody's sake. **take something into account/take account of something** to make allowances for something; to consider it as a factor, e.g. when making a decision.

account[2] *v* to think of in a certain way; to consider to be something. ✱ **account for 1** to give an explanation or reason for. **2** to be the sole or primary explanation for. **3** to bring about the defeat or destruction of.

accountable *adj* **1** (*often* + to/for) responsible; answerable. **2** able to be explained; explicable. ➤➤ **accountability** *n,* **accountably** *adv.*

accountancy *n* the profession or practice of accounting.

accountant *n* a person who practises and is usu qualified in accounting.

accounting *n* the recording, analysis, and verification of business and financial transactions.

accoutre (*NAm* **accouter**) *v* to provide with equipment, *esp* in the form of military costume and trappings; to fit out.

accoutrement (*NAm* **accouterment**) *n* **1** (*usu in pl*) an item of equipment, dress, etc. **2** (*also in pl*) a soldier's outfit excluding clothes and weapons.

accredit *v* (**accredited, accrediting**) **1a** to give official authorization to. **b** to send (*esp* an envoy) somewhere with credentials. **c** to vouch for as conforming to a standard. **2a** to credit (somebody) with something, *esp* a saying. **b** to attribute (*esp* a saying) to somebody. ➤➤ **accreditation** *n.*

accrete *v* to grow by accretion.

accretion *n* **1** increase in size caused by natural growth or the external adhesion or addition of matter. **2** something added or stuck on extraneously. ➤➤ **accretive** *adj.*

accrue *v* (**accrues, accrued, accruing**) **1a** (*often* + to) to come as an increase or addition. **b** to be periodically accumulated. **2** to collect or accumulate (something). ➤➤ **accrual** *n.*

acculturate *v* to adopt the values of a different culture, or to cause (e.g. a social group) to do this. ➤➤ **acculturation** *n.*

accumulate *v* **1** to collect together gradually; to amass. **2** to increase in quantity or number. ➤➤ **accumulative** *adj,* **accumulatively** *adv.*

accumulation *n* **1** increase or growth caused *esp* by repeated or continuous addition. **2** something that has accumulated.

accumulator *n* **1** the part of a computer where numbers are added or stored. **2** *Brit* a rechargeable secondary electric cell. **3** *Brit* a bet whereby the winnings from one event are staked on the next.

accurate *adj* **1** conforming precisely to truth or a measurable standard; free from error. **2** hitting the intended target. ➤➤ **accuracy** *n,* **accurately** *adv.*

accursed *or* **accurst** *adj* **1** *literary* under a curse; ill-fated. **2** *informal* detestable; irritating. ➤➤ **accursedly** *adv,* **accursedness** *n.*

accusation *n* **1** a charge of wrongdoing; an allegation. **2** accusing or being accused.

accusative *adj* denoting a grammatical case expressing the direct object of a verb or of some prepositions. ➤➤ **accusative** *n.*

accusatory *adj* containing an accusation or expressing accusation.

accuse *v* (*often* + of) to charge with a fault or crime. ➤➤ **accuser** *n,* **accusing** *adj,* **accusingly** *adv.*

accused *n* (**the accused**) the defendant or defendants in a criminal case.

accustom *v* to make used to (something) through experience; to habituate.

accustomed *adj* **1** customary or habitual. **2** (+ to) in the habit of or used to (doing something).

AC/DC *abbr* **1** alternating current/direct current. **2** *informal* = BISEXUAL[1] (2).

ace[1] *n* **1** a playing card, face of a dice, or domino marked with one spot. **2** a shot, *esp* a service in tennis, that an opponent fails to reach. **3a** *informal* an expert or leading performer in a specified field. **b** a combat pilot who has brought down at least five enemy aircraft. **4** *chiefly NAm* in golf, a hole in one (see HOLE[1]). ✱ **ace up one's sleeve** an effective argument or resource held in reserve. **within an ace of** on the point of; very near to.

ace[2] *adj informal* excellent.

-aceous *suffix* forming adjectives, denoting: **1** characteristics or content: *herbaceous*. **2** a group of animals characterized by the form or feature specified: *cetaceous*. **3** a specified plant family: *rosaceous*.

acephalous *adj* lacking a head.

acer *n* an ornamental tree or shrub of the maple family with brightly coloured leaves with five pointed lobes.

acerbic *adj* **1** bitter or sour in taste. **2** sharp or vitriolic in speech, temper, or manner. ➤➤ **acerbically** *adv*, **acerbity** *n*.

acetaldehyde *n* a colourless volatile liquid ALDEHYDE used chiefly in the synthesis of other organic chemical compounds.

acetate *n* **1** *no longer in technical use* a salt or ester of acetic acid. **2a** = CELLULOSE ACETATE. **b** a textile fibre made from cellulose acetate. **c** an audio recording disc coated with cellulose acetate.

acetic acid *n no longer in technical use* a pungent liquid acid that is the major acid in vinegar.

acetone *n no longer in technical use* a volatile liquid KETONE used as a solvent, e.g. in varnishes, and in organic chemical synthesis.

acetylene *n* a colourless inflammable gas used *esp* as a fuel, e.g. in oxyacetylene torches, and in the synthesis of organic chemical compounds.

Achaean *n* **1** a native or inhabitant of Achaea in ancient Greece. **2** *literary* an ancient Greek. ➤➤ **Achaean** *adj*.

ache[1] *v* **1a** to suffer a dull persistent pain. **b** (*often* + for) to feel anguish or distress. **2** to yearn or long to do something. ➤➤ **aching** *adj*, **achingly** *adv*.

ache[2] *n* a dull persistent pain.

achene *n* a small dry one-seeded fruit that does not split open at maturity.

achieve *v* **1** to carry out successfully; to accomplish. **2** to obtain by effort; to win. ➤➤ **achievable** *adj*, **achiever** *n*.

achievement *n* **1** something accomplished, *esp* by resolve, persistence, or courage; a feat. **2** successful completion; accomplishment. **3** performance in a test or academic course.

Achilles' heel *n* somebody's only vulnerable point.

Achilles tendon *n* the strong tendon joining the muscles in the calf to the heelbone.

achondroplasia *n* the failure of normal development of cartilage in humans, resulting in dwarfism. ➤➤ **achondroplastic** *adj*.

achromatic *adj* **1** transmitting light without dispersing it into its constituent colours. **2** possessing no hue; neutral. **3** in music, having no sharps or flats. ➤➤ **achromatically** *adv*, **achromaticity** *n*, **achromatism** *n*.

achy *adj* (**-ier, -iest**) afflicted with aches.

acid[1] *adj* **1a** sour or sharp to the taste. **b** sharp or biting in speech, manner, or disposition; caustic. **2a** of or containing an acid. **b** of substances: having a pH of less than seven. **3** of a colour: piercingly intense. ➤➤ **acidity** *n*, **acidly** *adv*, **acidness** *n*.

acid[2] *n* **1** a sour, typically water-soluble compound with a pH of less than seven that turns litmus paper red and is capable of reacting with an alkali or other chemical base to form a salt: compare ALKALI, BASE[1] (6). **2** *slang* the hallucinogenic drug LSD. **3** = ACID HOUSE. ➤➤ **acidic** *adj*.

acid drop *n* a hard sharp-tasting sweet made with sugar and tartaric acid.

acid house *n* a style of very fast dance music with a lively beat that originated in the late 1980s.

acidify *v* (**-ies, -ied**) to make or become acid. ➤➤ **acidification** *n*.

acid jazz *n* a kind of dance music containing features of jazz and soul music.

acid rain *n* rain containing high levels of acid, *esp* sulphuric and nitric acid, caused by the release of pollution from burning fuel into the atmosphere.

acid rock *n* rock music marked by long passages of electronic musical effects intended to convey the atmosphere of drug-induced hallucinations.

acid test *n* a severe or crucial test, e.g. of value or suitability.

acidulate *v no longer in technical use* to make slightly acid. ➤➤ **acidulation** *n*.

acidulous *adj* somewhat acid in taste or manner; caustic. ➤➤ **acidulosity** *n*.

-acious *suffix* forming adjectives denoting: inclined to; having as a characteristic: *audacious*; *capacious*.

-acity *suffix* forming nouns corresponding to adjectives ending in *-acious*: *audacity*; *capacity*.

ack-ack *adj* anti-aircraft.

ackee *n* a red pear-shaped tropical fruit, which is edible when fully ripe and cooked.

acknowledge *v* **1** to admit to be true, valid, or real. **2a** to express gratitude or obligation for (a service or kindness). **b** to show recognition of (somebody or their presence), e.g. by smiling or nodding. **c** to confirm receipt of (a letter). ➤➤ **acknowledgeable** *adj*.

acknowledgment *or* **acknowledgement** *n* **1** acknowledging or being acknowledged. **2** something done or given in recognition of something received. **3** a declaration or avowal of a fact. **4** (*usu in pl*) a list of people to whom an author is indebted, usu appearing at the front of a book.

acme *n* the highest point or stage, *esp* a perfect representative of a specified class or thing.

acne *n* a skin disorder found *esp* among adolescents, characterized by red pustules, *esp* on the face and neck. ➤➤ **acned** *adj*.

acolyte *n* **1** somebody who attends or assists another; a follower. **2** an assistant performing minor duties in a service of worship.

aconite *n* **1** a poisonous plant of the buttercup family bearing spikes of usu white, bluish, or purplish flowers. **2** = WINTER ACONITE. ➤➤ **aconitic** *adj*.

acorn *n* the nut of the oak, a smooth hard oval fruit in a cuplike base.

acoustic[1] *or* **acoustical** *adj* **1** of sound, the sense of hearing, or acoustics. **2** of a musical instrument: having sound that is not electronically amplified. **3** deadening or absorbing sound. ➤➤ **acoustically** *adv*.

acoustic[2] *n* = ACOUSTICS (2).

acoustics *pl n* **1** (*used as sing. or pl*) the science of sound. **2** the properties of a room, hall, etc that govern the quality of sound heard. ➤➤ **acoustician** *n*.

acquaint *v* (+ with) to cause to know something; to make familiar with.

acquaintance *n* **1** personal knowledge; familiarity. **2** somebody one knows slightly. * **make the acquaintance of** to come to know (somebody); to meet (them). ➤➤ **acquaintanceship** *n.*

acquaintance rape *n* rape committed by a person known to the victim.

acquainted *adj* (*often* + with) of people: having met each other socially; on familiar but not intimate terms with each other.

acquiesce *v* (*often* + in) to submit or comply tacitly or passively. ➤➤ **acquiescence** *n,* **acquiescent** *adj.*

acquire *v* **1** to gain or come into possession of. **2** to gain as a new characteristic or ability. ➤➤ **acquirable** *adj,* **acquirement** *n,* **acquirer** *n.*

acquired taste *n* something that one may learn to like through increased experience of it, although at first it seems unpleasantly strange.

acquisition *n* **1** acquiring or gaining possession. **2** something or somebody acquired, *esp* to the advantage of the acquirer.

acquisitive *adj* keen or tending to acquire and own material possessions. ➤➤ **acquisitively** *adv,* **acquisitiveness** *n.*

acquit *v* (**acquitted, acquitting**) **1** (*often* + of) to free from responsibility or obligation; *specif* to declare not guilty. **2** to conduct (oneself) in a specified, usu favourable, manner. ➤➤ **acquittal** *n,* **acquitter** *n.*

acre *n* **1** a unit of area equal to 4840yd² (about 0.405ha). **2** (*in pl*) lands; fields. **3** *informal* (*in pl,* + of) great quantities. ➤➤ **acreage** *n.*

acrid *adj* **1** unpleasantly pungent. **2** violently bitter in manner or language; acrimonious. ➤➤ **acridity** *n,* **acridly** *adv.*

acrimonious *adj* characterized by personal hostility or bitterness. ➤➤ **acrimoniously** *adv,* **acrimoniousness** *n.*

acrimony *n* caustic sharpness of manner or language resulting from anger or ill nature.

acrobat *n* somebody who performs gymnastic feats requiring skilful control of the body. ➤➤ **acrobatic** *adj,* **acrobatically** *adv.*

acrobatics *pl n* **1** (*used as sing. or pl*) the art, performance, or activity of an acrobat. **2** a spectacular performance involving great agility.

acromegaly *n* abnormal enlargement of the hands, feet, and face caused by excessive production of growth hormone by the pituitary gland. ➤➤ **acromegalic** *adj and n.*

acronym *n* a word formed from the initial letters of other words, e.g. *Aids* from *acquired immune deficiency syndrome.*

acrophobia *n* abnormal dread of being at a great height. ➤➤ **acrophobic** *adj and n.*

acropolis *n* the citadel of an ancient Greek city.

across¹ *adv* **1** from one side to the other. **2** to or on the opposite side.

across² *prep* **1a** from one side to the other of. **b** on the opposite side of. **2** so as to intersect at an angle.

across the board *adv* so as to embrace all classes or categories. ➤➤ **across-the-board** *adj.*

acrostic *n* a composition, usu in verse, in which sets of letters, e.g. the first letter of each line, form a word or phrase.

acrylic¹ *adj* of acrylic acid or its derivatives.

acrylic² *n* **1a** = ACRYLIC RESIN. **b** a paint containing an acrylic resin. **c** a painting done in this paint. **2** = ACRYLIC FIBRE.

acrylic acid *n no longer in technical use* an unsaturated liquid acid used in the manufacture of acrylic resins and other plastics.

acrylic fibre *n* a synthetic textile fibre made from the chemical compound acrylonitrile and usu other polymers.

acrylic resin *n* a glasslike plastic made by causing acrylic acid to form a polymer.

ACT *abbr* Australian Capital Territory.

act¹ *n* **1** a thing done; a deed. **2** the process of doing something. **3** (*often* **Act**) **a** a formal record of something done or transacted. **b** = STATUTE (1). **c** a decree or edict. **4a** any of the principal divisions of a play or opera. **b** any of the successive parts or performances in an entertainment, e.g. a circus. **5** a display of affected behaviour; a pretence. * **be/get in on the act** to be or become involved in a situation or undertaking, *esp* for one's own advantage. **get one's act together** *informal* to organize one's affairs and become more efficient.

act² *v* **1** to take action; to do something. **2a** to behave in a specified way: *She acted generously.* **b** (+ as) to perform a specified function: *It acts as a lever.* **3** (+ for) to represent somebody in a legal case. **4** to produce an effect. **5** (+ on) to do something in response to advice or instructions. **6** to play a dramatic role on the stage, in a film, etc. **7** to behave like (somebody specified): *to act the fool.* **8** to feign or simulate (a feeling).

acting *adj* holding a temporary rank or position: *acting manager.*

actinic *adj* of radiant energy, *esp* visible and ultraviolet light: having the property by which chemical changes are produced. ➤➤ **actinism** *n.*

actinide *n* any of a series of 15 radioactive elements from actinium (atomic number 89) to lawrencium (atomic number 103).

actinium *n* a radioactive metallic element found *esp* in pitchblende.

action¹ *n* **1a** the state of functioning actively. **b** practical activity usu directed towards a particular aim. **c** energetic activity, initiative, or enterprise. **2** a voluntary act; a deed. **3** the events in a play or work of fiction. **4a** combat in war. **b** an engagement between troops or ships. **5a** an operating mechanism, e.g. of a gun or piano. **b** the manner in which something operates or moves. **6** a civil legal proceeding. **7** (**the action**) *informal* lively or productive activity. * **out of action** not working or functioning actively. **take action 1** to begin to act; to do something. **2** to begin legal proceedings.

action² *v* to take action on; to implement.

actionable *adj* giving grounds for an action at law. ➤➤ **actionably** *adv.*

action painting *n* abstract art in which paint is applied, e.g. by throwing, dripping, or smearing.

action replay *n* a recording of a televised incident played back, usu in slow motion, after the event.

action stations *pl n* **1** the positions taken up by members of the armed forces preparing for military action. **2** a state of readiness.

activate *v* **1** to cause to start operating. **2** to make active or reactive, or more so, e.g.: **a** to make radioactive. **b** to increase the rate of chemical reaction. ➤➤ **activation** *n,* **activator** *n.*

activated carbon *or* **activated charcoal** *n* powdered carbon chemically treated to increase its adsorptive properties, used chiefly for removing impurities, e.g. from alcohol.

active *adj* **1** moving, working, or operating, not at rest. **2a** marked by or requiring vigorous activity. **b** full of activity; busy. **3** characterized by practical action and involvement: *an active interest in politics.* **4a** having practical results; effective. **b** of a substance: capable of acting or reacting; activated. **5** of a volcano: liable to erupt; not extinct. **6** in grammar, of a verb form or voice: having as the subject the person or thing doing the action. **7** relating to full-time service, *esp* in the armed forces. **8** of an electronic device: using electrical power for amplifying or controlling an electrical signal. ➤➤ **actively** *adv,* **activeness** *n.*

active service *n* service in a combat area with the armed forces.

activism *n* a doctrine that emphasizes vigorous or militant action, e.g. the use of mass demonstrations, in controversial, *esp* political, causes. ➤➤ **activist** *n.*

activity *n* (*pl* **-ies**) **1** a state in which things are happening or being done. **2** vigorous or energetic action; liveliness. **3** a pursuit in which a person takes part for business or pleasure. **4** in chemistry, the capacity of a substance to react.

act of God *n* a sudden event, *esp* a catastrophe, brought about by uncontrollable natural forces.

actor *n* **1** a man or woman who represents a character in a dramatic production; *esp* a professional performer. **2** a participant in an event or situation.

act out *v* to represent or express (ideas or feelings) by actions.

actress *n* a female actor.

actual *adj* **1** existing in fact or reality; real. **2** existing or occurring at the time; current.

actual bodily harm *n* physical harm, less serious than grievous bodily harm, deliberately inflicted by one person on another.

actuality *n* (*pl* **-ies**) **1** the quality or state of being actual; reality. **2** (*also in pl*) an existing circumstance; a real fact.

actualize *or* **-ise** *v* to make (an idea, hope, etc) actual or real. ➤➤ **actualization** *n.*

actually *adv* **1** really; in fact. **2** at the present moment. **3** strange as it may seem; even.

actuary *n* (*pl* **-ies**) a statistician who calculates insurance risks and premiums. ➤➤ **actuarial** *adj,* **actuarially** *adv.*

actuate *v* **1** to put (a device or machine) into action. **2** to incite to action; to motivate. ➤➤ **actuation** *n,* **actuator** *n.*

act up *v informal* to behave badly or function unreliably.

acuity *n formal* keenness of mental or physical perception.

acumen *n* keen discernment or discrimination, *esp* in practical matters; shrewdness.

acupressure *n* the application of controlled pressure to the body at particular points, usu with the fingers, for therapeutic purposes, e.g. to relieve pain. Also called SHIATSU.

acupuncture *n* the practice, Chinese in origin, of puncturing the body at particular points with needles to cure disease, relieve pain, produce anaesthesia, etc. ➤➤ **acupuncturist** *n.*

acute *adj* **1a** marked by keen discernment or intellectual perception. **b** highly responsive to impressions or stimuli. **2** intensely felt or perceived. **3** said of an illness: having a sudden severe onset and short course: compare CHRONIC. **4** demanding urgent attention; severe. **5** of an angle: measuring less than 90°. **6** marked with an acute accent. ➤➤ **acutely** *adv,* **acuteness** *n.*

acute accent *n* a mark (´) placed over certain vowels in some languages, e.g. over *e* in French, to show a particular vowel quality or stress.

ACW *abbr* aircraftwoman.

-acy *suffix* forming nouns denoting an action, state, or quality: *advocacy; intricacy.*

AD *abbr* anno Domini, used to indicate that a year or century comes within the Christian era.

Usage note

AD *and* BC. *AD* is traditionally written before a number signifying a year: *AD 1625.* When referring to centuries, however, it is necessary to put *AD* at the end of the phrase: *in the third century AD. BC* always follows a date: *440 BC; the seventh century BC.*

ad *n informal* an advertisement.

ad- *or* **a-** *or* **ac-** *or* **af-** *or* **ag-** *or* **al-** *or* **ap-** *or* **ar-** *or* **as-** *or* **at-** *prefix* (a- before sc, sp, st; ac- before c, k, q; af- before f; ag- before g; al- before l; ap- before p; as- before s; at- before t) **1** denoting movement or direction. **2** denoting proximity.

adage *n* a maxim or proverb that embodies a commonly accepted observation.

adagio *adj and adv* of a piece of music: to be performed in a slow gentle tempo. ➤➤ **adagio** *n.*

adamant[1] *adj* refusing to change one's mind; unyielding. ➤➤ **adamantly** *adv.*

adamant[2] *n* a legendary stone of impenetrable hardness, sometimes identified with diamond.

adamantine *adj* impenetrably hard or unbreakable.

Adam's apple *n* the projection in the front of the neck, more prominent in men, formed by the largest cartilage of the larynx.

adapt *v* to make or become fitted for a new use, different circumstances, etc, often by modification. ➤➤ **adaptability** *n,* **adaptable** *adj,* **adaptive** *adj.*

adaptation *n* **1** adapting or being adapted. **2a** adjustment of a sense organ to the intensity or quality of stimulation. **b** modification of an organism, fitting it better for existence under the conditions of its environment. **3** a composition rewritten in a new form or for a different medium.

adapter *or* **adaptor** *n* **1** somebody who adapts something; *specif* the writer of an adaptation. **2a** a device for connecting two pieces of apparatus not orig intended to be joined. **b** a device for converting a tool to some new use. **c** a device for connecting several pieces of electrical apparatus to a single power point.

adaptogen *n* in alternative medicine, a usu herbal substance that helps the body adapt to stress.

ADC *abbr* **1** aide-de-camp. **2** analogue-digital converter.

add *v* **1a** to join to something else so as to bring about an increase or improvement. **b** to serve as an addition to something. **2** to say or write further. **3** (*often* + up) to combine into a single number. **4** to perform addition.

addendum *n* (*pl* **addenda**) (*also in pl*) a supplement to a book.

adder *n* a common European venomous viper that has a dark zigzag pattern along the back.

addict[1] *v* (*usu in passive*) **1** to cause to become dependent on a habit-forming drug. **2** to devote (oneself) to something habitually or obsessively. ➤➤ **addiction** *n,* **addictive** *adj.*

addict[2] *n* **1** somebody who is addicted to a drug. **2** an enthusiast or devotee.

addition *n* **1** the act or process of adding, *esp* adding numbers. **2** something or somebody added. ✱ **in addition** also; as well.

additional *adj* added, extra, or supplementary. ➤➤ **additionally** *adv.*

additive[1] *n* a substance added to another in relatively small amounts to impart desirable properties or suppress undesirable ones.

additive[2] *adj* of, characterized by, or produced by addition.

addle[1] *adj* **1** (*used in combinations*) confused or muddled: *addle-headed.* **2** *archaic* of an egg: rotten.

addle[2] *v* **1** to confuse or muddle, or to become confused or muddled. **2** of an egg: to make or become rotten.

address[1] *v* **1** to mark directions for delivery on (e.g. a letter or package). **2a** to speak or write directly to. **b** to communicate (something) directly to somebody. **3** to greet (somebody) by a prescribed form. **4a** to direct the efforts or attention of (oneself) to something. **b** to deal with or apply oneself to. ➤➤ **addressee** *n,* **addresser** *n.*

address[2] *n* **1a** a place where a person or organization may be communicated with. **b** a description of such a place in conventional form, e.g. written on an envelope. **2a** a location in the memory of a computer where particular information is stored. **b** the digits that identify such a location. **3** a prepared speech delivered to an audience.

adduce *v formal* to offer as an example, reason, or proof. ➤➤ **adducible** *adj,* **adduction** *n.*

add up *v* **1** to amount to something in total. **2** to come to the expected total. **3** *informal* to be internally consistent; to make sense.

adenine *n* a chemical compound that is one of the four bases coding genetic information in a DNA or RNA molecule: compare CYTOSINE, GUANINE, THYMINE, URACIL.

adenoid *n* (*usu in pl*) a mass of glandular tissue at the back of the pharynx that obstructs breathing when enlarged. ➤➤ **adenoidal** *adj.*

adenoma *n* (*pl* **adenomas** *or* **adenomata**) a benign tumour of a glandular structure or of glandular origin.

adenosine *n* a NUCLEOSIDE containing adenine and ribose that forms part of RNA.

adept[1] *adj* highly skilled or proficient. ➤➤ **adeptly** *adv,* **adeptness** *n.*

adept[2] *n* a highly skilled person.

adequate *adj* **1** sufficient for a specific requirement. **2** barely sufficient or satisfactory. ➤➤ **adequacy** *n,* **adequately** *adv.*

à deux *adj* of, for, or involving only two people.

ADHD *abbr* attention deficit hyperactivity disorder, a condition occurring mainly in children, characterized by impaired concentration, hyperactivity, and learning and behavioural difficulties.

adhere *v* **1** to stick or hold fast by gluing, suction, grasping, etc. **2a** to give continued support or loyalty to (e.g. a political party or religion). **b** (+ to) to observe or follow (something) exactly. ➤➤ **adherence** *n.*

adherent[1] *n* a supporter of a leader, cause, etc.

adherent[2] *adj* sticking or holding fast by or as if by gluing, suction, grasping, etc.

adhesion *n* **1a** the action or state of adhering. **b** in physics, the sticking together of unlike substances through molecular attraction: compare COHESION. **2** in medicine, an abnormal union of tissues that are usu separated in the body.

adhesive[1] *adj* causing adherence; sticky. ➤➤ **adhesively** *adv,* **adhesiveness** *n.*

adhesive[2] *n* an adhesive substance, e.g. glue.

ad hoc *adj and adv* for the particular purpose at hand only.

ad hominem *adj and adv* based on personal rather than intellectual grounds.

adiabatic *adj* of a thermodynamic process: occurring without loss or gain of heat. ➤➤ **adiabatically** *adv.*

adieu *interj and n* (*pl* **adieus** *or* **adieux**) *chiefly literary* goodbye.

ad infinitum *adv* without end or limit.

adipose *adj* containing animal fat; fatty. ➤➤ **adiposity** *n.*

adit *n* a nearly horizontal passage from the surface into a mine for access or drainage.

adj. *abbr* **1** adjective. **2** adjutant.

adjacent *adj* **1** (*often* + to) having a common boundary or border. **2** neighbouring or nearby. **3** of two angles: having the point from which the lines diverge and one side in common. ➤➤ **adjacency** *n,* **adjacently** *adv.*

adjective *n* a word that modifies a noun or pronoun by describing a particular characteristic of it. ➤➤ **adjectival** *adj,* **adjectivally** *adv.*

adjoin *v* of e.g. a building, room, or piece of land: to be next or joined to. ➤➤ **adjoining** *adj.*

adjourn *v* **1** to suspend (e.g. a session or meeting) until a later time. **2** to defer for later discussion or resolution. **3** *informal* to move to another place. ➤➤ **adjournment** *n.*

adjudge *v* **1** to declare or judge formally. **2** to award or grant judicially.

adjudicate *v* **1** to decide judicially. **2** to act as judge, e.g. in a competition. ➤➤ **adjudication** *n,* **adjudicative** *adj,* **adjudicator** *n.*

adjunct[1] *n* **1** something added as an incidental accompaniment. **2** in grammar, a word or phrase that is not one of the principal structural elements in a sentence. ➤➤ **adjunctive** *adj.*

adjunct[2] *adj* attached in a subordinate or temporary capacity; auxiliary.

adjure *v formal* to command, entreat, or advise solemnly to do something. ➤➤ **adjuration** *n,* **adjuratory** *adj.*

adjust *v* **1** to bring to a more satisfactory state by a minor change; to regulate, correct, or modify (it). **2** to adapt oneself, e.g. to a new environment or different conditions. **3** to determine the amount to be paid under an insurance policy in settlement of (a loss). ➤➤ **adjustability** *n,* **adjustable** *adj,* **adjuster** *n,* **adjustment** *n.*

adjutant *n* a military officer who assists a commanding officer and is responsible for correspondence and other administrative matters. ➤➤ **adjutancy** *n.*

adjuvant[1] *adj* of therapy: serving to enhance the effectiveness of medical treatment.

adjuvant[2] *n* something that makes medical treatment more effective, *esp* by enhancing the body's immune response.

ad lib *adv* **1** without restraint or limit; as desired. **2** without preparation; spontaneously.

ad-lib[1] *adj* spoken or performed without preparation; impromptu.

ad-lib[2] *v* (**ad-libbed, ad-libbing**) to say lines or a speech spontaneously and without preparation; to improvise.

ad-lib[3] *n* an improvised speech, line, or performance.

ad litem /ˌad 'lietem/ *adj* in law, acting on behalf of a minor.

administer *v* **1** to manage or supervise. **2a** to mete out or dispense (e.g. punishment or justice). **b** to give (a drug, medicine, etc) as a remedy. **3** in law, to supervise or direct the taking of (an oath). ➤➤ **administrable** *adj.*

administrate *v* to perform the office of administrator; to manage or supervise (something). ⪢ **administrative** *adj,* **administratively** *adv.*

administration *n* **1a** the business of organizing and running the day-to-day affairs of a corporate body. **b** a body of adminstrators. **2** the act of administering. **3a** a government. **b** *NAm* the term of office of a leader or government. **c** *NAm* a government agency. **4** in law, the management of a dead person's estate.

administrator *n* **1** somebody who administers the affairs of a government, business, or other institution. **2** in law, somebody who manages the estate of a deceased person or the property of an individual or company that is in financial difficulties.

admirable *adj* deserving the highest respect; excellent. ⪢ **admirably** *adv.*

admiral *n* **1** the commander-in-chief of a fleet or navy. **2** an officer in the Royal Navy or US Navy ranking below an admiral of the fleet or fleet admiral. ⪢ **admiralship** *n.*

Admiral of the Fleet *n* an officer of the highest rank in the Royal Navy.

admiralty *n* (*pl* **-ies**) (**Admiralty**) (*used as sing. or pl*) in Britain, the executive department formerly having authority over naval affairs.

admiration *n* **1** a feeling of delighted or astonished approval. **2** somebody or something that is admired.

admire *v* to think highly of; to have or express admiration for. ⪢ **admirer** *n,* **admiring** *adj,* **admiringly** *adv.*

admissible *adj* **1** capable of being allowed or accepted; permissible. **2** acceptable as legal evidence. **3** entitled or worthy to be allowed to enter. ⪢ **admissibility** *n.*

admission *n* **1** acknowledgment that a fact or allegation is true. **2a** allowing or being allowed to enter a place or become a member of a group. **b** a fee paid for admission. **c** a person admitted to a hospital. ⪢ **admissive** *adj.*

admit *v* (**admitted, admitting**) **1a** to concede as true or valid. **b** (+ to) to make an acknowledgment of something. **2a** to allow to enter a place or become a member of a group. **b** to take into a hospital for treatment. **3** (*often* + of) to allow or permit something.

admittance *n* **1** permission to enter a place. **2** access or entrance.

admittedly *adv* as must be admitted.

admix *v* to mix or blend. ⪢ **admixture** *n.*

admonish *v* **1** to reprove for remissness or error, *esp* gently. **2** to urge or warn. ⪢ **admonishment** *n,* **admonition** *n,* **admonitory** *adj.*

ad nauseam *adv* in an extremely tedious manner; annoyingly or sickeningly often.

ado *n* fussy bustling excitement, *esp* over unimportant things. ✻ **without more/further ado** without any further delay.

adobe *n* **1** a building brick of sun-dried earth and straw. **2** a heavy clay used in making adobe bricks.

adolescent[1] *adj* **1** of or in the period of life between puberty and maturity. **2** immature or puerile. ⪢ **adolescence** *n.*

adolescent[2] *n* somebody in the period of life between puberty and maturity.

Adonis *n* a strikingly handsome young man.

adopt *v* **1** to bring up (a child of other parents) as one's own child after certain legal formalities. **2** to take up and begin to use (e.g. a strategy). **3** to take over (e.g. a belief) from somebody else and use it as one's own. **4** to vote to accept (something). **5** of a constituency: to nominate (somebody) as a Parliamentary candidate. ⪢ **adoptable** *adj,* **adoptee** *n,* **adopter** *n,* **adoption** *n.*

adoptive *adj* adopting or acquired by adoption. ⪢ **adoptively** *adv.*

adorable *adj* sweetly lovable; charming. ⪢ **adorably** *adv.*

adore *v* **1** to regard with reverent admiration and devotion; to love greatly. **2** to worship or honour as a deity. **3** *informal* to like very much. ⪢ **adoration** *n,* **adorer** *n,* **adoring** *adj,* **adoringly** *adv.*

adorn *v* **1** to decorate, *esp* with ornaments. **2** to add to the pleasantness or attractiveness of. ⪢ **adornment** *n.*

adrenal *adj* **1** relating to or in the region of the kidneys. **2** of or derived from the adrenal glands. ⪢ **adrenally** *adv.*

adrenal gland *n* an endocrine gland near the front of each kidney that secretes steroid hormones and adrenalin.

adrenalin *or* **adrenaline** *n* a hormone produced by the adrenal gland, often in response to stress or excitement, that increases the heart rate and blood pressure.

adrift *adv and adj* **1** of a boat: afloat without power, steerage, or mooring and at the mercy of winds and currents. **2** drifting or aimless. ✻ **come adrift** to become unfastened or unstuck.

adroit *adj* **1** dexterous or skilful. **2** shrewd or resourceful in coping with difficulty or danger. ⪢ **adroitly** *adv,* **adroitness** *n.*

adsorb *v* to take up and hold (molecules of gases, liquids, etc) by adsorption. ⪢ **adsorbable** *adj,* **adsorbent** *adj and n.*

adsorption *n* the adhesion of an extremely thin layer of molecules of gases, liquids, etc to the surface of solids or liquids. ⪢ **adsorptive** *adj.*

aduki *or* **aduki bean** *n* see ADZUKI.

adulate *v* to flatter or admire (somebody) excessively or slavishly. ⪢ **adulation** *n,* **adulator** *n,* **adulatory** *adj.*

adult[1] *adj* **1** fully developed and mature; grown-up. **2** typical of or appropriate to adults. **3** considered suitable only for adults, usu because of pornographic content. ⪢ **adulthood** *n,* **adultness** *n.*

adult[2] *n* a grown-up person or animal; *esp* a human being of or past an age specified by law (in Britain, 18).

adulterate *v* to corrupt or make impure by the addition of a foreign or inferior substance. ⪢ **adulterant** *n and adj,* **adulteration** *n,* **adulterator** *n.*

adulterer *or* **adulteress** *n* a man or woman who commits adultery.

adultery *n* (*pl* **-ies**) voluntary sexual intercourse between a married person and somebody other than his or her spouse. ⪢ **adulterous** *adj,* **adulterously** *adv.*

adumbrate *v formal* **1** to outline broadly without details. **2** to foreshadow vaguely. ⪢ **adumbration** *n,* **adumbrative** *adj.*

adv. *abbr* **1** adverb. **2** adverbial.

advance[1] *v* **1a** to bring, move, or go forward in position or time. **b** (+ on) to approach in a threatening manner. **2a** to accelerate the growth or progress of. **b** to develop or make progress. **3** to raise in rank; to promote. **4** to supply (money or goods) ahead of time or as a loan. **5** to bring (an opinion or argument) forward for notice. ⪢ **advancer** *n.*

advance[2] *n* **1** a forward movement. **2a** progress in development; an improvement. **b** = ADVANCEMENT

(IA). **3** (*usu in pl*) a friendly or amorous approach. **4** money or goods supplied ahead of time or before a return is received. ✻ **in advance** beforehand.

advance[3] *adj* **1** made, sent, or provided ahead of time. **2** going or situated ahead of others.

advanced *adj* **1** far on in time or course. **2** beyond the elementary; more developed.

Advanced level *n* = A LEVEL.

Advanced Supplementary level *n* = AS LEVEL.

advancement *n* **1a** promotion to a higher rank or position. **b** furtherance towards perfection or completeness. **2** forward movement or progress.

advantage *n* **1** a factor or circumstance that makes something or somebody superior to others. **2** a benefit or gain, *esp* one resulting from some course of action. **3** the first point won in tennis after deuce. ✻ **take advantage of somebody or something 1** to use something to one's advantage or benefit; to profit by it. **2** to impose upon somebody, or their good nature; to exploit them or it. **to advantage** in a way that produces a favourable impression or effect.

advantageous *adj* providing an advantage; favourable. ➤➤ **advantageously** *adv.*

Advent *n* **1** the period beginning on the fourth Sunday before Christmas and ending at Christmas itself. **2** the coming of Christ to earth as a human being: compare INCARNATION (3). **3** (**advent**) a coming into being; an arrival.

Advent calendar *n* a large card with 24 numbered windows, one for each day of December up to Christmas Eve, which, when opened, reveal a small picture or gift.

Adventism *n* the doctrine that the second coming of Christ and the end of the world are near at hand. ➤➤ **Adventist** *adj and n.*

adventitious *adj* **1** coming accidentally or unexpectedly from another source; extraneous. **2** of part of a plant or animal: occurring sporadically or in an unusual place. ➤➤ **adventitiously** *adv,* **adventitiousness** *n.*

adventure *n* **1a** an undertaking involving danger and uncertainty of outcome. **b** an exciting or remarkable experience. **2** an enterprise involving financial risk. ➤➤ **adventuresome** *adj.*

adventure playground *n* a children's playground with interesting or exciting equipment for climbing, building, and other activities.

adventurer *or* **adventuress** *n* **1** somebody who enjoys taking part in adventures. **2** somebody who seeks wealth or position by unscrupulous means.

adventurism *n* risky improvisation, *esp* in politics. ➤➤ **adventurist** *n.*

adventurous *adj* prepared to take risks or try new experiences. ➤➤ **adventurously** *adv,* **adventurousness** *n.*

adverb *n* a word that modifies a verb, an adjective, another adverb, or a sentence, and that answers such questions as *how?*, *when?*, *where?*, etc.

adverbial[1] *adj* functioning as an adverb. ➤➤ **adverbially** *adv.*

adverbial[2] *n* a word or phrase that functions as an adverb.

adversarial *adj* involving opposition, hostility, or conflict; antagonistic.

adversary *n* (*pl* **-ies**) an enemy or opponent.

adverse *adj* **1** acting against or in a contrary direction. **2** unfavourable. ➤➤ **adversely** *adv,* **adverseness** *n.*

Usage note

adverse *or* **averse?** *Adverse* means 'acting against' or 'unfavourable' and is almost always used before a noun: *adverse criticism. Averse* means 'strongly opposed to or disliking', usually comes after a verb, and is followed by the preposition *to*: *I wouldn't be averse to giving it another try.*

adversity *n* (*pl* **-ies**) a condition of suffering, affliction, or hardship.

advert[1] *n chiefly Brit, informal* an advertisement.

advert[2] *v formal* (+ to) to make a casual reference in speech or writing.

advertise *v* **1a** to announce (e.g. an article for sale, a vacancy, or forthcoming event) publicly, *esp* in the press. **b** (+ for) to seek by means of advertising. **2** to encourage sales of (e.g. a product or service), *esp* by emphasizing its desirable qualities. **3** to draw attention to. ➤➤ **advertiser** *n,* **advertising** *n.*

advertisement *n* something published, broadcast, or displayed publicly to advertise a product, service, etc.

advertorial *n* an advertisement designed to look like an editorial feature.

advice *n* **1** recommendations regarding a decision or course of conduct. **2** an official notice concerning a business transaction.

advisable *adj* worthy of being recommended or done; prudent. ➤➤ **advisability** *n,* **advisably** *adv.*

advise *v* **1a** to give advice to. **b** to recommend. **2** to give information or notice to; to inform. ➤➤ **adviser** *n,* **advisor** *n.*

advised *adj* thought out; considered. ➤➤ **advisedly** *adv.*

advisory *adj* **1** having power to advise. **2** containing or giving advice.

advocaat /'advəkah/ *n* a sweet liqueur consisting chiefly of brandy and eggs.

advocate[1] *n* **1a** somebody who pleads the cause of another before a tribunal or court. **b** *Scot* = BARRISTER. **2** somebody who supports a cause or proposal.

advocate[2] *v* to recommend or plead in favour of (e.g. a cause or proposal). ➤➤ **advocacy** *n.*

adze (*NAm* **adz**) *n* a tool with a blade attached at right angles to a handle, used for cutting or shaping wood.

adzuki *or* **aduki** *n* (*pl* **adzukis** *or* **adukis**) **1** a plant of the pea family that is widely cultivated in Japan and China as a food crop. **2** (*also* **adzuki bean** *or* **aduki bean**) the small round edible dark red seed of the adzuki plant.

aegis *n* auspices, patronage, or sponsorship.

aegrotat *n* **1** an unclassified degree awarded in British universities to students prevented by illness from taking their examinations. **2** a certificate stating that a student is too ill to take an examination.

-aemia *or* **-haemia** (*NAm* **-emia** *or* **-hemia**) *comb. form* denoting: **1** the condition of having the specified blood type or abnormality: *leukaemia.* **2** the condition of having the specified thing in the blood: *uraemia.*

aeolian (*NAm* **eolian**) *adj* carried, deposited, or produced by the wind.

aeolian harp *n* a stringed musical instrument on which the wind produces varying harmonics over the same fundamental tone.

aeon *or* **eon** *n* **1** an immeasurably or indefinitely long period of time. **2** in astronomy, a period of 1000 million years. **3** a division of geological time that may be subdivided into eras.

aerate *v* **1** to combine, supply, or impregnate with a gas, *esp* air, oxygen, or carbon dioxide. **2** to make (a liquid) effervescent. » **aeration** *n,* **aerator** *n.*

aerated *adj Brit, informal* highly excited or upset.

aerial[1] *adj* **1a** existing, occurring, or situated in the air or atmosphere. **b** operating overhead on elevated cables or rails. **2a** of or involving aircraft. **b** by or from an aircraft. **3** lacking substance; thin. » **aerially** *adv.*

aerial[2] *n* a conductor, usu a metal rod or wire, designed to transmit or receive radio or television signals.

aerie *n* see EYRIE.

aero- *comb. form* denoting: **1** air; atmosphere. **2** gas. **3** aircraft.

aerobatics *pl n* (*used as sing. or pl*) the performance of stunts in an aircraft, usu for the entertainment of spectators. » **aerobatic** *adj.*

aerobic *adj* **1** to do with aerobics. **2** living or occurring only in the presence of oxygen.

aerobics *pl n* (*used as sing. or pl*) a system of physical exercises designed to improve respiration and circulation, usu done to music and resembling a dance routine.

aerodrome *n chiefly Brit* a small airport or airfield.

aerodynamics *pl n* **1** (*used as sing. or pl*) the dynamics of the motion of gases, e.g. air, and solid bodies moving through them. **2** the particular properties of a solid body that determine how fast and efficiently it can move through the air. » **aerodynamic** *adj,* **aerodynamically** *adv,* **aerodynamicist** *n.*

aerofoil *n chiefly Brit* a structure on an aircraft, car, etc designed to provide lift or steerage as the vehicle moves through the air.

aerogram *or* **aerogramme** *n* a sheet of airmail stationery that can be folded and sealed with the message inside and the address outside.

aeronautics *pl n* (*used as sing. or pl*) the science or practice of flight. » **aeronautical** *adj,* **aeronautically** *adv.*

aeroplane *n* an aircraft that is heavier than air, has fixed wings from which it derives its lift, and is mechanically propelled, e.g. by a propeller or jet engine.

aerosol *n* **1** a suspension of fine solid or liquid particles in gas. **2** a substance dispersed from a pressurized container as an aerosol. **3** a metal container for substances in aerosol form.

aerospace *n* **1a** the earth's atmosphere and the space beyond. **b** the branch of physical science dealing with aerospace. **2** the industry or technology involved in travel in aerospace.

aesthete (*NAm* **esthete**) *n* somebody who has a particular sensitivity to the beautiful in art or nature.

aesthetic[1] *or* **aesthetical** (*NAm* **esthetic** *or* **esthetical**) *adj* **1a** to do with aesthetics, beauty, or the appreciation of the beautiful. **b** artistic. **2** having a developed sense of beauty. » **aesthetically** *adv,* **aestheticism** *n.*

aesthetic[2] *n* a set of principles on which the work of an artist or artistic movement is based.

aesthetics (*NAm* **esthetics**) *pl n* **1** (*used as sing. or pl*) a branch of philosophy dealing with the nature of beauty and aesthetic taste. **2** the principles concerning the nature and understanding of beauty. » **aesthetician** *n.*

aestival (*NAm* **estival**) *adj formal* relating to summer.

aestivate (*NAm* **estivate**) *v* of animals, *esp* insects: to pass the summer in a state of torpor. » **aestivation** *n.*

aetiology (*NAm* **etiology**) *n* (*pl* **-ies,** *NAm* **-ies**) **1** the cause or origin of something, *esp* a disease or abnormal condition. **2** the study of all the causes of something, *esp* a disease. » **aetiologic** *adj,* **aetiological** *adj,* **aetiologically** *adv.*

af- *prefix* see AD-.

afar *adv* from, to, or at a great distance. ✱ **from afar** from a great distance.

AFC *abbr* **1** Air Force Cross. **2** Association Football Club. **3** automatic frequency control.

affable *adj* **1** pleasant and relaxed in talking to others. **2** characterized by ease and friendliness. » **affability** *n,* **affably** *adv.*

affair *n* **1a** a particular or personal concern. **b** (*in pl*) commercial, professional, or public business. **2a** a procedure, action, or occasion vaguely specified. **b** a social event; a party. **3** a love affair. **4** a matter causing public anxiety, controversy, or scandal. **5** *informal* an object or collection of objects vaguely specified.

affaire *n* a romantic or sexual relationship between two people who are not married to each other, often of significant but limited duration.

affect[1] *v* **1** to have a material effect on or produce an alteration in. **2** to act on (somebody or their feelings) so as to bring about a response.

Usage note

affect *or* **effect**? *Affect* is a verb that means 'to influence or change': *How will this affect my pension prospects? Effect* is most commonly used as a noun: *What effect will this have on my pension prospects?* It can also be used, slightly formally, as a verb meaning to 'bring about' or 'carry out': *The police effected an entry into the premises.*

affect[2] *v* **1a** to put on a pretence of (a quality). **b** to assume the character or attitude of. **2** to show a preference for or inclination to.

affect[3] *n* the conscious subjective aspect of an emotion that affects behaviour.

affectation *n* **1** an insincere display of a quality not really possessed. **2** a deliberately assumed peculiarity of speech or conduct.

affected *adj* **1** given to affectation; insincere or pretentious. **2** assumed artificially or falsely; pretended. » **affectedly** *adv,* **affectedness** *n.*

affecting *adj* evoking a strong emotional response; moving. » **affectingly** *adv.*

affection *n* **1** tender and lasting attachment; fondness. **2** (*also in pl*) emotion or feeling as compared with reason. » **affectional** *adj,* **affectionally** *adv.*

affectionate *adj* **1** having or feeling affection or warm regard; loving. **2** showing or resulting from affection; tender. » **affectionately** *adv.*

affective *adj* **1** expressing or to do with emotion. **2** arising from or influencing the conscious subjective aspect of emotion. » **affectively** *adv.*

afferent *adj* conducting something inwards, e.g. nervous impulses towards the brain: compare EFFERENT[1]. » **afferently** *adv.*

affiance *v literary* to promise (oneself or another) solemnly in marriage.

affidavit *n* a sworn written statement for use as judicial proof.

affiliate[1] *v* **1** (+ to/with) to attach (e.g. an organization) as a member or branch. **2** to connect or associate oneself with another, often in a dependent or subordinate position. » **affiliation** *n.*

affiliate[2] *n* an affiliated person or organization.

affinity *n* (*pl* **-ies**) **1a** a natural liking for somebody or an inclination to think and feel alike. **b** an attraction to or taste for something. **2** relationship by marriage. **3** resemblance based on relationship or causal connection. **4** a chemical attraction between substances, causing them to combine. **5** a relation between biological groups with similar structure and common ancestry.

affirm *v* **1a** to validate or confirm. **b** to state positively. **2** to assert (e.g. a judgment of a lower court) as valid. **3** to testify by affirmation. » **affirmable** *adj*, **affirmer** *n*.

affirmation *n* **1** something affirmed; a positive assertion. **2** a solemn declaration made by somebody who conscientiously declines taking an oath.

affirmative[1] *adj* asserting or agreeing that something is true or correct. » **affirmatively** *adv*.

affirmative[2] *n* a word, phrase, or statement expressing agreement or assent.

affirmative action *n NAm* = POSITIVE DISCRIMINATION.

affix[1] *v* **1** to attach physically. **2** to add in writing. » **affixable** *adj*, **affixation** *n*.

affix[2] *n* an addition to a word or root, usu at the beginning or end, producing another word with a related meaning; a prefix, suffix, or infix.

afflict *v* **1** to distress very severely, causing great suffering. **2** to cause serious problems or trouble to. » **afflictive** *adj*.

affliction *n* **1** great suffering. **2** a cause of persistent pain or distress.

affluent *adj* wealthy. » **affluence** *n*, **affluently** *adv*.

afford *v* **1 a** to be able to bear the cost of. **b** to be able to do without serious harm. **c** to be able to spare. **2** to provide or supply. » **affordability** *n*, **affordable** *adj*.

afforest *v* to establish a forest on (an area of land). » **afforestation** *n*.

affray *n* a brawl in a public place.

affront *v* to insult by openly disrespectful behaviour or language; to give offence to. » **affront** *n*.

Afghan *n* **1** a native or inhabitant of Afghanistan. **2** (**afghan**) **a** a blanket or shawl of coloured wool knitted or crocheted in strips or squares. **b** an embroidered sheepskin coat with a long shaggy pile on the inside. **3** (*also* **Afghan hound**) a tall hunting dog of a breed with silky thick hair. » **Afghan** *adj*.

afghani *n* (*pl* **afghanis**) the basic monetary unit of Afghanistan, divided into 100 puls.

aficionado /ə,fishyə'nahdoh/ *n* (*pl* **aficionados**) a devotee or fan.

afield *adv* away from home; abroad.

AFL *abbr* Australian Football League.

aflame *adj and adv* **1** on fire. **2** passionately aroused.

afloat *adj and adv* **1a** floating on the water. **b** on a boat or ship. **2** free of debt. **3** circulating about. **4** *informal* flooded with water.

aflutter *adj and adv* **1** fluttering. **2** nervously excited.

AFM *abbr* Air Force Medal.

afoot *adv and adj* **1** happening; astir. **2** on foot.

afore *adv, conj, and prep chiefly dialect* before.

aforementioned *adj* mentioned previously.

aforethought *adj formal* premeditated or deliberate.

a fortiori *adv* with still greater reason or certainty.

afraid *adj* **1** (*often* + of/to) filled with fear. **2** regretfully of the opinion.

afresh *adv* anew or again.

African *n* **1** a native or inhabitant of Africa. **2** a person of African descent, *esp* a black person. » **African** *adj*.

African-American *n* an American of black African descent. » **African-American** *adj*.

African violet *n* a tropical African plant with velvety leaves and showy purple, pink, or white flowers, grown as a houseplant.

Afrikaans *n* a language of S Africa developed from 17th-cent. Dutch.

Afrikaner *n* an Afrikaans-speaking S African of European, *esp* Dutch, descent.

Afro *n* (*pl* **Afros**) a hairstyle consisting of a round bushy mass of small curls.

Afro- *comb. form* **1** African. **2** African and.

Afro-American *n* = AFRICAN-AMERICAN. » **Afro-American** *adj*.

Afro-Caribbean *n* a West Indian person of black African descent. » **Afro-Caribbean** *adj*.

aft[1] *adv and adj* towards or in the stern of a ship or the tail of an aircraft.

aft[2] *adj* rearward; AFTER[4] (2).

after[1] *prep* **1a** behind in place or order. **b** next in importance to. **2** following in time; later than. **3** in search or pursuit of. **4** about; concerning. **5a** in accordance with. **b** in allusion to the name of. **c** in the characteristic manner of. **d** in imitation of.

after[2] *adv* **1** in the rear; behind. **2** afterwards.

after[3] *conj* later than the time when.

after[4] *adj* **1** *archaic* later or subsequent. **2** located towards the rear of a ship, aircraft, etc.

after all *adv* **1** in spite of everything. **2** it must be remembered.

afterbirth *n* the placenta and foetal membranes expelled after delivery of a baby.

afterburner *n* a device in a jet engine for providing extra power.

aftercare *n* care given to people discharged from a hospital, prison, or other institution.

aftereffect *n* an effect that follows its cause after an interval of time.

afterglow *n* **1** a glow remaining where a light source has disappeared, e.g. in the sky after sunset. **2** a vestige of past splendour, success, or happy emotion.

after-hours *adj and adv* after closing time.

afterimage *n* a sensation remaining after stimulation has ceased, *esp* a visual sensation.

afterlife *n* **1** an existence after death. **2** a later period in one's life.

aftermath *n* **1** the period immediately following an unpleasant or ruinous event. **2** a consequence or result of something unpleasant or undesirable.

afternoon *n* the time between noon and evening, or between lunchtime and the end of the normal working day. » **afternoon** *adj*.

afters *pl n Brit, informal* (*used as sing. or pl*) a dessert.

aftershave *n* a scented lotion for use on the face after shaving.

aftershock *n* a smaller shock occurring after the main shock of an earthquake.

aftertaste *n* **1** persistence of a flavour after eating or drinking. **2** persistence of an impression.

afterthought *n* **1** an idea occurring later. **2** something added later.

afterwards *or* **afterward** *adv* after that; subsequently.

afterword *n* = EPILOGUE (1).

Ag *abbr* the chemical symbol for silver.

ag- *prefix* see AD-.

Aga *n trademark* a large solid metal kitchen stove.

again *adv* **1** another time; once more. **2** so as to be as before. **3** on the other hand. **4** further; in addition. ✱ **again and again** often; repeatedly.

against *prep* **1a** in opposition or hostility to. **b** unfavourable to. **c** as a defence or protection from. **2** contrasted with. **3** in the direction of and in contact with. **4** in a direction opposite to the motion or course of; counter to. **5** in preparation or provision for. **6** in exchange for. ✱ **as against** compared with. **have something against** to have a reason for disliking (somebody).

agape[1] /ə'gayp/ *adj* **1** wide open; gaping. **2** in a state of wonder.

agape[2] /'agəpi, ə'gapay/ *n* **1** = LOVE FEAST. **2** Christian love. ⋙ **agapeic** *adj.*

agar *or* **agar jelly** *n* = AGAR-AGAR.

agar-agar *n* a gelatinous extract from any of various red algae, used in culture media, as a thickening agent in foods, etc.

agaric *n* a fungus, such as the common edible mushroom, that has an umbrella-shaped cap with radiating gills on the underside.

agate *n* a mineral used as a gem composed of quartz of various colours, often arranged in bands.

agave *n* an American plant of the daffodil family with spiny leaves and flowers in tall spreading flat clusters.

age[1] *n* **1a** the length of time a person has lived or a thing existed. **b** a stage of life. **2a** a period of past time dominated by a central figure or prominent feature. **b** a division of geological time, shorter than an epoch. **3** *informal* (*usu in pl*) a long time. ✱ **act one's age** to behave appropriately for one's age. **come of age** to reach legal adult status. **of an age** of a similar age.

age[2] *v* (**ageing** *or* **aging**) **1a** to become old; to show the effects of increasing age. **b** to cause to seem old. **2** to make or become mellow or mature; to ripen.

-age *suffix* **1** an aggregate or collection: *baggage*. **2a** an action or process: *haulage*. **b** a cumulative result: *mileage*. **c** a rate or amount: *dosage*. **3** a house or place: *orphanage*. **4** a condition or rank: *bondage*; *peerage*. **5** a fee or charge: *postage*.

aged /'ayjid/ *adj* **1** of an advanced age. **2** typical of old age. **3** /ayjd/ having attained a specified age. ⋙ **agedness** *n.*

ageism *or* **agism** *n* discrimination on grounds of age, *esp* of advanced age. ⋙ **ageist** *adj and n.*

ageless *adj* **1** never growing old or showing the effects of age. **2** timeless or eternal.

agency *n* (*pl* **-ies**) **1a** an establishment that does a particular type of business, usu on behalf of another. **b** an administrative department of a government. **2** the function or place of business of an agent. **3** intervention or instrumentality. **4** the power or force behind a certain phenomenon or effect.

agenda *n* **1** a list of items to be discussed or business to be transacted, e.g. at a meeting. **2** a plan of procedure; a programme.

agent *n* **1** a person who is authorized to act for or in the place of another, e.g. a business representative. **2a** a representative of a government. **b** a spy. **3a** something or somebody that produces an effect or exerts power. **b** a chemically, physically, or biologically active substance.

agent noun *n* a noun, *esp* one ending in *-er* or *-or* such as *teacher* or *alternator*, that denotes a person or thing that carries out the action of a verb.

agent provocateur /,ahzhonh prə,vokə'tuh/ *n* (*pl* **agents provocateurs**) a person employed to incite suspected people to some open action that will make them liable to punishment.

age of consent *n* the age at which one is legally competent to give consent; *specif* that at which a person may consent to sexual intercourse.

age-old *adj* having existed for a long time; ancient.

agglomerate[1] *v* to gather, or cause to gather, into a cluster or disorderly mass. ⋙ **agglomeration** *n.*

agglomerate[2] *n* **1** a disorderly mass or collection. **2** a rock composed of irregular volcanic fragments.

agglutinate *v* **1** to cause to stick together; to fasten together as if with glue. **2** to combine (words) into a compound; to attach (word elements, e.g. affixes and roots) together to form words. ⋙ **agglutination** *n.*

aggrandize *or* **-ise** *v* **1** to enhance the power, wealth, position, or reputation of. **2** to give a false air of greatness to. ⋙ **aggrandizement** *n,* **aggrandizer** *n.*

aggravate *v* **1** to make (something, e.g. an illness) worse or more severe. **2** *informal* to annoy or irritate (somebody). ⋙ **aggravating** *adj,* **aggravation** *n.*

Usage note

The oldest surviving meaning of *aggravate* is 'to make worse or more serious': *We ought not to do anything that might aggravate the situation.* Some traditionalists disapprove of the use to mean 'annoy'. This other meaning has, however, been well established for centuries.

aggravated *adj* said of an offence: made more serious, e.g. by violence.

aggregate[1] *adj* **1** formed by the collection of units or particles into a body, mass, or amount. **2** taking all units as a whole; total.

aggregate[2] *v* **1** to bring (units or particles) together into a mass or whole. **2** to amount to (a specified total). ⋙ **aggregation** *n,* **aggregational** *adj,* **aggregative** *adj.*

aggregate[3] *n* **1** a mass of loosely associated parts. **2** the whole amount; the sum total. **3a** a rock composed of closely packed mineral crystals or rock fragments. **b** sand, gravel, etc for mixing with cement to make concrete. ✱ **in the aggregate** considered as a whole; collectively.

aggression *n* **1** attack, violent hostility, or encroachment; *esp* unprovoked violation by one country of the territory of another. **2** a hostile attack; *esp* one made without just cause. **3** hostile, injurious, or destructive behaviour or outlook. ⋙ **aggressor** *n.*

aggressive *adj* **1a** showing or practising aggression. **b** ready to attack. **2** forceful, dynamic, or self-assertive. ⋙ **aggressively** *adv,* **aggressiveness** *n.*

aggrieved *adj* **1** showing or expressing resentment; hurt. **2** treated unfairly or unjustly. ⋙ **aggrievedly** *adv.*

aggro *n chiefly Brit, informal* **1** provocation or hostility. **2** deliberate aggression or violence.

aghast *adj* suddenly struck with terror or amazement; shocked.

agile *adj* **1** quick, easy, and graceful in movement. **2** mentally quick and resourceful. ⋙ **agilely** *adv,* **agility** *n.*

agism *n* see AGEISM.

agitate *v* **1** to trouble or excite the mind or feelings of; to disturb. **2** to shake or stir (something). **3** to work to arouse public feeling for or against a cause. ➤➤ **agitatedly** *adv,* **agitation** *n.*

agitator *n* **1** somebody who stirs up public feeling on controversial issues. **2** a device or apparatus for stirring or shaking.

agitprop *n* political propaganda, *esp* pro-communist propaganda in the arts.

aglet *n* a metal tag attached to the end of a lace, cord, or ribbon.

agley *adv chiefly Scot* awry or wrong.

AGM *abbr* annual general meeting, *esp* of a society or company.

agnail *n* **1** a sore or inflammation around a fingernail or toenail. **2** = HANGNAIL.

agnate *n* a relative whose kinship is traceable exclusively through the male line of descent; *broadly* any paternal relative. ➤➤ **agnate** *adj.*

agnostic *n* **1** somebody who believes that it is impossible to know whether God or any other supreme being exists or not. **2** somebody who is doubtful or non-committal on a particular question. ➤➤ **agnostic** *adj,* **agnosticism** *n.*

ago *adv* before now.

agog *adj* full of intense anticipation or excitement; eager.

a gogo *adj informal* (*used after a noun*) in abundance; galore.

agonize *or* **-ise** *v* **1** to suffer, or cause to suffer, agony or anguish. **2** to make a great effort. ➤➤ **agonized** *adj,* **agonizing** *adj.*

agony *n* (*pl* **-ies**) **1** intense and often prolonged physical pain or mental suffering; anguish. **2** the struggle that precedes death.

agony aunt *n* a journalist who replies to readers' questions about their personal problems in a magazine or newspaper.

agony column *n* a column in a magazine or newspaper in which readers' personal problems are discussed.

agora[1] /'agorə/ *n* (*pl* **agoras** *or* **agorae**) a gathering place for popular political assembly in ancient Greece.

agora[2] /agə'rah/ *n* (*pl* **agorot**) a unit of currency in Israel, worth 100th of a shekel.

agoraphobia *n* abnormal dread of being in open spaces or public places. ➤➤ **agoraphobe** *n,* **agoraphobic** *n and adj.*

agorot *n* pl of AGORA[2].

agrarian *adj* **1** to do with farmers, farming, or agricultural life and interests. **2** relating to fields, lands, or their tenure.

agree *v* **1** *chiefly Brit* to come to terms on (e.g. a price), usu after discussion; to accept by mutual consent. **2a** (*often* + to) to give assent. **b** to consent to do something. **3a** (*often* + with) to get along together. **b** (*often* + on) to decide together. **4** (*often* + with) to correspond or be consistent. **5** (+ with) to suit somebody's health or constitution. **6** (*often* + with) to correspond in grammatical gender, number, case, or person.

agreeable *adj* **1** to one's liking; pleasing. **2** willing to agree or consent. ➤➤ **agreeableness** *n,* **agreeably** *adv.*

agreed *adj* **1** arranged by mutual consent. **2** of the joint opinion.

agreement *n* **1a** harmony of opinion or feeling. **b** correspondence or consistency. **c** consent. **2a** a treaty, contract, or other set of terms or conditions. **b** a legally binding contract. **3** correspondence in grammatical gender, number, case, or person.

agribusiness *n* all the industries involved in farming.

agriculture *n* the theory and practice of cultivating and producing crops from the soil and of raising livestock. ➤➤ **agricultural** *adj,* **agriculturalist** *n,* **agriculturally** *adv,* **agriculturist** *n.*

agrimony *n* (*pl* **-ies**) a plant of the rose family with spikes of yellow flowers and fruits like burs.

agrochemical *n* a chemical used in agriculture, e.g. as an insecticide or fertilizer.

agronomy *n* a branch of agriculture dealing with crop production and soil management. ➤➤ **agronomic** *adj,* **agronomically** *adv,* **agronomist** *n.*

aground *adv and adj* on or onto the shore or the bottom of a body of water.

ague *n* **1** a malarial fever with regularly recurring attacks of chills and sweating. **2** a fit of shivering. ➤➤ **aguish** *adj.*

AH *abbr* used before a date that falls within the Muslim era.

ahead *adv and adj* **1a** in a forward direction. **b** in front. **2** in, into, or for the future. **3** in or towards a better position. ✱ **ahead of 1** in front or advance of. **2** better than.

ahistorical *or* **ahistoric** *adj* without regard for history or tradition; concerned only with the present.

ahoy *interj* used at sea as a greeting or warning.

AI *abbr* **1** artificial insemination. **2** artificial intelligence.

AID *abbr* artificial insemination by donor.

aid[1] *v* **1** to give assistance to; to help. **2** to bring about the accomplishment of; to facilitate. ➤➤ **aider** *n.*

aid[2] *n* **1a** help; assistance. **b** money, supplies, or other tangible means of assistance given *esp* to another country. **2a** something that helps or supports. **b** a helper. ✱ **in aid of 1** in order to help or support (something). **2** *Brit, informal* for the purpose of (something).

aide *n* **1** = AIDE-DE-CAMP. **2** *chiefly NAm* an assistant to a political leader.

aide-de-camp *n* (*pl* **aides-de-camp**) an officer in the armed forces acting as a personal assistant to a senior officer.

aide-mémoire /ayd mem'wah/ *n* (*pl* **aides-mémoire**) **1** an aid to the memory, e.g. a note or sketch. **2** a diplomatic memorandum.

Aids *or* **AIDS** *n* a disease of the immune system, caused by the virus HIV, usu leading to death from infections that the body is no longer able to resist.

aikido *n* a martial art with holds and throws similar to those of judo and using non-resistance to cause an opponent's own momentum to work against them.

ail *v archaic* **1** to give pain or trouble to. **2** to be unwell.

aileron *n* a movable surface or flap at the trailing edge of an aircraft wing used to control rolling and turning manoeuvres.

ailing *adj* **1** unwell or chronically ill. **2** in an unsatisfactory condition.

ailment *n* a mild illness.

aim[1] *v* **1a** to point a weapon, camera, etc at an object or person. **b** to direct (something) at or towards a specified target. **2** to intend or try (to do something).

aim[2] *n* **1** a clear intention or purpose. **2a** the pointing of a weapon at a target. **b** the ability to hit a target. ➤➤ **aimless** *adj,* **aimlessly** *adv,* **aimlessness** *n.*

ain't *contr non-standard* **1a** am not. **b** are not. **c** is not. **2a** have not. **b** has not.

aïoli *or* **aioli** /ie'ohli/ *n* a garlic-flavoured mayonnaise.

air[1] *n* **1a** the mixture of invisible odourless tasteless gases, mainly nitrogen and oxygen, that surrounds the earth. **b** one of the four elements of the alchemists, the others being earth, fire, and water. **2a** empty unconfined space. **b** nothingness. **3** the supposed medium of transmission of radio waves. **4a** the appearance or bearing of a person; demeanour. **b** (*in pl*) an artificial or affected manner; haughtiness. **5** a tune or melody. **6** a light breeze. **7** (*used before a noun*) involving aircraft or aviation. ✱ **in the air** being generally spread round or hinted at. **off (the) air** not or no longer broadcasting on radio or television. **on (the) air** broadcasting on radio or television. **take the air** to go out of doors for a walk. **up in the air** not yet settled; uncertain.

air[2] *v* **1** to expose to the open air for freshening, drying, etc. **2** to expose to warmth so as to remove dampness. **3** to expose (e.g. an opinion) to public notice.

air bag *n* a bag inside a motor vehicle designed to inflate automatically in the event of an impact, cushioning the occupants against injury.

air base *n* a base of operations for military aircraft.

air bed *n chiefly Brit* an inflatable mattress.

air bladder *n* a pouch containing air or gas, *esp* an organ that controls buoyancy in bony fishes.

airborne *adj* supported or transported by air; in-flight.

air brake *n* **1** a brake operated by compressed air. **2** a movable surface projected into the air for slowing an aircraft.

air brick *n* a building brick or metal or plastic box perforated to allow ventilation.

airbrush[1] *n* an atomizer for spraying paint.

airbrush[2] *v* **1** to paint or spray with an airbrush. **2** to alter (a photograph) using an airbrush. **3** to alter the record or reputation of (a person) in the public perception.

airburst *n* a detonation of a bomb in the air above its target.

air chief marshal *n* an officer in the Royal Air Force ranking below marshal of the Royal Air Force.

air commodore *n* an officer in the Royal Air Force ranking below air vice marshal.

air conditioning *n* an apparatus for controlling the temperature, humidity, and cleanness of the air in a building or vehicle. ⋙ **air-condition** *v*, **air-conditioned** *adj*, **air conditioner** *n*.

air-cool *v* to cool the cylinders of (an internal-combustion engine) directly by air. ⋙ **air-cooled** *adj*.

air corridor *n* an air route over a country along which aircraft are allowed to fly.

air cover *n* the use of military aircraft to protect ground or naval forces against attack.

aircraft *n* (*pl* **aircraft**) an aeroplane, helicopter, or other means of transport that can travel through the air.

aircraft carrier *n* a warship designed so that aircraft can be operated from it.

aircraftman *or* **aircraftwoman** *n* (*pl* **aircraftmen** *or* **aircraftwomen**) a person of the lowest rank in the Royal Air Force.

aircrew *n* (*used as sing. or pl*) the crew of an aircraft, including the pilot and stewards.

air cushion *n* **1** the layer of air between a hovercraft and the surface over which it moves. **2** an inflatable cushion.

airdrop[1] *n* a delivery of cargo or personnel by parachute from an aircraft.

airdrop[2] *v* (**airdropped, airdropping**) to deliver (cargo or personnel) by parachute.

Airedale *n* a large terrier of a breed with a hard wiry coat that is dark on the back and sides and tan elsewhere.

airer *n chiefly Brit* a freestanding framework for airing or drying clothes, linen, etc.

airfield *n* an area of land maintained for the landing and takeoff of aircraft.

air force *n* the branch of a country's armed forces for air warfare.

airframe *n* the structure of an aircraft or missile, without the engine and related parts.

airfreight *n* the transport of freight by air, or the charge for this. ⋙ **airfreight** *v*.

air guitar *n informal* the playing of an imaginary guitar, *esp* while listening to rock music.

air gun *n* **1** a gun that propels a projectile by compressed air. **2** a hand tool worked by compressed air or emitting a stream of hot air.

airhead *n slang* a stupid person.

air hostess *n* a female member of the cabin crew on a passenger aircraft.

airing *n* **1** exposure to air or warmth for ventilation or drying. **2** a walk or drive in the open air. **3** exposure to discussion or debate.

air-kiss *v* to make the motions of kissing without making contact. ⋙ **air kiss** *n*.

air lane *n* a path customarily followed by aeroplanes.

air letter *n* **1** an airmail letter. **2** = AEROGRAM.

airlift *n* the transport of cargo or passengers by air, usu to or from an otherwise inaccessible area. ⋙ **airlift** *v*.

airline *n* **1** an organization that provides regular public air transport. **2** a pipe or hose supplying air, usu under pressure.

airliner *n* a passenger aircraft operated by an airline.

air lock *n* **1** an airtight chamber, e.g. in a spacecraft or submerged vessel, that allows movement between two areas of different air pressure. **2** a stoppage of flow caused by the presence of air in circulating liquid.

airmail *n* mail transported by aircraft, or this system of transporting mail. ⋙ **airmail** *v*.

airman *or* **airwoman** *n* (*pl* **airmen** *or* **airwomen**) a civilian or military pilot, aircraft crew member, etc.

air marshal *n* an officer in the Royal Air Force ranking below air chief marshal.

Air Miles *pl n trademark* points that are awarded to those purchasing certain products, *esp* airline tickets, and that can be used to pay for air travel.

airmiss *n* a situation in which two aircraft in flight pass dangerously close to each other.

air pistol *n* a small air gun.

airplane *n chiefly NAm* = AEROPLANE.

airplay *n* the broadcasting of a particular recording, *esp* by a radio station, or a single instance of this.

air pocket *n* **1** a region of down-flowing or low-density air that causes an aircraft to drop suddenly. **2** a cavity or enclosure containing air, e.g. under water.

airport *n* a fully-equipped airfield, usu with runways and associated buildings, that is used as a base for the transport of passengers and cargo by air.

air quality *n* the relative freedom of the air in a place from pollution.

air rage *n* violence and aggression by an aircraft passenger.

air raid *n* an attack by armed aircraft on a surface target.

airscrew *n* an aircraft propeller.

air-sea rescue *n* the rescue of people in difficulties at sea by helicopter or other aircraft.

airship *n* a gas-filled lighter-than-air aircraft that has its own means of propulsion and steering system.

airsick *adj* suffering from the motion sickness associated with flying. ➤➤ **airsickness** *n.*

airspace *n* the area of the atmosphere above a nation and coming under its jurisdiction.

airspeed *n* the speed of an aircraft relative to the air.

airstrip *n* a strip of ground where aircraft can take off and land.

airtight *adj* **1** impermeable to air. **2** unassailable. ➤➤ **airtightness** *n.*

airtime *n* the broadcasting of something, e.g. a record or advertisement, on radio or television, or the duration of this.

air-to-air *adj* from one aircraft in flight to or at another.

air traffic control *n* a ground-based agency that controls the movement of aircraft in flight, or at takeoff or landing, by issuing instructions to pilots. ➤➤ **air traffic controller** *n.*

air vice-marshal *n* an officer in the Royal Air Force ranking below air marshal.

airwaves *pl n* the supposed medium of radio and television transmission.

airway *n* **1** a designated route along which aircraft fly. **2a** the passage through which air travels to the lungs. **b** a tube inserted in the throat to let an unconscious person breathe. **3** a passage for air in a mine.

airworthy *adj* of an aircraft: fit for operation in the air. ➤➤ **airworthiness** *n.*

airy *adj* (**-ier, -iest**) **1a** well-ventilated. **b** spacious. **2a** not having solid foundation; illusory. **b** showing lack of concern; flippant. **3** light and graceful. **4** delicately thin in texture. ➤➤ **airily** *adv,* **airiness** *n.*

airy-fairy *adj chiefly Brit* whimsically unrealistic.

aisle *n* **1a** a passage between rows of seats, e.g. in a church or theatre. **b** a passage between rows of shelving in a shop. **2** the side division of a church separated from the nave by columns. ✱ **lead somebody up the aisle** to get married to somebody. ➤➤ **aisled** *adj.*

ait *or* **eyot** *n Brit* a small island in a river.

aitch *n* the letter *h.*

aitchbone *n* the hipbone, *esp* of cattle, or the cut of beef containing this.

ajar *adj and adv* of a door: slightly open.

AK *abbr* Alaska (US postal abbreviation).

AKA *or* **aka** *abbr* also known as.

Akan *n* (*pl* **Akans** *or* **Akan**) **1** a member of a people living in Ghana, the Ivory Coast, and Togo. **2** the language of this people. ➤➤ **Akan** *adj.*

akimbo *adj and adv* of the arm: with the hand on the hip and the elbow turned outwards.

akin *adj* **1** descended from a common ancestor. **2** essentially similar, related, or compatible.

AL *abbr* Alabama (US postal abbreviation).

Al *abbr* the chemical symbol for aluminium.

al- *prefix* see AD-.

-al[1] *suffix* forming adjectives from nouns, denoting: character or type: *fictional.*

-al[2] *suffix* forming nouns from verbs, denoting: an action or process: *rehearsal.*

à la *prep* **1** in the manner of. **2** prepared, flavoured, or served with.

alabaster *n* a fine-textured, usu white and translucent, chalky stone often carved into ornaments. ➤➤ **alabaster** *adj,* **alabastrine** *adj.*

à la carte *adv and adj* according to a menu that prices each item separately: compare TABLE D'HÔTE.

alack *interj archaic* used to express sorrow or regret.

alacrity *n formal* promptness or cheerful readiness.

Aladdin's cave *n* a hoard of precious things.

à la mode *adj* fashionable or stylish.

alanine *n* an amino acid found in most proteins.

alarm[1] *n* **1** the fear resulting from the sudden sensing of danger. **2** a signal that warns or alerts, or an automatic device that produces such a signal. **3** = ALARM CLOCK.

alarm[2] *v* **1** to cause great fear or anxiety in. **2** to warn or alert. **3** to fit with an automatic alarm. ➤➤ **alarming** *adj,* **alarmingly** *adv.*

alarm clock *n* a clock that can be set to sound an alarm at a required time, used to wake somebody up.

alarmist *n* a person who needlessly alarms other people.

alarum *n archaic* an alarm or a call to arms.

alarums and excursions *pl n* clamour and confusion.

alas *interj* an exclamation used to express unhappiness, pity, or disappointment.

alb *n* a full-length white linen vestment, with long sleeves and a girdle, worn by a priest at Mass.

albacore *n* (*pl* **albacores** *or* **albacore**) a large tuna fish with long pectoral fins caught for canning.

Albanian *n* **1** a native or inhabitant of Albania. **2** the Indo-European language of Albania. ➤➤ **Albanian** *adj.*

albatross *n* (*pl* **albatrosses** *or* **albatross**) **1** a very large web-footed seabird with long narrow wings related to the petrels. **2** an encumbrance or handicap. **3** a golf score of three strokes less than par on a hole.

albedo *n* (*pl* **albedos**) the proportion of light or other electromagnetic radiation reflected by a surface or body, e.g. the moon or a cloud.

albeit *conj formal* even though.

albino *n* (*pl* **-os**) an organism with deficient pigmentation resulting in a white or translucent skin, white or colourless hair, and eyes with a pink pupil. ➤➤ **albinic** *adj,* **albinism** *n,* **albinotic** *adj.*

Albion *n literary* Britain or England.

album *n* **1** a book with blank pages used to hold or display a collection, e.g. of stamps or photographs. **2** a collection of recordings of different songs, etc, usu issued on a single CD, tape, or LP.

albumen *n* **1** the white of an egg. **2** = ALBUMIN.

albumin *n* a protein occuring in large quantities in blood plasma, milk, egg white, plant fluids, etc and coagulated by heat. ➤➤ **albuminous** *adj.*

alcazar *n* a Spanish fortress or palace built by the Moors.

alchemy *n* (*pl* **-ies**) **1** a medieval chemical science and philosophical doctrine that sought to turn base metals into gold, cure all diseases, and achieve immortality. **2** a mysterious, beautifying transformation. ➤➤ **alchemic** *adj,* **alchemical** *adj,* **alchemist** *n.*

alcheringa *n* a golden age recorded in the legends of certain Australian Aboriginal peoples as the time when their first ancestors were created.

alcohol *n* **1** a colourless inflammable liquid, the intoxicating agent in fermented and distilled drinks and also used as a solvent. **2** intoxicating drink containing alcohol. **3** any organic compound derived from hydrocarbons containing the hydroxyl group.

alcoholic[1] *adj* **1** containing or caused by alcohol. **2** affected with alcoholism. ➤➤ **alcoholically** *adv.*

alcoholic[2] *n* somebody affected with alcoholism.

alcoholism *n* excessive and usu compulsive consumption of alcoholic drinks, or the physical and psychological disorders associated with such dependence.

alcopop *n Brit, informal* a soft drink containing alcohol.

alcove *n* a niche, recess, or arched opening, e.g. in the wall of a room.

aldehyde *n* any of various highly reactive compounds, e.g. acetaldehyde, characterized by the group CHO. ➤➤ **aldehydic** *adj.*

al dente *adj* of pasta and vegetables: cooked but firm when bitten.

alder *n* a tree or shrub of the birch family with toothed leaves and catkins that grows in moist ground.

alderman *n* (*pl* **aldermen**) **1** in Britain until 1974, a senior member of a county or borough council elected by the other councillors. **2** a viceroy for an Anglo-Saxon king. **3** *NAm, Aus* an elected member of the governing body of a borough. ➤➤ **aldermanic** *adj.*

aldosterone *n* a steroid hormone produced by the adrenal cortex that affects the salt and water balance of the body.

ale *n* **1** beer. **2** an alcoholic drink made with malt and hops, usu stronger and heavier than beer.

aleatoric *adj* = ALEATORY.

aleatory *adj* **1** depending on chance. **2** relating to or based on luck, *esp* bad luck. **3** improvisatory or random in character.

alembic *n* **1** an apparatus formerly used in distillation. **2** a means of refining or transmuting.

alert[1] *adj* **1** watchful; aware. **2** active; brisk. ➤➤ **alertly** *adv,* **alertness** *n.*

alert[2] *n* **1** an alarm signal that warns of danger. **2** the danger period during which an alert is in effect. ✱ **on the alert** on the lookout, *esp* for danger or opportunity.

alert[3] *v* **1** to call to a state of readiness; to warn. **2** (*often* + to) to cause to be aware, e.g. of a need or responsibility.

A level *n* an examination generally taken at sixth-form level and used as a basis for determining university entrance.

Alexander technique *n* a therapy for improving general health and well-being by correcting posture and movement and relieving tension.

Alexandrian *adj* **1** relating to or characteristic of ancient or modern Alexandria. **2** = HELLENISTIC.

alexandrine *n* (*also* **Alexandrine**) a twelve-syllable verse line consisting of six iambic feet with a pause after the third. ➤➤ **alexandrine** *adj.*

alfalfa *n* a deep-rooted plant of the pea family that is widely grown for fodder: *Medicago sativa.*

alfresco *or* **al fresco** *adj and adv* taking place in the open air.

alga *n* (*pl* **algae** *or* **algas**) (*usu in pl*) any of a group of chiefly aquatic plants, e.g. seaweeds and pond scums, that lack differentiated stems, roots, and leaves and that often contain a brown or red pigment in addition to chlorophyll. ➤➤ **algal** *adj,* **algoid** *adj.*

algebra *n* a branch of mathematics in which letters, symbols, etc representing various entities are combined in equations and formulas. ➤➤ **algebraic** *adj,* **algebraist** *n.*

Algerian *n* a native or inhabitant of Algeria. ➤➤ **Algerian** *adj.*

-algia *comb. form* forming nouns, denoting: pain in the part of the body specified: *neuralgia.* ➤➤ **-algic** *adj.*

Algonkian *n* see ALGONQUIAN.

Algonkin *n* see ALGONQUIN.

Algonquian *or* **Algonkian** *n* **1** a group of Native American languages spoken *esp* in the eastern parts of Canada and the USA. **2** a member of any of the Native American peoples speaking Algonquian languages. **3** = ALGONQUIN (1), (2). ➤➤ **Algonquian** *adj.*

Algonquin *or* **Algonkin** *n* **1** a member of a Native American people living in the Ottawa river valley in Canada. **2** the dialect of Ojibwa spoken by the Algonquins. **3** = ALGONQUIAN (1), (2). ➤➤ **Algonquin** *adj.*

algorithm *n* a systematic procedure for solving a mathematical problem in a finite number of steps, often using a computer; *broadly* a step-by-step procedure for solving a problem or accomplishing some end. ➤➤ **algorithmic** *adj.*

alias[1] *adv* otherwise called or known as.

alias[2] *n* an assumed name.

alibi[1] *n* (*pl* **alibis**) **1** the plea of having been elsewhere when a crime was committed, or evidence supporting such a claim. **2** a plausible excuse, usu intended to avert blame or punishment.

alibi[2] *v* (**alibies, alibied, alibiing**) to provide (somebody) with an alibi or excuse.

Alice band *n* a headband worn to hold the hair back from the face.

alien[1] *adj* **1a** belonging to another person, place, or thing; strange. **b** foreign. **2** from another world; extraterrestrial. **3** (+ to) differing in nature or character, *esp* to the extent of being opposed.

alien[2] *n* **1** a foreign-born resident who has not been naturalized; *broadly* a foreign-born citizen. **2** a being from another world; an extraterrestrial. **3** a person, animal, or plant from another family, race, or species. ➤➤ **alienage** *n.*

alienable *adj* legally capable of being sold or transferred. ➤➤ **alienability** *n.*

alienate *v* **1** to make (*esp* a former friend or supporter) hostile or indifferent. **2** to cause (e.g. affection) to be withdrawn or diverted. **3** to convey or transfer (e.g. property or a right) to another. ➤➤ **alienator** *n.*

alienation *n* **1** withdrawal from or apathy towards one's former attachments or society in general. **2** a conveyance of property to another.

alienist *n* **1** *NAm* a specialist in legal aspects of psychiatry. **2** *archaic* somebody who treats mental disorders.

alight[1] *v* **1** to come down from something; to dismount or disembark. **2** to descend from the air and settle; to land. ➤➤ **alightment** *n.*

alight[2] *adj* **1** *chiefly Brit* on fire; ignited. **2** animated or alive.

align *v* **1** to bring into proper relative position, usu in a straight line. **2** to position (usu oneself) on the side of or against a party or cause. » **alignment** *n.*

alike[1] *adj* showing close resemblance without being identical.

alike[2] *adv* in the same manner, form, or degree; equally.

alimentary *adj* relating to nourishment or nutrition.

alimentary canal *n* the tubular passage that extends from the mouth to the anus and functions in the digestion and absorption of food.

alimony *n chiefly NAm* = MAINTENANCE (2).

A-line *adj* of a garment: shaped like the lower part of an A, with the bottom wider than the top.

aliphatic *adj* **1** of a chemical compound: having an open-chain rather than a cyclic structure: compare AROMATIC[1] (2). **2** of or derived from fat.

aliquot[1] *adj* **1** contained an exact number of times in another. **2** constituting a fraction of a whole.

aliquot[2] *n* **1** a small part that is contained an exact number of times in a whole. **2** a small sample, e.g. one taken from a mixture undergoing a chemical reaction to determine what changes have occurred.

alive *adj* **1** having life; not dead. **2a** still in existence or operation; active. **b** = LIVE[2] (3B). **3** (+ to) realizing the existence of; aware of. **4** marked by alertness; lively or animated. **5** showing much activity; swarming. » **aliveness** *n.*

alizarin *n* an orange or red dye formerly obtained from madder.

alkali *n* (*pl* **alkalis** *or* **alkalies**) **1** any of various soluble chemical bases, *esp* a hydroxide or carbonate of an alkali metal that combine with acids to form salts: compare ACID[2], BASE[1] (6). **2** a soluble chemical salt that is present in some soils of dry regions and prevents the growth of crops. » **alkalize** *v.*

alkaline *adj* containing or having the properties of an alkali; *specif* having a pH of more than seven. » **alkalinity** *n.*

alkaloid *n* any of numerous nitrogen-containing organic compounds, e.g. morphine, that are usu chemical bases, occur in plants, and are extensively used as drugs. » **alkaloidal** *adj.*

alkane *n* any of a series of saturated open-chain hydrocarbons, e.g. methane, ethane, propane, or butane.

alkene *n* any of a series of unsaturated double-bonded hydrocarbons, e.g. ethylene or propylene, in which the carbon atoms are arranged in a straight line.

alkyd *or* **alkyd resin** *n* any of numerous plastics produced by heating alcohols with acids and used to make paints and tough protective coatings.

alkyl *n* a univalent radical, e.g. methyl, derived from an alkane by removal of a hydrogen atom. » **alkylic** *adj.*

alkyne *n* any of a series of unsaturated triple-bonded hydrocarbons, e.g. acetylene, in which the carbon atoms are arranged in a straight line.

all[1] *adj* **1** the whole amount, quantity, or number of. **2** every. **3** any whatever. **4a** displaying only: *all attention.* **b** having or seeming to have some physical feature conspicuously or excessively: *be all ears.* * **all there** *informal* not mentally subnormal; alert or shrewd. **all very well** a formula used in rejection of advice or sympathy. **for all** in spite of.

all[2] *adv* **1** wholly or altogether. **2** to a supreme degree. **3** for each side: *three all.* * **all but** very nearly; almost. **all that** *chiefly in negatives and questions* very: *not all that hungry.* **all the** (+ compar) so much. **all too** emphatically so.

all[3] *pron* (*pl* **all**) **1** the whole number, quantity, or amount. **2** everybody; everything. * **all in all 1** generally; taking everything into account. **2** supremely important. **all the best** used as an expression of goodwill and usu farewell. **for all** to the extent that. **for all one is worth** with all one's might. **in all** in total. **one's all** one's greatest effort or total resources.

alla breve *adj and adv* of a piece of music: with two or four beats in a bar, a single beat being represented by a minim.

Allah *n* the name for God used by Muslims or in reference to the Islamic religion.

all-American *adj* representative of the ideals of the USA; typically or truly American.

allay *v* (**allays, allayed, allaying**) **1** to reduce the severity of (e.g. pain or grief). **2** to reduce or diminish (e.g. fear or suspicion).

All Blacks *pl n* the New Zealand Rugby Union team.

all clear *n* a signal that a danger has passed or that it is safe to proceed.

allegation *n* a statement made without proof or that has yet to be proved.

allege *v* to assert without proof or before proving. » **alleged** *adj,* **allegedly** *adv.*

allegiance *n* **1** dedication to or dutiful support of a person, group, or cause. **2** the obligation of subjects or citizens to their sovereign or government.

allegorical *or* **allegoric** *adj* constituting or characteristic of allegory. » **allegorically** *adv.*

allegory *n* (*pl* **-ies**) **1** the expression by means of symbolic figures and actions of truths or generalizations about human existence. **2** a story, poem, painting, etc that contains or consists of allegory. » **allegorist** *n,* **allegorization** *n,* **allegorize** *v.*

allegretto *adj and adv* of a piece of music: to be performed faster than andante but not as fast as allegro. » **allegretto** *n.*

allegro *adj and adv* of a piece of music: to be performed in a brisk lively manner. » **allegro** *n.*

allele *n* any of two or more genes that occur as alternatives at a given place on a chromosome and are responsible for variations in a hereditary characteristic, e.g. eye colour. » **allelic** *adj.*

allelomorph *n* = ALLELE. » **allelomorphic** *adj.*

alleluia *interj and n* see HALLELUJAH[1], HALLELUJAH[2].

allemande *n* **1** a 17th-cent. and 18th-cent. court or folk dance. **2** music for an allemande, often part of a suite.

all-embracing *adj* complete or sweeping.

Allen key *n trademark* a tool with a hexagonal end that is designed to turn a screw with a recess of this shape in the head.

allergen *n* a substance that induces allergy. » **allergenic** *adj.*

allergic *adj* **1** having an allergy to something. **2** of or inducing allergy. **3** *informal* averse to a practice.

allergy *n* (*pl* **-ies**) **1** extreme sensitivity, marked by sneezing, itching, skin rashes, etc, to substances that have no such effect on the average individual. **2** increased sensitivity to an antigen in response to a first exposure. **3** *informal* a feeling of aversion.

alleviate *v* to relieve (a troublesome situation, state of mind, etc). » **alleviation** *n,* **alleviative** *adj,* **alleviator** *n,* **alleviatory** *adj.*

alley[1] *n* (*pl* **-eys**) **1** a narrow back street or passageway between buildings. **2** a garden walk bordered by trees or a hedge. **3** = BOWLING ALLEY.

alley[2] *n* (*pl* **-eys**) a large or superior playing marble.

alley cat *n* a stray cat living in the streets of a town.

alleyway *n* = ALLEY[1] (1).

all found *adv chiefly Brit* with free food and lodging provided in addition to wages.

all fours *pl n* all four legs of a quadruped. ✻ **on all fours** on hands and knees.

alliance *n* **1** an association or bond between nations, groups, or individuals who agree to cooperate for mutual benefit. **2** a connection or relationship, *esp* by marriage. **3** a botanical category comprising a group of related plant families.

allied *adj* **1** joined in alliance by agreement or treaty. **2** in close association; united. **3a** related by resemblance or common properties. **b** related genetically. **4** (**Allied**) of the Allies.

Allies *pl n* **1** the nations, including Britain, Russia, and France, united against the Central European powers in World War I. **2** the nations, including Britain, the USA, and the Soviet Union, united against the Axis powers in World War II.

alligator *n* **1** a large American or Chinese aquatic reptile related to the crocodiles but with a broader head that does not taper towards the snout. **2** leather made from alligator hide.

alligator pear *n NAm* = AVOCADO.

all in *adj informal* tired out; exhausted.

all-in *adj* **1** *chiefly Brit* all-inclusive, *esp* including all costs. **2** *Brit* said of wrestling: having almost no holds barred.

alliteration *n* the repetition of initial consonant sounds in neighbouring words or syllables, e.g. '*th*reatening *th*rongs of *th*reshers'. ⋙ **alliterate** *v*, **alliterative** *adj*, **alliteratively** *adv*.

allium *n* any of a large genus of plants of the lily family including the onion, garlic, chives, leek, and shallot.

allocate *v* **1a** to apportion and distribute (e.g. money or responsibility) in shares. **b** to assign (something limited in supply) to. **2** to earmark or designate. ⋙ **allocable** *adj*, **allocatable** *adj*, **allocation** *n*, **allocator** *n*.

allopathy *n* conventional medical practice using treatments that produce effects different from those of the disease being treated. ⋙ **allopath** *n*, **allopathic** *adj*, **allopathically** *adv*, **allopathist** *n*.

allosaurus *n* a large two-footed flesh-eating dinosaur of the late Jurassic period.

allot *v* (**allotted, allotting**) **1** to assign (something to a person or thing); = ALLOCATE (1). **2** to earmark or designate (something). ⋙ **allotter** *n*.

allotment *n* **1** *Brit* a small plot of land let out to an individual, e.g. by a town council, for cultivation. **2** the act of allotting or a share allotted.

allotrope *n* any of the two or more different physical forms in which a substance can exist. ⋙ **allotropic** *adj*, **allotropically** *adv*, **allotropy** *n*.

all-out *adj* using maximum effort and resources. ⋙ **all out** *adv*.

allow *v* **1a** to permit (something, or somebody to do something). **b** to make it possible for (somebody to do something). **2** to assign (e.g. time or money) as a share or suitable amount. **3a** to admit as true or valid; to acknowledge. **b** (+ of) to admit the possibility of something. **4** (+ for) to make allowance for something. ⋙ **allowable** *adj*, **allowably** *adv*, **allowedly** *adv*.

allowance *n* **1a** a share or portion allotted or granted; a ration. **b** a sum paid to a person, usu at regular intervals. **c** an amount of income on which no tax is payable. **2a** permission or sanction. **b** acknowledgment. ✻ **make allowances for** to take into account mitigating circumstances.

alloy[1] *n* **1** a solid substance composed of a mixture of metals or of a metal with a non-metal. **2** a metal mixed with a more valuable metal. **3** an addition that impairs or debases something.

alloy[2] *v* **1** to mix (metals, or a metal with a non-metal) so as to form an alloy. **2** to reduce the purity or value of by addition.

all right[1] *adv* **1** well enough. **2** beyond doubt; certainly: *it's him all right!*

all right[2] *adj* **1** satisfactory or acceptable. **2** safe or well; in good condition or working order. **3** agreeable or pleasing.

all right[3] *interj* **1** a formula used for giving assent. **2** an exclamation used in indignant or menacing response.

all round *adv* **1** by, for, or to everyone present. **2** in every respect.

all-round *adj* **1** competent in many fields. **2** having general utility. **3** encompassing all aspects; comprehensive.

all-rounder *n* somebody who is competent in many fields; *specif* a cricketer who bats and bowls to a relatively high standard.

All Saints' Day *n* 1 November observed in Christian churches as a festival in honour of all the saints.

all-seater *adj Brit* of a sports stadium: having no places for standing spectators.

All Souls' Day *n* 2 November observed in Christian churches as a day of prayer for the souls of believers who have died.

allspice *n* a mildly pungent spice prepared from the berry of a W Indian tree belonging to the eucalyptus family.

all-star *adj* composed wholly or chiefly of stars of the theatre, cinema, etc.

all-time *adj* exceeding all others yet known.

all told *adv* altogether; with everything or everybody taken into account.

allude *v* (+ to) to make indirect, casual, or implicit reference.

all-up *adj* of an aircraft's weight: including everything necessary for operation.

allure[1] *v* to entice by charm or attraction. ⋙ **allurement** *n*, **alluring** *adj*.

allure[2] *n* power of attraction or fascination; charm.

allusion *n* **1** an implied or indirect reference, or the use of such references, *esp* in literature. **2** alluding or hinting. ⋙ **allusive** *adj*, **allusively** *adv*, **allusiveness** *n*.

alluvium *n* (*pl* **alluviums** *or* **alluvia**) clay, silt, or similar material deposited by running water. ⋙ **alluvial** *adj*.

ally[1] *v* (**-ies, -ied**) **1** to join or unite with, *esp* for common benefit. **2** (*usu in passive*) to combine with. **3** (+ to) to relate (something) by resemblance or common properties.

ally[2] *n* (*pl* **-ies**) **1** a state associated with another by treaty or league. **2** a person or group that helps, supports, or cooperates with another.

-ally *suffix* forming adverbs from adjectives that end in *-al*, with the meaning: in (such) a manner: *provisionally; logically*.

alma mater *n* a school, college, or university that one has attended.

almanac *or* **almanack** *n* an annual publication containing statistical and general information, often in tabular form, *esp* a publication containing astronomical and meteorological data for each day in a particular year.

Almighty *n* (**the Almighty**) a title for God.

almighty[1] *adj* **1** (*often* **Almighty**) having absolute power over all. **2** having relatively unlimited power. **3** *informal* great in extent, seriousness, force, etc. ⋙ **almightiest** *adj.*

almighty[2] *adv informal* to a great degree; very.

almond *n* an edible oval nut obtained from a small tree of the rose family, used in cookery and confectionery.

almond-eyed *adj* having narrow slanting eyes.

almoner *n* **1** a former name for a social worker attached to a British hospital. **2** somebody who distributed alms in former times.

almost *adv* very nearly but not exactly or entirely.

alms *pl n* (*used as sing. or pl*) money, food, etc given to help the poor, *esp* in former times. ⋙ **almsgiver** *n,* **almsgiving** *n.*

almshouse *n Brit* a house founded and financed by charity in which a poor person can live cheaply or free.

aloe *n* **1** a succulent plant of the lily family with thick leaves and tall spikes of flowers. **2** (*usu in pl, used as sing.*) the dried juice of the leaves of various aloes used *esp* as a laxative. **3** = CENTURY PLANT.

aloe vera *n* a jelly-like extract from the leaves of a species of aloe, used in cosmetic preparations and ointments.

aloft *adv* **1** at or to a higher place or a great height. **2** at or to the masthead or the upper rigging of a ship.

aloha *interj* a Hawaiian word used to express greeting or farewell.

alone *adj and adv* **1** considered without reference to any other. **2** separated from others; isolated. **3** exclusive of other factors. **4** free from interference. **5** without assistance. ⋙ **aloneness** *n.*

along[1] *prep* **1** over the length of or in a line parallel with. **2** in the course of: *along the way.* **3** in accordance with: *along these lines.*

along[2] *adv* **1** forward; on. **2** as a companion or a necessary or pleasant addition: *Can I bring a friend along?* **3** arriving at a particular place: *I'll be along in five minutes.* ✻ **all along** all the time. **along with** **1** in addition to. **2** in company with; simultaneously with.

alongshore *adv and adj* along the shore or coast.

alongside[1] *adv* along or at the side of something.

alongside[2] *prep* **1** (*also* + of) side by side with or along the side of. **2** (*also* + of) concurrently with.

aloof[1] *adv* at a distance; out of involvement.

aloof[2] *adj* distant in interest or feeling; reserved or unsympathetic. ⋙ **aloofly** *adv,* **aloofness** *n.*

alopecia *n* abnormal loss of hair in humans or loss of wool, feathers, etc in animals. ⋙ **alopecic** *adj.*

aloud *adv* with a normal speaking voice; not silently.

ALP *abbr* Australian Labor Party.

alp *n* **1** a high mountain. **2** in Switzerland, a mountainside pasture.

alpaca *n* (*pl* **alpacas** *or* **alpaca**) **1** a type of domesticated mammal, related to the llama, found in Peru. **2** the fine long wool of this mammal, or fabric made from this.

alpenhorn *n* a long straight wooden wind instrument used by Swiss herdsmen to call sheep and cattle, *esp* in the past. Also called ALPHORN.

alpenstock *n* a long staff with an iron point, used in hill climbing.

alpha[1] *n* **1** the first letter of the Greek alphabet (Α, α), equivalent to and transliterated as roman a. **2** a grade given to students showing the highest standard of work. **3** (*used before a noun*) in astronomy, denoting the brightest star of a constellation.

alpha[2] *adj informal* alphabetical.

alpha and omega *n* (**the alpha and omega**) the beginning and ending

alphabet *n* **1** a set of letters used to write a language, *esp* when arranged in a conventional order. **2** a system of signs and signals used in place of letters, e.g. a phonetic alphabet. **3** a set of basic principles about a subject. ⋙ **alphabetize** *v.*

alphabetical *or* **alphabetic** *adj* **1** using an alphabet. **2** in the order of the letters of the alphabet. ⋙ **alphabetically** *adv.*

alpha blocker *n* a drug that inhibits the type of nervous stimulation that causes constriction of the blood vessels.

alphameric *or* **alphamerical** *adj* alphanumeric. ⋙ **alphamerically** *adv.*

alphanumeric *or* **alphanumerical** *adj* **1** consisting of both letters and numbers, and often other symbols, such as punctuation marks or mathematical symbols. **2** of a letter, number, or symbol: belonging to an alphanumeric system. ⋙ **alphanumeric** *n,* **alphanumerically** *adv.*

alpha particle *n* a positively charged nuclear particle, identical with the nucleus of a helium atom, ejected at high speed from the nucleus of some radioactive substances when they decay: compare BETA PARTICLE.

alpha ray *n* a continuous narrow stream of alpha particles.

alpha rhythm *or* **alpha wave** *n* a variation in a record of the electrical activity of the brain of a frequency of about 10Hz, often associated with states of waking relaxation.

alpha test *n* a test of a piece of computer software that its manufacturer completes before the more demanding BETA TEST. ⋙ **alpha-test** *v.*

alpha wave *n* see ALPHA RHYTHM.

alphorn *n* = ALPENHORN.

alpine[1] *n* any of various plants that grow naturally in mountainous or northern parts of the northern hemisphere.

alpine[2] *adj* **1** (*often* **Alpine**) of or from the Alps. **2** of or like any high mountains. **3** growing in high mountain areas above the tree line. **4** (**Alpine**) of competitive ski events: featuring slalom and downhill racing: compare NORDIC[1].

alpinism *n* (*often* **Alpinism**) the climbing of high mountains, *esp* in the Alps. ⋙ **Alpinist** *n,* **alpinist** *n.*

already *adv* **1** before now or before a particular time. **2** previously. **3** before the expected time. **4** *chiefly NAm, informal* used as an intensifier or to express irritation, impatience, etc.

alright *adv, adj, and interj* = ALL RIGHT[1].

Usage note
The spelling *alright,* although fairly common, is still considered by many users of English, especially traditionalists, to be an incorrect spelling of *all right.*

Alsatian *n* **1** *chiefly Brit* a large dog of a wolflike breed originating in Germany, with a dense brownish or blackish coat, often used as a guard dog or by the police. Also called GERMAN SHEPHERD. **2** a person from Alsace in eastern France. ⋙ **Alsatian** *adj.*

also *adv* as well; additionally; besides.

also-ran *n* **1** an entrant that finishes outside the first three places in a race, *esp* a horse. **2** a person of no distinction or achievement.

altar *n* **1** a table on which the bread and wine used at communion are consecrated in Christian churches. **2** any table-like structure that serves as a centre of worship or ritual, e.g. on which sacrifices are offered or incense is burned in worship. ✻ **get/lead somebody to the altar** *informal* to succeed in marrying somebody.

altar boy *n* a boy who helps a priest during a service in a Christian church.

altarpiece *n* a work of art that decorates the space above and behind an altar.

alter *v* **1** to make or become different, *esp* in a way that involves only a slight change. **2** *chiefly NAm, euphem* to castrate or spay (an animal). ⋙ **alterable** *adj*, **alterably** *adv*, **alteration** *n*, **alterative** *adj*.

altercation *n* an angry discussion or quarrel.

alter ego *n* (*pl* **alter egos**) **1** a side of somebody's character that is different from their usual character. **2** a close and trusted friend.

alternate[1] *adj* **1** of two things: occurring by turns. **2** arranged one above or alongside the other; forming an alternating series. **3** every other; every second. **4** *chiefly NAm* = ALTERNATIVE[1] (1). ⋙ **alternately** *adv*.

Usage note

alternate *or* **alternative**? In British English *alternate* is an adjective and a verb, *alternative* is an adjective and a noun. *Alternate* means 'every other' (*Meetings take place on alternate Wednesdays*) or 'occurring by turns' (*alternate layers of stone and brick*). To *alternate* is 'to do something by turns': *They alternated between urging us to go faster and telling us to slow down*. An *alternative* is 'another different person or thing that could act as a replacement': *an alternative venue*. In American English, however, *alternate* is widely used as an adjective in the sense of *alternative* (*an alternate venue*) and as a noun to mean 'a deputy or substitute'.

alternate[2] *v* **1a** (*often* + with) of two things or people: to occur or do something by turns. **b** to interchange (one person or thing) with another. **2** (*often* + between) to change repeatedly from one state or action to another. ⋙ **alternation** *n*.

alternate[3] *n chiefly NAm* a substitute or deputy.

alternate angles *pl n* in mathematics, two equal angles formed on opposite sides and at opposite ends of a line that intersects two parallel lines.

alternating current *n* an electric current that reverses its direction at regularly recurring intervals: compare DIRECT CURRENT.

alternative[1] *adj* **1** able to be used instead of something else. **2** different from what is usual or traditional. **3** not accepting or demonstrating conventional social values. ⋙ **alternatively** *adv*.

Usage note

alternative *or* **alternate**? See note at ALTERNATE[1].

alternative[2] *n* **1** another different person or thing that could act as a replacement. **2** an opportunity to choose between two or more possibilities.

alternative energy *n* energy produced by methods that do not harm the environment, e.g. by using the power of the wind or the waves.

alternative medicine *n* any of a range of medical treatments that are not generally considered to be part of the conventional system of medicine, such as homoeopathy or shiatsu. Also called COMPLEMENTARY MEDICINE.

alternative therapy *n* = ALTERNATIVE MEDICINE.

alternator *n* an electric generator for producing alternating current.

although *conj* **1** in spite of the fact or possibility that; though. **2** but. **3** even if or even though.

altimeter *n* an instrument used for measuring altitude, *esp* by detecting changes in atmospheric pressure. ⋙ **altimetry** *n*.

altitude *n* the height of an object, e.g. an aircraft, or a place, *esp* above sea level. ⋙ **altitudinal** *adj*.

altitude sickness *n* a disorder affecting people, *esp* climbers, who breathe air at high altitudes with low oxygen concentrations. The symptoms are nausea, hyperventilation, dizziness, headache, and exhaustion.

Alt key *n* in computing, a keyboard key that is used in conjunction with another key or keys to give extra functions or special features.

alto *n* (*pl* **-os**) **1a** a female singer with a range below that of a soprano. **b** an adult male singer with a range above that of a tenor; a countertenor. **2** a musical instrument having a range below that of a soprano. **3** the second highest part in conventional four-part harmony. ⋙ **alto** *adj*.

altocumulus *n* (*pl* **altocumuli**) a large whitish globular cloud formation occurring at medium altitude.

altogether[1] *adv* **1** completely; thoroughly. **2** with everything taken into account. **3** in every way.

altogether[2] ✻ **in the altogether** *informal* naked.

altostratus *n* (*pl* **altostrati**) a cloud formation consisting of a continuous dark layer occurring at medium altitude.

altruism *n* unselfish regard for or devotion to the welfare of others. ⋙ **altruist** *n*, **altruistic** *adj*, **altruistically** *adv*.

alum *n* a sulphate of aluminium with potassium, used *esp* as an emetic and astringent.

alumina *n* = ALUMINIUM OXIDE.

aluminise *v* see ALUMINIZE.

aluminium (*NAm* **aluminum**) *n* a silver-white metallic chemical element that is light and easily shaped, conducts heat and electricity well, and is used *esp* in kitchen utensils and lightweight alloys.

aluminium oxide *n* a chemical compound that occurs naturally as corundum and in bauxite, used to produce aluminium and as an abrasive and an electrical insulator. Also called ALUMINA.

aluminize *or* **-ise** *v* to treat or coat with aluminium.

aluminosilicate *n* a silicate mineral in which some of the silicon is replaced by aluminium.

aluminous *adj* containing alum or aluminium.

alumna *n* (*pl* **alumnae**) a former female student of a particular school, college, or university.

alumnus *n* (*pl* **alumni**) a former male student of a particular school, college, or university.

alveolar[1] *adj* **1** of, resembling, or having alveoli or an alveolus. **2** of a consonant: articulated with the tip of the tongue touching or near the ridge of flesh behind the front teeth.

alveolar[2] *n* an alveolar consonant, e.g. *d*, *s*, or *t* in English.

alveolus *n* (*pl* **alveoli**) **1** a socket for a tooth. **2** an air cell of the lungs.

always *adv* **1a** at all times; continuously. **b** in all cases. **2** on every occasion; repeatedly. **3** forever; perpetually. **4** as a last resort.

alyssum *n* a Eurasian and African plant of the cabbage family that is grown in gardens for its clusters of small white or yellow flowers.

Alzheimer's disease /ˈalts·hieməz/ *n* a progressive disease involving the blood vessels of the brain and leading to premature senile dementia.

AM *abbr* amplitude modulation.

Am *abbr* the chemical symbol for americium.

am *v* first person sing. present of BE.

a.m. *abbr* ante meridiem, used to indicate the time between midnight and midday.

amah *n* a female servant in the Far East, *esp* a Chinese nursemaid.

amalgam *n* **1** an alloy of mercury with another metal, e.g. silver, used *esp* in making dental fillings. **2** a mixture of different elements.

amalgamate *v* **1** to unite in a mixture; to combine into a single body. **2** to combine or alloy (a metal) with mercury. ➤➤ **amalgamation** *n*, **amalgamator** *n*.

amanuensis *n* (*pl* **amanuenses**) somebody employed to write from dictation or to copy a manuscript.

amaranth *n* a herbaceous plant, grown in gardens for its showy purple flowers.

amaretti *pl n* small crisp Italian biscuits flavoured with almonds.

amaretto *n* (*pl* **amaretti**) an Italian liqueur flavoured with almonds.

amaryllis *n* a plant that grows from bulbs and has bright reddish or white lily-like flowers.

amass *v* **1** to collect for oneself; to accumulate. **2** to bring together into a mass. ➤➤ **amasser** *n*.

amateur[1] *n* **1** somebody who does something as a pastime rather than as a profession, *esp* a sportsman or sportswoman who does not compete for payment. **2** somebody who practises an art or science unskilfully. ➤➤ **amateurism** *n*.

amateur[2] *adj* **1** of or for amateurs rather than professionals. **2** not professional; inexpert.

amateurish *adj* not having or showing professional skill; done badly or carelessly. ➤➤ **amateur-ishly** *adv*, **amateurishness** *n*.

amatory *adj* of or expressing sexual love or desire.

amaze *v* to fill with wonder; to astound. ➤➤ **amazement** *n*.

amazing *adj* used as a generalized term of approval. ➤➤ **amazingly** *adv*.

Amazon *n* a tall strong or athletic woman.

Amazonian *adj* **1** of a woman: masculine or aggressive. **2** of the Amazon river.

ambassador *n* **1** a diplomat accredited to a foreign government or sovereign as a resident representative, or appointed for a special diplomatic assignment. **2** somebody who represents or promotes a quality. ➤➤ **ambassadorial** *adj*.

ambassadress *n* **1** a female ambassador. **2** the wife of an ambassador.

amber *n* **1** a hard yellow to brown translucent substance that is the fossilized resin of some extinct trees, used chiefly for ornaments and jewellery. **2** a yellowish brown colour. ➤➤ **amber** *adj*.

ambergris *n* a waxy substance found floating in tropical waters, which originates in the intestines of the sperm whale and is used in perfumery.

ambiance *n* see AMBIENCE.

ambidextrous *adj* able to use either hand with equal ease. ➤➤ **ambidexterity** *n*, **ambidextrously** *adv*, **ambidextrousness** *n*.

ambience *or* **ambiance** *n* a surrounding or pervading atmosphere that is characteristic of a place.

ambient *adj* relating to the immediate surroundings.

ambient music *n* music played in the background in supermarkets, restaurants, etc to create a pleasant atmosphere.

ambiguity *n* (*pl* **-ies**) **1** an ambiguous or imprecise word or expression. **2** uncertainty of meaning or significance.

ambiguous *adj* **1** capable of more than one interpretation. **2** vague, indistinct, or difficult to classify. ➤➤ **ambiguously** *adv*, **ambiguousness** *n*.

ambit *n* **1** a limiting range or distance. **2** the bounds or limits of a place. **3** a sphere of influence; a scope.

ambition *n* **1** a strong drive to attain status, wealth, or power. **2** a strong wish to achieve an objective.

ambitious *adj* **1** acting from or motivated by ambition. **2** showing ambition; advanced and difficult to achieve. ➤➤ **ambitiously** *adv*, **ambitiousness** *n*.

ambivalence *n* **1** the state of having two opposing and contradictory attitudes or feelings towards an object, person, etc. **2** uncertainty or indecisiveness in making a choice. ➤➤ **ambivalent** *adj*, **ambivalently** *adv*.

amble[1] *v* to move at a leisurely pace. ➤➤ **ambler** *n*.

amble[2] *n* a leisurely stroll.

ambrosia *n* **1** the food of the Greek and Roman gods. **2** something extremely pleasing to eat or smell. ➤➤ **ambrosial** *adj*.

ambulance *n* a vehicle equipped for transporting injured or sick people to and from hospital.

ambulance chaser *n chiefly NAm, informal* a lawyer who specializes in cases that involve suing for damages on behalf of people who have suffered personal injuries.

ambulant *adj formal* said of a patient: not confined to bed; able to walk.

ambulatory[1] *adj* **1** relating to or adapted for walking. **2** moving or movable from place to place; not fixed. **3** = AMBULANT.

ambulatory[2] *n* (*pl* **-ies**) a sheltered place for walking, *esp* a passage at the east end of a church.

ambuscade *n* an ambush.

ambush[1] *v* to attack from a hidden position.

ambush[2] *n* **1** the concealment of a military force or other group in order to carry out a surprise attack from a hidden position. **2** a surprise attack carried out by such a force.

ameliorate *v formal* to make or become better or more tolerable. ➤➤ **amelioration** *n*, **ameliorative** *adj*, **ameliorator** *n*.

amen *interj* used at the end of a prayer or to express a solemn avowal or a strong approval.

amenable *adj* **1** easily persuaded to yield or agree. **2** liable to be made to account for one's behaviour; answerable. **3** capable of being judged or tested. ➤➤ **amenability** *n*, **amenably** *adv*.

amend *v* **1** to make corrections to (e.g. a text). **2** to revise (a law, etc). ➤➤ **amendable** *adj*.

Usage note

amend *or* emend? To *amend* is a general word meaning to 'correct and improve': *She did her best to amend her behaviour. Emend* has a more limited use. It is used exclusively in relation to texts and means 'to remove errors or irregularities from'.

amendment *n* an alteration or addition proposed or effected by amending.

amends ✱ **make amends** to compensate for a loss or injury.

amenity *n* (*pl* **-ies**) (*usu in pl*) something, e.g. a public facility, that provides or enhances material comfort.

amenorrhoea (*NAm* **amenorrhea**) *n* abnormal absence of menstruation.

Amerasian *n* a person of mixed American and Asian parentage. ➤➤ **Amerasian** *adj.*

American *n* **1** a native or inhabitant of N, S or Central America. **2** a native or inhabitant of the USA. **3** the form of English used in the USA. ➤➤ **American** *adj.*

Americana *pl n* artefacts or ideas associated with the USA.

American Dream *n* (**the American Dream**) the ideals of democracy, freedom, and equality on which the USA was founded.

American Football *n* a football game played with an oval ball between teams of eleven players, involving kicking and running with the ball and forward passing.

American Indian *n dated* a member of any of the indigenous peoples of S or Central America.

Usage note

American Indian has been largely replaced by *Native American* as the preferred general name for a member of one of the indigenous peoples of, especially, North America. See also note at NATIVE AMERICAN.

Americanise *v* see AMERICANIZE.

Americanism *n* **1** a custom, belief, word, etc characteristic of the USA or of its citizens, culture, or language. **2** adherence or attachment to the USA and its culture.

Americanize *or* **-ise** *v* **1** to make (a country or people) conform to American customs or institutions. **2** to become American in character.

americium *n* a radioactive metallic chemical element produced by bombarding plutonium with neutrons.

Amerindian *n chiefly NAm* = NATIVE AMERICAN. ➤➤ **Amerind** *n*, **Amerindian** *adj.*

amethyst *n* a clear purple or violet variety of quartz that is much used as a gemstone.

Amharic *n* the Semitic language of the people of Ethiopia. ➤➤ **Amharic** *adj.*

amiable *adj* friendly and pleasant. ➤➤ **amiability** *n*, **amiably** *adv.*

amicable *adj* characterized by friendly goodwill; peaceable. ➤➤ **amicably** *adv.*

amice *n* a vestment made of an oblong piece of white cloth, worn by a priest round the neck and shoulders.

amid *prep formal* in or to the middle of (something); among (it).

amide *n* an organic compound containing the $-CONH_2$ group. Amides are white crystalline solids.

amidships *adv and adj* in or towards the part of a ship midway between the bow and the stern.

amidst *prep literary* = AMID.

amigo /ə'meegoh/ *n* (*pl* **-os**) *chiefly NAm, informal* a friend, *esp* in Spanish-speaking communities.

amine *n* a chemical compound that is a base derived from ammonia by replacement of hydrogen by one or more carbon- and hydrogen-containing groups with a valency of one.

amino acid *n* an organic acid containing the amino group NH_2 and a carboxyl group, *esp* any of the amino acids that are the chief components of proteins and are synthesized by living cells or are obtained as essential components of the diet.

amir *n* see EMIR.

Amish *pl n* the members of a strict Mennonite sect established in America in the 18th cent. ➤➤ **Amish** *adj.*

amiss *adv and adj* wrong; not in order. ✱ **not come/go amiss** to be apt or appropriate. **take it/something amiss** to be offended or upset by something.

amity *n* (*pl* **-ies**) friendship, *esp* friendly relations between nations.

ammeter *n* an instrument for measuring electric current in amperes.

ammo *n informal* ammunition.

ammonia *n* **1** a pungent colourless gas that is a chemical compound of nitrogen and hydrogen, is very soluble in water, forming an alkaline solution, and is used in the manufacture *esp* of fertilizers, synthetic fibres, and explosives. **2** a solution of ammonia in water used *esp* as a cleaning fluid. ➤➤ **ammoniacal** *adj.*

ammonite *n* **1** an extinct marine mollusc that was common during the Mesozoic era. **2** a flat spirally-coiled shell of one of these molluscs.

ammonium *n* an ion, NH_4^+, or chemical group, NH_4, derived from ammonia by combination with a hydrogen ion or atom.

ammunition *n* **1** projectiles that can be fired from a weapon, e.g. bullets or shells, or a collection or supply of these. **2** material used to defend or attack a point of view.

amnesia *n* loss of memory, often due to brain injury. ➤➤ **amnesiac** *adj and n*, **amnesic** *adj and n.*

amnesty[1] *n* (*pl* **-ies**) **1** a pardon granted to a large group of individuals, *esp* for political offences. **2** a suspension of a law for a fixed period during which no official action will be taken against people who admit to having broken the law, provided they satisfy certain conditions.

amnesty[2] *v* (**-ies, -ied**) to grant (somebody) an amnesty.

amnia *n* pl of AMNION.

amniocentesis *n* (*pl* **amniocenteses**) the insertion of a hollow needle into the uterus of a pregnant female, *esp* to obtain amniotic fluid from which various abnormalities in the developing foetus can be detected.

amnion *n* (*pl* **amnions** *or* **amnia**) a thin membrane forming a closed sac around the embryos of reptiles, birds, and mammals. ➤➤ **amniotic** *adj.*

amniotic fluid *n* the fluid surrounding the foetus in the uterus.

amoeba (*NAm* **ameba**) *n* (*pl* **amoebas** *or* **amoebae**, *NAm* **amebas** *or* **amebae**) a protozoan that has temporary finger-like extensions of protoplasm with which it feeds and moves, and is widely distributed in water and wet places. ➤➤ **amoebic** *adj*, **amoeboid** *adj.*

amok *or* **amuck** *adv* in a frenzied or confused state. ✱ **run amok 1** to rush about in a wild frenzy. **2** to get completely out of control.

among *or* **amongst** *prep* **1** in or through the midst of; surrounded by. **2** in company or association with. **3** by or through the whole group of. **4** in the number or class of. **5** used with more than two things or people: in shares to each of; between.

amontillado /ə,monti'lahdoh/ *n* (*pl* **-os**) a pale fairly dry sherry.

amoral *adj* **1** lying outside the sphere of moral principles or ethical judgments: compare IMMORAL. **2** of a person: having no understanding of or concern with morals. ➤➤ **amoralist** *n*, **amorality** *n.*

Usage note

amoral *or* **immoral**? An *immoral* person is one who breaks accepted standards of right and wrong. To be *amoral* means that one rejects the whole concept of morality or does not know or cannot know right from wrong.

amorous *adj* **1** of or relating to love. **2** moved by, inclined to, or indicative of love or desire. ➤➤ **amorously** *adv*, **amorousness** *n*.

amorphous *adj* **1** having no definite form; shapeless. **2** of rocks, etc: not crystalline.

amortize *or* **-ise** *v* **1** to pay off (e.g. a mortgage, debt, etc) gradually, usu by periodic instalments or contributions to a sinking fund. **2** to write off the initial cost of (an asset, *esp* in business) over an agreed period. ➤➤ **amortization** *n*.

amount[1] *v* **1** to be equal in number or quantity to. **2** to be equivalent in significance to.

amount[2] *n* **1** a collection of something considered as a unit; a quantity. **2** the total of two or more quantities.

amour /ə'maw, ə'mooə/ *n* a love affair, *esp* an illicit one.

amour propre /'proprə/ *n* self-esteem.

amp *n* **1** = AMPERE. **2** = AMPLIFIER (2).

amperage *n* the strength of an electric current expressed in amperes.

ampere /'ampeə/ *n* the basic SI unit of electric current.

ampersand *n* a sign (&) standing for the word *and*.

amphetamine *n* a synthetic drug that is a powerful stimulant of the central nervous system and that can be strongly addictive if abused.

amphibian *n* (*pl* **amphibians** *or* **amphibia**) **1** a frog, toad, newt, or other member of a class of cold-blooded vertebrates intermediate in many characteristics between fishes and reptiles and having gilled aquatic larvae and air-breathing adults. **2** an aeroplane, tank, etc adapted to operate on both land and water.

amphibious *adj* **1** able to live both on land and in water. **2** involving or trained for coordinated action of land, sea, and air forces organized for invasion. ➤➤ **amphibiously** *adv*.

amphibole *n* a silicate mineral, e.g. hornblende, that is an important constituent of many rocks.

amphitheatre (*NAm* **amphitheater**) *n* **1** an oval or circular building with rising tiers of seats ranged about an arena and used in ancient Greece and Rome, *esp* for contests and public spectacles. **2** a semicircular gallery in a theatre.

amphora *n* (*pl* **amphorae** *or* **amphoras**) a two-handled oval jar or vase with a narrow neck and base, orig used by the ancient Greeks and Romans for holding oil or wine: compare AMPULLA.

ample *adj* (**ampler, amplest**) **1** enough or more than enough. **2** fairly large or extensive.

amplifier *n* **1** an electronic device that makes sounds louder. **2** an electronic device used to increase voltage, current, or power.

amplify *v* (**-ies, -ied**) **1** to increase the volume of (sound) using an amplifier. **2** to increase the magnitude of (an electronical signal or other input of power). **3** to expand (e.g. a statement) or make it clearer by the use of detail, illustration, etc. ➤➤ **amplification** *n*.

amplitude *n* **1** largeness of dimensions or scope; abundance. **2** the extent of a vibration or oscillation measured from the average position to a maximum.

amplitude modulation *n* **1** a modulation of the amplitude of a wave, *esp* a radio carrier wave, by the characteristics of the signal carried. **2** a method of transmitting using this: compare FREQUENCY MODULATION, PHASE MODULATION.

amply *adv* generously; more than adequately.

ampoule (*NAm* **ampul** *or* **ampule**) *n* a sealed small bulbous glass vessel that is used to hold a sterile solution for hypodermic injection.

ampulla *n* (*pl* **ampullae**) **1** a bottle for consecrated oil, wine, etc. **2** a two-handled globular flask of glass or earthenware used *esp* by the ancient Romans to hold ointment, perfume, or wine: compare AMPHORA.

amputate *v* to remove (all or part of a limb) surgically. ➤➤ **amputation** *n*.

amputee *n* somebody who has had all or part of a limb amputated.

amuck *adv* see AMOK.

amulet *n* a natural object or a made ornament, item of jewellery, etc, often inscribed with a magic incantation or symbol, that is believed to bring a person good luck, protect them against evil, etc.

amuse *v* **1** to appeal to the sense of humour of. **2** to do something to entertain or interest. ➤➤ **amused** *adj*.

amusement *n* **1** the act or an instance of amusing, or the state of being amused. **2** a means of entertaining or occupying somebody; a pleasurable diversion. **3** a mechanical device or stall for entertainment at a fair, e.g. a roundabout or coconut shy.

amusement arcade *n chiefly Brit* a covered area with coin-operated games machines for recreation.

amusing *adj* entertaining, *esp* in way that makes one laugh; comical; funny. ➤➤ **amusingly** *adv*.

amyl *n* the former name for the pentyl group C_5H_{11}, derived from pentane by the removal of a hydrogen atom.

amylase *n* an enzyme that accelerates the breakdown of starch and glycogen, or their products, into simple sugars.

amyl nitrite *n* a yellowish liquid used as a treatment for angina and sometimes inhaled as a recreational drug.

an *indefinite article* used in place of *a* (see A[1]) before words with an initial vowel sound.

Usage note

an *or* a? See note at A[1].

an- *prefix* see A-[2], ANA-.

-an[1] *or* **-ean** *or* **-ian** *suffix* forming nouns, denoting: **1** somebody who comes from, belongs to, supports, etc a specified place, thing, or person: *Mancunian; republican*. **2** somebody skilled in or specializing in the subject specified: *phonetician*.

-an[2] *or* **-ean** *or* **-ian** *suffix* forming adjectives, with the meanings: **1** of or belonging to: *American; Christian*. **2** characteristic of; resembling: *Shavian*.

-an[3] *suffix* forming nouns, denoting: **1** an unsaturated carbon compound: *furan*. **2** a polymeric anhydride of the carbohydrate specified: *dextran*.

ana- *or* **an-** *prefix* **1** up or upwards: *anabasis*. **2** back or backwards: *anapaest*. **3** again: *anabaptism*.

-ana *or* **-iana** *suffix* forming pl ns, denoting: collected objects or information relating to or characteristic of the topic, period, place, or individual specified: *Victoriana*.

Anabaptism *n* the Anabaptist movement or its doctrine or practices.

Anabaptist *n* a member of a Protestant movement that was established in Zurich in 1524. Its chief distinguishing feature was its insistence on baptism or rebaptism of adult believers. ➤➤ **Anabaptist** *adj*.

anabolic steroid *n* a synthetic steroid hormone that causes a rapid increase in the size and weight of skeletal muscle; they are used legitimately in medicine and illegally to enhance the performance of athletes.

anabolism *n* an organism's synthesizing of proteins, fats, and other complex molecules from simpler molecules, with the accompanying storage of energy: compare CATABOLISM. ⋙ **anabolic** *adj.*

anachronism *n* **1** an error in chronology, *esp* the placing of people, events, objects, or customs in a period to which they do not in fact belong. **2** somebody or something that is chronologically out of place. ⋙ **anachronistic** *adj*, **anachronistically** *adv.*

anaconda *n* a large semiaquatic S American snake of the boa family that crushes its prey in its coils.

anaemia (*NAm* **anemia**) *n* a condition in which the blood is deficient in red blood cells, haemoglobin, or total volume, which results in pallor and a lack of energy.

anaemic (*NAm* **anemic**) *adj* **1** suffering from anaemia. **2** with an unhealthily pale complexion.

anaerobic *adj* living, active, or occurring in the absence of oxygen. ⋙ **anaerobically** *adv.*

anaesthesia (*NAm* **anesthesia**) *n* loss of sensation of pain, *esp* induced artificially, e.g. through the injection of drugs or the inhalation of gases.

anaesthesiology (*NAm* **anesthesiology**) *n* *chiefly NAm* = ANAESTHETICS. ⋙ **anaes-thesiologist** *n.*

anaesthetic[1] (*NAm* **anesthetic**) *n* a substance that produces anaesthesia, *esp* a drug or gas administered so that surgery can be carried out painlessly.

anaesthetic[2] (*NAm* **anesthetic**) *adj* of or capable of producing anaesthesia.

anaesthetics *pl n Brit* (*used as sing.*) the branch of medical science dealing with anaesthesia and anaesthetic substances.

anaesthetise *v* see ANAESTHETIZE.

anaesthetist (*NAm* **anesthetist**) *n* a doctor or other qualified person, who is specially trained in administering anaesthetics.

anaesthetize *or* **-ise** (*NAm* **anesthetize**) *v* to administer an anaesthetic to. ⋙ **anaesthetization** *n.*

anagram *n* a word or phrase made by rearranging the letters of another, e.g. *ladies* is an anagram of *ideals*.

anal *adj* **1** relating to or in the region of the anus. **2** in psychoanalysis, relating to or deriving from the stage of psychosexual development during which the child is *esp* concerned with its anal region and faeces, such fixation being linked to personality traits that include fussiness, etc: compare GENITAL, ORAL[1]; see ANAL RETENTIVE. ⋙ **anally** *adv.*

analeptic[1] *adj* of a medicine: stimulating the central nervous system; restorative.

analeptic[2] *n* an analeptic medicine.

analgesia *n* insensibility to pain without loss of consciousness.

analgesic[1] *n* a drug that relieves pain; a painkiller.

analgesic[2] *adj* relieving pain; painkilling.

analog *adj* **1** of a computer, etc: using data supplied in a stream of numbers represented by directly measurable quantities, e.g. voltages or mechanical rotations: compare DIGITAL. **2** of a clock or watch, etc: using a pointer or hands to indicate e.g. time rather than having an electronic display of numbers: compare DIGITAL. **3** of a way of recording sound: converting sound waves into a continuous electrical wave form: compare DIGITAL.

analogical *adj* **1** of or based on analogy. **2** expressing or implying an analogy.

analogous *adj* **1** (*often* + to/with) similar in some respects. **2** of plant or animal parts: similar in function but having evolved separately and distinctly. The wings of insects and the wings of birds are analogous structures. ⋙ **analogously** *adv.*

analogue[1] (*NAm* **analog**) *n* **1** something that is analogous or parallel to something else. **2** an organ or body part similar in function to that of another animal or plant but different in structure and origin: compare HOMOLOGUE.

analogue[2] *adj* = ANALOG.

analogy *n* (*pl* **-ies**) **1a** an explanation or illustration of something that uses a comparison with something similar. **b** (*often* + between) comparison for the purposes of explanation or illustration. **2** resemblance in some respects; similarity. ⋙ **analogical** *adj.*

anal retentive *n* in psychoanalysis, a person who has personality traits, such as fussiness, meanness with money, and obstinacy, considered to originate in habits or values associated with the anal stage of psychosexual development. ⋙ **anal-retentive** *adj.*

analysand *n* a person who is undergoing psychoanalysis.

analyse (*NAm* **analyze**) *v* **1** to make a close examination of (something) in order to determine its nature, content, or structure. **2** = PSYCHOANALYSE. ⋙ **analysable** *adj*, **analyser** *n.*

analysis *n* (*pl* **analyses**) **1** the examination and identification of the constituents of a complex whole and their relationship to one another. **2** the act or process of breaking something up into its constituent elements: compare SYNTHESIS. **3** = PSYCHOANALYSIS.

analyst *n* **1** a person who analyses or is skilled in analysis. **2** a psychoanalyst.

analytical *or* **analytic** *adj* **1** relating to or produced by analysis. **2** skilled in or using analysis, *esp* in reasoning. ⋙ **analytically** *adv.*

anamnesis *n* (*pl* **anamneses**) in psychology and psychoanalysis, the recalling to mind of past events and experiences.

anamorphic *adj* of a lens or the image produced by it: producing or having a different image magnification in each of two perpendicular directions, thereby either compressing wide-screen gauge to fit 35mm film or expanding 35mm film to fill a wide screen. ⋙ **anamorphosis** *n.*

anaphora *n* **1** the use of a grammatical substitute, e.g. a pronoun, to refer to a preceding word or phrase, e.g. the word *it* in the sentence *She bought some salmon because it was specially reduced.* **2** in rhetoric, the repetition of a word or phrase at the beginning of successive clauses, *esp* for effect. ⋙ **anaphoric** *adj.*

anaphylactic *adj* of or causing anaphylaxis.

anaphylactic shock *n* = ANAPHYLAXIS.

anaphylaxis *n* (*pl* **anaphylaxes**) a sometimes fatal reaction to drugs, insect venom, etc caused by hypersensitivity resulting from earlier contact.

anarchic *or* **anarchical** *adj* **1** advocating anarchy or likely to bring about anarchy. **2** not adhering to conventions or expectations. ⋙ **anarchically** *adv.*

anarchism *n* a political theory holding that all forms of governmental authority are undesirable and advocating a society based on voluntary cooperation.

anarchist *n* **1** somebody who attacks the established social order or laws; a revolutionary. **2** a believer in or promoter of anarchism, often one who favours overthrowing the established social order by violent means. ⋙ **anarchist** *adj,* **anarchistic** *adj.*

anarchy *n* **1a** absence of government. **b** a state of lawlessness or political disorder owing to the absence of governmental authority. **c** a utopian society with complete freedom and no government. **2** any state of confusion or chaos.

Anasazi *n* (*pl* **Anasazis** *or* **Anasazi**) a member of an ancient Native American people of Arizona, Colorado, New Mexico, and Utah.

anastomosis *n* (*pl* **anastomoses**) the interconnecting of parts or branches of streams, leaf veins, blood vessels, etc.

anathema *n* **1** somebody or something despised or unacceptable. **2** a ban or curse solemnly pronounced by ecclesiastical authority and accompanied by excommunication, or the person or thing that is the object of such a ban or curse.

anathematize *or* **-ise** *v* **1** to curse (somebody or something). **2** to proclaim an anathema on.

Anatolian *n* a native or inhabitant of Anatolia. ⋙ **Anatolian** *adj.*

anatomise *v* see ANATOMIZE.

anatomize *or* **-ise** *v* **1** to dissect (a corpse). **2** to analyse minutely and *esp* critically.

anatomy *n* (*pl* **-ies**) **1a** the branch of biology or medicine that deals with the structure of people, animals, and plants. **b** the art or practice of separating the parts of people, animals, and plants in order to ascertain their position, relations, structure, and function; dissection. **2** structural make-up, *esp* of an organism or part of it. **3** a detailed analysis of any kind. ⋙ **anatomical** *adj,* **anatomically** *adv,* **anatomist** *n.*

ANC *abbr* African National Congress.

-ance *suffix* forming nouns, denoting: **1** an action or process: *furtherance.* **2** an instance of a specified action or process: *performance.* **3** a quality or state: *brilliance.* **4** an instance of a specified quality or state: *protuberance.*

ancestor *n* **1** somebody from whom a person is descended, usu more distant than a grandparent. **2** an animal or plant from which a more recent species has evolved. **3** a device or type of technology from which something else develops or is developed. ⋙ **ancestress** *n.*

ancestral *adj* of or inherited from an ancestor. ⋙ **ancestrally** *adv.*

ancestry *n* (*pl* **-ies**) **1** a line of *esp* noble descent; a lineage. **2** (*used as sing. or pl*) one's ancestors as a group.

anchor[1] *n* a device dropped from a ship or boat to hold it in a particular place, typically a large metal hook that digs into the seabed.

anchor[2] *v* **1** to hold (a boat or ship) in place in the water by means of an anchor. **2** to secure firmly in place.

anchorage *n* **1** a place where boats and ships are anchored or can anchor. **2** the act or an instance of anchoring a boat or ship, or a charge for this.

anchorite *n* somebody who lives in seclusion, usu for religious reasons; a hermit.

anchorman *or* **anchorwoman** *n* (*pl* **anchormen** *or* **anchorwomen**) in television and radio broadcasting, a man or woman who links up with outside reporters from a central studio.

anchovy *n* (*pl* **anchovies** *or* **anchovy**) a common small fish that resembles a herring and is often used as a garnish.

ancien régime /,onsi·an ray'zheem/ *n* (*pl* **anciens régimes**) **1** the political and social system of France before the Revolution of 1789. **2** any system or arrangement which has been superseded.

ancient[1] *adj* **1** having existed for many years. **2** belonging to a remote period of history, *esp* from the time of the earliest known civilizations to the fall of the western Roman Empire in AD 476. **3** *informal* very old or old-fashioned. ⋙ **anciently** *adv.*

ancient[2] *n* **1** (**the ancients**) members of an ancient civilization, *esp* the ancient Greeks and Romans. **2** *archaic* an old person.

ancient lights *pl n* (*used as sing.*) a legally enforceable right to unobstructed daylight from an opening, e.g. a window, in a building.

Ancient of Days *n* (**the Ancient of Days**) a title given in the Bible to God: Daniel 7:9.

ancillary *adj* **1** giving support; auxiliary. **2** having a less important position or role; subordinate.

-ancy *suffix* forming nouns, denoting: a quality or state: *piquancy; expectancy.*

and *conj* **1** used to join coordinate sentence elements of the same class or function expressing addition or combination. **2a** used, *esp* in British English, before the numbers 1 to 99 after the numbers 100, 200, 300, etc. **b** plus. **3a** used to introduce a second clause expressing a sequence in time. **b** used to express consequence. **c** used to express contrast. **d** used to express supplementary explanation. **4** used to join repeated words expressing continuation or progression. **5** *informal* used instead of *to* after *come, go, run, try,* and *stop.*

-and *suffix* forming nouns, denoting: a person or thing treated in the way specified: *multiplicand.*

Andalusian *n* a native or inhabitant of Andalusia. ⋙ **Andalusian** *adj.*

andante *adj and adv* of a piece of music: to be performed moderately slowly. ⋙ **andante** *n.*

Andean *n* a native or inhabitant of the region of the Andes, a mountain range in S America. ⋙ **Andean** *adj.*

andiron *n* either of a pair of metal stands used on a hearth to support burning wood.

Andorran *n* a native or inhabitant of Andorra. ⋙ **Andorran** *adj.*

androgen *n* a hormone, such as testosterone, that influences the development of the male reproductive system.

androgyne *n* = HERMAPHRODITE.

androgynous *adj* **1** combining features that are typically male with features that are typically female and therefore of uncertain sex. **2** having characteristics of both the male and female forms; hermaphrodite. ⋙ **androgyny** *n.*

android *n* in science fiction, an automaton that looks and behaves like a human.

-ane *suffix* forming nouns, denoting: a saturated carbon compound: *methane.*

anecdotage *n* **1** anecdotes in general. **2** *humorous* old age accompanied by a tendency to tell too many stories.

anecdotal *adj* **1** existing in the form of an anecdote, *esp* as distinct from corroborated evidence or proof. **2** containing anecdotes or depicting an anecdote. ⋙ **anecdotally** *adv.*

anecdote *n* a usu short account of an interesting or amusing incident. ⋙ **anecdotalist** *n.*

anechoic *adj technical* free from echoes and reverberations.

anemometer *n* an instrument for measuring the force or speed of the wind.

anemone *n* **1** a plant of the buttercup family with divided leaves and brightly coloured flowers. **2** = SEA ANEMONE.

aneroid *adj* containing no liquid or operated without the use of liquid.

aneroid barometer *n* a barometer in which the action of atmospheric pressure in compressing an evacuated metal capsule is made to move a pointer.

aneurysm *or* **aneurism** *n* a permanent blood-filled swelling of a diseased blood vessel. ➤➤ **aneurysmal** *adj.*

anew *adv chiefly literary* **1** one more time; again. **2** in a new form or way.

angel *n* **1a** a spiritual being, usu depicted with wings, serving as God's intermediary or acting as a heavenly worshipper. **b** a representation of an angel as a human being with wings. **2** a very kind or loving person or a well-behaved child. **3** *informal* a financial backer of a theatrical venture or other enterprise. **4** a former English gold coin portraying St Michael killing a dragon.

angel cake (*NAm* **angel food cake**) *n* a pale very light sponge cake.

angel dust *n informal* the drug phencyclidine.

Angeleno *n* (*pl* **Angelenos**) a native or inhabitant of Los Angeles.

angelfish *n* (*pl* **angelfishes** *or* **angelfish**) a brightly coloured bony fish of warm seas that has a body that is narrow from side to side and deep from top to bottom.

angelic *adj* **1** of angels. **2** very pretty, kind, or well-behaved. ➤➤ **angelically** *adv.*

angelica *n* a plant related to the carrot and parsley, the candied stalks of which are used as a decoration on cakes and desserts.

Angelus *n* **1** a Roman Catholic devotion said at morning, noon, and evening to commemorate the Incarnation. **2** a bell rung to mark the time for saying the prayer.

anger[1] *n* a strong feeling of displeasure aroused by real or imagined offence or injustice and usu accompanied by the desire to retaliate.

anger[2] *v* to make or become angry.

angina *n* a disease marked by spasmodic attacks of intense chest pain.

angina pectoris *n* brief attacks of intense chest pain, *esp* on exertion, caused by deficient oxygenation of the heart muscles.

angiogram *n* an X-ray photograph of blood vessels.

angiography *n* **1** a technique for imaging blood and lymph vessels using an X-ray examination after a contrast medium that is opaque to radiation has been introduced. **2** an examination of this kind. ➤➤ **angiographic** *adj.*

angioplasty *n* (*pl* **-ies**) surgical repair of a blood vessel, *esp* the unblocking or widening of a blocked or narrowed artery, e.g. by means of a tiny balloon inflated inside the artery.

angiosperm *n* any of a large group of plants, including herbaceous plants, shrubs, grasses, and some trees, that produce flowers and reproduce by means of seeds enclosed within a carpel: compare GYMNOSPERM.

Angle *n* a member of a Germanic people who, along with the Saxons and Jutes, invaded England during the fifth cent. AD and settled there, mainly in northern and eastern parts of the country.

angle[1] *n* **1a** a geometric figure or space formed by two lines extending from the same point or by two surfaces diverging from the same line. **b** a measure of the inclination of two lines or surfaces that form an angle, expressed in degrees, minutes, and seconds. **2** a corner. **3a** a precise viewpoint from which something is observed, photographed, filmed, or considered; an aspect. **b** a special approach or technique for accomplishing an objective. ➤➤ **angled** *adj.*

angle[2] *v* **1a** to place, move, or direct in a sloping or slanting position. **b** to bend or shape into an angle. **2** to present (e.g. a news story) from a particular or prejudiced point of view; to slant. **3** to turn or proceed at an angle.

angle[3] *v* **1** to fish with a hook and line. **2** (*usu* + for) to use clever or devious means to attain or try to attain an objective, *esp* by making known indirectly or subtly what one wants. ➤➤ **angler** *n,* **angling** *n.*

angle bracket *n* **1** either of a pair of punctuation marks (<>) used to enclose text. Also called BRACKET[1] (I). **2** a metal bracket with arms set at right angles, used to support shelving, etc.

angle iron *n* a rolled steel structural member with an L-shaped cross-section.

angle of incidence *n* the angle between the direction of a moving body or ray of light where it meets a surface, and a perpendicular at that point.

anglepoise *n trademark* a lamp with a jointed support that can be moved into various positions.

anglerfish *n* (*pl* **anglerfishes** *or* **anglerfish**) a marine fish with a large flat head and wide mouth with a lure on the head that is used to attract smaller fishes.

Anglican[1] *adj* relating to the established episcopal Church of England and Churches of similar faith in communion with it. ➤➤ **Anglicanism** *n.*

Anglican[2] *n* a member of the Anglican Church.

anglicise *v* see ANGLICIZE.

Anglicism *n* **1** a characteristic feature of English occurring in another language. **2** adherence or attachment to England, English culture, etc. **3** the fact or quality of being English, *esp* typically so.

anglicize *or* **-ise** *v* **1** to make English in tastes or characteristics. **2** to adapt (a foreign word or phrase) to English usage. ➤➤ **anglicization** *n.*

Anglo- *comb. form* **1** English or British nation, people, or culture: *Anglophobia.* **2** English or British and: *Anglo-Irish.*

Anglo-Catholic *adj* relating to or denoting a High Church movement in Anglicanism fostering Catholic traditions of belief and forms of worship. ➤➤ **Anglo-Catholic** *n,* **Anglo-Catholicism** *n.*

Anglocentric *adj* based on or concentrating on England or Britain.

Anglo-Indian[1] *n* **1** a British person who lived for a long time in India, *esp* during the time when India was part of the British Empire. **2** a Eurasian of mixed British and Indian birth or descent.

Anglo-Indian[2] *adj* **1** relating to or denoting relations between Britain and India, *esp* during the period when India was a British colony. **2** relating to or denoting Anglo-Indians.

Anglo-Irish *adj* **1** relating to or denoting relations between Britain and Ireland. **2** relating to or denoting the English Protestant settlers in Ireland or their descendants. **3** of mixed English and Irish birth or descent.

Anglophile *n* somebody who is greatly interested in and admires England or Britain. ➤➤ **Anglophilia** *n.*

Anglophone *adj* consisting of, belonging, or relating to an English-speaking population or community.

Anglo-Saxon *n* **1** a member of the Germanic peoples who conquered England in the fifth cent. AD and formed the ruling group until the Norman conquest in 1066. **2** = OLD ENGLISH. **3** loosely, a white person of English or British descent or whose first language is English. **4** *informal* direct or indecent English speech or writing.

Angolan *n* a native or inhabitant of Angola. ➤➤ **Angolan** *adj.*

angora *n* **1** a cat, goat, or rabbit of a long-haired domestic breed. **2** a fabric or yarn made of Angora rabbit or goat hair.

angostura bark *n* the aromatic bitter bark of a S American tree of the rue family used as a flavouring.

Angostura bitters *n trademark* a bitter aromatic tonic added to alcoholic drinks as a flavouring.

angry *adj* (**-ier, -iest**) **1a** feeling or showing anger. **b** caused by or expressing anger. **2** painfully inflamed. ➤➤ **angrily** *adv.*

angst *n* anxiety and anguish, caused *esp* by considering the state of the world and the human condition.

angstrom *or* **ångström** *n* a unit of length equal to 10^{-10}m, used *esp* in measuring electromagnetic radiation wavelength.

anguish *n* extreme mental distress or physical pain.

anguished *adj* suffering or expressing anguish.

angular *adj* **1a** having one or more angles. **b** forming an angle; sharp-cornered. **c** placed, attached, etc at an angle. **2** measured by an angle or with reference to the rate at which an angle changes. **3** lean and bony. ➤➤ **angularity** *n,* **angularly** *adv.*

anhydrous *adj* containing no water.

aniline *n* a poisonous, colourless, oily liquid derived from coal tar and used chiefly in the manufacture of dyes and plastics.

anima *n* **1** an individual's true inner self: compare PERSONA. **2** in Jungian psychology, the inner feminine part of the male personality: compare ANIMUS.

animadvert *v formal* to comment, *esp* critically or adversely, on something. ➤➤ **animadversion** *n.*

animal *n* **1a** a living creature, typically differing from a plant in its capacity for spontaneous movement, and rapid response to stimulation. **b** any living creature apart from a human being. **c** a mammal, or a mammal or reptile, as opposed to a bird, fish, etc. **2a** a person considered as a purely physical being; a creature. **b** a coarse, unfeeling, or cruel person. **3** *informal* a person or thing of a particular kind.

animalcule *n* a minute usu microscopic organism, e.g. an amoeba.

animalism *n* **1** behaviour that demonstrates qualities thought to be typical of animals, *esp* lack of spiritual feeling. **2** preoccupation with the satisfaction of physical needs and urges; sensuality. ➤➤ **animalist** *n,* **animalistic** *adj.*

animality *n* **1** behaviour typical of animals. **2** behaviour in or characteristics of humans thought to be more typical of animals, e.g. a lack of spiritual feeling or rational thought.

animal liberation *n* the unauthorized freeing of animals from captivity by people who believe that animals should not be exploited by humans under any circumstances.

animal magnetism *n* **1** powerful physical charm or sexual attractiveness. **2** *dated* a force that some individuals are said to possess and by which a strong hypnotic influence can be exerted.

animate[1] *v* **1** to make lively and interesting. **2** to create or film using the techniques of animation. **3** to give life to. ➤➤ **animator** *n.*

animate[2] *adj* possessing life; alive.

animated *adj* **1** full of vigour and spirit; vivacious. **2** made using the techniques of animation, or appearing to move via these techniques. ➤➤ **animatedly** *adv.*

animation *n* **1** the state of being lively and full of energy and activity. **2** the technique of filming a sequence of drawings, computer images, or models in different positions so that, in the final film, the characters and other elements in them appear to be moving in a lifelike way.

animatronics *pl n* (*used as sing.*) a branch of theatre and film technology that combines the techniques of traditional puppetry with modern electronics to create animated special effects. ➤➤ **animatronic** *adj.*

anime /'ahneemay/ *n* a type of animation, orig from Japan, that deals with fantasy relating to the possibilities of modern technology.

animism *n* attribution of conscious life, spirits, or souls to nature or natural objects or phenomena. ➤➤ **animist** *n,* **animistic** *adj.*

animosity *n* (*pl* **-ies**) a strong feeling of hostility or resentment.

animus *n* **1** ill will or hostility; animosity. **2** in Jungian psychology, the inner masculine part of the female personality: compare ANIMA.

anion *n* a negatively charged ion, that moves towards the anode during electrolysis: compare CATION. ➤➤ **anionic** *adj.*

anise *n* a plant of the carrot family with aromatic seeds that have a liquorice-like flavour.

aniseed *n* the seed of anise used as a flavouring in food and drinks.

ankh *n* a cross that has a loop for its upper vertical arm, used in ancient Egypt as an emblem of life.

ankle *n* **1** the joint between the foot and the leg. **2** the part of the leg between the lower calf and this joint.

anklet *n* an ornamental band or chain worn round the ankle.

ankylosaur *n* a herbivorous dinosaur of the Cretaceous period with short legs and a heavy body covered in armoured plates.

ankylosis *n* (*pl* **ankyloses**) the fusing of the bones in a joint resulting in a stiff or immovable joint.

anna *n* a former money unit of India, Pakistan, Bangladesh, and Myanmar, worth one sixteenth of a rupee.

annalist *n* a writer of annals; a historian.

annals *pl n* **1** a record of events, activities, etc, arranged in yearly sequence. **2** historical records; chronicles. **3** records of the activities of an organization, e.g. a learned society.

annatto *n* (*pl* **-os**) a yellowish red dye made from the pulp that surrounds the seeds of a tropical tree.

anneal *v* to toughen or relieve internal stresses in (steel, glass, etc) by heating and usu gradual cooling.

annelid *n* an earthworm or leech that has a long segmented body.

annex[1] *v* **1** to add as an extra part; to append. **2** to incorporate (a country or other territory) within the domain of a state. ➤➤ **annexation** *n.*

annex[2] *or* **annexe** *n* **1** a separate or attached extra structure, *esp* a building providing extra accommodation. **2** something added as an extra part, *esp* an addition to a document.

annihilate *v* **1** to destroy entirely. **2** *informal* to defeat conclusively; to rout or thrash. ➤➤ **annihilation** *n,* **annihilator** *n.*

anniversary *n* (*pl* **-ies**) the date on which a notable event took place in a previous year, or the celebration of the event held on that date.

Anno Domini *adv* see AD.

annotate *v* to provide (e.g. a literary work) with critical or explanatory notes. ➤➤ **annotation** *n,* **annotative** *adj,* **annotator** *n.*

announce *v* **1** to make known publicly. **2a** to give notice of the arrival or presence of (somebody, e.g. a guest) or readiness of (something, e.g. dinner). **b** to indicate in advance; to foretell. ➤➤ **announcement** *n.*

announcer *n* a person who introduces television or radio programmes, makes commercial announcements, reads news summaries, or gives station identification.

annoy *v* **1** to make mildly angry; to irritate. **2** to bother repeatedly; to pester. **3** to be a source of irritation. ➤➤ **annoyance** *n,* **annoyed** *adj,* **annoying** *adj,* **annoyingly** *adv.*

annual[1] *adj* **1** covering or lasting for the period of a year. **2** occurring or performed once a year; yearly. **3** of a plant: completing the life cycle in one growing season: compare BIENNIAL, PERENNIAL[1]. ➤➤ **annually** *adv.*

annual[2] *n* **1** a publication that appears once a year. **2** an annual plant.

annuity *n* (*pl* **-ies**) an amount payable at specified intervals during a specified period, often a person's life.

annul *v* (**annulled, annulling**) **1** to declare (something, e.g. a marriage) legally invalid. **2** to cancel or abolish. ➤➤ **annulment** *n.*

annular *adj* in the shape of a ring.

annulate *adj* marked with rings or in the shape of a ring.

annunciation *n* **1** (**the Annunciation**) the announcement by the angel Gabriel to the Virgin Mary that she would be the mother of Jesus Christ, related in Luke 1:26–38. **2** a festival of the Christian Church commemorating this, held on Lady Day, 25 March.

annus horribilis *n* a year marked by misfortune or disaster.

annus mirabilis *n* a remarkable or wonderful year.

anode *n* the electrode by which electrons leave a device and enter an external circuit, e.g.: **a** the negative terminal of a battery: compare CATHODE. **b** the positive electrode in an electrolytic cell.

anodize *or* **-ise** *v* to subject (something metal) to electrolytic action by making it the anode of a cell in order to coat it with a protective or decorative film.

anodyne[1] *adj* mild or inoffensive to the point of being dull.

anodyne[2] *n* a painkilling drug.

anoint *v* **1** to put oil on the head or feet of (somebody) as part of a religious ceremony. **2** to confer an office on (a priest or monarch) by anointing them.

anomalous *adj* deviating from what is usual or expected; irregular. ➤➤ **anomalously** *adv,* **anomalousness** *n.*

anomaly *n* (*pl* **-ies**) something that deviates from what is usual or expected.

anomie *or* **anomy** *n* lack of moral or social standards of conduct and belief in an individual or community.

anon *adv archaic or informal* in a short while; soon.

anonymous *adj* **1** giving no name, or from somebody whose name is not known. **2** having no outstanding distinguishing features; nondescript. ➤➤ **anonymity** *n,* **anonymously** *adv.*

anopheles *n* (*pl* **anopheles**) a mosquito that transmits malaria to human beings.

anorak *n* **1** *chiefly Brit* a short weatherproof coat with a hood. **2** *Brit, informal* somebody with laughably unfashionable or boring hobbies.

anorectic *adj and n* see ANOREXIC[1], ANOREXIC[2].

anorexia *n* **1** = ANOREXIA NERVOSA. **2** prolonged loss of appetite.

anorexia nervosa *n* a psychological disorder characterized by an aversion to food induced by an obsessive desire to lose weight and sometimes resulting in life-threatening emaciation.

anorexic[1] *or* **anorectic** *adj* **1** suffering from anorexia nervosa. **2** extremely or unhealthily thin.

anorexic[2] *or* **anorectic** *n* a person suffering from anorexia nervosa.

another[1] *adj* **1** being a different or distinct one. **2** some other. **3** being one additional.

another[2] *pron* **1** an additional one. **2** a different one.

answer[1] *n* **1** a spoken or written reply to a question, remark, etc. **2** the correct solution to a mathematical, etc problem, or any of several solutions offered.

answer[2] *v* **1** to speak, write, or act in reply. **2** to act in response to a sound or other signal. **3a** to be responsible or accountable for something. **b** to make amends for something. **4** to correspond to something. **5** to be adequate or usable. **6** to reply to (something, e.g. a charge) in justification or explanation.

answerable *adj* (+ to/for) responsible to somebody for something.

answer back *v* to reply rudely.

answering machine *n* a device that responds to incoming telephone calls with a recorded message and records messages spoken by the callers.

answerphone *n* = ANSWERING MACHINE.

ant *n* an insect related to bees and wasps that lives in large social groups with a complex organization and hierarchy in which different castes perform specific duties.

-ant[1] *suffix* forming nouns, denoting: **1** somebody or something that performs the action specified: *claimant.* **2** a thing that causes the action or process specified: *decongestant.* **3** a thing that is used or acted on in the manner specified: *inhalant.*

-ant[2] *suffix* forming adjectives, with the meanings: **1** performing a specified action or being in the condition specified: *repentant.* **2** causing the action or process specified: *expectorant.*

antacid *n* a medicine that combats excessive acidity, *esp* in the stomach.

antagonise *v* see ANTAGONIZE.

antagonism *n* hostility or antipathy, *esp* when actively expressed.

antagonist *n* somebody who opposes or is hostile to another person; an adversary. ➤➤ **antagonistic** *adj.*

antagonize *or* **-ise** *v* to cause to become antagonistic.

Antarctic *adj* of the S Pole or the surrounding region.

ante[1] *n* (*pl* **antes**) **1** a poker stake usu put up before the deal. **2** *informal* the importance of something that is under discussion, *esp* something that is at stake.

ante[2] *v* (**antes, anteed** *or* **anted, anteing**) to put up (an ante): compare ANTE UP.

ante- *prefix* **1a** prior; before: *antecedent.* **b** prior to; earlier than: *antediluvian.* **2** situated before; anterior: *anteroom.*

anteater *n* a toothless mammal that feeds chiefly on ants and termites, such as the giant anteater which has a long snout and bushy tail.

antebellum *adj* existing before a war, *esp* the American Civil War.

antecedent[1] *n* **1** a preceding thing, event, or circumstance. **2** (*in pl*) family origins; ancestry. **3** a word, phrase, or clause functioning as a noun and referred to by a pronoun.

antecedent[2] *adj* earlier in time or order.

antechamber *n* = ANTEROOM.

antedate *v* **1** to precede in time. **2** to attach or assign (something, e.g. a document) to a date earlier than the true one *esp* in order to deceive.

antediluvian *adj* **1** belonging to the period before the flood described in the Bible. **2** laughably out-of-date; antiquated.

antelope *n* (*pl* **antelopes** *or* **antelope**) a fast-running hoofed mammal native to Africa and Asia.

antenatal *adj* relating to pregnancy, pregnant women, or unborn children.

antenna *n* **1** (*pl* **antennae** /-nee/) a movable segmented sense organ on the head of insects, crustaceans, and centipedes. **2** (*pl* **antennas** *or* **antennae** /-nee/) an aerial.

antepenultimate *adj* coming before the next to last; third from last.

ante-post *adj* of a bet, etc: placed before the day of a horse race, usu before all the runners are known.

anterior *adj* **1** before in time. **2** situated towards the front, *esp* towards the front of the body or near the head: compare POSTERIOR[1].

anteroom *n* an outer room that leads to another usu more important one, often used as a waiting room.

ante up *v chiefly NAm, informal* to pay what is due; to pay up: compare ANTE[2].

anthelmintic *adj* expelling or destroying parasitic worms, e.g. tapeworms.

anthem *n* **1** a song of praise or gladness, *esp* a solemn song sung as an expression of national identity. **2a** a set of religious responses that are sung as part of a church service; an antiphon. **b** a piece of church music set to a biblical text and sung by a choir as part of a church service. **3** any rousing or uplifting song. ➤➤ **anthemic** *adj.*

anther *n* in flowering plants, the organ at the tip of the stamen that contains and releases pollen.

anthill *n* a mound of soil, leaves, etc thrown up by ants or termites in digging their nest.

anthologize *or* **-ise** *v* **1** to compile (an anthology). **2** to publish (something, e.g. a poem) in an anthology.

anthology *n* (*pl* **-ies**) a collection of selected literary or musical pieces or passages. ➤➤ **anthologist** *n.*

anthracite *n* a hard variety of coal that burns slowly and with a non-luminous flame.

anthrax *n* an often fatal infectious disease of cattle and sheep caused by a spore-forming bacterium and capable of being transmitted to humans.

anthropogenic *adj* of or influenced by the impact of humans on nature. ➤➤ **anthropogenically** *adv.*

anthropoid *adj* resembling human beings in form or behaviour.

anthropology *n* the scientific study of human beings, *esp* in relation to physical characteristics, social relations and culture, and the origin and distribution of races. ➤➤ **anthropological** *adj,* **anthropologist** *n.*

anthropomorphic *adj* **1** having a human form or human attributes. **2** ascribing human characteristics to non-human things, e.g. to a god or animal. ➤➤ **anthropomorphism** *n.*

anthropophagi *n* pl of ANTHROPOPHAGUS.

anthropophagous *adj* feeding on human flesh; cannibalistic. ➤➤ **anthropophagy** *n.*

anthropophagus *n* (*pl* **anthropophagi**) a cannibal.

anti *prep and adj* opposed or antagonistic to something or somebody.

anti- *prefix* **1a** opposing or hostile to in opinion, sympathy, or practice: *anti-Semite.* **b** opposing in effect or activity; preventing: *antiseptic.* **c** being a rival: *antipope.* **2** combating or defending against: *anti-aircraft.* **3a** opposite in kind to: *anticlimax.* **b** of the same kind but situated opposite or in the opposite direction to: *antipodes.*

antibacterial *adj* directed or effective against bacteria.

antibiotic *n* a substance, such as penicillin, produced by a micro-organism and able in dilute solution to inhibit the growth of or kill micro-organisms, *esp* bacteria.

antibody *n* (*pl* **-ies**) a protein, e.g. a blood protein, that is produced by the body in response to a specific ANTIGEN (toxin, virus, etc).

Antichrist *n* (*often* **the Antichrist**) an enemy of Christ predicted to appear shortly before the end of the world.

anticipate *v* **1a** to foresee and deal with in advance; to forestall. **b** to act before (another person), *esp* so as to thwart their plans. **2** to discuss or think about in advance or too early. **3** to use or spend before the right or natural time. **4** to look forward to as certain; to expect. ➤➤ **anticipator** *n,* **anticipatory** *adj.*

anticipation *n* **1** the state of foreseeing or expecting something. **2** feelings of pleasurable expectation. **3** the foreseeing of something and the action taken to prepare for or forestall it.

anticlimax *n* an event that is strikingly less important or exciting than expected. ➤➤ **anticlimactic** *adj.*

anticline *n* an arch of stratified rock in which the layers bend downwards in opposite directions from the crest: compare SYNCLINE. ➤➤ **anticlinal** *adj.*

anticlockwise *adj and adv* in a direction opposite to that in which the hands of a clock rotate when viewed from the front.

anticoagulant *adj* having the effect of inhibiting the clotting of blood.

anticonvulsant[1] *adj* having the effect of controlling or preventing convulsions, *esp* epileptic convulsions.

anticonvulsant[2] *n* an anticonvulsant drug.

antics *pl n* silly, bizarre, or funny acts or behaviour.

anticyclone *n* a system of winds that rotates about a centre of high atmospheric pressure, usually associated with calm, fine weather. ➤➤ **anticyclonic** *adj.*

antidepressant[1] *adj* used to relieve mental depression.

antidepressant[2] *n* an antidepressant drug.

antidote *n* **1** a remedy that counteracts the effects of poison. **2** (*usu* + to) something that relieves or counteracts something regarded as unpleasant.

anti-emetic[1] *adj* of a drug or treatment: preventing vomiting.

anti-emetic[2] *n* an anti-emetic substance or treatment.

antifreeze *n* a substance added to a liquid, *esp* the water in a car radiator, to lower its freezing point.

antigen *n* a chemical, virus, etc that stimulates the production of an antibody when introduced into the body. ⋙ **antigenic** *adj.*

Antiguan *n* a native or inhabitant of the island of Antigua or the state of Antigua and Barbuda in the Caribbean. ⋙ **Antiguan** *adj.*

anti-hero *or* **anti-heroine** *n* (*pl* **anti-heroes** *or* **anti-heroines**) a man or woman who is a main character in a story, film, play, etc, but who lacks traditional heroic qualities, or whose circumstances do not allow for heroic action.

antihistamine *n* a drug that opposes the actions of histamine and is used *esp* for treating allergies and motion sickness.

anti-inflammatory *adj* of a drug: counteracting inflammation.

antilog *or* **antilogarithm** *n* the number corresponding to a given logarithm.

antimacassar *n* a cover put over the backs or arms of upholstered seats for decoration or protection, orig to protect the backs from soiling by men's hair oil.

antimatter *n* hypothetical matter composed of antiparticles.

antimony *n* a silver-white metallic chemical element used *esp* as a constituent of alloys to give added strength and hardness.

antinomian *n* a person who denies that moral laws apply to everyone, *esp* an adherent of the view that Christians whose salvation is preordained are freed from all moral restraints. ⋙ **antinomian** *adj,* **antinomianism** *n.*

antinomy *n* (*pl* **-ies**) *esp* in philosophy, a contradiction or conflict between two apparently valid principles; a paradox.

antioxidant *n* a substance that inhibits oxidation reactions, *esp* one added to foods to increase shelf life.

antiparticle *n* an elementary particle identical to another in mass but opposite to it in electric and magnetic properties that, when brought together with its counterpart, produces mutual annihilation.

antipasto *n* (*pl* **antipastos** *or* **antipasti**) an Italian hors d'oeuvre.

antipathetic *adj* **1** opposed in nature or character to something. **2** feeling or causing opposition or hostility.

antipathy *n* (*pl* **-ies**) (*often* + to) a deep-seated aversion or dislike; a distaste.

antipersonnel *adj* of a weapon: designed for use against people.

antiperspirant *n* a substance used to prevent or control perspiration.

antiphon *n* a verse, usu from Scripture, said or sung usu before and after a canticle, psalm, or psalm verse as part of a church service. ⋙ **antiphonal** *adj.*

antipodal *adj* **1** situated at the opposite side of the earth or moon. **2** diametrically opposite.

antipode *n* (*pl* **antipodes**) *chiefly NAm* the exact opposite or contrary.

Antipodes *pl n* (**the Antipodes**) from the point of view of inhabitants of the northern hemisphere, Australia and New Zealand. ⋙ **Antipodean** *adj and n.*

antipyretic *adj* of a drug or treatment: reducing fever.

antiquarian[1] *n* somebody who collects or studies ancient relics or old and rare books and works of art.

antiquarian[2] *adj* **1** of antiquarians or ancient relics. **2** said of books, prints, and other works of art: old and rare. ⋙ **antiquarianism** *n.*

antiquary *n* (*pl* **-ies**) = ANTIQUARIAN[1].

antiquated *adj* outmoded or discredited by reason of age; out-of-date.

antique[1] *adj* **1** made in an earlier period and therefore valuable. **2** suggesting the style of an earlier period or imitating the appearance of something old. **3** belonging to or surviving from earlier, *esp* classical, times; ancient.

antique[2] *n* a piece of furniture, decorative object, or work of art made in an earlier period and sought by collectors.

antiquity *n* (*pl* **-ies**) **1** ancient times, *esp* the period before the Middle Ages. **2** the quality of being ancient or of ancient lineage. **3** (*in pl*) relics or monuments of ancient times.

antirrhinum *n* (*pl* **antirrhinums**) a plant of the foxglove family, e.g. the snapdragon, with brightly-coloured flowers that have petals in the form of two lips.

antiscorbutic *adj* counteracting or preventing the development of scurvy.

anti-Semitism *n* hostility towards or discrimination against Jewish people. ⋙ **anti-Semite** *n,* **anti-Semitic** *adj.*

antiseptic[1] *adj* **1** preventing or inhibiting the growth of disease-causing micro-organisms, *esp* bacteria. **2a** scrupulously clean. **b** extremely neat or orderly, *esp* to the point of being bare or uninteresting.

antiseptic[2] *n* an antiseptic substance.

antiserum *n* (*pl* **antiserums** *or* **antisera**) a serum containing antibodies that attack a specific antigen, used in vaccination and in the treatment of disease.

antisocial *adj* **1a** *Brit* said of a person or behaviour: causing annoyance to others, *esp* remorselessly. **b** hostile or harmful to organized society. **2** tending to avoid the company of others; unsociable. ⋙ **antisocially** *adv.*

antithesis *n* (*pl* **antitheses**) **1** somebody or something that is a direct opposite. **2** a contrast of ideas expressed by a parallel arrangement of words, e.g. in 'action, not words'.

antithetical *adj* **1** directly opposed or contrary. **2** constituting or marked by antithesis.

antitoxin *n* an antibody capable of neutralizing the specific toxin that stimulated its production in the body, or a serum containing one.

antitrust *adj NAm* of laws: protecting trade from monopolies or unfair business practices.

antivenin *n* an antitoxin to a venom, or a serum containing one.

antivivisectionist *n* a person who opposes the use of live animals for scientific research. ⋙ **antivivisection** *adj,* **antivivisectionist** *adj.*

antler *n* one of a pair of branched horns of an animal of the deer family, which is shed periodically.

antonym *n* a word that means the opposite of another.

anus *n* the opening at the end of the alimentary canal through which solid waste matter leaves the body.

anvil *n* a heavy iron block on which metal is shaped by hammering.

anxiety *n* (*pl* **-ies**) **1** uneasiness of mind because of possible impending trouble or danger. **2** a cause of anxiety.

anxious *adj* **1** uneasy in the mind because of possible or impending trouble or danger. **2** causing anxiety; when anxiety is felt; worrying. **3** ardently or earnestly wishing to do something. ➤➤ **anxiously** *adv*, **anxiousness** *n*.

any[1] *adj* **1** one or some, no matter which. **2** one, some, or all; whatever, e.g.: **a** of whatever number or quantity even the smallest number or quantity of. **b** no matter how great. **c** no matter how ordinary or inadequate. **3** (*usu in negatives*) being an appreciable number, part, or amount of.

any[2] *pron* (*pl* **any**) **1** any person; anybody. **2a** any thing. **b** any part, quantity, or number.

Usage note

Any, as a pronoun, may be used with a verb in either the singular or the plural: *I need some glue – is there any left?*; *We sold most of them, and any that were unsold we gave away to friends.* There is sometimes a subtle distinction in the choice of a singular or plural verb. *Is any of these seats free?* would mean, specifically, 'any one', whereas one might ask, equally correctly, *Are any of these seats free?* to mean 'are some of them free?'.

any[3] *adv* to any extent or degree.

anybody *pron* any person.

anyhow *adv* **1** = ANYWAY. **2** in a haphazard manner.

anyone *pron* any person.

anything *pron* **1** any thing whatever. **2** any event, happening, etc. ✱ **anything but** not at all; far from.

anyway *adv* **1** in any case; inevitably. **2** used when resuming a narrative. **3** in spite of that; nevertheless.

anywhere[1] *adv* in, at, or to any place.

anywhere[2] *n* any place.

Anzac *n* **1** a soldier from Australia or New Zealand, *esp* in World War I. **2** *informal* any person from Australia or New Zealand.

a.o.b. *abbr* (*also* **AOB**) *chiefly Brit* any other business, used at the end of a meeting to refer to points not specified on the agenda.

aorta *n* (*pl* **aortas** *or* **aortae**) the main artery in the body, carrying oxygenated blood from the left side of the heart to be distributed by branch arteries throughout the body. ➤➤ **aortic** *adj*.

ap- *prefix* see AD-.

apace *adv* at a quick pace; swiftly.

Apache *n* (*pl* **Apaches** *or* **Apache**) a member of a group of Native American peoples of the SW USA.

apart *adv* **1a** at a distance from something or somebody else in space or time. **b** at a distance in character or quality. **2** so as to separate one from another. **3** excluded from consideration. **4** in or into two or more parts.

apart from *prep* **1** besides (something); in addition to (it). **2** except for (something).

apartheid /ə'paht·(h)ayt, -(h)iet/ *n* a policy of segregation and discrimination against non-whites in the Republic of S Africa, officially abandoned in 1992.

apartment *n* **1** *chiefly NAm* a flat. **2** a suite of rooms used for living quarters.

apathetic *adj* **1** having or showing little or no feeling; spiritless. **2** lacking interest or concern; indifferent. ➤➤ **apathetically** *adv*.

apathy *n* **1** lack of feeling or emotion; impassiveness. **2** lack of interest or concern; indifference.

apatosaurus *n* a large herbivorous dinosaur of the Jurassic and Cretaceous periods, with a long neck and tail, its hindlegs being longer than its forelegs, formerly called *brontosaurus*.

ape[1] *n* **1** a large tailless or short-tailed primate belonging to the group which includes gorillas, chimpanzees, orang-utans, and gibbons. **2** *informal* a large and clumsy or ill-mannered person.

ape[2] *v* to imitate closely but often clumsily and ineptly.

aperçu /apuh'sooh/ *n* (*pl* **aperçus**) a penetrating or enlightening comment.

aperient *n* a medicine that eases constipation; a laxative. ➤➤ **aperient** *adj*.

aperitif *n* an alcoholic drink taken before a meal to stimulate the appetite.

aperture *n* **1** an open space; a hole or gap. **2** the opening in a camera or other optical system through which the light passes, or the adjustable size of the opening.

APEX *abbr* (*also* **Apex**) Advance Purchase Excursion, an airline or rail ticket bought at a cheaper rate a minimum number of days before travelling.

apex *n* (*pl* **apexes** *or* **apices**) **1** the uppermost point of a triangle, cone, or pyramid. **2** the narrowed or pointed end or tip of something, e.g. a leaf. **3** the highest or culminating point, e.g. of a hierarchy, one's career, etc.

aphasia *n* loss of the power to use or understand words, usu resulting from brain damage. ➤➤ **aphasic** *n and adj*.

aphelion *n* (*pl* **aphelia**) the point in the path of a planet, comet, etc that is farthest from the sun: compare PERIHELION.

aphid *n* a small insect that sucks the juices of plants, e.g. a greenfly.

aphorism *n* a concise pithy phrase expressing a universal truth; an adage. ➤➤ **aphoristic** *adj*.

aphrodisiac *n* a food, drink, or drug that stimulates sexual desire.

apiarist *n* a beekeeper.

apiary *n* (*pl* **-ies**) a place where bees are kept in hives or colonies, *esp* for their honey.

apical *adj* situated at an apex or forming an apex.

apices *n* pl of APEX.

apiculture *n* the keeping of bees, *esp* on a large scale.

apiece *adv* for each one; individually.

aplenty *adj archaic or literary* enough and to spare; in abundance.

aplomb *n* complete composure or self-assurance; poise.

apnoea (*NAm* **apnea**) *n* temporary cessation of breathing, *esp* during sleep.

apocalypse *n* **1** a cataclysmic event. **2** (**the Apocalypse**) the ultimate destruction of the world, as depicted in the Book of Revelation in the Bible.

apocalyptic *adj* **1** momentous, overwhelming, or catastrophic. **2** relating to or resembling the biblical Apocalypse. ➤➤ **apocalyptically** *adv*.

Apocrypha *n* (**the Apocrypha**) (*used as sing. or pl*) books included in the SEPTUAGINT (Greek version of Old Testament) and VULGATE (St Jerome's Latin bible) but excluded from the Jewish and Protestant canons of the Old Testament.

apocryphal *adj* **1** of an account or story: of doubtful authenticity; probably not based on reality or fact. **2** (*often* **Apocryphal**) relating to the Apocrypha.

apogee *n* **1** the point farthest from the earth reached by the moon or a satellite in its orbit: compare PERIGEE. **2** the farthest or highest point; the culmination.

apolitical *adj* having no interest or involvement in political affairs.

apologetic *adj* regretfully acknowledging a fault or failure; contrite. ➤➤ **apologetically** *adv.*

apologetics *pl n* (*used as sing. or pl*) systematic reasoned argument in defence, e.g. of a doctrine.

apologia *n* a reasoned defence in speech or writing, *esp* of a faith, cause, or institution.

apologise *v* see APOLOGIZE.

apologist *n* a person who speaks or writes in defence of something.

apologize *or* **-ise** *v* (*often* + for) to make an apology.

apology *n* (*pl* **-ies**) **1** an admission of error or discourtesy accompanied by an expression of regret. **2** (+ for) a poor substitute; a specimen. **3** an excuse or explanation for, or vindication of, something; an apologia.

apophthegm (*NAm* **apothegm**) *n* a short, pithy, and instructive saying; a maxim.

apoplectic *adj* **1** relating to or causing apoplexy, or showing symptoms of apoplexy. **2** *informal* bursting with fury; extremely angry.

apoplexy *n* (*pl* **-ies**) **1** paralysis or loss of consciousness caused by a rupture or blockage in a blood vessel in the brain; a stroke. **2** *informal* speechless, incapacitating rage.

apoptosis *n* the natural death of cells in an organism.

aporia *n* an unresolvable position, *esp* in philosophy; an impasse.

apostasy *n* (*pl* **-ies**) renunciation of a religious faith or a previous loyalty.

apostate *n* a person who commits apostasy.

apostatize *or* **-ise** *v* to commit apostasy.

a posteriori *adj and adv* of argument or reasoning: proceeding from observed facts to their cause, or from the particular to the general; inductive or inductively: compare A PRIORI.

apostle *n* **1** (*often* **Apostle**) an early Christian teacher sent out to preach the gospel, *esp* one of the group made up of Jesus's original twelve disciples and Paul. **2** an advocate, early exponent, or ardent supporter of a system, movement, etc.

apostolate *n* the office, mission, or evangelistic work of an apostle.

apostolic *adj* **1** relating to an apostle or the New Testament apostles. **2** relating to the pope as the successor to the apostolic authority vested in St Peter.

apostrophe[1] *n* a punctuation mark (') used to indicate the omission of letters or figures, the possessive case, or the plural of letters or figures.

Usage note

The apostrophe is used before the letter *s* to mark a possessive (*Sharon's new car, the horse's feet, the children's toys*). It can cause problems when the last letter of the word to which it is attached is itself *s*. If the word is plural, the apostrophe is used on its own without another *s* (*the girls' shoes, the horses' feet*). If the word is singular, the usual modern practice is to add *'s* as normal if there is an extra s in speech (*Bridget Jones's Diary, Jesus's words to the Apostles*). It is not incorrect to add a simple apostrophe in such cases, and this is usual if there is not an extra s in speech (*Manasses' prayer, Socrates' submission to the law*). Note that an apostrophe should not be used before *s* to make ordinary words plural (the so-called 'grocer's apostrophe', as in *apple's 40p a pound*). It should only be used to make plural forms of letter and numbers (*a's, P's, 4's*) and is not always needed then (*1940s*).

apostrophe[2] *n* the rhetorical addressing of a person, usu absent, or a personified thing, as in *O death, where is thy sting? O grave, where is thy victory?*

apostrophize *or* **-ise** *v* to address (an absent person or a personified thing), *esp* as a rhetorical or poetic device.

apothecaries' measure *or* **apothecaries' weight** *n* the series of units of weight used formerly by pharmacists and based on the ounce of eight drachms and the drachm of three scruples or 60 grains.

apothecary *n* (*pl* **-ies**) *archaic* a pharmacist or pharmacy.

apotheosis *n* (*pl* **apotheoses**) **1** elevation to the status of a god; deification. **2** a supreme example of something at its most developed.

apotheosize *or* **-ise** *v* **1** to deify. **2** to glorify.

appal (*NAm* **appall**) *v* (**appalled, appalling**) to overcome with consternation, horror, or dismay. ➤➤ **appalling** *adj*, **appallingly** *adv.*

apparatchik /apəˈrachik/ *n* (*pl* **apparatchiks** *or* **apparatchiki**) **1** a member of a communist apparat. **2** a bureaucrat in any organization, *esp* one regarded as bedevilled by bureaucracy.

apparatus *n* (*pl* **apparatuses** *or* **apparatus**) **1** equipment designed for a particular use, or a single piece of such equipment. **2** the administrative bureaucracy of an organization, *esp* a political party.

apparel[1] *v* (**apparelled, apparelling,** *NAm* **appareled, appareling**) **1** *literary* to dress (somebody) or array them in something. **2** to clothe, cover, or adorn.

apparel[2] *n literary* garments or clothing.

apparent *adj* **1** easily seen or understood; evident. **2** seemingly real but not necessarily so. ➤➤ **apparently** *adv.*

apparition *n* **1** an unusual or unexpected sight; *esp* the appearance of a ghost. **2** a ghostly figure itself; a phantom.

appeal[1] *n* **1** the power of arousing a sympathetic response; attraction. **2** an earnest plea, e.g. for mercy; an entreaty. **3** a large-scale coordinated approach to the public for donations to a charity or cause. **4** an application, e.g. to a recognized authority, for corroboration, vindication, or decision. **5** a legal proceeding by which a case is brought to a higher court for review. **6** in cricket, a call by members of the fielding side, *esp* the bowler, for the umpire to declare a batsman out.

appeal[2] *v* (*often* + to) **1** to arouse a sympathetic response. **2** to make an earnest plea or request. **3** to call on another for corroboration, vindication, or decision. **4** to take a case to a higher court. **5** to make an appeal in cricket.

appealing *adj* having appeal; attractive. ➤➤ **appealingly** *adv.*

appear *v* **1a** to be or become visible. **b** to arrive. **2** to give the impression of being; to seem. **3** to come into public view. **4** to come formally before an authoritative body.

appearance *n* **1a** a visit or attendance that is seen or noticed by others. **b** participation in a performance, show, programme, etc on screen or on the stage. **2a** an outward aspect; a look. **b** an external show; a semblance. **c** (*in pl*) an outward or superficial look, *esp* one that hides the real situation. ✱ **keep up appearances** to maintain standards outwardly at least.

appease *v* **1** to pacify or calm. **2** to conciliate (*esp* an aggressor) by making concessions. **3** to assuage or allay (hunger, thirst, etc). ⪢ **appeasement** *n,* **appeaser** *n.*

appellant *n* a person who appeals against a judicial decision.

appellate *adj* of a court of law: relating to or recognizing appeals.

appellation *n literary* an identifying name or title.

appellation contrôlée /apə'lasyonh kontroh'lay/ *n* a government certification of a French wine guaranteeing that it originates from a specified geographical area and meets that locality's standards of production.

append *v formal* to attach or add, *esp* as a supplement, attachment, or appendix to a text.

appendage *n* **1** a limb or other subordinate or derivative body part. **2** something appended to something larger or more important.

appendicectomy *or* **appendectomy** *n* (*pl* **-ies**) surgical removal of the appendix.

appendices *n* pl of APPENDIX.

appendicitis *n* inflammation of the appendix.

appendix *n* **1** (*pl* **appendices** /-seez/) a supplement, e.g. containing explanatory or statistical material, attached at the end of a book or other piece of writing. **2** (*pl* **appendixes**) a narrow short blind tube that extends from the lower end of the large intestine.

appertain *v* (*usu* + to) to belong or be connected as a rightful or customary part, possession, or attribute; to pertain.

appetiser *n* see APPETIZER.

appetising *adj* see APPETIZING.

appetite *n* **1** a desire to satisfy an internal bodily need; *esp* a desire to eat. **2** a strong desire demanding satisfaction; an inclination. ⪢ **appetitive** *adj.*

appetizer *or* **appetiser** *n* a food or drink that stimulates the appetite, usu served before a meal.

appetizing *or* **appetising** *adj* appealing to the appetite, *esp* in appearance or aroma.

applaud to express approval (of somebody or something) by clapping, cheering, etc.

applause *n* approval or admiration expressed by clapping the hands.

apple *n* a round fruit with red or green skin and crisp white flesh. ✱ **the apple of one's eye** somebody or something greatly cherished [orig the pupil, once believed to be a solid ball, hence something equally precious and delicate]. **upset the apple cart** to ruin a scheme or plan.

apple-pie order *n informal* perfect order.

applet *n* in computing, a small application that runs within a larger program, or operates within a web page.

appliance *n* **1** an instrument or device designed for a particular use; *esp* a domestic machine, e.g. a food mixer, vacuum cleaner, or cooker. **2** *Brit* the process of applying something; application.

applicable *adj* able to be applied rightfully or suitably; appropriate or related. ⪢ **applicability** *n.*

applicant *n* a person who applies for something, e.g. a job.

application *n* **1** a request or petition, *esp* a formal request made in writing, e.g. to be considered for a job. **2a** an act of applying. **b** a use to which something is put. **3** capacity for practical use; relevance. **4** close attention; diligence. **5** a computer program that performs a particular function, e.g. word processing.

applicator *n* a device for applying a substance, e.g. medicine or polish.

applied *adj* put to practical use; *esp* applying general principles to solve definite problems.

appliqué[1] /ə'pleekay, aplee'kay/ *n* decorative work in which a cutout decoration is fastened, usu by sewing, to a larger piece of material.

appliqué[2] *v* (**appliqués, appliquéd, appliquéing**) to apply (e.g. a decoration or ornament) to a larger surface.

apply *v* (**-ies, -ied**) **1a** to bring to bear or put to use, *esp* for some practical purpose. **b** to lay or spread on a surface. **2** to devote (e.g. oneself) to something with close attention or diligence. **3** (*usu* + to) to have relevance. **4** to make a request, *esp* formally in writing.

appoint *v* **1** to select for an office or position. **2** *formal* to fix or name (something, e.g. a time) officially.

appointed *adj* **1** of a time or place: as previously decided for the event in question. **2** (*used in combinations*) equipped or furnished as specified.

appointee *n* a person who is appointed to a job or post.

appointment *n* **1** an act of appointing. **2** an office or position held by somebody who has been appointed to it rather than voted into it. **3** an arrangement for a meeting or other engagement. **4** (*in pl*) equipment or furnishings. ✱ **by appointment/by appointment to the Queen** selling a commodity or supplying a service to the Queen.

apportion *v* **1** to divide, distribute, or allot in just proportion or according to a plan. **2** to assign (blame). ⪢ **apportionment** *n.*

apposite *adj* highly pertinent or appropriate; apt.

apposition *n* **1** a grammatical construction in which two usu adjacent nouns or noun phrases both refer to the same person or thing and stand in the same syntactic relation to the rest of a sentence, as in 'She lives with *her son, an art historian*', '*My sister Jill* phoned'. **2** *technical* the placing of one thing side by side with another. ⪢ **appositive** *adj and n.*

appraisal *n* an act or instance of appraising, e.g. a valuation of property by an authorized person, or an assessment of a worker's performance.

appraise *v* **1** to evaluate the worth, significance, or status of. **2** to make a valuation of (property, etc) for tax purposes, etc. ⪢ **appraisee** *n,* **appraiser** *n.*

Usage note

appraise *or* **apprise**? To *appraise* is a fairly formal word meaning 'to assess' something or 'estimate its value': *appraise the damage caused by the fire.* To *apprise* is an even more formal word meaning 'to inform' and is followed by the preposition *of*: *She had already apprised us of her intentions.*

appreciable *adj* large enough to notice; substantial. ⪢ **appreciably** *adv.*

appreciate *v* **1** to recognize the value or importance of. **2** *informal* (*in negative contexts*) to be pleased at (something). **3** to esteem. **4** to realize or be aware of. **5** to increase in value. ⪢ **appreciative** *adj,* **appreciatively** *adv,* **appreciator** *n.*

appreciation *n* **1** sensitive awareness, *esp* recognition of aesthetic values. **2** admiration, approval, or gratitude. **3** an increase in value. **4** a judgment or evaluation; *esp* a favourable critical assessment.

apprehend *v* **1** *formal or literary* to arrest or seize (a suspected person, etc). **2** to understand or perceive.

apprehension *n* **1** anxiety or fear; nervous anticipation. **2** understanding; comprehension. **3** the arrest of a suspected person, etc.

apprehensive *adj* fearful, anxious, or uneasy. ➤➤ **apprehensively** *adv,* **apprehensiveness** *n.*

apprentice[1] *n* a person who is learning an art or trade, either from an employer to whom he or she is bound by contract, or by practical experience under skilled workers. ➤➤ **apprenticeship** *n.*

apprentice[2] *v* (*usu in passive*) to take on as an apprentice.

apprise *or* **apprize** *v formal* to inform of something.

Usage note

apprise *or* appraise? See note at APPRAISE.

approach[1] *v* **1a** to draw closer to. **b** to come very near to in quality, character, etc. **2a** to make advances to (somebody), *esp* with an offer of work or a request for support. **b** to begin to consider or deal with.

approach[2] *n* **1** an act or instance of approaching. **2** a means of access. **3** a manner or method of doing something, or the attitude behind this. **4** (*usu in pl*) an advance made to establish personal or business relations.

approachable *adj* not hostile or forbidding in manner and therefore easy to talk to or deal with. ➤➤ **approachability** *n.*

approbation *n* **1** approval, *esp* if formal or official; sanction. **2** praise; commendation. ➤➤ **approbative** *adj,* **approbatory** *adj.*

appropriate[1] *v* **1** to take exclusive possession of. **2** (*often* + to) to set (something, *esp* money) apart for a particular purpose or use. ➤➤ **appropriation** *n,* **appropriator** *n.*

appropriate[2] *adj* **1** suitable. **2** apt; fitting. ➤➤ **appropriately** *adv,* **appropriateness** *n.*

approval *n* **1** a favourable opinion or judgment. **2** formal or official permission. ✱ **on approval** of goods supplied commercially: able to be returned without payment if found unsatisfactory.

approve *v* **1** (*often* + of) to take a favourable view. **2** to give formal or official sanction to; to ratify. **3** to accept as satisfactory. ➤➤ **approvingly** *adv.*

approved school *n Brit* a former name for a boarding school for young offenders, now called a community home.

approximate[1] *adj* **1** nearly correct or exact. **2** of a term, etc: loose; inexact. ➤➤ **approximately** *adv.*

approximate[2] *v* **1** (*often* + to) to come close, *esp* in quality or character. **2** (*often* + to) to average out. **3** to make a guess. **4** to approach, *esp* in quality or number. ➤➤ **approximative** *adj,* **approximatively** *adv.*

approximation *n* **1** a roughly calculated amount; an estimate. **2** a loose or inexact account, description, etc. **3** the near approach of one thing to another so that they are approximately similar. **4** (+ to) something that is approximately similar to a certain thing.

appurtenance *n* (*also in pl*) an item that belongs to the equipment for something, *esp* a piece of furniture, fitting, household article, etc.

APR *abbr* annual or annualized percentage rate.

Apr. *abbr* April.

apraxia *n* loss or impairment of the ability to execute complex coordinated movements.

après-ski /,apray 'skee/ *n* social activity after a day's skiing.

apricot *n* an oval orange-coloured fruit with soft juicy yellow or orange flesh.

April *n* the fourth month of the year.

April Fools' Day *n* 1 April, characteristically marked by the playing of practical jokes.

a priori *adj and adv* relating to or derived by reasoning from self-evident propositions; deductive: compare A POSTERIORI.

apron *n* **1** a garment tied round the waist and used to protect clothing. **2 a** the part of a theatre stage that projects in front of the curtain. **b** the paved area by an airport terminal or in front of hangars, used for loading and moving aircraft. **3** a conveyor belt made of rubber or metal plates. ✱ **tied to somebody's apron strings** usu of a man: dominated by a woman, *esp* a mother or wife.

apropos /aprə'poh/ *prep* (*also* + of) concerning (something); with regard to (it).

apse *n* a projecting and usu rounded and vaulted part of a building, *esp* a church.

apsidal *adj* forming or in the form of an apse.

apt *adj* **1** likely, or having a tendency to do something. **2** suited to a purpose; relevant. **3** keenly intelligent and responsive. ➤➤ **aptly** *adv,* **aptness** *n.*

aptitude *n* **1** a natural ability or talent, *esp* for learning. **2** (*usu* + for) general fitness or suitability.

aqua- *comb. form* forming words, denoting: water: *aquaplane.*

aqualung *n* an underwater breathing apparatus consisting of cylinders of compressed air or oxygen carried on the back and connected to a face mask.

aquamarine *n* **1** a transparent blue to green beryl used as a gemstone: compare BERYL, EMERALD. **2** a pale blue to light greenish blue colour. ➤➤ **aquamarine** *adj.*

aquanaut *n* a diver who works inside and outside an underwater shelter.

aquaplane[1] *n* a board for riding on water, towed by a fast motorboat.

aquaplane[2] *v* **1** to ride on an aquaplane. **2** of a car: to go out of control by sliding on water lying on the surface of a wet road.

aqua regia *n* a mixture of nitric and hydrochloric acids that dissolves gold or platinum.

aquarelle *n* the technique of painting in thin usu transparent watercolours.

aquaria *n* pl of AQUARIUM.

aquarist *n* a person who keeps an aquarium.

aquarium *n* (*pl* **aquariums** *or* **aquaria**) a glass tank, artificial pond, etc in which living aquatic animals or plants are kept.

Aquarius *n* **1** in astronomy, a constellation (the Water Carrier) depicted as a man pouring water from a jar. **2** in astrology, the eleventh sign of the zodiac or a person born under this sign. ➤➤ **Aquarian** *adj and n.*

aquatic[1] *adj* **1** growing or living in water. **2** taking place in or on water.

aquatic[2] *n* an aquatic animal or plant.

aquatint *n* a print produced by a method of etching a printing plate that enables tones similar to watercolour washes to be reproduced.

aquavit *n* a colourless Scandinavian spirit made with potatoes and flavoured with caraway seeds.

aqua vitae /,akwə 'veetie, 'vie-/ *n* a strong alcoholic spirit, e.g. brandy or whisky.

aqueduct *n* a bridge-like structure, usu supported by arches, built to carry a canal across a valley.

aqueous *adj* of, resembling, or containing water.

aqueous humour *n* a transparent liquid occupying the space between the lens and the cornea of the eye.

aquifer *n* a water-bearing layer of permeable rock, sand, or gravel.

aquilegia *n* = COLUMBINE.

aquiline *adj* **1** relating to or like an eagle. **2** of the human nose: hooked.

AR *abbr* Arkansas (US postal abbreviation).

Ar *abbr* the chemical symbol for argon.

ar- *prefix* see AD-.

-ar[1] *suffix* forming adjectives from nouns, denoting: **1** nature or composition: *molecular; spectacular.* **2** resemblance: *oracular.*

-ar[2] *suffix* forming nouns, denoting: somebody who engages in a particular activity: *beggar; scholar.*

Arab *n* **1** a member of a Semitic people orig of the Arabian peninsula and now widespread throughout the Middle East and N Africa. **2** a typically intelligent, graceful, and swift horse of an Arabian stock. ➤➤ **Arab** *adj.*

arabesque *n* **1** a posture in ballet in which the dancer is supported on one leg with one arm extended forwards and the other arm and leg backwards. **2** a decorative design or style that combines natural motifs, e.g. flowers or foliage, to produce an intricate pattern. **3** a musical passage with a highly ornamental melody.

Arabian[1] *adj* relating to Arabia or its people.

Arabian[2] *n* **1** chiefly formerly, a native or inhabitant of Arabia. **2** an Arab horse.

Arabic *n* the Semitic language of the Arab peoples, now spoken in Arabia, Jordan, Lebanon, Syria, Iraq, Egypt, and parts of N Africa. ➤➤ **Arabic** *adj.*

arabica *n* coffee made from a bean that is widely grown in S America.

Arabic numeral *n* any of the number symbols 0, 1, 2, 3, 4, 5, 6, 7, 8, 9.

arable *adj* **1** of land: used or suitable for crop farming. **2** of crops: suitable for growing on arable land.

arachnid *n* an arthropod such as a spider, mite, tick, or scorpion, having a body that has two segments, the front segment bearing four pairs of legs. ➤➤ **arachnid** *adj.*

arachnophobia *n* irrational fear of spiders. ➤➤ **arachnophobe** *n*, **arachnophobic** *adj.*

arak *n* see ARRACK.

Aramaic *n* an ancient Semitic language of Syria and Upper Mesopotamia, still spoken by certain minorities, that was used as a lingua franca in SW Asia from the sixth cent. BC. ➤➤ **Aramaic** *adj.*

Aran *n* denoting a kind of thick knitwear characterized by cable stitching and lozenge patterns.

Arawak *n* (*pl* **Arawaks** *or* **Arawak**) **1** a member of a group of Native American people living chiefly on the coast of Guyana. **2** a family of languages spoken in parts of Central and S America. ➤➤ **Arawakan** *adj and n.*

arbiter *n* a person or agency with absolute power of judging and determining.

arbitrage /'ahbitrij, -trahzh/ *n* the simultaneous purchase and sale of the same or equivalent security in different markets in order to profit from price discrepancies.

arbitrageur /'ahbitrahzhə, -zhuh/ *n* a dealer on a stock exchange who specializes in arbitrage.

arbitrary *adj* **1** of a decision, judgment, etc: based not on reason so much as on whim or random choice. **2** of a sentence, penalty, etc: that can be imposed at the discretion of a court of law. **3** of a style of governing or rule: despotic or tyrannical. ➤➤ **arbitrarily** *adv*, **arbitrariness** *n.*

arbitrate *v* **1** to act as an arbitrator. **2** to submit for decision to an arbitrator.

arbitration *n* the settlement of a disputed issue by an arbitrator.

arbitrator *n* somebody chosen to settle differences between two parties in dispute.

arbor *n* **1** a spindle or axle of a wheel. **2** a shaft on which a workpiece, e.g. on a lathe, is mounted.

arboreal *adj* of, inhabiting, or relating to trees. ➤➤ **arboreality** *n*, **arboreally** *adv.*

arboretum *n* (*pl* **arboretums** *or* **arboreta**) a place where trees and shrubs are cultivated for study and display.

arboriculture *n* the cultivation of trees and shrubs.

arbour (*NAm* **arbor**) *n* a garden alcove formed by climbing plants or by branches.

arc[1] *n* **1** a continuous portion of a curve, e.g. of a circle or an ellipse. **2** the apparent path followed by a planet or other celestial body. **3** a sustained luminous discharge of electricity across a gap in a circuit or between electrodes.

arc[2] *v* (**arced, arcing**) **1** to form an arc or follow an arching or curving trajectory. **2** to form an electric arc.

arcade *n* **1** a long arched gallery or building. **2** a series of arches with their columns or piers. **3** a passageway or avenue, e.g. between shops. ➤➤ **arcading** *n.*

Arcadia *or* **Arcady** *n* an idealized rural region or scene of simple pleasure and quiet, the typical setting of Greek and Latin pastoral poetry. ➤➤ **Arcadian** *adj.*

arcana *n* pl of ARCANUM.

arcane *adj* **1** known or knowable only to a few people to whom secret information has been revealed; esoteric. **2** mysterious. ➤➤ **arcanely** *adv.*

arcanum *n* (*pl* **arcana**) a secret or mystery known only to those who have been initiated.

arch[1] *n* **1** a curved symmetrical structure spanning an opening and supporting, e.g. a ceiling, roof, wall, bridge, or other part above it. **2** the vaulted bony structure of the foot.

arch[2] *v* to form or bend (something) into an arch.

arch[3] *adj* of a look, manner, remark, etc: consciously sly or teasing; saucy or playful. ➤➤ **archly** *adv*, **archness** *n.*

arch- *prefix* **1** chief or principal: *archbishop.* **2** extreme; most fully embodying the qualities of a specified usu undesirable human type: *arch-rogue; arch-enemy.*

archaea /ah'keeə/ *pl n* a class of bacteria that live in extreme environments and are thought to represent the most ancient group of organisms still living.

Archaean (*NAm* **Archean**) *adj* of the earlier part of the Precambrian aeon, lasting from about 4600 to about 2500 million years ago, before the first living things appeared. ➤➤ **Archaean** *n.*

archaeology (*NAm* **archeology**) *n* the scientific study of material remains, *esp* artefacts and dwellings, of past human life and activities. ➤➤ **archaeologic** *adj*, **archaeological** *adj*, **archaeologist** *n.*

archaeopteryx *n* the oldest fossil bird of the late Jurassic period, which combined the wings and feathers of a bird with the teeth and bony tail of a dinosaur.

archaic *adj* **1** antiquated. **2** of vocabulary or expressions: no longer used in ordinary speech or writing. **3** of art, music, etc: belonging to an early period of development. ➤➤ **archaically** *adv.*

archaism *n* **1** an instance of archaic usage; *esp* an archaic word or expression. **2** the use of archaic diction or style. **3** something outmoded or old-fashioned.

archangel *n* a chief or principal angel. ➤➤ **archangelic** *adj.*

archbishop *n* a bishop at the head of an ecclesiastical province, or one of equivalent honorary rank.

archdeacon *n* a member of the clergy having the duty of assisting a diocesan bishop, *esp* in administrative work.

archduchess *n* **1** the wife or widow of an archduke. **2** a woman having the rank of archduke in her own right.

archduke *n* a principal duke, *esp* as a former title of the eldest son of the Emperor of Austria. ➤➤ **archducal** *adj,* **archduchy** *n.*

Archean *adj NAm* see ARCHAEAN.

arch-enemy *n* (*pl* **-ies**) one's most bitter enemy.

archer *n* a person who practises archery.

archerfish *n* (*pl* **archerfishes** *or* **archerfish**) a small fish that catches insects by stunning them with drops of water ejected from the mouth.

archery *n* the art, practice, skill, or sport of shooting arrows from a bow.

archetype *n* **1** an original pattern or model; a prototype. **2** a perfect example or model of something. ➤➤ **archetypal** *adj,* **archetypical** *adj.*

archiepiscopal *adj* relating to an archbishop. ➤➤ **archiepiscopacy** *n,* **archiepiscopate** *n.*

Archimedes' principle *n* in physics, a law stating that an object floating in a liquid displaces a weight of liquid equal to its own weight.

Archimedes' screw *n* a device for raising water, consisting of a tube bent spirally round an axis, or of a broad-threaded screw encased by a cylinder.

archipelago *n* (*pl* **-os** *or* **-oes**) a group of scattered islands.

architect *n* **1** a person who designs buildings and superintends their construction. **2** a person who originates or comprehensively plans a system, project, etc.

architectonic *adj* **1** relating to architecture or according with its principles. **2** resembling architecture in structure or organization. ➤➤ **architectonically** *adv.*

architectonics *pl n* (*used as sing. or pl*) **1** the art or science of architecture. **2** the systematic arrangement of knowledge.

architecture *n* **1** the art, practice, or profession of designing and erecting buildings. **2** a particular method or style of building. **3** the design and structure of anything. ➤➤ **architectural** *adj,* **architecturally** *adv.*

architrave *n* **1** in classical architecture, the lowest part of an ENTABLATURE (upper section supported on columns) resting immediately on the capital of the column. **2** the moulded frame round a rectangular recess or opening, e.g. a door or window.

archive[1] *n* **1** a collection of historical documents and records. **2** computer data transferred to a disk or tape for long-term storage. ➤➤ **archival** *adj.*

archive[2] *v* **1** to file or collect (e.g. records or documents) in an archive. **2** to transfer (computer data not needed for immediate access) to a tape or disk for long-term storage.

archivist *n* an official who organizes and is responsible for archives.

archosaur *n* a reptile of a class that includes the crocodiles and alligators.

archway *n* an arch with a passage running beneath it, or the passage itself.

-archy *comb. form* forming nouns, denoting: rule or government: *monarchy.*

arc lamp *n* a type of electric lamp that produces light by an arc made when a current passes between two incandescent electrodes surrounded by gas.

Arctic[1] *adj* **1** relating to the N Pole or the surrounding region. **2** (**arctic**) extremely cold.

Arctic[2] *n* (*usu* **the Arctic**) the regions surrounding the North Pole.

arcuate *adj* curved like a bow.

ardent *adj* **1** characterized by strength of feeling; eager or zealous. **2** *archaic or literary* burning; glowing. ➤➤ **ardency** *n,* **ardently** *adv.*

ardour (*NAm* **ardor**) *n* **1** intense feelings, often of passion or love. **2** great enthusiasm or zeal.

arduous *adj* difficult or strenuous. ➤➤ **arduously** *adv,* **arduousness** *n.*

are[1] *v* second person sing. present or pl present of BE.

are[2] *n* a metric unit of area equal to $100m^2$.

area *n* **1** the extent of a surface or plane figure measured in square units. **2** a piece of ground. **3** a particular space or surface, or one serving a special function. **4** the extent, range, or scope of a concept, operation, or activity; a field. **5** a sunken court or yard giving access to the basement of a building. ➤➤ **areal** *adj.*

area code *n* a set of numbers indicating a particular area of a country, dialled before individual subscriber numbers when making telephone calls to that area.

arena *n* **1** an enclosed area used for public entertainment usu consisting of a level area surrounded by tiered seating. **2** a sphere of interest or activity.

aren't *contr* **1** are not. **2** used in questions: am not.

areola *n* (*pl* **areolae**) a coloured ring, e.g. round the nipple. ➤➤ **areolar** *adj,* **areolate** *adj.*

arête /ə'ret, ə'rayt/ *n* a narrow sharp-crested mountain ridge.

argent *n* **1** used in heraldry: a silver or white colour. **2** *archaic or literary* the metal or colour silver. ➤➤ **argent** *adj.*

Argentine *n and adj* = ARGENTINIAN.

argentine *adj archaic* silver or silvery.

Argentinian *n* a native or inhabitant of Argentina. ➤➤ **Argentinian** *adj.*

arginine *n* an amino acid found in most proteins and essential in the nutrition of most vertebrates.

argon *n* a gaseous chemical element of the noble gas group found in the air and volcanic gases and used *esp* as a filler for vacuum tubes and electric light bulbs.

argosy *n* (*pl* **-ies**) *literary* a large merchant sailing ship.

argot *n* the jargon or slang that is peculiar to a particular group.

arguable *adj* **1** capable of being reasonably asserted or having a case made for it. **2** open to dispute; debatable. ➤➤ **arguably** *adv.*

argue *v* (**argues, argued, arguing**) **1** to give reasons for or against something; to reason. **2** to contend or disagree in words; to bicker or quarrel. ✱ **argue the toss** *chiefly Brit, informal* to dispute a decision that has already been made. ➤➤ **arguer** *n.*

argument *n* **1** a quarrel or disagreement. **2a** the act or process of arguing; debate. **b** a coherent series of reasons offered. **3** a reason given as a proof or refutation.

argumentation *n* the act or process of forming reasons and drawing conclusions and applying them to a case in discussion.

argumentative *adj* tending or liking to argue; disputatious. ➤➤ **argumentatively** *adv,* **argumentativeness** *n.*

argy-bargy *n chiefly Brit, informal* lively discussion or heated dispute.

argyle *n* a pattern on knitwear consisting of coloured lozenges on a plain background.

aria *n* an accompanied melody sung, e.g. in an opera, by one voice.

arid *adj* **1** of land: excessively dry, *esp* having insufficient rainfall to support agriculture; parched. **2** bleakly unproductive or unrewarding; barren. ➤➤ **aridity** *n,* **aridly** *adv,* **aridness** *n.*

Aries *n* **1** in astronomy, a constellation (the Ram) depicted as the ram with the golden fleece sought by Jason. **2** in astrology, the first sign of the zodiac or a person born under this sign. ➤➤ **Arian** *adj and n,* **Arien** *adj and n.*

aright *adv* rightly or correctly.

aril *n* an exterior covering of some seeds, typically hairy or fleshy, like those of yew, that develops after fertilization.

arise *v* (*past tense* **arose,** *past part.* **arisen**) **1a** to originate from a source. **b** (*often* + from) to come into being or to somebody's attention. **2** *literary or formal* to get up or rise.

aristocracy *n* (*pl* **-ies**) (*used as sing. or pl*) a usu hereditary nobility ranking socially above the ordinary or common people and below royalty.

aristocrat *n* a member of an aristocracy; *esp* a noble.

aristocratic *adj* belonging to or having the qualities of aristocracy. ➤➤ **aristocratically** *adv.*

Aristotelian *adj* relating to the Greek philosopher Aristotle (d.322 BC). ➤➤ **Aristotelian** *n.*

arithmetic *n* **1** a branch of mathematics that deals with real numbers and calculations made with them. **2** calculation using numbers. ➤➤ **arithmetic** *adj,* **arithmetical** *adj,* **arithmetically** *adv,* **arithmetician** *n.*

arithmetic progression *n* a sequence, e.g. 3, 5, 7, 9, in which the difference between any term and its predecessor is constant.

-arium *suffix* denoting: a thing or place relating to or connected with something: *planetarium.*

ark *n* **1** a ship, *esp* the one built by Noah to escape the Flood, or one built as a model of it. **2a** (**Ark/Ark of the Covenant**) the sacred chest containing the Ten Commandments, and representing to the Hebrews the presence of God among them. **b** (*also* **Holy Ark**) a repository for the scrolls of the Torah. ✱ **out of the ark** *informal* deplorably antiquated.

arm[1] *n* **1** either of the human upper limbs that extend from the shoulder, sometimes not including the hand and wrist. **2** a support, e.g. on a chair, for the elbow and forearm. **3** an inlet of water from the sea. **4** a functional division of a group or activity. ✱ **a baby/babe in arms** a child too young to walk. **arm in arm** with arms linked. **at arm's length** far enough away to avoid unwanted familiarity. **cost an arm and a leg** *informal* to be very expensive. **with open arms** with welcoming enthusiasm. ➤➤ **armless** *adj.*

arm[2] *v* **1** to supply or equip with weapons. **2** to provide with something that strengthens or protects. **3** to activate the fuse of (a bomb).

armada *n* a fleet of warships.

armadillo *n* (*pl* **-os**) a burrowing chiefly nocturnal S American mammal with a body and head encased in an armour of small bony plates.

Armageddon *n* **1** a final and conclusive battle between the forces of good and evil, as in the New Testament of the Bible. **2** a vast decisive conflict.

Armagnac *n* a dry brandy produced in the Gers district of France.

armament *n* **1** (*usu in pl*) the military strength, *esp* in arms and equipment, of a ship, fort, or combat unit, nation, etc. **2** the process of preparing for war.

armature *n* **1** the central rotating part of an electric motor or generator. **2** a bar of soft iron or steel placed across the poles of a horseshoe magnet to close the magnetic circuit. **3** the part of an electromagnetic device that moves or vibrates under the influence of a magnetic field. **4** the protective covering of a plant or animal. **5** *archaic* arms or armour.

armband *n* **1** a band of material, *esp* cloth, attached over the upper sleeve, usu denoting status or condition, e.g. mourning. **2** an inflatable plastic band worn round the upper arm by non-swimmers to keep them afloat.

armchair *n* **1** a chair with armrests, usu upholstered. **2** (*used before a noun*) dealing with matters from a theoretical rather than practical angle.

armed *adj* having or using a firearm.

armed forces *pl n* the military, naval, and air forces of a nation.

Armenian *n* **1** a member of a people living chiefly in Armenia in the Caucasus. **2** the Indo-European language of the Armenians. ➤➤ **Armenian** *adj.*

armful *n* (*pl* **armfuls**) **1** as much or as many as the arms will hold. **2** an amount being held in the arms.

armistice *n* a suspension of hostilities; a truce.

armlet *n* a band, e.g. of cloth or metal, worn round the upper arm.

armlock *n* a hold in which a person is restrained by having one arm bent behind the back.

armoire *n* a large usu decorative cupboard or wardrobe.

armorial *adj* relating to or bearing heraldic arms.

armory *n* heraldry.

armour (*NAm* **armor**) *n* **1a** a defensive covering for the body; *esp* a covering of metal or chain mail worn by medieval soldiers in combat. **b** a usu metallic protective covering, e.g. for a ship, aircraft, or car. **2** armoured forces and vehicles, e.g. tanks.

armoured (*NAm* **armored**) *adj* **1** of a vehicle: protected with armour plate. **2** of an army unit, etc: consisting of or equipped with vehicles protected with armour plate.

armourer (*NAm* **armorer**) *n* **1** a person who makes or looks after armour or arms. **2** a person who repairs, assembles, and tests firearms.

armour plate *n* a defensive covering of hard metal plates for combat vehicles and vessels. ➤➤ **armour-plated** *adj.*

armoury (*NAm* **armory**) *n* (*pl* **-ies**) **1** a collection of or place for storing arms and military equipment. **2** a collection of available resources.

armpit *n* the hollow beneath the junction of the arm and shoulder.

armrest *n* a support for the arm, *esp* one on a chair.

arms *n* **1** weapons, *esp* firearms. **2** the heraldic insignia of a group or body, e.g. a family, corporation, or country. ✱ **up in arms** angrily rebellious and protesting strongly.

arms race *n* a continuing rivalry between two countries that are potential adversaries, in which each tries to get and keep superiority in armaments.

arm wrestling *n* a contest in which two opponents sit opposite each other across a table, grip each other's hand with the elbows on its surface, and try to force each other's forearm down.

army *n* (*pl* **-ies**) **1** a large organized force for fighting on land. **2** a large crowd. **3** a body of people organized to advance a cause.

arnica *n* a plant of the daisy family with yellow or orange flower heads which yield an oil used in treating sprains and bruises.

aroha /'ahrohə/ *n NZ* love, affection, or compassion.

aroma *n* a distinctive, pervasive, and usu pleasant or savoury smell.

aromatherapy *n* the use of natural essential oils in a variety of treatments to relieve symptoms, promote healing, and reduce tension. ⋙ **aromatherapeutic** *adj*, **aromatherapist** *n*.

aromatic[1] *adj* **1a** fragrant. **b** having a strong *esp* pungent or spicy smell. **2** of a chemical compound: having a molecular structure containing a ring, *esp* containing a benzene ring or similar chemical group: compare ALIPHATIC. ⋙ **aromatically** *adv*.

aromatic[2] *n* an aromatic substance, plant, drug, or chemical compound.

arose *v* past tense of ARISE.

around[1] *adv* **1** used like ABOUT[1], in various senses, e.g.: **a** in the vicinity. **b** in various directions; to and fro. **c** used with verbs to convey purposelessness. **d** in existence. **e** *chiefly NAm* approximately. **2** *chiefly NAm* used like ROUND[2] in various senses, e.g.: **a** in a rough circle surrounding something or somebody. **b** from person to person. **c** so as to face the other way. **d** so as to move in a circle.

around[2] *prep* **1** used like ABOUT[2], ROUND[3] in various senses, e.g.: **a** here and there in (a place). **b** in all directions outwards from (oneself). **2** used like ROUND[3] in certain senses, e.g.: **a** so as to encircle (something). **b** *chiefly NAm* with a change of direction occasioned by (a corner, bend, or obstacle).

arouse *v* **1** to stimulate (a feeling) or evoke (a reaction or response). **2** to awaken (somebody) from sleep. **3** to rouse to action. **4** to excite sexually. ⋙ **arousal** *n*.

ARP *abbr* air-raid precautions.

arpeggio *n* (*pl* **-os**) a chord with notes that are played in succession, not simultaneously.

arquebus *or* **harquebus** *n* an early type of portable matchlock usu fired from a support, used in the 15th and 16th cents.

arrack *or* **arak** *n* an alcoholic spirit distilled in various Eastern countries from rice, the sap of the coco palm, etc.

arraign *v* to charge formally with an offence in a court of law. ⋙ **arraignment** *n*.

arrange *v* **1** to put in order or into sequence or relationship. **2** to make preparations for; to plan. **3** to adapt (a musical composition) by scoring it for different voices or instruments. **4** to make plans. ⋙ **arrangeable** *adj*, **arranger** *n*.

arrangement *n* **1** a preliminary measure; a preparation or plan. **2** an informal agreement or settlement, *esp* on personal, social, or political matters. **3** something made by arranging constituents or things together, or the way in which they are arranged. **4** an adaptation of a musical composition for different voices or instruments.

arrant *adj* usu intensifying contemptuous terms: complete; utter. ⋙ **arrantly** *adv*.

arras *n* (*pl* **arras**) a wall hanging or screen made of tapestry.

array[1] *v* **1** to set or place in order; to marshal. **2** to dress or decorate, *esp* in splendid or impressive clothes; to adorn.

array[2] *n* **1** an imposing collection or large number. **2** an orderly arrangement of things or people, *esp* troops. **3** *literary or archaic* clothing; apparel.

arrears *pl n* an unpaid or overdue debt. ✻ **in arrears 1** behind in the payment of a debt or the discharge of an obligation. **2** of rent or wages: paid at the end of a particular period.

arrest[1] *v* **1** to seize or capture, *esp* to take or keep in custody by authority of law. **2** to catch and fix or hold. **3a** to bring to a stop. **b** to make inactive.

arrest[2] *n* **1** the act of taking or detaining somebody in custody by authority of law. **2** a stoppage or cessation, e.g. of the function of an organ.

arresting *adj* catching the attention; striking. ⋙ **arrestingly** *adv*.

arrhythmia *n* an abnormal alteration in rhythm of the heartbeat. ⋙ **arrhythmic** *adj*.

arrival *n* **1** the act or time of arriving. **2** somebody or something that has arrived.

arrive *v* **1** to reach a destination. **2** to come. **3** to achieve success. ✻ **arrive at** to reach by effort or thought.

arriviste /aree'veest/ *n* a person who puts self-advancement above scruple; a climber or careerist.

arrogant *adj* having a feeling of superiority over others, as revealed in a haughty overbearing manner or in presumptuous claims. ⋙ **arrogance** *n*, **arrogantly** *adv*.

arrogate *v* to claim or take without justification. ⋙ **arrogation** *n*.

arrondissement /arən'deesmənt/ *n* **1** an administrative district of some large French cities, *esp* Paris. **2** a parliamentary division of a French department.

arrow[1] *n* **1** a projectile shot from a bow, usu having a slender shaft, a pointed head, and feathers at the end. **2** something shaped like an arrow; *esp* a mark or sign indicating direction.

arrow[2] *v* to move with speed and precision.

arrowroot *n* a tropical American plant with fleshy roots which yield a nutritive starch that is used as a thickening agent in cooking.

arroyo *n* (*pl* **-os**) *NAm* a gully or channel carved by running water.

arse *n Brit, coarse slang* **1** the buttocks: compare ASS[2]. **2** the anus.

arsenal *n* a store of weapons and ammunition.

arsenic *n* a steel-grey metalloid chemical element which forms many poisonous compounds. ⋙ **arsenical** *adj*, **arsenide** *n*.

arson *n* the criminal act of setting fire to property in order to cause destruction. ⋙ **arsonist** *n*.

art[1] *n* **1a** the conscious use of skill and creative imagination, *esp* in the production of aesthetic objects. **b** paintings, sculptures, and other works produced using skill and creative imagination. **c** any of the fine arts or graphic arts. **2a** a skill acquired by experience, study, or observation. **b** an activity which requires a combination of practical knowledge, judgment, and imagination. **3** (**the Arts**) the humanities as contrasted with science. **4** decorative or illustrative elements in books and other printed matter; artwork.

art[2] *v* archaic second person sing. present of BE.

art deco *n* a decorative style of the 1920s and 1930s characterized *esp* by bold geometric shapes and bright contrasting colours, and the use of new materials, e.g. plastic.

artefact *or* **artifact** *n* a product of human workmanship, e.g. a tool or a pot, often as a subject of archaeological study.

arterial *adj* **1** relating to or located in an artery. **2** denoting the bright red blood contained in an artery. **3** denoting a main road linking large cities and towns.

arteriole *n* a small branch of an artery connecting it with capillaries. ⋙ **arteriolar** *adj.*

arteriosclerosis *n* abnormal thickening and hardening of the arterial walls.

artery *n* (*pl* **-ies**) **1** any of the branching elastic-walled blood vessels that carry blood from the heart to the lungs and through the body: compare CAPILLARY[1], VEIN. **2** a main channel of transport or communication, *esp* a road, railway line, or river.

artesian well *n* a well sunk perpendicularly into sloping strata receiving water from a higher level than that of the well, so that the water reaches the surface under its own pressure, with little or no pumping.

artful *adj* clever in attaining an end, often by deceitful or indirect means; crafty. ⋙ **artfully** *adv,* **artfulness** *n.*

art house *n* a cinema specializing in films that do not have mass appeal, e.g. artistic or experimental films.

arthritic *adj* relating to or affected with arthritis. ⋙ **arthritic** *n.*

arthritis *n* an illness causing painful inflammation and stiffness of the joints.

arthropod *n* an invertebrate animal with a jointed body and limbs and usu an outer skin made of chitin, such as an insect, spider, or crustacean.

arthroscope *n* an instrument for examining or operating on the interior of a joint. ⋙ **arthroscopic** *adj,* **arthroscopy** *n.*

Arthurian *adj* relating to the legend of King Arthur and his royal court.

artichoke *n* (*also* **globe artichoke**) the flower head of a tall thistle-like plant, used as a vegetable.

article[1] *n* **1** a particular or separate object or thing, *esp* viewed as a member of a class of things. **2** a piece of non-fictional prose, usu forming an independent part of a magazine, newspaper, etc. **3** a separate clause, item, provision, or point in a text, document, etc. **4a** (*in pl*) a written agreement specifying conditions of apprenticeship. **b** a period of work with a firm undertaken by a trainee solicitor, architect, accountant, or surveyor. **5** a word or affix, e.g. *a, an,* and *the,* used with nouns to specify indefiniteness or definiteness: compare DEFINITE ARTICLE, INDEFINITE ARTICLE. ✱ **article of faith** a strongly held belief.

article[2] *v* to bind by articles, e.g. of apprenticeship.

articled clerk *n Brit* a trainee solicitor.

articular *adj* relating to a joint.

articulate[1] *adj* **1** expressing oneself clearly or effectively. **2** of speech or writing: clearly and intelligibly expressed. **3** having joints. ⋙ **articulacy** *n,* **articulately** *adv,* **articulateness** *n.*

articulate[2] *v* **1a** to say (words) clearly and distinctly. **b** to express (an idea) clearly and effectively. **2** to unite (a body part) with a joint. **3** of two bones: to fit together or interconnect to form a joint. ⋙ **articulation** *n.*

articulated *adj* **1** having joints; connected by joints. **2** *chiefly Brit* denoting a commercial vehicle with a tractor and trailer linked by a bar with a pivoting joint.

artifact *n* see ARTEFACT.

artifice *n* **1** an artful device, expedient, or stratagem; a trick. **2** clever or artful skill; ingenuity.

artificer *n* **1** a skilled or artistic worker or designer. **2** a military or naval mechanic.

artificial *adj* **1** made by human skill and labour, often to a natural model; synthetic. **2** of somebody's manner: lacking in natural quality; affected or insincere. ⋙ **artificiality** *n,* **artificially** *adv.*

artificial insemination *n* introduction of semen into the uterus or vagina by other than natural means.

artificial intelligence *n* a branch of computer science that aims to produce machines, e.g. robots or computers, that can emulate human behaviour, understanding, etc.

artificial respiration *n* the rhythmic forcing of air into and out of the lungs of somebody whose breathing has stopped.

artillery *n* (*pl* **-ies**) **1** large-calibre mounted firearms, e.g. guns and missile launchers. **2** (*used as sing. or pl*) a branch of an army armed with artillery.

artisan *n* a skilled manual worker.

artist *n* **1** a person who practises an imaginative art such as painting or sculpture. **2** a skilled performer; *esp* an artiste. **3** *informal* somebody who is proficient in a specified and usu dubious activity; an expert.

artiste /ah'teest/ *n* a skilled public performer, *esp* a musical or theatrical entertainer.

artistic *adj* **1** concerning or characteristic of art or artists. **2** showing imaginative skill in arrangement or execution. ⋙ **artistically** *adv.*

artistry *n* artistic quality or ability.

artless *adj* **1** free from artificiality or affectation; natural. **2** free from deceit, guile, or artifice. **3** clumsy. ⋙ **artlessly** *adv,* **artlessness** *n.*

art nouveau /,ah(t) nooh'voh/ *n* a decorative style of late 19th-cent. origin, characterized *esp* by flattened curves and plant motifs.

artsy *adj* (**-ier, -iest**) *NAm* = ARTY.

artwork *n* **1** paintings, drawings, and other works of art collectively. **2** the pictures and illustrations in a printed text.

arty *adj* (**-ier, -iest**) showily or pretentiously artistic. ⋙ **artiness** *n.*

arugula *n NAm* = ROCKET[3].

arum *n* an Old World plant with tiny, densely packed flowers enclosed in a large fleshy SPATHE (leaflike sheath), e.g. a cuckoopint.

arum lily *n* a lily-like African plant with a large SPATHE (leaflike sheath).

arvo *n* (*pl* **-os**) *Aus, NZ, informal* the afternoon.

-ary[1] *suffix* forming nouns, with the meanings: **1** belonging to or connected with something: *ovary.* **2** a place or repository for something: *library.*

-ary[2] *suffix* forming adjectives, with the meaning: relating to or connected with something: *military.*

Aryan *n* **1a** a member of a people speaking an Indo-European language, who appeared as invaders in N India in the second millennium BC. **b** the language of this people. **2** in Nazi ideology, a white non-Jewish person of typically Nordic features, held to be racially superior. ⋙ **Aryan** *adj.*

As *abbr* the chemical symbol for arsenic.

as[1] *adv* to the same degree or amount; equally; so.

as[2] *conj* **1** used in comparisons: *as deaf as a post; as many as 100.* **2** used to give a reason: *As it's raining, we'll stay indoors.* **3** in accordance with: *Do as I say.* **4** used to indicate an action occurring at the same time: *As we turned the corner, a wheel fell off.*

as[3] *prep* **1** in the capacity, role, state, etc of. **2** used with certain verbs of regarding and describing.

as- *prefix* see AD-.

asafoetida (*NAm* **asafetida**) *n* the fetid gum resin of various oriental plants of the carrot family. It is used in cookery, *esp* in India and the Middle East, to add flavour and aid digestion.

a.s.a.p. *abbr* as soon as possible.

asbestos *n* any of several minerals composed of thin flexible fibres, used to make non-combustible, non-conducting, or chemically resistant materials.

asbestosis *n* a disease of the body caused by the inhalation of asbestos particles.

ascend *v* **1** to move or slope gradually upwards; to rise. **2** to go or move up (something, e.g. a slope). **3** to rise from a lower level or degree. **4** to rise in pitch.

ascendancy *or* **ascendency** *n* controlling influence; domination.

ascendant[1] *or* **ascendent** *n* **1** the degree of the zodiac that rises above the eastern horizon at any moment, e.g. at one's birth. **2** a state or position of dominant power or importance.

ascendant[2] *or* **ascendent** *adj* **1** rising. **2** superior or dominant.

ascendency *n* see ASCENDANCY.

ascendent *n and adj* see ASCENDANT[1], ASCENDANT[2].

ascension *n* **1** the act of ascending. **2** (**Ascension**) in Christianity, Jesus Christ's ascent to heaven after rising from the dead.

ascent *n* **1a** the act of going, climbing, or travelling up. **b** a way up; an upward slope or path. **2** an advance in social status or reputation; progress.

ascertain *v* to find out or learn (something) with certainty. ⋙ **ascertainable** *adj*, **ascertainment** *n*.

ascetic *adj* **1** practising strict self-denial as a spiritual discipline. **2** austere in appearance, manner, or attitude. ⋙ **ascetic** *n*, **ascetically** *adv*, **asceticism** *n*.

ASCII *n* a computer code used for representing characters as binary numbers storable in a computer memory.

ascites /ə'sieteez/ *n* (*pl* **ascites**) the accumulation of fluid in the abdomen.

ascorbic acid *n* a compound occurring in citrus fruits and green vegetables that is essential in the diet for the maintenance of healthy connective tissue. Also called VITAMIN C.

ascribe *v* **1** to refer or attribute (something) to a supposed cause or source. **2** to attribute (a quality) to a person or thing. **3** to attribute (a work of art or literature) to somebody. ⋙ **ascribable** *adj*, **ascription** *n*.

asdic *n* an echo-sounding device for detecting submarines: compare SONAR.

aseptic *adj* **1** preventing infection. **2** free or freed from disease-causing micro-organisms.

asexual *adj* **1** having no sex organs, or apparently without sex. **2** produced without sexual action or differentiation. **3** without expression of or reference to sexual interest. ⋙ **asexuality** *n*, **asexually** *adv*.

as for *prep* concerning or in regard to (somebody or something).

ash[1] *n* **1** a tall pinnate-leaved tree of the olive family with tough elastic wood. **2** the ligature *æ* used in Old English.

ash[2] *n* **1** the solid residue left when material is thoroughly burned or oxidized. **2** (*in pl*) **a** the remains of something destroyed by fire. **b** the remains of a dead body after cremation or disintegration.

ashamed *adj* feeling shame, guilt, or disgrace. ⋙ **ashamedly** *adv*.

ash blonde *or* **ash blond** *adj* of hair: of a pale or silvery blonde colour.

ashcan *n NAm* a dustbin.

ashen *adj* deadly pale; blanched.

Ashes *pl n* (**the Ashes**) a trophy played for in a series of cricket Test matches between England and Australia.

Ashkenazi /ashkə'nahzi/ *n* (*pl* **Ashkenazim**) a Yiddish-speaking Jewish person from central Europe or with central European ancestry: compare SEPHARDI.

ashlar *n* **1** hewn or squared stone, or masonry consisting of such stone. **2** a thin squared and dressed stone for facing a wall of rubble or brick.

ashore *adv* on or to the shore.

ashram *n* a religious retreat or sanctuary, *esp* the retreat of a Hindu sage.

ashtray *n* a receptacle for tobacco ash and cigar and cigarette ends.

Ash Wednesday *n* the first day of Lent.

ashy *adj* (**-ier, -iest**) **1** of ashes. **2** = ASHEN.

Asian *adj* relating to or characteristic of the continent of Asia or its people. ⋙ **Asian** *n*.

Asiatic *adj* relating to Asia.

A-side *n* the main side of a vinyl record.

aside[1] *adv and adj* **1** to or towards the side. **2** out of the way. **3** in reserve for future use.

aside[2] *n* **1** an actor's speech supposedly not heard by other characters on stage. **2** a digression.

aside from *prep chiefly NAm* = APART FROM.

asinine *adj* lacking intelligence or common sense; stupid. ⋙ **asininity** *n*.

-asis *suffix* see -IASIS.

ask *v* **1a** to call on for an answer. **b** to put a question about (something). **c** to put or frame (a question). **2a** to make a request of. **b** to make a request for. **3** (*used in the continuous tenses*) to behave in such a way as to provoke (an unpleasant response). **4** to set as a price. **5** to invite. **6** to seek information. **7** to enquire after somebody's welfare. ✱ **a big ask** *Aus, NZ, informal* a steep demand; a tall order. **for the asking** with little or no outlay or effort.

askance ✱ **look askance at** to regard (something or someone) with disapproval or distrust.

askari /ə'skahri/ *n* (*pl* **askaris** *or* **askari**) an E African soldier or police officer.

askew *adv and adj* out of line; awry.

asking price *n* the price set by the seller.

ask out *v* to invite (somebody) to accompany one somewhere on a date.

aslant *prep, adv, and adj* in a slanting direction, or over or across (something) in a slanting direction.

asleep *adj* **1** in a state of sleep. **2** of a limb: lacking sensation; numb.

AS level *n* an examination intermediate between GCSE and A level.

asp *n* **1** a small viper that has an upturned snout. **2** a small African cobra.

asparagine *n* an amino acid that is found in most proteins.

asparagus *n* a spike-shaped shoot of a plant of the lily family, used as a vegetable.

aspartame *n* an artificial sweetener prepared from aspartic acid and phenylalanine.

aspartic acid *n* an amino acid found in most proteins.

aspect *n* **1a** a particular feature of a situation, plan, or point of view. **b** appearance to the eye or mind. **2a** a position facing a particular direction. **b** the side of a building facing a certain direction. ⋙ **aspectual** *adj*.

aspect ratio *n* **1** the ratio of an aerofoil's span to its mean chord. **2** the ratio of the width to the height of a screen or image, e.g. in television or the cinema.

aspen *n* a poplar with leaves that flutter in the lightest wind.

Asperger's syndrome *n* a slight psychiatric disorder related to autism, characterized by difficulty with social interaction and rather narrow preoccupations.

asperity *n* (*pl* **-ies**) **1** roughness of manner or temper; harshness. **2** roughness of surface; unevenness.

aspersion ✱ **cast aspersions on** to attack the reputation of; to defame.

asphalt *n* **1** a brown to black bituminous substance found in natural beds and also obtained as a residue in petroleum or coal tar refining. **2** an asphaltic composition used for surfacing roads and footpaths. ➤➤ **asphaltic** *adj.*

asphodel *n* an Old World plant of the lily family with long spikes of flowers.

asphyxia *n* a lack of oxygen in the body, usu caused by an interruption of breathing, resulting in unconsciousness or death.

asphyxiate *v* **1** to suffer a lack of oxygen in the body and become unconscious or die as a result. **2** to kill or make unconscious in this way. ➤➤ **asphyxiation** *n.*

aspic *n* a clear savoury jelly, e.g. of fish or meat stock.

aspidistra *n* an Asiatic plant of the lily family with large leaves, often grown as a house plant.

aspirate[1] *v* **1** to pronounce (a vowel, consonant, or word) with an *h*-sound. **2** to draw or remove (e.g. blood) by suction. **3** *technical* to inhale.

aspirate[2] *n* **1** an independent /h/ sound, or the character, *esp h*, representing this sound. **2** an aspirated consonant, e.g. the *p* of *pit*.

aspiration *n* **1** a strong desire to achieve something important; an ambition. **2** the pronunciation or addition of an aspirate. **3** the action of aspirating. ➤➤ **aspirational** *adj.*

aspirator *n* an apparatus for aspirating fluid, tissue, etc from the body.

aspire *v* (*usu* + to) to seek to attain or accomplish a particular goal. ➤➤ **aspirant** *n and adj,* **aspirer** *n,* **aspiring** *adj.*

aspirin *n* (*pl* **aspirin** *or* **aspirins**) the compound acetylsalicylic acid used in the form of a tablet for relief of pain and fever.

as regards *prep* with respect to or in regard to (somebody or something).

ass[1] *n* **1** either of two species of long-eared hardy gregarious mammals related to and smaller than the horse. **2** a stupid or obstinate person or thing.

ass[2] *n chiefly NAm* = ARSE.

assail *v* **1** to attack (somebody) violently with blows or words. **2** of a feeling: to prey on (somebody).

assailant *n* a person who carries out a physical attack; an attacker.

assassin *n* a murderer, *esp* of a political or religious leader.

assassinate *v* to kill (a political or religious leader) suddenly or secretly. ➤➤ **assassination** *n.*

assault[1] *n* **1** a violent physical or verbal attack. **2a** an attempt to do or immediate threat of doing unlawful personal violence. **b** rape or other physical attack of a sexual nature. **3** an attempt to attack a fortification by a sudden rush.

assault[2] *v* **1** to make an assault on. **2** to rape or sexually attack. ➤➤ **assaultive** *adj.*

assault and battery *n* the crime of attacking somebody physically and causing them bodily harm.

assault course *n* an obstacle course on which soldiers train for an assault.

assay[1] *n* analysis of an ore, drug, etc to determine the presence, absence, or quantity of one or more components.

assay[2] *v* **1a** to analyse (an ore, etc) for one or more valuable components. **b** to determine the purity of (gold, silver, or another precious metal). **2** *archaic* to attempt. ➤➤ **assayer** *n.*

assay office *n* **1** an office at which ores are assayed. **2** *Brit* an institution that awards a hallmark on articles of gold, silver, or platinum.

assegai *n* (*pl* **assegais**) a slender hardwood spear with an iron tip used by tribal societies in southern Africa.

assemblage *n* **1** a collection of people or things; a gathering or accumulation. **2** an artistic work consisting of a three-dimensional collage made from scraps or odds and ends.

assemble *v* **1** to bring together (a group of people or a collection of things) in a particular place or for a particular purpose. **2** to gather together; to convene. **3** to fit together the parts of (a kit, model, etc).

assembly *n* (*pl* **-ies**) **1** a company of people gathered together for a particular purpose; *specif* a regular gathering of staff and pupils of a school for announcements, etc. **2** (**Assembly**) a legislative or deliberative body. **3** the process of assembling or of being assembled. **4a** the fitting together of manufactured parts into a complete machine, structure, etc. **b** the collection of parts to be so assembled, or the finished structure.

assembly line *n* an arrangement of factory machines and equipment by means of which work passes through successive stages and operations until the product is assembled.

assent[1] *v* to agree to something. ➤➤ **assenter** *n,* **assentor** *n.*

assent[2] *n* **1** the act of agreeing; formal agreement. **2** acquiescence.

assert *v* **1** to state or declare forcefully. **2** to give positive demonstration of (a quality or attribute). **3** to insist on (a right or claim). ✱ **assert oneself** to compel recognition of one's individuality, authority, or rights.

assertion *n* **1** a declaration or positive statement. **2** the act of asserting.

assertive *adj* **1** characterized by bold assertion; dogmatic. **2** (*also* **self-assertive**) self-confident and firm in dealing with others and getting one's way. ➤➤ **assertively** *adv,* **assertiveness** *n.*

assess *v* **1** to determine the rate or amount of (a tax, claim for damages, etc). **2** (*often* + at) to make an official valuation of (property or income) for the purposes of taxation. **3** to estimate the quality or worth of; to evaluate. ➤➤ **assessable** *adj,* **assessment** *n,* **assessor** *n.*

asset *n* **1a** (*in pl*) the total property of a person, company, or institution; *esp* that part which can be used to pay debts. **b** a single item of property. **2** an advantage or resource.

asset-stripping *n* the practice of taking over an unsuccessful company and selling its assets separately at a profit.

asseverate *v formal* to affirm solemnly. ➤➤ **asseveration** *n.*

assiduity *n* **1** persistent application; diligence. **2** solicitous or obsequious attention to a person.

assiduous *adj* showing careful unremitting attention or persistent application; sedulous. ⋙ **assiduously** *adv,* **assiduousness** *n.*

assign *v* **1a** to allot (a task, place, accommodation, etc) to somebody. **b** to appoint to a particular charge. **2** to transfer (property) to another person, *esp* in trust or for the benefit of creditors. **3** to fix authoritatively (a date for a future event, etc). **4** to ascribe as the motive or reason. ⋙ **assignable** *adj,* **assigner** *n,* **assignor** *n.*

assignation *n* **1** the act of assigning. **2** a meeting, *esp* a secret one with a lover.

assignee *n* **1** a person to whom property or a right is legally transferred. **2** a person appointed to act for another.

assignment *n* **1a** a position, post, or job to which one is assigned. **b** a specified task or amount of work assigned by somebody in authority, *esp* a teacher or tutor. **2** the legal transfer of property or a document putting this into effect.

assimilate *v* **1a** to take in or absorb (a substance) into the system, *esp* as nourishment. **b** to absorb and understand (facts or information). **2a** to make (one thing) similar to another. **b** to absorb (e.g. immigrants) into a cultural tradition. **3** to become assimilated. ⋙ **assimilable** *adj,* **assimilation** *n,* **assimilative** *adj.*

assist[1] *v* to help (somebody); to give support.

assist[2] *n chiefly NAm* in baseball and other games, the action of a player who by throwing the ball enables a teammate to put an opponent out or score a goal.

assistance *n* the act of assisting or the help supplied; aid.

assistant *n* **1** a person who assists; a helper. **2** (*also* **shop assistant**) a person who serves customers in a shop, etc.

assize *n* (*usu in pl*) the periodical sessions of the courts formerly held in every English county for trial of civil and criminal cases.

associate[1] *v* **1** to involve (a person or group) with another, typically more powerful one, e.g. as a business partner or ally. **2** (*usu in passive*) to involve or connect (somebody or something) with something. **3** (*often* + with) to come together as partners, or mix socially as friends or companions. **4** to combine or join with other parts; to unite.

associate[2] *adj* **1** sharing a function or office with another. **2** having secondary or subordinate status.

associate[3] *n* **1** a fellow worker; a partner or colleague. **2** a person admitted to a subordinate degree of membership.

association *n* **1** an organization of people having a common interest; a society or league. **2** a link in memory, thought, or imagination with a thing or person; a connotation. **3** associating or being associated; *specif* the formation of mental connections between sensations, ideas, memories, etc. ⋙ **associational** *adj.*

Association Football *n* football played by teams of eleven players using a round ball which may be kicked and passed to another player but not handled, except by the goalkeepers.

associative *adj* **1** dependent on or acquired by association or learning. **2** denoting a mathematical operation that gives the same result regardless of the order of the elements. ⋙ **associatively** *adv,* **associativity** *n.*

assonance *n* **1** resemblance of sound in words or syllables. **2** repetition of the vowel sounds in two or more words, e.g. in *stony* and *holy,* or the consonant sounds, as an alternative to rhyme: compare CONSONANCE. ⋙ **assonant** *adj.*

assorted *adj* consisting of various kinds mixed together.

assortment *n* a mixed collection of various kinds of things or people.

assuage *v* **1** to lessen the intensity of (suffering, discomfort, etc). **2** to put an end to by satisfying; to appease or quench. ⋙ **assuagement** *n.*

assume *v* **1** to take (a supposition or hypothesis) as granted or true; to suppose (something) for the sake of argument. **2a** to take (a role etc) upon oneself; to undertake (a task or duty). **b** to invest oneself formally with (an office or its symbols). **3a** to pretend to feign (a certain attitude). **b** to adopt (a new name, identity, etc). **4** to acquire or grow to have (significance). **5** to seize or usurp (power or authority).

assumption *n* **1a** the supposition that something is true. **b** a fact or statement, e.g. a proposition, taken for granted. **2** the act of assuming. **3** the act of laying claim to or taking possession of something. **4a** the taking up of a person into heaven. **b** (**Assumption**) 15 August, observed by Christians in commemoration of the assumption of the Virgin Mary.

assurance *n* **1** the act of assuring; a positive declaration that something is the case. **2a** the quality or state of being sure or certain; freedom from doubt. **b** confidence of mind or manner; excessive self-confidence. **3** *chiefly Brit* life insurance.

Usage note

assurance *or* **insurance**? British English uses the term *assurance* to refer to a form of insurance in which money is bound to be paid out at the end of a fixed period of time or on the death of the insured person: *life assurance. Insurance* is the general term covering all instances where money will only be paid in particular circumstances: *house contents insurance; travel insurance.*

assure *v* **1** to inform (somebody) positively that something is the case. **2** to give confidence to; to reassure. **3** to guarantee the happening or attainment of; to ensure. **4** (*usu in passive*) to insure (life, safety, etc). ⋙ **assurer** *n.*

assured *adj* **1** characterized by self-confidence and expertise. **2** characterized by certainty; guaranteed. ⋙ **assuredly** *adv.*

Assyrian *n* a member of an ancient Semitic kingdom and people of Mesopotamia. ⋙ **Assyrian** *adj.*

astatine *n* a radioactive chemical element of the halogen group, similar to iodine and formed by radioactive decay or made artificially.

aster *n* a composite plant, often with a showy head and leafy stem, blooming chiefly in the autumn.

asterisk[1] *n* the sign (*) used as a reference mark, *esp* to denote the omission of letters or words or to show that something is doubtful or absent.

asterisk[2] *v* to mark with an asterisk; to star.

asterism *n* **1** a pattern of stars within a constellation. **2** three asterisks arranged in the form of a pyramid, used in a text to direct attention to a following passage.

astern *adv* behind or towards the stern of a ship or aircraft.

asteroid *n* a small planet in the form of a rocky body mostly between Mars and Jupiter.

asthma *n* an allergic condition marked by attacks of laboured breathing with wheezing, coughing, and a sense of constriction in the chest. ⋙ **asthmatic** *adj and n.*

astigmatism *n* a defect of an optical system, e.g. a lens or the eye, in which rays from a single point fail to meet in a focal point, resulting in patchy blurring of the image. ➤➤ **astigmatic** *adj.*

astilbe *n* a plant of the saxifrage family grown in gardens for its showy white or purple flowers.

astir *adj* **1** in a state of bustle or excitement. **2** out of bed; up.

astonish *v* to affect with sudden wonder or surprise. ➤➤ **astonished** *adj,* **astonishing** *adj,* **astonishingly** *adv,* **astonishment** *n.*

astound *v* to affect with bewilderment and wonder. ➤➤ **astounded** *adj,* **astounding** *adj,* **astoundingly** *adv.*

astr- *comb. form* see ASTRO-.

astrakhan /astra'kan/ *n* **1** karakul sheep wool of Russian origin. **2** a woollen fabric with curled and looped pile.

astral *adj* relating to or consisting of stars.

astray *adv* **1** off the right path or route. **2** in error; away from a proper or desirable course or development.

astride[1] *adv* with the legs wide apart.

astride[2] *prep* **1** on or above (something) and with one leg on each side of it. **2** extending over or across (something); spanning (something).

astringent[1] *adj* **1** of a lotion or other application: having a contracting and firming effect on the soft tissues of the body. **2** checking the flow of a bodily fluid, e.g. blood; styptic. **3** of wit or remarks: showing little sentiment or sympathy; dry or caustic. **4** sharply refreshing. ➤➤ **astringency** *n,* **astringently** *adv.*

astringent[2] *n* an astringent liquid.

astro- *or* **astr-** *comb. form* denoting: stars or the heavens; outer space: *astrophysics.*

astrodome *n* **1** a transparent dome in the roof of an aircraft, through which astronomical observations can be made. **2** *chiefly NAm* a sports stadium with a domed roof.

astrolabe *n* an instrument formerly used to show the positions of the planets and bright stars at any date and time.

astrology *n* the art or practice of determining the supposed influences of the planets and their motions on human affairs and human disposition. ➤➤ **astrologer** *n,* **astrological** *adj,* **astrologically** *adv.*

astronaut *n* a person trained to travel in space.

astronautics *pl n* (*used as sing. or pl*) the science of the construction and operation of vehicles for travel in space.

astronomer *n* a person who is skilled in or practises astronomy.

astronomical *or* **astronomic** *adj* **1** relating to astronomy. **2** *informal* enormously or inconceivably large. ➤➤ **astronomically** *adv.*

astronomical unit *n* a unit of length used in astronomy, equal to the mean distance of the earth from the sun, or about 149 million km (about 93 million mi).

astronomy *n* the scientific study of the stars, planets, and other bodies of the universe.

astrophysics *pl n* (*used as sing. or pl*) a branch of astronomy dealing with the physical nature of astronomical bodies and phenomena. ➤➤ **astrophysical** *adj,* **astrophysicist** *n.*

AstroTurf *n trademark* an artificial grasslike surface that is used for sports fields.

astute *adj* shrewd and perceptive. ➤➤ **astutely** *adv,* **astuteness** *n.*

asunder *adv literary* **1** into parts. **2** apart from each other in position.

as well *adv* **1** in addition; also. **2** with an effect that is the same or preferable.

as yet *adv* up to now, or up to the time mentioned.

asylum *n* **1** protection from arrest and extradition given by a nation to political refugees. **2** a place of retreat and security, or the refuge provided by it. **3** *dated* an institution for the care of the destitute or afflicted, *esp* the insane.

asymmetric *or* **asymmetrical** *adj* not symmetrical. ➤➤ **asymmetrically** *adv,* **asymmetry** *n.*

asymmetric bars *pl n* a pair of parallel wooden bars, one higher than the other, used for gymnastics exercises.

asymptomatic *adj* of a patient or a disorder: presenting no symptoms of disease.

asymptote *n* a straight line that is approached more and more closely by a curve but not met by it. ➤➤ **asymptotic** *adj,* **asymptotically** *adv.*

asynchronous *adj* not synchronous; proceeding at its own pace. ➤➤ **asynchronously** *adv.*

At *abbr* the chemical symbol for astatine.

at[1] *prep* **1** used to indicate position in or movement towards a place: *at the station.* **2** used to indicate a time: *at midnight.* **3** used to indicate a rate or value: *estimated at 5,000.* **4** used to express the object of an action: *Look at them!* **5** used to indicate a state: *at risk.* ✱ **at that** used to emphasize some striking aspect; too. **where it's at** see WHERE[2].

at[2] *n* (*pl* **at**) a unit of currency in Laos, worth 100th of a kip.

at- *prefix* see AD-.

at all *adv* used for emphasis with negatives or in questions.

atavism *n* **1** the recurrence in an organism of a form typical of ancestors more remote than the parents. **2** reversion to an earlier type. **3** an individual or character manifesting atavism; a throwback. ➤➤ **atavistic** *adj,* **atavistically** *adv.*

ataxia *n* an inability to coordinate voluntary muscular movements that is symptomatic of some nervous disorders. ➤➤ **ataxic** *adj.*

ATC *abbr* **1** air traffic control. **2** Air Training Corps.

ate *v* past tense of EAT.

-ate[1] *suffix* forming nouns, denoting: **1** the product of a specified process: *distillate.* **2** a chemical compound or complex ANION (negatively charged atom or group of atoms) derived from a specified compound or element: *ferrate.* **3** the salt or ester of a specified acid with a name ending in *-ic* and not beginning with *hydro-*: *sulphate.*

-ate[2] *suffix* forming nouns, denoting: **1** the office, function, or rank of the official or title-bearer specified: *consulate.* **2** an individual or group of people holding a specified office or rank or having the function specified: *electorate.*

-ate[3] *suffix* forming verbs, with the meanings: **1** to act in a specified way: *pontificate.* **2** to change the state or status of (somebody or something) in the way specified: *activate.* **3** to provide (somebody or something) with the thing specified: *pollinate.*

atelier *n* an artist's or designer's studio or workroom.

atheism *n* the belief or doctrine that there is no deity. ➤➤ **atheist** *n,* **atheistic** *adj,* **atheistical** *adj.*

atheling *n* an Anglo-Saxon prince or nobleman.

Athenian *n* a native or inhabitant of Athens. ➤➤ **Athenian** *adj.*

atherosclerosis *n* arteriosclerosis with the deposition of fatty substances on and fibrosis of the inner lining of the arteries. ➤➤ **atherosclerotic** *adj.*

athlete *n* a person who is trained or skilled in exercises, sports, etc that require physical strength, agility, or stamina, *esp* in athletics.

athlete's foot *n* a form of RINGWORM (fungal infection) of the feet affecting the skin between the toes.

athletic *adj* **1** relating to athletes or athletics. **2** characteristic of an athlete; vigorous or active. **3** aid of a person's build: slim, muscular, and well-proportioned. ➤➤ **athletically** *adv,* **athleticism** *n.*

athletics *pl n* (*used as sing. or pl*) **1** *Brit* competitive running, walking, throwing, and jumping sports collectively. **2** *NAm* exercises, sports, or games in general.

at home *n* a reception or party that one gives in one's own house.

athwart[1] *adv* across, *esp* in an oblique direction.

athwart[2] *prep* across (something).

-ation *suffix* forming nouns from verbs, denoting: the action, process, or result of doing something: *flirtation; computation.*

Atlantic *adj* of or found near the Atlantic Ocean.

atlas *n* **1** a book of maps, charts, or tables. **2** the topmost vertebra of the neck, supporting the skull.

ATM *abbr* automated teller machine.

atmosphere *n* **1** a mass of gas enveloping a celestial body, e.g. a planet; *esp* all the air surrounding the earth. **2** the air or climate of a locality. **3** a surrounding feeling or mood encountered in some ambience or environment. **4** a unit of pressure chosen to be a typical pressure of the air at sea level and equal to 101,325 newtons per square metre (about 14.7lb per square inch).

atmospheric *adj* **1** of, occurring in, or like the atmosphere. **2** having, marked by, or contributing aesthetic or emotional atmosphere. ➤➤ **atmospherically** *adv.*

atmospherics *pl n* electrical atmospheric phenomena, e.g. lightning, that produce audible disturbances in a radio receiver.

ATOC /'aytok/ *n* Association of Train Operating Companies.

ATOL *abbr* Air Travel Organizer's Licence.

atoll *n* a coral reef surrounding a lagoon.

atom *n* **1** the smallest particle of an element that can exist either alone or in combination, consisting of electrons, protons, and neutrons. **2** a tiny particle; a bit.

atom bomb *or* **atomic bomb** *n* a bomb whose violent explosive power is due to the sudden release of atomic energy derived from the splitting of the nuclei of plutonium, uranium, etc by neutrons in a very rapid chain reaction.

atomic *adj* **1** of or concerned with atoms, atom bombs, or atomic energy. **2** of a chemical element: existing as separate atoms. ➤➤ **atomically** *adv.*

atomic bomb *n* see ATOM BOMB.

atomic clock *n* a highly accurate type of clock that is regulated by the natural vibration frequencies of an atomic system, such as a beam of caesium atoms.

atomicity *n* **1** the state of consisting of atoms. **2** the number of atoms in the molecule of a gaseous element.

atomic mass *n* the mass of an atom expressed in atomic mass units.

atomic mass unit *n* a unit of mass used in atomic and nuclear physics, equal to one twelfth of the mass of an atom of carbon-12.

atomic number *n* the number of protons in the nucleus of an atom, which is characteristic of a chemical element and determines its place in the periodic table.

atomic theory *n* the theory that all material substances are composed of atoms of a relatively small number of types and all the atoms of the same type are identical.

atomic weight *n* a former name for RELATIVE ATOMIC MASS.

atomize *or* **-ise** *v* **1** to reduce (a solid or liquid) to minute particles or to a fine spray. **2** to reduce (something) to atoms or to small discrete units. ➤➤ **atomization** *n.*

atomizer *or* **atomiser** *n* an instrument for atomizing a perfume, disinfectant, etc.

atonal *adj* of a musical composition: organized without reference to a musical key and using the notes of the chromatic scale impartially. ➤➤ **atonality** *n.*

atone *v* to give satisfaction or make amends for a crime, sin, or deficiency.

atonement *n* **1** reparation for an offence or injury; satisfaction. **2** (**Atonement**) the expiation of humankind's original sin through the death of Christ.

atop *prep literary* at the top of or on top of (something).

atopy *n* a tendency to asthma, hay fever, dermatitis, and other allergies; hypersensitivity. ➤➤ **atopic** *adj.*

ATP *n* automatic train protection.

atrabilious *adj formal* ill-humoured or melancholic.

atrium *n* (*pl* **atria** *or* **atriums**) **1** an inner courtyard open to the sky; *specif* in a Roman house. **2** an anatomical cavity or passage; *specif* either of the two upper chambers of the heart that receive blood from the veins and force it into the ventricles (lower chambers; see VENTRICLE); = AURICLE (2). ➤➤ **atrial** *adj.*

atrocious *adj* **1** extremely wicked or cruel; barbaric. **2** *informal* horrifying; appalling. **3** *informal* of very poor quality. ➤➤ **atrociously** *adv,* **atrociousness** *n.*

atrocity *n* (*pl* **-ies**) **1** the quality of being atrocious; extreme wickedness. **2** something shocking or horrifying. **3** (*usu in pl*) a barbarically cruel act. **4** *informal* something ugly; an eyesore.

atrophy[1] *n* (*pl* **-ies**) **1a** the decrease in size or wasting away of a body part or tissue. **b** the arrested development or loss of a part or organ. **2** a wasting away or progressive decline of something, *esp* through lack of use; degeneration. ➤➤ **atrophic** *adj.*

atrophy[2] *v* (**-ies, -ied**) **1** to undergo atrophy; to waste away or degenerate. **2** to cause to undergo atrophy.

atropine *n* an alkaloid found in deadly nightshade and used in medicine to inhibit the parasympathetic nervous system, e.g. in order to dilate the pupils, or to inhibit salivation.

attach *v* **1** to fasten. **2** to ascribe or attribute. **3** to appoint (a person) to serve with an organization for special duties or for a temporary period. **4** to involve or include (a proviso, etc) in a deal etc. **5** to bind (somebody) to oneself by ties of affection. **6** *archaic* to seize (a person or property) by legal authority. **7** to bring (oneself) into an association with a person or group. ➤➤ **attachable** *adj.*

attaché /ə'tashay/ *n* a technical expert on a diplomatic staff.

attaché case *n* a small slim case used for carrying papers.

attached *adj* (+ to) feeling affection or liking for (a person, place, or thing).

attachment *n* **1** the process of attaching one thing, etc to another. **2** a device for attaching to a machine or implement; *esp* one that adds a function. **3a** being personally attached to somebody or something; fidelity. **b** (*often* + to) an affectionate regard for a person, place or thing, *esp* resulting from familiarity. **4** *Brit* a temporary posting or tour of duty in an organization or military unit other than that in which one is normally employed. **5** a computer file or set of data sent with an e-mail message.

attack[1] *v* **1** to set upon forcefully in order to damage, injure, or destroy; to assault. **2** to take the initiative against (the opposing team, etc) in a game or contest. **3** to assail with unfriendly or bitter words. **4** of a disease, etc: to begin to affect or to act on (the body or a part of it) injuriously. **5** to set to work on (a task, etc), *esp* vigorously. ⋙ **attacker** *n.*

attack[2] *n* **1** the act of attacking; an assault. **2** a belligerent or antagonistic action or verbal assault. **3** the beginning of destructive action, e.g. by a chemical agent. **4** a fit of sickness or disease, often of a recurrent type. **5a** an attempt to score or to gain ground in a game. **b** (**the attack**) (*used as sing. or pl*) the attacking players in a team or the positions occupied by them; *specif* the bowlers in a cricket team.

attain *v* **1** to achieve (an objective). **2** *formal* to reach (e.g. a certain age). ⋙ **attainability** *n,* **attainable** *adj.*

attainder *n* formerly, a penalty by which a person sentenced to death or outlawry on conviction for treason or felony forfeited property and civil rights.

attainment *n* something attained; an accomplishment.

attar *n* a fragrant essential oil or perfume obtained from rose petals.

attempt[1] *v* **1** to make an effort, or try (to do something) or to effect or accomplish (something), *esp* without success. **2a** to try to climb (a mountain or mountain face). **b** to try to better or break (a record).

attempt[2] *n* **1** (*often* + at) the act or an instance of attempting something; *esp* an unsuccessful effort. **2** (*often* + on) an effort to conquer a mountain or record. **3** an attack or assault.

attend *v* **1** to go to or be present at (an event or performance). **2** to go regularly to (school or another institution) for instruction, treatment etc. **3** of medical personnel: to look after or tend to (somebody needing treatment). **4** to look after in the role of servant, attendant, or companion. **5** of a bridesmaid or best man: to accompany or escort (a bride or bridegroom). **6** (+ to) to deal with a task, problem, etc. **7** (*often* + to) to listen or watch carefully; to pay attention to what is being said or done. **8** (+ on) to result from something. ⋙ **attender** *n.*

attendance *n* **1** the number of people attending an institution, event, etc. **2** the number of times a person attends an institution, etc, usu out of a possible maximum.

attendant[1] *adj formal* (*often* + on/upon) accompanying or following as a consequence.

attendant[2] *n* a person who attends another to perform a service; *esp* an employee who waits on or looks after customers, etc.

attendee *n* a person attending a conference or similar gathering; a delegate.

attention *n* **1** the activity of attending, *esp* through application of the mind, to an object of sense or thought. **2** consideration with a view to action. **3a** (*usu in pl*) an act of civility or courtesy, *esp* in courtship. **b** sympathetic consideration of the needs and wants of others. **4** usu as a command: a formal position of readiness assumed by a soldier, etc, standing with feet together and body erect. ⋙ **attentional** *adj.*

attention deficit hyperactivity disorder *n* see ADHD.

attentive *adj* **1** paying attention. **2** concerned for the welfare of somebody; solicitous. ⋙ **attentively** *adv,* **attentiveness** *n.*

attenuate *v* (*usu in passive*) **1** to weaken or lessen the force or strength of. **2** to cause to taper or diminish in width. ⋙ **attenuation** *n.*

attest *v* **1a** to affirm the truth or existence of. **b** to authenticate officially. **2** to be proof of or bear witness to. ⋙ **attestation** *n.*

Attic *adj* of Attica or Athens.

attic *n* a room or space immediately below the roof of a building.

attire[1] *n formal* dress or clothing.

attire[2] *v formal* (*usu in passive*) to dress (somebody).

attitude *n* **1** a feeling, emotion, or mental position, *esp* with regard to a topic, person, etc. **2** the arrangement of the parts of a body in sitting, standing, etc; a posture. **3** *chiefly NAm, informal* a confrontational or deliberately challenging manner in one's dealings, *esp* with those in authority; studied insolence. **4** the position of an aircraft or spacecraft relative to a particular point of reference such as the horizon. ⋙ **attitudinal** *adj.*

attitudinize *or* **-ise** *v* to assume an affected mental attitude; to pose.

atto- *comb. form* denoting: one million million millionth (10^{-18}) part.

attorney *n* (*pl* **-eys**) **1** a person who has legal authority to act for another. **2** *NAm* a lawyer.

Attorney General *n* (*pl* **Attorneys General** *or* **Attorney Generals**) the chief legal officer of a nation or state.

attract *v* **1** to have the power to draw (things) towards itself. **2** to fascinate or arouse the affection or sexual interest of. **3** to draw the interest of. **4** to become the focus of (notice or attention). **5** to be a reliable proposition for (funding or investment). **6** in law and insurance, to be liable for (tax, payments, etc). ⋙ **attractor** *n.*

attractant[1] *adj* of a pheromone or other substance: having the power to attract something, *esp* insects.

attractant[2] *n* something that attracts, *esp* a pheromone or other substance that attracts insects or animals.

attraction *n* **1** (*usu in pl*) a characteristic that arouses interest or admiration. **2** the ability to draw a response in the form of interest or affection. **3** an attractive quality or aspect. **4** something that draws or is intended to draw the crowds by appealing to their desires and tastes. **5** a force, e.g. between unlike electrical charges, unlike magnetic poles, or particles of matter, tending to resist separation. **6** personal charm.

attractive *adj* **1** having the power to attract. **2** good-looking or sexually interesting. **3** arousing interest or pleasure; charming. ⋙ **attractively** *adv,* **attractiveness** *n.*

attribute[1] *n* **1** a characteristic or quality of a person. **2** something associated with or belonging to a person or thing by virtue of which they are what they are; an inherent property or a customary accompaniment.

attribute[2] *v* **1a** to ascribe (something or its invention or origination) to, e.g. a certain person or age. **b** (+ to) to credit with a particular work of art or other piece of work. **2** (+ to) to put (a happening, etc) down to a particular circumstance, etc; to ascribe (something) to a cause or influence. ⋙ **attributable** *adj,* **attribution** *n.*

attributive *adj* in grammar, denoting an adjective or modifying noun that directly precedes a noun, as *city* does in *city streets*: compare PREDICATIVE. ⋙ **attributively** *adv.*

attrition *n* **1** the wearing away or grinding down of a surface, etc by friction; abrasion. **2** the process of weakening or exhausting e.g. an opponent by constant harassment or abuse. ⋙ **attritional** *adj.*

attune *v* **1** to cause or allow (people or their bodies) to become used, accustomed, or acclimatized to new circumstances. **2** (*often* + to) to train (the ear) to recognize and respond to certain sounds, etc. **3** to bring (things, people, etc) into harmony with each other.

atypical *adj* not typical; deviating from a specified type or pattern. ⋙ **atypically** *adv.*

Au *abbr* the chemical symbol for gold.

aubade /'ohbahd/ *n* a song, musical work, or poem associated with morning.

aubergine *n* a large purple oval fruit of a plant of the nightshade family, used as a vegetable.

aubrietia *n* a trailing rock plant of the mustard family, flowering in the spring.

auburn[1] *n* a reddish brown colour.

auburn[2] *adj* of hair: dark reddish brown in colour.

au courant /,oh kooh'ronh/ *adj* fully informed or up to date on developments, etc.

auction[1] *n* a public sale of property in which prospective buyers bid against one another and the sale is made to the buyer offering the highest bid.

auction[2] *v* (*often* + off) to sell (property) at an auction.

auctioneer *n* a person who conducts the bidding at an auction.

audacious *adj* **1a** intrepidly daring; adventurous. **b** recklessly bold; rash. **2** insolent or presumptuous. ⋙ **audaciously** *adv,* **audaciousness** *n,* **audacity** *n.*

audible *adj* capable of being heard; loud enough to be heard. ⋙ **audibility** *n,* **audibly** *adv.*

audience *n* **1** (*used as sing. or pl*) a group of listeners or spectators, e.g. at a theatre or concert performance or a formal lecture. **2a** a formal hearing or interview. **b** an opportunity of being heard.

audio[1] *adj* **1** relating to or denoting acoustic, mechanical, or electrical frequencies corresponding to those of audible sound waves, approximately 20 to 20,000Hz. **2a** relating to sound or its reproduction, *esp* high-fidelity reproduction. **b** relating to or used in the transmission or reception of sound: compare VIDEO[2].

audio[2] *n* the transmission, reception, or reproduction of sound.

audio- *comb. form* denoting: hearing or sound: *audiotape; audiovisual.*

audiology *n* the biology of hearing. ⋙ **audiological** *adj,* **audiologist** *n.*

audiotape *n* magnetic tape for recording sound.

audiotypist *n* a typist trained to type directly from a sound-recording or dictating machine.

audiovisual *adj* of teaching methods: using both hearing and sight.

audit[1] *n* a formal or official examination and verification of an account book by qualified accountants.

audit[2] *v* (**audited, auditing**) to perform an audit on (account books, etc).

audition[1] *n* a trial performance to assess the ability of a candidate for a performing role or an applicant for membership of an orchestra, choir, etc.

audition[2] *v* **1** to test (a performer) for a part, etc by means of an audition. **2** to give a trial performance before a group of selectors for a play, show, etc.

auditor *n* **1** a person authorized to perform an audit. **2** a person who hears; a listener.

auditorium *n* (*pl* **auditoria** *or* **auditoriums**) the part of a theatre, concert hall, etc where an audience sits.

auditory *adj* **1** relating to hearing. **2** received through the ear.

au fait /,oh 'fay/ *adj* fully informed about or familiar with (a particular matter or subject).

Aug. *abbr* August.

auger *n* a tool for boring holes in wood consisting of a shank with a central tapered screw and a pair of cutting lips with projecting spurs: compare GIMLET.

aught *pron archaic* (*in negative contexts*) anything at all.

augment *v* **1** to make or become greater, more numerous, larger, or more intense. **2** to render (a musical note) augmented. ⋙ **augmentation** *n.*

augmented *adj* of a musical interval: made a semitone greater than major or perfect.

au gratin /oh 'gratin/ *adj* (*used after a noun*) covered with breadcrumbs or grated cheese and browned under a grill: *cauliflower au gratin.*

augur[1] *n* a person believed able to foretell events by means of omens; a prophet or soothsayer; *specif* an official diviner of ancient Rome.

augur[2] *v* **1** to foretell (future events), *esp* from omens. **2** to give promise of or presage (some future state or event).

augury *n* (*pl* **-ies**) **1** the prediction of the future from omens or portents. **2** an omen or portent.

August *n* the eighth month of the year.

august *adj* marked by majestic dignity or solemn grandeur.

Augustan[1] *adj* **1** relating to Augustus Caesar (d.AD 14), first Roman emperor, or the literature of his reign. **2** relating to a period in art and literature that imitates the age of Augustus and is marked by refinement and elegance.

Augustan[2] *n* an artist or writer of the Augustan period.

Augustinian *n* a member of a monastic order based on the teachings of St Augustine of Hippo (d.430). ⋙ **Augustinian** *adj.*

auk *n* a diving seabird of the N hemisphere, with a short neck and black-and-white plumage, e.g. the puffin, guillemot, and razorbill.

auld *adj Scot* old.

auld lang syne *n* the good old times.

au naturel /oh natyoo'rel/ *adj and adv* in natural style or condition.

aunt *n* the sister of one's father or mother, or the wife of one's uncle.

Aunt Sally *n* (*pl* **-ies**) **1** an effigy of a woman at which objects are thrown at a fair. **2** an easy target of criticism or attack.

au pair /,oh 'peə/ *n* a young foreigner, *esp* a young woman, who does domestic work for a family in return for meals and accommodation and the opportunity to learn the language of the family.

aura *n* **1** a distinctive atmosphere surrounding a given source. **2** an emanation, invisible except to those with psychic powers, coming from a person or thing.

aural *adj* relating to the ear or the sense of hearing. ➤➤ **aurally** *adv.*

Usage note

aural *or* oral? These two words are pronounced the same and are easy to confuse. *Aural* relates to the ears and hearing and is connected with words such as *audible* and *audition*. *Oral* relates to the mouth and speaking, as in an *oral* examination.

aurar *n* pl of EYRIR.

aureate *adj literary* made of gold, or golden in colour.

aureole *or* **aureola** *n* **1** a radiant light surrounding the head or body of a representation of a holy figure: compare NIMBUS. **2** the halo surrounding the sun, moon, etc when seen through thin cloud; a corona.

au revoir /,oh rə'vwah/ *interj* goodbye.

auricle *n* **1** = PINNA. **2** *no longer in technical use* either ATRIUM (upper chamber) of the heart.

auricular *adj* **1** relating to the ear or the sense of hearing. **2** relating to the external ear or to the auricles of the heart. **3** ear-shaped.

aurochs *n* (*pl* **aurochs**) an extinct European ox held to be a wild ancestor of domestic cattle.

aurora *n* (*pl* **auroras** *or* **aurorae**) an atmospheric phenomenon occurring over the northern and southern magnetic poles, consisting of bands or streamers of coloured light passing across the sky.

aurora australis *n* the aurora of the S hemisphere.

aurora borealis *n* the aurora of the N hemisphere.

aurorae *n* pl of AURORA.

auscultation *n* the act of listening to the heart, lungs, etc as a medical diagnostic aid.

auspice *n archaic* a favourable prophetic sign. ✱ **under the auspices of** under the patronage or guidance of (a body or person).

auspicious *adj* affording a favourable auspice; propitious. ➤➤ **auspiciously** *adv,* **auspiciousness** *n.*

Aussie[1] *n informal* an Australian.

Aussie[2] *adj informal* Australian.

austere *adj* **1** stern and forbidding in appearance and manner. **2** rigidly abstemious; self-denying. **3** unadorned; simple. ➤➤ **austerely** *adv.*

austerity *n* (*pl* **austerities**) **1** enforced or extreme economy. **2** an austere act, manner, or attitude.

austral *adj technical* southern.

Australasian *n* a native or inhabitant of Australasia. ➤➤ **Australasian** *adj.*

Australian *n* a native or inhabitant of Australia. ➤➤ **Australian** *adj.*

Australian Rules football *n* a game played between two teams of 18 players on an oval field, using a ball similar to a rugby ball which may be passed by kicking or by striking it with the clenched fist.

australopithecine *n* an extinct southern African hominid with near-human teeth and a relatively small brain. ➤➤ **australopithecine** *adj.*

Austrian *n* a native or inhabitant of Austria. ➤➤ **Austrian** *adj.*

Austrian blind *n* a window blind of soft fabric that gathers into vertical ruches when raised.

aut- *or* **auto-** *comb. form* **1** self; same one; of or by oneself: *autobiography.* **2** automatic; self-acting; self-regulating: *autoclave.*

autarchy *n* (*pl* **-ies**) **1** absolute sovereignty; autocracy. **2** see AUTARKY. ➤➤ **autarchic** *adj,* **autarchical** *adj.*

autarky *or* **autarchy** *n* (*pl* **-ies**) **1** self-sufficiency and independence. **2** a state which is economically self-sufficient. ➤➤ **autarkic** *adj.*

auteur /oh'tuh/ *n* a film director whose personal style and views so distinctively influence the film under production that he or she is thought of as its overall creator.

authentic *adj* **1** worthy of belief as conforming to fact or reality; trustworthy. **2** not imaginary, false, or imitation; genuine. ➤➤ **authentically** *adv,* **authenticity** *n.*

authenticate *v* **1** to prove or declare (a document, signature, etc) genuine. **2** to corroborate (a story, etc) independently. ➤➤ **authentication** *n,* **authenticator** *n.*

author[1] *n* **1** the writer of a literary work. **2** a person whose profession is writing. **3** somebody or something that originates something or gives it existence; a source. ➤➤ **authorial** *adj,* **authorship** *n.*

author[2] *v* to be the writer of.

authoress *n* a female author.

authorise *v* see AUTHORIZE.

authoritarian[1] *adj* **1** of a régime: enforcing strict obedience to authority, as distinct from allowing independent decision-making. **2** of a person in a controlling position: dictatorial and tyrannical. ➤➤ **authoritarianism** *n.*

authoritarian[2] *n* a person in a position of control who brooks no opposition to his or her authority.

authoritative *adj* **1a** having or proceeding from authority; definitive; official. **b** entitled to credit or acceptance; reliable; conclusive. **2** commanding respect and obedience. ➤➤ **authoritatively** *adv,* **authoritativeness** *n.*

authority *n* (*pl* **-ies**) **1** the power to issue directives accompanied by the right to expect obedience. **2** (**the authorities**) people in command; *specif* a governmental or law-enforcing agency. **3** (*often* **Authority**) a governmental body that administers a public service or enterprise. **4** a citation used in defence or support of one's actions, opinions, or beliefs, or the source from which the citation is drawn. **5** an individual cited or appealed to as an expert.

authorize *or* **-ise** *v* **1** to invest (somebody) with authority or legal power or empower them to act in a certain way. **2** to give official permission for (a proceeding, etc); to sanction (an activity, etc). ➤➤ **authorization** *n.*

Authorized Version *n* an English version of the Bible prepared under James I, published in 1611, and widely used by Protestants.

autism *n* a disorder of childhood development marked by inability to form relationships with other people, those affected having only a limited understanding of themselves and others as individuals with independent personalities and thought processes. ➤➤ **autistic** *adj and n.*

auto-[1] *comb. form* see AUT-.

auto-[2] *comb. form* self-propelling; automotive: *autogiro.*

autobahn /'awtohbahn/ *n* a German motorway.

autobiography *n* (*pl* **-ies**) an account of one's own life written by oneself. ➤➤ **autobiographer** *n,* **autobiographic** *adj,* **autobiographical** *adj.*

autochthon *n* (*pl* **autochthons** *or* **autochthones**) **1** an aborigine or native. **2** an autochthonous plant, animal, etc. ⋙ **autochthonous** *adj.*

autoclave *n* an apparatus, e.g. for sterilizing, using superheated steam under pressure.

autocracy *n* (*pl* **-ies**) **1** government by an autocrat. **2** a community or state governed by autocracy.

autocrat *n* **1** a person who rules with unlimited power. **2** a dictatorial person. ⋙ **autocratic** *adj,* **autocratically** *adv.*

Autocue *n trademark* a device that enables a person being televised, e.g. a newsreader, to read a script without averting his or her eyes from the camera.

auto-da-fé /,awtoh dah 'fay/ *n* (*pl* **autos-da-fé**) the burning of a heretic; *esp* the ceremonial execution of somebody condemned by the Spanish Inquisition.

autodidact *n* a person who is self-taught. ⋙ **autodidactic** *adj.*

auto-erotism *or* **auto-eroticism** *n* sexual gratification obtained by oneself from one's own body. ⋙ **auto-erotic** *adj,* **auto-erotically** *adv.*

autogenic *adj technical* produced from the individual's own body; AUTOGENOUS.

autogenous *adj* originating or derived from sources within the same individual.

autogenous welding *n* the welding of metal parts by melting their edges together, as distinct from adding a welding agent.

autogiro *or* **autogyro** *n* (*pl* **-os**) an aircraft that resembles a helicopter and has a propeller for forward motion and a freely rotating horizontal rotor for lift.

autograph[1] *n* **1** a person's handwritten signature, *esp* that of a celebrity. **2** an original manuscript or work of art.

autograph[2] *v* to write one's signature in (a book, etc) or on (a page, etc).

autogyro *n* see AUTOGIRO.

autoimmune *adj* **1** of or caused by autoantibodies. **2** of a disease: caused by the production of large numbers of autoantibodies.

autolysis *n* the breakdown of all or part of a cell or tissue by self-produced enzymes. ⋙ **autolytic** *adj.*

automata *n* pl of AUTOMATON.

automate *v* **1** to convert (a system, etc) to largely automatic operation. **2** to undergo automation.

automated teller machine *n* = CASH DISPENSER.

automatic[1] *adj* **1a** acting or done spontaneously or unconsciously. **b** resembling an automaton; mechanical. **2** having a self-acting or self-regulating mechanism. **3** of a firearm: repeatedly ejecting the empty cartridge shell, introducing a new cartridge, and firing it. **4** happening as a matter of course. ⋙ **automatically** *adv,* **automaticity** *n.*

automatic[2] *n* an automatic machine or apparatus; *esp* an automatic vehicle or firearm.

automatic pilot *n* a device for automatically steering a ship, aircraft, or spacecraft.

automation *n* **1** the technique of making an apparatus, process, or system operate automatically. **2** automatic operation of an apparatus, process, or system by mechanical or electronic devices that take the place of human operators.

automatism *n* the unconscious or subconscious performance of actions.

automaton *n* (*pl* **automatons** *or* **automata**) **1a** a mechanism having its own power source. **b** a robot. **2** a machine or control mechanism designed to carry out a predetermined sequence of operations or respond to encoded instructions.

automobile *n chiefly NAm* a motor car.

automotive *adj* relating to motor vehicles.

autonomic *adj* **1** acting or occurring involuntarily. **2** relating to, affecting, or controlled by the autonomic nervous system.

autonomic nervous system *n* a part of the nervous system of vertebrates that serves and controls the involuntary action of the smooth muscle, cardiac muscle, and glandular tissue.

autonomous *adj* self-governing; independent. ⋙ **autonomously** *adv.*

autonomy *n* (*pl* **-ies**) **1** self-determined freedom and independence, *esp* moral independence. **2** self-government; *esp* the degree of political independence possessed by a minority group, territorial division, etc.

autopilot *n* = AUTOMATIC PILOT.

autopsy *n* (*pl* **-ies**) a postmortem examination.

autoroute *n* a French motorway.

autos-da-fé *n* pl of AUTO-DA-FÉ.

autostrada /'owtohstrahdə/ *n* (*pl* **autostradas** *or* **autostrade**) an Italian motorway.

autosuggestion *n* the influencing of one's own attitudes, behaviour, or physical condition by mental processes other than conscious thought.

autumn *n chiefly Brit* the season between summer and winter. ⋙ **autumnal** /aw'tumnəl/ *adj.*

auxiliary[1] *adj* **1** subsidiary. **2** kept in reserve; supplementary.

auxiliary[2] *n* (*pl* **-ies**) a person, group, or device serving or used in an auxiliary capacity.

auxiliary verb *n* in grammar, a verb such as *be, do,* or *have,* or a modal auxiliary verb, such as *will, shall, should, would, may,* or *might,* that helps another verb to form tenses, voices, and moods that cannot be indicated by INFLECTION (verb ending).

avail[1] *v* **1** to help or benefit (somebody or their cause). **2** to be of use or advantage. ✱ **avail oneself of** to make use of or take advantage of (an opportunity, facility, etc).

avail[2] *n* benefit; use. ✱ **be of little avail/no avail** to be in vain; to prove useless.

available *adj* **1** present or ready for immediate use. **2** accessible or obtainable. ⋙ **availability** *n.*

avalanche *n* **1** a large mass of snow or ice falling rapidly down a mountain. **2** a sudden overwhelming rush or accumulation of something.

avant-garde[1] /,avong 'gahd/ *n* (**the avant-garde**) the group of people who create or apply new ideas and techniques in any field, *esp* the arts. ⋙ **avant-gardism** *n,* **avant-gardist** *n.*

avant-garde[2] *adj* of ideas, works of art, etc: daringly modish or innovative.

avarice *n* excessive or insatiable desire for wealth or gain; cupidity. ⋙ **avaricious** *adj.*

avast *interj* a nautical command to stop or cease.

avatar *n* an earthly incarnation of a Hindu deity.

Ave Maria /mə'ree·ə/ *n* = HAIL MARY.

avenge *v* **1** to take vengeance on behalf of. **2** to exact satisfaction for (a wrong) by punishing the wrongdoer. ⋙ **avenger** *n.*

avenue *n* **1** a broad street or road. **2** a line of approach.

aver *v* (**averred, averring**) *formal* to declare positively.

average[1] *n* **1** a single value representative of a set of other values obtained by adding all the values together and dividing by the number of them. **2** a level, e.g. of intelligence, typical of a group, class, or series.

average[2] *adj* **1** in arithmetic and geometry, equalling a mean. **2a** about midway between extremes. **b** not out of the ordinary; common; typical. ➤➤ **averagely** *adv,* **averageness** *n.*

average[3] *v* **1** (*often* + out) to be, come, or bring to an average. **2** to do, get, or have (a certain amount) on average or as an average sum or quantity. **3** in arithmetic and geometry, to find the mean of (a set of values).

averse *adj* (*usu* + to) strongly opposed; disliking.

Usage note

averse *or* adverse? See note at ADVERSE.

aversion *n* a feeling of settled dislike for something; antipathy.

avert *v* **1** to turn away (the eyes, etc) in avoidance. **2** to see (trouble, etc) coming and ward it off; to avoid or prevent (a problem, etc).

avian *adj* relating to birds.

aviary *n* (*pl* **-ies**) a large high enclosure for keeping birds.

aviation *n* **1** the operation of aircraft. **2** aircraft manufacture, development, and design.

aviator *n dated* the pilot of an aircraft.

aviculture *n* the raising and care of birds, *esp* of wild birds in captivity. ➤➤ **avicultural** *adj,* **aviculturist** *n.*

avid *adj* urgently or greedily eager; keen. ➤➤ **avidity** *n,* **avidly** *adv.*

avionics *pl n* (*used as sing. or pl*) the development and production of electronic equipment for aircraft and space vehicles.

avocado *n* (*pl* **-os** *or* **-oes**) a pulpy green or purple pear-shaped fruit.

avocation *n* a subordinate occupation pursued in addition to one's vocation, *esp* for enjoyment; a hobby.

avocet *n* a black-and-white wading bird with webbed feet and a slender upward-curving bill.

avoid *v* **1** to keep away from or shun. **2** to prevent the occurrence of. **3** to refrain from (doing something). ➤➤ **avoidable** *adj,* **avoidably** *adv,* **avoidance** *n.*

avoirdupois /ˌavwahdooh'pwah, ˌavədə'poyz/ *or* **avoirdupois weight** *n* the series of units of weight based on the pound of 16 ounces and the ounce of 16 drams: compare TROY.

avow *v* **1** to declare with assurance. **2** to acknowledge (one's beliefs or views) openly, bluntly, and without shame. ➤➤ **avowal** *n,* **avowed** *adj,* **avowedly** *adv.*

avuncular *adj* kindly or genial like an uncle.

AWACS *abbr* airborne warning and control system.

await *v* **1** to wait for. **2** of events: to be in store for.

awake[1] *v* (*past tense* **awoke** *or* **awaked,** *past part.* **awoken**) **1** to emerge from sleep or a sleeplike state. **2** (*usu* + to) to become conscious or aware of something. **3** to arouse from sleep or a sleeplike state.

awake[2] *adj* **1** roused from sleep, or as if from sleep. **2** (*usu* + to) fully conscious of; aware of.

awaken *v* **1** to wake (somebody). **2** to wake up. **3** to stir up (a feeling). ➤➤ **awakening** *n and adj.*

award[1] *v* **1** to confer or bestow (a scholarship, prize, etc) as being deserved or needed. **2** to give (damages) by judicial decree.

award[2] *n* **1** something that is conferred or bestowed, *esp* on the basis of merit or need. **2** a final decision; *esp* the decision of arbitrators in a case submitted to them.

aware *adj* **1** (*often* + of) having or showing realization; conscious of something. **2** having kept oneself informed. ➤➤ **awareness** *n.*

awash *adj* (*used after a noun*) covered with water; flooded.

away[1] *adv* **1** on the way; along. **2** from here or there; hence; thence. **3a** in a secure place or manner. **b** in another direction; aside. **4** out of existence; to an end. **5a** on; uninterruptedly. **b** without hesitation or delay. **6** by a long distance or interval; far. **7** from one's possession.

away[2] *adj* of a football match, etc: played on an opponent's grounds.

awe[1] *n* an emotion compounded of dread, veneration, and wonder.

awe[2] *v* to inspire or fill with awe.

aweigh *adj* of an anchor: raised just clear of the bottom of a body of water.

awesome *adj* **1** inspiring awe. **2** *informal* excellent; great.

awful *adj* **1** extremely disagreeable or objectionable. **2** *informal* used as an intensive: *an awful headache.* **3** *archaic* inspiring awe. ➤➤ **awfulness** *n.*

awfully *adv* **1** *informal* used as an intensifier in favourable as well as unfavourable contexts: *awfully difficult.* **2** extremely disagreeably or objectionably.

awhile *adv* for a short time.

awkward *adj* **1** lacking dexterity or skill, *esp* in the use of hands; clumsy. **2** lacking ease or grace, e.g. of movement or expression. **3a** lacking social grace and assurance. **b** causing embarrassment. **4** poorly adapted for use or handling. **5** requiring caution. **6** deliberately obstructive. ➤➤ **awkwardly** *adv,* **awkwardness** *n.*

awl *n* a pointed instrument for marking surfaces or making small holes, e.g. in leather.

awn *n* any of the slender bristles at the end of the flower spikelet in some grasses, e.g. barley.

awning *n* a rooflike cover, often of canvas, used to protect something, e.g. a shop window or a ship's deck from sun or rain.

awoke *v* past tense of AWAKE[1].

awoken *v* past part. of AWAKE[1].

AWOL *adj* in the armed forces, absent without leave.

awry *adv and adj* **1** in a turned or twisted position or direction; askew. **2** out of the right or hoped-for course; amiss.

axe[1] (*NAm* **ax**) *n* **1** a tool that has a cutting edge parallel to the handle and is used for felling trees and chopping and splitting wood. **2** (**the axe**) drastic reduction or removal, e.g. of personnel. ✱ **get the axe 1** to be sacked; to be made redundant. **2** of a project: to be cut. **have an axe to grind** to have an ulterior, often selfish, purpose to pursue.

axe[2] (*NAm* **ax**) *v* to remove (personnel from employment or a project from a budget) abruptly.

axel *n* a jump in ice skating from one skate with one, two, or three and a half turns in the air and a return to the other skate.

axes *n* pl of AXIS.

axial *adj* **1** relating to or functioning as an axis. **2** situated round, in the direction of, or along an axis. ➤➤ **axially** *adv.*

axil *n* the angle between a branch or leaf and the axis from which it arises.

axiom *n* **1** a principle, rule, or maxim widely accepted on its intrinsic merit; a generally recognized truth. **2** a proposition regarded as a self-evident truth.

axiomatic *adj* of the nature of an axiom; self-evident.

axis *n* (*pl* **axes**) **1a** a straight line about which a body or a geometric figure rotates or may be supposed to rotate. **b** a straight line with respect to which a body or figure is symmetrical. **c** any of the reference lines of a coordinate system. **2** a partnership or alliance, e.g. the one between Germany and Italy in World War II.

axis deer *n* a white-spotted deer of India and other parts of S Asia. Also called CHITAL.

axle *n* **1** a shaft on or with which a wheel revolves. **2** a rod connecting a pair of wheels of a vehicle.

axolotl *n* a salamander of mountain lakes of Mexico that matures sexually in the larval stage.

axon *n* a long projecting part of a nerve cell that conducts impulses away from the cell body. ➤➤ **axonal** *adj.*

ay *interj and n* see AYE[1], AYE[2].

ayah /'ie·ə/ *n* a native nurse or maid in India.

ayatollah /ie·ə'tolə/ *n* a leader of Iranian Shiite Islam.

aye[1] *or* **ay** *interj archaic or dialect* **1** yes. **2** used as the correct formal response to a naval order.

aye[2] *or* **ay** *n* an affirmative vote or voter.

aye[3] *adv archaic or Scot* always; ever; continually.

Ayurveda /ahyooə'vaydə, ie·ooə'veedə/ *n* the traditional Hindu system of medicine based mainly on herbal remedies, homoeopathy, and naturopathy. ➤➤ **Ayurvedic** *adj.*

AZ *abbr* Arizona (US postal abbreviation).

azalea *n* a rhododendron with funnel-shaped flowers and deciduous leaves.

Azerbaijani /,azəbie'jahni/ *n* (*pl* **Azerbaijanis**) a native or inhabitant of Azerbaijan. ➤➤ **Azerbaijani** *adj.*

azimuth *n* **1** an arc of the horizon expressed as the clockwise angle measured between a fixed point, e.g. true north or true south and the vertical circle passing through the centre of an object. **2** horizontal direction. ➤➤ **azimuthal** *adj.*

azo dye *n* any of numerous versatile dyes containing azo groups.

Aztec *n* a member of the Nahuatlan people that founded the Mexican empire conquered by Cortes in 1519.

azure[1] *adj* of a deep blue colour.

azure[2] *n* **1** sky blue. **2** in heraldry, blue.

B

B[1] *or* **b** *n* (*pl* **B's** *or* **Bs** *or* **b's**) **1** the second letter of the English alphabet. **2** a mark or grade rating a student's work as good but short of excellent. **3** in music, the seventh note of the diatonic scale of C major. **4** in the ABO system of human blood classification, a type containing the B antigen. **5** *euphem* used for any offensive word beginning with the letter *b*.

B[2] *abbr* **1** in chess, bishop. **2** used on lead pencils: black.

B[3] *abbr* the chemical symbol for boron.

b *abbr* **1** born. **2** in cricket, bowled by. **3** in cricket, bye.

BA *abbr* **1** Bachelor of Arts. **2** British Airways.

Ba *abbr* the chemical symbol for barium.

baa[1] *v* (**baas, baaed** *or* **baa'd, baaing**) to make the bleat of a sheep.

baa[2] *n* (*pl* **baas**) the characteristic bleating sound of a sheep.

baba *n* a rich cake leavened with yeast, usu soaked with a rum and sugar syrup.

babble[1] *v* **1a** to utter meaningless or unintelligible sounds. **b** to talk foolishly; to chatter. **2** of a stream: to make a continuous murmuring or bubbling sound. » **babbler** *n.*

babble[2] *n* **1** meaningless or unintelligible sounds. **2** the murmuring or bubbling sound of a stream, etc.

babe *n* **1** *chiefly literary* an infant or baby. **2** *informal* a girl or woman, *esp* one regarded as sexually attractive.

babel *n* a scene of noise or confusion, *esp* from many voices.

baboon *n* a large African and Asian monkey that has a long doglike muzzle and a medium-length tail.

babushka /bə'booshkə/ *n* an elderly Russian woman.

baby[1] *n* (*pl* **-ies**) **1a** a very young child, *esp* one in the first year or two after birth; an infant. **b** a very young animal or unborn animal. **2** (*used before a noun*) comparatively small of its type: *baby carrots.* **3** a childish or immature person. **4** a person or thing for which one feels special responsibility or pride. **5** *informal* an affectionate form of address for a person, *esp* a girl or woman. ✱ **throw the baby out with the bathwater** to get rid of or reject something useful along with other things that are not wanted or not useful. » **babyhood** *n,* **babyish** *adj.*

baby[2] *v* (**-ies, -ied**) to tend or indulge with often excessive or inappropriate care.

baby bond *n* a savings scheme in which money is invested on behalf of a baby or child and matures when the child reaches adulthood.

baby boom *n* a rapid increase in the birthrate. » **baby boomer** *n.*

Babylonian[1] *adj* relating to Babylon or ancient Babylonia.

Babylonian[2] *n* a native or inhabitant of ancient Babylonia or Babylon.

babysit *v* (**babysitting,** *past tense and past part.* **babysat**) to care for a child, usu for a short period while the parents are out. » **babysitter** *n.*

babywalker *n* = WALKER (2).

baccalaureate *n* **1** the academic degree of bachelor. **2** a qualification allowing students to enter higher education, or the examinations for this.

baccarat /'bakərah/ *n* a card game in which three hands are dealt and players may bet on either or both hands against the dealer's.

bacchanal *n* **1a** a devotee of Bacchus, *esp* one who celebrates the Bacchanalia. **b** a reveller. **2** drunken revelry or carousal; bacchanalia.

bacchanalia *pl n* (*used as sing. or pl*) **1** (**Bacchanalia**) a Roman festival of Bacchus celebrated with dancing, song, and revelry. **2** a drunken feast; an orgy. » **bacchanalian** *adj.*

bacchant *n* (*pl* **bacchants** *or* **bacchantes**) a priest or follower of Bacchus.

bacchante *n* a priestess or female follower of Bacchus.

bacchantes *n* pl of BACCHANT.

baccy *n* (*pl* **-ies**) *chiefly Brit, informal* tobacco.

bachata /ba'chahtə/ *n* a style of country music from the Dominican Republic.

bachelor *n* **1a** an unmarried man. **b** a man past the usual age for marrying or one who seems unlikely to marry. **2** (*often* **Bachelor**) in degree titles: a recipient of what is usu the lowest degree conferred by a college or university. » **bachelorhood** *n.*

bacillary *adj* of or caused by bacilli.

bacilli *n* pl of BACILLUS.

bacillus *n* (*pl* **bacilli**) a usu rod-shaped bacterium, *esp* one that causes disease.

back[1] *n* **1a** the rear part of the human body, *esp* from the neck to the end of the spine. **b** the corresponding part of a quadruped or other animal. **2**

the side or surface behind the front or face, e.g. the rear part or the farther or reverse side. **3** a primarily defensive player in some team games, e.g. football, or the position of such a player. ✱ **back to back** facing in opposite directions with backs touching or close together. **back to front 1** in such a way that the back and the front are reversed in position. **2** in such a way that comprehensive knowledge is gained. **behind somebody's back** without a person's knowledge or permission; deceitfully or unfairly. **get/put somebody's back up** to annoy or irritate somebody. **put one's back into** to make a great effort in carrying out a task. **turn one's back on** to reject or deny (somebody or something). **with one's back to/against the wall** in a situation from which one cannot retreat and must either fight or be defeated. ⋙ **backless** *adj.*

back[2] *adv* **1a** to, towards, or at the rear. **b** in or into a reclining position. **2a** away, e.g. from the speaker. **b** in or into the past, ago. **c** nearer the beginning. **3a** to, towards, or in a place from which somebody or something came. **b** to or towards a former state. **c** in return or reply. ✱ **back and forth** backwards and forwards repeatedly.

back[3] *adj* **1** at or in the back. **2** distant from a central or main area; remote.

back[4] *v* **1** to support by giving material or moral assistance. **2** to provide a musical backing for (a singer, musician, or song). **3** to cause (a vehicle) to go backwards. **4a** to provide (something, e.g. a chair) with a back. **b** to be at or form the back of. **5** to place a bet on (a competitor in a race). **6** of the wind: to shift anticlockwise: compare VEER[1] (2). **7** (+ on/onto) said of a building: to have its back adjacent to or closely facing something specified. ⋙ **backer** *n.*

backbeat *n* in music, *esp* jazz, rock, or hip hop, an emphatic beat on one of the usu unaccented beats of the bar.

back bench *n* (*usu in pl*) any of the benches in Parliament on which non-ministerial members sit. ⋙ **back bench** *adj,* **back-bencher** *n.*

backbite *v* (*past tense* **backbit,** *past part.* **backbitten**) to say mean or spiteful things about (somebody). ⋙ **backbiter** *n,* **backbiting** *n.*

backblocks *pl n Aus, NZ* remote or culturally backward areas.

back boiler *n chiefly Brit* a domestic boiler fitted at the back of a coal or gas fire and heated by it.

backbone *n* **1** = SPINAL COLUMN. **2** the foundation or most substantial part of something. **3** a firm and resolute character.

backbreaking *adj* physically taxing or exhausting.

backchat *n chiefly Brit* impudent or argumentative talk made in reply.

backcloth *n* **1** *Brit* a painted cloth hung across the rear of a theatre stage. **2** = BACKGROUND (1A), (2A).

backcomb *v* to comb (the hair) against the direction of growth starting with the short underlying hairs in order to produce a bouffant effect.

backdate *v* **1** to apply (a measure or reward) retrospectively. **2** to date (a document) with an earlier date than the actual date.

back door *n* **1** a door at the rear of a building. **2** an indirect, underhand, or unfair means of access. ⋙ **backdoor** *adj.*

back down *v* to concede defeat or give up an argument or claim.

backdrop *n* = BACKCLOTH.

backfire *v* **1** of a vehicle or its engine: to undergo a premature explosion in a cylinder or in the exhaust system and make a loud bang as a result. **2** to have the reverse of the desired or expected effect, *esp* causing problems that seem to repay unkindness or malicious intent.

back-formation *n* the formation of a word by subtraction of an element from an existing word, or a word formed in this way, e.g. *burgle* from *burglar.*

backgammon *n* a board game for two players played with dice and counters in which each player tries to move his or her counters along the board and at the same time to block or capture his or her opponent's counters.

background *n* **1a** the scenery or ground behind something. **b** the part of a painting or photograph that depicts what lies behind objects in the foreground. **2a** the conditions that form the setting within which something is experienced. **b** information essential to the understanding of a problem or situation. **c** the total of a person's experience, knowledge, and education. **3** = BACKGROUND NOISE. **4** = BACKGROUND RADIATION. **5** in computing, low-priority tasks and processes performed by a computer without direct involvement of the operator.

background noise *n* intrusive sound or signals that interfere with received or recorded electronic signals.

background radiation *n* a low level of radiation found throughout the natural environment emanating from naturally occurring radioactive isotopes in the soil, etc.

backhand[1] *n* a stroke in tennis, squash, etc made with the back of the hand turned in the direction of movement.

backhand[2] *adv* with a backhand.

backhand[3] *v* to strike (a ball) with a backhand.

backhanded *adj* **1** using or made with a backhand. **2** of a compliment: ambiguous or ironic; apparently complimentary but with an uncomplimentary edge to it.

backhander *n* **1** a backhanded blow or stroke. **2** *informal* a bribe.

backing *n* **1a** support or aid, *esp* financial. **b** endorsement. **2** something forming a back or reverse side. **3** the musical or vocal accompaniment to a song or singer.

backlash *n* **1** a sudden violent backward movement or reaction. **2** a strong adverse reaction, e.g. to a recent political or social development.

backlist *n* a list of a publishing company's publications that are still in print.

backlog *n* an accumulation of tasks not performed, orders unfulfilled, or materials not processed.

backlot *n* an outdoor area near a film studio, where exterior scenes are shot.

back off *v* to retreat or shy away from a confrontation.

back out *v* to withdraw from a commitment or contest.

backpack[1] *n* = RUCKSACK.

backpack[2] *v* to travel or hike carrying food and equipment in a backpack. ⋙ **backpacker** *n.*

back passage *n chiefly Brit, euphem* the rectum.

backpedal *v* (**backpedalled, backpedalling,** *NAm* **backpedaled, backpedaling**) **1** to pedal the pedals of a bicycle in the opposite direction to normal, e.g. in order to slow down or brake. **2** to back down from or reverse a previous opinion or stand.

backroom *adj* **1** relating to a directing group that exercises its authority in an inconspicuous and indirect way. **2** relating to somebody who works behind the scenes, doing work that is often not publicly acknowledged.

back room *n* a place where work is carried out, decisions are made, etc in secret.

backscratching *n informal* doing favours for people in return for favours received, often in a secretive or underhanded way.

back-seat driver *n informal* a car passenger who offers unwanted advice to the driver.

backside *n informal* the buttocks.

backslapping *n* excessive cordiality or good fellowship.

backslash *n* a diagonal line that slopes backwards (\).

backslide *v* (*past tense* **backslid,** *past part.* **backslid** *or* **backslidden**) to lapse morally or in the practice of religion. ➤➤ **backslider** *n,* **backsliding** *n.*

backspace[1] *v* to press a key on a typewriter or computer keyboard which causes the carriage or cursor to move back one space.

backspace[2] *n* the key on a typewriter or computer keyboard which when pressed causes the carriage or cursor to move back one space.

backspin *n* spin of a ball in a direction opposite to that of the ball's forward motion: compare TOPSPIN.

backstabbing *n* harmful or disloyal behaviour towards a friend. ➤➤ **backstabber** *n,* **backstabbing** *adj.*

backstage[1] *adv* in or to an area out of view of a theatre audience.

backstage[2] *adj* **1** of or occurring in the parts of a theatre that cannot be seen by the audience. **2** of the inner working or operation, e.g. of an organization.

backstairs[1] *pl n* stairs at the back of a building, in some buildings, *esp* formerly, for private use or for the use of servants.

backstairs[2] *or* **backstair** *adj* **1** secret or furtive. **2** sordid or scandalous.

backstitch[1] *n* a method of hand sewing in which each new stitch is formed by inserting the needle a stitch length behind and bringing it out a stitch length in front of the end of the previous stitch.

backstitch[2] *v* to sew (something) using backstitch.

backstreet[1] *n* a street, usu small and narrow, that is not a main street or attached to a main street in a town.

backstreet[2] *adj* made, done, or acting illegally or surreptitiously.

backstroke *n* a swimming stroke executed on the back using reverse overarm strokes and kicking movements of the feet.

back-to-back *n* (*pl* **back-to-backs**) a two-storey terraced house built with its back against the back of a parallel terrace.

backtrack *v* **1** to retrace a path or course. **2** to reverse one's position or stand.

backup *n* **1** somebody or something that serves as a substitute or alternative. **2** somebody or something that gives support if called upon. **3** in computing, the process of backing up data, or a copy of data made in this way.

back up *v* **1a** to support in an argument or proposal. **b** to give support to (an argument, etc). **2** in computing, to make a security copy of (data, a file, etc). **3** of traffic: to form an increasing queue behind a hazard or congestion.

backward *adj* **1a** directed or turned backwards. **b** done or executed backwards. **2** affected by a developmental disability. **3** diffident or shy. ➤➤ **backwardly** *adv,* **backwardness** *n.*

backwards (*NAm* **backward**) *adv* **1** towards the back. **2** with the back foremost. **3** in a reverse direction or towards the beginning. **4** perfectly; thoroughly. **5** towards the past. **6** towards or into a worse state. ✱ **bend/fall/lean over backwards** to make extreme efforts, *esp* in order to please or conciliate somebody.

backwash *n* **1** a backward movement in air, water, etc produced by a propelling force, e.g. the motion of oars. **2** the backward movement of a receding wave.

backwater *n* **1** a stagnant pool or inlet kept filled by the opposing current of a river. **2** a place or condition that is isolated or backward, *esp* culturally or intellectually.

backwoods *n chiefly NAm* **1** (*usu* **the backwoods**) (*used as sing. or pl*) heavily forested and uncultivated areas where few people live. **2** a remote or culturally backward area.

backwoodsman *n* (*pl* **backwoodsmen**) *chiefly NAm* somebody who lives in the backwoods, or who has the skills and knowledge to survive in the backwoods.

back yard *n* **1** a yard at the back of one's house. **2** *NAm* a back garden. **3** any area close to one's home, etc about which one feels some concern or responsibility.

bacon *n* meat cut from the cured and often smoked side of a pig. ✱ **bring home the bacon 1** to achieve success. **2** to provide whatever is necessary for living, etc. **save somebody's bacon** *informal* to save somebody from serious danger or difficulty.

BACS *abbr* Bankers Automated Clearing Services, a system of processing computerized payments.

bacteria *n* pl of BACTERIUM.

Usage note

Bacteria is a plural noun and takes a plural verb. One single micro-organism is a *bacterium.*

bactericide *n* a substance that kills bacteria. ➤➤ **bactericidal** *adj.*

bacteriology *n* **1** a science that deals with bacteria. **2** bacterial life and phenomena. ➤➤ **bacteriological** *adj,* **bacteriologically** *adv,* **bacteriologist** *n.*

bacterium *n* (*pl* **bacteria**) any of a group of unicellular microscopic organisms that live in soil, water, organic matter, or the bodies of plants and animals. They are important to human beings because of their chemical effects and because many of them cause diseases. ➤➤ **bacterial** *adj.*

Bactrian camel *n* one of two species of camel, having two humps.

bad *adj* (**worse, worst**) **1a** failing to reach an acceptable standard; poor or inadequate. **b** unfavourable. **c** no longer acceptable or usable, because of decay or disrepair. **2a** morally objectionable. **b** mischievous or disobedient. **3** (*often* + at) unskilful or incompetent. **4** disagreeable or unpleasant. **5a** (+ for) injurious or harmful. **b** worse than usual; severe. **6** incorrect or faulty. **7a** suffering pain or distress; unwell. **b** unhealthy or diseased. **8** (*often* + about) regretful or remorseful. **9** of a debt: not collectible; not going to be paid. **10** (**badder, baddest**) *chiefly NAm, informal* excellent or admirable. ✱ **in bad faith** with dishonest intentions. **not bad** *informal* quite good. **too bad 1** *informal* regrettable; unfortunate. **2** *informal* said dismissively or philosophically, unfortunate but unable to be changed and therefore to be accepted. ➤➤ **badness** *n.*

bad blood *n* ill feeling or bitterness.

baddie *or* **baddy** *n* (*pl* **-ies**) *informal* somebody or something bad or dangerous, e.g. an opponent of the hero in fiction or the cinema.

bade *v* past tense of BID[1].

badge *n* **1** a device or token, *esp* of membership in a society or group. **2** an emblem awarded for a particular accomplishment.

badger[1] *n* either of two species of sturdy burrowing nocturnal mammals widely distributed in the northern hemisphere, typically black or dark grey with white striped facial markings.

badger[2] *v* to harass or annoy persistently.

bad hair day *n informal* a day on which everything goes wrong.

badinage *n* playful repartee; banter.

badlands *pl n chiefly NAm* a barren region marked by extensive rock erosion with fantastic hill formations and deep ravines.

badly *adv* **1** in an unsatisfactory, incorrect, unsuitable, etc way. **2** unkindly; cruelly. **3** unsuccessfully. **4** severely. **5** very much. ✱ **badly off** not having enough money.

badminton *n* a court game played with light long-handled rackets and a shuttlecock that is volleyed over a net.

badmouth *v informal* to criticize or speak badly of.

bad-tempered *adj* angry, or easily made angry.

baffle[1] *v* to throw into puzzled confusion; to perplex. ⋙ **bafflement** *n,* **baffling** *adj,* **bafflingly** *adv.*

baffle[2] *n* **1** a device, e.g. a plate, wall, or screen, to deflect, check, or regulate flow, e.g. of a fluid or light. **2** a structure that reduces the exchange of sound waves between the front and back of a loudspeaker.

bag[1] *n* **1a** a usu flexible container for holding, storing, or carrying something. **b** a handbag or shoulder bag. **2** something resembling a bag, *esp* a sagging in cloth or a sagging of the skin under the eyes. **3a** a quantity of game taken or permitted to be taken. **b** spoils or loot. **4** *chiefly Brit, informal* (*in pl*) a great deal; lots. **5** *informal, derog* a woman regarded dismissively. **6** *informal* something that somebody particularly likes or does. ✱ **in the bag** *informal* as good as achieved, or already certain before formally decided or declared. ⋙ **bagful** (*pl* **bagfuls**) *n.*

bag[2] *v* (**bagged, bagging**) **1** to swell out; to bulge. **2** to hang loosely. **3** to put into a bag. **4a** to get possession of. **b** *informal* to steal. **c** to take (animals) as game. ✱ **bags I/bags** *Brit, informal* a phrase used, *esp* by children, in claiming something or the right to do something. ⋙ **bagger** *n.*

bagasse *n* the residue of sugarcane, grapes, etc left after a product, e.g. juice, has been extracted.

bagatelle *n* **1** something unimportant or of little value. **2** a game in which balls must be put into or through cups or arches at one end of an oblong table with pins as obstacles.

bagel /'baygl/ *n* a hard glazed ring-shaped bread roll.

baggage *n* **1** luggage, *esp* for travel by sea or air. **2** the sum of a person's earlier experiences or knowledge regarded as a hindrance to or influence on their response to subsequent events and conditions. **3** *dated* an impudent girl or young woman.

baggy *adj* (**-ier, -iest**) loose, puffed out, or hanging like a bag.

bag lady *n informal* a homeless woman who lives on the streets and carries all her belongings in shopping bags.

bagman *n* (*pl* **bagmen**) **1** *chiefly Brit, dated* a sales representative; a travelling salesman. **2** *chiefly NAm* a person who collects or distributes dishonestly or illegally gained money on behalf of another.

bagpipe *n* (*also in pl*) a wind instrument consisting of a mouth tube, chanter, and drone pipes, sounded by the pressure of wind emitted from a leather bag squeezed by the player. ⋙ **bagpiper** *n.*

baguette /ba'get/ *n* a long thin French loaf.

bah *interj* used to express disdain.

Baha'i *n* (*pl* **Baha'is**) **1** a religious movement originating in Iran in the 19th cent. and emphasizing the spiritual unity of humankind and all religions. **2** an adherent of this religion.

Bahamian *n* a native or inhabitant of the Bahamas. ⋙ **Bahamian** *adj.*

Bahraini *n* (*pl* **Bahrainis**) a native or inhabitant of Bahrain. ⋙ **Bahraini** *adj.*

baht /baht/ *n* (*pl* **bahts** *or* **baht**) the basic monetary unit of Thailand.

Bahutu *n* pl of HUTU.

bail[1] *n* **1** security deposited as a guarantee that somebody temporarily freed from custody will return to stand trial. **2** temporary release on bail. ✱ **go/stand bail** to act as or provide security for somebody who has been freed from custody temporarily. **jump bail** of somebody who has been released on bail: to fail to appear for trial.

bail[2] *v* **1** to release on bail. **2** (*often* + out) to procure the release of (a person in custody) by giving bail.

bail[3] *n* **1** in cricket, either of the two crosspieces that lie on the stumps to form the wicket. **2a** *chiefly Brit* a partition for separating animals. **b** *Aus, NZ* a device for holding a cow's head when it is being milked. **3** a bar for holding paper steady on a typewriter or printer.

bail[4] *or* **bale** *v* **1** (*usu* + out) to clear (water) from a boat by collecting it in a bail, bucket etc and throwing it over the side. **2** (*usu* + out) to parachute from an aircraft. **3** (*usu* + out) to flee a difficult or dangerous situation, often leaving others in trouble or with onerous responsibilities.

bailey *n* (*pl* **-eys**) the outer wall of a castle.

Bailey bridge *n* a prefabricated bridge built from interchangeable latticed steel panels.

bailiff *n* **1** *chiefly Brit* an official employed by a sheriff to serve writs, seize property, make arrests, etc. **2** *chiefly Brit* somebody who manages an estate or farm, or who acts as the agent of a landlord.

bailiwick *n* the area of jurisdiction of a bailiff.

bail out *or* **bale out** *v* to help out of a predicament or free from difficulty.

bail up *v Aus, NZ* **1** to secure (a cow's head) in a bail during milking. **2** to make (somebody) a captive, either by force, e.g. in order to rob them, or by engaging them in conversation.

Baily's beads *pl n* a chain of bright points of light that appears round the edge of the moon just before and just after a total solar eclipse, caused by sunlight shining between mountains at the edge of the moon.

bain-marie /,banh mə'ree/ *n* (*pl* **bains-marie** *or* **bain-maries**) a vessel of hot or boiling water into which another vessel, containing food, is placed, in order to cook or heat the food gently.

bairn *n chiefly Scot, N Eng* a child.

bait[1] *n* **1a** something used in luring an animal, *esp* to a hook or trap. **b** a poisonous material placed where it will be eaten by pests. **2** see BATE.

bait[2] *v* **1** to provoke, tease, or exasperate with unjust, nagging, or persistent remarks. **2** to harass (e.g. a chained animal) with dogs, usu for sport. **3** to provide with bait.

baiza /'biezah/ *n* (*pl* **baiza** *or* **baizas**) a unit of currency in Oman, worth 1000th of a rial.

baize *n* a woollen cloth resembling felt used chiefly as a covering, *esp* for billiard tables and card tables.

bake[1] *v* **1** to cook (food) by dry heat, *esp* in an oven. **2** to dry or harden (something, *esp* clay articles) by subjecting it to heat. **3** to become baked. **4** to become extremely hot. ➤➤ **baker** *n.*

bake[2] *n* a batch of baked food, or a dish containing baked ingredients.

baked Alaska *n* a baked dessert consisting of a meringue case filled with sponge cake and ice cream.

baked beans *pl n* baked haricot beans, *esp* as sold tinned in tomato sauce.

Bakelite *n trademark* any of various synthetic resins and plastics.

baker's dozen *n* thirteen.

bakery *n* (*pl* **-ies**) a place for baking or selling baked goods, *esp* bread and cakes.

Bakewell tart *n Brit* an almond sponge tart lined with jam.

baking powder *n* a powder that consists of a bicarbonate and an acid substance, often cream of tartar, used in place of yeast as a raising agent.

baking soda *n* = SODIUM BICARBONATE.

baklava /'bahkləvah, 'bak-/ *n* a sweet rich dessert of Turkish origin, made of thin layers of pastry containing nuts and honey.

baksheesh *n esp* in the Middle East, money given as a tip or bribe or as alms.

balaclava *n* a knitted pull-on hood that covers the ears, neck, and throat.

balafon /'baləfon/ *n* a large W African xylophone.

balalaika /balə'liekə/ *n* a musical instrument of Russian origin, having a triangular body and usu three strings.

balance[1] *n* **1a** the ability to retain one's physical equilibrium. **b** stability produced by even distribution of weight on each side of a vertical axis. **c** mental and emotional steadiness. **d** an aesthetically pleasing integration of elements. **2a** equilibrium between contrasting, opposing, or interacting elements. **b** equality between the totals of the two sides of an account. **3a** the difference between credits and debits in an account, or a statement of this. **b** something left over; a remainder. **c** an amount in excess, *esp* on the credit side of an account. **4** the weight or force of one side in excess of another. **5a** an instrument for weighing, traditionally a centrally-supported beam that has two scalepans of equal weight suspended from its ends. **b** any device that measures weight and force. ✱ **in the balance** in an uncertain critical position, *esp* with the fate or outcome about to be determined. **on balance** all things considered. ➤➤ **balanced** *adj.*

balance[2] *v* **1** to be or become balanced or established in balance. **2** to bring to a state or position of balance. **3** to compare the relative importance, value, force, or weight of; to ponder. **4** of accounts, etc: to have the debit and credit totals equal. **5a** to equal or equalize (two or more things) in weight, number, or proportion. **b** to counterbalance or offset. ➤➤ **balancer** *n.*

balance of payments *n* the difference over a period of time between a country's payments to and receipts from abroad.

balance of power *n* **1** an equilibrium of power sufficient to prevent one nation from imposing its will upon another. **2** a situation in which one group is in a position to support either of two other groups.

balance of trade *n* the difference in value between a country's imports and exports.

balance sheet *n* a statement of an organization's financial condition at a given date.

balboa /bal'boh·ə/ *n* the basic monetary unit of Panama.

balcony *n* (*pl* **-ies**) **1** a platform built out from the wall of a building and enclosed by a railing or low wall. **2** a gallery inside a building, e.g. a theatre. ➤➤ **balconied** *adj.*

bald *adj* **1a** with a scalp on which some or all of the hair has fallen out, has been shaved off, or has not yet grown. **b** of a tyre: having little or no tread. **c** lacking a natural or normal covering, e.g. of vegetation or nap. **2** blunt and unadorned or undisguised. **3** of an animal: marked with white, *esp* on the head or face. ➤➤ **baldish** *adj,* **baldly** *adv,* **baldness** *n.*

baldachin *or* **baldaquin** *n* **1** a cloth canopy fixed or carried over an important person or a sacred object. **2** an ornamental structure resembling a canopy, *esp* over an altar or shrine in a Christian church.

bald eagle *n* an eagle of N America that has a white head and neck when mature and eats fish and carrion.

balderdash *n* nonsense, often used as a general expression of disagreement.

balding *adj* becoming bald.

baldric *n* an often ornamented belt worn over one shoulder and across the body to support a sword, bugle, etc.

bale[1] *n* a large bundle of goods, *esp* a large closely pressed package of merchandise bound and usu wrapped for storage or transportation.

bale[2] *v* to tie (goods) into bales or bundles. ➤➤ **baler** *n.*

bale[3] *noun and v Brit* see BAIL[4].

baleen *n* = WHALEBONE.

baleen whale *n* a large whale that has whalebone plates instead of teeth, used to filter krill from large volumes of sea water.

baleful *adj* **1** deadly or pernicious in influence. **2** gloomily threatening; menacing. ➤➤ **balefully** *adv,* **balefulness** *n.*

bale out *v Brit* see BAIL OUT.

Balinese *n* (*pl* **Balinese**) a native or inhabitant of Bali. ➤➤ **Balinese** *adj.*

balk[1] (*Brit* **baulk**) *v* **1** (*usu* + at) to stop short and refuse to proceed. **2** (*often* + at) to refuse abruptly. **3** to check or stop by an obstacle; to thwart.

balk[2] (*Brit* **baulk**) *n* a roughly squared beam of timber.

Balkan *adj* relating to the Balkan Peninsula in SE Europe, or to the countries occupying it.

Balkanize *or* **-ise** *v* to divide (a region) into smaller and often mutually hostile units. ➤➤ **Balkanization** *n.*

Balkans *pl n* (**the Balkans**) the Balkan Peninsula or the countries occupying it.

ball[1] *n* **1a** a solid or hollow spherical or egg-shaped object, *esp* one used in a game or sport. **b** a delivery or play of the ball in cricket, baseball, etc. **c** *chiefly NAm* any game in which a ball is thrown, kicked, or struck, *esp* baseball. **2** *coarse slang* **a** (*usu in pl*) a testicle. **b** (*in pl*) nonsense. ✱ **on the ball** knowledgeable and competent; alert. **start/set/keep the ball rolling** to begin or continue something. **the ball is in your, his, etc court** it is up to you, him, etc to make the next move.

ball[2] *v* to form or gather into a ball.

ball[3] *n* a large formal gathering for social dancing. ✱ **have a ball** *informal* to enjoy oneself.

ballad *n* **1** a rhythmic poem of a kind that was orig sung by a strolling minstrel. **2** a slow, romantic or sentimental popular song, *esp* one that tells a story. ➤➤ **balladeer** *n*, **balladry** *n*.

ballade /ba'lahd/ *n* **1** a fixed verse form of usu three stanzas with recurrent rhymes, a short concluding verse, and an identical refrain for each part. **2** a musical composition, *esp* for piano, intended to suggest a narrative ballad.

ball-and-socket joint *n* a joint in which a rounded part moves within a cuplike socket so as to allow free movement in many directions.

ballast *n* **1a** heavy material carried in a ship to improve stability. **b** heavy material that is carried on a balloon or airship to steady it and can be jettisoned to control the rate of descent. **2** gravel or broken stone laid in a bed for railway lines or the lower layer of roads. **3** a device used to stabilize the current in an electrical circuit.

ball bearing *n* a bearing in which hardened steel balls roll with minimal friction in a groove between a shaft and a support, or any of the balls in such a bearing.

ballboy *or* **ballgirl** *n* a boy or girl who retrieves balls for the players during a tennis match.

ballcock *n* an automatic valve, *esp* in a cistern, controlled by the rise and fall of a float at the end of a lever.

ballerina *n* a female ballet dancer.

ballet *n* **1** a form of artistic dancing in which the graceful flowing movements are based on conventional positions and steps. **2** a theatrical art form using ballet dancing, music, and scenery to convey a story, theme, or atmosphere. ➤➤ **balletic** *adj*.

balletomane *n* a devotee of ballet.

ball game *n* **1** a game played with a ball. **2** *informal* a situation or set of circumstances.

ballgirl *n* see BALLBOY.

ballistic *adj* **1** of ballistics. **2** relating to projectiles that move under their own momentum and the force of gravity. **3** *informal* violently and uncontrollably angry; furious.

ballistic missile *n* a missile propelled and guided in ascent but falling freely in descent.

ballistics *pl n* **1** (*used as sing. or pl*) the science of the motion of projectiles in flight. **2** the particular properties of a firearm or projectile.

ballocks *pl n* see BOLLOCKS.

balloon[1] *n* **1a** a baglike container filled with hot air or a gas lighter than air so as to rise and float in the atmosphere. **b** an inflatable usu brightly coloured rubber bag used as a toy. **2** a line enclosing words spoken or thought by a character, *esp* in a cartoon. ✱ **when the balloon goes up** *informal* when the trouble starts or the action begins.

balloon[2] *v* **1** to ascend or travel in a balloon. **2** (*often* + out) to swell or puff out; to expand. **3** to increase rapidly. ➤➤ **ballooning** *n*, **balloonist** *n*.

balloon angioplasty *n* a medical operation in which a CATHETER (tubular device) with a balloon at the end of it is inserted into a vein or artery, the balloon then being inflated to unblock or widen the blood vessel.

ballot[1] *n* **1** a vote in which votes are recorded and cast in secret. **2** the system of casting votes in secret. **3** the number of votes cast.

ballot[2] *v* (**balloted, balloting**) **1** (*often* + for) to vote by ballot, or decide something in this way. **2** to ask (somebody) to vote.

ballpark[1] *n NAm* a park in which ball games, *esp* baseball, are played. ✱ **in the ballpark/in the right ballpark** *informal* roughly accurate.

ballpark[2] *adj informal* approximate.

ballpoint *or* **ballpoint pen** *n* a pen having as the writing point a small rotating metal ball.

ballroom *n* a large room for dances.

ballroom dancing *n* a usu formal type of dancing done *esp* by couples.

balls up (*NAm* **ball up**) *v coarse slang* to ruin or make a mess of (e.g. a task).

balls-up (*NAm* **ball-up**) *n coarse slang* a muddle; a bungled task or activity.

ballsy *adj* (**-ier, -iest**) *chiefly NAm, informal* spirited or courageous.

ball up *v NAm* see BALLS UP.

ball-up *n NAm* see BALLS-UP.

bally *adj and adv Brit, euphem* = BLOODY[1], BLOODY[3]

ballyhoo *n* (*pl* **ballyhoos**) **1** a noisy demonstration or talk. **2** flamboyant, exaggerated, or sensational advertising or promotion.

balm *n* **1** an aromatic and medicinal resin. **2** something that soothes, relieves, or heals physically or emotionally.

balmy *adj* (**-ier, -iest**) of weather: pleasantly mild.

baloney *or* **boloney** *n* (*pl* **-eys**) nonsense.

balsa *n* (*also* **balsa wood**) the strong very light wood of a tropical American tree.

balsam *n* **1** an oily and resinous substance released by various plants, or a medicinal preparation containing it. **2** an annual plant with watery juice, e.g. touch-me-not. ➤➤ **balsamic** *adj*.

balsamic vinegar *n* a dark Italian vinegar made from the juice of white grapes and matured in wooden casks.

balti /'balti, 'bawlti/ *n* (*pl* **baltis**) a style of Indian cooking in which the food is cooked and served in a dish that resembles a small wok.

Baltic[1] *adj* **1** of the Baltic Sea or the countries that lie on its shores. **2** of a branch of the Indo-European languages including Latvian, Lithuanian, and Old Prussian.

Baltic[2] *n* the Baltic languages.

baluster *n* an upright rounded, square, or vase-shaped support, *esp* for the rail of a staircase balustrade.

balustrade *n* a row of balusters topped by a rail, *esp* one that runs along the edge of a balcony or bridge. ➤➤ **balustraded** *adj*.

bambino /bam'beenoh/ *n* (*pl* **bambinos** *or* **bambini**) *informal* a young child.

bamboo *n* (*pl* **bamboos**) a tropical giant grass with strong hollow stems used for building, furniture, or utensils.

bamboozle *v* **1** to deceive by trickery. **2** to confuse or mystify.

ban[1] *v* (**banned, banning**) to prohibit or forbid, *esp* by legal means or social pressure.

ban[2] *n* a legal or social prohibition.

ban[3] /bahn/ *n* (*pl* **bani**) a unit of currency in Romania, worth 100th of a leu.

banal *adj* lacking originality or novelty; dull. ➤➤ **banality** *n*, **banally** *adv*.

banana *n* an elongated usu tapering fruit with soft pulpy flesh enclosed in a soft usu yellow rind that grows in bunches.

banana republic *n derog* a small tropical country that is politically unstable and economically underdeveloped.

bananas *adj informal* mad or angry.

banana split *n* a dish composed of banana, ice cream, nuts, and whipped cream.

band[1] *n* **1** a narrow strip serving chiefly as decoration, *esp* a narrow strip of material applied as trimming to an article of dress. **2** a strip distinguishable in some way, e.g. by colour, texture, or composition. **3** an elongated surface or section with parallel or roughly parallel sides. **4** a strip or belt serving to join or hold things together or to transmit motion between pulleys or wheels. **5** a more or less well-defined range of wavelengths, frequencies, or energies of light waves, radio waves, sound waves, etc. **6** *Brit* a group of pupils assessed as being of broadly similar ability: compare STREAM[1] (5), SET[3] (3). **7** in computing, one or more tracks on a compact or floppy disk. ➤➤ **banding** *n.*

band[2] *v* **1** (*often* + together) to unite for a common purpose. **2** to fasten a band to or tie up with a band. **3** to mark with a band. **4** *Brit* to divide (pupils) into bands.

band[3] *n* (*used as sing. or pl*) **1** a group of people, animals, or things. **2** a group of musicians playing jazz, pop, rock, or marching music.

bandage[1] *n* a strip of fabric used to dress and bind up wounds.

bandage[2] *v* to bind, dress, or cover (a wound or other injury) with a bandage.

bandanna *n* a large colourful patterned handkerchief.

b and b *abbr* (*often* **B and B**) *Brit* bed and breakfast.

bandbox *n* a usu cylindrical box of cardboard or thin wood used *esp* for holding hats.

bandeau /'bandoh/ *n* (*pl* **bandeaux**) **1** a band of material worn round the head to keep the hair in place. **2** a tight strapless top worn by women.

banderilla /bandə'ree(l)yə/ *n* a decorated barbed dart thrust into the neck or shoulders of the bull in a bullfight.

banderillero /,bandəree(l)'yeəroh/ *n* (*pl* **-os**) a bullfighter whose task is to thrust banderillas into a bull's neck or shoulders in a bullfight.

bandicoot *n* **1** (*also* **bandicoot rat**) either of two large rats found in India, Sri Lanka, and SE Asia. **2** a small insect- and plant-eating marsupial mammal of Australia, Tasmania, and New Guinea.

bandit *n* (*pl* **bandits** *or* **banditti**) an outlaw, *esp* a member of a band of armed robbers or marauders. ➤➤ **banditry** *n.*

bandog *n* a dog that is a cross between a pit bull terrier and a mastiff, rottweiler, or Rhodesian Ridgeback.

bandolier *or* **bandoleer** *n* a belt worn over the shoulder and across the chest with pockets or loops for cartridges.

band saw *n* a power saw consisting of an endless steel blade running over pulleys.

bandstand *n* a usu roofed stand or platform for a brass band to perform on outdoors.

bandwagon *n* **1** a wagon for carrying a band in a parade. **2** a party, faction, or cause that attracts adherents by its timeliness, momentum, etc.

bandwidth *n* a range of frequencies used in radio transmission and telecommunications.

bandy[1] *v* (**-ies, -ied**) **1** to exchange (words) in an argumentative, careless, or light-hearted manner. **2** (*often* + about) to use or make reference to in a glib or offhand manner.

bandy[2] *adj* (**-ier, -iest**) of a person's legs: bowed.

bane *n* a cause of death, ruin, or trouble.

bang[1] *v* **1** to strike sharply; to bump. **2** to knock, beat, or strike hard, often with a loud sharp or metallic noise. **3** to cause to make a loud sharp or metallic noise. **4** *coarse slang* of a person: to have sexual intercourse with. **5** to move about noisily.

bang[2] *n* **1** a resounding blow; a thump. **2** a sudden loud noise. **3** a quick or impressive burst of energy or activity. **4** *coarse slang* an act of sexual intercourse. ✱ **bang goes...** *informal* that is the end of (something, e.g. a plan or hope).

bang[3] *adv informal* **1** right or directly. **2** exactly. ✱ **bang on** *Brit, informal* just right; just what is needed.

bang[4] *n chiefly NAm* (*usu in pl*) a short squarely-cut fringe of hair.

bang away *v informal* (*often* + at) to work with persistent determined effort.

banger *n Brit* **1** a firework that explodes with a loud bang. **2** *informal* a sausage. **3** *informal* an old usu dilapidated car.

Bangladeshi *n* (*pl* **Bangladeshi** *or* **Bangladeshis**) a native or inhabitant of Bangladesh. ➤➤ **Bangladeshi** *adj.*

bangle *n* a rigid usu ornamental bracelet.

bang on *v Brit, informal* to talk at length and forcefully about something.

bangra *or* **bhangra** /'bangrə/ *n* a form of traditional Punjabi folk music, sometimes now performed as a form of fusion music influenced by rock and rap.

bang up *v chiefly Brit, informal* to imprison.

bang-up *adj NAm, informal* first-rate; excellent.

bani *n* pl of BAN[3].

banian *n* see BANYAN.

banish *v* **1** to require (somebody) by authority to leave a place, *esp* a country. **2** to dispel (e.g. an unpleasant thought) from one's mind. ➤➤ **banishment** *n.*

banister *or* **bannister** *n* **1** (*also in pl*) a handrail with its upright supports guarding the edge of a staircase. **2** an upright support of such a handrail.

banjo *n* (*pl* **-os** *or* **-oes**) a stringed musical instrument with a round flat body, long neck and usu four or five strings. ➤➤ **banjoist** *n.*

bank[1] *n* **1a** a mound, pile, or ridge, e.g. of earth or snow. **b** a piled-up mass of cloud or fog. **2a** the rising ground bordering a lake or river or forming the embankment along a road or railway. **b** a slope. **3** the lateral inward tilt of a surface along a curve or of a vehicle, *esp* an aircraft, when following a curved path.

bank[2] *v* **1** (*often* + up) to rise in or form a bank. **2** of an aircraft: to incline laterally. **3** to surround with a bank. **4** to build (a road or railway) with the outer edge of a curve higher than the inner.

bank[3] *n* **1** an establishment for keeping, lending, exchanging, or issuing money and for the transmission of funds. **2** (**the bank**) the money, chips, etc held by the bank or banker for use in a gambling game. **3** a collection of something kept available for use when needed. **4** a container for collecting paper, glass, etc for recycling.

bank[4] *v* to deposit (money) in a bank. ✱ **bank on** to depend or rely on.

bank[5] *n* **1** a group or series of objects arranged close together in a row or tier. **2** a row of keys on a typewriter or computer keyboard.

bankable *adj* **1** acceptable to or at a bank. **2** regarded as a likely or certain source of profit, *esp* because tending to attract large cinema audiences.

bank card *n* = CHEQUE CARD.

banker[1] *n* **1** somebody who engages in the business of banking, *esp* a senior bank executive. **2** the player who keeps the bank in various games.

banker[2] *n Aus, NZ* a river that has overflowed its banks.

bank holiday *n* a public holiday in the British Isles on which banks and some businesses are closed.

banking[1] *n* the business of a bank or a banker.

banking[2] *n* = BANK[1] (2).

banknote *n* money in paper form.

bank rate *n* = BASE RATE.

bankroll[1] *n* **1** a roll of banknotes. **2** *NAm* a supply of money; funds.

bankroll[2] *v* to supply the money required for (something) to function or operate; to finance.

bankrupt[1] *adj* **1** reduced to a state of financial ruin, *esp* legally declared insolvent. **2a** broken or ruined. **b** (+ of/in) devoid of or totally lacking in (a quality, skill, etc).

bankrupt[2] *n* an insolvent person whose estate is administered under the bankruptcy laws for the benefit of his or her creditors.

bankrupt[3] *v* to reduce (a person or organization) to bankruptcy.

bankruptcy *n* (*pl* **-ies**) **1** being bankrupt. **2** utter failure, or total absence of something desired or required.

banksia *n* an Australian evergreen tree or shrub with tough leathery leaves and yellow flowers.

banner[1] *n* **1a** a usu square or oblong flag bearing heraldic arms. **b** an ensign displaying a distinctive or symbolic device or legend, *esp* one presented as an award of honour or distinction. **2** a strip of cloth on which a message, slogan, or sign is painted.

banner[2] *adj NAm* distinguished from all others, *esp* in excellence: *a banner year for business.*

bannister *n* see BANISTER.

bannock *n Scot, N Eng* a round flat loaf of unleavened bread made with oatmeal or barley meal.

banns *pl n* the public announcement in church of a proposed marriage.

banoffi pie *or* **banoffee pie** *n* a pie made with bananas, toffee, and cream.

banquet[1] *n* a large and elaborate ceremonial meal often in honour of a person; a feast.

banquet[2] *v* (**banqueted, banqueting**) to provide or entertain with a banquet.

banquette /bang'ket/ *n* a built-in upholstered bench along a wall.

banshee *n* a female spirit in Gaelic folklore whose wailing warns of approaching death in a household.

bantam *n* a small domestic fowl.

bantamweight *n* a weight in boxing and amateur wrestling between flyweight and featherweight.

banter[1] *n* teasing or badgering; badinage.

banter[2] *v* to speak or act playfully or wittily.

Bantu *n* (*pl* **Bantus** *or* **Bantu**) **1** *derog* a member of a group of indigenous peoples of central and southern Africa. **2** a group of languages spoken by these peoples. ➤➤ **Bantu** *adj.*

banyan *or* **banian** *n* an Indian tree of the fig family with branches that send out shoots which grow down to the soil and root to form secondary trunks.

banzai /ban'zie/ *interj* a Japanese cheer or battle cry.

baobab *n* an Old World tropical tree with a thick trunk and an edible acid fruit resembling a gourd.

bap *n Brit* a soft bread roll with a thin crust and often dusted with flour.

baptise *v* see BAPTIZE.

baptism *n* the ritual use of water for purification, *esp* in the Christian sacrament of admission to the church. ➤➤ **baptismal** *adj.*

baptism of fire *n* an initial experience, e.g. a soldier's first battle, that is a severe ordeal.

Baptist *adj* belonging or relating to the Baptist Church, a Protestant denomination which baptizes full adult believers rather than babies or children. ➤➤ **Baptist** *n.*

baptistery *or* **baptistry** *n* (*pl* **-ies**) a part of a church or formerly a separate building used for baptism.

baptize *or* **-ise** *v* **1** to administer baptism to. **2** to give a name to, *esp* at baptism; to christen.

bar[1] *n* **1** a straight piece, e.g. of wood or metal, that is longer than it is wide and has any of various uses, e.g. as a lever, support, or fastening. **2** something that obstructs or prevents passage, progress, or action. **3** in a court of law, the dock or the railing that encloses the dock. **4** (*usu* **the Bar**) **a** *Brit* (*used as sing. or pl*) the whole body of barristers. **b** *Brit* the profession of barrister. **c** *NAm* the legal profession. **5** a straight stripe, band, or line much longer than it is wide, e.g. a strip of metal attached to a military medal to indicate an additional award of the medal. **6a** a counter at which food or *esp* alcoholic drinks are served. **b** a room or establishment whose main feature is a bar for the serving of alcoholic drinks. **c** a place where goods, *esp* a specified commodity, are sold or served across a counter or a service provided. **7** in music, a group of notes and rests that add up to a prescribed time value, bounded on each side on the staff by a bar line, or the bar line itself. ✱ **be called to the Bar** *Brit* to become a barrister. **behind bars** in prison.

bar[2] *v* (**barred, barring**) **1** to fasten (e.g. a door) with a bar. **2** to shut in or out by or as if by bars. **3** to prevent or forbid. ➤➤ **barred** *adj.*

bar[3] *prep* = EXCEPT[1].

bar[4] *n* a unit of pressure equal to 100,000 newtons per square metre (about 14.5lb per square inch).

barathea *n* a fabric with a rough pebbly texture, used for coats and jackets.

barb *n* **1** a sharp projection extending backwards from the point of an arrow, fishhook, etc, and preventing easy extraction. **2** a biting or pointedly critical remark or comment. ➤➤ **barbless** *adj.*

Barbadian *n* a native or inhabitant of Barbados. ➤➤ **Barbadian** *adj.*

barbarian *n* **1** a person belonging to a land, culture, or people regarded as uncivilized or inferior to and more savage than one's own. **2** somebody regarded as lacking refinement, learning, or artistic or literary culture. ➤➤ **barbarian** *adj.*

barbaric *adj* **1** vicious and cruel. **2** unsophisticated or uncivilized. ➤➤ **barbarically** *adv.*

barbarism *n* **1** a word, action, or idea that is unacceptable by contemporary standards, or the use of such words, actions, or ideas. **2** primitive or unsophisticated social or intellectual condition. **3** barbarous cruelty.

barbarity *n* (*pl* **-ies**) = BARBARISM (2), (3).

barbarous *adj* **1** lacking culture or refinement. **2** mercilessly harsh or cruel. **3** with no system of social organization; uncivilized. ➤➤ **barbarously** *adv.*

barbecue[1] *n* **1** an outdoor, often portable fireplace over which meat and fish are roasted or grilled. **2** a meal or social gathering in the open air at which barbecued food is served.

barbecue[2] *v* (**barbecues, barbecued, barbecuing**) to roast or grill (food) on a barbecue.

barbed *adj* **1** having barbs. **2** characterized by pointed and biting criticism or sarcasm.

barbed wire *n* twisted wires armed with sharp points set at intervals along it.

barbel[1] *n* a European freshwater fish with four barbels (tactile organs; see BARBEL[2]) on its upper jaw.

barbel[2] *n* a slender tactile projecting organ on the lips of certain fishes, e.g. catfish, used in locating food.

barbell *n* a bar with adjustable weighted discs attached to each end that is used for exercise and in weight-lifting.

barber[1] *n* a person who cuts and styles men's hair and shaves or trims beards.

barber[2] *v* to cut or trim (a man's hair or beard).

barberry *n* (*pl* **-ies**) a shrub that has spines, yellow flowers, and oval red berries.

barbershop *n* unaccompanied vocal harmonizing of popular songs, *esp* by a male quartet.

barber's pole *n* a red and white striped pole traditionally fixed to the front of a barber's shop.

barbican *n* a defensive structure, *esp* a tower at a gate or bridge.

bar billiards *n* a form of billiards using a small table with holes in the playing area instead of side pockets and obstacles in the form of small upright pegs.

barbiturate *n* **1** a salt or ester of barbituric acid. **2** any of several derivatives of barbituric acid, e.g. thiopentone and phenobarbitone, that are used *esp* in the treatment of epilepsy and were formerly widely used in sleeping pills.

barbituric acid *n* an organic acid used in the manufacture of barbiturate drugs and plastics.

Barbour *n trademark* a waxed cotton jacket or coat.

bar chart *n* = BAR GRAPH.

bar code *n* a code printed on the label of a product for sale consisting of parallel lines of varying thickness that can be read by an electronic scanner to automatically register a price on a cash register or for automatic stock control.

bard[1] *n* **1** *archaic or literary* somebody, *esp* a Celtic poet-singer, who composed, sang, or recited verses about heroes and their deeds. **2** any poet, *esp* one recognized or honoured at an eisteddfod. **3** (**the Bard**) an epithet for Shakespeare. ➤➤ **bardic** *adj.*

bard[2] *or* **barde** *v* to cover (meat to be roasted) with strips of pork fat or bacon to add flavour and seal in moisture.

bare[1] *adj* **1** lacking a natural, usual, or appropriate covering, *esp* clothing. **2** open to view; exposed. **3** unfurnished or empty. **4a** having nothing left over or added; mere. **b** not disguised or embellished in any way. ✱ **with one's bare hands** without tools or weapons. ➤➤ **bareness** *n.*

bare[2] *v* to reveal (something, *esp* body parts normally covered up, or thoughts or feelings normally kept private). ✱ **bare one's teeth** to draw back the lips and show the teeth, e.g. in a snarl.

bareback *or* **barebacked** *adv and adj* on the bare back of a horse without a saddle.

barefaced *adj* lacking scruples; shameless.

barely *adv* **1** only just; hardly. **2** in a meagre manner; scantily. **3** not quite; hardly.

barf *v chiefly NAm, informal* to vomit.

bargain[1] *n* **1** an advantageous purchase, or something bought at an advantageous price. **2** an agreement between parties concerning the terms of a transaction between them or the course of action each pursues in respect to the other. ✱ **into the bargain** in addition; what is more.

bargain[2] *v* (*often* + with) to negotiate over the terms of a purchase, agreement, or contract. ✱ **bargain for** to be prepared for. **bargain on** to expect. ➤➤ **bargainer** *n.*

barge[1] *n* **1** a flat-bottomed boat used chiefly for the transport of goods on inland waterways or between ships and the shore. **2** a long, flat-bottomed, usu brightly decorated boat used on canals and rivers as a pleasure craft or sometimes as a dwelling.

barge[2] *v* **1** to move in a headlong or clumsy fashion. **2** (+ in/into) to intrude, *esp* noisily or clumsily.

bargeboard *n* an often ornamented board attached to the sloping edge of a gabled roof.

bargee *n Brit* somebody who works on a barge.

bargepole *n* a long thick pole for propelling a barge. ✱ **he/she etc wouldn't touch (something or somebody) with a bargepole** *informal* he, she, etc wouldn't have anything to do with something or somebody under any circumstances.

bar graph *n* a graph or diagram in which the frequency with which an item occurs is represented by the length of a vertical bar.

barite *n* see BARYTES.

baritone *n* **1** a male singer having a voice between base and tenor. **2** a musical instrument having a range below that of tenor.

barium *n* a silver-white soft metallic chemical element of the alkaline-earth group.

barium meal *n* a solution of barium sulphate swallowed by a patient to make the stomach or intestines visible in X-ray pictures.

bark[1] *v* **1** to make the short loud cry characteristic of a dog. **2** to speak in a curt, loud, and usu angry tone; to snap loudly. ✱ **bark up the wrong tree** to proceed under a misapprehension.

bark[2] *n* the sound made by a barking dog. ✱ **his/her etc bark is worse than his/her etc bite** he, she, etc is less fierce than he, she, etc seems.

bark[3] *n* the tough exterior covering of a woody root or stem.

bark[4] *v* **1** to scrape the skin of (a part of the body, e.g. the knee or shin) by accident. **2** to remove some or all of the bark from (a tree).

bark[5] *n* **1** *NAm* see BARQUE. **2** *literary* a boat of any kind.

barker *n* a person who stands outside a circus, fair, etc and shouts to encourage people to go in.

barking *or* **barking mad** *adj Brit, informal* completely mad.

barley *n* (*pl* **-eys**) a widely cultivated cereal grass used to make malt, in foods, e.g. breakfast cereals and soups, and to feed cattle.

barley sugar *n* a brittle semi-transparent amber-coloured sweet made of boiled sugar.

barley water *n* a non-alcoholic drink made by boiling barley in water, often flavoured with fruit.

barley wine *n* a type of strong sweet ale.

barm *n* yeast formed during the fermenting of beer.

barman *or* **barmaid** *n* (*pl* **barmen** *or* **barmaids**) somebody who serves drinks in a bar.

bar mitzvah /bah 'mitsvə/ *n* the religious ceremony marking a Jewish boy's reaching the age of 13, when adult religious duties and responsibilities are assumed.

barmy *adj* (**-ier, -iest**) *informal* foolish or slightly mad. ➤➤ **barmily** *adv,* **barminess** *n.*

barn *n* a large farm building for storage, *esp* of feed, harvested grain etc.

barnacle *n* a marine crustacean that is free-swimming as a larva but fixed to rocks or floating objects as an adult. ➤➤ **barnacled** *adj.*

barnacle goose *n* a European goose with a white face and black neck that breeds in the Arctic.

barn dance *n* **1** a country dance, *esp* a round dance or a square dance with called instructions. **2** a social gathering for such dances.

barnet *n Brit, informal* a person's hair.

barney *n* (*pl* **-eys**) *Brit, informal* a quarrel or row.

barn owl *n* an owl with a distinctive heart-shaped face that nests *esp* in barns and other buildings.

barnstorm *v chiefly NAm* **1** to tour rural districts staging theatrical performances. **2** to travel from place to place making brief stops, e.g. in the course of a political campaign.

barnyard *n NAm* = FARMYARD.

barograph *n* a barometer that records its readings, e.g. as a line on a graph.

barometer *n* **1** an instrument for determining the pressure of the atmosphere and hence for assisting in predicting the weather or measuring the height of an ascent. **2** something that registers fluctuations, e.g. in public opinion. ⋙ **barometric** *adj.*

baron *n* **1a** a member of the lowest rank of the peerage in Britain. **b** formerly, a feudal tenant who received his rights and title directly from the sovereign in return for military or other honourable service. **2** a man of great power or influence in a specified field of activity.

baronage *n* (*used as sing. or pl*) **1** barons collectively. **2** the nobility; the peerage.

baroness *n* **1** the wife or widow of a baron. **2** a woman having the rank of a baron in her own right.

baronet *n* the holder of a rank of honour below a baron and above a knight. ⋙ **baronetcy** *n.*

baronial *adj* **1** of or befitting a baron or the baronage. **2** stately and spacious.

baron of beef *n* a cut of beef consisting of two sirloins joined at the backbone.

barony *n* (*pl* **-ies**) the domain or rank of a baron.

baroque[1] *adj* **1** of a style of art, architecture, and music prevalent *esp* in the 17th cent. that is marked by extravagant forms and elaborate and sometimes grotesque ornamentation. **2** extravagantly intricate or recherché.

baroque[2] *n* the baroque style in art, architecture, and music.

barouche /bə'roohsh/ *n* a four-wheeled horse-drawn carriage with a high driver's seat at the front and a folding top over the rear seats.

barque (*NAm* **bark**) *n* **1** a sailing vessel with the rearmost of usu three masts fore-and-aft rigged and the others square-rigged. **2** *literary* a boat.

barrack[1] *n* (*usu in pl*) a set or area of buildings providing accommodation for soldiers.

barrack[2] *v* to accommodate (soldiers) in barracks.

barrack[3] *v* **1** *chiefly Brit* to jeer or scoff at (a player or performer). **2** *chiefly Aus, NZ* (*usu* + for) to root or cheer, e.g. for a team.

barrack-room lawyer *n* an opinionated person who persistently and pettily argues over details without having the knowledge or authority to do so.

barracouta *n* (*pl* **barracoutas** *or* **barracouta**) a large food fish of Pacific seas.

barracuda *n* (*pl* **barracudas** *or* **barracuda**) a predatory fish of warm seas.

barrage[1] *n* **1** a wide-ranging bombardment of intensive artillery fire, intended to hinder enemy action. **2** a rapid and overwhelming series of questions or complaints. **3** *Brit* an artificial dam placed in a watercourse or estuary.

barrage[2] *v* to overwhelm with questions or complaints.

barrage balloon *n* a large tethered balloon used to support wires or nets to prevent the approach of low-flying enemy aircraft.

barramundi *n* (*pl* **barramundis** *or* **barramundies** *or* **barramundi**) an Australian freshwater fish used for food.

barre *n* a horizontal handrail used by ballet dancers while exercising.

barrel[1] *n* **1** an approximately cylindrical container, *esp* for liquids, with bulging sides and flat ends constructed from wooden staves bound together with hoops. **2** a unit of volume variously reckoned at between 30 and 40 gallons (135 and 180l), e.g. a barrel of oil is 35 gallons (159l), and a barrel of beer 36 gallons (164l). **3** the tube of a gun, from which the bullet, etc is fired. ✻ **over a barrel** *informal* at a disadvantage or in a position of helplessness.

barrel[2] *v* (**barrelled, barrelling,** *NAm* **barreled, barreling**) **1** to put or pack (something, *esp* a liquid) in a barrel. **2** *chiefly NAm, informal* to move at a high speed.

barrel organ *n* a musical instrument consisting of a revolving cylinder studded with pegs that open a series of valves to admit air from a bellows to a set of pipes.

barrel vault *n* an arched roof, ceiling, etc having the form of a half cylinder unbroken by joins.

barren *adj* **1** incapable of producing offspring. **2** of a tree: habitually failing to fruit. **3** of land: not productive, *esp* producing inferior or scanty vegetation. **4** lacking in or devoid of (a quality, etc). **5** lacking interest, information, or charm. ⋙ **barrenness** *n.*

barrette *n NAm* a hair-slide.

barricade[1] *n* an obstruction thrown up across a passage, often a street, to hold back a perceived enemy.

barricade[2] *v* to block off or defend (a place) with a barricade.

barrier *n* **1** a fence, bar, or other object that separates, demarcates, or serves as a barricade. **2** something immaterial that impedes or separates.

barrier cream *n* a cream for protecting the skin, e.g. from intensive sunlight or chemicals that cause irritation.

barrier method *n* the use of a mechanical barrier, e.g. a condom or diaphragm, to prevent conception.

barrier reef *n* a coral reef roughly parallel to a shore and separated from it by a lagoon.

barring *prep* = EXCEPT[1].

barrio *n* (*pl* **-os**) **1** a Spanish-speaking neighbourhood in a city or town in the USA, *esp* in the Southwest. **2** in a Spanish-speaking country, a quarter or district of a city or town.

barrister *n* (*also* **barrister-at-law**) *Brit* a lawyer who has the right to plead as an advocate in an English or Welsh superior court: compare SOLICITOR.

barrow[1] *n* a cart with a shallow box body, two wheels, and shafts for pushing it, used e.g. by street and market traders.

barrow[2] *n* a large mound of earth or stones over an ancient grave; a tumulus.

Bart *abbr* baronet.

bartender *n chiefly NAm* = BARMAN.

barter[1] *v* to trade by exchanging (commodities) without the use of money.

barter[2] *n* the carrying on of trade by bartering.

baryon *n* any of a group of elementary particles, e.g. a neutron, that are fermions (see FERMION) and have a mass equal to or greater than that of the proton.

barytes /bə'rieteez/ *or* **baryte** *or* **barite** *n* naturally occurring barium sulphate.

basal *adj* of, situated at, or forming the base.

basal metabolic rate *n* the rate at which heat is given off by an organism at complete rest.

basalt *n* a dense to fine-grained dark igneous rock consisting essentially of a feldspar and usu pyroxene. ➤➤ **basaltic** *adj.*

bascule *n* **1** a counterbalancing apparatus. **2** (*also* **bascule bridge**) a bridge with sections that are raised and lowered using counterweights on the principle of the seesaw.

base[1] *n* **1a** the bottom of something, *esp* a support or foundation. **b** the lower part of a wall, pier, or column considered as a separate architectural feature. **c** a side or face of a geometrical figure on which it is regarded as standing. **d** that part of an organ by which it is attached to another structure nearer the centre of a living organism. **2** the fundamental part of something; a basis on which other activities or institutions depend. **3a** a centre from which a start is made in an activity or from which operations proceed. **b** the locality or installations on which a military force relies for supplies or from which it starts operations. **c** the number with reference to which a number system is constructed. **4a** a main ingredient. **b** a supporting or carrying ingredient. **5a** the starting place or goal in various games. **b** any of the stations at each of the four corners of the inner part of a baseball field to which a batter must run in turn in order to score a run. **6** any of various typically water-soluble and acrid or salty-tasting chemical compounds that are capable of taking up a hydrogen ion from or donating an unshared pair of electrons to an acid to form a salt: compare ALKALI, ACID[2].

base[2] *v* **1** to make, form, or serve as a base for. **2** (*usu* + on/upon) to use as a base or basis for; to found. **3** (*usu* + in/at) to have (a place) as an operational base.

base[3] *adj* **1a** lacking higher values; degrading. **b** lacking or showing a lack of moral values such as honour, chivalry, or loyalty. **2a** of a metal: of comparatively low value and having relatively inferior properties, e.g. poor resistance to corrosion: compare NOBLE[1] (5). **b** of a coin: containing a larger than usual proportion of base metals. **3** *archaic* lowly. ➤➤ **basely** *adv,* **baseness** *n.*

baseball *n* a game played with a bat and ball between two teams of nine players each on a large field centring on four bases arranged in a diamond that mark the course a batter must run to score.

baseball cap *n* a close-fitting round cap of light material with a large peak.

base-jumping *n* (*also* **BASE jumping**) parachuting from fixed objects such as buildings, bridges, and mountains. ➤➤ **base-jumper** *n.*

baseless *adj* not supported by evidence or fact; unfounded. ➤➤ **baselessly** *adv,* **baselessness** *n.*

baseline *n* **1** a basis or starting point for measurements or comparisons. **2** the back line at each end of a court in tennis, badminton, etc.

basement *n* the part of a building that is wholly or partly below ground level.

base metal *n* a common and relatively cheap metal such as iron or copper, as opposed to e.g. gold and silver.

base rate *n* the rate of interest, set by the Bank of England, used by major British banks as a basis for calculating charges on loans and interest on deposits.

bases[1] *n* pl of BASE[1].

bases[2] *n* pl of BASIS.

bash[1] *v informal* **1** to strike violently, or to injure or damage by striking. **2** (*often* + up) to make a violent physical attack on. ➤➤ **basher** *n.*

bash[2] *n informal* **1** a forceful blow. **2** *chiefly Brit* (*often* + at) an attempt. **3** a party.

bashful *adj* **1** socially shy or timid. **2** characterized by extreme sensitiveness or self-consciousness. ➤➤ **bashfully** *adv,* **bashfulness** *n.*

BASIC *n* a high-level computer language designed for teaching programming to beginners.

basic[1] *adj* **1a** forming the base or essence; fundamental. **b** simple; elementary. **2a** serving as the minimum basis or starting point. **b** simple; without embellishment; of a low but acceptable standard. **3a** having the character of a chemical base. **b** alkaline.

basic[2] *n* (*usu in pl*) something basic; a fundamental.

basically *adv* **1a** essentially; fundamentally: *The plan is basically sound.* **b** in fact: *That's basically all there is to it.* **c** *informal* generally; without being specific: *We were basically thinking of some time in March.* **2** in a simple or unsophisticated way.

basil *n* an aromatic plant of the mint family whose leaves are widely used as a herb in cooking.

basilar *adj* of or situated at the base of something, e.g. the skull.

basilica *n* **1** an oblong building used in ancient Rome as a place of assembly or as a lawcourt. **2** an early Christian church similar to a Roman basilica. ➤➤ **basilican** *adj.*

basilisk *n* **1** a mythical reptile whose breath and glance were fatal. **2** a crested tropical American lizard related to the iguanas.

basin *n* **1a** a rounded open fairly shallow container, used *esp* for holding water for washing. **b** a bowl used *esp* for holding, mixing, or cooking food. **2** a partly enclosed area of water providing shelter for ships; a dock. **3a** a depression in the surface of the land or ocean floor. **b** the region drained by a river and its tributaries. ➤➤ **basinal** *adj,* **basined** *adj,* **basinful** *n.*

basis *n* (*pl* **bases**) **1** a physical or intellectual foundation, *esp* a principle governing a course of action. **2** the principal component of something.

bask *v* **1** to lie enjoying pleasant warmth or sunshine. **2** (*usu* + in) to enjoy somebody's favour or approval.

basket *n* **1** a rigid receptacle for carrying e.g. shopping or produce made of interwoven strips of wicker or wood, or of plastic or wire mesh. **2a** a net, open at the bottom and suspended from a metal ring, that constitutes the goal in basketball. **b** a goal scored in basketball. **3** a collection or group. **4** *Brit, euphem* = BASTARD[1] (2). ➤➤ **basketful** *n.*

basketball *n* **1** an indoor court game between two teams of five players who score goals by tossing a large ball through a raised basket. **2** the ball used in basketball.

basket case *n informal* **1** somebody who has had all four limbs amputated. **2** somebody or something regarded as worn out or useless.

basket chair *n* a wickerwork armchair.

basketry *or* **basketwork** *n* **1** the art or craft of making baskets or objects woven like baskets or woven objects. **2** baskets collectively.

basking shark *n* a large species of shark that often lies near the water surface, feeding on plankton.

basmati rice *n* long-grain rice of high quality with a delicate flavour.

Basque *n* **1** a member of a people inhabiting the W Pyrenees. **2** the language of the Basques. ➤➤ **Basque** *adj.*

basque *n* **1** the lower part of a bodice, that extends a little below the waist. **2** a close-fitting bodice for women.

bas-relief *n* sculptural relief in which the design projects very slightly from the surrounding surface: compare HIGH RELIEF.

bass[1] *n* (*pl* **basses** *or* **bass**) an edible spiny-finned marine and freshwater fish.

bass[2] *n* **1** a male singer with a voice of the lowest range. **2** (*used before a noun*) a musical instrument having the lowest range. **3** a double bass or bass guitar. **4** the lower portion of the audio frequency range considered *esp* in relation to its electronic reproduction. ➤➤ **bassist** *n.*

bass[3] *adj* **1** of low pitch. **2** deep or grave in tone.

bass clef *n* in musical notation, a clef placing the F below middle C on the fourth line of the staff.

basset *or* **basset hound** *n* a hunting dog of a short-legged breed with a long body and very long ears.

bassi *n* pl of BASSO.

bassinet *n* a baby's basketlike cradle, e.g. of wickerwork or plastic, often with a hood over one end.

basso *n* (*pl* **bassos** *or* **bassi**) a bass voice or singer.

bassoon *n* a large woodwind musical instrument with a double reed and a usual range two octaves lower than the oboe. ➤➤ **bassoonist** *n.*

basso profundo *n* (*pl* **basso profundos** *or* **bassi profundi**) a singer with an exceptionally low bass singing voice.

bast *n* a strong woody fibre obtained chiefly from the phloem of certain plants, used for making ropes and mats.

bastard[1] *n* **1** *offensive or archaic* an illegitimate child. **2** *informal* **a** an offensive or disagreeable person, often used as a general term of abuse. **b** a person of a specified type: *lucky bastard.* ➤➤ **bastardly** *adj.*

bastard[2] *adj* **1** *offensive or archaic* illegitimate. **2** of an inferior or less typical type. **3** lacking genuineness or authority; false.

bastardize *or* **-ise** *v* **1** *archaic* to declare illegitimate. **2** to debase. ➤➤ **bastardization** *n.*

bastardy *n formal or archaic* illegitimacy.

baste[1] *v* to sew temporarily; to tack. ➤➤ **baster** *n,* **basting** *n.*

baste[2] *v* to moisten (e.g. meat) at intervals with melted butter, dripping, etc during cooking, *esp* roasting. ➤➤ **baster** *n,* **basting** *n.*

baste[3] *v* to beat severely or soundly; to thrash. ➤➤ **basting** *n.*

bastinado /basti'naydoh/ *n* (*pl* **-oes**) a form of punishment or torture by beating the soles of the feet with a stick. ➤➤ **bastinado** *v.*

bastion *n* **1** a projecting part of a fortification. **2** something or somebody considered as providing defence or protection: *a bastion of press freedom.* ➤➤ **bastioned** *adj.*

bat[1] *n* **1** a usu wooden implement used for hitting the ball in cricket, baseball, table tennis, etc. **2a** a batsman or batswoman. **b** a turn at batting in cricket, baseball, etc. **3** a hand-held implement shaped like a table-tennis bat for guiding aircraft when landing or taxiing. ✱ **off one's own bat** through one's own efforts, *esp* without being prompted.

bat[2] *v* (**batted, batting**) **1** to strike or hit with, or as if with, a bat. **2** to take one's turn at batting, e.g. in cricket or baseball.

bat[3] *n* **1** a nocturnal flying mammal with forelimbs modified to form wings. **2** (**old bat**) *derog* a foolish or disagreeable old woman. ✱ **have bats in the belfry** to be mad or eccentric.

bat[4] *v* (**batted, batting**) to blink (an eye), *esp* in surprise or emotion. ✱ **not bat an eyelid** not to be at all surprised or disconcerted.

batch[1] *n* **1** a quantity of goods produced or prepared, e.g. baked, at one time. **2** a group of jobs to be run on a computer at one time with the same program. **3** a group of people or things; a lot.

batch[2] *v* to gather together or process as a batch.

batch file *n* a computer file containing a series of commands to be processed by a computer in sequence.

bate *or* **bait** *n informal* a rage or temper.

bated ✱ **with bated breath** expectantly, *esp* in nervous anticipation.

bath[1] *n* **1** a large open container for bathing in, *esp* one that is permanently fixed in a bathroom. **2a** a washing of all or part of the body in water or steam. **b** water used for bathing. **3** a liquid used for a special purpose, e.g. developing photographic film, or the vat or tank holding it. **4** (*usu in pl*) **a** a building containing a room or series of rooms designed for bathing. **b** = SWIMMING POOL.

bath[2] *v Brit* to take or give (somebody) a bath.

Bath bun *n* a sweet yeast-leavened bun containing dried fruit and topped with sugar crystals.

bath chair *n* an old-fashioned usu hooded wheelchair.

bathe[1] *v* **1a** to take a bath. **b** *NAm* to bath (somebody). **2** *chiefly Brit* to swim, e.g. in the sea or a river, for pleasure. **3** to wash, moisten, or clean with water or other liquid, e.g. a liquid medicament. **4** to suffuse, *esp* with light. ➤➤ **bather** *n.*

bathe[2] *n Brit* an act of bathing, *esp* in the sea.

bathing costume *n Brit* = SWIMMING COSTUME.

bathing machine *n* formerly, a hut on wheels that was pulled to the water's edge, for bathing from.

bathing suit *n* = SWIMMING COSTUME.

batholith *n* a large dome-shaped mass of igneous rock formed at a great depth below the earth's surface. ➤➤ **batholithic** *adj.*

bathos *n* a sudden descent from something serious or high-minded to something commonplace or trivial. ➤➤ **bathetic** *adj,* **bathetically** *adv.*

bathrobe *n* a loose usu absorbent robe, e.g. made of towelling, worn before and after having a bath.

bathroom *n* **1** a room containing a bath or shower and usu a washbasin and toilet. **2** *NAm* a toilet.

bath salts *pl n* (*used as sing. or pl*) a usu coloured compound for perfuming or softening bathwater.

bathyscaphe *or* **bathyscaph** *n* a navigable submersible ship for deep-sea exploration.

bathysphere *n* a strongly built diving sphere for deep-sea observation.

batik *n* an orig Indonesian method of hand-printing by coating with wax the parts to be left undyed.

batiste *n* a fine soft sheer fabric of plain weave made of various fibres.

batman *n* (*pl* **batmen**) a British officer's servant.

bat mitzvah *n* the religious ceremony marking a Jewish girl's reaching the age of 13, when religious responsibilities are assumed.

baton *n* **1** a small stick with which a conductor directs a band or orchestra. **2** a stick passed by the runners in a relay team. **3** a short stick carried as a symbol of rank, *esp* by a senior military officer. **4** a police officer's truncheon. **5** the long metal rod twirled by a drum major or majorette.

baton charge *n* a charge by police or troops wielding batons.

baton round *n* = PLASTIC BULLET.

batrachian *n* a frog, toad, or other vertebrate amphibian animal. ➤➤ **batrachian** *adj.*

bats *adj chiefly Brit, informal* mad; crazy.

batsman *or* **batswoman** *n* (*pl* **batsmen** *or* **batswomen**) somebody who bats or is batting, *esp* in cricket. ➤➤ **batsmanship** *n.*

battalion *n* (*also in pl, used as sing. or pl*) **1** a military unit composed of a headquarters and two or more companies. **2** a large number of troops, people, or things.

batten[1] *n* a thin narrow strip of squared timber, plastic, or metal.

batten[2] *v* (**battened, battening**) (*often* + down) to fasten (*esp* a ship's hatches) with battens.

batten[3] *v* (**battened, battening**) (+ on/upon) to thrive or grow prosperous, *esp* at the expense of somebody or something.

battenberg *n* an oblong sponge cake covered in marzipan with a cross-section of pink and yellow squares.

batter[1] *v* to strike heavily and repeatedly; to break or damage with heavy persistent blows.

batter[2] *n* a mixture of flour, egg, and milk or water, used for coating fish, making pancakes, etc.

batter[3] *n* in baseball, etc, the player who is batting.

battered[1] *adj* of food: fried in batter.

battered[2] *adj* **1** of an object: old and damaged or worn. **2** of a person: injured by repeated violent abuse.

battering ram *n* a large wooden beam with a head of iron, formerly used for beating down walls.

battery *n* (*pl* **-ies**) **1** two or more cells connected together to provide an electric current. **2a** (*often* + of) a number of similar things connected, or used together. **b** *chiefly Brit* a large number of small cages in which egg-laying hens are kept. **3** the unlawful application of any degree of force to a person without their consent. **4a** (*usu* + of) a grouping of similar artillery guns, e.g. for tactical purposes. **b** a fortified gun emplacement.

battle[1] *n* **1** a hostile encounter between armies, warships, aircraft, etc. **2** a combat between two people. **3** an extended struggle or controversy.

battle[2] *v* **1** to fight vigorously. **2** to try with great energy and determination to do something; to struggle. ➤➤ **battler** *n.*

battle-axe *n* **1** a large axe with a broad head, used formerly in warfare. **2** a quarrelsome domineering woman.

battle cruiser *n* a large heavily-armed warship faster than a battleship.

battledress *n* the uniform worn by soldiers in battle.

battlefield *or* **battleground** *n* a piece of ground where a battle is fought.

battlement *n* a parapet with indentations that surmounts a wall and is used for defence or decoration. ➤➤ **battlemented** *adj.*

battle royal *n* (*pl* **battles royal** *or* **battle royals**) a violent struggle or heated dispute.

battleship *n* the largest and most heavily armed and armoured type of warship.

batty *adj* (**-ier, -iest**) *informal* mentally unstable; crazy. ➤➤ **battiness** *n.*

bauble *n* **1** a trinket or trifle. **2** a jester's staff.

baud *n* (*pl* **baud** *or* **bauds**) a unit of data transmission speed equal to one bit of data per second.

Bauhaus *adj* characteristic of a German school of design, established in 1919, noted for synthesizing technology, craftsmanship, and design aesthetics.

baulk[1] *v Brit* see BALK[1].

baulk[2] *n Brit* see BALK[2].

bauxite *n* a mineral that is an impure mixture of aluminium oxides and hydroxides, and the principal ore of aluminium. ➤➤ **bauxitic** *adj.*

Bavarian *n* a native or inhabitant of Bavaria, a region in S Germany. ➤➤ **Bavarian** *adj.*

bavarois *or* **bavaroise** *n* a cold dessert made from flavoured and moulded custard.

bawd *n* a woman who keeps a house of prostitution; a madam.

bawdy[1] *adj* (**-ier, -iest**) boisterously or humorously indecent. ➤➤ **bawdily** *adv,* **bawdiness** *n.*

bawdy[2] *n* suggestive, coarse, or obscene language.

bawl *v* **1** to yell or bellow. **2** to cry or wail. ➤➤ **bawl** *n,* **bawler** *n.*

bawl out *v chiefly NAm, informal* to reprimand loudly or severely.

bay[1] *n* a wide curving inlet of a sea or lake.

bay[2] *n* a small evergreen Mediterranean tree of the laurel family with leaves used for flavour in cooking.

bay[3] *n* **1** a special area, division, or compartment within a larger structure: *a loading bay.* **2a** a structure projecting from the wall of a building. **b** = BAY WINDOW. **c** a section of wall between two columns or buttresses.

bay[4] *adj* of a horse: reddish brown.

bay[5] *n* a horse with a reddish brown body and black mane, tail, and points.

bay[6] *v* **1** of dogs and wolves: to bark fiercely. **2** (+ for) to demand insistently: *baying for his blood.* ✱ **at bay** trapped and forced to confront danger head on. **hold/keep at bay** to prevent from coming close to or overwhelming one.

bay leaf *n* the leaf of the European laurel used dried in cooking.

bayonet[1] *n* a blade attached to the muzzle of a firearm and used in hand-to-hand combat.

bayonet[2] *v* (**bayoneted, bayoneting**) to stab with a bayonet.

bayonet fitting *n* a fitting in which something, *esp* a light bulb, is held fast by being pushed in and twisted to one side.

bayou *n* (*pl* **bayous**) a sluggish marshy tributary of a river or lake, *esp* in the southern USA.

bay rum *n* a fragrant cosmetic and medicinal liquid from the oil of the leaves of a W Indian tree of the myrtle family.

bay window *n* a window or series of windows projecting outwards from the wall.

bazaar *n* **1** a market, *esp* in the Orient, consisting of rows of shops or stalls selling miscellaneous goods. **2** a fair for the sale of miscellaneous articles, *esp* for charitable purposes.

bazooka *n* a short-range antitank rocket launcher.

BBC *abbr* British Broadcasting Corporation.

BBQ *abbr* barbecue.

BBS *abbr* in computing, bulletin board system.

BC *abbr* **1** used after a date: before Christ. **2** British Columbia.

Usage note

BC *and* AD. See note at AD.

BCD *abbr* binary-coded decimal.

BCE *abbr* before the Common Era, used with cultural neutrality to indicate dates that are BC in Christian reckoning.

BCG vaccine *n* a vaccine used to protect people against tuberculosis.

BD *abbr* Bachelor of Divinity.

BDS *abbr* Bachelor of Dental Surgery.

Be *abbr* the chemical symbol for beryllium.

be *v* (*first person sing. present tense* **am,** *second person sing. present tense* **are,** *third person sing. present tense* **is,** *pl present tense* **are,** *present subjunctive* **be,** *present part.* **being,** *first and third person sing. past tense* **was,** *second person sing. past tense and pl past tense* **were,** *past subjunctive* **were,** *past part.* **been**) **1** to exist or be present; to have a particular location. **2** to occur in time. **3** to have a specified state, function, or value: *The leaves are green.* **4** used instead of *go* or *come* in the perfect tense: *I've been to New York.* ➤ ***verb aux.*** **1** used with the present participle to form continuous or progressive tenses. **2** used with the past participle of transitive verbs to form the passive voice. **3** used with *to* and an infinitive to express future action or a command: *They are to marry next month; You are not to worry.* ✱ **be oneself** to behave normally or naturally. **not be oneself 1** to feel unwell. **2** to behave abnormally.

be- *prefix* **1** on; round; all over: *besmear.* **2** to a great or greater degree; thoroughly: *befuddle.* **3** wearing (a specified article of dress): *bewigged.* **4** about; across: *bestride.* **5** to make; to cause to be: *belittle.*

beach[1] *n* a seashore or lakeshore, often gently sloping and usu covered by sand or pebbles.

beach[2] *v* to run or drive (a boat) ashore.

beachcomber *n* a person who searches along a shore for useful or saleable flotsam and jetsam.

beachhead *n* an area on a hostile shore occupied to secure further landing of troops and supplies.

beacon *n* **1** a signal fire commonly on a hill, tower, or pole. **2a** a signal mark used to guide shipping. **b** a radio transmitter emitting signals for the guidance of aircraft. **3** a source of light or inspiration. **4** *Brit* a high conspicuous hill.

bead[1] *n* **1** a small ball, e.g. of wood or glass, pierced for threading on a string or wire. **2** a small ball-shaped body, *esp* a drop of liquid. **3** a small metal knob on a firearm used as a front sight. **4** a projecting rim, band, or moulding, e.g. on a door. ✱ **draw a bead on** to take aim at. ▶▶ **beaded** *adj,* **beading** *n.*

bead[2] *v* **1** to adorn or cover (clothing, etc) with beads or beading. **2** to string together like beads.

beadle *n* a minor parish official whose duties include ushering and preserving order at services.

beady *adj* (**-ier, -iest**) of eyes: small, round, and shiny with interest or greed.

beagle *n* a hound of a breed with short legs and a smooth coat.

beagling *n* hunting on foot with beagles. ▶▶ **beagler** *n.*

beak *n* **1** the rigid projecting mouth structures of birds and some animals, e.g. a turtle. **2** a metal-tipped beam projecting from the bow of an ancient galley for ramming an enemy ship. **3** *chiefly Brit, informal* **a** a magistrate. **b** a schoolteacher. ▶▶ **beaked** *adj.*

beaker *n* **1** a large drinking cup with a wide mouth; a mug. **2** a cylindrical flat-bottomed vessel, usu with a pouring lip, used *esp* by chemists and pharmacists.

be-all and end-all *n* (**the be-all and end-all**) the chief factor; the essential element.

beam[1] *n* **1a** a long piece of heavy timber suitable for use in building. **b** a bar for balancing on in gymnastic exercises. **2a** the width of a ship at its widest part. **b** used in indicating position: the side of a ship: *on the starboard beam.* **3a** a ray or shaft of radiation, *esp* light. **b** a collection of rays or particles moving in nearly parallel paths: *an electron beam.* **4a** a radio signal transmitted continuously in one direction as an aircraft navigation aid. **b** the course indicated by this. ✱ **broad in the beam** *informal* having wide hips. **off beam/off the beam** wrong; irrelevant. **on her beam-ends** of a ship: about to capsize. **on the beam** proceeding or operating correctly.

beam[2] *v* **1** to smile with joy. **2** to aim (a broadcast) by directional aerials. **3** to emit (light, etc) in beams or as a beam.

bean *n* **1** a seed of a climbing plant, growing in a pod and used as a vegetable. **2** *informal* **a** the smallest possible amount of money. **b** a valueless item. **3** *informal, dated* somebody's head. ✱ **full of beans** full of vigour; very energetic.

beanbag *n* **1** a small fabric bag filled with beans, used in games or as a toy. **2** a large, loosely stuffed cushion usu containing granules or fragments of plastic foam, used as an informal low chair.

bean curd *n* a soft cheeselike food prepared from soya-bean milk.

beanfeast *n Brit, informal* a festivity or celebration.

beanie *n* a small round hat worn on the back of the head.

beano *n* (*pl* **-os**) *Brit, informal* a beanfeast.

beanpole *n informal* a very tall thin person.

bean sprouts *pl n* the sprouts of bean seeds, *esp* of the mung bean, used as a vegetable.

bear[1] *n* (*pl* **bears** *or* **bear**) **1** a large heavy mammal with long shaggy hair and a short tail. **2** a surly, uncouth, or shambling person. **3** a person who sells securities or commodities in expectation of a fall in price: compare BULL[1].

bear[2] *v* (*past tense* **bore,** *past part.* **borne**) **1** to carry or transport. **2** to show (a feeling). **3** to conduct (oneself) in a particular way: *She bore herself with dignity.* **4** to have or show as a feature: *He bears the scars of a failed marriage.* **5** to have (a name). **6a** to give birth to. **b** of a plant or tree: to produce (fruit or flowers). **7a** to support the weight of. **b** to tolerate. **c** to sustain or incur: *to bear the cost.* **8** to go in a specified direction: *to bear right.* **9** (+ on) to be relevant to something. **10** to produce fruit. **11** (+ with) to show patience or indulgence towards somebody: *Bear with me a little longer.* ✱ **bear fruit** to have good results. **bring to bear 1** to make use of. **2** to aim a gun. ▶▶ **bearable** *adj,* **bearably** *adv.*

bearbaiting *n* the practice of setting dogs on a captive bear, which was formerly a popular entertainment.

beard[1] *n* **1** the hair that grows on the lower part of a man's face, usu excluding the moustache. **2** a hairy or bristly appendage or tuft, e.g. on a goat's chin. ▶▶ **bearded** *adj,* **beardless** *adj.*

beard[2] *v* to confront with boldness, resolution, and often effrontery; to defy.

bear down *v* of a woman in childbirth: to exert concentrated downward pressure in an effort to expel the baby from the womb. ✱ **bear down on 1** to come towards (somebody) purposefully or threateningly. **2** to weigh heavily on (something).

bearer *n* **1** a porter. **2** a plant yielding fruit. **3** a person holding an order for payment, *esp* a bank note or cheque.

bear garden *n* a scene of great noise or tumult.

bear hug *n* a rough tight embrace.

bearing *n* **1** the manner in which one stands, moves, or conducts oneself. **2** (*also in pl*) a machine part in which another part turns or slides. **3a** the compass direction of a course or of one point with respect to another. **b** (*in pl*) comprehension of one's position, environment, or situation. **c** (*usu* + on) connection or relevance to something. **4** an emblem or figure on a heraldic shield.

bearish *adj* **1a** bad-tempered. **b** clumsy or rough. **2** marked by or fearful of falling prices, e.g. in a stock market: compare BULLISH. ➤➤ **bearishness** *n.*

bear market *n* a stock market in which prices are falling.

Béarnaise sauce /bayə'nayz/ *n* a rich sauce made with butter and egg yolks, and flavoured with wine, onion, and tarragon.

bear out *v* to confirm or substantiate.

bearskin *n* an article made of the skin of a bear; *esp* a tall black military hat worn by the Brigade of Guards.

bear up *v* to summon up courage, resolution, or strength.

beast *n* **1** an animal, *esp* a farm animal or a large wild animal. **2** a contemptible person.

beastly[1] *adj* (**-ier, -iest**) **1** abominable or disagreeable. **2** bestial. ➤➤ **beastliness** *n.*

beastly[2] *adv informal* very.

beast of burden *n* an animal employed to carry heavy material or perform heavy work.

beat[1] *v* (*past tense* **beat,** *past part.* **beaten**) **1a** (*often* + up) to hit (somebody) repeatedly, *esp* so as to inflict pain. **b** to strike repeatedly in order to produce music or a signal. **c** to mix (food) by stirring. **d** to range over in order to rouse game. **e** to shape or flatten thin by repeated blows. **2a** to overcome or defeat. **b** to surpass. **c** to prevail despite: *to beat the clock.* **3** of a heart or pulse: to pulsate. **4** *informal* to bewilder or baffle (somebody). **5** of a bird's wing: to strike the air. ✱ **beat about the bush** to fail to come to the point in conversation. **beat a retreat** to withdraw quickly. **beat down** to make (somebody) reduce the price of something. **beat it** *informal* to hurry away. **beat off** to repel. **beat somebody to it** to act ahead of somebody. **off the beaten track 1** of a place: remote or isolated. **2** not well-known. ➤➤ **beatable** *adj,* **beater** *n.*

beat[2] *n* **1a** a pulsation or throb. **b** a sound produced by beating, or as if by beating. **2a** metrical or rhythmic stress in poetry or music. **b** the tempo indicated to a musical performer. **3** an area or route regularly patrolled, *esp* by a police officer.

beat[3] *adj informal* exhausted.

beatbox *n informal* a drum machine.

beat generation *n* a movement among young people in the 1950s and early 1960s, *esp* in the USA, whose members rejected conventional values in favour of a more liberated, often communal, lifestyle.

beatific *adj* **1** blissfully happy. **2** enjoying the peace and happiness of heaven. ➤➤ **beatifically** *adv.*

beatify *v* (**-ies, -ied**) to authorize the veneration of (a dead person) by Roman Catholics by giving the title 'Blessed'. ➤➤ **beatification** *n.*

beatitude *n* **1** a state of utmost bliss. **2** any of a series of sayings of Jesus beginning 'Blessed are' in the Authorized Version of the Bible.

beatnik *n* a person in the 1950s and 1960s who rejected the attitudes of established society.

beat up *v* to assault and harm by repeated punching, kicking, etc.

beat-up *adj informal* dilapidated or worn out.

beau *n* (*pl* **beaux** *or* **beaus**) **1** *chiefly NAm* a boyfriend. **2** any eligible young male acquaintance. **3** *archaic* a dandy.

Beaufort scale *n* a scale indicating the force of the wind by numbers from 0 (calm) to 12 (hurricane).

Beaujolais /'bohzhəlay/ *n* a chiefly red table wine made in southern Burgundy in France.

Beaujolais nouveau /,bohzhəlay nooh'voh/ *n* Beaujolais wine sold in the year of its production.

beau monde /boh 'mond/ *n* fashionable people.

beauteous *adj archaic* beautiful. ➤➤ **beauteousness** *n.*

beautician *n* somebody who gives beauty treatments.

beautiful *adj* **1** producing aesthetic or sensual pleasure. **2** generally enjoyable and good; excellent. ➤➤ **beautifully** *adv.*

beautify *v* (**-ies, -ied**) to make beautiful. ➤➤ **beautification** *n,* **beautifier** *n.*

beauty *n* (*pl* **-ies**) **1** a quality that gives pleasure to the senses or satisfies the aesthetic demands of the mind; loveliness. **2** a beautiful person or thing; *esp* a beautiful woman. **3** a brilliant or extreme example of something. **4** a particularly advantageous or excellent quality.

beauty parlour *n* = BEAUTY SALON.

beauty queen *n* a young woman who wins a beauty contest.

beauty salon *n* an establishment offering professional beauty treatments, e.g. hairdressing and manicures, *esp* for women.

beauty sleep *n* sleep considered as being beneficial to a person's beauty.

beauty spot *n* **1** a beautiful scenic area. **2** a mole, or an artificial mole worn on the face.

beaux *n* pl of BEAU.

beaver[1] *n* (*pl* **beavers** *or* **beaver**) **1** a large semiaquatic rodent with webbed hind feet and a broad flat tail that builds dams and underwater lodges. **2a** the fur of the beaver. **b** a hat made of beaver fur or a fabric imitation.

beaver[2] *v* (*also* + away) to work energetically.

bebop *n* jazz characterized by unusual chord structures, syncopated rhythm, and harmonic complexity and innovation. Also called BOP[3]. ➤➤ **bebopper** *n.*

becalm *v* (*usu in passive*) to keep (a ship) motionless by lack of wind.

became *v* past tense of BECOME.

because[1] *conj* **1** for the reason that; since. **2** and the proof is that.

because[2] *adv informal* because of something forgotten or unmentionable.

because of *prep* **1** as a result of. **2** for the sake of.

béchamel /'bayshəmel/ *n* a white sauce made with roux and milk in which vegetables and herbs have been infused.

beck[1] *n N Eng* a brook; *esp* a pebbly mountain stream.

beck[2] ✱ **at somebody's beck and call** in continual readiness to obey somebody.

beckon *v* **1** to summon or signal, typically with a wave or nod. **2** to appear inviting.

become *v* (*past tense* **became,** *past part.* **become**) **1** to come to be. **2** to suit or be suitable to (somebody). ✱ **become of** to happen to.

becoming *adj* suitable or fitting; *esp* attractively suitable. ➤➤ **becomingly** *adv.*

becquerel *n* the SI unit of radiation activity equal to one unit of disintegration per second.

BEd *abbr* Bachelor of Education.

bed[1] *n* **1a** a place for resting or sleeping, *esp* a piece of furniture usu including a bedstead, mattress, and bedding. **b** a place of sexual relations, or lovemaking. **c** sleep, or a time for sleeping. **2** a plot of ground, *esp* in a garden, prepared for plants. **3** the bottom of a body of water. **4** a supporting surface or structure; *esp* the foundation that supports a road or railway. **5** = STRATUM. ✱ **get out of bed on the wrong side** to be bad-tempered all day. **go to bed with** to have sexual intercourse with.

bed[2] *v* (**bedded, bedding**) **1a** (*often* + down) to provide with a bed. **b** (*often* + down) to go to bed. **2** to go to bed with for sexual intercourse. **3a** to embed. **b** (*often* + out) to plant (flowers, vegetables, etc) in beds.

bed and breakfast *n Brit* a night's lodging and breakfast the following morning.

bedazzle *v* to dazzle. ⋙ **bedazzlement** *n.*

bed-blocking *n* the occupying of hospital beds by patients who do not actually need hospital care because there is no alternative care available.

bedbug *n* a wingless bloodsucking bug that sometimes infests beds.

bedclothes *pl n* the covers, e.g. sheets and blankets, used on a bed.

beddable *adj informal* sexually attractive.

bedding *n* **1** = BEDCLOTHES. **2** a bottom layer; a foundation. **3** material used as a bed for livestock.

bedding plant *n* a plant appropriate or adapted for culture in open-air beds.

bedeck *v* to adorn.

bedevil *v* (**bedevilled, bedevilling,** *NAm* **bedeviled, bedeviling**) to be a continual problem or nuisance to. ⋙ **bedevilment** *n.*

bedfellow *n* **1** a person who shares a bed. **2** a close associate; an ally.

bedlam *n* a place or state of uproar and confusion.

bed linen *n* the sheets and pillowcases used on a bed.

bed of roses *n* a place or situation of agreeable ease.

Bedouin *or* **Beduin** *n* (*pl* **Bedouins** *or* **Beduins** *or* **Bedouin** *or* **Beduin**) a nomadic Arab of the Arabian, Syrian, or N African deserts.

bedpan *n* a shallow vessel used by a person in bed for urination or defecation.

bedpost *n* a post of a bedstead, often turned or carved.

bedraggled *adj* looking limp and untidy, *esp* after being made wet.

bedridden *adj* confined to bed, e.g. by illness.

bedrock *n* **1** the solid rock underlying unconsolidated surface materials, e.g. soil. **2** the basis of something.

bedroll *n chiefly NAm* bedding, *esp* that used for sleeping in the open, rolled up for carrying.

bedroom *n* **1** a room with a bed, intended primarily for sleeping. **2** (*used before a noun*) suggestive of or inviting sexual relations.

Beds *abbr* Bedfordshire.

bedside *adj* **1** of or conducted at the bedside. **2** suitable for a person in bed.

bedside manner *n* the manner with which a doctor deals with patients.

bed-sit *n Brit, informal* a bed-sitter.

bed-sitter *n Brit* a single room serving as both bedroom and sitting room.

bed-sitting-room *n Brit* a bed-sitter.

bedsore *n* a sore caused by prolonged pressure on the tissue of a bedridden invalid.

bedspread *n* an ornamental cloth cover for a bed.

bedstead *n* the framework of a bed.

bedstraw *n* a plant of the madder family with angled stems and small flowers.

Beduin *n* see BEDOUIN.

bed-wetting *n* involuntary discharge of urine during sleep. ⋙ **bed-wetter** *n.*

bee *n* **1** a social four-winged insect with a hairy body and sting, often kept in a hive for the honey that it produces. **2** *chiefly NAm* a gathering of people for a specified purpose: *a sewing bee.* ✱ **bee in one's bonnet** an obsession about a specified subject or idea.

Beeb *n Brit* the BBC.

beech *n* (*pl* **beeches** *or* **beech**) a hardwood deciduous tree with smooth grey bark and small edible triangular nuts. ⋙ **beechen** *adj.*

beech mast *n* the nuts of the beech when lying on the ground.

bee eater *n* a brightly coloured insect-eating bird with a slender bill.

beef[1] *n* (*pl* **beefs**) **1a** meat from a bullock, cow, or bull. **b** (*pl* **beeves,** *NAm* **beefs**) a full-grown ox, cow, or bull, *esp* when fattened for food. **2** *informal* muscular flesh; brawn. **3** *informal* a complaint.

beef[2] *v* **1** *informal* (*usu* + up) to add weight, strength, or power to. **2** *informal* to complain.

beefburger *n* a hamburger.

beefcake *n informal* a photographic display of muscular male physiques; compare CHEESECAKE (2).

beefeater *n* a Yeoman of the Guard.

beef tea *n* a hot drink made from beef extract.

beef tomato *n* a very large variety of tomato.

beef Wellington *n* a fillet of beef covered with pâté de foie gras and baked in a casing of pastry.

beefy *adj* (**-ier, -iest**) **1** tasting of beef. **2** brawny or powerful. ⋙ **beefiness** *n.*

beehive *n* **1** a structure for housing a colony of bees. **2** a conical lacquered hairstyle, fashionable for women in the 1960s.

beeline ✱ **make a beeline** take a straight direct course.

Beelzebub *n* a devil or the Devil.

been *v* past part. of BE.

beep[1] *n* a sound, e.g. from a horn or electronic device, that serves as a signal or warning.

beep[2] *v* **1** to sound a horn. **2** to make a beep. ⋙ **beeper** *n.*

beer *n* **1** an alcoholic drink brewed from fermented malt flavoured with hops. **2** a carbonated non-alcoholic or slightly alcoholic drink, flavoured with roots or other plant parts.

beer and skittles *pl n* (*used as sing. or pl*) pleasure and enjoyment.

beer garden *n* a garden or open area, attached to a pub or bar, where customers can eat and drink.

beery *adj* (**-ier, -iest**) **1** affected or caused by beer. **2** smelling or tasting of beer.

bee's knees ✱ **the bee's knees** *informal* somebody or something that is outstandingly good.

beestings *pl n* (*used as sing.*) colostrum, *esp* of a cow.

beeswax *n* a yellowish plastic substance secreted by bees, used by them for constructing honeycombs and by humans as a wood polish.

beeswing *n* a thin crust of tartar that forms on old wine.

beet *n* **1** any of several species of plants with a swollen root used as a vegetable, a source of sugar, or for forage. **2** *NAm* beetroot.

beetle[1] *n* an insect with four wings, of which the front pair are modified into stiff coverings that protect the back pair at rest.

beetle[2] *v Brit, informal* (*often* + off) to move swiftly.

beetle[3] *n* a heavy wooden tool for hammering or ramming.

beetle-browed *adj* with thick, overhanging eyebrows.

beetling *adj* prominent and overhanging.

beetroot *n* (*pl* **beetroots** *or* **beetroot**) *chiefly Brit* a cultivated beet with a red edible root that is a common salad vegetable.

beeves *n* pl of BEEF[1] (1B).

BEF *abbr* British Expeditionary Force.

befall *v* (*past tense* **befell**, *past part.* **befallen**) to happen to, *esp* as if by fate.

befit *v* (**befitted, befitting**) to be proper or becoming to. ⋙ **befitting** *adj*, **befittingly** *adv.*

befog *v* (**befogged, befogging**) **1** to confuse. **2** to make foggy; to obscure.

before[1] *adv* **1** earlier in time; previously. **2** so as to be in advance of others; ahead.

before[2] *prep* **1** in front of. **2** earlier than. **3** in a higher or more important position than. **4** in preference to.

before[3] *conj* **1** earlier than the time when. **2** rather than.

beforehand *adv and adj* **1** in anticipation. **2** ahead of time.

befriend *v* to become a friend of purposely; to show kindness and understanding to.

befuddle *v* **1** to muddle or stupefy with drink. **2** to confuse or perplex. ⋙ **befuddlement** *n.*

beg *v* (**begged, begging**) **1** to ask for alms or charity. **2a** to ask for earnestly. **b** to ask (somebody) earnestly to do something. **3** of a dog: to sit up and hold out the forepaws. ✻ **beg the question** to assume something as established or proved without justification. **go begging** to be available but in little demand.

began *v* past tense of BEGIN.

beget *v* (**begetting**, *past tense* **begot**, *archaic* **begat**, *past part.* **begotten**) **1** *archaic* to be the father. **2** *literary* to cause. ⋙ **begetter** *n.*

beggar[1] *n* **1** a person who lives by asking for money, food, etc. **2** a pauper. **3** *informal* a person of the kind specified.

beggar[2] *v* **1** to reduce to beggary. **2** to exceed the resources or abilities of.

beggarly *adj* contemptibly mean or paltry. ⋙ **beggarliness** *n.*

beggar-my-neighbour *n* a card game based on luck in which the object is to acquire all the cards held by the other players.

beggary *n* extreme poverty.

begin *v* (**beginning**, *past tense* **began**, *past part.* **begun**) **1** to do the first part of an action; to start. **2** to bring or come into existence. **3** (+ with) to have as a starting point. **4** to come first in. **5** (*usu in negative contexts*) to manage in the least degree (to do something): *I can't begin to explain it all.* ⋙ **beginner** *n.*

beginning *n* **1** the point at which something begins. **2** the first part. **3** the origin or source. **4** (*usu in pl*) a rudimentary stage or early period.

begone *v* (*usu in imperative*) to go away.

begonia *n* a tropical plant widely cultivated as an ornamental garden and house plant.

begorra *interj Irish* used as a mild oath.

begot *v* past tense of BEGET.

begotten *v* past part. of BEGET.

begrudge *v* **1** to give only very reluctantly. **2** to envy (somebody) the pleasure or enjoyment of something. ⋙ **begrudgingly** *adv.*

beguile *v* **1** to please or persuade by charm or wiles. **2** (*usu* + into) to deceive or hoodwink. **3** to while (the time) away, *esp* by some agreeable occupation. ⋙ **beguilement** *n*, **beguiler** *n*, **beguilingly** *adv.*

beguine *n* a vigorous popular W Indian dance.

begum *n* used as a title in some Muslim countries: a woman of high rank.

begun *v* past part. of BEGIN.

behalf ✻ **on behalf of** in the interest of; as a representative of.

behave *v* **1** to act in a specified way. **2** to conduct oneself properly.

behaviour (*NAm* **behavior**) *n* the way in which a person or animal acts or something, e.g. a machine, functions. ⋙ **behavioural** *adj.*

behaviourism *n* a theory that the proper concern of psychology is the objective study of behaviour and that information derived from introspection is not admissible psychological evidence.

behead *v* to execute (somebody) by cutting off their head.

beheld *v* past tense and past part. of BEHOLD.

behemoth *n* a huge and monstrous creature or thing.

behest *n* a command or urgent request.

behind[1] *adv* **1a** in a place or time now departed from. **b** in or towards the back. **2a** in a secondary or inferior position. **b** (*usu* + in/with) in arrears. **c** (*usu* + with) late.

behind[2] *prep* **1** at or to the rear of. **2a** remaining after (somebody who has departed). **b** obscured by. **3a** less advanced than: *behind the rest of the class.* **b** not keeping up with: *behind schedule.* **4** responsible for: *I know who's behind this.* **5** supporting and helping: *solidly behind the candidate.*

behind[3] *n informal* the buttocks.

behindhand *adj* **1a** (*usu* + with) behind schedule. **b** (*usu* + in/with) in arrears. **2** lagging behind the times; backward.

behold *v* (*past tense and past part.* **beheld**) **1** to see. **2** *archaic* used in the imperative to call attention. ⋙ **beholder** *n.*

beholden *adj* (+ to) under an obligation for a favour or gift; indebted.

behove (*NAm* **behoove**) *v* to be necessary or advantageous for.

beige *adj* of a yellowish grey colour. ⋙ **beige** *n.*

being *n* **1a** the state of having existence. **b** life. **2** the essential qualities of a person or thing. **3** a living thing; *esp* a person.

bejewelled (*NAm* **bejeweled**) *adj* decorated with jewels.

belabour (*NAm* **belabor**) *v* **1** to deal with in excessive detail. **2a** to strike repeatedly. **b** to attack verbally.

Belarussian *or* **Belarusian** *n* see BELORUSSIAN.

belated *adj* delayed beyond the usual time. ⋙ **belatedly** *adv*, **belatedness** *n.*

belay[1] *v* (**belays, belayed**) **1a** to secure (a rope) by winding it round a support. **b** to secure (somebody) at the end of a rope. **2** (*usu in imperative*) to stop; to leave off.

belay² *n* **1** in mountain climbing, an act of belaying a rope or person. **2a** a belayed rope. **b** something to which a belayed rope is attached.

bel canto *n* operatic singing stressing purity of tone production and an agile vocal technique.

belch¹ *v* **1** to expel gas from the stomach through the mouth. **2** (*often* + out) **a** said of smoke, steam, etc: to gush. **b** to emit (smoke, steam, etc) violently.

belch² *n* a sudden expulsion of gas from the stomach through the mouth.

beldam *or* **beldame** *n archaic* an old woman.

beleaguer *v* **1** to harass. **2** to besiege.

belemnite *n* a conical fossil shell of an extinct mollusc.

belfry *n* (*pl* **-ies**) **1** a bell tower, *esp* attached to a church. **2** a room in which a bell is hung in a bell tower.

Belgian *n* a native or inhabitant of Belgium. ⋙ **Belgian** *adj.*

Belial *n* the Devil.

belie *v* (**belies, belied, belying**) **1** to give a false impression of. **2** to show to be false.

belief *n* **1** something believed; *specif* a tenet held by a group. **2** conviction of the truth of a statement or the reality of a being or phenomenon. **3** trust in somebody or something.

believe *v* **1** to consider (something) to be true or (somebody) to be telling the truth. **2** to hold as an opinion; to think. **3a** (*often* + in) to have a firm religious faith. **b** (*often* + in) to have a firm conviction as to the reality or goodness of something. ⋙ **believable** *adj*, **believer** *n.*

Belisha beacon *n Brit* a flashing light in an amber globe mounted on a black-and-white-striped pole that marks a zebra crossing.

belittle *v* to undermine the value of. ⋙ **belittlement** *n*, **belittler** *n.*

Belizean *n* a native or inhabitant of Belize. ⋙ **Belizean** *adj.*

bell¹ *n* **1** a hollow metallic device that gives forth a ringing sound when struck. **2** the sound of a bell as a signal. **3** a half-hour subdivision of a watch on ship-board, indicated by the strokes of a bell. **4** a bell-shaped object, e.g. the corolla of a flower, or the flared end of a wind instrument. ✱ **bells and whistles** attractive additional features. **give somebody a bell** *Brit* to telephone somebody.

bell² *v* to take the form of a bell; to flare.

belladonna *n* **1** deadly nightshade. **2** an extract of deadly nightshade containing atropine.

bell-bottoms *pl n* trousers with wide flaring bottoms. ⋙ **bell-bottom** *adj.*

bellboy *n chiefly NAm* a porter or page in a hotel.

bell curve *n* in mathematics, a graph of a normal distribution.

belle *n* a popular and attractive young woman.

belle époque /bel ay'pok/ *n* the time immediately before World War I, regarded as a time of elegance and prosperity.

belles lettres /,bel 'letrə, 'letə/ *pl n* (*used as sing. or pl*) literature that has no practical or informative function, *esp* of a light, entertaining, sophisticated nature. ⋙ **belletrist** *n.*

bellflower *n* = CAMPANULA.

bellicose *adj* fond of quarrels or fighting; aggressive. ⋙ **bellicosity** *n.*

belligerence *or* **belligerency** *n* **1** an aggressive attitude or disposition. **2** the state of being at war.

belligerent¹ *adj* **1** engaged in war. **2** assertive or combative. ⋙ **belligerently** *adv.*

belligerent² *n* a country or person engaged in war.

bell jar *n* a bell-shaped glass vessel that is designed to cover objects or to contain gases or a vacuum.

bell metal *n* bronze with a high tin content, used for bells.

bellow¹ *v* **1** to make the loud deep hollow sound characteristic of a bull. **2** to shout in a deep voice.

bellow² *n* **1** a bellowing sound. **2** a loud deep shout.

bellows *pl n* (*used as sing.*) **1** a device with handles and pleated expandable sides used to create a current of air, *esp* to fan a fire. **2** a pleated expandable part in e.g. a camera.

bellwether *n* **1** a male sheep that leads the flock. **2** a leader or trendsetter.

belly¹ *n* (*pl* **-ies**) **1a** the abdomen. **b** the undersurface of an animal's body. **c** the stomach and associated organs. **2** an internal cavity; the interior. **3** a surface or object curved or rounded like a human belly.

belly² *v* (**-ies, -ied**) (*often* + out) to swell or fill.

bellyache¹ *n* colic.

bellyache² *v informal* to complain whiningly or peevishly. ⋙ **bellyacher** *n.*

belly button *n informal* = NAVEL .

belly dance *n* a solo dance originating in the Middle East, performed by women and emphasizing movements of the belly. ⋙ **belly dancer** *n.*

belly flop *n* a dive into water in which the front of the body strikes flat against the surface.

bellyful *n* (*pl* **bellyfuls**) *informal* an excessive amount.

belly laugh *n* a deep hearty laugh.

belong *v* **1** (+ to) to be somebody's property. **2** to be in a proper situation, e.g. according to ability or social qualification, or a proper position or place. **3** (+ to) to be attached by birth, allegiance, or membership. **4** (+ to) to be an attribute or function of a person or thing.

belongings *pl n* possessions.

Belorussian *or* **Belarussian** *or* **Belarusian** *or* **Byelorussian** *n* **1** a native or inhabitant of Belarus (Belorussia) in eastern Europe. **2** the Slavonic language of the Belorussians. ⋙ **Belorussian** *adj.*

beloved¹ *adj* dearly loved.

beloved² *n* a dearly loved person.

below¹ *adv* **1** in or to a lower place, floor, or deck. **2** less than the number or amount specified. **3** lower down on the same page or on a following page.

below² *prep* **1** in or to a lower place than. **2** inferior to, e.g. in rank. **3** not suitable to the rank of; = BENEATH¹. **4** covered by; underneath. **5** downstream from. **6** less than.

Bel Paese *n* a mild creamy Italian cheese with a dark yellow rind.

belt¹ *n* **1** a strip of material, *esp* leather, worn round the waist to hold something, e.g. clothing or a weapon. **2** an endless band of material for transmitting motion and power or conveying objects. **3** an area characterized by some distinctive feature, e.g. of culture, geology, or life forms. ✱ **below the belt** in an unfair way. **belt and braces** *Brit* offering double security; taking no chances. **tighten one's belt** to reduce expenditure or consumption. **under one's belt** as part of one's experience; successfully attained or accomplished. ⋙ **belted** *adj.*

belt² *v* **1** to fasten with a belt. **2** *informal* to strike or hit (somebody). **3** *informal* (*usu* + out) to sing (a song) in a forceful manner or style. **4** *informal* to move or act in a vigorous or violent manner.

belt³ *n informal* a jarring blow; a whack.

belter *n informal* **1** an excellent person or thing. **2** a song that is suitable for belting out.

belt up *v Brit, informal* = SHUT UP.

beltway *n chiefly NAm* a ring road.

beluga *n* **1** a white sturgeon of the Black Sea that provides caviar. **2** a small whale that is white when adult.

belvedere *n* a turret, cupola, etc placed *esp* on the roof of a house to command an extensive view.

BEM *abbr* British Empire Medal.

bemoan *v* to express regret, displeasure, or deep grief over.

bemuse *v* to make confused; to bewilder. ➤➤ **bemusedly** *adv,* **bemusement** *n.*

ben *n Scot* used in place names: a mountain or hill.

bench *n* **1** a long seat for two or more people. **2** (*often* **the Bench**) a judge's seat in court. **3a** (*used as sing. or pl*) the judges or magistrates hearing a particular case. **b** (*used as sing. or pl*) judges or magistrates collectively. **4** a long worktable. **5** (**the bench**) seating for substitute players at e.g. a football match.

bencher *n Brit* any of the chief or governing members of any of the Inns of Court.

benchmark *n* **1** a point of reference, e.g. a mark indicating height above sea level, from which measurements may be made, *esp* in surveying. **2** something that serves as a standard for assessing others.

bench press *n* a weightlifting exercise in which a person lies on their back on a bench and lifts a weight with both arms.

bend¹ *v* (*past tense and past part.* **bent**) **1** to move into or out of a curve or angle. **2a** to make submissive; to subdue. **b** to incline the body, *esp* in submission; to bow. **3** (*often* + to) to yield or compromise. **4** to direct (oneself or one's attention) strenuously or with interest. **5** to alter or modify (a rule) to make it more acceptable, *esp* to oneself.

bend² *n* **1** a curved part, *esp* of a road or stream. **2** (**the bends**) (*used as sing. or pl*) = DECOMPRESSION SICKNESS. ✱ **round the bend** *informal* mad or crazy.

bend³ *n* any of various knots for fastening one rope to another or to an object.

bender *n informal* **1** a drinking spree. **2** a homosexual man. **3** a temporary shelter made from branches bent over and covered with plastic or canvas.

bend sinister *n* in heraldry, a band across a shield from top right to bottom left, supposedly a sign of bastardy.

beneath¹ *prep* **1a** in or to a lower position than. **b** directly under. **2** not suitable to; unworthy of. **3** under the control or influence of.

beneath² *adv* in or to a lower position; below.

Benedictine *n* **1** a member of a religious order following the rule of St Benedict and devoted *esp* to scholarship. **2** *trademark* a brandy-based liqueur made orig by French Benedictine monks. ➤➤ **Benedictine** *adj.*

benediction *n* a blessing; *esp* the short blessing with which public worship is concluded.

benefaction *n* a benefit conferred; *esp* a charitable donation.

benefactor *or* **benefactress** *n* a man or woman who gives aid; *esp* one who makes a gift or bequest to a person, institution, etc.

benefice *n* an ecclesiastical office to which an income is attached. ➤➤ **beneficed** *adj.*

beneficent *adj* doing or producing good; *esp* performing acts of kindness and charity. ➤➤ **beneficence** *n,* **beneficently** *adv.*

beneficial *adj* conferring benefits; conducive to personal or social well-being. ➤➤ **beneficially** *adv.*

beneficiary *n* (*pl* **-ies**) a person who benefits from something, *esp* a trust, will, or insurance policy.

benefit¹ *n* **1a** something that promotes well-being; an advantage. **b** good or welfare. **2** (*also in pl*) **a** financial help provided by the state in time of need, e.g. sickness, old age, or unemployment. **b** a payment provided under a pension scheme or insurance policy. **3** a game or social event to raise funds for a person or cause.

benefit² *v* (**benefited, benefiting,** *NAm* **benefitted, benefitting**) **1** to be useful or profitable to. **2** to receive benefit.

benefit of clergy *n* **1** the former clerical privilege of being tried in an ecclesiastical court. **2** *humorous* the ministration or sanction of the church.

benefit of the doubt *n* the assumption that somebody is correct or innocent in the absence of proof to the contrary.

benevolent *adj* **1** disposed to do good; charitable. **2** characterized by goodwill. ➤➤ **benevolence** *n,* **benevolently** *adv.*

BEng *abbr* Bachelor of Engineering.

Bengali *n* **1** a native or inhabitant of Bengal. **2** the modern Indic language of the people of Bengal. ➤➤ **Bengali** *adj.*

benighted *adj* intellectually, morally, or socially unenlightened. ➤➤ **benightedness** *n.*

benign *adj* **1** gentle or gracious. **2** favourable or mild. **3** of a tumour: not malignant. ➤➤ **benignity** *n,* **benignly** *adv.*

benignant *adj* = BENIGN. ➤➤ **benignancy** *n,* **benignantly** *adv.*

Beninese *n* a native or inhabitant of Benin. ➤➤ **Beninese** *adj.*

bent¹ *v* past tense and past part. of BEND¹.

bent² *adj* **1** not straight or even; curved. **2** (+ on) determined to **3** *Brit, informal* homosexual. **4** *Brit, informal* corrupt; dishonest.

bent³ *n* **1** a strong inclination or interest; a bias. **2** a special ability or talent.

bent⁴ *n* a species of grass used for pasture and lawns.

benthos *n* the organisms that live on or at the bottom of bodies of water. ➤➤ **benthic** *adj.*

bentonite *n* an absorbent clay used *esp* to give bulk to paper, drugs, etc.

benumb *v* to make (a person or body part) inactive or numb.

Benzedrine *n trademark* a type of amphetamine.

benzene *n* an inflammable liquid hydrocarbon found in petroleum and used as a solvent. ➤➤ **benzenoid** *adj.*

benzine *n* a volatile inflammable petroleum distillate used *esp* as a solvent or motor fuel.

benzodiazepine *n* any of several chemically related synthetic drugs widely used as tranquillizers.

benzoic acid *n* an organic acid used *esp* as a food preservative.

bequeath *v* **1** to leave (personal property) by will. **2** to transmit; to hand down. ⋙ **bequeathal** *n.*

bequest *n* **1** the act of bequeathing. **2** a legacy.

berate *v* (*often* + for) to scold or condemn vehemently.

Berber *n* **1** a member of a Caucasian people of northern Africa. **2** an Afro-Asiatic language spoken by these people. ⋙ **Berber** *adj.*

berceuse *n* a lullaby or a musical composition in this style.

bereave *v* (*past part.* **bereaved** *or* **bereft**) **1** (**be bereaved**) to suffer loss by the death of a loved person. **2** *literary* to deprive of something held dear. ⋙ **bereavement** *n.*

bereft *adj* deprived or robbed of; completely without.

beret *n* a cap with a tight headband, a soft full flat top, and no peak.

bergamot *n* a pear-shaped orange with a rind that yields an essential oil used in perfumery.

beriberi *n* a deficiency disease marked by degeneration of the nerves, caused by a lack of vitamin B_1.

berk *n Brit, slang* see BURK.

berkelium *n* a radioactive metallic chemical element that is artificially produced.

Berks *abbr* Berkshire.

berm *or* **berme** *n* **1** a raised bank of earth or sand used as a fortification. **2** a narrow raised path beside a road, canal, etc.

Bermudan *or* **Bermudian** *n* a native or inhabitant of Bermuda. ⋙ **Bermudan** *adj,* **Bermudian** *adj.*

Bermuda shorts *pl n* knee-length shorts.

berry *n* (*pl* **-ies**) **1a** a small, pulpy, and usu edible fruit without a stone. **b** in botany, a simple fruit, e.g. a currant, grape, tomato, or banana, with a pulpy or fleshy pericarp. **2** an egg of a fish or lobster.

berserk[1] *n* an ancient Scandinavian warrior who fought in a wild frenzy.

berserk[2] ✱ **go berserk** to become frenzied, *esp* with anger; to become crazed.

berserker *n* = BERSERK[1].

berth[1] *n* **1** a place for sleeping, e.g. a bunk, *esp* on a ship or train. **2** an allotted place for a ship when at anchor or at a wharf. ✱ **give a wide berth to** to remain at a safe distance from.

berth[2] *v* **1** of a ship: to dock. **2** to allot a berth to.

beryl *n* a green, yellow, pink, or white mineral, used as a gemstone: compare AQUAMARINE, EMERALD.

beryllium *n* a steel-grey light metallic chemical element.

beseech *v* (*past tense and past part.* **beseeched** *or* **besought**) **1** to ask (somebody) earnestly to do something. **2** to beg for (something) urgently or anxiously. ⋙ **beseechingly** *adv.*

beset *v* (**besetting,** *past tense and past part.* **beset**) **1** to trouble constantly. **2** to surround and attack. ⋙ **besetment** *n.*

besetting *adj* constantly causing temptation or difficulty; continuously present.

beside *prep* **1a** by the side of. **b** in comparison with. **c** unconnected with; wide of. **2** besides. ✱ **beside oneself** in a state of extreme agitation or excitement.

besides[1] *adv* **1** as an additional factor or circumstance. **2** moreover.

besides[2] *prep* **1** other than. **2** as an addition to.

besiege *v* **1** to surround (a place) with armed forces. **2a** to crowd round (somebody). **b** to press (somebody) with questions, requests, etc. ⋙ **besieger** *n.*

besmirch *v* to sully or soil.

besom *n* a broom, *esp* one made of twigs.

besotted *adj* **1** infatuated. **2** drunk or intoxicated.

besought *v* past tense and past part. of BESEECH.

bespatter *v* to spatter.

bespeak *v* (*past tense* **bespoke,** *past part.* **bespoken**) *formal* **1** to indicate or signify. **2** to order beforehand. **3** *archaic* to speak to or address (somebody).

bespectacled *adj* wearing glasses.

bespoke[1] *adj Brit* **1** made-to-measure. **2** dealing in or producing articles that are made to measure.

bespoke[2] *v* past tense of BESPEAK.

bespoken *v* past part. of BESPEAK.

Bessemer process *n* a steelmaking process in which air is blasted through molten pig iron to oxidize impurities.

best[1] *adj* **1** of the highest quality or most excellent type. **2** most appropriate or advisable. ✱ **the best part of** most of something.

best[2] *adv* **1** in the best manner; to the best extent or degree. **2** as a preference or ideal. ✱ **had best** would be well advised to do something.

best[3] *n* (**the best**) what is most excellent or desirable. ✱ **at best** using the most favourable interpretation or in the most favourable circumstances. **for the best 1** advantageous in the long term. **2** having good intentions. **get the best of** to defeat (somebody) or get an advantage over them. **make the best of** to cope with (an unfavourable situation) so as to get some advantage from it. **the best of three/five/etc.** a greater number of games won in a series, bringing overall victory.

best[4] *v* to outdo or outwit (somebody).

best before date *n* a date stamped on food packaging to indicate the date by which it should be used.

best boy *n* an assistant to a gaffer or key grip in a film or television studio.

best end *n Brit* a cut of lamb or other meat from the lower end of the neck.

bestial *adj* **1** marked by brutal or inhuman instincts or desires; *specif* sexually depraved. **2** of beasts. ⋙ **bestially** *adv.*

bestiality *n* bestial behaviour; *specif* sexual relations between a human being and an animal.

bestiary *n* (*pl* **-ies**) an allegorical or moralizing work of medieval times dealing with real or imaginary animals.

bestir *v* (**bestirred, bestirring**) to rouse (oneself) to action.

best man *n* a male friend or relative chosen to attend the bridegroom at his wedding.

bestow *v* (*usu* + on/upon) to present as a gift or honour. ⋙ **bestowal** *n.*

bestrew *v* (*past tense* **bestrewed,** *past part.* **bestrewed** *or* **bestrewn**) *literary* to scatter or lie scattered over.

bestride *v* (*past tense* **bestrode,** *past part.* **bestridden**) **1** to ride or stand astride. **2** to tower over; to dominate.

bestseller *n* a book or other product that achieves a high level of sales. ⋙ **bestselling** *adj.*

bet[1] *n* **1a** the act of risking a sum of money or other stake on the forecast outcome of a future event, e.g. a race or contest. **b** a stake. **c** an outcome or result on which a stake is gambled. **2** an opinion or belief. **3a** *informal* a plan of action; a course. **b** a person or thing likely to be successful.

bet² *v* (**betting,** *past tense and past part.* **bet** *or* **betted**) **1** (*usu* + on/against) to stake (an amount of money) as a bet. **2** to make a bet with. **3** *informal* to be convinced that. ✱ **you bet** *informal* you may be sure; certainly.

beta *n* **1** the second letter of the Greek alphabet (Β, β), equivalent to roman b. **2** = B¹ (2).

beta-blocker *n* a drug that inhibits the action of adrenalin and similar compounds and is used *esp* to treat high blood pressure.

beta decay *n* radioactive decay of an atomic nucleus with the emission of an electron or positron.

betake *v* (*past tense* **betook,** *past part.* **betaken**) *literary* (+ to) to take (oneself) off somewhere.

beta particle *n* an electron or positron emitted from the nucleus of an atom during beta decay: compare ALPHA PARTICLE.

beta test *n* a test of a machine or a piece of software, carried out by somebody other than the manufacturer before it is sold to the public: compare ALPHA TEST.

betatron *n* an accelerator in which electrons are propelled by the inductive action of a rapidly varying magnetic field.

betel *n* a climbing pepper whose leaves are chewed together with betel nut and lime, *esp* by SE Asians as a mild stimulant.

betel nut *n* the astringent seed of the betel palm.

bête noire *n* (*pl* **bêtes noires**) a person or thing strongly detested.

bethink *v* (*past tense and past part.* **bethought**) *formal or archaic* to remind (oneself) of something.

betide *v formal or literary* to happen, *esp* as if by fate. ✱ **woe betide** used as a warning of retribution or punishment.

bêtise *n* (*pl* **bêtises**) an act of stupidity.

betoken *v* **1** to show. **2** to presage or portend.

betony *n* (*pl* **-ies**) a plant of the mint family with purple flowers.

betook *v* past tense of BETAKE.

betray *v* **1** to give up or reveal (somebody or something) to an enemy by treachery. **2** to be disloyal to. **3a** to show (one's feelings, etc) inadvertently. **b** to be an outward sign of (an inner feeling). **c** to disclose (a secret), deliberately or unintentionally, in violation of confidence. ➤➤ **betrayal** *n,* **betrayer** *n.*

betroth *v* (**be betrothed**) *formal* to be engaged to be married. ➤➤ **betrothal** *n.*

betrothed *n* the person to whom one is betrothed.

better¹ *adj* **1** of a higher quality. **2** more appropriate or advisable. **3** improved in health; partly or wholly recovered from an injury. ✱ **better off** enjoying better circumstances, *esp* financially. **go one better** to improve slightly on what somebody else has achieved. **the better part of** most or nearly all of something.

better² *adv* **1** in a way that is more excellent or desirable. **2** to a greater degree; more. **3** more wisely or usefully. ✱ **had better** would be well advised (to do something).

better³ *n* **1** (**the better**) what is more excellent or desirable. **2** *dated* (*usu in pl*) one's superiors, *esp* in rank or ability. ✱ **for better or worse/or for worse** whether the outcome is good or bad. **get the better of** to overcome or defeat (somebody).

better⁴ *v* **1** to surpass or improve on. **2** to make more tolerable or acceptable. ✱ **better oneself** to improve one's living conditions or social status.

better half *n informal* a spouse or partner.

betterment *n* improvement.

betting shop *n Brit* a bookmaker's shop.

between¹ *prep* **1a** through the common action of. **b** in shares to each of. **2a** in or into the time or space that separates. **b** in intermediate relation to. **3** from one to the other of (two places). ✱ **between you and me** in confidence.

Usage note

between you and me. Like other prepositions, *between* is followed by the object form of the personal pronoun, not the subject form: *We divided it between us* (not *between we*). It is incorrect to say *between you and I*; the grammatically correct form is *between you and me.*

between² *adv* in or into an intermediate space or interval.

betwixt *adv and prep archaic* between. ✱ **betwixt and between** in a midway position; neither one thing nor the other.

bevel¹ *n* **1** in carpentry: a sloping or slanting edge or surface, usu between two other surfaces meeting at right angles. **2** an instrument consisting of two arms jointed together and opening to any angle, for drawing angles or adjusting surfaces to be given a bevel.

bevel² *v* (**bevelled, bevelling,** *NAm* **beveled, beveling**) to cut or shape to a bevel.

beverage *n* a liquid for drinking; *esp* one that is not water.

bevvy *n* (*pl* **-ies**) *Brit, informal* an alcoholic drink.

bevy *n* (*pl* **-ies**) a group or collection, *esp* of young women.

bewail *v* to express deep sorrow for.

beware *v* (*usu in imperative*) to be wary of (something).

bewilder *v* to perplex or confuse, *esp* by a complexity, variety, or multitude of objects or considerations. ➤➤ **bewilderingly** *adv,* **bewilderment** *n.*

bewitch *v* **1** to attract as if by the power of witchcraft. **2** to cast a spell over. ➤➤ **bewitchingly** *adv.*

bey *n* a provincial governor in the Ottoman Empire.

beyond¹ *prep* **1** on or to the farther side of; at a greater distance than. **2a** out of the reach of. **b** in a degree or amount surpassing. **c** out of the comprehension of. **3** = BESIDES². **4** later than.

beyond² *adv* on or to the farther side.

beyond³ *n* (**the beyond**) something that lies outside the scope of ordinary experience; *specif* life after death.

bezel *n* **1** the faceted portion, *esp* the upper one, of a gem. **2** a rim or groove that holds a transparent covering of a watch, clock, headlight, etc.

bezique *n* a card game for two people that is played with a double pack of 64 cards, including the seven to ace only in each suit.

Bh *abbr* the chemical symbol for bohrium.

bhaji *or* **bhajee** *n* a spicy Indian vegetable fritter.

bhang *n* a mild form of cannabis used *esp* in India.

bhangra /ˈbaŋgrə/ *n* see BANGRA.

bhp *abbr* brake horsepower.

Bhutanese *n* a native or inhabitant of Bhutan. ➤➤ **Bhutanese** *adj.*

Bi *abbr* the chemical symbol for bismuth.

bi- *or* **bin-** *prefix* **1a** two: *bilingual.* **b** appearing or occurring every two: *bimonthly.* **c** into two parts: *bisect.* **2** appearing or occurring twice in: *biweekly.*

biannual *adj* occurring twice a year: compare BIENNIAL. ➤➤ **biannually** *adv.*

bias¹ *n* **1** an inclination to favour or disfavour certain people or things, *esp* a personal prejudice. **2**

(**the bias**) a line diagonal to the grain of a fabric, often used in the cutting of garments for smoother fit. **3a** the tendency of a bowl to take a curved path when rolled. **b** the weighting that causes this. **4** a voltage applied to an electronic device, e.g. the grid of a thermionic valve, to enable it to function normally.

bias[2] *v* (**biased** *or* **biassed, biasing** *or* **biassing**) **1** to give a prejudiced outlook to. **2** to influence unfairly.

bias binding *n* a narrow folded ribbon of fabric used for hemming and for decoration.

biathlon *n* an athletic contest consisting of combined cross-country skiing and rifle shooting.

bib *n* **1** a covering, e.g. of cloth or plastic, placed over a child's front to protect the clothes. **2** a small rectangular section of a garment extending above the waist.

bib and tucker ✱ **one's best bib and tucker** *informal* one's best clothes.

bibelot /'bib(ə)loh/ *n* (*pl* **bibelots** /-loh(z)/) a small ornament or decorative object; a trinket or curio.

bible *n* **1a** (**the Bible**) the sacred book of Christians, comprising the Old Testament and the New Testament. **b** the Jewish scriptures. **c** any book containing the sacred writings of a religion. **2** an authoritative book.

Bible Belt *n* an area characterized by religious fundamentalism, *esp* in the southern USA.

biblical *adj* of or in accord with the Bible. ➤➤ **biblically** *adv.*

bibliography *n* (*pl* **-ies**) **1** a list of the works referred to in a text or consulted by its author. **2** a list of writings relating to a particular topic, written by a particular author, issued by a particular publisher, etc. **3** the history or description of writings and publications. ➤➤ **bibliographer** *n*, **bibliographic** *adj*, **bibliographical** *adj*, **bibliographically** *adv.*

bibliomania *n* excessive enthusiasm for books.

bibliophile *n* a lover or collector of books. ➤➤ **bibliophilic** *adj*, **bibliophilism** *n*, **bibliophily** *n.*

bibulous *adj* prone to over-indulgence in alcoholic drinks. ➤➤ **bibulously** *adv*, **bibulousness** *n.*

bicameral *adj* having two legislative chambers. ➤➤ **bicameralism** *n.*

bicarb *n informal* = SODIUM BICARBONATE.

bicarbonate *n* an acid carbonate; *esp* SODIUM BICARBONATE.

bicentenary *n* (*pl* **-ies**) the celebration of a 200th anniversary.

biceps *n* **1** the large muscle at the front of the upper arm that bends the arm at the elbow. **2** any muscle attached in two places at one end.

bicker *v* to engage in petulant or petty argument. ➤➤ **bickerer** *n.*

bicuspid[1] *adj* said *esp* of a tooth: having or ending in two points.

bicuspid[2] *n* a tooth with two points.

bicycle[1] *n* a two wheeled pedal-driven vehicle with handlebars and a saddle. ➤➤ **bicycler** *n*, **bicyclist** *n.*

bicycle[2] *v* to ride a bicycle.

bicyclic *adj* in chemistry, consisting of or arranged in two cycles or circles.

bid[1] *v* (**bidding,** *past tense* **bid** *or* **bade,** *past part.* **bid** *or* **bidden**) **1a** to offer (a price) for payment or acceptance, e.g. at an auction. **b** to make a bid of or in (a suit at cards). **2** to make an attempt to do something. **3a** *archaic* to issue an order to. **b** to invite to come. **4** *archaic* to give expression to. ✱ **bid fair** to seem likely; to show promise. ➤➤ **bidder** *n.*

bid[2] *n* **1** a statement of what one will give or take for something; *esp* an offer of a price. **2** an opportunity to bid. **3** an attempt to win or achieve something. **4** in cards, an announcement of the number of tricks to be won, suit to be played in, etc.

biddable *adj* easily led or controlled; docile. ➤➤ **biddability** *n.*

bidden *v* past part. of BID[1].

bidding *n* order or command.

biddy *n* (*pl* **-ies**) *informal* a woman.

bide *v archaic or dialect* to remain a while; to stay. ✱ **bide one's time** to wait patiently for an opportunity to act.

bidet *n* a low fixture used *esp* for bathing the external genitals and the anus.

Biedermeier *or* **Biedermaier** *adj* denoting a conventional and restrained style of furniture and interior decoration in 19th-cent. Germany.

biennial *adj* **1** occurring every two years: compare BIANNUAL. **2** said of a plant: growing vegetatively during the first year and fruiting and dying during the second: compare ANNUAL[1], PERENNIAL[1]. ➤➤ **biennial** *n*, **biennially** *adv.*

bier *n* a stand on which a corpse or coffin is placed.

biff[1] *n informal* a whack or blow.

biff[2] *v informal* to give (somebody) a whack or blow.

bifid *adj* divided into two equal lobes or parts by a central cleft. ➤➤ **bifidity** *n*, **bifidly** *adv.*

bifocal *adj* **1** having two focal lengths. **2** having one part that corrects for near vision and one for distant vision.

bifocals *pl n* glasses with bifocal lenses.

bifurcate[1] *v* to divide into two branches or parts. ➤➤ **bifurcation** *n.*

bifurcate[2] *adj* divided into two branches or parts.

big[1] *adj* (**bigger, biggest**) **1a** large in size, amount, or number. **b** large and important in influence, standing, or wealth. **2a** elder. **b** older or grown-up. **3** of great force or intensity. **4a** pretentious or boastful. **b** *often ironic* magnanimous or generous. **5** *informal* popular. ✱ **in a big way** *informal* very much or very greatly. **too big for one's boots** arrogant or conceited. ➤➤ **biggish** *adj*, **bigness** *n.*

big[2] *adv informal* **1a** outstandingly. **b** on a grand scale. **2** pretentiously or boastfully. ✱ **talk big** to talk boastfully. **think big** to be ambitious.

bigamy *n* the crime of going through a marriage ceremony with one person while legally married to another. ➤➤ **bigamist** *n*, **bigamous** *adj*, **bigamously** *adv.*

Big Apple *n* (**the Big Apple**) *chiefly NAm, informal* New York City.

big band *n* a large jazz orchestra, *esp* playing swing music from the 1930s and 1940s.

big bang *n* **1** in cosmology, the theoretical explosion of material from which the universe originated. **2** a sudden reorganization or change.

Big Brother *n* a ruthless all-powerful government or its leader.

big cat *n* a large member of the cat family, such as a lion or leopard.

big cheese *n informal* an important person; a boss.

big deal *interj informal* used to show that one is not impressed by something.

big dipper *n* **1** (*often* **Big Dipper**) *Brit* = ROLLER COASTER. **2** (**the Big Dipper**) *NAm* = PLOUGH[1] (2).

big end *n Brit* the end of an engine's connecting rod nearest the crankpin.

Bigfoot *n* (*pl* **Bigfeet**) = SASQUATCH.

big game *n* large animals hunted or fished for sport.

bighead *n informal* a conceited person. ⋙ **big-headed** *adj*, **bigheadedness** *n*.

bighearted *adj* generous and kindly. ⋙ **bigheartedly** *adv*, **bigheartedness** *n*.

bighorn *n* (*pl* **bighorns** *or* **bighorn**) a wild sheep of mountainous parts of western N America, the male of which has large curved horns.

bight *n* **1** a bend of a river, coast, mountain chain, etc. **2** the middle part of a slack rope.

bigmouth *n informal* a loudmouthed or indiscreet person. ⋙ **bigmouthed** *adj*.

big name *n* a very famous or important performer or personage. ⋙ **big-name** *adj*.

big noise *n informal* an important person.

bigot *n* somebody who is obstinately or intolerantly devoted to their own religion, opinion, etc. ⋙ **bigoted** *adj*, **bigotedly** *adv*, **bigotry** *n*.

big screen *n* the cinema, or cinema screen, as opposed to television.

big shot *n informal* an important person.

big time[1] *n* (*usu* **the big time**) *informal* success, *esp* in show business. ⋙ **big-time** *adj*, **big-timer** *n*.

big time[2] *adv informal* to a very great extent or degree.

big top *n* (*usu* **the big top**) the main tent of a circus.

big wheel *n* **1** (*often* **the big wheel**) a fairground amusement device consisting of a large upright power-driven wheel carrying seats round its rim that remain horizontal while the wheel turns. **2** *chiefly NAm* = BIG SHOT.

bigwig *n informal* = BIG SHOT.

bijou[1] *n* (*pl* **bijous** *or* **bijoux**) a small dainty usu ornamental piece of delicate workmanship; a jewel.

bijou[2] *adj* said *esp* of a house: small and attractively elegant.

bijoux *n* pl of BIJOU[1].

bike[1] *n informal* **1** a bicycle. **2** a motorcycle.

bike[2] *v* to ride a bicycle or motorcycle.

biker *n* **1** a motorcyclist, *esp* a member of a gang of motorcyclists. **2** a person who rides a bicycle.

bikini *n* **1** a woman's brief two-piece garment worn for swimming or sunbathing. **2** (*also in pl*) a pair of woman's very brief underpants.

bilateral *adj* **1** having two sides. **2** = BIPARTITE (2). ⋙ **bilateralism** *n*, **bilaterally** *adv*, **bilateralness** *n*.

bilberry *n* (*pl* **-ies**) a bluish edible soft fruit produced by a dwarf shrub of the heath family that grows on moorland.

Bildungsroman *n* a novel that deals with the development of a person's character during youth.

bile *n* **1** a fluid secreted by the liver into the intestines to aid the digestion of fats. **2** a tendency to become angry; irritability.

bile duct *n* the duct by which bile passes from the liver or gall bladder to the duodenum.

bilge *n* **1a** the lowest part of a ship's hull between the keel and the vertical sides. **b** (*also in pl*) the space inside this part of the hull. **2** = BILGE WATER. **3** *informal* nonsense.

bilge water *n* dirty water that collects in the bilge of a ship.

bilharzia *n* **1** = SCHISTOSOME. **2** = SCHISTOSOMIASIS. ⋙ **bilharzial** *adj*.

bilingual *adj* **1** able to use two languages fluently. **2** using or expressed in two languages. ⋙ **bilingualism** *n*, **bilingually** *adv*.

bilious *adj* **1** suffering from vomiting or a feeling of nausea. **2** *informal* of colours: extremely distasteful; sickly. **3** peevish or ill-natured. **4** relating to bile. ⋙ **biliously** *adv*, **biliousness** *n*.

bilk *v* **1** to cheat (somebody), *esp* by swindling them out of money. **2** (*usu* + of) to avoid paying (somebody) what is due to them. ⋙ **bilker** *n*.

Bill *n* (*usu* **the Bill**) *Brit, informal* the police.

bill[1] *n* **1a** the charges made for goods or services. **b** an itemized statement of charges. **2** a draft of a law presented to a law-making body such as Parliament. **3a** a written or printed notice advertising an event. **b** a programme of entertainment. **4** *chiefly NAm* = BANKNOTE. ✱ **fill/fit the bill** to serve the required purpose or be suitable.

bill[2] *v* **1** to submit a bill of charges to. **2** (+ as) to announce or proclaim to be something. **3** to advertise, *esp* by posters or placards.

bill[3] *n* **1a** the hard mouthparts of a bird; a beak. **b** the similar mouthparts of an animal such as a turtle or platypus. **2** a narrow piece of land projecting into the sea.

bill[4] *v* said of birds, *esp* doves: to stroke each other's bills in courtship. ✱ **bill and coo** said of people, *esp* lovers: to caress and talk lovingly.

billabong *n Aus* **1** a blind channel leading out from a river. **2** a backwater forming a stagnant pool.

billboard *n chiefly NAm* = HOARDING (1).

billet[1] *n* **1** a place (e.g. a private home) where soldiers are provided with board and lodging. **2** a position or job.

billet[2] *v* (**billeted, billeting**) (*often* + on) to provide (e.g. soldiers) with a billet.

billet[3] *n* **1** a small thick piece of wood (e.g. for firewood). **2** a usu small bar of iron, steel, etc.

billet-doux /,bili 'dooh, ,beeyay/ *n* (*pl* **billets-doux**) a love letter.

billfold *n NAm* = WALLET (1).

billhook *n* a cutting or pruning tool with a blade with a hooked point.

billiards *pl n* (*used as sing.*) a game played with three balls, in which scores are made by causing the cue ball to hit the other two balls in succession: compare POOL[2], SNOOKER[1]. ⋙ **billiard** *adj*.

billiard table *n* a long rectangular table with a smooth surface covered in green cloth and six pockets at the corners and along its sides, used for playing billiards and similar games.

billing *n* **1** advertising: *advance billing*. **2** the relative prominence given to a name (e.g. of an actor) in advertising programmes.

billion *n* **1** a thousand millions or 1,000,000,000 (10^9). **2** *Brit, dated* a million millions or 1,000,000,000,000 (10^{12}). **3** (*also in pl*) an indefinitely large number. ⋙ **billion** *adj*, **billionth** *adj and n*.

billionaire *n* somebody whose wealth is estimated at a billion or more units of money (e.g. pounds or dollars).

bill of exchange *n* a written order from one person to another to pay a specified sum of money to a designated person.

bill of fare *n* = MENU (1).

bill of health *n* **1** a certificate given to a ship's captain indicating the state of health of the crew and the condition of the port with regard to infectious diseases. **2** a usu satisfactory report about some condition or situation.

bill of lading *n* a receipt signed usu by the agent or owner of a ship listing goods to be shipped.

Bill of Rights *n* a summary in law of fundamental rights and privileges guaranteed by the state.

billow[1] *n* **1** a great wave, *esp* in the open sea. **2** a rolling swirling mass (e.g. of flame or smoke). ➤➤ **billowy** *adj.*

billow[2] *v* to rise, roll, or swell out in billows.

billposter *n* somebody who pastes up advertisements and public notices on hoardings. ➤➤ **billposting** *n.*

billsticker *n* = BILLPOSTER. ➤➤ **billsticking** *n.*

billy *n* (*pl* **-ies**) a metal can with an arched handle and a lid, used for outdoor cooking.

billy goat *n informal* a male goat.

bimbo *n* (*pl* **-os**) *informal, derog* an attractive but unintelligent person, *esp* a woman.

bimetallic *adj* composed of two different metals, *esp* ones that expand by different amounts when heated.

bimetallic strip *n* a device functioning as a switch, consisting of strips of two metals which expand by different amounts when heated, causing the device to change shape.

bimonthly *adj* **1** occurring, appearing, etc every two months. **2** occurring, appearing, etc twice a month. ➤➤ **bimonthly** *adv and n.*

bin[1] *n* **1** *Brit* a container for rubbish. **2** a container used for storage (e.g. of flour, grain, bread, or coal). **3** a partitioned stand for storing and ageing bottles of wine.

bin[2] *v* (**binned, binning**) **1** to dispose of as rubbish. **2** to discard (an idea, etc). **3** to put or store (*esp* bottled wine) in a bin.

bin- *comb. form* see BI-.

binary[1] *adj* **1a** relating to a system of numbers that has two as its base and uses only the digits 0 and 1. **b** involving a choice of two alternatives (e.g. on or off, yes or no). **2** consisting of or marked by two things or parts.

binary[2] *n* (*pl* **-ies**) **1** something made of two things or parts. **2** = BINARY STAR.

binary star *n* a system of two stars that revolve round each other.

bind[1] *v* (*past tense and past part.* **bound**) **1a** (*also* + up) to tie together, or make secure by tying. **b** to tie (someone) up. **2** to put (somebody) under an obligation or legal requirement. **3** (*often* + up) to enclose (something) by wrapping something else around it; *esp* to bandage (a wound, etc). **4** to stick together. **5** to make (somebody) feel attached to somebody else, e.g. through gratitude or affection. **6** to make (e.g. an agreement or bargain) firm or sure. **7** to strengthen or decorate with a band or binding. **8** to apply a binding to (a book). **9** to form a cohesive mass. **10** to become unable to move or operate freely. **11** *informal* to complain.

bind[2] *n informal* a nuisance or bore. ✻ **in a bind** *chiefly NAm, informal* in trouble or difficulty.

binder *n* **1** a usu detachable cover (e.g. for holding sheets of paper). **2** a person who binds books. **3** something (e.g. tar or cement) that makes loose substances stick together. **4** a harvesting machine that binds straw into bundles.

bindery *n* (*pl* **-ies**) a place where books are bound.

bindi *n* (*pl* **bindis**) a decorative mark in the middle of the forehead, worn *esp* by Indian women.

binding[1] *n* **1** a material or device that is used to bind something. **2** a covering that fastens the leaves of a book together. **3** a narrow strip of fabric used to finish raw edges.

binding[2] *adj* (*often* + on) imposing an obligation. ➤➤ **bindingly** *adv.*

bind over *v* to impose a specific legal obligation on.

bindweed *n* a twining plant such as convolvulus, with a widespread root system and trumpet-shaped flowers that is a nuisance to gardeners.

bin end *n* one of the last bottles from a particular bin or consignment of wine.

binge[1] *n informal* a session of unrestrained indulgence in something; *esp* a drinking bout.

binge[2] *v* (**binged, bingeing**) *informal* to indulge in a binge, *esp* of eating or drinking.

bingo[1] *interj* **1** used to express the suddenness of an event, or announce the successful completion of a task. **2** used to show that one has won a game of bingo.

bingo[2] *n* a game played with cards with numbered squares. As numbers are called out at random, the corresponding squares are covered, a game being won by covering all one's squares.

binnacle *n* a case, stand, etc containing a ship's compass.

binocular *adj* relating to or using both eyes.

binoculars *pl n* an optical instrument for viewing things at a distance consisting of two small telescopes fixed side by side.

binomial[1] *n* **1** a mathematical expression consisting of two terms connected by a plus sign or minus sign. **2** a Latin name for a species consisting of two parts, the name of its genus followed by another name that designates it specifically. ➤➤ **binomially** *adv.*

binomial[2] *adj* consisting of two terms or names.

binomial distribution *n* in statistics, a probability distribution each of whose values corresponds to the probability that a specific combination of two types of possible event will occur in a given proportion of statistical trials.

bint *n Brit, chiefly derog* a girl or woman.

bio *n* (*pl* **-os**) *informal* a biography or autobiography.

bio- *comb. form* denoting: **1** life. **2** living organisms or tissue.

biochemistry *n* chemistry dealing with the chemical compounds and processes that occur in living organisms. ➤➤ **biochemical** *adj,* **biochemically** *adv,* **biochemist** *n.*

biochip *n* a device made with biological molecules that functions in the same way as a silicon chip.

biocide *n* a substance, such as DDT, that kills many different living organisms. ➤➤ **biocidal** *adj.*

biodegradable *adj* capable of being broken down into simpler harmless products by the action of living organisms, such as bacteria. ➤➤ **biodegradability** *n,* **biodegradation** *n.*

biodiesel *n* a fuel made from organic products that will drive a diesel engine.

biodiversity *n* the number and diversity of distinct living species within the world or a particular environment.

bioethics *pl n* (*used as sing.*) the study of the ethical aspects of various techniques (e.g. genetic engineering and birth control) involving human intervention in biological processes.

biofeedback *n* the technique of making involuntary bodily processes perceptible to the senses so that they can be affected by conscious mental control.

bioflavonoid *n* any of a group of chemical compounds occurring in plants that decrease the fragility of the blood capillaries.

biofuel *n* a fuel made from renewable, organic sources.

biogas *n* gas, *esp* methane, obtained from processing biological waste and used as fuel.

biogenic *adj* produced by living organisms. ➤➤ **biogenicity** *n*.

biogeography *n* a branch of biology that deals with the geographical distribution of animals and plants. ➤➤ **biogeographical** *adj*.

biography *n* (*pl* **-ies**) **1** a usu written account of a person's life. **2** biographical writing as a literary genre. ➤➤ **biographer** *n*, **biographic** *adj*, **biographical** *adj*, **biographically** *adv*.

biohazard *n* a danger to health or the environment caused by biological research.

bioinformatics *pl n* (*used as sing. or pl*) the application of data collection and processing methods to the analysis of complex biological phenomena such as genetic codes.

biol. *abbr* **1** biological. **2** biology.

biological *adj* **1** relating to biology, life, or living organisms. **2** acting on or produced by living organisms. **3** containing a plant or animal product; *specif* being a detergent (e.g. a washing powder) containing an enzyme. ➤➤ **biologically** *adv*.

biological clock *n* the inherent timing mechanism responsible for various cyclic responses, e.g. changes in hormone levels, of living beings.

biological control *n* control of pests by interference with their ecological environment, usu by means of natural enemies.

biological warfare *n* warfare involving the use of living organisms, *esp* ones that cause disease, or of chemicals harmful to plants.

biology *n* **1** a science that deals with the life processes of living organisms. **2a** the plant and animal life of a region or environment. **b** the physical structure, processes, and functions of a particular organism or group. ➤➤ **biologist** *n*.

bioluminescence *n* the emission of light by living organisms. ➤➤ **bioluminescent** *adj*.

biomass *n* **1** the amount of living matter present in a region, e.g. in a unit area or volume of habitat. **2** organic materials or waste used as fuel.

biome *n* a major type of ecological community.

biomorph *n* **1** an object or ornament representing a living creature. **2** a computer graphic depicting a living organism.

bionic *adj* **1** denoting an artificial part designed to replace or simulate a living part such as a limb. **2** *not used technically* having exceptional abilities or powers. ➤➤ **bionically** *adv*.

bionics *pl n* (*used as sing. or pl*) **1** a science concerned with the application of biological systems to engineering problems. **2** the use of mechanical parts or artificial substances to replace or simulate damaged or missing parts of a living organism.

biophysics *pl n* (*used as sing. or pl*) a branch of science concerned with the application of physics to biological problems. ➤➤ **biophysical** *adj*, **biophysicist** *n*.

biopic *n* a film based on the life of a well-known person.

biopsy *n* (*pl* **-ies**) the removal and examination of tissue, cells, or fluids from the living body.

biorhythm *n* (*usu in pl*) a supposed periodic fluctuation in the biological activity of a living thing that affects mood, behaviour, and performance. ➤➤ **biorhythmic** *adj*, **biorhythmically** *adv*.

BIOS *abbr* Basic Input-Output System, a set of computer instructions controlling input and output functions in the firmware of a computer.

biosphere *n* the entirety of those areas of the earth's surface and atmosphere in which life exists.

biosynthesis *n* (*pl* **biosyntheses**) the production of a chemical compound by a living organism. ➤➤ **biosynthetic** *adj*, **biosynthetically** *adv*.

biota *n* the flora and fauna of a region.

biotechnology *n* the use of living cells or microorganisms, such as bacteria, in industry and technology to manufacture drugs and chemicals, create energy, destroy waste matter, etc. ➤➤ **biotechnological** *adj*, **biotechnologically** *adv*, **biotechnologist** *n*.

bioterrorism /bie·oh'terrərizm/ *n* terrorism using forms of biological warfare, such as the use of organisms that cause disease. ➤➤ **bioterrorist** *n*.

biotic *adj* relating to life, living organisms, or the effect living organisms have on each other.

biotin *n* a growth-controlling vitamin of the vitamin B complex found *esp* in yeast, liver, and egg yolk.

biotype *n* a group of organisms whose genetic make-up is identical.

bipartisan *adj* involving two political parties. ➤➤ **bipartisanship** *n*.

bipartite *adj* **1** consisting of two parts. **2** of a treaty, contract, etc between two parties: affecting both parties in the same way. ➤➤ **bipartitely** *adv*, **bipartition** *n*.

biped *n* a two-footed animal. ➤➤ **bipedal** *adj*.

biplane *n* an aeroplane with two pairs of wings, one placed above the other.

bipolar *adj* **1** having two poles, e.g. positive and negative electrical poles. **2** characterized by two opposed statements, views, natures, etc. ➤➤ **bipolarity** *n*.

birch[1] *n* **1** a deciduous tree with a layered outer bark that peels readily. **2a** a birch rod or bundle of twigs for flogging. **b** (**the birch**) punishment by flogging with a birch. ➤➤ **birchen** *adj*.

birch[2] *v* to whip with a birch.

bird *n* **1** any of a class of warm-blooded vertebrates whose bodies are covered with feathers and whose forelimbs are modified as wings. **2a** *chiefly informal* a person, *esp* somebody slightly odd. **b** *chiefly Brit, informal* a girl. **3** *Brit, informal* a period of imprisonment. ✱ **birds of a feather** people of similar characters, tastes, or interests. **for the birds** *informal* trivial or worthless. **give somebody/get the bird** *chiefly Brit, informal* to hiss or jeer at somebody, or to be hissed or jeered at. **the bird has flown** the person whom one expected to find or capture has escaped. **the birds and the bees** *informal, humorous* the facts of sex and sexual reproduction, *esp* in a form suitable for children. ➤➤ **birdlike** *adj*.

birdbrain *n informal* a silly or stupid person. ➤➤ **birdbrained** *adj*.

bird dog *n NAm* a gundog trained to hunt or retrieve birds.

birdie[1] *n* **1** used *esp* by or to children: a bird, *esp* a small bird. **2** a golf score of one stroke less than par on a hole.

birdie[2] *v* (**birdies, birdied, birdieing** *or* **birdying**) to play (a hole in golf) in one stroke under par.

birdlime *n* a sticky substance smeared on twigs to snare small birds.

bird of paradise *n* a bird of the New Guinea area, the males of which have brilliantly coloured plumage.

bird of passage *n* **1** a migratory bird. **2** a person who leads a wandering or unsettled life.

bird of prey *n* a hawk, vulture, or other bird that feeds on carrion or on meat taken by hunting.

bird's-eye view *n* **1** a view from above. **2** a brief and general summary.

birdshot *n* very small pellets designed for shooting birds.

bird's nest soup *n* in Chinese cooking, a soup made with gelatinous material formed of dried saliva from the nests of Asiatic swifts.

birdstrike *n* a collision between a bird and an aircraft.

bird table *n* a table, usu on a pole, on which food is put out for wild birds.

bird-watching *n* the observation or identification of birds in their natural environment, *esp* as a hobby. ➤➤ **bird-watcher** *n.*

bireme *n* an ancient galley with two banks of oars.

biretta *n* a square cap with three ridges on top worn by clergy, *esp* in the Roman Catholic Church.

biriani *or* **biryani** *n* a spicy Indian dish that consists of saffron-flavoured rice mixed with meat, fish, etc.

Biro *n* (*pl* **-os**) *trademark* a kind of ballpoint pen.

birr *n* the basic monetary unit of Ethiopia.

birth *n* **1** the emergence of a new individual from the body of its parent. **2** the fact of being born, *esp* at a particular time or place. **3** family origin and social status. **4** a beginning or start. ✱ **give birth (to) 1** to produce (a baby) as a mother. **2** to cause the development or creation of.

birth certificate *n* an official record of somebody's parentage and date and place of birth.

birth control *n* control of the number of children born; *broadly* contraception.

birthday *n* an anniversary of the day a person was born.

birthday suit *n humorous* a state of nakedness.

birthing *n* giving birth, *esp* by methods which aim not to interfere with the natural birth process.

birthing pool *n* a large circular bath in which a woman may sit to give birth.

birthmark *n* a blemish existing on the skin at birth and usu remaining permanently.

birth mother *n* the woman who gives birth to a child, as opposed to an adoptive mother.

birthplace *n* the place of somebody's birth or where something originated.

birthrate *n* the number of live births per unit of population.

birthright *n* something to which a person is entitled by being born into a particular family, nation, etc.

birthstone *n* a gemstone associated symbolically with the month of one's birth.

biryani *n* see BIRIANI.

bis *adv* in music, an instruction to a player or singer to repeat a passage.

biscuit[1] *n* **1** *Brit* a small dry bakery product, either sweet or savoury, usu crisp in texture, eaten as or with a snack. **2** a light yellowish brown colour. **3** earthenware or porcelain after the first firing and before glazing. ✱ **take the biscuit** *Brit, informal* to be the most astonishing or preposterous thing one has heard or seen.

biscuit[2] *adj* light yellowish brown.

bisect *v* to divide into two *esp* equal parts. ➤➤ **bisection** *n,* **bisector** *n.*

bisexual[1] *adj* **1** sexually attracted to both sexes. **2** possessing characteristics of both sexes. ➤➤ **bisexuality** *n,* **bisexually** *adv.*

bisexual[2] *n* a bisexual person.

bishop *n* **1** a senior member of the clergy with authority to ordain and confirm and typically governing a diocese. **2** in chess, either of two pieces of each colour allowed to move diagonally across the board. ➤➤ **bishophood** *n.*

bishopric *n* **1** a diocese. **2** the office of bishop.

bismuth *n* a heavy brittle reddish white metallic element used in alloys. ➤➤ **bismuthic** *adj.*

bison *n* (*pl* **bison**) **1** a large shaggy-maned bovine mammal now nearly extinct. **2** = BUFFALO (1).

bisque[1] *n* a thick cream soup (e.g. of shellfish or game).

bisque[2] *n* = BISCUIT[1] (3).

bistable *adj* having two stable states, e.g. off or on.

bistro *n* (*pl* **-os**) a small bar or restaurant.

bisulphate *n* a salt or ester of sulphuric acid, containing the group HSO_4.

bit[1] *n* **1a** a small piece or quantity of anything. **b** a part or section. **2** *informal* **a** (**a bit**) a brief period. **b** (**a bit**) a short distance. **3** *informal* everything appropriate to or associated with a given way of life, sphere of activity, role, etc: *the whole marriage bit.* **4a** a small coin. **b** *NAm, informal* a monetary unit worth of a US dollar. **5** *informal* a young woman, *esp* an attractive one. ✱ **a bit** *informal* somewhat; rather. **a bit much** more than one wants to put up with. **bit by bit** by small amounts; little by little. **bit on the side 1** *informal* a casual sexual relationship with somebody other than one's partner. **2** *informal* somebody with whom one has such a relationship. **bits and pieces/bobs** miscellaneous things of little value or substance. **do one's bit** *Brit* to make one's personal contribution to a task or cause. **to bits 1** into pieces. **2** to a great extent.

bit[2] *n* a unit of computer information equivalent to the result of a choice between two alternatives (e.g. *on* or *off*).

bit[3] *n* **1** a bar of metal attached to the bridle and inserted in the mouth of a horse. **2** a replaceable drilling, boring, etc part of a tool. **3** the part of a key that enters the lock and acts on the bolt and tumblers. ✱ **get/have/take the bit between one's teeth** to begin to do something in a determined manner, or refuse to stop doing something.

bit[4] *v* past tense and past part. of BITE[1].

bitch[1] *n* **1** the female of the dog or similar animals. **2** *slang* a spiteful and domineering woman. **3** *informal* something difficult, trying, or unpleasant. **4** *informal* a complaint or act of complaining.

bitch[2] *v informal* **1** to make malicious or spiteful comments. **2** to complain.

bitchy *adj* (**-ier, -iest**) *informal* malicious or spiteful. ➤➤ **bitchily** *adv,* **bitchiness** *n.*

bite[1] *v* (*past tense* **bit**, *past part.* **bitten** *or* **bit**) **1a** to seize with the teeth or jaws. **b** to sting with a fang or other specialized part of the body. **2** to remove with the teeth. **3** to take a strong hold of; to grip. **4** *informal* to annoy or worry (somebody). **5** of fish: to take a bait. **6** of a person: to accept an offer, etc. **7** of sanctions, etc: to have an effect. ✱ **be bitten by/with something** to have great enthusiasm for. **bite off more than one can chew** to undertake to do more than one can successfully manage. **bite one's tongue** to stop oneself with an effort from saying something. **bite somebody's head off** to speak to or scold somebody angrily. **bite the bullet** to endure stoically something unpleasant that cannot be avoided. **bite the dust 1** to fall dead, *esp* in a fight. **2** to collapse or be destroyed. **bite the**

hand that feeds one to deliberately injure a benefactor. **once bitten, twice shy** somebody who has had an unpleasant experience will be more cautious the next time. ➤➤ **biter** *n.*

bite² *n* **1a** the act of biting. **b** a wound made by biting. **2a** the amount of food taken with one bite. **b** a snack. **3** a fish nibbling or taking the bait. **4** the grip by which purchase is obtained. **5** a sharp incisive quality or effect. **6** sharpness or pungency of taste. ✱ **put the bite on** *informal* to borrow or extort money from.

biting *adj* **1** strong and icy. **2** sarcastic. ➤➤ **bitingly** *adv.*

bitmap *n* a representation in a computer's memory of an image presented on a computer screen, in which each pixel is represented by one or more bits of information. ➤➤ **bitmap** *v.*

bit part *n* a small acting part, usu with spoken lines.

bit player *n* an actor who plays bit parts.

bitstream *n* a continuous succession of bits (see BIT²) of data.

bitten *v* past part. of BITE¹.

bitter¹ *adj* **1** having a sharp taste that is usu more disagreeable than sourness. **2a** intense or severe. **b** showing or stemming from great dislike or resentment. **c** very cold. **3** characterized by or causing severe grief or regret. ➤➤ **bitterish** *adj,* **bitterly** *adv,* **bitterness** *n.*

bitter² *n* **1** (*in pl, used as sing. or pl*) a solution of bitter plant products used *esp* in preparing mixed drinks. **2** *Brit* a bitter beer heavily flavoured with hops.

bitter end *n* (**the bitter end**) the very end, however painful or calamitous.

bitter lemon *n* a sharp-tasting non-alcoholic fizzy drink flavoured with lemon.

bittern *n* a small or medium-sized heron with a characteristic booming cry.

bittersweet¹ *adj* **1** bitter and sweet at the same time. **2** pleasant but with elements of suffering or regret. ➤➤ **bittersweetly** *adv,* **bittersweetness** *n.*

bittersweet² *n* = WOODY NIGHTSHADE.

bitty *adj* (**-ier, -iest**) scrappy or disjointed. ➤➤ **bittily** *adv.*

bitumen *n* a viscous mixture of hydrocarbons, e.g. tar, that occur naturally or as residues after heating petroleum, coal, etc, used *esp* in surfacing roads. ➤➤ **bituminous** *adj.*

bituminous coal *n* a black or dark brown form of coal that gives a lot of heat but is also a major cause of air pollution.

bivalve¹ *adj* of a mollusc: having a shell composed of two valves.

bivalve² *n* any of a class of aquatic molluscs having a shell composed of two valves.

bivouac¹ *n* a usu temporary encampment under little or no shelter.

bivouac² *v* (**bivouacked, bivouacking**) to make a bivouac; to camp.

biweekly *adj* issued or occurring every two weeks, or twice a week. ➤➤ **biweekly** *adv and n.*

biyearly *adj* occurring every two years, or twice a year. ➤➤ **biyearly** *adv.*

biz *n informal* = BUSINESS.

bizarre *adj* **1** odd or eccentric. **2** involving sensational contrasts or incongruities. ➤➤ **bizarrely** *adv,* **bizarreness** *n.*

Bk *abbr* the chemical symbol for berkelium.

blab¹ *v* (**blabbed, blabbing**) **1** to reveal (a secret). **2** to talk indiscreetly or thoughtlessly. ➤➤ **blabber** *n.*

blab² *n* somebody who blabs.

blabber¹ *v* (**blabbered, blabbering**) **1** to babble. **2** to say (something) indiscreetly. ➤➤ **blabberer** *n.*

blabber² *n informal* **1** indiscreet or idle chatter. **2** somebody who reveals a secret.

blabbermouth *n* somebody who talks too much or indiscreetly.

black¹ *adj* **1** of the colour of coal, the darkest colour from its absorption of all light. **2** (*often* **Black**) **a** having dark skin pigmentation; *esp* being African, African-American, or Australian Aboriginal in origin. **b** relating to black people or culture. **3** dirty or soiled. **4** of coffee or tea: served without milk or cream. **5a** thoroughly sinister or evil. **b** indicative of hostility or disapproval. **6a** gloomy. **b** marked by disaster. **7** showing a profit: compare RED¹ (5). **8** characterized by grim or grotesque humour. **9** bought, sold, or operating illegally and *esp* in contravention of official economic regulations. ➤➤ **blackish** *adj,* **blackly** *adv,* **blackness** *n.*

black² *n* **1** a black colour. **2** (*often* **Black**) somebody who belongs to a dark-skinned race, *esp* a person of African, African-American, or Australian Aboriginal origins. **3a** the dark-coloured pieces in a board game (e.g. chess) for two players. **b** the player by whom these are played. ✱ **in the black** financially in credit; solvent; making a profit.

Usage note

black, Negro, *and* **coloured**. The word *black* (without a capital letter) is currently the most widely accepted non-offensive word for people of African or African-American origin. The terms *Negro* and *coloured* are no longer felt to be acceptable by black people themselves.

black³ *v* **1** to make black. **2** *chiefly Brit* to declare (e.g. a business or industry) subject to boycott by trade-union members.

blackamoor *n archaic, offensive* = BLACK¹ (2A).

black-and-blue *adj* darkly discoloured from blood that has leaked under the skin by bruising.

Black and Tan *n* a member of the Royal Irish Constabulary formed to resist the armed movement for Irish independence in 1921.

black and white *n* **1** writing or print. **2** black-and-white reproduction of visual images, *esp* by photography or television. **3** an uncompromising separation into good or bad, right or wrong, etc.

black-and-white *adj* **1** reproducing visual images in black, white, and tones of grey rather than in colours. **2** evaluating things as either all good or all bad, etc.

black art *n* = BLACK MAGIC.

blackball *v* **1** to vote against (somebody, *esp* a candidate for membership of a club). **2** to ostracize.

black bean *n* a black soya or kidney bean.

black belt *n* the black belt worn by a person who has been rated as an expert in judo, karate, etc.

blackberry¹ *n* (*pl* **-ies**) a usu black raspberry-like edible fruit that grows on a prickly shrub of the rose family.

blackberry² *v* (**-ies, -ied**) to pick blackberries.

blackbird *n* **1** a common Old World thrush, the male of which is black with an orange beak and eye rim. **2** any of several species of American birds, the males of which have black plumage.

blackboard *n* a hard smooth usu dark surface used *esp* in schools for writing on with chalk.

black book *n* a book containing a list of those to be punished, blacklisted, etc. ✱ **in somebody's black books** *informal* in trouble with somebody, or out of favour with them.

black bottom *n* a popular dance of the 1920s, originating in the USA, involving rotation of the hips.

black box *n* = FLIGHT RECORDER.

blackcap *n* a small Old World warbler, the male of which has a black crown.

Black Country *n* (**the Black Country**) the industrial area in the West Midlands of England.

blackcurrant *n* a small black edible soft fruit.

Black Death *n* (*usu* **the Black Death**) a form of plague epidemic in Europe and Asia in the 14th cent., or the catastrophic outbreak of this plague in Europe between 1347 and 1350.

black economy *n* (*often* **the black economy**) business activity that is carried on unofficially or illegally, *esp* to avoid taxation.

blacken *v* **1** to become or make dark or black. **2** to injure or destroy (somebody's reputation). ➤➤ **blackener** *n*.

black eye *n* a discoloration of the skin round the eye from bruising.

blackface *n* make-up for a non-black actor or performer playing a black role.

blackfly *n* (*pl* **blackflies** *or* **blackfly**) any of several small dark-coloured insects, *esp* a black blood-sucking gnat or a black aphid parasitic on various agricultural and garden plants.

Blackfoot *n* (*pl* **Blackfoot** *or* **Blackfeet**) a member of a confederacy of Native American peoples of the NW plains of the USA.

black friar *n* a Dominican friar.

black gold *n* crude oil.

blackguard *n often humorous* a coarse or unscrupulous person; a scoundrel. ➤➤ **blackguardism** *n*, **blackguardly** *adj and adv*.

blackhead *n* a small usu dark-coloured oily plug blocking the duct of a sebaceous gland, *esp* on the face.

black hole *n* **1** a celestial body, prob formed from a collapsed star, with a very intense gravitational field, from which no radiation can escape. **2** *informal* a place or situation where something (e.g. money) can disappear without leaving a trace.

black ice *n Brit* transparent slippery ice (e.g. on a road).

blacking *n* **1** a paste, polish, etc applied to an object to make it black. **2** a boycotting of business, industry, etc by trade-union members.

blackjack *n* **1** = PONTOON². **2** *NAm* a cosh.

blackleg¹ *n chiefly Brit* a worker acting in opposition to union policies, *esp* by working during a strike.

blackleg² *v* (**blacklegged, blacklegging**) *chiefly Brit* to work during a strike.

black light *n* invisible ultraviolet or infrared light.

blacklist¹ *n* a list of people or organizations who are disapproved of or are to be punished or boycotted.

blacklist² *v* to put on a blacklist.

black magic *n* magic performed with the aim of harming or killing somebody or something, *esp* with the supposed aid of evil spirits.

blackmail¹ *n* **1** extortion by threats, *esp* to expose secrets that would lead to loss of reputation, prosecution, etc. **2** political, industrial, or moral pressure to do something that is considered undesirable.

blackmail² *v* (*often* + into) to subject to blackmail; to force or persuade to do something through blackmail. ➤➤ **blackmailer** *n*.

Black Maria *n* an enclosed motor vehicle used by police to carry prisoners.

black mark *n* a supposed mark indicating somebody's censure or disapproval.

black market *n* illicit trade in commodities or currencies in violation of official regulations, e.g. rationing. ➤➤ **black marketeer** *n*.

Black Mass *n* a travesty of the Christian mass ascribed to worshippers of Satan.

blackout *n* **1** a period of darkness enforced as a precaution against air raids, or caused by a failure of electrical power. **2** a temporary loss of consciousness, vision, or memory. **3** a holding back or suppression of something. **4** a usu temporary loss of radio signal, e.g. during the re-entry of a spacecraft.

Black Panther *n* a member of a militant organization of US blacks.

Black Power *n* the mobilization of the political and economic power of US blacks, *esp* to further racial equality.

black pudding *n chiefly Brit* a very dark sausage made from suet and a large proportion of pigs' blood: compare WHITE PUDDING.

Black Rod *n* in Britain, the principal usher of the House of Lords.

black sheep *n* a disreputable member of a respectable group, family, etc.

Blackshirt *n* a member of a fascist organization with a black shirt as part of its uniform.

blacksmith *n* somebody who works iron, *esp* at a forge. ➤➤ **blacksmithing** *n*.

black spot *n Brit* a stretch of road on which accidents occur frequently.

black swan *n* a swan with black outer feathers and a red beak originally native to Australia.

blackthorn *n* a spiny European shrub of the rose family with hard wood and small white flowers.

black tie *n* **1** a black bow tie worn with a dinner jacket. **2** an ordinary tie of black material, worn as a sign of mourning.

black-tie *adj* of e.g. a dinner: requiring the wearing of semiformal evening dress by men including a dinner jacket and a black bow tie: compare WHITE TIE.

black up *v* to put on black make-up, *esp* in order to play the role of a black character.

blackwater fever *n* a severe form of malaria in which the urine becomes dark-coloured.

black widow *n* a venomous New World spider of which the female is black with an hourglass-shaped red mark on the underside of the abdomen.

bladder *n* **1a** a membranous sac in animals that serves as the receptacle of a liquid, *esp* urine. **b** a hollow balloon-like part in e.g. a frond of seaweed. **2** a bag filled with a liquid or gas (e.g. the air-filled rubber bag inside a football).

bladderwort *n* an aquatic plant with bladder-like floats or insect traps.

bladderwrack *n* a common brown seaweed with air bladders in its fronds, used as a manure and also as a source of iodine.

blade *n* **1** the cutting part of a knife, razor, etc with a sharpened edge or edges. **2** a long narrow leaf, *esp* of a grass, cereal, etc. **3** the runner of an ice skate. **4a** the broad flattened part of an oar, paddle, bat, etc. **b** an arm of a propeller, electric fan, etc. **5** the broad flat part of a machine, e.g. a bulldozer, that comes into contact with material to be moved. **6** used chiefly in naming cuts of meat: a broad flat body part, *esp* the shoulder blade. **7** *literary* **a** a sword or swordsman. **b** *archaic or humorous* a dashing lively man. ➤➤ **bladed** *adj.*

blag[1] *n Brit, informal* **1** a mugging or armed robbery. **2** a bluff.

blag[2] *v* (**blagged, blagging**) **1** *Brit, informal* **a** to rob, *esp* with violence. **b** to steal. **2** to bluff. ➤➤ **blagger** *n.*

blah *or* **blah-blah** *n informal* silly or pretentious chatter or nonsense.

Blairism *n* the policies associated with Tony Blair, British Labour leader and prime minister from 1997, *esp* regarded as a modified form of traditional socialism. ➤➤ **Blairite** *n.*

blame[1] *v* **1** to hold responsible for wrongdoing or an undesirable state of affairs. **2** to find fault with. ✱ **be to blame** (*often* + for) to be responsible for wrongdoing or an undesirable state of affairs. ➤➤ **blamable** *adj,* **blamably** *adv,* **blameable** *adj,* **blameably** *adv,* **blamer** *n.*

blame[2] *n* **1** (*often* + for) responsibility for wrongdoing or an undesirable state of affairs. **2** disapproval or reproach, or an expression of it. ➤➤ **blameless** *adj,* **blamelessly** *adv,* **blamelessness** *n,* **blameworthy** *adj.*

blanch *v* **1** to make or become pale. **2** to scald (almonds) to remove the skin. **3** to prepare (vegetables), e.g. for freezing, by plunging them briefly in boiling water. ➤➤ **blancher** *n.*

blancmange *n* a sweetened and flavoured dessert made from cornflour and milk.

Blanco *n trademark* a substance used *esp* in the armed forces to whiten or colour belts and webbing. ➤➤ **blanco** *v.*

bland *adj* **1a** soothing. **b** showing no emotion or anxiety. **2a** not irritating or stimulating. **b** without character or excitement; dull or insipid. **c** of food: with little flavour or texture. ➤➤ **blandly** *adv,* **blandness** *n.*

blandishment *n* (*usu in pl*) **1** a coaxing or flattering act or utterance. **2** an enticement or attraction.

blank[1] *adj* **1a** with nothing marked, written, printed, or recorded on it. **b** not filled in. **2a** dazed or nonplussed. **b** expressionless. **c** temporarily without memory or understanding. **3** absolute or unqualified. ➤➤ **blankly** *adv,* **blankness** *n.*

blank[2] *n* **1** an empty space, e.g. one to be filled in on a form. **2a** a void, without thought, memory, or understanding. **b** a vacant or uneventful period. **3a** a piece of material prepared to be made into something, e.g. a key or coin. **b** = BLANK CARTRIDGE. ✱ **draw a blank** to obtain no positive results.

blank cartridge *n* a cartridge loaded with powder but no bullet.

blank cheque *n* **1** a signed cheque with the amount unspecified. **2** complete freedom of action.

blanket[1] *n* **1** a large thick usu rectangular piece of fabric used *esp* as a bed covering, or as a body covering, e.g. for a horse. **2** a thick covering or layer. ✱ **born on the wrong side of the blanket** *informal* illegitimate.

blanket[2] *v* (**blanketed, blanketing**) to cover with a heavy layer of something.

blanket[3] *adj* applicable in all instances or to all members of a group or class.

blanket bath *n* a wash given to a bedridden person.

blanket stitch *n* a widely spaced loop stitch used *esp* round the edges of thick fabrics instead of hemming.

blankety *adj informal, euphem* a substitute for any adjectival swearword.

blank out *v* **1** to erase (something, e.g. a memory) from one's mind. **2** to make blank.

blank verse *n* unrhymed verse, *esp* in iambic pentameters.

blanquette *n* a stew of white meat, e.g. veal, in a white sauce.

blare[1] *v* **1** to emit loud and harsh sound. **2** to proclaim (something) loudly or sensationally.

blare[2] *n* a loud harsh sound.

blarney *n* **1** smooth wheedling talk; flattery. **2** nonsense.

blasé /'blahzay/ *adj* indifferent to pleasure or excitement as a result of real or pretended over-familiarity.

blaspheme *v* to speak of or use the name of (God or something sacred) with impiety. ➤➤ **blasphemer** *n.*

blasphemy *n* (*pl* **-ies**) **1** contempt or lack of reverence for God or something sacred. **2** something considered disrespectful to God or sacred things. ➤➤ **blasphemous** *adj,* **blasphemously** *adv,* **blasphemousness** *n.*

blast[1] *n* **1a** an explosion or violent detonation. **b** a violent wave of increased atmospheric pressure produced by an explosion or detonation. **2** a violent gust of wind. **3** a violent outburst. **4** the sound produced by air blown through a wind instrument or whistle. ✱ **full blast/at full blast** at top speed, full capacity, etc.

blast[2] *v* **1a** to shatter, remove, or open with an explosive. **b** to destroy (hopes, etc). **2a** to denounce vigorously. **b** to curse or damn. **3** to hit (e.g. a ball) vigorously and effectively. **4** to cause (a plant) to shrivel or wither. ➤➤ **blaster** *n,* **blasting** *n and adj.*

blast[3] *interj Brit, informal* used to express annoyance.

blasted *adj informal* infuriating or detestable.

blast furnace *n* a furnace, *esp* for converting iron ore into iron, in which combustion is forced by a current of air under pressure.

blast off *v* of rocket-propelled missiles and vehicles: to leave the ground or launch-pad; to take off. ➤➤ **blast-off** *n.*

blatant *adj* **1** completely or crassly obvious. **2** unashamed. ➤➤ **blatancy** *n,* **blatantly** *adv.*

blather[1] *n* foolish voluble talk.

blather[2] *v* (**blathered, blathering**) to talk foolishly or volubly. ➤➤ **blatherer** *n.*

blaze[1] *n* **1a** an intensely burning flame or fire. **b** intense direct light. **2a** a dazzling display. **b** brilliance. **3** a sudden outburst. **4** (*in pl*) a euphemism for HELL. ✱ **like blazes** *informal* very hard, fast, etc.

blaze[2] *v* **1a** to burn intensely. **b** to shine brightly. **2** to be conspicuously brilliant. **3** (+ away) to shoot rapidly and repeatedly. ➤➤ **blazingly** *adv.*

blaze[3] *n* **1** a broad white mark on the face of an animal, *esp* a horse. **2** a trail marker, *esp* a mark made on a tree by cutting off a piece of the bark.

blaze[4] *v* to mark (e.g. a trail) with blazes. ✱ **blaze a trail** to lead or be a pioneer in some activity.

blazer *n* a jacket, *esp* with patch pockets, worn for casual wear or as part of a school uniform.

blaze up *v* **1** to begin to burn fiercely. **2** to quickly become very angry.

blazon[1] *n* **1** = COAT OF ARMS. **2** the proper formal description of heraldic arms or charges.

blazon[2] *v* (**blazoned, blazoning**) **1** to proclaim widely. **2** to describe (heraldic arms or charges) in technical terms. ➤➤ **blazoner** *n,* **blazoning** *n.*

bleach[1] *v* **1** to remove colour or stains from (e.g. fabric). **2** to make or become whiter or lighter, *esp* by the physical or chemical removal of colour. ⋙ **bleachable** *adj*, **bleacher** *n.*

bleach[2] *n* a strong chemical substance used in bleaching.

bleachers *pl n* (*usu* **the bleachers**) *NAm* a usu uncovered stand of tiered planks providing inexpensive seating for spectators, e.g. at a sports event.

bleaching powder *n* a white powder consisting chiefly of calcium hydroxide, used as a bleach, disinfectant, or deodorant.

bleak *adj* **1** exposed, barren, and often windswept. **2** cold or raw. **3a** lacking in warmth or kindness. **b** not hopeful or encouraging. **4** severely simple or austere. ⋙ **bleakish** *adj*, **bleakly** *adv*, **bleakness** *n.*

bleary *adj* (**-ier, -iest**) **1** of the eyes or vision: dull or dimmed, *esp* from fatigue or sleep. **2** poorly outlined or defined. ⋙ **blear** *v*, **blearily** *adv*, **bleariness** *n.*

bleat[1] *v* **1** to make the cry characteristic of a sheep or goat. **2a** to talk complainingly or with a whine. **b** to blather. ⋙ **bleater** *n*, **bleating** *adj and n*, **bleatingly** *adv.*

bleat[2] *n* **1** the cry of a sheep or goat. **2** a feeble whining complaint.

bleb *n* **1** a small blister. **2** an air bubble.

bleed[1] *v* (*past tense and past part.* **bled**) **1a** to emit or lose blood. **b** in old-fashioned medicine, to remove or draw blood from. **2** (+ for) to feel anguish, pain, or sympathy. **3** of colour, dye, etc: to flow over onto an adjoining area. **4** to be printed so as to run off an edge of a page after trimming. **5a** to extort money from. **b** to drain the vitality or lifeblood from. **6** to let out some or all of a liquid or gas from a container.

bleed[2] *n* an act or instance of bleeding, *esp* by a haemophiliac.

bleeder *n Brit, informal* **1** a person or thing regarded as a nuisance, worthless, or objectionable. **2** a haemophiliac.

bleeding *adj and adv informal* = BLOODY[1], BLOODY[3].

bleeding edge *n* the very forefront *esp* of technological advance.

bleeding heart *n* **1** *informal derog* somebody who is considered to show excessive sympathy for e.g. victims of injustice or ill-treatment. **2** a plant of the fumitory family with usu red or pink heart-shaped flowers.

bleep[1] *n* **1** a short high-pitched sound, e.g. from electronic equipment. **2** = BLEEPER.

bleep[2] *v* **1** to call by means of a bleeper. **2** (*usu* + out) to replace (recorded words) with a bleep. **3** to emit a bleep.

bleeper *n* a portable radio receiver that emits a bleep as a signal that the wearer is required.

blemish[1] *n* **1** a flaw, stain, or disfiguring mark. **2** a defect of character.

blemish[2] *v* to spoil the perfection or appearance of.

blench *v* to draw back or flinch from lack of courage.

blend[1] *v* **1** to mix, *esp* to combine separate constituents so that they cannot be distinguished. **2** to prepare (e.g. tea or whisky) by thoroughly intermingling different varieties or grades. **3a** (*often* + in) to produce a harmonious effect. **b** to fit in well.

blend[2] *n* a mixture, *esp* a harmonious one.

blender *n* an electric appliance for grinding or mixing; a liquidizer.

blenny *n* (*pl* **-ies**) a scaleless sea fish with long spiny fins, mostly found in coastal waters.

blepharitis *n* inflammation of the eyelids.

bless *v* (*past tense and past part.* **blessed** *or* **blest**) **1** to consecrate by a religious rite, *esp* by making the sign of the cross. **2** to invoke divine care for. **3** to praise or glorify (God). **4a** to confer prosperity or happiness on. **b** to endow with a talent, asset, advantage, etc. ✱ **bless you!/God bless you! 1** words traditionally said to somebody who has just sneezed. **2** an exclamation of surprise, thanks, etc.

blessed *adj* **1a** (*often* **Blessed**) holy; venerated. **b** (**Blessed**) used as a title for a beatified person. **2a** bringing pleasure or contentment. **b** used to express annoyance. **3** /blest/ enjoying the bliss of heaven. ⋙ **blessedly** *adv*, **blessedness** *n.*

blessing *n* **1a** the invocation of God's favour upon a person. **b** the words used in such an invocation. **2** approval. **3** something conducive to happiness or welfare. ✱ **a blessing in disguise** an apparent misfortune that is found in the end to be beneficial.

blest *v* past tense and past part. of BLESS.

blether *v* **1** to talk nonsense or talk volubly; to BLATHER[2]. **2** *chiefly Scot, informal* to have a friendly chat with somebody. ⋙ **blether** *n*, **bletherer** *n.*

blew *v* past tense of BLOW[1], BLOW[4].

blewits *n* (*pl* **blewits**) an edible mushroom that has a lilac-coloured cap and stem when young.

blight[1] *n* **1a** a disease of plants resulting in withering. **b** an organism that causes this. **2** something that impairs or destroys. **3** a condition of disorder or decay.

blight[2] *v* **1** to affect (e.g. a plant) with blight. **2** to impair or destroy.

blighter *n chiefly Brit, informal* a person or thing regarded as irritating, troublesome, or pitiable.

Blighty *n informal* used *esp* by British soldiers in World War I: Britain.

blimey *interj chiefly Brit, informal* used to express surprise.

blimp *n* **1** a non-rigid airship. **2** (*usu* **Blimp**) a pompous person with out-of-date views. **3** *NAm, informal, offensive* a very fat person. ⋙ **blimpish** *adj*, **blimpishly** *adv*, **blimpishness** *n.*

blind[1] *adj* **1a** unable to see; sightless. **b** of or for sightless people. **2a** (*often* + to) unable to perceive clearly or judge rationally. **b** acting or done without control or judgment. **3** without sight or knowledge of anything that could serve for guidance beforehand. **4** performed solely by the use of instruments within an aircraft. **5** having only one opening or outlet. **6** *informal* the slightest. ✱ **(as) blind as a bat** completely, or almost totally, blind. **turn a blind eye** to refuse to take action against somebody's mistakes or wrongdoing. ⋙ **blindly** *adv*, **blindness** *n.*

blind[2] *v* **1** to make blind. **2** (*often* + to) to rob of judgment or discernment. ✱ **blind with science** to overwhelm with a display of usu technical knowledge.

blind[3] *n* **1** a flexible screen for covering a window, e.g. a strip of cloth mounted on a roller. **2** a cover or subterfuge. **3** *NAm* = HIDE[2].

blind[4] *adv* **1** to the point of insensibility. **2** without seeing outside an aircraft. ✱ **bake blind** to bake (a pastry case) without a filling.

blind alley *n* **1** = CUL-DE-SAC. **2** a fruitless or mistaken course or direction.

blind date *n* **1** a date between people who have not previously met. **2** a participant in such a meeting.

blinder *n* **1** *Brit, informal* something outstanding, *esp* an outstanding piece of play. **2** *NAm* = BLINKER[1] (3).

blindfold[1] *v* to cover the eyes of (somebody) with a piece of material to prevent them from seeing.

blindfold[2] *n* a piece of cloth tied around the head to prevent a person seeing.

blindfold[3] *adj and adv* **1** wearing a blindfold. **2** without careful thought.

blinding *adj* **1** said of light: so bright as to make seeing difficult or impossible. **2** *informal* **a** outstanding or extraordinary, *esp* in showing supreme skill. **b** extremely obvious; glaring. ➤➤ **blindingly** *adv.*

blindman's buff *n* a group game in which a blindfolded player tries to catch and identify any of the other players.

blind side *n* the side on which one cannot see danger, etc.

blind spot *n* **1a** the point in the retina where the optic nerve enters and that is not sensitive to light. **b** a part of a visual field that cannot be seen. **2** an area in which one lacks knowledge or discrimination. **3** a locality in which radio reception is poorer than in the surrounding area.

blind trust *n* a trust that manages the financial affairs of a person in public office without that person knowing the details of its financial dealings.

blindworm *n* = SLOWWORM.

blini *or* **bliny** *or* **blinis** *pl n* in Russian cooking, small pancakes made with yeast and buckwheat flour, usu served with sour cream.

blink[1] *v* **1** to close and open the eyes involuntarily. **2** to shine intermittently. **3a** (+ at) to condone or ignore. **b** to look with surprise or dismay at.

blink[2] *n* a usu involuntary shutting and opening of the eye. ✱ **on the blink** *informal* not working properly.

blinker[1] *n* **1** a warning or signalling light that flashes on and off. **2** (*in pl*) something that restricts understanding or awareness. **3** *chiefly Brit* either of two flaps, one on each side of a horse's bridle, allowing only frontal vision.

blinker[2] *v* **1** to put blinkers on (a horse). **2** to restrict or lessen the understanding or awareness of. ➤➤ **blinkered** *adj.*

blinking *adj and adv Brit, euphem* = BLOODY[1], BLOODY[3].

bliny *pl n* see BLINI.

blip[1] *n* **1** a bleep. **2** an image on a radar screen. **3** a brief, and sometimes unwelcome, deviation from the norm; an aberration.

blip[2] *v* (**blipped, blipping**) to deviate briefly from the norm.

blipvert *n* a very brief television advertisement.

bliss *n* **1** complete happiness. **2** paradise or heaven. ➤➤ **blissful** *adj,* **blissfully** *adv,* **blissfulness** *n.*

blissed out *adj informal* completely happy.

blister[1] *n* **1** a raised part of the outer skin containing watery liquid. **2** a bubble or raised spot, e.g. in paint or wallpaper. ➤➤ **blistery** *adj.*

blister[2] *v* to make or become affected with a blister or blisters.

blistering *adj* **1** extremely intense or severe. **2** of speed: extremely fast. ➤➤ **blisteringly** *adv.*

blister pack *n* a pack for small manufactured items, consisting of a transparent covering fastened to a cardboard backing.

blithe *adj* **1** light-hearted, merry or cheerful. **2** casual or heedless. ➤➤ **blithely** *adv,* **blitheness** *n.*

blithering *adj informal* **1** stupid. **2** talking nonsense; babbling.

BLitt *abbr* Bachelor of Letters.

blitz[1] *n* **1** a period of intensive action. **2a** an intensive aerial bombardment. **b** (**the Blitz**) the bombardment of British cities by the German air force in 1940 and 1941.

blitz[2] *v* **1** to deal with in a short, intensive period of action. **2** to attack in an intensive aerial bombardment.

blitzkrieg *n* a violent surprise campaign conducted by coordinated air and ground forces.

blizzard *n* **1a** a severe snowstorm. **b** an intensely strong cold wind filled with fine snow. **2** an overwhelming rush or deluge. ➤➤ **blizzardy** *adj.*

bloat *v* **1** to make or become swollen with gas or liquid. **2** to enlarge beyond the normal or necessary size. ➤➤ **bloated** *adj.*

bloater *n* a large herring or mackerel lightly salted and briefly smoked.

blob[1] *n* **1** a small drop of liquid or of a viscous substance. **2** something ill-defined or amorphous. ➤➤ **blobby** *adj.*

blob[2] *v* (**blobbed, blobbing**) to apply (a liquid such as paint) in the form of blobs.

bloc *n* a combination of parties or nations for a common purpose.

block[1] *n* **1** a quantity or section of things dealt with as a unit. **2** a large building divided into separate functional units. **3** a rectangular area in a town enclosed by streets and usu occupied by buildings. **4** a compact solid piece of material such as wood or stone, *esp* when specially shaped to serve a particular purpose. **5** *Brit* a thick pad of paper. **6a** an obstacle or blockage. **b** a psychological factor that prevents normal functioning, reactions, etc. **7** an action intended to halt an opponent's manoeuvre in sports. **8** the metal casting that contains the cylinders of an internal-combustion engine. **9** a wooden or metal case enclosing one or more pulleys. **10** *informal* the head.

block[2] *v* **1a** (*often* + up) to be a barrier that obstructs (a passage, road, pipe, etc). **b** to hinder the movement or progress of. **2** to shut (something) off from view. **3** to stop or obstruct (an opponent or ball) with one's body. **4** to prevent the normal functioning of. ➤➤ **blocker** *n.*

blockade[1] *n* the surrounding of a particular enemy area, *esp* a port, to prevent passage of people or supplies.

blockade[2] *v* to subject to a blockade. ➤➤ **blockader** *n.*

blockage *n* something that causes e.g. a pipe to be blocked.

block and tackle *n* an arrangement of pulley blocks with associated rope or cable for hoisting or hauling.

blockbuster *n informal* somebody or something particularly outstanding or effective. ➤➤ **blockbusting** *adj.*

block capitals *pl n* plain capital letters.

blockhead *n* an extremely dull or stupid person. ➤➤ **blockheaded** *adj.*

blockhouse *n* **1** an observation post built to withstand heat, blast, radiation, etc. **2** a small fort. **3** a building built with logs or squared timber.

block in *v* **1** to sketch the outlines of. **2** to keep in by means of a barrier or obstruction.

blockish *adj* **1** stupid or lacking in imagination. **2** dull or lacking in energy.

block letters *pl n* = BLOCK CAPITALS.

block off *v* to prevent access to or passage through.

block out *v* **1** to prevent the passage of (light, sound, etc). **2** to exclude (a memory) from one's consciousness. **3** to sketch the outlines of.

block release *n* a short course of full-time study for which a worker is released by his or her employer: compare DAY RELEASE.

block vote *n* a single vote cast by a representative of a large group and given a relative value proportional to the number of people in that group. Also called CARD VOTE.

bloke *n chiefly Brit, informal* a man.

blokeish *or* **blokish** *adj informal* stereotypically male, *esp* hearty and boisterous, inclined to show off, etc.

blonde[1] *or* **blond** *adj* **1** *esp* of hair: of a golden or pale yellowish brown colour. **2** having blonde hair and usu a fairly pale skin. ➤➤ **blondish** *adj.*

blonde[2] *or* **blond** *n* **1** somebody, *esp* a woman, with blond hair. **2** a light yellowish brown to dark greyish yellow colour.

blood[1] *n* **1** the red fluid that circulates in the arteries and veins of a vertebrate animal, carrying nourishment and oxygen to all parts of the body. **2a** lifeblood; life. **b** bloodshed; murder. **3a** human lineage, *esp* the royal lineage. **b** descent from parents, family background, or ancestors. **4** *archaic* a dashing lively *esp* young man; a rake. ✱ **after/out for somebody's blood** wanting revenge on somebody. **in one's blood** being an inherent or supposedly inherited part of a person's character or life. **make one's blood boil** to make one very angry. **make one's blood run cold** to horrify one. **one's blood is up** one is ready for a fight.

blood[2] *v* **1** to mark the face of (an inexperienced fox hunter) with the blood of the fox. **2** to give an initiating experience to.

blood-and-thunder *adj informal* violently melodramatic.

bloodbath *n* a great slaughter; a massacre.

blood brother *n* either of two men pledged to mutual loyalty, *esp* by a ceremonial mingling of each other's blood. ➤➤ **blood brotherhood** *n.*

blood count *n* the number of blood cells in a definite volume of blood.

bloodcurdling *adj* arousing horror. ➤➤ **bloodcurdlingly** *adv.*

blood doping *n* the (illegal) practice of injecting an athlete with a quantity of specially oxygenated blood just before an event in an attempt to improve performance.

blood feud *n* a murderous feud between clans or families.

blood group *n* any of the classes into which human beings can be separated on the basis of the presence or absence of specific antigens in their blood. Also called BLOOD TYPE.

bloodhound *n* a large powerful hound remarkable for its acuteness of smell and poor sight.

bloodless *adj* **1** deficient in blood. **2** not accompanied by the shedding of blood. **3** lacking in spirit or vitality. **4** lacking in human feeling. ➤➤ **bloodlessly** *adv,* **bloodlessness** *n.*

bloodletting *n* **1** = BLOODSHED. **2** = PHLEBOTOMY.

bloodline *n* a group of related individuals, *esp* with distinctive characteristics.

bloodlust *n* an intense desire to shed blood or kill.

blood money *n* **1** money paid for murder. **2** money paid to the next of kin of a person who has been killed.

blood orange *n* a type of eating orange that has red and orange flesh and a reddish skin.

blood plasma *n* = PLASMA (1B).

blood poisoning *n* = SEPTICAEMIA.

blood pressure *n* pressure exerted by the blood on the walls of the blood vessels, *esp* arteries, that varies with the age and health of the individual.

blood relation *n* a person related by birth or descent, as opposed to by marriage.

blood relative *n* = BLOOD RELATION.

bloodshed *n* **1** the shedding of blood. **2** the taking of life.

bloodshot *adj* of an eye: having the white part tinged with red.

blood sport *n derog* a field sport, e.g. fox-hunting or beagling, in which animals are killed.

bloodstock *n* (*used as sing. or pl*) thoroughbred horses, *esp* when used for racing.

bloodstream *n* the flowing blood in a circulatory system.

bloodsucker *n* **1** a person who extorts money from another. **2** an animal or insect that sucks blood, *esp* a leech. ➤➤ **bloodsucking** *adj.*

blood sugar *n* the amount of glucose in the blood.

bloodthirsty *adj* eager for bloodshed. ➤➤ **bloodthirstily** *adv,* **bloodthirstiness** *n.*

blood type *n* = BLOOD GROUP.

blood vessel *n* any of the tubes through which blood circulates in an animal; a vein, artery, or capillary.

bloody[1] *adj* (**-ier, -iest**) **1** *informal* used as an intensifier *esp* to express annoyance. **2** smeared with blood. **3** accompanied by bloodshed. **4a** murderous or bloodthirsty. **b** *informal* unkind or unpleasant. ➤➤ **bloodily** *adv,* **bloodiness** *n.*

bloody[2] *v* (**-ies, -ied**) to make bloody.

bloody[3] *adv informal* used as an intensifier.

Bloody Mary *n* (*pl* **Bloody Marys**) a cocktail consisting chiefly of vodka and tomato juice.

bloody-minded *adj* deliberately obstructive or unhelpful. ➤➤ **bloody-mindedly** *adv,* **bloody-mindedness** *n.*

bloom[1] *n* **1a** a flower. **b** the state of having flowers. **2** a time of beauty, freshness, and vigour. **3** a rosy or healthy appearance, *esp* on the cheeks. **4** a delicate powdery coating on some fruits and leaves. ➤➤ **bloomy** *adj.*

bloom[2] *v* **1a** to produce or yield flowers. **b** to support abundant plant life. **2** to flourish.

bloomer *n* **1** *informal* a stupid or embarrassing blunder. **2** *chiefly Brit* a large longish glazed loaf marked with diagonal cuts across the top.

bloomers *pl n* **1** *informal* knickers. **2** a costume worn formerly by women, consisting of a short skirt and long loose trousers gathered closely about the ankles. **3** full loose knickers gathered at the knee, formerly worn by women.

blooming *adj* **1** flourishing. **2** *chiefly Brit, euphem* used as a generalized intensifier, usu expressing annoyance. ➤➤ **blooming** *adv.*

blooper *n NAm, informal* an embarrassing public blunder.

blossom[1] *n* **1** the flower of a plant, *esp* the flower that produces edible fruits. **2a** the mass of flowers on a single plant, *esp* a tree or shrub. **b** the state of having flowers. ➤➤ **blossomy** *adj.*

blossom[2] *v* (**blossomed, blossoming**) **1** to bloom. **2** to develop in a promising or satisfying way.

blot[1] *n* **1** a disfiguring mark, *esp* a spot of ink or other liquid. **2** a fault or bad act.

blot[2] *v* (**blotted, blotting**) **1** to spot or stain *esp* with ink. **2** to dry (e.g. ink or spilt liquid) with an absorbing agent such as blotting paper. **3** to spoil (e.g. one's reputation) by committing an error or wrongdoing. ✱ **blot one's copybook** to mar one's previously good record or standing.

blotch[1] *n* an irregular spot or mark, e.g. of colour or ink. ⋙ **blotchily** *adv*, **blotchy** *adj*.

blotch[2] *v* to make a blotch or blotches.

blot out *v* **1** to obscure or eclipse. **2** to shut out from one's consciousness. **3** to destroy totally.

blotter *n* a piece of blotting paper.

blotting paper *n* a spongy unsized paper used to absorb ink.

blotto *adj Brit, informal* extremely drunk.

blouse[1] *n* **1** a usu loose-fitting woman's upper garment that resembles a shirt. **2** a battledress jacket.

blouse[2] *v* to make (e.g. part of a piece of clothing) fall in folds.

blouson *n* a short loose jacket or blouse usu closely fitted at the waist.

blow[1] *v* (*past tense* **blew**, *past part.* **blown**) **1** said of air, wind, etc: to move perceptibly or audibly. **2** to move or be carried by the wind or a current of air. **3** to send a current of air through the mouth or nose. **4a** to force air through (a musical instrument) to produce a sound. **b** of a wind instrument: to make a sound. **5** of a tyre: to lose the air inside it through a rupture of the casing. **6** of an electric fuse or a valve: to melt or break when overloaded. **7a** *informal* to explode or detonate. **b** to burst or destroy (something) with explosives. **8** to shape (e.g. glass or bubbles) by the action of blown air. **9** *informal* to lose (a chance of success, etc) by failing to use an opportunity. **10** *informal* to spend (money) extravagantly. **11** *informal* to reveal (a secret or disguise). **12** *informal* to leave hurriedly. ✱ **blow hot and cold** to vary unpredictably in one's support for something; to vacillate. **blow one's own trumpet** to praise oneself; to boast. **blow one's top** *informal* to lose one's temper. **blow somebody's mind 1** *informal* to amaze. **2** *informal* to cause to hallucinate. **blow the gaff** *Brit, slang* to reveal a secret, *esp* something discreditable. **blow the whistle on 1** *informal* to reveal (*esp* a wrongdoing). **2** *informal* to inform against. **I'll be blowed/I'm blowed** an expression of surprise or refusal.

blow[2] *n* **1** a strong wind or windy storm. **2** *informal* a walk or other outing in the fresh air.

blow[3] *n* **1** a hard hit delivered with the hand or fist, a weapon, tool, or other object. **2** a shock or misfortune. ✱ **at one blow** in a single action. **come to blows** to start fighting; to end up as a fight.

blow[4] *v* (*past tense* **blew**, *past part.* **blown**) to cause (e.g. flowers or blossom) to open out, usu just before dropping.

blow away *v informal* **1** to kill with a gun. **2** to defeat thoroughly. **3** to impress.

blow-by-blow *adj* minutely detailed.

blow-dry *v* (**-ies, -ied**) to dry and style (the hair) with a hairdrier. ⋙ **blow-drier** *n*, **blow-dry** *n*.

blower *n* **1** a device for producing a current of air or gas. **2** *Brit, informal* the telephone.

blowfish *n* = GLOBEFISH.

blowfly *n* (*pl* **-ies**) a two-winged fly that deposits eggs or maggots *esp* on meat or in wounds.

blowhard *n NAm, informal* a braggart.

blowhole *n* **1** a nostril in the top of the head of a whale, porpoise, or dolphin. **2** a hole in the ice to which aquatic mammals, e.g. seals, come to breathe. **3** an opening for letting out air or other gas.

blow in *v* **1** *informal* to arrive casually or unexpectedly. **2** to break inwards because of an explosion.

blow-job *n coarse slang* an act of FELLATIO.

blowlamp *n* a small portable burner that produces an intense flame and has a pressurized fuel tank.

blown[1] *v* past part. of BLOW[1], BLOW[4].

blown[2] *adj* **1** swollen. **2** = FLYBLOWN .

blow off *v informal* **1** to lose one's temper suddenly. **2** to break wind noisily.

blowout *n* **1** *informal* a large meal or other lavish entertainment. **2** a bursting of e.g. a tyre. **3** an uncontrolled eruption of an oil or gas well. **4** the melting of a fuse.

blow out *v* **1** to extinguish or be extinguished by a breath or gust of air. **2** to break outwards because of an explosion. **3** of an oil or gas well: to erupt out of control. **4** of a storm: to dissipate itself blowing.

blow over *v* **1** of a storm: to pass by; to stop. **2** of a difficulty: to pass by without lasting ill-effects.

blowpipe *n* **1** a tube for propelling a projectile, e.g. a dart, by blowing. **2** a long metal tube used to shape glass by blowing.

blowsy *or* **blowzy** *adj* (**-ier, -iest**) **1** having a coarse ruddy complexion. **2** *esp* of a woman: slovenly in appearance and usu fat. ⋙ **blowsily** *adv*, **blowsiness** *n*.

blowtorch *n* = BLOWLAMP.

blow up *v* **1** to shatter or destroy by an explosion. **2** to exaggerate to an unreasonable extent. **3** to inflate with air or gas. **4** to make an enlargement of (a photograph). **5** *informal* to reprimand angrily. **6** *informal* to become violently angry. **7a** of a storm or wind: to start to develop or strengthen. **b** to arise or develop unexpectedly. ✱ **blow up in one's face** said of an action or plan: to fail disastrously with adverse effects for its originator. ⋙ **blowup** *n*.

blowy *adj* (**-ier, -iest**) windy.

blowzy *adj* see BLOWSY.

BLT *n informal* a bacon, lettuce, and tomato sandwich.

blub *v* (**blubbed, blubbing**) *informal* = BLUBBER[2].

blubber[1] *n* **1** the fat of large marine mammals, *esp* whales. **2** *informal* body fat. ⋙ **blubbery** *adj*.

blubber[2] *v informal* to weep noisily.

bludge[1] *v Aus, NZ, informal* **1** to scrounge. **2** to avoid a task, etc. ⋙ **bludger** *n*.

bludge[2] *n Aus, NZ, informal* an easy task; a doddle.

bludgeon[1] *n* a short club used as a weapon.

bludgeon[2] *v* **1** to hit or beat with a bludgeon. **2** (*also* + into) to force or persuade to do something by aggressive argument.

blue[1] *adj* **1** of the colour of a clear sky, between green and indigo in the spectrum. **2** discoloured through cold, anger, bruising, or fear. **3a** low in spirits. **b** depressing or dismal. **4a** obscene or pornographic. **b** off-colour or risqué. **5** *Brit* supporting the Conservative Party. ✱ **once in a blue moon** very rarely. **until one is blue in the face** unsuccessfully for ever. ⋙ **bluely** *adv*, **blueness** *n*.

blue[2] *n* **1** a blue colour. **2** a blue preparation used to whiten clothes in laundering. **3** (*often* **Blue**) *Brit* somebody who has played in a sporting contest between Oxford and Cambridge universities. **4** *Aus, NZ, informal* a quarrel or row. ✱ **out of the blue** without warning; unexpectedly.

blue[3] *v* (**blues, blued, blueing** *or* **bluing**) *Brit, informal* to spend (money) lavishly and wastefully.

blue baby *n* a baby born with skin of a bluish tint, usu from a congenital heart defect.

bluebell *n* a plant of the lily family bearing blue bell-shaped flowers.

blueberry *n* (*pl* **-ies**) an edible blue or blackish soft fruit produced by a shrub of the heath family.

bluebird *n* a small N American songbird with blue plumage on its head, back, and tail.

blue blood *n* high or noble birth. ➤➤ **blue-blooded** *adj.*

blue book *n* an official parliamentary report or document.

bluebottle *n* a blowfly whose body is iridescent blue.

blue cheese *n* cheese marked with veins of greenish blue mould.

blue chip *n* a high-quality stock regarded as a very sound investment. ➤➤ **blue-chip** *adj.*

blue-collar *adj* relating to the class of manual wage-earning employees whose duties often call for the wearing of work clothes or protective clothing: compare WHITE-COLLAR.

blue-eyed boy *n often derog* a favourite.

bluefish *n* (*pl* **bluefishes** *or* **bluefish**) an active voracious blue-coloured fish that is found in all warm seas and is popular as a game fish.

bluegrass *n* **1** a type of country music played on unamplified stringed instruments. **2** bluish green meadow grass used as fodder and for lawns.

blue-green alga *n* = CYANOBACTERIUM.

blue heeler *n* a dog of an Australian breed with a blue-speckled coat mainly used for controlling cattle.

blue murder ✱ **cry/scream/yell blue murder** *informal* to make a loud noise of fear, pain, etc.

blue note *n* a flattened third or seventh note used in a chord *esp* in jazz and blues.

blue-pencil *v* to edit (a manuscript, film, etc), *esp* by deleting parts considered indecent.

Blue Peter *n* a blue signal flag with a white square in the centre, used to indicate that a merchant vessel is ready to sail.

blueprint *n* **1a** a photographic print in white on a bright blue ground, used *esp* for copying maps and plans. **b** a design plan. **2** a detailed programme of action.

blue riband *n* = BLUE RIBBON.

blue ribbon *n* a ribbon of blue fabric worn as an honour or award, *esp* by members of the Order of the Garter.

blues *n* (*pl* **blues**) **1** (**the blues**) (*used as sing. or pl*) low spirits; melancholy. **2a** (*often* **the blues**) (*usu used as sing.*) a melancholy style of music which originated among American blacks in the early 20th cent. **b** a song or piece of music in this style. ➤➤ **bluesy** *adj.*

blue-sky *adj* having no specific practical application; pure or theoretical.

bluestocking *n derog* a woman with intellectual or literary interests.

blue tit *n* a widely distributed European tit that has a bright blue crown and a mostly yellow underside.

blue whale *n* a slate-blue-coloured whale that is the largest living animal and is found *esp* in northern European waters.

bluff[1] *v* **1** to deceive by pretence or an outward appearance of strength, confidence, etc. **2** to deceive (an opponent) in cards by a bold bet on an inferior hand. ➤➤ **bluffer** *n.*

bluff[2] *n* an act or instance of bluffing. ✱ **call somebody's bluff** to challenge (somebody) to prove a claim one believes to be untrue.

bluff[3] *adj* **1** good-naturedly frank and outspoken. **2** rising steeply with a broad, flat, or rounded front. ➤➤ **bluffly** *adv,* **bluffness** *n.*

bluff[4] *n* a high steep bank; a cliff.

blunder[1] *v* **1** to move unsteadily or confusedly. **2a** to make a blunder. **b** to mismanage (something). ➤➤ **blunderer** *n,* **blunderingly** *adv.*

blunder[2] *n* a gross error or mistake resulting from stupidity, ignorance, or carelessness.

blunderbuss *n* an obsolete short firearm with a large bore and usu a flaring muzzle.

blunt[1] *adj* **1a** having an edge or point that is not sharp. **b** without an edge or point. **2a** aggressively outspoken. **b** direct or straightforward. **3** insensitive; dull. ➤➤ **bluntly** *adv,* **bluntness** *n.*

blunt[2] *v* **1** to make less sharp. **2** to make less forceful or severe.

blur[1] *n* **1** a smear or stain. **2** something vague or indistinct. ➤➤ **blurriness** *n,* **blurry** *adj.*

blur[2] *v* (**blurred, blurring**) **1** to obscure or blemish by smearing. **2** to make or become indistinct or confused. ➤➤ **blurringly** *adv.*

blurb *n* a short publicity notice, *esp* on a book cover.

blurt out *v* to utter abruptly and impulsively.

blush[1] *v* **1** to become red in the face, *esp* from shame, modesty, or embarrassment. **2** to feel shame or embarrassment. ➤➤ **blushingly** *adv.*

blush[2] *n* **1** a reddening of the face, *esp* from shame, confusion, or embarrassment. **2** a red or rosy tint. ✱ **at first blush** when first seen; as a first impression. **spare somebody's blushes** to avoid embarrassing (somebody), *esp* by not praising them publicly. ➤➤ **blushful** *adj.*

blusher *n* a cream or powder for adding colour to the cheeks.

bluster[1] *v* **1** to talk or act in a noisily self-assertive manner. **2** to blow in stormy gusts. ➤➤ **blusterer** *n,* **blusteringly** *adv.*

bluster[2] *n* loudly boastful or empty threatening talk. ➤➤ **blusterous** *adj,* **blustery** *adj.*

BM *abbr* **1** Bachelor of Medicine. **2** British Museum.

BMA *abbr* British Medical Association.

B-movie *n* a low-budget film shown, *esp* formerly, as a supporting item in a cinema programme.

BMus *abbr* Bachelor of Music.

BMX *n* **1** the sport of cross-country or stunt riding on a specially designed bicycle. **2** a bicycle with a strong frame and small wheels designed for use in BMX.

BO *n* a disagreeable smell, *esp* of stale perspiration, given off by a person's body.

bo *interj* = BOO[1].

boa *n* **1** a large snake, e.g. the boa constrictor, anaconda, or python, that crushes its prey. **2** a long fluffy scarf of fur, feathers, or delicate fabric.

boa constrictor *n* a tropical American boa that reaches a length of 3m (about 10ft) or more.

boar *n* **1a** an uncastrated male pig. **b** the male of any of several mammals, e.g. a guinea pig or badger. **2** = WILD BOAR. ➤➤ **boarish** *adj.*

board[1] *n* **1a** a long thin narrow piece of sawn timber. **b** (**the boards**) the stage. **2** a flat piece of material designed for a special purpose, e.g. for playing board games or for use as a blackboard or noticeboard. **3** (*used as sing. or pl*) a group of people having managerial or investigatory powers. **4a** a wood pulp or composition material formed into stiff flat rectangular sheets. **b** = CARDBOARD[1]. **5** daily meals, *esp* when provided in return for payment. ✱ **go by the board** to be neglected; to go out of use. **on board** aboard. **take something on board** *Brit, informal* to grasp, accept, or take account of (an idea, etc). ➤➤ **boardlike** *adj.*

board[2] *v* **1** to go aboard (e.g. a ship, train, aircraft, or bus). **2** to come alongside (a ship), usu in order to attack it. **3** (+ over/up) to cover with boards. **4** to provide with regular meals and usu lodging for a fixed price. **5** to take one's meals, usu as a paying customer.

boarder *n* **1** a lodger. **2** a resident pupil at a boarding school. **3** somebody who boards a ship, *esp* in an attack.

board game *n* any game that is played by moving pieces on a specially patterned board, e.g. chess, draughts, or snakes and ladders.

boarding card *n* = BOARDING PASS.

boarding house *n* a lodging house that supplies meals.

boarding pass *n* a document given to a passenger, usu in exchange for a ticket, that enables him or her to board an aircraft or ship.

boarding school *n* a school at which meals and lodging are provided.

boardroom *n* a room in which the meetings of a board of directors are held.

boardsailing *n* = WIND-SURFING.

boardwalk *n NAm* a walk often constructed of planking, usu beside the sea.

boast[1] *n* **1** an act of boasting. **2** a cause for pride. ➤➤ **boastful** *adj*, **boastfully** *adv*, **boastfulness** *n*.

boast[2] *v* **1** (*often* + of/about) to praise oneself; to talk with excessive pride about one's abilities, achievements, etc. **2** to have or display (something that is considered notable or a source of pride). ➤➤ **boaster** *n*.

boat[1] *n* **1** a small open vessel or craft for travelling across water. **2** a boat-shaped utensil or dish. ✱ **in the same boat** in the same situation or predicament.

boat[2] *v* to use a boat, *esp* for recreation. ➤➤ **boating** *n*.

boatel *or* **botel** *n* a waterside hotel with berths to accommodate people travelling by boat.

boater *n* a stiff straw hat with a shallow flat crown and a brim.

boathook *n* a pole with a hook at one end, used *esp* for fending off or holding boats alongside.

boatload *n* the quantity of cargo or passengers that a boat is carrying or can carry.

boatman *n* (*pl* **boatmen**) a person who works with, looks after, or hires out boats, *esp* pleasure boats.

boat people *pl n* refugees, *esp* from Vietnam, who set sail in boats to find a country that is willing to admit them.

boatswain *or* **bosun** *or* **bo's'n** *n* a petty officer on a merchant vessel or warrant officer in the navy who is responsible *esp* for routine maintenance of the ship's structure.

boat train *n* an express train that takes people to or from a ship.

bob[1] *v* (**bobbed, bobbing**) **1** to move down and up briefly or repeatedly. **2** to curtsy briefly. **3** (+ for) to try to seize a suspended or floating apple, etc with the teeth.

bob[2] *n* a short quick down-and-up motion.

bob[3] *n* **1** a short straight hairstyle for women, with the hair cut evenly at about chin level, so that it swings loosely. **2** = FLOAT[1] (IA). **3** a hanging ball or weight on a plumb line or kite's tail.

bob[4] *v* (**bobbed, bobbing**) **1** to cut shorter; *esp* to crop (a horse's tail). **2** to cut (hair) in a bob.

bob[5] *n* (*pl* **bob**) *Brit, informal* a shilling.

bobbin *n* a cylinder or spindle on which yarn or thread is wound, for use in sewing, spinning, or lacemaking.

bobble[1] *v* to move jerkily down and up briefly or repeatedly.

bobble[2] *n* **1** a small fluffy ball, e.g. of wool, used for ornament or trimming. **2** a bobbling movement.

bobby *n* (*pl* **-ies**) *Brit, informal, dated* a police officer.

bobcat *n* a common N American lynx with reddish fur and dark spots.

bobsled *n NAm* = BOBSLEIGH. ➤➤ **bobsledding** *n*.

bobsleigh *n chiefly Brit* a large sledge with mechanisms for steering and braking, used for racing down an embanked ice-covered slope, as a winter-sports event. ➤➤ **bobsleighing** *n*.

bobtail *n* a bobbed tail, or a horse or dog with a bobbed tail.

Boche /bosh/ *n* (**the Boche**) *informal, dated* Germans, *esp* German soldiers.

bod *n informal* **1** a person's body. **2** *chiefly Brit* a person.

bodacious *adj NAm, informal* outstanding or impressive.

bode *v* to presage or foreshadow (*esp* evil or misfortune). ✱ **bode ill/well for** to be a bad or good sign for (the future, or some future plan).

bodega /boh'deega, boh'daygə/ *n* a storehouse for wine in a Spanish-speaking country, or a shop that sells wine.

bodge *v Brit, informal* to make or repair clumsily; to botch. ➤➤ **bodger** *n*.

bodhran /'bowrahn, bow'rahn/ *n* a small Irish drum held in one hand and beaten with a short two-headed stick.

bodice *n* **1** the upper part of a woman's dress, from neck to waist. **2** formerly, a woman's corset-like garment, laced at the front, worn over a blouse or as an undergarment.

bodice-ripper *n informal, humorous* a romantic novel or film with a high content of excitement, sex, and violence, typically in a historical setting.

bodiless *adj* **1** lacking a body, or lacking body. **2** incorporeal; insubstantial.

bodily[1] *adj* **1** relating to or belonging to the body. **2** physical or actual, as distinct from spiritual.

bodily[2] *adv* **1** involving the whole body. **2** in bodily form; in the flesh.

bodkin *n* **1** a blunt thick needle with a large eye used to draw tape or ribbon through a loop or hem. **2** formerly, a long ornamental hairpin.

body *n* (*pl* **-ies**) **1** the physical structure, made up of bones, flesh and organs, that constitutes a person or animal. **2** a corpse. **3** the main part of a human or animal body; the trunk as distinct from the head and limbs. **4** a woman's garment for the trunk, usu of opaque stretchy material, fastening between the legs. **5** the main, central, or principal part of something, e.g. the nave of a church. **6** a mass or expanse, *esp* of water. **7** any of the objects in the heavens, that is, the sun, moon, or stars. **8** a material object. **9** (*used as sing. or pl*) a group of people or things, e.g. a fighting unit or a group of individuals organized for some purpose. **10a** compactness or firmness of texture. **b** fullness, e.g. of hair. **c** comparative richness of flavour in wine. ✱ **keep body and soul together** to stay alive. **over my dead body** *informal* not if I can help it.

body bag *n* a bag in which a dead body, e.g. that of a soldier killed in action, is placed for transportation.

body blow *n* **1** a hard punch on the body. **2** a serious setback.

bodyboard *n* a short surfboard.

body-building *n* the practice of strengthening the body and developing a conspicuously muscular physique through weightlifting and diet. ➤➤ **body-builder** *n.*

body clock *n* = BIOLOGICAL CLOCK.

body double *n* a person whose body substitutes for a film actor, *esp* during stunt scenes.

bodyguard *n* an escort whose duty is to protect a person from bodily harm.

body language *n* the expressing of feelings, *esp* unconsciously, by looks, movement, and posture.

body politic *n* (**the body politic**) a group of people under a single government.

body-popping *n* a solo dance form of the 1980s typified by jerky robot-like movements.

body shop *n* a workshop where repairs are made to the bodywork of vehicles.

body-snatcher *n* formerly, a person who dug up corpses illegally for dissection in medical schools, etc.

body stocking *n* a very light one-piece garment covering the trunk, with or without sleeves or legs, worn *esp* by dancers.

body suit *n* = BODY (4).

bodysurf *v* to surf without a surfboard by planing on the chest and stomach. ➤➤ **bodysurfer** *n.*

body-warmer *n* a padded and usu quilted sleeveless waist-length jacket.

bodywork *n* the structure or form of a vehicle body.

Boer /'bawə, 'boh·ə/ *n* a S African of Dutch descent. ➤➤ **Boer** *adj.*

boff[1] *v NAm, informal* **1** to hit or punch. **2** to have sexual intercourse with.

boff[2] *n NAm, informal* **1** a blow. **2** an act of sexual intercourse.

boffin *n chiefly Brit, informal* a scientific expert; *esp* one involved in technological research.

boffo *adj NAm, informal* used mostly in show-business contexts: highly successful.

bog *n* **1** wet spongy poorly-drained ground, or an area of this. **2** *Brit, informal* = TOILET (1). ➤➤ **bogginess** *n,* **boggy** *adj.*

bog down *v* (**bogged down, bogging down**) (*usu in passive*) **1** to cause (a vehicle) to sink into mud or a bog, so that it can progress no further. **2** to cause (a person or project) to get stuck and fail to progress.

bogey[1] *or* **bogy** *n* (*pl* **-eys** *or* **-ies**) **1** a golf score of one stroke over par on a hole. **2** a spectre; a ghost. **3** a source of recurring fear, perplexity, or harassment; = BUGBEAR. **4** *Brit, informal* a piece of dried nasal mucus.

bogey[2] *v* (**bogeys, bogeyed**) in golf, to play (a hole) in one stroke over par.

bogeyman *or* **bogyman** *n* (*pl* **bogeymen** *or* **bogymen**) a monstrous figure invented to threaten children with, so as to frighten them into obedience.

boggle *v informal* (+ at) to hesitate to do something because of doubt, fear, or scruples. ✱ **the mind boggles** used in mock bewilderment or ironic speculation: goodness knows; I haven't a clue.

bogie *or* **bogy** *n* (*pl* **-ies**) *chiefly Brit* **1** a swivelling framework with one or more pairs of wheels and springs to carry and guide one end of a railway vehicle. **2** a low four-wheeled truck.

bog-standard *adj informal, derog* of the ordinary or regular standard, without refinements.

bogus *adj* spurious, sham. ➤➤ **bogusly** *adv,* **bogusness** *n.*

bogy *n* see BOGEY[1], BOGIE.

bogyman *n* see BOGEYMAN.

Bohemian *n* **1** a native or inhabitant of Bohemia. **2** a person, typically a writer or artist, living an unconventional life. ➤➤ **Bohemian** *adj,* **Bohemianism** *n.*

bohrium *n* a radioactive metallic chemical element artificially produced by atomic collisions at high energy.

boil[1] *v* **1a** of a fluid: to reach a temperature, when heated, at which it bubbles and changes into vapour. **b** of a vessel: to contain a fluid that is boiling. **2** of disturbed water: to bubble or foam violently; to churn. **3** to become furious. **4** to undergo the action of a boiling liquid. **5** to subject (food, etc) to the action of a boiling liquid. **6** to heat (a kettle, etc) till its contents boil.

boil[2] *n* **1** (**the boil**) the act or state of boiling; = BOILING POINT. **2** a state of excitement or activity.

boil[3] *n* a localized pus-filled swelling of the skin resulting from infection of a hair follicle.

boil down *v* to amount in essence to a certain thing.

boiled sweet *n Brit* a sweet of boiled sugar, usu fruit-flavoured.

boiler *n* **1** a tank in which water is heated or domestic hot water is stored. **2** the part of a steam generator in which water is converted into steam under pressure. **3** *Brit, informal* a chicken suitable for boiling rather than roasting.

boilerplate *n* **1** rolled steel plate used *esp* in the construction of boilers. **2** *chiefly NAm* **a** journalistic material syndicated to various newspapers, formerly distributed as stereotype plates. **b** speech or writing that merely repeats or rehashes doctrine, etc uncritically. **c** fixed strings of wording for use *esp* in word-processing documents, e.g. clauses in legal contracts.

boiler suit *n chiefly Brit* a one-piece work garment combining shirt and trousers, worn over clothing to protect it; = OVERALL[2].

boiling *adj* **1** at or near boiling point. **2** *informal* very hot.

boiling point *n* the temperature at which a liquid boils.

boil over *v* **1** of milk or other fluid: to overflow while boiling. **2** to become so angry that one loses one's temper.

boisterous *adj* **1** noisily and cheerfully rough. **2** of the wind, weather, or water: stormy or wild. ➤➤ **boisterously** *adv,* **boisterousness** *n.*

bola /'bohlə/ *or* **bolas** /'bohləs/ *n* (*pl* **bolas** *or* **bolases**) a S American weapon consisting of two or more heavy balls attached to the ends of a cord for hurling at and entangling an animal.

bold[1] *adj* **1** showing or requiring a fearless adventurous spirit. **2** impudent; presumptuous. **3** departing from convention or tradition. **4** standing out prominently; conspicuous. **5** set, printed, etc in a thickened form of a typeface. ✱ **as bold as brass** with brazen self-assurance; without a hint of shame. ➤➤ **boldly** *adv,* **boldness** *n.*

bold[2] *n* a bold typeface.

bole *n* the trunk of a tree.

bolero /bə'leəroh/ *n* (*pl* **-os**) **1** a type of Spanish dance in moderate triple time. **2** (/'boləroh/) a woman's short jacket open at the front.

boletus *n* (*pl* **boletuses**) a fleshy mushroom or toadstool with a rounded cap that has pores rather than gills on its undersurface, some species of which are edible.

bolide *n* a large bright meteor of a type that tends to explode.

bolivar *n* (*pl* **bolivars** *or* **bolivares**) the basic monetary unit of Venezuela.

Bolivian *n* a native or inhabitant of Bolivia. ➤➤ **Bolivian** *adj.*

boliviano *n* (*pl* **-os**) the basic monetary unit of Bolivia.

boll *n* the seed pod of cotton or similar plants.

bollard *n* **1** *Brit* a short post, e.g. on a kerb or traffic island, to guide vehicles or prevent their access. **2** a post on a wharf round which to fasten mooring lines.

bollock *v Brit, coarse slang* to reprimand severely.

bollocking *n Brit, coarse slang* a severe reprimand.

bollocks *or* **ballocks** *pl n Brit, coarse slang* **1** a man's testicles. **2** (*used as sing. or pl*) often used as an interjection: utter rubbish; complete nonsense.

bollworm *n* a moth larva that feeds on cotton bolls.

Bollywood *n informal* the Indian film industry.

bologna /bə'lohnyə/ *n* a large smoked sausage made of beef, veal, and pork.

bolometer *n* a very sensitive electrical instrument used in the detection and measurement of heat radiation. ➤➤ **bolometric** *adj.*

boloney *n* see BALONEY.

bolo tie *n NAm* a long cord worn round the neck, fastened with an ornamental clasp.

Bolshevik *n* **1** a member of the more radical wing of the Russian Social Democratic party that seized power in Russia in 1917 and became the Communist party in 1918. **2** *derog* a former term for a Communist, *esp* a Russian Communist. ➤➤ **Bolshevik** *adj,* **Bolshevism** *n,* **Bolshevist** *n.*

bolshie *or* **bolshy** *adj* (**-ier**, **-iest**) *Brit, informal* obstinate and argumentative; stubbornly uncooperative. ➤➤ **bolshiness** *n.*

bolster[1] *n* **1** a long pillow or cushion placed across the head of a bed. **2** a structural part, e.g. in machinery, that eliminates friction or provides support.

bolster[2] *v* (*often* + up) to give support to or reinforce. ➤➤ **bolsterer** *n.*

bolt[1] *n* **1a** a sliding bar or rod used to fasten a door. **b** the part of a lock that is shot or withdrawn by the key. **2a** a metal rod or pin for fastening objects together. **b** a screw-bolt with a head suitable for turning with a spanner. **3** a rod or bar that closes the breech of a breech-loading firearm. **4** a roll of cloth or wallpaper of a standard length. **5a** a short stout blunt-headed arrow shot from a crossbow. **b** a lightning stroke; a thunderbolt. ✱ **bolt from the blue** a totally unexpected and typically unwelcome happening or development. **have shot one's bolt** *informal* to have used up the resources at one's command to no avail.

bolt[2] *v* **1** (*also* + for) to move rapidly; to dash. **2** to dart off or away; to flee. **3** of plants: to produce seed prematurely. **4** to secure (a door, etc) with a bolt. **5** to attach or fasten (one part of a machine, etc) to another with bolts. **6** to swallow (food) hastily or without chewing. ➤➤ **bolter** *n.*

bolt[3] *adv* rigidly.

bolt[4] *n* an escape attempt; a dash or run. ✱ **make a bolt for** to dash towards (a door, etc).

bolt-hole *n chiefly Brit* a means of rapid escape or place of refuge.

bolus *n* (*pl* **boluses**) **1** a large pill. **2** a soft mass of food that has been chewed but not swallowed. **3** a single dose of a drug.

bomb[1] *n* **1** an explosive or incendiary device, typically detonated by impact or a timing mechanism and usu dropped from aircraft, thrown or placed by hand, or fired from a mortar. **2** (**the bomb**) the atom bomb or hydrogen bomb, or nuclear weapons in general. ✱ **cost a bomb** *Brit, informal* to be very expensive. **go down a bomb** *Brit, informal* to be received enthusiastically. **go like a bomb** *informal* to go very fast. **make a bomb** *Brit, informal* to make a lot of money.

bomb[2] *v* **1** to drop bombs on (a place) or detonate a bomb in (a building, etc). **2** *informal* of a show, etc: to be a disastrous failure. **3** *Brit, informal* to go very fast.

bombard[1] *v* **1** to attack (a place or position) with heavy artillery or with bombs. **2** (*usu* + with) to direct an unremitting flow of questions or facts at. **3** to subject (a substance) to the impact of electrons, alpha rays, or other rapidly moving particles. ➤➤ **bombardment** *n.*

bombard[2] *n* a cannon used in late medieval times to hurl large stones.

bombardier *n* **1** a non-commissioned officer in the British artillery. **2** a US bomber-crew member who aims and releases the bombs.

bombardier beetle *n* a beetle that can detonate an acrid vapour in the form of a fine mist in the direction of a predator.

bombast *n* pretentious inflated speech or writing. ➤➤ **bombastic** *adj,* **bombastically** *adv.*

Bombay duck *n* a small fish found off S Asian coasts and eaten dried and salted with curry. Also called BUMMALO.

Bombay mix *n* a spicy snack of Indian origin, consisting of a mixture of nuts, lentils, etc.

bombazine *n* a silk fabric woven in twill weave and dyed black.

bombe /bomb/ *n* a frozen dessert made in a round or cone-shaped mould.

bombed *adj* **1** damaged or destroyed by bombs. **2** *informal* heavily under the influence of alcohol or drugs.

bomber *n* **1** an aircraft designed for dropping bombs. **2** somebody who throws or plants bombs. **3** *informal* a large cigarette containing cannabis.

bomber jacket *n* a short jacket with elasticated waistband and cuffs, usu with a zipped front.

bombinate *v literary* to buzz or drone.

bombora *n Aus* a dangerous reef, or the sea breaking over it.

bombshell *n* **1** an astounding or devastating occurrence or piece of news. **2** *informal* a stunning girl or woman.

bona fide /,bohnə 'fiedi/ *adj* genuine.

bona fides /,bohnə 'fiediz/ *n* **1** honest intentions; sincerity. **2** *informal* (*used as pl*) documentary evidence supporting one's claim to be a certain thing; one's credentials.

bonanza *n* **1** an exceptionally large and rich mass of ore in a mine. **2** widely enjoyed wealth or prosperity resulting from something proving unexpectedly profitable.

bonbon *n* a sweet.

bonce *n Brit, informal* the head.

bond[1] *n* **1** something, e.g. a fetter, that binds or restrains. **2** a force of attraction by means of which atoms, ions, or groups of atoms are held together in a molecule or crystal. **3a** an adhesive or cementing material. **b** the adhesion achieved between surfaces cemented together. **4** something that unites or binds. **5** a binding agreement, *esp*: **a** a legally enforceable agreement to pay. **b** a certificate of intention to pay the holder a specified sum, with or without other interest, on a specified date. **6a** the system of overlapping bricks in a wall. **b** a term used for any of the various patterns for overlapping bricks. ✱ **in bond** of dutiable goods: retained in a bonded warehouse pending payment of duty.

bond² *v* **1a** to stick or cause (surfaces) to stick firmly. **b** to hold (atoms) together in a molecule or crystal by chemical bonds. **2** to overlap (bricks, etc) for solidity of construction. **3** to put (goods) in bond until duties and taxes are paid. **4** of two people, *esp* a mother and newborn child: to form a strong close emotional bond.

bondage *n* **1** the tenure or service of a villein, serf, or slave. **2** slavery or serfdom. **3** a form of sexual gratification involving the physical restraint of one partner.

bonded *adj* **1** denoting items that are imported but held without payment of customs duty. **2** composed of two or more layers of fabric held together by an adhesive. **3** bound by a legal agreement.

bonded warehouse *n* a warehouse in which imported goods are retained awaiting payment of duty or re-export.

bond paper *n* writing paper of superior quality.

bondsman *n* (*pl* **bondsmen**) **1** somebody who is legally responsible for the payment of a bond. **2** a slave or serf.

bone¹ *n* **1a** the rigid material, made up largely of calcium salts, of which the adult skeleton of most vertebrate animals is chiefly composed. **b** any of the hard structures consisting of this, that together compose the skeleton. **2a** baleen, ivory, or another hard substance resembling bone. **b** any structure composed of this. **3** a strip of whalebone or steel used to stiffen a corset or dress. ✱ **feel in one's bones** to know (something) instinctively or intuitively. **have a bone to pick with** *informal* to have a cause of complaint against (somebody), calling for mutual discussion and settlement. **make no bones about** to have no hesitation in (doing or saying something potentially embarrassing or hurtful). **near/close to the bone** of a remark: risqué, indecent, or too close to the truth. **on the bone** of meat: with the bones left in it. **to the bone** reduced to the essentials. ⋙ **boneless** *adj.*

bone² *v* to remove the bones from (fish or meat).

bone china *n* a type of translucent and durable white hard-paste porcelain.

bone-dry *adj* containing no moisture; completely or excessively dry.

bonehead *n informal* a stupid person.

bone-idle *adj* lazy through and through.

bone meal *n* fertilizer or feed made of crushed or ground bone.

boner *n* **1** *informal* an embarrassing blunder; a howler. **2** *chiefly NAm, coarse slang* a penile erection.

bone-shaker *n Brit, informal* **1** an early bicycle with solid tyres. **2** an old vehicle.

bone up *v informal* (+ on) to try to master necessary information in a short time, *esp* for a special purpose.

bonfire *n* a large fire built in the open air.

Bonfire Night *n* = GUY FAWKES NIGHT.

bongo *n* (*pl* **-os** *or* **-oes**) either of a pair of small tuned drums played with the hands.

bonhomie /ˈbonəmee, bonəˈmee/ *n* good-natured friendliness.

bonito /bəˈneetoh/ *n* (*pl* **-os**) a medium-sized tuna with dark stripes.

bonk¹ *v informal* **1** to hit, usu not very hard. **2** *Brit* to have sexual intercourse with.

bonk² *n informal* **1** a light blow or hit. **2** *Brit* an act of sexual intercourse.

bonkers *adj Brit, informal* mad or crazy.

bon mot /ˌbon ˈmoh/ *n* (*pl* **bons mots**) a witticism.

bonnet *n* **1** a cloth or straw hat for a woman or child, tied under the chin. **2** *chiefly Scot* a soft brimless cap. **3** *Brit* the hinged metal covering over the engine of a motor vehicle. ⋙ **bonneted** *adj.*

bonny *adj* (**-ier, -iest**) *chiefly Scot, N Eng* **1** attractive or comely. **2** substantial; considerable. ⋙ **bonnily** *adv,* **bonniness** *n.*

bonsai /ˈbonsie/ *n* (*pl* **bonsai**) the art of growing dwarfed varieties of trees.

bonus *n* (*pl* **bonuses**) **1** something given in addition to what is usual or strictly due. **2** *chiefly Brit* an extra dividend distributed to shareholders out of profits. **3** money or an equivalent given in addition to an employee's usual remuneration, usu for good performance. **4** an unlooked-for and welcome plus or extra.

bon vivant /ˌbonh veeˈvonh/ *n* (*pl* **bon vivants** *or* **bons vivants**) a person with cultivated and refined tastes, *esp* in regard to food and drink.

bon viveur /ˌbonh veeˈvuh/ *n* (*pl* **bon viveurs** *or* **bons viveurs**) *chiefly Brit* = BON VIVANT.

bon voyage /bon vwahˈyahj, -ˈyahzh/ *interj* said to somebody embarking on a journey: farewell.

bony *adj* (**-ier, -iest**) **1** consisting of or resembling bone. **2a** full of bones. **b** having large or prominent bones. **3** skinny or scrawny. ⋙ **boniness** *n.*

bony fish *n* a fish with a bony rather than a cartilaginous skeleton such as the salmon, carp, herring, etc.

bonzer *adj Aus, NZ, informal* excellent; especially good.

boo¹ *interj* used to express contempt or disapproval or to startle or frighten.

boo² *v* (**boos, booed, booing**) to show scorn or disapproval by shouting 'boo!'.

boob¹ *n* **1** *Brit, informal* a stupid mistake; a blunder. **2** *NAm* a stupid person.

boob² *v Brit, informal* to make a stupid mistake.

boob³ *n informal* a woman's breast.

booboo *n* (*pl* **-os**) *informal* an embarrassing blunder.

boob tube¹ *n informal* a woman's tube-like garment made of stretchy material.

boob tube² *n NAm, informal* a television set.

booby¹ *n* (*pl* **-ies**) **1** *informal* an awkward foolish person. **2** a small gannet of tropical seas with brightly coloured feet.

booby² *n* (*pl* **-ies**) *informal* a woman's breast.

booby prize *n* an award for the poorest performance in a contest.

booby trap *n* **1** a trap for the unwary or unsuspecting. **2** a harmless-looking object concealing an explosive device that is set to explode by remote control or if touched.

booby-trap *v* (**booby-trapped, booby-trapping**) to set a booby trap in or on.

boodle *n informal* money, *esp* when stolen or used for bribery.

boogie¹ *n* **1** = BOOGIE-WOOGIE. **2** *informal* a dance to rock music.

boogie² *v* (**boogies, boogied, boogieing**) *informal* to dance to rock music.

boogie board *n* a type of short surfboard that the rider can lie on.

boogie-woogie *n* a style of playing blues on the piano characterized by a steady rhythmic bass and a simple, often improvised, melody.

boohai /boo'hie/ ✻ **up the boohai** *NZ, informal* completely lost or astray.

book[1] *n* **1** a set of written, printed, lined, or blank sheets bound together. **2** a long written or printed composition, *esp* a literary one. **3** a major division of a treatise or literary work. **4** (*in pl*) journals, ledgers, etc recording business accounts. **5** (**the Book**) the Bible. **6** a small folder containing a quantity of stamps, tickets, matches, etc, for detaching as required for use. **7** the bets registered by a bookmaker. **8** the number of tricks a card player or side must win before any trick can have scoring value. ✻ **bring to book** to punish or reprimand (an offender). **by the book** by following previously laid down instructions and not using personal initiative. **in my book** in my opinion. **in somebody's good/bad books** in favour or disfavour with somebody. **on the books** included in a list of clients, members, or employees. **take a leaf out of somebody's book** to copy or imitate somebody's behaviour. **throw the book at 1** to charge (a misdoer) with all the offences that can be found. **2** to reprimand severely or comprehensively.

book[2] *v* **1a** to reserve (seats, tickets, accommodation, etc) in advance. **b** to hire the services of (an organization, etc) in advance. **2a** of a police officer, etc: to take the name of (a driver, etc) with a view to prosecution. **b** to enter the name of (a rugby or football player) in a book for a violation of the rules, usu involving foul play. ➤➤ **booker** *n*, **booking** *n*.

bookable *adj* **1** *chiefly Brit* of theatre seats, tickets, etc: that may be reserved in advance. **2** of an offence in football or rugby: that makes a player liable to be booked by a referee.

bookbinding *n* the craft or trade of binding books. ➤➤ **bookbinder** *n*.

bookcase *n* a piece of furniture consisting of a set of shelves to hold books.

book club *n* an association that offers books to its members at a discount.

bookend *n* a support placed at the end of a row of books.

bookie *n informal* a bookmaker.

book in *v* **1** to reserve a room at a hotel. **2** to register one's arrival somewhere, *esp* at a hotel.

bookish *adj* **1** fond of reading and studying. **2** of language: literary as opposed to colloquial. ➤➤ **bookishly** *adv*, **bookishness** *n*.

bookkeeper *n* a person who records the accounts or transactions of a business. ➤➤ **bookkeeping** *n*.

booklet *n* a small book with a paper cover and comparatively few pages, usu containing information about a particular subject; a pamphlet.

bookmaker *n* a person who determines odds and receives and pays off bets. ➤➤ **bookmaking** *n*.

bookmark *n* **1** a strip of card or leather, or a similar device, used to mark a place in a book. **2** a computing facility whereby the address of a file, web page, etc is recorded for quick future access.

bookplate *n* a label placed inside the cover of a book, bearing the owner's name.

book token *n Brit* a gift token exchangeable for books.

book value *n* the value of a company's buildings, machinery, vehicles, etc that is recognized by the government for accounting and tax purposes, allowing for depreciation: compare MARKET VALUE.

bookworm *n informal* a person unusually fond of reading and study.

Boolean *adj* relating to or denoting a system in logic that symbolically represents certain relationships between entities, e.g. sets, propositions, or states of computer logic circuits.

boom[1] *n* **1** a booming sound or cry. **2a** the rapid expansion and development of a town or region. **b** a rapid and widespread expansion of economic activity. ✻ **boom and bust** over-rapid commercial expansion followed by collapse.

boom[2] *v* **1** to make a deep hollow sound or cry. **2** to experience a rapid increase in activity or market success.

boom[3] *n* **1** a spar at the foot of the mainsail in a fore-and-aft rig that is attached at its fore end to the mast. **2** a long movable arm used to manipulate a microphone. **3** a floating barrier across a river or enclosing an area of water, e.g. to keep logs together, confine an oil spill, etc. **4** a cable or line of spars extended across a river or the mouth of a harbour as a barrier to navigation.

boomerang[1] *n* a bent piece of wood shaped so that it returns to its thrower, used by Australian aboriginals as a hunting weapon.

boomerang[2] *v* of a plan: to recoil on the utterer or originator, *esp* with unpleasant effects.

boon *n* **1** a timely benefit; a blessing. **2** *archaic* a benefit or favour.

boon companion *n* a close and congenial friend.

boondocks *pl n NAm, informal* **1** (**the boondocks**) rough country filled with dense brush. **2** (**the boondocks**) a remote or rural area.

boondoggle[1] *n NAm, informal* a trivial, time-wasting, or dishonest task.

boondoggle[2] *v NAm, informal* to engage in trivial or money-wasting tasks so as to appear busy.

boonies *pl n* (**the boonies**) *NAm, informal* = BOONDOCKS.

boor *n* a coarse or insensitive person. ➤➤ **boorish** *adj*, **boorishly** *adv*, **boorishness** *n*.

boost[1] *v* **1** to increase or raise the level of. **2** to encourage or give a fillip to (somebody's pride, confidence, or morale). **3a** to increase (a physical quantity, e.g. voltage). **b** to amplify (an electrical signal). **4** to push (somebody) from behind or below to help them.

boost[2] *n* **1** an increase in amount. **2** an upward thrust, a fillip. **3** a push from below or behind to assist progress.

booster *n* **1** (*also* **booster shot**) a supplementary dose of vaccine increasing or renewing the effectiveness of an earlier dose. **2** an auxiliary engine which assists a rocket or spacecraft at take-off by providing a large thrust for a short time. **3** a device that increases voltage or amplifies an electrical signal.

boot[1] *n* **1** a piece of footwear that extends above the ankle, sometimes up to the knee. **2** *informal* a kick. **3** *Brit* the luggage compartment of a motor car. ✻ **get the boot** *informal* to get the sack. **give somebody the boot** *informal* to sack somebody. **put the boot in** *chiefly Brit, informal* to kick somebody or treat them cruelly or unfairly, *esp* when they are already in a vulnerable position. **the boot is on the other foot** the situation is the other way round. ➤➤ **booted** *adj*.

boot[2] *v* **1** to kick (somebody). **2** *informal* (+ out) to eject or discharge (a person) summarily. **3** = BOOT UP. ➤➤ **bootable** *adj*.

boot[3] ✻ **to boot** besides; as well.

bootblack *n* formerly, a person who cleaned and shone shoes.

bootboy *n informal* a rowdy or violent youth, *esp* one wearing heavy boots.

boot camp *n NAm* a basic training camp for recruits to the navy and marines.

bootee *or* **bootie** *n* **1** an infant's boot-shaped sock. **2** a short boot.

booth *n* **1** a stall or stand for the sale or exhibition of goods. **2** a small enclosure affording privacy, e.g. for telephoning, vote-casting, etc.

bootie *n* see BOOTEE.

bootlace *n Brit* a long stout shoelace.

bootleg[1] *adj* **1** of alcoholic drink or recordings: smuggled or illegally produced. **2** of trousers: having legs that flare slightly at the bottom, for wearing over boots. ➤➤ **bootleg** *n.*

bootleg[2] *v* (**bootlegged, bootlegging**) **1** to manufacture, sell, or transport for sale (alcoholic drink, etc) contrary to law. **2** to record, reproduce, or sell (popular music) without authorization. ➤➤ **bootlegger** *n*, **bootlegging** *n.*

bootless *adj archaic* useless or unprofitable.

bootlick *v informal* to attempt to gain favour by a cringing or flattering manner. ➤➤ **bootlicker** *n.*

bootstrap *n* **1** a looped tab at the back of a boot, used for pulling the boot on with. **2** the procedure of starting up a computer in such a way that its operating programs load automatically. ✱ **pull oneself up by one's bootstraps** to improve one's lot through one's own efforts.

boot up *v* to start up (a computer).

booty *n* (*pl* **-ies**) **1** plunder taken, e.g. in war. **2** a rich gain or prize.

booze[1] *n informal* intoxicating drink, *esp* spirits.

booze[2] *v informal* to drink intoxicating liquor to excess.

boozer *n informal* **1** a person who drinks excessively. **2** *Brit* a public house.

booze-up *n informal* a drunken party or a drinking spree.

boozy *adj* (**-ier, -iest**) *informal* **1** characterized by much intake of alcohol. **2** given to drinking heavily. ➤➤ **boozily** *adv.*

bop[1] *n chiefly Brit, informal* **1** a dance to popular music. **2** a disco or dance.

bop[2] *v* (**bopped, bopping**) *informal* to dance to popular music. ➤➤ **bopper** *n.*

bop[3] *n* = BEBOP.

bop[4] *v* (**bopped, bopping**) *informal* to punch smartly.

bop[5] *n informal* a punch.

bora *n* a violent cold northerly wind of the Adriatic.

boracic *adj* **1** = BORIC. **2** *Brit, informal* penniless; = SKINT.

borage *n* a coarse hairy blue-flowered European herb.

borax *n* natural or synthetic hydrated sodium borate used *esp* as a flux, cleansing agent, and water-softener.

Bordeaux /baw'doh/ *n* (*pl* **Bordeaux**) a red or white wine of the Bordeaux region of France.

bordello *n* (*pl* **-os**) *chiefly NAm* a brothel.

border[1] *n* **1** an outer part or edge. **2** a boundary or frontier. **3** a narrow bed of planted ground, e.g. beside a path. **4** an ornamental design at the edge of something, e.g. printed matter, fabric, or a rug.

border[2] *v* **1** to form a border along the edge of. **2** of a country or region: to adjoin (another country or region). **3** (+ on) to be close to a feeling or state.

borderer *n* a person who lives in a border area between two countries.

borderline *adj* **1** verging on one or other place, stake, or concept without being definitely assignable to either. **2** not quite meeting accepted standards, e.g. of morality or good taste.

border line *n* a line of demarcation.

bore[1] *v* **1** to make (a hole) in something using a drill. **2** to hollow out (a gun barrel). ➤➤ **borer** *n.*

bore[2] *n* **1a** an interior cylindrical cavity. **b** the barrel of a gun. **2a** the size of a hole. **b** the interior diameter of a tube; calibre.

bore[3] *n* a tedious person, situation, or thing.

bore[4] *v* to weary (somebody) by being dull or monotonous. ➤➤ **bored** *adj*, **boring** *adj.*

bore[5] *n* a tidal flood that moves swiftly in the form of a steep-fronted wave up an estuary, etc.

bore[6] *v* past tense of BEAR[2].

Boreal *adj* relating to the coniferous forest belt growing in northern and mountainous parts of the northern hemisphere.

boredom *n* the state of being bored.

borehole *n* a hole drilled in the earth to obtain water, oil, etc.

boric *adj* relating to or containing boron.

boric acid *n* a white crystalline solid acid used *esp* as a weak antiseptic.

boride *n* a binary compound of boron, usu with a more electropositive element or radical.

borlotti bean *n* a speckled pink kidney bean that turns brown when cooked.

born *adj* **1a** brought into existence by, or as if by, birth. **b** (*used in combinations*) by birth; native: *British-born.* **2** having a specified character, situation, or destiny from birth. **3** (+ of) resulting from (e.g. a feeling or cause): *wisdom born of experience.* ✱ **born and bred** by birth and training; through and through. **never in all my born days** never in my whole life. **not born yesterday** sufficiently knowing about the ways of the world.

born-again *adj* having undergone a conversion, *esp* to evangelical Christianity.

borne[1] *v* past part. of BEAR[2].

borne[2] *adj* (*used in combinations*) carried by something specified: *airborne.*

Bornean *n* a native or inhabitant of Borneo. ➤➤ **Bornean** *adj.*

boron *n* a metalloid chemical element found in nature only in combination.

boronia *n* a sweet-scented Australian shrub, cultivated for the cut-flower trade.

borough *n* **1** an urban area in Britain with powers of local self-government granted by royal charter. **2** any of the local-government areas that together with the City of London comprise Greater London. **3** a municipal corporation in certain states of the USA. **4** any of the five political divisions of New York City.

borrow *v* **1a** to take or receive (something) with the implied or expressed intention of returning it to its owner or the place where it belongs. **b** to get (a sum of money) from a bank, etc, under an arrangement to pay it back, usu with interest. **2a** to appropriate or adopt for a temporary period. **b** to take (ideas, etc) from somebody else. **c** to introduce (words from another language) into one's own. **3** in arithmetic, to take (one) from the number of the next highest power of ten when the number being subtracted from is less than the number to be subtracted. ✱ **living on borrowed time** continuing to live in spite of being terminally ill. ➤➤ **borrower** *n.*

Usage note
See note at LEND.

borscht *or* **borsch** *n* a soup of Russian origin, made primarily from beetroots and served hot or cold, often with sour cream.

Borstal *n Brit* formerly, a penal institution providing training for young offenders.

borzoi /'bawzoy, baw'zoy/ *n* a dog of a large long-haired breed developed in Russia.

bosh *n informal* nonsense.

bosky *adj* (**-ier, -iest**) *literary* full of trees; wooded.

bo's'n *n* see BOATSWAIN.

Bosnian *n* a native or inhabitant of Bosnia. ➤➤ **Bosnian** *adj.*

bosom *n* **1** the front of the human chest; *esp* the female breasts. **2** the breast considered as the centre of secret thoughts and emotions. **3** the deep heart or centre of something. ✱ **in the bosom of one's family** safely surrounded by one's loved ones.

bosom companion *n* = BOSOM FRIEND.

bosom friend *n* an intimate friend.

bosomy *adj* having large breasts.

boson *n* a particle, e.g. a photon, meson, or alpha particle, whose spin is either zero or an integral number.

boss[1] *n informal* a person who exercises control or authority; *specif* somebody who directs or supervises workers.

boss[2] *v informal* **1** to act as director or supervisor of (the staff of an organization, etc). **2** (*usu* + about/around) to give orders to in a domineering manner.

boss[3] *adj NAm, informal* first-rate or excellent.

boss[4] *n* **1** a stud or knob projecting from the centre of a shield. **2** a carved ornament concealing the intersection of the ribs of a vault or panelled ceiling. **3** the enlarged part of a shaft, on which a wheel is mounted. **4** the middle part of a propeller.

bossa nova *n* a Brazilian dance similar to the samba.

boss-eyed *adj Brit, informal* having a squint; cross-eyed.

bossy *adj* (**-ier, -iest**) *informal* domineering or dictatorial. ➤➤ **bossily** *adv,* **bossiness** *n.*

bossyboots *n Brit, informal* a bossy or domineering person.

bosun *n* see BOATSWAIN.

bot *n* a computer program that runs automatically, used for example as a labour-saving tool for getting information from data.

botanic *adj* = BOTANICAL.

botanical *adj* relating to plants or botany. ➤➤ **botanically** *adv.*

botanic garden *n* (*also in pl*) a place in which plant collections are grown for display and scientific study.

botany *n* a branch of biology dealing with plant life. ➤➤ **botanist** *n.*

botch[1] *v informal* **1** to repair, patch, or assemble in a makeshift or inept way. **2** to foul up or bungle hopelessly. ➤➤ **botcher** *n.*

botch[2] *n informal* something botched; a mess.

botel *n* see BOATEL.

both[1] *adj* being the two; affecting or involving the one as well as the other. ✱ **have it both ways** to exploit or profit from each of a pair of contradictory positions, circumstances, etc, or to maintain two contradictory views simultaneously.

both[2] *pron* the one as well as the other.

both[3] *conj* used to indicate and stress the inclusion of each of two things specified by coordinated words or word groups.

bother[1] *v* **1** to disturb, pester, or distract. **2** to cause to be troubled or perplexed. **3** to cause (somebody) discomfort or pain. **4** (*usu in negative contexts*) to take the trouble to do something. **5** (*usu in negative contexts*) to concern oneself about something.

bother[2] *n* **1** trouble, *esp* involving violence. **2** difficulty or problems. **3** unnecessary fuss or effort. **4** something that is a nuisance or requires a lot of attention.

bother[3] *interj* (*also* **bother it**) used as a mild expression of annoyance.

bothersome *adj* causing bother; annoying.

bothy *n* (*pl* **-ies**) *Scot* **1** a small outbuilding on a farm which formerly provided accommodation for farmworkers. **2** a small hut in the mountains which provides shelter for mountaineers and hill-walkers.

bo tree *n* the pipal tree.

botrytis *n* a rot-causing fungus which is encouraged to form on grapes used for certain wines; = NOBLE ROT.

Botswanan *n* a native or inhabitant of Botswana. ➤➤ **Botswanan** *adj.*

bottle[1] *n* **1** a rigid or semirigid container, *esp* for liquids, usu of glass or plastic, with a comparatively narrow neck or mouth. **2** *Brit, informal* courage. ✱ **hit the bottle** *informal* to start drinking alcohol heavily.

bottle[2] *v* **1** to put (liquid, *esp* wine or milk) into a bottle. **2** *Brit* to preserve (fruit, etc) by storage in glass jars. ✱ **bottle it** *Brit, informal* to lose one's nerve; = BOTTLE OUT.

bottle bank *n* a large container in which people can deposit empty glass bottles for recycling.

bottlebrush *n* **1** a brush with a cylindrical head for cleaning bottles. **2** an Australasian shrub of the eucalyptus family with spikes of brightly coloured, *esp* red, flowers.

bottle-feed *v* (*past tense and past part.* **bottle-fed**) to feed (an infant) by means of a bottle.

bottle-green *adj* of a very dark green colour. ➤➤ **bottle green** *n.*

bottleneck *n* **1** the neck of a bottle. **2** a narrow stretch of road where the flow of traffic is impeded, so that frequent hold-ups result.

bottle out *v Brit, informal* to lose one's nerve and back out of a plan, challenge, etc.

bottle up *v* to confine or restrain (one's emotions).

bottom[1] *n* **1a** the underside of something. **b** a surface on which something rests. **c** *chiefly Brit* the buttocks or rump. **2a** the lowest, deepest, or farthest part or place. **b** the lowest position or last place in order of precedence. **c** (*also in pl*) the lower part of a two-piece garment. ✱ **at bottom** basically, really. **be at the bottom of** to be the real cause of (a situation, problem, etc). **bottoms up!** *informal* used as a toast before starting to drink: cheers! **from the bottom of one's heart** with fervent sincerity. **get to the bottom of** to find out the truth, source, or basis of (a situation, problem, etc). **the bottom falls out of the market, etc** the market, etc collapses suddenly.

bottom[2] *v* **1** of a submarine: to reach the sea bed. **2** *Aus, NZ* to excavate (a mine) to the depth of the mineral-bearing strata.

bottom[3] *adj* relating to or situated at the bottom or lower part of something. ➤➤ **bottommost** *adj.*

bottom drawer *n Brit, dated* a young woman's collection of clothes and household articles, kept in anticipation of her marriage.

bottomless *adj* **1** extremely deep. **2** boundless or unlimited.

bottom line *n* **1** (**the bottom line**) the last line of figures in a financial report showing the final profit or loss. **2** (**the bottom line**) *informal* the one important criterion that decides viability.

bottom out *v* of a situation: to sink to a lowest point and then level out.

botty *n* (*pl* **-ies**) *Brit, informal* the bottom or buttocks.

botulism *n* acute, often fatal, food poisoning caused by a toxin in food, *esp* incompletely sterilized food preserved in an airtight container.

bouclé /'boohklay/ *n* an uneven yarn of three plies, one of which forms loops at intervals.

boudoir /'boohdwah/ *n* a woman's dressing room, bedroom, or private sitting room.

bouffant[1] /'boohfong/ *adj* puffed out: *bouffant hair; bouffant sleeves.*

bouffant[2] *n* a bouffant hairstyle.

bougainvillea *or* **bougainvillaea** *n* an ornamental tropical climbing plant with brilliant purple or red floral bracts.

bough *n* a main branch of a tree.

bought *v* past tense and past part. of BUY[1].

bouillabaisse /booh·yə'bes/ *n* a highly seasoned fish stew made with at least two kinds of fish.

bouillon /'boohyong/ *n* a thin clear soup made usu from lean beef.

boulder *n* a large stone or mass of rock. ➤➤ **bouldery** *adj.*

boulder clay *n* a glacial deposit of pebbles, rock, etc in clay.

boule *n* (*also in pl, used as sing.*) an orig French game similar to bowls in which metal balls are thrown or rolled.

boulevard *n* a broad avenue, usu lined by trees.

boulle *n* see BUHL.

bounce[1] *v* **1** to cause (a ball, etc) to rebound. **2** to rebound after striking the ground or other surface. **3** to move violently, noisily, or with a springing step. **4** *informal* to return (a cheque) as not good because of lack of funds in the payer's account. **5** *informal* of a cheque: to be returned by a bank as not good. **6** *Brit, informal* to coerce into doing something. **7** *chiefly NAm, informal* to dismiss; fire. ✱ **bounce something off somebody** *informal* to see what somebody's reactions are to an idea, etc.

bounce[2] *n* **1a** a sudden leap or bound. **b** a rebound. **2** verve, liveliness. **3** the quality of bouncing well; springiness.

bounce back *v* to recover quickly from a blow or defeat.

bouncer *n* a person employed in a nightclub or other public place to restrain or remove disorderly people.

bouncing *adj* enjoying good health; robust: *a bouncing baby.*

bouncy *adj* (**-ier, -iest**) **1** that bounces readily. **2** buoyant; exuberant. ➤➤ **bouncily** *adv,* **bounciness** *n.*

bouncy castle *n* a large inflatable play structure with a base and sides, typically in the shape of a castle, set up outdoors for children to jump around on.

bound[1] *adj* (*also used in combinations*) going or intending to go somewhere specified: *bound for home; the northbound carriageway.*

bound[2] *n* (*usu in pl, used as sing. or pl*) **1** a limiting line; a boundary. **2** something that limits or restrains. ✱ **out of bounds 1** outside the permitted limits. **2** of the ball in team sport, etc: outside the area of play.

bound[3] *v* (*usu in passive*) **1** to set limits to. **2** to form the boundary of (a country, region, etc).

bound[4] *adj* **1a** (*usu used in combinations*) confined to a place: *house-bound.* **b** certain or sure (to do something). **2** (*also used in combinations*) placed under legal or moral obligation (to do something): *We are duty-bound to assist him.* ✱ **bound up with** closely connected with or dependent on (something). **I'll be bound** I bet; I'll warrant. **I'm bound to say** I must admit.

bound[5] *n* **1** a leap or jump. **2** a bounce.

bound[6] *v* **1** to move by leaping. **2** to rebound or bounce.

bound[7] *v* past tense and past part. of BIND[1].

boundary *n* (*pl* **-ies**) **1** something, *esp* a dividing line, that indicates or fixes a limit or extent. **2** a border or frontier. **3** a stroke in cricket that sends the ball over the limits of the field, or the score of four or six made by this.

bounden ✱ **bounden duty** an obligatory or binding responsibility.

bounder *n Brit, dated, informal* a man who behaves badly; a cad.

boundless *adj* limitless. ➤➤ **boundlessly** *adv,* **boundlessness** *n.*

bounteous *adj* giving or given freely. ➤➤ **bounteously** *adv,* **bounteousness** *n.*

bountiful *adj* **1** generous; liberal. **2** abundant; plentiful. ➤➤ **bountifully** *adv.*

bounty *n* (*pl* **-ies**) **1** a financial inducement or reward, *esp* when offered by a government for an act or service, e.g. for the capture of a criminal or outlaw, or the killing of unwanted animals. **2** *literary* something given generously. **3** *literary* generosity.

bounty-hunter *n* a person who tracks down outlaws or wanted criminals for a reward.

bouquet *n* **1** a bunch of flowers fastened together. **2** a distinctive and characteristic fragrance, e.g. of wine.

bouquet garni /'gahni/ *n* a small bunch of herbs, e.g. thyme, parsley, and a bay leaf, for use in flavouring stews and soups.

bourbon *n* **1** a whisky distilled from a mash made up of not less than 51% maize plus malt and rye. **2** *Brit* a chocolate-flavoured biscuit with a filling of chocolate cream.

bourgeois[1] /'booəzhwah, 'bawzhwah/ *n* (*pl* **bourgeois**) **1** a middle-class person. **2** (*in pl*) the bourgeoisie.

bourgeois[2] *adj* **1** middle-class. **2** characterized by a narrow-minded concern for material interests and respectability. **3** capitalist.

bourgeoisie /booəzhwah'zee/ *n* (*used as sing. or pl*) the middle class.

bourn[1] *n* a small stream.

bourn[2] *or* **bourne** *n literary* **1** a boundary or limit. **2** a goal or destination.

bourrée /'booray/ *n* **1** a 17th-cent. French dance usu in duple time. **2** in ballet, a series of small steps with the feet close together.

bourse *n* a stock exchange of continental Europe.

bout *n* **1** a spell of activity. **2** a boxing or wrestling match. **3** an outbreak or attack of illness, fever, etc.

boutique *n* a small fashionable shop selling specialized goods, *esp* clothes, or a small shop within a large department store.

bouzouki /boo'zoohki/ *n* (*pl* **bouzoukis**) a long-necked Greek stringed musical instrument that resembles a mandolin.

bovine[1] *adj* **1** relating to cattle. **2** like an ox or cow, e.g. in being slow, stolid, or dull. ➤➤ **bovinely** *adv.*

bovine[2] *n* an ox or related animal.

bovine spongiform encephalopathy *n* see BSE.

Bovril *n trademark* a concentrated beef extract.

bovver *n Brit, informal* rowdy or violent disturbance.

bow[1] *v* **1** to submit or yield to something or somebody. **2** (*also* + down) to bend the head, body, or knee in respect, submission, or greeting. ✱ **bow and scrape** to act in an obsequious manner.

bow[2] *n* a bending of the head or body in respect, submission, or greeting. ✱ **take a bow** to acknowledge applause or praise.

bow[3] *n* **1** a weapon for shooting arrows, consisting of a strip of wood, fibreglass, or other flexible material held bent by a strong cord connecting the two ends. **2** a knot that can be pulled undone, tied with two loops and two free ends, used for shoelaces, etc. **3** an implement for playing a violin, etc consisting of a resilient wooden rod with horsehairs stretched from end to end.

bow[4] *v* **1a** to bend or curve, or cause to bend into a curve. **b** (*also* + down) to weigh down or oppress. **2** to play (a stringed instrument) with a bow.

bow[5] *n* (*also in pl*) the forward part of a ship. ✱ **shot across the bows** a gesture intended as a sharp warning.

bowdlerize *or* **-ise** *v* to expurgate (a book, etc) by omitting or modifying parts considered too indecent or offensive for family reading.

bowel *n* **1a** (*in pl*) the intestines. **b** the large intestine or the small intestine. **2** (*in pl*) the innermost parts of something.

bowel movement *n* the action of discharging faeces from the body; defecation.

bower *n* **1** an attractive dwelling or retreat. **2** a shelter made e.g. in a garden with tree boughs or vines twisted together. **3** *literary* a boudoir.

bowerbird *n* a songbird of Australia and New Guinea, the male of which builds a bower-like chamber or passage arched over with twigs and grasses, often adorned with bright-coloured feathers and shells, to attract the female.

bow-fronted *n* having an outward curving front.

bowie knife *n* a stout hunting knife with a sharpened part on the back edge curved concavely to the point.

bowl[1] *n* **1** a round hollow vessel used *esp* for holding liquids or food or for mixing food. **2a** the hollow of a spoon or tobacco pipe. **b** the receptacle of a toilet. **3a** a bowl-shaped geographical region or formation. **b** *NAm* a bowl-shaped structure; *esp* a sports stadium.

bowl[2] *n* **1** a ball used in bowls that is weighted or shaped to give it a bias. **2** a ball used in skittles or tenpin bowling. **3** (*in pl, used as sing.*) a game played typically outdoors on a green, in which bowls are rolled at a target jack in an attempt to bring them nearer to it than one's opponent's bowls.

bowl[3] *v* **1a** to roll (a ball) in bowling. **b** to score by bowling. **2a** to deliver (a ball) to a batsman in cricket. **b** of a bowler: to dismiss (a batsman in cricket) by breaking the wicket. **3** (*often* + along) to in a vehicle smoothly and rapidly.

bowlegged *adj* having legs that are bowed outwards at the knees; bandy-legged.

bowler[1] *n* the person who bowls in a team sport; *specif* in cricket, a member of the fielding side who bowls regularly as a specialist.

bowler[2] *n* (*also* **bowler hat**) a stiff felt hat with a rounded crown and a narrow brim.

bowline *n* **1** a rope attached to a square sail that is used to keep the windward edge of the sail taut and at a steady angle to the wind. **2** a knot used to form a non-slipping loop at the end of a rope.

bowling *n* any of several games in which balls are rolled at one or more objects.

bowling alley *n* a long narrow enclosure or lane with a smooth floor for bowling or playing skittles.

bowling green *n* a smooth close-cut area of turf for playing bowls.

bowl out *v* to dismiss all the members of (the batting side) in cricket.

bowl over *v* **1** to bump into, or cause something to bump into (a person) so as to knock them down. **2** *informal* to overwhelm with surprise.

bow out *v* to retire or withdraw.

bowser *n* **1a** a tanker for refuelling aircraft. **b** any tanker delivering fuel. **2** *Aus* a petrol pump.

bowsprit *n* a spar projecting forward from the bow of a ship.

Bow-Street runner *n* a member of a police force in London in the early 19th cent.

bow tie *n* a short tie fastened in a bow, *esp* a small black one for use with formal evening dress.

bow window *n* a curved bay window.

bowyer *n* a person who makes or sells bows for archery.

box[1] *n* **1** a rigid container, typically rectangular, having sides, a bottom, and usu a lid. **2** (**the box**) *chiefly Brit, informal* television. **3** a small compartment, e.g. for a group of spectators in a theatre, for transporting a horse, or for housing a public telephone, etc. **4** a square or oblong division or storage compartment. **5** = POST OFFICE BOX. **6** a shield to protect the genitals, worn *esp* by batsmen and wicket-keepers in cricket. **7** a square or rectangle containing, or to be filled in with, information, e.g. on a proforma, or on a computer screen. **8** a grid marked out on the road, e.g. at a junction, for guiding traffic. **9** = PENALTY AREA.

box[2] *v* **1** (*often* + up) to enclose in a box. **2** (+ in) **a** to build a box round (pipes, etc). **b** to enclose or confine; to hem in. ✱ **box the compass** to name the 32 points of the compass in their order.

box[3] *v* **1** to engage in boxing. **2** to slap (somebody's ears) with the hand. ✱ **box clever** *Brit, informal* to outdo an opponent by cunning.

box[4] *n* a punch or slap, *esp* on the ear.

box[5] *n* an evergreen shrub or small tree used *esp* for hedges.

boxcar *n NAm* an enclosed goods wagon on a train.

boxer[1] *n* a person who engages in the sport of boxing.

boxer[2] *n* a dog of a breed having a compact medium-sized body, short hair, and a flat pug-like face.

boxer shorts *pl n* men's loose-fitting underpants.

box girder *n* a hollow rectangular girder.

boxing *n* the art of attack and defence with the fists, practised as a sport.

Boxing Day *n* 26 December, observed as a public holiday in Britain.

box junction *n* a road junction at which a pattern of crosshatched yellow lines on the road warns the road-user not to enter until their exit is clear.

box number *n* the number of a box or pigeon hole at a newspaper or post office where arrangements are made for replies to advertisements or other mail to be sent.

box office *n* an office, e.g. in a theatre, where tickets of admission are sold.

box pleat *n* a pleat made by forming two folded edges, one facing right and the other left.

boxroom *n Brit* a small storage room in a house.

boxy *adj* (**-ier, -iest**) **1** resembling a box; box-like. **2** of clothing, *esp* a jacket: square-cut; chunky. **3** of a room: cramped or poky.

boy[1] *n* **1** a male child from birth to puberty. **2** (**the boys**) *informal* a man's male friends, work colleagues, team mates, etc. ➤➤ **boyhood** *n,* **boyish** *adj,* **boyishly** *adv,* **boyishness** *n.*

boy[2] *interj* (*also* **oh boy**) *chiefly NAm* an exclamation of surprise, delight, excitement, etc.

boyar *n* a member of the pre-imperial Russian aristocracy.

boycott[1] *v* to engage in a concerted refusal to have dealings with (a person, shop, organization, etc) or buy (certain goods), usu to express disapproval or to force acceptance of certain conditions.

boycott[2] *n* an act of boycotting.

boyfriend *n* a frequent or regular male companion; a male lover.

Boyle's law *n* a law in chemistry: the volume of a fixed mass of gas is inversely proportional to the pressure at a constant temperature.

boyo *n* (*pl* **-os**) *Irish and Welsh, informal* a boy or lad.

Boy Scout *n dated* a Scout.

boysenberry *n* (*pl* **-ies**) a large raspberry-like fruit.

bozo *n* (*pl* **-os**) *NAm, informal* a thick-witted person.

BP *abbr* **1** used after dates, *esp* in geology and archaeology: before the present. **2** blood pressure. **3** British Petroleum.

Bq *abbr* becquerel.

Br *abbr* the chemical symbol for bromine.

bra *n* a woman's closely fitting undergarment with cups for supporting the breasts. ➤➤ **braless** *adj.*

brace[1] *n* **1** an appliance for supporting a weak leg or other body part. **2** a dental fitting worn to correct irregular teeth. **3** a diagonal piece of structural material that serves to strengthen. **4** a rope attached to a yard on a ship that swings the yard horizontally to trim the sail. **5a** a mark ({ or }) used to connect words or items to be considered together. **b** this mark connecting two or more musical staves the parts of which are to be performed simultaneously. **6** (*pl* **brace**) two of a kind; a pair. **7** (*also* **brace and bit**) a crank-shaped instrument for using with and turning a drilling bit.

brace[2] *v* **1a** to prepare (oneself, or a part of one's body) for receiving an impact. **b** to prepare or steel (oneself). **2** to turn (a sail yard) by means of a brace. **3** to fit or support (a limb, the front teeth, etc) with a brace.

bracelet *n* an ornamental band or chain worn round the wrist.

braces *pl n Brit* a pair of elasticated straps attached to the waistband of trousers and worn over the shoulders, for holding the trousers up.

brachiopod *n* a marine invertebrate animal with a shell composed of two halves hinged together.

brachiosaurus *n* a huge plant-eating dinosaur.

bracing *adj* refreshing or invigorating. ➤➤ **bracingly** *adv.*

bracken *n* a common large coarse fern *esp* of moorland areas.

bracket[1] *n* **1** either of a pair of marks ( ), [ ], < >, or { }, used to enclose matter in writing or printing. **2** any of a graded series of social groups. **3** an overhanging projecting fixture or strut that supports a load or strengthens an angle.

bracket[2] *v* (**bracketed, bracketing**) **1** to place (written or printed matter) within brackets. **2** (+ together) to put (two or more people or things) in the same category or associate them mentally. **3** to attach or support (a beam, overhanging part, etc) with brackets.

brackish *adj* of water: slightly salty. ➤➤ **brackishness** *n.*

bract *n* a small leaf near a flower or floral axis.

brad *n* a thin wedged-shaped nail having a slight projection at the top of one side instead of a head.

bradawl *n* an awl; *esp* one used by a woodworker.

brae *n Scot* a hillside, steep river bank, or steep hill on a road.

brag[1] *v* (**bragged, bragging**) to talk boastfully. ➤➤ **bragger** *n.*

brag[2] *n* **1** a card game resembling poker. **2** a boastful statement.

braggadocio /bragə'dochioh, -'dokioh/ *n* empty boasting.

braggart *n* a loud arrogant boaster.

Brahma *n* = BRAHMAN (2).

Brahman *n* (*pl* **Brahmans**) **1** (*also* **Brahmin**) a Hindu of the highest caste traditionally assigned to the priesthood: compare KSHATRIYA, SUDRA, VAISYA. **2** the impersonal ground of all being in Hinduism. Also called BRAHMA.

Brahmin *n* **1** = BRAHMAN (1). **2** *NAm* an intellectually and socially cultivated but aloof person. ➤➤ **Brahminical** *adj.*

braid[1] *v* **1** *chiefly NAm* to plait (the hair). **2** (*usu in passive*) to ornament (clothing, etc) with ribbon or braid.

braid[2] *n* **1** a narrow strip of fabric, *esp* plaited cord or ribbon, used for trimming. **2a** a length of plaited hair. **b** a very narrow plait of hair with coloured threads interlaced and decorative beads at the end.

braille *n* (*also* **Braille**) a system of writing or printing for the blind that uses characters made up of raised dots.

brain[1] *n* **1** the portion of the central nervous system that constitutes the organ of thought and neural coordination, is enclosed within the skull, and is continuous with the spinal cord. **2a** (*in pl*) intellectual endowment; intelligence. **b** *informal* a very intelligent or intellectual person. **c** (**the brain/the brains**) *informal* the chief planner of an organization or enterprise; the mastermind. ✱ **have something on the brain** *informal* to have a snatch of music, song, or verse constantly recurring in one's head. **rack/wrack one's brains** to make a great mental effort; to think hard. ➤➤ **brained** *adj.*

brain[2] *v informal* to hit hard on the head.

brainbox *n Brit, informal* a very intelligent person.

brainchild *n* something that is the product of a specified person's creative imagination.

brain-dead *adj* **1** having suffered brain death. **2** *informal* totally lacking in intelligence.

brain death *n* the death of a human being determined by the assessment that their brain has irreversibly ceased to function.

brain drain *n* (**the brain drain**) *informal* loss of highly qualified workers and professionals through emigration.

brainiac *n NAm, informal* a very intelligent or intellectual person.

brainless *adj* stupid; foolish. ▸▸ **brainlessly** *adv,* **brainlessness** *n.*

brainpan *n chiefly NAm, informal* the skull.

brain stem *n* the part of the brain comprising the medulla oblongata, the midbrain, and the pons.

brainstorm *n* **1** *informal* a transitory disturbance in the brain, resulting in uncharacteristic behaviour or a lapse in concentration; a mental aberration. **2** an instance of brainstorming.

brainstorming *n* a problem-solving technique that involves the spontaneous contribution of ideas from all members of a group.

brains trust *n chiefly Brit* a group of expert advisers assembled to answer questions of immediate or current interest in public or on radio or television.

brainteaser *n informal* a logical or mathematical puzzle.

brainwash *v* to attempt systematically to instil beliefs into (somebody), often in place of beliefs already held.

brain wave *n* **1** a rhythmic fluctuation of voltage between parts of the brain. **2** *informal* a sudden bright idea.

brainy *adj* (**-ier, -iest**) *informal* intelligent; clever. ▸▸ **braininess** *n.*

braise *v* to cook (meat, etc) slowly by first sautéeing it in hot fat and then simmering it gently in very little liquid in a closed container.

brake[1] *n* (*also in pl*) a device for slowing down or stopping a vehicle, usu by friction against the wheels.

brake[2] *v* to operate, manage, or apply a brake, *esp* on a vehicle.

brake[3] *n literary* a thicket.

brake[4] *n* an open horse-drawn four-wheeled carriage.

brake[5] *n* **1** a toothed instrument used for crushing flax and hemp. **2** (*also* **brake harrow**) a machine formerly used for breaking up large clumps of earth.

brake drum *n* in a drum brake, the short broad cylinder attached to the wheel, against which the brake shoe presses.

brake horsepower *n* the useful power of an engine as calculated from the resistance to a brake or dynamometer applied to the shaft or flywheel.

brake shoe *n* in a drum brake, a long curved block that presses on the drum.

bramble *n* **1** a prickly rambling shrub of the rose family, *esp* a blackberry. **2** *chiefly Brit* the fruit of this shrub. ▸▸ **brambly** *adj.*

brambling *n* a brightly coloured Old World finch.

Bramley *n* (*pl* **-eys**) a large green variety of cooking apple.

bran *n* the broken husk of cereal grain separated from the flour or meal by sifting.

branch[1] *n* **1** a secondary woody shoot arising from the trunk of a tree, or from a bough, or from the main axis of a shrub. **2a** *chiefly NAm* the tributary of a river. **b** a side road or way. **3** a distinct part of a complex whole, e.g.: **a** a division of a family descending from a particular ancestor. **b** a distinct section of a particular subject of study. **c** a division or separate part of an organization.

branch[2] *v* **1** to put forth branches. **2** to spring out, e.g. from a main stem.

branch out *v* to extend one's activities or try new experiences.

brand[1] *n* **1** a class of goods identified by name as the product of a single firm or manufacturer. **2** a mark made by burning with a hot iron, or with a stamp or stencil, to identify manufacture or quality or to designate ownership, e.g. of cattle. **3** a charred or smouldering piece of wood.

brand[2] *v* **1** to mark (goods, cattle, slaves, or criminals) with a brand. **2** to stigmatize (somebody, or their conduct).

brandish *v* to shake or wave (a weapon, etc) menacingly or ostentatiously.

brandling *n* a red earthworm with brighter-coloured rings, found in manure and used as angling bait.

brand name *n* the name or trademark that a manufacturer gives to a product or range of products; = TRADE NAME.

brand-new *adj* conspicuously new and unused.

brandy *n* (*pl* **-ies**) a spirit made by distilling wine or fermented fruit juice.

brandy butter *n Brit* a hard sauce served *esp* with Christmas pudding, made by beating butter with sugar and brandy.

brandy snap *n* a very thin cylindrical ginger biscuit sometimes flavoured with brandy.

bran tub *n Brit* a tub filled with bran, with small wrapped presents concealed within it; = LUCKY DIP.

brash *adj* **1** aggressively or insensitively self-assertive; impudent. **2** tastelessly showy. ▸▸ **brashly** *adv,* **brashness** *n.*

brass *n* **1** an alloy of copper and zinc. **2a** the brass instruments of an orchestra or band. **b** *Brit* a brass memorial tablet, *esp* set into the wall or floor of a church. **c** a round flat brass ornament for attaching to a horse's harness. **3** (*also* **the top brass**) *informal* the senior office-bearers; the people in authority. **4** *Brit, informal* money. ▸▸ **brass** *adj.*

brass band *n* a band consisting, or chiefly consisting, of brass and percussion instruments.

brassed off *adj Brit, informal* miserably bored, dissatisfied, or fed up.

brasserie *n* a small informal French-style restaurant.

brass hat *n Brit, informal* a high-ranking military officer.

brassica *n* a plant of the mustard family that includes many important vegetables and crop plants, e.g. cabbage, turnip, mustard, and rape.

brassiere *n formal* the full form of BRA.

brass rubbing *n* the activity of taking an impression from an engraved brass plaque by rubbing a sheet of paper laid over it, or an impression taken in this way.

brass tacks *pl n informal* details of immediate practical importance. ✱ **get down to brass tacks** to tackle the real or practical issues.

brassy *adj* (**-ier, -iest**) **1** shamelessly bold; brazen. **2** resembling brass, *esp* in colour.

brat *n informal* a child, *esp* an ill-disciplined one. ▸▸ **brattish** *adj.*

bratpack *n informal* **1** a group of precociously successful and fashionable young performers, writers, etc. **2** a group of self-important and ill-mannered young people. ▸▸ **bratpacker** *n.*

bratwurst /ˈbrahtvoohst/ *n* a German sausage, usu of pork, for frying.

bravado *n* swaggering conduct intended to impress or deceive people.

brave[1] *adj* courageous; fearless. ▸▸ **bravely** *adv.*

brave[2] *v* to face or endure (unpleasant or dangerous conditions) with courage.

brave[3] *n dated* a Native N American warrior.

bravery *n* courage or valour.

bravo[1] *interj* used *esp* by audience members to applaud a performer: well done!

bravo[2] *n* (*pl* **-os** *or* **-oes**) a villain or desperado; *esp* a hired assassin.

bravura /brəˈv(y)ooərə/ *n* **1** a flamboyant brilliant style, *esp* in the performance of a musical piece requiring technical expertise. **2** a display of flamboyant recklessness.

braw *adj Scot* fine or beautiful.

brawl[1] *v* to quarrel or fight noisily. ⋙ **brawler** *n.*

brawl[2] *n* a noisy quarrel or fight.

brawn *n* **1** muscular strength. **2** *Brit* pork trimmings, *esp* the meat from a pig's head, boiled, chopped, and pressed into a mould.

brawny *adj* (**-ier, -iest**) muscular; strong.

Braxton Hicks contractions *pl n* irregular weak contractions of the muscles of the uterus that occur during pregnancy.

bray *v* to utter the loud harsh cry of a donkey. ⋙ **bray** *n.*

braze *v* to solder (metals) with an alloy, e.g. of brass and silver, that melts on contact with the heated metals being joined. ⋙ **braze** *n.*

brazen[1] *adj* **1** shamelessly or contemptuously bold. **2** *literary* resembling or made of brass. ⋙ **brazenly** *adv.*

brazen[2] ✱ **brazen it out** to face danger, trouble, or criticism with defiance or impudence.

brazier[1] *n* **1** a receptacle or stand for holding burning coals. **2** *NAm* a barbecue.

brazier[2] *n* a person who works in brass.

Brazilian *n* a native or inhabitant of Brazil. ⋙ **Brazilian** *adj.*

brazil nut *n* a roughly triangular oily edible nut.

breach[1] *n* **1** infringement or violation, e.g. of a law, obligation, or standard. **2** a gap, e.g. in a wall, made by battering. **3** a break in customarily friendly relations. ✱ **step into the breach** to replace somebody who has been prevented from doing a certain job, *esp* at short notice.

breach[2] *v* **1** to make a breach in (a barrier). **2** to break or violate (an agreement, etc).

breach of promise *n* violation of a promise, *esp* to marry somebody.

breach of the peace *n* an instance of disorderly conduct causing a public disturbance, treated as a criminal offence.

bread *n* **1** a food consisting essentially of flour or meal which is baked and usu leavened, *esp* with yeast. **2** *informal* money. ✱ **cast one's bread upon the waters** to do good without expectation of thanks or reward. **know which side one's bread is buttered** to know where one's best interest lies.

bread and butter *n* one's means of sustenance or livelihood.

bread and circuses *n* political measures or policies aimed at pleasing large numbers of people.

breadcrumb *n* a small fragment of bread.

breadfruit *n* a large starchy fruit that has white flesh with a breadlike texture.

breadline *n NAm* a queue of people waiting to receive food given in charity. ✱ **on the breadline** *Brit* earning no more than the minimum for survival.

bread sauce *n* a spicy sauce made with breadcrumbs, milk, and onion, traditionally served with turkey.

breadth *n* **1** the distance from side to side of something; = WIDTH (1A). **2a** wide range or scope; catholicity. **b** liberality of views or taste.

breadwinner *n* the member of a family whose earnings are their chief means of support.

break[1] *v* (*past tense* **broke**, *past part.* **broken**) **1** to damage or be damaged by separating into pieces after being struck or dropped etc. **2** to stop working, or to cause (a machine) to stop working. **3** to fracture (a limb), or to become fractured. **4a** to fail to keep (a promise or agreement). **b** to fail to observe (a law or rule). **5a** to defeat (an opponent) thoroughly. **b** to crush the spirit of (a person). **6** to reduce the impact of (a fall). **7** to interrupt (a journey) for a rest or diversion. **8** to exceed or surpass (a record). **9** to resolve or discover the secret of (a code). **10a** to make (news) known to people. **b** of news: to become known: *The story broke on Sunday morning.* **11** of the day: to begin at dawn. **12a** of weather: to change, *esp* after a settled period. **b** of a storm: to develop suddenly. **13a** of a person: to give way under pressure. **b** of a person's health: to fail. **14** of a boy's voice: to deepen at puberty. **15** to make the first stroke in a game of snooker, billiards, or pool. ✱ **break cover** of a person or animal on the run. to emerge from concealment **break even** to recoup an initial investment or outlay. **break into 1** to start an activity: *The horse broke into a gallop; to break into song.* **2** to assume an expression: *to break into a grin.* **break loose** to escape. **break rank** of soldiers: to move out of formation. **break serve/service** in tennis, to win a game against the server. **break the back of** to complete the most difficult part of (a task). **break the bank** to cause financial ruin. **break the ice** to do or say something that overcomes the initial reserve of a person or group. **break wind** to release gas from the anus. **break with 1** to end a relationship with (somebody) after a quarrel. **2** to do something different from (a custom or tradition).

break[2] *n* **1** an act or action of breaking. **2** a gap. **3** a respite from work or duty. **4** a brief holiday. **5** the action or act of breaking in, out, or forth. **6** a dash or rush. **7** *informal* an opportunity or a stroke of good luck. **8** (*also* **break of service**) the action or an instance of breaking an opponent's service at tennis. **9** a sequence of successful shots or strokes, e.g. in snooker, or a score thus made. **10** a short ornamental passage between phrases in jazz. ✱ **break of day** dawn. **give me/us a break!** *informal* used to express impatient irritation: spare me!

breakable *adj* capable of being broken; fragile.

breakage *n* **1** (*usu in pl*) something broken. **2** allowance for things broken, e.g. in transit.

breakaway *n* **1** somebody or something that breaks away. **2** a breaking away, e.g. from a group or tradition; a withdrawing.

break away *v* **1** to escape. **2** to separate from the main group.

break-dance *v* to perform break dancing. ⋙ **break dancer** *n.*

break dancing *n* an athletic form of street dance developed in the 1980s by African Americans, in which performers spin on head and shoulders.

breakdown *n* **1** a failure to function. **2** a physical, mental, or nervous collapse. **3** the process of decomposing. **4** a division into categories; a classification. **5** a whole analysed into parts; *specif* an account in which the transactions are recorded under various categories.

break down *v* **1a** of a machine or vehicle: to stop working suddenly. **b** of an agreement, talks, etc: to fail or become unworkable. **2** of a person: to give way to feelings, to show distress. **3** to cause (a door, etc) to collapse by breaking or shattering it. **4** to separate (a substance) into its components or elements.

breaker *n* **1** a wave breaking into foam. **2** a person or machine that breaks something.

breakfast[1] *n* the first meal of the day, *esp* when taken in the morning.

breakfast[2] *v* to have breakfast.

break in *v* **1** to enter a building by force. **2** to intrude or interrupt. **3a** to train (a horse) to carry a rider. **b** to use (new shoes) until they become comfortable.

break-in *n* an act of forcing an entry into a building, usu with the intention of committing burglary.

breakneck *adj* denoting a dangerously fast pace.

break off *v* **1** to detach something, or to become detached. **2** to stop something abruptly. **3** to discontinue (a connection or relationship).

break out *v* **1** of something unwelcome: to start suddenly. **2** to escape from confinement. **3** (+ in) to become infected with a skin eruption.

breakthrough *n* a sudden advance, *esp* in knowledge or technique.

breakthrough bleeding *n* irregular bleeding from the uterus occurring between menstrual periods.

break up *v* **1** to bring or come to an end. **2** to break (something) into pieces. **3a** of a meeting or group: to finish an activity and disperse. **b** *Brit* to end a school term.

breakwater *n* an offshore structure, e.g. a wall used to protect a harbour or beach from the force of waves.

bream *n* (*pl* **breams** *or* **bream**) a silvery European freshwater fish related to the carp, with a deep narrow body.

breast[1] *n* **1** either of two protuberant milk-producing glandular organs situated on the front of the chest in the human female and some other mammals. **2a** the front part of the body between the neck and the abdomen; the chest. **b** the corresponding part of an animal's body.

breast[2] *v* **1** to contend with or confront resolutely. **2** to meet or lean against with the breast or front.

breastbone *n* = STERNUM.

breast-feed *v* (*past tense and past part.* **breast-fed**) to feed (a baby) with milk from the breast rather than with formula milk.

breastplate *n* a metal plate worn as defensive armour for the chest.

breaststroke *n* a swimming stroke executed on the front by thrusting the arms forwards while kicking outwards and backwards with the legs, then sweeping the arms backwards.

breastwork *n* a temporary fortification, usu consisting of a wall of earth built to about chest height.

breath *n* **1** air inhaled and exhaled in breathing. **2** an act of breathing. **3** a slight movement of air. **4** a slight indication; a suggestion. ✱ **catch one's breath 1** to rest long enough to restore normal breathing. **2** to stop breathing briefly, usu under the influence of strong emotion. **out of breath** breathing very rapidly, e.g. from strenuous exercise. **under one's breath** in a whisper.

breathable *adj* **1** suitable for breathing. **2** allowing air to pass through; porous.

breathalyse (*NAm* **breathalyze**) *v* to test (a driver) for the level of alcohol in exhaled breath, using a breathalyser.

breathalyser (*NAm* **breathalyzer**) *n* a device used to test the alcohol content in the blood of a motorist.

breatharian *n* somebody who believes that people can train themselves to live on air and light, without needing food or water.

breathe *v* **1** to draw air into and expel it from the lungs. **2** to let air or moisture out. **3** of wine: to be exposed to the beneficial effects of air after being kept in a bottle. **4a** to utter or express. **b** to make manifest; to display: *The novel breathes despair.* ✱ **breathe down somebody's neck** to keep somebody under constant or too close surveillance.

breather *n informal* a break in activity for rest or relief.

breathing space *n* a pause in a period of activity, *esp* for rest and recuperation.

breathless *adj* **1** not breathing, *esp* holding one's breath due to excitement or suspense. **2a** gasping for breath, e.g. after strenuous exercise. **b** gripping or intense. ➤➤ **breathlessly** *adv*, **breathlessness** *n*.

breathtaking *adj* hugely impressive, exciting, or thrilling. ➤➤ **breathtakingly** *adv*.

breath test *n Brit* a test made with a breathalyser.

breathy *adj* (**-ier, -iest**) characterized or accompanied by the audible passage of breath. ➤➤ **breathily** *adv*, **breathiness** *n*.

breccia /'breki·ə, 'brechi·ə/ *n* a rock consisting of angular fragments embedded in sand, clay, etc.

bred *v* past tense and past part. of BREED[1].

breech *n* the part of a firearm at the rear of the barrel.

breech birth *n* a birth in which the feet or the buttocks of the baby appear first.

breeches *pl n* knee-length trousers, usu closely fastened at the lower edges.

breeches buoy *n* a life-saving apparatus in the form of a pair of canvas breeches hung from a lifebuoy running on a rope leading from a ship in distress to a rescue ship or to the shore.

breed[1] *v* (*past tense and past part.* **bred**) **1** to produce offspring by sexual union. **2** to propagate (plants or animals) sexually and usu under controlled conditions. **3** to produce or engender. **4** to inculcate by training.

breed[2] *n* **1** a group of animals or plants, often specially selected, visibly similar in most characteristics. **2** a class or kind.

breeder *n* **1** an animal or plant kept for propagation. **2** a person engaged in the breeding of a specified animal or plant. **3** = BREEDER REACTOR.

breeder reactor *n* a nuclear reactor in which more radioactive fuel is produced than is consumed.

breeding *n* **1** behaviour, *esp* when it shows good manners. **2** ancestry.

breeze[1] *n* **1** a light gentle wind. **2** *chiefly NAm, informal* something easily done; a cinch.

breeze[2] *v* to come in or into, or move along, swiftly and casually or nonchalantly.

breeze-block *n* a rectangular building block made of an ashy residue from coke or charcoal mixed with sand and cement.

breezy *adj* (**-ier, -iest**) **1** quite windy; fresh. **2** brisk or lively. **3** carefree or careless; insouciant. ➤➤ **breezily** *adv*, **breeziness** *n*.

Bren gun *n* a gas-operated magazine-fed light machine gun.

brethren *n* used in formal address and to refer to members of a religious order or a society: pl of BROTHER[1].

Breton *n* **1** a native or inhabitant of Brittany. **2** the Celtic language of the Bretons. ➤➤ **Breton** *adj*.

breve *n* **1** a musical note with the time value of two semibreves or four minims. **2** a curved mark (˘) placed over a vowel in some languages to show a short or unstressed vowel or syllable.

brevet *n* a commission giving a military officer higher nominal rank than that for which he or she receives pay.

breviary *n* (*pl* **-ies**) (*often* **Breviary**) a book containing the prayers, hymns, psalms, and readings for the canonical hours.

brevity *n* **1** the quality of being brief, *esp* shortness of duration. **2** expression in few words; conciseness.

brew[1] *v* **1** to prepare (e.g. beer or ale) by steeping, boiling, and fermentation or by infusion and fermentation. **2** to prepare (e.g. tea) by infusion in hot water. **3** (*often* + up) to contrive or plot (something). **4** (*often* + up) to be in the process of formation. ➤➤ **brewer** *n.*

brew[2] *n* **1** a brewed beverage. **2** a product of brewing.

brewery *n* (*pl* **-ies**) a place in which beer or ale is brewed commercially.

briar[1] *n* see BRIER[1].

briar[2] *n* **1** see BRIER[2]. **2** a tobacco pipe made from the root of a brier.

bribe[1] *v* to induce or influence by bribery.

bribe[2] *n* something, *esp* money, given or promised to influence somebody's judgment or conduct.

bribery *n* the act or practice of giving or taking a bribe.

bric-a-brac *n* miscellaneous small articles, usu of ornamental or sentimental value; curios.

brick[1] *n* **1** a rectangular block of baked clay and sand used for building or paving purposes. **2** a small block used as a children's toy. **3** *Brit, informal, dated* a reliable or undaunted person; a stalwart.

brick[2] *v* (+ up) to close, face, or pave with bricks.

brickbat *n* **1** a piece of something hard used as a missile. **2** a critical remark.

brickie *n Brit, informal* a bricklayer.

bricklayer *n* a person who is employed to lay bricks.

brick red *adj* of a reddish brown colour. ➤➤ **brick red** *n.*

bricolage /brikə'lahzh/ *n* something made using a mixture of materials, or the effect created by this.

bridal *adj* of or for a bride or wedding.

bride *n* a woman at the time of her wedding.

bridegroom *n* a man at the time of his wedding.

bridesmaid *n* an unmarried woman or girl who attends a bride.

bridge[1] *n* **1** a structure spanning a gap or obstacle, e.g. a river, and supporting a roadway, railway, canal, or path. **2a** the upper bony part of the nose. **b** an arch serving to raise the strings of a musical instrument. **c** a raised platform on a ship from which the captain and officers control it. **3** a partial denture permanently attached to adjacent natural teeth, filling a gap. **4** a musical passage or phrase linking two unrelated themes or tunes.

bridge[2] *v* **1** to make a bridge over or across (something, e.g. a river). **2** to bring together people or things that are separated by (something). ➤➤ **bridgeable** *adj.*

bridge[3] *n* a card game related to whist for usu four players in two partnerships in which players bid for the right to name a trump suit and try to win tricks.

bridgehead *n* **1** a fortification protecting the end of a bridge nearest an enemy. **2** an advanced position, usu beyond a bridge, seized or targeted in hostile territory as a foothold for further advance.

bridge roll *n* a small finger-shaped soft roll.

bridging loan *n* a short-term loan made to somebody awaiting finalization of a long-term loan or mortgage.

bridle[1] *n* a framework of leather straps buckled together round the head of a horse or other draught or riding animal, including the bit and reins, used to direct and control it.

bridle[2] *v* **1** to put a bridle on (an animal). **2** to restrain or control (something). **3** to show hostility or resentment in response to a perceived affront to pride or dignity.

bridle path *n* a track or right of way suitable for horse riding.

bridleway *n* = BRIDLE PATH.

Brie /bree/ *n* a large round cream-coloured soft cheese that becomes runny as it ripens.

brief[1] *adj* **1** short in duration or extent. **2** expressed in few words; concise. ➤➤ **briefly** *adv.*

brief[2] *n* **1a** a set of instructions outlining what is required, and usu setting limits to one's powers, e.g. in negotiating. **b** a statement of a client's case drawn up for the instruction of legal counsel. **c** *Brit, informal* a barrister or solicitor assigned to somebody. **2** a papal directive, less binding than a BULL[2]. ✱ **hold a brief for** *Brit* to be retained as counsel for.

brief[3] *v* to provide with final instructions or necessary information.

briefcase *n* a flat rectangular case for carrying papers or books.

briefing *n* a meeting to give out final instructions or necessary information.

briefs *pl n* short underpants for men or women.

brier[1] *or* **briar** *n* a plant with woody and thorny or prickly stems, *esp* a wild plant of the rose family.

brier[2] *or* **briar** *n* a HEATH (plant) of S Europe with a root used for making pipes.

brig[1] *n* a two-masted square-rigged sailing ship.

brig[2] *n* a prison in the US Navy.

brig[3] *n Scot* a bridge.

brigade *n* **1** a large section of an army usu composed of a headquarters, several fighting units, e.g. infantry battalions or armoured regiments, and supporting units. **2** *informal* a group of people who have a particular point of view: *the anti-abortion brigade.*

brigadier *n* an officer in the British Army and the Royal Marines ranking below a major general.

brigadier general *n* an officer in the US army, air force, and marines ranking below a major general.

brigalow *n Aus* a species of acacia forming thick scrub.

brigand *n* somebody who lives by plunder, usu as a member of a gang of marauding thieves; a bandit. ➤➤ **brigandage** *n.*

brigantine *n* a two-masted square-rigged sailing ship differing from a brig in not carrying a square mainsail.

bright *adj* **1a** radiating or reflecting light; shining. **b** radiant with happiness, animation, or good fortune. **2** of a colour: of high saturation or brilliance. **3a** quick to learn or understand; intelligent. **b** lively and charming. **c** successful, or promising success or good fortune. ✱ **bright spark** an intelligent person. ➤➤ **brightly** *adv,* **brightness** *n.*

brighten *v* (*often* + up) to become or make bright or brighter.

Bright's disease *n* a kidney disease marked by albumin in the urine.

brill *n* (*pl* **brill**) a European flatfish related to the turbot.

brilliant *adj* **1** very bright, *esp* sparkling or glittering with light. **2a** having great intellectual ability. **b** strikingly impressive or distinctive. **3** *Brit, informal* of high quality; good. ⯮ **brilliance** *n,* **brilliancy** *n,* **brilliantly** *adv.*

brim[1] *n* **1** the edge or rim of something, *esp* a container. **2** the projecting rim of a hat.

brim[2] *v* (**brimmed, brimming**) to be full to the brim.

brimful *adj* full to the brim, *esp* about to overflow.

brimstone *n* **1** *archaic* = SULPHUR . **2** a yellow butterfly common in Britain and N Europe.

brindled *or* **brindle** *adj* of an animal: having dark streaks or flecks on a grey or tawny background.

brine *n* **1** a solution of water and common salt. **2** sea water.

bring *v* (*past tense and past part.* **brought**) **1** to carry or convey to a place or person. **2** to cause to reach a particular condition: *Bring the water to the boil.* **3** to force (oneself) to do something. **4** to cause to occur; to lead to: *Winter brings snow and ice.* **5** to present or initiate. ✻ **bring to bear** to apply or put to use.

bring about *v* to cause (something) to happen.

bring and buy sale *n Brit* a sale of donated goods, held to raise money for charity.

bring around *v NAm* see BRING ROUND.

bring down *v* **1** to reduce (e.g. a price). **2** to cause (a government) to lose power.

bring forth *v formal* **1a** to bear (produce). **b** to give birth to (offspring). **2** to offer or present.

bring forward *v* **1** to schedule for an earlier time. **2** to propose (an idea or plan) for consideration.

bring in *v* **1** to earn (an amount of income). **2** to introduce (a measure).

bring off *v* to achieve (something) successfully.

bring on *v* **1** to cause (a feeling or symptom) to occur. **2** to help (somebody or something) to make progress.

bring out *v* **1** to publish or market (a new publication or product). **2** to encourage (somebody) to be less reticent. **3** to make (something) more clearly visible or noticeable. **4** to emphasize (something).

bring round (*NAm* **bring around**) *v* **1** to persuade (somebody) to adopt a particular opinion. **2** to revive (somebody) who has been unconscious.

bring to *v* **1** = BRING ROUND (2). **2** to cause (a boat) to lie to or stop moving.

bring up *v* to educate and look after (a child) until adulthood.

brink *n* **1** an edge, *esp* the edge at the top of a steep place. **2** the point at which something is about to happen; the verge.

brinkmanship *n* the art of going to the very brink of conflict, danger, etc before drawing back, as a tactic to intimidate an enemy into conceding or backing down.

briny[1] *n* (**the briny**) *Brit, informal* sea water, or the sea itself.

briny[2] *adj* (**-ier, -iest**) of brine; salty.

brio *n* enthusiasm and liveliness; verve.

brioche *n* a light, slightly sweet bread roll made with a rich yeast dough.

briquette *or* **briquet** *n* a compacted block, e.g. a block of coal-dust used as fuel for a barbecue.

brisk *adj* **1** energetic and fast. **2** fresh and invigorating. **3** sharp in tone or manner. ⯮ **briskly** *adv,* **briskness** *n.*

brisket *n* a joint of beef cut from the breast.

brisling *n* (*pl* **brislings** *or* **brisling**) a small herring that resembles a sardine and is processed in the same way.

bristle[1] *n* **1** a short stiff coarse hair or filament. **2** a material consisting of natural rather than synthetic filaments, used to make artists' brushes.

bristle[2] *v* **1a** to rise and stand stiffly erect. **b** of an animal: to raise the bristles, e.g. in anger. **2** to take on an aggressive attitude or appearance, e.g. in response to an insult or criticism. **3** to be filled or thickly covered with something suggestive of bristles.

bristly *adj* (**-ier, -iest**) **1a** consisting of or resembling bristles. **b** thickly covered with bristles. **2** tending to bristle easily; belligerent.

Bristol fashion *adj Brit, informal, dated* in good order; spick-and-span.

bristols *pl n Brit, slang, dated* a woman's breasts.

Brit *n informal* a British person.

Britannia *n* Great Britain or the British Empire personified in the form of a seated female figure wearing a helmet and carrying a trident.

Britannic *adj dated* British.

British[1] *n* (**the British**) (*used as pl*) the people of Britain.

British[2] *adj* of Britain, its people, or the variety of the English language that they speak. ⯮ **Britishness** *n.*

Britisher *n chiefly NAm, informal* a British person.

British Summer Time *n* time one hour ahead of Greenwich Mean Time that is used in Britain during the summer and is the same as Central European Time: compare DAYLIGHT SAVING TIME.

British thermal unit *n* the quantity of heat required to raise the temperature of 1lb of water by 1°F under standard conditions.

Briton *n* **1** a native or inhabitant of Britain. **2** a member of any of the peoples inhabiting Britain before the Anglo-Saxon invasions.

brittle[1] *adj* **1** easily broken or cracked. **2** light and thin in tone; sharp. **3** lacking warmth or depth of feeling. ⯮ **brittleness** *n.*

brittle[2] *n* a sweet made with caramelized sugar and nuts.

brittle bone disease *n* = OSTEOPOROSIS.

broach *v* **1** to open up (a subject) for discussion. **2** to pierce (a container, *esp* a cask or bottle) prior to using the contents; to tap.

broad[1] *adj* **1a** large in size or extent from side to side or between limits. **b** of a specified size in width. **2** widely applicable or applied; general. **3** relating to main points or features rather than to details. **4** easily understood or noticed; obvious. **5** extending far and wide; vast. **6** dialectal, *esp* in pronunciation. **7** marked by lack of restraint or delicacy; coarse. ✻ **broad daylight** full daylight. ⯮ **broadly** *adv,* **broadness** *n.*

broad[2] *n NAm, informal* a woman.

broad bean *n* a large flat seed of a leguminous plant, used as a vegetable.

broad-brush *adj* dealing with main elements rather than details; general.

broadcast[1] *v* (*past tense* **broadcast,** *past part.* **broadcast** *or* **broadcasted**) **1** to transmit (a television or radio programme). **2** to make (something) widely known. **3** to scatter or sow (seed) over a broad area. ⯮ **broadcaster** *n.*

broadcast[2] *n* a single radio or television programme.

Broad Church *adj* relating to a liberal form of Anglicanism that flourished in the late 19th cent.

broadcloth *n* a woollen or worsted fabric with a smooth lustrous finish and dense texture.

broaden *v* to become or make broad or broader.

broad gauge *n* a size of railway track that is wider than the standard.

broad-leaved *or* **broadleaf** *adj* having broad leaves, *esp* not coniferous.

broadloom *n* a carpet woven on a wide loom.

broad-minded *adj* tolerant of varied views, unconventional behaviour, etc; liberal. ➤➤ **broad-mindedly** *adv*, **broad-mindedness** *n*.

broadsheet *n* **1** a large-format newspaper. **2** a large sheet of paper printed on one side only.

broadside[1] *n* **1a** the simultaneous firing of all the guns on one side of a ship. **b** a forceful verbal or written attack. **2** the side of a ship above the waterline.

broadside[2] *adv* with the broadside or broader side towards a given object or point; sideways.

broadsword *n* a sword with a broad blade for cutting rather than thrusting.

Brobdingnagian *adj* of colossal size; towering.

brocade *n* a rich usu silk fabric woven with raised patterns often in gold or silver thread. ➤➤ **brocaded** *adj*.

broccoli *n* a green or purplish flower head of a plant of the cabbage family, used as a vegetable.

brochette /bro'shet, broh'shet/ *n* a skewer of roasted or grilled food.

brochure *n* a small pamphlet containing advertising or promotional material.

broderie anglaise /,brohdəri 'ongglez, ong'glez/ *n* openwork embroidery, usu in white thread, on white fine cloth.

brogue[1] *n* a stout shoe characterized by decorative perforations on the uppers.

brogue[2] *n* a dialect or regional pronunciation, *esp* an Irish accent.

broil *v* **1** *NAm* to grill (food). **2** to become extremely hot.

broiler *n* **1** a bird suitable for grilling, *esp* a young chicken. **2** *NAm* a grill.

broke[1] *v* past tense of BREAK[1].

broke[2] *adj informal* with no money at all; penniless.

broken[1] *v* past part. of BREAK[1].

broken[2] *adj* lacking fluency: *broken English*. ➤➤ **brokenly** *adv*, **brokenness** *n*.

broken-down *adj* **1** in a state of disrepair; dilapidated. **2** spiritually or physically ill or exhausted.

brokenhearted *adj* overcome by sorrow or grief.

broken home *n* a family that has been adversely affected or disrupted by marital separation or divorce.

broker[1] *n* **1** an agent who negotiates contracts of purchase and sale, *esp* in the financial and insurance sectors. **2** somebody who acts as an intermediary, e.g. in a business deal or political negotiation.

broker[2] *v* to negotiate or settle (e.g. a deal) as a broker.

brokerage *n* **1** the business of a broker. **2** the fee or commission for transacting business as a broker.

broker-dealer *n* a person or firm combining the functions of stockbroker and stockjobber.

broking *n Brit* = BROKERAGE (I).

brolga *n* a large grey Australian bird that is a species of crane.

brolly *n* (*pl* **-ies**) *Brit, informal* an umbrella.

bromeliad *n* a tropical American plant including the pineapple and various ornamental plants with fleshy spiky leaves.

bromide *n* **1** a chemical compound of bromine with another element or radical. **2** *dated* a compound such as potassium bromide, formerly used as a sedative. **3** a commonplace or hackneyed statement or notion.

bromine *n* a non-metallic chemical element of the halogen group, usu occurring as a deep red corrosive toxic liquid with a pungent, often irritating vapour.

bronchi *n* pl of BRONCHUS.

bronchial *adj* relating to or in the region of the bronchi or the smaller tubes branching off them in the lungs.

bronchiole *n* a minute thin-walled branch of a bronchus.

bronchitis *n* acute or chronic inflammation of the bronchial tubes accompanied by a cough and catarrh. ➤➤ **bronchitic** *adj and n*.

bronchopneumonia *n* pneumonia affecting many widely scattered but small areas of lung tissue.

bronchoscope *n* a tubular, usu flexible, illuminated instrument used for inspecting or passing instruments into the bronchi.

bronchus *n* (*pl* **bronchi**) either of the two main branches of the windpipe that lead into the lungs.

bronco *n* (*pl* **-os**) a wild or partially broken horse of western N America, *esp* a mustang.

brontosaurus *or* **brontosaur** *n dated* an apatosaurus.

bronze[1] *n* **1** any of various copper-base alloys, *esp* one containing a high proportion of tin. **2** a sculpture or artefact made of bronze. **3** a yellowish brown colour. ➤➤ **bronze** *adj*, **bronzy** *adj*.

bronze[2] *v* **1** to give the appearance of bronze to. **2** to make brown or suntanned.

Bronze Age *n* (**the Bronze Age**) the period of human history characterized by the use of bronze or copper tools and weapons, coming between the Stone Age and the Iron Age.

bronze medal *n* a medal of bronze awarded to somebody who comes third in a competition, *esp* in athletics or other sports. ➤➤ **bronze medallist** *n*.

brooch *n* an ornament worn on clothing and fastened by means of a pin.

brood[1] *n* **1** young birds, insects, etc hatched or cared for at one time. **2** *humorous or derog* the children in one family.

brood[2] *v* **1** of a bird: to sit on eggs in order to hatch them. **2** to dwell gloomily on, or worry over or about something. **3** to hover or seem to hover menacingly.

brood[3] *adj* of an animal: kept for breeding.

brooder *n* a heated house or other structure used for raising young birds.

broody *adj* (**-ier, -iest**) **1** of a hen: being in a state of readiness to brood eggs. **2** *informal* of a woman: feeling a strong desire or urge to be a mother. **3** tending to be occupied with thoughts, *esp* depressing thoughts; introspective. ➤➤ **broodily** *adv*, **broodiness** *n*.

brook[1] *n* a stream. ➤➤ **brooklet** *n*.

brook[2] *v formal* (*in negative contexts*) to tolerate; to stand for: *She would brook no interference with her plans*.

broom *n* **1** a long-handled brush for sweeping. **2** a shrub of the pea family with long slender branches, small leaves, and usu showy yellow flowers.

broomrape *n* a plant that grows as a parasite on the roots of other plants.

broomstick *n* the long thin handle of a broom, or the whole broom when ridden by a witch in children's stories.

bros. *or* **Bros.** *abbr* brothers.

brose *n chiefly Scot* a porridge made with boiling liquid and oatmeal.

broth *n* **1a** the stock in which meat, fish, cereal grains, or vegetables have been cooked. **b** a thin soup made from stock. **2** a liquid medium for culturing *esp* bacteria.

brothel *n* a premises in which the services of prostitutes can be bought.

brother[1] *n* **1** a male having the same parents as another person. **2** *NAm, informal* a black man. **3** (*pl* **brothers** *or* **brethren**) a fellow member of a trade union or fellow member of an all-male club or society. **4** (*pl* **brothers** *or* **brethren**) a member of a men's religious order who is not in holy orders. **5** (*pl* **brothers** *or* **brethren**) used as a title in some evangelical denominations: a fellow male member of the Christian Church. ⪢ **brotherly** *adj.*

brother[2] *interj* used to express surprise, despair, etc.

brotherhood *n* **1** the quality or state of being brothers. **2a** an association, e.g. a religious body, founded for a particular purpose. **b** fellowship between all human beings, or the idea of it.

brother-in-law *n* (*pl* **brothers-in-law**) **1** the brother of one's husband or wife. **2** the husband of one's sister.

brougham *n* **1** a light closed four-wheeled horse-drawn carriage in which the driver sits high up at the front. **2** a large car with an open compartment for the driver.

brought *v* past tense and past part. of BRING.

brouhaha *n* a scene of noisy confusion or protest; an uproar.

brow *n* **1a** the forehead. **b** an eyebrow. **2** the top or edge of a hill, cliff, etc.

browbeat *v* (*past tense* **browbeat,** *past part.* **browbeaten**) to intimidate, coerce, or bully by a persistently threatening or dominating manner.

browlift *n* a cosmetic operation to raise the position of low eyebrows.

brown[1] *adj* **1** of the colour of wood or soil, between red and yellow in hue. **2** of dark or tanned complexion. **3** of foodstuffs: partially or wholly unrefined, or made with such ingredients. **4** of bread: made with wholemeal or wheatmeal flour, or a mixture of either of these and a proportion of white flour. ⪢ **brownness** *n.*

brown[2] *n* a brown colour. ⪢ **brownish** *adj,* **browny** *adj.*

brown[3] *v* to make (e.g. meat) brown by cooking, or to become brown.

brown ale *n Brit* a sweet, dark, heavily malted beer.

brown bear *n* a large and fierce bear that is predominantly brown in colour, found in the forests of Europe, Asia, and N America.

brown belt *n* a rating of expertise below that of a black belt in judo, karate, etc.

brown coal *n* = LIGNITE.

brown dwarf *n* a cool faint star with a mass less than about one tenth of that of the sun.

browned-off *adj informal* annoyed or disheartened; = FED UP.

brownfield *adj* relating to or located in urban areas where buildings previously existed and have since been demolished.

brown goods *pl n* electrical consumer goods, e.g. television sets, hi-fi systems, and home computers, that are chiefly used for recreation: compare WHITE GOODS.

Brownian motion *n* a random movement of microscopic particles suspended in liquids or gases resulting from the impact of molecules of the liquid or gas surrounding the particles.

brownie *n* **1** (**Brownie**) a member of the most junior section of the Guide movement for girls aged from seven to ten. **2** a small square or rectangle of rich chocolate cake containing nuts. **3** a good-natured goblin believed to perform household chores at night.

Brownie Guide *n Brit* = BROWNIE (I).

brownie point *n informal* a mark of merit gained in the eyes of somebody else for having done something helpful or kind.

browning *n Brit* a substance, e.g. caramelized sugar, used to give a brown colour to soups and gravies.

brown-nose[1] *v NAm, informal* to behave in a servile and flattering manner towards.

brown-nose[2] *n NAm, informal* a servile and flattering person; a crawler.

brown-noser *n* = BROWN-NOSE[2].

brownout *n chiefly NAm* a temporary dimming of electric lights, e.g. in a city, caused by a reduction of power.

brown owl *n* a tawny owl.

brown rice *n* rice that has been hulled but not polished, so that it retains the germ and bran.

brown sauce *n Brit* a commercially prepared condiment with a dark brown colour and a strong taste of vinegar.

Brownshirt *n* a Nazi stormtrooper.

brownstone *n NAm* a building, usu an apartment block, made of a reddish brown sandstone, or this kind of sandstone itself.

brown sugar *n* unrefined or partially refined sugar.

brown trout *n* a speckled trout which is the common native species in Europe, widely fished and used for food.

browse[1] *v* **1** to read or search idly through a book or mass of things, e.g. in a shop, in the hope of finding something interesting. **2** of animals: to nibble at leaves, grass, or other vegetation. **3** in computing, to look at (the contents of a file, disk, directory, or web site). ⪢ **browsable** *adj.*

browse[2] *n* a period of time spent browsing.

browser *n* **1** a customer in a shop who is merely browsing. **2** an animal that browses. **3** a computer program used for finding and viewing information on the World Wide Web.

brucellosis *n* a serious long-lasting infectious disease affecting cattle, often causing miscarriage in pregnant cattle, and humans, causing fever, pain, and swelling of the joints.

bruise[1] *n* **1** an injury involving rupture of small blood vessels and discoloration without a break in the skin. **2** an injury to plant tissue involving underlying damage and discoloration without a break in the skin.

bruise[2] *v* **1** to inflict a bruise on (somebody, or a part of somebody's body). **2** to be damaged by a bruise.

bruiser *n informal* a large burly person, *esp* a man.

bruit *v literary* (*often* + abroad) to spread (a report or rumour).

brumby *n* (*pl* **-ies**) *Aus* a wild or unbroken horse.

brume *n literary* mist or fog. ⋙ **brumous** *adj.*

Brummy *or* **Brummie** *n* (*pl* **-ies**) *Brit, informal* a native or inhabitant of Birmingham. ⋙ **Brummie** *adj,* **Brummy** *adj.*

brunch *n* a meal, usu taken in the middle of the morning, that combines a late breakfast and an early lunch.

Bruneian *n* a native or inhabitant of Brunei. ⋙ **Bruneian** *adj.*

brunette (*NAm* **brunet**) *n* a girl or woman with dark brown hair.

brunt *n* the principal force, e.g. of an attack or a blow.

bruschetta /broo'sketə/ *n* thick slices of bread flavoured with garlic and olive oil and toasted.

brush[1] *n* **1** an implement composed of filaments of hair, bristle, nylon, or wire set into a firm piece of material and used for grooming hair, painting, sweeping, or scrubbing. **2** an act of brushing. **3** a quick light touch or momentary contact in passing. **4** a conductor, e.g. a piece of carbon or braided copper wire, that makes electrical contact between a stationary and a moving part. **5** the bushy tail of a fox.

brush[2] *v* **1a** to apply a brush to (something, e.g. hair). **b** to apply (something, e.g. paint) with a brush. **2** (+ away/off) to remove with sweeping strokes. **3** to touch or pass lightly over or across (something).

brush[3] *n* **1** scrub vegetation, or land covered with it. **2** *chiefly NAm, Aus* = BRUSHWOOD.

brush[4] *n* a brief antagonistic encounter or skirmish.

brush aside *v* = BRUSH OFF .

brushed *adj* **1** of a fabric: with the nap raised to give a softer texture. **2** of metal: having a surface that does not reflect light.

brush off *v* to reject in an offhand way; to dismiss.

brushtail *n* an Australian possum with a long prehensile tail.

brush up *v* (*often* + on) to renew one's skill in: *She'll have to brush up on her French.*

brushwood *n* twigs or small branches, *esp* when cut or broken.

brusque *adj* blunt or abrupt in manner or speech, often to the point of rudeness. ⋙ **brusquely** *adv,* **brusqueness** *n.*

Brussels sprout *or* **Brussel sprout** *n* a bud of a plant of the cabbage family, used as a vegetable.

brut /brooht/ *adj* of champagne: very dry.

brutal *adj* **1** cruel and cold-blooded. **2** harsh or severe. **3** unpleasantly accurate and incisive. ⋙ **brutalism** *n,* **brutality** *n,* **brutally** *adv.*

brutalise *v* see BRUTALIZE.

brutalize *or* **-ise** *v* **1** to make brutal, unfeeling, or inhuman. **2** to treat brutally. ⋙ **brutalization** *n.*

brute[1] *n* **1** a brutal person. **2** an animal, *esp* when its animal qualities are contrasted to human qualities. ⋙ **brutish** *adj.*

brute[2] *adj* **1** purely physical. **2a** cruel or savage. **b** not working by reason; mindless.

bryony *n* (*pl* **-ies**) a climbing plant of the cucumber family with large leaves and red or black fruit.

bryophyte *n* any of a division of nonflowering plants comprising the mosses and liverworts.

bryozoan *n* an aquatic invertebrate animal that reproduces by budding and lives permanently attached to rocks, seaweed, etc.

BS *abbr* **1** Bachelor of Surgery. **2** British Standard.

BSc *abbr* Bachelor of Science.

BSE *abbr* bovine spongiform encephalopathy, a fatal disease of cattle affecting their central nervous system.

BSI *abbr* British Standards Institution.

B-side *n* the less important side of a vinyl record.

BSL *abbr* British Sign Language.

BST *abbr* **1** bovine somatotrophin (an additive in cattle feed). **2** British Summer Time.

BT *abbr* British Telecom.

Btu *or* **BTU** *abbr* British thermal unit.

bubble[1] *n* **1** a usu small body of gas within a liquid or solid. **2** a thin, spherical, usu transparent, film of liquid inflated with air or vapour. **3** a transparent dome.

bubble[2] *v* **1** to form or produce bubbles. **2** to make a sound like the bubbles rising in liquid. **3** to be highly excited or overflowing with a feeling.

bubble and squeak *n Brit* a dish consisting of usu leftover potato, cabbage, and sometimes meat, fried together.

bubble bath *n* a perfumed preparation that produces foam when added to water.

bubble gum *n* chewing gum that can be blown into large bubbles.

bubble memory *n* in computing, a kind of memory formerly used to permit a large amount of information to be stored as tiny areas of magnetization in a semiconductor.

bubble wrap *n* wrapping material in the form of sheets of plastic with air pockets at regular intervals.

bubbly[1] *adj* (**-ier, -iest**) **1** full of bubbles. **2** overflowing with good spirits or liveliness; vivacious.

bubbly[2] *n informal* champagne, or any sparkling wine.

bubo *n* (*pl* **-oes**) an inflamed swelling of a lymph gland, *esp* in the groin or armpit. ⋙ **bubonic** *adj.*

bubonic plague *n* a highly infectious and fatal form of plague characterized by the formation of buboes: compare PLAGUE[1].

buccal *adj technical* relating to or in the region of the cheeks or the mouth.

buccaneer *n* **1** a pirate, *esp* one preying on Spanish ships and settlements in the W Indies in the 17th cent. **2** an unscrupulous adventurer, *esp* in politics or business. ⋙ **buccaneering** *adj.*

buck[1] *n* **1a** a male animal, *esp* a male deer, antelope, rabbit, or rat. **b** *SAfr* an antelope. **2** *archaic* a dandy.

buck[2] *v* **1** of a horse or mule: to spring into the air with the back curved and come down with the forelegs stiff and the head lowered. **2** to fight against or refuse to comply with; to oppose.

buck[3] *n* a plunging leap by a horse or mule.

buck[4] *n NAm, Aus, NZ, informal* a dollar.

buck[5] *n* an object formerly used in poker to mark the next player to deal. ✱ **pass the buck** *informal* to shift a responsibility to somebody else. **the buck stops here** *informal* the responsibility cannot be shifted to somebody else.

buckboard *n NAm* a four-wheeled horse-drawn vehicle with the seat mounted on a sprung platform fixed between the front and back wheels.

bucket[1] *n* **1** a large open container, usu round, with tapering sides, a flat bottom, and a handle on top, used *esp* for holding or carrying liquids. **2a** the scoop of an excavating machine. **b** any of the scooped-out blades on the rim of a waterwheel. **c** any of the vanes of a turbine rotor. **3** *informal* (*in pl*) large quantities. ➤➤ **bucketful** (*pl* **bucketfuls**) *n*.

bucket² *v* (**bucketed, bucketing**) to move about jerkily or recklessly.

bucket down *v Brit* of rain: to fall heavily.

bucket seat *n* an individual seat in a vehicle with a rounded back and sides that extend slightly forward.

bucket shop *n informal* **1** *Brit* a travel agent selling low-priced air tickets, that operates on the edge of the law and may default on its commitments to its customers. **2** a dishonest stockbroking firm that speculates and gambles on stocks and commodities using the funds of its clients.

buckeye *n* a N American tree or shrub with large red or white flowers and sticky buds.

buckhorn *n* horn from a buck used *esp* for knife-handles.

buckjumper *n Aus, NZ* an often untamed horse given to bucking.

buckle¹ *n* a fastening consisting of a rigid rim, usu with a hinged pin, used to join together two loose ends of a belt or strap.

buckle² *v* **1** to fasten (e.g. a belt) with a buckle. **2** to cause (e.g. metal) to bend, give way, or crumple. **3** to bend or warp. **4** to give up a struggle or abandon resistance; to yield.

buckle down *v* to apply oneself vigorously.

buckler *n* a small round shield held by a handle at arm's length.

Buckley's *n Aus, NZ, informal* a remote chance.

buckram *n* a fabric stiffened for use as an interlining in garments, and in bookbinding.

Bucks *abbr* Buckinghamshire.

buck's fizz *n Brit* a drink of champagne mixed with orange juice.

buckshee *adj chiefly Brit, informal* without charge; free.

buckshot *n* a coarse lead shot used *esp* for shooting large animals.

buckskin *n* **1** a soft pliable usu suede-finished leather. **2** thick heavy cotton or woollen fabric with a smooth finish.

buckthorn *n* a thorny tree or shrub with berries that were formerly used as a laxative.

bucktooth *n* a large projecting front tooth. ➤➤ **buck-toothed** *adj*.

buck up *v* **1** to become encouraged or more cheerful. **2** to hurry up. **3** to raise the morale or spirits of. ✱ **buck up one's ideas** to take a more serious and positive approach.

buckwheat *n* an Asian plant of the dock family that has pinkish white flowers and triangular edible seeds used to make flour.

bucolic *adj* **1** relating to shepherds; pastoral. **2** of the countryside or rural life.

bud¹ *n* **1** a small protuberance on the stem of a plant that develops into a flower, leaf, or shoot. **2** an outgrowth of an organism, e.g. a yeast, that becomes a new individual.

bud² *v* (**budded, budding**) **1** of a plant: to produce buds. **2** to begin to grow or develop. **3** to reproduce asexually by forming buds.

Buddhism *n* a religion or philosophy that developed in India out of the teaching of Gautama Buddha, maintaining that one can be liberated from the suffering inherent in life by ridding oneself of desire and self-delusion. ➤➤ **Buddhist** *n and adj*.

budding *adj* in an early and usu promising stage of development: *a budding playwright.*

buddleia *n* a shrub or tree with showy clusters of usu yellow or violet flowers, many of which are attractive to butterflies.

buddy *n* (*pl* **-ies**) *chiefly NAm, informal* a friend, colleague, or partner.

budge *v* (*usu in negative contexts*) **1** to move or make (somebody or something) move. **2** to change or make (somebody) change an opinion or abandon a standpoint.

budgerigar *n* a small Australian bird that is often kept in captivity, typically light green with yellow and black markings.

budget¹ *n* **1** a statement of a financial position for a definite period of time. **2** (**the Budget**) a statement of the British government's financial position presented annually to the British parliament by the Chancellor of the Exchequer. **3** the amount of money available for or required for a particular purpose. **4** (*used before a noun*) designed or suitable for people with a limited income or a limited amount of money to spend. ➤➤ **budgetary** *adj*.

budget² *v* (**budgeted, budgeting**) to plan or provide for the use of (e.g. money, time, or personnel) in detail.

budgie *n informal* a budgerigar.

buff¹ *n* **1** a pale yellowish brown colour. **2** a strong supple oil-tanned leather produced chiefly from cattle hides. **3** *informal* somebody who has a keen interest in and wide knowledge of a specified subject; an enthusiast. ✱ **in the buff** *informal* naked.

buff² *adj* of a pale yellowish brown colour.

buff³ *v* **1** to polish or shine. **2** to give a velvety surface like that of buff to (leather).

buffalo *n* (*pl* **buffaloes** *or* **buffalo**) **1** a large shaggy N American wild ox with short horns, heavy forequarters, and a large muscular hump. Also called BISON. **2** a large African ox with a short mane and large horns that curve outwards and backwards.

buffer¹ *n* **1** a spring-loaded metal disc on a railway vehicle or at the end of a railway track. **2** a device that serves to protect something, or to cushion against shock. **3** a chemical substance capable in solution of neutralizing both acids and bases and thereby maintaining original acidity or basicity. **4** a temporary storage area in a computer, *esp* one that accepts information at one rate and delivers it at another.

buffer² *n Brit, informal* a silly or ineffectual man.

buffer solution *n* = BUFFER¹ (3).

buffet¹ *n* **1** a meal set out on tables or a sideboard for diners to help themselves. **2** a counter for refreshments. **3** a sideboard or cupboard often used for the display of tableware.

buffet² *v* (**buffeted, buffeting**) to strike (something) repeatedly; to batter: *The waves buffeted the shore.*

buffet car *n Brit* a railway carriage with a counter at which snacks and drinks can be bought.

buffeting *n* the shaking or vibrating of an aircraft or part of an aircraft caused by irregular air currents.

buffoon *n* **1** a person who behaves ludicrously in order to amuse others; a clown. **2** a noisy, clumsy, or incompetent fool. ➤➤ **buffoonery** *n*.

bug¹ *n* **1** *technical* an insect with mouthparts that enable it to pierce and suck. **2** any creeping or crawling insect commonly considered unpleasant or a pest, e.g. a bedbug. **3** *informal* any micro-organism, *esp* a disease-producing bacterium, or a disease caused by it. **4** an unexpected defect or imperfection. **5** a fault in a computer program. **6**

informal a temporary enthusiasm; a craze. **7** a concealed listening device.

bug[2] *v* (**bugged, bugging**) **1** *informal* to bother or annoy. **2** to plant a concealed listening device in (a place).

bugaboo *n* (*pl* **-os**) *chiefly NAm* a source of often imaginary fear or anxiety.

bugbear *n* a source of persistent dread, concern, or difficulty.

bug-eyed *adj* with eyes that protrude.

bugger[1] *n coarse slang* **1a** a disagreeable or contemptible person, *esp* a man or boy. **b** a person of a specified kind. **2** *chiefly Brit* a cause of annoyance or difficulty. **3** a man who has anal intercourse.

bugger[2] *v coarse slang* **1** (*often* + up) to damage or ruin (something), usu because of incompetence. **2** *Brit* (+ around/about) to cause (somebody) problems, *esp* by being deliberately evasive or misleading. **3** to have anal intercourse with. **4** used interjectionally to express contempt or annoyance.

bugger all *n Brit, coarse slang* nothing.

bugger off *v Brit, coarse slang* to go away.

buggery *n* anal intercourse.

buggy *n* (*pl* **-ies**) **1** a lightweight foldable pushchair. **2** a motor vehicle of basic design, *esp* one for use on beaches or a lunar exploration vehicle. **3** a light one-horse carriage.

bugle[1] *n* a valveless brass musical instrument that resembles a small trumpet, used *esp* for military calls.

bugle[2] *v* to sound a bugle. ➤➤ **bugler** *n.*

bugle[3] *n* a European annual plant of the mint family that has spikes of usu blue flowers.

bugloss *n* a coarse hairy plant of the borage family that grows mainly in dry and sandy areas.

buhl *or* **boulle** /boohl/ *n* inlaid decoration of tortoiseshell or ornamental metalwork, e.g. brass, used in cabinetwork.

build[1] *v* (*past tense and past part.* **built**) **1** to construct by putting together materials gradually into a composite whole. **2** (+ on) to develop (a concept, scheme, or relationship) according to specified principles. **3** to increase gradually in size or intensity. ➤➤ **builder** *n.*

build[2] *n* the physical proportions of a person or animal, *esp* a person's figure of a usu specified type: *an athletic build.*

build in *v* to construct or develop as an integral part.

building *n* **1** a permanent structure usu having walls and a roof. **2** the business or act of assembling materials into a structure.

building society *n* an organization providing its members with financial services similar to those of a bank, *esp* investment accounts and loans in the form of mortgages.

buildup *n* **1** a gradual increase. **2** praise or publicity, *esp* given in advance.

build up *v* **1** to accumulate or develop. **2** to develop (something) gradually by increments.

built[1] *v* past tense and past part. of BUILD[1].

built[2] *adj* proportioned or formed in a specified way.

built-in *adj* **1** forming an integral part of a structure. **2** existing naturally or as a basic or essential feature; intrinsic.

built-up *adj* of an area: in which many houses and other buildings are situated.

bulb *n* **1** a short stem base of a plant, with one or more buds enclosed in overlapping membranous or fleshy leaves, that is formed underground as a resting stage in the plant's development: compare CORM, TUBER. **2** a light bulb. **3** a part shaped like a bulb, e.g. the mercury reservoir of a thermometer.

bulbil *n* in botany, a small or secondary bulb, *esp* a bud that grows in the angle between the stem and the leaf or in place of flowers on some plants and is capable of producing a new plant.

bulbous *adj* **1** resembling a bulb, *esp* in roundness. **2** growing from or bearing bulbs.

bulgar *n* see BULGUR.

Bulgarian *n* **1** a native or inhabitant of Bulgaria. **2** the Slavonic language of this people. ➤➤ **Bulgarian** *adj.*

bulge[1] *n* **1** a swelling or convex curve on a surface, usu caused by pressure from within or below. **2** *informal* a sudden and usu temporary expansion, e.g. in population. ➤➤ **bulging** *adj*, **bulgy** *adj.*

bulge[2] *v* to swell or curve outwards.

bulgur *or* **bulgar** *n* wheat grain that has been parboiled, dried, and broken into pieces, popular in Middle Eastern cookery; cracked wheat.

bulimia *n* an emotional disorder in which the sufferer follows periods of compulsive overeating with periods of fasting or self-induced vomiting, often accompanied by depression. ➤➤ **bulimic** *adj and n.*

bulimia nervosa *n* = BULIMIA.

bulk[1] *n* **1** thickness, volume, size, or extent, *esp* when great. **2** a large, heavy, or substantial mass. **3** (+ of) the main or greater part. **4** dietary fibre; roughage. ✱ **in bulk** in large amounts or quantities.

bulk[2] *v* **1** (*often* + out) to cause to swell or to be thicker or fuller; to pad: *I had to bulk the text out to 20,000 words.* **2** to appear as a factor; to loom: *It is a consideration that bulks large in everyone's thinking.*

bulk[3] *adj* of materials: bought or sold in large quantities, usu unpackaged.

bulkhead *n* a partition or wall separating compartments, e.g. in an aircraft or ship.

bulky *adj* (**-ier, -iest**) having too much bulk, *esp* unwieldy or cumbersome.

bull[1] *n* **1a** an adult male bovine animal. **b** an adult male elephant, whale, or other large animal. **2** somebody who buys securities or commodities in expectation of a price rise or who acts to effect such a rise: compare BEAR[1]. **3** *Brit* a bull's-eye. ✱ **like a bull in a china shop** clumsy or tactless. **take the bull by the horns** to face up to a problem.

bull[2] *n* a papal edict.

bull[3] *n informal* nonsense.

bull bar *n* a protective metal grille fitted to the front of a vehicle.

bulldog *n* a sturdy breed of dog with widely separated forelegs, a short neck, and a wide head with a projecting lower jaw.

bulldog clip *n Brit, trademark* a large clip used to clamp sheets of paper together.

bulldoze *v* **1** to move, clear, demolish, or level with a bulldozer. **2** to force (*esp* one's way) insensitively or ruthlessly. **3** *informal* (*often* + into) to bully or intimidate somebody.

bulldozer *n* an earth-moving vehicle fitted with caterpillar tracks, with a broad blunt horizontal blade at one end, mounted on a pivoting arm.

bullet *n* **1** a small round or elongated projectile designed to be fired from a pistol, rifle, or other firearm. **2** in printing, a large dot used to introduce each of several lines or passages of text, e.g. points in a list. **3** (**the bullet**) *informal* dismissal from employment.

bulletin *n* **1** a brief public notice, *esp* a brief news item. **2** a short programme of news items on radio or television. **3** a journal published at regular intervals, *esp* the journal of an institution or association.

bulletin board *n* **1** *NAm* a noticeboard. **2** a computer-based information exchange system that authorized users can access by direct telephone communication.

bullet train *n informal* a Japanese high-speed train.

bullfight *n* a spectacle in an arena in which bulls are ceremonially fought with, and in Hispanic tradition killed, for public entertainment. ➤➤ **bullfighter** *n*, **bullfighting** *n*.

bullfinch *n* a European finch, the male of which has a rosy red breast and throat, a blue-grey back, and a black cap, chin, tail, and wings.

bullfrog *n* a large frog with a deep croak, native to N America.

bullheaded *adj* stupidly stubborn; headstrong.

bullhorn *n chiefly NAm* a megaphone.

bullion *n* gold or silver in bars that has not been minted.

bullish *adj* **1** marked by, tending to cause, or hopeful of rising prices, e.g. in a stock market: compare BEARISH. **2** energetically optimistic or enterprising. ➤➤ **bullishly** *adv*, **bullishness** *n*.

bull market *n* a stock market characterized by rising share prices.

bullock *n* a young castrated bull.

bullring *n* an arena for bullfights.

bull's-eye *n* **1** the centre of a target, or a shot that hits it. **2** a very hard round usu peppermint sweet.

bullshit[1] *n coarse slang* nonsense.

bullshit[2] *v* (**bullshitting,** *past tense and past part.* **bullshit** *or* **bullshitted**) *coarse slang* to talk loudly or confidently about something of which one has no knowledge. ➤➤ **bullshitter** *n*.

bull terrier *n* a short-haired breed of terrier, a cross between a bulldog and a breed of terrier.

bully[1] *n* (*pl* **-ies**) a browbeating person, *esp* somebody who is habitually cruel to other weaker people.

bully[2] *v* (**-ies, -ied**) to intimidate with persistently aggressive or violent behaviour, or by using threats of violence.

bully[3] *n* (*pl* **-ies**) in hockey, a procedure for starting play in a match, in which two opposing players face each other and alternately strike the ground and the opponent's stick three times before attempting to gain possession of the ball.

bully[4] *adj and interj* used, sometimes ironically, as a general expression of approval: excellent.

bully[5] *v* (**-ies, -ied**) (+ off) to start or restart a hockey match with a bully.

bully[6] *n* = BULLY BEEF.

bully beef *n informal* beef that has been preserved with salt and tinned.

bully-off *n* (*pl* **bully-offs**) = BULLY[3].

bulrush *n* **1** an annual or perennial grasslike plant that grows in wet areas and is a variety of sedge. **2** either of two plants that have a tall stem topped with a thick furry spike of densely packed flowers and are varieties of reedmace.

bulwark *n* **1a** a solid wall-like structure built, e.g. around a fort, for defence; a rampart. **b** a breakwater or seawall. **2** (*usu in pl*) the side of a ship above the upper deck.

bum[1] *n Brit, informal* the buttocks.

bum[2] *adj informal* bad, wrong, or worthless: *bum advice.*

bum[3] *n NAm, informal* **1** an idler or loafer. **2** a homeless person who lives on the streets. **3** an incompetent person. **4** somebody who devotes his or her time to a specified recreational activity: *a beach bum.*

bum[4] *v* (**bummed, bumming**) **1** *chiefly NAm, informal* (+ around) to spend time idly. **2** *informal* to obtain by begging; to cadge.

bum bag *n Brit, informal* a small bag for personal belongings, attached to a belt worn around the waist.

bumble[1] *v* **1** to speak in a faltering or rambling manner. **2** (*often* + along) to move or act in a clumsy or incompetent manner. ➤➤ **bumbler** *n*.

bumble[2] *v* of an insect: to drone.

bumblebee *n* a large hairy bee with a deep loud hum.

bumf *or* **bumph** *n chiefly Brit, informal* documents, brochures, and other paperwork regarded as superfluous or unwanted.

bummalo *n* (*pl* **bummalo**) = BOMBAY DUCK.

bummer[1] *n informal* an unpleasant experience, *esp* a piece of bad luck or a bad reaction to a hallucinogenic drug.

bummer[2] *n NAm* = BUM[3] (1).

bump[1] *v* **1** to strike or knock with force. **2** to injure or damage (something) by striking it on something hard, usu accidentally. **3** to collide with. **4** to dislodge with a jolt. **5** to move in a series of bumps, e.g. in a vehicle along an uneven road. ✱ **bump into** to meet (somebody) unexpectedly or by chance.

bump[2] *n* **1** a sudden forceful blow or jolt. **2** a swelling or protuberance.

bumper[1] *n* a metal, rubber, or plastic bar fitted at either end of a motor vehicle for absorbing shock or minimizing damage in collision.

bumper[2] *adj* unusually large or fine.

bumper[3] *n archaic* a brimming cup or glass.

bumper car *n* a car used in dodgems.

bumph *n* see BUMF.

bumpkin *n* an awkward and unsophisticated person, *esp* from the country.

bump off *v informal* to murder.

bumptious *adj* self-assertive in a presumptuous manner; overbearing. ➤➤ **bumptiously** *adv*, **bumptiousness** *n*.

bump up *v informal* to raise or increase (something, e.g. a price).

bumpy *adj* (**-ier, -iest**) **1** having or covered with bumps; uneven. **2** marked by jolts. ➤➤ **bumpily** *adv*, **bumpiness** *n*.

bum's rush *n NAm, informal* forcible ejection from a place or dismissal from a position: *They gave him the bum's rush.*

bun *n* **1** a small round bread roll or cake. **2** a tight knot of hair worn on the back of the head. **3** *NAm, informal* (*in pl*) buttocks. ✱ **have a bun in the oven** *informal* to be pregnant.

bunch[1] *n* **1** a compact group formed by a number of things of the same kind, *esp* when growing or loosely held together; a cluster. **2** *informal* a group of people. ➤➤ **bunchy** *adj*.

bunch[2] *v* (*often* + up) to form (people or things) into a group or cluster.

bundle[1] *n* **1** a collection of things held loosely together. **2** a small band of mostly parallel nerve or other fibres. **3** *informal* a sizable sum of money. ✱ **go a bundle on** *Brit, informal* (*usu in negative contexts*) to like or enjoy.

bundle[2] *v* **1** to make (things) into a bundle or package. **2** *informal* to hustle or hurry (somebody) unceremoniously. **3** (+ into) to hastily deposit or stuff into a suitcase, box, drawer, etc.

bundle up *v* to dress (somebody) warmly.

bun-fight *n Brit, informal* a social gathering at which food is served, *esp* a tea party.

bung[1] *n* a stopper in the hole of a cask.

bung[2] *v* **1** (*often* + up) to plug, block, or close with, or as if with, a bung. **2** *chiefly Brit, informal* to throw, toss, or put.

bung[3] *n Brit, informal* a bribe.

bung[4] *adj Aus, NZ, informal* **1** broken or useless. **2** dead. ✱ **go bung 1** to die. **2** to fail.

bungalow *n* a single-storeyed house.

bungee *n* an elasticated rope used to secure objects and in the sport of bungee jumping.

bungee jumping *n* the activity or sport of diving from a high place, e.g. a bridge or a crane, with the feet attached to a bungee designed to pull the jumper up just before he or she would hit the ground. ⋙ **bungee jump** *n.*

bungle[1] *v* to perform or handle clumsily; to botch. ⋙ **bungler** *n,* **bungling** *adj.*

bungle[2] *n* something done clumsily; a botch.

bunion *n* an inflamed swelling at the side of the foot on the first joint of the big toe.

bunk[1] *n* **1** a built-in bed, e.g. on a ship, that is often one of a tier of berths. **2** a bunk bed.

bunk[2] *v* (*often* + down) to sleep or bed down, *esp* in a makeshift bed.

bunk[3] *n informal, dated* nonsense.

bunk[4] ✱ **do a bunk** *chiefly Brit, informal* to make a hurried departure, *esp* in order to escape.

bunk bed *n* either of two single beds constructed so as to sit one above the other.

bunker[1] *n* **1** a bin or compartment for storage, *esp* one for storing coal or other fuel. **2** a protective embankment or dugout, *esp* a fortified chamber built of reinforced concrete and set mostly below ground. **3** a golf course hazard that is an area of sand-covered bare ground with one or more embankments.

bunker[2] *v* to place or store (*esp* fuel) in a bunker.

bunkhouse *n NAm* a rough simple building providing sleeping quarters, e.g. for workers on a ranch.

bunk off *v chiefly Brit, informal* to play truant from school.

bunny *n* (*pl* **-ies**) *informal* used by or to children: a rabbit.

bunny girl *n* a nightclub hostess who wears a costume that includes a stylized rabbit's tail and ears.

Bunsen burner *n* a gas burner in which air is mixed with the gas to produce an intensely hot blue flame.

bunting[1] *n* a bird that has a short strong beak and is related to the finches.

bunting[2] *n* flags, pennants, streamers, and other decorations collectively.

bunyip *n Aus* a mythical monster that is supposed to inhabit swamps in remote parts of Australia.

buoy[1] *n* a distinctively shaped and marked float moored to the bottom of a body of water, as a navigational aid to mark a channel or hazard, or for mooring a ship.

buoy[2] *v* **1a** (+ up) to keep (something) afloat. **b** (+ up) to support or sustain. **2** (+ up) to raise the spirits of.

buoyant *adj* **1** capable of floating. **2** cheerful or resilient. **3** of prices or business activity: maintaining a satisfactorily high level. ⋙ **buoyancy** *n,* **buoyantly** *adv.*

BUPA *abbr* British United Provident Association, a private health insurance company.

bur *n* see BURR[1] (1).

burble[1] *v* **1** to make a bubbling sound; to gurgle. **2** to speak rapidly or ramblingly; to prattle.

burble[2] *n* **1** a burbling sound. **2** rapid or rambling speech.

burbot *n* (*pl* **burbots** *or* **burbot**) a freshwater fish of the cod family that has barbels on its mouth.

burden[1] *n* **1** something that is carried; a load. **2** something, e.g. a responsibility or debt, regarded as oppressive or wearisome; an encumbrance. **3** capacity for carrying cargo.

burden[2] *v* to give (somebody) a burden of some kind to bear.

burden[3] *n* **1** the chorus or refrain of a song or poem. **2** a central topic; a theme.

burden of proof *n* the duty of proving an assertion.

burdensome *adj* imposing or constituting a burden; oppressive.

burdock *n* a sturdy plant of the daisy family that has prickly purple spherical flower heads similar to those of the thistles.

bureau /'byooəroh/ *n* (*pl* **bureaus** *or* **bureaux**) **1a** a specialized administrative unit, *esp* a government department. **b** an office or agency where information or contacts are provided, *esp* one offering a public service. **2a** *Brit* a writing desk with drawers and a sloping top. **b** *NAm* a low chest of drawers.

bureaucracy *n* (*pl* **-ies**) **1** government characterized by specialization of functions, adherence to fixed rules, and a hierarchy of authority. **2** any administrative system that is marked by excessive officialism. ⋙ **bureaucratic** *adj.*

bureaucrat *n* **1** a member of a bureaucracy, *esp* a government official. **2** any official or representative who rigidly adheres to inflexible rules or procedures.

bureaucratize *or* **-ise** *v* to make bureaucratic. ⋙ **bureaucratization** *n.*

bureau de change /də 'shonzh/ *n* (*pl* **bureaux de change**) an office or part of a bank where money can be changed into other currencies.

bureaux *n* pl of BUREAU.

bureaux de change *n* pl of BUREAU DE CHANGE.

burette (*NAm* **buret**) *n* a graduated glass tube with a small hole at the bottom that is opened and closed by a tap, used for dispensing measured quantities of liquid.

burgeon *v* **1** to send forth new growth, e.g. buds or branches. **2** to grow and expand rapidly.

burger *n* = HAMBURGER.

burgess *n* **1** *archaic* a citizen of a British borough. **2** formerly, a Member of Parliament for a borough, city, or university.

burgh *n* **1** *archaic* a borough. **2** a town in Scotland that has a charter.

burgher *n archaic* an inhabitant of an *esp* medieval borough or a town.

burglar *n* somebody who commits burglary.

burglarize *or* **-ise** *v NAm* to burgle (a building or person).

burglary *n* (*pl* **-ies**) the offence of unlawfully entering a building with criminal intent, *esp* to steal.

burgle *v* to commit an act of burglary in (a building) or against (a person).

Burgundy *n* (*pl* **-ies**) a red or white table wine from the Burgundy region of France.

burgundy *adj* of a deep purplish red colour. ➤➤ **burgundy** *n.*

burial *n* the burying of a dead body.

burin *n* **1** an engraver's steel cutting tool. **2** a prehistoric flint tool with a bevelled point.

burk *or* **berk** *n Brit, slang* a stupid person.

Burkinan *n* a native or inhabitant of Burkina Faso. ➤➤ **Burkinan** *adj.*

burl *n* **1** a knot or lump in thread or cloth. **2** *NAm* a hard rounded outgrowth on a tree.

burlap *n* a coarse heavy plain-woven fabric, usu of jute or hemp, used for sacking.

burlesque[1] *n* **1** a literary or dramatic work that uses exaggeration or imitation to ridicule. **2** *NAm* a stage show usu consisting of short turns, comic sketches, and striptease acts.

burlesque[2] *v* (**burlesques, burlesqued, burlesquing**) to imitate in a humorous or derisive manner; to mock.

burly *adj* (**-ier, -iest**) strongly and heavily built. ➤➤ **burliness** *n.*

Burman *n* (*pl* **Burmans**) = BURMESE. ➤➤ **Burman** *adj.*

Burmese *n* (*pl* **Burmese**) a native or inhabitant of Myanmar. ➤➤ **Burmese** *adj.*

Burmese cat *n* a cat of a breed resembling the Siamese cat but of solid and darker colour.

burn[1] *v* (*past and past part.* **burned** *or* **burnt**) **1** to undergo or cause to undergo combustion by fire. **2** to injure or damage by exposure to fire or heat, or to become charred, scorched, or destroyed in this way. **3** of a fire: to consume fuel and give off heat, light, and gases. **4** to use as fuel. **5** of the skin: to become reddened and sore from exposure to heat. **6** (+ with) to experience a strong emotion or desire. **7** *informal* to drive very fast. ✱ **burn one's bridges/boats** to commit oneself to a course of action that cannot be reversed. **burn one's fingers** see FINGER[1]. **burn the candle at both ends** to be active at night as well as by day. **burn the midnight oil** to work or study far into the night.

burn[2] *n* an injury or damage resulting from burning.

burn[3] *n chiefly Scot* a small stream.

burner *n* the part of a fuel-burning device, e.g. a stove or furnace, where the flame is produced.

burning *adj* **1a** on fire. **b** ardent or intense. **2** of fundamental importance; urgent. ➤➤ **burningly** *adv.*

burnish[1] *v* to make (something, *esp* metal) shiny or lustrous, *esp* by rubbing; to polish. ➤➤ **burnisher** *n.*

burnish[2] *n* a shine or lustre.

burnous (*NAm* **burnoose**) /buh'noohs/ *n* a hooded cloak traditionally worn by Arabs and Moors.

burnout *n* **1** a condition of extreme exhaustion and disillusionment caused by overwork and stress. **2** the moment at which a jet or rocket engine uses up its fuel and ceases to operate.

burn out *v* **1** of a fuse or other electrical device: to cease to conduct electricity when the filament has melted. **2** to become exhausted from overwork or stress.

burnt *v chiefly Brit* past tense and past part. of BURN[1].

burp[1] *n informal* a belch.

burp[2] *v* **1** *informal* to belch. **2** to relieve the indigestion of (a baby) by patting or rubbing its back.

burr[1] *n* **1** (*also* **bur**) a rough or prickly covering of a fruit or seed. **2** a thin rough edge left after cutting or shaping metal, plastic, etc. **3** the rolled pronunciation of /r/ made at the back of the throat or the front of the mouth. **4** a small drill, e.g. one used by a dentist or surgeon. **5** a rough whirring sound.

burr[2] *v* **1** to make a whirring sound. **2** to form a rough or projecting edge on (metal).

burrito *n* (*pl* **-os**) a tortilla rolled round a savoury filling and baked.

burro *n* (*pl* **-os**) *chiefly NAm* a small donkey used as a pack animal.

burrow[1] *n* a hole or excavation in the ground made by a rabbit, fox, etc.

burrow[2] *v* **1** to construct or excavate (e.g. a hole or passage) by tunnelling. **2** to conceal oneself in, or as if in, a burrow. **3** to make a search as if by digging. ➤➤ **burrower** *n.*

bursa *n* (*pl* **bursas** *or* **bursae**) a small sac or pouch in the body, *esp* a fluid-filled sac between a tendon and a bone.

bursar *n* **1** *chiefly Brit* an officer, e.g. of a monastery or college, in charge of funds. **2** *Scot* the holder of a bursary.

bursary *n* (*pl* **-ies**) a grant of money awarded to a student; a scholarship.

bursitis *n* inflammation of a bursa of the knee, shoulder, elbow, or other joint.

burst[1] *v* (*past tense and past part.* **burst**) **1** to break or cause to break suddenly and violently apart or into pieces. **2a** to give vent suddenly to a repressed emotion: *He burst into tears.* **b** to begin suddenly and forcefully: *They burst into song.* **3** to emerge or appear suddenly: *She burst out of the house.* **4** (+ with) to be filled to breaking point or to the point of overflowing.

burst[2] *n* **1** a sudden usu temporary outbreak or eruption. **2** a sudden, usu brief, intense effort or exertion; a spurt. **3** a volley of shots from a usu automatic firearm.

burst out *v* **1** to begin suddenly. **2** to exclaim suddenly.

burton ✱ **go for a burton** *Brit, informal* to be broken, destroyed, or ruined.

Burundian *n* a native or inhabitant of Burundi. ➤➤ **Burundian** *adj.*

bury *v* (**-ies, -ied**) **1** to place (a corpse) in the earth or a tomb with the appropriate funeral rites. **2** to hide or dispose of (something) by depositing it in the earth. **3** to cover from view; to conceal. **4** (+ in) to submerge or engross (somebody, *esp* oneself). ✱ **bury the hatchet** to settle a disagreement and become reconciled [from the custom among Native Americans of burying all weapons during peace negotiations].

bus[1] *n* (*pl* **buses,** *NAm* **busses**) **1** a large motor-driven passenger vehicle operating usu according to a timetable along a fixed route. **2** a conductor or an assembly of conductors connected to several similar circuits in an electrical or electronic system, e.g. one that carries data from one part of a computer to another.

bus[2] *v* (**bused** *or* **bussed, busing** *or* **bussing**) **1** to travel by bus. **2** to transport (people) by bus. **3** *NAm* to work as a busboy.

busboy *n NAm* a waiter.

busby *n* (*pl* **-ies**) **1** a military full-dress fur hat that has a small bag hanging one side, worn *esp* by hussars. **2** *informal* the bearskin worn by the Brigade of Guards.

bush[1] *n* **1a** a shrub, *esp* one with a woody stem and branches that grow thickly from it at a low level. **b** a dense thicket of shrubs. **2** (*usu* **the bush**) a large uncleared or sparsely settled area, e.g. in Africa or Australia. **3** *coarse slang* the pubic hair.

bush[2] *v* to grow thickly or spread like a bush.

bush[3] *or* **bushing** *n* **1** a cylindrical lining for an opening through which a shaft passes, e.g. in a car's suspension system. **2** an electrically insulated lining for a hole through which a wire passes.

bush baby *n* a small active nocturnal tree-dwelling African primate with large eyes and ears, and a long tail and hind limbs.

bushed *adj informal* **1** exhausted. **2** *chiefly Aus* lost, *esp* in the bush.

bushel *n* **1** a British unit of volume used for grain and other dry goods and for liquids, equal to 8 imperial gallons (about 36.4l). **2** a US unit of volume used for dry goods, equal to 64 US pints (about 30.3l). ✱ **hide one's light under a bushel** see HIDE[1].

Bushido /boohshi'doh/ *n* the Japanese code of chivalry that originated with the Samurai warriors, valuing honour above life, and stressing loyalty to the feudal lord or emperor.

bushing *n* see BUSH[3].

bushman *n* (*pl* **bushmen**) **1** (**Bushman**) a member of a race of nomadic hunting people of southern Africa. **2** *dated* the San languages spoken by these peoples. **3** *chiefly Aus* somebody who lives in the bush.

bushranger *n* **1** *NAm* somebody who lives in a sparsely populated uncultivated or forested area. **2** *Aus* an outlaw living in the bush.

bush telegraph *n* the rapid unofficial communication of news by word of mouth.

bushwhack *v* **1** *NAm, Aus, NZ* to clear a path through thick woods by chopping down bushes and low branches. **2** *NAm, Aus, NZ* to live or hide out in the woods. **3** to ambush. ➤➤ **bushwhacker** *n.*

bush-whacked *adj* exhausted.

bushy[1] *adj* (**-ier, -iest**) **1** growing thickly or densely. **2** full of or overgrown with bushes. ➤➤ **bushily** *adv,* **bushiness** *n.*

bushy[2] *n* (*pl* **-ies**) *Aus, NZ, informal* somebody who lives in the bush.

business *n* **1a** a commercial activity engaged in as a means of livelihood. **b** one's regular employment, profession, or trade. **c** a commercial or industrial enterprise or commercial and industrial enterprises as a whole. **d** custom. **2** an immediate task or objective; a mission. **3** an affair of some kind; a matter. **4** personal concern. **5** movements or actions performed by an actor. **6** (**the business**) *informal* excellent, or precisely what is needed. ✱ **like nobody's business** extraordinarily well or rapidly. **mean business** to speak or act with serious intent.

business end *n informal* the end of a tool, machine, etc that performs the work.

businesslike *adj* efficient and systematic.

businessman *or* **businesswoman** *n* (*pl* **businessmen** *or* **businesswomen**) a man or woman who is professionally engaged in commercial transactions, *esp* in an executive capacity.

busk *v* to sing or play an instrument in the street in order to earn money. ➤➤ **busker** *n.*

buskin *n* formerly, a laced boot reaching halfway up the calf or to the knee, e.g. the high thick-soled boot worn by actors in ancient Athenian tragedy.

busman *n* (*pl* **busmen**) a bus driver.

busman's holiday *n* a holiday spent doing the kind of thing one normally does at work.

bust[1] *n* **1** a woman's breasts. **2** a sculpture of the upper part of the human figure including the head, neck, and usu shoulders.

bust[2] *v* (*past tense and past part.* **busted** *or* **bust**) *informal* **1** to break or smash (something) or make it inoperative. **2** to burst or become inoperative through breakage or wear; to break down. **3** *chiefly NAm* **a** to arrest (somebody). **b** to raid (a place). **4** *NAm* to demote (somebody), *esp* to a lower military rank.

bust[3] *adj informal* **1** broken. **2** bankrupt.

bust[4] *n informal* **1** a police raid or arrest. **2** a period of economic collapse.

bustard *n* a large long-legged and long-necked game bird that builds nests on the ground, has a slow stately walk, and is capable of powerful swift flight when alarmed.

buster *n chiefly NAm, informal* used as an often disrespectful form of address to a man or boy.

bustier /'boostiay/ *n* an article of women's clothing similar to a bodice, worn as a top.

bustle[1] *v* **1** to move briskly and often with an ostentatious show of activity or purpose. **2** to be full of people and activity. ➤➤ **bustling** *adj.*

bustle[2] *n* noisy and energetic activity.

bustle[3] *n* a pad or framework worn formerly to expand and support fullness at the back of a woman's skirt.

bust-up *n informal* a quarrel or brawl.

busty *adj* (**-ier, -iest**) *informal* of a woman: having large breasts.

busy[1] *adj* (**-ier, -iest**) **1** engaged in an activity and giving it full attention; occupied. **2** full of activity; bustling. **3** full or too full of detail. ➤➤ **busily** *adv,* **busyness** *n.*

busy[2] *v* (**-ies, -ied**) to make (*esp* oneself) busy; to occupy (*esp* oneself).

busybody *n* (*pl* **-ies**) a meddlesome or inquisitive person.

busy lizzie *n* a common house plant that bears usu pink, scarlet, or crimson flowers almost continuously.

but[1] *conj* **1** used to join coordinate sentence elements of the same class or function expressing contrast: on the other hand: *I meant to tell you but you weren't here.* **2** and nevertheless; yet: *They were poor but proud.* **3** used to introduce an expression of protest or enthusiasm: *But that's ridiculous!* **4** *formal* were it not; save: *He would have collapsed but for your help.*

but[2] *prep* **1** with the exception of (something or somebody); barring (them): *We're all here but Mary.* **2** other than (something): *This letter is nothing but an insult.* **3** not counting (something): *They live in the next house but two.*

but[3] *adv* **1** only or merely. **2** *NE Eng, Aus* however or though: *It's pouring with rain, warm but.*

but[4] *n* a doubt or objection.

butane *n* an inflammable gas obtained usu from petroleum or natural gas and used *esp* as a fuel, e.g. in cigarette lighters.

butch *adj informal* of a woman or homosexual man: aggressively masculine in appearance or behaviour.

butcher[1] *n* **1a** a person who slaughters animals bred for meat or cuts up and prepares them for sale. **b** somebody who sells or deals in meat. **2** somebody who kills people ruthlessly or brutally. ✱ **have/take a butcher's** *Brit, slang* to have a look [rhyming slang *butcher's hook* 'look'].

butcher[2] *v* **1** to slaughter and prepare (an animal) for sale. **2** to kill (people) ruthlessly or indiscriminately. **3** to spoil or ruin by clumsy or unthinking treatment. ➤➤ **butchery** *n.*

butcher-bird *n* a bird of the shrike family that often impales its prey on thorns.

butler *n* the chief male servant of a large household.

butt[1] *v* to strike or shove with the head or horns.

butt[2] *n* a blow or thrust with the head or horns.

butt[3] *n* **1** the thicker or handle end of a tool or weapon. **2** the unsmoked remnant of a cigar or cigarette. **3** *NAm, informal* the buttocks.

butt[4] *n* **1** an object of abuse or ridicule; a victim. **2a** a target used in archery or rifle practice. **b** (*in pl*) a shooting range for archery or rifle practice. **c** a low mound, wall, etc from behind which hunters shoot at game birds.

butt[5] *v* **1** to place end to end or side to side without overlapping. **2** to join (pieces, e.g. of wood) by means of a butt joint. **3** (+ against/on to) to abut.

butt[6] *n* a large barrel for water, wine, or beer.

butte /byooht/ *n NAm or technical* an isolated hill with steep sides, usually with a smaller summit area than a mesa.

butter[1] *n* a pale yellow solid substance that is used as food, e.g. for spreading on bread and in baking, made by churning milk or cream. ✻ **look as if butter wouldn't melt (in one's mouth)** to have an innocent or meek appearance that may well be deceptive.

butter[2] *v* to spread or coat with butter.

butter bean *n* a large dried lima bean.

buttercream *n* a creamy icing or cake filling made with butter and icing sugar.

buttercup *n* a plant with usu bright yellow flowers that commonly grows in fields and as a weed.

butterfat *n* the natural fat of milk and chief constituent of butter.

butterfingers *n* (*pl* **butterfingers**) *informal* somebody who tends to drop things.

butterfly *n* (*pl* **-ies**) **1** a slender-bodied insect that flies by day and has large, broad, often brightly coloured wings and long thin antennae. **2** a frivolous person, *esp* one chiefly occupied with the pursuit of pleasure. **3** a swimming stroke executed on the front by moving both arms together forwards out of the water and then sweeping them back through the water while kicking the legs up and down together. **4** *informal* (*in pl*) queasiness caused by nervous tension.

butterfly effect *n* the progressive production of a vast and far-reaching effect by a small and apparently insignificant cause.

butterfly nut *n* = WING NUT.

butter icing *n* = BUTTERCREAM.

buttermilk *n* **1** the liquid left after butter has been churned from milk or cream. **2** fermented, slightly sour milk made by the addition of suitable bacteria to milk.

butter muslin *n Brit* thin muslin with a fine mesh, orig used to wrap butter.

butternut squash *n* a pear-shaped winter squash with a pale rind.

butterscotch *n* a brittle toffee made from brown sugar, syrup, butter, and water.

butter up *v informal* to charm with lavish flattery; to cajole.

buttery[1] *n* (*pl* **-ies**) *Brit* a room in a college in which food and drink are sold.

buttery[2] *adj* similar to or containing butter. ➤➤ **butteriness** *n.*

buttie *n* see BUTTY.

butt in *v* **1** to meddle or intrude. **2** to interrupt.

butt joint *n* a joint made by placing the ends or sides of the parts together without overlap and often with reinforcement.

buttock *n* the back of a hip that forms one of the two fleshy parts on which a person sits.

button[1] *n* **1** a small knob or disc secured to an article, e.g. of clothing, and used as a fastener by passing it through a buttonhole or loop. **2** *chiefly NAm* a badge bearing a design or slogan. **3** a knob on an item of electrical or electronic equipment that is pressed to activate a function. **4** a guard on the tip of a fencing foil. ✻ **on the button** *informal* with absolute precision; exactly.

button[2] *v* (*often* + up) to close or fasten (something) with buttons.

button-down *adj* of a collar: having the ends fastened to the garment with buttons.

buttonhole[1] *n* **1** a slit or loop in the edge of a piece of material, through which a button is passed. **2** *Brit* a flower worn in a buttonhole or pinned to the lapel.

buttonhole[2] *v informal* to detain in conversation.

button mushroom *n* an immature whole mushroom.

button-through *adj Brit* of a garment: fastened from the top to the bottom with buttons.

buttress[1] *n* **1** a supporting structure built against a wall or building to provide reinforcement. **2** a projecting part of a mountain, *esp* on a rock cliff.

buttress[2] *v* **1** to support (a wall) with a buttress. **2** to give support or strength to (something, e.g. an argument).

butty *or* **buttie** *n* (*pl* **-ies**) *Brit, informal* a sandwich.

butut /booh'tooht/ *n* a unit of currency in The Gambia, worth 100th of a dalasi.

butyl *n* any of various chemical groups derived from butane.

buxom *adj* of a woman: with an attractively rounded figure and large breasts.

buy[1] *v* (*past tense and past part.* **bought**) **1** to become the owner of (something) by paying or agreeing to pay money for it. **2** to obtain (something), often by some sacrifice. **3** *informal* to believe or accept (something said or proposed).

buy[2] *n informal* a purchase.

buyer *n* somebody who buys something, *esp* a person who selects and buys stock to be sold in a shop or other business.

buyer's market *n* a market in which supply exceeds demand, buyers have a wide range of choice, and prices tend to be low: compare SELLER'S MARKET.

buyout *n* the purchase of all the shares in a business, or a controlling proportion of them, *esp* by its managers.

buy out *v* **1** to buy the shares or controlling interest of (a company). **2** to buy the share of (somebody) to get control of a company. **3** to free (somebody, *esp* oneself) from military service by payment.

buzz[1] *v* **1** to make a continuous low humming sound like that of a bee. **2** to be filled with the murmur of voices, or with gossip or rumours. **3** to make a signal with a buzzer. **4** to move in a hurried, energetic, or busy manner. **5** to summon (somebody) or signal (somebody or something) with a buzzer. **6** *informal* to fly over or close to (somebody or something) in order to threaten or warn them.

buzz[2] *n* **1** a continuous low humming sound. **2** a confused murmur or flurry of activity. **3** *informal* rumour or gossip. **4** a signal conveyed by a buzzer or bell. **5** *informal* a telephone call. **6** *informal* a pleasant stimulation; a kick.

buzzard *n* **1** *chiefly Brit* a large European hawk with broad rounded wings and a soaring flight. **2** *chiefly NAm* a large bird of prey, e.g. the turkey buzzard.

buzz cut *n* a crew cut.

buzzer *n* an electrical signalling device that makes a buzzing sound.

buzz off *v informal* to go away.

buzz saw *n NAm* a circular saw.

buzzword *n informal* a usu technical word or phrase that has become fashionable and is frequently bandied about.

BVM *abbr* Blessed Virgin Mary.

b/w *abbr* black and white.

bwana *n* often used in former times by an E African person to a European settler: master or boss.

by[1] *prep* **1** in proximity to (somebody or something); near (them): *standing by the window.* **2a** through, or through the medium of (something); via (it): *Enter by the door.* **b** up to and then beyond (somebody or something); past (them): *The bullet went right by him.* **3a** in the circumstances of (something); during (it): *She studies by night.* **b** not later than (a time): *I was in bed by two.* **4** through the instrumentality or use of (something): *I travel by bus.* **5** through the action or creation of (somebody): *a trio by Mozart.* **6a** in conformity with (something): *You must act by the rules.* **b** in terms of (something): *They pay by the hour.* **7** to the amount or extent of (something): *better by far.* **8** in successive units or increments of (something): *by inches.* **9** used in multiplication: *Multiply ten by four.* **10** used in measurements: *a room 4m by 5m.* ✻ **by oneself 1** unaccompanied. **2** unaided.

by[2] *adv* past.

by- *or* **bye-** *prefix* incidental or secondary: *by-election.*

by and by *adv* soon.

by and large *adv* on the whole.

by-blow *n Brit, dated* an illegitimate child.

bye[1] *n* **1** the passage to the next round of a tournament allowed to a competitor who has no opponent or whose opponent has withdrawn. **2** in cricket, a run scored off a ball that passes the batsman without striking the bat or body. ✻ **by the bye** by the way.

bye[2] *interj informal* used as an expression of farewell.

bye- *prefix* see BY-.

bye-bye *interj informal* used as an expression of farewell.

byelaw *n* see BYLAW.

by-election *n Brit* a special election held between regular elections to fill a vacancy that has arisen unexpectedly.

bye-line *n informal* = BY-LINE (2).

Byelorussian *n* see BELORUSSIAN.

bygone[1] *adj* belonging to an earlier time.

bygone[2] ✻ **let bygones be bygones** to forgive and forget past quarrels.

bylaw *or* **byelaw** *n* **1** a law or regulation made by a local authority and having effect only within an area controlled by the authority. **2** a rule concerning the affairs of a club, company, etc.

by-line *n* **1** the author's name printed with a newspaper or magazine article. **2** a goal line.

bypass[1] *n* **1** a road built so that through traffic can avoid a town centre. **2** a channel carrying a fluid round a part and back to the main stream. **3** a passage created surgically between two blood vessels to divert blood from one part to another.

bypass[2] *v* **1** to avoid (something, e.g. a town centre) by means of a bypass. **2** to neglect or ignore (something or somebody), usu intentionally.

byplay *n* action engaged in on the side while the main action proceeds, e.g. during a film or play.

by-product *n* **1** something produced, e.g. in manufacturing, in addition to a principal product. **2** a secondary and sometimes unexpected result.

byre *n Brit* a cow shed.

byroad *n* a secondary road.

Byronic *adj* characteristic of Lord Byron (d.1824) or his writings, *esp* in displaying a self-conscious romanticism.

bystander *n* somebody present but not involved in a situation or event.

byte *n* in computing, a string of eight adjacent bits (binary digits) that is capable of representing numbers from 0 to 255, processed by a computer as a unit.

byway *n* a little-used road.

byword *n* **1** a proverb. **2** somebody or something taken as representing some usu bad quality.

Byzantine[1] *adj* **1** of the ancient city of Byzantium or its empire. **2** of or in a style of architecture developed in the Byzantine Empire in the fourth to sixth cents. **3** complex to the point of being confusing or obscure. **4** characterized by trickery and deception.

Byzantine[2] *n* a native or inhabitant of Byzantium.

C

C[1] *or* **c** *n* (*pl* **C's** *or* **Cs** *or* **c's**) **1** the third letter of the English alphabet. **2** a mark or grade rating a student's work as fair or mediocre in quality. **3** in music, the first note of the diatonic scale of C major. **4** the Roman numeral for 100.

C[2] *abbr* **1** Cape (on maps). **2** Celsius. **3** centigrade. **4** century. **5** in Britain, Conservative. **6** coulomb.

C[3] *abbr* the chemical symbol for carbon.

© *symbol* copyright.

c *abbr* **1** in cricket, caught by. **2** cent. **3** century. **4** circa. **5** in physics, the speed of light in a vacuum.

CA *abbr* California (US postal abbreviation).

Ca *abbr* the chemical symbol for calcium.

ca *abbr* circa.

CAA *abbr Brit* Civil Aviation Authority.

CAB *abbr* Citizens' Advice Bureau.

cab *n* **1** a taxi. **2** the part of a locomotive, truck, crane, etc that houses the driver and operating controls. **3** in former times, a horse-drawn carriage used for hire.

cabal *n* a clandestine or unofficial faction, *esp* in political intrigue.

Word history

The word *cabal* orig meant 'secret', soon extended to 'secret meeting' and 'clandestine group'. The latter was particularly applied to a committee of the privy council, which in 1670 had five members whose initials spelt the word *cabal*: Clifford, Arlington, Buckingham, Ashley, and Lauderdale.

cabala *or* **cabbala** *or* **kabbala** *or* **kabbalah** *n* (*often* **Cabala**) a system of esoteric Jewish belief based on the extraction of hidden meanings and predictions from the Old Testament and other texts. ➤➤ **cabalism** *n*, **cabalist** *n*, **cabalistic** *adj.*

cabaret /'kabəray/ *n* **1** a stage show or series of acts provided at a nightclub, restaurant, etc. **2** a nightclub or other venue providing such entertainment.

cabbage *n* **1** the leaves of a cultivated plant with a short stem and a dense round head, used as a vegetable. **2a** *derog* somebody who has lost control of their mental and usu physical faculties as the result of illness, brain damage, or an accident. **b** *informal* an inactive or apathetic person.

cabbage white *n* a largely white butterfly whose caterpillars feed on cabbage plants.

cabbala *n* see CABALA.

cabby *or* **cabbie** *n* (*pl* **-ies**) *informal* a taxi driver.

caber *n* a roughly trimmed tree trunk that is thrown in the Scottish sport of tossing the caber.

Cabernet Franc /,kabənay 'fronh/ *n* a variety of grape related to Cabernet Sauvignon, or the wine produced from it.

Cabernet Sauvignon /,kabənay sohvi'nyonh/ *n* a variety of grape widely used in the production of dry red wine, or the wine produced from it.

cabin *n* **1a** a private room or compartment on a ship or boat for passengers or crew. **b** a compartment in an aircraft for cargo, crew, or passengers. **2** a small usu single-storeyed dwelling of simple construction, *esp* one made of wood.

cabin boy *n* a boy employed as a servant on board a ship.

cabin class *n* a class of accommodation on a passenger ship superior to tourist class and inferior to first class.

cabin cruiser *n* a large private motorboat with living accommodation.

cabinet *n* **1a** a case or cupboard usu with doors, shelves, and compartments for storing or displaying articles. **b** an upright case housing a radio, television, etc. **2** (*often* **Cabinet**) (*used as sing. or pl*). **a** in Britain, a body consisting of the prime minister and senior ministers who together formulate government policy. **b** in the USA, the heads of the executive departments of government collectively. ➤➤ **cabinetry** *n.*

cabinetmaker *n* a craftsman who makes fine furniture in wood.

cabin fever *n chiefly NAm, informal* depression or irritability resulting from a long period spent in cramped quarters or otherwise confined.

cable[1] *n* **1a** a strong thick rope, *esp* one over 8cm (3in.) in thickness. **b** a wire rope or metal chain of great strength, *esp* one connected to a ship's anchor. **2** an assembly of electrical wires insulated from each other and surrounded by a sheath. **3** = CABLEGRAM. **4** a nautical unit of length equal to 608ft (about 185m) in Britain and 720ft (about 219m) in the USA.

cable[2] *v dated* to communicate with or inform by cablegram.

cable car *n* any of a series of cabins suspended from an overhead cable along which they are pulled, *esp* to transport passengers up and down a mountainside.

cablegram *n* a telegram sent by an underwater cable.

cable stitch *n* a knitting stitch that produces a twisted ropelike pattern.

cable television *n* a television broadcasting system in which subscribers receive programmes via a cable, rather than by aerial.

cabochon /ˈkabəshon/ *n* a highly polished gem cut in a dome-shaped form without facets.

caboodle ✻ **the whole caboodle** *informal* the whole lot.

caboose *n* **1** *archaic* a ship's galley, *esp* when housed in a cabin on the deck. **2** *NAm* a wagon attached to a goods train, usu at the rear, mainly for the crew to eat and sleep in.

cabriole *n* (*also* **cabriole leg**) a curved furniture leg, often ending in an ornamental foot, characteristic of the early 18th cent.

cabriolet /ˌkabriohˈlay/ *n* **1** a light two-wheeled carriage with a hood, pulled by a single horse. **2** a car with a folding or removable roof; a convertible.

cacao *n* (*pl* **-os**) the fatty seeds of a S American tree that are used in making cocoa, chocolate, and cocoa butter; a cocoa bean.

cache[1] *n* **1** a hiding place, *esp* for provisions or weapons. **2** = CACHE MEMORY.

cache[2] *v* to place, hide, or store in a cache.

cache memory *n* a small computer memory that keeps frequently used data within the central processing unit so that it can be accessed at a higher speed than from main memory.

cache-sexe *n* a small garment worn to cover only the genitals.

cachet *n* **1** prestige, or a characteristic feature or quality that confers prestige. **2** a seal on a document, *esp* one used as a mark of official approval. **3** a capsule of rice paper or flour paste containing an unpleasant-tasting medicine.

cachexia *n* general physical wasting and malnutrition, usu associated with chronic disease. ⪢ **cachectic** *adj.*

cacique /kəˈseek/ *n* **1** a Native American chief in an area in which Spanish culture is predominant. **2** a local political leader in Spain and Latin America.

cack *n Brit, informal* excrement.

cack-handed *adj Brit, informal* **1** awkward or clumsy. **2** *derog* left-handed.

cackle[1] *v* **1** to make the sharp squawking noise or cry of a hen. **2** to talk noisily about trivialities; to chatter.

cackle[2] *n* **1** a cackling noise made by a hen. **2** a cackling laugh. ✻ **cut the cackle** *informal* to stop talking.

cacophony *n* (*pl* **-ies**) a harsh or discordant combination or confusion of sounds. ⪢ **cacophonous** *adj.*

cactus *n* (*pl* **cacti** *or* **cactuses**) a plant that has fleshy stems and scales or spines instead of leaves, often bears brightly coloured flowers, and is found *esp* in deserts and other dry areas.

CAD *abbr* computer-aided design.

cad *n dated* an unscrupulous or dishonourable man. ⪢ **caddish** *adj.*

cadaver *n* a corpse, *esp* one intended for dissection.

cadaverous *adj* **1** resembling a corpse, *esp* in being unhealthily pale or thin. **2** gaunt or haggard.

CADCAM *abbr* computer-aided design and manufacture.

caddie[1] *or* **caddy** *n* (*pl* **-ies**) somebody who carries a golfer's clubs and may also give other assistance or advice.

caddie[2] *or* **caddy** *v* (**-ies, -ied**) to act or work as a golfer's caddie.

caddis fly *n* an insect with four membranous wings, long thin antennae with many joints, and aquatic larvae.

caddy[1] *n* (*pl* **-ies**) a small container, *esp* a box or tin used for holding tea.

caddy[2] *n* see CADDIE[1].

caddy[3] *v* see CADDIE[2].

cadence *n* **1a** the rhythmic flow and intonations of speech. **b** the rhythm of poetry or prose. **2** in music, a sequence of chords moving to a harmonic close or point of rest and giving the sense of harmonic completion. **3** the beat, time, or measure of a rhythmical motion or activity. ⪢ **cadenced** *adj.*

cadenza *n* a technically showy, sometimes improvised, solo passage in a concerto.

cadet *n* **1** somebody training to be an officer in the armed forces or the police force. **2** a young person receiving basic military training, *esp* at school. **3** *formal or archaic* a younger son. ⪢ **cadetship** *n.*

cadge *v informal* to ask for and get (something) by imposing on somebody's hospitality or good nature. ⪢ **cadger** *n.*

cadmium *n* a bluish white soft metallic chemical element used *esp* in protective platings and batteries, and in alloys for making tramway wires and electric fuses.

cadmium yellow *n* a vivid yellow colour, or a pigment of this colour containing cadmium sulphide.

cadre *n* **1** a permanent group of trained people forming the nucleus of a military force or other organization, capable of rapid expansion if required. **2** a group of activists working for the Communist Party or a similar cause.

caduceus *n* (*pl* **caducei**) the symbolic staff of an ancient Greek or Roman herald, with two entwined snakes and two wings at the top, carried by the messenger god Hermes or Mercury.

caeca *n* pl of CAECUM.

caecilian *n* a mainly tropical burrowing amphibian animal that resembles a worm.

caecum (*NAm* **cecum**) *n* (*pl* **caeca,** *NAm* **ceca**) the pouch in which the large intestine begins and into which the ileum of the small intestine opens from one side. ⪢ **caecal** *adj.*

Caerphilly *n* a mild white moist cheese.

Caesar *n* used as a title for a Roman emperor, *esp* those from Augustus to Hadrian.

Caesarean[1] *or* **Caesarian** *adj* relating to any of the Caesars.

Caesarean[2] (*NAm* **Cesarean**) *n* a surgical operation carried out to deliver a baby, involving an incision of the abdominal and uterine walls.

Caesarean section (*NAm* **Cesarean section**) *n* = CAESAREAN[2].

Caesarian *adj* see CAESAREAN[1].

caesium (*NAm* **cesium**) *n* a silver-white soft metallic chemical element of the alkali metal group that is used in photoelectric cells and atomic clocks.

caesura *n* (*pl* **caesuras** *or* **caesurae**) **1** a break or pause in a line of verse, usu at or near the middle. **2** in classical Greek or Latin verse, a break within a metrical FOOT[1] (unit comprising fixed combination of syllables) caused by the ending of a word.

café *n* **1** *chiefly Brit* a small restaurant serving light meals and usu non-alcoholic drinks. **2** *NAm* a bar or nightclub.

cafeteria *n* a restaurant in which the customers serve themselves or are served at a counter.

cafetière /kaf'tyeə/ *n* a coffee pot with a plunger inside that is used to push the grounds to the bottom of the pot before the coffee is poured.

caffeine *n* a chemical compound that occurs naturally in tea and coffee and acts as a stimulant and DIURETIC[2] (substance that increases the production of urine). ➤➤ **caffeinated** *adj.*

caffè latte /,kafay 'latay/ *n* a drink made by adding a little espresso coffee to frothy steamed milk.

caftan *n* see KAFTAN.

cage[1] *n* **1** a box or enclosure of open construction, usu with bars or netting, for confining or carrying animals. **2** the moving enclosed platform of a lift.

cage[2] *v* **1** to put or keep (e.g. an animal) in a cage. **2** to confine (somebody) as if in a cage.

cagey *or* **cagy** *adj* (**-ier, -iest**) *informal* hesitant about committing oneself, communicating one's intentions, etc. ➤➤ **cageyness** *n,* **cagily** *adv,* **caginess** *n.*

cagoule *or* **kagoul** *n* a lightweight waterproof jacket with a hood, *esp* one that is pulled over the head rather than fastened with a zip.

cagy *adj* see CAGEY.

cahoots ✱ **in cahoots** *informal* working together secretly, *esp* with some dishonest or evil intention.

CAI *abbr* **1** computer-aided instruction. **2** computer-assisted instruction.

caiman *n* see CAYMAN.

Cainozoic *adj and n* see CENOZOIC.

caïque /kie'eek/ *n* **1** a small sailing vessel used in the E Mediterranean. **2** a light rowing boat used on the Bosphorus.

cairn *n* **1** a pile of stones built as a memorial or landmark, e.g. at the top of a mountain. **2** = CAIRN TERRIER.

cairn terrier *n* a terrier of a breed originating in Scotland, having a small compact body and coarse hair.

caisson /'kays(ə)n, kə'soohn/ *n* **1** a watertight chamber, usu with a supply of compressed air, used to house people doing construction work under water. **2** a watertight structure used to keep water in or out of a dock, harbour, etc.

caitiff *n archaic or literary* a cowardly or despicable person.

cajole *v* to persuade with flattery or deception; to coax. ➤➤ **cajolery** *n.*

Cajun *n* a descendant of the French Canadians who settled in Louisiana in the 18th cent. ➤➤ **Cajun** *adj.*

cake[1] *n* **1** any of various sweet foods made from a basic mixture of flour and sugar, usu with fat, eggs, and a raising agent, and typically baked in a round, square, or oblong mould. **2** (*usu in combination*) a flattened usu round mass of fried or baked savoury food: *a fishcake.* ✱ **go/sell like hot cakes** to sell extremely quickly; to be very popular.

cake[2] *v* **1** to cover with a layer of something solid or semi-solid; to encrust. **2** to form or harden into a mass.

cakehole *n Brit, informal* the mouth.

cakewalk *n* **1** a dance characterized by stylish walking steps and figures and typically involving high strutting movements. **2** *informal* an easy task.

CAL *abbr* **1** computer-aided learning. **2** computer-assisted learning.

Cal. *abbr* large calorie.

cal. *abbr* small calorie.

calabash *n* something made from the hollowed-out and dried skin of a flask-shaped tropical fruit, e.g. a water container or a tobacco pipe.

calaboose *n NAm, informal* a jail.

calabrese *n* a type of sprouting broccoli.

calamari *pl n* squid served as food.

calamine *n* a pink powder of zinc oxide or carbonate with a small amount of ferric oxide, used in soothing or cooling lotions.

calamity *n* (*pl* **-ies**) an extremely grave event; a disaster. ➤➤ **calamitous** *adj,* **calamitously** *adv.*

calando *adj and adv* of a piece of music: to be performed with gradually increasing speed and volume.

calash *or* **calèche** *n* **1** a light horse-drawn carriage with a folding top and small wheels. **2** a hood on a framework worn by women over high elaborate wigs in the 18th cent.

calcareous *adj* containing or consisting of calcium compounds, *esp* calcium carbonate.

calceolaria *n* a tropical American plant of the foxglove family with brightly coloured pouch-shaped flowers.

calces *n* pl of CALX.

calciferol *n* a synthetic vitamin D used to treat rickets and as a rat poison; vitamin D_2.

calciferous *adj* producing or containing calcium carbonate.

calcify *v* (**-ies, -ied**) **1** to harden (something, e.g. body tissue) by the deposition of calcium carbonate or other calcium compounds. **2** to convert (something) into a solid compound of calcium. **3** to become calcified. ➤➤ **calcification** *n.*

calcine *v* to heat (*esp* a metal ore or other inorganic material) to a high temperature, usu in order to cause it to lose water, combine with oxygen, or turn to powder. ➤➤ **calcination** *n.*

calcite *n* calcium carbonate in the form of limestone, chalk, marble, etc.

calcium *n* a silver-white metallic chemical element of the alkaline-earth group found in nature only in combination.

calcium carbonate *n* a chemical compound that occurs naturally in bones and shells and as chalk, marble, limestone, etc, and is used industrially in cement, fertilizers, and animal feed.

calculate *v* **1** to determine by mathematical processes. **2** to reckon by exercise of practical judgment; to estimate. **3** (+ on) to count or rely on (doing something). ➤➤ **calculable** *adj.*

calculated *adj* **1** shrewdly planned or contrived to accomplish a purpose. **2** intentional; deliberate. ➤➤ **calculatedly** *adv.*

calculating *adj* marked by shrewd consideration of one's own interests; scheming. ➤➤ **calculatingly** *adv.*

calculation *n* **1** the process or result of calculating something. **2** an act of calculating something. **3** studied care in planning, *esp* to promote one's own interests.

calculator *n* a machine for performing mathematical operations, *esp* a small hand-held electronic device.

calculi *n* pl of CALCULUS.

calculus *n* **1** (*pl* **calculi**) a hard stony mass, e.g. of cholesterol, that forms abnormally in the kidney, gall bladder, or other hollow organ or tube. **2** (*pl* **calculuses**) a branch of mathematics, comprising differential and integral calculus, that deals with rates of change of functions and the ideas of limits and has applications to the calculation of arcs, areas, volumes, etc.

caldera *n* a wide volcanic crater formed by violent eruption followed by subsidence of the central part of the volcano.

caldron *n* see CAULDRON.

calèche *n* see CALASH.

Caledonian *adj* relating to Scotland, *esp* to the Scottish Highlands or ancient Scotland.

calendar *n* **1** a system for fixing the beginning, length, and divisions of the year and arranging days and longer divisions of time, e.g. weeks and months, in a definite order. **2** a table or set of tables displaying the days of one year. **3** a chronological list of events or activities.

calender *n* a machine for pressing cloth, rubber, paper, etc between rollers or plates, e.g. to produce a smooth or glossy surface.

calends *or* **kalends** *pl n* (*used as sing. or pl*) the first day of each month in the ancient Roman calendar: compare IDES, NONES.

calendula *n* a plant of the daisy family with orange or yellow flowers, e.g. the pot marigold.

calf[1] *n* (*pl* **calves** *or* **calfs**) **1a** the young of the domestic cow or any other bovine mammal, e.g. the bison. **b** the young of some other large animals, e.g. the elephant or whale. **2** a mass of floating ice detached from an iceberg, a glacier that runs into the sea, etc.

calf[2] *n* (*pl* **calves**) the fleshy back part of the leg below the knee.

calf love *n* = PUPPY LOVE.

caliber *n NAm* see CALIBRE.

calibrate *v* **1** to determine the correct reading of (an arbitrary or inaccurate scale or instrument) by comparison with a standard. **2** to determine, adjust, or mark the graduations of (e.g. a thermometer). **3** to measure the diameter of (e.g. a gun barrel). ➤➤ **calibration** *n*, **calibrator** *n*.

calibre (*NAm* **caliber**) *n* **1** the internal diameter of a hollow cylinder, *esp* a gun barrel. **2** the external diameter of a round or cylindrical object, *esp* a bullet, shell, or other projectile. **3a** degree of mental capacity or moral quality. **b** degree of excellence or importance.

calico *n* (*pl* **-oes** *or* **-os**) **1** white or unbleached cotton cloth of medium weight, orig imported from India. **2** *NAm* any brightly printed cotton fabric.

calif *n* see CALIPH.

califate *n* see CALIPHATE.

Californian *n* a native or inhabitant of the US state of California. ➤➤ **Californian** *adj*.

California poppy *n* a N American plant of the poppy family with bright yellow or orange flowers.

californium *n* a radioactive metallic chemical element that is artificially produced by bombarding curium 244 and americium 243 with neutrons.

caliper *n NAm* see CALLIPER.

caliph *or* **calif** *n* in former times, a secular and spiritual head of Islam claiming descent from Muhammad. ➤➤ **caliphal** *adj*.

caliphate *or* **califate** *n* the position of caliph or the area ruled by a caliph.

calisthenics *pl n NAm* see CALLISTHENICS.

calk[1] *v* see CAULK[1].

calk[2] *n* see CAULK[2].

call[1] *v* **1a** to cry out loudly or distinctly. **b** to cry out to (somebody) to attract their attention or make them come. **2** of a bird or animal: to utter a characteristic note or cry. **3** to telephone. **4** to summon people to come to (a meeting). **5** to summon (a witness) to be present in court to give evidence. **6** to use a particular name or description for: *We call her Kitty; I call that generous.* **7** (*often* + in/by/round) to make a short visit. **8** of a train, etc: to stop at a particular place. ✻ **call for 1** to need or demand. **2** to stop to collect. **call in/into question** to express doubts about. **call on/upon** to require (somebody) to do something. **call the shots/tune** to be in control. **call to account** to demand an explanation from. ➤➤ **caller** *n*.

call[2] *n* **1a** an act of calling with the voice. **b** the cry of an animal, e.g. a bird. **2** a request or command to come or assemble. **3a** a demand or request. **b** need or justification: *There was no call for such rudeness.* **4** a strong inner prompting to a course of action, e.g. a divine vocation; a calling. **5** a short usu formal visit. **6** an act of telephoning somebody. **7** a usu vocal ruling made by an official of a sports contest. ✻ **on call 1** ready to respond to a summons or command, *esp* outside normal hours of duty. **2** of a loan: repayable on demand.

call centre *n* an office or department handling telephone calls received from customers of a company or other organization.

call girl *n* a prostitute who accepts appointments by telephone.

calligraphy *n* the art of producing beautiful or elegant handwriting, or the handwriting itself. ➤➤ **calligrapher** *n*, **calligraphic** *adj*.

call in *v* **1** to summon (somebody) for help or consultation. **2** to demand repayment of (a loan).

calling *n* **1** a strong inner impulse towards a particular course of action. **2** a profession or occupation.

calling card *n* a visiting card.

calliope *n NAm* a keyboard musical instrument resembling an organ and consisting of a series of whistles sounded by steam or compressed air.

calliper (*NAm* **caliper**) *n* **1** (*usu in pl*) a measuring instrument with two hinged arms that can be adjusted to determine thickness, diameter, or distance between surfaces. **2** a support for the human leg extending from the knee or thigh to the foot.

callipygian *adj literary* having well-shaped attractive buttocks.

callisthenics (*NAm* **calisthenics**) *pl n* (*used as sing. or pl*) systematic rhythmic bodily exercises, usu performed without apparatus.

call off *v* **1** to cancel (a plan or arrangement). **2** to give a command to (an animal) to leave somebody alone.

call of nature *n euphem* the urge to urinate or defecate.

callosity *n* (*pl* **-ies**) *technical* an area of marked or abnormal hardness and thickness on skin, bark, etc.

callous *adj* feeling no sympathy for others; cruelly unsympathetic. ➤➤ **callously** *adv*, **callousness** *n*.

call out *v* **1** to call loudly. **2** to summon to action.

callow *adj* lacking adult attitudes; immature. ➤➤ **callowly** *adv*, **callowness** *n*.

call sign *n* the combination of letters and numbers assigned to a radio operator or station for identification.

call up *v* **1** to summon (somebody) for military service or some other duty. **2** to bring to mind.

call-up *n* an order to report for military service.

callus *n* (*pl* **calluses**) **1** a hard thickened area on skin or bark. **2** soft tissue that forms over a wounded or cut plant surface.

calm[1] *adj* **1** free from anger, nervousness, excitement, etc. **2** marked by the absence of wind or rough water; still. ➤➤ **calmly** *adv*, **calmness** *n*.

calm[2] *n* **1** an emotional state free from anger, nervousness, excitement, etc. **2** the absence of wind or rough water; stillness.

calm[3] *v* (*often* + down) to become or make (somebody or something) calm.

calmative *adj* of a drug: having a calming effect; sedative.

calomel *n* a white tasteless powder consisting largely of mercurous chloride, used medicinally, e.g. as a purgative.

Calor gas *n trademark* butane gas in liquid form that is contained in portable cylinders and used as a fuel.

caloric *adj* of heat or calories.

calorie *or* **calory** *n* (*pl* **-ies**) **1** the quantity of heat required to raise the temperature of 1g of water by 1°C under standard conditions, equal to 4.1868 joules. Also called SMALL CALORIE. **2** the amount of heat required to raise the temperature of 1kg of water by 1°C under standard conditions. Also called KILOCALORIE, LARGE CALORIE.

calorific *adj* **1** relating to the energy-producing content of food, fuel, etc. **2** high in calories.

calorimeter *n* a device for measuring heat taken up or given out, e.g. during a chemical reaction. ➤➤ **calorimetric** *adj*, **calorimetry** *n*.

calory *n* see CALORIE.

caltrop *or* **caltrap** *n* **1** = WATER CHESTNUT (2). **2** a device with four metal points arranged so that one always projects upwards, used to hinder enemy horses, vehicles, etc.

calumet *n* a long highly ornamented pipe smoked by Native Americans, *esp* on ceremonial occasions in token of peace.

calumniate *v formal* to maliciously make false statements about (somebody). ➤➤ **calumniation** *n*, **calumniator** *n*.

calumny[1] *n* (*pl* **-ies**) **1** a false charge or misrepresentation maliciously calculated to damage another person's reputation. **2** the making of such a false charge or misrepresentation. ➤➤ **calumnious** *adj*.

calumny[2] *v* (**-ies, -ied**) *formal* to calumniate.

Calvados *n* apple brandy made in the Calvados department of Normandy.

calve *v* **1** of a cow, whale, etc: to give birth to (a calf). **2** of an iceberg, glacier, etc: to release (a floating mass of ice).

calves[1] *n* pl of CALF[1].

calves[2] *n* pl of CALF[2].

Calvinism *n* the Christian doctrines of John Calvin (d.1564) and his followers, marked by emphasis on the doctrine of predestination. ➤➤ **Calvinist** *n and adj*, **Calvinistic** *adj*.

calx *n* (*pl* **calxes** *or* **calces**) the crumbly residue left when a metal or mineral has been subjected to intense heat.

calyces *n* pl of CALYX.

calypso *n* (*pl* **-os**) a style of West Indian music in which improvised lyrics, usu satirizing current events, are sung to music with a syncopated rhythm.

calyx *n* (*pl* **calyxes** *or* **calyces**) **1** the outer usu green or leafy part of a flower, consisting of a ring of sepals that protect the developing bud. **2** any cup-shaped body part.

calzone /kalt'sohnay/ *n* (*pl* **calzoni** *or* **calzones**) a pizza base folded over a generous filling.

CAM *abbr* computer-aided manufacture.

cam *n* a mechanical device, e.g. a wheel or shaft with a projecting part, that transforms circular motion into intermittent or back-and-forth motion.

camaraderie *n* a spirit of good humour and trust among friends.

camber[1] *n* **1** a slight arching or upward sloping from the sides to the middle of a road, deck, beam, etc. **2** the degree to which an aircraft wing or other aerofoil curves up from its front edge and down again to its back edge. **3** a positioning of the wheels of a motor vehicle so that they are closer together at the bottom than at the top.

camber[2] *v* **1** to curve upwards in the middle. **2** to cause (e.g. a road or deck) to curve in this way.

cambium *n* (*pl* **cambiums** *or* **cambia**) a thin layer of cells between the XYLEM (water-conducting tissue) and PHLOEM (food-conducting tissue) of many plants that divides to form more xylem and phloem as the plant grows.

Cambodian *n* **1** a native or inhabitant of Cambodia. **2** the official language of Cambodia; Khmer. ➤➤ **Cambodian** *adj*.

Cambrian *adj* **1** Welsh. **2** of the earliest geological period of the Palaeozoic era, lasting from about 570 to about 510 million years ago, and marked by the presence of every type of invertebrate animal. ➤➤ **Cambrian** *n*.

cambric *n* a fine white linen or cotton fabric.

Cambs *abbr* Cambridgeshire.

camcorder *n* a video camera with a built-in video recorder.

came *v* past tense of COME[1].

camel *n* either of two large RUMINANT[1] (cud-chewing) mammals with humped backs and long necks used for riding and for carrying goods in desert regions: **a** the one-humped Arabian camel; the dromedary. **b** the two-humped Bactrian camel.

camel hair *n* **1** soft silky cloth made from the hair of a camel, sometimes mixed with wool, usu light tan in colour. **2** the hair of a camel or a substitute for it, used *esp* in paintbrushes.

camellia *n* a shrub with glossy evergreen leaves and showy roselike flowers.

camelopard *n archaic* a giraffe.

Camembert /'kaməmbeə/ *n* a round soft cheese with a thin greyish white rind.

cameo *n* (*pl* **-os**) **1** a piece of stone carved with a contrasting raised design, especially a head in profile in a piece of jewellery. **2** a short piece of writing that highlights a plot or character. **3** a small dramatic role played by a well-known actor.

camera *n* a device for recording still or moving images, using light-sensitive film or electronic array to produce a still photograph, cinema film, or video signal. ✱ **in camera** in private, often in a judge's private rooms.

camera obscura *n* a darkened box or room with an aperture through which light from outside enters through an optical system to form an image of the exterior view on a flat surface, e.g. a screen, inside.

camera-ready *adj* of artwork, typeset material, etc: ready to be photographed without alteration for reproduction.

Cameroonian *n* a native or inhabitant of Cameroon. ➤➤ **Cameroonian** *adj*.

camiknickers *pl n Brit* a women's one-piece undergarment that combines a camisole and knickers.

camisole *n* a short bodice worn as an undergarment by women.

camomile *or* **chamomile** *n* a strong-scented plant of the daisy family with leaves and flowers that are used medicinally, *esp* in herbal remedies.

camouflage[1] *n* **1** the disguising of military or other equipment or installations with nets, paint, foliage, etc. **2** animal markings, colouring, etc that match the natural surroundings and conceal the animal from predators. **3** concealment by means of disguise.

camouflage[2] *v* to conceal or disguise by camouflage.

camp[1] *n* **1a** an area of ground on which tents or other temporary shelters are erected. **b** a place where troops are housed or trained. **c** a place with temporary accommodation and other facilities, e.g. for holidaymakers, prisoners, etc. **2** (*used as sing. or pl*) a group of people who share a particular view, e.g. members of a political party or supporters of a particular doctrine: *split into two camps.* **3** an ancient or prehistoric fortified site.

camp[2] *v* **1** to pitch or occupy a camp. **2** to live temporarily in a tent or other outdoor accommodation, e.g. on holiday. ⋙ **camping** *n.*

camp[3] *adj informal* **1** exaggeratedly effeminate. **2** deliberately and outrageously affected or inappropriate, in order to amuse. ⋙ **campy** *adj.*

camp[4] ✻ **camp it up** *informal* to act or behave in an exaggeratedly theatrical or effeminate manner that is intended to be amusing.

camp[5] *n* a camp style of acting or way of behaving.

campaign[1] *n* **1** a series of coordinated events or operations designed to bring about a particular result, *esp* a social or political objective. **2** a connected series of military operations forming a distinct phase of a war.

campaign[2] *v* to go on, engage in, or conduct a campaign. ⋙ **campaigner** *n.*

campanile /kampə'neeli/ *n* (*pl* **campaniles** *or* **campanili**) a bell tower, *esp* one that is freestanding.

campanology *n* the art of bell ringing. ⋙ **campanological** *adj,* **campanologist** *n.*

campanula *n* a plant of the harebell family with bell-shaped blue, white, or purple flowers. Also called BELLFLOWER.

camp bed *n* a small collapsible bed, usu of fabric stretched over a lightweight frame.

camper *n* **1** a person who stays temporarily in a tent, caravan, etc, or at a holiday camp. **2** a motor vehicle equipped for use as temporary accommodation, e.g. while holidaying.

camper van *n* = CAMPER (2).

camp follower *n* **1** a civilian, *esp* a prostitute, who follows or works in a military unit. **2** somebody who is temporarily attached to a group, *esp* for opportunistic reasons.

camphor *n* a gummy fragrant chemical compound obtained from the wood and bark of the camphor tree and used as a liniment and insect repellent.

campion *n* a plant of the carnation family with delicate red, pink, or white flowers.

campo *n* (*pl* **-os**) a type of grassland plain in S America.

campsite *n* an area of land set aside for tents, caravans, etc and often having toilets and other facilities for holidaymakers.

campus *n* (*pl* **campuses**) **1** the grounds and buildings of a university. **2** *NAm* the grounds of a school, college, etc.

campylobacter *n* a rod-shaped bacterium that causes food poisoning and gastroenteritis.

camshaft *n* a shaft to which a cam is attached.

can[1] *v aux* (*third person sing. present tense* **can,** *past tense* **could**) **1** to be able to; to know how to. **2** to have permission to; may. **3** to have a certain tendency or likelihood: *It can be cold at night.* **4** used in the negative to express surprise or disbelief: *They cannot be serious.*

can[2] *n* **1** a usu cylindrical metal container in which food or drink is sealed for sale or long-term storage; a tin. **2** *NAm, informal* a toilet. **3** *chiefly NAm, informal* jail. ✻ **in the can** of a film, videotape, etc: completed and ready for release.

can[3] *v* (**canned, canning**) **1** to pack or preserve (*esp* food or drink) in a can. **2** *chiefly NAm, informal* to put a stop or end to (something). ⋙ **canner** *n.*

Canada goose *n* a wild goose that is grey and brown with a black head and neck and a white patch under the throat, introduced into Europe from N America.

Canadian *n* a native or inhabitant of Canada. ⋙ **Canadian** *adj,* **Canadianism** *n.*

canaille /kə'nayəl, kə'nie/ *n derog* (*used as sing. or pl*) the common people; the rabble.

canal *n* **1** an artificial waterway for commercial vessels and pleasure boats. **2** any channel or watercourse used for drainage, for irrigation, or to convey water for power. **3** a tubular passage in an animal or plant; a duct.

canalize *or* **-ise** *v* **1** to provide (an area) with a canal or canals. **2** to convert (a river) into a canal. **3** to direct (something, e.g. a flow of liquid or gas) into a preferred channel or outlet. ⋙ **canalization** *n.*

canapé *n* an appetizer consisting of a small piece of bread, biscuit, pastry, etc with a savoury topping.

canard *n* a false or unfounded report or story; a hoax.

canary *n* (*pl* **-ies**) a small usu yellow finch native to the Canary Islands, widely kept as a cage bird.

canary yellow *adj* of a vivid yellow colour. ⋙ **canary yellow** *n.*

canasta *n* a card game resembling rummy usu for four players using two full packs plus jokers.

cancan *n* an energetic stage dance performed by women, often in a row, who kick their legs high while holding up the front of their skirt.

cancel *v* (**cancelled, cancelling,** *NAm* **canceled, canceling**) **1** to decide that (something arranged) will not take place, usu without intending to reschedule it. **2** to make void; to annul or revoke. **3** to deface (e.g. a postage stamp), usu with a set of lines, so as to prevent reuse. **4** (*often* + out) to match in force or effect; to counterbalance or offset. ⋙ **cancellation** *n,* **canceller** *n.*

cancer *n* **1a** a malignant tumour that develops when cells multiply in an unlimited way. **b** the medical condition that is characterized by the presence of such a tumour or tumours. **2** a spreading evil in a person, society, etc. **3** (**Cancer**) in astronomy, a constellation (the Crab) depicted as a crab crushed beneath Hercules' foot. **4** (**Cancer**) in astrology, the fourth sign of the zodiac or a person born under this sign. ⋙ **Cancerian** *adj and n,* **cancerous** *adj.*

candela *n* the basic SI unit of luminous intensity.

candelabrum *or* **candelabra** *n* (*pl* **candelabra** *or* **candelabrums** *or* **candelabras**) a branched candlestick or lamp with several lights.

candescent *adj formal* glowing or dazzling with heat. ⋙ **candescence** *n.*

candid *adj* indicating or suggesting complete sincerity; frank or open. ⋙ **candidly** *adv,* **candidness** *n.*

candida *n* a parasitic fungus that resembles yeast, including the fungus that causes THRUSH[2].

candidate *n* **1** somebody who is competing with others for something, e.g. a job, a political position, or an award. **2** somebody who is taking an examination. **3** somebody or something regarded as suitable for something, or likely to suffer something. ➤➤ **candidacy** *n,* **candidature** *n.*

candle *n* a usu long slender cylindrical mass of tallow or wax enclosing a wick that is burned to give light. ✱ **not hold a candle to** to be much inferior to (something else). **not worth the candle** not worth the effort, or not justified by the result.

Candlemas *n* a Christian feast commemorating the presentation of Christ in the temple and the purification of the Virgin Mary, observed on 2 February.

candlepower *n* luminous intensity expressed in candelas.

candlestick *n* a holder with a socket for a candle.

candlewick *n* a fabric made with thick soft cotton yarn cut in a raised tufted pattern, used *esp* for bedspreads.

candour (*NAm* **candor**) *n* sincerity or honesty of expression; frankness or openness.

candy[1] *n* (*pl* **-ies**) **1** crystallized sugar formed by boiling down sugar syrup. **2** *chiefly NAm* sweets.

candy[2] *v* (**-ies, -ied**) to encrust or glaze (e.g. fruit or fruit peel) with sugar by cooking it in a heavy syrup.

candy floss *n Brit* **1** a light fluffy mass of spun sugar, usu wound round a stick as a sweet. **2** something attractive but insubstantial.

candy-striped *adj* of fabric: with a regular pattern of usu narrow stripes of colour, often pink, on a white background.

candytuft *n* a plant of the mustard family cultivated for its white, pink, or purple flowers.

cane[1] *n* **1a** a hollow or pithy usu flexible jointed stem of some reeds and grasses, e.g. bamboo. **b** any of various tall woody grasses or reeds, *esp* sugarcane. **c** a long woody flowering or fruiting stem, *esp* of a raspberry. **2a** a walking stick, *esp* one made from a cane. **b** a cane or rod used to give beatings, or the punishment so inflicted. **c** a length of split rattan used in basketry, wickerwork, etc.

cane[2] *v* to beat (somebody) with a cane. ➤➤ **caner** *n,* **caning** *n.*

canine[1] *adj* **1** resembling or being a dog or a member of the dog family. **2** of or being any of the four conical pointed teeth lying between the incisor and the first premolar on each side of both jaws.

canine[2] *n* **1** a canine tooth. **2** a canine animal.

canister *n* a small usu metal container, e.g. a box or tin for holding tea or shot.

canker[1] *n* **1** an ulcer or spreading sore, *esp* one affecting the mouth. **2a** an area of dead tissue or an open wound in a plant. **b** any of various inflammatory diseases of animals, e.g. an ear disease of dogs, cats, and rabbits, or a disease of horses that softens the underside of the hooves. **3** a source of spreading corruption or evil. ➤➤ **cankerous** *adj.*

canker[2] *v* **1** to corrupt or undermine. **2** to infect or become infected with canker.

canna *n* a tropical plant grown for its bright red or yellow flowers and decorative leaves.

cannabis *n* the dried leaves and flowering tops of female hemp plants, which yield a dark resin and are sometimes smoked or eaten for their intoxicating effect.

canned *adj* **1** recorded for mechanical or electronic reproduction, *esp* prerecorded for addition to a soundtrack or a videotape. **2** sold or preserved in a can; tinned. **3** *informal* drunk.

cannellini bean *n* a white haricot bean used in Italian cooking.

cannelloni *pl n* (*used as sing. or pl*) large tubular rolls of pasta served with a filling, e.g. of meat, vegetables, or cheese.

cannery *n* (*pl* **-ies**) a factory for canning foods.

cannibal *n* a human being who eats human flesh. ➤➤ **cannibalism** *n,* **cannibalistic** *adj.*

cannibalize *or* **-ise** *v* to dismantle (e.g. a machine) in order to provide spare parts for others. ➤➤ **cannibalization** *n.*

cannon[1] *n* (*pl* **cannons** *or* **cannon**) **1** a large gun mounted on a carriage, used formerly in warfare. **2** an automatic shell-firing gun mounted *esp* in an aircraft.

cannon[2] *v* **1** (+ into) to collide with. **2** (+ off) to collide with and be deflected off (something).

cannonade[1] *n* a burst or period of continuous heavy artillery fire.

cannonade[2] *v* to attack (e.g. troops) with a cannonade.

cannonball *n* a round solid missile made for firing from the type of cannon used in former times.

cannon bone *n* the leg bone between the hock joint and the fetlock of a horse or other hoofed mammal.

cannon fodder *n* soldiers regarded merely as material to be expended in battle.

cannot *contr* can not.

cannula *n* (*pl* **cannulas** *or* **cannulae**) a small tube for inserting into a body cavity or duct, e.g. for draining off fluid or for introducing medicine.

canny *adj* (**-ier, -iest**) **1** cautious and shrewd; astute. **2** *NE Eng* pleasant or attractive. ➤➤ **cannily** *adv,* **canniness** *n.*

canoe[1] *n* a long light narrow boat with pointed ends and curved sides usu propelled with a paddle.

canoe[2] *v* (**canoes, canoed, canoeing**) to travel in or paddle a canoe. ➤➤ **canoeist** *n.*

can of worms *n informal* a potentially awkward or complicated matter, situation, etc.

canon[1] *n* **1** a regulation or dogma decreed by a church council. **2a** an accepted principle, rule, or criterion. **b** a body of principles, rules, or standards. **3a** an authoritative list of books accepted as Holy Scripture. **b** the authentic works of a writer. **4** a musical composition for two or more vocal or instrumental parts in which the melody is repeated by the voices or instruments entering in succession and overlapping.

canon[2] *n* **1** a clergyman belonging to the chapter of a cathedral or collegiate church. **2** = CANON REGULAR.

canonic *adj* = CANONICAL.

canonical *adj* **1** of a canon, *esp* an ecclesiastical or musical one. **2a** conforming to a general rule; orthodox. **b** conforming to CANON LAW. **3** accepted as forming part of the canon of Holy Scripture or of a writer's works. **4** of a cathedral chapter. ➤➤ **canonically** *adv.*

canonicals *pl n* the vestments prescribed by canon for an officiating clergyman.

canonize *or* **-ise** *v* **1** to recognize (somebody) officially as a saint. **2** to give official sanction or approval to (something), *esp* by ecclesiastical authority. ➤➤ **canonization** *n.*

canon law *n* the codified law governing a church.

canon regular *n* (*pl* **canons regular**) a member of any of several Roman Catholic institutes of priests belonging to a religious order and living in a community.

canonry *n* (*pl* **-ies**) **1** the office of a canon. **2** the endowment that financially supports a canon.

canoodle *v informal* to kiss and cuddle amorously with somebody.

canopy[1] *n* (*pl* **-ies**) **1a** a cloth covering suspended over a bed. **b** a cover, often of cloth, fixed or carried above a person of high rank or a sacred object. **c** an awning or marquee. **2** an ornamental rooflike structure. **3** the lifting or supporting surface of a parachute. **4** the uppermost layer of a forest, composed of spreading leafy branches.

canopy[2] *v* (**-ies, -ied**) to cover with a canopy, or as if with a canopy.

cant[1] *n* **1** the insincere or hypocritical expression of platitudes or sentiments, *esp* those suggesting piety. **2** the jargon of a specific group of people; *specif* the slang used by thieves, beggars, etc. **3** set or stock phrases.

cant[2] *v dated* to speak in cant or jargon.

cant[3] *n* **1** an oblique or slanting surface. **2** an inclination from a given line; a slope.

cant[4] *v* to be or cause (something) to be at an angle; to tilt or slope.

can't *contr* can not.

Cantab. *abbr* used with academic awards: of Cambridge.

cantabile /kan'tahbili, -lay/ *adj and adv* of a piece of music: to be performed in a singing manner.

cantaloupe *or* **cantaloup** *n* a MUSKMELON (type of cultivated melon) with a hard ridged rind and orange flesh.

cantankerous *adj* ill-natured or quarrelsome. ⋙ **cantankerously** *adv*, **cantankerousness** *n*.

cantata *n* a choral composition, often a musical setting of a religious text, comprising choruses, solos, recitatives, and interludes.

canteen *n* **1** a dining hall, *esp* in a school or factory. **2** *Brit* a partitioned box for holding cutlery. **3** a small flask used by a soldier, traveller, etc to carry drinking water.

canter[1] *n* a three-beat gait of a horse or similar animal that is smoother and slower than a gallop. ✱ **at a canter** easily; with little or no effort.

canter[2] *v* to progress or ride at a canter.

Canterbury bell *n* a tall European plant cultivated for its large showy bell-shaped flowers.

canticle *n* any of several songs, e.g. the Magnificat, taken from the Bible and used in services of worship.

cantilever[1] *n* **1** a projecting beam or member supported at only one end. **2** a bracket-shaped member supporting a balcony or a cornice.

cantilever[2] *v* to support with a cantilever.

canto *n* (*pl* **-os**) a major division of a long poem.

canton *n* a small territorial division of a country, e.g. any of the states of the Swiss confederation. ⋙ **cantonal** *adj*.

Cantonese *n* (*pl* **Cantonese**) **1** a native or inhabitant of Canton, city in China. **2** the dialect of Chinese spoken in and around Canton. ⋙ **Cantonese** *adj*.

cantonment *n* a group of structures providing temporary or permanent accommodation for troops; a military camp or situation.

cantor *n* **1** a singer who leads the choir or congregation in Christian church services. **2** a synagogue official who sings or chants liturgical music and leads the congregation in prayer.

Canuck *n chiefly NAm, informal* a Canadian, *esp* a French Canadian.

canvas[1] *n* (*pl* **canvases** *or* **canvasses**) **1** a strong closely woven cloth, usu of linen, hemp, or cotton, used for clothing, sails, tents, etc. **2** a cloth surface suitable for painting on in oils. **3** in rowing, either end of a racing boat, orig covered with canvas. **4** the floor of a boxing or wrestling ring. ✱ **under canvas 1** in a tent. **2** under sail.

canvas[2] *v* (**canvassed, canvassing,** *NAm* **canvased, canvasing**) to cover or line with canvas.

canvass[1] *v* **1** to visit (e.g. voters) in order to solicit political support or to ascertain opinions. **2** to discuss or debate (something). ⋙ **canvasser** *n*.

canvass[2] *n* the act of canvassing.

canyon *n* a deep valley or gorge.

canyoning *n* the sport of jumping into a mountain stream in protective clothing and being carried along by the water through rapids and down falls.

CAP *abbr* Common Agricultural Policy.

cap[1] *n* **1a** a soft close-fitting head covering without a brim and often with a peak. **b** *chiefly Brit* a head covering awarded to a member of a sports team. **2** the PILEUS (upper dome-shaped part) of a mushroom or toadstool. **3** something that serves as a cover or protection, *esp* for the end or top of an object. **4** an upper financial limit. **5** a small container holding an explosive charge, e.g. for a toy pistol or for priming the charge in a firearm. **6** *Brit* = DUTCH CAP. **7** an artificial substitute or protective covering for the external part of a tooth. ✱ **cap in hand** in a deferential manner. **set one's cap at** *dated* of a woman: to try to attract (a particular man), *esp* with a view to marriage. ⋙ **capful** (*pl* **capfuls**) *n*.

cap[2] *v* (**capped, capping**) **1** to provide or protect with a cap. **2** to form a cap over; to crown. **3a** *chiefly Brit* to select (a player) for a sports team. **b** *chiefly Scot, NZ* to award an academic degree to. **4a** to follow (something) with a more impressive or significant example; to outdo. **b** to put the finishing touch to. **5** to impose an upper financial limit on (e.g. a tax or charge). ✱ **to cap it all** as the last and usu most infuriating, outrageous, etc of a series of events.

capability *n* (*pl* **-ies**) **1** being capable. **2** a feature or faculty capable of development; potential.

capable *adj* **1** able or competent. **2** (+ of) having the required attributes or inclination to perform (a specified deed or action). **3** (+ of) susceptible of (something). ⋙ **capably** *adv*.

capacious *adj* able to hold a great deal; roomy. ⋙ **capaciously** *adv*, **capaciousness** *n*.

capacitance *n* **1** the ability of a conductor or system of conductors and insulators to store electric charge. **2** the measure of this ability, equal to the ratio of the charge induced to the potential difference.

capacitate *v* **1** to make legally competent. **2** to make capable; to qualify. ⋙ **capacitation** *n*.

capacitor *n* a component in an electrical circuit that provides capacitance and usu consists of an insulator sandwiched between two oppositely charged conductors.

capacity *n* (*pl* **-ies**) **1a** the maximum amount that can be contained or produced. **b** (*used before a noun*) being such a maximum amount: *a capacity crowd*. **2a** ability or talent. **b** power or potential. **3** a position or role assigned or assumed. **4** the quantity of electricity that a battery, motor, etc can deliver under particular conditions.

caparison[1] *n* an ornamental covering for a horse, *esp* for a warhorse in former times.

caparison[2] *v* to put a caparison on (something or somebody).

cape[1] *n* a sleeveless outer garment, or part of a garment, that fits closely at the neck, hangs loosely from the shoulders, and is usu shorter than a cloak. ⋙ **caped** *adj*.

cape[2] *n* a point or area of land jutting out into water as a headland or promontory.

Cape gooseberry *n* the edible yellow fruit of a tropical plant of the potato family.

capelin *or* **caplin** *n* a small food fish of northern seas related to the smelts.

caper[1] *v* to leap about in a playful or carefree way; to prance.

caper[2] *n* **1** a playful or carefree leap. **2** a high-spirited escapade; a prank. **3** *informal* a frivolous, disreputable, dangerous, or illegal activity or enterprise.

caper[3] *n* (*usu in pl*) a greenish flower bud or young berry of a Mediterranean shrub, which is pickled and used as a seasoning, garnish, etc.

capercaillie *or* **capercailzie** *n* the largest grouse of Europe, Asia, and Africa, found *esp* in N European forests.

capillarity *n* the phenomenon in which the surface of a liquid in contact with a solid, e.g. in a fine-bore tube, is raised or lowered depending on the relative attraction of the molecules of the liquid for each other and for those of the solid.

capillary[1] *n* (*pl* **-ies**) a capillary tube or passage, *esp* any of the smallest blood vessels connecting arterioles (small arteries; see ARTERIOLE) with venules (small veins; see VENULE): compare ARTERY, VEIN.

capillary[2] *adj* **1a** resembling a hair, *esp* in slender elongated form. **b** of a tube, passage, etc: having a very fine bore. **2** of capillaries or capillarity.

capillary action *n* = CAPILLARITY.

capital[1] *n* **1** a city serving as a seat of government. **2a** wealth or goods used to produce further wealth or goods. **b** the excess of the assets of a business over its liabilities. **3** a capital letter. ✱ **make capital out of** to turn (a situation) to one's advantage.

capital[2] *adj* **1** punishable by death. **2** of a letter: of the series used to begin sentences or proper names, e.g. *A, B, C* rather than *a, b, c*. **3** *dated* excellent. ➤➤ **capitally** *adv.*

capital[3] *n* the uppermost part of an architectural column.

capital gain *n* (*usu in pl, used as sing.*) the profit from the sale of an asset, e.g. a house.

capital goods *pl n* goods used in producing other commodities rather than for sale to consumers.

capitalise *v* see CAPITALIZE.

capitalism *n* an economic system characterized by the profit motive and by private ownership and control of the means of production, distribution, and exchange. ➤➤ **capitalist** *n and adj*, **capitalistic** *adj.*

capitalist *n* **1** a person with capital, *esp* invested in business; *broadly* a very wealthy person. **2** a person who favours capitalism.

capitalize *or* **-ise** *v* **1** (+ on) to gain by turning (something) to advantage. **2** to supply capital for (somebody or something). **3** to convert (something) into capital. **4** to write or print (e.g. a word) in capitals or with an initial capital. ➤➤ **capitalization** *n.*

capital punishment *n* the legal killing of criminals as punishment for their crimes; the death penalty.

capital sum *n* a lump sum of money, *esp* payable under an insurance policy.

capital transfer tax *n* in Britain, between 1975 and 1986, a tax levied on the estate of a dead person: compare DEATH DUTY, INHERITANCE TAX.

capitation *n* a payment or charge based on a fixed amount per person.

capitol *n* **1** (**Capitol**) the building in which the US Congress meets in Washington DC. **2** a building in which a US state legislative body meets.

capitulate *v* **1** to surrender, often after negotiation of terms. **2** to cease resisting; to acquiesce. ➤➤ **capitulation** *n*, **capitulator** *n.*

caplet *n trademark* a medicinal tablet, usu oval in shape, with a hard smooth soluble outer coating.

caplin *n* see CAPELIN.

capo *n* (*pl* **-os**) a movable bar attached to the fingerboard of a guitar or similar musical instrument to raise the pitch of all the strings uniformly.

capon *n* a castrated male chicken fattened for eating.

cappuccino /kapoo'cheenoh/ *n* (*pl* **-os**) frothy coffee made with espresso and steamed milk.

caprice *n* a sudden and seemingly unmotivated change of mind.

capricious *adj* governed or characterized by caprice; apt to change suddenly or unpredictably. ➤➤ **capriciously** *adv*, **capriciousness** *n.*

Capricorn *n* **1** (*also* **Capricornus**) in astronomy, a constellation (the Goat) depicted as a creature resembling a goat with the tail of a fish. **2** in astrology, the tenth sign of the zodiac or a person born under this sign. ➤➤ **Capricornian** *adj and n.*

caprine *adj* of or resembling a goat.

capri pants *pl n* tight-fitting trousers that taper down to the ankle, worn by women.

capsicum *n* a many-seeded fleshy fruit of a tropical plant of the nightshade family, used as a vegetable.

capsize *v* **1** to cause (a boat) to overturn. **2** of a boat: to overturn.

capstan *n* **1** a mechanical device consisting of an upright drum round which a rope, cable, etc is wound, used for moving or raising heavy weights. **2** a rotating shaft that drives tape at a constant speed in a tape recorder.

capstone *n* = COPINGSTONE.

capsule *n* **1** a gelatin shell enclosing a drug for swallowing. **2** a detachable pressurized compartment, *esp* in a spacecraft or aircraft, containing crew and controls. **3** a compact usu rounded container. **4** a dry fruit composed of two or more carpels (female reproductive organs; see CARPEL) that burst open spontaneously when mature to release their seeds. ➤➤ **capsular** *adj*, **capsulate** *adj.*

captain[1] *n* **1a** a person in command of a ship or boat. **b** a pilot of a civil aircraft. **2a** in the Royal Navy and US Navy, an officer ranking below a commodore and above a commander. **b** in the army, marines, and some air forces, an officer ranking below a major and above a lieutenant. **3** a leader of a team, *esp* a sports team. **4** *NAm* a fire or police officer. ➤➤ **captaincy** *n.*

captain[2] *v* to be captain of.

caption[1] *n* **1** a comment or description accompanying a pictorial illustration. **2** a subtitle or other piece of textual information on a film or television screen.

caption[2] *v* to supply a caption or captions for.

captious *adj* having or showing an ill-natured inclination to find fault and raise objections. ➤➤ **captiously** *adv*, **captiousness** *n.*

captivate *v* to fascinate or charm irresistibly. ➤➤ **captivating** *adj*, **captivation** *n.*

captive[1] *adj* **1a** taken and held prisoner, *esp* by an enemy in war. **b** kept within bounds; confined. **2** in a situation that makes departure or inattention difficult. ➤➤ **captivity** *n.*

captive[2] *n* somebody who is taken and held prisoner.

captor *n* somebody who takes and holds another captive.

capture[1] *n* **1** the act of gaining control or possession. **2** somebody or something that has been captured. **3** the collection and storing of data by computer.

capture[2] *v* **1** to take (a person, animal, or place) captive. **2** to represent or preserve in words, pictures, etc. **3** to remove (e.g. a chess piece) from the playing board according to the rules of a game. **4** to store (data) in a computer.

capuchin *n* **1** (**Capuchin**) a member of a strict branch of the Franciscan order of missionary friars. **2** a hooded cloak worn by women in former times. **3** a S American monkey with hair on its crown shaped like a monk's cowl.

capybara *n* (*pl* **capybaras**) a mainly aquatic S American rodent with no tail that resembles a large guinea pig.

car *n* **1** a usu four-wheeled motor vehicle designed for transporting a small number of people and typically propelled by an internal-combustion engine. **2** a railway carriage, *esp* one used for a specific purpose.

carabiner *n* see KARABINER.

carabiniere /ˌkarəbiˈnyeəri/ *n* (*pl* **carabinieri**) a member of the Italian national police force.

caracal *n* a medium-sized wild cat of Africa and Asia that has long legs and sharply pointed ears with black tufts.

caracul *n* see KARAKUL.

carafe *n* a glass container, typically with a flaring lip and open top, used to hold water or wine at table.

carambola *n* a greenish yellow fruit with a sweet-sour taste and a distinctive lobed appearance that gives it a star-shaped cross-section. Also called STARFRUIT.

caramel *n* **1** a dark brown substance obtained by heating sugar and used as a colouring and flavouring agent. **2** a chewy soft toffee.

caramelize *or* **-ise** *v* to change (sugar or the sugar content of a food) into caramel.

carapace *n* a hard case, e.g. of chitin, covering the back or part of the back of a turtle, crab, etc.

carat *n* **1** a unit of weight used for precious stones equal to 200mg. **2** (*NAm chiefly* **karat**) a unit of fineness for gold equal to one twenty-fourth part of pure gold in an alloy.

caravan *n* **1a** *Brit* an enclosed or covered vehicle designed to be towed by a car or horse and to serve as a dwelling when parked. **b** *NAm* a covered truck. **2a** (*used as sing. or pl*) a company of travellers, often with pack animals, on a journey through desert or hostile regions. **b** a group of vehicles travelling together. ➤➤ **caravanner** *n*, **caravanning** *n*.

caravanserai (*NAm* **caravansary**) *n* (*pl* **caravanserais** *or* **caravansaries**) **1** a large inn in Eastern countries that is built round a courtyard and used as a resting place for travellers and their animals. **2** a group of travellers; a caravan.

caravel *or* **carvel** *n* a small Spanish and Portuguese ship of the 15th and 16th cents.

caraway *n* the seeds of an aromatic plant of the carrot family with white flowers, used in cookery.

carbide *n* a chemical compound of carbon usu with a metallic element.

carbine *n* **1** a short light automatic or semiautomatic rifle. **2** a short light rifle or musket orig carried by cavalry.

carbohydrate *n* any of various compounds of carbon, hydrogen, and oxygen, e.g. sugars, starches, and celluloses, often formed by plants and constituting a major class of energy-providing animal foods.

carbolic acid *n* = PHENOL (1).

carbon *n* a non-metallic chemical element occurring naturally as diamond, graphite, etc or forming a constituent of coal, petroleum, limestone and other carbonates, and organic compounds.

carbonara *n* a pasta dish served with a sauce containing ham, cheese, cream, and eggs.

carbonate[1] *n* a salt or ester of carbonic acid.

carbonate[2] *v* **1** to convert (something) into a carbonate. **2** to impregnate (a drink) with carbon dioxide. ➤➤ **carbonation** *n*.

carbon black *n* any of various black substances consisting of very small particles of carbon that are obtained usu as soot and are used as pigments.

carbon copy *n* **1** a copy made with carbon paper. **2** a duplicate or exact replica.

carbon dating *n* the determination of the age of ancient organic material, e.g. wood or fossil bones, by recording the deterioration of carbon 14 in the material.

carbon dioxide *n* a heavy colourless gas that does not support combustion, is formed *esp* by the burning and decomposition of organic substances, and is absorbed from the air by plants in photosynthesis.

carbon fibre *n* a strong lightweight material made from filaments of pure carbon.

carbonic *adj* relating to carbon or carbon dioxide.

carbonic acid *n* a weak acid that is a solution of carbon dioxide in water.

carboniferous *adj* **1** producing or containing carbon or coal. **2** (**Carboniferous**) of the fifth geological period of the Palaeozoic era, lasting from about 363 million to about 290 million years ago, and marked by the formation of coal deposits. ➤➤ **Carboniferous** *n*.

carbonize *or* **-ise** *v* **1** to convert into carbon or a carbon-containing residue. **2** to become carbonized. ➤➤ **carbonization** *n*.

carbon monoxide *n* a very toxic gas with no colour or odour, formed as a product of the incomplete combustion of carbon.

carbon paper *n* thin paper coated on one side with dark pigment that is placed between two sheets of paper to make a copy.

carbon steel *n* a steel with characteristics that are determined by the amount of carbon it contains.

carbon tax *n* a tax on fossil fuels, e.g. petrol, with the aim of reducing their use in order to protect the environment.

carbonyl *n* a chemical group occurring in aldehydes, ketones and carboxylic acids.

car boot sale *n Brit* a sale of miscellaneous secondhand articles from cars parked on a designated site.

Carborundum *n trademark* any of various abrasive materials.

carboxyl *n* a chemical group that is typical of acidic organic chemical compounds.

carboxylic acid *n* an organic acid, e.g. acetic acid, containing one or more carboxyl groups.

carboy *n* a large usu spherical container for corrosive liquids, often in a protective frame.

carbuncle *n* **1** a painful boil-like inflammation of the skin and deeper tissues with several openings for the discharge of pus. **2** a red gemstone, usu a garnet, cut in a domed shape without facets. ➤➤ **carbuncular** *adj.*

carburet *v* (**carburetted, carburetting,** *NAm* **carbureted, carbureting**) to combine or enrich (e.g. a gas) with carbon or carbon compounds.

carburettor *or* **carburetter** (*NAm* **carburetor**) *n* an apparatus for supplying an internal-combustion engine with a fixed quantity of vaporized fuel mixed with air in an explosive mixture.

carcass *or* **carcase** *n* **1** a dead body, *esp* the body of an animal slaughtered for meat. **2** the decaying or worthless remains of a structure. **3** a framework, *esp* the framework of a tyre as distinct from the tread.

carcinogen *n* something, e.g. a chemical compound, that causes cancer. ➤➤ **carcinogenesis** *n,* **carcinogenic** *adj,* **carcinogenicity** *n.*

carcinoma *n* (*pl* **carcinomas** *or* **carcinomata**) a cancerous tumour originating in the EPITHELIUM (tissue covering an external surface or lining a body cavity). ➤➤ **carcinomatous** *adj.*

card[1] *n* **1** thin cardboard or stiff paper. **2a** a postcard. **b** a greetings card. **c** a visiting card. **3a** a playing card. **b** (*in pl, used as sing. or pl*) a game played with cards. **4** a rectangular piece of plastic, usu having machine-readable information about the holder and used to obtain credit, withdraw cash, etc. **5** *Brit, informal* (*in pl*) the official documents relating to an employee's income tax, national insurance, etc, held by their employer. **6** *informal* an amusing or eccentric person. ✱ **a card up one's sleeve** a secret plan or asset kept in reserve until needed. **get/ask for one's cards** *Brit, informal* to be dismissed/resign from employment. **on the cards** quite possible; likely to occur. **put/lay one's cards on the table** to divulge or declare one's intentions, position, etc.

card[2] *n* an implement or machine for carding fibres or raising a nap on cloth.

card[3] *v* to cleanse and disentangle (fibres) with a toothed implement or machine preparatory to spinning. ➤➤ **carder** *n.*

cardamom *n* the aromatic fruit of a plant of the ginger family, containing seeds used as a spice or condiment.

cardboard[1] *n* a thick stiff material made from the same ingredients as paper and used for boxes, packaging, etc.

cardboard[2] *adj* **1** made of cardboard. **2** unreal or insubstantial.

cardboard city *n* a place where many homeless people sleep in makeshift shelters, e.g. cardboard boxes.

card-carrying *adj* **1** being a fully paid-up member, *esp* of a political party or trade union. **2** dedicated or committed to a cause.

cardiac *adj* relating to or in the region of the heart.

cardie *or* **cardy** *n* (*pl* **-ies**) *informal* a cardigan.

cardigan *n* a knitted garment with sleeves for the upper body that opens down the front and is usu fastened with buttons.

cardinal[1] *n* **1** a member of a body of high officials of the Roman Catholic Church whose powers include the election of a new pope. **2** a deep scarlet colour. **3** a finch of the USA, the male of which has bright red plumage. ➤➤ **cardinalate** *n,* **cardinalship** *n.*

cardinal[2] *adj* of primary importance; fundamental. ➤➤ **cardinally** *adv.*

cardinal number *n* a number, e.g. one, two, three, that is used in simple counting and that indicates how many items there are in a set: compare ORDINAL NUMBER.

cardinal point *n* any of the four principal compass points: north, south, east, and west.

cardinal virtue *n* any of the four traditionally defined natural virtues, i.e. prudence, justice, temperance, and fortitude.

card index *n Brit* a filing or cataloguing system in which each item is entered on a separate card.

cardiogram *n* the curve or tracing made by a cardiograph.

cardiograph *n* an instrument that registers movements of the heart in the form of a graph. ➤➤ **cardiographer** *n,* **cardiography** *n.*

cardiology *n* the branch of medical science concerned with the heart, its diseases, and their treatment. ➤➤ **cardiological** *adj,* **cardiologist** *n.*

cardiopulmonary *adj* relating to or in the region of the heart and lungs.

cardiovascular *adj* relating to or in the region of the heart and blood vessels.

cardoon *n* a large plant of the daisy family that is related to the globe artichoke and cultivated for its edible root and leafstalks.

cardsharp *n* a person who habitually cheats at cards.

cardsharper *n* = CARDSHARP.

card vote *n* = BLOCK VOTE.

cardy *n* see CARDIE.

care[1] *n* **1a** anxiety. **b** a cause for anxiety. **2** close attention; effort. **3a** charge; supervision. **b** *Brit* legal responsibility for or guardianship of children by a local authority. **c** a sense of loving protectiveness or solicitude. **d** attention to or provision for the welfare, maintenance, etc of somebody or something. ✱ **care of** at the address of. **take care** to be careful or watchful; to exercise caution or prudence. **take care of 1** to attend to. **2** to deal with. **3** to look after.

care[2] *v* **1a** to be concerned about (something or somebody). **b** to feel trouble or anxiety: *She doesn't care if she hurts people's feelings.* **2** to have a liking or taste for: *I don't care for brandy.* **3** to give care: *caring for the sick.* **4** to wish (to do something): *if you care to go.*

careen *v* **1** to cause (e.g. a boat) to lean over to one side. **2** to clean, caulk, or repair (a boat) in this position. **3** of a boat: to lean over to one side; to heel over. **4** *chiefly NAm* = CAREER[2].

career[1] *n* **1** a field of employment in which one expects to spend a significant part of one's working life, *esp* a field requiring special qualifications or training and having opportunities for advancement. **2** (*used before a noun*) of or engaged in an occupation that offers a long-term series of opportunities for advancement, usu within some specified organization or business: *a career diplomat.*

career[2] *v* to move swiftly in an uncontrolled fashion.

careerist *n* somebody who is intent on advancing their career, often at the expense of personal integrity. ➤➤ **careerism** *n.*

career woman *n* a woman who puts advancement in her career or profession before marriage or motherhood.

carefree *adj* free from anxiety or responsibility. ➤➤ **carefreeness** *n.*

careful *adj* **1** exercising or taking care. **2a** marked by attentive concern. **b** cautious; prudent. ➤➤ **carefully** *adv,* **carefulness** *n.*

careless *adj* **1** not taking care. **2** unstudied; spontaneous: *careless grace.* **3a** free from care; untroubled: *careless days.* **b** indifferent; unconcerned:

careless of the consequences. ➤➤ **carelessly** *adv,* **carelessness** *n.*

carer *n Brit* a person who looks after somebody who is ill, elderly, or disabled, *esp* in the home.

caress[1] *n* **1** a gentle or loving touch or stroke. **2** a kiss.

caress[2] *v* to touch or stroke lightly and lovingly. ➤➤ **caressingly** *adv.*

caret *n* a mark (^) or (⅄) used on written or printed matter to indicate an insertion to be made.

caretaker *n* **1** a person who takes care of the house or land of an owner. **2** a person who looks after a usu large public building, e.g. a school. **3** somebody or something temporarily installed in office.

careworn *adj* showing the effects of grief or anxiety.

cargo *n* (*pl* **-oes** *or* **-os**) the goods conveyed in a ship, aircraft, or vehicle; freight.

Carib *n* (*pl* **Caribs** *or* **Carib**) **1** a member of a Native American people of northern S America and the Lesser Antilles. **2** the language of the Caribs.

Caribbean *adj* of the Caribbean Sea and its islands, *esp* the W Indies.

caribou *n* (*pl* **caribous** *or* **caribou**) a large N American deer that has broad branching antlers and is related to the reindeer.

caricature[1] *n* **1** exaggeration of personal features or characteristics, often to a ludicrous or grotesque degree. **2** a representation, *esp* in literature or art, that makes use of such exaggeration for comic or satirical effect. ➤➤ **caricatural** *adj,* **caricaturist** *n.*

caricature[2] *v* to make a caricature of; to represent in caricature.

caries *n* (*pl* **caries**) progressive decay of a tooth or bone, caused by micro-organisms.

carillon *n* a set of tuned bells sounded by hammers controlled from a keyboard.

carjacking *n* the act or an instance of hijacking a car. ➤➤ **carjacker** *n.*

Carlovingian *adj* = CAROLINGIAN.

Carmelite *n* a member of a Roman Catholic order of mendicant friars or a corresponding order of nuns. ➤➤ **Carmelite** *adj.*

carminative[1] *adj* causing expulsion of gas from the digestive tract to relieve flatulence.

carminative[2] *n* a carminative drug.

carmine *n* a rich crimson or scarlet pigment.

carnage *n* great slaughter, e.g. in battle.

carnal *adj* of or given to physical, *esp* sexual, pleasures and appetites. ➤➤ **carnality** *n,* **carnally** *adv.*

carnal knowledge *n* used *esp* as a legal term: sexual intercourse.

carnation *n* **1** a cultivated variety of the clove pink with fragrant typically red, pink, or white flowers. **2** a light red or pink colour.

carnelian *n* see CORNELIAN.

carnival *n* **1** a period or instance of public merrymaking or feasting. **2a** a festival. **b** a travelling circus or funfair.

carnivore *n* a flesh-eating mammal.

carnivorous *adj* **1** of an animal: feeding on flesh. **2** of a plant: feeding on nutrients obtained from animal tissue, *esp* insects. ➤➤ **carnivorously** *adv,* **carnivorousness** *n.*

carnosaur *n* a large flesh-eating dinosaur of a group that walked on two legs, including tyrannosaurus and allosaurus.

carob *n* the edible dark-coloured pod of a Mediterranean evergreen tree, used for animal fodder and as the source of a chocolate substitute.

carol[1] *n* a Christmas song or hymn.

carol[2] *v* (**carolled, carolling,** *NAm* **caroled, caroling**) **1** to sing (something), *esp* joyfully. **2** to sing carols, *esp* at Christmas. ➤➤ **caroller** *n.*

Carolingian *adj* of a medieval Frankish dynasty, named after Charles Martel, that ruled in France, Germany, and Italy. ➤➤ **Carolingian** *n.*

carotene *n* any of several orange or red plant pigments, found *esp* in carrots, that are converted to vitamin A in the body.

carotenoid *n* a carotene or similar pigment occurring in plants and some animal tissues.

carotid *adj* of or being either of the pair of arteries that supply the head with blood.

carousal *n* = CAROUSE[2].

carouse[1] *v* to take part in a drinking spree or drunken revel. ➤➤ **carouser** *n.*

carouse[2] *n* a drunken revel.

carousel *or* **carrousel** *n* **1** *chiefly NAm* a merry-go-round. **2** a rotating stand or delivery system, e.g. for slides in a projector or for baggage at an airport.

carp[1] *n* (*pl* **carps** *or* **carp**) a large soft-finned freshwater fish often farmed for food.

carp[2] *v informal* (+ at) to find fault or complain querulously and often unnecessarily. ➤➤ **carper** *n.*

carpaccio /kah'pachioh/ *n* an Italian delicacy comprising thin slices of raw meat or fish served with a dressing.

carpal[1] *adj* of or forming part of the wrist.

carpal[2] *n* a carpal bone.

carpal tunnel syndrome *n* a condition caused by pressure on the nerve passing through the wrist and resulting in pain and tingling in the hand and fingers.

carpe diem /kahpay 'dee·em/ *interj* enjoy the pleasures of the moment without concern for the future.

carpel *n* the female reproductive organ of a flowering plant, which consists of an ovary attached to a STIGMA (pollen-receiving structure) by a thin tubular STYLE[1]. ➤➤ **carpellary** *adj.*

carpenter[1] *n* a woodworker, *esp* one who builds or repairs large-scale structural woodwork. ➤➤ **carpentry** *n.*

carpenter[2] *v* to make by carpentry.

carpenter trousers *pl n* trousers that have several pockets and loops on the legs.

carpet[1] *n* **1** a floor covering made of a heavy woven or felted material. **2** a covering that resembles a carpet. ✱ **on the carpet** before an authority for censure or reprimand.

carpet[2] *v* (**carpeted, carpeting**) **1** to cover with a carpet or as if with a carpet. **2** *informal* to reprimand.

carpetbag *n* a travelling bag made of carpet-like fabric.

carpetbagger *n* **1** in the USA in former times, a Northerner who went to the South after the American Civil War in search of personal gain. **2** an opportunist.

carpet bomb *v* to drop bombs on (an area) so as to cause extensive uniform damage.

carpet slipper *n* a slipper for indoor wear.

car phone *n* a cellular phone for use in a motor vehicle.

carpi *n* pl of CARPUS.

carport *n* an open-sided shelter for cars, attached to a house.

carpus *n* (*pl* **carpi**) the wrist, or the bones that form the wrist.

carrack *n* a large square-rigged trading vessel of the 14th to 17th cents.

carrageen *or* **carragheen** *n* a dark purple branching edible seaweed found on the coasts of N Europe and N America.

carragheen *n* see CARRAGEEN.

carrel *n* a partitioned area or cubicle used for individual study, *esp* in a library.

carriage *n* **1** *Brit* a railway passenger vehicle; a coach. **2** a wheeled vehicle, *esp* a horse-drawn passenger vehicle. **3** a movable part of a machine that supports some other part. **4a** the act of carrying or conveying something, *esp* items of merchandise. **b** the price or cost of this. **5** the manner of bearing the body; posture.

carriage clock *n* a small clock enclosed in a glass-sided metal frame, usu with a handle at the top.

carriageway *n Brit* the part of a road used by vehicular traffic, often consisting of several lanes; see LANE (2).

carrier *n* **1** a bearer or messenger. **2** an individual or organization that undertakes to transport goods, messages, people, etc for payment. **3a** a container for carrying something. **b** a device or mechanism that carries something. **4** a bearer and transmitter of a causative agent of disease, *esp* a person or animal that is immune to the disease.

carrier bag *n Brit* a usu disposable bag of plastic or thick paper used for carrying shopping.

carrier pigeon *n* a homing pigeon used to carry messages.

carrion *n* **1** (*also used before a noun*) dead and putrefying flesh. **2** something corrupt or rotten.

carrion crow *n* the common European black crow.

carrot *n* **1** a long orange root of a plant with feathery leaves, used as a vegetable. **2** a promised and often illusory reward or advantage: *He offered them the carrot of promotion.* ➤➤ **carroty** *adj.*

carrousel *n* see CAROUSEL.

carry[1] *v* (**-ies, -ied**) **1** to move or transport from one place to another. **2** to wear or have on one's person. **3** to support the weight of. **4** to bear or transmit (a disease). **5** to accept (blame or responsibility). **6** to have as a consequence or attribute: *The offence carries a heavy penalty.* **7** to hold (oneself) in a specified manner: *He carries himself well.* **8** to maintain (a plan or undertaking) by personal effort. **9a** to win acceptance of (a proposal). **b** to persuade (somebody) to accept something. **10** to develop (an idea) to a particular point. **11** to broadcast or publish (a feature or story). **12** of sounds: to be audible at a distance. ✻ **be/get carried away** to become emotional or lose self-control. **carry all before one** to win against all opposition. **carry the can** *informal* to accept blame or responsibility. **carry the day** to win or prevail.

carry[2] *n* (*pl* **-ies**) the act or a method of carrying.

carryall *n NAm* = HOLDALL.

carrycot *n chiefly Brit* a small lightweight boxlike bed with two handles, in which a baby can be carried.

carry forward *v* in accounting, to transfer a total to a new column or account.

carrying-on *n* (*pl* **carryings-on**) *informal* rowdy, excited, or improper behaviour.

carry off *v* **1** to take away, *esp* by force. **2** to perform (something) successfully. **3** of a disease: to cause the death of.

carry on *v* **1** to conduct or manage (an undertaking). **2** to continuein an activity. **3** *informal* to behave in a rowdy or improper manner. **4** *Brit, informal* to have a love affair.

carry-on *n Brit, informal* a fuss or to-do.

carry out *v* to perform or implement (an idea or task).

carry over *v* **1** to postpone. **2** = CARRY FORWARD.

carry through *v* to complete (a task).

cart[1] *n* **1** a heavy two-wheeled or four-wheeled vehicle used for transporting loads. **2** a small wheeled vehicle. ✻ **put the cart before the horse** to do things in the reverse of the normal order.

cart[2] *v* **1** to carry or convey (something or somebody) in a cart. **2** *informal* (+ off) to take or drag (somebody) away without ceremony or by force. **3** *informal* to carry (*esp* something heavy) by hand. ➤➤ **carter** *n.*

carte blanche /,kaht 'blonhsh/ *n* full discretionary power.

cartel *n* an association of independent commercial enterprises designed to limit competition, e.g. by regulating prices.

Cartesian[1] *adj* relating to the philosophy of René Descartes (d.1650). ➤➤ **Cartesianism** *n.*

Cartesian[2] *n* a follower of René Descartes.

Cartesian coordinate *n* (*usu in pl*) any of a set of numbers fixing the position of a point by its distance from each of two or three lines or planes at right angles to one another.

Carthaginian *n* a native or inhabitant of the ancient city of Carthage in N Africa. ➤➤ **Carthaginian** *adj.*

carthorse *n* a large strong horse bred or used for pulling heavy loads.

Carthusian *n* a member of an austere contemplative order of monks or nuns founded by St Bruno in 1084. ➤➤ **Carthusian** *adj.*

cartilage *n* a translucent firm elastic tissue that makes up most of the skeleton of very young vertebrates and becomes mostly converted into bone in adult higher vertebrates, e.g. mammals, remaining in structures such as the external ear and the larynx. ➤➤ **cartilaginous** *adj.*

cartilaginous fish *n* any of a major group of fishes comprising all those with a cartilaginous rather than a bony skeleton, and including the sharks, dogfishes, and rays.

cartography *n* the art, science, or technology of drawing or compiling maps and charts. ➤➤ **cartographer** *n,* **cartographic** *adj.*

carton *n* a box or container made of cardboard, plastic, etc.

cartoon[1] *n* **1** a satirical drawing commenting on public and usu political matters. **2** = STRIP CARTOON. **3** a film that creates the illusion of movement by photographing successive positional changes, e.g. characters in drawings. **4** a preparatory design, drawing, or painting.

cartoon[2] *v* to draw a cartoon of (something or somebody). ➤➤ **cartoonist** *n.*

cartouche *n* **1** a scroll-shaped ornamental tablet, drawing, or architectural feature. **2** an oval or oblong outline, e.g. on ancient Egyptian monuments, enclosing a ruler's name.

cartridge *n* **1** a tube containing the charge and a bullet or shot for a firearm or an explosive charge for blasting. **2** a case holding magnetic tape, photographic film, etc, or a quantity of ink, designed for easy insertion into a device. **3** the part of the arm of a record player holding the stylus.

cartridge paper *n* thick paper with a rough surface, e.g. for drawing.

cartwheel *n* **1** a sideways handspring with arms and legs extended. **2** a wheel of a cart.

cartwright *n* somebody who makes and repairs carts.

carve *v* **1a** to cut (e.g. wood or stone) so as to shape it. **b** to produce (a statue, design, etc) by cutting. **2** (*often* + out) to make or acquire (a career, reputation, etc) through one's own efforts. **3** to cut (food, *esp* meat) into pieces or slices. ⯮ **carving** *n.*

carvel *n* see CARAVEL.

carvel-built *adj* of a boat: built with the planks meeting flush at the seams: compare CLINKER-BUILT.

carver *n* **1a** a long sharp knife used for carving meat. **b** (*in pl*) a knife and fork used for carving and serving meat. **2** *Brit* a chair with armrests forming part of a set of dining-room chairs.

carvery *n* (*pl* **-ies**) *chiefly Brit* a buffet-style restaurant where the customers' choice of roast meat is carved in their presence.

carve up *v* **1** to divide (something) into parts or shares. **2** *Brit, informal* to overtake (a vehicle or its driver) in an aggressive manner.

car wash *n* an automatic machine for washing cars, consisting of large revolving brushes through which water and soap are sprayed.

caryatid *n* (*pl* **caryatids** *or* **caryatides**) an architectural column in the form of a draped female figure used to support an entablature.

Casanova *n* a promiscuous and unscrupulous male lover.

casbah *n* see KASBAH.

cascade[1] *n* **1** a steep small fall of water, *esp* one of a series of such falls. **2** a series or succession of stages, processes, etc in which each item derives from, is triggered by, or acts on the product of the one before. **3** an arrangement of fabric, e.g. lace, that falls in a wavy or zigzag line. **4** something falling or rushing forth in profusion.

cascade[2] *v* to fall or pour in a cascade, or as if in a cascade.

cascara *n* the dried bark of a buckthorn tree or shrub of the Pacific coast of the USA, used as a mild laxative. Also called CASCARA SAGRADA.

cascara sagrada *n* = CASCARA .

case[1] *n* **1a** a set of circumstances or conditions; a situation. **b** a situation or object requiring investigation or action. **2** a form of a noun, pronoun, or adjective indicating its grammatical relation to other words. **3a** a suit or action that reaches a court of law. **b** the evidence supporting a conclusion. **c** an argument, *esp* one that is convincing. **4a** an instance that directs attention to a situation or exhibits it in action; an example. **b** a patient suffering from a specific condition. **c** a person or family receiving the attention or services of a social worker. ✱ **in case** for use in or as a precaution against the event that: *In case of fire, press the alarm button.*

case[2] *n* **1** a box or receptacle for holding something. **2** *chiefly Brit* a suitcase. **3** a box together with its contents: *a case of champagne.* **4** an outer covering. **5** a shallow divided tray for holding printing type.

case[3] *v* **1** to enclose in a case; to encase. **2** *informal* to inspect or study (e.g. a house), *esp* with intent to rob it.

casebook *n* a book containing records of illustrative cases for reference, e.g. in law or medicine.

case-harden *v* **1** to harden the surface of (iron or steel). **2** to make (somebody) callous. ⯮ **case-hardened** *adj.*

case history *n* a record of history and relevant details, e.g. of individual behaviour or condition, *esp* for use in analysis or diagnosis.

casein *n* a protein in milk that is precipitated by lactic acid or rennet, is the chief constituent of cheese, and is used in making paints or plastics.

case law *n* law established by previous judicial decisions.

case load *n* the number of cases handled in a particular period, e.g. by a court or clinic.

casement *n* a window that opens on hinges at the side.

case-sensitive *adj* in computing, sensitive to the difference between upper-case and lower-case letters.

case study *n* an analysis of a person or community based on details concerning development, environment, etc.

casework *n* social work involving direct consideration of the problems of individual people or families. ⯮ **caseworker** *n.*

cash[1] *n* **1** money in the form of notes and coins, *esp* when immediately available; ready money. **2** money or its equivalent paid promptly at the time of purchase. ⯮ **cashable** *adj,* **cashless** *adj.*

cash[2] *v* to pay or obtain cash for (a cheque, money order, etc).

cash-and-carry *n* a system by which the purchaser pays for goods at wholesale rate and takes them away immediately.

cashback *n* **1** an arrangement by which customers can obtain cash from a shop when paying for their purchases by debit card. **2** a discount or cash refund offered as an incentive to purchase.

cashbook *n* a book in which a record is kept of all money received and paid out.

cash card *n* a card that is issued by a bank or building society and allows the holder to operate a cash dispenser.

cash cow *n informal* a business or product from which liquid assets can be easily and consistently derived.

cash crop *n* a crop, e.g. cotton or sugar beet, produced for sale rather than for use by the grower.

cash desk *n* a desk, e.g. in a shop, where payment for purchases is made.

cash dispenser *n* an electronic machine from which cash can be withdrawn by inserting a cash card or credit card and keying in a personal identification number.

cashew *n* the edible kidney-shaped nut of a tropical American tree.

cash flow *n* the flow of money into and out of a business; the pattern of income and expenditure.

cashier[1] *n* a person employed to handle cash or deal with payment and receipts in a shop, bank, etc.

cashier[2] *v* to dismiss (somebody), usu with dishonour, *esp* from service in the armed forces.

cash in *v* **1** to convert (something) into cash. **2** (*usu* + on) to exploit (a financial or other advantage).

cashmere *n* fine wool from the undercoat of the Kashmir goat.

cashpoint *n Brit* = CASH DISPENSER.

cash register *n* a machine with a drawer for cash that is used in shops etc to record and display the amount of a sale and the money received.

cash up *v Brit* to add up the day's takings at the close of business.

casing *n* **1** an outer cover or shell, *esp* for protection. **2** an enclosing frame round a door or window opening.

casino *n* (*pl* **-os**) a building or room used for gambling.

cask *n* a barrel-shaped container, usu for holding liquids.

casket *n* **1** a small chest or box, usu ornamental, e.g. for jewels. **2** *chiefly NAm* a coffin.

Cassandra *n* a person who predicts misfortune or disaster.

cassata /kə'sahtə/ *n* ice cream containing fruit and nuts.

cassava *n* the fleshy edible rootstock of a tropical plant of the spurge family, used as food.

casserole[1] *n* **1** a heatproof covered dish in which food may be cooked, usu slowly in an oven, and served. **2** the savoury food cooked and served in a casserole.

casserole[2] *v* to cook (food) slowly in a casserole.

cassette *n* **1** a small case containing magnetic tape that can be inserted into a recording or playback device. **2** a lightproof container holding film that can be inserted into a camera.

cassia *n* **1** = SENNA (1). **2** a coarse cinnamon bark obtained from a tropical Asian tree.

cassis *n* a sweet purple liqueur made from blackcurrants.

cassock *n* an ankle-length garment worn *esp* by the Roman Catholic and Anglican clergy.

cassoulet /'kasəlay/ *n* a stew of haricot beans and mixed meats.

cassowary *n* (*pl* **-ies**) a large flightless bird that is closely related to the emu, found in New Guinea and Australia.

cast[1] *v* (*past and past part.* **cast**) **1** to cause (something) to move by forcibly throwing it. **2** to direct (something): *Cast your mind back to last year.* **3** to send forth or emit (something): *The fire casts a warm glow.* **4** to cause (something) to fall on or affect something or somebody: *The results cast doubt on our theory.* **5** to cause (a spell) to have an effect. **6** to deposit (a vote) formally. **7** to throw off or away; to discard or shed. **8** to assign the parts for (a play, film, etc) or select (an actor) for a particular role. **9** to arrange (facts, figures, etc) into a suitable form or order. **10a** to shape (metal, plastic, etc) by pouring it into a mould and letting it harden. **b** to form (an object) in this way. **11** to throw out a line and bait with a fishing rod. **12** (+ about/around) to look or search. ⋙ **casting** *n.*

cast[2] *n* **1** (*used as sing. or pl*) the set of performers in a dramatic production. **2a** a reproduction, e.g. of a statue, formed by casting. **b** an impression taken from an object with a molten or plastic substance. **c** = PLASTER[1] (3). **3** the act or an instance of casting something, e.g. a fishing line. **4** a slight squint in the eye. **5** something shed, ejected, or discarded, e.g. the excrement of an earthworm or a pellet regurgitated by a bird. **6** a shape or appearance.

castanet *n* (*usu in pl*) either of a pair of small wooden or plastic shells clicked together in the hand, *esp* by flamenco dancers.

castaway *n* a person who is cast adrift or ashore as a result of a shipwreck or as a punishment.

cast away *v* (*usu in passive*) to shipwreck or maroon (somebody or something).

cast down *v* (*usu in passive*) to depress (somebody).

caste *n* **1** any of the hereditary social groups in Hinduism that restrict the occupations of their members and their association with members of other castes. **2** a social class.

castellated *adj* having battlements like a castle. ⋙ **castellation** *n.*

caster *n* **1** see CASTOR. **2** somebody or something that casts.

caster sugar *or* **castor sugar** *n* finely granulated white sugar.

castigate *v formal* to punish or reprimand severely. ⋙ **castigation** *n,* **castigator** *n.*

Castilian *n* **1** a native or inhabitant of Castile, region and former kingdom of Spain. **2** the Spanish dialect of Castile, or the official and literary language of Spain based on it. ⋙ **Castilian** *adj.*

casting vote *n* a deciding vote cast by a presiding officer in the event of a tie.

cast iron *n* a hard brittle alloy of iron, carbon, and silicon, cast in a mould.

cast-iron *adj* **1** made of cast iron. **2a** capable of withstanding great strain; strong or unyielding. **b** impossible to disprove or falsify.

castle[1] *n* **1** a large fortified building or set of buildings. **2** = ROOK[3].

castle[2] *v* in chess, to move (a king) two squares towards a rook and then place the rook on the square passed over by the king.

castle in Spain *n* = CASTLE IN THE AIR.

castle in the air *n* (*usu in pl*) an impractical scheme; a daydream.

castoff *n* (*also in pl*) a cast-off article, e.g. a piece of clothing.

cast off *v* **1** to unfasten or untie a boat or a line. **2** to finish a knitted article by casting off all the stitches.

cast-off *adj* given up or discarded, *esp* because outgrown or no longer wanted.

cast on *verb trans or intrans* to place a stitch or stitches on a knitting needle, *esp* for beginning a knitted article.

castor *or* **caster** *n* **1** a small wheel set in a swivel mounting on the base of a piece of furniture, machinery, etc. **2** a container with a perforated top for sprinkling powdered or granulated foods.

castor oil *n* a pale viscous oil obtained from the seeds of the castor-oil plant, used *esp* as a laxative.

castor-oil plant *n* a tropical plant of the spurge family widely grown for its oil-rich beans.

castor sugar *n* see CASTER SUGAR.

castrate *v* **1** to remove the testes of (a male animal). **2** to deprive (somebody or something) of vitality or effect. ⋙ **castration** *n,* **castrator** *n.*

castrato *n* (*pl* **castrati**) a male singer castrated prepuberty to preserve the high range of his voice.

casual[1] *adj* **1** subject to, resulting from, or occurring by chance. **2a** occurring without regularity; occasional: *casual work.* **b** employed for irregular periods. **3a** feeling or showing little concern; nonchalant or offhand. **b** informal, *esp* designed for informal wear: *casual clothes.* ⋙ **casually** *adv,* **casualness** *n.*

casual[2] *n* **1** a casual or migratory worker. **2** (*in pl*) casual clothes or shoes.

casualty *n* (*pl* **-ies**) **1** a member of a military force killed or wounded in action. **2** a person or thing injured, lost, or destroyed. **3** the accident and emergency department of a hospital.

casuarina *n* an Australian and SE Asian tree that has thin drooping jointed twigs and yields a heavy hard wood.

casuist *n* a person skilled in or given to casuistry. ⋙ **casuistic** *adj,* **casuistical** *adj.*

casuistry *n* **1** a method or doctrine dealing with cases of conscience and the resolution of conflicting moral obligations. **2** the false application of general principles to particular instances, *esp* with regard to morals or law.

casus belli /ˌkahsoos ˈbelee/ *n* (*pl* **casus belli**) an event or action that brings about a war.

CAT *abbr* **1** computer-aided testing. **2** computerized axial tomography.

cat *n* **1a** a small furry flesh-eating mammal kept as a pet or for catching rats and mice. **b** any of a family of carnivores that includes the domestic cat, lion, tiger, leopard, jaguar, cougar, lynx, and cheetah. **2** *informal* a malicious woman. ✱ **let the cat out of the bag** to divulge a secret, *esp* inadvertently. **like a cat on a hot tin roof/on hot bricks** very agitated or uneasy. **put/set the cat among the pigeons** to do or say something that causes trouble. ➤➤ **catlike** *adj.*

cata- *or* **cat-** *prefix* **1** down: *catabolism.* **2** wrong: *catachresis.* **3** completely: *cataclysm.* **4** against: *catatonia.*

catabolism *or* **katabolism** *n* destructive metabolism involving the release of energy and resulting in the breakdown of complex materials, e.g. glucose: compare ANABOLISM. ➤➤ **catabolic** *adj.*

catachresis *n* (*pl* **catachreses**) use of the wrong word for the context.

cataclysm *n* **1** a violent geological change of the earth's surface. **2** a momentous event marked by violent upheaval and destruction. ➤➤ **cataclysmal** *adj,* **cataclysmic** *adj,* **cataclysmically** *adv.*

catacomb *n* (*also in pl*) **1** a galleried subterranean cemetery with recesses for tombs. **2** an underground passageway or group of passageways; a labyrinth.

catafalque *n* an ornamental structure supporting or bearing a coffin, e.g. while the body lies in state.

Catalan *n* **1** a native or inhabitant of Catalonia, region of NW Spain. **2** the Romance language of Catalonia, Valencia, and the Balearic islands. ➤➤ **Catalan** *adj.*

catalepsy *n* a trancelike state associated with schizophrenia in which the body remains rigid and immobile for prolonged periods. ➤➤ **cataleptic** *adj and n.*

catalogue[1] (*NAm* **catalog**) *n* **1** a complete list of items arranged systematically with descriptive details, or a brochure or book containing such a list. **2** a list or series.

catalogue[2] (*NAm* **catalog**) *v* (**catalogues, catalogued, cataloguing,** *NAm* **catalogs, cataloged, cataloging**) **1** to enter (an item) in a catalogue. **2** to make a catalogue of (a collection of things).

catalpa *n* an American and Asian tree of the jacaranda family with heart-shaped leaves and pale showy flowers.

catalyse (*NAm* **catalyze**) *v* to bring about the catalysis of (a chemical reaction).

catalysis *n* (*pl* **catalyses**) a change, *esp* an increase, in the rate of a chemical reaction induced by a catalyst.

catalyst *n* **1** a substance that changes, *esp* increases, the rate of a chemical reaction but itself remains chemically unchanged. **2** somebody or something whose action inspires further and usu more important events.

catalytic *adj* causing or involving catalysis.

catalytic converter *n* a device in a motor vehicle that uses catalysts to reduce the poisonous and polluting substances in exhaust fumes.

catalyze *v NAm* see CATALYSE.

catamaran *n* a boat with twin hulls side by side.

catamite *n archaic* a boy kept for homosexual intercourse.

Word history

Catamitus, Latin name of Ganymede. Ganymede was a beautiful young Trojan prince who was carried off by Zeus and made cupbearer to the gods.

cataplexy *n* sudden temporary paralysis following a strong emotional stimulus, e.g. shock.

catapult[1] *n* **1** *chiefly Brit* a Y-shaped stick with a piece of elastic material fixed between the two prongs, used for shooting small objects, e.g. stones. **2** in former times, a military device used for hurling missiles. **3** a device for launching an aircraft at flying speed, e.g. from an aircraft carrier.

catapult[2] *v* **1** to throw or launch (a missile) by means of a catapult. **2** to move or cause (somebody or something) to move suddenly or abruptly.

cataract *n* **1** a waterfall, *esp* a large one descending steeply or in steps. **2** a clouding of the lens of the eye or its enclosing membrane, obstructing the passage of light.

catarrh *n* inflammation of a mucous membrane, *esp* in the human nose and throat, or the resulting excessive discharge of mucus. ➤➤ **catarrhal** *adj.*

catastrophe *n* a momentous, tragic, and unexpected event of extreme severity. ➤➤ **catastrophic** *adj,* **catastrophically** *adv.*

catatonia *n* **1** a form of schizophrenia, marked by catalepsy. **2** = CATALEPSY. ➤➤ **catatonic** *adj and n.*

catboat *n* a sailing boat with a mast positioned close to the bows and a single sail.

cat burglar *n* a burglar who enters buildings by skilful or daring feats of climbing.

catcall[1] *n* a loud or raucous cry expressing disapproval.

catcall[2] *v* to utter a catcall.

catch[1] *v* (*past tense and past part.* **caught**) **1a** to capture or seize (a person or an animal), *esp* after pursuit. **b** to take or entangle (a person or an animal) in a snare, or as if in a snare. **c** to discover (somebody) unexpectedly. **d** to become or cause to become entangled, fastened, or stuck. **2a** to intercept and keep hold of (a moving object), *esp* in the hands. **b** to dismiss (a batsman in cricket) by catching the ball after it has been hit and before it has touched the ground. **c** to seize (something): *Catch hold of the railing.* **d** to take in and retain (something): *a barrel to catch rainwater.* **3a** to contract or become infected with (a disease). **b** to hit or strike. **c** to be struck or affected by. **4** to attract or arrest (somebody's attention). **5** to take or get momentarily or quickly. **6** to be in time for. **7** to grasp with the senses or the mind. **8** to capture a likeness of. **9** of a fire: to start to burn. ✱ **catch sight of** to see (something or somebody) suddenly or momentarily. ➤➤ **catchable** *adj,* **catcher** *n.*

catch[2] *n* **1a** something caught, *esp* the total quantity caught at one time. **b** the act or an instance of catching. **2** a game in which a ball is thrown and caught. **3** something that retains or fastens something. **4** a concealed difficulty; a snag. **5** *informal* an eligible marriage partner. **6** a break in the voice, *esp* one caused by emotion.

catch-22 *n* a predicament from which a victim is unable to extricate himself or herself because the means of escape depends on mutually exclusive prior conditions.

catchall *n* something intended to include or cover miscellaneous cases, items, circumstances, etc.

catch crop *n* a crop planted between the rows of the main crop or grown between the harvesting of one crop and the planting of another.

catching *adj* infectious; contagious.

catchment area *n* **1** the area from which a river, lake, reservoir, etc gets its water. **2** a geographical area from which people are drawn to attend a particular school, hospital, etc.

catch on *v* **1** to become popular. **2** *informal* (*often* + to) to understand or become aware.

catch out *v* to expose or detect in wrongdoing or error.

catchpenny *adj derog* designed to sell quickly and cheaply by superficial appeal, showiness, sensationalism, etc.

catchphrase *n* a phrase that enjoys often short-lived popularity; *specif* one associated with a particular person or group.

catchup *n NAm* see KETCHUP.

catch up *v* **1** to succeed in reaching or drawing level with (somebody ahead). **2** to complete (work or commitments) that remain or are overdue. ✱ **be/get caught up in** to become involved or engrossed in (an activity).

catchword *n* **1** a word or expression associated with some school of thought or political movement; a slogan. **2** a word printed under the last line of a page that duplicates the first word of the following page.

catchy *adj* (**-ier, -iest**) easy to remember and reproduce.

catechesis *n* (*pl* **catecheses**) oral instruction of somebody preparing to become a member of a Christian Church.

catechetical *adj* **1** relating to catechesis. **2** relating to a system of teaching, *esp* religious instruction, by question and answer.

catechise *v* see CATECHIZE.

catechism *n* **1** instruction by question and answer. **2** a manual for systematic teaching; *specif* a summary of religious doctrine in the form of questions and answers.

catechize *or* **-ise** *v* to teach (somebody) systematically, *esp* by using question and answer; *specif* to give (them) religious instruction in such a manner. ➤➤ **catechist** *n.*

catechumen *n* a person receiving instruction in Christian doctrine and discipline before admission to membership of a church.

categoric *adj* = CATEGORICAL.

categorical *adj* absolute; unqualified. ➤➤ **categorically** *adv.*

categorize *or* **-ise** *v* to put into a category; to classify. ➤➤ **categorization** *n.*

category *n* (*pl* **-ies**) **1** a division within a system of classification. **2** a general or fundamental form or class of terms, things, or ideas, e.g. in philosophy.

catenary *n* (*pl* **-ies**) the curve formed by a perfectly flexible cord of uniform density and cross section hanging freely from two fixed points. ➤➤ **catenary** *adj.*

cater *v* **1** (*often* + for) to provide and serve a supply of prepared food. **2** (+ for/to) to supply what is required or desired by (somebody or something). ➤➤ **caterer** *n,* **catering** *n.*

catercorner *adv and adj NAm* in a diagonally opposite position.

cater-cornered *adv and adj* = CATERCORNER.

Caterpillar *n trademark* **1** a tractor or other vehicle designed to travel over rough or soft ground and propelled by two endless metal belts. **2** either of the endless metal belts used to propel such a vehicle.

caterpillar *n* a wormlike larva; *specif* the larva of a butterfly or moth.

caterwaul[1] *v* to make a loud wailing cry.

caterwaul[2] *n* a loud wailing cry.

catfish *n* (*pl* **catfishes** *or* **catfish**) a large-headed fish with barbels (tactile organs; see BARBEL[2]) round the mouth.

cat flap *n* a small hinged flap in the lower part of a door through which a cat may pass.

catgut *n* a tough cord usu made from sheep intestines and used *esp* for the strings of musical instruments and sports rackets.

catharsis *n* (*pl* **catharses**) **1** purification or purgation of the emotions through drama. **2** the process of bringing repressed ideas and feelings to consciousness and expressing them, *esp* during psychoanalysis. ➤➤ **cathartic** *adj,* **cathartically** *adv.*

cathedral *n* a church that is the official seat of a diocesan bishop.

Catherine wheel *n* a firework in the form of a flat coil that spins as it burns.

catheter *n* a flexible tubular device for insertion into a hollow body part, e.g. the bladder, usu to draw off or inject fluids or to keep a passage open.

catheterize *or* **-ise** *v* to introduce a catheter into (a hollow body part). ➤➤ **catheterization** *n.*

cathode *n* **1** the electrode by which electrons leave an external circuit and enter a device, e.g.: **a** the positive terminal of a battery: compare ANODE. **b** the negative electrode in an electrolytic cell. **2** the electrode in a thermionic valve or similar electronic device that emits the electrons.

cathode ray *n* a beam of high-speed electrons projected from the heated cathode of a vacuum tube.

cathode-ray tube *n* a vacuum tube in which a beam of electrons is projected onto a fluorescent screen to provide a spot of light that produces a visual display, e.g. a television picture.

Catholic *n* a member of the Roman Catholic Church.

catholic *adj* **1a** comprehensive; universal. **b** broad in sympathies, tastes, or interests. **2** (**Catholic**) **a** Roman Catholic. **b** of or forming the entire body of worshippers that constitutes the Christian Church. ➤➤ **Catholicism** *n.*

Catholicise *v* see CATHOLICIZE.

catholicity *n* **1** liberality of sentiments or views. **2** universality; comprehensiveness.

Catholicize *or* **-ise** *v* to become converted or convert (a person or group) to Catholicism.

cation *n* a positively charged ion that moves towards the cathode during electrolysis: compare ANION. ➤➤ **cationic** *adj.*

catkin *n* a densely crowded spike of flowers without petals hanging from a tree, e.g. a willow or hazel.

catmint *n* a blue-flowered plant of the mint family with small pale purple-spotted flowers and a strong scent that is attractive to cats.

catnap[1] *n* a brief period of sleep, *esp* during the day.

catnap[2] *v* (**catnapped, catnapping**) to have a catnap.

catnip *n* = CATMINT.

cat-o'-nine-tails *n* (*pl* **cat-o'-nine-tails**) a flogging whip made of nine knotted cords fastened to a handle.

cat's cradle *n* a game in which different patterns are formed in a loop of string held between the hands.

Catseye *n trademark* each of a series of small reflecting studs set in the road to mark the middle or edge of the carriageway.

cat's-eye *n* (*pl* **cat's-eyes**) any of various gems, e.g. a chrysoberyl or a chalcedony, that reflect a narrow band of light from within.

cat's-paw *n* (*pl* **cat's-paws**) somebody used by another as a tool or dupe.

cat's pyjamas *pl n* = CAT'S WHISKERS.

catsuit *n* a tightly fitting one-piece garment combining top and trousers.

catsup *n NAm* = KETCHUP.

cat's whisker *n* a fine wire used as a metallic electrode in a crystal radio receiver.

cat's whiskers *pl n* (**the cat's whiskers**) *informal* an excellent person or thing.

cattery *n* (*pl* **-ies**) a place for the breeding or care of cats.

cattle *pl n* bovine animals, e.g. cows or oxen, *esp* those reared for domestic use.

cattle cake *n* cattle food in a concentrated compressed form.

cattle grid *n Brit* a shallow ditch in a road covered by parallel bars spaced far enough apart to prevent livestock but not wheeled vehicles from crossing.

catty *adj* (**-ier, -iest**) spiteful; malicious. ➤➤ **cattily** *adv,* **cattiness** *n.*

CATV *abbr* community antenna television.

catwalk *n* **1** a narrow stage extending into the audience at a fashion show. **2** a narrow walkway, e.g. round a piece of machinery.

Caucasian *adj* **1** of the white race of humankind as classified according to physical features. **2** of the Caucasus or its inhabitants. ➤➤ **Caucasian** *n.*

caucus *n* (*pl* **caucuses**) **1** a closed political meeting to decide on policy, select candidates, etc. **2** a group of people forming a faction within a larger body or organization, *esp* a political party.

caudal *adj* **1** of or resembling a tail. **2** relating to or in the region of the hind part of the body. ➤➤ **caudally** *adv.*

caught *v* past tense of CATCH[1].

caul *n* the inner foetal membrane of higher vertebrate animals, e.g. humans, *esp* when covering the head at birth.

cauldron *or* **caldron** *n* a large open metal pot used for cooking over an open fire.

cauliflower *n* the flower head of a plant of the cabbage family, used as a vegetable.

cauliflower ear *n* an ear thickened and deformed through injury, e.g. from repeated blows in boxing.

caulk[1] *or* **calk** *v* **1** to stop up and make watertight (the seams of a boat, cracks in wood, etc) by filling or sealing them with a waterproof material. **2** to make (a boat or ship) watertight in this way. ➤➤ **caulker** *n.*

caulk[2] *or* **calk** *n* waterproof material used as a filler and sealant.

causal *adj* **1** of or being a cause. **2** expressing or indicating a cause or causation. ➤➤ **causally** *adv.*

causality *n* (*pl* **-ies**) **1** the relationship between a cause and its effect. **2** the principle that everything has a cause.

causation *n* **1** the act or process of causing. **2** the relationship between cause and effect.

causative *adj* **1** effective or operating as a cause or agent. **2** in grammar, expressing causation.

cause[1] *n* **1a** somebody or something that brings about an effect or result. **b** a reason for an action or condition; a motive. **2a** a ground for legal action. **b** a suit or action that reaches a court of law. **3** a principle or movement worth defending or supporting. ➤➤ **causeless** *adj.*

cause[2] *v* to serve as the cause of (something).

cause célèbre *n* (*pl* **causes célèbres**) a legal case or controversial issue that excites widespread interest.

causeway *n* a raised road or path, *esp* across wet ground or water.

caustic[1] *adj* **1** capable of destroying or eating away by chemical action; corrosive. **2** bitterly sarcastic or cutting. ➤➤ **caustically** *adv,* **causticity** *n.*

caustic[2] *n* a caustic substance.

caustic soda *n* = SODIUM HYDROXIDE.

cauterize *or* **-ise** *v* to sear or burn (a wound or body tissue) with a cautery, *esp* in order to stop bleeding or destroy infection. ➤➤ **cauterization** *n.*

cautery *n* (*pl* **-ies**) **1** the act of cauterizing a wound or body tissue. **2** an instrument, e.g. a hot iron, or a caustic chemical used in cauterization.

caution[1] *n* **1** prudent forethought intended to minimize risk; care. **2** a warning or admonishment; *specif* an official warning given to somebody who has committed a minor offence.

caution[2] *v* **1** to warn or advise caution to. **2** to warn (somebody under arrest) that their words will be recorded and may be used in evidence. **3** to admonish or reprove (somebody); *specif* to give (them) an official warning.

cautionary *adj* serving or intended to serve as a warning.

cautious *adj* careful; prudent. ➤➤ **cautiously** *adv,* **cautiousness** *n.*

cava *n* a sparkling white wine produced in Spain by the champagne method.

cavalcade *n* a procession, *esp* one of people on horseback or in carriages or other vehicles.

cavalier[1] *n* **1** a gallant gentleman of former times, *esp* one in attendance on a lady. **2** (**Cavalier**) a supporter of Charles I of England, *esp* during the Civil War.

cavalier[2] *adj* offhand or dismissive with regard to important matters, other people's feelings, etc. ➤➤ **cavalierly** *adv.*

cavalry *n* (*pl* **-ies**) (*used as sing. or pl*) a branch of an army consisting of mounted troops or armoured vehicles. ➤➤ **cavalryman** *n.*

cavalry twill *n* a strong fabric woven in a double twill and used orig for riding breeches.

cave[1] *n* a natural chamber, usu underground or in the side of a hill or cliff, with an opening on the surface.

cave[2] *v* **1** to form a cave in or under; to hollow out. **2** to explore underground systems of caves or potholes. ➤➤ **caver** *n.*

caveat *n formal* a cautionary statement or warning.

caveat emptor *n* the principle in commerce stating that buyers who purchase goods without a guarantee take the risk of quality upon themselves.

cave in *v* **1** to fall in or collapse. **2** *informal* to cease to resist; to submit.

caveman *n* (*pl* **cavemen**) somebody who lives in a cave, *esp* a cave dweller of the Stone Age.

cavern *n* a large usu underground chamber or cave. ➤➤ **cavernous** *adj,* **cavernously** *adv.*

caviar *or* **caviare** *n* the salted roe of large fish, e.g. sturgeon, eaten as a delicacy.

cavil[1] *v* (**cavilled, cavilling,** *NAm* **caviled, caviling**) (*often* + at) to raise trivial and frivolous objections. ➤➤ **caviller** *n.*

cavil[2] *n* a trivial or frivolous objection.

cavitation *n* the formation of cavities in something.

cavity *n* (*pl* **-ies**) an empty or hollowed-out space within a mass; *specif* a decaying hollow in a tooth.

cavity wall *n* a wall built in two thicknesses with an insulating air space between them.

cavort *v* to prance or leap about.

cavy *n* (*pl* **-ies**) a short-tailed S American rodent such as the guinea pig.

caw *v* to utter the harsh raucous cry of the crow. ➤➤ **caw** *n.*

cayenne *n* = CAYENNE PEPPER.

cayenne pepper *n* a pungent red condiment consisting of the ground dried pods and seeds of hot peppers: compare CHILLI, PAPRIKA.

cayman *or* **caiman** *n* (*pl* **caymans** *or* **cayman**) a Central and S American reptile of the crocodile family closely related to the alligators.

Cayuga *n* (*pl* **Cayugas** *or* **Cayuga**) a member of a Native American people formerly inhabiting New York State.

Cayuse *n* (*pl* **Cayuses** *or* **Cayuse**) a member of a Native American people of Oregon and Washington.

CB *abbr* **1** in radio, citizens' band. **2** *Brit* Companion of the (Order of the) Bath.

CBE *abbr Brit* Commander of the (Order of the) British Empire.

CBI *abbr* Confederation of British Industry.

CC *abbr* **1** City Council. **2** County Council. **3** Cricket Club.

cc *abbr* **1** carbon copy. **2** cubic centimetre.

CCTV *abbr* closed-circuit television.

CD *abbr* **1** compact disc. **2** diplomatic corps.

Cd *abbr* the chemical symbol for cadmium.

cd *abbr* candela.

CD-I *abbr* compact disc interactive.

CD player *n* a piece of audio equipment for playing compact discs.

CD-ROM *n* a compact disc on which very large amounts of data can be stored for use by a computer.

CDT *abbr* **1** Central daylight time. **2** craft, design, and technology.

CDV *abbr* CD video.

CD video *n* a system for the recording and reproduction of high-quality sound synchronized with video images on a compact disc.

CE *abbr* **1** Church of England. **2** Common Era. **3** Council of Europe.

Ce *abbr* the chemical symbol for cerium.

ceanothus *n* a shrub or small tree of the buckthorn family that is grown for its showy clusters of blue or white flowers.

cease[1] *v* to come or bring to an end; to terminate.

cease[2] *n* stopping; cessation.

cease-fire *n* a suspension of active hostilities.

ceaseless *adj* continuing endlessly; constant. ➤➤ **ceaselessly** *adv.*

ceca *n NAm* pl of CECUM.

cecum *n NAm* see CAECUM.

cedar *n* a usu tall evergreen coniferous tree of the pine family, with fragrant durable wood.

cede *v* to yield or surrender (e.g. territory), usu by treaty.

cedi *n* (*pl* **cedi**) the basic monetary unit of Ghana.

cedilla *n* a mark (¸) placed under a letter to show an alteration of its usual pronunciation, e.g. under *c* in French to change its sound from the /k/ of *café* to the /s/ of *façade.*

Ceefax *n trademark* a service provided by the BBC transmitting information in the form of printed text on a television set.

ceilidh *n* a party, e.g. after a wedding, with traditional country dancing and music, *esp* in Scotland or Ireland.

ceiling *n* **1** the overhead inside surface of a room. **2** an upper prescribed limit. **3** a prescribed or actual maximum height at which an aircraft can fly.

celandine *n* **1** a common yellow-flowered European perennial plant of the buttercup family. Also called LESSER CELANDINE. **2** a yellow-flowered biennial plant of the poppy family. Also called GREATER CELANDINE.

celebrant *n* **1** the priest officiating at the Eucharist. **2** somebody who is celebrating something.

celebrate *v* **1a** to mark (a special occasion) with festivities or suspension of routine activities. **b** to mark (a holy day or feast day) ceremonially. **2** to perform (a sacrament or solemn ceremony) publicly and with appropriate rites. **3** to hold (something) up for public acclaim; to extol (it). ➤➤ **celebration** *n,* **celebrator** *n,* **celebratory** *adj.*

celebrated *adj* widely known or acclaimed; famous.

celebrity *n* (*pl* **-ies**) **1** a well-known and widely acclaimed person. **2** the state of being famous.

celeriac *n* a type of celery grown for its thickened edible root.

celerity *n formal* rapidity of motion or action.

celery *n* a European plant of the carrot family with leafstalks that are eaten raw or cooked as a vegetable.

celesta *or* **celeste** *n* a keyboard musical instrument with hammers that strike steel plates producing a tinkling bell-like sound.

celestial *adj* **1** of or suggesting heaven or divinity; divine. **2** of or in the sky. ➤➤ **celestially** *adv.*

celestial equator *n* the great circle on the celestial sphere midway between the two points round which the daily rotation of the stars appears to take place.

celestial pole *n* either of the two points on the celestial sphere round which the daily rotation of the stars appears to take place.

celestial sphere *n* an imaginary sphere of infinite radius against which the celestial bodies appear to be projected.

celiac *adj NAm* see COELIAC.

celibate[1] *adj* **1** abstaining from sexual intercourse, *esp* because of a religious vow. **2** unmarried. ➤➤ **celibacy** *n.*

celibate[2] *n* a celibate person.

cell *n* **1** a small room in a prison or in a convent or monastery. **2** the smallest structural unit of living matter, consisting of a nucleus surrounded by CYTOPLASM (jelly-like material) and bounded by a membrane. **3** a small compartment, or a bounded space, e.g. a compartment of a honeycomb or a receptacle for seeds in a plant. **4** the primary unit of a political, *esp* subversive, organization. **5** a vessel containing electrodes and an electrolyte either for generating electricity by chemical action or for use in electrolysis. **6** a basic subdivision of a computer memory that is addressable and can hold one unit, e.g. a word, of a computer's basic operating data.

cellar *n* **1** an underground room, *esp* one used for storage. **2** a stock of wine.

cell division *n* the process by which two daughter cells are formed from a parent cell.

Cellnet *n trademark* a cellular radio network for users of mobile phones.

cello *n* (*pl* **-os**) a stringed musical instrument of the violin family that is held between the player's knees, supported on the ground by an adjustable metal spike. ⋙ **cellist** *n.*

Cellophane *n trademark* thin transparent sheets of cellulose, used *esp* for wrapping goods.

cellphone *n* a mobile phone for use in a cellular radio system.

cellular *adj* **1** relating to or consisting of cells. **2** containing cavities; porous. **3** having a very open weave. **4** relating to or used in a cellular radio system.

cellular radio *n* a communications system for mobile phones in which an area is divided into regions, each with its own transmitter.

cellulite *n* a type of body fat, possibly caused by water retention, that produces a dimpled effect on the skin, e.g. of the thigh.

cellulitis *n* inflammation of body tissue, *esp* below the surface of the skin.

celluloid *n* **1** (**Celluloid**) *trademark* a tough inflammable thermoplastic that is composed mainly of cellulose nitrate and camphor and was formerly used to coat film. **2** film for the cinema.

cellulose *n* **1** a carbohydrate made up of glucose units that constitutes the chief part of plant cell walls and is the raw material of many manufactured goods, e.g. paper, rayon, and cellophane. **2** paint or lacquer of which the main constituent is cellulose nitrate or acetate.

cellulose acetate *n* a chemical compound formed by the action of acetic acid on cellulose and used for making textile fibres, packaging sheets, photographic films, and varnishes.

cell wall *n* the firm outer layer, formed usu from cellulose, that encloses and supports most plant cells.

Celsius *adj* of or being a scale of temperature on which water freezes at 0° and boils at 100° under standard conditions.

Usage note

Celsius *or* centigrade? *Celsius* has been internationally adopted as the name of the temperature scale and is always used, for example, in giving weather forecasts. *Centigrade* is no longer in technical use.

Celt *or* **Kelt** *n* **1** a member of a division of the early Indo-European peoples extending at various times from the British Isles and Spain to Asia Minor. **2** a native or inhabitant of Highland Scotland, Ireland, Wales, Cornwall, the Isle of Man, or Brittany.

Celtic[1] *or* **Keltic** *adj* of the Celts or their languages.

Celtic[2] *or* **Keltic** *n* a branch of Indo-European languages comprising Welsh, Cornish, Breton, Irish and Scottish Gaelic, and Manx.

cement[1] *n* **1a** a powder containing lime and clay that is used as the binding agent in mortar and concrete. **b** concrete or mortar. **2** a substance used for sticking objects together.

cement[2] *v* **1** to join (things) together firmly by the application of cement or a similar substance. **2** to make (e.g. a relationship) firm and strong.

cementation *n* the process of heating a solid surrounded by a powder so that the solid is changed by chemical combination with the powder, *esp* the heating of iron surrounded by charcoal to make steel.

cemetery *n* (*pl* **-ies**) a burial ground, *esp* one not in a churchyard.

cenobite *n NAm* see COENOBITE.

cenotaph *n* a tomb or monument erected in honour of a dead person or group of people whose remains are elsewhere.

Cenozoic *or* **Cainozoic** *adj* a geological era (extending from the end of the Mesozoic era until the present time, and including the Tertiary and Quaternary periods) lasting from about 65 million years ago to the present, and marked *esp* by a rapid evolution of mammals, birds, and flowering plants. ⋙ **Cenozoic** *n.*

censer *n* a covered incense burner swung on chains during certain religious rituals.

censor[1] *n* an official who examines publications, films, letters, etc and has the power to suppress objectionable, e.g. obscene or libellous, matter.

censor[2] *v* to examine and remove objectionable matter from (e.g. a publication, film, letter). ⋙ **censorship** *n.*

censorious *adj* severely critical; given to censure. ⋙ **censoriously** *adv,* **censoriousness** *n.*

censure[1] *n* **1** a judgment involving condemnation. **2** the act of blaming or condemning sternly.

censure[2] *v* to find fault with and criticize (somebody) as blameworthy. ⋙ **censurable** *adj.*

census *n* (*pl* **censuses**) a periodic counting of the population and gathering of related statistics, e.g. age, sex, or social class, carried out by a government.

cent *n* a unit of currency worth 100th of the basic monetary unit of certain countries, e.g. the dollar.

centas *n* (*pl* **centas** *or* **centai**) a unit of currency in Lithuania, worth 100th of a litas.

centaur *n* any of a race of mythological creatures with the head, arms, and upper body of a man, and the lower body and back legs of a horse.

centavo *n* (*pl* **-os**) a unit of currency worth 100th of the basic monetary unit of certain Spanish- or Portuguese-speaking countries.

centenarian[1] *n* somebody who is 100 years old or older.

centenarian[2] *adj* at least 100 years old.

centenary[1] *n* (*pl* **-ies**) a 100th anniversary, or a celebration marking this.

centenary[2] *adj* **1** relating to a 100th anniversary or a period of 100 years. **2** occurring every 100 years.

centennial[1] *adj* **1** marking a 100th anniversary. **2** occurring every 100 years. **3** relating to or lasting for a period of 100 years. ⋙ **centennially** *adv.*

centennial[2] *n* = CENTENARY[1].

center *noun and v NAm* see CENTRE[1], CENTRE[2].

centésimo *n* (*pl* **-os**) a unit of currency worth 100th of the basic monetary unit of Panama and Uruguay.

centi- *comb. form* **1** hundred: *centipede.* **2** one hundredth part: *centimetre.*

centigrade *adj* of or being a scale of 100 degrees, *esp* the Celsius scale of temperature.

Usage note

centigrade *or* Celsius? See note at CELSIUS.

centigram *n* a metric unit of mass equal to 100th of a gram.

centilitre (*NAm* **centiliter**) *n* a metric unit of capacity equal to 100th of a litre (about 0.35fl oz).

centime *n* a unit of currency worth 100th of the basic monetary unit of France and certain French-speaking countries.

centimetre (*NAm* **centimeter**) *n* a metric unit of length equal to 100th of a metre (about 0.4in.).

centimo *n* (*pl* **-os**) a unit of currency worth 100th of the basic monetary unit of Spain and certain Spanish-speaking countries.

centipede *n* a long invertebrate animal with a flattened body divided into many segments, each bearing one pair of legs.

cento *n* (*pl* **centones** *or* **centos**) a literary work made up of quotations from other works.

centr- *or* **centri-** *or* **centro-** *comb. form* centre.

central *adj* **1a** at or near the centre. **b** easily accessible; convenient. **2** of primary importance; principal. **3** having overall power or control. ➤➤ **centrality** *n,* **centrally** *adv.*

Central America *n* the isthmus between North America and South America and the countries it contains, e.g. Guatemala, Nicaragua, and Costa Rica. ➤➤ **Central American** *adj.*

central bank *n* the main banking institution of a country, dealing mainly with government or interbank transactions.

Central European Time *n* the standard time, one hour ahead of Greenwich Mean Time, used by most countries of continental Europe.

central heating *n* a system in which heat is produced at a central source, e.g. a boiler, and carried by pipes to radiators or air vents throughout a building.

centralise *v* see CENTRALIZE.

centralism *n* the principle of concentrating power in a central authority. ➤➤ **centralist** *n and adj,* **centralistic** *adj.*

centralize *or* **-ise** *v* to bring (power, authority, administration, etc) under central control. ➤➤ **centralization** *n.*

central nervous system *n* the part of the nervous system, consisting of the brain and spinal cord, that coordinates bodily functions.

central processing unit *n* the part of a computer system that controls operations and carries out software commands.

central reservation *n* a strip in the middle of a road, *esp* a motorway or dual carriageway, that is usu covered with grass or tarmac.

centre[1] (*NAm* **center**) *n* **1** the middle point or part of something, *specif* the point lying at the same distance from both ends of a line, all sides of a polygon, or all points on the circumference of a circle. **2a** a place, *esp* a building, in which a particular activity is concentrated. **b** the part of a town or city where most of the shops, banks, offices, etc are situated. **c** a focus on which interest is concentrated. **d** a source from which something originates. **3** (*often* **Centre**) a group, party, etc holding moderate political views. **4a** in some sports, e.g. football or hockey, a player occupying a middle position in the forward line. **b** an instance of passing the ball from the side to the middle of a pitch or field.

centre[2] *v* **1** (+ on/round/around) to have as a centre; to focus on. **2** to place or fix in or at a centre or central area. **3** in sports, to pass (e.g. a ball or puck) from either side towards the middle of the playing area.

centre back *n* a player or position in football in the middle of the defence.

centreboard *n* a retractable keel used *esp* in small sailing boats.

centred *adj* **1** at or in the centre. **2** *chiefly NAm* of a person: emotionally stable.

centrefold *n* the two facing pages in the centre of a newspaper or magazine, or an illustration covering them.

centre forward *n* a player or position in hockey, football, etc in the middle of the forward line.

centre half *n* a player or position in hockey, football, etc in the middle of the halfback line.

centre of gravity *n* the point from which the whole weight of a body may be considered to act.

centre of mass *n* the point at which the entire mass of a body or system of bodies may be considered as concentrated.

centrepiece *n* **1** an ornament, e.g. a flower arrangement, placed in the centre of a table. **2** the most important or outstanding item.

centre spread *n* = CENTREFOLD.

centre stage *n* **1** the centre of a theatre stage. **2** a position of prominence; the focus of attention.

centre three-quarter *n* either of the two players or positions in rugby in the middle of the three-quarter-back line.

centri- *comb. form* see CENTR-.

-centric *comb. form* forming adjectives, with the meanings: **1** having the specified thing as a centre: *heliocentric.* **2** having the specified thing as one's central point of view or interest: *Eurocentric.*

centrifugal *adj* **1** proceeding or acting in a direction away from a centre: compare CENTRIPETAL (I). **2** using centrifugal force. **3** tending away from centralization; separatist. ➤➤ **centrifugally** *adv.*

centrifugal force *n* the force that appears to act on an object moving along a circular path and that acts outwardly from the centre of rotation.

centrifuge *n* a rotating machine that uses centrifugal force to separate substances of different densities, remove moisture, or simulate gravitational effects. ➤➤ **centrifuge** *v.*

centripetal *adj* **1** proceeding or acting in a direction towards a centre or axis: compare CENTRIFUGAL (I). **2** tending towards centralization; unifying. ➤➤ **centripetally** *adv.*

centripetal force *n* the force that is necessary to keep an object moving in a circular path and that is directed inwards towards the centre of rotation.

centrist *n* (*often* **Centrist**) a member of a moderate political party; *broadly* somebody holding moderate political views. ➤➤ **centrism** *n.*

centro- *comb. form* see CENTR-.

centuple *v* to make or become 100 times as great or as many. ➤➤ **centuple** *adj,* **centuple** *n.*

centurion *n* **1** an officer commanding an ancient Roman century. **2** somebody who scores a century in cricket.

century *n* (*pl* **centuries**) **1** a period of 100 years, *esp* reckoned forwards or backwards from the conventional date of the birth of Christ. **2** 100 runs made by a cricketer in one innings. **3** a subdivision of an ancient Roman legion orig consisting of 100 men.

century plant *n* a Mexican agave with long lance-shaped leaves that matures and flowers once after many years of growth and then dies.

CEO *abbr* Chief Executive Officer.

cep *n* an edible fungus with a shiny brown cap and white sponge-like underside.

cephalic *adj* **1** relating to the head. **2** situated on, in, or near the head. ➤➤ **cephalically** *adv.*

cephalopod *n* any of a class of molluscs including the squids, cuttlefishes, and octopuses, that have muscular tentacles around the head and highly developed eyes. ➤➤ **cephalopod** *adj.*

ceramic[1] *adj* **1** relating to a product, e.g. porcelain or brick, made from clay or similar material by firing at high temperatures. **2** relating to the manufacture of ceramic articles.

ceramic[2] *n* **1** (*in pl, used as sing.*) the art or process of making ceramic articles. **2** a product of ceramic manufacture. ⋙ **ceramicist** *n.*

ceratopsian *n* any of a group of horned plant-eating dinosaurs, including triceratops, that walked on four legs and had a protective bony frill around the neck.

cereal *n* **1a** a plant, e.g. wheat or rice, yielding grain suitable for food. **b** the edible grain of such a plant. **2** a food made from grain and usu eaten with milk at breakfast.

Usage note
cereal *or* **serial**? These two words, which are pronounced the same, are sometimes confused. *Cereal* refers to grain and food (*breakfast cereal; cereal crops*). The word derives from the name of the Roman goddess of corn and agriculture *Ceres*, which is why it is spelt with two *e's*. *Serial* derives from the word *series* and refers to things that happen in a series: *a serial killer; a TV serial.*

cerebellum *n* (*pl* **cerebellums** *or* **cerebella**) a large part of the back of the brain that projects outwards and is concerned with coordinating muscles and maintaining balance. ⋙ **cerebellar** *adj.*

cerebr- *or* **cerebro-** *comb. form* **1** brain; cerebrum: *cerebrate.* **2** of the brain or cerebrum and: *cerebrospinal.*

cerebra *n* pl of CEREBRUM.

cerebral *adj* **1a** of the brain. **b** of the cerebrum. **2a** appealing to the intellect. **b** primarily intellectual in nature. ⋙ **cerebrally** *adv.*

cerebral haemorrhage *n* bleeding from an artery of the brain, which may cause a stroke.

cerebral palsy *n* a disability resulting from damage to the brain before or during birth and characterized by speech disturbance and lack of muscular coordination.

cerebrate *v formal* to use the mind; to think. ⋙ **cerebration** *n.*

cerebro- *comb. form* see CEREBR-.

cerebrospinal *adj* of the brain and spinal cord.

cerebrospinal fluid *n* a watery liquid that fills the spaces between the membranes that surround the spinal cord and the brain.

cerebrovascular *adj* of the brain and the blood vessels supplying it.

cerebrum *n* (*pl* **cerebrums** *or* **cerebra**) the expanded front portion of the brain that in higher mammals is considered to be the seat of conscious mental processes.

cerecloth *n* waxed cloth formerly used for wrapping a dead body.

cerement *n archaic* (*usu in pl*) a shroud for the dead.

ceremonial[1] *adj* marked by or used in ceremony. ⋙ **ceremonialism** *n,* **ceremonialist** *n,* **ceremonially** *adv.*

Usage note
ceremonial *or* **ceremonious**? *Ceremonial* indicates that an occasion is a ceremony or that a thing is used in ceremonies: *a ceremonial wreath-laying; ceremonial robes. Ceremonious* describes the elaborate and formal manner in which something is done: *a ceremonious bow.*

ceremonial[2] *n* **1** an action involving ceremony. **2** a prescribed system of formalities or rituals.

ceremonious *adj* **1** devoted to form and ceremony; punctilious. **2** = CEREMONIAL[1]. ⋙ **ceremoniously** *adv,* **ceremoniousness** *n.*

Usage note
ceremonious *or* **ceremonial**? See note at CEREMONIAL[1].

ceremony *n* (*pl* **-ies**) **1** a formal act or series of acts prescribed by ritual, protocol, or convention. **2a** established procedures of civility or politeness. **b** exaggeratedly polite, correct, or formal behaviour. ✱ **stand on ceremony** to act in a formally correct manner.

cereology *n* the study of crop circles. ⋙ **cereologist** *n.*

cerise *adj* of a light purplish red colour. ⋙ **cerise** *n.*

cerium *n* a grey soft metallic chemical element, the most abundant of the rare-earth group, that is used to make lighter flints.

CERN *abbr* European Organization for Nuclear Research.

cert *n Brit, informal* a certainty, *esp* a horse that is sure to win a race.

cert. *abbr* **1** certificate. **2** certified. **3** certify.

certain[1] *adj* **1** assured in mind; convinced. **2a** established beyond doubt or question. **b** dependable. **3a** inevitable. **b** incapable of failing; destined. **4a** of a known but unspecified character, quantity, or degree: *The house has a certain charm.* **b** named but not known: *a certain Mr Brown.* **c** moderate: *to a certain extent.* ✱ **for certain** without doubt; assuredly.

certain[2] *pron* some; unspecified ones.

certainly *adv* **1** undoubtedly. **2** yes; of course.

certainty *n* (*pl* **-ies**) **1a** something indisputable or inevitable. **b** somebody or something that cannot fail. **2** the quality or state of being certain. ✱ **for a certainty** without doubt.

CertEd *abbr Brit* Certificate in Education.

certifiable *adj* **1** able to be certified. **2** *informal* insane.

certificate[1] *n* a document containing an official statement; *esp* one declaring the status or qualifications of the holder.

certificate[2] *v* to authorize or provide with a certificate. ⋙ **certification** *n,* **certificatory** *adj.*

certify *v* (**-ies, -ied**) **1a** to confirm, *esp* officially in writing. **b** to declare officially to be true or up to a standard. **c** to declare officially to be insane. **2** to award a certificate or licence to.

certiorari *n* a writ of a superior court calling for the records of proceedings in an inferior court.

certitude *n* the state of being or feeling certain.

cerulean *adj literary* deep sky blue in colour. ⋙ **cerulean** *n.*

cervelat *n* a smoked sausage made from pork and beef.

cervical *adj* **1** of a cervix, *esp* the cervix of the uterus. **2** of the neck.

cervical smear *n* a test for the early detection of cancer in which cells from the cervix of the uterus are examined under a microscope.

cervices *n* pl of CERVIX.

cervine *adj* of or resembling deer.

cervix *n* (*pl* **cervices** *or* **cervixes**) **1** a constricted portion of an organ or body part, *esp* the narrow outer end of the uterus. **2** the neck.

Cesarean *n NAm* see CAESAREAN[2].

cesium *n NAm* see CAESIUM.

cessation *n* a temporary or final stop; an ending.

cession *n* the act or an instance of yielding rights or property, *esp* territory.

cesspit *n* **1** a pit for the disposal of refuse, *esp* sewage. **2** a corrupt or squalid place.

cesspool *n* **1** an underground basin for liquid waste, e.g. household sewage. **2** a corrupt or squalid place.

cestode *n* any of a subclass of parasitic flatworms including the tapeworms, usu living in the intestines. ➤➤ **cestode** *adj.*

CET *abbr* Central European Time.

cetacean *n* any of an order of mammals, including the whales, dolphins, and porpoises, with a fish-like body and paddle-shaped forelimbs. ➤➤ **cetacean** *adj,* **cetaceous** *adj.*

ceteris paribus *adv formal* all other things being equal.

CF *abbr* cystic fibrosis.

Cf *abbr* the chemical symbol for californium.

cf. *abbr* compare.

c/f *abbr* carried forward.

CFC *abbr* chlorofluorocarbon.

CFE *abbr* College of Further Education.

CFS *abbr* chronic fatigue syndrome.

cg *abbr* centigram.

CGS *abbr Brit* Chief of General Staff.

CGT *abbr* capital gains tax.

CH *abbr* **1** central heating. **2** Companion of Honour.

ch *abbr* **1** chapter. **2** in chess, check. **3** church.

cha *n* see CHAR[5].

Chablis *n* (*pl* **Chablis**) a dry white table wine produced in northern Burgundy.

cha-cha *or* **cha-cha-cha** *n* (*pl* **cha-chas** *or* **cha-cha-chas**) a fast rhythmic ballroom dance of Latin American origin. ➤➤ **cha-cha** *v,* **cha-cha-cha** *v.*

chaconne *n* **1** a musical composition typically consisting of variations on a repeated succession of chords. **2** an old Spanish dance tune resembling the passacaglia.

chad *n* in US elections, a punched out section of a voter's ballot paper, indicating the choice of candidate.

Chadian *n* a native or inhabitant of Chad. ➤➤ **Chadian** *adj.*

chador *or* **chadar** *n* a large cloth serving as a veil and head covering worn *esp* by some Muslim women as a sign of religious orthodoxy.

chafe[1] *v* **1a** to make or become sore by rubbing. **b** to rub (something) so as to wear it away. **2** to warm (part of the body) by rubbing. **3** to feel irritation or discontent; fret.

chafe[2] *n* injury or wear caused by friction.

chafer *n* any of numerous species of large beetles, e.g. the cockchafer, whose larvae do great damage to plant roots.

chaff[1] *n* **1** the husks and other debris separated from the seed in threshing grain. **2** chopped straw, hay, etc used for animal feed. **3** worthless matter. ➤➤ **chaffy** *adj.*

chaff[2] *n* light jesting talk; banter.

chaff[3] *v* to tease good-naturedly.

chaffinch *n* a European finch with a reddish breast, a bluish head, and white wing bars.

chafing dish *n* a dish for cooking or keeping food warm, *esp* over a spirit burner at the table.

chagrin[1] *n* mental distress caused by humiliation, disappointment, or failure.

chagrin[2] *v* (**chagrined, chagrining**) (*usu in passive*) to disappoint or annoy.

chain[1] *n* **1a** a series of usu metal links or rings connected to one another and used e.g. for support, restraining prisoners, or as jewellery or a badge of office. **b** a unit of length equal to 66ft (about 20.12m). **c** a measuring instrument of 100 links used in surveying. **2a** a series of linked or connected things. **b** a group of e.g. shops or hotels under the same ownership. **c** a number of atoms or chemical groups united like links in a chain.

chain[2] *v* (*often* + up/down) to fasten, restrict, or confine with, or as if with, a chain.

chain gang *n* (*used as sing. or pl*) a gang of convicts chained together, usu while doing hard labour outside prison.

chain letter *n* a letter requesting the recipient to send copies of it to a specified number of other people who should then repeat the process.

chain mail *n* flexible armour made of interlinked metal rings.

chain reaction *n* **1** a series of related events, each one initiating the next. **2** a self-sustaining chemical or nuclear reaction yielding energy or products that cause further reactions of the same kind.

chain saw *n* a portable power saw that has teeth linked together to form a continuous revolving chain.

chain-smoke *v* to smoke continually, usu lighting one cigarette from the butt of the previous one. ➤➤ **chain-smoker** *n.*

chain stitch *n* an ornamental embroidery or crochet stitch that resembles the links of a chain.

chain store *n* any of several shops under the same ownership and selling the same lines of goods.

chair[1] *n* **1** a seat for one person, usu with four legs and a back and sometimes with arms. **2a** a professorship. **b** a chairman or chairwoman. **3** (**the chair**) *NAm* = ELECTRIC CHAIR. **4** a deep-grooved metal block fastened to a railway sleeper to hold a rail in place.

chair[2] *v* **1** to preside as chairman or chairwoman of (a meeting, committee, etc). **2** *chiefly Brit* to carry shoulder-high in acclaim.

chair lift *n* a ski lift with seats for passengers.

chairman *or* **chairwoman** *n* (*pl* **chairmen** *or* **chairwomen**) somebody who presides over or heads a meeting, committee, organization, or board of directors. ➤➤ **chairmanship** *n.*

chairperson *n* (*pl* **chairpersons**) a chairman or chairwoman.

chaise *n* a light horse-drawn carriage, usu with two wheels and a folding top.

chaise longue *n* (*pl* **chaise longues** *or* **chaises longues**) a low sofa with a partial backrest and only one armrest, for reclining on.

chakra *n* in yoga, a centre of spiritual power in the human body.

chalcedony *n* (*pl* **-ies**) a translucent quartz, often pale blue or grey in colour, used as a gemstone. ➤➤ **chalcedonic** *adj.*

chalet *n* **1** a small usu wooden house with a steeply sloping roof and widely overhanging eaves, common in rural Switzerland. **2** a small house or hut used *esp* for temporary accommodation, e.g. at a holiday camp.

chalice *n* **1** *literary* a drinking cup; a goblet. **2** a gold or silver cup used to hold the wine at Communion in some Christian churches.

chalk[1] *n* **1** a soft white, grey, or buff limestone composed chiefly of the shells of small marine organisms. **2** a short stick of chalk or chalky material, often coloured, used *esp* for writing and drawing. ✱ **as alike/different as chalk and cheese** very different from each other. **not by a long chalk** by no means; definitely not. ⋙ **chalky** *adj.*

chalk² *v* **1** (*often* + up) to write or draw with chalk. **2** to rub, mark, or whiten with chalk.

chalk and talk *n* teaching by traditional methods of talking in front of a class and using a blackboard.

chalkboard *n NAm* = BLACKBOARD.

chalkface *n* the classroom, considered as the workplace of teachers.

chalk up *v* **1** to attain or achieve. **2** to ascribe or credit; *specif* to charge to an account.

challenge¹ *v* **1** to invite or call to fight or compete. **2** to dispute (something), *esp* as being unjust, invalid, or outmoded. **3** to question formally the legality or legal qualifications of (e.g. a juror). **4** to order to halt and provide proof of identity. **5** to test the skill of (somebody) in a stimulating way. ⋙ **challengeable** *adj,* **challenger** *n,* **challenging** *adj.*

challenge² *n* **1** an invitation or summons to fight or compete; *specif* a call to a duel. **2a** a calling to account or into question. **b** a command given by a sentry to halt and prove identity. **c** a formal objection to a juror or jury. **3** something demanding or stimulating.

challenged *adj euphem* (*usu used in combinations*) lacking or deficient in the specified physical or mental attribute.

challis *n* a lightweight soft clothing fabric made of cotton, wool, or synthetic yarn.

chalybeate *adj* of water: impregnated with iron-containing chemical compounds.

chamber *n* **1** a natural or artificial enclosed space or cavity. **2** a legislative or judicial body, *esp* either of two houses of a legislature, or a hall used by such a body. **3a** a reception room in an official or state building. **b** *archaic* a room, *esp* a bedroom. **c** (*in pl*) a set of rooms used by a group of barristers. **d** (*usu in pl*) a room where a judge hears private cases. **4** the part of a gun that holds the charge or cartridge. **5** (*used before a noun*) relating to or involving a small group of musical instruments or a small orchestra.

chamberlain *n* **1** a chief officer of a royal or noble household. **2** a treasurer, e.g. of a corporation.

chambermaid *n* a woman who cleans bedrooms and makes beds, *esp* in a hotel.

chamber music *n* music written for a small group of instruments.

Chamber of Commerce *n* an association of business people to promote commercial and industrial interests in the community.

chamber of horrors *n* a place where objects of macabre interest, e.g. instruments of torture, are exhibited; *broadly* any horrifying or frightening place, situation, etc.

chamber pot *n* a bowl-shaped receptacle for urine and faeces, used chiefly in the bedroom.

chambray *n* a lightweight clothing fabric with coloured warp and white weft yarns.

chambré /'shombray/ *adj* said of wine: at or brought to room temperature.

chameleon *n* **1** an African and Eurasian lizard with a long tongue, a grasping tail, eyeballs that move independently, and the ability to change the colour of its skin. **2** somebody or something changeable; *specif* a fickle person. ⋙ **chameleonic** *adj.*

chamfer *n* an edge cut back from a right angle to form a narrow flat surface with two oblique angles. ⋙ **chamfer** *v.*

chammy *or* **shammy** *n* = CHAMOIS (2).

chamois *n* (*pl* **chamois**) **1** a small goatlike antelope of Europe and the Caucasus. **2** a soft pliant leather prepared from the skin of the chamois or sheep, used *esp* as a cloth for polishing.

chamomile *n* see CAMOMILE.

champ¹ *v* **1** to munch (food) noisily. **2** to make biting or gnashing movements. ✱ **champ at the bit** to show impatience or eagerness.

champ² *n informal* a champion, *esp* in a sport or game.

champagne *n* **1** a white sparkling wine made in the former province of Champagne in France. **2** a pale golden cream colour.

champers *n Brit, informal* champagne.

champion¹ *n* **1** the winner of a competitive event, usu the overall winner after a series of contests. **2** a militant supporter of, or fighter for, a cause or person. **3** in former times, somebody who did battle on behalf of another, *esp* in a tournament.

champion² *v* (**championed, championing**) to protect or fight for as a champion.

champion³ *adj chiefly N Eng, informal* superb; splendid.

championship *n* **1a** a contest held to determine a champion. **b** the position or title of champion. **2** the act of championing; defence.

chance¹ *n* **1a** the incalculable element in existence that renders events unpredictable. **b** an event without an observable cause. **2a** a situation favouring some purpose; an opportunity. **b** an opportunity of scoring a goal in football or dismissing a batsman in cricket. **3a** the possibility of a specified or favourable outcome in an uncertain situation. **b** (*in pl*) the more likely indications. ✱ **by chance** accidentally; without planning or intention. **take a chance/chances** to do something risky or dangerous.

chance² *adj* accidental or casual; happening by chance.

chance³ *v* **1** to take place or come about by chance. **2** (+ on/upon) to find by chance. **3** to take a risk with. ✱ **chance it** *informal* to do something knowing that it is risky. **chance one's arm** *informal* to risk something with little chance of success.

chancel *n* the part of a church containing the altar and seats for the clergy and choir.

chancellery *or* **chancellory** *n* (*pl* **-ies**) the position, department, or official residence of a chancellor.

chancellor *n* **1** the titular head of a British university. **2** the chief minister of state in some European countries. **3a** = CHANCELLOR OF THE EXCHEQUER. **b** = LORD CHANCELLOR. ⋙ **chancellorship** *n.*

Chancellor of the Duchy of Lancaster *n* a British government minister who has no direct responsibility for a government department but is usu a member of the cabinet.

Chancellor of the Exchequer *n* a member of the British cabinet in charge of public finances.

chancellory *n* see CHANCELLERY.

chancer *n Brit, informal* an unprincipled person; an opportunist.

Chancery *n* a division of the High Court having jurisdiction over causes in equity.

Chancery Division *n* = CHANCERY.

chancre *n* an initial sore or ulcer of some diseases, e.g. syphilis. ⋙ **chancrous** *adj.*

chancroid *n* a bacterial venereal disease causing ulceration in the genital area, or an ulcer so caused. ⋙ **chancroidal** *adj.*

chancy *adj* (**-ier, -iest**) uncertain in outcome or prospect; risky. ⋙ **chancily** *adj,* **chanciness** *n.*

chandelier *n* a branched ornamental lighting fixture suspended from a ceiling.

chandler *n* a retail dealer in supplies and equipment of a specified kind.

chandlery *n* (*pl* **-ies**) the business, shop, or merchandise of a chandler.

change[1] *v* **1** to make or become different. **2** to replace (one thing) with another. **3** to convert or transform (something) into something else. **4** to give (money of one currency) in exchange for an equivalent amount in another currency. **5** to select (a new gear) in a motor vehicle. **6** to put on fresh clothes. ✱ **change hands** to become the property of somebody else. **change the subject** to begin talking about something different during a conversation.

change[2] *n* **1a** an alteration. **b** a substitution. **c** variety or novelty. **2** an alternative set, *esp* of clothes. **3a** money returned when a payment exceeds the amount due. **b** coins of low denominations. **4** an order in which a set of bells is struck in change ringing. **5** (**the change**) the menopause. ✱ **for a change 1** for the sake of variety. **2** in contrast to what normally happens. **get no change out of** *informal* to fail to get information from, exploit, or outwit (somebody). ⋙ **changeful** *adj*, **changeless** *adj*, **changelessness** *n*.

changeable *adj* **1** likely to vary. **2** capable of being altered or exchanged. **3** fickle. ⋙ **changeability** *n*, **changeableness** *n*, **changeably** *adv*.

changeling *n* a child believed to have been left in place of a human child by fairies.

change of heart *n* a complete reversal in attitude.

change of life *n* (**the change of life**) the menopause.

change-over *n* a conversion to a different system or function.

change ringing *n* the art of ringing a set of tuned bells in continually varying order.

channel[1] *n* **1a** the bed where a stream of water runs. **b** the deeper navigable part of a river, harbour, or strait. **c** a narrow region of sea between two land masses. **d** (**the Channel**) the English Channel separating Britain and France. **2** a path along which information passes or can be communicated. **3a** a band of frequencies of sufficient width for a transmission, e.g. from a radio or television station. **b** a television station. **4** a usu tubular passage, *esp* for liquids. **5** a long gutter, groove, or furrow.

channel[2] *v* (**channelled, channelling,** *NAm* **channeled, channeling**) **1** to direct towards a particular purpose. **2** to convey through a channel. **3** to form or wear a channel in.

channel-hop *v* (**channel-hopped, channel-hopping**) *informal* to change television channels repeatedly using a remote control device.

chant[1] *v* to utter (e.g. a slogan), sing, or recite in a rhythmic monotonous tone.

chant[2] *n* **1a** a repetitive melody used for liturgical singing in which as many syllables are assigned to each note as required. **b** a psalm or canticle sung in this way. **2** a rhythmic monotonous utterance, recitation, or song.

chanter *n* the reed pipe with finger holes on which the melody is played on a bagpipe.

chanterelle *n* an edible yellow mushroom with a funnel-shaped cap and a pleasant smell.

chanteuse /shon'tuhz/ *n* (*pl* **chanteuses** /shon'tuhz/) a female nightclub or cabaret singer.

chantry *n* (*pl* **-ies**) a chapel or altar founded under an endowment for the chanting of masses for the founder's soul.

chanty *n* = SHANTY[2].

Chanukah *n* see HANUKKAH.

chaos *n* **1a** a state of utter confusion. **b** a confused mass. **2** (*often* **Chaos**) the confused unorganized state of original matter before the creation of distinct forms: compare COSMOS. ⋙ **chaotic** *adj*, **chaotically** *adv*.

chaos theory *n* a scientific theory relating to the irregular and unpredictable behaviour of complex systems that nevertheless have an underlying order.

chap[1] *n informal* a man; a fellow.

chap[2] *v* (**chapped, chapping**) to cause (the skin) to open in slits or cracks, usu by exposure to wind, cold, or dryness.

chaparral *n* in the USA, a dense area of shrubs or dwarf trees, *esp* evergreen oaks.

chapati *or* **chapatti** *n* in Indian cookery, a thin unleavened usu round bread.

chapbook *n* a small book formerly sold by pedlars, containing ballads, tales, etc.

chapel[1] *n* **1a** a place of worship serving a residence or institution. **b** a room or bay in a church for prayer or minor religious services. **2** a place of worship used by a Nonconformist Christian group. **3** (*used as sing. or pl*) the members of a trade union, *esp* in a printing or publishing house.

chapel[2] *adj chiefly Brit* belonging to a Nonconformist church.

chaperon[1] *or* **chaperone** *n* an older woman who accompanies a younger woman on social occasions to ensure propriety.

chaperon[2] *or* **chaperone** *v* (**chaperoned, chaperoning**) to act as chaperon to; to escort. ⋙ **chaperonage** *n*.

chaplain *n* a clergyman officially attached to a branch of the armed forces, an institution, a family, etc. ⋙ **chaplaincy** *n*.

chaplet *n* **1** a wreath to be worn on the head. **2** a string of prayer beads; one third of the rosary. **3** a beaded moulding. ⋙ **chapleted** *adj*.

chapman *n* (*pl* **chapmen**) *archaic* an itinerant pedlar; a trader.

chaps *pl n* leather leggings worn over the trousers, *esp* by N American ranch hands.

chaptalize *or* **-ise** *v* to add sugar to (the juice of wine grapes). ⋙ **chaptalization** *n*.

chapter *n* **1a** a major division of a book. **b** a significant unit or sequence of events. **2a** the canons of a cathedral or collegiate church, or the members of a religious house. **b** a regular meeting of a religious chapter. **3** a local branch of a society or fraternity.

chapter and verse *n* a full specification of the source of a piece of information.

char[1] *v* (**charred, charring**) to burn slightly; to scorch and blacken.

char[2] *or* **charr** *n* (*pl* **chars** *or* **charrs** *or* **char** *or* **charr**) any of several species of freshwater and sea fishes related to the trout and salmon.

char[3] *v* (**charred, charring**) to work as a cleaning woman, *esp* in a private house.

char[4] *n Brit, informal* = CHARWOMAN.

char[5] *or* **cha** *n Brit, informal* = TEA (1B).

charabanc /'sharəbang/ *n Brit, dated* a motor coach used for sightseeing.

character *n* **1a** the mental or moral qualities that distinguish a particular person. **b** the distinctive qualities characteristic of something; its main or essential nature. **2a** any of the people portrayed in a novel, film, play, etc. **b** *informal* a person, *esp* one marked by notable or conspicuous traits. **3** good reputation. **4** moral strength; integrity. **5** a written testimonial of a person's qualities. **6** a symbol, e.g. a letter, numeral, or punctuation mark, used in writing or printing. ✱ **in/out of character** in/not in accord with a person's usual qualities, traits, or behaviour. ⯮ **characterful** *adj*, **characterless** *adj*.

character actor *n* an actor capable of playing unusual or eccentric personalities often markedly different in age.

characterise *v* see CHARACTERIZE.

characteristic[1] *adj* serving to reveal individual character and distinguish one person or thing from another; typical. ⯮ **characteristically** *adv*.

characteristic[2] *n* a distinguishing trait, quality, or property.

characterize *or* **-ise** *v* **1** to describe the character or quality of. **2** to be a characteristic of; to distinguish. ⯮ **characterization** *n*.

character witness *n* a person who gives evidence concerning the reputation, conduct, and moral nature of somebody involved in a legal action.

charade *n* **1** (*in pl, used as sing. or pl*) a game in which one team acts out a word or phrase syllable by syllable while the other tries to guess what is being represented. **2** a ridiculous pretence.

charbroil *v NAm* = BARBECUE[2].

charcoal *n* **1** a black porous carbon prepared by partly burning wood. **2a** fine charcoal used in pencil form for drawing. **b** a drawing done with charcoal. **3** (*also* **charcoal grey**) a very dark grey colour.

charcuterie /shah'koohtəri/ *n* **1** cooked cold meats. **2** a shop selling cooked cold meats.

chard *n* a beet with large dark green leaves and succulent stalks that are often cooked as a vegetable. Also called SEA KALE (2).

Chardonnay *n* a variety of grape used to produce dry white wines, or the wine produced from it.

Charentais *n* a small round melon with a yellowish green rind and faintly scented orange flesh.

charge[1] *v* **1a** to set or ask (a price or fee). **b** to ask payment of (a person). **c** to record (an item) as an expense, debt, obligation, or liability. **2** to accuse (somebody) formally of having committed an offence. **3** to rush violently forward, *esp* in order to attack. **4a** to load or fill (something) to capacity or so that it is ready for use. **b** (*often* + up) to restore the active materials in (a battery) by the application of a current. **c** to fill (somebody or something) with passionate emotion, feeling, etc. ✱ **charge with** to entrust with (a task or responsibility). ⯮ **chargeable** *adj*.

charge[2] *n* **1** the price demanded or paid for something. **2** an accusation, indictment, or statement of complaint. **3** an instruction or command. **4a** an obligation or requirement. **b** control, supervision, or custody. **c** somebody or something committed to the care of another. **5** a violent rush forwards, *esp* in attack. **6a** the quantity that something is intended to receive and hold, *esp* the quantity of explosive for a gun or cannon. **b** a basic property of matter responsible for electrical activity and characterized as negative or positive. **c** a definite quantity of electricity, *esp* the quantity held by a battery. ✱ **in charge** in control or command. **in charge of** responsible for. **take charge** (*often* + of) to assume care, custody, command or control.

charge card *n* a card, usu provided by a shop, authorizing the purchase of goods or services that are charged to the holder's account with the shop.

chargé d'affaires /ˌshahzhay da'feə/ *n* (*pl* **chargés d'affaires** /ˌshahzhay da'feə(z)/) **1** a diplomat who substitutes for an ambassador or minister in their absence. **2** a diplomatic representative inferior in rank to an ambassador.

chargehand *n Brit* a worker in charge of a group of other workers or a particular piece of work.

charge nurse *n* a nurse in charge of a hospital ward, *esp* a male nurse: compare SISTER (4).

charger[1] *n* **1** a horse for battle or parade. **2** a device used to charge a battery.

charger[2] *n* a large flat meat dish used in former times.

chargrill *v* to grill (food) quickly over charcoal.

chariot *n* a two-wheeled horse-drawn vehicle of ancient times used in warfare and racing. ⯮ **charioteer** *n*.

charisma *n* (*pl* **charismata**) **1** the special magnetic appeal, charm, or power of an individual, e.g. a political leader, that inspires popular loyalty and enthusiasm. **2** an extraordinary power divinely given to a Christian.

charismatic *adj* **1** having charisma. **2** relating to a group within a Christian church whose members display charismatic powers, e.g. speaking in tongues. **3** said of a power or gift: divinely given to a Christian. ⯮ **charismatically** *n*.

charitable *adj* **1a** liberal in giving to the poor; generous. **b** of or giving charity. **2** merciful or kind in judging others; lenient. ⯮ **charitableness** *n*, **charitably** *adv*.

charity *n* (*pl* **-ies**) **1a** kindly generosity and helpfulness, shown *esp* to those in need. **b** an institution engaged in helping those in need. **c** money or other help given to those in need. **2** benevolent goodwill towards or love of humanity. **3** lenient judgment of others.

charlady *n* (*pl* **-ies**) *Brit* = CHARWOMAN.

charlatan *n* somebody who pretends to have special knowledge or ability; a quack. ⯮ **charlatanism** *n*, **charlatanry** *n*.

charleston *n* a lively ballroom dance, popular in the 1920s, in which the knees are turned inwards and heels are swung sharply outwards on each step. ⯮ **charleston** *v*.

charlie *n* **1** an absurd or stupid person; a fool. **2** *informal* cocaine.

charlotte *n* a hot baked dessert consisting of fruit layered or covered with breadcrumbs or sponge cake.

charm[1] *n* **1a** the quality of fascinating, alluring, or delighting others. **b** (*also in pl*) a particularly pleasing or attractive quality or feature. **2** something, e.g. an act or phrase, believed to have magic power. **3** something worn to ward off evil or to ensure good fortune. **4** a small ornament worn on a bracelet or chain. ✱ **like a charm** perfectly. ⯮ **charmless** *adj*.

charm[2] *v* **1a** to fascinate or delight by means of attractive qualities or manner. **b** to gain (something) or influence (somebody) by the use of personal charm. **2a** to affect by magic or as if by supernatural powers. **b** to control (an animal) by the use of rituals, e.g. the playing of music, held to have magical powers. ⯮ **charmer** *n*.

charmed[1] *adj* free of any difficulty or misfortune as if protected by supernatural powers.

charmed[2] *interj dated* used to express pleasure at meeting somebody for the first time.

charming[1] *adj* extremely pleasing or delightful; entrancing. ⯮ **charmingly** *adv*.

charming[2] *interj* used ironically to express disapproval or displeasure, *esp* in response to rudeness.

charm offensive *n* a campaign to achieve a particular goal, *esp* in politics, by the strategic use of charm.

charnel house *n* a building or chamber in which dead bodies or bones are deposited.

Charolais *n* (*pl* **Charolais**) an animal of a French breed of large white cattle used primarily for beef and crossbreeding.

charpoy *n* a lightweight Indian bedstead.

charr *n* see CHAR².

chart¹ *n* **1a** a map used for navigation by sea or air. **b** an outline map showing the geographical distribution of something, e.g. climatic variations. **2a** a sheet giving information in the form of a table or graph. **b** (**the charts**) a list of best-selling popular records produced weekly.

chart² *v* **1** to make a chart of (an area, *esp* of the sea). **2** to display, mark, or record (something) on a chart. **3** to outline (the course or progress of something).

charter¹ *n* **1a** a document that creates and defines the rights of a city, educational or professional institution, or company. **b** = CONSTITUTION (I). **2** a special privilege, immunity, or exemption. **3a** a total or partial lease of a ship, aeroplane, etc for a particular use or group of people. **b** (*used before a noun*) relating to such a lease: *charter flights.*

charter² *v* **1** to grant a charter to. **2** to hire or lease (something) for usu exclusive and temporary use. ➤➤ **charterer** *n.*

chartered *n* having passed the examinations or satisfied other requirements for membership of a professional institution.

Chartism *n* the principles and practices of a 19th-cent. English political movement whose principal aim was to reform the electoral system. ➤➤ **Chartist** *n.*

chartreuse *n* **1** an aromatic liqueur, usu green or yellow in colour. **2** a brilliant yellowish green colour.

charwoman *n* (*pl* **charwomen**) a cleaning woman; *esp* one employed in a private house.

chary *adj* (**-ier, -iest**) **1** cautious, *esp* wary of taking risks. **2** slow to grant or accept. ➤➤ **charily** *adv,* **chariness** *n.*

chase¹ *v* **1** to follow rapidly or persistently. **2** to cause to depart or flee. **3** *chiefly Brit* (+ up) to investigate (a matter) or contact (a person, company, etc) in order to obtain information or hasten results. **4** *informal* to attempt to establish a romantic or sexual relationship with. **5** to rush.

chase² *n* **1a** the act or an instance of chasing; pursuit. **b** (**the chase**) hunting. **2** a tract of unenclosed land set aside for the breeding of animals for hunting and fishing. ✱ **give chase** to go in pursuit.

chase³ *v* to ornament with raised or incised work, e.g. by engraving or inlaying.

chaser *n* **1** an alcoholic drink taken immediately after another that is milder or stronger, e.g. beer after spirits. **2** a horse used in steeplechasing.

chasm *n* **1** a deep cleft in the earth. **2** an apparently unbridgeable gap. ➤➤ **chasmic** *adj.*

chassé /'shasay/ *n* a sliding dance step. ➤➤ **chassé** *v.*

chasseur *adj* (*used after a noun*) cooked in a sauce made with wine and mushrooms.

Chassid *n* see HASID.

chassis *n* (*pl* **chassis**) **1** a supporting framework for the body of a vehicle, e.g. a car. **2** the frame on which the electrical parts of a radio, television, etc are mounted.

chaste *adj* **1** abstinent from sexual intercourse, or from unlawful or immoral sexual intercourse. **2** pure in thought and behaviour; modest. **3** severely simple in design or execution; austere. ➤➤ **chastely** *adv,* **chasteness** *n.*

chasten *v* **1** to correct by punishment or suffering; to discipline. **2** to subdue or restrain. ➤➤ **chastener** *n.*

chastise *v* **1** to inflict punishment on, *esp* by beating. **2** to subject to severe reproof or criticism. ➤➤ **chastisement** *n,* **chastiser** *n.*

chastity *n* **1** the state of being chaste; purity. **2a** abstinence from sexual intercourse, *esp* extramarital sexual intercourse. **b** virginity.

chastity belt *n* a device consisting of a belt with an attachment passing between the legs, used in former times to prevent a woman from having sexual intercourse.

chasuble *n* a sleeveless outer vestment worn by the officiating priest at mass.

chat¹ *v* (**chatted, chatting**) to talk in an informal or familiar manner.

chat² *n* **1** light familiar talk. **2** a friendly conversation.

château /'shatoh/ *n* (*pl* **châteaus** *or* **châteaux**) **1** a feudal castle or large country house in France. **2** a French vineyard estate.

chatelaine /'shatəlayn/ *n* **1** the mistress of a castle or large house. **2** a clasp with a short chain formerly used to attach small articles, e.g. keys, to a woman's belt.

chatline *n* a telephone service that people call to join in a general conversation with other users of the service.

chat room *n* a facility on the Internet where people with similar interests can exchange messages, views, etc.

chat show *n* a television or radio programme in which people, *esp* celebrities, are interviewed informally or engage in discussion.

chattel *n* an item of personal property.

chatter¹ *v* **1** to talk idly, incessantly, or fast. **2** said of birds and other animals: to produce rapid successive inarticulate sounds suggestive of language. **3** of teeth: to click together repeatedly or uncontrollably, e.g. from cold. ➤➤ **chatterer** *n.*

chatter² *n* **1** the sound or action of chattering. **2** idle talk; prattle.

chatterbox *n informal* somebody who talks incessantly.

chattering classes *pl n informal, derog* the educated section of society considered as always talking about political and cultural issues.

chatty *adj* (**-ier, -iest**) *informal* **1** fond of chatting; talkative. **2** having the style and content of light familiar conversation. ➤➤ **chattily** *adv,* **chattiness** *n.*

chat up *v Brit, informal* to engage (somebody) in friendly conversation flirtatiously or for an ulterior motive.

chauffeur¹ *or* **chauffeuse** *n* a person employed to drive a private car or similar motor vehicle.

chauffeur² *v* to act as driver or chauffeur while transporting (somebody).

chauvinism *n* **1** excessive or blind patriotism. **2** undue belief in the superiority of one's own group, cause, etc. ➤➤ **chauvinist** *n and adj,* **chauvinistic** *adj,* **chauvinistically** *adv.*

ChB *abbr* Bachelor of Surgery.

cheap¹ *adj* **1a** relatively low in price, *esp* lower than the market price or the real value. **b** charging a low price. **2a** of inferior quality or worth. **b** contemptible because of lack of any fine or redeeming qualities. **3a** gained with little effort. **b** gained by contemptible means. **4** *NAm* miserly or stingy. ⋙ **cheapish** *adj*, **cheaply** *adv*, **cheapness** *n*.

cheap² *adv* at or for a low price; cheaply.

cheap³ ✱ **on the cheap** at minimum expense; cheaply.

cheapen *v* (**cheapened, cheapening**) **1** to make or become cheap or cheaper in price or value. **2** to make less estimable or tawdry and inferior.

cheap-jack *adj* **1** inferior, cheap, or worthless. **2** characterized by unscrupulous opportunism.

cheapo *adj informal* inexpensive and often of inferior quality.

cheapskate *n informal* (*often before a noun*) a miserly or stingy person.

cheat¹ *v* **1** to violate rules dishonestly, e.g. at a game or in an examination. **2** to deceive, trick, or swindle. **3** to deprive (somebody) of something valuable, *esp* by deceit or fraud. **4** to avoid, defeat the purpose of, or blunt the effects of. **5** (+ on) to be sexually unfaithful to. ⋙ **cheater** *n*.

cheat² *n* **1** somebody who cheats. **2** a trick or fraud.

Chechen *n* **1** a native or inhabitant of Chechnya in the Caucasus. **2** the Caucasian language of the Chechens. ⋙ **Chechen** *adj*.

check¹ *n* **1** an inspection, test, or verification. **2** a sudden stoppage of the forward progress of something. **3** somebody or something that arrests, limits, or restrains. **4** (*often used as an interj*) in chess, exposure of a king to an attack from which it must be protected or moved to safety. **5a** a pattern of squares, usu of alternating colours, or a square in such a pattern. **b** a fabric woven or printed with such a design. **6** *NAm* see CHEQUE. **7a** *chiefly NAm* a ticket or token showing ownership or indicating payment made. **b** *NAm* a bill, *esp* for food and drink in a restaurant. **8** *NAm* = TICK¹ (1). ✱ **in check** under restraint or control.

check² *v* **1a** to inspect for satisfactory condition, accuracy, safety, or performance. **b** to verify. **c** to compare against a source, original, or authority. **2a** to slow or bring to a stop. **b** to block the progress of. **c** to restrain or diminish the force of. **3** *chiefly NAm* (*often* + in) to note or mark (e.g. an item on a list) with a tick. **4** *chiefly NAm* (*often* + in) to leave or accept (something) for safekeeping in a cloakroom or left-luggage office. **5** *chiefly NAm* (*often* + out) to correspond point for point; to tally. ✱ **check into** to check in at (a hotel etc). **check up on** to make thorough inquiries about. ⋙ **checkable** *adj*, **checker** *n*.

checked *adj* marked with a pattern of squares, *esp* of alternating colours.

checker¹ *n* **1** *informal* see CHEQUER¹. **2** *NAm* a piece used in the game of draughts.

checker² *v NAm* see CHEQUER².

checkerboard *n NAm* = CHESSBOARD.

checkered *adj NAm* see CHEQUERED.

checkers *pl n NAm* = DRAUGHTS.

check in *v* **1** to report one's presence or arrival, *esp* to arrive and register at a hotel or airport. **2** to deposit (luggage) for transport, *esp* by air. ⋙ **check-in** *n*.

checklist *n* a list of things, people, etc, *esp* a complete list of checks to be made or tasks to be done.

checkmate *n* **1a** (*often used as an interj*) the act of putting a chess opponent's king in check from which escape is impossible and thereby winning the game. **b** the situation of a king in this position. **2** complete defeat. ⋙ **checkmate** *v*.

checkout *n* **1** a cash desk equipped with a cash register in a self-service shop. **2** the act of checking out of a hotel etc.

check out *v* **1** to complete the formalities for leaving a hotel etc. **2** to cause the removal of (something) to be recorded.

checkpoint *n* a location where inspection, e.g. of people or vehicles crossing a border, may take place.

checkup *n* an examination, *esp* a general medical or dental examination.

Cheddar *n* a hard smooth-textured cheese with a flavour that ranges from mild to strong as the cheese matures.

cheek¹ *n* **1** the fleshy side of the face below the eye and above and to the side of the mouth. **2** insolent boldness; impudence. **3** *informal* a buttock. ✱ **cheek by jowl** very close together. **turn the other cheek** to respond to injury or unkindness with patience; to forgo retaliation [from Christ's instruction 'whosoever shall smite thee on thy right cheek, turn to him the other also' (Matthew 5:39).

cheek² *v informal* to speak rudely or impudently to (somebody).

cheekbone *n* the bone forming the prominence below the eye.

cheeky *adj* (**-ier, -iest**) impudent or insolent. ⋙ **cheekily** *adv*, **cheekiness** *n*.

cheep *n* a faint shrill sound characteristic of a young bird. ⋙ **cheep** *v*.

cheer¹ *n* **1** a shout of joy, congratulation, or encouragement. **2** happiness; gaiety.

cheer² *v* **1a** to shout with joy, in applause, or in triumph. **b** to applaud or acclaim by shouting. **c** to encourage or urge on by shouts. **2** (*often* + up) to make or become happier or more hopeful.

cheerful *adj* **1a** full of good spirits; happy. **b** ungrudging. **2** conducive to good spirits; likely to dispel gloom. ⋙ **cheerfully** *adv*, **cheerfulness** *n*.

cheerio *interj chiefly Brit* used as an informal farewell or drinking toast.

cheerleader *n* somebody who leads organized cheering, *esp* at N American sports events.

cheerless *adj* gloomy or miserable. ⋙ **cheerlessly** *adv*, **cheerlessness** *n*.

cheers *interj* used as a drinking toast and sometimes as an informal farewell or expression of thanks.

cheery *adj* (**-ier, -iest**) marked by or causing good spirits; cheerful. ⋙ **cheerily** *adv*, **cheeriness** *n*.

cheese *n* **1a** a food consisting of coagulated, compressed, and usu ripened milk curds. **b** a cake of cheese, often cylindrical in shape. **2** a fruit preserve with the consistency of cream cheese.

cheeseboard *n* **1** a board on which cheese is served. **2** a selection of cheeses served as a course of a meal.

cheeseburger *n* a burger with a slice of cheese on top, usu in a soft bread roll.

cheesecake *n* **1** a baked or refrigerated dessert consisting of a soft filling, usu containing cheese, on a biscuit or pastry base. **2** *informal* a photographic display of shapely and scantily clothed women: compare BEEFCAKE.

cheesecloth *n* a lightweight loosely woven cotton fabric.

cheesed off *adj chiefly Brit, informal* annoyed or bored; fed up.

cheeseparing¹ *n* miserly or petty economizing; stinginess.

cheeseparing[2] *adj* miserly or stingy.

cheese plant *n* = SWISS CHEESE PLANT.

cheese straw *n* a stick of pastry flavoured with cheese, eaten as a snack.

cheesy *adj* (**-ier, -iest**) **1** resembling cheese in smell, taste, appearance, or consistency. **2** *informal* of a smile: very broad and often insincere. **3** *informal* of poor quality and lacking in good taste.

cheetah *n* a long-legged spotted African cat that resembles a small leopard and is the fastest land animal.

chef *n* a skilled cook; *esp* the chief cook in a restaurant or hotel.

chef d'oeuvre /shay 'duhvrə/ *n* (*pl* **chefs d'oeuvre** /shay 'duhvrə/) a masterpiece, *esp* in art or literature.

chela *n* (*pl* **chelae**) a pincerlike claw of a crustacean, e.g. a crab, or an arachnid, e.g. a scorpion. ➤➤ **chelate** *adj.*

Chelsea bun *n* a sweet bun made with yeast and dried fruit, e.g. currants, raisins, etc, and shaped in a flat coil.

Chelsea pensioner *n* a veteran or disabled soldier living at the Chelsea Royal Hospital.

chemical[1] *adj* **1** of, used in, or produced by chemistry. **2** using, involving, or made from chemicals. ➤➤ **chemically** *adv.*

chemical[2] *n* a substance obtained by a chemical process or used to produce a chemical effect.

chemical engineering *n* engineering dealing with the industrial application of chemistry. ➤➤ **chemical engineer** *n.*

chemin de fer /shə,manh də 'feə/ *n* a card game resembling baccarat in which only two hands are dealt and any number of players may bet against the dealer.

chemise *n* **1** a woman's loose-fitting undergarment. **2** a loose straight-hanging dress without a waist.

chemist *n* **1** somebody who is trained in chemistry. **2** *Brit* a pharmacist. **3** *Brit* a retail shop where medicines and other articles, e.g. cosmetics and films, are sold.

chemistry *n* (*pl* **-ies**) **1** a science that deals with the composition, structure, and properties of substances and the transformations they undergo. **2** the composition and chemical properties of a substance. **3** an instinctive affinity or attraction between people.

chemotherapy *n* the use of chemical agents in the treatment or control of disease, *esp* cancer. ➤➤ **chemotherapist** *n.*

chenille *n* **1** a soft velvety yarn of silk, cotton, wool, or synthetic fibre with a long pile. **2** a fabric made from this yarn.

cheongsam *n* a dress with a slit skirt and a mandarin collar worn *esp* by Chinese women.

cheque (*NAm* **check**) *n chiefly Brit* a written order for a bank to pay money as instructed or the printed form on which it is written.

chequebook *n* a book containing unwritten cheques.

chequebook journalism *n* sensationalist journalism consisting of exclusive reports acquired by paying large amounts of money, e.g. to friends and relations of people in the public eye.

cheque card *n* a card guaranteeing that the holder's cheques up to a specified amount will be honoured by the issuing bank.

chequer[1] (*NAm* **checker**) *n* (*also in pl*) = CHECK[1] (5A).

chequer[2] (*NAm* **checker**) *v* to variegate with different colours or shades, *esp* to mark it with squares of alternating colours.

chequered (*NAm* **checkered**) *adj* characterized by variations in fortune.

cherish *v* **1a** to hold dear; to feel or show affection for. **b** to keep or cultivate with care and affection; to nurture. **2** to keep in the mind with hope or affection. ➤➤ **cherishable** *adj.*

chernozem *n* a dark-coloured humus-rich soil found in temperate to cool climates, *esp* in the Russian steppes.

Cherokee *n* (*pl* **Cherokees** *or* **Cherokee**) **1** a member of a Native N American people orig of Tennessee and N Carolina. **2** the Iroquoian language of this people. ➤➤ **Cherokee** *adj.*

cheroot *n* a cigar cut square at both ends.

cherry *n* (*pl* **-ies**) **1a** a smooth yellow to deep red or blackish fruit with sweet flesh and a hard stone. **b** a tree and shrub of the rose family that bears this fruit and often has ornamental flowers. **2** a bright red colour. **3** *informal* virginity. ➤➤ **cherry** *adj.*

cherry brandy *n* a sweet liqueur in which cherries have been steeped.

cherry-pick *v informal* to select the most desirable things or people and ignore other items or members of the group.

cherry tomato *n* a very small tomato with a strong sweet flavour.

chert *n* a rock resembling flint and consisting essentially of quartz. ➤➤ **cherty** *adj.*

cherub *n* **1** (*pl* **cherubim**) a biblical attendant of God or of a holy place, often represented as a being with large wings, a human head, and an animal body. **2** (*pl* **cherubs**) **a** a beautiful usu winged and chubby child in painting and sculpture. **b** an innocent-looking usu chubby and pretty person, *esp* a child. ➤➤ **cherubic** *adj,* **cherubically** *adv.*

chervil *n* an aromatic plant of the carrot family with leaves that are used as a herb or a salad vegetable.

Ches. *abbr* Cheshire.

Cheshire cheese *n* a white or pinkish orange cheese with a crumbly texture.

chess *n* a board game for two players who have 16 pieces each and try to get the opposing king into a position called CHECKMATE (a direct attack from which the king cannot escape).

chessboard *n* a board used in chess, draughts, etc that is divided into 64 equal squares of two alternating colours.

chessman *n* (*pl* **chessmen**) any of the pieces used by each player in the game of chess.

chest *n* **1a** a box with a lid used *esp* for the safekeeping of belongings. **b** a small cupboard used *esp* for storing medicines or first-aid supplies. **2a** the part of the body enclosed by the ribs and breastbone. **b** the front of the body from the neck to the waist. ✱ **get something off one's chest** to relieve the burden of a problem, worry etc by talking about it. ➤➤ **chestful** *n.*

chesterfield *n* **1** a heavily padded usu leather sofa with arms and back of the same height. **2** a man's semifitted overcoat with a velvet collar.

chestnut *n* **1a** an edible nut with shiny brown skin, often eaten roasted, that grows inside a spiny case. **b** the tree of the beech family that produces this nut. **2** a reddish brown colour. **3** = HORSE CHESTNUT. **4** a chestnut-coloured horse. **5** *informal* an often repeated joke or story; *broadly* anything repeated excessively. ➤➤ **chestnut** *adj.*

chest of drawers *n* a piece of furniture containing a set of drawers.

chesty *adj* (**-ier, -iest**) **1** inclined to or suffering from catarrh. **2** *informal* having prominent breasts. ➤➤ **chestiness** *n.*

chetrum *n* (*pl* **chetrums** *or* **chetrum**) a unit of currency in Bhutan, worth 100th of a ngultrum.

cheval glass /shə'val/ *n* a full-length mirror in a frame by which it may be tilted.

chevalier /shevə'liə/ *n* **1** a member of any of various orders of merit, e.g. the French Legion of Honour. **2** a chivalrous man. **3** *archaic* a knight.

Cheviot *n* a sheep of a hardy hornless breed originally from the Cheviot Hills on the border between England and Scotland.

chèvre *n* a soft goat's-milk cheese.

chevron *n* **1** a V shape or V-shaped object, e.g.: **a** a sleeve badge indicating the wearer's rank. **b** a V-shaped heraldic design with the point uppermost. **2** (*in pl*) a row of horizontal black and white V-shaped stripes indicating that a road bends sharply.

chevrotain *n* a small deer-like mammal with tusks found in tropical Asia and W Africa.

chew[1] *v* (*also* + on, up) to crush, grind, or gnaw with the teeth. ✱ **chew the fat/rag** *informal* to make friendly conversation; to chat or gossip. ➤➤ **chewable** *adj,* **chewer** *n,* **chewiness** *n,* **chewy** *adj.*

chew[2] *n* **1** the act of chewing. **2** something for chewing, e.g. a chewy sweet or something made for a pet dog to chew.

chewing gum *n* a flavoured sweetened substance, e.g. chicle, for chewing.

chew over *v informal* to think about (something) carefully.

Cheyenne *n* (*pl* **Cheyennes** *or* **Cheyenne**) **1** a Native American people of the western plains of the USA, or a member of this people. **2** the Algonquian language of this people.

chez /shay/ *prep* at or to the home of.

chi[1] *n* the 22nd letter of the Greek alphabet (X, χ), equivalent to roman ch.

chi[2] *or* **ch'i** *or* **qi** *n* in traditional Chinese medicine, philosophy, and martial arts, the life-force or energy that flows within an individual's body.

Chianti *n* a dry red Italian table wine.

chiaroscuro *n* (*pl* **-os**) **1** pictorial representation in terms of light and shade. **2** the arrangement or treatment of light and shade in a painting.

chiasma *n* (*pl* **chiasmas** *or* **chiasmata**) an anatomical cross-shaped configuration, e.g. one between paired chromatids considered to be the point where genetic material is exchanged.

chiasmus *n* (*pl* **chiasmi**) inversion of the relationship between the elements of parallel phrases, e.g. as in Goldsmith's *to stop too fearful, and too faint to go,* or an example of this. ➤➤ **chiastic** *adj.*

chic[1] *adj* (**chicer, chicest**) having or showing elegance and sophistication, *esp* of dress or manner. ➤➤ **chicly** *adv,* **chicness** *n.*

chic[2] *n* elegance and sophistication.

Chicana *n* (*pl* **Chicanas**) *NAm* an American woman or girl of Mexican origin or descent.

chicane[1] *n* **1** a series of tight turns in opposite directions in an otherwise straight stretch of a road-racing course. **2** a hand of cards containing no trumps.

chicane[2] *v* **1** to deceive (somebody) by the use of chicanery. **2** to use chicanery.

chicanery *n* (*pl* **-ies**) **1** deception by the use of fallacious or irrelevant arguments. **2** a piece of sharp practice or legal trickery.

Chicano *n* (*pl* **Chicanos**) *NAm* an American man or boy of Mexican origin or descent.

chichi *adj* **1** showy, frilly, or elaborate. **2** unnecessarily elaborate or affected.

chick *n* **1a** a young bird. **b** a newly hatched chicken. **2** *informal, dated* a young woman.

chickadee *n* a crestless N American songbird of the tit family.

chicken[1] *n* **1** the common domestic fowl, *esp* when young. **2** *informal* **a** an informal contest in which the participants put themselves in danger to see who is brave. **b** a coward. ✱ **he/she is no chicken/spring chicken** he/she is no longer young.

chicken[2] *adj informal* scared to do something.

chicken feed *n informal* a small and insignificant amount, *esp* of money.

chicken-hearted *adj* timid; cowardly.

chicken-livered *adj* = CHICKEN-HEARTED.

chicken out *v informal* (*often* + of) to lose one's nerve.

chickenpox *n* an infectious virus disease, *esp* of children, that is marked by mild fever and a rash of small blisters.

chicken wire *n* a light galvanized wire netting with a hexagonal mesh.

chick-pea *n* the hard edible seed of an Asiatic plant.

chickweed *n* a small-leaved plant of the pink family that occurs commonly as a weed.

chicle *n* a gum from the latex of the sapodilla, used as the chief ingredient of chewing gum.

chicory *n* (*pl* **-ies**) **1** a blue-flowered European perennial plant of the daisy family, widely cultivated for its edible thick roots and as a salad plant. **2** the ground roasted root of this plant, used as a coffee additive.

chide *v* (*past tense* **chided** *or* **chid,** *past part.* **chided** *or* **chidden**) to rebuke angrily; to scold. ➤➤ **chider** *n,* **chidingly** *adv.*

chief[1] *n* the head of a body of people or an organization; a leader. ➤➤ **chiefdom** *n.*

chief[2] *adj* **1** of the highest rank or office; head. **2** of greatest importance or influence; main.

chief constable *n* the principal officer of a British police force.

chiefly *adv* **1** most importantly; principally or especially. **2** for the most part; mostly or mainly.

chief of staff *n* the senior officer of an armed forces staff serving a commander.

chieftain *n* a chief, *esp* of a band, tribe, or clan. ➤➤ **chieftaincy** *n,* **chieftainship** *n.*

chiffchaff *n* a small greenish European warbler.

chiffon *n* a sheer fabric of silk, etc.

chiffonier *n* **1** a high narrow chest of drawers. **2** a low sideboard often with a shelf or shelves above it.

chigger *n* = CHIGOE.

chignon *n* a smooth knot of hair worn *esp* at the nape of the neck.

chigoe *n* a tropical flea, the female of which burrows under the skin.

Chihuahua *n* a dog of a very small breed of Mexican origin with a round head and large ears.

chilblain *n* an inflammatory sore, *esp* on the feet or hands, caused by exposure to cold. ➤➤ **chilblained** *adj.*

child *n* (*pl* **children**) **1** a young person, *esp* between infancy and youth. **2** an unborn or recently born person. **3** a son or daughter. **4** a childlike or childish person. **5** (+ of) a person who is strongly influenced by another or by a place or state of affairs. ✱ **with child** of a woman: PREGNANT. ➤➤ **childless** *adj*, **childlessness** *n*.

childbed *n archaic* = CHILDBIRTH.

child benefit *n* a state allowance paid weekly or monthly to a parent for each child in the family.

childbirth *n* the action or process of giving birth to a child or children.

childhood *n* the state or period of being a child.

childish *adj* **1** of or befitting a child or childhood. **2** marked by or suggestive of immaturity. ➤➤ **childishly** *adv*, **childishness** *n*.

childlike *adj* marked by the innocence and trust associated with children.

childminder *n chiefly Brit* a person who looks after other people's children, *esp* in their own home, when the parents are at work. ➤➤ **childminding** *n*.

childproof *adj* not liable to damage or misuse by children; *specif* designed to be impossible for children to open.

children *n* pl of CHILD.

child's play *n* an extremely simple task or act.

Chilean *n* a native or inhabitant of Chile. ➤➤ **Chilean** *adj*.

chili *n NAm* see CHILLI.

chiliasm *n* = millenarianism (see MILLENARIAN). ➤➤ **chiliast** *n*, **chiliastic** *adj*.

chill[1] *v* **1a** to make or become cold or chilly. **b** to make (food or drink) cool, *esp* without freezing. **2a** to frighten or horrify. **b** to dispirit. **3** *informal* = CHILL OUT. ➤➤ **chillingly** *adv*.

chill[2] *n* **1a** a disagreeable sensation of coldness. **b** a feverish cold, causing shivering, etc. **2** a moderate but disagreeable degree of cold. **3** coldness of manner.

chill[3] *adj* = CHILLY (1), (2).

chiller *n* **1** something that chills something or somebody. **2** a terrifying film or story, usu with a supernatural element; a SPINE-CHILLER.

chilli (*NAm* **chili**) *n* (*pl* **chillies**, *NAm* **chilies**) **1** the pod of a hot pepper used either whole or ground as a pungent condiment: compare PAPRIKA. **2** = CHILLI POWDER. **3** = CHILLI CON CARNE.

chilli con carne *n* a spiced Mexican stew of minced beef and beans, strongly seasoned with chillies or chilli powder.

chilli powder *n* a reddish powder made from ground chillies mixed with other spices, used as a flavouring.

chill out *v informal* to relax.

chillum *n* a pipe used for smoking cannabis.

chilly *adj* (**-ier, -iest**) **1** noticeably cold, *esp* unpleasantly so. **2** lacking warmth of feeling; distant or unfriendly. ➤➤ **chilliness** *n*.

Chiltern Hundreds *pl n* a nominal office for which an MP applies in order to resign his or her seat.

chimaera *n* see CHIMERA.

chime[1] *n* **1a** a musically tuned set of bells. **b** a set of objects, e.g. hanging metal bars or tubes, that sound like bells when struck. **2** (*usu in pl*) **a** the sound of a set of bells. **b** a musical sound like that of bells.

chime[2] *v* **1a** to make a musical ringing sound. **b** to signal or indicate (the time) by chiming. **2** (*usu* + together/with) to be or act in accord. ➤➤ **chimer** *n*.

chime in *v* **1** to break into a conversation or discussion, *esp* in order to express an opinion. **2** to combine harmoniously with a person or policy.

chimera *or* **chimaera** *n* (*pl* **chimeras** *or* **chimaeras**) **1** (**Chimera, Chimaera**) in Greek mythology, a fire-breathing female monster with a lion's head, a goat's body, and a serpent's tail. **2** an illusion or fabrication of the mind, *esp* an unrealizable dream. **3** an organism with tissues from various genetic sources. ➤➤ **chimeric** *adj*, **chimerical** *adj*, **chimerically** *adv*.

chimney *n* (*pl* **chimneys**) **1** a vertical structure in a building for carrying off smoke; *esp* the part extending above a roof. **2** a structure through which smoke and gases, e.g. from a furnace or steam engine, are discharged. **3** a glass tube shielding a flame, e.g. of an oil lamp. **4** a narrow cleft, vent, etc, e.g. in rock.

chimney breast *n* the wall that encloses a chimney and projects into a room.

chimneypiece *n Brit* = MANTELPIECE.

chimney pot *n* a pipe, usu made of earthenware, at the top of a chimney.

chimney stack *n* **1** a chimney rising above a roof. **2** a tall usu circular chimney serving a factory, power station, etc.

chimney sweep *n* somebody whose occupation is cleaning soot from chimney flues.

chimp *n informal* = CHIMPANZEE.

chimpanzee *n* an anthropoid ape of equatorial Africa with predominantly black coloration.

chin[1] *n* the lower portion of the face lying below the lower lip and including the prominence of the lower jaw. ✱ **keep one's chin up** to remain cheerful in trying circumstances. **take it on the chin** to accept (a difficult situation) bravely or stoically.

chin[2] *v* (**chinned, chinning**) **1** *informal* to hit on the chin. **2** in gymnastics, to raise one's chin to the level of (e.g. a bar) by pulling oneself up with one's arms.

china *n* **1** porcelain. **2** crockery.

china clay *n* = KAOLIN.

chinagraph *n* a pencil that will write on china or glass.

chinagraph pencil *n* = CHINAGRAPH.

Chinaman *n* (*pl* **Chinamen**) *dated or offensive* a Chinese man.

China syndrome *n* a hypothetical disastrous consequence of the meltdown of a nuclear reactor, in which the molten nuclear core burns its way deep into the earth's crust.

China tea *n* smoke-cured tea made from a tea plant grown in China.

Chinatown *n* the Chinese quarter of a city.

chinaware *n* tableware made of china.

chinchilla *n* **1a** a S American rodent the size of a large squirrel. **b** its soft pearly-grey fur. **2a** a breed of domestic rabbit with long white or greyish fur. **b** a breed of cat with similar fur.

chin-chin *interj Brit* used as an informal greeting, farewell, or toast.

Chindit *n* a member of an Allied force fighting behind Japanese lines in Burma (now Union of Myanmar) during WWII.

chine[1] *n* **1a** the backbone, *esp* of an animal. **b** a cut of meat including the whole or part of the backbone. **2** a mountain ridge. **3** the intersection of the bottom and sides of a boat.

chine[2] *v* to separate the backbone from the ribs of (a joint of meat).

chine[3] *n Brit* a steep-sided ravine, *esp* in Dorset or the Isle of Wight.

Chinese *n* (*pl* **Chinese**) **1** a native or inhabitant of China. **2** a group of related Sino-Tibetan languages spoken by the people of China, *esp* Mandarin. ➤➤ **Chinese** *adj*.

Chinese cabbage *n* either of two Asian varieties of cabbage widely used in oriental cookery.

Chinese chequers (*NAm* **Chinese checkers**) *pl n* (*used as sing.*) a board game in which each player tries to be the first to transfer a set of pegs or marbles across a star-shaped board by single moves or jumps.

Chinese lantern *n* **1** a collapsible lantern of thin coloured paper. **2** a plant, related to the nightshade and petunia, with thin-walled seed cases that are a brilliant orange-red when mature.

Chinese leaves *pl n* a CHINESE CABBAGE or its leaves used as a salad vegetable.

Chinese puzzle *n* an intricate or ingenious puzzle.

Chinese wall *n* **1** an apparently insurmountable barrier, *esp* a serious obstacle to understanding. **2** a code of practice prohibiting the exchange of sensitive information among different departments of a financial institution.

Chinese whispers *pl n* a game in which a message is whispered around a circle of people, the fun being to see how distorted the message becomes in the process.

Chink *n offensive or derog* a Chinese person.

chink[1] *n* **1** a small slit or fissure. **2** a means of evasion or escape; a loophole.

chink[2] *n* a short sharp metallic sound.

chink[3] *v* to make a sharp light metallic or ringing sound.

chinless *adj Brit, informal, derog* lacking firmness of purpose; ineffectual.

chinless wonder *n Brit, informal, derog* a person, *esp* a male of the upper classes, who is weak and foolish.

chino *n* (*pl* **chinos**) **1** a cotton twill fabric, usu khaki-coloured. **2** (*in pl*) trousers made of chino.

chinoiserie /shee'nwahzəri/ *n* **1** a style in art and interior design that copies Chinese features or motifs. **2** an object or a decoration in this style.

Chinook *n* (*pl* **Chinooks** *or collectively* **Chinook**) **1** a member of a Native American people of Oregon. **2** the language of this people. ➤➤ **Chinook** *adj.*

chinook *n* **1** a warm moist southwesterly wind of the NW coast of the USA. **2** a warm dry westerly wind of the E slopes of the Rocky Mountains.

Chinook Jargon *n* a mixture of Chinook and other Native American languages, French, and English, formerly used as a lingua franca in the NW USA and in W Canada and Alaska.

chintz *n* a printed plain-weave fabric, usu of glazed cotton.

chintzy *adj* (**chintzier, chintziest**) **1** made or decorated with chintz. **2** gaudy; cheap. ➤➤ **chintziness** *n.*

chinwag *n informal* a conversation or chat.

chip[1] *n* **1** a small thin flat piece, e.g. of wood or stone, cut or flaked off. **2** a flaw left after a chip is removed. **3a** *chiefly Brit* a strip of potato fried in deep fat. **b** *NAm, Aus* = CRISP[2]. **4** a counter used as a token for money in gambling games. **5** an integrated circuit or the small piece of semiconductor, *esp* silicon, on which it is constructed. **6a** = CHIP SHOT. **b** in football, rugby, etc, a kick in which the ball is lifted into the air and travels over a short distance. ✱ **a chip off the old block** a person who resembles either of their parents. **a chip on one's shoulder** a challenging, belligerent, or embittered attitude. **have had one's chips** *informal* to be beaten, doomed, dead, etc. **when the chips are down** when the crucial or critical point has been reached.

chip[2] *v* (**chipped, chipping**) **1a** (*often* + off/away) to cut or break (a small piece) from something. **b** to break off in small pieces. **2** to kick or hit (a ball, pass, etc) in a short high arc. **3** *Brit* to cut (potatoes) into chips.

chipboard *n* a board made from compressed wood chips and glue, used e.g. for flooring.

chip in *v informal* **1** to contribute. **2** *Brit* to interrupt or add a comment to a conversation between other people.

chipmunk *n* a small striped American squirrel.

chipolata *n* a small sausage.

Chippendale *adj* of an 18th-cent. English furniture style characterized by graceful outline and fine ornamentation.

chipper *adj informal* cheerful; bright.

chipping *n* (*usu in pl*) a fragment of stone used in surfacing roads.

chippy[1] *n* (*pl* **chippies**) *Brit, informal* **1** a shop selling fish and chips. **2** a carpenter.

chippy[2] *adj* (**-ier, -iest**) touchy; sensitive.

chip shot *n* a short shot in golf that lofts the ball to the green and allows it to roll.

chiral *adj* of a crystal or molecule: not able to be superimposed on its mirror image. ➤➤ **chirality** *n.*

chirography *n* handwriting; penmanship. ➤➤ **chirographer** *n,* **chirographic** *adj,* **chirographical** *adj.*

chiromancy *n* = PALMISTRY. ➤➤ **chiromancer** *n.*

chiropody *n* the care and treatment of the human foot in health and disease. ➤➤ **chiropodist** *n.*

chiropractic *n* a system of healing disease that employs manipulation and adjustment of body structures, e.g. the spinal column. ➤➤ **chiropractor** *n.*

chirp[1] *v* **1** of a small bird or insect: to make a short shrill sound. **2** to say (something) in a lively or cheerful manner.

chirp[2] *n* the short shrill sound of a small bird or insect, or a sound resembling this.

chirpy *adj* (**-ier, -iest**) *informal* lively; cheerful. ➤➤ **chirpily** *adv,* **chirpiness** *n.*

chirr[1] *v* said of a grasshopper, etc: to make a characteristic trilled sound.

chirr[2] *n* the trilled sound of a grasshopper, etc.

chirrup[1] *v* said *esp* of a bird: to chirp. ➤➤ **chirrupy** *adj.*

chirrup[2] *n* a chirp.

chisel[1] *n* a metal tool with a cutting edge at the end of a blade, used in shaping wood, stone, or metal.

chisel[2] *v* (**chiselled, chiselling,** *NAm* **chiseled, chiseling**) **1** to cut or work with a chisel. **2** *informal* **a** to trick or cheat. **b** to obtain by cheating. ➤➤ **chiseller** *n.*

chiselled (*NAm* **chiseled**) *adj* sharply defined; clear-cut.

chit[1] *n* an immature, often disrespectful, young woman, *esp* one of slight build.

chit[2] *n* a small slip of paper with writing on it, *esp* an order for goods or a note of money owed.

chital *n* = AXIS DEER.

chitchat[1] *n informal* small talk; gossip.

chitchat[2] *v* (**chitchatted, chitchatting**) *informal* to make small talk; to gossip.

chitin *n* a horny substance that forms part of the hard outer covering of *esp* insects and crustaceans. ➤➤ **chitinous** *adj.*

chiton *n* **1** any of a class of marine molluscs with a shell of many plates. **2** a knee-length woollen tunic worn in ancient Greece.

chitterling *n* (*usu in pl*) a section of the smaller intestines of pigs, *esp* when prepared as food.

chivalrous *adj* **1a** honourable; generous. **b** graciously courteous and considerate, *esp* to women. **2** having the characteristics of a knight, e.g. valour or gallantry. ➤➤ **chivalrously** *adv,* **chivalrousness** *n.*

chivalry *n* **1** the spirit or customs of medieval knighthood. **2a** the qualities, e.g. courage, integrity, and consideration, of an ideal knight; chivalrous conduct. **b** courteous behaviour, *esp* towards women. ➤➤ **chivalric** *adj.*

chive *n* (*usu in pl*) a perennial plant related to the onion whose long thin leaves are used to flavour and garnish food.

chivvy *or* **chivy** *v* (**-ies, -ied**) *informal* (*often* + up/along) to harass or pester (somebody) to get them to start doing something or go faster.

chlamydia *n* (*pl* **chlamydia** *or* **chlamydiae**) a micro-organism that is an intracellular parasite causing infections of the eye and the urinogenital system.

chloral *n* = CHLORAL HYDRATE.

chloral hydrate *n* a synthetic drug used as a sedative and hypnotic.

chlorate *n* a salt containing the radical ClO_3.

chloride *n* a compound of chlorine with another element or radical, *esp* a salt or ester of hydrochloric acid.

chlorinate *v* to treat or cause to combine with chlorine. ➤➤ **chlorination** *n,* **chlorinator** *n.*

chlorine *n* a chemical element of the halogen group that is a pungent dense greenish yellow gas.

chlorofluorocarbon *n* a compound methane-based gas containing chlorine and fluorine used as a refrigerant or a propellant in aerosol cans, and held responsible for damage to the earth's ozone layer.

chloroform[1] *n* a colourless volatile liquid used *esp* as a solvent and formerly as a general anaesthetic.

chloroform[2] *v* to administer chloroform to, *esp* so as to produce unconsciousness.

chlorophyll (*NAm also* **chlorophyl**) *n* the green photosynthetic colouring matter of plants. ➤➤ **chlorophyllous** *adj.*

chloroplast *n* a chlorophyll-containing part that is the site of photosynthesis and starch formation in plant cells.

chlorosis *n* **1** an iron-deficiency anaemia of young girls characterized by a greenish colour of the skin. **2** a diseased condition in green plants marked by yellowing or blanching. ➤➤ **chlorotic** *adj.*

ChM *abbr* Master of Surgery.

chocaholic *n* see CHOCOHOLIC.

choc-ice *n Brit* a bar of ice cream covered in chocolate.

chock[1] *n* a wedge or block placed under a door, barrel, wheel, etc to prevent movement.

chock[2] *v* **1** to secure with chocks. **2** to raise or support (a boat, etc) on blocks.

chock-a-block *adj and adv* tightly packed; in a very crowded condition.

chocker *adj Brit, informal* **1** absolutely full; chock-a-block. **2** *dated* annoyed; fed up.

chock-full *adv* as full as possible.

chocoholic *or* **chocaholic** *n* somebody who is addicted to or extremely fond of chocolate.

chocolate[1] *n* **1** a food prepared from ground roasted cacao seeds, usu sweetened or flavoured. **2** a sweet made or coated with chocolate. **3** a beverage made by mixing chocolate with hot water or milk. **4** dark brown. ➤➤ **chocolatey** *adj,* **chocolaty** *adj.*

chocolate[2] *adj* dark brown.

chocolate-box *adj* superficially pretty or sentimental.

Choctaw *n* (*pl* **Choctaws** *or collectively* **Choctaw**) **1** a member of a Native American people of Mississippi, Alabama, and Louisiana. **2** the language of this people.

choice[1] *n* **1** the act of choosing. **2** the power of choosing. **3a** somebody or something chosen. **b** the best part; the elite. **4** a sufficient number and variety to choose among.

choice[2] *adj* **1** of high quality. **2** selected with care; well chosen. **3** of language, etc: vulgar; rude; obscene. ➤➤ **choicely** *adv,* **choiceness** *n.*

choir *n* **1** (*used as sing. or pl*) **a** an organized group of singers. **b** a group of instruments of the same type playing together. **2** the part of the chancel of a church between the sanctuary and the nave.

choirboy *or* **choirgirl** *n* a boy or girl singer in a choir, *esp* in church.

choke[1] *v* **1a** to stop normal breathing by compressing or obstructing the windpipe, or by poisoning available air. **b** to become unable to breathe e.g. because of an obstruction in the windpipe. **2a** (*often* + back/down) to suppress (e.g. tears) or prevent the expression of (e.g. emotion). **b** (*also* + up) to make or become speechless with emotion. **3a** to restrain the growth or activity of (a plant, etc). **b** to obstruct or become obstructed by filling up or clogging. **4** to enrich the fuel mixture of (a petrol engine) by partially shutting off the air intake of the carburettor.

choke[2] *n* **1** the act or sound of choking. **2** a valve in the carburettor of a petrol engine for controlling the amount of air in a fuel-air mixture. **3** = INDUCTOR.

choke[3] *n* the inedible fibrous central part of a globe artichoke.

choked *adj informal* **1** *Brit* angry or resentful. **2** emotionally moved; touched.

chokedamp *n* a nonexplosive gas containing carbon dioxide that occurs in mines and is incapable of supporting animal life or a flame.

choker *n* **1** a short necklace or decorative band that fits closely round the throat. **2** a high stiff collar, *esp* a clerical collar.

chokey *or* **choky** *n* (*pl* **chokeys** *or* **chokies**) *Brit, slang* = PRISON.

choko *n* (*pl* **-os**) *Aus, NZ* a succulent green or white pear-shaped fruit that tastes like cucumber and is used as a vegetable.

choky *n* see CHOKEY.

cholecalciferol *n* naturally occurring vitamin D (vitamin D_3), found in most fish liver oils and formed in the skin of human beings on exposure to sunlight.

choler *n formal* anger; irascibility.

cholera *n* an often fatal epidemic disease caused by a bacterium and marked by severe gastrointestinal disorders. ➤➤ **choleraic** *adj.*

choleric *adj formal* angry; irate.

cholesterol *n* a steroid, present in animal and plant cells, that is a possible factor in hardening of the arteries.

choli *n* (*pl* **cholis**) a short-sleeved close-fitting bodice worn under a sari.

chomp *v* to chew noisily. ➤➤ **chomp** *n.*

Chomskyan *or* **Chomskian** *adj* characteristic of the work or theories of Noam Chomsky (b.1928), US linguist who argues that linguistics is an integral part of psychology and philosophy. ➤➤ **Chomskyan** *n*, **Chomskian** *n*.

chook *n Aus, NZ* a chicken or fowl.

choose *v* (*past tense* **chose**, *past part.* **chosen**) **1** to decide on and take (somebody or something) when offered several alternatives. **2a** to decide (to do something). **b** to wish (to do something). ➤➤ **chooser** *n*.

choosy *or* **choosey** *adj* (**-ier, -iest**) fastidiously selective; particular. ➤➤ **choosily** *adv*, **choosiness** *n*.

chop[1] *v* (**chopped, chopping**) **1a** (*usu* + off/down) to cut into or sever (something), usu by a blow or repeated blows of a sharp instrument. **b** (*often* + up) to cut into pieces. **2** to dispense with ruthlessly or reduce drastically. **3a** to strike (a ball) so as to impart backspin. **b** to strike (an opponent, etc) with a short, sharp blow, *esp* with the side of the hand.

chop[2] *n* **1** a forceful, usu slanting, blow or stroke with an axe or cleaver or with the side of the hand. **2** a small cut of meat often including part of a rib. **3** (**the chop**) *informal* an abrupt dismissal or discontinuation.

chop[3] *v* (**chopped, chopping**) *esp* of the wind: to change direction. ✻ **chop and change** *Brit* to keep changing one's mind, plans, etc. **chop logic** to argue with minute oversubtle distinctions.

chop-chop *adv and interj informal* without delay; quickly.

chopper *n* **1** *Brit* a short-handled axe or cleaver. **2** *informal* a helicopter. **3** *informal* (*in pl*) teeth. **4** *informal* a customized motorcycle, *esp* one with high handlebars. **5** *coarse slang* a penis.

choppy *adj* (**-ier, -iest**) of the sea or other expanse of water: rough with small waves. ➤➤ **choppiness** *n*.

chops *pl n* jaws, or the fleshy covering of the jaws. ✻ **lick one's chops** *informal* to show that one is looking forward to something with great pleasure.

chopstick *n* either of two slender sticks held between thumb and fingers, used chiefly in oriental countries to lift food to the mouth.

chop suey *n* a Chinese-style dish of shredded meat or chicken with bean sprouts and other vegetables, usu served with rice and soy sauce.

choral *adj* accompanied with or designed for singing, *esp* by a choir. ➤➤ **chorally** *adv*.

chorale *n* **1** a traditional hymn or psalm, usu German, for singing in church. **2** *chiefly NAm* (*used as sing. or pl*) a chorus or choir.

chord[1] *n* a combination of notes sounded together.

chord[2] *n* **1** = CORD[1] (2). **2** a straight line joining two points on the circumference of a circle. **3** the straight line joining the leading and trailing edges of an aerofoil. **4** in building either of the two outside members of a truss. ✻ **strike/touch a chord** produce a sympathetic or emotional response in somebody.

chordal *adj* **1** of or suggesting a chord. **2** relating to music characterized more by harmony than by counterpoint.

chordate *n* any of a large phylum of animals, including the vertebrates, that have at some stage of development a notochord, a central nervous system along the back, and gill clefts. ➤➤ **chordate** *adj*.

chore *n* **1** a routine task or job, *esp* a household one. **2** a difficult, disagreeable, or boring, task.

chorea *n* a nervous disorder marked by spasmodic movements of limbs and facial muscles and by lack of coordination.

choreograph *v* to compose or arrange the steps and dances for (a ballet or piece of music). ➤➤ **choreographer** *n*.

choreography *n* **1** the composition and arrangement of a ballet or other dance for the stage. **2** stage dancing as distinguished from social or ballroom dancing. ➤➤ **choreographic** *adj*, **choreographically** *adv*.

choric *adj* in the style of a chorus, *esp* a Greek chorus.

chorion *n* the outer embryonic membrane of higher vertebrates. ➤➤ **chorionic** *adj*.

chorister *n* a singer in a choir; *specif* a choirboy or choirgirl.

chorizo *n* (*pl* **chorizos**) a dried pork sausage highly seasoned with paprika, pimientos, garlic, and spices.

chortle *v* to laugh or chuckle, *esp* in satisfaction or exultation. ➤➤ **chortle** *n*, **chortler** *n*.

chorus[1] *n* **1a** (*used as sing. or pl*) an organized company of singers; *specif* the singers who sing the choral parts of e.g. an opera. **b** a group of dancers and singers supporting the featured players in a musical or revue. **c** a composition sung by a chorus. **2** a section of a song or hymn repeated at intervals, *esp* after each verse. **3** something uttered simultaneously by a number of people. **4a** a character, e.g. in Elizabethan drama, who comments on the action. **b** a group of singers and dancers, e.g. in Greek drama, who comment on the action. ✻ **in chorus** in unison.

chorus[2] *v* (**choruses, chorused, chorusing**) to sing or utter (something) in chorus.

chorus girl *n* a young woman who sings or dances in the chorus of a musical, cabaret, etc.

chose *v* past tense of CHOOSE.

chosen *v* past part. of CHOOSE.

chough *n* a bird of the crow family found in Europe and Asia that has red legs and glossy black plumage.

choux pastry *n* a light pastry made with an egg-enriched dough, used for profiteroles, eclairs, etc.

chow[1] *n informal* food.

chow[2] *or* **chow chow** *n* a dog of a breed having a blue-black tongue, a heavy coat, and a broad head.

chowder *n* a thick soup or stew made with clams or other seafood.

chow mein *n* a Chinese-style dish of fried noodles usu mixed with shredded meat or poultry and vegetables.

chrism *n* consecrated oil used in Greek and Roman Catholic churches, *esp* in baptism, confirmation, and ordination.

Christ[1] *n* = MESSIAH (1); a title given by Christians to Jesus. ➤➤ **Christlike** *adj*.

Christ[2] *interj informal* an exclamation of surprise, horror, etc.

Christadelphian *n* a member of a millenarian and fundamentalist Christian sect that claims to follow the practices of the earliest disciples. ➤➤ **Christadelphian** *adj*.

christen *v* **1** = BAPTIZE. **2** to give a name to, *esp* to name at baptism. **3** *informal* to use (something) for the first time.

Christendom *n* the community of people or nations professing Christianity.

christening *n* **1** the ceremony of baptizing and naming a child. **2** any event in which something is given a name or used for the first time.

Christian[1] *n* **1a** an adherent of Christianity. **b** a member of a Christian denomination, *esp* by baptism. **2** *informal* a good or kind person regardless of religion.

Christian[2] *adj* **1** of or consistent with Christianity or Christians. **2** *informal* commendably decent or generous. ⋙ **Christianize** *v*, **Christianise** *v*, **Christianly** *adv*.

Christian era *n* (**the Christian era**) the period dating from the birth of Christ.

Christianity *n* **1** the religion based on the life and teachings of Jesus Christ and the Bible. **2** conformity to the Christian religion, or a branch of it.

Christian name *n* **1** a name given at christening or confirmation. **2** a forename.

Christian Science *n* a religion founded by Mary Baker Eddy d.1910, that includes a practice of spiritual healing. ⋙ **Christian Scientist** *n*.

Christingle *n* an orange stuck with a lighted candle held by children at a Protestant religious service during Advent symbolizing Christ as the light of the world.

Christmas *n* **1** a festival of the Christian Church commemorating the birth of Christ and usu observed as a public holiday, celebrated on 25 December. **2** the festival season from Christmas Eve till the Epiphany on 6 January. ⋙ **Christmassy** *adj*.

Christmas box *n Brit* a small gift, usu of money, given at Christmas to e.g. postmen or tradespeople for their services throughout the year.

Christmas cake *n* a rich fruit cake covered in almond paste and icing, eaten at Christmas.

Christmas Eve *n* the day before Christmas day; *specif* the evening of that day.

Christmas pudding *n* a rich steamed pudding containing dried fruit, candied peel, spices, brandy, etc, traditionally eaten at Christmas.

Christmas rose *n* a European plant of the buttercup family that flowers in winter and has white or purplish flowers.

Christmas tree *n* an evergreen or artificial tree decorated with lights, tinsel, etc at Christmas.

chromakey *n* a digital technique by which a block of a particular colour in a video image can be replaced by another colour or image.

chromate *n* a salt or ester of chromic acid.

chromatic *adj* **1** relating to colour sensation or intensity of colour. **2a** of or giving all the notes of the chromatic scale. **b** characterized by frequent use of intervals or notes outside the diatonic scale. ⋙ **chromatically** *adv*, **chromaticism** *n*.

chromatic scale *n* a musical scale consisting entirely of semitones.

chromatid *n* either of the paired strands of a chromosome.

chromatin *n* a complex of DNA with proteins that forms the chromosomes in the cell nucleus and is readily stained.

chromatography *n* the separation of chemicals from a mixture by passing it through a substance, e.g. paper, which adsorbs the chemicals to differing extents. ⋙ **chromatograph** *n*, **chromatographic** *adj*.

chrome *n* **1** chromium, or a pigment formed from it. **2** a plating of chromium.

-chrome *comb. form* forming nouns and adjectives, with the meanings: **1** coloured; coloured thing. **2** colouring matter.

chrome yellow *n* a yellow pigment consisting essentially of lead chromate.

chromite *n* a mineral that consists of a magnetic oxide of iron and chromium.

chromium *n* a blue-white metallic chemical element found naturally only in combination and used *esp* in alloys and in electroplating.

chromosome *n* any of the gene-carrying bodies that contain DNA and protein and are found in the cell nucleus. ⋙ **chromosomal** *adj*.

chromosphere *n* the lower layer of the sun's atmosphere that is immediately above the PHOTOSPHERE (luminous surface). ⋙ **chromospheric** *adj*.

chronic *adj* **1a** of an illness: marked by long duration or frequent recurrence: compare ACUTE. **b** suffering from a chronic disease. **2a** always present or encountered, *esp* constantly troubling. **b** habitual; persistent. **3** *Brit, informal* bad; terrible. ⋙ **chronically** *adv*, **chronicity** *n*.

chronic fatigue syndrome *n* a condition, whose cause is unknown, characterized by extreme and long-lasting tiredness, often accompanied by muscle and joint pains, weakness, slight fever, sore throat, and depression.

chronicle[1] *n* **1** a continuous and detailed historical account of events arranged chronologically without analysis or interpretation. **2** a narrative.

chronicle[2] *v* to record (events) in or as if in a chronicle. ⋙ **chronicler** *n*.

chronograph *n* an instrument for accurately measuring and recording time intervals. ⋙ **chronographic** *adj*.

chronological *adj* of or arranged in or according to the order of time. ⋙ **chronologically** *adv*.

chronology *n* (*pl* **-ies**) **1** a method for setting past events in order of occurrence, or the scientific study or use of such a method. **2** an arrangement in order of occurrence; *specif* such an arrangement presented in tabular or list form. ⋙ **chronologist** *n*.

chronometer *n* an instrument for measuring time, *esp* one designed to keep time with great accuracy.

chronometry *n* the science of accurate time measurement. ⋙ **chronometric** *adj*, **chronometrical** *adj*, **chronometrically** *adv*.

chrysalis *n* (*pl* **chrysalises** *or* **chrysalides**) **1** a pupa, *esp* of a butterfly or moth, or the case enclosing it. **2** a sheltered state or stage of being or growth.

chrysanthemum *n* a garden plant with a brightly coloured often double flower head.

chthonian *adj* = CHTHONIC.

chthonic *adj* of the underworld; infernal.

chub *n* (*pl* **chubs** *or* **chub**) a European freshwater fish of the carp family.

Chubb *n trademark* a type of lock with a device for jamming the bolt if an attempt is made to pick it.

chubby *adj* (**-ier, -iest**) plump. ⋙ **chubbiness** *n*.

chuck[1] *v* **1** *informal* **a** to toss or throw. **b** (*often* + out/away) to discard. **2** *informal (+ in)* to leave or give up (something or somebody). **3** to pat or tap. ✱ **chuck it down** *informal* to rain heavily.

chuck[2] *n* **1** a pat or nudge under the chin. **2** *informal* a throw. **3** (**the chuck**) *Brit, informal*. **a** dismissal. **b** rejection by a partner in a relationship.

chuck[3] *n* **1** a cut of beef that includes most of the neck and the area about the shoulder blade. **2** a device for holding a workpiece, e.g. for turning on a lathe, or a tool, e.g. in a drill.

chuck[4] *n dialect* a term of endearment.

chuckle[1] *v* to laugh inwardly or quietly.

chuckle[2] *n* an inward or quiet laugh.

chucklehead *n informal* a stupid person. ⋙ **chuckleheaded** *adj*.

chuck out *v informal* to eject (somebody) from a place or an office. ⋙ **chucker-out** *n.*

chuck steak *n* = CHUCK³ (1).

chuck up *v informal* **1** to discontinue or give up (something). **2** to vomit.

chuck wagon *n NAm* a wagon carrying a stove and provisions for cooking, e.g. on a ranch.

chuff *v* to produce or move with the sound made by a steam engine releasing steam regularly. ⋙ **chuff** *n.*

chuffed *adj Brit, informal* pleased.

chug *v* (**chugged, chugging**) to move with the repetitive dull explosive sound made by a labouring engine. ⋙ **chug** *n.*

chukka *n* **1** see CHUKKER. **2** (*also* **chukka boot**) an ankle-length leather boot worn for playing polo.

chukker *or* **chukka** *n* any of the periods of play in a polo game.

chum *n informal, dated* a close friend; a mate.

chummy *adj* (**-ier, -iest**) *informal* friendly; intimate. ⋙ **chummily** *adv,* **chumminess** *n.*

chump *n* **1** a cut of lamb, mutton, or pork taken from between the loin and hindleg. **2** *informal* a fool; a stupid person. ✱ **off one's chump** *Brit, slang* crazy; mad.

chum up *v* (**chummed, chumming**) *dated* (*often* + with) to form a friendship, *esp* a close one.

chunder *v* (**chundered, chundering**) *chiefly Aus, informal* to vomit.

chunk *n* **1** a lump, *esp* of a firm or hard material, e.g. wood. **2** *informal* a fairly large quantity.

chunky *adj* (**-ier, -iest**) **1** broad and heavy; stocky. **2** filled with chunks. **3** of materials, clothes, etc: thick and heavy. ⋙ **chunkiness** *n.*

Chunnel *n* (**the Chunnel**) *informal* the railway tunnel under the English Channel.

chunter *v Brit, informal* to talk or mutter incessantly and usu complainingly.

church *n* **1** a building for public Christian worship. **2a** (**the Church**) the whole body of Christians. **b** = DENOMINATION (1). **3** (**the church**) the clerical profession. ⋙ **churchly** *adj,* **churchman** *n,* **churchwoman** *n.*

Church Commissioner *n* a member of a body of trustees responsible for overseeing and administering the finances, investments, and properties of the Church of England.

Church of England *n* the established episcopal church of England.

Church of Scotland *n* the main Presbyterian denomination in Scotland.

churchwarden *n* **1** either of two lay parish officials in Anglican churches with responsibility *esp* for parish property and alms. **2** *Brit* a long-stemmed clay tobacco pipe.

churchy *adj* (**-ier, -iest**) marked by strict conformity or zealous adherence to the forms or beliefs of a church. ⋙ **churchiness** *n.*

churchyard *n* an enclosed piece of ground surrounding a church; *esp* one used as a burial ground.

churinga *n* (*pl* **churinga** *or* **churingas**) among Australian aborigines, a sacred stone amulet or similar object.

churl *n* **1** a rude ill-bred person. **2** *archaic* a rustic or country person.

churlish *adj* **1** rudely uncooperative; surly. **2** lacking refinement or sensitivity. ⋙ **churlishly** *adv,* **churlishness** *n.*

churn¹ *n* **1** a vessel in which milk or cream is agitated to make butter. **2** *Brit* a large metal container for transporting milk.

churn² *v* **1** to agitate (milk or cream) in order to make butter. **2a** to stir or agitate (liquid) violently. **b** to be in violent motion.

churn out *v chiefly informal* to produce (something) prolifically and mechanically, usu without great concern for quality.

churn rate *n* the rate of turnover of a business in staff, clients, etc.

churr *v* to make a vibrant or whirring noise characteristic of certain insects and birds, e.g. the partridge. ⋙ **churr** *n.*

chute *n* **1** an inclined plane or channel down which things may pass. **2** a slide into a swimming pool. **3** a waterfall, rapid, etc. **4** *informal* a parachute. **5** *Scot* = SLIDE² (1A).

chutney *n* (*pl* **chutneys**) a thick condiment or relish of Indian origin that contains fruits, sugar, vinegar, and spices.

chutzpah *n informal* brazen audacity.

chyle *n* a milky liquid produced during intestinal absorption of fats. ⋙ **chylous** *adj.*

chyme *n* the semifluid mass of partly digested food expelled by the stomach into the duodenum. ⋙ **chymous** *adj.*

Ci *abbr* curie.

CIA *abbr NAm* Central Intelligence Agency.

ciabatta /chə'bahtə/ *n* (*pl* **ciabattas** *or* **ciabatte**) a type of flattish white Italian bread made with olive oil.

ciao *interj* used to express greeting or farewell.

cicada /si'kahdə/ *n* (*pl* **cicadas** *or* **cicadae**) an insect with large transparent wings, the male of which produces a shrill singing noise.

cicatrice *n* = CICATRIX.

cicatrices *n* pl of CICATRIX.

cicatrise *v* see CICATRIZE.

cicatrix /'sikətriks/ *n* (*pl* **cicatrices** /-'trieseez/) **1** a scar resulting after a flesh wound has healed. **2** a mark left on a stem after the fall of a leaf or bract. ⋙ **cicatricial** *adj.*

cicatrize *or* **-ise** *v* **1** = SCAR². **2** to heal by forming a scar. ⋙ **cicatrization** *n.*

cicerone /sisə'rohni, chichə-/ *n* (*pl* **cicerones** *or* **ciceroni**) **1** a person who acts as a guide to antiquities. **2** a guide or mentor.

cichlid *n* a tropical freshwater fish with spiny fins.

CID *abbr Brit* Criminal Investigation Department.

-cide *comb. form* forming nouns, denoting: a type of killing, or somebody or something that kills: *homicide*; *suicide.* ⋙ **-cidal** *comb. form.*

cider *n* **1** fermented, often sparkling, apple juice. **2** *NAm* an unfermented apple-juice drink.

c.i.f. *abbr* cost, insurance, and freight.

cig *n informal* a cigarette.

cigar *n* a roll of tobacco leaf for smoking.

cigarette (*NAm also* **cigaret**) *n* a narrow cylinder of cut tobacco enclosed in paper for smoking.

cigarette card *n* a small oblong card with a picture on one side and information on the other, formerly given away in a packet of cigarettes.

cigarillo *n* (*pl* **-os**) a very small cigar.

ciggie *or* **ciggy** *n* (*pl* **-ies**) *informal* a cigarette.

cilia *n* pl of CILIUM.

cilium *n* (*pl* **cilia**) **1** a minute hairlike part that beats rapidly to move a single-celled organism along. **2** an eyelash. ⋙ **ciliary** *adj,* **ciliate** *adj,* **ciliated** *adj,* **ciliation** *n.*

C-in-C *abbr* Commander-in-Chief.

cinch *n informal* **1a** something certain to happen. **b** a task performed with ease. **2** *NAm* = GIRTH (2).

cinchona *n* **1** a S American tree of the madder family. **2** its dried bark which contains quinine. **3** a drug made from this bark.

cinder *n* a piece of partly burned material, e.g. coal, that will burn further but will not flame. ➤➤ **cindery** *adj.*

cine- *comb. form* **1** moving pictures. **2** relating to the cinema.

cineaste *or* **cineast** *n* a devotee of the cinema.

cinecamera *or* **ciné camera** *n* a simple hand-held camera for making amateur films.

cinefilm *or* **ciné film** *n* film for making moving pictures on cinecameras.

cinema *n* **1** *chiefly Brit* a theatre where films are shown. **2** (**the cinema**) films considered as an art form, entertainment, or industry.

cinematic *adj* **1** made and presented as a film. **2** of or suitable for the making of films. ➤➤ **cinematically** *adv.*

cinematograph *n chiefly Brit* a film camera or projector.

cinematography *n* the art or science of cinema photography. ➤➤ **cinematographer** *n,* **cinematographic** *adj,* **cinematographically** *adv.*

cinema vérité *n* the art or technique of film-making so as to convey documentary-style realism.

cineraria *n* a composite pot plant with heart-shaped leaves and clusters of bright flower heads.

cinerarium *n* (*pl* **cineraria**) a place where the ashes of the cremated dead are kept. ➤➤ **cinerary** *adj.*

cinnabar *n* **1** naturally occurring red mercuric sulphide. **2** a European moth with greyish black fore wings marked with red and clear reddish pink hind wings.

cinnabar moth *n* = CINNABAR (2).

cinnamon *n* **1** a spice obtained from the dried bark of an Asian tree of the laurel family. **2** a light yellowish brown.

cinquecento /chingkwi'chentoh/ *n* (*often* **Cinquecento**) the 16th cent., *esp* in Italian art.

cinquefoil *n* **1** a plant of the rose family with five-lobed leaves. **2** in architecture, a design enclosed by five joined arcs arranged in a circle.

Cinque Ports *pl n* orig five and now seven towns on the SE coast of England with ancient privileges because of their importance in naval defence.

cipher[1] *or* **cypher** *n* **1a** a method of transforming a text in order to conceal its meaning; a code. **b** a key to a code. **2** a combination of symbolic letters, *esp* a monogram. **3a** *archaic* = ZERO[1] (1). **b** a nonentity.

cipher[2] *or* **cypher** *v* to encode.

circa *prep* used *esp* with dates: at, in, or of approximately.

circadian *adj* occurring in approximately day-long periods or cycles, e.g. of biological activity or function.

circle[1] *n* **1a** a shape in the form of a closed curved line every point of which is equidistant from the centre. **b** something in the form of a circle. **2** a balcony or tier of seats in a theatre. **3** (*used as sing. or pl*) a group of people sharing a common interest, activity, or leader. ✱ **come/turn full circle** to return to the position or condition in which the thing in question started. **go/run round in circles** to be frantically active without making any progress.

circle[2] *v* **1** to move in a circle. **2** to enclose in a circle. ➤➤ **circler** *n.*

circlet *n* something in the form of a little circle, *esp* a circular ornament.

Circlip *n trademark* a clip that encircles a tubular fitting and is held in place by its natural tension.

circs *pl n chiefly Brit, informal* circumstances.

circuit[1] *n* **1** a closed loop encompassing an area, or the area enclosed. **2a** a course round a periphery. **b** a racetrack. **c** the act of going round such a course or a racetrack. **3** a regular tour, e.g. by a judge, round an assigned area or territory. **4a** a complete path of an electric current. **b** an array of electrical components connected so as to allow the passage of current. **c** a two-way communication path between points, e.g. in a computer. **5a** a regular series of sports competitions in which the same competitors take part. **b** a set of physical exercises to be performed one after the other.

circuit[2] *v* to make a circuit round (something).

circuit breaker *n* a switch that automatically interrupts an electric circuit under an infrequent abnormal condition.

circuitous *adj* indirect in route or method; roundabout. ➤➤ **circuitously** *adv,* **circuitousness** *n,* **circuity** *n.*

circuitry *n* (*pl* **-ies**) electrical circuits, or a system of circuits.

circular[1] *adj* **1** having the form of a circle. **2** marked by the fallacy of assuming something which is to be demonstrated. **3** of a letter or advertising material: intended for circulation to a number of people, e.g. by mail. ➤➤ **circularity** *n,* **circularly** *adv.*

circular[2] *n* a paper, e.g. a leaflet or advertisement, intended for wide distribution.

circularize *or* **circularise** *v* **1** to send circulars to. **2** to publicize by means of circulars. ➤➤ **circularization** *n.*

circular saw *n* a power-driven saw that has its teeth set on the edge of a revolving metal disc.

circulate *v* **1** to move in a circle, circuit, or orbit, *esp* to follow a course that returns to the starting point. **2a** to flow without obstruction. **b** to become well known or widespread. **c** to go from group to group at a social gathering. **d** of a newspaper, etc: to be sold or distributed. ➤➤ **circulative** *adj,* **circulator** *n,* **circulatory** *adj.*

circulating library *n* a small library which moves from one place to another, e.g. between hospitals.

circulation *n* **1** orderly movement through a circuit, *esp* the movement of blood through the vessels of the body induced by the pumping action of the heart. **2a** passage or transmission from person to person or place to place, *esp* the interchange of currency. **b** the average number of copies of a publication sold over a given period. ✱ **out of circulation** not participating in social life.

circum- *prefix* round; about.

circumambient *adj formal or literary* on all sides; encompassing. ➤➤ **circumambience** *n,* **circumambiently** *adv.*

circumcise *v* to cut off all or part of the foreskin of (a male) or the clitoris of (a female). ➤➤ **circumcision** *n.*

circumference *n* **1** the perimeter of a circle. **2** the external boundary or surface of a figure or object. ➤➤ **circumferential** *adj,* **circumferentially** *adv.*

circumflex *n* a mark (ˆ) or (˜), placed over a vowel in some languages to show length, contraction, or a particular vowel quality.

circumlocution *n* **1** the use of an unnecessarily large number of words to express an idea. **2** evasive language. ⋙ **circumlocutory** *adj.*

circumnavigate *v* to travel completely round the earth, *esp* by sea or air. ⋙ **circumnavigation** *n,* **circumnavigator** *n.*

circumpolar *adj* **1** surrounding or found near a pole of the earth. **2** of a celestial body: continually visible above the horizon at a particular latitude.

circumscribe *v* **1** to restrict the range or activity of. **2** to draw round (a geometrical figure) so as to touch it at as many points as possible. ⋙ **circumscription** *n.*

circumspect *adj* careful to consider all circumstances and possible consequences; prudent. ⋙ **circumspection** *n,* **circumspectly** *adv.*

circumstance *n* **1a** (*usu in pl, used as sing. or pl*) the situation one finds oneself in and for which one is not responsible: *a victim of circumstances.* **b** (*in pl*) one's situation with regard to material or financial welfare. **2** a fact or detail pertinent to an event, story, etc; an incident viewed as part of a narrative or course of events. ✻ **in/under no circumstances** on no account; never. **in/under the circumstances** because of the conditions; considering the situation.

circumstantial *adj* **1** of evidence: tending to prove a fact indirectly by proving other related events or circumstances. **2** pertinent but not essential; incidental. **3** abounding in factual details. ⋙ **circumstantiality** *n,* **circumstantially** *adv.*

circumvent *v* **1** to find a way round (a problem), *esp* by ingenuity. **2** to evade (e.g. an enemy), *esp* by means of a stratagem. ⋙ **circumvention** *n.*

circus *n* (*pl* **circuses**) **1a** an entertainment in which a variety of performers, e.g. acrobats and clowns, and performing animals are involved in a series of unrelated acts. **b** a busy scene of noisy or frivolous action. **2** (**Circus**) *Brit* usu in proper names: a large open road junction in a town partly surrounded by a circle of buildings. **3** a large circular or oval stadium used *esp* for sports contests or spectacles.

cirque /suhk/ *n* a deep steep-walled glacially excavated hollow on a mountain flank.

cirrhosis *n* (*pl* **cirrhoses**) hardening, *esp* of the liver, caused by excessive formation of connective tissue. ⋙ **cirrhotic** *adj and n.*

cirri *n* pl of CIRRUS.

cirrocumulus *n* (*pl* **cirrocumuli**) a cloud formation consisting of small white rounded masses occurring at high altitude, usu in a mackerel sky.

cirrostratus *n* (*pl* **cirrostrati**) a cloud formation consisting of a uniform layer of high stratus clouds that are darker than cirrus.

cirrus *n* (*pl* **cirri**) **1** a wispy white cloud formation occurring at high altitudes. **2** *technical* **a** = TENDRIL . **b** a slender, usu flexible, animal appendage.

CIS *abbr* Commonwealth of Independent States, a successor to the USSR.

cisalpine *adj* south of the Alps.

cisco *n* (*pl* **-oes** *or* **-os**) a herring-like North American freshwater food fish of the salmon family.

cissy[1] *or* **sissy** *n* (*pl* **-ies**) *Brit, informal* **1** an effeminate boy or man. **2** a cowardly person.

cissy[2] *or* **sissy** *adj* (**-ier, -iest**) *Brit, informal* **1** effeminate. **2** cowardly.

Cistercian *n* a member of an austere Benedictine order founded by St Robert of Molesme in 1098 at Cîteaux in France. ⋙ **Cistercian** *adj.*

cistern *n* **1** a water reservoir for a toilet. **2** a tank at the top of a house or building. **3** *chiefly NAm* a tank, usu underground, for storing rainwater.

cistus *n* a shrub of the rockrose family with large red or white flowers.

citadel *n* a fortress, *esp* one that commands a city.

citation *n* **1a** an act of quoting. **b** a quotation. **2** a mention, *esp* of something praiseworthy; *specif* specific reference in a military dispatch to meritorious conduct. **3** *chiefly NAm* an official summons to appear before a court of law. ⋙ **citational** *adj.*

cite *v* **1** to quote by way of example, precedent, or proof. **2** to refer to or name, *esp* to mention formally in commendation or praise. **3** to call upon to appear before a court of law. ⋙ **citable** *adj.*

cithara *n* an ancient Greek stringed instrument of the lyre family.

citified *or* **cityfied** *adj often derog* having adopted city ways. ⋙ **citification** *n.*

citizen *n* **1** a member of a state, *esp* a native or naturalized one. **2** an inhabitant of a city or town. ⋙ **citizenship** *n.*

citizenry *n* (*pl* **-ies**) *formal* (*used as sing. or pl*) the whole body of citizens.

Citizens' Advice Bureau *n* in Britain, an office at which members of the public can get information about their civil rights, the law, etc.

citizen's arrest *n* a legally permitted arrest by a member of the public.

Citizens' Band *n* a system of radio communication by which private individuals, *esp* drivers, can transmit messages to one another.

citric acid *n* an acid occurring in lemons, limes, etc, used as a flavouring.

citrine[1] *adj* resembling a lemon, *esp* in colour.

citrine[2] *n* semiprecious yellow quartz.

citron *n* a fruit like the lemon but larger and with a thicker rind.

citronella *n* a fragrant oil used in perfumery and as an insect repellent, derived from a S Asian grass.

citrus *n* (*pl* **citruses**) any of a genus of thorny trees grown in warm regions for their edible thick-rinded juicy fruit, e.g. the orange or lemon.

cittern *n* a plucked stringed musical instrument with an oval belly and back and wire strings, popular *esp* in Renaissance England.

city *n* (*pl* **-ies**) **1a** a large town. **b** *Brit* a town that has a cathedral or has had city status conferred on it by charter. **c** *NAm* a chartered municipality, usu a large one. **2** (**the City**) *Brit.* **a** the financial and commercial area of London. **b** (*used as sing. or pl*) influential financial interests of the British economy.

city desk *n* **1** *Brit* the department dealing with the financial section of a journal or newspaper. **2** *NAm* the section of a newspaper office in charge of local news.

city father *n* an important official or prominent citizen of a city.

city hall *n NAm* **1** the chief administrative building of a city. **2** (*often* **City Hall**) the administration of a city.

cityscape *n* a view of a city, or its pictorial representation.

city slicker *n NAm, informal* = SLICKER (2B).

city-state *n* an autonomous state consisting of a city and surrounding territory, e.g. in ancient Greece or medieval Italy.

city technology college *n* a British secondary school providing a science-based education in an inner-city area.

civet *n* **1** a musky-smelling substance extracted from a pouch near the sexual organs of the civet cat and used in perfumery. **2** = CIVET CAT.

civet cat *n* a flesh-eating mammal of Africa, Asia, and S Europe with a long body and short legs.

civic *adj* of a citizen, a city, or citizenship. ➤➤ **civically** *adv.*

civic centre *n Brit* an area where the chief public buildings of a town are situated, or the buildings themselves.

civics *pl n* (*used as sing. or pl*) a social science dealing with the rights and duties of citizens.

civil *adj* **1** adequately courteous and polite; not rude. **2** of or involving the general public as opposed to e.g. the military or clergy. **3** relating to private rights as distinct from criminal proceedings. ➤➤ **civilly** *adv.*

civil defence *n* (*often* **Civil Defence**) protective measures organized by and for civilians against hostile attack, *esp* from the air, or natural disaster.

civil disobedience *n* refusal to obey governmental demands, e.g. payment of tax, as a means of protest.

civil engineer *n* an engineer who deals with the design and construction of large-scale public works, e.g. roads or bridges. ➤➤ **civil engineering** *n.*

civilian *n* somebody who is not in the army, navy, air force, or other uniformed public body. ➤➤ **civilian** *adj.*

civility *n* (*pl* **-ies**) **1** courtesy; politeness. **2** (*usu in pl*) a polite act or remark.

civilization *or* **-isation** *n* **1a** a relatively high level of cultural and technological development. **b** the culture characteristic of a particular time or place. **2** the process of becoming civilized. **3** *often humorous* life in a place that offers the comforts of the modern world.

civilize *or* **-ise** *v* **1** to bring to a technically and socially advanced stage of development. **2** to educate or refine (somebody). ➤➤ **civilizable** *adj,* **civilized** *adj,* **civilizer** *n.*

civil law *n* **1** the body of private law developed from Roman law as distinct from common law. **2** law as it applies to private citizens and their dealings rather than to crime.

civil liberty *n* a right or freedom of the individual citizen in relation to the state, e.g. freedom of speech. ➤➤ **civil libertarian** *n.*

civil list *n* (**the civil list**) an annual allowance by Parliament for the household expenses of the monarch and royal family.

civil marriage *n* a marriage involving a civil contract but no religious rite.

civil rights *pl n* civil liberties, *esp* those of status equality between races or groups.

civil servant *n* a member of a civil service.

civil service *n* (*used as sing. or pl*) the administrative service of a government or international agency, exclusive of the armed forces and the judiciary.

civil war *n* war between opposing groups of citizens of the same country.

civvies *or* **civies** *pl n informal* civilian as distinguished from military clothes.

civvy street *n* (*often* **Civvy Street**) *Brit, informal* civilian life, as opposed to life in the services.

CJD *abbr* Creutzfeldt-Jakob disease.

Cl *abbr* the chemical symbol for chlorine.

cl *abbr* centilitre.

clack[1] *v* **1** to make an abrupt striking sound or sounds. **2** *informal* to chatter. ➤➤ **clacker** *n.*

clack[2] *n* **1** a sound of clacking. **2** *informal* rapid continuous talk; chatter.

clad[1] *v* past tense and past part. of CLOTHE.

clad[2] *v* past tense and past part. of CLAD[4].

clad[3] *adj* covered or clothed.

clad[4] *v* (**cladded** *or* **clad, cladding**) to cover (a surface) with cladding.

cladding *n* a thin covering or overlay, e.g. of stone on a building or metal on a metal core.

clade *n technical* a group of organisms, e.g. all animals with backbones, that includes all the descendants of a single common ancestor. ➤➤ **cladism** *n,* **cladistic** *adj.*

cladistics *pl n* (*used as sing. or pl*) a theory that the sharing of a unique characteristic, e.g. the hair of mammals, by a group of organisms indicates their descent from a single common ancestor.

claim[1] *v* **1a** to ask for, *esp* as a right. **b** to require or demand. **2** to take as the rightful owner. **3** to assert; to maintain without proof. **4** to end (somebody's life). **5** (+ for) to make a claim under the terms of e.g. an insurance policy. ➤➤ **claimable** *adj,* **claimer** *n.*

claim[2] *n* **1** a demand for something due, or believed to be due. **2a** (+ to/on) a right or title to something. **b** an assertion open to challenge. **3** something claimed, *esp* a tract of land staked out.

claimant *n* (*also* + to) somebody who asserts a right or entitlement, e.g. to a title or a benefit.

clairvoyance *n* the ability to perceive matters beyond the range of ordinary perception. ➤➤ **clairvoyant** *adj and n.*

clam *n* a large marine mollusc eaten as food, with a burrowing foot and noted for tightly closing the two halves of its shell.

clamber *v* to climb awkwardly or with difficulty. ➤➤ **clamberer** *n.*

clammy *adj* (**-ier, -iest**) **1** damp, clinging, and usu rather cold. **2** of the weather: humid. ➤➤ **clammily** *adv,* **clamminess** *n.*

clamour[1] (*NAm* **clamor**) *n* **1** noisy shouting. **2** a loud continuous noise. **3** (*often* + against/for) insistent public expression, e.g. of support or protest. ➤➤ **clamorous** *adj,* **clamorously** *adv,* **clamorousness** *n.*

clamour[2] (*NAm* **clamor**) *v* **1** to make a din. **2** (*usu* + against/for) to make one's wishes or views known loudly and insistently.

clamp[1] *n* **1** a device that holds or compresses two or more things firmly together. **2** = WHEEL CLAMP.

clamp[2] *v* **1** to fasten with a clamp. **2** to hold tightly. **3** to wheel-clamp (a vehicle). ➤➤ **clamper** *n.*

clamp[3] *n Brit* a heap of potatoes, turnips, etc covered over with straw or earth.

clamp down *v* to impose or strengthen restrictions on something or somebody. ➤➤ **clampdown** *n.*

clam up *v* (**clammed up, clamming up**) *informal* to become silent.

clan *n* **1a** all the people belonging to a particular family group of Scottish descent and sharing a common surname. **b** a group of people related by family. **2** a close-knit group united by a common interest or common characteristics. ➤➤ **clansman** *n,* **clanswoman** *n.*

clandestine *adj* held in or conducted with secrecy; surreptitious. ➤➤ **clandestinely** *adv.*

clang *v* to make a loud metallic ringing sound. ➤➤ **clang** *n.*

clanger *n Brit, informal* a blunder.

clangour (*NAm* **clangor**) *n* a resounding clang or series of clangs. ➤➤ **clangorous** *adj,* **clangorously** *adv.*

clank *v* to make a sharp brief metallic sound or a series of such sounds. ➤➤ **clank** *n,* **clankingly** *adv.*

clannish *adj* tending to associate only with a select group of similar background, status, or interests. ➤➤ **clannishly** *adv,* **clannishness** *n.*

clap[1] *v* (**clapped, clapping**) **1a** to strike (the hands) together repeatedly, usu in applause. **b** to applaud (a person or an act). **2** to strike (somebody) with the flat of the hand in a friendly way. **3a** to place, put, or set (something or somebody) in a certain place or condition, *esp* energetically. **b** to impose (e.g. a restriction). **4** of a bird: to flap (the wings) noisily. ✱ **clap eyes on** see EYE[1]. **clap hold of** *informal* to seize suddenly and energetically.

clap[2] *n* **1** the sound of clapping hands, *esp* applause. **2** a loud sharp percussive noise, *esp* of thunder. **3** a friendly slap.

clap[3] *n* (*often* **the clap**) *slang* = SEXUALLY TRANSMITTED DISEASE, *esp* gonorrhoea.

clapboard *n NAm* = WEATHERBOARD (1).

clapped out *adj chiefly Brit, informal* old and worn-out; liable to break down irreparably.

clapper *n* the tongue of a bell. ✱ **go/run like the clappers** *Brit, informal* to move as fast as possible.

clapperboard *n* a hinged board that is held before the camera and banged together to mark the beginning and end of each take in a film.

claptrap *n informal* pretentious nonsense; rubbish.

claque *n* (*used as sing. or pl*) **1** a group hired to applaud at a performance. **2** a group of self-interested obsequious flatterers.

claret *n* **1** a dry red Bordeaux wine. **2** a dark purplish red colour. ➤➤ **claret** *adj.*

clarify *v* (**-ies, -ied**) **1** to make or become understandable or free from confusion. **2a** to make (a liquid, etc) clear by freeing it from suspended matter. **b** to melt (butter) to make it clear. ➤➤ **clarification** *n,* **clarificatory** *adj,* **clarifier** *n.*

clarinet *n* a woodwind musical instrument with a single reed, a cylindrical tube flared at the end, and holes stopped by keys. ➤➤ **clarinettist** *n.*

clarion[1] *n* a medieval trumpet, or the sound of one.

clarion[2] *adj* loud and clear.

clarity *n* the quality or state of being clear.

clarsach *n* the ancient small harp of Ireland and Scotland.

clash[1] *n* **1** a noisy, usu metallic, sound of collision. **2a** a hostile encounter. **b** a sharp conflict.

clash[2] *v* **1** to make a clash. **2a** (*often* + with) to come into conflict. **b** (*often* + with) to form a displeasing combination; not to match. **c** said of opinions, etc: to be incompatible or irreconcilable. ➤➤ **clasher** *n.*

clasp[1] *n* **1** a device for holding objects or parts of something together. **2** an embrace. **3** a device, e.g. a bar, attached to a medal ribbon to indicate the action or campaign at which the bearer was present.

clasp[2] *v* **1** to fasten with a clasp. **2** to enclose and hold with the arms; to embrace. **3** to seize with the hand; to grasp. ➤➤ **clasper** *n.*

clasp knife *n* a large single-bladed folding knife having a catch to hold the blade open.

class[1] *n* **1a** (*used as sing. or pl*) a group in society sharing the same economic or social status. **b** the system of differentiating society by classes. **c** *informal* high quality; elegance. **2a** (*used as sing. or pl*) a body of students meeting regularly with a teacher to study the same subject. **b** a lesson. **c** *NAm* the students who graduate in a particular year. **3** a distinct group of objects or organisms sharing common characteristics. **4a** a division or rating based on grade or quality. **b** *Brit* a level of university honours degree.

class[2] *v* to classify or grade.

class[3] *adj informal* very good; excellent; classy.

class action *n chiefly NAm* a lawsuit undertaken, often by a single litigant, on behalf of a group.

class-conscious *adj* **1** actively aware of one's common status with others in a particular class. **2** taking part in class war. ➤➤ **class-consciousness** *n.*

classic[1] *adj* **1a** serving as a standard of excellence. **b** both traditional and enduring. **c** simply and elegantly tailored so as to remain in fashion year after year. **2** being an archetypal example of some particular thing or occurrence.

Usage note

classic *or* **classical**? Something described as *classic* either sets a standard of excellence (*a classic recording*) or perfectly illustrates a particular phenomenon (*a classic case of mistaken identity*). *Classical* generally refers to ancient Greece and Rome (*classical antiquity*), to serious music (*classical composers such as Beethoven and Mozart*) or to formerly authoritative forms when contrasted with modern ones (*classical mechanics as opposed to quantum mechanics*).

classic[2] *n* **1** (*in pl*) **a** (**the classics**) literary works of ancient Greece or Rome. **b** (*often* **Classics**) Greek and Latin literature, history, and philosophy considered as an academic subject. **2** a work of lasting excellence, or the author of one. **3** a classic example; an archetype. **4** in Britain, any of five flat races for horses, the Derby, the Oaks, the St Leger, the One Thousand Guineas, and the Two Thousand Guineas.

classical *adj* **1** of or influenced by the ancient Greek and Roman world, or its art and culture. **2a** relating to music of the late 18th and early 19th cents characterized by simplicity, objectivity, and proportion. **b** relating to music in the European tradition that includes such forms as chamber music, opera, and symphony as distinguished from folk, popular music, or jazz. **3a** both authoritative and traditional. **b** constituting an early and highly influential approach to a subject that thereafter becomes standard. ➤➤ **classicality** *n,* **classically** *adj.*

Usage note

classical *or* **classic**? See note at CLASSIC[1].

classicism *n* **1** adherence to traditional standards that are considered to have universal and lasting worth. **2** the principles or style embodied in classical literature, art, or architecture.

classicist *n* **1** an advocate or student of classicism. **2** a scholar or student of Classics.

classification *n* **1** systematic arrangement in groups according to established criteria. **2** a class or category. ➤➤ **classificatory** *adj.*

classified *adj* **1** of information, a document, etc: withheld from general circulation for reasons of national or military security. **2** of a road: given a classification as a motorway, an A-road, or a B-road, according to its relative size and importance.

classified ad *n* (*usu in pl*) an advertisement in a newspaper or periodical, usu in small type and grouped according to subject.

classify *v* (**-ies, -ied**) **1a** to arrange in classes. **b** (*often* + as) to assign to a category. **2** to designate (a document, information, etc) as secret. ➤➤ **classifiable** *adj,* **classifier** *n.*

classless *adj* **1** free from class distinction. **2** belonging to no particular social class. ➤➤ **classlessness** *n.*

classroom *n* a room where classes are held, *esp* in a school.

class struggle *n* (*often* **the class struggle**) in Marxist theory, the struggle for economic and political power between the workers and the capitalists and ruling class in a capitalist society.

classy *adj* (**-ier, -iest**) *informal* elegant; stylish. ➤➤ **classiness** *n.*

clatter *v* **1** to make a loud rattling or banging noise. **2** to move or go with a loud rattling or banging noise. ➤➤ **clatter** *n,* **clatterer** *n,* **clatteringly** *adv.*

clause *n* **1** a string of words containing a subject and predicate and functioning either as a sentence or as part of a sentence. **2** a distinct article or condition in a formal document. ➤➤ **clausal** *adj.*

claustrophobia *n* abnormal dread of being in closed or confined spaces. ➤➤ **claustrophobe** *n.*

claustrophobic *adj* **1** suffering from claustrophobia. **2** of a place or situation: making one feel uncomfortable, as if suffering from claustrophobia.

clavichord *n* an early keyboard musical instrument, with strings that are struck by small brass blades.

clavicle *n* a shoulder bone typically linking the shoulder blade and breastbone in humans and other vertebrates; the collarbone. ➤➤ **clavicular** *adj.*

claw[1] *n* **1** a sharp curved nail on an animal's toe. **2** a pincer-like organ on the end of some limbs of a lobster, scorpion, or similar arthropod. **3** something, e.g. the forked end of a claw hammer, resembling a claw. ➤➤ **clawed** *adj,* **clawless** *adj.*

claw[2] *v* to rake, seize or dig with, or as if with, claws.

claw back *v* **1** to get or take back with difficulty or harshness. **2** to take (money) back, *esp* by taxation. ➤➤ **claw-back** *n.*

claw hammer *n* a hammer with one end of the head forked for pulling out nails.

clay *n* **1a** an earthy material, soft when moist but hard when fired, used for making brick, tile, and pottery, or soil composed chiefly of this. **b** thick and clinging earth or mud. **2** the human body as distinguished from the spirit. ➤➤ **clayey** *adj,* **clayish** *adj.*

claymore *n* a large two-edged broadsword formerly used by Scottish Highlanders.

clay pigeon *n* a saucer-shaped object, usu made of baked clay, thrown into the air as a target for shooting at with a shotgun for sport.

clean[1] *adj* **1a** free or relatively free from dirt. **b** habitually keeping oneself clean. **2a** free from contamination, pollution, infection, or disease. **b** producing little or no radioactive fallout. **3a** free from illegal, immoral, or disreputable activities. **b** not risqué, smutty, or obscene. **c** of a driving licence: free from endorsements or penalty points. **d** *NAm, informal* carrying no concealed weapons, illegal drugs, etc. **4** observing the rules; fair. **5** thorough; complete: *a clean break with the past.* **6a** of a sheet of paper, etc: unused; without anything on it. **b** of a copy: legible and with few corrections or alterations. **7a** characterized by clarity, precision, or deftness. **b** not jagged; smooth. ✱ **a clean sheet/slate** a situation in which no record is kept of past errors, previous decisions, etc. **a clean sweep 1** the removal of everything and everyone that is not wanted. **2** the winning of all prizes, etc. **make a clean breast of it** to make a full confession. ➤➤ **cleanly** *adv,* **cleanness** *n.*

clean[2] *adv* **1** all the way; completely. **2a** so as to leave something clean. **b** in a fair manner; according to the rules.

clean[3] *v* **1** to make clean. **2a** (*often* + out) to strip or empty (something). **b** (*often* + out) to deprive (somebody) of money or possessions. **3** to be cleanable. ➤➤ **cleanable** *adj.*

clean[4] *n* an act of cleaning away dirt.

clean-cut *adj* **1** sharply defined; clear. **2** of a person: clean and neat in appearance.

cleaner *n* **1** somebody whose occupation is cleaning rooms or clothes. **2** a substance, implement, or machine for cleaning. ✱ **take to the cleaners** *informal* to rob or defraud.

cleanliness *n* fastidiousness in keeping things or one's person clean. ➤➤ **cleanly** *adj.*

cleanse *v* **1** to clean thoroughly, e.g. with a lotion or cleanser. **2** to free from something undesirable or corrupting. **3** to make ritually pure. ➤➤ **cleanser** *n.*

clean-shaven *adj* with the hair of the beard and moustache shaved off.

clean up *v* **1** to make clean. **2** *informal* to make a large gain, e.g. in business or gambling. ➤➤ **clean-up** *n.*

clear[1] *adj* **1** easy to understand, not complicated or ambiguous. **2a** easily visible. **b** easily audible. **3a** transparent. **b** of the air or sky: free from cloud, mist, or dust. **4a** free from obstructions. **b** (+ of) not touching. **c** (+ of) no longer troubled by. **5a** of somebody's thinking: not vague; incisive. **b** free from doubt; sure. **6a** free from blemishes, disease, or pollution. **b** free from guilt. **7a** of income, profit: net. **b** full: *six clear days.*

clear[2] *adv* **1** clearly. **2** *chiefly NAm* all the way.

clear[3] *v* **1a** to free from obstructions or unwanted material. **b** to evacuate (an area, a building). **2** (*often* + off/up/away) to remove or dispose of (something) that is no longer wanted. **3** in football, to kick (the ball) away from the goal as a defensive measure. **4** to free from accusation or blame. **5a** (*often* + off) to settle or discharge (a debt, etc). **b** to deal with (work) until it is finished or settled. **c** to earn (a certain sum of money) without deduction. **d** to put (a cheque) through a clearing house. **6** to authorize or cause to be authorized. **7** to go over (an obstacle) without touching it. **8** to make or become transparent or translucent. **9** (*often* + up) of the weather: to become free from rain, mist, etc. ✱ **clear the air** to remove tension or hostility by open discussion. **clear the decks** to prepare for action. ➤➤ **clearable** *adj,* **clearer** *n.*

clearance *n* **1** the removal of obstructions. **2** the clear *esp* vertical space between objects. **3** authorization. **4** (*also* **clearance sale**) a sale to clear out stock. **5** in football, a kick to clear the ball.

clear-cut *adj* **1** sharply outlined; distinct. **2** free from ambiguity or uncertainty.

clearheaded *adj* **1** not confused; sensible; rational. **2** having no illusions about a state of affairs; realistic.

clearing *n* an area of land cleared of wood and brush.

clearing bank *n* a bank that is a member of a clearing house.

clearing house *n* **1** an establishment maintained by banks for settling mutual claims and accounts. **2** an agency for collecting, classifying, and distributing something, *esp* information.

clear off *v informal* to go away.

clear out *v* **1** to use or empty all the contents of. **2** *informal* to go away; to leave a place. ➤➤ **clear-out** *n.*

clear-sighted *adj* CLEARHEADED (2), *esp* having perceptive insight.

clear up *v* **1a** to remove (a mess, etc). **b** to tidy (a room, etc) by removing unwanted things. **2** to provide a solution or explanation for (a problem or mystery). **3** of an illness, etc: to be cured or alleviated.

clearway *n Brit* a road on which vehicles may stop only in an emergency.

cleat *n* **1** a projecting piece, e.g. on the bottom of a shoe, that provides a grip. **2a** a wedge-shaped piece serving as a support or check. **b** a wooden or metal fitting, usu with two projecting horns, round which a rope may be made fast.

cleavage *n* **1** the space between a woman's breasts. **2** a division. **3** = CELL DIVISION. **4** the property of a crystal or rock, e.g. slate, of splitting along definite planes.

cleave[1] *v* (*past tense* **clove** *or* **cleft** *or* **cleaved,** *past part.* **cloven** *or* **cleft** *or* **cleaved**) **1** to split, *esp* along the grain. **2** to create (a path) through something as if by cutting. ➤➤ **cleavable** *adj.*

cleave[2] *v* (*past tense* **cleaved**) **1** (+ to) to stick firmly and loyally. **2** (+ to) to be devoted.

cleaver *n* a butcher's chopping implement with a heavy rectangular blade.

clef *n* a sign placed on a musical stave to indicate the pitch represented by the notes following it.

cleft[1] *n* **1** a space or opening made by splitting. **2** a V-shaped indented formation; a hollow between ridges or protuberances.

cleft[2] *v* past tense and past part. of CLEAVE[1].

cleft lip *n* = HARELIP.

cleft palate *n* a congenital fissure of the roof of the mouth.

cleft stick *n chiefly Brit* a dilemma.

clematis *n* a climbing plant of the buttercup family with three leaflets on each leaf and white, pink, or purple flowers.

clement *adj* **1** of the weather: pleasantly mild. **2** inclined to be merciful; lenient. ➤➤ **clemency** *n.*

clementine *n* a small citrus fruit, with pink-tinged flesh, that is a cross between an orange and a tangerine.

clench *v* **1** to close or hold (the fists, teeth, etc) together tightly. **2** to grip or clutch firmly. **3** of a set of muscles: to contract suddenly.

clerestory *n* (*pl* **-ies**) *esp* in church architecture, the part of an outside wall that rises above an adjoining roof.

clergy *n* (*used as sing. or pl*) the group of people ordained to act as priests or ministers in an organized religion *esp* a Christian church.

clergyman *or* **clergywoman** *n* (*pl* **clergymen** *or* **clergywomen**) an ordained minister.

cleric *n* a member of the Christian clergy, or a minister or leader from another religion.

clerical *adj* **1** involving office work of a fairly routine kind, such as typing, copying, and filing. **2** relating to or characteristic of the clergy. ➤➤ **clerically** *adv.*

clerical collar *n* a narrow stiff upright white collar worn by clergymen.

clerical error *n* a mistake in a document made when it was being written or copied out.

clerihew *n* a witty pseudo-biographical four-line verse.

clerk[1] *n* **1a** somebody whose occupation is keeping records or accounts or doing general office work. **b** an official who keeps records and does administrative work for a council or court. **2** *NAm* **a** a shop assistant. **b** a hotel receptionist. ➤➤ **clerkly** *adj,* **clerkship** *n.*

clerk[2] *v* to act or work as a clerk.

clever *adj* (**cleverer, cleverest**) **1a** mentally quick and resourceful; intelligent. **b** characterized by intelligence or ingenuity. **2** skilful or adroit with the hands or body. ➤➤ **cleverly** *adv,* **cleverness** *n.*

clever-clever *adj derog* over-ingenious, or trying too hard to be or appear clever.

clever clogs *n* = CLEVER DICK.

clever dick *n Brit, informal* a person who is ostentatiously or annoyingly clever.

clew[1] *n* **1a** the lower corner of a square sail. **b** a metal loop attached to this. **2** (*in pl*) the cords for hanging a hammock.

clew[2] *v* to haul (a sail) up or down by ropes through the clews.

cliché *n* **1** a hackneyed phrase or expression, or the idea expressed by it. **2** a hackneyed theme or situation. ➤➤ **clichéd** *adj,* **cliché'd** *adj.*

click[1] *n* **1** a light sharp sound made, for example, when one metal or plastic part locks into another. **2** a sharp speech sound in some languages. **3** in computing, an action of pressing and releasing a button on a mouse.

click[2] *v* **1** to produce or make (something) produce a click. **2a** in computing, to press and release (a button on a mouse). **b** (*often* + on) in computing, to carry out an operation by moving the pointer on the screen over (something) and pressing the mouse button. **3** *informal* **a** (*often* + with) to strike up an immediately warm friendship with somebody. **b** (*usu* + with) to become successful or popular. **4** *Brit* to cause sudden insight or recognition. ➤➤ **clicker** *n.*

client *n* **1a** somebody who receives the advice or services of a professional person or organization. **b** a customer. **2a** a person for whom a social worker has responsibility. **b** a patient of a particular doctor or hospital. **3a** in computing, a computer to which data is provided by a server. **b** in computing, a program used to contact another computer or a network and request data from it. ➤➤ **clientage** *n,* **cliental** *adj.*

clientele *n* (*used as sing. or pl*) a body of clients.

cliff *n* a very steep high face of rock, earth, ice, etc. ➤➤ **cliffy** *adj.*

cliffhanger *n* a story, or an episode in a story, that ends in extreme suspense; any suspenseful situation. ➤➤ **cliff-hanging** *adj.*

climacteric[1] *adj* **1** of crucial importance, or having vital consequences or implications. **2** relating to or being a climacteric.

climacteric[2] *n* **1** a major turning point or critical stage; *specif* one supposed to occur at intervals of seven years. **2** the menopause, or a corresponding period in males.

climactic *adj* causing or forming a climax. ➤➤ **climactically** *adv.*

climate *n* **1a** the average weather conditions over a period of years as shown by temperature, wind, rain, etc. **b** a region of the earth having a particular type of weather conditions. **2** the prevailing state of affairs or feelings of a group or period. ➤➤ **climatic** *adj,* **climatical** *adj,* **climatically** *adv,* **climatological** *adj,* **climatology** *n.*

climate control *n* = AIR CONDITIONING.

climax[1] *n* **1** the highest point or point of maximum intensity or highest dramatic tension. **2** = ORGASM.

climax[2] *v* to come or bring to a climax.

climb[1] *v* **1a** to go up or down a more or less vertical surface using the hands to grasp or give support. **b** of a plant: to ascend while growing, e.g. by twining. **2a** to go gradually upwards; to rise. **b** to slope upwards. **3** to increase in amount or value. **4** to get into or out of clothing, a confined space, etc, usu with effort. **5** to go up mountains for sport. ➤➤ **climbable** *adj.*

climb² *n* **1** an ascent by climbing. **2a** a route taken by climbers. **b** a steep slope or ascent. **3** an increase, *esp* a sudden one, in amount or value.

climb down *v* to withdraw from a position in an argument; to back down. ➤➤ **climbdown** *n.*

climber *n* **1** a person who climbs hills or mountains. **2** a climbing plant. **3** *chiefly Brit* = SOCIAL CLIMBER.

climbing frame *n Brit* a framework for children to climb on.

climbing wall *n* a wall fitted with artificial hand- and footholds to provide practice in rock climbing.

clime *n chiefly literary* (*usu in pl*) = CLIMATE (1B).

clinch¹ *v* **1** to make final; to settle. **2a** to turn over or flatten the protruding pointed end of (e.g. a driven nail). **b** to fasten (something) in this way. **3a** in boxing or wrestling, to hold an opponent at close quarters. **b** *informal* to embrace or hug somebody.

clinch² *n* **1** in boxing or wrestling, an act or instance of clinching. **2a** *informal* an embrace. **b** a fastening by means of a clinched nail, rivet, or bolt.

clincher *n informal* a decisive fact, argument, act, or remark.

cline *n* a graded series of differences shown by a group of related organisms; *broadly* a continuum. ➤➤ **clinal** *adj.*

-cline *comb. form* forming nouns, denoting: a slope.

cling *v* (*past tense and past part.* **clung**) **1a** (+ to/onto) to hold on tightly or tenaciously. **b** (+ to/onto) to stick as if glued firmly. **2a** to have a strong emotional attachment or dependence. **b** (+ to) to remain stubbornly attached to or convinced of. ➤➤ **clingy** *adj.*

clingfilm *n* a thin transparent plastic film used to wrap foodstuffs in and keep them fresh.

clinic *n* **1a** a place where treatment or advice is given in a specified area of medicine. **b** part of a hospital where medical treatment is given to outpatients. **2** a bedside class for medical students in which patients are examined and discussed. **3a** a meeting where an expert or person in authority discusses people's problems with them. **b** a session in which skills or knowledge are taught by an expert, *esp* remedially.

clinical *adj* **1** based on direct observation of a patient or a group of patients. **2** analytic or detached. **3** of a room, surroundings, etc: severely plain and functional. ➤➤ **clinically** *adv.*

clinical psychology *n* the branch of psychology concerned with the diagnosis and treatment of mental illness.

clinician *n* somebody qualified in clinical medicine, psychiatry, etc as distinguished from somebody specializing in laboratory or research techniques.

clink¹ *v* to make a slight sharp short metallic sound. ➤➤ **clink** *n.*

clink² *n slang* prison.

clinker *n* **1** stony matter fused by fire; slag. **2** a vitrified brick.

clinker-built *adj* of a boat: having the lower edge of each external plank or plate overlapping the upper edge of the one below it: compare CARVEL-BUILT.

clip¹ *v* (**clipped, clipping**) **1** to clasp or fasten with a clip. **2** (*often* + on) to be or become attached by means of a clip.

clip² *n* **1** a device that grips or holds objects together or in position. **2** a piece of jewellery held in position by a spring clip. **3** a device to hold cartridges that is inserted into a magazine of an automatic firearm.

clip³ *v* (**clipped, clipping**) **1** to cut (hair or wool) with shears. **2** to cut off the end or outer part of. **3** to abbreviate (letters or words) in speech or writing. **4** *informal* to hit with a glancing blow; *also* to hit smartly.

clip⁴ *n* **1** an act of clipping, or the manner in which something is clipped. **2** a section of filmed material, *esp* an excerpt from a feature film. **3** *informal* a sharp blow. **4** *informal* a rapid pace or speed.

clip art *n* in computing, ready-drawn pictures, symbols, etc provided in software programs for users to insert into their own documents.

clipboard *n* **1** a small writing board with a spring clip for holding papers. **2** a temporary storage area in word-processing programs where removed or copied data is held.

clip-clop *v* (**clip-clopped, clip-clopping**) *informal* to make the rhythmic repeated sound characteristic of horses' hooves. ➤➤ **clip-clop** *n.*

clip joint *n informal* a nightclub or bar that defrauds, overcharges, etc.

clip-on *adj* incorporating a clip for easy fastening to something else.

clip-ons *pl n* **1** sunglasses that clip onto spectacles. **2** earrings that clip onto ears.

clipped *adj* said of a person's way of speaking: tersely quick and distinct.

clipper *n* **1** (*usu in pl*) an implement for trimming hair or nails. **2** a fast sailing ship.

clipping *n chiefly NAm* a piece cut or trimmed from something, e.g. from a newspaper.

clique *n* (*used as sing. or pl*) a highly exclusive and often aloof group of people held together by common interests, views, etc. ➤➤ **cliquey** *adj,* **cliquish** *adj.*

clitoridectomy *n* (*pl* **-ies**) surgical removal of the clitoris; female circumcision.

clitoris *n* a mainly internal erectile organ at the front or top part of the vulva that is a centre of sexual sensation in females. ➤➤ **clitoral** *adj.*

cloaca *n* (*pl* **cloacae**) the chamber into which the intestinal, urinary, and generative canals discharge, *esp* in birds, reptiles, amphibians, and many fishes. ➤➤ **cloacal** *adj.*

cloak¹ *n* **1** a long sleeveless outer garment that usu fastens at the neck and hangs loosely from the shoulders. **2** something that conceals; a pretence or disguise.

cloak² *v* to cover or hide with, or as if with, a cloak.

cloak-and-dagger *adj* involving melodramatic intrigue and usu espionage.

cloakroom *n* **1** a room in which outdoor clothing or luggage may be left. **2** *chiefly Brit, euphem* a room with a toilet.

clobber¹ *n Brit, informal* gear, paraphernalia; *esp* clothes worn for a usu specified purpose or function.

clobber² *v informal* **1** to hit with force. **2** to defeat overwhelmingly.

cloche *n* **1** a translucent cover used for protecting outdoor plants. **2** a woman's soft close-fitting hat with rounded crown and narrow brim.

clock¹ *n* **1** a device with a dial and hands or a digital display for indicating or measuring time. **2** *informal* a recording or metering device, *esp* a speedometer or milometer. **3** *Brit, informal* a person's face. **4** *Brit* the fluffy head of a dandelion when it has gone to seed. ✱ **against the clock** within a strictly limited space of time. **round the clock** continuously all day and night. **turn back the clock** to revert to a past state or condition.

clock[2] *v* **1** *esp* in sports, to time with a stopwatch or electric timing device. **2a** to register (a time, distance, or speed) on a mechanical recording device. **b** *Brit, informal* (*often* + up) to attain (a time, speed, etc) or achieve (a victory, success, etc). **3** *informal* to hit. **4** *Brit, informal* to see or observe. **5** *Brit, informal* to turn back the milometer of (a vehicle) illegally.

clock[3] *n* an ornamental pattern on the outside ankle of a stocking or sock.

clock in *v* to record the time of one's arrival at work by means of a time clock.

clock off *v* = CLOCK OUT.

clock on *v* = CLOCK IN.

clock out *v* to record the time of one's departure from work by means of a time clock.

clock speed *n* in computing, the speed at which a processor is able to perform its operations, usu measured in megahertz.

clock-watcher *n* a person who keeps close watch on the time in order not to work a moment longer than he or she has to. ➤➤ **clock-watching** *n.*

clockwise *adv* in the direction in which the hands of a clock rotate as viewed from in front. ➤➤ **clockwise** *adj.*

clockwork *n* a mechanism like that of a mechanical clock with toothed gearwheels and powered by a coiled spring. ✻ **like clockwork** smoothly and with no hitches.

clod *n* **1** a lump of earth or clay. **2** an oaf or dolt. ➤➤ **cloddish** *adj,* **cloddishly** *adv,* **cloddishness** *n,* **cloddy** *adj.*

clodhopper *n informal* **1** a large heavy shoe. **2** an awkward or clumsy person. ➤➤ **clodhopping** *adj.*

clog[1] *n* **1** a shoe, sandal, etc with a thick wooden sole. **2** an impediment or encumbrance.

clog[2] *v* (**clogged, clogging**) **1** (*often* + up) to block or become blocked *esp* with sticky or matted material. **2** to halt or retard the operation or growth of. ➤➤ **cloggy** *adj.*

cloisonné /'klwazonay, klwah'zonay/ *n* a style of enamel decoration in which the enamel is fired in raised sections separated by fine wire or thin metal strips.

cloister[1] *n* **1** a covered passage with arches or columns on the inner side, along the wall of a courtyard in a church, monastery, college, etc. **2** (**the cloister**) the monastic life. ➤➤ **cloistral** *adj.*

cloister[2] *v* to seclude (somebody or oneself) from the world.

cloistered *adj* **1a** kept apart or sheltered from everyday life. **b** suggestive of the seclusion of a monastic cloister. **2** surrounded with a cloister.

clomp *v* to tread clumsily; to clump.

clone[1] *n* **1** an asexually produced individual identical to its parent. **2** *informal* an exact or very close copy of somebody or something. ➤➤ **clonal** *adj.*

clone[2] *v* **1** to cause (a cell or organism) to grow as a clone. **2** to make a clone or a very close copy of.

clonk *v* **1** to make a dull heavy thumping sound like a hard object hitting a hard but hollow surface. **2** *informal* to hit (somebody or something). ➤➤ **clonk** *n.*

clop *n* a sound made by a hoof or shoe on a hard surface. ➤➤ **clop** *v.*

close[1] *adj* **1** near in space or time. **2** of relatives: near in relationship. **3** intimate or affectionate. **4a** of a connection: strong. **b** of a resemblance: showing only small variations. **5** having little space in between; dense. **6** of a haircut: very short. **7** fitting neatly or tightly. **8** of a game or contest: evenly contested. **9** very careful and concentrated. **10** of the weather, or a room or building: hot and stuffy; airless. **11a** secretive or reticent. **b** not generous, *esp* with money; mean. ✻ **close to home** see HOME[1]. ➤➤ **closely** *adv,* **closeness** *n.*

close[2] *adv* (**closer, closest**) in or into a close position or manner; near. ✻ **close on** almost. **come close to doing something** almost to do something.

close[3] *n* **1** *Brit* a road closed at one end. **2** *Brit* the precinct of a cathedral.

close[4] *v* **1a** to move something in a position to cover an opening. **b** to cover or shut (something that is open). **c** to become covered, or in a position that covers an opening: *The door slowly closed.* **2** to prevent access to (a road or entrance). **3** to bring or come to an end. **4a** (*often* + down) of a business, etc: to suspend or stop operations. **b** of a shop: to stop trading for the day. **5** (*often* + on/in on) to come closer to (somebody), *esp* in order to challenge them.

close[5] *n* the end or conclusion of something.

close call *n* a narrow escape.

closed *adj* **1a** not open. **b** not allowing entry; blocked. **2a** of a system or society: forming a self-contained unit; self-sufficient. **b** limited or restricted. **3** of a curve: fully enclosing an area. ✻ **behind closed doors** in secret.

closed-circuit television *n* a television system or installation in which the signal is transmitted by wire to a limited number of receivers, usu in one location.

closed shop *n* an establishment which employs only union members: compare OPEN SHOP.

close-fisted *adj* not generous with money; mean.

close harmony *n* harmony using chords in which the notes are close together.

close-hauled *adj and adv* of a ship: with the sails set for sailing as near directly into the wind as possible.

close in *v* **1** (*often* + on) to approach and surround a place. **2** to become progressively darker in the evenings towards the winter solstice.

close-knit *adj* bound together by strong ties of familiarity and affection.

close quarters *pl n* (*usu* + at) immediate contact or short range.

close season *n Brit* **1** a period during which it is illegal to kill or catch certain game or fish. **2** a period of the year when there is no play in a particular sport.

close shave *n informal* a narrow escape.

closet[1] *n* **1** a small or private room. **2** *archaic* = WATER CLOSET. **3** *chiefly NAm* a cupboard. ✻ **come out of the closet** to declare oneself to be a homosexual.

closet[2] *v* (**closeted, closeting**) **1** to take (somebody) into a private place for a secret interview. **2** to shut (oneself) up in a closet, or as if in a closet.

closet[3] *adj* being privately but not overtly as specified; secret.

close up *v* to become closer together.

close-up *n* a photograph or film shot taken at close range.

clostridium *n* (*pl* **clostridia**) a spore-forming soil or intestinal bacterium that causes gas gangrene, tetanus, and other diseases. ➤➤ **clostridial** *adj.*

closure *n* **1** the act of closing or the state of being closed. **2** the closing of debate in a legislative body, *esp* by calling for a vote. **3** a device that closes or seals a container.

clot[1] *n* **1a** a roundish viscous lump formed by coagulation of a portion of liquid, e.g. cream. **b** a coagulated mass produced by clotting of blood. **2** *Brit, informal* a stupid person.

clot[2] *v* (**clotted, clotting**) to become a clot; to form clots or cause (a liquid) to clot.

cloth *n* (*pl* **cloths**) **1** a pliable material made usu by weaving, felting, or knitting natural or synthetic fibres and filaments. **2** a piece of cloth adapted for a particular purpose. **3** a profession or calling distinguished by its dress; *specif* the clergy.

cloth-cap *adj Brit, informal* working-class.

clothe *v* (*past tense and past part.* **clothed** *or* **clad**) **1** to cover with clothing. **2** to provide with clothes.

cloth-eared *adj Brit, informal* irritatingly deficient in hearing.

clothes *pl n* articles of material worn to cover the body, for warmth, protection, or decoration.

clotheshorse *n* a frame on which to hang clothes, *esp* for drying or airing indoors.

clothesline *n* a line on which clothes may be hung to dry, *esp* outdoors.

clothes moth *n* a small yellowish or buff-coloured moth whose larvae eat wool, fur, hair, or feathers.

clothes peg *n* a clip or forked device used for holding clothes or washing on a line.

clothespin *n NAm* = CLOTHES PEG.

clothier *n* somebody who makes or sells cloth or clothing.

clothing *n* = CLOTHES.

clotted cream *n* a thick cream made by slowly heating whole milk and then skimming the cooled cream from the top.

clotting factor *n* any of a number of substances, including Factor 8, which is needed in the blood to allow clotting.

cloud[1] *n* **1a** a visible mass of particles of water or ice at a usu great height in the air. **b** a light filmy, puffy, or billowy mass seeming to float in the air. **2** a great crowd or multitude; a swarm, *esp* of insects. **3** something that obscures or blemishes or causes a feeling of gloom. ✱ **on cloud nine** *informal* feeling extremely elated or happy. **under a cloud** under suspicion or in a bad mood. **with one's head in the clouds** out of touch with reality. ➤➤ **cloudless** *adj*, **cloudlet** *n*.

cloud[2] *v* **1** (+ over/up) to grow cloudy. **2a** of facial features: to become troubled, apprehensive, etc. **b** to become blurred, dubious, or ominous. **3a** to envelop or obscure with a cloud, or as if with a cloud. **b** to make opaque or murky by condensation, smoke, etc. **4** to make unclear or confused.

cloudburst *n* a sudden very heavy fall of rain.

cloud-cuckoo-land *n* a utopian world that exists only in the mind of someone who is resolutely idealistic and impractical.

cloudy *adj* (**-ier, -iest**) **1a** of the sky: overcast with clouds. **b** of the weather: characterized by overcast skies and little sunshine. **2** not clear or transparent. **3** anxious or gloomy. ➤➤ **cloudily** *adv*, **cloudiness** *n*.

clout[1] *n* **1** *informal* a blow or hit. **2** *informal* influence; *esp* effective political power. **3** *chiefly N Eng, Scot dialect* a piece of cloth, *esp* a piece of cloth or rag.

clout[2] *v informal* to hit forcefully.

clove[1] *n* any of the small bulbs, e.g. in garlic, developed as parts of a larger bulb.

clove[2] *n* the dried unopened flower bud of a tropical tree, shaped like a small brown spike, used as a spice and for making oil.

clove[3] *v* past tense of CLEAVE[1].

clove hitch *n* a knot used to secure a rope temporarily to a spar or another rope.

cloven *v* past part. of CLEAVE[1].

cloven foot *n* a foot, e.g. of a sheep, divided into two parts at the end farthest from the body. ➤➤ **cloven-footed** *adj*.

cloven hoof *n* **1** = CLOVEN FOOT. **2** the sign of Satan or the devil. ➤➤ **cloven-hoofed** *adj*.

clove oil *n* an aromatic oil obtained from clove flowers and used medicinally, *esp* in dentistry, to relieve pain.

clover *n* a leguminous fodder plant with leaves that have three leaflets and flowers in dense heads. ✱ **in clover** in prosperity or in pleasant circumstances.

clown[1] *n* **1** an entertainer who wears a grotesquely comic costume and makeup; *specif* a traditionally dressed comedy performer in a circus. **2** somebody who habitually acts in a ridiculously comical way or plays the fool; a joker. ➤➤ **clownish** *adj*.

clown[2] *v* (*usu* + about/around) to act as or like a clown.

cloy *v* **1** to make weary or satiated with an excess, usu of something orig pleasing. **2** to cause a feeling of distaste or excess. ➤➤ **cloying** *adj*, **cloyingly** *adv*.

cloze test *n* an educational test in which the reader has to replace words that have been deleted from a text.

club[1] *n* **1** an association of people with a common interest or who jointly engage in a particular activity. **2a** an association of people that has premises available for members to stay, eat, or socialize. **b** the meeting place or premises of a club. **3** = NIGHTCLUB. **4a** a heavy stick thicker at one end than the other and used as a hand weapon. **b** in golf and other games, a stick or bat used to hit a ball. **5a** a playing card marked with one or more black figures in the shape of a cloverleaf. **b** (*in pl, used as sing. or pl*) the suit comprising cards identified by this figure.

club[2] *v* (**clubbed, clubbing**) **1** to beat or strike (a person or an animal) with a club, or as if with a club. **2** (+ together) to combine to share a common expense or object. **3** *informal* to go to nightclubs.

clubbable *or* **clubable** *adj* sociable.

clubber *n* somebody who frequents nightclubs.

club car *n NAm* a lounge car on a train.

club class *n Brit* a class of air travel between first class and economy class, used *esp* by business travellers.

club foot *n* a misshapen foot twisted out of position from birth.

clubhouse *n* **1** a house occupied by a club or used for club activities. **2** a building that has changing rooms and social facilities for a sports club.

club moss *n* a primitive vascular plant.

clubroot *n* a disease of cabbages and related plants characterized by swellings or distortions of the root.

club sandwich *n* a sandwich of three slices of bread with two layers of filling.

club soda *n NAm* soda water.

cluck *v* **1** to make the guttural sound of a hen. **2** *informal* (+ over) to express fussy interest or concern. ➤➤ **cluck** *n*.

clucky *adj* (**-ier, -iest**) **1** of a hen: sitting on or ready to sit on eggs. **2** *Aus, informal* of a woman: obsessed with children; broody.

clue[1] *n* **1** something that helps to solve a problem or mystery. **2** a cryptic phrase or anagram that has to be solved as part of a crossword puzzle. ✱ **not have a clue 1** to know nothing. **2** to be incompetent.

clue[2] *v* (**clues, clued, clueing** *or* **cluing**) *informal* (*usu* + in/up) to inform (somebody) of something.

clued-up *adj* well informed.

clueless *adj Brit, informal* hopelessly ignorant or lacking in ability, knowledge, or common sense. ⋙ **cluelessness** *n.*

clump[1] *n* **1** a compact group of things of the same kind, *esp* trees or bushes; a cluster. **2** a compact mass. **3** a heavy tramping sound. ⋙ **clumpy** *adj.*

clump[2] *v* **1** to tread clumsily and noisily. **2** to form clumps.

clumsy *adj* (**-ier, -iest**) **1a** awkward and ungraceful in movement or action. **b** lacking tact or subtlety. **2** awkwardly or poorly made; unwieldy. ⋙ **clumsily** *adv,* **clumsiness** *n.*

clung *v* past tense and past part. of CLING.

Cluniac *adj* of the monastery of Cluny and the reformed Benedictine order founded there in 910.

clunk *v* to make a soft metallic sound or a heavy thump. ⋙ **clunk** *n.*

cluster[1] *n* **1** a compact group formed by a number of similar things or people; a bunch. **2** a group of faint stars or galaxies that appear close together.

cluster[2] *v* **1** to collect (people or things) into a cluster. **2** (*often* + about/around) to grow or assemble in a cluster.

cluster bomb *n* a bomb that explodes to release many smaller usu incendiary or fragmentation missiles.

clutch[1] *v* **1** to grasp or hold tightly or suddenly. **2** (*often* + at) to seek to grasp and hold.

clutch[2] *n* **1a** the claws or a hand in the act of grasping or seizing firmly. **b** (*in pl*) control or possession. **2a** a coupling used to connect and disconnect a driving and a driven part of a mechanism. **b** a lever or pedal operating such a clutch, *esp* in a motor vehicle.

clutch[3] *n* **1** a nest of eggs or a brood of chicks. **2** a group of people or things.

clutch bag *n* a small handbag with no handle.

clutter[1] *v* (*often* + up) to fill or cover (a surface or room) with scattered or disordered things.

clutter[2] *n* **1** a crowded or confused mass or collection. **2** scattered or disordered material.

Cm *abbr* the chemical symbol for curium.

cm *abbr* centimetre.

CMG *abbr Brit* Companion of the Order of St Michael and St George.

CMV *abbr* cytomegalovirus.

CNAA *abbr* Council for National Academic Awards.

CND *abbr* Campaign for Nuclear Disarmament.

CNN *abbr* Cable News Network.

CNS *abbr* central nervous system.

CO *abbr* **1** Colorado (US postal abbreviation). **2** commanding officer.

Co *abbr* the chemical symbol for cobalt.

co. *or* **Co.** *abbr* **1** company. **2** county.

c/o *abbr* care of.

co- *prefix* **1** with or together: *coexist; co-education.* **2** sharing: *co-author; co-pilot.*

coach[1] *n* **1** *chiefly Brit* **a** a usu single-deck bus used for long-distance or charter work. **b** a railway carriage. **2** a large, usu closed, four-wheeled horse-drawn carriage. **3a** somebody who instructs or trains a performer, sportsperson, etc. **b** a private tutor.

coach[2] *v* **1** to train (somebody) intensively by instruction, demonstration, and practice. **2** to act as coach to (a person or team). **3** to travel in a coach.

coach-built *adj* of a vehicle body: built to individual requirements by craftsmen. ⋙ **coachbuilder** *n.*

coachwork *n* the bodywork of a road or rail vehicle.

coagulant *n* something that produces coagulation.

coagulate[1] *v* **1** to cause (a fluid) to become viscous or thickened into a coherent mass. **2** to become viscous; to curdle or clot. ⋙ **coagulable** *adj,* **coagulation** *n,* **coagulator** *n.*

coagulate[2] *n* a substance produced by coagulation.

coal *n* **1** a black solid combustible mineral, mined from the ground, consisting chiefly of carbonized vegetable matter and widely used as a natural fuel. **2** a small piece of this. ✱ **coals to Newcastle** something taken or sent to a place that already has plenty of it. ⋙ **coaly** *adj.*

coalesce *v* to unite into a whole; to fuse. ⋙ **coalescence** *n,* **coalescent** *adj.*

coalface *n* the exposed seam ready to be worked in a coalmine. ✱ **at the coalface** engaged in practical or hard physical work; *esp* as opposed to theoretical or managerial work.

coalfield *n* a region in which deposits of coal occur.

coal gas *n* gas made from burning coal; *esp* gas made by carbonizing bituminous coal and used for heating and lighting.

coalition *n* (*used as sing. or pl*) a temporary alliance, e.g. of political parties, for joint action such as forming a government. ⋙ **coalitionist** *n.*

coalmine *n* a mine from which coal is extracted. ⋙ **coalminer** *n,* **coalmining** *n.*

coal tar *n* tar obtained by the distilling of bituminous coal and used *esp* in making dyes and drugs.

coal tit *n* a small black-crowned European tit with a white patch on the neck.

coaming *n* a raised frame, e.g. round a hatchway in the deck of a ship, to keep out water.

coarse *adj* **1** rough in texture or tone. **2** composed of relatively large particles. **3a** crude or unrefined in taste, manners, or language; common. **b** of language: vulgar or obscene. **4** of ordinary or inferior quality or value. ⋙ **coarsely** *adv,* **coarseness** *n.*

coarse fish *n chiefly Brit* any freshwater fish not belonging to the salmon family. ⋙ **coarse fishing** *n.*

coarsen *v* to make or become coarse.

coast[1] *n* **1a** the edge of a landmass or country where it reaches the sea. **b** the land near a shore; the seashore. **2** an instance of travelling in a vehicle without the use of power. ✱ **the coast is clear** there is no danger, or the danger is past. ⋙ **coastal** *adj.*

coast[2] *v* **1a** to slide, glide, etc downhill by the force of gravity. **b** to move along without, or as if without, further application of propulsive power. **c** to proceed easily without making any special effort or becoming greatly involved or concerned. **2** to sail along the shore.

coaster *n* **1** a small vessel trading from port to port along a coast. **2** a small mat used, *esp* under a drinks glass, to protect a surface.

coastguard *n* a force responsible for maintaining lookout posts round the coast of a country, for mounting rescues at sea, preventing smuggling, etc.

coastline *n* a coast, *esp* considered with respect to its shape or characteristics.

coat[1] *n* **1** an outer garment that has sleeves and usu opens the full length of the centre front. **2** the external covering of an animal. **3** a protective layer; a coating. ➤➤ **coated** *adj.*

coat[2] *v* to cover or spread with a protective or enclosing layer.

coati *n* (*pl* **coatis**) a tropical American mammal related to the raccoon but with a longer body and tail and a long flexible snout.

coatimundi *n* (*pl* **coatimundis**) = COATI.

coating *n* a layer of one substance covering another.

coat of arms *n* (*pl* **coats of arms**) a set of distinctive heraldic shapes or representations, usu depicted on a shield, that is the central part of a heraldic achievement.

coat of mail *n* a garment of overlapping metal scales or chain mail formerly worn as armour.

coat tails *pl n* two long tapering skirts at the back of a man's tailcoat. ✱ **on somebody's coat tails** with the help, usu undeserved, of somebody else.

co-author[1] *n* a joint or associate author.

co-author[2] *v* to be a joint author of (a book, article, etc).

coax *v* **1** to influence or gently urge by caresses or flattery; to wheedle. **2** to extract or gain by means of gentle urging or flattery: *I coaxed an answer out of her.* **3** to manipulate with great perseverance and skill towards a desired condition: *He spent hours coaxing his hair into a quiff.*

coaxial *adj* **1** mounted on a common axis. **2** using or connected to a coaxial cable. ➤➤ **coaxially** *adv.*

coaxial cable *n* a conductor for high-frequency electrical signals, e.g. telephone or television signals, consisting of a tube of electrically conducting material containing and insulated from a central conducting wire.

cob *n* **1** a male swan. **2a** = CORNCOB . **b** = COBNUT. **3** a horse of a short-legged stocky breed. **4** *Brit* a small rounded usu crusty loaf.

cobalt *n* a silver-white magnetic metallic chemical element used in many alloys.

cobalt blue *n* a greenish blue pigment consisting essentially of cobalt oxide and alumina.

cobber *n Aus, informal* a man's male friend; a mate.

cobble[1] *v* **1** to repair or make (*esp* shoes). **2** (+ together) to make or assemble roughly or hastily.

cobble[2] *n* a naturally rounded stone of a size suitable for paving a street.

cobble[3] *v* to pave (a road) with cobblestones.

cobbler *n* **1** a mender or maker of leather goods, *esp* shoes. **2** *Brit, slang* (*in pl*) often used interjectionally: nonsense, rubbish. **3a** *NAm* a deep-dish fruit pie with a thick crust. **b** *Brit* a dish of stewed meat with a topping of scones.

cobblestone *n* = COBBLE[2]. ➤➤ **cobblestoned** *adj.*

cobnut *n* the nut of a European hazel tree.

Cobol *or* **COBOL** *n* a high-level computer language designed for business applications.

cobra *n* a venomous Asiatic and African snake that has grooved fangs and when excited expands the skin of the neck into a hood.

cobweb *n* a spider's web or the material from which it is spun. ➤➤ **cobwebbed** *adj,* **cobwebby** *adj.*

coca *n* a S American shrub with yellow flowers whose leaves contain cocaine and other alkaloids.

Coca-Cola *n trademark* a brand of cola.

cocaine *n* an alkaloid that is obtained from coca leaves, has been used as a local anaesthetic, and is a common drug of abuse that can result in psychological dependence.

cocci *n* pl of COCCUS.

coccus *n* (*pl* **cocci**) a spherical bacterium. ➤➤ **coccal** *adj,* **coccoid** *adj.*

coccyx *n* (*pl* **coccyges** *or* **coccyxes**) the small triangular bone at the end of the spinal column below the sacrum in human beings and the tailless apes. ➤➤ **coccygeal** *adj.*

cochineal *n* a red dyestuff consisting of the dried bodies of female cochineal insects, used *esp* as a colouring agent for food.

cochineal insect *n* a small bright red insect that feeds on cacti.

cochlea *n* (*pl* **cochleas** *or* **cochleae**) a coiled part of the inner ear of higher vertebrates that is filled with liquid through which sound waves are transmitted to the auditory nerve. ➤➤ **cochlear** *adj.*

cock[1] *n* **1** the male, *esp* the adult male, of various birds; *specif* the domestic fowl. **2** a device, e.g. a tap or valve, for regulating the flow of a liquid. **3** the hammer of a firearm, or its position when cocked ready for firing. **4** *Brit* used as a term of informal address to a man: pal. **5** *coarse slang* the penis. **6** *Brit, informal* nonsense, rubbish.

cock[2] *v* **1** to turn, tip, or tilt (something), usu to one side. **2** to draw back and set the hammer of (a firearm) for firing. **3** to turn up (e.g. the brim of a hat). ✱ **cock a snook** to react with disdain or defiance.

cockabully *n* (*pl* **-ies**) a small blunt-nosed freshwater fish found in New Zealand.

cockade *n* a rosette or knot of ribbon worn on the hat as a badge. ➤➤ **cockaded** *adj.*

cock-a-doodle-doo *interj* used to represent the crowing of a cockerel.

cock-a-hoop *adj informal* triumphantly boastful; exulting. ➤➤ **cock-a-hoop** *adv.*

cock-a-leekie *n* a chicken and leek soup.

cock-and-bull story *n* an incredible and apparently fabricated story.

cockatiel *n* a small grey Australian parrot with a crested yellow head.

cockatoo *n* (*pl* **cockatoos**) a large noisy chiefly Australasian parrot with a crest and brightly coloured plumage.

cockatrice *n* **1** a mythical creature, half snake and half cock, hatched from a cock's egg and able to kill with a look. **2** in heraldry, an animal with a dragon's tail and the body of a cock.

cockchafer *n* a large European beetle destructive to vegetation.

cockcrow *n literary* dawn.

cocked hat *n* a hat with a brim turned up at three places to give a three-cornered shape. ✱ **knock into a cocked hat** *informal* to defeat or surpass completely.

cockerel *n* a young male domestic fowl.

cocker spaniel *n* a small spaniel with long ears and silky coat.

cock-eyed *adj informal* **1a** askew or awry. **b** somewhat foolish or mad: *a cock-eyed scheme.* **2** having a squint.

cockfighting *n* the setting of specially bred cocks, usu fitted with metal spurs, to fight each other for public entertainment. ➤➤ **cockfight** *n.*

cockle[1] *n* a common edible bivalve mollusc with a ribbed shell. ✱ **warm the cockles of one's heart** to give one a feeling of pleasure mixed with slightly sentimental tenderness.

cockle² *v* to wrinkle or pucker or cause (e.g. fabric) to wrinkle.

cockleshell *n* **1** the shell of a cockle, scallop, or similar mollusc. **2** a light flimsy boat.

cockney *n* (*pl* **-eys**) **1** a native of London and now *esp* of the East End of London; traditionally somebody born within the sound of the bells of St Mary-le-Bow. **2** the dialect of London, *esp* the East End of London.

cockpit *n* **1a** a space in the fuselage of an aeroplane for the pilot and crew. **b** the driver's compartment in a racing or sports car. **2** a pit or enclosure for cockfights.

cockroach *n* an insect resembling a beetle that has a flattened body and long antennae.

cockscomb *n* the comb of a domestic fowl or related bird.

cocksure *adj informal* = COCKY. ➤➤ **cocksureness** *n.*

cocktail *n* **1a** a drink of mixed spirits or of spirits mixed with flavourings. **b** something resembling or suggesting such a drink; *esp* a mixture of diverse elements. **2a** a dish served as a starter usu consisting of seafood or fruit with a sauce. **b** a dish of finely chopped mixed fruits. **3** (*used before a noun*) suitable for social occasions involving cocktails.

cock up *v chiefly Brit, coarse slang* to spoil by bungling or incompetence. ➤➤ **cock-up** *n.*

cocky *adj* (**-ier, -iest**) *informal* marked by arrogant overconfidence or presumptuousness. ➤➤ **cockily** *adv,* **cockiness** *n.*

cocoa *n* **1** powdered ground roasted cacao seeds from which some fat has been removed. **2** a hot drink made by mixing cocoa with milk.

cocoa bean *n* the seed of the cacao tree.

cocoa butter *n* a pale vegetable fat with a low melting point obtained from cacao seeds.

coco de mer /kohkoh də 'meə/ *n* a tall palm tree of the Seychelles that produces a large nut.

coconut *n* the large oval fruit of the coconut palm with an outer fibrous husk that yields coir and a nut containing thick edible white flesh and sweet milk.

coconut ice *n* a coconut sweet with the consistency of fudge that is usu coloured pink or white.

coconut milk *n* **1** the sweet juice contained in the coconut. **2** a liquid obtained from the flesh of the coconut by pressing or boiling, used in Asian cookery.

coconut palm *n* a tall American tropical palm tree that produces coconuts.

coconut shy *n* a stall at a funfair where people throw balls at coconuts on stands.

cocoon¹ *n* **1** a silk envelope which an insect larva forms about itself and in which it passes the pupa stage. **2** a protective covering like a cocoon, e.g. for an aeroplane in storage. **3** a sheltered or insulated state of existence.

cocoon² *v* to wrap or envelop in a cocoon, or as if in a cocoon.

cocotte *n* a small ovenproof dish in which an individual portion of a particular dish is cooked and served.

COD *abbr* cash on delivery.

cod¹ *n* (*pl* **cods** *or* **cod**) a large, grey soft-finned fish with barbels (tactile organs; see BARBEL²) that is a major food fish.

cod² *n Brit, informal, dated* nonsense.

cod³ *v* (**codded, codding**) *Brit, informal* to trick or kid.

cod⁴ *n* a trick or hoax.

coda *n* **1** a concluding section to a piece of music that is formally distinct from its main structure. **2** something that serves to round out or conclude something.

coddle *v* **1** to cook (*esp* eggs) slowly in a liquid just below the boiling point. **2** to treat (a person or animal) with extreme care; to pamper. ➤➤ **coddler** *n.*

code¹ *n* **1** a system of letters, numbers, words, or symbols used to represent and replace those conveying the plain meaning of a text and to keep its contents secret. **2a** a system of letters, symbols, etc that enables information to be communicated briefly. **b** a system of numbers, symbols, etc that conveys information or instructions to a computer. **3a** a systematic body of laws, *esp* one established by statutes. **b** a set of rules or principles governing the behaviour of a particular group or individual. ➤➤ **coded** *adj.*

code² *v* to put (words) into the form or symbols of a code. ➤➤ **coder** *n.*

codeine *n* a derivative of morphine that is given orally to relieve pain and coughing.

co-dependency *n* a state of mutual dependency, *esp* a situation where somebody comes to rely psychologically on a person he or she is caring for. ➤➤ **co-dependent** *adj and n.*

codex *n* (*pl* **codices**) a manuscript book, *esp* of biblical or classical texts.

codger *n informal* an old and mildly eccentric man.

codices *n* pl of CODEX.

codicil *n* a modifying clause added to a will.

codify *v* (**-ies, -ied**) to collect and arrange (e.g. laws or rules) in a systematic form. ➤➤ **codification** *n,* **codifier** *n.*

codling¹ *n* a young cod.

codling² *n* any of several elongated greenish cooking apples.

codling moth *n* a small moth whose larva lives in apples, pears, etc.

cod-liver oil *n* an oil obtained from the liver of the cod and closely related fishes and used as a source of vitamins A and D.

codpiece *n* a flap or bag concealing an opening in the front of men's breeches, *esp* in the 15th and 16th cent.

codswallop *n chiefly Brit, informal* nonsense.

co-ed *n NAm* a female student in a co-educational institution. ➤➤ **co-ed** *adj.*

co-education *n* the education of students of both sexes at the same institution. ➤➤ **co-educational** *adj.*

coefficient *n* **1** a constant, usu a number, placed before the variable factor or factors in an algebraic expression and multiplying them. **2** a number that serves as a measure of some property or characteristic, e.g. of a device or process.

coelacanth *n* a fish with fleshy pectoral fins, known only from fossils until a living specimen was caught in S African waters in 1938.

coelenterate *n* any of a phylum of invertebrate animals including the corals, sea anemones, and jellyfishes. ➤➤ **coelenterate** *adj.*

coeliac (*NAm* **celiac**) *adj* to do with or in the region of the abdominal cavity.

coeliac disease *n* defective digestion of fats in the intestines, *esp* in young children.

coelurosaur *n* a small flesh-eating dinosaur that walked on two legs and is believed to be an ancestor of the birds.

coenobite (*NAm* **cenobite**) *n* a member of a monastic community. ➤➤ **coenobitic** *adj.*

coenzyme *n* a nonprotein compound that combines with a protein to form an active enzyme and whose activity cannot be destroyed by heat.

coequal *adj* equal with one another. ➤➤ **coequal** *n,* **coequality** *n.*

coerce *v* **1** (*often* + into) to compel (somebody) to do something by force or threats. **2** to restrain or dominate by authority or force. ➤➤ **coercion** *n,* **coercive** *adj.*

coeval *adj* of the same or equal age, antiquity, or duration. ➤➤ **coeval** *n.*

coexist *v* **1** to exist together or at the same time. **2** to live in peace with each other. ➤➤ **coexistence** *n,* **coexistent** *adj.*

coextensive *adj* having the same scope or boundaries in space or time.

C of E *abbr* **1** Church of England. **2** Council of Europe.

coffee *n* **1** a drink made from the roasted seeds of a large African evergreen shrub or small tree. **2** these seeds either green or roasted.

coffee table *n* a low table usu placed in a living room.

coffee-table *adj* of a book: large and lavishly produced, e.g. with extensive use of full-colour illustrations.

coffer *n* **1** a chest or box; *esp* a strongbox. **2** (*usu in pl*) a treasury or exchequer. **3** a recessed decorative panel in a vault, ceiling, etc.

cofferdam *n* a watertight enclosure from which water is pumped to allow construction or repair, e.g. of a pier or ship's hull.

coffin[1] *n* a box or chest for the burial of a corpse.

coffin[2] *v* to enclose or place in a coffin.

cog[1] *n* a tooth on the rim of a wheel or gear. ➤➤ **cogged** *adj.*

cog[2] *n* = TENON.

cogent *adj* of an argument or evidence: appealing forcibly to the mind or reason; convincing. ➤➤ **cogency** *n,* **cogently** *adv.*

cogitate *v formal* to ponder, usu intently and objectively; to meditate. ➤➤ **cogitation** *n,* **cogitative** *adj,* **cogitator** *n.*

cognac /'konyak/ *n* a French brandy, *specif* one from the departments of Charente and Charente-Maritime distilled from white wine.

cognate[1] *adj* **1** related by blood, *esp* on the mother's side. **2** related by derivation or borrowing or by descent from the same ancestral language. **3** of the same or similar nature.

cognate[2] *n* a word that is cognate with another.

cognisance *n* see COGNIZANCE.

cognisant *adj* see COGNIZANT.

cognition *n* the mental act or process of acquiring knowledge that involves the processing of sensory information and includes perception, awareness, and judgment. ➤➤ **cognitional** *adj.*

cognitive *adj* relating to cognition. ➤➤ **cognitively** *adv.*

cognitive therapy *n* a method of treating psychological disorders that encourages patients to face up to and resolve their own distorted ways of thinking about themselves and the world.

cognizance *or* **cognisance** *n formal or technical* **1** the ability to perceive or understand. **2** notice or heed.

cognizant *or* **cognisant** *adj formal or technical* having special or certain knowledge, often from first-hand sources.

cognomen *n* (*pl* **cognomens** *or* **cognomina**) a surname, *esp* the family (and usu third) name of a citizen of ancient Rome.

cognoscente /konyoh'shenti/ *n* (*pl* **cognoscenti**) a person having or claiming expert knowledge; a connoisseur.

cohabit *v* (**cohabited, cohabiting**) to live or exist together, *esp* as husband and wife. ➤➤ **cohabitant** *n,* **cohabitation** *n,* **cohabitee** *n.*

cohere *v* **1** to hold together firmly as parts of the same whole. **2** to be logically or aesthetically consistent.

coherent *adj* **1** able to speak clearly and make oneself understood. **2a** logically consistent. **b** showing a unity of thought or purpose. **3** having the quality of cohering. ➤➤ **coherence** *n,* **coherently** *adv.*

cohesion *n* **1** the fact or state of being coherent, *esp* acting or working together effectively as a unit. **2** the act of cohering. ➤➤ **cohesive** *adj,* **cohesively** *adv,* **cohesiveness** *n.*

cohort *n* **1** a group of soldiers; esp a division of a Roman legion. **2** a group of individuals having age, class membership, or other statistical factors in common in a study of the population. **3** *chiefly NAm* a companion or accomplice.

coif[1] *n* a close-fitting cap worn by nuns under a veil.

coif[2] *v* (**coiffed, coiffing,** *NAm* **coifed, coifing**) to arrange (hair) by brushing, combing, or curling.

coiffeur /kwah'fuh/ *n* a hairdresser.

coiffeuse /kwah'fuhz/ *n* a female hairdresser.

coiffure *n* a hairstyle. ➤➤ **coiffured** *adj.*

coign of vantage *n formal* an advantageous position.

coil[1] *v* **1** to wind (something long) into rings or spirals. **2** to move in a circular, spiral, or winding course. **3** to form, or lie in, a coil.

coil[2] *n* **1** a length of rope, cable, etc gathered into a series of loops. **2a** a number of turns of wire, *esp* in spiral form, usu for electromagnetic effect or for providing electrical resistance. **b** an electrical coil that supplies a high voltage to the spark plugs of an internal-combustion engine. **3** an intrauterine contraceptive device in the form of a metal or plastic coil.

coin[1] *n* **1** a usu thin round piece of metal issued as money. **2** metal money.

coin[2] *v* **1a** to make (a coin), *esp* by stamping; to mint. **b** to convert (metal) into coins. **2** to create or invent (a word or phrase). **3** to make or earn (money) rapidly and in large quantity.

coinage *n* **1a** coins collectively. **b** the coins in use as money in a particular country. **2a** the act of coining or inventing something. **b** something, e.g. a word, that is made up or invented.

coincide *v* **1** (*often* + with) to occur at the same time or in the same place. **2** (*often* + with) to correspond in nature, character, function, or position. **3** (*often* + with) to be in accord or agreement; to concur.

coincidence *n* **1a** the chance occurrence at the same time or place of two or more events that appear to be related or similar. **b** a particular incident in which two or more events happen, by chance, simultaneously. **2** the act or condition of coinciding; a correspondence. ➤➤ **coincidental** *adj,* **coincidentally** *adv.*

coincident *adj* **1** occupying the same space or time; coinciding. **2** of similar nature; harmonious.

coiner *n chiefly Brit* somebody who makes counterfeit coins.

Cointreau /'kwontroh/ *n trademark* a colourless liqueur flavoured with oranges.

coir *n* a stiff coarse fibre from the husk of a coconut.

coitus *n technical* the natural conveying of semen to the female reproductive tract; sexual intercourse. ➤➤ **coital** *adj.*

coitus interruptus *n* coitus which is purposely interrupted in order to prevent ejaculation of sperm into the vagina.

cojones /kə'hohnayz/ *pl n chiefly NAm, informal* **1** the testicles. **2** courage.

Coke *n trademark* short for Coca-Cola.

coke[1] *n* a solid porous fuel that remains after gases have been driven from coal by heating.

coke[2] *v* to convert (coal) into coke.

coke[3] *n slang* cocaine.

Col. *abbr* Colonel.

col *n* a depression or pass in a mountain ridge or range.

col- *prefix* see COM-.

cola *or* **kola** *n* **1** a carbonated soft drink flavoured with extract from coca leaves, kola nut, sugar, caramel, and acid and aromatic substances. **2** a small W African tree that has seeds containing caffeine.

colander *or* **cullender** *n* a perforated bowl-shaped utensil for washing or draining food.

cola nut *n* see KOLA NUT.

colcannon *n* an Irish dish of potatoes and cabbage boiled and mashed together.

colchicum *n* (*pl* **colchicums**) **1** an African and Eurasian plant of the lily family with flowers that resemble crocuses. **2** the dried corm or dried ripe seeds of the meadow saffron, used in medicine.

cold[1] *adj* **1** having a low temperature. **2** of food: previously cooked but served cold. **3** made cold; refrigerated. **4a** characterized by lack of feeling or sociability; unemotional; unresponsive. **b** unfriendly or hostile. **5a** depressing or cheerless. **b** producing a sensation of cold; chilling. **6** of a colour: producing an impression of being cool; *specif* in the range blue to green. **7a** dead. **b** unconscious. **8a** retaining only faint scents, traces, or clues. **b** far from a goal, object, or solution sought. **9** unprepared. ✱ **give somebody the cold shoulder** to be unfriendly towards somebody. **in cold blood** with premeditation; deliberately. **in the cold light of day** when a situation is considered soberly and objectively. **leave somebody cold** to fail to excite or impress somebody. ➤➤ **coldly** *adv,* **coldness** *n.*

cold[2] *n* **1a** a condition of low temperature. **b** cold weather. **2** bodily sensation produced by relative lack of heat; chill. **3** an infection characterized by a sore throat, runny nose and cough. ✱ **out in the cold** ignored or neglected.

cold[3] *adv* **1** with utter finality; absolutely. **2** without any preparation.

cold-blooded *adj* **1a** done or acting without consideration or compunction; ruthless. **b** concerned only with the facts; emotionless. **2** having a body temperature not internally regulated but approximating to that of the environment: compare WARM-BLOODED. ➤➤ **cold-bloodedly** *adv,* **cold-bloodedness** *n.*

cold call *n* an unsolicited visit or phone call made by a salesperson to a prospective customer.

cold-call *v* to make a cold call to (somebody).

cold chisel *n* a chisel made of steel of a strength and temper suitable for chipping or cutting cold metal.

cold comfort *n* something intended to console or compensate somebody for a loss or disappointment but inadequate for the purpose.

cold cream *n* a thick oily often perfumed cream for cleansing and soothing the skin.

cold cuts *pl n* sliced assorted cold cooked meats.

cold feet *pl n informal* fear or doubt strong enough to prevent a planned course of action.

cold frame *n* a usu glass-covered frame without artificial heat used to protect plants and seedlings.

cold fusion *n* the supposed production of energy by nuclear fusion at ordinary temperatures, without the application of great heat and pressure.

cold-hearted *adj* marked by lack of sympathy or sensitivity. ➤➤ **cold-heartedly** *adv,* **cold-heartedness** *n.*

cold sore *n* a group of blisters appearing round or inside the mouth, caused by an infection with herpes simplex.

cold start *n* **1** an act of starting something, *esp* an engine or a machine, without preparation. **2** in computing, the reloading of a program.

cold-start *v* to start (something) in this way.

cold sweat *n* concurrent perspiration and chill, usu associated with fear or pain.

cold turkey *n informal* **1** the abrupt complete cessation of the use of an addictive narcotic drug by an addict. **2** the shivering, nausea, feelings of fear, etc resulting from this.

cold war *n* **1** a conflict carried on by methods short of military action. **2** (**the Cold War**) the period of intense rivalry and hostility between the Western and Soviet blocs between 1945 and 1989.

cole *n* cabbage, broccoli, kohlrabi, or a related edible plant of the cabbage family.

coleopteran *n* any of an order of beetles typically with shell-like forewings. ➤➤ **coleopteran** *adj,* **coleopterous** *adj.*

coleslaw *n* a salad of raw sliced or chopped white cabbage.

coleus *n* (*pl* **coleuses**) a plant of the mint family grown for its brightly coloured and variegated foliage.

coley *n* (*pl* **coleys** *or* **coley**) *Brit* a N Atlantic food fish closely related to the cod.

colic *n* a paroxysm of abdominal pain localized in the intestines or other hollow organ and caused by spasm, obstruction, or twisting. ➤➤ **colicky** *adj.*

coliform *adj* of the rod-shaped bacteria that are normally present in the intestines of vertebrate animals.

coliseum *or* **colosseum** *n* a large building, e.g. a stadium or theatre, used for public entertainments.

colitis *n* inflammation of the colon.

collaborate *v* **1** to work together or to work with somebody else on a common project or with a common aim. **2** to cooperate with an enemy of one's country. ➤➤ **collaboration** *n,* **collaborative** *adj,* **collaboratively** *adv,* **collaborator** *n.*

collaborationism *n* collaboration with an enemy. ➤➤ **collaborationist** *adj and n.*

collage *n* **1** a composition made of pieces of paper, wood, cloth, etc fixed to a surface. **2** an assembly of diverse fragments.

collagen *n* an insoluble protein that occurs as fibres in connective tissue, e.g. tendons, and in bones, and yields gelatin and glue on prolonged heating with water.

collapsar *n* an old star that has collapsed; *esp* a black hole.

collapse[1] *v* **1** to fall down or break down completely; to disintegrate. **2** to fall inward and become flat abruptly and completely, e.g. through compression. **3** to fail suddenly and completely. **4** to suffer a breakdown through exhaustion or disease; *esp* to fall helpless or unconscious. **5** to fold down into a more compact shape. **6** to cause (something) to collapse. ➤➤ **collapsible** *adj.*

collapse[2] *n* **1** an instance of collapsing. **2** total failure or breakdown.

collar[1] *n* **1** a band of fabric that serves to finish or decorate the neckline of a garment. **2** a band fitted about the neck of an animal. **3** a protective or supportive device worn round the neck. **4** something resembling a collar, e.g. a ring or round flange to restrain motion or hold something in place. **5** a cut of bacon from the neck of a pig. ➤➤ **collared** *adj,* **collarless** *adj.*

collar[2] *v informal* to seize by the collar or neck; to apprehend.

collarbone *n* the clavicle.

collate *v* **1** to collect and compare (information, statements, etc) carefully in order to verify them and often to integrate them or arrange them in order. **2** to assemble (pages) in proper order. ➤➤ **collator** *n.*

collateral[1] *adj* **1** accompanying as secondary or subordinate. **2** belonging to the same ancestral stock but not in a direct line of descent. **3** parallel or corresponding in position, time, or significance. ➤➤ **collaterally** *adv.*

collateral[2] *n* **1** property pledged by a borrower to protect the interests of the lender. **2** a collateral relative.

collateral damage *n* unintended destruction or casualties in non-military areas caused by a military operation.

collation *n* **1** the act, process, or result of collating. **2** a light meal; *esp* one allowed on fast days in place of lunch or supper.

colleague *n* a fellow worker, *esp* in a profession.

collect[1] *v* **1a** to bring (things) together. **b** to gather or exact (things) from a number of sources. **c** to come together in a band, group, or mass; to gather. **2a** to fetch (something) from a place. **b** to provide transport or an escort for (somebody). **3** to gain or regain control of (something): *He tried to collect his thoughts.* **4** to claim as due and receive possession or payment of: *She is entitled to collect social security.*

collect[2] *n* **1** a short prayer comprising an invocation, petition, and conclusion. **2** a prayer preceding the Epistle read at Communion.

collect[3] *adj and adv NAm* of a telephone call: to be paid for by the receiver.

collectable[1] *or* **collectible** *adj* **1** able to be collected. **2** worth making a collection of or putting into a collection; of interest to a collector.

collectable[2] *or* **collectible** *n* an object that is worth collecting.

collected *adj* **1** exhibiting calmness and composure. **2** assembled from a number of sources.

collectible *adj and n* see COLLECTABLE[1], COLLECTABLE[2].

collection *n* **1** the act or process of collecting. **2** something collected, *esp* an accumulation of objects gathered for study or exhibition. **3** a range of similar products, e.g. garments, presented to the public.

collective[1] *adj* **1** denoting a number of individuals considered as one group. **2** of, made, or held in common by a group of individuals. **3** collectivized. ➤➤ **collectively** *adv,* **collectivity** *n.*

collective[2] *n* **1** (*used as sing. or pl*) a collective body; a group. **2** a cooperative organization; *specif* a collective farm.

collective bargaining *n* negotiation between an employer and union representatives usu on wages and working conditions.

collective farm *n* a large farm that is worked jointly by a group of people, but is usually owned and supervised by the state.

collective noun *n* in grammar, a noun that denotes a number of individuals considered as one group.

collectivise *v* see COLLECTIVIZE.

collectivism *n* a political or economic theory advocating collective control, *esp* over production and distribution. ➤➤ **collectivist** *adj and n.*

collectivize *or* **-ise** *v* to organize (something) under collective control. ➤➤ **collectivization** *n.*

collector *n* **1** somebody who collects things of a certain type. **2** an official who collects money.

colleen *n Irish* a girl or young woman.

college *n* **1** a building used for an educational or religious purpose. **2a** a self-governing endowed constituent body of a university offering instruction and often living quarters but not granting degrees. **b** an institution offering vocational or technical instruction. **3** an organized body of people engaged in a common pursuit.

collegial *adj* **1** = COLLEGIATE (1), (2). **2** characterized by equal sharing of authority, *esp* by Roman Catholic bishops.

collegian *n* a member of a college.

collegiate *adj* **1** relating to a collegiate church. **2** relating to or comprising a college. **3** = COLLEGIAL (2).

collegiate church *n* a church other than a cathedral that has a chapter of canons.

collide *v* **1** to come together forcibly. **2** to come into conflict.

collie *n* a large dog with a pointed nose and long hair belonging to a breed orig used to herd sheep.

collier *n* **1** a coal miner. **2** a ship for transporting coal.

colliery *n* (*pl* **-ies**) a coal mine and its associated buildings.

collimate *v* **1** to make (e.g. rays of light) parallel. **2** to adjust the line of sight of (a telescope, theodolite, etc). ➤➤ **collimation** *n,* **collimator** *n.*

collinear *adj* of points: lying on or passing through the same straight line. ➤➤ **collinearity** *n.*

collision *n* an act or instance of colliding; a clash. ➤➤ **collisional** *adj.*

collocate[1] *v* **1** *formal* to set or arrange (things) in a particular place or position, *esp* side by side. **2** (*often* + with) of a linguistic element: to form part of a collocation.

collocate[2] *n* a word that is typically, or very frequently, used in conjunction with another word.

collocation *n* the act or result of placing or arranging together; *specif* a combination of two or more words or other linguistic elements that is well established by usage.

colloid *n* **1** a substance composed of particles that are too small to be seen with a light microscope but too large to form a true solution and that will typically diffract a beam of light. **2** a gelatinous substance found in tissues, *esp* in disease. ➤➤ **colloidal** *adj.*

colloquia *n* pl of COLLOQUIUM.

colloquial *adj* used in or using the style of familiar and informal conversation; conversational. ➤➤ **colloquially** *adv.*

colloquialism *n* a colloquial expression.

colloquium *n* (*pl* **colloquiums** *or* **colloquia**) a conference or seminar.

colloquy *n* (*pl* **-ies**) **1** a formal conversation or dialogue. **2** a religious conference.

collude *v* to cooperate with somebody in secret; to conspire or plot.

collusion *n* secret agreement or cooperation for an illegal or deceitful purpose. ⋙ **collusive** *adj.*

collywobbles *pl n informal* **1** (*usu* **the collywobbles**) stomachache. **2** (*usu* **the collywobbles**) qualms or butterflies.

colobus monkey *n* a long-tailed African monkey that lives in trees, eats leaves, and has long silky fur.

cologne *n* scented toilet water.

Colombian *n* a native or inhabitant of Colombia. ⋙ **Colombian** *adj.*

colon[1] *n* the part of the large intestine that extends from the caecum to the rectum. ⋙ **colonic** *adj.*

colon[2] *n* a punctuation mark (:) used to introduce a quotation, a list of items, or an expansion or explanation of words earlier in the sentence.

colón *n* (*pl* **colones**) the basic monetary unit of Costa Rica and El Salvador.

colonel *n* an officer in the army or US air force ranking below brigadier or brigadier general. ⋙ **colonelcy** *n.*

colones *n* pl of COLÓN.

colonial[1] *adj* **1** relating to or characteristic of a colony. **2** (*often* **Colonial**) made or prevailing in America before 1776. **3** possessing or composed of colonies. ⋙ **colonially** *adv.*

colonial[2] *n* a member or inhabitant of a colony.

colonialism *n* **1** control by a state over a dependent area or people. **2** a policy based on this. ⋙ **colonialist** *n and adj.*

colonic irrigation *n* the injection of fluid into the colon via the anus as a cleansing or therapeutic operation.

colonise *v* see COLONIZE.

colonist *n* a member or inhabitant of a colony.

colonize *or* **-ise** *v* **1** to establish a colony in (a place) or extend colonial control over (an indigenous people). **2** of plants and animals: to come into and begin to live and breed in (a new area or environment). **3** *often humorous* to take over and occupy (e.g. a room). ⋙ **colonization** *n,* **colonizer** *n.*

colonnade *n* a row of columns placed at regular intervals, usu supporting an entablature and often a roof. ⋙ **colonnaded** *adj.*

colonoscope *n* a long medical instrument with which the colon can be examined and operated upon. ⋙ **colonoscopy** *n.*

colony *n* (*pl* **-ies**) **1a** a body of settlers living in a new territory but subject to control by the parent state. **b** their territory. **2a** a group of individuals with common interests or origins living close together. **b** the area occupied by such a group. **3** a group of people segregated from the general public. **4** a distinguishable localized population within a species.

colophon *n* an identifying symbol used by a printer or publisher.

color *v and n NAm* see COLOUR[1] and COLOUR[2].

Colorado beetle *n* a black-and-yellow striped beetle that feeds on the leaves of the potato.

coloration (*Brit also* **colouration**) *n* **1** colouring or complexion. **2** use or choice of colours, e.g. by an artist. **3** an arrangement or range of colours.

coloratura *n* **1** elaborate embellishment in vocal music. **2** a singer who uses such embellishment.

colored *adj and n NAm* see COLOURED[1], COLOURED[2].

colorful *adj NAm* see COLOURFUL.

coloring *adj NAm* see COLOURING.

colorist *n NAm* see COLOURIST.

colorless *adj NAm* see COLOURLESS.

colossal *adj* of very great size or degree. ⋙ **colossally** *adv.*

colosseum *n* see COLISEUM.

colossus *n* (*pl* **colossuses** *or* **colossi**) **1** a statue of gigantic size, often in particular reference to the Colossus of Rhodes of antiquity, erroneously believed to bestride the harbour. **2** somebody or something remarkably preeminent.

colostomy *n* (*pl* **-ies**) the surgical formation of an artificial anus in the wall of the abdomen after a shortening of the colon.

colostrum *n* the milk that is secreted for a few days after giving birth and is characterized by high protein and antibody content.

colour[1] (*NAm* **color**) *n* **1a** the visual sensation, e.g. of redness, blueness, etc, caused by the wavelength of perceived light that enables one to differentiate otherwise identical objects. **b** the property of objects and light sources that enables them to be described as green, yellow, brown, etc. **2a** a hue, e.g. red or blue, or hues in general, *esp* as opposed to black, white, and grey. **b** a substance, e.g. a pigment used in painting, that gives colour when applied to an object. **3** the use or combination of colours, e.g. by painters. **4a** the skin pigmentation characteristic of a particular race. **b** skin pigmentation other than white. **5** the tint characteristic of good health. **6** (*usu in pl*) **a** an identifying badge, pennant, or flag, e.g. of a ship or regiment. **b** coloured clothing distinguishing somebody, e.g. as a member of a usu specified group. **7** vitality or interest. ✱ **show (oneself in) one's true colours** to reveal one's true nature or character. **with flying colours** see FLYING.

colour[2] *v* **1** to give colour to. **2 a** to misrepresent or distort. **b** to influence or affect. **3** to take on or impart colour; *specif* to blush. ⋙ **colourant** *n.*

colouration *n Brit* see COLORATION.

colour-blind *adj* unable or partially unable to distinguish one or more colours. ⋙ **colour blindness** *n.*

coloured[1] (*NAm* **colored**) *adj* **1** having colour. **2** marked by exaggeration or bias. **3** *offensive* **a** of a race other than the white; *esp* BLACK[1] (2). **b** (*often* **Coloured**) of S Africans: of mixed race.

coloured[2] *n* (*often* **Coloured**) *offensive* a person of mixed descent.

Usage note

Negro, black, *and* **coloured.** See note at BLACK[2].

colourfast *adj* having colour that will not fade or run.

colourful (*NAm* **colorful**) *adj* **1** having striking colours. **2** full of variety or interest. **3** of language: coarse or vulgar. ⋙ **colourfully** *adv,* **colourfulness** *n.*

colouring (*NAm* **coloring**) *n* **1a** applying colours. **b** the effect produced by combining or applying colours. **2** something that produces colour. **3a** natural colour. **b** complexion.

colourist (*NAm* **colorist**) *n* somebody, *esp* a painter, who colours or deals with colour.

colourless (*NAm* **colorless**) *adj* **1** lacking colour; pallid. **2** dull or uninteresting.

colour scheme *n* a systematic combination of colours.

colour sergeant *n* **1** the senior sergeant in a British infantry company. **2** a non-commissioned officer of the highest rank in the Royal Marines.

colour supplement *n Brit* an illustrated colour magazine published as a supplement to a newspaper.

colourway *n* = COLOUR SCHEME.

colposcope *n* an instrument for examining the cervix and vagina. ⋙ **colposcopy** *n.*

colt *n* **1** a young male horse that is either sexually immature or has not attained an arbitrarily designated age. **2** a novice; *esp* a cricketer or rugby player in a junior team.

colter *n NAm* see COULTER.

coltish *adj* **1** frisky or playful. **2** of or resembling a colt.

coltsfoot *n* (*pl* **coltsfoots**) a composite plant with yellow flower heads.

colubrine *adj* relating to or resembling a snake.

columbine *n* a plant of the buttercup family with showy spurred flowers. Also called AQUILEGIA.

column *n* **1** a pillar that usu consists of a round shaft, a capital, and a base. **2** a rod or shaft used to control the operations of a machine or vehicle. **3** a long narrow formation of soldiers, vehicles, etc in rows. **4a** a vertical arrangement of items or a vertical section of printing on a page. **b** a special and usu regular feature in a newspaper or periodical. ⋙ **columnar** *adj,* **columned** *adj.*

columnist *n* somebody who writes a newspaper or magazine column.

com- *or* **col-** *or* **con-** *or* **cor-** *prefix* with, together or jointly: *commingle; correlation.*

coma *n* a state of deep unconsciousness caused by disease, injury, etc.

Comanche *n* (*pl* **Comanches** *or* **Comanche**) a member of a Native American people who live over an area ranging from Wyoming and Nebraska into New Mexico and NW Texas.

comatose *adj* **1** in a state of coma. **2** characterized by lethargy and sluggishness; torpid.

comb[1] *n* **1a** a toothed instrument used for adjusting or holding the hair. **b** a toothed device used in handling or ordering textile fibres. **2** a fleshy crest on the head of a domestic fowl or a related bird. **3** a honeycomb.

comb[2] *v* **1** to draw a comb through (the hair) for the purpose of arranging it. **2** to prepare (e.g. wool or cotton) for use in manufacturing by cleaning and arranging its fibres with a comb. **3** to search or examine systematically.

combat[1] *n* **1** a fight or contest between individuals or groups. **2** active fighting in a war.

combat[2] *v* (**combated, combating,** *NAm* **combatted, combatting**) to struggle against (something); *esp* to strive to reduce or eliminate (something): *strategies to combat inflation.*

combatant[1] *n* a person, nation, etc that is an active participant in combat.

combatant[2] *adj* actively participating in combat.

combat fatigue *n* = SHELL SHOCK.

combative *adj* marked by eagerness to fight or contend. ⋙ **combatively** *adv,* **combativeness** *n.*

combat trousers *pl n* loose-fitting trousers, usu made of strong cotton, with patch pockets on the back and on the legs.

combe *n Brit* see COOMB.

comber *n* **1** a long heavy wave; a roller. **2** somebody or something that combs.

combination *n* **1** a process of combining, *esp* to form a chemical compound. **2** a result or product of combining. **3** in mathematics, any of the different sets of a specified number of individuals that can be chosen from a group and are considered without regard to order within the set: compare PERMUTATION. **4** the sequence of letters or numbers that will open a combination lock. ⋙ **combinational** *adj.*

combination lock *n* a lock with a mechanism operated by the selection of a specific combination of letters or numbers.

combine[1] *v* **1a** to bring (people or things) into such close relationship as to obscure individual characters; to merge. **b** to unite or cause (substances) to unite into a chemical compound. **2** to cause (people or things) to mix together. **3** to possess (certain qualities) in combination. **4** to act together. **5** to become one.

combine[2] *n* **1** a combination of people or organizations, *esp* in industry or commerce, to further their interests. **2** = COMBINE HARVESTER.

combine harvester *n* a harvesting machine that cuts, threshes, and cleans grain while moving over a field.

combining form *n* in grammar, a linguistic form, e.g. *Franco-,* that cannot stand alone but forms compounds with other forms.

comb jelly *n* a marine animal resembling a jellyfish that uses comblike plates of fused filaments (cilia; see CILIUM) for propulsion.

combo *n* (*pl* **-os**) *informal* **1** a small jazz or dance band. **2** *chiefly NAm* any combination.

combust *v* to burn (something).

combustible[1] *adj* **1** capable of being set on fire. **2** easily excited. ⋙ **combustibility** *n.*

combustible[2] *n* a substance that is capable of being set on fire.

combustion *n* **1** an act or instance of burning. **2** a chemical reaction, *esp* an oxidation, in which light and heat are evolved; the process of burning.

come[1] *v* (*past tense* **came,** *past part.* **come**) **1** to move in a direction towards the speaker. **2** to arrive or occur: *The time has come.* **3** to happen: *No harm will come to you.* **4a** to become: *The knot came loose.* **b** to reach a certain position or limit: *The dress came down to her ankles; He came third in the final.* **5** to be available in a specified form: *It comes in a range of colours.* **6** *informal* to have an orgasm. ✱ **come across 1** to produce a specified impression: *His ideas didn't come across very well.* **2** to meet or find by chance. **come by** to manage to get. **come clean** *informal* to admit everything. **come into** to inherit (money or property). **come of** to result from. **come off it** *informal* an expression of disbelief. **come over** to affect (somebody) suddenly and strangely. **come to 1** to recover consciousness. **2** to reach a total: *The cost comes to £100.* **come to pass** *literary* to happen. **come upon** to meet (somebody) by chance.

come[2] *interj* used to express encouragement or to urge reconsideration.

come[3] *n informal* semen.

come about *v* **1** to occur; to take place. **2** of a ship: to change course.

comeback *n* **1** a return to a former state or condition. **2** a means of redress. **3** *informal* a sharp or witty reply; a retort.

come back *v* **1** to return to memory. **2** to regain a former position or reputation. **3** *NAm* to reply or retort.

comedian *n* **1** an actor who plays comic roles. **2** a person, *esp* a professional entertainer, who aims to be amusing.

comedic *adj* of comedy.

comedienne *n* **1** an actress who plays comic roles. **2** a woman, *esp* a professional entertainer, who aims to be amusing.

comedown *n informal* **1** a striking descent in rank or dignity. **2** a disappointment.

come down *v* **1** of a price, etc: to decrease. **2** of an aircraft: to land or crash. **3** to express a specified opinion. ✻ **come down on** to criticize or punish. **come down to** to amount to in the end.

comedy *n* (*pl* **-ies**) **1** a drama of light and amusing character, typically with a happy ending. **2** a ludicrous or farcical event or series of events. **3** the comic aspect of something.

comedy of manners *n* a comedy that portrays satirically the manners and fashions of a particular class or set of people.

come-hither *adj informal* sexually inviting.

come in *v* **1** to function as specified: *This will come in handy.* **2** of news, etc: to become known. **3** of income: to be received. **4** of a competitor: to finish as specified: *He came in last.*

comely *adj* (**-ier, -iest**) of pleasing appearance; not plain. ➤➤ **comeliness** *n.*

come off *v* **1** to succeed. **2** to finish in a specified way: *to come off best.* **3** to become detached.

come on *v* **1** to advance or begin by degrees: *Darkness came on.* **2** to make an entrance, *esp* on a stage.

come-on *n* **1** *informal* an instance of sexually provocative enticement. **2** an attraction or enticement, e.g. in sales promotion, to induce an action.

come out *v* **1** to be published or made public. **2** to declare oneself in favour of or opposed to something. **3** of a photograph: to appear satisfactory or as specified. **4** to end up as specified. **5** to declare one's homosexuality. **6** *Brit, dated* to make one's first appearance in society as a debutante. ✻ **come out in** of the skin: to be covered in (a rash, spots, etc). **come out with** to say (something) surprising or unexpected.

come over *v* **1** to make a casual visit. **2** to change from one side or opinion to another. **3** to be affected by a feeling: *She came over all peculiar.* **4** to produce a specified impression.

come round *v* **1** to recover consciousness. **2** to be persuaded to adopt a particular opinion. **3** of a date or time: to approach again.

comestible *n formal* (*usu in pl*) food.

comet *n* a celestial body that typically follows a highly elliptical orbit round the sun and consists of an icy nucleus surrounded by a cloud of gas and dust, some of which trails away from the sun to form long tails. ➤➤ **cometary** *adj.*

come through *v* **1** to survive. **2** of a radio signal, etc: to be received clearly.

come up *v* of a situation, difficulty, etc: to arise or occur unexpectedly. ✻ **come up against** to encounter (a difficulty). **come up with** to produce (something needed).

comeuppance *n informal* a deserved rebuke or penalty.

comfit *n archaic* a sweetmeat consisting of a nut, piece of fruit, etc preserved with sugar.

comfort[1] *n* **1** consolation or encouragement in time of trouble or worry, or somebody or something that provides this. **2** contented well-being. ➤➤ **comfortless** *adj.*

comfort[2] *v* **1** to cheer (somebody) up. **2** to ease the grief or trouble of; to console. ➤➤ **comforting** *adj,* **comfortingly** *adv.*

comfortable *adj* **1a** providing or enjoying physical comfort. **b** providing or enjoying contentment and security. **2a** causing no worry or doubt. **b** free from stress or tension. **c** free from pain or discomfort. **3** easy. ➤➤ **comfortably** *adv.*

comforter *n* **1** somebody who gives comfort. **2** *Brit* a baby's dummy. **3** *NAm* a quilt.

comfort station *n NAm, euphem* a public toilet.

comfrey *n* (*pl* **-eys**) a tall plant of the borage family, with coarse hairy leaves that are much used in herbal medicine.

comfy *adj* (**-ier, -iest**) *informal* comfortable.

comic[1] *adj* **1** of or marked by comedy. **2** causing laughter or amusement; funny.

comic[2] *n* **1** a comedian. **2** a magazine consisting mainly of strip cartoon stories.

comical *adj* exciting laughter, *esp* because of a startlingly or unexpectedly humorous impact. ➤➤ **comically** *adv.*

comic opera *n* opera with humorous episodes and usu some spoken dialogue and a sentimental plot.

comic strip *n* a strip cartoon.

comity *n* (*pl* **-ies**) **1** a loose widespread community. **2** = COMITY OF NATIONS. **3** *formal* harmony or fellowship.

comity of nations *n* the courtesy and friendship of nations, marked *esp* by recognition of each other's laws.

comma *n* **1** a punctuation mark (,) used to separate parts of a sentence and items in a list. **2** a butterfly with a silvery comma-shaped mark on the underside of the hind wing.

command[1] *v* **1** to direct (somebody) authoritatively; to order (somebody). **2a** to have at one's immediate disposal. **b** to be able to ask for and receive. **c** to overlook or dominate from a strategic position. **d** to have military command of (troops) as senior officer.

command[2] *n* **1a** an order given. **b** (*used before a noun*) done on command or request. **2** an electrical signal that actuates a device, or the activation of a device by means of such a signal. **3a** the ability or power to control; mastery. **b** the authority or right to command. **c** facility in use. **4** (*used as sing. or pl*) the unit, personnel, etc under a commander.

commandant *n* a commanding officer.

command economy *n* see PLANNED ECONOMY.

commandeer *v* **1** to seize for military purposes. **2** to take arbitrary or forcible possession of.

commander *n* **1** a commanding officer. **2** the presiding officer of a society or organization. **3** an officer in the Royal Navy or the US Navy ranking below a captain.

commander-in-chief *n* (*pl* **commanders-in-chief**) an officer who is in supreme command of an armed force.

commanding *adj* **1** having command; being in charge. **2** deserving or expecting respect and obedience. **3** dominating or having priority. ➤➤ **commandingly** *adv.*

command language *n* in computing, a simplified language that enables the operator to enter sets of commands.

commandment *n* something commanded; *specif* any of the biblical Ten Commandments.

command module *n* a part of a spacecraft designed to carry the crew, the main communication equipment, and the equipment for re-entry.

commando *n* (*pl* **-os**) **1** a soldier trained to carry out surprise raids. **2** a unit of such soldiers.

command paper *n Brit* a government report laid before Parliament at the command of the crown.

command performance *n* a performance of a play, film, etc for a member of the royal family.

commedia dell'arte /kə,maydi·ə del 'ahti/ *n* Italian comedy of the 16th–18th cents, improvised from standardized situations and stock characters.

comme il faut /,kom eel 'foh/ *adj* conforming to accepted standards; proper.

commemorate *v* **1** to call (an event or person) to formal remembrance. **2** to mark (an event or a person) by some ceremony or observation; to observe. **3** of a plaque, monument, etc: to serve as a memorial of (somebody or something). ⋙ **commemoration** *n*, **commemorative** *adj*.

commence *v* to start or begin (something).

commencement *n* **1** a beginning. **2** *NAm* a day on which degrees or diplomas are conferred by a school or college.

commend *v* **1** to praise or express approval of. **2** to recommend as worthy of confidence or notice. **3** to entrust to somebody for care or preservation. **4** (+ to) to pass on the good wishes of. ⋙ **commendable** *adj*, **commendably** *adv*, **commendation** *n*, **commendatory** *adj*.

commensal[1] *adj* living in a state of commensalism.

commensal[2] *n* an organism living in a state of commensalism.

commensalism *n* the association of two species whereby one species obtains benefits, e.g. food or protection, from the association without the other species being harmed.

commensurable *adj* (*often* + with/to) having a common measure; *esp* divisible by a common unit an integral number of times.

commensurate *adj* **1** (*usu* + with) equal, or approximately equal in measure or extent; coextensive. **2** (*often* + to/with) corresponding in size, extent, amount, or degree; proportionate. ⋙ **commensurately** *adv*.

comment[1] *n* **1** an observation or remark expressing an opinion or attitude. **2** discussion, *esp* of a topical issue.

comment[2] *v* **1** (*often* + on/upon) to make a comment. **2** (*often* + on/upon) to explain or interpret something by comment.

commentary *n* (*pl* **-ies**) **1** a systematic series of explanations or interpretations, e.g. of a piece of writing. **2** a series of spoken remarks and comments used as a broadcast description of some event.

commentate *v* (*often* + on) to act as a commentator; *esp* to give a broadcast commentary.

commentator *n* a person who provides a commentary; *specif* somebody who reports and discusses news or sports events on radio or television.

commerce *n* **1** the exchange or buying and selling of commodities, *esp* on a large scale. **2** *dated* the exchange of ideas or sentiments.

commercial[1] *adj* **1** engaged in work designed for the market. **2** of or characteristic of commerce. **3a** having or being a good financial prospect. **b** producing work to a standard determined only by market criteria. **4a** viewed with regard to profit. **b** designed for a large market. **5** supported by advertisers. ⋙ **commercially** *adv*.

commercial[2] *n* an advertisement broadcast on radio or television.

commercialise *v* see COMMERCIALIZE.

commercialism *n* **1** commercial spirit, institutions, or methods. **2** excessive emphasis on profit.

commercialize *or* **-ise** *v* **1** to make commercial. **2** to exploit for profit. ⋙ **commercialization** *n*.

commie *n informal, derog* a communist.

commingle *v literary* to combine or mix (something).

comminute *v* to reduce to minute particles; to pulverize. ⋙ **comminution** *n*.

commis /'komi/ *n* (*pl* **commis**) (*used before a noun*) a junior or assistant in a hotel, catering establishment, etc: *a commis chef*.

commiserate *v* (+ with) to feel or express sympathy; to condole. ⋙ **commiseration** *n*.

commissar *n* a Communist party official assigned to a military unit to teach party principles and ideals.

commissariat *n* the department of an army that organizes food supplies.

commissary *n* (*pl* **-ies**) **1** an officer in charge of military supplies. **2** a bishop's deputy. **3** *NAm* a restaurant, *esp* on a military base or in a film studio. **4** *NAm* a store selling equipment and food supplies.

commission[1] *n* **1** an authorization or command to act in a prescribed manner or to perform prescribed acts; a charge. **2** (*used as sing. or pl*) a group of people directed to perform some duty. **3** a fee, *esp* a percentage, paid to an agent or employee for transacting a piece of business or performing a service. **4a** a formal warrant granting various powers. **b** military rank above a certain level, or a certificate conferring such rank. **5** an act of committing something. **6** authority to act as agent for another, or something to be done by an agent. ✱ **in commission 1** of a ship: ready for active service. **2** of a machine, etc: in use or in condition for use. **on commission** with commission serving as partial or full pay for work done. **out of commission 1** of a ship: out of active service or use. **2** of a machine, etc: out of working order.

commission[2] *v* **1a** to order or appoint (somebody) to perform a task or function. **b** to order (a task) to be done. **2** to confer a formal commission on (a member of the armed forces). **3** to put (a ship) in commission. **4** to put (equipment or machinery) into working order.

commissionaire *n chiefly Brit* a uniformed attendant at a cinema, theatre, etc.

commissioner *n* **1** a member or the head of a commission. **2** the government representative in a district, province, etc.

Commissioner for oaths *n Brit* a solicitor authorized to administer oaths or affirmations or to take affidavits.

commissure *n* **1** the place where two parts are joined; a closure. **2** a connecting band of nerve tissue in the brain or spinal cord.

commit *v* (**committed, committing**) **1** to carry out (a crime, sin, etc). **2a** to obligate or bind (oneself or somebody else) to a course of action or a set of beliefs. **b** to assign (somebody or something) to some particular course or use. **3a** to entrust (something or somebody) to somebody's care. **b** to place in a prison or psychiatric hospital.

commitment *n* **1a** an agreement or pledge to do something in the future. **b** something pledged. **c** loyalty to a system of thought or action. **2** an act of committing to a charge or trust; *esp* a consignment to an institution.

committal *n* **1** the consigning of somebody to prison or a psychiatric hospital, or for trial. **2** the burial of a body.

committee *n* **1** (*used as sing. or pl*) a body of people delegated to organize or administrate a society, event, etc. **2** (*used as sing. or pl*) a body of people delegated to report on or investigate some matter. **3** formerly, somebody entrusted with the charge of a mentally ill or mentally handicapped person.

committee stage *n* the stage in British parliamentary procedure when a bill is discussed in detail in committee.

commode *n* **1** a boxlike structure or chair with a removable seat covering a chamber pot. **2** a low chest of drawers.

commodious *adj formal* comfortably or conveniently spacious; roomy.

commodity *n* (*pl* **-ies**) **1** something that can be bought and sold. **2** something useful or valuable.

commodore *n* **1** the senior captain of a merchant shipping line. **2** the chief officer of a yacht club.

common[1] *adj* **1a** occurring or appearing frequently; familiar. **b** of the familiar kind. **2a** widespread or general. **b** characterized by a lack of privilege or special status. **c** simply satisfying accustomed criteria and no more; elementary. **3** lacking refinement. **4a** belonging to or shared by two or more individuals or by all members of a group. **b** belonging equally to two or more quantities. **5** of the community at large; public. **6** in grammar, belonging to a gender that includes masculine and feminine. ✱ **common or garden** ordinary or everyday. ⋙ **commonly** *adv,* **commonness** *n.*

Usage note

common, mutual, *or* reciprocal? See note at MUTUAL.

common[2] *n* **1a** an expanse of undeveloped land available for recreation. **b** undivided land used *esp* for pasture. **2** a religious service suitable for any of various festivals. **3** (*also* **right of common**) in law, a right which somebody may have on another person's land. ✱ **in common 1** of shared interests, attitudes, or experience; shared together. **2** used jointly.

commonality *n* (*pl* **-ies**) **1** possession of common features or attributes or of some degree of standardization; commonness. **2** a common feature or attribute. **3** (**the commonality**) = COMMONALTY.

commonalty *n* (**the commonalty**) the common people, or the political estate formed by them.

common denominator *n* **1** in mathematics, a number into which the denominators of several fractions can be divided with no remainder. **2** a common trait or theme.

commoner *n* a member of the common people; somebody not of noble rank.

Common Era *n* the Christian era.

common law *n* **1** the body of uncodified English law that forms the basis of the English legal system. **2** (*used before a noun*) recognized in law without solemnization of marriage: *his common law wife.*

common market *n* **1** an economic unit formed to remove trade barriers among its members. **2** (**the Common Market**) an informal name for the European Economic Community (now the European Union).

common noun *n* a noun that may occur with limiting modifiers, e.g. *a* or *an, some, every,* and *my,* and that designates any one of a class of beings or things.

commonplace[1] *adj* routinely found; ordinary or unremarkable.

commonplace[2] *n* **1** an obvious or trite observation. **2** something taken for granted.

common room *n chiefly Brit* a room in a school or college for the recreational use of the staff or students.

commons *pl n* **1** (**the Commons**) the House of Commons. **2** the common people, *esp* thought of as a political group. **3** *archaic* shared food or provisions; rations.

common sense *n* sound and prudent judgment. ⋙ **commonsensical** *adj.*

common time *n* the musical metre marked by four crotchets per bar.

commonweal *n archaic* **1** the general welfare. **2** a commonwealth.

commonwealth *n* **1** an independent state; a republic. **2** (**the Commonwealth**) an association consisting of Britain and states that were formerly British colonies. **3** (**the Commonwealth**) the British state from 1649 to 1660. **4** (**the commonwealth**) *archaic* a political unit founded on law and united by agreement of the people for the common good.

Commonwealth of Nations *n* = COMMONWEALTH (2).

commotion *n* **1** a disturbance or tumult. **2** noisy confusion and bustle.

communal *adj* **1** shared or used in common by members of a group or community. **2** of a community. **3** of a commune or communes. ⋙ **communality** *n,* **communally** *adv.*

communard *n* **1** (**Communard**) a person who participated in the Commune of Paris in 1871. **2** a person who lives in a commune.

commune[1] *n* **1** a community of unrelated individuals or families organized on a communal basis. **2** the smallest administrative district of a number of European countries.

commune[2] *v* (*usu* + with) to communicate intimately.

communicable *adj* of a disease: transmittable.

communicant *n* a church member who receives or is entitled to receive Communion.

communicate *v* **1** to convey knowledge of or information about (something); to make (something) known. **2** to cause (something) to pass from one person to another. **3** of rooms: to give access to each other; to connect. **4** to receive Communion. ⋙ **communicator** *n.*

communication *n* **1** the exchange of information, or the use of a common system of symbols, signs, behaviour, etc for this. **2** a verbal or written message. **3** (*in pl*) **a** a system, e.g. of telephones, for communicating. **b** a system of routes for moving troops, supplies, etc. **4** (*in pl, used as sing. or pl*) techniques for the effective transmission of information, ideas, etc. ⋙ **communicational** *adj.*

communication cord *n Brit* a chain or handle in a railway carriage that may be pulled in an emergency to sound an alarm.

communicative *adj* tending to communicate; talkative. ⋙ **communicatively** *adv.*

communion *n* **1** (*often* **Communion**) the religious service celebrating the Eucharist in Protestant churches, or the act of receiving the Eucharist. **2** intimate fellowship or rapport. **3** a body of Christians having a common faith and discipline.

communiqué *n* an official announcement; a bulletin.

communism *n* **1a** a theory advocating elimination of private property. **b** a system in which goods are held in common and are available to all as needed. **2** (**Communism**) a doctrine based on revolutionary Marxian socialism and Marxism-Leninism that was the official ideology of the former Soviet Union. ⋙ **communist** *n and adj,* **communistic** *adj.*

communitarian[1] *adj* of or based on social organization in small communes.

communitarian[2] *n* a supporter of social organization in small collectivist communities. ⋙ **communitarianism** *n.*

community *n* (*pl* **-ies**) **1** (*used as sing. or pl*) **a** a group of people living in a particular area. **b** all the interacting populations of various living organisms in a particular area. **c** a group of individuals with some common characteristic, e.g. profession, religion, or status. **d** a body of people or nations having a common history or common interests. **2** society in general.

community care *n* the provision of care, e.g. nursing, to enable people to stay in their own community rather than in a hospital or institution.

community centre *n* a building or group of buildings for the educational and recreational activities of a community.

community service *n* unpaid work undertaken for the benefit of the community, *esp* by a convicted person under a judicial order.

commutate *v* to reverse the direction of (an electric current); *esp* to convert (alternating current) to direct current.

commutation *n* **1** an act or process of commuting. **2** the process of converting an alternating current to a direct current. **3** the substitution by executive authority of a legal penalty less severe than that imposed judicially.

commutative *adj* **1** of a binary operation: denoting the combination of elements that produces a result that is independent of the order in which the elements are taken. **2** of or showing commutation.

commutator *n* a device for reversing the direction of an electric current; *esp* a device on a motor or generator that converts alternating current to direct current.

commute *v* **1** to travel back and forth regularly, e.g. between home and work. **2** of two mathematical operators: to give a commutative result. **3** (*usu* + to) to exchange (a penalty) for another less severe. **4** to convert (e.g. a payment) into another form. ➤➤ **commutable** *adj,* **commuter** *n.*

compact[1] *adj* **1** having parts or units closely packed or joined. **2** occupying a small volume because of efficient use of space. ➤➤ **compactly** *adv,* **compactness** *n.*

compact[2] *v* **1** to press (something) together; to compress. **2** to knit or draw together; to combine or consolidate. ➤➤ **compaction** *n,* **compactor** *n.*

compact[3] *n* **1** a small slim case for face powder. **2** *NAm* a medium-sized motor car.

compact[4] *n* an agreement or contract.

compact disc *n* a small plastic aluminium-coated disc on which sound or information is stored in digital form in microscopic pits that can be read by a laser beam.

compadre *n chiefly NAm, informal* a companion.

companion *n* **1** a person who accompanies another; a comrade. **2** something belonging to a pair or set of matching things. **3** a person employed to live with and provide company and service for somebody. **4** a member of the lowest rank of certain orders of knighthood. ➤➤ **companionship** *n.*

companionable *adj* marked by or suggestive of companionship; sociable. ➤➤ **companionably** *adv.*

companionate marriage *n* a proposed form of marriage in which the partners would be treated as equals.

companionway *n* a ship's stairway from one deck to another.

company *n* (*pl* **-ies**) **1** (*used as sing. or pl*) an association of people for carrying on a commercial or industrial enterprise. **2a** friendly association with another; fellowship. **b** companions or associates. **c** (*used as sing. or pl*) visitors or guests. **3** (*used as sing. or pl*) **a** a group of people or things. **b** a unit of soldiers composed usu of a headquarters and two or more platoons. **c** an organization of musical or dramatic performers. ✱ **keep company with** to spend time with. **keep somebody company** to provide somebody with companionship.

comparable *adj* **1** (*often* + with/to) capable of or suitable for comparison. **2** approximately equivalent; similar. ➤➤ **comparability** *n,* **comparably** *adv.*

comparative[1] *adj* **1** considered as if in comparison to something else as a standard; relative. **2** involving comparison between different branches of a subject. **3** in grammar, of or constituting the degree of comparison expressing increase in quality, quantity, or relation: compare SUPERLATIVE[1] (2). ➤➤ **comparatively** *adv.*

comparative[2] *n* the comparative degree or form in a language.

comparator *n* in engineering, a device for comparing something with a similar thing or with a standard measure.

compare[1] *v* **1** (*usu* + to) to represent (something or somebody) as similar to another thing or person. **2** (*often* + to/with) to examine the character or qualities of (something or somebody), *esp* in order to discover resemblances or differences. **3** (+ with) to bear being compared. **4** (+ with) to be equal or alike. ✱ **compare notes** to exchange information or opinions.

compare[2] *n* comparison.

comparison *n* **1a** the representing of one thing or person as similar to or like another. **b** an examination of two or more items to establish similarities and dissimilarities. **2** identity or similarity of features.

compartment *n* **1** any of the parts into which an enclosed space is divided. **2** a separate division or section. ➤➤ **compartmental** *adj,* **compartmentally** *adv.*

compartmentalize *or* **-ise** *v* to separate (things) into isolated compartments, or to keep (something) in isolated categories. ➤➤ **compartmentalization** *n.*

compass[1] *n* **1a** an instrument that indicates directions, typically by means of a freely-turning needle pointing to magnetic north. **b** (*usu in pl, used as sing.*) an instrument for drawing circles or transferring measurements that consists of two legs joined at one end by a pivot. **2** range or scope.

compass[2] *v archaic* **1a** to encompass. **b** to travel entirely round (a place). **2** to achieve; to bring about.

compassion *n* sympathetic consciousness of others' distress together with a desire to alleviate it.

compassionate *adj* **1** having or showing compassion; sympathetic. **2** granted because of unusual, distressing circumstances affecting an individual: *compassionate leave.* ➤➤ **compassionately** *adv.*

compatible *adj* **1** (*often* + with) capable of existing or living together in harmony. **2** of equipment: able to be used in combination without modification. **3** consistent. ➤➤ **compatibility** *n,* **compatibly** *adv.*

compatriot *n* a person from the same country.

compeer *n formal* an equal or peer.

compel *v* (**compelled, compelling**) **1** to drive or force (somebody) irresistibly to do something. **2** to cause (something) to occur by overwhelming pressure.

compelling *adj* having an irresistible power of attraction. ➤➤ **compellingly** *adv.*

compendia *n* pl of COMPENDIUM.

compendious *adj formal* comprehensive but relatively brief. ➤➤ **compendiously** *adv*, **compendiousness** *n*.

compendium *n* (*pl* **compendiums** *or* **compendia**) **1** a brief summary of a larger work or of a field of knowledge; an abstract. **2** a collection of indoor games and puzzles.

compensate *v* **1** (*often* + for) to make amends to, *esp* by appropriate payment. **2** to have an equal and opposite effect to; to counterbalance. **3** (+ for) to supply an equivalent. ➤➤ **compensator** *n*, **compensatory** *adj*.

compensation *n* **1** a recompense; *specif* payment for damage or loss. **2a** increased functioning or development of one organ to compensate for a defect in another. **b** the alleviation of feelings of inferiority, frustration, failure, etc in one field by increased endeavour in another.

compere[1] *n Brit* the presenter of a radio or television programme, *esp* a light entertainment programme.

compere[2] *v Brit* to present or introduce (a show).

compete *v* (*often* + with) to strive consciously or unconsciously for an objective, or to be in a state of rivalry.

competence *or* **competency** *n* (*pl* **competences** *or* **competencies**) **1** the quality or state of being competent. **2** *formal* a sufficiency of means for the necessities and conveniences of life.

competent *adj* **1a** having requisite or adequate ability. **b** showing clear signs of production by a competent agent, e.g. a worker or writer. **2** legally qualified to deal with a particular matter. ➤➤ **competently** *adv*.

competition *n* **1** the act or process of competing; rivalry. **2a** an organized test of comparative skill, performance, etc. **b** (*used as sing. or pl*) the others competing with one.

competitive *adj* **1** relating to, characterized by, or based on competition. **2** of wages and prices: at least as good as those offered by competitors. **3** inclined or desiring to compete. ➤➤ **competitively** *adv*, **competitiveness** *n*.

competitor *n* somebody or something that competes; a rival.

compilation *n* **1** compiling. **2** something compiled.

compile *v* **1** to collect (material) into one work. **2** to compose (a book, etc) out of materials from other documents. **3** in computing, to translate (e.g. a program) using a compiler.

compiler *n* **1** a computer program that translates instructions written in a high-level symbolic language into machine code. **2** a person who compiles a book, etc.

complacency *or* **complacence** *n* self-satisfaction accompanied by unawareness of actual dangers or deficiencies.

complacent *adj* self-satisfied. ➤➤ **complacently** *adv*.

complain *v* **1** to express feelings of discontent. **2** to announce that one has a pain or symptom. ➤➤ **complainer** *n*, **complainingly** *adv*.

complainant *n* in law, the party in a legal action or proceeding who makes a complaint.

complaint *n* **1** an expression of discontent. **2a** something that is the cause or subject of protest or outcry. **b** a bodily ailment or disease.

complaisant *adj* **1** marked by an inclination to please or comply. **2** tending to consent to others' wishes. ➤➤ **complaisance** *n*.

compleat *adj archaic* complete, *esp* having a complete range of relevant qualities.

complement[1] *n* **1a** something that fills up or completes a whole, or adds extra features to enhance it. **b** the quantity required to make something complete; *specif* a group of people or things. **c** either of two mutually completing parts; a counterpart. **2** in grammar, an added word or expression by which a predication is made complete, e.g. *president* in the sentence *They elected him president*. **3** in geometry, an angle or arc that when added to a given angle or arc equals 90°.

Usage note

complement *or* compliment? See note at COMPLIMENT[1].

complement[2] *v* to be complementary to: *The flower complemented her dress.*

complementary *adj* **1** serving to fill out or complete. **2** mutually supplying each other's lack. **3** using or relating to complementary medicine. ➤➤ **complementarity** *n*.

complementary angle *n* either of two angles that have the sum of 90°.

complementary colour *n* either of a pair of contrasting colours that produce a neutral colour when combined.

complementary medicine *n* = ALTERNATIVE MEDICINE.

complete[1] *adj* **1** having all necessary parts, elements, or steps. **2** whole or concluded. **3a** fully carried out; thorough. **b** total or absolute. **4** thoroughly competent; highly proficient: *the complete interviewer*. ➤➤ **completely** *adv*, **completeness** *n*.

complete[2] *v* **1** to bring to an end; *esp* to bring to a perfected state. **2a** to make whole or perfect. **b** to mark the end of. **c** to execute or fulfil. **d** to enter information on (a form). **3** to carry out all the legal requirements for transfer of a property. ➤➤ **completion** *n*.

completist *n* somebody who has an obsession with collecting everything belonging to a particular set.

complex[1] *adj* **1** composed of two or more parts. **2** hard to separate, analyse, or solve; intricate. ➤➤ **complexity** *n*, **complexly** *adv*.

complex[2] *n* **1** a whole made up of complicated or interrelated parts. **2a** a group of repressed related desires and memories that usu adversely affects personality and behaviour. **b** *informal* an exaggerated reaction to or anxiety about something.

complexion *n* **1** the appearance of the skin, *esp* of the face. **2** the overall aspect or character of something. ➤➤ **complexioned** *adj*.

complex number *n* a number containing both real and imaginary parts.

compliance *n* **1** the act or process of complying with the wishes of others. **2** a disposition to yield to others. ➤➤ **compliant** *adj*, **compliantly** *adv*.

complicate *v* to make complex or difficult.

complicated *adj* **1** difficult to analyse, understand, or explain. **2** consisting of parts intricately combined.

complication *n* **1a** intricacy or complexity. **b** an instance of making difficult, involved, or intricate. **c** a complex or intricate feature or element. **d** a factor or issue that occurs unexpectedly and changes existing plans, methods, or attitudes. **2** a secondary disease or condition developing in the course of a primary disease or condition.

complicit *adj* participating in a wrongful act.

complicity *n* association or participation in a wrongful act.

compliment[1] *n* **1** an expression of esteem, affection, or admiration; *esp* a flattering remark. **2** (*in pl*) best wishes; regards.

Usage note

compliment *or* **complement**? These two words are easily confused. An expression of admiration is a *compliment*. A *complement* is an accompaniment to something that sets off its good qualities, the full number of something, or a word or expression that completes a predicate. The verbs *compliment* and *complement* work in the same way.

compliment[2] *v* (*often* + on) to pay a compliment to.

complimentary *adj* **1** expressing or containing a compliment: *a complimentary remark.* **2** given free as a courtesy or favour: *complimentary tickets.* ➤➤ **complimentarily** *adv.*

compline *n* the last of the daily religious services making up the Divine Office, said before retiring at night.

comply *v* (**-ies, -ied**) **1** (*usu* + with) to conform or adapt one's actions to somebody else's wishes or to a rule. **2** (*usu* + with) to meet a certain standard.

component[1] *n* a constituent part, *esp* of a machine.

component[2] *adj* of parts: serving or helping to constitute; constituent.

comport *v formal* to behave (oneself) in a manner that conforms with what is right or expected.

comportment *n informal* bearing or demeanour.

compose *v* **1a** to create by mental or artistic labour; to produce. **b** to formulate and write (a piece of music). **2a** to form (something) by putting it together. **b** (*usu in passive*) to form the substance of (something); to make (it) up. **c** to arrange (type) for printing; to set. **3** to free (oneself) from agitation; to calm or settle (oneself).

composed *adj* free from agitation; collected.

composer *n* a person who writes music.

composite[1] /'kompəzit/ *adj* **1** made up of distinct parts. **2** combining the typical or essential characteristics of individuals making up a group. **3** (**Composite**) of a Roman order of architecture that combines Ionic with Corinthian. **4** /'kompəziet/ of or belonging to a family of plants typically having florets arranged in dense heads that resemble single flowers.

composite[2] *n* **1** a composite building material. **2** /'kompəziet/a motion or proposal created from several related motions for the purpose of discussion.

composition *n* **1a** a piece of writing. **b** a written piece of music. **2** a product of mixing or combining various elements or ingredients. **3** the factors or parts which go to make something, or the way in which the factors or parts make up the whole. **4** the act or process of composing; *specif* arrangement into proper proportion or relation and artistic form. ➤➤ **compositional** *adj.*

compositor *n* somebody who sets type.

compos mentis *adj* of sound mind, memory, and understanding.

compost[1] *n* a mixture of decayed organic matter used for fertilizing and conditioning land.

compost[2] *v* **1** to convert (plant debris, etc) to compost. **2** to treat with compost.

composter *n* a barrel or similar container in which organic matter is collected for composting.

composure *n* calmness or repose, *esp* of mind, bearing, or appearance.

compote *n* fruit cooked in syrup and usu served cold.

compound[1] *n* **1** something formed by a union of elements or parts. **2** in chemistry, a distinct substance formed by combination of chemical elements in fixed proportion by mass. **3** a word consisting of components that are words, combining forms, or affixes, e.g. *houseboat* or *anthropology*.

compound[2] *adj* **1** composed of or resulting from union of many similar separate elements or parts. **2** involving or used in a combination.

compound[3] *v* **1** to put together (parts) so as to form a whole; to combine. **2** to form (something, e.g. a medicine) by combining parts. **3a** to pay (interest) on both the accumulated interest and the principal. **b** to add to (something bad); to augment. **4** in law, to agree for a consideration not to prosecute (an offence). ➤➤ **compounder** *n.*

compound[4] *n* a fenced or walled-in area containing a group of buildings, *esp* residences.

compound fracture *n* a bone fracture produced in such a way as to form an open wound.

compound interest *n* interest computed on the principal plus accumulated interest.

compound time *n* in music, a tempo with two or more groups of simple time units in each bar.

comprehend *v* **1** to grasp the nature, significance, or meaning of; to understand. **2** *formal* to include: *The park comprehends all of the land beyond the river.*

comprehensible *adj* capable of being comprehended; intelligible. ➤➤ **comprehensibility** *n,* **comprehensibly** *adv.*

comprehension *n* **1a** grasping with the intellect; understanding. **b** the capacity for understanding fully. **2** *Brit* a school exercise testing understanding of a passage.

comprehensive[1] *adj* **1** covering completely or broadly; inclusive. **2** having or exhibiting wide mental grasp. **3** *Brit* of or being the principle of educating in one unified school nearly all children above the age of eleven from a given area regardless of ability. ➤➤ **comprehensively** *adv,* **comprehensiveness** *n.*

comprehensive[2] *n Brit* a comprehensive school.

compress[1] *v* **1** to press or squeeze together. **2** to reduce in size or volume as if by squeezing. **3** in computing, to reduce (a file) to the smallest size possible, e.g. so that it will take up less memory or fit onto a disk. ➤➤ **compressibility** *n,* **compressible** *adj.*

compress[2] *n* a pad pressed on a body part, e.g. to ease the pain and swelling of a bruise.

compressed air *n* air under pressure greater than that of the atmosphere.

compression *n* **1** the action of compressing or being compressed. **2** the process of compressing the fuel mixture in a cylinder of an internal-combustion engine.

compressor *n* **1** something that compresses. **2** a machine for compressing gases.

comprise *v* **1** to be made up of: *The family comprised two adults and three children.* **2** to make up or constitute.

Usage note

Comprise is a difficult word to use. There are two rules to remember. First, a whole *comprises* (consists of or is composed of) its parts; the parts *make up* or *constitute* the whole, but do not *comprise* it: *The meal comprised no less than fifteen courses.* Second, *comprise* should not be followed by *of,* even when it is used in the passive.

compromise[1] *n* **1** a settlement reached by compromise. **2** the settling of differences through arbitration or through consent reached by mutual concessions.

compromise[2] *v* **1** to come to agreement by mutual concession. **2** to expose (somebody or something) to discredit or danger. **3** *archaic* to adjust or settle (a disagreement) by mutual concessions. ➤➤ **compromiser** *n.*

compromising *adj* likely to lead to discredit or scandal.

comptroller *n* a public finance officer.

compulsion *n* **1a** compelling or being compelled. **b** a force or agency that compels. **2** a strong impulse to perform an irrational act.

compulsive *adj* of, caused by, like, or suffering from a psychological compulsion or obsession. ➤➤ **compulsively** *adv,* **compulsiveness** *n.*

compulsory *adj* **1** mandatory or enforced. **2** involving compulsion or obligation; coercive. ➤➤ **compulsorily** *adv.*

compulsory purchase *n Brit* the compulsory purchase of private land for public use or development.

compunction *n* **1** anxiety arising from awareness of guilt; remorse. **2** a twinge of misgiving; a scruple. ➤➤ **compunctious** *adj.*

computation *n* **1** calculating, or a system of calculating. **2** the use or operation of a computer. ➤➤ **computational** *adj.*

compute *v* to determine (a quantity or number), *esp* by mathematical means, or by means of a computer. ➤➤ **computable** *adj.*

computer *n* a programmable electronic device that can store, retrieve, and process data.

computer-aided design *n* industrial design using computer graphics to construct models.

computerate *adj informal* computer-literate.

computerize *or* **-ise** *v* **1** to equip (an office, company, etc) with computers. **2** to carry out or conduct by means of a computer. ➤➤ **computerization** *n.*

computer language *n* an artificial language used to program a computer.

computer-literate *adj* able to use a computer competently. ➤➤ **computer literacy** *n.*

computer science *n* the study of the construction, operation, and use of computers.

comrade *n* **1a** an intimate friend or associate; a companion. **b** a fellow soldier. **2** a fellow communist. ➤➤ **comradely** *adj,* **comradeship** *n.*

con[1] *n informal* a confidence trick.

con[2] *v* (**conned, conning**) *informal* to swindle or trick.

con[3] *n informal* a convict.

con[4] *n* the opposing or negative position, or somebody holding it: compare PRO[1].

con[5] *adv* on the negative side; in opposition: compare PRO[2].

con[6] (*NAm* **conn**) *v* (**conned, conning**) to conduct or direct the steering of (a ship).

con- *prefix* see COM-.

concatenate *v formal or technical* to link (things) together in a series or chain. ➤➤ **concatenation** *n.*

concave *adj* hollowed or rounded inwards like the inside of a bowl: compare CONVEX. ➤➤ **concavely** *adv,* **concavity** *n.*

conceal *v* **1** to place out of sight. **2** (*often* + from) to prevent disclosure or recognition of. ➤➤ **concealer** *n,* **concealment** *n.*

concede *v* **1a** to accept as true, valid, or accurate. **b** to acknowledge grudgingly or hesitantly. **2** to grant or yield (a right or privilege). **3** to allow (e.g. a goal or point) involuntarily.

conceit *n* **1** excessively high opinion of oneself. **2** *literary* **a** a fanciful idea. **b** an elaborate and cleverly expressed figure of speech.

conceited *adj* having an excessively high opinion of oneself.

conceivable *adj* capable of being conceived; imaginable. ➤➤ **conceivably** *adv.*

conceive *v* **1** to become pregnant with (a baby). **2a** to cause (something) to originate in one's mind. **b** to form a conception of; to visualize.

concentrate[1] *v* **1a** to bring or direct (one's mind or attention) towards a common centre or objective; to focus. **b** to gather (something) into one body, mass, or force. **2** to make (a solution) less dilute. **3** (*often* + on/upon) to concentrate one's powers, efforts, or attention. ➤➤ **concentrator** *n.*

concentrate[2] *n* something concentrated; *esp* a feed for animals rich in digestible nutrients.

concentration *n* **1** direction of attention to a single object. **2** a concentrated mass or thing. **3** the relative amount of a substance in a mixture or a solution.

concentration camp *n* a camp where political prisoners, refugees, etc are confined; *esp* any of the Nazi camps during World War II.

concentric *adj* of a shape: having a common centre. ➤➤ **concentrically** *adv,* **concentricity** *n.*

concept *n* **1** something conceived in the mind; a thought or notion. **2** (*used before a noun*) developed to test or implement new ideas: *a concept car.* ➤➤ **conceptual** *adj,* **conceptually** *adv.*

conception *n* **1** conceiving or being conceived. **2** a general idea; a concept. **3** the originating of something in the mind.

conceptualize *or* **-ise** *v* to form a concept of. ➤➤ **conceptualization** *n.*

concern[1] *v* **1** to relate to; to be about: *The novel concerns three soldiers.* **2** to have an influence on (somebody); to involve: *The problem concerns us all.* **3** to be a care, trouble, or distress to. **4** to engage or occupy (oneself).

concern[2] *n* **1** something that relates or belongs to one. **2** a worry. **3** a matter for consideration. **4** a business or manufacturing organization or establishment.

concerned *adj* **1** anxious. **2** (*used after a noun*) involved, *esp* culpably involved: *The police arrested the men concerned.*

concerning *prep* relating to (something); with reference to (something).

concert[1] *n* **1** a public performance of music or dancing. **2** agreement. ✱ **in concert 1** working together. **2** of a musician: performing live.

concert[2] *v* to establish (a plan) by agreement between those involved.

concerted *adj* **1** planned or done together; combined. **2** performed in unison.

concerti *n* pl of CONCERTO.

concertina[1] *n* a small hexagonal musical instrument of the accordion family.

concertina[2] *v* (**concertinas, concertinaed** *or* **concertina'd, concertinaing**) to collapse or fold up.

concerto *n* (*pl* **concertos** *or* **concerti**) a piece for one or more soloists and orchestra, usu with three contrasting movements.

concert pitch *n* **1** in music, a tuning standard of usu 440 Hertz for A above middle C. **2** a high state of fitness or readiness.

concession *n* **1** the act or an instance of conceding. **2** a reduced price or fare for people in certain categories. **3** a grant of land, property, or a right made in return for services or for a particular use. **4a** a small shop or business that is allowed to operate on the premises of a larger business. **b** the right to operate such a concession. ➤➤ **concessionary** *adj*, **concessive** *adj*.

concessionaire *n* the owner or beneficiary of a concession.

conch *n* (*pl* **conchs** *or* **conches**) a large marine gastropod mollusc with a spiral shell.

conchology *n* the study of shells. ➤➤ **conchologist** *n*.

concierge *n* somebody who is employed as a doorkeeper, caretaker, etc, *esp* in France.

conciliate *v* **1** to appease or pacify. **2** *formal* to reconcile (people). ➤➤ **conciliation** *n*, **conciliative** *adj*, **conciliator** *n*, **conciliatory** *adj*.

concise *adj* brief and clear, without unnecessary details. ➤➤ **concisely** *adv*, **conciseness** *n*, **concision** *n*.

conclave *n* **1** a private meeting or secret assembly. **2** the assembly of Roman Catholic cardinals secluded while electing a pope.

conclude *v* **1** to bring or come to an end, *esp* in a particular way or with a particular action. **2a** to arrive at (an opinion) as a logically necessary inference. **b** to decide (something). **c** to come to an agreement on (something); to settle.

conclusion *n* **1** an act or instance of concluding. **2** a final summing up, e.g. of an essay. **3** a reasoned judgment; an inference. **4** a result or outcome.

conclusive *adj* putting an end to debate or question, *esp* by reason of irrefutability. ➤➤ **conclusively** *adv*, **conclusiveness** *n*.

concoct *v* **1** to prepare (e.g. a meal) by combining diverse ingredients. **2** to devise or invent (e.g. a story). ➤➤ **concocter** *n*, **concoction** *n*.

concomitant[1] *adj formal* accompanying, *esp* in a subordinate or incidental way. ➤➤ **concomitance** *n*, **concomitantly** *adv*.

concomitant[2] *n* something that accompanies or is collaterally connected with something else.

concord *n* **1** a state of agreement; harmony. **2** a treaty or covenant.

concordance *n* **1** an alphabetical index of the principal words in a book or an author's works, with their immediate contexts. **2** *formal* agreement.

concordant *adj* **1** in agreement. **2** harmonious.

concordat *n* a compact or covenant; *specif* one between a pope and a sovereign or government.

concourse *n* **1a** an open space where roads or paths meet. **b** an open space or main hall, e.g. in a station. **2** *formal* a coming or gathering together.

concrete[1] *adj* **1** real or tangible. **2** specific or particular. **3** characterized by or belonging to immediate experience of actual things or events. ➤➤ **concretely** *adv*, **concreteness** *n*.

concrete[2] *n* a hard strong building material made by mixing cement, sand, and gravel with sufficient water to cause the cement to set and bind the entire mass.

concrete[3] *v* to cover, form, or set with concrete.

concretion *n* **1** a hard, usu inorganic, mass formed abnormally in a living body. **2** a mass of deposited mineral matter in rock.

concubine *n* in a polygamous society, a woman who lives with a man as his wife; *esp* a woman who lives with a man in addition to his lawful wife or wives.

concupiscence *n formal* strong desire; *esp* lust. ➤➤ **concupiscent** *adj*.

concur *v* (**concurred, concurring**) **1** (*often* + with) to express agreement. **2** of events: to happen together; to coincide.

concurrent *adj* **1** operating or occurring at the same time. **2** in mathematics, of lines: convergent; *specif* having a common point. ➤➤ **concurrence** *n*, **concurrently** *adv*.

concuss *v* to affect with concussion.

concussion *n* **1** a jarring injury to the brain, often resulting in unconsciousness, caused by a hard blow. **2** a hard blow or collision. ➤➤ **concussive** *adj*.

condemn *v* **1** to declare (a person or an action) to be utterly reprehensible, wrong, or evil, usu after considering evidence. **2a** to prescribe punishment for; *specif* to sentence to death. **b** (*usu* + to) to sentence or doom. **3** to declare unfit for use. ➤➤ **condemnable** /kən'demnəbl/ *adj*, **condemnation** /kondem'naysh(ə)n/ *n*, **condemnatory** /kən'demnət(ə)ri/ *adj*.

condensate *n* a liquid product of condensation.

condensation *n* **1** droplets of water formed, e.g. on a window, when water vapour in the air cools and becomes liquid. **2** the change from a vapour or a gas to a liquid. **3** something that has been condensed, e.g. an abridgment of a literary work.

condense *v* **1** to make denser or more compact; to compress. **2** to undergo condensation.

condensed milk *n* milk thickened by evaporation and sweetened.

condenser *n* **1a** an apparatus for condensing gas or vapour. **b** a lens or mirror used to concentrate light on an object. **2** a capacitor.

condescend *v* **1** to waive the privileges of rank. **2** to descend to less formal or dignified action or speech. ➤➤ **condescending** *adj*, **condescendingly** *adv*, **condescension** *n*.

condign *adj literary* well-deserved; merited: *condign praise*.

condiment *n* a flavouring for food, such as pepper or mustard.

condition[1] *n* **1** a favourable or unfavourable state of something. **2a** a usu defective state of health or appearance. **b** a state of physical fitness or readiness for use. **c** (*in pl*) attendant circumstances. **3** something essential to the appearance or occurrence of something else; a prerequisite. ✱ **on condition that** providing that.

condition[2] *v* **1a** to adapt or modify (a person or animal) to a surrounding culture. **b** to modify (something) so that an act or response previously associated with one stimulus becomes associated with another. **2** to put into a proper or desired state for work or use. **3** to give a certain condition to. **4** to use conditioner on (the hair). **5** to put a condition on.

conditional[1] *adj* **1** subject to, implying, or dependent on a condition. **2** in grammar, expressing a condition, often with the word 'if'. ➤➤ **conditionality** *n*, **conditionally** *adv*.

conditional[2] *n* in grammar, a conditional clause or mood.

conditioner *n* a substance applied to the hair, fabric, etc, to improve the condition.

condo *n* (*pl* **-os**) *NAm, informal* a condominium.

condole *v* (+ with) to express sympathetic sorrow.

condolence *n* **1** sympathy with somebody in sorrow. **2** (*also in pl*) an expression of sympathy.

condom *n* a rubber sheath worn over the penis during sexual intercourse to prevent conception or sexually transmitted disease.

condominium *n* (*pl* **condominiums**) **1** joint sovereignty by two or more nations, or a territory under joint sovereignty. **2** *NAm* **a** an individually owned unit in a multi-unit structure, e.g. a block of flats. **b** a block of individually owned flats.

condone *v* to pardon or overlook (an offence) voluntarily. ➤➤ **condonation** *n.*

condor *n* a very large vulture of the high Andes with a bare head and neck.

conduce *v formal* (+ to) to lead or contribute to a particular and usu desirable result.

conducive *adj* (+ to) likely to bring about a certain desirable result.

conduct[1] *n* **1** a mode or standard of personal behaviour, *esp* as based on moral principles. **2** the act or manner of carrying on or directing an operation, etc; management.

conduct[2] *v* **1** to guide or escort (somebody) somewhere. **2a** to carry on or direct (an operation) from a position of command or control. **b** to carry out (an exercise or operation). **3a** to convey (water or other fluid material) in a channel, pipe, etc. **b** to act as a medium for transmitting (heat or light). **4** to behave (oneself) in a specified manner. **5** to direct the performance or execution of (a musical work or group of musicians). ➤➤ **conductive** *adj.*

conductance *n* the ability of a material to conduct electricity.

conduction *n* **1** the transfer of heat from an area of higher temperature to one of lower temperature in a conducting medium. **2** the transmission of sound or electricity through a medium. **3** = CONDUCTIVITY.

conductivity *n* (*pl* **-ies**) the ability of a material to conduct or transmit heat or electricity, or the degree of this.

conductor *n* **1** a person who directs the performance of an orchestra or other group of musicians. **2** a substance or body capable of transmitting electricity, heat, sound, etc. **3a** *esp* formerly, a collector of fares on a bus or tram. **b** *chiefly NAm* a guard in charge of a train. ➤➤ **conductorship** *n.*

conductress *n esp* formerly, a female collector of fares on a bus or tram.

conduit *n* **1** a channel through which something, e.g. a fluid, is conveyed. **2** a pipe, tube, or tile for protecting electric wires or cables. **3** an agency of communication or transmission.

cone *n* **1** the tapering fruit of a coniferous tree. **2** in solid geometry: **a** a solid generated by rotating a right-angled triangle about a side other than its hypotenuse. **b** a solid figure tapering evenly to a point from a circular base. **3** a plastic cone-shaped portable marker set up on a road surface to re-route traffic. **4** a crisp cone-shaped wafer for holding a portion of ice cream. **5** the apex of a volcano. **6** any of the relatively short light-receptors in the retina of vertebrates that are sensitive to bright light and function in colour vision: compare ROD (5).

coney *n* = CONY.

confab *n informal* a chat or discussion.

confabulate *v formal* **1** to chat. **2** to hold a discussion. ➤➤ **confabulation** *n.*

confect *v* to put together or prepare (an elaborate dish, artistic work, etc) from assorted ingredients or materials.

confection *n* **1** an elaborately prepared item of sweet food. **2** an elaborately contrived article of dress, e.g. a woman's hat.

confectioner *n* a manufacturer of or dealer in confectionery.

confectionery *n* (*pl* **-ies**) sweets and chocolate.

confederacy *n* (*pl* **-ies**) **1** a league or compact for mutual support or common action; an alliance of independent states. **2** (**the Confederacy**) the eleven southern states that withdrew from the USA in 1860 and 1861.

confederate[1] *adj* **1** united in a league; allied. **2** (**Confederate**) belonging or relating to the Confederacy.

confederate[2] *n* **1** an ally or accomplice. **2** (**Confederate**) an adherent of the Confederacy.

confederate[3] *v* **1** to unite (states, bodies, etc) in a confederacy. **2** to band together to form a confederacy.

confederation *n* **1** a league or alliance. **2** a union of self-governing states under the minimal control of a central authority. **3** the act of forming such a union or league.

confer *v* (**conferred, conferring**) **1** to bestow (an honour, award, or title) on somebody. **2** (*often* + with) to come together to compare views or take counsel; to consult. ➤➤ **conferral** *n,* **conferrer** *n.*

conferee *or* **conferree** *n* **1** a person on whom an award, etc is conferred. **2** a person who is conferred with on some matter. **3** any of the participants or delegates attending a conference.

conference *n* **1a** a usu formal interchange of views; a consultation. **b** a discussion held between people linked by telephone or computer. **2** a meeting of people, e.g. members of a certain profession, for the discussion of matters of common concern. **3** a representative assembly or administrative organization of an organization, association, etc.

conferree *n* see CONFEREE.

confess *v* **1a** to make known or admit (wrongdoing, etc on one's part). **b** to acknowledge (a fact), *esp* reluctantly. **2** of a priest: to receive the confession of (a penitent). **3** to acknowledge one's sins or the state of one's conscience to God or a priest.

confessedly *adv* by confession; admittedly.

confession *n* **1a** an acknowledgement of a fault, etc. **b** (*in pl*) revelations of a private nature about one's life. **2** a formal or written acknowledgment of guilt by a person accused of an offence. **3** in the Roman Catholic Church, a disclosure of one's sins in confidence to a priest, or the procedure of attending a church for this purpose. **4** a formal statement of religious beliefs. ➤➤ **confessional** *adj,* **confessionally** *adv.*

confessional *n* **1** the enclosed cubicle in a church where a priest hears confessions. **2** the practice of confessing to a priest.

confessor *n* **1** in the Roman Catholic Church a priest who hears confessions and gives absolution. **2** a person who makes a confession.

confetti *n* (*used as sing.*) small bits of coloured paper for throwing at celebrations, *esp* weddings.

confidant *or* **confidante** *n* a male or female friend to whom one entrusts one's secrets; an intimate.

confide *v* **1** (+ in) to impart one's secrets and other private matters to somebody. **2** to tell (something) confidentially. **3** *dated* to entrust (something) to somebody's care.

confidence *n* **1** a consciousness of one's powers being sufficient, or a feeling of reliance on one's circumstances; self-assurance. **2** faith or trust in something or somebody. **3** certainty or strong expectation. **4** something said or written in confidence; a secret. ✱ **in somebody's confidence** on intimate enough terms with somebody for them to tell one their private concerns. **take somebody into**

one's confidence to tell somebody something in private.

confidence game *n NAm* = CONFIDENCE TRICK.

confidence trick *n* a swindle performed by somebody pretending to be something they are not. ➤➤ **confidence trickster** *n.*

confident *adj* **1** characterized by assurance; self-reliant. **2** (*also* + of) full of conviction; certain. ➤➤ **confidently** *adv.*

confidential *adj* **1** of information: intended to be kept secret. **2** characterized by intimacy or willingness to confide. **3** of a secretary or assistant: entrusted with private or confidential information. ➤➤ **confidentiality** *n,* **confidentially** *adv.*

configuration *n* **1a** an arrangement of parts, *esp* as relative one to another. **b** the figure, contour, pattern, workings, etc, produced by such an arrangement. **2** the process of configuring a computer program or system, or the resulting set-up. ➤➤ **configurational** *adj.*

configure *v* **1** to give (a thing or things) a certain shape, pattern or configuration. **2** to set up (a computer system along with its peripherals, or a computer program) to operate according to a certain pattern or sequence. ➤➤ **configurable** *adj.*

confine *v* **1** (*often* + to) to restrict or keep within certain limits. **2** to shut (somebody) up. **3** (+ to) of an illness, etc: to keep (somebody) in bed, a wheelchair, etc. **4** *dated* to keep (a woman) indoors or in bed around the time of childbirth. ➤➤ **confinement** *n.*

confines *pl n* limits or boundaries.

confirm *v* **1** to establish or give official notice of the correctness of (a report, fear, etc). **2** (+ in) to vindicate or strengthen (somebody) in a belief, etc. **3** to be evidence of or prove. **4** to commit oneself definitely to (a booking, arrangement, etc). **5** to administer the rite of confirmation to (a candidate). ➤➤ **confirmatory** *adj.*

confirmation *n* **1** confirming proof; corroboration. **2** the confirming of a booking, arrangement, etc. **3** a religious ceremony admitting a person to full membership of a Christian church.

confirmed *adj* **1** being so fixed in habit or attitude as to be unlikely to change. **2** having been admitted to full membership of a Christian church through confirmation.

confiscate *v* **1** to seize (somebody's property) by authority. **2** to appropriate (somebody's land) and add it to the public treasury as a penalty. ➤➤ **confiscation** *n,* **confiscator** *n,* **confiscatory** *adj.*

confit *n* a dish of meat, typically duck or goose, cooked slowly in its own fat.

conflagration *n* a fire, *esp* a large and disastrous one.

conflate *v* to combine or fuse (two or more things, ideas, etc) into one. ➤➤ **conflation** *n.*

conflict[1] *n* **1** a sharp disagreement or clash. **2** mental struggle resulting from incompatible impulses. **3** a hostile encounter, e.g. a fight or war.

conflict[2] *v* to be incompatible or in opposition to each other; to clash.

conflicting *adj* being in conflict or opposition; incompatible.

confluence *n* **1** a coming or flowing together; a meeting or gathering at one point. **2** the union of two or more streams, or the place where this occurs. ➤➤ **confluent** *adj.*

conform *v* **1** to be obedient or compliant; *esp* to adapt oneself to prevailing standards or customs. **2** (+ to/with) to accord with a certain standard or pattern.

conformable *adj* consistent with, or corresponding to (a certain mood, type, etc).

conformance *n* = CONFORMITY.

conformation *n* the way in which something is formed; shape or structure. ➤➤ **conformational** *adj.*

conformist *n* a person who conforms to the orthodox view or accepted social practice. ➤➤ **conformism** *n,* **conformist** *adj.*

conformity *n* **1** correspondence or accordance with a certain model or standard. **2** (+ to) behaviour that is in compliance with a convention or specified requirements. **3** similarity in form.

confound *v* **1** to surprise or disconcert. **2** to prove (an argument, prediction, etc) wrong. **3** to defeat or overthrow (somebody or their plans).

confounded *adj dated* used to express annoyance: damned. ➤➤ **confoundedly** *adv.*

confraternity *n* (*pl* **-ies**) a brotherhood devoted to a religious or charitable cause.

confrère *n* a colleague or a fellow member of one's profession.

confront *v* **1** of a problem, etc: to lie before (somebody). **2** to have (something) before one to face or tackle. **3** to face up to (a problem or an opponent) and prepare to tackle them. **4** to present (somebody) with irrefutable and unwelcome facts, etc. ➤➤ **confrontation** *n,* **confrontational** *adj.*

Confucianism *n* a system of social and moral teachings founded by the Chinese philosopher Confucius (d.479 BC), emphasizing harmonious behaviour and human sympathy. ➤➤ **Confucian** *n and adj,* **Confucianist** *n and adj.*

confuse *v* **1** to bewilder or perplex. **2** to muddle or befuddle (a person or their mind). **3** to make more incomprehensible. **4** (*often* + with) to muddle (two or more usu similar things) or mistake (one thing) for another. ➤➤ **confusable** *adj,* **confusion** *n.*

confused *adj* **1** unable to sort out one's thoughts or emotions; bewildered. **2** muddled in one's mind, usu because of old age. **3** disorganized or muddled. **4** composed of a bewildering mixture of elements. ➤➤ **confusedly** *adv.*

confusing *adj* tending to cause mental confusion or bewilderment. ➤➤ **confusingly** *adv.*

confute *v* **1** to defeat thoroughly in argument. **2** to refute (an argument) conclusively. ➤➤ **confutation** *n.*

conga *n* **1** a dance involving three steps followed by a kick, performed by a group, usu in single file. **2** a tall narrow bass drum beaten with the hands.

congeal *v* to pass from a fluid to a solid state in the process of cooking or freezing; to coagulate. ➤➤ **congelation** *n.*

congener *n* **1** a member of the same taxonomic genus as another plant or animal. **2** somebody or something resembling another in nature or action. ➤➤ **congeneric** *adj.*

congenial *adj* **1** pleasant; *esp* agreeably suited to one's nature or tastes. **2** suited to or fitting in well with something. ➤➤ **congeniality** *n,* **congenially** *adv.*

congenital *adj* **1** of a disease or abnormality: existing at or dating from birth. **2** *informal* having an ingrained tendency to be a certain thing: *He's a congenital liar.* ➤➤ **congenitally** *adv.*

conger *n* a large edible sea eel.

conger eel *n* = CONGER.

congeries *n* (*pl* **congeries**) an accumulation or aggregation.

congested *adj* **1** overcrowded, e.g. with people or traffic. **2** of the lungs or respiratory system: filled with mucus, so as to make breathing difficult. **3** of other parts of the body: over-full of blood. ➤➤ **congestion** *n,* **congestive** *adj.*

conglomerate[1] *v* to gather into a mass; to accumulate. ➤➤ **conglomeration** *n,* **conglomerative** *adj.*

conglomerate[2] *n* **1** a composite mixture; *specif* a type of rock composed of variously-sized rounded fragments in a cement-like bed. **2** a widely diversified business company formed through successive acquisitions of other firms. ➤➤ **conglomerate** *adj.*

Congolese *n* (*pl* **Congolese**) **1** a native or inhabitant of the Congo, or the Democratic Republic of Congo, formerly Zaïre. **2** any of the Bantu languages spoken in the Congo area. ➤➤ **Congolese** *adj.*

congratulate *v* (+ on) to express one's pleasure to (somebody) at their success or good fortune. ➤➤ **congratulation** *n,* **congratulatory** *adj.*

congratulations *pl n and interj* an expression of pleasure at somebody's success or good fortune.

congregant *n* a member of a congregation.

congregate *v* **1** to gather together. **2** (*usu in passive*) to assemble (people or things) together.

congregation *n* **1** an assembly of people, *esp* gathered for religious worship. **2** a religious community; *esp* an organized body of believers in a particular locality. **3** congregating or being congregated. ➤➤ **congregational** *adj.*

Congregationalism *n* a Protestant denomination in which each church is governed by the assembly of the local congregation. ➤➤ **Congregationalist** *n and adj.*

congress *n* **1** a formal meeting or programme of meetings between delegates. **2a** the supreme legislative body of a nation. **b** (**Congress**) the supreme legislative body of the USA. **3** *formal* the act or action of coming together and meeting. ➤➤ **congressional** *adj.*

congressman *or* **congresswoman** *n* (*pl* **congressmen** *or* **congresswomen**) a man or woman who is a member of a congress.

congruent *adj* **1** = CONGRUOUS. **2** geometrically identical; equal in size and shape. ➤➤ **congruence** *n,* **congruently** *adv.*

congruous *adj* (+ with) in agreement, harmony, or accordance with something. ➤➤ **congruity** *n,* **congruously** *adv,* **congruousness** *n.*

conic[1] *adj* **1** relating to cones. **2** having the shape of a cone.

conic[2] *n* = CONIC SECTION.

conical *adj* **1** having the shape of a cone. **2** relating to cones. ➤➤ **conically** *adv.*

conic section *n* any of the closed or open curves produced by the intersection of a plane with a cone, that is, the circle, ellipse, parabola, or hyperbola.

conifer *n* a tree or shrub, e.g. the pine, cypress, and yew, that bear ovules naked on the surface of scales, e.g. in cones, rather than enclosed in an ovary. ➤➤ **coniferous** *adj.*

conjecture[1] *n* **1** the drawing of conclusions from incomplete evidence. **2** a conclusion reached by surmise or guesswork. ➤➤ **conjectural** *adj.*

conjecture[2] *v* **1** to guess. **2** to form conjectures.

conjoin *v formal* to unite or join (people or things) together.

conjoint *adj* involving two or more in combination; joint or united.

conjugal *adj* relating to the married state or married people and their relationship.

conjugal rights *pl n* the rights implied by and involved in the marriage relationship, *esp* the right of sexual intercourse between husband and wife.

conjugate[1] *v* **1** to give in prescribed order the various inflectional forms of (a verb). **2** to join or combine (two substances), *esp* reversibly. **3** to become joined together. **4** of reproductive cells: to pair and fuse. ➤➤ **conjugation** *n.*

conjugate[2] *adj* **1** joined together, *esp* in pairs; coupled. **2** of words: derived from the same root and therefore usu alike in meaning.

conjugate[3] *n* something conjugate; a product of conjugating.

conjunct[1] *adj* joint or united.

conjunct[2] *n* **1** each of two or more combined or associated things. **2** in grammar, an adverb such as *therefore* or *however*, that connects sentences, etc.

conjunction *n* **1** in grammar, a word such as *and, or, but, if,* or *when*, that joins together sentences, clauses, phrases, or words. **2** the process of joining, or state of being joined. **3** in astrology, the apparent meeting or passing of two or more planets in the same part of the sky. **4** occurrence together in time or space; concurrence. ✱ **in conjunction with** combined with.

conjunctiva *n* the mucous membrane that lines the inner surface of the eyelids and part of the eyeball. ➤➤ **conjunctival** *adj.*

conjunctive[1] *adj* **1** connective. **2** in grammar, behaving as a conjunction.

conjunctive[2] *n* in grammar, a conjunction.

conjunctivitis *n* inflammation of the CONJUNCTIVA (membrane lining the eyelid), *esp* a contagious type with overproduction of mucus, causing eyelashes to adhere.

conjuncture *n* a combination of circumstances or events usu producing a crisis.

conjure *v* **1** (+ up) to produce from one's imagination or by using one's creative powers. **2** (+ up) of a word, sensation, etc: to evoke (ideas, images, etc). **3** *archaic* to summon (spirits, demons, etc) by means of a magic ritual. **4** *archaic* to beg or implore (somebody) to do something. **5** to perform conjuring tricks. ➤➤ **conjuring** *n.*

conjurer *or* **conjuror** *n* a person who performs tricks by sleight of hand or illusion.

conjuring trick *n* a trick using sleight of hand that deceives the eye or apparently defies nature.

conjuror *n* see CONJURER.

conk *n informal Brit* the nose.

conker *n* **1** the large hard shiny brown nut of the horse chestnut. **2** *Brit* (*in pl, used as sing.*) a game in which each player in turn swings a conker on a string to try to break one held by their opponent.

conk out *v informal* **1** of a motor vehicle, a machine, or body part: to break down. **2** of a person: to collapse, die, or fall asleep.

conman *n* (*pl* **conmen**) *informal* a person who uses confidence tricks to cheat others; a swindler.

conn *v NAm* see CON[6].

connect *v* **1** to link (two things) together. **2** (*often* + with) to associate (two things) mentally. **3** to constitute a link between (two things). **4** to link (two callers) by telephone. **5** (*often* + with) to be joined. **6** (*often* + with) of a train, bus, etc: to be timed to reach its destination in time for passengers to transfer to another train, bus, etc. **7** *informal* (*also* + with) of a hit or shot: to find its target. ➤➤ **connector** *n.*

connecting rod *n* a rod that transmits power from a part of a machine in reciprocating motion, e.g. a piston, to another that is rotating, e.g. a crankshaft.

connection (*Brit* **connexion**) *n* **1** something that connects; a link. **2** a relationship or association. **3** a train, bus, plane, etc, that one is scheduled to transfer to. **4** (*also in pl*) somebody connected to one by friendship, professional interests, etc. ✱ **in connection with** with relation to. **in this/that connection** in reference to this or that.

connective *adj* tending or serving to connect. ▸▸ **connectively** *adv*, **connectivity** *n*.

connective tissue *n* any of various tissues, e.g. bone or cartilage, that pervade, support, and bind together other tissues and organs.

connexion *n Brit* see CONNECTION.

conning tower *n* a raised observation tower, usu incorporating an entrance on the deck of a submarine.

connive *v* **1** (*often* + in/at) to pretend ignorance of or fail to take action against something one ought to oppose. **2** (*often* + with) to cooperate secretly or have a secret understanding; to conspire. ▸▸ **connivance** *n*, **conniver** *n*.

conniving *adj* scheming or coldly manipulative.

connoisseur /konə'suh/ *n* an expert judge in matters of taste or appreciation, e.g. of art or food. ▸▸ **connoisseurship** *n*.

connotation *n* (*also in pl*) something suggested by a word as distinct from its direct meaning. ▸▸ **connotational** *adj*.

connote *v* **1** of a word, etc: to convey (a range of ideas or feelings) in addition to its exact explicit meaning. **2** of a fact or circumstance: to imply or indicate as a logically essential attribute of something. ▸▸ **connotative** *adj*.

connubial *adj* concerning marriage or the relationship between husband and wife.

conquer *v* **1** to gain control over or subjugate (a country, etc or its people). **2** to overcome by force of arms, or vanquish (an army or general). **3** to master (a personal problem or weakness). **4** to climb and reach the summit of (a mountain). ▸▸ **conquerable** *adj*, **conqueror** *n*.

conquest *n* **1** the act or process of conquering. **2** (*also in pl*) **a** something conquered; *esp* territory appropriated in war. **b** a person who has been won over, *esp* by love or sexual attraction.

conquistador *n* (*pl* **conquistadores** *or* **conquistadors**) a conqueror; *specif* any of the Spanish conquerors of America.

consanguineous *adj* of the same blood or origin; *specif* descended from the same ancestor. ▸▸ **consanguinity** *n*.

conscience *n* the consciousness of the moral quality of one's own conduct or intentions, together with a feeling of obligation to refrain from doing wrong. ✱ **in all conscience** by any standard of fairness. ▸▸ **conscienceless** *adj*.

conscientious *adj* **1** governed by or conforming to the dictates of conscience; scrupulous. **2** meticulous or careful, *esp* in one's work; hard-working. ▸▸ **conscientiously** *adv*, **conscientiousness** *n*.

conscientious objector *n* a person who refuses to serve in the armed forces or bear arms, *esp* on moral or religious grounds.

conscious[1] *adj* **1** aware of one's surroundings and responding to them normally; awake. **2** (+ of) aware of something. **3** (+ of) recognizing a feeling in oneself. **4** (+ of) painfully aware of, or sensitive about something. **5** self-conscious; put-on. **6** deliberate. **7** (*used in combinations*) showing concern for the thing specified: *bargain-conscious shoppers*. ▸▸ **consciously** *adv*.

conscious[2] *n* in Freudian psychology, the part of the mind's workings that one is aware of.

consciousness *n* **1** the state of being conscious. **2** the state of knowing about or being conscious of something. **3** (*often as comb. form*) concern about a specific matter or area of activity: *political consciousness*.

conscript[1] *n* a person who has been conscripted.

conscript[2] *v* to enlist (somebody) compulsorily, *esp* for military service. ▸▸ **conscription** *n*.

consecrate *v* **1** to make or declare (a church, etc) sacred by a solemn ceremony. **2** to prepare (bread and wine used at communion) to be received as Christ's body and blood. **3** to ordain to a religious office, *esp* that of bishop. ▸▸ **consecration** *n*.

consecutive *adj* **1** following one after the other in order without gaps. **2** in grammar, denoting a clause expressing result. ▸▸ **consecutively** *adv*.

consensual *adj* relating to consent or consensus. ▸▸ **consensually** *adv*.

consensus *n* **1** general agreement; unanimity. **2** the judgment arrived at by most of those concerned.

consent[1] *v* **1** to give assent or approval to something; to agree to it. **2** to agree (to do something).

consent[2] *n* compliance in or approval of what is done or proposed by another; acquiescence.

consequence *n* **1** a result or effect. **2** importance or relevance. **3** *dated* social importance.

consequent *adj* **1** *formal* (+ to) following as a result or effect. **2** observing logical sequence; rational. ▸▸ **consequential** *adj*.

consequently *adv* as a result; in view of the foregoing.

conservancy *n* (*pl* **-ies**) **1a** conservation. **b** an organization designated to conserve and protect the environment. **c** an area protected by such a body. **2** *Brit* a board regulating a river or port.

conservation *n* **1** careful preservation and protection, *esp* of a natural resource, the quality of the environment, or a plant or animal species, to prevent exploitation or destruction. **2** the preservation of historic or archaeological artefacts or sites. **3** in physics, the conserving of a quantity. ▸▸ **conservational** *adj*, **conservationist** *n*.

conservatism *n* **1** the disposition to preserve what is established, or a political philosophy based on this. **2** (**Conservatism**) the principles and policies of a Conservative party. **3** the tendency to prefer an existing situation to change.

conservative[1] *adj* **1a** relating to or denoting a philosophy of conservatism; traditional. **b** (**Conservative**) relating to or constituting a British political party associated with support of established institutions and opposed to radical change. **2a** moderate; cautious: *a conservative estimate*. **b** characterized by or relating to traditional norms of taste, style, or manners: *a conservative suit*. ▸▸ **conservatively** *adv*.

conservative[2] *n* **1** (**Conservative**) a supporter of a Conservative party. **2** a person who keeps to traditional methods or views.

conservatoire *n* a school specializing in any one of the fine arts.

conservator *n* **1** a museum official responsible for the care, restoration, etc of exhibits. **2** an official charged with the protection of something affecting public welfare and interests, e.g. as a member of a conservancy.

conservatory *n* (*pl* **-ies**) **1** a greenhouse, usu forming a room of a house, for growing or displaying ornamental plants. **2** *chiefly NAm* a specialist academy in one of the arts; = CONSERVATOIRE.

conserve[1] *v* **1a** to keep (something, such as wildlife) in a state of safety or wholeness. **b** to avoid wasteful or destructive use of (a resource). **2** to preserve (fruit, etc), *esp* with sugar. **3** to maintain (mass, energy, momentum, etc) at a constant level during a process of chemical or physical change.

conserve[2] *n* a preserve of fruit boiled with sugar that is used like jam.

consider *v* **1** to think about carefully. **2** to deem or judge (something or someone to be something). **3** to have sympathetic regard for (somebody, their wishes, etc). **4** to look at (something) appraisingly. **5** to bear in mind.

considerable *adj* **1** worth consideration; significant. **2** large in extent or degree. ⋙ **considerably** *adv.*

considerate *adj* showing concern for the rights and feelings of others. ⋙ **considerately** *adv.*

consideration *n* **1** careful thought. **2** a factor taken into account in making a decision, etc. **3** the bearing of something in mind. **4** concern for others; considerateness. **5** a payment for a service. ✻ **in consideration of** in return for (a service, etc).

considering[1] *prep* taking (something) into account: *He did well considering his limitations.*

considering[2] *conj* in view of the fact that (something is the case): *Considering he was new at the job, he did quite well.*

considering[3] *adv informal* all things considered: *You did pretty well, considering.*

consign *v* **1** to entrust (something) to somebody's care. **2** to send or address (something) to an agent to be cared for or sold. **3** to commit (something) to a place where it will be got rid of. ⋙ **consignor** *n.*

consignee *n* a person to whom something is consigned.

consignment *n* a batch of goods for delivery.

consist *v* **1** (+ in) to lie or reside in something: *Liberty consists in the absence of obstructions* — A E Housman. **2** (+ of) to be made up or composed of one or several things: *Breakfast consisted of cereal, milk, and fruit.*

consistency *or* **consistence** *n* (*pl* **consistencies** *or* **consistences**) **1** the degree of thickness, viscosity, or firmness of a substance. **2** the quality of being mutually consistent, or of not being contradictory. **3** the quality of not varying over a period of time.

consistent *adj* **1** (*often* + with) in agreement; not contradictory. **2** not varying over a period of time. **3** hanging together logically; not self-contradictory. **4** (+ with) fitting in with (certain conjectural circumstances). ⋙ **consistently** *adv.*

consistory *n* (*pl* **-ies**) a church tribunal or governing body; *esp* one made up of the pope and cardinals.

consistory court *n* a diocesan court in the Church of England.

consolation *n* **1** comfort given to or received by somebody who has suffered loss or disappointment. **2** something that affords comfort.

consolation prize *n* a prize given to somebody who just fails to gain a major prize in a contest.

console[1] *v* to comfort or serve to comfort (somebody) in their grief or disappointment. ⋙ **consolingly** *adv.*

console[2] *n* **1** a control panel, or switchboard, or a cabinet or other unit in which a control panel is mounted. **2** an electronic device dedicated to playing computerized video games using a television set as display. **3** the desk containing the keyboards, stops, etc of an organ. **4** a carved bracket projecting from a wall to support a shelf or cornice.

consolidate *v* **1** to strengthen or make more solid and stable. **2** to cause to solidify or form a compact mass. **3** to combine (several elements) into a unit. ⋙ **consolidation** *n,* **consolidator** *n.*

consommé *n* a thin clear soup made from meat broth.

consonance *n* **1a** in verse, etc, correspondence or recurrence of sounds, *esp* consonant sounds, as in *shall surely follow*: compare ASSONANCE. **b** a harmonious combination of musical notes: compare DISSONANCE. **2** *formal* harmony or agreement.

consonant[1] *n* **1** any of a class of speech sounds, e.g. /p/, /g/, /n/, /l/, /s/, /r/, characterized by constriction or closure at one or more points in the breath channel. **2** a letter or symbol representing any of these sounds. ⋙ **consonantal** *adj.*

consonant[2] *adj formal* (+ with) in agreement or harmony with. ⋙ **consonantly** *adv.*

consort[1] *n* **1** a husband or wife, *esp* that of a reigning monarch. **2** a companion. **3** a ship acting as escort.

consort[2] *n* a group of musicians performing together, *esp* playing early music.

consort[3] *v formal* (+ with) to keep company with certain people.

consortium *n* (*pl* **consortia** *or* **consortiums**) a temporary combination of businesses providing or bidding for services for a project.

conspectus *n* a survey or summary; *esp* a brief one providing an overall view.

conspicuous *adj* **1** obvious to the eye or mind. **2** attracting attention; striking. ⋙ **conspicuously** *adv.*

conspicuous consumption *n* lavish or wasteful spending thought to enhance social prestige.

conspiracy *n* (*pl* **-ies**) **1** the activity of conspiring together. **2** the offence of conspiring to do something criminal or illegal. **3** an agreement reached by a group of conspirators; a plot.

conspiracy theory *n* a theory that an otherwise unexplained event was caused by the secret concerted action of powerful individuals or groups, rather than by a combination of circumstances.

conspirator *n* a person who conspires; a plotter. ⋙ **conspiratorial** *adj,* **conspiratorially** *adv.*

conspire *v* **1** to plot secretly with others, *esp* to do something wrong or illegal. **2** to act together as if deliberately, with undesirable results.

constable *n Brit* a police officer.

constabulary *n* (*pl* **-ies**) (*used as sing. or pl*) the police force of a district or country.

constant[1] *adj* **1** characterized by steadfast resolution or faithfulness; exhibiting constancy of mind or attachment. **2** invariable or uniform. **3** continually occurring or recurring; regular. ⋙ **constancy** *n,* **constantly** *adv.*

constant[2] *n* something with an invariable or unchanging value, e.g.: **a** a number that has a fixed value in a given situation or universally or that is characteristic of some substance or instrument. **b** a number that is assumed not to change value in a given mathematical discussion.

constellation *n* any of 88 arbitrary configurations of stars supposed to fill the outlines of usu mythical figures.

consternation *n* amazed dismay that throws one into confusion.

constipate *v* (*usu in passive*) to cause constipation in.

constipation *n* abnormally delayed or infrequent passage of faeces, *esp* when these are hard and compacted.

constituency *n* (*pl* **-ies**) an electoral district or the body of voters resident in it.

constituent[1] *n* **1** an essential part; a component. **2** a member of an MP's constituency.

constituent[2] *adj* **1** serving to form or make up a unit or whole; component. **2** having the power to frame or amend a constitution.

constitute *v* **1** of a group of people or things: to compose (something) together. **2** to be or amount to: *Does this constitute a breach of the peace?* **3** to establish or set up (an organization, etc). **4** to give legal form to (an assembly, court, etc).

constitution *n* **1** the fundamental principles and laws of a nation, state, or social group that guarantee certain rights to the people in it, determine the powers and duties of the government, and state how the government is appointed and what its structure will be. **2** the act of establishing, making, or setting up. **3** the make-up of something in terms of the elements of which it consists; composition. **4** the physical and mental make-up of a person.

constitutional *adj* **1** in accordance with or authorized by the constitution of a state or society. **2** regulated by or ruling according to a constitution. **3** relating to the constitution of a state. **4** relating to the fundamental make-up of something; essential. **5** relating to the constitution of body or mind. ➤➤ **constitutionality** *n*, **constitutionally** *adv*.

constitutive *adj* **1** having the power to enact or establish something. **2** forming a constituent part of something. ➤➤ **constitutively** *adv*.

constrain *v* **1** of circumstances: to force (somebody) to do something. **2** to inhibit (something).

constrained *adj* of conversation, smiles, etc: forced or unnatural, e.g. as a result of embarrassment. ➤➤ **constrainedly** *adv*.

constraint *n* **1** the state of being forced into a course of action. **2** a constraining force; a check. **3** inhibition that represses one's natural freedom of behaviour; embarrassment.

constrict *v* **1a** to make (a passage or opening) narrow. **b** to compress or squeeze (a nerve, etc). **2** to limit or inhibit. ➤➤ **constriction** *n*, **constrictive** *adj*.

constrictor *n* **1** a muscle that contracts a cavity or orifice or compresses an organ. **2** a snake, e.g. a boa or python, that kills prey by compressing it in its coils.

construct[1] *v* **1** to make, build, or erect. **2** to build up (a theory or hypothesis) from pieces of evidence. ➤➤ **constructor** *n*.

construct[2] *n* **1** something constructed or formulated. **2** a product of thought; an idea or concept.

construction *n* **1** the activity of building, or the process of being built. **2** a building or other structure. ✻ **put a certain construction on** to interpret (somebody's behaviour or words) in a certain way. ➤➤ **constructional** *adj*.

constructive *adj* **1** relating to or involved in construction. **2** of criticism, etc: offering ideas for improvement; positive rather than negative and destructive. **3** inferred rather than explicit. ➤➤ **constructively** *adv*, **constructiveness** *n*.

construe *v* (**construes, construed, construing**) to interpret (words, actions, evidence, etc) in a certain way. ➤➤ **construable** *adj*, **construal** *n*.

consubstantiation *n* in Christian theology, the Lutheran doctrine of the actual presence and combination of the body and blood of Christ with the bread and wine used at Communion.

consul *n* **1** an official appointed by a government to reside in a foreign country and look after the interests of citizens of the appointing country. **2** either of two elected chief magistrates of the Roman republic. ➤➤ **consular** *adj*, **consulship** *n*.

consulate *n* **1** the premises where a consul works. **2** government by consuls. **3** the period of office of a consul.

consult *v* **1** to ask the advice or opinion of (a doctor or other professional). **2** to look up (a reference book, etc). **3** to deliberate together; to confer. **4** to serve as a consultant; to give consultations. ➤➤ **consultation** *n*, **consultative** *adj*, **consultee** *n*.

consultancy *n* (*pl* **-ies**) **1** an agency that provides consulting services. **2** the post of a consultant.

consultant *n* **1** an expert who gives professional advice or services. **2** the most senior grade of British hospital doctor.

consumables *pl n* food or provisions.

consume *v* **1** to ingest (food or drink). **2** to use or use up (a fuel or other resource). **3** of fire: to destroy completely. **4** (*usu in passive*) of an emotion, *esp* an unworthy one: to obsess the heart or mind of (somebody). ➤➤ **consumable** *adj*, **consuming** *adj*.

consumer *n* a customer for goods or services.

consumerism *n* **1** the promotion and protection of the consumer's interests. **2** the theory that an increasing consumption of goods is economically desirable. ➤➤ **consumerist** *n and adj*.

consummate[1] *adj* **1** of the practiser of an art: extremely skilled and accomplished. **2** of the highest degree. ➤➤ **consummately** *adv*.

consummate[2] *v* **1** to make (a marriage) complete by sexual intercourse. **2** to finish (e.g. a business deal). ➤➤ **consummation** *n*, **consummator** *n*.

consumption *n* **1** the act of consuming or process of being consumed. **2** an amount consumed. **3** *dated* a wasting disease, *esp* tuberculosis of the lungs.

consumptive[1] *adj dated* affected with consumption, *esp* of the lungs.

consumptive[2] *n dated* someone suffering from consumption.

contact[1] *n* **1** the action or condition of physically touching. **2** meeting or communication. **3** a useful business acquaintance or relationship. **4** any of the people who have been in association with an infected person. **5a** the junction of two electrical conductors. **b** a part of an electrical device for such a junction. **6** (*used before a noun*) caused by or involving touch: *contact dermatitis*. **7** (*in pl*) contact lenses.

contact[2] *v* to communicate with (somebody). ➤➤ **contactable** *adj*.

contact lens *n* a thin lens designed to fit over the cornea of the eye, *esp* for the correction of a visual defect.

contact print *n* a photographic print made with a negative in contact with a photographic paper, plate, or film.

contact sport *n* any sport that of its nature brings participants into direct physical contact, such as wrestling or rugby.

contagion *n* the transmission of a disease from one person to another by contact.

contagious *adj* **1** of a disease: communicable by contact; catching. **2** of a person: suffering from a contagion and likely to communicate it; infectious. **3** of somebody's mood or attitude: tending to communicate itself to others; infectious. ➤➤ **contagiously** *adv*, **contagiousness** *n*.

contain *v* **1** to have or hold (something) within itself. **2** to comprise or include: *The bill contained some new clauses.* **3** to keep (something) within limits: *The flood waters could not be contained.* **4** to check or halt: *They tried to contain the spread of the infection.*

5 to restrain or control (oneself or one's excitement). ⋙ **containable** *adj.*

container *n* **1** an object, such as a box or tin, that contains things. **2** a metal packing case for the transport of goods, usu forming a single load for a lorry or railway wagon.

containerize *or* **-ise** *v* **1** to transport (goods) in containers. **2** to convert (a port or goods-transporting system) to the use of containers.

containment *n* the action of keeping something under control, *esp* of preventing the expansion of a hostile power or ideology.

contaminate *v* **1** to render impure or unfit for use through contact with or the admixture of a polluting or poisonous substance. **2** to make radioactive through exposure to a radioactive substance. **3** to destroy the purity and innocence of (somebody or something) through unwholesome or undesirable influences. ⋙ **contaminant** *n,* **contamination** *n,* **contaminative** *adj,* **contaminator** *n.*

contemn *v archaic* to despise or treat with contempt. ⋙ **contemner** *n.*

contemplate *v* **1** to consider or meditate on. **2** to look at attentively. **3** (*usu in negative contexts*) to envisage with equanimity. **4** to consider as a course of action. ⋙ **contemplator** *n.*

contemplation *n* **1** the activity of contemplating. **2** meditation on spiritual things as a private devotion.

contemplative[1] *adj* **1** relating to or involving contemplation. **2** denoting a religious order devoted to prayer and penance. ⋙ **contemplatively** *adv.*

contemplative[2] *n* a person who practises contemplation, *esp* as a member of a religious order.

contemporaneous *adj* existing during or happening during the same period of time. ⋙ **contemporaneity** *n,* **contemporaneously** *adv,* **contemporaneousness** *n.*

contemporary[1] *adj* **1** happening, existing, or coming into being during the same period of time. **2** reflecting today's design or fashion trends; modern.

contemporary[2] *n* (*pl* **-ies**) a person who is contemporary with the person in question, *esp* somebody of the same age.

contempt *n* **1** the feeling one has towards someone or something that one despises or has no respect for. **2** (**contempt of court**) wilful disobedience to or open disrespect for a court. ✱ **beneath contempt** utterly despicable. **hold somebody/something in contempt** to despise somebody or something.

contemptible *adj* deserving contempt. ⋙ **contemptibly** *adv.*

contemptuous *adj* manifesting or expressing contempt. ⋙ **contemptuously** *adv,* **contemptuousness** *n.*

contend *v* **1** to strive or vie in contest or rivalry. **2** (+ with) to try to overcome difficulties. **3** to strive in debate; to argue. **4** to maintain or assert (something). ⋙ **contender** *n.*

content[1] *adj* happy or satisfied. ✱ **not content with** in spite of having achieved something. ⋙ **contentment** *n.*

content[2] *v* to satisfy (somebody) or appease their desires. ✱ **content oneself with** to accept (something that is less than one really wants).

content[3] *n* a state of happy satisfaction; *esp* freedom from care or discomfort. ✱ **to one's heart's content** as much as one wants.

content[4] *n* **1** (*in pl*) the things that are contained in something. **2** (*also* **table of contents**) (*in pl*) the topics and material advertised as treated in a written work. **3** the matter dealt with in a literary work, lecture, etc, as distinct from its form or style of presentation. **4** the amount or proportion of a specified material contained in something.

contented *adj* **1** satisfied with one's situation, status, etc; happy. **2** reflecting such satisfaction. ⋙ **contentedly** *adv,* **contentedness** *n.*

contention *n* **1** rivalry or competition. **2** disagreement or argument. **3** a point advanced or maintained in a debate or argument. ✱ **in contention** contending for a prize, etc.

contentious *adj* **1** exhibiting a tendency to quarrels and disputes. **2** likely to cause contention. **3** denoting a legal case involving a dispute between parties. ⋙ **contentiously** *adv,* **contentiousness** *n.*

conterminous *adj* see COTERMINOUS. ⋙ **conterminously** *adv.*

contest[1] *n* **1** a struggle for superiority or victory. **2** a competition or competitive event.

contest[2] *v* **1** to stand as a candidate in (an election) or for (an elected post). **2** to dispute (a will, claim, decision, etc), sometimes through the law. **3** (+ with/against) to strive or vie. ⋙ **contestable** *adj,* **contester** *n.*

contestant *n* **1** one of the participants in a contest. **2** a person who contests an award or decision.

context *n* **1** the parts surrounding a written or spoken word or passage that can throw light on its meaning. **2** the interrelated conditions in which something exists or occurs. ⋙ **contextual** *adj,* **contextually** *adv.*

contextualize *or* **-ise** *v* to put (something) into its appropriate context. ⋙ **contextualization** *n.*

contiguous *adj* **1** in actual contact. **2** touching along a boundary or at a point; adjacent. **3** next or near in time or sequence. ⋙ **contiguity** *n,* **contiguously** *adv.*

continent[1] *n* **1** any of the great divisions of land on the globe, that is, Europe, Asia, Africa, N and S America, Australia, and Antarctica. **2** (**the Continent**) the continent of Europe, as distinguished from the British Isles.

continent[2] *adj* **1** exercising self-restraint. **2** able to control the passing of urine and faeces. ⋙ **continence** *n,* **continently** *adv.*

continental[1] *adj* relating to or characteristic of a continent, *esp* Europe.

continental[2] *n* an inhabitant of a continent, *esp* Europe.

continental breakfast *n* a light breakfast, typically of bread rolls with preserves and coffee.

continental climate *n* the climate typical of the interior of a continent, with hot summers, cold winters, and comparatively little rainfall.

continental day *n Brit* a school day that starts in the early morning and ends in the early afternoon, without a long midday break.

continental drift *n* the drifting apart of the continents across the earth's surface from a single solid land mass over geological time.

continental quilt *n Brit* = DUVET.

continental shelf *n* the gently sloping part of the ocean floor that borders a continent and ends in a steeper slope to the ocean depths.

contingency *n* (*pl* **-ies**) **1** an event, especially an undesirable one, that may occur but cannot be definitely predicted; an eventuality. **2** the absence of certainty in the occurrence of events.

contingent[1] *adj* **1** happening by or subject to chance or unforeseen causes. **2** happening as a secondary rather than direct consequence. **3** not logically necessary. **4** (+ on/upon) dependent on or conditioned by something. ➤➤ **contingently** *adv.*

contingent[2] *n* a quota or share, *esp* of people supplied from or representative of an area, group, or military force.

continua *n* pl of CONTINUUM.

continual *adj* **1** continuing indefinitely without interruption: *living in continual fear.* **2** recurring in steady rapid succession: *continual interruptions.* ➤➤ **continually** *adv.*

Usage note

continual *or* **continuous**? The classic illustration of the difference between these two closely related adjectives compares a dripping tap (*continual* – occurring constantly, again and again and again with breaks in between) with a flowing tap (*continuous* – continuing in an unbroken stream). It follows from this that *continual* is generally the word to use with a plural noun (*continual interruptions; continual requests for this record*), whereas either word may accompany a singular noun: *a continual* (constantly renewed) or *continuous* (unceasing) *bombardment by the enemy*.

continuance *n* **1** the act or process of continuing. **2** the time during which an arrangement, etc lasts or is in force.

continuation *n* **1** the process of continuing or of being continued. **2** resumption after an interruption. **3** something that continues, increases, or adds to something.

continue *v* **1a** to maintain (a condition, course, or action) without interruption; to carry on (doing something). **b** to resume (an activity) after interruption. **2** to remain in existence; to endure. **3** to remain in a place or condition; to stay. **4** to say (something) further. ➤➤ **continuer** *n.*

continuity *n* (*pl* **-ies**) **1a** uninterrupted connection, succession, or union. **b** persistence without essential change. **c** uninterrupted duration in time. **2 a** a film script or scenario giving the details of the sequence of individual shots. **b** speech or music used to link parts of a radio or television programme.

continuo *n* a bass part for a keyboard instrument written as a succession of bass notes with figures that indicate the required chords, used as an accompaniment in baroque music.

continuous *adj* uninterrupted; unbroken: *a continuous stream of phone calls; a continuous line.* ➤➤ **continuously** *adv,* **continuousness** *n.*

Usage note

continuous *or* **continual**? See note at CONTINUAL.

continuous assessment *n* appraisal of a student's work throughout a course as a means of awarding their final mark or degree.

continuum *n* (*pl* **continua**) **1** a continuous homogeneous extent or succession, such that adjacent parts are not distinguishable one from the other. **2** a sequence of minute gradations between extremes.

contort *v* **1** to twist (something) out of shape. **2** of a face or features: to twist in fury, agony, etc. ➤➤ **contortion** *n.*

contortionist *n* an acrobat who specializes in unnatural, *esp* convoluted, body postures.

contour[1] *n* **1** an outline, *esp* of a curving or irregular figure, or a line representing this. **2** a line, e.g. on a map, connecting points of equal elevation or height.

contour[2] *v* **1a** to shape the contour or outline of. **b** to shape so as to fit contours. **2** to construct (a road, etc) in conformity to a contour. **3** of a road, etc: to follow the contours of (a natural feature). **4** to enter the contours on (a map, etc).

contour line *n* = CONTOUR[1] (2).

contra- *prefix* **1** against: *contraception.* **2** contrary; contrasting: *contradistinction.* **3** pitched below normal: *contrabass.*

contraband *n* **1** goods or merchandise whose import, export, or possession is forbidden. **2** smuggled goods. ➤➤ **contraband** *adj.*

contraception *n* prevention of conception or impregnation, *esp* by artificial means.

contraceptive[1] *adj* denoting a method, device, or drug used to prevent conception.

contraceptive[2] *n* a contraceptive method, device, or drug.

contract[1] *n* **1a** a legally binding agreement between two or more people or parties. **b** a document stating the terms of such an agreement. **2** *informal* an arrangement for the murder of somebody by a hired killer.

contract[2] *v* **1a** to establish or undertake by contract. **b** to transfer or convey by contract. **2** to catch (a disease). **3** to incur (a debt). **4** to knit or wrinkle (one's brows) when frowning. **5** to reduce (something) to a smaller size by squeezing or forcing it together. **6** to draw together or tighten, so as to shorten or become reduced in size. **7** to shorten (a word) by omitting one or more sounds or letters.

contractable *adj* of a disease or habit: that can be caught or passed on.

contract bridge *n* a form of the card game bridge, which differs from auction bridge in that overtricks do not count towards game bonuses.

contractible *adj* **1** of tissues, etc: that can contract. **2** of a word or name: that can be shortened.

contractile *adj* having the ability to contract or cause contraction. ➤➤ **contractility** *n.*

contract in *v Brit* to agree to be included in a particular scheme.

contraction *n* **1** the contracting of a muscle or muscle fibre. **2** a shortening of a word, syllable, or word group, or the resultant short form. ➤➤ **contractive** *adj.*

contractor *n* a person who contracts to perform work, *esp* building work, or to provide supplies.

contract out *v* to opt not to be included in a particular scheme.

contractual *adj* relating to or constituting a contract. ➤➤ **contractually** *adv.*

contradict *v* **1** to state the contrary of (a statement or speaker). **2** to deny the truthfulness of (a statement or speaker). ➤➤ **contradictor** *n.*

contradiction *n* **1** the act of contradicting. **2** an expression or proposition containing contradictory parts; logical inconsistency. **3** opposition of factors inherent in a system or situation. ✱ **contradiction in terms** a group of words or a concept that associates incompatible elements.

contradictory *adj* **1** constituting a contradiction; incompatible or inconsistent. **2** of a person: inclined to contradict. **3** of a pair of propositions: logically such that one and only one must be true: compare CONTRARY[1]. ➤➤ **contradictorily** *adv,* **contradictoriness** *n.*

contradistinction *n* a distinction made between things by contrasting their different qualities.

contraflow *n* a temporary two-way traffic-flow system introduced on one carriageway of a motorway, etc while the other is closed off.

contraindicate *v* to render (a treatment or procedure) inadvisable. ➤➤ **contraindication** *n.*

contralto *n* (*pl* **-os**) a singer having the lowest female singing voice.

contraption *n* a newfangled or complicated device; a gadget.

contrapuntal *adj* relating to musical counterpoint. ➤➤ **contrapuntally** *adv.*

contrariety *n* opposition or inconsistency between two things.

contrariwise *adv* **1** conversely; vice versa. **2** on the contrary. **3** in contrast; on the other hand.

contrary[1] *adj* **1** completely different or opposed in nature. **2** /kən'treəri, 'kontrəri/ obstinately self-willed; inclined to oppose the wishes of others. **3** of the wind or weather: unfavourable. **4** /kən'treəri/ opposite in position or direction. ➤➤ **contrarily** *adv,* **contrariness** *n.*

contrary[2] ✱ **on/quite the contrary** just the opposite; no. **to the contrary 1** to the opposite effect. **2** notwithstanding.

contrary to *prep* in opposition to (something).

contrast[1] *n* **1a** juxtaposition of dissimilar elements, e.g. colour or emotion, in a work of art. **b** degree of difference between the lightest and darkest parts of a photograph, television picture, etc. **2** comparison of similar objects to set off their dissimilar qualities. **3** a person or thing against which another may be contrasted. ➤➤ **contrastive** *adj,* **contrastively** *adv.*

contrast[2] *v* **1** (+ with) to exhibit contrast. **2** to put (two things or people) in contrast. **3** to compare (two things) in respect to differences. ➤➤ **contrastable** *adj,* **contrasting** *adj,* **contrastingly** *adv.*

contravene *v* to act, or be, contrary to (a law, agreement, principle, etc). ➤➤ **contravener** *n.*

contravention *n* a violation or infringement. ✱ **in contravention of** in such a manner as to infringe (a law or principle).

contretemps /'konhtrətonh, 'kon-/ *n* (*pl* **contretemps**) a minor disagreement or confrontation.

contribute *v* **1** to give (money, etc) in common with others for a common cause. **2** to supply (an article, etc) for a publication. **3** (+ to) to help bring about an end or result. ➤➤ **contribution** *n,* **contributive** *adj,* **contributor** *n.*

Usage note

Contribute is usually pronounced with the stress on the second syllable *-trib-*. Pronunciation with the stress on the first syllable *con-* is disliked by many people.

contributory *adj* **1** having helped to cause something. **2** denoting a pension scheme or insurance plan that is contributed to by both employers and employees. **3** contributing to a common fund or enterprise.

con trick *n informal* = CONFIDENCE TRICK.

contrite *adj* grieving and penitent for one's sin or shortcomings. ➤➤ **contritely** *adv,* **contriteness** *n.*

contrition *n* sorrow for one's sins, arising *esp* from the love of God rather than fear of punishment.

contrivance *n* **1** the process of contriving something. **2** something contrived, e.g. a mechanical device or a clever ploy. **3** rather too obvious artificiality in achieving an effect.

contrive *v* **1a** to devise or plan (something). **b** to create in an inventive or resourceful manner. **2a** to bring about or manage. **b** to manage (to do something stupid). ➤➤ **contrivable** *adj,* **contriver** *n.*

contrived *adj* of artistic or literary effects, language, etc: unnatural or forced.

control[1] *v* (**controlled, controlling**) **1** to supervise and direct (something). **2** to operate (a machine). **3** to restrain (oneself or one's emotions). **4** to regulate (the finances of an organization, etc). ➤➤ **controllability** *n,* **controllable** *adj,* **controller** *n.*

control[2] *n* **1** power or authority to control. **2** the activity or situation of controlling. **3** direction, regulation, and coordination of business activities. **4** mastery in the use of a tool, technique, or artistic medium. **5** restraint or reserve. **6** a checking device. **7a** = CONTROL EXPERIMENT. **b** in a control experiment, a subject not given the treatment under trial, for purposes of comparison. **8** (*in pl*) the devices and mechanisms used to regulate or guide the operation of a machine, apparatus, or system. **9** (*used as sing. or pl*) an organization that directs a space flight. ✱ **in control** in control or command. **out of control** dangerously unrestrained. **under control** being properly supervised and regulated.

control character *n* in computing, a keyboard character that is not printed, but initiates an operation or controls a device.

control experiment *n* an experiment or trial in which parallel testing is carried out on a CONTROL[2] (a subject not given the treatment under trial).

control key *n* a key on a computer keyboard that another key causes to emit a command sequence when pressed simultaneously with it.

controlling interest *n* sufficient share ownership in a company to have control over policy.

control tower *n* a tall airport building from which movements of aircraft are controlled.

control unit *n* a section of the central processing unit in a computer that controls the movement of information between the memory, the arithmetic and logic unit, and other registers in order to execute a program.

controversial *adj* tending to cause controversy. ➤➤ **controversialist** *n,* **controversially** *adv.*

controversy *n* (*pl* **-ies**) **1** debate or disagreement, *esp* in public or in the media. **2** a dispute over a specific issue.

Usage note

The traditional pronunciation of *controversy* places the stress on the first syllable *con-*. In British English the stress is frequently placed on the second syllable *-trov-*. All modern British dictionaries accept this pronunciation, but many traditionalists dislike it.

controvert *v formal* to deny or dispute the truth of. ➤➤ **controvertible** *adj.*

contumacious *adj formal* stubbornly disobedient; rebellious. ➤➤ **contumaciously** *adv,* **contumacy** *n.*

contumely *n formal* abusive and contemptuous language or treatment.

contuse *v* to injure (part of the body) without breaking the skin; to bruise.

contusion *n* a bruise.

conundrum *n* (*pl* **conundrums**) **1** a riddle; *esp* one whose answer is or involves a pun. **2** an intricate and difficult problem.

conurbation *n* a vast urban area, formed when the suburbs of a large city coalesce with nearby towns.

convalesce *v* to recover gradually after sickness or weakness. ➤➤ **convalescence** *n,* **convalescent** *adj and n.*

convect *v* to circulate (warm air) by convection.

convection *n* the transfer of heat by the circulatory motion that occurs in a gas or liquid at a non-uniform temperature owing to the variation of density with temperature. ➤➤ **convectional** *adj,* **convective** *adj.*

convector *n* a heating unit from which heated air circulates by convection.

convene *v* to assemble or cause (a committee, etc) to assemble for a meeting, etc.

convener *n* see CONVENOR.

convenience *n* **1** ease of use or access; handiness. **2** one's personal comfort or advantage. **3** an appliance or service conducive to comfort. **4** *Brit* = PUBLIC CONVENIENCE. ✱ **at one's convenience** when it suits one to do something.

convenience food *n* commercially prepared food requiring little or no further preparation before eating.

convenient *adj* **1** suited to personal comfort or to easy use. **2** suited to a particular situation. **3** near at hand; easily accessible. ➤➤ **conveniently** *adv.*

convenor *or* **convener** *n* **1** *chiefly Brit* a member of a group, *esp* a committee, responsible for calling meetings. **2** an elected union official responsible for coordinating the work of shop stewards in an establishment.

convent *n* **1** a local community of a religious order or congregation; *esp* an establishment of nuns. **2** a school attached to a convent, at which the majority of teachers are nuns.

conventicle *n* formerly, an irregular or unlawful assembly or meeting, *esp* of dissenters (people not conforming to the Church of England; see DISSENTER), for religious worship.

convention *n* **1** accepted social custom or practice, or a specific form or use. **2** a generally agreed principle or practice. **3** an agreement between states that regulates matters affecting all of them. **4** an assembly of people met for a common purpose; a conference. **5** a meeting of the delegates of a US political party for the purpose of formulating policies and selecting candidates for office. **6** an established artistic technique or practice.

conventional *adj* **1a** conforming to or sanctioned by convention. **b** lacking originality or individuality. **2** of warfare: not using atom bombs or hydrogen bombs. ➤➤ **conventionalism** *n*, **conventionalist** *n*, **conventionality** *n*, **conventionally** *adv.*

conventionalize *or* **-ise** *v* to make conventional.

converge *v* **1** of lines: to move together towards a common point and finally meet. **2** (+ on/upon) to come together in a common interest or focus. ➤➤ **convergence** *n*, **convergent** *adj.*

conversant *adj* (+ with) fully acquainted or familiar with facts, principles, etc.

conversation *n* **1** informal verbal exchange of feelings, opinions, or ideas. **2** an instance of this. ➤➤ **conversational** *adj*, **conversationally** *adv.*

conversationalist *n* a person who enjoys or excels in conversation.

converse[1] *v* to exchange thoughts and opinions in speech; to talk. ➤➤ **converser** *n.*

converse[2] *adj* reversed in order, relation, or action; opposite. ➤➤ **conversely** *adv.*

converse[3] *n* a situation, fact, etc that is the opposite of something else.

conversion *n* **1** the converting of something or its converted state. **2** something converted from one use to another. **3a** the alteration of a building to a different purpose. **b** a building so altered. **4** a definite and decisive adoption of a religious faith, or an experience that prompts this or is associated with it. **5** in rugby or American football, an opportunity to score extra points awarded after a try or touchdown, or the score that results from this.

convert[1] *v* **1** to change (something) from one form or function to another, e.g. to make structural alterations to (a building or part of a building). **2** to alter the physical or chemical nature or properties of (something), *esp* in manufacturing. **3** to exchange (e.g. a security or bond) for something of equivalent value. **4a** to win (somebody) over from one persuasion or party to another. **b** to experience or cause (somebody) to experience a religious conversion. **5a** in rugby, to complete (a try) by successfully kicking a conversion. **b** in American football, to complete (a touchdown) by successfully kicking a conversion. ➤➤ **converter** *n*, **convertor** *n.*

convert[2] *n* a person who has been converted, *esp* one who has undergone a religious conversion.

convertible[1] *adj* **1** capable of being converted. **2** of a car: having a top that may be lowered or removed. ➤➤ **convertibility** *n.*

convertible[2] *n* a convertible car.

convex *adj* curved or rounded outwards like the outside of a bowl: compare CONCAVE. ➤➤ **convexity** *n*, **convexly** *adv.*

convey *v* **1** to take or carry from one place to another. **2** to impart or communicate (e.g. a feeling or idea). **3** in law, to transfer (property or the rights to property) to another person. ➤➤ **conveyable** *adj*, **conveyer** *n*, **conveyor** *n.*

conveyance *n* **1** the conveying of something. **2** a means of transport; a vehicle. **3** a document by which rights to property are transferred, or the transfer itself. ➤➤ **conveyancer** *n*, **conveyancing** *n.*

conveyor belt *n* a mechanical apparatus for carrying articles, in the form of an endless moving belt or set of linked plates.

convict[1] *v* to find or prove (somebody) to be guilty of a crime.

convict[2] *n* a person who has been found guilty and is serving a prison sentence.

conviction *n* **1a** a strongly held persuasion or belief. **b** the state of being convinced. **2** the convicting of somebody, or the state of being convicted, *esp* in judicial proceedings.

convince *v* **1** to cause to believe or accept something. **2** to persuade to a course of action. ➤➤ **convincer** *n*, **convincible** *adj.*

convincing *adj* **1** removing doubt or disbelief; plausible. **2** of a victory, etc: secured easily and by a large margin. ➤➤ **convincingly** *adv.*

convivial *adj* **1** sociable or friendly. **2** occupied with or fond of eating, drinking, and good company. ➤➤ **conviviality** *n*, **convivially** *adv.*

convocation *n* **1** either of the two provincial assemblies of bishops and representative clergy of the Church of England (Canterbury and York). **2** *Brit* a legislative assembly of a university. **3** the act of calling people together. ➤➤ **convocational** *adj.*

convoke *v formal* to call (a formal meeting).

convoluted *adj* **1** complex and difficult to understand or unravel; involved. **2** *technical* having twists or coils. ➤➤ **convolutedly** *adv.*

convolution *n* **1** a twist or coil. **2** something intricate or complicated. ➤➤ **convolutional** *adj.*

convolvulus *n* (*pl* **convolvuluses**) a trailing or twining plant of the bindweed family, many of which have trumpet-shaped flowers and broadly triangular leaves.

convoy[1] *n* (*used as sing. or pl*) a group of ships, military vehicles, etc moving together, *esp* with a protective escort. ✱ **in convoy** travelling together.

convoy[2] *v* to accompany or escort (something or somebody in transit) for protection.

convulsant[1] *adj* of a drug: causing convulsions.

convulsant[2] *n* a convulsant drug.

convulse *v* **1** to cause (a person) to be shaken violently by spasms, e.g. of rage, laughter, etc. **2** to be convulsed. ⋙ **convulsive** *adj*, **convulsively** *adv*.

convulsion *n* **1** an abnormal violent and involuntary contraction or series of contractions of the muscles. **2** a violent disturbance. **3** (*in pl*) an uncontrolled fit of laughter.

cony *or* **coney** *n* (*pl* **conies** *or* **coneys**) a rabbit.

coo *v* (**coos, cooed, cooing**) **1** to make the low soft cry characteristic of a dove or pigeon, or a sound similar to it. **2** to talk lovingly or appreciatively. ⋙ **coo** *n*.

cooee *interj informal* used to make one's presence known or to attract somebody's attention at a distance. ✻ **within cooee** *Aus, NZ* in earshot.

cook[1] *v* **1** to prepare (food) for eating by a heating process. **2** of food: to undergo the process of being cooked. **3** to subject (something) to the action of heat or fire. **4** *informal* to falsify (e.g. financial accounts) in order to deceive. ✻ **cook somebody's goose** *informal* to ruin somebody's plans irretrievably.

cook[2] *n* a person who prepares food for eating, *esp* as a job.

cook-chill *n Brit* a method of preparing food in which dishes are pre-cooked and quickly chilled for reheating later. ⋙ **cook-chill** *adj*.

cooker *n Brit* **1** an appliance for cooking, typically consisting of an oven, hot plates or rings, and a grill fixed in position. **2** *informal* a variety of fruit, *esp* an apple, not usu eaten raw.

cookery *n* (*pl* **-ies**) **1** the art or practice of cooking. **2** *NAm* a kitchen.

cookhouse *n* a kitchen set up outdoors, e.g. at a campsite.

cookie *n* **1** *NAm* a sweet biscuit. **2** *informal* a person of a specified type: *a tough cookie*. **3** in computing, a string of data relating to a particular web site, downloaded to a user's hard disk and accessed whenever he or she visits that site. ✻ **the way the cookie crumbles** *chiefly NAm, informal* what inevitably happens.

cookout *n NAm* an outing at which food is cooked and served in the open.

Cook's tour *n informal* a quick tour in which attractions are viewed briefly and cursorily.

cook up *v informal* to concoct or improvise.

cool[1] *adj* **1** moderately cold; lacking in warmth. **2** bringing or suggesting relief from heat. **3** lacking friendliness or enthusiasm. **4** dispassionately calm and self-controlled. **5** *informal* used as an intensive: *We made a cool million*. **6** *informal* fashionable or attractive. **7** *informal* very good. ⋙ **coolish** *adj*, **coolly** *adv*, **coolness** *n*.

cool[2] *v* to make or become cool. ✻ **cool it** *informal* to become calm or quiet; to relax. **cool one's heels** to wait or be kept waiting for a long time.

cool[3] *n* **1** a cool atmosphere or place. **2** *informal* poise or composure. **3** *informal* the quality of being impressively fashionable or attractive. ✻ **keep/lose one's cool** *informal* to stay, or fail to stay, calm and composed.

coolabah *or* **coolibah** *n* a eucalyptus or gum tree that typically grows near rivers and streams.

coolant *n* a liquid or gas used in cooling, *esp* in an engine.

cool down *v* to allow a violent emotion, e.g. rage, to pass.

cooler *n* **1a** a container for cooling liquids. **b** *NAm* a refrigerator. **c** an insulated container for food or drink. **2** (**the cooler**) *informal* prison or a prison cell. **3** a drink consisting of wine, fruit juice, and soda water.

coolibah *n* see COOLABAH.

coolie *n* **1** *dated* an unskilled labourer or porter, usu in or from the Far East. **2** *offensive* somebody from India.

coolie hat *n* a shallow conical hat, usu of straw.

cooling-off period *n* an interval to allow passions to cool, to permit negotiation between parties, or to allow a recently signed contract to be cancelled.

cooling tower *n* a tall wide concrete tower in which steam from an industrial process is allowed to condense.

coomb *or* **coombe** *or* **combe** *n Brit* a valley or basin, *esp* on a hillside or running up from the coast.

coon *n* **1** *NAm* a raccoon. **2** *informal, offensive* a black person.

coop[1] *n* a cage or small enclosure for housing poultry.

coop[2] *v* (*usu* + up) to confine (a person or animal) in a restricted space.

co-op *n informal* a cooperative enterprise.

cooper *n* a person who makes or repairs barrels, casks, etc. ⋙ **cooperage** *n*.

cooperate *or* **co-operate** *v* **1** to act or work with another person or other people for a common purpose. **2** to do or agree to what is asked. ⋙ **cooperation** *n*, **cooperator** *n*.

cooperative[1] *or* **co-operative** *adj* **1** showing cooperation or a willingness to work with others. **2** of, or organized as, a cooperative. ⋙ **cooperatively** *adv*, **cooperativeness** *n*.

cooperative[2] *or* **co-operative** *n* an enterprise or organization owned by and operated for the benefit of those using its services.

co-opt *v* **1** of a committee or other body: to choose or elect (somebody) as a member. **2** to take (e.g. a faction or movement) into a larger group; to assimilate. **3** to take (something) and use it as one's own; to appropriate. ⋙ **co-optation** *n*, **co-option** *n*, **co-optive** *adj*.

coordinate[1] *or* **co-ordinate** *v* **1** to combine (diverse elements) into a common action, movement or condition; to harmonize. **2** to combine or act together harmoniously. ⋙ **coordinative** *adj*, **coordinator** *n*.

coordinate[2] *or* **co-ordinate** *n* **1** in mathematics, any of a set of numbers used in specifying the location of a point on a line, on a surface, or in space. **2** (*in pl*) outer garments, usu separates, in harmonizing colours and materials.

coordinate[3] *or* **co-ordinate** *adj* equal in rank, quality, or significance.

coordinated *or* **co-ordinated** *adj* able to move one's body efficiently and usu gracefully in sports, gymnastics, etc.

coordination *or* **co-ordination** *n* **1** the act or action of coordinating. **2** the state of being coordinate or coordinated.

coot *n* (*pl* **coot**) **1** a water bird with dark plumage and a white bill. **2** *informal* a foolish or eccentric person.

cop[1] *n informal* a police officer. ✻ **not much cop** *Brit, informal* fairly bad; worthless.

cop[2] *v* (**copped, copping**) *informal* **1** to capture or arrest. **2** to suffer (something). ✻ **cop a plea** *NAm, informal* to plea bargain. **cop hold of** *Brit, informal* to hold onto. **cop it 1** *Brit, informal* to be in serious trouble. **2** *Brit, informal* to be killed.

copal *n* a resin from various tropical trees used in varnishes.

cope[1] *v* to deal with something effectively.

cope[2] *n* a long ecclesiastical vestment resembling a cape, worn on special occasions.

cope[3] *v* to supply (e.g. a wall) with a coping.

copeck *n* see KOPECK.

Copernican system *n* the theory put forward by the Polish astronomer Nicolaus Copernicus (d.1543) that the earth rotates daily on its axis and the planets revolve in orbits round the sun: compare PTOLEMAIC SYSTEM.

copier *n* a machine for making copies, *esp* a photocopier.

co-pilot *n* a qualified aircraft pilot who assists or relieves the pilot but is not in command.

coping *n* the final, usu sloping, course of brick, stone, etc on the top of a wall.

copingstone *n* a stone forming part of a coping.

copious *adj* **1** yielding something in abundance; plentiful. **2** present in large quantities, or taking place on a large scale. ➤➤ **copiously** *adv*, **copiousness** *n*.

cop off *v informal* to have a casual sexual encounter with somebody.

copolymer *n* a POLYMER (large molecule composed of many repeating subunits) in which two or more chemically different subunits are present. ➤➤ **copolymeric** *adj*.

cop out *v informal* to avoid an unwanted responsibility or fail to fulfil a commitment.

cop-out *n informal* the act or an instance of copping out.

copper[1] *n* **1** a common reddish metallic chemical element that is ductile and malleable and one of the best conductors of heat and electricity, and is used for electrical wiring and as a constituent of certain alloys. **2** the colour of copper. **3** *Brit* a coin or token made of copper or bronze and usu of low value. **4** *Brit* a large metal vessel used, *esp* formerly, for boiling laundry. ➤➤ **coppery** *adj*.

copper[2] *adj* of the reddish colour of copper.

copper[3] *v* to coat or sheathe with copper.

copper[4] *n Brit, informal* a police officer.

copper beech *n* a variety of beech tree with copper-coloured leaves.

copper-bottomed *adj Brit* completely safe; reliable: *a copper-bottomed currency*.

copperplate *n* **1** a style of fine handwriting that is marked by lines of sharply contrasting thickness. **2** an engraved or etched copper printing plate, or a print made from such a plate.

copper sulphate (*NAm* **copper sulfate**) *n* a chemical compound that usu occurs chemically associated with water in the form of blue crystals but also occurs as a white powder when free from water.

coppice[1] *n* a thicket, grove, etc of small trees in which the trees are regularly cut back to promote growth and supply wood for poles and firewood.

coppice[2] *v* to cut back (trees) to produce a dense growth of small trees.

copra *n* dried coconut kernels yielding coconut oil.

coprolite *n* fossil excrement.

coprophilia *n* a marked, *esp* sexual, interest in excrement and defecation.

copse *n* a coppice.

Copt *n* **1** a member of a people descended from the ancient Egyptians. **2** a member of the Coptic Church.

Coptic[1] *n* the Afro-Asiatic language of the Copts, which is no longer spoken but survives in the liturgy of the Coptic Church.

Coptic[2] *adj* of or relating to the Copts, the Coptic language, or the Coptic Church.

Coptic Church *n* the ancient branch of the Christian Church that developed in Egypt and survives today.

copula *n* a verb, e.g. a form of *be* or *seem*, that links a subject and a complement, as in the sentence *She became rich*. ➤➤ **copular** *adj*.

copulate *v* to engage in sexual intercourse. ➤➤ **copulation** *n*, **copulatory** *adj*.

copy[1] *n* (*pl* **-ies**) **1** an imitation, transcript, or reproduction of an original work. **2** a single specimen of a printed book, CD, etc. **3** material ready to be printed. **4** written material as distinct from illustrations or other graphic material. **5** newsworthy material.

copy[2] *v* (**-ies, -ied**) **1** to make a copy of. **2** to make a copy of (somebody else's work); to imitate. **3** to model oneself on.

copybook *n* **1** a book formerly used in teaching handwriting, containing models for imitation. **2** *(used before a noun)* completely correct and conforming to established standards: *a copybook display*.

copycat *n informal* **1** somebody who slavishly imitates the behaviour or practices of another. **2** (*used before a noun*) imitating something else: *copycat murders*.

copy-edit *v* (**copy-edited, copy-editing**) to prepare (manuscript copy) for printing, *esp* by correcting errors and making the style consistent throughout. ➤➤ **copy editor** *n*.

copyist *n* **1** a person who makes written copies of documents. **2** a person who imitates the work of others, e.g. somebody who copies works of art.

copyright[1] *n* the exclusive legal right to reproduce, publish, and sell a literary, musical, or artistic work for a fixed number of years.

copyright[2] *v* to secure a copyright on (a literary, musical, or artistic work).

copy typist *n* a typist who types up written notes or drafts.

copywriter *n* a writer of advertising or publicity copy.

coq au vin /kok oh 'van/ *n* a dish of chicken cooked in red wine with bacon and shallots.

coquette *n* a woman who flirts with men. ➤➤ **coquetry** *n*, **coquettish** *adj*, **coquettishly** *adv*, **coquettishness** *n*.

cor- *prefix* see COM-.

coracle *n* a small round boat made by covering a wicker frame with waterproof material.

coral *n* **1a** a hard substance, usu containing calcium, produced by certain marine invertebrate animals. **b** a rich red precious type of coral. **2** a deep orange-pink colour. ➤➤ **coral** *adj*.

coralline *adj* of or like coral.

cor anglais /,kawr 'ongglay, kawr ong'glay/ *n* (*pl* **cors anglais**) a woodwind musical instrument with a double reed similar to, and with a range a fifth lower than, the oboe.

corbel[1] *n* a stone or brick projection from a wall which supports a weight, *esp* one stepped upwards and outwards.

corbel[2] *v* (**corbelled, corbelling,** *NAm* **corbeled, corbeling**) to supply (a wall) with a corbel, or lay (stone or brick) in the form of a corbel.

cord[1] *n* **1** a length of long thin flexible material consisting of several strands, e.g. of thread or yarn, woven or twisted together, or such material in general. **2** an anatomical structure, e.g. a nerve, resembling a cord. **3** an electric flex. **4a** corduroy. **b** (*in *pl*) trousers made of corduroy. **5** a unit of cut wood usu equal to $3.63m^3$ ($128ft^3$).

cord[2] *v* to provide or bind with a cord, or connect with a cord.

cordate *adj* heart-shaped.

corded *adj* **1** striped or ribbed with cord; twilled. **2** bound or fastened with cords. **3** of a muscle: ridged.

cordial[1] *adj* **1** warmly and genially affable. **2** sincerely or deeply felt. ⋙ **cordiality** *n,* **cordially** *adv.*

cordial[2] *n* **1** *Brit* a non-alcoholic sweetened fruit drink. **2** *NAm* a liqueur. **3** a stimulating medicine.

cordite *n* a smokeless explosive made from nitroglycerine, guncotton, and petroleum jelly.

cordless *adj* of an electrical device: operating without direct connection to the mains supply or power source.

cordoba *n* the basic monetary unit of Nicaragua.

cordon[1] *n* **1** (*used as sing. or pl*) a line of troops, police, etc enclosing an area and preventing access to it. **2** a plant, *esp* a fruit tree, trained to a single stem by pruning off all side shoots.

cordon[2] *v* (+ off) to form a protective or restrictive cordon round (an area).

cordon bleu[1] /,kawdonh 'bluh/ *adj* of cookery: of the highest standard.

cordon bleu[2] *n* (*pl* **cordons bleus**) a person with a high degree of skill or distinction in cookery, *esp* in classical French cuisine.

cordon sanitaire *n* (*pl* **cordons sanitaires**) **1** a barrier round an infected region, policed to prevent the spread of infection. **2** a buffer zone.

corduroy *n* a durable usu cotton pile fabric with lengthways ribs.

cordwainer *n Brit, archaic* a shoemaker.

cordwood *n* wood piled or sold in cords.

core[1] *n* **1** the usu inedible central part of some fruits; *esp* the papery parts encasing the seeds in fruit such as apples and pears. **2a** the essential or central part of something. **b** the inmost or most intimate part. **3** the central part of a planet, *esp* the earth, which has physical properties that are different from those of the surrounding parts. **4** the part of a nuclear reactor that contains the rods of fuel and in which the energy-producing reaction occurs.

core[2] *v* to remove a core from (a fruit). ⋙ **corer** *n.*

coreopsis *n* a plant of the daisy family, widely grown for its showy yellow or yellow and red flowers.

co-respondent *or* **corespondent** *n* a person alleged to have committed adultery with the respondent in a divorce case.

core subject *n* a school subject that is compulsory, *esp* for pupils at each key stage of the National Curriculum in British schools.

core time *n Brit* the period of each day which is a compulsory working period for employees on flexitime.

corgi *n* (*pl* **corgis**) a short-legged dog of a breed with a fox-like head, orig developed in Wales. Also called WELSH CORGI.

coriander *n* an aromatic plant of the carrot family cultivated for its leaves and seeds that are used as a flavouring in cooking.

Corinthian *adj* **1** relating to the modern city or the ancient city-state of Corinth. **2** denoting the lightest and most ornate of the three Greek orders of architecture characterized by its bell-shaped CAPITAL[3] (upper part of a column) enveloped with large spiny acanthus leaves: compare DORIC[1], IONIC. ⋙ **Corinthian** *n.*

Coriolis force *n* a force arising as a result of the earth's rotation that deflects moving objects, e.g. projectiles or air currents, to the right in the northern hemisphere and to the left in the southern hemisphere.

cork[1] *n* **1** the elastic tough outer tissue of the cork oak used for stoppers and insulation. **2** a cork stopper for a bottle. **3** an angling float made from cork.

cork[2] *v* to fit or close (something, *esp* a bottle) with a cork.

corkage *n* a charge made in a restaurant for serving wine brought in by a customer.

corked *adj* of wine: having an unpleasant smell and taste as a result of being kept in a bottle sealed with a leaky cork.

cork oak *n* a S European and N African oak with bark that yields cork.

corkscrew[1] *n* an implement for removing corks from bottles, typically consisting of a pointed spiral piece of metal attached to a handle.

corkscrew[2] *v* to move or twist in a spiral.

corm *n* a rounded thick underground plant stem base with buds and scaly leaves that stores food and produces new shoots each year: compare BULB, TUBER.

cormorant *n* a common dark-coloured European seabird with a long neck, hooked bill, webbed feet, and white throat and cheeks.

Corn *abbr* Cornwall.

corn[1] *n* **1** *chiefly Brit* the important cereal crop of a particular region, usu wheat, barley, or oats in Britain. **2** *NAm, Aus, NZ* maize. **3** *informal* something corny.

corn[2] *v* to preserve or season (food) with salt or brine.

corn[3] *n* a local hardening and thickening of skin, e.g. on the top of a toe.

corncob *n* the core on which the edible kernels of sweet corn are arranged.

corncrake *n* a common Eurasian bird of the rail family with a short bill, tan-coloured speckled plumage, and a reddish tail.

corn dolly *n Brit* an article of woven straw, orig having ritual significance but now used for decoration.

cornea *n* the hard transparent membrane of the eyeball that covers the iris and pupil. ⋙ **corneal** *adj.*

corned beef *n* chopped and pressed beef that has been preserved in brine.

cornelian *or* **carnelian** *n* a hard reddish form of the mineral chalcedony, used in jewellery.

corner[1] *n* **1a** the point where converging lines, edges, or sides meet; an angle. **b** the place of intersection of two streets or roads. **2a** the area of a playing field or court near the intersection of the sideline and the goal line or baseline. **b** any of the four angles of a boxing or wrestling ring, *esp* one in which a fighter rests between rounds. **3a** a private or remote place. **b** a difficult or embarrassing situation; a position from which escape or retreat is difficult or impossible. **4** = CORNER KICK. **5** in economics, control or ownership of enough of the available supply of a commodity to allow manipulation of the price. ✱ **in somebody's corner** on somebody's side.

corner[2] *v* **1a** to drive (a person or animal) into a corner. **b** to detain (somebody); *esp* to force (somebody) into conversation. **2** to gain control of (an economic market) by acquiring a substantial supply of a commodity. **3** to turn corners.

corner kick *n* in football, a free kick that is taken from the corner of the field and is awarded to the attacking team when a member of the defending team has sent the ball behind his or her own goal line.

corner shop *n Brit* a small shop selling food, household supplies, and sometimes newspapers and magazines.

cornerstone *n* **1** a block of stone forming a part of a corner or angle in a wall, *esp* one forming the base of a corner and often laid ceremonially to mark the beginning of construction. **2** the most basic element of something; a foundation.

cornet *n* **1** a brass musical instrument with finger-operated valves to vary the pitch. It resembles a trumpet but has a shorter tube and less brilliant tone. **2** *Brit* an ice cream cone. ➤➤ **cornetist** *n*, **cornettist** *n*.

corn exchange *n* a building in which corn was formerly traded.

cornflakes *pl n* toasted flakes of maize eaten as a breakfast cereal.

cornflour *n Brit* a finely ground flour made from maize, rice, etc and used as a thickening agent in cooking.

cornflower *n* a European plant with narrow leaves and delicate blue, purple, or white flowers that resemble daisies.

cornice *n* **1** an ornamental projecting piece that forms the top edge of a building, pillar, etc. **2** an ornamental plaster moulding between the wall and ceiling of a room. ➤➤ **corniced** *adj*, **cornicing** *n*.

corniche *n* a road built along a coast, *esp* along the face of a cliff.

Cornish[1] *n* the Celtic language of Cornwall.

Cornish[2] *adj* of or from Cornwall or the Cornish language.

Cornish pasty *n Brit* a pasty consisting of a circular piece of pastry folded over a savoury filling of meat, potato, and vegetables.

cornucopia *n* **1** a goat's horn overflowing with flowers, fruit, and corn, used to symbolize abundance. **2** an inexhaustible store; an abundance. ➤➤ **cornucopian** *adj*.

corny *adj* (**-ier, -iest**) *informal* **1** tiresomely simple and sentimental; trite. **2** unoriginal and overused; hackneyed. ➤➤ **cornily** *adv*, **corniness** *n*.

corolla *n* the petals of a flower collectively, constituting the inner floral envelope.

corollary *n* (*pl* **-ies**) **1** in logic, a direct conclusion from a proved proposition. **2** something that naturally follows or accompanies something else. ➤➤ **corollary** *adj*.

corona[1] *n* (*pl* **coronas** *or* **coronae**) **1a** a usu coloured circle of usu diffracted light seen round and close to a luminous celestial body, e.g. the sun or moon. **b** the tenuous outermost part of the atmosphere of the sun and other stars appearing as a halo round the moon's black disc during a total eclipse of the sun. **2** the upper portion of a bodily part, e.g. a tooth or the skull. **3** in botany, a circular appendage on the inner side of the corolla in the daffodil, jonquil, and similar flowers.

corona[2] *n* a long straight-sided cigar of uniform thickness.

coronae *n* pl of CORONA[1].

coronal *adj* of a corona or crown.

coronary[1] *adj* relating to or in the region of the arteries and veins that supply and encircle the heart.

coronary[2] *n* (*pl* **-ies**) = CORONARY THROMBOSIS.

coronary thrombosis *n* the blocking of an artery of the heart by a blood clot, usu causing death of heart muscle tissue.

coronation *n* the act or ceremony of crowning a sovereign or his or her consort.

coroner *n* a public officer whose principal duty is to enquire into the cause of any death which there is reason to suppose might not be due to natural causes.

coronet *n* **1** a small crown. **2** an ornamental wreath or band for the head.

corpora *n* pl of CORPUS.

corporal[1] *n* a non-commissioned officer in the British and US armies, Royal Air Force, Royal Marines, and US Marines, ranking below a sergeant.

corporal[2] *adj* of or affecting the body.

corporal punishment *n* physical punishment, e.g. caning.

corpora lutea *n* pl of CORPUS LUTEUM.

corporate *adj* **1** relating to companies or the people, *esp* the executives, who work in them. **2** in law, forming a company; incorporated. **3** of or belonging to a unified body of individuals. ➤➤ **corporately** *adv*.

corporation *n* **1** a body made up of more than one person which is formed and authorized by law to act as a single person with its own legal identity, rights, and duties. **2** (*used as sing. or pl*) the municipal authorities of a British town or city.

corporation tax *n* tax levied on the profits of companies.

corporatism *n* the organization of a society into corporations serving as organs of political representation, e.g. in Fascist Italy. ➤➤ **corporatist** *adj and n*.

corporeal *adj* **1** having or relating to a physical material body; not spiritual. **2** not immaterial or intangible; substantial. ➤➤ **corporeality** *n*.

corps *n* (*pl* **corps**) **1** (*used as sing. or pl*) an army unit usu consisting of two or more divisions organized for a particular purpose. **2** a body of people engaged in a specific activity: *the diplomatic corps*.

corps de ballet /,kaw də 'balay, *NAm* ba'lay/ *n* (*pl* **corps de ballet**) (*used as sing. or pl*) the members of a ballet company.

corpse[1] *n* a dead body, *esp* a dead human body.

corpse[2] *v informal* to stifle laughter with difficulty, e.g. on a solemn occasion or while acting in a play.

corpulent *adj* excessively fat; obese. ➤➤ **corpulence** *n*.

corpus *n* (*pl* **corpora** *or* **corpuses**) **1** a collection or body of writings or works, *esp* of a particular kind or on a particular subject. **2** a body of spoken or written language for linguistic study.

Corpus Christi *n* a Christian feast in honour of the Eucharist, observed on the Thursday after Trinity Sunday.

corpuscle *n* **1** a living cell, *esp* a blood cell. **2** any of various very small multicellular parts of an organism. ➤➤ **corpuscular** *adj*.

corpus delicti *n* in law, the body of facts showing that a breach of the law has taken place, *esp* the body of the victim in a case of murder.

corpus luteum *n* (*pl* **corpora lutea**) a reddish yellow mass of hormone-secreting tissue that forms in the ovary of a mammal after ovulation and quickly returns to its original state if the ovum is not fertilized.

corral[1] *n NAm* **1** a pen or enclosure for confining livestock. **2** formerly, a ring of covered wagons around a camp to provide protection against potential attack.

corral[2] *v* (**corralled, corralling**) **1** *chiefly NAm* to enclose (livestock) in a corral. **2** *NAm* to arrange (wagons) so as to form a corral. **3** to collect (people) together.

correct[1] *adj* **1** true or right. **2** conforming to an approved or conventional standard. **3** conforming to a specified ideology: *politically correct.* ➤➤ **correctly** *adv,* **correctness** *n.*

correct[2] *v* **1a** to make or set right; to amend. **b** to alter or adjust so as to remove an error or imperfection. **2** to point out the faults in (a piece of writing). **3** *archaic* to punish (e.g. a child) with a view to reforming or improving them. ➤➤ **correctable** *adj,* **correction** *n,* **corrector** *n.*

correctional *adj NAm* relating to prisons or other places or methods of punishment.

correction fluid *n* a white or coloured liquid used to cover an error in writing or typing.

corrective *adj* intended to correct. ➤➤ **corrective** *n,* **correctively** *adv.*

correlate[1] *v* **1** to have a reciprocal or mutual relationship. **2** to establish a mutual or reciprocal relation between (things). **3** to bring (things) together for the purposes of comparison.

correlate[2] *n* in philosophy, either of two things related in such a way that one directly implies the other, e.g. husband and wife.

correlation *n* **1** a mutual or reciprocal relationship between things. **2** in statistics, an association between two variables such that a change in one implies a proportionate change in the other. **3** the act or an instance of correlating two things.

correlative[1] *adj* **1** naturally related; corresponding. **2** of words or parts of words: grammatically related and regularly used together, e.g. *neither* and *nor*.

correlative[2] *n* a correlative word.

correspond *v* **1a** to conform or be compatible; to match. **b** to be equivalent or similar. **2** to communicate by exchanging letters.

correspondence *n* **1** letters, or communication by letter. **2a** the agreement of things with one another. **b** a particular similarity.

correspondence course *n* a course of study in which students send and receive material by post.

correspondent[1] *n* **1** a person who contributes news or comment to a publication or radio or television network. **2** a person who communicates with another by letter.

correspondent[2] *adj* **1** similar. **2** conforming to something or agreeing with it.

corrida /ko'reedhə, -də/ *n* a bullfight.

corridor *n* **1** a passage onto which compartments or rooms open. **2** a narrow strip of land through foreign-held territory. **3** a restricted path for air traffic. **4** a strip of land that by geographical characteristics is distinct from its surroundings. ✱ **the corridors of power** the highest levels of administration in government, business, etc.

corrie *n Scot* a steep-sided glacially excavated hollow in the side of a mountain.

corrigendum *n* (*pl* **corrigenda**) an error in a printed work.

corroborate *v* to support (e.g. a claim or an opinion) with evidence or authority. ➤➤ **corroboration** *n,* **corroborative** *adj,* **corroborator** *n,* **corroboratory** *adj.*

corroboree *n* an Australian Aboriginal ceremony with songs and symbolic dances to celebrate important events.

corrode *v* **1** to eat or wear (*esp* metal) away gradually by chemical action. **2** to weaken or destroy gradually, as if by chemical action. **3** to undergo corroding. ➤➤ **corrosion** *n.*

corrosive[1] *adj* **1** causing corrosion. **2** harmful or destructive, *esp* insidiously so. ➤➤ **corrosively** *adv,* **corrosiveness** *n.*

corrosive[2] *n* a substance, *esp* an acid, that causes corrosion.

corrugate *v* to fold or become folded into alternating ridges and grooves. ➤➤ **corrugated** *adj,* **corrugation** *n.*

corrupt[1] *adj* **1a** open to or characterized by bribery or other improper conduct. **b** morally degenerate and perverted; depraved. **2a** of computer data: damaged in a way that may make the program, file, etc unusable. **b** of a text: containing errors. **3** *archaic* tainted. ➤➤ **corruptly** *adv.*

corrupt[2] *v* **1** to make (somebody or something) corrupt. **2a** to alter (a manuscript, text, etc) from the original or correct form or version. **b** to damage (computer data). **3** *archaic* to taint or make putrid. ➤➤ **corrupter** *n,* **corruptible** *adj,* **corruption** *n,* **corruptive** *adj.*

corsage *n* **1** an arrangement of flowers worn by a woman, pinned to a dress or a lapel. **2** the bodice of an evening dress.

corsair *n* a pirate, *esp* a privateer of the Barbary coast.

corselette *or* **corselet** *n* a one-piece undergarment combining girdle and bra.

corset *n* **1** a stiffened or elasticated supporting undergarment for women, extending from beneath the bust to below the hips, designed to give shape to the figure. **2** a similar garment worn by men and women to give support in cases of injury, *esp* to the back. ➤➤ **corseted** *adj,* **corsetry** *n.*

Corsican *n* **1** a native or inhabitant of Corsica. **2** the language of Corsica. ➤➤ **Corsican** *adj.*

cortège *n* a procession, *esp* a funeral procession.

cortex *n* (*pl* **cortices**) the outer part of an organ of the body, *esp* the outer layer of grey matter of the brain.

cortical *adj* **1** of or consisting of a cortex. **2** involving or resulting from the action or condition of the cerebral cortex.

cortices *n* pl of CORTEX.

corticosteroid *n* **1** any of several steroids, e.g. cortisone, produced by the cortex of the adrenal gland. **2** a synthetic drug with actions similar to those of natural corticosteroids.

cortisone *n* a steroid hormone that is produced by the cortex of the adrenal gland and is used, in synthetic form, as a treatment for various conditions, e.g. skin disorders.

corundum *n* a very hard natural or synthetic mineral that consists of aluminium oxide and is used as an abrasive and a gemstone.

coruscate *v literary* to give off flashes of light; to sparkle. ➤➤ **coruscation** *n.*

corvette *n* a small highly manoeuvrable armed escort ship.

corvine *adj* of or resembling a crow.

corybantic *adj* wildly ecstatic.

corymb *n* a flower that grows in the form of a flat-topped cluster; *specif* one in which the flower stalks are attached at different levels on the main axis.

coryza *n* a short-lasting infectious inflammation of the upper respiratory tract, *esp* the common cold.

cos[1] *n* (*also* **cos lettuce**) a crisp long-leaved variety of lettuce.

cos² *abbr* cosine.

cosec *abbr* cosecant.

cosecant *n* in mathematics, the trigonometric function that is the reciprocal of the sine.

cosh¹ *n Brit* a short heavy rod often enclosed in a softer material and used as a hand weapon.

cosh² *v Brit* to strike with a cosh.

cosignatory *or* **co-signatory** *n* (*pl* **-ies**) a joint signer of a document or treaty.

cosine *n* in mathematics, the trigonometric function that for an acute angle in a right-angled triangle is the ratio between the side adjacent to the angle and the hypotenuse: compare SINE, TANGENT¹.

cosmetic¹ *n* a preparation designed to be applied to the skin or hair to improve its appearance or texture.

cosmetic² *adj* **1** of or intended to improve beauty, e.g. of the hair or complexion. **2** intended to improve the outward appearance only, often in order to conceal underlying or fundamental shortcomings. ➤➤ **cosmetically** *adv.*

cosmic *adj* **1** of the universe in contrast to the earth alone. **2** relating to the region of space that lies outside the earth's atmosphere. ➤➤ **cosmical** *adj,* **cosmically** *adv.*

cosmic dust *n* very fine particles of solid matter in any part of the universe.

cosmic ray *n* (*usu in pl*) a stream of high energy radiation reaching the earth from outer space.

cosmogony *n* (*pl* **-ies**) the study of the creation or origin of the universe, or of a particular part of it. ➤➤ **cosmogonic** *adj,* **cosmogonist** *n.*

cosmography *n* (*pl* **-ies**) **1** the branch of science dealing with the constitution of the universe, *esp* of the solar system. **2** a general description of the world or the universe. ➤➤ **cosmographer** *n,* **cosmographic** *adj.*

cosmology *n* (*pl* **-ies**) **1** the branch of astronomy dealing with the origin, structure, and space-time relationships of the universe. **2** a theoretical account of the nature of the universe. ➤➤ **cosmological** *adj,* **cosmologist** *n.*

cosmonaut *n* a Russian astronaut.

cosmopolitan¹ *adj* **1** composed of people or elements from many parts of the world. **2** marked by a sophistication that comes from wide and often international experience. **3** having worldwide rather than provincial scope or bearing. ➤➤ **cosmopolitanism** *n.*

cosmopolitan² *n* a cosmopolitan person.

cosmos *n* the universe, *esp* when regarded as an orderly system: compare CHAOS (2).

Cossack *n* **1** a member of a people of S Russia and the Ukraine famous for their horseriding skill. **2** a member of a unit of Cossack cavalrymen who fought under the Russian tsars.

cosset *v* (**cosseted, cosseting**) to treat (a person or animal) with great or excessive indulgence and protection; to pamper.

cost¹ *n* **1** the price paid or charged for something. **2** the expenditure, e.g. of effort or sacrifice, made to achieve an objective. **3** the loss or penalty incurred in gaining something. **4** (*in pl*) expenses incurred in litigation, *esp* those ordered by the court to be paid to the successful party. ✱ **at all costs** regardless of the price or difficulties. **at any cost** regardless of the price or difficulties. **at cost** at the price paid by the retailer. **to one's cost** to one's disadvantage or loss.

cost² *v* (*past tense and past part.* **cost**) **1** to have a price of (a specified amount). **2** *informal* to have a high price for (somebody). **3** to cause (somebody) to pay, suffer, or lose something: *Frequent absences cost him his job.* **4** (*past tense and past part.* **costed**) to estimate or set the cost of.

co-star¹ *n* a star who has equal billing with another leading performer in a film or play.

co-star² *v* (**co-starred, co-starring**) **1** to appear as a co-star in a film or play. **2** to feature (an actor) as a co-star.

Costa Rican *n* a native or inhabitant of Costa Rica. ➤➤ **Costa Rican** *adj.*

cost-effective *adj* economically worthwhile. ➤➤ **cost-effectiveness** *n.*

costermonger *n Brit, dated* a person who sells fruit or vegetables from a street barrow or stall.

costive *adj* affected with constipation. ➤➤ **costiveness** *n.*

costly *adj* (**-ier, -iest**) **1** expensive or valuable. **2** made at great expense or with considerable sacrifice. ➤➤ **costliness** *n.*

cost of living *n* the cost of purchasing those goods and services that are regarded as necessary for maintaining an acceptable standard of living.

cost price *n* the price paid by a retailer for an article of merchandise to be resold.

costume¹ *n* a set of garments belonging to a specific time, place, or character, worn in order to assume a particular role, e.g. in a play or as fancy dress.

costume² *v* **1** to provide with a costume. **2** to design costumes for (a play, film, or other performance).

costume drama *n* a film or television drama set in a particular historical period.

costume jewellery *n* inexpensive jewellery, orig of a kind typically worn attached to clothing rather than on the body.

costumier (*NAm* **costumer**) *n* a person who deals in or makes costumes, e.g. for theatrical productions.

cosy¹ (*NAm* **cozy**) *adj* (**-ier, -iest**) **1** enjoying or affording warmth and comfort; snug. **2** marked by the intimacy of the family or a close group. **3a** *informal, derog* suggesting close association or connivance: *a cosy agreement.* **b** complacent: *cosy morality.* ➤➤ **cosily** *adv,* **cosiness** *n.*

cosy² (*NAm* **cozy**) *n* (*pl* **-ies**) a cover, *esp* for a teapot, designed to keep the contents hot.

cosy up (*NAm* **cozy up**) *v* (**-ies, -ied**) *informal* (*usu* + to) to attempt to gain friendship or intimacy, *esp* in an ingratiating and self-serving way.

cot¹ *n Brit* a small bed for a baby or young child, with high enclosing sides consisting of vertical bars.

cot² *n* **1** *archaic* a small house or cottage. **2** a shelter for sheep, birds, etc; a cote.

cot³ *abbr* cotangent.

cotangent *n* in mathematics, the trigonometric function that is the reciprocal of the tangent.

cot death *n Brit* the death of a baby or very young child during sleep, from no apparent disease.

cote *n* a shed or coop for small domestic animals, *esp* pigeons.

coterie *n* a small and usu exclusive group of people with a unifying common interest or purpose.

coterminous *or* **conterminous** *adj* **1** having the same boundaries. **2** having the same scope or lasting the same time.

cotillion *n* **1** an elaborate 18th-cent. French dance with frequent changing of partners. **2** *NAm* a formal ball.

cotoneaster *n* a flowering shrub of the rose family, with small white flowers followed by red or black berries.

cottage[1] *n* a small simple house, *esp* in the country. ➤➤ **cottagey** *adj.*

cottage[2] *v informal* of men: to engage in homosexual activity in a public toilet. ➤➤ **cottaging** *n.*

cottage cheese *n* a soft white mild-tasting cheese made from the curds of skimmed milk.

cottage hospital *n Brit* a small hospital without resident doctors.

cottage industry *n* an industry with a work force consisting of family units working at home with their own equipment.

cottage loaf *n* a loaf of bread formed by placing a small round mass of dough on top of a larger one.

cottage pie *n Brit* a shepherd's pie *esp* made with minced beef.

cottager *n* somebody who lives in a cottage.

cottar *or* **cotter** *n* in Scotland and Ireland formerly, a person occupying a cottage, usu in return for services.

cotter pin *n* **1** a pin for fastening parts of a machine or other mechanism together. **2** a split pin that passes through the holes in two or more parts and is spread open at its ends to secure the fastening.

cotton *n* **1** a soft usu white fibrous substance composed of the hairs surrounding the seeds of a tropical and subtropical plant. **2a** fabric made of cotton. **b** yarn spun from cotton. ➤➤ **cottony** *adj.*

cotton bud *n Brit* a short plastic stick with a small wad of cotton wool on each end, used for cleaning ears, etc and for removing make-up.

cotton gin *n* a machine for separating the seeds, seed cases, and waste material from cotton.

cotton on *v informal* (*often* + to) to become aware of something, usu after initially not realizing it.

cotton wool *n* **1** *Brit* fluffy fabric in balls or pads, orig made from raw cotton, used for cleaning wounds, removing make-up, etc. **2** *NAm* raw cotton.

cotyledon *n* the first leaf or either of the first pair of leaves developed by the embryo of a seed plant.

couch[1] *n* **1** a long upholstered piece of furniture for sitting or lying on, either with a back and armrests or with a low back and raised head-end. **2** a long upholstered seat with a headrest for patients to lie on during medical examination or psychoanalysis.

couch[2] *v* **1** to phrase in a specified manner: *The letter was couched in hostile terms.* **2** of an animal: to lie down to sleep. **3** *literary* to lie in ambush.

couch[3] *n* = COUCH GRASS.

couchette *n* **1** a railway carriage that has seats which convert into bunks. **2** a bunk in a railway carriage.

couch grass *n* a grass that spreads rapidly by long creeping underground stems.

couch potato *n informal* an inactive person, *esp* somebody who spends a lot of time watching television.

cougar *n* (*pl* **cougars** *or* **cougar**) *NAm* a puma.

cough[1] *v* **1** to expel air from the lungs suddenly with an explosive noise. **2** to make a noise like that of coughing. **3** *Brit, informal* to reveal information.

cough[2] *n* **1** a condition marked by repeated or frequent coughing. **2** an act or sound of coughing. ➤➤ **cougher** *n.*

cough mixture *n Brit* any of various medicated liquids used to relieve coughing.

cough up *v* **1** to expel (e.g. mucus) by coughing. **2** *informal* to produce or hand over (e.g. money or information) unwillingly.

could *v aux* the past tense of CAN[1], used: **1** to express possibility in the past: *He realized he could go.* **2** to express a condition: *He said he would go if he could.* **3** to express a possibility: *You could be right.* **4** as a polite form in the present: *Could you do this for me?* **5** to express expectation or obligation: *You could at least apologize.*

couldn't *contr* could not.

coulis /koo'lee/ *n* (*pl* **coulis**) a thin sauce made from puréed fruit or vegetables.

coulomb *n* the SI unit of electric charge, equal to the charge transported in one second by a current of one ampere.

coulter (*NAm* **colter**) *n* a blade attached to the beam of a plough that makes a vertical cut in the ground in front of the ploughshare.

council *n* **1a** (*used as sing. or pl*) an elected or appointed body with administrative, legislative, or advisory powers. **b** (*used as sing. or pl*) a locally-elected body having power over a district, county, parish, etc. **2** *Brit (used before a noun)* provided and often subsidized by a local authority: *council housing.*

councillor (*NAm* **councilor**) *n* a member of a council.

council tax *n* a tax based on the value of property, paid by householders in Britain as a way of funding the provision of services by their local authority.

counsel[1] *n* **1a** advice, *esp* when given following consultation. **b** *archaic* deliberation or consultation itself. **2a** (*pl* **counsel**) a barrister engaged in the trial of a case in court. **b** (*pl* **counsel**) a lawyer appointed to advise a client. ✱ **keep one's own counsel** to keep one's thoughts or intentions to oneself.

counsel[2] *v* (**counselled, counselling,** *NAm* **counseled, counseling**) **1** to advise. **2** to give (somebody) help with psychological, social, or personal problems. ➤➤ **counselling** *n.*

counsellor (*NAm* **counselor**) *n* **1** a person who gives professional advice or guidance. **2** a senior diplomatic officer. **3** *NAm* a person who has supervisory duties at a summer camp for children. **4** *NAm, Irish* a lawyer; *specif* a barrister.

count[1] *v* **1** to find the total number of. **2** to include in a tallying and reckoning. **3** to be thought of or think of (somebody or something) as having a particular quality or fulfil a particular role: *Count yourself lucky.* **4** to include or exclude as if by counting: *You can count me in.* **5** to name the numbers in order by units or groups. **6** to have value or significance. ✱ **count on 1** to look forward to (something) as certain. **2** to rely on (somebody). ➤➤ **countable** *adj.*

count[2] *n* **1a** the act or process of counting. **b** a total obtained by counting. **2a** in law, an allegation in an indictment. **b** a specific point under consideration; an issue. **3** in boxing, the calling out of the seconds from one to ten when a boxer has been knocked down. ✱ **out for the count** in boxing, having been knocked down and staying down for a count of ten.

count[3] *n* a European nobleman corresponding in rank to a British earl.

countdown *n* **1** a continuous counting backwards to zero of the time remaining before an event, *esp* the launching of a rocket. **2** the remaining time before an important event.

count down *v* to count backwards to zero, *esp* to show the time remaining before the launch of a rocket.

countenance[1] *n* **1** a person's face, *esp* as an indication of mood or character. **2** *formal* moral support or approval. ✱ **keep one's countenance** to keep calm and composed.

countenance[2] *v* to consider or allow.

counter[1] *n* **1** a level surface, e.g. a table, over which transactions are conducted or food is served. **2** a small disc used in counting or in games. **3** something of value in bargaining; an asset. **4** a person or machine that counts. ✱ **over the counter** without a prescription. **under the counter** by surreptitious means, often in an illicit and private manner.

counter[2] *v* **1** to act in opposition to; to oppose. **2** to meet attacks or arguments with defensive or retaliatory steps. **3** in boxing or fencing, to attack while warding off a blow.

counter[3] *adv* (+ to) in an opposite, contrary, or wrong direction.

counter[4] *n* something that counters something else.

counter[5] *adj* opposite, or showing opposition.

counter- *prefix* **1a** opposing or retaliatory: *counteroffensive.* **b** in the opposite direction: *counterpoise.* **2** complementary or corresponding: *counterpart.* **3** duplicate or substitute: *counterfoil.*

counteract *v* to lessen or neutralize the usu ill effects of (something) by an opposing action. ➤➤ **counteraction** *n,* **counteractive** *adj.*

counterattack[1] *or* **counter-attack** *n* an attack made in reply to an enemy's attack.

counterattack[2] *or* **counter-attack** *v* to make a counterattack.

counterattraction *or* **counter-attraction** *n* an attraction that competes with another.

counterbalance[1] *n* **1** a weight that balances another. **2** a force or influence that offsets or checks an opposing force.

counterbalance[2] *v* to oppose or balance with an equal weight or force.

counterblast *n* often as the title of a militant writing: an energetic and often vociferous reaction or response.

counterclockwise *adj and adv NAm* anticlockwise.

counterculture *n* a way of life with values that run counter to established social norms.

counterespionage *or* **counter-espionage** *n* espionage directed towards detecting and thwarting enemy espionage.

counterfeit[1] *adj* made in imitation of something else with intent to deceive or defraud.

counterfeit[2] *n* a forgery.

counterfeit[3] *v* to imitate or copy closely, *esp* with intent to deceive or defraud. ➤➤ **counterfeiter** *n.*

counterfoil *n chiefly Brit* the part of a cheque, ticket, etc that is kept as a record or receipt.

counterinsurgency *or* **counter-insurgency** *n* organized military activity designed to suppress rebellion.

counterintelligence *or* **counter-intelligence** *n* organized activity designed to block an enemy's sources of information; counterespionage.

counterintuitive *or* **counter-intuitive** *adj* going against common sense or what one might expect.

countermand[1] *v* **1** to revoke (a command) by a contrary order. **2** to order back (e.g. troops) by a superseding contrary order.

countermand[2] *n* a contrary order revoking an earlier one.

countermeasure *n* a measure designed to counter another action or state of affairs.

counteroffensive *n* a military offensive undertaken from a previously defensive position.

counterpart *n* a person or thing with the same function or characteristics as another; an equivalent.

counterpoint[1] *n* **1a** the combination of two or more independent melodies into a single harmonic texture. **b** one or more independent melodies added above or below a given melody. **2a** the use of contrast or interplay of elements in a work of art. **b** a complementing or contrasting idea.

counterpoint[2] *v* **1** to compose or arrange (a musical work) in counterpoint. **2** to set off or emphasize by contrast or juxtaposition.

counterpoise[1] *n* **1** a force, influence, etc that acts as a counterbalance. **2** a counterbalance.

counterpoise[2] *v* to balance (something); to act as a contrast to (something).

counterproductive *adj* having effects that are the opposite to those intended.

Counter-Reformation *n* the reform movement in the Roman Catholic Church in the 16th and 17th cents, in response to the Protestant Reformation.

counterrevolution *or* **counter-revolution** *n* a revolution directed towards overthrowing the system established by a previous revolution. ➤➤ **counterrevolutionary** *adj and n.*

countersign *v* to add one's signature to (a document) as a witness of another signature.

countersink *v* (*past tense and past part.* **countersunk**) **1** to enlarge (a hole), *esp* by bevelling, so that the head of a bolt, screw, etc will fit below or level with the surface. **2** to set the head of (e.g. a screw) below or level with the surface.

countertenor *n* a male singer having a voice higher than tenor.

countervail *v* to counterbalance the effect of; to offset.

counterweight *n* a counterbalance.

countess *n* **1** the wife or widow of an earl or count. **2** a woman who has the rank of earl or count in her own right.

countless *adj* too numerous to be counted; innumerable.

count noun *n* in grammar, a noun, e.g. *bean* or *sheet*, that forms a plural and can be used with a number or the indefinite article: compare MASS NOUN.

countrified *or* **countryfied** *adj* rural in style or manner, *esp* lacking the sophistication of the city.

country *n* (*pl* **-ies**) **1** a political state or nation or its territory. **2** rural as opposed to urban areas; countryside. **3** an indefinite usu extended expanse of land; a region. ✱ **go to the country** *Brit* to dissolve Parliament and have a general election.

country and western *n* country music.

country club *n* a sporting or social club set in a rural area.

country cousin *n* somebody who is unaccustomed to or confused by city life.

country dance *n* any of various folk dances typically arranged in square or circular figures or in two long rows with dancers facing their partners.

countryfied *adj* see COUNTRIFIED.

countryman *or* **countrywoman** *n* (*pl* **countrymen** *or* **countrywomen**) **1** a man or woman who lives in the country or has country ways. **2** a man or woman who comes from the same country as oneself; a compatriot.

country music *n* music derived from or imitating the folk style of the southern or western USA, typically featuring acoustic guitars, simple melodies, and narrative lyrics.

countryside *n* a rural area.

county *n* (*pl* **-ies**) **1** a territorial division of Britain and Ireland constituting the chief unit for administrative, judicial, and political purposes. **2** the largest local government unit in various countries, e.g. the USA. **3** *Brit* (*used before a noun*) characteristic of or belonging to the English landed gentry: *a county accent.*

county council *n* an elected government body responsible for the administration of a county. ➤➤ **county councillor** *n.*

county court *n* a local civil court in England which is presided over by a judge and deals with relatively minor claims.

county seat *n NAm* = COUNTY TOWN.

county town *n chiefly Brit* a town that is the seat of the government of a county.

coup /kooh/ *n* (*pl* **coups**) **1** = COUP D'ÉTAT. **2** a brilliant, sudden, and usu highly successful stroke or act.

coup de grâce /ˌkooh də 'grahs, 'gras/ *n* (*pl* **coups de grâce**) a fatal blow or shot administered to end the suffering of a mortally wounded person or animal.

coup d'état /ˌkooh day'tah/ *n* (*pl* **coups d'état**) the violent overthrow of an existing government by a small group of rebels.

coupe *n* **1** a small shallow dish with a stem. **2** a cold dessert of fruit and ice cream served in a coupe.

coupé *n* a two-door car that has a fixed roof and a sloping rear.

couple[1] *n* **1** two things considered together; a pair. **2** (*used as sing. or pl*) two people paired together; *esp* two people who are married or living together. **3** *informal* an indefinite small number; a few. **4** in mechanics, two equal and opposite forces that act along parallel lines and cause rotation. ➤➤ **coupledom** *n.*

couple[2] *v* **1** to unite or link (one thing) with another. **2** to fasten (e.g. railway carriages) together; to connect. **3** to copulate. ➤➤ **coupler** *n.*

couplet *n* a unit of two successive, usu rhyming, lines of verse.

coupling *n* a device that serves to connect the ends of adjacent parts or objects, e.g. electrical circuits or railway carriages.

coupon *n* **1** a ticket or voucher that entitles the holder to something, e.g. a discount or a share in rationed food. **2** a part of a printed advertisement to be cut off for use as an order or enquiry form. **3** a printed entry form for a competition, *esp* the football pools.

courage *n* mental or moral strength to confront and withstand danger, fear, or difficulty; bravery. ✱ **have the courage of one's convictions** to be brave enough to do what one thinks is right, irrespective of the obstacles in one's way.

courageous *adj* having or showing courage; brave. ➤➤ **courageously** *adv,* **courageousness** *n.*

courgette *n Brit* a variety of small vegetable marrow used as a vegetable.

courier[1] *n* **1** a person whose job is collecting and delivering parcels, papers, etc. **2** a person employed by a holiday company to assist tourists abroad.

courier[2] *v* to send (e.g. a parcel) by courier.

course[1] *n* **1** the path over which something moves. **2** the direction of travel, *esp* of an aircraft, usu measured as a clockwise angle from north. **3** a movement or progression in space or time. **4a** the usual procedure or normal action of something. **b** a chosen manner of conducting oneself; a plan of action. **5** a series of lessons or lectures relating to a subject. **6** a part of a meal served at one time. **7** a particular medical treatment administered over a designated period. **8** an area of land marked out for a particular sport, e.g. a racecourse or golf course. **9** a continuous horizontal layer of brick or masonry throughout a wall.

course[2] *v* **1** of a liquid: to run or flow. **2** to hunt or pursue (e.g. hares) with dogs that follow by sight rather than smell.

coursebook *n Brit* a textbook for students that covers a particular syllabus.

courser *n literary* a swift powerful horse; a charger.

coursework *n* work done by a student on a course, *esp* for a course marked by continuous assessment.

court[1] *n* **1a** an official assembly of people authorized to hear judicial cases. **b** a place in which a such a court is held. **2** a rectangular space walled or marked off for playing lawn tennis, squash, etc. **3** a space enclosed wholly or partly by buildings or circumscribed by a single building. **4a** (*used as sing. or pl*) the family and retinue or total body of courtiers of a sovereign. **b** the residence or establishment of a sovereign. **5** (*used as sing. or pl*) the body of members of an assembly or board with legislative or administrative powers. ✱ **out of court** without having a court hearing.

court[2] *v* **1a** *dated* to seek the affections of; to woo. **b** of an animal: to perform actions to attract (a mate). **2** to seek to win the favour or support of. **3** to act so as to invite or provoke (a specified outcome).

court card *n Brit* a king, queen, or jack in a pack of cards.

court circular *n Brit* a daily report of the engagements and other activities of the members of the royal family.

courteous *adj* showing respect and consideration for others; polite. ➤➤ **courteously** *adv,* **courteousness** *n.*

courtesan *n* a prostitute, *esp* one with a wealthy or upper-class clientele.

courtesy *n* (*pl* **-ies**) **1** courteous behaviour. **2** a courteous act or expression. **3** (*used before a noun*) done or provided by way of courtesy: *a courtesy call.* ✱ **by courtesy of/courtesy of** through the kindness, generosity, or permission granted by (a person or organization).

courtesy light *n* a small light inside a motor vehicle that comes on when a door is opened.

courtesy title *n* a title given to somebody, e.g. the son or daughter of a peer, which is without legal validity but commonly accepted.

courthouse *n* **1** a building in which a court of law is held. **2** the administrative building of a US county.

courtier *n* an attendant or companion to a king or queen.

courtly *adj* (**-ier, -iest**) elegant and refined. ➤➤ **courtliness** *n.*

court-martial[1] *n* (*pl* **courts-martial** *or* **court-martials**) **1** a court of commissioned officers that tries members of the armed forces. **2** a trial by such a court.

court-martial[2] *v* (**court-martialled, court-martialling,** *NAm* **court-martialed, court-martialing**) to try by court-martial.

court of law *n* = COURT[1] (1A).

court order *n* an order issuing from a court of law that requires a person to do or abstain from doing a specified act.

courtroom *n* a room in which the sessions of a court of law are held.

courtship *n* **1** a period of courting. **2** the courting rituals of animals. **3** the process of courting favour.

court shoe *n Brit* a plain high-heeled woman's shoe with no fastenings.

courtyard *n* an open court or enclosure adjacent to a building.

couscous *n* a N African dish of crushed or coarsely ground wheat steamed and served with meat or vegetables.

cousin *n* **1** a child of one's uncle or aunt. **2** a kinsman or relative. ➤➤ **cousinly** *adj,* **cousinship** *n.*

couture *n* the business of designing and making fashionable custom-made women's clothing.

couturier *or* **couturière** *n* a man or woman who makes and sells couture clothes.

couvade *n* a custom among some peoples by which a father takes to his bed at the birth of his child as if bearing it himself.

couverture *n* chocolate containing a high percentage of cocoa butter, used by chefs for coating or decorating confectionery.

covalent *adj* of chemical bonds: created by shared electrons or pairs of electrons between combining atoms. ➤➤ **covalence** *n,* **covalency** *n,* **covalently** *adv.*

cove[1] *n* **1** a small sheltered inlet or bay. **2** a concave architectural moulding, *esp* at the point where a wall meets a ceiling or floor.

cove[2] *v* to fit (a wall or ceiling) with a cove.

coven *n* (*used as sing. or pl*) a group or gathering of witches.

covenant[1] *n* **1** a solemn agreement; a contract. **2** a contract that binds a person to make regular payments of money to a charitable organization. **3** in the Bible, an agreement between God and the Israelites. ➤➤ **convenantal** *adj.*

covenant[2] *v* **1** to enter into a covenant. **2** to agree to or promise (something) by entering into a covenant.

Coventry ✱ **send to Coventry** to exclude or ostracize.

cover[1] *v* **1** to place or set a cover or covering over (something). **2** to hide (something) from sight or knowledge; to conceal. **3** to lie or spread over (something); to envelop. **4** to include, consider, or take into account; to treat. **5** to report news about (something). **6** to have as one's territory or field of activity. **7** to extend thickly or conspicuously over the surface of. **8** to pass over (a distance); to traverse. **9a** to insure (something). **b** to provide protection against or compensation for (loss, risk, etc). **10** to make sufficient provision for (a demand or charge) by means of a reserve or deposit. **11a** to protect (somebody) by being in a position to fire at an attacker. **b** to hold (somebody) within range of an aimed firearm. **12** in sport, to mark (a member of an opposing team) in order to obstruct a play. **13** of a male animal: to copulate with (a female animal). **14** to record a cover version of (a song). **15** (+ for) to act as a substitute or replacement for somebody during an absence. **16** (+ for) to provide an alibi for somebody who is absent or doing something wrong. ✱ **cover one's back** *informal* to try to make sure that one won't be blamed for something. **cover one's tracks** to conceal evidence of one's past actions. ➤➤ **covering** *n.*

cover[2] *n* **1** a lid or top. **2** an overlay or outer layer, e.g. for protection. **3** a protective covering, e.g. a binding or jacket, for a book. **4** a position or situation affording shelter from attack. **5** natural shelter, e.g. undergrowth, for an animal, or the materials that provide such shelter. **6** the protection offered by a force, e.g. of aircraft, supporting a military operation. **7** something that conceals or obscures. **8** a pretext or disguise. **9** *Brit* protection under an insurance policy. **10** a single place setting in a restaurant. **11** = COVER VERSION.

coverage *n* **1** an area or amount covered. **2** inclusion within the scope of discussion or reporting. **3** the number or percentage of people reached by a communications medium.

cover charge *n* a charge for service made by a restaurant or nightclub.

cover crop *n* a crop, e.g. clover, planted in otherwise bare fields to enrich the soil and prevent erosion.

covering letter *n* a letter containing an explanation of or additional information about an accompanying item.

coverlet *n* a bedspread.

cover note *n Brit* a provisional insurance document providing cover between acceptance of a risk and issue of a full policy.

covert[1] *adj* not openly shown or acknowledged; secret. ➤➤ **covertly** *adv,* **covertness** *n.*

covert[2] *n* **1** a thicket providing cover for game. **2** a feather covering the bases of the wing or tail feathers of a bird.

cover-up *n* a device or course of action that conceals an error or a crime.

cover version *n* a new version of a pop song previously recorded by another artist.

covet *v* (**coveted, coveting**) to long to have (something that belongs to somebody else). ➤➤ **covetable** *adj.*

covetous *adj* showing an inordinate desire to have something, *esp* somebody else's wealth or possessions. ➤➤ **covetously** *adv,* **covetousness** *n.*

covey *n* (*pl* **-eys**) a small flock of birds, *esp* grouse or partridge.

coving *n* = COVE[1] (2).

cow[1] *n* **1** the mature female animal of cattle, *esp* domestic cattle. **2** a mature female of various other animals, e.g. the whale, seal, or moose. **3** *informal* a woman, *esp* an unpleasant one. **4** *Aus, NZ, informal* a cause of annoyance or difficulty. ✱ **till the cows come home** for ever.

cow[2] *v* to intimidate with threats or a show of strength.

coward *n* somebody who lacks courage or resolve. ➤➤ **cowardice** *n,* **cowardliness** *n,* **cowardly** *adj.*

cowbell *n* a bell hung round the neck of a cow.

cowboy *n* **1** a man who tends or drives cattle, *esp* a cattle ranch hand in N America. **2** *informal* a person who employs irregular or unscrupulous methods, *esp* a tradesman who is incompetent or dishonest.

cowcatcher *n chiefly NAm* an apparatus on the front of a locomotive for removing obstacles from the track.

cower *v* to crouch down or shrink away, e.g. in fear, from something menacing.

cowherd *n* a person who tends cows.

cowl *n* **1** a hood or long hooded cloak, *esp* of a monk. **2a** a chimney covering designed to improve ventilation. **b** a cowling. ➤➤ **cowled** *adj.*

cowlick *n* a tuft of hair that sticks up, *esp* over the forehead.

cowling *n* a removable metal covering over an engine, *esp* in an aircraft.

cow parsley *n* a coarse tall plant of the carrot family with clusters of tiny white flowers and leaves that resemble those of parsley.

cowpat *n* a small heap of cow dung.

cowpoke *n NAm, informal* a cowboy.

cowpox *n* a mild viral disease of cows causing vesicles on the udders, that when communicated to humans gives protection against smallpox.

cowpuncher *n NAm, informal* a cowboy.

cowrie *or* **cowry** *n* (*pl* **-ies**) **1** a marine gastropod mollusc with a glossy and often brightly coloured shell **2** the shell of a cowrie, formerly used as money in parts of Africa and Asia.

cowslip *n* a common European plant of the primrose family with fragrant yellow flowers.

Cox *n* a variety of green eating apple with a red tinge.

cox[1] *n* a coxswain. ⋙ **coxless** *adj.*

cox[2] *v* to be cox of (a boat).

coxcomb *n archaic* **1** a conceited foolish person; a fop. **2** the comb of a domestic fowl.

Cox's orange pippin *n* = Cox.

coxswain *n* **1** the steersman of a racing rowing boat who usu directs the crew. **2** a sailor who commands and usu steers a ship's boat.

coy *adj* (**coyer, coyest**) **1a** affectedly shy. **b** provocatively playful or coquettish. **2** showing reluctance to reveal details, *esp* over a sensitive issue. ⋙ **coyly** *adv,* **coyness** *n.*

coyote *n* (*pl* **coyotes** *or* **coyote**) a predatory wild dog of N America, of wolflike appearance.

coypu *n* (*pl* **coypus** *or* **coypu**) a S American semi-aquatic beaver-like rodent with webbed feet, farmed for its fur.

cozen *v archaic or literary* to deceive, trick, or beguile.

cozy[1] *adj* (**-ier, -iest**) *NAm* see COSY[1].

cozy[2] *n* (*pl* **-ies**) *NAm* see COSY[2].

cozy up *v NAm* see COSY UP.

CP *abbr* Communist Party.

CPR *abbr* cardiopulmonary resuscitation.

CPS *abbr* in England and Wales, Crown Prosecution Service.

cps *abbr* **1** in computing, characters per second. **2** cycles per second.

CPU *abbr* central processing unit.

CPVE *abbr Brit* Certificate of Pre-Vocational Education.

Cr *abbr* the chemical symbol for chromium.

crab[1] *n* **1** a crustacean found chiefly by the sea, with a short broad flattened shell and the front pair of limbs forming pincers. **2** (*in pl*) infestation with crab lice. ⋙ **crablike** *adj.*

crab[2] *v* (**crabbed, crabbing**) **1** to move sideways or obliquely like a crab. **2** to go fishing for crabs. ⋙ **crabber** *n.*

crab apple *n* a small wild sour apple.

crabbed *adj* **1** morose or peevish; = CRABBY. **2** of writing: difficult to read or understand.

crabby *adj* (**-ier, -iest**) cross; ill-tempered.

crabgrass *n* a grass with freely rooting creeping stems that grows as a weed in lawns.

crab louse *n* (*also in pl*) a sucking louse that infests human body hair, e.g. in the pubic area.

crab stick *n* a stick of compressed fish meat flavoured with crab.

crabwise *adv* **1** sideways. **2** in a sidling or cautiously indirect manner.

crack[1] *v* **1** to make or cause (something) to make a sudden sharp noise. **2** to break or split apart. **3** to break (something) with a crack. **4** to tell (a joke). **5** to puzzle out and expose or solve (e.g. a code or mystery). **6** to break into (a safe). **7** of the voice: to change pitch suddenly. **8** to collapse emotionally under stress.

crack[2] *n* **1** a sudden sharp loud noise. **2** a line or narrow opening; a fissure or chink. **3** a sharp resounding blow. **4** *informal* a witty remark; a quip. **5** *informal* an attempt or try at something. **6** (**the crack**) *dialect, informal* conversation, *esp* amusing conversation. **7** (*also* **crack cocaine**) *slang* a purified, potent, and highly addictive variety of cocaine, in the form of white pellets that are smoked by users. ✱ **at the crack of dawn** very early in the morning.

crack[3] *adj informal* of superior quality or ability: *a crack shot.*

crackbrained *adj informal* idiotic; crazy.

crackdown *n informal* an act or instance of cracking down.

crack down *v informal* (+ on) to take regulatory or disciplinary action against.

cracked *adj* **1** broken in such a way as to produce cracks. **2** *informal* mentally disordered; crazy.

cracked wheat *n* whole wheat that has been cut or crushed into small pieces and boiled and dried; = BULGUR.

cracker *n* **1** a paper and cardboard tube that makes a cracking noise when pulled sharply apart and usu contains a toy and a paper hat, used *esp* at Christmas. **2** a firecracker. **3** a thin savoury biscuit. **4** *Brit, informal* something or somebody exceptional.

cracker-barrel *adj NAm* homespun; unsophisticated.

crackerjack *n chiefly NAm, informal* somebody or something of marked excellence.

crackers *adj chiefly Brit, informal* mad; crazy.

cracking *adv informal, dated* used as an approving intensive: *a cracking good story.*

crackle[1] *v* to make a series of small cracking noises.

crackle[2] *n* **1** the noise of repeated small cracks or reports. **2** a network of fine cracks on an otherwise smooth surface. ⋙ **crackly** *adj.*

crackling *n* the crisp skin of roast meat, *esp* pork.

cracknel *n* a hard brittle biscuit or sweet.

crack on *v informal* to make speedy progress with a task, etc.

crackpot[1] *n informal* (*often before another noun*) somebody with eccentric ideas.

crackpot[2] *adj informal* eccentric or cranky.

crack up *v informal* **1** to undergo a physical or mental collapse. **2** to laugh uncontrollably. ✱ **not all it's cracked up to be** *informal* not as good as one has been led to expect.

-cracy *comb. form* forming nouns, denoting: rule or government: *democracy.*

cradle[1] *n* **1a** a baby's bed or cot, usu on rockers. **b** a framework of wood or metal used as a support, scaffold, etc. **2** a place of origin: *An English gentleman who had lived some years in this region [of Switzerland] said it was the cradle of compulsory education* — Mark Twain.

cradle[2] *v* **1** to place or keep in a cradle. **2** to shelter or hold protectively.

cradle-snatcher *n informal* a person who is romantically or sexually involved with a much younger person.

craft[1] *n* **1a** an activity or trade requiring manual dexterity or artistic skill. **b** a trade or profession. **2** (*often in combination*) skill in planning, making, or executing something; dexterity: *stagecraft.* **3** (*pl* **craft** *or* **crafts**) a boat, aircraft, or spacecraft. **4** skill in deceiving to gain an end.

craft[2] *v* to form or construct using skill and dexterity.

craftsman *or* **craftswoman** *n* (*pl* **craftsmen** *or* **craftswomen**) **1** a man or woman who practises a skilled trade or handicraft. **2** a person who displays a high degree of manual dexterity or artistic skill. ▶▶ **craftsmanship** *n.*

crafty *adj* (**-ier, -iest**) showing subtlety and guile. ▶▶ **craftily** *adv,* **craftiness** *n.*

crag *n* a steep rugged rock or cliff.

craggy *adj* (**-ier, -iest**) rough; rugged. ▶▶ **cragginess** *n.*

crake *n* a short-billed rail, e.g. the corncrake.

cram *v* (**crammed, cramming**) **1** to pack or jam (a container) tight. **2** (+ in/into) to thrust (something) forcefully into something. **3** *informal* to eat (something) voraciously; to bolt (one's food). **4** to study hastily and intensively for an examination.

crammer *n Brit, informal* a school that prepares students intensively for an examination.

cramp[1] *n* **1** a painful involuntary spasmodic contraction of a muscle. **2** (*in pl*) severe abdominal pain, e.g. in menstruation.

cramp[2] *n* **1** a usu metal device bent at the ends and used to hold timbers or blocks of stone together. **2** a clamp.

cramp[3] *v* **1** to affect with cramp. **2** to confine or restrain. **3** to fasten or hold with a clamp. ✱ **cramp somebody's style** to be an inhibiting influence on them.

cramped *adj* **1** of conditions or accommodation: too small or crowded for comfort. **2** of handwriting: small and hard to read.

cramp-iron *n* = CRAMP[2] (1).

crampon *n* a metal frame with spikes that is fixed to the sole of a boot for climbing slopes of ice or hard snow.

cranberry *n* (*pl* **-ies**) a red acid berry, used in making sauces and jellies.

crane[1] *n* **1** a machine for moving heavy weights by means of a projecting swinging arm or a hoisting apparatus supported on an overhead track. **2** a tall wading bird, typically with white or grey plumage.

crane[2] *v* **1** to stretch (one's neck), *esp* in order to see better. **2** to raise or lift by a crane.

crane fly *n* a long-legged slender fly that resembles a large mosquito but does not bite.

cranesbill *n* a plant with lobed leaves and pink or purple five-petalled flowers.

crania *n* pl of CRANIUM.

cranium *n* (*pl* **craniums** *or* **crania**) the skull; *specif* the part that encloses the brain. ▶▶ **cranial** *adj.*

crank[1] *n* **1** a part of an axle or shaft bent at right angles by which reciprocating motion is changed into circular motion or vice versa. **2** an eccentric person.

crank[2] *v* **1** (*often* + up) to turn a crank, or to start (an engine) using a crank. **2** (+ up) to increase (something, e.g. the volume of a sound) in intensity.

crankcase *n* the housing of a crankshaft.

crankpin *n* the pin which forms the handle of a crank or to which the connecting rod is attached.

crankshaft *n* a shaft driven by or driving a crank.

cranky *adj* (**-ier, -iest**) **1** *informal* odd; eccentric. **2** *NAm* bad-tempered. **3** of machinery: working erratically. ▶▶ **crankily** *adv,* **crankiness** *n.*

cranny *n* (*pl* **-ies**) a small crack or slit; a chink.

crap[1] *n coarse slang* **1** sometimes used as an interjection: nonsense; rubbish. **2a** excrement. **b** the act or an instance of defecating.

crap[2] *v* (**crapped, crapping**) *coarse slang* to defecate.

crap[3] *adj coarse slang* worthless; of poor quality.

crape *n* **1** any crinkly material; = CREPE (1). **2** black silk or artificial silk, from which mourning clothes were formerly made.

crappy *adj* (**-ier, -iest**) *coarse slang* of very poor quality.

craps *pl n* (*used as sing. or pl*) a gambling game played with two dice where players try to throw a seven or eleven.

crapulent *adj literary* crapulous. ▶▶ **crapulence** *n.*

crapulous *adj literary* **1** suffering the effects of excessive drinking of alcohol. **2** characterized by excessive indulgence, *esp* in alcohol.

crash[1] *v* **1** to break or smash (something) violently and noisily. **2** to make or cause (something) to make a crashing sound. **3** to damage (an aircraft) in landing or (a vehicle) by collision. **4** to be involved in a crash. **5** to move or force (one's way) somewhere noisily. **6** to cause (a computer system or program) to fail. **7** of a computer system or program: to become completely inoperative. **8** of shares: to fall suddenly in value. **9** *informal* to enter (a party, etc) without invitation or payment. **10** *informal* (*also* + out) to spend the night; to go to sleep.

crash[2] *n* **1a** a loud noise. **b** the noise of things smashing. **2** the act or an instance of crashing; a violent collision. **3** a sudden decline or failure, e.g. of a business.

crash[3] *adj* designed to achieve an intended result in the shortest possible time: *a crash diet.*

crash dive *n* a steep descent in an aircraft.

crash-dive *v* of an aircraft or submarine: to descend or dive steeply and quickly.

crash helmet *n* a helmet worn to protect the head in the event of an accident.

crash-land *v* of an aircraft or pilot: to land under emergency conditions, usu with some damage to the craft. ▶▶ **crash landing** *n.*

crash pad *n informal* a place where free temporary sleeping accommodation is available.

crash team *n* a medical team equipped to deal at a moment's notice with cardiac arrest.

crash-test *v* to crash (a new vehicle) deliberately in controlled conditions so as to assess its strength under impact.

crashworthiness *n* the capacity of a vehicle to protect its occupants in a collision.

crass *adj* insensitive; coarse. ▶▶ **crassly** *adv,* **crassness** *n.*

-crat *comb. form* forming nouns, denoting: an advocate or partisan of a specified form of government: *democrat.* ▶▶ **-cratic** *comb. form.*

crate[1] *n* **1** a framework or box, usu wooden, for holding goods, e.g. fruit, bottles, etc. **2** *informal* an old dilapidated car, aeroplane, etc.

crate[2] *v* to pack (something) in a crate.

crater[1] *n* **1a** a bowl-shaped depression forming the mouth of a volcano. **b** a bowl-shaped depression formed by the impact of a meteorite. **2** a hole in the ground made by an explosion.

crater[2] *v* to form craters in.

-cratic *comb. form* see -CRAT.

cravat *n* a decorative band or scarf worn round the neck by men.

crave *v* **1** to have a strong or urgent desire for (something): *The sufferer craves water but cannot drink.* **2** *formal* to ask for or beg (something) earnestly: *I crave the court's indulgence.*

craven *adj* completely lacking in courage; cowardly. ➤➤ **cravenly** *adv*, **cravenness** *n.*

craving *n* a great desire or longing.

craw *n* the crop of a bird or insect. ✱ **stick in one's craw** to be difficult to swallow, do, accept, or utter.

crawfish *n* (*pl* **crawfish**) *chiefly NAm* a crayfish.

crawl[1] *v* **1** to move slowly on hands and knees or by dragging the body using the arms. **2** to move or progress slowly or laboriously. **3** to be alive or swarming with creeping things, or as if with creeping things. **4** to have the sensation of insects crawling over one: *It made her flesh crawl.* **5** *informal* (*often* + to) to behave in a servile manner.

crawl[2] *n* **1a** the act or an instance of crawling. **b** slow or laborious motion. **2** the fastest swimming stroke, executed lying on the front and consisting of alternating overarm strokes combined with kicks with alternate legs.

crawler *n* **1** *Brit, informal* a servile person. **2** a vehicle, e.g. a crane, that travels on caterpillar tracks. **3** a heavy slow-moving vehicle. **4** a computer program that scans the World Wide Web so as to compile an index of data.

crayfish *n* (*pl* **crayfish** *or* **crayfishes**) a freshwater crustacean resembling the lobster but usu much smaller.

crayon[1] *n* a stick of coloured chalk or wax used for writing or drawing.

crayon[2] *v* to draw or colour (something) with a crayon.

craze[1] *v* **1** (*usu as past part.*) to madden or send crazy. **2** to develop a mesh of fine cracks.

craze[2] *n* an exaggerated and often short-lived enthusiasm; a fad.

crazy[1] *adj* (**-ier, -iest**) *informal* **1** mad; insane. **2a** impractical: *a crazy idea.* **b** unusual; eccentric. **3** (+ about) extremely enthusiastic about or very fond of (somebody or something). **4** spectacularly precarious: *The door was hanging at a crazy angle.* ➤➤ **crazily** *adv*, **craziness** *n.*

crazy[2] *n* (*pl* **-ies**) *chiefly NAm, informal* an insane person.

crazy paving *n* a paved surface made up of irregularly shaped paving stones.

CRC *abbr* camera-ready copy.

creak[1] *v* to make a prolonged grating or squeaking noise.

creak[2] *n* a prolonged rasping, grating, or squeaking noise, e.g. of an unoiled hinge. ➤➤ **creakily** *adv*, **creaky** *adj.*

cream[1] *n* **1a** the yellowish part of milk containing butterfat, which forms a surface layer when milk is allowed to stand. **b** this separated as a distinct commodity. **2a** a food prepared with or resembling cream. **b** a biscuit, chocolate, etc filled with whipped cream or a soft preparation resembling it. **c** an emulsified medicinal or cosmetic preparation: *hand cream.* **3** (**the cream**) (+ of) the choicest part: *The cream of the Scottish nobility.* **4** a pale yellowish white colour. ➤➤ **creamily** *adv*, **creaminess** *n*, **creamy** *adj.*

cream[2] *v* **1a** to prepare (food) with a cream sauce. **b** to mash (vegetables) with added milk or cream. **2** to work or blend (butter and sugar) to the consistency of cream. **3** *NAm, informal* to defeat completely.

cream[3] *adj* of a pale yellowish white colour.

cream cheese *n* a mild white soft unripened cheese made from whole milk enriched with cream.

cream cracker *n Brit* a crisp thin savoury biscuit.

creamer *n* **1** a device for separating cream from milk. **2** a powdered cream substitute for use in coffee. **3** *NAm* a small jug for serving cream.

creamery *n* (*pl* **-ies**) an establishment where butter and cheese are made or where milk and milk products are prepared or sold.

cream off *v* to select and remove (the choicest part or items) from the main body.

cream of tartar *n* potassium hydrogen tartrate occurring as a white powder and used in baking powder.

cream puff *n* **1** a cake consisting of choux pastry filled with cream. **2** *chiefly NAm, informal* an ineffectual person.

cream sherry *n* a full-bodied sweet sherry.

cream soda *n* a soft fizzy drink flavoured with vanilla.

cream tea *n Brit* afternoon tea at which scones are served with whipped or clotted cream and jam.

crease[1] *n* **1a** a mark made in fabric, paper, etc by crumpling or crushing. **b** a ridge made, e.g. in a trouser leg, by folding and pressing. **2** a line marked on a cricket pitch, e.g. in front of the stumps or in line with the wickets.

crease[2] *v* **1** to crush or crumple (cloth or paper) or fold and press it. **2** to become creased. **3** *chiefly Brit, informal* (*often* + up) to double up or cause (somebody) to double up with laughter.

create *v* **1** to bring into existence. **2a** to produce or cause: *His accomplice created a diversion.* **b** to invest (somebody) with a new form, office, or rank. **3** to make, design, or invent. **4** *Brit, informal* to make a loud fuss about something.

creatine *n* a compound present in the body that is produced during the metabolism of protein and has a part in supplying energy for muscle contraction.

creation *n* **1a** something created. **b** an original work of art. **c** the world. **2** (**the Creation**) the act of bringing the world into ordered existence.

creationist *n* an adherent of a theory that all forms of life were created simultaneously by God and did not evolve from earlier forms. ➤➤ **creationism** *n*, **creationist** *adj.*

creative *adj* **1** showing the ability or power to create; given to creating. **2** having the quality of something imaginatively created. **3** containing misleading inventions designed to falsify or conceal the facts: *creative accounting.* ➤➤ **creatively** *adv*, **creativeness** *n*, **creativity** *n.*

creator *n* **1** a person who creates, usu by bringing something new or original into being. **2** (**the Creator**) God.

creature *n* **1a** a lower animal. **b** an animate being, *esp* a non-human one. **2** a human being; a person. **3** a person who is the servile dependant or tool of another.

creature comforts *pl n* material things that give bodily comfort.

crèche *n Brit* a centre where young children are looked after while their parents are at work, shopping, etc.

cred *n Brit, informal* street credibility.

credal *or* **creedal** *adj* relating to a creed.

credence *n* acceptance of something as true or real.

credential *n* (*usu in pl, used as sing.*) something, *esp* a letter, that gives proof of identity, status, or authority.

credibility *n* **1** the quality of being believable. **2** trust or belief in somebody based on their track record. **3** = STREET CREDIBILITY.

credible *adj* offering reasonable grounds for belief. ➤➤ **credibly** *adv.*

credit[1] *n* **1** a source of honour or repute. **2** acknowledgment; approval. **3** influence derived from enjoying the confidence of others; standing. **4** credence. **5a** the balance in a person's favour in an account. **b** an amount or sum placed at a person's disposal by a bank and usu to be repaid with interest. **c** time given for payment for goods or services provided but not immediately paid for. **d** an entry on the right-hand side of an account constituting an addition to a revenue, net worth, or liability account. **6** (*usu in pl*) an acknowledgment of a contributor by name that appears at the beginning or end of a film or television programme. **7a** recognition that a student has fulfilled a course requirement. **b** *Brit* the passing of an examination at a level well above the minimum though not with distinction. ✱ **do somebody credit/do credit to somebody** of a quality, etc that somebody evinces: to show somebody in a worthy light. **in credit** of a bank account: having money in it. **on credit** with the cost charged to one's account and paid later. **take credit for** to claim responsibility for (something satisfactory). **to somebody's credit** as a creditable effort in difficult circumstances.

credit[2] *v* (**credited, crediting**) **1** to believe (something). **2a** to enter (an amount) on the credit side of an account. **b** to place an amount to the credit of (an account): compare DEBIT[2]. **3a** (+ with) to ascribe some favourable characteristic to (somebody). **b** (+ to) to attribute (e.g. an invention, a saying, etc) to some person.

creditable *adj* of a performance or effort: deserving acknowledgment even if not successful; very respectable. ➤➤ **creditability** *n,* **creditably** *adv.*

credit card *n* a card allowing the holder to obtain goods and services on credit.

creditor *n* a person to whom a debt is owed.

credit transfer *n* a transfer of money directly from one bank account to another.

credit union *n* a cooperative association of people who save money in a common fund and make loans to members at a low rate of interest.

creditworthy *adj* qualifying for commercial credit. ➤➤ **creditworthiness** *n.*

credo *n* (*pl* **-os**) **1** a creed. **2** (**Credo**) a musical setting of the creed in a sung mass.

credulity *n* undue willingness to believe; gullibility.

credulous *adj* ready to believe, *esp* on slight evidence. ➤➤ **credulously** *adv,* **credulousness** *n.*

Cree *n* (*pl* **Crees** *or* **Cree**) a member of a Native American people of Manitoba and Saskatchewan. ➤➤ **Cree** *adj.*

creed *n* **1** a set of religious beliefs. **2** a tenet or set of tenets. **3** a conventionalized statement of religious belief.

creedal *adj* see CREDAL.

Creek *n* (*pl* **Creek**) a member of a confederacy of Native American peoples of Alabama, Georgia, and Florida.

creek *n* **1** *chiefly Brit* a small narrow inlet of a lake, sea, etc. **2** *chiefly NAm, Aus* a brook. ✱ **up the creek 1** *informal* in trouble. **2** *informal* wrong; mistaken.

creel *n* a wickerwork container, e.g. for newly caught fish.

creep[1] *v* (*past tense and past part.* **crept**) **1** to move along with the body prone and close to the ground; to crawl. **2** to go very slowly. **3** to move cautiously or quietly so as to escape notice. **4** (+ into) to become increasingly evident as an element in somebody's manner, etc. **5** *informal* to behave in a servile manner. **6** of a plant: to spread or grow over a surface by clinging or rooting at intervals.

creep[2] *n* **1** a creeping movement. **2** *Brit, informal* an ingratiatingly servile person. **3** *informal* a contemptuous term for a person one dislikes, *esp* a man. ✱ **give one the creeps** *informal* to repel one; to make one's flesh creep.

creeper *n* **1** a creeping plant. **2** a shoe with a thick crepe sole that allows the wearer to pad about silently.

creepy *adj* (**-ier, -iest**) **1** producing a sensation of shivery apprehension. **2** *informal* slightly sinister or unpleasant. ➤➤ **creepily** *adv,* **creepiness** *n.*

creepy-crawly *n* (*pl* **-ies**) *Brit, informal* a small creeping or scuttling creature, e.g. a spider.

creese *n* = KRIS.

cremate *v* to reduce (a dead body) to ashes by burning. ➤➤ **cremation** *n.*

crematorium *n* (*pl* **crematoriums** *or* **crematoria**) a place where dead bodies are cremated.

crème brûlée /,krem brooh'lay/ *n* a thick custard made with eggs and cream and topped with caramelized sugar.

crème caramel /,krem karə'mel/ *n* an egg custard made in an oven dish lined with caramel.

crème de la crème /,krem də lah 'krem/ *n* (**the crème de la crème**) the finest of the finest; the most exclusive set.

crème de menthe /,krem də 'month/ *n* a sweet green or white mint-flavoured liqueur.

crème fraîche /,krem 'fresh/ *n* a type of slightly fermented thick cream.

crenellated *adj* having battlements.

crenellation *n* an indentation in a battlement.

Creole *n* **1** a person of European descent in the W Indies or Spanish America. **2** a white descendant of early French or Spanish settlers of the Gulf States of the USA. **3** a person of mixed French or Spanish and black descent. ➤➤ **Creole** *adj.*

creole *n* a language based on two or more languages, *esp* one developed through the interaction of a local language, e.g. an African tongue spoken in the W Indies, with a European one: compare PIDGIN.

creosote[1] *n* **1** a brownish oily liquid obtained from coal tar and used as a wood preservative. **2** a clear or yellowish oily liquid obtained from wood tar and used as an antiseptic.

creosote[2] *v* to treat with creosote.

crepe *or* **crêpe** *n* **1** (*also* **crape**) a light crinkled fabric woven from any of various fibres. **2** a small very thin pancake. **3** = CREPE RUBBER. ➤➤ **crepey** *adj,* **crepy** *adj.*

crepe de Chine /,krayp də 'sheen/ *n* a soft fine crepe, orig of silk.

crepe paper *n* thin paper with a crinkled or puckered texture.

crepe rubber *n* crude or synthetic rubber in the form of crinkled sheets, used *esp* for shoe soles.

crêpe suzette *n* (*pl* **crêpes suzette**) a thin pancake in a hot sauce that is sprinkled with a liqueur, e.g. cognac, and set alight for serving.

crept *v* past tense and past part. of CREEP[1].

crepuscular *adj formal* relating to or resembling twilight.

crescendo[1] *n* (*pl* **crescendos** *or* **crescendi**) **1** a gradual increase; *esp* a gradual increase in volume in a musical passage. **2** a crescendo musical passage.

crescendo[2] *adj and adv* of a piece of music: to be performed with an increase in volume.

crescendo[3] *v* (**crescendoes, crescendoed, crescendoing**) to increase in force or volume.

crescent *n* **1** the figure of the moon at any stage between new moon and first quarter or last quarter and the succeeding new moon. **2** something shaped like a crescent. **3** *Brit* a curved street.

cress *n* a plant of the mustard family that has mildly pungent leaves and is used in salads and as a garnish.

crest[1] *n* **1a** a showy tuft or projection on the head of an animal, *esp* a bird. **b** a plume, emblem, etc worn on a knight's helmet. **c** a symbol of a family, office, etc, that appears as a figure above the shield in a coat of arms. **2** the ridge or top, *esp* of a wave, roof, or mountain. ✱ **on the crest of a wave** enjoying great success. ➤➤ **crested** *adj.*

crest[2] *v* to reach the crest of (a hill, ridge, wave, etc).

crestfallen *adj* disheartened or dejected.

Cretaceous *adj* of the last geological period of the Mesozoic era, lasting from about 146 million to about 65 million years ago, and marked by the dominance of dinosaurs. ➤➤ **Cretaceous** *n.*

Cretan *n* a native or inhabitant of the island of Crete. ➤➤ **Cretan** *adj.*

cretin *n* **1** somebody afflicted with cretinism. **2** *offensive* an imbecile; an idiot. ➤➤ **cretinous** *adj.*

cretinism *n* congenital physical stunting and mental retardation caused by severe deficiency of the thyroid hormone in infancy.

cretonne *n* a strong unglazed cotton or linen cloth used for curtains and upholstery.

Creutzfeldt-Jakob disease /kroytsfelt 'yakob/ *n* (*often* **CJD**) a progressive disease of middle age, characterized by dementia, muscular wasting, spasticity, and involuntary movements, believed to be caused by a PRION (infectious protein particle). ✱ **new variant Creutzfeldt-Jakob disease** (*often* **new variant CJD**) a form of the disease characterized by early onset, thought to be the human variety of BSE.

crevasse *n* a deep fissure in a glacier.

crevice *n* a narrow opening resulting from a split or crack.

crew[1] *n* (*used as sing. or pl*) **1a** the personnel of a ship or boat, excluding the captain and officers. **b** the people who work on an aircraft or train. **2** *informal, derog* a number of people temporarily associated. ➤➤ **crewman** *n.*

crew[2] *v chiefly Brit* past tense of CROW[2].

crew[3] *v* **1** to serve as a member of a crew on (a ship, aircraft, etc). **2** to provide with a crew.

crew cut *n* a very short bristly haircut.

crewel *n* loosely twisted worsted yarn used in embroidery and tapestry.

crew neck *n* a round flat neckline on a knitted pullover.

crib[1] *n* **1** *chiefly NAm* a child's cot with barred or slatted sides. **2** a cattle stall. **3** a manger or rack for animal fodder. **4** a literal translation of a text, *esp* one used surreptitiously by students. **5** *NAm* an apartment. **6** the card game cribbage. **7** *Aus, NZ, informal* a snack.

crib[2] *v* (**cribbed, cribbing**) **1** to copy (somebody else's work) without permission or acknowledgment. **2** *archaic* to steal (something). ➤➤ **cribber** *n.*

cribbage *n* a card game for two to four players who each try to form various counting combinations of cards.

crick[1] *n* a painful spasmodic condition of the muscles of the neck, back, etc.

crick[2] *v* to cause a crick in (the neck, etc).

cricket[1] *n* a game played with a bat and ball on a large field with two wickets near its centre by two sides of eleven players each who try to score runs by hitting the ball and running between the wickets. ✱ **not cricket** *Brit, informal* against the dictates of fair play; not honourable. ➤➤ **cricketer** *n.*

cricket[2] *n* a leaping insect noted for the chirping sounds produced by the male.

cri de coeur /kree də 'kuh/ *n* (*pl* **cris de coeur**) a passionate plea or protest.

cried *v* past tense and past part. of CRY[1].

crier *n* an officer who makes announcements in a court.

crime *n* **1** violation of law, or an instance of this, punishable by the state. **2** a grave offence, *esp* against morality. **3** criminal activity. **4** *informal* something deplorable or disgraceful.

crime passionnel /,kreem pasyo'nel/ *n* (*pl* **crimes passionnels**) a crime, usu murder, prompted by sexual jealousy.

criminal[1] *adj* **1** involving or constituting a crime. **2** relating to crime or its punishment. **3** guilty of crime. **4** *informal* disgraceful; deplorable. ➤➤ **criminality** *n,* **criminally** *adv.*

criminal[2] *n* a person who has committed or been convicted of a crime.

criminalize *or* **-ise** *v* **1** to make (an activity) illegal. **2** to outlaw the activities of (a person) and so turn them into a criminal.

criminology *n* the study of crime, criminals, and penal treatment. ➤➤ **criminological** *adj,* **criminologist** *n.*

crimp[1] *v* **1** to make (the hair) wavy or curly. **2** to roll or curl the edge of (a steel panel, etc). **3** to pinch or press (material) together in order to seal or join it. ➤➤ **crimper** *n.*

crimp[2] *n* **1** a rolled, folded, or compressed edge. **2** a tight curl or wave in the hair.

Crimplene *n trademark* a textured continuous-filament polyester yarn.

crimson[1] *adj* of a deep purplish red colour. ➤➤ **crimson** *n.*

crimson[2] *v literary* **1** to become crimson. **2** to blush.

cringe[1] *v* **1** to shrink or cower in fear. **2** to adopt a cowering posture expressive of humility. **3** (*often* + to) to behave with fawning self-abasement. **4** to feel acute embarrassment.

cringe[2] *n* the act or an instance of cringing.

cringeworthy *adj informal* embarrassingly awful.

crinkle[1] *v* **1** to wrinkle. **2** to cause (something) to crinkle.

crinkle[2] *n* a wrinkle. ➤➤ **crinkly** *adj.*

crinoline *n* a full skirt as worn by women in the 19th cent., or a padded or hooped petticoat supporting it.

cripple[1] *n* **1** *offensive* a lame or partly disabled person. **2** a person who is impaired in a non-physical way: *an emotional cripple.*

cripple[2] *v* **1** to make (somebody) a cripple. **2** to impair (somebody) mentally, emotionally, etc. **3** to hamper or severely limit (a person, operation, etc).

crisis *n* (*pl* **crises**) **1** a time of acute difficulty or danger, *esp* on a national or international scale. **2** the turning point for better or worse in an acute disease, e.g. pneumonia.

crisp[1] *adj* **1a** easily crumbled; brittle. **b** desirably firm and fresh: *crisp lettuce leaves.* **2** sharp, clean-cut, and clear: *a crisp illustration.* **3** decisive; sharp: *a crisp manner.* **4** of the weather: briskly cold; fresh; *esp* frosty. ➤➤ **crisply** *adv,* **crispness** *n.*

crisp[2] *n Brit* a thin slice of flavoured or salted fried potato.

crisp[3] *v* **1** to make or keep (food) crisp. **2** *archaic* to curl or crimp (hair).

crispbread *n* a plain dry unsweetened biscuit made from crushed grain, e.g. rye.

crisper *n* a compartment at the bottom of a refrigerator for keeping vegetables fresh.

crispy *adj* (**-ier, -iest**) **1** firm and fresh. **2** made crisp by deep frying. ➤➤ **crispiness** *n.*

crisscross[1] *n* a crisscrossed pattern.

crisscross[2] *adj* marked or characterized by a crisscrossing pattern or network.

crisscross[3] *v* **1** to pass back and forth through or over (a place). **2** to mark with intersecting lines.

criterion *n* (*pl* **criteria**) a standard on which a judgment or decision may be based. ➤➤ **criterial** *adj.*

Usage note

criterion *and* **criteria**. *Criteria* is the plural form of *criterion.* A phrase such as *this criteria* is incorrect. If a thing is judged by such and such *criteria,* then more than one standard of judgment is being applied to it: *The criteria by which schools will be judged to have succeeded or failed are set out in the report.*

critic *n* **1** a person who evaluates works of art, literature, or music. **2** a person who tends to judge harshly or to be over-critical of minor faults.

critical *adj* **1a** inclined to criticize severely and unfavourably. **b** consisting of or involving criticism. **c** exercising or involving careful judgment or judicious evaluation. **2a** relating to or denoting a measurement, point, etc at which some quality, property, or phenomenon undergoes a marked change. **b** crucial; decisive. **c** being in or approaching a state of crisis. **3** of a nuclear reactor: sustaining an energy-producing chain reaction. ➤➤ **critically** *adv.*

critical mass *n* the minimum mass of fissile material that can sustain a nuclear chain reaction.

critical path *n* a sequence of activities that forms part of a complex activity, the timing of which determines the expected completion time of the complex activity.

criticise *v* see CRITICIZE.

criticism *n* **1a** the act of criticizing, usu unfavourably. **b** a critical observation or remark. **c** a detailed or reasoned assessment; a critique. **2** the art or act of analysing and evaluating the fine arts, literature, or literary documents.

criticize *or* **-ise** *v* **1** to find fault with (somebody or something). **2** to consider the merits and demerits of (a literary or artistic work) and judge or evaluate it accordingly.

critique[1] *n* a critical estimate or discussion, e.g. an article or essay.

critique[2] *v* (**critiques, critiqued, critiquing**) to analyse or criticize (something).

critter *n dialect* a creature.

croak *v* **1a** to give the characteristic cry of a frog or crow. **b** to speak in a hoarse throaty voice. **2** *informal* to die. ➤➤ **croak** *n,* **croaker** *n,* **croaky** *adj.*

Croat *n* = CROATIAN.

Croatian *n* **1** a native or inhabitant of Croatia. **2** the form of Serbo-Croatian spoken by the Croatians and written in the Roman alphabet. ➤➤ **Croatian** *adj.*

crochet[1] *n* crocheted work.

crochet[2] *v* (**crocheted, crocheting**) to make (a garment or design) by drawing a single continuous yarn or thread into a pattern of interlocked loops using a hooked needle.

croci *n* pl of CROCUS.

crock[1] *n Brit, informal* **1** an elderly infirm person. **2** an old broken-down vehicle.

crock[2] *n* **1** a thick earthenware pot or jar. **2** an item of crockery. **3** *chiefly NAm, informal* a lie or piece of nonsense.

crock[3] *v informal* **1** (*also* + up) to injure or disable (somebody or something). **2** *NAm* to make drunk.

crockery *n* earthenware or china tableware.

crocodile *n* **1** a tropical or subtropical large voracious semi-aquatic reptile with a thick skin and long body. **2** (*often before a noun*) the skin of a crocodile, leather prepared from this, or an imitation of it. **3** *Brit* a line of people, e.g. schoolchildren, walking in pairs.

crocodile clip *n* a peg-like metal clip with long notched edges, used for joining wires or making other electrical connections.

crocodile tears *pl n* false or affected tears; hypocritical sorrow.

crocus *n* (*pl* **crocuses** *or* **croci**) an early-flowering plant of the iris family bearing a single brightly-coloured flower.

Croesus *n* a fabulously wealthy person.

croft *n* **1** *Brit* a small enclosed field usu adjoining a house. **2** a small farm, *esp* in Scotland, worked by a tenant. ➤➤ **crofter** *n.*

crofting *n Brit* the system of working the land as crofts.

Crohn's disease *n* a chronic inflammatory disease of the bowel, causing scarring and thickening of the bowel wall, fistulae, and abscesses.

croissant *n* a flaky rich crescent-shaped roll of bread or yeast-leavened pastry.

Cro-Magnon *n* (*used before a noun*) denoting a tall erect race of human beings who appeared about 35,000 years ago, and flourished from the Upper Palaeolithic to Neolithic period.

cromlech *n* **1** *no longer used technically* in Wales, a megalithic burial chamber consisting of a flat stone laid on upright ones; = DOLMEN. **2** in Brittany, a circle of standing stones.

crone *n* a withered old woman.

crony *n* (*pl* **-ies**) *informal, often derog* a close friend, *esp* of long standing.

cronyism *n* favouritism shown to friends, *esp* in making political appointments.

crook[1] *n* **1** an implement or part of something having a bent or hooked shape. **2a** a shepherd's staff. **b** a bishop's crozier. **3** a bend or curve. **4** *informal* a person given to criminal practices; a thief or swindler.

crook[2] *v* **1** to bend (something). **2** to curve or wind.

crook[3] *adj Aus, NZ, informal* **1** ill; sick. **2** not in correct working order. **3** bad; unpleasant.

crookback *n archaic* a hunchback.

crooked *adj* **1** having a crook or curve; bent. **2** *informal* not morally straightforward; dishonest. **3** *Aus, NZ, informal* bad-tempered; angry. ➤➤ **crookedly** *adv,* **crookedness** *n.*

croon[1] *v* to sing, usu sentimental popular songs, in a low or soft voice. ➤➤ **crooner** *n.*

croon[2] *n* a crooning voice or tone.

crop[1] *n* **1** a plant product that can be grown and harvested extensively, or the total production of it. **2** a group or quantity appearing at any one time: *a new crop of students.* **3** a riding whip. **4** a short haircut. **5** a pouched enlargement of the gullet of many birds in which food is stored and prepared for digestion.

crop[2] *v* (**cropped, cropping**) **1a** to cut (hair) short. **b** of an animal: to graze on (grass, etc). **c** to cut and harvest (mature plant produce). **d** to trim (a photograph). **2a** to grow (something) as a crop. **b** to plant (land) so as to bear a crop. **3** to yield or bear a crop.

crop circle *n* a ring or other pattern of flattened corn appearing within a field of standing corn.

crop-dusting *n* the spraying of crops from the air with fertilizer, insecticide, or fungicide in powdered form.

cropper[1] *n* a plant that yields a crop of a usu specified quality or amount.

cropper[2] ✱ **come a cropper 1** *informal* to have a fall. **2** *informal* to suffer a severe reversal.

crop top *n* a woman's close-fitting garment cut short beneath the bust to leave the midriff bare.

crop up *v informal* to happen or appear unexpectedly or casually.

croque-monsieur /krok mə'syuh/ *n* a cheese and ham sandwich grilled or fried.

croquet[1] *n* **1** a game in which wooden balls are driven by mallets through a series of hoops set out on a lawn. **2** the driving away of an opponent's croquet ball by striking one's own ball placed against it.

croquet[2] *v* (**croqueted, croqueting**) to drive away (an opponent's croquet ball) by striking one's own ball placed against it.

croquette *n* a small piece of minced meat, vegetable, etc coated with breadcrumbs and fried in deep fat.

crosier *or* **crozier** *n* a staff resembling a shepherd's crook, carried by bishops as a symbol of office.

cross[1] *n* **1a** a figure formed by two intersecting lines (+ or x). **b** the figure (x) used to mark something wrong in a school exercise, etc, or to represent a kiss in a letter, etc. **2a** an upright stake with a transverse beam used, *esp* by the ancient Romans, for execution. **b** (**the Cross**) in Christianity, the cross on which Jesus was crucified. **c** a monument in the form of a cross. **d** a badge or decoration shaped like a cross. **3a** the crossing of dissimilar individuals, or the resulting hybrid. **b** somebody or something that combines characteristics of two different types or individuals. **4** the act of crossing the ball in football. ✱ **at cross purposes** misunderstanding each other or having different objectives. **have one's cross to bear** to have personal troubles to bear like everybody else [from the practice of making someone condemned to crucifixion carry his cross to the place of execution]. **make the sign of the cross** as an act of reverence, to indicate the shape of the Cross, gesturing towards one's forehead, centre body, and each shoulder in turn. **on the cross** on the bias; diagonally.

cross[2] *v* **1a** to lie or be situated across each other or across (something). **b** to intersect (something). **c** to pass simultaneously in opposite directions. **2** to go across (e.g. a road, river, or boundary). **3a** (+ off/out/through) to cancel (an item) by drawing a line across it. **b** to draw two parallel lines across (a cheque) so as to allow only direct payment into a bank account, not encashment. **c** to finish off (a letter *t* or *f*) with the horizontal bar. **4a** in sitting, to position (one's legs) so that one thigh is resting on the other. **b** to fold (one's arms) or place them crosswise. **5** to make the sign of the cross in front of (oneself). **6** to oppose or frustrate (somebody). **7** to hybridize (an animal or plant) by causing it to interbreed with one of a different kind. **8** to kick or pass (the ball) across the field in football. ✱ **cross my heart** used to guarantee the truth of what one is saying. **cross somebody's palm with silver** *often humorous* to pay them to tell one's fortune or perform some other service. **cross swords** (*often* + with) to come into conflict. **cross the floor** *Brit* to join the opposing party, or change parties, in Parliament. **get one's lines or wires crossed** *informal* to misunderstand something. ➤➤ **crosser** *n.*

cross[3] *adj* **1** angry; annoyed. **2** irritable; grumpy. ➤➤ **crossly** *adv,* **crossness** *n.*

crossbar *n* a transverse bar, e.g. between goalposts.

cross bench *n* any of the benches in the House of Lords for members who belong to neither government nor opposition parties. ➤➤ **crossbencher** *n.*

crossbill *n* a finch whose bill has a strongly curved crossed tip, adapted for extracting seeds from fir cones.

crossbow *n* a short bow mounted crosswise near the end of a wooden support and used, *esp* formerly, to fire bolts and stones.

crossbreed[1] *v* (*past tense and past part.* **crossbred**) to hybridize or cross (two varieties or breeds of the same species).

crossbreed[2] *n* a hybrid.

cross-check[1] *v* to check (information) for validity or accuracy by reference to more than one source.

cross-check[2] *n* a check by reference to more than one source.

cross-country[1] *adj and adv* **1** proceeding over countryside rather than by roads. **2** of a race: held over the countryside instead of over a track.

cross-country[2] *n* cross-country running, horse-riding, etc.

cross-cultural *adj* **1** embracing different cultures. **2** drawing a comparison between different cultures.

crosscurrent *n* **1** a current in a river or the sea that flows across the main current. **2** a conflicting tendency.

crosscut *v* to cut across the grain of (wood).

crosscut saw *n* a saw designed to cut across the grain of wood.

cross-dresser *n* a transvestite. ➤➤ **cross-dressing** *n.*

crosse *n* a long-handled stick with a shallow triangular net of leather thongs at the end, used in lacrosse.

crossed *adj* of a telephone line: connected in error to two or more telephones.

cross-examine *v* to question (a witness in a law court) closely in order to check answers or elicit new information. ➤➤ **cross-examination** *n.*

cross-eye *n* **1** a squint in which the eye turns towards the nose. **2** (*in pl*) eyes that squint inwards. ➤➤ **cross-eyed** *adj.*

cross-fertilization *or* **cross-fertilisation** *n* **1a** fertilization by the joining of ova with pollen or sperm from a different individual. **b** cross-pollination. **2** interaction, *esp* of a broadening or productive nature.

crossfire *n* **1** firing from two or more points in crossing directions. **2** rapid or heated interchange.

cross-grained *adj* **1** of timber: having the grain or fibres running diagonally, transversely, or irregularly. **2** of a person: difficult to deal with; intractable.

cross hair *n* a fine wire or thread, usu one of two, seen through the eyepiece of an optical instrument and used as a reference.

crosshatch *v* to shade with a series of intersecting parallel lines. ⋙ **cross-hatching** *n.*

crossing *n* **1** a journey across something, e.g. a strip of sea, a mountain range, etc. **2a** part of a road marked by studs, stripes, etc, where pedestrians may cross. **b** a place where a railway crosses a road. **c** a place where roads, etc cross each other.

cross-legged *adv and adj* of a person seated *esp* on the floor: with ankles crossed and knees bent outwards.

cross-match *v* to determine the compatibility of (a donor's and a recipient's blood) before transfusion.

crossover[1] *n* **1a** a crossing on a street or over a river. **b** a short track joining two adjacent railway lines. **2** the act or an instance of changing the style of popular music, *esp* to broaden its appeal, or of combining styles.

crossover[2] *adj* **1** representing a crossover in popular music. **2** having or combining two or more styles, functions, etc.

crosspatch *n informal* a bad-tempered person.

crosspiece *n* a transverse beam, joist, or bar.

crossply *adj* of a tyre: having the cords arranged crosswise to strengthen the tread.

cross-pollination *n* the transfer of pollen from one flower to the stigma of another.

cross-question *v* **1** to cross-examine (a witness). **2** to question (somebody) intensively.

cross-reference *n* an indication at one place, e.g. in a book or filing system, of the existence of relevant information at another place.

crossroad *n* (*usu in pl, used as sing. or pl*) **1** the place where two or more roads intersect. **2** a crucial point or stage, *esp* where a decision must be made.

cross-section *n* **1** a surface made by cutting across something, *esp* at right angles to its length, or a drawing of one. **2** a representative sample.

cross-sell *v* (*past tense and past part.* **cross-sold**) to sell (an additional product or service) to a client or customer who has already purchased some product or service.

cross-stitch[1] *n* a stitch in the shape of an X formed by crossing one stitch over another, or needlework using such a stitch.

cross-stitch[2] *v* to sew (something) using cross-stitches.

cross-talk *n* **1** unwanted signals in a communications channel or storage location that come from another channel or storage location. **2** rapid witty exchanges; repartee.

crosstie *n NAm* a railway sleeper.

crosstrees *pl n* a pair of horizontal crosspieces on a mast to which supporting ropes are attached.

crosswalk *n NAm, Aus* a specially paved or marked path for pedestrians crossing a street or road.

crossways *adv* crosswise; diagonally.

crosswind *n* a wind blowing in a direction not parallel to the course of a vehicle, aircraft, etc.

crosswise *adv* so as to cross something; across.

crossword *n* a puzzle in which words are entered horizontally and vertically in a pattern of numbered squares in answer to correspondingly numbered clues.

crostini *pl n* small pieces of toast or fried bread with a savoury topping, served as canapés.

crotch *n* **1** the angle between the inner thighs where they meet the human body. **2** a fork in a tree. ⋙ **crotched** *adj.*

crotchet *n Brit* a musical note with the time value of half a minim or two quavers.

crotchety *adj informal* bad-tempered or irritable.

crouch[1] *v* to lower the body by bending one's knees and bending the upper body forward.

crouch[2] *n* a crouching position.

croup[1] *n* inflammation of the larynx and trachea in children and babies, causing laboured, rasping breathing.

croup[2] *n* the rump or hindquarters, *esp* of a horse.

croupier *n* a person in a casino who collects and pays out bets at the gaming tables.

crouton *n* a small cube of crisp bread served with soup or used as a garnish.

Crow *n* (*pl* **Crow** *or* **Crows**) a member of a Native American people of the region between the Platte and Yellowstone rivers.

crow[1] *n* **1** a large bird with glossy plumage, a heavy beak, rounded wings, and a raucous cry. **2** *informal* an ugly old woman. ✱ **as the crow flies** in a direct line, usu as distinct from the overland route. **eat crow** *NAm, informal* to be forced to accept humiliation or defeat; to eat humble pie.

crow[2] *v* (*past tense* **crowed** *or* **crew,** *past part.* **crowed**) **1** to make the shrill long-drawn-out cry of a cock. **2** to utter sounds of happiness or pleasure. **3a** (+ over) to triumph over somebody in their defeat. **b** (*often* + over/about) to brag about one's success. ⋙ **crow** *n.*

crowbar *n* an iron or steel bar for use as a lever that is wedge-shaped at the working end.

crowd[1] *n* **1a** (*used as sing. or pl*) a large number of people gathered together without order; a throng. **b** a mass of spectators. **2** (**the crowd**) people in general. **3** a large number of things close together and in disorder; a huddle. **4** a specified social group: *He got in with a bad crowd.*

crowd[2] *v* **1** (*often* + round) to press close. **2** to collect in numbers; to throng. **3a** to fill (a place) by pressing or thronging together. **b** to force or thrust (objects) into a small space. **4** (+ off/out of) of a throng: to push (others) out of the way. **5** to press close to or jostle (somebody).

crowded *adj* **1** filled with numerous people or things. **2** full of events: *her crowded engagement diary.*

crowd out *v* to exclude (somebody or something) by depriving them of space or attention.

crowdpuller *n chiefly Brit, informal* somebody or something that attracts a large audience.

crowfoot *n* an aquatic plant of the buttercup family, with lobed leaves shaped like a crow's foot.

crown[1] *n* **1** a gold and jewel-encrusted headdress worn as a symbol of sovereignty. **2** (**the Crown**) **a** the government under a constitutional monarchy. **b** the sovereign as head of state, or sovereignty. **3** a reward of victory or mark of honour; *esp* the title representing the championship in a sport. **4** a wreath, band, or circular ornament for the head, *esp* worn as a symbol of victory. **5a** the topmost part of the skull or head. **b** the summit of a slope, mountain, etc. **c** the part of a hat or cap that covers the crown of the head. **d** the part of a tooth visible outside the gum, or an artificial substitute or covering for it. **6** the high point or culmination. **7** a British coin worth 25 pence (formerly five shillings), now minted only for a commemorative purpose.

crown[2] *v* **1** to place a crown on the head of (somebody), *esp* as a symbol of investiture. **2** to recognize (somebody), usu officially, as the leader in a particular field, *esp* a sport. **3** *literary* to surmount (something). **4** to bring to a successful conclusion. **5** to put an artificial crown on (a tooth). **6** *informal* to hit on the head. **7** of a baby's head: to appear in the vaginal opening fully, before emerging.

Crown Colony *n* a colony of the Commonwealth over which the British government retains some control.

Crown Court *n* a local criminal court in England and Wales having jurisdiction over serious offences.

Crown Derby *n* a type of porcelain manufactured in Derby from the mid 18th to mid 19th cent., typically stamped with a D surmounted by a crown.

crowned head *n* a king or queen.

crown glass *n* a glass of relatively low refractive index, used *esp* in lenses.

crown green *n Brit* a bowling green which slopes downwards slightly from its centre to its outer edge.

crown imperial *n* a tall garden plant of the lily family, with usu orange bell-shaped flowers.

crown jewels *pl n* the jewels, e.g. crown and sceptre, belonging to a sovereign's regalia.

crown prince *n* a male heir to a crown or throne.

crown princess *n* **1** the wife of a crown prince. **2** a female heir to a crown or throne.

Crown Prosecution Service *n* In England and Wales, a body that conducts all prosecutions initiated by the police.

crown saw *n* a saw with teeth at the edge of a hollow cylinder that is used to cut circular holes.

crown wheel *n* a gearwheel of the kind used in motor vehicles, whose teeth are at right angles to its face.

crow's-foot *n* (*pl* **crow's-feet**) (*usu in pl*) any of the wrinkles round the outer corners of the eyes.

crow's nest *n* a high lookout platform on a ship's mast.

crozier *n* see CROSIER.

CRT *abbr* cathode-ray tube.

cru *n* (*pl* **crus**) in France, a vineyard or group of vineyards that produces fine wines.

cruces *n* pl of CRUX.

crucial *adj* **1** essential to the resolving of a crisis. **2** of the greatest importance or significance. **3** *informal* wonderful or excellent. ⋙ **crucially** *adv.*

cruciate *adj* cross-shaped or arranged in the form of a cross: *cruciate ligaments.* ⋙ **cruciately** *adv.*

crucible *n* **1** a vessel for melting a substance at a very high temperature. **2** a severe test. **3** a situation in which interacting influences produce something new.

crucifer *n* any of several species of plants of the mustard family, including the cabbage, stock, cress, etc. ⋙ **cruciferous** *adj.*

crucifix *n* a representation of Christ on the cross.

crucifixion *n* **1** the act of crucifying. **2** (**Crucifixion**) the crucifying of Christ.

cruciform *adj* forming a cross. ⋙ **cruciformly** *adv.*

crucify *v* (**-ies, -ied**) **1** to execute (somebody) by fastening their hands and feet to a cross and leaving them to die. **2** to cause anguish or agony to. **3** *informal* to defeat decisively. **4** to criticize or ridicule unmercifully.

crud *n informal* **1** filth, grease, etc. **2** rubbish; nonsense. ⋙ **cruddy** *adj.*

crude[1] *adj* **1** existing in a natural state and unaltered by processing. **2** of language, behaviour, etc: vulgar; gross. **3** rough or inexpert. ⋙ **crudely** *adv,* **crudeness** *n,* **crudity** *n.*

crude[2] *n* a substance, *esp* petroleum, in its natural unprocessed state.

crudités /'kroohditay/ *pl n* small pieces of raw vegetables served as an hors d'oeuvre, usu with a dip.

cruel *adj* (**crueller, cruellest,** *NAm* **crueler, cruelest**) **1** liking to inflict pain or suffering; pitiless. **2** painful. ⋙ **cruelly** *adv,* **cruelness** *n.*

cruelty *n* (*pl* **-ies**) **1** the quality of being cruel. **2** cruel behaviour, or an instance of it.

cruet *n* **1** *Brit* a small container for holding salt, pepper, mustard, etc at table. **2** *Brit* a set of cruets on a stand. **3** a vessel to hold wine or water for the Eucharist.

cruise[1] *v* **1** to travel by sea for pleasure. **2** to go about without any definite destination. **3** of an aircraft or vehicle: to travel at an efficient or economical steady speed. **4** to make progress easily. **5** *informal* to search for a sexual partner, *esp* a homosexual one.

cruise[2] *n* a sea voyage for pleasure.

cruise control *n* a control in a motor vehicle that can be operated to maintain a constant speed without the use of the accelerator pedal.

cruise missile *n* a long-distance low-flying missile that is guided by an inbuilt computerized navigation system.

cruiser *n* **1** a yacht or motor boat with passenger accommodation. **2** a large fast lightly armoured warship. **3** *NAm* a police patrol car.

cruiserweight *n chiefly Brit* = LIGHT-HEAVYWEIGHT.

crumb[1] *n* **1** a small fragment of bread, cake, biscuit, or cheese. **2** a small amount. **3** the soft inner part of a loaf of bread.

crumb[2] *v* **1** to cover (food) with crumbs. **2** to break up (food) into crumbs.

crumble[1] *v* **1** to break into small pieces. **2** to disintegrate. ⋙ **crumbly** *adj.*

crumble[2] *n* a dessert of stewed fruit topped with a crumbly mixture of fat, flour, and sugar.

crumbs *interj chiefly Brit, informal* used to express surprise or consternation.

crumby *adj* see CRUMMY.

crumhorn *n* see KRUMMHORN.

crummy *or* **crumby** *adj* (**-ier, -iest**) *informal* **1** disagreeable; inferior; squalid. **2** ill. ⋙ **crummily** *adv,* **crumminess** *n.*

crumpet *n* **1** a small round unsweetened cake that is usu toasted before serving. **2** *Brit, informal, offensive* women collectively as sexual objects.

crumple[1] *v* **1** to crush out of shape. **2** to make or become creased or wrinkled. **3** to collapse.

crumple[2] *n* a wrinkle or crease made by crumpling.

crumple zone *n* a part of a motor vehicle designed to buckle on absorbing the force of an impact, thus protecting the passenger area.

crunch[1] *v* **1** to chew or bite (something) with a noisy crushing sound. **2** to make a crushing sound. **3** to move with a crushing sound.

crunch[2] *n* **1** an act or sound of crunching. **2** (**the crunch**) *informal* the decisive situation or moment.

crunchy *adj* (**-ier, -iest**) crisp; brittle. ⋙ **crunchiness** *n.*

crupper *n* a leather loop passing under a horse's tail and buckled to the saddle to prevent the saddle from slipping forwards.

crural *adj* relating to the leg or thigh.

crusade[1] *n* **1** (*usu* **the Crusades**) any of the medieval Christian military expeditions to win the Holy Land from the Muslims. **2** a reforming enterprise undertaken with zeal and enthusiasm.

crusade[2] *v* to engage in a crusade. ➤➤ **crusader** *n.*

cruse *n archaic* a small earthenware jar or pot for holding oil, water, etc.

crush[1] *v* **1** to deform or flatten by compression. **2** to reduce to particles by pounding or grinding. **3** to subdue or overwhelm. ➤➤ **crushable** *adj,* **crusher** *n,* **crushing** *adj,* **crushingly** *adv.*

crush[2] *n* **1** a crowding together of many people. **2** a soft drink made from the juice of pressed fruit. **3** *informal* an infatuation, *esp* with somebody unsuitable or unattainable.

crush bar *n* a bar in a theatre where drinks can be bought in the interval.

crush barrier *n Brit* a barrier erected to control crowds.

crushed velvet *n* velvet with an irregular nap that gives the fabric the appearance of having been squashed.

crust[1] *n* **1a** the hardened exterior of bread. **b** a piece of bread grown dry or hard. **2** the pastry cover of a pie. **3** a hard or brittle surface layer. **4** the outer rocky layer of the earth. **5** a deposit built up on the inside of a wine bottle.

crust[2] *v* to form a crust on.

crustacean *n* any of a large group of mostly aquatic arthropods, including the lobsters, crabs, and woodlice. ➤➤ **crustacean** *adj,* **crustaceous** *adj.*

crusty[1] *adj* (**-ier, -iest**) **1** having a hard well-baked crust. **2** surly; uncivil. ➤➤ **crustily** *adv,* **crustiness** *n.*

crusty[2] *n* (*pl* **-ies**) *informal* a young person of unkempt appearance who follows an alternative lifestyle, often involving squatting.

crutch *n* **1a** a staff of wood or metal used to support an injured person in walking. **b** any prop or support. **2** the crotch, or the part of a garment that covers it.

crux *n* (*pl* **cruxes** *or* **cruces**) **1** an essential or decisive point. **2** a puzzling or difficult problem.

cry[1] *v* (**-ies, -ied**) **1** to weep or sob. **2** to call loudly; to shout. **3** of a bird or animal: to utter a characteristic call. **4** *informal* (+ out for) to require or suggest strongly a certain treatment, remedy, etc. ✱ **cry for the moon** to want the unattainable. **for crying out loud** *informal* used to express exasperation and annoyance.

cry[2] *n* (*pl* **-ies**) **1** a spell of weeping. **2** an inarticulate utterance of distress, rage, pain, etc. **3** a loud shout. **4** a general public demand or complaint. **5** the characteristic call of an animal or bird. ✱ **in full cry** in pursuit.

cry- *or* **cryo-** *comb. form* denoting very low temperature or freezing: *cryogenics.*

crybaby *n* (*pl* **-ies**) *informal* a person who cries or complains too easily or frequently.

crying ✱ **a crying shame** a shocking thing.

cryo- *comb. form* see CRY-.

cry off *v* **1** to call off (an agreement, etc). **2** *chiefly Brit* to withdraw; to back out.

cryogenics *pl n* (*used as sing. or pl*) the physics of the production and effects of very low temperatures. ➤➤ **cryogenic** *adj.*

cryonics *pl n* (*used as sing. or pl*) the procedure by which a dead body is preserved by freezing in the hope of restoration to life and health at some future time when medical science will have advanced. ➤➤ **cryonic** *adj.*

cryostat *n* an apparatus for maintaining a constant low temperature.

cryosurgery *n* surgery in which extreme chilling is used to destroy or cut tissue.

crypt *n* a chamber, e.g. a vault, wholly or partly underground; *esp* a vault under the main floor of a church.

crypt- *or* **crypto-** *comb. form* **1** hidden; obscure: *cryptogenic.* **2** secret; unavowed: *cryptography.*

cryptic *adj* **1** secret; occult. **2** intended to be obscure or mysterious. **3** serving to conceal. ➤➤ **cryptically** *adv.*

crypto- *comb. form* see CRYPT-.

cryptobiosis *n* a state in which the metabolic activity of an organism is temporarily undetectable. ➤➤ **cryptobiotic** *adj.*

cryptogam *n dated* a plant, e.g. a fern, moss, fungus, lichen, or alga, reproducing by means of spores and not producing flowers or seed. ➤➤ **cryptogamic** *adj,* **cryptogamous** *adj.*

cryptogenic *adj* of obscure or unknown origin.

cryptogram *n* a communication in code.

cryptography *n* **1** secret writing; cryptic symbolization. **2** the preparation of cryptograms or codes. ➤➤ **cryptographer** *n,* **cryptographic** *adj.*

cryptology *n* **1** the scientific study of codes. **2** the art of devising a code. ➤➤ **cryptologic** *adj,* **cryptological** *adj,* **cryptologist** *n.*

cryptonym *n* a code name. ➤➤ **cryptonymous** *adj,* **cryptonymy** *n.*

cryptosporidium *n* a parasitic protozoan that can be transmitted from animals to human beings, causing intestinal disorders.

cryptozoology *n* the study of animals, e.g. the yeti, which are generally believed to be extinct or mythical. ➤➤ **cryptozoologist** *n.*

crystal[1] *n* **1** a piece of a solid material with a naturally regular geometrical structure and plane faces that are symmetrically arranged. **2** a clear transparent mineral, *esp* colourless quartz. **3** a clear colourless glass of superior quality. **4** the transparent cover over a watch or clock dial.

crystal[2] *adj* **1** made or composed of crystal. **2** clear; lucid.

crystal ball *n* **1** a glass or crystal sphere traditionally used by fortune-tellers. **2** a means or method of predicting future events.

crystal-clear *adj* perfectly clear.

crystal-gazing *n* **1** the art or practice of concentrating on a crystal ball to aid divination. **2** the attempt to predict future events or make difficult judgments, *esp* without adequate data. ➤➤ **crystal-gazer** *n.*

crystall- *or* **crystallo-** *comb. form* denoting crystal: *crystallography.*

crystalline *adj* **1** composed of crystal or crystals. **2** having the form or structure of a crystal. **3** like crystal in transparency or clarity. ➤➤ **crystallinity** *n.*

crystalline lens *n* the lens of the eye.

crystallise *v* see CRYSTALLIZE.

crystallize *or* **-ise** *v* **1** to cause (a substance) to form crystals or assume crystalline form. **2** to cause (a thought or idea) to take a definite form. **3** to coat or impregnate (fruit, etc) with sugar. **4** to become crystallized. ⋙ **crystallization** *n,* **crystallized** *adj.*

crystallo- *comb. form* see CRYSTALL-.

crystallography *n* the science dealing with the forms and structures of crystals. ⋙ **crystallographer** *n,* **crystallographic** *adj,* **crystallographically** *adv.*

crystal set *n* a simple early form of radio receiver that has no amplifier or source of power and uses a crystal detector to convert radio signals into sound when passed through an earphone.

crystal system *n* any of the six or seven categories into which a crystal is placed according to the arrangement of its atoms.

Cs *abbr* the chemical symbol for caesium.

c/s *abbr* cycles per second.

CSA *abbr* Child Support Agency.

CS gas *n* a gas that causes irritation and watering of the eyes when dispersed in the air as a means of controlling riots.

CST *abbr NAm, Can* Central Standard Time.

CT *abbr* **1** computerized *or* computed tomography. **2** Connecticut (US postal abbreviation).

ct *abbr* **1** carat. **2** cent. **3** (*often* **Ct**) court.

CTC *abbr* City Technology College.

CTS *abbr* carpal tunnel syndrome.

CU *abbr* **1** Christian Union. **2** in computing, control unit.

Cu *abbr* the chemical symbol for copper.

cu. *abbr* cubic.

cub[1] *n* **1** the young of a flesh-eating mammal, e.g. a fox, bear, or lion. **2** (**Cub**) = CUB SCOUT. **3** *dated* a young man.

cub[2] *v* (**cubbed, cubbing**) to give birth to cubs.

cubage *n* cubic capacity or contents.

Cuban *n* a native or inhabitant of Cuba. ⋙ **Cuban** *adj.*

Cuban heel *n* a broad medium-high heel on a shoe or boot.

cubature *n* **1** the determination of the volume of a solid. **2** cubic contents or capacity.

cubby *n* (*pl* **-ies**) *chiefly NAm* a snug space or room, e.g. one used as a children's play area; = CUBBY-HOLE.

cubbyhole *n* a small room or enclosed space.

cube[1] *n* **1** a three-dimensional shape or block with six equal square faces. **2** the result of multiplying a number by its square, represented by a superscript number 3.

cube[2] *v* **1** to raise (a number) to the third power by multiplying it by its square. **2** to cut (food) into small cubes; = DICE[2]. ⋙ **cuber** *n.*

cube root *n* the number that, when cubed, produces the given number.

cubic *adj* **1** cube-shaped. **2** three-dimensional. **3** used before a unit of length: denoting a volume equal to that of a cube whose edges are of the specified unit. **4** relating to or involving the cube of a quantity. ⋙ **cubical** *adj,* **cubically** *adv.*

cubicle *n* a small partitioned space or compartment.

cubiform *adj* cube-shaped.

cubism *n* a 20th-cent. art movement that abandoned perspective represented from a single viewpoint by displaying several aspects of the same object simultaneously through the device of interlocking planes. ⋙ **cubist** *adj,* **cubist** *n,* **cubistic** *adj.*

cubit *n* any of various ancient units of length based on the length of the forearm from the elbow to the tip of the middle finger.

cuboid[1] *adj* cube-shaped. ⋙ **cuboidal** *adj.*

cuboid[2] *n* **1** a three-dimensional shape having six rectangular faces at right angles to each other. **2** an approximately cube-shaped bone in the ankle.

cub reporter *n informal, dated* a junior newspaper reporter.

Cub Scout *n* a member of a junior section of the Scout Association.

cuckold[1] *n* a man whose wife is adulterous, traditionally a figure of fun.

cuckold[2] *v* to make a cuckold of (a married man) by having an adulterous relationship. ⋙ **cuckoldry** *n.*

cuckoo[1] *n* (*pl* **cuckoos**) **1** a greyish brown European bird that lays its eggs in the nests of other birds. **2** the characteristic two-note call of the male cuckoo.

cuckoo[2] *adj informal* insane; crazy.

cuckoo clock *n* a clock containing a mechanical cuckoo on a spring, that shoots out on the hour and delivers the appropriate number of cuckoo calls.

cuckoopint *n* a European arum that has a pale green leaflike bract surrounding tiny purple flowers, and bears a cluster of red berries.

cuckoo spit *n* a frothy secretion exuded on plants by the larva of a froghopper.

cucumber *n* the long green edible fruit of a climbing plant, eaten raw as a salad vegetable. ✱ **as cool as a cucumber** perfectly calm and composed.

cud *n* food brought up into the mouth by a ruminating animal from its first stomach to be chewed again. ✱ **chew the cud 1** of a ruminant animal: to re-chew partly digested food. **2** to turn things over in the mind; to ruminate.

cuddle[1] *v* **1** to hold (a person, soft toy, etc) close for warmth or comfort or in affection. **2** (*often* + up to) to lie close; to nestle or snuggle.

cuddle[2] *n* an act of cuddling.

cuddly *adj* (**-ier, -iest**) **1** attractively soft and plump. **2** enjoying a cuddle.

cudgel[1] *n* a short heavy club. ✱ **take up the cudgels** to engage vigorously in a defence.

cudgel[2] *v* (**cudgelled, cudgelling,** *NAm* **cudgeled, cudgeling**) to beat with or as if with a cudgel. ✱ **cudgel one's brains** to make a supreme effort of cogitation or recollection.

cue[1] *n* **1a** a signal to a performer to begin a specific speech or action. **b** a signal or hint prompting action. **2** in psychology, a feature of something that determines the way in which it is perceived. **3** a facility in video or audio equipment for feeding a recording through at high speed and picking it up at a preselected point. ✱ **on cue** at exactly the right time.

cue[2] *v* (**cuing, cueing**) **1** to give a cue to; to prompt. **2** to set audio or video equipment to play (a preselected section of a recording).

cue[3] *n* a long tapering rod for striking the ball in billiards, snooker, etc. ⋙ **cueist** *n.*

cue[4] *v* (**cuing, cueing**) to strike (a ball) with a cue.

cue ball *n* the ball in billiards, snooker, etc that is struck by a cue.

cue card *n* a card held up alongside a television camera for a person to read from while appearing to be looking into the camera.

cuff[1] *n* **1** a fold or band at the end of a sleeve which encircles the wrist. **2** *chiefly NAm* a turned-up hem of a trouser leg. **3** *informal (usu in pl)* a handcuff.

✱ **off the cuff** speaking without preparation, as though from notes hastily made on one's shirt cuff. ⋙ **cuffed** *adj.*

cuff[2] *v* to strike (somebody), *esp* with or as if with the palm of the hand.

cuff[3] *n* a blow with the hand.

cuff link *n* an ornamental device consisting of two linked parts used to fasten a shirt cuff.

cui bono /kwee 'bonoh/ *phrase* a principle that probable responsibility for an act or event lies with somebody having something to gain.

cuirass /kwi'ras/ *n* formerly, a piece of armour consisting of a joined backplate and breastplate.

cuirassier /kwirə'siə/ *n* formerly, a cavalry soldier wearing a cuirass.

cuisine /kwi'zeen/ *n* a manner of preparing or cooking food, *esp* as typical of a certain country or region.

cul-de-sac *n* (*pl* **culs-de-sac** *or* **cul-de-sacs**) a street, usu residential, closed at one end.

-cule *suffix* forming nouns, denoting: a small example of the thing specified: *animalcule.*

culinary *adj* relating to the kitchen or cookery.

cull *v* **1** to control the size of a population of (animals) by killing a limited number. **2** to identify and remove the rejects from (a flock, herd, etc) for slaughter. **3** to select (a body of people or things) from a source or a range of sources. ⋙ **cull** *n,* **culler** *n.*

cullender *n* see COLANDER.

cullet *n* broken or waste glass added to new material in glass manufacture, to increase the rate of melting and as a means of recycling glass.

culminate *v* **1** (*often* + in) to reach the highest or a climactic or decisive point. **2** of a celestial body: to be at the meridian; to be directly overhead. ⋙ **culmination** *n.*

culottes /kyoo'lots/ *pl n* women's knee-length shorts, cut very full so as to resemble a skirt.

culpable *adj* meriting condemnation or blame. ⋙ **culpability** *n,* **culpably** *adv.*

culprit *n* a person who is guilty of a crime or a fault.

Word history

Anglo-French *cul* (abbr of *culpable* CULPABLE) + *prest, prit* ready. In English courts after the Norman Conquest, a prisoner's plea was answered by the clerk of the crown, who said *culpable* (guilty) and that he was *prest* (ready) to proceed with the prosecution. The formula *cul. prest* or *cul. prit,* entered on the official record of proceedings, was later mistakenly taken as a single word referring to the prisoner.

cult *n* **1a** a system of religious beliefs and ritual, or its adherents. **b** a religion regarded as unorthodox or spurious, or its adherents. **2** (*often before a noun*) great devotion among a group to a particular person, idea, or thing. ⋙ **cultic** *adj,* **cultish** *adj,* **cultism** *n,* **cultist** *n.*

cultigen *n* a plant species that is known only in cultivation, with no known wild forebear.

cultivar *n* a plant variety that has been developed in cultivation by selective breeding from natural species.

cultivate *v* **1** to prepare or use (land) for the growing of crops. **2** to grow (a plant or crop), *esp* on a large scale. **3** to grow (bacteria, tissue, etc) in a culture. **4** to improve or refine (one's mind) through study, edifying pursuits, etc. **5** to affect (a manner, etc) with assiduous practice. **6** to encourage or foster the friendship of (a person, *esp* who can be useful to one). ⋙ **cultivatable** *adj,* **cultivation** *n.*

cultivated *adj* refined; educated.

cultivator *n* an implement to break up the soil while crops are growing.

cultural *adj* **1** relating to education and the arts. **2** relating to a society's culture and traditions. ⋙ **culturally** *adv.*

culture[1] *n* **1** the development of the mind, *esp* by education. **2** intellectual and artistic enlightenment as distinguished from vocational and technical skills. **3a** the customary beliefs, social forms, etc of a racial, religious, or social group. **b** the socially transmitted pattern of human behaviour that includes thought, speech, action, institutions, and artefacts. **4** the cultivation of living cells, viruses, etc in prepared nutrient media, or a product of this. **5** the cultivation of plants or crops.

culture[2] *v* **1** to grow (bacteria, viruses, etc) in a culture. **2** to start a culture from (a specimen, etc).

-culture *comb. form* forming nouns, denoting: the cultivation or tending of the thing specified: *viticulture.*

cultured *adj* cultivated.

cultured pearl *n* a natural pearl grown under controlled conditions by inserting a foreign body into the oyster.

culture shock *n* psychological and social disorientation caused by confrontation with a new or alien culture.

culture vulture *n humorous* a person who has an avid, sometimes uncritical, interest in culture.

culvert *n* a small tunnel that allows water to pass under a road, railway, etc.

cum *prep* with; combined with; along with: *a lounge-cum-dining room.*

cumber *v dated* **1** to clutter up (a place or surface). **2** to burden or hamper (somebody).

Cumberland sauce *n* a spicy sauce made from redcurrant jelly and served with game, turkey, etc.

Cumberland sausage *n Brit* a large coarse type of sausage.

cumbersome *adj* unwieldy because of heaviness and bulk. ⋙ **cumbersomely** *adv,* **cumbersomeness** *n.*

cumbrous *adj literary* cumbersome; unwieldy. ⋙ **cumbrously** *adv,* **cumbrousness** *n.*

cumin *or* **cummin** /'kumin/ *n* the aromatic seeds of a plant of the carrot family, used as a flavouring.

cummerbund *n* a broad waist sash worn *esp* with men's formal evening wear.

cummin *n* see CUMIN.

cumquat *n* see KUMQUAT.

cumulate[1] *v* to accumulate. ⋙ **cumulation** *n.*

cumulate[2] *adj* accumulated.

cumulative *adj* increasing by successive additions. ⋙ **cumulatively** *adv,* **cumulativeness** *n.*

cumuli *n* pl of CUMULUS.

cumulonimbus *n* (*pl* **cumulonimbi**) a cumulus cloud formation, often in the shape of an anvil, occurring at low altitude but extending to great heights and characteristic of thunderstorms.

cumulus *n* (*pl* **cumuli**) a massive cloud formation with a flat base and rounded outlines often piled up like a mountain, occurring at low altitude.

cuneiform[1] /'kyoohnifawm/ *adj* **1** wedge-shaped. **2** composed of or written in the wedge-shaped characters used in ancient Assyrian, Babylonian, and Persian inscriptions.

cuneiform[2] *n* cuneiform writing.

cunnilingus *n* oral stimulation of the vulva or clitoris.

cunning[1] *adj* **1** devious; crafty. **2** dexterous; ingenious. **3** *NAm* prettily appealing; cute. ➤➤ **cunningly** *adv,* **cunningness** *n.*

cunning[2] *n* **1** craftiness; slyness. **2** skill; dexterity; ingenuity.

cunt *n taboo* **1** the female genitals. **2** an abusive term for a person one dislikes.

cup[1] *n* **1** a small bowl-shaped drinking vessel with a handle on one side. **2** an ornamental metal cup with two handles offered as a prize, or a competition with a cup as a prize. **3a** something resembling a cup, e.g. a plant or body part. **b** either of two parts of a bra that are shaped to fit over the breasts. **c** in golf, the hole on a putting green, or its metal lining. **4** any of various alcoholic cold drinks made from mixed ingredients. **5** *chiefly NAm* the capacity of a cup of standard size, used as a measurement; = CUPFUL (2). ✱ **in one's cups** *informal* drunk. **one's cup of tea** *informal* what is thoroughly congenial to one. ➤➤ **cuplike** *adj.*

cup[2] *v* **(cupped, cupping) 1** to curve (one's hands) into the shape of a cup. **2** to curve one's hands round (something).

cupboard /'kubəd/ *n* a piece of furniture with a door or doors and usu shelves, used for storage.

cupboard love *n* insincere love professed in order to get something.

cup cake *n* a small cake baked in a cup-shaped container and covered with a thick layer of icing.

cupel *n* a small shallow porous cup used to separate gold and silver from lead. ➤➤ **cupel** *v,* **cupellation** *n.*

cup final *n* the final match that decides the winner of a competition for a cup.

cupful *n* (*pl* **cupfuls**) **1** as much as a cup will hold. **2** *chiefly NAm* a unit of measure equal to 8fl oz (0.227l).

cupid *n* **1** **(Cupid)**in Roman mythology, the god of sexual love, depicted as a winged naked boy holding a bow and arrow. **2** a representation of Cupid in art.

cupidity *n* inordinate desire for wealth or possessions; avarice; greed.

Cupid's bow *n* the double curve made by the edge of a person's top lip, reminiscent of the bow traditionally carried by Cupid.

cupola /'kyoohpələ/ *n* (*pl* **cupolas**) **1** a small domed structure built on top of a roof. **2** a domed gun turret on a tank, warship, etc. **3** a vertical cylindrical furnace for melting pig iron, orig domed.

cuppa *n* (*pl* **cuppas**) *chiefly Brit, informal* a cup of tea.

cupr- *or* **cupri-** *or* **cupro-** *comb. form* denoting copper: *cupreous; cupro-nickel.*

cuprammonium rayon *n* a rayon made from cellulose dissolved in a copper solution containing ammonia.

cupreous *adj archaic or literary* resembling copper; coppery.

cupri- *comb. form* see CUPR-.

cupro /'kyoohproh/ *n* = CUPRAMMONIUM RAYON.

cupro- *comb. form* see CUPR-.

cupro-nickel *n* an alloy of copper and nickel, used *esp* in British silver coins.

cur *n* **1** a mongrel or inferior dog. **2** *informal* a surly or cowardly fellow.

curaçao /kyooərə'soh/ *n* a liqueur flavoured with the peel of bitter oranges.

curacy *n* (*pl* **-ies**) the office or term of office of a curate.

curare *or* **curari** *n* **1** a highly toxic plant extract used by S American Indians as arrow poison. **2** an alkaloid extracted from a plant and used medicinally as a muscle relaxant.

curate[1] *n* **1** a clergyman serving as assistant, e.g. to a rector, in a parish. **2** *archaic* a clergyman in charge of a parish.

curate[2] *v* to manage (a museum, exhibition, etc) as a curator. ➤➤ **curation** *n.*

curate's egg *n Brit* something with both good and bad parts.

Word history

from a cartoon depicting a curate who, given a stale egg by his bishop, declared that parts of it were excellent.

curative[1] *adj* relating to or used in the cure of diseases. ➤➤ **curatively** *adv.*

curative[2] *n* a medicine or agent used to cure something.

curator *n* a person in charge of a museum, art gallery, exhibition etc. ➤➤ **curatorial** *adj,* **curatorship** *n.*

curb[1] *n* **1** a check or restraint. **2** a chain or strap used to restrain a horse, attached to the sides of the bit and passing below the lower jaw, or the bit to which it is attached. **3** *chiefly NAm* = KERB.

curb[2] *v* **1** to check or control. **2** to put a curb on (a horse).

curd *n* **1** (*also in pl*) the thick part of coagulated milk used as a food or made into cheese. **2** a rich thick fruit preserve made with eggs, sugar, and butter. **3** the edible head of a cauliflower or a similar related plant. ➤➤ **curdy** *adj.*

curd cheese *n* a smooth sharp-tasting soft cheese made from the curds of skimmed milk.

curdle *v* **1** to cause (milk or a soft mixture) to separate into solid curds or lumps and liquid. **2** to separate in this manner. ✱ **make one's blood curdle** to fill one with dread.

cure[1] *n* **1a** a drug, treatment, etc that gives relief or recovery from a disease. **b** relief or recovery from a disease. **2** something that corrects a harmful or troublesome situation; a remedy. **3** a process or method of curing meat, hardening concrete, etc. **4a** a spiritual or pastoral charge. **b** a parish. ➤➤ **cureless** *adj.*

cure[2] *v* **1** to restore (somebody) to health. **2** to bring about recovery from (an illness or other disorder). **3** to rectify (a harmful or troublesome situation). **4** to free (somebody) from something objectionable or harmful. **5a** to preserve (meat, fish, etc) by salting, drying, smoking, etc. **b** to harden (rubber, plastic, concrete, etc) by a chemical process. **6** to undergo a curing or hardening process. ➤➤ **curability** *n,* **curable** *adj,* **curableness** *n,* **curer** *n.*

curé /'kyooəray/ *n* a parish priest in France or another French-speaking country.

cure-all *n* a remedy for all ills; a panacea.

curet *n* see CURETTE[1].

curettage /kyoo'retij, kyooəri'tahzh/ *n* a surgical scraping or cleaning, e.g. of the womb, by means of a curette.

curette[1] *or* **curet** *n* a scoop, loop, or ring used in curettage.

curette[2] *v* to perform curettage on.

curfew *n* **1** a regulation requiring the withdrawal of all or particular people from the streets by a stated time. **2** a signal for a curfew, the time at which it begins, or the period during which it is in effect.

Curia *n* the administration and governmental apparatus of the Roman Catholic Church. ➤➤ **Curial** *adj.*

curie *n* a unit of radioactivity equal to 3.7×10^{10} disintegrations per second.

curio *n* (*pl* **-os**) an object that is considered novel, rare, or bizarre.

curiosity *n* (*pl* **-ies**) **1** desire to know. **2** inquisitiveness or nosiness. **3** a strange, interesting, or rare object, custom, fact, etc.

curious *adj* **1** eager to investigate and learn. **2** inquisitive or nosy. **3** strange, novel, or odd. ➤➤ **curiously** *adv,* **curiousness** *n.*

curium *n* a radioactive metallic chemical element produced by bombarding plutonium with high speed particles.

curl[1] *v* **1** to form (*esp* hair) into waves or coils. **2** to form, adopt, or grow in a curved, twisted, or spiral shape. **3** to move or progress in curves or spirals. **4** to play the game of curling. ✱ **curl one's lip** to lift the corner of one's mouth in a sneer; to sneer. **make one's hair curl** to horrify one.

curl[2] *n* **1** a curled lock of hair. **2** something with a spiral or winding form; a coil. **3** a curling movement.

curler *n* **1** a small cylinder on which hair is wound for curling; a roller. **2** a person who plays the game of curling.

curlew *n* (*pl* **curlews** *or* **curlew**) any of various wading birds with long legs and a long slender down-curved bill.

curlicue *n* a decorative curve or flourish, e.g. in handwriting.

curling *n* a game in which two teams of four players each slide heavy round flat-bottomed stones over ice towards a target circle marked on the ice.

curling irons *pl n* = CURLING TONGS.

curling tongs *pl n* a rod-shaped instrument with a hinged clamp that is heated to curl locks of hair wound round it.

curly *adj* (**-ier, -iest**) tending to curl; having curls. ➤➤ **curliness** *n.*

curly endive *n* a variety of endive with curled leaves.

curmudgeon *n* a crusty ill-tempered or miserly person, *esp* an old man. ➤➤ **curmudgeonly** *adj.*

currach *or* **curragh** /'kurə, 'kurəkh/ *n* a coracle.

currant *n* **1** a small seedless dried grape used in cookery. **2** a shrub of the gooseberry family bearing a redcurrant, blackcurrant, or similar fruit.

Usage note

currant *or* current? See note at CURRENT[1].

currawong *n* an Australian songbird similar to a crow, with black, grey, and white plumage.

currency *n* (*pl* **-ies**) **1** a system of money that is in circulation as a medium of exchange. **2** general use, acceptance, or prevalence, or the state of being in general use, etc.

current[1] *adj* **1** occurring now or belonging to the present time. **2** valid as a medium of exchange. **3** generally accepted, used, or practised at the moment. ➤➤ **currently** *adv,* **currentness** *n.*

Usage note

current *or* **currant**? *Current* with an *e* has a wide range of meanings: *current affairs; the current month;* also *electric current; strong currents make swimming dangerous* (see CURRENT[2]). *Currant* with an *a* is a fresh or dried berry: *redcurrants; currants and raisins.*

current[2] *n* **1a** the part of a body of water, air, etc that moves continuously in a certain direction. **b** the swiftest part of a stream. **2a** a flow of electricity resulting from the movement of electrically charged particles. **b** a quantity, usu measured in amperes, representing the rate of such flow. **3** a tendency to follow a certain or specified course.

current account *n Brit* a bank account against which cheques may be drawn and on which interest is usu not payable.

current assets *pl n* cash, or assets that will convert to cash in the current year: compare FIXED ASSETS.

curricle *n* a light, open carriage drawn by two horses harnessed side by side.

curricula *n* pl of CURRICULUM.

curricula vitae *n* pl of CURRICULUM VITAE.

curriculum *n* (*pl* **curricula** *or* **curriculums**) the courses offered by an educational institution or followed by an individual or group. ➤➤ **curricular** *adj.*

curriculum vitae /'veetie/ *n* (*pl* **curricula vitae**) a summary of somebody's career and qualifications, *esp* as relevant to a job application.

curry[1] *v* (**-ies, -ied**) **1** to groom the coat of (a horse) with a currycomb. **2** to dress (tanned leather). ✱ **curry favour** to seek to gain favour by flattery or attention; to ingratiate oneself. ➤➤ **currier** *n.*

curry[2] *n* (*pl* **-ies**) a food or dish seasoned with a mixture of spices or curry powder.

curry[3] *v* (**-ies, -ied**) to flavour or cook (food) with curry powder or sauce.

currycomb *n* a metal comb with rows of teeth or serrated ridges, used *esp* to curry horses.

curry powder *n* a condiment consisting of several pungent ground spices, e.g. cayenne pepper and turmeric.

curse[1] *n* **1a** an appeal to a deity that invokes harm or injury on another. **b** a swearword or other offensive expression used in anger. **2** an evil or misfortune that comes or seems to come as retribution. **3** a cause of misfortune. **4** (**the curse**) *informal, dated* menstruation.

curse[2] *v* **1** to call upon supernatural power to cause harm or injury to; to doom or damn. **2** to use profanely insolent language against. **3** to bring evil upon; to afflict with something. **4** to utter curses; to swear.

cursed /'kuhsid, kuhst/ *or* **curst** *adj* **1** *informal, dated* under or deserving a curse. **2** *archaic* vicious, cantankerous, or contrary. ➤➤ **cursedly** *adv,* **cursedness** *n.*

cursive *adj* of handwriting: having the characters joined in each word. ➤➤ **cursive** *n,* **cursively** *adv,* **cursiveness** *n.*

cursor *n* **1** a movable pointer on a visual display unit, radar screen, etc for indicating the specific position that will be immediately affected by input. **2** a transparent slide with a reference hairline for precisely locating marks on a scientific instrument, e.g. a slide rule.

cursory *adj* rapid and often superficial; hasty. ➤➤ **cursorily** *adv,* **cursoriness** *n.*

curst *adj archaic* see CURSED.

curt *adj* characterized by rude or peremptory shortness; brusque. ➤➤ **curtly** *adv,* **curtness** *n.*

curtail *v* to cut short; to limit. ➤➤ **curtailer** *n,* **curtailment** *n.*

curtain[1] *n* **1** a hanging fabric screen that can usu be drawn back or up, *esp* one used at a window or to separate the stage from the auditorium of a theatre. **2** the ascent or opening of a stage curtain or its descent or closing. **3** *informal (in pl)* the end; *esp* death. **4** a device or agency that conceals or acts as a barrier. **5a** a castle wall between two neighbouring bastions. **b** an exterior wall that carries no load.

curtain[2] *v* **1** to furnish (a window or opening) with curtains. **2** to veil or shut off with, or as if with, a curtain.

curtain call *n* an appearance by a performer on stage after the end of a play, opera, etc in response to the applause of the audience.

curtain-raiser *n* **1** a short play presented before the main full-length drama. **2** a short preliminary to a main event.

curtain wall *n* = CURTAIN[1] (5).

curtsy[1] *or* **curtsey** *n* (*pl* **-ies**) a gesture of respect performed by a woman or girl by putting one leg behind the other, flexing the knees, and dropping the head.

curtsy[2] *or* **curtsey** *v* (**-ies, -ied**) to make a curtsy.

curvaceous *adj* of a woman: having a pleasingly well-developed figure with attractive curves.

curvature *n* **1a** the circumstance of being curved. **b** the degree to which something is curved. **2** an abnormal curving, e.g. of the spine.

curve[1] *v* to have or cause to make a turn, change, or deviation from a straight line without sharp breaks or angularity.

curve[2] *n* **1** a curving line or surface. **2** a representation on a graph of a varying quantity. ➤➤ **curvy** *adj.*

curvet[1] *n* **1** a prancing leap of a horse in which all legs are in the air at once, the forelegs being raised first. **2** a graceful leap.

curvet[2] *v* (**curvetted, curvetting,** *NAm also* **curveted, curveting**) to make a curvet.

curvilinear *adj* consisting of or bounded by curved lines. ➤➤ **curvilinearity** *n,* **curvilinearly** *adv.*

cusec *n* a unit of flow used *esp* for water, equal to one cubic foot per second.

cushion[1] *n* **1** a soft pillow or padded bag, *esp* one used for sitting, leaning, or kneeling on. **2** a pad along the inside of the rim of a billiard table off which balls bounce. **3** something serving to mitigate the effects of disturbances or disorders. ➤➤ **cushiony** *adj.*

cushion[2] *v* **1** to furnish with a cushion or cushions. **2a** to mitigate the effects of (something unpleasant). **b** to protect (somebody or something) against force or shock.

Cushitic *n* a branch of the Afro-Asiatic language family comprising various languages of E Africa, *esp* Ethiopia and Somalia. ➤➤ **Cushitic** *adj.*

cushy *adj* (**-ier, -iest**) *informal* entailing little hardship or effort; easy. ➤➤ **cushiness** *n.*

cusp *n* **1** either horn of a crescent moon. **2** a pointed projection formed by or arising from the intersection of two arcs, e.g. in Gothic tracery: compare FOIL[1] (2). **3** a point on the grinding surface of a tooth. **4** the initial point of an astrological house. ✱ **on the cusp** in transition between one state and another. ➤➤ **cuspate** *adj.*

cuspidor *n* a spittoon.

cuss[1] *n informal* **1** a curse. **2** a fellow.

cuss[2] *v informal* to curse.

cussed /'kusid/ *adj informal* obstinate; cantankerous. ➤➤ **cussedly** *adv,* **cussedness** *n.*

custard *n* a semisolid baked mixture or pouring sauce made with milk and eggs or a commercial preparation of coloured cornflour, usu sweetened with sugar.

custard apple *n* a large tropical fruit with sweet yellow pulp.

custard pie *n* **1** an open pastry case containing baked custard. **2** this type of pie or an artificial substitute used in slapstick comedy for throwing at somebody's face.

custodial *adj* **1** of a sentence imposed by a judge: involving detention, usu in prison. **2** relating to guardianship or custody.

custodian *n* a person who guards and protects or maintains; *esp* a curator. ➤➤ **custodianship** *n.*

custody *n* **1** the state of being cared for or guarded; guardianship. **2** imprisonment; detention. **3** the act or right of caring for a minor, *esp* when granted by a court of law.

custom *n* **1a** an established socially accepted practice. **b** long-established practice having the force of law. **c** the usual practice of an individual. **2** (*in pl*) **a** duties imposed on imports or exports. **b** (*used as sing. or pl*) the agency, establishment, or procedure for collecting such duties. **3** *chiefly Brit* business patronage.

customary *adj* established by or according to custom; usual. ➤➤ **customarily** *adv,* **customariness** *n.*

custom-built *adj* built to individual specifications.

customer *n* **1** a person who purchases a commodity or service. **2** an individual, usu having some specified distinctive trait.

customhouse *n* see CUSTOMSHOUSE.

customize *or* **-ise** *v* **1** to build, fit, or alter (something) according to individual specifications. **2** to program (computer keys) to perform some dedicated task.

custom-made *adj* made to individual specifications.

customshouse *or* **customhouse** *n* a building where customs are collected.

customs union *n* an agreement between two or more states to allow free trade between themselves but to impose a common external tariff on imports from non-member states.

cut[1] *v* (**cutting,** *past tense and past part.* **cut**) **1a** to penetrate or make an opening in (something) with a sharp object. **b** to injure or wound in this way. **2** to shorten, divide, or detach by cutting. **3** to make or shape something by cutting. **4** to be able to cut or to be cut easily: *Cheese cuts easily.* **5a** to reduce the amount of something, *esp* of money: *to cut taxes.* **b** to shorten or edit (a piece of writing). **6** to break or interrupt (a flow, supply, etc). **7** of a line: to cut or intersect (another line). **8** to divide (a pack of cards) into two parts. **9** to ignore (an acquaintance) deliberately or spitefully. **10** to switch off an engine or machine. **11a** to stop filming or recording. **b** to change from one sound or image to another. **12a** to move swiftly: *The yacht cut through the water.* **b** to go by a shorter route. **13** *NAm* to dilute (a drink). ✱ **cut and run** to make a speedy or undignified escape from an awkward situation. **cut a tooth** of a baby: to produce a new tooth. **cut both ways 1** of a statement: to be equally valid for and against an argument. **2** of a procedure: to have advantages and disadvantages. **cut corners** to do something cheaply or quickly by making risky economies. **cut it fine** see FINE[1]. **cut no ice** to fail to impress or make a difference. **cut one's teeth** to get early experience of an activity. **cut short** to interrupt (a speaker).

cut[2] *n* **1** something cut or cut off. **2** a piece from a meat carcass. **3** *informal* a share. **4a** an opening made with an edged instrument. **b** a gash or wound. **5** a reduction or paring. **6** a sharp blow or stroke. **7** an abrupt transition from one sound or image to another in film, radio, or television. **8** the style in which something is cut or shaped, e.g. a garment or the hair. **9** a version of an edited film. ✱ **a cut above** superior to or of higher quality or rank than. **cut and thrust** a competitive and stimulating environment.

cut-and-dried *adj* of a situation: completely decided; not open to further discussion.

cut-and-paste *n* a word-processing technique in which a portion of text can be deleted and reinserted in a different position.

cutaneous *adj* relating to or affecting the skin.

cutaway *adj* having parts cut away or absent.

cutback *n* a reduction or decrease.

cut back *v* **1** to reduce expenditure. **2** to prune (a plant).

cut down *v* **1** to make (something growing) fall by cutting through it. **2** to reduce or restrict an activity, expenditure, etc.

cute *adj* **1** *informal* attractive or pretty, *esp* in a dainty or delicate way. **2** sexually attractive. **3** shrewd; knowing. ➤➤ **cutely** *adv*, **cuteness** *n*.

cutes *n* pl of CUTIS.

cutesy *adj* (**-ier, -iest**) odiously sweet or cute.

cut glass *n* glass ornamented with patterns cut into its surface by an abrasive wheel and then polished.

cuticle *n* **1** dead or horny skin; *esp* the skin surrounding the base and sides of a fingernail or toenail. **2** the thick or horny epidermis of an animal. **3** a thin fatty film on the external surface of a plant. **4** the outer layer of a hair. ➤➤ **cuticular** *adj*.

cut in *v* **1** to interrupt. **2** to pull in too closely after overtaking a vehicle. **3** of a device: to start functioning automatically. **4** to include (somebody) in a deal or payment.

cutis *n* (*pl* **cutes** *or* **cutises**) the true skin; = DERMIS.

cutlass *n* a short curved sword, *esp* as used formerly by sailors.

cutler *n* a person who deals in, makes, or repairs cutlery.

cutlery *n* knives, forks, and spoons for cutting and eating food.

cutlet *n* **1** a small slice of meat from the neck, or a burger of minced food in this shape. **2** a cross-sectional slice from between the head and centre of a large fish.

cutoff *n* **1** the process of cutting something off, or a device for doing this. **2** (*often before a noun*) a stopping-point or limit for something. **3** (*in pl*) shorts made from a pair of jeans by cutting the legs off at the thigh.

cut off *v* **1** to remove by cutting. **2** to stop the supply of. **3** to block access to (a place). **4** to disconnect (somebody) during a telephone call. **5** to disinherit.

cutout *n* **1** something cut out. **2** a device that cuts out; *esp* one that is operated automatically by an excessive electric current.

cut out[1] *v* **1** to make by cutting from a larger piece. **2** to eliminate or exclude. **3** to stop doing (something). **4** of an engine: to stop operating. ✱ **cut it out** *informal* to stop doing something.

cut out[2] *adj* (*usu in negative contexts*) naturally fitted or suited.

cut-price *adj* selling or sold at a discount.

cutpurse *n archaic* a purse-stealer; a pickpocket.

cutter *n* **1a** a person whose work is cutting or involves cutting, e.g. of cloth or film. **b** an instrument or machine that cuts. **2a** a ship's boat for carrying stores or passengers. **b** a light fast boat.

cutthroat[1] *n dated* a murderous thug.

cutthroat[2] *adj* **1** murderous; cruel. **2** ruthless; unprincipled.

cutthroat razor *n Brit* a razor with a rigid blade hinged to a case that forms a handle when open.

cutting[1] *n* **1** something cut off or out. **2** a part of a plant capable of developing into a new plant. **3** an excavation, *esp* through high ground, for a canal, road, etc. **4** *Brit* an item cut out of a publication. *NAm* Also called CLIPPING.

cutting[2] *adj* **1** designed for cutting; sharp or edged. **2** of a remark: likely to wound the feelings of another; sarcastic. **3** of wind: strong and piercingly cold. ➤➤ **cuttingly** *adv*.

cutting edge *n* the most advanced point, where important action is taken. ➤➤ **cutting-edge** *adj*.

cuttlebone *n* the internal shell of the cuttlefish used as a mineral supplement for cage birds.

cuttlefish *n* (*pl* **cuttlefishes** *or* **cuttlefish**) a marine mollusc related to the squid, having ten arms and a hard internal shell.

cut up[1] *v* **1** to cut into pieces. **2** to criticize harshly. **3** *informal* of a driver: to swerve in front of (another driver). ✱ **cut up rough** to behave aggressively.

cut up[2] *adj informal* deeply distressed; grieved.

cutwater *n* the foremost part of a ship's bow.

cutworm *n* a nocturnal caterpillar that feeds on plant stems near ground level.

cuvée /'kyoohvay/ *n* a blend or batch of wine, *esp* champagne.

CV *abbr* curriculum vitae.

CVO *abbr Brit* Commander of the Royal Victorian Order.

CVS *abbr* chorionic villus sampling, a test for foetal abnormality.

cwm /koohm/ *n* a basin-shaped hollow in a mountain, *esp* in Wales; = CIRQUE .

cwt *abbr* hundredweight.

-cy *suffix* forming nouns, denoting: **1** an action or practice: *piracy*. **2** a rank or office: *papacy*. **3** a body or class: *magistracy*. **4** a quality or state: *accuracy*.

cyan *n* a greenish blue colour.

cyan- *or* **cyano-** *comb. form* **1** dark blue; blue: *cyanosis*. **2** denoting cyanide: *cyanogen*.

cyanic *adj* **1** relating to or containing CYANOGEN. **2** of a blue or bluish colour.

cyanide *n* an extremely poisonous salt of HYDROCYANIC ACID.

cyano- *comb. form* see CYAN-.

cyanobacterium *n* (*pl* **cyanobacteria**) any of a group of blue-pigmented micro-organisms capable of PHOTOSYNTHESIS (using light to synthesize organic compounds, as plants do) and formerly regarded as algae; = BLUE-GREEN ALGA.

cyanocobalamin *n* a water-soluble vitamin containing cobalt, that occurs *esp* in liver and whose lack or malabsorption results in pernicious anaemia; vitamin B_{12}.

cyanogen *n* a colourless inflammable extremely poisonous gas made from hydrogen cyanide.

cyanosis *n* bluish or purplish discoloration of the skin due to deficient oxygenation of the blood. ➤➤ **cyanotic** *adj*.

cyber- *comb. form* denoting information technology, *esp* the Internet: *cybercafé*.

cybercafé *n* a café that offers the public access to information technology, *esp* the Internet, for a fee.

cyber cop *n informal* a member of a police unit set up to counter cyber-crime.

cyber-crime *n* computer-based crime such as hacking, financial fraud and the dissemination of illegal pornography.

cybernation *n* the automatic control of a process or operation, e.g. in manufacturing, by means of computers. ⋙ **cybernated** *adj.*

cybernetics *pl n* (*used as sing. or pl*) the comparative study of the automatic control systems formed by the nervous system and brain and by mechanical-electrical communication systems. ⋙ **cybernetic** *adj.*

cyberphobia *n* fear or distrust of information technology, *esp* the Internet.

cyberpunk *n* **1** a genre of science fiction which envisages a bleak and violent future society in which the world is controlled by a computer network. **2** a creator or devotee of cyberpunk.

cybersex *n* sexual activity on the Internet involving the use of pornographic websites, sexual titillation in chat rooms, etc.

cyberspace *n* the notional environment in which on-line communication takes place.

cybersquatter *n* somebody who registers an Internet domain name that is likely to be wanted by another person, a business organization, etc in the hope of selling it to them at a profit.

cyberterrorism *n* politically motivated disruptive or destructive attacks on computer systems and databases via the Internet.

cyborg *n* an unemotional fictional character that is part human and part machine.

cycad /'siekad/ *n* any of a genus of tropical trees resembling palms.

cycl- *or* **cyclo-** *comb. form* **1** denoting a circle: *cyclorama.* **2** having a cyclic molecular structure: *cyclamate.*

cyclamate /'sikləmayt, 'sie-/ *n* a synthetic compound used, *esp* formerly, as an artificial sweetener.

cyclamen /'sikləmən/ *n* (*pl* **cyclamen** *or* **cyclamens**) a plant of the primrose family with drooping pink, red, or white flowers.

cycle[1] *n* **1a** a series of related events happening in a regularly repeated order, or the time needed to complete it. **b** one complete performance of a periodic process, e.g. a vibration or electrical oscillation. **2** a group of poems, plays, novels, operas, or songs on a central theme. **3** a bicycle.

cycle[2] *v* **1** to ride a bicycle. **2a** to pass through a cycle. **b** to recur in cycles. ⋙ **cycling** *n.*

cyclic *adj* **1** of a cycle. **2** of a chemical compound: containing a ring of atoms.

cyclical *adj* = CYCLIC.

cyclist *n* a person who rides a bicycle.

cyclo- *comb. form* see CYCL-.

cyclohexane *n* a cyclic hydrocarbon found in petroleum and used *esp* as a solvent and in organic synthesis.

cycloid[1] *n* a curve resembling a series of arches traced by a point on the circumference of a circle that is rolling along a straight line. ⋙ **cycloidal** *adj.*

cycloid[2] *adj* circular; *esp* arranged or progressing in circles.

cyclometer *n* a device designed to record the revolutions of a wheel and often the distance travelled by a wheeled vehicle, *esp* a bicycle.

cyclone *n* **1** a storm or system of winds that rotates about a centre of low atmospheric pressure and often brings abundant rain. **2** a tornado. **3** a region of low atmospheric pressure; = LOW[2] (2). ⋙ **cyclonic** *adj,* **cyclonically** *adv.*

cyclopaedia *n* see CYCLOPEDIA.

cyclopean *adj* **1** of or resembling a Cyclops. **2** denoting a style of masonry of ancient Greece, using massive blocks of undressed stone.

cyclopedia *or* **cyclopaedia** *n archaic* an encyclopedia. ⋙ **cyclopedic** *adj.*

Cyclops *n* (*pl* **Cyclopses** *or* **Cyclopes** /-peez/) **1** in Greek mythology, a member of a race of savage giants with a single eye in the centre of the forehead. **2** (**cyclops**) a tiny predatory crustacean with a cylindrical body and a single eye.

cyclorama *n* (*pl* **cycloramas**) **1** a scene painted on the interior wall of a cylindrical room, appearing in natural perspective to a central observer. **2** in the theatre, a cloth or wall curved in an arc at the back of the stage, often painted to represent the sky.

cyclosporin *n* a drug that suppresses the immune response and is used to prevent rejection after transplant surgery.

cyclotron *n* a particle accelerator in which protons, ions, etc are propelled by an alternating electric field in a constant magnetic field.

cyder *n Brit, archaic* = CIDER.

cygnet *n* a young swan.

cylinder *n* **1a** a three-dimensional shape or surface traced by a straight line moving in a circle parallel to a fixed straight line. **b** a hollow or solid object with the shape of a cylinder and a circular or oval cross-section. **2a** the piston chamber in a steam or internal-combustion engine. **b** any of various rotating parts, e.g. in printing presses. **c** a metal container for gas under pressure.

cylinder block *n* the metal moulding that contains the cylinders of an internal-combustion engine.

cylinder head *n* the top cover of the CYLINDER BLOCK of an internal-combustion engine, providing a gas-tight seal.

cylindric *adj* = CYLINDRICAL.

cylindrical *adj* having the shape of a cylinder. ⋙ **cylindrically** *adv.*

cymbal *n* a percussion instrument consisting of a concave brass plate that produces a clashing tone when struck with a drumstick or against another cymbal. ⋙ **cymbalist** *n.*

cyme *n* an inflorescence in which the main stem bears the central and first-opening flower with subsequent flowers developing from side shoots: compare RACEME. ⋙ **cymose** *adj,* **cymosely** *adv.*

Cymric /'kimrik/ *adj dated* denoting the Welsh language or Welsh culture.

cynic /'sinik/ *n* **1a** a person who doubts the existence of human sincerity or of any motive other than self-interest. **b** a person who is habitually pessimistic or sardonic. **2** (**Cynic**) an adherent of an ancient Greek school of philosophers who held that virtue is the highest good and lies in mastering one's desires. ⋙ **cynical** *adj,* **cynically** *adv,* **cynicism** *n.*

cynosure /'sinəzyooə, 'sie-/ *n* a centre of attraction, interest, or attention.

cypher[1] *n* see CIPHER[1].

cypher[2] *v* see CIPHER[2].

cypress *n* an evergreen tree with aromatic overlapping leaves resembling scales.

Cypriot /'sipri·ət/ *or* **Cypriote** /-oht/ *n* **1** a native or inhabitant of Cyprus. **2** the form of Greek spoken on Cyprus. ⋙ **Cypriot** *adj.*

Cyrillic *adj* denoting an alphabet used for writing various Slavic languages, e.g. Old Church Slavonic, Russian, and Bulgarian. ⋙ **Cyrillic** *n.*

cyst *n* **1** a closed sac, e.g. of watery liquid or gas, *esp* one developing abnormally in a plant or animal. **2a** a micro-organism in a resting or spore stage, or a capsule formed about it. **b** a resistant cover formed about a parasite when inside the host. ➤➤ **cystoid** *adj and n.*

cyst- *or* **cysto-** *comb. form* denoting a bladder or sac: *cystectomy.*

cystectomy *n* (*pl* **-ies**) surgical removal of the urinary bladder, the gall bladder, or a diseased cyst.

cysteine *n* a sulphur-containing amino acid found in many proteins and readily convertible to cystine.

cystic *adj* **1** containing a cyst or cysts. **2** of the urinary or gall bladder. **3** enclosed in a cyst.

cystic fibrosis *n* a common hereditary disease appearing in early childhood and marked *esp* by faulty digestion and difficulty in breathing.

cystine *n* an oxidized form of cysteine.

cystitis *n* inflammation of the urinary bladder, causing frequency of urination, accompanied by a burning sensation.

cysto- *comb. form* see CYST-.

cyt- *or* **cyto-** *comb. form* denoting a cell: *cytology.*

-cyte *comb. form* forming nouns, denoting: a cell.

cyto- *comb. form* see CYT-.

cytogenetics *pl n* (*used as sing. or pl*) a branch of genetics that investigates the structure of chromosomes in relation to heredity and variation. ➤➤ **cytogenetic** *adj.*

cytology *n* the biology of the structure, function, multiplication, pathology, etc of cells. ➤➤ **cytological** *adj,* **cytologically** *adv,* **cytologist** *n.*

cytolysis *n* the dissolution or disintegration of cells, usu associated with disease. ➤➤ **cytolytic** *adj.*

cytomegalovirus *adj* any of a large group of DNA-containing viruses that are widely distributed in human beings and that cause enlargement of infected cells.

cytoplasm *n* the substance of a plant or animal cell outside the nucleus. ➤➤ **cytoplasmic** *adj,* **cytoplasmically** *adv.*

cytosine *n* a chemical compound that is one of the four bases whose order in a DNA or RNA chain codes genetic information: compare ADENINE, GUANINE, THYMINE, URACIL.

cytotoxin *n* a substance with a toxic effect on cells. ➤➤ **cytotoxic** *adj,* **cytotoxicity** *n.*

czar *n* see TSAR.

czarevich *n* see TSAREVITCH.

czarina *n* see TSARINA.

Czech /chek/ *n* **1** a native or inhabitant of the former country of Czechoslovakia or of the Czech Republic. **2** the Slavonic language of the Czechs. ➤➤ **Czech** *adj.*

Czechoslovak *or* **Czechoslovakian** *n* a native or inhabitant of the former country of Czechoslovakia, separated since 1993 into the two independent countries of the Czech Republic and Slovakia. ➤➤ **Czechoslovakian** *n.*

D[1] *or* **d** *n* (*pl* **D's** *or* **Ds** *or* **d's**) **1** the fourth letter of the English alphabet. **2** a mark or grade rating a student's work as below average. **3** in music, the second note of the diatonic scale of C major. **4** the Roman numeral for 500.

D[2] *abbr* **1** *NAm* Democrat. **2** *NAm* Democratic. **3** depth (of an object). **4** dimensional (used after a number). **5** dimensions (used after a number). **6** drawn (used in tables of match results).

D[3] *abbr* the chemical symbol for deuterium.

d *abbr* **1** daughter. **2** deci-. **3** departs (used in timetables). **4** died. **5** *Brit* pence (before decimalization). **6** *Brit* penny (before decimalization).

'd *contr* **1** had. **2** would.

DA *abbr NAm* district attorney.

D/A *abbr* in electronics, digital to analogue.

da *abbr* deca-.

dab[1] *v* (**dabbed, dabbing**) **1** to touch lightly and usu repeatedly, *esp* with a cloth, brush, etc. **2** to apply (a liquid or powder) with light strokes.

dab[2] *n* **1** a small amount of something soft or moist. **2** a gentle touch or stroke. **3** *Brit, informal* (*in pl*) fingerprints.

dab[3] *n* a common brown flatfish found *esp* in the North Atlantic.

dabble *v* **1** to dip (e.g. the fingers or toes) in water. **2** (*often* + in) to work or concern oneself superficially. ➤➤ **dabbler** *n.*

dabchick *n* the little grebe.

dab hand *n Brit, informal* a person who is skilful at something; an expert.

da capo /dah 'kahpoh/ *adj and adv* used as a direction in music: repeat or repeated from the beginning: compare DAL SEGNO.

dace *n* (*pl* **dace**) a small slender freshwater European fish.

dacha *or* **datcha** /'dahchə/ *n* (*pl* **dachas** *or* **datchas**) a Russian country cottage, *esp* one used as a holiday home.

dachshund /'daksənd/ *n* a dog of a breed originating in Germany, having a long body, short legs, and long drooping ears.

dacoit /də'koyt/ *n* in India and Union of Myanmar (formerly Burma), a member of an armed gang of robbers.

dactyl *n* a metrical foot consisting of one long and two short, or one stressed and two unstressed, syllables, e.g. in *tenderly*. ➤➤ **dactylic** *adj.*

dad *n informal* one's father.

Dada /'dahdah/ *n* an early 20th-cent. movement in art and literature based on deliberate irrationality and negation of traditional artistic values. ➤➤ **Dadaism** *n,* **Dadaist** *n and adj,* **Dadaistic** *adj.*

daddy *n* (*pl* **-ies**) *informal* one's father.

daddy longlegs *n* (*pl* **daddy longlegs**) **1** *Brit* = CRANE FLY. **2** *NAm* = HARVESTMAN.

dado /'daydoh/ *n* (*pl* **-os** *or* **-oes**) **1** the lower part of an interior wall when decorated differently from the upper part. **2** in architecture, the part of a pedestal or plinth between the base and the cornice.

dado rail *n* a decorative moulding attached to an interior wall, usu at the height of the windowsills.

daemon /'deemən/ *or* **daimon** /'diemohn/ *n* **1** a supernatural being of Greek mythology; a demigod. **2** an attendant power or spirit; a genius. **3** *archaic* = DEMON[1] (I). ➤➤ **daemonic** *adj.*

daffodil *n* a bulb-producing plant with yellow flowers that have elongated trumpet-shaped centres.

daffy *adj* (**-ier, -iest**) *informal* crazy or foolish. ➤➤ **daffiness** *n.*

daft *adj chiefly Brit, informal* silly or foolish.

dag[1] *n Aus, NZ* a piece of matted or manure-coated wool on a sheep's hindquarters.

dag[2] *n Aus, NZ, informal* **1** somebody who is dowdy or unfashionable. **2** somebody who has a conservative attitude.

dagger *n* **1** a short sharp pointed weapon for stabbing. **2** in printing, a sign (†) used as a reference mark or to indicate a death date; an obelus. ✱ **at daggers drawn** in bitter conflict. **look daggers at** to look angrily at; to glare at.

daggy *adj* (**-ier, -iest**) *Aus, NZ, informal* **1** slovenly. **2** dowdy or unfashionably dressed.

dago *n* (*pl* **-os** *or* **-oes**) *informal, offensive* a person of Italian, Spanish, or Portuguese birth or descent.

daguerreotype *or* **daguerrotype** /də'gerətiep/ *n* an early photograph produced on a silver or a silver-covered copper plate.

dahlia /'dayli·ə, 'daylyə/ *n* an ornamental garden plant with showy flower heads and roots that form tubers.

daikon /'diek(ə)n, 'diekon/ *n* = MOOLI.

Dáil /doyl, diel/ *or* **Dáil Éireann** /'eərən/ *n* the lower house of parliament in the Republic of Ireland: compare SEANAD ÉIREANN.

daily[1] *adj* **1** of or occurring every day or every weekday. **2** of a newspaper: issued every weekday.

daily[2] *adv* every day.

daily[3] *n* (*pl* **-ies**) **1** *informal* a newspaper published daily from Monday to Saturday. **2** *Brit, dated* a cleaning woman who works on a daily basis.

daimon *n* see DAEMON.

dainty[1] *adj* (**-ier, -iest**) **1** delicately beautiful. **2** graceful; elegant. **3** fastidious, *esp* about food. ➤➤ **daintily** *adv,* **daintiness** *n.*

dainty[2] *n* (*pl* **-ies**) something particularly nice to eat; a delicacy.

daiquiri /'dakiri/ *n* (*pl* **daiquiris**) a cocktail made of rum, lime juice, and sugar.

dairy *n* (*pl* **-ies**) **1** a place where milk is processed and butter or cheese is made. **2** an establishment for the sale or distribution of milk and milk products. **3** (*used before a noun*) of or containing milk, butter, or cheese. **4** (*used before a noun*) involved in the production of milk. ➤➤ **dairying** *n.*

dairymaid *n archaic* a woman employed in a dairy.

dairyman *n* (*pl* **dairymen**) a man who runs a dairy farm or who works in a dairy.

dais /'day·is/ *n* a raised platform in a hall or large room, e.g. for a speaker using a lectern.

daisy *n* (*pl* **-ies**) a common European plant bearing flowers with yellow centres and white rays. ✱ **pushing up the daisies** *informal* dead and in one's grave.

daisy chain *n* **1** a string of daisies threaded together through their stalks. **2** in computing, a way of linking hardware in a linear series using cables.

daisy-chain *v* in computing, to connect (hardware) in a linear series using cables.

daisy wheel *n* a device in a typewriter or printer that is shaped like a wheel with a different character at the end of each spoke.

Dakota *n* (*pl* **Dakotas** *or collectively* **Dakota**) **1** a member of a Native American people of the N Mississippi valley. **2** the Siouan language of this people. ➤➤ **Dakotan** *adj.*

dal *n* see DHAL.

Dalai Lama *n* the spiritual head of Tibetan Buddhism. Until 1959, the Dalai Lama was the ruler of Tibet.

dalasi /dah'lahsi/ *n* (*pl* **dalasis** *or* **dalasi**) the basic monetary unit of the Gambia.

dale *n* a valley.

Dalit /'dahlit/ *n* in India, a member of the lowest caste in the traditional caste system: compare SCHEDULED CASTE, UNTOUCHABLE[2].

dally *v* (**-ies, -ied**) **1** to waste time; to dawdle. **2a** (+ with) to act playfully or flirtatiously with somebody. **b** (+ with) to deal lightly or casually with something. ➤➤ **dalliance** *n.*

Dalmatian *n* **1** a large dog of a breed having a white short-haired coat with black or brown spots. **2** a native or inhabitant of Dalmatia. ➤➤ **Dalmatian** *adj.*

dal segno *adj and adv* used as a direction in music: return to the sign that marks the beginning of a section to be repeated: compare DA CAPO.

dalton *n* = ATOMIC MASS UNIT.

dam[1] *n* a barrier built across a watercourse to hold back and raise the level of the water, *esp* to form a reservoir.

dam[2] *v* (**dammed, damming**) **1** to build a dam across (a river or lake). **2** to block or stop (e.g. a flow of water).

dam[3] *n* a female parent of a domestic animal.

damage[1] *n* **1** loss or harm resulting from injury to somebody or something. **2** (*in pl*) compensation in money imposed by law for loss or injury. ✱ **what's the damage?** how much is the cost?

damage[2] *v* **1** to cause damage to. **2** to become damaged. ➤➤ **damaging** *adj,* **damagingly** *adv.*

Damascene[1] *n* a native or inhabitant of Damascus, capital of Syria.

Damascene[2] *adj* **1** of or relating to Damascus. **2** of or like St Paul's conversion, which happened on the road to Damascus. **3** relating to the art of damascening metal.

damascene *v* to ornament (e.g. iron or steel) with wavy patterns like those of watered silk or with inlaid work of precious metals.

damask[1] *n* a reversible lustrous fabric having a plain background woven with patterns.

damask[2] *adj* of the colour of a damask rose; greyish pink.

damask rose *n* a large fragrant greyish pink rose.

dame *n* **1** (**Dame**) in the UK, a title given to a woman who has been awarded an order of knighthood, e.g. the Order of the British Empire. **2** *archaic* an elderly woman. **3** *Brit* a comic ill-tempered old woman in a pantomime, usu played by a male actor. **4** *NAm, informal* a woman.

damn[1] *v* **1** to condemn to a punishment or fate; *esp* to condemn to hell. **2** to condemn by public criticism. **3** to curse. ✱ **damn with faint praise** to praise in such a way that it seems like criticism.

damn[2] *n* (*usu in negative contexts*) the slightest bit.

damn[3] *adj informal* used as an intensive. ✱ **damn all** *Brit, informal* nothing at all. **damn well** *informal* beyond doubt or question; certainly.

damn[4] *interj informal* used to express annoyance.

damnable /'damnəbl/ *adj* **1** very bad; detestable. **2** deserving damnation. ➤➤ **damnably** *adv.*

damnation[1] /dam'naysh(ə)n/ *n* condemnation to hell.

damnation[2] *interj* used to express annoyance.

damned *adj* (**damnedest**) *informal* used as an intensive.

damnedest ✱ **do one's damnedest** *informal* to try one's best to do something.

damnify /'damnifie/ *v* (**-ies, -ied**) in law, to cause loss or damage to (somebody). ➤➤ **damnification** *n.*

damning *adj* causing or leading to condemnation or ruin. ➤➤ **damningly** *adv.*

damp[1] *adj* slightly or moderately wet. ➤➤ **dampish** *adj,* **damply** *adv,* **dampness** *n.*

damp[2] *n* moisture or humidity.

damp[3] *v* **1** to make damp. **2** (*often* + down) to diminish the activity or intensity of. **3** (*often* + down) to reduce the air supply to (a fire) so that it becomes less intense. **4** in physics, to decrease the amplitude of (an oscillation or wave) progressively. **5** in music, to decrease the vibration of (the strings of an instrument).

damp course *n* a horizontal damp-resistant layer near the ground in a masonry wall.

dampen *v* **1** to make damp. **2** to check or diminish the activity or vigour of (*esp* feelings). **3** to decrease the vibration or oscillation of (e.g. sound waves). ➤➤ **dampener** *n.*

damper *n* **1** in music, a small felted block which stops the vibration of a piano string. **2** a device, e.g. a shock absorber, designed to reduce vibration or oscillation. **3** a valve or plate in the flue of a furnace for regulating the draught. ✱ **put a damper on** to have a dulling or deadening influence on.

damp-proof[1] *adj* impervious to damp.

damp-proof[2] *v* to make (a wall or building) impervious to damp by means of a damp course.

damp-proof course *n* = DAMP COURSE.

damp squib *n Brit* something that ends feebly, *esp* after a promising start.

damsel *n archaic or literary* a young unmarried woman.

damselfish *n* (*pl* **damselfishes** *or* **damselfish**) a small brightly coloured marine fish of tropical and warm seas.

damselfly *n* (*pl* **-ies**) a slender insect related to the dragonfly, having wings that are folded above the body.

damson *n* a small purple fruit similar to a plum.

dan *n* any of the ten levels of expertise in judo or karate, or a person who has achieved a specified level.

dance[1] *v* **1** to move the body in a rhythmic way, *esp* in time to music. **2** to move quickly and lightly. ✱ **dance attendance on** to attend to the needs of; to try to please. **dance to somebody's tune** to do what somebody wants. ➤➤ **danceable** *adj*, **dancer** *n*, **dancing** *n*.

dance[2] *n* **1** a series of steps and bodily movements, usu in time to music. **2** a social gathering at which dancing takes place. **3** a piece of music for dancing to. **4** = DANCE MUSIC (2). ✱ **lead somebody a merry dance** to cause somebody a lot of trouble.

dance floor *n* a separate part of the floor in a disco, nightclub, etc where people can dance.

dance music *n* **1** music for dancing to. **2** rhythmic electronic music played in clubs.

D and C *abbr* dilatation and curettage, a gynaecological procedure in which the womb is gently stretched open to allow its temporary lining to be scraped clean.

dandelion *n* a plant of the daisy family with yellow flowers and downy seed heads.

dandelion clock *n* the downy seed head of a dandelion.

dander ✱ **get/have one's dander up** *informal* to lose one's temper.

dandify *v* (**-ies, -ied**) to make (somebody) resemble a dandy.

dandle *v* to move (a baby or small child) up and down in one's arms or on one's knee in affectionate play.

dandruff *n* dead skin that comes off the scalp in small white or greyish scales. ➤➤ **dandruffy** *adj*.

dandy[1] *n* (*pl* **-ies**) **1** a man who is overly concerned with looking fashionable. **2** *informal, dated* something excellent in its class. ➤➤ **dandyish** *adj*, **dandyism** *n*.

dandy[2] *adj* (**-ier, -iest**) *chiefly NAm, informal* very good; first-rate.

Dane *n* a native or inhabitant of Denmark.

danger *n* **1** exposure to the possibility of injury, pain, or loss. **2** a case or cause of danger. **3** a possibility.

danger list *n Brit* a list of hospital patients who are critically ill.

danger money *n* extra payment for dangerous work.

dangerous *adj* **1** able or likely to do harm or inflict injury. **2** involving danger; risky or perilous. ➤➤ **dangerously** *adv*, **dangerousness** *n*.

dangle *v* **1** to hang or swing loosely. **2** to cause to dangle. **3** to offer enticingly. ➤➤ **dangler** *n*, **dangly** *adj*.

Danish[1] *adj* from or relating to Denmark.

Danish[2] *n* the Scandinavian language spoken in Denmark.

Danish blue *n* a white Danish cheese with blue veins and a strong flavour.

Danish pastry *n* a small cake made from a rich yeast dough with a sweet filling.

dank *adj* unpleasantly moist or wet. ➤➤ **dankly** *adv*, **dankness** *n*.

daphne *n* a small ornamental shrub with evergreen leaves and fragrant bell-shaped pinkish flowers.

daphnia *n* (*pl* **daphnia**) a minute freshwater crustacean used as food for aquarium fish.

dapper *adj* of a man: neat and spruce in dress and demeanour. ➤➤ **dapperly** *adv*, **dapperness** *n*.

dapple[1] *v* to mark (a surface) with rounded patches of varying shade.

dapple[2] *n* **1** a spot or patch of a colour different from its background. **2** a dappled horse or other animal.

dapple-grey *n* a horse with a grey coat marked with spots of a darker colour. ➤➤ **dapple-grey** *adj*.

Darby and Joan *n chiefly Brit* a happily married elderly couple.

Darby and Joan club *n Brit* a club for elderly people.

dare[1] *v* (*third person sing. present tense before an expressed or implied infinitive without 'to'* **dare**) **1** to have sufficient courage or boldness to do something. **2** to challenge (somebody) to do something. ✱ **how dare you?** used to express anger. **I dare say/daresay** it is likely or probable that. ➤➤ **darer** *n*.

dare[2] *n* a challenge to do something bold or rash.

daredevil *n* somebody who is recklessly bold. ➤➤ **daredevilry** *n*.

daren't *contr* dare not.

daring[1] *adj* adventurously bold in action or thought. ➤➤ **daringly** *adv*.

daring[2] *n* adventurous boldness.

dariole *n* a small cup-shaped mould in which a single portion of a sweet or savoury dish is cooked and served.

Darjeeling *n* a high-quality tea grown in the mountainous districts of N India.

dark[1] *adj* **1** with little or no light. **2a** wholly or partially black. **b** of a colour: not light or pale. **3** of the hair or complexion: not fair. **4** secret or mysterious. **5a** sinister or evil. **b** dismal or sad. **6** remote or uncivilized: *darkest Peru*. ➤➤ **darkish** *adj*, **darkly** *adv*, **darkness** *n*.

dark[2] *n* **1a** the absence of light; darkness. **b** night or nightfall. **2** a dark or deep colour. ✱ **in the dark** in ignorance.

Dark Ages *pl n* **1** the period of European history from the fall of the Roman Empire in the West (AD 476) to about 1000, typically perceived as a time devoid of culture or learning. **2** any period seen as similarly deprived.

dark chocolate *n* chocolate that is dark in colour and slightly bitter; plain chocolate.

darken *v* **1** to make or become dark or darker. **2** to spoil or blight. **3** to make or become unhappy, angry, or pessimistic. ✱ **darken somebody's door** (*usu in negative contexts*) to come to visit somebody. ➤➤ **darkener** *n*.

dark horse *n* **1** somebody or something that is little known but is likely to succeed, *esp* a competitor in a race or contest. **2** a secretive person.

darkie *n* see DARKY.

darkling *adj literary* of or in the dark.

dark matter *n* invisible and unidentified matter that is believed by astronomers to account for up to 90% of the universe's mass.

darkroom *n* a room with subdued light for handling and processing photographic materials.

darksome *adj literary* dark.

darky *or* **darkie** *n* (*pl* **-ies**) *offensive* a black person.

darling[1] *n* **1** used as an affectionate form of address. **2** a dearly loved person. **3** a favourite.

darling[2] *adj* **1** dearly loved; favourite. **2** charming.

darn[1] *v* to mend (knitted material) with interwoven stitches across a hole. ⋙ **darning** *n.*

darn[2] *n* a darned area of a garment.

darn[3] *v informal, euphem* = DAMN[1] (3).

darn[4] *adj informal, euphem* = DAMN[3].

darned *adj informal, euphem* = DAMNED.

darnel *n* a grass that is a common weed in fields of grain.

darning needle *n* a long needle with a large eye for use in darning.

dart[1] *n* **1** a small projectile with a pointed shaft and flights of feather or plastic, used as a weapon or in the game of darts. **2** a stitched tapering fold put in a garment to shape it to the figure. **3** a quick movement or dash.

dart[2] *v* to move suddenly or rapidly.

dartboard *n* a circular target used in the game of darts, marked into sections that have different scores.

darter *n* **1** a fish-eating bird that has a long slender neck and flies with darting movements. **2** a small, brightly coloured freshwater fish of N America.

darts *pl n* (*usu used as sing.*) an indoor game in which darts are thrown at a dartboard to score points.

Darwinism *n* a theory of evolution developed by Charles Darwin, based on the concept of natural selection. ⋙ **Darwinian** *n and adj,* **Darwinist** *n and adj.*

dash[1] *v* **1** to move with speed or haste. **2** to hurl or strike with great force. **3** to destroy or ruin (a hope or plan).

dash[2] *n* **1** a punctuation mark (—) used to indicate a break or an omission. **2** in Morse code, a signal of relatively long duration: compare DOT[1] (4). **3** a speedy or hasty movement or journey. **4** *chiefly NAm* a sprint. **5** a small amount of a substance. **6** liveliness of style and action; panache. **7** = DASHBOARD.

dash[3] *interj Brit, informal, dated* used to express annoyance.

dashboard *n* a panel containing dials and controls in a car or other vehicle.

dashiki /də'sheeki/ *n* (*pl* **dashikis**) a loose brightly coloured shirt without buttons, traditionally worn by men in W Africa.

dashing *adj* **1** marked by vigorous action; spirited. **2** smart and stylish in dress and manners. ⋙ **dashingly** *adv.*

dash off *v* to complete or execute (e.g. writing or drawing) hastily.

dastard *n archaic* a coward, *esp* one who commits malicious acts.

dastardly *adj dated* despicably malicious or cowardly. ⋙ **dastardliness** *n.*

dasyure /'dasiyooə/ *n* a tree-dwelling flesh-eating marsupial mammal of Australia and Tasmania resembling a large weasel. Also called QUOLL.

DAT *abbr* digital audiotape.

data *pl n* **1** (*used as sing. or pl*) factual information used as a basis for reasoning, discussion, or calculation. **2** (*used as sing. or pl*) in computing, any numbers, characters, etc that a computer can use.

Usage note

Data is, strictly speaking, a plural noun with the singular form datum, but it is increasingly used as a singular mass noun like information or news: The data is currently being processed.

databank *n* a collection of computer data organized for rapid search and retrieval.

database *n* a set of data held in structured form by a computer.

datable *or* **dateable** *adj* able to be given a particular date.

data capture *n* in computing, the act of collecting data and converting it into a form that a computer can use.

data compression *n* in computing, the reorganization or restructuring of data so that it takes up less storage space.

data processing *n* the entering, storing, and maintaining of data, *esp* by a computer. ⋙ **data processor** *n.*

data protection *n Brit* legal protection of the privacy and security of information stored in computers.

datcha *n* see DACHA.

date[1] *n* **1** a particular day of the month or year, identified by a number. **2** the time at which a particular event has occurred or will occur. **3** the period of time to which something belongs. **4** *informal* **a** an appointment, *esp* a romantic or social engagement. **b** a person with whom one has arranged such an appointment. **5** a show or concert, *esp* one that is part of a series being performed in different venues. ✱ **to date** until the present moment.

date[2] *v* **1** to determine the date of. **2** to mark with a date. **3** *informal* **a** to go on a date or dates with. **b** to go out on dates. **4** to have been in existence for a specified time: *coins dating from Anglo-Saxon times.* **5** to become old-fashioned.

date[3] *n* a small brown oval fruit with a long thin stone and a sweet taste, eaten fresh or dried.

dateable *adj* see DATABLE.

dated *adj* out of date or old-fashioned.

dateless *adj* **1** having no date. **2** timeless.

Date Line *n* = INTERNATIONAL DATE LINE.

date palm *n* a tall tropical palm tree that bears dates.

date rape *n* the rape of somebody while on a date.

date stamp *n* a device for stamping a date, or the mark it makes. ⋙ **date-stamp** *v.*

dating agency *n* an agency that arranges introductions for people seeking a companion or partner.

dative[1] *adj* in Greek, Latin, German, etc: denoting a grammatical case expressing an indirect object.

dative[2] *n* the dative case or a word in this case.

datum *n* (*pl* **data**) **1** something, e.g. a fixed point or assumed value, used as a basis for measuring or calculating. **2** something given or admitted, *esp* as a basis for reasoning or drawing conclusions.

daub[1] *v* **1** to cover or smear (a surface) with a soft adhesive or dirty substance. **2** to apply (e.g. colouring material) crudely to a surface. ⋙ **dauber** *n.*

daub[2] *n* **1** in building, *esp* formerly, a mixture of plaster or clay and straw, used with WATTLE (interwoven sticks) to form a wall. **2** something daubed on; a smear. **3** a crude painting.

daube *n* a stew of meat, *esp* beef, braised in wine.

daughter *n* **1a** a girl or woman having the relation of child to parent. **b** a female descendant. **2** a woman having a specified origin or affiliation: *a daughter of the Church.* ⯮⯮ **daughterhood** *n,* **daughterly** *adj.*

daughter-in-law *n* (*pl* **daughters-in-law**) the wife of one's son.

daunt *v* to discourage or dishearten. ⯮⯮ **daunting** *adj,* **dauntingly** *adv.*

dauntless *adj* courageous and fearless. ⯮⯮ **dauntlessly** *adv,* **dauntlessness** *n.*

dauphin /'dohfanh/ *n* used, formerly, as a title: the eldest son of a king of France.

daven /'dahv(ə)n/ *v* in Judaism, to recite the prayers of the liturgies, or to lead the prayers.

davenport *n* **1** *Brit* a writing desk with a sloping top and drawers. **2** *NAm* a large upholstered sofa, *esp* one that converts into a bed.

davit *n* a projecting arm, similar to a crane, used on a vessel for lowering equipment, e.g. a lifeboat.

Davy Jones's locker *n informal* the bottom of the sea, regarded as the resting place of the drowned.

Davy lamp *n* an oil-burning lamp, formerly used in mines, with a wire mesh around the flame to minimize the risk of explosions.

dawdle *v* **1** to move slowly or lackadaisically. **2** to spend time idly. ⯮⯮ **dawdler** *n.*

dawn[1] *n* **1** the first appearance of light in the morning. **2** a first appearance; a beginning.

dawn[2] *v* **1** to begin to grow light as the sun rises. **2** to begin to appear or develop. **3** (*usu* + on) to begin to be perceived or understood by somebody.

dawn chorus *n* the singing of large numbers of birds at dawn.

day *n* **1** a period of 24 hours beginning at midnight, corresponding to one rotation of the earth on its axis. **2** the time when it is light, when the sun is above the horizon between one night and the next. **3** the time established by usage or law for work, school, etc. **4** (*also in pl*) a specified time or period. **5** a day set aside for a particular activity. ✻ **any day 1** *informal* at any time. **2** *informal* soon. **3** *informal* used to express a preference: in any circumstances. **at the end of the day** *informal* when one considers everything. **call it a day** to decide to stop work or another activity for the time being. **day and night** at all times. **day in, day out** for a seemingly endless number of days in a row. **one day/one of these days** at some future time. **that will be the day** *informal* used to express a view that something is not likely to happen. **these days** in the present times.

Dayak *n* see DYAK.

daybed *n* **1** a narrow bed or couch for rest or sleep during the day. **2** *NAm* a sofa that can be converted into a bed.

dayboy *n Brit* a boy who attends a boarding school during the day but lives at home.

daybreak *n* dawn.

day-care centre *n* = DAY CENTRE.

day centre *n* a place providing supervision and facilities for elderly or handicapped people during the day.

daydream[1] *n* **1** a pleasant fantasy or reverie indulged in while one is awake. **2** an idle scheme or plan that is unlikely to be fulfilled.

daydream[2] *v* to have a daydream. ⯮⯮ **daydreamer** *n.*

daygirl *n Brit* a girl who attends a boarding school during the day but lives at home.

daylight *n* **1** the light of the sun during the day; sunshine. **2** dawn. **3** *informal* (*in pl*) consciousness; wits: *You scared the living daylights out of me.* ✻ **see daylight** to understand something that has been obscure.

daylight robbery *n Brit, informal* exorbitant pricing or charging.

daylight saving time *n chiefly NAm* time set usu one hour ahead of standard time and used *esp* during the summer: compare BRITISH SUMMER TIME.

day lily *n* a Eurasian plant of the lily family with large red, orange, or yellow flowers that last only one day.

Day of Atonement *n* = YOM KIPPUR.

Day of Judgment *n* = JUDGMENT DAY.

day release *n* a system in Britain whereby employees are allowed days off work to attend educational courses: compare BLOCK RELEASE.

day return *n Brit* a ticket sold at a reduced fare for a return journey completed on the same day.

day room *n* a living room in a hospital or other institution, for the use of people during the day.

day school *n* **1** a private school for students living at home. **2** a school that holds classes during the day rather than the evening.

dayspring *n literary* dawn.

day surgery *n* surgery that can be carried out without the patient staying overnight in the hospital.

daytime *n* the time when it is light, between sunrise and sunset.

day-to-day *adj* **1** happening every day; regular or routine. **2** providing for a day at a time with little thought for the future.

day trip *n* a journey or outing that is completed in one day, *esp* one made for pleasure. ⯮⯮ **day tripper** *n.*

daze[1] *v* to stupefy or stun, *esp* by a blow or shock. ⯮⯮ **dazedly** /'dayzidli/ *adv.*

daze[2] *n* a state of confusion or shock.

dazzle[1] *v* **1** to blind temporarily by sudden bright light. **2** to impress deeply or overwhelm with brilliance. ⯮⯮ **dazzler** *n,* **dazzling** *adj,* **dazzlingly** *adv.*

dazzle[2] *n* sudden blinding brightness.

dB *abbr* decibel(s).

Db *abbr* the chemical symbol for dubnium.

DBE *abbr* Dame Commander of the Order of the British Empire.

DBS *abbr* **1** direct broadcasting by satellite. **2** direct broadcasting satellite.

DC *abbr* **1** in music, da capo. **2** direct current. **3** District of Columbia (US postal abbreviation).

DCB *abbr Brit* Dame Commander of the Order of the Bath.

DCC *abbr* digital compact cassette.

DCM *abbr Brit* Distinguished Conduct Medal.

DCMG *abbr Brit* Dame Commander of the Order of St Michael and St George.

DCVO *abbr Brit* Dame Commander of the Royal Victorian Order.

DD *abbr* **1** direct debit. **2** Doctor of Divinity.

D-day *n* **1** 6 June 1944, the day on which the Allies began the invasion of France in World War II. **2** a day set for launching or beginning anything.

DDT *n* dichlorodiphenyltrichloroethane, a synthetic insecticide that tends to accumulate in food chains and is poisonous to many vertebrates.

DE *abbr* Delaware (US postal abbreviation).

de- *prefix* **1** denoting the opposite of a specified action: *decompose.* **2** denoting removal of something: *decapitate.* **3** a reduction in something: *devalue.*

deacon *n* **1** in Catholic, Anglican, and Orthodox Churches, an ordained minister ranking below a priest. **2** in various Protestant Churches, a lay minister with administrative and sometimes spiritual duties. ➤➤ **deaconship** *n.*

deaconess *n* in some Churches, a woman with the duties of a deacon.

deactivate *v* to make (e.g. a bomb or a virus) inactive or ineffective. ➤➤ **deactivation** *n,* **deactivator** *n.*

dead[1] *adj* **1** no longer alive. **2** having no living things: *a dead planet.* **3a** of a body part: lacking feeling; numb. **b** unfeeling or unresponsive. **4** no longer working. **5** no longer used, active, or relevant. **6** of a bottle or glass: empty or finished with. **7** *informal* lacking in activity or interest; dull. **8** complete or absolute. ✱ **dead as a dodo/doornail** utterly dead. **dead from the neck up** *informal* stupid. **dead on one's feet** *informal* very tired. **dead to the world** *informal* asleep or otherwise unaware of one's surroundings. ➤➤ **deadness** *n.*

dead[2] *n* **1** the state of being dead. **2** the time when something is at its most complete: *the dead of night.*

dead[3] *adv* **1** absolutely or exactly. **2** *Brit, informal* very.

deadbeat *n informal* **1** an idle person; a loafer. **2** *NAm* somebody who consistently fails to pay debts.

dead beat *adj informal* very tired; exhausted.

deadbolt *n* a bolt that is operated directly by a key or knob rather than having a spring mechanism.

dead centre *n* **1** either of the two positions at the ends of a stroke when a crank and connecting rod are directly in line. **2** the exact centre.

dead duck *n informal* somebody or something that is unlikely to succeed.

deaden *v* **1** to reduce the resonance of (a sound). **2a** to reduce the sensation of (e.g. pain). **b** to deprive (e.g. a part of the body) of sensation. **3** to deprive of liveliness or excitement. **4** to make insensitive. ➤➤ **deadener** *n.*

dead end *n* **1** an end of a street or passage without an exit. **2** a situation or course of action that leads no further.

dead hand *n* an oppressive influence.

deadhead[1] *v chiefly Brit* to remove dead flower heads from (a plant).

deadhead[2] *n* **1** *informal* somebody who is boring or stupid. **2** *chiefly Brit* a dead flower head.

dead heat *n* an inconclusive finish to a race, in which the fastest time is achieved by more than one competitor.

dead letter *n* **1** a law or treaty that has lost its force without being formally repealed or abolished. **2** a letter that cannot be delivered or returned because it lacks adequate directions.

deadline *n* **1** a date or time before which something must be done. **2** a boundary beyond which it is not possible or permitted to pass.

Word history

The word was coined in the Confederate prisoner of war camp, Andersonville, during the American Civil War (1861–5), when a line was marked out a little distance from the perimeter wire fence and the instruction was given that any prisoner crossing the line should be shot on sight.

deadlock[1] *n* **1** a situation in which no progress can be made because of conflicting views or circumstances; a standstill. **2** *Brit* a lock that can be opened and shut only by a key.

deadlock[2] *v* **1** to bring (negotiations, etc) to a standstill. **2** *Brit* to lock (e.g. a door) with a deadlock.

dead loss *n* a totally useless person or thing.

deadly[1] *adj* (**-ier, -iest**) **1** likely or able to cause death. **2** aiming to kill or destroy. **3** unerring. **4** *informal* dull or boring. **5** intense or extreme. ➤➤ **deadliness** *n.*

deadly[2] *adv* **1** suggesting death. **2** extremely.

deadly nightshade *n* a European poisonous nightshade that has dull purple flowers and black berries.

deadly sin *n* in Christian belief, any of the seven sins of pride, covetousness, lust, anger, gluttony, envy, and sloth, held to lead to damnation.

dead man's handle *n* a handle that requires constant pressure to allow operation, e.g. of a train, and automatically applies the brakes if the driver lets go.

deadnettle *n* a European or Asian plant of the mint family, resembling a stinging nettle but without stinging hairs.

deadpan *adj and adv* without feeling or expression.

dead reckoning *n* the calculation of the position of a ship or aircraft from the record of the course and distance travelled, without the use of external navigational aids.

dead ringer *n* a person or thing strongly resembling another.

deadweight *n* **1** the unrelieved weight of an inert person or object. **2** a ship's total weight including cargo, fuel, stores, crew, and passengers.

deadwood *n* useless people or things.

deaf *adj* **1** lacking or deficient in the sense of hearing. **2** (+ to) unwilling to hear or listen to; not to be persuaded by. ✱ **fall on deaf ears** to be ignored or unheeded. **turn a deaf ear** to refuse to listen. ➤➤ **deafness** *n.*

deaf aid *n Brit* a hearing aid.

deaf-blind *adj* severely deficient in both hearing and vision.

deafen *v* to overpower with noise.

deafening *adj* extremely loud. ➤➤ **deafeningly** *adv.*

deaf-mute *n offensive* somebody who is unable to hear or speak.

deal[1] *v* (*past tense and past part.* **dealt** /delt/) **1** to distribute (cards) to players in a game. **2** (+ out) to distribute or apportion. **3** to administer or inflict (e.g. a blow). **4** (*often* + in) to sell or trade in something commercially. **5** *informal* to buy and sell drugs illegally. ✱ **deal with 1a** to take action with regard to. **b** to cope with. **2** to be concerned with (a theme or subject). **3** to have business relations with.

deal[2] *n* **1** an advantageous bargain or transaction. **2** a particular kind of treatment. **3** the process of distributing cards to players in a game. ✱ **a good/great deal 1** a lot. **2** considerably.

deal[3] *n* fir or pine timber, or a sawn piece of this.

dealer *n* **1** a person who deals in goods or services. **2** a person who deals in shares, securities, etc, and for whom somebody else acts as an agent. **3** somebody who deals in illegal drugs; a pusher. **4** somebody who deals playing cards. ➤➤ **dealership** *n.*

dealings *pl n* business or personal relationships.

dealt *v* past tense and past part. of DEAL[1].

dean[1] *n* **1** the head of the chapter of a collegiate or cathedral church. **2** = RURAL DEAN. **3** the head of a university division, faculty, or school. **4** a college or secondary school administrator in charge of guidance and discipline. ⋙ **deanery** *n.*

dean² *or* **dene** *n Brit* usu in place names: a narrow wooded valley with a stream running through it.

dear¹ *adj* **1** much loved; precious or cherished. **2** used as a polite form of address in letters. **3** expensive. **4** sweet; appealing. ✱ **for dear life** desperately; as if to escape death. ⋙ **dearness** *n.*

dear² *n* **1** used as an affectionate form of address. **2** a lovable person.

dear³ *adv* at a high cost; dearly.

dear⁴ *interj* used to express annoyance or dismay.

dearest¹ *adj* **1** most loved or cherished. **2** most expensive.

dearest² *n* used as an affectionate form of address.

Dear John *or* **Dear John letter** *n informal* a letter written by a woman to a man to break off a relationship or engagement.

dearly *adv* **1** very much. **2** at a great cost.

dearth *n* an inadequate supply; a scarcity.

death *n* **1a** the end of life. **b** an instance of dying. **2** the state of being dead. **3** (**Death**) death personified, usu represented as a skeleton with a scythe. **4** extinction or disappearance. ✱ **at death's door** seriously ill. **be the death of** *often humorous* to cause the death of. **like death warmed up** *informal* looking very pale and ill. **to death** beyond all acceptable limits; excessively: *I was bored to death.* ⋙ **deathlike** *adj.*

deathbed *n* the bed in which a person is dying or has died. ✱ **on one's deathbed** near the point of death.

death camp *n* a prison camp in which large numbers of people are put to death or die.

death cap *n* a poisonous toadstool with a pale green cap and milky white gills.

death certificate *n* an official document issued by a doctor, stating the time and cause of a person's death.

death duty *n* in Britain until 1975, a tax levied on the estate of a dead person: compare CAPITAL TRANSFER TAX, INHERITANCE TAX.

death knell *n* **1** the ringing of a bell to mark a person's death. **2** an indication of the end of something.

deathless *adj* immortal; lasting for ever. ⋙ **deathlessness** *n.*

deathly *adj* (**-ier, -iest**) **1** suggestive of death. **2** *archaic or literary* fatal.

death mask *n* a cast taken from the face of a dead person.

death penalty *n* punishment of a crime by death.

death rate *n* the number of deaths per 1000 people in a population per year.

death rattle *n* a gurgling sound produced by air passing through mucus in the lungs and throat of a dying person.

death row *n* a part of a prison containing the cells of those condemned to death.

death's-head moth *n* a large European hawkmoth with skull-shaped markings on its back.

death toll *n* the number of people or animals dying as a result of something.

death trap *n* a potentially lethal structure or place.

death warrant *n* a warrant for the execution of a death sentence.

deathwatch beetle *n* a small beetle common in old buildings, where it bores into woodwork making an ominous ticking sound.

death wish *n* a usu unconscious desire for one's own death.

deb *n informal* a debutante.

debacle /di'bahkəl/ *n* a complete failure; a fiasco.

debag *v* (**debagged, debagging**) *Brit, informal* to remove the trousers of (somebody) as a joke or punishment.

debar *v* (**debarred, debarring**) (+ from) to bar from having or doing something; to preclude. ⋙ **debarment** *n.*

debark *v* to disembark. ⋙ **debarkation** *n.*

debase *v* **1** to lower in status, esteem, quality, or character. **2a** to reduce the intrinsic value of (a coin). **b** to reduce the exchange value of (a monetary unit). ⋙ **debasement** *n,* **debaser** *n.*

debatable *adj* open to debate; questionable. ⋙ **debatably** *adv.*

debate¹ *n* **1** a formal discussion of a motion. **2** an argument or controversy.

debate² *v* **1** to discuss a question by considering opposed arguments. **2** to argue about. **3** to consider (a matter) from different viewpoints. ⋙ **debater** *n.*

debauch¹ *v* to cause to become morally impure; to corrupt. ⋙ **debauched** *adj,* **debaucher** *n.*

debauch² *n* an episode of indulgence in sensual pleasures.

debauchee *n* somebody given to debauchery.

debauchery *n* excessive indulgence in sensual pleasures.

debenture *n Brit* a loan secured on the assets of a company in respect of which the company must pay a fixed interest before any dividends are paid to its own shareholders.

debilitate *v* to impair the strength of; to enfeeble. ⋙ **debilitation** *n,* **debilitative** *adj.*

debility *n* weakness or infirmity.

debit¹ *n* **1** an entry in an account recording money owed. **2** a charge against a bank account.

debit² *v* (**debited, debiting**) **1** to record (an amount) as a debit. **2** of a bank: to take (a sum of money) from an account as payment: compare CREDIT².

debit card *n* a card issued by a bank enabling purchases to be charged directly to the holder's account.

debonair *adj* **1** suave or urbane. **2** light-hearted or nonchalant. ⋙ **debonairly** *adv.*

debouch *v* to emerge or issue from a narrow place into a wider place.

debouchment *n* a mouth or outlet, *esp* of a river.

debrief *v* to interrogate (a soldier, diplomat, etc) after a mission. ⋙ **debriefer** *n,* **debriefing** *n.*

debris /'debri/ *n* **1** the remains of something broken down. **2** an accumulation of fragments of rock. **3** accumulated rubbish or waste.

debt *n* **1** something owed, *esp* money; an obligation. **2** the state of owing something, *esp* money or gratitude.

debt of honour *n* a debt that cannot be legally enforced but is regarded as morally binding.

debtor *n* somebody who owes a debt.

debug *v* (**debugged, debugging**) **1** to eliminate errors or malfunctions in (e.g. a computer program). **2** to remove a concealed microphone or wiretapping device from (a room or building). ⋙ **debugger** *n.*

debunk *v* **1** to expose the falseness of (a statement or idea). **2** to expose the reputation of (somebody) to ridicule. ⋙ **debunker** *n.*

debut[1] /'dayb(y)ooh/ *n* **1** a first public appearance. **2** *dated* a formal entrance into society. **3** (*used before a noun*) denoting a first recording, book, etc.

debut[2] *v* (**debuted, debuting**) to make a debut.

debutant *n* somebody making a debut.

debutante *n* a woman making a debut; *esp* an aristocratic young woman making her formal entrance into society.

Dec. *abbr* December.

deca- *or* **dec-** *comb. form* denoting ten: *decagon.*

decade *n* **1** a period of ten years. **2** a group, set, or sequence of ten. ➤➤ **decadal** *adj.*

decadence *n* **1** a period or process of moral or cultural decline. **2** self-indulgence, *esp* the unrestrained gratification of one's desires.

decadent *adj* **1** marked by moral or cultural decline. **2** self-indulgent in an uninhibited or immoral way. ➤➤ **decadently** *adv.*

decaffeinate *v* to remove most of the caffeine from (e.g. coffee or tea). ➤➤ **decaffeinated** *adj,* **decaffeination** *n.*

decagon *n* a polygon with ten angles and ten sides. ➤➤ **decagonal** *adj.*

decahedron *n* (*pl* **decahedra** *or* **decahedrons**) a polyhedron with ten faces. ➤➤ **decahedral** *adj.*

decal /'deekal, 'dekəl/ *n chiefly NAm* a design or picture on prepared paper for transfer to another surface; a transfer.

decalcify *v* (**-ies, -ied**) to remove calcium or calcium compounds from (bones, teeth, soil, etc). ➤➤ **decalcification** *n,* **decalcifier** *n.*

decalitre (*NAm* **decaliter** *or* **dekaliter**) *n* a metric unit of capacity equal to ten litres (about 2.2gall).

Decalogue *n* the Ten Commandments.

decametre (*NAm* **decameter** *or* **dekameter**) *n* a metric unit of length equal to 10m (about 10.94yd).

decamp *v* to depart secretly or suddenly; to abscond. ➤➤ **decampment** *n.*

decanal *adj* of a dean or deanery.

decant *v* **1** to pour (liquid) gradually from one vessel into another, *esp* without disturbing the sediment. **2** *informal* to transfer from one place to another.

decanter *n* an ornamental glass bottle into which an alcoholic drink, *esp* wine, is decanted.

decapitate *v* to cut off the head of. ➤➤ **decapitation** *n,* **decapitator** *n.*

decapod *n* any of a group of crustaceans, including the shrimps, lobsters, and crabs, having stalked eyes and five pairs of legs. ➤➤ **decapod** *adj.*

decarbonize *or* **-ise** *v* to remove carbon from (e.g. an engine). ➤➤ **decarbonization** *n,* **decarbonizer** *n.*

decasyllabic *adj* consisting of ten syllables.

decathlon *n* an athletic contest in which each competitor takes part in ten events: the 100m, 400m and 1500m races, the 110m high hurdles, and the javelin, discus, shot put, pole vault, high jump, and long jump. ➤➤ **decathlete** *n.*

decay[1] *v* **1** to rot or decompose because of the action of bacteria or fungi. **2** to decrease gradually in soundness or vigour; to deteriorate. **3** in physics, to undergo radioactive decay.

decay[2] *n* **1** the state or process of decaying. **2** the product of decay; rot or decomposition.

decease[1] *n formal* death.

decease[2] *v archaic* to die.

deceased[1] *n* (*pl* **deceased**) (**the deceased**) *formal* used to refer to somebody who has recently died.

deceased[2] *adj formal* recently dead.

deceit *n* **1** the act or practice of deceiving; deception. **2** an attempt to deceive. **3** the quality of being deceitful.

deceitful *adj* having a tendency or disposition to deceive; dishonest: *a deceitful child.* ➤➤ **deceitfully** *adv,* **deceitfulness** *n.*

Usage note

deceitful *or* **deceptive**? Generally speaking, only people can be described as *deceitful. Deceptive* is applied to things.

deceive *v* to cause to accept as true what is false; to delude. ➤➤ **deceivable** *adj,* **deceiver** *n.*

decelerate *v* to move or cause to move at decreasing speed. ➤➤ **deceleration** *n,* **decelerator** *n.*

December *n* the twelfth month of the year.

decency *n* (*pl* **-ies**) **1** behaviour that conforms to normal standards of morality, respectability, or civility. **2a** (*usu in pl*) a standard of propriety. **b** (*in pl*) the things considered necessary for an adequate standard of living.

decennial *adj* **1** lasting for ten years. **2** occurring every ten years. ➤➤ **decennial** *n,* **decennially** *adv.*

decent *adj* **1** conforming to normal standards of propriety, good taste, or morality. **2a** adequate or satisfactory. **b** *chiefly Brit, informal* obliging; considerate. **3** *informal* sufficiently clothed to be seen by somebody without impropriety. ➤➤ **decently** *adv.*

decentralize *or* **-ise** *v* to redistribute functions and powers from a central authority to regional authorities. ➤➤ **decentralist** *n and adj,* **decentralization** *n.*

deception *n* **1** the act of deceiving or the state of being deceived. **2** something that deceives; a trick.

deceptive *adj* tending or having the power to deceive; misleading: *Appearances can be deceptive.* ➤➤ **deceptively** *adv,* **deceptiveness** *n.*

Usage note

deceptive *or* **deceitful**? See note at DECEITFUL.

deci- *comb. form* denoting one tenth part of (the unit specified): *decilitre.*

decibel *n* **1** a unit for expressing the intensity of sounds. **2** a unit for expressing the power of an electric or acoustic signal.

decide *v* **1** to make a definite choice or come to a firm conclusion. **2** to make a judgment. **3** to influence (somebody) to make a choice or resolution. **4** to settle the outcome of. ➤➤ **decidable** *adj.*

decided *adj* **1** unquestionable. **2** free from doubt or hesitation. ➤➤ **decidedly** *adv,* **decidedness** *n.*

decider *n* a point or goal, or an additional contest, that decides the winner of a competition.

deciduous *adj* **1** of a tree: having leaves that are shed seasonally: compare EVERGREEN[1] (1). **2** of leaves, teeth, etc: shed at a particular stage in development. ➤➤ **deciduousness** *n.*

decigram *n* a metric unit of mass equal to one tenth of a gram (0.0035oz).

decilitre (*NAm* **deciliter**) *n* a metric unit of capacity equal to one tenth of a litre (about 0.18pt).

decimal[1] *adj* **1a** based on the number ten. **b** subdivided into units which are tenths, hundredths, etc of another unit. **c** expressed in a decimal fraction. **2** using a decimal system: *decimal currency.* ➤➤ **decimally** *adv.*

decimal[2] *n* a fraction that is expressed by writing a dot followed by digits for the number of tenths, hundredths, etc.

decimal fraction *n* = DECIMAL[2].

decimalize *or* **-ise** *v* **1** to express (a number) as a decimal. **2** to convert (e.g. currency) to a decimal system. ➤➤ **decimalization** *n.*

decimal place *n* the position of a digit to the right of a decimal point.

decimal point *n* the dot placed to the left of a decimal fraction, often between it and a whole number.

decimate *v* **1** to kill a large number of people from among (a group or population). **2** to destroy a large part of (something). ⋙ **decimation** *n*, **decimator** *n*.

Usage note

Historically, the word *decimate* refers to the practice in the Roman army of killing every tenth man in a mutinous unit in order to ensure loyalty of the rest. The word is now generally accepted as meaning 'kill or destroy a large number or part of something', but should not be used as a substitute for *annihilate* or *exterminate*.

decimetre (*NAm* **decimeter**) *n* a metric unit of length equal to one tenth of a metre (about 3.9in.).

decipher *v* **1** to convert (something coded) into intelligible form; to decode. **2** to make out the meaning of (something obscure). ⋙ **decipherable** *adj*, **decipherment** *n*.

decision *n* **1a** a choice or conclusion reached after considering various alternatives. **b** the act or process of deciding. **2** promptness and firmness in deciding.

decisive *adj* **1** of crucial importance in determining the outcome of something. **2** unambiguously settling an issue; conclusive. **3** having or showing the ability to make clear or firm decisions. ⋙ **decisively** *adv*, **decisiveness** *n*.

deck[1] *n* **1** a platform in a ship dividing the hull horizontally; *specif* the upper platform, open to the air. **2** something resembling the deck of a ship, e.g. the floor of a bus. **3a** the upper operating surface of a record player with the turntable on it. **b** = TAPE DECK. **4** *NAm* a pack of playing cards. **5** (**the deck**) *informal* the ground or floor. ✱ **clear the decks** to remove all objects or obstacles from an area or surface, *esp* in order to prepare for another activity.

deck[2] *v* **1** (*often* + out) to decorate or adorn. **2** *informal* to hit hard; to floor. **3** to add a deck to (a vessel).

deck chair *n* an adjustable folding chair made of canvas stretched over a wooden frame.

-decker *comb. form* forming nouns or adjectives, denoting: objects with the number of levels or layers specified: *a double-decker bus*.

deckhand *n* a seaman who performs manual duties.

decking *n* **1** an arrangement of planks forming a platform, e.g. in a garden. **2** material used to make a deck or decking.

deckle edge *n* a rough untrimmed edge of paper. ⋙ **deckle-edged** *adj*.

declaim *v* **1** to speak loudly and with dramatic or rhetorical expression. **2** to speak pompously or bombastically. ⋙ **declaimer** *n*.

declamation *n* **1** the art or act of declaiming. **2** a declamatory speech.

declamatory *adj* impassioned, rhetorical, or bombastic.

declaration *n* **1a** an emphatic announcement or formal statement. **b** a document containing a formal statement. **2** the act or an instance of declaring.

declarative *adj* **1** of a sentence: constituting a statement rather than a command or a question. **2** making a declaration. ⋙ **declaratively** *adv*.

declaratory *adj* serving to declare, set forth, or explain.

declare *v* **1** to make known formally or explicitly. **2** to make evident; to show. **3** to state emphatically; to affirm. **4** to make a full statement of (something taxable or dutiable): *I have nothing to declare except my genius* — Oscar Wilde. **5** of a cricket captain or team: to announce a decision to end the team's innings before all the batsmen are out. ✱ **declare war** to commence hostilities; *specif* to make a formal declaration of intention to go to war. ⋙ **declarable** *adj*, **declarer** *n*.

déclassé /day'klasay/ *adj* brought down to a lower social class or status.

declassify *v* (**-ies**, **-ied**) to declare (e.g. documents, information) no longer secret. ⋙ **declassification** *n*.

declension *n* **1** a schematic arrangement of noun, adjective, or pronoun inflections. **2** a class of nouns or adjectives having the same type of inflectional forms.

declination *n* **1** the angular distance, e.g. of a star, N or S from the celestial equator. **2** the angle between a compass needle and the geographical meridian, equal to the difference between magnetic and true north.

decline[1] *v* **1a** to become gradually less strong, effective, or good. **b** to become smaller or fewer in number; to diminish. **2** to refuse, *esp* courteously. **3a** to slope downwards; to descend. **b** to bend down; to droop. **4a** of a celestial body: to sink towards setting. **b** to draw towards a close; to wane. **5** in grammar, to list the inflectional forms of (a noun, pronoun, or adjective) in the prescribed order. ⋙ **declinable** *adj*, **decliner** *n*.

decline[2] *n* **1** a gradual reduction or change for the worse. **2** the period during which something is approaching its end.

declivity *n* (*pl* **-ies**) *formal* a descending slope. ⋙ **declivitous** *adj*.

declutch *v* to disengage the clutch of a motor vehicle or other machine.

decoction *n* **1** the extraction of the essence of a substance by boiling. **2** the concentrated liquor extracted.

decode *v* **1** to convert (a coded message) into intelligible language. **2** to convert (e.g. computer characters or electrical signals) from one coded form to another. ⋙ **decoder** *n*.

decoke *v Brit* to remove carbon deposits from (e.g. an internal-combustion engine).

décolletage /daykol'tahzh/ *n* the low-cut neckline of a dress.

décolleté[1] /daykol'tay, day'koltay/ *adj* of a dress: low-necked.

décolleté[2] *n* = DÉCOLLETAGE.

decolonize *or* **-ise** *v* to free from colonial status; to grant independence to. ⋙ **decolonization** *n*.

decommission *v* **1** to remove (a ship, weapon, etc) from service. **2** to shut down and abandon (a nuclear reactor).

decompose *v* **1** to decay or rot. **2** to separate into constituent parts, elements, atoms, etc. ⋙ **decomposition** *n*.

decompress *v* **1** to release from pressure or compression. **2** to expand (computer data) to its normal size after it has been compressed. ⋙ **decompression** *n*.

decompression chamber *n* a chamber in which air pressure can be gradually reduced to normal, used *esp* by deep-sea divers returning to the surface.

decompression sickness *n* a condition suffered *esp* by deep-sea divers, caused by the expansion of nitrogen bubbles in the blood and tissue after a rapid transfer from a pressurized environment.

decongestant *n* something, e.g. a drug, that relieves congestion. ➤➤ **decongestant** *adj.*

deconsecrate *v* to declare (a building or area) to be no longer sacred and return it to secular use. ➤➤ **deconsecration** *n.*

deconstruct *v* **1** to analyse (e.g. a film or text) by deconstruction. **2** to take to pieces; to dismantle. ➤➤ **deconstructive** *adj.*

deconstruction *n* a critical technique, e.g. in literary or film criticism, in which the implied unity of a work of art is dismantled to reveal a variety of possible interpretations. ➤➤ **deconstructionism** *n,* **deconstructionist** *n and adj.*

decontaminate *v* to rid of contamination, e.g. radioactivity. ➤➤ **decontamination** *n.*

decontextualize *or* **-ise** *v* to remove (something) from its context and consider it in isolation. ➤➤ **decontextualization** *n.*

decontrol *v* (**decontrolled, decontrolling**) to end control of (e.g. commodity prices). ➤➤ **decontrol** *n.*

decor *or* **décor** *n* **1** the style and layout of interior decoration and furnishings. **2** a stage setting.

decorate *v* **1a** to give (something) a more attractive appearance by adding colour or ornament. **b** to apply paint, wallpaper, etc to the surfaces of (a room or building). **2** to award a medal or other mark of honour to (somebody).

Decorated *adj* denoting a style of Gothic architecture prevalent in Britain from the late 13th to the mid 14th cent., characterized by elaborate ornamentation.

decoration *n* **1** the act or process of decorating. **2** an ornament. **3** a badge of honour, e.g. a medal.

decorative *adj* serving to decorate; ornamental. ➤➤ **decoratively** *adv,* **decorativeness** *n.*

decorator *n* somebody whose job is painting and wallpapering rooms or buildings.

decorous *adj* marked by propriety and good taste; decent or restrained. ➤➤ **decorously** *adv,* **decorousness** *n.*

decorum *n* behaviour that is in accordance with propriety and good taste.

decoupage /daykooh'pahzh/ *n* the art of applying decorative cutouts, e.g. of paper, to a surface.

decoy[1] *n* **1** something used to lure a person or animal into a trap. **2** somebody or something used to divert the attention, e.g. of an enemy. **3** a pond into which wildfowl are lured for capture.

decoy[2] *v* to lure by or as if by a decoy.

decrease[1] *v* to make or become progressively less in size, amount, number, or intensity. ➤➤ **decreasingly** *adv.*

decrease[2] *n* **1** the process of decreasing. **2** the amount by which something decreases.

decree[1] *n* **1** an order, *esp* one having legal force. **2** a judicial decision, *esp* in an equity, probate, or divorce court.

decree[2] *v* (**decrees, decreed, decreeing**) to command or impose by decree.

decree absolute *n* a decree making a divorce final.

decree nisi /'niesie/ *n* a provisional decree of divorce that is made absolute after a fixed period unless cause to the contrary is shown.

decrement *n* **1** a gradual decrease in quality or quantity. **2** the quantity lost by diminution or waste. **3** in physics, a measure of the amount by which an oscillator damps the oscillation of the alternating current that it produces, expressed as a ratio of successive amplitudes.

decrepit *adj* **1** weakened, *esp* by the infirmities of old age. **2a** worn-out. **b** fallen into ruin or disrepair. ➤➤ **decrepitude** *n.*

decretal /di'kreetl/ *n* an authoritative papal decision on a point of canon law.

decriminalize *or* **-ise** *v* to stop treating as a criminal offence; to legalize. ➤➤ **decriminalization** *n.*

decry *v* (**-ies, -ied**) to express strong disapproval of. ➤➤ **decrier** *n.*

decrypt *v* to decode (a cryptogram), *esp* without prior knowledge of the key. ➤➤ **decryption** *n.*

dedicate *v* **1** to make a solemn long-term commitment of (oneself or one's time) to a particular goal or way of life. **2a** to set apart for a specific use or purpose. **b** to set (e.g. a building) apart for a sacred purpose, e.g. the worship of God or the commemoration of a saint. **3** to inscribe or address (a book, song, etc) to somebody as a mark of esteem or affection. ➤➤ **dedicatee** *n,* **dedicative** *adj,* **dedicator** *n,* **dedicatory** *adj.*

dedicated *adj* **1** devoted to a cause, ideal, or purpose; zealous. **2** given over to a particular purpose. ➤➤ **dedicatedly** *adv.*

dedication *n* **1** the act of dedicating something. **2** words used to dedicate a book, song, etc to somebody. **3** commitment to achieving a particular purpose, ideal, etc.

deduce *v* to establish (a fact, the truth, etc) by reasoning and making use of the information available; *specif* to infer (a conclusion) from a general principle. ➤➤ **deducible** *adj.*

deduct *v* to subtract (an amount) from a total.

deductible *adj* that can be deducted, *esp* from income before taxation. ➤➤ **deductibility** *n.*

deduction *n* **1a** the act or an instance of deducting. **b** an amount that is or may be deducted. **2a** the act or practice of deducing. **b** a conclusion reached by the process of deducing. ➤➤ **deductive** *adj,* **deductively** *adv.*

deed[1] *n* **1** something that is done; an action. **2** an illustrious act or action; a feat or exploit. **3** in law, a document containing a transfer, bargain, or contract.

deed[2] *v NAm* to convey or transfer (e.g. property) by deed.

deed of covenant *n Brit* an agreement to pay a certain amount of money regularly, *esp* one that enables the recipient to reclaim the tax paid on the sum.

deed poll *n* (*pl* **deeds poll**) a deed made and executed by one party only, often used to change a person's name.

deejay *n informal* a disc jockey.

deem *v formal* to judge or consider to be as specified.

deemster *n* a High Court judge in the Isle of Man.

deep[1] *adj* **1a** extending far downwards, inwards, or back from a surface or area. **b** having a specified extension in this direction. **2a** of a colour: high in saturation and low in lightness; dark. **b** of a sound: having a low pitch. **3a** intellectually demanding or difficult to understand. **b** capable of serious and significant thought. **4** intense or extreme. **5** *informal* cunning or devious. **6** remote in time or space. **7** in sport, near or towards the outer limits of the playing area. ✱ **go off the deep end 1** to become very excited or angry. **2** *chiefly NAm* to enter recklessly on a course of action. **in deep water** in difficulty or distress; unable to manage. ➤➤ **deeply** *adv,* **deepness** *n.*

deep[2] *adv* **1** at or to a great depth. **2** in a deep position in sport. **3** far back in space or time.

deep[3] *n* **1a** (**the deep**) the sea. **b** any of the very deep portions of a body of water, *esp* the sea. **2** a vast or immeasurable extent; an abyss. **3** the middle or most intense part. **4** in cricket, the part of the playing area near the boundary and far from the batsman.

deepen *v* to make or become deeper or more profound.

deep freeze *n* a freezer.

deep-freeze *v* (*past tense* **deep-froze,** *past part.* **deep-frozen**) to freeze or store (e.g. food) in a freezer.

deep-fry *v* (**-ies, -ied**) to fry (food) by complete immersion in hot fat or oil. ➤➤ **deep-fryer** *n.*

deep-laid *adj* carefully and cunningly contrived.

deep-rooted *adj* firmly established; held or felt with great intensity or conviction.

deep sea *n* (*used before a noun*) of or in the deeper parts of the sea.

deep-seated *adj* firmly established and difficult to change or remove.

deep space *n* space well beyond the limits of the earth's atmosphere, including space outside the solar system.

deep vein thrombosis *n* the development of a blood clot in a deep-lying vein in the calf or thigh, caused especially by injury or inactivity, and sometimes giving rise to a pulmonary embolism.

deer *n* (*pl* **deers** *or* **deer**) a ruminant mammal that usu bears antlers, *esp* in the male.

deerhound *n* a tall dog of a rough-coated breed resembling the greyhound.

deerstalker *n* a close-fitting hat with peaks at the front and the back and ear-flaps.

de-escalate *v* **1** to reduce the intensity, extent, or scope of. **2** to decrease in intensity, extent, or scope. ➤➤ **de-escalation** *n.*

def *adj slang* excellent.

deface *v* to spoil the external appearance of. ➤➤ **defaceable** *adj,* **defacement** *n,* **defacer** *n.*

de facto[1] /day 'faktoh/ *adv* in reality; actually.

de facto[2] *adj* existing in fact; effective: compare DE JURE.

defalcate *v formal* to embezzle. ➤➤ **defalcation** *n,* **defalcator** *n.*

defame *v* to injure the reputation of (somebody) by libel or slander. ➤➤ **defamation** *n,* **defamatory** *adj,* **defamer** *n.*

default[1] *n* **1** failure to do something required by duty or law, e.g. to pay debts or to appear in a court. **2** failure to be present; absence. **3** an option or setting that has been pre-selected, e.g. in computing, and that remains in effect until it is overridden or cancelled. ✱ **by default** in the absence of an alternative. **in default of** in the absence of.

default[2] *v* **1** (*often* + on) to fail to meet an obligation, *esp* a financial one. **2** to fail to appear in court. **3** to revert to a pre-selected option or setting.

defaulter *n* **1** somebody who defaults. **2** *Brit* a member of the armed forces who commits a military offence.

defeasible *adj* capable of being annulled. ➤➤ **defeasibility** *n.*

defeat[1] *v* **1** to win a victory over. **2** to frustrate (e.g. a hope). **3** in law, to nullify.

defeat[2] *n* **1a** failure to win, or to achieve an aim. **b** a contest, battle, etc in which one is the loser. **2** the act or an instance of defeating somebody or something.

defeatism *n* acceptance of or resignation to defeat. ➤➤ **defeatist** *n and adj.*

defecate *v* to discharge faeces from the bowels. ➤➤ **defecation** *n,* **defecator** *n,* **defecatory** *adj.*

defect[1] *n* **1** an imperfection that impairs the worth or usefulness of something; a fault or shortcoming. **2** a deficiency.

defect[2] *v* to desert a cause or party, often in favour of another. ➤➤ **defection** *n,* **defector** *n.*

defective *adj* **1** having a defect and unable to function properly; faulty: *defective brakes.* **2** in grammar, lacking one or more of the usual inflections. ➤➤ **defectively** *adv,* **defectiveness** *n.*

Usage note

defective *or* **deficient**? These two words are close together in meaning and can sometimes be used to describe the same thing, but there is a significant difference between them. *Defective* is applied to functioning things that fail to function properly: a *defective* component is faulty and does not work: *defective brakes. Deficient* primarily means 'lacking' or 'inadequate': *a diet deficient in the vitamins necessary for healthy growth.*

defence (*NAm* **defense**) *n* **1a** the act or an instance of defending. **b** a means or method of defending. **2a** an argument in support or justification. **b** a defendant's answer or strategy. **3** (*in pl*) a defensive structure. **4** (*used as sing. or pl*) **a** a defending party or group, e.g. in a court of law. **b** in sport, defending players or moves. **5** the military resources of a country. ➤➤ **defenceless** *adj,* **defencelessly** *adv,* **defencelessness** *n.*

defence mechanism *n* **1** a reaction used by a living organism to defend itself against bacteria and viruses. **2** a mental process that prevents the entry of unacceptable or painful thoughts into consciousness.

defend *v* **1a** to protect from attack. **b** to attempt to retain (a military position, sporting title, or parliamentary seat) in the face of efforts by others to gain it. **2** to maintain (something) by argument in the face of opposition or criticism. **3** in sport, to attempt to prevent an opponent from scoring, e.g. by protecting a goal. **4** to act as legal representative in court for. ➤➤ **defendable** *adj,* **defender** *n.*

defendant *n* a party against whom a criminal charge or civil claim is made: compare PLAINTIFF.

defenestration *n chiefly humorous* the act of throwing somebody out of a window.

defensible *adj* capable of being defended by argument or in a war. ➤➤ **defensibility** *n,* **defensibly** *adv.*

defensive *adj* **1a** serving to defend. **b** devoted to resisting or preventing aggression, attack, criticism, etc. **2** sensitive to anticipated criticism and eager to defend one's own actions or views. ✱ **on the defensive** having to defend oneself against attack or criticism. ➤➤ **defensively** *adv,* **defensiveness** *n.*

defer[1] *v* (**deferred, deferring**) to postpone (an action, decision, etc). ➤➤ **deferment** *n,* **deferrable** *adj,* **deferral** *n.*

defer[2] *v* (**deferred, deferring**) (*usu* + to) to acknowledge somebody else's superiority or allow their opinion to prevail.

deference *n* **1** the respect due to a superior or an elder. **2** compliance with the wishes or opinion of another.

deferential *adj* **1** showing or expressing deference; respectful. **2** showing or expressing excessive deference; obsequious. ➤➤ **deferentially** *adv.*

defiance *n* bold resistance or disobedience. ➤➤ **defiant** *adj,* **defiantly** *adv.*

defibrillation *n* the restoration of the normal regular beating and rhythm of the heart.

defibrillator *n* an apparatus used to apply an electric current to the heart to restore its normal rhythm.

deficiency *n* (*pl* **-ies**) **1** being deficient; inadequacy. **2** a lack or shortage.

deficiency disease *n* a disease caused by a lack of essential vitamins, minerals, etc in the diet.

deficient *adj* **1** (*usu* + in) lacking in some necessary quality or element: *a diet deficient in minerals.* **2** not up to a normal standard or complement; inadequate. ➤➤ **deficiently** *adv.*

Usage note
deficient *or* **defective**? See note at DEFECTIVE.

deficit *n* **1** a deficiency in amount or quality. **2** an excess of expenditure over revenue or of liabilities over assets.

defilade[1] *v* to arrange (fortifications) so as to protect the lines from enemy fire.

defilade[2] *n* the act or process of defilading.

defile[1] *v* to make unclean or impure. ➤➤ **defilement** *n,* **defiler** *n.*

defile[2] *n* a narrow passage or gorge.

define *v* **1a** to describe the essential quality or nature of; to identify. **b** to set forth the meaning of (e.g. a word). **2a** to fix or mark the limits of; to demarcate. **b** to make clear or precise in outline. ➤➤ **definable** *adj,* **definer** *n.*

definite *adj* **1a** free of all ambiguity or uncertainty. **b** clearly apparent; unquestionable. **2** having distinct or certain limits. ➤➤ **definitely** *adv,* **definiteness** *n.*

Usage note
definite *or* **definitive**? These two words are sometimes confused. Both *definite* and *definitive* suggest that something is unlikely to be changed: a *definite* answer is clear, firm, and unambiguous; a *definite* date is one that has been decided on and fixed by the people involved. *Definitive* has connotations of being authoritative and conclusive: the *definitive* answer to a problem is one that solves it once and for all. If someone writes a *definitive* biography or plays the *definitive* Hamlet, that person's book or performance becomes the standard by which all later ones are judged.

definite article *n* in grammar, a word (*the* in English) that designates an immediately identifiable person or thing: compare INDEFINITE ARTICLE.

definition *n* **1** a statement of what a word or phrase means. **2** the act or an instance of defining. **3a** distinctness of outline or detail, e.g. in a photograph. **b** clarity of musical sound in reproduction. ➤➤ **definitional** *adj.*

definitive[1] *adj* **1a** serving to provide a final solution. **b** serving to define something. **2** authoritative and apparently exhaustive. **3** issued as one of the normal postage stamps of a country, rather than for commemorative purposes. ➤➤ **definitively** *adv.*

Usage note
definitive *or* **definite**? See note at DEFINITE.

definitive[2] *n* a definitive postage stamp.

deflate *v* **1** to release air or gas from (e.g. a balloon or a tyre). **2** to reduce (somebody) in self-confidence or self-importance, *esp* suddenly. **3** to cause deflation in (an economy or price levels). ➤➤ **deflator** *n.*

deflation *n* **1a** the act or an instance of deflating. **b** the state of being deflated. **2a** a contraction in the volume of available money and credit, and a resulting decline in economic activity, *esp* as a result of government policy. **b** a decline in the general level of prices. ➤➤ **deflationary** *adj,* **deflationist** *n and adj.*

deflect *v* to turn from a straight course or fixed purpose. ➤➤ **deflective** *adj,* **deflector** *n.*

deflection *or* **deflexion** *n* **1** the act of deflecting or the condition of being deflected. **2** the amount by which something is deflected.

defloration *n* deflowering or being deflowered.

deflower *v dated or literary* to deprive (a woman) of her virginity.

defoliant *n* a chemical applied to plants to cause the leaves to drop off prematurely.

defoliate *v* to deprive (a tree or an area) of leaves, *esp* prematurely or as a tactic in warfare. ➤➤ **defoliation** *n,* **defoliator** *n.*

deforest *v* to clear (an area) of forests. ➤➤ **deforestation** *n.*

deform *v* **1** to spoil the form or appearance of. **2** to make ugly or monstrous. **3** to become misshapen or changed in shape, *esp* by stress. ➤➤ **deformable** *adj,* **deformation** *n,* **deformational** *adj.*

deformed *adj* distorted or unshapely in form.

deformity *n* (*pl* **-ies**) **1a** the state of being deformed. **b** a deformed person or thing. **2** a physical blemish or distortion; a disfigurement. **3** a moral or aesthetic flaw or defect.

defraud *v* to cheat (somebody) of something, *esp* money. ➤➤ **defrauder** *n.*

defray *v* to provide for the payment of (an expense). ➤➤ **defrayable** *adj,* **defrayal** *n,* **defrayment** *n.*

defrock *v* to unfrock (e.g. a priest).

defrost *v* **1** to thaw out (food) from a frozen state. **2** to free (a refrigerator or freezer) from ice.

deft *adj* marked by facility and skill; nimble. ➤➤ **deftly** *n,* **deftness** *n.*

defunct *adj* **1** no longer existing or in use. **2** dead; extinct.

defuse *v* **1** to remove the fuse from (a mine, bomb, etc). **2** to make (a situation) less harmful, potent, or tense.

defy *v* (**-ies, -ied**) **1** to resist by refusing to obey. **2** to challenge to do something considered impossible; to dare. **3** to resist attempts at (something). ➤➤ **defier** *n.*

dégagé /dayga'zhay/ *adj* **1** free and easy in manner; nonchalant; unconcerned. **2** politically uncommitted.

degauss *v* to demagnetize, *esp* to demagnetize (a steel ship) as a protection against magnetic mines. ➤➤ **degausser** *n.*

degenerate[1] *adj* having sunk to a lower and usu morally or physically corrupt state. ➤➤ **degeneracy** *n,* **degenerately** *adv.*

degenerate[2] *n* a degenerate person.

degenerate[3] *v* to pass from a higher to a lower state; to deteriorate. ➤➤ **degeneration** *n,* **degenerative** *adj.*

deglaze *v* to add wine, cream, stock, etc to (a pan in which food has been cooked) in order to dilute the residue and make a sauce.

degradation *n* **1a** the process of degrading or being degraded. **b** a humiliating action or condition. **2** a state of physical or moral debasement or squalor. **3** a gradual loss of quality or deterioration in performance.

degrade *v* **1** to cause to lose self-respect or the respect of others; to demean. **2** to reduce the quality of. **3** *archaic* to lower in grade, rank, or status; to demote. **4** in chemistry, to decompose (a compound). **5** in geology, to wear (rocks) down by erosion. **6** to decompose or disintegrate. ➤➤ **degradable** *adj*, **degrader** *n*.

degrading *adj* humiliating; debasing. ➤➤ **degradingly** *adv*.

degree *n* **1a** the extent or measure of an action, condition, or relation. **b** an amount or measure. **2a** a division or interval of a scale of measurement; *specif* a unit for measuring temperature. **b** a 360th part of the circumference of a circle. **3** a stage in a process or order of classification. **4** an academic title conferred *esp* on university students. **5** rank or status. **6** in law, a measure of guilt or negligence. **7** in medicine, a measure of damage caused to tissue by burning. ✱ **by degrees** gradually. **to a degree 1** to some extent; somewhat. **2** to a remarkable extent.

de haut en bas /də ˌoh on(h) 'bah/ *adj and adv* with a superior or condescending manner.

dehisce *v* of seedpods, etc: to split open; to discharge the contents by splitting. ➤➤ **dehiscence** *n*, **dehiscent** *adj*.

dehumanize *or* **-ise** *v* to deprive of human qualities or personality. ➤➤ **dehumanization** *n*.

dehumidify *v* (**-ies, -ied**) to remove moisture from (e.g. air). ➤➤ **dehumidification** *n*, **dehumidifier** *n*.

dehydrate *v* **1** to remove water from (a chemical compound, foodstuff, etc). **2** to cause to lose water or body fluids. ➤➤ **dehydrated** *adj*, **dehydration** *n*, **dehydrator** *n*.

de-ice *v* to keep free from ice or rid of ice.

de-icer *n* **1** a substance used to remove ice or frost from a windscreen. **2** a device used to remove ice from, or prevent the formation of ice on, the outer surface of an aircraft.

dei ex machina *n* pl of DEUS EX MACHINA.

deify /'deeifie, 'day-/ *v* (**-ies, -ied**) **1** to make a god of. **2** to take as an object of worship. ➤➤ **deification** *n*.

deign *v* to see fit to act in a less dignified, haughty, or indifferent way than usual; to condescend.

de-industrialization *or* **-isation** *n* the loss of industrial capability or strength.

deionize *or* **-ise** *v* to remove ions from (*esp* water). ➤➤ **deionization** *n*, **deionizer** *n*.

deism /'deeiz(ə)m, 'day-/ *n* a movement or system of thought advocating natural religion based on human reason rather than revelation; *specif* a doctrine asserting that God created the universe but does not intervene in its functioning. ➤➤ **deist** *n*, **deistic** *adj*, **deistical** *adj*, **deistically** *adv*.

deity /'deeiti, 'day-/ *n* (*pl* **-ies**) **1** a god or goddess. **2a** the rank or essential nature of a god. **b** (**the Deity**) the Supreme Being; God. **3** somebody exalted or revered as supremely good or powerful.

déjà vu /ˌdayzhah 'vooh/ *n* **1** the illusion of remembering scenes and events when they are experienced for the first time. **2** something excessively or unpleasantly familiar.

dejected *adj* cast down in spirits; depressed. ➤➤ **dejectedly** *adv*.

dejection *n* lowness of spirits; depression or melancholy.

de jure /di 'jooəri/ *adv and adj* by right, *esp* full legal right: compare DE FACTO².

dekko *n Brit, informal* a look or glance.

Del. *abbr* Delaware.

Delaware *n* a member of a Native American people of New Jersey and eastern Pennsylvania.

delay¹ *n* **1** the act or an instance of delaying or being delayed. **2** the time during which something is delayed.

delay² *v* **1** to leave or put off to a later time; to postpone. **2** to stop, detain, or hinder for a time. **3** to fail to act or move immediately. ➤➤ **delayer** *n*.

dele¹ /'deeli/ *v* (**deles, deled, deleing**) in printing, to delete (e.g. a character) from typeset matter.

dele² *n* any of several proofreading marks used to indicate a deletion from a text.

delectable *adj* **1** highly pleasing; delightful. **2** of food: delicious. ➤➤ **delectability** *n*, **delectableness** *n*, **delectably** *adv*.

delectation *n formal* delight or enjoyment.

delegacy *n* (*pl* **-ies**) **1a** the act of delegating. **b** an appointment as delegate. **2** (*used as sing. or pl*) a body of delegates; a board.

delegate¹ *n* **1** a person delegated to represent or act for somebody else, e.g. at a conference. **2** a representative of a territory of the USA in the House of Representatives.

delegate² *v* **1** to entrust (e.g. a duty or responsibility) to another. **2** to appoint (somebody) as one's representative. **3** to assign responsibility or authority to other people.

delegation *n* **1** (*used as sing. or pl*) a group of people chosen to represent others. **2** the act of delegating or the process of being delegated.

delete *v* to eliminate by crossing out, cutting out, or erasing. ➤➤ **deletion** *n*.

deleterious /deli'tiəri·əs/ *adj formal* harmful or detrimental. ➤➤ **deleteriously** *adv*, **deleteriousness** *n*.

delft *n* glazed Dutch earthenware with blue and white or polychrome decoration.

delftware *n* = DELFT.

deli *n* (*pl* **delis**) *informal* = DELICATESSEN .

deliberate¹ *adj* **1** characterized by awareness of the nature of the action involved and of its consequences; intentional or wilful. **2** resulting from careful and thorough consideration. **3** slow or unhurried. ➤➤ **deliberately** *adv*, **deliberateness** *n*.

deliberate² *v* to ponder and often discuss carefully and thoroughly before reaching a decision. ➤➤ **deliberator** *n*.

deliberation *n* **1a** careful and serious thought. **b** a discussion and consideration of pros and cons. **2** slow and careful movement or action. ➤➤ **deliberative** *adj*, **deliberatively** *adv*, **deliberativeness** *n*.

delicacy *n* (*pl* **-ies**) **1** something pleasing to eat that is considered rare or luxurious. **2a** daintiness. **b** frailty or fragility. **3a** refined sensibility in feeling or conduct; tact. **b** avoidance of anything offensive or disturbing; squeamishness. **4** precise and refined perception or discrimination.

delicate *adj* **1a** very finely made. **b** easily damaged; fragile. **2a** pleasing to the senses in a mild or subtle way. **b** dainty. **3a** marked by extreme precision. **b** having or showing extreme sensitivity. **4** requiring meticulously careful treatment. **5** marked by or requiring tact. **6** weak or sickly. **7** fastidious or squeamish. ➤➤ **delicately** *adv*, **delicateness** *n*.

delicatessen *n* a shop where delicacies and foreign foods, e.g. cooked meats, are sold.

delicious *adj* **1** highly pleasing to the sense of taste. **2** affording great pleasure; delightful. ➤➤ **deliciously** *adv*, **deliciousness** *n*.

delight¹ *v* **1** to take great pleasure in doing something. **2** to give enjoyment or satisfaction to.

delight² *n* **1** great pleasure or satisfaction; joy. **2** something that gives great pleasure.

delighted *adj* highly pleased. ➤➤ **delightedly** *adv*.

delightful *adj* highly pleasing; charming. ⋙ **delightfully** *adv,* **delightfulness** *n.*

delimit *v* (**delimited, delimiting**) to fix the limits of. ⋙ **delimitation** *n.*

delineate *v* **1** to draw lines in the shape of; to portray. **2** to describe in sharp or vivid detail. ⋙ **delineation** *n.*

delinquency *n* (*pl* **-ies**) **1** antisocial or illegal conduct, *esp* by young people. **2** an offence or crime. **3** failure to fulfil one's obligations.

delinquent[1] *n* somebody who has behaved in an antisocial or criminal way, *esp* a young person.

delinquent[2] *adj* **1** guilty of wrongdoing or of neglect of duty. **2** marked by delinquency. ⋙ **delinquently** *adv.*

deliquesce *v* **1** to melt away. **2** of a compound: to dissolve gradually in water attracted and absorbed from the air. ⋙ **deliquescence** *n,* **deliquescent** *adj.*

delirious *adj* **1** suffering from or characteristic of delirium. **2** wildly joyful; ecstatic. ⋙ **deliriously** *adv,* **deliriousness** *n.*

delirium *n* **1** confusion, disordered speech, hallucinations, etc, occurring as a mental disturbance. **2** frenzied excitement or emotion.

delirium tremens *n* a violent delirium with tremors induced by chronic alcoholism.

deliver *v* **1a** to bring or take to a specified place or person. **b** (*often* + up) to hand over formally; to surrender. **2** to guide (e.g. a blow) to an intended target. **3** to utter or announce (a speech, verdict, etc) formally. **4** to set (somebody) free. **5a** to assist in the birth of (a baby). **b** to assist (a woman) in giving birth. **6** (*often* **be delivered of**) to give birth to (a baby). **7** to take goods purchased or ordered to customers' homes. **8** *informal* to produce the promised, desired, or expected results. ✱ **deliver the goods** *informal* to do what has been promised. ⋙ **deliverable** *adj,* **deliverer** *n.*

deliverance *n* **1** liberation or rescue. **2** *formal* an opinion or verdict expressed publicly.

delivery *n* (*pl* **-ies**) **1a** the act or an instance of delivering something. **b** something delivered at one time. **2** the act of giving birth. **3** the manner or style in which a speech is spoken. **4** an instance of throwing or bowling, *esp* in cricket. **5** liberation or rescue.

dell *n* a small secluded hollow or valley, *esp* in a forest.

delouse *v* to remove lice from (a person or an animal).

Delphic *adj* **1** (*also* **delphic**) of an utterance: ambiguous, obscure, or enigmatic. **2** relating to ancient Delphi or its oracle. ⋙ **delphically** *adv.*

delphinium *n* (*pl* **delphiniums**) a garden plant of the buttercup family with deeply cut leaves and blue or purple flowers in showy spikes.

delta *n* **1** a triangular alluvial deposit at the mouth of a river. **2** the fourth letter of the Greek alphabet (Δ, δ), equivalent to roman d. ⋙ **deltaic** *adj.*

delta rhythm *n* the electrical activity of the brain during deep sleep.

delta wave *n* = DELTA RHYTHM.

delta wing *n* an approximately triangular aircraft wing with a nearly straight rearmost edge.

deltiology *n* the hobby of collecting and studying postcards. ⋙ **deltiologist** *n.*

deltoid *n* a large triangular muscle covering the shoulder joint and acting to raise the arm to the side.

delude *v* to mislead the mind or judgment of; to deceive or trick. ⋙ **deluder** *n.*

deluge[1] *n* **1** a great flood. **2** (**the Deluge**) the Flood recorded in the Old Testament (Genesis 6:8). **3** a drenching fall of rain. **4** an overwhelming amount or number.

deluge[2] *v* **1** to overwhelm or swamp (somebody). **2** to flood (something).

delusion *n* **1a** a false belief or impression. **b** a mental state characterized by false beliefs that persist despite the contrary evidence of fact. **2** the act of deluding or the state of being deluded. ⋙ **delusional** *adj.*

delusive *adj* giving a false impression; misleading or deceptive. ⋙ **delusively** *adv,* **delusiveness** *n.*

delusory *adj* = DELUSIVE.

de luxe *adj* notably luxurious or elegant; of a superior quality.

delve *v* **1** to make a careful or detailed search for information. **2** to reach inside something and search about in it; to rummage. **3** *archaic* to dig.

Dem. *abbr NAm* **1** Democrat. **2** Democratic.

demagnetize *or* **-ise** *v* to remove magnetic properties or a magnetic field from. ⋙ **demagnetization** *n,* **demagnetizer** *n.*

demagogue (*NAm* **demagog**) *n* **1** an agitator who makes use of popular prejudices in order to gain power. **2** a leader of the common people in ancient times. ⋙ **demagogic** *adj,* **demagoguery** *n,* **demagogy** *n.*

demand[1] *n* **1a** an act of demanding; a claim. **b** (*in pl*) requirements. **2** desire or need. **3** in economics, the quantity of a commodity or service wanted at a specified price and time: compare SUPPLY[2]. ✱ **in demand** sought after; popular. **on demand** whenever the demand is made.

demand[2] *v* **1** to ask for in an authoritative or peremptory way; to claim as due or just. **2** to call for urgently or insistently. **3** to require. ⋙ **demander** *n.*

demanding *adj* **1** needing much effort or skill; exacting. **2** difficult to please, *esp* requiring hard work or high standards from other people. ⋙ **demandingly** *adv.*

demarcate *v* **1** to mark the limits of. **2** to set (things) apart; to separate.

demarcation *or* **demarkation** *n* **1** the marking of limits or boundaries. **2** *Brit* the separation of areas of work to be carried out by members of particular trade unions.

Word history

The word was orig used in the phrase *line of demarcation* (translating Spanish *linea de demarcación* and Portuguese *linha de demarcação*), a line fixed by the pope in 1493 which separated Spanish and Portuguese territories in the New World.

dematerialize *or* **-ise** *v* to lose material form or qualities; to vanish.

demean[1] *v* to degrade or debase (somebody or oneself).

demean[2] *v archaic* to behave or conduct (oneself).

demeanour (*NAm* **demeanor**) *n* behaviour towards others; outward manner.

demented *adj* insane; crazy. ⋙ **dementedly** *adv,* **dementedness** *n.*

dementia *n* a state of chronic impairment of mental functions caused by damage to or deterioration of the brain and characterized by memory failure and personality changes.

dementia praecox /'preekoks/ *n* = SCHIZOPHRENIA.

demerara sugar *n* brown crystallized unrefined cane sugar from the W Indies.

demerge *v* to split up (a conglomerate formed by a previous merger) into separate companies. ➤➤ **demerger** *n.*

demerit *n* **1** a quality that deserves blame or lacks merit; a fault or defect. **2** *NAm* a bad mark given to an offender.

demersal *adj* of fish: living near the bottom of the sea: compare PELAGIC.

demesne /di'mayn, di'meen/ *n* **1** land surrounding a manor that is occupied by the owner and not held by tenants. **2** legal possession of land as one's own. **3** landed property; an estate. **4** a region or realm.

demi- *prefix* **1** half: *demisemiquaver.* **2** denoting a person or thing partly belonging to the specified class: *demigod.*

demigod *or* **demigoddess** *n* **1a** a mythological superhuman being with less power than a god. **b** an offspring of a union between a mortal and a god. **2** a person so outstanding that they seem to approach the divine.

demijohn *n* a large narrow-necked bottle.

demilitarize *or* **-ise** *v* to strip (an area) of military forces, weapons, etc. ➤➤ **demilitarization** *n.*

demimondaine *n* a woman of the demimonde.

demimonde *n* (*used as sing. or pl*) **1** a class of women, *esp* in the 19th cent., who were on the fringes of respectable society, generally consisting of courtesans and kept women. **2** a group engaged in activity of doubtful legality or propriety.

demineralize *or* **-ise** *v* to remove the mineral matter from (e.g. water). ➤➤ **demineralization** *n.*

demi-pension /demi'ponhsyonh/ *n* in French-speaking countries, hotel accommodation providing bed, breakfast and a main meal per day; = HALF-BOARD.

demise *n* **1a** *technical or euphem* death. **b** the end of something, e.g. an industry or enterprise. **2a** the conveyance of an estate by a will or lease. **b** the transfer of sovereignty by succession or inheritance.

demi-sec /demi'sek/ *adj* of wine: medium dry.

demisemiquaver *n* a musical note with the time value of half a semiquaver or a quarter of a quaver.

demist *v Brit* to remove mist from (e.g. a car windscreen). ➤➤ **demister** *n.*

demiurge *n* **1** a deity who, according to the philosophy of Plato, is the creator of the material universe. **2** a Gnostic deity who is the creator of the material world but is inferior to the supreme being. ➤➤ **demiurgic** *adj,* **demiurgical** *adj.*

demi-vegetarian *n* a person who avoids red meat but occasionally eats white meat and fish.

demo *n* (*pl* **demos**) **1** *informal* **a** = DEMONSTRATION (2). **b** (*used before a noun*) used for the purposes of demonstration. **c** a version of a computer game or piece of recorded music used for demonstration purposes. **2** (**Demo**) *NAm* = DEMOCRAT (2).

demob[1] *v* (**demobbed, demobbing**) *chiefly Brit, informal* to demobilize (troops).

demob[2] *n chiefly Brit, informal* demobilization.

demobilize *or* **-ise** *v* to disband (troops) or to release (somebody) at the end of a period of military service. ➤➤ **demobilization** *n.*

democracy *n* (*pl* **-ies**) **1a** a form of government in which the supreme power is exercised by the people, usu through a system of representation involving free elections. **b** a state governed in this way. **2** the absence of class distinctions or privileges in a society. **3** control of a group by its own members or the will of a majority of them.

democrat *n* **1** an adherent of democracy. **2** (**Democrat**) a member of the Democratic party of the USA.

democratic *adj* **1** of or favouring democracy or social equality. **2** (*often* **Democratic**) denoting a political party of the USA associated with policies of social reform and internationalism. ➤➤ **democratically** *adv.*

democratize *or* **-ise** *v* to make (a state or organization) democratic. ➤➤ **democratization** *n,* **democratizer** *n.*

démodé /daymoh'day/ *adj* no longer fashionable; out-of-date.

demodulate *v* to extract information, e.g. a video signal, from (a modulated carrier wave). ➤➤ **demodulation** *n,* **demodulator** *n.*

demographic timebomb *n* a marked increase or decrease in the present birthrate that is expected to cause very serious social problems in the future.

demography *n* the statistical study of human populations, *esp* with reference to size and density, distribution, and vital statistics. ➤➤ **demographer** *n,* **demographic** *adj,* **demographically** *adv.*

demoiselle /demwah'zel/ *n archaic or literary* a young lady.

demolish *v* **1** to destroy, smash, or tear down. **2** to defeat or refute (an argument). **3** *informal* to devour (food). ➤➤ **demolisher** *n.*

demolition *n* the act or an instance of demolishing. ➤➤ **demolitionist** *n.*

demon[1] *n* **1a** an evil supernatural being; a devil. **b** an evil or cruel person. **2a** somebody who has unusual drive or effectiveness. **b** (*used before a noun*) very forceful or enthusiastic. **3** *Aus, NZ* a police officer, *esp* in plain clothes. **4** = DAEMON (1), (2).

demon[2] *n* in computing, a background process that performs operations such as spooling.

demonetize *or* **-ise** *v* to stop using (a metal) as a money standard. ➤➤ **demonetization** *n.*

demoniac[1] *adj* **1** = DEMONIC. **2** possessed or influenced by a demon. ➤➤ **demoniacally** *adv.*

demoniac[2] *n* somebody regarded as possessed by a demon.

demoniacal *adj* = DEMONIAC[1].

demonic *adj* **1** of or resembling a demon or evil spirit. **2** intense or frenzied. ➤➤ **demonically** *adv.*

demonize *or* **-ise** *v* to make (somebody or something) seem evil or wicked. ➤➤ **demonization** *n.*

demonolatry *n* the worship of demons.

demonology *n* the study of or belief in demons. ➤➤ **demonologist** *n.*

demonstrable *adj* capable of being demonstrated. ➤➤ **demonstrability** *n,* **demonstrably** *adv.*

demonstrate *v* **1** to show (something) clearly. **2** to prove or make clear by reasoning, evidence, or example. **3** to give a demonstration of (an action or process). **4** to show the merits of (e.g. a car) to a prospective buyer. **5** to take part in a demonstration. ➤➤ **demonstrator** *n.*

demonstration *n* **1** the act or an instance of demonstrating. **2** a mass meeting, procession, etc to display group feelings, e.g. about grievances or political issues.

demonstrative[1] *adj* **1a** inclined to display feelings openly. **b** expressing a feeling or intention clearly. **2** (+ of) demonstrating something to be real or true. **3** of a pronoun or determiner: pointing out the particular person or thing referred to and distinguishing him, her, or it from others of the same class. ⪢ **demonstratively** *adv,* **demonstrativeness** *n.*

demonstrative[2] *n* in grammar, a demonstrative word or morpheme.

demoralize *or* **-ise** *v* to weaken the morale or self-respect of; to discourage or dispirit. ⪢ **demoralization** *n,* **demoralizing** *adj.*

demote *v* to reduce to a lower grade or rank. ⪢ **demotion** *n.*

demotic[1] *adj* **1** of language: typical of the common people; popular. **2** denoting or written in the language spoken in modern Greece.

demotic[2] *n* **1** demotic language. **2** demotic Greek.

demotivate *v* to make (somebody) less motivated to do something. ⪢ **demotivation** *n.*

demount *v* **1** to remove (e.g. a gun) from a mounting. **2** to disassemble or dismantle. ⪢ **demountable** *adj.*

demur[1] *v* (**demurred, demurring**) to show hesitation or to raise doubts or objections about accepting something. ⪢ **demurral** *n.*

demur[2] *n* hesitation or objection.

demure *adj* (**demurer, demurest**) **1** reserved or modest. **2** affectedly modest, shy, or serious; coy. ⪢ **demurely** *adv,* **demureness** *n.*

demurrer *n* a legal objection that assumes the truth of the matter alleged by the opponent, but asserts that it is insufficient in law to sustain the opponent's claim.

demutualize *or* **-ise** *v* **1** of a building society or insurance company: to change from being run on mutual principles to being a public limited company. **2** to change (e.g. a building society) in this way. ⪢ **demutualization** *n.*

demystify *v* (**-ies, -ied**) to eliminate the mystery from; to clarify. ⪢ **demystification** *n.*

demythologize *or* **-ise** *v* to eliminate the mythical elements or associations of (a belief, tradition, etc).

den *n* **1** the lair of a wild, usu predatory, animal. **2** a centre of secret, *esp* unlawful, activity: *an opium den.* **3** a comfortable usu secluded room.

denar /'deenə/ *n* the basic monetary unit of Macedonia.

denarii /di'neəriie/ *n* pl of DENARIUS.

denarius /di'neəri·əs/ *n* (*pl* **denarii**) a small silver coin of ancient Rome.

denary *adj* of a system of numbers having ten as its base; decimal.

denationalize *or* **-ise** *v* **1** to remove (something) from ownership or control by the state. **2** to divest (a person or a country) of national status, character, or rights. ⪢ **denationalization** *n.*

denature *v* **1** to take away the natural qualities of (something or somebody). **2a** to modify (e.g. a protein) by heat, acid, etc so that some of the original structure of the molecule is lost and its properties are changed. **b** to make (alcohol) unfit for drinking, e.g. by adding an obnoxious substance. ⪢ **denaturation** *n.*

dendrite *n* a branching extension from a nerve cell that conducts impulses towards the cell body. ⪢ **dendritic** *adj.*

dendrochronology *n* the dating of events and variations in climate by comparative study of the annual growth rings in wood. ⪢ **dendrochronological** *adj,* **dendrochronologist** *n.*

dene *n* see DEAN[2].

dengue /'denggi/ *n* an infectious short-lasting viral disease transmitted by mosquitoes and characterized by a headache and pain in the joints.

deni /'deeni/ *n* (*pl* **deni**) a unit of currency in Macedonia, worth 100th of a denar.

deniable *adj* capable of being denied.

denial *n* **1** a refusal to satisfy a request or desire. **2a** a refusal to admit the truth or reality, e.g. of a statement or charge. **b** an assertion that an allegation is false. **3** a refusal to acknowledge somebody or something; a disavowal. **4** self-denial. **5** in psychology, an unconscious refusal to acknowledge feelings or thoughts that may be painful.

denier *n* a unit of fineness for silk, rayon, or nylon yarn equal to the fineness of a yarn weighing 1g for each 9000m.

denigrate *v* to make negative or critical statements, usu unjustly, about (somebody or something). ⪢ **denigration** *n,* **denigrator** *n,* **denigratory** *adj.*

denim *n* **1** a firm durable twilled usu blue cotton fabric used for jeans and work clothes. **2** *informal* (*in pl*) denim clothes; *esp* blue jeans.

denizen *n* **1** *literary or humorous* an inhabitant or resident. **2** somebody who is allowed to live in a foreign country.

denominate *v formal* to give a name to (somebody or something).

denomination *n* **1** a religious organization or sect. **2** a grade or degree in a series of values or sizes, e.g. of money. **3** a name or designation; *esp* a general name for a category.

denominational *adj* belonging or relating to a particular religious denomination.

denominationalism *n* the narrowly exclusive emphasizing of denominational differences.

denominator *n* the part of a vulgar fraction that is below the line and that indicates how many parts the numerator is divided into; a divisor.

denotation *n* **1** an act or process of denoting. **2** a meaning; *esp* a direct specific meaning as distinct from a suggested or implied meaning. **3** a denoting term; a name. **4** a sign or indication.

denote *v* **1** to signify or indicate: *Their swollen bellies denote starvation.* **2** to be a sign or mark for; to symbolize: *Red denotes danger.* **3** to have the meaning of or mean (something). ⪢ **denotative** *adj.*

denouement /day'noohmonh/ *n* the final part of a literary work in which all the complications of the plot are resolved.

denounce *v* **1** to condemn (somebody), *esp* publicly, as deserving censure or punishment. **2** to inform against or accuse. ⪢ **denouncement** *n,* **denouncer** *n.*

dense *adj* **1** marked by high density, compactness, or crowding together of parts. **2** *informal* dull; stupid. **3** demanding concentration if it is to be followed or understood: *dense prose.* ⪢ **densely** *adv,* **denseness** *n.*

density *n* (*pl* **-ies**) **1** the quantity or state of being dense. **2a** the mass of a substance or distribution of a quantity per unit of volume or space. **b** the average number of individuals or units per unit of space.

dent[1] *n* **1** a depression or hollow made by a blow or by pressure. **2** an adverse effect.

dent[2] *v* to make a dent in or on.

dental *adj* **1** relating to the teeth or to dentistry. **2** of a consonant: articulated with the tip or blade of the tongue against or near the upper front teeth, e.g. the sound 'th' in English.

dental floss *n* a waxed thread used to clean between the teeth.

dental surgeon *n* = DENTIST.

dentate *adj* having teeth or pointed conical projections: *a dentate leaf.*

dentifrice *n* a powder, paste, or liquid for cleaning the teeth.

dentil *n* any of a series of small projecting rectangular blocks, *esp* under a cornice on a building.

dentine (*NAm* **dentin**) *n* a calcium-containing material, similar to but harder and denser than bone, of which the principal mass of a tooth is composed.

dentist *n* somebody who treats diseases, malformations, and injuries to the teeth, mouth, etc and who makes and inserts false teeth. ➤➤ **dentistry** *n.*

dentition *n* **1** the number, kind, and arrangement of a human being's or animal's teeth. **2** the emergence of teeth from the gums.

denture *n* **1** an artificial replacement for one or more teeth. **2** (*in pl*) a set of false teeth.

denude *v* **1a** to strip (something) of all covering. **b** to lay (an area) bare by erosion. **2** to remove an important possession or quality from (somebody or something). ➤➤ **denudation** *n.*

denunciate *v* = DENOUNCE. ➤➤ **denunciator** *n,* **denunciatory** *adj.*

denunciation *n* the act or an instance of denouncing; public condemnation.

deny *v* (**-ies, -ied**) **1** to declare to be untrue or invalid; to refuse to accept. **2a** to refuse to give or permit something to. **b** to refuse to grant (e.g. a request or access). **3** to disown or repudiate (somebody or something). ✱ **deny oneself** to refrain ascetically from self-indulgence or pleasure.

deodorant *n* a preparation that destroys or masks unpleasant smells.

deodorize *or* **-ise** *v* to remove or mask the unpleasant smell of (something). ➤➤ **deodorizer** *n.*

deoxygenate *v* to remove oxygen from. ➤➤ **deoxygenation** *n.*

deoxyribonucleic acid *n* see DNA.

depart *v* **1** (*usu* + from) to go away; to leave. **2** (*usu* + for) to set out. **3** (*usu* + from) to turn aside; to deviate. **4** to die.

departed *adj euphem* having died, *esp* recently.

department *n* **1a** a major division of a government. **b** a division of an institution or business that provides a specified service or deals with a specified subject. **2** a major administrative subdivision, e.g. in France. **3** *informal* **a** a distinct sphere, e.g. of activity or thought; an area of responsibility. **b** a particular aspect, *esp* of somebody's physical or mental makeup: *rather deficient in the brains department.* ➤➤ **departmental** *adj,* **departmentally** *adv.*

departmentalize *or* **-ise** *v* to divide (something) into departments.

department store *n* a large shop selling a wide variety of goods in different sections.

departure *n* the act or an instance of departing.

depend *v* **1** (*usu* + on/upon) to be determined by or based on some condition or action. **2** (*usu* + on/upon) to place reliance or trust in (a claim, statement, etc). **3** (+ on/upon) to rely on (somebody) for assistance, financial support, etc.

dependable *adj* reliable or trustworthy. ➤➤ **dependability** *n,* **dependably** *adv.*

dependance *n NAm* see DEPENDENCE.

dependant (*NAm* **dependent**) *n* a person who relies on another person, *esp* for financial support.

Usage note

dependant *or* dependent? In British English *dependent* is an adjective and *dependant* is a noun meaning 'a dependent person'. In American English the form *dependent* is generally used both as an adjective and noun.

dependence (*NAm* **dependance**) *n* **1** the fact of being wholly determined by or based on something else. **2** the fact of needing somebody or something else in order to be able to live or function satisfactorily. **3** reliance or trust. **4** a psychological or physiological need for a drug; addiction or habituation.

dependency *n* (*pl* **-ies**) **1** a territorial unit under the jurisdiction of a nation but not formally annexed to it. **2** something that is dependent on something else. **3** dependence.

dependent[1] *adj* **1** relying on somebody or something else for support or help: *She was dependent on her mother for support.* **2** (*often* + on/upon) determined or conditioned by somebody else; contingent. **3** subject to the jurisdiction of e.g. another state; subordinate. **4** having a need for something, e.g. a drug. **5** in grammar, = SUBORDINATE[1]. ➤➤ **dependently** *adv.*

Usage note

dependent *or* dependant? See note at DEPENDANT.

dependent[2] *n NAm* see DEPENDANT.

depersonalize *or* **-ise** *v* to deprive (somebody or something) of the sense of personal identity. ➤➤ **depersonalization** *n.*

depict *v* **1** to represent by a picture. **2** to describe. ➤➤ **depiction** *n.*

depilate *v* to remove hair from (a part of the body). ➤➤ **depilation** *n,* **depilator** *n.*

depilatory *n* (*pl* **-ies**) a cream, wax, or lotion for removing hair, wool, or bristles. ➤➤ **depilatory** *adj.*

deplete *v* **1** to lessen (something) markedly in quantity, content, power, or value. **2** to empty (something) wholly or partially. ➤➤ **depletion** *n.*

depleted uranium *n* a dense form of uranium, less radioactive than the enriched uranium used in power stations and nuclear weapons, that is used in the tips or cores of some artillery shells and projectiles.

deplorable *adj* **1** extremely bad. **2** lamentable. ➤➤ **deplorably** *adv.*

deplore *v* to regret or disapprove of (something) strongly.

deploy *v* **1** to spread out (e.g. troops or ships); *esp* in battle formation. **2** to put to use; to bring into action. **3** of troops: to move into position ready for action. ➤➤ **deployment** *n.*

depoliticize *or* **-ise** *v* to make (something) nonpolitical. ➤➤ **depoliticization** *n.*

deponent *n* somebody who gives evidence, *esp* written evidence, under oath.

depopulate *v* to reduce greatly the population of (an area). ➤➤ **depopulation** *n.*

deport *v* **1** to expel (e.g. an alien) legally from a country; to exile (somebody). **2** *formal* to behave or conduct (oneself) in a specified manner. ➤➤ **deportation** *n.*

deportee *n* a person who has been deported or is under sentence of deportation.

deportment *n Brit* the manner in which one stands, sits, or walks; posture.

depose *v* **1** to remove from a position of authority, e.g. a throne. **2** to testify (something) under oath or by affidavit. **3** to bear witness.

deposit[1] *v* (**deposited, depositing**) **1a** to place (something) for safekeeping or as a pledge. **b** to put (money) in a bank. **2a** to lay down (something); to place (something). **b** to let fall (e.g. sediment). ➤➤ **depositor** *n.*

deposit² *n* **1a** money given as a pledge or down payment. **b** money or valuables deposited in a bank. **2** a depository. **3** something laid down; *esp* matter deposited by a natural process.

deposit account *n chiefly Brit* an account, e.g. in a bank, on which interest is usu payable and from which withdrawals can be made usu only by prior arrangement.

depositary *n* (*pl* **-ies**) a person to whom something is entrusted.

deposition *n* **1** the removal of somebody from a position of authority. **2** a usu written and sworn statement presented as evidence. **3** an act or process of depositing.

depository *n* (*pl* **-ies**) **1** a place where something is deposited, *esp* for safekeeping; a storehouse. **2** a trustee; a depositary.

depot *n* **1a** *Brit* a place where buses or trains are kept when not in use or taken for maintenance. **b** *NAm* a railway or bus station. **2** a place for storing goods; a storehouse. **3** a place for the reception and training of military recruits; a regimental headquarters.

deprave *v* to corrupt morally; to pervert. ➤➤ **depraved** *adj,* **depravity** *n.*

deprecate *v* **1** to express disapproval of (something or somebody), *esp* mildly or regretfully: *She deprecated their lack of courtesy toward the old lady.* **2** to disparage or depreciate (something). ➤➤ **deprecatingly** *adv,* **deprecation** *n.*

Usage note

deprecate *or* **depreciate**? The difference in meaning between these two words is becoming eroded. The distinction between expressing disapproval and belittling or disparaging is sometimes so fine that the words *deprecate* and *depreciate* are increasingly being used interchangeably.

deprecatory *adj* **1** apologetic. **2** disapproving.

depreciate *v* **1** to lower the price or estimated value of. **2** to lessen in value; to fall. **3** to belittle or disparage (somebody or something): *My efforts were depreciated and I was made to feel useless.* ➤➤ **depreciation** *n,* **depreciative** *adj,* **depreciatory** *adj.*

Usage note

depreciate *or* **deprecate**? See note at DEPRECATE.

depredation *n* (*usu in pl*) an act of plundering, pillage, or robbery.

depress *v* **1** to sadden or dispirit. **2** to lessen the activity or strength of. **3** to decrease the market value or marketability of. **4** to push or press (something) down.

depressant *n* something, e.g. a drug, that depresses function or activity. ➤➤ **depressant** *adj.*

depressed *adj* **1** low in spirits; sad, *esp* suffering from depression. **2** suffering from economic depression.

depression *n* **1** a mental disorder marked by inactivity, difficulty in thinking and concentration, and *esp* by sadness or dejection. **2** an unhappy state or mood; dejection. **3** a lowering of activity, vitality, amount, force, etc. **4** a period of low general economic activity marked by rising levels of unemployment. **5** a lowered or sunken place or part; a hollow. **6** an atmospheric low. **7** the act of depressing.

depressive¹ *adj* **1** tending to depress. **2** characterized by or liable to psychological depression.

depressive² *n* somebody who suffers from periods of psychological depression.

depressurize *or* **-ise** *v* to cause the pressure of a gas to drop within (a container or vehicle). ➤➤ **depressurization** *n.*

deprivation *n* **1a** the state of being without or of being denied something, *esp* something vital to one's well-being. **b** lack of basic necessities such as food or shelter; hardship. **2** the act or an instance of depriving somebody of something.

deprive *v* **1** (*usu* + of) to prevent (somebody) from making use of or benefiting from something. **2** (*usu* + of) to take something away from (somebody).

deprived *adj* lacking the necessities of life or a good environment.

deprogramme (*NAm* **deprogram**) *v* to free (somebody) from the effects of intensive short-term conditioning, e.g. that received by a convert to a religious group.

dept *abbr* department.

depth *n* **1** the quality of being deep; deepness. **2a** the perpendicular measurement downwards from a surface. **b** the distance from front to back. **3** a part that is far from the outside or surface. **4** a profound or intense state, e.g. of thought or feeling: *the depths of despair.* **5** the worst, most intensive, or severest part: *the depths of winter.* **6** the degree of intensity: *depth of a colour.* **7** the quality of being profound, e.g. in insight, or full, e.g. of knowledge. **8** (*in pl*) a deep place in a body of water. ✱ **out of one's depth 1** in water that is deeper than one's height. **2** beyond one's ability to understand. ➤➤ **depthless** *adj.*

depth charge *n* an explosive projectile for use underwater, *esp* against submarines.

deputation *n* (*used as sing. or pl*) a small group of people chosen to represent the members of a larger, usu unofficial group.

depute¹ *v* **1** to appoint (somebody) to act as a deputy. **2** to delegate (something).

depute² *n Scot* a deputy.

deputize *or* **-ise** *v* (*usu* + for) to act as a deputy.

deputy *n* (*pl* **-ies**) **1** a person, e.g. a second-in-command, appointed as a substitute with power to act for another. **2** a member of the lower house of some legislative assemblies.

deracinate *v formal or literary* to uproot (something). ➤➤ **deracination** *n.*

derail *v* **1** to cause (a train) to leave the rails. **2** to throw off course. ➤➤ **derailment** *n.*

derailleur *n* a mechanism for changing gear on a bicycle, by moving the chain from one set of exposed gears to another.

derange *v* **1** to disturb the operation or functions of; to disarrange. **2** to make insane. ➤➤ **derangement** *n.*

deranged *adj* mad or insane.

derby *n* (*pl* **-ies**) **1** (**the Derby**) a flat race for three-year-old horses held annually at Epsom in England. **2** a usu informal race or contest for a specified category of contestant: *a donkey derby.* **3** a sporting match against a major local rival. **4** *chiefly NAm* a bowler hat.

deregulate *v* **1** to remove from legal jurisdiction by law. **2** to remove from government control or management. ➤➤ **deregulation** *n,* **deregulatory** *adj.*

derelict¹ *adj* **1** left to decay; abandoned or ruined. **2** *chiefly NAm* lacking a sense of duty; negligent.

derelict² *n* **1** a down-and-out. **2** something voluntarily abandoned, e.g. a ship.

dereliction *n* **1a** conscious neglect. **b** a fault or shortcoming. **2** abandonment or being abandoned, *esp* when this is intentional.

derestrict *v* to cancel or remove a restriction, *esp* a speed limit, from (something). ⋙ **derestriction** *n.*

deride *v* to mock or scorn (something).

de rigueur /də ri'guh/ *adj* required by fashion, etiquette, or custom.

derision *n* scorn or ridicule.

derisive *adj* showing derision; mocking or scornful: *derisive jeers.* ⋙ **derisively** *adv,* **derisiveness** *n.*

derisory *adj* **1** ridiculously small and inadequate: *a derisory pay offer.* **2** derisive.

derivation *n* **1a** the fact of being obtained or originating from a particular source. **b** the act or an instance of deriving. **2** the history or formation of a word from another word or root. ⋙ **derivational** *adj.*

derivative[1] *adj* **1** made up of derived elements; not original. **2** formed by derivation. ⋙ **derivatively** *adv.*

derivative[2] *n* **1** something derived, e.g. a word formed by derivation. **2** in mathematics, the limit of the ratio of the change in a function to the corresponding change in its independent variable as the latter change approaches zero. **3** a financial product, such as a futures contract, linked to a commodity, currency, etc and dependent on the value of that for its own value.

derive *v* **1** to obtain or receive, *esp* from a specified source. **2** to infer or deduce. **3** to form (something) by derivation. **4** (+ from) to come as a derivative. ⋙ **derivable** *adj.*

dermatitis *n* a disease or inflammation of the skin.

dermatology *n* the branch of medicine dealing with the skin and skin diseases. ⋙ **dermatological** *adj,* **dermatologically** *adv,* **dermatologist** *n.*

dermis *n* **1** the skin. **2** the sensitive vascular inner layer of the skin. ⋙ **dermal** *adj.*

dernier cri /ˌdeəniay 'kree/ *n* the latest fashion.

derogate *v formal* **1** (+ from) to take away a desirable aspect or feature; to detract. **2** (+ from) to deviate or go astray from (e.g. a principle or standard). **3** to express a negative opinion of; to disparage. ⋙ **derogation** *n.*

derogatory *adj* expressing a low opinion; insulting or disparaging. ⋙ **derogatorily** *adv.*

derrick *n* **1** a hoisting apparatus employing a tackle rigged at the end of a beam. **2** a framework over an oil well or similar hole, for supporting drilling tackle.

derrière *n euphem or humorous* the buttocks.

derring-do *n archaic or literary* daring action.

Word history

from Middle English *dorring don* daring to do. Spenser used it in *The Shephearde's Calendar* (1579) and the *Faerie Queen* in the meaning 'chivalry' and Sir Walter Scott revived it in *Ivanhoe* in the meaning 'desperate courage'.

derris *n* a preparation of the roots and stems of a tropical climbing plant, used as an insecticide.

derv *n* fuel oil for diesel engines.

dervish *n* a member of a Muslim religious order noted for devotional exercises, e.g. bodily movements leading to a trance.

desalinate *v* to remove salt from (sea water). ⋙ **desalination** *n.*

descale *v* to remove scale deposits from (pipes, kettles, etc).

descant[1] *n* a counterpoint superimposed on a simple melody and usu sung by some or all of the sopranos.

descant[2] *v* (+ on/upon) to talk or write at considerable length.

descant recorder *n chiefly Brit* the member of the recorder family with a range of two octaves above the C above middle C.

descend *v* **1a** to pass from a higher to a lower level. **b** to incline, lead, or extend downwards. **2** to pass, move, or extend down, or down along (something). **3** (+ from) to derive or come from; to have as an ancestor. **4** to pass by inheritance. **5a** (+ on/upon) to make a sudden attack or be suddenly inflicted on somebody. **b** *chiefly humorous* (+ on/upon) to make a sudden disconcerting visit or appearance. **6** (+ to) to sink in status or dignity; to stoop. ⋙ **descender** *n.*

descendant (*NAm* **descendent**) *n* somebody or something descended or deriving from somebody or something else.

descent *n* **1** the act or process of descending. **2** a downward inclination; a slope. **3a** derivation from an ancestor; birth or lineage. **b** a transmission from a usu earlier source; a derivation. **4** a sudden hostile raid or attack.

describe *v* **1** to give an account of (something) in words. **2** to trace the outline of. ⋙ **describable** *adj,* **describer** *n.*

description *n* **1** an account intended to convey a mental image of something experienced. **2** a kind or sort: *people of every description.*

descriptive *adj* **1** serving to describe, *esp* vividly. **2** characterized by description. **3** in linguistics, serving to describe the structure of a language at a particular time without making value judgments and usu excluding historical and comparative data. ⋙ **descriptively** *adv,* **descriptiveness** *n.*

descry *v* (**-ies, -ied**) *formal* to notice or see, *esp* at a distance.

desecrate *v* **1** to violate the sanctity of (something sacred). **2** to treat (a sacred place) irreverently or contemptuously. ⋙ **desecration** *n,* **desecrator** *n.*

desegregate *v* to eliminate racial segregation in (e.g. a school). ⋙ **desegregation** *n.*

deselect *v* **1** to drop (somebody) from a team or group. **2** of a constituency political party in Britain: to refuse to readopt (somebody) as a parliamentary candidate. ⋙ **deselection** *n.*

desensitize *or* **-ise** *v* **1** to make (somebody) less sensitive or responsive to feelings or situations, e.g. to the suffering of others. **2** to make (somebody previously sensitive) insensitive or nonreactive to a sensitizing agent. ⋙ **desensitization** *n.*

desert[1] *n* **1a** a barren region incapable of supporting much life. **b** an uninhabited place; a place of solitude; a wilderness. **2** an area or place that is deprived of or devoid of something important: *a cultural desert.*

Usage note

desert *or* **dessert**? The noun *desert* has the stress on the first syllable, and the related verb *desert* has the stress on the second syllable. Do not confuse these with *dessert,* which is a noun with a different meaning and has the stress on the second syllable.

desert[2] *n* (*usu in pl*) deserved reward or punishment: *She got her just deserts.*

desert[3] *v* **1** to leave (somebody or something), usu without intending to return. **2** to abandon or forsake (somebody). **3** to quit one's post, military service, etc without leave or justification. ⋙ **deserter** *n,* **desertion** *n.*

desertification *n* the reduction of fertile land to barren land or desert, *esp* as a result of overuse and poor irrigation.

deserve *v* to be worthy of or suitable for (some recompense or treatment). ⯮ **deservedly** *adv.*

deserving *adj* meriting something, *esp* financial aid.

desex *v* **1** to castrate or spay (an animal). **2** to desexualize (somebody).

desexualize *or* **-ise** *v* to deprive (somebody) of sexuality, sexual power, or the qualities appropriate to one or other sex.

déshabillé /dayza'beeay/ *or* **deshabille** /-'beel, disə'beel/ *n* the state of being only partially or carelessly dressed.

desiccate *v* **1** to dry (something) up. **2** to preserve (a food) by drying; to dehydrate. ⯮ **desiccation** *n.*

desiderata *n* pl of DESIDERATUM.

desideratum *n* (*pl* **desiderata**) *formal* something desired as necessary.

design[1] *v* **1a** to conceive and plan out in the mind. **b** to devise for a specific function or end. **2a** to draw the plans for (e.g. a building). **b** to create or execute according to a plan.

design[2] *n* **1** a drawing, plan, or pattern showing the details of how something is to be constructed. **2** the act of producing such a plan. **3** a decorative pattern. **4** the arrangement of the elements of a work of art or artefact. **5a** a particular purpose held in view. **b** deliberate purposeful planning. **6** a mental plan or scheme. **7** (*in pl,* + on) dishonest, hostile, or acquisitive intent.

designate[1] *v* **1** to nominate for a specified purpose, office, or duty. **2** to call (somebody or something) by a distinctive name or title. ⯮ **designator** *n.*

designate[2] *adj* chosen for an office but not yet installed: *ambassador designate.*

designation *n* **1** a distinguishing name or title. **2** the act of indicating or identifying.

designedly *adv* on purpose.

designer *n* **1** somebody who designs; *esp* somebody who creates the design of a manufactured object. **2** (*used before a noun*) **a** made by a well-known fashion designer: *designer jeans.* **b** worn or used by people who want to seem fashionable: *designer stubble.* **3** (*used before a noun*) altered by genetic engineering: *a designer virus that attacks caterpillars.*

designer drug *n* a synthetic drug that has effects similar to those of an illegal narcotic but can be made legally.

designing *adj* crafty or scheming.

desirable *adj* **1** worth seeking or doing as advantageous or beneficial. **2** causing desire; attractive, *esp* sexually. ⯮ **desirability** *n,* **desirableness** *n,* **desirably** *adv.*

desire[1] *v* **1** to long or hope for. **2** to express a wish for; to request. **3** to wish to have sexual relations with. **4** *archaic or formal* to express a wish to (somebody).

desire[2] *n* **1** a longing or craving; *esp* a sexual longing. **2** a formal request or petition. **3** something desired.

desirous *adj formal* (*usu* + of/to) eagerly wanting; desiring.

desist *v formal* (*often* + from) to cease to proceed or act.

desk *n* **1a** a table with a sloping or horizontal surface and often drawers and compartments, designed *esp* for writing and reading. **b** a table, counter, or booth at which cashiers, clerks, etc work. **c** a music stand, *esp* as shared by two players in an orchestra, or the position shared by two such players. **2** a division of an organization specializing in a usu specified type or phase of activity, *esp* a section of the editorial staff of a newspaper or news programme.

de-skill *v* **1** to remove or diminish the element of skill in (a job) by the introduction of automation. **2** to deprive (a worker) of a chance to use their skill, through changes in manufacturing patterns or processes.

desk job *n* a clerical or administrative job.

desk rage *n* = OFFICE RAGE.

desktop[1] *n* **1** the working surface of a desk. **2** a desktop computer. **3** the visible screen produced on a VDU by computer software, on which icons, the cursor, etc are displayed.

desktop[2] *adj* **1** of a compact size suitable for use on a desk or table. **2** of or using a compact computer system that can fit on a desk, usu comprising a keyboard, VDU, microcomputer, and printer, as opposed e.g. to a laptop or hand-held portable computer.

desktop publishing *n* the production of printed material by a desktop system comprising a personal computer, software, and a laser printer.

desolate[1] *adj* **1** deserted; uninhabited. **2** barren; lifeless. **3** devastated; laid waste. **4** forlorn or hopeless; extremely unhappy. ⯮ **desolately** *adv.*

desolate[2] *v* **1** to deprive (a place) of inhabitants. **2** to lay waste to (a place). **3** to make (somebody) feel forlorn or extremely unhappy. ⯮ **desolation** *n.*

despair[1] *v* (*often* + of) to lose all hope or confidence. ⯮ **despairing** *adj,* **despairingly** *adv.*

despair[2] *n* **1** utter loss of hope. **2** (**the despair of**) a cause of hopelessness or great exasperation.

despatch[1] *v* see DISPATCH[1].

despatch[2] *n* see DISPATCH[2].

desperado *n* (*pl* **-oes** *or* **-os**) *dated* a reckless or violent criminal.

desperate *adj* **1** in despair because beyond or almost beyond hope. **2a** reckless because of despair. **b** undertaken as a last resort. **3** (*often* + for) suffering extreme need or anxiety. **4** fraught with extreme danger or impending disaster. **5** violent or dangerous. **6** *informal* of the weather, etc: very bad; severe.

desperately *adv* **1** in a desperate manner; in despair or desperation. **2** *informal* extremely.

desperation *n* **1** loss of hope and surrender to despair. **2** extreme recklessness caused by hopelessness.

despicable *adj* morally contemptible. ⯮ **despicably** *adv.*

despise *v* to regard with contempt or distaste. ⯮ **despiser** *n.*

despite *prep* notwithstanding; in spite of. ✱ **despite oneself** in spite of one's intentions, wishes, character, etc.

despoil *v* to plunder or pillage (a place). ⯮ **despoiler** *n.*

despoliation *n* the act or an instance of plundering or being plundered.

despondent *adj* feeling extreme discouragement or dejection. ⯮ **despondency** *n,* **despondently** *adv.*

despot *n* **1** a ruler with absolute power. **2** a person exercising power abusively or tyrannically. ⯮ **despotic** *adj,* **despotically** *adv,* **despotism** *n.*

des. res. *n Brit, informal* a house with desirable characteristics.

dessert *n* a sweet course or dish served at the end of a meal.

Usage note

dessert *or* desert? See note at DESERT[1].

dessertspoon *n* a spoon intermediate in size between a teaspoon and a tablespoon and used for eating dessert.

dessert wine *n* a sweet wine often served with dessert.

destabilize *or* **-ise** *v* to make (a government or the economy of a country, etc) unstable. ➤➤ **destabilization** *n.*

destination *n* a place which is set for the end of a journey or to which something is sent.

destine *v* (*usu in passive*) **1** (+ for) to designate or dedicate (something or somebody) in advance; to set (something or somebody) apart for a specified purpose or goal: *She believed she was destined for great things.* **2** (*usu* + for) to direct (something) to a place: *At the harbour there was freight destined for various English ports.*

destiny *n* (*pl* **-ies**) **1** the power or agency held to determine the course of events; fate. **2** something to which a person or thing is destined; their fate or fortune. **3** a predetermined course of events.

destitute *adj* **1** lacking the basic necessities of life; extremely poor. **2** (+ of) lacking something necessary or desirable. ➤➤ **destitution** *n.*

destrier *n archaic* a war-horse or charger.

destroy *v* **1** to demolish or ruin. **2a** to put an end to (somebody); to kill. **b** to kill (an animal) humanely. **3** to make ineffective; to neutralize.

destroyer *n* **1** somebody or something that destroys. **2** a fast multi-purpose warship smaller than a cruiser.

destruct *v* to destroy (something or somebody, *esp* a missile or rocket of one's own, e.g. on grounds of safety). ➤➤ **destructibility** *n,* **destructible** *adj,* **destructor** *n.*

destruction *n* **1** the act or an instance of destroying or being destroyed. **2** a cause of ruin or downfall.

destructive *adj* **1a** causing destruction. **b** designed or tending to destroy. **2** of criticism, etc: pointing out faults and failings without offering ideas for improvement; not constructive. ➤➤ **destructively** *adv,* **destructiveness** *n.*

desuetude *n formal* discontinuance from use; disuse.

desultory *adj* **1** passing aimlessly from one subject or activity to another. **2** random; haphazard; happening on and off. ➤➤ **desultorily** *adv,* **desultoriness** *n.*

detach *v* **1** to separate (something), *esp* from a larger mass and usu without causing damage. **2** to separate (something) from a parent organization or larger group for a special purpose. **3** to keep (oneself) emotionally detached from something. ➤➤ **detachability** *n,* **detachable** *adj.*

detached *adj* **1** of a house: standing by itself; not sharing any wall with another building. **2** of a person: free from prejudice or emotional involvement; aloof. **3** separate; not connected. ➤➤ **detachedly** *adv.*

detachment *n* **1a** freedom from bias or emotional involvement. **b** indifference to worldly concerns. **2** (*used as sing. or pl*) a body of troops, ships, etc separated from the main body for a special mission. **3** the act or an instance of detaching; separation.

detail[1] *n* **1a** a part considered separately from the whole. **b** (*usu in pl*) an individual relevant part or fact. **c** a small and subordinate part; *specif* part of a work of art considered or reproduced in isolation. **2** extended treatment of or attention to particular items. **3** (*used as sing. or pl*) a small military detachment selected for a particular task. ✱ **in detail** item by item; thoroughly.

detail[2] *v* **1** to report (something) in detail. **2** to assign (somebody) to a particular task or place.

detailed *adj* marked by abundant detail or thorough treatment.

detain *v* **1** to delay (somebody); to hold (somebody) back. **2** to hold or retain (somebody) in custody, or as if in custody. ➤➤ **detainer** *n,* **detainment** *n.*

detainee *n* a person held in custody, *esp* for political reasons.

detect *v* **1** to discover the existence or discern the presence of (something or somebody). **2** to discover (a crime or criminal). ➤➤ **detectable** *adj,* **detection** *n.*

detective *n* a police officer or other person engaged in investigating crimes, detecting lawbreakers, etc.

detector *n* a device used to detect the presence of radiation, particles, or physical substances or objects.

détente *or* **detente** *n* a relaxation of strained relations, e.g. between ideologically opposed nations.

detention *n* **1** the act or an instance of detaining or being detained, *esp* in custody. **2** *chiefly Brit* the act or an instance of keeping in a pupil after school hours as a punishment.

detention centre *n* an institution for the detention of young offenders for short periods.

deter *v* (**deterred, deterring**) **1** (*often* + from) to discourage or prevent (somebody) from acting. **2** to prevent (something) happening; to discourage people from doing (something).

detergent[1] *n* a cleansing agent; *specif* any of various synthetic water-soluble compounds that are chemically different from soaps but have similar cleansing properties.

detergent[2] *adj* cleaning or cleansing.

deteriorate *v* to grow worse. ➤➤ **deterioration** *n.*

determinant *n* **1** something that determines, fixes, or conditions. **2** something that is inherited and produces a genetic effect, *esp* a gene. **3** in mathematics: **a** an array of symbols or numbers written in the form of a square matrix bordered on either side by a vertical line. **b** a value assigned to a determinant obtained by manipulating its elements according to a certain rule. ➤➤ **determinant** *adj.*

determinate *adj* **1** fixed; established. **2** conclusively determined; definitive. ➤➤ **determinacy** *n.*

determination *n* **1a** firm intention. **b** the ability to make and act on firm decisions; resoluteness. **2** the act or an instance of determining something. **3** a judicial decision settling a dispute.

determine *v* **1a** to fix conclusively or authoritatively. **b** to settle or decide (something). **2a** to fix beforehand. **b** to regulate. **3** to ascertain the intent, nature, or scope of. ➤➤ **determinable** *adj.*

determined *adj* firm; resolute. ➤➤ **determinedly** *adv.*

determiner *n* **1** something or somebody that determines. **2** a word that limits the meaning of a noun and comes before a descriptive adjective modifying the same noun, e.g. *his* in 'his new car'.

determinism *n* a doctrine that all phenomena are determined by preceding occurrences, *esp* the doctrine that all human acts, choices, etc are causally determined and that free will is illusory. ⋙ **determinist** *n and adj*, **deterministic** *adj*.

deterrent[1] *n* something that deters; *specif* a weapon that is held in readiness by one nation or alliance in order to deter another from attacking.

deterrent[2] *adj* serving to deter. ⋙ **deterrence** *n*.

detest *v* to feel intense dislike for; to loathe.

detestable *adj* arousing or deserving intense dislike; hateful.

detestation *n* extreme dislike; abhorrence.

dethrone *v* **1** to depose (a monarch). **2** to depose or remove from a position of power or authority. ⋙ **dethronement** *n*.

detonate *v* **1** to cause (a bomb, etc) to explode with sudden violence. **2** of a bomb, etc: to explode. ⋙ **detonation** *n*.

detonator *n* a device used for detonating a high explosive.

detour[1] *n* a roundabout way that is an alternative to a shorter or planned route.

detour[2] *v* to make a detour.

detox[1] *n informal* detoxification.

detox[2] *v* = DETOXIFY.

detoxicate *v* = DETOXIFY. ⋙ **detoxication** *n*.

detoxify *v* (**-ies, -ied**) **1** to remove a poison or toxin from (something or somebody). **2** to treat (somebody) for dependency on alcohol or drugs. ⋙ **detoxification** *n*.

DETR *abbr Brit* Department of the Environment, Transport, and the Regions.

detract *v* (+ from) to take away something desirable from something; to make something less valuable, interesting, etc. ⋙ **detraction** *n*.

detractor *n* a person who denigrates somebody or their ideas or beliefs.

detrain *v* **1** to alight from a railway train. **2** to remove (somebody or something) from a train.

detriment *n* injury or damage, or a cause of this.

detrimental *adj* harmful, damaging. ⋙ **detrimentally** *adv*.

detritus *n* **1** loose material, e.g. rock fragments or organic particles, produced by disintegration. **2** debris or waste material. ⋙ **detrital** *adj*.

de trop /də 'troh/ *adj* not wanted or needed; superfluous.

detumescence *n* subsidence or diminution of swelling. ⋙ **detumescent** *adj*.

detune *v* **1** to cause (a musical instrument) to be out of tune. **2** to adjust (the engine of a motor vehicle) so that performance and efficiency are reduced.

deuce *n* **1** a playing card or the face of a dice representing the number two. **2** a tie in a game, e.g. tennis, after which a side must score two consecutive clear points to win. **3** *informal* (*used as an interjection or intensive*) **a** (**the deuce**) the devil; the dickens. **b** something very bad or remarkable of its kind.

deus ex machina /,dayəs eks 'makinə/ *n* (*pl* **dei ex machina**) somebody or something, e.g. in fiction or drama, that appears or is introduced suddenly and unexpectedly and provides a contrived solution to an apparently insoluble difficulty.

Word history

In Greek theatre actors representing gods were suspended above the stage on a kind of crane, by which they could be lowered to intervene in the action and bring about the denouement.

deuterium *n* the hydrogen isotope that is twice the mass of ordinary hydrogen.

Deutschmark /'doychmahk/ *or* **Deutsche Mark** /'doychə mahk/ *n* the basic monetary unit of Germany.

devaluation *n* **1** a reduction in the exchange value of a currency. **2** a lessening, *esp* of status or stature.

devalue *v* **1** to reduce the exchange value of (money). **2** to lessen the value or reputation of (something or somebody). **3** to institute devaluation.

devastate *v* **1** to reduce (a place) to ruin; to lay waste. **2** to have a shattering effect on (somebody); to overwhelm (somebody), e.g. with grief or horror. ⋙ **devastation** *n*, **devastator** *n*.

devastating *adj* **1** causing great destruction. **2** shocking; horrifying. **3** *informal* extremely attractive or impressive. ⋙ **devastatingly** *adv*.

develop *v* (**developed, developing**) **1a** to go through a process of natural growth, differentiation, or evolution by successive changes. **b** to evolve; to grow. **2a** to promote the growth of (something). **b** to build on or change the use of (a tract of land). **3** to cause (something) to grow, mature, or increase. **4** to become gradually visible or apparent. **5a** to unfold (an idea) gradually or in detail. **b** to show signs of (an illness). **c** to subject (exposed photographic material) to chemicals, in order to produce a visible image. **6** to bring out the possibilities of (something). **7** to acquire (something) gradually: *He developed a taste for good wine.* ⋙ **developable** *adj*.

developed *adj* of a country: having achieved a high economic level of industrialization and a high standard of living.

developer *n* **1** a chemical used to develop exposed photographic materials. **2** a person who develops real estate, *esp* somebody who improves and subdivides land and builds and sells houses on it.

developing *adj* of a country: underdeveloped.

development *n* **1a** the act or an instance of developing or being developed. **b** the result of this, e.g. an innovation or new product. **2** something which changes a situation. **3** an area of new building. ⋙ **developmental** *adj*, **developmentally** *adv*.

deviant[1] *adj* **1** deviating, *esp* from a norm. **2** characterized by deviation. ⋙ **deviance** *n*, **deviancy** *n*.

deviant[2] *n* a person whose behaviour differs markedly from the norm, *esp* with regard to their sexual or social behaviour.

deviate *v* to stray, *esp* from a principle or accepted norm, or from a straight course.

deviation *n* **1** departure from accepted norms of behaviour, *esp* sexual or social behaviour. **2** departure from an established party line. **3** the difference between a value in a frequency distribution and a fixed number. **4** the act or an instance of deviating.

device *n* **1** a piece of equipment or a mechanism designed for a special purpose or function. **2** a scheme to trick or deceive. **3** something elaborate or intricate in design. ✱ **leave somebody to their own devices** to leave somebody alone to do as they please.

devil[1] *n* **1** (*usu* **the Devil**) the supreme spirit of evil in Jewish and Christian belief. **2** a malignant spirit; a demon. **3** an extremely cruel or wicked person; a fiend. **4** a high-spirited or reckless person. **5** *informal* a person of the specified type: *You're a lucky devil.* **6a** (**the devil**) *informal* something provoking, difficult, or trying. **b** used as an interjection or intensive. ✱ **between the devil and the deep blue sea** faced with two equally unwelcome alternatives. **give the devil his due** to give desired credit to an opponent or an unpleasant person. **go**

to the devil 1 to fail completely; to be ruined. **2** to become depraved. **3** said in anger, rejection, etc: to go away. **like the devil** *informal* with great speed, intensity, etc. **play the devil with** to cause damage or disruption to (something). **speak/talk of the devil** said when somebody appears who has just been mentioned [from the proverb *talk of the devil and he's sure to appear*]. **the devil to pay** a lot of trouble.

devil² *v* (**devilled, devilling,** *NAm* **deviled, deviling**) to season (food) highly, *esp* with peppery condiments.

devilish *adj* of or characteristic of a devil; wicked. ⯮ **devilishly** *adv*, **devilishness** *n*.

devil-may-care *adj* heedless of authority or convention.

devilment *n* wild mischief.

devilry *n* (*pl* **-ies**) **1** mischief, or an act of mischief. **2** action performed with the help of the devil; witchcraft.

devil's advocate *n* a person who champions the less accepted or approved cause, *esp* for the sake of argument.

devil's food cake *n chiefly NAm* a rich dark chocolate cake.

devious *adj* **1** of a person: not straightforward or wholly sincere. **2** tortuously underhand. **3** roundabout or circuitous. ⯮ **deviously** *adv*, **deviousness** *n*.

devise *v* **1a** to formulate (a plan) in the mind; to invent. **b** to plan or plot (something). **2** to give or leave (real property) by will. ⯮ **deviser** *n*.

devitalize *or* **-ise** *v* to deprive (somebody) of life, vigour, or effectiveness. ⯮ **devitalization** *n*.

devoid *adj* (+ of) not having or using; lacking.

devolution *n* the surrender of functions and powers to regional or local authorities by a central government. ⯮ **devolutionary** *adj*, **devolutionist** *n*.

devolve *v* **1** (*usu* + on/upon/to) to transfer (property or a responsibility or duty) from one person to another; to hand down. **2** (*usu* + on/upon/to) to surrender (power) by devolution. **3** (*usu* + on/upon/to) to pass by transmission or succession. **4** (*usu* + on/upon/to) to fall or be passed, usu as an obligation or responsibility.

Devonian *adj* **1** of Devon. **2** of the fourth geological period of the Palaeozoic era, lasting from about 409 million to about 363 million years ago, and marked by the first appearance of insects and amphibians. ⯮ **Devonian** *n*.

devoré *n* a velvet fabric having a pattern etched with acid.

devote *v* **1** (+ to) to set (something) apart for a special purpose. **2** (+ to) to give (oneself) over wholly to something or somebody.

devoted *adj* **1** very loving. **2** loyally attached. **3** giving a lot of time, effort, etc to something; dedicated. ⯮ **devotedly** *adv*.

devotee *n* **1** a keen follower or supporter; an enthusiast. **2** a deeply religious person.

devotion *n* **1a** great love, affection, or dedication. **b** the act or an instance of devoting or being devoted. **2a** religious zeal; piety. **b** (*usu in pl*) a special act of prayer or supplication. ⯮ **devotional** *adj*.

devour *v* **1** to eat (food) up greedily or ravenously. **2** *literary* to swallow up; to consume. **3** (*usu in passive*) of a feeling: to preoccupy or absorb (somebody). **4** to take in eagerly through the mind or senses. ⯮ **devourer** *n*.

devout *adj* **1** devoted to religion; pious. **2** sincere; genuine: *a devout hope*. ⯮ **devoutly** *adv*, **devoutness** *n*.

dew *n* **1** moisture that condenses on the surfaces of cool bodies, *esp* at night. **2** any minute droplets of moisture, e.g. tears or sweat.

dewberry *n* (*pl* **-ies**) the berry of a shrub resembling the blackberry.

Dewey decimal classification *n* a book classification whereby main classes are shown by a three-digit number and subdivisions by numbers after a decimal point.

dewlap *n* a hanging fold of skin under the neck of an animal, e.g. a cow.

dew point *n* the temperature of the air at which dew begins to be deposited.

dewy *adj* (**-ier, -iest**) moist with dew, or as if with dew.

dewy-eyed *adj* naively credulous or trusting.

Dexedrine *n trademark* a preparation of the stimulatory drug dextroamphetamine sulphate.

dexter *adj* of or on the right-hand side of a heraldic shield from the bearer's point of view: compare SINISTER (3).

dexterity *n* **1** skill and ease in using the hands. **2** physical or mental nimbleness or agility.

dexterous *or* **dextrous** *adj* **1** skilful with the hands. **2** mentally adroit. ⯮ **dexterously** *adv*.

dextral¹ *adj* **1** of or inclined to the right. **2** right-handed.

dextral² *n* somebody who is right-handed.

dextrose *n* a form of glucose.

dextrous *adj* see DEXTEROUS.

DFC *abbr Brit* Distinguished Flying Cross.

DfEE *abbr* Department for Education and Employment.

DFM *abbr Brit* Distinguished Flying Medal.

DG *abbr* director-general.

dhal *or* **dal** *n* a puree made from the seeds of a plant of the pea family.

dhansak *n* an Indian dish *esp* of chicken or lamb, cooked in a thick sauce with lentils and spices.

dharma *n* in Hinduism and Buddhism, the fundamental concept of law, both natural and moral, based on the principle of everything in the universe acting according to its essential nature or proper station.

dhobi *n* (*pl* **dhobis**) an Indian washerman or washerwoman.

dhoti *n* (*pl* **dhotis**) a loincloth worn by Hindu men.

dhow *n* an Arab lateen-rigged (with triangular sail set at an angle: see LATEEN) boat, usu having a long overhanging bow and a high poop.

dhurrie *n* an Indian woven rug, typically of thick coarse cotton yarn.

DI *abbr* **1** Detective Inspector. **2** donor insemination.

di-¹ *comb. form* twice; twofold; double: *dicotyledon*.

di-² *prefix* see DIA-.

dia- *or* **di-** *prefix* **1** through: *dielectric*. **2** across: *diameter*.

diabetes *n* any of various abnormal conditions characterized by the secretion and excretion of excessive amounts of urine, *esp* diabetes mellitus.

diabetes mellitus *n* a form of diabetes in which not enough insulin is produced or there is increased resistance to its action, characterized by abnormally great amounts of sugar in the blood and urine.

diabetic¹ *adj* affected with diabetes.

diabetic² *n* a person affected with diabetes.

diabolic *adj* of or characteristic of the devil; fiendish. ⯮ **diabolically** *adv.*

diabolical *adj* **1** of the devil. **2** *chiefly Brit, informal* dreadful; appalling. ⯮ **diabolically** *adv.*

diabolism *n* dealings with, possession by, or worship of the devil. ⯮ **diabolist** *n.*

diabolo *n* (*pl* **-os**) **1** a game in which a two-headed top is balanced and spun on a string stretched between two sticks. **2** the two-headed top used in the game of diabolo.

diachronic *adj* of or dealing with the historical development of phenomena, *esp* language: compare SYNCHRONIC. ⯮ **diachronically** *adv,* **diachrony** *n.*

diaconal *adj* of a deacon or deaconess.

diaconate *n* **1** the office of a deacon or deaconess. **2** the body of deacons or deaconesses.

diacritic *n* a mark near or through an orthographic or phonetic character or combination of characters indicating a changed phonetic value. ⯮ **diacritical** *adj.*

diadem *n* a crown; *specif* a headband worn as a badge of royalty.

diaeresis (*NAm* **dieresis**) *n* (*pl* **diaereses,** *NAm* **diereses**) a mark (¨) placed over a vowel to indicate pronunciation as a separate syllable, e.g. in *naïve.*

diagnose *v* **1** to recognize (a disease, etc) by signs and symptoms. **2** to make a diagnosis. ⯮ **diagnosable** *adj.*

diagnosis *n* (*pl* **diagnoses**) **1** the art or act of identifying a disease from its signs and symptoms, or a statement resulting from this. **2** the investigation of the cause or nature of a problem or phenomenon, or a statement resulting from this.

diagnostic[1] *adj* of or involving diagnosis. ⯮ **diagnostically** *adv.*

diagnostic[2] *n* (*also in pl, used as sing. or pl*) the art or practice of diagnosis. ⯮ **diagnostician** *n.*

diagonal[1] *adj* **1** of a line: running in an oblique direction from a reference line, e.g. the vertical. **2** joining two nonadjacent angles of a polygon or polyhedron. ⯮ **diagonally** *adv.*

diagonal[2] *n* a diagonal line.

diagram[1] *n* **1** a line drawing made for mathematical or scientific purposes. **2** a drawing or design that shows the arrangement and relations, e.g. of parts. ⯮ **diagrammatic** *adj,* **diagrammatically** *adv.*

diagram[2] *v* (**diagrammed, diagramming,** *NAm* **diagramed, diagraming**) to represent in the form of a diagram.

dial[1] *n* **1** the graduated face of a timepiece. **2a** a face on which some measurement is registered, usu by means of numbers and a pointer. **b** a sometimes disc-shaped control or indicator on an electrical or mechanical device.

dial[2] *v* (**dialled, dialling,** *NAm* **dialed, dialing**) **1** to operate a dial so as to select (a telephone number, etc). **2** to indicate or control by means of a dial. **3** to make a call on a dial telephone. ⯮ **dialler** *n.*

dialect *n* **1** a regional, social, or subordinate variety of a language, usu differing distinctively in grammar and vocabulary from the standard language. **2** a variant of a computer programming language. ⯮ **dialectal** *adj.*

dialectic *n* **1** (*usu in pl, used as sing. or pl*) a systematic reasoning, exposition, or argument that juxtaposes opposed or contradictory ideas and seeks to resolve their conflict. **2** the dialectical tension or opposition between two interacting forces or elements. **3** (*usu in pl, used as sing. or pl*) development through the stages of thesis, antithesis, and synthesis in accordance with Hegel's logic or systems derived from it. ⯮ **dialectic** *adj,* **dialectical** *adj,* **dialectically** *adv.*

dialectical materialism *n* the Marxist theory that the material basis of a reality constantly changes in a dialectical process that is independent of thought.

dialectician *n* somebody who is skilled in or practises dialectic.

dialectology *n* the study of dialect. ⯮ **dialectological** *adj,* **dialectologist** *n.*

dialling code *n* the part of a telephone number that refers to an exchange rather than an individual subscriber.

dialling tone *n* a sound heard over a telephone indicating that a number may be dialled.

dialog *n NAm* see DIALOGUE.

dialog box *n NAm* see DIALOGUE BOX.

dialogic *adj* of or characterized by dialogue.

dialogical *adj* = DIALOGIC.

dialogue (*NAm* **dialog**) *n* **1** a conversation between two or more people or between a person and a computer. **2** the conversational element of literary or dramatic composition. **3** discussion or negotiation between two nations, factions, groups, etc with conflicting interests.

dialogue box (*NAm* **dialog box**) *n* a small window on a computer screen that prompts a response from the user.

dial tone *n NAm* = DIALLING TONE.

dialyse (*NAm* **dialyze**) *v* to subject (a person, blood, etc) to dialysis.

dialysis *n* (*pl* **dialyses**) the separation of substances in solution by means of their unequal diffusion through semipermeable membranes, *esp* the purification of blood by such means.

dialyze *v NAm* see DIALYSE.

diamanté *n* **1** sparkling particles, *esp* powdered crystal, or cloth or other material decorated with these. **2** (*used before a noun*) decorated with diamanté.

diameter *n* **1** a line passing through the centre of a geometrical figure or body. **2** the length of a straight line through the centre of an object, e.g. a circle. **3** the thickness or width of something round, e.g. a pole or hole.

diametric *adj* **1** completely opposed or opposite. **2** of or constituting a diameter. ⯮ **diametrically** *adv.*

diametrical *adj* = DIAMETRIC.

diamond[1] *n* **1** a very hard crystalline carbon, or a piece of it, which is highly valued as a precious stone and used industrially as an abrasive and in rock drills. **2** a square or rhombus orientated so that the diagonals are horizontal and vertical. **3a** a playing card marked with one or more red diamond-shaped figures. **b** (*in pl, used as sing. or pl*) the suit comprising cards identified by this figure. ⯮ **diamondiferous** *adj.*

diamond[2] *adj* of a 60th or, less often, 75th anniversary: *They're celebrating their diamond wedding.*

diamorphine *n* heroin.

dianthus *n* (*pl* **dianthuses** *or* **dianthi**) = PINK[3].

diapason *n* **1** a principal organ stop extending through the range of the instrument. **2** a full deep burst of harmonious sound.

diaper[1] *n* **1** *chiefly NAm* a nappy. **2** a soft, usu white, linen or cotton fabric used for tablecloths or towels. **3** an ornamental pattern consisting of one or more small repeated units of design, e.g. geometric figures.

diaper[2] *v* **1** to put a diaper on (a baby). **2** to ornament (something) with diaper designs.

diaphanous *adj* of fabrics: so fine as to be almost transparent.

diaphragm *n* **1** the partition separating the chest and abdominal cavities in mammals. **2** a dividing membrane or thin partition, *esp* in a tube. **3** = DUTCH CAP. **4** a device that limits the amount of light entering an optical system. **5** a thin flexible disc that is free to vibrate, e.g. in an earphone. ➤➤ **diaphragmatic** /-frag'matik/ *adj.*

diarist *n* somebody who keeps a diary.

diarrhoea (*NAm* **diarrhea**) *n* abnormally frequent intestinal evacuations with more or less fluid faeces. ➤➤ **diarrhoeal** *adj,* **diarrhoeic** *adj.*

diary *n* (*pl* **-ies**) **1** a book containing a daily record of personal experiences or observations. **2** *chiefly Brit* a book with dates marked in which memoranda can be noted.

Diaspora *n* **1a** (**the Diaspora**) (*used as sing. or pl*) the Jews living outside Palestine or modern Israel. **b** the settling, or area of settlement, of Jews outside Palestine after the Babylonian exile. **2** (*also* **diaspora**) a dispersion or migration, e.g. of people orig coming from the same country or having a common culture.

diastole *n* the dilation of the cavities of the heart during which they fill with blood: compare SYSTOLE. ➤➤ **diastolic** *adj.*

diathermy *n* the generation of heat in tissue by electric currents for medical or surgical purposes.

diatom *n* a minute single-celled alga with a hard shell-like skeleton composed of silica. ➤➤ **diatomaceous** *adj.*

diatomic *adj* consisting of two atoms.

diatonic *adj* relating to a major or minor musical scale of eight notes to the octave without chromatic deviation.

diatribe *n* a lengthy piece of bitter and abusive criticism.

diazepam *n* a synthetic tranquillizer that is also used as a sedative and muscle relaxant, *esp* before surgical operations.

dibber *n* a dibble.

dibble *n* a small pointed hand implement used to make holes in the ground for plants, seeds, or bulbs.

dibs *pl n* **1** *informal* money, *esp* in small amounts. **2** *chiefly NAm, informal* (+ on) the right to have first choice.

dice[1] *n* (*pl* **dice**) **1** a small cube that is marked on each face with from one to six spots used to determine arbitrary values in various games. **2** (*usu in pl*) small cubical pieces of food. ✱ **no dice** *informal* of no avail; no use.

Usage note

dice *and* **die**. Strictly and historically speaking, *dice* is the plural of *die*. The use of *dice* to mean a single small cube is, however, long established and perfectly acceptable. *Dice* therefore is both the singular and plural form: *to throw the dice* could refer to one or more cubes.

dice[2] *v* to cut (food) into small cubes. ✱ **dice with death** to take a big risk.

dicey *adj* (**dicier, diciest**) *informal* risky; unpredictable.

dichotomize *or* **-ise** *v* to divide (something) into two usu mutually exclusive parts or groups.

dichotomy *n* (*pl* **-ies**) a division into two mutually exclusive or contradictory groups or things, or a contrast between them. ➤➤ **dichotomous** *adj.*

dick *n* **1** *coarse slang* the penis. **2** *coarse slang* a contemptible person.

dickens *n* (**the dickens**) *informal* (*used as an interjection or intensive*) devil; deuce.

Dickensian *adj* characteristic of the novels of Charles Dickens (d.1870), *esp* in relation to the social conditions of the Victorian age they describe.

dicker *v* **1** to bargain or haggle. **2** to hesitate or dither.

dickhead *n coarse slang* a stupid or incompetent person.

dicky *adj* (**-ier, -iest**) *Brit, informal* in a weak or unsound condition.

dicotyledon *n* any of a class of flowering plants that have two cotyledons (leaves produced by a germinating seed: see COTYLEDON).

dicta *n* pl of DICTUM.

Dictaphone *n trademark* a dictating machine.

dictate[1] *v* **1** to speak or act with authority; to prescribe. **2** to speak or read (a letter, etc) for a person to transcribe or for a machine to record. **3** to impose, pronounce, or specify (something) with authority. ➤➤ **dictation** *n.*

dictate[2] *n* **1** an authoritative rule, prescription, or command. **2** (*usu in pl*) a ruling principle.

dictator *n* an absolute ruler, *esp* one who has seized power unconstitutionally and uses it oppressively. ➤➤ **dictatorial** *adj.*

dictatorship *n* a state or form of government where absolute power is concentrated in one person or a small clique.

diction *n* **1** choice of words, *esp* with regard to correctness or clearness. **2** pronunciation and enunciation of words in speaking or singing.

dictionary *n* (*pl* **-ies**) **1** a reference book containing words and usu phrases, usu alphabetically arranged, together with information about them, *esp* their forms, pronunciations, and meanings. **2** a reference book giving for words or phrases of one language equivalents in another language.

dictum *n* (*pl* **dicta** *or* **dictums**) **1** an authoritative statement on some topic; a pronouncement. **2** = OBITER DICTUM (1).

did *v* past tense of DO[1].

didactic *adj* **1** intended to teach something, *esp* a moral lesson. **2** having a tendency to teach in an authoritarian manner. ➤➤ **didactically** *adv,* **didacticism** *n.*

diddicoy *n* see DIDICOI.

diddle *v informal* to cheat or swindle (somebody).

diddly-squat *or* **doodly-squat** *n NAm, informal* nothing.

didgeridoo *n* (*pl* **didgeridoos**) an Australian wind instrument consisting of a long wooden tube.

didicoi *or* **diddicoy** *n* (*pl* **didicois** *or* **diddicoys**) *dialect* an itinerant tinker, traveller, etc who is not a true Romany.

didn't *contr* did not.

didst *v archaic* second person sing. past tense of DO[1].

die[1] *v* (**dies, died, dying**) **1** to stop living; to undergo the ending of physical life. **2a** to pass out of existence, to cease. **b** to be forgotten. **3** (*also* + for) to long keenly or desperately. **4** (+ of) to be almost overwhelmed with (e.g. boredom). ✱ **die hard** of habits or attitudes: to take a long time to change or disappear. **never say die** *informal* never give up. **to die for** *informal* excellent or desirable.

die[2] *n* **1** (*pl* **dice**) a dice. **2** (*pl* **dies**) any of various tools or devices for giving a desired form or finish to a material or for impressing an object or material.

✱ **the die is cast** the irrevocable decision or step has been taken.

Usage note

die *and* dice. See note at DICE[1].

die away *v* to become weaker or fainter and then disappear.

dieback *n* a condition in woody plants in which young shoots are killed as a result of frost damage, pollution, or fungal infection.

die-cast *v* (*past tense and past part.* **die-cast**) to make (an object) by forcing molten plastic, metal, etc into a die.

diecious *adj NAm* see DIOECIOUS.

die down *v* to diminish or subside.

die-hard *n* **1** a person who strongly resists change. **2** (*used before a noun*) strongly resisting change: *a die-hard conservative.*

die-in *n* the act of simulated death by a large number of people, as a form of public protest.

dielectric[1] *adj* able to transmit an electrical effect by electrostatic induction but not by conduction.

dielectric[2] *n* a dielectric substance; an insulator.

die off *v* to die one by one, sometimes until none exist.

die out *v* **1** to become extinct. **2** to disappear; to cease to exist, be done, etc.

dieresis *n NAm* see DIAERESIS.

diesel *n* **1** a diesel engine, or a vehicle driven by one. **2** a heavy mineral oil used as fuel in diesel engines.

diesel engine *n* an internal-combustion engine in which fuel is ignited by air compressed to a sufficiently high temperature.

diesel oil *n* = DIESEL (2).

diet[1] *n* **1** the food and drink habitually taken by a group, animal, or individual. **2** the kind and amount of food prescribed for a person for a special purpose, e.g. losing weight. **3** (*used before a noun*) of food or drinks: low in calories or fat content. ➤➤ **dietary** *adj.*

diet[2] *v* (**dieted, dieting**) to eat and drink sparingly or according to prescribed rules, *esp* in order to lose weight. ➤➤ **dieter** *n.*

diet[3] *n* any of various national or provincial legislatures.

dietary fibre *n* the fibrous content of food that helps digestion and is present in large amounts in roughage.

dietetic *adj* **1** of diet. **2** adapted for use in special diets. ➤➤ **dietetically** *adv.*

dietetics *pl n* (*used as sing. or pl*) the application of the principles of nutrition to feeding.

dietitian *or* **dietician** *n* a specialist in dietetics.

differ *v* **1** (+ from) to be unlike; to be distinct from. **2** of people: to disagree.

difference *n* **1a** unlikeness between two or more people or things. **b** the degree or amount by which things differ. **2** a disagreement or dispute; dissension. **3** the degree or amount by which things differ in quantity or measure; *specif* a remainder. **4** a significant change in or effect on a situation.

different *adj* **1** partly or totally unlike; dissimilar. **2** *informal* unusual; special. **3a** distinct. **b** other. ➤➤ **differently** *adv,* **differentness** *n.*

Usage note

different from/to/than. The combination preferred by traditionalists is *different from.* Most modern authorities on British English accept *different to* as an alternative, at least in anything but very formal writing. *Different than* is in widespread use in American English but is not usually acceptable when followed by a noun.

differentia *n* (*pl* **differentiae**) the mark or feature that distinguishes one member of a general class from another.

differential[1] *adj* **1a** of or constituting a difference. **b** based on or resulting from a differential. **2** in physics, of quantitative differences, or producing effects by reason of quantitative differences. **3** in mathematics, relating to a differential or differentiation. ➤➤ **differentially** *adv.*

differential[2] *n* **1** the amount of a difference between comparable individuals or classes; *specif* the amount by which the remuneration of distinct types of worker differs. **2** in mathematics, the product of the derivative of a function of one variable with the increment of the independent variable. **3** = DIFFERENTIAL GEAR.

differential calculus *n* a branch of mathematics dealing chiefly with the rate of change of functions with respect to their variables.

differential equation *n* an equation containing differentials or derivatives of functions.

differential gear *n* an arrangement of gears in a vehicle that allows one of the wheels imparting motion to turn, e.g. in going round a corner, faster than the other.

differentiate *v* **1** to mark or show a difference in (things). **2** to cause differentiation of (something) in the course of development. **3** to obtain the mathematical derivative of (a function, etc). **4** to become distinct or different in character. ➤➤ **differentiable** *adj,* **differentiator** *n.*

differentiation *n* **1** the act or an instance of differentiating. **2** development into more complex, numerous, or varied forms. **3a** modification of body parts for performance of particular functions. **b** all the processes whereby apparently similar cells, tissues, and structures attain their adult forms and functions.

difficult *adj* **1** hard to do, make, carry out, or understand. **2** hard to deal with, manage, or please.

difficulty *n* (*pl* **-ies**) **1** the state of being difficult. **2** an obstacle or impediment. **3** (*usu in pl*) a cause of trouble or embarrassment, *esp* of a financial nature. **4** a disagreement.

diffident *adj* lacking in self-confidence; reserved; unassertive. ➤➤ **diffidence** *n,* **diffidently** *adv.*

diffract *v* to cause (a beam of light) to become a set of light and dark or coloured bands in passing by the edge of an opaque body, through narrow slits, etc. ➤➤ **diffraction** *n,* **diffractive** *adj.*

diffuse[1] *adj* **1** not concentrated or localized; scattered. **2** lacking conciseness; verbose. ➤➤ **diffusely** *adv.*

diffuse[2] *v* **1** to spread out or cause (something) to spread or become transmitted. **2** to undergo diffusion. ➤➤ **diffuser** *n,* **diffusive** *adj.*

diffusion *n* **1** the act or an instance of diffusing or being diffused. **2a** the process whereby particles of liquids, gases, or solids intermingle as the result of their spontaneous movement. **b** reflection of light by a rough reflecting surface.

dig[1] *v* (**digging,** *past tense and past part.* **dug**) **1a** to turn up, loosen, or remove earth. **b** to hollow out (a hole or tunnel) by removing earth; to excavate. **c** (+ for) to look for something by digging. **2** to bring to the surface by digging, or as if by digging; to unearth. **3** to poke or prod. **4** *slang, dated* to understand or appreciate (something).

dig[2] *n* **1a** a thrust or poke. **b** *informal* a cutting or snide remark. **2** an archaeological excavation site. **3** *chiefly Brit, informal* (*in pl*) lodgings.

digerati *pl n informal* experts in information technology.

digest[1] *v* **1** to convert (food) into a form the body can use. **2** to soften or decompose or extract soluble ingredients from (a substance) by heat and moisture or chemicals. **3** to assimilate (something) mentally. ➤➤ **digestible** *adj.*

digest[2] *n* **1** a literary abridgment. **2** a systematic compilation of laws.

digestif /dizhes'teef/ *n* a drink taken after a meal as an aid to digestion.

digestion *n* the process or power of digesting something, *esp* food.

digestive[1] *n* **1** something that aids digestion. **2** *Brit* = DIGESTIVE BISCUIT.

digestive[2] *adj* relating to digestion.

digestive biscuit *n Brit* a slightly sweet biscuit made from wholemeal flour.

digger *n* **1** somebody or something that digs. **2** a tool or machine for digging.

diggings *pl n* a place of excavating, *esp* for ore, metals, or precious stones.

dight *v archaic* to dress or adorn (somebody or something).

dig in *v* **1** of a soldier: to dig defensive positions. **2** *informal* to hold stubbornly to a position. **3** *informal* to begin eating. ✱ **dig one's heels in** *informal* to refuse to move or change one's mind.

digit *n* **1a** any of the Arabic numerals from one to nine, usu also including 0. **b** any of the elements that combine to form numbers in a system other than the decimal system. **2** a finger or toe.

digital *adj* **1a** relating to calculation or data storage using discrete values rather than continuously variable ones. **b** relating to data presented, stored, or manipulated in the form of numerical digits. **c** of a computer: operating with numbers expressed as discrete pulses representing digits, usu in the form of binary notation: compare ANALOG. **d** of a clock or watch, etc: presenting information in the form of numerical digits rather than by a pointer moving round a dial: compare ANALOG. **e** of a way of recording sound: involving the conversion of sounds into digital form so that background noise and distortion are reduced: compare ANALOG. **2** of or relating to fingers or toes. ➤➤ **digitally** *adv.*

digital audiotape *n* magnetic tape that records and stores sound in digital form.

digital camera *n* a camera which produces digital images that can be stored on a computer, displayed on a screen, and printed.

digital compact cassette *n* a magnetic tape cassette on which sound can be recorded in digital form.

digital divide *n* the gap in educational potential, earning potential, etc that exists between those who have access to computing facilities and the Internet and those who do not.

digitalin *n* a compound obtained from digitalis and used in the treatment of heart disease.

digitalis *n* the dried leaf of the common foxglove, containing several compounds which are important as drugs used as powerful heart stimulants.

digitalize *or* **-ise** *v* to digitize (data, etc).

digital recording *n* a recording process in which sound or images are converted into numbers and stored for reproduction.

digital television *n* television in which the picture information is transmitted in digital form and decoded at the receiver.

digital versatile disc *n* = DIGITAL VIDEO DISC.

digital video disc *n* a type of high-capacity optical compact disc that can store a much larger quantity of video, audio, or other information than a conventional compact disc.

digitigrade *adj* of a mammal: walking on the toes with the back of the foot more or less raised: compare PLANTIGRADE.

digitize *or* **-ise** *v* to put (data, etc) into digital notation. ➤➤ **digitization** *n,* **digitizer** *n.*

dignified *adj* showing or having dignity.

dignify *v* (**-ies, -ied**) to confer dignity or distinction on (something or somebody).

dignitary *n* (*pl* **-ies**) a person of high rank or holding a position of dignity or honour.

dignity *n* **1** being worthy or esteemed. **2** high rank or position. **3** a high opinion of oneself; self-esteem. **4** stillness of manner; gravity. ✱ **beneath one's dignity** not worthy of being done by somebody as important as one considers oneself to be. **stand on one's dignity** to demand to be treated with respect.

dig out *v* **1** to remove by digging. **2** to search for and find.

digraph *n* a group of two successive letters, with the phonetic value of a single sound, e.g. *sh* or *th.*

digress *v* to turn aside, *esp* from the main subject in writing or speaking. ➤➤ **digression** *n,* **digressive** *adj.*

dig up *v* **1a** to find or produce by digging. **b** to remove by digging. **2** to discover by searching.

dihedral[1] *adj* having or contained by two flat surfaces.

dihedral[2] *n* **1** the angle between two intersecting planes or faces of a solid. **2** the angle between an upwardly inclined wing of an aircraft and a horizontal line.

dike[1] *n* see DYKE[1].

dike[2] *v* see DYKE[2].

dike[3] *n informal, derog* see DYKE[3].

diktat *n* a harsh settlement or ruling imposed by a victor or authority.

dilapidated *adj* decayed or fallen into partial ruin, *esp* through neglect or misuse. ➤➤ **dilapidation** *n.*

dilatation *n* **1** the condition of being stretched beyond normal dimensions. **2** = DILATION (2).

dilatation and curettage *n* = D AND C.

dilate *v* **1** to distend (something). **2** to become wide. **3** (+ on/upon) to comment at length on.

dilation *n* **1a** the act or an instance of dilating or being dilated. **b** the state of being dilated. **2** the stretching or enlarging of an organ or other part of the body.

dilator *n* **1** a muscle that contracts to dilate an organ or other part of the body. **2** a surgical instrument used in dilation.

dilatory *adj* **1** tending or intended to cause delay. **2** slow, tardy. ➤➤ **dilatorily** *adv,* **dilatoriness** *n.*

dildo *n* (*pl* **-os** *or* **-oes**) an object serving as an artificial penis for inserting into the vagina for sexual stimulation.

dilemma *n* **1a** a situation involving choice between two equally unsatisfactory alternatives. **b** *informal* a problem seemingly incapable of a satisfactory solution. **2** an argument in which an opponent's position is refuted by being shown to lead to two or more unacceptable alternatives.

Usage note

Strictly, a *dilemma* refers to a situation in which one is faced by two, and only two, equally unpleasant alternatives. *Dilemma* ought not to be used if there is an open choice as to how to deal with a problem or if the alternatives faced are not unpleasant.

dilettante /dili'tanti/ *n* (*pl* **dilettantes** *or* **dilettanti**) a person with a superficial interest in an art or a branch of knowledge. ➤➤ **dilettantish** *adj,* **dilettantism** *n.*

diligence[1] *n* steady application and effort.

diligence[2] *n* a stagecoach, *esp* one formerly used in France.

diligent *adj* showing steady application and effort. ➤➤ **diligently** *adv.*

dill *n* a European plant with aromatic foliage and seeds, both of which are used in flavouring foods, e.g. pickles.

dill pickle *n* a small pickled cucumber seasoned with dill.

dilly bag *n* an Australian mesh bag of native grass or fibres.

dillydally *v* (**-ies, -ied**) *informal* to waste time by loitering; to dawdle.

dilophosaurus *n* a meat-eating dinosaur of the early Jurassic period that walked on two legs and had two thin semicircular crests on its head.

diluent[1] *n* an agent for diluting.

diluent[2] *adj* making thinner or less concentrated; diluting.

dilute[1] *v* **1** to make (a liquid) thinner or more liquid by adding another liquid. **2** to diminish the strength, force, brilliance, etc of. ➤➤ **diluter** *n,* **dilution** *n,* **dilutive** *adj.*

dilute[2] *adj* weak; diluted.

dim[1] *adj* (**dimmer, dimmest**) **1** giving out a weak or insufficient light. **2** seen indistinctly. **3** not seeing clearly. **4** *informal* lacking intelligence; stupid. **5** not remembered clearly. ✱ **take a dim view of** to have an unfavourable or pessimistic attitude to (something). ➤➤ **dimly** *adv,* **dimness** *n.*

dim[2] *v* (**dimmed, dimming**) **1** to make or become dim. **2** *NAm* to dip (a vehicle's headlights).

dime *n* a coin worth a tenth of a US dollar. ✱ **a dime a dozen** *NAm, informal* very cheap.

dimension *n* **1a** (*in pl*) size in one or all directions. **b** (*usu in pl*) the range over which something extends; the scope. **2** an aspect. **3a** extension in one direction; *specif* any of three or four coordinates determining a position in space or in space and time. **b** (*usu in pl*) any of the fundamental quantities, *specif* mass, length, and time, which combine to make a derived unit. ➤➤ **dimensional** *adj.*

dimer *n* a compound formed by the union of two radicals or two molecules of a simpler compound. ➤➤ **dimeric** *adj.*

dimerize *or* **-ise** *v* to combine with (a similar molecule) to form a dimer. ➤➤ **dimerization** *n.*

dimetrodon *n* a large meat-eating reptile of the Permian period that had four short legs and a large sail-like flap along its back.

diminish *v* **1** to cause (something) to be or appear less. **2** to reduce (a person or thing) in standing or perceived worth. **3** to become gradually less; to dwindle. **4** to taper.

diminished responsibility *n* limitation of a person's criminal responsibility due to mental abnormality or instability.

diminishing returns *pl n* a rate of yield that beyond a certain point fails to increase in proportion to additional investments of labour or capital.

diminuendo *adj and adv* of a piece of music: to be performed with a decrease in volume.

diminution *n* a diminishing or decrease.

diminutive[1] *adj* **1** exceptionally small; tiny. **2** of certain affixes, e.g. *-ling*, and words formed with them, e.g. *duckling*: indicating small size and sometimes lovableness or triviality. ➤➤ **diminutively** *adv,* **diminutiveness** *n.*

diminutive[2] *n* a diminutive word, affix, or name.

dimity *n* (*pl* **-ies**) a corded cotton fabric woven with checks or stripes.

dimmer *n* **1** a device for regulating the brightness of electric lighting. **2** *NAm* a dipped headlight on a vehicle.

dimmer switch *n* = DIMMER (1).

dimorphism *n* the occurrence, combination, or existence of two distinct forms, e.g. of a species or the leaves of a plant. ➤➤ **dimorphic** *adj,* **dimorphous** *adj.*

dimple[1] *n* **1** a slight natural indentation in the cheek or another part of the human body. **2** a depression or indentation on a surface. ➤➤ **dimply** *adj.*

dimple[2] *v* **1** to mark (something) with dimples. **2** to form dimples, e.g. by smiling.

dim sum *n* Chinese food consisting of small pieces of meat or vegetable wrapped in pastry and fried or steamed.

dimwit *n informal* a stupid or mentally slow person. ➤➤ **dim-witted** *adj,* **dim-wittedly** *adv,* **dim-wittedness** *n.*

DIN *abbr* German Industrial Standards.

din[1] *n* a loud continued discordant noise.

din[2] *v* (**dinned, dinning**) to make a din. ✱ **din something into** to instil something into (somebody) by perpetual repetition.

dinar /'deenah/ *n* the basic monetary unit of certain N African and Middle Eastern countries, of Bosnia-Herzegovina, and Yugoslavia.

dine *v* **1** to eat dinner. **2** to entertain (somebody) to dinner. ✱ **dine out on** to be socially in demand as a result of (an amusing or interesting story one has to tell).

diner *n* **1** somebody who is dining. **2a** *NAm* a small restaurant, often beside the road. **b** *chiefly NAm* a dining car.

dinette *n* a small room or part of a room set aside for eating meals in.

ding *v* to make or cause (e.g. a bell) to make a ringing sound. ➤➤ **ding** *n.*

dingbat *n* an eccentric or stupid person.

dingdong[1] *n* **1** the ringing sound produced by repeated strokes, *esp* on a bell. **2** *Brit, informal* a rapid heated exchange of words or blows.

dingdong[2] *adj* **1** of or resembling the sound of a bell. **2** *Brit, informal* with the advantage, e.g. in an argument or fight, passing continually back and forth from one participant, side, etc to the other.

dinghy *n* (*pl* **-ies**) **1** a small boat often carried on a ship and used as a lifeboat or to transport passengers to and from shore. **2** a small open sailing boat. **3** a rubber life raft.

dingle *n* a small narrow wooded valley.

dingo *n* (*pl* **-oes** *or* **-os**) a wild dog of Australia.

dingy *adj* (**-ier, -iest**) **1** dirty; discoloured. **2** shabby; squalid. ➤➤ **dingily** *adv,* **dinginess** *n.*

dining car *n* a railway carriage where meals are served.

dinkum *adj Aus, NZ, informal* real or genuine.

dinky *adj* (**-ier, -iest**) *informal* **1** *chiefly Brit* neat and dainty. **2** *chiefly NAm* small; insignificant.

dinner *n* **1** the principal meal of the day taken either in the evening or at midday. **2** a formal evening meal or banquet.

dinner jacket *n* a jacket, usu black, for men's semiformal evening wear.

dinner lady *n Brit, informal* a woman who serves meals and supervises children during mealtimes at school.

dinosaur *n* **1** any of a group of extinct, typically very large reptiles of the Mesozoic era, most of which lived on the land. **2** a person or organization that is outdated and unwilling or unable to adapt to change.

dint[1] *n archaic* a blow or stroke. ✱ **by dint of** by means or application of.

dint[2] *v* **1** to make a dent in. **2** to drive (something) in with force.

diocese *n* the area under the jurisdiction of a bishop. ➤➤ **diocesan** *adj.*

diode *n* **1** a semiconductor device having only two terminals. **2** a thermionic valve having only an anode and a cathode.

dioecious (*NAm* **diecious**) *adj* having male and female reproductive organs in different individuals: compare MONOECIOUS.

Dionysiac *adj* = DIONYSIAN.

Dionysian *adj* **1** of or relating to Dionysus, the Greek god of wine. **2** frenzied; orgiastic.

dioptre (*NAm* **diopter**) *n* a unit of measurement of the refractive power of lenses equal to the reciprocal of the focal length in metres.

dioptric *adj* **1** causing or serving to cause the convergence or divergence of a beam of light; refractive. **2** produced by means of refraction.

dioptrics *pl n* (*used as sing. or pl*) the branch of optics concerned with the refraction of light.

diorama *n* **1** a scenic representation in which an artificially lit translucent painting is viewed through an opening. **2a** a three-dimensional representation in which miniature modelled figures, buildings, etc are displayed against a painted background. **b** a life-size museum exhibit of an animal or bird in realistic natural surroundings against a painted background.

diorite *n* a medium- to coarse-grained intrusive igneous rock rich in plagioclase. ➤➤ **dioritic** *adj.*

dioxide *n* an oxide containing two atoms of oxygen.

dioxin *n* any of a group of poisonous chemical compounds produced as by-products during the manufacture of certain herbicides or during burning at high temperatures.

DIP *abbr* **1** document image processing. **2** Dual Inline Package.

Dip. *abbr* Diploma.

dip[1] *v* (**dipped, dipping**) **1a** to plunge or immerse (something or somebody) in a liquid. **b** to immerse (a sheep, etc) in an antiseptic or parasite-killing solution, or (wood, grain, etc) in a preservative. **c** to moisten, cool, dye, or coat (something) by immersion. **2** to lift up (water, grain etc) by scooping or ladling. **3** to lower (something) and then raise it again. **4** to lower (the beam of a vehicle's headlights) so as to reduce glare. **5** (+ in/into) to reach (a hand, etc) into a container, *esp* so as to take something out. **6** to drop or decrease suddenly, often only temporarily and by a small amount. **7a** to slope down. **b** to incline downward from the plane of the horizon. ✱ **dip into 1** to make inroads into (something) for funds or supplies. **2** to read (something) superficially or in a random manner.

dip[2] *n* **1** the act or an instance of dipping or being dipped. **2** a brief bathe. **3** a sauce or soft mixture into which food is dipped before being eaten. **4** a brief drop followed by a rise. **5a** a hollow or depression. **b** a short downward slope, e.g. in a road, followed by a rise.

diphtheria *n* an acute infectious disease caused by a bacterium and marked by fever and the formation of a false membrane, *esp* in the throat, causing difficulty in breathing.

diphthong *n* a gliding monosyllabic vowel sound, e.g. /oy/ in *toy*, that starts at the articulatory position for one vowel and moves to the position of another.

diplodocus *n* a large plant-eating dinosaur with a long neck and long tail.

diploid *adj* of a cell or organism: having double the basic number of chromosomes arranged in homologous pairs: compare HAPLOID, POLYPLOID[1].

diploma *n* a certificate of a qualification, usu in a more specialized subject or at a lower level than a degree.

diplomacy *n* **1** the art and practice of conducting international relations. **2** skill and tact in handling affairs or dealing with people.

diplomat *n* **1** a person, e.g. an ambassador, employed in diplomacy. **2** a person skilled in dealing with people tactfully and adroitly.

diplomatic *adj* **1** of diplomats or international relations. **2** employing tact and conciliation. ➤➤ **diplomatically** *adv.*

diplomatic bag *n chiefly Brit* a bag or container in which official mail is sent, exempt from customs inspection, to or from an embassy.

diplomatic corps *n* the whole body of diplomats representing foreign governments in a country.

diplomatic immunity *n* the exemption from local laws and taxes accorded to diplomatic staff abroad.

dipole *n* **1** a pair of equal and opposite electric charges, or magnetic poles of opposite sign, separated by a small distance. **2** a radio aerial consisting of two horizontal rods in line, with their ends slightly separated. ➤➤ **dipolar** *adj.*

dipper *n* **1** somebody or something that dips. **2** a small bird somewhat resembling a blackbird that swims underwater in rivers and streams to feed. **3** something, e.g. a long-handled cup, used for dipping.

dippy *adj* (**-ier, -iest**) *informal* crazy; eccentric.

dipsomania *n* acute and relatively short-lived bouts of craving for alcohol. ➤➤ **dipsomaniac** *n.*

dipstick *n* **1** a graduated rod for measuring the depth of a liquid, e.g. the oil in a car's engine. **2** *informal* a stupid or contemptible person.

dipteran *n* any of an order of insects that has a single pair of wings. ➤➤ **dipteran** *adj,* **dipterous** *adj.*

diptych *n* a painting or carving done on two hinged panels and used *esp* as an altarpiece.

dire *adj* **1** warning of disaster; ominous. **2** desperately urgent. **3** *informal* dreadful; awful. ➤➤ **direly** *adv,* **direness** *n.*

direct[1] *v* **1a** to control and regulate the activities or course of. **b** to control the organization and performance of (a film, play, or broadcast). **c** to order or instruct (somebody) with authority. **2** to show or point out the way for (somebody). **3** to cause (something) to turn, move, point, or follow a straight course. **4** to address or aim (a remark).

direct[2] *adj* **1a** going from one point to another in time or space without deviation or interruption; straight. **b** going by the shortest way. **2a** stemming immediately from a source, cause, or reason. **b** passing in a straight line of descent from parent to offspring. **3** frank; straightforward. **4** operating without an intervening agency. ➤➤ **directness** *n.*

direct[3] *adv* **1** from point to point without deviation; by the shortest way. **2** without an intervening agency or stage.

direct access *n* a fast method of finding data in a storage medium, *esp* on magnetic disk or in random-access memory, where the access time is independent of the location of the data: compare SEQUENTIAL ACCESS.

direct action *n* action that seeks to achieve an end by the most immediately effective means, e.g. a boycott or strike.

direct current *n* an electric current flowing in one direction only, *esp* such a current that is substantially constant in value: compare ALTERNATING CURRENT.

direct debit *n* an order to a bank to accept charges for amounts not specified in advance on an account from another named account at specified times.

direction *n* **1a** the line or course along which somebody or something moves or is aimed. **b** the point towards which somebody or something faces. **2a** the act or an instance of directing or being directed. **b** guidance or supervision of action. **c** the act, art, or technique of directing an orchestra, film, or theatrical production. **3** (*in pl*) explicit instructions on how to do something or get to a place. ➤➤ **directional** *adj*, **directionless** *adj*.

directive[1] *n* an authoritative instruction issued by a high-level body or official.

directive[2] *adj* **1** serving to direct, guide, or influence. **2** serving to provide a direction.

directly[1] *adv* **1** in a direct manner. **2** without delay; immediately.

directly[2] *conj chiefly Brit, informal* immediately after; as soon as.

direct mail *n* unsolicited advertising material posted by a company to potential customers.

direct object *n* a grammatical object representing the primary goal or the result of the action of a verb, e.g. *me* in 'He hit me' and *a house* in 'We built a house'.

director *n* **1** the head of an organized group or administrative unit. **2** a member of a governing board entrusted with the overall direction of a company. **3** somebody who has responsibility for supervising the artistic and technical aspects of a film or play. ➤➤ **directorial** *adj*, **directorship** *n*.

directorate *n* (*used as sing. or pl*) a board of directors, e.g. of a company.

director-general *n* (*pl* **directors-general** *or* **director-generals**) the senior director of a large organization.

directory *n* (*pl* **-ies**) **1** an alphabetical or classified list, e.g. of names, addresses, telephone numbers, etc. **2** on a computer, a list of the files contained in a disk.

directory assistance *n NAm* = DIRECTORY ENQUIRIES.

directory enquiries *pl n* (*used as sing. or pl*) a telephone service providing enquirers with the telephone numbers of people and organizations.

direct speech *n* in grammar, the exact words uttered by a person to somebody as opposed to their words in the form in which they are reported or referred to, e.g. *I told you so* as opposed to *I said I'd told him so*.

direct tax *n* a tax on income or resources exacted directly from the person, organization, etc on whom it is levied.

dirge *n* **1** a song or hymn of grief or lamentation, *esp* intended to accompany funeral or memorial rites. **2** a slow mournful song or piece of music.

dirham /'diərəm, 'diəhəm/ *n* **1** the basic monetary unit of Morocco and the United Arab Emirates. **2a** a unit of currency in Libya, worth 1000th of a dinar. **b** a unit of currency in Qatar, worth 100th of a riyal.

dirigible *n* an airship.

dirigisme *n chiefly derog* state control of the economy and social institutions. ➤➤ **dirigiste** *adj*.

dirk *n* a long straight-bladed dagger, formerly used by Scottish Highlanders.

dirndl *n* **1** (*also* **dirndl skirt**) a full skirt with a tight waistband. **2** a traditional Alpine style of woman's dress with a tight bodice and a dirndl skirt.

dirt *n* **1a** a filthy or soiling substance, e.g. mud or grime. **b** *informal* excrement. **2** earth; soil. **3** *informal* **a** obscene or pornographic speech or writing. **b** scandalous or malicious gossip. ✱ **treat like dirt** *informal* to treat (somebody) very badly, as if they are of no value or significance.

dirt bike *n* a motorcycle designed for riding across country or on unmade roads.

dirt cheap *adj and adv informal* at a very low price.

dirt track *n* a track of earth, cinders, etc used for motorcycle races or flat races.

dirty[1] *adj* (**-ier, -iest**) **1a** not clean or pure; marked or contaminated with dirt. **b** causing somebody or something to become soiled or covered with dirt. **2a** base; sordid. **b** unsportsmanlike; unfair. **c** low; despicable: *a dirty trick*. **3a** indecent; obscene: *dirty language*. **b** involving illicit sexual activity: *a dirty weekend*. **4** of the weather: rough or stormy. **5** of a colour: not clear and bright; dull. **6** conveying resentment or disgust: *She gave him a dirty look*. ✱ **do the dirty on** to play a mean or treacherous trick on (somebody). ➤➤ **dirtily** *adv*, **dirtiness** *n*.

dirty[2] *v* (**-ies, -ied**) to make or become dirty.

dirty[3] *adv* **1** *informal* very. **2a** in an unfair or underhanded manner. **b** using obscene or indecent language.

dirty old man *n informal* an elderly man who shows an interest in sex that is considered lewd or immoral or distasteful in a person of his age.

dirty word *n* **1** an obscene word or swearword. **2** *informal* something somebody has a strong dislike of: *Effort is a dirty word in his book*.

dirty work *n informal* behaviour or an act that is unfair, treacherous, or criminal.

dis *or* **diss** *v* (**dissed, dissing**) *informal, chiefly NAm* to insult; to speak to in a disrespectful manner.

dis- *prefix* **1a** to do the opposite of (a specified action): *disappear*. **b** to deprive of or remove (something specified) from: *disarm*. **c** to exclude or expel from: *disbar*. **2** opposite or absence of: *disbelief*. **3** not: *dishonest*. **4** completely: *disgruntled*.

disability *n* (*pl* **-ies**) **1** the condition of being disabled; *specif* inability to do something because of physical or mental impairment. **2** something that disables; a handicap.

disable *v* **1** to make (somebody or something) incapable or ineffective. **2** to deprive (somebody or something) of physical soundness; to cripple. ➤➤ **disablement** *n*.

disabled *adj* **1** having physical disabilities. **2** having been made incapable of operating.

disabuse *v* (*usu* + of) to free (somebody) from a mistaken impression or judgment.

disaccharide *n* any of a class of sugars, e.g. sucrose, which, on hydrolysis, yield two MONOSACCHARIDE (simple sugar) molecules.

disadvantage[1] *n* **1a** an unfavourable or prejudicial situation. **b** somebody or something which causes one to be in an unfavourable condition or position; a handicap. **2** loss or damage, *esp* to reputation or finances. ⋙ **disadvantageous** *adj.*

disadvantage[2] *v* to place at a disadvantage.

disadvantaged *adj* underprivileged, *esp* socially.

disaffected *adj* discontented and resentful, *esp* towards authority. ⋙ **disaffection** *n.*

disagree *v* **1** (*often* + with) to differ in opinion. **2** to be unlike or at variance with. **3** (+ with) to have a bad effect on.

disagreeable *adj* **1** unpleasant; objectionable. **2** peevish; ill-tempered. ⋙ **disagreeably** *adv.*

disagreement *n* **1** a difference of opinion; an argument. **2** a lack of correspondence; a disparity.

disallow *v* **1** to refuse to allow; to prohibit. **2** to refuse to admit or recognize the truth or validity of. ⋙ **disallowance** *n.*

disambiguate *v* to remove possible ambiguity from (a phrase, sentence, etc). ⋙ **disambiguation** *n.*

disappear *v* **1** to pass from view suddenly or gradually. **2** to cease to be or to be known. **3** *informal* to leave or depart, *esp* secretly. **4** to cause (somebody) to disappear from their home or from society by imprisoning or killing them secretly. ⋙ **disappearance** *n.*

disapplication *n* in British education, exemption from the requirements of the National Curriculum.

disappoint *v* to fail to meet the expectation or hope of (somebody), or to sadden (somebody) by so doing. ⋙ **disappointing** *adj,* **disappointingly** *adv.*

disappointed *adj* defeated in expectation or hope; thwarted. ⋙ **disappointedly** *adv.*

disappointment *n* **1** the act or an instance of disappointing or being disappointed. **2** somebody or something that disappoints.

disapprobation *n formal* disapproval.

disapproval *n* unfavourable opinion; censure.

disapprove *v* **1** to have or express an unfavourable opinion of (something or somebody). **2** to refuse approval to (something); to reject. ⋙ **disapproving** *adj,* **disapprovingly** *adv.*

disarm *v* **1a** to deprive (somebody) of a weapon or weapons. **b** to deprive (a country or force) of a means of attack or defence. **c** to make (a bomb, etc) harmless, *esp* by removing a fuse or warhead. **2** to lay aside arms. **3** to reduce or abolish weapons and armed forces. **4** to dispel the hostility or suspicion of.

disarmament *n* the relinquishment or reduction of weapons and armed forces.

disarming *adj* allaying criticism or hostility. ⋙ **disarmingly** *adv.*

disarrange *v* to disturb the arrangement or order of.

disarray[1] *n* a lack of order or sequence; disorder.

disarray[2] *v* to throw or place into disorder.

disassemble *v* to take (a machine, etc) apart. ⋙ **disassembly** *n.*

disassembler *n* somebody or something that disassembles something; *specif* a computer program that translates something written in machine code into assembly language.

disassociate *v* = DISSOCIATE. ⋙ **disassociation** *n.*

disaster *n* **1a** a sudden event bringing great damage, loss, or destruction. **b** an unfortunate occurrence; a calamity. **2** *informal* a failure. ⋙ **disastrous** *adj,* **disastrously** *adv.*

disavow *v formal* to deny knowledge of or responsibility for; to repudiate. ⋙ **disavowal** *n.*

disband *v* **1** of a group: to break up and separate; to disperse. **2** to break up (a group).

disbar *v* (**disbarred, disbarring**) to deprive (a barrister) of the right to practise; to expel from the bar. ⋙ **disbarment** *n.*

disbelief *n* mental rejection of something as untrue.

disbelieve *v* **1** to reject or withhold belief. **2** to believe that (somebody) is not speaking the truth. ⋙ **disbeliever** *n,* **disbelieving** *adj.*

disburden *v* **1** to unburden (oneself or one's mind). **2** to unload (something).

disburse *v* to pay out (money), *esp* from a fund. ⋙ **disbursal** *n,* **disbursement** *n,* **disburser** *n.*

disc (*NAm* **disk**) *n* **1a** a thin flat circular object. **b** an apparently flat figure or surface, e.g. of a planet. **2** a disk for a computer. **3** any of the cartilaginous discs between the spinal vertebrae.

Usage note

disc *or* disk? *Disc* is the correct spelling of the word in British English, except in the context of computers where the usual American English spelling *disk* is generally preferred.

discard[1] *v* to get rid of (something or somebody) as useless or superfluous.

discard[2] *n* somebody or something discarded.

disc brake *n* a brake that operates by the friction of pads pressing against the sides of a rotating disc.

disc camera *n* a camera using film contained on a disc that rotates in the camera after each exposure.

discern *v* **1** to detect with one of the senses, *esp* vision. **2** to perceive or recognize mentally. ⋙ **discernible** *adj,* **discernibly** *adv.*

discerning *adj* showing insight and understanding; discriminating. ⋙ **discernment** *n.*

discharge[1] *v* **1a** to dismiss from employment or service. **b** to release from custody or care. **2a** to fulfil (a debt or obligation) by performing an appropriate action. **b** to release from an obligation. **3a** to send or pour out (a liquid or gas); to emit. **b** to shoot (a firearm). **4** to annul (an order of court) legally. **5** to remove an electric charge from (something) or reduce the electric charge of (something). ⋙ **discharger** *n.*

discharge[2] *n* **1** the act or an instance of discharging. **2** something that is discharged or emitted. **3** a brief flow of an electric charge through a gas, usu with associated light emission. ⋙ **discharger** *n.*

disciple *n* **1** a person who learns from a teacher or instructor; a pupil or follower. **2** any of the followers of Christ during his life on earth; *esp* any of Christ's twelve appointed followers. ⋙ **discipleship** *n.*

disciplinarian *n* a person who enforces or advocates strict discipline or order.

discipline[1] *n* **1a** order obtained by enforcing obedience, e.g. in a school or army. **b** self-control. **2** training of the mind and character designed to produce obedience and self-control. **3** punishment or chastisement. **4** a field of study. ⋙ **disciplinary** *adj.*

discipline[2] *v* **1** to punish or penalize (a person or animal) for the sake of discipline. **2** to train (a person or animal) by instruction and exercise, *esp* in obedience and self-control. **3** to bring (a group, e.g. troops) under control.

disc jockey *n* a person who plays and introduces recorded music on a radio programme or at a nightclub or party.

disclaim *v* **1** to deny or disavow. **2** to renounce a legal claim to (property). **3** to make a disclaimer.

disclaimer *n* **1** a denial or repudiation. **2a** a denial of legal responsibility. **b** a renunciation of a legal claim.

disclose *v* **1** to make (information) known; to reveal (information) to public knowledge. **2** to expose to view. ➤➤ **discloser** *n.*

disclosure *n* **1** something disclosed; a revelation. **2** the act or an instance of disclosing or exposing.

disco *n* (*pl* **-os**) *informal* **1** a discotheque. **2** a type of soul-based dance music.

discography *n* (*pl* **-ies**) **1** a descriptive list of recordings, *esp* by a particular artist or band. **2** the study of recorded music. ➤➤ **discographer** *n.*

discoid *adj* resembling a disc or discus; disc-shaped. ➤➤ **discoidal** *adj.*

discolour (*NAm* **discolor**) *v* **1** to cause to change colour for the worse; to stain. **2** to become discoloured. ➤➤ **discoloration** *n,* **discolouration** *n.*

discombobulate *v NAm, informal* to upset or confuse (somebody).

discomfit *v* (**discomfited, discomfiting**) **1** to cause perplexity and embarrassment to; to disconcert. **2** to frustrate the plans of; to thwart. ➤➤ **discomfiture** *n.*

discomfort[1] *n* mental or physical unease, or something causing this.

discomfort[2] *v* to make (somebody) uncomfortable or uneasy.

discommode *v* to inconvenience (somebody). ➤➤ **discommodious** *adj.*

discompose *v formal* to disturb the composure of (somebody). ➤➤ **discomposure** *n.*

disconcert *v* to disturb the composure of (somebody); to fluster. ➤➤ **disconcerted** *adj,* **disconcerting** *adj,* **disconcertingly** *adv.*

disconnect *v* **1** to break the connection of (something), e.g. to a power supply. **2a** to cut off the supply of (e.g. electricity or the telephone). **b** to cut off the supply of e.g. electricity or the telephone to (a person, etc). **3** to cut (somebody) off during a telephone call. **4** to become disconnected or be able to be disconnected. ➤➤ **disconnection** *n.*

disconnected *adj* **1** disjointed or incoherent. **2** not connected; having been disconnected.

disconsolate *adj* dejected; downcast. ➤➤ **disconsolately** *adv.*

discontent[1] *n* lack of contentment; dissatisfaction.

discontent[2] *v* to make discontented.

discontent[3] *adj* = DISCONTENTED.

discontented *adj* restlessly unhappy; dissatisfied. ➤➤ **discontentment** *n.*

discontinue *v* (**discontinues, discontinued, discontinuing**) **1** to cease or stop (something). **2** to cease production of. **3** to come to an end. ➤➤ **discontinuation** *n.*

discontinuous *adj* lacking sequence, coherence, or continuity. ➤➤ **discontinuity** *n.*

discord *n* **1** lack of agreement or harmony; conflict. **2a** a combination of musical sounds that strikes the ear very harshly; dissonance. **b** a harsh unpleasant combination of sounds.

discordant *adj* **1** relating to a discord; dissonant. **2** disagreeing; at variance. ➤➤ **discordance** *n,* **discordancy** *n,* **discordantly** *adv.*

discotheque *n* a nightclub for dancing to recorded music.

discount[1] *n* **1** a reduction made from the gross amount or value of something, e.g. a reduction in the price of goods or a reduction in the amount due on a debt, etc when paid promptly or before the specified date. **2** (*used before a noun*) selling goods or services at a discount, or relating to such goods and services.

discount[2] *v* **1a** to make a deduction from (a price). **b** to sell or offer for sale at a discount. **c** to buy or sell (a bill of exchange) before maturity at below the stated price. **2a** to leave (something) out of account as unreliable or irrelevant; to disregard. **b** to underestimate the importance of; to minimize.

discountenance *v* **1** to abash or disconcert. **2** *formal* to discourage (something or somebody) by showing disapproval.

discount house *n chiefly Brit* an organization whose business is discounting bills of exchange before their due date.

discount rate *n* **1** the interest on an annual basis deducted in advance on a loan, e.g. a bank loan. **2** the charge levied by a central bank for advances and rediscounts.

discourage *v* **1** to deprive of confidence; to dishearten. **2a** to hinder or deter (somebody) from doing something. **b** to attempt to prevent (something), *esp* by showing disapproval of it or taking some action to counter it. ➤➤ **discouragement** *n,* **discouraging** *adj,* **discouragingly** *adv.*

discourse[1] *n* **1** talk, conversation, or continuous text, *esp* with regard to logical flow and progression. **2** a formal speech or piece of writing.

discourse[2] *v literary* **1** (+ on/upon) to express one's ideas in speech or writing. **2** (*also* + on/upon) to talk or converse.

discourteous *adj* rude or impolite; lacking in manners or consideration for others. ➤➤ **discourteously** *adv,* **discourteousness** *n.*

discourtesy *n* (*pl* **-ies**) rudeness, incivility, or an instance of either.

discover *v* **1** to find by searching or by chance. **2** to be the first to see, find, or know about (something). **3** to realize or find out (a fact). ➤➤ **discoverable** *adj,* **discoverer** *n.*

discovery *n* (*pl* **-ies**) **1** the act or process of discovering or revealing something; the process of being discovered or revealed. **2a** somebody or something discovered. **b** a divulgence or revelation. **3** in law, an obligatory disclosure of documents or facts by a party to a legal action.

discredit[1] *v* (**discredited, discrediting**) **1** to reject (a story or statement) as untrue. **2** to cast doubt on the authority or reputation of (a person or their ideas, work, etc).

discredit[2] *n* **1** loss of credit or reputation. **2** a person or thing that brings disgrace.

discreditable *adj* bringing discredit or disgrace; shameful. ➤➤ **discreditably** *adv.*

discreet *adj* **1** judicious in speech or conduct; *esp* capable of maintaining a prudent silence. **2** subtle; trying not to attract attention. **3** unpretentious or modest; showing quiet good taste. ➤➤ **discreetly** *adv,* **discreetness** *n.*

Usage note

discreet *or* **discrete**? Though they are pronounced the same and look very similar, these two words have distinct and different meanings. When used of people, *discreet* means 'careful, reliable, and not likely to gossip' (*Can we rely on her to be discreet?*): when used about actions, it means 'unlikely to attract attention' (*We have made a few discreet inquiries*). *Discrete* is a more technical word meaning 'separate' or 'individually distinct': *The process can be broken down into a number of discrete stages.*

discrepancy *n* (*pl* **-ies**) **1** the state of being at variance, or of not agreeing. **2** an instance of inconsistency between two accounts, etc. ➤➤ **discrepant** *adj.*

discrete *adj* **1** individually distinct. **2** consisting of distinct or unconnected elements; discontinuous. ➤➤ **discretely** *adv,* **discreteness** *n.*

Usage note

discrete *or* discreet? See note at DISCREET.

discretion *n* **1** the quality of being discreet, e.g. in employing self-control, and in safeguarding the dignity and privacy of others. **2** the freedom to act as one sees fit in any particular situation.

discretionary *adj* **1** left to or exercised at one's own discretion. **2** subject to the discretion of another.

discretionary income *n* what remains of one's income after obligatory charges and basic living expenses have been deducted.

discriminate[1] *v* **1a** (+ between) to make a distinction between (two things). **b** to show good judgment or discernment. **2** (+ against) to treat (somebody) differently and *esp* unfavourably on the grounds of race, sex, religion, etc. ➤➤ **discriminable** *adj,* **discriminably** *adv.*

discriminate[2] *adj* showing discrimination.

discriminating *adj* **1** discerning or judicious in matters of taste, etc. **2** observant of fine differences and distinctions. ➤➤ **discriminatingly** *adv.*

discrimination *n* **1** prejudicial treatment, e.g. on the grounds of race or sex. **2** the recognition or appreciation of the difference between one thing and another. **3** discernment and good judgment, *esp* in matters of taste.

discriminative *adj* = DISCRIMINATORY.

discriminatory *adj* showing discrimination, *esp* of an unfavourable kind. ➤➤ **discriminatorily** *adv.*

discursive *adj* **1** of a person's writing or lecturing style, etc: passing unmethodically from one topic to another; digressive. **2** relating to discourse of various kinds. ➤➤ **discursively** *adv,* **discursiveness** *n.*

discus *n* a solid disc that is thicker in the centre than at the edge, thrown as an event in ancient Greek games and in modern athletic contests.

discuss *v* **1** to consider or examine (a topic) in speech or writing. **2** to talk about (an issue, problem, etc) so as to make decisions. ➤➤ **discussable** *adj,* **discussant** *n.*

discussion *n* **1** consideration of a question in open debate or conversation. **2** a conversation or debate about something.

disdain[1] *n* the feeling one has for something one despises; contempt or scorn.

disdain[2] *v* **1** to regard (a person or thing) with disdain. **2** to refuse (to do something) because of disdain.

disdainful *adj* feeling or showing disdain; superior. ➤➤ **disdainfully** *adv,* **disdainfulness** *n.*

disease *n* a condition of a living animal or plant body, or of a specific part of one, that impairs the performance of a vital function. ➤➤ **diseased** *adj.*

diseconomy *n* (*pl* **-ies**) **1** a lack of economy. **2** an increase in costs, or a factor responsible for this.

disembark *v* to alight from a ship, plane, etc. ➤➤ **disembarkation** *n.*

disembarrass *v formal* (*usu* + of) to free (somebody) from something troublesome or superfluous.

disembodied *adj* **1** denoting a soul existing apart from the body it inhabited. **2** coming from an invisible source: *a disembodied voice.*

disembowel *v* (**disembowelled, disembowelling,** *NAm* **disemboweled, disemboweling**) to remove the bowels or entrails of or eviscerate (a person or animal). ➤➤ **disembowelment** *n.*

disempower *v* to deprive (a person or group) of initiative or confidence. ➤➤ **disempowerment** *n.*

disenchant *v* to rid (somebody) of an illusion; to disillusion. ➤➤ **disenchanted** *adj,* **disenchantingly** *adj,* **disenchantingly** *adv,* **disenchantment** *n.*

disenfranchise *v* **1** to deprive (a person) of any citizen's rights, *esp* that of voting. **2** to deprive (a place) of the right to send representatives to an elected body. ➤➤ **disenfranchisement** *n.*

disengage *v* **1** to release or detach (somebody, *esp* oneself, or a part of one) from something that holds, engages, or entangles. **2** to remove (troops) from combat areas. **3** of troops or combatants: to withdraw, or retire from engagement. ➤➤ **disengagement** *n.*

disentangle *v* **1** to free (somebody or something) from entanglements. **2** to unravel (tangled wool, string, etc).

disequilibrium *n* loss or lack of equilibrium.

disestablish *v* to deprive (*esp* a national Church) of established status. ➤➤ **disestablishment** *n.*

disfavour[1] (*NAm* **disfavor**) *n* **1** disapproval or dislike. **2** the state of being disapproved of.

disfavour[2] *v* to regard or treat (a person or thing) with disfavour.

disfigure *v* to mar or spoil the appearance or quality of (somebody or something). ➤➤ **disfigurement** *n.*

disgorge *v* **1** to vomit (food) from the stomach. **2** to discharge (a load or contents). **3** to give up (dishonestly acquired funds) on request or under pressure.

disgrace[1] *v* **1** to bring reproach or shame to (somebody) through unacceptable conduct. **2** to cause (somebody) to lose favour or standing, *esp* as a consequence of dishonourable behaviour.

disgrace[2] *n* **1** loss of favour, honour, or respect; shame. **2** somebody or something shameful.

disgraceful *adj* shameful or shocking. ➤➤ **disgracefully** *adv,* **disgracefulness** *n.*

disgruntled *adj* aggrieved and dissatisfied. ➤➤ **disgruntlement** *n.*

disguise[1] *v* **1** to change the appearance or nature of (a person or thing) in order to conceal their identity. **2** to hide the true state or character of.

disguise[2] *n* **1** a costume or other means of disguising oneself or concealing one's identity. **2** the state of being disguised.

disgust[1] *n* **1** the loathing or revulsion one feels for something that sickens one, or that one cannot bear. **2** the indignation one feels at a moral outrage.

disgust[2] *v* to arouse repugnance or indignation in (somebody). ➤➤ **disgusted** *adj,* **disgustedly** *adv,* **disgusting** *adj,* **disgustingly** *adv,* **disgustingness** *n.*

dish[1] *n* **1a** a shallow open often circular vessel used *esp* for holding or serving food. **b** (**the dishes**) the utensils and tableware used in preparing, serving, and eating a meal. **2** a type of food prepared in a particular way. **3** something resembling a dish in shape. **4** *informal* an attractive person. ➤➤ **dishful** (*pl* **dishfuls**) *n.*

dish[2] *v* **1** *chiefly Brit, informal* to ruin or spoil (a person or their hopes). **2** *NAm* to gossip. ✱ **dish the dirt** *informal* to spread gossip.

dishabille /disə'beel/ *n* = DÉSHABILLÉ.

disharmony *n* lack of harmony; discord. ➤➤ **disharmonious** *adj.*

dishcloth *n* a cloth for washing or drying dishes.

dishearten *v* to discourage or cause to lose enthusiasm or morale. ➤➤ **disheartening** *adj*, **dishearteningly** *adv*.

dishevelled (*NAm* **disheveled**) *adj* of a person's hair or appearance: unkempt or untidy.

dishonest *adj* not honest, truthful, or sincere; deceitful. ➤➤ **dishonestly** *adv*, **dishonesty** *n*.

dishonor *n and v NAm* see DISHONOUR[1], DISHONOUR[2].

dishonorable *adj NAm* see DISHONOURABLE.

dishonour[1] (*NAm* **dishonor**) *n* **1** loss of honour or reputation. **2** a state of shame or disgrace. **3** an insult or affront.

dishonour[2] (*NAm* **dishonor**) *v* **1** to treat (a person, or a thing deserving respect) in a degrading or disrespectful manner. **2** to bring shame on (somebody). **3** of a bank, etc: to refuse to accept or pay (a cheque, etc).

dishonourable (*NAm* **dishonorable**) *adj* base or shameful; discreditable. ➤➤ **dishonourably** *adv*.

dish out *v* **1** to serve out (food) from a dish, pan, etc. **2** *informal* to give or distribute (advice, criticism, etc) freely.

dish up *v* **1** to serve (food) onto dishes from a pan, etc. **2** to produce or present (facts or information).

dishwasher *n* **1** an electrical machine that washes dishes. **2** a person employed to wash dishes.

dishy *adj* (**-ier, -iest**) *chiefly Brit, informal* of a person, *esp* a man: attractive.

disillusion[1] *n* the state of being disillusioned or disabused; loss of a cherished ideal or belief.

disillusion[2] *v* to reveal the unpleasant truth about somebody or something admired to (somebody); to disenchant. ➤➤ **disillusioned** *adj*, **disillusionment** *n*.

disincentive *n* something that discourages action or effort; a deterrent.

disinclination *n* unwillingness to do something.

disinclined *adj* unwilling to do something.

disinfect *v* to cleanse (a place, etc) of infection, *esp* by destroying harmful micro-organisms. ➤➤ **disinfection** *n*.

disinfectant *n* a chemical that destroys harmful micro-organisms. ➤➤ **disinfectant** *adj*.

disinflation *n* a reduction of the rate of inflation. ➤➤ **disinflationary** *adj*.

disinformation *n* deliberately false or misleading information, e.g. supplied to an enemy.

disingenuous *adj* insincere, especially in pretending ignorance of something one knows about; falsely naïve. ➤➤ **disingenuously** *adv*, **disingenuousness** *n*.

disinherit *v* (**disinherited, disinheriting**) to deprive (an heir) of the right to inherit, *esp* by altering one's will. ➤➤ **disinheritance** *n*.

disintegrate *v* **1** to break into fragments or constituent elements. **2** to lose unity or cohesion. ➤➤ **disintegrative** *adj*, **disintegrator** *n*.

disintegration *n* **1** the act or an instance of disintegrating. **2** the process by which a nucleus or other subatomic particle emits radioactive particles or divides into smaller units.

disinter *v* (**disinterred, disinterring**) **1** to remove (somebody's corpse) from a grave or tomb. **2** to bring to light or unearth (something hidden or forgotten). ➤➤ **disinterment** *n*.

disinterest *n* **1** lack of self-interest; impartiality. **2** *non-standard* lack of interest; apathy.

disinterested *adj* **1** free from selfish motive or interest; impartial. **2** *non-standard* uninterested. ➤➤ **disinterestedly** *adv*, **disinterestedness** *n*.

Usage note

disinterested *or* **uninterested**? *Disinterested* does not mean the same as *uninterested*. A *disinterested* observer is somebody who is not on anybody's side; an *uninterested* observer simply does not care about what is going on.

disintermediation *n* the practice in corporate finance of borrowing money directly from lenders, e.g. by issuing bonds, instead of using an intermediary, e.g. a bank.

disinvest *v* to reduce or terminate investment.

disinvestment *n* reduction or termination of investment, *esp* by realizing assets or not replacing capital equipment.

disjoint *v* to disturb the orderly structure or arrangement of.

disjointed *adj* lacking orderly sequence; incoherent. ➤➤ **disjointedly** *adv*, **disjointedness** *n*.

disjunction *n* **1** a lack of coordination; a mismatch. **2** a cleavage or separation.

disjunctive *adj* **1** lacking coordination or cohesiveness. **2** of a conjunction, e.g. *or* or *but*: expressing an alternative or opposition between the meanings of the words connected by it.

disk *n* **1a** (*Brit also* **disc**) a round flat plate coated with a magnetic substance on which data for a computer is stored. **b** a computer storage device consisting of a stack of disks rotating at high speed, each disk having its own head to read and write data. **2** *chiefly NAm* = DISC.

Usage note

disk *or* **disc**? See note at DISC.

disk drive *n* a device that enables a computer to transfer data to and retrieve it from magnetic disks.

diskette *n* = FLOPPY DISK.

disk-operating system *n* the part of a computer's operating system that reads and writes data to and from disk drives.

disk pack *n* = DISK (1B).

dislike[1] *n* **1** a feeling of aversion or disapproval. **2** something one has an aversion for.

dislike[2] *v* to regard (somebody or something) with dislike. ➤➤ **dislikable** *adj*, **dislikeable** *adj*.

dislocate *v* **1** to displace (a bone) from its normal articulation. **2** to disrupt the normal order or organization of (a timetable, etc). **3** to put (machinery) out of order. ➤➤ **dislocation** *n*.

dislodge *v* to force (something or somebody) out of a fixed or entrenched position. ➤➤ **dislodgement** *n*.

disloyal *adj* not loyal to obligations or ties; unfaithful. ➤➤ **disloyally** *adv*, **disloyalty** *n*.

dismal *adj* **1** causing or expressing gloom or sadness. **2** *informal* incompetent. ➤➤ **dismally** *adv*, **dismalness** *n*.

dismantle *v* to take to pieces. ➤➤ **dismantlement** *n*, **dismantler** *n*.

dismast *v* to remove or break off the mast of (a ship).

dismay[1] *v* to fill (somebody) with consternation or sadness.

dismay[2] *n* consternation or sadness.

dismember *v* **1** to cut or tear off the limbs of (a person or animal). **2** to divide up (a territory, etc) into parts. ➤➤ **dismembered** *adj*, **dismemberment** *n*.

dismiss *v* **1** to order or allow (somebody) to leave; to send away. **2** to discharge from employment or service. **3** to put (a suggestion, etc) out of one's mind or reject it as unworthy of serious consideration. **4** of a judge: to refuse a further hearing to (a court case). **5** in cricket, to bowl out (a batsman or side). ⋙ **dismissal** *n,* **dismissible** *adj.*

dismissive *adj* **1** of somebody's attitude to something: disparaging or disdainful. **2** serving to dismiss a topic, etc. ⋙ **dismissively** *adv,* **dismissiveness** *n.*

dismount *v* **1** to alight from a horse, bicycle, etc. **2** to make (a computer disk or disk drive) unavailable for use. **3** to remove (a cannon, etc) from a mounting or support.

disobedient *adj* refusing or failing to obey. ⋙ **disobedience** *n,* **disobediently** *adv.*

disobey *v* to fail to obey (somebody, an order, etc).

disoblige *v* **1** to act counter to the wishes of. **2** *informal* to inconvenience.

disorder[1] *v* (*usu in passive*) to disrupt or upset (something).

disorder[2] *n* **1** lack of order; confusion. **2** breach of the peace or public order. **3** an abnormal physical or mental condition; an ailment.

disorderly *adj* **1** untidy or disarranged. **2** unruly, violent, or disruptive of public order. ⋙ **disorderliness** *n.*

disorderly house *n* in law, a brothel.

disorganise *v* see DISORGANIZE.

disorganised *adj* see DISORGANIZED.

disorganize *or* **-ise** *v* to disrupt (an arrangement, system, etc). ⋙ **disorganization** *n.*

disorganized *or* **disorganised** *adj* **1** lacking coherence or system. **2** of a person: unmethodical.

disorient *v chiefly NAm* = DISORIENTATE.

disorientate *v* **1** (*usu in passive*) to deprive (somebody) of the normal sense of position, relationship, or identity. **2** to confuse (somebody). ⋙ **disorientated** *adj,* **disorientation** *n.*

disown *v* **1** to refuse to acknowledge (a relative, *esp* one's own child) as one's own. **2** to repudiate any connection with (principles or beliefs that other people might associate one with).

disparage *v* to speak slightingly of or belittle (somebody or something). ⋙ **disparagement** *n,* **disparaging** *adj,* **disparagingly** *adv.*

disparate *adj* quite separate and distinct. ⋙ **disparately** *adv,* **disparateness** *n.*

disparity *n* (*pl* **-ies**) difference or inequality, or an instance of this.

dispassionate *adj* not influenced by strong feeling; impartial. ⋙ **dispassion** *n,* **dispassionately** *adv.*

dispatch[1] *or* **despatch** *v* **1a** to send (a letter, etc) somewhere. **b** to send (personnel) to carry out a particular, usu official, task. **2a** to carry out or complete (a task) rapidly or efficiently. **b** *informal* to consume or make short work of (food or drink). **3** *euphem* to kill (somebody), *esp* with quick efficiency. ⋙ **dispatcher** *n.*

dispatch[2] *or* **despatch** *n* **1** a message; *esp* an important official diplomatic or military message. **2** a news item sent in by a correspondent to a newspaper. **3** promptness and efficiency. **4** the act of dispatching.

dispatch box *n* **1** a case or container for carrying dispatches or documents, *esp* concerning affairs of state. **2** (**the Dispatch Box**) either of a pair of boxes in front of the Speaker's or Lord Chancellor's seat in the British Parliament, from which ministers speak.

dispatch case *n* = DISPATCH BOX (1).

dispatch rider *n* a motorcyclist carrying urgent dispatches.

dispel *v* (**dispelled, dispelling**) to drive away or disperse (fears, doubts, depression, etc).

dispensable *adj* that can be dispensed with; inessential.

dispensary *n* (*pl* **-ies**) **1** a part of a hospital or chemist's shop where drugs, medical supplies, etc are dispensed. **2** a clinic where medical, dental, or veterinary aid is provided.

dispensation *n* **1** an exemption from a law, vow, etc; *specif* permission to disregard or break a rule of Roman Catholic Church law. **2** the act or an instance of dispensing. **3** a particular religious system, *esp* considered as controlling human affairs during a specified period. ⋙ **dispensational** *adj.*

dispense *v* **1** to deal out or distribute in portions. **2** to prepare and give out (drugs, medicine, etc on prescription). **3** to administer (law or justice). **4a** (+ with) to get rid of or discard. **b** (+ with) to do without (something).

dispenser *n* **1** a container or machine that dispenses items, e.g. of food, or fixed quantities, e.g. of drink. **2** a person who dispenses medicines.

dispersant *n* a liquid or gas used to disperse and stabilize fine particles of a substance in a particular medium.

disperse *v* **1** to spread or distribute (something) widely. **2** to break up (a crowd, etc). **3** to cause (fog, etc) to evaporate or vanish. **4** to break up (something) into fine particles. **5** in physics, to separate (light) into its constituent wavelengths. **6** to break up in random fashion. **7** to become dispersed; to dissipate or vanish. ⋙ **dispersal** *n,* **disperser** *n,* **dispersible** *adj,* **dispersive** *adj.*

dispersion *n* **1** the act or an instance of dispersing, or the state of being dispersed. **2** (**the Dispersion**) the scattering of Jews outside Israel; = DIASPORA.

dispirit *v* (**dispirited, dispiriting**) to dishearten or discourage. ⋙ **dispiritedly** *adv,* **dispiritedness** *n,* **dispiriting** *adj.*

displace *v* **1** to replace or take the place of. **2a** to remove (something) from or force it out of its usual or proper place. **b** to remove (somebody) from office. **c** to force (somebody) to leave their home or country because of war, revolution, etc. ⋙ **displaceable** *adj.*

displacement *n* **1** the action of displacing or process of being displaced. **2** the volume or weight of water displaced by a ship of equal weight floating in it, used as a measure of the ship's size. **3** the difference between the initial position of a body and any later position. **4** in psychoanalysis, the transfer of emotions from the object that orig evoked them to a substitute, e.g. in dreams.

display[1] *v* **1** to set out (a collection of things) for public viewing. **2** to expose (something) to view, e.g. by spreading it out. **3** of a computer, etc: to show (information) on screen. **4** to demonstrate (a quality). **5** to make a deliberate play of (something one prides oneself on) to impress others. **6** of a bird, reptile, or fish: to go through a ritual of showy behaviour in order to attract a mate.

display[2] *n* **1** a public presentation in the form of a performance or exhibition. **2** the displaying of something, e.g. the demonstration of a quality or of a type of behaviour. **3** ostentation; showing off. **4** an electronic device for presenting pictures or data on screen.

displease *v* to annoy or upset. ⋙ **displeased** *adj,* **displeasing** *adj,* **displeasingly** *adv.*

displeasure *n* disapproval or annoyance.

disport *v archaic* **1** to divert or amuse (oneself) actively. **2** to frolic or gambol.

disposable[1] *adj* **1** designed to be used once and then thrown away. **2** of financial resources: available for use. ➤➤ **disposability** *n.*

disposable[2] *n* (*usu in pl*) a disposable article.

disposable income *n* what is left of one's income after taxes and social-security charges have been paid.

disposal *n* the action or process of getting rid of something. ✱ **at one's disposal** available for one's use.

dispose *v* **1** to put (things or personnel) in position. **2** to give (somebody) a tendency towards something: *Faulty diet disposes one to sickness.* **3** (+ of) to transfer (a possession) to somebody else or sell it on. **4** to get rid of (rubbish or waste).

disposed *adj* **1** (*usu in negative contexts*) inclined or willing to do something. **2** inclined a certain way in one's attitude to somebody or something.

disposition *n* **1** a person's temperamental makeup. **2** a tendency or inclination. **3** the action of arranging people or things in a certain way, or the result of this.

dispossess *v* **1** to deprive of possession or occupancy. **2** in football, etc, to deprive (an opponent) of the ball. ➤➤ **dispossession** *n.*

dispossessed *adj* deprived of homes, possessions, and security.

disproof *n* **1** the act or an instance of disproving. **2** evidence that disproves.

disproportion *n* lack of proportion, symmetry, or proper relation. ➤➤ **disproportional** *adj,* **disproportionally** *adv.*

disproportionate *adj* out of proportion. ➤➤ **disproportionately** *adv.*

disprove *v* to prove (a statement, etc) to be false. ➤➤ **disprovable** *adj.*

disputable *adj* open to doubt or debate; questionable. ➤➤ **disputably** *adv.*

disputation *n* debate or argument.

disputatious *adj* inclined to dispute; argumentative. ➤➤ **disputatiously** *adv,* **disputatiousness** *n.*

dispute[1] *v* **1** (*often* + about) to argue, *esp* angrily and persistently. **2** to make (something) the subject of disputation. **3** to call (a statement, etc) into question. **4** to struggle over or contest (a reigning or leading position). ➤➤ **disputant** *n,* **disputative** *adj.*

dispute[2] *n* **1** controversy or debate. **2** a quarrel or disagreement. **3** a disagreement with management over pay, etc.

disqualify *v* (**-ies, -ied**) **1** to make or declare (somebody) unfit or unsuitable to do something. **2** to declare (somebody) ineligible, e.g. for a prize, because of violation of the rules. ➤➤ **disqualification** *n.*

disquiet[1] *n* anxiety or worry.

disquiet[2] *v* (**disquieted, disquieting**) to make uneasy or worried. ➤➤ **disquieted** *adj,* **disquieting** *adj.*

disquietude *n formal* disquiet or anxiety.

disquisition *n* a long or elaborate discussion or essay on a subject.

disregard[1] *v* to pay no attention to.

disregard[2] *n* lack of attention or regard; neglect.

disrepair *n* the state of being in need of repair.

disreputable *adj* **1** having a bad reputation; not respectable. **2** of clothing, etc: dirty or untidy in appearance.

disrepute *n* lack of good reputation or respectability.

disrespect[1] *n* lack of respect or politeness. ➤➤ **disrespectful** *adj,* **disrespectfully** *adv.*

disrespect[2] *v chiefly NAm* to show disrespect for or insult.

disrobe *v* **1** *formal* to take off ceremonial clothing. **2** to undress.

disrupt *v* **1** to throw into disorder. **2** to interrupt the continuity of (a schedule, etc). ➤➤ **disrupter** *n,* **disruption** *n,* **disruptive** *adj,* **disruptively** *adv,* **disruptiveness** *n,* **disruptor** *n.*

diss *v* see DIS.

dissatisfaction *n* lack of satisfaction; discontent.

dissatisfy *v* (**-ies, -ied**) to disappoint or fail to satisfy (somebody). ➤➤ **dissatisfied** *adj.*

dissect *v* **1** to cut (an animal or plant) into pieces, *esp* for scientific examination. **2** to analyse and interpret (a literary work, etc) in detail. ➤➤ **dissection** *n,* **dissector** *n.*

dissected *adj* **1** of a leaf: cut deeply into several fine lobes. **2** of a plateau: sliced by gorges.

dissemble *v* **1** to conceal facts, intentions, or feelings under some pretence. **2** to hide (something) under a false appearance. ➤➤ **dissembler** *n.*

disseminate *v* to spread (ideas, information, etc) about freely or widely. ➤➤ **dissemination** *n,* **disseminator** *n.*

dissension *n* disagreement in opinion that makes for discord.

dissent[1] *v* **1** to differ in opinion. **2** to reject the doctrines of an established Church. **3** to withhold assent. ➤➤ **dissenter** *n.*

dissent[2] *n* difference of opinion; *esp* religious or political nonconformity.

Dissenter *n* formerly, a person who refuses to conform to the established, usu Anglican, Church; = NONCONFORMIST (2).

dissentient[1] *adj* disagreeing or dissenting, *esp* from a majority view.

dissentient[2] *n* a person who dissents, *esp* from a majority view.

dissertation *n* a long detailed written treatment of a subject; *specif* one submitted for a degree, diploma, etc.

disservice *n* an action or deed which works to somebody's disadvantage.

dissident[1] *n* a person who disagrees strongly or rebelliously with the policies of the government or with established opinion. ➤➤ **dissidence** *n.*

dissident[2] *adj* disagreeing, *esp* strongly or rebelliously, with an opinion or group.

dissimilar *adj* not similar; unlike. ➤➤ **dissimilarity** *n,* **dissimilarly** *adv.*

dissimulate *v* to conceal one's real feelings or motives, or disguise them. ➤➤ **dissimulation** *n,* **dissimulator** *n.*

dissipate *v* **1** to dispel or cause to disappear or scatter. **2** to spend or use up (money, energy, etc) aimlessly or foolishly. **3** to cause (energy) to be lost on its conversion to heat. **4** to separate and scatter, or fade away and vanish. ➤➤ **dissipater** *n,* **dissipative** *adj,* **dissipator** *n.*

dissipated *adj* given to dissipation; dissolute.

dissipation *n* **1** the process of dissipating or of being dissipated. **2** dissolute living; debauchery; *esp* excessive indulgence in alcohol. **3** wasteful expenditure.

dissociate *v* **1** to declare (oneself) aloof from association or union with somebody or something else.

2 to separate (two ideas) in the mind. ⋙ **dissociative** *adj.*

dissociation *n* **1** the process of dissociating or of being dissociated. **2** in psychiatry, the separation of a more or less autonomous group of ideas or activities from the mainstream of consciousness, *esp* in cases of mental disorder.

dissoluble *adj* capable of being dissolved, disconnected, or undone. ⋙ **dissolubility** *n.*

dissolute *adj* morally unrestrained; debauched. ⋙ **dissolutely** *adv,* **dissoluteness** *n.*

dissolution *n* **1** the act or an instance of dissolving. **2** the termination of an association or union, *esp* a marriage. **3** the breaking up or dispersal of a group, assembly, etc. **4** dissolute behaviour or lifestyle. **5** disintegration or decay.

dissolve *v* **1a** to terminate (a partnership, *esp* a marriage) officially. **b** to dismiss or break up (an assembly, etc). **2a** to pass or cause (a substance) to pass into solution. **b** to become fluid or to melt or liquefy (a substance). **3** to fade out (one film or television scene) whilst fading in another. **4** to fade away; to disperse. **5** (*usu* + into) to be emotionally overcome. ⋙ **dissolvable** *adj,* **dissolver** *n.*

dissonance *n* **1** in music, an unresolved note or chord, *esp* an interval not included in a major or minor triad or its inversions; the sound made by this. **2** a combination of discordant sounds: compare CONSONANCE. **3** lack of harmony or agreement; a clash. ⋙ **dissonant** *adj,* **dissonantly** *adv.*

dissuade *v* (+ from) to deter or discourage from a course of action by persuasion. ⋙ **dissuasion** *n,* **dissuasive** *adj.*

dissyllable *n* see DISYLLABLE.

dissymmetry *n* **1** lack of symmetry. **2** mirror-image symmetry, as between an object and its mirror image, or between the left and right hands.

distaff *n* **1** in spinning, a staff for holding the flax, wool, etc that is to be spun. **2** woman's work or domain. **3** = DISTAFF SIDE.

distaff side *n* the female side of a family.

distal *adj* of an anatomical part: far from the centre or point of attachment or origin; terminal: compare PROXIMAL. ⋙ **distally** *adv.*

distance[1] *n* **1** the space between two points or places, or the length of this. **2** a far-off point. **3** wide separation or remoteness. **4** (*often* **distance in time**) an interval or time gap. **5** aloofness or reserve in a relationship between people. **6** *Brit* in horse-racing, a gap of more than 20 lengths between two finishers. ✱ **go the distance** to keep going until the end of a contest, etc. **keep one's distance 1** to maintain a coolness or reserve; to avoid getting involved. **2** to preserve a physical gap between oneself and another person, etc. **keep somebody at a distance** to treat somebody with reserve. **the middle distance** the area between foreground and distance. **within striking distance of** very close to (a point that represents one's destination or goal).

distance[2] *v* **1** to separate (one person from another) or make them less close. **2** to keep (oneself) aloof from a situation, etc.

distance learning *n* the activity of studying at home, e.g. for a degree, sometimes with the support of occasional local tutorials.

distance runner *n* a runner who takes part in long-distance or middle-distance races.

distant *adj* **1** a certain distance away. **2** remote in space or time. **3** not closely related. **4** reserved or aloof in personal relationships; cold. **5** of somebody's eyes or expression: abstracted from the immediate present. ⋙ **distantly** *adv.*

distaste *n* a dislike of or aversion to something.

distasteful *adj* causing distaste; offensive. ⋙ **distastefully** *adv,* **distastefulness** *n.*

distemper[1] *n* a viral disease of certain animals, *esp* dogs, with fever and coughing and sometimes disturbance of the nervous systems.

distemper[2] *n* **1** a method of painting in which pigments are mixed with white or yolk of egg or size, *esp* for mural decoration. **2** the paint used in the distemper process.

distemper[3] *v* to paint (something) in or with distemper.

distend *v* to swell or cause (a part of the body, e.g. the belly) to swell from internal pressure. ⋙ **distended** *adj,* **distensibility** *n,* **distensible** *adj,* **distension** *n.*

distil (*NAm* **distill**) *v* (**distilled, distilling**) **1** to produce (a liquid) in purified form by heating it till it evaporates as steam, and cooling it till it again becomes liquid. **2** to make (whisky or other spirits) by this method. **3** (+ out/off) to obtain, or separate (a volatile ingredient) by heating. **4** to derive (ideas, a written work, etc) from a body of previously amassed material. **5** to extract the essential matter from (previously amassed material). ⋙ **distillation** *n.*

distillate *n* **1** a product of distillation. **2** a concentrated form.

distiller *n* a person or company that makes alcohol, *esp* spirits, by distilling.

distillery *n* (*pl* **-ies**) the works where whisky or another spirit is distilled.

distinct *adj* **1** different or separate: *'Courage' has a meaning distinct from 'bravery'.* **2** readily perceptible to the senses or mind; clear: *The image remained distinct in her memory.* **3** definite: *a distinct possibility of rain.* ⋙ **distinctness** *n.*

Usage note

distinct *or* **distinctive**? These two words are sometimes confused. *Distinct* means 'separate and different', 'clear', or 'clearly noticeable': *a distinct air of unease; The word has two distinct meanings.* Something that is *distinctive* has its own special or unmistakable character: *a distinctive flavour.*

distinction *n* **1** a discrimination made between things that are similar but not the same. **2** a division resulting from discrimination. **3** outstanding merit or special talent. **4** the highest level of excellence in passing an exam.

distinctive *adj* clearly marking somebody or something as different from others; characteristic: *a very distinctive voice.* ⋙ **distinctively** *adv,* **distinctiveness** *n.*

Usage note

distinctive *or* **distinct**? See note at DISTINCT.

distinctly *adv* **1** clearly. **2** definitely. **3** very or remarkably.

distinguish *v* **1** to perceive as being separate or different. **2** (*often* + from) to recognize a difference between (one thing) and another: *You are old enough to distinguish right from wrong.* **3** (+ between) to recognize the difference between (two or more things): *You are old enough to distinguish between right and wrong.* **4** to separate (things or people) into kinds, classes, or categories. **5** to define (something) or list its characteristics. **6** of a feature, etc: to serve to identify (a person or thing). **7** to do something to make (oneself) notable, *esp* achieve something worthy. ⋙ **distinguishable** *adj.*

distinguished *adj* **1** characterized by eminence or excellence. **2** dignified in manner or appearance.

distort *v* **1** to alter the true meaning of or misrepresent (words, a statement, etc). **2** to cause to take on an unnatural or abnormal shape. **3** to reproduce or broadcast (radio sound, a television picture, etc) poorly or inaccurately owing to a change in the wave form of the original signal. ➤➤ **distorted** *adj,* **distortion** *n.*

distract *v* **1** to draw (somebody or their attention) away from the task in hand, etc. **2** to divert (somebody). ➤➤ **distracting** *adj.*

distracted *adj* **1** not able to concentrate on the matter in hand, etc. **2** agitated. ➤➤ **distractedly** *adv,* **distractedness** *n.*

distraction *n* **1** something that distracts one's attention. **2** an amusement or activity. ✱ **drive somebody to distraction** of a constant irritation, etc: to reduce somebody to a state of nervous agitation.

distrain *v* **1** to seize the property of (a debtor) in compensation for money owed. **2** to seize (property) in compensation for money owed.

distraint *n* the act of distraining.

distrait /di'stray/ *adj* absentminded.

distraught *adj* mentally agitated; frantic.

distress[1] *n* **1** mental or physical anguish. **2** hardship or suffering caused *esp* by lack of money or the necessities of life. **3** a state of danger or desperate need. **4** a medical condition in which there is strain on the vital functions, *esp* difficulty in breathing. **5** = DISTRAINT. ➤➤ **distressful** *adj.*

distress[2] *v* **1** to cause distress to (somebody). **2** to simulate marks of usage, wear and tear, etc on (new furniture, etc) to give an appearance of antiquity. ➤➤ **distressing** *adj,* **distressingly** *adv.*

distressed *adj* **1** suffering distress. **2** impoverished.

distributary *n* (*pl* **-ies**) a river branch flowing from and never returning to the main stream, as in a delta.

distribute *v* **1** to divide or apportion among a number of recipients. **2** (*usu in passive*) to disperse or scatter (something) over an area. **3** to supply (goods) to the shops or outlets that are to sell them to consumers. ➤➤ **distributable** *adj.*

distributed logic *n* a computer system in which processing is shared between many processors linked by a network or bus.

distributed system *n* a network of linked computers.

distribution *n* **1** the act or an instance of distributing. **2a** the position, arrangement, or frequency of occurrence, e.g. of the members of a group, over an area or throughout a space or unit of time. **b** the natural geographical range of an organism. **3** in statistics, the set of possible values of a variable presented in terms of frequency. ➤➤ **distributional** *adj.*

distributive *adj* **1** relating to or concerned with distribution. **2** in grammar, denoting a pronoun or determiner such as *each, either, every,* or *none,* that refers singly and without exception to all the members of a group. ➤➤ **distributively** *adv.*

distributor *n* **1** somebody or something that distributes. **2** a person employed to manage the distribution of goods. **3** an apparatus for directing current to the sparking plugs of an internal-combustion engine.

district *n* **1** a territorial division made *esp* for administrative purposes; *specif* in Britain, a division of a region or county that elects its own councillors. **2** an area or region with a specified character or feature.

district attorney *n* the prosecuting officer of a judicial district in the USA.

district nurse *n* in Britain, a qualified nurse, employed by a local authority, who visits and treats patients in their own homes.

distrust[1] *n* suspicion or lack of trust. ➤➤ **distrustful** *adj,* **distrustfully** *adv,* **distrustfulness** *n.*

distrust[2] *v* to regard (somebody or something) as untrustworthy or unreliable.

disturb *v* **1** to break in upon (somebody) or interrupt them. **2** to alter the position or arrangement of. **3** to destroy the peace of mind or composure of. **4** to put to inconvenience. **5** to disrupt the calm tenor of. ➤➤ **disturbing** *adj,* **disturbingly** *adv.*

disturbance *n* **1** the act or an instance of disturbing. **2** an interruption. **3** in law, a riot or outbreak of public disorder. **4** a small earthquake.

disturbed *adj* suffering from emotional or mental instability.

disunite *v* to divide or separate (people or things). ➤➤ **disunited** *adj.*

disunity *n* lack of unity; dissension.

disuse *n* the state of no longer being used.

disused *adj* no longer used; abandoned.

disyllable *or* **dissyllable** *n* a word, metrical foot, etc consisting of two syllables. ➤➤ **dissyllabic** *adj,* **disyllabic** *adj.*

ditch[1] *n* a long narrow excavation dug in the earth for defence, drainage, irrigation, etc.

ditch[2] *v* **1** to dig ditches throughout (an area) for drainage, etc. **2** to make a forced landing of (an aircraft) on water. **3** of a pilot: to come down in the sea. **4** *informal* to get rid of or abandon (a plan, project, etc). ➤➤ **ditcher** *n.*

dither[1] *v* to act nervously or indecisively; to vacillate. ➤➤ **ditherer** *n.*

dither[2] *n* a state of indecision or nervous excitement. ➤➤ **dithery** *adj.*

dithyramb *n* **1** a rapturous Greek hymn in honour of Bacchus. **2** a short poem or other piece of writing in a rapturous or exalted style. ➤➤ **dithyrambic** /-'rambik/ *adj.*

ditsy *adj* (**-ier, -iest**) see DITZY.

ditto *n* **1** used to avoid repeating a word: a thing mentioned previously or above; the same. **2** a mark (,, or ") used as a sign indicating repetition usu of a word directly above in a previous line.

ditto mark *n* = DITTO (2).

ditty *n* (*pl* **-ies**) a short simple song.

ditz *n NAm, informal* a ditzy person; a scatterbrain.

ditzy *or* **ditsy** *adj* (**-ier, -iest**) *chiefly NAm, informal* silly or scatterbrained. ➤➤ **ditziness** *n.*

diuretic[1] *adj* of a drug: acting to increase the flow of urine.

diuretic[2] *n* a diuretic medicine.

diurnal *adj* **1** having a daily cycle. **2** occurring during the day or daily. **3** of flowers: opening during the day and closing at night. **4** of animals: active during the day. ➤➤ **diurnally** *adv.*

diva /'deevə/ *n* (*pl* **divas** *or* **dive**) a principal female opera singer; = PRIMA DONNA (1).

Divali /di'vahli/ *n* see DIWALI.

divan *n* **1** a long low couch, usu without arms or back, placed against a wall. **2** a bed of a similar style without a head or foot board.

dive[1] *v* (*past tense and past part.* **dived** *or NAm* **dove**) **1** to plunge into water headfirst, with arms extended forward. **2** to swim underwater using breathing equipment. **3** of a submarine: to submerge. **4** of a bird or an aircraft: to descend steeply through the air. **5** of prices or profits: to plummet. **6** (+ into) to plunge one's hand into (a container, etc). **7** (+ into) to plunge into (some activity). **8** (+ for) to dash for (cover or shelter). **9** to lunge.

dive² *n* **1** a headlong plunge into water. **2** the submerging of a submarine. **3** a steep descent by an aircraft. **4** a sharp decline. **5** *informal* a disreputable bar or meeting place. **6** a ploy in football in which a player falls over deliberately and ostentatiously after being tackled in order to give the effect of having been fouled.

dive³ /'deevee/ *n* pl of DIVA.

dive-bomb *v* to bomb (a place) from an aeroplane while making a steep dive towards the target. ➤➤ **dive-bomber** *n.*

diver *n* **1** a person who dives as a competitive sport. **2** a person who works or explores underwater for long periods, either carrying a supply of air in cylinders or having it sent from the surface. **3** a large fish-eating diving bird that has its legs placed far back under its body and as a result has a clumsy floundering gait on land.

diverge *v* **1** to move in different directions from a common point. **2** (*often* + from) to differ in character, form, or opinion. **3** to turn aside from a course or norm. ➤➤ **divergence** *n.*

divergent *adj* diverging or differing from each other. ➤➤ **divergently** *adv.*

divers *adj archaic* various.

diverse *adj* **1** different or unlike. **2** varied or assorted. ➤➤ **diversely** *adv,* **diverseness** *n.*

diversify *v* (**-ies, -ied**) **1** to make (things) diverse or vary them. **2** to divide (investment of funds, etc) among different securities to reduce risk. **3** of a company: to engage in varied business operations or lines of production in order to reduce risk. ➤➤ **diversification** *n.*

diversion *n* **1** a turning aside from a course or activity. **2** a detour designated for traffic when the usual route is closed. **3** an amusement or pastime. **4** something that draws the attention away from the main scene of activity or operations. ➤➤ **diversionary** *adj.*

diversity *n* (*pl* **-ies**) **1** the condition of being different or having differences. **2** a variety or assortment.

divert *v* **1a** to redirect (something) from one course or use to another. **b** to distract. **2** to entertain or amuse (somebody).

diverticula *n* pl of DIVERTICULUM.

diverticulitis *n* inflammation of a diverticulum, *esp* in the large bowel, causing pain and difficulty with bowel movements.

diverticulum *n* (*pl* **diverticula**) a pocket or closed branch opening off a main passage, *esp* an abnormal pouch opening off the intestine.

divertimento *n* (*pl* **divertimenti** *or* **divertimentos**) an instrumental chamber work in several movements and usu light in character.

diverting *adj* amusing; entertaining.

divertissement /di'vuhtismənt/ *n* (*pl* **divertissements**) **1a** a ballet or ballet suite serving as an interlude. **b** a virtuoso solo dance within a ballet. **2** a diversion or entertainment.

divest *v* **1** (+ of) to deprive or dispossess (somebody) of property, authority, title, etc. **2a** (+ of) to rid or free (oneself) of something oppressive. **b** (+ of) to relieve (oneself) of clothing. **3** to strip (something) of an attribute, etc. **4** to take away (property or vested rights) from somebody. **5** to sell off (subsidiary companies) or dispose of (investments).

divestiture *or* **divesture** *n* **1** the compulsory transfer of title or disposal of interests on government order. **2** the selling off of subsidiary companies, or withdrawal from investment; = DISINVESTMENT.

divestment *n* **1** the act of divesting. **2** = DIVESTITURE.

divesture *n* = DIVESTITURE.

divi *n* see DIVVY¹.

divide¹ *v* **1** to separate into parts, branches, groups, etc. **2** to split (people, things, etc) into two or more parts or groups. **3** to split (a territory) into areas. **4** to separate (something) into categories. **5** to share (something) between recipients. **6** to be what separates (one thing and another). **7** to be the issue that provokes disagreement in (a body) or between (parties). **8** in mathematics, to operate on (a number) to find out how many times it contains a smaller number. **9** in mathematics, of a number: to allow of division without a remainder. **10** of a legislative body: to separate into groups for voting. ➤➤ **dividable** *adj.*

divide² *n* a line of division; a split.

dividend *n* **1a** a sum of money to be divided and distributed, *esp* the part of a company's profits payable to shareholders. **b** an individual shareholder's portion of this. **2** (*usu in pl*) a reward or benefit. **3** in mathematics, a number to be divided by another.

divider *n* **1** (*in pl*) a compasslike instrument with two pointed ends used for measuring or marking off lines, angles, etc. **2** a partition or screen used to separate parts of a room.

divination *n* **1** the art or practice that seeks to foresee the future or discover hidden knowledge, e.g. by using supernatural powers. **2** unusual insight or perception, or an instance of this. ➤➤ **divinatory** *adj.*

divine¹ *adj* **1a** being a god or goddess. **b** of or from God or a god. **2** *informal* delightful or superb. ➤➤ **divinely** *adv,* **divineness** *n.*

divine² *n* a clergyman; *esp* one skilled in theology.

divine³ *v* **1** to discover, perceive, or foresee intuitively or by supernatural means. **2** to discover or locate (water or minerals) by means of a divining rod. ➤➤ **diviner** *n.*

Divine Office *n* the prescribed forms of prayer and ritual for daily worship used by Roman Catholic priests.

divine right *n* **1** the right of a sovereign to rule, held to derive directly from God. **2** a right which cannot be transferred.

diving bell *n* a bell-shaped metal container open only at the bottom and supplied with compressed air through a tube, in which a person can be let down under water.

diving board *n* a springboard or platform projecting over a swimming pool, from which people can dive into the water.

diving duck *n* a duck that frequents deep waters and obtains its food by diving.

diving suit *n* a diver's waterproof suit with a helmet that is supplied with a mixture of gases suitable for breathing pumped through a tube.

divining rod *n* a forked rod or twig believed to dip downwards when held over ground concealing water or minerals.

divinity *n* (*pl* **-ies**) **1** the quality or state of being divine. **2a** (**the Divinity**) God. **b** a male or female deity. **3** theology.

divisible *adj* **1** capable of being divided. **2** of a number: that can be divided by another without remainder. ➤➤ **divisibility** *n.*

division *n* **1** the action of dividing or process of being divided. **2** any of the parts into which a whole is divided. **3** (*used as sing. or pl*) **a** a major army formation that can act independently. **b** a naval unit under a single command. **4** an administrative or operating unit of an organization. **5** a group of organisms forming part of a larger group; *specif* a primary category of the plant kingdom equivalent to a phylum of the animal kingdom. **6** a competitive class or category, e.g. of a football league. **7** something that divides, separates, or marks off; a dividing line. **8** disagreement or disunity. **9** the physical separation of the members of a parliamentary body voting for and against a question. ➤➤ **divisional** *adj.*

division bell *n* a bell rung in the British Parliament to warn that a vote is about to take place.

division of labour *n* the distribution of various parts of the process of production among different people to increase efficiency.

division sign *n* the symbol (÷) used to indicate the mathematical operation of division.

divisive *adj* tending to cause disunity or dissension. ➤➤ **divisively** *adv,* **divisiveness** *n.*

divisor *n* in mathematics, the number by which the number or quantity undergoing division is divided.

divorce[1] *n* **1** a legal dissolution of a marriage, or the decree ratifying this. **2** a separation or dissociation.

divorce[2] *v* **1** to end marriage with (one's spouse) by divorce. **2** to separate or dissociate (one thing) from another.

divorcee /divaw'see/ *n* a divorced person.

divot *n* a piece of turf, *esp* one struck out of the ground in making a golf shot.

divulge *v* to make known or reveal (a confidence or secret). ➤➤ **divulgence** *n.*

divvy[1] *n* (*pl* **-ies**) *Brit, informal* a dividend, *esp* one paid by a cooperative society.

divvy[2] *v* (**-ies, -ied**) *informal* (*usu* + up) to divide or share (something).

Diwali /di'wahli/ *or* **Divali** /di'vahli/ *n* the Hindu or Sikh Festival of Lights, celebrating the end of the monsoon.

Dixie *n informal* the Southern states of the USA.

dixie *n* (*pl* **-ies**) a large metal pot in which food and drink is made or carried by soldiers or campers.

dixieland *n* jazz music in duple time characterized by collective improvisation.

DIY *n chiefly Brit* **1** amateur repair, maintenance, and building work around the home. **2** (*used before a noun*) of materials and equipment needed for this.

dizzy[1] *adj* (**-ier, -iest**) **1a** experiencing a whirling sensation in the head and a tendency to lose balance. **b** mentally confused. **2** *informal* foolish or silly. ✱ **the dizzy heights** *informal* the pinnacle of power, success, or importance. ➤➤ **dizzily** *adv,* **dizziness** *n.*

dizzy[2] *v* (**-ies, -ied**) to make dizzy; to bewilder.

DJ *n* (*pl* **DJs**) **1** = DISC JOCKEY. **2** = DINNER JACKET.

djellaba *or* **jellaba** /jə'lahbə, 'jeləbə/ *n* a long loose outer garment with full sleeves and a hood, traditionally worn by Arabs.

Djiboutian /ji'boohti·ən/ *n* a native or inhabitant of Djibouti. ➤➤ **Djiboutian** *adj.*

djin *or* **djinn** /jin/ *n* (*pl* **djin** *or* **djinn**) see JINN.

dl *abbr* decilitre.

DLitt *abbr* Doctor of Letters.

DM *abbr* Deutschmark.

dm *abbr* decimetre.

DMA *abbr* in computing, direct memory access.

D-Mark *abbr* Deutschmark.

DMs *pl n* Doc Martens.

DMus *abbr* Doctor of Music.

DNA *n* deoxyribonucleic acid, which occurs in the nuclei of cells, is the material that makes up genes, and consists of long chains typically paired in a double helix.

DNA fingerprinting *n* genetic fingerprinting.

DNA profiling *n* genetic fingerprinting.

D-notice *n* an official request, e.g. to a newspaper, that certain information be withheld from publication for security reasons.

do[1] *v* (*past tense* **did,** *past part.* **done**) **1** to effect or perform (an action or activity). **2** to make or provide. **3** to work on (something): *Shall we do the garden?* **4** to have a particular effect: *A rest will do you good.* **5** to work at (something) for a living or as a course of study: *What subject does she do?* **6** to be adequate or acceptable: *These will do quite well.* **7a** to achieve (a particular speed). **b** to serve (a number of years) in prison. ➤ *v aux* **1** used to form questions and negative statements: *I did not agree; Do you like this place?* **2** used for emphasis: *I do hope you can come.* **3** used as a substitute for a verb already mentioned: *I am earning more than I did last year.* ✱ **could do with** need or would like: *We could do with some peace.* **do away with** *informal* abolish or kill. **do by** to treat (somebody) in a specified way. **do for** to be enough or adequate for. **do out of** to deprive of something. **do without** to manage in spite of not having (something). **have done with** to finish with or have no further concern with. **to do with** concerned with.

do[2] *n* (*pl* **dos** *or* **do's**) **1** (*usu in pl*) something one ought to do: *I gave her a list of dos and don'ts.* **2** *chiefly Brit, informal* a party or festive occasion.

do[3] *or* **doh** *n* in music, the first note of a major scale in the tonic sol-fa system.

do. *abbr* ditto.

DOA *abbr* used chiefly in hospitals: dead on arrival.

dob *v* (**dobbed, dobbing**) *Aus, informal* (*often* + in) to inform on.

Doberman *or* **Dobermann** *n* (*in full* **Doberman pinscher** /'pinshə/) a guard dog of a short-haired medium-sized breed originating in Germany.

dobra /'dohbrə/ *n* the basic monetary unit of São Tomé and Principe.

DOC *abbr* of wines: Denominaziòne d'Origine Contròllata.

doc *n* sometimes used as an informal term of address: a doctor.

docent *n* **1** a lecturer in some US colleges and universities. **2** a guide in a museum, art gallery, etc.

docile *adj* easily led or managed; tractable. ➤➤ **docilely** *adv,* **docility** *n.*

dock[1] *n* a coarse weed, the leaves of which are used to alleviate nettle stings.

dock[2] *v* **1a** to remove part of the tail of (a horse). **b** to cut (an animal's tail) short. **2** to make a deduction from (wages). **3** to take away (a specified amount) from wages, a score etc.

dock[3] *n* **1** an artificially enclosed body of water in a port or harbour, where a ship can moor for unloading, repair work, etc. **2** (**the docks**) the area of such enclosures, together with wharves, sheds, etc.

dock[4] *v* **1a** to bring (a ship) into dock. **b** of a ship: to come or go into a dock. **2a** to join (two spacecraft) together while in space. **b** of spacecraft: to join together while in space.

dock[5] *n* the prisoner's enclosure in a criminal court. ✱ **in the dock** on trial.

docker *n* a person who is employed in loading and unloading ships.

docket[1] *n* **1** a document recording the contents of a shipment or the payment of customs duties. **2** a label attached to goods bearing identification or instructions. **3** a receipt.

docket[2] *v* (**docketed, docketing**) to put a docket on (a consignment, etc).

docking station *n* an adapter that enables a laptop computer to be connected to a monitor, keyboard, and extra disk drives.

dockland *n Brit* (*also in pl*) the district around the docks in a large port.

dockyard *n* a place or enclosure in which ships are built or repaired.

Doc Martens *pl n* (*also informal* **Docs**) *trademark* tough-looking laced shoes or boots with thick lightweight rubber soles.

doctor[1] *n* **1** a person qualified to practise medicine; a physician or surgeon. **2** a holder of the highest academic degree conferred by a university. **3** *informal* a person who is skilled in repairing or treating a usu specified type of machine, vehicle, etc. **4** *Aus, NZ* a cook on board ship or at a station or camp. ✱ **go for the doctor** *Aus, NZ* to make a supreme effort. **just what the doctor ordered** just the thing needed. ⋙ **doctorly** *adj*, **doctorship** *n*.

doctor[2] *v* **1a** to give medical treatment to. **b** to repair or mend. **2a** to adapt or modify (something) for a desired end. **b** to alter (evidence or statistics) in a dishonest way. **3** *euphem* to castrate or spay (a dog or cat).

doctoral *adj* relating to a doctorate.

doctorate *n* the highest academic degree, awarded by a university for original postgraduate research presented as a thesis.

Doctor of Philosophy *n* a person who has a doctorate, usu in any subject other than law, medicine, or theology.

doctrinaire *adj* concerned with abstract theory to the exclusion of practical considerations.

doctrine *n* a principle or the body of principles in a branch of knowledge or system of belief. ⋙ **doctrinal** /dok'trienl/ *adj*, **doctrinally** *adv*.

docudrama *n* a play, film, etc in which factual incidents are presented in dramatized form.

document[1] *n* an original or official paper, or electronic record, that gives information about or proof of something. ⋙ **documental** *adj*.

document[2] *v* **1** to record (e.g. an event) in detail, with eye-witness reports, photographs, etc. **2** to support (a hypothesis or statement) with authoritative references.

documentary[1] *adj* **1** consisting of documents; contained or certified in writing. **2** presenting or based on factual material. ⋙ **documentarily** *adv*.

documentary[2] *n* (*pl* **-ies**) a broadcast or film that presents a factual account using a variety of techniques.

documentation *n* **1** written instructions, plans, specifications, etc. **2** documents provided in evidence or support for a claim, etc.

document case *n* a light flat leather or plastic case, usu lockable, for carrying papers.

docusoap *n* a documentary series of television programmes following the lives of a particular group of people over a period of time.

dodder[1] *v* **1** to walk feebly and unsteadily. **2** to tremble or shake from weakness or age. ⋙ **dodderer** *n*.

dodder[2] *n* a parasitic leafless plant of the bindweed family having suckers for attachment to the host plant.

doddering *adj* weak, shaky, and slow, *esp* because of old age.

doddery *adj* = DODDERING.

doddle *n chiefly Brit, informal* a very easy task.

dodeca- *or* **dodec-** *comb. form* twelve: *dodecahedron*.

dodecagon *n* a polygon with twelve angles and twelve sides. ⋙ **dodecagonal** *adj*.

dodecahedron *n* (*pl* **dodecahedrons** *or* **dodecahedra**) a polyhedron with twelve faces. ⋙ **dodecahedral** *adj*.

dodge[1] *v* **1** to shift position suddenly, e.g. to avoid a blow or a pursuer. **2** to evade (a duty, etc) usu by subterfuge. **3** to avoid (a blow, etc) by a sudden or repeated shift of position.

dodge[2] *n* **1** a sudden movement to avoid something. **2** a clever device to evade something or deceive somebody.

dodgem *or* **dodgem car** *n* a small electric car designed to be steered about and bumped into others as a funfair amusement.

dodger *n* (*often used in combinations*) a person who uses clever and often dishonest methods, e.g. to avoid payment or responsibility: *a tax-dodger; a draft-dodger*.

dodgy *adj* (**-ier, -iest**) *chiefly Brit, informal* **1** shady or dishonest. **2** risky or dangerous. **3** liable to collapse, fail, or break down.

dodo *n* (*pl* **-oes** *or* **-os**) a large extinct flightless bird that formerly lived on the island of Mauritius.

do down *v* to disparage or criticize.

DOE *abbr Brit* formerly, Department of the Environment.

doe *n* (*pl* **does** *or* **doe**) **1** the adult female fallow deer. **2** the adult female of any of various mammals, e.g. the rabbit.

doer *n* one who takes action or participates actively, rather than theorizing.

does *v* third person sing. present tense of DO[1].

doesn't *contr* does not.

doff *v* **1** to take off (one's hat) in greeting or as a sign of respect. **2** to remove (any item of clothing).

dog[1] *n* **1a** a four-legged flesh-eating domesticated mammal occurring in a great variety of breeds. **b** any of a family of carnivores to which the dog belongs, e.g. a wolf, jackal, coyote, or fox. **c** (*often used before a noun*) a male dog, wolf, fox, etc. **2** *chiefly NAm, informal* something inferior of its kind. **3** *informal, dated* a fellow. **4** *derog* an unattractive woman. **5** (**the dogs**) greyhound racing. ✱ **go to the dogs** *informal* to decline or deteriorate. **turn dog on** *Aus, NZ, informal* to betray or inform on. ⋙ **dogdom** *n*, **doggish** *adj*, **doglike** *adj*.

dog[2] *v* (**dogged, dogging**) **1** to pursue (somebody) closely like a dog; to hound. **2** of something unwanted: to haunt (somebody).

dog biscuit *n* a hard dry biscuit for dogs.

dogcart *n* a light horse-drawn two-wheeled carriage with two seats set back to back.

dog collar *n informal* = CLERICAL COLLAR.

dog days *pl n chiefly poetic* the hottest days in the year.

doge /dohj/ *n* the chief magistrate of the former republics of Venice and Genoa.

dog-eared *adj* **1** of a book: having pages with turned-down corners. **2** worn or shabby.

dog-eat-dog *adj* of business, etc: marked by ruthless self-interest; aggressively competitive.

dog-end *n informal* a cigarette end.

dogfight *n* **1** a viciously fought contest. **2** a fight between aircraft, usu at close quarters. ➤➤ **dogfighting** *n.*

dogfish *n* (*pl* **dogfishes** *or* **dogfish**) a small long-tailed shark.

dog fund *n* an investment fund that is not providing a good return.

dogged /'dogid/ *adj* stubbornly determined. ➤➤ **doggedly** *adv,* **doggedness** *n.*

doggerel *n* **1** verse that is loosely styled and irregular in measure, *esp* for comic effect. **2** verse that lacks any poetic quality.

doggie *n* see DOGGY².

doggie bag *n* see DOGGY BAG.

doggo ✱ **lie doggo** to lie low and stay motionless, to avoid detection.

doggone *adj and adv chiefly NAm, euphem* damned.

doggy¹ *adj* (**-ier, -iest**) *informal* **1** of or resembling a dog. **2** fond of dogs.

doggy² *or* **doggie** *n* (*pl* **-ies**) used *esp* by or to children: a dog.

doggy bag *or* **doggie bag** *n* a bag for carrying home leftover food from a meal eaten in a restaurant, etc.

doggy paddle *n* = DOG PADDLE.

doghouse *n chiefly NAm* a dog kennel. ✱ **in the doghouse** *informal* in a state of disfavour.

dog in the manger *n* a person who selfishly deprives others of something of no use to themselves.

dog Latin *n* spurious or debased Latin.

dogleg *n* a sharp bend, e.g. in a road.

dogma *n* **1** an authoritative tenet or principle. **2** a body of doctrines formally and authoritatively stated by a Church.

dogmatic *adj* **1** of statements or opinions: insisted on as if authoritative. **2** said of a person: inclined to make dogmatic statements. **3** of dogma. ➤➤ **dogmatically** *adv,* **dogmaticalness** *n.*

dogmatics *pl n* (*used as sing. or pl*) a branch of theology that seeks to interpret the dogmas of a religious faith.

dogmatism *n* unwarranted assertion of opinion. ➤➤ **dogmatist** *n.*

do-gooder *n* an earnest, but often naive or ineffectual, humanitarian or reformer. ➤➤ **do-goodery** *n.*

dog paddle *n* an elementary form of swimming in which the arms paddle and the legs kick.

dog-paddle *v* to do the dog paddle.

dog rose *n* a common European wild rose with pink or white flowers.

dogsbody *n* (*pl* **-ies**) *chiefly Brit, informal* a person who carries out routine or menial work at the behest of others.

dog's breakfast *n* = DOG'S DINNER.

dog's chance *n* (*in negative contexts*) any chance at all.

dog's dinner *n informal* a horrible mess. ✱ **done up like a dog's dinner** overelaborately dressed or made up.

dog's life *n informal* a miserable drab existence.

Dog Star *n* Sirius, the brightest star in the sky.

dogstooth check *n* = HOUNDSTOOTH CHECK.

dog-tag *n NAm, informal* an identification disc for military personnel.

dog-tired *n informal* extremely tired.

dogtooth *n* an architectural moulding or ornamentation consisting of a series of four leaves radiating from a raised centre.

dogtrot *n* a quick easy gait suggesting that of a dog.

dog violet *n* a European wild violet with purple or blue flowers.

dogwatch *n* either of two short watches, 4–6 and 6–8 p.m. on a ship.

dogwood *n* a tree or shrub with heads of small flowers, berries, and hard wood.

DoH *abbr Brit* Department of Health.

doh *n* see DO³.

doily *or* **doyley** *or* **doyly** *n* (*pl* **doilies** *or* **doylies**) a small decorative lacy mat of paper, cloth, or plastic, *esp* one placed under cakes, biscuits, etc on a plate.

do in *v informal* **1** to kill (somebody). **2** to exhaust (somebody).

doing *n* **1** the result of somebody's activity: *This must be your doing.* **2** (*in pl*) things that are done or that occur; activities.

doings *n* (*pl* **doings** *or* **doingses**) *chiefly Brit, informal* (*used as sing.*) a word used to refer to an unspecified fitting, tool, etc.

do-it-yourself *n* full form of DIY. ➤➤ **do-it-yourselfer** *n.*

dojo *n* (*pl* **-os**) a school for training in various martial arts.

Dolby *n trademark* **1** a sound-recording technique or system that reduces unwanted noise by electronic processing. **2** a stereophonic sound system used for cinema and television.

dolce far niente /,dolchay fah 'nyenti/ *n* carefree idleness.

Dolcelatte /dolchə'latay/ *n trademark* a creamy blue-veined Italian cheese.

dolce vita /,dolchi 'veetah/ *n* a life of indolence and self-indulgence.

doldrums *pl n* (**the doldrums**) an equatorial region of the Atlantic ocean where calms, squalls, and light shifting winds prevail. ✱ **in the doldrums 1** in a state of depression. **2** of the economy: in a state of stagnation or slump.

dole *n Brit, informal* the government unemployment benefit. ✱ **on the dole** receiving unemployment benefit.

doleful *adj* sad or mournful. ➤➤ **dolefully** *adv,* **dolefulness** *n.*

dole out *v* to give, distribute, or deliver.

dolerite /'doləriet/ *n* a fine-grained or medium-grained dark igneous rock, *esp* a coarse basalt. ➤➤ **doleritic** *adj.*

doll *n* **1** a child's toy in the form of a human being, *esp* a child or baby. **2** *informal* a term for an attractive person, *esp* a woman.

dollar *n* the basic monetary unit of the USA, Canada, Australia, and various other countries. ✱ **bet your bottom dollar** *informal* to be virtually certain.

dollar diplomacy *n* diplomacy used by a country to promote its financial or commercial interests abroad and hence to strengthen its power.

dollop¹ *n* a soft shapeless blob; *esp* a serving of food.

dollop² *v* (**dolloped, dolloping**) (+ out) to serve out (food) carelessly or clumsily.

doll's house *n* a child's small-scale toy house.

doll up *v informal* (*usu in passive*) to dress (oneself) prettily or showily.

dolly *n* (*pl* **-ies**) **1** a child's word for DOLL (1). **2** in cricket, an easy catch. **3a** a platform on wheels or castors for moving heavy objects. **b** a wheeled platform for a film or television camera.

dolly bird *n chiefly Brit* an attractive, stylish, and lively girl, *esp* an empty-headed one.

dolly mixtures *pl n* an assortment of miniature sweets, typically in various pastel shades.

dolma *n* (*pl* **dolmas** *or* **dolmades** /dohl'mahdiz/) a vine leaf or cabbage leaf stuffed with a savoury filling.

dolman sleeve *n* a sleeve very wide at the armhole and tight at the wrist, often cut in one piece with the bodice.

dolmen *n* a prehistoric monument consisting of two or more upright stones supporting a horizontal slab.

dolomite *n* **1** calcium magnesium carbonate occurring as a mineral. **2** a limestone-like rock consisting mainly of the mineral dolomite. ➤➤ **dolomitic** *adj.*

dolorous *adj literary* causing or expressing misery or grief. ➤➤ **dolorously** *adv,* **dolorousness** *n.*

dolour (*NAm* **dolor**) *n* mental suffering or anguish.

dolphin *n* a small gregarious toothed marine whale with the snout elongated into a beak.

dolphinarium *n* (*pl* **dolphinariums** *or* **dolphinaria**) an establishment where dolphins are trained to perform in public in a large pool.

dolt *n* an extremely dull or stupid person. ➤➤ **doltish** *adj,* **doltishly** *adv,* **doltishness** *n.*

Dom *n* **1** used as a title for Benedictine, Carthusian, and Cistercian monks and some Roman Catholic priests. **2** used formerly as a title preceding the Christian name of a Portuguese or Brazilian man of rank.

-dom *suffix* forming nouns, denoting: **1a** rank or office: *dukedom.* **b** realm or jurisdiction: *kingdom.* **2** state: *freedom.* **3** a group or class of people: *officialdom.*

domain *n* **1** a territory over which control is exercised. **2** a sphere of influence or activity. **3** the set of values to which a variable is limited. **4** in computing, a group of Internet locations having addresses with the same suffix. **5** *Aus, NZ* a public park or recreation ground.

domain name *n* the combination of letters, words, and punctuation that specifies the location of a web site on the Internet.

dome *n* **1** a hemispherical roof or vault. **2** a dome-shaped structure. **3** the top part of the head. ➤➤ **domical** *adj,* **domelike** *adj.*

domed *adj* **1** of a building: having a dome. **2** of somebody's forehead: high and rounded.

Domesday Book /'doohmzday/ *n* a record of a survey of English lands made by order of William I about 1086.

domestic[1] *adj* **1** of, for, or devoted to the home or the family. **2** of one's own country; not foreign. **3** of an animal: tame, or bred by human beings for some specific purpose, e.g. food or hunting. ➤➤ **domestically** *adv.*

domestic[2] *n* **1** a person employed to do household tasks. **2** *informal* a fight or dispute between members of a family, *esp* one causing a disturbance.

domesticate *v* **1** to bring (an animal) under human control for some specific purpose, e.g. for carrying loads, hunting, or food. **2** to cultivate (a plant) for use as food. ➤➤ **domesticable** *adj,* **domestication** *n.*

domestic help *n* = DOMESTIC[2] (1).

domesticity *n* home or family life, or devotion to this.

domestic worker *n* = DOMESTIC[2] (1).

domicile[1] *n* a home; *esp* a person's permanent and principal home for legal purposes.

domicile[2] *v* (*usu in passive*) to establish in or provide with a domicile.

domiciliary *adj* of or taking place in the home.

dominant[1] *adj* **1** commanding, controlling, or prevailing over all others. **2** of a position: commanding a view from a superior height. **3** denoting the one of a pair of genes determining contrasting inherited characteristics that predominates: compare RECESSIVE[1]. ➤➤ **dominance** *n,* **dominancy** *n,* **dominantly** *adv.*

dominant[2] *n* a dominant gene or trait.

dominate *v* **1** to exert controlling influence or power over. **2** to overlook from a superior height. ➤➤ **domination** *n,* **dominative** *adj,* **dominator** *n.*

dominatrix /domi'naytriks/ *n* (*pl* **dominatrixes** *or* **dominatrices** /-triseez/) a woman who takes an aggressively or sadistically dominant role in sexual interaction.

domineer *v* to exercise arbitrary or overbearing control. ➤➤ **domineering** *adj,* **domineeringly** *adv.*

dominical *adj* **1** relating to Jesus Christ. **2** relating to Sunday.

Dominican[1] *n* a member of a preaching order of mendicant friars founded by St Dominic in 1215. ➤➤ **Dominican** *adj.*

Dominican[2] *n* a native or inhabitant of the Dominican Republic. ➤➤ **Dominican** *adj.*

Dominican[3] *n* a native or inhabitant of Dominica. ➤➤ **Dominican** *adj.*

dominion *n* **1** the power or right to rule; sovereignty. **2** the territory of a ruler. **3** absolute ownership. **4** (*often* **Dominion**) *esp* formerly, a self-governing nation of the Commonwealth other than the United Kingdom.

domino *n* (*pl* **-oes** *or* **-os**) **1** a flat rectangular block with a face divided into two equal parts that are either blank or bear from one to six dots arranged as on dice faces. **2** (*in pl, usu used as sing.*) any of several games played with a set of 28 dominoes.

domino effect *n* a series of causally related events following one after another, precipitated by some significant initial happening, like a line of dominoes collapsing in sequence.

don[1] *n* **1** a university teacher, *esp* a senior member of staff at Oxford or Cambridge. **2a** a Spanish nobleman or gentleman. **b** (**Don**) a title preceding the forename of a Spanish man, *esp* one of rank. **3** *informal* the head of a Mafia family.

don[2] *v* (**donned, donning**) to put on (an item of clothing).

Doña /'donyə/ *n* a title preceding the forename of a Spanish woman, *esp* one of rank.

donate *v* **1** to make a gift of (something, e.g. money), *esp* to a public or charitable cause. **2** to give or allow the removal of (blood, semen, organs, etc) for use in the medical treatment of others. ➤➤ **donator** *n.*

donation *n* **1** the act of donating. **2** something donated, *esp* money.

done[1] *v* past part. of DO[1].

done[2] *adj* **1** socially acceptable or expected. **2** completed. **3** of food: cooked sufficiently. **4** physically exhausted. **5** *informal* arrested or imprisoned. ✱ **done for 1** dead or close to death. **2** doomed to failure or defeat; ruined. **done in** *informal* physically exhausted.

done[3] *interj* used in acceptance of a deal or bet.

donee *n* a recipient of a gift or donation.

doner kebab /'dohnə, 'donə/ *n* slices of spiced lamb or other meat cut from a large block grilled on a spit.

dong[1] *v* to make the deep sound of a large heavy bell. ➤➤ **dong** *n.*

dong[2] *n* the basic monetary unit of Vietnam.

donga *n SAfr, Aus, NZ* a narrow steep-sided ravine formed by erosion.

dongle *n* in computing, a security device that, when plugged into a computer, allows a particular program to run.

donjon *n* a massive inner tower in a medieval castle.

Don Juan /don 'jooh·ən, 'wahn/ *n* a man who attempts to seduce many women; a lady-killer.

donkey *n* (*pl* **-eys**) **1** a domesticated animal of the horse family that has long ears and is used to carry loads. **2** a stupid or obstinate person. ✱ **talk the hind leg off a donkey** *Brit, informal* to talk endlessly.

donkey engine *n* a small, usu portable, auxiliary engine.

donkey jacket *n* a thick hip-length hard-wearing jacket, usu dark blue and with a strip of leather or plastic across the shoulders.

donkey's years *pl n chiefly Brit, informal* a very long time.

donkeywork *n informal* hard, monotonous, and routine work.

donna *n* (*pl* **donne** /'donay/) **1** an Italian woman, *esp* one of rank. **2** (**Donna**) a title preceding the forename of an Italian woman.

donnish *adj* characteristic of a university don, *esp* in being pedantic.

donor *n* **1** a person who donates something. **2a** in chemistry, an atom that combines with another and provides the two electrons that are shared to make the bond. **b** in physics, an impurity that is added to a semiconductor to increase the number of mobile electrons.

donor card *n* a card carried by people who wish to donate organs or other body parts for transplant in the event of their death.

don't[1] *contr* do not.

don't[2] *n* (*usu in pl*) something that is prohibited: *a list of dos and don'ts.*

doodah *n Brit, informal* a small article whose name is unknown or forgotten.

doodle[1] *v* to draw or scribble in a bored or aimless manner. ➤➤ **doodler** *n.*

doodle[2] *n* an aimless scribble, design, or sketch.

doodlebug *n Brit, informal* = FLYING BOMB.

doodly-squat *n* see DIDDLY-SQUAT.

doofer *n informal* a gadget whose name is unknown or has been forgotten.

doolally *adj informal* crazy; temporarily mad.

Word history

from *doolally tap* Indian army slang for *Deolali tap*, from *Deolali* a town near Bombay + *tap* fever. British soldiers returning home were sent to Deolali to await embarkation and supposedly went mad with boredom.

doom[1] *n* **1a** destiny, *esp* an unhappy or terrible fate. **b** unavoidable death or destruction. **2** judgment or condemnation.

doom[2] *v* **1** to cause to fail or be ruined. **2** to destine or condemn.

doomsday *n* **1** = JUDGMENT DAY. **2** some remote point in the future.

doomster *n informal* a person given to forebodings and predictions of impending calamity.

door *n* **1a** a hinged or sliding panel by which the entrance to a building, room, or vehicle is closed and opened. **b** a similar part of a piece of furniture. **2** a means of access. ✱ **lay something at somebody's door** to charge somebody as being responsible for something. **out of doors** in or into the open air.

doorbell *n* a bell at the entrance to a building, rung to summon somebody inside to open the door.

do-or-die *adj* requiring or having the determination to face a danger or challenge without flinching.

door furniture *n* handles, knockers, and other fixtures that can be fitted to doors.

doorkeeper *n* a person who guards the main door to a building and lets people in and out.

doorman *n* (*pl* **doormen**) a person employed to stand at the entrance to a hotel, theatre, etc and assist people going in or out, e.g. by calling taxis.

doormat *n* **1** a mat placed at a doorway for wiping dirt from the shoes. **2** *informal* a person who submits to bullying and indignities without complaint or resistance.

doorstep[1] *n* **1** a step in front of an outer door. **2** *Brit, informal* a very thick slice of bread. ✱ **on one's/the doorstep** conveniently nearby.

doorstep[2] *v* (**doorstepped, doorstepping**) **1** to call at every residence in an area as a political canvasser, salesperson, etc. **2** of a journalist: to seek information from or photographs of by waiting outside somebody's house or by more intrusive tactics. ➤➤ **doorstepper** *n.*

doorstop *n* a device for holding a door open or preventing it from opening too far.

doorway *n* an entrance into a building or room that is closed by means of a door.

do over *v informal* **1** to attack and injure (somebody). **2** to redecorate (a house, room, etc).

doo-wop *n* a style of popular music featuring close harmony singing, often using nonsense words made to sound like musical instruments, backed by a stylized form of rhythm and blues.

dopamine *n* a compound that occurs as a neurotransmitter in the brain and as an intermediate compound in the synthesis of adrenalin in body tissue.

dopant *n* in electronics, a substance added in small amounts to a pure semiconductor material to produce a desired electrical effect.

dope[1] *n* **1a** a preparation given illegally to a racehorse, greyhound, etc to make it run faster or slower. **b** *slang* marijuana, opium, or another illegal drug. **2** *informal* a stupid person. **3** *informal* information, *esp* from a reliable source.

dope[2] *v* **1** to administer an illegal or narcotic drug to. **2** to add an impurity to (a semiconductor) so as to give the required electrical properties. ➤➤ **doper** *n.*

dopey *or* **dopy** *adj* (**-ier, -iest**) **1** stupefied, e.g. by sleep or the effects of a drug. **2** *informal* stupid. ➤➤ **dopily** *adv,* **dopiness** *n.*

doppelgänger /'doplgengə, -gangə/ *n* a ghostly counterpart of a living person.

Doppler effect *n* a change in the apparent frequency of sound, light, or other waves when there is relative motion between the source and the observer.

Doppler shift *n* = DOPPLER EFFECT.

dopy *adj* see DOPEY.

dorado *n* (*pl* **dorados** *or* **dorado**) a freshwater game fish, with a golden-coloured body and red fins, that lives in South American rivers.

Dorian *n* a member of an ancient Hellenic people that settled chiefly in the Peloponnesus and Crete. ➤➤ **Dorian** *adj.*

Doric[1] *adj* **1** of the Dorians or their language. **2** of or denoting the oldest and simplest of the three Greek orders of architecture, characterized by fluted columns and a plain capital: compare IONIC, CORINTHIAN.

Doric[2] *n* a dialect of ancient Greek spoken by the Dorians.

dork *n chiefly NAm, slang* a stupid or contemptible person. ➤➤ **dorky** *adj.*

dorm *n informal* = DORMITORY (1).

dormant *adj* **1** asleep or inactive, e.g. during hibernation. **2a** temporarily showing no signs of external activity. **b** temporarily in abeyance. **3** of a plant or plant part: not actively growing but protected from the environment. ➤➤ **dormancy** *n.*

dormer *or* **dormer window** *n* a window set vertically in a structure projecting through a sloping roof.

dormice *n* pl of DORMOUSE.

dormitory *n* (*pl* **-ies**) **1** a large room containing a number of beds, e.g. in a boarding school. **2** (*often used before a noun*) a residential community from which the inhabitants commute to their places of employment.

dormouse *n* (*pl* **dormice**) a small rodent that resembles a mouse with a long bushy tail.

dorsal *adj* relating to or in the region of the back or top surface of something: compare VENTRAL. ➤➤ **dorsally** *adv.*

dory[1] *n* (*pl* **-ies**) a small boat.

dory[2] *n* see JOHN DORY.

DOS *abbr* disk-operating system.

dosage *n* the amount of a dose of medicine or radiation.

dose[1] *n* **1a** a measured quantity of medicine to be taken at one time. **b** a quantity of radiation administered or absorbed. **2** *informal* an infection with a sexually transmitted disease. ✻ **like a dose of salts** *Brit, informal* very quickly.

dose[2] *v* **1** to give a dose of medicine to. **2** to prescribe, dispense, or administer (medicine) in doses.

do-se-do *n* see DO-SI-DO.

dosh *n Brit, informal* money.

do-si-do *or* **do-se-do** /dohsee'doh, -zee-/ *n* (*pl* **-os**) a movement in country dancing that involves two dancers advancing towards each other, passing back to back, and returning to their own places.

dosimeter *n* a device for measuring doses of X-rays or radioactivity. ➤➤ **dosimetric** *adj,* **dosimetry** *n.*

doss[1] *n chiefly Brit, informal* **1** a crude or makeshift bed, *esp* one in a dosshouse. **2** a short sleep. **3** a very easy task.

doss[2] *v chiefly Brit, informal* (*often* + down) to sleep rough or in a makeshift bed.

dosser *n* **1** *chiefly Brit* a person who sleeps in dosshouses; a homeless person. **2** = DOSSHOUSE.

dosshouse *n chiefly Brit* a hostel for people with no fixed address and little or no money.

dossier /'dosi·ə, 'dosiay/ *n* a file of papers containing a detailed report or information.

dost /dust/ *v archaic* present second person sing. of DO[1].

dot[1] *n* **1** a small spot or mark. **2** a small round mark used in writing or printing, e.g. over the letter *i*, as a full stop or decimal point, after a note or rest in music increasing the time value by one half, or to separate the different parts of the domain name in an Internet address. **3** a very small amount. **4** in Morse code, a signal of relatively short duration: compare DASH[2] (2). ✻ **on the dot** exactly; precisely. **the year dot** *Brit, informal* a very long time ago.

dot[2] *v* (**dotted, dotting**) **1** to mark with a dot or dots. **2** to scatter with small marks, amounts, or objects positioned at random. ✻ **dot the i's and cross the t's** **1** *informal* to pay minute attention to detail. **2** to put the finishing touches to something.

dotage *n* a state or period of mental decline in old age.

dotard *n* a feeble-minded old person.

dotcom *n* = DOT COM COMPANY.

dot com company *n* (*pl* **dot com companies**) a company that operates exclusively or chiefly on the Internet and that usu has a domain name ending in the suffix .com, which identifies it as a commercial organization.

dote *v* (+ on/upon) to show excessive or foolish fondness for. ➤➤ **doter** *n,* **doting** *adj,* **dotingly** *adv.*

doth /duth/ *v archaic* present third person sing. of DO[1].

dot-matrix printer *n* a printer that uses a rectangular array of needles for printing and forms each character from dots printed by a particular set of needles in the array.

dotted line *n* a line of dots or short dashes on paper, *esp* to indicate the place where a signature or some other information should be added.

dotterel *n* a Eurasian plover with a distinctive white breast band during the summer months.

dotty *adj* (**-ier, -iest**) *informal* **1** crazy; mad. **2** eccentric or absurd, often in an endearing way. **3** (*usu* + about) extremely or excessively fond of somebody or something. ➤➤ **dottily** *adv,* **dottiness** *n.*

double[1] *adj* **1** twofold; dual. **2** consisting of two, usu combined, similar members or parts. **3** of twice the usual size, quantity, etc. **4** designed or intended for two people. **5** folded in two. **6a** marked by duplicity; deceitful: *a double life.* **b** having two interpretations; ambiguous: *a double meaning.* **7** of a plant or flower: having more than the normal number of petals or sepals: compare SINGLE[1]. ➤➤ **doubleness** *n,* **doubly** *adv.*

double[2] *n* **1** something twice the usual amount, number, size, etc, *esp* a double measure of spirits. **2** somebody who closely resembles another person. **3** somebody who takes the place of an actor in scenes calling for special skills or qualities. **4** two wins, e.g. in races on the same day or championships in the same year. **5** the outermost narrow ring on a dartboard or a throw that lands there, counting double the stated score. ✻ **at the double** very quickly; with great haste.

double[3] *adv* **1** to twice the extent or amount. **2** two together.

double[4] *v* **1** to make or become twice as much or as many. **2a** to fold into two thicknesses. **b** (+ up/over) to stoop or bend over, or cause (somebody) to do this, e.g. in pain or laughter. **3** to sail around (a headland). **4** (+ back) to turn back on one's course. **5a** (+ as) to serve the additional purpose of (something). **b** (+ for) to be a stand-in or substitute for (somebody). ➤➤ **doubler** *n.*

double act *n* an act that involves two performers, *esp* two comedians.

double agent *n* a spy pretending to serve one government while actually serving another.

double-barrelled *adj* **1** of a firearm: having two barrels. **2** of a surname: having two parts, usu joined by a hyphen.

double bass *n* the largest stringed musical instrument of the violin family, tuned a fifth below the cello.

double bed *n* a bed for two people.

double bill *n* an entertainment featuring two main acts, bands, etc of equal status.

double bind *n* a dilemma, *esp* a situation where any choice made will have unpleasant consequences.

double-blind *adj* denoting an experimental procedure in which neither the subjects nor the experimenters know the make-up of the test group and control group during the actual course of the experiments: compare SINGLE-BLIND.

double bluff *n* an attempt to deceive somebody who expects to be bluffed by doing the opposite, e.g. by telling the truth instead of lying.

double boiler *n chiefly NAm* = DOUBLE SAUCEPAN.

double bond *n* a chemical bond between two atoms in a molecule involving two shared pairs of electrons.

double-book *v* to reserve (the same seat, room, etc) for two different people or groups at the same time.

double-breasted *adj* of a coat, jacket, etc: having a relatively large overlapping front, usu with two sets of buttons and buttonholes: compare SINGLE-BREASTED.

double-check *v* to check carefully for a second time.

double chin *n* a person's chin with a fleshy fold under it. ➤➤ **double-chinned** *adj.*

double cream *n* thick heavy cream that contains a relatively high proportion of fat and is suitable for whipping: compare SINGLE CREAM.

double-cross *v* to betray or cheat by an act of deceit or duplicity. ➤➤ **double-cross** *n,* **double-crosser** *n.*

double-dealing[1] *n* underhand or deceitful action. ➤➤ **double-dealer** *n.*

double-dealing[2] *adj* given to or marked by deceit or duplicity.

double-decker *n* something that has two levels or layers, *esp* a bus with seats on two floors.

double decomposition *n* a chemical reaction in which two different compounds exchange ions to form two new compounds.

double Dutch *n informal* unintelligible or nonsensical speech or writing; gibberish.

double-edged *adj* **1** of a knife, sword, etc: having two cutting edges. **2** having two purposes or effects. **3** of a remark: having two possible and often contradictory interpretations.

double entendre /,doohbl on'ton(h)dr/ *n* (*pl* **double entendres** /,doohbl on'ton(h)dr/) an ambiguous word or expression, one of whose meanings is usu risqué.

double entry *n* a method of bookkeeping that records both sides of a business transaction by debiting the amount of the transaction to one account and crediting it to another account.

double exposure *n* the act of exposing the same section of photographic film twice, resulting in superimposed images, or a photograph produced in this way.

double fault *n* two consecutive service faults in tennis, squash, etc, resulting in the loss of a point or of the service.

double figures *pl n* the range of numbers from 10 to 99.

double first *n Brit* a first-class honours degree in two university examinations or subjects.

double glazing *n* windows having two panes of glass separated by an air space, providing better heat and sound insulation than a single pane. ➤➤ **double-glaze** *v.*

Double Gloucester *n* a rich orange-coloured cheese with a firm smooth texture.

double helix *n* two parallel helices arranged round the same axis, *esp* two complementary DNA strands.

double jeopardy *n* the act of prosecuting a person for the same offence twice.

double-jointed *adj* of a person: having joints that permit an exceptional degree of flexibility in bending.

double negative *n* a syntactic construction containing two negatives and having a negative meaning, e.g. 'I didn't hear nothing' meaning 'I heard nothing'.

Usage note

The use of *not* together with another negative word to express a negative idea, as in *I don't know nothing,* is not standard English. Double negative forms should only be used when the intention is to express a positive idea: *a not unusual* (quite common) *request; I can't do nothing* (I must do something).

double-park *v* to park (a vehicle) beside a row of vehicles already parked parallel to the kerb.

double pneumonia *n* pneumonia affecting both lungs.

doubles *pl n* (*used as sing. or pl*) a game between two pairs of players, e.g. in tennis or badminton.

double saucepan *n Brit* two interlocking saucepans, the contents of the upper being cooked or heated by boiling water in the lower.

double-space *v* to type or print leaving alternate lines blank.

doublespeak *n* = DOUBLE-TALK.

double standard *n* a principle or code that applies more rigorously to one group than to another.

doublet *n* **1** a man's close-fitting jacket, with or without sleeves, worn *esp* in the 15th to 17th cents. **2** a pair of similar or identical things, or either of such a pair.

double take *n* a delayed reaction to a surprising or significant situation.

double-talk *n* involved and often deliberately ambiguous language.

doublethink *n* unconscious acceptance, or cynical propagation, of conflicting principles.

double time *n* payment of a worker at twice the normal wage rate.

double up *v* to share accommodation designed for one.

double vision *n* a disorder of vision in which two images of a single object are seen, e.g. because of unequal action of the eye muscles.

double whammy *n* two simultaneous blows or setbacks, often resulting from a single action or event.

doubloon *n* a former Spanish gold coin.

doubt[1] *v* **1** to be uncertain about; to feel inclined to disbelieve. **2** to consider (something) unlikely. **3** to distrust or lack confidence in (somebody). ➤➤ **doubter** *n*, **doubtingly** *adv*.

doubt[2] *n* **1** uncertainty. **2** an inclination not to believe something; a reservation. ✱ **no doubt** certainly; probably.

doubtful *adj* **1** causing doubt; open to question. **2a** lacking a definite opinion; unconvinced. **b** uncertain in outcome; not settled. **3** of questionable worth, honesty, or validity. ➤➤ **doubtfully** *adv*, **doubtfulness** *n*.

doubting Thomas *n* a person who habitually insists on having some kind of proof before accepting or believing things.

doubtless *adv* **1** without doubt; certainly. **2** probably. ➤➤ **doubtlessly** *adv*, **doubtlessness** *n*.

douche[1] /doohsh/ *n* **1** a jet of water or other fluid, directed on or into a part of the body, *esp* the vagina. **2** a device for giving a douche.

douche[2] *v* **1** to clean or treat (something) with a douche. **2** to shower or spray with water.

dough *n* **1** a mixture of flour and liquid that is stiff enough to knead or roll to make bread, pastry, etc. **2** *informal* money.

doughnut (*NAm also* **donut**) *n* a small round or ring-shaped cake that is made with a yeast dough, often filled with jam, and deep-fried.

doughty /'dowti/ *adj* (**-ier, -iest**) *chiefly literary or humorous* bold and resolute. ➤➤ **doughtily** *adv*, **doughtiness** *n*.

doughy *adj* (**-ier, -iest**) **1** unhealthily pale; pasty. **2** resembling dough in consistency. ➤➤ **doughiness** *n*.

Douglas fir *n* a tall tree of the pine family, with large hanging cones, that is extensively grown for its wood.

do up *v* **1** to wrap or fasten. **2** *informal* to repair or refurbish. ✱ **be done up** be dressed for an occasion.

dour /dooə, 'dowə/ *adj* **1** stern, severe, or harsh. **2** gloomy; sullen. ➤➤ **dourly** *adv*, **dourness** *n*.

douse *or* **dowse** *v* **1** to plunge into or drench with liquid. **2** to extinguish (a flame, light, etc). ➤➤ **douser** *n*.

dove[1] /duv/ *n* **1** a bird of the pigeon family that is usu smaller than the domestic pigeon. **2** an advocate of peace, negotiation, or compromise. ➤➤ **dovelike** *adj*, **dovish** *adj*.

dove[2] /dohv/ *v NAm* past tense of DIVE[1].

dovecot *or* **dovecote** *n* a small compartmented raised house or box for domestic pigeons.

Dover sole *n* a European marine flatfish highly valued for food.

dovetail[1] *n* a joint formed by fitting a projection with the flared shape of a dove's tail into a cavity of the same shape.

dovetail[2] *v* **1** to join (pieces of wood etc) by means of dovetails. **2** to fit together skilfully, neatly, or conveniently.

dowager *n* **1** a widow holding property or a title received from her deceased husband. **2** a dignified elderly woman.

dowdy *adj* (**-ier, -iest**) old-fashioned or dull in appearance, clothing etc. ➤➤ **dowdily** *adv*, **dowdiness** *n*.

dowel[1] *n* **1** a wooden or metal pin fitting into holes in adjacent pieces to hold them together. **2** rods of wood or metal for sawing into such pins.

dowel[2] *v* (**dowelled, dowelling,** *NAm* **doweled, doweling**) to fasten (pieces) together by dowels.

dowelling *n* = DOWEL[1] (2).

dower *n* **1** a widow's legal share during her life of her deceased husband's property. **2** *archaic* dowry.

dower house *n* a house provided for a widow, often on the estate of her deceased husband.

Dow-Jones index *n* an index of the prices of securities in the USA based on the daily average price of selected lists of shares.

down[1] *adv* **1a** at or towards a relatively low level or position. **b** in or into a lying or sitting position. **c** to or on the ground, surface, or bottom. **2a** in a direction conventionally the opposite of up. **b** in or towards the south. **c** *chiefly Brit* away from the capital of a country or from a university city. **3a** in or into a relatively low condition or status. **b** used to express opposition: *Down with the oppressors!* **c** *informal* to prison. **4a** in or into a state of reduced or relatively low intensity, heat, volume, etc. **b** to a lower amount, price, figure, or rank. **5a** so as to be recorded, *esp* on paper. **b** so as to be firmly held in position. **6** in cash on the spot, *esp* as an initial payment: *I paid £100 down.* **7** from an earlier time. **8a** so as to be flattened, reduced, eroded, concentrated, or diluted. **b** completely from top to bottom.

down[2] *adj* **1** directed or going downwards. **2** depressed; dejected. **3** of a computer system: temporarily out of action. **4** *chiefly Brit* travelling away from a large town or city. ✱ **down for** on the list to enter (e.g. a race or school). **down on** having a low opinion of or grudge against. **down to 1** attributed to. **2** the responsibility of.

down[3] *prep* **1a** in a downward direction along, through, towards, in, on, etc. **b** at or to a position further along. **2** *Brit, informal* down to; to: *I'm going down the shops.*

down[4] *v* **1** to cause to go or come down. **2** *informal* to drink or swallow quickly. ✱ **down tools** *chiefly Brit* to stop working.

down[5] *n* **1** a downward movement. **2** (*also in pl*) a period of depression, ill fortune, etc: *life's ups and downs.* ✱ **have a down on** to have a grudge against.

down[6] *n* **1a** the fine soft feathers that cover a young bird. **b** the finer softer layer of feathers below an adult bird's contour feathers. **c** fine soft feathers used to fill pillows, duvets, etc. **2** fine soft hairs, e.g. on a person's skin.

down[7] *n* (*usu in pl*) a region of undulating usu chalk uplands, *esp* in S England.

down-and-out[1] *adj* destitute and homeless.

down-and-out[2] *n* a destitute and homeless person.

downbeat[1] *n* the principally accented note of a bar of music, usu the first note.

downbeat[2] *adj* **1** pessimistic; gloomy. **2** relaxed; informal.

downcast *adj* **1** dejected or depressed. **2** directed downwards.

downer *n* **1** *informal* a depressing experience or situation. **2** *slang* a depressant drug, *esp* a barbiturate.

downfall *n* a sudden fall, e.g. from high rank or power, or a cause of such a fall.

downgrade *v* to lower in rank, value, or importance.

downhearted *adj* discouraged or dejected. ➤➤ **downheartedly** *adv*, **downheartedness** *n*.

downhill[1] *n* **1** a descending gradient. **2** a skiing race downhill against time.

downhill[2] *adv* towards the bottom of a hill or slope. ✱ **go downhill** to decline or deteriorate.

downhill[3] *adj* going or sloping downhill.

downland *n* undulating countryside, *esp* that of the downs.

downlink *n* a transmission path for radio signals from a spacecraft, satellite, etc to the earth.

download *v* to transfer (programs or data) from one computer to another, *esp* via a telephone line. ➤➤ **download** *n*, **downloadable** *adj*.

down-market[1] *adj* denoting, selling, or characteristic of goods designed to appeal to the lower end of a market.

down-market[2] *adv* towards the lower end of a market.

down payment *n* an initial payment for something bought on credit.

downpipe *n* a pipe for carrying rainwater from a roof or gutter to the ground or into a drain.

downplay *v* to treat (something) as being less significant than it is.

downpour *n* a heavy fall of rain.

downright[1] *adv* thoroughly; altogether.

downright[2] *adj* **1** absolute; thorough. **2** plain or blunt.

downriver *adv and adj* towards or nearer to the mouth of a river.

downshift *v* **1** *NAm* to put a vehicle into a lower gear. **2** to adopt a less stressful lifestyle.

downside *n* a drawback, shortcoming, or undesirable feature.

downsize *v* to reduce (something) in size, *esp* to reduce (a workforce) by redundancy.

Down's syndrome *n* a chromosomal disorder causing varying degrees of intellectual impairment and distinctive physical characteristics.

downstage *adv and adj* at the front of a theatrical stage, or towards the audience.

downstairs[1] *adv* down the stairs; on or to a lower floor.

downstairs[2] *adj* situated on a lower floor or the ground floor of a building.

downstairs[3] *pl n* (*used as sing.*) the lower floors or ground floor of a building.

downstream *adv and adj* in the direction of the flow of a stream.

downtime *n* time during which a computer, machine, etc is inoperative.

down-to-earth *adj* practical or realistic.

downtown[1] *adv and adj chiefly NAm* of, to, or in the lower part or main business district of a town or city.

downtown[2] *n chiefly NAm* the downtown area of a town or city.

downtrodden *adj* oppressed by those in power.

downturn *n* a downward turn, *esp* towards diminished economic or commercial activity.

down under[1] *adv informal* in or into Australia or New Zealand.

down under[2] *n informal* Australia or New Zealand.

downward *adj* moving or extending downwards. ➤➤ **downwardly** *adv*.

downwards *adv* **1** from a higher to a lower place or level; in the opposite direction from up. **2** from a higher to a lower condition, amount, rank, etc.

downwind *adv and adj* in the direction towards which the wind is blowing.

downy *adj* (**-ier, -iest**) resembling or covered in soft fluffy feathers or fine hairs.

dowry *n* (*pl* **-ies**) the money, goods, or estate that a woman brings to her husband in marriage.

dowse[1] *v* to search for hidden water or minerals with a divining rod. ➤➤ **dowser** *n*.

dowse[2] *v* see DOUSE.

doxology *n* (*pl* **-ies**) a liturgical expression of praise to God. ➤➤ **doxological** *adj*.

doxy *n* (*pl* **-ies**) *archaic* **1** a lover or mistress. **2** a prostitute.

doyen *or* **doyenne** *n* the most experienced, important, or highly respected member of a group: *the doyen of literary critics*.

doyley *or* **doyly** *n* see DOILY.

doze[1] *v* **1** to sleep lightly. **2** (+ off) to fall into a light sleep. ➤➤ **dozer** *n*.

doze[2] *n* a short light sleep.

dozen *n* (*pl* **dozens** *or* **dozen**) **1** a group of twelve. **2** an indefinitely large number. ✱ **talk nineteen to the dozen** *Brit* to talk non-stop and often very quickly. ➤➤ **dozen** *adj*, **dozenth** *adj*.

dozy *adj* (**-ier, -iest**) **1** drowsy; sleepy. **2** *chiefly Brit, informal* stupid and slow-witted. ➤➤ **dozily** *adv*, **doziness** *n*.

DP *abbr* data processing.

DPhil *abbr* Doctor of Philosophy.

dpi *abbr* in computing, dots per inch.

DPP *abbr* Director of Public Prosecutions.

Dr *abbr* **1** doctor. **2** in street names, Drive.

dr *abbr* **1** debtor. **2** drachm. **3** drachma. **4** dram. **5** drawer.

drab[1] *adj* (**drabber, drabbest**) **1** dull or cheerless. **2** of a dull brown or grey colour. ➤➤ **drably** *adv*, **drabness** *n*.

drab[2] *n* **1** *archaic* a slovenly woman. **2** *archaic* a prostitute.

drachm /dram/ *n* **1** a unit of measurement equal to one eighth of a fluid ounce. **2** a unit of apothecaries' weight equal to one eighth of an ounce (about 3.89g).

drachma /'drakmə/ *n* (*pl* **drachmas** *or* **drachmae**) **1** the basic monetary unit of Greece. **2** an ancient Greek silver coin.

draconian *adj* of laws, measures, etc: extremely severe; drastic.

Word history

Latin *Dracon-*, *Draco*, from Greek *Drakōn* seventh-cent. BC Athenian lawgiver. Draco's laws were notorious for their severity; the death penalty was prescribed for the most trivial offences.

draft[1] *n* **1a** a construction plan or technical drawing. **b** a preliminary sketch, outline, or version. **c** (*used before a noun*) constituting a preliminary version or sketch. **2** an order for the payment of money drawn by one person or bank on another. **3** a group of individuals selected for a particular job or purpose. **4** *chiefly NAm* conscription for military service.

draft[2] *v* **1** to produce a draft of (a letter, design, etc). **2a** to select for a particular job or purpose. **b** *NAm* to conscript for military service. ➤➤ **drafter** *n*.

draftee *n NAm* a person who is conscripted for military service.

draftsman *n* (*pl* **draftsmen**) somebody who draws up legal documents or other writings.

drag[1] *v* (**dragged, dragging**) **1a** to pull (something) along slowly or with difficulty. **b** to cause (something) to trail along a surface. **c** to move (something) across a computer screen, usu by means of a mouse. **2** to bring or obtain by force or compulsion. **3** to search (a body of water) with a large net, hook, or other device. **4** to trail along a surface. **5** to pass, move, or proceed laboriously or tediously. **6** *informal* (+ on) to draw smoke from (a cigarette, pipe, etc) into the mouth. ✻ **drag one's feet/heels** to act in a deliberately slow or ineffective manner.

drag[2] *n* **1a** something that retards motion, action, or progress. **b** the retarding force acting on a body moving through air, water, etc, parallel and opposite to the direction of motion. **2** the act or process of dragging. **3** *informal* a drawing into the mouth of cigarette, pipe, or cigar smoke. **4** *informal* **a** women's clothing worn by a man. **b** (*used before a noun*) of or featuring men who dress in women's clothing. **5** *informal* a dull or boring person or experience. **6** a device that is pulled along under water to search for objects. **7** an object drawn over the ground to leave a scented trail, e.g. for dogs to follow.

dragée /'drazhay/ *n* **1** a sugar-coated nut or fruit. **2** a small silver-coloured sugar ball for decorating cakes.

draggle *v* **1** to make wet and dirty, *esp* by trailing on the ground. **2** to straggle.

dragnet *n* **1** a net drawn along the bottom of a body of water or the ground to catch fish or small game. **2** a network of measures designed to lead to capture or discovery, e.g. of a criminal.

dragoman *n* (*pl* **dragomans** *or* **dragomen**) an interpreter, chiefly of Arabic, Turkish, or Persian.

dragon *n* **1** a mythical monster usu represented as a winged and scaly reptile with the power to breathe fire. **2** *informal* a very strict or formidable person, *esp* a woman. ✻ **chase the dragon** *informal* to take heroin by heating it and inhaling the fumes.

dragonfly *n* (*pl* **-ies**) a long slender-bodied insect having two pairs of intricately veined wings held outspread when at rest.

dragoon[1] *n* a member of a cavalry unit formerly composed of mounted infantrymen armed with carbines.

dragoon[2] *v* to force (somebody) to do something against their will.

drag out *v* to protract or lengthen unnecessarily.

drag queen *n informal* a man who dresses in women's clothes, *esp* one who wears flamboyant outfits.

drag race *n* an acceleration contest between cars over a short course. ⋙ **drag racer** *n*, **drag racing** *n*.

dragster *n* a car built or modified for use in a drag race.

drag up *v informal* to mention (an unpleasant topic) unnecessarily.

drain[1] *v* **1a** to draw off (liquid) gradually or completely. **b** of liquid: to flow off gradually or completely. **c** to make or become empty or dry by causing or allowing liquid to drain away. **d** to empty (e.g. a glass) by drinking the contents. **2a** to exhaust (somebody) physically or emotionally. **b** to deplete or empty (something) by gradually using up resources etc. ⋙ **drainer** *n*.

drain[2] *n* **1** a pipe or other means by which liquid is drained away. **2** a gradual outflow or withdrawal. **3** something that causes depletion; a burden. ✻ **go down the drain** to be wasted or to come to nothing.

drainage *n* **1** the act or process of draining. **2** a system of drains.

drainer *n* **1** a rack where washed dishes are left to dry. **2** = DRAINING BOARD.

draining board *n Brit* a usu grooved and slightly sloping surface at the side of a sink unit on which washed dishes are placed to drain.

drainpipe *n* a pipe that carries rainwater from a roof.

drainpipes *pl n* = DRAINPIPE TROUSERS.

drainpipe trousers *pl n* tight trousers with narrow legs.

drake *n* a male duck.

DRAM *abbr* dynamic random access memory.

dram[1] *n* **1** a unit of mass equal to one sixteenth of an ounce (about 1.77g). **2** *chiefly Scot* a tot of spirits, usu whisky.

dram[2] *n* the basic monetary unit of Armenia.

drama *n* **1** a composition in verse or prose intended for performance by actors; a play. **2a** plays collectively or as a genre. **b** (*used before a noun*) relating to plays or the theatre. **3** an exciting or emotionally charged situation or set of events.

dramatic *adj* **1** of or characteristic of drama or acting; theatrical. **2a** vivid or exciting. **b** striking in appearance or effect. ⋙ **dramatically** *adv*.

dramatics *pl n* **1** (*used as sing. or pl*) the study or practice of theatrical arts, e.g. acting and stage management. **2** dramatic behaviour, *esp* an exaggerated display of emotion.

dramatise *v* see DRAMATIZE.

dramatis personae *pl n* (*used as sing. or pl*) the characters or actors in a play, or a list of these.

dramatist *n* a writer of plays.

dramatize *or* **-ise** *v* **1** to adapt (e.g. a novel) for performance by actors. **2** to exaggerate the seriousness, excitement, etc of. ⋙ **dramatization** *n*.

dramaturgy *n* the art or technique of dramatic composition and theatrical representation. ⋙ **dramaturgic** *adj*, **dramaturgical** *adj*.

drank *v* past tense of DRINK[1].

drape[1] *v* **1** to cover or decorate with cloth or clothing hanging in loose folds or flowing lines. **2** to arrange (cloth, clothing, etc) in this way.

drape[2] *n* **1a** a piece of drapery. **b** *chiefly NAm* a curtain. **2** the way in which fabric or clothing hangs.

draper *n chiefly Brit, dated* a person who sells textile fabrics and haberdashery.

drapery *n* (*pl* **-ies**) **1a** cloth, clothing, curtains, etc arranged or hung in loose folds. **b** textile fabrics. **2** *Brit* the business or shop of a draper.

drastic *adj* radical in effect or action; severe. ⋙ **drastically** *adv*.

drat *interj* used to express annoyance. ⋙ **dratted** *adj*.

draught[1] (*NAm* **draft**) *n* **1** a current of air in an enclosed space. **2a** an act of drinking or inhaling, or a portion drunk or inhaled. **b** a portion prepared for drinking; a dose. **3** the act of drawing liquid, e.g. from a cask. **4** the depth of water a vessel requires to float in. **5** the act of drawing in a fishing net.

draught[2] (*NAm* **draft**) *adj* **1** of an animal: used for drawing loads. **2** of beer or cider: served from the barrel or cask.

draughtboard *n* = CHESSBOARD.

draughts *pl n Brit* (*used as sing. or pl*) a board game for two players each of whom moves twelve disc-shaped pieces diagonally across a chessboard.

draughtsman *or* **draughtswoman** (*NAm* **draftsman** *or* **draftswoman**) *n* (*pl* **draughtsmen** *or* **draughtswomen**) **1a** a person who draws technical plans and sketches. **b** an artist skilled in drawing. **2** = DRAFTSMAN. **3** *Brit* a disc-shaped piece used in draughts. ⋙ **draughtsmanship** *n*.

draughty (*NAm* **drafty**) *adj* (**-ier, -iest**) of a room, house, etc: having cold draughts blowing through it. ⋙ **draughtiness** *n*.

Dravidian /drə'vidi·ən/ *n* **1** a member of a group of indigenous peoples of S India and Sri Lanka. **2** any of several languages spoken by these peoples, including Tamil and Malayalam. ➤➤ **Dravidian** *adj.*

draw[1] *v* (*past tense* **drew,** *past part.* **drawn**) **1a** to produce (a picture, diagram, etc) by making lines on a surface. **b** to produce a likeness of (somebody or something) in this way. **2a** to pull or haul (a vehicle, etc). **b** to move (somebody) in a particular direction: *She drew him to one side.* **c** to pull (curtains) to an open or closed position. **3a** to bring out of a container, often with an effort: *to draw a sword.* **b** to extract (a tooth). **4** to take in (a breath). **5** to attract: *to draw the crowds.* **6** to bring about (a response): *to draw cheers.* **7** to reach (a conclusion). **8** to receive (a salary). **9** to take (money) from a bank account. **10** to take (cards) from a pack. **11** to take or be awarded (a random choice). **12** to have equal scores at the end of (a game). **13** to come or go steadily or gradually: *Night draws near.* ✱ **draw on/upon** to use as a source of supply. **draw the line** to fix a limit or boundary for an activity.

draw[2] *n* **1** a raffle, lottery, or drawing of lots. **2** a random selection, e.g. of opponents for a sporting contest. **3** a contest left undecided; a tie. **4** something that attracts public attention or a large audience. **5a** a sucking pull on something held between the lips. **b** the removing of a handgun from its holster in order to shoot.

drawback *n* an undesirable feature; a disadvantage.

drawbridge *n* a bridge that can be raised or let down in order to prevent or permit passage, e.g. one over a castle moat.

drawee *n* the person or organization from whose account money is taken when a cheque, draft, etc is presented for payment.

drawer *n* **1** /draw/ an open-topped storage box that slides out of a piece of furniture for access. **2** /'draw·ə/ **a** somebody who draws something. **b** the person or organization to whom money is paid when a cheque, draft, etc is presented for payment. **3** /drawz/ *dated or humorous* (*in pl*) knickers or underpants.

draw in *v* **1** of successive days: to grow shorter with the approach of winter. **2** of a train: to approach a station. **3** to entice (somebody) to take part.

drawing *n* **1a** the art or technique of representing an object, figure, or plan by means of lines. **b** a representation formed by drawing. **2** an amount drawn from a fund.

drawing board *n* **1** a board to which paper is attached for drawing on. **2** a planning stage.

drawing pin *n Brit* a pin with a broad flat head used *esp* to fasten sheets of paper to boards.

drawing room *n* a formal reception room.

drawl[1] *v* to speak slowly or lazily with vowels greatly prolonged.

drawl[2] *n* a drawling manner of speaking. ➤➤ **drawly** *adj.*

drawn[1] *v* past part. of DRAW[1].

drawn[2] *adj* **1** looking strained, tired, or ill. **2** of a game, competition, etc: ended in a draw.

draw off *v* to remove (liquid).

draw on *v* to approach: *Night draws on.*

draw out *v* **1** to extend in length or time. **2** to encourage (somebody) to speak freely. **3** of successive days: to grow longer at the end of winter.

drawstring *n* a string or tape, usu threaded through a casing, that can be pulled to close a bag, tighten clothes, etc.

draw up *v* **1** to prepare (a document or proposal). **2** to come to a halt.

dray[1] *n* a strong low cart or wagon without sides, used *esp* by brewers.

dray[2] *n* see DREY.

dread[1] *v* **1** to be extremely apprehensive about. **2** to fear greatly. ➤➤ **dreaded** *adj.*

dread[2] *n* **1** great fear, uneasiness, or apprehension. **2** *archaic* great reverence.

dread[3] *adj* greatly feared.

dreadful *adj* **1a** extremely unpleasant or shocking. **b** very disagreeable, e.g. through dullness or poor quality. **2** extreme. ➤➤ **dreadfully** *adv,* **dreadfulness** *n.*

dreadlocks *pl n* long matted, plaited, or tightly curled locks of hair worn *esp* by male Rastafarians.

dreadnought *n* a battleship whose main armament consists of big guns of the same calibre.

dream[1] *n* **1** a series of thoughts, images, or emotions occurring during sleep. **2** a state of absent-mindedness; a daydream. **3a** a strongly desired goal; an ambition. **b** (*used before a noun*) perfect. **4** something notable for its beauty, excellence, etc. ✱ **like a dream** *informal* very well, easily, successfully, etc. ➤➤ **dreamless** *adj,* **dreamlike** *adj.*

dream[2] *v* (*past tense and past part.* **dreamed** *or* **dreamt** /dremt/) **1** to have a dream. **2** to indulge in daydreams or fantasies. **3** to consider as a possibility; to imagine. ➤➤ **dreamer** *n.*

dreamt /dremt/ *v* past tense and past part. of DREAM[2].

dream up *v informal* to devise or invent.

dreamy *adj* (**-ier, -iest**) **1** pleasantly abstracted from immediate reality. **2** given to daydreaming or fantasy. **3** suggestive of a dream. **4** *informal* delightful; very pleasing or attractive. ➤➤ **dreamily** *adv,* **dreaminess** *n.*

dreary *adj* (**-ier, -iest**) causing feelings of cheerlessness or gloom; dull. ➤➤ **drearily** *adv,* **dreariness** *n.*

dredge[1] *n* **1** a machine for removing earth, mud, etc, usu by scooping or sucking. **2** a frame with an attached net for gathering fish, objects, etc from the bottom of a body of water.

dredge[2] *v* **1** (*often* + up/out) **a** to dig, gather, or remove with a dredge. **b** to deepen (e.g. a waterway) with a dredge. **2** *informal* (+ up) to bring to light by thorough searching. ➤➤ **dredger** *n.*

dredge[3] *v* to coat (food) by sprinkling with flour, sugar, etc. ➤➤ **dredger** *n.*

dregs *pl n* **1** sediment contained in a liquid or deposited by it. **2** the most undesirable part.

drench[1] *v* **1** to make thoroughly wet; to soak or saturate. **2** to administer a drench to (an animal).

drench[2] *n* a dose of liquid medicine.

Dresden *n* a type of ornate and delicately coloured German porcelain. ➤➤ **Dresden** *adj.*

dress[1] *v* **1a** to put clothes on (oneself or somebody else). **b** to put on clothing. **2** to make neater or more attractive by decorating, arranging, grooming, etc. **3a** to apply dressings or medicaments to (e.g. a wound). **b** to apply fertilizer to (soil, land, etc). **c** to finish the surface of (e.g. timber, stone, leather or textiles). **d** to add a dressing to (a salad). **4** to prepare for use or service, e.g. for cooking or eating. ✱ **dressed to kill** *informal* wearing clothes that are intended to make a dramatic impact.

dress[2] *n* **1** a one-piece outer garment including both top and skirt for a woman or girl. **2a** clothing, *esp* garments suitable for a particular occasion or appropriate to a specified time. **b** (*used before a* *noun*) denoting or suitable for an occasion requiring formal dress.

dressage /'dresahzh/ *n* **1** the performance by a trained horse of precise movements in response to its rider. **2** the art of riding and training a horse to give such a performance.

dress circle *n* the first or lowest curved tier of seats in a theatre.

dress down *v* **1** to reprove severely, often publicly. **2** to wear casual or less formal clothes. ➤➤ **dressing down** *n.*

dresser[1] *n* **1** a piece of kitchen furniture resembling a sideboard with a high back that has open shelves for holding or displaying dishes. **2** *chiefly NAm* a dressing table.

dresser[2] *n* **1** somebody who dresses in a specified way: *a fashionable dresser.* **2** somebody who looks after stage costumes and helps actors to dress.

dressing *n* **1a** a usu cold sauce for adding to food, *esp* salads. **b** *chiefly NAm* a seasoned mixture used as stuffing, e.g. for poultry. **2** material applied to cover a wound, sore, etc. **3** manure or compost to improve the growth of plants. **4** a substance used to stiffen fabrics in the finishing process.

dressing gown *n* a loose robe worn *esp* over nightclothes or when not fully dressed.

dressing room *n* **1** a room used chiefly for dressing, *esp* a room in a theatre for changing costumes. **2** a small room, often off a bedroom, where clothes, shoes, etc are kept.

dressing table *n* a table with drawers and a mirror for use while applying make-up, combing one's hair, etc.

dressmaker *n* a person, *esp* a woman, who makes clothes for female clients. ➤➤ **dressmaking** *n.*

dress rehearsal *n* a full rehearsal in costume and with stage props shortly before the first performance of a play, show, etc.

dress sense *n* taste in choosing and wearing clothes that fit well and suit the wearer.

dress shirt *n* a man's formal shirt, *esp* for wear with evening dress.

dress up *v* **1a** to dress in good, formal, or smart clothes. **b** to dress in a particular costume: *dressed up as pirates.* **2** to make more attractive or suitable for a formal occasion. **3** to cause to appear in a more favourable light.

dressy *adj* (**-ier, -iest**) of clothes: stylish, smart, or formal. ➤➤ **dressiness** *n.*

drew *v* past tense of DRAW[1].

drey *or* **dray** *n* (*pl* **dreys** *or* **drays**) a squirrel's nest.

dribble[1] *v* **1** to fall or flow in drops or in a thin intermittent stream. **2** to let saliva trickle from the mouth. **3** in football, hockey, basketball, etc, to propel (a ball) by successive slight taps or bounces. ➤➤ **dribbler** *n.*

dribble[2] *n* **1** a small trickling stream or flow. **2** a tiny or insignificant bit or quantity. **3** an act of dribbling in sport. ➤➤ **dribbly** *adj.*

dribs and drabs *pl n informal* small usu scattered amounts.

dried *v* past tense and past part. of DRY[2].

drier[1] *or* **dryer** *n* a machine for drying something, e.g. the hair or laundry.

drier[2] *adj* compar of DRY[1].

driest *adj* superl of DRY[1].

drift[1] *v* **1a** to be carried along by a current of water or air. **b** to move or float smoothly and effortlessly. **2** to move in a random, aimless, or casual way. **3** of snow, leaves, etc: to pile up under the force of wind or water. **4** to deviate from a set course, plan, or adjustment. **5** (+ apart) to lose contact or fail to keep in touch.

drift[2] *n* **1a** the motion or action of drifting. **b** a gradual shift in attitude, opinion, or emotion. **2a** the lateral motion of an aircraft or ship due to currents of air or water. **b** a deviation from a set course, plan, etc. **3a** a mass of snow, leaves, etc deposited by wind or water. **b** a deposit of clay, sand, gravel, and boulders transported by running water from a glacier. **4** a general underlying tendency or meaning. **5** *SAfr* a ford.

drifter *n* **1** somebody who travels or moves about aimlessly. **2** a coastal fishing boat equipped with drift nets.

drift ice *n* floating ice masses that drift with the currents in the sea.

drift net *n* a long fishing net having floats and weights to allow it to hang vertically and drift with the tide.

driftwood *n* wood floating on water or cast up on a shore or beach.

drill[1] *v* **1a** to make (a hole) by piercing action, *esp* with a drill. **b** to drill a hole in (something). **2a** to fix (something) in somebody's mind by repetitive instruction. **b** to train or exercise (somebody) in military drill. **3** *informal* to hit (e.g. a ball) to make it travel fast and straight. ➤➤ **driller** *n.*

drill[2] *n* **1** a tool with an edged or pointed end for making a hole in a solid substance by revolving or by a succession of blows. **2** military training in marching, the handling of arms, etc. **3** an exercise aimed at improving skill by regular practice. **4** *chiefly Brit, informal* the approved or correct procedure for accomplishing something efficiently.

drill[3] *n* **1** a shallow furrow into which seed is sown. **2** a planting implement that makes such furrows, drops in the seed, and covers it with earth.

drill[4] *v* to sow (seeds) by dropping them along a shallow furrow.

drill[5] *n* a durable cotton fabric in twill weave.

drill[6] *n* a W African baboon closely related to the mandrills.

drily *or* **dryly** *adv* **1** in a subtly or understatedly ironic or humorous way. **2** in a dry manner or condition.

drink[1] *v* (*past tense* **drank,** *past part.* **drunk**) **1** to swallow (a liquid), usu for refreshment or nourishment. **2** to join in (a toast) by raising one's glass and drinking from it. **3** to drink alcohol, *esp* habitually or to excess. **4** (+ in) to take in or receive avidly. ✱ **drink to** to drink a toast to. ➤➤ **drinkable** *adj.*

drink[2] *n* **1a** liquid suitable for drinking. **b** alcoholic drink. **2** a portion of liquid for drinking. **3** excessive consumption of alcohol. **4** (**the drink**) *informal* the sea.

drink-driving *n Brit* the crime of driving a vehicle while under the influence of alcohol. ➤➤ **drink-driver** *n.*

drinker *n* **1** somebody who drinks, *esp* one who drinks alcohol to excess. **2** a device that provides water for domestic animals or poultry.

drinking chocolate *n* **1** a mixture of cocoa powder, dried milk, and sugar. **2** a drink made by adding hot water to this mixture.

drinking fountain *n* a fixture with a nozzle that delivers a stream of water for drinking.

drip[1] *v* (**dripped, dripping**) **1a** to let (liquid) fall in drops. **b** of liquid: to fall in drops. **2** to let drops of liquid fall.

drip[2] *n* **1a** a drop of liquid. **b** the action or sound of falling in drops. **2** a projection for throwing off rainwater. **3a** a device used in medicine to administer a liquid, e.g. drugs or nutrients in solution, slowly into a vein. **b** a substance administered by means of a drip. **4** *informal* a weak or insipid person. ⋙ **dripless** *adj.*

drip-dry *v* of a fabric or garment: to dry with few or no creases when hung up dripping wet. ⋙ **drip-dry** *adj.*

drip-feed[1] *n* = DRIP[2] (3).

drip-feed[2] *v* to feed (a patient) by means of a drip.

dripping[1] *n* the fat that runs out from meat during roasting.

dripping[2] *adj* extremely wet.

drippy *adj* (**-ier, -iest**) **1** *informal* weak, insipid, or mawkish. **2** inclined to drip.

dripstone *n* **1** a stone projection, e.g. over a window, for throwing off rainwater. **2** calcium carbonate in the form of stalactites or stalagmites.

drive[1] *v* (*past tense* **drove,** *past part.* **driven**) **1** to control and direct the course of (a vehicle). **2** to transport (somebody) in a vehicle. **3** to propel or force something by physical force. **4** to cause (people or animals) to go in a certain direction. **5a** to apply pressure on (somebody) to act in a certain way: *They drove her to despair.* **b** to lead (somebody) to a certain emotional state: *It drives me crazy.* **6** to provide the energy or motive power for (a machine or engine). **7** to rush or dash with great speed: *rain driving against the window.* ✱ **be driving at** to be implying or suggesting.

drive[2] *n* **1** a journey or trip in a car. **2** a private road or surfaced path giving access from a public right of way to a building, *esp* a private house. **3a** a motivating instinctual need or acquired desire. **b** great zeal in pursuing one's ends. **4** a strong systematic group effort; a campaign. **5** the means for giving motion to a machine, vehicle, or part. **6** = DISK DRIVE. **7a** an attacking cricket stroke. **b** a long golf shot. **8** *Brit* a gathering of people to play a specified game: *a whist drive.* **9** a shoot in which the game is driven within the range of the guns.

drive-by *n* (*pl* **drive-bys**) *informal* a crime, *esp* a shooting, committed from a moving vehicle.

drive-in *adj* denoting a bank, cinema, restaurant, etc that people can use while remaining in their cars.

drivel[1] *v* (**drivelled, drivelling,** *NAm* **driveled, driveling**) **1** to talk foolish or childish nonsense. **2** *archaic* to let saliva dribble from the mouth or mucus run from the nose. ⋙ **driveller** *n.*

drivel[2] *n* foolish or childish nonsense.

driven *v* past part. of DRIVE[1].

driver *n* **1** somebody who drives a vehicle. **2** somebody who drives animals. **3** a golf club used to hit the ball long distances, *esp* from the tee. **4** an implement or mechanical part used for driving. **5** a piece of computer software that controls a piece of hardware. ✱ **in the driver's seat** in a position of authority or control. ⋙ **driverless** *adj.*

drive shaft *n* = PROPELLER SHAFT.

drive-time *n* a time in the morning or late afternoon when people are driving to and from work.

driveway *n* = DRIVE[2] (2).

driving *adj* **1** communicating power or force. **2** having great force. **3** acting with vigour; energetic. **4** of or used in the driving of a vehicle. ✱ **in the driving seat** in a position of authority or control.

driving range *n* an area having equipment for practising golf drives.

drizzle[1] *v* **1** to rain in very small drops or very lightly. **2** to let (liquid) fall in minute drops or a thin stream.

drizzle[2] *n* a fine misty rain. ⋙ **drizzly** *adj.*

drogue *n* **1** a small parachute for stabilizing or decelerating something or for pulling a larger parachute out of stowage. **2** = SEA ANCHOR.

droid *n* in science fiction, a robot.

droll *adj* humorous, whimsical, or amusing, *esp* in an odd way. ⋙ **drollery** *n,* **drollness** *n,* **drolly** *adv.*

-drome *comb. form* forming nouns, denoting: **1** something that runs in a specified direction: *palindrome.* **2** a place where a specified type of racing is held: *hippodrome.* **3** a large place where a specified activity goes on: *aerodrome.*

dromedary *n* (*pl* **-ies**) a one-humped camel of W Asia and N Africa.

drone[1] *n* **1** a male bee with no sting whose sole function is to mate with the queen. **2** somebody who lives off others. **3** a remote-controlled pilotless aircraft, missile, or ship. **4** a droning sound. **5** a pipe on a set of bagpipes that sounds a fixed continuous note. **6** an unvarying sustained bass note.

drone[2] *v* **1** to make a sustained deep murmuring or buzzing sound. **2** (*often* + on) to talk persistently and tediously in a monotonous tone.

drongo *n* (*pl* **-os** *or* **-oes**) an insect-eating songbird of tropical India, Africa, and Australia with glossy black plumage and a long forked tail.

drool *v* **1a** to secrete saliva in anticipation of food. **b** to let saliva dribble from the mouth. **2** (*often* + over) to make an excessive or effusive show of pleasure.

droop[1] *v* **1** to hang or bend downwards; to sag. **2** to become tired or depressed.

droop[2] *n* the condition or appearance of drooping. ⋙ **droopily** *adv,* **droopiness** *n,* **droopy** *adj.*

drop[1] *n* **1a** a round or pear-shaped mass of falling liquid. **b** the quantity of liquid that falls in such a mass. **2** (*in pl*) a dose of medicine measured or administered in drops. **3a** a minute quantity, *esp* of liquid. **b** a small quantity of drink, *esp* alcohol. **4** a small globular sweet or medicated lozenge. **5** the act or an instance of dropping; a fall, decrease, or decline. **6** the distance through which or the amount by which something drops. **7** a parachute descent, or the people or things dropped by parachute. ✱ **a drop in the ocean/a bucket** something much too small to have any effect. **at the drop of a hat** without hesitation; promptly.

drop[2] *v* (**dropped, dropping**) **1** to fall or cause to fall vertically. **2** to fall in a state of collapse or death. **3** to make or become weaker or less: *He dropped his voice; Production has dropped.* **4a** to cease to be of concern: *Let the matter drop.* **b** to give up or abandon (an idea, accusation, friendship, etc). **c** to interrupt (an activity). **5** to leave somebody out of (a team, etc). **6** to set down (passengers or cargo) from a vehicle, ship, etc. **7** to lose (a point or game) in a series. **8** to utter or mention casually: *to drop a hint.*

drop back *v* to move into a position further back or behind.

drop behind *v* to fail to keep up with the rest of a group.

drop curtain *n* a stage curtain that can be lowered and raised.

drop-dead *adv informal* impressively or extremely: *drop-dead gorgeous.*

drop goal *n* a score in rugby made by drop-kicking the ball over the goal's crossbar.

drop handlebars *pl n* lowered curving handlebars, *esp* on a racing bicycle.

drop kick *n* a kick made, e.g. in rugby, by dropping a ball to the ground and kicking it at the moment it starts to rebound. ⋙ **drop-kick** *v.*

drop leaf *n* a hinged flap on the side or end of a table that can be folded down.

droplet *n* a small drop of liquid.

drop off *v* **1** to fall asleep, *esp* unintentionally. **2** to become less.

drop-off *n* **1** a marked dwindling or decline. **2** *NAm* a very steep or perpendicular descent.

dropout *n* **1** somebody who withdraws from participation in conventional society. **2** a student who fails to complete a course of study. **3** a drop kick awarded to the defending team in rugby.

drop out *v* **1** to withdraw from an activity. **2** to adopt an alternative lifestyle.

dropper *n* a short glass tube fitted with a rubber bulb and used to measure or administer liquids in drops.

droppings *pl n* animal excrement, e.g. from mice, rabbits, or birds.

drop scone *n* a small round cake made by dropping a spoonful of batter onto a hot griddle. Also called SCOTCH PANCAKE.

drop shot *n* a delicate shot in tennis, badminton, squash, etc that drops abruptly after crossing the net or hitting a wall.

dropsy *n dated* = OEDEMA. ⋙ **dropsical** *adj.*

drosophila /dro'sofilə/ *n* (*pl* **drosophilas** *or* **drosophilae**) a small two-winged fruit fly extensively used in genetic research.

dross *n* **1** the scum on the surface of molten metal. **2** waste or rubbish.

drought /drowt/ *n* a prolonged period with little or no rainfall.

drove[1] *n* **1** a group of animals driven or moving together. **2** (*also in pl*) a crowd of people moving or acting together.

drove[2] *v* to drive (cattle, sheep, etc) over a long distance, usu to market. ⋙ **drover** *n.*

drove[3] *v* past tense of DRIVE[1].

drown *v* **1** to die or cause to die through suffocation by submersion in water. **2** to submerge, *esp* by a rise in the water level. **3** to wet thoroughly; to drench. **4** (*often* + out) to cause (a sound) not to be heard by making a loud noise. ✱ **drown one's sorrows** to attempt to forget one's problems by drinking alcohol.

drowse[1] *v* to sleep lightly; to doze.

drowse[2] *n* **1** the act or an instance of drowsing. **2** a state of drowsiness.

drowsy *adj* (**-ier, -iest**) **1** sleepy. **2** tending to induce sleepiness. **3** lazy or lethargic. ⋙ **drowsily** *adv,* **drowsiness** *n.*

drub *v* (**drubbed, drubbing**) **1** to beat severely. **2** to defeat decisively. ⋙ **drubbing** *n.*

drudge *n* a person who does hard, menial, or monotonous work.

drudgery *n* hard, menial, or monotonous work.

drug[1] *n* **1** a substance intended for use in the treatment or prevention of disease. **2** a substance that has a particular effect on the body, e.g. a stimulant. **3** something that causes addiction or habituation.

drug[2] *v* (**drugged, drugging**) **1** to administer a drug to. **2** to adulterate (e.g. a drink) with a drug.

drugget *n* a coarse durable cloth used chiefly as a floor covering.

druggie *or* **druggy** *n* (*pl* **-ies**) *informal* a drug addict. ⋙ **druggy** *adj.*

druggist *n* **1** somebody who deals in or dispenses drugs and medicines; a pharmacist. **2** *NAm* the owner or manager of a drugstore.

druggy *n* see DRUGGIE.

drugstore *n chiefly NAm* a pharmacy, *esp* one that also sells sweets, magazines, and refreshments.

druid *or* **druidess** *n* (*often* **Druid** *or* **Druidess**) a member of an ancient Celtic order of priests, often appearing in legends as magicians, or of a modern movement reviving this cult. ⋙ **druidic** *adj,* **druidical** *adj,* **druidism** *n.*

drum[1] *n* **1** a percussion instrument in the form of a hollow cylinder or hemisphere with a skin stretched over the opening that is played by beating with sticks or the hands. **2** the sound made by striking a drum, or any similar sound. **3** something resembling a drum in shape, e.g. a cylindrical container or mechanical part. ⋙ **drumlike** *adj.*

drum[2] *v* (**drummed, drumming**) **1** to beat a drum. **2** to make a succession of taps that produce drumlike sounds. **3** to throb or sound rhythmically. **4** to summon or enlist (somebody), orig by beating a drum. **5** (*usu* + into) to instil (an idea or lesson) by constant repetition.

drum and bass *n* a type of modern dance music characterized by fast insistent drum beats and low bass lines.

drumbeat *n* a stroke on a drum or its sound.

drumfire *n* continuous artillery fire that sounds like a rapid succession of drumbeats.

drumhead *n* the skin or other material stretched over the end of a drum.

drum kit *n* a set of drums and other percussion instruments usu played by a single player, e.g. in a rock band.

drumlin *n* an elongated or oval hill formed from glacial debris.

drum major *n* the marching leader of a band, *esp* a non-commissioned officer in charge of the corps of drums in a military band.

drum majorette *n* a girl or young woman who twirls a baton while leading or accompanying a procession or marching band.

drummer *n* **1** somebody who plays a drum. **2** *chiefly NAm* a travelling sales representative.

drum out *v* to dismiss (somebody) ignominiously, usu for some misdemeanour.

drum roll *n* a succession of drum beats played so quickly that they sound continuous.

drumstick *n* **1** a stick for beating a drum. **2** the part of a fowl's leg between the thigh and foot when cooked as food.

drum up *v* **1** to obtain by canvassing, soliciting, or persistent effort. **2** to invent or originate.

drunk[1] *v* past part. of DRINK[1].

drunk[2] *adj* under the influence of alcohol.

drunk[3] *n* a person who is drunk, *esp* habitually.

drunkard *n* a person who is habitually drunk.

drunken *adj* **1** = DRUNK[2]. **2a** given to habitual excessive use of alcohol. **b** of or resulting from alcoholic intoxication. ⋙ **drunkenly** *adv,* **drunkenness** *n.*

drupe *n* a fruit, e.g. a cherry or plum, that has a stone enclosed by a fleshy layer and is usu covered by a thin skin. ⋙ **drupaceous** *adj.*

drupel *n* = DRUPELET.

drupelet *n* any of the small drupes that together form a fruit such as a raspberry.

Druze *or* **Druse** *n* (*pl* **Druzes** *or* **Druses** *or* **Druze** *or* **Druse**) a member of a religious sect originating among Muslims and centred in the mountains of Lebanon and Syria.

dry[1] *adj* (**drier** *or* **dryer, driest** *or* **dryest**) **1a** free from moisture or liquid, *esp* water; not or no longer wet. **b** not in or under water. **c** having little rainfall or low humidity. **d** lacking water, natural moisture, or lubrication. **e** not or no longer yielding milk, oil, etc. **2** of bread, toast, etc: eaten without butter or other spread. **3** prohibiting the manufacture or sale of alcoholic drinks. **4** of wine, etc: not sweet. **5a** not showing enthusiasm or feeling; impassive. **b** uninteresting. **c** marked by a matter-of-fact, ironic, or terse manner of expression. ➤➤ **dryish** *adj,* **dryness** *n.*

dry[2] *v* (**-ies, -ied**) **1** to make or become dry. **2** to preserve by removing moisture. ➤➤ **dryable** *adj.*

dry[3] *n* (*pl* **dries** *or* **drys**) **1a** a dry place. **b** (**the dry**) *chiefly Aus* the dry season. **2** *Brit, informal* a Conservative politician who holds uncompromising views. **3** *NAm* somebody who supports a ban on the sale of alcoholic drinks; a prohibitionist.

dryad *n* a nymph of the woods in Greek mythology.

dry battery *n* an electric battery consisting of a single dry cell or two or more dry cells connected together.

dry cell *n* a battery cell whose electrolyte is not a liquid: compare WET CELL.

dry-clean *v* to clean (a fabric, garment, etc) with organic solvents rather than water. ➤➤ **dry cleaner** *n,* **dry cleaning** *n.*

dry dock *n* a dock from which the water can be pumped to allow ships to be repaired.

dryer *n* see DRIER[1].

dry fly *n* an artificial angling fly designed to float on the surface of the water.

dry goods *pl n* **1** solid as opposed to liquid commodities. **2** *NAm* textiles, clothing, haberdashery, etc, *esp* as distinguished from hardware and groceries.

dry ice *n* solidified carbon dioxide used *esp* as a refrigerant or to produce the theatrical effect of white mist.

dryly *adv* see DRILY.

dry measure *n* a series of units for measurement of the capacity of dry goods.

dry out *v* **1** to make or become dry. **2** *informal* to overcome an addiction to alcohol or drugs.

dry rot *n* **1** a decay of seasoned timber caused by fungi. **2** a fungus causing dry rot.

dry run *n* a practice exercise; a rehearsal or trial.

dry slope *n* an artificial ski slope covered with matting rather than snow.

drystone *adj* of a wall: constructed of stone without the use of mortar.

drysuit *n* a close-fitting waterproof suit worn over other clothing by participants in certain water sports: compare WET SUIT.

dry up *v* **1** to disappear by evaporation, draining, or the cutting off of a source of supply. **2** to wither or die. **3** to dry washed-up dishes by hand. **4** *informal* to stop talking.

DS *abbr* in music, dal segno.

DSC *abbr Brit* Distinguished Service Cross.

DSc *abbr* Doctor of Science.

DSM *abbr Brit* Distinguished Service Medal.

DSO *abbr Brit* Distinguished Service Order.

DSP *abbr* **1** digital signal processing. **2** digital signal processor.

DSS *abbr Brit* Department of Social Security.

DST *abbr* daylight saving time.

DTI *abbr Brit* Department of Trade and Industry.

DTP *abbr* desktop publishing.

dt's *or* **DT's** *pl n informal* = DELIRIUM TREMENS.

DU *abbr* depleted uranium.

dual *adj* **1** consisting of two parts or elements. **2** having a double character or nature. ➤➤ **duality** *n,* **dually** *adv.*

dual carriageway *n chiefly Brit* a road that has traffic travelling in two or more lanes in each direction, usu separated by a central reservation.

dualism *n* **1** the state of being dual. **2** a theory that considers reality to consist of two independent and fundamental principles, e.g. mind and matter. **3** a doctrine that the universe is ruled by the two opposing principles of good and evil. ➤➤ **dualist** *n,* **dualistic** *adj,* **dualistically** *adv.*

dual-purpose *adj* intended for or serving two purposes.

dub[1] *v* (**dubbed, dubbing**) **1a** to call by a descriptive unofficial name or nickname. **b** to confer knighthood on, *esp* by ceremonial touching on the shoulder with a sword. **2** to dress (leather) by rubbing it with grease.

dub[2] *v* **1a** to provide (a film, television broadcast, etc) with a new soundtrack, *esp* one in a different language. **b** to match (a soundtrack) to the pictures of a film. **c** (*often* + in) to add (commentary, sound effects, music, etc) to a film or to a radio or television broadcast. **2a** *chiefly Brit* to construct (a soundtrack) out of two or more different tracks, e.g. music, sound effects, or commentary: compare MIX[1]. **b** to transpose (a previous recording) to a new record. ➤➤ **dubbing** *n.*

dub[3] *n* **1** the act or an instance of dubbing. **2** a type of popular music that developed from reggae and is characterized by the use of sparse vocals and instruments that are electronically remixed.

dubbin[1] *n* a grease made of oil and tallow used for softening and waterproofing leather.

dubbin[2] *v* to apply dubbin to (leather).

dubiety /dyooh'bieiti/ *n* (*pl* **-ies**) *formal* **1** the state of being doubtful. **2** a matter of doubt.

dubious *adj* **1** giving rise to doubt; uncertain. **2** unsettled in opinion; undecided. **3** of questionable value, quality, or origin. ➤➤ **dubiously** *adv,* **dubiousness** *n.*

dubnium *n* an unstable radioactive metallic chemical element that is artificially produced by bombarding plutonium with high-energy atoms.

ducal *adj* of a duke or duchy. ➤➤ **ducally** *adv.*

ducat *n* **1** a usu gold coin formerly used in many European countries. **2** *informal* (*in pl*) money.

duchess *n* **1** the wife or widow of a duke. **2** a woman having the rank of a duke.

duchesse potatoes /'duchis, -ches, 'dooshes/ *pl n* mashed potatoes mixed with egg, butter, etc, piped on to a baking sheet and baked or browned under the grill.

duchy *n* (*pl* **-ies**) the territory of a duke or duchess; a dukedom.

duck[1] *n* (*pl* **ducks** *or* **duck**) **1** a swimming bird with a short neck, short legs, webbed feet, and a broad flat beak. **2** a female duck: compare DRAKE. **3** *chiefly Brit, informal* (*also in pl, used as sing.*) an affectionate term of address. ✱ **like water off a duck's back** of a remark, reprimand, etc: having no effect or impact at all.

duck[2] *v* **1** to lower one's head or body suddenly, e.g. to avoid being seen or hit. **2** to thrust momentarily under water. **3** to evade (a duty, question, responsibility, etc). ➤➤ **ducker** *n.*

duck[3] *n* the act or an instance of ducking, *esp* a sudden lowering of the head.

duck[4] *n* **1** a durable usu cotton fabric with a close weave. **2** (*in pl*) trousers made from this fabric.

duck[5] *n* a score of nought, *esp* in cricket.

duck-billed *adj* having a snout or jaws shaped like a duck's bill.

duck-billed platypus *n* = PLATYPUS.

duckboard *n* (*usu in pl*) a wooden board or slat used to make a path over wet or muddy ground.

ducking stool *n* a seat attached to a plank that was formerly used to punish offenders by plunging them into water.

duckling *n* a young duck.

ducks and drakes *pl n* (*treated as sing*) the pastime of skimming flat stones along the surface of calm water.

duck's arse (*NAm* **duck's ass**) *n informal* a man's hairstyle in which the hair is swept back and cut so as to droop at the nape of the neck in the shape of a duck's tail.

duckweed *n* a small free-floating stemless plant with small rounded leaves that often covers large areas of the surface of still water.

ducky[1] *adj* (**-ier, -iest**) *informal* delightful; sweet.

ducky[2] *n* (*pl* **-ies**) *Brit, informal* an affectionate term of address.

duct[1] *n* **1** a pipe, tube, or channel that conveys or carries air, power lines, telephone cables, etc. **2** a bodily tube or vessel that carries a glandular secretion. ➤➤ **ducting** *n.*

duct[2] *v* to convey through a duct.

ductile *adj* **1** of metals: capable of being drawn out or hammered thin. **2** capable of being easily moulded into a new form. **3** easily led or influenced; tractable. ➤➤ **ductility** *n.*

dud[1] *n informal* **1** something that fails to perform as it should. **2** a counterfeit or fake. **3** (*in pl*) clothes.

dud[2] *adj informal* ineffectual or counterfeit.

dude *n chiefly NAm, informal* **1** a man. **2** a man who wears fashionable or flashy clothes.

dude ranch *n* a cattle ranch in the western USA converted into a holiday centre, offering activities such as camping and riding.

dudgeon *n archaic* great resentment. ✻ **in high dudgeon** in a fit or state of great indignation, resentment, or anger.

due[1] *adj* **1a** owed or owing as a debt. **b** payable. **2a** owed or owing as a natural or moral right. **b** proper or appropriate. **c** regular or lawful: *due process of law.* **3** required or expected in the prearranged or normal course of events. ✻ **due to 1** ascribable to. **2** because of. **in due course** after a normal passage of time; in the expected or allocated time.

Usage note

due to *or* **owing to?** *Owing to* means 'because of' and *due to* means 'caused by': *Owing to circumstances beyond our control, the departure of the train has had to be delayed*; *The delay is due to circumstances beyond our control.* *Due* is an adjective and should either be attached to a noun or follow the verb *to be.*

due[2] *n* **1** something due or owed. **2** something that rightfully belongs to somebody. **3** (*in pl*) fees; charges. ✻ **give somebody their due** to give somebody the credit they deserve.

due[3] *adv* used before points of the compass: directly or exactly.

duel[1] *n* **1** a formal combat with weapons fought between two people in the presence of witnesses in order to settle a quarrel or point of honour. **2** a conflict or contest between usu evenly matched people, ideas, or forces.

duel[2] *v* (**duelled, duelling,** *NAm* **dueled, dueling**) to fight a duel. ➤➤ **dueller** *n,* **duellist** *n.*

duenna *n* an older woman serving as governess, companion, or chaperon to the younger ladies in a Spanish or Portuguese family.

duet *n* **1** a composition for two performers. **2** a performance by two musicians, singers, dancers, etc.

duff[1] *n* a boiled or steamed pudding, often containing dried fruit. ✻ **up the duff** *Brit, Aus, informal* pregnant.

duff[2] *adj Brit, informal* not working; worthless or useless.

duff[3] *v* **1** *Brit, informal* in golf, to mishit (a shot) by hitting the ground behind the ball. **2** *Aus, informal* to steal and change the brands on (cattle).

duffel *or* **duffle** *n* **1** a coarse heavy woollen material with a thick nap. **2** *NAm* personal belongings, equipment, etc, e.g. for camping or sport.

duffel bag *n* a cylindrical canvas bag closed by a drawstring.

duffel coat *n* a hooded coat made of duffel that is usu fastened with toggles.

duffer[1] *n informal* an incompetent, ineffectual, or clumsy person.

duffer[2] *n Aus, informal* somebody who duffs cattle.

duffle *n* see DUFFEL.

duff up *v Brit, informal* to beat (somebody) up.

dug[1] *v* past tense and past part. of DIG[1].

dug[2] *n* **1** an udder, teat or nipple. **2** *derog* a woman's breast.

dugong /'doohgong/ *n* a large aquatic plant-eating mammal of shallow tropical waters.

dugout *n* **1** a boat made by hollowing out a log. **2** a shelter dug in the ground or in a hillside, *esp* for troops. **3** a shelter at the side of a sports ground where trainers, managers, substitutes, etc sit during a match.

duiker /'diekə/ *n* (*pl* **duikers** *or* **duiker**) a small African antelope with short backward-pointing horns.

duke *n* **1** a nobleman of the highest hereditary rank, *esp* a member of the highest rank of the British peerage. **2** a sovereign ruler of a European duchy. **3** *informal* (*usu in pl*) a fist. ➤➤ **dukedom** *n.*

dulcet *adj* of sounds: sweetly pleasant or soothing.

dulcimer /'dulsimə/ *n* a musical instrument having strings of graduated length stretched over a sounding board and played by striking the strings with light hammers.

dull[1] *adj* **1** boring or uninteresting. **2** cloudy or overcast. **3** lacking brightness or intensity. **4** not resonant or ringing. **5a** slow in perception or understanding. **b** lacking activity or vivacity; listless or sluggish. ➤➤ **dullness** *n,* **dully** *adv,* **dulness** *n.*

dull[2] *v* to make or become dull.

dullard *n* a stupid or insensitive person.

duly *adv* in a due manner, time, or degree; properly.

dumb *adj* **1** lacking the power of speech; mute. **2** not expressed in uttered words. **3** unwilling or temporarily unable to speak. **4** *chiefly NAm, informal* stupid. **5** of a computer terminal: able to receive and display data but unable to modify or process it. ➤➤ **dumbly** *adv,* **dumbness** *n.*

dumbbell *n* **1** a short bar with adjustable weights at each end used for weight training. **2** *NAm, informal* a stupid person.

dumb down *v informal* to make or become less intellectual or less intellectually challenging.

dumbfound *or* **dumfound** *v* to strike dumb with astonishment; to amaze.

dumbo /'dumboh/ *n* (*pl* **-os**) *informal* a foolish or stupid person.

dumb show *n* **1** movements, signs, and gestures used in place of words. **2** a play or part of a play presented in this way.

dumbstruck *adj* dumbfounded.

dumb waiter *n* **1** a movable table or stand often with revolving shelves for holding food or dishes. **2** a small lift for conveying food and dishes, e.g. from the kitchen to the dining area of a restaurant.

dumdum *n* a bullet that expands on impact and inflicts a severe wound.

dum-dum *n informal* a stupid or silly person.

dumfound *v* see DUMBFOUND.

dummy[1] *n* (*pl* **-ies**) **1** an imitation or copy of something used as a substitute, for demonstration purposes, etc. **2a** a model of the human body used e.g. for fitting or displaying clothes. **b** a large puppet used by a ventriloquist. **3** *chiefly Brit* a rubber or plastic teat given to babies to suck in order to soothe them. **4** *informal* a dull or stupid person. **5** the act or an instance of deceiving an opponent in sports.

dummy[2] *adj* **1** resembling or being a dummy. **2** sham or artificial.

dummy[3] *v* (**-ies, -ied**) to deceive an opponent in sports by pretending to pass or release the ball.

dummy run *n* a rehearsal or trial run.

dump[1] *v* **1a** to unload or deposit (something unwanted, e.g. refuse). **b** to deposit or drop carelessly or heavily. **c** to get rid of unceremoniously or irresponsibly; to abandon. **2** to sell (goods) in quantity at a very low price, *esp* abroad at less than the market price at home. **3** to copy (computer data) to an external storage medium.

dump[2] *n* **1a** an accumulation of discarded materials, e.g. refuse. **b** a place where such materials are dumped. **2** an accumulation of military materials or the place where they are stored. **3** an instance of dumping data stored in a computer. **4** *informal* an unpleasant or dilapidated place.

dumper *n* **1** somebody or something that dumps. **2** = DUMPER TRUCK.

dumper truck *n* a lorry with a body that can be tilted to empty the contents.

dumpling *n* **1** a small round mass of dough cooked by boiling or steaming, often in a stew. **2** a dessert of fruit wrapped in dough and usu baked.

dumps *pl n informal* a gloomy state of mind; despondency.

dump truck *n* = DUMPER TRUCK.

dumpy *adj* (**-ier, -iest**) of a person: short and thick in build; squat. ⋙ **dumpiness** *n.*

dun[1] *adj* **1** of a brownish grey colour. **2** of a horse: having a variable colour between brownish grey and yellow.

dun[2] *n* **1** a dun horse. **2** a brownish grey colour.

dun[3] *v* (**dunned, dunning**) to make persistent demands on (somebody) for payment of a debt.

dun[4] *n* **1** a persistent creditor or debt collector. **2** an urgent request, *esp* a demand for payment.

dunce *n* a stupid person or slow learner.

Word history

from the name of John *Duns* Scotus d.1308, Scots theologian whose once accepted writings were ridiculed in the 16th cent. Followers of Duns Scotus, known as *Dunsmen* or *Dunses*, were regarded as dull pedants, and from this the word *dunce* came to mean 'slow learner'.

dunce's cap *n* a conical cap that slow learners at school were formerly forced to wear as a punishment or humiliation.

Dundee cake *n* a fruit cake decorated on top with almonds.

dunderhead *n* a stupid or slow-witted person. ⋙ **dunderheaded** *adj.*

dune *n* a hill or ridge of sand piled up by the wind.

dung *n* the excrement of an animal. ⋙ **dungy** *adj.*

dungaree *n* a heavy coarse durable cotton twill woven from coloured yarns, *esp* blue denim.

dungarees *pl n* a one-piece outer garment consisting of trousers and a bib with shoulder straps fastened to the waist at the back.

dung beetle *n* a beetle that rolls balls of dung in which to lay its eggs and on which the larvae feed.

dungeon *n* a dark underground prison or vault, *esp* in a castle.

dunghill *n* a heap of dung, e.g. in a farmyard.

dungworm *n* an earthworm found in dung, compost, etc that is used as fishing bait.

dunk[1] *v* **1** to dip (a biscuit, a piece of bread, etc) into liquid, e.g. a drink or soup, before eating it. **2** to submerge temporarily in water. **3** in basketball, to put (the ball) through the hoop from above in a slamming movement. ⋙ **dunker** *n.*

dunk[2] *n* **1** the act or an instance of dunking. **2** in basketball, a goal scored by dunking.

dunlin *n* (*pl* **dunlins** *or* **dunlin**) a small sandpiper with reddish brown upper parts and a white breast marked with a black patch in summer.

dunnage *n* **1** loose materials or padding used to prevent damage to cargo. **2** *informal* baggage or personal effects.

dunno *contr informal* don't know.

dunnock *n* a small dull-coloured European bird common in gardens, hedges, and bushy places. Also called HEDGE SPARROW.

dunny *n* (*pl* **-ies**) *chiefly Aus, NZ, informal* a toilet.

duo *n* (*pl* **-os**) **1** a pair of people or things, *esp* a pair of performers. **2** a composition for two performers; a duet.

duo- *comb. form* two: *duologue.*

duodecimal *adj* of a system of numbers that has twelve as its base.

duodecimo *n* (*pl* **-os**) a book format in which a folded sheet forms twelve leaves.

duodenum *n* (*pl* **duodena** *or* **duodenums**) the first part of the small intestine, extending from the stomach to the jejunum. ⋙ **duodenal** *adj.*

duologue *n* **1** a play or part of a play with only two speaking roles. **2** a dialogue between two people.

duopoly *n* (*pl* **-ies**) a market situation that is controlled by two sellers. ⋙ **duopolistic** *adj.*

dupe[1] *n* somebody who is easily deceived or cheated.

dupe[2] *v* to cheat or deceive. ⋙ **dupable** *adj,* **duper** *n,* **dupery** *n.*

dupion /'dyoohpi·ən/ *n* a rough silk fabric.

duple *adj* **1** having two elements; twofold. **2** of musical rhythm or time: marked by two, or a multiple of two, beats per bar.

duplex[1] *adj* **1** double; twofold. **2** of a system of communication: allowing transmission of signals in opposite directions simultaneously.

duplex[2] *n NAm* a house divided into two flats.

duplicate[1] *adj* **1** consisting of two corresponding or identical parts or examples. **2** being the same as another. **3** double.

duplicate[2] *n* **1** either of two things that exactly resemble each other. **2** a copy.

duplicate[3] *v* **1** to make or become duplicate. **2** to make an exact copy of. **3** to repeat or equal. ➤➤ **duplicable** *adj,* **duplication** *n.*

duplicator *n* a machine for making copies.

duplicity *n* malicious deception in thought, speech, or action. ➤➤ **duplicitous** *adj,* **duplicitously** *adv.*

duppy *n* (*pl* **-ies**) a ghost or spirit in W Indian folklore, usu a malevolent one.

durable *adj* able to exist or be used for a long time without significant deterioration. ➤➤ **durability** *n,* **durably** *adv.*

durables *pl n* consumer goods, e.g. household appliances, that are typically used repeatedly over a period of years without being replaced.

dura mater /,dyooərə 'mahtə, 'maytə/ *n* the tough outermost membrane that envelops the brain and spinal cord.

duramen *n* = HEARTWOOD.

durance *n archaic* imprisonment.

duration *n* the time during which something exists or lasts.

durbar *n* **1** a reception held in former times by an Indian prince or a British governor or viceroy in India. **2** the court of an Indian prince in former times.

duress *n* **1** compulsion by threat, violence, or imprisonment. **2** forcible restraint or restriction.

Durex *n* (*pl* **Durex** *or informal* **Durexes**) *trademark* a condom.

durian *n* a large oval tropical fruit with a prickly rind and pleasant-tasting but foul-smelling flesh.

during *prep* **1** throughout the whole duration of. **2** at some point in the course of.

durum *n* a hard wheat that yields a flour used to make pasta.

dusk *n* the darker part of twilight.

dusky *adj* (**-ier, -iest**) **1** somewhat dark in colour, *esp* dark-skinned. **2** shadowy; gloomy. ➤➤ **duskily** *adv,* **duskiness** *n.*

dust[1] *n* **1a** fine dry particles of any solid matter. **b** the fine particles of waste that settle on household surfaces. **2** the surface of the ground. **3** an act of dusting. ✱ **when/after/until the dust settles** when, etc things quieten down or return to normal. ➤➤ **dustless** *adj.*

dust[2] *v* **1** to make free of dust, e.g. by wiping or brushing. **2** (+ down/off) to prepare to use again, *esp* after a long period of disuse. **3** to sprinkle with fine particles.

dust bath *n* a bird's working dust into its feathers in order to clean them.

dustbin *n Brit* a large container for holding household refuse until collection.

dust bowl *n* a region that suffers from prolonged droughts and dust storms.

dustcart *n Brit* a vehicle for collecting household refuse.

dustcover *n* **1** = DUSTSHEET. **2** = DUST JACKET.

dust devil *n* a small whirlwind containing sand or dust.

duster *n* a cloth for removing dust from household surfaces.

dust jacket *n* a removable outer paper cover for a book.

dustman *n* (*pl* **dustmen**) *Brit* somebody employed to remove household refuse.

dustpan *n* a shovel-like utensil into which household dust and litter is swept.

dustsheet *n* a large sheet used as a cover to protect furniture, etc from dust.

dust storm *n* a strong dust-laden wind or whirlwind.

dust-up *n informal* a quarrel or fight.

dusty *adj* (**-ier, -iest**) **1** covered with dust. **2** consisting of dust; powdery. **3** resembling dust. **4** lacking vitality; dry. ✱ **give/get a dusty answer** to give or get an unhelpful or brusque reply. ➤➤ **dustily** *adv,* **dustiness** *n.*

Dutch *n* **1** (**the Dutch**) (*used as pl*) the people of the Netherlands. **2** the Germanic language of the people of the Netherlands. ✱ **go Dutch** to pay one's own share; to divide expenses equally. ➤➤ **Dutch** *adj.*

dutch *n Brit, informal* a person's wife, *esp* a Cockney's wife.

Dutch auction *n* an auction in which the bidding price is gradually reduced until a bid is received.

Dutch barn *n* a large barn with a curved roof and open sides used *esp* for storing hay.

Dutch cap *n* a moulded cap, usu of thin rubber, that fits over the cervix of the womb to act as a contraceptive barrier.

Dutch courage *n* confidence or courage induced by drinking alcohol.

Dutch elm disease *n* a fatal disease of elms caused by a fungus, spread by a beetle, and characterized by yellowing and withering of the leaves.

Dutch hoe *n* a garden hoe that is pushed rather than pulled.

Dutchman *or* **Dutchwoman** *n* (*pl* **Dutchmen** *or* **Dutchwomen**) a native or inhabitant of the Netherlands.

Dutch oven *n* **1** a heavy pot with a tight-fitting lid used for cooking stews, casseroles, etc. **2** a metal box used for roasting in front of an open fire.

Dutch treat *n* a meal or entertainment for which each person pays their own share.

Dutch uncle *n informal* somebody who advises or criticizes sternly and bluntly, but in a well-intentioned way.

dutiable *adj* subject to a duty.

dutiful *adj* filled with, motivated by, or expressive of a sense of duty. ➤➤ **dutifully** *adv,* **dutifulness** *n.*

duty *n* (*pl* **-ies**) **1a** a task, service, or function arising from one's position or job. **b** assigned military or official service or business. **2** a moral or legal obligation. **3** a tax, e.g. on imports or the transfer of property. ✱ **on/off duty** engaged or not engaged in one's usual work.

duty-bound *adj* obliged by duty, *esp* morally or legally.

duty-free *adj* **1** exempt from the payment of duty. **2** selling goods that are exempt from duty. ➤➤ **duty-free** *adv.*

duty-paid *adj* of goods: on which duty has been paid in the country of purchase.

duvet /'doohvay/ *n* a large quilt filled with feathers or synthetic fibre, used in place of an upper sheet and blankets.

duvet day *n informal* a tolerated absence from work for a trivial reason such as minor illness.

DVD *abbr* digital videodisc (or digital versatile disc), a disc with a large capacity for storing audio, video, or other information.

DVLA *abbr Brit* Driver and Vehicle Licensing Agency.

DVT *abbr* deep vein thrombosis.

dwarf[1] *n* (*pl* **dwarfs** *or* **dwarves**) **1** a person of abnormally small stature. **2a** an animal or plant that is much smaller than normal size. **b** (*used before a noun*) denoting such an animal or plant. **3** in mythology and folklore, a small human-like creature often depicted as having magical powers or skilled as a craftsman. **4** = DWARF STAR. ➤➤ **dwarfish** *adj.*

dwarf[2] *v* **1** to stunt the growth of. **2** to cause to appear smaller or less significant by comparison.

dwarfism *n* the condition of unusually small size or stunted growth.

dwarf star *n* a relatively small star of ordinary or low luminosity.

dwarves *n* pl of DWARF[1].

dweeb *n NAm, informal* a dull or ineffectual person.

dwell *v* (*past tense and past part.* **dwelt** *or* **dwelled**) **1** *formal* to live as a resident; to reside. **2** (*often* + in) to live or exist in a specified condition. ✱ **dwell on/upon** to think, write, or speak about at length. ➤➤ **dweller** *n.*

dwelling *n formal* a place, e.g. a house or flat, in which people live; a home.

dwelling place *n* = DWELLING.

dwelt *v* past tense and past part. of DWELL.

dwindle *v* to become steadily less in quantity or size.

Dy *abbr* the chemical symbol for dysprosium.

dyad *n technical* a pair or couple. ➤➤ **dyadic** *adj.*

Dyak *or* **Dayak** *n* (*pl* **Dyaks** *or* **Dayaks** *or collectively* **Dyak** *or* **Dayak**) **1** a member of a group of indigenous peoples inhabiting the interior of Borneo. **2** a group of Austronesian languages or dialects spoken by these peoples. ➤➤ **Dyak** *adj.*

dybbuk /'dibək/ *n* (*pl* **dybbukim** *or* **dybbuks**) in Jewish folklore, an evil spirit that inhabits the body of a living person.

dye[1] *n* **1** a substance used to colour something. **2** a colour or tint produced by dyeing.

dye[2] *v* (**dyes, dyed, dyeing**) to impart a new and often permanent colour to (something, e.g. fabric or hair) by impregnation with a dye. ➤➤ **dyer** *n.*

dyed-in-the-wool *adj* thoroughgoing, uncompromising, or unchanging.

dyestuff *n* = DYE[1] (I).

dying[1] *v* present part. of DIE[1].

dying[2] *adj* **1** made or occurring at the point of death. **2** final or last.

dyke[1] *or* **dike** *n* **1** a watercourse or ditch. **2** a bank, usu of earth, constructed to control or confine water. **3** a barrier preventing passage. **4** a raised causeway. **5** a wall-like body of rock that has flowed while molten into a fissure.

dyke[2] *or* **dike** *v* to surround or protect (land) with a dyke.

dyke[3] *or* **dike** *n informal, derog* a lesbian. ➤➤ **dykey** *adj.*

dynamic[1] *adj* **1a** of physical force or energy in motion: compare STATIC[1]. **b** of dynamics. **2a** marked by continuous activity or change. **b** energetic and forceful. **3** of computer memory: using devices that require periodic renewal to preserve the stored information. **4** relating to variation in sound intensity or volume in music. ➤➤ **dynamical** *adj,* **dynamically** *adv.*

dynamic[2] *n* a dynamic force.

dynamics *pl n* (*used as sing. or pl*) **1** the branch of mechanics that deals with forces and their relation to the motion of bodies. **2** a pattern of change or growth, or the forces that produce it. **3** variation and contrast in force or intensity, *esp* in music. ➤➤ **dynamicist** *n.*

dynamism *n* the quality of being energetic and forceful.

dynamite[1] *n* **1** a blasting explosive that is made of nitroglycerine absorbed in a porous material. **2** *informal* somebody or something that has a potentially dangerous or spectacular effect.

dynamite[2] *v* to blow up or destroy with dynamite.

dynamo *n* (*pl* **-os**) **1** a machine by which mechanical energy is converted into electrical energy. **2** *informal* a forceful energetic person.

dynamometer *n* an instrument for measuring power exerted, e.g. by an engine.

dynast *n* a ruler, *esp* a hereditary one.

dynasty *n* (*pl* **-ies**) **1** a succession of hereditary rulers, or the time during which they rule. **2** a powerful group or family that maintains its position for a considerable time. ➤➤ **dynastic** *adj,* **dynastically** *adv.*

dyne *n* a unit of force that would give a mass of one gram an acceleration of one centimetre per second per second, equivalent to 10^{-5} newtons.

dys- *prefix* **1** abnormal; impaired: *dysfunction.* **2** difficult; painful: *dysmenorrhoea.*

dysbiosis /,disbie'ohsis/ *n* an excess of harmful over beneficial micro-organisms in the gut.

dysentery /'dis(ə)ntri/ *n* an infection of the intestines characterized by severe diarrhoea, usu with passing of mucus and blood.

dysfunction *n* impaired or abnormal functioning.

dysfunctional *adj* **1** not functioning properly. **2** characterized by the breakdown of the usual forms of social behaviour, relationships, or interactions. ➤➤ **dysfunctionally** *adv.*

dyslexia *n* difficulties with reading, writing, spelling, and understanding symbols, caused by a neurological disorder. ➤➤ **dyslectic** *adj and n,* **dyslexic** *adj and n.*

dysmenorrhoea (*NAm* **dysmenorrhea**) /dis,menə'riə/ *n* a disorder in which menstruation is abnormally painful.

dyspepsia *n* indigestion.

dyspeptic *adj* **1** relating to or having dyspepsia. **2** ill-tempered. ➤➤ **dyspeptically** *adv.*

dysphagia /dis'fayji·ə/ *n* difficulty in swallowing, usu a symptom of a physiological disorder.

dysphasia *n* difficulty in using or understanding language caused by brain injury or disease or malfunction of the brain. ➤➤ **dysphasic** *n and adj.*

dysphoria *n* a state of feeling unwell, unhappy, or ill at ease. ➤➤ **dysphoric** *adj and n.*

dysplasia *n* abnormal growth or development of an organ, cells, tissue, etc. ➤➤ **dysplastic** *adj.*

dyspnoea (*NAm* **dyspnea**) /disp'nee·ə/ *n* difficult or laboured breathing. ➤➤ **dyspnoeic** *adj.*

dyspraxia *n* a brain disorder that causes problems with coordination and movement.

dysprosium *n* a silver-white soft metallic chemical element that is used to absorb neutrons in the control rods of a nuclear reactor.

dysthymia /dis'thiemi·ə/ *n* depression, anxiety, and other characteristics associated with introversion. ➤➤ **dysthymic** *adj and n.*

dystopia *n* an imaginary place that is depressingly wretched: compare UTOPIA. ➤➤ **dystopian** *adj.*

dystrophy *n* a disorder of the body characterized by wasting of organs or tissues, e.g. muscles or bones: compare MUSCULAR DYSTROPHY. ➤➤ **dystrophic** *adj.*

E e

E[1] *or* **e** *n* (*pl* **Es** *or* **E's** *or* **e's**) **1** the fifth letter of the English alphabet. **2** a mark or grade rating a student's work as poor. **3** in music, the third note of the diatonic scale of C major.

E[2] *abbr* **1** East. **2** Eastern. **3** English. **4** European.

E[3] *n* (*pl* **Es** *or* **E's**) **1** the drug Ecstasy. **2** a tablet of this drug.

E- *prefix* used before a series of digits: E number.

e-[1] *prefix* **1a** to deprive of: *emasculate.* **b** lacking; without: *edentate.* **2** out: *emanate.*

e-[2] *prefix* electronic: *e-commerce.*

each[1] *adj and pron* every one of two or more distinct individuals within a group considered separately. ✱ **each and every** all; every single.

each[2] *adv* to or for each; apiece.

each other *pron* (*not used as the subject of a verb*) each of two or more in reciprocal action or relation.

each way *adj and adv Brit* of a bet: backing a horse, dog, etc to win or to finish in the first two, three, or four in a race.

eager *adj* showing keen or impatient desire or interest. ➤➤ **eagerly** *adv,* **eagerness** *n.*

eagle *n* **1** a large bird of prey noted for its strength, size, keenness of vision, and powers of flight. **2** a golf score of two strokes less than par on a hole.

eagle eye *n* a close watch; careful attention.

eagle-eyed *adj* **1** having very good eyesight. **2** good at noticing details; observant.

eagle owl *n* the largest European owl, with prominent ear tufts and large orange eyes.

eaglet *n* a young eagle.

-ean *suffix* see -AN[1], -AN[2].

ear[1] *n* **1a** the organ of hearing and equilibrium in humans and other vertebrates. **b** the external part of this organ. **2** the sense or act of hearing. **3** sensitivity to musical tone and pitch. **4** sympathetic attention. **5** something resembling an ear in shape, function, or position. ✱ **be all ears** to listen very attentively. **have an ear to the ground** to be in receipt of information not generally known. **have somebody's ear** to have access to somebody so that one can give advice, make complaints, etc. **out on one's ear** thrown out of a job, home, etc with no possibility of returning. **somebody's ears are burning** somebody has a feeling that they are being talked about. **up to one's ears** very busy.

ear[2] *n* the fruiting spike of a cereal, including the seeds and protective structures.

earache *n* pain in the ear.

eardrum *n* = TYMPANIC MEMBRANE.

earful *n informal* a sharp verbal reprimand.

earhole *n* the ear, *esp* of a person.

earl *n* a member of the British peerage ranking below a marquess and above a viscount. ➤➤ **earldom** *n.*

Earl Grey *n* a black China tea scented with bergamot oil.

earlobe *n* the soft, fleshy, lower part of the ear.

early[1] *adv* (**-ier, -iest**) **1** before the usual, expected, or proper time. **2** at or near the beginning of a period of time or series.

early[2] *adj* (**-ier, -iest**) **1a** occurring before the usual time. **b** occurring in the near future. **2a** of, at, or occurring near the beginning of a period of time or series. **b** distant in past time. ✱ **at the earliest** not sooner than a specified date or time. **it's early days** it is too soon to be sure of an outcome, to expect a result, etc. ➤➤ **earliness** *n.*

Early English *adj* of an early Gothic style of architecture, prevalent in Britain from the late 12th to the late 13th cent., characterized by lancet windows and pointed arches.

early music *n* medieval and Renaissance music, sometimes also including baroque music, *esp* when performed in modern times on period instruments.

earmark[1] *n* **1** a mark of identification on the ear of an animal. **2** a distinguishing or identifying characteristic.

earmark[2] *v* **1** to mark (livestock) with an earmark. **2** to designate (e.g. funds) for a specific use or recipient.

earmuffs *pl n* a pair of ear coverings connected by a flexible band and worn as protection against cold or noise.

earn *v* **1** to receive (money) as return for work done or services rendered. **2** to bring in (money) as income. **3** to gain or deserve (a title, reward, etc) because of one's behaviour, qualities, or effort.

earned income *n* income from work one is paid for as opposed to income from shares, etc.

earner *n* **1** somebody who earns wages, etc. **2** *Brit, informal* something profitable.

earnest[1] *adj* determined and serious. ➤➤ **earnestly** *adv,* **earnestness** *n.*

earnest[2] ✱ **in earnest** serious or seriously; sincere or sincerely.

earnest[3] *n* **1** something of value, *esp* money, given by a buyer to a seller to seal a bargain. **2** a token of what is to come; a pledge.

earnings *pl n* money or other income earned.

earphone *n* a device attached to a radio, personal stereo, etc that converts electrical energy into sound waves and is worn over or inserted into the ear.

earpiece *n* a part of an instrument, e.g. a telephone, held to the ear for listening.

earpiercing *adj* distressingly loud and shrill.

ear-piercing *n* the making of a hole in the lobe or edge of the ear to allow earrings to be worn.

earplug *n* a device inserted into the outer opening of the ear for protection against water, loud noise, etc.

earring *n* an ornament that is attached to the lobe or edge of the ear.

earshot *n* the range within which something, *esp* the unaided voice, may be heard.

earsplitting *adj* distressingly loud.

earth[1] *n* **1** (*often* **Earth**) the planet on which we live, third in order from the sun. **2** land or solid ground as distinguished from sea and air. **3** the loose powdery material on the surface of the planet, in which plants grow; soil. **4** *chiefly Brit* **a** an electrical connection to the ground. **b** the terminal, e.g. in a plug, for this connection. **5** (**the earth**) *informal* a huge amount of money. **6** the lair of a fox, badger, etc. **7** one of the four elements of the alchemists, the others being fire, air, and water. ✱ **back down to earth** back to reality. **go to earth** to go into hiding. **on earth** used to intensify an interrogative pronoun: *Where on earth is it?* ➤➤ **earthward** *adj and adv*, **earthwards** *adv*.

earth[2] *v* **1** *chiefly Brit* to connect (an electrical device) to earth. **2a** to drive (e.g. a fox) to hiding in its lair. **b** of a hunted animal: to hide in its lair.

earthbound *adj* **1a** restricted to the earth. **b** heading or directed towards the planet earth. **2a** bound by worldly interests; lacking spiritual quality. **b** pedestrian or unimaginative.

earth closet *n* a toilet in which earth is used to cover excreta.

earthen *adj* made of earth or baked clay.

earthenware *n* ceramic ware made of slightly porous opaque clay fired at a low temperature: compare STONEWARE.

earthling *n* an inhabitant of the earth, *esp* in science fiction.

earthly *adj* **1a** characteristic of or belonging to the earth. **b** relating to human life on earth; worldly. **2** (*in negative or interrogative contexts*) possible: *There is no earthly reason for such behaviour.* ➤➤ **earthliness** *n*.

earth mother *n* **1** the female principle of fertility. **2** a woman who embodies the earth mother, *esp* in being generously proportioned and maternal.

earthquake *n* a sudden violent earth tremor caused by volcanic action or processes within the earth's crust.

earth science *n* any or all of the sciences, such as geology, that deal with physical aspects of the earth.

earthshattering *adj* having tremendous importance or a widespread often violent effect. ➤➤ **earthshatteringly** *adv*.

earthshine *n* sunlight reflected by the earth and illuminating the dark part of the moon.

earthwork *n* (*also in pl*) an embankment, fortification, etc made of earth.

earthworm *n* a widely distributed hermaphroditic worm that lives in the soil.

earthy *adj* (**-ier, -iest**) **1** consisting of or resembling earth or soil. **2** crude or coarse. ➤➤ **earthily** *adv*, **earthiness** *n*.

ear trumpet *n* a trumpet-shaped device held to the ear to improve hearing.

earwax *n* the yellow waxy secretion from the glands of the outer ear.

earwig[1] *n* a small insect with slender antennae and a pair of appendages resembling forceps.

Word history

Old English *ēarwicga*, from *ēare* EAR[1] + *wicga* insect. Earwigs were once thought to crawl into people's ears.

earwig[2] *v* (**earwigged, earwigging**) *informal* to eavesdrop.

ease[1] *n* **1a** freedom from pain or anxiety. **b** freedom from embarrassment or constraint; naturalness. **c** rest or relaxation. **2** facility or effortlessness. **3** easing or being eased. ✱ **at ease 1** free from pain or discomfort. **2** (*also* **at one's ease**) free from restraint or formality; relaxed. **3** used as a military command: standing with the feet apart and the hands behind the body. ➤➤ **easeful** *adj*, **easefully** *adv*.

ease[2] *v* **1a** to make (pain, suffering, etc) less severe or intense. **b** to free from something that causes pain or anxiety. **2** to make less difficult. **3** to manoeuvre gently or carefully in a specified way. **4** (*often* + off/up) to decrease in activity, intensity, severity, etc.

easel *n* a frame for supporting something, *esp* an artist's canvas.

easement *n* **1** a right in law to the limited use, for access, of another person's ground or property. **2** an act or means of easing or relieving.

easily *adv* **1** without difficulty. **2** without doubt; by far.

east[1] *n* **1** the direction 90° clockwise from north that is the general direction of sunrise. **2a** regions or countries lying to the east. **b** (*usu* **the East**) regions lying to the east of Europe. **c** (**the East**) formerly, the bloc of communist countries in eastern Europe. ➤➤ **eastbound** *adj and adv*.

east[2] *adj and adv* **1** at, towards, or coming from the east. **2** of the wind: blowing from the east. ✱ **east by north/south** in a position or direction between east and east-northeast (or east-southeast).

Easter *n* a Christian feast commemorating Christ's resurrection, observed on a Sunday between 21 March and 25 April.

Easter egg *n* a usu chocolate egg given as a present and eaten at Easter.

easterly[1] *adj and adv* **1** in an eastern position or direction. **2** of a wind: blowing from the east.

easterly[2] *n* (*pl* **-ies**) an easterly wind.

eastern *adj* **1** in or towards the east; inhabiting the east. **2** (*often* **Eastern**) of or stemming from Oriental traditions, in contrast with those of Europe or America. ➤➤ **easternmost** *adj*.

Eastern Church *n* **1** (*also* **Eastern Orthodox Church**) a Christian Church originating in the Eastern Roman Empire and forming the main Christian Churches in Greece, Russia, Serbia, etc. **2** (*also* **Eastern church**) a Christian Church of North Africa and the Middle East.

Eastertide *n* the period of time around Easter.

easting *n* **1** distance due east in longitude from the preceding point of measurement. **2** easterly progress.

east-northeast *n* the direction midway between east and northeast. ➤➤ **east-northeast** *adj and adv*.

east-southeast *n* the direction midway between east and southeast. ⪢ **east-southeast** *adj and adv.*

eastward *adj and adv* towards the east; in a direction going east. ⪢ **eastwards** *adv.*

easy[1] *adj* (**-ier, -iest**) **1** causing or involving little difficulty. **2a** marked by peace, comfort, or freedom from constraint. **b** not hurried or strenuous. **c** free from pain, annoyance, or anxiety. **3** *informal* readily persuaded to have sexual relations. **4** *chiefly Brit, informal* not having strong preferences on a particular issue. * **be easy on** to be lenient with (somebody). **easy on the eye** *informal* attractive. **easy on the ear** *informal* pleasant to listen to. ⪢ **easiness** *n.*

easy[2] *adv* **1** easily. **2** slowly or cautiously. * **go easy on** to deal leniently with (somebody). **take it easy 1** to relax or rest. **2** to remain calm.

easy-care *adj* of a material or item of clothing: easy to look after, clean, etc.

easy chair *n* a large usu upholstered armchair designed for comfort and relaxation.

easygoing *adj* **1a** taking life easily. **b** placid and tolerant. **2** unhurried, relaxed, or comfortable.

easy listening *n* music and song that is undemanding and pleasant to listen to.

easy meat *n chiefly Brit* somebody who is easily duped, imposed upon, or mastered.

easy street *n informal* a position of affluence.

eat *v* (*past tense* **ate,** *past part.* **eaten**) **1** to put (food) in the mouth and swallow it, usu after chewing it. **2a** (+ away/into/through) to destroy, erode, or corrode gradually. **b** (+ into) to use a great deal of (a limited resource). **3** *informal* to worry or annoy (somebody): *What's eating them?* * **eat one's heart out** to grieve bitterly, *esp* for something desired but unobtainable. **eat one's words** to retract what one has said, *esp* in an ignominious way. **eat out of somebody's hand** to do everything somebody asks. ⪢ **eater** *n.*

eatable *adj* suitable for eating.

Usage note

eatable *or* **edible**? Both *eatable* and *edible* mean 'reasonably pleasant to eat', but the primary meaning of *edible* is 'nonpoisonous': *Are these berries edible?*

eatables *pl n* food.

eaten *v* past part. of EAT.

eatery *n* (*pl* **-ies**) *informal* a restaurant.

eat in *v* to eat a meal at home, rather than in a restaurant, etc.

eating *adj* suitable for eating raw: *an eating apple.*

eat out *v* to eat a meal away from home, *esp* in a restaurant.

eats *pl n informal* food.

eat up *v* **1** to eat (food) completely. **2** to use up (money, resources, etc). **3** *informal* (*usu in passive*) to absorb or preoccupy (somebody): *He was eaten up by vanity.*

eau de cologne /,oh də kə'lohn/ *n* (*pl* **eaux de cologne** /,oh/) a variety of toilet water with a characteristic perfume.

eau-de-nil /,oh də 'neel/ *n* a pale slightly bluish green. ⪢ **eau-de-nil** *adj.*

eau de toilette /,oh də twah'let/ *n* (*pl* **eaux de toilette** /,oh/) = TOILET WATER.

eau-de-vie /,oh də 'vee/ *n* (*pl* **eaux-de-vie** /,oh/) = BRANDY.

eaux de cologne *n* pl of EAU DE COLOGNE.

eaux de toilette *n* pl of EAU DE TOILETTE.

eaux-de-vie *n* pl of EAU-DE-VIE.

eaves *pl n* the lower border of a roof that overhangs the wall.

eavesdrop *v* (**eavesdropped, eavesdropping**) to listen secretly to what is said in private. ⪢ **eavesdropper** *n.*

ebb[1] *n* the flowing out of the tide towards the sea. * **at a low ebb** at a low point; in a poor state.

ebb[2] *v* **1** of tidal water: to recede from the highest level. **2** (*often* + away) to decline or disappear gradually.

EBCDIC *n* a computer code consisting of 256 eight-bit characters that is used for representing data and to facilitate the exchange of information between a computer and other data processing equipment.

Ebola fever /ee'bohlə, ə-/ *n* an often fatal infectious viral disease characterized by internal bleeding and fever.

e-bomb *n* = ELECTRONIC BOMB.

ebonise *v* see EBONIZE.

ebonite *n* = VULCANITE.

ebonize *or* **-ise** *v* to colour (wood, furniture, etc) with a black or dark stain in imitation of ebony.

ebony *n* **1** a hard heavy black wood obtained from a tropical tree. **2** a dark brown or black colour. ⪢ **ebony** *adj.*

e-book *n* a text published in electronic rather than printed form.

ebullient *adj* **1** full of liveliness and enthusiasm; exuberant. **2** *archaic or literary* boiling or agitated. ⪢ **ebullience** *n,* **ebulliently** *adv.*

ebullition *n* **1** the act, process, or state of boiling or bubbling up. **2** *formal* a sudden violent outburst or display.

e-business *n* = E-COMMERCE.

EC *abbr* **1** East Central (London postcode). **2** European Commission. **3** European Community.

ec- *or* **eco-** *comb. form* **1** denoting habitat or environment: *ecotype.* **2** ecological: *ecotourism.*

e-cash *n* see E-MONEY.

eccentric[1] /ik'sentrik/ *adj* **1** deviating from established convention; odd. **2** not having the same centre. **3a** deviating from a circular path. **b** located elsewhere than at the geometrical centre, or having the axis or support so located. ⪢ **eccentrically** *adv,* **eccentricity** *n.*

eccentric[2] *n* **1** an eccentric person. **2** a mechanical device using eccentrically mounted parts to transform circular into reciprocating motion.

ecclesi- *or* **ecclesio-** *comb. form* denoting a church or the Church: *ecclesiology.*

ecclesiastic[1] /i,kleezi'astik/ *n* a member of the clergy.

ecclesiastic[2] *adj* = ECCLESIASTICAL.

ecclesiastical *adj* **1** relating to the Church. **2** suitable for use in a church. ⪢ **ecclesiastically** *adv.*

ecclesio- *comb. form* see ECCLESI-.

ecclesiology *n* **1** the study of church architecture and ornament. **2** theological doctrine relating to the Church. ⪢ **ecclesiological** *adj,* **ecclesiologist** *n.*

eccrine /'ekrin, 'ekrien, 'ekreen/ *adj* **1** of a gland: producing a liquid secretion without the loss of cytoplasm from the secreting cells. **2** of or produced by an eccrine gland.

ecdysis /'ekdisis/ *n* (*pl* **ecdyses** /-seez/) the moulting or shedding of an outer layer or skin, e.g. in insects and crustaceans.

ECG *abbr* **1** electrocardiogram. **2** electrocardiograph.

echelon /'eshəlon/ *n* **1** any of a series of levels or grades, e.g. of authority or responsibility, in some organized field of activity. **2** an arrangement, e.g. of troops or ships, resembling a series of steps.

echidna /i'kidnə/ *n* (*pl* **echidnas** *or* **echidnae** /-nee/) a spiny burrowing nocturnal mammal of Australia, Tasmania, and New Guinea that lays eggs, and feeds chiefly on ants. Also called SPINY ANTEATER.

echinacea /eki'naysi·ə/ *n* a preparation of the leaves and stems of a plant of the daisy family, thought to have medicinal value in strengthening the immune system.

echinoderm *n* any of a group of radially symmetrical marine animals including the starfishes, sea urchins, etc.

echo[1] /'ekoh/ *n* (*pl* **-oes**) **1** the repetition of a sound caused by the reflection of sound waves. **2** somebody or something that repeats or imitates another. **3a** the reflection by an object of transmitted radar signals. **b** a blip on a radar screen. ➤➤ **echoey** *adj*, **echoless** *adj*.

echo[2] *v* (**echoes, echoed, echoing**) **1** to resound with echoes. **2** to produce an echo. **3** to produce a continual effect. **4** to repeat or imitate (somebody or something). ➤➤ **echoer** *n*, **echoing** *adj*.

echocardiography *n* investigation of the action of the heart by means of ultrasound. ➤➤ **echocardiogram** *n*, **echocardiograph** *n*, **echocardiographic** *adj*.

echo chamber *n* a room with sound-reflecting walls used for making acoustic measurements and for producing echoing sound effects.

echogram *n* **1** a recording of the information produced by an echo sounder. **2** a display, e.g. on a screen, of the information obtained by echography. ➤➤ **echograph** *n*, **echographic** *adj*.

echography *n* investigation of the internal structures of the body by means of ultrasound.

echoic /e'koh·ik/ *adj* **1** relating to an echo. **2** onomatopoeic. ➤➤ **echoically** *adv*, **echoism** *n*.

echolocation /'ekohlohkaysh(ə)n/ *n* the location of distant or invisible objects by means of sound waves reflected back to the sender, e.g. a bat or submarine, by the objects.

echo sounder *n* an instrument that uses echolocation to determine depth in water.

éclair /i'kleə, ay'kleə/ *n* a small long cake of choux pastry that is filled with cream and usu topped with chocolate icing.

eclampsia *n* an attack of convulsions during pregnancy or childbirth. ➤➤ **eclamptic** *adj*.

éclat /ay'klah/ *n* **1** ostentatious display. **2** brilliant or conspicuous success or distinction. **3** acclaim or applause.

eclectic[1] *adj* selecting or composed of elements drawn from various sources, methods, or styles. ➤➤ **eclectically** *adv*, **eclecticism** *n*.

eclectic[2] *n* somebody who uses an eclectic method or approach.

eclipse[1] *n* **1** the total or partial obscuring of one celestial body by another, or the time when this happens. **2** a falling into obscurity or decay; a decline.

eclipse[2] *v* **1** to cause an eclipse of (a celestial body). **2** to surpass (a person, achievement, etc).

eclipse plumage *n* comparatively dull plumage occurring seasonally in ducks or other birds that adopt a distinct nuptial plumage.

ecliptic[1] *n* **1** the plane of the earth's orbit around the sun. **2** the projection of the plane of the earth's orbit on the celestial sphere.

ecliptic[2] *adj* relating to the ecliptic or an eclipse. ➤➤ **ecliptically** *adv*.

eclogue *n* a short poem, *esp* a pastoral dialogue.

eco- *comb. form* see EC-.

ecocide *n* destruction of the natural environment to the extent that it is unable to support life.

eco-friendly *adj* not harmful to the environment.

eco-labelling *n* the use of labels by manufacturers to identify products that satisfy certain environmental standards. ➤➤ **eco-label** *n*.

E. coli /'kohlie/ *n* a bacterium, *Escherichia coli*, that is found naturally in the intestines of humans and other animals and can sometimes cause severe food poisoning.

ecology *n* the interrelationship of living organisms and their environments, or the scientific study of this. ➤➤ **ecological** *adj*, **ecologically** *adv*, **ecologist** *n*.

e-commerce *n* the buying and selling of goods and services by computer, *esp* over the Internet.

econometrics *pl n* (*used as sing.*) the application of statistical methods to the study of economic data and problems. ➤➤ **econometric** *adj*, **econometrical** *adj*, **econometrically** *adv*, **econometrician** *n*, **econometrist** *n*.

economic *adj* **1** relating to economics or finance. **2** relating to an economy. **3** profitable: *It is not economic to reopen the mine.* **4** to do with practical or financial necessity. ➤➤ **economically** *adv*.

Usage note

economic *or* **economical?** *Economic* means 'relating to economics or an economy' (*an economic crisis; economic indicators*), 'reasonably profitable' (*If the price of tin were to rise, it might become economic to reopen the mine*), and 'not wasteful'. This final meaning overlaps with that of *economical* (*an economical* or *economic use of resources*). *Economical* is, however, far more widely and commonly used in this sense. A person who is thrifty or a machine that uses resources frugally should be described by preference as *economical*: *a very economical little car*.

economical *adj* **1** thrifty. **2** efficient; not wasting money, fuel, etc: *an economical little car.* ✱ **be economical with the truth** to lie, or be less than totally honest or open. ➤➤ **economically** *adv*.

Usage note

economical *or* **economic?** See note at ECONOMIC.

economics *pl n* **1** (*used as sing. or pl*) a social science concerned chiefly with the production, distribution, and consumption of goods and services. **2** economic aspect or significance. ➤➤ **economist** *n*.

economic sanctions *pl n* measures intended to have an adverse effect on the economy of another nation, often to force it to change some policy or comply with international law.

economize *or* **-ise** *v* (*often* + on) to practise economy; to be frugal or not wasteful. ➤➤ **economizer** *n*.

economy[1] *n* (*pl* **-ies**) **1a** thrifty and efficient use of material resources; frugality in expenditure. **b** an instance or means of economizing. **2** efficient and sparing use of nonmaterial resources, e.g. effort, language, or motion. **3** the structure of economic life in a country, area, or period; an economic system. **4** a cheaper standard of travel, *esp* by air, than first class.

economy[2] *adj* **1** designed to save money. **2** relating to travel in economy class.

economy class *n* = ECONOMY[1] (4).

economy-class syndrome *n* deep vein thrombosis caused by sitting for long periods of time in cramped conditions on aircraft on long flights.

economy of scale *n* a lowering of average production costs resulting from an increased scale of production.

ecosphere *n* the parts of the universe habitable by living organisms, *esp* the biosphere.

ecosystem *n* a community and its environment functioning as an ecological unit in nature.

ecoterrorist *n* a person who uses violence as part of an environmental campaign. ➤➤ **ecoterrorism** *n.*

ecotourism *n* tourism in unspoiled undeveloped regions that does not harm the environment and often generates revenue for conservation.

ecotype *n* a group maintained as a distinct population by ecological and geographical factors. ➤➤ **ecotypic** *adj,* **ecotypically** *adv.*

eco-warrior *n* a person who takes an active part in an environmental campaign.

ecru /'aykrooh, 'ekrooh/ *n* a pale fawn colour. ➤➤ **ecru** *adj.*

Ecstasy *n* an illegal drug taken recreationally for its strong stimulant and euphoric effects.

ecstasy *n* (*pl* **-ies**) **1a** a feeling of great joy or happiness. **b** a state of strong emotion. **2** a trance, *esp* a mystic or prophetic one.

ecstatic[1] *adj* **1** extremely happy or enthusiastic. **2** causing or in a state of ecstasy. ➤➤ **ecstatically** *adv.*

ecstatic[2] *n* somebody who is prone to ecstatic trancelike states.

ECT *abbr* electroconvulsive therapy.

ect- *or* **ecto-** *comb. form* outside or external.

ectoderm *n* the outermost of the three primary germ layers of an embryo, or a tissue derived from this. ➤➤ **ectodermal** *adj,* **ectodermic** *adj.*

ectomorph *n* a person having a light slender body build: compare ENDOMORPH, MESOMORPH. ➤➤ **ecto-morphic** *adj,* **ectomorphy** *n.*

-ectomy *comb. form* forming nouns, denoting: surgical removal of a specified part: *appendectomy.*

ectopic *adj* occurring in an abnormal position or in an unusual manner or form: *an ectopic pregnancy.* ➤➤ **ectopically** *adv.*

ectoplasm *n* a substance supposed to emanate from a spiritualist medium in a state of trance as the substance in which a spirit manifests itself. ➤➤ **ectoplasmic** *adj.*

ecu *or* **ECU** /ay'kyooh/ *n* a former money used within the European Community as a standard and for transactions between member states: compare EURO.

Ecuadorean *or* **Ecuadorian** *n* a native or inhabitant of Ecuador. ➤➤ **Ecuadorean** *adj.*

ecumenical *adj* **1** of or representing the whole of a body of Churches. **2** promoting or tending towards worldwide Christian unity or cooperation. ➤➤ **ecumenicalism** *n,* **ecumenically** *adv,* **ecumenism** *n,* **ecumenist** *n.*

eczema /'eksimə/ *n* an inflammatory condition of the skin characterized by itching and oozing blisters. ➤➤ **eczematous** *adj.*

-ed[1] *suffix* forming the past tense and past participle of regular weak verbs: *guarded.*

-ed[2] *suffix* forming adjectives with the meanings: **1** having; characterized by; provided with: *two-legged.* **2** wearing: *bowler-hatted.* **3** having the characteristics of: *bigoted.* ➤➤ **-edly** *adv.*

Edam *n* a mild yellow cheese of Dutch origin usu made in flattened balls coated with red wax.

eddo *n* = TARO.

eddy[1] *n* (*pl* **-ies**) a current of water, air, etc running contrary to the main current, *esp* a small whirlpool.

eddy[2] *v* (**-ies, -ied**) to move in an eddy or with circular motion.

edelweiss /'aydlvies/ *n* a small perennial plant that is covered in dense fine white hairs and grows high in the Alps.

Eden *n* **1** the garden where, according to the account in Genesis, Adam and Eve lived before the Fall. **2** = PARADISE (3).

edentate[1] *adj* having few or no teeth.

edentate[2] *n* any of a group of mammals, including the sloths, armadillos, and anteaters, that have few or no teeth.

edge[1] *n* **1a** the line where an object or area begins or ends; a border. **b** the narrow part adjacent to a border. **c** a line where two planes or two surfaces of a solid meet or cross. **2a** the cutting side of a blade. **b** the sharpness of a blade. **c** penetrating power; keenness or intensity. ✱ **have the edge on/over somebody** to have an advantage over somebody. **on edge** anxious or nervous. ➤➤ **edged** *adj,* **edgeless** *adj.*

edge[2] *v* **1** to provide with an edge. **2** to move or cause to move gradually or cautiously. ➤➤ **edger** *n.*

edgeways *adv* **1** with the edge foremost; sideways. **2** on, with, or towards the edge.

edgewise *adv* = EDGEWAYS.

edging *n* something that forms an edge or border.

edgy *adj* (**-ier, -iest**) tense, anxious, or irritable. ➤➤ **edgily** *adv,* **edginess** *n.*

EDI *abbr* electronic data interchange.

edible *adj* fit to be eaten as food. ➤➤ **edibility** *n,* **edibleness** *n.*

Usage note

edible *or* **eatable**? See note at EATABLE.

edibles *pl n* things that are eatable; food.

edict *n* an official public decree or command. ➤➤ **edictal** *adj.*

edifice *n* **1** a building, *esp* a large or massive structure. **2** a large abstract structure or organization.

edify *v* (**-ies, -ied**) to instruct and improve, *esp* in moral and spiritual knowledge. ➤➤ **edification** *n,* **edifying** *adj,* **edifyingly** *adv.*

edit[1] *v* (**edited, editing**) **1a** to prepare an edition of (a book, article, etc). **b** to assemble (e.g. a film or recording) by deleting, inserting, and rearranging material. **c** to alter (e.g. written material), *esp* to condense or improve it. **2** to direct the publication of (a periodical). ➤➤ **editable** *adj.*

edit[2] *n* an editorial change or correction.

edition *n* **1a** the form in which a text is published. **b** a number of copies published at one time or place. **2** a copy or version.

editor *n* **1** a person in overall charge of the content of a newspaper or magazine, a book containing material by various writers, or a radio or television programme. **2** a person who commissions or edits written material. **3** a person who edits films, recordings, etc. **4** a computer program that allows one to edit data. ➤➤ **editorship** *n.*

editorial[1] *adj* of or written by an editor. ➤➤ **editorially** *adv.*

editorial[2] *n* a newspaper or magazine article that gives the opinions of the editors or publishers.

editorialize *or* **-ise** *v* **1** to express an opinion in the form of an editorial. **2** to introduce personal opinion into an apparently objective report. ➤➤ **editorialization** *n*, **editorializer** *n*.

edit out *v* to remove (material) from a book, film, etc while editing it.

EDP *abbr* electronic data processing.

educate *v* **1** to provide schooling for. **2** to teach or instruct in academic, moral, or social matters. **3** to train or improve (a person's faculties, judgment, skills, etc). ➤➤ **educable** *adj*, **educatable** *adj*, **educative** *adj*, **educator** *n*.

educated *adj* **1** having an education, *esp* one beyond the average. **2a** appropriate to somebody educated. **b** based on some knowledge or experience: *an educated guess*.

education *n* **1a** the action or process of educating or of being educated. **b** a stage of such a process. **c** instruction in some subject. **2** the knowledge and development resulting from instruction. **3** the field of study that deals mainly with methods of teaching. **4** (**an education**) an experience that causes one to see things in a new way. ➤➤ **educational** *adj*, **educationally** *adv*.

educationalist *n* an educational theorist or administrator.

educationist *n* = EDUCATIONALIST.

educe *v formal* **1** to develop or bring out (something hitherto unrealized). **2** to arrive at (a conclusion) through a consideration of facts or evidence; to infer (something). ➤➤ **educible** *adj*, **eduction** *n*.

edutainment *n* entertainment which is designed to include some educational content.

Edwardian *adj* of the reign of Edward VII of England (1901–1910). ➤➤ **Edwardian** *n*.

-ee *suffix* forming nouns, denoting: **1** a person to whom a specified action is done: *trainee*. **2** a person who acts in a specified way: *escapee*.

EEC *abbr* European Economic Community.

EEG *abbr* **1** electroencephalogram. **2** electroencephalograph.

eel *n* a long snakelike fish with a smooth slimy skin and no pelvic fins. ➤➤ **eel-like** *adj*, **eely** *adj*.

eelgrass *n* **1** a freshwater plant that has very long narrow leaves and grows underwater. **2** a marine plant with long grasslike leaves.

eelworm *n* a nematode worm, *esp* one living free in the soil or as a parasite in plants.

e'en *adv chiefly literary* even.

e'er *adv chiefly literary* ever.

-eer *suffix* **1** forming nouns, denoting: a person engaged in (a specified occupation or activity): *auctioneer*. **2** forming verbs, with the meaning: to be involved in a specified activity: *electioneer*.

eerie *or* **eery** *adj* (**-ier, -iest**) frighteningly strange or gloomy; weird. ➤➤ **eerily** *adv*, **eeriness** *n*.

eff *v Brit, informal* a euphemism for 'fuck'. ✱ **eff and blind** *euphem* to utter obscenities and swearwords.

efface *v* **1** to eliminate or make indistinct by wearing away a surface; to erase. **2** to make (oneself) modestly or shyly inconspicuous. ➤➤ **effaceable** *adj*, **effacement** *n*, **effacer** *n*.

effect[1] *n* **1a** the result produced by a cause or action. **b** the extent to which a cause or action produces results. **c** power to bring about a result; efficacy. **2** the quality or state of being operative: *come into effect*. **3** (*in pl*) personal movable property; goods. **4** (*often in pl*) something designed to enhance the drama, realism, or impressiveness of something, *esp* in a play or film. **5** a scientific phenomenon named usu after its discoverer. ✱ **for effect** in order to impress. **in effect** for all practical purposes; actually although not appearing so. **take effect 1** to become operative. **2** to produce a result. **to that effect** with the same basic meaning.

Usage note

effect *or* affect? See note at AFFECT[1].

effect[2] *v* **1** to bring about, often by surmounting obstacles; to accomplish. **2** to put into effect; to carry out.

effective *adj* **1a** producing a decisive or desired effect. **b** impressive or striking. **2** ready for service or action. **3** actual or real. **4** in force; operative. ➤➤ **effectiveness** *n*.

effectively *adv* **1** in an effective manner; impressively. **2** for all practical purposes; in effect.

effectual *adj* **1** able to produce a desired effect; adequate, effective. **2** of a legal document: valid or binding. ➤➤ **effectuality** *n*, **effectually** *adv*, **effectualness** *n*.

effectuate *v* to carry out or bring about. ➤➤ **effectuation** *n*.

effeminate *adj* **1** of a man: having qualities usu thought of as feminine; not manly. **2** marked by an unbecoming delicacy or lack of vigour. ➤➤ **effeminacy** *n*, **effeminately** *adv*, **effeminateness** *n*.

effendi *n* (*pl* **effendis**) a title of respect for a man of property, authority, or education in an eastern Mediterranean country.

efferent[1] *adj* conducting outwards from a part or organ; *specif* conveying nervous impulses from the brain: compare AFFERENT. ➤➤ **efference** *n*, **efferently** *adv*.

efferent[2] *n* an efferent nerve.

effervesce *v* **1** of a liquid: to bubble and hiss as gas escapes. **2** to show liveliness or exhilaration. ➤➤ **effervescence** *n*, **effervescent** *adj*, **effervescently** *adv*.

effete *adj* marked by weakness and decadent over-refinement. ➤➤ **effetely** *adv*, **effeteness** *n*.

efficacious *adj* having the power to produce a desired effect. ➤➤ **efficaciously** *adv*, **efficaciousness** *n*, **efficacity** *n*, **efficacy** *n*.

efficient *adj* **1** of a person: able and practical; briskly competent. **2** productive of desired effects, *esp* with minimum waste. ➤➤ **efficiency** *n*, **efficiently** *adv*.

effigy *n* (*pl* **-ies**) an image or representation, *esp* of a person; *specif* a crude figure representing a hated person.

effing *adj and adv euphem* fucking.

effloresce *v* **1** to burst into flower. **2a** to change from crystals to a powder on exposure to air. **b** to form or become covered with a powdery covering. ➤➤ **efflorescence** *n*, **efflorescent** *adj*.

effluence *n* **1** something that flows out. **2** an action or process of flowing out.

effluent *n* something that flows out, *esp* smoke, liquid industrial refuse, sewage, etc discharged into the environment and causing pollution.

effluvium *n* (*pl* **effluvia, effluviums**) an offensive gas or smell, e.g. from rotting vegetation.

effort *n* **1** conscious exertion of physical or mental power. **2** a serious attempt; a try. **3** something produced by exertion or trying. ➤➤ **effortful** *adj*, **effortfully** *adv*, **effortless** *adj*, **effortlessly** *adv*, **effortlessness** *n*.

effrontery *n* (*pl* **-ies**) **1** the quality of being shamelessly bold; insolence. **2** an instance of insolent behaviour.

effulgence *n formal* radiant splendour; brilliance. ➤➤ **effulgent** *adj*, **effulgently** *adv*.

effusion *n* **1a** an act of emitting or pouring out. **b** something that is poured out. **2** an unrestrained expression of feelings in words.

effusive *adj* unduly emotionally demonstrative, *esp* in speech; gushing. ⋙ **effusively** *adv,* **effusiveness** *n.*

EFL *abbr* English as a foreign language.

EFT *abbr* electronic funds transfer.

eft *n* a newt.

EFTA *abbr* European Free Trade Association.

EFTPOS *abbr* electronic funds transfer at point of sale, a system in which a purchase is made by debit or credit card and the funds are transferred directly by computer to the seller's account.

e.g. *abbr* for example.

egalitarianism *n* a belief in social, political, and economic equality among human beings. ⋙ **egalitarian** *adj,* **egalitarian** *n*

egg *n* **1a** the hard-shelled oval reproductive body produced by a bird. **b** an animal reproductive body consisting of an ovum together with its nutritive and protective envelopes that is capable of developing into a new individual. **c** = OVUM. **2** the egg of domestic poultry, etc, used as food. **3** something resembling a hen's egg in shape. **4** *dated, informal* a person. ✻ **have egg on one's face** to be made to look foolish. **have/put all one's eggs in one basket** to be relying on one thing for success. ⋙ **eggy** *adj.*

egghead *n derog or humorous* an intellectual or highbrow. ⋙ **eggheaded** *adj.*

eggnog *n* a drink consisting of eggs beaten with sugar, milk or cream, and often spirits, e.g. rum or brandy.

egg on *v* to incite (somebody) to action.

eggplant *n chiefly NAm* = AUBERGINE.

eggshell[1] *n* the hard exterior covering of an egg.

eggshell[2] *adj* **1** *esp* of china: thin and fragile. **2** *esp* of paint: having only a slight sheen.

egg timer *n* an instrument like a small hourglass used for timing the boiling of eggs.

egg tooth *n* a prominence on the beak or nose of an unhatched bird or reptile that is used to break through the eggshell.

egg white *n* the clear viscous material that surrounds an egg yolk; = ALBUMEN.

eglantine *n* = SWEETBRIER.

EGM *abbr* extraordinary general meeting.

ego *n* (*pl* **egos**) **1a** SELF-ESTEEM . **b** excessive self-esteem. **2** in psychoanalytic theory, a part of the mind that encompasses memory and self-consciousness and mainly controls a person's behaviour and relations with reality: compare ID, SUPEREGO. **3** the self, *esp* as contrasted with another self or the world.

egocentric[1] *adj* self-centred or selfish. ⋙ **egocentrically** *adv,* **egocentricity** *n,* **egocentrism** *n.*

egocentric[2] *n* an egocentric person.

egoism *n* **1** a doctrine that individual self-interest is or should be the foundation of morality, or conduct based on this doctrine. **2** = EGOTISM. ⋙ **egoist** *n,* **egoistic** *adj,* **egoistically** *adv.*

Usage note

egoism *or* **egotism**? Both these words are ordinarily used as equivalents of self-centredness. But on the basis of their more technical uses (*egoism* being a philosophical belief in selfishness as the only real motive for action: *egotism* being self-obsession, for example the excessive use of *I, me,* and *myself* when speaking) *egoism* is best used for *self-seeking* and *egotism* for *self-importance.*

egomania *n* the quality of being extremely egocentric. ⋙ **egomaniac** *n,* **egomaniacal** *adj.*

egotism *n* **1** the practice of talking about oneself too much. **2** an extreme sense of self-importance. ⋙ **egotist** *n,* **egotistic** *adj,* **egotistically** *adv.*

Usage note

egotism *or* **egoism**? See note at EGOISM.

ego trip *n informal* an act or series of acts that selfishly enhances and satisfies one's ego. ⋙ **ego-trip** *v,* **ego-tripper** *n.*

egregious *adj* conspicuously or shockingly bad; flagrant. ⋙ **egregiously** *adv,* **egregiousness** *n.*

egress *n formal* **1** going or coming out. **2** a place or means of going out; an exit.

egret *n* a species of heron that has long plumes during the breeding season.

Egyptian *n* **1** a native or inhabitant of Egypt. **2** the Afro-Asiatic language of the ancient Egyptians to about the third cent. AD. ⋙ **Egyptian** *adj.*

Egyptology *n* the study of Egyptian antiquities. ⋙ **Egyptologist** *n.*

eh *interj* used to ask for confirmation or to express enquiry.

Eid *n* **1** = EID-UL-ADHA. **2** = EID-UL-FITR.

eider *n* (*pl* **eiders** *or* **eider**) **1** = EIDER DUCK. **2** = EIDERDOWN (1).

eiderdown *n* **1** the down of the eider duck. **2** *chiefly Brit* a thick warm quilt filled with eiderdown or other insulating material.

eider duck *n* a large northern sea duck with fine soft down that is used by the female to line the nest.

eidetic *adj* involving extraordinarily accurate and vivid recall of visual images. ⋙ **eidetically** *adv.*

Eid-ul-Adha /ˌeed ool ˈahdə/ *n* a Muslim festival that celebrates the faith and obedience of Abraham, and also marking the end of the annual pilgrimage to Mecca.

Eid-ul-Fitr /ˌeed ool ˈfeetə/ *n* a Muslim festival marking the end of the fast of Ramadan.

eight *n* **1** the number 8. **2** an eight-person racing boat or its crew. ✻ **be/have one over the eight** *informal* to have had too much to drink. ⋙ **eight** *adj,* **eightfold** *adj and adv.*

eighteen *adj and n* the number 18. ⋙ **eighteenth** *adj and n.*

eighth *adj and n* **1** having the position in a sequence corresponding to the number eight. **2** one of eight equal parts of something. **3** in music, = OCTAVE. ⋙ **eighthly** *adv.*

eighth note *n NAm* = QUAVER[2] (1).

eights *pl n* races for eight-oared rowing boats.

eightsome reel *n* a Scottish reel for eight dancers.

eighty *adj and n* (*pl* **-ies**) **1** the number 80. **2** (*in pl*) the numbers 80 to 89. ⋙ **eightieth** *adj and n.*

einsteinium *n* a radioactive metallic chemical element artificially produced from plutonium.

eirenic *or* **eirenical** *adj* see IRENIC.

eisteddfod *n* (*pl* **eisteddfods** *or* **eisteddfodau**) a Welsh-language competitive festival of the arts, *esp* music and poetry. ⋙ **eisteddfodic** *adj.*

either[1] *adj* **1** both of the two: *on either side of the path.* **2** being the one or the other of two: *Take either road.*

Usage note

Both pronunciations (ˈiedhə or ˈeedhə) are acceptable: British English tends to prefer the former, American English, the latter.

either[2] *pron* the one or the other: *I don't want either of them.*

either[3] *conj* used before two or more sentence elements of the same class or function joined usu by *or* to indicate that what immediately follows is the first of two or more alternatives: *Either that wallpaper goes, or I do* — Oscar Wilde.

either[4] *adv* used for emphasis after a negative or implied negation: for that matter; likewise: *I can't drive and I can't ride a bike either.*

either-or *adj* involving an unavoidable choice between only two possibilities. ➤➤ **either-or** *n.*

ejaculate[1] *v* **1** to eject (semen) from the body in orgasm. **2** *formal* to utter (something) suddenly and vehemently. ➤➤ **ejaculation** *n,* **ejaculative** *adj,* **ejaculator** *n,* **ejaculatory** *adj.*

ejaculate[2] *n* the semen released by a single ejaculation.

eject *v* **1a** to drive out, *esp* by physical force. **b** to emit forcefully. **2** to evict from property. **3** to escape from an aircraft by using the ejector seat. ➤➤ **ejectable** *adj,* **ejection** *n,* **ejective** *adj,* **ejector** *n.*

ejection seat *n* = EJECTOR SEAT.

ejector seat *n* an emergency escape seat that propels an occupant out and away from an aircraft by means of an explosive charge.

eke *adv archaic* also.

eke out *v* **1a** to make up for the deficiencies of; to supplement. **b** to make (a supply) last longer by using it frugally. **2** to make (e.g. a living) by laborious or precarious means.

elaborate[1] *adj* **1** planned or carried out with great care and attention to detail. **2** marked by complexity, wealth of detail, or ornateness. ➤➤ **elaborately** *adv,* **elaborateness** *n.*

elaborate[2] *v* **1** to work out (e.g. a plan) in detail. **2** (*often* + on) to go into detail; to add further information. ➤➤ **elaboration** *n,* **elaborative** *adj,* **elaborator** *n.*

élan *n* vigorous spirit or enthusiasm; verve.

eland *n* either of two large African antelopes that resemble oxen and have spirally twisted horns.

elapse *v* of a period of time: to pass by.

elastane *n* a synthetic stretchy fabric, used for tight-fitting clothing.

elastic[1] *adj* **1** made of elastic. **2** of a material: capable of resuming its former shape after being stretched, squashed, etc. **3** capable of recovering quickly, *esp* from depression or disappointment; buoyant or resilient. **4** readily changed, expanded, or contracted; flexible or adaptable. ➤➤ **elastically** *adv,* **elasticity** *n,* **elasticize** *v.*

elastic[2] *n* **1** easily stretched rubber, usu prepared in cords, strings, or bands. **2** an elastic fabric usu made of yarns containing rubber.

elasticated *adj* of fabric: made stretchy by the insertion or interweaving of elastic.

elastic band *n Brit* = RUBBER BAND.

elastin *n* a protein similar to collagen that is the chief component of elastic fibres of connective tissue.

elastomer *n* any of various elastic substances resembling rubber. ➤➤ **elastomeric** *adj.*

Elastoplast *n trademark* a type of elastic adhesive plaster.

elate *v* to fill with joy or pride. ➤➤ **elated** *adj,* **elatedly** *adv,* **elatedness** *n,* **elation** *n.*

elbow[1] *n* **1** the joint between the human forearm and upper arm. **2** something resembling an arm bent at the elbow, *esp* a pipe fitting. **3** (**the elbow**) *informal* an abrupt rejection or dismissal. ✱ **out at elbow/elbows** poor; shabbily dressed. **up to the elbows in/with** busily engaged in.

elbow[2] *v* **1a** to push or shove aside with one's elbow. **b** to strike with one's elbow. **2** to force (e.g. one's way) rudely or roughly by pushing with one's elbow.

elbow grease *n informal* hard physical effort.

elbowroom *n* adequate space or scope for movement, work, or operation.

elder[1] *adj* of earlier birth or greater age, *esp* than another related person or thing.

Usage note

elder *or* older? *Elder* is used only in comparing the ages of people (*my elder brother/sister*), and cannot be followed by *than* (*My brother is two years older* – not *elder* – *than I am*). *Older* is always used when describing things.

elder[2] *n* **1** somebody who is older. **2** somebody having authority by virtue of age and experience. **3** an official of the early Christian Church or of a Presbyterian, Quaker, etc congregation. ➤➤ **eldership** *n.*

elder[3] *n* a common shrub or small tree of the honeysuckle family with white flowers and black or red berries.

elderberry *n* (*pl* **-ies**) **1** the edible black or red berry of an elder. **2** an elder shrub or tree.

elderly *adj* rather old. ➤➤ **elderliness** *n.*

elder statesman *n* an eminent senior or retired member of a group whose advice is often sought unofficially.

eldest *adj* of the greatest age or seniority; oldest.

El Dorado *or* **eldorado** *n* a place of fabulous wealth, abundance, or opportunity.

eldritch *adj archaic or Scot* weird, uncanny, or unearthly.

elecampane *n* a large European composite plant with yellow flowers, whose root is used in herbal medicine as an expectorant and digestive.

elect[1] *v* **1** to select by vote for an office, position, or membership. **2** of God: to choose or predestine to receive salvation. **3** *formal* to choose or decide to do something. ➤➤ **electable** *adj.*

elect[2] *adj* **1** picked out in preference to others. **2** chosen for office or position but not yet installed.

election *n* **1** a procedure for electing somebody, e.g. to public office. **2** the act of electing somebody or the fact of being elected.

electioneer *v* to work for a candidate or party in an election. ➤➤ **electioneering** *n.*

elective[1] *adj* **1a** chosen or filled by popular election. **b** relating to elections. **2** that can be freely selected; optional. ➤➤ **electively** *adv,* **electiveness** *n.*

elective[2] *n chiefly NAm* an elective course or subject of study.

elector *n* **1** somebody voting or qualified to vote in an election. **2a** (*often* **Elector**) any of the German princes entitled to elect the Holy Roman Emperor. **b** a member of the electoral college in the USA. ➤➤ **electorship** *n.*

electoral *adj* relating to election, elections, or electors.

electoral college *n* **1** (*used as sing. or pl*) a body of electors chosen in each state to elect the president and vice-president of the USA. **2** any body of electors chosen by a larger body.

electoral register *n* = ELECTORAL ROLL.

electoral roll *n* the official list of those who are entitled to vote in an election.

electorate *n* **1** (*used as sing. or pl*) a body of electors. **2** *Aus, NZ* the area represented by a Member of Parliament. **3** (*often* **Electorate**) the territory, jurisdiction, etc of a German elector.

Electra complex *n* the OEDIPUS COMPLEX when it occurs in a female.

electric[1] *adj* **1a** of, producing, or produced by electricity. **b** operated by or using electricity. **2a** producing an intensely stimulating effect; thrilling. **b** (*often* + with) tense.

electric[2] *n* (*in pl*) electrical parts; electric circuitry.

electrical *adj* **1** of or connected with electricity. **2** = ELECTRIC[1] (1B). ➤➤ **electrically** *adv.*

electricals *pl n* electrical parts or electric circuitry; electrics.

electric blanket *n* a blanket containing an electric heating element that is used to warm a bed.

electric blue *adj and n* harshly bright slightly greenish blue.

electric chair *n* **1** a chair used in legal electrocution. **2** the penalty of death by electrocution.

electric eel *n* a large eel-shaped fish of the Orinoco and Amazon rivers that is capable of giving a severe electric shock.

electric eye *n* = PHOTOELECTRIC CELL.

electric fence *n* a fence consisting of an electrified wire or wires that gives an electric shock to any person or animal that touches it.

electric field *n* a portion of space in which a perceptible force is exerted on an electric charge.

electric guitar *n* a guitar with a pickup that converts string vibrations into electrical signals which are then passed through an electrical amplifier.

electrician *n* somebody who installs, operates, or repairs electrical equipment.

electricity *n* **1a** a form of energy derived from stationary or moving negatively or positively charged particles. **b** electric current or electric charge. **2** contagious excitement; tension.

electric ray *n* a round-bodied ray found in warm seas that can give electric shocks.

electric shock *n* a sudden stimulation of the nerves and convulsive contraction of the muscles caused by the passage of electricity through the body.

electric storm *n* a violent atmospheric disturbance usu accompanied by thunder and lightning.

electrify *v* (**-ies, -ied**) **1a** to charge with electricity. **b** to equip for the use of electric power. **c** to supply with electric power. **2** to excite or thrill. ➤➤ **electrification** *n,* **electrifier** *n.*

electrocardiogram *n* the tracing made by an electrocardiograph.

electrocardiograph *n* an instrument for recording the changes in electrical activity occurring during the heartbeat. ➤➤ **electrocardiographic** *adj,* **electrocardiography** *n.*

electroconvulsive therapy *n* a treatment for serious mental disorder, *esp* severe depression, in which a fit is induced by passing an electric current through the brain.

electrocute *v* to execute or kill by electric shock. ➤➤ **electrocution** *n.*

electrode *n* a conductor used to establish electrical contact with a non-metallic part of a circuit, e.g. the acid in a car battery.

electrodynamics *pl n* (*used as sing. or pl*) the branch of physics dealing with the effects arising from the interaction of electric currents with magnets or with other electric currents. ➤➤ **electrodynamic** *adj.*

electroencephalogram *n* the tracing made by an electroencephalograph.

electroencephalograph *n* an instrument for detecting and recording the electrical activity of the brain. ➤➤ **electroencephalography** *n,* **electroencephalographic** *adj.*

electrolyse (*NAm* **electrolyze**) *v* to subject to electrolysis. ➤➤ **electrolyser** *n.*

electrolysis *n* **1** the passage of an electric current through an electrolyte to generate a gas, deposit a metal on an electrode, etc. **2** the destruction of hair roots, warts, moles, etc by means of an electric current. ➤➤ **electrolytic** *adj.*

electrolyte *n* **1** a non-metallic electric conductor, e.g. a solution of a chemical salt, in which current is carried by the movement of ions. **2** the ions in cells, blood, etc, that regulate their electric charge and help control fluid levels in the body.

electrolyze *v NAm* see ELECTROLYSE.

electromagnet *n* a core of magnetizable material surrounded by a coil of wire through which an electric current is passed to make the core into a magnet.

electromagnetic *adj* of or produced by electromagnetism. ➤➤ **electromagnetically** *adv.*

electromagnetic radiation *n* radiation consisting of a series of electromagnetic waves.

electromagnetic wave *n* any of the waves produced by simultaneous variations in the intensities of electric and magnetic fields and that include radio waves, infrared, visible light, ultraviolet, X-rays, and gamma rays.

electromagnetism *n* **1** magnetism developed, e.g. in an electromagnet, by a current of electricity. **2** the branch of physics dealing with the interaction of electricity and magnetism.

electrometer *n* an instrument for detecting or measuring *esp* voltages or very low currents. ➤➤ **electrometric** *adj,* **electrometry** *n.*

electromotive *adj* producing or relating to an electric current.

electromotive force *n* the amount of energy derived from an electrical source, e.g. a cell or generator, per unit current of electricity passing round a circuit.

electromyograph *n* an instrument used for recording the electric waves associated with muscle activity, used *esp* in diagnosing disorders of the nerves and muscles. ➤➤ **electromyographic** *adj,* **electromyographically** *adv,* **electromyography** *n.*

electron *n* an elementary particle that carries a single negative electrical charge, that occurs in atoms outside the nucleus, and the overall movement of which constitutes electric current.

electron gun *n* the cathode and its surrounding assembly that emits a focused stream of electrons, e.g. in a cathode-ray tube.

electronic *adj* **1a** relating to electronics. **b** involving devices, e.g. transistors or microchips, in which a flow of electrons through a gas, vacuum, or semiconductor is controlled by a voltage. **c** involving computers or other electronic systems. **2** relating to electrons. ➤➤ **electronically** *adv.*

electronic bomb *n* a weapon, not yet in existence, that consists of an artillery shell containing a transmitter capable of sending out a powerful beam of energy that disrupts computers and other electronic systems.

electronic flash *n* in photography, an electronic device for producing a bright flash of light from a gas-discharge tube.

electronic funds transfer at point of sale *n* see EFTPOS.

electronic mail *n* = E-MAIL[1] (1).

electronic publishing *n* the publishing of texts in forms that can be accessed by a computer, *esp* on CD-ROMs.

electronics *pl n* **1** (*used as sing. or pl*) the branch of physics or technology dealing with the emission, behaviour, and effects of electrons in transistors, microchips, etc. **2** the circuits, devices, etc of a piece of electronic equipment.

electronic tag *n* an electronic monitoring device worn around the wrist or ankle by people convicted of or charged with a crime but not held in custody. ➤➤ **electronic tagging** *n.*

electronic virtual assistant *n* a computer-synthesized person with whom one can talk on the Internet, for example on an organization's customer helpline.

electron microscope *n* an instrument in which a beam of electrons is used to produce a highly magnified image of an object. ➤➤ **electron microscopy** *n.*

electron volt *n* a unit of energy equal to the energy gained by an electron in passing between two points between which there is a voltage difference of one volt.

electrophoresis *n* the movement of particles through a gel or other medium in which particles are suspended under the action of an applied electric field. ➤➤ **electrophoretic** *adj,* **electrophoretically** *adv.*

electroplate[1] *v* to plate (an object) with a continuous metallic coating by electrolysis. ➤➤ **electroplater** *n.*

electroplate[2] *n* articles that have been electroplated, *esp* with silver.

electroscope *n* an instrument for detecting the presence of an electric charge or determining whether it is positive or negative. ➤➤ **electroscopic** *adj.*

electroshock therapy *n* = ELECTROCONVULSIVE THERAPY.

electrostatic *adj* **1** of or producing static electricity. **2** relating to electrostatics.

electrostatics *pl n* (*used as sing. or pl*) the branch of physics dealing with stationary electric charges, *esp* the attraction between opposite and repulsion between identical charges.

electrotechnology *n* the use of electricity for technological purposes.

electrotherapy *n* treatment of disease by the use of electricity, e.g. to generate heat or stimulate muscular activity in tissues. ➤➤ **electrotherapeutic** *adj,* **electrotherapist** *n.*

electrum *n* a pale yellow alloy of gold and silver.

eleemosynary /ˌeli·əˈmosinəri/ *adj* of, supported by, or giving charity.

elegant *adj* **1** gracefully refined or dignified, e.g. in manners or style. **2** tastefully rich or luxurious, *esp* in design or ornamentation. **3** of ideas: simple and ingenious. ➤➤ **elegance** *n,* **elegantly** *adv.*

elegiac *adj* **1** relating to or characteristic of an elegy. **2** expressing sorrow, often for something now past. ➤➤ **elegiacally** *adv.*

elegize *or* **-ise** *v* **1** to write in elegiac style. **2** to write an elegy on (somebody or something). ➤➤ **elegist** *n.*

elegy *n* (*pl* **-ies**) **1** a song, poem, or other work expressing sorrow or lamentation, *esp* for a dead person. **2** a pensive or reflective poem that is usu nostalgic or melancholy.

element *n* **1** in chemistry, any of more than 100 fundamental substances that consist of atoms of only one kind and that singly or in combination constitute all matter. **2** any of the constituent parts that make up a whole. **3** (*in pl*) the simplest principles of a subject of study; the rudiments. **4** (*used as sing. or pl*) a specified group within a human community: *the criminal element.* **5** something present in a small quantity; a hint: *There is an element of truth in what he said.* **6** the part of an electric device, e.g. a heater or kettle, that contains the heating wire. **7a** any of the four substances, air, water, fire, and earth, formerly believed to compose the physical universe. **b** the state or sphere natural or suited to someone or something. **c** (*in pl*) forces of nature, *esp* violent or severe weather.

elemental *adj* **1** of or being a chemical element. **2** fundamental, basic, or essential. **3** of or resembling a powerful force of nature. ➤➤ **elementalism** *n.*

elementary *adj* **1** of or dealing with the basic elements of something; simple. **2** = ELEMENTAL (1). ➤➤ **elementarily** *adv,* **elementariness** *n.*

elementary particle *n* any of various simple subatomic constituents of matter, e.g. the electron, proton, or photon.

elementary school *n* **1** *Brit* formerly, a state school for children aged from 5 to 13 or 14. **2** *NAm* a state school for pupils in the first six or eight years of their education.

elephant *n* a very large mammal having a muscular trunk instead of a snout and two long ivory tusks. The African elephant is larger than the Indian elephant of S Asia, which has smaller ears and a humped back.

elephantiasis *n* enormous enlargement of tissues, typically those of a limb or the scrotum, caused by parasitic worms.

elephantine *adj* **1a** huge or massive. **b** clumsy or ponderous. **2** relating to an elephant.

elevate *v* **1** to lift up. **2** to raise in rank or status. **3** to raise the axis of (a gun) in order to increase its range.

elevated *adj* **1** raised above a surface. **2** on a high moral or intellectual plane; lofty.

elevation *n* **1** the height to which something is elevated, *esp* the height above sea level. **2** the act of elevating or the state of being elevated. **3** a representation drawn to scale of the front, back, or side of a building. **4** the ability of a ballet dancer or skater to leap and be apparently suspended in the air. ➤➤ **elevational** *adj.*

elevator *n* **1** *chiefly NAm* = LIFT[2] (1). **2a** an endless belt or chain conveyor with scoops or buckets for raising grain, liquids, etc. **b** *NAm* a building for elevating and storing grain. **3** a movable horizontal surface usu attached to the tailplane of an aircraft for controlling climb and descent. **4** a muscle that raises a part of the body.

eleven *n* **1** the number 11. **2** a cricket, football, or hockey team. ➤➤ **eleven** *adj,* **elevenfold** *adj and adv.*

eleven-plus *or* **11-plus** *n* an examination taken, *esp* formerly, at the age of 10–11 to determine which type of British state secondary education a child should receive.

elevenses *pl n Brit* (*used as sing. or pl*) light refreshment taken in the middle of the morning.

eleventh *adj and n* **1** having the position in a sequence corresponding to the number eleven. **2** one of eleven equal parts of something.

eleventh hour *n* (**the eleventh hour**) the latest possible time. ➤➤ **eleventh-hour** *adj.*

elf *n* (*pl* **elves**) a fairy, *esp* a small mischievous one. ➤➤ **elfish** *adj,* **elfishly** *adv.*

elfin *adj* of or resembling an elf, *esp* in being small, delicate, or mischievous.

elf-lock *n* (*usu in pl*) a tangled lock of hair.

elicit *v* (**elicited, eliciting**) (*often* + from) to call forth or draw out (e.g. a response or reaction), *esp* when the thing involved is latent, or given or shown reluctantly. ➤➤ **elicitation** *n,* **elicitor** *n.*

Usage note

elicit *or* **illicit**? These two words are sometimes confused. *Elicit* is a verb, usually followed by the preposition *from*, meaning 'to call or draw forth (something)': *We managed to elicit from him how he obtained the information. Illicit* is an adjective meaning 'illegal' or 'not allowed': *an illicit love affair.*

elide *v* to suppress (e.g. a vowel or syllable) by elision.

eligible *adj* **1** qualified to do or receive something. **2** worthy or desirable, *esp* as a marriage partner. ➤➤ **eligibility** *n,* **eligibly** *adv.*

eliminate *v* **1a** to get rid of completely. **b** to set aside as unimportant. **2** to kill (a person), *esp* so as to remove them as an obstacle. **3** to remove (a competitor, team, etc) from a competition, usu by defeat. ➤➤ **eliminable** *adj,* **elimination** *n,* **eliminative** *adj,* **eliminator** *n.*

elision *n* omission of a vowel or syllable in speech or writing, e.g. reducing *I am* to *I'm.*

elite *or* **élite** *n* **1** (*used as sing. or pl*) a relatively small and often powerful group that is considered to be intellectually, professionally, or socially superior. **2** a typewriter type producing twelve characters to the inch. ➤➤ **elite** *adj.*

elitism *or* **élitism** *n* **1a** the belief in leadership by an elite. **b** the belief that some people are superior to others and deserve special treatment. **2** consciousness of belonging to an elite. ➤➤ **elitist** *n and adj.*

elixir *n* **1** an alchemist's substance supposedly capable of changing base metals into gold. **2a** (*also* **elixir of life**) a substance held to be capable of prolonging life indefinitely. **b** a cure-all.

Elizabethan *adj* of the reign of Elizabeth I of England (1558–1603). ➤➤ **Elizabethan** *n.*

elk *n* (*pl* **elks** *or* **elk**) **1** the largest existing deer of Europe and Asia, of the same species as but smaller than the moose of N America. **2** *NAm* = WAPITI.

ell *n* a former English unit of length equal to 45in. (about 1.14m).

ellipse *n* **1** a two-dimensional closed curve generated by a point moving in such a way that the sum of its distances from two fixed points is constant; the intersection of a plane cutting obliquely through a cone: compare HYPERBOLA, PARABOLA. **2** = ELLIPSIS.

ellipsis *n* (*pl* **ellipses**) **1** the omission of one or more words needed to make a construction grammatically complete, as in *I took flowers, and my sister a book.* **2** marks or a mark (e.g. ... or *** or —), indicating the omission of letters or words.

ellipsoid *n* a solid or surface of which all the plane sections are ellipses or circles: compare HYPERBOLOID, PARABOLOID. ➤➤ **ellipsoidal** *adj.*

elliptic *adj* = ELLIPTICAL (1), (2A).

elliptical *adj* **1** of or shaped like an ellipse. **2a** of or marked by ellipsis. **b** of speech or writing: extremely or excessively concise, often resulting in obscurity or ambiguity. ➤➤ **elliptically** *adv,* **ellipticity** *n.*

elm *n* a large graceful tree with serrated leaves and small light disc-shaped fruits, producing hard heavy wood.

El Niño *n* a warming of the equatorial Pacific region that occurs every five to eight years and can have severe effects on the weather in other parts of the world.

elocution *n* the art of effective public speaking, *esp* of good diction. ➤➤ **elocutionary** *adj,* **elocutionist** *n.*

elongate *v* to make or become longer. ➤➤ **elongated** *adj,* **elongation** *n.*

elope *v* to run away secretly with a lover, usu with the intention of getting married or cohabiting. ➤➤ **elopement** *n,* **eloper** *n.*

eloquence *n* **1** fluent, forceful, and persuasive speech. **2** the art or power of using such speech.

eloquent *adj* **1** characterized by fluent, forceful, and persuasive use of language. **2** vividly or movingly expressive or revealing. ➤➤ **eloquently** *adv.*

else *adv* **1** different from or other than the person, place, manner, or time mentioned or understood: *somewhere else.* **2** also; besides: *There's nothing else to eat.* ✻ **or else 1** used to express a threat. **2** if not; otherwise.

elsewhere *adv* in or to another place.

ELT *abbr* English language teaching.

elucidate *v* to make clear, *esp* by explanation. ➤➤ **elucidation** *n,* **elucidative** *adj,* **elucidator** *n,* **elucidatory** *adj.*

elude *v* **1** to avoid cunningly or adroitly. **2** to escape the memory or notice of. ➤➤ **elusion** *n.*

elusive *adj* **1** difficult to find or catch. **2** difficult to remember or understand. ➤➤ **elusively** *adv,* **elusiveness** *n.*

elver *n* a young eel.

elves *n* pl of ELF.

elvish *adj* resembling an elf; elfish.

Elysium *n* (*pl* **Elysiums** *or* **Elysia**) **1** the home of the blessed after death in Greek mythology. **2** a place of bliss, happiness, or delight; a paradise. ➤➤ **Elysian** *adj.*

em *n* **1** in printing, a unit of width equal to the body of a piece of type bearing the letter M or the height of the type size. **2** = PICA (1).

em- *prefix* see EN-[1], EN-[2].

'em *pron* used in writing to suggest casual speech: them.

emaciate *v* to make or become excessively thin or feeble. ➤➤ **emaciated** *adj,* **emaciation** *n.*

e-mail[1] *or* **email** *n* **1** a system for transmitting messages from one computer to another via a local area network or through a modem and telephone line. **2** a message or messages sent in this way.

e-mail[2] *or* **email** *v* **1** to send (somebody) an e-mail. **2** to send (a message, document, etc) by e-mail.

emalangeni *n* pl of LILANGENI.

emanate *v* **1** to come out from a source. **2** to send out or give off.

emanation *n* **1** something that emanates or is produced by emanating. **2** a heavy gaseous element produced by radioactive disintegration. **3** the act of emanating. ➤➤ **emanational** *adj,* **emanative** *adj.*

emancipate *v* to free from slavery or from restrictions imposed by society or law. ➤➤ **emancipation** *n,* **emancipator** *n,* **emancipatory** *adj.*

emasculate *v* **1** to deprive of effectiveness or strength. **2a** to castrate. **b** to rob (a man) of his male identity or role. ➤➤ **emasculation** *n,* **emasculator** *n,* **emasculatory** *adj.*

embalm *v* to treat (a dead body) in order to protect it against decay. ⯮ **embalmer** *n*, **embalmment** *n*.

embankment *n* a raised structure to hold back water or to carry a road or railway.

embargo[1] *n* (*pl* **-oes**) **1** a government order prohibiting the departure or entry of commercial ships. **2** a legal prohibition on commerce. **3** a stoppage or prohibition.

embargo[2] *v* (**embargoes, embargoed, embargoing**) to place an embargo on (e.g. ships or commerce).

embark *v* **1** to go on board a ship or aircraft. **2** to make a start on something. ⯮ **embarkation** *n*.

embarrass *v* **1** to cause to experience a state of self-conscious distress. **2** to involve in financial difficulties, *esp* debt. ⯮ **embarrassed** *adj*, **embarrassedly** *adv*, **embarrassing** *adj*, **embarrassingly** *adv*, **embarrassment** *n*.

embassy *n* (*pl* **-ies**) **1** the official residence of an ambassador. **2** a diplomatic body headed by an ambassador.

embattled *adj* **1** hemmed in by adversaries, difficulties, etc. **2** prepared for or involved in battle. **3** having battlements or other fortifications.

embed *or* **imbed** *v* (**embedded** *or* **imbedded, embedding** *or* **imbedding**) **1** to place or fix firmly or deeply in surrounding matter. **2** to make an integral part of a whole. **3** to implant (e.g. an idea) in the mind.

embellish *v* **1** to make beautiful by adding ornaments; to decorate. **2** to make (speech or writing) more interesting by adding fictitious or exaggerated detail. ⯮ **embellisher** *n*, **embellishment** *n*.

ember *n* a glowing fragment of coal or wood in a dying fire.

Ember Day *n* in Anglican and Roman Catholic Churches, any of twelve days set aside for fasting and prayer.

embezzle *v* to appropriate (money or property entrusted to one's care) fraudulently to one's own use. ⯮ **embezzlement** *n*, **embezzler** *n*.

embitter *v* **1** to make (somebody) bitter. **2** to make (a bad situation or feeling) worse. ⯮ **embittered** *adj*, **embitterment** *n*.

emblazon *v* **1** to display conspicuously. **2** to decorate with a heraldic device or other emblem. ⯮ **emblazonment** *n*, **emblazonry** *n*.

emblem *n* **1** a design or symbol adopted and used as an identifying mark. **2** an object symbolizing another object or idea. ⯮ **emblematic** *adj*, **emblematize** *v*.

embody *v* (**-ies, -ied**) **1** to make (e.g. ideas or concepts) concrete and perceptible. **2** (+ in) to make (e.g. connected ideas or principles) a part of a body or system. **3** to represent (an idea or belief) in human or animal form; to personify. ⯮ **embodier** *n*, **embodiment** *n*.

embolden *v* to make bold or courageous.

emboli *n* pl of EMBOLUS.

embolism *n* **1** the sudden obstruction of a blood vessel by an embolus. **2** = EMBOLUS.

embolus *n* (*pl* **emboli**) a blood clot, air bubble, or other particle likely to cause an embolism. ⯮ **embolic** *adj*.

embonpoint *n euphem* plumpness or stoutness.

emboss *v* to carve, mould, or paint (a design, lettering, etc) in relief on a surface. ⯮ **embossed** *adj*, **embosser** *n*, **embossment** *n*.

embouchure *n* in music, the position and use of the lips and tongue in playing a wind instrument.

embrace[1] *v* **1** to take (somebody) in one's arms and hold them closely as a sign of affection. **2a** to take up (a cause or idea), *esp* readily or eagerly. **b** to accept (e.g. an opportunity) willingly or welcome (it). **3** to include as an integral part or element of a whole. ⯮ **embraceable** *adj*, **embracement** *n*, **embracer** *n*.

embrace[2] *n* the act or an instance of embracing.

embrasure *n* **1** a door or window aperture, *esp* one with angled sides. **2** an opening in a wall or parapet of a fortification to fire through.

embrocation *n* a liquid rubbed into the skin, *esp* to relieve pain.

embroider *v* **1a** to ornament (e.g. cloth or a garment) with decorative stitches. **b** to form (e.g. a design or pattern) in ornamental needlework. **2** to embellish with exaggerated or fictitious details. ⯮ **embroiderer** *n*.

embroidery *n* (*pl* **-ies**) **1** the art or process of embroidering designs. **2** embroidered work. **3** unnecessary additions or embellishments, *esp* to a narrative.

embroil *v* to involve in conflict or difficulties. ⯮ **embroilment** *n*.

embryo *n* (*pl* **-os**) **1a** an animal in the early stages of growth before birth or hatching. **b** an unborn human during the first eight weeks after conception. **2** a rudimentary plant within a seed. ✻ **in embryo** in an undeveloped state.

embryology *n* the study of the development of embryos. ⯮ **embryologic** *adj*, **embryological** *adj*, **embryologist** *n*.

embryonic *adj* **1** of or relating to an embryo. **2** in an early stage of development. ⯮ **embryonically** *adv*.

emcee[1] *n informal* a compere or master of ceremonies.

emcee[2] *v* (**emcees, emceed, emceeing**) *informal* to act as an emcee of.

emend *v* to remove errors or irregularities from (a text). ⯮ **emendable** *adj*, **emendation** *n*.

Usage note

emend *or* amend? See note at AMEND.

emerald *n* **1** a bright green variety of beryl used as a gemstone: compare AQUAMARINE, BERYL. **2** a bright green colour. ⯮ **emerald** *adj*.

emerge *v* **1** to come out into view. **2** to become manifest or known. **3** to survive a difficult or unpleasant experience. **4** to come into being or develop. ⯮ **emergence** *n*, **emerging** *adj*.

emergency *n* (*pl* **-ies**) **1a** an unforeseen occurrence that is potentially dangerous and calls for immediate action. **b** (*used before a noun*) resulting from or used in such a situation. **2** a patient who needs urgent treatment.

emergent *adj* emerging, *esp* in the early stages of formation or development.

emeritus *adj* retaining a title on an honorary basis after retirement.

emery *n* a dark granular mineral, consisting mainly of corundum, used for grinding and polishing.

emery board *n* a strip of cardboard or wood coated with powdered emery and used as a nail file.

emery paper *n* paper coated with emery powder for use as an abrasive.

emetic[1] *n* something that causes vomiting.

emetic[2] *adj* causing vomiting. ⯮ **emetically** *adv*.

EMF *abbr* European Monetary Fund.

emf *abbr* electromotive force.

-emia *comb. form NAm* see -AEMIA.

emigrant *n* a person who emigrates. ➤➤ **emigrant** *adj.*

emigrate *v* to leave one's home or country for permanent residence elsewhere. ➤➤ **emigration** *n.*

émigré *or* **emigré** /'emigray/ *n* a person who emigrates, *esp* for political reasons.

eminence *n* **1a** a position of prominence or superiority. **b** (**Eminence**) used as a title of a Roman Catholic cardinal. **2 a** a person of high rank or attainments. **b** a natural geographical elevation; a height.

éminence grise /,ayminonhs 'greez/ *n* (*pl* **éminences grises**) a person who exercises power indirectly through influence on somebody with titular authority.

eminent *adj* **1** conspicuous or notable. **2** highly regarded; distinguished. ➤➤ **eminently** *adv.*

emir *or* **amir** *n* a ruler of a Muslim state.

emirate *n* **1** the rank of an emir. **2** the territory ruled by an emir.

emissary *n* (*pl* **-ies**) a person sent on a mission to represent a government or head of state; an envoy.

emission *n* **1** the act or an instance of emitting. **2** something emitted, e.g. electromagnetic waves, electrons, fumes, bodily fluids, etc. ➤➤ **emissive** *adj.*

emit *v* (**emitted, emitting**) **1** to send out or give off (e.g. light, smoke, or radiation). **2** to make (a sound). ➤➤ **emitter** *n.*

Emmental *or* **Emmenthal** *n* a pale yellow Swiss cheese with many holes that form during ripening.

Emmy *n* (*pl* **Emmys**) in the USA, a statuette awarded annually for notable achievement in television.

emollient[1] *adj* **1** making soft or supple, or giving soothing relief, *esp* to the skin. **2** making a situation calmer.

emollient[2] *n* an emollient substance, e.g. lanolin.

emolument *n* the returns arising from office or employment; a salary or fee.

e-money *or* **e-cash** *n* money in the form of digitally encoded information used to make payments via the Internet or by special smart cards.

emote *v* to give expression to emotion, *esp* theatrically.

emoticon *n* a representation of a human face formed from keyboard characters, used in e-mail to express feelings.

emotion *n* **1a** a strong feeling, e.g. anger, fear, or joy. **b** such feelings considered collectively. **2** instinctive feelings or reactions, *esp* as opposed to reason. ➤➤ **emotionless** *adj.*

emotional *adj* **1** relating to the emotions. **2** feeling or expressing emotion. **3** inclined to show excessive emotion. **4** = EMOTIVE. ➤➤ **emotionalism** *n,* **emotionality** *n,* **emotionalize** *v,* **emotionally** *adv.*

Usage note

emotional *or* **emotive**? See note at EMOTIVE.

emotive *adj* arousing or appealing to emotion, *esp* as opposed to reason. ➤➤ **emotively** *adv,* **emotiveness** *n,* **emotivity** *n.*

Usage note

emotive *or* **emotional**? The main meaning of *emotive* is 'arousing strong feelings, appealing to the feelings (rather than reason)', whereas the core sense of *emotional* is 'feeling or expressing emotion'. By making an *emotional* speech a speaker would show how strongly he or she felt about something. But somebody making an *emotive* speech would be more interested in stirring up the crowd than expressing feeling.

empanada /empə'nahdə/ *n* in South American cooking, a turnover with a savoury filling that is baked or fried.

empanel *or* **impanel** *v* (**empanelled** *or* **impanelled, empanelling** *or* **impanelling,** *NAm* **empaneled** *or* **impaneled, empaneling** *or* **impaneling**) to enrol (somebody) on a panel list, *esp* for jury service. ➤➤ **empanelment** *n.*

empathize *or* **empathise** *v* (*usu* + with) to understand and share the feelings of another person.

empathy *n* the capacity for understanding and sharing another's feelings or ideas. ➤➤ **empathetic** *adj,* **empathetically** *adv,* **empathic** *adj.*

emperor *n* the supreme ruler of an empire. ➤➤ **emperorship** *n.*

emperor penguin *n* the largest known penguin, found only in the south polar region.

emphasis *n* (*pl* **emphases**) **1** force or intensity of expression that gives special importance to something in speaking or writing. **2** special consideration of or stress on something.

emphasize *or* **-ise** *v* **1a** to give emphasis to. **b** to draw attention to. **2** to make sharper or clearer in form or outline.

emphatic *adj* **1** spoken with or marked by emphasis. **2** tending to express oneself forcefully or take decisive action. **3** clear or definite. ➤➤ **emphatically** *adv.*

emphysema *n* a disorder of the lungs involving abnormal enlargement of the air sacs and causing breathlessness.

Empire *adj* characteristic of a style, e.g. of furniture or interior decoration, popular during the first French Empire (1804–15).

empire *n* **1a** a large group of countries under the authority of a single ruler or state. **b** an extensive territory or enterprise under the control of a single person or entity. **2** imperial sovereignty.

empire-builder *n* a person who seeks to extend their influence, e.g. within a business organization, by acquiring additional staff or areas of operation. ➤➤ **empire-building** *n.*

empire line *n* a style of women's dress having a high waistline and a low neckline, first popular in early 19th cent. France.

empirical *or* **empiric** *adj* based on observation, experience, or experiment rather than theory. ➤➤ **empirically** *adv.*

empiricism *n* **1** a theory that all knowledge is dependent on experience of the external world. **2** the practice of discovery by observation and experiment. ➤➤ **empiricist** *n.*

emplacement *n* a prepared position for guns or military equipment.

employ[1] *v* **1** to pay (somebody) wages or a salary in return for their work. **2** to give (somebody) a task or occupation. **3** to use (something) in a specified way or for a specific purpose. ➤➤ **employability** *n,* **employable** *adj.*

employ[2] *n* the state of being employed, *esp* for wages or a salary.

employee *n* somebody employed by another for wages or a salary.

employer *n* a person, company, or other organization that employs people.

employment *n* **1** the act of employing or the state of being employed. **2a** paid work. **b** a job or occupation.

emporium *n* (*pl* **emporiums** *or* **emporia**) a large shop or commercial centre.

empower *v* **1** to give official authority or legal power to. **2** to give (somebody) the strength and confidence to act on their own initiative. ➤➤ **empowerment** *n.*

empress *n* **1** the wife or widow of an emperor. **2** a woman having the rank of emperor in her own right.

empty[1] *adj* (**-ier, -iest**) **1a** containing nothing, *esp* lacking typical or expected contents. **b** not inhabited or frequented. **2a** lacking reality or substance; hollow. **b** lacking effect, value, or sincerity. **3** *informal* hungry. ➤➤ **emptily** *adv,* **emptiness** *n.*

empty[2] *v* (**-ies, -ied**) **1a** to remove the contents of. **b** to become empty. **2** to discharge or transfer (contents) by pouring or tipping them out. **3** to deprive or divest. ➤➤ **emptier** *n.*

empty[3] *n* (*pl* **-ies**) a bottle or other container that has been emptied.

empty-handed *adj* having or bringing nothing, *esp* because nothing has been gained or obtained.

empty-headed *adj* foolish or silly.

empty nester *n informal* a parent whose children have grown up and left home.

empyema *n* (*pl* **empyemata** *or* **empyemas**) the presence of pus in a body cavity, *esp* in the chest. ➤➤ **empyemic** *adj.*

empyrean *n* **1** the highest heavenly sphere in ancient and medieval cosmology. **2** *literary* the sky. ➤➤ **empyreal** *adj,* **empyrean** *adj.*

em rule *n* in printing, a long dash roughly the width of a letter M.

EMS *abbr* European Monetary System.

EMU *abbr* European monetary union.

emu *n* a swift-running flightless Australian bird, related to but smaller than the ostrich.

emulate *v* **1** to imitate closely, *esp* in order to equal. **2** to rival or compete with. ➤➤ **emulation** *n,* **emulative** *adj,* **emulator** *n.*

emulous *adj* ambitious or eager to emulate. ➤➤ **emulously** *adv.*

emulsifier *n* a food additive that stabilizes processed foods.

emulsify *v* (**-ies, -ied**) to convert (e.g. an oil) into an emulsion. ➤➤ **emulsifiable** *adj,* **emulsification** *n.*

emulsion *n* **1** a substance consisting of one liquid dispersed in droplets throughout another liquid. **2** a suspension of a silver compound in a gelatin solution for coating photographic plates, film, etc. **3** a type of paint in which the pigment is dispersed in an oil which forms an emulsion with water. ➤➤ **emulsive** *adj.*

en *n* in printing, a unit of width equal to the body of a piece of type bearing the letter N or half an em.

en-[1] *or* **em-** *prefix* **1 a** to put into or onto: *embed; enthrone.* **b** to provide with: *empower; endow.* **2** to cause to be: *enslave; enable.* **3** forming more intensive forms of verbs: *entangle.*

en-[2] *or* **em-** *prefix* denoting inclusion or involvement: *energy; empathy.*

-en[1] *or* **-n** *suffix* forming adjectives from nouns, with the meaning: made of or consisting of: *earthen; wooden.*

-en[2] *or* **-n** *suffix* forming verbs, with the meaning: to cause to be or have; to become: *sharpen; heighten.*

-en[3] *or* **-n** *suffix* forming past participles of verbs: *broken; worn.*

enable *v* **1** to provide with the means or opportunity to do something. **2** to make possible or practical.

enact *v* **1** to make (e.g. a bill) into law. **2** to act out or perform (a role, scene, etc). ➤➤ **enactable** *adj,* **enaction** *n,* **enactment** *n,* **enactor** *n.*

enamel[1] *n* **1** a usu opaque glassy coating applied to the surface of metal, glass, or pottery. **2** something enamelled. **3** a white substance consisting mainly of calcium that forms a thin hard layer capping the teeth. **4** a paint that dries with a glossy appearance. **5** *chiefly NAm* nail varnish.

enamel[2] *v* (**enamelled, enamelling,** *NAm* **enameled, enameling**) to cover or decorate with enamel. ➤➤ **enameller** *n,* **enamellist** *n,* **enamelwork** *n.*

enamour (*NAm* **enamor**) *v* (*usu in passive,* + of/with) to cause to love or like a person or thing: *I'm not enamoured with the colour scheme.*

enantiomer *n* = ENANTIOMORPH. ➤➤ **enantiomeric** *adj.*

enantiomorph *n* either of a pair of chemical compounds or crystals with structures that are a mirror-image of each other. ➤➤ **enantiomorphic** *adj,* **enantiomorphism** *n,* **enantiomorphous** *adj.*

en bloc /onh 'blok/ *adv and adj* all together; in a mass.

encamp *v* to set up a camp, or place (people) in a camp.

encampment *n* **1** the place where a group, e.g. a body of troops, is encamped. **2** the act of encamping or the state of being encamped.

encapsulate *v* **1** to express in a concise form. **2** to enclose in a capsule. ➤➤ **encapsulation** *n.*

encase *or* **incase** *v* to enclose in or as if in a case. ➤➤ **encasement** *n.*

encash *v Brit, formal* to pay or obtain cash for (e.g. a cheque). ➤➤ **encashable** *adj,* **encashment** *n.*

encaustic *n* **1** a paint made from pigment mixed with melted beeswax and fixed by heat after application. **2** a method involving the use of heat to fix or burn a colour onto or into a surface. ➤➤ **encaustic** *adj.*

-ence *suffix* forming nouns, denoting: **1** an action or process: *emergence.* **2** an instance of an action or process: *reference.* **3** a quality or state: *dependence.*

encephalitis *n* inflammation of the brain, usu caused by infection. ➤➤ **encephalitic** *adj.*

encephalogram *n* **1** an X-ray picture of the brain made by encephalography. **2** = ELECTROENCEPHALOGRAM.

encephalograph *n* **1** = ENCEPHALOGRAM. **2** = ELECTROENCEPHALOGRAPH.

encephalography *n* X-ray photography of the brain after some of the cerebrospinal fluid has been replaced by air or oxygen.

encephalomyelitis *n* inflammation of both the brain and spinal cord.

encephalopathy *n* (*pl* **-ies**) a disease of the brain, *esp* one involving alterations of brain structure.

enchant *v* **1** to cast a spell on; to bewitch. **2** to attract and move deeply; to delight. ➤➤ **enchanter** *n,* **enchantment** *n,* **enchantress** *n.*

enchanting *adj* charming; delightful. ➤➤ **enchantingly** *adv.*

enchilada *n* a Mexican dish consisting of a tortilla spread with a meat filling, rolled up, and covered with a chilli sauce.

encipher *v* to convert (a message) into a code. ➤➤ **encipherment** *n.*

encircle *v* **1** to form a circle round; to surround. **2** to move or pass completely round. ➤➤ **encirclement** *n.*

enclave *n* **1** a territorial or culturally distinct unit enclosed within foreign territory. **2** a distinct social or cultural group surrounded by a larger group.

enclose *or* **inclose** *v* **1** to include in a package or envelope, *esp* along with something else. **2** to shut in or surround completely.

enclosed order *n* a Christian religious community that avoids contacts with the outside world.

enclosure *or* **inclosure** *n* **1a** a fenced-off area of ground. **b** an area reserved for certain spectators in a sports ground. **2** something included with a letter in the same envelope or package. **3** *esp* in former times, the fencing in of common land in order to appropriate it for private use.

encode *v* to convert (a message) into code. ⋙ **encoder** *n.*

encomium *n* (*pl* **encomiums** *or* **encomia**) a usu formal expression of warm or high praise; a eulogy.

encompass *v* **1** to encircle or enclose. **2** to include, *esp* in a comprehensive manner. **3** *formal* to bring about. ⋙ **encompassment** *n.*

encore[1] *n* a performer's reappearance to give an additional or repeated performance at the request of the audience.

encore[2] *v* to call for an encore.

encore[3] *interj* used by an audience to call for an encore.

encounter[1] *v* **1** to meet, *esp* unexpectedly. **2** to be faced with.

encounter[2] *n* **1** a chance meeting. **2** a meeting or clash between hostile factions or people.

encounter group *n* a group of people who meet regularly to develop greater understanding of their own and one another's feelings.

encourage *v* **1** to inspire with confidence, spirit, or hope. **2** to spur on. **3** to give help, support, or approval to (e.g. a process or action). ⋙ **encouragement** *n,* **encourager** *n,* **encouraging** *adj,* **encouragingly** *adv.*

encroach *v* **1** (+ on/upon) to intrude gradually or by stealth on the possessions or rights of another. **2** (*often* + on/upon) to advance beyond the usual or proper limits. ⋙ **encroacher** *n,* **encroachment** *n.*

en croûte /ong 'krooht/ *adj* wrapped in pastry.

encrust *or* **incrust** *v* **1** to cover or overlay with a hard or decorative layer, e.g. of jewels or precious metal. **2** to form a crust. ⋙ **encrustation** *n.*

encrypt *v* to convert into code. ⋙ **encryption** *n.*

encumber *v* **1** to impede, hamper, or weigh (somebody or something) down. **2** to burden with a debt or legal claim.

encumbrance *n* **1** an impediment or burden. **2** a mortgage or other claim against property.

-ency *suffix* forming nouns, denoting: a quality or state: *despondency.*

encyclical *n* in the Roman Catholic Church, a letter from the pope to all bishops or to those in one country.

encyclopedia *or* **encyclopaedia** *n* a work containing general information on all branches of knowledge or comprehensive information on one branch, usu in articles arranged alphabetically.

encyclopedic *or* **encyclopaedic** *adj* **1** of or relating to an encyclopedia or its methods of treating a subject. **2** comprehensive. ⋙ **encyclopedically** *adv.*

encyclopedist *or* **encyclopaedist** *n* a person who compiles or contributes to an encyclopedia.

end[1] *n* **1** either of the parts farthest from the middle of something long. **2a** the point at which something stops happening, is completed, or ceases to exist. **b** the last part or section of something. **3** death or destruction. **4** a piece left over; a remnant. **5** an aim, goal, or purpose. **6** either half of a sports field, pitch, court, etc. **7** *informal* a particular part of an undertaking or organization: *the advertising end of the business.* **8** (**the end**) *informal* something or somebody particularly unpleasant. ✱ **at an end** **1** finished; completed. **2** exhausted; used up. **end on** with the end pointing towards one. **in the end** eventually. **keep one's end up** to maintain one's position or perform well in an argument, competition, etc. **make (both) ends meet** to cope financially. **no end** **1** exceedingly. **2** a vast amount; a huge quantity. **on end** **1** in an upright position. **2** without stopping.

end[2] *v* **1** to bring or come to an end. **2** to destroy. **3** (*often* + up) to reach a specified ultimate situation, condition, position, or rank. ✱ **end it all** to commit suicide.

end[3] *adj* final or ultimate.

end- *or* **endo-** *comb. form* within or inside: *endoskeleton.*

endanger *v* to put in danger. ⋙ **endangerment** *n.*

endangered *adj* at risk, *esp* threatened with extinction.

endear *v* (*often* + to) to cause to become beloved or admired. ⋙ **endearing** *adj,* **endearingly** *adv.*

endearment *n* a word or phrase expressing affection.

endeavour[1] (*NAm* **endeavor**) *v formal* to attempt (to do something) by exertion or effort.

endeavour[2] (*NAm* **endeavor**) *n* **1** serious determined effort. **2** an attempt, effort, or undertaking.

endemic *adj* **1** of a disease, prevalent within a particular area or group of people. **2** of a species, native and usu restricted to a particular region. ⋙ **endemically** *adv,* **endemicity** *n.*

end game *n* the final stage of a game, *esp* the stage of a chess game when only a few pieces remain on the board.

ending *n* **1** the final part of something, e.g. a book, film, etc. **2** one or more letters or syllables added to a word base, *esp* as an inflection.

endive *n* **1** a plant of the daisy family resembling a lettuce whose bitter leaves are used in salads. **2** *NAm* chicory used as a salad plant, *esp* its leaves.

endless *adj* **1** being or seeming without end. **2** extremely numerous. **3** of a belt, chain, etc: joined to itself at its ends. ⋙ **endlessly** *adv,* **endlessness** *n.*

endmost *adj* situated at the very end; farthest.

endo- *comb. form* see END-.

endocarditis *n* inflammation of the lining and valves of the heart.

endocrine *adj esp* of a gland: producing secretions that are discharged directly into the bloodstream.

endocrinology *n* the branch of physiology and medicine dealing with the endocrine glands. ⋙ **endocrinological** *adj,* **endocrinologist** *n.*

endoderm *n* **1** the innermost of the three germ layers of an embryo. **2** tissue derived from this germ layer. ⋙ **endodermal** *adj.*

endogenous *adj* **1** originating within the body. **2** having no direct or apparent external cause. ⋙ **endogenously** *adv,* **endogeny** *n.*

endometria *n* pl of ENDOMETRIUM.

endometriosis *n* the presence of endometrial tissue in places where it is not normally found, e.g. the ovary, often causing pain.

endometrium *n* (*pl* **endometria**) the mucous membrane lining the uterus. ⋙ **endometrial** *adj.*

endomorph *n* a person having a heavy rounded build, often with a marked tendency to become fat:

compare ECTOMORPH, MESOMORPH. ➤➤ **endomorphic** *adj,* **endomorphy** *n.*

endorphin *n* a natural painkiller secreted by the brain that resembles opium derivatives, e.g. morphine or heroin.

endorse *or* **indorse** *v* **1** to express approval of or support for, *esp* publicly. **2** to sign the back of (a cheque, bill, etc) as an instruction regarding payment, e.g. to another recipient. **3** *Brit* to record details of a motoring offence on (a driver's licence). ➤➤ **endorsable** *adj,* **endorsee** *n,* **endorser** *n.*

endorsement *or* **indorsement** *n* **1** the act or an instance of endorsing. **2** something that endorses, e.g. a signature. **3** *Brit* a record of a motoring offence entered on a driving licence. **4** a provision added to an insurance contract altering its scope or application.

endoscope *n* a medical instrument for looking inside a hollow organ, e.g. the intestine. ➤➤ **endoscopic** *adj,* **endoscopically** *adv,* **endoscopy** *n.*

endoskeleton *n* an internal skeleton in an animal. ➤➤ **endoskeletal** *adj.*

endosperm *n* plant tissue formed within the seed providing nutrition for the developing embryo. ➤➤ **endospermic** *adj,* **endospermous** *adj.*

endothelium *n* (*pl* **endothelia**) a tissue composed of a single layer of thin flattened cells that lines internal body cavities. ➤➤ **endothelial** *adj.*

endothermal *adj* = ENDOTHERMIC.

endothermic *adj* of a chemical reaction or compound: characterized by or formed with absorption of heat.

endow *v* **1** to provide with a continuing source of income, often by bequest. **2** to provide with an ability or attribute.

endowment *n* **1** the part of an institution's income derived from donations. **2** a natural quality with which a person is endowed. **3** (*used before a noun*) denoting a form of life insurance under which an agreed sum is paid to the policyholder at the end of a specified period or to another designated person if the policyholder dies within that period.

endowment mortgage *n* a mortgage that is paid back by the money received through an endowment policy.

endpaper *n* a folded sheet of paper pasted to the front or back inside cover of a book.

endue *or* **indue** *v formal* (*usu in passive,* + with) to provide with a quality or attribute.

endurance *n* the ability to withstand hardship, adversity, or stress.

endure *v* **1** to undergo (e.g. a hardship), *esp* without giving in. **2** to tolerate. **3** to continue in the same state; to last. ➤➤ **endurable** *adj.*

enduring *adj* lasting or durable. ➤➤ **enduringly** *adv,* **enduringness** *n.*

end user *n* the final recipient of goods or services produced by a complex process.

endways *adv and adj* **1** with the end forwards or towards the observer. **2** end to end.

endwise *adv and adj* = ENDWAYS.

ENE *abbr* east-northeast.

-ene *suffix* forming nouns, denoting: an unsaturated carbon compound, *esp* one with a double bond: *benzene; ethylene.*

enema *n* (*pl* **enemas** *or* **enemata**) an injection of liquid into the intestine by way of the anus, e.g. to ease constipation.

enemy *n* (*pl* **-ies**) **1** a person who is opposed to or actively seeking to harm somebody or something. **2** something harmful or deadly. **3** (*used as sing. or pl*) a nation or military force with whom one is at war.

energetic *adj* **1** marked by energy, activity, or vigour. **2** relating to energy. ➤➤ **energetically** *adv.*

energy *n* (*pl* **-ies**) **1** the natural strength and vitality required for action. **2** (*in pl*) physical and mental powers. **3** in physics, the capacity for doing work. **4** fuel and other sources of power, *esp* electricity.

enervate *v* to lessen the mental or physical strength or vitality of. ➤➤ **enervated** *adj,* **enervating** *adj,* **enervation** *n.*

en famille /onh fa'mee/ *adv* **1** all together as a family. **2** informally.

enfant terrible /,onfonh te'reeblə/ *n* (*pl* **enfants terribles**) a person whose outspoken remarks or unconventional actions cause embarrassment or controversy.

enfeeble *v* to make weak. ➤➤ **enfeeblement** *n.*

enfilade *n* gunfire directed along the length of an enemy battle line. ➤➤ **enfilade** *v.*

enfold *v* **1** (*usu* + in) to wrap up; to envelop. **2** to clasp in one's arms; to embrace (them).

enforce *v* **1** to cause (a rule or law) to be obeyed or carried out. **2** to give greater force to (e.g. an argument). **3** to impose or compel (e.g. obedience). ➤➤ **enforceability** *n,* **enforceable** *adj,* **enforced** *adj,* **enforcedly** *adv,* **enforcement** *n,* **enforcer** *n.*

enfranchise *v* **1** to give the right of voting to. **2** to set free, *esp* from slavery. ➤➤ **enfranchisement** *n.*

engage *v* **1** to attract and hold (somebody's thoughts, attention, affection, etc). **2a** (+ in) to participate or become involved. **b** to induce (somebody) to participate, *esp* in conversation. **3** to arrange to employ. **4** of a mechanical part: to interlock with (another part). **5** to begin a battle with (an enemy force). **6** to pledge or promise (to do something).

engagé /ongga'zhay/ *adj* actively involved in or committed to something, *esp* a political cause.

engaged *adj* **1** involved in activity; occupied. **2** pledged to be married. **3** *chiefly Brit* in use.

engagement *n* **1** an agreement to marry. **2a** a promise to be present at something; an appointment. **b** employment, *esp* for a limited period, e.g. as a performer. **3** a hostile encounter between military forces. **4** the act of engaging or the state of being engaged.

engaging *adj* attractive or pleasing. ➤➤ **engagingly** *adv,* **engagingness** *n.*

en garde *interj* in fencing, used to warn one's opponent to assume a defensive position.

engender *v* to cause to exist or develop; to produce.

engine *n* **1** a machine for converting any of various forms of energy into mechanical force and motion. **2** a railway locomotive. ➤➤ **engineless** *adj.*

engineer[1] *n* **1** a person who is trained or works in engineering. **2** a person who maintains or operates an engine or apparatus. **3** a soldier who carries out engineering work. **4** *NAm* a driver of a railway locomotive.

engineer[2] *v* **1** to design or construct as an engineer. **2** to produce (a product or organism) through biological manipulation. **3** to contrive or plan (something), usu with subtle skill and craft.

engineering *n* the application of science, mathematics, and technology to the design and construction of machines, structures, etc.

English *n* **1** the Germanic language spoken in Britain, the USA, and most Commonwealth countries.

2 (**the English**) (*used as pl*) the people of England. ➤➤ **English** *adj*, **Englishness** *n*.

English breakfast *n* a breakfast typically consisting of cereal, a hot cooked dish such as bacon and eggs, toast and marmalade, and tea or coffee.

Englishman *or* **Englishwoman** *n* (*pl* **Englishmen** *or* **Englishwomen**) a native or inhabitant of England.

English rose *n* a pretty English girl or woman with a smooth skin, fair complexion, and delicately pink cheeks.

Englishwoman *n* see ENGLISHMAN.

engorge *v* to make or become swollen or congested with blood, water, etc. ➤➤ **engorgement** *n*.

engraft *or* **ingraft** *v* **1** to graft (a shoot) onto a stock. **2** to insert or implant (something). ➤➤ **engraftation** *n*, **engraftment** *n*.

engrain *v* see INGRAIN.

engrained *adj* see INGRAINED. ➤➤ **engrainedly** *adv*.

engrave *v* **1** to cut (a design or lettering) on metal or stone, *esp* with a sharp tool. **2** to cut a design or lettering on (a hard surface). **3** to impress (something) deeply on somebody's mind. ➤➤ **engraver** *n*.

engraving *n* **1** a print made from an engraved printing surface. **2** the art of cutting designs on hard surfaces, *esp* to make prints.

engross *v* **1** to occupy all the time and attention of. **2** to prepare the final text of (an official document). ➤➤ **engrosser** *n*, **engrossment** *n*.

engulf *v* **1** to flow over and completely cover. **2** to overwhelm. ➤➤ **engulfment** *n*.

enhance *v* to improve the value, desirability, or attractiveness of. ➤➤ **enhancement** *n*, **enhancer** *n*.

enharmonic *adj* denoting notes with different names, e.g. A flat and G sharp, that sound the same on keyboard instruments but are slightly different on string and wind instruments. ➤➤ **enharmonically** *adv*.

enigma *n* somebody or something hard to understand or explain; a puzzle or mystery. ➤➤ **enigmatic** *adj*, **enigmatical** *adj*, **enigmatically** *adv*.

enjambment *or* **enjambement** /in'jam(b)mənt/ *n* the running over of a sentence from one verse or couplet into another.

enjoin *v formal* **1** to order (somebody) to do something. **2** to impose (a condition or course of action) on somebody. **3** to forbid (somebody) from doing something by law.

enjoy *v* **1** to take pleasure or satisfaction in. **2a** to have the use or benefit of. **b** to experience (something desirable). ✱ **enjoy oneself** to take pleasure in what one is doing; to have fun. ➤➤ **enjoyable** *adj*, **enjoyableness** *n*, **enjoyably** *adv*, **enjoyment** *n*.

enlarge *v* **1** to make or become larger. **2** to reproduce in a larger form, *esp* by making a photographic enlargement. **3** (*often* + on/upon) to speak or write at length; to elaborate. ➤➤ **enlarger** *n*.

enlargement *n* **1** a photographic print that is larger than the negative or larger than an earlier print. **2** the act of enlarging or the state of being enlarged.

enlighten *v* to give knowledge or spiritual insight to; to cause to understand.

enlightened *adj* rational, well-informed, and free from prejudice.

enlightenment *n* **1** (**the Enlightenment**) an 18th-cent. movement marked by a belief in universal human progress and the importance of reason and the sciences. **2** the act of enlightening or the state of being enlightened.

enlist *v* **1** to enrol for duty in the armed forces. **2a** to secure the support and aid of (somebody). **b** to secure and employ (resources, services, etc) in advancing a cause, interest, or venture. ➤➤ **enlister** *n*, **enlistment** *n*.

enlisted man *n* a member of the US armed forces ranking below a commissioned or warrant officer.

enliven *v* **1** to make more lively or interesting. **2** to make more cheerful or bright. ➤➤ **enlivenment** *n*.

en masse /onh 'mas/ *adv* in a body; as a whole.

enmesh *v* to catch or entangle in or as if in a net. ➤➤ **enmeshment** *n*.

enmity *n* (*pl* **-ies**) a feeling or state of hatred, hostility, or ill will, e.g. between rivals or enemies.

ennoble *v* **1** to make finer or more dignified. **2** to raise to the rank of the nobility. ➤➤ **ennoblement** *n*.

ennui *n* weariness and dissatisfaction resulting from lack of interest or boredom.

enology *n NAm* see OENOLOGY.

enophile *n NAm* see OENOPHILE.

enormity *n* (*pl* **-ies**) **1** the quality or state of being enormous. **2** great wickedness. **3** a terribly wicked or evil act.

enormous *adj* marked by extraordinarily great size, number, or degree. ➤➤ **enormously** *adv*, **enormousness** *n*.

enough[1] *adj* fully adequate in quantity, number, or degree.

enough[2] *adv* **1** to a fully adequate degree: *This hasn't been cooked long enough.* **2** to a tolerable or moderate degree: *He understands well enough.*

enough[3] *pron* (*pl* **enough**) a sufficient quantity or number.

en passant /onh pa'sonh/ *adv* in passing; by the way.

enprint *n* a standard size of photographic print produced from a negative.

enquire *or* **inquire** *v* **1** to seek information by questioning; to ask. **2** (*often* + into) to make an investigation. ✱ **enquire after** to ask about the health, etc of (somebody). ➤➤ **enquirer** *n*, **enquiring** *adj*, **enquiringly** *adv*.

Usage note

enquire *or* inquire? *Enquire* is the commoner British English spelling; *inquire* is generally used in American English.

enquiry *or* **inquiry** *n* (*pl* **-ies**) **1** a request for information. **2** a systematic investigation, *esp* of a matter of public concern.

enrage *v* to make very angry.

enrapture *v* to fill with delight.

enrich *v* **1** to make wealthy or wealthier. **2** to improve or enhance. **3a** to make (soil) more fertile. **b** to improve (a food) in nutritive value by adding nutrients. ➤➤ **enriched** *adj*, **enrichment** *n*.

enrol (*NAm* **enroll**) *v* (**enrolled, enrolling**) to enter on a list, roll, etc; *specif* to register as a member. ➤➤ **enrollee** *n*, **enroller** *n*.

enrolment (*NAm* **enrollment**) *n* **1** the act of enrolling or the state of being enrolled. **2** the number of people enrolled, *esp* at a school or college.

en route /on 'rooht/ *adv and adj* on or along the way.

en rule *n* in printing, a short dash measuring one en.

ensconce *v* to settle (e.g. oneself) comfortably or snugly.

ensemble[1] *n* **1** a group that works together as a whole, e.g.: **a** a complete outfit of matching garments. **b** (*used as sing. or pl*) a group of actors, players, singers, or dancers who perform together on a roughly equal footing. **c** a section involving all the performers. **2** the quality of togetherness in performance.

ensemble[2] *adv* all together.

enshrine *v* **1** to enclose in or as if in a shrine. **2** to preserve as sacred and protect from change. ⋙ **enshrinement** *n.*

enshroud *v* to cover and conceal completely.

ensign *n* **1** a flag that is flown, e.g. by a ship, as the symbol of nationality. **2** a commissioned officer of the lowest rank in the US navy or, formerly, in the British infantry. **3** in former times, a standard-bearer.

enslave *v* to reduce to slavery; to subjugate. ⋙ **enslavement** *n,* **enslaver** *n.*

ensnare *v* to catch in or as if in a snare. ⋙ **ensnarement** *n.*

ensue *v* (**ensues, ensued, ensuing**) to take place afterwards or as a result.

en suite /on 'sweet/ *adv and adj* of a room: opening off or into, and forming a single unit with, another room.

ensure *v* to make (something) sure or certain.

ENT *abbr* ear, nose, and throat.

-ent *suffix* **1** forming adjectives, with the meaning: performing a specified action or being in a specified condition: *astringent; convenient.* **2** forming nouns, denoting: an agent that performs a specified action or causes a specified process: *regent; nutrient.*

entablature *n* in classical architecture, the upper section of a wall or storey, usu supported on columns and consisting of an architrave, a frieze, and a cornice.

entail[1] *v* **1** to involve or imply as a necessary accompaniment or result. **2** to settle (property) so that sale is not permitted and inheritance is limited to a specified category of heirs. ⋙ **entailer** *n,* **entailment** *n.*

entail[2] *n* **1** an instance of entailing property. **2** property that has been entailed.

entangle *v* **1** to cause to become tangled, complicated, or confused. **2** to involve in a difficult situation. ⋙ **entanglement** *n,* **entangler** *n.*

entente *n* a friendly relationship between two or more countries; an informal international agreement.

enter *v* **1a** to go or come into (a place). **b** to pierce or penetrate (e.g. flesh). **c** to come onto the stage in a play. **2** to record (a piece of information) in a diary, account, computer file etc. **3** to become a member of or an active participant in (something). **4** to register as candidate in a competition. **5** (+ into/on/upon) to begin to embark on something. ✱ **enter into 1** to make oneself a party to or in (e.g. an agreement). **2** to play a part or be a factor in. **3** to participate or share in.

enteric *adj* relating to the intestines.

enteritis *n* inflammation of the intestines, *esp* the lower part of the small intestine, usu marked by diarrhoea.

enterprise *n* **1** a difficult or complicated project or undertaking. **2** a business organization. **3** readiness to engage in enterprises; boldness and initiative. ⋙ **enterpriser** *n.*

enterprising *adj* marked by boldness and initiative; resourceful. ⋙ **enterprisingly** *adv.*

entertain *v* **1** to give enjoyment or amusement to. **2** to show hospitality to. **3** to consider or have in one's mind (an idea, doubt, suggestion, etc). ⋙ **entertaining** *adj.*

entertainer *n* a person whose job is to entertain people, e.g. a singer or comedian.

entertainment *n* **1** something that is enjoyable to watch or take part in. **2** the act of entertaining somebody or something.

enthral (*NAm* **enthrall**) *v* (**enthralled, enthralling**) **1** to hold the complete interest and attention of; to captivate. **2** *archaic* to enslave. ⋙ **enthralment** *n.*

enthrone *v* **1** to place, *esp* ceremonially, on a throne. **2** to assign supreme virtue or value to. ⋙ **enthronement** *n.*

enthuse *v* **1** to make enthusiastic. **2** to show enthusiasm.

enthusiasm *n* **1** keen and eager interest and admiration. **2** an object of enthusiasm. **3** *archaic* excessive display of religious emotion.

enthusiast *n* **1** somebody ardently attached to a cause or pursuit. **2** somebody who is excessively zealous in their religious views. ⋙ **enthusiastic** *adj,* **enthusiastically** *adv.*

entice *v* to tempt or persuade by arousing hope or desire. ⋙ **enticement** *n,* **enticer** *n,* **enticing** *adj,* **enticingly** *adv.*

entire *adj* **1** having no element or part left out; whole. **2** total or absolute. **3** intact. ⋙ **entireness** *n.*

entirely *adv* **1** wholly or completely. **2** in an exclusive manner; solely.

entirety *n* **1** the state of being entire or complete. **2** the whole or total.

entitle *v* **1** to give a title to. **2** to give the right to do or have something. ⋙ **entitlement** *n.*

entity *n* (*pl* **-ies**) something that has separate and distinct existence.

entomb *v* **1** to place (e.g. a body) in a tomb. **2** to cover or hide as if in a tomb. ⋙ **entombment** *n.*

entomology *n* a branch of zoology that deals with insects. ⋙ **entomological** *adj,* **entomologist** *n.*

entourage *n* (*used as sing. or pl*) a group of attendants or associates, *esp* of a famous or important person.

entr'acte *n* **1** the interval between two acts of a play or opera. **2** a dance, piece of music, or dramatic entertainment performed in this interval.

entrails *pl n* internal parts, *esp* the intestines.

entrain *v* to board or put on board a train. ⋙ **entrainment** *n.*

entrance[1] /'entrəns/ *n* **1** the act or an instance of entering. **2** a means or place of entry. **3** power, right, or permission to enter.

entrance[2] /in'trahns/ *v* **1** to fill (somebody) with delight or wonder. **2** to put into a trance. ⋙ **entrancement** *n,* **entrancing** *adj.*

entrant *n* somebody who enters a contest, profession, etc.

entrap *v* (**entrapped, entrapping**) **1** to catch in or as if in a trap. **2** to lure or trick into making a compromising statement or committing a crime. ⋙ **entrapment** *n.*

entreat *v* **1** to beg or plead with (somebody). **2** to request (something) urgently or earnestly. ⋙ **entreatingly** *adv,* **entreatment** *n.*

entreaty *n* (*pl* **-ies**) a humble or heartfelt plea.

entrechat *n* a leap in which a ballet dancer repeatedly crosses his or her feet and beats them together.

entrecôte *n* a steak cut from a boned sirloin of beef.

entrée *or* **entree** *n* **1a** *chiefly Brit* a dish served between the fish and meat courses of a formal dinner or before the main course. **b** the principal dish of a meal. **2** right of entry or access.

entrench *or* **intrench** *v* **1** to establish (something) firmly and solidly, *esp* so that it is difficult to change. **2** to dig and occupy trenches, or place (troops) in trenches, for defence. ➤➤ **entrenchment** *n.*

entre nous /ˌontrə 'nooh/ *adv* between ourselves; confidentially.

entrepôt *n* a seaport, warehouse, or other intermediary centre of trade and transshipment.

entrepreneur *n* somebody who organizes, manages, and assumes the risks of a business or enterprise. ➤➤ **entrepreneurial** *adj,* **entrepreneurship** *n.*

entropy *n* **1** a measure of the amount of energy that is unavailable for doing work in a thermodynamic system. **2** the degree to which the particles of a thermodynamic system are randomly arranged, which gives a measure of the amount of disorder in the system. ➤➤ **entropic** *adj.*

entrust *or* **intrust** *v* **1** (+ with) to give (somebody) the responsibility to look after or deal with something. **2** (+ to) to put (something) into somebody's care. ➤➤ **entrustment** *n.*

entry *n* (*pl* **-ies**) **1** the act of entering; entrance. **2** the right or privilege of entering. **3** a door, gate, hall, or other place of entrance. **4a** a record made in a diary, account book, index, etc. **b** a headword in a reference book, often with the accompanying definition or article. **5** a person, thing, or group entered in a contest; an entrant.

entryism *n* the practice of infiltrating a political party in order to influence its policy from within. ➤➤ **entryist** *n and adj.*

entry-level *adj* denoting the basic model in a range of e.g. computers, designed for new users who may later progress to more sophisticated equipment.

Entryphone *n trademark* an intercom system at the entrance to a building, which visitors use to identify themselves.

entwine *v* to twine together or round.

E number *n* a number with the letter E in front of it, used in the lists of ingredients on food packaging to denote a particular additive.

enumerate *v* **1** to list or name one by one. **2** to count up. ➤➤ **enumerable** *adj,* **enumeration** *n,* **enumerative** *adj.*

enumerator *n Brit* a person employed to issue and collect census forms.

enunciate *v* **1** to articulate distinctly. **2** to state or formulate precisely or systematically. ➤➤ **enunciation** *n,* **enunciative** *adj,* **enunciator** *n.*

enure *v* see INURE.

enuresis *n* an involuntary discharge of urine. ➤➤ **enuretic** *adj and n.*

envelop *v* (**enveloped, enveloping**) to wrap or surround completely with or as if with a covering. ➤➤ **envelopment** *n.*

Usage note

envelop *or* **envelope**? These two words are related and sometimes confused. *Envelop* (always pronounced with the stress on the second syllable *-vel-*) is a verb: *Fog envelops the city; enveloped in a huge black cloak. Envelope* (always pronounced with the stress on the first syllable *en-*) is a noun: *She opened the sealed envelope and drew out the winner's name.*

envelope *n* **1** a flat container, usu of folded and gummed paper, e.g. for a letter. **2** a wrapper, cover, or casing, e.g. the gasbag of an airship. **3** an enclosing membrane or other natural covering. **4** the performance limits of a machine, aircraft, etc.

Usage note

envelope *or* envelop? See note at ENVELOP.

envenom *v* **1** to put poison into or onto. **2** to fill with bitterness.

enviable *adj* worthy of envy; highly desirable. ➤➤ **enviableness** *n,* **enviably** *adv.*

envious *adj* feeling or showing envy. ➤➤ **enviously** *adv,* **enviousness** *n.*

environ *v formal* to encircle or surround.

environment *n* **1** the objects or conditions by which somebody or something is surrounded. **2** the natural surroundings and other external factors that act upon an organism, an ecological community, or plant and animal life in general. ➤➤ **environmental** *adj,* **environmentally** *adv.*

environmentalism *n* **1** concern about the protection or quality of the natural environment. **2** a theory that views environment rather than heredity as the important factor in human development. ➤➤ **environmentalist** *n.*

environmentally-friendly *adj* causing or said to cause no harm to the environment.

environment-friendly *adj* = ENVIRONMENTALLY-FRIENDLY.

environs *pl n* the neighbourhood surrounding something, *esp* a town.

envisage *v* **1** to have a mental picture of; to visualize. **2** to consider as a possibility in the future.

envision *v chiefly NAm* = ENVISAGE.

envoy[1] *or* **envoi** *n* the concluding words of a poem, essay, or book; *specif* a short fixed final stanza of a ballad.

envoy[2] *n* **1** a diplomatic agent, *esp* one who ranks immediately below an ambassador. **2** a messenger or representative.

envy[1] *n* (*pl* **-ies**) **1** resentful or admiring awareness of, and a wish to possess, an advantage enjoyed by another. **2** an object of such a feeling.

envy[2] *v* (**-ies, -ied**) to be envious of. ➤➤ **envier** *n,* **envyingly** *adv.*

enwrap *or* **inwrap** *v* (**enwrapped** *or* **inwrapped, enwrapping** *or* **inwrapping**) to wrap or envelop.

Enzed *n Aus, NZ, informal* **1** New Zealand. **2** an inhabitant of New Zealand. ➤➤ **Enzedder** *n.*

enzyme *n* a complex protein produced by living cells that promotes specific biochemical reactions without undergoing change itself. ➤➤ **enzymatic** *adj,* **enzymic** *adj.*

EOC *abbr Brit* Equal Opportunities Commission.

Eocene *adj* of the second geological epoch of the Tertiary period, lasting from about 56.5 to about 35.5 million years ago, and marked *esp* by the first appearance of horses and other hoofed animals. ➤➤ **Eocene** *n.*

eolian *adj NAm* see AEOLIAN.

eon *n* see AEON.

EP[1] *n* a record or compact disc with a playing time greater than a normal single.

EP[2] *abbr* **1** electroplate. **2** European Parliament.

ep- *prefix* see EPI-.

EPA *abbr NAm* Environmental Protection Agency.

epaulette (*NAm* **epaulet**) *n* an ornamental strip or pad attached to the shoulder of a garment, *esp* a military uniform.

épée /'epay/ *n* a fencing or duelling sword having a bowl-shaped guard and a rigid tapering blade with no cutting edge. ➤➤ **épéeist** *n*.

ephedrine *n* an alkaloid drug obtained from a desert shrub or made synthetically that is used *esp* to relieve hay fever, asthma, and nasal congestion.

ephemera *pl n* items of short-lived duration, use, or interest, *esp* those that subsequently become collectible.

ephemeral *adj* **1** lasting a very short time. **2** lasting one day only. ➤➤ **ephemerality** *n*, **ephemerally** *adv*.

epi- *or* **ep-** *prefix* **1** outer; external: *epidermis*. **2** besides; in addition: *epilogue*. **3** over; above: *epigraph*. **4** on; upon: *epiphyte*. **5** after; later: *epigone*.

epic[1] *adj* **1** of an epic. **2a** extending beyond the usual or ordinary, *esp* in size or scope. **b** heroic. ➤➤ **epical** *adj*, **epically** *adv*.

epic[2] *n* **1** a long narrative poem recounting the deeds of a legendary or historical hero. **2** a novel, film, etc that resembles an epic in length or content.

epicanthic fold *n* a fold of the skin of the upper eyelid extending over the inner corner of the eye and found among Mongolian peoples.

epicene *adj* **1** having characteristics typical of both sexes; hermaphrodite. **2** lacking characteristics typical of either sex; sexless. **3** effeminate.

epicentre (*NAm* **epicenter**) *n* the part of the earth's surface directly above the place of origin of an earthquake. ➤➤ **epicentral** *adj*.

epicure *n* somebody with sensitive and discriminating tastes, *esp* in food or wine. ➤➤ **epicurism** *n*.

Epicurean[1] *n* **1** a follower of the doctrine of the materialist Greek philosopher Epicurus (d.270 BC) who taught that pleasure, in the form of mental serenity and freedom from pain, was the highest good. **2** (*often* **epicurean**) an epicure. ➤➤ **Epicureanism** *n*.

Epicurean[2] *adj* **1** relating to the Greek philosopher Epicurus or his doctrine. **2** (*often* **epicurean**) relating to or suitable for an epicure.

epicycle *n* a circle that itself moves round the circumference of a larger circle. ➤➤ **epicyclic** *adj*.

epidemic[1] *n* **1** an outbreak of a disease affecting many individuals within a population or region at the same time. **2** a widespread outbreak or sudden rapid spread, *esp* of something undesirable. ➤➤ **epidemical** *adj*, **epidemically** *adv*.

epidemic[2] *adj* very or excessively prevalent.

epidemiology *n* **1** a branch of medicine that deals with the incidence and control of disease in a population. **2** the factors controlling the presence or absence of disease. ➤➤ **epidemiological** *adj*, **epidemiologically** *adv*, **epidemiologist** *n*.

epidermis *n* **1** the outer insensitive layer of the skin of a vertebrate animal that covers the dermis. **2** a thin protective surface layer of cells in higher plants. ➤➤ **epidermal** *adj*, **epidermic** *adj*, **epidermoid** *adj*.

epidiascope *n* a projector for producing images of both opaque objects and transparencies.

epididymis *n* (*pl* **epididymides**) a mass of coiled tubes at the back of the testis in which sperm is stored. ➤➤ **epididymal** *adj*.

epidural[1] *adj* situated on or administered outside the DURA MATER (outermost membrane covering brain and spinal cord).

epidural[2] *n* an injection of a local anaesthetic into the lower portion of the canal housing the spinal cord, *esp* to reduce the pain of childbirth.

epifauna *n* aquatic animals living on a solid surface, *esp* a hard sea floor: compare INFAUNA. ➤➤ **epifaunal** *adj*.

epigenesis *n* **1** in biology, development of an organism by gradual production of different parts from a single undifferentiated cell, e.g. a fertilized egg. **2** change in the character of a rock owing to outside influences. ➤➤ **epigenetic** *adj*.

epiglottis *n* a thin plate of flexible cartilage at the root of the tongue that folds back to cover the entrance to the larynx during swallowing. ➤➤ **epiglottal** *adj*, **epiglottic** *adj*.

epigone *n* (*pl* **epigones** *or* **epigoni**) an inferior follower or imitator. ➤➤ **epigonic** *adj*, **epigonous** *adj*.

epigram *n* **1** a short witty or satirical poem. **2** a concise, witty, and often paradoxical remark or saying. ➤➤ **epigrammatic** *adj*, **epigrammatical** *adj*, **epigrammatically** *adv*, **epigrammatist** *n*.

epigraph *n* **1** an engraved inscription. **2** a quotation at the beginning of a book, chapter, etc, suggesting its theme. ➤➤ **epigraphic** *adj*.

epigraphy *n* **1** epigraphs collectively. **2** the study of inscriptions, *esp* ancient inscriptions. ➤➤ **epigrapher** *n*, **epigraphist** *n*.

epilation *n* the loss or removal of hair. ➤➤ **epilator** *n*.

epilepsy *n* a disorder marked by disturbed electrical rhythms of the brain and typically manifested by convulsive attacks and sometimes loss of consciousness. ➤➤ **epileptic** *adj*, **epileptic** *n*.

epilimnion *n* (*pl* **epilimnia**) the warm, less dense, oxygen-rich upper layer of water in a lake: compare HYPOLIMNION.

epilogue *n* **1** a concluding section of a literary work that often comments on the main theme or reveals the later fate of the characters. **2** a speech addressed to the audience by an actor at the end of a play.

epiphany *n* (*pl* **epiphanies**) **1** (**Epiphany**) **a** the coming of the Magi to see the infant Christ. **b** 6 January, observed as a festival in the Christian Church in commemoration of this. **2** a sudden revelation of the essential nature or meaning of something. ➤➤ **epiphanic** *adj*.

epiphenomenon *n* (*pl* **epiphenomena**) **1** a secondary phenomenon accompanying and caused by another. **2** a mental process regarded as an epiphenomenon of brain activity. **3** an unrelated or unexpected symptom occurring during the course of a disease. ➤➤ **epiphenomenal** *adj*.

epiphyte *n* a plant that derives its moisture and nutrients from the air and rain and grows on another plant. ➤➤ **epiphytal** *adj*, **epiphytic** *adj*.

episcopacy *n* (*pl* **episcopacies**) **1** government of the Church by bishops or by a hierarchy. **2** = EPISCOPATE.

episcopal *adj* **1** of a bishop. **2** governed by bishops. **3** (**Episcopal**) Anglican; *esp* of an Anglican Church that is not the official national Church, e.g. in the USA or Scotland. ➤➤ **episcopally** *adv*.

episcopalian[1] *adj* **1** of the episcopal form of Church government. **2** (**Episcopalian**) of the Episcopal Church. ➤➤ **episcopalianism** *n*.

episcopalian[2] *n* **1** an adherent of the episcopal form of Church government. **2** (**Episcopalian**) a member of the Episcopal Church.

episcopate *n* **1** the office or term of a bishop. **2** a body of bishops.

episiotomy *n* (*pl* **episiotomies**) surgical enlargement of the opening of the vagina during childbirth, to prevent tearing.

episode *n* **1** a distinct event that is part of a larger series, e.g. in history or in somebody's life. **2** an instalment of a serialized literary work, radio or television programme, etc.

episodic *adj* **1** made up of separate, *esp* loosely connected, episodes. **2** occasional or sporadic. ➤➤ **episodically** *adv.*

epistemology *n* the philosophical study of the nature, limits, and grounds of knowledge. ➤➤ **epistemological** *adj,* **epistemologically** *adv,* **epistemologist** *n.*

epistle *n* **1** a letter, *esp* a formal or lengthy one. **2** (**Epistle**) **a** any of the letters from the apostles adopted as books of the New Testament. **b** a reading from any of these books at a church service.

epistolary *adj* **1** of a letter. **2** carried on by letters. **3** written in the form of a series of letters.

epitaph *n* **1** a commemorative inscription on a tombstone or monument. **2** a brief statement commemorating a deceased person or past event.

epitaxy *n* the growth of one crystalline substance on another whose structure provides the orientation for that of the overlying layer. ➤➤ **epitaxial** *adj.*

epithalamium *n* (*pl* **epithalamiums** *or* **epithalamia**) a song or poem in celebration of a marriage. ➤➤ **epithalamic** *adj.*

epithelium *n* (*pl* **epithelia**) a thin layer of cellular tissue that covers an external or internal surface of the body, *esp* serving as a lining to hollow organs such as the intestines. ➤➤ **epithelial** *adj.*

epithet *n* **1** a descriptive word or phrase accompanying or replacing the name of a person or thing. **2** a disparaging word or phrase. ➤➤ **epithetic** *adj,* **epithetical** *adj.*

epitome *n* **1** a typical or ideal example. **2** a summary, *esp* of a literary work.

epitomize *or* **epitomise** *v* **1** to serve as a typical or ideal example of. **2** to summarize. ➤➤ **epitomist** *n,* **epitomization** *n.*

EPNS *abbr* electroplated nickel silver.

epoch *n* **1a** an extended period of time, usu characterized by a memorable series of events. **b** a division of geological time less than a period and greater than an age. **2** a memorable event or date; a turning point. ➤➤ **epochal** *adj.*

epoch-making *adj* uniquely or highly significant.

eponym *n* **1** a word or name, e.g. *cardigan* or *Hodgkin's disease,* derived from the name of a real or mythical person. **2** a person after whom something is named or believed to be named.

eponymous *adj* denoting a character in a film, book, etc, whose name is in its title.

EPOS *n* electronic point of sale, a system of recording every sale made in a shop, by means of bar coding and a laser scanner at the cash desk.

epoxide *n* an epoxy compound.

epoxy[1] *adj* of a chemical compound: containing a three-membered ring consisting of one oxygen and two carbon atoms.

epoxy[2] *n* (*pl* **-ies**) a substance containing an epoxy group, *esp* a tough resistant resin used as an adhesive or coating.

EPROM *abbr* erasable programmable read-only memory.

epsilon *n* the fifth letter of the Greek alphabet (Ε, ϵ), equivalent to roman e.

Epsom salts *pl n* hydrated magnesium sulphate used as a laxative.

equable *adj* **1** even-tempered or placid. **2** uniform or even, *esp* free from extremes or sudden changes. ➤➤ **equability** *n,* **equableness** *n,* **equably** *adv.*

Usage note

equable *or* **equitable**? These two words are sometimes confused. *Equable* means 'even-tempered' or 'free from extremes' and is frequently used to describe a person's character: *He has a very equable temperament. Equitable* means 'fair' or 'just': *an equitable system of taxation.*

equal[1] *adj* **1a** of the same quantity, size, degree, value, or status as another. **b** identical or equivalent for each member of a group, class, or society. **2** evenly balanced or matched. **3** (+ to) capable of meeting the requirements of (e.g. a situation or task).

equal[2] *n* somebody or something that is equal to another.

equal[3] *v* (**equalled, equalling,** *NAm* **equaled, equaling**) **1** to be equal, *esp* identical in value, to. **2** to achieve as much or reach the same standard as. **3** (*usu* + out) to become equal or identical.

equalise *v* see EQUALIZE.

equaliser *n* see EQUALIZER.

equality *n* the quality or state of being equal.

equalize *or* **equalise** *v* **1** to make equal. **2** to distribute evenly or uniformly. **3** to bring the scores level, e.g. in a football match. ➤➤ **equalization** *n.*

equalizer *or* **equaliser** *n* **1** somebody or something that makes things equal. **2** a goal, point, etc that brings the scores level in a game.

equally *adv* **1** in an equal or uniform manner; evenly. **2** to an equal degree; alike.

equal opportunity *n* (*also in pl*) nondiscrimination on the grounds of age, sex, race, etc, *esp* in the workplace.

equals sign *or* **equal sign** *n* a sign (=) indicating mathematical equality or logical equivalence.

equanimity *n* evenness of mind or temper, *esp* under stress. ➤➤ **equanimous** *adj.*

equate *v* **1** to treat or regard as equal, equivalent, or comparable. **2** to be or make equal or equivalent. ➤➤ **equatable** *adj.*

equation *n* **1** a statement of the equality of two mathematical or logical expressions. **2** an expression representing a chemical reaction quantitatively by means of chemical symbols. **3** a complex of variable factors. **4** the act of equating or the state of being equated. ➤➤ **equational** *adj,* **equationally** *adv.*

equator *n* **1** the notional circle around the earth that is equidistant from the two poles and divides the earth's surface into the northern and southern hemispheres. **2** = CELESTIAL EQUATOR.

equatorial *adj* **1** of, at, or near the equator of the earth. **2** of the climate: characterized by consistently high temperatures and rainfall throughout the year.

equerry *n* (*pl* **equerries**) **1** an officer of the British royal household in personal attendance on a member of the royal family. **2** formerly, an officer of a royal or noble household in charge of horses.

equestrian[1] *adj* **1** of horses or horse riding. **2** representing a person on horseback. ➤➤ **equestrianism** *n.*

equestrian[2] *n* a person who rides or performs on horseback.

equi- *comb. form* **1** equal: *equipoise.* **2** equally: *equidistant.*

equiangular *adj* having all, or all corresponding, angles equal.

equidistant *adj* equally distant. ➤➤ **equidistance** *n,* **equidistantly** *adv.*

equilibrate *v* to bring into or keep in equilibrium; to balance. ➤➤ **equilibration** *n.*

equilibria *n* pl of EQUILIBRIUM.

equilibrist *n* a person who performs balancing tricks, *esp* on a high wire.

equilibrium *n* (*pl* **equilibria**) **1** a state of balance between opposing forces, actions, or processes. **2a** a state of bodily or physical balance. **b** a calm and controlled intellectual or emotional state.

equine[1] *adj* of or resembling a horse or other member of the horse family. ➤➤ **equinely** *adv.*

equine[2] *n* a horse or other member of the horse family.

equinoctial *adj* **1** relating to or occurring at an equinox. **2** relating to the equator or celestial equator.

equinoctial point *n* = EQUINOX (2).

equinoctial year *n* = SOLAR YEAR.

equinox *n* **1** either of the two times each year, around 21 March and 23 September, when the sun crosses the equator and day and night are of equal length everywhere on earth. **2** either of the two points where the apparent path of the sun crosses the celestial equator.

equip *v* (**equipped, equipping**) **1** to provide with appropriate supplies. **2** to provide with the necessary abilities, intellectual capacity, emotional resources, etc. ➤➤ **equipper** *n.*

equipage *n* **1** *archaic* equipment. **2** formerly, a horse-drawn carriage with its servants.

equipment *n* **1** the articles, apparatus, or physical, mental, or emotional resources needed for a particular purpose. **2** the act of equipping somebody or something.

equipoise *n* **1** a state of equilibrium. **2** a counterbalance.

equitable *adj* **1** fair and just. **2** valid in equity as distinguished from law. ➤➤ **equitability** *n,* **equitableness** *n,* **equitably** *adv.*

Usage note

equitable *or* **equable**? See note at EQUABLE.

equitation *n formal* the act or art of riding on horseback.

equity *n* (*pl* **equities**) **1** justice according to natural law or right; fairness. **2** a system of justice orig developed on the basis of fairness to supplement the more rigid common law. **3** the value of a property, e.g. a mortgaged house, in excess of monetary claims against it. **4** (*usu in pl*) a share that does not bear fixed interest. **5** the value of shares issued by a company.

equivalent[1] *adj* **1** equal in force, amount, or value. **2** corresponding or virtually identical, *esp* in effect, function, or meaning. ➤➤ **equivalence** *n,* **equivalently** *adv.*

equivalent[2] *n* something or somebody that is equivalent.

equivocal *adj* **1** subject to two or more interpretations; ambiguous. **2** questionable or suspicious. ➤➤ **equivocality** *n,* **equivocally** *adv,* **equivocalness** *n.*

equivocate *v* to use equivocal language, *esp* with intent to deceive or avoid committing oneself. ➤➤ **equivocation** *n,* **equivocator** *n,* **equivocatory** *adj.*

ER *abbr* **1** *NAm* emergency room. **2** Queen Elizabeth.

Er *abbr* the chemical symbol for erbium.

er *interj* used to express hesitation or doubt.

-er[1] *suffix* forming the comparative of adjectives and adverbs: *hotter; quicker; unhappier.*

-er[2] *suffix* forming nouns, denoting: **1a** somebody or something that performs (the action specified): *recorder; eye-opener.* **b** something suitable for (the action specified): *broiler.* **2a** somebody or something associated with: *sixth-former.* **b** native or resident of: *Londoner.* **c** something that has: *threewheeler.*

era *n* **1** a historical period begun or typified by some distinctive figure or characteristic feature. **2** a major division of geological time that is subdivided into periods.

eradicate *v* to eliminate or do away with completely. ➤➤ **eradicable** *adj,* **eradication** *n,* **eradicative** *adj,* **eradicator** *n.*

erase *v* **1a** to obliterate or rub out (something written, painted, etc). **b** to remove (recorded matter) from a magnetic tape. **c** to delete (data) from a computer storage device. **2** to remove from existence or memory completely. ➤➤ **erasable** *adj,* **erasure** *n.*

eraser *n* something, e.g. a piece of rubber or a felt pad, used to erase pencil, chalk, etc marks.

Erastian *adj* of or advocating the doctrine of State supremacy over the Church in ecclesiastical affairs. ➤➤ **Erastian** *n,* **Erastianism** *n.*

erbium *n* a silver-white soft metallic chemical element of the rare-earth group.

ere *prep and conj literary* before.

erect[1] *adj* **1a** vertical in position; upright. **b** characterized by firm or rigid straightness, e.g. in bodily posture. **2** in a state of physiological erection. ➤➤ **erectly** *adv,* **erectness** *n.*

erect[2] *v* **1a** to build. **b** to fix in an upright position. **2** to establish; to set up. ➤➤ **erectable** *adj,* **erector** *n.*

erectile *adj* capable of undergoing physiological erection. ➤➤ **erectility** *n.*

erection *n* **1a** a process in which a previously limp body part, *esp* the penis, clitoris, or nipples, becomes firm through being dilated with blood, usu as a result of sexual stimulation. **b** an occurrence of this, *esp* in the penis. **2** something erected, *esp* a building. **3** the act of erecting something.

eremite *n* a Christian hermit or recluse. ➤➤ **eremitic** *adj,* **eremitical** *adj.*

erg *n* a unit of work or energy equal to the work done by a force of one dyne moving its point of application through one centimetre, equivalent to 10^{-7} joules.

ergo *adv* therefore or hence.

ergonomic *adj* designed to maximize productivity by minimizing effort and discomfort. ➤➤ **ergonomically** *adv.*

ergonomics *pl n* (*used as sing. or pl*) a science concerned with the relationship between human beings, machines and equipment and the working environment, and improving its efficiency. ➤➤ **ergonomist** *n.*

ergot *n* a disease of rye and other cereals caused by a fungus that produces a mass of dark threads in the ear of the plant. ➤➤ **ergotic** *adj.*

ergotism *n* a condition produced by eating grain or grain products infected with ergot and characterized by convulsions and gangrene of the fingers and toes.

erica *n* a low evergreen shrub of a genus that includes several species of heather and the heath family.

ericaceous *adj* **1** denoting a member of the family that includes the heaths, heathers, and rhododendrons. **2** of compost: suitable for plants that will not grow in limy soil, e.g. heathers and rhododendrons.

Erin *n archaic or literary* Ireland.

Erinys *n* (*pl* **Erinyes**) (*usu in pl*) = FURY (3).

Eritrean *n* a native or inhabitant of Eritrea. ⯮ **Eritrean** *adj.*

erk *n Brit, slang* a person holding the lowest rank in the air force or navy.

erl-king *n* in Germanic mythology, a malevolent being who carries children off to the realm of death.

ERM *abbr* exchange-rate mechanism.

ermine *n* (*pl* **ermines** *or* **ermine**) **1** a stoat that has a white winter coat usu with black on the tail. **2** the winter fur of this animal, used to trim ceremonial robes.

Ernie *n* in Britain, an electronic device used to draw the prizewinning numbers of Premium Bonds.

erode *v* **1** to wear away by the action of water, wind, glacial ice, etc. **2** to eat into slowly and destructively. **3** to diminish or destroy by degrees. ⯮ **erodible** *adj.*

erogenous *or* **erotogenic** *adj* of part of the body: sensitive to sexual stimulation.

Eros *n* **1** sexual love. **2** a desire for self-preservation and uninhibited enjoyment that in Freudian theory is one of two primal instincts.

erosion *n* eroding or being eroded. ⯮ **erosional** *adj,* **erosive** *adj.*

erotic *adj* concerned with or tending to arouse sexual desire. ⯮ **erotically** *adv.*

erotica *pl n* (*used as sing. or pl*) literature or art with an erotic theme or quality.

eroticise *v* see EROTICIZE.

eroticism *or* **erotism** *n* **1** an erotic quality or character. **2** sexual arousal or excitement. ⯮ **eroticist** *n.*

eroticize *or* **eroticise** *v* to give erotic qualities to. ⯮ **eroticization** *n.*

erotism *n* see EROTICISM.

erotogenic *adj* see EROGENOUS.

erotomania *n* **1** excessive sexual desire. **2** a psychiatric condition in which a person groundlessly believes that another person is in love with them. ⯮ **erotomaniac** *n.*

err *v* **1** to make a mistake. **2** to do wrong; to sin. ✱ **err on the side of** to show more (e.g. caution, generosity) than the situation strictly requires.

errand *n* **1** a short trip taken to attend to some business, often for somebody else. **2** the object or purpose of such a trip.

errant *adj* **1** *formal* doing wrong. **2** *formal* going astray. **3** *archaic* given to travelling, *esp* in search of adventure. ⯮ **errancy** *n,* **errantly** *adv,* **errantry** *n.*

errata *n* pl of ERRATUM.

erratic *adj* **1** characterized by lack of consistency or regularity; unpredictable. **2** having no fixed course. ⯮ **erratically** *adv,* **erraticism** *n.*

erratum *n* (*pl* **errata**) **1** an error in a printed work discovered after printing and shown with its correction. **2** (*in pl, used as sing. or pl*) a list of such errors and corrections inserted into a publication.

erroneous *adj* incorrect. ⯮ **erroneously** *adv,* **erroneousness** *n.*

error *n* **1a** a mistake or inaccuracy. **b** the state of being wrong in behaviour or beliefs. **2** the difference between an observed or calculated value and a true value, e.g. in statistics. ✱ **in error** by mistake. ⯮ **error-free** *adj,* **errorless** *adj.*

ersatz *adj* denoting an artificial and inferior substitute or imitation.

Erse *n* the Irish Gaelic language. ⯮ **Erse** *adj.*

erst *adv archaic* in the past; formerly.

erstwhile[1] *adj* former; previous.

erstwhile[2] *adv archaic* formerly; previously.

eruct *v formal* to belch. ⯮ **eructation** *n.*

erudite *adj* possessing or displaying extensive knowledge; learned. ⯮ **eruditely** *adv,* **erudition** *n.*

erupt *v* **1a** of a volcano: to release lava, steam, etc suddenly and usu violently. **b** to become suddenly active or violent; to explode. **c** to become violently angry. **2a** of a rash, spot, etc: to appear on the skin. **b** of a tooth: to emerge through the gum. ⯮ **eruptive** *adj.*

eruption *n* **1** the act of erupting. **2** a product of erupting, e.g. a rash or spot on the skin.

-ery *or* **-ry** *suffix* forming nouns, denoting: **1** quality of having (a specified mode of behaviour): *snobbery.* **2** art or practice of: *cookery; archery.* **3** place for doing, keeping, producing, or selling: *brewery; bakery.* **4a** collection or body of: *greenery.* **b** class of (specified goods): *ironmongery.* **5** state or condition of: *slavery.*

erysipelas *n* a feverish disease with intense deep red local inflammation of the skin, caused by infection by a streptococcal bacterium.

erythema *n* abnormal redness of the skin, usu occurring in patches, caused by widening of the blood vessels, e.g. after injury. ⯮ **erythematous** *adj.*

erythrocyte *n* any of the haemoglobin-containing cells that carry oxygen to the tissues and are responsible for the red colour of vertebrate blood; a red blood cell.

Es *abbr* the chemical symbol for einsteinium.

ESA *abbr* **1** *Brit* environmentally sensitive area. **2** European Space Agency.

escalade *n* an act of scaling the walls of a fortification with ladders.

escalate *v* to increase, or cause to increase, in amount, scope, intensity, or seriousness, usu rapidly. ⯮ **escalation** *n.*

escalator *n* a power-driven set of stairs on an endless belt that ascend or descend continuously.

escallonia *n* an evergreen shrub of the saxifrage family, grown as a garden ornamental.

escalope *or* **escallop** /ˈeskəlop/ *n* a thin boneless slice of meat coated with egg and breadcrumbs, and fried.

escapade *n* a wild, reckless, and often mischievous adventure, *esp* one that flouts rules or conventions.

escape[1] *v* **1a** to get away, *esp* from confinement or restraint. **b** of gases, liquids, etc: to leak out gradually. **2** to avoid a threatening evil, danger, etc. **3** to fail to be noticed or recalled by. **4** to be produced or uttered by, usu involuntarily. ⯮ **escapable** *adj,* **escapee** *n,* **escaper** *n.*

escape[2] *n* **1** the act or an instance of escaping. **2** a means of escape. **3** a key on a computer keyboard that is used e.g. to terminate or interrupt an operation.

escape clause *n* a clause in a contract setting out the conditions under which a party may be freed from its obligations under it.

escape key *n* = ESCAPE[2] (3).

escapement *n* **1** a device in a watch or clock that controls the motion of the cogwheels and delivers energy to the regulatory mechanism. **2** the mechanism of a typewriter that moves the carriage on one space when a key is struck. **3** a space left between the hammer and the strings of a piano that allows the strings to vibrate.

escape velocity *n* the minimum velocity that a moving body, e.g. a rocket, must have to escape from the gravitational field of the earth, moon, etc.

escape wheel *n* a notched wheel in the escapement of a watch or clock.

escapism *n* activity or entertainment intended to provide an escape from unpleasant reality or routine. ➤➤ **escapist** *adj and n.*

escapology *n* the theatrical art of escaping from restraints such as chains, handcuffs, or locked boxes. ➤➤ **escapologist** *n.*

escargot /e'skahgoh/ *n* (*pl* **escargots**) an edible snail, *esp* when prepared for eating.

escarpment *n* a long cliff or steep slope separating two comparatively level or more gently sloping surfaces.

eschatology *n* a branch of theology concerned with the ultimate destiny of the universe, *esp* Christian doctrine concerning death, judgment, heaven, and hell. ➤➤ **eschatological** *adj,* **eschatologist** *n.*

escheat *n* the reversion of property to a government or sovereign as a result of the owner's dying without heirs.

eschew *v formal* to avoid habitually, *esp* on moral or practical grounds.

escort[1] *n* **1** one or more people, cars, ships, etc accompanying somebody or something to give protection or show courtesy. **2** a person who accompanies another person socially, often in return for a fee.

escort[2] *v* to accompany as an escort.

escritoire /eskri'twah/ *n* a writing table or desk.

escrow *n* a deed, money, piece of property, etc deposited with somebody to be delivered to a designated person only upon the fulfilment of some condition. ✱ **in escrow** in trust as an escrow.

escudo *n* (*pl* **escudos**) the basic monetary unit of Portugal and Cape Verde.

esculent *adj formal* edible.

escutcheon *n* **1** a shield on which a coat of arms is displayed. **2** a protective or ornamental shield or plate, e.g. round a keyhole. ✱ **a blot on one's escutcheon** a stain on one's reputation. ➤➤ **escutcheoned** *adj.*

ESE *abbr* east-southeast.

-ese[1] *suffix* forming adjectives, with the meaning: of or originating in (a specified place or country): *Japanese.*

-ese[2] *suffix* (*pl* **-ese**) forming nouns, denoting: **1** inhabitant of: *Chinese.* **2a** language of: *Cantonese.* **b** *chiefly derog* speech, literary style, or diction peculiar to (the place, person, or group specified): *journalese.*

esker *or* **eskar** *n* a long narrow ridge of sand and gravel deposited by a stream flowing beneath a retreating glacier or ice sheet.

Eskimo *n* (*pl* **Eskimos** *or* **Eskimo**) **1** a member of any of a group of indigenous peoples of N Canada, Greenland, Alaska, and E Siberia. **2** either of the two main languages of these peoples, Inuit and Yupik. ➤➤ **Eskimoan** *adj.*

Usage note

Eskimo *or* Inuit? See note at INUIT.

ESL *abbr* English as a second language.

ESN *abbr* electronic serial number.

esoteric *adj* **1** understood by or restricted to a small group, *esp* of the specially initiated. **2** hard to understand. ➤➤ **esoterically** *adv,* **esotericism** *n.*

ESP *abbr* extrasensory perception.

espadrille *n* a flat sandal with a canvas upper and a rope sole.

espalier *n* **1** a fruit tree or ornamental shrub trained to grow flat against a railing, trellis, wall, etc. **2** a support on which such plants grow. ➤➤ **espalier** *v.*

esparto *n* either of two Spanish and Algerian grasses used *esp* to make rope, shoes, and paper.

especial *adj* **1** distinctively or particularly special. **2** unusually great or significant. **3** distinctly personal.

especially *adv* **1** in particular. **2** very much.

Usage note

especially *or* **specially**? *Especially* means both 'very' (*an especially nice surprise*) and 'in particular' (*I was impressed with all the performances, especially Nigel's*). *Specially* means 'in a special way' (*specially cooked using a totally new method*) and, more commonly, 'specifically, for a particular purpose' (*specially trained staff*). In the following sentence, however, either *especially* or *specially* could be used: *I made it especially* (or *specially*) *for you.*

Esperanto *n* an artificial international language largely based on words common to the chief European languages. ➤➤ **Esperantist** *n and adj.*

espionage *n* spying or the use of spies to obtain information.

esplanade *n* a level open stretch of paved or grassy ground, *esp* one designed for walking or driving along a shore.

espousal *n* the adoption or support of a cause or belief.

espouse *v* **1** to take up and support (a cause, belief, etc). **2** *archaic or formal* to marry. ➤➤ **espouser** *n.*

espresso *n* coffee brewed by forcing steam through finely ground coffee beans.

esprit /e'spree/ *n* vivacious cleverness or wit.

esprit de corps /də 'kaw/ *n* the spirit of fellowship, loyalty, and common purpose that unites the members of a group.

espy *v* (**-ies, -ied**) *literary* to catch sight of.

Esq. *abbr* Esquire.

-esque *suffix* forming adjectives, with the meaning: in the manner or style of; like: *statuesque; Kafkaesque.*

Esquimau *n* (*pl* **Esquimaux** *or* **Esquimau**) *archaic* = ESKIMO.

esquire *n* **1** *Brit* used instead of Mr as a man's courtesy title and usu placed in its abbreviated form after the surname. **2** formerly, a candidate for knighthood serving as attendant to a knight.

-ess *suffix* forming nouns, with the meaning: female: *actress; lioness.*

Usage note

With a few exceptions, the use of the feminizing suffix *-ess* (and similar suffixes such as *-ette* and *-trix*) has come to be seen as inappropriate, patronizing, or sexist in modern English. The 'male' term is treated as a neutral term with no sexual reference. A woman author should therefore be referred to as an *author,* not an *authoress,* a woman editor as an *editor,* not an *editress* or *editrix,* etc.

essay[1] *n* **1** a short piece of prose writing on a specific topic. **2** *formal* an effort or attempt. ➤➤ **essayist** *n,* **essayistic** *adj.*

essay[2] *v formal* to attempt.

essence *n* **1a** the real or ultimate nature of an individual being or thing, or its most important qualities, those that make it what it is. **b** somebody or something that embodies the fundamental nature of an idea, characteristic, etc. **2** an extract, essential oil, etc possessing the special qualities of a plant, drug, etc in concentrated form, or a preparation, e.g. a perfume or flavouring, made from such a substance. ✱ **in essence** basically, briefly, and most importantly. **of the essence** of the utmost importance.

essential[1] *adj* **1** of the utmost importance; necessary. **2** fundamental or inherent. **3** derived from or constituting an essence. ⯮ **essentiality** *n,* **essentially** *adv,* **essentialness** *n.*

essential[2] *n* something indispensable or fundamental.

essential element *n* a chemical element that is required for normal health or growth.

essential oil *n* a volatile oil that imparts a characteristic odour to a plant and is used *esp* in perfumes and flavourings.

Essex girl *n informal, derog* a stereotype of a young woman from Essex, SE England, as being vulgar, empty-headed, and promiscuous.

Essex man *n informal, derog* a stereotype of a man from Essex, SE England, as being affluent, vulgar, and right-wing.

est. *abbr* **1** established. **2** estimated.

-est[1] *suffix* forming the superlative of adjectives and adverbs: *nearest; dirtiest.*

-est[2] *or* **-st** *suffix* forming the archaic second person singular present of verbs (the form used with *thou*): *goest; canst.*

establish *v* **1** to make stable, secure, or permanent; to set on a firm basis. **2** to bring into existence. **3a** to place (somebody, e.g. oneself) in a permanent or firm position. **b** to gain full recognition or acceptance for. **4** to put beyond doubt; to prove. **5** to make (a Church or religion) a national institution supported by civil authority. **6** to cause (a plant) to grow in a place where it was previously absent. ⯮ **established** *adj,* **establisher** *n.*

establishment *n* **1** the act of establishing or the state of being established. **2a** a usu large organization or institution. **b** a place of business or residence with its furnishings and staff. **3** (**the Establishment**) (*used as sing. or pl*) the group of institutions and people held to control public life and to support the existing order of society.

establishmentarian *adj* of or favouring the established religion. ⯮ **establishmentarian** *n,* **establishmentarianism** *n.*

estate *n* **1** a large landed property, *esp* in the country, usu with a large house on it. **2** *Brit* **a** a part of an urban area devoted to a particular type of development. **b** a housing estate. **3** a property where wine is produced. **4a** the assets and liabilities left by somebody at death. **b** the whole of somebody's real or personal property. **5** a social or political class, e.g. the nobility, the clergy, or the commons (the three estates). **6** = ESTATE CAR.

estate agent *n chiefly Brit* an agent who is involved in the buying and selling of land and property, *esp* houses and flats. ⯮ **estate agency** *n.*

estate car *n Brit* a large motor car designed to carry passengers and bulky luggage, with a rear door opening onto a large luggage compartment.

estate duty *n* = DEATH DUTY.

esteem[1] *v* **1** to admire and respect. **2** *formal* to consider or deem.

esteem[2] *n* admiration and respect.

ester *n* a chemical compound formed by the reaction between an acid and an alcohol, usu with elimination of water.

esthete *n NAm* see AESTHETE.

esthetic *adj NAm* see AESTHETIC[1].

esthetics *pl n NAm* see AESTHETICS.

estimable *adj* worthy of esteem. ⯮ **estimableness** *n,* **estimably** *adv.*

estimate[1] *v* **1a** to determine roughly the size, value, or nature of. **b** to produce a statement of approximate cost. **2** to judge or conclude. ⯮ **estimative** *adj,* **estimator** *n.*

estimate[2] *n* **1a** a rough or approximate calculation. **b** a statement of the expected cost of a job. **2** an opinion or judgment of the nature, character, or quality of somebody or something.

estimation *n* **1a** the act or an instance of estimating. **b** the value, amount, or size arrived at by estimating. **2** = ESTIMATE[2] (2). **3** = ESTEEM[2].

estival *adj NAm* see AESTIVAL.

estivate *v NAm* see AESTIVATE.

Estonian *n* **1** a native or inhabitant of Estonia. **2** the Finno-Ugric language of Estonia. ⯮ **Estonian** *adj.*

estop *v* (**estopped, estopping**) in law, to impede, *esp* by estoppel.

estoppel *n* the legal principle that precludes people from denying or disproving facts they have previously stated to be true.

estradiol *n NAm* see OESTRADIOL.

estrange *v* (*often* + from) to alienate. ⯮ **estrangement** *n.*

estranged *adj* of a husband or wife: no longer living with his or her spouse.

estrogen *n NAm* see OESTROGEN.

estrus *n NAm* see OESTRUS.

estuary *n* (*pl* **-ies**) a sea inlet at the mouth of a river. ⯮ **estuarial** *adj,* **estuarine** *adj.*

Estuary English *n* a variety of British English used in London and neighbouring counties, containing the speech sounds of standard pronunciation modified by those of cockney and other local accents.

esurient *adj formal* hungry or greedy. ⯮ **esuriently** *adv.*

ET *abbr* extraterrestrial.

-et *suffix* forming nouns, denoting: **1** small or lesser kind of: *baronet.* **2** group of (the number specified): *octet.*

ETA *abbr* estimated time of arrival.

eta *n* the seventh letter of the Greek alphabet (Η, η), equivalent to roman ē.

e-tailer *n* a company that sells its product through the Internet. ⯮ **e-tailing** *n.*

et al *adv* and others.

etc *abbr* et cetera.

et cetera *adv* and other things, *esp* of the same kind; and so forth.

etceteras *pl n* unspecified additional items.

etch *v* **1** to produce (a picture or letters), *esp* on metal or glass, by the corrosive action of an acid. **2** to delineate or imprint clearly. ⯮ **etcher** *n.*

etching *n* **1** the art of producing pictures or designs by printing from an etched metal plate. **2** an impression from an etched plate.

ETD *abbr* estimated time of departure.

eternal *adj* **1** having infinite duration; everlasting. **2** *informal* incessant or interminable. **3** timeless. ⯮ **eternalize** *v,* **eternally** *adv,* **eternalness** *n.*

eternal triangle *n* a situation of conflict resulting from the emotional or sexual involvement of two people with one other person.

eternity *n* (*pl* **-ies**) **1** the quality or state of being eternal. **2** infinite time. **3** the eternal life after death. **4** *informal* a seemingly endless or immeasurable time.

eternity ring *n* a ring set with gemstones all around, usu given as a symbol of continuing or everlasting affection.

-eth[1] *or* **-th** *suffix* forming the archaic third person singular present of verbs: *goeth; doth.*

-eth[2] *suffix* see -TH[1].

ethane *n* a colourless, odourless gas of the alkane series of organic chemical compounds, obtained from petroleum or natural gas, and used *esp* as a fuel.

ethanol *n* = ALCOHOL (1).

ether *n* **1a** an inflammable liquid that vaporizes readily, used *esp* as a solvent and formerly as a general anaesthetic. **b** any of various organic compounds characterized by an oxygen atom attached to two alkyl groups. **2** *literary* the clear blue sky or upper regions of the atmosphere. **3** a medium formerly held to permeate all space and transmit electromagnetic waves, e.g. light and radio waves. ➤➤ **etheric** *adj.*

ethereal *adj* **1a** lacking material substance; intangible. **b** marked by unusual delicacy, lightness, and refinement. **2** *literary* celestial; heavenly. ➤➤ **ethereality** *n,* **etherealize** *v,* **ethereally** *adv,* **etherealness** *n.*

etherize *or* **etherise** *v* to treat or anaesthetize with ether. ➤➤ **etherization** *n,* **etherizer** *n.*

Ethernet *n trademark* a popular type of local area network connecting a number of computer systems.

ethic *n* **1** (*in pl, used as sing. or pl*) the principles of conduct governing an individual or a group. **2a** a set of moral principles or values. **b** (*in pl*) the moral uprightness of an action, judgment, etc. **3** (*in pl, used as sing.*) the study of the nature and basis of moral principles and judgments. ➤➤ **ethicist** *n.*

ethical *adj* **1** conforming to accepted, *esp* professional, standards of conduct or morality. **2** relating to ethics. **3** not connected with or investing in companies whose activities or products are felt to be harmful to society, the environment, etc. **4** of a drug: available to the general public only on prescription. ➤➤ **ethicality** *n,* **ethically** *adv,* **ethicalness** *n.*

Ethiopian *n* a native or inhabitant of Ethiopia and Eritrea. ➤➤ **Ethiopian** *adj.*

ethnic *adj* **1a** sharing or classed according to factors, e.g. race, culture, or language, held in common. **b** belonging to a particular group by birth or descent. **2** of a traditional, *esp* peasant or non-Western, culture. ➤➤ **ethnically** *adv,* **ethnicity** *n.*

ethnic cleansing *n* the systematic and often violent removal of all members of a particular ethnic group from a region or country.

ethnic minority *n* an ethnic group that constitutes a minority of the population of a country or region.

ethnocentric *adj* based on the attitude that one's own race, culture, etc is superior. ➤➤ **ethnocentrically** *adv,* **ethnocentricity** *n,* **ethnocentrism** *n.*

ethnography *n* the scientific description of races, peoples, cultures, etc. ➤➤ **ethnographer** *n,* **ethnographic** *adj,* **ethnographical** *adj,* **ethnographically** *adv.*

ethnology *n* a science that deals with races and peoples and their origin, distribution, relations, and characteristics. ➤➤ **ethnologic** *adj,* **ethnological** *adj,* **ethnologically** *adv,* **ethnologist** *n.*

ethos *n* the distinguishing character or guiding beliefs of a person, institution, etc.

ethyl *n* a chemical group (CH_3CH_2) derived from ethane.

ethyl alcohol *n* = ALCOHOL (1).

ethylene *n* a colourless inflammable gas found in coal gas and used *esp* in the synthesis of organic chemical compounds. ➤➤ **ethylenic** *adj.*

ethylene glycol *n* a thick liquid alcohol used *esp* as an antifreeze.

etiolate *v* **1** to bleach and alter the natural development of (a green plant) by excluding sunlight. **2** to make weak, pale, or sickly. ➤➤ **etiolation** *n.*

etiology *n NAm* see AETIOLOGY.

etiquette *n* the conventionally accepted standards of proper social or professional behaviour.

Etruscan *n* **1** a native or inhabitant of ancient Etruria. **2** the language used by the Etruscans. ➤➤ **Etruscan** *adj.*

et seq. *adv* **1** and the following one. **2** (*also* **et seqq.**) and the following ones.

-ette *suffix* forming nouns, with the meanings: **1** small or lesser kind of: *kitchenette.* **2** female: *usherette.* **3** imitation; substitute: *leatherette.*

étude /ay'toohd/ *n* a piece of music written primarily for the practice of a technique.

etyma *n* pl of ETYMON.

etymology *n* (*pl* **-ies**) the history of the origin and development of a word. ➤➤ **etymological** *adj,* **etymologically** *adv,* **etymologist** *n.*

etymon *n* (*pl* **etyma** *or* **etymons**) an earlier linguistic form from which later forms or words are derived.

EU *abbr* European Union.

Eu *abbr* the chemical symbol for europium.

eucalyptus *n* (*pl* **eucalyptuses** *or* **eucalypti**) **1** an Australasian evergreen tree of the myrtle family widely cultivated for its gum, resin, oil, and wood. **2** oil from the leaves of a eucalyptus tree, used medicinally.

eucaryote *n* see EUKARYOTE.

Eucharist *n* **1** the Christian sacrament in which consecrated bread and wine are consumed in accordance with Christ's injunctions at the Last Supper. **2** the consecrated bread and wine consumed in the Eucharist. ➤➤ **Eucharistic** *adj,* **Eucharistical** *adj.*

euchre[1] *n* a N American card game for two to four players, played with the 32 highest cards, the winner taking at least three out of five tricks.

euchre[2] *v* **1** to prevent from winning three tricks in euchre. **2** *NAm, informal* to cheat, trick, or outwit.

Euclidean *adj* (*also* **euclidean**) of the Greek mathematician Euclid (fl.300 BC), his geometry, or the three-dimensional space in which his geometry applies.

eugenics *pl n* (*used as sing. or pl*) a science dealing with the improvement of the hereditary qualities of a race or breed, e.g. by control of mating or careful selection of parents. ➤➤ **eugenic** *adj,* **eugenically** *adv,* **eugenicist** *n.*

eukaryote *or* **eucaryote** *n* any organism characterized by possessing cells with a nucleus, i.e. most living things except bacteria and some other minute forms: compare PROKARYOTE. ➤➤ **eukaryotic** *adj.*

eulogize *or* **eulogise** *v* to praise highly in speech or writing; to extol. ➤➤ **eulogizer** *n.*

eulogy *n* (*pl* **-ies**) **1** a speech or piece of writing in praise of somebody or something, *esp* of somebody who has recently died. **2** high praise. ➤➤ **eulogist** *n,* **eulogistic** *adj,* **eulogistically** *adv.*

Eumenides *pl n* a group of avenging Greek goddesses; the Furies.

eunuch *n* a castrated man.

euonymus *n* an evergreen shrub or small tree of a family including the spindle tree, typically having red fruits and hard wood.

eupepsia *n formal* **1** good digestion. **2** happiness or optimism. ➤➤ **eupeptic** *adj.*

euphemism *n* a mild, indirect, or vague expression substituted for an offensive or unpleasant one, e.g. *pass away* for *die.* ➤➤ **euphemistic** *adj,* **euphemistically** *adv.*

euphonious *adj* pleasing to the ear. ➤➤ **euphoniously** *adv.*

euphonium *n* a brass musical instrument resembling a tuba but smaller and having a higher range.

euphony *n* (*pl* **-ies**) **1** a pleasing or sweet sound, *esp* in speech. **2** the alteration of speech sounds for ease of pronunciation. ➤➤ **euphonic** *adj,* **euphonically** *adv.*

euphorbia *n* any of a genus of plants, including the spurges, that have a milky juice and usu green flowers.

euphoria *n* an intense or exaggerated feeling of well-being or elation. ➤➤ **euphoric** *adj,* **euphorically** *adv.*

Eurasian[1] *adj* **1** of mixed European and Asian origin. **2** of, growing in, or living in Europe and Asia.

Eurasian[2] *n* a person of mixed European and Asian origin.

eureka *interj* used to express triumph at a discovery.

eurhythmics (*NAm* **eurythmics**) *pl n* (*used as sing. or pl*) the art of harmonious bodily movement, *esp* through expressive timed movements in response to music.

Euro *adj informal* connected with Europe or the European Union.

euro *n* (*pl* **-os**) the single European currency used by some member countries of the European Union: compare ECU.

Eurobond *n* (*also* **eurobond**) a bond sold outside the country in whose currency it is issued.

Eurocentric *adj* concentrating on European issues, *esp* to the exclusion of those involving the rest of the world.

Eurocrat *n* (*also* **eurocrat**) *informal* a member of the administrative commission of the European Union.

Eurodollar *n* (*also* **eurodollar**) a US dollar held by a bank or other institution outside the USA, *esp* in Europe.

Euroland /'yooərohland/ *n* = EURO-ZONE.

Euro-MP *n* a Member of the European Parliament.

European[1] *adj* **1** of, from, or relating to Europe. **2** of European descent or origin. **3** relating to the European Union. ➤➤ **Europeanism** *n.*

European[2] *n* **1** a native or inhabitant of Europe or the mainland of Europe. **2** a person of European origin; a white person.

European Commission *n* the executive body of the European Union, which conducts economic relations with other countries or organizations.

European Council *n* an executive body of the European Union, made up of leaders of the member states.

European Currency Unit *n* = ECU.

European Union *n* an economic and political association of European states, including Austria, Belgium, Denmark, Finland, France, Germany, Greece, Ireland, Italy, Luxembourg, the Netherlands, Portugal, Spain, Sweden, and the UK.

Europhile *n* an admirer of Europe or the European Union.

europium *n* a silver-white metallic element of the rare-earth group.

Euro-sceptic *n* a person, *esp* a British politician, who is opposed to the European Union or the increase of its powers. ➤➤ **Euro-sceptic** *adj.*

Eurostar *n trademark* a high-speed rail service that links London with mainland Europe via the Channel Tunnel.

Eurotunnel *n trademark* the Channel Tunnel.

euro-zone /'yooərohzohn/ *n* the countries in which the euro is the official currency.

eurythmics *pl n NAm* see EURHYTHMICS.

Eustachian tube *n* (*also* **eustachian tube**) a tube connecting the middle ear with the throat, which allows the air pressure on both sides of the eardrum to be equalized.

eustasy *n* worldwide change of sea level brought about by movements of the sea bed, melting of ice sheets, etc. ➤➤ **eustatic** *adj.*

eutectic *adj* **1** denoting an alloy or other mixture that has the lowest possible melting or freezing point for a mixture of these constituents. **2** denoting the melting or freezing point of a eutectic alloy or mixture. ➤➤ **eutectic** *n.*

euthanasia *n* the act or practice of killing incurably sick or injured individuals for reasons of mercy.

eutrophic *adj* of a body of water: rich in dissolved nutrients, e.g. phosphates, but often shallow and seasonally deficient in oxygen: compare MESOTROPHIC, OLIGOTROPHIC. ➤➤ **eutrophication** *n,* **eutrophy** *n.*

eV *abbr* electron volt.

Eva /'eevə/ *n* = ELECTRONIC VIRTUAL ASSISTANT.

evacuate *v* **1a** to remove (a person or people) or withdraw, *esp* from a dangerous place. **b** to vacate (a dangerous place). **2** to discharge urine, faeces, etc from the body as waste. **3** to empty, *esp* to remove gas, water, etc from (something) to produce a vacuum in it. ➤➤ **evacuation** *n,* **evacuative** *adj.*

evacuee *n* a person evacuated from a dangerous place.

evade *v* **1** to get away from or avoid, *esp* by skill or deception. **2a** to avoid facing up to or answering. **b** to fail to pay (taxes, etc). ➤➤ **evadable** *adj,* **evader** *n.*

evaluate *v* to determine the amount, value, or significance of, *esp* by careful appraisal and study. ➤➤ **evaluation** *n,* **evaluative** *adj,* **evaluator** *n.*

evanescent *adj chiefly literary* tending to dissipate or vanish like vapour; ephemeral. ➤➤ **evanesce** *v,* **evanescence** *n.*

evangelical[1] *adj* **1** of or in accordance with the Christian message as presented in the four Gospels. **2** (*often* **Evangelical**) denoting a Protestant denomination emphasizing salvation by faith in the atoning death of Jesus Christ, personal conversion, and the authority of Scripture. **3a** marked by fundamentalism. **b** = LOW CHURCH. **4** evangelistic; zealous. ➤➤ **evangelicalism** *n,* **evangelically** *adv.*

evangelical[2] *n* (*often* **Evangelical**) a member of an evangelical denomination.

evangelise *v* see EVANGELIZE.

evangelism *n* **1** the spreading of the Christian gospel in an effort to bring about personal conversion. **2** militant or crusading zeal, *esp* in support of a cause.

evangelist *n* **1** (*often* **Evangelist**) a writer of any of the four Gospels. **2** a person who preaches the

Christian gospel and seeks to convert. **3** a person with crusading zeal. ➤➤ **evangelistic** *adj*, **evangelistically** *adv.*

evangelize *or* **evangelise** *v* to preach the Christian gospel to (somebody), *esp* with the intention of converting them to Christianity. ➤➤ **evangelization** *n*, **evangelizer** *n.*

evaporate *v* **1** to change from liquid to vapour. **2** to disappear or fade. ➤➤ **evaporable** *adj*, **evaporation** *n*, **evaporative** *adj*, **evaporator** *n.*

evaporated milk *n* unsweetened milk concentrated by partial evaporation, usu sold in tins.

evasion *n* the act, an instance, or a means of evading something or somebody.

evasive *adj* **1** intended to avoid something. **2** tending to avoid committing oneself; equivocal or indirect. ➤➤ **evasively** *adv*, **evasiveness** *n.*

eve *n* **1** the evening or the day before a special day, *esp* a religious holiday. **2** the period immediately preceding an event. **3** *chiefly literary* the evening.

even[1] *adj* **1a** having a horizontal surface; flat or level. **b** without break or irregularity; smooth. **c** in the same plane or line: *even with the ground.* **2a** without variation; uniform. **b** of a person's temper: calm; equable. **3a** equal. **b** fair. **c** in equilibrium; balanced. **4** of a number: exactly divisible by two. **5** fifty-fifty: *an even chance.* ✱ **be/get even with somebody** to have exacted or exact revenge on somebody. ➤➤ **evenly** *adv*, **evenness** *n.*

even[2] *v* (*often* + up/out) to make or become even. ➤➤ **evener** *n.*

even[3] *adv* **1** used to emphasize the contrast with a less strong possibility: *I can't even walk, let alone run.* **2** used to emphasize the comparative degree: *even better than last time.* **3** used to express nonfulfilment of expectation: *They didn't even apologize.* ✱ **even as** at the very time that. **even if** in spite of the possibility or fact that. **even now 1** at this very moment. **2** in spite of what has happened. **even so** in spite of that.

even[4] *n archaic or literary* the evening.

evenhanded *adj* fair; impartial. ➤➤ **evenhandedly** *adv*, **evenhandedness** *n.*

evening *n* **1a** the latter part of the day and the early part of the night. **b** an evening's activity or entertainment. **2** a late period, e.g. of somebody's life; the end.

evening dress *n* clothes for formal or semiformal evening occasions, *esp* a dress with a floor-length skirt.

evening primrose *n* a plant with pale yellow flowers that open in the evening and seeds that yield a medicinal oil.

evening star *n* the planet Venus, seen in the western sky at sunset.

even money *n* odds in betting that give the gambler the opportunity to win the sum staked.

evens *pl n Brit* = EVEN MONEY.

evensong *n* (*often* **Evensong**) the daily evening service of the Anglican Church.

event *n* **1a** a happening or occurrence, *esp* a noteworthy or important one. **b** a social occasion or activity. **2** any of the contests in a sporting programme. **3** a contingency or case. ✱ **after the event** after something happens or happened. **at all events** whatever may happen; anyway. **in the event** when something actually happens or happened. **in the event of/that** if the specified thing should happen. ➤➤ **eventless** *adj.*

eventful *adj* marked by noteworthy or exciting occurrences. ➤➤ **eventfully** *adv*, **eventfulness** *n.*

event horizon *n* in astronomy, the boundary of a black hole.

eventide *n chiefly literary* the evening.

eventing *n* the participation of a horse or rider in an equestrian competition, *esp* a three-day event. ➤➤ **eventer** *n.*

eventual *adj* taking place at an unspecified later time; ultimately resulting. ➤➤ **eventually** *adv.*

eventuality *n* (*pl* **-ies**) a possible, *esp* unwelcome, event or outcome.

eventuate *v formal* to result. ➤➤ **eventuation** *n.*

ever *adv* **1** (*often in negatives and questions*) at any time. **2** (*often in combination*) always: *an ever-growing need.* **3** used as an intensive: *ever since Monday; why ever not?* ✱ **ever so/such** *chiefly Brit, informal* used as an intensive.

Usage note

ever *and* **-ever**. *Whoever, however, whatever,* etc are written as one word when they mean 'any person who', 'in whichever way', or 'no matter what': *Whoever told you that is a liar.* But when *ever* is used in the intensifying sense of 'on earth', the two words are written separately: *Who ever can it be?*; *What ever did he mean by that?*

evergreen[1] *adj* **1** having leaves that remain green and functional throughout the year: compare DECIDUOUS (1). **2** always retaining freshness, interest, or popularity.

evergreen[2] *n* an evergreen plant.

everlasting *adj* **1** lasting or enduring for all time. **2** continuing for a long or indefinite time. **3** tediously persistent. **4** of a plant: retaining its form or colour for a long time when dried. ➤➤ **everlasting** *n*, **everlastingly** *adv*, **everlastingness** *n.*

evermore *adv archaic or literary* always; forever.

evert *v* to turn outward or inside out. ➤➤ **eversible** *adj*, **eversion** *n.*

every *adj* **1** all, without exception, of a group larger than two. **2** each or all possible: *She was given every chance.* **3** once in each: *Change the oil every 5000 miles.* ✱ **every bit as** just as; equally. **every now and then/again** at intervals; occasionally. **every other** each alternate. **every so often/every once in a while** at intervals; occasionally.

everybody *pron* every person.

everyday *adj* encountered or used routinely or typically; ordinary. ➤➤ **everydayness** *n.*

everyman *n* the typical or ordinary human being; = MAN IN THE STREET.

everyone *pron* every person.

everything *pron* **1a** all that exists. **b** all that is necessary or that relates to the subject. **2** something of the greatest importance; all that counts: *He meant everything to her.*

everywhere *adv* in, at, or to every place or the whole place.

every which way *adv NAm* in every direction; all over the place.

evict *v* to force out or expel, *esp* to remove (a tenant) from rented accommodation or land by a legal process. ➤➤ **eviction** *n*, **evictor** *n.*

evidence[1] *n* **1** an outward sign; an indication. **2** something that gives reason for believing or agreeing with something; *specif* information used, e.g. by a court, to arrive at the truth. ✱ **in evidence** to be seen; conspicuous. **turn King's/Queen's evidence** *Brit* said of an accomplice: to testify for the prosecution in court. ➤➤ **evidential** *adj*, **evidentially** *adv*, **evidentiary** *adj.*

evidence[2] *v* to offer evidence of; to show.

evident *adj* clear to the vision or understanding.

evidently *adv* **1** clearly; obviously. **2** on the basis of available evidence; as seems evident.

evil[1] *adj* **1a** not good morally; sinful or wicked. **b** associated with the Devil. **2a** causing discomfort or repulsion; offensive: *an evil smell.* **b** disagreeable: *an evil temper.* **3** pernicious or harmful. ⋙ **evilly** *adv,* **evilness** *n.*

evil[2] *n* **1a** wickedness; sin. **b** a force, *esp* of supernatural origin, doing moral harm and opposed to goodness. **2** something that is *esp* socially harmful or morally wrong.

evildoer *n* somebody who does evil. ⋙ **evildoing** *n.*

evil eye *n* a look believed to be capable of inflicting harm.

evince *v formal* to show clearly; to reveal. ⋙ **evincible** *adj.*

eviscerate *v* to disembowel. ⋙ **evisceration** *n.*

evocation *n* the act or an instance of evoking something.

evocative *adj* evoking something, e.g. a memory or image, strongly or poignantly. ⋙ **evocatively** *adv,* **evocativeness** *n.*

evoke *v* **1** to call forth. **2** to bring to mind or recollection. **3** to summon (a spirit, etc) by invocation. ⋙ **evoker** *n.*

evolution *n* **1** a theory that the various existing types of animals and plants are derived from preexisting types by natural selection. **2a** a process of change and development, *esp* from a lower state to a higher state. **b** a process of gradual and relatively peaceful social, political, economic, etc advance. **3** in chemistry, the action of forming and giving something off; emission. **4** a set of prescribed movements, e.g. in a dance. ⋙ **evolutional** *adj,* **evolutionary** *adj.*

evolutionism *n* the theory of the evolution of animals and plants by natural selection, or belief in this theory. ⋙ **evolutionist** *n and adj.*

evolve *v* **1** to work out or develop gradually. **2** to produce (e.g. an organ) by natural evolutionary processes. **3** in chemistry, to give off (gas, heat, etc). ⋙ **evolvable** *adj,* **evolvement** *n.*

ewe *n* the female of the sheep or a related animal.

ewer *n* a wide-mouthed pitcher or jug, *esp* one used formerly to hold water for washing.

ex[1] *prep* **1** from a specified place or source. **2a** said of shares etc: without an indicated value or right. **b** free of charges until the time of removal from (a place): *ex dock.*

ex[2] *n informal* a former spouse, boyfriend, or girlfriend.

ex-[1] *prefix* **1** out of; outside: *exclude; exodus.* **2** to cause to be: *exacerbate; exalt.* **3** to deprive of: *expropriate; excommunicate.* **4** former: *the ex-president.*

ex-[2] *prefix* see EXO-.

exa- *comb. form* forming words, denoting: million million million (10^{18}).

exacerbate *v* to make worse; to aggravate. ⋙ **exacerbation** *n.*

exact[1] *adj* **1** marked by complete accordance with fact; precise or accurate. **2** marked by thorough consideration or minute measurement of small factual details. ⋙ **exactitude** *n,* **exactness** *n.*

exact[2] *v* to demand and obtain by force, threats, etc. ⋙ **exactable** *adj,* **exacter** *n,* **exactor** *n.*

exacting *adj* making rigorous demands, *esp* requiring careful attention and precise accuracy. ⋙ **exactingly** *adv,* **exactingness** *n.*

exaction *n* **1** the act or an instance of exacting something; extortion. **2** something exacted, *esp* a fee or contribution demanded with severity or injustice.

exactly *adv* **1** altogether; entirely. **2** used to express complete agreement: *'He must have cheated.' 'Exactly'.*

exaggerate *v* **1** to say or believe that (something) is greater, better, etc than it is. **2** to make greater or more pronounced than normal; to overemphasize. ⋙ **exaggeratedly** *adv,* **exaggeration** *n.*

exalt *v* **1** to raise (something or somebody) high, *esp* in rank, power, or character. **2** to praise (somebody or something) highly; to glorify.

exaltation *n* **1** an intense or excessive sense of well-being, power, or importance. **2** the act or an instance of exalting.

exam *n* an examination, *esp* one associated with a course of study.

examination *n* **1** the act or an instance of examining. **2** an exercise, e.g. a set of questions, designed to test knowledge or proficiency, *esp* during or at the end of a course of study. **3** a formal interrogation, e.g. in a law court.

examine *v* **1a** to inspect closely. **b** to investigate the health of (a patient). **2a** to test the knowledge, proficiency, etc of (somebody), *esp* by a set of written or oral questions. **b** to interrogate (a witness, etc) closely. ⋙ **examinee** *n,* **examiner** *n.*

example *n* **1** something representative of all of the group or type to which it belongs. **2** somebody or something that may be copied by other people. **3** a punishment inflicted as a warning to others, or the recipient of such a punishment. **4** a problem to be solved to illustrate a rule, e.g. in arithmetic. ✱ **for example** as an example or illustration.

exasperate *v* to anger or irritate intensely. ⋙ **exasperating** *adj,* **exasperation** *n.*

ex cathedra *adv and adj* **1** with authority. **2** in the Roman Catholic Church, with papal authority and therefore infallibly true.

excavate *v* **1** to form a cavity or hole in. **2** to form (something, e.g. a hole or tunnel) by hollowing or digging. **3** to dig out and remove (something, e.g. soil or earth). **4** to expose to view by digging away a covering. **5** to make holes or expose things by digging. ⋙ **excavation** *n,* **excavator** *n.*

exceed *v* **1** to be greater than or superior to (something). **2** to act or go beyond the limits of. **3** to extend beyond.

exceedingly *adv* very; extremely.

excel *v* (**excelled, excelling**) (*often* + at/in) to be superior to or surpass all others. ✱ **excel oneself** to do something particularly well, *esp* better than ever before.

excellence *n* **1** the state of being excellent. **2** (**Excellence**) = EXCELLENCY .

excellency *n* (*pl* **-ies**) (**Excellency**) used as a title for certain high dignitaries of State and Church.

excellent *adj* outstandingly good. ⋙ **excellently** *adv.*

except[1] *prep* with the exclusion or exception of (something or somebody). ✱ **except for 1** with the exception of (something or somebody). **2** but for (something or somebody).

except[2] *conj* only; but: *I would go except it's too far.*

except[3] *v* to take or leave out (somebody or something) from a number or a whole; to exclude.

excepting *prep* = EXCEPT[1].

exception *n* **1** the act or an instance of excepting somebody or something; exclusion. **2** somebody or something excepted, *esp* a case to which a rule does not apply. **3** question or objection. ✱ **take exception to** to object to (something).

exceptionable *adj* likely to cause objection; objectionable.

Usage note

exceptionable *or* **exceptional**? See note at EXCEPTIONAL.

exceptional *adj* **1** forming an exception; unusual. **2** not average; superior. ➤➤ **exceptionally** *adv.*

Usage note

exceptional *or* **exceptionable**? These two words are sometimes confused. *Exceptional* means 'extremely unusual' (*only under exceptional circumstances*) or 'outstanding' (*an exceptional student*). *Exceptionable* is a formal word meaning 'objectionable', 'offensive': *I was not the only one who found her remarks exceptionable.* See also note at UNEXCEPTIONAL.

excerpt[1] *n* a passage taken from a book, musical composition, etc, e.g. for quoting or performing.

excerpt[2] *v* to take (a passage) from something for quoting, copying, or performing.

excess *n* **1** an amount that is more than normal, prescribed, or desirable. **2** (*also in pl*) undue or immoderate indulgence; intemperance. **3** an amount an insured person agrees to pay towards a claim made on an insurance policy in return for a lower premium. **4a** (*used before a noun*) denoting an amount that is more than normal, etc: *excess baggage.* **b** underpaid: *excess postage.* ✱ **in excess of** more than.

excessive *adj* exceeding normal, proper, or desirable limits. ➤➤ **excessively** *adv,* **excessiveness** *n.*

exchange[1] *n* **1a** the act of giving one thing for another; a swap or transaction. **b** something given or received in exchange. **2** a brief interchange of words or blows. **3** change or conversion of one currency into another. **4 a** an organized market for trading in securities or commodities. **b** a centre or device controlling the connection of telephone calls between many different lines.

exchange[2] *v* **1a** to give (something) in return for something received as an equivalent. **b** of two parties: to give and receive (things of the same type). **2** to replace (goods) by other goods. ➤➤ **exchangeable** *adj,* **exchanger** *n.*

exchange rate *n* the price at which one currency may be exchanged for another.

exchequer *n* **1** (*often* **Exchequer**) *Brit* the department of state in charge of the national revenue. **2** a national or royal treasury.

excise[1] *n* an internal tax levied on the manufacture, sale, or consumption of a commodity within a country.

excise[2] *v* **1** to remove (something) by cutting it out, *esp* surgically. **2** to remove or delete (something, e.g. a passage of text). ➤➤ **excision** *n.*

exciseman *n* (*pl* **excisemen**) formerly, an officer who inspected and rated articles liable to excise, collected the money payable, and prevented smuggling.

excitable *adj* capable of being readily roused into a state of excitement or irritability. ➤➤ **excitability** *n,* **excitably** *adv.*

excite *v* **1a** to rouse (somebody) to strong, *esp* pleasurable, feeling. **b** to arouse (an emotional response). **c** to provoke or stir up (action, e.g. a rebellion). **2** to increase the activity of or produce a response in (an organ, tissue, etc); to stimulate. **3a** to induce a magnetic field or electric current in. **b** to induce (a magnetic field or an electric current). **4** to raise (an atom or a molecule) to a higher energy level. ➤➤ **excitation** *n,* **excitatory** *adj,* **excitement** *n,* **exciting** *adj,* **excitingly** *adv.*

excited *adj* **1** happy and emotionally aroused. **2** worried or agitated. **3** of an atom, molecule, etc: raised to a higher energy level. ➤➤ **excitedly** *adv.*

exclaim *v* to cry out or speak sharply, passionately, or vehemently.

exclamation *n* **1** the act or an instance of exclaiming. **2** the words exclaimed. ➤➤ **exclamatory** *adj.*

exclamation mark *n* a punctuation mark (!) principally used after an interjection or exclamation.

exclamation point *n NAm* = EXCLAMATION MARK.

exclosure *n* an area from which wild animals or other intruders are excluded, *esp* by fencing.

exclude *v* **1** to bar (somebody or something) from participation or inclusion. **2** to shut (somebody or something) out. **3** to expel (somebody), *esp* from a place or position previously occupied. ➤➤ **excludable** *adj,* **excluder** *n.*

exclusion *n* **1** the act or an instance of excluding somebody or something. **2** something that is not covered by a contract, insurance policy, etc. ➤➤ **exclusionary** *adj.*

exclusive[1] *adj* **1a** excluding or having the power to exclude. **b** limiting or limited to possession, control, use, etc by a single individual, group, etc: *an exclusive interview.* **2a** excluding others, *esp* those considered to be inferior, from participation, membership, or entry. **b** snobbishly aloof. **3** stylish and expensive. **4a** whole or undivided: *He gave her his exclusive attention.* **b** functioning independently and without assistance or interference; sole: *exclusive jurisdiction.* **5** not inclusive: *Monday to Friday exclusive.* ➤➤ **exclusively** *adv,* **exclusiveness** *n,* **exclusivity** *n.*

exclusive[2] *n* an interview, article, etc published by only one newspaper or broadcast by only one television channel or radio station.

excommunicate[1] *v* to deprive (somebody) officially of the rights of church membership. ➤➤ **excommunication** *n.*

excommunicate[2] *adj* excommunicated.

excommunicate[3] *n* a person who is excommunicated.

ex-con *n informal* a former convict.

excoriate *v* **1a** to wear away the skin of (somebody or something). **b** to abrade or wear away (skin, etc). **2** *formal* to censure scathingly. ➤➤ **excoriation** *n.*

excrement *n* faeces. ➤➤ **excremental** *adj.*

excrescence *n* **1** an excessive or abnormal outgrowth or enlargement. **2** *literary* an ugly or undesirable thing.

excreta *pl n* (*used as sing. or pl*) excrement.

excrete *v* to separate and discharge (waste) from the body or from living tissue. ➤➤ **excretion** *n,* **excretory** *adj.*

excruciating *adj* **1** causing great pain or anguish; agonizing or tormenting. **2** very intense; extreme. **3** very bad, irritating, or tedious. ➤➤ **excruciatingly** *adv.*

exculpate *v* to clear (somebody) from alleged fault, blame, or guilt. ➤➤ **exculpation** *n,* **exculpatory** *adj.*

excursion *n* **1** a short pleasure trip, e.g. for sightseeing. **2** (*used before a noun*) of or offered at a reduced rate for such a trip: *an excursion ticket.* ➤➤ **excursionist** *n.*

excursus *n* (*pl* **excursus** *or* **excursuses**) an appendix or digression that contains further discussion of some point or topic.

excuse[1] *v* **1a** to forgive entirely. **b** to overlook as unimportant. **2a** to seek pardon or make apology for. **b** to try to remove blame from (somebody, e.g. oneself). **3** to be an acceptable reason for; to justify. **4** to allow to leave; to dismiss. **5** *Brit* (*usu in passive*) to free from a duty. ✱ **be excused** *euphem* to go to the toilet. **excuse me** used to attract somebody's attention, to apologize for an interruption or mistake, or to ask to be allowed to pass. ⋙ **excusable** *adj*, **excusably** *adv*.

excuse[2] *n* **1a** something offered as grounds for being excused. **b** a false reason given in explanation of an action etc. **2** (*in pl*) an expression of regret for failure to do something or for one's absence. **3** *informal* a very poor example.

ex-directory *adj Brit* intentionally not listed in a telephone directory.

execrable *adj* detestable or appalling. ⋙ **execrably** *adv*

execrate *v* **1** to detest utterly; to abhor. **2** to declare (somebody or something) to be evil or detestable; to denounce. ⋙ **execration** *n*.

execute *v* **1** to carry out fully; to put completely into effect. **2** to put to death as a punishment. **3** to make or produce (a work of art, etc), *esp* by carrying out a design. **4** to do what is required to make (something) legally effective or valid. **5** to play or perform (something, e.g. a musical piece). **6** in computing, to run (a file, program, etc). ⋙ **executable** *adj*, **execution** *n*.

executioner *n* a person legally appointed to perform capital punishment.

executive[1] *adj* **1a** concerned with making and carrying out laws, decisions, etc. **b** concerned with the detailed application of policy or law rather than its formulation. **2** of, for, or being an executive. ⋙ **executively** *adv*.

executive[2] *n* **1** a person who holds a position of administrative or managerial responsibility. **2** a person or group that controls or directs an organization. **3** the executive branch of a government.

executor *n* a person appointed to carry out the provisions of another person's will.

executrix *n* (*pl* **executrices**) a female executor.

exegesis *n* (*pl* **exegeses**) an explanation or critical interpretation of a text, *esp* a biblical text. ⋙ **exegetic** *adj*, **exegetical** *adj*.

exegete *n* a person who practises exegesis.

exempla *n* pl of EXEMPLUM.

exemplar *n* somebody or something that serves as a typical or ideal example or model.

exemplary *adj* **1** deserving imitation; commendable. **2** of a punishment: serving as a warning. **3** serving as an example, instance, or illustration.

exemplify *v* (**-ies, -ied**) **1** to show or illustrate by example. **2** to be an instance of or serve as an example of; to typify or embody. ⋙ **exemplification** *n*.

exemplum *n* (*pl* **exempla**) an example, *esp* an anecdote or story that illustrates a moral point or supports an argument.

exempt[1] *adj* free from some liability or requirement to which others are subject.

exempt[2] *v* to make (somebody or something) exempt; to excuse. ⋙ **exemption** *n*.

exequy *n* (*pl* **-ies**) *formal* (*usu in pl*) a funeral ceremony.

exercise[1] *n* **1a** regular or repeated use of a part of the body, the senses, or the powers of the mind. **b** physical exertion for the sake of developing and maintaining bodily fitness. **2** something performed or practised in order to develop, improve, or display a specific power or skill. **3** something done for a particular purpose. **4** a manoeuvre or drill carried out for training and discipline. **5** the use of a specified power or right.

exercise[2] *v* **1** to engage in physical exertion for the sake of fitness. **2a** to use (a part of the body) repeatedly in order to strengthen or develop it. **b** to give exercise to (somebody or something). **3** to make (something) effective in action; to use or exert (it): *She chose to exercise her right to remain silent.* **4a** to engage the attention and effort of (somebody or something). **b** to cause anxiety, alarm, or indignation in. ⋙ **exercisable** *adj*, **exerciser** *n*.

exercise bike *n* a stationary piece of equipment that is pedalled like a bicycle for physical exercise.

exercise book *n* a booklet of blank, usu lined, pages used for written work in schools.

exert *v* **1** to bring (strength or authority) to bear, *esp* with sustained effort; to employ or wield. **2** to take upon (oneself) the effort of doing something. ⋙ **exertion** *n*.

exeunt *v* (*third person pl pres*) used as a stage direction to specify that all or certain named characters leave the stage.

exfoliant *n* a gently abrasive skin cream or cleaning device that removes dead skin cells.

exfoliate *v* **1** to cast (skin or bark) off in scales, layers, etc. **2** to remove surface cells, layers, etc from (the skin). **3** to shed scales, surface body cells, etc. ⋙ **exfoliation** *n*, **exfoliative** *adj*.

ex gratia /'grayshə/ *adj and adv* as a favour; not compelled by legal right.

exhale *v* **1** to breathe (something) out. **2** to give forth (gas or vapour); to emit. **3** to emit breath or vapour. ⋙ **exhalation** *n*.

exhaust[1] *v* **1a** to tire (somebody) out. **b** to consume entirely; to use up. **2a** to develop or deal with (a subject) to the fullest possible extent. **b** to try out the whole number of (possibilities, etc). **3a** to draw off or let out completely. **b** to empty by drawing off the contents; *specif* to create a vacuum in. ⋙ **exhauster** *n*, **exhaustible** *adj*, **exhausting** *adj*.

exhaust[2] *n* **1** used gas or vapour expelled from an engine. **2** the emission of such gases. **3** the pipe or system of parts through which such gases escape.

exhaustion *n* **1** extreme tiredness. **2** the act or an instance of exhausting.

exhaustive *adj* comprehensive; thorough. ⋙ **exhaustively** *adv*, **exhaustiveness** *n*.

exhibit[1] *v* (**exhibited, exhibiting**) **1** to show (a work of art, etc) publicly, *esp* for purposes of competition or information. **2** to show or display (a feeling, symptom, etc) outwardly, *esp* by visible signs or actions; to reveal or manifest. ⋙ **exhibitor** *n*.

exhibit[2] *n* **1** something exhibited. **2** something produced as evidence in a court of law.

exhibition *n* **1** a public showing, e.g. of works of art or objects of manufacture. **2** the act or an instance of exhibiting. **3** *Brit* a grant awarded, usu on merit, by a school or university to a student. ✱ **make an exhibition of oneself** to behave foolishly in public.

exhibitionism *n* **1** the act or practice of behaving so as to attract attention to oneself. **2** a compulsion to commit acts of indecent exposure. ⋙ **exhibitionist** *n*, **exhibitionistic** *adj*.

exhilarate *v* **1** to make (somebody) very happy or cheerful. **2** to enliven or invigorate (somebody). ⋙ **exhilarating** *adj*, **exhilaration** *n*.

exhort *v* to urge or advise (somebody) strongly. ⋙ **exhortation** *n*.

exhume *v* to disinter (something buried, *esp* a dead body). ⋙ **exhumation** *n*.

exigence *n* = EXIGENCY.

exigency *n* (*pl* **-ies**) *formal* **1** an exigent state of affairs; an emergency. **2** (*usu in pl*) such need or necessity as belongs to the occasion; a requirement.

exigent *adj formal* **1** requiring immediate aid or action. **2** exacting; demanding.

exiguous *adj formal* excessively scanty; inadequate; meagre.

exile[1] *n* **1** enforced or voluntary absence from one's country or home. **2** somebody who goes or is sent into exile. ➤➤ **exilic** *adj.*

exile[2] *v* to send into exile.

exist *v* **1a** to have being in the real world; to be. **b** to have being in specified conditions. **2a** to have life or the functions of vitality. **b** to live at an inferior level or under adverse circumstances.

existence *n* **1** the state or fact of existing or being. **2** a manner of living or being.

existent *adj* having being; existing.

existential *adj* **1** of, affirming, or grounded in existence. **2** of or relating to existentialism. ➤➤ **existentially** *adv.*

existentialism *n* a philosophical movement characterized by enquiry into human beings' experience of themselves in relation to the world, *esp* with reference to their freedom, responsibility, and isolation. ➤➤ **existentialist** *n and adj.*

exit[1] *v* (**exited, exiting**) **1** (*third person sing. pres*) used as a stage direction to specify that a certain character leaves the stage. **2** of an actor: to leave the stage. **3** to leave or depart. **4** in computing, to leave or terminate (a program, process, or system).

exit[2] *n* **1** a way out of a room, building, or other enclosed space. **2** the act of going out or away. **3** a departure of a performer from the stage. **4** a point at which vehicles can leave a major road, roundabout, etc.

exit poll *n* a survey of voting trends conducted by questioning people as they leave a polling station after voting in an election.

exo- *or* **ex-** *prefix* outside; outer: *exoskeleton.*

exobiology *n* the study of extraterrestrial plants and animals. ➤➤ **exobiological** *adj,* **exobiologist** *n.*

exocrine *adj* of a gland: producing secretions that are discharged through a duct.

exodus *n* **1** (**Exodus**) the second book of the Old Testament, relating the flight of the Israelites from their captivity in Egypt. **2** a mass departure; an emigration.

ex officio *adv and adj* by virtue or because of an office.

exogenous *adj* originating from the outside; due to external causes. ➤➤ **exogenously** *adv.*

exonerate *v* **1** to free from blame; to exculpate. **2** (*often* + from) to relieve of a responsibility or obligation. ➤➤ **exoneration** *n.*

exorbitant *adj* of prices, demands, etc: much greater than is reasonable; excessive. ➤➤ **exorbitance** *n,* **exorbitantly** *adv.*

exorcize *or* **-ise** *v* **1** to expel (an evil spirit) by solemn command, e.g. in a religious ceremony. **2** to free (a person or place) of an evil spirit. **3** to get rid of (an unpleasant thought or emotion) as if by exorcism. ➤➤ **exorcism** *n,* **exorcist** *n.*

exoskeleton *n* **1** a hard external supportive covering of an animal, e.g. a lobster or beetle. **2** a type of powered suit being developed for soldiers in order to enable them to carry larger weapons and heavier loads, to march faster and over longer distances, to communicate better, etc than is currently possible. ➤➤ **exoskeletal** *adj.*

exothermal *adj* = EXOTHERMIC.

exothermic *adj* of a chemical reaction or compound: characterized by or formed with the evolution of heat.

exotic[1] *adj* **1** introduced from another country; not native to the place where found. **2** strikingly or excitingly different or unusual. ➤➤ **exotically** *adv,* **exoticism** *n.*

exotic[2] *n* an exotic plant or animal.

exotica *pl n* exotic things, *esp* literary or artistic items with an exotic theme or quality.

expand *v* **1** to increase the size, extent, number, volume, or scope of. **2** to become larger, greater, etc. **3** to unfold or open out. **4** to express in detail or in full. **5** (*often* + on) to speak or write at length; to enlarge. **6** to grow genial; to become more sociable. ➤➤ **expandable** *adj,* **expander** *n.*

expanded *adj* of a plastic, resin, etc: having gas introduced during manufacture to produce a light cellular structure.

expanded metal *n* sheet metal cut and expanded into an open mesh, used e.g. for reinforcement.

expanse *n* **1** something spread out, *esp* over a wide area. **2** the extent to which something is spread out.

expansible *adj* able to expand or be expanded; expandable.

expansion *n* the act or an instance of expanding. ➤➤ **expansionary** *adj.*

expansionism *n* a policy of economic or territorial expansion. ➤➤ **expansionist** *n and adj.*

expansion joint *n* a joint that has a gap to allow for thermal expansion of the sections.

expansive *adj* **1** having a capacity or tendency to expand or cause expansion. **2** freely communicative; genial or effusive. **3** having a wide expanse or extent. **4** characterized by extravagance or magnificence of scale. ➤➤ **expansively** *adv,* **expansiveness** *n.*

expansivity *n* the amount that a substance or body expands when its temperature is increased by one degree.

expat *n and adj informal* = EXPATRIATE².

expatiate *v* (*usu* + on/upon) to speak or write at length or in detail on. ➤➤ **expatiation** *n.*

expatriate[1] *v* **1** to exile or banish. **2** to withdraw (oneself) from residence in one's native country. ➤➤ **expatriation** *n.*

expatriate[2] *n* a person who lives outside their native country. ➤➤ **expatriate** *adj.*

expect *v* **1a** to consider (an event) probable or certain. **b** to consider reasonable, due, or necessary. **c** to consider (somebody) bound in duty or obligated. **2a** to anticipate, look forward to, or be waiting for. **b** to be waiting or prepared for the arrival of (somebody). **3** to suppose or think (something). ✱ **be expecting** *informal* to be pregnant. ➤➤ **expectable** *adj.*

expectance *n* = EXPECTANCY.

expectancy *n* (*pl* **-ies**) **1** = EXPECTATION (1), (2). **2** the expected amount, number, or length of something.

expectant *adj* **1** having, showing, or characterized by expectation. **2** of a woman: pregnant. ➤➤ **expectantly** *adv.*

expectation *n* **1** the state of expecting something; a mood of anticipation. **2** hopeful anticipation of a desired event. **3** (*also in pl*) something expected.

expectorant *n* a medicine, drug, or other agent that promotes expectoration.

expectorate *v* **1** to eject (phlegm or similar matter) from the throat or lungs by coughing or spitting. **2** to spit (saliva, etc). ➤➤ **expectoration** *n*.

expedient[1] *adj* **1** suitable for achieving a particular end. **2** characterized by concern with what is opportune or advantageous rather than what is right, just, or moral. ➤➤ **expedience** *n*, **expediency** *n*, **expediently** *adv*.

Usage note

expedient *or* **expeditious**? *Expedient* means 'useful or convenient in the circumstances (often disregarding moral considerations)': *It might be expedient to deny any knowledge of the plan.* It is sometimes confused with *expeditious*, which is a formal word meaning 'quick and efficient': *the most expeditious method of sending supplies.*

expedient[2] *n* a means to an end, *esp* one devised or used in case of urgent need.

expedite *v formal* **1** to execute (something) promptly. **2** to hasten the process or progress of; to facilitate. ➤➤ **expediter** *n*, **expeditor** *n*.

expedition *n* **1a** a journey or excursion undertaken for a specific purpose, e.g. for war or exploration. **b** (*used as sing. or pl*) the group of people making such an expedition. **2** *formal* efficient promptness; speed. ➤➤ **expeditionary** *adj*.

expeditious *adj formal* speedy; prompt and efficient. ➤➤ **expeditiously** *adv*, **expeditiousness** *n*.

Usage note

expeditious *or* **expedient**? See note at EXPEDIENT[1].

expel *v* (**expelled, expelling**) **1** to drive or force (something) out. **2** to cut (somebody) off from membership of a school, society, etc. ➤➤ **expellable** *adj*, **expellee** *n*, **expeller** *n*.

expend *v* **1** to consume (time, care, or attention) by use; to use up. **2** *formal* to spend or pay out (money).

expendable *adj* **1** normally used up in service; not intended to be kept or re-used. **2** regarded as available for sacrifice or destruction in order to accomplish an objective. ➤➤ **expendability** *n*, **expendably** *adv*.

expenditure *n* **1** the act or an instance of spending money. **2** the amount of money spent.

expense *n* **1a** something expended to secure a benefit or bring about a result. **b** financial burden or outlay. **c** (*in pl*) the charges incurred by an employee in performing their duties. **2** a cause or occasion of high expenditure. ✱ **at somebody's expense** in a manner that causes somebody to be ridiculed. **at the expense of** to the detriment of.

expense account *n* an account of expenses reimbursable to an employee.

expensive *adj* **1** commanding a high price; costly. **2** involving great expense. ➤➤ **expensively** *adv*, **expensiveness** *n*.

experience[1] *n* **1a** direct participation or observation. **b** the knowledge, skill, or practice derived from such experience, *esp* over a period of time. **2** something personally encountered or undergone. **3** the sum total of conscious events that make up an individual life or the collective past of a community, nation, etc.

experience[2] *v* to have experience of.

experienced *adj* skilful or wise as a result of experience of a particular activity or of life in general.

experiential *adj* based on or derived from experience; empirical. ➤➤ **experientially** *adv*.

experiment[1] *n* **1** an operation carried out under controlled conditions in order to test or establish a hypothesis or to illustrate a known law. **2** a tentative procedure or policy that has not been tried before. **3** the act or an instance of experimenting.

experiment[2] *v* to carry out an experiment or experiments. ➤➤ **experimentation** *n*, **experimenter** *n*.

experimental *adj* **1** based on or derived from an experiment or experiments. **2** used as a means of or having the characteristics of an experiment. **3** innovative. **4** provisional or tentative. ➤➤ **experimentalism** *n*, **experimentalist** *n*, **experimentally** *adv*.

expert[1] *adj* having or showing special skill or knowledge derived from training or experience. ➤➤ **expertly** *adv*, **expertness** *n*.

expert[2] *n* a person who has special skill or knowledge in a particular field.

expertise *n* skill in or knowledge of a particular field.

expert system *n* a computer program that contains specialized knowledge elicited from human experts on a particular subject and can use it to deduce solutions to novel problems.

expiate *v* **1a** to eradicate the guilt incurred by (a sin, etc). **b** to pay the penalty for (a crime, etc). **2** to make amends for. ➤➤ **expiable** *adj*, **expiation** *n*, **expiator** *n*, **expiatory** *adj*.

expire *v* **1** to come to an end; to cease to be valid. **2** *formal* to die. **3** to breathe (air) out from the lungs. ➤➤ **expiration** *n*, **expiratory** *adj*.

expiry *n* (*pl* **-ies**) **1** a termination, *esp* of a time or period fixed by law, contract, or agreement. **2** *archaic* death.

explain *v* **1** to make plain or understandable, *esp* by giving details. **2** to give the reason for or cause of. ✱ **explain oneself** to clarify one's statements or the reasons for one's conduct. ➤➤ **explainable** *adj*, **explainer** *n*, **explanation** *n*.

explain away *v* to minimize the significance of (errors or unpleasant facts) by making excuses.

explanatory *adj* serving to explain. ➤➤ **explanatorily** *adv*.

expletive *n* an exclamatory word or phrase; *specif* one that is obscene or profane.

explicable *adj* capable of being explained. ➤➤ **explicably** *adv*.

explicate *v formal* **1** to give a detailed explanation of. **2** to develop the implications of (a theory, etc). **3** to analyse (a literary work, etc). ➤➤ **explication** *n*, **explicative** *adj*, **explicator** *n*, **explicatory** *adj*.

explicit *adj* **1** clear and unambiguous. **2** graphically frank or detailed. **3** fully developed or formulated. ➤➤ **explicitly** *adv*, **explicitness** *n*.

explode *v* **1a** to undergo a rapid chemical or nuclear reaction with the production of noise, heat, and violent expansion of gases. **b** to burst violently as a result of pressure. **c** to expand suddenly. **2** to give expression to sudden, violent, and usu noisy emotion. **3** to cause to explode or burst noisily. **4** to demonstrate the falsity of (a belief or theory) or the non-existence of (a theoretical entity). ➤➤ **exploder** *n*.

exploded *adj* of a drawing, diagram, etc: showing the parts separated but in correct relationship to each other.

exploit[1] *n* a deed or act, *esp* a notable or heroic one.

exploit[2] *v* **1** to use or develop (resources, materials, etc) fully, *esp* for profit or advantage. **2** to take unfair advantage of (somebody) for financial or other gain. ➤➤ **exploitable** *adj*, **exploitation** *n*, **exploitative** *adj*, **exploiter** *n*, **exploitive** *adj*.

explore *v* **1** to travel into or through (an unfamiliar place), *esp* for purposes of geographical or scientific discovery. **2** to examine or enquire into thoroughly. **3** to examine (something, e.g. a part of the body) minutely, *esp* for diagnostic purposes. ⋙ **exploration** *n,* **explorative** *adj,* **exploratory** *adj,* **explorer** *n.*

explosion *n* **1** the act or an instance of exploding. **2a** a rapid large-scale expansion, increase, or upheaval. **b** a sudden violent outburst of emotion.

explosive[1] *adj* **1** capable of exploding or likely to explode. **2** tending or threatening to burst forth with sudden violence or noise. **3** tending to arouse strong reactions; controversial. ⋙ **explosively** *adv,* **explosiveness** *n.*

explosive[2] *n* an explosive substance.

exponent *n* **1a** somebody or something that expounds or interprets. **b** somebody or something that advocates or exemplifies something. **c** a skilled performer, artist, etc. **2** a symbol written above and to the right of a mathematical expression to indicate the number of times a quantity is multiplied by itself, e.g. $2^3 = 2 \times 2 \times 2$.

exponential *adj* **1** involving a variable in an exponent, e.g. 10^x. **2a** expressed in terms of exponential functions. **b** increasing with accelerating rapidity. ⋙ **exponentially** *adv.*

exponential function *n* a mathematical function in which an independent variable appears in an exponent.

export[1] *v* **1** to carry or send (a commodity) to another country for purposes of trade. **2** to take or spread (an idea, custom, etc) abroad. **3** in computing, to transfer (data) from one program or application for use in another. ⋙ **exportability** *n,* **exportable** *adj,* **exportation** *n,* **exporter** *n.*

export[2] *n* **1** something exported. **2** the act or an instance of exporting.

expose *v* **1** to lay (something) open to view; to uncover or display. **2** to deprive (somebody or something) of shelter or protection; to lay (somebody or something) open to attack, danger, etc. **3** to subject (a photographic film, plate, or paper) to the action of light, X-rays, etc. **4** to bring (something shameful) to public notice. ✻ **expose oneself** to engage in indecent exposure. ⋙ **exposer** *n.*

exposé *n* **1** a formal recital or exposition of facts; a statement. **2** an exposure of something discreditable.

exposed *adj* **1** open to view, to inclement weather, etc. **2** vulnerable to danger or criticism.

exposition *n* **1** the art or practice of expounding or explaining something, e.g. a text. **2** a large public exhibition or show, e.g. of industrial products. **3** the first part of a musical composition in which the themes are presented. ⋙ **expositional** *adj.*

expositor *n* a person who expounds or explains something; a commentator.

expository *adj* descriptive; explanatory.

ex post facto *adj and adv* with retrospective application, action, or effect.

expostulate *v formal* to remonstrate or reason earnestly with (somebody), *esp* in order to dissuade them. ⋙ **expostulation** *n,* **expostulatory** *adj.*

exposure *n* **1a** the act or an instance of being exposed, *esp* to something harmful or unpleasant. **b** the condition arising from lack of protection from cold weather. **2a** the act or an instance of exposing a sensitized photographic film, plate, or paper, or the product of the light intensity multiplied by the duration of such an exposure. **b** a section of a film with one picture on it. **3** a disclosure, *esp* of a weakness or of something shameful or criminal. **4** presentation or exposition, *esp* to the public by means of the mass media.

expound *v* to set forth (an idea, theory, etc), *esp* in careful or elaborate detail; to state or explain. ⋙ **expounder** *n.*

express[1] *v* **1a** to show or represent, *esp* in words; to state. **b** to make known the opinions, feelings, etc of (oneself). **c** to represent by a sign or symbol. **2** to force out (air or liquid) by pressure. **3** to send by express. ⋙ **expresser** *n,* **expressible** *adj.*

express[2] *adj* **1** firmly and explicitly stated: *He disobeyed my express orders.* **2** of a particular sort; specific: *She came for that express purpose.* **3a** travelling at high speed, usu with few stops along the way, or suitable for such travel: *an express train.* **b** *Brit* designated to be delivered without delay by special messenger: *express mail.*

express[3] *adv* by express.

express[4] *n* **1** an express vehicle, *esp* a train. **2** *Brit* an express delivery service.

expression *n* **1a** the act or an instance of expressing. **b** a significant word or phrase. **c** an outward manifestation or symbol. **d** a look on somebody's face that indicates their feelings. **e** a mathematical or logical symbol or combination of symbols. **2** a means or manner of expressing something. ⋙ **expressional** *adj,* **expressionless** *adj.*

expressionism *n* a mode of expression in art, literature, or music that attempts to depict subjective emotions and responses to objects and events. ⋙ **expressionist** *n and adj,* **expressionistic** *adj.*

expressive *adj* **1** (+ of) serving to express or represent something. **2** full of expression. **3** full of meaning; significant. ⋙ **expressively** *adv,* **expressiveness** *n,* **expressivity** *n.*

expressly *adv* **1** explicitly. **2** for an express purpose; specially.

expresso *n* (*pl* **-os**) = ESPRESSO.

expressway *n chiefly NAm* a motorway.

expropriate *v* **1** to deprive of possession, occupancy, or owner's rights. **2** to transfer (the property of another) to one's own possession. **3** to take possession of (personal property) for public use. ⋙ **expropriation** *n,* **expropriator** *n.*

expulsion *n* the act or an instance of expelling. ⋙ **expulsive** *adj.*

expunge *v formal* **1** to delete or erase (words, passages, etc). **2** to blot out or obliterate. ⋙ **expunger** *n.*

expurgate *v* to rid (something) of something morally offensive, *esp* to remove objectionable parts from (a text) before publication or presentation. ⋙ **expurgation** *n,* **expurgator** *n,* **expurgatory** *adj.*

exquisite *adj* **1** marked by flawless, beautiful, and usu delicate craftsmanship. **2** extremely beautiful; delightful. **3** keenly sensitive, *esp* in feeling; discriminating. **4** acute or intense. ⋙ **exquisitely** *adv,* **exquisiteness** *n.*

ex-serviceman *or* **ex-servicewoman** *n* (*pl* **ex-servicemen** *or* **ex-servicewomen**) *chiefly Brit* a former member of the armed forces.

extant *adj* still or currently existing.

extemporaneous *adj* spoken, done, etc on the spur of the moment and without preparation; impromptu. ⋙ **extemporaneously** *adv,* **extemporaneousness** *n.*

extemporary *adj* = EXTEMPORANEOUS. ⋙ **extemporarily** *adv,* **extemporariness** *n.*

extempore /ik'stempəri/ *adj and adv* spoken or done in an extemporaneous manner.

extemporize *or* **-ise** *v* to speak or perform something extemporaneously; to improvise. ⋙ **extemporization** *n.*

extend *v* **1a** to lengthen or enlarge (something): *The house has been extended.* **b** to prolong (something) in time: *They have extended the deadline.* **2** to stretch out in distance, space, time, or scope. **3a** to spread or stretch (something) forth: *She extended her arm.* **b** to stretch (something) out to its fullest length. **4** to give or offer; to proffer: *extending aid to the needy.* ⋙ **extendability** *n,* **extendable** *adj,* **extendibility** *n,* **extendible** *adj,* **extensibility** *n,* **extensible** *adj.*

extended family *n* a family unit that includes three or more generations of near relatives in addition to a nuclear family, *esp* living in one household or close together.

extender *n* **1** somebody or something that extends something. **2** a substance added to a product to increase its bulk or improve its physical properties.

extensile *adj* capable of being extended.

extension *n* **1a** the act or an instance of extending. **b** something extended. **2a** a part added to make something longer or larger, e.g. an extra room or rooms added to a building. **b** an extra telephone connected to the principal line. **c** a length of electric cable that enables an appliance to be connected to a distant socket. **3** the characters following the dot in a filename created by DOS-based software, identifying the type of file. ⋙ **extensional** *adj.*

extensive *adj* **1** having wide or considerable extent. **2** of or being farming in which large areas of land are used with minimum expenditure and labour. ⋙ **extensively** *adv,* **extensiveness** *n.*

extensor *n* a muscle that extends or straightens a part of the body, *esp* a limb: compare FLEXOR.

extent *n* **1** the range or distance over which something extends. **2** the point or limit to which something extends.

extenuate *v* **1** to lessen the seriousness or extent of (a crime, etc), *esp* by providing a reason or excuses. **2** to make (somebody) thin or emaciated. ⋙ **extenuation** *n,* **extenuator** *n,* **extenuatory** *adj.*

exterior[1] *adj* **1** on the outside or an outside surface; external. **2** suitable for use on outside surfaces. ⋙ **exteriorly** *adv.*

exterior[2] *n* **1a** an exterior part or surface; outside. **b** an outward manner or appearance. **2** a representation of an outdoor scene.

exterminate *v* to destroy (something) completely, *esp* to kill all of (a population of pests, etc). ⋙ **extermination** *n,* **exterminator** *n,* **exterminatory** *adj.*

external[1] *adj* **1** of, on, or intended for the outside or an outer part. **2** situated outside, apart, or beyond. **3a** arising or acting from outside. **b** of dealings with foreign countries. ⋙ **externally** *adv.*

external[2] *n* (*usu in pl*) an external feature or aspect.

external ear *n* the parts of an ear between the eardrum and the exterior, including the parts on the outside of the head.

externalize *or* **-ise** *v* **1** to make external or externally visible. **2** to attribute (a feeling, event, etc) to causes outside the self; to rationalize. ⋙ **externalization** *n.*

extinct *adj* **1** no longer existing as a species. **2a** no longer burning; extinguished. **b** no longer active: *an extinct volcano.*

extinction *n* the act or an instance of making extinct or extinguishing.

extinguish *v* **1a** to cause to cease burning; to quench (a flame, fire, etc). **b** to put out (a light). **c** to bring to an end; to destroy completely: *Hope for their safety was slowly extinguished.* **2a** to make (a claim, etc) void. **b** to abolish (a debt) by payment. ⋙ **extinguishable** *adj,* **extinguisher** *n,* **extinguishment** *n.*

extirpate *v* **1** to remove or destroy completely as if by uprooting; to annihilate. **2** to cut out by surgery. ⋙ **extirpation** *n,* **extirpator** *n.*

extol (*NAm* **extoll**) *v* (**extolled, extolling**) to praise highly; to glorify. ⋙ **extoller** *n,* **extolment** *n.*

extort *v* to obtain (money or a confession) from somebody by force or threats. ⋙ **extorter** *n,* **extortion** *n,* **extortioner** *n,* **extortionist** *n,* **extortive** *adj.*

extortionate *adj* **1** of a price: excessive or exorbitant. **2** using or characterized by extortion. ⋙ **extortionately** *adv.*

extra[1] *adj* more than is due, usual, or necessary; additional.

extra[2] *n* **1** something extra or additional, e.g. an added charge or an item for which such a charge is made. **2** somebody extra or additional; *specif* somebody hired to act in a group scene in a film or stage production.

extra[3] *adv* beyond or above the usual size, extent, or amount.

extra- *prefix* outside; beyond: *extramural.*

extract[1] *v* **1** to pull out, draw forth, or obtain, *esp* against resistance or with effort. **2** to withdraw (a juice, etc) or separate (a constituent of a mixture, etc) by a physical or chemical process. **3** to take (a passage) from something for quoting, copying or performing. ⋙ **extractability** *n,* **extractable** *adj,* **extractive** *adj.*

extract[2] *n* **1** a passage taken from a book, musical composition, etc, e.g. for quoting or performing. **2** a solution or concentrate of the essential constituents of a complex material, e.g. an aromatic plant, prepared by extraction.

extraction *n* **1** the act or an instance of extracting. **2** ancestry or origin. **3** something extracted.

extractor *n* **1** a device used to extract something, e.g. juice. **2** = EXTRACTOR FAN.

extractor fan *n* a type of ventilator, usu electrically driven, designed to expel fumes, stale air, etc.

extracurricular *adj* **1** not falling within the scope of a regular school or college curriculum. **2** lying outside one's normal activities.

extradite *v* **1** to hand (somebody) over for extradition. **2** to obtain the extradition of (a criminal suspect or fugitive). ⋙ **extraditable** *adj.*

extradition *n* the surrender of an alleged criminal by one state to another having the power by law to try the charge.

extramarital *adj* of sexual relations: occurring outside marriage; adulterous.

extramural *adj* **1** outside the walls or boundaries of a place or organization. **2** *chiefly Brit* for students of a university, college, etc who do not attend on a full-time basis. ⋙ **extramurally** *adv.*

extraneous *adj* **1** not forming an essential or vital part; irrelevant. **2** on or coming from the outside. ⋙ **extraneously** *adv,* **extraneousness** *n.*

extraordinaire *adj* (*used after a noun*) outstanding: *a chef extraordinaire.*

extraordinary *adj* **1a** going beyond what is usual, regular, or customary. **b** highly exceptional; remarkable. **2** (*also used after a noun*) on or for a special function or service: *an ambassador extraordinary; an extraordinary general meeting.* ⋙ **extraordinarily** *adv,* **extraordinariness** *n.*

extrapolate *v* **1** in mathematics, to predict (a value of a variable at a given point) by extending a line or curve plotted on a graph from known values at previous points. **2a** to use or extend (known data or experience) in order to surmise or work out something unknown. **b** to predict by extrapolating known data or experience. ⋙ **extrapolation** *n,* **extrapolative** *adj,* **extrapolator** *n.*

extrasensory *adj* residing beyond or outside the ordinary physical senses.

extrasensory perception *n* the faculty of perception by means other than the known senses, e.g. by telepathy and clairvoyance.

extraterrestrial[1] *adj* of or from outside the earth or its atmosphere.

extraterrestrial[2] *n* an extraterrestrial being.

extra time *n* a period of playing time added to the end of a match to resolve a draw.

extravagant *adj* **1a** wasteful, *esp* of money. **b** profuse. **2** unreasonably high in price; exorbitant. **3a** lacking in moderation and restraint; excessive. **b** excessively elaborate or showy. ⋙ **extravagance** *n,* **extravagancy** *n,* **extravagantly** *adv.*

extravaganza *n* a lavish or spectacular show or event.

extravert *n and adj* see EXTROVERT.

extra virgin *adj* of olive oil: extracted by the first cold pressing of the olives and therefore of the highest quality.

extreme[1] *adj* **1a** existing in a very high degree: *extreme poverty.* **b** going to great or exaggerated lengths; not moderate: *an extreme right-winger.* **c** exceeding the usual or expected; severe: *extreme measures.* **2** situated at the farthest possible point from a centre or the nearest to an end: *the extreme north of the country.* **3a** most advanced or thoroughgoing: *the extreme avant-garde.* **b** maximum: *the extreme penalty.* ⋙ **extremely** *adv,* **extremeness** *n.*

extreme[2] *n* **1** something situated at or marking a point at one end or the other of a range. **2** (*also in pl*) a very pronounced or extreme degree. **3** (*also in pl*) an extreme measure or expedient.

extreme sports *pl n* sports such as base-jumping, bungee jumping, and canyoning which offer a high level of excitement but which also involve a certain element of danger.

extreme unction *n* the Roman Catholic and Eastern Orthodox sacrament of anointing and praying over a sick or dying person.

extremism *n* advocacy of extreme political measures; radicalism. ⋙ **extremist** *n and adj.*

extremity *n* (*pl* **-ies**) **1a** the furthest or most extreme part or point. **b** the greatest or most extreme degree. **2** (*also in pl*) a limb or the end of a limb, *esp* a human hand or foot. **3** extreme misfortune or danger of destruction or death. **4** (*also in pl*) a drastic or desperate act or measure.

extricate *v* to disentangle (something, somebody, or oneself), *esp* with considerable effort. ⋙ **extricable** *adj,* **extrication** *n.*

extrinsic *adj* **1** not forming part of or belonging to a thing; extraneous. **2** originating from or on the outside. ⋙ **extrinsically** *adv.*

extrovert *or* **extravert** *n* **1** a person whose attention and interests are directed wholly or predominantly towards what is outside the self: compare INTROVERT. **2** a sociable, gregarious, or outgoing person: compare INTROVERT. ⋙ **extroversion** *n,* **extrovert** *adj,* **extroverted** *adj.*

extrude *v* **1** to force or push (something) out. **2** to shape (metal, plastic, etc) by forcing it through a die. ⋙ **extrudable** *adj,* **extruder** *n,* **extrusion** *n.*

extrusive *adj* of a rock: formed by crystallization of lava forced out at the earth's surface.

exuberant *adj* **1a** joyously unrestrained and enthusiastic. **b** lavish and flamboyant. **2** abundant or luxuriant. ⋙ **exuberance** *n,* **exuberantly** *adv.*

exudate *n* exuded matter.

exude *v* **1** to ooze out or allow or cause (a liquid or smell) to ooze or spread out in all directions. **2** to display (a quality, feeling, etc) in abundance. ⋙ **exudation** *n.*

exult *v* to be extremely joyful; to rejoice openly. ⋙ **exultancy** *n,* **exultant** *adj,* **exultantly** *adv,* **exultation** *n.*

exurb *n NAm* a prosperous district outside a city and usu beyond its suburbs. ⋙ **exurban** *adj.*

ex-voto *n* (*pl* **-os**) an offering given in fulfilment of a vow or in gratitude or devotion.

-ey *suffix* see -Y[1].

eyas *n* a young hawk.

eye[1] *n* **1a** an organ of sight; *esp* a nearly spherical liquid-filled organ that is lined with a light-sensitive retina and housed in a bony socket in the skull. **b** the faculty of seeing with the eyes: *a keen eye for detail.* **c** the faculty of intellectual or aesthetic perception or appreciation: *an eye for beauty.* **2 a** the hole through the head of a needle. **b** a loop, *esp* one of metal into which a hook is inserted or one at the end of a rope. **c** an undeveloped bud, e.g. on a potato. **d** a circular mark, e.g. on a peacock's tail. **3** a calm area in the centre of a storm, hurricane, etc. ✱ **all eyes** watching closely. **an eye for an eye** retaliation in kind [from God's commandments to the Israelites on just retribution (Exodus 21:24)]. **close/shut one's eyes to** to ignore deliberately. **get/keep one's eye in** *Brit* to get into or keep in practice. **have eyes for** to be interested in (somebody or something). **have one's eye on 1** to watch (somebody or something), *esp* constantly and attentively. **2** to have as an objective. **in the eye/eyes of** in the judgment or opinion of. **keep an/one's eye on** to watch (somebody or something) carefully. **keep one's eyes open/peeled/skinned** to be on the alert; to be watchful. **make eyes at** to ogle. **more than meets the eye** more than is at first obvious or apparent. **one in the eye for** a disappointment or setback for. **put somebody's eye/eyes out** to make somebody blind in one or both eyes, e.g. by pushing or poking them. **see eye to eye** to have a common viewpoint; to agree. **set/clap/lay eyes on** to catch sight of; to see. **with an eye to** to having as an aim or purpose. **with one's eyes open** in a state of full awareness of the problems, difficulties, etc that a situation will present.

eye[2] *v* (**eyes, eyed, eyeing** *or* **eying**) to fix the eyes on (something or somebody).

eyeball[1] *n* the more or less spherical capsule of the eye of a vertebrate animal formed by the SCLERA (white outer coat) and the CORNEA (transparent membrane at the front), together with the structures they contain. ✱ **eyeball to eyeball** *informal* face to face, *esp* with hostility.

eyeball[2] *v chiefly NAm, informal* to look at intently.

eyebath *n* a small oval cup specially shaped for applying liquid remedies to the eye.

eyebright *n* a tiny plant of the foxglove family with very small white or violet flowers.

eyebrow *n* the ridge over the eye or the line of hair that grows on it. ✱ **raise an eyebrow** to show surprise. **raise eyebrows** to cause surprise. **up to one's eyebrows** deeply involved.

eye-catching *adj* strikingly visually attractive.

eye contact *n* a meeting of eyes when two people look directly at each other.

eyeful *n informal* **1** a pleasing sight; *specif* an attractive person. **2** a look or gaze.

eyeglass *n* **1** a lens worn to aid vision; *specif* a monocle. **2** *chiefly NAm* (*in pl*) glasses; spectacles.

eyelash *n* the fringe of hair edging the eyelid or a single hair of this fringe.

eyelet *n* **1** a small reinforced hole designed so that a cord, lace, etc may be passed through it. **2** a small typically metal ring to reinforce an eyelet; a grommet.

eye level *n* the height at which the eyes are looking straight ahead.

eyelid *n* a movable lid of skin and muscle that can be closed over the eyeball.

eyeliner *n* a cosmetic for emphasizing the outline of the eyes.

eye-opener *n informal* something surprising and revelatory.

eyepiece *n* the lens or combination of lenses looked through at the eye end in an optical instrument.

eyeshade *n* a small shield that shades the eyes from strong light and is fastened to the head with a headband.

eye shadow *n* a coloured cream or powder applied to the eyelids to accentuate the eyes.

eyesight *n* the power of seeing or the ability to see.

eyesore *n* something offensive to the sight, *esp* an ugly building.

eyetooth *n* (*pl* **eyeteeth**) a canine tooth of the upper jaw. ❋ **give one's eyeteeth for** to do anything in order to obtain or achieve.

eye up *v informal* to look at (somebody) in order to assess their sexual attractiveness.

eyewash *n* **1** *informal* deceptive statements or actions; rubbish or nonsense. **2** lotion for the eyes.

eyewitness *n* a person who sees an occurrence and can bear witness to it, e.g. in a court of law.

eyot *n* see AIT.

eyrie *or* **aerie** *n* the nest of a bird, *esp* a bird of prey, on a cliff or a mountain top.

eyrir /'ayriə/ *n* (*pl* **aurar**) a unit of currency in Iceland, worth 100th of a króna.

e-zine *n* a magazine, newsletter, fanzine, etc published on the Internet.

F[1] *or* **f** *n* (*pl* **F's** *or* **Fs** *or* **f's**) **1** the sixth letter of the English alphabet. **2** in music, the fourth note of the diatonic scale of C major.

F[2] *abbr* **1** Fahrenheit. **2** farad(s). **3** female. **4** *Brit* used on pencils: fine. **5** in physics, force. **6** franc.

F[3] *abbr* the chemical symbol for fluorine.

f[1] *abbr* **1** in grammar, feminine. **2** folio. **3** following (page). **4** in music, forte. **5** furlong(s).

f[2] *symbol* **1** focal length. **2** in electronics, frequency. **3** in mathematics, function.

FA *abbr* **1** Fanny Adams. **2** in Britain, Football Association.

fa *or* **fah** *n* in music, the fourth note of a major scale in the tonic sol-fa system.

fab *adj informal* fabulous or great.

Fabian[1] *n* a member of a socialist society founded in Britain in 1884 to work for the gradual establishment of socialism. ▶▶ **Fabianism** *n*, **Fabianist** *n*.

Fabian[2] *adj* **1** of or relating to the Fabians. **2** using a cautious, gradual strategy to wear down an enemy.

fable *n* **1** a story intended to convey a moral; *esp* one in which animals speak and act like human beings. **2a** a legendary story of supernatural happenings. **b** myths or legendary tales collectively.

fabled *adj* **1** told or celebrated in fables; legendary. **2** fictitious or imaginary.

fabric *n* **1** a pliable material made by weaving, knitting, etc; cloth. **2a** the basic structure or framework of a building, *esp* the floor, walls, and roof. **b** the underlying structure of something abstract, e.g. a society or way of life.

fabricate *v* **1** to invent or create (e.g. a story), *esp* in order to deceive. **2** to construct or manufacture (a product) from many parts. ▶▶ **fabrication** *n*, **fabricator** *n*.

fabulist *n* **1** a person who composes fables. **2** a person who tells lies.

fabulous *adj* **1** resembling things told of in fables, *esp* in incredible or exaggerated quality; extraordinary. **2** *informal* marvellous or great. **3** told in or based on fable. ▶▶ **fabulously** *adv*, **fabulousness** *n*.

facade *or* **façade** *n* **1** a face, *esp* the front or principal face, of a building. **2** a false or superficial appearance.

face[1] *n* **1a** the front part of the human head from the chin to the forehead. **b** the part of an animal that corresponds to the human face. **2** a facial expression, *esp* a grimace. **3a** a front, upper, or outer surface. **b** in geometry, each of the plane surfaces of a solid. **c** the side of a mountain or cliff. **4** one aspect of something. ✻ **if one's face fits** *Brit* if one is suitable, e.g. for a particular job. **in the face/in face of** in opposition to; despite. **on the face of it** at first glance; apparently. **put a bold/brave face on something** to pretend that something unpleasant is really all right. **set one's face against** to be resolutely opposed to. **to somebody's face** in somebody's presence; frankly.

face[2] *v* **1** to have the face or front turned in a specific direction or towards (something). **2** to meet or deal with (a situation or problem) firmly and without evasion; to confront. **3** to have (something unpleasant) to come; to have the prospect of. **4** to cover the front or surface of. ✻ **face the music** to confront and endure the unpleasant consequences of one's actions. **face up to** to confront (a difficulty or problem) without shrinking.

facecloth *n* a cloth for washing the face; a flannel.

face down *v* to prevail against (somebody) by defiant confrontation.

faceless *adj* lacking identity; anonymous. ▶▶ **facelessness** *n*.

face-lift *n* plastic surgery to remove signs of ageing, e.g. wrinkles or sagging skin.

face mask *n* **1** a mask worn over the nose and mouth for protection. **2** a face-pack.

face off *v* **1** *chiefly NAm* to confront somebody, e.g. before a fight. **2** in lacrosse or ice hockey, to start play with a face-off.

face-off *n* **1** *chiefly NAm* a confrontation between hostile parties. **2** in lacrosse or ice hockey, a method of putting a ball or puck in play in which two opposing players stand facing each other and on a signal attempt to gain control of the ball or puck.

face-pack *n chiefly Brit* a cream, paste, etc applied to the face to improve the complexion and remove impurities.

face paint *n* brightly coloured paint for decorating the face.

faceplate *n* **1** a disc fixed with its face at right angles to the driven spindle of a lathe, to which the article being worked on is attached. **2** the glass panel at the front of a diving helmet or space helmet. **3** in electronics, the front part of a cathode-ray tube carrying the phosphor screen.

face-saving *adj* serving to preserve one's dignity or reputation. ▶▶ **face-saver** *n*.

facet *n* **1** a plane surface, e.g. of a cut gem. **2** one aspect of something.

facetious *adj* **1** inappropriately lacking seriousness in manner; flippant. **2** intended to be amusing. ➤➤ **facetiously** *adv,* **facetiousness** *n.*

face to face *adv* **1** of two people: looking directly at each other. **2** in confrontation with somebody or something.

face value *n* **1** the value indicated on the face of a postage stamp, a share certificate, etc, *esp* when this differs from the actual value. **2** the apparent value or significance.

facia[1] *n chiefly Brit* see FASCIA[1].

facia[2] *n* see FASCIA[2].

facial[1] *adj* relating to or in the region of the face. ➤➤ **facially** *adv.*

facial[2] *n* a beauty treatment for the face.

facile *adj* **1** indicating a lack of thought; superficial and glib. **2** easily or readily accomplished or performed. ➤➤ **facilely** *adv,* **facileness** *n.*

facilitate *v* to make (e.g. a task) easier. ➤➤ **facilitation** *n,* **facilitative** *adj,* **facilitator** *n.*

facility *n* (*pl* **-ies**) **1** a building, piece of equipment or resource designed to provide a particular service. **2** an ability to do something easily; an aptitude. **3** ease in doing or performing something.

facing *n* **1** a lining at the edge of a garment, for stiffening or ornament. **2** an ornamental or protective layer applied to a wall.

facsimile[1] *n* an exact copy, *esp* of printed material.

facsimile[2] *v* (**facsimiles, facsimiled, facsimileing**) to make a facsimile of.

fact *n* **1** an actual event or occurrence. **2** a piece of information. **3** in law, an actual or alleged event or state as distinguished from its legal effect. ✱ **after the fact** in law, after a criminal act has been committed. **before the fact** in law, before a criminal act has been committed. **in fact** as a matter of fact. **in point of fact** as a matter of fact.

faction[1] *n* a party or minority group within a party, *esp* one that is seen as divisive. ➤➤ **factional** *adj,* **factionalism** *n,* **factionally** *adv.*

faction[2] *n* in literature and cinema, the dramatized reconstruction of real historical situations or events.

factious *adj* caused by or inclined to dissension. ➤➤ **factiously** *adv,* **factiousness** *n.*

factitious *adj* produced artificially; sham or unreal. ➤➤ **factitiously** *adv,* **factitiousness** *n.*

fact of life *n* (*pl* **facts of life**) **1** something that exists and must be taken into consideration. **2** (**the facts of life**) details of the processes and behaviour involved in sex and reproduction.

factoid *n* **1** something that is widely accepted as a fact but is not really true. **2** *NAm* a snippet of factual information.

factor[1] *n* **1** a condition, force, or fact that actively contributes to a result. **2** in mathematics, one of two or more numbers or quantities that can be multiplied together to produce a given number or quantity. **3** formerly, in biology, a gene. **4** in physiology, a substance in the blood that causes it to clot. **5a** a person who acts for another; an agent. **b** *chiefly Scot* a land agent.

factor[2] *v* (**factored, factoring**) to express (a number) as the product of factors. ✱ **factor in/out** to include or exclude as a factor when considering a matter. ➤➤ **factorable** *adj.*

Factor 8 *n* a protein in the blood that is involved in clotting. A deficiency of this protein is one of the causes of haemophilia.

factorial[1] *n* in mathematics, the product of all the positive integers from one to a given positive integer.

factorial[2] *adj* of a factor or a factorial. ➤➤ **factorially** *adv.*

factorize *or* **-ise** *v* **1** to calculate the factors of (a number). **2** of a number: to be able to be expressed in terms of its factors. ➤➤ **factorization** *n.*

factory *n* (*pl* **-ies**) a building or set of buildings containing machinery used for manufacturing.

factory farming *n* a system of agriculture, used *esp* in milk, egg, or meat production, that uses intensive production methods.

factory floor *n* the workers in a factory or company as distinct from the management.

factotum *n* (*pl* **factotums**) a person employed to carry out many types of work.

factual *adj* restricted to or based on fact. ➤➤ **factuality** *n,* **factually** *adv,* **factualness** *n.*

faculty *n* (*pl* **-ies**) **1** an inherent capability, power, or function of the body. **2** a natural aptitude; a talent. **3a** *chiefly Brit* a group of related subject departments in a university. **b** *NAm* (*used as sing. or pl*) the staff of an educational institution.

fad *n* **1** a short-lived practice or interest; a craze. **2** an idiosyncratic taste or habit. ➤➤ **faddish** *adj,* **faddishness** *n,* **faddism** *n,* **faddist** *n.*

faddy *adj* (**-ier, -iest**) *Brit* having idiosyncratic likes and dislikes about food. ➤➤ **faddily** *adv,* **faddiness** *n.*

fade[1] *v* **1** to disappear gradually; to vanish. **2** to lose or cause to lose freshness or brilliance of colour. **3a** of an image on a screen: to come gradually in and out of view. **b** of an electronic sound: to increase or decrease in volume or strength.

fade[2] *n* the act or an instance of fading.

fader *n* a device used to cause audio or video signals to gradually appear or disappear.

faeces (*NAm* **feces**) *pl n* bodily waste discharged through the anus. ➤➤ **faecal** *adj.*

faerie *or* **faery** *n literary* fairyland.

Faeroese *or* **Faroese** *n* (*pl* **Faeroese**) **1** a native or inhabitant of the Faeroe Islands. **2** the Germanic language of the Faeroese. ➤➤ **Faeroese** *adj.*

faery *n* see FAERIE.

faff[1] *v Brit, informal* (+ about/around) to waste time over trifles; to fuss or dither.

faff[2] *n Brit, informal* fuss or dithering.

fag[1] *n Brit, informal* a cigarette.

fag[2] *n chiefly Brit, informal* **1** a tiring or boring task. **2** a public school pupil who acts as servant to an older pupil.

fag[3] *v* (**fagged, fagging**) *chiefly Brit, informal* **1** to work hard. **2** to act as a fag, *esp* in a public school.

fag[4] *n NAm, informal, derog* a male homosexual. ➤➤ **faggy** *adj.*

fag end *n chiefly Brit, informal* **1** a cigarette end. **2** a worn-out end; a remnant.

fagged out *adj chiefly Brit, informal* tired or exhausted.

faggot *n* **1** *Brit* a round mass of minced meat, e.g. pig's liver, mixed with herbs and usu breadcrumbs. **2** (*NAm* **fagot**) a bundle of sticks used as fuel. **3** *chiefly NAm, informal, derog* a male homosexual.

faggoting (*NAm* **fagoting**) *n* embroidery in which some of the horizontal threads are tied in the middle to form hourglass shapes.

fagot *n NAm* see FAGGOT.

fagoting *n NAm* see FAGGOTING.

fah *n* see FA.

Fahr. *abbr* Fahrenheit.

Fahrenheit *adj* of or being a scale of temperature on which water freezes at 32° and boils at 212° under standard conditions.

faience *or* **faïence** /fie'ahns, fie'onhs/ *n* tin-glazed decorated earthenware.

fail[1] *v* **1** to be unsuccessful at something. **2** to neglect to do something. **3a** to stop functioning. **b** to be or become insufficient or inadequate. **4a** to lose strength; to weaken. **b** to fade or die away. **5** to become bankrupt or insolvent. **6a** to be unsuccessful in passing (a test, examination, or interview). **b** to be unable to reach the quality or standard required by (a test, inspection, etc). **c** to judge (a candidate in an examination) as being unsuccessful. **7a** to disappoint the expectations or trust of (somebody). **b** to let (somebody) down.

fail[2] *n* a mark indicating the failing of an examination. ✱ **without fail** without exception.

failing[1] *n* a defect in character.

failing[2] *prep* in absence or default of (something).

failsafe *adj* **1** of a machine: designed to return automatically to a safe condition, e.g. to switch itself off, in the event of failure or breakdown. **2** foolproof.

failure *n* **1a** lack of success. **b** an unsuccessful or disappointing person or thing. **2a** the act or an instance of failing to perform a duty or expected action. **b** the act or an instance of failing to function normally.

fain[1] *adv archaic* with pleasure.

fain[2] *adj archaic* **1** willing. **2** compelled.

faint[1] *adj* **1** lacking distinctness, volume, or brightness. **2** slight. **3** weak and dizzy as if about to lose consciousness. ➤➤ **faintly** *adv*, **faintness** *n*.

faint[2] *v* to lose consciousness briefly, because of a temporary decrease in the blood supply to the brain, e.g. through exhaustion or shock.

faint[3] *n* a brief loss of consciousness.

faint-hearted *adj* lacking courage or resolution; timid.

fair[1] *adj* **1** free from favouritism or prejudice; honest or just. **2** conforming with the established rules; allowed. **3** of hair or complexion: light in colour. **4** moderately good or large; adequate. **5a** of weather: fine. **b** of wind: favourable. **6** *archaic* beautiful. ✱ **fair enough** *informal* used to agree that something is reasonable. ➤➤ **fairish** *adj*, **fairness** *n*.

fair[2] *adv* **1** in a fair way. **2** *dialect* fairly; completely.

fair[3] *n* **1** a fete or fun fair. **2** an exhibition designed to acquaint people with a product. **3** a gathering of buyers and sellers: *a sheep fair.*

fair and square *adv* **1** in an honest manner. **2** exactly or directly.

fair copy *n* a piece of work written or printed again after corrections have been made.

fair dos *pl n Brit, informal* fair treatment.

fairer sex *n* = FAIR SEX.

fair game *n* somebody or something open to legitimate attack or ridicule.

fairground *n* an area where outdoor fairs, circuses, or exhibitions are held.

fair-haired *adj* **1** having blond hair. **2** *NAm* favourite.

fairing[1] *n* a smooth structure intended to reduce drag or air resistance, e.g. on a car or aircraft.

fairing[2] *n Brit, archaic* a present bought or given at a fair.

Fair Isle *n* a style of knitting having horizontal, characteristically patterned bands worked in two or more colours against a plain background.

fairly *adv* **1** impartially or honestly. **2** in a proper or legal manner. **3** quite. **4** positively.

fair-minded *adj* just or unprejudiced.

fair play *n* equitable or impartial treatment; justice.

fair sex *n* (**the fair sex**) *dated* women.

fair trade *n* trade that supports producers in developing countries by making sure that they receive fair wages.

fairway *n* **1** the mown part of a golf course between a tee and a green. **2** a navigable channel in a river, bay, or harbour.

fair-weather friend *n* a friend who is present or loyal only in untroubled times.

fairy *n* (*pl* **-ies**) **1** a small mythical being in human form with magical powers. **2** *informal, derog* a male homosexual.

fairy cake *n Brit* a very small iced sponge cake.

fairy floss *n Aus* candy floss.

fairy godmother *n* in fairy stories, a woman who comes to the aid of the heroine or hero.

fairyland *n* **1** the land of fairies. **2** a place of magical charm.

fairy lights *pl n chiefly Brit* small coloured electric lights hung up for decoration.

fairy ring *n* a ring of dark vegetation on the ground caused by fungi growing outwards in a circle from an initial point.

fairy story *n* **1** a children's story featuring magical or imaginary places and characters. **2** a made-up story, *esp* one designed to mislead.

fairy tale *n* **1** a fairy story. **2a** (*used before a noun*) marked by apparently magical success or good fortune: *a fairy tale start to his career.* **b** (*used before a noun*) marked by great beauty or perfection: *a fairy tale wedding dress.*

fait accompli /,fayt ə'kompli/ *n* (*pl* **faits accomplis** /,fayts ə'kompli/) something already accomplished and considered irreversible.

faith *n* **1** complete confidence or belief in something, *esp* without objective proof. **2a** a particular system of religious beliefs. **b** belief in the traditional doctrines of a religion.

faithful[1] *adj* **1** showing faith; *specif* loyal to one's spouse or partner in having no sexual relations outside the relationship. **2** true to the facts or to an original; accurate. ➤➤ **faithfulness** *n*.

faithful[2] *n* (*used as pl*) (**the faithful**) the body of adherents of a religion.

faithfully *adv* in a faithful way. ✱ **yours faithfully** *chiefly Brit* used to end a formal letter when the writer does not know the recipient's name.

faith healing *n* the cure of illnesses by prayer and faith, rather than medical treatment. ➤➤ **faith healer** *n*.

faithless *adj* **1** lacking faith, e.g. to a spouse or partner; disloyal or untrustworthy. **2** lacking religious faith. ➤➤ **faithlessly** *adv*, **faithlessness** *n*.

faits accomplis /,fayts ə'kompli/ *n* pl of FAIT ACCOMPLI.

fajitas /fə'heetəz/ *pl n* a Mexican dish consisting of small pieces of cooked spiced meat and vegetables, topped with grated cheese and wrapped in a tortilla.

fake[1] *adj* counterfeit or phoney.

fake[2] *n* **1** a worthless imitation passed off as genuine. **2** an impostor or charlatan.

fake[3] *v* **1** to forge or counterfeit. **2** to feign (e.g. an illness or emotion). ➤➤ **faker** *n*, **fakery** *n*.

fakir *n* **1** a Muslim mendicant. **2** an itinerant Hindu ascetic holy man.

falafel *or* **felafel** *n* a Middle Eastern snack made of ground chick-peas and spices, formed into balls and deep-fried.

falcon *n* **1** a hawk distinguished by long wings. **2** in falconry, a female falcon, *esp* a peregrine: compare TERCEL.

falconer *n* a person who hunts with hawks or who breeds or trains hawks for hunting.

falconry *n* the art of training falcons or the sport of using falcons to pursue game.

falderal *n* = FOLDEROL.

fall[1] *v* (*past tense* **fell**, *past part.* **fallen**) **1** to descend freely by the force of gravity. **2** to lose one's balance and collapse to the ground. **3** to hang down. **4a** of a place: to be defeated or captured. **b** of a government: to lose office. **5** to become less or weaker. **6** to pass into a new state or condition: *to fall in love; to fall into disrepair.* **7** to occur at a specified time: *Christmas falls on a Monday.* **8** to come within the scope or limits of something. ✻ **fall for 1** *informal* to fall in love with. **2** *informal* to be deceived by (a trick, etc). **fall into place** to begin to make sense or progress. **fall on** to attack suddenly or fiercely. **fall over oneself to do something** *informal* to make great efforts. **fall short** to fail to achieve a goal or target. **fall to** to be the responsibility of.

fall[2] *n* **1** the act or an instance of falling. **2** something that falls or has fallen. **3** *NAm* autumn. **4** a drop in height. **5** (*usu in pl, used as sing.*) a large and steep waterfall. **6** a downward slope. **7** a decrease in size, quantity, degree, or value. **8** a loss of greatness or power; a collapse or defeat.

fall about *v informal* to laugh uncontrollably.

fallacy *n* (*pl* **-ies**) **1** a false idea. **2** in logic, an argument failing to satisfy the conditions of valid inference. ➤➤ **fallacious** *adj.*

fall away *v* **1** to withdraw friendship or support. **2** of land: to slope down.

fallback *n* **1** something on which one can fall back; a reserve or replacement. **2** a reduction.

fall back *v* to retreat. ✻ **fall back on** to have recourse to, *esp* in difficult circumstances.

fall behind *v* to fail to keep up with the rest of a group.

fall down *v* **1** to collapse or drop to the ground. **2** to fail to meet expectations.

fallen[1] *v* past part. of FALL[1].

fallen[2] *adj* **1** *dated* of a woman: dishonoured from having had sexual relations outside marriage. **2** killed in battle.

faller *n* **1** *Brit* somebody or something that falls, e.g. a horse that falls at a fence. **2** *NAm* a person who fells trees.

fall guy *n informal* a scapegoat.

fallible *adj* capable of being or likely to be wrong. ➤➤ **fallibility** *n,* **fallibly** *adv.*

fall in *v* **1** of a structure: to sink or collapse inward. **2** of a soldier: to take a place in a formation. ✻ **fall in with 1** to concur with (an arrangement). **2** to encounter and join (a group).

falling-out *n* a disagreement or quarrel.

falling star *n* a meteor.

fall line *n* **1** the natural slope of a hill, e.g. one used for skiing, straight down from top to bottom. **2** in geography, an imaginary line at a boundary between a higher region and a plain. Rapids and waterfalls often occur at the point where a river crosses this line.

falloff *n* a decline, *esp* in quantity or quality.

fall off *v* **1** to become detached and drop to the ground. **2** to become less or weaker.

Fallopian tube *n* either of the pair of tubes conducting the egg from the ovary to the uterus in female mammals.

fallout *n* **1** polluting particles, *esp* radioactive particles resulting from a nuclear explosion, descending through the atmosphere. **2** secondary results or products.

fall out *v* **1** to have a disagreement. **2** to happen in a certain way. **3** of a soldier: to leave a place in a formation.

fallow[1] *adj* **1** of land: left unsown after ploughing. **2** dormant or inactive. **3** of a sow: not pregnant. ➤➤ **fallowness** *n.*

fallow[2] *n* ploughed and harrowed land that is allowed to lie idle during the growing season.

fallow deer *n* a small European deer with broad antlers and a pale yellow coat spotted with white in the summer.

fall through *v* of a plan: to fail to be carried out.

fall to *v* to begin doing something vigorously.

false *adj* **1** not based on reality; untrue or incorrect. **2** not according to law or rules; invalid. **3a** intended to deceive; artificial. **b** illusory: *The weapon gave him a false sense of security.* **4** disloyal or treacherous. ➤➤ **falsely** *adv,* **falseness** *n,* **falsity** *n.*

false alarm *n* a warning given about something that proves to be groundless.

false dawn *n* light that appears just before sunrise.

false economy *n* a measure carried out to save money but which actually wastes it.

falsehood *n* **1** an untrue statement; a lie. **2** absence of truth or accuracy; falsity.

false memory *n* an apparent memory of something that did not really happen, e.g. of sexual abuse in childhood, perhaps prompted by suggestion during psychoanalysis.

false pretences *pl n* acts or appearances intended to deceive.

false start *n* an early, incorrect start by a competitor in a race.

false step *n* **1** a stumble or slip. **2** an unwise action; a mistake.

falsetto *n* (*pl* **-os**) in music, the technique of artificially producing a high male singing voice that extends above the range of the singer's full voice.

falsies *pl n informal* pads of foam rubber or other material worn inside a woman's clothing to increase the apparent size of the breasts.

falsify *v* (**-ies, -ied**) **1** to make (information, etc) false by fraudulent alteration. **2** to prove or declare (a statement, etc) false. ➤➤ **falsifiable** *adj,* **falsification** *n.*

Falstaffian *adj* fat, jolly, and somewhat disreputable.

falter *v* **1a** to hesitate in purpose or action; to waver. **b** to lose strength, purpose, or effectiveness; to weaken. **2** to walk or move unsteadily or hesitatingly; to stumble. **3** to speak brokenly or weakly; to stammer. ➤➤ **falterer** *n,* **faltering** *adj,* **falteringly** *adv.*

fame *n* the state of being famous; renown or recognition.

famed *adj* famous.

familial *adj* characteristic of or relating to a family or its members.

familiar[1] *adj* **1** frequently seen or experienced; common or well-known. **2** (+ with) having knowledge of. **3a** close or intimate. **b** too intimate and unrestrained; presumptuous. ➤➤ **familiarity** *n,* **familiarly** *adv.*

familiar[2] *n* **1** an intimate associate; a companion. **2** a familiar spirit.

familiarize *or* **-ise** *v* (+ with) to make (somebody) familiar with something. ➤➤ **familiarization** *n.*

familiar spirit *n* a spirit or demon that waits on a witch.

family *n* (*pl* **-ies**) **1** (*used as sing. or pl*) **a** a group of people living under one roof; *esp* a group comprising one set of parents and their own or adopted children. **b** a social group comprising one or more parents and one or more generations of their offspring. **c** somebody's children. **2** a group of people of common ancestry or deriving from a common stock. **3** a group of related languages descended from a single ancestral language. **4** in biology, a category in the classification of organisms ranking above genus and below order. **5** a closely related group. **6** (*used before a noun*) of or suitable for a family or all of its members: *family entertainment.* ✱ **in the family way** *informal* pregnant.

family credit *n* in Britain, a state payment for families with a low income and one or more dependent children.

family name *n* a surname.

family planning *n* the control of the timing and number of babies born in a family, *esp* with the use of contraception.

family therapy *n* a form of psychotherapy in which all the members of a family participate.

family tree *n* a diagram of a genealogy.

family values *pl n* standards of morality, discipline, etc, thought of as being associated with the traditional family unit.

famine *n* **1** an extreme scarcity of food. **2** *archaic* a ravenous appetite.

famish *v archaic* to suffer or cause to suffer severely from hunger.

famished *adj informal* very hungry.

famous *adj* **1** well-known. **2** *informal, dated* excellent or first-rate. ➤➤ **famousness** *n.*

famously *adv* **1** as is well-known. **2** *informal* very well.

fan[1] *n* **1** a device, usu a series of vanes radiating from a hub rotated by a motor, for producing a current of air. **2** a folding circular or semicircular device that is waved to and fro by hand to produce a cooling current of air.

fan[2] *v* (**fanned, fanning**) **1** to cause a current of air to blow on (somebody or something). **2** to drive (something) away by waving. **3** to spread out or cause to spread out in the shape of a fan. **4** to increase the intensity of (a fire) by agitating the air around it. **5** to stir up or stimulate (e.g. an emotion).

fan[3] *n* an enthusiastic supporter or admirer, e.g. of a sport or celebrity.

fanatic *n* **1** a person who is excessively and often uncritically enthusiastic, *esp* about a religion or cause. **2** *informal* a person who is excessively keen on a hobby, sport, etc. ➤➤ **fanatic** *adj,* **fanatical** *adj,* **fanatically** *adv,* **fanaticism** *n.*

fan belt *n* in an internal-combustion engine, an endless belt driving a cooling fan for a radiator.

fancier *n* a person who breeds a specified animal or grows a specified plant for points of excellence, e.g. for showing.

fanciful *adj* **1** given to or guided by fancy or imagination rather than by reason and experience; unrealistic. **2** existing in fancy only; imaginary. **3** marked by fancy or whim; *specif* elaborate or contrived. ➤➤ **fancifully** *adv,* **fancifulness** *n.*

fan club *n* an organized group of people who are enthusiastic supporters or admirers of the same celebrity, team, etc.

fancy[1] *v* (**-ies, -ied**) **1a** to have a fancy for (somebody or something); to like or desire. **b** to consider (somebody or something) likely to do well. **2** to believe (something) without knowledge or evidence. **3** *informal* (*usu in imperative*) to form a conception of; to imagine. ✱ **fancy oneself** *informal* to have a high opinion of one's own worth, ability, etc. ➤➤ **fanciable** *adj.*

fancy[2] *adj* (**-ier, -iest**) **1a** not plain or ordinary, and *esp* of a fine quality. **b** ornamental. **c** highly decorated or decorative. **2** based on fancy or the imagination; whimsical. **3** *informal* extravagant or exorbitant. ➤➤ **fancily** *adv,* **fanciness** *n.*

fancy[3] *n* (*pl* **-ies**) **1** a liking based on whim rather than reason; an inclination. **2a** a notion or whim. **b** a mental image or representation of something. **3a** imagination, *esp* of a capricious or delusive sort. **b** the power of mental conception and representation, used in artistic expression, e.g. by a poet. **4** a small iced cake.

fancy dress *n* unusual or amusing dress, e.g. representing a historical or fictional character.

fancy-free *adj* free to do what one wants, *esp* because not involved in an amorous relationship. ✱ **footloose and fancy-free** see FOOTLOOSE.

fancy man *n informal, derog* a woman's, *esp* a married woman's, lover.

fancy woman *n informal, derog* a man's, *esp* a married man's, lover.

fandango *n* (*pl* **-os**) a lively Spanish dance in triple time, usu performed by a couple to the accompaniment of guitar and castanets.

fanfare *n* **1** a flourish of brass instruments, *esp* trumpets, usu for a ceremonial occasion. **2** a showy outward display.

fang *n* **1** a tooth by which an animal's prey is seized and held or torn. **2** any of the long hollow or grooved teeth of a venomous snake. **3** any of the clawlike structures around the mouth of a spider. ➤➤ **fanged** *adj.*

fanlight *n* a window, *esp* a semicircular one, with radiating divisions over a door or window.

fanny *n* (*pl* **-ies**) **1** *Brit, coarse slang* the female genitals. **2** *NAm, informal* the buttocks.

Fanny Adams *or* **sweet Fanny Adams** *n Brit, informal* absolutely nothing.

Word history

orig a nautical term for tinned meat, named after a murder victim whose body was cut up into small pieces. The current sense is partly a euphemism for *fuck all.*

fantail *n* **1** a fan-shaped tail or end. **2** a domestic pigeon having a broad rounded tail. ➤➤ **fan-tailed** *adj.*

fantasia *n* a free instrumental or literary composition not in strict form, comprising familiar tunes.

fantasize *or* **-ise** *v* (*often* + about) to indulge in reverie; to create or develop imaginative and often fantastic views or ideas. ➤➤ **fantasist** *n.*

fantastic *adj* **1a** unreal or imaginary. **b** so extreme as to challenge belief; incredible. **2** marked by extravagant fantasy or eccentricity; unrealistic. **3** *informal* wonderful; eccentric. ➤➤ **fantastical** *adj,* **fantastically** *adv.*

fantasy *n* (*pl* **-ies**) **1** an extravagant mental image or daydream, or the power or process of creating one, e.g. in response to a psychological need. **2a** a fantastic design or idea. **b** imaginative fiction or drama characterized by strange, unrealistic, or grotesque elements. **3** unrestricted creative imagination; fancy.

fanzine *n* a magazine for fans, *esp* of a particular sports team or pop star.

FAO *abbr* for the attention of.

FAQ *abbr* in computing, frequently asked question.

far[1] *adv* (**farther, further, farthest, furthest**) **1** to or at a considerable distance in space or time: *They wandered far into the woods; I worked far into the night.* **2a** by a broad interval: *the far distant hills.* **b** (+ from) in total contrast to: *Far from criticizing you, I'm delighted.* **3** to or at an extent or degree: *As far as I know, she won't be coming.* **4a** to or at a considerable distance or degree: *A bright student will go far.* **b** very much: *far too hot.* ✱ **a far cry from** something totally different to something else. **by far** by a considerable margin. **far and away** by a considerable margin. **far and near/wide** in every direction; everywhere. **far be it from me** used to express reluctance to say or do something. **far gone 1** in a very poor or serious state because of drink, injury, etc. **2** of a period of time: far advanced. **go too far** to go beyond what is acceptable. **how far** to what extent, degree, or distance. **in so far as** = INSOFAR AS. **so far 1** up to the present. **2** to a given extent, degree, or distance.

far[2] *adj* (**farther** *or* **further, farthest** *or* **furthest**) **1** remote in space, time, or degree: *in the far distance.* **2** long: *a far journey.* **3** being the more distant of two: *the far side of the lake.* **4** of a political position: extreme.

farad *n* the SI unit of electrical capacitance.

faraway *adj* **1** situated far away; lying at a great distance; remote. **2** dreamy or abstracted.

farce *n* **1** a comedy with an improbable plot that is concerned more with situation than characterization. **2** the broad humour characteristic of farce. **3** a ridiculous or nonsensical situation. **4** a travesty; a mockery.

farceur *n* a writer or actor of farce.

farcical *adj* of or resembling a farce, *esp* unintentionally; ludicrous or absurd. ➤➤ **farcically** *adv.*

fardel *n archaic* a bundle.

fare[1] *n* **1a** the price charged to transport somebody. **b** a paying passenger. **2** food provided for a meal.

fare[2] *v* **1** *formal* **a** to get along; to succeed or do. **b** to happen. **2** *archaic* to travel.

Far East *n* the countries in Asia east of India, including China, Japan, Korea, and Indochina. ➤➤ **Far Eastern** *adj.*

farewell[1] *interj archaic* goodbye.

farewell[2] *n* an act of departure or leave-taking.

farfalle /fah'falay/ *pl n* pasta in the shape of bows.

farfetched *adj* not easily or naturally deduced; improbable.

far-flung *adj* **1** remote. **2** widely spread or distributed.

farina *n* a starchy flour or fine meal of vegetable matter, e.g. cereal grains, used chiefly as a cereal or for making puddings.

farinaceous *adj* **1** containing or rich in starch; starchy. **2** having a mealy texture or surface.

farl *n Scot* a small thin triangular cake or biscuit sometimes made with oatmeal.

farm[1] *n* **1a** an area of land devoted to growing crops or raising domestic animals and worked or managed as a single unit. **b** a group of buildings associated with a farm, *esp* a farmhouse. **2a** something resembling a farm, *esp* in housing a large number of individuals under farm-like conditions. **b** an area of water used to breed or produce fish, shellfish, etc commercially. **3** a place for the processing or storage of something: *a sewage farm.*

farm[2] *v* **1** to engage in the production of crops or livestock. **2a** to cultivate or rear (crops or livestock) on a farm. **b** to manage and cultivate (land) as farmland or as a farm. ➤➤ **farmed** *adj,* **farming** *n.*

farmer *n* somebody who cultivates land or crops or raises livestock.

farmhand *n* a farm worker.

farmhouse *n* a dwelling house on a farm.

farm out *v* **1** to turn (work) over to somebody for performance or use, usu on contract. **2** to put (children, etc) into somebody's care in return for a fee.

farmstead *n* the buildings and adjacent areas of a farm.

farmyard *n* the area round or enclosed by farm buildings.

faro *n* a gambling game in which players bet on the value of the next card to be dealt.

Faroese *n* see FAEROESE.

farouche *adj* shy or unpolished.

farrago *n* (*pl* **-oes** *or* **-os**) a confused collection; a hotchpotch.

far-reaching *adj* having a wide range, influence, or effect.

farrier *n* a blacksmith who shoes horses. ➤➤ **farriery** *n.*

farrow[1] *n* a litter of pigs.

farrow[2] *v* of a sow: to give birth to (piglets).

farseeing *adj* = FARSIGHTED (1).

Farsi *n* the modern Persian language, the official language of Iran.

farsighted *adj* **1** having foresight or good judgment; sagacious. **2** *NAm* longsighted.

fart[1] *v informal* to expel wind from the anus.

fart[2] *n informal* **1** an expulsion of intestinal wind. **2** a boring or unpleasant person.

fart about *v chiefly Brit, informal* to spend time in pointless or worthless activity.

fart around *v* = FART ABOUT.

farther[1] *adv* **1** at or to a greater distance or more advanced point. **2** to a greater degree or extent; = FURTHER[1] (1).

Usage note

farther *or* **further**? These two words are sometimes confused. When referring to physical distance, *farther* and *further* are equally correct: *Penzance lies farther* (or *further*) *west than Truro.* In abstract and figurative senses, *further* is the preferred form: *of no further use*; *closed until further notice.* As a verb, only *further* is used: *to further God's purposes.*

farther[2] *adj* **1a** more distant; remoter. **b** being the more distant of two; = FAR[2] (3). **2** extending beyond what exists or has happened; = FURTHER[2] (1).

farthermost *adj* most distant; farthest.

farthest[1] *adj* most distant in space or time.

farthest[2] *adv* **1** to or at the greatest distance in space, time, or degree. **2** by the greatest degree or extent; most.

farthing *n* a former British unit of currency worth a quarter of an old penny, or a coin representing this.

farthingale *n* a petticoat consisting of a framework of hoops, formerly worn to expand a skirt at the hip line.

fasces *pl n* (*used as sing. or pl*) a bundle of rods containing an axe with a projecting blade carried before ancient Roman magistrates as a badge of authority.

fascia[1] (*chiefly Brit* **facia**) *n* **1a** a flat horizontal piece, e.g. of stone or board, under projecting eaves. **b** a nameplate over the front of a shop. **2** *chiefly Brit* the dashboard of a motor car. ⋙ **fascial** *adj.*

fascia[2] *or* **facia** *n* (*pl* **fasciae**) a sheet of connective tissue covering or binding together body structures.

fascicle *n* a division of a book published in parts.

fascinate *v* **1** to attract (somebody) strongly, *esp* by arousing interest or curiosity; to captivate. **2** to transfix (somebody or something) by an irresistible mental power. ⋙ **fascinating** *adj,* **fascinatingly** *adv,* **fascination** *n.*

fascism *n* **1** a political philosophy, movement, or regime that is aggressively nationalistic and stands for a centralized autocratic government headed by a dictatorial leader, severe regimentation, and forcible suppression of opposition. **2** *informal* brutal dictatorial control. ⋙ **fascist** *n and adj,* **fascistic** *adj.*

fash *v chiefly Scot* to vex (oneself).

fashion[1] *n* **1a** a prevailing and often short-lived custom or style. **b** the prevailing style or custom, *esp* in dress. **c** the business of fashion design and production. **2** a manner or way. ✱ **after a fashion** in an approximate or rough way. **in fashion** fashionable. **out of fashion** not fashionable.

fashion[2] *v* to give shape or form to (something) *esp* by using ingenuity; to mould or construct.

fashionable *adj* **1** conforming to the latest custom or fashion. **2** of the world of fashion; used or patronized by people of fashion. ⋙ **fashionably** *adv.*

fashionista *n informal* a person who follows or writes about the latest fashions in clothing.

fashion victim *n informal* somebody who dresses according to the latest fashion regardless of suitability or cost.

fast[1] *adj* **1** moving or able to move rapidly; swift. **2a** taking a comparatively short time. **b** accomplished quickly. **c** having or being a high photographic speed. **3** indicating in advance of what is correct: *The clock was fast.* **4a** (*often used in combinations*) resistant to change from destructive action, fading, etc. **b** of a colour: permanently dyed; not liable to fade. **5** firmly fixed or attached. **6** of a woman: forward or promiscuous. **7** *informal* dishonest, shady, or acquired by dishonest means or with little effort: *trying to make a fast buck.*

fast[2] *adv* **1a** in a rapid manner; quickly. **b** in quick succession. **2** ahead of a correct time or posted schedule. **3** in a firm or fixed manner. **4** sound or deeply.

fast[3] *v* to abstain from some or all foods or meals, e.g. for religious reasons.

fast[4] *n* an act or time of fasting.

fastback *n* a motor car with a roof sloping backward to or nearly to the bumper.

fast breeder reactor *n* a nuclear reactor in which fast neutrons are used to cause fission with the release of energy, and more fissionable material is produced than is used.

fasten *v* **1** to attach or secure, *esp* by pinning, tying, or nailing. **2** to fix or direct (something) steadily. **3** (+ on) to attach or impose (something) on somebody. **4** to become fixed. ✱ **fasten on/upon/onto 1** to focus attention on. **2** to take a firm grip or hold on.

fastener *n* somebody or something that fastens, *esp* a means of fastening clothing, etc.

fastening *n* something that fastens; a fastener.

fast food *n* **1** take-away food that is available on demand rather than being prepared individually for each customer. **2** frozen or packaged food that can be prepared and served quickly.

fast-forward[1] *n* an operating facility on a video or tape recorder that causes the tape to be wound forward very quickly without being played.

fast-forward[2] *v* to wind (a video, cassette tape, or other recording) quickly forward.

fastidious *adj* **1** excessively difficult to satisfy or please. **2** showing or demanding great delicacy or care. ⋙ **fastidiously** *adv,* **fastidiousness** *n.*

fastigiate *adj* **1** of a plant: having upright, usu clustered, branches. **2** of body parts or organs: united in a cone-shaped bundle.

fastness *n* **1a** the quality of being fixed. **b** the quality of being colourfast. **2** a fortified, secure, or remote place.

fast track *n* a method or procedure that gets quick results or rapid promotion.

fast-track *v* **1** to deal with (something) as a priority. **2** to promote (somebody) rapidly.

fat[1] *n* **1** greasy or oily matter, or animal tissue consisting chiefly of cells distended with greasy or oily matter. **2** fatness; being fat. **3a** any of numerous compounds of carbon, hydrogen, and oxygen that are a major class of energy-rich food and are soluble in organic solvents but not in water. **b** a solid or semisolid fat as distinguished from an oil. ⋙ **fatless** *adj.*

fat[2] *adj* (**fatter, fattest**) **1** having an unusually large amount of fat; plump or obese. **2** of a farm animal: fattened for market. **3** well filled out; thick or big: *a fat book.* **4** richly rewarding or profitable; substantial: *a fat part in a play.* **5** *informal* practically non-existent: *A fat chance you've got!* ⋙ **fatly** *adv,* **fatness** *n,* **fattish** *adj.*

fat[3] *v* (**fatted, fatting**) *archaic* to fatten (a person or an animal). ✱ **kill the fatted calf** to put on a celebration.

fatal *adj* **1a** causing death. **b** bringing ruin: *a fatal mistake.* **c** *informal* productive of disagreeable or contrary results. **2** fateful or decisive. **3** like fate in proceeding according to a fixed sequence; inevitable. ⋙ **fatally** *adv.*

fatalism *n* the belief that all events are predetermined and outside the control of human beings. ⋙ **fatalist** *n,* **fatalistic** *adj.*

fatality *n* (*pl* **-ies**) **1a** death resulting from a disaster. **b** somebody who experiences or is subject to a fatal outcome, e.g. somebody killed in an accident. **2a** the quality or state of causing death or destruction. **b** the quality or condition of being destined for disaster.

fat cat *n derog* a wealthy, privileged, and usu influential person.

fate[1] *n* **1** the power beyond human control that determines events; destiny. **2a** an outcome or end, *esp* one that is adverse and inevitable. **b** the expected result of normal development. **3a** a destiny apparently determined by fate. **b** a disaster, *esp* death.

fate[2] *v* (*usu in passive*) to destine (somebody or something); to doom: *The plan was fated to fail.*

fateful *adj* **1** having momentous and often unpleasant, catastrophic, or deadly consequences; decisive: *that fateful day.* **2** controlled by fate; foreordained. **3** having a quality of ominous prophecy: *a fateful remark.* ⋙ **fatefully** *adv,* **fatefulness** *n.*

Fates *pl n* (**the Fates**) in classical mythology, the three goddesses who determine the course of human life.

fathead *n informal* a slow-witted or stupid person.

father[1] *n* **1** a male parent of a child. **2** a forefather. **3** (**Father** *or* **the Father**) **a** God. **b** the first person of the Trinity. **4** used *esp* as a title in the Roman Catholic Church: a priest of the regular clergy. **5** somebody who originates or institutes something. ⋙ **fatherhood** *n*, **fatherless** *adj*.

father² *v* to beget (offspring).

Father Christmas *n* an old man with a white beard and red suit believed by children to deliver their presents at Christmas time.

father-in-law *n* (*pl* **fathers-in-law**) the father of one's husband or wife.

fatherland *n* one's native land.

fatherly *adj* **1** of or characteristic of a father. **2** resembling a father, e.g. in care or affection. ⋙ **fatherliness** *n*.

Father's Day *n* the third Sunday in June, on which fathers are honoured.

fathom¹ *n* a unit of length used *esp* for measuring the depth of water, equal to 6ft (about 1.83m).

fathom² *v* **1** (*often* + out) to penetrate and come to understand. **2** to measure the depth of (water) by a sounding line. ⋙ **fathomable** *adj*, **fathomless** *adj*.

fatigue¹ *n* **1** physical or nervous exhaustion. **2** the tendency of a material to break under repeated stress. **3a** manual or menial military work. **b** (*in pl*) the uniform or work clothing worn on fatigue.

fatigue² *v* (**fatigues, fatigued, fatiguing**) **1** to weary or exhaust (somebody). **2** to induce a condition of fatigue in (a material, etc).

fatso *n* (*pl* **-oes**) *informal* often used as a derog form of address: a fat person.

fatten *v* **1** (*often* + up) to become or make (a person or animal) fat or plump. **2** to become fat.

fatty¹ *adj* (**-ier, -iest**) **1a** containing large amounts of fat. **b** fat. **2** oily; greasy. **3** derived from or chemically related to fat. ⋙ **fattiness** *n*.

fatty² *n* (*pl* **-ies**) *informal* a fat person.

fatty acid *n* any of numerous organic acids with one carboxyl group, e.g. acetic acid, including many that occur naturally in fats, waxes, and essential oils.

fatty degeneration *n* deterioration in an organ of the body such as the heart or liver, caused by accumulation of fat in the cells of the organ.

fatuous *adj* complacently or inanely foolish; idiotic. ⋙ **fatuity** *n*, **fatuously** *adv*, **fatuousness** *n*.

fatwa *n* a formal legal opinion delivered by an Islamic religious authority.

faucet *n chiefly NAm* a tap.

fault¹ *n* **1** a failing, imperfection, or defect. **2a** misdemeanour or mistake. **b** an action, *esp* a service that does not land in the prescribed area, which loses a rally in tennis, squash, etc. **3** responsibility for wrongdoing or failure. **4a** a fracture in the earth's crust accompanied by displacement, e.g. of the strata, along the fracture line. **b** a rupture of rock structures due to strain. ✱ **at fault** in the wrong; liable for blame. **to a fault** to an excessive degree. ⋙ **faultless** *adj*, **faultlessly** *adv*, **faultlessness** *n*.

fault² *v* **1** to find a fault in. **2** to produce a geological fault in (the earth's crust).

faulty *adj* (**-ier, -iest**) having a fault, blemish, or defect; imperfect. ⋙ **faultily** *adv*, **faultiness** *n*.

faun *n* a figure of Roman mythology similar to the satyr, with a human body and the horns and legs of a goat.

fauna *n* (*pl* **faunas** *or* **faunae**) the animal life of a region, period, or special environment: compare FLORA. ⋙ **faunal** *adj*.

Faustian *adj* relating to the German magician and astrologer Johann Faust (d.*c*.1540), said to have sold his soul to the devil in return for knowledge and power.

faute de mieux /ˌfoht də ˈmyuh/ *adv* for lack of something more suitable or desirable.

Fauve /fohv/ *n* an exponent of Fauvism.

Fauvism *n* a 20th-cent. art movement characterized by pure and vivid colour and a free treatment of form. ⋙ **Fauvist** *n and adj*.

faux-naïf¹ /ˌfoh nahˈeef/ *adj* affecting a childlike innocence or simplicity.

faux-naïf² *n* somebody who affects a childlike innocence.

faux pas /ˌfoh ˈpah/ *n* (*pl* **faux pas** /ˌfoh ˈpahz/) a social blunder.

favor *n and v NAm* see FAVOUR¹, FAVOUR².

favorable *adj NAm* see FAVOURABLE.

favorite *n and adj NAm* see FAVOURITE¹, FAVOURITE².

favour¹ (*NAm* **favor**) *n* **1a** approving consideration or attention; approbation. **b** partiality or favouritism. **2** friendly regard shown towards another, *esp* by a superior. **3** kindness, or an act of kindness beyond what is expected or due. **4a** *archaic* a token of allegiance or love, usu worn conspicuously. **b** a small gift given to a guest, *esp* at a wedding reception. ✱ **in favour of 1** in agreement or sympathy with; on the side of. **2** to the advantage of. **3** in order to choose (something); out of preference for.

favour² (*NAm* **favor**) *v* **1a** to regard or treat with favour. **b** (+ by/with) to do a favour or kindness for; to oblige. **2** to show partiality towards; to prefer. **3** *informal* to look like (a relation). **4** to treat (*esp* an injured limb) gently or carefully.

favourable (*NAm* **favorable**) *adj* **1a** expressing or winning approval, or giving a result in one's favour. **b** disposed to favour; partial. **2** successful. ⋙ **favourably** *adv*.

favourite¹ (*NAm* **favorite**) *n* **1** somebody or something favoured or preferred above others. **2** the competitor judged most likely to win.

favourite² (*NAm* **favorite**) *adj* constituting a favourite; most liked.

favouritism (*NAm* **favoritism**) *n* the showing of unfair favour; partiality.

fawn¹ *n* **1** a young deer. **2** a light greyish brown colour. ⋙ **fawn** *adj*.

fawn² *v* **1** (+ on/upon) to court favour with somebody by acting in a servilely flattering manner. **2** (+ on/upon) of a dog, etc: to show affection to somebody. ⋙ **fawning** *adj*.

fax¹ *n* **1** a facsimile message. **2** a facsimile machine.

fax² *v* **1** to send a fax to. **2** to send (a message) by fax.

fay *n literary* a fairy.

fayre *n* = FAIR³.

faze *v informal* to disturb the composure of; to disconcert or daunt.

FBI *abbr NAm* Federal Bureau of Investigation.

FC *abbr* Football Club.

FCO *abbr Brit* Foreign and Commonwealth Office.

FE *abbr Brit* further education.

Fe *abbr* the chemical symbol for iron.

fealty *n* (*pl* **-ies**) formerly, fidelity to one's feudal lord.

fear¹ *n* **1** an unpleasant, often strong, emotion caused by anticipation or awareness of danger. **2** anxiety or solicitude. **3** reason for alarm; danger. ✱ **put the fear of God into somebody** to frighten somebody. **without fear or favour** with complete impartiality. ⋙ **fearless** *adj*, **fearlessly** *adv*, **fearlessness** *n*.

fear² *v* **1** to be afraid of (somebody or something). **2** to believe (something) with regret. **3** *archaic* to have a reverential awe of (God). **4** (+ for) to be afraid or apprehensive.

fearful *adj* **1a** full of fear of something; afraid. **b** showing or arising from fear. **2** causing or likely to cause fear. **3** *informal* extremely bad, large, or intense. ➤➤ **fearfully** *adv,* **fearfulness** *n.*

fearsome *adj* **1** causing fear. **2** awesome. ➤➤ **fearsomely** *adv.*

feasible *adj* **1** capable of being done or carried out. **2** *informal* reasonable or likely. ➤➤ **feasibility** *n,* **feasibly** *adv.*

Usage note

Feasible means 'able to be done or capable of being dealt with': *a feasible project*. Its use to mean 'likely' or 'probable' (*a feasible explanation of the events*) is best avoided in formal contexts.

feast¹ *n* **1** an elaborate meal, sometimes accompanied by a ceremony or entertainment; a banquet. **2** a periodic religious observance commemorating an event or honouring a deity, saint, person, or thing.

feast² *v* to have or take part in a feast. ✱ **feast one's eyes on** to look appreciatively at (something or somebody). ➤➤ **feaster** *n.*

feat *n* **1** a notable and *esp* courageous act or deed. **2** an act or product of skill, endurance, or ingenuity.

feather¹ *n* any of the light horny outgrowths that form the external covering of a bird's body, consisting of a shaft with two sets of interlocking barbs. ✱ **a feather in one's cap** a deserved honour or mark of distinction in which one can take pride. ➤➤ **feathery** *adj.*

feather² *v* **1** to turn (an oar blade) almost horizontal when lifting it from the water. **2** to change the angle at which (a propeller blade) meets the air so as to have the minimum wind resistance. ✱ **feather one's nest** to provide for oneself, *esp* dishonestly, through a job in which one is trusted.

featherbed *v* (**featherbedded, featherbedding**) **1** to cushion or protect from hardship, worry, etc; to pamper. **2** to assist (an industry, etc) with government subsidies.

feather bed *n* a feather mattress.

featherbrain *n* a foolish scatterbrained person. ➤➤ **featherbrained** *adj.*

feathering *n* **1a** plumage. **b** the feathers of an arrow. **2** a fringe of hair, e.g. on the legs of a dog or cart horse.

featherweight *n* **1** a weight in boxing and wrestling between lightweight and bantamweight. **2** an ineffective or unimportant person or thing.

feature¹ *n* **1** a prominent or distinctive part or characteristic. **2a** a part of the face. **b** (*in pl*) the face. **3a** a full-length film, *esp* the main film on a cinema programme. **b** a distinctive article, story, or special section in a newspaper or magazine. ➤➤ **featureless** *adj.*

feature² *v* **1** to give special prominence to (a story), e.g. in a performance or newspaper. **2** to have (something or somebody) as a characteristic or feature. **3** (+ in) to play an important part; to be a feature.

feature film *n* = FEATURE¹ (3A).

Feb. *abbr* February.

febrifuge *n* a drug that alleviates fever.

febrile *adj* of fever; feverish.

February *n* (*pl* **-ies**) the second month of the year.

feces *pl n NAm* see FAECES.

feckless *adj* **1** ineffectual; weak. **2** worthless; irresponsible. ➤➤ **fecklessly** *adv,* **fecklessness** *n.*

feculent *adj formal* foul with impurities or excrement.

fecund *adj* **1** fruitful in offspring or vegetation; prolific. **2** very intellectually productive or inventive to a marked degree. ➤➤ **fecundity** *n.*

fecundate *v* **1** *archaic* to make (a woman or female animal) fertile; to impregnate. **2** *literary* to make fecund. ➤➤ **fecundation** *n.*

fed¹ *v* past tense and past part. of FEED¹.

fed² *n* (*often* **Fed**) *NAm, informal* a federal agent or officer.

federal *adj* **1a** formed by agreement between political units that surrender their individual sovereignty to a central authority but retain limited powers of government, or of or constituting a government so formed. **b** of the central government of a federation as distinguished from those of the constituent units. **2** of or loyal to the federal government of the USA in the American Civil War. ➤➤ **federalism** *n,* **federalist** *n and adj,* **federally** *adv.*

Federal Reserve System *n* in the USA, a banking system that consists of twelve Federal Reserve Banks plus their member banks.

federate *v* **1** to join (states, etc) in a federation. **2** of states, etc: to join a federation. ➤➤ **federate** *adj.*

federation *n* **1 a** a country formed by the federation of separate states. **b** a union of organizations. **2** the act or an instance of federating, *esp* the formation of a federal union.

fedora *n* a low felt hat with the crown creased lengthways.

fed up *adj informal* discontented or bored.

fee *n* **1** (*also in pl*) a sum of money paid *esp* for entrance or for a professional service. **2** (*usu in pl*) money paid for education.

feeble *adj* **1** lacking in strength or endurance; weak. **2** deficient in authority, force, or effect. ➤➤ **feebleness** *n,* **feebly** *adv.*

feebleminded *adj* foolish or stupid.

feed¹ *v* (*past tense and past part.* **fed**) **1a** to give food to (a person or an animal). **b** to give (something) to a person or animal as food. **c** to produce or provide food for (people). **2** to provide something essential to the growth, sustenance, maintenance, or operation of (something). **3a** to satisfy or gratify (a feeling, etc). **b** to support or encourage (somebody's ambition, dislike, etc). **4** to supply for use, consumption, or processing, *esp* in a continuous manner. **5** to supply (a signal or power) to an electronic circuit. **6** to be moved into a machine or opening gradually. **7** to act as a feed for (a comedian, etc). **8** (*usu* + off/on/upon) to consume food; to eat. **9** (*usu* + off/on/upon) to become nourished or satisfied as if by food.

feed² *n* **1** the act or an instance of feeding or eating. **2** a mixture or preparation of food for livestock. **3a** material supplied, e.g. to a furnace. **b** a mechanism by which the action of feeding is effected. **4** a performer who supplies cues for another performer's lines or actions.

feedback *n* **1** information about the results of an action or process, usu in response to a request. **2** the return to the input of a part of the output of a machine, system, or process, e.g. noise fed back to a microphone. **3** the modifying influence of the results or effects of a process, *esp* a biological process, on another stage in the same process.

feeder *n* **1** a person or animal that feeds, *esp* in a stated way. **2** a device or apparatus for supplying food, e.g. to a caged animal or bird. **3a** a device feeding material into or through a machine. **b** a heavy wire conductor supplying electricity to a point of an electric distribution system. **c** a transmission line running from a radio transmitter to an antenna. **d** a road, railway, airline, or aircraft that links remote areas with the main transport system.

feedstock *n* raw material supplied to a machine or processing plant.

feel[1] *v* (*past tense and past part.* **felt**) **1a** to handle or touch (something) in order to examine or explore it. **b** to perceive by a physical sensation coming from discrete end organs, e.g. of the skin or muscles. **2** to experience actively or passively; to be affected by. **3** (*often* + out) to find, ascertain, or explore by cautious trial: *They felt out the opposition.* **4a** to be aware of (something) without direct experience or by drawing conclusions from the evidence available. **b** to believe or think. **5a** to receive or be able to receive the sensation of touch. **b** to search for something by using the sense of touch. **6a** to have or be conscious of an inward impression, state of mind, or physical condition: *She feels much better now.* **b** to believe oneself to be (something): *I did feel stupid.* **7** (+ for) to have sympathy or pity for. ✻ **feel like 1** to wish for; to be in the mood for. **2** to resemble or seem to be (something) on the evidence of touch. **feel up to** to be well enough or fit enough to.

feel[2] *n* **1** the sense of feeling; touch. **2** sensation or feeling. **3a** the quality of a thing as imparted through touch. **b** typical or peculiar quality or atmosphere. **4** intuitive skill, knowledge, or ability for something.

feeler *n* **1** a tactile appendage, e.g. a tentacle, of an animal. **2** (*usu in pl*) something, e.g. a proposal, ventured to ascertain the views of others.

feeler gauge *n* a set of thin steel strips of various known thicknesses by which small gaps may be measured.

feel-good *adj informal* inducing a feeling of well-being.

feeling[1] *n* **1a** an emotional state or reaction. **b** (*in pl*) susceptibility to impression; sensibility. **2** a conscious recognition; a sense. **3a** an opinion or belief, *esp* when unreasoned; a sentiment. **b** a presentiment. **4** generalized bodily consciousness, sensation, or awareness. **5** capacity to respond emotionally, *esp* with the higher emotions. **6** = FEEL[2] (3). **7** = FEEL[2] (4).

feeling[2] *adj* **1** expressing emotion or sensitivity. **2a** having the capacity to feel or respond emotionally; sensitive. **b** easily moved emotionally; sympathetic. ➤➤ **feelingly** *adv.*

feet *n* pl of FOOT[1].

feign *v* **1** to give a false appearance or impression of (something) deliberately. **2** to pretend (something).

feint[1] *n* a mock blow or attack directed towards a point away from the point one really intends to attack.

feint[2] *v* to make a feint.

feint[3] *adj* of rulings on paper: faint or pale.

feisty *adj* (**-ier, -iest**) *informal* **1** spirited and determined. **2** touchy or quarrelsome.

felafel *n* see FALAFEL.

feldspar *or* **felspar** *n* any of a group of minerals that consist of aluminium silicates with either potassium, sodium, calcium, or barium, an essential constituent of nearly all crystalline rocks.

felicitations *pl n* congratulations.

felicitous *adj formal* very well suited or expressed; apt. ➤➤ **felicitously** *adv,* **felicitousness** *n.*

felicity *n* (*pl* **-ies**) *formal* **1** great happiness, or something causing great happiness. **2** a felicitous faculty or quality, *esp* in art or language; aptness. **3** a felicitous expression.

feline[1] *adj* **1** of cats or the cat family. **2** resembling a cat; having the characteristics generally attributed to cats.

feline[2] *n* a cat; a member of the cat family.

fell[1] *v* past tense of FALL[1].

fell[2] *v* **1** to cut, beat, or knock (something) down. **2** to knock down or kill (somebody). **3** to turn under and sew down the raw edges of (a seam). ➤➤ **feller** *n.*

fell[3] *n* (*also in pl*) a steep rugged stretch of high moorland, *esp* in northern England and Scotland.

fell[4] *adj literary* **1** fierce or cruel. **2** very destructive; deadly. ✻ **at one fell swoop** all at once, or with a single concentrated effort.

fellate *v* to perform fellatio on. ➤➤ **fellator** *n.*

fellatio *n* oral stimulation of the penis.

felloe *or* **felly** *n* (*pl* **felloes** *or* **fellies**) the exterior rim of a spoked wheel, or a segment of it.

fellow *n* **1** *informal* a man or a boy. **2a** an equal in rank, power, or character; a peer. **b** either of a pair; a mate. **3a** (*usu in pl*) a comrade or associate. **b** (*used before a noun*) being a companion or associate; belonging to the same group: *fellow travellers.* **4** *Brit* a member of an incorporated literary or scientific society. **5** an incorporated member of a collegiate foundation.

fellow feeling *n* a feeling of community of interest or of mutual understanding; *specif* sympathy.

fellowship *n* **1** the condition of friendly relations between people; companionship. **2a** community of interest or experience. **b** the state of being a fellow or associate. **3** (*used as sing. or pl*) a group of people with similar interests; an association. **4** the position of a fellow, e.g. of a university.

fellow traveller *n* a non-member who sympathizes with and often furthers the ideals and programme of an organized group, *esp* the Communist party.

felly *n* (*pl* **-ies**) see FELLOE.

felon *n* somebody who has committed a felony.

felony *n* (*pl* **-ies**) a grave crime, e.g. murder or arson, that was formerly regarded in law as more serious than a misdemeanour. ➤➤ **felonious** *adj,* **feloniously** *adv,* **feloniousness** *n.*

felspar *n* see FELDSPAR.

felt[1] *n* a nonwoven cloth made by compressing wool or fur, often mixed with natural or synthetic fibres.

felt[2] *v* **1** to make (wool, etc) into felt, or to cover with felt. **2** to become matted or cause (something) to stick and mat together.

felt[3] *v* past tense and past part. of FEEL[1].

felt-tipped pen *n* = FELT-TIP PEN.

felt-tip pen *n* a pen with a soft felt tip through which ink flows.

felucca *n* a narrow lateen-rigged sailing ship, chiefly of the Mediterranean area.

fem /fem/ *n* see FEMME.

female[1] *adj* **1** relating to or denoting the sex that bears offspring or produces eggs. **2** of a plant or flower: having an ovary but no stamens. **3** designed with a hollow part for receiving a corresponding male part. ➤➤ **femaleness** *n.*

female[2] *n* a female animal, person, or plant.

female circumcision *n* the practice, traditional in some ethnic groups, of removing the clitoris of young or adolescent girls, sometimes also involving the removal of the labia and the sewing up of part of the vagina.

feminine[1] *adj* **1** of or being a female person. **2** characteristic of, appropriate to, or peculiar to women; womanly. **3** of or belonging to the gender that normally includes most words or grammatical forms referring to females. ⋙ **femininely** *adv*, **femininity** *n*.

feminine[2] *n* the feminine gender, or a word or morpheme of this gender.

feminise *v* see FEMINIZE.

feminism *n* the advocacy or furtherance of women's rights, interests, and equality with men. ⋙ **feminist** *n and adj*.

feminize *or* **-ise** *v* **1** to give a feminine quality to. **2** to cause (a male or castrated female) to take on feminine characteristics, e.g. by administration of hormones. ⋙ **feminization** *n*.

femme *or* **fem** /fem/ *n informal* a lesbian who adopts a passive role and extreme feminine characteristics.

femme fatale /ˌfam fəˈtahl/ *n* (*pl* **femmes fatales**) a seductive and usu mysterious woman, *esp* one who lures men into dangerous or compromising situations.

femora *n* pl of FEMUR.

femto- *comb. form* one thousand million millionth (10^{-15}) part of: *femtoampere*.

femur *n* (*pl* **femurs** *or* **femora**) the bone of the hind or lower limb nearest the body; the thighbone. ⋙ **femoral** *adj*.

fen[1] *n* **1a** an area of low marshy or flooded land. **b** such an area when artificially drained. **2** (**the Fens**) a fertile agricultural district of eastern England consisting of land reclaimed from the Wash. ⋙ **fenny** *adj*.

fen[2] *n* (*pl* **fen**) a unit of currency in China, worth 100th of a yuan.

fence[1] *n* **1a** a barrier, e.g. of wire or boards, intended to prevent escape or intrusion or to mark a boundary. **b** an upright obstacle to be jumped by a horse, e.g. in showjumping or steeplechasing. **c** a protective guard on a tool or piece of machinery. **2** *informal* a receiver of stolen goods. ✻ **sit on the fence** to adopt a position of neutrality or indecision.

fence[2] *v* **1a** (*usu* + in) to enclose (an area) with a fence. **b** (*usu* + off) to separate (an area) off with a fence. **2** *informal* to receive or sell (stolen goods). **3a** to practise fencing. **b** to use tactics of attack and defence, e.g. thrusting and parrying, resembling those of fencing. ⋙ **fencer** *n*.

fencing *n* **1** the art of attack and defence with a sword, e.g. the foil, épée, or sabre. **2** fences, or material used for building them.

fend *v* (+ for) to provide a livelihood for somebody, *esp* oneself; to look after oneself.

fender *n* **1** a cushion, e.g. of rope or wood, hung over the side of a ship to absorb impact. **2** a low metal guard for a fire, used to confine the coals. **3** *NAm* a wing or mudguard.

fend off *v* to keep or ward off; to repel.

fenestration *n* **1** the arrangement of windows in a building. **2** an opening in a surface, e.g. a wall or membrane. **3** the operation of cutting an opening in the bony labyrinth between the inner ear and tympanum as a treatment for deafness.

feng shui /ˌfung ˈshway, ˌfeng ˈshooh·i/ *n* in Chinese philosophy, a system of rules governing the placement and arrangement of a building, room, etc, according to the flow of energy in the environment, so as to bring good fortune.

Fenian *n* a member of a secret Irish and Irish-American organization of the 19th cent., dedicated to the overthrow of British rule in Ireland.

fennel *n* a European plant of the carrot family cultivated for its aromatic seeds and foliage.

fennig *n* a unit of currency in Bosnia-Herzegovina, worth 100th of a convertible marka.

fenugreek *n* a leguminous Asiatic plant whose aromatic seeds are used as a flavouring.

feral *adj* **1a** not domesticated or cultivated; = WILD[1]. **b** having escaped from domestication and become wild. **2** of or suggestive of a wild beast; savage.

ferment[1] *v* **1** to undergo or cause (a substance) to undergo fermentation. **2** to cause (a state of agitation). ⋙ **fermentable** *adj*, **fermenter** *n*.

ferment[2] *n* a state of unrest or upheaval; agitation or tumult.

fermentation *n* an enzymatically controlled anaerobic breakdown of an energy-rich compound, e.g. a carbohydrate to carbon dioxide and alcohol, or an enzymatically controlled transformation of an organic compound. ⋙ **fermentative** *adj*.

fermion *n* a particle, e.g. an electron, that interacts with other particles in a way described by physicists Fermi and Dirac.

fermium *n* a radioactive metallic chemical element that is artificially produced.

fern *n* (*pl* **ferns** *or* **fern**) a flowerless seedless plant that has a root, stem, and leaflike fronds and reproduces by spores. ⋙ **fernery** *n*, **ferny** *adj*.

ferocious *adj* extremely fierce or violent. ⋙ **ferociously** *adv*, **ferociousness** *n*, **ferocity** *n*.

-ferous *or* **-iferous** *comb. form* forming adjectives, with the meaning: bearing or containing: *carboniferous*.

ferret[1] *n* **1** a partially domesticated European polecat, *esp* an albino, used for hunting small rodents, e.g. rats, or kept as a pet. **2** *informal* an active and persistent search. ⋙ **ferrety** *adj*.

ferret[2] *v* (**ferreted, ferreting**) **1** *informal* (+ about/around) to search about or around. **2** to hunt with ferrets. ⋙ **ferreter** *n*.

ferret out *v informal* to find (information) and bring it to light by searching.

ferric *adj* of, containing, or being iron with a valency of three.

Ferris wheel *n chiefly NAm* = BIG WHEEL.

ferrite *n* any of several magnetic substances of high magnetic permeability consisting mainly of an iron oxide.

ferroconcrete *n* = REINFORCED CONCRETE.

ferroelectric *adj* of or being a crystalline substance having spontaneous electric polarization reversible by an electric field. ⋙ **ferroelectricity** *n*.

ferromagnetic *adj* of or being a substance, *esp* iron, characterized by strong magnetization in which all the magnetic ions are polarized in the same direction. ⋙ **ferromagnetism** *n*.

ferrous *adj* of, containing, or being iron with a valency of two.

ferruginous *adj* **1** of or containing iron. **2** resembling iron rust in colour.

ferrule *n* **1** a ring or cap, usu of metal, strengthening a cane, tool handle, etc. **2** a short tube or bush for making a tight joint, e.g. between pipes.

ferry[1] *v* (**-ies, -ied**) **1** to carry (somebody) by boat, hovercraft, etc over a body of water. **2** to convey (somebody) by car, etc from one place to another.

ferry[2] *n* (*pl* **-ies**) a boat, etc providing a regular service for carrying passengers, vehicles, or goods across a body of water, e.g. a river.

ferryman *n* (*pl* **ferrymen**) somebody who operates a ferry.

fertile *adj* **1a** capable of producing or bearing fruit, *esp* in great quantities; productive. **b** capable of sustaining abundant plant growth. **c** characterized by great resourcefulness and activity; inventive: *a fertile imagination.* **2a** capable of breeding or reproducing. **b** capable of growing or developing: *a fertile egg.* **c** affording abundant possibilities for development: *a fertile area for research.* ➤➤ **fertility** *n.*

fertilise *v* see FERTILIZE.

fertiliser *n* see FERTILIZER.

fertility drug *n* a drug which treats infertility in women by stimulating the release of ova from the ovaries.

fertilize *or* **-ise** *v* **1a** to make (an ovule, egg, etc) capable of developing into a new individual by uniting with a male germ cell. **b** to apply a fertilizer to (soil) or nutrients to (water). **2** to make (something) fertile by insemination, impregnation, or pollination. ➤➤ **fertilization** *n.*

fertilizer *or* **fertiliser** *n* a substance, e.g. manure, used to make soil more fertile.

fervent *adj* exhibiting deep sincere emotion; ardent. ➤➤ **fervency** *n,* **fervently** *adv.*

fervid *adj* passionately intense; ardent. ➤➤ **fervidly** *adv.*

fervour (*NAm* **fervor**) *n* the quality or state of being fervent or fervid.

fescue *n* any of several species of tufted grasses, some of which are important fodder grasses and a few used as lawn grasses.

festal *adj* = FESTIVE.

fester *v* **1** of a wound: to generate pus. **2** of food, etc: to putrefy or rot. **3** of a feeling, etc: to rankle. **4** of a problem, situation, etc: to become worse; to intensify.

festival *n* **1a** a time marked by special, e.g. customary, celebration. **b** a religious feast. **2** a programme or season of cultural events or entertainment.

festive *adj* **1** of or suitable for a feast or festival, *esp* Christmas and New Year. **2** joyous or merry. ➤➤ **festively** *adv,* **festiveness** *n.*

festivity *n* (*pl* **-ies**) **1** (*also in pl*) festive activity; a party or celebration. **2** a festival.

festoon[1] *n* a decorative chain or strip hanging between two points, or an ornament representing this.

festoon[2] *v* **1** to hang or form festoons round (a room, etc). **2** to cover (something) profusely and gaily with decorations.

festschrift /'festshrift/ *n* (*pl* **festschrifts** *or* **festschriften**) a volume of writings by various authors presented as a tribute or memorial, *esp* to a scholar.

feta *n* a firm white Greek cheese made of sheep's or goat's milk and cured in brine.

fetal *adj* = foetal (see FOETUS).

fetch[1] *v* **1** to go or come after (something or somebody) and bring or take them back. **2a** to cause (somebody) to come; to bring. **b** to reach (a specified price) as profit or return. **3** *informal* to strike or deal (a blow, slap, etc). ✱ **fetch and carry** to perform simple tasks or run errands for somebody. ➤➤ **fetcher** *n.*

fetch[2] *n* the act or an instance of fetching.

fetching *adj* attractive or becoming. ➤➤ **fetchingly** *adv.*

fetch up *v* **1** *informal* to come to rest or arrive. **2** *informal* to vomit (food, etc).

fete[1] *or* **fête** *n* **1** *Brit* an outdoor bazaar or other entertainment, usu held to raise money for a particular purpose. **2** *chiefly NAm* a festival.

fete[2] *or* **fête** *v* (*usu in passive*) to honour or commemorate (somebody or something) with ceremony.

fetid *or* **foetid** *adj* having a heavy offensive smell; stinking.

fetish *n* **1a** an object believed among a primitive people to have magical power. **b** an object regarded with superstitious trust or reverence. **2** a form of sexual desire and gratification related to an object or bodily part. **3** an object of irrational reverence or obsessive devotion.

fetishism *n* **1** the displacement of erotic interest and satisfaction to a fetish. **2** belief in magical fetishes. ➤➤ **fetishist** *n,* **fetishistic** *adj.*

fetlock *n* **1** a projection bearing a tuft of hair on the back of the leg above the hoof of an animal of the horse family. **2** the joint of the limb or tuft of hair at the fetlock.

fetor *n formal* a strong offensive smell.

fetter[1] *n* **1** a shackle for the feet. **2** (*usu in pl*) something that confines; a restraint.

fetter[2] *v* **1** to put fetters on (somebody). **2** to shackle or restrain.

fettle *n* a state of physical or mental fitness or order; condition.

fettuccine /fetə'cheeni/ *pl n* (*used as sing. or pl*) pasta in narrow ribbons.

fetus *n* see FOETUS.

Usage note

foetus *or* fetus? See note at FOETUS.

feud[1] *n* a lasting state of hostilities, *esp* between families or clans, marked by violent attacks for the purpose of revenge.

feud[2] *v* to carry on a feud.

feudal *adj* of feudalism. ➤➤ **feudally** *adv.*

feudalism *n* a medieval system of political organization involving the relationship of lord to vassal with all land held in exchange for service, homage, the service of tenants under arms and in court, wardship, and forfeiture.

fever *n* **1** a rise of body temperature above the normal, or any of various diseases characterized by such a rise in temperature. **2** a state of intense emotion or activity. ➤➤ **feverish** *adj,* **feverishly** *adv,* **feverishness** *n.*

fevered *adj* **1** hot or flushed owing to fever or agitation. **2** extremely fast or active, and usu agitated or excited: *a fevered imagination.*

feverfew *n* a perennial European composite plant with white-yellow flowers.

fever pitch *n* a state of intense excitement and agitation.

few[1] *adj* **1** amounting to only a small number. **2** (**a few**) at least some though not many. ✱ **few and far between** scarce; rare. **not a few** quite a lot.

few[2] *n* **1** (*pl*) not many: *Few of his stories were true.* **2** (**a few**) at least some though not many. **3** (**the few**) a select or exclusive group of people; an elite.

fewer *adj* comparative of FEW[1].

Usage note

fewer *or* less? The general rule is to use *fewer* with plural nouns (*fewer people, fewer books*) and *less* with singular nouns (*less time, less work, less sugar*). More precisely, *fewer* is used with people or things that can be counted (*fewer than 100 people came to the meeting*) and *less* is used with quantities and numbers that give a quantity or size: *less than two years ago*. The use of *less* with plural nouns should be avoided: *fewer opportunities*, not *less opportunities*.

fey *adj* **1** marked by an otherworldly and irresponsible air. **2** able to see into the future or to see spirits. ➤➤ **feyness** *n*.

fez *n* (*pl* **fezzes**) a red brimless hat shaped like a truncated cone with a tassel, worn by men in southern and eastern Mediterranean countries.

ff *abbr* **1** folios. **2** following, e.g. pages. **3** fortissimo.

fiancé *or* **fiancée** *n* a man or woman to whom a person is engaged to be married.

fiasco *n* (*pl* **-os**) a complete and ignominious failure.

fiat *n* an authoritative and often arbitrary order; a decree.

fib[1] *n informal* a trivial or childish lie.

fib[2] *v* (**fibbed, fibbing**) *informal* to tell a trivial or childish lie. ➤➤ **fibber** *n*.

fiber *n NAm* see FIBRE.

Fibonacci number /feebə'nahchi/ *n* a number in the Fibonacci sequence 1, 1, 2, 3, 5, 8, 13, 21, ...

Fibonacci sequence *n* an infinite sequence of integers in which every term after the second is the sum of the two preceding terms.

fibre (*NAm* **fiber**) *n* **1a** an elongated tapering plant cell with thick walls. **b** = NERVE FIBRE. **c** any of the filaments composing most of the intercellular matrix of connective tissue. **d** any of the elongated contractile cells of muscle tissue. **e** a slender natural or manufactured thread or filament, e.g. of wool, cotton, or asbestos. **2** material made of fibres. **3** = DIETARY FIBRE. **4** strength or fortitude.

fibreboard *n* a material made by compressing fibres of wood, etc into stiff boards.

fibreglass *n* **1** glass in fibrous form used in making various products, e.g. textiles and insulation materials. **2** a combination of synthetic resins and fibreglass.

fibre optics *pl n* (*used as sing. or pl*) the use of very thin bundles of glass or plastic fibres that transmit light throughout their length by internal reflections and are used, e.g. for transmitting optical signals. ➤➤ **fibre-optic** *adj*.

fibrescope *n* a flexible instrument using fibre optics for examining inaccessible areas, e.g. the lining of the stomach.

fibril *n* a small filament or fibre. ➤➤ **fibrillar** *adj*.

fibrillate *v* to undergo or cause (something) to undergo fibrillation.

fibrillation *n* **1** the forming of fibres or fibrils. **2** very rapid irregular contractions of muscle fibres of the heart resulting in a lack of synchronization between heartbeat and pulse.

fibrin *n* a fibrous protein formed from fibrinogen by the action of thrombin, *esp* in the clotting of blood. ➤➤ **fibrinous** *adj*.

fibrinogen *n* a blood plasma protein that is produced in the liver and is converted into fibrin during clotting of blood.

fibroblast *n* a cell giving rise to connective tissue which secretes collagen.

fibroid[1] *adj* resembling, forming, or consisting of fibrous tissue.

fibroid[2] *n* a benign tumour made up of fibrous and muscular tissue that occurs *esp* in the uterine wall.

fibroma *n* (*pl* **fibromas** *or* **fibromata**) a benign tumour consisting mainly of fibrous tissue.

fibrosis *n* the abnormal increase of fibrous tissue in an organ or part of the body. ➤➤ **fibrotic** *adj*.

fibrous *adj* containing or consisting of fibres.

fibula *n* (*pl* **fibulae** *or* **fibulas**) the outer and usu smaller of the two bones of the hind limb of higher vertebrates between the knee and ankle.

-fic *suffix* forming adjectives, with the meaning: making or causing: *horrific*; *pacific*.

fichu /'feeshooh/ *n* a woman's light triangular scarf draped over the shoulders and fastened at the bosom.

fickle *adj* lacking steadfastness or constancy; capricious. ➤➤ **fickleness** *n*.

fiction *n* **1a** literature, e.g. novels or short stories, describing imaginary people and events. **b** something invented by the imagination; *specif* an invented story. **2** the action of feigning or creating with the imagination. **3** an assumption of a possibility as a fact, irrespective of the question of its truth. ➤➤ **fictional** *adj*, **fictionality** *n*, **fictionally** *adv*, **fictionist** *n*.

Usage note

fictional *or* fictitious? These two words are sometimes confused. *Fictional* means 'of fiction': *fictional heroes*; *fictitious* means 'not real or genuine; false': *He gave a fictitious name to the police*.

fictionalize *or* **-ise** *v* to make into or treat in the manner of fiction. ➤➤ **fictionalization** *n*.

fictitious *adj* **1** of a name: false; assumed. **2** not genuinely felt; feigned. **3** found or described in fiction. ➤➤ **fictitiously** *adv*, **fictitiousness** *n*.

Usage note

fictitious *or* fictional? See note at FICTION.

fictive *adj* **1** not genuinely felt; = FICTITIOUS (2). **2** of or capable of imaginative creation.

ficus /'feekəs/ *n* (*pl* **ficus**) a tropical plant of the genus that includes the fig tree.

fiddle[1] *n* **1** *informal* a violin. **2** *Brit, informal* a dishonest practice; a swindle. **3** *Brit, informal* an activity involving intricate manipulation.

fiddle[2] *v informal* **1** to move one's hands or fingers restlessly. **2** *Brit* to falsify (accounts, etc), *esp* so as to gain financial advantage. **3** *Brit* to get or contrive (something) by cheating or deception. ✱ **fiddle with** *informal* to tamper or meddle with (something). ➤➤ **fiddler** *n*.

fiddle-faddle *n informal* often used as an exclamation: nonsense.

fiddler crab *n* a burrowing crab of which the male has one claw much enlarged.

fiddlesticks *pl n informal* used as an exclamation: nonsense.

fiddling *adj informal* **1** trifling or petty. **2** *Brit* = FIDDLY.

fiddly *adj* (**-ier, -iest**) *Brit, informal* finicky or intricate.

fideism *n* reliance on faith rather than reason, *esp* in metaphysics.

fidelity *n* **1a** the quality or state of being faithful; loyalty. **b** accuracy in details; exactness. **2** the degree of similarity between some reproduced material and its original source.

fidget[1] *v* (**fidgeted, fidgeting**) to move or act restlessly or nervously. ➤➤ **fidgety** *adj*.

fidget[2] *n* **1** somebody who fidgets. **2** (*usu in pl*) uneasiness or restlessness shown by nervous movements.

fiducial *adj* taken as a standard of reference: *a fiducial mark*.

fiduciary[1] *adj* of or having the nature of a trust.

fiduciary[2] *n* (*pl* **-ies**) somebody who is entrusted to hold or manage property for another.

fie *interj archaic* used to express disgust or shock.

fief *n* **1** formerly, a feudal estate. **2** something over which somebody has rights or exercises control. ➤➤ **fiefdom** *n.*

field[1] *n* **1a** an area of open land surrounded by a hedge or fence and used for cultivation or pasture. **b** an area of land containing a natural resource. **c** the place where a battle is fought, or a battle itself. **d** a large unbroken expanse, e.g. of ice. **2** an area constructed, equipped, or marked for sports. **3a** an area or division of an activity. **b** an area of knowledge or expertise. **4** (*used before a noun*) working or for use in the field: *field artillery.* **5** (**the field**) the participants in a sports activity, *esp* with the exception of the favourite or winner. **6** a region or space in which a given effect, e.g. magnetism, exists. **7** the area visible for observation through an optical instrument. **8** an area, e.g. a region of a computer disk store, in which a particular type of information is recorded. ✻ **take the field** of a sports team: to go onto a playing field.

field[2] *v* **1a** to stop and pick up (a batted ball). **b** to deal with (a question) by giving an impromptu answer. **2a** to put (a team) into the field of play. **b** to put (troops) into the field of battle. **3** to play as a fielder in cricket, baseball, etc. ➤➤ **fielder** *n.*

field day *n* **1** a time of unusual pleasure and unrestrained action. **2a** a day for military exercises or manoeuvres. **b** an outdoor meeting or social gathering.

field event *n* an athletic event, e.g. discus, javelin, or jumping, other than a race.

fieldfare *n* a medium-sized Eurasian thrush with an ash-coloured head and chestnut wings.

field glasses *pl n* an optical instrument consisting of two telescope-like parts on a single frame with a focusing device.

field hockey *n chiefly NAm* hockey.

field hospital *n* a temporary hospital established for emergency treatment in a combat zone.

field marshal *n* an officer of the highest rank in the British army.

field mouse *n* any of several species of mice that inhabit fields.

field mushroom *n* the common edible mushroom.

field officer *n* a commissioned army officer of the rank of colonel, lieutenant colonel, or major.

field sport *n* an open-air sport, e.g. hunting or shooting, involving the pursuit of animals.

field test *n* = FIELD TRIAL.

field-test *v* to submit (something) to a field test.

field trial *n* (*usu in pl*) a test for a new design, variety of plant, etc under authentic working or growing conditions, rather than in the laboratory, workshop, or greenhouse.

field trip *n* a visit made by students for first-hand observation, e.g. to a farm or a museum.

fieldwork *n* **1** work done in the field, e.g. by students, to gain practical experience through first-hand observation. **2** the gathering of data in anthropology, sociology, etc through the observation or interviewing of subjects in the field.

fiend *n* **1a** a demon. **b** (**the Fiend**) the Devil; Satan. **c** a person of great wickedness or cruelty. **2** *informal* somebody greatly or excessively devoted to a specified activity or thing; a fanatic or devotee: *a fresh-air fiend.* **3** *informal* a person who uses immoderate quantities of something specified; an addict: *a dope fiend.*

fiendish *adj* **1** extremely cruel or wicked. **2** *informal* extremely bad, unpleasant, or difficult. **3** *informal* ingeniously clever or complex. ➤➤ **fiendishly** *adv,* **fiendishness** *n.*

fierce *adj* **1** violently hostile or aggressive; combative or pugnacious. **2a** lacking restraint or control; violent or heated. **b** extremely intense or severe. **3** furiously active or determined. **4** of a mechanism: operating with a sharp and powerful action. ➤➤ **fiercely** *adv,* **fierceness** *n.*

fiery *adj* (**-ier, -iest**) **1a** consisting of fire. **b** burning or blazing. **c** liable to catch fire or explode. **2** of food: very hot. **3** of the colour of fire, *esp* red. **4a** full of or exuding strong emotion or spirit; passionate. **b** easily provoked; irascible. ➤➤ **fierily** *adv,* **fieriness** *n.*

fiesta *n* **1** in Spain and Latin America, a saint's day, often celebrated with processions and dances. **2** a festive occasion; a celebration.

FIFA *abbr* International Football Federation.

fife *n* a small flute used chiefly in military bands.

fifteen *adj and n* **1** the number 15. **2** (*used as sing. or pl*) a Rugby Union football team. ➤➤ **fifteenth** *adj and n.*

fifth *adj and n* **1** having the position in a sequence corresponding to the number five. **2** one of five equal parts of something. **3** in music, an interval of five degrees of a diatonic scale, or the combination of two notes at such an interval. ✻ **take the fifth** in the USA, to refuse to testify as a witness against oneself, in accordance with the Fifth Amendment to the Constitution. ➤➤ **fifthly** *adv.*

fifth column *n* a group within a nation or faction that sympathizes with and works secretly for an enemy or rival. ➤➤ **fifth columnist** *n.*

fifty *adj and n* (*pl* **-ies**) **1** the number 50. **2** (*in pl*) the numbers 50 to 59. ➤➤ **fiftieth** *adj and n.*

fifty-fifty[1] *adv* evenly; equally.

fifty-fifty[2] *adj* half favourable and half unfavourable; even.

fig[1] *n* **1** a fleshy pear-shaped or oblong edible fruit with many seeds. **2** a contemptibly worthless trifle: *It's not worth a fig.*

fig[2] *n informal* dress; array: *All belted and plumed, and in full military fig* — De Quincey.

fight[1] *v* (*past tense and past part.* **fought**) **1a** (*also* + for/against) to contend in battle or physical combat, *esp* to strive to overcome a person by blows or weapons. **b** to disagree verbally; to argue. **2** (*often* + for/against) to strive or struggle. **3** to contend against (somebody) in or as if in battle or physical combat. **4** to attempt to prevent the success, effectiveness, or development of (somebody or something). **5** to wage (a war). **6** to struggle to endure or surmount (a difficulty). **7a** to make (one's way) by fighting, or as if by fighting. **b** (*usu* + back/down) to control (something) with a struggle: *She fought down her fear.* ✻ **fight shy of** to avoid facing or getting (something).

fight[2] *n* **1a** an act of fighting; a battle or combat. **b** a verbal disagreement; an argument. **2** a protracted struggle for an objective. **3** strength or disposition for fighting; pugnacity. ✻ **fight or flight** the natural response to stress or threat, in which the body prepares itself to oppose a source of stress or threat or to flee from it.

fight back *v* to struggle to recover from a losing or disadvantageous position; to resist. ➤➤ **fightback** *n.*

fighter *n* **1** somebody or something that fights. **2** a fast manoeuvrable aeroplane designed to destroy enemy aircraft.

fighting chance *n* (**a fighting chance**) a small chance that may be realized through struggle.

fighting fit *adj* very fit; in good health.

fight off *v* to ward off by fighting, or as if by fighting; to repel.

fig leaf *n* **1** a leaf of a fig tree. **2** a representation of such a leaf positioned so as to conceal the genitals on a statue, etc.

figment *n* something fabricated or imagined.

figuration *n* **1** the creation or representation of an allegorical or symbolic figure. **2** a form or outline. **3** in music, ornamentation of a passage by using musical figures.

figurative *adj* **1** characterized by or using figures of speech, *esp* metaphor. **2a** representing by a figure or likeness; emblematic. **b** representational. ➤➤ **figuratively** *adv*, **figurativeness** *n*.

figure[1] *n* **1** a number symbol, *esp* an Arabic one. **2** bodily shape or form, *esp* a slim shape. **3a** a personage or personality. **b** a representative or substitute. **4a** the graphic representation of a human or animal form. **b** a diagram or pictorial illustration in a text. **c** a geometrical diagram or shape. **5** an appearance made; an impression produced, *esp* a favourable one. **6** a short musical phrase.

figure[2] *v* **1** (*often* + in) to take an important or conspicuous part. **2** to calculate. **3** *informal* to seem reasonable or expected. **4** *chiefly NAm, informal* to regard or consider (something). **5** to represent (somebody or something) by a figure or outline; to portray. ✱ **figure on** *NAm, informal* to take into consideration, e.g. in planning.

figurehead *n* **1** an ornamental carved figure on a ship's bow. **2** a head or chief in name only.

figure of speech *n* a form of expression, e.g. a hyperbole or metaphor, used to convey meaning or heighten effect.

figure out *v informal* **1** to discover or determine. **2** to solve or fathom (something or somebody).

figure skating *n* skating in which the skater outlines distinctive circular patterns based on the figure eight. ➤➤ **figure skater** *n*.

figurine *n* a statuette.

Fijian *n* a member of the Melanesian people of the Fiji Islands. ➤➤ **Fijian** *adj*.

filagree[1] *n* see FILIGREE[1].

filagree[2] *v* see FILIGREE[2].

filament *n* **1** a single thread or a thin flexible threadlike object or part. **2** a slender conductor in an electric light bulb, made incandescent by the passage of an electric current. **3** the stalk of a stamen that bears the anther. ➤➤ **filamentary** *adj*, **filamentous** *adj*.

filariasis *n* (*pl* **filariases**) infestation with or a disease, e.g. elephantiasis, caused by threadlike nematode worms.

filbert *n* a sweet thick-shelled variety of hazelnut.

filch *v informal* to steal (something of small value); to pilfer.

file[1] *n* **1** a folder, cabinet, etc in which papers are kept in order. **2** a collection of papers or publications on a subject, usu arranged or classified. **3** a collection of related data records, e.g. for a computer.

file[2] *v* **1** to arrange (papers, etc) in order, e.g. alphabetically, for preservation and reference. **2** to submit or record (a lawsuit, etc) officially. ➤➤ **filing** *n*.

file[3] *n* **1** a row of people, animals, or things arranged one behind the other. **2** any of the rows of squares that extend across a chessboard from white's side to black's side: compare RANK[1] (5).

file[4] *v* to march or proceed in file.

file[5] *n* a tool, usu of hardened steel, with many cutting ridges for shaping or smoothing objects or surfaces.

file[6] *v* to rub or smooth with a file.

file manager *n* a computer program that allows a user to organize and handle files and directories.

filename *n* a sequence of characters and/or spaces which identifies a computer file.

file server *n* the main computer in a network that stores programs and files that are to be accessed by other computers in the network.

filet *n NAm* see FILLET[1].

filet mignon /ˌfilay miˈnyon/ *n* (*pl* **filets mignons**) a small steak cut from the centre of a beef fillet.

filial *adj* of or befitting a son or daughter, *esp* in his or her relationship to a parent. ➤➤ **filially** *adv*.

filibuster[1] *n chiefly NAm* the use of extreme delaying tactics in a legislative assembly.

filibuster[2] *v chiefly NAm* to engage in delaying tactics.

filicide *n* **1** the act of murdering one's son or daughter. **2** a person who commits filicide.

filigree[1] *or* **filagree** *n* ornamental openwork of delicate or intricate design.

filigree[2] *or* **filagree** *v* to decorate with filigree. ➤➤ **filigreed** *adj*.

filing *n* (*usu in pl*) a metal fragment rubbed off in filing.

Filipina *n* a female native or inhabitant of the Philippine Islands.

Filipino *n* (*pl* **-os**) **1** a male native or inhabitant of the Philippine Islands. **2** the official language of the Philippine Islands. ➤➤ **Filipino** *adj*.

fill[1] *v* **1a** (*often* + up) to put into (something) as much as can be held or conveniently contained. **b** to supply (something) with a full complement. **c** (*often* + up) to stop up or plug (a hole or gap). **2a** to feed or satiate (somebody). **b** to satisfy or fulfil (a need or requirement). **3a** to occupy the whole of (a place). **b** to spread through (a place). **c** to occupy (time). **4a** to hold and perform the duties of (an office). **b** to place a person in (a vacancy). **5** (*often* + up) to become full or obstructed. ✱ **fill somebody's shoes** to take over somebody's job or responsibilities.

fill[2] *n* **1** as much as one can eat or drink. **2** as much as one can bear.

filler[1] *n* **1** a substance added to a product, e.g. to increase bulk or strength. **2** a composition or material used to fill holes before painting or varnishing. **3** material used to fill extra space in a page of a newspaper or magazine. **4** an utterance inserted into speech to occupy time.

filler[2] *n* (*pl* **fillers** *or* **filler**) a unit of currency in Hungary, worth 100th of a forint.

fillet[1] (*NAm* **filet**) *n* **1a** a fleshy boneless piece of meat cut from the hind loin or upper hind leg. **b** a long slice of boneless fish. **2** a ribbon or narrow strip of material used *esp* as a headband. **3** a narrow flat architectural moulding.

fillet[2] *v* (**filleted, filleting**) **1** to remove the bones from (a fish). **2** to cut (meat or fish) into fillets.

fill in *v* **1** *Brit* to add what is necessary to complete (a form). **2** (*often* + on) to give (somebody) information. **3** (*often* + for) to act as a temporary substitute.

filling *n* something used to fill a cavity, container, or depression.

filling station *n* a retail establishment for selling fuel, oil, etc to motorists.

fillip *n* something that arouses or boosts; a stimulus.

fill out *v* **1** to become fatter. **2** *chiefly NAm* to complete (a form).

filly *n* (*pl* **-ies**) **1** a young female horse, usu of less than four years. **2** *informal* a young woman; a girl.

film[1] *n* **1a** a roll or strip of plastic coated with a light-sensitive emulsion for taking photographs. **b** a thin flexible transparent sheet, e.g. of plastic, used as a wrapping. **2a** a series of pictures recorded on film for the cinema and projected rapidly onto a screen so as to create the illusion of movement. **b** a representation, e.g. of an incident or story, on film. **c** (*also in pl*) the cinema. **3** a thin layer, skin, or covering.

film[2] *v* **1** to make a film of. **2** (*often* + over) to become covered with a film of something.

filmic *adj* relating to the cinema.

film noir *n* a style of film-making developed in the 1940s, with a plot involving suspense, mystery, crime, and corruption, and a bleak, often shadowy, setting.

filmography *n* (*pl* **-ies**) a list of films of a prominent film figure or on a particular topic.

film star *n* a famous and popular film actor or actress.

filmstrip *n* a strip of film containing photographs, diagrams, or graphic matter for still projection.

filmy *adj* (**-ier, -iest**) **1** of, resembling, or composed of film; gauzy. **2** covered with a mist or film; hazy. ⋙ **filminess** *n.*

filo *or* **phyllo** /ˈfeeloh/ *n* a flaky pastry made with extremely thin sheets of dough.

Filofax *n trademark* a loose-leaf personal organizer.

fils *n* (*pl* **fils**) a unit of currency in some countries of the Middle East, worth 1000th of a dinar in Bahrain, Iraq, Jordan, and Kuwait; 100th of a dirham in the United Arab Emirates; and 100th of a rial in Yemen.

filter[1] *n* **1** a porous article or mass, e.g. of paper, sand, etc, through which a gas or liquid is passed to separate out matter in suspension. **2** an apparatus containing a filter medium, such as a car's oil filter or the filter tip of a cigarette. **3** a device or material for suppressing or minimizing waves or oscillations of certain frequencies, e.g. of electricity, light, or sound. **4** *Brit* a traffic signal at a road junction consisting of a green arrow which allows traffic to turn left or right when the main signals are red.

filter[2] *v* **1** to subject (a substance) to the action of a filter. **2** to pass or move through a filter, or as if through a filter. **3** of information: to become known over a period of time. **4** *Brit* of traffic: to turn left or right in the direction of the green arrow while the main lights are still red. ⋙ **filterable** *adj,* **filtrable** *adj,* **filtration** *n.*

filter feeder *n* an animal, e.g. a blue whale, adapted to filtering minute organisms or other food from water that passes through its system.

filter paper *n* porous paper used for filtering.

filter tip *n* a cigarette tip of porous material that filters the smoke before it enters the smoker's mouth. ⋙ **filter-tipped** *adj.*

filth *n* **1** foul or putrid matter, *esp* dirt or refuse. **2** something loathsome or vile, *esp* obscene or pornographic material. **3** (**the filth**) *Brit, informal, derog* (*used as sing. or pl*) the police.

filthy *adj* (**-ier, -iest**) **1** covered with or containing filth; offensively dirty. **2** vile, evil, or lewd. **3** *informal* of the weather: stormy. **4** *informal* of books or magazines: pornographic. ✻ **filthy lucre** *literary or humorous* money. **filthy rich** obscenely wealthy. ⋙ **filthily** *adv,* **filthiness** *n.*

filtrate *n* material that has passed through a filter.

fin *n* **1** a flattened appendage of an aquatic animal, e.g. a fish or whale, used in propelling or guiding the body. **2** a flattened projecting, often movable, part attached to the underside of a vessel, e.g. a submarine, to give it stability or to improve its controllability. **3** a vertical aerofoil attached to an aircraft for directional stability. **4** = FLIPPER (2). ⋙ **finned** *adj.*

finable *or* **fineable** *adj* of an offence: liable to a fine.

finagle *v informal* to manage to obtain (something) using trickery or persistence. ⋙ **finagler** *n.*

final[1] *adj* **1** being the last; occurring at the end. **2** not to be altered or undone; conclusive. **3** relating to the ultimate object or result of a process.

final[2] *n* **1a** a deciding match, game, etc in a sport or competition. **b** (*in pl*) a round made up of these. **2** (*in pl*) the last and usu most important series of examinations in an academic or professional course.

finale *n* **1a** a final scene or number in a show or an opera. **b** the last and often most spectacular item in a public performance. **2** the last section of an instrumental musical composition.

finalise *v* see FINALIZE.

finalist *n* **1** a contestant in the finals of a competition. **2** a person sitting finals (important college or university exams; see FINAL[2] (2)).

finality *n* **1** the condition of being final. **2** a determined air or tone that admits of no further argument.

finalize *or* **-ise** *v* **1** to put (plans or arrangements) in final or finished form. **2** to give final approval to (an agreement or transaction). ⋙ **finalization** *n.*

finally *adv* **1** after some time, or period of difficulty; eventually. **2** as the last in a series of things. **3** used to introduce a final point: lastly.

final solution *n* (*often* **Final Solution**) the Nazi euphemism for the policy of exterminating all the Jews in Europe during WWII.

finance[1] *n* **1** the system that includes the circulation of money and involves banking, credit, and investment. **2** the science of the management of funds. **3** (*in pl*) resources of money. **4** the obtaining of funds.

finance[2] *v* to raise or provide money for (a project or a person).

finance company *n* a company that specializes in arranging or financing hire purchase.

finance house *n* = FINANCE COMPANY.

financial *adj* relating to finance, finances, or money. ⋙ **financially** *adv.*

financial year *n* in the UK, the tax and accounting year that runs from 6 April of one year to 5 April of the following year.

financier *n* a person employed or engaged in large-scale finance or investment.

finch *n* any of numerous species of songbirds with short stout conical beaks adapted for crushing seeds.

find[1] *v* (*past tense and past part.* **found**) **1a** to come upon or encounter (something or somebody), *esp* accidentally. **b** to become aware of (something). **c** to know, discover, or recognize (something) to be present in something or native to an area: *Iodine is found in seaweed.* **2** to come upon, discover, or obtain (a person or thing) by searching, effort, or experiment. **3** to attain or reach (a level, etc): *Water finds its own level.* **4** to perceive (oneself) to be in a specified place or condition: *He found himself in a dilemma.* **5** to discover (a person or thing) to have a specified quality, attribute, etc: *I found her sympathetic.* **6** of a jury: to pronounce (a defendant) guilty or innocent after deliberation. ✻ **find fault** (*often* + with) to criticize unfavourably. **find it in one's heart** to be hard-hearted enough (to do something hurtful). **find one's feet** to gain confidence with experience. ➤➤ **findable** *adj.*

find[2] *n* somebody or something found; *esp* a valuable object or talented person discovered.

finder *n* **1** a person who finds something. **2** a small astronomical telescope attached to a larger telescope for finding an object. ✱ **finders keepers (losers weepers)** *informal* the person who finds something has the right to keep it.

fin de siècle /ˌfan də see'eklə/ *n* **1** the end of a century, *esp* the 19th cent. **2** (**fin-de-siècle**) (*used before a noun*) relating to or characteristic of the close of a century, *esp* the 19th cent. and its literary and artistic climate of sophisticated decadence and world-weariness.

finding *n* (*also in pl*) the result of an investigation, piece of research, or judicial enquiry.

find out *v* **1** to learn or discover by study, observation, or search. **2** to detect (a person) in an offence.

fine[1] *adj* **1** superior in quality; excellent. **2** wonderful; splendid. **3** dry and usu sunny. **4** well; in good health or spirits. **5** OK; all right. **6** characterized by elegance or refinement. **7** performed with extreme care and accuracy. **8** narrow in gauge or width; not thick or coarse. **9** consisting of relatively small particles. **10** very small. **11** keen; sharp. **12** having a delicate or subtle quality. **13** subtle or sensitive in perception or discrimination. ✱ **cut it fine** to leave it dangerously close to the deadline before doing something. **not to put too fine a point on it** to speak bluntly or plainly. **one fine day** one of these days; at some unspecified time. **one's finest hour** one's moment of glory or greatest achievement. ➤➤ **finely** *adv,* **fineness** *n.*

fine[2] *adv* **1** *informal* satisfactorily; well; OK. **2** into small parts; finely.

fine[3] *v* **1** (*often* + down) to purify or clarify (beer or wine). **2** (*often* + down) to make finer in quality or size by paring, trimming, or editing.

fine[4] *n* a sum payable as punishment for an offence.

fine[5] *v* to punish by imposing a fine.

fineable *adj* see FINABLE.

fine art *n* (*also in pl*) any of the arts appreciated primarily for aesthetic qualities, such as painting or sculpture.

fine print *n* very small print, typically that on a guarantee or insurance certificate.

finery *n* elaborate or special clothes, jewellery, or decoration.

fines herbes /ˌfeenz 'eəb/ *pl n* a mixture of finely chopped herbs used *esp* as a seasoning.

finespun *adj* **1** of a yarn, fabric, etc: delicate. **2** made or developed with extreme care or delicacy.

finesse[1] *n* **1** refinement or delicacy of workmanship. **2** skilful and subtle handling of a situation; adroitness. **3** *esp* in bridge and whist, the withholding of one's highest card in the hope that a lower card will take the trick.

finesse[2] *v* **1a** to bring about (a tricky manoeuvre, etc) by finesse. **b** to avoid blame or trouble by adroit manipulation of (a situation, facts, etc). **2** to play (a card) in a finesse.

fine-tooth comb *n* a comb with narrow teeth set very close together. ✱ **go over/through something with a fine-tooth comb** to search something very thoroughly.

fine-toothed comb *n* = FINE-TOOTH COMB.

fine-tune *v* to make minute adjustments to, in order to optimize performance or results.

finger[1] *n* **1** any of the five parts at the end of the hand or forelimb, *esp* one other than the thumb. **2** something that resembles a finger, *esp* in being long, narrow, and often tapering in shape. **3** the breadth of a finger, *esp* when used as a measure of alcoholic drink. ✱ **be all fingers and thumbs** to be clumsy in handling something. **get one's fingers burned/burn one's fingers** to suffer for one's efforts or temerity. **have a finger in the/every pie** to be involved or have an interest in something or everything. **have/keep one's finger on the pulse** to ensure one is aware of the latest developments or trends. **keep one's fingers crossed** to hope for the best. **not lay a finger on** to avoid touching or interfering with in the slightest. **not lift a finger** to make not the slightest effort to help, etc. **pull/take one's finger out** *Brit, informal* to start working hard; to get going. **put one's finger on something** to identify something, *esp* a problem or the cause of a difficulty, etc. **put the finger on somebody** *informal* to identify somebody, *esp* as having committed a crime. **twist somebody round one's little finger** to be able to get what one wants from somebody. **work one's fingers to the bone** to wear oneself out with laborious manual work. ➤➤ **fingerless** *adj,* **fingerlike** *adj.*

finger[2] *v* (**fingered, fingering**) **1** to touch, feel, or handle. **2a** *chiefly NAm, informal* to inform on. **b** (*often* + for) to select (somebody) for a certain role, etc. **3** to mark fingerings on (a music score) as a guide to playing.

fingerboard *n* the part of a stringed instrument against which the fingers press the strings to vary the pitch.

finger bowl *n* a small bowl of water for rinsing the fingers at table.

finger food *n* food that can be picked up in the fingers and eaten easily at receptions, drinks parties, etc.

fingering *n* the use or position of the fingers in sounding notes on an instrument, or the marking indicating this on the score.

fingernail *n* the thin horny plate on the upper surface at the tip of a finger.

finger paints *pl n* thick paints in various colours, intended to be applied with the fingers rather than a brush, *esp* by children.

fingerpick[1] *v* to play (a stringed instrument such as a guitar) with the fingernails, or with plectrums attached to the fingertips. ➤➤ **fingerpicker** *n.*

fingerpick[2] *n* a plectrum worn on a fingertip.

fingerplate *n* a metal or porcelain plate fastened to a door, usu above the handle, to protect the door surface from finger marks.

fingerpost *n* a signpost that gives directions, distance, etc on signs resembling a pointing finger.

fingerprint[1] *n* **1** an ink impression of the lines upon the fingertip taken for purposes of identification. **2** any set of characteristics that can be used to identify something.

fingerprint[2] *v* to take an inked impression of the fingerprints of (somebody), *esp* for identification purposes.

fingerstall *n* a protective cover for an injured finger.

fingertip *n* **1** the end joint of a finger or the soft part at the end of a finger. **2** (*used before a noun*) **a** activated by the use of a fingertip. **b** using, or as if using, the fingertips; extremely thorough. ✱ **at one's fingertips** *esp* of information: readily accessible to one. **to one's fingertips** through and through.

finial *n* **1** an ornament forming an upper extremity of a spire, gable, pinnacle, etc, *esp* in Gothic architecture. **2** an ornament, e.g. a decorative knob on the top or end of an object such as a piece of furniture.

finical *adj* finicky. ⋙ **finically** *adv*, **finicalness** *n.*

finicky *adj* **1** excessively exacting in taste or standards; fussy. **2** requiring delicate attention to detail. ⋙ **finickiness** *n.*

fining *n* (*also in pl*) a substance used for clarifying beer or wine.

finis /'finis/ *n* used *esp* to mark the end of a book or film: the end.

finish[1] *v* **1a** to end or terminate. **b** to stop (doing something). **2** (*often* + off/up) to eat, drink, use, or dispose of (something) entirely. **3a** (*also* + off) to complete or perfect (something). **b** to provide (a product) with a finish; *esp* to put a final coat or surface on (something). **c** to neaten (the raw edge of a piece of sewing) by oversewing or facing, to prevent fraying. **4a** to ruin, terminally damage, or put an end to (something). **b** *informal* (*also* + off) to bring about the death of (somebody). **c** *informal* to exhaust (somebody) utterly. **5** (*often* + up) to arrive or end up in a specified place or state. **6** to end a competition, etc in a specified place or order. ✱ **finish with 1** to have no further need of (a tool, etc that one has been using). **2** to break off relations with (a person, group, etc). ⋙ **finisher** *n.*

finish[2] *n* **1a** the final stage of something; the end. **b** the end of a race or the place designated for this. **2 a** the final treatment or coating of a surface, or a material such as varnish used for this. **b** the texture or appearance of a surface, *esp* after a coating has been applied. **c** the relative neatness of workmanship on a finished product. **d** polish or refinement. ✱ **fight to the finish** a struggle that ends with the death or total defeat of one of the contestants.

finishing school *n* a private school, usu for girls of school-leaving age, that trains its students in social refinement.

finishing touch *n* (*also in pl*) something done or added as a last detail to enhance the presentation of a piece of work, etc.

finite *adj* **1** having definable limits. **2** subject to limitations, *esp* those imposed by the laws of nature. **3** of a verb form: showing distinction of grammatical person and number, and tense, as distinct from the base form. ⋙ **finite** *n*, **finitely** *adv*, **finiteness** *n*, **finitude** *n.*

finito /fi'neetoh/ *adj informal* completely finished; all over.

fink[1] *n NAm, derog* **1** an informer. **2** a general term of abuse for a person one dislikes.

fink[2] *v NAm, informal* **1** (+ on) to inform on somebody. **2** (+ out) to renege on an undertaking or promise.

Finn *n* a native or inhabitant of Finland.

finnan haddie *n chiefly Scot, informal* = FINNAN HADDOCK.

finnan haddock *n* a haddock that is split and smoked until pale yellow.

Finnish *n* **1** the language of the people of Finland, Karelia, and parts of Sweden and Norway. **2** (**the Finnish**) (*used as pl*) the people of Finland; the Finns. ⋙ **Finnish** *adj.*

fino /'feenoh/ *n* (*pl* **finos**) a light-coloured dry sherry.

fiord *n* see FJORD.

fipple *n* the block fitted into the mouthpiece of a whistle, recorder, or flageolet.

fir *n* an evergreen tree of the pine family that has flat needle-shaped leaves and erect cones.

fir cone *n* the fruit of a conifer, covered with overlapping woody scales.

fire[1] *n* **1a** a phenomenon in which burning is manifested in the production of flame, light, heat, and usu smoke. **b** a mass of burning fuel, e.g. in a fireplace or furnace. **c** a destructive burning e.g. of a building or forest. **2** *Brit* a small domestic heater using gas or electricity. **3** intense energy or emotion, *esp* passionate enthusiasm. **4a** the discharge of guns. **b** criticism or verbal attack. **5** one of the four elements of the alchemists, the others being air, earth, and water. ✱ **catch fire** to begin to burn. **fight fire with fire** to use similar methods to those used against one. **go through fire and water** to endure great hardship. **hang fire 1** of a gun: be slow to fire. **2** to hesitate or delay. **on fire 1** burning. **2** eager or enthusiastic. **open/cease fire** to begin/stop shooting a weapon. **play with fire** to take foolhardy risks. **set fire to/set on fire** to start (something) burning, *esp* accidentally or maliciously. **set the world (***Brit also* **the Thames) on fire** (*usu in negative contexts*) to achieve something remarkable. **under fire 1** being shot at. **2** being harshly criticized.

fire[2] *v* **1a** to discharge (a gun or other firearm). **b** to discharge (a bullet or other projectile) from a gun or other weapon. **c** to direct (questions, commands, etc) in quick succession at somebody. **2** to dismiss (an employee). **3** to supply (a heating system, furnace, or power station) with fuel. **4** to set fire to (something). **5** to bake (pottery, ceramics, or bricks) in a kiln. **6** to kindle or stimulate (somebody's imagination). **7** (*also* + up) to inspire or fill with enthusiasm. **8** of an internal-combustion engine: to burst into life on ignition of its fuel. ✱ **fire away** *informal* go ahead; say what you have to say. **fire on all (four) cylinders** to function with maximum effectiveness. ⋙ **firer** *n*, **firing** *n.*

fire alarm *n* a device such as a bell, hooter, or siren, that is activated to give warning of a fire.

fire and brimstone *n* (*used as sing. or pl*) a terrible fate or punishment.

firearm *n* a portable gun, *esp* a pistol or rifle.

fireball *n* **1** a spherical mass of fire or flame. **2** a large brilliant meteor. **3** the bright cloud of vapour and dust created by a nuclear explosion. **4** *informal* a highly energetic person.

fire blanket *n* a blanket of non-flammable material, *esp* fibreglass, used for smothering flames.

fire blight *n* a highly infectious disease of apples, pears, and related fruits caused by a bacterium that gives the leaves a blackened scorched appearance.

firebomb[1] *n* an incendiary bomb.

firebomb[2] *v* to attack or damage with a firebomb.

firebrand *n* **1** a piece of burning material, *esp* wood. **2** a person who creates unrest or strife; an agitator or troublemaker.

firebreak *n* a strip of cleared or unplanted land intended to check a forest or grass fire.

firebrick *n* a brick that is resistant to high temperatures and is used for lining furnaces, fireplaces, etc.

fire brigade *n* an organization for preventing or extinguishing fires, *esp* one maintained in Britain by local government.

firebug *n informal* a pyromaniac; an arsonist.

fireclay *n* clay that is resistant to high temperatures and is used *esp* for firebricks and crucibles.

firecracker *n* a small firework that explodes with a series of bangs and jumps.

firedamp *n* a combustible mine gas consisting chiefly of methane that forms a highly explosive mixture when combined with air.

firedog *n* either of a pair of metal stands for burning logs in a fireplace; = ANDIRON.

fire door *n* **1** a fire-resistant connecting door inside a building, designed to prevent the spread of fire. **2** an emergency exit, *esp* one that can easily be opened from inside.

fire drill *n* a practice drill in extinguishing or escaping from fires.

fire-eater *n* **1** a performer who gives the impression of swallowing fire. **2** *dated* a person who is quarrelsome or violent. ➤➤ **fire-eating** *n and adj.*

fire engine *n* a vehicle that carries firefighting equipment and a team of firefighters.

fire escape *n* a device, *esp* an external staircase, for escape from a burning building.

fire-extinguisher *n* an apparatus for putting out fires with chemicals.

firefight *n* a fight involving guns as distinct from bombs or other weapons.

firefighter *n* a person trained to fight and extinguish fires. ➤➤ **firefighting** *n.*

firefly *n* (*pl* **-ies**) any of several species of night-flying beetles that produce a bright intermittent light.

fireguard *n* **1** a protective metal framework placed in front of an open fire. **2** *NAm* = FIREBREAK.

firehouse *n NAm* = FIRE STATION.

fire irons *pl n* utensils, e.g. tongs, poker, and shovel, for tending a household fire.

firelighter *n* a piece of inflammable material used to help light a fire, *esp* in a grate.

fireman *n* (*pl* **firemen**) **1** a person trained and employed to extinguish fires. **2** a person who tends or feeds fires or furnaces, e.g. on a steam ship or steam engine.

fireplace *n* a usu framed opening made at the base of a chimney to hold a domestic fire; a hearth.

firepower *n* the capacity, e.g. of a military unit, to deliver effective fire on a target.

fire practice *n Brit* = FIRE DRILL.

fireproof[1] *adj* able to withstand fire or high temperatures.

fireproof[2] *v* to make fireproof.

fire-raising *n Brit* arson. ➤➤ **fire-raiser** *n.*

fire sale *n* **1** a sale at bargain prices of goods that have survived a fire on commercial premises. **2** a quick sale of goods at bargain prices, e.g. when the seller faces bankruptcy or closure.

fire screen *n* **1** a light often ornamental screen placed in front of a fireplace when there is no fire in the grate. **2** *chiefly NAm* = FIREGUARD (1).

fireside *n* **1** a place near the fire or hearth. **2** (*used before a noun*) taking place at, or having the cosiness and intimacy associated with, the fireside.

fire station *n* a building where fire engines and firefighting apparatus are kept and where firefighters are on duty.

firestorm *n* a huge uncontrollable fire that is typically started by bombs and is sustained by its power to draw in strong currents of air.

firetrap *n* a building that is difficult to escape from in case of fire or that does not have adequate fire escapes, fire-extinguishers, etc.

fire-walking *n* the activity, *esp* as a religious rite, of walking barefoot over hot stones or ashes. ➤➤ **fire-walker** *n.*

fire wall *n* **1** a fireproof wall within a building. **2** a safeguard to ensure that the banking and share-dealing activities of a financial company are kept separate. **3** in computing, a software device that protects sensitive areas of a network, etc from unauthorized access.

fire-watcher *n* somebody who watches for the outbreak of fire, e.g. during an air raid. ➤➤ **fire-watching** *n.*

firewater *n informal* strong alcoholic drink.

fireweed *n* rosebay willowherb.

firewood *n* wood used or cut for fuel.

firework *n* **1a** a device containing explosive material that goes off with dramatic light and sound effects when ignited. **b** (*in pl*) a display of fireworks. **2** (*in pl*) **a** a display of temper or a clash of wills. **b** a sparkling display of brilliance, e.g. in oratory or repartee.

firing line *n* the battle line from which fire is discharged against the enemy. ✱ **in the firing line** in the forefront of an activity, *esp* one involving risk, difficulty, or criticism.

firing squad *n* a detachment of soldiers detailed to fire a salute at a military burial or to carry out an execution.

firkin *n chiefly dated* a small wooden tub or cask used for storing liquids, butter, or fish.

firm[1] *adj* **1** solidly or securely fixed; stable. **2** of a surface or structure: not yielding to pressure; solid and compact. **3** having a sustained strength. **4** of an opinion or principle: unchanging; steadfast. **5** of friends: having a strong and constant relationship. **6** of a decision or arrangement: settled or definite. **7** resolute in dealing with people or situations. ✱ **a firm hand** strong control or guidance. **hold/stand firm** to remain steadfast and unyielding. **on firm ground** sure of one's position in a dispute, etc. ➤➤ **firmish** *adj,* **firmly** *adv,* **firmness** *n.*

firm[2] *v* **1** to make solid, compact, or secure. **2** (*also* + up) to settle (an agreement, arrangement, etc) or put it into final form.

firm[3] *n* **1** a business partnership of two or more people. **2** any business unit or enterprise.

firmament *n* the vault or arch of the sky; the heavens. ➤➤ **firmamental** *adj.*

firmware *n* computer programs that are stored in a read-only memory and cannot be altered or erased, constituting permanent software.

first[1] *adj* **1** having the position in a sequence corresponding to the number one. **2** preceding all the rest; earliest. **3** in the top or winning place. **4** most important and, therefore, taking precedence. ✱ **first thing** early tomorrow morning or early next day. **first things first** everything in its due order. **not have the first idea/notion** to have not the slightest idea. **of the first order** of the most excellent or outstanding kind.

first[2] *adv* **1** before anybody or anything else. **2** by way of introduction or preliminary; to start with. **3** for the first time. ✱ **come first 1** to win or be top. **2** to take precedence. **feet/head first** with the feet or head leading. **first and last** always and most importantly. **first come first served** people will be dealt with in the order in which they arrive. **first of all** before doing anything else. **first off** *informal* to start with; firstly.

first[3] *noun and pron* **1a** a person, thing, or group, that is first. **b** a thing that has never happened, been done, or been experienced before. **2** the first and lowest forward gear of a motor vehicle; bottom gear. **3** in Britain, a first-class honours degree. ✱ **at first** at the beginning; to start with; initially. **first past the post 1** winning by reaching the finishing post first. **2** (**first-past-the-post**) (*used before a noun*) denoting the electoral system in which the candidate with a simple majority wins. **from the first** from the very beginning.

first aid *n* emergency treatment given to an ill or injured person before full medical aid can be obtained. ➤➤ **first-aider** *n.*

first base *n chiefly NAm* (*usu in negative contexts*) the first step or stage in a course of action.

firstborn *adj* born before all others; eldest. ➤➤ **firstborn** *n.*

first class *n* **1** the first or highest group in a system of classification. **2** the highest class of travel accommodation, e.g. on a train, plane, or ship. **3** *Brit* the highest class in the assessment of the results of a university degree examination.

first-class *adj and adv* **1** in the first class. **2** of mail: for delivery as fast as possible.

first cousin *n* a child of one's uncle or aunt; = COUSIN (1). ✱ **first cousin once removed** see REMOVED.

first-day cover *n* a special envelope with a newly issued postage stamp or stamps postmarked on the first day of issue.

first-degree *adj chiefly NAm* denoting the most serious form of a particular criminal offence, *esp* murder.

first-degree burn *n* a mild burn characterized by heat, pain, and reddening of the burned surface but without blistering or charring.

first-degree relative *n* one's parent, sibling, or child.

first floor *n* **1** *Brit* the floor immediately above the ground floor. **2** *NAm* = GROUND FLOOR.

first-foot[1] *n esp* in Scotland, the first person to cross one's threshold in the New Year.

first-foot[2] *v* (**first-footed, first-footing**) to be the first person to cross the threshold of (somebody) in the New Year. ➤➤ **first-footer** *n,* **first-footing** *n.*

first fruits *pl n* **1** the first agricultural products of a season, *esp* a selection of these offered to God in thanksgiving. **2** the earliest products or results of an enterprise.

first-hand *adj* coming directly from the original source or personal experience. ✱ **at first hand** directly; without an intermediary. ➤➤ **first-hand** *adv.*

first lady *n* (*often* **First Lady**) the wife or female partner of a US president or other head of state.

first lieutenant *n* **1** a naval officer in executive charge of a ship. **2** in the US army, air force, or marines, a rank immediately below captain.

firstly *adv* used to introduce a first point: in the first place; first.

first mate *n* on a merchant ship, the officer second in command to the master.

First Minister *n* the chief executive of the Scottish Parliament or the Northern Ireland Assembly.

first name *n* the personal or given name that usu stands first in a person's full name. ✱ **on first-name terms** said of two or more people: having an informal relationship.

first night *n* the first public performance of a play, ballet, show, etc.

first officer *n* **1** on a merchant ship, = FIRST MATE. **2** on an aircraft, the crew member who is second in command to the captain.

first person *n* in grammar, the term used to refer to the speaker or speakers, represented by the pronouns *I* or *we,* and to the verb forms appropriate to these: compare PERSON (3), SECOND PERSON, THIRD PERSON.

first principles *pl n* the fundamental principles or assumptions that underlie a theory, set of beliefs, etc.

first-rate *adj* of the best class or finest quality; excellent. ➤➤ **first-rater** *n.*

first reading *n* the first submitting of a bill before a legislative assembly, to allow its introduction.

first refusal *n* the right of accepting or refusing something before it is offered to others.

first school *n* a primary school for children between five and eight.

First Secretary *n* the chief executive of the National Assembly for Wales.

first-strike *adj* denoting nuclear weapons or an initial nuclear attack designed to destroy the enemy's power to retaliate.

first-string *adj* of a member of a sports team, group, etc: having a regular place, not used as a substitute.

first water *n* the highest quality of gemstone. ✱ **of the first water** *sometimes ironic* of the most outstanding kind.

First World *n* the industrialized nations of the world, including N America, the countries of W Europe, Japan, Australia, and New Zealand: compare SECOND WORLD, THIRD WORLD (1).

firth *n* a sea inlet or estuary, *esp* in Scotland.

fiscal *adj* **1** relating to taxation, public revenues, or public debt. **2** *chiefly NAm* relating to finance generally. ➤➤ **fiscally** *adv.*

fiscal year *n NAm* = FINANCIAL YEAR.

fish[1] *n* (*pl* **fishes** *or* **fish**) **1a** a cold-blooded aquatic vertebrate with an elongated scaly body, fins, and gills. **b** the flesh of a fish used as food. **2** a person, *esp* one of a specified, often eccentric, nature. ✱ **a big fish in a little pond** an important person but only in a small community. **a fish out of water** a person who is uneasy or uncomfortable through being unsuited to the position he or she is in. **have other/bigger fish to fry** to have other, *esp* more important, things to do. ➤➤ **fishless** *adj,* **fishlike** *adj.*

fish[2] *v* **1** to try to catch fish, e.g. with a hook and line or a net. **2** to feel about in the interior of a container for something. **3** (*often* + for) to try to obtain something, *esp* by using cunning or devious means.

fish[3] *n* **1** a flat piece of wood or iron fixed lengthways to a beam, etc, or across a joint, to add strength. **2** a curved piece of wood lashed to a split mast or boom, serving as a temporary splint.

fishbowl *n* a round glass bowl that fish, *esp* pet goldfish, are kept in.

fishcake *n* a usu circular portion of flaked fish mixed with mashed potato, coated with breadcrumbs and fried.

fisher *n* **1** a large brown woodland marten of N America. **2** *archaic* a fisherman.

fisherfolk *n* (*used as pl*) people who live in a community that is dependent on fishing.

fisherman *or* **fisherwoman** *n* (*pl* **fishermen** *or* **fisherwomen**) a person who engages in fishing as an occupation or for pleasure.

fishery *n* (*pl* **-ies**) **1** the activity or business of catching fish and other sea animals. **2** a place or establishment for catching fish and other sea animals.

fish-eye *adj* denoting a wide-angle photographic lens that has a highly curved protruding front and covers an angle up to 180°.

fish farm *n* a tract of water where fish or shellfish are reared and bred commercially.

fish finger *n* a small oblong of flaked fish coated with breadcrumbs or batter.

fishing line *n* a strong silk or nylon thread with a baited hook attached to it, used for catching fish.

fishing rod *n* a tapering rod with a reel, used with an attached line and hook for catching fish.

fish kettle *n* a usu deep long oval vessel used for cooking fish.

fish knife *n* a knife with a broad, blunt, usu decorated blade for eating or serving fish.

fish ladder *n* a series of pools arranged like steps by which fish can pass over a dam or waterfall when going upstream.

fish meal *n* ground dried fish used as fertilizer and animal food.

fishmonger *n chiefly Brit* a person or shop that sells raw food fish.

fishnet *n* **1** a coarse open-mesh fabric. **2** (*used before a noun*) made of this fabric.

fish out *v* **1** to draw out of a body of liquid or out of a cavity. **2** to exhaust the supply of fish in (a body of water).

fishplate *n* a usu metal plate used to make a joint between consecutive rails on a railway line.

fish slice *n* a kitchen implement with a broad blade and long handle used *esp* for turning or lifting food in frying.

fishtail[1] *n* a manoeuvre that involves swinging an aircraft's tail from side to side to reduce speed for landing.

fishtail[2] *v* **1** to perform a fishtail. **2a** of a motor vehicle: to swing its rear end from side to side when out of control. **b** of a driver: to cause a vehicle's rear end to swing from side to side.

fishwife *n* (*pl* **fishwives**) a vulgar, abusive, or loud-mouthed woman.

fishy *adj* (**-ier, -iest**) **1** resembling fish, *esp* in taste or smell. **2** *informal* creating doubt or suspicion; questionable. ➤➤ **fishily** *adv,* **fishiness** *n.*

fissile *adj* **1** of rock: capable of being easily split. **2** of an atom or element: capable of undergoing nuclear fission. ➤➤ **fissility** *n.*

fission[1] *n* **1** a splitting or breaking up into parts. **2** in biology, asexual reproduction by spontaneous division into two or more parts each of which grows into a complete organism. **3** the splitting of an atomic nucleus with the release of large amounts of energy. ➤➤ **fissional** *adj.*

fission[2] *v esp* of an atom: to undergo fission. ➤➤ **fissionability** *n,* **fissionable** *adj.*

fission bomb *n* = ATOM BOMB.

fissiparous *adj* **1** of an organism: reproducing by fission. **2a** of an organization, etc: inclined to division. **b** inclined to cause division; divisive. ➤➤ **fissiparity** *n,* **fissiparously** *adv,* **fissiparousness** *n.*

fissure[1] *n* **1** a narrow, long, and deep opening, e.g. in rock. **2** a natural cleft between body parts or in the substance of an organ, e.g. the brain.

fissure[2] *v* to break into fissures. ➤➤ **fissured** *adj.*

fist *n* the hand clenched with the fingers doubled into the palm and the thumb across the fingers. ✱ **make a fair/poor fist of/at something** *informal* to make a creditable or ineffectual attempt at something. ➤➤ **fistful** *n.*

fisticuffs *pl n dated or humorous* the activity of fighting with the fists.

fistula *n* (*pl* **fistulas** *or* **fistulae**) an abnormal or surgically made passage from an abscess or hollow organ to the body surface or between hollow organs.

fit[1] *adj* (**fitter, fittest**) **1a** adapted or suited to a purpose. **b** in a suitable state. **2** strong and healthy. **3** acceptable from a particular viewpoint, e.g. of competence, morality, or qualifications; worthy. **4** *informal* likely to; so as to be likely to: *We walked till we were fit to drop.* **5** *Brit, informal* of a person: attractive. ✱ **fit as a fiddle/flea** in excellent health. **fit to be tied** *informal* extremely angry. **fit to bust** *informal* with huge vigour. **see/think fit** to consider it proper or advisable. ➤➤ **fitly** *adv,* **fitness** *n.*

fit[2] *v* (**fitting,** *past tense and past part.* **fitted** *or NAm* **fit**) **1** to be the right size or shape for. **2a** to insert or adjust (something) so that it is correctly in position. **b** to install (a device or component). **c** to supply with equipment. **3** to match or correspond to: *a theory that fits all the facts.* **4** to make (somebody) suitable for something. **5** to find time for (activities): *too much to fit into one day.* ✱ **fit to be tied** *informal* very angry.

fit[3] *n* the manner in which something fits, e.g. a piece of clothing, or things fit together.

fit[4] *n* **1** a sudden violent attack of a disease, e.g. epilepsy, *esp* when accompanied by convulsions or unconsciousness. **2** a spell or attack of something difficult to control: *a coughing fit.* **3** a sudden outburst of a specified activity: *a fit of letter-writing.* ✱ **by/in fits and starts** in an impulsive or irregular manner. **have/throw a fit** to be extremely shocked or horrified. **in fits** *informal* laughing uncontrollably.

fitful *adj* spasmodic or intermittent. ➤➤ **fitfully** *adv,* **fitfulness** *n.*

fit in *v* **1** to make space for. **2** to be compatible or suitable.

fitment *n* **1** a piece of equipment; *esp* an item of built-in furniture. **2** (*also in pl*) a small detachable usu standard part; = FITTING[2] (2).

fit out *v* to supply with the necessary equipment.

fitted *adj* **1** of carpets, sheets, or clothes: made to fit the shape that is to be covered closely. **2a** of cupboards, kitchen units, etc: built so as to fit a particular space and fixed there. **b** of a kitchen: having fitted units, shelves, and working surfaces. **3** (+ for/to) suitable, adapted, or qualified for something.

fitter *n* a person who assembles or repairs machinery or appliances.

fitting[1] *adj* appropriate to the situation. ➤➤ **fittingly** *adv,* **fittingness** *n.*

fitting[2] *n* **1** an act of trying on clothes which are being made or altered. **2** a small often standardized part. **3** (*in pl*) items, e.g. carpets, curtains, etc, fitted in a property, that the owner is entitled to remove if the property is sold: compare FIXTURE (1B). **4** the act or an instance of installing or securing something.

fitting room *n* a room or cubicle in a shop where one can try on clothes before buying them.

fit up *v* **1** to provide with equipment. **2** *Brit, informal* to incriminate (somebody).

five *n* the number 5. ✱ **take five** *informal* to have a short break or rest. ➤➤ **five** *adj,* **fivefold** *adj and adv.*

five-and-dime *n NAm* a store selling inexpensive household goods and personal requirements.

five-and-dime store *n NAm* = FIVE-AND-DIME.

five-a-side *n* a form of football with five players on each side.

five-o'clock shadow *n* a just visible growth of beard.

fiver *n informal* **1** *Brit* a five-pound note. **2** *NAm* a five-dollar bill.

fives *pl n* (*used as sing.*) a game in which players use their hands or small bats to hit a ball in a walled court.

five-spice *n* a powdered blend of five spices, usu cinnamon, cloves, fennel seeds, peppercorns, and star anise, used in Chinese cuisine.

five-star *adj* of accommodation, etc: of the highest standard or quality.

fix[1] *v* **1** to position and attach firmly. **2** to make firm, stable or permanent, e.g. to change (a substance) into a stable chemical compound. **3** to decide upon or establish (a date, price, etc). **4a** (*often* + with) to gaze intently at (somebody). **b** to direct (one's eyes) steadily somewhere. **5a** to make (something) possible. **b** to arrange (to do something). **c** *NAm* to be about to (do something). **6a** to repair or mend (something). **b** *NAm* to set (something) in order. **7** *chiefly NAm* to get (something) ready, *esp* to prepare (food or drink). **8** *informal* to get even with (somebody). **9** to influence (e.g. a jury or the outcome of something) by illicit means. **10** *informal* to inject oneself with (a narcotic drug). ⋙ **fixable** *adj*, **fixer** *n*.

fix[2] *n* **1** *informal* a position of difficulty or embarrassment. **2** *informal* **a** the act of injecting a narcotic drug. **b** a single dose of a narcotic drug. **c** *chiefly humorous* a reviving experience of something exciting or pleasurable. ✱ **get a fix on 1** to determine the position of (a ship, etc) using bearings, observation, radio, etc. **2** *informal* to discover or understand the basic nature of.

fixate *v* to focus one's eyes or attention on. ✱ **be fixated on** to have an obsessive preoccupation with.

fixation *n* **1** (*also* + on/with) an attachment to or preoccupation with, *esp* if obsessive or unhealthy. **2** concentration of the gaze on something, *esp* words in reading. **3a** *esp* in plant biology, the process of fixing something chemically. **b** the use of a chemical to stabilize a specimen, e.g. before examination under a microscope.

fixative *n* a fixing substance used e.g. to prevent a perfume evaporating too quickly or *esp* to protect drawings. ⋙ **fixative** *adj*.

fixed *adj* **1** securely placed or fastened. **2** stationary. **3** not capable of change or variation; settled. **4a** intent. **b** of a smile: unvarying and artificial. **5** arranged or determined dishonestly. ✱ **how one is fixed** *informal* (*often* + for) what one's position is, *esp* financially. ⋙ **fixedly** *adv*, **fixedness** *n*.

fixed assets *pl n* business assets, such as land, large-scale machinery, buildings, etc, that are put to long-term use and are not readily converted into cash: compare CURRENT ASSETS.

fixed charge *n* **1** a regularly recurring expense, e.g. rent, taxes, or interest. **2** = FIXED COSTS. **3** a loan or liability for which specific assets of the borrowing company serve as security: compare FLOATING CHARGE.

fixed costs *pl n* costs such as maintenance and rent that do not vary along with product or output: compare OVERHEAD[3], VARIABLE COST.

fixed odds *pl n* in betting, e.g. on the results of football matches, the system of offering a predetermined amount per unit stake for a certain result or combination of results.

fixed-wing *adj* denoting the conventional type of aircraft as distinct from the helicopter type with rotating blades.

fixings *pl n* **1** *Brit* the fasteners such as nails, screws, nuts, and bolts, needed for a repair or construction job. **2** *NAm* trimmings.

fixity *n* the quality or state of being fixed or stable.

fixture *n* **1a** a household appliance or piece of equipment, e.g. a bath or toilet, that is fixed in position. **b** (*in pl*) items, e.g. sanitary ware, kitchen cupboards, worktops, etc, fixed in a property, that the owner is not entitled to remove if the property is sold: compare FITTING[2] (3). **2** *informal* somebody or something invariably present in a specified setting. **3** *chiefly Brit* a sporting event scheduled for a certain date or time.

fix up *v* **1** to provide with something. **2** to organize or arrange. **3** to adapt, repair, or do up (a place) for a certain purpose.

fizgig *n* **1** *Aus, informal* a police informer. **2** *archaic* a flirtatious young woman.

fizz[1] *v* **1** to make a hissing or sputtering sound. **2** of a liquid: to produce bubbles of gas.

fizz[2] *n* **1** the act or sound of fizzing. **2** spirit or liveliness. **3a** *informal* an effervescent drink, e.g. sparkling wine. **b** the effervescence of sparkling wine, etc.

fizzer *n informal* **1** *Brit* something that is successful or sparkles. **2** *Aus, NZ* something that is a fiasco or dismal failure.

fizzle *v* to make a weak fizzing sound. ⋙ **fizzle** *n*.

fizzle out *v informal* to fail or end feebly, *esp* after a promising start.

fizzy *adj* (**-ier, -iest**) **1** of a drink: effervescent. **2** of somebody's personality: exuberant or sparkling. ⋙ **fizzily** *adv*, **fizziness** *n*.

fjord *or* **fiord** *n* a narrow inlet of the sea, *esp* one between steep cliffs that was formed by the action of glaciers, e.g. in Norway or New Zealand.

FL *abbr* **1** Florida (US postal abbreviation). **2** Flight Lieutenant.

fl. *abbr* **1** floor. **2** floruit. **3** fluid.

flab *n informal* soft loose body tissue.

flabbergast *v informal* (*usu in passive*) to overwhelm with shock or astonishment.

flabby *adj* (**-ier, -iest**) **1a** of flesh: lacking resilience or firmness. **b** of a person or body part: having flesh like this. **2** ineffective or feeble. ⋙ **flabbily** *adv*, **flabbiness** *n*.

flaccid /'flaksid, 'flasid/ *adj* **1a** lacking normal or youthful firmness; flabby. **b** soft; hanging limply. **2** lacking vigour or force. ⋙ **flaccidity** *n*, **flaccidly** *adv*.

flack[1] *n NAm, informal* a person who provides publicity, *esp* a press agent. ⋙ **flackery** *n*.

flack[2] *v NAm, informal* to promote or publicize.

flack[3] *n* see FLAK.

flag[1] *n* **1** a usu rectangular piece of fabric of distinctive design used as an identifying symbol, e.g. of a nation, or as a signalling device, *esp* one flown from a single vertical staff. **2** a flag-shaped marker indicating a hole on a golf course, or a smaller device for pinpointing positions on a map. **3** a small paper flag on a pin, given *esp* formerly, as a badge to contributors to a charity on a flag day. **4** something, e.g. a strip of paper inserted into an opening of a book or a piece of coding inserted into a computer file, used as a marker. ✱ **fly the flag** of a ship: to be registered in a specific country and sail under its flag. See also FLAG OF CONVENIENCE. **keep the flag flying** to continue to represent or promote the interests of one's country, organization, etc. **put the flags/flag out** to celebrate.

flag[2] *v* (**flagged, flagging**) **1** to mark (a page, word, or passage) with a paper strip or sticker or with a piece of coding. **2** to direct (e.g. the driver of a vehicle, competitor in a race, etc) somewhere by signalling with the hands or a flag. ⋙ **flagger** *n*.

flag[3] *v* (**flagged, flagging**) **1** to grow tired; to lose energy. **2** to become feeble, less interesting, or less active; to decline.

flag[4] *n* = FLAGSTONE .

flag[5] *n* any of various plants that have long bladelike leaves and grow near water or on damp ground.

flag day *n* a day on which a charity holds a street collection, usu giving contributors paper badges, formerly in the form of flags.

flag down *v* to direct (a driver or vehicle) to stop by signalling with the hands.

flagella *n* pl of FLAGELLUM.

flagellant *n* **1** a person who scourges himself or herself as a public penance. **2** a person who responds sexually to being beaten or to beating another person. ➤➤ **flagellant** *adj*, **flagellantism** *n*.

flagellate[1] *v* to whip or flog (somebody), *esp* as a religious punishment or for sexual gratification. ➤➤ **flagellation** *n*, **flagellator** *n*, **flagellatory** *adj*.

flagellate[2] *n* a minute single-celled animal that swims by means of a flagellum or flagella. ➤➤ **flagellate** *adj*.

flagellum *n* (*pl* **flagella** *or* **flagellums**) a minute whip-like projection by means of which protozoans, spermatozoa, and bacteria swim. ➤➤ **flagellar** *adj*.

flageolet[1] *n* a small recorder-like instrument with four finger holes and two thumb holes.

flageolet[2] *n* = FRENCH BEAN.

flagitious *adj* very wicked, *esp* criminally so; villainous. ➤➤ **flagitiously** *adv*, **flagitiousness** *n*.

flag of convenience *n* the flag of a country under which a ship is registered in order to avoid the taxes and regulations of the ship-owner's home country.

flagon *n* **1** a large usu metal or pottery vessel with a handle and spout and often a lid, used *esp* for holding liquids at table. **2** a large squat short-necked bottle, often with one or two ear-shaped handles, in which cider, wine, etc are sold.

flagpole *n* a tall pole on which to hoist a flag.

flagrant *adj* conspicuous; outrageous. ➤➤ **flagrance** *n*, **flagrancy** *n*, **flagrantly** *adv*.

flagship *n* **1** the ship that carries the commander of a fleet and flies his or her flag. **2** something that is considered the pride of an organization.

flagstaff *n* (*pl* **flagstaffs** *or* **flagstaves**) = FLAGPOLE.

flagstone *n* a flat slab of stone used for paving. ➤➤ **flagstoned** *adj*.

flag-waving *n informal* a passionate appeal to patriotic or partisan sentiment; jingoism. ➤➤ **flag-waver** *n*.

flail[1] *n* a threshing implement consisting of a stout short free-swinging stick attached to a wooden handle.

flail[2] *v* **1** (*often* + about/around) to wave one's arms and legs about violently. **2** of the arms: to wave about violently.

flair *n* **1** (+ for) a natural aptitude, ability, or talent for a certain thing. **2** style, originality, and taste.

flak *or* **flack** *n* **1** the fire from anti-aircraft guns. **2** *informal* heavy criticism or opposition.

flake[1] *n* **1** a small loose particle. **2** a thin flattened piece or layer; a chip. **3** a pipe tobacco of small irregularly cut pieces. **4** *NAm, informal* a crazy person.

flake[2] *v* **1** (+ off) to come away in flakes. **2** to separate or break up into flakes. ➤➤ **flaker** *n*.

flake out *v informal* to collapse or fall asleep from exhaustion.

flak jacket *n* a jacket of heavy fabric containing shields, e.g. of metal or plastic, for protection, *esp* against enemy fire.

flaky *adj* (**-ier, -iest**) **1** consisting of flakes. **2** tending to flake. **3** *chiefly NAm, informal* eccentric; daft; crazy. ➤➤ **flakily** *adv*, **flakiness** *n*.

flaky pastry *n* rich pastry composed of numerous very thin layers, used for pies, tarts, etc.

flambé[1] *adj* (*used after a noun*) of food: sprinkled with brandy, rum, etc and ignited.

flambé[2] *v* (**flambés, flambéed, flambéing**) to sprinkle (food) with brandy, rum, etc and ignite it.

flambeau *n* (*pl* **flambeaux** *or* **flambeaus**) **1** a flaming torch. **2** a large ornamental branched candlestick.

flamboyant *adj* **1** given to dashing display or ostentatious exuberance. **2** of e.g. clothing: colourful or exotic. **3** ornate; florid. ➤➤ **flamboyance** *n*, **flamboyancy** *n*, **flamboyantly** *adv*.

flame[1] *n* **1** a bright mass of burning gas coming from something that is on fire. **2** the fierce intensity or ardour of an emotion, etc. **3** a brilliant reddish orange colour. **4** *informal* an abusive message sent by e-mail or appearing on the notice board of a newsgroup, etc. ✱ **old flame** a former lover. ➤➤ **flameless** *adj*, **flamelike** *adj*, **flamy** *adj*.

flame[2] *v* **1a** to burn vigorously; to blaze. **b** to apply a flame to or set alight. **2** of an emotion: to be felt or displayed with intensity. **3** of the face or cheeks: to grow fiery red with anger or embarrassment. **4** to send an abusive message by e-mail or other electronic means.

flamenco *n* (*pl* **-os**) a vivacious style of Spanish guitar music, often accompanied by singing, dancing, and hand clapping.

flameout *n* **1** the failure of a jet engine in flight caused by its flame being extinguished. **2** *chiefly NAm, informal* any spectacular failure. ➤➤ **flame out** *v*.

flameproof *adj* **1** of fabric: rendered non-flammable by treatment. **2** of cookware: suitable for use in an oven or on a hob.

flamethrower *n* a weapon that expels a burning stream of liquid.

flame tree *n* an ornamental tree with vivid scarlet flowers.

flaming *adj* **1** emitting flames or on fire; blazing. **2** brilliantly hot or bright. **3** full of fury or ardour. **4** *informal* used to express irritation. ➤➤ **flamingly** *adv*.

flamingo *n* (*pl* **-os** *or* **-oes**) a web-footed wading bird with long legs and neck, curved beak, and rosy-white plumage with scarlet and black markings.

flammable *adj* easily set on fire; = INFLAMMABLE[1]. ➤➤ **flammability** *n*.

Usage note

flammable *or* **inflammable**? Although *flammable* and *inflammable* appear to be opposites, they have the same meaning. But since *inflammable* may seem to mean 'not flammable' (from the prefix *in-* meaning 'not') *flammable* is increasingly preferred, especially in technical contexts. The preferred negative is *non-flammable*.

flan *n* a pastry or cake case containing a sweet or savoury filling.

flâneur *n* an aimless person; an idler.

flange *n* a projecting rib or rim on something *esp* for strengthening or guiding it. ➤➤ **flanged** *adj*, **flangeless** *adj*.

flank[1] *n* **1** the side of a person or animal between the ribs and the hip. **2** the side of something large, such as a mountain. **3** the right or left of a formation of troops or ships. **4** = WING[1] (7B).

flank[2] *v* (*usu in passive*) to be at the side of.

flanker *n* **1** in rugby, an attacking player positioned on the outside of the second row of the scrum. Also called WING FORWARD. **2** in American football, an offensive back at the outside of an end. **3** a military fortification for protecting a flank.

flannel[1] *n* **1a** a twilled loosely woven wool or worsted fabric with a slightly napped surface. **b** (*in pl*) garments, *esp* trousers, made of flannel. **2** *Brit* a small square of towelling used for washing, *esp* the face; = FACECLOTH. **3** *chiefly Brit, informal* talk that is intended to deceive or to disguise a lack of knowledge or understanding. ➤➤ **flannelly** *adj.*

flannel[2] *v* (**flannelled, flannelling,** *NAm* **flanneled, flanneling**) *chiefly Brit, informal* to speak or write vacuously or flatteringly, *esp* with intent to deceive or conceal one's ignorance.

flannelette *n* a napped cotton fabric resembling flannel.

flap[1] *n* **1** something flexible or hinged, and usu thin, that hangs loose or covers an opening, e.g.: **a** an extended part forming a closure, e.g. of an envelope or carton. **b** a movable control surface on an aircraft wing for increasing lift during takeoff or drag during landing. **2** a flapping movement. **3** *informal* a state of excitement or panicky confusion. ➤➤ **flappy** *adj.*

flap[2] *v* (**flapped, flapping**) **1** to shake (e.g. a piece paper or cloth) or be shaken up and down or from side to side, usu creating a noise. **2** of a bird or bat: to move its wings up and down in flight. **3** *informal* to get into a panic.

flapjack *n* **1** a thick soft biscuit made with oats and syrup. **2** *NAm* a pancake.

flapper *n informal* a fashionable young woman of the 1920s, *esp* one flouting the conventions of her mother's generation.

flare[1] *v* **1** to shine or blaze with a sudden flame. **2** (*usu* + up) to become suddenly angry. **3** (*usu* + up) of violence, etc: to break out. **4** (*usu* + out) of trousers, sleeves, etc: to get wider towards the hem. **5** to ignite and burn off (waste gas, etc). ➤➤ **flareup** *n.*

flare[2] *n* **1** a sudden unsteady glaring light or flame. **2** a device producing a very bright light, used to signal, illuminate, or attract attention. **3** a sudden outburst, *esp* of anger. **4** a temporary outburst of gas and radiation from a small area of the sun's surface. Also called SOLAR FLARE. **5** a flame that burns off unwanted gas at an oil refinery or oil well. **6a** a gradual widening of a skirt, trouser leg, sleeve, etc towards the hem. **b** (*in pl*) flared trousers.

flarepath *n* an illuminated area enabling aircraft to land or take off in low visibility.

flash[1] *v* **1** to shine with or cause to shine with a bright light briefly or intermittently. **2a** to move or pass very quickly. **b** to direct (a smile, look, etc) briefly at somebody. **c** to broadcast (a message) instantaneously. **3a** to show (something) quickly or briefly. **b** to display (something) ostentatiously. **4** *informal* of a man: to show his genitals in public.

flash[2] *n* **1** a sudden burst of light. **2** a sudden burst of perception, emotion, etc. **3** a camera attachment that produces a flash of light for indoor photography. **4** a fleeting glimpse or appearance. **5** a quick-spreading flame or intense outburst of radiant heat, e.g. from a nuclear explosion. **6** an armband or piece of coloured cloth worn on a uniform as a distinguishing symbol. ✻ **flash in the pan** a sudden success that cannot be repeated [from the firing of the gunpowder in the pan of a musket]. **in a flash** very quickly.

flash[3] *adj* **1** *informal* vulgarly ostentatious. **2** *esp* of a process such as freezing: carried out very quickly.

flashback *n* **1** an interruption of the chronological sequence in a book, play, or film to show earlier events. **2** a sudden memory of a past event, often of a traumatic experience.

flashboard *n* a board projecting above the top of a dam to increase its height and therefore capacity.

flashbulb *n* an electric bulb used in a flashgun.

flash burn *n* a burn resulting from momentary exposure to intense radiant heat.

flash card *n* a card that has a word or words on it, used in some methods of teaching reading.

flash flood *n* a brief but heavy local flood usu resulting from rainfall.

flashgun *n* a device for holding and operating a photographic flashlight.

flashing *n* sheet metal used in waterproofing a roof or the angle between a vertical surface and a roof.

flashlight *n* **1** a sudden bright artificial light used in taking photographic pictures. **2** *chiefly NAm* an electric torch.

flash memory *n* computer memory that retains data in the absence of a power supply.

flashover *n* **1** an intense electrical arc produced by an accidental short circuit. **2** a sudden airborne transmission of fire to another object under conditions of intense heat.

flash point *n* **1** the temperature at which vapour from a volatile substance ignites. **2** a point in a situation or a place at which violence or anger erupts.

flashy *adj* (**-ier, -iest**) **1** ostentatious or flamboyant, *esp* beyond the bounds of good taste. **2** superficially brilliant. ➤➤ **flashily** *adv,* **flashiness** *n.*

flask *n* **1** a conical or spherical usu glass container with a narrow neck used for wine or in a laboratory. **2** a broad flat bottle, usu of metal or leather-covered glass, used to carry alcohol on the person; = HIP FLASK. **3** = VACUUM FLASK. **4** a lead-lined container for nuclear waste.

flat[1] *adj* (**flatter, flattest**) **1** of a surface: **a** horizontal; not sloping. **b** broad and smooth, without raised or hollow areas. **2** having a broad surface and little thickness. **3a** of shoes: without a raised heel. **b** of shoe heels: low. **4a** clearly unmistakable; downright: *a flat denial.* **b** fixed: *a flat rate.* **5a** lacking animation; dull or monotonous. **b** having lost effervescence or sparkle. **6a** of a tyre: lacking air; deflated. **b** of a battery: completely or partially discharged. **7a** of a musical note: lowered a semitone in pitch. **b** lower than the proper musical pitch. ✻ **that's flat** *informal* that's final; there's to be no more argument. ➤➤ **flatness** *n,* **flattish** *adj.*

flat[2] *n* **1** a flat part or surface. **2** (*in pl*) **a** an area of level ground; a plain. **b** mudflats. **3** *chiefly NAm (in pl)* shoes with no heel or a low heel. **4a** a musical note one semitone lower than a specified or particular note. **b** the character (♭) indicating this. **5** a flat piece of theatrical scenery. **6** a flat tyre. **7** (*often* **the Flat**) the flat-racing season. ✻ **on the flat 1** on level ground; not uphill or downhill. **2** (**on the Flat**) of a horse race: run on a course without jumps.

flat[3] *adv* **1a** on or against a flat surface. **b** so as to be spread out; at full length. **2** below the proper musical pitch. **3** *informal* **a** completely: *flat broke.* **b** absolutely and emphatically: *turn an offer down flat.* **4** not an instant longer; exactly: *in ten seconds flat.* ✻ **fall flat** to fail to achieve the intended effect. **flat out** as hard or fast as possible.

flat[4] *n* a self-contained set of rooms within a larger building used as a dwelling. ➤➤ **flatlet** *n.*

flatbed *adj* **1** denoting a printing press in which the assembled type is carried on a horizontal surface. **2** *chiefly NAm* denoting a truck or lorry with a flat sideless load-carrying platform. **3** denoting a scanner or plotter with a flat glass surface on which documents are placed.

flat feet *pl n* (*used as pl or sing.*) a condition in which the arches of the insteps are flattened so that the soles rest entirely on the ground.

flat file *n* **1** a computer file from which all word-processing and formatting characters have been removed. **2** a computer file containing records with no embedded or hierarchical structure.

flatfish *n* (*pl* **flatfishes** *or* **flatfish**) a marine fish, e.g. a flounder or sole, that swims on one side and has both eyes on the upper surface of its horizontally flattened body.

flat-footed *adj* **1** affected with flat feet. **2** *informal* **a** inept; clumsy. **b** complete; unequivocal. **c** off guard or unprepared. ➤➤ **flat-footedly** *adv,* **flat-footedness** *n.*

flatiron *n* an iron heated in the fire or on a stove, formerly used for pressing laundry.

flatline *v informal* **1** of a person: to die. **2** of a plan, project, etc: to fail or be ineffectual. ➤➤ **flatliner** *n.*

flatly *adv* **1** emphatically and without compromise. **2** expressionlessly; tonelessly.

flatmate *n Brit* a person who shares a flat with one.

flatpack *n chiefly Brit* (*used before a noun*) denoting furniture or equipment that is sold in pieces packed into a flat box, for assembly by the purchaser. ➤➤ **flatpacked** *adj.*

flat race *n* a race for horses on a course without jumps. ➤➤ **flat racing** *n.*

flat spin *n* **1** an aerial manoeuvre or flight condition consisting of a spin in which the aircraft is roughly horizontal. **2** *informal* a state of extreme agitation.

flatten *v* **1** (*also* + out) to make or become flat or flatter. **2** to press (oneself) flush against a surface. **3a** to raze to the ground. **b** to knock to the ground with a blow. **c** to overcome, subdue, or crush (somebody). **4** to lower (a note) in pitch, *esp* by a semitone. ➤➤ **flattener** *n.*

flatter *v* **1** to praise excessively, *esp* from motives of self-interest. **2** (*usu in passive*) to make (somebody) feel valued or sought-after. **3** of a painting or photograph: to portray or represent (the subject) over-favourably. **4** to display (a person or thing) to advantage. **5** to deceive (oneself), *esp* by believing that something is better or more favourable than it actually is. ➤➤ **flatterer** *n,* **flatteringly** *adv.*

flattery *n* (*pl* **-ies**) **1** the act or an instance of flattering. **2** insincere or excessive praise.

flattie *or* **flatty** *n* (*pl* **-ies**) a low-heeled shoe.

flatulent *adj* **1** suffering from or characterized by an excessive accumulation of gas in the alimentary canal. **2** of a speech, piece of writing, etc: pompous or pretentious. ➤➤ **flatulence** *n,* **flatulency** *n,* **flatulently** *adv.*

flatus *n* gas generated in the stomach or intestines.

flatware *n* **1** *NAm* cutlery. **2** relatively flat items of crockery such as plates and saucers.

flatworm *n* any of various parasitic and free-living worms, e.g. a tapeworm or fluke, that have flattened, as distinct from rounded, bodies.

flaunt *v* to display or parade ostentatiously or impudently. ✱ **if you've got it, flaunt it** don't be modest about your attributes, *esp* physical ones; put them on display. ➤➤ **flaunter** *n,* **flauntingly** *adv,* **flaunty** *adj.*

Usage note

flaunt *or* **flout**? These two words are often confused. To *flaunt* means 'to display ostentatiously': *to flaunt one's wealth*; *flout* means 'to treat with contemptuous disregard': *flout one's parents' wishes.* Phrases such as *to flaunt the rules* and *to flaunt convention* are wrong.

flautist *n* a person who plays a flute.

flavonoid *n* any of a group of naturally occurring aromatic chemical compounds that are found *esp* as plant pigments.

flavor *n and v NAm* see FLAVOUR[1], FLAVOUR[2].

flavoring *n NAm* see FLAVOURING.

flavour[1] (*NAm* **flavor**) *n* **1** the blend of taste and smell sensations evoked by a substance in the mouth. **2** a characteristic or predominant quality. **3** a representative sample of something. **4** *NAm* = FLAVOURING. **5** in particle physics, any of the five distinguishing properties of quarks (see QUARK[1]). ✱ **flavour of the month** a person or thing that is currently fashionable. ➤➤ **flavourful** *adj,* **flavourless** *adj,* **flavoursome** *adj.*

flavour[2] (*NAm* **flavor**) *v* to give or add flavour to (something). ➤➤ **flavoured** *adj.*

flavouring (*NAm* **flavoring**) *n* any substance used to give a stronger, different, or pleasanter flavour to food.

flaw[1] *n* **1** a blemish or imperfection. **2** a usu hidden defect, e.g. a crack, that may cause failure under stress. **3** a weakness in reasoning, etc. **4** a fault in a legal paper that may invalidate it. ➤➤ **flawless** *adj,* **flawlessly** *adv,* **flawlessness** *n.*

flaw[2] *v* to make or become blemished or imperfect.

flax *n* **1** a slender erect blue-flowered plant cultivated for its strong woody fibre and seeds (see LINSEED). **2** the fibre of the flax plant, *esp* when prepared for spinning.

flaxen *adj* **1** made of flax. **2** of hair: having a pale soft straw colour.

flaxseed *n* = LINSEED.

flay *v* **1** to strip off the skin. **2** to whip savagely. **3** to criticize or censure harshly. ➤➤ **flayer** *n.*

flea *n* a wingless bloodsucking jumping insect that feeds on warm-blooded animals. ✱ **a flea in one's ear** a sharp or embarrassing reprimand. **fit as a flea** see FIT[1].

fleabite *n informal* a trifling problem or expense.

flea-bitten *adj* **1** covered in flea bites or infested with fleas. **2** *informal* shabby; run-down.

flea collar *n* a dog's or cat's collar impregnated with insecticide and worn to kill or repel fleas.

fleadh *n* a festival of Celtic music, dancing, and culture.

flea market *n* a usu open-air market selling secondhand articles and antiques.

fleapit *n chiefly Brit, informal or humorous* a shabby cinema or theatre.

flèche /flesh/ *n* a slender usu wooden spire rising from the ridge of a roof.

fleck[1] *n* **1** a small spot or mark, *esp* of colour. **2** a grain or particle.

fleck[2] *v* to cover with small spots or marks.

flection *n* see FLEXION.

fled *v* past tense and past part. of FLEE.

fledge *v* **1** to rear (a young bird) until ready for flight or independent activity. **2** of a young bird: to develop wing feathers ready for flight. ➤➤ **fledged** *adj.*

fledgling *or* **fledgeling** *n* **1** a young bird that has just fledged. **2** (*used before a noun*) **a** inexperienced. **b** in its infancy.

flee *v* (**flees, fleeing,** *past tense and past part.* **fled**) **1** to run away from danger, evil, etc. **2** *literary* to pass away swiftly; to vanish.

fleece[1] *n* **1** the coat of wool covering a sheep or similar animal. **2** a soft bulky deep-piled fabric used chiefly for lining coats. **3** a jacket or pull-on top made of a synthetic fabric with a thick warm pile. ➤➤ **fleecy** *adj.*

fleece[2] *v informal* to strip of money or property, usu by fraud or extortion; *esp* to overcharge.

fleer[1] *v archaic* (*often* + at) to mock, *esp* in a crude, coarse manner.

fleer[2] *n archaic* a mocking look or remark.

fleet[1] *n* **1** a number of warships under a single command. **2** (*often* **the Fleet**) a country's navy. **3** a group of ships, aircraft, lorries, etc operating together or owned or operated under one management.

fleet[2] *adj* quick and nimble. ⋙ **fleetly** *adv,* **fleetness** *n.*

fleet[3] *v chiefly literary* to fly swiftly; to pass rapidly.

Fleet Air Arm *n* the branch of the Royal Navy that maintains and operates naval aircraft.

fleeting *adj* passing swiftly; transitory. ⋙ **fleetingly** *adv,* **fleetingness** *n.*

Fleet Street *n* the British press, *esp* newspaper journalism or the people working in the industry.

Fleming *n* **1** a native or inhabitant of Flanders, a region lying on the North Sea coasts of the Netherlands, Belgium, and France. **2** a member of the Flemish-speaking people of Belgium: compare WALLOON.

Flemish *n* **1** (**the Flemish**) (*used as pl*) the people of Flanders. **2** the Germanic language of the people of Flanders. ⋙ **Flemish** *adj.*

flense *or* **flench** *v* to strip (e.g. a whale) of blubber or skin.

flesh *n* **1** the soft, *esp* muscular, parts of the body of an animal, *esp* a vertebrate, as distinguished from visceral structures, bone, hide, etc. **2** the edible parts of an animal, *esp* its muscular tissue. **3** a pulpy part of a plant or fruit, *esp* if edible. **4a** the physical being of humans. **b** the physical or sensual aspect of human nature. ✱ **go the way of all flesh** to die. **in the flesh** in bodily form; in person. **make somebody's flesh creep/crawl** to cause revulsion in somebody. **one's own flesh/flesh and blood** one's own kindred or stock. **press the flesh** *informal esp* of a politician: to meet and shake hands with numerous people. ⋙ **fleshless** *adj.*

flesh-colour *adj* of a pinkish white colour with a slight yellow tint. ⋙ **flesh-colour** *n,* **flesh-coloured** *adj.*

fleshings *pl n* flesh-coloured tights worn by dancers and actors.

fleshly *adj* (**-ier, -iest**) belonging or relating to the body; carnal; sensual.

flesh out *v* to develop or expand (e.g. an idea, proposal) through fuller treatment or discussion.

fleshpot *n* **1** (*usu in pl*) a place that offers sensual or sexual forms of entertainment. **2** (**the fleshpots**) bodily comfort or good living; luxury.

flesh wound *n* an injury involving penetration of body muscle without damage to bones or internal organs.

fleshy *adj* (**-ier, -iest**) **1a** plump or thickset; corpulent. **b** consisting of or resembling flesh. **2** of a plant or fruit: succulent or pulpy. ⋙ **fleshiness** *n.*

fleur-de-lis *or* **fleur-de-lys** *n* (*pl* **fleurs-de-lis** *or* **fleurs-de-lys**) in art and heraldry, a stylized representation of three lily petals, usu bound together at their bases.

flew *v* past tense of FLY[1].

flex[1] *v* **1a** to bend (*esp* a limb or joint). **b** to contract or tense (a muscle or muscles) so as to flex a limb or joint. **2** of something pliable: to bend and revert to an original position or shape.

flex[2] *n chiefly Brit* a length of flexible insulated electrical cable used in connecting an electrical appliance to a socket.

flexible *adj* **1** capable of being bent. **2** yielding to influence; willing to adapt or fit in with others. **3** capable of changing in response to new conditions; versatile. ⋙ **flexibility** *n,* **flexibly** *adv.*

flexion *or* **flection** *n* the action of flexing *esp* a joint, or the condition or process of being flexed.

flexitime (*NAm* **flextime**) *n* a system whereby employees work a set total of hours per week or month but can choose daily starting and finishing times.

flexor *n* a muscle that contracts to bend a joint: compare EXTENSOR.

flextime *n NAm* see FLEXITIME.

flexuous *adj* bending and curving; sinuous. ⋙ **flexuously** *adv.*

flibbertigibbet *n informal* a silly, irresponsible person, *esp* one who chatters on or who flits from one thing to another.

flick[1] *n* **1** a light jerky movement or blow. **2** a quick-release movement of a finger against the thumb, used for propelling small objects away.

flick[2] *v* **1** to strike lightly or remove with a quick sharp motion. **2** to cause (something) to move with a flick of the fingers. **3** to move lightly or jerkily; to dart. ✱ **flick through** to look at or read (a book, etc) cursorily, turning the pages quickly.

flick[3] *n informal* **1** a cinema film. **2** (**the flicks**) the cinema.

flicker[1] *v* **1** of a light: to vary in intensity. **2** of a flame or candle: to burn fitfully or with a fluctuating light. **3** to move irregularly or unsteadily. **4** to appear or be present irregularly or indistinctly. ⋙ **flickering** *n and adj,* **flickeringly** *adv.*

flicker[2] *n* **1** the act or an instance of flickering. **2** a momentary quickening or stirring. ⋙ **flickery** *adj.*

flick knife *n* a pocket knife with a blade that is stored in the handle and springs out when a button is pressed.

flier *n* see FLYER.

flight[1] *n* **1** the act of flying. **2** a journey through air or space, *esp* a journey made in an aircraft. **3** the trajectory of a projectile, e.g. a struck or bowled ball. **4** swift movement. **5a** a flock of birds flying together. **b** in the airforce, a unit of six or so aircraft operating together. **6a** a continuous series of stairs from one landing or floor to another. **b** a series of locks taking a canal up an ascent. **7** any of the vanes or feathers at the tail of a dart, arrow, etc that provide stability. ✱ **flight of fancy/the imagination** a piece of originality or inventiveness. **take flight** of a bird: to leave the ground, a perch, etc and fly off.

flight[2] *n* the act or an instance of fleeing. ✱ **put to flight** to cause to flee. **take (to) flight** to flee.

flight attendant *n* a person employed to look after the needs of passengers onboard a commercial aircraft.

flight deck *n* **1** the compartment housing the controls and the crew who operate them in an aircraft. **2** the deck of a ship used for the takeoff and landing of aircraft.

flight feather *n* any of the large stiff feathers of a bird's wing or tail that are important in providing lift and control for flight.

flightless *adj* of a bird or insect: naturally unable to fly. ⋙ **flightlessness** *n.*

flight lieutenant *n* in the Royal Air Force, an officer ranking below squadron leader and above flying officer.

flight path *n* the course taken by an aircraft, spacecraft, etc, usu fixed in advance.

flight plan *n* a statement, usu written, of the details of an intended flight.

flight recorder *n* a robust device fitted to an aircraft that records details of its flight, *esp* for use in investigating accidents.

flight sergeant *n* in the Royal Air Force, a non-commissioned officer ranking below warrant officer and above sergeant.

flighty *adj* (**-ier, -iest**) of a person: irresponsible, silly, flirtatious, or inclined to be restless. ⋙ **flightily** *adv,* **flightiness** *n.*

flimflam[1] *n informal* **1** deception or trickery. **2** nonsense; humbug. ⋙ **flimflammery** *n.*

flimflam[2] *v* (**flimflammed, flimflamming**) to deceive, cheat, or trick. ⋙ **flimflammer** *n.*

flimsy[1] *adj* (**-ier, -iest**) **1a** not built to last; insubstantial. **b** thin and light. **2** of an excuse, reason, etc: implausible; unconvincing. ⋙ **flimsily** *adj,* **flimsiness** *n.*

flimsy[2] *n* (*pl* **-ies**) **1** lightweight paper used *esp* for multiple copies. **2** a document, or a copy of one, printed on this paper.

flinch[1] *v* **1** to make a nervous shrinking movement, *esp* in response to fear, pain, threats, etc. **2** (+ from) to avoid contact with something or be averse or unwilling to do something. ⋙ **flinchingly** *adv.*

flinch[2] *n* the act or an instance of flinching.

flinders *pl n* splinters or fragments.

fling[1] *v* (*past tense and past part.* **flung**) **1** to throw or hurl, *esp* with force or recklessness. **2** to send or put somewhere unceremoniously. **3** (+ into) to involve (oneself) energetically in an activity. **4** to move in a hasty or violent manner.

fling[2] *n* **1** a period devoted to self-indulgence. **2** *informal* a brief sexual relationship with somebody. **3** a vigorous Scottish reel or dance.

flint *n* **1** a hard quartz found *esp* in chalk or limestone. **2** a piece of this material chipped or flaked in antiquity to form a tool or weapon. **3** a material, e.g. an alloy of iron and cerium, used for producing a spark, e.g. in a cigarette lighter. ⋙ **flintlike** *adj.*

flintlock *n* a gun, used in the 17th and 18th cents, in which the charge is ignited by sparks struck from flint.

flinty *adj* (**-ier, -iest**) **1** of stone or other material: resembling flint. **2** of a person, facial expression, or an attitude: hard, unsympathetic, or unyielding. ⋙ **flintily** *adv,* **flintiness** *n.*

flip[1] *v* (**flipped, flipping**) **1** to toss (something) with a sharp movement, *esp* so that it turns over in the air. **2** to turn over, *esp* lightly or easily. **3** to propel with a flick of the fingers. **4** *informal* to lose one's sanity or self-control. ✻ **flip one's lid** (*also NAm* **flip one's wig**) *informal* to go crazy; to lose one's self-control. **flip through** to turn the pages of (a book, magazine, etc) quickly or casually.

flip[2] *n* **1** the act or an instance of flipping. **2** a somersault, *esp* when performed in the air. **3** an alcoholic drink with beaten eggs added to it.

flip[3] *adj* (**flipper, flippest**) *informal* of a person, remark, etc: flippant; impertinent.

flip chart *n* a large pad of paper mounted on a stand and used as a visual aid during a presentation, the sheets being flipped backwards over the top after display.

flip-flop[1] *n* **1** *chiefly NAm* a backward handspring. **2** *NAm, informal* a sudden about-turn in policy; = VOLTE-FACE (1). **3** a circuit, e.g. in a computer, capable of assuming either of two stable states. **4** a rubber sandal consisting of a sole and two diagonal straps anchored between the big toe and the second toe.

flip-flop[2] *v* (**flip-flopped, flip-flopping**) to move with repeated flapping sound or movements.

flippant *adj* of a person, attitude, remark, etc: not showing proper respect or seriousness. ⋙ **flippancy** *n,* **flippantly** *adv.*

flipper *n* **1** a broad flat limb, e.g. of a seal, adapted for swimming. **2** a flat rubber shoe with the front expanded into a paddle, used for underwater swimming.

flipping *adj informal* used for emphasis or to express irritation.

flip side *n informal* **1** the side of a gramophone record which is not the principal marketing attraction. **2** the less familiar side of a person, situation, etc, *esp* if less acceptable or more sinister.

flirt[1] *v* to show sexual interest in or make advances to somebody in a playful way. ✻ **flirt with 1** to show superficial or casual interest in. **2** to risk (danger, death, etc), *esp* deliberately and as a means of obtaining excitement. ⋙ **flirtatious** *adj,* **flirtatiously** *adv,* **flirty** *adj.*

flirt[2] *n* a person who flirts, *esp* somebody who flirts regularly or blatantly.

flirtation *n* **1** the activity of flirting with somebody, or with an idea, etc. **2** a short-lived romantic or sexual relationship. **3** (*often* + with) a brief foray into some area of activity or thought.

flit[1] *v* (**flitted, flitting**) **1a** to move or fly lightly and quickly. **b** to pass quickly or irregularly from one thing to another. **2** *chiefly Scot, N Eng* to move house. **3** *Brit* to escape or abscond in order to avoid problems or obligations.

flit[2] *n* **1** *chiefly Scot, N Eng* the act or an instance of moving house. **2** *Brit* a hurried departure, *esp* in order to avoid problems or obligations.

flitch *n* **1** a salted and often smoked side of pork. **2** a longitudinal section of a log.

flitter *v* to move about in a random, restless, or agitated way. ⋙ **flitter** *n.*

float[1] *n* **1** something buoyant or hollow that floats, e.g.: **a** a cork or other device used to keep the baited end of a fishing line afloat. **b** a hollow ball at the end of a lever in a cistern, tank, or boiler that regulates the liquid level. **c** a sac containing air or gas in the body of a plant or animal. **2** a tool for smoothing a surface of plaster, concrete, etc. **3a** a platform of a lorry supporting an exhibit in a parade. **b** an electrically powered delivery vehicle. **4** a soft drink with a scoop of ice cream floating in it. **5** a sum of money available for giving change at a stall, in a shop, etc.

float[2] *v* **1** to rest on the surface of or be suspended in a fluid. **2a** to drift on or through a liquid, or move gently in an air current. **b** to wander aimlessly. **c** in sport, to send (a ball) on a high smooth flight. **3** to lack firmness of aim or commitment. **4** to present (e.g. an idea) for acceptance or rejection. **5** of a currency: to find a level in the international exchange market in response to the law of supply and demand, without artificial support or control. **6** to offer the shares of (a company) for the first time for sale on the stock market. ✻ **float somebody's boat** *informal* to excite or interest somebody, *esp* sexually. ⋙ **floatability** *n,* **floatable** *adj,* **floater** *n.*

floatation *n* see FLOTATION.

floatation tank *n* see FLOTATION TANK.

float chamber *n* the petrol reservoir in a carburettor, in which the level is kept constant by a floating valve.

float glass *n* a flat polished glass made by floating a continuous ribbon of molten glass over a liquid metal bath.

floating charge *n* a loan or liability for which the total assets of the borrowing company serve as security: compare FIXED CHARGE.

floating-point *adj* denoting a mathematical notation in which a value is represented by a number multiplied by a power of the number base.

floating rib *n* a rib, e.g. any of the lowest two pairs in human beings, that has no attachment to the sternum.

floating voter *n* a person who does not always vote for the same party.

floaty *adj* (**-ier, -iest**) of a fabric: light and flimsy.

flob *v* (**flobbed, flobbing**) *Brit, informal* to spit. ➤➤ **flob** *n.*

floccinaucinihilipilification *n chiefly humorous* the act of contemptuously dismissing something or of treating something as worthless.

flocculate *v technical* to form a flocculent mass. ➤➤ **flocculant** *n,* **flocculation** *n.*

flocculent *adj* **1** resembling wool, *esp* in having a loose fluffy texture. **2** made up of small woolly clumps. ➤➤ **flocculence** *n.*

flock[1] *n* **1** (*used as sing. or pl*) a group of birds or mammals assembled or herded together. **2** (*also in pl*) a large group. **3** a Christian church congregation, *esp* when considered as being under the charge of a specified minister, priest, etc.

flock[2] *v* to gather or move in a crowd.

flock[3] *n* **1** a tuft of wool or cotton fibre. **2** woollen or cotton refuse used for stuffing furniture, mattresses, etc. **3** very short or pulverized fibre used *esp* to form a velvety pattern on cloth or paper. ➤➤ **flocky** *adj.*

flock[4] *v* to decorate (a fabric or wallpaper) with flock. ➤➤ **flocking** *n.*

flock wallpaper *n* wallpaper with a raised pattern produced by dusting powdered wool over the partially sized surface.

floe *n* a sheet of floating ice, *esp* on the sea.

flog *v* (**flogged, flogging**) **1** to beat severely with a rod, whip, etc. **2** *informal* to repeat (something) so frequently as to make it uninteresting. **3** *Brit, informal* to sell or offer for sale. ✱ **flog a dead horse** to waste time or energy on worn-out or previously settled issues. ➤➤ **flogger** *n.*

flokati *n* (*pl* **flokatis**) a Greek hand-woven rug with a shaggy pile.

flood[1] *n* **1a** an overflowing of a body of water, *esp* onto land that is normally dry. **b** (**the Flood**) the biblical flooding of the earth caused by God as a punishment for human wickedness. **2** the inflow of water associated with a rising tide. **3** *literary* a body of water such as a river or the sea. **4** an overwhelming quantity or volume. **5** = FLOODLIGHT[1].

flood[2] *v* **1a** to cover with, or become submerged under, water that has overflowed. **b** of a river: to rise and overflow its banks. **2a** to come out, move along, arrive etc in a continuous stream or overwhelming quantities. **b** of sound, light, etc: to fill or suffuse (a place) throughout. **3a** to oversupply (a market). **b** to supply (a carburettor or engine) with too much fuel. ✱ **be flooded out 1** be forced to leave one's home because of flooding. **2** be faced with overwhelming quantities of something.

floodgate *n* **1** a gate for shutting out or admitting water. **2** (*also in pl*) something that acts as a barrier to a potentially overwhelming flow.

floodlight[1] *n* a lamp producing a broad bright beam of light for artificially illuminating e.g. a theatre stage or a sports arena.

floodlight[2] *v* (*past tense and past part.* **floodlit**) to illuminate with floodlights. ➤➤ **floodlit** *adj.*

floodplain *n* a low-lying area beside a river that is composed of sedimentary deposits and is subject to periodic flooding.

flood tide *n* the tide while flowing in or at its highest point.

floor[1] *n* **1** the lower surface of a room, hallway, etc. **2** the bottom inside surface of a hollow structure, e.g. a cave or bodily part. **3** a storey of a building. **4** (**the floor**) **a** the part of a legislative or other assembly in which members sit and speak. **b** the members of an assembly, people attending a meeting, etc. **5** an area in a stock exchange where trading is done. **6** a lower limit or minimum for wages or prices. ✱ **get/have/be given the floor** to be granted the right to speak in an assembly. **take the floor 1** to stand up, e.g. in a meeting, to make a formal speech. **2** to begin dancing.

floor[2] *v* **1** to fit with a floor. **2a** to knock to the floor or ground. **b** of a question, etc: to confuse or disconcert (somebody).

floorboard *n* a long board or plank forming part of a floor.

floor manager *n* **1** in a store, an overseer of sales staff; = SHOPWALKER. **2** the stage manager of a television programme.

floor show *n* a series of acts presented in a nightclub.

floozy *or* **floozie** *or* **floosie** *n* (*pl* **-ies**) *informal* a disreputable or promiscuous woman or girl.

flop[1] *v* (**flopped, flopping**) **1** to swing or hang loosely but heavily. **2** to move or drop in a heavy, clumsy, or relaxed manner. **3** *informal* to relax completely; to slump. **4** *informal* to fail completely.

flop[2] *n* **1** a flopping motion, or the sound of this. **2** *informal* a complete failure.

flophouse *n chiefly NAm, informal* = DOSSHOUSE.

floppy[1] *adj* (**-ier, -iest**) limp and tending to hang loosely. ➤➤ **floppily** *adv,* **floppiness** *n.*

floppy[2] *n* (*pl* **-ies**) *informal* = FLOPPY DISK.

floppy disk *n* in computing, a flexible disk coated with a magnetic substance, used for storing data. Also called DISKETTE.

flora *n* (*pl* **floras** *or* **florae**) **1** the plant life of a region, period, or special environment: compare FAUNA. **2** the bacteria or fungi, whether normal or pathological, occurring in or on a bodily organ.

floral *adj* **1** relating to or composed of flowers. **2** relating to flora. ➤➤ **florally** *adv.*

Florentine[1] *adj* **1** relating to or belonging to the Italian city of Florence. **2** (*usu* **florentine**) (*used after a noun*) denoting a dish of food containing spinach or served on a bed of spinach.

Florentine[2] *n* **1** a native or inhabitant of Florence. **2** (**florentine**) a hard sweet biscuit with a chocolate coated base and topped with nuts and pieces of crystallized fruit.

florescence *n formal* a state or period of flourishing or flowering. ➤➤ **florescent** *adj.*

floret *n* **1** any of the small flowers forming the head of a composite plant. **2** any of the individual flowering stems making up a cauliflower or broccoli head.

floribunda *n* a plant, *esp* a hybrid rose, that produces sprays or clusters of flowers, as distinct from single flowers.

floriculture *n* the cultivation and management of ornamental and flowering plants. ➤➤ **floricultural** *adj,* **floriculturally** *adv,* **floriculturist** *n.*

florid *adj* **1** tinged with red; ruddy. **2** excessively flowery or ornate in style. ➤➤ **floridity** *n,* **floridly** *adv,* **floridness** *n.*

floriferous *adj* of a plant: producing or capable of producing flowers, *esp* in abundance. ➤➤ **floriferously** *adv,* **floriferousness** *n.*

florin *n* **1** a former British or Commonwealth coin worth two shillings. **2** any of various former gold coins of European countries, *esp* a Dutch guilder.

florist *n* a person or shop that sells cut flowers and floral arrangements. ➤➤ **floristry** *n.*

floruit /'floroo·it/ *n* used to indicate the date or period when the person in question, *esp* a historical figure whose birth and death dates are unknown, lived, worked, or was most active.

floss[1] *n* **1** waste or short silk, *esp* from the outer part of a silkworm's cocoon. **2** soft thread of silk or mercerized cotton for embroidery. **3** soft thread, often waxed, for cleaning between the teeth. **4** silky plant fibres, *esp* on maize cobs or cotton bolls.

floss[2] *v* to clean one's teeth with dental floss.

flossy *adj* (**-ier, -iest**) **1** composed of or resembling floss. **2** *chiefly NAm, informal* ornate, *esp* in a vulgar, tasteless, or superficial way; flashy.

flotation *or* **floatation** *n* **1** the act, process, or state of floating. **2** the process of launching a company on the stock market by offering shares for the first time.

flotation tank *or* **floatation tank** *n* a pod-like chamber containing a small amount of mineral-rich water that a person floats in as a form of stress-relief therapy.

flotilla *n* a small fleet of ships, *esp* warships.

flotsam *n* **1** floating wreckage, *esp* of a ship or its cargo: compare JETSAM. **2** a collective term for vagrants and homeless or destitute people. ✱ **flotsam and jetsam** accumulated odds and ends.

flounce[1] *v* (*often* + out/off/about/away) to move in a violent or exaggerated fashion, *esp* to emphasize one's anger. ➤➤ **flouncy** *adj.*

flounce[2] *n* the act or an instance of flouncing.

flounce[3] *n* a wide gathered strip of fabric attached by the gathered edge, e.g. to the hem of a skirt or dress. ➤➤ **flounced** *adj,* **flouncy** *adj.*

flounder[1] *n* (*pl* **flounders** *or* **flounder**) any of various flatfishes including some marine food fishes.

flounder[2] *v* **1** to stagger or thrash about ineffectually in soft mud or water. **2** to behave or speak in a blundering or incompetent way, as a result of being at a loss. ➤➤ **flounder** *n.*

Usage note

flounder *or* **founder**? *Flounder* means to struggle to move; *founder* when referring to a ship means 'to sink' and when referring to an animal means 'to go lame'. In their extended senses, *founder* implies complete failure: *The plans foundered after attempts to raise money failed*; while someone who *flounders* is struggling awkwardly: *flounder through a speech*.

flour[1] *n* **1** finely ground meal, *esp* of wheat. **2** a fine soft powder.

flour[2] *v* to coat with flour.

flourish[1] *v* **1** to grow luxuriantly; to thrive. **2** to achieve success; to prosper. **3** to be in good health. **4** to reach a height of activity, development, or influence at a specified date or during a specified period. **5** to wave or brandish with dramatic gestures. ➤➤ **flourisher** *n.*

flourish[2] *n* **1a** a decorative embellishment, *esp* a flowing curve on handwriting, scrollwork, etc. **b** an ostentatious piece of language or passage in a speech or written text. **2** an ostentatious or dramatic gesture or action. **3a** a fanfare on a brass instrument, *esp* a trumpet. **b** an ornate or florid passage in a piece of music.

floury *adj* (**-ier, -iest**) **1** resembling flour. **2** covered with flour. **3** of a potato: having a light fluffy texture when cooked. ➤➤ **flouriness** *n.*

flout *v* **1** to treat (something, *esp* a convention or rule of behaviour) with contemptuous disregard. **2** *archaic* to mock or insult. ➤➤ **flouter** *n.*

Usage note

flout *or* **flaunt**? See note at FLAUNT.

flow[1] *v* **1** of water or other liquid: to move or pour steadily and continuously. **2** of a river or stream: to move in a certain direction. **3** of the tide: to move towards the land; to rise: compare EBB[1]. **4** of gas or electricity: to pass along pipes or cables. **5** of crowds, traffic, etc: to move steadily along. **6** of long hair, loose clothing, etc: to swing or stream gracefully. **7** of ideas or words: **a** to come easily to one as one speaks or writes. **b** to have a smooth graceful continuity. **8** of conversation: to be animated and lively. **9** to proceed from, or be the result or outcome of something. **10** of rock or other solid material: to deform under stress without cracking or rupturing. ✱ **be flowing with** to have a plentiful supply of (something). ➤➤ **flowing** *adj,* **flowingly** *adv.*

flow[2] *n* **1** the action of flowing, *esp* moving along steadily or issuing forth in a stream. **2** the rising of the tide: compare EBB[1]. ✱ **go with the flow** to be content to be carried along by events, current thinking, etc.

flow chart *n* a diagram consisting of a set of symbols, e.g. rectangles or diamonds, and connecting lines, that shows the step-by-step progression through a usu complicated procedure or system.

flow diagram *n* = FLOW CHART.

flower[1] *n* **1a** a reproductive structure in a plant that typically consists of a shortened stem bearing leaves modified to form coloured petals, sepals, carpels or stamens and has a scent. **b** a plant that produces a reproductive structure of this kind. **2a** the finest or most perfect part or example of something. **b** the finest, most vigorous period; the prime. **c** a state of blooming or flourishing. ➤➤ **flowerless** *adj,* **flower-like** *adj.*

flower[2] *v* **1** of a plant: to produce flowers; to blossom. **2** to develop and flourish. ➤➤ **flowerer** *n,* **flowering** *adj and n.*

flowered *adj* having a pattern of flowers.

flower head *n* a rounded or flattened cluster of densely packed stalkless flowers at the top of a stem, having the appearance of a single flower.

flowerpot *n* an earthenware or plastic container in which to grow plants.

flower power *n* a movement of the late 1960s which promoted peace and love as forces to change the world and used flowers as its symbols.

flowery *adj* **1** relating to, full of, or patterned with flowers. **2** containing or using highly ornate language. ➤➤ **floweriness** *n.*

flown *v* past part. of FLY[1].

flow sheet *n* = FLOW CHART.

flu *n* influenza.

flub *v* (**flubbed, flubbing**) *NAm, informal* **1** to botch or bungle (something). **2** to blunder. ➤➤ **flub** *n.*

fluctuate *v* **1** to rise and fall; to swing back and forth. **2** to change continually and often irregularly. ➤➤ **fluctuation** *n.*

flue *n* **1** a channel in a chimney for flame and smoke. **2** a pipe for conveying heat, e.g. to water in a steam boiler.

fluence *n Brit, informal* magical power or influence.

fluent *adj* **1a** able to speak, write, read, etc without difficulty. **b** of somebody's command of a language: effortless and competent. **2** effortlessly smooth and rapid; polished. **3** flowing or capable of flowing; = FLUID² (1). ⋙ **fluency** *n,* **fluently** *adv.*

fluff¹ *n* **1a** small loose bits of waste material, e.g. hairs and threads, that stick to clothes, carpets, etc. **b** soft light fur, down, etc. **2** *informal* a blunder, *esp* in performance. ✱ **bit of fluff** *informal* an attractive young woman, *esp* considered as being frivolous or as lacking intelligence.

fluff² *v* **1** (+ out/up) to make (something) fuller, plumper, or fluffier. **2** *informal* to make a mistake, or do (something) badly, *esp* to forget (one's lines) in a play.

fluffy *adj* (**-ier, -iest**) **1** like or covered with fluff. **2** of whipped foods, etc: light and soft or airy. ⋙ **fluffily** *adv,* **fluffiness** *n.*

flugelhorn *n* a valved brass musical instrument resembling a cornet.

fluid¹ *n* **1** a substance, *esp* a liquid or gas, that can flow freely, has no fixed shape, yields to pressure, and conforms to the shape of its container. **2** a liquid in the body of an animal or plant. ⋙ **fluidal** *adj.*

fluid² *adj* **1** of liquids, gases, etc: capable of flowing. **2a** of a form or shape: likely or tending to change or move; not fixed. **b** of plans, etc: not yet definite; capable of alteration or adaptation. **3** of a style of movement: smooth or easy; effortlessly graceful. ⋙ **fluidity** *n,* **fluidly** *adv,* **fluidness** *n.*

fluid mechanics *pl n* (*used as sing.*) the branch of engineering that studies the mechanical properties and flow of liquids; = HYDRAULICS.

fluid ounce (*NAm* **fluidounce**) *n* **1** a British unit of liquid capacity equal to one twentieth of an imperial pint (about 28.4ml). **2** a US unit of liquid capacity equal to one sixteenth of a US pint (about 29.54ml).

fluke¹ *n* **1** any of various parasitic flatworms, e.g. a liver fluke. **2** *chiefly NAm* a flatfish, *esp* a flounder.

fluke² *n* **1** the part of an anchor that digs into the sea, river, etc bottom. **2** a barbed end, e.g. of a harpoon. **3** either of the lobes of a whale's tail.

fluke³ *n* **1** an accidental success, and therefore one unlikely to be repeated. **2** a strange or lucky coincidence. ⋙ **flukey** *adj,* **fluky** *adj.*

fluke⁴ *v* to achieve or gain by accident or luck.

flume *n* **1** an inclined water channel, *esp* one for conveying floating logs. **2** an amusement-park chute with a shallow stream of water flowing down it, or one of tubular design at a swimming pool.

flummery *n* (*pl* **-ies**) **1** *informal* pretentious humbug. **2** a sweet dish typically made with flour or oatmeal, eggs, honey, and cream.

flummox *v* to bewilder or confuse completely.

flump *v* to move or drop with a dull heavy sound. ⋙ **flump** *n.*

flung *v* past tense and past part. of FLING¹.

flunk *v chiefly NAm, informal* **1** to fail, or to fail (somebody), *esp* in an examination or course. **2** (+ out) to be turned out of a school or college for failure.

flunky *or* **flunkey** *n* (*pl* **-ies** *or* **-eys**) **1** a person performing menial duties. **2** a yes-man; a servile follower. **3** a liveried servant. ⋙ **flunkeyism** *n.*

fluoresce *v* to glow with fluorescence. ⋙ **fluorescer** *n.*

fluorescence *n* **1** the emitting of electromagnetic radiation, usu as visible light, as a result of the simultaneous absorption of radiation of shorter wavelength. **2** the light or other radiation emitted in this process.

fluorescent *adj* **1** of or having fluorescence. **2** bright and glowing as a result of fluorescence. **3** brightly colourful.

fluorescent lamp *n* a tubular electric lamp with a coating of fluorescent material on its inner surface.

fluoridate *v* to add a fluoride to (e.g. drinking water) to prevent tooth decay. ⋙ **fluoridation** *n.*

fluoride *n* a compound of fluorine, *esp* one added to toothpaste or drinking water to prevent tooth decay.

fluorinate *v* **1** to treat or combine with fluorine or a compound of fluorine. **2** = FLUORIDATE. ⋙ **fluorination** *n.*

fluorine *n* a non-metallic chemical element of the halogen group that normally occurs as a pale yellowish toxic gas.

fluorite *n* = FLUORSPAR.

fluorocarbon *n* a chemically inert compound containing carbon and fluorine, used chiefly as a lubricant, refrigerant, or in making resins and plastics.

fluoroscope *n* an instrument with a screen coated with a fluorescent substance, used for observing the internal structure of an opaque object, e.g. the living body, by means of X-rays. ⋙ **fluoroscopic** *adj,* **fluoroscopically** *adv,* **fluoroscopy** *n.*

fluorspar *n* a mineral consisting of calcium fluoride, the chief source of fluorine and also used in glass-making and as a flux in the manufacture and refining of metals.

flurry¹ *n* (*pl* **-ies**) **1a** a gust of wind. **b** a brief fall of snow or rain, or a quantity of something such as leaves, blown by a light wind. **2** a state of nervous excitement or bustle. **3** a short-lived outburst of activity.

flurry² *v* (**-ies, -ied**) to make or become agitated and confused.

flush¹ *n* **1a** a tinge of red, *esp* in the cheeks; a blush. **b** the act or an instance of flushing. **c** a fresh and vigorous state. **2** a transitory sensation of extreme heat, e.g. a hot flush. **3a** a surge of emotion. **b** a sudden increase, *esp* of new plant growth. **4a** a sudden flow, *esp* of water. **b** the cleansing of something, e.g. a toilet, with a flow of water. **c** *Brit* a device for flushing toilets or drains.

flush² *v* **1a** to glow, or cause to glow, brightly with a ruddy or rosy colour. **b** to blush. **2a** to cause liquid to flow over or through (e.g. a toilet), *esp* to cleanse it. **b** to dispose of (e.g. waste) by carrying it away on a stream of liquid. ✱ **be flushed with** to feel proud of and excited by. ⋙ **flusher** *n.*

flush³ *adj* **1a** forming a continuous edge or plane surface; level. **b** arranged edge to edge so as to fit snugly. **2** *informal* having a plentiful supply of money. ⋙ **flush** *adv,* **flushness** *n.*

flush⁴ *v* to make flush.

flush⁵ *v* **1** to cause (*esp* a game bird) to take flight suddenly. **2** (*often* + out) to force (somebody) to leave a place of concealment.

flush⁶ *n* a hand of playing cards, *esp* in a gambling game such as poker, all of the same suit.

fluster¹ *v* to make or become agitated, nervous, or confused. ⋙ **flustered** *adj.*

fluster² *n* a state of agitated confusion.

flute¹ *n* **1** a high-pitched woodwind musical instrument that consists of a cylindrical tube with finger holes stopped at one end, held horizontally and played by blowing air across a side hole. **2a** a grooved pleat or frill on a garment, upholstery, etc. **b** any of the vertical parallel grooves on the shaft of a classical column. **3** a tall narrow wineglass. ⋙ **flutelike** *adj,* **fluty** *adj.*

flute[2] *v* **1** to utter (something) with a flutelike sound; to produce (a flutelike sound). **2** to form flutes in (a column, garment, etc). ➤➤ **fluter** *n.*

fluting *n* a series of parallel grooves or pleats.

flutist *n chiefly NAm* = FLAUTIST.

flutter[1] *v* **1** to flap the wings rapidly. **2a** to move or fall with quick wavering or flapping motions. **b** to beat or vibrate in irregular spasms. **3** to move about or behave in an agitated aimless manner. ➤➤ **flutterer** *n.*

flutter[2] *n* **1** the act or an instance of fluttering. **2a** a state of nervous confusion, excitement, or commotion. **b** abnormal spasmodic fluttering of the heart, etc. **3** a distortion in reproduced sound similar to but at a faster rate than WOW[4]. **4** *chiefly Brit* a small gamble or bet. ➤➤ **fluttery** *adj.*

fluvial *adj* relating to, found in, or living in or near a stream or river.

flux[1] *n* **1a** a continuous flow or flowing. **b** an influx. **2** continual change; fluctuation. **3a** a substance used to promote fusion of metals, e.g. in soldering or brazing. **b** a substance used in smelting ores and refining metals to promote melting and remove impurities. **4a** the rate of transfer of a fluid, particles, or energy across a given surface. **b** the strength of the forces acting in an area of an electric or magnetic field. **5** *archaic* an abnormal flowing of fluid, *esp* excrement, from the body.

flux[2] *v* to treat (e.g. metal to be soldered) with a flux.

fly[1] *v* (**-ies, -ied, flew, flown**) **1a** to move in or through the air by means of wings. **b** to move through the air or space. **c** to float or wave in the air. **2a** to operate (an aircraft or spacecraft) in flight. **b** to transport in an aircraft, or travel by aircraft. **3a** to move or pass swiftly. **b** to pass suddenly and violently into a specified state: *He flew into a rage.* **4** *informal* to depart in haste; to dash. **5a** to take flight; to flee. **b** *literary* to fade and disappear; to vanish. ✻ **fly a kite** *informal* to take action to gauge public opinion on some matter. **fly at** to make a sudden verbal or physical attack on. **fly in the face of 1** to act in open defiance or disobedience of (e.g. somebody's orders). **2** to be contrary to (a belief, common sense, etc). **fly off the handle** *informal* to become very angry, *esp* without any warning. ➤➤ **flyable** *adj,* **flying** *n.*

fly[2] *n* (*pl* **-ies**) **1a** an opening in a garment, etc concealed by a fold of cloth extending over the fastener. **b** (*usu in pl*) such an opening in the front of a pair of trousers. **2** (*in pl*) the space over a stage where scenery and equipment can be hung. **3** = FLY SHEET (1). **4** (*pl also* **flys**) *chiefly Brit* a light covered horse-drawn carriage.

fly[3] *n* (*pl* **flies**) **1** any of a large order of insects having two membranous wings and mouthparts adapted for piercing and sucking. **2** any of various winged insects that are not true flies. **3** a natural or artificial fly attached to a fishhook for use as bait. ✻ **fly in the ointment** a detracting factor or element. **fly on the wall** somebody who watches others while not being noticed himself or herself. **there are no flies on** there is little or no possibility of deceiving or cheating (him, her, etc).

fly[4] *adj* (**flyer, flyest**) *chiefly Brit, informal* clever and worldly-wise, *esp* in being able to use people or situations to gain advantages.

fly agaric *n* a poisonous toadstool usu with a bright red cap with small white scaly patches.

flyaway *adj esp* of the hair: tending not to stay in place.

flyblown *adj* infested with the eggs or young larvae of a flesh fly or blowfly.

flyby *n* (*pl* **flybys**) a flight of a spacecraft close to a celestial body, *esp* to obtain scientific data.

fly-by-night *adj* **1** given to making a quick profit, usu by disreputable or irresponsible acts; untrustworthy. **2** transitory; passing.

fly-by-wire *adj* denoting a control system for an aircraft that is electronic rather than mechanical and largely run by computer.

flycatcher *n* any of various species of small birds that feed on insects caught while flying.

flyer *or* **flier** *n* **1** a person or thing that flies or moves very fast. **2a** a passenger on an aircraft. **b** a pilot. **3** a small leaflet or handbill, *esp* one advertising an event, product, etc. **4** *informal* a fast or auspicious start, *esp* a flying start in athletics.

fly-fishing *n* fishing, e.g. for salmon or trout, using a rod and artificial flies as bait. ➤➤ **fly-fish** *v.*

fly-half *n* = STAND-OFF HALF.

flying *adj* **1** moving in the air or capable of doing so. **2a** rapidly moving. **b** very brief; hasty. **c** passing quickly. ✻ **with flying colours** with complete or eminent success.

flying boat *n* a seaplane with a hull adapted for floating.

flying bomb *n* a pilotless aircraft carrying explosives, *esp* a V-1.

flying buttress *n* a projecting arched structure that supports a wall or building.

flying doctor *n* a doctor who visits patients in remote areas by aeroplane, *esp* in Australia.

flying fish *n* a tropical fish that has long pectoral fins and is able to glide some distance through the air.

flying fox *n* any of various fruit-eating bats with foxlike faces, found in Africa, Asia, and Australia.

flying officer *n* an officer in the Royal Air Force ranking below a flight lieutenant.

flying picket *n* a person who travels to picket a place of work other than his or her own.

flying saucer *n* any of various unidentified flying objects reported as being saucer- or disc-shaped and believed by many to come from outer space.

flying squad *n* (*often* **Flying Squad**) a group of police ready to move or act swiftly in an emergency.

flying start *n* **1** a start to a race in which the participants are already moving when they cross the starting line. **2** a privileged or successful beginning, *esp* one that gives somebody an advantage over others.

flying wing *n* an aircraft in the shape of a large wing with no fuselage and often no tailplane.

flyleaf *n* (*pl* **flyleaves**) a blank page at the beginning or end of a book that is fastened to the cover.

flyover *n* **1** *Brit* a crossing of two roads, railways, etc at different levels, or the upper level of such a crossing. **2** *chiefly NAm* = FLYPAST.

flypaper *n* paper coated with a sticky, often poisonous, substance that is hung indoors to attract and kill flies.

flypast *n Brit* a ceremonial usu low-altitude flight by aircraft over an important person or a public gathering.

flyposting *n* the unauthorized placing of advertising or political material, e.g. posters, in public places. ➤➤ **flyposter** *n.*

fly sheet *n* **1** an outer protective sheet covering a tent or a flap at the entrance to a tent. **2** a small pamphlet or circular.

flyspeck *n* a tiny spot of fly excrement. ➤➤ **flyspecked** *adj.*

fly-tip *v Brit* to dump (waste) illegally. ➤➤ **fly-tipper** *n,* **fly-tipping** *n.*

flyweight *n* a weight in boxing and wrestling between light flyweight and bantamweight.

flywheel *n* a wheel with a heavy rim that when revolving can either reduce speed fluctuations in the rotation of an engine or store energy.

FM[1] *adj* denoting a broadcasting or receiving system using frequency modulation and usu noted for lack of interference.

FM[2] *abbr* Field Marshal.

Fm *abbr* the chemical symbol for fermium.

fm *abbr* fathom.

FMD *abbr* foot-and-mouth disease.

f-number *n* the ratio of the focal length of the lens to the diameter of the aperture in a camera.

FO *abbr* **1** Flying Officer. **2** Foreign Office.

fo. *abbr* folio.

foal[1] *n* a young animal of the horse family.

foal[2] *v* of a mare: to give birth to a foal.

foam[1] *n* **1a** a light frothy mass of fine bubbles formed in or on the surface of a liquid. **b** any substance in the form of a light frothy mass of bubbles. **2** a material in a lightweight cellular form resulting from introduction of gas bubbles during manufacture. **3** *literary* the sea. ➤➤ **foaminess** *n,* **foamless** *adj,* **foamy** *adj.*

foam[2] *v* to produce or form foam. ✱ **foam at the mouth** to be very angry.

fob *n* **1** a tag or tab attached to a key ring. **2** a small pocket on or near the waistband of trousers, orig for holding a watch. **3** a short strap or chain attached to a watch carried in a fob or a waistcoat pocket.

fob off *v* (**fobbed, fobbing**) **1** (+ with) to put (somebody) off with a trick or excuse. **2** (+ on) to pass or offer (something spurious or inferior) as genuine or perfect.

fob pocket *n* = FOB (2).

fob watch *n* a large circular watch usu attached to a strap or chain in e.g. a waistcoat pocket.

focaccia /fə'kachə/ *n* (*pl* **focaccias**) a round flat Italian bread made with olive oil and topped with herbs.

focal *adj* **1** of or having a focus. **2** located at a focus. ➤➤ **focally** *adv.*

focal length *n* the distance between the optical centre of a lens or mirror and the focal point.

focal point *n* **1** the focus for a beam of incident rays parallel to the axis of a lens or mirror. **2** a centre of activity or attention.

foci *n* pl of FOCUS[1].

fo'c'sle *n* see FORECASTLE.

focus[1] *n* (*pl* **focuses** *or* **foci**) **1a** a point at which rays of e.g. light, heat, or sound converge. **b** the point at which an object must be placed for an image formed by a lens or mirror to be sharp. **2a** = FOCAL LENGTH. **b** adjustment, e.g. of the eye, necessary for distinct vision. **3** a centre of activity or attention. **4** a localized area of disease or the chief site of a generalized disease. **5a** a fixed point that together with a straight line forms a reference system for generating a conic section in plane geometry. **b** either of two fixed points used in generating an ellipse or hyperbola. **6** the place of origin of an earthquake. ✱ **in focus** having or giving the proper sharpness of outline due to good focusing. **out of focus** not in focus.

focus[2] *v* (**focused** *or* **focussed, focusing** *or* **focussing**) **1a** to adjust (e.g. a camera or telescope) so as to obtain a sharp image. **b** to become able to see clearly. **2** to concentrate one's thoughts or attention, a discussion, etc on. **3** of rays: to converge on a point. ➤➤ **focuser** *n.*

focus group *n* a number of people gathered together to discuss e.g. a new product or policy, so that others can benefit from their opinions and assessments of it.

fodder *n* **1** food for cattle, horses, sheep, or other domestic animals, *esp* coarse food such as hay. **2** something used to supply a constant demand: *computer fodder.*

foe *n literary* an enemy or adversary.

foehn *n* see FÖHN.

foetid *adj* see FETID.

foetus *or* **fetus** *n* (*pl* **foetuses** *or* **fetuses**) an unborn or unhatched vertebrate; *specif* a developing human from usu seven weeks after conception to birth, from the time of appearance of bone cells in the cartilage. ➤➤ **foetal** *adj.*

Usage note

foetus *or* fetus? *Foetus* was the usual British spelling until the late 20th cent., *fetus* being used in American English. *Fetus* is now the only spelling in technical use, and is increasingly found in popular writing in British English.

fog[1] *n* **1** fine particles of water or anything similar suspended in the lower atmosphere causing a lessening of visibility. **2a** a state of confusion or bewilderment. **b** something that confuses or obscures. **3** cloudiness on a developed photograph caused by chemical action or radiation, e.g. from X-rays.

fog[2] *v* (**fogged, fogging**) **1** to cover or obscure with fog, condensation, or anything similar. **2** to make (e.g. an argument) confused or confusing. **3** to produce fog on (e.g. a photographic film) during development.

fogey *or* **fogy** *n* (*pl* **fogeys** *or* **fogies**) a person with old-fashioned ideas. ➤➤ **fogeyish** *adj,* **fogeyism** *n.*

foggy *adj* (**-ier, -iest**) **1a** thick with fog. **b** covered or made opaque by moisture or grime. **2** vague; confused. ✱ **not have the foggiest (idea)** *chiefly Brit, informal* to have no idea at all. ➤➤ **foggily** *adv,* **fogginess** *n.*

foghorn *n* **1** a horn sounded in a fog to give warning to ships. **2** *informal* a loud deep voice.

fogy *n* see FOGEY.

föhn *or* **foehn** *n* a warm dry wind that descends the leeward side of a mountain range, *esp* the Alps.

foible *n* a minor weakness or shortcoming in personal character or behaviour; a quirk.

foie gras *n* **1** the fatted liver of an animal, *esp* a goose, used in making pâté. **2** *informal* = PÂTÉ DE FOIE GRAS.

foil[1] *n* **1** very thin sheet metal. **2** somebody or something that serves as a contrast to another, e.g. in a comedy duo.

foil[2] *v* **1** to prevent (somebody) from attaining an end. **2** to frustrate or defeat (an attempt, etc).

foil[3] *n* a light fencing sword with a circular guard and a flexible blade tipped with a button.

foist *v* (*usu* + off on/on/upon) to force acceptance of (something or somebody unwanted) by somebody.

fold[1] *v* **1** (*often* + over) to lay one part of (something) over another part. **2a** (*often* + up) to reduce the length or bulk of (something) by doubling it over. **b** (*often* + up) to become folded or be capable of being folded. **3a** to clasp (e.g. one's arms) together. **b** to bring (e.g. wings) to rest close to the body. **4a** to clasp closely; to embrace. **b** to wrap or envelop. **5** (+ in/into) to gently incorporate (a food ingredient) into a mixture without thorough stirring or beating. **6** *informal* (*often* + up) to fail completely, *esp* to stop production or operation. ➤➤ **foldable** *adj.*

fold[2] *n* **1** a doubling or folding over of e.g. material, or a crease made in this way. **2** a part doubled or laid over another part; a pleat. **3** something that is loosely folded or draped, or a hollow or sagging part, e.g. of skin, that is formed in this way. **4a** a bend in rock strata produced usu by compression. **b** *chiefly Brit* an undulation in the landscape.

fold[3] *n* **1** an enclosure for sheep. **2** (**the fold**) (*used as sing. or pl*) a group of people adhering to a common faith, belief, or enthusiasm.

-fold *suffix* **1** forming adjectives or adverbs, with the meaning: multiplied by the number specified: *a tenfold increase.* **2** forming adjectives, with the meaning: having a given number of parts: *the three-fold aspect of the problem.*

foldaway *adj* designed to fold out of the way or out of sight.

folder *n* **1** a folded cover or large envelope for holding or filing loose papers. **2** a computer directory containing a number of files.

folderol *n* **1** a useless ornament; a trifle. **2** nonsense.

folding money *n informal* money in the form of bank notes.

foldout *n* a folded insert in a publication larger in size than the page.

foley *n* (*pl* **foleys**) in film-making, a person who adds sound effects to a film at the post-production stage.

foliage *n* the leaves of a plant or clump of plants. ➤➤ **foliaged** *adj.*

foliar *adj technical* of a leaf or leaves.

foliate[1] *adj* **1** (*often in combination*) having leaves or leaflets. **2** leaf-shaped.

foliate[2] *v* **1** to beat (metal) into a leaf or thin foil. **2** to number the leaves of (e.g. a manuscript): compare PAGINATE. **3** to decorate (e.g. an arch or pedestal) with leaflike designs. **4** of a plant: to produce leaves. ➤➤ **foliation** *n.*

folic acid *n* a vitamin of the vitamin B complex that is found *esp* in green leafy vegetables and liver. A lack of it results in anaemia.

folie à deux *n* (*pl* **folies à deux**) the presence of the same or similar delusional ideas in two closely associated people.

folio *n* (*pl* **-os**) **1a** a sheet of paper folded once, or the size of each of the two leaves so formed. **b** a book printed on pages of this size. **2a** a leaf of a manuscript or book. **b** a page or leaf number. **3** a case or folder for loose papers.

folk *n* **1** *informal* **a** (*also* **folks**) (*used as pl*) people; people in general. **b** (*also* **folks**) (*used as pl*) the members of one's own family or community. **c** (*in pl*) used when addressing a group of people: everyone. **2** = FOLK MUSIC. **3** (*used before a noun*) relating to or originating from the common people who preserve the ancient traditions and culture of a nation. ➤➤ **folkish** *adj.*

folk dance *n* a traditional dance of a people or region. ➤➤ **folk dancer** *n,* **folk dancing** *n.*

folk etymology *n* **1** the transformation of words so as to bring them into an apparent relationship with other more familiar words, e.g. the change of Spanish *cucaracha* to *cockroach.* **2** an explanation of the origin of a word or phrase that is popularly held to be true, but is actually erroneous.

folkie *or* **folky** *n* (*pl* **-ies**) *informal* a folk music enthusiast.

folklore *n* **1** the traditional customs and beliefs of a people preserved by oral tradition. **2** the stories, etc attached to a particular place, group, etc. ➤➤ **folkloric** *adj,* **folklorist** *n.*

folk memory *n* the collective memory of a people enshrining ancient events, customs, stories, etc.

folk music *n* the traditional music and songs of a people or region.

folk song *n* **1** a traditional song of a people or region. **2** a contemporary song in a similar style. ➤➤ **folksinger** *n,* **folksinging** *n.*

folksy *adj* (**-ier, -iest**) *informal* **1** informal or familiar in manner or style. **2** having or affecting a lack of sophistication. ➤➤ **folksily** *adv,* **folksiness** *n.*

folk tale *n* an anonymous traditional story that is transmitted orally.

folkway *n* a traditional social custom.

folky *n* see FOLKIE.

follicle *n* a small anatomical cavity or deep narrow depression, e.g. the tubular sheath surrounding the root of a hair. ➤➤ **follicular** *adj,* **folliculate** *adj,* **folliculated** *adj.*

follow *v* **1a** to go or come after. **b** to go after (somebody or something) in order to observe them or watch their movements. **2a** to accept as a guide or leader. **b** to obey or act in accordance with (rules or instructions). **3** to copy or imitate. **4** to walk or proceed along (a path or route). **5a** to engage in (an activity) as a calling or way of life. **b** to undertake (a course of action). **6a** to come or take place after in time or order. **b** (+ with) to cause (something) to be followed by something else. **7** (*often* + from) to come into existence or take place as a result of. **8a** to watch the progress of. **b** to be a supporter of (a sport, team, etc). **9** to understand the meaning or logic of (e.g. an argument, or the person making it). ✱ **follow one's nose 1** to go in a straight or obvious course. **2** to do what one instinctively feels to be right. **follow suit 1** to play a card of the same suit as the card led. **2** to follow an example set.

follower *n* **1a** somebody who follows the opinions or teachings of another. **b** a fan or supporter. **2a** a servant or attendant. **b** *archaic* a male admirer.

following[1] *adj* **1** next after. **2** now to be stated. **3** of a wind: blowing in the direction in which something is travelling.

following[2] *n* (*used as sing. or pl*) **1** (**the following**) something that comes immediately after or below in writing or speech. **2** a group of followers, adherents, or partisans.

following[3] *prep* subsequent to.

follow-my-leader *n Brit* a game in which the actions of a designated leader must be copied by the other players.

follow on *v* **1** (*often* + from) to continue. **2** (*often* + from) to come as a consequence. **3** of a side in cricket: to be made to bat again immediately after failing to reach a certain score in the first innings. ➤➤ **follow-on** *n.*

follow-the-leader *n NAm* = FOLLOW-MY-LEADER.

follow through *v* **1** to continue the movement of a stroke after a ball has been struck. **2** to pursue or complete (an activity or process).

follow up *v* **1** to continue or enquire into (something) further. **2** to maintain contact with (a person) in order to give them further advice or treatment. ➤➤ **follow-up** *n.*

folly *n* (*pl* **-ies**) **1** a lack of good sense or prudence. **2** a foolish act or idea. **3** foolish actions or conduct. **4** a usu fanciful building built *esp* for scenic effect or to satisfy a whim.

foment *v* **1** to incite or promote the growth or development of (trouble, rebellion, etc). **2** to treat (a part of the body) with moist heat, e.g. for easing pain. ➤➤ **fomentation** *n,* **fomenter** *n.*

fond *adj* **1a** (+ of) having an affection or liking for: *fond of music.* **b** (+ of) having an inclination or predisposition for: *fond of arguing.* **2a** affectionate; loving. **b** foolishly tender; indulgent. **3** cherished. **4** foolish; naive. ⋙ **fondly** *adv,* **fondness** *n.*

fondant *n* a soft creamy preparation of flavoured sugar and water, or a sweet made from this.

fondle *v* to handle or caress tenderly and lovingly or erotically. ⋙ **fondler** *n.*

fondue *n* a dish in which small pieces of food are dipped in a hot liquid, e.g. oil or a sauce of melted cheese, at the table.

font¹ *n* a receptacle in a church for the water used in baptism. ⋙ **fontal** *adj.*

font² *n* = FOUNT².

fontanelle (*NAm* **fontanel**) *n* any of the spaces closed by membranous structures between the parietal bones of the skull of an infant or foetus.

food *n* **1** material taken into the body of a living organism and used to provide energy and sustain processes essential for life. **2** something that sustains or supplies: *food for thought.*

food chain *n* a hierarchical arrangement of organisms ordered according to each organism's use of the next as a food source.

foodie *or* **foody** *n* (*pl* **-ies**) *informal* a person who takes a keen interest in food, *esp* in rare or exotic dishes; a gourmet.

food poisoning *n* an acute gastrointestinal disorder caused by the toxic products of bacteria or by chemical residues in food.

foodstuff *n* a substance with food value, *esp* the raw material of food before or after processing.

foody *n* see FOODIE.

fool¹ *n* **1** a person lacking in prudence, common sense, or understanding. **2** a jester employed by a royal or noble household. ✱ **act/play the fool** to deliberately behave in an amusingly or irritatingly foolish manner. **be no/nobody's fool** to be wise or shrewd. **make a fool of somebody** to make somebody look foolish. **make a fool of oneself** to behave in a way or do something that leads to embarrassment. ⋙ **foolery** *n.*

fool² *v* **1** to trick or deceive. **2** to say or do something as a joke. **3** to behave in a silly or irresponsible way. **4** (+ with) to meddle or tamper thoughtlessly or ignorantly with something.

fool³ *adj NAm, informal* foolish or silly.

fool⁴ *n chiefly Brit* a cold dessert made from whipped cream or custard and fruit pureé.

fool about *v* **1** to behave in a silly or irresponsible way. **2** to spend time idly or aimlessly. **3** *chiefly NAm* (*often* + with) to have a casual sexual relationship with somebody.

fool around *v* = FOOL ABOUT.

foolhardy *adj* (**-ier, -iest**) foolishly adventurous and bold; rash. ⋙ **foolhardily** *adv,* **foolhardiness** *n.*

foolish *adj* **1** unwise; silly. **2** absurd; ridiculous. ⋙ **foolishly** *adv,* **foolishness** *n.*

foolproof *adj* so simple or reliable as to leave no opportunity for error, misuse, or failure.

foolscap *n chiefly Brit* a size of paper usu 17 × 13in. (432 × 343mm).

fool's errand *n* a needless or fruitless task or activity.

fool's gold *n* = IRON PYRITES.

fool's paradise *n* a state of illusory happiness.

foot¹ *n* (*pl* **feet**) **1** the end part of the leg on which an animal or person stands. **2** (*pl also* **foot**) a unit of length equal to 0.305m (12in.). **3a** the lower edge or lowest part; the bottom. **b** the end of something that is opposite the head or top: *the foot of the bed.* **4** the basic unit of verse metre consisting of a combination of stressed and unstressed or long and short syllables. **5** *chiefly Brit* (*used as sing. or pl*) the infantry. ✱ **a foot in the door** a position from which progress may be made. **fall/land on one's feet** to be successful or happy, *esp* after overcoming difficulties. **feet of clay** a flaw or weakness in somebody who is otherwise perfect. **get/start off on the right/wrong foot** to start a job, relationship, etc well or badly. **have/keep one's feet on the ground** to have or keep a sensible, practical attitude to life. **my foot** *informal* an expression of disbelief. **not put a foot wrong** to make no mistakes at all. **on/by foot** walking or running, as opposed to using transport. **one foot in the grave** *informal* close to death, *esp* because of old age or illness. **put one's best foot forward** to make every effort; to do one's best. **put one's foot down 1** to take a firm stand. **2** *informal* to press on the accelerator of a vehicle in order to go faster. **put one's foot in it** to make an embarrassing blunder. **run/rush somebody off their feet** (*usu in passive*) to keep somebody very busy. **set foot** (+ in/inside/on) to go into (a building or an area), often for the first time. **under foot** on the ground; under a person's feet. **under somebody's feet** in somebody's way. ⋙ **footless** *adj.*

foot² *v* to pay (e.g. a bill). ✱ **foot it 1** to travel on foot; to walk. **2** to dance.

footage *n* **1** length or quantity expressed in feet. **2** a length of cinema or television film.

foot-and-mouth disease *n* a infectious virus disease of cattle, sheep, pigs, and goats, characterized by small ulcers in the mouth, about the hoofs, and on the udder and teats.

football *n* **1a** any of several games that involve kicking a ball, *esp* Association Football in the UK or American football in the US, played between two teams on a field with goalposts at each end. **b** the inflated round or oval ball used in any of these games. **2** something treated as a basis for contention rather than on its intrinsic merits. ⋙ **footballer** *n.*

-footer *comb. form* forming nouns, denoting: **1** somebody or something that is a specified number of feet in height, length, or breadth. **2** a person who has a preference for or greater skill with the foot specified.

footfall *n* the sound of a footstep.

foot fault *n* a fault in tennis, squash, etc made when a server's feet are not behind the baseline. ⋙ **foot-fault** *v.*

foothill *n* a hill at the foot of mountains.

foothold *n* **1** = FOOTING (1). **2** an established position or basis from which to progress.

footie *n* see FOOTY.

footing *n* **1** a stable position or placing of or for the feet. **2a** an established position. **b** a position or rank in relation to others. **3** (*also in pl*) an enlargement at the lower end of a foundation, wall, or column to distribute the load, or a trench dug to accommodate this.

footle *v informal* (*often* + about/around) to waste time in aimless or fruitless activity.

footlights *pl n* a row of lights set across the front of a stage floor.

footling *adj informal* **1** bungling or inept. **2a** unimportant or trivial. **b** pettily fussy.

footloose *adj* having no ties; free to go or do as one pleases.

footman *n* (*pl* **footmen**) a servant in livery hired chiefly to wait on or receive visitors, etc.

footnote *n* **1** a note of reference, explanation, or comment typically placed at the bottom of a printed page. **2** something subordinately related to a larger event or work.

footpad *n archaic* somebody who robs pedestrians on foot.

footpath *n* **1** a narrow path for people on foot, e.g. in the country. **2** a pavement.

footplate *n Brit* the platform on which the crew stand in a locomotive.

footprint *n* **1** an impression made by a foot or shoe. **2** the area on the earth's surface covered by the transmissions of a communications satellite. **3** the space on a desk occupied by an electronic device such as a computer.

Footsie *n* an index showing the prices on the London Stock Exchange of the shares of the hundred largest public companies in Britain.

footsie *n informal* the act of surreptitiously and playfully touching, *esp* the feet, as an indication of romantic or sexual interest.

footslog[1] *v* (**footslogged, footslogging**) to march or tramp laboriously. ➤➤ **footslogger** *n.*

footslog[2] *n* a long and tiring walk, hike, or march.

foot soldier *n* **1** an infantry soldier. **2** a lowly but indispensable worker or member of an organization.

footsore *adj* having sore or tender feet, *esp* from much walking. ➤➤ **footsoreness** *n.*

footstep *n* **1a** the sound of a step or tread. **b** the distance covered by a step. **2** = FOOTPRINT (1). ✱ **follow in somebody's footsteps** to do what another person has done before, e.g. in following the same career.

footstool *n* a low stool used to support the feet.

footwear *n* shoes, boots, etc collectively.

footwork *n* the control and placing of the feet in sport or dancing.

footy *or* **footie** *n Brit, informal* football.

foo yong *or* **fu yong** *n* a Chinese-style dish, similar to a vegetable omelette.

fop *n* a man who is overly concerned about his clothes, hair, appearance, etc; a dandy. ➤➤ **foppery** *n,* **foppish** *adj,* **foppishly** *adv,* **foppishness** *n.*

for[1] *prep* **1a** used to indicate purpose or reason: *for money.* **b** used to indicate goal or direction, intention, or desire: *head for home.* **2** as being or constituting: *for breakfast.* **3** because of: *cry for joy.* **4a** in place of. **b** on behalf of; representing. **c** in support of; in favour of. **5** considered as; considering: *tall for her age.* **6** with respect to; concerning: *a stickler for detail.* **7** used to indicate cost, payment, equivalence, or correlation: *work for nothing.* **8** used to indicate duration of time or extent of space. ✱ **for it** *chiefly Brit, informal* likely to get into trouble. **Oh for...** used in expressions of, often exasperated, desire.

for[2] *conj* **1** and the reason is that. **2** because.

for[3] *adj* being in favour of a motion or measure.

for. *abbr* **1** foreign. **2** forest. **3** forestry.

for- *prefix* denoting: **1** prohibition or exclusion: *forbid.* **2** omission, refraining, or neglect: *forgo; forget.*

fora *n* pl of FORUM.

forage[1] *n* **1** food for animals, *esp* when taken by browsing or grazing, e.g. hay or straw. **2a** the act or an instance of foraging for provisions. **b** a search.

forage[2] *v* **1a** to wander in search of forage or food. **b** (*usu* + for) to make a search; to rummage. **2** to obtain (food) by foraging. ➤➤ **forager** *n.*

forage cap *n* a cap worn by infantry soldiers as part of their undress uniform.

foramen *n* (*pl* **foramina** *or* **foramens**) a small anatomical opening or perforation. ➤➤ **foraminal** *adj.*

foraminifer *n* (*pl* **foraminifera** *or* **foraminifers**) an amoeba-like single-celled organism usu having a hard perforated calcium-containing shell. ➤➤ **foraminiferal** *adj,* **foraminiferous** *adj.*

forasmuch as *conj archaic or formal* used e.g. in official proclamations or legal documents: in view of the fact that; since.

foray[1] *v* to make a raid or incursion. ➤➤ **forayer** *n.*

foray[2] *n* **1** a sudden invasion, attack, or raid. **2** a brief excursion or attempt, *esp* outside one's accustomed sphere.

forbad *v* past tense of FORBID.

forbade *v* past tense of FORBID.

forbear[1] *v* (*past tense* **forbore,** *past part.* **forborne**) **1** to hold oneself back from (doing something), *esp* with an effort. **2** (+ from) to hold back or abstain.

Usage note

forbear *or* forebear? The verb that means 'refrain from' is spelt *forbear,* with *bear* stressed; the noun that means 'ancestor' is spelt either *forebear* or *forbear,* with *for(e)* stressed.

forbear[2] *n* see FOREBEAR.

forbearance *n* **1** patience; self-restraint. **2** leniency.

forbid *v* (**forbidding,** *past tense* **forbade** *or* **forbad,** *past part.* **forbidden**) **1a** to refuse to allow. **b** to refuse access to (somewhere) or use of (something). **2** to make impracticable; to hinder or prevent. ✱ **God/Heaven forbid** used to express a strong wish that something does not happen. ➤➤ **forbidder** *n.*

forbidden fruit *n* (*used as sing. or pl*) something that is very tempting but not allowed.

forbidding *adj* **1** having a menacing or dangerous appearance. **2** unfriendly. ➤➤ **forbiddingly** *adv,* **forbiddingness** *n.*

forbore *v* past tense of FORBEAR[1].

forborne *v* past part. of FORBEAR[1].

force[1] *n* **1a** strength or energy exerted or brought to bear; active power. **b** moral or mental strength, or somebody showing this. **c** capacity to persuade or convince. **d** legal validity; operative effect. **2a** a body, e.g. of troops or ships, assigned to a military purpose. **b** (*in pl*) the armed services of a nation or commander. **3a** a body of people or things fulfilling some function: *labour force.* **b** (*often* **the Force**) = POLICE[1] (1). **c** an individual or group having the power of effective action. **4** violence, compulsion, or constraint exerted on or against a person or thing. **5** an agency that if applied to a free body results chiefly in an acceleration of the body and sometimes in elastic deformation and other effects. **6** (**Force**) a measure of wind strength as expressed by a number on the Beaufort scale. ✱ **by force of** by means of; using. **in force 1** in great numbers. **2** valid; operative.

force[2] *v* **1a** to compel (somebody) to do something. **b** to bring (something) about by compulsion, violence, or a great effort, or through natural or logical necessity. **2a** to press or drive (something) with a violent effort. **b** to break open (a door, lock, etc). **c** to make (one's way) with a violent effort into or through something. **3** to impose or thrust (something) on. **4a** to produce (e.g. a laugh) with an unnatural effort. **b** to strain (e.g. one's voice). **5** to hasten the growth of (a plant). ✱ **force somebody's hand** to cause somebody to act or reveal their intentions prematurely. **force the issue** to compel a decision, action, etc to be taken. ➤➤ **forceable** *adj,* **forcer** *n.*

forced *adj* **1** unnatural or produced only with effort. **2** made because of an emergency: *forced landing.* **3** done under pressure or compulsion: *forced labour.* **4** made at great speed without rest: *forced march.* ➤➤ **forcedly** *adv.*

force-feed *v* (*past tense and past part.* **force-fed**) to feed (e.g. a person on hunger strike or with an eating disorder) against their will.

force field *n* chiefly in science fiction, an invisible barrier that is impermeable to alien life forms, weaponry such as energy beams, etc.

forceful *adj* possessing or filled with force; powerful; intense; effective. ➤➤ **forcefully** *adv,* **forcefulness** *n.*

force-land *v* to land (an aircraft) involuntarily or in an emergency.

force majeure /,faws ma'zhuh/ *n* **1** an unavoidable event that in law excuses a party from fulfilling a contract. **2** overwhelming force or superiority.

forcemeat *n* a savoury highly seasoned stuffing, *esp* of breadcrumbs and meat.

force of habit *n* behaviour made involuntary or automatic by repetition.

forceps *n* (*pl* **forceps**) **1** (*usu in pl*) an instrument used, e.g. in surgery and watchmaking, for grasping, holding firmly, or pulling. **2** a large instrument of this type used to clasp a baby's head to assist in its delivery.

forcible *adj* **1** effected by force used against opposition or resistance. **2** powerful; forceful. ➤➤ **forcibleness** *n,* **forcibly** *adv.*

ford[1] *n* a shallow part of a river or other body of water that can be crossed by wading, in a vehicle, etc.

ford[2] *v* to cross (a river, stream, etc) at a ford. ➤➤ **fordable** *adj.*

fore[1] *adj and adv* situated in, towards, or adjacent to the front, *esp* of a ship.

fore[2] *n* something that occupies a forward position; a front part. ✱ **to the fore** in or into a position of prominence.

fore[3] *interj* used by a golfer to warn anyone in the probable line of flight of the ball.

fore- *comb. form* **1** occurring, etc earlier or beforehand: *foresee; forefather.* **2 a** situated at the front; in front: *foreleg; foreground.* **b** a front part: *forearm.*

fore and aft *adv* **1** from bow to stern; lengthways. **2** at or towards both the bow and stern of a ship.

fore-and-aft *adj* **1** running or acting in the general line of the length of a construction, *esp* a ship. **2a** of a sail: set lengthways in the direction of the bow and stern. **b** of a ship: having fore-and-aft sails. ➤➤ **fore-and-after** *n.*

forearm[1] /'fawrahm/ *n* the human arm between the elbow and the wrist.

forearm[2] /faw'rahm/ *v* to prepare (oneself or others) against attack, etc.

forebear *or* **forbear** *n* an ancestor or forefather.

Usage note

forebear *or* forbear? See note at FORBEAR[1].

forebode *v archaic or literary* **1** to foretell or portend (something bad that is to happen). **2** to have a premonition of (evil, misfortune, etc). ➤➤ **foreboder** *n.*

foreboding[1] *n* an omen, prediction, or presentiment of coming evil.

foreboding[2] *adj* presaging evil; ominous. ➤➤ **forebodingly** *adv.*

forebrain *n* the front part of the brain.

forecast[1] *v* (*past tense and past part.* **forecast** *or* **forecasted**) to estimate or predict (some future event or condition), *esp* as a result of study and analysis of available data. ➤➤ **forecaster** *n.*

forecast[2] *n* a prediction of a future happening or condition, *esp* of the weather.

forecastle *or* **fo'c'sle** *n* **1** a short raised deck at the bow of a ship. **2** a forward part of a merchant ship where the living quarters are situated.

foreclose *v* **1** to take away the right to redeem (e.g. a mortgage), usu because of nonpayment; to repossess (property) in this way. **2** to rule out (a possible action). ➤➤ **foreclosure** *n.*

forecourt *n* **1** an open or paved area in front of a building, *esp* a petrol station. **2** the part of a court in some racket games lying between the net and the service line.

foredoom *v* (*usu in passive*) to doom (somebody or something) beforehand, *esp* to failure.

forefather *n* an ancestor.

forefeet *n* pl of FOREFOOT.

forefinger *n* the finger next to the thumb.

forefoot *n* (*pl* **forefeet**) the front foot of a four-footed animal.

forefront *n* the foremost part or place; the vanguard.

foregather *or* **forgather** *v formal* to come together or assemble.

forego *v* see FORGO.

foregoing *adj* going before; immediately preceding.

foregone conclusion *n* an inevitable result; a certainty.

foreground *n* **1** the part of a picture or view nearest to the spectator. **2** a position of prominence; the forefront. ➤➤ **foreground** *v.*

forehand *n* a stroke in tennis, squash, etc made with the palm of the hand turned in the direction of movement. ➤➤ **forehand** *adj,* **forehand** *adv.*

forehead *n* the part of the face above the eyes.

foreign *adj* **1** born in, belonging to, or characteristic of some place or country other than one's own or the one under consideration. **2** concerned with or dealing with other nations. **3** occurring in an abnormal situation in the living body and commonly introduced from outside. **4a** (*usu* + to) alien in character; not characteristic of (somebody or something). **b** (+ to) not connected or relevant. ➤➤ **foreignness** *n.*

foreigner *n* **1** a person belonging to or owing allegiance to a foreign country. **2** a stranger or outsider.

foreign exchange *n* **1** foreign currency. **2** the buying and selling of foreign currency.

foreign legion *n* (*also* **Foreign Legion**) a body of foreign volunteers serving within a regular national army, *esp* that of France.

foreign secretary *n* (*also* **Foreign Secretary**) the government minister with responsibility for foreign affairs.

foreknowledge *n* knowledge of an event before it happens.

foreland *n* **1** a promontory or headland. **2** an area of land in front of a body of water or other prominent feature.

foreleg *n* a front leg, *esp* of a quadruped.

forelock *n* a lock of hair growing just above the forehead. ✱ **touch/tug one's forelock** to make a gesture that indicates one's social inferiority to another person, *esp* by raising a hand to one's forehead.

foreman *n* (*pl* **foremen**) **1** the chairman and spokesman of a jury. **2** a senior male worker who supervises a group of workers.

foremast *n* the mast nearest the bow of a ship, or the lower part of it.

foremost[1] *adj* **1** first in a series or progression. **2** of first rank or position; preeminent.

foremost[2] *adv* most importantly.

forename *n* a name that precedes a person's surname.

forenoon *n* morning, *esp* the hours of daylight before midday.

forensic *adj* **1** relating to or denoting the scientific investigation of crime. **2** belonging to or used in courts of law. ➤➤ **forensically** *adv.*

forensic medicine *n* a science that deals with the application of medical facts and methods to criminal investigations and legal problems.

forensics *pl n* **1** scientific tests, methods, etc involved in investigating crime. **2** (*used as sing. or pl*) the department or people involved in this.

foreordain *v* of a god, fate, etc: to predestine (somebody or something) to something. ➤➤ **foreordination** *n.*

foreplay *n* erotic stimulation preceding sexual intercourse.

forequarters *pl n* the front legs, shoulders, etc of a quadruped.

forerun *v* (**forerunning,** *past tense* **foreran,** *past part.* **forerun**) *literary* **1** to go before. **2** to act as an indication or warning of.

forerunner *n* **1** a sign or symptom that gives advance warning of something. **2** = PROTOTYPE (1).

foresail *n* the main sail on the foremast of a ship.

foresee *v* (*past tense* **foresaw,** *past part.* **foreseen**) to be aware of (e.g. a development or event) beforehand. ➤➤ **foreseeable** *adj,* **foreseeably** *adv,* **foreseer** *n.*

foreshadow *v* to indicate or suggest beforehand (what is to come). ➤➤ **foreshadower** *n.*

foresheet *n* **1** the controlling rope attached to a foresail. **2** (*in pl*) the forward part of an open boat.

foreshore *n* **1a** the part of a seashore between high-tide and low-tide marks. **b** the land just above the high-water mark. **2** a strip of land bordering a body of water.

foreshorten *v* (**foreshortened, foreshortening**) **1** to shorten (a detail in a drawing or painting) so as to create an illusion of depth. **2** to make more compact in scale or time.

foresight *n* **1** the ability to foresee things; prescience. **2** prudence due to the ability to foresee future events or conditions. **3** the sight nearest the muzzle on a firearm. ➤➤ **foresighted** *adj,* **foresightedly** *adv,* **foresightedness** *n.*

foreskin *n* the fold of skin that covers the glans of the penis.

forest[1] *n* **1** a dense growth of trees and underbrush covering a large tract of land. **2** something resembling a profusion of trees. **3** a tract of wooded land in Britain formerly owned by the sovereign and used for hunting game.

forest[2] *v* to cover (a tract of land) with trees or forest. ➤➤ **forestation** *n.*

forestall *v* **1** to hinder or prevent by taking measures or action in advance. **2** to get ahead of or anticipate. ➤➤ **forestaller** *n,* **forestalment** *n.*

forestay *n* a stay from the top of the foremast to the bow of a ship.

forester *n* **1** a person trained in forestry. **2** a person or animal that inhabits forest land.

forestry *n* **1** the scientific study or practice of cultivating or managing forests. **2** forest land.

foretaste *n* **1** an advance indication or warning. **2** an anticipatory sampling.

foretell *v* (*past tense and past part.* **foretold**) to predict (a coming event, etc). ➤➤ **foreteller** *n.*

forethought *n* **1** the act of thinking or planning out in advance. **2** consideration for the future.

foretoken[1] *n* a premonitory sign.

foretoken[2] *v* to indicate or warn of (something) in advance.

foretold *v* past tense and past part. of FORETELL.

foretop *n* a platform at the top of a ship's foremast.

forever *adv* **1** (*also* **for ever**) for all future time; indefinitely. **2** persistently; incessantly. **3** a long time.

forewarn *v* to warn in advance. ➤➤ **forewarner** *n.*

forewent *v* past tense of FOREGO.

foreword *n* a preface, *esp* one written by somebody other than the author of the text.

forfeit[1] *n* **1** something lost, taken away, or imposed as a penalty. **2** the loss or forfeiting of something, *esp* of civil rights. **3a** (*in pl, used as sing. or pl*) a game in which making a mistake has to be redeemed by performing a task such as singing a song. **b** a task performed in the game of forfeits.

forfeit[2] *v* (**forfeited, forfeiting**) to lose the right to (a privilege, etc) because of some error, offence, or crime. ➤➤ **forfeitable** *adj,* **forfeiter** *n,* **forfeiture** *n.*

forfeit[3] *adj* forfeited or subject to forfeiture.

forfend *v* **1** *archaic* to forbid (something). **2** *NAm* to defend, protect, or secure (something). ✱ **Heaven/God forfend** *archaic or humorous* used to express a hope that something does not happen.

forgather *v* see FOREGATHER.

forgave *v* past tense of FORGIVE.

forge[1] *n* an open furnace where metal, *esp* iron, is heated and worked, or a workshop with such a furnace.

forge[2] *v* **1** to shape (metal or a metal object) by heating and hammering or with a press. **2** to form or bring into being, *esp* by an expenditure of effort. **3** to counterfeit (*esp* a signature, document, or bank note). ➤➤ **forgeable** *adj,* **forger** *n.*

forge[3] *v* to move forwards slowly and steadily but with effort.

forge ahead *v* to move with a sudden increase of speed and power.

forgery *n* (*pl* **-ies**) **1a** the act or an instance of forging. **b** forging as a crime. **2** a forged document, bank note, etc.

forget *v* (**forgetting,** *past tense* **forgot,** *past part.* **forgotten,** *or archaic or NAm* **forgot**) **1** to be unable to remember. **2** to fail to give attention to; to disregard. **3a** to disregard intentionally; to overlook. **b** to reject the possibility of. ✱ **forget it! 1** reject that possibility or hope. **2** think nothing of it; it's not important. **forget oneself 1** to lose one's temper or self-control. **2** to act unsuitably or unworthily. ➤➤ **forgettable** *adj,* **forgetter** *n.*

forgetful *adj* likely or apt to forget. ➤➤ **forgetfully** *adv,* **forgetfulness** *n.*

forget-me-not *n* a small low-growing plant of the borage family with bright blue flowers usu arranged in a spike.

forgive *v* (*past tense* **forgave,** *past part.* **forgiven**) **1** to stop feeling angry about (something) or resentful towards (somebody). **2** to pardon (somebody, an offence, etc). ➤➤ **forgivable** *adj,* **forgivably** *adv,* **forgiver** *n.*

forgiveness *n* forgiving or being forgiven; pardon.

forgiving *adj* willing or able to forgive. ➤➤ **forgivingly** *adv.*

forgo *or* **forego** *v* (**forgoes** *or* **foregoes, forgoing** *or* **foregoing,** *past tense* **forwent** *or* **forewent,** *past part.* **forgone** *or* **foregone**) to abstain or refrain from (something desirable).

forgot *v* **1** past tense of FORGET. **2** *archaic or NAm* past part. of FORGOT.

forgotten *v* past part. of FORGOT.

forint *n* the basic monetary unit of Hungary.

fork[1] *n* **1** a tool or implement with two or more prongs set on the end of a handle, e.g.: **a** an agricultural or gardening tool for digging, carrying, etc. **b** a small implement for eating or serving food. **2** either of two forked supports for a bicycle or motorcycle wheel. **3a** a division into branches, or a place where this happens. **b** any of the branches into which something forks. ➤➤ **forkful** *n.*

fork[2] *v* **1** to divide into two or more branches. **2** to make a turn into one of the branches of a fork. **3** *informal* (+ out/up) to make a payment or contribution. **4** to raise, dig, or work (something) with a fork.

forked *adj* having one end divided into two or more branches or points.

forked lightning *n* lightning that is seen as a branching or zigzag line in the sky.

forklift *n* a vehicle for hoisting and transporting heavy objects by means of steel prongs inserted under the load.

forklift truck *n* = FORKLIFT.

forlorn *adj* **1** sad and lonely because of isolation or desertion. **2** nearly hopeless. ➤➤ **forlornly** *adv,* **forlornness** *n.*

forlorn hope *n* **1** a desperate or extremely difficult enterprise. **2** a hope or desire that persists despite the knowledge that it is unlikely to materialize.

form[1] *n* **1a** the shape and structure of something as distinguished from its material or content. **b** a body, e.g. of a person, *esp* in its external appearance or as distinguished from the face. **c** a kind or variety. **2a** an established or correct method of proceeding or behaving. **b** a prescribed and set order of words. **3** a printed or typed document with blank spaces for insertion of required information. **4** a long seat without a back; a bench. **5** something, e.g. shuttering, that holds, supports, and determines the shape of something. **6** *chiefly Brit* (*used as sing. or pl*) a school class organized for the work of a particular year. **7a** the past performances of a competitor, racehorse, greyhound, etc considered as a guide to future performance. **b** condition suitable for performing well, *esp* in sports. **8** *Brit, informal* a criminal record. ➤➤ **formless** *adj,* **formlessly** *adv,* **formlessness** *n.*

form[2] *v* **1a** to give shape or existence to. **b** to mould into a particular shape. **c** to create or establish. **2a** to come into existence; to take shape. **b** to serve to make up or constitute. **3a** to join together as (a group). **b** to arrange or be arranged in (a shape). **4** to influence (somebody) strongly through experience, instruction, etc.

formal *adj* **1a** characterized by dignity, ceremoniousness, and the observance of correct procedure. **b** suitable for a formal occasion. **2** done in accordance with established procedure; official. **3** of language: grammatically precise and elevated above the colloquial or everyday. **4** relating to outward form or internal organization as opposed to content. **5** arranged in a symmetrical or orderly pattern. ➤➤ **formally** *adv,* **formalness** *n.*

formaldehyde *n* a pungent irritating gas used chiefly as a disinfectant and preservative and in chemical synthesis.

formalin *n* a clear aqueous solution of formaldehyde.

formalise *v* see FORMALIZE.

formalism *n* **1** strict or excessive adherence to prescribed or external forms, often without regard to their content, inner significance, moral value, etc. **2** the structure of a logical, mathematical, or scientific argument as opposed to its content. ➤➤ **formalist** *n and adj,* **formalistic** *adj,* **formalistically** *adv.*

formality *n* (*pl* **-ies**) **1** the quality or state of being formal. **2** observance of formal or conventional rules; ceremony. **3a** an established form or procedure that is required or conventional. **b** something required by rule or custom but which has little real significance.

formalize *or* **formalise** *v* **1** to give formal status or approval to. **2** to give (something) a definite shape. ➤➤ **formalization** *n.*

format[1] *n* **1** the shape, size, and general make-up, e.g. of a book. **2** the general plan of organization or arrangement. **3** in computing, the structure of data e.g. held on a disk or displayed on a screen.

format[2] *v* (**formatted, formatting**) **1** to arrange (material, e.g. a book or data) in a particular format. **2** in computing, to prepare (a floppy disk, etc) to receive data. ➤➤ **formatting** *n.*

formation *n* **1** giving form or shape to something, or taking form. **2** the manner in which a thing is formed or arranged; structure. **3** (*used as sing. or pl*) a group of people or things arranged in some prescribed manner or for a particular purpose. ➤➤ **formational** *adj.*

formative *adj* giving or capable of giving form to something, *esp* having a significant influence on the growth or development of somebody or something. ➤➤ **formatively** *adv,* **formativeness** *n.*

former[1] *adj* **1** of or occurring in the past. **2** having been previously or once. **3** denoting the first of two things mentioned or understood.

former[2] *n* (*pl* **former**) the first mentioned.

Usage note

former *and* **latter**. The *former* refers back to the first of two previously mentioned things or people, the *latter* to the second. They should never be used when more than two things are listed. In that case use *first, first-named, second, last* etc.

former[3] *n chiefly Brit* (*usu in combination*) a member of a specified school form or year.

formerly *adv* at an earlier time; previously.

Formica *n trademark* a laminated plastic used to make heat-resistant surfaces, *esp* for worktops, tables, etc.

formic acid *n* a pungent corrosive liquid acid naturally produced by ants.

formication *n* a hallucinatory feeling as if insects were crawling over one's skin.

formidable *adj* **1** causing fear. **2** difficult to overcome. **3** of a person: tending to inspire respect or awe; discouraging approach by others. ➤➤ **formidableness** *n,* **formidably** *adv.*

form letter *n* a letter in a standardized format, to which pertinent details such as people's names and addresses can be added.

formula *n* (*pl* **formulas** *or* **formulae**) **1a** a set form of words for use in a ceremony or ritual. **b** a set form or method, e.g. of writing, often followed uncritically. **2a** a fact, rule, or principle expressed in symbols, e.g. in mathematics. **b** a symbolic expression of the chemical composition of a substance. **3a** a recipe or the list of ingredients in it. **b** liquid baby food made from milk or soya. **4** a method or procedure for bringing something about. **5** (**Formula**) a classification of racing cars (Formula One, Two, etc) specifying *esp* size, weight, and engine capacity. ➤➤ **formulaic** *adj*, **formulaically** *adv*.

formulary *n* (*pl* **-ies**) **1** a book or other collection of stated and prescribed forms, e.g. of prayers. **2** a book containing a list of medicinal substances and formulas.

formulate *v* **1** to state (something) as a formula or reduce it to a formula. **2** to devise or develop (a policy, plan, product, etc). ➤➤ **formulation** *n*, **formulator** *n*.

form up *v* of e.g. soldiers, Scouts: to arrange themselves in, or cause them to take up, a particular formation.

formwork *n* a wooden structure that holds concrete in place and in shape while it hardens.

fornicate *v formal or humorous* to commit fornication. ➤➤ **fornicator** *n*.

fornication *n formal or humorous* voluntary sexual intercourse outside marriage.

forsake *v* (**forsaking**, *past tense* **forsook**, *past part.* **forsaken**) **1** to renounce (e.g. something once cherished), often for ever. **2** to desert or abandon (somebody).

forsaken *adj* **1** of a place: completely deserted. **2** of a person: left absolutely alone or helpless. ➤➤ **forsakenly** *adv*, **forsakenness** *n*.

forsook *v* past tense of FORSAKE.

forsooth *adv archaic or humorous* indeed; actually; no less.

forswear *v* (*past tense* **forswore**, *past part.* **forsworn**) **1** to solemnly renounce (something). **2** to perjure (oneself).

forsythia *n* an ornamental shrub of the olive family with bright yellow bell-shaped flowers that appear in early spring before the leaves.

fort *n* a fortified building or strongly fortified place maintained for defence. ✱ **hold the fort** to take charge of something for somebody or deputize temporarily.

forte[1] /'fawtay/ *n* something at which a person excels; a person's strong point.

forte[2] /'fawti, 'fawtay/ *adv and adj* of a piece of music: to be performed in a loud and often forceful manner. ➤➤ **forte** *n*.

Fortean *adj* relating to or denoting the paranormal or paranormal phenomena.

fortepiano *n* an early type of piano in use in the late 18th and early 19th centuries.

forth *adv chiefly archaic* **1** onwards in time, place, or order; forwards. **2** out; into notice or view. **3** away from a centre. ✱ **and so forth** and so on; and other related things.

forthcoming *adj* **1** about to occur or appear. **2a** made available. **b** willing to give information; responsive.

forthright *adj* going straight to the point without ambiguity or hesitation. ➤➤ **forthrightly** *adv*, **forthrightness** *n*.

forthwith *adv* immediately.

fortification *n* **1a** the act or an instance of fortifying. **b** the science or art of providing defensive works. **2** something that fortifies, defends, or strengthens, *esp* works erected to defend a place or position.

fortify *v* (**-ies, -ied**) **1** to strengthen and secure (a place, etc) by military defences. **2** to give strength, courage, or endurance to. **3** to add (e.g. alcohol to wine or vitamins to food) to strengthen or enrich it. ➤➤ **fortifiable** *adj*, **fortifier** *n*.

fortissimo *adj and adv* of a piece of music: to be performed in a very loud manner.

fortitude *n* courage or endurance, *esp* in the face of pain or adversity.

fortnight *n chiefly Brit* two weeks.

fortnightly[1] *adj* occurring or appearing once a fortnight.

fortnightly[2] *adv chiefly Brit* once in a fortnight; every fortnight.

fortnightly[3] *n* (*pl* **-ies**) a publication issued fortnightly.

fortress *n* a fortified place, *esp* a large and permanent fortification, sometimes including a town.

fortuitous *adj* **1** occurring by chance. **2** *informal* fortunate; lucky. ➤➤ **fortuitously** *adv*, **fortuitousness** *n*, **fortuity** *n*.

Usage note

fortuitous *or* **fortunate**? Primarily, and from its origins, *fortuitous* means 'occurring by chance': *I had no idea she was going to be there; our meeting was entirely fortuitous.* In modern writing and speech *fortuitous* has also come to mean 'happening by good fortune': *The event could not have happened at a more fortuitous time.* This is a usage that traditionalists seek to avoid.

fortunate *adj* **1** unexpectedly bringing something good; auspicious. **2** lucky. ➤➤ **fortunateness** *n*.

Usage note

fortunate *or* **fortuitous**? See note at FORTUITOUS.

fortunately *adv* **1** in a fortunate manner; luckily. **2** as was fortunate in the circumstances.

fortune *n* **1** a large quantity of money, or of money and possessions. **2** luck, destiny, or fate, often personified, as a force affecting human affairs. **3a** one's future destiny. **b** (*in pl*) the experiences good and bad that a person or thing undergoes. ✱ **a small fortune** a large amount of money.

fortune cookie *n NAm* a biscuit containing a slip of paper with a prediction, proverb, or joke printed on it.

fortune-teller *n* a person who claims to foretell future events. ➤➤ **fortune-telling** *n and adj*.

forty *adj and n* (*pl* **-ies**) **1** the number 40. **2** (*in pl*) the numbers 40 to 49. ➤➤ **fortieth** *adj and n*.

forty-five *n* (*usu* **45**) a gramophone record that plays at 45 revolutions per minute.

forty winks *pl n informal* (*used as sing. or pl*) a short sleep; a nap.

forum *n* (*pl* **forums** *or* **fora**) **1a** a public meeting place for open discussion. **b** an event, broadcast, or medium where views may be aired and debated. **2** *chiefly NAm* a court or tribunal. **3** the marketplace or public place of an ancient Roman city which formed the centre for judicial and public business.

forward[1] *adj* **1** in the direction in which one is facing or moving. **2** (*also* + of) located at or nearer to the front, *esp* of a ship or aircraft. **3a** lacking modesty or reserve; brash, assertive, or impudent. **b** advanced in physical or mental development; precocious. **4** advanced in what is being or needs to be done. **5** for the future. ➤➤ **forwardly** *adv*, **forwardness** *n*.

forward[2] *adv* **1a** towards what is ahead or in front. **b** into the future. **2** to an earlier time. **3** into prominence or open view.

forward[3] *n* in hockey, football, etc, an attacking player stationed at or near the front of his or her side or team.

forward[4] *v* **1a** to send. **b** to send onwards from an intermediate point in transit. **2** to help onwards; to promote. ➤➤ **forwarder** *n.*

forwards *adv* = FORWARD[2] (1A).

forwent *v* past tense of FORGO.

fosse *or* **foss** *n* a ditch or moat, *esp* one that forms part of a fortification.

fossick *v* **1** *Aus, NZ* to search for gold, *esp* by picking over abandoned workings. **2** (*usu* + about/around/for) to search or rummage for something. ➤➤ **fossicker** *n.*

fossil *n* **1** the petrified remains of an animal or plant of a past geological age, preserved in the earth's crust. **2a** a person with outmoded views. **b** an outdated viewpoint or custom that has become rigidly fixed. ➤➤ **fossiliferous** *adj*, **fossilization** *n*, **fossilize** *v.*

fossil fuel *n* a fuel, e.g. coal, that is extracted from the earth and derived from the remains of living things.

foster[1] *v* **1** to promote the growth or development of (friendship, trade, etc). **2a** to give parental care to (a child with whom one has no blood or legal ties) in one's home. **b** *Brit* to place (a child) in a foster home. **3** to cherish (a hope, etc). ➤➤ **fosterage** *n*, **fosterer** *n*, **fostering** *n.*

foster[2] *adj* providing or receiving care in a family home though not related by blood or legal ties.

fought *v* past tense and past part. of FIGHT[1].

foul[1] *adj* **1** offensive to the smell or taste; disgusting. **2** morally or spiritually evil. **3** particularly unpleasant, disagreeable, or distressing. **4** obscene or abusive. **5** infringing the rules, *esp* in a game or sport. **6a** filled or covered with dirty or offensive matter; polluted. **b** (*often* + with) clogged or choked with a foreign substance. ✱ **fall/run foul of 1** to come into conflict with. **2** to collide with. ➤➤ **foully** *adv*, **foulness** *n.*

foul[2] *n* **1** an infringement of the rules in a game or sport. **2** an entanglement or collision in angling, sailing, etc.

foul[3] *v* **1** to make dirty; to pollute. **2** in sport, to commit a foul. **3a** to obstruct or block (e.g. a drain). **b** to entangle or collide with (e.g. a boat).

foulard *n* a lightweight plain-woven or twilled silk, or silk and cotton, fabric.

foulmouthed *adj* using obscene, profane, or abusive language.

foul play *n* **1** violence, *esp* murder. **2** play that infringes the rules in a game or sport.

foul up *v* **1a** to make a mistake or do something badly. **b** to spoil or confuse (something) by making mistakes. **2** to entangle or block. ➤➤ **foul-up** *n.*

found[1] *v* past tense and past part. of FIND[1].

found[2] *v* **1** to establish (e.g. an institution). **2** (*often* + on/upon) to set or ground (e.g. a plan, a system of thought) on something sure or solid.

found[3] *v* **1** to melt (metal) and pour it into a mould. **2** to make or shape (something metal) in this way.

foundation *n* **1** (*also in pl*) an underlying natural or prepared base or support, *esp* the masonry substructure on which a building rests. **2a** the basis or principle underlying something. **b** a reason or justification. **3** the act of establishing something, e.g. an institution or colony. **4** an organization or institution established by endowment with provision for future maintenance. **5** a cream, lotion, etc applied to the face as a base for other make-up. ➤➤ **foundational** *adj*, **foundationally** *adv*, **foundationless** *adj.*

foundation course *n* a basic general course, e.g. as taught in the first year at certain universities.

foundation garment *n* a girdle, corset, or other supporting undergarment.

foundation stone *n* a stone in the foundation of a building, *esp* when laid with public ceremony.

founder[1] *n* a person who establishes an institution, colony, etc.

founder[2] *n* a person who owns, manages, or works in a foundry.

founder[3] *v* **1** of a ship: to sink. **2** of e.g. a plan, project, or arrangement: to fail. **3** of a horse: to stumble or go lame.

Usage note

founder *or* flounder? See note at FLOUNDER[2].

founding father *n* **1** a founder. **2** (**Founding Father**) a member of the American Constitutional Convention of 1787.

foundling *n* an infant found abandoned by unknown parents.

foundry *n* (*pl* **-ies**) a place for casting metals.

fount[1] *n* **1** *literary* a fountain or spring. **2** a source.

fount[2] *or* **font** *n* in printing: a complete set of characters for printing in one style.

fountain[1] *n* **1** an artificially produced jet of water, or the structure providing this. **2** a spring of water issuing from the ground. **3** a source.

fountain[2] *v* to flow or spout like or in a fountain.

fountainhead *n* a principal source.

fountain pen *n* a pen with a reservoir or cartridge that automatically feeds the nib with ink.

four *n* **1** the number 4. **2** a four-person racing boat or its crew. **3** a shot in cricket that crosses the boundary after having hit the ground and scores four runs: compare SIX. ➤➤ **four** *adj*, **fourfold** *adj and adv.*

four-by-four *or* **4x4** *n* a motor vehicle equipped with a transmission system that sends power directly to all four wheels.

four-dimensional *adj* denoting something that exists in four dimensions, usu length, breadth, and depth, plus time.

four-eyes *n* (*pl* **four-eyes**) *informal, derog* a person who wears glasses. ➤➤ **four-eyed** *adj.*

Fourier series *n* an infinite series in which the terms are constants multiplied by sine or cosine functions, used in the analysis of periodic functions such as simple harmonic motion.

four-in-hand *n* a team of four horses driven by one person, or a vehicle drawn by such a team.

four-leaf clover *n* a clover leaf that has four leaflets instead of three and is believed to bring good luck.

four-leaved clover *n* = FOUR-LEAF CLOVER.

four-letter word *n* a vulgar or obscene word made up of four letters.

four-poster *n* a bed with four tall corner posts designed to support curtains or a canopy.

fourscore *n and adj dated* eighty.

foursome *n* a group of four people or things.

foursquare[1] *adj* **1** bold and resolute. **2** solid; squarely based.

foursquare[2] *adv* **1** in a solidly based and steady way. **2** resolutely.

four-stroke *adj* denoting an internal-combustion engine with a cycle of four strokes, usu intake, compression, combustion, and exhaust.

fourteen *adj and n* the number 14. ➤➤ **fourteenth** *adj and n.*

fourth *adj and n* **1** having the position in a sequence corresponding to the number four. **2** one of four equal parts of something. **3** the fourth and sometimes highest forward gear of a motor vehicle. **4** in music, an interval of four degrees of a diatonic scale, or the combination of two notes at such an interval. ⋙ **fourthly** *adv.*

fourth dimension *n* time considered as a dimension in addition to length, breadth, and depth. ⋙ **fourth-dimensional** *adj.*

fourth estate *n* (**the Fourth Estate**) journalists; the press.

Fourth World *n* (*used as sing. or pl*) the poorest and most underdeveloped nations of the world: compare THIRD WORLD.

four-wheel drive *n* **1** a transmission system in a motor vehicle that sends power directly to all four wheels. **2** a vehicle equipped with this type of transmission system.

fovea /'fohvi·ə/ *n* (*pl* **foveae** /'fohvi·ee, 'fohviie/) a small anatomical pit, e.g. in the retina of the eye. ⋙ **foveal** *adj,* **foveate** *adj.*

fowl[1] *n* (*pl* **fowls** *or* **fowl**) **1** a domestic bird such as a chicken, turkey, or duck, *esp* an adult hen. **2** = WILDFOWL.

fowl[2] *v* to hunt, catch, or kill wildfowl. ⋙ **fowler** *n,* **fowling** *n.*

fox[1] *n* (*pl* **foxes** *or* **fox**) **1a** a flesh-eating mammal of the dog family with a pointed muzzle, large erect ears, and a long bushy tail. **b** the fur of a fox. **2** a clever crafty person. **3** *NAm, informal* a physically attractive woman. ⋙ **foxlike** *adj.*

fox[2] *v* to outwit or baffle (somebody).

foxed *adj* of a document, book, etc: discoloured with brown spots.

foxglove *n* a common tall European wild or garden plant with attractive white or purple tubular flowers.

foxhole *n* a pit dug, usu hastily, for individual cover against enemy fire.

foxhound *n* a hound of a breed developed to hunt foxes, having a short-haired coat.

fox-hunting *n* the practice of hunting foxes usu on horseback, with a pack of hounds.

foxtail *n* a grass with spikes resembling the tail of a fox.

fox terrier *n* a small terrier of a breed formerly used to dig out foxes, having a short-haired or wire-haired coat.

foxtrot[1] *n* a ballroom dance that includes slow walking and quick running steps.

foxtrot[2] *v* (**foxtrotted, foxtrotting**) to dance a foxtrot.

foxy *adj* (**-ier, -iest**) **1** cunningly shrewd. **2** *NAm, informal* of a woman: physically attractive. **3** fox-like. ⋙ **foxily** *adv,* **foxiness** *n.*

foyer *n* an anteroom or lobby, e.g. of a theatre, or an entrance hallway.

Fr *abbr* the chemical symbol for francium.

Fr. *abbr* Father.

fr. *abbr* franc(s).

Fra *n* used as a title preceding the name of an Italian monk or friar: brother.

fracas *n* (*pl* **fracas,** *NAm* **fracases**) a noisy quarrel; a brawl.

fractal *n* an irregular geometric shape or pattern that can be successively subdivided into parts which are smaller copies of the whole. ⋙ **fractal** *adj.*

fraction *n* **1a** a number that is not a whole number, most often a number less than one, e.g. ¾, ⅝, 0.234. **b** a small portion, amount, or section. **2** in chemistry, any of several portions, e.g. of a distillate, separable by fractionation.

fractional *adj* **1** relating to or being a fraction. **2** relatively small; inconsiderable. **3** in chemistry, relating to or being a process for separating components of a mixture through differences in physical or chemical properties. ⋙ **fractionally** *adv.*

fractionalize *or* **-ise** *v* to divide (something) into separate parts. ⋙ **fractionalization** *n.*

fractionate *v* to separate (a compound mixture) into its different components. ⋙ **fractionation** *n.*

fractious *adj* irritable and restless; hard to control. ⋙ **fractiously** *adv,* **fractiousness** *n.*

fracture[1] *n* **1a** a break in or the breaking of something, *esp* hard tissue such as bone. **b** a split, division, or breach. **2** the appearance of the surface of a mineral or rock that has been recently broken.

fracture[2] *v* **1** to cause a fracture in (e.g. a bone). **2** to undergo fracture. **3** to damage or destroy (something) as if by breaking it apart. **4** to break up or split into separate parts.

fragile *adj* **1** easily broken or shattered; flimsy; brittle. **2** not secure or firmly founded; vulnerable. **3** light or delicate. **4** physically weak or weakened. ⋙ **fragilely** *adv,* **fragility** *n.*

fragment[1] *n* an incomplete, broken off, or detached part; a bit or scrap. ⋙ **fragmentary** *adj.*

fragment[2] *v* **1** to fall to pieces. **2** to break (something) up or apart into fragments. ⋙ **fragmentation** *n.*

fragmentation bomb *n* a bomb or shell that, when it explodes, sprays deadly fragments of its casing in all directions.

fragmentation grenade *n* = FRAGMENTATION BOMB.

fragrance *n* **1** a sweet or pleasant smell. **2** a perfume or aftershave. ⋙ **fragranced** *adj.*

fragrant *adj* smelling sweet or pleasant. ⋙ **fragrantly** *adv.*

frail *adj* **1** physically weak; delicate. **2** easily broken or destroyed. ⋙ **frailly** *adv,* **frailness** *n.*

frailty *n* (*pl* **-ies**) **1** being frail. **2** a moral or physical fault due to weakness.

frame[1] *n* **1** a structure that gives shape or strength, e.g. to a building. **2a** an open case or structure made for admitting, enclosing, or supporting something. **b** a rigid surrounding structure in which a painting, photograph, etc is placed for display. **3a** the rigid part of a bicycle or other vehicle. **b** (*in pl*) the outer structure of a pair of glasses that holds the lenses. **4** the physical structure of the human body; the physique. **5** a single picture of the series on a length of film. **6** a limiting, typical, or *esp* appropriate set of circumstances; a framework: *within the frame of our society and culture.* **7a** in snooker or bowling, one round of play. **b** in snooker, the triangular piece of wood used to place the balls on the table. ✱ **in the frame 1** under consideration for a particular purpose, appointment, etc. **2** wanted or suspected by the police.

frame[2] *v* **1** to place (a picture) in a frame. **2a** to plan or work out; to formulate. **b** to shape or construct. **3** to fit or adjust for a purpose; to arrange. **4** *informal* to make up evidence against (an innocent person); to incriminate (somebody) falsely. ⋙ **framed** *adj,* **frameless** *adj,* **framer** *n.*

frame house *n* a house with a wooden framework.

frame of mind *n* a particular mental or emotional state.

frame of reference *n* **1** a set or system of facts or ideas serving to orient or give particular meaning to a statement, a point of view, etc. **2** an arbitrary set of axes used as a reference to describe the position or motion of something or to formulate physical laws.

frame-up *n informal* a conspiracy to incriminate somebody falsely.

framework *n* **1** a skeletal, openwork, or structural frame. **2** a basic structure, e.g. of ideas.

franc *n* the basic monetary unit of France, Belgium, Switzerland, and certain other French-speaking countries.

franchise[1] *n* **1** (*usu* **the franchise**) the right to vote. **2a** the right granted to an individual or group to market a company's goods or services in a particular territory. **b** a business or service to which such a right has been granted. **3** any special privilege or right. ➤➤ **franchisee** *n,* **franchiser** *n,* **franchisor** *n.*

franchise[2] *v* **1** to grant a franchise to (a person or company). **2** to grant a franchise for (goods or services).

Franciscan *n* a friar of an order founded by St Francis of Assisi in 1209. ➤➤ **Franciscan** *adj.*

francium *n* a radioactive metallic chemical element of the alkali metal group that occurs naturally in uranium and thorium ores, and is artificially produced by bombarding thorium with protons.

Franco- *comb. form* **1** the French nation, people, or culture: *Francophile.* **2** French and: *Franco-German.*

francolin *n* a game bird of S Asia and Africa resembling a partridge.

Francophile *n* somebody who is markedly friendly to France or French culture.

Francophone[1] *adj* French-speaking.

Francophone[2] *n* somebody who speaks French.

frangible *adj formal* readily or easily broken; fragile.

frangipane *n* an almond-flavoured pastry or cream.

frangipani *n* (*pl* **frangipanis** *or* **frangipani**) **1** a tropical American shrub or small tree of the periwinkle family. **2** a perfume derived from or imitating the odour of the flower of the red jasmine.

franglais /'fronglay/ *n* French with a considerable number of words borrowed from English.

Frank *n* a member of a W Germanic people who established themselves in the Netherlands, Gaul, and on the Rhine in the third and fourth cents. ➤➤ **Frankish** *adj.*

frank[1] *adj* **1** marked by forthright and sincere expression. **2** undisguised. ➤➤ **frankness** *n.*

frank[2] *v* **1** to mark (a piece of mail) with an official signature or sign indicating that the postal charges need not be paid. **2** to send (a piece of mail) without charge. ➤➤ **franker** *n,* **franking** *n.*

frank[3] *n* a signature or mark used to frank a piece of mail.

Frankenstein food *n slang* food consisting of or containing genetically modified substances.

Frankenstein's monster *n* a creation that ruins its creator.

Word history

named after Baron *Frankenstein,* hero of the novel *Frankenstein* by Mary Shelley d.1851, English novelist. In the novel Frankenstein creates a human monster who destroys him.

frankfurter *n* a cured cooked sausage usu made from beef and pork.

frankincense *n* a fragrant gum resin chiefly from E African or Arabian trees which is burned as incense.

franklin *n* a medieval English landowner of free but not noble birth.

frankly *adv* **1** to tell the truth; actually. **2** in a frank manner.

frantic *adj* **1** emotionally out of control. **2** marked by fast and nervous or anxiety-driven activity. ➤➤ **frantically** *adv,* **franticly** *adv,* **franticness** *n.*

frappé[1] *n* a drink that is chilled or partly frozen.

frappé[2] *adj* of a drink: chilled or partly frozen.

Frascati *n* a usu white wine of the Frascati region of Italy.

frass *n* excrement or debris left by larvae or adult insects, *esp* after boring into wood.

fraternal *adj* **1a** relating to or involving brothers; brotherly. **b** relating to or being a fraternity or society. **2** of twins: derived from two ova: compare IDENTICAL (3). ➤➤ **fraternalism** *n,* **fraternally** *adv.*

fraternise *v* see FRATERNIZE.

fraternity *n* (*pl* **-ies**) **1** (*used as sing. or pl*) a group of people associated or formally organized for a common purpose or interest, e.g.: **a** a guild or religious order of brothers. **b** a club for male students in some US universities: compare SORORITY. **2** brotherliness.

fraternize *or* **-ise** *v* (*usu* + with) to associate or mingle on friendly terms. ➤➤ **fraternization** *n,* **fraternizer** *n.*

fratricide *n* **1** the act of killing one's brother or sister. **2** somebody who does this. ➤➤ **fratricidal** *adj.*

Frau /frow/ *n* (*pl* **Frauen**) used as a title equivalent to Mrs: a German-speaking married woman or widow.

fraud *n* **1a** deception, *esp* for unlawful gain. **b** an act of deception; a trick. **2a** a person who is not what he or she pretends to be; an impostor. **b** something that is not what it seems or is represented to be.

fraudster *n* somebody who commits a fraud.

fraudulent *adj* characterized by or involving fraud; dishonest. ➤➤ **fraudulence** *n,* **fraudulently** *adv.*

Frauen /'frowən/ *n* pl of FRAU.

fraught *adj* **1** (+ with) filled or charged with (something specified). **2** characterized by anxieties and tensions.

Fräulein /'froylien/ *n* used as a title equivalent to Miss: an unmarried German-speaking woman.

fray[1] *v* **1** of fabric or rope: to become worn, *esp* to start showing loose ragged threads at the edges. **2** to separate the threads at the edge of (e.g. fabric). **3** of a person's temper or nerves: to become strained so that one has difficulty maintaining self-control.

fray[2] *n* **1** (**the fray**) a dispute or competition. **2** a brawl or fight.

frazzle[1] *v informal* to put (somebody) in a state of extreme physical or nervous fatigue.

frazzle[2] ✱ **to a frazzle** *informal* completely; utterly: *burnt to a frazzle.*

freak[1] *n* **1** a person, animal, or plant with a physical abnormality. **2** a person seen as being highly unconventional, *esp* in dress or ideas. **3a** a highly unusual and unforeseeable event or phenomenon. **b** (*used before a noun*) occurring unexpectedly and under most unusual circumstances: *a freak accident.* **4** *informal* an ardent enthusiast: *a sci-fi freak.* ➤➤ **freakish** *adj,* **freakishly** *adv,* **freakishness** *n.*

freak[2] *v informal* = FREAK OUT.

freak out *v informal* **1** to behave in an irrational, uncontrolled, or unconventional manner as if under the influence of drugs. **2** to put (somebody) into a state of intense excitement or agitation.

freaky *adj* (**-ier, -iest**) *informal* very or disturbingly strange. ➤➤ **freakily** *adv*, **freakiness** *n*.

freckle[1] *n* a small brownish spot on the skin increasing in number and intensity on exposure to sunlight. ➤➤ **freckly** *adj*.

freckle[2] *v* to become marked or mark (a surface) with freckles or small spots.

free[1] *adj* (**freer, freest**) **1a** not subject to the control or domination of another. **b** not bound, confined, or detained by force. **2** exempt, relieved, or released, *esp* from an unpleasant or unwanted condition or obligation. **3a** having no obligations or commitments. **b** not taken up with obligations or commitments. **4a** not obstructed or impeded, clear. **b** not being used or occupied. **5** not hampered or restricted; unfettered. **6** not costing or charging anything. **7a** (*usu* + with) lavish or unrestrained. **b** outspoken or too familiar. **8a** not determined by external influences. **b** voluntary or spontaneous. **9** of a translation: not literal or exact. **10** (*used in combinations*) free from: *duty-free*. ✱ **free and easy** marked by informality and lack of constraint; casual. **give somebody a free hand** to give somebody complete freedom of action. **make free with** to make use of (something) without restraint and usu without respecting the wishes of the person it actually belongs to. ➤➤ **freely** *adv*, **freeness** *n*.

free[2] *adv* **1** in a free manner. **2** without charge.

free[3] *v* (**frees, freed, freeing**) **1** to cause (somebody or something) to be free; to release. **2** (*often* + up) to make available.

free association *n* a psychoanalytical technique used to reveal unconscious mental processes, in which the patient expresses the thoughts or responses spontaneously elicited by key words used by the psychoanalyst.

freebase[1] *n* purified cocaine produced by mixing with ether or ammonia, heating, and evaporation.

freebase[2] *v* to smoke (freebased cocaine).

freebie *n informal* something, e.g. a gift or service, offered free.

freeboard *n* the vertical distance between the waterline and the deck of a ship.

freebooter *n* a pirate or plunderer.

freeborn *adj* not born in slavery.

Free Church *n chiefly Brit* a British Nonconformist Church.

freedom *n* **1 a** the absence of necessity or constraint in choice or action. **b** liberation from slavery, imprisonment, or restraint. **2** (+ from) being exempt or released from something onerous. **3a** (+ of) unrestricted use of something. **b** the full rights and privileges of a citizen of a city, granted as an honour to a distinguished person. **4** a right or privilege, *esp* political.

freedom fighter *n* somebody engaged in militant action against established rule, *esp* against a government seen as illegal or repressive.

free enterprise *n* an economic system that relies on private business operating competitively for profit to satisfy consumer demands and in which government action is restricted.

free fall *n* **1** unrestrained motion in a gravitational field. **2** the part of a parachute jump before the parachute opens.

free-fall *v* to fall in a fast or uncontrolled way, *esp* during a parachute jump before the parachute opens.

free-for-all *n* **1** a fight or competition open to all comers and usu with no rules. **2** an often vociferous quarrel or argument involving several participants.

free-form *adj* of an art form: not having a fixed outline or structure; spontaneous.

freehand *adj and adv* done without the aid of drawing or measuring instruments.

free-handed *adj* openhanded or generous.

freehold *n* **1** a form of ownership of land or property that gives owners the unconditional right to dispose of it as they will. **2** a property held by this form of tenure. ➤➤ **freeholder** *n*.

free house *n* a public house in Britain that is entitled to sell drinks supplied by more than one brewery.

free kick *n* in football or rugby, an unhindered kick awarded because of a breach of the rules by an opponent.

freelance[1] *n* a person who pursues a profession without long-term contractual commitments to any one employer. ➤➤ **freelance** *adj and adv*.

freelance[2] *v* to act as a freelance.

freelancer *n* = FREELANCE[1].

freeload *v informal* to take advantage of somebody else's generosity or hospitality without sharing in the cost or responsibility involved. ➤➤ **freeloader** *n*.

free love *n* the concept or practice of sexual relations without being faithful to one partner.

freeman *n* (*pl* **freemen**) **1** formerly, somebody who is no longer a slave. **2** somebody who has been granted the freedom of a city.

free market *n* an economic market operating by free competition.

Freemason *n* a member of a secret fraternity called Free and Accepted Masons who offer each other support and friendship. ➤➤ **Freemasonry** *n*.

free port *n* **1** a port that can be used by ships of all nations on equal terms. **2** an enclosed port or port area where goods can be received and re-exported free of customs duty.

free radical *n* an atom or a group of atoms having at least one unpaired electron and participating in various reactions.

free-range *adj* **1** of farm animals, *esp* poultry: reared in the open air and allowed to move about. **2** of eggs: produced by free-range hens.

freesia *n* a sweet-scented African plant of the iris family with red, white, yellow, or purple flowers.

freestanding *adj* standing alone, not attached to or supported by something else.

freestyle *n* **1** (*often used before a noun*) a competition in which a contestant uses a style of his or her choice. **2** = CRAWL[2] (2).

freethinker *n* a person who forms opinions on the basis of reason; *esp* one who rejects religious dogma.

free trade *n* trade based on the unrestricted international exchange of goods.

free verse *n* verse without rhyme or a fixed metrical form.

free vote *n chiefly Brit* a vote in Parliament not subject to party instructions.

freeware *n* computer software that is available for people to use without charge.

freeway *n NAm* a motorway or highway without tolls.

freewheel[1] *n* a device fitted to a vehicle wheel allowing it to move freely when the motive power is removed, e.g. when a cyclist stops pedalling.

freewheel[2] *v* to coast freely without power from the pedals of a bicycle or engine of a vehicle. ⋙ **freewheeler** *n.*

freewheeling *adj* moving, living, or drifting along freely or irresponsibly.

free will *n* the power of choosing, *esp* of making moral choices, independently of divine necessity or causal law.

freeze[1] *v* (*past tense* **froze,** *past part.* **frozen**) **1** to become congealed into a solid, e.g. ice, by cold. **2** to convert (e.g. water) from a liquid to a solid by cold. **3** to become or make chilled with cold. **4** to stick solidly by freezing, or as if by freezing. **5** to preserve (e.g. food) by freezing the water content and maintaining at a temperature below 0°C. **6** to become or cause to become clogged with ice. **7** to become fixed or motionless; *esp* to abruptly cease acting or speaking. **8** of a computer screen: to stop working temporarily due to a fault, lack of memory, or other problem. **9** to anaesthetize (a part of the body) by cold, or as if by cold. **10** to cause to become fixed or unalterable. ⋙ **freezable** *adj.*

freeze[2] *n* **1** freezing cold weather. **2** an act or period of freezing something.

freeze-dry *v* (**-ies, -ied**) to dehydrate (e.g. food) while in a frozen state in a vacuum, *esp* for preservation.

freeze-frame *n* **1** a frame of a film that is repeated so as to give the illusion of a static picture. **2** the function on a video camera or recorder that enables a static picture to be produced.

freeze out *v informal* to deliberately ignore or fail to respond to (somebody).

freezer *n* an insulated cabinet or room for storing frozen food or for freezing food rapidly.

freezing *adj* **1** *informal* very cold. **2** below 0°C.

freezing point *n* the temperature at which a liquid solidifies.

freight[1] *n* **1** goods transported commercially. **2** the transport of goods commercially, *esp* at the ordinary or comparatively slower rate.

freight[2] *v* to load (*esp* a ship) with goods for transport.

freightage *n* = FREIGHT[1].

freighter *n* **1** a ship or aircraft used chiefly to carry freight. **2** a person or company that charters or loads a ship.

French[1] *adj* relating to France, its people, or their language. ⋙ **Frenchness** *n.*

French[2] *n* **1** the language of France and parts of Belgium, Switzerland, Canada, and Africa. **2** (**the French**) (*used as pl*) the people of France. ✱ **excuse/pardon my French** excuse these swear words.

French bean *n chiefly Brit* a slender edible green pod of a common bean plant, used as a vegetable.

French bread *n* crusty white bread made in long thin loaves.

French Canadian *n* a French-speaking Canadian, *esp* one of French descent. ⋙ **French Canadian** *adj.*

French chalk *n* a soft white granular variety of soapstone used for drawing lines on cloth and as a dry lubricant.

French cricket *n* a children's game in which one player has a bat, and any other player may bowl at the batter's legs.

French dressing *n* a salad dressing of oil, vinegar, and seasonings.

french fries *pl n chiefly NAm* chips.

French horn *n* a spiral-shaped brass musical instrument with a convoluted tube that flares outwards at the end.

frenchify *v* (**-ies, -ied**) (*also* **Frenchify**) to make (somebody or something) French in qualities or typical practices.

French kiss *n* a kiss made with open mouths and usu with tongue-to-tongue contact.

French knickers *pl n* wide-legged underpants for women.

French letter *n Brit, informal* a condom.

Frenchman *n* (*pl* **Frenchmen**) a native or inhabitant of France.

French polish *n* a solution of shellac used as a wood polish.

French-polish *v* to apply French polish to (wood or furniture) in order to obtain a high gloss finish.

French stick *n* a long thin loaf of French bread.

French toast *n* **1** sliced bread dipped in a mixture of egg and milk and fried. **2** *Brit* sliced bread buttered on one side and toasted on the other.

French windows *pl n Brit* a pair of doors with full length glazing, often opening onto a garden.

Frenchwoman *n* (*pl* **Frenchwomen**) a female native or inhabitant of France.

frenetic *adj* frenzied or frantic. ⋙ **frenetically** *adv.*

frenzied *adj* marked by uncontrolled activity or emotion or wild haste; frantic. ⋙ **frenziedly** *adv.*

frenzy *n* (*pl* **-ies**) **1** a state of extreme agitation or intense uncontrolled emotion. **2** a spell of wild, compulsive, or agitated behaviour.

frequency *n* (*pl* **-ies**) **1** the fact or condition of occurring frequently. **2** the number of repetitions of an event over a particular period of time. **3a** the number of complete alternations per second of an alternating current of electricity. **b** the number of complete oscillations per second of an electromagnetic wave. **4** the number of sound waves per second produced by a sounding body.

frequency distribution *n* in statistics, an arrangement of data showing the frequency of the occurrence of the values of a variable.

frequency modulation *n* a modulation of the frequency of a wave, *esp* a radio carrier wave, in accordance with the instantaneous value of some signal waveform: compare AMPLITUDE MODULATION, PHASE MODULATION.

frequent[1] *adj* **1** often repeated or occurring. **2** habitual or persistent. ⋙ **frequently** *adv.*

frequent[2] *v* to be in or visit (a place) often or habitually. ⋙ **frequenter** *n.*

fresco *n* (*pl* **-oes** *or* **-os**) a painting made by the application of watercolours to moist plaster.

fresh[1] *adj* **1** new or recent. **2** original or different. **3a** of food: not tinned or frozen. **b** not stale, sour or decayed. **4** of water: not salty. **5** free from taint; clean and pure. **6a** of weather: cool and windy. **b** of wind: rather strong; invigorating. **7** refreshed and alert. **8a** of a complexion: clear and healthy-looking. **b** of colours: not faded; bright. **9** not worn or rumpled; clean. **10a** newly come or arrived. **b** inexperienced. **11** *informal* too forward or disrespectful; presumptuous, *esp* in a sexual way. ⋙ **freshly** *adv,* **freshness** *n.*

fresh[2] *adv* just recently; newly.

freshen *v* **1** to become fresh or fresher. **2** of wind: to increase in strength. **3** (**freshen up**) to make (oneself) fresher or more comfortable. **4** to refresh (e.g. a drink).

fresher *n chiefly Brit, informal* a student in the first year at college or university.

freshet *n* **1** a stream of fresh water flowing into salt water. **2** a great rise or overflowing of a stream caused by heavy rains or melted snow.

freshman *n* (*pl* **freshmen**) a student in the first year at college or university.

freshwater *adj* relating to or living in fresh water.

fret[1] *v* (**fretted, fretting**) **1** to be vexed or worried. **2a** to eat or gnaw into (something); to corrode. **b** to rub or chafe (something).

fret[2] *n* a state of mental agitation or irritation.

fret[3] *n* in art or architecture, an ornamental pattern or decoration consisting of small straight bars intersecting usu at right angles.

fret[4] *v* (**fretted, fretting**) to decorate (e.g. a ceiling) with embossed or carved patterns.

fret[5] *n* any of a series of ridges fixed across the fingerboard of a stringed musical instrument, e.g. a guitar. ➤➤ **fretless** *adj.*

fretful *adj* tending to fret; in a fret. ➤➤ **fretfully** *adv,* **fretfulness** *n.*

fretsaw *n* a fine-toothed saw with a narrow blade held under tension in a frame and used for cutting intricate patterns in thin wood.

fretwork *n* ornamental openwork, *esp* in thin wood.

Freudian[1] *adj* relating or conforming to the psychoanalytic theories or practices of the Austrian neurologist Sigmund Freud (d.1939).

Freudian[2] *n* somebody who believes in or uses the ideas of Sigmund Freud. ➤➤ **Freudianism** *n.*

Freudian slip *n* a slip of the tongue that is held to reveal some unconscious aspect of the speaker's mind.

Fri. *abbr* Friday.

friable *adj* easily crumbled. ➤➤ **friability** *n.*

friar *n* a member of a religious order combining monastic life with outside religious activity.

friary *n* (*pl* **-ies**) a building housing a community of friars.

fricassee[1] *n* a dish of small pieces of stewed chicken, rabbit, etc served in a white sauce.

fricassee[2] *v* (**fricassees, fricasseed, fricasseeing**) to stew (chicken, etc) in white sauce.

fricative *n* a consonant, e.g. *f, th, sh,* made by forcing air through a narrow opening formed by placing the tongue or lip close to another part of the mouth, or by constricting the pharynx.

friction *n* **1a** the rubbing of one body against another. **b** resistance to relative motion between two bodies in contact. **2** disagreement between two people or parties of opposing views. ➤➤ **frictional** *adj,* **frictionless** *adj.*

Friday *n* the day of the week following Thursday.

fridge *n chiefly Brit* a refrigerator.

fridge-freezer *n* a unit consisting of a separate refrigerator and freezer.

fried *v* past tense and past part. of FRY[1].

friend *n* **1** a person whose company and attitudes one finds sympathetic and to whom one is not closely related. **2** somebody or something of the same nation, party, or group. **3** somebody or something that favours or encourages something, e.g. a charity. **4** (**Friend**) a Quaker. ✱ **make friends 1** to acquire friends. **2** to become friendly. ➤➤ **friendless** *adj,* **friendship** *n.*

friendly[1] *adj* (**-ier, -iest**) **1** like a friend; kind. **2** not hostile. **3** inclined to be favourable. **4** (*used in combinations*) adapted to the needs of; helpful to: *child-friendly restaurants.* ➤➤ **friendliness** *n.*

friendly[2] *n* (*pl* **-ies**) *chiefly Brit* a match played for practice or pleasure and not as part of a competition.

friendly fire *n* in warfare, weapon fire that injures or kills one's own soldiers.

friendly society *n Brit* a mutual insurance association providing its subscribers with benefits during sickness, unemployment, and old age.

fries *pl n chiefly NAm* chips, *esp* thin ones.

Friesian *n Brit* an animal of a black-and-white breed of dairy cattle originating in N Holland and Friesland.

frieze *n* **1** a sculptured or ornamented band, e.g. on a building. **2** in architecture, the part of an entablature between the architrave and the cornice.

frig *v* (**frigged, frigging**) *coarse slang* to have sexual intercourse with or masturbate (somebody).

frigate *n* **1** *Brit* a warship smaller than a destroyer. **2** formerly, a square-rigged warship next in size below a ship of the line.

frigate bird *n* a strong-winged seabird with a forked tail and a long bill, noted for the habit of snatching food from other birds.

fright *n* **1** fear excited by sudden danger or shock. **2** *informal* something unsightly, strange, or shocking.

frighten *v* **1** to make (somebody) afraid; to scare. **2** to force (somebody) by frightening them: *I frightened them into confessing; The cat frightened the robin away.* ➤➤ **frightened** *adj,* **frightening** *adj,* **frighteningly** *adv.*

frightener *n* somebody or something frightening. ✱ **put the frighteners on** *Brit, informal* to intimidate.

frightful *adj* **1** causing intense fear, shock, or horror. **2** *informal* unpleasant or difficult. ➤➤ **frightfully** *adv,* **frightfulness** *n.*

frigid *adj* **1a** intensely cold. **b** *formal* unenthusiastic or unfriendly. **2** *esp* of a woman: abnormally averse to sexual contact, *esp* intercourse. ➤➤ **frigidity** *n,* **frigidly** *adv,* **frigidness** *n.*

frill *n* **1** a gathered or pleated fabric edging used on clothing or as ornament. **2** a ruff of hair, skin, or feathers round the neck of an animal or bird. **3** something decorative but not essential; a luxury. ➤➤ **frilled** *adj,* **frilliness** *n,* **frilly** *adj.*

fringe[1] *n* **1** an ornamental border, e.g. on a curtain or garment, consisting of straight or twisted threads or tassels. **2a** something resembling a fringe; a border. **b** *chiefly Brit* the hair that falls over the forehead. **3** something marginal, additional, or secondary. **4** (*used as sing. or pl*) an unconventional or extremist group.

fringe[2] *v* **1** to provide or decorate (e.g. material) with a fringe. **2** to serve as a fringe for (something).

fringe benefit *n* a benefit, e.g. a pension, granted by an employer to an employee in addition to basic wages.

frippery *n* (*pl* **-ies**) **1** non-essential ornamentation, *esp* of a showy kind. **2** affected elegance; ostentation.

Frisbee *n trademark* a plastic disc thrown between players by a flip of the wrist.

frisée *n* curly endive.

Frisian *n* **1** a native or inhabitant of Friesland or the Frisian islands. **2** the language of the Frisian people. ➤➤ **Frisian** *adj.*

frisk[1] *v* **1** *informal* to search (a person) for something by running the hand over their clothing. **2** to leap, skip, or dance in a lively or playful way.

frisk² *n* **1** *informal* an act of frisking somebody. **2** a gambol or romp.

frisky *adj* (**-ier, -iest**) lively or playful. ➤➤ **friskily** *adv,* **friskiness** *n.*

frisson *n* a shudder or thrill.

fritillary *n* (*pl* **-ies**) **1** a plant of the lily family with mottled or chequered bell-shaped flowers. **2** a butterfly that is orange with black spots.

frittata *n* an unfolded omelette usu containing vegetables, cheese, and seasonings.

fritter¹ *n* a piece of fried batter containing fruit, meat, etc.

fritter² *v* (*usu* + away) to waste (e.g. money or time) bit by bit.

frivolous *adj* **1** lacking in seriousness; irresponsibly self-indulgent. **2** lacking practicality or serious purpose; unimportant. ➤➤ **frivolity** *n,* **frivolously** *adv,* **frivolousness** *n.*

frizz¹ *v* of hair: to form a mass of tight curls.

frizz² *n* hair in a mass of small tight curls.

frizzle¹ *v* to fry (e.g. bacon) until crisp and curled.

frizzle² *v* to frizz or curl (the hair).

frizzle³ *n* a tight curl in the hair.

frizzy *adj* (**-ier, -iest**) of hair: in small tight curls. ➤➤ **frizziness** *n.*

fro *adv* see TO².

frock *n* **1** *Brit* a woman's or girl's dress. **2** a loose garment, *esp* a monk's or friar's habit.

frock coat *n* a usu double-breasted coat with knee-length skirts worn by men, *esp* in the 19th cent.

frog¹ *n* **1** a tailless largely aquatic leaping amphibian with a smooth skin and webbed feet. **2** (**Frog**) *informal, derog* a French person. ✱ **have a frog in one's throat** to have a hoarse voice. ➤➤ **froggy** *adj.*

frog² *n* **1** a loop attached to a belt to hold a weapon or tool. **2** a usu ornamental braiding, consisting of a button and a loop, for fastening the front of a garment.

frog³ *n* the triangular elastic horny pad in the middle of the sole of a horse's foot.

froghopper *n* a leaping insect whose larvae secrete froth.

frogman *n* (*pl* **frogmen**) a person equipped with face mask, flippers, rubber suit, etc and an air supply for swimming underwater for extended periods.

frogmarch *v* to force (a person) to move forwards by holding his or her arms firmly from behind.

frogspawn *n* a gelatinous mass of frogs' eggs.

frolic¹ *v* (**frolicked, frolicking**) to play and run about happily.

frolic² *n* **1** a playful expression of high spirits; gaiety. **2** a light-hearted entertainment or game. ➤➤ **frolicsome** *adj.*

from *prep* **1** used to indicate a starting point, e.g.: **a** a place where a physical movement or action begins: *They came here from the city.* **b** a starting point in measuring or reckoning: *These cost from £5 to £10.* **2** used to indicate separation or removal: *Take a glass from the cupboard.* **3** used to indicate a source, cause, or basis: *He suffers from gout.*

fromage frais /ˌfromahzh 'fray/ *n* a soft smooth fresh cheese that is low in fat.

frond *n* a leaf, *esp* of a palm or fern.

front¹ *n* **1** the part or surface of something that usually faces forward. **2** the part of the human body opposite to the back. **3** a face of a building, *esp* the side that contains the main entrance. **4a** a line of battle. **b** (*often* **Front**) a zone of conflict between armies. **5** a movement linking divergent elements to achieve certain common objectives; *esp* a political coalition. **6** a particular situation or sphere of activity. **7** in meteorology, the boundary between two dissimilar air masses. **8** a person, group, or thing used to mask the identity or true character of something, *esp* something illegal. **9** demeanour or bearing, *esp* in the face of a challenge or danger. ✱ **in front of 1** directly ahead of. **2** in the presence of. **up front** as payment in advance.

front² *v* **1** to face towards. **2** to be in front of (something). **3a** to act as a front for (something). **b** to supply a front for (something). **4a** to lead (e.g. a band or group). **b** to present (a television programme).

front³ *adj* of or situated at the front.

frontage *n* **1** the front face of a building. **2** the land between the front of a building and the street.

frontal *adj* **1** relating to, situated at, or showing the front. **2** relating or adjacent to the forehead. ➤➤ **frontally** *adv.*

frontal lobe *n* the front lobe of either cerebral hemisphere.

front bench *n Brit* either of two rows of benches in the House of Commons on which party leaders sit. ➤➤ **frontbencher** *n.*

front-end¹ *adj* **1** required or provided at the beginning of a project. **2** of a computer program: relating to the user interface of the system.

front-end² *n* the software or hardware of a computer that takes in and processes the raw data.

frontier *n* **1** a border between two countries. **2** *NAm* a region that forms the margin of settled or developed territory. **3** (*also in pl*) the boundary between the known and the unknown.

frontiersman *or* **frontierswoman** *n* (*pl* **frontiersmen** *or* **frontierswomen**) a man or woman living on the frontier, *esp* of settled territory.

frontispiece *n* an illustration preceding and usu facing the title page of a book or magazine.

front line *n* a military front.

front man *n* a person serving as a front or figurehead.

front of house *n* the parts of a theatre accessible to the public, e.g. the auditorium and foyer.

front-runner *n* the leading contestant in a competition.

frost¹ *n* **1** a covering of minute ice crystals formed on a cold surface when the temperature falls below freezing. **2** a period of freezing weather.

frost² *v* **1** to cover or be covered with frost, or as if with frost. **2** *chiefly NAm* to ice (a cake). **3** (*often* + over) to freeze.

frostbite *n* gangrene or other local damage caused by a partial freezing of some part of the body.

frosted *adj* **1** covered with frost. **2** of glass: having a slightly roughened surface, making it hard to see through. **3** having a frosty or sparkling sheen.

frosting *n* **1** a dull or roughened finish on metal or glass. **2a** *Brit* thick fluffy cooked icing. **b** *chiefly NAm* icing.

frosty *adj* (**-ier, -iest**) **1** marked by or producing frost; freezing. **2** covered with frost; hoary. **3** marked by coolness or extreme reserve in manner. ➤➤ **frostily** *adv,* **frostiness** *n.*

froth¹ *n* **1a** a mass of bubbles formed on or in a liquid; foam. **b** a foamy saliva sometimes accompanying disease, e.g. rabies. **2** something insubstantial or of little value.

froth² *v* **1** (*often* + up) to cause (a liquid) to foam. **2** (*often* + up) to produce or emit froth. ➤➤ **frothily** *adv,* **frothy** *adj.*

frottage /'frotahzh/ *n* **1** in art, the technique or process of creating an image of an object by rubbing on a sheet of paper placed over it. **2** the practice of rubbing against somebody in a crowd as a way of getting sexual pleasure.

froufrou *n* **1** a rustling sound, *esp* of a woman's dress. **2** frilly ornamentation.

froward *adj archaic* habitually disobedient or contrary.

frown[1] *v* **1** to contract the brow in a frown. **2** (*often* + on/upon) to give evidence of displeasure or disapproval.

frown[2] *n* **1** a wrinkling of the brow in displeasure, concentration, or puzzlement. **2** an expression of displeasure.

frowst[1] *v chiefly Brit, informal* to remain indoors in a hot airless room.

frowst[2] *n chiefly Brit, informal* a stuffy atmosphere.

frowsty *adj* (**-ier, -iest**) *chiefly Brit* lacking fresh air; stuffy.

frowzy *or* **frowsy** *adj* (**-ier, -iest**) having a slovenly or uncared-for appearance.

froze *v* past tense of FREEZE[1].

frozen *v* past part. of FREEZE[1].

FRS *abbr Brit* Fellow of the Royal Society.

fructify *v* (**-ies, -ied**) *formal* **1** to bear fruit. **2** to make fruitful or productive.

fructose *n* a very sweet sugar that occurs in fruit juices and honey.

frugal *adj* economical in the expenditure of resources; sparing. ➤➤ **frugality** *n*, **frugally** *adv.*

frugivore *n* an animal that feeds on fruit. ➤➤ **frugivorous** *adj.*

fruit[1] *n* **1** the usu edible reproductive body of a seed plant; *esp* one having a sweet pulp associated with the seed, e.g. an apple or pear. **2** in botany, a product of fertilization in a plant with its modified skins or attached structures; *specif* the ripened ovary of a flowering plant together with its contents. **3** (*also in pl*) the effect or consequence of an action or operation, *esp* a favourable one. **4** *chiefly NAm, informal, offensive* a male homosexual.

fruit[2] *v* to bear fruit.

fruitarian *n* somebody whose diet consists of fruit.

fruit bat *n* a large fruit-eating bat found in warm regions of Africa and Eurasia.

fruitcake *n* **1** a rich usu dark cake containing nuts and dried fruit. **2** *Brit, informal* a crazy or eccentric person.

fruiterer *n chiefly Brit* a person who sells fruit.

fruit fly *n* a small fly whose larvae feed on fruit or decaying vegetable matter.

fruitful *adj* **1** yielding or producing a great deal of fruit; fertile. **2** having beneficial results; productive. ➤➤ **fruitfully** *adv*, **fruitfulness** *n.*

fruiting body *n* a plant organ, e.g. in lichens and mosses, specialized for producing spores.

fruition *n* **1** the realization or fulfilment of a project. **2** bearing fruit.

fruitless *adj* **1** useless or unsuccessful. **2** lacking or not bearing fruit. ➤➤ **fruitlessly** *adv*, **fruitlessness** *n.*

fruit machine *n Brit* a coin-operated gambling machine that pays out according to different combinations of symbols visible on wheels.

fruit salad *n* a dessert consisting of a mixture of chopped pieces of fruit.

fruit sugar *n* = FRUCTOSE.

fruity *adj* (**-ier, -iest**) **1** resembling or having the flavour of fruit. **2** of a voice: marked by richness and depth; mellow. **3** *chiefly Brit, informal* amusing in a sexually suggestive way. ➤➤ **fruitiness** *n.*

frump *n* a dowdy unattractive girl or woman. ➤➤ **frumpish** *adj*, **frumpy** *adj.*

frustrate *v* **1a** to prevent (somebody) from carrying out a plan or intention; to foil. **b** to prevent (a plan) from being carried out or (a hope) from being realized. **2** to induce feelings of discouragement and vexation in. ➤➤ **frustrated** *adj*, **frustrating** *adj*, **frustratingly** *adv*, **frustration** *n.*

fry[1] *v* (**-ies, -ied**) **1** to cook (food) in hot oil or fat, *esp* in a pan over direct heat. **2** of food: to cook in hot oil or fat. **3** *informal* of a person: to feel very hot or to burn in the sun.

fry[2] *n* (*pl* **-ies**) a dish of fried food.

fry[3] *pl n* recently hatched fishes.

fryer *n* a deep vessel for frying foods.

frying pan *n* a shallow metal pan with a handle, used for frying food. ✱ **out of the frying pan into the fire** clear of one difficulty only to fall into a greater one.

fry-up *n Brit, informal* a dish or meal consisting of fried food.

f-stop *n* a camera lens aperture setting indicated by an f-number.

ft *abbr* **1** feet. **2** foot.

FTP *abbr* in computing, file transfer protocol.

FTSE index *n* an index of relative share prices on the London Stock Exchange, published in the *Financial Times*.

fuchsia *n* **1** a decorative shrub with hanging flowers with flared petals usu in deep pinks, reds, and purples. **2** a vivid reddish purple colour.

fuci *n* pl of FUCUS.

fuck[1] *v taboo* **1** to have sexual intercourse with. **2** to spoil or ruin. ➤➤ **fucker** *n.*

fuck[2] *n taboo* **1** an act of sexual intercourse. **2** a sexual partner.

fuck[3] *interj taboo* used to express annoyance or impatience.

fuck about *v taboo* **1** to waste time; to mess about. **2** to treat badly; to mess about.

fuck all *n Brit, taboo* nothing at all.

fuck around *v taboo* = FUCK ABOUT.

fuck off *v taboo* to go away.

fuck up *v taboo* **1** to spoil or ruin. **2** to do psychological damage to.

fucus *n* (*pl* **fuci**) a seaweed with greenish brown leathery fronds used in the kelp industry. ➤➤ **fucoid** *adj.*

fuddle *v* to make drunk or confused.

fuddy-duddy *n* (*pl* **-ies**) *informal* a person who is old-fashioned, pompous, or unimaginative.

fudge[1] *n* **1** a soft creamy sweet made of sugar, milk, and butter. **2** a decision, agreement, or statement that evades the central and most difficult issues.

fudge[2] *v* **1** to present (e.g. facts or figures) in a misleading way. **2** to fail to come to grips with (a problem or issue).

fuehrer *n* see FÜHRER.

fuel[1] *n* **1a** a material used to produce heat or power by combustion. **b** a material from which atomic energy can be liberated, *esp* in a nuclear reactor. **2a** a source of sustenance, strength, or encouragement. **b** material providing nutrition; food.

fuel[2] *v* (**fuelled, fuelling,** *NAm* **fueled, fueling**) **1** to provide (e.g. a machine or vehicle) with fuel. **2**

to support or stimulate (e.g. an emotion or activity).

fuel cell *n* a cell that continuously changes chemical energy to electrical energy.

fuel injection *n* the introduction of liquid fuel under pressure directly into the cylinders of an internal-combustion engine, without using a carburettor. ➤➤ **fuel-injected** *adj.*

fug *n Brit, informal* the stuffy atmosphere of a poorly ventilated space. ➤➤ **fuggy** *adj.*

fugal *adj* in the style of a musical fugue.

fugitive[1] *n* a person who flees or tries to escape.

fugitive[2] *adj* **1** running away or trying to escape. **2** elusive or fleeting; ephemeral.

fugu *n* a poisonous pufferfish eaten as a delicacy in Japan.

fugue *n* **1** a musical composition in which one or two themes are repeated or imitated by successively entering voices, instruments, or parts and are developed by a continuous interweaving. **2** in psychiatry, a disturbed state characterized by loss of memory and by the patient's disappearance from home.

führer *or* **fuehrer** *n* a leader exercising tyrannical authority, *esp* Hitler, leader of the Nazis in Germany.

-ful[1] *suffix* **1** forming adjectives from nouns, with the meaning: full of: *colourful.* **2** forming adjectives from nouns, with the meaning: characterized by: *peaceful.* **3** forming adjectives from nouns, with the meaning: having the qualities of: *masterful.* **4** forming adjectives from verbs, with the meaning: tending to or able to: *mournful.*

-ful[2] *suffix* forming nouns from nouns, denoting: number or amount that (the thing specified) holds or can hold: *a roomful.*

fulcrum *n* (*pl* **fulcrums** *or* **fulcra**) the support about which a lever turns.

fulfil (*NAm* **fulfill**) *v* (**fulfilled, fulfilling**) **1a** to cause to happen as appointed or predicted. **b** to put (e.g. an order) into effect; to carry out. **2** to measure up to (a requirement or condition); to satisfy. **3** to develop the full potential of (somebody or something). ➤➤ **fulfilled** *adj,* **fulfilling** *adj,* **fulfilment** *n.*

full[1] *adj* **1** containing as much or as many as is possible or normal. **2a** complete, *esp* in detail, number, or duration. **b** not lacking in any essential; perfect. **3** (+ of) possessing or containing a great number or amount of. **4** at the highest or greatest degree; maximum. **5a** of somebody's figure or face: rounded in outline; plump. **b** of a garment: having an abundance of material. **6a** of a sound: having volume or depth. **b** of a colour: rich and strong. **7a** (*often* + of) with the attention completely occupied by something. **b** (*often* + of) filled with and expressing excited anticipation or pleasure. ✱ **full of oneself** self-satisfied and conceited. **full up** completely full. **in full flight 1** fleeing as fast as possible. **2** in top operating form. **in full flow** speaking fluently and animatedly. **in full swing** at a high level of activity. ➤➤ **fullness** *n,* **fulness** *n.*

full[2] *adv* **1** very. **2** exactly or squarely.

full[3] *n* (**the full**) the highest or fullest state, extent, or degree. ✱ **in full** completely or entirely.

full[4] *v* to cleanse and finish (woollen cloth) by moistening, heating, and pressing. ➤➤ **fuller** *n.*

fullback *n* a primarily defensive player in football, rugby, etc, usu stationed nearest the defended goal.

full-blooded *adj* **1** of unmixed ancestry; purebred. **2** forceful or vigorous; hearty.

full-blown *adj* fully developed or mature; complete.

full board *n Brit* accommodation at a guest house or hotel with all meals included.

full-bodied *adj* marked by richness and fullness, *esp* of flavour.

full dress *n* **1** the style of dress prescribed for ceremonial or formal social occasions. **2** (*used before a noun*) requiring full dress; formal.

fullerene *n* a form of carbon in which the 60 carbon atoms form rings arranged in a spherical shape.

fuller's earth *n* a clayey substance used in fulling cloth and as a catalyst.

full-face *adj* **1** covering the whole face: *a full-face crash helmet.* **2** showing the whole face: *a full-face photograph.*

full-fledged *adj NAm* see FULLY-FLEDGED.

full-frontal *adj* **1** exposing the whole front of the body, including the genitals. **2** without concealment or restraint.

full house *n* **1** a full theatre or other venue. **2** in poker, a hand containing three of a kind and a pair. **3** in bingo, a winning set of numbers.

full monty *n* (**the full monty**) *Brit, informal* everything needed or wanted; the whole thing or the whole lot.

full moon *n* the moon when its whole apparent disc is illuminated.

full-motion video *n* video data that is stored digitally to be used on a computer screen, e.g. in a computer game or presentation.

full nelson *n* a wrestling hold in which both arms are thrust under the corresponding arms of an opponent and the hands clasped behind the opponent's head: compare HALF NELSON.

full-on *adj informal* unrestrained or intense; explicit.

full-scale *adj* **1** identical to an original in proportion and size. **2** involving full use of available resources.

full stop *n* a punctuation mark (.) used to mark the end of a sentence or abbreviation.

full time[1] *n* **1** the amount of time considered the normal or standard amount for working during a given period, *esp* a week. **2** the end of e.g. a football match.

full time[2] *adv* on a full-time basis.

full-time *adj* employed for or involving full time. ➤➤ **full-timer** *n.*

fully *adv* **1** completely. **2** at least.

-fully *suffix* forming adverbs from adjectives ending in *-ful*: *mournfully.*

fully-fashioned *adj* of clothing: shaped and seamed so that it fits the body.

fully-fledged (*NAm* **full-fledged**) *adj* **1** of a bird: having fully developed feathers and able to fly. **2** having attained complete status.

fulmar *n* a grey and white seabird of colder regions closely related to the petrels.

fulminant *adj* = FULMINATING (2).

fulminate *v* **1a** (*usu* + against/at) to criticize or denounce something vehemently. **b** to be furiously indignant; to feel enraged. **2** to make a sudden loud noise; to explode. ➤➤ **fulmination** *n,* **fulminator** *n.*

fulminating *adj* **1** exploding with a vivid flash. **2** of a disease or infection: coming on suddenly with great severity.

fulsome *adj* **1** unnecessarily effusive or obsequious. **2** overabundant or copious. ➤➤ **fulsomely** *adv,* **fulsomeness** *n.*

Usage note

In its standard modern meaning, *fulsome* is a strongly uncomplimentary word. *Fulsome praise* is embarrassingly excessive or insincerely flattering. Though *fulsome* derives originally from a word meaning 'abundant', its use in a positive sense to mean 'copious', 'very full', or 'lavish' should be avoided for fear of misunderstanding.

fumarole *n* a hole in a volcanic region from which hot vapours are emitted.

fumble[1] *v* **1** to grope for or handle something clumsily or awkwardly. **2** (*often* + about/around) to make awkward attempts to do or find something. **3** to feel or handle (e.g. a ball) clumsily. **4** to deal with (something) awkwardly or clumsily. ➤➤ **fumbler** *n,* **fumblingly** *adv.*

fumble[2] *n* an act of fumbling.

fume[1] *n* (*also in pl*) an irritating or offensive smoke, vapour, or gas. ➤➤ **fumy** *adj.*

fume[2] *v* **1** to emit fumes. **2** to be in a state of excited irritation or anger. **3** to expose (e.g. wood) to or treat (something) with fumes. ➤➤ **fuming** *adj.*

fumigate *v* to apply smoke, vapour, or gas to (an area), *esp* in order to disinfect it or destroy pests. ➤➤ **fumigant** *n,* **fumigation** *n,* **fumigator** *n.*

fumitory *n* (*pl* **-ies**) an erect or climbing plant with purple or white flowers.

fun[1] *n* **1a** amusement or enjoyment. **b** a cause of this. **2** good humour. ✱ **in fun** not intending harm or to be taken seriously. **make fun of/poke fun at** to make (somebody or something) an object of amusement or ridicule.

fun[2] *adj chiefly NAm, informal* providing entertainment or enjoyment.

function[1] *n* **1** the purpose of a person or thing, or for which a thing exists, or what a person or thing characteristically does. **2** an elaborate or formal ceremony or social gathering. **3** a mathematical relationship between each element of one set and at least one element of the same or another set. **4** a quality, trait, or fact dependent on and varying with another. **5** a facility on a computer or similar device that carries out a particular operation. ➤➤ **functionless** *adj.*

function[2] *v* **1** to have a function; to serve. **2** to operate.

functional *adj* **1** designed or developed for practical use without ornamentation. **2** capable of performing a function. **3** connected with or being a function. **4** of disease: affecting physiological or psychological functions but not organic structure. ➤➤ **functionality** *n,* **functionally** *adv.*

functionalism *n* a theory or practice that emphasizes practical utility or functional relations to the exclusion of ornamentation. ➤➤ **functionalist** *n and adj.*

functionary *n* (*pl* **-ies**) somebody who serves in a certain function; an official or bureaucrat.

function key *n* a keyboard key, e.g. on a calculator or computer, which controls a command or action sequence.

fund[1] *n* **1** a sum of money whose principal or interest is set apart for a specific objective. **2** (*in pl*) an available supply of money. **3** an available quantity of material or intangible resources.

fund[2] *v* to provide funds for.

fundament *n* **1** an underlying theory or principle. **2** *euphem* the buttocks.

fundamental[1] *adj* **1** of central importance; principal. **2** of the essential structure, function, or facts of something; radical. ➤➤ **fundamentally** *adv.*

fundamental[2] *n* **1** a minimum constituent without which a thing or system would not be what it is. **2** in music, the lowest note of a chord in normal position.

fundamentalism *n* **1a** a belief in the literal truth of the Bible. **b** (*often* **Fundamentalism**) a movement in 20th-cent. Protestantism emphasizing such belief. **2** a movement stressing strict adherence to a set of basic principles or beliefs, *esp* in religion. ➤➤ **fundamentalist** *n and adj.*

fundholding *n* a system formerly used in Britain in which general practitioners controlled their own budgets. ➤➤ **fundholder** *n.*

fund-raiser *n* **1** somebody who works to raise funds for a cause. **2** an event held to raise funds for a cause. ➤➤ **fund-raising** *n.*

funeral *n* a formal and ceremonial disposing of a dead body, *esp* by burial or cremation. ✱ **be somebody's funeral** *informal* to be somebody's own problem or fault.

funeral director *n* = UNDERTAKER.

funeral parlour *n* an undertaker's establishment.

funerary *adj* used for or associated with burial.

funereal *adj* gloomy or solemn.

fun fair *n chiefly Brit* a usu outdoor show offering amusements, e.g. sideshows and rides.

fungi *n* pl of FUNGUS.

fungible *adj* in law, of movable goods: such that one specimen may be used in place of another in the fulfilment of a contract.

fungicide *n* a substance used for destroying or preventing fungus. ➤➤ **fungicidal** *adj.*

fungous *adj* **1** relating to or like a fungus or fungi. **2** caused by a fungus.

fungus *n* (*pl* **fungi** *or* **funguses**) any of a major group of organisms lacking chlorophyll and including moulds, rusts, mildews, smuts, mushrooms, and toadstools; reproduction involves minute spores. ➤➤ **fungal** *adj,* **fungoid** *adj.*

funicular[1] *n* a cable railway on a steep slope in which an ascending carriage counterbalances a descending carriage.

funicular[2] *adj* of a railway: dependent on a rope or cable to draw the carriages.

funk[1] *n informal* **1** a state of paralysing fear. **2** a fit of inability to face difficulty.

funk[2] *v informal* to avoid doing or facing (something) because of lack of determination.

funk[3] *n* funky music.

funky *adj* (**-ier, -iest**) **1** *informal* having an earthy unsophisticated style and feeling, as in the blues; soulful. **2** *informal* said of clothes: original and stylish. ➤➤ **funkily** *adv,* **funkiness** *n.*

funnel[1] *n* **1** a utensil having the shape of a hollow cone with a tube extending from the smaller end, designed to direct liquids or powders into a small opening. **2** a shaft, stack, or flue for ventilation or the escape of smoke or steam.

funnel[2] *v* (**funnelled, funnelling,** *NAm* **funneled, funneling**) **1** to pass through a funnel, or as if through a funnel. **2** to move (something) to a focal point or into a central channel.

funnel web *n* a spider that builds a tube-shaped web; *esp* an extremely poisonous large black Australian spider.

funny[1] *adj* (**-ier, -iest**) **1** causing amusement and laughter; seeking or intended to amuse. **2** peculiar, strange, or odd. **3** involving deception or dishonesty. **4** unwilling to be helpful; difficult. **5** *informal* slightly unwell. ➤➤ **funnily** *adv,* **funniness** *n.*

funny² *n* (*pl* **-ies**) **1** *informal* (*usu in pl*) a comic strip or comic section in a periodical. **2** *informal* a joke.

funny bone *n* the place at the back of the elbow where the nerve supplying the hand and forearm rests against the bone.

funny farm *n informal* a psychiatric hospital.

fun run *n informal* a long-distance run, *esp* to raise money for charity.

fur¹ *n* **1** the hairy coat of a mammal, *esp* when fine, soft, and thick. **2a** a piece of the dressed pelt of an animal used to make, trim, or line garments. **b** an article of clothing made of or with fur. **3** a coating of dead cells on the tongue of somebody who is unwell. **4** a coating formed in vessels, e.g. kettles or pipes, by deposition of scale from hard water. ✱ **make the fur fly** to cause an argument or a scene. ➤➤ **furred** *adj.*

fur² *v* (**furred, furring**) (*often* + up) to become coated or clogged, or to coat or clog (e.g. a pipe) with fur.

furbelow *n* **1** a flounce on women's clothing. **2** something showy or superfluous.

furious *adj* **1** exhibiting or goaded by uncontrollable anger. **2a** having a stormy or turbulent appearance. **b** marked by noise, excitement, or activity. **3** intense. ➤➤ **furiously** *adv,* **furiousness** *n.*

furl *v* to fold or roll (e.g. a sail or umbrella) close to or round something. ➤➤ **furled** *adj.*

furlong *n* a unit of length equal to 220 yards (about 0.2km).

furlough¹ *n* a leave of absence from duty granted *esp* to a soldier.

furlough² *v chiefly NAm* to grant a furlough to (e.g. a soldier).

furnace *n* an enclosed apparatus in which heat is produced, e.g. for heating a building or reducing ore.

furnish *v* **1a** to provide, supply, or give (something). **b** to provide or supply (somebody) with what they need. **2** to equip (a room, flat, etc) with furniture. ➤➤ **furnished** *adj,* **furnisher** *n.*

furnishing *n* **1** (*in pl*) articles of furniture and fittings used to make a room comfortable. **2** (*used before a noun*) denoting material used for carpets, cushions, etc.

furniture *n* **1** the movable articles, e.g. tables, chairs, and beds, that make an area suitable for living in or use. **2** accessories: *door furniture.*

furore (*NAm* **furor**) *n* an outburst of general excitement or indignation.

furrier *n* a fur dealer.

furrow¹ *n* **1** a trench in the earth made by a plough. **2** a groove. **3** a deep wrinkle.

furrow² *v* **1** to make a furrow or line in (a surface). **2** to become grooved or wrinkled.

furry *adj* (**-ier, -iest**) like, made of, or covered with fur. ➤➤ **furriness** *n.*

fur seal *n* an eared seal that has a double coat with a dense soft underfur.

further¹ *adv* **1** to a greater degree or extent. **2** moreover. **3** = FARTHER¹ (I).

Usage note
further *or* farther? See note at FARTHER¹.

further² *adj* **1** extending beyond what exists or has happened; additional. **2** coming after the one referred to. **3** = FARTHER² (I).

further³ *v* to bring (something) closer to fulfilment, realization, or success. ➤➤ **furtherance** *n.*

further education *n Brit* vocational, cultural, or recreational education for people who have left school.

furthermore *adv* in addition to what precedes; moreover.

furthermost *adj* most distant.

further to *prep formal* in response to and following on from.

furthest¹ *adj* most distant in space or time.

furthest² *adv* **1** to or at the greatest distance in space, time, or degree. **2** by the greatest degree or extent; most.

furtive *adj* expressive of or done by stealth; surreptitious or sly. ➤➤ **furtively** *adv,* **furtiveness** *n.*

fury *n* (*pl* **-ies**) **1a** intense, disordered, and often destructive rage. **b** a fit of intense rage. **2** wild disordered force or activity. **3** (**Fury**) any of the three avenging deities who in Greek mythology punished crimes.

furze *n* = GORSE.

fuse¹ *n* **1** a combustible substance enclosed in a cord or cable for setting off an explosive charge by transmitting fire to it. **2** (*NAm* **fuze**) the detonating device for setting off the charge in a projectile, bomb, etc.

fuse² (*NAm* **fuze**) *v* to equip (a bomb) with a fuse.

fuse³ *v* **1** to blend (two things) thoroughly, e.g. by melting together. **2** to become blended by melting together, or as if by melting together. **3** to reduce (a material) to a liquid or plastic state by heat; to melt. **4** to cause (e.g. a light bulb) to fail by fusing. **5** of an electrical appliance: to fail because of the melting of a fuse. **6** to equip (e.g. a plug) with an electrical fuse.

fuse⁴ *n* an electrical safety device that includes a wire or strip of fusible metal that melts and interrupts the circuit when the current exceeds a particular value.

fuselage *n* the central body portion of an aeroplane designed to accommodate the crew and the passengers or cargo.

fusible *adj* able, or easily able, to be fused or melted.

fusil *n* a light flintlock musket.

fusilier (*NAm* **fusileer**) *n* a member of a British regiment formerly armed with fusils.

fusillade *n* **1** a number of shots fired simultaneously or in rapid succession. **2** a spirited outburst, *esp* of criticism.

fusilli /fyooh'zili/ *pl n* (*used as sing. or pl*) spiral-shaped pasta.

fusion *n* **1** the act or process of fusing. **2** the union of light atomic nuclei to form heavier nuclei, resulting in the release of enormous quantities of energy. **3** a union formed when two things fuse; a merging. **4** a blend of two or more styles, e.g. in music, cookery, or design.

fuss¹ *n* **1** needless or useless bustle or excitement. **2a** a state of agitation, *esp* over a trivial matter. **b** an objection or protest.

fuss² *v* **1** to pay close or undue attention to small details. **2** (*usu* + with) to keep touching or moving something anxiously or unnecessarily. **3** to become upset; to worry. **4** to agitate or upset (somebody). ✱ **not fussed** *Brit, informal* with no strong feelings about something, *esp* a choice of alternatives; not bothered. ➤➤ **fusser** *n.*

fusspot *n informal* a person who fusses about trifles.

fussy *adj* (**-ier, -iest**) **1a** showing too much concern over details. **b** fastidious. **2** having too much or too detailed ornamentation. ➤➤ **fussily** *adv,* **fussiness** *n.*

fustian *n* a strong cotton or linen fabric, e.g. corduroy or moleskin, usu having a pile face and twill weave.

fusty *adj* (**-ier, -iest**) **1** stale or musty from being left undisturbed for a long time. **2** rigidly old-fashioned or reactionary. ➤➤ **fustily** *adv,* **fustiness** *n.*

futile *adj* completely ineffective; pointless. ➤➤ **futilely** *adv,* **futility** *n.*

futon *n* a thick padded quilt that is laid on the floor or on a frame to serve as a bed.

future[1] *n* **1a** (**the future**) time that is to come. **b** that which is going to occur. **2** a likelihood of success. **3a** in grammar, the verb tense that expresses action or state in the future. **b** a verb form in this tense. **4** (*in pl*) something, e.g. a bulk commodity, bought for future acceptance or sold for future delivery. ✱ **in future** from now on.

future[2] *adj* **1** that is to be. **2** of or constituting the future tense.

future perfect *n* a verb tense, e.g. *will have finished,* expressing completion of an action at or before a future time.

future-proof *adj* not likely to become obsolete.

future shock *n* a sense of confusion and powerlessness caused by the effect on daily life of rapid technological and social changes.

futurism *n* **1** (*often* **Futurism**) a movement in art, music, and literature begun in Italy about 1910 and seeking to express the dynamic energy and movement of mechanical processes. **2** a point of view that finds meaning or fulfilment in the future rather than in the past or present. ➤➤ **futurist** *n and adj.*

futuristic *adj* to do with a vision of the future; *esp* in being revolutionary or technologically advanced. ➤➤ **futuristically** *adv.*

futurity *n* (*pl* **-ies**) **1** the future. **2** a future event or prospect.

futurology *n* the forecasting of the future from current trends in society. ➤➤ **futurologist** *n.*

fu yong *n* see FOO YONG.

fuze *noun and v NAm* see FUSE[1] (2) and FUSE[2].

fuzz[1] *n* **1** fine light particles or fibres, e.g. of down or fluff. **2** a blur. **3** a distortion in sound, e.g. on a radio.

fuzz[2] *v* **1** of hair: to become fuzzy or frizzy. **2** to make (e.g. a picture) fuzzy or blurred.

fuzz[3] *n* (**the fuzz**) *informal* the police.

fuzzy *adj* (**-ier, -iest**) **1** marked by or giving a suggestion of fuzz. **2** not clear; indistinct. ➤➤ **fuzzily** *adv,* **fuzziness** *n.*

fuzzy logic *n* a system of logic that allows for degrees of uncertainty, rather than depending on absolute truth-values, and that is used to make human thought processes or imprecise information accessible to computers.

FWD *or* **f.w.d.** *abbr* **1** four-wheel drive. **2** front-wheel drive.

f-word *n euphem* the word 'fuck'.

FX *abbr* used in film-making: special effects.

-fy *or* **-ify** *suffix* forming verbs, with the meanings: **1** to become or cause to be: *purify.* **2** to fill with: *horrify.* **3** to give the characteristics of; to make similar to: *countrify.* **4** to engage in (a specified activity): *speechify.*

G[1] *or* **g** *n* (*pl* **G's** *or* **Gs** *or* **g's**) **1** the seventh letter of the English alphabet. **2** in music, the fifth note of the diatonic scale of C major.

G[2] *abbr* **1** giga-. **2** *NAm, informal* grand ($1000). **3** gravitational constant.

g *abbr* **1** gas. **2** gram(s). **3** gravity, or acceleration due to gravity.

GA *abbr* Georgia (US postal abbreviation).

Ga *abbr* the chemical symbol for gallium.

gab[1] *v* (**gabbed, gabbing**) *informal* to chatter or blab.

gab[2] *n informal* idle talk.

gabardine *n* see GABERDINE.

gabble[1] *v* to talk rapidly or unintelligibly; to jabber. ➤➤ **gabbler** *n.*

gabble[2] *n* rapid or unintelligible talk.

gabbro *n* (*pl* **-os**) a coarse-grained, dark-coloured igneous rock composed of a calcium-containing feldspar and iron and magnesium minerals. ➤➤ **gabbroic** *adj.*

gabby *adj* (**-ier, -iest**) *informal* talkative or garrulous.

gaberdine *or* **gabardine** *n* **1** a firm durable fabric, e.g. of wool or rayon, woven with diagonal ribs on the right side. **2** *chiefly Brit* a waterproof coat made of gaberdine.

gable *n* **1** the vertical triangular section of wall between two slopes of a pitched roof. **2** a triangular part used as a decoration over a window or door. ➤➤ **gabled** *adj.*

Gabonese *n* (*pl* **Gabonese**) a native or inhabitant of Gabon. ➤➤ **Gabonese** *adj.*

gad *v* (**gadded, gadding**) (+ about/around) to go or travel in an aimless or restless manner or in search of pleasure.

gadabout *n informal* a person who goes from place to place in search of pleasure.

Gadarene *adj* headlong or precipitate.

gadfly *n* (*pl* **-ies**) **1** a fly, e.g. a horsefly or botfly, that bites or annoys livestock. **2** an annoying person who provokes others, *esp* by persistent irritating criticism.

gadget *n* a usu small and often novel mechanical or electronic device. ➤➤ **gadgetry** *n.*

gadolinium *n* a silvery metallic chemical element of the rare-earth group.

gadroon *n* an elaborate convex moulding used in architecture and as a decoration on silverware. ➤➤ **gadrooning** *n.*

gadzooks *interj archaic* used as a mild oath.

Gael *n* a Gaelic-speaking inhabitant of Scotland or Ireland.

Gaelic *n* the Celtic languages of Ireland, the Isle of Man, and Scotland. ➤➤ **Gaelic** *adj.*

Gaelic coffee *n* = IRISH COFFEE.

gaff[1] *n* **1a** a pole with a hook for holding or landing heavy fish. **b** a spear or spearhead for killing fish or turtles. **2** a spar on which the head of a fore-and-aft sail is extended.

gaff[2] *v* to strike or secure (e.g. a fish) with a gaff.

gaff[3] *n Brit, informal* a house, flat, or other dwelling place.

gaff[4] ✱ **blow the gaff** see BLOW[1].

gaffe *n* a social or tactical blunder; a faux pas.

gaffer *n* **1** *Brit* the chief lighting electrician in a film or television studio. **2** *Brit, informal* a foreman or overseer. **3** *Brit, informal* an old man.

gag[1] *v* (**gagged, gagging**) **1** to put a gag in the mouth of (somebody) to prevent speech. **2** to prevent (somebody) from having free speech or expression. **3** to heave or retch.

gag[2] *n* **1** something thrust into the mouth to keep it open or prevent speech or outcry. **2** a joke or humorous story. **3** a check to free speech.

gaga *adj informal* **1** senile. **2** slightly mad.

gage[1] *n archaic* **1** a token of defiance; *specif* a glove, cap, etc thrown on the ground in former times as a challenge to a fight. **2** something deposited as a pledge of performance.

gage[2] *v archaic* to pledge (something) as a gage.

gage[3] *n NAm* see GAUGE[1].

gage[4] *v NAm* see GAUGE[2].

gage[5] *n* a greengage.

gaggle *n* **1** a flock of geese. **2** *informal* a typically noisy or talkative group or cluster.

Gaia *n* the earth and all living things on it considered as an organic whole, with the different parts interacting to promote survival and stability.

gaiety *n* (*pl* **-ies**) **1** the quality of being cheerful or merry. **2** merrymaking; festive activity.

gaijin /gie'jin/ *n* (*pl* **gaijin**) in Japan, a foreigner.

gaillardia *n* a plant of the daisy family with showy flowers that have a purple centre surrounded by yellow, reddish orange, or white.

gaily *adv* **1** cheerfully or merrily. **2** with bright colours.

gain[1] *v* **1** to get possession of or win (something good), usu by industry, merit, or craft. **2a** to increase a lead over or catch up a rival by (*esp* time or distance). **b** to get (something) by a natural development or process. **c** to acquire. **d** to arrive at (a place). **3** to increase in (e.g. speed). **4** to get advantage; to profit. **5** of a watch or clock: to run fast. ▶▶ **gainer** *n.*

gain[2] *n* **1** resources or advantage acquired or increased; a profit. **2** the obtaining of profit or possessions. **3** an increase in amount, magnitude, or degree.

gainful *adj* profitable. ▶▶ **gainfully** *adv.*

gainsay *v* (*third person sing. present* **gainsays,** *past tense and past part.* **gainsaid**) *formal* to deny or dispute (e.g. an allegation). ▶▶ **gainsayer** *n.*

gait *n* **1** a manner of walking or moving on foot. **2** a sequence of foot movements, e.g. a walk, trot, or canter, by which a horse moves forwards.

gaiter *n* (*usu in pl*) **1** a cloth or leather legging worn by men. **2** a climber's legging of tough nylon canvas for the lower leg and boot upper, for preventing snow from getting into the top of the boots.

gal *n informal* a girl.

gal. *abbr* see GALL..

gala *n* **1** a festive gathering, *esp* one that marks a special occasion. **2** *Brit* a special sports meeting. **3** (*used before a noun*) marking or being a special occasion: *a gala performance.*

galactic *adj* of a galaxy, *esp* the Milky Way galaxy.

galactic equator *n* the circle of the celestial sphere lying in the plane that bisects the band of the Milky Way.

galactose *n* a sugar that is less soluble and less sweet than glucose.

galago *n* (*pl* **-os**) = BUSH BABY.

galah *n* an Australian cockatoo with a rose-coloured breast and a grey back, kept as a cage bird but seen as a pest in wheat-growing areas.

galangal *or* **galingale** *n* a plant of the ginger family with an aromatic rhizome used in Asian cookery.

galantine *n* a cold dish of boned and usu stuffed cooked meat glazed with aspic.

Galatian *n* a native or inhabitant of Galatia, an ancient Roman province in Asia Minor. ▶▶ **Galatian** *adj.*

galaxy *n* (*pl* **-ies**) **1a** a system composed chiefly of stars, dust, and gas. **b** (**the Galaxy**) the Milky Way. **2** an assemblage of brilliant or notable people or things.

gale *n* **1** a strong wind. **2** a noisy outburst of laughter.

galena *n* lead sulphide occurring as a bluish grey mineral.

Galilean *adj* of or developed by the Italian physicist and astronomer Galileo Galilei (d.1642).

galingale *n* **1** a sedge with an aromatic root. **2** see GALANGAL.

gall[1] *n* **1** brazen and insolent audacity; impudence. **2a** *archaic* bile. **b** something bitter to endure. **c** rancour or bitterness.

gall[2] *n* **1** a cause or state of exasperation. **2** a skin sore caused by rubbing.

gall[3] *v* **1** to cause feelings of mortification and irritation in (somebody). **2** to wear (something) away by rubbing; to chafe.

gall[4] *n* a diseased swelling of plant tissue produced by infection with fungi, insect parasites, etc.

gall. *or* **gal.** *abbr* gallon(s).

gallant[1] *adj* **1** nobly chivalrous and brave. **2** courteously and elaborately attentive, *esp* to women. **3** *archaic* showy in dress. ▶▶ **gallantly** *adv.*

gallant[2] *n* a man of fashion who is particularly attentive to women.

gallantry *n* (*pl* **-ies**) **1** spirited and conspicuous bravery. **2** courteous attention to a lady. **3** (*in pl*) gallant words or actions.

gall bladder *n* a membranous muscular sac in which bile from the liver is stored.

galleon *n* a heavy square-rigged sailing ship of the 15th cent. to early 18th cent. used for war or commerce.

gallery *n* (*pl* **-ies**) **1** a room or building devoted to the exhibition of works of art. **2** a balcony projecting from one or more interior walls of a hall, auditorium, or church. **3** the occupants of a balcony, e.g. in a theatre. **4** the spectators at a golf or tennis tournament match. **5** a long and narrow passage, room, or corridor. **6** a horizontal subterranean passage in a cave or military mining system. ✱ **play to the gallery** to act in a way calculated to win popular support or approval. ▶▶ **galleried** *adj.*

galley *n* (*pl* **-eys**) **1** a large low usu single-decked ship propelled by oars and sails. **2** a kitchen on a ship or aircraft. **3** in printing, a proof in the form of a long sheet.

galley proof *n* = GALLEY (3).

galliard *n* a lively dance in triple time that was popular in the 16th cent.

Gallic *adj* of or characteristic of Gaul or France.

Gallicise *v* see GALLICIZE.

Gallicism *n* a characteristic French word or expression occurring in another language.

Gallicize *or* **-ise** *v* to cause (somebody or something) to conform to a French mode or idiom.

gallimaufry *n* (*pl* **-ies**) a medley or jumble.

galling *adj* markedly irritating or vexing; deeply mortifying.

gallium *n* a rare bluish white metallic chemical element that is soft and melts just above room temperature.

gallivant *v* to travel energetically or roam about for pleasure.

gallon *n* **1** a unit of liquid capacity equal to eight pints (about 4.546l). **2** a unit of liquid capacity in the USA equal to 0.83 imperial gallon (3.79l). **3** *informal (in pl)* large quantities.

gallop[1] *n* **1** a fast bounding gait of a quadruped; *specif* the fastest natural four-beat gait of the horse. **2** a ride or run at a gallop.

gallop[2] *v* (**galloped, galloping**) **1** to go or ride at a gallop. **2** to read, talk, or proceed at great speed. ▶▶ **galloper** *n.*

gallows *n* (*pl* **gallows** *or* **gallowses**) **1** a frame, usu of two upright posts and a crosspiece, for hanging criminals. **2** (**the gallows**) the punishment of hanging.

gallows humour *n* grim humour that makes fun of a very serious or terrifying situation.

gallstone *n* a rounded solid mass of cholesterol and calcium salts formed in the gall bladder or bile ducts.

Gallup poll *n* a survey of public opinion used as a means of forecasting something, e.g. an election result.

galore *adj* (*used after a noun*) abundant or plentiful: *bargains galore.*

galosh *n* a rubber overshoe.

galumph *v informal* to stride along or bound around with exuberant din.

galvanic *adj* **1** of, being, or producing a direct current of electricity resulting from chemical action. **2** having an electric effect; stimulating vigorous activity or vitality. ➤➤ **galvanically** *adv.*

galvanize *or* **-ise** *v* **1** to stimulate, rouse, or excite (somebody) as if by the action of an electric current. **2** to coat (iron or steel) with zinc as a protection from rust. ➤➤ **galvanization** *n,* **galvanizer** *n.*

galvanometer *n* an instrument for detecting or measuring a small electric current. ➤➤ **galvanometric** *adj.*

Gamay *n* a variety of grape used in the production of red wine, *esp* Beaujolais, or the wine produced from it.

Gambian *n* a native or inhabitant of Gambia. ➤➤ **Gambian** *adj.*

gambit *n* **1** a calculated move; a stratagem. **2** a remark intended to start a conversation or make a telling point. **3** a chess opening, *esp* one in which a player risks minor pieces to gain an advantage.

gamble[1] *v* **1a** to play a game of chance for money or property. **b** to bet or risk something on an uncertain outcome. **2** to take on a business risk with the expectation of gain; to speculate. **3** to risk (e.g. money) by gambling; to wager. ➤➤ **gambler** *n.*

gamble[2] *n* **1** something involving an element of risk. **2** an act of gambling.

gamboge *n* a gum resin from some SE Asian trees, used as a yellow pigment.

gambol[1] *v* (**gambolled, gambolling,** *NAm* **gamboled, gamboling**) to skip or leap about in play.

gambol[2] *n* a skipping or leaping about in play.

gambrel *n* **1** *Brit* a roof that has sloping ends and sides, and a ridge in a small vertical triangular gable at each end. **2** *NAm* a roof that has two sides with a double slope, with the lower slope steeper than the upper one.

game[1] *n* **1** an activity engaged in for diversion or amusement. **2** a physical or mental competition conducted according to rules with the participants in direct opposition to each other. **3** a division of a larger contest. **4** the number of points necessary to win a game. **5** (*often* **Games**) organized sports, *esp* athletics. **6** the equipment used for a particular game. **7** a computer game. **8a** a course or plan consisting of manoeuvres directed towards some end. **b** a specified type of activity seen as competitive or governed by rules, and pursued for financial gain. **9a** animals under pursuit or taken in hunting; *esp* wild mammals, birds, and fish. **b** the edible flesh of game animals, e.g. deer and pheasant. ✻ **on the game** *Brit, informal* working as a prostitute. **the game is up** the crime, plot, etc has been discovered or exposed.

game[2] *v* **1** to play for money; to gamble. **2** to play computer games. ➤➤ **gamer** *n.*

game[3] *adj* **1** ready to take risks or try something new. **2** having a resolute unyielding spirit. ➤➤ **gamely** *adv,* **gameness** *n.*

game[4] *adj* of somebody's leg: crippled or lame.

game fish *n* any fish sought by anglers for sport, e.g. salmon, trout, and whitefish.

gamekeeper *n* somebody who has charge of the breeding and protection of game animals or birds on a private estate.

gamelan *n* a flute, string, and percussion orchestra of SE Asia.

game plan *n* a strategy for winning a game or achieving an objective by a series of steps, e.g. in politics.

game point *n* a situation in tennis, badminton, etc in which one player or side will win the game by winning the next point.

game show *n* a television programme in which the participants play games for prizes.

gamesmanship *n* the art or practice of winning games by means other than superior skill without actually violating the rules.

gamester *n* somebody who plays games, *esp* a gambler.

gamete *n* a mature germ cell with a single set of chromosomes, capable of fusing with another gamete of the other sex to form a zygote from which a new organism develops. ➤➤ **gametic** *adj.*

game theory *n* the rigorous analysis of strategy, e.g. in a business or military situation, where there is a conflict of interest.

gametophyte *n* the haploid phase of a plant of a species that exhibits alternation of generations, e.g. a moss or fern, which develops from asexual spores and bears sex organs that produce the gametes.

gamey *adj* see GAMY.

gamine *n* a girl or woman having an elfin impish appeal. ➤➤ **gamine** *adj.*

gamma *n* the third letter of the Greek alphabet (Γ, γ), equivalent to roman g.

gamma globulin *n* any of several immunoglobulins in blood or serum including most antibodies.

gamma radiation *n* radiation composed of gamma rays.

gamma rays *pl n* streams of high-energy electromagnetic radiation that have a shorter wavelength than X-rays and are emitted in the radioactive decay of some unstable atomic nuclei.

gammon *n* **1** ham that has been smoked or cured. **2** the lower end of a side of bacon, removed from the carcass after curing with salt.

gammy *adj* (**-ier, -iest**) *Brit, informal* of somebody's leg: injured or lame.

gamut *n* **1** an entire range or series. **2** the whole series of recognized musical notes. ✻ **run the gamut** to go through the whole range of something.

Word history

late Latin *gamma ut*, lowest note in medieval scale of music, from *gamma*, applied to the lowest note G on the bass clef + *ut*, applied to the first note of a hexachord, the notes of which were named after syllables of a Latin hymn: Ut *queant laxis re*sonare *fibris Mi*ra *gestorum fa*muli *tuorum, Sol*ve *polluti la*bii *reatum, Sancte Johannes*. In the 18th cent. DOH replaced *ut*, SOH replaced *sol*, and another note, named *si* from the initials of *Sancte Johannes*, was added to the scale; *si* was later changed to TE to avoid having two notes with the same initial letter. In the 20th cent. *me* became a common spelling for MI[1], reflecting its pronunciation.

gamy *or* **gamey** *adj* (**-ier, -iest**) having the strong flavour or smell of game that has been hung until high. ➤➤ **gaminess** *n.*

gander[1] *n* an adult male goose.

gander[2] *n informal* a look or glance.

gang[1] *n* **1** a group of people associating for criminal or disreputable ends. **2** a group of people working together, e.g. as labourers. **3** a group of adolescents who spend leisure time together. **4** a series of switches or devices arranged to act together.

gang[2] *v* **1** (+ together) to move or act as a gang. **2** to assemble or operate (e.g. mechanical parts) simultaneously as a group.

gang[3] *v Scot* to go.

gang-bang *n coarse slang* **1** the rape of somebody by a succession of men on one occasion. **2** sexual intercourse involving several people; an orgy.

ganger *n Brit* the foreman of a gang of labourers.

ganglia *n* pl of GANGLION.

gangling *adj* tall, thin, and awkward in movement.

ganglion *n* (*pl* **ganglia** *or* **ganglions**) **1** a small cyst on a joint membrane or tendon sheath. **2** a mass of nerve cells outside the brain or spinal cord. ➤➤ **ganglionic** *adj.*

gangly *adj* = GANGLING.

gangplank *n* a movable board or plank used to board a ship from a quay or another ship.

gangrene[1] *n* death of soft tissues in a localized area of the body, due to loss of blood supply. ➤➤ **gangrenous** *adj.*

gangrene[2] *v* to become gangrenous.

gangsta *n NAm, slang* **1** a member of a black street gang. **2** a kind of rap music, often with lyrics about gang warfare and fighting.

gangster *n* a member of a criminal gang. ➤➤ **gangsterism** *n.*

gang up *v* (*often* + on/against) to combine as a group for a specific purpose, *esp* a disreputable one.

gangway[1] *n* **1** a passageway; *esp* a temporary way constructed from planks. **2a** the opening in a ship's side or rail through which the ship is boarded. **b** a gangplank. **3** *Brit* a narrow passage between sections of seats in a theatre, storage bays in a warehouse, etc.

gangway[2] *interj* used when trying to make one's way round an obstacle: make way!

ganja *n* cannabis.

gannet *n* **1** a large white fish-eating seabird, breeding in large colonies mainly on offshore islands. **2** *Brit, informal* a greedy person.

gantlet *n chiefly NAm* a gauntlet.

gantry *n* (*pl* **-ies**) a frame structure raised on side supports that spans over or round something and is used for railway signals, as a travelling crane, etc.

gaol *n and v Brit* see JAIL[1], JAIL[2].

gaoler *n* see JAILER.

gap *n* **1** a break in a barrier, e.g. a wall or hedge. **2** an empty space between two objects or two parts of an object. **3** a break in continuity; an interval. **4** a disparity or difference. **5a** a mountain pass. **b** a ravine. ➤➤ **gapped** *adj,* **gappy** *adj.*

gape[1] *v* **1a** to open the mouth wide. **b** to open or part widely. **2** to gaze stupidly or in openmouthed surprise or wonder. ➤➤ **gaping** *adj.*

gape[2] *n* **1** an act of gaping; *esp* an openmouthed stare. **2** the average width of the open mouth or beak.

gap year *n* a year's break that somebody takes between leaving school and starting further education.

gar *n* = GARFISH (2).

garage[1] *n* **1** a building for the shelter of motor vehicles. **2** an establishment for providing essential services, e.g. the supply of petrol or repair work to motor vehicles. **3** a style of house music with a soul influence.

garage[2] *v* to keep or put (a car) in a garage.

garage sale *n* a sale of secondhand furniture and household goods, held in the seller's garage or house.

garam masala /ˌgarəm məˈsahlə/ *n* an aromatic mixture of ground coriander, cumin, cinnamon, etc used *esp* in curries.

garb[1] *n* a style of clothing; dress.

garb[2] *v* to dress (somebody).

garbage *n* **1** *chiefly NAm* rubbish or waste. **2** worthless writing or speech. ✱ **garbage in, garbage out** *informal* invalid or poor data put in to a computer will produce equally poor output.

garble[1] *v* to distort or confuse (a message), giving a false impression of the facts. ➤➤ **garbler** *n.*

garble[2] *n* a garbled message.

garçon /gah'sonh/ *n* a waiter in a French restaurant.

garda *n* (*pl* **gardai**) **1** (*often* **Garda**) (*used as sing. or pl*) the Irish police. **2** a member of the garda.

garden[1] *n* **1** *Brit* a plot of ground where herbs, fruits, vegetables, or typically flowers are cultivated. **2** a public recreation area or park. **3** (*used before a noun*) found in, or suitable for, a garden. ✱ **lead somebody up the garden path** to mislead or deceive somebody.

garden[2] *v* to work in, cultivate, or lay out a garden. ➤➤ **gardener** *n.*

garden centre *n* an establishment selling equipment for gardens or gardening.

garden city *n* a planned town with spacious residential areas including public parks.

gardenia *n* an Old World tropical tree or shrub with showy fragrant white or yellow flowers.

garden party *n* a usu formal party held on the lawns of a garden.

garderobe *n* **1** a part of a medieval building used as a privy. **2** a wardrobe or private room in a medieval building.

garfish *n* (*pl* **garfishes** *or* **garfish**) **1** a fish of European and N Atlantic waters with a long body and elongated jaws. **2** *NAm* a similar freshwater fish.

garganey *n* (*pl* **garganeys** *or* **garganey**) a small European duck, the male of which has a broad white stripe over the eye.

gargantuan *adj* gigantic or colossal.

gargle[1] *v* to cleanse one's mouth or throat by blowing through a liquid held in the mouth.

gargle[2] *n* **1** a liquid used in gargling. **2** a bubbling liquid sound produced by gargling.

gargoyle *n* a spout in the form of a grotesque human or animal figure projecting from a roof gutter to throw rainwater clear of a building.

garibaldi *n* (*pl* **garibaldis**) *Brit* a biscuit with a layer of currants in it.

garish *adj* excessively and gaudily bright or vivid. ➤➤ **garishly** *adv,* **garishness** *n.*

garland[1] *n* **1** a wreath of flowers or leaves worn as an ornament or sign of distinction. **2** *archaic* an anthology of verse or prose.

garland[2] *v* to crown or deck with a garland.

garlic *n* the pungent compound bulb of a plant of the lily family, used as a flavouring in cookery. ➤➤ **garlicky** *adj.*

garment *n* an article of clothing.

garner[1] *n archaic* a granary or grain bin.

garner[2] *v* **1** to collect (e.g. evidence or information). **2** *archaic* to gather or store (e.g. grain).

garnet *n* a hard brittle silicate mineral used as an abrasive, and in its transparent deep red form as a gem.

garnish[1] *v* **1** to decorate or embellish (*esp* food). **2** in law, to serve (somebody) with a garnishment.

garnish[2] *n* an embellishment, *esp* an edible savoury or decorative addition to a dish.

garnishment *n* a judicial warning to a debtor not to pay his or her debt to anyone other than the appropriate third party.

garotte *n and v NAm* see GARROTTE[1], GARROTTE[2].

garret *n* a small room just under the roof of a house.

garrison[1] *n* **1** a body of troops stationed in a fortified town or place to defend it. **2** a town or place in which troops are stationed.

garrison[2] *v* to station troops in (a place).

garrotte[1] (*NAm* **garotte** *or* **garrote**) *n* an iron collar or a wire or cord used for strangling somebody.

garrotte[2] (*NAm* **garotte** *or* **garrote**) *v* to execute or kill with a garrotte.

garrulous *adj* excessively talkative. ➤➤ **garrulity** *n,* **garrulously** *adv,* **garrulousness** *n.*

garter *n* **1** a band worn to hold up a stocking or sock. **2** *NAm* = SUSPENDER (1). ➤➤ **gartered** *adj.*

garter snake *n* **1** a harmless longitudinally striped American snake. **2** a venomous African snake.

garter stitch *n* the ribbed pattern formed by using only a plain knit stitch.

garth *n* **1** the open space bounded by a cloister. **2** *archaic* a small yard or enclosure.

gas[1] *n* (*pl* **gases** *or* **gasses**) **1** a fluid substance, e.g. air, that has neither independent shape nor volume and tends to expand indefinitely. **2a** a gas or gaseous mixture used to produce general anaesthesia, as a fuel, etc. **b** a substance, e.g. tear gas or mustard gas, that can be used to produce a poisonous, asphyxiating, or irritant atmosphere. **3** *NAm, informal* petrol. **4** *informal* an enjoyable or amusing person or thing. **5** *NAm* flatulence.

gas[2] *v* (**gassed, gassing**) **1** to poison or otherwise affect (a person or animal) adversely with gas. **2** *NAm, informal* (+ up) to fill the tank of (a motor vehicle) with petrol. **3** *informal* to talk idly.

gasbag *n informal* an idle talker.

gas chamber *n* a chamber in which prisoners are executed or animals killed by poison gas.

Gascon *n* a native or inhabitant of Gascony in France. ➤➤ **Gascon** *adj.*

gaseous *adj* having the form or nature of a gas. ➤➤ **gaseousness** *n.*

gash[1] *v* to injure with a deep long cut or cleft.

gash[2] *n* a deep long cut, *esp* in flesh.

gasify *v* (**-ies, -ied**) **1** to change (a solid or liquid) into gas. **2** to become a gas. ➤➤ **gasification** *n.*

gasket *n* a specially shaped piece of sealing material for ensuring that a joint does not leak liquid or gas.

gaslight *n* light from a gas flame or gas lighting fixture. ➤➤ **gaslit** *adj.*

gas mask *n* a mask connected to a chemical air filter and used as a protection against noxious fumes or gases.

gasoline *or* **gasolene** *n NAm* petrol.

gasometer *n* a large cylindrical storage container for gas.

gasp[1] *v* **1** to catch the breath suddenly and audibly, e.g. with shock. **2** to breathe laboriously. **3** (+ for) to crave.

gasp[2] *n* an audible catching of the breath.

gas-permeable *adj* of a contact lens: allowing oxygen to reach the surface of the eye.

gassy *adj* (**-ier, -iest**) **1** full of, containing, or like gas. **2** *informal* full of boastful or insincere talk. ➤➤ **gassiness** *n.*

gasteropod *n* = GASTROPOD.

gastrectomy *n* (*pl* **-ies**) surgical removal of all or part of the stomach.

gastric *adj* relating to or in the region of the stomach.

gastric flu *n* a disorder of the stomach or intestinal tract, causing nausea and diarrhoea.

gastric juice *n* a thin acidic digestive liquid secreted by glands in the lining of the stomach.

gastritis *n* inflammation of the membrane lining the stomach.

gastroenteritis *n* inflammation of the lining of the stomach and the intestines, usu causing painful diarrhoea.

gastroenterology *n* the study of the diseases and abnormalities of the stomach and intestines. ➤➤ **gastroenterological** *adj,* **gastroenterologist** *n.*

gastrointestinal *adj* relating to or in the region of both the stomach and intestine.

gastronome *n* an epicure or gourmet.

gastronomy *n* the art or science of good eating. ➤➤ **gastronomic** *adj.*

gastropod *n* any of a large class of molluscs including the snails, usu with a distinct head bearing sensory organs.

gastroscope *n* an instrument for looking at the interior of the stomach. ➤➤ **gastroscopic** *adj,* **gastroscopy** *n.*

gas turbine *n* an internal-combustion engine in which turbine blades are driven by hot gases, the pressure and velocity of which are intensified by compressed air introduced into the combustion chamber.

gasworks *n* (*pl* **gasworks**) (*used as sing.*) a plant for manufacturing gas.

gat *v archaic* past tense of GET.

gate[1] *n* **1** the usu hinged frame or door that closes an opening in a wall or fence. **2** a city or castle entrance, often with defensive structures. **3a** a numbered exit from an airport building to the airfield. **b** either of a pair of barriers that let water in and out of a lock or close a road at a level crossing. **4** an electronic device, e.g. in a computer, that produces a defined output for every combination of input conditions. **5** the number of spectators at a sporting event. ➤➤ **gated** *adj.*

gate[2] *v Brit* to punish (a student) by confinement to the premises of a school or college.

gateau *n* (*pl* **gateaux** *or* **gateaus**) a rich often filled elaborate cream cake.

gate-crash *v* to enter or attend (a party) without a ticket or invitation. ➤➤ **gate-crasher** *n.*

gatefold *n* a large folded page inserted in a book, journal, etc; *esp* one with a single fold.

gatehouse *n* **1** a structure above or beside a gate, e.g. of a city wall or castle, often used in former times as a guardroom or prison. **2** a lodge at the entrance to the grounds of a large house.

gatekeeper *n* somebody who guards a gate.

gateleg table *n* a table with drop leaves supported by two movable legs.

gatepost *n* the post on which a gate is hung or against which it closes.

gateway *n* **1** an opening for a gate. **2** in computing, a piece of hardware or software used to connect networks. **3** a point of entry or access.

gather[1] *v* **1** to bring (things) together; to collect. **2** to come together in a body. **3** to pick or harvest (flowers, crops, etc). **4a** to summon up (e.g. nerves or courage). **b** to accumulate (speed). **c** to prepare (e.g. oneself) for an effort. **5a** to clasp (somebody), e.g. to oneself, in an embrace. **b** to pull (fabric) together, *esp* along a line of stitching, to create small tucks. **6** to reach a conclusion intuitively from hints or through inferences. ▸▸ **gatherer** *n.*

gather² *n* something gathered; *esp* a tuck in cloth made by gathering.

gathering *n* an assembly or meeting.

Gatling gun *n* an early machine gun with a revolving cluster of barrels fired once each per revolution.

GATT *abbr* General Agreement on Tariffs and Trade.

gauche *adj* lacking social experience or grace. ▸▸ **gauchely** *adv,* **gaucheness** *n.*

gaucherie *n* tactless or awkward manner or behaviour, or an instance of this.

gaucho *n* (*pl* **-os**) a cowboy of the pampas regions in S America.

gaudy¹ *adj* (**-ier, -iest**) ostentatiously or tastelessly and brightly ornamented. ▸▸ **gaudily** *adv,* **gaudiness** *n.*

gaudy² *n* (*pl* **-ies**) *Brit* a feast, *esp* a dinner for ex-students, in some universities.

gauge¹ (*NAm* **gage**) *n* **1** an instrument for measuring or testing something, e.g. a dimension or quantity. **2a** the thickness of a thin sheet of metal, plastic, film, etc. **b** the diameter of wire, a hypodermic needle, a screw, etc. **3** a measure of the size of the bore of a shotgun. **4** the distance between the rails of a railway, wheels on an axle, etc.

gauge² (*NAm* **gage**) *v* **1** to measure exactly the size, dimensions, capacity, or contents of. **2** to estimate or judge (something). **3** to check (something) for conformity to specifications or limits. ▸▸ **gaugeable** *adj,* **gauger** *n.*

Gaul *n* a native or inhabitant of ancient Gaul.

Gauleiter /'gowlietə/ *n* **1** an official in charge of a district in Nazi Germany. **2** (*also* **gauleiter**) an arrogant henchman or subordinate.

Gaulish *n* the Celtic language of the ancient Gauls. ▸▸ **Gaulish** *adj.*

Gaullism *n* the political principles and policies of the French political leader Charles de Gaulle (d.1970). ▸▸ **Gaullist** *adj and n.*

gaunt *adj* **1** excessively thin and angular, *esp* from hunger or suffering. **2** of a place: barren or desolate. ▸▸ **gauntly** *adv,* **gauntness** *n.*

gauntlet¹ *n* **1** a strong protective glove with a wide extension above the wrist, used *esp* for sports and in industry. **2** a glove formerly worn with medieval armour. ✱ **take up the gauntlet** to accept a challenge. **throw down the gauntlet** to issue a challenge.

gauntlet² *n* **1** a double file of men armed with weapons with which to strike at somebody made to run between them, used formerly as a military punishment. **2** criticism or an ordeal or test. ✱ **run the gauntlet 1** to have to suffer criticism or a testing experience. **2** formerly, to have to run through a gauntlet as a punishment.

gauss *n* (*pl* **gauss** *or* **gausses**) a unit of magnetic induction equal to 10^{-4} tesla.

gauze *n* **1** a thin often transparent fabric used chiefly for clothing or draperies. **2** a loosely woven cotton surgical dressing. **3** a fine mesh of metal or plastic filaments. ▸▸ **gauzy** *adj.*

gave *v* past tense of GIVE¹.

gavel *n* a small mallet with which a chairman, judge, or auctioneer commands attention or confirms a vote, sale, etc.

gavial *n* a large Indian crocodile.

gavotte *n* an 18th-cent. dance in which the feet are raised rather than slid.

gawk¹ *v* to gawp. ▸▸ **gawker** *n.*

gawk² *n* a clumsy awkward person. ▸▸ **gawkish** *adj.*

gawky *adj* (**-ier, -iest**) awkward and lanky. ▸▸ **gawkily** *adv,* **gawkiness** *n.*

gawp *v Brit, informal* to gape or stare stupidly. ▸▸ **gawper** *n.*

gay¹ *adj* **1** homosexual. **2** for or relating to homosexuals. **3** *dated* bright or attractive. **4** *dated* happily excited; carefree. ▸▸ **gayness** *n.*

Usage note

The primary meaning of *gay* in contemporary English is 'homosexual'. Before the 1960s, in standard usage, *gay* was an adjective meaning 'cheerful' or 'bright'. These senses are still sometimes used, but care should be taken when using the word with these meanings to avoid misunderstanding.

gay² *n* a homosexual; *esp* a man.

gaze¹ *v* to fix the eyes in a steady and intent look. ▸▸ **gazer** *n.*

gaze² *n* a fixed intent look.

gazebo *n* (*pl* **-os** *or* **-oes**) a freestanding structure, e.g. a summerhouse, placed to command a view.

gazelle *n* (*pl* **gazelles** *or* **gazelle**) a small, graceful, and swift antelope noted for its soft lustrous eyes.

gazette¹ *n* a newspaper or journal, *esp* an official one.

gazette² *v Brit* to publish or report (news, military appointments, etc) in an official gazette.

gazetteer *n* a dictionary of place names.

gazpacho *n* (*pl* **-os**) a Spanish cold soup containing tomatoes, olive oil, garlic, and peppers.

gazump *v Brit* to thwart (a would-be house purchaser) by raising the price after agreeing to sell at a certain price. ▸▸ **gazumper** *n.*

GB *abbr* **1** (*also* **Gb**) gigabyte(s). **2** Great Britain.

GBE *abbr* Knight or Dame Grand Cross of the Order of the British Empire.

GBH *abbr Brit* grievous bodily harm.

GC *abbr* George Cross.

GCB *abbr Brit* Knight or Dame Grand Cross of the Order of the Bath.

GCHQ *abbr Brit* Government Communications Headquarters.

GCMG *abbr Brit* Knight or Dame Grand Cross of the Order of St Michael and St George.

GCSE *abbr Brit* General Certificate of Secondary Education.

GCVO *abbr Brit* Knight or Dame Grand Cross of the Royal Victorian Order.

Gd *abbr* the chemical symbol for gadolinium.

GDP *abbr* gross domestic product.

GDR *abbr* German Democratic Republic.

Ge *abbr* the chemical symbol for germanium.

gean *n* a wild sweet cherry.

gear¹ *n* **1** a toothed wheel that is one of a set of interlocking wheels. **2a** any of two or more adjustments of a transmission, e.g. of a bicycle or motor vehicle, that determine direction of travel or ratio of engine speed to vehicle speed. **b** working relation, position, or adjustment. **3** a mechanism that performs a specific function in a complete machine. **4** a set of equipment usu for a particular purpose. **5** *informal* clothing.

gear² *v* **1** to provide (machinery) with gears or connect it by gearing. **2** (+ to) to adjust (something) so as to match, blend with, or satisfy something. **3** of machinery: to be in or come into gear.

gearbox *n* a protective casing enclosing a set of *esp* car gears, or the gears so enclosed.

gear lever *n* a control, *esp* a rod, on a gear-changing mechanism, e.g. a gearbox, used to engage the different gears.

gearshift *n NAm* = GEAR LEVER.

gearstick *n* = GEAR LEVER.

gear up *v* **1** to make (something) ready for effective operation. **2** to put (e.g. oneself) into a state of anxious excitement or nervous anticipation.

gearwheel *n* a toothed wheel that engages another piece of a mechanism; a cogwheel.

gecko *n* (*pl* **-os** *or* **-oes**) a small chiefly tropical lizard able to walk on vertical or overhanging surfaces.

gee *interj NAm, informal* used as an exclamation of surprise or enthusiasm.

gee-gee *n Brit, informal* used by or to children: a horse.

geek *n informal* **1** somebody who is unfashionable or socially awkward. **2** somebody who is obsessively interested in computers and technology. ➤➤ **geeky** *adj.*

geek chic *n informal* = TECHNO-CLOTHING.

geese *n* pl of GOOSE[1].

gee up *v informal* **1** to stir (somebody) to greater activity. **2** to encourage (e.g. a horse) to go faster.

gee-up *interj* used as a direction, *esp* to a horse: move ahead; go faster.

gee whiz *interj chiefly NAm, informal* gee.

geezer *n informal* a man.

gefilte fish /gə'filtə/ *n* a dish consisting of fish, breadcrumbs, eggs, and seasoning shaped into balls or ovals and boiled in a fish stock.

Geiger counter *n* an electronic instrument for detecting the presence and intensity of ionizing radiations, e.g. particles from a radioactive substance.

geisha /'gayshə/ *n* (*pl* **geisha** *or* **geishas**) a Japanese girl who is trained to provide entertaining and light-hearted company, *esp* for a man or a group of men.

gel[1] *n* **1** a jelly-like substance, e.g. a hair gel or shaving gel. **2** a COLLOID (non-crystalline substance) composed of a liquid evenly dispersed in a solid.

gel[2] *v* (**gelled, gelling**) **1** to change into a gel; to set. **2** (*NAm* **jell**) of an idea, plan, etc: to take shape or become definite. **3** (*NAm* **jell**) of a group of people: to get on well together. **4** to put gel on (the hair).

gelatin *or* **gelatine** *n* a glutinous material obtained from animal tissues by boiling; *esp* a protein used in food, e.g. to set jellies, and photography.

gelatinize *or* **-ise** *v* **1** to convert (a substance) into a jelly or jelly-like form. **2** to coat or treat with gelatine. **3** to become jelly-like in consistency or change into a jelly. ➤➤ **gelatinization** *n.*

gelatinous *adj* resembling gelatin or jelly, *esp* in consistency; viscous.

geld *v* to castrate (a male animal).

gelding *n* a castrated male horse.

gelid *adj* extremely cold; icy.

gelignite *n* a dynamite in which the adsorbent base is a mixture of potassium or sodium nitrate usu with wood pulp.

gem *n* **1** a precious or sometimes semiprecious stone, *esp* when cut and polished for use in jewellery. **2** somebody or something highly prized or much beloved.

Gemini *n* **1** in astronomy, a constellation (the Twins) depicted as the twins Castor and Pollux. **2** in astrology, the third sign of the zodiac or a person born under this sign. ➤➤ **Geminian** *adj and n.*

gemsbok *n* (*pl* **gemsboks** *or* **gemsbok**) a large and strikingly marked oryx with long straight horns, formerly abundant in southern Africa.

gemstone *n* a mineral or petrified material used as a gem.

gen *n Brit, informal* the correct or complete information.

-gen *comb. form* forming nouns, denoting: something that produces something: *carcinogen.*

gendarme /'zhondahm/ *n* a member of a corps of armed police, *esp* in France.

gendarmerie *or* **gendarmery** /'zhondahməri, zhon'dah-/ *n* (*used as sing. or pl*) a body of gendarmes, or their headquarters.

gender *n* **1a** a system of subdivision within a grammatical class of a language, e.g. noun or verb, partly based on sexual characteristics, that determines agreement with and selection of other words or grammatical forms. **b** a subclass within such a system. **2** sex; the state of being male or female. ➤➤ **gendered** *adj.*

Usage note

gender *and* **sex**. Efforts have been made in recent years to enforce a distinction between *gender* and *sex*, using *gender* to refer to femaleness or maleness in cultural, social, and linguistic contexts and *sex* in biological ones.

gendering *n* the discriminatory use of different standards in assessing men and women in similar activities.

gene *n* a unit of inheritance that is carried on a chromosome, controls transmission of hereditary characters, and consists of DNA or, in some viruses, RNA.

genealogy *n* (*pl* **-ies**) **1** the descent of a person, family, or group from an ancestor or from older forms. **2** the study of family pedigrees. ➤➤ **genealogical** *adj,* **genealogist** *n.*

gene pool *n* the whole body of genes in an interbreeding population.

genera *n* pl of GENUS.

general[1] *adj* **1** of, involving, or applicable to every member of a class, kind, or group. **2a** applicable to or characteristic of the majority of individuals involved; prevalent. **b** concerned or dealing with universal rather than particular aspects. **3** holding superior rank or taking precedence over others similarly titled: *the general manager.* ✱ **in general** usually; for the most part.

general[2] *n* an officer in the British and US armies and the US air force ranking below a field marshal, general of the army, or general of the air force.

general anaesthetic *n* an anaesthetic that causes loss of consciousness and lack of sensation over the whole body.

general election *n* an election in which candidates are elected in all constituencies of a nation or state.

generalise *v* see GENERALIZE.

generalissimo *n* (*pl* **-os**) the supreme commander of several armies acting together or of a nation's armed forces.

generalist *n* somebody whose skills, interests, etc extend to several different fields or activities.

generality *n* (*pl* **-ies**) **1** a generalization. **2** total applicability. **3** the quality or state of being general. **4** (**the generality**) the greatest part; the majority.

generalize *or* **-ise** *v* **1** to make vague or indefinite statements that do not take adequate account of the facts. **2** to make (something) more general or widespread. **3** to derive or induce (a general conception or principle) from particulars; to infer. ⋙ **generalizable** *adj*, **generalization** *n*, **generalizer** *n*.

generally *adv* **1** without regard to specific instances. **2** usually; as a rule. **3** collectively; as a whole.

general practitioner *n* a medical doctor who treats all types of disease and is usu the first doctor consulted by a patient. ⋙ **general practice** *n*.

general-purpose *adj* suitable to be used for two or more basic purposes.

general staff *n* (*used as sing. or pl*) a group of officers who aid a commander.

general strike *n* a strike in all or many of the industries of a region or country.

generate *v* **1** to bring (something) into existence. **2** to originate (e.g. energy) by a physical process. **3** to be the cause of (a situation, action, or state of mind): *The stories generated a good deal of suspense.* ⋙ **generable** *adj*.

generation *n* **1a** (*used as sing. or pl*) a group of individuals born and living at the same time. **b** a group of living organisms constituting a single step in the line of descent from an ancestor. **c** a type or class of objects usu developed from an earlier type. **2** the average time between the birth of parents and that of their offspring, usu considered to be about 30 years. **3a** the producing of offspring; procreation. **b** the process of coming or bringing into being; production or origination. ⋙ **generational** *adj*.

generation gap *n* the difference in ideas and interests between older and younger people, *esp* considered as causing a mutual lack of understanding.

generation X *n* the generation of people who were born between the mid 1960s and the mid 1970s, seen as being well-educated but having no direction in life.

generative *adj* having the power or function of generating, producing, reproducing, etc.

generator *n* **1** a machine by which mechanical energy is changed into electrical energy. **2** an apparatus for producing a vapour or gas. **3** a person or thing that generates.

generic *adj* **1** characteristic of or applied to a whole group or class; general. **2** not having a trademark. **3** having the rank of a biological genus. ⋙ **generically** *adv*.

generous *adj* **1** liberal in giving e.g. money or help. **2** magnanimous and kindly. **3** marked by abundance, ample proportions, or richness. ⋙ **generosity** *n*, **generously** *adv*.

geneses *n* pl of GENESIS.

Genesis *n* the first book of the Old Testament.

genesis *n* (*pl* **geneses**) the origin or coming into being of something.

gene therapy *n* the correction of genetic defects by the replacement or supplementation of affected cells with genetically corrected cells, or with normal genes.

genetic *adj* **1a** of or involving genetics. **b** of or involving genes. **2** of or determined by the origin or development of something. ⋙ **genetical** *adj*, **genetically** *adv*.

genetically modified *adj* of food: containing an ingredient that has had its genetic structure modified, e.g. to make it grow better or have greater resistance to pests.

genetic code *n* the triplet sequences of bases in DNA or RNA strands that form the biochemical basis of heredity and determine the specific amino acid sequences in proteins.

genetic counselling *n* advice given to prospective parents about the chances of their conceiving children with hereditary disorders.

genetic engineering *n* the artificial manipulation of the genetic constitution of living things for experimental or industrial purposes.

genetic fingerprint *n* a unique pattern of repeated DNA sequences in the genetic make-up of an individual that can be used to identify that individual. ⋙ **genetic fingerprinting** *n*.

genetic map *n* the arrangement of genes on a chromosome.

genetics *pl n* **1** (*used as sing.*) a branch of biology that deals with the mechanisms and structures involved in the heredity and variation of organisms. **2** (*used as sing. or pl*) the genetic make-up of an organism, type, or condition. ⋙ **geneticist** *n*.

genial *adj* **1** cheerfully good-tempered; kindly. **2** *literary* of the weather: mild. ⋙ **geniality** *n*, **genially** *adv*.

-genic *comb. form* forming adjectives, with the meanings: **1** producing or produced by: *pathogenic; allergenic*. **2** well-suited to or suitable for: *photogenic*.

genie *n* (*pl* **genies** *or* **genii**) a jinn or spirit in stories who can be summoned to grant wishes.

genii *n* **1** pl of GENIE. **2** pl of GENIUS.

genital *adj* **1** relating to or in the region of the genitalia. **2** in psychoanalysis, of or characterized by the final stage of sexual development in which oral and anal impulses are replaced by gratification obtained from sexual relationships: compare ANAL, ORAL[1]. ⋙ **genitally** *adv*.

genitalia *pl n* the external reproductive and sexual organs.

genitals *pl n* the genitalia.

genitive[1] *adj* denoting a grammatical case expressing a relationship of possessor or source.

genitive[2] *n* the genitive case or a word in this case.

genitourinary *adj* to do with the genital and urinary organs.

genius *n* (*pl* **geniuses**) **1** a person endowed with extraordinary intellectual power; *specif* a person of a very high intelligence. **2** extraordinary intellectual power, *esp* as displayed in creative activity. **3** (*pl* **genii**) a spirit, *esp* in Arabic folklore. **4** a special, distinctive, or identifying character or spirit.

genoa *n* a large jib which partly overlaps a ship's mainsail.

genocide *n* the deliberate murder of a racial or cultural group. ⋙ **genocidal** *adj*.

genome *n* **1** the complete single or basic set of chromosomes characteristic of a particular kind of organism. **2** a single set of an organism's chromosomes with the genes they contain. ⋙ **genomic** *adj*.

genotype *n* the genetic constitution of an individual or group: compare PHENOTYPE. ⋙ **genotypic** *adj*.

-genous *comb. form* forming adjectives, with the meanings: **1** producing or yielding: *erogenous*. **2** produced by or originating in: *endogenous*.

genre *n* a category of artistic, musical, or literary composition characterized by a particular style or content.

genre painting *n* painting that depicts scenes or events from everyday life.

gent *n* *informal* a gentleman.

genteel *adj* **1** of or appropriate to the status or manners of the gentry or upper class. **2** polite. ⋙ **genteelly** *adv.*

gentian *n* a plant with smooth leaves and showy usu blue flowers found *esp* in mountainous regions.

gentian violet *n* a violet dye used as a biological stain and as a skin disinfectant in the treatment of boils, ulcers, etc.

gentile[1] *n* (*often* **Gentile**) a person of a non-Jewish nation or of non-Jewish faith.

gentile[2] *adj* (*often* **Gentile**) of the nations at large as distinguished from the Jews.

gentility *n* **1** genteel attitudes, behaviour, or activity. **2** superior social status or prestige indicated by manners, possessions, etc.

gentle *adj* (**gentler, gentlest**) **1** of a person: kind and mild; not harsh or violent. **2** soft or delicate. **3** of a breeze: moderate. **4** of a slope: gradual. **5** *archaic* honourable, distinguished. ⋙ **gentleness** *n,* **gently** *adv.*

gentlefolk *or* **gentlefolks** *pl n archaic* people of good family and breeding.

gentleman *n* (*pl* **gentlemen**) **1a** a man who is chivalrous and honourable. **b** a man belonging to the landed gentry or nobility. **2** in polite or formal reference: a man. ⋙ **gentlemanly** *adj.*

gentleman's agreement *n* an unwritten agreement that is secured only by the honour of the participants and is not legally enforceable.

gentlewoman *n* (*pl* **gentlewomen**) *archaic* a woman of noble or gentle birth.

gentrification *n* the purchase and renovation, by middle-class people, of urban and run-down properties that are traditionally inhabited by working-class people.

gentrify *v* (**-ies, -ied**) to change (a property or area) by gentrification. ⋙ **gentrifier** *n.*

gentry *n* (*used as sing. or pl*) the upper class, or those regarded as constituting it in local society.

gents *n* (*pl* **gents**) *Brit, informal* a public lavatory for men.

genuflect *v* to bend the knee, *esp* in worship or as a gesture of respect to sacred objects. ⋙ **genuflection** *n.*

genuine *adj* **1** actually produced by or proceeding from the alleged source or author or having the reputed qualities or character. **2** free from pretence; sincere. ⋙ **genuinely** *adv,* **genuineness** *n.*

gen up *v* (**genned, genning**) *Brit, informal* (+ on) to find information; to learn about something.

genus *n* (*pl* **genera**) **1** a category in the classification of living things ranking between family and species. **2** a class divided into several subordinate classes.

-geny *comb. form* forming nouns, denoting: origin, development, or mode of production: *ontogeny.*

geo- *comb. form* **1** earth, or the earth's surface: *geodesic.* **2** geographical; geography and: *geopolitics.*

geocentric *adj* **1** having or relating to the earth as centre: compare HELIOCENTRIC. **2** measured from or observed as if from the earth's centre.

geochemistry *n* the study of the chemical composition of and chemical changes in the crust of the earth. ⋙ **geochemical** *adj,* **geochemist** *n.*

geode *n* **1** a cavity lined with crystals or mineral matter. **2** a rounded stone having such a cavity.

geodesic[1] *adj* **1** made of light straight structural elements mostly in tension. **2** geodetic.

geodesic[2] *n* the shortest line on a given surface between two points.

geodesy *n* a branch of applied mathematics that determines the exact positions of points and the shape and area of large portions of the earth's surface. ⋙ **geodesist** *n.*

geodetic[1] *adj* **1** of or determined by geodesy. **2** relating to the geometry of geodetic lines.

geodetic[2] *n* a geodesic on the earth's surface.

geodetic line *n* = GEODETIC[2].

geographical *adj* to do with geography. ⋙ **geographic** *adj,* **geographically** *adv.*

geographical mile *n* a nautical mile (1853.2m).

geography *n* **1** a science that deals with the earth and its life; *esp* the description of land, sea, air, and the distribution of plant and animal life including human beings and their industries. **2** the geographical features of an area. ⋙ **geographer** *n.*

geology *n* **1** a science that deals with the origin, structure, composition, and history of the earth, *esp* as recorded in rocks. **2** the geological features of an area. ⋙ **geologic** *adj,* **geological** *adj,* **geologically** *adv,* **geologist** *n.*

geomagnetism *n* **1** the magnetic field of the earth. **2** the branch of geology that deals with this. ⋙ **geomagnetic** *adj.*

geomancy *n* **1** divination by means of configurations of earth or by dots jotted down hastily at random. **2** the supposed discovery and mystical interpretation of the disposition and alignment of prominent landscape features and sacred sites. ⋙ **geomantic** *adj.*

geometric *adj* **1a** of or according to geometry or its laws. **b** increasing in a geometric progression. **2** using, being, or decorated with patterns formed from straight and curved lines. ⋙ **geometrical** *adj,* **geometrically** *adv.*

geometric mean *n* the nth root of the product of n numbers, e.g. the square root of two numbers.

geometric progression *n* a sequence, e.g. one, ½, ¼, in which the ratio of any term to its predecessor is constant.

geometry *n* (*pl* **-ies**) **1a** a branch of mathematics that deals with the measurement, properties, and relationships of points, lines, angles, surfaces, and solids. **b** a particular type or system of geometry. **2** a surface shape, e.g. of a crystal. **3** an arrangement of objects or parts that suggests geometrical figures. ⋙ **geometrician** *n.*

geomorphology *n* the geology of the structure and formation of the features of the surface of the earth. ⋙ **geomorphological** *adj,* **geomorphologist** *n.*

geophysics *pl n* (*used as sing.*) the physics of the earth including meteorology, oceanography, seismology, etc. ⋙ **geophysical** *adj,* **geophysicist** *n.*

geopolitics *pl n* (*used as sing.*) the study of the influence of geography, economics, and demography on politics. ⋙ **geopolitical** *adj.*

Geordie *n Brit, informal* a native or inhabitant of Tyneside.

georgette *n* a thin strong crepe fabric of silk or of other material with a dull pebbly surface.

Georgian[1] *adj* of the reigns of the first four King Georges of Britain (1714–1830).

Georgian[2] *n* **1** a native or inhabitant of Georgia in the Caucasus. **2** the national language of Georgia. ⋙ **Georgian** *adj.*

geostationary *adj* of an artificial satellite: travelling above the equator at the same speed as the earth rotates, so remaining above the same place.

geosynchronous *adj* = GEOSTATIONARY.

geothermal *adj* of or produced by the heat of the earth's interior.

geranium *n* **1** a plant with radially symmetrical pinkish to blue flowers. **2** a pelargonium.

gerbera *n* a plant of the daisy family, with tufted leaves and showy yellow, pink, or orange flowers.

gerbil *n* an African or Asian burrowing desert rodent with long hind legs adapted for leaping.

geriatric[1] *adj* **1** of or for geriatrics, the aged, or the process of ageing. **2** *informal, derog* aged or decrepit.

geriatric[2] *n* an elderly person.

geriatrics *pl n* (*used as sing. or pl*) a branch of medicine that deals with old age and the diseases associated with old age. ➤➤ **geriatrician** *n.*

germ *n* **1** a micro-organism, *esp* one that causes disease. **2** a small mass of cells capable of developing into an organism or one of its points. **3** the embryo of a cereal grain that is usu separated from the starchy endosperm during milling. **4** the rudimentary state from which something develops.

German *n* **1** a native or inhabitant of Germany. **2** the language of Germany, Austria, and parts of Switzerland. ➤➤ **German** *adj.*

germane *adj* relevant and appropriate.

Germanic[1] *adj* **1** relating to Germanic. **2** characteristic of the Germanic-speaking peoples. **3** characteristic of the German people.

Germanic[2] *n* **1** a branch of the Indo-European language family containing English, German, Dutch, Afrikaans, Flemish, Frisian, the Scandinavian languages, and Gothic. **2** Proto-Germanic, the unrecorded early language from which these languages developed.

germanium *n* a greyish white metalloid chemical element that resembles silicon, occurs naturally in sulphide ores, and is used as a semiconductor.

German measles *pl n* (*used as sing.*) = RUBELLA.

German shepherd *n* = ALSATIAN (1).

German silver *n* = NICKEL SILVER.

germ cell *n* an egg or sperm cell, or any of the cells from which they develop.

germicide *n* a substance that kills germs. ➤➤ **germicidal** *adj.*

germinal *adj* **1** of or having the characteristics of a germ cell or early embryo. **2a** in the earliest stage of development. **b** creative or seminal.

germinate *v* **1** to begin to grow; to sprout. **2** to come into being; to evolve. ➤➤ **germination** *n.*

germ warfare *n* the use of germs to spread disease as a form of warfare.

gerontocracy *n* (*pl* **-ies**) **1** a society in which a group of old men or a council of elders dominates or exercises control. **2** rule by old men. ➤➤ **gerontocratic** *adj.*

gerontology *n* the biology and medicine of ageing and the problems of the aged. ➤➤ **gerontological** *adj,* **gerontologist** *n.*

gerrymander *v* to divide (an area) into election districts to give one political party an electoral advantage.

Word history

named after Elbridge *Gerry* d.1814, US statesman + SALAMANDER; from the shape of an election district formed during Gerry's governorship of Massachusetts, which favoured his own party. A map of the district, with wings, claws, and teeth added, was published in a Boston newspaper in 1812.

gerund *n* **1** a verbal noun in Latin that expresses generalized or uncompleted action and is used in all cases but the nominative. **2** the English verbal noun ending in *-ing* that has the function of a noun and at the same time shows certain verbal features, e.g. *singing* in *He likes singing* and in *Singing chorales is fun.*

gesso *n* (*pl* **-oes**) plaster of Paris or gypsum mixed with glue for use in painting or making bas-reliefs.

gestalt /gəˈshtalt/ *n* (*pl* **gestalten** *or* **gestalts**) a structure, pattern, etc, e.g. a melody, that as an object of perception constitutes a functional unit with properties not derivable from the sum of its parts.

Gestalt psychology *n* the study of perception and behaviour using the theory that perceptions, reactions, etc are gestalts.

Gestapo /gəˈshtahpoh, gəˈstahpoh/ *n* the secret police organization operating against suspected traitors in Nazi Germany.

gestate *v* **1** to carry (a foetus) in gestation. **2** of a foetus: to be in the process of gestation.

gestation *n* **1** the carrying of young in the uterus; pregnancy. **2** conception and development, *esp* in the mind.

gesticulate *v* to make expressive gestures, *esp* when speaking. ➤➤ **gesticulation** *n.*

gesture[1] *n* **1a** a movement, usu of the body or limbs, that expresses or emphasizes an idea, sentiment, or attitude. **b** the use of gestures. **2** something said or done for its effect on the attitudes of others or to convey a feeling, e.g. friendliness. ➤➤ **gestural** *adj.*

gesture[2] *v* **1** to make a gesture. **2** to express (something) with a gesture.

get *v* (**getting,** *past tense* **got,** *past part.* **got** *or NAm or archaic* **gotten**) **1** to gain possession of; to obtain or receive. **2** to seek out and bring: *Get me a pencil.* **3** to capture (somebody). **4** to succeed in achieving. **5** to prepare or get ready: *I'll get you a meal.* **6** to establish communication with: *Can you get her on the phone?* **7a** to become affected by (an illness). **b** to suffer or undergo: *to get a reprimand.* **8** to cause (something or somebody) to come into a certain condition: *I must get my shoes mended; Get these people out of the house.* **9** to persuade or induce: *Why not get him to help you?* **10a** to become: *to get drunk.* **b** used as a verbal auxiliary instead of *be* to form the passive: *They were in danger of getting trapped by the tide.* **11** to travel by (a form of public transport): *I'll get the train next time.* **12** to succeed in coming or going: *Where did they get to?* **13** to manage to do something, *esp* by effort: *She never got to drive the car.* **14** *informal* to hear or understand (something said): *I'm afraid I didn't quite get that.* **15** *informal* to punish or harm (somebody). ✱ **get at 1** to reach or gain access to. **2** *informal* to imply: *What is he getting at?* **3** *informal* to criticize or tease. **4** *informal* to bribe.

get about *v* **1** of news: to be circulated. **2** of a person: to be well enough to walk.

get across *v* to make clear or convincing.

get along *v* **1** to manage. **2** to be or remain on congenial terms.

getaway *n* a departure or escape.

get away *v* to escape. ✱ **get away with** to avoid punishment or blame for.

get back *v* to return. ✱ **get back at** to retaliate against (somebody).

get by *v* to manage with difficulty or limited resources.

get down *v* **1** to leave or descend from a vehicle. **2** to depress (somebody). **3** to record in writing. ✱ **get down to** to start to give attention to (an activity).

get in *v* **1** to be admitted to a place. **2** to be elected to office or come to power. **3** of a train, etc: to arrive at its destination.

get off *v* **1** to start or leave. **2** to escape danger or punishment. **3** to go to sleep. **4** to leave work.

✱ **get off with** *informal* to have a sexual relationship with.

get on *v* **1** = GET ALONG. **2** to succeed. ✱ **be getting on for** to be approaching (a specified age, time, distance, etc).

get out *v* **1** to emerge or escape. **2** of a secret, etc: to become known. ✱ **get out of** to escape responsibility for.

get over *v* **1** to overcome (a difficulty). **2** to recover from (an illness or bad experience). **3** to succeed in communicating (an idea, etc).

get round *v* **1** to persuade (somebody) to do what you want. **2** to evade (a law or responsibility). ✱ **get round to** to make a start eventually on (a task, etc).

get through *v* **1** to reach the end of (an ordeal). **2** to use up (a supply). **3** to overcome difficulties to reach a destination. **4** to make contact by telephone. ✱ **get through to** to make oneself understood by.

get together *v* to assemble or come together for a social purpose or to cooperate.

get-together *n* an informal social gathering or meeting.

get up *v* **1a** to rise from a sitting or lying position. **b** to rise from bed in the morning. **2** of the wind: to become stronger. ✱ **get up to** *Brit, informal* to be involved in (something wrong, mischievous, etc).

get-up *n informal* an outfit or costume.

gewgaw *n* something showy but worthless; a bauble or trinket.

Gewürztraminer /gə'vooətstrəmeenə/ *n* a variety of grape used in the production of white wine, or the wine produced from it.

geyser *n* **1** a spring that intermittently throws out jets of heated water and steam. **2** *Brit* an apparatus with a boiler in which water is rapidly heated by a gas flame and may be stored.

Ghanaian *n* a native or inhabitant of Ghana. ➤➤ **Ghanaian** *adj.*

gharial *n* = GAVIAL.

ghastly *adj* (**-ier, -iest**) **1a** terrifyingly horrible. **b** *informal* intensely unpleasant, disagreeable, or objectionable. **2** pale and wan. ➤➤ **ghastliness** *n.*

ghat /gawt/ *n* **1** a broad flight of steps providing access to an Indian river. **2** a mountain pass, *esp* in India.

GHB *abbr* (sodium) gammahydroxybutyrate, used as an anaesthetic and a designer drug.

ghee *n* a clarified butter used in Indian cooking.

gherkin *n* the small immature fruit of the cucumber, used for pickling.

ghetto *n* (*pl* **-os** *or* **-oes**) **1** an area of a city, *esp* a slum area, in which a minority group live because of social, legal, or economic pressures. **2** part of a city in which Jews formerly lived.

ghetto blaster *n informal* a large portable radio, usu incorporating a cassette or CD player.

ghettoize *or* **-ise** *v* **1** to force (a group of people) to live in a ghetto, or as if in a ghetto because of their customs, beliefs, or social class. **2** to cause (an area) to become a ghetto. ➤➤ **ghettoization** *n.*

Ghibelline *n* a member of a political party in medieval Italy supporting the German emperors: compare GUELF.

ghillie *n* see GILLIE.

ghost[1] *n* **1** a disembodied soul; *esp* the soul of a dead person haunting the living. **2** a faint shadowy trace. **3** a false image in a photographic negative or on a television screen. ✱ **give up the ghost** to die.

ghost[2] *v* to ghostwrite (e.g. a book).

ghostly *adj* (**-ier, -iest**) of, like, or being a ghost; spectral. ➤➤ **ghostliness** *n.*

ghost town *n* a once-flourishing but now deserted town.

ghostwrite *v* (*past tense* **ghostwrote,** *past part.* **ghostwritten**) to write (e.g. a speech) for another person, who is the presumed author. ➤➤ **ghostwriter** *n.*

ghoul *n* **1** an evil being of Arabic legend, *esp* one that robs graves and feeds on corpses. **2** an evil spirit or ghost. **3** a person who enjoys the macabre. ➤➤ **ghoulish** *adj,* **ghoulishly** *adv,* **ghoulishness** *n.*

GHQ *abbr* General Headquarters.

GI *n* (*pl* **GI's** *or* **GIs**) a member of the US army, *esp* a private.

giant[1] *n* **1** a legendary being, like a human in shape, but having great size and strength. **2** an extraordinarily large person, animal, or plant.

giant[2] *adj* extremely large.

giantess *n* a female giant.

giant-killer *n* a person or team that defeats an apparently far superior opponent.

giant panda *n* = PANDA.

giant star *n* a star of great brightness and enormous size that is reaching the end of its life.

giardiasis *n* an infection of the small intestine that can cause diarrhoea, caused by a microscopic parasite.

gibber *v* to make rapid, inarticulate, and usu incomprehensible utterances.

gibberish *n* unintelligible or meaningless language.

gibbet[1] *n* **1** a gallows. **2** an upright post with an arm, used formerly for hanging the bodies of executed criminals as a warning.

gibbet[2] *v* (**gibbeted, gibbeting**) **1** to hang (somebody) on a gibbet. **2** to execute by hanging.

gibbon *n* a small tailless tree-dwelling ape of SE Asia.

gibbous *adj* of the moon: seen with more than half but not all of the apparent disc illuminated.

gibe *verb and n* see JIBE[1], JIBE[2].

giblets *pl n* a fowl's heart, liver, or other edible internal organs.

Gibraltarian *n* a native or inhabitant of Gibraltar. ➤➤ **Gibraltarian** *adj.*

giddy[1] *adj* (**-ier, -iest**) **1a** feeling a sensation of unsteadiness and lack of balance as if everything is whirling round; dizzy. **b** causing dizziness. **2** lightheartedly frivolous. ➤➤ **giddily** *adv,* **giddiness** *n.*

giddy[2] *v* (**-ies, -ied**) to make (somebody) feel giddy.

GIF *abbr* in computing, graphic interchange format, a format for image files.

GIFT *abbr* gamete intrafallopian transfer, a technique for the treatment of infertile women, in which eggs and sperm are injected into the fallopian tubes.

gift[1] *n* **1** something freely given by one person to another; a present or donation. **2** a natural capacity or talent. **3** *Brit, informal* something obtained easily. ✱ **gift of the gab** *informal* the ability to talk glibly and persuasively.

gift[2] *v* **1** to give as a gift. **2** to present with a gift.

gifted *adj* **1** having or revealing great natural ability. **2** highly intelligent. ➤➤ **giftedness** *n.*

gift token *n Brit* a voucher redeemable for merchandise to the stated amount.

gift wrap *n* decorative wrapping paper.

gift-wrap *v* (**gift-wrapped, gift-wrapping**) to wrap (a gift) decoratively.

gig[1] *n* **1** a light two-wheeled carriage pulled by a horse. **2** a long light ship's boat propelled by oars, sails, etc.

gig[2] *n informal* a musician's engagement for a specified time; *esp* such an engagement for one performance.

gig[3] *v* (**gigged, gigging**) *informal* to perform a gig.

giga- *comb. form* **1** a factor of one thousand million (10^9): *gigavolt.* **2** in computing, a factor of 2^{30}: *gigabyte.*

gigabyte *n* in computing, a quantity of data equal to one thousand million (10^9) or (more accurately) 2^{30} bytes.

gigaflop *n* in computing, a unit of speed equal to one thousand million flops.

gigantic *adj* unusually great or enormous. ➤➤ **gigantically** *adv.*

gigantism *n* development of a plant or animal to abnormally large size.

giggle[1] *v* to laugh with repeated short catches of the breath or in a silly manner. ➤➤ **giggler** *n.*

giggle[2] *n* **1** an act or instance of giggling. **2** *Brit, informal* something amusing. ➤➤ **giggly** *adj.*

GIGO *abbr* in computing, garbage in, garbage out.

gigolo *n* (*pl* **-os**) **1** a man paid by a usu older woman for companionship or sex. **2** a professional dancing partner or male escort.

gigot *n* a leg of meat, e.g. lamb.

gild *v* (*past tense and past part.* **gilded** *or* **gilt**) **1** to overlay with a thin covering of gold. **2** to give an attractive but often deceptive appearance to. ✱ **gild the lily** to add unnecessary ornamentation to something already beautiful. ➤➤ **gilder** *n,* **gilding** *n.*

gilet *n* a loose waistcoat.

gill[1] *n* **1** an organ, *esp* of a fish, for oxygenating blood using the oxygen dissolved in water. **2** any of the radiating plates forming the undersurface of the cap of some fungi, e.g. mushrooms. **3** (*in pl*) the flesh under or about the chin or jaws.

gill[2] *n* a unit of liquid capacity equal to a quarter of a pint.

gill[3] *n* **1** *Brit* a ravine. **2** a narrow mountain stream or rivulet.

gillie *or* **ghillie** *n* an attendant to somebody who is hunting or fishing in Scotland.

gillyflower *or* **gilliflower** *n* any of several plants having clove-scented flowers, e.g. a wallflower or stock.

gilt[1] *adj* covered with gold or gilt; of the colour of gold.

gilt[2] *n* **1** gold leaf or gold paint laid on a surface. **2** superficial brilliance; surface attraction. **3** (*in pl*) gilt-edged securities. ✱ **take the gilt off the gingerbread** to make something less attractive [because gingerbread was traditionally sold at fairs decorated with 'Dutch gold', an alloy of copper and bronze].

gilt[3] *n* a young female pig.

gilt[4] *v* past tense and past part. of GILD.

gilt-edged *adj* of government securities: traded on the Stock Exchange and having a guaranteed fixed interest rate.

gimbal *n* (*also* **gimbals**) (*used as sing.*) a device that allows a ship's compass, stove, etc to remain level when its support is tipped.

gimcrack[1] *adj* showy but unsubstantial; shoddy. ➤➤ **gimcrackery** *n.*

gimcrack[2] *n* a showy unsubstantial object of little use or value.

gimlet *n* a tool for boring small holes in wood, usu consisting of a crosswise handle fitted to a tapered screw: compare AUGER.

gimmick *n* a scheme, device, or object devised to gain attention or publicity. ➤➤ **gimmickry** *n,* **gimmicky** *adj.*

gimp *n* **1** an ornamental flat braid or round cord used as a trimming. **2** the thread used to fill in ornamental details, e.g. flowers, in lace.

gin[1] *n* a spirit made by distilling grain flavoured with juniper berries.

gin[2] *n* **1** = COTTON GIN. **2** a machine for raising or moving heavy weights. **3** a snare or trap for game.

gin[3] *v* (**ginned, ginning**) to separate (cotton fibre) from seeds and waste material.

ginger *n* **1a** the dried and ground rhizome of a tropical plant, used as a spice. **b** the rhizome itself, which has a strong hot taste and is used in cooking, candied as a sweet, or preserved in syrup. **2** a reddish brown or yellowish brown colour. **3** high spirit; vigour. ➤➤ **gingery** *adj.*

ginger ale *n* a sweet yellowish carbonated non-alcoholic drink flavoured with ginger.

ginger beer *n* **1** a weak alcoholic effervescent drink of milky appearance, made by the fermentation of ginger and syrup. **2** a similar non-alcoholic commercial preparation.

gingerbread *n* a thick biscuit or cake made with treacle or syrup and flavoured with ginger. ✱ **take the gilt off the gingerbread** see GILT[2].

ginger group *n Brit* a pressure group, e.g. within a political party, urging stronger action.

gingerly[1] *adv* very cautiously or carefully.

gingerly[2] *adj* very cautious or careful. ➤➤ **gingerliness** *n.*

ginger up *v* to stir (somebody or something) to activity; to vitalize.

gingham *n* a lightweight fabric usu woven from dyed cotton yarn to give a checked design.

gingival *adj* relating to or in the region of the gums.

gingivitis *n* inflammation of the gums.

ginkgo *or* **gingko** *n* (*pl* **-oes**) a showy Chinese tree that has fan-shaped leaves and yellow fruit and is often grown for ornament.

ginormous *adj Brit, informal* exceptionally large.

gin rummy *n* a form of rummy for two players in which both are dealt ten cards and may end play when the value of their unmatched cards is less than ten.

ginseng *n* the aromatic root of a Chinese or N American plant of the ivy family, widely valued as a tonic.

gip *n* see GYP[1].

gipsy *n* see GYPSY.

gipsy moth *n* see GYPSY MOTH.

giraffe *n* (*pl* **giraffes** *or* **giraffe**) a large African ruminant mammal, the tallest living four-legged animal, that has a very long neck and a fawn or cream coat marked with brown or black patches.

gird *v* (*past tense and past part.* **girded** *or* **girt**) to encircle or bind with a flexible band, e.g. a belt. ✱ **gird (up) one's loins** to prepare for action; to muster one's resources.

girder *n* a horizontal main structural member, e.g. in a building or bridge, that supports vertical loads.

girdle[1] *n* **1** a belt or cord encircling the body, usu at the waist. **2** a woman's tightly fitting undergarment that extends from the waist to below the hips.

girdle[2] *v* to encircle (something or somebody) with a girdle, or as if with a girdle.

girdle[3] *n Scot, N Eng dialect* = GRIDDLE[1].

girl *n* **1a** a female child. **b** a young unmarried woman. **2** a girlfriend. ➤➤ **girlhood** *n,* **girlish** *adj,* **girlishly** *adv,* **girlishness** *n.*

girlfriend *n* **1** a frequent or regular female companion with whom somebody is romantically or sexually involved. **2** a female friend.

Girl Guide *n chiefly Brit* = GUIDE[1] (4).

girlie[1] *or* **girly** *adj* **1** featuring nude or scantily clothed young women. **2** *chiefly derog* suitable for or like a young girl, *esp* affectedly so.

girlie[2] *or* **girly** *n* (*pl* **-ies**) *informal* a girl or young woman.

girl scout *n NAm* = GUIDE[1] (4).

girly[1] *adj* = GIRLIE[1].

girly[2] *n* = GIRLIE[2].

girn *or* **gurn** *v Brit* to pull a grotesque face. ➤➤ **girner** *n.*

giro *n* (*pl* **-os**) **1** a computerized low-cost system of money transfer comparable to a current account. **2** *informal* a giro cheque or payment, *esp* a social security benefit.

girt *v* past tense and past part. of GIRD.

girth *n* **1** a measurement round something, e.g. a tree trunk or somebody's waist. **2** a strap that passes under the body of a horse or other animal to fasten a saddle on its back.

gismo *n* see GIZMO.

gist *n* the main point of a matter; essence.

git *n chiefly Brit, informal* a worthless or contemptible person.

gîte /zheet/ *n* a furnished house in France that is rented to holidaymakers.

give[1] *v* (*past tense* **gave,** *past part.* **given**) **1** to transfer the possession or use of (something) to another person. **2a** to offer (advice, a promise, etc). **b** to express or propose (a reason, argument, etc). **c** to present (an appearance). **3** to provide or organize: *to give a party.* **4** to cause somebody to experience or suffer (something): *You gave me a fright; She gave the child a rebuke.* **5** to utter (a sound). **6** to yield as a product: *Cows give milk.* **7** to allow or concede: *I'll give you that game.* **8** to collapse or yield under physical or emotional pressure. ✱ **give or take** allowing for a specified margin of error. **give way 1** to concede a right of way. **2** to collapse or yield under pressure. ➤➤ **giver** *n.*

give[2] *n* the capacity or tendency to yield to pressure; resilience or elasticity.

give-and-take *n* the practice of making mutual concessions.

giveaway *n* **1** an unintentional revelation or betrayal. **2** something given free or at a reduced price.

give away *v* **1** to make a present of. **2** to betray. **3** to reveal (a secret). **4** to concede (an advantage) to an opponent. ✱ **give the game/show away** to unwittingly reveal a secret.

give in *v* **1** to yield or surrender. **2** to concede an argument or fight.

given[1] *v* past part. of GIVE[1].

given[2] *adj* **1** prone; disposed. **2a** fixed; specified. **b** assumed as actual or hypothetical.

given[3] *n* a known or accepted fact.

given name *n chiefly NAm* = FORENAME.

give off *v* to emit (something unpleasant).

give out *v* **1** to issue or distribute. **2** of a supply: to come to an end.

give over *v* **1** to deliver to somebody's care. **2** to stop or desist.

give up *v* **1** to abandon an activity and concede failure. **2** to discontinue (a habit). **3** to surrender (somebody or oneself) as a prisoner.

gizmo *or* **gismo** *n* (*pl* **-os**) *informal* a gadget, *esp* one whose name is unknown or has been forgotten.

gizzard *n* **1** an enlargement of the digestive tract of birds, that has thick muscular walls and usu contains small stones or grit for breaking up and grinding food. **2** a thickened or enlarged part of the digestive tract in some invertebrate animals, e.g. an insect or earthworm, that is similar in function to the gizzard of a bird.

glacé *adj* **1** of a food, *esp* fruit: coated with a glaze; candied. **2** of fabric, leather, etc: finished with a smooth glossy surface.

glacé icing *n* a smooth icing made from icing sugar and water.

glacial *adj* **1a** extremely cold. **b** lacking warmth or cordiality. **2** of or produced by glaciers. **3** resembling ice in appearance, *esp* when frozen. ➤➤ **glacially** *adv.*

glacial period *n* any period of the earth's history when the surface of the planet was extensively covered with ice sheets.

glaciate *v* **1** to cover (land, etc) with ice or a glacier. **2** to subject (rock, etc) to the action or effects of glaciers. ➤➤ **glaciation** *n.*

glacier *n* a large body of ice moving slowly down a slope or spreading outwards on a land surface.

glaciology *n* the study of glaciers. ➤➤ **glaciological** *adj,* **glaciologist** *n.*

glad *adj* (**gladder, gladdest**) **1** expressing or experiencing pleasure, joy, or delight. **2** causing happiness and joy. **3** (+ of) grateful for; pleased to have. ➤➤ **gladly** *adv,* **gladness** *n.*

gladden *v* to make (somebody or something) glad.

glade *n* an open space in a wood or forest.

glad hand *n informal* a warm welcome or greeting, often prompted by ulterior motives.

glad-hand *v* to extend a glad hand. ➤➤ **glad-hander** *n.*

gladiator *n* a man trained to fight another man or wild animals in a public arena for the entertainment of ancient Romans. ➤➤ **gladiatorial** *adj.*

gladiolus *n* (*pl* **gladioli** *or* **gladioluses**) a plant of the iris family with erect sword-shaped leaves and spikes of brilliantly coloured irregular flowers.

glad rags *pl n informal* smart clothes worn for a party or other special occasion.

Gladstone bag *n* a travelling bag with flexible sides on a hinged frame that opens flat into two equal compartments.

Glagolitic *adj* relating to or denoting an alphabet formerly used for some Slavic languages.

Glam. *abbr* Glamorgan.

glam[1] *adj informal* glamorous.

glam[2] *n informal* **1** glamour. **2** = GLAM ROCK.

glam[3] *v* (**glammed, glamming**) (*often* + up) to dress or decorate (somebody, oneself, or something) in a glamorous way.

glamor *n NAm* see GLAMOUR.

glamorize *or* **-ise** *or* **glamourize** *or* **-ise** *v* **1** to make (something or somebody) glamorous. **2** to romanticize (something). ➤➤ **glamorization** *n.*

glamour (*NAm* **glamor**) *n* **1** a romantic, exciting, and often illusory attractiveness. **2** alluring or fascinating beauty. ➤➤ **glamorous** *adj,* **glamorously** *adv.*

glamourize *or* **-ise** *v* see GLAMORIZE.

glam rock *n* a style of popular music, prominent in the UK during the 1970s, characterized by singalong tunes performed by bands wearing outrageous clothes and flamboyant make-up.

glance[1] *v* **1a** (*usu* + at) to take a quick look. **b** of the eyes: to move swiftly from one thing to another. **2** (*often* + off) to strike a surface obliquely in such a way as to go off at an angle.

glance[2] *n* a quick or cursory look.

glancing *adj* having a slanting direction; deflected.

gland *n* **1** an organ of the body that selectively removes materials from the blood, alters them, and secretes them for further use or for elimination. **2** a bodily structure that resembles a gland but does not secrete, e.g. a lymph node.

glanders *pl n* (*used as sing. or pl*) a contagious bacterial disease, *esp* of horses, in which mucus is discharged profusely from the nostrils.

glandes *n* pl of GLANS.

glandular *adj* relating to, affecting, or produced by a gland or glands.

glandular fever *n* = INFECTIOUS MONONUCLEOSIS.

glans *n* (*pl* **glandes**) the rounded mass of tissue at the end of the penis or clitoris.

glare[1] *v* **1** to stare angrily or fiercely. **2** to shine with a harsh uncomfortably brilliant light.

glare[2] *n* **1** an angry or fierce stare. **2** a harsh uncomfortably bright light; *specif* painfully bright sunlight.

glaring *adj* obtrusively evident. ➤➤ **glaringly** *adv.*

glasnost *n* the willingness of an organization, orig the government of the former USSR, to be open about its affairs and invite public scrutiny and debate.

glass[1] *n* **1** a hard brittle usu transparent or translucent substance formed by melting sand or some other form of silica with metallic oxides and other ingredients and cooling the mixture rapidly. **2 a** a glass drinking vessel. **b** a mirror. **c** a barometer. **d** an optical instrument, e.g. a magnifying glass, for viewing objects not easily seen. ➤➤ **glassful** (*pl* **glassfuls**) *n,* **glassware** *n.*

glass[2] *v* to enclose, cover, or fit with glass.

glass-blowing *n* the art or process of shaping a mass of semi-molten glass by blowing air into it through a tube.

glass ceiling *n* a hypothetical barrier to career advancement, *esp* one caused by sexism or racism.

glasses *pl n* a pair of glass lenses in a frame worn in front of the eyes to correct defects of vision or for protection.

glass fibre *n* = FIBREGLASS.

glasshouse *n chiefly Brit* **1** a greenhouse. **2** *informal* a military prison or place of detention.

glasspaper *n* paper to which a thin layer of powdered glass has been glued for use as an abrasive.

glass wool *n* glass fibres in a mass resembling wool used for insulation, filtering, packing, etc.

glassy *adj* (**-ier, -iest**) **1** resembling glass. **2** dull or lifeless. ➤➤ **glassily** *adv,* **glassiness** *n.*

Glaswegian *n* a native or inhabitant of Glasgow. ➤➤ **Glaswegian** *adj.*

glaucoma *n* increased pressure within the eyeball causing damage to the retina and gradual impairment or loss of vision.

glaucous *adj* **1** of plants or plant parts: of a dull blue or bluish green colour. **2** of a leaf or fruit: having a powdery or waxy coating giving a frosted appearance.

glaze[1] *v* **1** to provide or fit (e.g. a window frame) with glass. **2** to coat (e.g. food or pottery) with a glaze. **3** to give a smooth glossy surface to. **4** (*often* + over) to become dull or lifeless. ➤➤ **glazer** *n,* **glazing** *n.*

glaze[2] *n* **1** a liquid preparation that sets or hardens to give a glossy coating to food. **2** a vitreous coating made chiefly from a mixture of oxides and used to seal or decorate pottery. **3** a transparent or translucent colour applied to a painted or printed surface to modify its tone. **4** a smooth glossy or lustrous surface or finish.

glazier *n* a person who fits glass, *esp* into windows and doors, as an occupation.

gleam[1] *n* **1a** a short-lived appearance of reflected, subdued, or partly obscured light. **b** a small bright light. **2** a brief or faint indication of emotion, etc.

gleam[2] *v* **1** to shine, *esp* with reflected light. **2** to appear briefly or faintly. ➤➤ **gleaming** *adj.*

glean *v* **1** to gather grain left by reapers. **2** to gather (e.g. information) bit by bit. ➤➤ **gleaner** *n.*

gleanings *pl n* things acquired by gleaning.

glebe *n* in former times, land belonging or yielding revenue to a church or clergyman.

glee *n* **1** a feeling of merry high-spirited joy or delight. **2** an unaccompanied song for three or more usu male solo voices.

gleeful *adj* full of glee; merry or triumphant. ➤➤ **gleefully** *adv,* **gleefulness** *n.*

glen *n* a narrow valley, *esp* in Scotland or Ireland.

glib *adj* (**glibber, glibbest**) **1** showing little forethought or preparation; lacking depth and substance. **2** marked by ease and fluency in speaking or writing, often to the point of being superficial or dishonest. ➤➤ **glibly** *adv,* **glibness** *n.*

glide[1] *v* **1** to move noiselessly in a smooth, continuous, and effortless manner. **2** to pass gradually and imperceptibly. **3a** of an aircraft: to fly without the use of engines. **b** to fly in a glider. ➤➤ **gliding** *adj and n.*

glide[2] *n* **1** the act or an instance of gliding. **2** in music, = PORTAMENTO.

glide path *n* the path of descent of an aircraft in landing.

glider *n* **1** an aircraft similar to an aeroplane but without an engine. **2** a person or thing that glides.

glimmer[1] *v* to shine faintly or unsteadily. ➤➤ **glimmering** *adj and n.*

glimmer[2] *n* **1** a feeble or unsteady light. **2a** a dim perception or faint idea. **b** a small sign or amount: *a glimmer of intelligence.*

glimpse[1] *v* to see briefly or partially.

glimpse[2] *n* a brief or partial view or look.

glint[1] *v* **1** to shine with tiny bright flashes, *esp* by reflection. **2** of rays of light: to strike a reflecting surface obliquely and dart out at an angle.

glint[2] *n* **1** a tiny bright flash of usu reflected light. **2** a brief or faint manifestation.

glissade[1] /gli'sahd, gli'sayd/ *n* **1** a slide down a snow- or ice-covered slope, usu in a standing or squatting position. **2** a gliding step in ballet.

glissade[2] *v* to perform a glissade.

glissando *n* (*pl* **glissandi** *or* **glissandos**) in music, a rapid sliding up or down the scale.

glisten[1] *v* to shine, usu by reflection, with a sparkling radiance or with the lustre of a wet or oily surface.

glisten[2] *n* a sheen or sparkle, *esp* a light reflected from something wet or oily.

glister[1] *v chiefly literary* = GLITTER[1].

glister[2] *n chiefly literary* = GLITTER[2].

glitch *n informal* a technical hitch; a temporary malfunction or setback.

glitter[1] *v* **1** to shine by reflection in bright flashes, with a metallic lustre, or with a glassy brilliance. **2** to have an enticing brilliance: *The world continues to offer glittering prizes to those who have stout hearts and sharp swords* — F E Smith.

glitter[2] *n* **1** bright shimmering reflected light or metallic lustre. **2** small glittering particles used for ornamentation. **3** something that is brilliantly attractive, sometimes in a superficial way. ➤➤ **glittery** *adj.*

glitterati /glitə'rahti/ *pl n informal* celebrated and fashionable people, *esp* those in the world of entertainment.

glitz *n informal* superficial glamour.

glitzy *adj* (**-ier, -iest**) *informal* glamorous, *esp* in a superficial, overstated, or ironic way. ➤➤ **glitzily** *adv,* **glitziness** *n.*

gloaming *n* (**the gloaming**) *literary* twilight or dusk.

gloat[1] *v* (*often* + over) to think or talk about something, *esp* one's own achievements or another person's misfortunes, with great and often malicious satisfaction or relish. ➤➤ **gloater** *n,* **gloatingly** *adv.*

gloat[2] *n* the act or an instance of gloating.

glob *n chiefly informal* a blob, *esp* of a semiliquid substance.

global *adj* **1** of or involving the entire world. **2** general; comprehensive. **3** operating on or applying to the whole of a computer file or program. **4** spherical. ➤➤ **globally** *adv.*

globalize *or* **-ise** *v* to make international or worldwide in scope or application. ➤➤ **globalization** *n.*

Global Positioning System *n* a system of 24 satellites orbiting the earth that allows someone with an appropriate receiver to establish their exact geographical location, altitude, and speed and direction of travel.

global village *n* the world viewed as an integrated system in which all the constituent parts are interdependent and linked, *esp* by modern technology.

global warming *n* an increase in the average temperature of the earth's atmosphere that is believed to be caused by the greenhouse effect.

globe *n* **1a** a spherical representation of the earth. **b** (**the globe**) the world; the earth. **2** something spherical or rounded, e.g. a glass bowl or light. ➤➤ **globoid** *adj,* **globose** *adj.*

globe artichoke *n* = ARTICHOKE.

globefish *n* (*pl* **globefishes** *or* **globefish**) a tropical marine fish that can distend its body to a globular form, *esp* as a form of defence. Also called BLOWFISH, PUFFER FISH.

globetrotter *n informal* somebody who travels widely. ➤➤ **globetrotting** *n and adj.*

globular *adj* **1** having the shape of a globe; spherical. **2** having or consisting of globules. ➤➤ **globularity** *n,* **globularly** *adv.*

globule *n* a tiny globe or ball, e.g. of liquid or melted solid. ➤➤ **globulous** *adj.*

globulin *n* any of a group of widely occurring proteins that are soluble in dilute salt solutions.

glockenspiel /'glokənspeel, -shpeel/ *n* a percussion instrument consisting of a series of graduated metal bars played with two hammers.

gloom *n* **1** partial or total darkness. **2** a state or atmosphere of despondency.

gloomy *adj* (**-ier, -iest**) **1** dismally or depressingly dark. **2** feeling or causing despondency. ➤➤ **gloomily** *adv,* **gloominess** *n.*

gloop (*NAm* **glop**) *n informal* a sticky or messy semiliquid substance or mixture. ➤➤ **gloopy** *adj.*

glorified *adj* appearing or made to appear more special, important, etc than is really the case: *a glorified salesman.*

glorify *v* (**-ies, -ied**) **1** to bestow honour, praise, or admiration on. **2** to give glory to (God), e.g. in worship. **3** to shed radiance or splendour on. ➤➤ **glorification** *n,* **glorifier** *n.*

glorious *adj* **1** possessing, deserving, or conferring glory. **2** marked by great beauty, splendour, or excellence. ➤➤ **gloriously** *adv,* **gloriousness** *n.*

glory[1] *n* (*pl* **-ies**) **1a** praise, honour, or distinction granted by common consent; renown. **b** worshipful praise, honour, and thanksgiving. **2** something that secures praise or renown. **3** splendour or magnificence. ✱ **in (all) its/his/her/their glory** *informal* in a state of great pride, satisfaction, happiness, etc.

glory[2] *v* (**-ies, -ied**) **1** (*often* + in) to rejoice proudly. **2** *informal* (*often* + in) to have or take great pride or pleasure.

glory box *n Aus, NZ* = BOTTOM DRAWER.

glory hole *n informal* a cupboard or small room used for storage, *esp* one that is often untidy.

Glos. *abbr* Gloucestershire.

gloss[1] *n* **1a** surface lustre or sheen. **b** something that gives this: *lip gloss.* **2** a deceptively attractive outer appearance. **3a** paint to which varnish has been added to give a shiny finish. **b** (*used before a noun*) relating to or denoting such paint.

gloss[2] *v* to give a gloss to. ➤➤ **glosser** *n.*

gloss[3] *n* **1** a brief explanation or translation of a difficult word or expression. **2** a deliberately false or misleading interpretation.

gloss[4] *v* to supply a gloss or glosses for (a word, text, etc).

glossary *n* (*pl* **-ies**) a list of terms, e.g. those used in a particular text or in a specialized field, usu with their meanings.

glossolalia *n* the phenomenon of ecstatic speaking in usu incomprehensible language, *esp* in evangelical Christianity or as a symptom of a mental disorder.

gloss over *v* **1** to make (something wrong) appear right and acceptable. **2** to veil or hide (something undesirable) by rapid or superficial treatment.

glossy[1] *adj* (**-ier, -iest**) **1** having a lustre or sheen. **2** superficially attractive in a sophisticated manner. ➤➤ **glossily** *adv,* **glossiness** *n.*

glossy[2] *n* (*pl* **-ies**) *informal* a magazine expensively produced on glossy paper with many colour photographs and often having a fashionable or sophisticated content.

glottal *adj* of or produced by the glottis.

glottal stop *n* a speech sound produced by closure and sudden reopening of the glottis, as heard between the two syllables in a Cockney pronunciation of *butter.*

glottis *n* (*pl* **glottises** *or* **glottides** /'glotideez/) *technical* the slit-like space between the two vocal cords in the larynx.

glove *n* a close-fitting covering for the hand having separate sections for each of the fingers and the thumb, worn for warmth, fashion, or protection. ✱ **fit like a glove** of clothes: to be a perfect fit. ➤➤ **gloved** *adj.*

glove box *n* **1** *chiefly Brit* = GLOVE COMPARTMENT. **2** a sealed compartment that has holes with gloves attached for handling dangerous materials inside the compartment.

glove compartment *n* a small storage compartment in the dashboard of a motor vehicle.

glove puppet *n* a puppet, usu made of fabric, worn on the hand and animated by moving the fingers.

glover *n* a person who makes or sells gloves.

glow[1] *v* **1** to shine with the steady light produced by intense heat without flames. **2a** to have or experience a sensation of heat. **b** of the complexion, etc: to have a strong, healthy, *esp* red, colour. **c** to show great pleasure or satisfaction: *a glowing report.* ➤➤ **glowingly** *adv.*

glow[2] *n* **1** the state of glowing, or the light so produced. **2** brightness or warmth of colour. **3a** a sensation of warmth. **b** warmth of feeling or emotion.

glower[1] *v* to look or stare with sullen annoyance or anger. ➤➤ **gloweringly** *adv.*

glower[2] *n* a sullen or angry look or stare.

glow-worm *n* a larva or wingless female of a beetle that emits light from the abdomen.

gloxinia *n* a tropical plant widely cultivated for its attractive white or purple bell-shaped flowers.

gloze *v archaic* **1** to explain away. **2** to use flattering or fawning language.

glucose *n* a simple sugar that occurs widely in nature and is the usual form in which carbohydrate is absorbed and used in the body by animals.

glue[1] *n* a substance used for sticking things together, *esp* one obtained by boiling animal hides, bones, etc; an adhesive. ➤➤ **glue-like** *adj*, **gluey** *adj.*

glue[2] *v* (**glues, glued, gluing** *or* **glueing**) **1** to cause to stick tightly with glue. **2** to fix (the eyes, one's attention, etc) steadily or with deep concentration.

glue ear *n* a condition in which an accumulation of a sticky substance in the middle ear impairs hearing, *esp* in children.

glue-sniffing *n* the practice of breathing in the fumes from various kinds of glue as an intoxicant. ➤➤ **glue-sniffer** *n.*

glug[1] *v* (**glugged, glugging**) **1** to pour in such a way as to make a gurgling noise. **2** to drink quickly and often noisily. ➤➤ **gluggable** *adj.*

glug[2] *n* the act or sound of glugging.

glum *adj* (**glummer, glummest**) **1** broodingly morose. **2** dreary; gloomy. ➤➤ **glumly** *adv*, **glumness** *n.*

gluon *n* an elementary particle held to be responsible for the force that binds quarks together.

glut[1] *n* an excessive supply of something that exceeds market demand.

glut[2] *v* (**glutted, glutting**) **1** to fill or feed beyond capacity. **2** to flood (the market) with goods so that supply exceeds demand.

glutamate *n* a salt or ester of glutamic acid.

glutamic acid *n* an acidic amino acid found in most proteins.

glutamine /'gloohtəmeen, -min/ *n* an amino acid found in many proteins that breaks down to yield glutamic acid and ammonia.

glutei *n* pl of GLUTEUS.

gluten *n* a protein substance, *esp* of wheat flour, that gives dough its cohesive and elastic properties. ➤➤ **glutenous** *adj.*

gluteus /'gloohti·əs/ *n* (*pl* **glutei** /'gloohtiie/) any of the three large muscles of the buttock. ➤➤ **gluteal** *adj.*

glutinous *adj* resembling glue; sticky. ➤➤ **glutinously** *adv*, **glutinousness** *n.*

glutton *n* **1** a habitually greedy and voracious eater and drinker. **2** somebody who has a great liking for something. ✱ **a glutton for punishment** a person who is keen to take on difficult or unpleasant tasks, etc. ➤➤ **gluttonous** *adj.*

gluttony *n* habitual greed or excess in eating or drinking.

glyc- *or* **glyco-** *comb. form* denoting sugar: *glycoside.*

glycerin *or* **glycerine** *n* = GLYCEROL.

glycerol *n* a sweet syrupy alcohol usu obtained from fats and used *esp* as a solvent and plasticizer.

glycine *n* a sweet amino acid found in most proteins.

glyco- *comb. form* see GLYC-.

glycogen *n* a substance that is the chief form in which carbohydrate is stored in body tissue. ➤➤ **glycogenic** *adj.*

glycol *n* = ETHYLENE GLYCOL.

glycolysis /glie'koləsis/ *n* the partial oxidation of a carbohydrate, e.g. glucose, by enzymes, releasing a little energy in the cell. ➤➤ **glycolytic** *adj.*

glycoprotein *n* a protein containing one or more carbohydrate groups.

glycoside *n* a chemical compound in which a sugar is attached by an oxygen or nitrogen atom to a nonsugar group.

glyph *n* **1** a symbolic figure or character usu incised or carved in relief. **2** a symbol, e.g. on a road sign or in computer graphics, that conveys information without using words. **3** an ornamental vertical groove in architecture. ➤➤ **glyphic** *adj.*

GM *abbr* **1** general manager. **2** genetically modified. **3** George Medal. **4** *Brit* of a school: grant-maintained.

gm *abbr* gram.

G-man *n informal* **1** *NAm* a special agent of the Federal Bureau of Investigation. **2** *Irish* a political detective.

GMO *abbr* genetically modified organism.

GMT *abbr* Greenwich Mean Time.

gnarled *adj* **1** of a tree: full of or covered with knots or lumps. **2** of hands, etc: rough and twisted, *esp* with age.

gnarly *adj* (**-ier, -iest**) **1** gnarled. **2** *chiefly NAm, informal* of an undertaking, problem, etc: difficult or tricky.

gnash *v* to strike or grind (the teeth) together.

gnashers *pl n Brit, informal* teeth.

gnat *n* a small two-winged fly that bites.

gnaw *v* **1a** to bite or chew on with the teeth, *esp* to wear away by persistent nibbling. **b** to make (e.g. a hole) by gnawing. **2** to affect as if by continuous eating away. **3** to destroy or affect something by or as if by gnawing. ➤➤ **gnawer** *n.*

gnawing *adj* persistently worrying or distressing.

gneiss /nies/ *n* a metamorphic rock usu composed of light bands of feldspar and quartz alternating with dark bands of mica or hornblende. ➤➤ **gneissic** *adj.*

gnocchi /'n(y)oki/ *pl n* small dumplings made from flour, semolina, or potatoes.

gnome *n* **1** in folklore, a dwarf who lives under the earth and guards treasure. **2** a garden ornament in the form of a gnome. **3** an international banker considered to have great power over the financial sector of national economies: *the gnomes of Zurich.* ▶▶ **gnomish** *adj.*

gnomic /'nohmik, 'nomik/ *adj* **1** characterized by or in the form of short wise sayings. **2** mysterious or enigmatic. ▶▶ **gnomically** *adv.*

gnomon *n* a fixed projecting part that casts a shadow on the face of a sundial, indicating the time.

gnosis *n* secret knowledge of spiritual truth available only to the initiated. ▶▶ **gnostic** *adj.*

Gnosticism *n* a religious movement of the late pre-Christian and early Christian era, distinguished by the conviction that matter is evil and that emancipation comes through esoteric spiritual knowledge. ▶▶ **Gnostic** *n and adj.*

GNP *abbr* gross national product.

gnu *n* (*pl* **gnus** *or* **gnu**) a large African antelope with an oxlike head, a short mane, and horns that curve downward and outward.

GNVQ *abbr Brit* General National Vocational Qualification.

go[1] *v* (*past tense* **went,** *past part.* **gone**) **1a** to proceed on a course; to travel. **b** to move out of or away from a place; to leave. **2a** used with a further verb to express purpose: *I'll go and look.* **b** to make an expedition for a specified activity. **c** to attend a specified institution habitually. **3** to extend. **4** to be in or arrive at a specified state or condition. **5a** to become lost, consumed, or spent. **b** to disappear. **c** to elapse. **d** to be got rid of, e.g. by sale or removal. **e** to fail or give way. **6a** (*often* + on) to happen or progress. **b** to turn out, *esp* in a specified manner. **7a** to begin, maintain, or perform an action or motion. **b** to function in a proper or specified way. **c** to make a characteristic noise. **8a** to be known or identified as specified. **b** to be sung or played in a specified manner. **9** to act or be in accordance or harmony. **10** (+ an infinitive) to be about, intending, or destined: *Is it going to rain?* **11** (+ with) to be compatible or harmonize with. **12a** to be capable of passing, extending, or being contained or inserted. **b** to belong. **13** to be acceptable, satisfactory, or adequate. **14** *informal* to empty the bladder or bowels. **15** to emit (a sound). **16** *Brit, informal* to say. ✱ **go about** to undertake or begin to tackle. **go after** to seek or pursue. **go ahead 1** to begin. **2** to continue; to advance or proceed. **go at** to undertake (e.g. a task) energetically. **go back on** to fail to keep (e.g. a promise). **go for 1** to try to gain. **2** to choose, favour, or accept. **3** to have an interest in or liking for. **4** to attack. **5** to apply to. **go into 1** of a number: to be contained in (another number). **2** to investigate. **3** to explain in depth. **go it alone** to act alone, *esp* courageously. **go missing** *chiefly Brit* to disappear. **go off** *informal* to stop liking or begin to dislike. **go one better** to outdo or surpass another. **go out of one's way** to take extra trouble. **go over 1** to examine, inspect, or check. **2** to repeat. **3** to study or revise. **go through 1** to subject to thorough examination, study, or discussion. **2** to experience or undergo (something difficult or unpleasant). **3** to spend, use, or exhaust. **go west** *informal* to die or become destroyed or expended. **go with 1** to accompany. **2** to be the romantic or sexual companion of. **go without** to be deprived of. **leave/let go** to stop holding. **to go** *chiefly NAm, informal* of prepared food and drink: to be taken away for consumption off the premises.

go[2] *n* (*pl* **goes**) **1a** a turn in an activity, e.g. a game. **b** an attempt, a try. **c** a chance; an opportunity. **2a** energy; vigour. **b** vigorous activity: *It's all go!* **3** a spell of activity. ✱ **have a go at** to attack, *esp* verbally; to criticize. **make a go of** to be successful in (e.g. a business venture). **no go** *informal* to no avail; useless. **on the go** *informal* constantly or restlessly active.

go[3] *n* a Japanese board game of capture and territorial domination played by two players with counters on a board covered in a grid.

goad[1] *n* **1** a pointed rod used to urge on an animal. **2** something that stimulates somebody into action.

goad[2] *v* **1** to drive (e.g. cattle) with a goad. **2** to incite or urge (somebody) by nagging or persistent annoyance.

go-ahead[1] *adj* energetic and progressive.

go-ahead[2] *n* (**the go-ahead**) a signal or permission to proceed.

goal *n* **1a** in sport, an area or object into which players must put a ball, etc to score points. **b** an instance of putting a ball, etc into a goal. **c** the position of a player defending a goal. **2** an end towards which effort is directed; an aim or objective. **3** the destination of a journey. ▶▶ **goalless** *adj.*

goalie *n informal* a goalkeeper.

goalkeeper *n* a player who defends the goal in football, hockey, lacrosse, etc. ▶▶ **goalkeeping** *n.*

goal kick *n* **1** a free kick in football awarded to the defending side when the ball is sent over the goal line by an opposing player. **2** in rugby, an attempt to kick a goal. ▶▶ **goal-kicker** *n,* **goal-kicking** *n.*

goal line *n* a line at either end of a playing area on which a goal or goal post is situated.

go along *v* **1** to move along; to proceed. **2** to go or travel as a companion. ✱ **go along with** to agree or cooperate with.

goalpost *n* either of usu two vertical posts with or without a crossbar that constitute the goal in football, rugby, etc. ✱ **move the goalposts** to change the rules, conditions, etc that pertain to something, *esp* in order to gain a personal advantage.

goanna *n* a large Australian lizard.

goat *n* **1** a long-legged agile ruminant mammal with backward-curving horns, a short tail, and usu straight hair. **2** *informal* a lecherous man. **3** *informal* a foolish person. ✱ **get somebody's goat** *informal* to annoy or irritate somebody. ▶▶ **goatish** *adj,* **goaty** *adj.*

goatee *n* a small beard covering only the bottom of the chin.

goatherd *n* somebody who tends goats.

goatskin *n* **1** the skin of a goat or the leather made from this. **2** a container or other article made from goatskin.

goatsucker *n* = NIGHTJAR.

gob[1] *n* **1** a shapeless or sticky lump. **2** *NAm* (*usu in pl*) a large amount.

gob[2] *v* (**gobbed, gobbing**) *chiefly Brit, informal* to spit.

gob[3] *n Brit, informal* the mouth.

gobbet *n* a piece or portion.

gobble[1] *v* **1** to swallow or eat greedily or noisily. **2** (*often* + up) to take, use, or read quickly or eagerly. ▶▶ **gobbler** *n.*

gobble[2] *v* to make the guttural sound of a male turkey or a similar sound. ▶▶ **gobbler** *n.*

gobble[3] *n* a gobbling sound.

gobbledygook *or* **gobbledegook** *n* wordy and generally unintelligible jargon.

go-between *n* an intermediary or agent.

goblet *n* **1** a drinking vessel that has a rounded bowl, a foot, and a stem. **2** the part of a liquidizer in which food is liquidized or ground by means of rotating blades.

goblin *n* a grotesque mischievous elf.

gobshite *n chiefly Irish, coarse slang* a stupid or contemptible person.

gobsmacked *adj Brit, informal* utterly taken aback; overwhelmed with astonishment.

gobstopper *n* a large round hard sweet.

goby *n* (*pl* **gobies** *or* **goby**) a small spiny-finned fish with the pelvic fins united to form a sucking disc.

go by *v* to pass.

go-cart *n* see GO-KART.

god[1] *n* **1** (**God**) the supreme or ultimate reality; the being whom people worship as creator and ruler of the universe. **2** a being or object believed to have more than natural attributes and powers and to require human worship. **3** a very influential person. **4** somebody or something of supreme value. **5** (**the gods**) the highest gallery in a theatre, usu with the cheapest seats. ➤➤ **godhood** *n,* **godlike** *adj.*

god[2] *or* **God** *interj* used to express astonishment, exasperation, etc.

god-awful *adj informal* extremely unpleasant.

godchild *n* (*pl* **godchildren**) somebody for whom another person becomes godparent at baptism.

goddamn *or* **goddam** *or* **goddamned** *adj and adv* damned.

goddaughter *n* a female godchild.

goddess *n* **1** a female deity. **2** a woman whose great charm or beauty arouses adoration.

godet /goh'det, 'gohday/ *n* an inset, usu triangular in shape, inserted into a garment to give fullness or flare.

godetia /gə'deeshə/ *n* an American plant of the fuchsia family widely grown for its attractive white, pink, or red flowers.

godfather *n* **1** a male godparent. **2** the leader of a criminal organization, *esp* the Mafia.

God-fearing *adj* devout.

godforsaken *adj* **1** remote; desolate. **2** neglected or miserable.

godhead *n* **1** divine nature or essence. **2** (**the Godhead**) the supreme being; God.

godless *adj* **1** not acknowledging a deity; impious. **2** wicked. ➤➤ **godlessness** *n.*

godly *adj* (**-ier, -iest**) **1** divine. **2** pious; devout. ➤➤ **godliness** *n.*

godmother *n* a female godparent.

godown /'gohdown/ *n* a warehouse in an Asian country, *esp* India.

go down *v* **1** to decline or decrease. **2** of the sun: to go below the horizon. **3a** of a ship or aircraft: to sink or crash. **b** to undergo defeat. **c** of a computer system or program: to become inoperative; to crash. **4a** to be received in a specified way. **b** to come to be remembered, *esp* by posterity. **5** (*often* + with) to become ill.

godparent *n* somebody who undertakes responsibility for the religious education and spiritual welfare of another person at baptism.

godsend *n* a desirable or needed person, thing, or event, *esp* one that comes at just the right time.

God's gift *n informal, chiefly ironic* the best person or thing, *esp* somebody who considers himself or herself supremely attractive, competent, etc.

godson *n* a male godchild.

godsquad *n chiefly derog* any religious, usu Christian, group that is thought to be overly pious or zealously evangelical.

godwit *n* a wading bird with a long upward-curving bill.

goer *n* **1** (*usu in combination*) a regular attender of something specified: *a theatregoer.* **2** *informal* somebody or something that moves or does things fast. **3** *informal* a sexually active person. **4** *Aus* a proposal or idea that is acceptable or feasible.

goes *v* third person present sing. of GO[1].

gofer *n informal* somebody who runs errands or carries messages for others.

goffer[1] *v* to crimp, wave, or flute (e.g. a lace edging), *esp* with a heated iron.

goffer[2] *n* an iron or other tool used for goffering.

go-getter *n* an aggressively enterprising person. ➤➤ **go-getting** *adj.*

goggle *v* to stare with wide or bulging eyes.

goggle-box *n Brit, informal* a television set.

goggle-eyed *adj and adv* with the eyes wide or bulging, in amazement or fascination.

goggles *pl n* protective glasses set in a flexible frame that fits snugly against the face.

go-go dancer *n* a female dancer employed to entertain by dancing in a modern usu erotic style, e.g. in a disco, pub, or nightclub. ➤➤ **go-go dance** *n,* **go-go dancing** *n.*

go in *v* **1** to enter. **2** of the sun, etc: to become obscured by a cloud. ✱ **go in for 1** to engage in (an activity), *esp* for enjoyment. **2** to enter and compete in (e.g. a test or race).

going[1] *n* **1** the condition of the ground, e.g. for horse racing. **2** advance; progress.

going[2] *adj* **1a** living; existing: *the best novelist going.* **b** available; to be had. **2a** current; prevailing. **b** profitable or thriving: *a going concern.*

going-over *n* (*pl* **goings-over**) **1** a thorough examination or investigation. **2** a severe scolding or beating.

goings-on *pl n* **1** actions or events. **2** irregular or reprehensible happenings or conduct.

goitre (*NAm* **goiter**) /'goytə/ *n* an abnormal enlargement of the thyroid gland visible as a swelling of the front of the neck. ➤➤ **goitred** *adj,* **goitrous** *adj.*

go-kart *or* **go-cart** *n* a small racing car used in karting.

gold *n* **1a** a yellow precious metallic element that is soft and easily worked, and is used *esp* in jewellery and as a currency reserve. **b** (*used before a noun*) made of or containing gold. **2a** gold coins. **b** money. **c** gold as a commodity. **3** a deep metallic yellow colour.

goldcrest *n* a very small olive-green European bird that has a bright yellow crown with a black border.

gold digger *n informal* a woman who uses her charms and sexual attraction to extract money or gifts from men.

gold disc *n* a music award in the form of a framed gold record given to an artist, group, etc, for sales in excess of a particular figure.

gold dust *n* gold in the form of very fine particles. ✱ **like gold dust** very rare or valuable.

golden *adj* **1** consisting of or containing gold. **2a** of the colour of gold. **b** of hair: having a colour between blond and ginger. **3** prosperous; flourishing. **4** favourable; advantageous. **5** marking a 50th anniversary. ➤➤ **goldenly** *adv,* **goldenness** *n.*

golden age *n* **1** a period of great happiness, prosperity, or achievement. **2** a period of time when a particular art form, type of music, etc was flourishing.

golden boy *n* a man or boy who is very successful, has great potential, or is highly favoured.

Golden Delicious *n* a variety of eating apple with a greenish yellow skin and sweet juicy flesh.

golden eagle *n* a large eagle of the northern hemisphere with brownish yellow tips on the head and neck feathers.

goldeneye *n* (*pl* **goldeneyes** *or* **goldeneye**) a large-headed diving duck of northern regions, the male of which is strikingly marked in black and white and has yellow eyes.

golden girl *n* a woman or girl who is very successful, has great potential, or is highly favoured.

golden goose *n* a source of continuing prosperity that must be handled with restraint.

golden handcuffs *pl n informal* a series of payments or other benefits given to an employee as an inducement to remain with a company.

golden handshake *n informal* a large sum of money given to an employee on leaving a company, *esp* on retirement.

golden hello *n informal* a substantial payment given to a person after they have agreed to join a company, often used to induce a person to leave a rival organization.

golden mean *n* the medium between extremes; moderation.

golden oldie *n informal* a hit song from the past that is still popular.

golden parachute *n informal* a substantial payment guaranteed to a business executive in the event of dismissal or demotion, *esp* following a takeover or merger.

golden retriever *n* a retriever of a medium-sized gold-coloured breed.

golden rice *n* a pale-yellow form of rice genetically modified to produce grains containing betacarotene in order to counteract vitamin-A deficiency.

goldenrod *n* a plant of the daisy family with heads of small yellow flowers often clustered in branching spikes.

golden rule *n* **1** a guiding principle. **2** a moral principle requiring that one treat others as one would wish to be treated by them.

golden share *n* a share in a company that is sufficient to prevent a takeover.

golden syrup *n* a pale yellow syrup derived from cane sugar and used in cooking.

goldfield *n* a district in which gold-bearing minerals occur.

goldfinch *n* a small red, black, yellow, and white European finch.

goldfish *n* (*pl* **goldfishes** *or* **goldfish**) a small golden-yellow or orange-red fish related to the carps and widely kept in aquariums and ponds.

goldfish bowl *n chiefly Brit* **1** a small usu spherical tank for keeping goldfish in. **2** *informal* any place or situation that affords little or no privacy.

gold leaf *n* gold beaten into very thin sheets and used *esp* for gilding.

gold medal *n* a medal of gold awarded to somebody who comes first in a competition or race. ⋙ **gold medallist** *n.*

gold mine *n* **1** an extremely profitable enterprise, business, etc. **2** a rich source of something desired. **3** a place where gold is mined. ⋙ **gold miner** *n.*

gold plate *n* **1** a thin coating of gold on another metal. **2** articles that are made of or plated with gold.

gold-plate *v* to cover (metal, etc) with a thin layer of gold.

gold reserve *n* gold held by a central bank, e.g. to protect a nation's currency or to meet international payments.

gold rush *n* a rush of people to newly discovered goldfields in pursuit of riches.

goldsmith *n* somebody who makes or deals in articles of gold.

gold standard *n* a monetary system in which the basic unit of currency is defined by a stated quantity of gold of a fixed purity.

golem /'gohləm/ *n* **1** a clay figure of Hebrew folklore supernaturally endowed with life. **2** something, e.g. a robot, resembling a golem.

golf *n* a game in which players using long-shafted clubs attempt to hit a small ball into each of the holes on a course with as few strokes as possible.

golf ball *n* **1** a small hard ball used in golf. **2** a metal sphere that carries the characters in some electric typewriters.

golf club *n* **1** any of a set of clubs with long shafts and shaped metal or wooden heads used to strike the ball in golf. **2** an association of golf players or their clubhouse.

golf course *n* an area of land laid out for golf having a series of 9 or 18 holes and usu various natural or artificial hazards.

golfing *n* the sport of playing golf. ⋙ **golfer** *n.*

golf links *pl n* (*used as sing. or pl*) a golf course, *esp* one near the sea.

golliwog *n* a soft doll with a black face, often dressed in colourful clothes.

golly[1] *interj* used to express surprise.

golly[2] *n* (*pl* **-ies**) = GOLLIWOG.

-gon *comb. form* forming nouns, denoting: a geometrical figure having the number of angles specified: *decagon.*

gonad /'gohnad/ *n* a primary sex gland in which egg or sperm cells are produced, e.g. the ovaries or testes. ⋙ **gonadal** *adj.*

gonadotrophin *n* a hormone that acts on or stimulates the gonads.

gonadotropin *n* = GONADOTROPHIN.

gondola *n* **1** a long narrow flat-bottomed boat used on the canals of Venice. **2a** an enclosure suspended from a balloon for carrying passengers or instruments. **b** a cabin suspended from a cable for transporting passengers, e.g. up a ski slope. **3** a fixture approachable from all sides used in self-service retail shops to display merchandise.

gondolier *n* somebody who propels a gondola.

gone[1] *v* past part. of GO[1].

gone[2] *adj* **1a** past; ended. **b** used up. **2** intoxicated with drugs, alcohol, etc. **3** pregnant by a specified length of time.

gone[3] *adv Brit* later or older than: *It's gone three o'clock.*

goner *n informal* **1** a hopeless or irretrievable person or thing. **2** a dead person.

gong[1] *n* **1** a disc-shaped percussion instrument that produces a resounding tone when struck, usu with a padded hammer. **2** *Brit, informal* a medal or decoration.

gong[2] *v* **1** to strike a gong. **2** to make the resonant sound of a gong.

gonna *contr informal* going to.

gonorrhoea (*NAm* **gonorrhea**) /gonə'ri·ə/ *n* a sexually transmitted disease in which there is inflammation of the mucous membranes of the genital tracts. ⋙ **gonorrhoeal** *adj.*

-gony *comb. form* forming nouns, denoting: origin; reproduction; manner of coming into being: *cosmogony.*

gonzo *adj NAm, informal* **1** bizarre; crazy. **2** denoting a highly subjective or eccentric style of journalism.

goo *n informal* **1** a sticky substance. **2** cloying sentimentality.

good[1] *adj* (**better, best**) **1a** of a favourable or desirable character or tendency. **b** of a high standard. **c** agreeable; pleasant. **d** (+ for) beneficial to the health or character of. **2a** morally commendable; virtuous. **b** well-behaved. **3** (*often* + at) competent; skilful. **4a** suitable; fit. **b** free from injury or disease. **c** not rotten; fresh. **5a** kind; benevolent. **b** reputable; *specif* upper-class. **6a** well-founded; true. **b** correct; conforming to a standard. **c** legally valid. **7a** adequate; satisfactory. **b** thorough; full. **8** at least: *a good hour later.* **9** used in expressions of greeting and farewell. ✻ **all in good time** in due course. **as good as** virtually; in effect: *as good as dead.* **good for/on you!** well done! **in good faith** with honest or sincere intentions. **make good 1** to be successful in life. **2** *chiefly Brit* to repair (something). **3** to provide compensation for (a loss, expense, etc). **4** to fulfil (a promise, etc). ➤➤ **goodish** *adj.*

good[2] *n* **1a** something good; merit or use. **b** the quality of being good. **2** benefit; advantage. **3a** (*usu in pl*) personal property. **b** (*usu in pl*) wares; merchandise. **c** (*in pl, used before a noun*) relating to the transport of merchandise, *esp* by rail. **4** *informal* (*in pl, used as sing. or pl*) the desired or necessary article: *They came up with the goods.* ✻ **do somebody/something good** to be beneficial to somebody or something. **for good** forever; permanently. **to the good 1** for the best; beneficial. **2** in a position of net gain or profit.

goodbye[1] (*NAm* **goodby**) *interj* used to express farewell.

goodbye[2] (*NAm* **goodby**) *n* (*pl* **goodbyes** *or NAm* **goodbys**) a concluding remark or gesture at parting.

good-for-nothing[1] *adj* of no value; worthless.

good-for-nothing[2] *n* an idle worthless person.

Good Friday *n* the Friday before Easter Sunday, observed in the Christian Church as the anniversary of the crucifixion of Christ.

good-hearted *adj* having a kindly generous disposition. ➤➤ **good-heartedness** *n.*

good-humoured *adj* good-natured; cheerful. ➤➤ **good-humouredly** *adv.*

goodie *n* see GOODY[1].

good-looking *adj* having a pleasing or attractive appearance. ➤➤ **good-looker** *n.*

goodly *adj* (**-ier, -iest**) **1** significantly large in amount; considerable. **2** *archaic* pleasantly attractive. ➤➤ **goodliness** *n.*

good-natured *adj* having or showing a pleasant and cooperative disposition. ➤➤ **good-naturedly** *adv.*

goodness[1] *n* **1** the quality or state of being good. **2** the nutritious or beneficial part of something.

goodness[2] *interj* used to express surprise.

good offices *pl n* power or action that helps somebody out of a difficulty.

Good Samaritan *n* = SAMARITAN (2A).

goods and chattels *pl n* all the things belonging to a person.

good-tempered *adj* having an even temper; not easily annoyed.

good-time *adj* of a person, *esp* a young woman: devoted to the pursuit of pleasure.

goodwill *n* **1** a kindly feeling of approval and support; benevolent interest or concern. **2a** cheerful consent. **b** willing effort. **3** the favour or prestige that a business has acquired beyond the mere value of what it sells.

good word *n* a favourable statement.

goody[1] *or* **goodie** *n* (*pl* **-ies**) *informal* **1** (*usu in pl*) something particularly attractive or desirable. **2** a good person or hero, *esp* in a film or book.

goody[2] *interj informal* used, *esp* by children, to express pleasure or delight.

goody-goody *n* (*pl* **goody-goodies**) *informal* somebody who is affectedly or ingratiatingly prim or virtuous. ➤➤ **goody-goody** *adj.*

gooey *adj* (**gooier, gooiest**) **1** soft and sticky. **2** cloyingly sentimental.

goof[1] *n informal* **1** a ridiculous or stupid person. **2** *chiefly NAm* a blunder.

goof[2] *v* **1** (*often* + about/around) to fool around. **2** *chiefly NAm, informal* to make a foolish mistake; to blunder.

go off *v* **1** to explode. **2** of food: to begin to decompose. **3** to follow a specified course; to proceed.

goofy *adj* (**-ier, -iest**) *informal* **1** *chiefly NAm* silly; foolish. **2** *chiefly Brit* of teeth: protruding. ➤➤ **goofily** *adv,* **goofiness** *n.*

googly *n* (*pl* **-ies**) in cricket, a slow ball bowled so that it turns the opposite way to that expected on bouncing.

googol *n* the figure 1 followed by 100 zeros; 10^{100}.

gook *n chiefly NAm, informal* a foreigner, *esp* somebody of southeast Asian origin or descent.

gooly *or* **goolie** *n* (*pl* **-ies**) *Brit, informal* a testicle.

goon *n informal* **1** somebody who behaves in a silly or foolish manner. **2** *chiefly NAm* somebody hired to terrorize or eliminate opponents; a bully or thug.

go on *v* **1** to continue; to carry on. **2a** to proceed by or as if by a logical step. **b** of time: to pass. **3** to take place; to happen. **4a** to talk, *esp* in an effusive manner. **b** (*often* + at) to criticize or nag somebody constantly. ✻ **go on! 1** used to encourage somebody. **2** used to express disbelief.

goosander *n* (*pl* **goosanders** *or* **goosander**) a duck of the northern hemisphere, the male of which has a black back, pinkish white underparts, and a greenish black head.

goose[1] *n* (*pl* **geese**) **1a** a large water bird with a long neck and webbed feet. **b** the female of such a bird: compare GANDER[1]. **2** *informal* a foolish person.

goose[2] *v informal* to poke (somebody) on the bottom.

gooseberry *n* (*pl* **-ies**) **1** a small round edible green or yellow fruit with soft prickly skin and acid flesh. **2** an unwanted companion to two lovers.

gooseflesh *n* a bristling bumpy condition of the skin accompanying erection of its hairs, usu caused by cold or fear.

gooseneck *n* something, e.g. a joint or pipe, that is curved like the neck of a goose or U-shaped.

goose pimples *pl n* = GOOSEFLESH.

goose step *n* a straight-legged marching step with the legs swung high. ➤➤ **goose-step** *v.*

go out *v* **1a** to go to social events, entertainments, etc. **b** (+ with) to spend time regularly with somebody in a romantic relationship. **2a** to become extinguished. **b** of the tide: to ebb. **c** to play the last card of one's hand.

go over *v* **1** to become converted, e.g. to a religion or political party. **2** to be received in a specified way.

gopher *n* **1** an American burrowing rodent that is the size of a large rat and has large cheek pouches.

2 a small ground squirrel of the N American prairies, closely related to the chipmunk. **3** in computing, an early form of Internet search engine.

gopik /'gohpik/ *n* (*pl* **gopik** *or* **gopiks**) a unit of currency in Azerbaijan, worth 100th of a manat.

gorblimey *interj Brit, informal* used to express surprise or indignation.

Gordian knot *n* an intricate problem, *esp* one insoluble in its own terms.

Word history
named after *Gordius*, King of Phrygia, who tied an intricate knot that supposedly could be undone only by the future ruler of Asia, and which Alexander the Great cut with his sword.

gore[1] *n* thick or clotted blood, *esp* blood that has been shed as a result of violence.

gore[2] *v* of an animal, *esp* a bull: to pierce or wound with a horn or tusk.

gore[3] *n* a tapering or triangular piece of material used to give shape to something, e.g. a garment or sail.

gore[4] *v* to give shape to (a garment, sail, etc) by inserting a gore or gores. ⋙ **gored** *adj.*

gorge[1] *n* **1** a narrow steep-walled valley, often with a stream flowing through it. **2** the contents of the stomach. **3** *archaic* the throat. ✱ **one's gorge rises** one is disgusted, sickened, or nauseated.

gorge[2] *v* **1** to eat hungrily or greedily. **2** to stuff (oneself) with food. ⋙ **gorger** *n.*

gorgeous *adj* **1** splendidly beautiful or magnificent. **2** *informal* very fine or pleasant. ⋙ **gorgeously** *adv,* **gorgeousness** *n.*

gorget /'gawjit/ *n* **1** a piece of armour protecting the throat. **2** a part of a wimple covering the throat and shoulders. **3** a band or patch of colour on a bird's or other animal's throat.

gorgio /'gawji·oh/ *n* (*pl* **-os**) used *esp* by gypsies: somebody who is not a gypsy.

gorgon *n* **1** (**Gorgon**) any of three sisters in Greek mythology who had live snakes in place of hair and who could turn anybody who looked at them to stone. **2** a repulsive or formidable woman.

Gorgonzola /gawgən'zohlə/ *n* a blue-veined strongly flavoured Italian cheese.

gorilla *n* **1** a large anthropoid ape of western equatorial Africa. **2** *informal* an ugly, heavily-built, or brutal man.

gormandize *or* **-ise** *or* **gourmandize** *or* **gourmandise** *v* **1** to eat voraciously. **2** to enjoy good food. ⋙ **gormandizer** *n.*

gormless *adj Brit, informal* lacking understanding and intelligence; stupid. ⋙ **gormlessly** *adv,* **gormlessness** *n.*

go round *v* **1** to spread or circulate. **2** to satisfy demand; to meet the need.

gorse *n* an evergreen European shrub having yellow flowers and green spines in place of leaves. ⋙ **gorsy** *adj.*

gory *adj* (**-ier, -iest**) **1** full of violence and bloodshed. **2** covered with blood. ✱ **(all) the gory details** *informal, often humorous* the explicit or most intimate details of something. ⋙ **gorily** *adv,* **goriness** *n.*

gosh *interj* used to express surprise.

goshawk /'gos·hawk/ *n* a long-tailed hawk with short rounded wings.

gosling /'gozling/ *n* a young goose.

go-slow *n Brit* a deliberate slowing down of production by workers as a means of forcing management to comply with their demands.

gospel *n* **1a** (*often* **Gospel**) the teachings of Jesus Christ or the message of the life, death, and resurrection. **b** (*usu* **Gospel**) any of the first four books of the New Testament relating these teachings and this message. **2a** something accepted as a guiding principle. **b** something so authoritative as not to be questioned. **3** a type of religious music that has its roots in black American culture and is associated with fervent Christian evangelism.

gospel music *n* = GOSPEL (3).

gossamer *n* **1** a film of cobwebs floating in the air in calm clear weather. **2** very fine gauze or silk. **3** (*used before a noun*) light, delicate, or insubstantial.

gossip[1] *n* **1** somebody who habitually reveals facts concerning other people, *esp* sensational or unsubstantiated facts. **2a** the facts related by a gossip or the act of talking about them. **b** a chatty talk. ⋙ **gossipy** *adj.*

Word history
Old English *godsibb* godparent, baptismal sponsor, from *god* + *sibb* kinsman, from *sibb* related. Because of the close relationship between parent and godparent, the word gossip gradually came to mean 'person with whom one shares news and idle talk'. The extension of the word to the idle talk itself is first recorded in the early 19th cent.

gossip[2] *v* (**gossiped, gossiping**) **1** to relate or discuss gossip. **2** to engage in casual conversation. ⋙ **gossiper** *n.*

gossip column *n* a column in a newspaper relating gossip about well-known people. ⋙ **gossip columnist** *n.*

got *v* past tense and past part. of GET.

Goth *n* **1** a member of a Germanic people that invaded parts of the Roman Empire between the third and fifth cent. AD. **2** (*often* **goth**) **a** a style of rock music that evolved from punk rock in the 1980s and is characterized by guitar-based rhythms and references to the occult. **b** a person who dresses mainly in black and who enjoys this type of music.

Gothic[1] *adj* **1** relating to the Goths or their language. **2** denoting a style of architecture of the 12th to the 16th cent. characterized by vaulting and pointed arches. **3** (*often* **gothic**) of or resembling a genre of fiction of the late 18th and early 19th cent. dealing with macabre or mysterious events in remote and desolate settings. **4** denoting a form of type or lettering with a heavy thick face and angular outlines used *esp* by the earliest European printers. ⋙ **Gothicism** *n.*

Gothic[2] *n* **1** the extinct E Germanic language spoken by the ancient Goths. **2** the Gothic architectural style.

go through *v* of a plan or proposal: to receive approval or sanction. ✱ **go through with** to continue resolutely with.

gotten *v NAm* past part. of GET.

gouache /goo'ahsh/ *n* **1** a method of painting with opaque watercolours that have been ground in water and mixed with a gum preparation. **2** paint or a painting produced in this way.

Gouda /'gowdə/ *n* a mild cheese of Dutch origin that is usu in the form of a disc coated in yellow wax.

gouge[1] /gowj/ *v* **1** to make (an uneven hole, dent, etc) in a surface. **2** (+ out) to force out roughly or violently: *They gouged out his eyes.* ⋙ **gouger** *n.*

gouge[2] *n* **1** a chisel with a curved cross section and a sharpened edge on the concave side of the blade. **2** a groove or cavity made by gouging.

goujon /'goohzhonh/ *n* a small strip of fish, chicken, etc, often coated in batter or breadcrumbs and deep-fried.

goulash /'goohlash/ *n* a meat stew of Hungarian origin made usu with beef or veal and highly seasoned with paprika.

go under *v* to be destroyed or defeated; to fail.

go up *v* **1** to increase. **2** to burst into flames.

gourami /'gooərəmi/ *n* (*pl* **gouramis** *or* **gourami**) a small brightly coloured fish often kept in an aquarium.

gourd *n* **1** the fleshy inedible fruit of a climbing plant, having a hard rind used to make vessels and utensils. **2** a cup, bottle, or other article made from a gourd.

gourde *n* the basic monetary unit of Haiti.

gourmand *n* somebody who is excessively fond of or heartily interested in food and drink. ➤➤ **gourmandism** *n.*

gourmet /'gawmay, 'gooəmay/ *n* **1** a connoisseur of food and drink. **2** (*used before a noun*) suitable for a gourmet.

gout /gowt/ *n* **1** a metabolic disorder that results in crystals of uric acid compounds being deposited in the joints, *esp* of the big toe, causing painful inflammation. **2** *archaic, literary* a blob or splash, e.g. of blood. ➤➤ **goutiness** *n,* **gouty** *adj.*

govern *v* **1** to control and direct the making and administration of policy in (a state, organization, etc). **2a** to control or strongly influence. **b** to hold in check; to restrain. **c** to serve as a deciding principle for. **3** of a word: to require (another word or group of words) to be in a specified grammatical case. ➤➤ **governability** *n,* **governable** *adj.*

governance *n formal* the action or manner of governing.

governess *n* a woman entrusted with the teaching and often supervision of a child in a private household.

government *n* **1** (*used as sing. or pl*) the body of people that governs a state, nation, or other political unit. **2** the act or process of governing. **3** the office or function of a governing body. **4** the system of rule by which a political unit is governed. ➤➤ **governmental** *adj.*

governor *n* **1a** a ruler, chief executive, or nominal head of a political unit. **b** the most senior administrator of an institution or organization, e.g. a prison. **c** a member of a body that controls an institution, e.g. a school. **d** the representative of the British Crown in a colony. **2** *informal* somebody, e.g. a father or employer, in a position of authority. **3** a device that automatically controls the supply of fuel, steam, etc to a machine. ➤➤ **governorate** *n,* **governorship** *n.*

governor general *n* (*pl* **governors general** *or* **governor generals**) a governor of high rank, *esp* one representing the British Crown in a Commonwealth country. ➤➤ **governor generalship** *n.*

gown[1] *n* **1a** a loose flowing robe worn *esp* by a professional or academic person when acting in an official capacity. **b** a woman's dress, *esp* one that is elegant or formal. **c** a protective outer garment worn in an operating theatre. **2** the body of students and staff of a college or university: *town and gown.*

gown[2] *v* (*usu in passive*) to dress in a gown.

goy *n* (*pl* **goyim** *or* **goys**) *offensive* used by Jews to refer to somebody who is not a Jew; a Gentile. ➤➤ **goyish** *adj.*

GP *abbr* **1** general practitioner. **2** Grand Prix.

GPS *abbr* Global Positioning System.

gr. *abbr* **1** grain. **2** gram. **3** gross.

grab[1] *v* (**grabbed, grabbing**) **1** to take or seize hastily or by a sudden snatching motion. **2** to obtain unscrupulously or opportunistically. **3** *informal* to forcefully engage the attention of; to impress: *It doesn't really grab me.* ➤➤ **grabber** *n.*

grab[2] *n* **1a** a sudden snatch. **b** an unlawful or unscrupulous seizure. **2** a mechanical device for clutching an object. ✱ **up for grabs** *informal* available for anyone to take or win.

grab bag *n chiefly NAm* = LUCKY DIP.

grace[1] *n* **1a** ease and suppleness of movement or bearing. **b** a charming or attractive trait. **2a** a temporary exemption; a reprieve. **b** (*also in pl*) approval; favour. **3a** unmerited divine assistance given to human beings. **b** a state of being pleasing to God. **4** a short prayer at a meal asking a blessing or giving thanks. **5** (**Her/His/Your Grace**) used as a title for a duke, duchess, or archbishop. **6** consideration; decency: *She had the grace to blush.* ✱ **with bad/good grace** unwillingly or willingly.

grace[2] *v* **1** (+ with) to favour or confer honour on (somebody or an event) with one's presence. **2** to adorn or embellish.

grace-and-favour *adj Brit* denoting a house, flat, etc in which somebody is allowed to live rent-free as a special privilege granted by the sovereign or government.

graceful *adj* having or displaying grace or elegance in form or movement. ➤➤ **gracefully** *adv,* **gracefulness** *n.*

graceless *adj* **1** lacking a sense of propriety. **2** devoid of elegance; awkward. ➤➤ **gracelessly** *adv,* **gracelessness** *n.*

grace note *n* a musical note added as an ornament.

Graces *pl n* (**the Graces, the Three Graces**) in Greek mythology, the three sister goddesses believed to personify and endow charm, grace, and beauty.

gracious[1] *adj* **1a** marked by kindness and courtesy. **b** having those qualities, e.g. comfort and elegance, made possible by wealth. **2** of divine grace. ➤➤ **graciously** *adv,* **graciousness** *n.*

gracious[2] *interj* used to express surprise.

grackle *n* **1** an Asian starling or mynah. **2** an American songbird with shiny black plumage.

gradation *n* **1a** a series forming successive stages. **b** a step or place in such a series. **2** a gradual passing from one shade or tone to another, e.g. in a painting. ➤➤ **gradational** *adj.*

grade[1] *n* **1** a position in a scale of ranks or qualities. **2** a mark indicating a degree of accomplishment at school. **3** a class of things of the same stage or degree. **4** *NAm* a group of pupils at the same level; a class or year. **5** a gradient. ✱ **make the grade** to reach the expected standard or an acceptable level; to succeed.

grade[2] *v* **1a** to sort according to quality. **b** to arrange in a scale or series. **2** to assign a grade to. **3** to level off (a road) to a smooth horizontal or sloping surface. **4** to pass from one stage or level to another, often by scarcely perceptible degrees.

grade crossing *n chiefly NAm* = LEVEL CROSSING.

grader *n* **1** a person or thing that grades. **2** a machine for levelling something, *esp* one used in constructing roads. **3** (*used in combination*) a student in a specified school grade: *a fifth grader.*

grade school *n NAm* a primary or elementary school.

gradient *n* **1a** the degree of inclination of a slope. **b** a sloping road or railway. **2** change in the value of a quantity with respect to the change in another quantity.

gradual *adj* **1** proceeding or happening by small steps or degrees, usu over a long period. **2** of a slope: not steep. ➤➤ **gradually** *adv,* **gradualness** *n.*

gradualism *n* the policy of approaching a desired end by gradual stages. ➤➤ **gradualist** *n and adj*, **gradualistic** *adj*.

graduand *n Brit* somebody who is about to receive an academic degree.

graduate[1] *n* **1** the holder of a first academic degree. **2** *chiefly NAm* somebody who has been awarded a high school diploma.

graduate[2] *v* **1** to mark (e.g. an instrument or vessel) with degrees of measurement. **2a** to receive an academic degree. **b** *NAm* to receive a high school diploma. **3** to move up to a higher stage of proficiency or prestige. **4** to change gradually. ➤➤ **graduator** *n*.

graduate school *n NAm* a place or period of postgraduate study.

graduation *n* **1** a mark, e.g. on an instrument or vessel, indicating a degree of measurement. **2** the award or acceptance of a degree or diploma, or a ceremony at which this takes place.

Graeco- (*NAm* **Greco-**) *comb. form* **1** denoting the Greek nation, people, or culture. **2** Greek and: *Graeco-Roman*.

graffiti *pl n* (*used as sing. or pl*) unauthorized drawings or writing painted in a public place, *esp* on a wall.

Usage note

Graffiti is a plural noun, but the singular form (*graffito*) is rare. *Graffiti* is commonly used with a singular verb, *esp* to refer to the drawings or writing collectively.

graft[1] *v* **1** to cause (a plant cutting) to unite with a growing plant. **2** to attach or add. **3** to implant (living tissue) surgically. **4** to use one's position improperly to one's own advantage. ➤➤ **grafter** *n*.

graft[2] *n* **1a** a grafted plant cutting. **b** the point of insertion of such a cutting. **2a** a surgical operation in which living tissue is grafted. **b** the living tissue so grafted. **3a** the improper use of one's position to one's own advantage. **b** something, *esp* money, acquired in this way.

graft[3] *v Brit, informal* to work hard. ➤➤ **grafter** *n*.

graft[4] *n Brit, informal* hard work.

graham *adj NAm* denoting wholemeal flour or something made from it.

Grail *n* = HOLY GRAIL.

grain[1] *n* **1a** a seed or fruit of a cereal plant. **b** such seeds or fruits considered collectively. **c** cereals or similar food plants considered collectively. **2a** a small hard particle, e.g. of sand or salt. **b** the least amount possible. **c** a particle of photographic emulsion. **3** a granular or grainy surface, nature, or appearance. **4** the arrangement of the fibres, particles, etc in wood, rock, fabric, etc. **5** a unit of weight based on the weight of a grain of wheat, equal to approximately 0.065 gram. ✱ **be/go against the grain** to be contrary to one's inclination, disposition, or feeling. ➤➤ **grainless** *adj*.

grain[2] *v* **1** to form into grains; to granulate. **2** to give a roughened texture or surface to. ➤➤ **grainer** *n*.

grainy *adj* (**-ier, -iest**) **1** consisting of or resembling grains; granular. **2** having or resembling the grain of wood. **3** of a photograph: having poor definition because the particles of emulsion are large and visible. ➤➤ **graininess** *n*.

gram *or* **gramme** *n* a metric unit of mass equal to one thousandth of a kilogram (about 0.04oz).

-gram *comb. form* forming nouns, denoting: **1** drawing; writing; record: *ideogram*. **2** a jocular greeting delivered on a special occasion: *kissogram*.

graminivorous *adj* of an animal: feeding on grass.

grammar *n* **1** the study of the classes of words, their inflections, and their functions and relations in the sentence. **2** the characteristic system of inflections and syntax of a language. **3** a grammar textbook. **4** speech or writing evaluated according to its conformity to grammatical rules. **5** the principles or rules of an art or science.

grammarian *n* a person who studies, writes about, or has expert knowledge of grammar.

grammar school *n* **1** *Brit* a secondary school providing an academic type of education from the age of 11 to 18. **2** *NAm* a primary or elementary school.

grammatical *adj* **1** relating to grammar. **2** conforming to the rules of grammar. ➤➤ **grammaticality** *n*, **grammatically** *adv*.

gramme *n* see GRAM.

Grammy *n* (*pl* **Grammys**) a statuette presented annually by the American National Academy of Recording Arts and Sciences for notable achievement in the recording industry.

gramophone *n Brit, dated* a record player.

gramps *n informal* one's grandfather.

grampus *n* **1** a marine animal that resembles a dolphin but with a bulbous head. **2** the killer whale or any small whale.

gran *n chiefly Brit, informal* one's grandmother.

granadilla *n* the egg-shaped, purple-skinned, many-seeded edible fruit of a passionflower.

granary *n* (*pl* **-ies**) **1** a storehouse for threshed grain. **2** a region producing grain in abundance. **3** *trademark* (*used before a noun*) denoting bread and other bakery products that contain malted wheat grains.

grand[1] *adj* **1a** large and striking in size, extent, or conception. **b** characterized by magnificence or opulence; sumptuous. **2** extremely dignified and proud. **3** intended to impress. **4** having more importance than others; principal. **5** *Brit, informal* very good; wonderful. ➤➤ **grandly** *adv*, **grandness** *n*.

grand[2] *n* **1** = GRAND PIANO. **2** *informal* **a** *Brit* a thousand pounds. **b** *NAm* a thousand dollars.

grandad *or* **granddad** *n* **1** *informal* one's grandfather. **2** (*used before a noun*) denoting a garment, *esp* a shirt, with an upright collar in the form of a narrow band.

grandam *or* **grandame** *n archaic* = GRANDMOTHER.

grandchild *n* a child of one's son or daughter.

granddad *n* see GRANDAD.

granddaughter *n* a daughter of one's son or daughter.

grand duchess *n* **1** the wife or widow of a grand duke. **2** a woman who has the rank of a grand duke in her own right.

grand duchy *n* the territory of a grand duke or grand duchess.

grand duke *n* **1** the sovereign ruler of any of various European states. **2** a son or male descendant of a Russian tsar.

grande dame /,grond 'dahm/ *n* **1** the most eminent and experienced woman in a particular field. **2** a usu elderly and dignified woman of high rank or standing.

grandee *n* **1** a Spanish or Portuguese nobleman of the highest rank. **2** any senior or high-ranking man.

grandeur *n* **1** the quality of being large or impressive; magnificence. **2** personal greatness marked by nobility, dignity, or power.

grandfather *n* **1** the father of one's father or mother. **2** a male ancestor. ➤➤ **grandfatherly** *adj.*

grandfather clock *n* a tall pendulum clock standing directly on the floor.

Grand Guignol /ˌgronh gee'nyol/ *n* a type of sensational or melodramatic entertainment featuring the gruesome or horrible. ➤➤ **Grand Guignol** *adj.*

grandiloquence *n* high-sounding or pompously eloquent speech or writing; bombast. ➤➤ **grandiloquent** *adj,* **grandiloquently** *adv.*

grandiose *adj* **1** characterized by the affectation of grandeur or by absurd exaggeration. **2** impressive because of uncommon largeness, scope, or ambitiousness. ➤➤ **grandiosely** *adv,* **grandioseness** *n,* **grandiosity** *n.*

grand jury *n* a jury in the USA that examines accusations and decides whether a case will go to trial.

grand larceny *n NAm* theft of property of a value greater than a sum specified by US law.

grandma *n informal* one's grandmother.

grand mal *n* a severe form of epilepsy involving muscle spasms and prolonged unconsciousness, or an attack of it: compare PETIT MAL.

grand master *n* **1** a chess player who has consistently scored highly in international competition. **2** (**Grand Master**) a title given to the head of various societies and orders, e.g. the Freemasons, and to senior exponents of some martial arts.

grandmother *n* **1** the mother of one's father or mother. **2** a female ancestor. ➤➤ **grandmotherly** *adj.*

grandmother clock *n* a smaller version of a grandfather clock.

Grand National *n* a major British steeplechase for horses that is run annually at Aintree near Liverpool.

grand opera *n* opera with a serious dramatic plot and with all the dialogue sung, not spoken.

grandpa *n informal* one's grandfather.

grandparent *n* a parent of one's father or mother. ➤➤ **grandparenthood** *n.*

grand piano *n* a large piano with a horizontal frame and strings.

grand prix /ˌgronh 'pree/ *n* (*pl* **grands prix**) **1** any of a series of long-distance motor races held consecutively in different countries. **2** a major competitive event in various other sports.

grandsire *n archaic* = GRANDFATHER.

grand slam *n* **1** the winning of all the major tournaments in a particular sport in a given year, or of all the games in a tournament. **2** in bridge, the winning of all 13 tricks by one player or side.

grandson *n* a son of one's son or daughter.

grandstand *n* **1** a usu roofed stand for spectators at a racecourse, stadium, etc in the best position for viewing the contest. **2** (*used before a noun*) giving an ideal viewing position.

grandstand finish *n* a particularly exciting end to a race or competition.

grand total *n* the final or complete amount or figure after lesser items have been added together.

grand tour *n* **1** an extended tour of the cultural sites of Europe, formerly part of the education of young British gentlemen. **2** an extensive and usu educational tour.

grange *n* **1** a large country house, often with many outbuildings. **2** *archaic* a barn or granary.

graniferous *adj* producing grain or similar seeds.

granita /grə'neetə/ *n* a coarse-grained water ice.

granite *n* a very hard granular igneous rock formed of quartz, feldspar, and mica and used *esp* for building. ➤➤ **granitic** *adj.*

granivorous *adj* of animals: feeding on seeds or grain.

granny *or* **grannie** *n* (*pl* **-ies**) **1** *informal* one's grandmother. **2** = GRANNY KNOT.

granny bond *n Brit* a savings bond, formerly available only to those over a certain age, which is guaranteed to maintain its value in line with the rate of inflation.

granny flat *n Brit* a part of a house converted into an independent dwelling, usu to accommodate an elderly relative.

granny knot *n* a reef knot crossed the wrong way and therefore not secure.

Granny Smith *n* a large green variety of dessert apple.

granny specs *pl n informal* glasses with small circular lenses and metal frames.

granola *n NAm* a breakfast dish resembling muesli.

grant[1] *v* **1a** to consent to carry out or fulfil (e.g. a wish or request). **b** to give as a right, privilege, or favour. **2** to bestow or transfer (something, e.g. a title or property) formally. **3a** to be willing to concede (something). **b** to assume to be true. ✱ **take somebody or something for granted 1** to assume to be true, real, or certain to occur. **2** to value too lightly. ➤➤ **grantee** *n,* **granter** *n,* **grantor** *n.*

grant[2] *n* **1** an amount of money given by a government or other body for a particular purpose. **2a** the act or an instance of granting. **b** a transfer of property or the property so transferred.

granted *adv* admittedly.

grant-in-aid *n* (*pl* **grants-in-aid**) **1** a grant or subsidy paid by a central to a local government to fund a public project. **2** a grant to a school or individual for a project.

grant-maintained *adj* denoting a British state school funded directly by the Department of Education and run by its governors and head teacher rather than by a local education authority.

gran turismo *adj* = GT.

granular *adj* consisting of granules, or having a grainy texture or appearance. ➤➤ **granularity** *n.*

granulate *v* **1** to form or crystallize into grains or granules. **2** to make or become rough or granular in appearance or texture. **3** of a wound: to form minute grainy particles laced with tiny blood vessels as part of the process of healing. ➤➤ **granulated** *adj,* **granulation** *n.*

granule *n* a small hard particle.

grape *n* **1** a smooth-skinned juicy green or purple berry that grows in clusters on a grapevine, eaten as a fruit or fermented to produce wine. **2** (**the grape**) *informal* wine. ➤➤ **grapy** *adj.*

grapefruit *n* a large round citrus fruit with a bitter yellow rind and a somewhat acid juicy pulp.

grape hyacinth *n* a small plant of the lily family with clusters of usu blue flowers.

grapeshot *n* ammunition for cannons, in the form of small iron balls shot in clusters.

grapevine *n* **1** a vine on which grapes grow. **2** (**the grapevine**) *informal* a secret or unofficial means of circulating information or gossip, *esp* word of mouth.

graph[1] *n* a diagram expressing a relation between quantities or variables, typically a line joining points plotted in relation to a vertical and a horizontal axis.

graph[2] *v* to plot or represent on a graph.

-graph *comb. form* forming nouns, denoting: **1** something written or represented: *monograph.* **2** an instrument for recording or transmitting something: *telegraph.*

graphic[1] *or* **graphical** *adj* **1** formed by writing, drawing, or engraving. **2** marked by clear and vivid description; explicit. **3** of methods of producing pictures or the pictorial arts. **4** of computer graphics. **5** represented by a graph. ➤➤ **graphically** *adv.*

graphic[2] *n* **1** a picture, map, or graph used for illustration or demonstration. **2** a graphic representation displayed by a computer.

graphical *adj* = GRAPHIC[1].

graphical user interface *n* any visual means by which a computer user gives instructions to the computer (e.g. icons on the screen).

graphic arts *pl n* the fine and applied arts of representation, decoration, and writing or printing on flat surfaces.

graphic design *n* the art of combining text and illustration in the design of printed matter. ➤➤ **graphic designer** *n.*

graphic equalizer *n* an electronic device for adjusting the level of certain frequencies in a recording system.

graphic novel *n* a work of literature in the form of a comic strip.

graphics *pl n* **1a** (*used as sing. or pl*) the art or science of drawing an object on a two-dimensional surface according to mathematical rules of projection. **b** designs (e.g. advertising posters) containing both typographical and pictorial elements. **2a** the images on a computer screen. **b** (*used as sing. or pl*) the use of computers to create and manipulate images, e.g. in television and films.

graphite *n* a soft black lustrous form of carbon that is used in lead pencils, as a lubricant, and in lightweight sports equipment. ➤➤ **graphitic** *adj.*

grapho- *comb. form* denoting writing: *graphology.*

graphology *n* **1** the study of handwriting, *esp* for the purpose of character analysis. **2** the study of writing systems and the symbols used in them. ➤➤ **graphological** *adj,* **graphologist** *n.*

graph paper *n* paper printed with small squares for drawing graphs and diagrams.

-graphy *comb. form* forming nouns, denoting: **1** writing or representation in a particular manner, on a particular subject, etc: *biography.* **2** the art or science of: *choreography.* ➤➤ **-grapher** *comb. form,* **-graphic** *comb. form,* **-graphical** *comb. form.*

grapnel *n* **1** a device with several claws or hooks radiating from a central stem that is hurled with a line attached in order to hook onto a ship, the top of a wall, etc. **2** a small anchor with several hooks used for anchoring small boats.

grappa *n* an Italian spirit distilled from the fermented remains of grapes after the juice has been extracted for making wine.

grapple[1] *v* **1** (*often* + with) to engage in hand-to-hand fighting; to wrestle. **2** (+ with) to struggle to deal successfully with something. **3** *archaic or literary* to seize or attach firmly with or as if with a grapnel. ➤➤ **grappler** *n.*

grapple[2] *n* **1** a hand-to-hand struggle. **2** a grapnel.

grappling iron *n* = GRAPNEL (1).

graptolite *n* an extinct fossil marine animal from the Palaeozoic era.

grasp[1] *v* **1** to take hold of eagerly with the fingers or arms. **2** to take advantage of enthusiastically. **3** to succeed in understanding; to comprehend. ➤➤ **graspable** *adj,* **grasper** *n.*

grasp[2] *n* **1** a firm hold. **2** control or power. **3** the ability or opportunity to seize or attain something: *Success was just beyond his grasp.* **4** understanding or ability to understand.

grasping *adj* eager for material possessions; greedy. ➤➤ **graspingly** *adv,* **graspingness** *n.*

grass[1] *n* **1a** a plant with slender leaves and green flowers in small spikes or clusters. **b** grass leaves or plants collectively. **2** an area covered in growing grass. **3** vegetation or land suitable or used for grazing animals. **4** *slang* marijuana. **5** *Brit, slang* a police informer. ✱ **let the grass grow under one's feet** to delay before taking action. **put/send out to grass** to cause to enter usu enforced retirement. ➤➤ **grasslike** *adj.*

grass[2] *v* **1** to feed (livestock) on grass. **2** to cover or seed (an area) with grass. **3** *Brit, slang* (*often* + on) to inform the police about wrongdoing committed by somebody.

grasshopper *n* a plant-eating insect with hind legs that are adapted for leaping and produce a chirping noise when rubbed together.

grass roots *pl n* (*used as sing. or pl*) **1** society at the local level as distinguished from the centres of political leadership. **2** the fundamental level or source. ➤➤ **grass-roots** *adj.*

grass snake *n* a nonpoisonous European snake with two yellow or orange patches forming a collar behind its head.

grass widow *n* a woman whose husband is temporarily away often or for long periods.

grass widower *n* a man whose wife is temporarily away.

grassy *adj* (**-ier, -iest**) **1** consisting of or covered with grass. **2** having the texture or smell of grass.

grat *v* past tense of GREET[2].

grate[1] *n* **1a** a frame or bed of metal bars that holds the fuel in a fireplace, stove, or furnace. **b** a fireplace. **2** = GRATING[1].

grate[2] *v* **1** to reduce (a hard food) to small particles by rubbing it on something rough. **2** to gnash or grind (teeth) noisily. **3** to rub or rasp noisily. **4** to cause irritation; to jar. ➤➤ **grater** *n.*

grateful *adj* feeling or expressing thanks. ➤➤ **gratefully** *adv,* **gratefulness** *n.*

graticule *n* **1** a network or scale visible on the eyepiece of a telescope, microscope, etc and used in locating or measuring objects. **2** the network of latitude and longitude lines on which a map is drawn.

gratify *v* (**-ies, -ied**) **1** to give pleasure or satisfaction to. **2** to give in to or to satisfy (an urge, whim, etc). ➤➤ **gratification** *n,* **gratifier** *n,* **gratifyingly** *adv.*

gratin /'gratanh/ *n* a dish cooked with a topping of breadcrumbs or grated cheese that has formed a brown crust.

grating[1] *n* **1** a framework of parallel bars or crossbars, e.g. covering a window. **2** a set of close parallel lines or bars ruled on a polished surface to produce optical spectra by diffraction.

grating[2] *adj* of sounds: with an annoyingly harsh quality; rasping.

gratis /'gratis, 'grah-/ *adv and adj* without charge; free.

gratitude *n* the state or feeling of being grateful; thankfulness.

gratuitous *adj* **1** not called for by the circumstances; unwarranted. **2** costing nothing; free. ➤➤ **gratuitously** *adv,* **gratuitousness** *n.*

gratuity *n* (*pl* **-ies**) **1** a small sum of money given in return for or in anticipation of some service; a tip. **2** a sum of money given to someone when they retire, *esp* from the armed services.

gravadlax *n* = GRAVLAX.

gravamen /grə'vaymen/ *n* (*pl* **gravamens** *or* **gravamina** /grə'vaminə/) the most significant part of a complaint or legal grievance.

grave[1] *n* **1a** a pit excavated for the burial of a body. **b** a tomb. **2** (**the grave**) *literary* death. ✱ **turn in one's grave** used to suggest that a dead person would strongly disapprove of something if he or she knew about it: *Your grandmother would turn in her grave if she saw you dressed like that.*

grave[2] *adj* **1a** requiring serious consideration; important. **b** likely to produce great harm or danger. **2** solemn and dignified. ⋙ **gravely** *adv*, **graveness** *n*.

grave[3] *v* (*past part.* **graven** *or* **graved**) **1** *archaic* to engrave. **2** *literary* to fix in the mind.

grave[4] /grahv/ *n* a mark (`) placed over a vowel in some languages to show that it is pronounced in a particular way.

gravel[1] *n* loose fragments of rock or small stones, often used to surface roads and paths.

gravel[2] *v* (**gravelled, gravelling,** *NAm* **graveled, graveling**) to cover or spread (a surface, e.g. a road) with gravel.

gravelly *adj* **1** like, containing, or covered with gravel. **2** harsh-sounding; grating.

graven image *n* an idol, usu carved from wood or stone.

graver *n* any of various tools (e.g. a burin) used in engraving.

Graves /grahv/ *n* (*pl* **Graves** /grahv/) a dry white or occasionally red wine produced in the Graves district of the Bordeaux region of France.

gravestone *n* a stone over or at one end of a grave, usu inscribed with details of the dead person.

graveyard *n* an area of ground used for burials, usu beside a church.

graveyard shift *n* *NAm, informal* the working shift that starts late at night and finishes early in the morning; the night shift.

gravi- *comb. form* heavy or weight: *gravimeter.*

gravid *adj* = PREGNANT. ⋙ **gravidity** *n*, **gravidly** *adv.*

gravimeter *n* a weighing instrument for measuring variations in gravity on the earth, moon, etc.

gravimetric *adj* **1** relating to the measurement of density or weight. **2** relating to the measurement of a gravitational field using a gravimeter. ⋙ **gravimetry** *n*.

gravitas /'gravitas/ *n* a solemn and serious quality or manner.

gravitate *v* to move under the influence of gravitation. ✱ **gravitate towards** to move or be drawn gradually and steadily towards.

gravitation *n* the natural force of mutual attraction between objects or particles, or the movement caused by this force. ⋙ **gravitational** *adj*, **gravitationally** *adv.*

gravitational constant *n* in Newton's law of gravity, the factor that relates gravity to the mass of and distance between bodies under the influence of the force of gravity.

gravitational field *n* a property of the region of space surrounding a body (e.g. a planet) that exerts a force of attraction on nearby bodies.

gravity *n* **1** the force that attracts objects towards the earth, or towards any body that has mass. **2** the quality of being heavy; weight. **3a** dignity or sobriety of bearing. **b** significance, *esp* seriousness.

gravlax *n* filleted salmon which has been seasoned and pressed, and is usu eaten raw.

gravure *n* **1** the process of printing from an engraved plate made of copper or wood. **2** = PHOTOGRAVURE.

gravy *n* **1** the fat and juices from cooked meat, thickened and seasoned and used as a sauce. **2** *informal* something of benefit that is obtained easily and sometimes unexpectedly.

gravy boat *n* a small boat-shaped vessel used for pouring gravy or other sauces.

gravy train *n* *informal* a much exploited source of easy money.

gray *n* the SI unit of ionizing radiation equal to an absorbed dose of one joule per kilogram.

grayling *n* (*pl* **graylings** *or* **grayling**) a silvery freshwater fish resembling a trout.

graze[1] *v* **1a** of animals: to feed on growing grass and other green plants. **b** to put (animals) out to graze. **2** *informal* to eat snacks frequently, instead of eating meals at regular times. **3** *informal* to sample things, e.g. television channels, casually and irregularly. ⋙ **grazer** *n*.

graze[2] *v* **1** to abrade or scratch, usu by glancing contact. **2** to touch lightly in passing.

graze[3] *n* an abrasion, *esp* of the skin, made by a scraping along a surface.

grazier *n* **1** somebody who grazes cattle, usu for beef production. **2** *Aus* a sheep farmer.

grazing *n* vegetation or land for animals to feed on.

grease[1] *n* **1** a thick oily substance, *esp* one used as a lubricant. **2** animal fat used in cooking, or produced when meat is cooked. **3** oily wool as it comes from the sheep. ⋙ **greaseless** *adj.*

grease[2] *v* **1** to smear or lubricate with grease. **2** to hasten or ease the process or progress of. ✱ **grease somebody's palm** to bribe somebody.

grease gun *n* a tool for releasing a controlled amount of lubricant.

grease monkey *n* *informal* a mechanic.

greasepaint *n* theatrical make-up.

greaseproof paper *n* paper resistant to penetration by grease, oil, etc and used *esp* for wrapping food.

greaser *n* **1** somebody whose work involves greasing machinery, *esp* a motor mechanic. **2** *informal* a long-haired man belonging to a motorcycle gang. **3** *NAm, informal, offensive* a Mexican or other person of Latin American origin.

greasy *adj* (**-ier, -iest**) **1a** smeared or soiled with grease. **b** oily in appearance or texture. **2** containing an unusual or unpalatable amount of grease. **3** insincerely polite or fawning in a distasteful way. ⋙ **greasily** *adv*, **greasiness** *n*.

great[1] *adj* **1** notably large in size or number. **2a** extreme in amount or degree. **b** of importance; significant. **3a** eminent or distinguished. **b** aristocratic or grand. **4** denoting the largest or most important of several; main or principal. **5** (*chiefly in combination*) removed in a family relationship by one stage further: *great-grandfather.* **6a** remarkably skilled: *a great organizer.* **b** enthusiastic: *a great fan.* **7** *informal* used as a generalized term of approval. ⋙ **great** *adv*, **greatly** *adv*, **greatness** *n*.

great[2] *n* (*pl* **great** *or* **greats**) (*usu in pl*) somebody who is eminent in a particular field.

great ape *n* any of the more advanced anthropoid apes, e.g. the gorilla.

great-aunt *n* an aunt of one's father or mother.

great circle *n* a circle formed on the surface of a sphere, e.g. the earth, by the intersection of a plane that passes through the centre of the sphere.

greatcoat *n* a heavy overcoat.

great crested grebe *n* a large diving water bird found in Europe, Africa, and Asia that has black projecting ear tufts in the breeding season.

Great Dane *n* a dog of a massive powerful smooth-coated breed with long legs.

greater *adj* (*often* **Greater**) consisting of a central city together with adjacent areas that are geographically or administratively connected with it.

greater celandine *n* = CELANDINE (2).

greathearted *adj* generous in spirit; magnanimous. ⋙ **greatheartedly** *adv,* **greatheartedness** *n.*

great-nephew *n* a grandson of one's brother or sister.

great-niece *n* a granddaughter of one's brother or sister.

Greats *pl n* the course and final BA examination in classics at Oxford University.

great tit *n* a large common black, white, and yellow Eurasian and N African tit.

great-uncle *n* an uncle of one's father or mother.

Great War *n* the first World War, 1914 to 1918.

greave *n* a piece of armour for the leg below the knee.

grebe *n* a swimming or diving bird with lobed rather than webbed toes.

Grecian *adj* relating to ancient Greece. ⋙ **Grecian** *n.*

Greco- *comb. form NAm* see GRAECO-.

greed *n* **1** excessive desire for or consumption of food. **2** excessive desire to acquire or possess things; avarice.

greedy *adj* (**-ier, -iest**) **1** consuming something, *esp* food, in excessive amounts. **2** having a great or excessive desire or need for something. ⋙ **greedily** *adv,* **greediness** *n.*

Greek *n* **1** a native or inhabitant of Greece. **2** the language of the people of ancient Greece or modern Greece. **3** *informal* something unintelligible: *It's all Greek to me.* ⋙ **Greek** *adj.*

Greek cross *n* a cross with four equal arms intersecting at right angles.

Greek Orthodox Church *n* the branch of the Orthodox Church that uses Greek in its liturgy and is the national Church of Greece.

green[1] *adj* **1** of the colour of grass, between blue and yellow in the spectrum. **2a** covered by grass or other green growth or foliage. **b** of food: consisting of green plants. **c** of fruit: not ripened. **d** of wood, leather, etc: not matured or seasoned. **3** of a person: **a** looking pale or sickly. **b** envious or jealous. **c** inexperienced or naive. **4a** relating to or beneficial to the natural environment. **b** concerned about environmental issues and supporting policies aimed at protecting the environment. **5** in the EU, denoting a unit of exchange with a special rate, used for paying agricultural producers. ⋙ **greenish** *adj,* **greenness** *n.*

green[2] *n* **1** a green colour. **2** (*in pl*) green vegetables. **3** an area of open grass for public use in a village or town. **4** a smooth area of grass for a special purpose, *esp* bowling or putting. **5** a member or supporter of an environmentalist party or group.

green[3] *v* **1** to make or become green. **2** to make more environmentally aware or less harmful to the environment.

greenback *n NAm, informal* a dollar.

green bean *n* the narrow green edible pod of any of various beans, e.g. the French bean or the runner bean.

green belt *n* an area of parks, farmland, etc encircling an urban area and usu subject to restrictions on new building.

green card *n* **1** an international certificate of motor insurance for UK drivers. **2** a permit allowing a foreign person to settle permanently and work in the USA.

greenery *n* green foliage or plants.

green-eyed monster *n* jealousy.

greenfield *adj* **1** consisting of land not previously built on. **2** not previously developed or exploited.

greenfinch *n* a common European finch with green and yellow plumage.

green fingers *pl n* an unusual ability to make plants grow. ⋙ **green-fingered** *adj.*

greenfly *n* (*pl* **greenflies** *or* **greenfly**) *Brit* a green aphid that is destructive to plants.

greengage *n* a small round greenish cultivated plum.

greengrocer *n chiefly Brit* a retailer of fresh vegetables and fruit. ⋙ **greengrocery** *n.*

greenhorn *n* an inexperienced or unsophisticated person, *esp* somebody who is easily cheated.

greenhouse *n* a building or enclosure with glass walls and a glass roof for the cultivation or protection of plants.

greenhouse effect *n* the warming of the lower layers of the atmosphere by absorption and reradiation of solar radiation that cannot escape through the build-up of carbon dioxide and other pollutants in the atmosphere.

greenhouse gas *n* a gas, *esp* carbon dioxide or methane, that contributes to the greenhouse effect.

greenkeeper *n* somebody who is responsible for the maintenance of a golf course or a bowling green.

Greenlander *n* a native or inhabitant of Greenland.

green light *n* authority or permission to undertake a project.

Green Paper *n chiefly Brit* a set of proposals issued by the government for public comment.

green pepper *n* a green unripe fruit of the sweet pepper plant, eaten raw or cooked as a vegetable.

green revolution *n* a process of rapid development and improvement in agriculture due to extensive use of artificial fertilizers and high-yielding plant strains.

greenroom *n* a room in a theatre or concert hall where performers can relax when not on stage.

greensand *n* a greenish form of sandstone coloured by the dull green silicates of iron and potassium.

greenshank *n* a European wading bird of the sandpiper family with olive-green legs and feet.

greenstick fracture *n* a fracture in a young person in which the bone is partly broken and partly bent.

greenstone *n* **1** a dark green compact rock. **2** a variety of jade found in New Zealand.

greensward *n archaic or literary* turf that is green with growing grass.

green tea *n* tea that is light in colour from incomplete fermentation of the leaf before firing.

green thumb *n NAm* = GREEN FINGERS. ⋙ **green-thumbed** *adj.*

greenware *n* pottery that has not been fired.

Greenwich Mean Time /'grenich/ *n* the mean solar time of the meridian of zero longitude that passes through Greenwich, used as the primary point of reference for standard time throughout the world.

greenwood *n archaic or literary* a forest with trees that are in full leaf.

greet[1] *v* **1** to acknowledge the presence or arrival of (somebody) with gestures or words. **2** to meet or react to in a specified manner. **3** to be perceived by: *the sight that greeted her eyes.* ⋙ **greeter** *n.*

greet[2] *v* (*past tense* **grat,** *past part.* **grutten**) *Scot* to weep or lament.

greeting *n* **1** a phrase or gesture expressing welcome or recognition on meeting. **2** (*usu in pl*) an expression of good wishes; regards.

greetings card *n* a card containing a message of goodwill usu sent or given on some special occasion.

gregarious *adj* **1** of people: having a liking for companionship; sociable. **2a** of animals: tending to associate with others of the same kind. **b** of a plant: growing in a cluster or a colony. ⋙ **gregariously** *adv,* **gregariousness** *n.*

Gregorian calendar *n* a revision of the Julian Calendar introduced in 1582 by Pope Gregory XIII and now in general use.

Gregorian chant *n* a rhythmically free liturgical chant in unison practised in the Roman Catholic Church.

gremlin *n* a mischievous creature said to cause the unexplained malfunctioning of machinery or equipment.

Grenache /grə'nash/ *n* a variety of grape used in the production of red and rosé wine, or a wine produced from it, *esp* a sweet dessert wine.

grenade *n* a small bomb that is thrown by hand or fired from a launcher.

Grenadian *n* a native or inhabitant of Grenada. ⋙ **Grenadian** *adj.*

grenadier *n* **1** a member of a regiment or corps formerly specially trained in the use of grenades. **2** (*often* **Grenadier**) in Britain, a member of the Grenadier Guards, the first regiment of the royal household infantry.

grenadine /'grenədeen/ *n* a syrup flavoured with pomegranates and used in mixed drinks.

grew *v* past tense of GROW.

grey[1] (*NAm* **gray**) *adj* **1** of a colour that is intermediate between black and white, like that of ash or a rain cloud. **2a** lacking sunshine or brightness; dull. **b** intermediate or unclear in position, condition, or character. **3** of hair: turning white with age. **4** without colour or character; nondescript. ⋙ **greyish** *adj,* **greyness** *n.*

grey[2] (*NAm* **gray**) *n* **1** a grey colour. **2** a horse with white hair but dark skin.

grey[3] (*NAm* **gray**) *v* to make or become grey.

grey area *n* **1** an intermediate zone between two others that has some of the qualities of each. **2** a subject or situation that is imprecisely defined or difficult to categorize.

greybeard *n* an old man.

Grey Friar *n* a Franciscan friar.

greyhound *n* a dog of a tall slender smooth-coated breed, characterized by swiftness and used for coursing and racing.

greylag *n* a common grey Eurasian wild goose with pink legs.

grey market *n* trade in goods or commodities that is underhand and usu involves profiteering, but is not illegal.

grey matter *n* **1** brownish grey nerve tissue in the brain and spinal cord. **2** *informal* brains or intellect.

grey seal *n* a large greyish seal of N Atlantic coasts.

grey squirrel *n* a common squirrel with grey fur that causes severe damage to deciduous trees.

grid *n* **1** a framework of parallel metal bars covering an opening, *esp* a drain; a grating. **2** a network of uniformly spaced intersecting horizontal and perpendicular lines, e.g. for locating points on a map. **3** a network of conductors for the distribution of electricity. **4** the starting positions of vehicles on a racetrack. ⋙ **gridded** *adj.*

griddle[1] *n* a flat metal pan or plate on which food is cooked by dry heat.

griddle[2] *v* to cook (food) on a griddle.

gridiron *n* **1** a framework of metal bars on which food is placed to be cooked; a grill. **2** any arrangement of horizontal and perpendicular lines or elements; a grid. **3** *informal* **a** an American football field. **b** the game of American football.

gridlock *n* **1** a severe traffic jam affecting a whole area with intersecting streets. **2** a point in a dispute or negotiations where the positions adopted by the parties involved make further progress impossible. ⋙ **gridlocked** *adj.*

grief *n* **1** deep distress, *esp* that caused by bereavement. **2** *informal* trouble of any kind. ✱ **come to grief** to end badly; to fail. **good grief!** an exclamation of surprise, annoyance, or alarm. ⋙ **griefless** *adj.*

grievance *n* **1** a cause of resentment or of dissatisfaction, constituting grounds for protest or complaint. **2** the formal expression of a grievance; a complaint.

grieve *v* **1** (*often* + for) to feel or express grief, *esp* over a bereavement. **2** to cause to suffer grief; to distress. ⋙ **griever** *n.*

grievous *adj* **1** causing or characterized by severe pain or sorrow. **2** of great seriousness; grave. ⋙ **grievously** *adv,* **grievousness** *n.*

grievous bodily harm *n* serious physical harm done to a person in an attack, for which the attacker may be charged in a court of law.

griffin *or* **griffon** *or* **gryphon** *n* a mythical animal with the head and wings of an eagle and the body and tail of a lion.

griffon *n* **1** see GRIFFIN. **2** = GRIFFON VULTURE. **3** a terrier of a small wire-haired breed originating in Belgium.

griffon vulture *n* a large vulture of Europe, Asia, or Africa with brown plumage.

grill[1] *n* **1** a cooking utensil consisting of a set of parallel bars on which food is exposed to heat. **2** *Brit* an apparatus on a cooker under which food is cooked or browned by radiant heat. **3** an article or dish of grilled food. **4** an informal restaurant. **5** see GRILLE.

grill[2] *v* **1** to cook (food) on or under a grill by radiant heat. **2** *informal* to subject to intense questioning. ⋙ **griller** *n.*

grille *or* **grill** *n* a grating forming a barrier or screen; *specif* an ornamental metal one at the front end of a motor vehicle.

grillroom *n* = GRILL[1] (4).

grilse *n* (*pl* **grilse**) a young mature salmon returning from the sea to spawn for the first time.

grim *adj* (**grimmer, grimmest**) **1** forbidding in disposition or appearance. **2** not flinching from a plan or intention; unyielding. **3** ghastly or sinister in character. **4** *informal* unpleasant in some way; nasty. ⋙ **grimly** *adv,* **grimness** *n.*

grimace¹ *n* a distorted facial expression, usu of disgust, anger, or pain.

grimace² *v* to express pain, disapproval, or disgust by twisting one's face. ➤➤ **grimacer** *n.*

grimalkin *n* **1** *archaic* an old female cat. **2** a spiteful or bad-tempered old woman.

grime¹ *n* dirt, *esp* when sticking to or ingrained in a surface. ➤➤ **griminess** *n,* **grimy** *adj.*

grime² *v* to cover or soil with grime.

grin¹ *v* (**grinned, grinning**) **1** to smile broadly, usu in a self-satisfied way. **2** to smile in a fierce or sinister way, showing the teeth. ✱ **grin and bear it** to put up with an unpleasant experience in a stoical way. ➤➤ **grinner** *n.*

grin² *n* **1** a broad smile. **2** a sinister smile.

grind¹ *v* (*past tense and past part.* **ground**) **1** to reduce to powder or small fragments by crushing. **2** to polish, sharpen, or wear down by friction. **3** to rub, press, or twist harshly. **4** to operate or produce by turning a crank. **5** to move with difficulty or friction, *esp* so as to make a grating noise. **6** (*often* + away) to work monotonously, *esp* to study hard. **7** to rotate the hips in an erotic manner. ✱ **grind to a halt** to stop in a noisy, jarring, or disconcerting way. ➤➤ **grinder** *n,* **grindingly** *adv.*

grind² *n* **1** dreary monotonous labour or routine. **2** an act of grinding.

grind down *v* to subject to domineering treatment; to oppress.

grind out *v derog* to produce (something, *esp* something of inferior quality) in a mechanical way.

grindstone *n* **1** = MILLSTONE (1). **2** a flat circular stone or abrasive disc that revolves on an axle and is used for grinding, polishing, sharpening, etc.

gringo *n* (*pl* **-os**) an English-speaking foreigner in Spain or Latin America.

grip¹ *v* (**gripped, gripping**) **1** to seize or hold firmly. **2** to attract and hold the interest of. ➤➤ **gripper** *n,* **gripping** *adj.*

grip² *n* **1a** a strong or tenacious grasp. **b** a particular manner of gripping. **2a** control, mastery, or power. **b** understanding or the ability to understand. **3** a part or device that grips. **4** a part by which something is grasped, *esp* a handle. **5** somebody who handles scenery, props, lighting, etc in a theatre or camera equipment in a film or television studio. **6** a travelling bag; a holdall. ✱ **come/get to grips with 1** to set about dealing with. **2** to grapple or wrestle with. **3** to begin to understand. **lose one's grip** to be unable any longer to deal with things effectively.

gripe¹ *v* **1** to cause to feel sharp intestinal pain. **2** *informal* to complain persistently. ➤➤ **griper** *n.*

gripe² *n* **1** (*usu in pl*) a stabbing spasmodic intestinal pain. **2** *informal* a grievance or complaint, *esp* one regarded as trivial or unjustified.

gripe water *n* a liquid preparation given to babies to aid digestion.

grisaille /gri'zayl/ *n* a method of decorative painting in tones of grey, designed to produce a three-dimensional effect.

gris-gris /'gree gree/ *n* (*pl* **gris-gris**) **1** an African amulet or spell. **2** the use of such spells or amulets.

grisly *adj* (**-ier, -iest**) inspiring horror, intense fear, or disgust. ➤➤ **grisliness** *n.*

grissini /gri'seeni/ *pl n* thin, Italian-style breadsticks.

grist *n* **1a** grain for grinding. **b** a batch of grain ground at one time. **2** crushed malt used to make a brewing mash. ✱ **grist to the mill** something that can be put to use or profit.

gristle *n* tough cartilaginous or fibrous matter in cooked meat. ➤➤ **gristly** *adj.*

grit¹ *n* **1** small hard particles of stone or coarse sand. **2** *informal* firmness of mind or spirit; determination.

grit² *v* (**gritted, gritting**) **1** to cover or spread (*esp* an icy road surface) with grit. **2** to clench (one's teeth) as a sign of determination or stoical firmness.

grits *pl n* (*used as sing. or pl*) *NAm* coarsely ground maize with the husks removed, boiled with water or milk and eaten as a breakfast dish, usu with butter.

gritty *adj* (**-ier, -iest**) **1** courageously persistent or determined. **2** not flinching from dealing with unpleasantness; uncompromising. **3** resembling or containing grit. ➤➤ **grittily** *adv,* **grittiness** *n.*

grizzle *v informal* **1** *Brit, dated* of a child: to cry quietly and fretfully. **2** (*often* + about) to complain in a self-pitying way.

grizzled *adj* sprinkled or streaked with grey.

grizzly *n* (*pl* **-ies**) a very large bear that lives in the highlands of western N America and has brownish fur streaked with white on its back.

grizzly bear *n* = GRIZZLY.

groan¹ *v* **1** to utter a deep moan. **2** to creak under strain. ➤➤ **groaner** *n.*

groan² *n* **1** a deep moaning sound. **2** a creaking sound.

groat *n* a former British coin worth four old pence.

groats *pl n* hulled grain broken into fragments.

grocer *n* a dealer in staple foodstuffs, household supplies, and usu fruit, vegetables, and dairy products.

groceries *pl n* foodstuffs and other general items sold by a grocer or in a supermarket.

grocery *n* a grocer's shop or business.

grockle *n Brit, informal, derog* a tourist or other visitor viewed disparagingly by the locals.

grog *n* **1** an alcoholic spirit, usu rum, mixed with water. **2** *informal* alcohol in general, *esp* spirits.

groggy *adj* (**-ier, -iest**) weak and dazed, *esp* owing to illness or tiredness. ➤➤ **groggily** *adv,* **grogginess** *n.*

grogram *n* a coarse loosely woven fabric of silk, often with mohair or wool.

groin *n* **1a** the area of the body between the lower abdomen and the inner part of the thigh. **b** *euphem* the genitals. **2** in architecture, the line along which two intersecting vaults meet. **3** *chiefly NAm* = GROYNE.

grommet *n* **1** an eyelet of firm material to strengthen or protect an opening, e.g. a hole that rope or cable passes through. **2** a small plastic tube inserted in the ear to drain off fluid.

groom¹ *n* **1** somebody who is in charge of the care of horses. **2** a bridegroom.

groom² *v* **1** to clean and care for (e.g. a horse or dog), *esp* by brushing its coat. **2** to make (oneself or one's appearance) neat or attractive. **3** to get (somebody) ready for a specific role or task, e.g. by training. ➤➤ **groomer** *n.*

groove¹ *n* **1a** a long narrow channel or depression cut into wood, stone, etc. **b** the continuous spiral track on a record, whose irregularities correspond to the recorded sounds. **2** a fixed routine; a rut. ✱ **in the groove 1** *informal* performing at one's peak. **2** *dated, informal* having an enjoyable time.

groove² *v* **1** to make a groove in. **2** *dated, informal* to dance to or perform popular music. ➤➤ **groover** *n.*

groovy *adj* (**-ier, -iest**) *dated, informal* fashionably attractive or exciting.

grope[1] *v* **1** to search or feel about blindly or uncertainly, *esp* with the hands. **2** to fondle for sexual pleasure, *esp* in a clumsy or unwelcome manner. ➤➤ **groper** *n.*

grope[2] *n* an act of groping.

groper *n* = GROUPER.

grosbeak /'grohsbeek/ *n* a finch or other songbird of Europe or America with a large thick conical beak.

groschen /'grohsh(ə)n/ *n* (*pl* **groschen**) a unit of currency in Austria, worth 100th of a schilling.

grosgrain /'grohgrayn/ *n* a strong closely woven corded fabric, usu of silk or rayon and with crosswise ribs.

gros point /'groh poynt/ *n* needlepoint embroidery worked on canvas across double threads in large diagonal stitches or cross-stitches.

gross[1] *adj* **1** glaringly noticeable or objectionable; flagrant. **2a** constituting an overall total before deductions (e.g. for taxes) are made: compare NET[3]. **b** of weight: including both the object in question and any incidentals, e.g. packaging or load. **3** coarse or vulgar. **4** *informal* disgustingly unpleasant; repulsive. **5** big or bulky, *esp* excessively overweight. ➤➤ **grossly** *adv,* **grossness** *n.*

gross[2] *n* an overall total before deductions.

gross[3] *v* **1a** to earn or bring in (an overall total) before deductions. **b** (+ up) to convert (a net amount) to a gross amount by adding tax, etc that has been deducted. **2** *informal* (+ out) to make (somebody) feel disgusted or repelled. ➤➤ **grosser** *n.*

gross[4] *n* (*pl* **gross**) a group of twelve dozen things.

gross domestic product *n* the total value of the goods and services produced in a country during a year, excluding income from investments abroad.

gross national product *n* the total value of the goods and services produced in a country during a year, including income from investments abroad.

grosz /grosh/ *n* (*pl* **groszy**) a unit of currency in Poland, worth 100th of a zloty.

grot[1] *n informal* something unpleasant, *esp* dirt.

grot[2] *n archaic, literary* = GROTTO.

grotesque[1] *adj* **1** amusingly or repellently unnatural or ugly in appearance. **2** absurdly incongruous or inappropriate. **3** of the grotesque style in art. ➤➤ **grotesquely** *adv,* **grotesqueness** *n.*

grotesque[2] *n* **1** a style of decorative art in which incongruous or fantastic human and animal forms are interwoven with natural motifs (e.g. foliage). **2** a grotesque person or thing.

grotesquerie *or* **grotesquery** *n* (*pl* **grotesqueries**) **1** something grotesque. **2** the quality of being grotesque; grotesqueness.

grotto *n* (*pl* **-oes** *or* **-os**) a small cave, *esp* one in a picturesque setting.

grotty *adj* (**-ier, -iest**) *Brit, informal* **1** unpleasant; nasty. **2** of poor quality. **3** not healthy; unwell. ➤➤ **grottily** *adv,* **grottiness** *n.*

grouch[1] *n* **1** a bad-tempered complaint. **2** a habitually irritable or complaining person. ➤➤ **grouchiness** *n,* **grouchy** *adj.*

grouch[2] *v* to complain annoyingly or habitually.

ground[1] *n* **1a** the surface of the earth. **b** soil or earth. **2** land of a particular type. **3** an area of land used for a particular purpose. **4** (*in pl*) the area around and belonging to a large building. **5** an area of knowledge or special interest. **6** (*also in pl*) a basis for belief, action, or argument. **7a** a background. **b** a prepared underlying surface on which something is to be added or applied. **8** (*in pl*) ground coffee beans after brewing. **9** *NAm* an electrical earth. ✱ **gain ground** to become more popular or widely accepted. **gain ground on** to begin to catch up with or overtake. **give ground** to withdraw before superior force; to retreat. **go to ground 1** to go into hiding. **2** of a fox: to enter its burrow. **off the ground** started and in progress. **on the ground** in the area or at the level where practical work takes place. **run into the ground** to tire out with heavy work or wear out with much use.

ground[2] *v* **1** to bring to or place on the ground. **2a** (*usu in passive*) to provide a reason or justification for. **b** to instruct in the fundamentals of a subject. **3a** to forbid (a pilot or aircraft) to fly. **b** *informal* to give (a child) the punishment of having to stay at home. **4** *NAm* to earth (an electrical appliance). **5** of a ship: to run aground.

ground[3] *v* past tense and past part. of GRIND[1].

groundbait *n* bait scattered on the water so as to attract fish.

ground-breaking *adj* introducing entirely new developments or methods; pioneering.

ground control *n* (*taking sing. or pl verb*) the equipment and operators that control or communicate with aircraft from the ground.

ground cover *n* low-growing plants that grow in a spreading fashion.

ground elder *n* a European plant that has creeping white underground stems and is commonly found growing as a weed on cultivated ground.

ground floor *n* the floor of a house on a level with the ground.

ground frost *n* a temperature below freezing on the ground, harmful to low-growing vegetation.

ground glass *n* **1** glass with a light-diffusing surface produced by etching or grinding that makes it translucent but not transparent. **2** glass ground into a powder, for use in abrasives.

groundhog *n NAm* = WOODCHUCK.

grounding *n* fundamental training in a field of knowledge.

ground ivy *n* a trailing plant of the mint family with bluish purple flowers.

groundless *adj* having no basis in fact or reason; unjustified. ➤➤ **groundlessly** *adv,* **groundlessness** *n.*

groundling *n* **1** a spectator who stood in the pit of an Elizabethan theatre. **2** somebody regarded as being of low status.

groundnut *n chiefly Brit* = PEANUT.

ground plan *n* **1** a plan of the ground floor of a building. **2** a first or basic plan.

ground rent *n* the rent paid by the owner of a building to the owner of the land that it is built on.

ground rule *n* a basic rule of procedure.

groundsel *n* a European plant of the daisy family that has small yellow flower heads and is a common weed.

groundsheet *n* a waterproof sheet placed on the ground (e.g. in a tent).

groundsman *n* (*pl* **groundsmen**) somebody who tends a playing field, *esp* a cricket pitch.

ground speed *n* the speed of an aircraft relative to the ground.

ground squirrel *n* a burrowing N American rodent, e.g. the chipmunk.

groundswell *n* **1** a sea swell caused by an often distant gale or ground tremor. **2** a rapid and spontaneous build-up of public opinion.

groundwater *n* underground water in soil and rocks that supplies wells and springs.

groundwork *n* work done to provide a foundation or basis.

ground zero *n* the point on the surface of the earth at or directly below or above the centre of a nuclear explosion.

group[1] *n* **1** (*used as sing. or pl*) a number of people or things gathered together or regarded as forming a single unit. **2** a small band of musicians, *esp* playing pop music. **3** an operational and administrative unit in an air force. **4** a number of business companies under the same ownership. **5a** an assemblage of atoms forming part of a molecule; a radical. **b** all the chemical elements forming one of the vertical columns of the periodic table.

group[2] *v* **1** to form or combine in a group. **2** (*often* + under/with) to assign to a group; to classify.

group captain *n* in the RAF, an officer who is senior to a wing commander and junior to an air commodore.

grouper *n* (*pl* **groupers** *or* **grouper**) a large fish of the sea bass family found in tropical seas.

groupie *n* an ardent female fan who follows a famous person, *esp* a rock star, on tour, often in the hope of striking up a sexual relationship.

grouping *n* a set of people or things combined in a group.

group practice *n* a medical practice run by a group of associated general practitioners.

group therapy *n* the treatment of several individuals with similar psychological problems simultaneously through group discussion and mutual aid.

groupware *n* computer software that enables a network of users to share information and other resources.

grouse[1] *n* (*pl* **grouse**) a game bird with a plump body and strong feathered legs.

grouse[2] *v informal* to complain, *esp* annoyingly or without reason; to grumble. ⋙ **grouser** *n.*

grouse[3] *n informal* a complaint.

grout[1] *n* **1** (*also* **grouting**) a thin mortar used for filling spaces, *esp* the gaps between wall or floor tiles. **2** (*usu in pl*) sediment of any kind at the bottom of a container.

grout[2] *v* to fill up the spaces between (tiles) with grout. ⋙ **grouter** *n.*

grove *n* a small wood or group of trees.

grovel *v* (**grovelled, grovelling,** *NAm* **groveled, groveling**) **1** to lie or creep with the body prostrate to show subservience or abasement. **2** to abase or humble oneself in order to earn forgiveness or favour. ⋙ **groveller** *n,* **grovellingly** *adv.*

grow *v* (*past tense* **grew,** *past part.* **grown**) **1** of an organism: to increase in size and develop to maturity. **2** to increase or expand. **3** to become gradually. **4** to cause (a plant, fruit, or vegetables, etc) to grow; to cultivate. **5** to develop (something) as a natural product of growing. ⋙ **grower** *n.*

growbag *n* a large bag of compost designed to be laid flat and used as a container for planting.

growing pains *pl n* **1** pains felt in the muscles and joints of growing children, *esp* in the legs. **2** problems that are experienced in the early stages of a new project.

grow into *v* to become big enough to fit (a piece of clothing).

growl *v* **1a** to utter a deep sound in the throat that expresses hostility. **b** to speak in an angry or hostile way. **2** to make a continuous low sound: *Thunder growled in the dark sky.* ⋙ **growl** *n.*

growler *n* **1** a small iceberg. **2** a person or animal that growls.

grown *v* past part. of GROW.

grown-up *adj* fully mature; adult. ⋙ **grown-up** *n.*

grow on *v* to become gradually more pleasing to.

grow out of *v* **1** to become too big to fit (a piece of clothing). **2** to become too mature or too accomplished to get enjoyment or satisfaction from.

growth *n* **1a** the process of growing. **b** progressive development. **2** an increase or expansion. **3a** something that grows or has grown. **b** a tumour or other abnormal tissue formation. **4** (*used before a noun*) growing rapidly: *a growth industry.*

growth hormone *n* **1** a hormone secreted by the pituitary gland in vertebrates that regulates growth. **2** a plant substance that promotes growth.

growth ring *n* a layer of wood, shell, etc produced by a plant or animal during a particular period of growth.

grow up *v* of a person: to develop towards or arrive at a mature state.

groyne (*NAm* **groin**) *n* a wall-like structure built out from a shore, *esp* to check erosion of the beach; a breakwater.

GRP *abbr* glass-reinforced plastic.

grub[1] *v* (**grubbed, grubbing**) **1a** to dig in the ground, *esp* for something that is difficult to find or extract. **b** (*usu* + up) to dig (something) up or out. **2** to search about; to rummage. ⋙ **grubber** *n.*

grub[2] *n* **1** a soft thick wormlike larva of an insect. **2** *informal* food.

grubby *adj* (**-ier, -iest**) **1** dirty; grimy. **2** disreputable or sordid. ⋙ **grubbily** *adv,* **grubbiness** *n.*

grub-screw *n* a headless screw.

Grub Street *n* the world or lifestyle of struggling journalists and literary hacks.

grudge[1] *v* **1** to be unwilling or reluctant to give or admit (something). **2** to feel resentful towards (somebody) who has something that you envy: *I don't grudge him his success.* ⋙ **grudger** *n.*

grudge[2] *n* a feeling of deep-seated resentment or ill will.

grudging *adj* offered or given only unwillingly; reluctant. ⋙ **grudgingly** *adv.*

gruel *n* thin porridge.

gruelling (*NAm* **grueling**) *adj* taxing or demanding to the point of exhaustion; punishing.

gruesome *adj* inspiring horror or repulsion; ghastly. ⋙ **gruesomely** *adv,* **gruesomeness** *n.*

gruff *adj* **1** brusque or stern in manner or speech. **2** deep and harsh. ⋙ **gruffly** *adv,* **gruffness** *n.*

grumble[1] *v* **1** to mutter discontentedly or in complaint. **2** to rumble. ⋙ **grumbler** *n,* **grumbly** *adj.*

grumble[2] *n* **1** the sound of grumbling. **2** a complaint or cause of complaint.

grumbling *adj* causing intermittent pain or discomfort.

grummet *n* = GROMMET.

grump[1] *n* **1** (*usu in pl*) a fit of ill humour or sulkiness. **2** a grumpy person.

grump[2] *v* to grumble or sulk; to be grumpy.

grumpy *adj* (**-ier, -iest**) moodily cross; surly. ⋙ **grumpily** *adv,* **grumpiness** *n.*

grunge *n* **1** *informal* dirt. **2** a style of rock music that features markedly discordant guitar and a sneering and listless vocal style. **3** a fashion style in which layers of clothing give a deliberately careless and uncoordinated appearance. ⋙ **grungy** *adj.*

grunt[1] *v* **1** to utter the deep short guttural sound typical of a pig. **2** to utter a similar sound, e.g. in reluctant agreement or during strenuous exertion. ⋙ **grunter** *n.*

grunt[2] *n* **1** a grunting sound. **2** *NAm, informal* **a** an infantryman in the US Army or Marines. **b** a person who does unskilled or routine work.

grutten *v* past part. of GREET[2].

Gruyère /'groohyeə/ *n* a Swiss cheese with smaller holes and a slightly fuller flavour than Emmenthal.

gryphon *n* see GRIFFIN.

GSOH *abbr* good sense of humour.

G spot *n* a small area near the front of the vagina that is highly erogenous in some women.

G-string *n* a small piece of cloth, leather, etc covering the genitals and held in place by thongs, elastic, etc passed round the hips and between the buttocks.

G suit *n* a suit designed to counteract the physiological effects of high acceleration in an aircraft or spacecraft.

GSVQ *abbr* General Scottish Vocational Qualification.

GT *adj* denoting a saloon car with a sporty appearance and performance but enough comfort to make it suitable for long journeys.

guacamole /gwahkə'mohli/ *n* a dip or hors d'oeuvre made of mashed avocado mixed with tomato and chilli.

guanaco /gwah'nahkoh/ *n* (*pl* **guanacos** *or* **guanaco**) a S American mammal that has a soft thick fawn-coloured coat and resembles a llama.

guanine *n* a chemical compound that is one of the four bases coding genetic information in a DNA or RNA molecule: compare ADENINE, CYTOSINE, THYMINE, URACIL.

guano *n* a phosphate-rich substance consisting chiefly of the excrement of seabirds and used as a fertilizer, or an artificial fertilizer that resembles it.

guarani *n* **1** (**Guarani**) a member of a Native South American people inhabiting Bolivia, Paraguay, and S Brazil. **2** (**Guarani**) the language spoken by this people. **3** the basic monetary unit of Paraguay.

guarantee[1] *n* **1a** an assurance of the quality of a product, work, etc, accompanied by a promise to replace it or refund money paid for it if it proves defective. **b** a document containing an assurance of this kind. **2** an agreement or written undertaking by which one person accepts responsibility for another's obligations, *esp* debts, in case of default. **3** an assurance that something will happen. **4** something given as security; a pledge. **5** a guarantor.

guarantee[2] *v* (**guaranteed, guaranteeing**) **1** to provide a guarantee of replacement or repayment with respect to (a product, work, etc). **2a** to undertake to do (something). **b** to give an assurance relating to (something). **3** to undertake to answer for the debt or default of (somebody).

guarantor *n* somebody who makes or gives a guarantee.

guaranty *n* **1** = GUARANTEE[1] (2). **2** something offered as security by a person making a guaranty.

guard[1] *n* **1** the act or duty of protecting or defending or of preventing escape. **2** a person or group who performs this duty. **3** (*in pl*) = HOUSEHOLD TROOPS. **4** a protective or safety device, e.g. on a machine to prevent injury. **5a** a defensive position in boxing, fencing, etc. **b** in cricket, the position of the batsman relative to the wicket when waiting to receive the ball. **6** a state of readiness to deal with adverse events; vigilance: *They caught me off guard.* **7** *Brit* the person in charge of the carriages, passengers, etc in a railway train.

guard[2] *v* **1** to protect from danger, *esp* by watchful attention. **2** to watch over so as to prevent escape, entry, etc. **3** to keep in check; to restrain. ✱ **guard against** to attempt to prevent by taking precautions. ⋙ **guarder** *n.*

guarded *adj* marked by caution. ⋙ **guardedly** *adv,* **guardedness** *n.*

guardhouse *n* a building used by soldiers on guard duty or as a prison.

guardian *n* **1** somebody or something that guards or protects. **2** somebody entrusted by law with the care of a person who is of unsound mind, not of age, etc. ⋙ **guardianship** *n.*

guardian angel *n* **1** a person's special protector. **2** an angel who is thought to watch over a particular person.

guardrail *n* a railing that protects people from falling from a high place.

guardroom *n* a room serving as a guardhouse.

guardsman *n* (*pl* **guardsmen**) a member of a military body such as the Household Troops in the British Army or the US National Guard.

guard's van *n Brit* a railway wagon or carriage for the use of the guard.

guar gum *n* a gum produced from the ground seeds of a plant of the pea family, used as a thickening agent and as a sizing material.

Guatemalan *n* a native or inhabitant of Guatemala. ⋙ **Guatemalan** *adj.*

guava /'gwahvə/ *n* a yellow edible tropical fruit with pink aromatic flesh.

gubbins *pl n Brit, informal* **1** (*used as sing.*) an object whose name is unknown or forgotten; a thingamajig. **2** (*used as sing. or pl*) a miscellaneous collection of objects, often associated with something specified.

gubernatorial *adj* relating to or belonging to a governor, *esp* a governor of a US state.

gudgeon[1] *n* **1** a pivot or spindle. **2** the socket into which the pins of a hinge fit. **3** a socket into which the rudder of a boat fits. **4** a pin that holds two blocks together.

gudgeon[2] *n* (*pl* **gudgeons** *or* **gudgeon**) a small European freshwater fish used *esp* for food or bait.

gudgeon pin *n* a metal pin linking the piston and connecting rod in an internal-combustion engine.

guelder rose /'geldə/ *n* a shrub of the honeysuckle family with clusters of fragrant white flowers.

Guelf *or* **Guelph** /gwelf/ *n* a member of a political party in medieval Italy which opposed the German emperors: compare GHIBELLINE.

guenon /gə'non/ *n* (*pl* **guenons** *or* **guenon**) a long-tailed tree-dwelling African monkey.

guerilla *n* see GUERRILLA.

guernsey *n* **1** (*often* **Guernsey**) an animal of a fawn-and-white breed of dairy cattle originating in Guernsey in the Channel Islands. **2** a thick knitted jersey traditionally worn by sailors.

guerrilla *or* **guerilla** *n* a member of a small independent fighting force which engages in sabotage, unexpected assaults, etc, usu with a political objective.

guess[1] *v* **1** to estimate or judge without sufficient knowledge or information for an accurate assessment. **2** to arrive at a correct conclusion about (something) by conjecture, chance, or intuition.

3 *chiefly NAm, informal* to believe or suppose. ➤➤ **guessable** *adj,* **guesser** *n.*

guess² *n* an opinion or estimate arrived at by guessing.

guesstimate¹ *n informal* an estimate made without adequate information.

guesstimate² *v* to make a guesstimate of.

guesswork *n* the act of guessing, or a judgment based on a guess.

guest¹ *n* **1a** a person entertained in one's home. **b** a person taken out and entertained at another's expense. **2** a person who pays to stay at a hotel, etc. **3** somebody who is present by invitation: *one of the guests on tonight's show.*

guest² *v* to appear as a guest, e.g. on a TV show.

guest beer *n* a draught beer that is on sale in a pub for a limited period only.

guesthouse *n* a private house used to accommodate paying guests.

guest worker *n* an immigrant worker who is a temporary resident of a country and is usu employed in an unskilled job.

guff *n informal* foolish talk or ideas; nonsense.

guffaw¹ *n* a loud or boisterous laugh.

guffaw² *v* to laugh loudly or boisterously.

GUI *abbr* graphical user interface.

guidance *n* **1** advice or instructions on how to do something. **2** the process of controlling the course of something as it moves.

guide¹ *n* **1a** somebody who leads or directs another or others. **b** somebody who shows and explains places of interest to travellers, tourists, etc. **2a** a book providing information about a place, activity, etc. **b** a principle that directs somebody's conduct or course of life. **3** a device or mark for positioning or directing the motion of something. **4** (**Guide**) *chiefly Brit* a member of a worldwide movement of girls founded with the aim of forming character and teaching good citizenship.

guide² *v* **1** to lead or direct (somebody) along a route or to a place. **2** to control and direct the movement of. **3** to give advice or instructions to (somebody) regarding behaviour, an appropriate course of action, etc. ➤➤ **guidable** *adj,* **guider** *n.*

guidebook *n* a book of information for travellers.

guided missile *n* a missile whose course in flight is controlled electronically from the ground or by an inbuilt device.

guide dog *n* a dog trained to lead a blind person.

guideline *n* a recommendation as to policy or conduct.

Guider *n* an adult leader of a Guide company or Brownie pack.

guild *n* (*used as sing. or pl*) **1** an association of people with similar interests or pursuits. **2** a medieval association of merchants or craftsmen.

guilder *n* (*pl* **guilders** *or* **guilder**) the basic monetary unit of the Netherlands and Surinam.

guildhall *n* **1** a hall where a guild or corporation assembles, or used to assemble. **2** in some British towns, the town hall.

guile *n* deceitful cunning; duplicity. ➤➤ **guileful** *adj,* **guilefully** *adv,* **guileless** *adj,* **guilelessly** *adv.*

guillemot /'gilimot/ *n* (*pl* **guillemots** *or* **guillemot**) a sea bird of the auk family that has black-and-white plumage.

guillotine¹ /'giləteen/ *n* **1** a machine for beheading with a heavy blade that slides down between grooved posts. **2** an instrument (e.g. a paper cutter) that works like a guillotine. **3** limitation of the discussion of legislative business by the imposition of a time limit.

Word history

French *guillotine*, named after Joseph *Guillotin* d.1814, French physician. Joseph Guillotin did not invent the guillotine, but he was a leading advocate of this method of execution, on both humanitarian and egalitarian grounds, since decapitation had previously been a privileged method of execution for nobles.

guillotine² *v* to behead, cut, or limit by means of a guillotine.

guilt *n* **1** the fact of having committed an offence, *esp* a crime. **2** feelings of being at fault or to blame. ➤➤ **guiltless** *adj.*

guilt trip *n informal* a period of suffering strong but sometimes unwarranted feelings of guilt, or a self-indulgent display of guilt and remorse.

guilty *adj* (**-ier, -iest**) **1a** responsible for an offence or wrongdoing. **b** found to have committed a crime by a judge, jury, etc after a trial. **2a** suggesting guilt. **b** feeling guilt. ➤➤ **guiltily** *adv,* **guiltiness** *n.*

guinea *n* **1** a former British gold coin worth 21 shillings. **2** a money unit worth £1.05, used *esp* in setting professional fees and in the auction trade.

guinea fowl *n* a W African bird with white-speckled slate-coloured plumage, related to the pheasant and widely kept for food.

guinea hen *n* a female guinea fowl.

Guinean *n* a native or inhabitant of Guinea. ➤➤ **Guinean** *adj.*

guinea pig *n* **1** a small stout-bodied nearly tailless rodent often kept as a pet. **2** somebody or something used as a subject of research or experimentation.

guipure /gi'pyooə/ *n* a heavy decorative lace with large patterns on a fabric foundation.

guise *n* **1** assumed appearance; semblance. **2** external appearance; aspect.

guitar *n* a stringed musical instrument with a flat body, a long fretted neck, and six or twelve strings played by plucking. ➤➤ **guitarist** *n.*

Gujarati *or* **Gujerati** /goojə'rahti/ *n* **1** a member of a people of the state of Gujarat in W India. **2** the language spoken by this people. ➤➤ **Gujarati** *adj.*

Gulag *n* the penal system of labour camps in the former Soviet Union, or one of these camps.

gulch *n chiefly NAm* a ravine, *esp* with a fast-flowing river running through it.

gulden *n* (*pl* **guldens** *or* **gulden**) = GUILDER.

gules /gyoohlz/ *n* the colour red on coats of arms and other heraldic emblems.

gulf *n* **1** a partially landlocked part of the sea, usu larger than a bay. **2** a deep chasm; an abyss. **3** an unbridgeable gap.

Gulf War Syndrome *n* a medical condition that affects some veterans of the 1991 Gulf War, with symptoms of chronic fatigue, recurrent headaches, and skin disorders.

gull¹ *n* a sea bird with long wings, webbed feet, and largely white, grey, or black plumage.

gull² *v dated* to trick or deceive (somebody).

gull³ *n archaic* a person who is easily tricked or deceived; a dupe.

Gullah *n* **1** a member of a people of African descent living mainly on the islands and coast of S Carolina, Georgia, and NE Florida. **2** the English dialect spoken by this people, heavily influenced by W African languages. ➤➤ **Gullah** *adj.*

gullet *n* the oesophagus or throat.

gulley *n* see GULLY.

gullible *adj* easily tricked or deceived. ⋙ **gullibility** *n.*

gull-wing *adj* **1** of a car door: hinged at the top and opening upwards. **2** of an aircraft wing: slanting upwards from the fuselage for a short distance with a long horizontal outer section.

gully *or* **gulley** *n* (*pl* **-ies** *or* **-eys**) **1** a trench worn in the earth by running water. **2** a deep gutter or drain. **3** in cricket, a fielding position close to the batsman on the off side and between point and the slips.

gulp[1] *v* **1** (*often* + down) to swallow (something) hurriedly or greedily. **2** to make a sudden swallowing movement as if surprised or nervous.

gulp[2] *n* **1** a swallowing sound or action. **2** the amount swallowed in a gulp.

gum[1] *n* the parts of the jaws from which the teeth grow, or the tissue that surrounds the teeth.

gum[2] *n* **1** a plant substance that is sticky or gelatinous when moist but hardens on drying. **2** a soft glue used for sticking paper and other lightweight materials. **3a** *informal* chewing gum. **b** a hard gelatinous sweet.

gum[3] *v* (**gummed, gumming**) to smear or stick with or as if with gum. ⋙ **gummer** *n.*

gum[4] ✱ **by gum** *dated, informal* a mild oath.

gum arabic *n* a water-soluble gum obtained from acacia plants and used in the manufacture of adhesives and in pharmacy.

gumbo *n* **1** a meat and vegetable soup thickened with okra pods, a popular dish in Cajun cooking. **2** *NAm* = OKRA .

gumboil *n* an abscess in the gum.

gumboot *n* a strong waterproof rubber boot reaching usu to the knee.

gumdrop *n* a hard jellylike sweet.

gummy[1] *adj* (**-ier, -iest**) **1** containing or covered with gum. **2** viscous or sticky. ⋙ **gumminess** *n.*

gummy[2] *adj* (**-ier, -iest**) with gums showing clearly, usu because of the absence of teeth.

gumption *n* **1** the intelligence and courage to take action; initiative. **2** shrewd practical common sense.

gum resin *n* a mixture of gum and resin obtained from a plant.

gumshield *n* a device worn in the mouth by sports players to protect their teeth.

gumshoe *n chiefly NAm, informal* a detective.

gum tree *n* any tree that exudes a gum, *esp* a eucalyptus tree. ✱ **up a gum tree** *informal* in a difficult situation.

gum turpentine *n* = TURPENTINE (1).

gum up *v informal* to prevent or impede the proper working of.

gun[1] *n* **1** a weapon that discharges a bullet or shell through a metal tube; a firearm. **2** somebody who carries or is skilled with a gun, e.g. a hunter or a hired killer. **3** a device that releases a controlled amount of something, e.g. grease or glue, and is operated like a firearm. ✱ **go great guns** to be working at great speed or very effectively. **jump the gun** to move or act before the proper time. **stick to one's guns** to refuse to change one's intentions or opinion in spite of opposition.

gun[2] *v* (**gunned, gunning**) *informal* to press hard on the accelerator to make (a vehicle or engine) go or run faster. ✱ **be gunning for** to be intent on finding, criticizing, punishing, or killing (somebody).

gunboat *n* a relatively heavily armed ship of shallow draught.

gunboat diplomacy *n* the high-handed threat or use of naval or military power.

guncotton *n* an explosive chemical compound consisting of cellulose nitrate with a high nitrogen content.

gundog *n* a dog trained to locate or retrieve game for hunters.

gun down *v* to kill (somebody) by shooting them, usu in cold blood.

gunfire *n* the firing of guns, or the noise they make.

gunge *n Brit, informal* any unpleasant, dirty, or sticky substance. ⋙ **gunged** *adj,* **gungy** *adj.*

gung ho *adj* extremely or excessively enthusiastic, *esp* for fighting or warfare.

gunk *n informal* any unpleasant, dirty, or sticky substance; gunge.

gunlock *n* the mechanism for igniting the charge of a firearm.

gunman *n* (*pl* **gunmen**) a man armed with a gun, *esp* a professional killer.

gunmetal *n* **1** a greyish form of bronze formerly used for cannons. **2** a bluish grey colour. ⋙ **gunmetal** *adj.*

gunnel[1] *n* see GUNWALE.

gunnel[2] *n* a small long N Atlantic fish resembling an eel.

gunner *n* **1** a soldier or airman who operates a gun, *specif* a private in the Royal Artillery. **2** somebody who hunts with a gun.

gunnery *n* the science of the flight of projectiles and of the effective use of guns.

gunpoint ✱ **at gunpoint** while threatening somebody, or being threatened, with the use of a gun.

gunpowder *n* an explosive mixture of potassium nitrate, charcoal, and sulphur formerly used in firearms and still used in blasting.

gunrunner *n* somebody who carries or deals in contraband arms and ammunition. ⋙ **gunrunning** *n.*

gunship *n* a heavily armed helicopter used to attack targets on the ground.

gunshot *n* **1** a shot or projectile fired from a gun. **2** the range of a gun.

gun-shy *adj* of a dog: afraid of the sound of a gun.

gunslinger *n informal* somebody who carries a gun, *esp* a cowboy in the Wild West.

gunsmith *n* somebody who designs, makes, or repairs firearms.

gunwale *or* **gunnel** *n* the upper edge of a ship's or boat's side.

gunyah *n Aus* a hut built by Australian aboriginals in the bush.

guppy *n* (*pl* **guppies** *or* **guppy**) a small fish that is native to the W Indies and S America and is a popular aquarium fish.

gurdwara *n* a Sikh place of worship.

gurgle *v* **1** to make a low-pitched bubbling sound. **2** of water: to flow or move with such a sound. ⋙ **gurgle** *n.*

Gurkha *n* **1** a member of any of several Nepalese peoples. **2** a Gurkha serving in the British or Indian army.

gurn *v* see GIRN.

gurnard *n* (*pl* **gurnards** *or* **gurnard**) a fish with a large armoured head and three pairs of pectoral fins used to walk along the sea floor.

gurney *n NAm* a wheeled stretcher of the kind used in hospitals to transport patients.

guru *n* (*pl* **gurus**) **1** a Hindu or Sikh personal religious teacher and spiritual guide. **2a** any spiritual and intellectual guide; a mentor. **b** *informal* an acknowledged leader or expert.

gush[1] *v* **1** to flow out copiously or violently. **2** to emit in a sudden copious flow. **3** to make an effusive display of sentiment or enthusiasm. ⋙ **gushing** *adj.*

gush[2] *n* **1** a sudden outpouring. **2** an effusive display of sentiment or enthusiasm.

gusher *n* **1** an oil well with a copious natural flow. **2** somebody who talks effusively.

gushy *adj* (**-ier, -iest**) marked by effusive often affected sentiment or enthusiasm. ⋙ **gushily** *adv.*

gusset *n* **1** a piece of material inserted in a seam (e.g. the crotch of an undergarment) to provide reinforcement or allow for movement. **2** a plate or bracket for strengthening a join in a structure.

gust[1] *n* **1** a sudden brief rush of wind. **2** a sudden outburst; a surge. ⋙ **gusty** *adj.*

gust[2] *v* to blow in gusts.

gustation *n formal* the action of tasting, or the sense of taste.

gustatory *adj* of the sense of taste.

gusto *n* enthusiastic and vigorous enjoyment or vitality.

gut[1] *n* **1** (*also in pl*) **a** the belly or abdomen. **b** the intestine. **2** (*often used before a noun*) the part of a person that responds emotionally or instinctively: *a gut feeling.* **3** = CATGUT. **4** *informal* (*in pl*) the inner essential parts. **5** *informal* (*in pl*) courage or determination. ✻ **bust a gut** *informal* to make a great effort. **hate somebody's guts** *informal* to hate somebody with great intensity.

gut[2] *v* (**gutted, gutting**) **1** to remove the intestines of (*esp* an animal); to disembowel. **2a** to destroy the inside of (*esp* a building). **b** to destroy the essential power or effectiveness of.

gutless *adj informal* lacking courage; cowardly. ⋙ **gutlessness** *n.*

gutsy *adj* (**-ier, -iest**) *informal* courageous. ⋙ **gutsiness** *n.*

gutta-percha *n* a tough plastic substance obtained from the latex of Malaysian trees and used in golfballs, waterproofing materials, and electrical insulation.

gutted *adj Brit, informal* deeply disappointed or disheartened.

gutter[1] *n* **1a** a trough just below the eaves of a roof or at the side of a street to catch and carry off water. **b** a trough or groove to catch or direct something, e.g. at the side of a bowling alley. **2** (**the gutter**) the lowest level or condition of human life.

gutter[2] *v* **1a** of a candle: to burn unevenly so that melted wax runs down one side. **b** of a flame: to burn fitfully or feebly. **2** to cut or wear gutters in.

guttering *n* the gutters on the roof of a building collectively.

gutter press *n* the section of the national press that is marked by extreme vulgarity or sensationalism.

guttersnipe *n dated* a deprived child living in poverty and usu dressed in ragged clothes.

guttural[1] *adj* **1** of a sound: formed or pronounced in the throat. **2** featuring guttural sounds prominently. ⋙ **gutturally** *adv.*

guttural[2] *n* a guttural consonant or speech sound.

guv *n Brit, informal* sir, used as a form of address.

guvnor *n informal* = GUV.

guy[1] *n* a rope, chain, etc used to secure something (e.g. a tent).

guy[2] *v* to secure with guys.

guy[3] *n* **1** *informal* a man. **2** a humorous effigy of a man burned in Britain on Guy Fawkes Night.

guy[4] *v dated* to make fun of; to ridicule.

Guyanese *n* (*pl* **Guyanese**) a native or inhabitant of Guayana. ⋙ **Guyanese** *adj.*

Guy Fawkes Night *n* 5 November, observed in Britain with fireworks and bonfires in commemoration of the arrest of Guy Fawkes in 1605 for attempting to blow up the Houses of Parliament.

guzzle *v* to consume greedily. ⋙ **guzzler** *n.*

Gy *abbr* gray.

gybe (*NAm* **jibe**) *v* **1** to change a ship's course by taking the stern through the wind. **2** of a sail: to swing violently from one side of a boat to the other when running before the wind. ⋙ **gybe** *n.*

gym *n* **1** a gymnasium. **2** gymnastics.

gymkhana *n* a local sporting event featuring competitions and displays relating to horse riding.

gymn- *or* **gymno-** *comb. form* naked; bare: *gymnosperm.*

gymnasium *n* (*pl* **gymnasiums** *or* **gymnasia**) a large room or separate building used for indoor sports and gymnastic activities.

gymnast *n* somebody trained in gymnastics.

gymnastics *pl n* **1** (*used as sing.*) physical exercises developing or displaying bodily strength and coordination. **2** (*used as pl*) exercises in intellectual or physical dexterity. ⋙ **gymnastic** *adj.*

gymno- *comb. form* see GYMN-.

gymnosperm *n* any of a group of woody plants (e.g. conifers) that produce naked seeds not enclosed in an ovary: compare ANGIOSPERM.

gymslip *n chiefly Brit* a girl's tunic or pinafore dress worn, *esp* formerly, as part of a school uniform.

gyn- *or* **gyno-** *comb. form* denoting women: *gynophobia.*

gynaecology (*NAm* **gynecology**) /gienə'koləji/ *n* a branch of medicine that deals with diseases and disorders of women, *esp* of the female reproductive system. ⋙ **gynaecological** *adj,* **gynaecologist** *n.*

gyno- *comb. form* see GYN-.

gynoecium /jie'neesi·əm, gie-/ *n* (*pl* **gynoecia**) all the female parts of a flower collectively.

gynophobia /jienə'fohbi·ə/ *n* extreme fear of women.

-gynous *comb. form* forming adjectives, denoting: female parts or organs: *androgynous.* ⋙ **-gyny** *comb. form.*

gyp[1] *or* **gip** ✻ **give somebody gyp** *Brit, informal* to cause (somebody) pain or discomfort.

gyp[2] *v* (**gypped, gypping**) *NAm, informal* to cheat.

gyp[3] *n NAm, informal* a fraud or swindle.

gypsophila /jip'sofilə/ *n* a plant of the pink family that has clusters of small delicate flowers.

gypsum *n* hydrated calcium sulphate occurring as a mineral and used *esp* in plaster of Paris.

gypsy *or* **gipsy** *n* (*pl* **-ies**) a member of the Romany people, a largely nomadic people who retain an itinerant lifestyle in modern societies.

Word history

by shortening and alteration from EGYPTIAN. When gypsies first came to Europe they claimed to be from a country called 'Little Egypt'.

gypsy moth *or* **gipsy moth** *n* a large European moth that is brown in the male and white in the female.

gyr- *or* **gyro-** *comb. form* **1** denoting a circle, spiral, or rotation: *gyrate*. **2** denoting a gyroscope: *gyrocompass*.

gyrate *v* **1** to move or cause to move with a circular or spiral motion. **2** to dance wildly or erotically. ≫ **gyration** *n*, **gyrator** *n*.

gyratory[1] *adj* moving with a circular or spiral motion.

gyratory[2] *n* (*pl* **-ies**) a traffic-control system resembling a large complex roundabout.

gyre[1] *v literary* to move with a swirling or rotating motion; to gyrate.

gyre[2] *n literary* a swirling or rotating motion.

gyrfalcon /ˈjuhfawlkən/ *n* a large and powerful Arctic falcon.

gyro *n* (*pl* **-os**) *informal* **1** a gyroscope. **2** a gyrocompass.

gyro- *comb. form* see GYR-.

gyrocompass *n* a compass in which the horizontal axis of a constantly spinning gyroscope always points to true north.

gyroscope *n* a device containing a wheel that is mounted to spin rapidly about an axis and is free to turn in any direction so that it maintains the same orientation. ≫ **gyroscopic** *adj*.

gyve *n* a fetter or shackle.

H

H[1] *or* **h** *n* (*pl* **H's** *or* **Hs** *or* **h's**) the eighth letter of the English alphabet.

H[2] *abbr* **1** used on lead pencils: hard. **2** *informal* heroin. **3** henry. **4** hospital.

H[3] *abbr* the chemical symbol for hydrogen.

h *abbr* **1** height. **2** high. **3** hour.

ha[1] *abbr* hectare.

ha[2] *or* **hah** *interj* used to express surprise, joy, triumph, etc.

habeas corpus /,haybi·əs 'kawpəs/ *n* a judicial writ requiring a detained person to be brought before a court so that the legality of their detention may be examined.

haberdasher *n* **1** *Brit* a dealer in buttons, thread, and other small articles used in sewing. **2** *NAm* a dealer in shirts, ties, and other minor articles of menswear.

haberdashery *n* (*pl* **-ies**) **1** goods sold by a haberdasher. **2** a haberdasher's shop.

habergeon /'habəjən/ *n* formerly, a sleeveless chain mail coat or jacket.

habiliment *n archaic or literary* (*usu in pl*) an article of clothing.

habit[1] *n* **1** a settled tendency, usual manner, or acquired pattern of behaviour. **2** an addiction, *esp* to drugs. **3** characteristic mode of growth or appearance, e.g. of a plant or crystal. **4** a characteristic costume, *esp* the long dress-like garment worn by a monk or nun.

habit[2] *v* (**habited, habiting**) *archaic (often as past part.)* to clothe or dress.

habitable *adj* capable of being lived in. ➤➤ **habitability** *n,* **habitableness** *n.*

habitant *n* **1** /abitonh/ a French settler in Louisiana or Quebec. **2** /'habitənt/ *archaic* an inhabitant or resident.

habitat *n* **1** the place or type of place where a plant or animal naturally grows or lives. **2** one's preferred surroundings.

habitation *n* **1** the inhabiting of a place; occupancy. **2** *formal or literary* a residence or home.

habit-forming *adj* of a drug, etc: addictive.

habitual *adj* **1** having the nature of a habit. **2** doing something by force of habit. **3** in accordance with habit; customary. ➤➤ **habitually** *adv,* **habitualness** *n.*

habituate *v* (+ to) to make or become used to something. ➤➤ **habituation** *n.*

habitué /hə'bityooay/ *n* a person who frequents a specified place.

haboob *n* in N Africa, a sandstorm.

háček /'hahchek/ *n* a mark (ˇ) placed over a letter in some languages, e.g. over *c* in Czech, to modify the sound of the letter.

hachure /ha'shyooə/ *n* **1** (*in pl*) short parallel lines used on a map to indicate sloping land. **2** the shading produced by such lines.

hacienda /hasi'endə/ *n* in a Spanish-speaking country, a large estate or the main house of such an estate.

hack[1] *v* **1** to cut with repeated irregular or unskilful blows. **2** in football or rugby, to commit the foul of kicking (an opposing player) on the shins. **3** *informal* (*used with a negative*) to bear or tolerate: *He couldn't hack it.* **4** *dated* to cough repeatedly in a short dry manner: *a hacking cough.* **5** to gain unauthorized access to a computer system. ➤➤ **hacker** *n.*

hack[2] *n* **1** a hacking blow. **2** a kick on the shins in rugby or football. **3** a mattock, pick, or similar tool. **4** *informal* an act of computer hacking.

hack[3] *n* **1** a person who produces mediocre work, *esp* writing, for financial gain. **2a** a riding horse let out for hire. **b** a worn-out old horse. **3** a ride on a horse. **4** *NAm* a taxi. ➤➤ **hackery** *n.*

hack[4] *adj* **1** done by or characteristic of a hack. **2** hackneyed; trite.

hack[5] *v* to ride a horse at an ordinary pace, *esp* over roads. ➤➤ **hacker** *n.*

hacking jacket *n* a tweed jacket with slits at the side, often worn for riding.

hackle *n* **1a** (*in pl*) the erectile hairs along the neck and back of an animal, *esp* a dog. **b** a long narrow feather on the neck of a domestic cock or other bird. **2** an artificial fishing fly made from a cock's hackles. **3** a steel comb with long teeth for dressing flax or hemp.

hackney[1] *n* a horse of a compact English breed with a high leg action.

Word history

Middle English *hakeney,* prob from *Hakeneye* Hackney, borough of London, where many horses were formerly pastured. The word orig denoted an ordinary riding horse, later shortened to *hack.* Such horses were often hired out for riding or driving, hence *hackney carriage,* which is still the official term for a taxi.

hackney[2] *adj esp* formerly, kept for public hire: *a hackney carriage.*

hackneyed *adj* lacking in freshness or originality; meaningless because used too often.

hacksaw *n* a fine-toothed saw, *esp* for cutting metal.

had *v* past tense and past part. of HAVE[1].

haddock *n* (*pl* **haddocks** *or* **haddock**) a silver-grey food fish of the N Atlantic, usu smaller than the cod.

Hades /'haydeez/ *n* **1** in Greek mythology, the underground abode of the dead. **2** (*often* **hades**) *euphem* hell.

Hadith /hə'deeth/ *n* the body of traditions relating to Muhammad and his companions.

hadj *n* see HAJJ.

hadji *n* see HAJJI.

hadn't *contr* had not.

hadron *n* an elementary particle that takes part in strong interactions. ➤➤ **hadronic** *adj.*

hadst *v* archaic second person sing. past tense of HAVE[1].

haem- *or* **haemo-** (*NAm* **hem-** *or* **hemo-**) *comb. form* denoting blood: *haemophilia.*

haemal (*NAm* **hemal**) *adj* **1** relating to the blood. **2** of or situated on the same side of the spinal cord as the heart.

haematite (*NAm* **hematite**) *n* iron oxide occurring as a crystalline or red earthy mineral.

haematology (*NAm* **hematology**) *n* the study of diseases of the blood and blood-forming organs. ➤➤ **haematological** *adj,* **haematologist** *n.*

haematoma (*NAm* **hematoma**) *n* (*pl* **haematomas** *or* **haematomata**) a tumour or swelling containing blood.

haematuria (*NAm* **hematuria**) *n* the abnormal presence of blood or blood cells in the urine.

-haemia *comb. form* = -AEMIA.

haemo- *comb. form* see HAEM-.

haemodialysis (*NAm* **hemodialysis**) *n* (*pl* **haemodialyses**) the purification of the blood by dialysis, in cases of kidney failure.

haemoglobin (*NAm* **hemoglobin**) *n* a protein containing iron that occurs in the red blood cells of vertebrates and transports oxygen from the lungs to the body tissues.

haemolysis (*NAm* **hemolysis**) *n* the dissolution of red blood cells with release of haemoglobin. ➤➤ **haemolytic** *adj.*

haemophilia (*NAm* **hemophilia**) *n* delayed clotting of the blood with consequent difficulty in controlling bleeding, occurring as a hereditary defect, usu in males. ➤➤ **haemophiliac** *n and adj,* **haemophilic** *adj.*

haemorrhage[1] (*NAm* **hemorrhage**) *n* **1** a loss of blood from a ruptured blood vessel. **2** a continuous and severe depletion of a resource. ➤➤ **haemorrhagic** *adj.*

haemorrhage[2] (*NAm* **hemorrhage**) *v* **1** to bleed profusely from a ruptured blood vessel. **2** to expend or lose (a resource) at a disastrous rate. **3** to disappear rapidly.

haemorrhoid (*NAm* **hemorrhoid**) *n* (*usu in pl*) a mass of dilated veins in swollen tissue in the region of the anus.

haemostasis (*NAm* **hemostasis**) *n* the arrest of bleeding. ➤➤ **haemostatic** *adj.*

haeremai /hierə'mie/ *interj NZ* welcome.

hafiz /'hahfiz/ *n* used as a title: a Muslim who knows the Koran by heart.

hafnium *n* a silvery metallic element that is used in tungsten alloys for filaments.

haft[1] *n* the handle of a weapon or tool.

haft[2] *v* to fit (a weapon or tool) with a haft.

hag[1] *n* **1** a witch. **2** an ugly or ill-natured old woman. ➤➤ **haggish** *adj.*

hag[2] *n Scot, N Eng* a bog, or a firm spot in a bog.

hagfish *n* (*pl* **hagfishes** *or* **hagfish**) a jawless marine eel-like vertebrate with a sucking mouth surrounded with barbels that feeds on dead or dying fishes by boring into their bodies.

haggard *adj* **1** having a worn or gaunt appearance, *esp* through anxiety, illness, or lack of sleep. **2** of a hawk: already mature before being caught and trained. ➤➤ **haggardness** *n.*

haggis *n* (*pl* **haggis** *or* **haggises**) a Scottish dish that consists of minced sheep's or calf's offal with suet, oatmeal, and seasonings, and traditionally boiled in the stomach of the animal.

haggle *v* to bargain or wrangle. ➤➤ **haggler** *n.*

hagi- *or* **hagio-** *comb. form* denoting saints: *hagiography.*

hagiography *n* (*pl* **-ies**) **1** biography of saints or venerated people. **2** an idealizing or idolizing biography. ➤➤ **hagiographer** *n,* **hagiographic** *adj,* **hagiographical** *adj.*

hagiolatry *n* **1** the worship of saints. **2** excessive veneration of any celebrated person. ➤➤ **hagiolater** *n,* **hagiolatrous** *adj.*

hagiology *n* literature dealing with venerated people or writings. ➤➤ **hagiological** *adj,* **hagiologically** *adv.*

hah *interj* see HA[2].

ha-ha[1] *interj* used to express or represent laughter.

ha-ha[2] *n* a fence or retaining wall sunk into a ditch and used as a boundary to a park or grounds, so as to give an uninterrupted view.

haiku /'hiekooh/ *n* (*pl* **haiku** *or* **haikus**) an unrhymed Japanese verse form of three lines containing five, seven, and five syllables respectively, or a poem written in this form.

hail[1] *n* **1** precipitation in the form of small particles of clear ice or compacted snow. **2** a shower of things coming fast and furiously.

hail[2] *v* **1** to precipitate hail. **2** to pour down or strike like hail.

hail[3] *v* **1a** to salute or greet (somebody). **b** to greet with enthusiastic approval; to acclaim: *He has been hailed as the new John Lennon.* **2** to summon (a taxi) by calling. ✱ **hail from** to be a native or resident of (a place). ➤➤ **hailer** *n.*

hail[4] *interj archaic* used as a respectful salutation, sometimes by way of acclamation.

hail[5] *n* a call to attract attention. ✱ **within hail** within earshot; within shouting distance.

hail-fellow-well-met *adj* heartily and often excessively informal from the first moment of meeting.

Hail Mary *n* (*pl* **Hail Marys**) a Roman Catholic prayer to the Virgin Mary that consists of salutations and a plea for her intercession.

hailstone *n* a pellet of hail.

hair *n* **1a** a slender threadlike outgrowth on the surface of an animal. **b** a structure resembling a hair, e.g. on a plant. **c** a coating of hairs, *esp* on the human head or an animal's body. **2** a hair's breadth. ✱ **hair of the dog** an alcoholic drink taken to cure a hangover. **in somebody's hair** persistently annoying or distracting somebody. **keep your hair on!** *Brit, informal* calm down! **let one's hair down** to relax and enjoy oneself. **make**

somebody's hair stand on end to give somebody a fright. **not turn a hair** to give not the least indication of surprise or alarm. ⯮ **hairless** *adj,* **hairlike** *adj.*

hair ball *n* a compact mass of hair formed in the stomach of an animal, e.g. a cat, that cleans its coat by licking.

hairbrush *n* a brush for the hair.

haircut *n* a cutting and shaping of the hair, or the style in which hair is cut.

hairdo *n* (*pl* **-os**) *informal* a hairstyle.

hairdresser *n* a person whose occupation is cutting and styling people's hair. ⯮ **hairdressing** *n.*

hairdryer *or* **hairdrier** *n* an electrical appliance for drying the hair by blowing it with warm air.

hairgrip *n Brit* a flat hairpin with prongs that close together.

hairline *n* **1** the line above the forehead beyond which hair grows. **2** (*often used before a noun*) a very fine line; *esp* a fine crack.

hairnet *n* a loosely woven net that is worn over the hair to keep it in place.

hairpiece *n* a section of false hair worn to enhance a hairstyle or make a person's natural hair seem more plentiful.

hairpin *n* **1** a two-pronged U-shaped pin of thin wire for holding the hair in place. **2** (*often used before a noun*) a sharp bend in a road.

hair-raising *adj* causing terror, astonishment, or horror.

hair's breadth *n* a very small distance or margin.

hair shirt *n* a shirt of coarse cloth formerly worn next to the skin by ascetics or penitent sinners.

hair-slide *n Brit* a decorative clip for the hair.

hairsplitting *n* argument over unimportant differences and points of detail; quibbling.

hairspray *n* a substance sprayed onto the hair to hold a style.

hairspring *n* a slender spiral spring that regulates the motion of the balance wheel of a watch.

hairstyle *n* a way in which the hair is cut or arranged. ⯮ **hairstyling** *n,* **hairstylist** *n.*

hair trigger *n* a trigger so adjusted that very slight pressure will fire the gun.

hairy *adj* (**-ier, -iest**) **1** covered with hair or material like hair. **2** *informal* **a** frighteningly dangerous. **b** alarmingly difficult. ⯮ **hairiness** *n.*

Haitian /'haysh(ə)n, hie'eeshən/ *n* **1** a native or inhabitant of Haiti. **2** (*also* **Haitian Creole**) the language of Haiti. ⯮ **Haitian** *adj.*

hajj *or* **hadj** *n* the pilgrimage to Mecca prescribed as a religious duty for Muslims.

hajji *or* **hadji** *n* used as a title: a Muslim who has made a pilgrimage to Mecca.

haka /'hahkə/ *n* a ceremonial Maori chant and war dance.

hake *n* (*pl* **hakes** *or* **hake**) a large marine food fish related to the cod.

halal *or* **hallal** /hə'lahl/ *n* (*often used before a noun*) meat from an animal slaughtered according to Islamic law.

halala *or* **halalah** /hə'lahlə/ *n* (*pl* **halala** *or* **halalas**) a unit of currency in Saudi Arabia, worth 100th of a riyal.

halberd *n* a long-handled weapon combining a spear and battle-axe, used *esp* in the 15th and 16th cents. ⯮ **halberdier** *n.*

halcyon *adj* denoting a time, *esp* past, of idyllic tranquillity.

hale[1] *adj* free from defect, disease, or infirmity; sound.

hale[2] *v archaic* to haul or drag.

haler /'hahlə/ *n* (*pl* **halers** *or* **haleru**) a unit of currency in the Czech Republic and Slovakia, worth 100th of a koruna.

half[1] *n* (*pl* **halves**) **1** the fraction $^1/_2$ or 0.5. **2** either of two equal parts into which something is divisible or divided. **3** either of two equal periods of a match or performance. **4 a** *Brit, informal* half a pint, *esp* of beer. **b** *informal* a child's ticket. **5** = HALFBACK. ✻ **go halves** *informal* to pay half each. **not do things by halves** *informal* to go in for things with enthusiasm. **too clever, etc, by half** *informal* too clever, etc for one's own good; far too clever, etc.

half[2] *adj* **1** denoting or amounting to half, or one of two equal parts, of something. **2** falling short of the full or complete thing: *a half smile.*

half[3] *adv* **1** in an equal part or degree. **2a** to the extent of a half. **b** incompletely: *half-remembered stories.* **c** almost: *half dead.* ✻ **half a chance** *informal* the slightest opportunity. **half past two/three, etc** thirty minutes past two, three, etc. **not half 1** *dated, informal* **a** used as an emphatic positive, often as an interjection. **b** not at all: *not half bad.* **2** not nearly: *not half finished.*

half-a-crown *n* = HALF CROWN.

half a dozen *n* **1** a set of six. **2** several.

half-and-half *adj and adv* approximately half one thing and half another.

half-arsed *adj coarse slang* ineffectual or incompetent.

halfback *n* a player in rugby, football, hockey, etc positioned immediately behind the forward line.

half-baked *adj* showing a lack of forethought or judgment; foolish.

half-binding *n* a type of bookbinding using two materials, with the better or stronger material on the spine and corners. ⯮ **half-bound** *adj.*

half blood *n* **1a** the relationship between people having only one parent in common. **b** a person so related to another. **2** *offensive* a half-breed. ⯮ **half-blooded** *adj.*

half-board *n Brit* provision of bed, breakfast, and evening meal, e.g. by a hotel.

half-breed *n offensive* a person with parents of different races. ⯮ **half-breed** *adj.*

half brother *n* a brother related through one parent only.

half-caste *n offensive* a person with parents of different races. ⯮ **half-caste** *adj.*

half-century *n* (*pl* **half-centuries**) **1** a period of 50 years. **2** in cricket, a score of 50.

half cock *n* the position of the hammer of a firearm when partly retracted and held by the safety catch so that it cannot be operated by a pull on the trigger. ✻ **go off at half cock** to move into action without adequate preparation, and risk failure.

half-cocked *adj* lacking adequate preparation or forethought.

half crown *n* a former British silver coin worth two shillings and sixpence.

half-cut *adj Brit, informal* somewhat drunk.

half-dozen *n* = HALF A DOZEN.

half-hardy *adj* of a plant: able to withstand a moderately low temperature but injured by severe frost.

halfhearted *adj* lacking enthusiasm or effort. ⯮ **halfheartedly** *adv,* **halfheartedness** *n.*

half-holiday *n* a holiday of half a day.

half hour *n* **1** a period of 30 minutes. **2** the middle point of an hour. ➤➤ **half-hourly** *adv and adj.*

half-inch *v Brit, slang* to steal (something).

half-landing *n* a landing halfway up a flight of stairs.

half-life *n* **1** the time required for half of the atoms of a radioactive substance to become disintegrated. **2** the time required for the concentration of a drug or other substance in an organism to be reduced to half by natural processes.

half-light *n* dim greyish light, e.g. at dusk.

half-mast *n* **1** the position of a flag lowered halfway down the staff as a mark of mourning. **2** *humorous* the position of a garment when not fully pulled up.

half measures *pl n* (*in negative contexts*) a partial, half-hearted, or weak line of action.

half-moon *n* **1** the figure of the moon when half its disc is illuminated. **2** something like a half-moon in shape.

half nelson *n* a wrestling hold in which one arm is thrust under the corresponding arm of an opponent and the hand placed on the back of the opponent's neck: compare FULL NELSON.

half note *n chiefly NAm* a minim.

halfpenny *or* **ha'penny** /'haypni/ *n* (*pl* **halfpennies** *or* **halfpence** *or* **ha'pennies**) **1** a former British bronze coin representing one half of a penny. **2** a small amount.

halfpennyworth *n* **1** formerly, as much as could be bought for one halfpenny. **2** *Brit, informal* (*in negative contexts*) the least amount.

half sister *n* a sister related through one parent only.

half term *n Brit* a short holiday taken about halfway through a school term.

half-timbered *adj* of a building: constructed of timber framework with spaces filled in by brickwork or plaster.

halftime *n* an intermission marking the completion of half of a game or contest.

half-title *n* the title of a book standing alone on a right-hand page immediately preceding the title page.

halftone *n* **1** a photoengraving made from an image photographed through a screen and then etched so that the details of the image are reproduced in dots. **2** *chiefly NAm* in music, a semitone.

half-track *n* a vehicle with a drive system of an endless chain or track at the back and wheels at the front.

half-truth *n* a statement that is only partially true; *esp* one intended to deceive.

half-volley *n* **1** a shot in tennis made at a ball just after it has bounced. **2** an easily hit delivery of the ball in cricket that bounces closer than intended to the batsman.

halfway *adj and adv* **1** midway between two points. **2** (*usu in negative contexts*) in the least; minimally.

halfway house *n* **1** a halfway point or place; *esp* a compromise. **2** a house, hostel, etc for former residents of institutions, e.g. psychiatric patients, that is designed to help them readjust to living in the community.

half-wit *n informal* a foolish or stupid person. ➤➤ **half-witted** *adj.*

half year *n* a six-month period. ➤➤ **half-yearly** *adj and adv.*

halibut *n* (*pl* **halibuts** *or* **halibut**) a large, dark green flatfish of the N Atlantic, used as food.

halide *n* a binary compound of a halogen and another element or radical.

halite *n* the mineral sodium chloride; = ROCK SALT.

halitosis *n* the condition of having offensive-smelling breath.

hall *n* **1** the entrance room or passage of a building. **2** *NAm* a corridor or passage in a building. **3** a large room for public assembly or entertainment. **4a** the common dining room of a college or university. **b** a building used by a college or university for some special purpose. **5** the chief living room in a medieval house or castle. **6** *Brit* the manor house of a landed proprietor.

hallal *n* see HALAL.

hallelujah[1] *or* **alleluia** *interj* used to express praise, joy, or thanks.

hallelujah[2] *or* **alleluia** *n* a shout or song used to express praise, joy, etc.

halliard *n* see HALYARD.

hallmark[1] *n* **1** in Britain, an official mark stamped on gold and silver articles after an assay test to testify to their purity. **2** a distinguishing characteristic or object.

hallmark[2] *v* to stamp (a gold or silver article) with a hallmark.

hallo *interj* = HELLO.

Hall of Fame *n chiefly NAm* a group of famous or illustrious individuals in a particular field.

hall of residence *n* (*also* **halls of residence**) a building on a university or college campus with living and sleeping facilities for students.

halloo *interj* = HOLLO.

hallow *v* **1** to make (something) holy or set it apart for holy use. **2** (*usu as past part.*) to revere or venerate (a person, thing, place, etc).

Halloween *or* **Hallowe'en** *n* 31 October, the eve of All Saints' Day.

hallucinate *v* to have hallucinations. ➤➤ **hallucinator** *n.*

hallucination *n* the perception of something apparently real to the perceiver but which has no objective reality, or the image, object, etc perceived. ➤➤ **hallucinatory** *adj.*

hallucinogen *n* a substance, e.g. LSD, that induces hallucinations. ➤➤ **hallucinogenic** *adj.*

hallway *n* an entrance hall or corridor.

halo[1] *n* (*pl* **-oes** *or* **-os**) **1** in art, a circle of light surrounding the head or placed over it, in depictions of Christ or the saints. **2** a circle of light appearing to surround the sun or moon and resulting from refraction or reflection of light by ice particles in the earth's atmosphere.

halo[2] *v* (**-oes, -oed**) to surround (somebody or something) with a halo, or as if with a halo.

halogen *n* **1** any of the five elements fluorine, chlorine, bromine, iodine, and astatine, that form group VII B of the periodic table. **2** (*used before a noun*) denoting a lamp or a heat source that has a filament surrounded by halogen vapour.

halon *n* any of several bromine-based chemical compounds that were formerly widely used in fire extinguishers.

halt[1] *v* to come or bring to a stop.

halt[2] *n* **1** a stop or interruption, *esp* a temporary one. **2** *Brit* a railway stopping place, without normal station facilities, for local trains. ✻ **call a halt to** to demand a stop to (an activity, etc).

halt[3] *adj archaic* lame.

halt[4] *v archaic or literary* to walk with a limp.

halter[1] *n* **1** a rope or strap for leading or tying an animal. **2** a U-shaped strap passing behind the neck, holding up the bodice of a woman's dress; = HALTER NECK. **3** *archaic* a noose for hanging criminals.

halter² *v* to put a halter on (an animal).

halter neck *n* a neckline formed by a strap passing from the front of a garment round the neck and leaving the shoulders and upper back bare.

halting *adj* hesitant or faltering. ➤➤ **haltingly** *adv.*

halvah *or* **halva** *n* a sweet confection of crushed sesame seeds mixed with honey.

halve *v* **1** to divide (something) into two equal parts. **2** to share (something) equally. **3** to reduce (an amount) to a half.

halves *n* pl of HALF¹.

halyard *or* **halliard** *n* a rope or tackle for hoisting or lowering a sail, etc.

ham¹ *n* **1** the meat of the rear end of a bacon pig, *esp* the thigh, when removed from the carcass before curing with salt. **2** (*usu in pl*) a buttock with its associated thigh.

ham² *n* **1** an inexpert though showy performer, *esp* an actor who overplays clumsily. **2** an amateur radio operator.

ham³ *v* (**hammed, hamming**) *informal* to overplay a part.

hamadryad *n* in classical mythology, a nymph who inhabits a tree and dies when it dies.

hamburger *n* a round flat cake of minced beef, fried or grilled and usu served in a bread roll.

ham-fisted *adj informal* lacking dexterity with the hands; clumsy.

ham-handed *adj* = HAM-FISTED.

hamlet *n* a small village, *esp*, in Britain, one without its own church.

hammer¹ *n* **1** a hand tool consisting of a solid head set crosswise on a handle, used to strike a blow, e.g. to drive in a nail. **2a** a lever with a striking head for ringing a bell or striking a gong. **b** the part of the mechanism of a modern gun whose action ignites the cartridge. **c** an auctioneer's mallet. **3** a metal sphere weighing about 7.3kg (16lb), attached by a flexible wire to a handle and thrown as far as possible, as an athletic contest. ✱ **come/go under the hammer** to be sold by auction. **hammer and tongs** with determination and vigour.

hammer² *v* **1** to beat or drive (something) with repeated blows of a hammer. **2a** (+ away at) to reiterate an opinion or attitude. **b** to apply oneself vigorously to something. **3** (*often* + into) to force (somebody) into compliance by repeated threats, etc. **4** *informal* to beat (a person or team) decisively. ✱ **hammer something into** to make (somebody) learn or remember something by continual repetition.

hammer and sickle *n* an emblem consisting of a crossed hammer and sickle used chiefly as a symbol of Communism.

hammer beam *n* either of the short horizontal beams or cantilevers to support either end of an arch or principal rafter in a roof truss.

hammerhead *n* a medium-sized shark with eyes at the ends of bulging projections on each side of the flattened head, so as to have the appearance of a double-headed hammer.

hammerlock *n* a wrestling hold in which an opponent's arm is held bent behind their back.

hammer out *v* to produce or bring about through lengthy discussion.

hammertoe *n* a deformity of the toe, giving it the appearance of an inverted V, usu resulting from ill-fitting footwear.

hammock *n* a hanging bed, usu made of netting or canvas and suspended by cords at each end.

hammy *adj* (**-ier, -iest**) *informal* characterized by clumsy overacting.

hamper¹ *v* **1** to restrict the movement or operation of (somebody). **2** to interfere with the progress of (something).

hamper² *n* **1** a large basket with a cover for packing, storing, or transporting food, etc. **2** a selection of festive fare contained in a hamper, presented as a gift.

hamster *n* a small Eurasian rodent with very large cheek pouches, often kept as a pet.

hamstring¹ *n* **1** any of the five tendons at the back of the human knee. **2** a large tendon above and behind the hock of a horse or other four-legged animal.

hamstring² *v* (*past tense and past part.* **hamstrung**) **1** to cripple (a person or animal) by cutting the leg tendons. **2** to restrict (somebody) severely or render them powerless.

Han *n* the Chinese people; ethnic Chinese, as distinct from Mongolians, Manchus, etc.

hand¹ *n* **1** the end of the arm beyond the wrist. **2** an indicator or pointer on a dial. **3** (*in pl*) **a** possession. **b** control or supervision. **4** a pledge, *esp* of betrothal or marriage. **5** handwriting. **6** a unit of measure equal to about 102mm (4in.) used *esp* for the height of a horse. **7** a round of applause. **8** assistance or aid. **9** a player in a card or board game, or the cards or pieces held by them. **10** a person employed at manual labour or general tasks. **11** (*used before a noun*) **a** for use in the hand: *a hand grenade.* **b** for carrying personally: *hand luggage.* **c** operated by hand: *a hand drill.* ✱ **an old hand** somebody with much experience. **at hand** near in time or place. **by hand** with the hands, rather than mechanically. **give/lend a hand** to help. **go hand in hand** to be closely linked. **hand in glove** in close collaboration or cooperation. **hand in hand 1** holding hands. **2** in close cooperation. **hand to mouth** satisfying one's immediate needs only. **have/take a hand in something** to have an instrumental part in something. **in hand** being done; in progress. **off hand** without checking or investigating. **on hand 1** ready to use. **2** in attendance; present. **on one's hands** in one's possession, care, or management. **on the one hand ... on the other hand** a formula for presenting contraries. **out of hand 1** out of control. **2** without delay; without reflection or consideration. **to hand** available and ready for use. **turn one's hand to** to try doing (something practical). **wait on somebody hand and foot** to attend to their every need. **win hands down** *informal* to win with ease.

hand² *v* **1** to give or pass (something) to somebody with the hand or hands. **2** to lead or assist (somebody) somewhere with the hand. ✱ **hand it to** to give credit to (somebody).

handbag *n Brit* a bag designed for carrying small personal articles and money, carried usu by women.

handball *n* **1** a game resembling fives and played in a walled court or against a single wall. **2** the offence of handling the ball in football.

handbill *n* a small printed sheet to be distributed, e.g. for advertising, by hand.

handbook *n* a short reference book, *esp* on a particular subject.

hand brake *n* a hand-operated brake in a motor vehicle, used to hold a vehicle that is already stationary.

h and c *abbr Brit* of water: hot and cold.

handcraft¹ *n* = HANDICRAFT.

handcraft[2] *v* to fashion (an object) by handicraft.

handcuff *v* to apply handcuffs to (somebody); to manacle.

handcuffs *pl n* a pair of metal rings, usu connected by a chain or bar, for locking round prisoners' wrists.

hand down *v* **1** to transmit (a possession, skill, etc) in succession; to bequeath. **2** to give (an outgrown article of clothing) to a younger member of one's family. **3** to deliver (a judgment) in court.

handful *n* (*pl* **handfuls**) **1** an amount held in the hand, or as much or as many as the hand will grasp. **2** a small quantity or number. **3** *informal* a child or animal that is difficult to control.

handgun *n* a firearm held and fired with one hand.

hand-held *adj* of a computer, camera, etc: small enough to be used while held in the hand.

handhold *n* something to hold onto for support, e.g. in mountain climbing.

handicap[1] *n* **1** a disability or disadvantage that makes achievement unusually difficult. **2a** an artificial advantage or disadvantage given to contestants so that all have a more equal chance of winning. **b** the number of strokes by which a golfer on average exceeds par for a course. **c** the extra weight assigned to a racehorse as a handicap.

handicap[2] *v* (**handicapped, handicapping**) **1** to assign handicaps to (people or horses). **2** to put at a disadvantage.

handicapped *adj* **1** *dated, sometimes offensive* affected by physical or mental disability. **2** of a golfer or other participant in a competition: assigned a disadvantage at the start of play, a race, etc.

handicraft *n* **1** manual skill, or an occupation requiring it. **2** an article or articles fashioned by handicraft.

handiwork *n* **1** work done personally. **2** work done by the hands, or the product of such work.

handkerchief *n* (*pl* **handkerchiefs** *or* **handkerchieves**) a small piece of cloth used for blowing the nose.

handle[1] *n* **1** a part that is designed to be grasped by the hand. **2** *informal* one's name or nickname. **3** *informal* any means of coming to grips with something.

handle[2] *v* **1** to try or examine (something), e.g. by touching or moving it with the hand. **2a** to deal with (a subject, idea, etc) in speech or writing, or as a work of art. **b** to manage or be in charge of (something). **3** to deal with (somebody or something). **4** to engage in the buying, selling, or distributing of (a commodity). **5** of a vehicle, etc: to respond to the controls in a specified way. ➤➤ **handling** *n.*

handlebar *n* (*also in pl*) a bar, *esp* on a cycle or scooter, for steering.

handlebar moustache *n* a long heavy moustache that curves upwards at each end.

handler *n* **1** (*usu in combination*) a person who handles or deals with a specified thing. **2** a person who is in immediate physical charge of an animal. **3a** a boxer's personal trainer, also acting as a second. **b** *informal* a performer's manager or publicity agent.

handmade *adj* made by hand rather than by machine.

handmaid *n* = HANDMAIDEN.

handmaiden *n* **1** *archaic* a female servant. **2** something whose essential function is to serve or assist.

hand-me-down *n* a garment or other possession that has been passed on to one, *esp* by an older sibling.

handout *n* **1** something, e.g. food, clothing, or money, distributed free, *esp* to people in need. **2** a folder or sheet of information for free distribution.

hand out *v* to give (something) freely to a group of people.

handover *n* an act of transferring something, *esp* power or responsibility, from one person or group to another.

handpick *v* to select (somebody or something) personally and carefully.

handset *n* **1** the part of a telephone that contains the mouthpiece and earpiece. **2** the remote-control device for a television set, video recorder, etc.

hands-free *adj* of a telephone, etc: able to be used without being held in the hands.

handshake *n* a clasping and shaking of each other's hand by two people, e.g. in greeting or agreement.

hands-off *adj* of management style: encouraging a degree of autonomy and keeping free of involvement as far as possible.

handsome *adj* **1a** of a man: having a pleasing appearance; good-looking. **b** of a woman: attractive in a dignified statuesque way. **2** of a building, room, etc: well-proportioned; stately. **3** considerable or sizable. **4** generous, gracious, or liberal. ➤➤ **handsomely** *adv,* **handsomeness** *n.*

hands-on *adj* involving direct personal participation or practical experience.

handspring *n* an acrobatic movement in which one turns one's body forward or backward in a full circle from a standing position and lands first on the hands and then on the feet.

handstand *n* an act of supporting and balancing the body upside down on the hands with the legs in the air.

hand-to-hand *adj* involving physical contact; very close.

handwriting *n* writing done by hand; *esp* the style of writing peculiar to a particular person.

handwritten *adj* of a letter, etc: written by hand.

handy *adj* (**-ier, -iest**) **1a** convenient for use; useful. **b** of a vessel or vehicle: easily handled. **2** conveniently near. **3** clever in using the hands, *esp* in a variety of practical ways. ➤➤ **handily** *adv,* **handiness** *n.*

handyman *n* (*pl* **handymen**) **1** a man who does odd jobs. **2** a man who is competent in a variety of skills or repair work.

hang[1] *v* (*past tense and past part.* **hung**) **1a** to fasten (something) to an elevated point by the top so that the lower part is free; to suspend (something). **b** to remain fastened at the top so that the lower part is free; to dangle. **c** (*past tense and past part.* **hanged**) to suspend (somebody) by the neck until dead, usu as a form of capital punishment, or to die in this way. **d** to fasten (a door, window, etc) on a point of suspension so as to allow free motion within given limits. **e** to suspend (meat, *esp* game) before cooking to make the flesh tender and develop the flavour. **2** to fasten (wallpaper) to a wall, e.g. with paste. **3** to display (a picture), e.g. in a gallery. **4** to remain poised or stationary in the air. **5** to stay on; to persist. **6** (+ over) to be imminent; to impend; to be a threat to somebody. **7** to fall or droop from a tense or taut position. **8** (+ up/upon) to depend on something. ✱ **hang fire** see FIRE[1].

Usage note

hanged *or* **hung**? *Hung* is the correct form of the past tense and past participle of *to hang,* except in the sense 'to execute by hanging'. In this sense the form *hanged* (*was hanged at Tyburn*) is preferable, although *hung* is often found (*hung, drawn and quartered*).

hang[2] *n* the manner in which a thing hangs. ✱ **get the hang of** *informal* to learn how to use, or deal with (something).

hang about *v Brit* **1** to wait or stay, usu without purpose or activity. **2** (+ with) to associate or be friendly with somebody.

hangar *n* a shed; *esp* a large shed for housing aircraft.

hang around *v* = HANG ABOUT.

hang back *v* to be reluctant to move or act; to hesitate.

hangdog *adj* ashamed or abject.

hanger *n* **1** a piece of shaped wire, plastic, or wood, surmounted by a hook, for hanging clothes on. **2** (*usu in combinations*) a person who hangs something.

hanger-on *n* (*pl* **hangers-on**) a sycophantic follower or associate of a person, group, etc.

hang-glider *n* a glider that resembles a kite and is controlled by the body movements of the harnessed person suspended beneath it. ⋙ **hang-gliding** *n.*

hangi *n* (*pl* **hangis**) *NZ* a Maori oven in the form of an open-air cooking pit, or the food produced in such an oven.

hanging *n* **1** execution by suspension from a noose. **2** a covering, e.g. a tapestry, for a wall.

hanging valley *n* a valley ending in a steeply descending cliff face.

hangman *n* (*pl* **hangmen**) a man who hangs a condemned person; a public executioner.

hangnail *n* a bit of skin hanging loose at the side or root of a fingernail.

hang on *v* **1** to keep hold; to hold onto something. **2** *informal* to persist tenaciously. **3a** *informal* to wait for a short time. **b** to remain on the telephone.

hangout *n informal* a place where one is often to be seen.

hang out *v informal* to spend time in a leisurely or idle way. ✱ **let it all hang out** *informal* to relax and enjoy oneself, without inhibitions.

hangover *n* **1** the disagreeable physical effects following heavy consumption of alcohol, e.g. headache and nausea. **2** something, e.g. a custom, that remains from the past.

hang up *v* to end a telephone conversation by replacing the receiver.

hang-up *n informal* a source of mental or emotional difficulty.

hank *n* a coil or loop of yarn, rope, hair, or wire.

hanker *v* (+ after/for) to desire something strongly or persistently. ⋙ **hankering** *n.*

hankie *or* **hanky** *n* (*pl* **-ies**) *informal* a handkerchief.

hanky-panky *n informal* mildly improper or deceitful behaviour.

Hanoverian *adj* of the British royal house that reigned from 1714 to 1901. ⋙ **Hanoverian** *n.*

Hansard *n* the official report of Parliamentary proceedings.

Hansen's disease *n* leprosy.

hansom *n* a light two-wheeled covered carriage seating two, with the driver's seat high up at the back.

hansom cab *n* = HANSOM.

hantavirus *n* (*pl* **hantaviruses**) any of a genus of viruses carried by rodents that can be transmitted to humans, causing fever, haemorrhage, and kidney or respiratory damage.

Hants *abbr* Hampshire.

Hanukkah *or* **Chanukah** *n* an eight-day Jewish festival falling in December and commemorating the rededication of the Temple of Jerusalem in 165 BC.

hap *n archaic* **1** a happening or occurrence. **2** chance or fortune.

ha'penny *n* (*pl* **-ies**) a halfpenny.

haphazard *adj* lacking any method, plan, or order; aimless. ⋙ **haphazardly** *adv,* **haphazardness** *n.*

hapless *adj* luckless; unfortunate. ⋙ **haplessly** *adv,* **haplessness** *n.*

haplography *n* a written haplology, e.g. *repetive* for *repetitive*.

haploid *adj* having a single and unpaired set of chromosomes: compare DIPLOID, POLYPLOID[1].

haplology *n* contraction of a word by the omission of one or more similar sounds or syllables in pronunciation, e.g. /'liebri/ for 'library'.

happen *v* **1** to take place; to occur. **2** to occur or do something by chance. **3** to be the case. ✱ **happen on/upon** *literary* to encounter (something or somebody) by chance.

happening[1] *n* **1** something that happens; an occurrence. **2** an unscripted or improvised public performance in which the audience participates.

happening[2] *adj informal* exciting and fashionable.

happenstance *n NAm* a circumstance regarded as due to chance.

happy *adj* (**-ier, -iest**) **1a** enjoying or expressing pleasure and contentment. **b** glad; pleased. **2** favoured by luck or fortune; fortunate. **3** well adapted or fitting; felicitous. **4** (*usu in combination*) impulsively quick or overinclined to use something: *trigger-happy*. ⋙ **happily** *adv,* **happiness** *n.*

happy-go-lucky *adj* blithely unconcerned; carefree.

happy hour *n* a limited period of the day during which drinks are sold in a bar, pub, etc at reduced prices.

happy hunting ground *n informal* a choice or profitable area of activity.

hapten *n* a small separable part of an antigen that reacts specifically with an antibody.

haptic *adj technical* relating to or based on the sense of touch.

hara-kiri *n* suicide by ritual disembowelment, formerly practised by the Japanese samurai when disgraced.

harangue[1] *n* a lengthy, ranting, censorious speech or piece of writing.

harangue[2] *v* to lecture (somebody) at length in a sententious or censorious manner.

harass *v* to annoy or worry (somebody) persistently. ⋙ **harassed** *adj,* **harasser** *n,* **harassment** *n.*

Usage note

harass *and* **harassment**. The traditional and still predominant British pronunciation of these words places the stress on the first syllable *ha-*. In modern American English the stress has moved to the second syllable. This pronunciation is gaining ground in Britain, but is disliked by some traditionalists.

harbinger *n literary* a person or thing that signals or heralds a future event, change, etc; a precursor or forerunner.

harbour[1] (*NAm* **harbor**) *n* a port or coastal inlet providing shelter and safe anchorage for ships.

harbour[2] (*NAm* **harbor**) *v* **1** to have or keep (thoughts or feelings) in the mind. **2** to give shelter or refuge to (somebody). **3** to be the home or habitat of; to contain: *These cracks can harbour dangerous bacteria.*

hard[1] *adj* **1** not easily penetrated or yielding to pressure; firm. **2a** physically fit; able to cope with stress; tough. **b** revealing no weakness. **3a** consisting of metal as distinct from paper. **b** of currency: stable in value, or soundly backed and readily convertible into foreign currencies without large discounts. **4a** demanding energy or stamina. **b** expending great energy or effort. **c** oppressive or exacting. **d** harsh or severe. **e** forceful or violent. **f** lacking consideration or compassion. **5** difficult to endure. **6a** not speculative or conjectural; factual. **b** close or searching. **7** difficult to understand, explain, or answer. **8** firm or definite. **9a** of a drink: containing a high percentage of alcohol. **b** of water: containing salts of calcium, magnesium, etc that inhibit lathering with soap. **10a** of a drug: addictive and gravely detrimental to health. **b** of pornography: hard-core. ✻ **hard going 1** arduous. **2** difficult to understand. **hard lines** an expression of sympathy or condolence. **hard of hearing** rather deaf. **no hard feelings** no offence taken. ➤➤ **hardness** *n.*

hard[2] *adv* **1a** with great or maximum effort or energy; strenuously. **b** in a violent manner; fiercely. **c** used in nautical directions: to the full extent. **d** in a searching or concentrated manner. **2** in a firm manner; tightly. ✻ **be hard put to it** to have difficulty. **feel hard done by** to think oneself unfairly treated. **hard on/upon** immediately after (something). **hard up** *informal* short of money.

hard-and-fast *adj* fixed or strict.

hardback *n* a book bound in stiff covers.

hard-bitten *adj* steeled by difficult experience; tough.

hardboard *n* composition board made by compressing shredded wood chips.

hard-boiled *adj* **1** of an egg: cooked to the point at which both white and yolk have solidified. **2** of a person: devoid of sentimentality; tough.

hard cash *n* money in the form of coin or bank notes as opposed to cheques or credit.

hard copy *n* a paper copy of data held on computer.

hardcore *n* **1** *Brit* compacted rubble or clinker used *esp* as a foundation for roads, paving, or floors. **2** a revived form of punk rock originating in the 1980s.

hard core *n* (*used as sing. or pl*) the unyielding or uncompromising members that form the nucleus of a group.

hard-core *adj* **1** constituting a hard core. **2** of pornography: extremely explicit; *esp* showing real rather than simulated sexual acts.

hard disk *n* a rigid magnetic disk permanently installed in a computer, with a large storage capacity for data.

hard drive *n* = HARD DISK.

harden *v* to make or become hard or harder. ➤➤ **hardened** *adj,* **hardener** *n.*

hard hat *n* a protective hat made of rigid material, e.g. metal or fibreglass, and worn *esp* by construction workers.

hardheaded *adj* sober or realistic. ➤➤ **hardheadedly** *adv,* **hardheadedness** *n.*

hardhearted *adj* lacking in sympathetic understanding; unfeeling. ➤➤ **hardheartedly** *adv,* **hardheartedness** *n.*

hard-hitting *adj* vigorous or effective.

hard labour *n* compulsory labour as part of prison discipline.

hard-line *adj* advocating or involving a persistently firm course of action; unyielding. ➤➤ **hard-liner** *n.*

hardly *adv* **1a** not in the least: *That news is hardly surprising.* **b** used as a response: certainly not!: *'You won't change your mind?' 'Hardly!'.* **2** only just; barely: *I hardly knew her.* **3** with difficulty; painfully: *I could hardly walk.*

hard-nosed *adj informal* **1** sober or realistic. **2** hard-bitten; stubborn.

hard-on *n* (*pl* **hard-ons**) *coarse slang* an erection of the penis.

hard palate *n* the bony front part of the palate forming the roof of the mouth.

hardpan *n* a hard compact soil layer.

hard-pressed *adj* **1** in difficulties. **2** of troops, etc: closely pursued or under fire.

hard rock *n* basic rock music played with a heavy beat.

hard sell *n* aggressive high-pressure salesmanship.

hardship *n* suffering or privation.

hard shoulder *n Brit* either of two surfaced strips alongside a motorway, on which stopping is allowed only in an emergency.

hardstanding *n Brit* a hard-surfaced area on which vehicles may park.

hardtack *n archaic* a ship's biscuit.

hardtop *n* a motor car with a rigid top.

hardware *n* **1** the physical components, e.g. electronic and electrical devices, of a computer or other electronically controlled device: compare SOFTWARE. **2** items sold by an ironmonger such as household tools and gardening equipment. **3** heavy military equipment such as tanks and missiles.

hard-wired *adj* in computing: **a** denoting an electronic circuit whose functions and operations are determined by its physical construction rather than by programming. **b** controlled by such a circuit.

hardwood *n* **1** a broad-leaved as distinguished from a coniferous tree. **2** the wood of such a tree.

hardy *adj* (**-ier, -iest**) **1** inured to fatigue or hardships; tough. **2** of a plant: capable of withstanding adverse conditions; *esp* capable of living outdoors over winter without artificial protection. ➤➤ **hardily** *adv,* **hardiness** *n.*

hare[1] *n* a swift long-eared mammal like a large rabbit with long hind legs. ✻ **run with the hare and hunt with the hounds** to remain on good terms with both sides.

hare[2] *v informal* to run fast.

harebell *n* a slender plant with blue bell-shaped flowers that grows on heaths and in open woodlands.

harebrained *adj* flighty or foolish.

Hare Krishna *n* **1** a missionary Hindu cult characterized by the public chanting of a psalm taken from the sacred writings of Hinduism and beginning 'Hare Krishna'. **2** a member of this cult.

harelip *n* a split in the upper lip like that of a hare occurring as a congenital deformity, often in association with a cleft palate. ➤➤ **harelipped** *adj.*

harem *n* **1a** a secluded part of a house allotted to women in a Muslim household. **b** (*used as sing. or* *pl*) the women occupying a harem. **2** used with reference to polygamous animals: a group of females associated with one male.

haricot *n* a type of French bean with white edible seeds that can be dried and stored.

harissa *n* a spicy paste used in N African cookery.

hark *v archaic or literary* (*usu in imperative*) to listen. ✱ **hark at so-and-so!** used disparagingly to draw attention to a foolish or pompous comment, etc.

hark back *v* (+ to) to return to an earlier topic or circumstance.

harken *v* see HEARKEN.

Harlequin *n* a mute character in traditional pantomime, in mask and lozenge-patterned costume.

harlequin *adj* of a pattern: consisting of coloured lozenges or brightly variegated.

harlequinade *n* a part of a play or pantomime in which Harlequin has a leading role.

harlot *n archaic* a female prostitute. ➤➤ **harlotry** *n.*

harm[1] *n* **1** physical or mental damage; injury. **2** mischief or wrong. ✱ **out of harm's way** safe from danger. ➤➤ **harmful** *adj,* **harmfully** *adv,* **harmfulness** *n.*

harm[2] *v* **1** to damage (something) or injure (somebody). **2** to have a deleterious effect on (something).

harmattan *n* a dry dust-laden wind that blows off the desert onto the Atlantic coast of Africa from December to February.

harmless *adj* lacking capacity or intent to injure. ➤➤ **harmlessly** *adv,* **harmlessness** *n.*

harmonic[1] *adj* **1** relating to musical harmony, a harmonic, or harmonics. **2** pleasing to the ear; harmonious. **3** in mathematics, expressible in terms of sine or cosine functions. ➤➤ **harmonically** *adv.*

harmonic[2] *n* a flutelike overtone produced on a stringed instrument by touching a vibrating string at a point, e.g. the midpoint, which divides it into halves, thirds, etc.

harmonica *n* a small rectangular wind instrument with free reeds recessed in air slots from which notes are sounded by breathing out and in.

harmonic progression *n* **1** in music, the sequence of chord changes that represents the harmonic structure of a composition, etc. **2** in mathematics, a sequence whose terms are the reciprocals of an arithmetic progression.

harmonious *adj* **1** musically concordant. **2** having the parts arranged so as to produce a pleasing effect. **3** of relations between people: characterized by mutual respect and amicable cooperation. ➤➤ **harmoniously** *adv,* **harmoniousness** *n.*

harmonise *v* see HARMONIZE.

harmonium *n* a musical instrument of the reed organ family in which pedals operate a bellows that forces air through free reeds.

harmonize *or* **-ise** *v* **1** to play or sing in harmony. **2** (*often* + with) to be in harmony or keeping. **3** to provide (a tune) with harmony. **4** to bring (differing things) into consonance or accord. ➤➤ **harmonization** *n.*

harmony *n* (*pl* **-ies**) **1a** the pleasant-sounding combination of simultaneous musical notes in a chord. **b** the structure of music with respect to the composition and progression of chords, or the science of the structure of music in this respect. **2a** pleasing or congruent arrangement of parts. **b** agreement or accord.

harness[1] *n* **1a** the gear of a draught animal other than a yoke. **b** *archaic* military equipment for a knight. **2** something that resembles a harness, e.g. in holding or fastening something. ✱ **in harness 1** in one's usual work, surroundings, or routine. **2** in close association.

harness[2] *v* **1a** to put a harness on (a horse, etc). **b** to attach (a wagon, etc) by means of a harness. **2** to utilize (something); *esp* to convert (a natural force) into energy.

harp[1] *n* a stringed musical instrument with strings stretched across an open triangular frame, plucked with the fingers. ➤➤ **harper** *n,* **harpist** *n.*

harp[2] *v* (+ on) to dwell on or return to a subject tediously or monotonously.

harpoon[1] *n* a barbed spear used in hunting large fish or whales. ➤➤ **harpooner** *n.*

harpoon[2] *v* to spear (a large fish or whale) with a harpoon. ➤➤ **harpooner** *n.*

harpsichord *n* a keyboard musical instrument having a horizontal frame and strings and producing notes by the action of quills or leather points plucking the strings. ➤➤ **harpsichordist** *n.*

harpy *n* (*pl* **-ies**) **1** (**Harpy**) a rapacious creature of Greek mythology with the head of a woman and the body of a bird. **2** *derog* a rapacious woman.

harquebus *n* see ARQUEBUS.

harridan *n* an ill-tempered unpleasant woman.

harrier[1] *n* a hunting dog resembling a small foxhound and used for hunting hares.

harrier[2] *n* a slender hawk with long angled wings.

Harris tweed *n trademark* a loosely woven tweed made in the Outer Hebrides.

harrow[1] *n* a cultivating implement set with spikes, spring teeth, or discs and drawn over the ground to pulverize and smooth the soil.

harrow[2] *v* **1** to cultivate (ground or land) with a harrow. **2** to cause distress to (somebody).

harrumph *v* to make a guttural sound as if clearing the throat, *esp* as a sign of disapproval.

harry *v* (**-ies, -ied**) **1** to make a destructive raid on (enemy territory). **2** to harass or torment (somebody).

harsh *adj* **1** disagreeable or painful to the senses. **2** lacking in aesthetic appeal or refinement; crude. **3** unduly exacting; severe. **4** of a climate, conditions, etc: unpleasant; difficult to endure. **5** having too strong or rough an effect. ➤➤ **harshen** *v,* **harshly** *adv,* **harshness** *n.*

hart *n* the male of the red deer, *esp* when over five years old.

hartebeest *n* a large African antelope with ridged horns that project upward and outward.

harum-scarum *adj informal* reckless or irresponsible.

harvest[1] *n* **1** the gathering in of agricultural crops, or the season when this is done. **2** a mature crop, or the yield of a crop, of grain, fruit, etc.

harvest[2] *v* **1** to gather in (a crop); to reap. **2** to gather (a natural product) as if by harvesting. ➤➤ **harvestable** *adj,* **harvester** *n.*

harvest home *n* **1** the gathering in of the harvest, or the time of this. **2** a festival at the close of harvest.

harvestman *n* (*pl* **harvestmen**) an arachnid with a small rounded body and very long slender legs.

harvest moon *n* the full moon nearest the time of the September equinox.

harvest mouse *n* a small European field mouse that nests in cornfields.

has *v* third person sing. present of HAVE[1].

has-been *n informal* somebody or something that has passed the peak of success or popularity.

hash[1] *n* **1** a dish consisting chiefly of reheated cooked chopped food, *esp* meat. **2** *informal* a muddle; a jumble. ✱ **make a hash of something** *informal* to do something incompetently.

hash[2] *v* to chop (meat, potatoes, etc) into small pieces.

hash[3] *n informal* hashish.

hash[4] *n* the symbol #.

hash browns *pl n* cooked potatoes that have been chopped or mashed and fried in hot oil or fat until browned.

hashish *n* the resin from the flowering tops of the female hemp plant, smoked or chewed for its intoxicating effect.

Hasid *or* **Chassid** *n* (*pl* **Hasidim** *or* **Chassidim**) a member of a Jewish mystical sect founded in Poland about 1750 in opposition to formalistic ritualism. ➤➤ **Hasidic** *adj,* **Hasidism** *n.*

haslet *n* the edible entrails, e.g. the liver, of an animal, *esp* a pig, cooked and compressed into a meat loaf.

hasn't *contr* has not.

hasp *n* a device for fastening; *esp* a hinged metal strap that fits over a metal loop and is secured by a pin or padlock.

hassium *n* a very unstable chemical element artificially produced by high-energy atomic collisions.

hassle[1] *n informal* **1** a difficult or trying situation. **2** harassment.

hassle[2] *v informal* to subject (somebody) to persistent harassment.

hassock *n chiefly Brit* a cushion for kneeling on in church.

hast *v* archaic present second person sing. of HAVE[1].

haste *n* **1** rapidity of motion; swiftness. **2** rash or headlong speed; precipitateness.

hasten *v* **1** to accelerate (something). **2** to move or act quickly; to hurry.

hasty *adj* (**-ier, -iest**) **1** done or made in a hurry. **2** precipitate; rash. ➤➤ **hastily** *adv,* **hastiness** *n.*

hat *n* a covering for the head, *esp* one with a shaped crown and brim. ✱ **keep something under one's hat** to keep something a secret. **pick out of a hat** to select (e.g. a name) at random. **take one's hat off to somebody** to give somebody due credit. **talk through one's hat** *informal* to voice irrational or erroneous ideas, *esp* in attempting to appear knowledgeable. **throw one's hat into the ring** to offer to take up a challenge. ➤➤ **hatless** *adj.*

hatband *n* a band made of fabric, leather, etc round the crown of a hat just above the brim.

hatch[1] *n* **1** a small door or opening, e.g. in a wall or aircraft. **2** an opening in the deck of a ship or in the floor or roof of a building, or a cover over such an opening. ✱ **down the hatch!** *informal* an expression of encouragement to drink up.

hatch[2] *v* **1** of young: to emerge from an egg or pupa. **2** to cause (young) to emerge from an egg. **3** of an egg: to open and release young. **4** to incubate (an egg). **5** of a female bird: to incubate eggs; to brood. **6** to devise or originate (a plot or plan), usu conspiratorially.

hatch[3] *n* a brood of young produced by hatching.

hatch[4] *v* to mark (a drawing, map, or engraving) with fine closely spaced parallel lines to show eminences and depressions. ➤➤ **hatching** *n.*

hatchback *n* a car with an upward-opening hatch giving entry to the luggage and passenger compartment.

hatchery *n* (*pl* **-ies**) a place for hatching eggs, *esp* fish eggs.

hatchet *n* a short-handled axe.

hatchet-faced *adj* grimly sharp-featured.

hatchet job *n informal* a vicious or damaging attack on a person or their work.

hatchet man *n informal* **1** a person hired for murder, coercion, or attack. **2** a vicious or merciless critic.

hatchling *n* a recently hatched animal.

hatchway *n* **1** a passage giving access, e.g. to a lower deck in a ship. **2** an opening in a ship's deck, etc, or a covering over such an opening.

hate[1] *v* to feel extreme enmity or aversion towards (somebody or something). ✱ **hate somebody's guts** see GUT[1]. ➤➤ **hatable** *adj,* **hateable** *adj,* **hater** *n.*

hate[2] *n* **1** intense hostility or dislike; loathing. **2** *informal* an object of hatred.

hateful *adj* deserving or arousing hate. ➤➤ **hatefully** *adv,* **hatefulness** *n.*

hath *v* archaic third person sing. present of HAVE[1].

hatha yoga *n* a system of yoga consisting of physical exercises and breath control.

hatred *n* intense dislike or hate.

hatter *n* a person who makes and sells hats.

hat trick *n* three successes by one person or side, usu in a sporting activity; *specif* the dismissing of three batsmen with three consecutive balls by a bowler in cricket.

hauberk *n* a tunic of chain mail worn as defensive armour, *esp* from the 12th to the 14th cent.

haughty *adj* (**-ier, -iest**) disdainfully proud; arrogant. ➤➤ **haughtily** *adv,* **haughtiness** *n.*

haul[1] *v* **1** to pull with effort; to drag. **2** to transport (goods) in a vehicle, *esp* a lorry. ✱ **haul somebody over the coals** to give somebody a severe reprimand.

haul[2] *n* **1a** an amount gathered or acquired, *esp* illegally; booty or spoils. **b** a seizure by the authorities of illicit goods. **c** the fish taken in a single draught of a net. **2** the distance or route to be travelled, or over which a load is to be transported.

haulage *n* the act or process of hauling.

haulier (*NAm* **hauler**) *n* a person or commercial establishment whose business is transport by lorry.

haulm *n* **1** a plant stem. **2** the stems or tops of potatoes, peas, beans, etc, after the crop has been gathered.

haunch *n* **1** the human hip. **2a** (*in pl*) the back legs of a four-legged animal; the hindquarters. **b** the back half of the side of a slaughtered animal; a hindquarter.

haunt[1] *v* **1** of a ghost: **a** to visit (a person). **b** to inhabit (a place). **2** of a person: to visit (a place) often. **3a** to recur constantly and spontaneously to (somebody). **b** to reappear continually in (something); to pervade. ➤➤ **haunter** *n.*

haunt[2] *n* a place habitually frequented.

haunted *adj* **1** of a building: inhabited by a ghost. **2** worried or anguished.

haunting *adj* **1** of concerns, memories, etc: constantly recurring to one; persistent. **2** poignantly evocative. ➤➤ **hauntingly** *adv.*

hausfrau /'howsfrow/ *n* a German housewife.

hautboy *or* **hautbois** *n archaic* an oboe.

haute couture /,oht kooh'tyooə/ *n* the designing and making of highly fashionable clothes by leading fashion houses.

haute cuisine /kwi'zeen/ *n* cooking of a high standard, *esp* following French methods.

hauteur *n* arrogance or haughtiness.

Havana *n* a cigar made in Cuba or from tobacco grown in Cuba.

have[1] *v* (*past tense and past part.* **had**) **1** to own or possess as property. **2** to exercise or display (a feeling or quality). **3a** to experience or undergo (e.g. an illness). **b** to engage in an activity: *to have a swim; to have a look.* **c** to eat or drink: *Will you have some tea?* **4** to receive or be given: *I've had some news.* **5** to get (something) done or to get (somebody) to do something: *We'll soon have it finished; Please have them come in.* **6a** to accommodate or be the host of: *Thank you for having us.* **b** to arrange or organize: *to have a party.* **7** to give birth to. ➤ *v aux* used with a past participle to form the perfect, pluperfect, and future perfect tenses of verbs. ✱ **be had** *informal* to be the victim of a deception. **have (got) it in for** *informal* to behave in a vindictive way towards. **have had it 1** *informal* to have missed one's chance. **2** *informal* to be useless or beyond repair. **have it out** *informal* to settle a disagreement openly.

have[2] ✱ **the haves and have-nots** *informal* wealthy people and poor people.

have-a-go *adj Brit, informal* of a member of the public: actively attempting to stop somebody who is committing a crime.

haven *n* **1** a place of safety or refuge. **2** a harbour or port.

have-not *n* see HAVE[2].

haven't *contr* have not.

have on *v* **1** to be wearing. **2** to have planned or organized (an event). **3** *informal* to deceive or tease (somebody).

haver *v* **1** *Scot* to talk nonsense. **2** *chiefly Brit* to be indecisive; to hesitate.

haversack *n* a knapsack.

have up *v informal* to bring before the authorities to answer a charge.

havoc *n* **1** widespread destruction; devastation. **2** great confusion and disorder; chaos. ✱ **cry havoc** *archaic* to give an army the signal to plunder. **play havoc with something** to disrupt something.

haw[1] *n* the red berry of the hawthorn.

haw[2] ✱ **hum and haw** see HUM[1].

Hawaiian *n* **1** a native or inhabitant of Hawaii. **2** the language of Hawaii. ➤➤ **Hawaiian** *adj.*

hawfinch *n* a large Eurasian finch with a large bill.

hawk[1] *n* **1** a medium-sized bird of prey with short rounded wings and a long tail, that hunts during the day. **2** a person who takes a militant attitude; a supporter of a warlike policy. ➤➤ **hawkish** *adj.*

hawk[2] *v* to hunt game with a trained hawk.

hawk[3] *v* to offer (goods) for sale in the street.

hawk[4] *v* **1** to utter a harsh guttural sound in clearing the throat. **2** to raise (phlegm) by hawking.

hawker *n* a person who hawks wares.

hawkmoth *n* a stout-bodied moth with long narrow forewings.

hawkweed *n* a plant of the daisy family with red, orange, or yellow dandelion-like heads.

hawser *n* a large rope, *esp* one used on a ship.

hawthorn *n* a spiny shrub of the rose family with white or pink flowers and small red fruits.

hay[1] *n* grass that has been mown and dried for fodder. ✱ **hit the hay** *informal* to go to bed. **make hay while the sun shines** to utilize an opportunity fully while it lasts.

hay[2] *v* to cut, cure, and store grass for hay.

haycock *n* a small conical pile of hay in a field.

hay fever *n* nasal catarrh and conjunctivitis occurring usu in the spring and summer through allergy to pollen.

haymaker *n* **1** a person who tosses and spreads hay to dry after cutting. **2** *informal* a powerful swinging blow, e.g. in boxing. **3** a machine that breaks or bends hay so that it dries more rapidly. ➤➤ **haymaking** *n.*

hayrick *n* a haystack.

hayseed *n* grass seed from hay.

haystack *n* a large constructed pile of hay, usu protected by thatch.

haywire *adj informal* out of control; erratic.

hazard[1] *n* **1a** a risk or peril. **b** a source of danger. **c** *chiefly archaic or literary* chance; accident; uncertainty. **2** a golf-course obstacle, e.g. a bunker. **3** a game of chance played with two dice.

hazard[2] *v* **1** to venture (an estimate, guess, etc). **2** to expose (something) to danger.

hazard lights *pl n* a vehicle's right and left indicator lights when flashing simultaneously, operated to warn that the vehicle is temporarily obstructing traffic.

hazardous *adj* **1** involving or exposing one to risk, e.g. of loss or harm. **2** depending on hazard or chance. ➤➤ **hazardously** *adv,* **hazardousness** *n.*

haze *n* **1** vapour, dust, smoke, etc causing a slight decrease in the air's transparency. **2** vagueness or confusion of mental perception.

hazel *n* **1** a small tree of the birch family, bearing edible nuts in autumn and catkins in spring. **2** a yellowish light to strong brown, *esp* as an eye colour. ➤➤ **hazel** *adj.*

hazelnut *n* the small round hard-shelled edible nut of the hazel.

hazy *adj* (**-ier, -iest**) **1** obscured or cloudy. **2** vague or indefinite. ➤➤ **hazily** *adv,* **haziness** *n.*

HB *abbr* used as a designation of medium grade on lead pencils: hard black.

hb *abbr* hardback.

H-bomb *n* a hydrogen bomb.

HC *abbr* **1** *Brit* House of Commons. **2** hydrocarbon.

HDTV *abbr* high-definition television.

HE *abbr* high explosive.

He *abbr* the chemical symbol for helium.

he[1] *pron* **1** used to refer to a male person or creature, previously mentioned, who is neither speaker nor hearer. **2** used in a generic sense or when the sex of the person is unspecified: **a** *archaic or literary* to mean 'anyone', followed by a relative clause. **b** *dated* to refer back to an indefinite pronoun or common-gender noun (now superseded by *he or she* or *they*).

he[2] *n* (*also in combination*) a male person or creature.

head[1] *n* **1** the upper or foremost division of the human body containing the brain, the chief sense organs, and the face, also clearly demarcated in most other animals. **2** (*in pl, used as sing. or pl*) the obverse of a coin, typically bearing the head of the monarch or president. **3a** a person or individual. **b** (*with pl meaning*) used in counting livestock. **4a** the end that is upper, higher, or opposite the foot. **b** the source of a stream, river, etc. **5** a director or leader, e.g. a school principal. **6a** a rounded or flattened cluster of flowers. **b** the foliaged part of a plant, *esp* when consisting of a compact mass of leaves or fruits. **7a** the uppermost extremity or projecting part of an object; the top. **b** the striking or operational part of a weapon, tool, implement, etc. **c** the flattened or rounded end of a nail, tack, screw, etc. **8a** a body of water kept in reserve at a height. **b** a mass of water in motion. **9a** the difference in height between two points in a body of liquid, or the pressure resulting from this. **b** the pressure of a fluid. **10** the foam or froth that rises on a fermenting or effervescing liquid, *esp* beer. **11a** a part of a machine or machine tool containing a device, e.g. a cutter or drill, or the part of an apparatus that performs the chief or a particular function. **b** any of at least two electromagnetic components which bear on the magnetic tape in a tape recorder, such that one can erase recorded material if desired and another may either record or play back. ✱ **above/over somebody's head** too difficult for somebody to understand. **bang/knock people's heads together** to deal summarily with people who persist in arguing and refusing to cooperate with each other. **come to a head** to arrive at a crisis. **get a head start** to secure an advantage for oneself at the outset of a competition, etc. **get one's head down 1** *informal* to get some sleep. **2** *informal* to start concentrating on a task. **give somebody their head** to give somebody scope to act on their own initiative. **go over somebody's head** to ignore the person immediately senior to somebody in a hierarchy and appeal, complain, etc to somebody in higher authority. **go to somebody's head 1** of alcohol: to make somebody intoxicated or dizzy. **2** of fame or success: to make somebody conceited or overconfident. **have a head/good head for something** to have an aptitude for, or an ability to cope with, something. **head over heels 1** so as to execute a somersault. **2** helplessly. **keep one's head** to keep emotionally and intellectually cool, and act the more effectively as a result. **keep one's head above water** to remain solvent; *broadly* to stay out of difficulty. **laugh/talk/shout/bawl one's head off** to laugh, talk, etc with inordinate vigour and vociferousness. **lose one's head** to panic or behave irrationally. **not make head or tail of something** to make no sense of something. **off one's head** *informal* crazy or mad. **turn somebody's head** to make somebody conceited. **with one's head in the clouds** in a dreamy state of mind. ➤➤ **headless** *adj.*

head[2] *adj* principal or chief.

head[3] *v* **1** to be at the head of (a movement, etc); to lead. **2a** to put something as the heading to (a list, paragraph, etc). **b** to stand as the first or leading member or item of (a list, catalogue, etc). **3** to drive (a football, etc) with the head. **4** to move in a specified direction.

headache *n* **1** a sustained pain in the head. **2** *informal* something that causes worry or difficulty. ➤➤ **headachy** *adj.*

headband *n* a band, typically of stretch fabric, worn round the head, *esp* to keep hair or sweat out of the eyes.

headbanger *n Brit, informal* a person who shakes their head violently and rhythmically to the beat of loud rock music, *esp* heavy metal.

headboard *n* a board forming the head of a bed.

headbutt[1] *v* to strike (somebody) with the head.

headbutt[2] *n* a blow with the head.

head case *n informal* a mad person; an eccentric.

headcount *n* a count of the number of people present.

headdress *n* any elaborate covering for the head, e.g. one worn ceremonially.

header *n* **1** a shot or pass in football made by heading the ball. **2** *informal* a headfirst fall or dive. **3** a brick or stone laid in a wall with its end towards the face of the wall. **4** a raised water tank that maintains fluid pressure in a plumbing system, etc. **5** a line of text appearing at the top of each page of a book, etc.

header tank *n* = HEADER (4).

headfirst *adv and adj* with the head foremost; headlong.

headgear *n* clothing for the head, *esp* hats.

headhunter *n* **1** a member of a people that collects the decapitated heads of defeated enemies. **2** a person who identifies and recruits personnel to fill business positions, *esp* at senior levels and from other firms. ➤➤ **headhunting** *n.*

heading *n* **1** an inscription, headline, or title standing at the top or beginning of a letter, chapter, etc. **2** the compass direction in which a ship or aircraft points. **3** in mining, a horizontal tunnel; = DRIFT[2] (4). **4** the top edge of a curtain, extending above the hooks suspending it.

headlamp *n* a headlight.

headland *n* a point of high land jutting out into the sea.

headlight *n* the main light mounted on the front of a motor vehicle.

headline[1] *n* **1** a title printed in large type above a newspaper story or article. **2** *Brit* (*in pl*) a summary given at the beginning or end of a news broadcast.

headline[2] *v* **1** to provide (an article or story) with a headline. **2** to be a star performer in (a show).

headlock *n* a wrestling hold in which one arm is locked around the opponent's head.

headlong *adv and adj* **1** headfirst. **2** without pause or delay.

head louse *n* a louse that lives on the human scalp.

headman *n* (*pl* **headmen**) a chief of a tribe or community.

headmaster *or* **headmistress** *n chiefly Brit* a head teacher.

head off *v* to stop the progress of (a person, animal, or developing crisis, etc), block them, or turn them aside by taking preventive action.

head of state *n* the titular head of a state, e.g. a monarch, as distinguished from the head of government, e.g. a prime minister.

head-on *adv and adj* **1** with the head or front making the initial contact. **2** in direct opposition.

headphones *pl n* a pair of earphones held over the ears by a band worn on the head.

headpiece *n* **1** a protective covering, e.g. a helmet, for the head. **2** the part of a halter or bridle that fits over a horse's head behind its ears.

headquartered *adj* having headquarters in a specified place.

headquarters *n* (*pl* **headquarters**) (*used as sing. or pl*) **1** a place from which a military commander exercises command. **2** the administrative centre of an enterprise.

headrest *n* a support for the head; *esp* a cushioned pad supporting the head in a vehicle.

headroom *n* vertical space, e.g. beneath a bridge, sufficient to allow passage or unrestricted movement.

headscarf *n* (*pl* **headscarves** *or* **headscarfs**) a scarf worn on the head.

headset *n* an attachment for holding earphones and a microphone to one's head.

headship *n* the position or office of a head, e.g. a head teacher.

headstone *n* a memorial stone placed at the head of a grave.

headstrong *adj* wilful or obstinate.

head teacher *n chiefly Brit* the teacher in charge of a school.

head-to-head *adj and adv* of competition, disputes, etc: involving direct confrontation between parties.

headwater *n* the upper part or source of a river.

headway *n* **1** advance or progress. **2** motion in a forward direction.

headwind *n* a wind blowing in a direction opposite to a course, *esp* that of a ship or aircraft.

headword *n* a word or term placed at the beginning of a chapter, an encyclopedia or dictionary entry, etc.

headwork *n* mental effort; thinking.

heady *adj* (**-ier, -iest**) **1** of alcoholic drinks: tending to make one giddy or exhilarated; intoxicating. **2** exciting or exhilarating. ➤➤ **headily** *adv,* **headiness** *n.*

heal *v* **1a** to restore (somebody) to health. **b** to make (a wound, etc) sound or whole. **2a** to make (pain or sorrow) less acute. **b** to mend (a breach between friends, etc). **3** to return to a sound or healthy state. ➤➤ **healer** *n,* **healing** *adj and n.*

health *n* **1a** soundness of body, mind, or spirit. **b** the general condition of the body. **2** condition or state generally.

health centre *n Brit* an establishment providing a variety of local medical services.

health farm *n* a residential establishment that provides treatments and regimes for people wishing to improve their health.

health food *n* organically grown untreated food containing no synthetic ingredients and eaten for the health-giving properties credited to it.

healthful *adj* **1** beneficial to the health of body or mind. **2** enjoying good health.

health visitor *n Brit* a nurse employed by a local authority to visit people and advise them on health matters.

healthy *adj* (**-ier, -iest**) **1** enjoying or showing health and vigour of body, mind, or spirit. **2** conducive to good health. **3** prosperous or flourishing. **4** of one's bank balance, profits, etc: reassuringly substantial. ➤➤ **healthily** *adv,* **healthiness** *n.*

heap[1] *n* **1** a collection of things lying one on top of another; a pile. **2** *informal* (*in pl*) a great number or large quantity; a lot. **3** *informal* an old or dilapidated car or building.

heap[2] *v* **1a** (*often* + up) to throw or lay (things) in a heap; to accumulate. **b** to form (something) into a heap. **2a** (*often* + with) to supply (somebody) abundantly with something. **b** to bestow (things) lavishly or in large quantities on somebody.

hear *v* (*past tense and past part.* **heard**) **1** to perceive (sound) with the ear. **2** to learn (something) by hearing. **3** (*also* + out) to listen to (somebody) with attention; to heed. **4** to give a legal or official hearing to (a case, complaint, etc). **5** (+ of/about) to gain information; to learn. ✻ **hear from** to receive a communication from (somebody). **hear! hear!** an expression indicating approval, e.g. during a speech. **hear of** (*in negative contexts*) to entertain the idea of (something). ➤➤ **hearer** *n.*

hearing *n* **1a** the one of the five basic physical senses by which waves received by the ear are interpreted by the brain as sounds varying in pitch, intensity, and timbre. **b** earshot. **2a** an opportunity to be heard. **b** a trial in court.

hearing aid *n* an electronic device worn by a person with defective hearing for amplifying sound before it reaches the ears.

hearing dog *n* a dog kept by a deaf person that is trained to alert them to any sound such as the telephone, doorbell, or an alarm.

hearken *or* **harken** *v archaic* (*usu* + to) to listen.

hearsay *n* something heard from somebody else; rumour.

hearse *n* a vehicle for transporting a coffin at a funeral.

heart *n* **1** a hollow muscular organ that uses rhythmic contractions to maintain the circulation of the blood. **2** the essential or most vital part. **3** a conventionalized representation of a heart. **4** the breast. **5a** a playing card marked with one or more red heart-shaped figures. **b** (*in pl*) the suit comprising cards identified by this figure. **6a** tenderness or compassion. **b** love or affections. **c** courage or spirit. **d** one's innermost character or feelings. ✻ **by heart** by rote or from memory. **have one's heart in one's mouth** to be worried, frightened, or excited. **have one's heart in the right place** to mean well; to have good intentions. **take heart** to gain courage or confidence. **take something to heart** to be deeply affected by something, e.g. what somebody says. **wear one's heart on one's sleeve** to show one's feelings and emotions.

heartache *n* mental anguish; sorrow.

heart attack *n* = CORONARY THROMBOSIS.

heartbeat *n* **1** a single complete pulsation of the heart. **2** a driving impulse.

heartbreak *n* intense grief or distress. ➤➤ **heartbreaker** *n.*

heartbreaking *adj* causing intense sorrow or distress. ➤➤ **heartbreakingly** *adv.*

heartbroken *adj* overcome by sorrow.

heartburn *n* a burning pain behind the lower part of the breastbone, usu caused by regurgitation of acid from the stomach into the gullet.

hearten *v* to cheer or encourage (somebody). ➤➤ **heartening** *adj,* **hearteningly** *adv.*

heart failure *n* **1** a condition in which the heart is unable to pump blood at an adequate rate or in adequate volume. **2** sudden stopping of the heartbeat causing death.

heartfelt *adj* deeply felt; earnest or sincere.

hearth *n* **1** a brick, stone, or cement area in front of the floor of a fireplace, often used as a symbol representing home and family life. **2** the lowest section of a metal-processing furnace.

hearthrug *n* a rug placed in front of a fireplace.

hearthstone *n* the stone forming a hearth.

heartily *adv* **1** in a hearty manner; wholeheartedly or vigorously. **2** thoroughly.

heartland *n* a central or important region.

heartless *adj* unfeeling or cruel. ➤➤ **heartlessly** *adv,* **heartlessness** *n.*

heart-lung machine *n* a mechanical pump used during heart surgery to divert the blood away from the heart and maintain the circulation and respiration.

heart-rending *adj* causing great sorrow.

heart-searching *n* close examination of one's motives or feelings.

heartsease *n* a wild European pansy with small variously coloured flowers, often violet and yellow.

heartsick *adj* deeply disappointed or despondent, *esp* from loss of love.

heartsore *adj* = HEARTSICK.

heart-stopping *adj* tense or thrilling.

heartstrings *pl n* the deepest emotions or affections.

heart-throb *n informal* a good-looking man.

heart-to-heart[1] *adj* sincere and intimate.

heart-to-heart[2] *n* a frank or intimate talk.

heart-warming *adj* inspiring sympathetic feeling; cheering.

heartwood *n* the nonliving central wood in a tree, which is usu darker and denser than the surrounding sapwood.

hearty *adj* (**-ier, -iest**) **1** vigorous or enthusiastic. **2** sincere; heartfelt. **3** robustly healthy. **4** of food: substantial or abundant. ➤➤ **heartiness** *n.*

heat[1] *n* **1a** the state of being hot; warmth. **b** in physics, the form of energy associated with the random motions of the molecules, atoms, etc of which matter is composed, transmitted by conduction, convection, or radiation. **c** a source or level of heat. **2** intensity of feeling or reaction. **3** a single round of a contest that has two or more rounds for each contestant. **4** *informal* pressure or criticism. ✻ **in the heat of the moment** while angry, excited, etc; without thinking. **on/in heat** of a female mammal: ready for sexual intercourse; in oestrus.

heat[2] *v* **1** (*often* + up) to make or become warm or hot. **2** (+ up) to become more exciting or intense.

heated *adj* marked by anger or passion. ➤➤ **heatedly** *adv.*

heater *n* a device that gives off heat, *esp* an apparatus for heating air or water.

heath *n* **1** *chiefly Brit* a large area of level uncultivated land, usu with poor peaty soil and plants such as heather and gorse. **2** an evergreen shrub that thrives on barren soil, with needlelike leaves and small pink or purple flowers. ➤➤ **heathy** *adj.*

heathen *n* (*pl* **heathens** *or* **heathen**) *derog* somebody who does not acknowledge the God of Judaism, Christianity, or Islam. ➤➤ **heathen** *adj,* **heathendom** *n,* **heathenish** *adj,* **heathenism** *n.*

heather *n* a common northern heath with purplish pink flowers.

heathery *adj* **1** of or resembling heather. **2** having flecks of various colours.

Heath Robinson *adj Brit* of a mechanical device: impractically complicated in design.

Word history

named after *W. Heath Robinson* d.1944, English cartoonist famous for his drawings of absurdly ingenious machines.

heating *n* **1** a system for supplying heat to a building. **2** the heat supplied by such a system.

heat-seeking *adj* of a missile: having a guiding apparatus that homes in on heat, *esp* the hot exhaust gases from an aircraft or rocket.

heatstroke *n* overheating of the body resulting from prolonged exposure to high temperature and leading in serious cases to collapse or death.

heat-treat *v* to treat (a metal or alloy) by heating and cooling in a way that will produce desired properties, e.g. hardness. ➤➤ **heat treatment** *n.*

heat wave *n* a prolonged period of unusually hot weather.

heave[1] *v* (*past tense and past part.* **heaved** *or* **hove**) **1** to lift or pull (something heavy), *esp* with great effort. **2** *informal* to throw (something heavy). **3** to utter (a sigh). **4** to rise and fall rhythmically. **5** to retch. ✻ **heave in sight/into view** to come into view. ➤➤ **heaver** *n.*

heave[2] *n* an act of heaving.

heave-ho[1] *interj* used as a cry when lifting something heavy.

heave-ho[2] *n* (**the heave-ho**) *informal* dismissal from a job.

heaven *n* **1** in some beliefs, the dwelling place of God or the gods; the place where good people go when they die. **2** (**the heavens**) *literary* the expanse of space that surrounds the earth like a dome; the sky. **3** *informal* a place or condition of complete happiness. **4** (*also in pl*) used in exclamations to mean 'God'. ✻ **move heaven and earth** to do everything that one can.

heavenly *adj* **1a** relating to heaven or the sky. **b** suggesting the blessed state of heaven; divine. **2** *informal* delightful.

heavenly body *n* a planet, star, or other body in space.

heaven-sent *adj* timely or providential.

heavenward *adj and adv* directed towards heaven or the sky. ➤➤ **heavenwards** *adv.*

heave to *v* to bring (a ship) to a stop by adjusting the sails against the wind, or to stop in this way.

heavily *adv* **1** slowly and laboriously; dully. **2** to a great degree; severely.

heaving *adj Brit, informal* of a place: extremely crowded.

heavy[1] *adj* (**-ier, -iest**) **1a** having great weight; difficult to carry, move, or lift. **b** large or heavy of its kind. **c** having great density; thick or solid. **2** of food: digested with difficulty, usu because of excessive richness. **3** of ground or soil: full of clay and inclined to hold water. **4** not delicate. **5** slow or sluggish; clumsy. **6** falling with force; powerful. **7** loud and dull in sound. **8a** of an unusually large amount, degree, or force: *heavy traffic; a heavy drinker.* **b** (+ on) using something in large quantities. **9** of industry: producing heavy goods, e.g. coal, steel, or machinery. **10a** needing physical effort and strength. **b** demanding or oppressive. **c** needing considerable mental effort to read or understand. **d** of weighty import; serious or dull. **11** of rock music: loud and having a strong rhythm. **12** *informal* **a** emotionally difficult. **b** strict or severe. ✻ **heavy going** difficult to understand or deal with. **with a heavy hand 1** with little mercy; sternly. **2** without grace; clumsily. ➤➤ **heaviness** *n,* **heavyish** *adj.*

heavy[2] *n* (*pl* **-ies**) **1** *informal* somebody hired to compel or deter by means of threats or physical violence. **2** *informal* somebody of importance or significance.

heavy-duty *adj* **1** able or designed to withstand unusual strain or wear. **2** *informal* more substantial or intensive than usual.

heavy-handed *adj* **1** clumsy or awkward. **2** oppressive or harsh.

heavy-hearted *adj* despondent or melancholy.

heavy hydrogen *n* = DEUTERIUM.

heavy metal *n* **1** a metal with a high relative density or high relative atomic weight. **2** a type of highly-amplified rock music.

heavy petting *n* sexual contact between two people that involves touching the genitals but not intercourse.

heavy water *n* water enriched *esp* with deuterium, used to slow down nuclear reactions.

heavyweight[1] *n* **1** the heaviest weight in boxing and wrestling. **2** *informal* an important or influential person.

heavyweight[2] *adj* **1** of above average weight. **2** *informal* important or influential.

hebdomadal *adj formal* weekly.

hebe *n* an evergreen shrub cultivated for its decorative leaves and usu white or purplish flowers.

Hebraic *adj* relating to the Hebrews or the Hebrew language.

Hebraist *n* a specialist in Hebrew and Hebraic studies.

Hebrew *n* **1** a member or descendant of any of a group of ancient N Semitic peoples including the

Israelites, *esp* an Israelite. **2** the language of the ancient Hebrews, or the revived form of it spoken in modern Israel. **3** *offensive* a Jew. ➤➤ **Hebrew** *adj.*

Hebridean *n* a native or inhabitant of the Hebrides. ➤➤ **Hebridean** *adj.*

hecatomb *n* **1** an ancient Greek and Roman sacrifice of 100 oxen or cattle. **2** the sacrifice or slaughter of many victims.

heck *interj* used to express annoyance, surprise, etc, or as an intensive.

heckle[1] *v* to interrupt and try to disconcert (e.g. a speaker) with comments or jeers. ➤➤ **heckler** *n.*

heckle[2] *n* a heckling comment or jeer.

hect- *or* **hecto-** *comb. form* hundred: *hectogram.*

hectare *n* a metric unit of area equal to 10,000 square metres (2.471 acres).

hectic *adj* filled with excitement or feverish activity. ➤➤ **hectically** *adv.*

hecto- *comb. form* see HECT-.

hectogram *or* **hectogramme** *n* a metric unit of mass equal to 100g.

hectolitre (*NAm* **hectoliter**) *n* a metric unit of capacity equal to 100l.

hectometre (*NAm* **hectometer**) *n* a metric unit of length equal to 100m.

hector *v* to intimidate (somebody) by bullying or blustering. ➤➤ **hectoring** *adj.*

he'd *contr* **1** he had. **2** he would.

hedge[1] *n* **1** a boundary formed by a dense row of shrubs or low trees. **2** a means of protection or defence, e.g. an asset held as protection against financial loss. **3** a deliberately non-committal or evasive use of language. ➤➤ **hedging** *n.*

hedge[2] *v* **1** to enclose or protect (an area) with a hedge. **2** to limit or qualify (e.g. a statement). **3** to protect oneself against losing (e.g. an investment), *esp* by making counterbalancing transactions. **4** to avoid committing oneself, *esp* by making evasive statements. ✱ **hedge one's bets** to cover oneself by supporting two sides, courses of action, etc. ➤➤ **hedger** *n.*

hedgehog *n* a small spine-covered mammal that eats insects and is active at night.

hedgehop *v* (**hedgehopped, hedgehopping**) to fly an aircraft close to the ground and rise over obstacles as they appear.

hedgerow *n* a row of shrubs or trees surrounding a field.

hedge sparrow *n* = DUNNOCK.

hedonism *n* **1** the pursuit of personal pleasure, *esp* sensual pleasure. **2** in philosophy, the doctrine that personal pleasure is the sole or chief good. ➤➤ **hedonist** *n*, **hedonistic** *adj.*

-hedra *comb. form* pl of -HEDRON.

-hedral *comb. form* forming adjectives, with the meaning: having the type of surface or number of surfaces specified: *dihedral.*

-hedron *comb. form* (*pl* **-hedrons** *or* **-hedra**) forming nouns, denoting: a crystal or geometrical figure having the type of surface or number of surfaces specified: *pentahedron.*

heebie-jeebies *pl n* (**the heebie-jeebies**) *informal* a state of nervousness or anxiety.

heed[1] *v* to pay close attention to (somebody or something).

heed[2] *n* careful attention; notice. ➤➤ **heedful** *adj.*

heedless *adj* inconsiderate or thoughtless. ➤➤ **heedlessly** *adv*, **heedlessness** *n.*

hee-haw *v* to make the sound of a donkey braying. ➤➤ **hee-haw** *n.*

heel[1] *n* **1** the back of the foot below the ankle. **2** the part of the palm of the hand nearest the wrist. **3** the part of an article of footwear that covers or supports the heel. ✱ **down at heel** in or into a run-down or shabby condition. **on/hot on the heels of** immediately following; closely behind. **take to one's heels** to run away. **to heel 1** used in training a dog: close behind. **2** into agreement or line; under control. ➤➤ **heeled** *adj*, **heelless** *adj.*

heel[2] *v* **1** to supply (e.g. a shoe) with a heel, *esp* to replace its heel. **2** of a dog: to walk close behind the person in charge of it.

heel[3] *v* of a ship: to tilt to one side.

heel[4] *n* a tilt to one side, or the extent of this.

heel[5] *v* (+ in) to plant (cuttings or plants) temporarily before setting in the final growing position.

heelball *n* a mixture of wax and lampblack used to polish the heels of footwear and to take brass or stone rubbings.

heft *v* **1** to heave up; to hoist. **2** to test the weight of (something) by lifting.

hefty *adj* (**-ier, -iest**) large, heavy, or powerful. ➤➤ **heftily** *adv*, **heftiness** *n.*

Hegelian *adj* relating to the German philosopher Georg Hegel (d.1831) or his philosophy equating mind and nature. ➤➤ **Hegelian** *n*, **Hegelianism** *n.*

hegemony *n* (*pl* **-ies**) domination or leadership of one nation, group, etc over others. ➤➤ **hegemonic** *adj.*

Hegira *or* **Hejira** /'hejirə/ *or* **Hijra** /'hijrə/ *n* the flight of Muhammad from Mecca to Medina in AD 622, the event marking the beginning of the Muslim era.

heifer *n* a young cow, *esp* one that has not had more than one calf.

heigh-ho *interj* used to express boredom, weariness, or happiness.

height *n* **1** the distance from the bottom to the top of something or somebody standing upright. **2** the elevation above a level. **3** the quality of being tall or high. **4a** (*usu in pl*) a piece of land, e.g. a hill or plateau, rising to a considerable degree above the surrounding country. **b** a high point or position. **5** the highest or most extreme point; the zenith.

heighten *v* **1** to increase the amount or degree of (something). **2** to intensify, or to deepen or intensify (something). **3** to make higher; to elevate. **4** to become great or greater in amount, degree, or extent.

heinous *adj* hatefully or shockingly evil; abominable. ➤➤ **heinously** *adv*, **heinousness** *n.*

heir *n* **1** a person who inherits or is entitled to succeed to an estate or rank. **2** a person who receives or is entitled to receive some position, role, or quality passed on from a parent or predecessor. ➤➤ **heirship** *n.*

heir apparent *n* (*pl* **heirs apparent**) **1** an heir who cannot be displaced so long as he or she outlives the person from whom he or she is to inherit. **2** a person whose succession, *esp* to a position or role, appears certain under existing circumstances.

heiress *n* a female heir, *esp* to great wealth.

heirloom *n* a piece of valuable property handed down within a family for generations.

heir presumptive *n* (*pl* **heirs presumptive**) an heir who can be displaced only by the birth of a child with a superior claim.

heist[1] *n chiefly NAm, informal* a robbery.

heist[2] *v chiefly NAm, informal* to steal (something).

Hejira *n* see HEGIRA.

held *v* past tense and past part. of HOLD[1].

heldentenor *n* (*often* **Heldentenor**) a powerful tenor voice suited to heroic roles, or a singer with this voice.

helical *adj* having the form of a helix; spiral. ⋙ **helically** *adv.*

helices *n* pl of HELIX.

helichrysum *n* a plant of the daisy family grown for its flowers that retain their shape and colour when dried.

helicopter *n* an aircraft which derives both lift and propulsive power from a set of horizontally rotating rotors or vanes and is capable of vertical takeoff and landing.

heliocentric *adj* **1** having or relating to the sun as a centre: compare GEOCENTRIC. **2** in astronomy, referred to, measured from, or as if observed from the sun's centre.

heliograph *n* **1** an apparatus for signalling using the sun's rays reflected from a mirror. **2** a telescope adapted for photographing the sun. ⋙ **heliographic** *adj.*

heliosphere *n* in astronomy, the region of space around the sun through which the effect of the solar wind extends. ⋙ **heliospheric** *adj.*

heliotrope *n* a plant of the borage family, *esp* a S American variety cultivated for its fragrant purplish flowers.

helipad *n* a place where helicopters can land and take off.

heliport *n* an airport for helicopters.

heli-skiing *n* skiing at a remote centre that is reached by helicopter.

helium *n* a gaseous chemical element of the noble gas group found in natural gases, and used *esp* for inflating balloons and in low-temperature research.

helix *n* (*pl* **helices** *or* **helixes**) something spiral in form.

hell *n* **1** a place regarded in some beliefs as a place of torment and punishment for souls of the dead, and as the abode of devils and demons. **2** a place or state of torment, misery, or wickedness. **3** used in exclamations or for emphasis. ✱ **come hell or high water** regardless of opposition or difficulties. **for the hell of it** *informal* for the fun of it. **get hell** *informal* to be severely scolded. **give somebody hell 1** *informal* to scold somebody severely. **2** *informal* to make somebody's life difficult. **hell to pay** *informal* serious trouble. **like hell 1** *informal* very hard or much. **2** *informal* used to intensify denial of a statement. **play (merry) hell** *informal* to cause disruption or damage. **what the hell** it doesn't matter.

he'll *contr* **1** he shall. **2** he will.

hell-bent *adj* stubbornly and often recklessly determined.

hellcat *n* a spiteful ill-tempered woman.

hellebore *n* a showy-flowered plant of the buttercup family having poisonous parts.

helleborine *n* a plant of the orchid family found mainly in woodland.

Hellene *n* a Greek.

Hellenic[1] *adj* **1** Greek. **2** in archaeology, of or relating to Greek culture between the Iron Age and the Classical period (1050–323 BC).

Hellenic[2] *n* the Greek language in its classical or modern form.

Hellenise *v* see HELLENIZE.

Hellenism *n* the culture and ideals associated with ancient Greece, or devotion to the imitation of these. ⋙ **Hellenist** *n.*

Hellenistic *adj* relating to Greek history, culture, or art from the death of Alexander the Great in 323 BC to the defeat of Antony and Cleopatra in 31 BC.

Hellenize *or* **-ise** *v* to conform or make (something) conform to Greek or Hellenistic form or culture.

hellfire *n* **1** punishment in hell, imagined as eternal fire. **2** (*used before a noun*) denoting preaching that emphasizes eternal punishment.

hell-for-leather *adv and adj* at full speed.

hellhole *n* a place of extreme discomfort, squalor, or evil.

hellhound *n* a fiend in the form of a dog.

hellish[1] *adj* of or resembling hell; diabolical. ⋙ **hellishly** *adv,* **hellishness** *n.*

hellish[2] *adv Brit, informal* extremely.

hello *or* **hallo** *or* **hullo** *interj* **1** used as a greeting or in answering the telephone. **2** *Brit* used to express surprise or to attract attention.

hellraiser *n* a person who acts in a wild or drunken manner.

Hell's Angel *n* a member of a motorcycle gang associated with lawless and sometimes violent behaviour.

hell's bells *interj informal* used to express irritation or impatience.

helm[1] *n* **1** a tiller or wheel controlling the steering of a ship. **2** (**the helm**) the position of control; the head.

helm[2] *v* **1** to steer (a ship). **2** to manage or direct (e.g. a company).

helm[3] *n archaic* a helmet.

helmet *n* any of various protective head coverings, *esp* made of a hard material to resist impact. ⋙ **helmeted** *adj.*

helminth *n* a parasitic worm, *esp* one living in the intestines of an animal. ⋙ **helminthic** *adj.*

helmsman *n* (*pl* **helmsmen**) a person steering a ship.

helot *n* **1** (**Helot**) a serf in ancient Sparta. **2** a serf or slave.

help[1] *v* **1** to give assistance or support to (somebody). **2a** to be of use to (somebody or something); to benefit. **b** to further the advancement of (something); to promote. **3a** to refrain from (doing something). **b** to keep from occurring; to prevent. **c** to restrain (oneself) from taking action. **4** to remedy or relieve (something). **5** to serve with food or drink, *esp* at a meal. **6** to enable (somebody) to move in a specified direction. **7** to appropriate something for (oneself), *esp* dishonestly. ✱ **so help me (God)** used to show that one is sincere and determined. ⋙ **helper** *n.*

help[2] *n* **1** aid or assistance. **2** remedy or relief. **3** somebody hired to do work, *esp* housework. **4** in computing, a system that provides information about a particular choice or action.

helpful *adj* of service or assistance; useful. ⋙ **helpfully** *adv,* **helpfulness** *n.*

helping *n* a serving of food.

helpless *adj* **1** lacking protection or support; defenceless. **2** lacking strength or effectiveness; powerless. **3** lacking control or restraint. ⋙ **helplessly** *adv,* **helplessness** *n.*

helpline *n* a telephone service provided by an organization offering advice and information.

helpmate *n* a companion and helper, *esp* a spouse.

helpmeet *n archaic* = HELPMATE.

helter-skelter[1] *adj and adv* in a hurried and disorderly manner.

helter-skelter[2] *n Brit* a spiral slide at a fairground.

helve *n* the handle of a weapon or tool.

Helvetian *adj* Swiss. ➤➤ **Helvetian** *n.*

hem[1] *n* the border of a cloth article when turned back and stitched down, *esp* the bottom edge of a garment finished in this manner.

hem[2] *v* (**hemmed, hemming**) **1a** to finish (e.g. a skirt) with a hem. **b** to border or edge. **2** (+ in/about) to enclose or confine.

hem[3] *interj* used to indicate a pause in speaking, or the sound made by clearing the throat.

hem[4] ✱ **hem and haw** to equivocate.

hem- *or* **hemo-** *comb. form NAm* see HAEM-.

hemal *adj NAm* see HAEMAL.

he-man *n* (*pl* **he-men**) *informal* a strong masculine man.

hemi- *prefix* half: *hemisphere.*

-hemia *comb. form NAm* see -AEMIA.

hemidemisemiquaver *n chiefly Brit* a musical note with the time value of half a demisemiquaver.

hemiparesis *n* = HEMIPLEGIA.

hemiplegia *n* paralysis of one side of the body. ➤➤ **hemiplegic** *adj and n.*

hemisphere *n* **1** either of two half spheres formed by a plane that passes through a sphere's centre. **2** the northern or southern half of the earth divided by the equator or the eastern or western half divided by a MERIDIAN (imaginary circle passing through both poles). **3** either of the two halves of the cerebrum of the brain. ➤➤ **hemispheric** *adj,* **hemispherical** *adj.*

hemline *n* the line formed by the lower hemmed edge of a garment, *esp* a dress.

hemlock *n* **1** a poisonous plant of the parsley family with small white flowers. **2** a poisonous drink made from this plant.

hemo- *comb. form NAm* see HAEM-.

hemp *n* **1** a tall widely cultivated Asiatic plant. **2** the fibre of hemp, used for making rope and fabrics. **3** the intoxicating drug cannabis, obtained from hemp.

hen *n* **1** a female bird, *esp* a domestic fowl. **2** (*in pl*) domestic fowls.

henbane *n* a poisonous foul-smelling African and Eurasian plant of the nightshade family having sticky hairy toothed leaves and yielding the drugs hyoscyamine and scopolamine.

hence *adv* **1** because of a preceding fact or premise. **2** from this time; later than now. **3** (*also* **from hence**) *archaic* from here; away.

henceforth *adv* from this time or point on.

henceforward *adv* henceforth.

henchman *n* (*pl* **henchmen**) a follower or supporter, *esp* one who is willing to be unscrupulous or dishonest.

Word history

Middle English *hengestman* groom, from Old English *hengest* stallion + MAN[1]. Sir Walter Scott revived it in the early 19th cent. to mean the principal attendant of a Highland chief, and its meaning broadened to refer to a follower of any important person, later acquiring derogatory overtones.

hendeca- *comb. form* eleven: *hendecagon.*

hendecagon *n* a polygon with eleven angles and eleven sides.

hendiadys *n* the expression of an idea by the use of two independent words connected by *and,* e.g. *nice and cool* instead of *nicely cool* or *grace and favour* instead of *gracious favour.*

henge *n* a prehistoric monument consisting of a circular structure made of wood or stones.

henna[1] *n* a reddish brown dye obtained from the leaves of a tropical shrub and used to colour the hair or as a body decoration.

henna[2] *v* (**hennas, hennaed, hennaing**) to dye or tint (*esp* hair) with henna.

hen night *n Brit, informal* a party for women, held for a woman who is about to get married.

hen party *n informal* a party for women only.

henpecked *adj* cowed by persistent nagging.

henry *n* (*pl* **henrys** *or* **henries**) the SI unit of electrical inductance equal to the self-inductance of a closed circuit in which the variation in current of one amp per second results in an induced electromotive force of one volt.

heparin *n* a POLYSACCHARIDE (complex sugar) that is found in the liver and other tissues, and is injected to slow the clotting of blood, *esp* in the treatment of thrombosis.

hepatic *adj* relating to or in the region of the liver.

hepatitis *n* a disease marked by inflammation of the liver.

hepatitis A *n* a form of viral hepatitis transmitted by contaminated food and drink.

hepatitis B *n* a severe and sometimes fatal form of viral hepatitis usu transmitted through infected blood or contaminated hypodermic syringes.

hepatitis C *n* a severe form of viral hepatitis transmitted through infected blood.

hepta- *or* **hept-** *comb. form* seven: *heptathlon.*

heptagon *n* a polygon with seven angles and seven sides.

heptahedron *n* (*pl* **heptahedrons** *or* **heptahedra**) a polyhedron with seven faces.

heptathlon *n* an athletic contest for women in which each contestant takes part in seven events. ➤➤ **heptathlete** *n.*

her[1] *adj* **1** belonging to or associated with her. **2** used in titles: *Her Majesty.*

her[2] *pron* used as the objective case: she.

herald[1] *n* **1** formerly, an official crier or messenger. **2** formerly, a person who officiated at tournaments. **3** somebody or something that conveys news or proclaims; an announcer. **4** an officer responsible for recording names, pedigrees, and armorial bearings or tracing genealogies. **5** in Britain, an officer of arms ranking above a pursuivant and below a king of arms.

herald[2] *v* **1** to give notice of; to announce. **2** to be a sign of the arrival of.

heraldic *adj* relating to a herald or heraldry. ➤➤ **heraldically** *adv.*

heraldry *n* **1** the system of identifying individuals by hereditary insignia, or the practice of granting, classifying, and creating these. **2** the study of the history, display, and description of heraldry and heraldic insignia, or the heraldic symbols themselves.

herb *n* **1** any aromatic plant used to flavour food or in medicine or perfume. **2** a seed plant that does not develop permanent woody tissue and dies down at the end of a growing season. ➤➤ **herby** *adj.*

herbaceous *adj* of, being, or having the characteristics of a herb (in the botanical sense).

herbaceous border *n* a permanent flower border of hardy, usu perennial, herbaceous plants.

herbage *n* herbaceous plants, e.g. grass, *esp* when used for grazing.

herbal[1] *adj* relating to or made of herbs.

herbal[2] *n* a book about plants, *esp* describing their medicinal qualities.

herbalist *n* somebody who grows or sells herbs, *esp* for medicines. ➤➤ **herbalism** *n*.

herbarium *n* (*pl* **herbaria**) a collection of dried plant specimens usu mounted and systematically arranged for reference.

herbicide *n* a chemical used to destroy or inhibit plant growth.

herbivore *n* a plant-eating animal. ➤➤ **herbivorous** *adj*.

herculean *adj* (*often* **Herculean**) requiring or showing immense effort or strength.

Hercynian *adj* of a geological period of the Upper Palaeozoic era, marked by the formation of major European mountain ranges.

herd[1] *n* **1** a number of animals of one kind kept together or living as a group, *esp* cattle. **2** *derog* (*used as sing. or pl*) a large group of people.

herd[2] *v* **1** to assemble or move in a herd or group. **2** to keep or move (animals) together. ➤➤ **herder** *n*.

herd instinct *n* the tendency of people or animals to follow the behaviour of the majority.

herdsman *n* (*pl* **herdsmen**) a manager, breeder, or tender of livestock.

here[1] *adv* **1** in or at this place. **2** to this place or position. **3** used when introducing, offering, or drawing attention to something. **4** at or in this point or particular. ✱ **here goes** used to express resolution at the outset of a bold act. **here's to** used when drinking a toast. **neither here nor there** of no consequence; irrelevant.

here[2] *interj* **1** used in answering a roll call. **2** used to attract attention.

hereabouts *or* **hereabout** *adv* in this vicinity.

hereafter[1] *adv formal* **1** after this. **2** in some future time or state. **3** after death.

hereafter[2] *n* (**the hereafter**) life after death.

here and now *n* (**the here and now**) the immediate present.

here and there *adv* in one place and another.

hereby *adv formal* by this means or pronouncement.

hereditary *adj* **1** received by, based on, or relating to inheritance. **2** having title through inheritance. **3** genetically transmitted or transmissible from parent to offspring. ➤➤ **hereditarily** *adv*.

heredity *n* **1** the transmission of qualities from ancestor to descendant through a mechanism lying primarily in the genes. **2** the sum of the qualities and potentialities genetically derived from one's ancestors.

Hereford *n* an animal of an English breed of red hardy beef cattle with white faces and markings.

herein *adv formal* in this document, matter, etc.

hereinafter *adv formal* in the following part of this writing or document.

hereof *adv formal* of this document.

heresiarch *n* the originator or chief advocate of a heresy.

heresy *n* (*pl* **-ies**) **1** a religious belief or doctrine contrary to or incompatible with an explicit Church dogma, *esp* Christian doctrine. **2** adherence to an opinion or doctrine contrary to generally accepted belief.

heretic *n* a person who dissents from established Church dogma, or from an accepted belief. ➤➤ **heretical** *adj*, **heretically** *adv*.

hereto *adv formal* to this matter or document.

heretofore *adv formal* up to this time; hitherto.

hereunder *adv formal* under or in accordance with this writing or document.

hereupon *adv archaic* **1** on this matter. **2** immediately after this.

herewith *adv formal* with this; enclosed in this.

heritable *adj* capable of being inherited. ➤➤ **heritability** *n*, **heritably** *adv*.

heritage *n* **1** property that descends to an heir; an inheritance. **2** something valuable transmitted by or acquired from a predecessor or predecessors; a legacy. **3** a country's history and traditions. **4** (*used before a noun*) relating to or presenting a country's history and traditions, *esp* in an attractive and nostalgic way: *a heritage centre*.

heritor *n* an inheritor.

hermaphrodite *n* **1** a human or animal having both male and female reproductive organs and secondary sexual characteristics. **2** in botany, a plant with both male and female organs (stamens and pistils) in the same flower. ➤➤ **hermaphroditic** *adj*, **hermaphroditism** *n*.

hermeneutic *adj* relating to the interpretation of literary texts or the Bible; interpretative. ➤➤ **hermeneutical** *adj*.

hermeneutics *pl n* (*used as sing. or pl*) the study of the principles and methodology of interpretation, *esp* of the Bible or literary texts.

hermetic *adj* **1** of a seal: airtight. **2** impervious to external influences. **3** (*often* **Hermetic**) abstruse or recondite. ➤➤ **hermetically** *adv*, **hermeticism** *n*.

hermit *n* **1** a person who retires from society and lives in solitude, *esp* for religious reasons. **2** a recluse. ➤➤ **hermitic** *adj*.

hermitage *n* a place where one or more hermits live.

hermit crab *n* a ten-legged crustacean that has a soft abdomen and occupies the empty shell of a gastropod mollusc.

hernia *n* (*pl* **hernias** *or* **herniae**) a protrusion of part of an organ, usu the intestine, through a wall of its enclosing cavity. ➤➤ **herniated** *adj*, **herniation** *n*.

hero *n* (*pl* **-oes**) **1** a person, *esp* a man, admired for special courage, nobility, or great achievements. **2** the principal male character in a literary or dramatic work. **3** a mythological or legendary figure, often of divine descent, endowed with great strength or ability.

heroic *adj* **1** showing courage. **2** of heroes or heroines. **3** grand; impressive. ➤➤ **heroically** *adv*.

heroic couplet *n* two rhyming lines of verse, each of which consists of five iambic feet.

heroics *pl n* extravagantly grand behaviour or language.

heroin *n* a strongly physiologically addictive narcotic drug made from morphine. It is used in medicine to relieve severe pain.

heroine *n* **1** a woman admired for special courage, nobility, or great achievements. **2** the principal female character in a literary or dramatic work. **3** a mythological or legendary woman, often of divine descent, endowed with great strength or ability.

heroism *n* heroic conduct or qualities, *esp* extreme courage.

heron *n* (*pl* **herons** *or* **heron**) a long-necked long-legged wading bird with a long tapering bill and large wings.

heronry *n* (*pl* **-ies**) a breeding colony of herons.

hero worship *n* **1** veneration of a hero. **2** foolish or excessive admiration for somebody.

hero-worship *v* (**hero-worshipped, hero-worshipping,** *NAm* **hero-worshiped, hero-worshiping**) to feel great or excessive admiration for (somebody).

herpes *n* an inflammatory virus disease of the skin, *esp* herpes simplex. ⯮ **herpetic** *adj.*

herpes simplex *n* a virus disease marked by groups of watery blisters on the skin or mucous membranes, e.g. of the mouth, lips, or genitals.

herpes zoster *n* = SHINGLES.

herpetology *n* the branch of zoology dealing with reptiles and amphibians. ⯮ **herpetological** *adj,* **herpetologist** *n.*

Herr /heə/ *n* (*pl* **Herren**) used of or to a German-speaking man as a title equivalent to *Mr.*

Herrenvolk /'herənfolk/ *n* a master race; *specif* the German people as regarded by the Nazis.

herring *n* (*pl* **herrings** *or* **herring**) a valuable silvery food fish that is abundant in the N Atlantic.

herringbone *n* a pattern made up of rows of parallel lines with any two adjacent rows slanting in opposite directions, *esp* a twilled fabric decorated with this pattern.

herring gull *n* a large gull of the northern hemisphere that is largely white with a blue-grey mantle and dark wing tips.

hers *pron* the one or ones that belong to or are associated with her. ✻ **of hers** belonging to or associated with her: *friends of hers.*

herself *pron* used reflexively or for emphasis to refer to a female person or animal that is the subject of the clause: *The girl has hurt herself; She herself said it.*

Herts *abbr* Hertfordshire.

hertz *n* (*pl* **hertz**) the SI unit of frequency, equal to one cycle per second.

he's *contr* **1** he has. **2** he is.

hesitant *adj* tending to hesitate; irresolute. ⯮ **hesitance** *n,* **hesitancy** *n,* **hesitantly** *adv.*

hesitate *v* **1** to hold back, *esp* in doubt or indecision. **2** to be reluctant or unwilling to do something. ⯮ **hesitation** *n.*

hessian *n* a coarse heavy plain-weave fabric, usu of jute or hemp, used *esp* for sacking.

heter- *or* **hetero-** *comb. form* other or different: *heteromorphic.*

heterocyclic *adj* in chemistry, of, characterized by, or being a ring composed of atoms of more than one kind.

heterodox *adj* **1** contrary to or different from established doctrines or opinions, *esp* in matters of religion. **2** holding opinions or doctrines which are not orthodox. ⯮ **heterodoxy** *n.*

heterodyne *adj* of a radio signal, receiver, etc: combining two similar radio frequencies to produce a lower frequency or beat.

heterogeneous *adj* consisting of dissimilar ingredients or constituents; disparate. ⯮ **heterogeneity** *n,* **heterogeneously** *adv,* **heterogeneousness** *n.*

heteromorphic *adj* in biology, exhibiting diversity of form or forms. ⯮ **heteromorph** *n,* **heteromorphism** *n.*

heterosexism *n* discrimination against a person on the grounds of his or her homosexuality. ⯮ **heterosexist** *adj.*

heterosexual¹ *adj* **1** having a sexual preference for members of the opposite sex. **2** of a relationship: between a man and a woman. ⯮ **heterosexuality** *n,* **heterosexually** *adv.*

heterosexual² *n* a person who is heterosexual.

het up *adj informal* angry or upset.

heuristic¹ *adj* **1** allowing people to learn for themselves. **2** denoting problem-solving techniques that proceed by trial and error. ⯮ **heuristically** *adv.*

heuristic² *n* a heuristic method or procedure.

heuristics *pl n* (*used as sing. or pl*) the study or practice of heuristic methods or procedures.

hew *v* (*past part.* **hewed** *or* **hewn**) **1** to strike, chop, or fell (e.g. wood) with blows of a heavy cutting instrument. **2** (*often* + out) to give form or shape to (something) with heavy cutting blows. ⯮ **hewer** *n.*

hex¹ *v chiefly NAm* to cast a spell on (somebody); to bewitch.

hex² *n chiefly NAm* **1** a magic spell or jinx. **2** a witch.

hexa- *or* **hex-** *comb. form* six: *hexagon.*

hexadecimal *adj* of or being a number system with a base of 16.

hexagon *n* a polygon with six angles and six sides. ⯮ **hexagonal** *adj.*

hexagram *n* a six-pointed star drawn by extending the sides of a regular hexagon.

hexahedron *n* (*pl* **hexahedrons** *or* **hexahedra**) a polyhedron with six faces. ⯮ **hexahedral** *adj.*

hexameter *n* a line of verse consisting of six metrical feet.

hexane *n* a volatile liquid that is a member of the alkane series of organic chemical compounds and is found in petroleum.

hexose *n* a MONOSACCHARIDE (simple sugar), e.g. glucose, containing six carbon atoms in the molecule.

hey *interj* used to call attention or to express enquiry, surprise, etc.

heyday *n* the period of one's greatest vigour, prosperity, or fame.

hey presto *interj* used, *esp* by conjurers, as an expression of triumph or satisfaction on completing or demonstrating something.

HF *abbr* high frequency.

Hf *abbr* the chemical symbol for hafnium.

HFC *abbr* hydrofluorocarbon.

Hg *abbr* the chemical symbol for mercury.

hg *abbr* hectogram(s).

HGH *abbr* human growth hormone.

HGV *abbr Brit* heavy goods vehicle.

HH *abbr* used on lead pencils: double hard.

H-hour *n* an hour set for launching or beginning something, e.g. an attack.

HI *abbr* Hawaii (US postal abbreviation).

hi *interj informal* used to attract attention or as a greeting.

hiatal hernia *n* = HIATUS HERNIA.

hiatus *n* (*pl* **hiatuses**) a break or gap in continuity.

hiatus hernia *n* a hernia in which part of the stomach protrudes through the oesophageal opening of the diaphragm.

Hib *n* a bacterium that can cause a serious infection, *esp* in young children, that can lead to meningitis and pneumonia.

hibachi *n* (*pl* **hibachis**) a portable charcoal-burning brazier or barbecue.

hibernal *adj* of or occurring in winter; wintry.

hibernate *v* of an animal or plant: to pass the winter in a dormant or resting state. ⯮ **hibernation** *n,* **hibernator** *n.*

Hibernian *adj* used *esp* in names: Irish. ⯮ **Hibernian** *n.*

hibiscus *n* a plant, shrub, or small tree of the mallow family with large showy flowers.

hiccup[1] *or* **hiccough** *n* **1** a spasmodic involuntary inhalation with closure of the glottis (opening between the throat and windpipe) accompanied by a characteristic sharp sound. **2** (*in pl*) an attack of hiccuping. **3** a brief interruption or breakdown; a hitch.

hiccup[2] *or* **hiccough** *v* (**hiccuped** *or* **hiccupped, hiccuping** *or* **hiccupping**) to make a hiccuping sound, or be affected with hiccups.

hickey *n* (*pl* **-eys**) in printing, a blemish.

hickory *n* (*pl* **hickories** *or* **hickory**) a N American hardwood tree of the walnut family, having sweet edible nuts and tough pale wood.

hid *v* past tense of HIDE[1].

hidden *v* past part. of HIDE[1].

hidden agenda *n* a concealed motive behind the ostensible purpose of an action.

hide[1] *v* (*past tense* **hid**, *past part.* **hidden**) **1** to put out of sight; to conceal. **2** to conceal oneself. **3** to keep secret. ✱ **hide one's light under a bushel** to be modest about one's own success. ⋙ **hider** *n.*

hide[2] *n Brit* a camouflaged hut or other shelter used for observation of wildlife or game.

hide[3] *n* the raw or dressed skin of an animal. ✱ **hide or hair** the least vestige or trace.

hide-and-seek *n* a children's game in which several players hide and one player then hunts for them.

hideaway *n* a retreat or hideout.

hidebound *adj* narrow or inflexible in character.

hideous *adj* **1** exceedingly ugly; repulsive. **2** very unpleasant; disgusting. ⋙ **hideously** *adv,* **hideousness** *n.*

hideout *n* a place of refuge or concealment, *esp* a hiding place used by a criminal.

hidey-hole *or* **hidy-hole** *n informal* a hiding place.

hiding[1] *n* **1** a beating or thrashing. **2** *informal* a severe defeat. ✱ **be on a hiding to nothing** *Brit* to be engaged in an enterprise that can only end in failure.

hiding[2] *n* a state, act, or place of concealment.

hidy-hole *n* see HIDEY-HOLE.

hie *v* (**hies, hied, hying** *or* **hieing**) *archaic* to hurry.

hierarch *n* **1** a religious leader in a position of authority, e.g. an archbishop. **2** a person with a high position in a hierarchy.

hierarchy *n* (*pl* **-ies**) **1a** a system in which people or groups are ranked according to their status or authority. **b** (**the hierarchy**) people in authority; the people at the top of a hierarchy. **c** a system in which things are ranked according to importance, e.g. the arrangement of plants into classes, species, etc. **2** (**the hierarchy**) the clergy in the Catholic Church or an episcopal Church organized according to rank. **3** in theology, the organization of heavenly beings, e.g. angels, into ranks. ⋙ **hierarchic** *adj,* **hierarchical** *adj,* **hierarchically** *adv.*

hieratic *adj* of or characteristic of a priest, *esp* in dignity or stateliness of manner. ⋙ **hieratically** *adv.*

hieroglyph *n* a pictorial character used in hieroglyphics.

hieroglyphic *adj* **1** relating to or using a system of writing mainly in hieroglyphs. **2** difficult to decipher. ⋙ **hieroglyphical** *adj.*

hieroglyphics *pl n* **1** (*used as sing. or pl*) a system of hieroglyphic writing; *specif* the picture script of various ancient peoples such as the Egyptians. **2** something like hieroglyphics, *esp* in being difficult to decipher.

hierophant *n* **1** a priest in ancient Greece responsible for initiation rites to sacred mysteries. **2** an interpreter of esoteric knowledge. ⋙ **hierophantic** *adj.*

hi-fi *n* (*pl* **hi-fis**) *informal* **1** equipment for the high-fidelity reproduction of sound. **2** (*used before a noun*) high fidelity.

higgledy-piggledy *adv and adj* in confusion; topsy-turvy.

high[1] *adj* **1a** extending upwards for a considerable or above average distance. **b** situated at a considerable height above the ground or above sea level. **c** having a specified elevation; tall. **2** of greater degree, amount, cost, value, or content than average. **3** foremost in rank, dignity, or standing. **4** elevated in pitch, resulting from a fast speed of vibration in the sound source. **5** forcible or strong. **6a** of food: beginning to go bad. **b** of meat, *esp* game: slightly decomposed and ready to cook. **7** *informal* **a** showing elation or excitement. **b** intoxicated by alcohol or a drug. ✱ **high time** the time at which something should happen. **on one's high horse** stubbornly or disdainfully proud. **the high ground** a position of advantage or superiority.

high[2] *adv* **1** at or to a high place, altitude, or degree. **2** highly. **3** of a sound: at or to a high pitch.

high[3] *n* **1** a high point or level. **2** a region of high atmospheric pressure. **3** *informal* a state of ecstasy or euphoria, *esp* one produced by a drug. ✱ **on high** in or to a high place, *esp* heaven.

high altar *n* the principal altar in a church.

high and dry *adv* **1** stranded by the sea; out of the water. **2** in a helpless or abandoned situation.

high and low *adv* everywhere.

high-and-mighty *adj informal* arrogant or imperious.

highball *n NAm* a drink of spirits, e.g. whisky, and water or a carbonated beverage, served with ice in a tall glass.

highboy *n NAm* = TALLBOY .

highbrow *adj* having or showing refined intellectual and cultural interests.

high chair *n* a child's chair with long legs, a footrest, and usu a feeding tray.

High Church *n* a movement or tendency in the Anglican Church that favours aspects of Roman Catholicism in liturgy, ceremonial, and dogma.

high-coloured *adj* of the complexion: ruddy or florid.

high command *n* the commander-in-chief and high-ranking officers of a country's army, navy, and air force.

high commissioner *n* an ambassadorial representative of one Commonwealth country stationed in another.

high court *n* **1** a supreme judicial court. **2** (**High Court**) the lower branch of the Supreme Court of England and Wales, consisting of the Queen's Bench Division, the Chancery Division, and the Family Division. **3** (**High Court**) the superior criminal court of Scotland.

High Court of Justice *n* = HIGH COURT (2).

high-definition television *n* an advanced television system that has far more horizontal lines per frame than the conventional system and produces a much sharper and clearer image.

Higher *n* in Scotland, the advanced level of the Scottish Certificate of Education.

higher *adj* **1** relatively high in position, rank, or order. **2** more advanced in the scale of evolutionary development.

higher education *n* education beyond the secondary level, at a college or university.

higher mathematics *pl n* (*usu used as sing.*) mathematics involving advanced abstract ideas such as number theory and topology.

highest common factor *n* the largest integer that can be divided exactly into each of two or more integers.

high explosive *n* a powerful explosive, e.g. TNT, that explodes with extreme rapidity.

highfalutin *or* **highfaluting** *adj informal* pretentious or pompous.

high fashion *n* = HAUTE COUTURE.

high fidelity *n* the faithful reproduction of sound.

high finance *n* large and complex financial operations.

high-flier *or* **high-flyer** *n* a person who shows extreme ambition or outstanding promise.

high-flown *adj* **1** excessively ambitious or extravagant. **2** of language: excessively elaborate or in-flated; pretentious.

high-flyer *n* see HIGH-FLIER.

high frequency *n* a radio frequency between 3 and 30 megahertz.

high gear *n* a gear giving a high ratio of propeller-shaft to engine-shaft speed and hence a high speed of travel.

High German *n* German as orig spoken in S Germany and now in standard use throughout the country.

high-handed *adj* overbearingly arbitrary or inconsiderate.

high-hat *n* a top hat.

high-impact *adj* of physical exercise, *esp* aerobics: making stressful demands on the body.

high jinks *pl n* high-spirited fun and games.

high jump *n* an athletic field event in which contestants jump over a high bar suspended between uprights. ✻ **for the high jump** *Brit, informal* about to receive a severe reprimand or punishment. ➤➤ **high jumper** *n.*

highland *n* **1** (*also in pl*) high or mountainous land. **2** (**the Highlands**) the northwest mountainous part of Scotland. ➤➤ **highlander** *n,* **highlandman** *n.*

Highland cattle *pl n* animals of a Scottish breed of shaggy-haired beef cattle with long horns.

Highland dress *n* the traditional clothing of the Scottish Highlands, including the kilt, plaid, and sporran.

Highland fling *n* a lively solo Scottish folk dance.

high-level *adj* **1** occurring, done, or placed at a high level. **2** of high importance or rank. **3** of a computer language: having each word equal to several machine code instructions so as to be more easily understood by humans.

high life *n* luxurious living associated with the rich.

highlight[1] *n* **1** an event or detail of special significance or interest. **2** the lightest spot or area, e.g. in a painting or photograph. **3** (*usu in pl*) a contrasting brighter part in the hair produced by tinting some of the strands.

highlight[2] *v* **1a** to focus attention on (something); to emphasize. **b** to emphasize (e.g. a figure) with light tones in painting, photography, etc. **c** to mark (part of a text) with a highlighter. **2** to give highlights to (hair).

highlighter *n* **1** a fluorescent marker pen used to overlay transparent colour on part of a text. **2** white or sparkling cosmetic cream or powder used to emphasize the cheeks, eyes, etc.

highly *adv* **1** to a high degree; extremely. **2** with approval; favourably.

highly-strung *adj Brit* extremely nervous or sensitive.

High Mass *n* in the Roman Catholic and Anglican Churches, an elaborate sung mass.

high-minded *adj* having or marked by elevated principles and feelings.

Highness *n* **1** used as a title for a person of exalted rank, e.g. a king or prince. **2** (**highness**) the quality or state of being high.

high-octane *adj* **1** of petrol: having a high octane number and hence good antiknock properties. **2** intense or dynamic.

high-powered *adj informal* having great drive or energy; dynamic.

high priest *n* **1** a chief priest, *esp* of the ancient Jewish Levitical priesthood traditionally traced from Aaron. **2** the head or chief exponent of a movement.

high priestess *n* **1** a chief priestess. **2** the female head or chief exponent of a movement.

high relief *n* sculptural relief in which at least half of the circumference of the design stands out from the surrounding surface: compare BAS-RELIEF.

high-rise *adj* of a building: constructed with a large number of storeys.

highroad *n* **1** *chiefly Brit* a main road. **2** the easiest course.

high school *n* **1** in the USA, a secondary school. **2** in Britain, usu in names: an independent or grammar school.

high seas *pl n* (**the high seas**) the part of a sea or ocean outside territorial waters.

high season *n Brit* a period when the number of visitors to a holiday resort is at a peak and prices are higher.

high-spirited *adj* of a person or animal: characterized by a bold or lively spirit.

high spirits *pl n* a cheerful or vivacious state of mind.

highspot *n* the most important or enjoyable feature of something.

high street *n Brit* **1** a main or principal street of a town, *esp* containing shops and other businesses. **2** (*used before a noun*) having branches in many towns: *the high street banks.*

high-strung *adj NAm* = HIGHLY-STRUNG.

high table *n* (*often* **High Table**) *Brit* a table in a dining hall, usu on a platform, used by people of high rank, *esp* the masters and fellows of a college.

high tea *n Brit* a fairly substantial early evening meal at which tea is served.

high tech *n* = HIGH TECHNOLOGY.

high-tech *or* **hi-tech** *adj* **1** using or requiring high technology. **2** of a style of interior decoration: involving the use of industrial building materials, fittings, etc.

high technology *n* advanced technological processes, *esp* in electronics.

high-tension *adj* having a high voltage, or relating to apparatus to be used at high voltage.

high tide *n* the tide when the water reaches its highest level, or the time of this.

high-tops *pl n* sports shoes with a soft sole and an upper that extends above the ankle.

high treason *n* see TREASON (1).

high water *n* = HIGH TIDE.

high-water mark *n* a mark showing the highest level reached by the surface of a body of water.

highway *n* **1** a public road. **2** *chiefly NAm* a main road.

highwayman *n* (*pl* **highwaymen**) formerly, a robber of travellers on a road, *esp* one on horseback.

high wire *n* a tightrope high above the ground.

hijack[1] *v* **1** to seize control of (a vehicle or aircraft) by force while it is in transit. **2** to steal, rob, or kidnap (something or somebody) as if by hijacking. ⋙ **hijacker** *n.*

hijack[2] *n* the act or an instance of hijacking.

Hijra *n* see HEGIRA.

hike[1] *n* **1** a long walk in the country. **2** a big increase or rise, *esp* in prices or wages.

hike[2] *v* **1** to go on a hike. **2** (*usu* + up) to pull or lift (something) up. **3** (*usu* + up) to raise (prices, wages, etc). ⋙ **hiker** *n.*

hilarious *adj* extremely funny. ⋙ **hilariously** *adv.*

hilarity *n* mirth or merriment.

hill *n* a usu rounded natural rise of land lower than a mountain. ✱ **over the hill** *informal* past one's prime; too old. ⋙ **hilly** *adj.*

hillfort *n* a fortified hilltop characteristic of Iron Age settlements in W Europe.

hillock *n* a small hill. ⋙ **hillocky** *adj.*

hill station *n* a town or settlement in the low mountains of N India, often established by the British as a place for officials and their families to stay during the hot season.

hilt *n* the handle of a sword, dagger, or knife. ✱ **to the hilt** completely.

him *pron* used as the objective case: he.

Himalayan *adj* of or relating to the Himalayas.

himself *pron* used reflexively or for emphasis to refer to a male person or animal that is the subject of the clause: *The boy has hurt himself; He himself said it.*

hind[1] *adj* situated at the back or behind; rear.

hind[2] *n* (*pl* **hinds** *or* **hind**) a female deer, *esp* a red deer.

hind[3] *n archaic* **1** a farm worker. **2** a peasant.

hinder[1] *v* to retard or obstruct the progress of (something or somebody); to hamper.

hinder[2] *adj* situated behind or at the rear; posterior.

Hindi *n* the language of N India, used as an official language of India. ⋙ **Hindi** *adj.*

hindmost *adj* furthest back; last.

hindquarter *n* **1** the back half of a side of the carcass of a quadruped. **2** (*in pl*) the hind legs and adjoining parts of a quadruped.

hindrance *n* **1** the act of hindering. **2** an impediment or obstacle.

hindsight *n* the grasp or understanding of a situation that one has only after it has occurred.

Hindu *n* an adherent of Hinduism. ⋙ **Hindu** *adj.*

Hinduism *n* a major religious faith of the Indian subcontinent, which involves belief in the illusory nature of the physical universe and in cycles of reincarnation, and the worship of many gods.

Hindustani[1] *n* **1** a group of Indic dialects of N India and Pakistan of which Hindi and Urdu are considered the main written forms. **2** the dialect of Hindi spoken in Delhi, used throughout India as a lingua franca.

Hindustani[2] *adj* relating to Hindustan (northern India), its people, or the Hindustani language.

hinge[1] *n* a jointed or flexible device on which a swinging part, e.g. a door or lid, turns.

hinge[2] *v* (**hingeing** *or* **hinging**) **1** to attach (something) by a hinge. **2** (+ on) to depend or turn on a single consideration or point.

hinny *n* (*pl* **-ies**) a hybrid offspring of a stallion and a female ass: compare MULE[1].

hint[1] *n* **1** a brief practical suggestion or piece of advice. **2** an indirect or veiled statement; an insinuation. **3** (+ of) a slight indication or trace.

hint[2] *v* (*often* + at) to indicate something indirectly or by allusion; to suggest it.

hinterland *n* **1** a region lying inland from a coast or away from a major river. **2** a region remote from urban or cultural centres.

hip[1] *n* **1** the projecting region at each side of the lower or rear part of the mammalian trunk formed by the pelvis and upper part of the thigh. **2** an external angle between two adjacent sloping sides of a roof. ⋙ **hipped** *adj.*

hip[2] *n* the ripened fruit of a rose. Also called ROSE-HIP.

hip[3] *interj* used to begin a cheer.

hip[4] *adj* (**hipper, hippest**) *informal* **1** keenly aware of or interested in the latest trends or fashions. **2** (+ to) aware of what is happening. ⋙ **hipness** *n.*

hip bath *n* a portable bath in which one sits rather than lies.

hipbone *n* the large bone that forms half of the pelvis in mammals.

hip flask *n* a flat flask for spirits, that can be carried in a hip pocket.

hip hop *n* a style of popular music in which the spoken word or 'rap' is accompanied by music with a regular heavy beat, and effects are produced by manipulating records on turntables.

hippie *or* **hippy** *n* (*pl* **-ies**) a person who rejects established values, advocates non-violence, and dresses unconventionally. ⋙ **hippiedom** *n,* **hippiness** *n,* **hippyish** *adj.*

hippo *n* (*pl* **hippos** *or* **hippo**) *informal* a hippopotamus.

hippocampus *n* (*pl* **hippocampi**) in anatomy, a curved elongated ridge of nervous tissue inside each hemisphere of the brain. It is part of the limbic system, the structures of the brain concerned with emotion and motivation.

Hippocratic oath *n* an oath embodying a code of medical ethics.

hippodrome *n* **1** usu in names: a music hall, theatre, etc. **2** an arena for equestrian performances or chariot races in ancient Greece or Rome.

hippopotamus *n* (*pl* **hippopotamuses** *or* **hippopotami**) a large chiefly aquatic mammal, with an extremely large head and mouth, thick hairless skin, and short legs.

hippy[1] *n* (*pl* **-ies**) see HIPPIE.

hippy[2] *adj* of a woman: having large hips.

hipster *n informal* somebody who is unusually aware of and interested in new and unconventional patterns, *esp* in jazz.

hipsters *pl n Brit* trousers that hang from the hips rather than the waist.

hire[1] *v* **1a** to obtain the temporary use of (something) for an agreed sum. **b** to engage the services of (somebody) for a set sum. **2** (+ out) to grant the services of (somebody) or temporary use of (something) for a fixed sum. ⋙ **hireable** *adj*, **hirer** *n*.

hire² *n* **1** payment for the temporary use of something. **2** hiring or being hired. **3** *NAm* somebody who has been hired. ✱ **for/on hire** available to be hired.

hireling *n derog* a person who works for payment, *esp* for purely mercenary motives.

hire purchase *n Brit* a system whereby a customer may take possession of goods after paying an initial deposit and then pay the remainder of the price in regular instalments over a specific period.

hirsute *adj formal* very hairy. ⋙ **hirsuteness** *n*.

hirsutism *n* excessive growth of hair.

his¹ *adj* **1** belonging to or associated with a male person or animal already known or mentioned. **2** used in titles: *His Majesty*.

his² *pron* the one or ones that belong to or are associated with him. ✱ **of his** belonging to or associated with him: *friends of his*.

Hispanic¹ *adj* relating to Spain, Portugal, or Latin America, or to Spanish-speaking people. ⋙ **Hispanicist** *n*, **Hispanist** *n*.

Hispanic² *n* a Spanish-speaking person of Latin American descent living in the USA.

hiss¹ *v* **1** to make a sharp voiceless sound like a prolonged *s*, *esp* in disapproval. **2** to utter something with a hiss.

hiss² *n* **1** a hissing sound. **2** electrical interference; noise.

histamine *n* a chemical compound that transmits nerve impulses between nerves of the autonomic nervous system. The release of this compound, usu after injury or in the presence of an allergen, causes an allergic reaction. ⋙ **histaminic** *adj*.

histidine *n* an amino acid that is a chemical base and is found in most proteins.

histology *n* the branch of anatomy that deals with the organization and microscopic structure of animal and plant tissues. ⋙ **histological** *adj*, **histologist** *n*.

histopathology *n* the branch of pathology concerned with the tissue changes accompanying disease. ⋙ **histopathological** *adj*, **histopathologist** *n*.

historian *n* a student or expert in history.

historic *adj* **1** famous or important in history, or likely to be so: *a historic occasion*. **2** in grammar, of a tense: expressive of past time.

Usage note

historic *or* **historical**? These two words are sometimes confused. A *historic* event is one that is very important or memorable and thought likely to be recorded as such in history. A *historical* event is any event that took place in the past.

historical *adj* **1** relating to history and past events. **2** belonging to the past. **3** dealing with or representing the events of history: *a historical novel*. **4** relating to changes over a period of time; diachronic: *historical linguistics*. ⋙ **historically** *adv*.

Usage note

historical *or* **historic**? See note at HISTORIC.

historicism *n* **1** a theory that emphasizes the importance of history as a standard of value or determiner of events. **2** excessive emphasis on past styles, e.g. in art and architecture. ⋙ **historicist** *adj and n*.

historicity *n* historical authenticity.

historic present *n* in grammar, the present tense used to relate past events.

historiography *n* **1** the writing of history. **2** the principles of historical writing. ⋙ **historiographer** *n*, **historiographic** *adj*, **historiographical** *adj*.

history *n* (*pl* **-ies**) **1** a branch of knowledge that records and interprets past events. **2** past events as a whole. **3** an account of past events. **4** a person's medical, sociological, etc background. **5** an unusual or interesting past. ✱ **be history** *informal* to be finished, dead, etc.

histrionic *adj* **1** deliberately affected; theatrical. **2** *formal* of actors, acting, or the theatre. ⋙ **histrionically** *adv*.

histrionics *pl n* (*used as sing. or pl*) the deliberate display of emotion for effect.

hit¹ *v* (**hitting**, *past tense and past part.* **hit**) **1** to aim a blow at (somebody or something) with the hand or an implement. **2** to come or bring into violent contact with something else: *The car hit a tree; She hit her head on the door*. **3a** to propel (a ball, etc) with a blow. **b** to reach (a target). **4** to harm or have a detrimental effect on: *a region hit by famine*. **5** *informal* to arrive at (a place). ✱ **hit it off** *informal* to enjoy one another's company. **hit on** to arrive at (a solution) by chance or unexpectedly. **hit the ground running** *informal* to be fully ready to start on an undertaking when the time comes. **hit the road** *informal* to start on a journey. **hit the roof** *informal* to become extremely angry.

hit² *n* **1** a blow, *esp* one that meets its target. **2a** something that enjoys great success. **b** a person who is popular. **3a** in computing, a successful match when a database is being searched for a particular item. **b** a visit to a site on the Internet. **4** *informal* a dose of a substance, e.g. a drug.

hit-and-miss *adj* = HIT-OR-MISS.

hit-and-run *adj* of a road accident: involving a driver who does not stop after causing damage or injury.

hitch¹ *v* **1** to move (something) by jerks. **2** to catch or fasten by a hook or knot. **3** *informal* to solicit and obtain (a free lift) in a passing vehicle, or to travel in this way. ✱ **get hitched** *informal* to get married.

hitch² *n* **1** a sudden halt or obstruction; a stoppage. **2** a knot used for a temporary fastening. **3** *informal* an act of hitchhiking.

hitcher *n* a hitchhiker.

hitchhike *v* to travel by obtaining free lifts in passing vehicles. ⋙ **hitchhiker** *n*.

hi-tech *adj* see HIGH-TECH.

hither *adv archaic or literary* to or towards this place.

hither and thither *adv* in all directions.

hitherto *adv* up to this time; until now.

Hitler *n* an autocratic or dictatorial person. ⋙ **Hitlerian** *adj*.

Hitlerism *n* the nationalistic and totalitarian principles and policies of the German political leader Adolf Hitler (d.1945).

hit list *n* a list of people or organizations to be killed or eliminated.

hitman *n* (*pl* **hitmen**) *informal* a hired assassin.

hit-or-miss *adj* lacking method or consistency of procedure; haphazard.

hit out *v* to act or speak aggressively or critically.

Hittite *n* **1** a member of a people that established an empire in Asia Minor and Syria in the second millennium BC. **2** the language of this people. ⋙ **Hittite** *adj*.

HIV *abbr* human immunodeficiency virus, a RETROVIRUS (virus containing ribonucleic acid) that breaks down the human body's immune system and is the cause of Aids.

hive[1] *n* **1** a beehive. **2** a place full of busy occupants.

hive[2] *v* to collect (bees) into a hive.

hive off *v chiefly Brit* to separate (something) from a group or larger unit; *specif* to assign (e.g. assets or responsibilities) to a subsidiary company or agency.

hives *pl n* (*used as sing. or pl*) = URTICARIA.

HIV-positive *adj* having tested positively for the presence of HIV.

HL *abbr Brit* House of Lords.

hl *abbr* hectolitre(s).

HM *abbr* His/Her Majesty.

hm *abbr* hectometre(s).

HMG *abbr Brit* His/Her Majesty's Government.

HMI *abbr Brit* formerly, His/Her Majesty's Inspector (of Schools).

HMS *abbr* His/Her Majesty's Ship.

HMSO *abbr Brit* His/Her Majesty's Stationery Office.

HNC *abbr Brit* Higher National Certificate.

HND *abbr Brit* Higher National Diploma.

Ho *abbr* the chemical symbol for holmium.

hoagie *n chiefly NAm* a long roll split and filled with meat, cheese, etc.

hoar[1] *n archaic or literary* = HOARFROST.

hoar[2] *adj archaic or literary* grey with age; hoary.

hoard[1] *n* **1** an often secret supply, e.g. of money or food, stored up for preservation or future use. **2** a store of useful information or facts.

Usage note

hoard *or* **horde**? These two words are pronounced the same but have different meanings. A *hoard* is a store or collection, often of valuable things (*a pirate's hoard*). A *horde* is a large and sometimes unruly group of people (*resorts overrun by hordes of tourists*).

hoard[2] *v* to accumulate (a hoard). ➤➤ **hoarder** *n.*

hoarding *n Brit* **1** a large board designed to carry outdoor advertising. **2** a temporary fence put round a building site.

hoarfrost *n* a covering of minute ice crystals that forms on the ground, trees, etc.

hoarhound *n* see HOREHOUND.

hoarse *adj* **1** of a voice: rough or harsh in sound; grating. **2** having a hoarse voice. ➤➤ **hoarsely** *adv,* **hoarseness** *n.*

hoarsen *v* to become or make hoarse.

hoary *adj* (**-ier, -iest**) **1a** grey or white with age. **b** having greyish or whitish hair. **2** impressively or venerably old; ancient. **3** hackneyed. ➤➤ **hoariness** *n.*

hoax[1] *n* an act of deception; a trick or practical joke.

hoax[2] *v* to play a trick on; to deceive. ➤➤ **hoaxer** *n.*

hob *n* **1** *Brit* a horizontal surface, either on a cooker or installed as a separate unit, that contains heating areas on which pans are placed. **2** a ledge near a fireplace on which something may be kept warm. **3** a cutting tool used to make gear wheels or screw threads.

hobbit *n* a member of an imaginary race of genial hole-dwellers that resemble small human beings.

hobble[1] *v* **1** to walk along unsteadily or with difficulty. **2** to fasten together the legs of (a horse) to prevent straying; to fetter. **3** to impede or hamper the progress of (somebody or something). ➤➤ **hobbler** *n.*

hobble[2] *n* **1** a hobbling movement. **2** something, e.g. a rope, used to hobble a horse.

hobby[1] *n* (*pl* **-ies**) **1** a leisure activity or pastime engaged in for interest or recreation. **2** an early type of bicycle without pedals.

hobby[2] *n* (*pl* **-ies**) a small falcon of Asia, Africa, and Europe that catches small birds while in flight.

hobbyhorse *n* **1** a toy consisting of an imitation horse's head attached to one end of a stick. **2** a rocking horse. **3** a favourite topic or preoccupation.

hobbyist *n* a person with a particular hobby.

hobgoblin *n* a mischievous goblin.

hobnail *n* a short large-headed nail for studding the soles of shoes or boots. ➤➤ **hobnailed** *adj.*

hobnob *v* (**hobnobbed, hobnobbing**) *informal* (+ with) to socialize or chat with somebody.

hobo *n* (*pl* **-oes** *or* **-os**) *NAm* a tramp or vagrant.

Hobson's choice *n* an apparently free choice which offers no real alternative.

hock[1] *n* **1** the joint of the hind limb of a horse or related quadruped that corresponds to the ankle in human beings. **2** a knuckle of meat.

hock[2] *n Brit* a dry to medium-dry or sometimes sweet white table wine produced in the Rhine valley.

hock[3] *v informal* to pawn (something).

hock[4] ✻ **in hock 1** of an object: having been pawned. **2** of a person: in debt.

hockey *n* a game played between teams of eleven players who try to get a small hard ball into a goal using a stick curved at the lower end.

hocus-pocus *n* deliberately nonsensical words, e.g. as uttered by a conjurer, usu intended to obscure or deceive.

hod *n* **1** a trough mounted on a pole handle for carrying mortar, bricks, etc. **2** a coal scuttle, *esp* a tall one used to shovel fuel directly onto a fire.

hodgepodge *n NAm* see HOTCHPOTCH.

Hodgkin's disease *n* a malignant disease characterized by progressive anaemia with enlargement of the lymph glands, spleen, and liver.

hoe[1] *n* an implement with a long handle and flat blade, used for tilling, weeding, etc.

hoe[2] *v* **1** to weed or cultivate (land or a crop) with a hoe. **2** to remove (weeds) by hoeing. ➤➤ **hoer** *n.*

hoedown *n NAm* a square dance, or a gathering featuring square dances.

hog[1] *n* **1a** *Brit* a castrated male pig raised for slaughter. **b** *chiefly NAm* a domestic pig. **2** *informal* a gluttonous person. ✻ **go the whole hog** *informal* to do something thoroughly. ➤➤ **hoggish** *adj.*

hog[2] *v* (**hogged, hogging**) *informal* to appropriate a selfish or excessive share of (something); to monopolize. ➤➤ **hogger** *n.*

hogback *n* see HOGSBACK.

hogget *n* **1** *Brit* a young sheep. **2** *NZ* a lamb that has been weaned but not yet shorn.

Hogmanay *n* in Scotland, New Year's Eve.

hogsback *or* **hogback** *n* a ridge with a sharp summit and steeply sloping sides.

hogshead *n* **1** a large cask or barrel. **2** any of several measures of capacity, *esp* a measure of 52 imperial gallons (about 238l).

hog-tie *v* (**hog-ties, hog-tied, hog-tying**) *NAm* **1** to tie together all four feet of (an animal) or the hands and feet of (a person). **2** to impede or thwart (somebody).

hogwash *n informal* nonsensical talk.

hogweed *n* a tall foul-smelling plant of the carrot family, with large leaves and broad heads of white or pinkish flowers.

hoick *v Brit, informal* to lift or pull abruptly; to yank.

hoiden *n* see HOYDEN.

hoi polloi *pl n* (**the hoi polloi**) the common people; the masses.

hoisin sauce *n* a thick dark red sauce used in Chinese cookery as a sweet and spicy flavouring.

hoist[1] *v* to raise into position, *esp* by means of tackle. ⋙ **hoister** *n.*

hoist[2] *n* **1** an apparatus for hoisting something. **2** the act of hoisting; a lift. **3a** the end of a flag next to the staff. **b** a group of flags used as a signal.

hoity-toity *adj* haughty or self-important.

hokey cokey *n* a dance performed by a large group of people in a circle, who sing a song with lyrics that specify the actions.

hokey-pokey *n NAm* = HOKEY COKEY.

hoki *n* a food fish of the waters south of New Zealand, related to the hake.

hokum *n informal* **1** pretentious nonsense. **2** a technique, e.g. the use of sentimentality, designed to captivate the audience of a play, film, etc.

hol- *or* **holo-** *comb. form* complete or completely: *holocaust; holographic.*

hold[1] *v* (*past tense and past part.* **held**) **1** to have or support something in the hands of arms. **2** to embrace. **3** to detain (somebody). **4** of a container: to contain or be able to contain. **5** to keep in a specified position: *A wedge will hold the door open.* **6** to occupy (a position or job). **7** to maintain (a belief). **8** to consider (somebody) to be to blame for something: *They hold you responsible.* **9** to organize (a meeting, party, etc). **10** to take part in (a conversation). **11a** to maintain a condition or position. **b** to withstand a strain. **12** to keep a telephone connection: *Please hold.* ✻ **hold forth** to speak at length or tediously. **hold good** to be true or valid. **hold one's own** to maintain one's position in the face of opposition or difficulty. **hold somebody to something** to make somebody honour a commitment or promise. **hold something against somebody** to have a grudge against somebody. **hold to** to remain faithful to (a principle). ⋙ **holdable** *adj,* **holder** *n.*

hold[2] *n* **1** a manner of grasping something or somebody; a grip. **2** something that may be grasped as a support. **3** influence or control. ✻ **on hold** held in a state of postponement or temporary inactivity. **take hold 1** (*often* + of) to grasp, grip, or seize something. **2** to become attached or established; to take effect.

hold[3] *n* the cargo compartment of a ship or plane.

holdall *n Brit* a bag or case for miscellaneous articles.

hold back *v* **1** to impede or inhibit (somebody). **2** to keep (tears or laughter) in check. **3** to hesitate.

hold down *v* to keep and manage well in (a job, etc).

hold in *v* to keep (feelings) in check.

holding *n* **1** a piece of land held by somebody *esp* as a tenant. **2** (*in pl*) one's financial assets, *esp* in the form of land or securities.

holding company *n* a company whose primary business is holding a controlling interest in the shares of other companies.

holding pattern *n* the circling flightpath around an airport that an aircraft keeps to while waiting for permission to land.

hold off *v* **1** to keep (an attacker or challenge) at a distance. **2** to delay (action). **3** of bad weather: not to occur after all.

hold on *v* **1** to persevere despite difficulties. **2** to wait. ✻ **hold on to** to keep possession of.

hold out *v* **1** to survive or persevere despite difficulties. **2** to offer (hope). **3** to continue to be enough. ✻ **hold out for** to insist on (something) as part of an agreement. **hold out on** to withhold information from (somebody).

hold over *v* to postpone (an event).

holdup *n* **1** an armed robbery. **2** a delay, or the cause of this. **3** (*in pl*) a stocking with an elasticated top for gripping the thigh that stays up without suspenders.

hold up *v* **1** to delay (a person or activity). **2** to rob at gunpoint. **3** to present as a good example of something.

hole[1] *n* **1** a hollow in something solid; a pit or cavity. **2** a gap or opening right through something. **3** in golf, a lined cylindrical cavity in a putting green into which the ball is to be played. **4** *informal* a small or unpleasant place. **5** *informal* an awkward situation. ✻ **hole in one** in golf, a shot from a tee that lands in the hole. **hole in the heart** a congenital heart defect in the form of an abnormal opening in the SEPTUM (partition) dividing the left and right sides of the heart, resulting in inadequate oxygenation of the blood. **hole in the wall 1** *informal* a poky little establishment. **2** *Brit* an automatic cash machine set into the external wall of a bank, etc. **make a hole in** to use up a lot of (a supply of money, food, or other resource).

hole[2] *v* **1** to make a hole in (something); *specif* to pierce the side of (a vessel). **2** in golf, to putt (the ball) into a hole.

hole-and-corner *adj* clandestine; underhand.

hole up *v informal* (*usu* + in) to hide oneself in a confined place.

Holi *n* a Hindu festival celebrated in the spring.

holiday[1] *n* **1** *chiefly Brit* a period taken as leave or a break from one's normal occupation, *esp* if spent away from home. **2** an official day of leave from work, such as a religious festival or a day of celebration.

holiday[2] *v* to take or spend a holiday.

holiday camp *n* an establishment for holidaymakers, usu with accommodation in chalets and facilities for a variety of sports and entertainments.

holidaymaker *n* a person who is going somewhere for a holiday, or is on holiday in a particular resort.

holier-than-thou *adj* having an air of superior piety or morality; self-righteous.

holily *adv* in a holy manner.

holiness *n* **1** the quality of being holy. **2** (**His/Your Holiness**) a title for the Pope, Orthodox patriarchs, and the Dalai Lama.

holism *n* **1** a view of the universe, and *esp* living nature, as being composed of interacting wholes that are more than simply the sum of their parts. **2** in alternative medicine, the practice of trying to treat the whole person, not merely their symptoms. ⋙ **holistic** *adj.*

hollandaise sauce *n* a rich sauce served with salmon, trout, etc.

holler *v NAm* to shout.

hollo *interj archaic* a cry used to attract attention or as a call of encouragement.

hollow[1] *adj* **1** having a recessed surface; curved inwards; concave; sunken. **2** having a cavity within. **3** echoing like a sound made in or by beating on an empty container; muffled. **4a** of an achievement: deceptively lacking in real value or significance. **b** of a vow or promise: insincere; not to be trusted. ✱ **beat somebody hollow** to defeat somebody thoroughly. ⋙ **hollowly** *adv*, **hollowness** *n*.

hollow[2] *v* (*usu* + out) to make hollow or form by hollowing.

hollow[3] *n* **1** a depressed or hollow part of a surface; *esp* a small valley or basin. **2** an unfilled space; a cavity.

holly *n* (*pl* **-ies**) a tree or shrub with thick glossy spiny-edged leaves and bright red berries.

hollyhock *n* a tall plant of the mallow family with large coarse rounded leaves and tall spikes of showy flowers.

holmium *n* a silver-white metallic chemical element of the rare-earth group that occurs naturally in various rare-earth minerals and forms highly magnetic compounds.

holm oak *n* a S European evergreen oak with glossy dark-green leaves.

holo- *comb. form* see HOL-.

holocaust *n* **1** an instance of wholesale destruction or loss of life. **2** (**the Holocaust**) the genocidal persecution of European Jewry by Hitler and the Nazi party during World War II.

Holocene *adj* of the present geological epoch, the second epoch of the Quaternary period, which began 10,000 years ago and followed the Pleistocene epoch. ⋙ **Holocene** *n*.

hologram *n* **1** a pattern produced by the interference between one part of a split beam of coherent light, e.g. from a laser, and the other part of the same beam reflected off an object. **2** a photographic reproduction of this pattern that when suitably illuminated produces a three-dimensional picture. ⋙ **holographic** *adj*, **holography** *n*.

holograph *n* a document wholly in the handwriting of its author.

hols *pl n Brit, informal* holidays.

holster *n* a leather holder for a pistol, usu worn on a belt.

holt *n* a den or lair, *esp* of an otter.

holy *adj* (**-ier, -iest**) **1** set apart to the service of God or a god; sacred. **2** characterized by perfection and transcendence; commanding absolute adoration and reverence. **3** spiritually pure; godly.

Holy Communion *n* the celebration of the Eucharist; = COMMUNION (1).

holy day *n* a day set aside for special religious observance.

Holy Father *n* (**the Holy Father**) the pope.

Holy Ghost *n* (**the Holy Ghost**) = the HOLY SPIRIT.

Holy Grail *n* the cup or platter used, according to medieval legend, by Christ at the Last Supper, which became the object of knightly quests.

holy of holies *n* **1** in Jewish history, the innermost and most sacred chamber of the Jewish tabernacle and temple. **2** any place or thing considered sacred.

holy orders *pl n* the office of a Christian minister.

Holy Roman Empire *n* a loose confederation of mainly German and Italian territories, representing the western part of the Roman Empire, as revived by Charlemagne in 800, that existed until 1806.

Holy Scripture *n* the sacred writings pertaining to Christianity embodied in the Bible.

Holy See *n* (**the Holy See**) the papacy.

Holy Spirit *n* (**the Holy Spirit**) the third person of the Trinity.

holy war *n* a war that is undertaken in the name of religion, either to defend or to promote a religious cause.

holy water *n* water that has been blessed by a priest for symbolic use in purification rituals.

Holy Week *n* the week before Easter during which the last days of Christ's life are commemorated.

holy writ *n* **1** (*often* **Holy Writ**) = HOLY SCRIPTURE. **2** a writing or utterance of unquestionable authority.

hom- *or* **homo-** *comb. form* **1** one and the same; similar: *homograph*. **2** relating to homosexual love: *homophobia*.

homage *n* reverential regard; deference.

homburg *n* a felt hat with a stiff curled brim and a high crown creased lengthways.

home[1] *n* **1** the place where one lives permanently. **2** the place of origin of something. **3** an establishment providing residence and care, *esp* for children, the elderly, or those physically or mentally unfit to look after themselves. **4** the finishing point in a race. **5** in board games, etc, a place where one is safe from attack. **6** (**Home**) in computing, the beginning of the line or file one is in. ✱ **at home** relaxed and comfortable. **close/near to home** of a comment, etc: too accurate for comfort.

home[2] *adv* **1** to or at the place where one lives. **2** to one's family or residence from somewhere else. **3** to one's ultimate objective, e.g. a finishing line. **4** into place; into position. ✱ **bring home to somebody** to make somebody aware of (a fact or circumstance). **come home to roost** of past misdeeds: to rebound upon the perpetrator. **drive/hammer home** to express (a point) forcibly, so as to convince one's hearers. **hit/strike home 1** of somebody's words: to have the effect intended by the speaker. **2** of the point or significance of a situation: to be truly understood. **home and dry** *chiefly Brit* having reached one's objective [from horse-racing, when the winner is so far ahead that it can be rubbed down before the other runners finish].

home[3] *adj* **1a** relating to one's home; domestic. **b** done, used, etc in the home. **2** denoting the headquarters or centre of operations. **3a** of a team or player: belonging to the ground where a sporting fixture is held. **b** of a match: played on a team's own ground. **4** relating to or belonging to one's own country; domestic.

home[4] *v* **1** of a bird or animal: to return to its base by means of instinct. **2** to provide (a domestic pet) with a home. ✱ **home in on 1** (*also* **home on to**) of a missile: to find (its target) automatically by electronic programming, automatic navigational aids, etc. **2** to concentrate one's critical attention on (particular weaknesses in an opponent's argument, etc).

home brew *n* an alcoholic drink, e.g. beer, made at home.

homecoming *n* a returning home.

home economics *pl n* (*used as sing. or pl*) a school subject teaching the skills needed for running a household.

home farm *n* a farm attached to and supplying produce to a large country house.

homegrown *adj* produced in or characteristic of the home country or region.

Home Guard *n* the volunteer citizen army recruited early in World War II to defend the UK against invasion.

home help *n Brit* a person employed to carry out household chores.

homeland *n* **1** one's native land. **2** in S Africa, formerly, an area reserved for black people.

homeless *adj* of a person: having no place to live. ➤➤ **homelessness** *n*.

homely *adj* (**-ier, -iest**) **1** commonplace; familiar. **2** *esp* of a woman: having a warm, affectionate, and sympathetic personality. **3** simple; unpretentious. **4** *chiefly NAm* not good-looking; plain. ➤➤ **homeliness** *n*.

homemade *adj* **1** made in the home, on the premises, or by one's own efforts. **2** made in crude or amateurish fashion.

homemaker *n* the member of a household who takes the chief responsibility for its housekeeping.

home movie *n* an amateur film made with a video camera or a cinecamera.

Home Office *n* the government office concerned with internal affairs.

homeopath *or* **homoeopath** *n* somebody who practises homeopathy.

homeopathy *or* **homoeopathy** *n* a system of complementary medicine in which diseases are treated by administering minute doses of substances that produce symptoms like those of the disease. ➤➤ **homeopathic** *adj*.

homeostasis *or* **homoeostasis** *n* the physiological maintenance of relatively constant conditions, e.g. constant internal temperature, within the body in the face of changing external conditions. ➤➤ **homeostatic** *adj*.

homeotherm *or* **homoiotherm** *n* an organism that maintains its body temperature approximately constant despite changes in external temperature; a warm-blooded organism. ➤➤ **homeothermic** *adj*.

home page *n* on the World Wide Web, a first page of information designed to introduce an individual or a concern.

home plate *n* in baseball, a rubber slab at which a batter stands.

Homeric *adj* **1** relating to or characteristic of the ancient Greek poet Homer, his age, or his writings. **2** of epic proportions; heroic.

home rule *n* limited self-government by the people of a dependent political unit.

home run *n* in baseball, a hit that enables the batter to make a complete circuit of the bases and score a run.

Home Secretary *n* a government minister for internal affairs.

homesick *adj* longing for home and family while absent from them. ➤➤ **homesickness** *n*.

homespun[1] *adj* **1** made of HOMESPUN[2] or from cloth spun or woven at home. **2** lacking sophistication; simple.

homespun[2] *n* a loosely woven woollen or linen fabric orig made from yarn spun at home.

homestead *n* **1** a house and adjoining land occupied by a family. **2** in N America, an area of land formerly granted to a settler. **3** *Aus, NZ* the owner's living quarters on a sheep or cattle station. ➤➤ **homesteader** *n*, **homesteading** *n*.

home straight *n* (**the home straight**) straight final part of a racecourse, usu opposite the grandstand.

home stretch *n* **1** (**the home stretch**) *chiefly NAm* = HOME STRAIGHT. **2** (**the home stretch**) the final stage of a project, etc.

home truth *n* (*also in pl*) an unpleasant but true fact about one's character or situation.

home unit *n Aus, NZ* a self-contained owner-occupied flat that is one of several within a building.

homeward *adj* heading towards home.

homewards (*NAm* **homeward**) *adv* towards home. ➤➤ **homeward-bound** *adj*.

homework *n* **1** school work that a pupil is given to do at home. **2** work done in one's own home for pay. **3** preparatory reading or research, e.g. for a discussion.

homeworker *n* a person who earns a living from work done at home.

homey *adj* see HOMY.

homicide *n* **1** murder. **2** a murderer. ➤➤ **homicidal** *adj*.

homiletics *pl n* (*used as sing. or pl*) the art of writing sermons and preaching. ➤➤ **homilectic** *adj*.

homily *n* (*pl* **homilies**) **1** a sermon intended for spiritual guidance. **2** a talking-to on moral conduct. ➤➤ **homilist** *n*.

homing *adj* **1** denoting a bird, etc that can find its way home after travelling long distances. **2** denoting a missile that is capable of locating its target electronically.

homing pigeon *n* a domesticated pigeon bred for its homing instinct, often used as a racer.

hominid *n* any of a family of two-legged primate mammals comprising humans and their extinct immediate ancestors. ➤➤ **hominid** *adj*.

hominoid[1] *adj* **1** resembling or related to man. **2** relating to or belonging to the primates, comprising humans and the anthropoid apes.

hominoid[2] *n* a hominoid mammal.

hominy *n* crushed or coarsely ground husked maize, *esp* when boiled with water or milk to make GRITS.

Homo *n* a genus of primate mammals including recent man, *Homo sapiens*, and various extinct ancestors.

homo *n* (*pl* **-os**) *informal, chiefly derog* a homosexual.

homo- *comb. form* see HOM-.

homoeopath *n* see HOMEOPATH.

homoeopathy *n* see HOMEOPATHY.

homoeostasis *n* see HOMEOSTASIS.

homoerotic *adj* relating to sexual desire aroused by or centred on a person of one's own sex. ➤➤ **homoeroticism** *n*.

homogeneous /homəˈjeeni·əs/ *adj* **1** of the same or a similar kind. **2** of uniform structure or composition throughout. ➤➤ **homogeneity** *n*, **homogeneously** *adv*, **homogeneousness** *n*.

homogenize *or* **-ise** *v* **1** to make or become uniform throughout, or make (different things) similar. **2a** to reduce the particles of (a substance) so that they are uniformly small and evenly distributed. **b** to break up the fat globules of (milk) into fine particles, so that the cream does not rise. ➤➤ **homogenization** *n*, **homogenized** *adj*, **homogenizer** *n*.

homograft *n* a graft of tissue taken from a donor of the same species as the recipient.

homograph *n* any of two or more words spelt alike but different in meaning, derivation, or pronunciation, e.g. the noun *conduct* and the verb *conduct*. ➤➤ **homographic** *adj*.

homoiotherm *n* see HOMEOTHERM.

homolog *n NAm* see HOMOLOGUE.

homologate *v* **1** to sanction, allow, or approve *esp* officially. **2** to approve (an engine or vehicle) for sale or for a certain class of racing. ⋙ **homologation** *n.*

homologous *adj* **1** of geometrical figures or their parts: having the same relative position, value, or structure. **2** of organs: corresponding in structure, position, and embryologic or evolutionary origin, but different in function. **3** of chemical compounds: belonging to a chemical series, e.g. the alkanes. **4** of a tissue graft: derived from an organism of the same species. ⋙ **homologize** *v,* **homology** *n.*

homologue (*NAm* **homolog**) *n* a homologous organ, chemical compound, or geometrical figure: compare ANALOGUE[1].

homomorphy *n* similarity of biological form, sometimes with different fundamental structure or origin. ⋙ **homomorphic** *adj,* **homomorphism** *n.*

homonym *n* any of two or more words that have the same spelling and pronunciation but different meanings and origins, as with the noun and the verb *bear.* ⋙ **homonymic** *adj,* **homonymous** *adj,* **homonymously** *adv,* **homonymy** *n.*

homophobia *n* intense and unreasoning hatred of homosexuality and homosexuals. ⋙ **homophobe** *n,* **homophobic** *adj.*

homophone *n* **1** any of two or more words pronounced alike but different in meaning, derivation, or spelling, e.g. *to, too,* and *two.* **2** any of two or more characters or groups pronounced the same, e.g. *ph* and *f.* ⋙ **homophonous** *adj.*

homophonic *adj* denoting music in which the parts move rhythmically in step with one another. ⋙ **homophonically** *adv,* **homophony** *n.*

Homo sapiens *n* the species of primate that comprises human beings, the only extant species of the genus *Homo.*

homosexual *n* a person who has a sexual preference for members of their own sex. ⋙ **homosexual** *adj,* **homosexuality** *n,* **homosexually** *adv.*

homosocial *adj* relating to interaction between members of the same sex, *esp* between men.

homunculus *n* (*pl* **homunculi**) a little man; a manikin or dwarf.

homy *or* **homey** *adj* (**homier, homiest**) *informal* **1** cosy, comfortable, and homelike. **2** unpretentious or unsophisticated.

Hon. *abbr* used as a title: Honourable.

hon. *abbr* **1** honorary. **2** honour. **3** honourable.

honcho *n* (*pl* **-os**) *chiefly NAm, informal* an important man; a boss.

Honduran *n* a native or inhabitant of Honduras. ⋙ **Honduran** *adj.*

hone[1] *v* **1** to sharpen (a blade, tool, etc) with a whetstone. **2** (*usu in passive*) to make keener, more sharply focused, or more effective.

hone[2] *n* a whetstone, *esp* a fine one for sharpening razors.

honest *adj* **1** free of deceit; sincere; truthful. **2a** free of any intention to do wrong; morally good. **b** morally right. **3** earned fairly, through hard work. **4** simple and unpretentious. **5** *archaic* of a woman: chaste. ✱ **make an honest woman of** *dated or humorous* to save the reputation of (a woman, *esp* formerly an unmarried pregnant woman) by marrying her. **to be honest** used to introduce a candid statement, admission, etc.

honest broker *n* a neutral mediator.

honestly *adv* **1** with honesty or integrity. **2** used for emphasis in averring something: frankly.

honest-to-God *adj informal* real, genuine, or authentic.

honest-to-goodness *adj* simple, ordinary, or straightforward.

honesty *n* **1a** upright and straightforward conduct; integrity. **b** sincerity; truthfulness. **2** a European plant of the mustard family with large broad smooth translucent seed pods.

honey *n* **1** a sweet sticky pale golden liquid formed from the nectar of flowers in the HONEY SAC of various bees and used as a food. **2** *chiefly NAm* used in affectionate address: sweetheart; dear. **3** *informal* a superlative example.

honey badger *n* = RATEL.

honeybee *n* any honey-producing bee that lives in a more or less organized community.

honeycomb[1] *n* **1** a mass of six-sided wax cells built by honeybees in their nest to contain their brood and stores of honey. **2** any cellular structure resembling this, or one riddled with cavities.

honeycomb[2] *v* (*usu in passive*) **1** to cause to be full of cavities like a honeycomb. **2** to burrow or penetrate into every part of.

honeydew *n* a sweet deposit secreted on the leaves of plants usu by aphids.

honeydew melon *n* a pale smooth-skinned MUSKMELON with pale greenish sweet flesh.

honeyed *or* **honied** *adj literary* of words or tone: sweet and agreeable or soft and soothing.

honeymoon[1] *n* **1** the period immediately following marriage, *esp* when taken as a holiday by the married couple. **2** a period of unusual harmony following the establishment of a new relationship, e.g. that of a new government with the public.

honeymoon[2] *v* said of a newly married couple: to have a honeymoon. ⋙ **honeymooner** *n.*

honeypot *n* **1** a jar of or for honey. **2** a place with many attractions that draw visitors in large numbers, or with financial possibilities that draw investors, etc.

honey sac *n* a distension of the oesophagus of a bee in which honey is produced.

honeysuckle *n* a climbing shrub usu with showy yellow and pink sweet-smelling flowers rich in nectar.

honeytrap *n informal* a stratagem for luring somebody to a compromising sexual assignation, *esp* with a view to blackmailing them.

hongi *n NZ* amongst the Maoris, the action of pressing noses together as a form of greeting.

honied *adj* see HONEYED.

honk[1] *v* **1** of a driver: to sound one's horn. **2** to make the characteristic cry of a goose. **3** *Brit, informal* to vomit. ⋙ **honker** *n.*

honk[2] *n* a honking sound.

honkie *or* **honky** *n* (*pl* **honkies**) *chiefly NAm, derog* used by Blacks: a white man.

honky-tonk *n* **1** a form of ragtime piano playing. **2** *chiefly NAm, informal* a cheap nightclub or dance hall. ⋙ **honky-tonk** *adj.*

honor[1] *n NAm* see HONOUR[1].

honor[2] *v NAm* see HONOUR[2].

honorable *adj NAm* see HONOURABLE.

honorarium *n* (*pl* **honorariums** *or* **honoraria**) a payment in recognition of professional services that are nominally given free.

honorary *adj* **1a** of a degree, doctorate, etc: conferred in recognition of achievement, without the usual obligations. **b** awarded a degree in this manner. **2** of an office-bearer: unpaid or voluntary. ⋙ **honorarily** *adv.*

honorific[1] *adj* **1** conferring or conveying honour. **2** belonging to a class of grammatical forms, e.g. in

Chinese and Japanese, used in speaking to or about a social superior. ➤➤ **honorifically** *adv.*

honorific[2] *n* **1** an honorific expression. **2** a respectful title or form of address, such as *Your/His Excellence.*

honour[1] (*NAm* **honor**) *n* **1a** public recognition or fame. **b** a person who brings credit or recognition. **c** an award or distinction conferred for achievement or excellence. **2a** one's sense of morality and justice. **b** one's good name or reputation. **3** a privilege. **4** (*in pl*) the highest academic standard in a degree course or examination. **5a** in whist, an ace, king, queen, or jack of the trump suit. **b** (*in pl*) in bridge, these cards and the ten, or the four aces when there are no trumps. **6** (**Your/His Honour**) used as a title of respectful address or reference to a holder of high office, *esp* a judge in court. **7** *dated* chastity or purity, *esp* that of a woman. ✱ **do the honours** *informal or humorous* to perform a social duty, *esp* to serve guests with food or drink. **in honour bound** (*also* **honour bound**) morally obliged to do or not do something. **in honour of** as a mark of respect for (a person or occasion). **on one's honour** morally obliged to do or not do something.

honour[2] (*NAm* **honor**) *v* **1** to regard with deep respect. **2a** to confer a mark of distinction on. **b** to confer distinction on by being present at (an event) or with (people). **3a** to do what is required under (an agreement or commitment). **b** to accept and make payment in respect of (a bill, debt, cheque, etc).

honourable (*NAm* **honorable**) *adj* **1** characterized by a sense of honour. **2** worthy of respect. **3** (*often* **Honourable**) used as a title for the children of certain British noblemen and various government officials, and as a respectful epithet for fellow Members of Parliament.

honourable mention *n* a distinction awarded, e.g. in a contest or exhibition, for work of exceptional merit that has not obtained a prize.

honours list *n* a twice yearly list of people to be honoured by the British sovereign for their public service.

honour system *n* the system of relying on honesty as the only form of control available, e.g. where a payment or an examination is unsupervised.

hooch *or* **hootch** *n NAm, informal* spirits, *esp* when inferior or illicitly made or obtained.

hood[1] *n* **1** a covering for the top and back of the head and neck that is usu attached to the neckline of a garment. **2** an ornamental scarf worn over an academic gown indicating the wearer's university and degree. **3** a folding waterproof top cover for an open car, pram, etc. **4** a cover or canopy, e.g. over a cooker, for carrying off fumes, smoke, etc. **5** *NAm* = BONNET (3). ➤➤ **hoodless** *adj,* **hoodlike** *adj.*

hood[2] *v* **1** to cover or protect with or as if with a hood. **2** to drop one's eyelids halfway over (one's eyes). ➤➤ **hooded** *adj.*

hood[3] *n NAm, informal* a hoodlum or gangster.

-hood *suffix* forming nouns, denoting: **1** the state or condition of: *likelihood; parenthood.* **2** an instance of something: *a falsehood.* **3** (*used as sing. or pl*) a body or class of people sharing (a specified character or state): *brotherhood; priesthood.*

hoodlum *n* a thug or gangster. ➤➤ **hoodlumish** *adj.*

hoodoo[1] *n* (*pl* **-os**) **1** voodoo. **2** a malign influence that haunts one, *esp* that prevents one achieving winning form in a sport. ➤➤ **hoodooism** *n.*

hoodoo[2] *v* (**hoodoos, hoodooed, hoodooing**) *chiefly NAm* to cast an evil spell on or bring bad luck to.

hoodwink *v chiefly informal* to deceive or delude. ➤➤ **hoodwinker** *n.*

hooey *n informal* nonsense.

hoof[1] *n* (*pl* **hooves** *or* **hoofs**) **1** a curved horny casing on the end of the foot of a horse, cow, or similar mammal. **2** the whole foot of such a mammal. ✱ **on the hoof 1** of a meat animal: before being butchered; while still alive. **2** *informal* while moving around and doing other things. **3** *informal* quickly or extempore; without much thought. ➤➤ **hoofed** *adj.*

hoof[2] *v informal* to kick (a ball, etc). ✱ **hoof it 1** *informal* to go somewhere on foot. **2** *informal* to dance.

hoofer *n NAm, informal* a professional dancer.

hoo-ha *n chiefly informal* a fuss; a to-do.

hook[1] *n* **1** a curved or bent metal or plastic device for hanging things on, attaching things to, or gripping. **2** a bent and barbed metal device for catching fish. **3** part of a presentation, e.g. a television documentary, that serves to gain the attention and interest of the audience. **4** a repeated melodic phrase in a popular musical composition. **5** a sickle. **6a** in golf, the flight of a ball that deviates from a straight course in a direction opposite to the player's dominant hand: compare SLICE[1]. **b** in cricket, an attacking leg-side stroke played with a horizontal bat aimed at a ball of higher than waist height. **7** in boxing, a short blow delivered with a circular motion while the elbow remains bent and rigid. ✱ **by hook or by crook** by any possible means. **get one's hooks into** *informal* to grab or get hold of (somebody or something). **hook, line, and sinker** completely. **off the hook 1** *informal* freed from a difficulty or embarrassment. **2** of a telephone receiver: not on its base. **sling one's hook** *Brit, informal* to leave. ➤➤ **hooklike** *adj.*

hook[2] *v* **1** to attach (one thing to another) by means of a hook or hooks. **2** (+ round/over) to crook or bend (e.g. an arm or leg) round something. **3** to get hold of or catch (something) with a hook or hooked implement. **4** in cricket or golf, to play a hook.

hookah *n* an oriental pipe for smoking tobacco, marijuana, etc, consisting of a flexible tube attached to a container of water, through which cooled smoke is inhaled: compare NARGHILE.

hook and eye *n* a fastening device used chiefly on garments that consists of a hook that links with a bar or loop.

hooked *adj* **1** shaped like a hook. **2** fitted with a hook. **3** *informal* **a** (*often* + on) addicted to drugs. **b** (*often* + on) very enthusiastic or compulsively attached to something specified.

hooker *n* **1** in rugby, a player stationed in the middle of the front row of the scrum. **2** *informal* a woman prostitute.

hookey *n* see HOOKY.

hook nose *n* a nose with a prominent, angled bridge; an aquiline nose.

hookup *n* a temporary linking up of broadcasting stations for a special broadcast, or of electronic equipment for a particular purpose.

hook up *v* to connect or link (radio stations or electronic equipment), or to be connected.

hookworm *n* **1** a parasitic nematode worm with strong mouth hooks for attaching to the host's intestinal lining. **2** infestation by hookworms.

hooky *or* **hookey** ✱ **play hooky** *NAm, Aus, NZ, informal* to play truant.

hooligan *n* a violent, aggressive, vandalistic, or troublemaking young person. ➤➤ **hooliganism** *n.*

hoon *n Aus, NZ, informal* **1** a pimp. **2** a lout.

hoop[1] *n* **1** a large circular strip of rigid material, used: **a** for holding together the staves of a barrel. **b** for bowling along the ground or exercising with. **c** formerly, for expanding a woman's skirt. **2** a circular figure or object. **3** an arch through which balls must be hit in croquet. **4** a horizontal band of contrasting colour round a cap or sports shirt. ✱ **be put/go through the hoops** to undergo a demanding series of tests.

hoop[2] *v* to encircle, bind, or fasten with or as if with a hoop. ➤➤ **hooped** *adj,* **hooper** *n.*

hoop-la *n* **1** *Brit* a game, *esp* at a fairground, in which prizes are won by tossing rings over them. **2** *NAm* **a** fuss; noise. **b** nonsense.

hoopoe /'hoohpooh, 'hoohpoh/ *n* a Eurasian and N African bird with pale pinkish brown plumage, a long erectile crest, and a slender downward-curving bill.

hooray *interj* = HURRAY.

Hooray Henry *or* **Hooray** *n* (*pl* **Hooray Henries** *or* **Henrys**) *informal* a well-off upper-class young man who behaves in a noisy insensitive way.

hoosegow *n chiefly NAm, informal* a jail.

hoot[1] *v* **1a** to make the characteristic cry of an owl. **b** to sound the horn, etc of a vehicle, *esp* as a warning. **2** to utter a loud derisive shout. **3** *informal* to laugh loudly.

hoot[2] *n* **1** a hooting sound. **2** *informal* a source of laughter or amusement. ✱ **not care/give a hoot/two hoots** not to care in the least.

hootch *n* see HOOCH.

hootenanny *or* **hootnanny** *n* (*pl* **hootenannies** *or* **hootnannies**) an informal gathering with entertainment by folksingers, usu with the audience singing along.

hooter *n* **1** *chiefly Brit* a device, e.g. the horn of a car, for producing a loud hooting noise. **2** *dated, informal* the nose.

hootnanny *n* see HOOTENANNY.

Hoover *n trademark* a vacuum cleaner.

hoover *v* **1** to clean using a vacuum cleaner. **2** to suck up (dust, debris, etc) with a vacuum cleaner.

hooves *n* pl of HOOF[1].

hop[1] *v* (**hopped, hopping**) **1a** of a frog, etc: to move by a quick springy leap or in a series of leaps. **b** of a human being: to jump on one foot. **c** of a bird: to jump with both feet. **2** to make a quick trip, *esp* by air. **3** to board or leave a vehicle. **4** to jump over. ✱ **hop it!/hop off!** *Brit, informal* go away! **hopping mad** *informal* absolutely furious. **hop (off) the twig/stick** *Brit, informal* to depart or to die.

hop[2] *n* **1** a short leap, *esp* on one leg. **2** a short or long flight between two landings. **3** *informal* a dance. ✱ **catch somebody on the hop** *informal* to find somebody unprepared. **hop, skip/step, and jump** formerly, the triple jump.

hop[3] *n* **1** a climbing plant of the hemp family with cone-shaped catkins. **2a** (*in pl*) the ripe dried catkins of a hop used *esp* in the brewing process to impart a bitter flavour to beer. **b** *Aus, NZ, informal* beer. ➤➤ **hoppy** *adj.*

hop[4] *v* (**hopped, hopping**) to impregnate (beer) with hops. ✱ **be hopped up** *informal* to be in a state of intoxication from or as if from a narcotic drug.

hope[1] *v* **1** to desire or trust that (something is or may be the case). **2** to desire and expect (to do something). **3** (+ for) to be eager for (something). ✱ **hope against hope** to hope for something when there is virtually no possibility of it.

hope[2] *n* **1** (*also in pl*) the feeling that what one wants to happen can happen. **2** a chance that the desired thing may happen. **3** (*in pl*) the things one wants to happen. **4** a person or thing that one is depending on for something.

hope chest *n NAm* a chest in which a woman accumulates household linen, etc in preparation for marriage; = BOTTOM DRAWER.

hopeful[1] *adj* **1** full of hope. **2** inspiring hope. ➤➤ **hopefulness** *n.*

hopeful[2] *n* a person who hopes to, or is likely to, succeed.

hopefully *adv* **1** in a hopeful manner. **2** *informal* it is hoped; I hope.

Usage note

Though the use of *hopefully* in sentences such as *Hopefully, they'll be home before it gets dark* is still decried by traditionalists in Britain and America, it has generally established itself as part of normal usage. However, it is probably better to limit it to informal or spoken contexts.

hopeless *adj* **1** having no expectation of success; despairing. **2** unable to be carried out, dealt with, or solved. **3** *chiefly informal* incompetent or useless. ➤➤ **hopelessly** *adv,* **hopelessness** *n.*

Hopi *n* (*pl* **Hopis** *or* **Hopi**) **1** a member of a Native American people of NE Arizona. **2** the language of the Hopis. ➤➤ **Hopi** *adj.*

hoplite *n* a heavily armed infantry soldier of ancient Greece.

hopper *n* **1** somebody or something that hops. **2** a leaping insect; *specif* an immature hopping form of an insect. **3** a receptacle, *esp* funnel-shaped, for the discharging or temporary storage of grain, coal, etc.

hopsack *n* **1** a coarse material for making sacks. **2** a firm rough-surfaced clothing fabric woven in basket weave.

hopscotch *n* a children's game in which a player tosses an object, e.g. a stone, into areas of a figure outlined on the ground and hops through the figure and back to regain the object.

horde *n* **1** *usu derog* (*also in pl*) a crowd or swarm. **2** a nomadic tribe or army, *esp* of Asian origin.

Usage note

horde *or* hoard? See note at HOARD[1].

horehound *or* **hoarhound** *n* a strong-smelling plant of the mint family with downy leaves and bitter juice, used medicinally.

horizon *n* **1** the apparent junction of earth and sky. **2** (*also in pl*) one's range of perception, experience, or knowledge. **3a** a geological or archaeological layer of a particular time, usu identified by distinctive fossils or artefacts. **b** any of the reasonably distinct soil or subsoil layers in a vertical section of land. ✱ **on the horizon** of an event: due shortly.

horizontal[1] *adj* **1** at right angles to the vertical; parallel to the earth's surface; level. **2** *humorous* lying flat, *esp* in bed. **3** applying uniformly to all members of a group. ➤➤ **horizontality** *n,* **horizontally** *adv.*

horizontal[2] *n* a horizontal line or structure.

hormone *n* **1** a product of living cells that usu circulates in body liquids, e.g. the blood or sap, and produces a specific effect on the activity of cells remote from its point of origin. **2** a synthetic substance that imitates the action of a natural hormone. ➤➤ **hormonal** *adj,* **hormonally** *adv.*

hormone replacement therapy *n* the treatment of women with the hormone oestrogen to counteract adverse effects of the menopause, and to help prevent osteoporosis.

horn *n* **1** any of the usu paired bony projecting parts on the head of cattle, deer, and similar hoofed mammals. **2** a solid pointed part consisting of keratin attached to the nasal bone of a rhinoceros. **3** the tough fibrous material that forms the horns and hooves of animals. **4** something shaped like a horn, e.g. either of the curved ends of a crescent. **5a** = FRENCH HORN. **b** a wind instrument used in a jazz band; *esp* a trumpet. **c** a device, e.g. on a motor car, for making loud warning noises. ✻ **draw in one's horns** to reduce one's activities or spending. **on the horns of a dilemma** faced with two equally undesirable alternatives. **toot/blow one's own horn** *NAm, informal* to sing one's own praises; to blow one's own trumpet. ⋙ **horned** *adj,* **hornist** *n,* **hornless** *adj,* **hornlike** *adj.*

hornbeam *n* a tree of the hazel family with smooth grey bark and hard white wood.

hornbill *n* a large Old World bird with an enormous horn-shaped bill.

hornblende *n* a dark mineral consisting chiefly of silicates of calcium, magnesium, and iron, present in many igneous and metamorphic rocks. ⋙ **hornblendic** *adj.*

hornet *n* a large wasp with black and yellow bands on the abdomen and a powerful sting. ✻ **stir up a hornets' nest** to provoke an angry reaction.

horn in *v informal* to intrude on something.

horn of plenty *n* a cornucopia.

hornpipe *n* a lively British folk dance typically associated with sailors, or a piece of music for dancing it to.

horn-rims *pl n* glasses with horn rims. ⋙ **horn-rimmed** *adj.*

hornswoggle *v informal* to hoax or outwit.

horny *adj* (**-ier, -iest**) **1** composed of or resembling horn. **2** *informal* sexually aroused; randy. ⋙ **horniness** *n.*

horology *n* **1** the science of measuring time. **2** the art of constructing instruments for indicating time. ⋙ **horologer** *n,* **horologic** *adj,* **horological** *adj,* **horologist** *n.*

horoscope *n* **1** a diagram of the relative positions of planets and signs of the zodiac at a specific time, *esp* somebody's birth. **2** an astrological forecast based on this, made for a particular person, or one presented, e.g. in a newspaper column, for people born under a certain zodiac sign.

horrendous *adj* dreadful or horrible. ⋙ **horrendously** *adv.*

horrible *adj* **1** causing, or of a nature to cause, horror. **2** *chiefly informal* extremely unpleasant or disagreeable. ⋙ **horribleness** *n,* **horribly** *adv.*

horrid *adj* **1** horrible; shocking. **2** *informal* repulsive; nasty. ⋙ **horridly** *adv,* **horridness** *n.*

horrific *adj* arousing horror; horrifying. ⋙ **horrifically** *adv.*

horrify *v* (**-ies, -ied**) **1** to cause to feel horror. **2** to shock or fill with distaste. ⋙ **horrification** *n,* **horrified** *adj,* **horrifiedly** *adv,* **horrifying** *adj,* **horrifyingly** *adv.*

horror *n* **1a** intense fear, dread, or dismay. **b** intense aversion or repugnance. **2a** the quality of inspiring horror. **b** an unpleasant or ugly person or thing. **3** (**the horrors**) *informal* a state of horror, depression, or apprehension.

hors de combat /ˌaw də ˈkombah/ *adv and adj* out of the fight; disabled.

hors d'oeuvre /ˌaw ˈduhv/ *n* (*pl* **hors d'oeuvres** *or* **hors d'oeuvre**) any of various savoury foods usu served as appetizers.

horse[1] *n* **1** a large solid-hoofed four-footed mammal, domesticated by humans since prehistoric times and used as a beast of burden, a draught animal, or for riding. **2** a male horse; a stallion or gelding. **3** a four-legged frame for supporting something, e.g. planks. **4a** = POMMEL HORSE. **b** = VAULTING HORSE. **5** (*used as sing. or pl*) cavalry. **6** *slang* heroin. ✻ **from the horse's mouth** of information: from the original source; first-hand. **hold one's horses** to postpone action; to restrain oneself. **horses for courses** different people or things suit different needs. ⋙ **horseless** *adj,* **horselike** *adj.*

horse[2] *v informal* (*usu* + around/about) to engage in horseplay.

horseback[1] ✻ **on horseback** mounted on a horse.

horseback[2] *adj and adv* mounted on a horse; on horseback.

horsebox *n* a lorry or closed trailer for transporting horses.

horse chestnut *n* **1** a large tree with five-lobed leaves and erect conical clusters of showy flowers. **2** the large glossy brown nut of this tree, enclosed in a spiny case; = CONKER.

horseflesh *n* **1** horses collectively. **2** horse meat.

horsefly *n* (*pl* **-ies**) any of numerous species of large swift flies, the females of which suck blood.

Horse Guards *pl n* a mounted regiment forming part of the British household cavalry.

horsehair *n* **1** the hair of a horse, *esp* from its mane or tail. **2** padding made from this, used in upholstery.

horse latitudes *pl n* either of two high-pressure belts in the latitudes 30°–35°N and 30°–35°S with weather characterized by calms and light changeable winds.

horse laugh *n* a loud boisterous laugh.

horseless carriage *n archaic* a motor car.

horseman *n* (*pl* **horsemen**) a rider on horseback, *esp* a skilled one. ⋙ **horsemanship** *n.*

horseplay *n* rough or boisterous play.

horsepower *n* an imperial unit of power equal to about 746 watts.

horseradish *n* **1** a tall coarse white-flowered plant of the mustard family. **2** the pungent root of the horseradish or a condiment prepared from it.

horse sense *n* = COMMON SENSE.

horseshit *n chiefly NAm, coarse slang* = BULLSHIT[1].

horseshoe *n* **1** a shoe for horses, usu consisting of a narrow U-shaped plate of iron fitting the rim of the hoof, traditionally a lucky symbol. **2** something resembling this, such as a bend in a road or river.

horsetail *n* a flowerless plant with a hollow jointed stem, related to the ferns.

horse-trading *n* negotiation accompanied by hard bargaining and reciprocal concessions. ⋙ **horse-trader** *n.*

horsewhip[1] *n* a long whip used for controlling horses.

horsewhip[2] *v* (**horsewhipped, horsewhipping**) to flog with or as if with a horsewhip.

horsewoman *n* (*pl* **horsewomen**) a female rider on horseback, *esp* a skilled one. ⋙ **horsewomanship** *n.*

horsey *or* **horsy** *adj* (**-ier, -iest**) **1** relating to or resembling a horse. **2** very interested in horses, horse-riding, or horse racing. ⋙ **horsily** *adv,* **horsiness** *n.*

horst *n* a geological term denoting a block of the earth's crust higher than and separated by faults from adjacent blocks.

horsy *adj* see HORSEY.

hortative *or* **hortatory** *adj formal* giving encouragement. ➤➤ **hortatively** *adv.*

horticulture *n* the science and art of growing fruits, vegetables, and flowers. ➤➤ **horticultural** *adj,* **horticulturally** *adv,* **horticulturist** *n.*

hosanna *interj and n* a cry of acclamation and adoration.

hose[1] *n* **1** (*pl* **hose**) (*usu in pl*) till the late 16th cent., close-fitting covering for the leg and foot. **2** (*pl* **hose**) (*usu in pl*) from the mid 16th cent., short pouched breeches reaching to the knee. **3** (*pl* **hose**) *NAm* (*in pl*) tights or stockings. **4** (*pl* **hoses**) a flexible tube for conveying fluids, e.g. from a tap, or in a car engine.

hose[2] *v* (*often* + down) to spray, water, or wash (something) with a hose.

hosepipe *n* a length of hose for conveying water, e.g. for watering plants or putting out fires.

hosier *n* a person or business that sells socks, stockings, and tights.

hosiery *n* a collective term for socks, stockings, and tights.

hospice *n* **1** *Brit* a nursing home, *esp* for terminally ill patients. **2** formerly, a place of shelter for travellers or the destitute, often run by a religious order.

hospitable *adj* **1** offering a generous and cordial welcome to guests or strangers. **2** offering a pleasant or sustaining environment. **3** readily receptive. ➤➤ **hospitably** *adv.*

hospital *n* **1** an institution where the sick or injured are given medical care. **2** a repair shop for specified small objects. **3** formerly, a charitable institution, e.g. for the needy, aged, infirm, or young.

hospital corner *n* in bed-making, a way of securing the sheet round the corner of the mattress with a neat diagonal fold, used in hospitals.

hospitaler *n NAm* see HOSPITALLER.

hospitalise *v* see HOSPITALIZE.

hospitality *n* **1** hospitable treatment or reception. **2** (*used before a noun*) where guests are entertained and usu offered free drinks.

hospitalize *or* **-ise** *v* to place in a hospital as a patient. ➤➤ **hospitalization** *n.*

hospitaller (*NAm* **hospitaler**) *n* a person, *esp* a member of a charitable religious order devoted to hospital or ambulance services.

hospital trust *n* in Britain, an autonomous trust within the National Health Service, established to run a hospital or group of hospitals that has withdrawn from local-authority management.

host[1] *n* **1a** a person who receives or entertains guests socially or officially. **b** an innkeeper. **c** a person or establishment, etc that provides facilities for an event or function. **2a** a living animal or plant on or in which a parasite or smaller organism lives. **b** an individual into which a tissue or part is transplanted from another. **3** a compere on a radio or television programme. **4** a computer that provides services to others linked up to it, e.g. access to the databases stored in it.

host[2] *v* **1** to act as host at or of (a reception, etc). **2** to act as compere of (a broadcast show, etc).

host[3] *n* **1** (*also in pl*) a very large number; a multitude. **2** *chiefly literary or archaic* an army.

host[4] *or* **Host** *n* the bread consecrated in the Eucharist.

hosta *n* an Asian perennial plant of the lily family that is cultivated for its variegated foliage and spikes of lilac, mauve, or white flowers.

hostage *n* a person held captive by one party to ensure that promises are kept or demands met by another party. ✱ **hostage to fortune** a commitment that lays one open to the risk of failure, attack, etc, if things go the wrong way.

hostel *n* **1** *chiefly Brit* a supervised residential home, e.g.: **a** an establishment providing accommodation for nurses, students, etc. **b** an institution for junior offenders, ex-offenders, etc, encouraging social adaptation. **2** = YOUTH HOSTEL.

hostelling (*NAm* **hosteling**) *n* the holidaying activity of travelling from place to place staying in youth hostels. ➤➤ **hosteller** *n.*

hostelry *n* (*pl* **-ies**) an inn; a hotel.

hostess *n* **1** a woman who entertains socially or acts as host. **2a** a female employee on a ship, aeroplane, etc who attends to the needs of passengers; STEWARDESS. **b** a woman who acts as a companion to male patrons, *esp* in a nightclub; *also* a prostitute.

hostile *adj* **1** relating to or constituting an enemy. **2** antagonistic; unfriendly. **3** of a takeover: not endorsed by the company being bought. **4** of a witness: whose evidence is detrimental to the case of the party calling them. ➤➤ **hostilely** *adv.*

hostility *n* (*pl* **-ies**) **1** (*in pl*) overt acts of warfare. **2** antagonism, opposition, or resistance.

hot[1] *adj* (**hotter, hottest**) **1a** having a relatively high temperature. **b** of food: cooked in the oven, etc and served immediately. **2** uncomfortable because of surrounding heat, thick clothes, etc. **3a** of somebody's temper: easily provoked. **b** sexually aroused or sexually arousing. **4** of a taste: pungent, peppery, or spicy. **5a** of intense and immediate interest. **b** currently popular or retailing fast. **6** *informal* **a** recently stolen and too easily identifiable to dispose of easily. **b** of a person: wanted by the police. **7a** (+ on) knowledgeable about (something). **b** (+ on) strict about rules, standards, etc. **8** fancied by everyone to win. **9a** *informal* radioactive; *also* dealing with dangerously radioactive material. **b** *chiefly NAm, informal* electrically live. ✱ **have the hots for** *informal* to desire sexually. **hot under the collar** *informal* angry or irritated. **in hot water** in trouble. **make it/things hot for** *informal* to create trouble for (somebody). **not so hot/not very hot** *informal* not very good. ➤➤ **hotness** *n,* **hottish** *adj.*

hot[2] *v* (**hotted, hotting**) **1** *informal* (+ up) to heat (food, etc). **2** (+ up) to get more intensive, faster, more exciting, etc.

hot air *n informal* empty talk.

hotbed *n* **1** a bed of soil heated *esp* by fermenting manure and used for forcing or raising seedlings. **2** an environment that favours rapid growth or development, *esp* of something specified.

hot-blooded *adj* excitable; passionate. ➤➤ **hotbloodedness** *n.*

hot button *n NAm, informal* a highly sensitive issue.

hotchpotch (*NAm* **hodgepodge**) *n* a mixture composed of many unrelated parts; a jumble.

hot cross bun *n* a spicy bun leavened with yeast, with a pastry cross on top, eaten *esp* on Good Friday.

hot desking *n* in an office, etc, the system of assigning desks on a temporary or rotation system, rather than allocating them on a permanent basis to particular employees.

hotdog *v* (**hotdogged, hotdogging**) *NAm, informal* to perform stunts, *esp* while skiing, surfing, or skateboarding. ➤➤ **hotdogger** *n.*

hot dog[1] *n* **1** a frankfurter or other sausage heated and served in a bread roll. **2** *NAm, informal* a performer of skiing, surfing, or skateboarding stunts.

hot dog[2] *interj NAm, informal* an expression of admiring approval.

hotel *n* an establishment that provides meals and temporary accommodation for the public, *esp* for people travelling away from home.

hotelier *n* the proprietor or manager of a hotel.

hot flash *n NAm* = HOT FLUSH.

hot flush *n* a sudden brief flushing and sensation of heat, usu associated with an imbalance of endocrine hormones occurring *esp* at the menopause.

hotfoot[1] *adv* in haste.

hotfoot[2] ✱ **hotfoot it** *informal* to hurry.

hot gospel *n informal* zealous evangelism or revivalism, *esp* now in the form of fervent preaching with communal praying and singing. ⋙ **hot-gospeller** *n,* **hot-gospelling** *n.*

hothead *n* a hotheaded person.

hotheaded *adj* fiery; impetuous. ⋙ **hotheadedly** *adv,* **hotheadedness** *n.*

hothouse[1] *n* **1** a heated greenhouse, *esp* for tropical plants. **2** an environment that promotes rapid, *esp* over-rapid growth or development.

hothouse[2] *v* to speed up the education of (particular children), advancing them intellectually beyond the normal level for their age.

hot key *n* in computing, a key or combination of keys that has been programmed to carry out a certain series of commands.

hot line *n* a direct telephone line kept in constant readiness for immediate communication, e.g. between heads of state.

hot link *n* in computing, a HYPERLINK (shortcut to additional information in another file) in a HYPERTEXT document.

hotly *adv* in a passionate or fiery manner.

hotpants *pl n* women's very brief tight-fitting shorts that were fashionable *esp* in the early 1970s.

hot plate *n* a metal plate or spiral, usu on an electric cooker, on which food can be heated and cooked.

hot pot *n Brit* a stew of mutton, lamb, or beef and potato cooked in a casserole.

hot potato *n informal* a controversial or sensitive question or issue.

hot rod *n* a motor vehicle rebuilt or modified for high speed and fast acceleration.

hot-rod *v* (**hot-rodded, hot-rodding**) **1** to modify (a motor vehicle) for high speed and fast acceleration. **2** to drive a hot rod.

hot seat *n informal* **1** (**the hot seat**) a position involving risk, embarrassment, or responsibility for decision-making. **2** *chiefly NAm* = ELECTRIC CHAIR.

hot shoe *n* a socket in a camera for accessories, through which there is direct electrical contact with a flashgun, for flash synchronization.

hotshot *n informal* a showily successful or important person. ⋙ **hotshot** *adj.*

hot spot *n* **1** an area of potential danger, where violence may break out; a trouble spot. **2** *informal* a much-frequented nightclub or disco. **3** a local area of greater heat or greater activity.

hot stuff *n informal* **1** a description used of somebody or something of outstanding ability or quality. **2** somebody or something that is sexually exciting.

hot-tempered *adj* inclined to lose one's temper easily.

Hottentot *n offensive* see KHOIKHOI.

hot ticket *n informal* a person or thing that is very much sought after.

hotting *n Brit, informal* the act of performing dangerous manoeuvres in a stolen car.

hot-water bottle *n* a flattish rubber container that is filled with hot water and used *esp* to warm a bed.

hot-wire *v* to start (a vehicle) by bypassing the ignition switch.

Houdini *n* a term for somebody who is adroit at escaping from confinement or from desperate situations.

hoummos *n* see HUMMUS.

hound[1] *n* **1** a dog; *esp* a dog of a hunting breed that tracks prey by scent. **2** a mean or despicable person, *esp* a man. **3** an untiring enthusiast for something.

hound[2] *v* to pursue or harass persistently. ⋙ **hounder** *n.*

houndstooth check *or* **hound's-tooth check** *n* a small broken-check textile pattern.

hour *n* **1** the 24th part of a day; a period of 60 minutes. **2a** the time reckoned in hours and minutes by the clock; *esp* the beginning of each full hour. **b** a particular point in time. **3** a fixed or customary period of time set aside for a specified purpose. **4** (*in pl*) the period during which a business, etc is operational. ✱ **after/out of hours** outside normal working hours. **keep early/late hours** to get up and go to bed early or late. **on the hour** at an exact hour, *esp* every hour. **the early/small hours** the period between midnight and dawn. **till all hours** until very late at night.

hourglass *n* **1** an instrument for measuring time consisting of two glass bulbs joined by a narrow neck from the uppermost of which a quantity of sand runs into the lower in the space of an hour. **2** (*used before a noun*) describing a shapely female silhouette, with a narrow waist.

hour hand *n* the short hand that marks the hours on the face of a watch or clock.

houri *n* (*pl* **houris**) **1** any of the female virgin attendants of the blessed in the Muslim paradise. **2** a voluptuously beautiful young woman.

hourly[1] *adv* **1** at or during every hour. **2** any time now. **3** by the hour.

hourly[2] *adj* **1** occurring or done every hour. **2** constant. **3** reckoned by the hour.

house[1] /hows/ *n* (*pl* **houses** /'howziz/) **1** a building designed for people to live in. **2** (*used in combinations*) a building in which animals live or things are stored: *the henhouse; the boathouse.* **3** (*used in com-binations*) a building or establishment with a particular purpose: *an opera house.* **4a** (*used in combinations*) a specific type of business company: *a publishing house.* **b** (*used before a noun*) relating to or produced for a particular organization or establishment: *house magazine.* **5a** a legislative or deliberative assembly, *esp* as one of two chambers. **b** the building or room where such an assembly meets. **6** a community of monks or nuns, or the building they live in. **7** any of several units into which a large school may be divided for social purposes, internal competitions, etc. **8** a family, *esp* an important or ancient one. **9** the area occupied by the audience in a theatre or cinema, or the audience itself. **10** in astrology, any of the twelve equal sectors into which the celestial sphere is divided. **11** (**House**) = HOUSE MUSIC. ✱ **bring the house down** to receive rapturous applause from an audience. **get on like a house on fire** *informal* to get on very well with somebody. **go round the houses** to go by a long indirect route. **keep house** to run a household. **on the house** at the expense of an establishment or its management. **put/set one's house in order** to put one's affairs straight. ⋙ **houseful** *n,* **houseless** *adj.*

house² /howz/ *v* **1a** to provide (a person) with accommodation. **b** to provide (things) with storage space. **2** to contain (something).

house arrest *n* confinement in one's place of residence instead of prison.

houseboat *n* a moored boat that is fitted out as a home.

housebound *adj* confined to the house, e.g. because of illness.

housebreak *v chiefly NAm* = HOUSETRAIN. ➤➤ **housebroken** *adj*.

housebreaking *n* an act of breaking into and entering somebody's house with a criminal purpose. ➤➤ **housebreaker** *n*.

housecoat *n* **1** a woman's light dressing gown for wear round the house. **2** a short overall.

housefather *n* a man in charge of a group of young people living in care, e.g. in a children's home.

housefly *n* (*pl* **-ies**) a fly found in most parts of the world that frequents houses and carries disease.

household *n* (*used as sing. or pl*) a dwelling and all the people who live together in it, considered as a unit.

household cavalry *n* a cavalry regiment appointed to guard a sovereign or his or her residence.

householder *n* a person who occupies a dwelling as owner or tenant.

household name *or* **household word** *n* a person or thing that everyone has heard of.

household troops *pl n* troops appointed to guard a sovereign or his or her residence.

household word *n* see HOUSEHOLD NAME.

house-hunting *n* the activity of looking for a house or flat to buy or rent. ➤➤ **house-hunter** *n*.

house husband *n* a man who lives with his wife or partner and performs the household tasks traditionally done by the housewife.

housekeeper *n* somebody employed to take charge of the running of a house.

housekeeping *n* **1a** the day-to-day running of a house and household affairs. **b** money allotted or used for this. **2** the general management of an organization which ensures its smooth running.

houseleek *n* any of several species of Eurasian plants with pink flowers that grow *esp* on walls and roofs.

house lights *pl n* the lights that illuminate the auditorium of a theatre.

housemaid *n* a female servant employed to do housework.

housemaid's knee *n* a swelling over the knee due to an enlargement of the fluid-filled sac in the front of the kneecap.

houseman *n* (*pl* **housemen**) *Brit* a resident junior doctor in a hospital; = HOUSE OFFICER.

house martin *n* a European martin with blue-black plumage and white rump that nests on cliffs and under the eaves of houses.

housemaster *or* **housemistress** *n* a teacher in charge of a house at a boarding school.

housemother *n* a woman in charge of a group of young people living in care, e.g. in a children's home.

house mouse *n* a common grey-brown mouse that lives and breeds in and around buildings.

house music *n* pop music with a strong fast beat which is chiefly instrumental with occasional repeated phrases of song or speech.

house of assembly *n* a legislative body or the lower house of such a body in various British colonies, protectorates, countries of the Commonwealth, etc.

House of Commons *n* the lower house of the British and Canadian parliaments.

house officer *n Brit* a newly qualified doctor resident in a hospital, usu receiving training from a senior physician or surgeon by working as a member of their team.

house of God *n* a church or other place of religious worship.

house of ill fame *n* = HOUSE OF ILL REPUTE.

house of ill repute *n euphem* a brothel.

House of Keys *n* in the Isle of Man, the lower, elected house of the Manx parliament.

House of Lords *n* **1** in Britain, the upper house of Parliament. **2** in Britain, the body of Law Lords that constitutes the highest court of appeal.

House of Representatives *n* the lower house of the US Congress or Australian Parliament.

house party *n* a party lasting for a day or more, held typically at a large country house.

houseplant *n* a plant grown or kept indoors.

house-proud *adj* careful about the management and appearance of one's house.

houseroom ✱ **not give something houseroom** *Brit* not to want or not to be interested in something at all.

house-sit *v* (**house-sat, house-sitting**) to live in somebody's house and look after it while they are away. ➤➤ **house-sitter** *n*.

house sparrow *n* a brown Eurasian sparrow that lives in or near human settlements.

house style *n* the rules for punctuation, spelling, etc followed by a particular publishing house, journal, etc.

house-to-house *adj* of enquiries or searches: systematically including every house in an area.

housetop *n* a roof. ✱ **from the housetops** for all to hear; publicly.

housetrain *v chiefly Brit* to train (a pet) to defecate and urinate outdoors, or in the indoor receptacle provided. ➤➤ **housetrained** *adj*.

housewarming *n* a party to celebrate moving into a new house or premises.

housewife *n* (*pl* **housewives**) **1** a woman, usu married, who runs a house. **2** /ˈhuzif/ a small container for needlework articles, e.g. thread. ➤➤ **housewifely** *adj*, **housewifery** *n*.

house wine *n* a wine that appears unnamed on a restaurant's wine list and is sold at a lower price than those that are named.

housework *n* the work, e.g. cleaning, involved in maintaining a house.

housey-housey *n Brit, dated* = BINGO².

housing *n* **1a** houses or dwelling-places collectively. **b** the provision of these. **2** a protective cover for machinery, sensitive instruments, etc.

housing association *n Brit* a non-profitmaking society that constructs, renovates, and helps tenants to rent or buy housing.

housing estate *n Brit* a planned area of housing, *esp* one that is self-contained, with its own shops and other amenities.

hove *v* past tense and past part. of HEAVE¹.

hovel *n* a small squalid dwelling, *esp* in a poor state of repair.

hover¹ *v* **1** of a bird, insect, or helicopter: to keep itself in one place in the air. **2** to hang in the air. **3**

to linger or wait restlessly around a place. **4** to be in a state of uncertainty, irresolution, or suspense, or on the borderline between two states. ⋙ **hoverer** *n.*

hover² *n* the act or an instance of hovering.

hovercraft *n* (*pl* **hovercraft**) a vehicle supported on a cushion of air provided by fans and designed to travel over both land and sea.

hoverfly *n* (*pl* **-ies**) any of numerous species of brightly coloured flies that hover in the air.

hoverport *n* a place where passengers embark on and disembark from hovercraft.

how¹ *adv* **1** in what way or manner, or by what means. **2** used to enquire about the state of somebody's health or the state or progress of something: *How are you?* **3** (*used before an adverb or adjective*) to what extent or degree: *How seriously hurt is she?* **4** (*used before an adverb or adjective*) used intensively in exclamations: *How odd!* ✱ **and how** *informal* used for emphasis. **how about** used to make suggestions. **how come** how does it happen; why is it? **how do you do** used as a formal greeting between people meeting for the first time. **how ever** used to ask emphatically. **how much** used to ask about cost or other amounts. **how now** *archaic* used to summon, greet, or challenge. **how's that 1** used to call attention or invite comment. **2** = HOWZAT.

how² *conj* **1** introducing a clause after asking or telling verbs, etc: **a** in what manner, state, to what degree, etc: *Tell me how it's done.* **b** that: *She kept telling me how nobody understood her.* **2** as; however.

how³ *interj* used as a greeting by Native Americans, or in humorous imitation of them.

howbeit¹ *adv archaic* however.

howbeit² *conj archaic* although.

howdah *n* a canopied seat on the back of an elephant or camel.

how-do-you-do *or* **how d'ye do** *n informal* a confused or embarrassing situation.

howdy *interj chiefly NAm, informal* hello.

how d'ye do *n* see HOW-DO-YOU-DO.

however¹ *conj* **1** in whatever manner or way; as. **2** (*used esp before adjectives, adverbs, or pronouns*) no matter how.

however² *adv* **1** be that as it may; nevertheless. **2** used emphatically: = HOW¹; how ever.

howitzer *n* a short cannon usu with a medium muzzle velocity and a relatively high trajectory.

howk *v chiefly Scot* (*usu* + out) to dig (something) out.

howl¹ *v* **1** to yell or shriek long and loud e.g. with pain or laughter. **2** to cry or sob loudly and without restraint. **3** *esp* of dogs, wolves, etc: to make a loud sustained doleful cry. **4** of wind: to make a sustained wailing sound. **5** to utter with a loud sustained cry.

howl² *n* **1** a howling sound. **2** in electronics, a high-pitched sound in a loudspeaker caused by feedback.

howl down *v* to express one's disapproval of (a speaker or their views) by shouting in order to prevent them from being heard.

howler *n informal* a stupid and comic blunder.

howling *adj informal* great or extreme.

howsoever¹ *adv formal or archaic* to whatever extent.

howsoever² *conj formal or archaic* in whatever way.

howzat *interj* used in cricket as an appeal to the umpire to give the batsman out; how's that.

hoy¹ *interj* used in attracting attention or in driving animals.

hoy² *n* a small fore-and-aft rigged coaster.

hoya *n* a climbing evergreen plant with waxy flowers, native to SE Asia and cultivated as a greenhouse plant.

hoyden *or* **hoiden** *n* a boisterous girl. ⋙ **hoydenish** *adj.*

HP *abbr* **1** (*also* **hp**) high pressure. **2** (*also* **hp**) hire purchase. **3** (*also* **hp**) horsepower.

HQ *abbr* headquarters.

HR *abbr* human resources.

hr *abbr* hour.

HRH *abbr* His/Her Royal Highness.

HRT *abbr* hormone replacement therapy.

hryvna *n* the basic monetary unit of Ukraine.

Hs *abbr* the chemical symbol for hassium.

HST *abbr* high-speed train.

HTML *abbr* hypertext markup language, a system for presenting text for use on a network, e.g. the Internet, with provision for accessing related material in other parts of the network.

HTTP *abbr* hypertext transfer protocol, the system for transferring hypertext documents over the Internet.

hub *n* **1** the central part of a wheel, propeller, or fan, through which the axle passes. **2** the focal point of activity.

hubbub *n* a noisy confusion; uproar.

hubby *n* (*pl* **-ies**) *informal* one's husband.

hubcap *n* a removable metal cap placed over the hub of a wheel.

hubris *n* overweening pride, usu leading to retribution. ⋙ **hubristic** *adj.*

huckleberry *n* (*pl* **-ies**) **1** an edible dark blue or black berry that grows on an American shrub of the heath family. **2** = BLUEBERRY.

huckster¹ *n* **1** a hawker or pedlar. **2** *chiefly NAm* a person who uses aggressive methods to sell or publicize something. ⋙ **hucksterism** *n.*

huckster² *v* (**huckstered, huckstering**) *chiefly NAm* **1** to haggle. **2** to promote or advertise (something), *esp* in an aggressive or underhand manner.

huddle¹ *v* (*usu in passive*) **1** (*often* + together) to gather in a closely-packed group. **2** to curl up or crouch.

huddle² *n* **1** a closely-packed group; a bunch. **2** a secretive or conspiratorial meeting.

hue *n* **1a** the attribute of colours that permits them to be classed as red, yellow, green, blue, or an intermediate between any adjacent pair of these colours. **b** a colour or shade. **2** a complexion or aspect. ⋙ **hueless** *adj.*

hue and cry *n* **1** formerly, a cry used when in pursuit of a criminal. **2** a clamour of alarm or protest; an outcry.

huff¹ *v* **1** to emit loud puffs, e.g. of breath or steam. **2** to make empty threats. **3** in draughts, to take (an opponent's piece) as a penalty for failing to make a compulsory capture. ✱ **huffing and puffing** bluster.

huff² ✱ **in a huff** in a piqued and resentful mood.

huffish *adj* = HUFFY.

huffy *adj* (**-ier, -iest**) **1** sulky or petulant. **2** easily offended; touchy. ⋙ **huffily** *adv,* **huffiness** *n.*

hug¹ *v* (**hugged, hugging**) **1** to hold or embrace tightly in one's arms. **2** to move parallel and in close proximity to. ⋙ **huggable** *adj.*

hug² *n* a tight clasp or embrace.

huge *adj* great in size, scale, degree, or scope; enormous. ⋙ **hugely** *adv,* **hugeness** *n.*

hugely *adv* very much; enormously.

hugger-mugger[1] *n* **1** secrecy. **2** confusion or muddle.

hugger-mugger[2] *adj and adv* **1** in secrecy. **2** in confusion.

Huguenot *n* a member of the French Protestant Church, *esp* of the 16th and 17th cents. ⋙ **Huguenot** *adj,* **Huguenotic** *adj,* **Huguenotism** *n.*

huh *interj* used to express surprise, disapproval, or enquiry.

hui *n NZ* a large social or ceremonial gathering of Maoris.

hula *or* **hula-hula** *n* a Polynesian dance involving swaying of the hips.

hula hoop *n* a light plastic or cane hoop that can be made to spin round the waist by gyrating the body.

hula-hula *n* see HULA.

hulk *n* **1a** the hull of a ship that is no longer seaworthy and is used as a storehouse or, *esp* formerly, as a prison. **b** an abandoned wreck or shell, *esp* of a vessel. **2** a person, creature, or thing that is bulky or unwieldy.

hulking *adj informal* bulky; massive.

hull[1] *n* **1** the main frame or body of a ship, excluding the superstructure and fittings. **2a** the outer covering of a fruit or seed; = HUSK[1]. **b** the calyx that surrounds some fruits, e.g. the strawberry.

hull[2] *v* **1** to remove the hulls of (fruit, seeds, etc). **2** to hit or pierce the hull of (a ship). ⋙ **huller** *n.*

hullabaloo *n* (*pl* **-os**) *informal* a confused noise; uproar.

hullo *interj chiefly Brit* see HELLO.

hum[1] *v* (**hummed, humming**) **1** to utter a prolonged /m/ sound. **2** to make the characteristic droning noise of an insect in flight. **3** to sing with the lips closed and without articulation. **4** *informal* to be lively or active. **5** *informal* to have an offensive smell. ✱ **hum and haw/ha** to show indecision, or to equivocate. ⋙ **hummable** *n,* **hummer** *n.*

hum[2] *n* a humming sound.

hum[3] *interj* used to express hesitation, uncertainty, disagreement, etc.

human[1] *adj* **1** relating to or characteristic of people. **2** typical of people considered as fallible and imperfect beings. **3** having the good attributes, e.g. kindness and compassion, thought to be characteristic of people. ⋙ **humanly** *adv,* **humanness** *n.*

human[2] *n* a man, woman, or child; a person.

human being *n* = HUMAN[2].

humane *adj* **1a** marked by compassion or consideration for other human beings or animals. **b** causing the minimum pain possible. **2** characterized by broad humanistic culture; liberal. ⋙ **humanely** *adv,* **humaneness** *n.*

human interest *n* the aspect of a news story that concerns the personal experiences and feelings of individual people, readily exploitable by the media.

humanise *v* see HUMANIZE.

humanism *n* **1a** a cultural movement, dominant during the Renaissance, characterized by a revival of classical learning and a shift of emphasis from religious to secular concerns. **b** literary culture. **2** a philosophy that asserts the intrinsic worth of human beings and that usu rejects religious belief. ⋙ **humanist** *n and adj,* **humanistic** *adj,* **humanistically** *adv.*

humanitarian[1] *adj* **1** relating to the promotion of human welfare, or the relief of human suffering. **2** of a disaster: involving human suffering on a large scale.

humanitarian[2] *n* a person who promotes human welfare and social reform; a philanthropist. ⋙ **humanitarianism** *n.*

humanity *n* (*pl* **-ies**) **1** humankind. **2** the quality or state of being human. **3** the quality of being humane. **4** (*in pl*) the cultural branches of learning.

humanize *or* **-ise** *v* **1** to give (something) a human quality or character. **2** to make (a person) humane. ⋙ **humanization** *n.*

humankind *n* (*used as sing. or pl*) human beings collectively.

human nature *n* the innate and acquired behavioural patterns, motives, attitudes, ideas, etc characteristic of human beings.

humanoid[1] *adj* having human form or characteristics.

humanoid[2] *n* in science fiction, a being with human form or characteristics.

human resources *pl n* **1** (*used with a pl verb*) = PERSONNEL . **2** (*used with a sing. verb*) = PERSONNEL .

human rights *pl n* the rights to which all human beings are entitled, including the rights to liberty, freedom of speech, and equality.

humble[1] *adj* **1** having a low opinion of oneself; unassertive. **2** marked by deference or submission. **3** ranking low in a hierarchy or scale. **4** modest or unpretentious. ⋙ **humbleness** *n,* **humbly** *adv.*

humble[2] *v* **1** to make humble in spirit or manner. **2** to defeat decisively; to destroy the power, independence, or prestige of. **3** to sacrifice one's pride and abase (oneself).

humble-bee *n* = BUMBLEBEE.

humble pie ✱ **eat humble pie** to abase oneself by apologizing.

humbug[1] *n* **1** pretence or deception, *esp* of a hypocritical kind. **2** a hypocritical impostor or sham. **3** drivel or nonsense. **4** *Brit* a hard peppermint-flavoured striped sweet made from boiled sugar. ⋙ **humbuggery** *n.*

humbug[2] *v* (**humbugged, humbugging**) to deceive with a hoax.

humdinger *n informal* an excellent or remarkable person or thing.

humdrum[1] *adj* monotonous or dull.

humdrum[2] *n* (**the humdrum**) monotonous or dull people or situations.

humectant[1] *n* a substance, such as glycerin, that promotes retention of moisture.

humectant[2] *adj* promoting retention of moisture.

humerus *n* (*pl* **humeri**) the long bone of the upper arm or forelimb extending from the shoulder to the elbow.

humid *adj* containing or characterized by perceptible moisture. ⋙ **humidity** *n,* **humidly** *adv.*

humidify *v* (**-ies, -ied**) (*usu in passive*) to increase the amount of moisture in (air). ⋙ **humidification** *n,* **humidifier** *n.*

humidor *n* a case or room in which cigars or tobacco can be kept moist.

humiliate *v* to make (somebody) feel worthless or robbed of their dignity or self-respect. ⋙ **humiliation** *n.*

humility *n* the quality or state of being humble.

hummingbird *n* a tiny brightly coloured tropical American bird with a slender bill and narrow wings that beat rapidly making a humming sound.

hummock *n* a hillock. ⋙ **hummocky** *adj.*

hummus *or* **hoummous** *n* a puree made from chick-peas and sesame seed paste, served as an appetizer or salad.

humongous *or* **humungous** *adj chiefly NAm, informal* very large; huge. ⋙ **humongously** *adv.*

humor *n and v NAm* see HUMOUR[1], HUMOUR[2].

humoral *adj* relating to a bodily fluid or secretion, or to blood serum and the antibodies circulating in it.

humoresque *n* a musical composition that is whimsical or fanciful in character.

humorist *n* a person specializing in or noted for humour in speech, writing, or acting. ⋙ **humoristic** *adj.*

humorous *adj* characterized by or expressing humour. ⋙ **humorously** *adv,* **humorousness** *n.*

humour[1] (*NAm* **humor**) *n* **1a** a comic or amusing quality. **b** things that are intended to be comic or amusing; wit. **2** a state of mind; temper. **3** *dated or archaic* a liquid or secretion in an animal or plant body, *esp* any of the four fluids, bile or choler, black bile or melancholy, blood, and phlegm, regarded in medieval physiology as determining by their relative proportions a person's health and temperament. ✱ **out of humour** in a bad temper. ⋙ **humourless** *adj,* **humourlessness** *n.*

humour[2] (*NAm* **humor**) *v* to comply with the mood or wishes of.

hump[1] *n* **1** a humped or crooked back. **2** a fleshy protuberance on the back of a camel, bison, etc. **3** a mound or knoll. ✱ **get the hump** *Brit, informal* to have a fit of sulking or depression. **over the hump** *informal* past the most difficult phase. ⋙ **humped** *adj,* **humpless** *adj.*

hump[2] *v* **1** to form or curve (the back) into a hump. **2** *chiefly Brit* to carry (something cumbersome) with difficulty. **3** *coarse slang* to have sexual intercourse with.

humpback *n* = HUNCHBACK. ⋙ **humpbacked** *adj.*

humpback bridge *n Brit* a narrow bridge rising and falling steeply from a central hump.

humph *interj and n* a gruntlike sound used to express doubt or contempt.

humungous *adj* see HUMONGOUS.

humus *n* a brown or black organic soil material resulting from partial decomposition of plant or animal matter.

Hun *n* **1** a member of a nomadic Mongolian people who overran a large part of central and E Europe under Attila during the fourth and fifth cents AD. **2** (*also collectively* **the Hun**) *derog* a German; *esp* a German soldier in World War I or II. ⋙ **Hunnish** *adj.*

hunch[1] *v* **1** to assume a bent or crooked posture. **2** to arch (one's shoulders).

hunch[2] *n* a strong intuitive feeling.

hunchback *n* **1** a humped back. **2** *offensive* a person with a humped back. ⋙ **hunchbacked** *adj.*

hundred *n* (*pl* **hundreds** *or* **hundred**) **1** (**a/one hundred**) the number 100. **2** (*in pl*) the numbers 100 to 999. **3a** (**the sixteen hundreds, etc**) (*in pl*) the hundred years of a specified century. **b** the first nine years of a specified century. **4** *informal* (*in pl*) a very large number. **5** a historical subdivision of some English and American counties, with its own court. ✱ **a hundred to one** in all probability. **one/a-hundred-per-cent** with complete conviction; wholeheartedly. **twenty, etc hundred hours** a verbal representation of 20.00, etc, that is, 8.00 p.m., etc, in the 24-hour system. ⋙ **hundred** *adj,* **hundredfold** *adj and adv,* **hundredth** *adj and n.*

hundreds and thousands *pl n* tiny strips of sugar of assorted bright colours, used *esp* for cake decoration.

hundredweight *n* (*pl* **hundredweights** *or* **hundredweight**) **1** a British unit of weight equal to 112lb (about 50.80kg). **2** *NAm* a US unit of weight equal to 100lb (about 45.36kg). **3** a unit of weight equal to about 50kg.

hung *v* past tense and past part. of HANG[1]. ✱ **hung up** *informal* in a state of anxiety, *esp* of an emotional nature. **hung up on** *informal* obsessed with (somebody or something).

Usage note

hung *or* hanged? See note at HANG[1].

Hungarian *n* **1** a native or inhabitant of Hungary. **2** the Finno-Ugric language of Hungary. ⋙ **Hungarian** *adj.*

hunger[1] *n* **1a** a craving or urgent need for food. **b** the unpleasant sensation or weakened condition arising from this. **2** a strong desire; a craving.

hunger[2] *v* (**hungered, hungering**) **1** to feel or suffer hunger. **2** (+ for/after) to have an eager desire for something.

hunger strike *n* refusal, as an act of protest, to eat enough to sustain life. ⋙ **hunger-striker** *n.*

hung jury *n* a jury that fails to reach a verdict.

hung over *adj* suffering from a hangover.

hung parliament *n* a parliament in which no party holds an overall majority.

hungry *adj* (**-ier, -iest**) **1** feeling hunger. **2** characterized by or indicating hunger or longing. **3** eager or avid for something. ⋙ **hungrily** *adv,* **hungriness** *n.*

hunk *n* **1** a large lump or piece of something. **2** *informal* a sexually attractive, usu muscular man. ⋙ **hunky** *adj.*

hunker *v* **1** (*usu* + down) to squat or crouch. **2** (*usu* + down) to take refuge or hide somewhere. ⋙ **hunkered** *adj.*

hunkers *pl n informal* the haunches.

hunky-dory *adj informal* perfectly satisfying; as one would wish.

hunt[1] *v* **1a** to pursue (a wild animal) for food or enjoyment. **b** of an animal: to chase and kill (prey). **2** of the police: to pursue (a suspect, etc) with intent to capture. **3** (+ for) to attempt to find something. **4** of a device, machine, etc: to run alternately fast and slowly. ⋙ **hunting** *n.*

hunt[2] *n* **1** the act or an instance of hunting. **2a** (*used as sing. or pl*) a group of mounted hunters and their hounds. **b** the area hunted.

hunt down *v* to pursue in order to capture, attack, or kill.

hunted *adj* of somebody's look or expression: suggestive of being harried or persecuted.

hunter *n* **1a** somebody who hunts game, *esp* with hounds. **b** a fast strong horse used in hunting. **2** a watch with a hinged metal cover to protect it.

hunter-gatherer *n* in anthropology, a member of a nomadic people living by hunting, fishing, and gathering fruit, etc, as distinct from staying in one place and cultivating the soil.

hunter-killer *adj* denoting a submarine or other vessel equipped to locate and destroy enemy vessels.

hunter's moon *n* the first full moon after harvest moon.

hunting crop *n* a short riding whip with an angled handle and looped thong, used by fox-hunters.

hunting ground *n* an area of fruitful search or exploitation.

hunting pink *n* the red colour of the coats worn by fox-hunters.

Huntington's chorea *n* a hereditary fatal brain disorder that develops usu in middle age and is characterized by spasmodic movement and nervous degeneration.

hunt saboteur *n* a person who tries to disrupt fox hunts.

huntsman *n* (*pl* **huntsmen**) **1** a person who hunts. **2** a person who trains and looks after the hounds of a hunt.

hurdle[1] *n* **1** a portable framework, usu of interlaced branches and stakes, used *esp* for enclosing land or livestock. **2a** a light barrier jumped by athletes, horses, dogs, etc in certain races. **b** (*in pl, used as sing. or pl*) any of various races over hurdles. **3** a barrier, obstacle, or testing experience.

hurdle[2] *v* **1** to jump over (a barrier, etc), *esp* while running. **2** to run in hurdle races. ➤➤ **hurdler** *n*, **hurdling** *n*.

hurdy-gurdy *n* (*pl* **hurdy-gurdies**) **1** a BARREL ORGAN or other musical instrument in which the sound is produced by turning a crank. **2** a medieval stringed instrument on which music was produced by turning a wheel and pressing keys.

hurl[1] *v* **1** to throw, drive, or thrust violently somewhere. **2** (*usu* + at) to utter or shout (abuse, etc) violently at somebody. ➤➤ **hurler** *n*.

hurl[2] *n* **1** an act of hurling something somewhere. **2** *Scot* a ride in a car.

hurley *n* **1** a stick for playing the game of hurling. **2** = HURLING.

hurling *n* an Irish field game resembling hockey played between two teams of 15 players each.

hurly-burly *n* an uproar or commotion.

Huron *n* (*pl* **Huron**) a member of a confederacy of Native American tribes formerly living east of Lake Huron.

hurrah *interj* = HURRAY.

hurray *or* **hooray** *interj* used as a cheer to express joy, approval, or encouragement.

hurricane *n* a usu tropical cyclone with a wind having a speed of greater than 117km/h (73mph).

hurricane lamp *n* a candlestick or oil lamp equipped with a glass chimney to protect the flame.

hurry[1] *v* (**-ies, -ied**) **1** (*often* + up) to go somewhere, or do something, as quickly as possible. **2** (*often* + up) to make (a person or pro-cess) go faster. **3** to rush (somebody) somewhere. ➤➤ **hurried** *adj*, **hurriedly** *adv*, **hurrier** *n*.

hurry[2] *n* haste or rush. ✱ **in a hurry** in haste; rushed. **in no hurry 1** not needing to hurry. **2** *informal* reluctant to do something. **not do something in a hurry** *informal* to be unlikely or reluctant to do something.

hurt[1] *v* (**hurting**, *past tense and past part.* **hurt**) **1a** to do something that causes pain or injury to. **b** to be painful. **2** to offend or upset. **3** to damage the interests of.

hurt[2] *adj* **1** injured. **2** upset or offended.

hurt[3] *n* **1** the emotional distress caused by an unpleasant experience or somebody's cruelty. **2** *archaic* harm. **3** *archaic* a wound.

hurtful *adj* of words or behaviour: causing pain or distress; intended to hurt feelings. ➤➤ **hurtfully** *adv*, **hurtfulness** *n*.

hurtle *v* to move somewhere rapidly or precipitately.

husband[1] *n* the man to whom a woman is married. ➤➤ **husbandhood** *n*, **husbandless** *adj*, **husbandly** *adj*.

husband[2] *v* to conserve or make the most economical use of (a resource, etc). ➤➤ **husbander** *n*.

husbandman *n* (*pl* **husbandmen**) *archaic* a farmer.

husbandry *n* **1** the judicious management of resources. **2** farming, *esp* of domestic animals.

hush[1] *v* **1** to quieten (a crying baby, etc). **2** often used as an exclamation: to stop making a noise. ➤➤ **hushed** *adj*.

hush[2] *n* a silence or calm, *esp* following noise.

hush-hush *adj informal* secret or confidential.

hush money *n* money paid secretly to prevent disclosure of damaging information.

hush up *v* to keep secret or suppress.

husk[1] *n* **1** a dry or membranous outer covering, e.g. a shell or pod, of a seed or fruit. **2** a useless outer layer of something.

husk[2] *v* to strip the husk from (a fruit, seed, etc).

husky[1] *adj* (**-ier, -iest**) hoarse; breathy. ➤➤ **huskily** *adv*, **huskiness** *n*.

husky[2] *adj* (**-ier, -iest**) *informal* burly or hefty.

husky[3] *n* (*pl* **-ies**) a powerful sledge dog with a broad chest and a shaggy outer coat, native to Greenland and Labrador.

huss *n Brit* a dogfish.

hussar *n* **1** a Hungarian horseman of the 15th cent. **2** (*often* **Hussar**) a member of any of various European cavalry regiments.

Hussite *n* a member of the Bohemian religious movement led by John Huss. ➤➤ **Hussite** *adj*.

hussy *n* (*pl* **-ies**) *derog* an impudent or promiscuous woman or girl.

hustings *pl n* (*used as sing. or pl*) **1** a place where election speeches are made. **2** the proceedings of an election campaign.

Word history

Old English *hūsting* deliberative assembly, from Old Norse *hūsthing*, formed from *hūs* house + *thing* assembly. From the 12th cent. onwards *husting* or *hustings* referred to a court held in the Guildhall, London by the Lord Mayor and the Aldermen, hence to the platform on which these dignitaries sat; the current senses date from the 18th cent.

hustle[1] *v* **1** to push or convey roughly, forcibly, or hurriedly. **2** to force (somebody) into doing something. **3** *informal* to swindle or cheat (somebody) out of something. **4** to hasten or hurry. **5** *chiefly NAm* to make strenuous, often dishonest, efforts to secure money or business. **6** *chiefly NAm* to engage in prostitution. ➤➤ **hustler** *n*.

hustle[2] *n* the act or an instance of hustling.

hut *n* a small, often temporary, dwelling of simple construction. ➤➤ **hutlike** *adj*.

hutch *n* **1** a pen or cage for a small animal, e.g. a rabbit. **2** *informal, derog* a shack or shanty.

Hutu /'hoohtooh/ *n* (*pl* **Hutus** *or collectively* **Hutu** *or* **Bahutu**) a member of the Bantu-speaking people that constitute the majority of the population of Rwanda and Burundi: compare TUTSI. ➤➤ **Hutu** *adj*.

huzzah *or* **huzza** *interj* = HURRAY.

hwyl /'hooh·il/ *n Welsh* emotional intensity or passion, e.g. in speaking or recitation.

hyacinth *n* **1** a common garden plant with fragrant blue, pink, or white flowers that grow in spikes. **2** a colour varying from light violet to mid-purple. **3** = JACINTH. ⋙ **hyacinth** *adj,* **hyacinthine** *adj.*

hyaena *n* see HYENA.

hyalin *n* a clear glassy substance found in degenerating body tissues.

hyaline *adj* **1** relating to glass. **2** of biological materials or structures: transparent or nearly so; consisting of HYALIN. **3** of a mineral: glassy; vitreous.

hyalite *n* a colourless or translucent opal.

hybrid *n* **1** an offspring of two animals or plants of different races, breeds, varieties, etc, e.g. a mule. **2** something heterogeneous in origin or composition. **3** a word, e.g. *television,* made up of elements from different languages. ⋙ **hybridism** *n,* **hybridist** *n,* **hybridity** *n.*

hybridize *or* **-ise** *v* to produce, or cause to produce, hybrids; to interbreed. ⋙ **hybridization** *n,* **hybridizer** *n.*

hydr- *or* **hydro-** *comb. form* **1a** water: *hydroelectric.* **b** liquid: *hydrometer.* **2** hydrogen; containing or combined with hydrogen: *hydrocarbon.*

hydra *n* **1** a small tubular freshwater polyp with a mouth surrounded by tentacles. **2** a persistent evil that is not easily overcome.

hydrangea *n* a shrub that produces large clusters of white, pink, or pale blue flowers.

hydrant *n* a discharge pipe with a valve and nozzle from which water may be drawn from a main.

hydrate[1] /'hiedrayt/ *n* a compound formed by the union of water with another substance.

hydrate[2] /hie'drayt, 'hiedrayt/ *v* to cause (a substance) to take up or combine with water or its constituent elements. ⋙ **hydratable** *adj,* **hydration** *n,* **hydrator** *n.*

hydraulic *adj* **1a** relating to liquid, *esp* water, in motion. **b** operated by the transmission of pressure in a liquid being forced through pipes, tubes, etc. **2** of cement: hardening or setting under water. ⋙ **hydraulically** *adv.*

hydraulics *pl n* (*used as sing.*) a branch of physics that deals with the practical applications of liquid in motion.

hydride *n* a compound of hydrogen usu with a less electronegative element or radical.

hydro *n* (*pl* **-os**) *Brit* a hotel or establishment formerly providing facilities for hydropathic treatment.

hydro- *comb. form* see HYDR-.

hydrocarbon *n* an organic compound, e.g. benzene, containing only carbon and hydrogen.

hydrocephalus *or* **hydrocephaly** *n* an abnormal increase in the amount of cerebrospinal fluid within the brain cavity accompanied by enlargement of the skull and brain atrophy. ⋙ **hydrocephalic** *adj.*

hydrochloric acid *n* a solution of hydrogen chloride in water that is a strong corrosive acid and is naturally present in the gastric juice.

hydrochloride *n* a compound of hydrochloric acid, *esp* with an organic chemical base, e.g. an alkaloid.

hydrocortisone *n* a steroid hormone produced by the cortex of the adrenal gland and used *esp* in the treatment of rheumatoid arthritis.

hydrocyanic acid *n* a solution of hydrogen cyanide in water that is a highly poisonous weak acid.

hydrodynamics *pl n* (*used as sing. or pl*) a science that deals with the motion of fluids and the forces acting on solid bodies immersed in them. ⋙ **hydrodynamic** *adj,* **hydrodynamicist** *n.*

hydroelectric *adj* relating to the production of electricity by waterpower. ⋙ **hydroelectrically** *adv,* **hydroelectricity** *n.*

hydrofoil *n* **1** a ship or boat fitted with an aerofoil-like device that lifts the hull out of the water at speed. **2** the aerofoil-like device itself.

hydrogen *n* the simplest and lightest of the chemical elements, normally occurring as a highly flammable gas. ⋙ **hydrogenous** *adj.*

hydrogenate *v* to combine or treat with hydrogen. ⋙ **hydrogenation** *n.*

hydrogen bomb *n* a bomb whose enormous explosive power is due to the sudden release of atomic energy resulting from the fusion of hydrogen nuclei.

hydrogen bond *n* an electrostatic chemical bond consisting of a hydrogen atom bonded to two small electronegative atoms, e.g. oxygen or nitrogen.

hydrogen cyanide *n* **1** a poisonous gaseous compound that has the smell of bitter almonds. **2** = HYDROCYANIC ACID.

hydrogen peroxide *n* an unstable compound used *esp* as an oxidizing and bleaching agent, an antiseptic, and a rocket propellant.

hydrogen sulphide *n* an inflammable poisonous gas that has a smell of rotten eggs and is formed in putrefying matter.

hydrogeology *n* the branch of geology dealing with underground water and with the geological aspects of surface water.

hydrography *n* the description, measurement, and mapping of bodies of water, e.g. seas. ⋙ **hydrographer** *n,* **hydrographic** *adj,* **hydrographically** *adv.*

hydroid *n* any member of an order of marine invertebrates that includes the hydras and many corals. ⋙ **hydroid** *adj.*

hydrokinetic *adj* relating to the motions of liquids or the forces that produce or affect such motions. ⋙ **hydrokinetically** *adv,* **hydrokinetics** *pl n.*

hydrology *n* a science dealing with the properties, distribution, and circulation of the water of the earth's surface. ⋙ **hydrologic** *adj,* **hydrological** *adj,* **hydrologically** *adv,* **hydrologist** *n.*

hydrolyse (*NAm* **hydrolyze**) *v* to subject (a substance) to hydrolysis. ⋙ **hydrolysable** *adj.*

hydrolysis *n* chemical breakdown involving splitting of a bond and addition of the elements of water. ⋙ **hydrolytic** *adj,* **hydrolytically** *adv.*

hydrolyze *v NAm* see HYDROLYSE.

hydromassage *n* massage performed using jets of water.

hydromechanics *pl n* (*used as sing. or pl*) the mechanics of fluids; = HYDRODYNAMICS.

hydrometer *n* an instrument for determining relative densities of solutions and hence their strength. ⋙ **hydrometric** *adj,* **hydrometrical** *adj,* **hydrometry** *n.*

hydropathy *n* the use of water in treating diseases; = HYDROTHERAPY. ⋙ **hydropathic** *adj,* **hydropathically** *adv.*

hydrophilic *adj* able to dissolve in, mix with, or be wetted by water easily. ⋙ **hydrophilicity** *n.*

hydrophobia *n* **1** abnormal dread of water. **2** = RABIES.

hydrophobic *adj* **1** characteristic of or suffering from hydrophobia. **2** unable to mix with or dissolve in water. ⋙ **hydrophobicity** *n.*

hydrophone *n* an instrument for listening to sound transmitted through water.

hydroplane[1] *n* **1** a speedboat fitted with hydrofoils or a stepped bottom so that the hull is raised out of the water when moving at speed. **2** a horizontal surface on a submarine's hull, used to control movement upward or downward.

hydroplane[2] *v* **1** to skim over the water with the hull largely clear of the surface. **2** *chiefly NAm* = AQUAPLANE[2] (2). ➤➤ **hydroplaner** *n.*

hydroponics *pl n* (*used as sing. or pl*) the growing of plants in liquid, sand, or gravel containing nutrient solutions rather than soil. ➤➤ **hydroponic** *adj,* **hydroponically** *adv.*

hydrosphere *n* all the waters (liquid or frozen) at the earth's surface, including soil and ground water. ➤➤ **hydrospheric** *adj.*

hydrostatic *adj* relating to liquids at rest, or the pressure exerted by them. ➤➤ **hydrostatically** *adv,* **hydrostatics** *pl n.*

hydrotherapy *n* the use of water in the treatment of disease; *esp* treatment using exercise in heated water.

hydrothermal *adj* relating to or caused by the action of hot water, *esp* on the earth's crust. ➤➤ **hydrothermally** *adv.*

hydrous *adj* containing water (chemically combined with other atoms or molecules).

hydroxide *n* a compound of hydroxyl with an element or radical.

hydroxyl *n* the univalent group or radical OH consisting of one hydrogen atom and one oxygen atom that is characteristic of hydroxides, alcohols, etc. ➤➤ **hydroxylic** *adj.*

hyena *or* **hyaena** *n* a doglike nocturnal carnivorous mammal of Asia and Africa, with front legs longer than the rear legs, and an erect mane.

hygiene *n* conditions or practices, *esp* cleanliness, conducive to the establishment and maintenance of health.

hygienic *adj* clean and conducive to the establishment and maintenance of health. ➤➤ **hygienically** *adv.*

hygienist *n* a person who is trained in the theory and practice of hygiene.

hygrometer *n* an instrument for measuring the humidity of the atmosphere. ➤➤ **hygrometric** *adj,* **hygrometry** *n.*

hygroscope *n* an instrument that shows changes in humidity, e.g. of the atmosphere.

hygroscopic *adj* of a substance: readily taking up and retaining moisture, e.g. from the air. ➤➤ **hygroscopically** *adv,* **hygroscopicity** *n.*

hying *v* present part. of HIE.

hymen *n* a fold of mucous membrane partly closing the opening of the vagina until it is ruptured, usu on the first occurrence of sexual intercourse. ➤➤ **hymenal** *adj.*

hymeneal *adj literary* nuptial.

hymenopteran *or* **hymenopteron** *n* any of an order of highly specialized usu stinging insects including the bees, wasps, or ants, that often associate in large colonies and have usu four membranous wings. ➤➤ **hymenopteran** *adj,* **hymenopterous** *adj.*

hymn[1] *n* **1** a song of praise to God; *esp* a metrical composition that can be included in a religious service. **2** a song of praise or joy. ➤➤ **hymnic** *adj.*

hymn[2] *v* to praise or worship (somebody, *esp* God, or something) in hymns.

hymnal[1] *n* a book or a collection of church hymns.

hymnal[2] *adj* of or relating to hymns.

hymnary *n* (*pl* **-ies**) = HYMNAL[1].

hymnody *n* (*pl* **-ies**) the singing or writing of hymns. ➤➤ **hymnodist** *n.*

hyoid *adj* relating to the hyoid bone.

hyoid bone *n* a complex of joined bones situated at the base of the tongue and supporting the tongue and its muscles.

hyoscine *n* an alkaloid found in various plants of the nightshade family that has effects on the nervous system similar to those of atropine.

hyp- *prefix* see HYPO-.

hype[1] *v informal* (*also* + up) to publicize or promote (a new product, forthcoming event, etc) intensively, *esp* making extravagant or exaggerated claims for it.

hype[2] *n informal* **1** intensive advertising or publicity for something, often involving making exaggerated or misleading claims for it. **2** a swindle, deception, or hoax.

hype[3] *v informal* (+ up) to stimulate or excite (a person or group), *esp* artificially. ➤➤ **hyped-up** *adj.*

hyper *adj informal* over-excited; overwrought.

hyper- *prefix* forming words, with the meanings: **1a** excessively: *hyperactive.* **b** excessive: *hypertension.* **2** above; beyond: *hypertext.*

Usage note

hyper- *or* hypo-? *Hyper-* means 'excessively' or 'higher than normal': *hypercritical, hypersensitive*; *hypertension* is abnormally high blood pressure. *Hypo-* means 'below' or 'less than normal': a *hypodermic* needle pierces beneath the skin, *hypotension* is abnormally low blood pressure.

hyperacid *adj esp* of the stomach: secreting more acid than is normal. ➤➤ **hyperacidity** *n.*

hyperactive *adj* **1** of a child: persistently active and disinclined to rest, sometimes behaving disruptively. **2** excessively or abnormally active. ➤➤ **hyperactivity** *n.*

hyperaemia *or* **hyperemia** *n* excess of blood in a body part.

hyperbaric *adj* of or using greater than normal pressure, *esp* of oxygen. ➤➤ **hyperbarically** *adv.*

hyperbaton *n* an inversion of word order for emphatic effect, as in *Temper tantrums I can do without.*

hyperbola *n* (*pl* **hyperbolas** *or* **hyperbolae**) a plane curve generated by a point so moving that the difference of its distances from two fixed points is a constant; the intersection of a double right circular cone with a plane that cuts both halves of the cone: compare ELLIPSE, PARABOLA.

hyperbole *n* deliberate extravagant exaggeration, used for effect, as in: *wade through oceans of blood.* ➤➤ **hyperbolist** *n.*

hyperbolic[1] *adj* relating to, characterized by, or given to hyperbole. ➤➤ **hyperbolically** *adv.*

hyperbolic[2] *adj* relating to or analogous to a hyperbola.

hyperboloid *n* a surface, some plane sections of which are hyperbolas and no plane sections of which are parabolas: compare ELLIPSOID, PARABOLOID.

hyperborean[1] *adj* **1** relating to an extreme northern region. **2** relating to any of the Arctic peoples.

hyperborean[2] *n* **1** an inhabitant of a cool northern climate. **2** (**Hyperborean**) in Greek mythology, a member of a people who worshipped Apollo and lived in a sunny land beyond the north wind.

hypercorrection *n* a mistake in speech or writing resulting from an overzealous attempt to be correct or well-bred, e.g. the wrong use of the subject form in *between you and I* where the object form *you and me* is needed. ⋙ **hypercorrect** *adj.*

hypercritical *adj* excessively critical; gratuitously faultfinding.

hyperdrive *n* in science fiction, a type of rocket drive that supposedly propels spacecraft through hyperspace.

hyperemia *n* see HYPERAEMIA.

hyperglycaemia *or* **hyperglycemia** *n* excess of sugar in the blood, e.g. in diabetes mellitus. ⋙ **hyperglycaemic** *adj.*

hypericum *n* any of a genus of shrubs with yellow five-petalled flowers, including SAINT JOHN'S WORT and ROSE OF SHARON.

hyperinflation *n* very rapid growth in the rate of inflation in an economy. ⋙ **hyperinflationary** *adj.*

hyperkinetic *adj* relating to or characterized by abnormally increased, usu uncontrollable, muscular movement. ⋙ **hyperkinesis** *n.*

hyperlink *n* a link to another file or location from a HYPERTEXT document, that is activated by clicking on a highlighted word, icon, etc in the document.

hypermarket *n* a very large self-service retail store selling a wide range of household and consumer goods.

hypermedia *n* hypertext software that enables the user to combine text and graphics with audio and video on a computer.

hypermetropia *or* **hypermetropy** *n* long-sightedness: compare MYOPIA. ⋙ **hypermetropic** *adj,* **hypermetropical** *adj.*

hyperreal *adj* **1** arrestingly or startlingly real. **2** of a simulation, etc: imitating reality in an exaggerated way. **3** of art: extremely realistic. ⋙ **hyperrealism** *n,* **hyperrealistic** *adj,* **hyperreality** *n.*

hypersensitive *adj* abnormally susceptible, e.g. to a drug or antigen. ⋙ **hypersensitiveness** *n,* **hypersensitivity** *n.*

hypersonic *adj* **1** denoting a speed five times that of the speed of sound, or greater. **2** denoting sound frequencies above a thousand million hertz. ⋙ **hypersonically** *adv.*

hyperspace *n* **1** space of more than three dimensions. **2** in science fiction, a hypothetical space-time continuum allowing faster-than-light travel. ⋙ **hyperspatial** *adj.*

hypertension *n* abnormally high blood pressure, or the physiological condition accompanying it. ⋙ **hypertensive** *adj and n.*

hypertext *n* a type of computerized document that contains active cross-references, called hyperlinks, which, when activated by a mouse, transfer the reader to another part of the document or to another document.

hypertext link *n* = HYPERLINK.

hyperthermia *n* very high body temperature. ⋙ **hyperthermic** *adj.*

hyperthyroidism *n* excessive activity of the thyroid gland, or the condition of increased metabolic and heart rate, nervousness, etc resulting from it: compare HYPOTHYROIDISM. ⋙ **hyperthyroid** *adj.*

hypertonic *adj* **1** having excessive muscular tone or tension. **2** having a higher concentration than a surrounding medium or a liquid under comparison: compare HYPOTONIC, ISOTONIC. ⋙ **hypertonia** *n,* **hypertonicity** *n.*

hypertrophy *n* excessive increase in bulk of an organ or part. ⋙ **hypertrophic** *adj,* **hypertrophied** *adj.*

hyperventilate *v* to breathe excessively fast and deep, often leading to dizziness. ⋙ **hyperventilation** *n.*

hypha *n* (*pl* **hyphae**) any of the threads that make up the MYCELIUM (vegetative part) of a fungus. ⋙ **hyphal** *adj.*

hyphen[1] *n* a punctuation mark (-) used to join words to show that they are to be understood as a combination or have a syntactic relationship, or to divide a word at a line end.

hyphen[2] *v* (**hyphened, hyphening**) = HYPHENATE.

hyphenate *v* to join or separate with a hyphen. ⋙ **hyphenation** *n.*

hypn- *or* **hypno-** *comb. form* **1** sleep: *hypnagogic.* **2** hypnotism: *hypnotherapy.*

hypnagogic *or* **hypnogogic** *adj* relating to the drowsiness preceding sleep: compare HYPNOPOMPIC.

hypno- *comb form* see HYPN-.

hypnogogic *adj* see HYPNAGOGIC.

hypnopompic *adj* relating to the semiconsciousness preceding waking: compare HYPNAGOGIC.

hypnosis *n* (*pl* **hypnoses**) **1** a condition resembling sleep, induced by a person to whose suggestions the subject is then markedly susceptible. **2** = HYPNOTISM.

hypnotherapy *n* the treatment of mental or physical disease, compulsive behaviour, etc using hypnosis. ⋙ **hypnotherapist** *n.*

hypnotic[1] *adj* **1** tending to produce sleep; soporific. **2** relating to hypnosis or hypnotism. ⋙ **hypnotically** *adv.*

hypnotic[2] *n* **1** a drug or other substance that induces sleep. **2** a person or animal that is or can be hypnotized.

hypnotise *v* see HYPNOTIZE.

hypnotism *n* the act of inducing hypnosis. ⋙ **hypnotist** *n.*

hypnotize *or* **-ise** *v* **1** to induce hypnosis in. **2** to attract and hold the attention of; to fascinate. ⋙ **hypnotizable** *adj,* **hypnotization** *n.*

hypo[1] *n* sodium thiosulphate, used as a fixing agent in photography.

hypo[2] *n* (*pl* **-os**) *informal* = HYPODERMIC[2].

hypo[3] *n* (*pl* **-os**) *informal* an attack of HYPOGLYCAEMIA.

hypo[4] *adj informal* of a diabetic: suffering from HYPOGLYCAEMIA.

hypo- *or* **hyp-** *prefix* **1** under; beneath: *hypodermic.* **2** less than normal or normally: *hypotension.*

Usage note

hypo- *or* hyper-? See note at HYPER-.

hypoallergenic *adj* of cosmetics: specially formulated so as to be unlikely to cause an allergic reaction.

hypocaust *n* an ancient Roman central heating system with an underground furnace and flues.

hypochondria *n* morbid concern about one's health.

Word history

from Greek *hypochondria,* neuter pl of *hypochondrios* relating to the soft parts below the cartilaginous ribs. This area was formerly thought to be the seat of melancholy and anxiety.

hypochondriac *n* a person who is affected by hypochondria. ⋙ **hypochondriac** *adj,* **hypochondriacal** *adj.*

hypocorism *n* **1** a pet name. **2** the practice of using pet names. ⋙ **hypocoristic** *adj.*

hypocotyl *n* the part of a plant embryo or seedling below the COTYLEDON (embryonic leaf or group of leaves).

hypocrisy *n* (*pl* **-ies**) the pretence of possessing virtues, beliefs, or qualities that one does not really have, *esp* in matters of religion or morality.

hypocrite *n* a person given to hypocrisy. ⋙ **hypocritical** *adj*, **hypocritically** *adv*.

hypodermic[1] *adj* **1** relating to the parts immediately beneath the skin. **2** of a syringe or needle: used to inject drugs beneath the skin. ⋙ **hypodermically** *adv*.

hypodermic[2] *n* a hypodermic syringe, hypodermic needle, or hypodermic injection.

hypoglycaemia *or* **hypoglycemia** *n* an abnormally low amount of sugar in the blood, or the condition resulting from this, involving confusion, headache, and sometimes convulsion and coma. ⋙ **hypoglycaemic** *adj*.

hypolimnion *n* (*pl* **hypolimnia**) the cold lower layer of water in a lake, usu rich in nutrients and low in oxygen: compare EPILIMNION.

hypomania *n* a mild form of mania, often characterized by hyperactivity, overexcitement, or excessive optimism. ⋙ **hypomanic** *adj*.

hypostasis *n* (*pl* **hypostases**) **1** the settling of blood in the lower parts of an organ or body, *esp* due to impaired circulation or death. **2** the substance or essential nature of an individual. **3** in Christian theology: **a** any of the three persons of the Trinity. **b** the person of Christ, combining divine and human nature. ⋙ **hypostatic** *adj*.

hypostasize *or* **-ise** *v* to think of (a concept) as having concrete reality, or reify it. ⋙ **hypostasization** *n*.

hypostyle *n* a building that has the roof resting on a grid of columns. ⋙ **hypostyle** *adj*.

hypotension *n* abnormally low blood pressure. ⋙ **hypotensive** *adj and n*.

hypotenuse *n* the side of a right-angled triangle that is opposite the right angle.

hypothalamus *n* (*pl* **hypothalami**) a part of the brain that lies beneath the thalamus and includes centres that regulate body temperature, appetite, and other autonomic functions. ⋙ **hypothalamic** *adj*.

hypothecate *v* **1** to pledge (property) by law as security for a debt. **2** to commit (tax revenue) from a specific source to a specific purpose, e.g. revenue from road tax to road improvements. ⋙ **hypothecation** *n*.

hypothermia *n* abnormally low body temperature. ⋙ **hypothermic** *adj*.

hypothesis *n* (*pl* **hypotheses**) **1** a proposed possible explanation for a phenomenon, set of circumstances, etc; a theory. **2** a proposition assumed for the sake of argument.

hypothesize *or* **-ise** *v* **1** to propose or assume as a hypothesis. **2** to form hypotheses.

hypothetical *adj* **1** *esp* in logic, involving hypothesis or a condition. **2** relating to or depending on supposition; conjectural. ⋙ **hypothetically** *adv*.

hypothyroidism *n* deficient activity of the thyroid gland, or the condition of lowered metabolic rate, lethargy, etc resulting from this: compare HYPERTHYROIDISM. ⋙ **hypothyroid** *adj*.

hypotonic *adj* **1** having deficient muscular tone or tension. **2** having a lower concentration than a surrounding medium or a liquid under comparison: compare HYPERTONIC, ISOTONIC. ⋙ **hypotonia** *n*, **hypotonically** *adv*, **hypotonicity** *n*.

hypoventilation *n* an abnormally slow rate of breathing, with a resultant accumulation of carbon dioxide in the blood.

hypoxia *n* a deficiency of oxygen reaching the tissues of the body. ⋙ **hypoxic** *adj*.

hypsilophodont *n* a small bipedal swift-running herbivorous dinosaur of the Jurassic and Cretaceous periods.

hyraces *n* pl of HYRAX.

hyrax *n* (*pl* **hyraxes** *or* **hyraces**) a small thickset short-legged mammal with feet with soft pads and broad nails.

hyssop *n* **1** a Eurasian plant of the mint family with aromatic leaves. **2** in biblical references, a plant used in purificatory rites by the ancient Hebrews.

hysterectomy *n* (*pl* **-ies**) surgical removal of the uterus.

hysteresis *n* a delay in the production of an effect by a cause; *esp* an apparent lag in the values of resulting magnetization in a magnetic material due to a changing magnetizing force. ⋙ **hysteretic** *adj*.

hysteria *n* **1** a mental disorder marked by emotional excitability and disturbances, e.g. paralysis, of the normal bodily processes. **2** unmanageable emotional excess, *esp* fits of laughing or weeping.

hysteric[1] *n* **1** a person who suffers from hysteria. **2** (*in pl, used as sing. or pl*) an attack of hysteria, *esp* with uncontrollable laughing or crying. ✱ **in hysterics** *informal* laughing vociferously.

hysteric[2] *adj* = HYSTERICAL.

hysterical *adj* **1** relating to or associated with hysteria. **2** suffering from or as if from hysteria. **3** *informal* very funny.

Hz *abbr* hertz.

i

I[1] *or* **i** *n* (*pl* **I's** *or* **Is** *or* **i's**) **1** the ninth letter of the English alphabet. **2** the Roman numeral for one.

I[2] *pron* the word used by a person who is speaking or writing to refer to himself or herself.

I[3] *abbr* **1** Institute or Institution. **2** International. **3** Island or Isle.

I[4] *abbr* the chemical symbol for iodine.

IA *abbr* Iowa (US postal abbreviation).

IAEA *abbr* International Atomic Energy Agency.

iamb *or* **iambus** *n* (*pl* **iambs** *or* **iambuses** *or* **iambi**) a metrical foot consisting of one short or unstressed syllable followed by one long or stressed syllable.

iambic[1] *n* **1** an iamb. **2** (*in pl*) verse written in iambs.

iambic[2] *adj* denoting verse or metre that is predominantly in iambs.

iambus *n* see IAMB.

-ian *suffix* see -AN[1], -AN[2].

-iana *suffix* see -ANA.

IAP *abbr* Internet access provider.

-iasis *or* **-asis** *suffix* forming nouns, denoting: a disease or diseased condition: *psoriasis*.

IATA *abbr* International Air Transport Association.

iatrogenic *adj* of a disease or condition: induced inadvertently by medical treatment. ⋙ **iatrogenesis** *n*, **iatrogenically** *adv*, **iatrogenicity** *n*.

IB *abbr* International Baccalaureate.

IBA *abbr* Independent Broadcasting Authority.

I-beam *n* an iron or steel beam or girder that is I-shaped in cross-section.

Iberian *n* **1a** a native or inhabitant of Spain or Portugal. **b** a member of any of the peoples that, in ancient times, inhabited Spain and Portugal. **2** either of the extinct Romance or Celtic languages of the ancient Iberians. ⋙ **Iberian** *adj*.

ibex *n* (*pl* **ibexes** *or* **ibices** *or* **ibex**) a wild goat living chiefly in high mountain areas of Europe, Asia, and N Africa and having large ridged backward-curving horns.

ibid. *abbr* = IBIDEM.

ibidem *adv* in the same book, chapter, passage, etc, used to reference a work that has been previously mentioned.

ibis *n* (*pl* **ibises** *or* **ibis**) a long-legged wading bird with a long neck and a long slender downward-curving bill.

-ible *suffix* see -ABLE.

IBM *abbr* International Business Machines.

Ibo *n* see IGBO.

IBS *abbr* irritable bowel syndrome.

ibuprofen *n* a synthetic drug that is used to relieve pain and reduce inflammation.

IC *n* **1** integrated circuit. **2** internal-combustion.

i/c *abbr* **1** in charge (of). **2** internal-combustion.

-ic[1] *suffix* forming adjectives from nouns, with the meanings: **1** having the character or form of: *panoramic*; *runic*. **2a** characteristic of or associated with: *Homeric*; *quixotic*. **b** related to, derived from, or containing: *alcoholic*. **3** affected with: *allergic*. **4** characterized by; producing: *analgesic*. **5** having a valency relatively higher than in compounds or ions named with an adjective ending in *-ous*: *ferric*; *mercuric*. ⋙ **-ically** *suffix*.

-ic[2] *suffix* forming nouns, denoting: **1** a person having a given character or nature: *fanatic*. **2** a person affected by something: *alcoholic*. **3** something that produces an effect: *emetic*.

-ical *suffix* forming adjectives from nouns with meanings similar to those of -IC[1]. ⋙ **-ically** *suffix*.

-ically *suffix* see -IC[1], -ICAL.

ICBM *abbr* intercontinental ballistic missile.

ICC *abbr* International Cricket Council.

ice[1] *n* **1a** frozen water. **b** a sheet, stretch, or covering of ice. **c** a substance reduced to a solid state by cold. **2** a frozen dessert such as ICE CREAM or WATER ICE. **3** *informal* a diamond or diamonds. ✱ **on ice** in abeyance; in reserve for later use. **on thin ice** perilously close to doing or saying something that will lead to trouble, danger, etc. ⋙ **iceless** *adj*.

ice[2] *v* **1** to cover (e.g. a cake) with icing or with something similar. **2a** to convert (something) into ice. **b** to supply or chill (e.g. a drink) with ice. **3** (*often* + over/up) to become covered or clogged with ice. **4** *chiefly NAm, informal* to kill (somebody), *esp* to murder (them).

ice age *n* **1** a time of widespread glaciation. **2** (**the Ice Age**) the Pleistocene glacial epoch.

ice axe *n* a combination pick and adze with a spiked handle used in climbing on snow or ice.

ice bag *n* = ICE PACK (2).

ice beer *n* a type of lager with a high alcohol content that is brewed at very low temperatures.

iceberg *n* **1** a large floating mass of ice detached from a glacier. **2** *chiefly NAm, informal* an emotionally cold person. ✱ **the tip of an/the iceberg** the small visible or known part of something much larger, *esp* something that is potentially troublesome, problematic, etc.

iceberg lettuce *n* a variety of lettuce with a round head of crisp close-packed leaves.

iceblink *n* a glare in the sky over a sheet of ice, caused by the reflection of light.

icebox *n* **1** *Brit* the freezing compartment of a refrigerator. **2** *NAm* a refrigerator. **3** a container that is chilled by means of ice, used for keeping food and drink, etc cold.

icebreaker *n* **1** a ship equipped to make and maintain a channel through ice. **2** something or somebody that breaks down feelings of reserve, awkwardness, or formality in a social situation.

ice cap *n* a permanent cover of ice over an area of land such as the peak of a mountain or a polar region of a planet.

ice cream *n* a sweet flavoured frozen food made from milk, cream, or custard.

ice dancing *n* a form of ice skating with movements based on those of ballroom dancing. ⋙ **ice dance** *n*, **ice dancer** *n*.

ice field *n* **1** an extensive sheet of sea ice. **2** a flat expanse of ice covering an area of land.

ice floe *n* a sheet of floating ice, *esp* on the sea.

ice hockey *n* a game resembling hockey played on an ice rink by two teams of six players who try to drive a PUCK[1] into the opposing side's goal.

ice house *n esp* formerly, a building in which ice is made or stored.

Icelander *n* a native or inhabitant of Iceland.

Icelandic *n* the N Germanic language of the people of Iceland. ⋙ **Icelandic** *adj*.

ice lolly *n Brit* a shaped portion of ice cream or, more usually, a flavoured piece of ice on a stick.

Iceni /ie'seenie/ *pl n* an ancient British people whose lands were in East Anglia and rebelled against the Romans under Boudicca (Boadicea).

ice pack *n* **1** an expanse of PACK ICE. **2** a bag of ice for applying cold to a part of the body, e.g. to reduce swelling or lower temperature.

ice pick *n* **1** a spiked hand tool for chipping ice off a larger block. **2** a small pick used by mountaineers for splitting ice.

ice skate *n* a shoe with a metal runner attached for skating on ice.

ice-skate *v* to glide over ice wearing ice skates, *esp* as a sport or pastime. ⋙ **ice skater** *n*, **ice skating** *n*.

IChemE *abbr* Institute of Chemical Engineers.

I Ching *n* an ancient Chinese book mainly used for divination by means of 64 hexagrams that are believed to provide information that can be interpreted to answer questions relevant to everyday life and future events.

ichneumon *n* **1** any of numerous species of four-winged insects with long antennae, whose larvae are parasites of other insect larvae, *esp* caterpillars. **2** a large mongoose that lives in Africa and southern Europe and has grey fur with black tail tufts.

ichor *n* **1** *archaic* a thin watery or blood-tinged discharge. **2** a fluid that flowed like blood in the veins of the ancient Greek gods. ⋙ **ichorous** *adj*.

ichthyology *n* the branch of zoology that deals with fish. ⋙ **ichthyological** *adj*, **ichthyologically** *adv*, **ichthyologist** *n*.

ichthyosaur *or* **ichthyosaurus** *n* any of various extinct marine reptiles with fish-shaped bodies, paddle-like flippers, and long snouts. ⋙ **ichthyosaurian** *adj and n*.

ICI *abbr* Imperial Chemical Industries.

-ician *suffix* forming nouns, denoting: a specialist in or practitioner of a specified subject or occupation: *beautician*; *technician*.

icicle *n* a hanging tapering mass of ice formed by the freezing of dripping water.

icing *n* **1** *chiefly Brit* a sweet, creamy or hard decorative coating for cakes, biscuits, etc, usu made with icing sugar and water, butter, or egg white. **2** the formation of ice, e.g. on a ship in freezing conditions. ✱ **the icing on the cake** a desirable but inessential addition.

icing sugar *n chiefly Brit* finely powdered sugar used in making icing and sweets.

icky *adj* (**-ier, -iest**) *informal* **1** disgustingly sticky. **2** cloying; sentimental. ⋙ **ickiness** *n*.

icon *n* **1** (*also* **ikon**) a religious image, e.g. of Christ, the Virgin Mary, or a saint, typically painted on a small wooden panel and used as an aid to devotion in the Eastern Orthodox churches. **2** a pictorial representation; an image or symbol. **3** somebody who is an object of uncritical devotion; an idol. **4** in computing, a picture or symbol displayed on a screen to show a program option or a facility available to the user. ⋙ **iconic** *adj*, **iconically** *adv*, **iconicity** *n*.

iconify *v* (**-ies, -ied**) in computing, to reduce a screen window to an icon.

iconoclast *n* **1** a person who attacks established beliefs or institutions. **2** a person who destroys religious images or opposes their veneration. ⋙ **iconoclasm** *n*, **iconoclastic** *adj*, **iconoclastically** *adv*.

iconography *n* (*pl* **-ies**) **1** pictorial material relating to or illustrating a subject. **2** the traditional or conventional images or symbols associated with a subject, *esp* a religious or legendary subject. **3** the imagery or symbolism of a work of art, an artist, or a body of art, or the use of such imagery or symbolism. ⋙ **iconographer** *n*, **iconographic** *adj*, **iconographical** *adj*, **iconographically** *adv*.

iconology *n* the study of icons or of artistic symbolism. ⋙ **iconological** *adj*, **iconologist** *n*.

iconostasis *n* (*pl* **iconostases**) a screen or partition with doors and tiers of icons separating the sanctuary from the nave in Eastern churches.

icosahedron *n* (*pl* **icosahedrons** *or* **icosahedra**) a polyhedron with 20 faces, *esp* one with equal triangular faces. ⋙ **icosahedral** *adj*.

-ics *suffix* forming plural nouns, denoting: **1** a branch of study, knowledge, skill, or practice: *linguistics*. **2** actions or mode of behaviour: *histrionics*; *acrobatics*. **3** operations or phenomena relating to something: *mechanics*.

ICU *abbr* intensive care unit.

icy *adj* (**-ier, -iest**) **1a** covered with, full of, or consisting of ice. **b** intensely cold. **c** resembling ice. **2** characterized by personal coldness; hostile. ⋙ **icily** *adv*, **iciness** *n*.

ID[1] *abbr* **1** Idaho (US postal abbreviation). **2** identification. **3** identity.

ID[2] *v* (**IDs, IDed, IDing**) *informal* to identify or check the identity of.

Id *n* = EID.

I'd *contr* **1** I had. **2** I should. **3** I would.

id *n* in psychoanalytic theory, the division of the mind that is completely unconscious and is the source of psychic energy derived from instinctual needs and drives: compare EGO, SUPEREGO.

id. *abbr* = IDEM.

-id *suffix* see -IDE.

-ide *or* **-id** *suffix* forming nouns, denoting: **1** a binary chemical compound: *sulphide*. **2** a chemical compound derived from a specified compound: *glucoside*. **3** a member of a class of related compounds or elements: *lanthanide*.

idea *n* **1a** a thought, concept, or image actually or potentially present in the mind. **b** a formulated thought or opinion. **2** a belief. **3** an indefinite or vague impression. **4** a plan of action. **5** an individual's conception of the perfect or typical example of something specified. **6** the central meaning or aim of a particular action or situation. ✱ **get ideas** to have inappropriate, undesirable, or unrealistic desires or expectations. **give somebody ideas** to cause somebody to get ideas. **have no idea** not to know at all. **that's the idea** *informal* that's right. **the very idea!** *informal* that is ridiculous, unreasonable, etc. ➤➤ **idealess** *adj.*

idea hamster *n informal* a creative person who has many new ideas.

ideal[1] *n* **1** a principle or standard of moral, aesthetic, etc excellence to be aspired to. **2** a person or thing that embodies such a standard or is regarded as perfect.

ideal[2] *adj* **1a** perfect. **b** embodying an ideal. **2** existing only in the mind, *esp* as an ideal that cannot be found in real life. **3** relating to or constituting mental images, ideas, or conceptions. ➤➤ **idealness** *n.*

idealise *v* see IDEALIZE.

idealism *n* **1** the practice of living according to one's ideals. **2** the representation of things in ideal forms. **3** in philosophy, a theory that material objects have no reality and only mental acts, perceptions, sensations, and ideas, can truly be said to exist. ➤➤ **idealist** *n,* **idealistic** *adj,* **idealistically** *adv.*

idealize *or* **idealise** *v* **1** to attribute qualities of excellence or perfection to. **2** to represent in an ideal form. ➤➤ **idealization** *n,* **idealizer** *n.*

ideally *adv* **1** in accordance with an ideal; perfectly. **2** for best results.

idée fixe /ˌeeday 'feeks/ *n* (*pl* **idées fixes**) a fixed or obsessive idea.

idem /'idem, 'iedem/ *pron* the same, used in citations to indicate that a book, author, etc is the same as the one just mentioned.

identical *adj* **1** the very same: *the identical place we stopped at before.* **2** (*often* + to/with) being very similar or exactly alike: *wearing identical green outfits.* **3** of twins, triplets, etc: derived from a single ovum and therefore very similar in appearance: compare FRATERNAL (2). ➤➤ **identically** *adv.*

identification *n* **1** the act or process of identifying or being identified. **2** evidence of identity.

identification parade *n chiefly Brit* a line-up of people arranged by the police to see whether a witness can identify a suspect.

identify *v* (**-ies, -ied**) **1a** to establish the identity of. **b** to discover by observation or analysis. **2a** to consider (two or more things) to be identical. **b** (+ with) to equate or link (somebody, oneself, or something) with another person or thing. **3** (*usu* + with) to consider that one shares the same qualities or experiences as somebody else. ➤➤ **identifiable** *adj,* **identifiably** *adv,* **identifier** *n.*

Identikit[1] *n* **1** *trademark* a set of alternative facial features used by the police to build up a likeness, *esp* of a suspect, using witnesses' descriptions. **2** a likeness constructed in this way.

Identikit[2] *adj* **1** of a picture of a suspect, etc: produced by Identikit. **2** (*usu* **identikit**) like many others of the same type.

identity *n* (*pl* **-ies**) **1a** who or what somebody or something is. **b** the individual characteristics that define a person or thing or by which a person or thing can be recognized. **2** the condition of being exactly alike; sameness. **3a** an algebraic equation that remains true whatever values are substituted for the symbols, e.g. $(x+y)^2 = x^2 + 2xy + y^2$. **b** = IDENTITY OPERATION. **c** = IDENTITY ELEMENT.

identity element *n* in mathematics, an element that leaves any element of the set to which it belongs unchanged when combined with it by a specified mathematical operation.

identity operation *n* a mathematical operation involving the combination of an identity element with another element in the same set.

identity parade *n* = IDENTIFICATION PARADE.

identity theft *n* the fraudulent use of another person's personal data, such as a bank account number, credit card number, PIN number, or telephone number, especially in order to purchase goods and services at their expense: compare SHOULDER SURFING.

ideogram *n* a symbol used to represent a thing or idea, e.g. (&) or (+). ➤➤ **ideogrammatic** *adj,* **ideogrammic** *adj.*

ideograph *n* = IDEOGRAM. ➤➤ **ideographic** *adj,* **ideographically** *adv.*

ideologue *n* **1** a strong advocate or adherent of a particular ideology. **2** a theorist, *esp* one who shows little concern for practicalities.

ideology *n* (*pl* **-ies**) **1** a systematic body of ideas underlying a social, political, or cultural programme. **2** a manner of thinking characteristic of an individual, group, or culture. ➤➤ **ideological** *adj,* **ideologically** *adv,* **ideologist** *n.*

ides *pl n* (*used as sing. or pl*) in the ancient Roman calendar, the 15th day of March, May, July, or October or the 13th day of any other month, or the week preceding any of these dates: compare CALENDS, NONES.

idiocy *n* (*pl* **-ies**) **1** foolishness. **2** something notably stupid or foolish.

idiolect *n* the language or speech pattern of an individual. ➤➤ **idiolectal** *adj,* **idiolectic** *adj.*

idiom *n* **1** an expression that has become established in a language and that has a meaning that cannot be derived from the meanings of its individual elements, e.g. *have bats in one's belfry* meaning to be mad or eccentric. **2a** the language peculiar to a people or to a district, community, or class. **b** the syntactic, grammatical, or structural form peculiar to a language. **3** a characteristic style or form of artistic expression.

idiomatic *adj* denoting, relating, or conforming to idioms or an idiom. ➤➤ **idiomatically** *adv,* **idiomaticity** *n.*

idiosyncrasy *n* (*pl* **-ies**) **1** a characteristic of thought or behaviour peculiar to an individual or group; an eccentricity. **2** characteristic peculiarity of habit or structure. ➤➤ **idiosyncratic** *adj,* **idiosyncratically** *adv.*

idiot *n* **1** a silly or foolish person. **2** *dated* a person with severe learning difficulties. ➤➤ **idiotic** *adj,* **idiotically** *adv.*

idiot savant /ˌidi·ət 'savənt/ *n* (*pl* **idiots savants** *or* **idiot savants**) a person who is considered to have a psychological or psychiatric disorder or some form of learning difficulty but who also exhibits exceptional skill or brilliance in some field.

idle[1] *adj* (**idler, idlest**) **1a** not occupied or employed. **b** not in use or operation. **2** lazy. **3** having no particular purpose or value: *idle curiosity.* **4** groundless: *idle rumour.* **5** without force or effect: *idle threats.* ➤➤ **idleness** *n,* **idly** *adv.*

idle[2] *v* **1** to spend time doing nothing. **2** *esp* of an engine: to run without being connected to the part, e.g. the wheels of a car, that is driven, so that no useful work is done. ⋙ **idler** *n.*

idol *n* **1a** an image or representation, e.g. of a god, used as an object of worship. **b** a false god. **2** an object of passionate or excessive devotion.

idolatry *n* **1** the worship of an idol or idols. **2** excessive attachment or devotion to something. ⋙ **idolater** *n,* **idolatrous** *adj,* **idolatrously** *adv,* **idolatrousness** *n.*

idolize *or* **idolise** *v* to love or admire to excess. ⋙ **idolization** *n,* **idolizer** *n.*

idyll *or* **idyl** *n* **1** a time or situation of peace and happiness. **2** a simple work in poetry or prose describing peaceful rustic life or pastoral scenes. ⋙ **idyllic** *adj,* **idyllically** *adv.*

i.e. *abbr* that is to say.

-ie *suffix* see -Y[4].

IF *abbr* intermediate frequency.

if[1] *conj* **1a** in the event that. **b** supposing. **c** on condition that. **2** whether. **3** used to introduce an exclamation expressing a wish: *If only you'd waited!* **4** even if; although. **5** used after expressions of emotion: that: *I don't care if she is cross!* **6** used to introduce expressions, usu in the negative, of surprise, dismay, etc: *Blow me if he didn't hand in his notice right there and then.* ✱ **if anything** used to suggest tentatively or tactfully that something is or could be the case: *It's if anything a bit too colourful.* **if not 1** if that is not so. **2** perhaps to the point of being: *It was unwise, if not downright idiotic.*

Usage note

if *and* **whether.** *If* and *whether* can often be used interchangeably: *He asked if* (or *whether*) *he could come too. Whether* should be preferred in more formal writing, however, and where using *if* could be ambiguous. *Let me know if he calls* could mean 'tell me that he's calling, when and if he calls' or 'tell me (afterwards) whether he called or not'.

if[2] *n* **1** a condition or stipulation. **2** a supposition.

IFA *abbr* independent financial adviser.

-iferous *comb. form* see -FEROUS.

iffy *adj* (**-ier, -iest**) *informal* **1** full of uncertainties. **2** of doubtful probability, legality, or morality. ⋙ **iffiness** *n.*

-ify *suffix* see -FY.

Igbo *n* (*pl* **Igbos** *or* **Igbo**) **1** a member of an indigenous people inhabiting southeastern Nigeria. **2** (*usu* **Igbo**) the Kwa language spoken by this people. ⋙ **Igbo** *adj.*

igloo *n* (*pl* **igloos**) an Inuit dwelling, usu made of snow blocks and in the shape of a dome.

igneous *adj* of rocks: formed by the flow or solidification of molten rock from the earth's core.

ignite *v* **1a** to set fire to, or to catch fire. **b** to cause (a fuel mixture) to burn. **2a** to arouse (an emotion, *esp* passion). **b** to cause or start (e.g. a riot or protest), *esp* suddenly. ⋙ **ignitability** *n,* **ignitable** *adj,* **igniter** *n.*

ignition *n* **1** the act or an instance of igniting or the state of being ignited. **2a** the process of igniting a fuel mixture, e.g. in an internal-combustion engine. **b** a device that effects this.

ignoble *adj* **1** base; dishonourable. **2** *formal* of low birth or humble origin. ⋙ **ignobility** *n,* **ignobleness** *n,* **ignobly** *adv.*

ignominious *adj* **1** marked by or causing disgrace or discredit. **2** humiliating; degrading. ⋙ **ignominiously** *adv,* **ignominiousness** *n.*

ignominy *n* (*pl* **-ies**) deep personal humiliation and disgrace, or a cause of this.

ignoramus *n* (*pl* **ignoramuses**) an ignorant or stupid person.

ignorant *adj* **1** having or showing a general lack of knowledge or education. **2** (*often* + of) uninformed about or unaware of a specified subject, etc. **3** *chiefly informal* lacking social training; impolite. ⋙ **ignorance** *n,* **ignorantly** *adv.*

ignore *v* to refuse or fail to take notice of; to disregard deliberately. ⋙ **ignorable** *adj,* **ignorer** *n.*

iguana *n* a large plant-eating, usu dark-coloured, tropical American lizard with a serrated or spiny crest on its back.

iguanodon *n* a large long-tailed plant-eating dinosaur from the late Jurassic and early Cretaceous periods.

IHS *abbr* used as a Christian symbol and monogram to indicate Jesus.

ikat *n* **1** a fabric, traditionally made in Asia, in which the threads are tied and dyed before weaving, so that a distinctive blurred pattern is produced. **2** the technique of producing such fabric.

ikebana *n* the Japanese art of flower-arranging that emphasizes form and balance in accordance with strict rules.

ikon *n* see ICON (1).

IL *abbr* Illinois (US postal abbreviation).

il- *prefix* see IN-[1], IN-[2].

-il *suffix* see -ILE.

ilang-ilang *n* see YLANG-YLANG.

-ile *or* **-il** *suffix* **1** forming adjectives and nouns, denoting: a part or relationship: *percentile.* **2** forming adjectives, with the meaning: denoting, relating to, capable of, etc: *fragile.*

ilea *n* pl of ILEUM.

ileum *n* (*pl* **ilea**) the last division of the small intestine extending between the jejunum and the caecum. ⋙ **ileac** *adj,* **ileal** *adj.*

ilex *n* (*pl* **ilexes**) **1** = HOLM OAK. **2** any of a genus of trees or shrubs including the holly.

ilia *n* pl of ILIUM.

ilium *n* (*pl* **ilia**) the uppermost and largest of the three principal bones that form either half of the pelvis.

ilk *n* sort or kind. ✱ **of that ilk** *chiefly Scot, dated* from or of the place or landed estate of the same name (as that of the person mentioned).

I'll *contr* I will or I shall.

ill[1] *adj* **1a** not in good health. **b** nauseated. **2** causing discomfort or inconvenience; disagreeable: *ill effects.* **3** malevolent; hostile. **4** unlucky or disadvantageous. **5** harsh. ✱ **ill at ease** uneasy or uncomfortable. **take it ill** to resent something.

ill[2] *adv* (**worse, worst**) (*often used in combinations*) **1** hardly; scarcely: *can ill afford.* **2a** in an unfortunate manner; badly or unluckily. **b** in a faulty, imperfect, or unpleasant manner. **3** unfavourably; critically.

ill[3] *n* **1a** an ailment or illness. **b** misfortune or trouble, or a misfortune or trouble. **2** the opposite of good; evil.

ill-advised *adj* **1** unwise. **2** showing lack of proper thought or planning or sound advice. ⋙ **ill-advisedly** *adv.*

ill-assorted *adj* not matching or not well matched; incompatible.

ill-bred *adj* having or showing bad upbringing; impolite. ⋙ **ill-breeding** *n.*

ill-considered *adj* = ILL-ADVISED.

ill-disposed *adj* (*often* + to/towards) unfriendly; unsympathetic.

illegal[1] *adj* **1** not authorized by law. **2** contrary to established rules, e.g. of a game. ⋙ **illegality** *n*, **illegally** *adv*.

illegal[2] *n chiefly NAm* an illegal immigrant.

illegible *adj* of handwriting, printed text, etc: unable to be read or deciphered. ⋙ **illegibility** *n*, **illegibly** *adv*.

illegitimate *adj* **1** illegal; not allowed by law or rules. **2** of a child: born to parents who are not lawfully married to each other. **3** wrongly deduced or inferred. ⋙ **illegitimacy** *n*, **illegitimately** *adv*.

ill-fated *adj* suffering, leading to, or destined for misfortune; unlucky.

ill-favoured (*NAm* **ill-favored**) *adj* **1** unattractive in physical appearance. **2** offensive; objectionable.

ill-gotten *adj* acquired by illicit or improper means.

ill humoured *adj* surly; irritable; bad-tempered. ⋙ **ill humour** *n*.

illiberal *adj* **1** of a person, views, attitude, etc: **a** not broad-minded; bigoted. **b** opposed to liberalism. **2** not generous; mean. ⋙ **illiberalism** *n*, **illiberality** *n*, **illiberally** *adv*, **illiberalness** *n*.

illicit *adj* not permitted by law, rules, or custom. ⋙ **illicitly** *adv*, **illicitness** *n*.

Usage note

illicit *or* elicit? See note at ELICIT.

illimitable *adj* without limits; measureless. ⋙ **illimitability** *n*, **illimitableness** *n*, **illimitably** *adv*.

illiterate[1] *adj* **1** unable to read or write. **2** showing a lack of education, e.g. by the use of poor grammar and spelling. **3** showing a lack of knowledge in a particular field. ⋙ **illiteracy** *n*, **illiterately** *adv*, **illiterateness** *n*.

illiterate[2] *n* an illiterate person.

ill-mannered *adj* having bad manners. ⋙ **ill-manneredly** *adv*, **ill-manneredness** *n*.

ill-natured *adj* having or showing a disagreeable disposition; surly. ⋙ **ill-naturedly** *adv*, **ill-naturedness** *n*.

illness *n* **1** a disease, period of sickness, or other indisposition. **2** an unhealthy condition of the body or mind.

illogical *adj* **1** contrary to the principles of logic. **2** devoid of logic; senseless. ⋙ **illogicality** *n*, **illogically** *adv*, **illogicalness** *n*.

ill-starred *adj* ill-fated; unlucky.

ill-tempered *adj* bad-tempered; surly. ⋙ **ill-temperedly** *adv*, **ill-temperedness** *n*.

ill-timed *adj* badly timed; inopportune.

ill-treat *v* to treat cruelly or improperly. ⋙ **ill-treatment** *n*.

illuminance *n* the amount of light per unit area of a surface on which it falls.

illuminate *v* **1a** to cast light on; to fill (e.g. a place) with light. **b** to decorate (e.g. a building) with lights. **2** to decorate (a manuscript) with elaborate initial letters or marginal designs in gold, silver, and brilliant colours. **3** to elucidate or clarify (something). ⋙ **illuminating** *adj*, **illuminatingly** *adv*, **illuminative** *adj*, **illuminator** *n*.

illuminati *pl n* (*sing.* **illuminato**) **1** people who are or claim to be unusually enlightened. **2** (**Illuminati**) any of various groups claiming special religious enlightenment.

illumination *n* **1** the act or an instance of illuminating or the state of being illuminated. **2** (*also in pl*) decorative lighting or lighting effects.

illuminato *n* sing. of ILLUMINATI.

illumine *v literary* to illuminate. ⋙ **illuminable** *adj*..

ill-use *v* to treat (somebody or something) harshly or unkindly. ⋙ **ill-usage** *or* **ill-use** *n*.

illusion *n* **1a** a false impression or belief. **b** something that deceives or misleads intellectually. **2** a misleading image presented to the vision. ✱ **be under the illusion that** to have the mistaken belief that. ⋙ **illusional** *adj*.

illusionism *n* the use of perspective or shading to create the illusion of reality, *esp* in a work of art.

illusionist *n* a conjuror or magician. ⋙ **illusionistic** *adj*.

illusive *adj chiefly literary* deceptive; illusory. ⋙ **illusively** *adv*, **illusiveness** *n*.

illusory *adj* deceptive; unreal. ⋙ **illusorily** *adv*, **illusoriness** *n*.

illustrate *v* **1** to provide (e.g. a book) with pictures or other visual material. **2** to clarify, explain, or demonstrate (something), *esp* by using examples, analogy, etc. **3** to be an example of. ⋙ **illustrator** *n*.

illustration *n* **1a** a picture or diagram that helps to make something clear or attractive. **b** something such as an example, analogy, etc that explains or clarifies something. **2** the act or an instance of illustrating or the fact of being illustrated. ⋙ **illustrational** *adj*.

illustrative *adj* serving or intended to illustrate. ⋙ **illustratively** *adv*.

illustrious *adj* **1** admired and well-known, *esp* for something done in the past; eminent. **2** of an action, etc: impressive and publicly acclaimed. ⋙ **illustriously** *adv*, **illustriousness** *n*.

ill will *n* unfriendly feeling; animosity or enmity.

I'm *contr* I am.

im- *prefix* see IN-[1], IN-[2].

i-mag /'iemag/ *n* a magazine published on the Internet.

image[1] *n* **1a** exact likeness. **b** a person who strikingly resembles another specified person. **2a** a reproduction, e.g. a portrait or statue, of the form of a person or thing. **b** an idol. **3a** the optical counterpart of an object produced by a lens, mirror, etc or an electronic device. **b** a likeness of an object produced on a photographic material. **4a** a mental picture of something not actually present. **b** an idea or concept. **5** a conception created in the minds of people, *esp* the general public. **6** a figure of speech, *esp* a metaphor or simile. ⋙ **imageless** *adj*.

image[2] *v* **1** to form an image of (somebody or something) in one's mind. **2a** to create a representation of. **b** to represent symbolically. ⋙ **imageable** *adj*.

image enhancement *n* a method of improving the definition of a picture by means of a computer program which detects and amplifies strong changes in contrast, so making images sharper.

imagery *n* (*pl* **-ies**) **1a** figurative language. **b** visual symbols. **2** mental images, *esp* the products of imagination.

imaginable *adj* capable of being thought of or believed. ⋙ **imaginably** *adv*.

imaginary *adj* **1** existing only in imagination; lacking factual reality. **2** in mathematics, expressed in terms of or relating to the square root of minus one. ⋙ **imaginarily** *adv*, **imaginariness** *n*.

imaginary number *n* = COMPLEX NUMBER.

imagination *n* **1** the act or power of forming a mental image of something not present to the senses or never before wholly perceived in reality.

2a creative ability. **b** resourcefulness; inventiveness.

imaginative *adj* **1** of or characterized by imagination. **2a** creative. **b** resourceful; inventive. **3** given to imagining; having a lively imagination. ⪢ **imaginatively** *adv,* **imaginativeness** *n.*

imagine *v* **1** to suppose or think. **2** to believe (something) without sufficient basis. **3** to form a mental image of (something not present). ⪢ **imaginer** *n.*

imagines *n* pl of IMAGO.

imagism *or* **Imagism** *n* a 20th-cent. movement in poetry advocating the expression of ideas and emotions through clear precise images. ⪢ **imagist** *n and adj,* **imagistic** *adj,* **imagistically** *adv.*

imago *n* (*pl* **imagoes** *or* **imagines**) **1** an insect in its final mature state. **2** in psychoanalysis, a subconscious idealized mental image of a person, *esp* a parent, seen as having an influence on a person's behaviour.

imam *n* **1** the leader of prayer in a mosque: compare MUEZZIN. **2** (**Imam**) a leader held by Shiite Muslims to be a divinely appointed successor of Muhammad. ⪢ **imamate** *n.*

IMAX *n trademark* a system for projecting cinematic film that gives images approximately ten times larger than those of standard 35mm film.

imbalance *n* **1** lack of functional balance. **2** a lack of proportion or numerical balance.

imbecile[1] *n* **1** *informal* a fool or idiot. **2** *dated* a person of very low intelligence. ⪢ **imbecilic** *adj,* **imbecilically** *adv,* **imbecility** *n.*

imbecile[2] *adj informal* very stupid. ⪢ **imbecilely** *adv.*

imbed *v* see EMBED.

imbibe *v* **1** *chiefly formal or humorous* **a** to drink (*esp* alcohol). **b** to take in (something) as if drinking it. **2** to receive (e.g. ideas) into the mind and retain them; to assimilate. ⪢ **imbiber** *n.*

imbricate *adj* **1** having scales, sepals, etc that overlap each other in regular order. **2** overlapping. ⪢ **imbricately** *adv,* **imbrication** *n.*

imbroglio *n* (*pl* **-os**) **1** an intricate or complicated situation, e.g. in a drama. **2** a confused or complicated misunderstanding or disagreement.

imbue *v* (**-ues, -ued**) of a feeling, ideal, principle, etc: to be a pervasive presence in.

IMF *abbr* International Monetary Fund.

IMHO *abbr* in my humble opinion, used *esp* in e-mail messages.

imitate *v* **1** to follow as a pattern, model, or example. **2** to mimic (somebody or something), *esp* for humorous effect. **3** to reproduce or simulate. ⪢ **imitable** *adj,* **imitator** *n.*

imitation *n* **1** the act or an instance of imitating. **2a** something produced as a copy; a counterfeit. **b** (*used before a noun*) denoting something that is not genuine; fake. ⪢ **imitational** *adj.*

imitative *adj* **1** marked by or given to imitation; imitating. **2** of a word: reflecting the sound it represents; onomatopoeic. ⪢ **imitatively** *adv,* **imitativeness** *n.*

immaculate *adj* **1** spotlessly clean and very tidy. **2** free from flaw or error. **3** without blemish; pure. **4** free from sin. ⪢ **immaculacy** *n,* **immaculately** *adv,* **immaculateness** *n.*

Immaculate Conception *n* **1** in the Roman Catholic Church, the doctrine that, from the moment she was conceived, the Virgin Mary was without taint of original sin. **2** a feast commemorating the Immaculate Conception, observed on 8 December.

immanent *adj* **1** existing within something; indwelling; inherent. **2** e.g. of God: always present in nature or the universe: compare TRANSCENDENT. ⪢ **immanence** *n,* **immanency** *n,* **immanently** *adv.*

immaterial *adj* **1** unimportant or not relevant. **2** not consisting of matter; incorporeal; spiritual, *esp* as distinct from being physical. ⪢ **immateriality** *n,* **immaterially** *adv,* **immaterialness** *n.*

immature *adj* **1** lacking complete growth, differentiation, or development; not yet fully developed. **2a** exhibiting less than an expected degree of maturity, wisdom, sense, etc. **b** not having arrived at a definitive form or state. ⪢ **immaturely** *adv,* **immatureness** *n,* **immaturity** *n.*

immeasurable *adj* unable to be measured, *esp* because of extreme size or extent. ⪢ **immeasurability** *n,* **immeasurableness** *n,* **immeasurably** *adv.*

immediate *adj* **1a** occurring at once or likely to occur very shortly. **b** current; most in need of attention or action. **2** next in line or relationship. **3** in close or direct physical proximity. **4** acting without any intervening agency or factor. ⪢ **immediacy** *n,* **immediateness** *n.*

immediately[1] *adv* **1** without delay. **2** in direct relation or proximity; directly.

immediately[2] *conj chiefly Brit* as soon as.

immemorial *adj* extending beyond the reach of memory, record, or tradition. ⪢ **immemorially** *adv.*

immense *adj* **1** very great, *esp* in size, degree, or extent. **2** *informal* very good. ⪢ **immensely** *adv,* **immenseness** *n,* **immensity** *n.*

immerse *v* **1** to plunge (somebody or something) completely into a fluid. **2** to engross or absorb (oneself) in something. ⪢ **immersible** *adj.*

immersion *n* **1** the act or an instance of immersing or being immersed. **2** *chiefly NAm* a method of teaching a foreign language by placing the student in a situation where only the foreign language is spoken.

immersion heater *n* an electrical apparatus for heating a liquid in which it is immersed, *esp* an electric water-heater fixed inside a domestic hot-water storage tank.

immigrant *n* **1** a person who comes to a country to take up permanent residence. **2** a plant or animal that becomes established in an area where it was previously unknown.

immigrate *v* **1** to come into a country of which one is not a native to take up permanent residence. **2** of a plant or animal: to become established in an area where it was previously unknown. ⪢ **immigration** *n,* **immigrational** *adj.*

imminent *adj* about to take place; impending *esp* in a threatening way. ⪢ **imminence** *n,* **imminently** *adv.*

immiscible *adj* of two or more different liquids: incapable of being thoroughly mixed together. ⪢ **immiscibility** *n,* **immiscibly** *adv.*

immobile *adj* **1** incapable of being moved. **2** motionless. ⪢ **immobility** *n.*

immobilize *or* **-ise** *v* **1** to prevent from moving freely, effectively, or normally. **2** to prevent or restrict (somebody or a body part) from moving by mechanical means or by strict bed rest, as a treatment to encourage healing. ⪢ **immobilization** *n,* **immobilizer** *n.*

immoderate *adj* lacking moderation; excessive. ⪢ **immoderately** *adv,* **immoderateness** *n,* **immoderation** *n.*

immodest *adj* **1** not conforming to the accepted or expected standards, *esp* of sexual propriety. **2** bold; shameless. ⋙ **immodestly** *adv,* **immodesty** *n.*

immolate *v* to kill or offer as a sacrificial victim, *esp* by burning. ⋙ **immolation** *n,* **immolator** *n.*

immoral *adj* **1** not conforming to conventional or expected moral standards, e.g. in sexual matters or business: compare AMORAL. **2** gained by corrupt or immoral means. ⋙ **immorality** *n,* **immorally** *adv.*

Usage note
immoral *or* amoral? See note at AMORAL.

immortal[1] *adj* **1** living for ever. **2** enduring for ever; imperishable. **3** having enduring fame. ⋙ **immortality** *n,* **immortally** *adv.*

immortal[2] *n* **1a** a person or being that lives for ever. **b** (*often* **Immortal**) (*usu in pl*) any of the gods of classical Greece and Rome. **2** a person of lasting fame.

immortalize *or* **-ise** *v* to give everlasting fame or notoriety to, *esp* through a work of art, film, or literary work, etc. ⋙ **immortalization** *n.*

immortelle *n* a flower that retains its shape and colour for a long time when dried.

immovable *or* **immoveable** *adj* **1** not moving, not able to be moved, or not intended to be moved. **2** steadfast; unyielding. **3** in law, denoting property, such as land and buildings, that cannot be moved. ⋙ **immovability** *n,* **immovableness** *n,* **immovably** *adv.*

immune *adj* **1a** (*often* + to) not susceptible to something, *esp* having high resistance to a disease. **b** (*often* + to/from) not liable to be affected by something bad. **2a** having or producing antibodies to a corresponding antigen. **b** concerned with or involving immunity. **3** (*often* + from) free or exempt.

immune response *n* an integrated bodily response to the presence of foreign matter, *esp* a disease-causing antigen, that results in the production of lymphocytes.

immune system *n* the various cells and tissues in humans and other vertebrate animals which enable them to respond to invading micro-organisms, parasites, etc and protect the body from infection.

immunise *v* see IMMUNIZE.

immunity *n* (*pl* **-ies**) **1** (*often* + from/to) the state of being immune. **2** (*often* + against/to) the ability to resist the effects or development of a disease-causing parasite, *esp* a micro-organism.

immunize *or* **-ise** *v* to make immune, *esp* by inoculation. ⋙ **immunization** *n,* **immunizer** *n.*

immunodeficiency *n* (*pl* **-ies**) any deficiency in the body's ability to mount an effective immune response, often resulting in infections. ⋙ **immunodeficient** *adj.*

immunoglobulin *n* a protein antibody that is made up of light and heavy amino acid chains and usu binds specifically to a particular antigen.

immunology *n* the branch of biology that deals with the phenomena and causes of immunity. ⋙ **immunologic** *adj,* **immunological** *adj,* **immunologically** *adv,* **immunologist** *n.*

immunosuppression *n* suppression, e.g. by drugs, of natural immune responses, *esp* when deliberately induced to help to prevent rejection of a transplanted organ. ⋙ **immunosuppressant** *n and adj,* **immunosuppressed** *adj.*

immunosuppressive[1] *adj* of a drug or treatment: having the ability to suppress the body's natural response to attack any foreign matter and used *esp* to help to prevent rejection of a transplanted organ.

immunosuppressive[2] *n* an immunosuppressive drug.

immunotherapy *n* treatment of or preventive measures against disease by stimulating or altering the immune response.

immure *v* **1** to enclose within walls or as if within walls; to imprison. **2** to shut (oneself) away from other people. ⋙ **immurement** *n.*

immutable *adj* not capable of or susceptible to change. ⋙ **immutability** *n,* **immutableness** *n,* **immutably** *adv.*

imp *n* **1** a small demon. **2** a mischievous child.

impact[1] /'impakt/ *n* **1a** a striking of one body against another. **b** a violent contact or collision or the impetus produced by this. **c** force or impetus. **2** a strong or powerful effect or impression.

impact[2] /im'pakt/ *v* **1** to fix or press firmly e.g. by packing or wedging. **2** to make contact, *esp* forcefully. **3** to have a strong effect or make a great impression on somebody or something. ⋙ **impactive** *adj.*

impacted *adj* **1** of a tooth: not able to grow into its proper position because of a lack of space in the jaw or obstruction by bone or other teeth. **2** of a fracture: with the broken ends of the bone wedged together.

impair *v* to diminish in quality, strength, or amount. ⋙ **impairer** *n,* **impairment** *n.*

impaired *adj* suffering from a disability of a particular kind: *visually impaired.*

impala *n* (*pl* **impalas** *or* **impala**) a large brownish African antelope noted for its ability to make long graceful leaps, having lyre-shaped horns in the male.

impale *v* **1** to pierce with something pointed. **2** to torture or kill by piercing with a sharp stake. ⋙ **impalement** *n.*

impalpable *adj* **1** incapable of being sensed by the touch; intangible. **2** not easily discerned or grasped by the mind. ⋙ **impalpability** *n,* **impalpably** *adv.*

impanel *v* see EMPANEL. ⋙ **impanelment** *n.*

impart *v* **1** to make known or disclose (information, etc). **2** to give or bestow. ⋙ **impartable** *adj,* **impartation** *n,* **impartment** *n.*

impartial *adj* not having or showing any favouritism, *esp* towards rivals; not biased. ⋙ **impartiality** *n,* **impartially** *adv,* **impartialness** *n.*

impassable *adj* of a road, etc: incapable of being passed, traversed, or surmounted. ⋙ **impassability** *n,* **impassableness** *n,* **impassably** *adv.*

impasse *n* **1** a deadlock or stalemate. **2** a predicament from which there is no obvious escape.

impassioned *adj* filled with passion or zeal; showing great warmth or intensity of feeling.

impassive *adj* **1** incapable of emotion. **2** showing no feeling or emotion. ⋙ **impassively** *adv,* **impassiveness** *n,* **impassivity** *n.*

impasto *n* (*pl* **impastos**) **1** in art, the technique or process of applying paint so thickly that it stands out from the canvas, etc. **2** paint that has been applied in this way. ⋙ **impastoed** *adj.*

impatiens *n* any of various plants, including the BUSY LIZZIE, that have exploding seed pods.

impatient *adj* **1a** lacking patience; quickly roused to anger or exasperation by delays, incompetence, incomprehension, etc. **b** (+ of) intolerant. **2** (*often* + to/for) eagerly desirous; anxious. ⋙ **impatience** *n,* **impatiently** *adv.*

impeach *v* **1a** *Brit* to charge with a serious crime against the state. **b** *NAm* to charge (a serving public official) with misconduct. **2** to cast doubt on or challenge the credibility or validity of (e.g. a person's honesty). ➤➤ **impeachable** *adj,* **impeachment** *n.*

impeccable *adj* free from fault or blemish; flawless. ➤➤ **impeccability** *n,* **impeccably** *adv.*

impecunious *adj* having very little or no money. ➤➤ **impecuniosity** *n,* **impecuniously** *adv,* **impecuniousness** *n.*

impedance *n* the opposition in an electrical circuit to the flow of an alternating current that is analogous to the opposition of an electrical resistance to the flow of a direct current.

impede *v* to interfere with or retard the progress of. ➤➤ **impeder** *n.*

impediment *n* **1** (*often* + to) something that impedes. **2** a physiological speech defect, e.g. a stammer or lisp. **3** (*pl* **impediments** *or* **impedimenta**) in law, something that obstructs the making or finalizing of a contract, *esp* a marriage contract.

impedimenta *pl n* **1** unwieldy baggage or equipment. **2** things that impede; encumbrances.

impel *v* (**impelled, impelling**) **1** to urge forward or force into action. **2** to propel or drive forward. ➤➤ **impeller** *n.*

impending *adj* about to happen.

impenetrable *adj* **1a** incapable of being penetrated or pierced. **b** not open to intellectual influences or ideas. **2** incapable of being comprehended. ➤➤ **impenetrability** *n,* **impenetrableness** *n,* **impenetrably** *adv.*

impenitent *adj* feeling or showing no regret or shame, e.g. about a wicked deed, bad behaviour, etc; unrepentant. ➤➤ **impenitence** *n,* **impenitency** *n,* **impenitently** *adv.*

imperative[1] *adj* **1** very urgent or important; not to be avoided. **2** commanding; showing authority. **3** denoting the grammatical mood that expresses command, e.g. the verb *stop* in *Stop that at once!* ➤➤ **imperatively** *adv,* **imperativeness** *n.*

imperative[2] *n* **1** an obligatory, necessary, or urgent act or duty. **2** the imperative mood or a verb form expressing this mood.

imperceptible *adj* **1** extremely slight, gradual, or subtle. **2a** not perceptible by the mind or senses. **b** too small to be perceptible. ➤➤ **imperceptibility** *n,* **imperceptibly** *adv.*

imperfect[1] *adj* **1** flawed, defective, or incomplete; not perfect. **2** relating to or denoting a verb tense expressing a continuing state or an incomplete action, *esp* in the past. ➤➤ **imperfectly** *adv,* **imperfectness** *n.*

imperfect[2] *n* the imperfect tense or a verb form expressing it.

imperfection *n* **1** the quality or state of being imperfect. **2** a fault or blemish.

imperial *adj* **1a** of or befitting an empire, emperor, or empress. **b** of the former British Empire. **2a** sovereign; royal. **b** regal, imperious, or majestic. **3** belonging to an official nonmetric British series of weights and measures such as the pound and the pint. ➤➤ **imperially** *adv,* **imperialness** *n.*

imperialism *n* **1** the policy, practice, or advocacy of extending the power and dominion of a nation, *esp* by territorial acquisition. **2** any unacceptable extension or attempted extension of power or influence. ➤➤ **imperialist** *n and adj,* **imperialistic** *adj,* **imperialistically** *adv.*

imperil *v* (**imperilled, imperilling,** *NAm* **imperiled, imperiling**) to put in danger or at risk of harm. ➤➤ **imperilment** *n.*

imperious *adj* marked by arrogant assurance; domineering. ➤➤ **imperiously** *adv,* **imperiousness** *n.*

imperishable *adj* **1** not subject to decay or deterioration; not perishable. **2** enduring permanently. ➤➤ **imperishability** *n,* **imperishableness** *n,* **imperishably** *adv.*

impermanent *adj* transient; not permanent or lasting. ➤➤ **impermanence** *n,* **impermanency** *n,* **impermanently** *adv.*

impermeable *adj* of a substance, membrane, etc: not permitting something, *esp* a fluid, to pass through. ➤➤ **impermeability** *n,* **impermeableness** *n,* **impermeably** *adv.*

impersonal *adj* **1a** not showing, influenced by, or involving personal feelings or opinions; objective or unbiased. **b** cold, formal, or detached. **2a** of a verb: used to express an action that has no definite subject, the subject in English usu being *it,* e.g. *rained* in *it rained.* **b** of a pronoun: not referring to a particular person, e.g. *it* in *it rained.* ➤➤ **impersonality** *n,* **impersonally** *adv.*

impersonate *v* to pretend to be (somebody), either for entertainment or as an act of deception. ➤➤ **impersonation** *n,* **impersonator** *n.*

impertinent *adj* **1** rude; insolent. **2** *formal* irrelevant; lacking pertinence. ➤➤ **impertinence** *n,* **impertinency** *n,* **impertinently** *adv.*

imperturbable *adj* marked by great calm and composure. ➤➤ **imperturbability** *n,* **imperturbableness** *n,* **imperturbably** *adv.*

impervious *adj* **1** (+ to) not capable of being affected or disturbed by something. **2** (*often* + to) not allowing a fluid to pass through; impermeable. ➤➤ **imperviously** *adv,* **imperviousness** *n.*

impetigo /impəˈtiegoh/ *n* a contagious bacterial skin disease characterized by blisters and pustules. ➤➤ **impetiginous** *adj.*

impetuous *adj* **1a** acting or done with impulsiveness or rashness. **b** impulsive or rash by nature. **2** *literary* marked by forceful and violent movement. ➤➤ **impetuosity** *n,* **impetuously** *adv,* **impetuousness** *n.*

impetus *n* **1a** a driving force. **b** an incentive or stimulus. **2** in physics, the energy possessed by a moving body.

impi *n* (*pl* **impis**) formerly in South Africa, a band or regiment of Zulu warriors.

impiety *n* (*pl* **-ies**) a lack of reverence or an irreverent act.

impinge *v* **1** to encroach or infringe on something. **2** (+ on/upon) to make an impression. ➤➤ **impingement** *n,* **impinger** *n.*

impious *adj* lacking in reverence or proper respect, e.g. for God; irreverent. ➤➤ **impiously** *adv,* **impiousness** *n.*

impish *adj* mischievous. ➤➤ **impishly** *adv,* **impishness** *n.*

implacable *adj* **1** not capable of being appeased or pacified. **2** unrelenting; never stopping, weakening, or changing. ➤➤ **implacability** *n,* **implacableness** *n,* **implacably** *adv.*

implant[1] *v* **1** to fix or set securely or deeply. **2** to set (e.g. an idea or principle) permanently in somebody's consciousness. **3** to insert (e.g. artificial tissue, a hormone, etc) in a living organism. ➤➤ **implantable** *adj,* **implantation** *n,* **implanter** *n.*

implant[2] *n* something, e.g. a graft or hormone pellet, implanted in the tissue of a living organism.

implausible *adj* of a story, excuse, etc: unlikely to be true; not plausible. ➤➤ **implausibility** *n,* **implausibly** *adv.*

implement[1] *n* a utensil or tool, *esp* one with a specified purpose.

implement[2] *v* to put (plans, orders, etc) into effect. ➤➤ **implementation** *n*, **implementer** *n*.

implicate *v* **1a** (*often* + in) to show that (somebody, oneself, or something) has a connection with something, *esp* to show that (a person) is involved in a crime, wrongdoing, etc. **b** to involve (something) in the way something else is or operates. **2** to involve (something) as a consequence or inference; to imply.

implication *n* **1a** the act or an instance of implicating or being implicated. **b** (*usu* + in) incriminating involvement. **2** the act or an instance of implying or being implied. **3** something implied. ➤➤ **implicative** *adj*.

implicit *adj* **1a** implied rather than directly stated. **b** (+ in) present but underlying rather than explicit. **2** unquestioning; absolute: *implicit obedience*. ➤➤ **implicitly** *adv*, **implicitness** *n*.

implode *v* to collapse inwards suddenly, or cause to do this. ➤➤ **implosion** *n*, **implosive** *adj*.

implore *v* to beg (somebody) to do something. ➤➤ **imploring** *adj*, **imploringly** *adv*.

imply *v* (**-ies, -ied**) **1** to express indirectly; to hint at: *His silence implied consent*. **2** to involve as a necessary or potential consequence.

Usage note

imply *or* **infer**? These two words are sometimes confused, though they are in fact opposite in meaning. To *imply* something is to suggest it by what you say without stating it explicitly: *She implied that I was untrustworthy*. To *infer* something is to deduce it from what someone says, even though they have not explicitly said as much: *I inferred from her remark that she thought me untrustworthy*.

impolite *adj* not having or showing good manners. ➤➤ **impolitely** *adv*, **impoliteness** *n*.

impolitic *adj* unwise or ill-advised.

imponderable[1] *adj* incapable of being precisely evaluated or assessed.

imponderable[2] *n* something whose effect is hard or impossible to calculate.

import[1] *v* **1** to bring (something) in from a foreign or external source, *esp* to bring (e.g. merchandise) in from abroad. **2** in computing, to transfer (a file, data, etc) from one computer, database, or package to another. **3** *formal or archaic* to signify. ➤➤ **importable** *adj*, **importation** *n*, **importer** *n*.

import[2] *n* **1** something imported, *esp* merchandise from abroad. **2** the act or an instance of importing. **3** *formal* meaning or significance. **4** *formal* importance.

important *adj* **1** of considerable significance or consequence. **2** having high rank or social standing. ➤➤ **importance** *n*, **importantly** *adv*.

importunate *adj* **1** very persistent in making requests or demands. **2** made persistently. ➤➤ **importunately** *adv*.

importune *v* **1** to make persistent demands of (somebody). **2** to solicit (somebody) for purposes of prostitution. ➤➤ **importunity** *n*.

impose *v* **1a** (*often* + on/upon) to establish or apply (something, e.g. a tax, fine, rule, etc) as compulsory. **b** (*often* + on/upon) to establish (something) by force. **2** to force (oneself) into the company or on the attention of another. **3** (*often* + on/upon) to be an excessive requirement or burden.

imposing *adj* impressive because of size, bearing, or grandeur. ➤➤ **imposingly** *adv*.

imposition *n* **1** the act or an instance of imposing. **2a** a levy or tax. **b** an excessive or unwarranted requirement or burden.

impossible *adj* **1** incapable of being or occurring; not possible. **2** extremely undesirable or difficult to put up with or deal with. ➤➤ **impossibility** *n*, **impossibly** *adv*.

impost *n* **1** a tax. **2** in horse-racing, the weight that a horse must carry as a handicap.

impostor *or* **imposter** *n* a person who assumes a false identity or title for fraudulent purposes.

imposture *n* fraud or deception, or an instance of this.

impotent *adj* **1** lacking in efficacy, strength, or vigour. **2** of an adult male: unable to perform sexual intercourse through an inability to attain or maintain an erection of the penis. ➤➤ **impotence** *n*, **impotency** *n*, **impotently** *adv*.

impound *v* **1a** to shut up (an animal) in a pound. **b** to take legal possession of (something, e.g. evidence from a crime scene, an illegally parked vehicle, etc). **2** to collect and confine (water) in a dam or reservoir. ➤➤ **impoundment** *n*.

impoverish *v* **1** to make (somebody) poor. **2** to deprive (somebody or something) of strength, richness, or fertility. ➤➤ **impoverishment** *n*.

impracticable *adj* incapable of being put into effect or carried out: *We soon realized that the plan was impracticable*. ➤➤ **impracticability** *n*, **impracticably** *adv*.

Usage note

impracticable *or* **impractical**? See note at IMPRACTICAL.

impractical *adj* **1a** incapable of dealing sensibly with practical matters, *esp* financial matters. **b** not good at doing practical things, *esp* manual tasks. **2** *chiefly NAm* not able to be put into effect or carried out. ➤➤ **impracticality** *n*, **impractically** *adv*.

Usage note

impractical *or* **impracticable**? These two words are very close in meaning, but it is useful to distinguish between them. A plan that is *impractical* may be fine in theory but is difficult to carry out or of little use in practice. An *impracticable* plan is, quite simply, impossible to carry out. A person can be described as *impractical* ('not good at ordinary tasks' or 'not down-to-earth'), but not as *impracticable*.

imprecation *n* a curse.

imprecise *adj* inexact, vague, or inaccurate. ➤➤ **imprecisely** *adv*, **imprecision** *n*.

impregnable *adj* **1** incapable of being taken by assault. **2** beyond criticism or question. **3** strong or unassailable: *an impregnable belief in his own superiority*. ➤➤ **impregnability** *n*, **impregnably** *adv*.

impregnate *v* **1a** to make (a female person or animal) pregnant; to fertilize. **b** to introduce sperm cells into (an ovum). **2a** (+ with) to soak or saturate with something. **b** of a quality, emotion, etc: to fill or be a dominant presence in (speech or writing). ➤➤ **impregnation** *n*.

impresario *n* (*pl* **-os**) a person who organizes, finances, or sponsors a public entertainment, e.g. a concert.

impress[1] *v* **1a** (*often* + by/with) to produce a deep and usu favourable impression on. **b** (*usu* + on) to fix (e.g. an idea or thought) strongly or deeply in the mind or memory. **2a** to apply (something) with pressure so as to imprint it on something. **b** to mark (something) by pressure or stamping.

impress[2] *n* **1** the act of impressing. **2** a mark made by pressure. **3** an impression or effect.

impress[3] *v* formerly, to force (a man) into service in the army or navy. ⋙ **impressment** *n.*

impression *n* **1** an influence or effect on the mind or senses. **2a** (*also in pl*) a thought or opinion. **b** (*also in pl*) a telling image impressed on the mind or senses. **c** a notion or recollection, *esp* one that is vague or subjective. **3a** an effect produced by some action or effort. **b** a characteristic, trait, or feature resulting from some influence. **4** an imitation of a person, animal, etc; *esp* as a form of entertainment. **5** the act or process of impressing. **6** a stamp, form, or figure produced by physical contact. **7a** in printing, a single instance of the meeting of a printing surface and the material being printed. **b** a print or copy so made. **c** all the copies of a book printed for issue at a single time.

impressionable *adj* easily influenced. ⋙ **impressionability** *n.*

impressionism *n* **1** (*often* **Impressionism**) an art movement, begun in late 19th-cent. France, that tries to convey the visual effects of actual reflected light on natural usu outdoor subjects. **2** literary depiction that seeks to convey a general subjective impression rather than a detailed re-creation of reality. **3** a style of musical composition designed to create impressions and moods through rich and varied harmonies and tones.

impressionist *n* **1** (*often* **Impressionist**) a person, e.g. a painter, who practises the theories of impressionism. **2** an entertainer who does impressions.

impressionistic *adj* **1** based on or involving subjective impression as distinct from knowledge, fact, or systematic thought. **2** (*usu* **Impressionistic**) relating to or denoting impressionism, *esp* in art. ⋙ **impressionistically** *adv.*

impressive *adj* stirring deep feelings, *esp* of awe or admiration. ⋙ **impressively** *adv,* **impressiveness** *n.*

imprimatur *n* **1** a licence granted by Roman Catholic episcopal authority to print or publish. **2** sanction or approval.

imprint[1] *n* **1** a mark made by pressure. **2a** a publisher's name printed at the foot of a title-page, or a printer's name on any publication. **b** a brand name under which a range of books are published.

imprint[2] *v* **1a** to make (a mark) on something by pressure. **b** to make a mark on (something) by pressure. **2** to fix (an image, etc) indelibly or permanently in the mind, memory, etc. **3** to cause (a young animal, chick, etc) to undergo imprinting. **4** (*usu* + on) of a young animal, chick, etc: to undergo imprinting.

imprinting *n* a behaviour pattern rapidly established early in the life of an animal that involves attachment to an object or other animal, *esp* the animal's mother, seen just after birth or hatching.

imprison *v* to put in prison or confine as if in a prison. ⋙ **imprisonment** *n.*

improbable *adj* unlikely to be true or to occur. ⋙ **improbability** *n,* **improbably** *adv.*

impromptu[1] *adj* made or done on the spur of the moment; unplanned or not rehearsed. ⋙ **impromptu** *adv.*

impromptu[2] *n* (*pl* **impromptus**) a musical composition suggesting improvisation.

improper *adj* **1** not in accordance with propriety or modesty; indecent. **2** not suitable or appropriate. **3** not in accordance with fact, truth, or normal or correct procedure. ⋙ **improperly** *adv.*

improper fraction *n* a fraction whose numerator is larger than the denominator.

impropriety *n* (*pl* **-ies**) **1** an absence of accepted standards of decency. **2** an improper act or remark.

improve *v* **1** to enhance in value or quality; to make better. **2** to advance or make good progress. **3** (*usu* + on/upon) to produce or achieve something better than a previous version, result, etc. ⋙ **improvability** *n,* **improvable** *adj,* **improver** *n.*

improvement *n* **1** the act or an instance of improving or being improved. **2** an increase in value or excellence, or something that brings this about.

improvident *adj* lacking foresight, *esp* in not providing for the future. ⋙ **improvidence** *n,* **improvidently** *adv.*

improvise *v* **1** to make or provide (something) using what is available. **2** to compose or perform (music, poetry, drama, etc) impromptu or without a set script or musical score. ⋙ **improvisation** *n,* **improvisational** *adj,* **improvisatory** *adj,* **improviser** *n.*

imprudent *adj* lacking discretion or caution. ⋙ **imprudence** *n,* **imprudently** *adv.*

impudent *adj* showing contemptuous or cocky boldness or disrespect. ⋙ **impudence** *n,* **impudently** *adv.*

impugn *v* to call into question or dispute the validity or integrity of (something said or done).

impulse *n* **1** a sudden spontaneous inclination or desire to do something. **2a** a force that produces motion suddenly. **b** inspiration or stimulus. **3a** an impelling or driving force. **b** a wave of electrical energy transmitted through tissues, *esp* nerve fibres and muscles, that results in physiological activity or inhibition. **4** in physics, the product of the average value of a force and the time during which it acts, being a quantity equal to the change in momentum produced by the force.

impulsion *n* **1** a strong urge, desire, or inclination. **2** a motivating factor. **3** an impelling or driving force.

impulsive *adj* **1** acting or done on the basis of a sudden whim or desire. **2** having the power of driving or propelling. **3** acting or lasting only momentarily. ⋙ **impulsively** *adv,* **impulsiveness** *n,* **impulsivity** *n.*

impunity *n* exemption or freedom from punishment, harm, or retribution.

impure *adj* **1** not pure, *esp* as a result of contamination. **2** morally wrong. **3** ritually unclean. **4** mixed, *esp* adulterated or tainted.

impurity *n* (*pl* **-ies**) **1** the quality or state of being impure. **2** something that is impure or that makes something else impure.

impute *v* to attribute (*esp* something bad) to somebody, often unjustly. ⋙ **imputable** *adj,* **imputation** *n.*

IN *abbr* Indiana (US postal abbreviation).

In *abbr* the chemical symbol for indium.

in[1] *prep* **1** used to indicate location within or inside something three-dimensional: *It's in the cupboard.* **2** used to indicate location more generally: *in the garden.* **3** used to indicate location in time: *in 1959.* **4** = INTO (IA). **5a** used to indicate a means, instrument, or medium of expression: *drawn in pencil.* **b** used to describe a person's clothing: *a girl in red.* **6** used to indicate qualification, manner, circumstance, or condition: *in public; in pain.* **7** used to indicate occupation or membership: *a job in insurance.* **8** used to indicate relevance or reference: *equal in distance; said in reply.* **9a** used to indicate division, arrangement, or quantity: *standing in a circle.* **b** used to indicate the larger member of a ratio: *a tax of 40p in the £.* ✱ **in that** for the reason that; because: *It's of limited use in that it has no lid.*

in[2] *adv* used to indicate: **a** movement to or towards the inside or centre: *come in out of the rain.* **b**

incorporation: *mix in the flour.* **c** movement to or towards home, the shore, a destination, etc: *Three ships came sailing in.* **d** presence at a particular place, *esp* at one's home or business: *be in for lunch.* **e** concealment: *The sun went in.* ✱ **be in for** to be certain to experience (usu something undesirable). **in on** having a share in or knowledge of something.

in[3] *adj* extremely fashionable.

in. *abbr* inch.

in-[1] *or* **il-** *or* **im-** *or* **ir-** *prefix* not: *inaccurate; irresponsibility.*

in-[2] *or* **il-** *or* **im-** *or* **ir-** *prefix* in, into, or towards: *influx; immersion.*

inability *n* lack of sufficient power or capacity.

in absentia *adv* in the absence of the specified person.

inaccessible *adj* **1** difficult or impossible to reach. **2** difficult or impossible to understand. ⋙ **inaccessibility** *n,* **inaccessibly** *adv.*

inaccurate *adj* faulty or imprecise. ⋙ **inaccuracy** *n,* **inaccurately** *adv.*

inaction *n* lack of action or activity.

inactivate *v* **1** to cause (something, *esp* a machine) to stop operating. **2** to render (something) chemically or biologically inactive. ⋙ **inactivation** *n,* **inactivator** *n.*

inactive *adj* **1** not given to action or effort. **2** out of use; not functioning. ⋙ **inactivity** *n.*

inadequate *adj* **1** not adequate; lacking the required or expected quantity or quality. **2** not capable; unable to cope. ⋙ **inadequacy** *n,* **inadequately** *adv.*

inadmissible *adj esp* of evidence in a court of law: invalid. ⋙ **inadmissibility** *n.*

inadvertent *adj* **1** heedless, inattentive, or lacking in care or consideration. **2** unintentional. ⋙ **inadvertence** *n,* **inadvertently** *adv.*

inadvisable *adj esp* of a course of action: likely to have unwanted or unpleasant consequences; unwise. ⋙ **inadvisability** *n.*

inalienable *adj* incapable of being removed or surrendered. ⋙ **inalienability** *n,* **inalienably** *adv.*

inamorata *n* a female romantic or sexual partner.

inamorato *n* (*pl* **-os**) a male romantic or sexual partner.

inane *adj* senseless or unintelligent. ⋙ **inanely** *adv,* **inaneness** *n,* **inanity** *n.*

inanimate *adj* **1** without life or spirit, *esp* in contrast to living things. **2** lacking consciousness or power of motion.

inanition *n formal* exhaustion due to lack of food.

inapplicable *adj* not appropriate or relevant. ⋙ **inapplicability** *n.*

inapposite *adj* not suitable or pertinent.

inappropriate *adj* not appropriate or suitable. ⋙ **inappropriately** *adv,* **inappropriateness** *n.*

inapt *adj* **1** not suitable or appropriate. **2** lacking skill or ability. ⋙ **inaptitude** *n,* **inaptly** *adv.*

inarticulate *adj* **1a** unable to speak or to express one's ideas or feelings coherently or effectively. **b** not coherently or effectively expressed. **c** not understandable as spoken words. **2** not jointed or hinged. ⋙ **inarticulacy** *n,* **inarticulately** *adv,* **inarticulateness** *n.*

inasmuch as *conj* **1** = INSOFAR AS. **2** in view of the fact that; because.

inattention *n* failure to pay attention; disregard. ⋙ **inattentive** *adj.*

inaudible *adj* unable to be heard. ⋙ **inaudibility** *n,* **inaudibly** *adv.*

inaugurate *v* **1a** to induct (somebody) ceremonially into office. **b** to open (e.g. a new building) ceremonially. **2** to mark the beginning or introduction of (a new system, project, etc). ⋙ **inaugural** *adj,* **inauguration** *n,* **inaugurator** *n.*

inauspicious *adj* not promising future success. ⋙ **inauspiciously** *adv,* **inauspiciousness** *n.*

inboard *adj and adv* within or towards the centre line of a ship, aircraft, etc.

inborn *adj* **1** forming part of the natural make-up of somebody or something. **2** existing from birth; congenital.

inbred *adj* **1** rooted and deeply ingrained in the nature of somebody or something. **2** subjected to or produced by inbreeding.

inbreed *v* (*past tense and past part.* **inbred**) **1** to cause (closely related individuals) to breed with each other, *esp* over a number of generations. **2** to produce (offspring) in this way. ⋙ **inbreeding** *n.*

inbuilt *adj* built-in; inherent or integral.

Inc. *abbr chiefly NAm* incorporated.

Inca *n* **1** a member of an indigenous South American people who lived in the region of the central Andes before the Spanish conquest. **2** a ruler of this people. ⋙ **Incan** *adj.*

incalculable *adj* **1** too great or numerous to be calculated. **2** unable to be predicted or estimated. ⋙ **incalculability** *n,* **incalculably** *adv.*

incandescent *adj* **1** white, glowing, or luminous with intense heat. **2** *informal* extremely angry. ⋙ **incandescence** *n,* **incandescently** *adv.*

incandescent lamp *n* a lamp in which an electrically heated filament gives off light.

incantation *n* **1** the use of spoken or sung spells in magic ritual. **2** a formula used in incantation. ⋙ **incantatory** *adj.*

incapable *adj* **1** (*usu* + of) lacking the capacity, ability, etc to do or admit of something. **2** unfit, *esp* because of illness or the effects of alcohol or drugs. ⋙ **incapability** *n.*

incapacitate *v* to prevent (somebody or something) from functioning or operating properly; to disable. ⋙ **incapacitation** *n.*

incapacity *n* (*pl* **-ies**) **1** lack of ability or power. **2** legal disqualification.

incarcerate *v* to imprison or confine (somebody). ⋙ **incarceration** *n.*

incarnate[1] *adj* (*used after a noun*) **1** invested with a human nature and form: *Satan incarnate.* **2** personified or typified: *evil incarnate.*

incarnate[2] *v* **1** to give (e.g. a deity) bodily or human form. **2** to be a representative or typical example of (an abstract concept or quality).

incarnation *n* **1** the embodiment of a deity or spirit in an earthly form. **2** somebody or something that is a representative or typical example of an abstract concept or quality. **3** (**Incarnation**) in Christian belief, the manifestation of Christ in human form: compare ADVENT (2). **4** any of several successive bodily manifestations or lives.

incase *v* see ENCASE.

incautious *adj* lacking care or caution; rash. ⋙ **incaution** *n,* **incautiously** *adv.*

incendiary[1] *adj* **1** relating to the deliberate burning of property. **2** tending to inflame or stir up trouble. **3** of a device or substance: able or designed to ignite spontaneously on contact. ⋙ **incendiarism** *n.*

incendiary[2] *n* (*pl* **-ies**) an incendiary substance or device, e.g. a bomb.

incense[1] *n* a substance, such as aromatic spices, gum, etc, used to produce a fragrant smell when burned.

incense[2] *v* to perfume with incense.

incense[3] *v* to arouse (a person or group) to extreme anger or indignation.

incentive *n* something that motivates somebody or spurs them on.

incentivize *or* **-ise** *v* to stimulate or motivate (e.g. employees) by offering an incentive.

inception *n* the act or an instance of beginning a process or undertaking.

incertitude *n* uncertainty; doubt.

incessant *adj* usu of something unpleasant or undesirable: continuing without interruption. ➤➤ **incessantly** *adv.*

incest *n* sexual intercourse between people so closely related that they are forbidden by law to marry.

incestuous *adj* **1** relating to, guilty of, or involving incest. **2** excessively or unhealthily close to or shut off from outside influences. ➤➤ **incestuously** *adv.*

inch[1] *n* **1** a unit of length equal to one twelfth of a foot (about 2.54cm). **2** a small amount or distance: *They came within an inch of scoring.* **3** a fall of rain or snow that would cover a level surface to the depth of one inch. ✻ **every inch** to the utmost degree: *He looks every inch a winner.* **within an inch of one's life** almost to the point of death; very thoroughly or soundly: *He shook her within an inch of her life.*

inch[2] *v* to move slowly.

inchoate *adj* only partly in existence or operation, *esp* imperfectly formed or formulated: *an inchoate longing.* ➤➤ **inchoately** *adv.*

inchworm *n* = LOOPER.

incidence *n* **1** the rate of occurrence or the extent of influence that something has. **2** the arrival of something, e.g. a projectile or a ray of light, at a surface.

incident[1] *n* **1** something that happens; an event or occurrence. **2a** an occurrence that is a cause of conflict or disagreement. **b** a violent act or exchange.

incident[2] *adj* **1** (*usu* + to) relating to, accompanying, or resulting from something. **2** *esp* of light: falling on or striking a surface.

incidental[1] *adj* **1** occurring merely by chance. **2** (*often* + to) occurring or likely to ensue as a minor consequence or accompaniment.

incidental[2] *n* something incidental, *esp* a minor expense or an insignificant event.

incidentally *adv* **1** by the way. **2** by chance.

incidental music *n* background music in a play, film, etc.

incinerate *v* to burn (something) to ashes. ➤➤ **incineration** *n.*

incinerator *n* a furnace or container for incinerating waste materials.

incipient *adj* just beginning to come into being or to become apparent. ➤➤ **incipience** *n,* **incipiently** *adv.*

incise *v* **1** to cut into (something). **2a** to carve letters, designs, etc into (something). **b** to carve (e.g. an inscription) into a surface.

incision *n* **1** a cut, *esp* one made in a surgical operation. **2** the act or process of cutting into something.

incisive *adj* **1** having or showing sharp intelligence. **2** impressively direct and decisive. ➤➤ **incisively** *adv,* **incisiveness** *n.*

incisor *n* a cutting tooth, *esp* one of the front teeth in mammals.

incite *v* **1** to move (a person or group) to action. **2** to encourage (violence, unlawful behaviour, etc). ➤➤ **incitement** *n,* **inciter** *n.*

incivility *n* (*pl* **-ies**) rudeness or discourtesy.

inclement *adj* of the weather: unpleasant, *esp* cold and wet. ➤➤ **inclemency** *n.*

inclination *n* **1** a particular tendency, propensity, or urge, *esp* a liking. **2a** a deviation from the vertical or horizontal, or the degree of this. **b** a slope. **c** the angle between two lines or planes.

incline[1] *v* **1** to influence or dispose (somebody) to a specified action or way of thinking. **2** to cause to lean or slope. **3** to slope or slant; to deviate from the horizontal or vertical. **4** to drop, nod, or bend (the head), e.g. as a gesture of agreement. ✻ **inclined to 1** having a tendency to (do or be something). **2** in favour of (doing something).

incline[2] *n* an inclined surface; a slope.

inclined plane *n* a plane surface that makes an angle with the horizontal.

inclose *v* see ENCLOSE.

inclosure *n* see ENCLOSURE.

include *v* **1** to take in, contain, or consider (something or somebody) as a part of a larger group or whole. **2** to add or put in (something or somebody).

including *prep* with the inclusion of: *The room costs £40 including breakfast.*

inclusion *n* **1** the act or process of including or being included. **2** something or somebody that is included.

inclusive *adj* **1** including or intended to include all or the specified items, costs, or services. **2** including the stated limits or extremes. **3** broad in orientation or scope. ➤➤ **inclusively** *adv,* **inclusiveness** *n.*

incognito[1] *adv and adj* with one's identity concealed; in disguise or under a false name.

incognito[2] *n* (*pl* **-os**) the disguise or false name of somebody who is incognito.

incoherent *adj* **1** not clearly intelligible; inarticulate. **2** lacking in logical connection. **3** in physics, denoting waves of the same frequency that are different in phase. ➤➤ **incoherence** *n,* **incoherency** *n,* **incoherently** *adv.*

incombustible *adj* incapable of being ignited or burned.

income *n* money received from work, property, or investment, *esp* regularly or over a specified time.

incomer *n* a person who moves into an area.

income support *n Brit* a social security payment made to people on low incomes.

income tax *n* a tax levied on personal income.

incoming *adj* **1** arriving, coming in, or being received. **2** taking on a role or office.

incomings *pl n* income or revenue.

incommensurable *adj* **1** lacking a common basis of comparison; incapable of being compared. **2** in mathematics, having no common factor. ➤➤ **incommensurability** *n.*

incommensurate *adj* **1** (*usu* + with) disproportionate to something, *esp* in being more or less than is expected or appropriate. **2** = INCOMMENSURABLE (1). ➤➤ **incommensurateness** *n.*

incommode *v formal* to inconvenience or trouble (somebody).

incommodious *adj formal* inconvenient or uncomfortable, *esp* from being too small.

incommunicado *adv and adj* without means of communication, e.g. while in solitary confinement or voluntary seclusion.

incomparable *adj* **1** beyond comparison; matchless. **2** not suitable for comparison. ➤➤ **incomparability** *n,* **incomparably** *adv.*

incompatible *adj* **1** of two or more people: unable to live or work together, *esp* because of opposing views, temperaments, etc. **2** unable to exist together. **3** unsuitable for use together. ➤➤ **incompatibility** *n.*

incompetent[1] *adj* **1** lacking the qualities, skill, experience, etc needed for effective action. **2** not legally qualified. ➤➤ **incompetence** *n,* **incompetency** *n,* **incompetently** *adv.*

incompetent[2] *n* an incompetent person.

incomplete *adj* not complete. ➤➤ **incompletely** *adv,* **incompleteness** *n,* **incompletion** *n.*

incomprehensible *adj* impossible to understand; unintelligible. ➤➤ **incomprehensibility** *n,* **incomprehensibly** *adv,* **incomprehension** *n.*

inconceivable *adj* unimaginable or unbelievable. ➤➤ **inconceivably** *adv.*

inconclusive *adj* leading to no conclusion or definite result. ➤➤ **inconclusively** *adv,* **inconclusiveness** *n.*

incongruent *adj* **1** = INCONGRUOUS. **2** said of some chemical processes involving melting or dissolution: affecting different alloys or other substances in different ways. **3** in geometry, not congruent. ➤➤ **incongruence** *n,* **incongruently** *adv.*

incongruous *adj* out of place. ➤➤ **incongruity** *n,* **incongruously** *adv.*

inconsequent *adj* **1** lacking reasonable sequence; illogical. **2** irrelevant. ➤➤ **inconsequence** *n,* **inconsequently** *adv.*

inconsequential *adj* **1** irrelevant. **2** of no significance; unimportant. ➤➤ **inconsequentiality** *n,* **inconsequentially** *adv.*

inconsiderable *adj* **1** insignificant or trivial. **2** small in size, amount, etc.

inconsiderate *adj* having or showing a lack of care for others; thoughtless. ➤➤ **inconsiderately** *adv,* **inconsiderateness** *n.*

inconsistent *adj* **1** containing conflicting or contradictory elements. **2** not consistent. ➤➤ **inconsistency** *n,* **inconsistently** *adv.*

inconsolable *adj* incapable of being consoled; brokenhearted. ➤➤ **inconsolably** *adv.*

inconspicuous *adj* not readily noticeable. ➤➤ **inconspicuously** *adv,* **inconspicuousness** *n.*

inconstant *adj* likely to change frequently without apparent reason. ➤➤ **inconstancy** *n.*

incontestable *adj* indisputable. ➤➤ **incontestably** *adv.*

incontinent *adj* **1** suffering from a lack of control over urination or defecation. **2** lacking self-restraint, *esp* sexually. ➤➤ **incontinence** *n,* **incontinently** *adv.*

incontrovertible *adj* not able to be denied, disputed, or challenged. ➤➤ **incontrovertibly** *adv.*

inconvenience[1] *n* **1** the state of being difficult, troublesome, or annoying. **2** a cause or instance of inconvenience. ➤➤ **inconvenient** *adj,* **inconveniently** *adv.*

inconvenience[2] *v* to cause (somebody or something) inconvenience.

incorporate[1] *v* **1a** to make (something) a usu indistinguishable part of a larger whole. **b** to admit (an organization) to membership of a corporate body. **2a** to combine (parts) thoroughly to form a consistent whole. **b** to form (a company, organization, etc) into a legal corporation. ➤➤ **incorporation** *n,* **incorporative** *adj,* **incorporator** *n.*

incorporate[2] *adj* **1** united in one body. **2** formed into a legal corporation.

incorporeal *adj* having no material body or form.

incorrect *adj* **1** inaccurate; factually wrong. **2** not in accordance with an established norm; improper. ➤➤ **incorrectly** *adv,* **incorrectness** *n.*

incorrigible *adj* **1** incapable of being corrected or improved, *esp* incurably bad. **2** unwilling or unlikely to change. ➤➤ **incorrigibility** *n,* **incorrigibly** *adv.*

incorruptible *adj* **1** incapable of being bribed or morally corrupted. **2** not subject to decay or dissolution. ➤➤ **incorruptibility** *n.*

increase[1] *v* to make or become progressively greater in size, amount, number, or intensity. ➤➤ **increasing** *adj,* **increasingly** *adv.*

increase[2] *n* the act or an instance of increasing.

incredible *adj* **1** too extraordinary and improbable to be believed; amazing or astonishing. **2** *informal* excellent; outstanding. ➤➤ **incredibility** *n,* **incredibly** *adv.*

incredulous *adj* unwilling or unable to believe something. ➤➤ **incredulity** *n,* **incredulously** *adv,* **incredulousness** *n.*

increment *n* **1** an increase, *esp* in quantity or value, or the amount of this. **2** any of a series of regular consecutive increases or additions. ➤➤ **incremental** *adj,* **incrementally** *adv.*

incriminate *v* to suggest or demonstrate that (somebody) is guilty of a crime or other wrongdoing. ➤➤ **incrimination** *n,* **incriminatory** *adj.*

in-crowd *n* (**the in-crowd**) *informal* people who are considered to be, or who consider themselves to be, particularly popular or fashionable.

incrust *v* see ENCRUST.

incubate *v* **1** of a bird: to sit on (eggs) so as to hatch them by the warmth of the body. **2** to maintain (something) under conditions favourable for hatching, development, growth, etc. **3** to develop (a disease), *esp* without any noticeable symptoms. ➤➤ **incubation** *n.*

incubator *n* **1** an apparatus in which a premature or sick baby is kept under controlled conditions until it is able to survive independently. **2** an apparatus in which eggs are hatched artificially. **3** an apparatus in which bacteria etc are grown under controlled conditions.

incubus *n* (*pl* **incubuses** *or* **incubi**) **1** a male demon believed to have sexual intercourse with women in their sleep: compare SUCCUBUS. **2** *archaic* a nightmare.

inculcate *v* to teach or instil (something) by frequent repetition or warning. ➤➤ **inculcation** *n.*

incumbency *n* the sphere of action or period of office of an incumbent.

incumbent[1] *n* the holder of an office.

incumbent[2] *adj* **1** (+ on/upon) imposed as a duty or obligation on somebody. **2** holding a specified office.

incunabulum *n* (*pl* **incunabula**) a book printed before 1501.

incur *v* (**incurred, incurring**) to become liable or subject to (something unpleasant or unwanted).

incurable[1] *adj esp* of a disease: not able to be cured or treated. ➤➤ **incurability** *n,* **incurably** *adv.*

incurable[2] *n* a person with an incurable disease.

incurious *adj* lacking curiosity; uninterested. ≫ **incuriosity** *n*, **incuriously** *adv.*

incursion *n* a sudden or brief invasion into another's territory.

indebted *adj* **1** owing gratitude or recognition to another. **2** owing money. ≫ **indebtedness** *n.*

indecent *adj* **1** improper or unseemly. **2** morally offensive. ≫ **indecency** *n*, **indecently** *adv.*

indecent assault *n* a criminal offence of sexual assault that does not involve rape.

indecent exposure *n* the criminal offence of publicly exposing one's genitals.

indecipherable *adj* **1** of handwriting: impossible to read. **2** of a code: unable to be solved or understood.

indecision *n* wavering between two or more possible courses of action.

indecisive *adj* **1** marked by or prone to indecision. **2** giving an uncertain result. ≫ **indecisively** *adv*, **indecisiveness** *n.*

indecorum *n* failure to conform to acceptable standards of behaviour, taste, etc; impropriety. ≫ **indecorous** *adj*, **indecorously** *adv.*

indeed *adv* **1** used as an intensifier or for emphasis: *It has been very cold indeed.* **2** used to introduce additional information: actually: *I don't mind, indeed I'm pleased; if indeed they come at all.* **3** used to express irony, contempt, disbelief, or surprise: *Does she indeed!*

indefatigable *adj* tireless or unflagging. ≫ **indefatigably** *adv.*

indefensible *adj* not capable of being justified or excused. ≫ **indefensibly** *adv.*

indefinable *adj* incapable of being precisely described or analysed. ≫ **indefinably** *adv.*

indefinite *adj* **1** not precise; vague or unsettled. **2** having no exact limits. **3** of a word, phrase, etc: not identifying any particular person or thing. ≫ **indefinitely** *adv*, **indefiniteness** *n.*

indefinite article *n* in grammar, a word, e.g. *a*, *an*, or *some* in English, that refers to an unspecified person or thing: compare DEFINITE ARTICLE.

indefinite pronoun *n* in grammar, a pronoun, e.g. *somebody* or *anything* in English, that refers to an unspecified person or thing.

indelible *adj* **1a** of a mark, stain, etc: incapable of being removed or erased. **b** of ink: designed to make marks that cannot be removed or erased. **2** of a memory: not able to be forgotten. ≫ **indelibly** *adv.*

indelicate *adj* **1** of a remark: almost indecent or offensive. **2** lacking in good manners, taste, or sensitivity. ≫ **indelicacy** *n*, **indelicately** *adv.*

indemnify *v* (**-ies, -ied**) **1** to secure (somebody or something) against harm, loss, or liability. **2** to compensate (somebody) for harm or loss. ≫ **indemnification** *n*, **indemnifier** *n.*

indemnity *n* (*pl* **-ies**) **1** security against harm, loss, or liability. **2** exemption from incurred penalties or liabilities. **3** compensation for harm, loss, or damage.

indent[1] *v* **1** to set (a line of text, a paragraph, etc) in from the margin. **2** to notch the edge of (something). **3** *chiefly Brit* to make an official requisition or order for something. ≫ **indenter** *n*, **indentor** *n.*

indent[2] *n* **1** = INDENTATION. **2** = INDENTURE[1]. **3** *chiefly Brit* an official requisition or order.

indent[3] *v* to make a dent or depression in (a surface).

indentation *n* **1a** an angular cut or series of cuts in an edge. **b** a deep recess. **2** the blank space produced by indenting a line of text, etc. **3** the act of indenting or the state of being indented.

indenture[1] *n* **1a** an indented document, *esp* an agreement, contract, etc. **b** (*also in pl*) a contract binding somebody, *esp* an apprentice, to work for another. **2a** a formal certificate, e.g. an inventory or voucher, prepared for purposes of control. **b** a document stating the terms under which a security is issued. ≫ **indentureship** *n.*

indenture[2] *v* to bind (an apprentice) by an indenture.

independent[1] *adj* **1a** not connected with or relying on something else. **b** not controlled by others. **c** having or providing enough money to live on, *esp* without working. **2** of a country: self-governing and free of external control. ≫ **independence** *n*, **independency** *n*, **independently** *adv.*

independent[2] *n* somebody who is independent.

in-depth *adj* comprehensively detailed and thorough.

indescribable *adj* **1** unable to be put into words. **2** beyond adequate description. ≫ **indescribably** *adv.*

indestructible *adj* impossible to destroy. ≫ **indestructibility** *n*, **indestructibly** *adv.*

indeterminable *adj* incapable of being definitely decided or ascertained.

indeterminate *adj* **1** not definitely or precisely determined or fixed; vague. **2a** of mathematical equations: having an infinite number of solutions. **b** being a mathematical expression of undefined value. ≫ **indeterminacy** *n*, **indeterminately** *adv.*

index[1] *n* (*pl* **indexes** *or* **indices**) **1a** an alphabetical list of names, topics, etc mentioned in a printed work indicating the page number or numbers where the items appear. **b** any systematic guide or list to aid reference, e.g. a catalogue of publications. **2** a device, e.g. a pointer on a scale, that indicates a value or quantity. **3** something that indicates or demonstrates a fact or circumstance. **4** a mathematical figure, letter, or expression, *esp* an exponent. **5** a number derived from a series of observations and used as an indicator or measure.

Usage note

indexes *or* **indices**? The plural of *index* in its common sense of an alphabetical list or catalogue is *indexes*. In technical uses, e.g. in mathematics and economics, the plural is more commonly *indices*: *indices of economic progress.*

index[2] *v* **1a** to provide (e.g. a book) with an index. **b** to list (an item) in an index. **2** to cause (something, e.g. a pension) to be index-linked. ≫ **indexer** *n.*

indexation *n* the act or process of making something, e.g. a pension, index-linked.

index finger *n* = FOREFINGER.

index-linked *adj* increasing or decreasing in proportion to a rise or fall in an index, *esp* the cost-of-living index.

India ink *n NAm* see INDIAN INK.

Indiaman *n* (*pl* **Indiamen**) a ship, *esp* a sailing ship, formerly used in trade with India or the E Indies.

Indian *n* **1** a native or inhabitant of India. **2** *dated, offensive* a member of any of the indigenous peoples of N, Central, or S America. ≫ **Indian** *adj.*

Indian club *n* a club shaped like a large bottle that is swung, often in pairs, for gymnastic exercise.

Indian ink (*NAm* **India ink**) *n Brit* an ink made from a solid black pigment and used in drawing and lettering.

Indian summer *n* a period of warm weather in late autumn or early winter.

India rubber *n* = RUBBER[1] (1).

indicate *v* **1** to point to or point out (something or somebody). **2** to be a sign or symptom of. **3** (*usu in passive*) to demonstrate or suggest the necessity or advisability of. **4** to state or express briefly or indirectly; to suggest. **5** of a driver: to show an intention to change direction by flashing an indicator. ➤➤ **indication** *n.*

indicative[1] *adj* **1** (*usu* + of) serving to indicate. **2** in grammar, of or being the mood that represents the denoted act or state as an objective fact. ➤➤ **indicatively** *adv.*

indicative[2] *n* the indicative mood or a verb form expressing this.

indicator *n* **1a** a hand or needle on a graduated instrument. **b** an instrument for giving visual readings attached to a machine or apparatus. **c** a flashing light or other device on a vehicle that is used to show the driver's intention to change direction. **d** a screen at a railway station or airport showing details of arrivals and departures. **2** a substance that shows, *esp* by change of colour, the condition of a solution, the presence of a particular material, or the end point of a chemical reaction.

indices *n* pl of INDEX[1].

Usage note

indices *or* **indexes**? See note at INDEX[1].

indict *v* to charge with an offence, *esp* a serious crime. ➤➤ **indictable** *adj,* **indictee** *n,* **indicter** *n.*

indictable offence *n* a serious crime that must be tried before a jury.

indictment *n* **1** a formal written accusation by a prosecuting authority. **2** grounds for severe censure or condemnation of something.

indie *n informal* (*used before a noun*) relating to or produced by a small independent film or record company.

indifferent *adj* **1** mediocre or poor. **2** (*often* + to) not interested or concerned. ➤➤ **indifference** *n,* **indifferently** *adv.*

indigenize *or* **-ise** *v* to make (something introduced from elsewhere) less alien.

indigenous *adj* originating, growing, or living naturally in a particular region or environment; native. ➤➤ **indigenously** *adv,* **indigenousness** *n.*

indigent[1] *adj* very needy or poor. ➤➤ **indigence** *n.*

indigent[2] *n* an indigent person.

indigestible *adj* **1** not able to be digested or difficult to digest. **2** difficult to understand, read, etc. ➤➤ **indigestibility** *n,* **indigestibly** *adv.*

indigestion *n* pain or discomfort resulting from difficulty in digesting something.

indignant *adj* filled with or marked by indignation. ➤➤ **indignantly** *adv.*

indignation *n* anger aroused by something judged unjust, unworthy, or mean.

indignity *n* (*pl* **-ies**) **1** an act that causes a loss of dignity or self-respect. **2** humiliating treatment.

indigo *n* (*pl* **-ies** *or* **-oes**) **1** a dark greyish blue colour, between blue and violet in the spectrum. **2** a dark blue dye formerly obtained from plants and now made artificially. ➤➤ **indigo** *adj.*

indirect *adj* **1a** deviating from a direct line or course; circuitous. **b** not going straight to the point. **2** not being a direct cause or consequence of something. **3** not straightforward or open; evasive or deceitful. ➤➤ **indirection** *n,* **indirectly** *adv,* **indirectness** *n.*

indirect object *n* a grammatical object representing a person or thing that is indirectly affected by the action of a transitive verb, e.g. *her* in *I gave her the book.*

indirect question *n* in grammar, a question in indirect speech, e.g. *He asked if I'd ever been to New York before.*

indirect speech *n* in grammar, the reporting of something previously said with appropriate changes of tense, person, etc, e.g. *I told him I'd never been to New York before.*

indirect tax *n* a tax levied on goods, services, etc and paid indirectly by a person or organization purchasing these goods or services at an increased price.

indiscernible *adj* **1** not able to be perceived or recognized. **2** not recognizable as separate or distinct. ➤➤ **indiscernibly** *adv.*

indiscipline *n* lack of discipline.

indiscreet *adj* not discreet, *esp* in revealing secret or private things. ➤➤ **indiscreetly** *adv.*

indiscretion *n* lack of discretion, or an act or remark that shows this.

indiscriminate *adj* **1** not marked by careful distinction; random. **2** lacking in discrimination and discernment. ➤➤ **indiscriminately** *adv,* **indiscriminateness** *n.*

indispensable *adj* essential; not able to be done without. ➤➤ **indispensability** *n,* **indispensableness** *n,* **indispensably** *adv.*

indisposed *adj* **1** slightly ill. **2** (*usu* + to) averse or unwilling to do something. ➤➤ **indisposition** *n.*

indisputable *adj* incontestable; not able to be denied or called into question. ➤➤ **indisputability** *n,* **indisputably** *adv.*

indissoluble *adj* incapable of being dissolved, undone, or annulled. ➤➤ **indissolubility** *n,* **indissolubly** *adv.*

indistinct *adj* **1** not sharply outlined; not clearly seen. **2** vague or uncertain. ➤➤ **indistinctly** *adv,* **indistinctness** *n.*

indistinguishable *adj* (*usu* + from) incapable of being clearly identified as different; identical. ➤➤ **indistinguishably** *adv.*

indium *n* a rare silvery soft metallic chemical element that occurs naturally in zinc blendes, and is used in electroplating and as a semi-conductor.

individual[1] *adj* **1** relating to or intended for a single person or thing. **2** existing as a distinct entity; separate. **3** having unusual or distinguishing features, traits, etc. ➤➤ **individually** *adv.*

individual[2] *n* **1** a particular person or thing, *esp* as distinguished from a group or from others in a group. **2** a person who has unusual or distinguishing characteristics.

individualise *v* see INDIVIDUALIZE.

individualism *n* **1** independent self-reliance. **2a** a doctrine that bases morality on the interests of the individual. **b** a social theory maintaining the political and economic independence of the individual and stressing individual initiative. ➤➤ **individualist** *n and adj,* **individualistic** *adj.*

individuality *n* **1** the quality of being distinctive or unique. **2** separate or distinct existence.

individualize *or* **-ise** *v* to make (something) individual; to adapt (something) to a purpose.

individuate *v* to give individuality or individual form to (somebody or something); to differentiate or distinguish. ➤➤ **individuation** *n.*

indivisible *adj* **1** not able to be separated or divided. **2** of a number: not able to be divided by another number without leaving a remainder. ⋙ **indivisibility** *n,* **indivisibly** *adv.*

Indo-Chinese *n* (*pl* **Indo-Chinese**) a native or inhabitant of Indochina. ⋙ **Indo-Chinese** *adj.*

indoctrinate *v* to teach (a person or group) to accept a view, ideology, etc uncritically, *esp* by systematic repetition. ⋙ **indoctrination** *n,* **indoctrinator** *n.*

Indo-European *n* a family of languages spoken in most of Europe, Asia as far as N India, and N and S America. ⋙ **Indo-European** *adj.*

indolent *adj* averse to activity, effort, or movement; lazy. ⋙ **indolence** *n,* **indolently** *adv.*

indomitable *adj* incapable of being subdued. ⋙ **indomitability** *n,* **indomitably** *adv.*

Indonesian *n* **1** a native or inhabitant of Indonesia or the Malay archipelago. **2** the language of the Indonesians. ⋙ **Indonesian** *adj.*

indoor *adj* **1** relating to the interior of a building. **2** done, situated, or belonging indoors.

indoors *adv* inside or into a building.

indorse *v* see ENDORSE.

indorsement *n* see ENDORSEMENT.

indrawn *adj* **1** drawn in. **2** aloof, reserved, or introspective.

indubitable *adj* too evident to be doubted or called into question. ⋙ **indubitably** *adv.*

induce *v* **1** to persuade or influence (somebody) to do something. **2a** to cause or bring about. **b** to cause (labour) to begin, *esp* by the use of drugs. **c** to produce (an electric charge, magnetism, etc) by induction. ⋙ **inducer** *n,* **inducible** *adj.*

inducement *n* **1** something that induces, *esp* a motive or consideration that encourages somebody to do something. **2** *euphem* a bribe.

induct *v* **1** to install (somebody) formally into office. **2** to introduce or initiate (somebody). **3** *NAm* to enrol (somebody) for military training or service. ⋙ **inductee** *n.*

inductance *n* a property of an electric circuit by which an electromotive force is induced in it by a variation of current, either in the circuit itself or in a neighbouring circuit.

induction *n* **1** the act or process of inducting, *esp* of installing somebody formally into office. **2** the act or an instance of reasoning from particular premises to a general conclusion, or a conclusion reached by such reasoning. **3** the act or process of inducing something, *esp* labour. **4a** the production of an electric charge, magnetism, or an electromotive force in an object by the proximity of, but not contact with, a similarly energized body. **b** the process of drawing the fuel-air mixture from the carburettor into the combustion chamber of an internal-combustion engine.

induction coil *n* a transformer, used *esp* in the ignition systems of road vehicles, that produces intermittent pulses of high-voltage alternating current from low-voltage direct current.

induction loop system *or* **induction loop** *n* in public buildings, a system of sound distribution within a designated area encircled by a loop of wire that sends out electromagnetic signals which are picked up by people wearing hearing aids or earphones.

inductive *adj* **1** relating to or employing logical or mathematical induction. **2** relating to or involving electrical or magnetic induction. **3** relating to or possessing inductance. ⋙ **inductively** *adv,* **inductiveness** *n.*

inductor *n* a component that is included in an electrical circuit to provide inductance, *esp* one that consists of a coiled conductor.

indue *v* see ENDUE.

indulge *v* **1a** to give free rein to (a taste, desire, etc). **b** to allow (oneself) to do or have something pleasurable or gratifying. **2** to treat with great or excessive leniency, generosity, etc; to pamper or spoil. ⋙ **indulger** *n.*

indulgence *n* **1** the act or an instance of indulging. **2** something indulged in; a luxury. **3** leniency or tolerance. **4** in the Roman Catholic Church, remission of all or part of the punishment that is due, *esp* in purgatory, for pardoned sins.

indulgent *adj* indulging or characterized by indulgence. ⋙ **indulgently** *adv.*

industrial *adj* relating to, characterized by, or used in industry. ⋙ **industrially** *adv.*

industrial action *n* a strike, go-slow, work-to-rule, etc by a body of workers, *esp* in industry.

industrial archaeology *n* the scientific study of the products and remains of past industrial activity.

industrial estate *n chiefly Brit* an area, often on the edge of a city or town, designed for industries and businesses.

industrialise *v* see INDUSTRIALIZE.

industrialism *n* an economic or social organization in which manufacturing industries, *esp* large-scale mechanized industries, are dominant.

industrialist *n* somebody who is engaged in the management of an industry.

industrialize *or* **-ise** *v* **1** to develop industries extensively in (a region). **2** of a region: to become industrialized. ⋙ **industrialization** *n.*

industrial park *n NAm* = INDUSTRIAL ESTATE.

industrial relations *pl n* the dealings or relationships between the management of a business or industrial enterprise and the employees or their trade unions.

industrial-strength *adj* very strong or powerful.

industrious *adj* conscientious and hard-working. ⋙ **industriously** *adv,* **industriousness** *n.*

industry *n* (*pl* **-ies**) **1a** economic activity that is concerned with the manufacture of goods, the processing of raw materials, construction work, etc. **b** a specified branch of this. **2** hard-working diligence.

-ine[1] *suffix* forming adjectives, denoting: **1** resemblance: *saturnine.* **2** membership of a group, *esp* a genus or family of animals: *canine.* **3** composition: *crystalline.*

-ine[2] *suffix* forming nouns, denoting: **1a** a chemical compound: *gasoline.* **b** a carbon compound, e.g. an amino acid or alkaloid, that is a chemical base and contains nitrogen: *morphine.* **c** a mixture of compounds, e.g. of hydrocarbons: *kerosine.* **2** a feminine form: *heroine.*

inebriate[1] *v esp* of alcohol: to intoxicate. ⋙ **inebriation** *n,* **inebriety** *n.*

inebriate[2] *adj* drunk, *esp* habitually.

inedible *adj* not fit to be eaten.

ineducable *adj* incapable of being educated, *esp* because of low intelligence or disruptive behaviour.

ineffable *adj* **1** too great or intense to be expressed; inexpressible. **2** too sacred to be uttered. ⋙ **ineffability** *n,* **ineffably** *adv.*

ineffective *adj* **1** not producing an effect or the intended effect. **2** not capable of performing efficiently or achieving results. ⋙ **ineffectively** *adv,* **ineffectiveness** *n.*

ineffectual *adj* **1** unable to get things done; weak in character. **2** not producing or not able to produce an effect or the proper or intended effect. ⋙ **ineffectuality** *n,* **ineffectually** *adv,* **ineffectualness** *n.*

inefficient *adj* failing to work, operate, etc in a capable or economical way. ⋙ **inefficiency** *n,* **inefficiently** *adv.*

inelastic *adj* inflexible; unyielding. ⋙ **inelasticity** *n.*

inelegant *adj* lacking in refinement, grace, or good taste. ⋙ **inelegance** *n,* **inelegantly** *adv.*

ineligible *adj* not qualified or able to receive or do something. ⋙ **ineligibility** *n.*

ineluctable *adj formal* unavoidable; inescapable. ⋙ **ineluctability** *n,* **ineluctably** *adv.*

inept *adj* incompetent or clumsy. ⋙ **ineptitude** *n,* **ineptly** *adv,* **ineptness** *n.*

inequality *n* (*pl* **-ies**) the state or an instance of being unequal; lack of equality.

inequitable *adj* unfair or unjust. ⋙ **inequitably** *adv.*

inequity *n* (*pl* **-ies**) injustice or unfairness.

ineradicable *adj* incapable of being eradicated. ⋙ **ineradicably** *adv.*

inert *adj* **1** lacking the power to move. **2** lacking active chemical or biological properties. **3** not moving; inactive or indolent. ⋙ **inertly** *adv,* **inertness** *n.*

inert gas *n* = NOBLE GAS.

inertia *n* **1** a tendency to resist motion, exertion, or change. **2** in physics, a property of matter by which it remains at rest or in uniform motion in the same straight line unless acted on by some external force. ⋙ **inertial** *adj.*

inertia-reel seat belt *n* a seat belt that allows steady unwinding but resists a sudden sharp jerk by locking the drum.

inescapable *adj* incapable of being avoided, ignored, or denied. ⋙ **inescapability** *n,* **inescapably** *adv.*

inessential[1] *adj* not absolutely necessary.

inessential[2] *n* something that is not absolutely necessary.

inestimable *adj* **1** too great in number or amount to be estimated. **2** too valuable or excellent to be measured. ⋙ **inestimably** *adv.*

inevitable[1] *adj* incapable of being avoided; bound to happen. ⋙ **inevitability** *n,* **inevitably** *adv.*

inevitable[2] *n* (**the inevitable**) something that is unavoidable or bound to happen.

inexact *adj* not precisely correct or true. ⋙ **inexactitude** *n,* **inexactly** *adv,* **inexactness** *n.*

inexcusable *adj* too bad to be excused or justified. ⋙ **inexcusably** *adv.*

inexhaustible *adj* **1** of a supply: incapable of being used up. **2** of a person: tireless. ⋙ **inexhaustibility** *n,* **inexhaustibly** *adv.*

inexorable *adj* **1** not to be persuaded or moved by entreaty. **2** continuing inevitably; unable to be averted. ⋙ **inexorability** *n,* **inexorably** *adv.*

inexpensive *adj* reasonable in price; cheap. ⋙ **inexpensively** *adv,* **inexpensiveness** *n.*

inexperience *n* lack of experience. ⋙ **inexperienced** *adj.*

inexpert *adj* unskilled or lacking knowledge. ⋙ **inexpertly** *adv.*

inexplicable *adj* incapable of being explained or accounted for. ⋙ **inexplicability** *n,* **inexplicably** *adv.*

inexpressible *adj* not able to be expressed. ⋙ **inexpressibly** *adv.*

inexpressive *adj* lacking expression or meaning. ⋙ **inexpressively** *adv,* **inexpressiveness** *n.*

inextinguishable *adj* unable to be extinguished or suppressed.

in extremis *adv* **1** in extremely difficult circumstances. **2** at the point of death.

inextricable *adj* **1** of a difficult situation: impossible to escape from. **2** incapable of being disentangled, untied, or separated. ⋙ **inextricably** *adv.*

infallible *adj* **1** incapable of error. **2** not liable to fail; known to be effective. ⋙ **infallibility** *n,* **infallibly** *adv.*

infamous *adj* **1** having a bad reputation; notorious. **2** disgraceful. ⋙ **infamously** *adv.*

infamy *n* (*pl* **-ies**) **1** disrepute brought about by something grossly criminal, shocking, or brutal. **2** an extreme and publicly known criminal or evil act.

infancy *n* (*pl* **-ies**) **1** early childhood. **2** a beginning or early period of existence.

infant *n* **1** a child in the first period of life. **2** *Brit* a child at school between the ages of five and seven or eight.

infanta *n* a daughter of a Spanish or Portuguese monarch.

infanticide *n* the act of killing an infant. ⋙ **infanticidal** *adj.*

infantile *adj* **1** relating to or suitable for infants or infancy. **2** *derog* childish or immature. ⋙ **infantility** *n.*

infantilism *n* **1** the persistence or retention of childish physical, mental, or emotional qualities in adult life. **2** childish behaviour.

infantry *n* (*used as sing. or pl*) soldiers trained and equipped to fight on foot.

infantryman *n* (*pl* **infantrymen**) an infantry soldier.

infarct *n* an area of dead tissue, e.g. in the heart or other organ, resulting from obstruction of the blood circulation in that area.

infarction *n* the development of an infarct.

infatuate *v* to inspire (somebody) with powerful but often superficial or short-lived feelings of love, desire, etc. ⋙ **infatuation** *n.*

infauna *n* aquatic animals living on the bottom, *esp* in a soft sea bed: compare EPIFAUNA.

infect *v* **1** to contaminate (e.g. air or food) with an agent that causes disease. **2a** to pass on a disease or an agent that causes disease to (somebody or something). **b** of a pathogenic organism: to invade (an individual or organ) and cause a disease. **3** of a computer virus: to invade and damage (a system, program, file, etc). **4** to corrupt or taint. ⋙ **infector** *n.*

infection *n* **1** a contagious or infectious disease, or an agent that causes this. **2** the act of infecting or the state of being infected.

infectious *adj* **1a** of a disease: caused and communicable by infection with a micro-organism, e.g. a bacterium or virus. **b** of a micro-organism: capable of causing disease. **2** readily spread or communicated to others. ⋙ **infectiously** *adv,* **infectiousness** *n.*

infectious mononucleosis *n* an acute infectious disease characterized by fever, swollen and painful lymph glands, and an increase in the number of lymphocytes in the blood; glandular fever.

infective *adj* of a micro-organism: capable of causing or likely to cause disease.

infelicitous *adj* not apt; not suitably chosen for the occasion. ⋙ **infelicitously** *adv.*

infelicity *n* (*pl* **-ies**) **1** an infelicitous act or remark. **2** *archaic* misfortune; unhappiness.

infer *v* (**inferred, inferring**) to derive (something) as a conclusion from evidence or premises as opposed to what is explicitly stated. ➤➤ **inferable** *adj,* **inferrable** *adj.*

Usage note

infer *or* imply? See note at IMPLY.

inference *n* **1** the act or process of inferring. **2** something inferred, *esp* a conclusion arrived at by considering the available evidence or premises.

inferential *adj* deduced or deducible by inference.

inferior[1] *adj* **1** of low or lower degree or rank. **2** of little or less importance, value, or merit. **3** situated at a lower position. **4** of a letter or other character: positioned below the line; subscript. ➤➤ **inferiority** *n.*

inferior[2] *n* a person who is lower in rank, standing, ability, etc than another or others.

inferiority complex *n* a sense of personal inferiority, either actual or imagined, often resulting in timidity or aggressiveness.

infernal *adj* **1** of or relating to hell. **2** *informal* dreadful; awful. ➤➤ **infernally** *adv.*

inferno *n* (*pl* **-os**) **1** a place or a state that resembles or suggests hell, *esp* in intense heat or raging fire. **2** (*often* **the Inferno**) hell.

infertile *adj* **1** not capable of producing offspring; sterile. **2** of land: not capable of sustaining vegetation, *esp* crops; barren. ➤➤ **infertility** *n.*

infest *v* **1** to spread or swarm in or over (something) in a troublesome or undesirable manner. **2** to live in or on (a host) as a parasite. ➤➤ **infestation** *n.*

infibulate *v* to partially close the vagina, the labia, or the foreskin by means of a clasp, stitches, etc. ➤➤ **infibulation** *n.*

infidel *n* **1** somebody who opposes or does not believe in a particular religion, *esp* Christianity or Islam. **2** somebody who acknowledges no religious belief.

infidelity *n* (*pl* **-ies**) **1** unfaithfulness or disloyalty, *esp* in marital or sexual matters. **2** lack of belief in a religion.

infield[1] *n* the area of a cricket or baseball field near the wickets or bounded by the bases, or the fielding positions stationed there. ➤➤ **infielder** *n.*

infield[2] *adv* away from the edge of a playing field.

infighting *n* prolonged and often bitter dissension among members of a group or organization. ➤➤ **infighter** *n.*

infill[1] *v* to fill in (a gap). ➤➤ **infilling** *n.*

infill[2] *n* **1** material used to fill a gap. **2** houses built between those already standing.

infiltrate *v* **1** to enter or become established in (e.g. an organization) gradually or unobtrusively, often with a hostile intention. **2** of a fluid: to pass into or through (a substance) by filtering or permeating. ➤➤ **infiltration** *n,* **infiltrator** *n.*

infinite *adj* **1** subject to or having no limitations or boundaries in time, space, number, etc. **2** great, immense, or extreme. ➤➤ **infinitely** *adv,* **infiniteness** *n,* **infinitude** *n.*

infinitesimal *adj* immeasurably or incalculably small. ➤➤ **infinitesimally** *adv.*

infinitesimal calculus *n* = CALCULUS (2).

infinitive *n* the base form of a verb, without inflection, in English sometimes preceded by the particle *to* (e.g. *go, take, to go, to take*).

infinity *n* (*pl* **-ies**) **1a** the quality of being infinite. **b** unlimited extent of time, space, etc. **2** a very great number or amount. **3** in mathematics, a value greater than that of any finite quantity. **4** a distance so great that the rays of light from a point or source at that distance may be regarded as parallel.

infirm *adj* physically feeble, *esp* from age.

infirmary *n* (*pl* **-ies**) usu in proper names: a hospital.

infirmity *n* (*pl* **-ies**) **1** the state of being infirm. **2** a disease or mental weakness.

in flagrante delicto /in flə'granti di'liktoh/ *adv* in the very act of committing a misdeed; red-handed.

inflame *v* **1a** to excite or arouse passion or strong feeling in (a person or group). **b** to make (e.g. an emotion or dispute) more heated or violent; to intensify. **2** to cause inflammation in (body tissue).

inflammable[1] *adj* capable of being easily ignited and of burning rapidly; flammable. ➤➤ **inflammability** *n.*

Usage note

inflammable *or* flammable? See note at FLAMMABLE.

inflammable[2] *n* something that is inflammable.

inflammation *n* a response to injury or infection of body tissues marked by local redness, heat, swelling, and pain.

inflammatory *adj* **1** tending to arouse strong feeling, *esp* anger, outrage, etc. **2** accompanied by or tending to cause inflammation.

inflatable[1] *adj* capable of being inflated.

inflatable[2] *n* an inflatable boat, toy, etc.

inflate *v* **1** to swell or distend (something, e.g. a balloon or the lungs) with air or gas. **2** to expand or increase (something) abnormally or excessively. **3** to cause inflation in (e.g. prices or the economy).

inflated *adj* **1** of speech, writing, opinions, etc: bombastic or exaggerated. **2** expanded or increased to an abnormal or excessive volume or level. **3** swollen or distended.

inflation *n* **1** a substantial and continuing rise in the general level of prices, caused by or causing an increase in the supply of money and credit or an expansion of the economy. **2** the act of inflating or the state of being inflated. ➤➤ **inflationary** *adj.*

inflationism *n* the policy of economic inflation, *esp* through expansion of currency or bank deposits. ➤➤ **inflationist** *n and adj.*

inflect *v* **1** to change the form or ending of (a word) by inflection. **2** to become modified by inflection. **3** to vary the pitch of (a voice or note). **4** *technical* to bend (a line, etc) from a normal or straight course. ➤➤ **inflective** *adj.*

inflection *or* **inflexion** *n* **1** in grammar, a change in the form of a word to show its case, gender, number, tense, etc. **2** variation in pitch or loudness of the voice. **3** in mathematics, change of curvature from concave to convex or vice versa. ➤➤ **inflectional** *adj,* **inflectionally** *adv,* **inflectionless** *adj.*

inflexible *adj* **1a** incapable of or resistant to change. **b** not variable to suit a particular circumstance. **2** rigidly firm; not able to be bent. ➤➤ **inflexibility** *n,* **inflexibly** *adv.*

inflexion *n Brit* see INFLECTION.

inflict *v* (*usu* + on) to force or impose (something unpleasant or painful) on somebody. ➤➤ **infliction** *n.*

in-flight *adj* done, occurring, or provided during flight in an aircraft.

inflorescence *n* **1a** a flower-bearing stem, including stalks and branches, or the arrangement of flowers on a stem. **b** a flower cluster or a solitary flower. **2** the budding and unfolding of blossoms; flowering.

inflow *n* **1** the act or process of flowing in. **2** something, e.g. liquid, money, or traffic, that flows, moves, or comes in.

influence[1] *n* **1** the act, power, or capacity of causing or producing an effect on somebody or something, *esp* in indirect or intangible ways, or the effect itself. **2** the power to achieve something desired by using wealth or position. **3** somebody or something that has or exerts influence, *esp* in matters of morality and behaviour. ✱ **under the influence** *informal* drunk.

influence[2] *v* to affect (somebody or something), *esp* by indirect or intangible means.

influential *adj* exerting or possessing influence. ➤➤ **influentially** *adv.*

influenza *n* a highly infectious viral disease characterized by fever, severe aches and pains, and inflammation of the mucous membranes lining the respiratory passages; flu. ➤➤ **influenzal** *adj.*

influx *n* **1** an arrival of people or things in large numbers. **2** an inflow, *esp* of water into a sea, lake, or river, or the mouth of a tributary where this occurs.

infomercial *n* a television or video commercial in the form of a short documentary.

inform *v* **1** to communicate knowledge or information to. **2** to impart an essential quality or character to. **3** (*usu* + against/on) to give the police or other authorities information about a criminal or crime.

informal *adj* **1** marked by an absence of formality or ceremony. **2** of language: relating or belonging to a style appropriate to conversation rather than formal writing. ➤➤ **informality** *n,* **informally** *adv.*

informal vote *n Aus, NZ* a spoiled or invalid ballot paper.

informant *n* **1** a person who gives somebody information about something. **2** = INFORMER .

information *n* **1** knowledge obtained from investigation, study, or instruction. **2** facts or data, *esp* pertaining to a particular subject or regarded as significant. **3** news. **4** a signal or sequence of symbols, e.g. in a radio transmission or computing, that represents data. ➤➤ **informational** *adj.*

information superhighway *n* an electronic network of information such as the Internet.

information technology *n* the use of computers, telecommunications, etc in electronically processing, storing, retrieving, and sending information.

informative *adj* conveying information; instructive. ➤➤ **informatively** *adv,* **informativeness** *n.*

informed *adj* **1** possessing or based on possession of information. **2** knowledgeable about matters of contemporary interest.

informer *n* a person who gives information about a criminal or crime to the police.

infotainment *n* educational or serious topics presented on television in an accessible and entertaining format.

infra- *prefix* below: *infrasonic.*

infraction *n* a violation or infringement, *esp* of a law or a person's rights.

infra dig *adj informal* beneath one's dignity; demeaning or humiliating.

infrared *n* electromagnetic radiation lying outside the visible spectrum, with a wavelength between red light and microwaves, and commonly perceived as heat. ➤➤ **infrared** *adj.*

infrasonic *adj* relating to or denoting sound waves or vibrations with a frequency below the lower threshold of human hearing.

infrasound *n* infrasonic sound waves or vibrations.

infrastructure *n* **1** the permanent features, e.g. road and rail networks, power supplies, educational institutions, etc, necessary for a country's economic well-being. **2** an underlying foundation or basic framework.

infrequent *adj* not occurring often; rare. ➤➤ **infrequency** *n,* **infrequently** *adv.*

infringe *v* **1** to encroach on (a right or privilege). **2** to violate (a law, agreement, etc). ➤➤ **infringement** *n,* **infringer** *n.*

infuriate *v* to make (a person or animal) furious; to anger or enrage. ➤➤ **infuriating** *adj,* **infuriatingly** *adv.*

infuse *v* **1** to steep (tea, herbs, etc) in liquid without boiling so as to extract the flavour, soluble properties, etc. **2** to imbue or pervade. **3** to instil (a quality or value) in somebody or something. **4** in medicine, to cause (a liquid, *esp* blood or plasma) to flow gradually into a person, vein, etc. ➤➤ **infuser** *n.*

infusible *adj* very difficult or impossible to fuse or melt. ➤➤ **infusibility** *n.*

infusion *n* **1** the process of infusing. **2** in medicine, the continuous slow introduction of a solution, *esp* blood or plasma, into a person, vein, etc. **3** an extract obtained by infusing.

-ing[1] *suffix* forming the present participle of verbs, or participial adjectives: *making; gruelling.*

-ing[2] *suffix* forming nouns, denoting: **1** an action or process, or a result of it: *running; a meeting.* **2** an activity or occupation: *banking.* **3** materials used in an activity: *scaffolding.* **4** a collection of things: *shipping.*

ingenious *adj* marked by originality, resourcefulness, and cleverness: *an ingenious method of recycling household waste.* ➤➤ **ingeniously** *adv,* **ingeniousness** *n.*

Usage note

ingenious *or* **ingenuous**? These two words are easy to confuse. *Ingenious* means 'clever' or 'effective', especially in an original or surprising way: *an ingenious method of recycling household waste. Ingenuous* means 'innocent', 'artless', or 'guileless': *too ingenuous to imagine that they might not mean what they said.*

ingenue *or* **ingénue** /anzhay'nooh/ *n* a naive or artless young woman.

ingenuity *n* resourcefulness, cleverness, or inventiveness.

ingenuous *adj* **1** showing innocent or childlike simplicity. **2** frank; candid. ➤➤ **ingenuously** *adv,* **ingenuousness** *n.*

Usage note

ingenuous *or* **ingenious**? See note at INGENIOUS.

ingest *v* to take (food or drink) into the body. ➤➤ **ingestion** *n,* **ingestive** *adj.*

inglenook *n* an alcove by a large open fireplace.

inglorious *adj* shameful; ignominious. ➤➤ **ingloriously** *adv,* **ingloriousness** *n.*

ingoing *adj* entering.

ingot *n* a mass of cast metal, often in the shape of a bar or brick.

ingraft *v* see ENGRAFT.

ingrain *or* **engrain** *v* to implant (an idea, moral value, etc) in a person's mind.

ingrained *or* **engrained** *adj* **1** of a habit, moral value, etc: firmly and deeply implanted; deep-rooted. **2** of dirt, stains, etc: thoroughly worked into something. **3** having a firmly established attitude or belief. ➤➤ **ingrainedly** *adv.*

ingrate[1] *n formal* an ungrateful person.

ingrate[2] *adj archaic* ungrateful.

ingratiate *v* to gain favour for (e.g. oneself) by deliberate effort. ➤➤ **ingratiating** *adj,* **ingratiatingly** *adv,* **ingratiation** *n.*

ingratitude *n* forgetfulness or scant recognition of kindness received; lack of gratitude.

ingredient *n* something that forms a component part of a compound, combination, or mixture, *esp* any of the edible substances that are combined in the preparation of food.

ingress *n* **1** the act or an instance of entering, e.g. the entering of a substance into a place where it is not wanted. **2** the right of entrance or access. **3** a way in; an entrance.

in-group *n* a select group within a larger unit, which does not readily admit outsiders.

ingrowing *adj esp* of a toenail: having the free tip or edge embedded in the flesh.

ingrown *adj* **1** inward-looking in activities or interests; withdrawn. **2** having developed naturally. **3** *esp* of a toenail: ingrowing.

ingrowth *n* **1** the act or an instance of growing inwards. **2** something that grows in or into a space.

inguinal *adj* relating to or in the region of the groin.

inhabit *v* (**inhabited, inhabiting**) to occupy (a place) permanently; to live in (a place). ➤➤ **inhabitable** *adj,* **inhabitant** *n,* **inhabitation** *n.*

inhalant *n* something, e.g. a medication, that is inhaled.

inhalation *n* **1** the act or an instance of inhaling. **2** an inward breath.

inhale *v* **1** to breathe in. **2** to breathe (something, e.g. a perfume) in.

inhaler *n* a device used for inhaling a medication, e.g. to relieve asthma.

inhere *v* (+ in) to be inherent; to reside.

inherent *adj* forming an essential and indivisible part of something; innate. ➤➤ **inherently** *adv.*

inherit *v* (**inherited, inheriting**) **1** to receive (property) from an ancestor at his or her death, either by succession or under the terms of a will. **2** to receive (something, e.g. a physical attribute) by genetic transmission. **3** to come to possess (something) because it was left by a predecessor. ➤➤ **inheritor** *n.*

inheritable *adj* **1** capable of being inherited. **2** capable of inheriting.

inheritance *n* **1a** the act or an instance of inheriting property. **b** property that is or may be inherited. **2** something acquired or derived from the past, e.g. from a predecessor.

inheritance tax *n* in the UK, a tax levied on inherited property and money above a certain value: compare CAPITAL TRANSFER TAX, DEATH DUTY.

inhibit *v* (**inhibited, inhibiting**) **1** to discourage (somebody) from free or spontaneous activity, *esp* by psychological or social controls. **2** (+ from) to prohibit (somebody) from doing something. **3** to restrain (e.g. an impulse). **4** to prevent or lessen (a chemical reaction). ➤➤ **inhibited** *adj,* **inhibitive** *adj,* **inhibitory** *adj.*

inhibiter *n* see INHIBITOR.

inhibition *n* **1** a psychological restraint on the way somebody thinks or behaves. **2a** the act or an instance of inhibiting or being inhibited. **b** something that forbids, debars, or restricts.

inhibitor *or* **inhibiter** *n* **1** somebody or something that inhibits. **2** something that slows or interferes with a chemical reaction or a physiological process.

inhospitable *adj* **1** of a person: not friendly or welcoming. **2** of a place, climate, etc: providing no shelter or means of support; hard to live in. ➤➤ **inhospitableness** *n,* **inhospitably** *adv,* **inhospitality** *n.*

in-house[1] *adj* of or carried on within a group or organization, *esp* without the help of freelancers.

in-house[2] *adv* within a group or organization.

inhuman *adj* **1** failing to conform to basic human needs; austere. **2** extremely cruel; barbarous. **3** not human in nature or quality. ➤➤ **inhumanly** *adv.*

inhumane *adj* completely lacking in kindness or compassion; cruel. ➤➤ **inhumanely** *adv.*

inhumanity *n* (*pl* **-ies**) pitiless or cruel nature or behaviour.

inhume *v formal* to bury (a body). ➤➤ **inhumation** *n.*

inimical *adj* **1** hostile or indicating hostility. **2** adverse in tendency, influence, or effects; harmful. ➤➤ **inimically** *adv.*

inimitable *adj* so good or extraordinary that no others can match it; unique. ➤➤ **inimitability** *n,* **inimitably** *adv.*

iniquity *n* (*pl* **-ies**) **1** lack of justice or moral rectitude; wickedness. **2** a wicked act; a sin. ➤➤ **iniquitous** *adj.*

initial[1] *adj* **1** existing at the beginning. **2** placed at the beginning; first. ➤➤ **initially** *adv.*

initial[2] *n* **1** the first letter of a name. **2** (*in pl*) the first letter of each word in a full name.

initial[3] *v* (**initialled, initialling,** *NAm* **initialed, initialing**) to put initials on (something), usu as an indication of ownership or authorization.

initialize *or* **-ise** *v* to prepare (computer hardware or software) for operation by setting its configuration to a known state.

initiate[1] *v* **1** to cause or allow to begin; to start. **2** to instil with the rudiments or principles of something complex or obscure. **3** to grant (somebody) membership of an organization or society, traditionally by formal rites. ➤➤ **initiation** *n,* **initiatory** *adj.*

initiate[2] *n* somebody who has undergone initiation.

initiative *n* **1** energy or resourcefulness displayed in being the first to act or in acting without being prompted; enterprise. **2a** a first or new step, *esp* in the attainment of an end or goal. **b** the right to take the first step or to act first. * **on one's own initiative** without being prompted.

initiator *n* **1** somebody or something that initiates. **2** a chemical that starts a chain reaction. **3** an explosive used in detonators.

inject *v* **1a** to force a fluid into the body of (somebody) using a syringe. **b** to force (a fluid) in in this way. **c** to throw, drive, or force (something) somewhere. **2** to introduce as an element or factor. ➤➤ **injectable** *adj,* **injector** *n.*

injection *n* **1** something, e.g. a medication, that is injected into a person's body using a syringe. **2a** the act or an instance of injecting or being injected. **b** = FUEL INJECTION.

injection moulding *n* the manufacture of rubber or plastic articles by injecting heated material into a mould.

in-joke *n* a joke that is understood only by people who belong to a particular clique.

injudicious *adj* showing a lack of judgment; unwise. ➤➤ **injudiciously** *adv,* **injudiciousness** *n.*

injunction *n* **1** a court order requiring somebody to do or refrain from doing a particular act. **2** a firm warning or an order. ⋙ **injunctive** *adj.*

injure *v* **1** to inflict bodily harm on (somebody, a part of the body, etc). **2** to impair the soundness of (e.g. somebody's health). **3** to inflict damage or loss on.

injurious *adj* **1** inflicting or tending to inflict injury. **2** of language: abusive or insulting. ⋙ **injuriously** *adv,* **injuriousness** *n.*

injury *n* (*pl* **-ies**) **1** a physical hurt caused to somebody. **2** damage or loss sustained.

injury time *n* time added onto the end of a match in football, rugby, etc to compensate for time lost through injuries to players.

injustice *n* **1** the absence of justice; unfairness. **2** an unjust act or state of affairs.

ink[1] *n* **1** a coloured liquid used for writing and printing. **2** the black secretion of a squid or similar cephalopod mollusc that hides it from a predator or prey. ⋙ **inkiness** *n,* **inky** *adj.*

ink[2] *v* **1** to apply ink to (something, e.g. a printing plate). **2** to write (something) in ink.

ink cap *n* a toadstool with a cap that melts into an inky fluid after the spores have matured.

ink-jet printer *n* a computer printer that prints by means of droplets of ink released from a bank of tiny jets.

inkling *n* **1** a slight knowledge or vague idea; a suspicion. **2** a faint indication; a hint.

inkwell *n* a container for ink, *esp* one set into a hole in a desktop.

INLA *abbr* Irish National Liberation Army.

inlaid *v* past tense and past part. of INLAY[1].

inland[1] *adv* into or towards the interior part of a country, away from the coast.

inland[2] *adj* **1** of the interior of a country. **2** *chiefly Brit* not foreign; domestic.

inland[3] *n* the interior of a country.

inlander *n* somebody who lives inland.

Inland Revenue *n* the government department responsible for collecting taxes in Britain.

in-law *n informal* a relative by marriage.

inlay[1] *v* (*past tense and past part.* **inlaid**) **1** to set into a surface for decoration or reinforcement. **2** to decorate with inlaid material.

inlay[2] *n* **1** inlaid work or a decorative inlaid pattern. **2** a dental filling shaped to fit a cavity.

inlet *n* **1** a usu long and narrow recess in a shoreline, or a water passage between two land areas. **2** a means of entry, *esp* an opening for fluid to enter. **3** something set in, e.g. a piece of material inserted into clothing.

in-line skates *pl n* roller skates on which the wheels are fixed in line with each other along the length of the boot.

in loco parentis *adv* in the place of and having the responsibilities of a parent.

inmate *n* somebody occupying an institution, *esp* a prison or hospital.

in memoriam *prep and adv* in memory of (somebody).

inmost *adj* furthest within.

inn *n* a pub, *esp* one that can or used to provide accommodation.

innards *pl n informal* **1** the internal organs of a human being or animal, *esp* the intestines. **2** the internal parts of a structure or mechanism.

innate *adj* **1** existing in or belonging to an individual from birth. **2** existing as a basic and inseparable part; inherent. **3** originating in the mind before and independently of experience; instinctive; unlearned. ⋙ **innately** *adv,* **innateness** *n.*

inner[1] *adj* **1a** situated inside something; internal. **b** situated near to a centre, *esp* of influence: *an inner circle of government ministers.* **2** relating to the mind or soul. **3** unexpressed; private.

inner[2] *n* the ring on a target next to the bull's-eye.

inner bar *n* (**the inner bar**) all the barristers who collectively form the Queen's or King's counsel.

inner city *n* a usu older and more densely populated central section of a city, *esp* such an area that suffers social and economic problems.

inner ear *n* the innermost part of the ear from which sound waves are transmitted to the brain as nerve impulses.

innermost *adj* **1** most inward or central. **2** most secret and private.

inner tube *n* an inflatable tube inside the casing of a pneumatic tyre.

inning *n* in baseball, a team's turn at batting, or a division of a game consisting of a turn at batting for each team.

innings *n* (*pl* **innings**) **1** in cricket, any of the alternating divisions of a match during which one side bats and the other bowls. **2** *chiefly Brit, informal* the duration of somebody's life.

innkeeper *n* the landlord or landlady of an inn.

innocent[1] *adj* **1a** free from guilt or sin; pure. **b** harmless in effect or intention. **c** (*often* + of) free from legal guilt. **2a** not aware; ignorant. **b** not crafty or scheming in nature; ingenuous. ⋙ **innocence** *n,* **innocently** *adv.*

innocent[2] *n* somebody who is innocent.

innocuous *adj* **1** having no harmful effects; harmless. **2** unlikely to provoke or offend; inoffensive. ⋙ **innocuously** *adv,* **innocuousness** *n.*

innovate *v* to make changes by introducing something new, e.g. new practices or ideas. ⋙ **innovation** *n,* **innovative** *adj,* **innovator** *n,* **innovatory** *adj.*

Inns of Court *pl n* four societies of students and barristers in London which have the exclusive right of admission to the English Bar.

innuendo *n* (*pl* **-os** *or* **-oes**) an obliquely worded comment, typically suggestive or subtly disparaging.

innumerable *adj* too many to be counted. ⋙ **innumerably** *adv.*

innumerate[1] *adj Brit* having no knowledge even of basic arithmetic and not able to use numbers effectively. ⋙ **innumeracy** *n.*

innumerate[2] *n* an innumerate person.

inoculate *v* **1** to introduce a disease-causing organism into the body of (somebody) in order to induce immunity; to vaccinate (them). **2** to introduce a micro-organism into (an animal) for testing purposes. **3** to introduce (e.g. a micro-organism) into a culture, animal, etc. ⋙ **inoculable** *adj,* **inoculation** *n,* **inoculator** *n.*

inoffensive *adj* **1** not causing any harm; innocuous. **2** not objectionable. ⋙ **inoffensively** *adv,* **inoffensiveness** *n.*

inoperable *adj* **1** not suitable for treatment by surgery. **2** not likely to work or be successful; impracticable. ⋙ **inoperability** *n,* **inoperably** *adv.*

inoperative *adj* not functioning, or having no effect.

inopportune *adj* happening at an awkward or unwelcome time; inconvenient. ⋙ **inopportunely** *adv,* **inopportuneness** *n.*

inordinate *adj* going beyond reasonable limits; excessive. ➤➤ **inordinately** *adv.*

inorganic *adj* **1a** being or composed of matter other than plant or animal; mineral. **b** relating to or dealt with by a branch of chemistry concerned with inorganic substances. **2** not arising through natural growth; artificial. ➤➤ **inorganically** *adv.*

inpatient *n* a hospital patient who lives at a hospital while undergoing treatment there.

input[1] *n* **1a** something, e.g. energy, material, or data, supplied to a machine or system. **b** an amount of anything coming or put in. **2** work, suggestions, advice, etc that somebody contributes; a contribution. **3** the point in a system, machine, etc at which an input, e.g. of energy, material, or data, is made. **4** the act or an instance of putting something in.

input[2] *v* (**inputting,** *past tense and past part.* **input** *or* **inputted**) to enter (data) into a computer.

inquest *n* **1** a judicial enquiry, *esp* by a coroner, into the cause of a death. **2** an enquiry or investigation, *esp* into something that has failed.

inquire *v* see ENQUIRE.

Usage note

inquire *or* enquire? See note at ENQUIRE.

inquiry *n* see ENQUIRY.

inquisition *n* **1** a ruthless investigation or examination. **2** *formal* a judicial or official enquiry. ➤➤ **inquisitional** *adj.*

inquisitive *adj* **1** unduly curious about the affairs of others. **2** eager for knowledge or understanding. ➤➤ **inquisitively** *adv,* **inquisitiveness** *n.*

inquisitor *n* somebody who makes enquiries or asks questions, *esp* harshly or with hostility. ➤➤ **inquisitorial** *adj.*

inquorate *adj formal* not having a quorum; not quorate.

in re /,in 'ray/ *prep* in the matter of.

inroad *n* **1** a serious or forcible encroachment or intrusion. **2** a raid.

inrush *n* a crowding or flooding in. ➤➤ **inrushing** *n and adj.*

insalubrious *adj* not conducive to good health; unhealthy.

ins and outs *pl n* characteristic peculiarities and complexities; ramifications.

insane *adj* **1** *dated, offensive* suffering from a mental illness or psychological disorder. **2** *dated, offensive* intended for mentally ill people. **3** utterly absurd. ➤➤ **insanely** *adv,* **insanity** *n.*

insanitary *adj* very dirty, *esp* unclean enough to endanger health.

insatiable *adj* incapable of being satisfied. ➤➤ **insatiability** *n,* **insatiably** *adv.*

inscribe *v* **1a** to write, engrave, or print (something), *esp* as a lasting record. **b** to write, engrave, or print on. **2** to address or dedicate (*esp* a book) to somebody by a handwritten note on the inside. **3** in geometry, to draw (a figure) within a figure, usu so that they touch but do not intersect. ➤➤ **inscriber** *n.*

inscription *n* **1** a handwritten dedication in a book or on a work of art. **2** any written or engraved form of words, e.g. on a statue or a coin. **3** the act or an instance of inscribing. ➤➤ **inscriptional** *adj,* **inscriptive** *adj.*

inscrutable *adj* hard to interpret or understand; enigmatic. ➤➤ **inscrutability** *n,* **inscrutably** *adv.*

insect *n* an invertebrate animal with a well-defined head, thorax, and abdomen, three pairs of legs, and typically one or two pairs of wings.

insectarium *n* (*pl* **insectariums** *or* **insectaria**) a place where insects are kept or reared.

insectary *n* (*pl* **insectaries**) = INSECTARIUM.

insecticide *n* a substance that destroys insects. ➤➤ **insecticidal** *adj.*

insectile *adj* resembling an insect.

insectivore *n* **1** a mammal of an order that is nocturnal and eats insects, such as a mole, shrew, or hedgehog. **2** an insect-eating plant or animal. ➤➤ **insectivorous** *adj.*

insecure *adj* **1a** lacking in self-confidence. **b** feeling afraid or anxious. **2** lacking adequate protection or guarantee. **3** not firmly fixed or supported. **4** not stable or well-adjusted. ➤➤ **insecurely** *adv,* **insecurity** *n.*

inselberg *n* a single steep-sided hill on a plateau.

inseminate *v* to introduce semen into (a woman or female animal). ➤➤ **insemination** *n,* **inseminator** *n.*

insensate *adj* **1** not capable of feeling; insentient. **2** lacking in human feeling; insensitive. **3** senseless; foolish. ➤➤ **insensately** *adv.*

insensible *adj* **1** bereft of feeling or sensation, e.g.: **a** having lost consciousness; unconscious. **b** lacking or deprived of sensory perception. **2** lacking concern or awareness; indifferent. **3** incapable of being felt or sensed; imperceptible. ➤➤ **insensibility** *n,* **insensibly** *adv.*

insensitive *adj* **1** failing to respond to or sympathize with the needs or feelings of others; callous. **2** (+ to) not physically or chemically sensitive. ➤➤ **insensitively** *adv,* **insensitiveness** *n,* **insensitivity** *n.*

insentient *adj* not endowed with the capacity to perceive; inanimate. ➤➤ **insentience** *n.*

inseparable *adj* **1** incapable of being separated. **2** always seen or found together. ➤➤ **inseparability** *n,* **inseparably** *adv.*

insert[1] *v* **1** to put or thrust (something) in through an opening. **2** to introduce (something) into the body of something, e.g. text. **3** to set (something) into a position between two parts, e.g. by sewing it. ➤➤ **inserter** *n.*

insert[2] *n* **1** a piece of written or printed material placed between the pages of a book or magazine. **2** = INSET[1] (2).

insertion *n* **1** the act or an instance of inserting. **2** something inserted in a text. **3** embroidery or needlework inserted as a decoration between two pieces of fabric. **4** a single appearance of an advertisement in a newspaper or magazine.

in-service *adj* of training: undertaken during the course of work.

inset[1] *n* **1** a small illustration set within a larger one. **2** a piece of cloth set into a garment for decoration, shaping, etc. **3** = INSERT[2] (1).

inset[2] *v* (**insetting,** *past tense and past part.* **inset** *or* **insetted**) to insert as an inset.

inshore *adj and adv* towards the shore, or operating near the shore.

inside[1] *n* **1** an inner side or surface. **2** an interior or internal part. **3** (*usu in pl*) the stomach or the intestines. **4** a position of confidence or of access to confidential information. **5** the side of a pavement farthest from the road. ✱ **inside out 1** with the inner surface on the outside. **2** in a very thorough manner: *She knows her subject inside out.*

inside[2] *adj* **1** of, on, near, or towards the inside: *an inside toilet.* **2** on the inner side of a curve or near the side of the road nearest the kerb or hard shoulder: *the inside lane.* **3** coming from, carried out by, etc somebody within an organization or with access to personal information: *an inside job.*

inside[3] *prep* **1a** in or into the interior of. **b** on the inner side of. **c** closer to the centre than. **2** within: *inside an hour.*

inside[4] *adv* **1** to or on the inner side. **2** in or into the interior. **3** indoors. **4** within somebody's body or mind. **5** *chiefly Brit, informal* in or into prison.

inside leg *n* the length of the leg from the crotch to the inside of the ankle.

insider *n* somebody recognized or accepted as a member of a group, *esp* somebody who has access to confidential information or is in a position of power.

insider dealing *n* the illegal exploitation of confidential information in buying or selling securities at a price which would have been materially affected if that information had been made public.

insider trading *n* = INSIDER DEALING.

insidious *adj* **1** acting gradually and imperceptibly but with very harmful consequences. **2** of a disease: developing so gradually as to be well established before becoming apparent. ➤➤ **insidiously** *adv,* **insidiousness** *n.*

insight *n* **1** the ability to discern the true or underlying nature of something. **2** an explanation or understanding that displays this ability. ➤➤ **insightful** *adj.*

insignia *n* (*pl* **insignia, insignias**) **1** a badge of authority or honour. **2** *literary* a sign or token of something.

insignificant *adj* **1** too unimportant to be worth consideration; inconsequential. **2** very small in size, amount, or number. ➤➤ **insignificance** *n,* **insignificantly** *adv.*

insincere *adj* not expressing feelings or opinions honestly. ➤➤ **insincerely** *adv,* **insincerity** *n.*

insinuate *v* **1** to introduce (an idea) or suggest (something unpleasant) in a subtle or oblique manner. **2** (+ into) to gain acceptance for (e.g. oneself) by crafty or stealthy means. **3** to insert or squeeze in (oneself, a remark, etc) somewhere. ➤➤ **insinuating** *adj,* **insinuator** *n.*

insinuation *n* **1** the act or an instance of insinuating. **2** a sly and usu derogatory reference.

insipid *adj* **1** lacking flavour; tasteless. **2** with no interesting or stimulating qualities; dull. ➤➤ **insipidity** *n,* **insipidly** *adv,* **insipidness** *n.*

insist *v* **1** (*usu* + on/upon) to state wishes or requirements forcefully, accepting no refusal or compromise. **2** (*usu* + on/upon) to take a resolute stand. **3** to maintain (something) persistently.

insistent *adj* **1** insisting forcefully or repeatedly; emphatic. **2** demanding attention. ➤➤ **insistence** *n,* **insistently** *adv.*

in situ *adv and adj* in the natural, original, or permanent position.

insobriety *n* lack of moderation, *esp* in drinking.

insofar as *conj* to the extent or degree that.

insolation *n technical* exposure to the sun's rays.

insole *n* **1** a shaped strip that is placed inside a shoe or boot for warmth or comfort. **2** a fixed inside sole of a shoe or boot.

insolent *adj* showing disrespectful rudeness; impudent. ➤➤ **insolence** *n,* **insolently** *adv.*

insoluble *adj* **1** incapable of being dissolved in liquid. **2** impossible to solve or explain. ➤➤ **insolubility** *n,* **insolubly** *adv.*

insolvent[1] *adj* **1** unable to pay debts as they fall due. **2** relating to or for the relief of people or companies that are insolvents. ➤➤ **insolvency** *n.*

insolvent[2] *n* somebody who is insolvent.

insomnia *n* prolonged inability to obtain adequate or uninterrupted sleep. ➤➤ **insomniac** *adj and n.*

insomuch as *conj* to such a degree that.

insomuch that *conj* = INSOMUCH AS.

insouciance *n* light-hearted unconcern; nonchalance. ➤➤ **insouciant** *adj,* **insouciantly** *adv.*

inspect *v* **1** to examine (something or somebody) closely and critically; to scrutinize. **2** to view or examine officially. ➤➤ **inspection** *n.*

inspector *n* **1** an official who carries out examinations in order to assess whether standards are being met or established rules and practices followed. **2** a police officer ranking immediately above a sergeant. ➤➤ **inspectorate** *n,* **inspectorship** *n.*

inspiration *n* **1** the action or power of stimulating the intellect or emotions. **2** an inspiring agent or influence. **3** an inspired idea. **4** the drawing of air into the lungs; inhalation. ➤➤ **inspirational** *adj.*

inspiratory *adj* relating to inspiration.

inspire *v* **1** to have an animating or uplifting influence on (somebody). **2** to act as a stimulus for (somebody or something). **3** (+ with) to cause to feel a particular emotion. **4** *formal* to breathe in. ➤➤ **inspirer** *n,* **inspiring** *adj.*

inspired *adj* **1** characterized, given or created by inspiration. **2** having been inhaled.

inspirit *v* (**inspirited, inspiriting**) to motivate or encourage. ➤➤ **inspiriting** *adj,* **inspiritingly** *adv.*

inspissate *v* to make thick or thicker, *esp* by condensation.

instability *n* (*pl* **-ies**) lack of stability, *esp* emotional or mental stability.

install (*NAm* **instal**) *v* **1** to place in position for use or service. **2** to establish (somebody) in a specified place, condition, or status. **3** to induct (somebody) into an office, rank, or order, *esp* with ceremonies or formalities. ➤➤ **installer** *n.*

installation *n* **1** the act or an instance of installing or being installed. **2** a device or piece of equipment fitted in place to perform some specified function. **3** a military base or establishment. **4** a large-scale work of art that is assembled in the gallery where it is exhibited.

instalment (*NAm* **installment**) *n* **1** any of the parts into which a debt is divided when payment is made at intervals. **2a** any of several parts, e.g. of a publication, presented at intervals. **b** a single part of a serial story.

instance[1] *n* **1** an example cited as an illustration or proof. **2** a situation viewed as one stage in a process or series of events. ✱ **for instance** as an example.

instance[2] *v* to put forward as a case or example; to cite.

instant[1] *n* **1** a very brief period of time; a second. **2** a precise point in time, *esp* separating two states.

instant[2] *adj* **1** immediate. **2** of food: prepared for easy final preparation. **3** *formal* demanding or urgent.

instantaneous *adj* **1** occurring or acting instantly; immediate. **2** occurring or present at a particular instant. ➤➤ **instantaneity** *n,* **instantaneously** *adv,* **instantaneousness** *n.*

instantiate *v* to represent (something abstract) by a concrete example. ➤➤ **instantiation** *n.*

instantly *adv* at once; immediately.

instate *v* to establish (somebody) in a rank or office.

instead *adv* as a substitute or alternative.

instead of *prep* as a substitute for or alternative to.

instep *n* the arched middle portion of the human foot, or the upper surface of it.

instigate *v* **1** to initiate (a course of action or procedure, e.g. a legal investigation). **2** to provoke or incite (somebody) to do something. ➤➤ **instigation** *n*, **instigator** *n*.

instil (*NAm* **instill**) *v* (**instilled, instilling**) **1** (+ in/into) to impart gradually. **2** to cause to enter drop by drop. ➤➤ **instillation** *n*.

instinct[1] *n* **1** a natural or inherent way of acting or thinking. **2** an animal's largely inheritable tendency to respond in a particular way without reason. ➤➤ **instinctual** *adj*.

instinct[2] *adj formal* (+ with) imbued or infused with something.

instinctive *adj* **1** relating to or prompted by instinct. **2** arising spontaneously and being independent of judgment or will. ➤➤ **instinctively** *adv*.

institute[1] *n* an organization for the promotion of a particular cause or for the carrying on of research or education in a particular field.

institute[2] *v* **1** to originate and establish. **2** *archaic* to appoint (somebody) to an official position.

institution *n* **1** an established organization or body, e.g. a university or hospital. **2** an established practice in a culture. **3** a familiar activity or object. **4** *dated* a psychiatric hospital or unit. ➤➤ **institutional** *adj*.

institutionalize *or* **-ise** *v* **1** to establish as a custom or regular practice. **2a** to put or keep in an institution, *esp* a psychiatric hospital. **b** to cause to acquire personality traits typical of people in an institution, *esp* a lack of independent thought or action. ➤➤ **institutionalization** *n*.

instruct *v* **1** to teach (somebody), *esp* in a non-academic discipline. **2** to direct (somebody) authoritatively; to command. **3** to engage (a lawyer, *specif* a barrister) for a case. **4** to inform (somebody) of something.

instruction *n* **1** (*usu in pl*) **a** an order or command. **b** advice on how to do something, or a manual outlining the procedure for doing it. **2** a code that tells a computer to perform a particular operation. **3** teaching or training. ➤➤ **instructional** *adj*.

instructive *adj* giving useful information or advice. ➤➤ **instructively** *adv*.

instructor *n* **1** a teacher, *esp* of a technical or practical subject. **2** *NAm* a college teacher below professorial rank. ➤➤ **instructorship** *n*.

instrument *n* **1** an implement, tool, or device designed *esp* for delicate work or measurement. **2** a device used to produce music. **3** an electrical or mechanical device used in navigating an aircraft, ship, or vehicle. **4** a formal legal document. **5a** a means whereby something is achieved or furthered. **b** somebody who is used by a person to achieve their usu dishonourable ends; a dupe.

instrumental[1] *adj* **1** (+ in) serving as an instrument, means, agent, or tool. **2** relating to, composed for, or performed on a musical instrument, *esp* as distinct from the human voice. ➤➤ **instrumentality** *n*, **instrumentally** *adv*.

instrumental[2] *n* a musical composition or passage for instruments but not voice.

instrumentalist *n* a player of a musical instrument.

instrumentation *n* **1** the instruments specified for the performance of a musical composition. **2** the set of navigation instruments on an aeroplane, ship, etc.

insubordinate *adj* unwilling to submit to authority; disobedient. ➤➤ **insubordination** *n*.

insubstantial *adj* **1** lacking firmness or solidity; flimsy. **2** lacking substance or material nature; imaginary or unreal. ➤➤ **insubstantiality** *n*.

insufferable *adj* too bad or unpleasant to put up with; intolerable. ➤➤ **insufferably** *adv*.

insufficient *adj* deficient in power, capacity, or competence; inadequate. ➤➤ **insufficiency** *n*, **insufficiently** *adv*.

insular *adj* **1** relating to islands or in the form of an island. **2a** cut off from other people or the wider community. **b** lacking in breadth of outlook or in liberalism; narrow-minded. ➤➤ **insularity** *n*.

insulate *v* **1** to separate (something) from conducting bodies by means of nonconductors so as to prevent the transfer or loss of electricity, heat, or sound. **2** to place or confine (somebody) in a situation that is detached from the wider world, *esp* to protect them from harsh realities. ➤➤ **insulant** *n*, **insulator** *n*.

insulating tape *n* a form of adhesive tape that can be wrapped around exposed electrical wires or connections to insulate them.

insulation *n* **1** material used in insulating. **2** the act or an instance of insulating or being insulated.

insulin *n* a pancreatic hormone that is essential for regulating the level of glucose in the blood.

insult[1] *v* to treat with insolence, indignity, or contempt, usu causing offence.

insult[2] *n* a remark, gesture, etc that insults.

insuperable *adj* incapable of being surmounted, overcome, or passed over. ➤➤ **insuperably** *adv*.

insupportable *adj* **1** impossible to tolerate; unendurable. **2** incapable of being supported or sustained. ➤➤ **insupportably** *adv*.

insurance *n* **1a** a contract whereby one party undertakes to indemnify another against loss by a particular contingency or risk, or the protection offered by such a contract. **b** the premium demanded under such a contract. **c** the sum for which something is insured. **2** the business of insuring people or property. **3** the act or an instance of insuring somebody or something.

Usage note
insurance *or* assurance? See note at ASSURANCE.

insure *v* **1** to give, take, or procure insurance on (a property, etc) or for (an owner). **2** (+ against) to protect (somebody) from something unpleasant. **3** *chiefly NAm* to ensure. ➤➤ **insurable** *adj*, **insurer** *n*.

insurgent[1] *n* somebody who revolts against civil authority or an established government. ➤➤ **insurgence** *n*, **insurgency** *n*.

insurgent[2] *adj* rising in opposition to civil authority or established leadership; rebellious.

insurmountable *adj* too great or difficult to conquer; insuperable. ➤➤ **insurmountably** *adv*.

insurrection *n* a revolt against civil authority or established government. ➤➤ **insurrectionary** *adj*, **insurrectionist** *n and adj*.

insusceptible *adj* not susceptible. ➤➤ **insusceptibility** *n*.

intact *adj* not harmed or damaged; whole.

intaglio /in'tahlioh/ *n* (*pl* **-os**) **1** an incised or engraved design made in hard material, *esp* stone, and sunk below the surface of the material. **2** something, e.g. a gem, carved in intaglio.

intake *n* **1** an opening through which liquid or gas enters an enclosure or system; an inlet. **2a** (*used as sing. or pl*) an amount or number taken in. **b** the act or an instance of taking in.

intangible[1] *adj* **1** not able to be perceived by touch. **2** not clear or definite; vague. ➤➤ **intangibility** *n,* **intangibly** *adv.*

intangible[2] *n* something intangible.

intarsia *n* **1** elaborate inlaid mosaic work in wood. **2** a geometric knitting pattern resembling intarsia, or a method of knitting that produces this.

integer *n* a whole number.

integral[1] *adj* **1** essential to completeness; constituent. **2** lacking nothing essential; whole. **3** formed as a unit with another part. **4** relating to a mathematical integer, integral, or integration. ➤➤ **integrally** *adv.*

Usage note

Modern dictionaries of both British and American English accept two ways of pronouncing *integral*: with the stress on the first syllable *in-*, or, less commonly, with the stress on the second syllable *-teg-*.

integral[2] *n* a mathematical expression which is essentially the sum of a large number of infinitely small quantities, and one form of which can be used to find the area under a given curve.

integral calculus *n* a branch of mathematics dealing with methods of finding integrals and with their applications.

integrand *n* a mathematical expression to be integrated.

integrate *v* **1** to form or blend (separate elements) into a whole. **2a** to combine (things) together or (one thing) with something else. **b** (+ into) to incorporate (somebody or something) into a larger unit. **3** in mathematics, to find the integral of (e.g. a function or differential equation). **4** to become integrated. ➤➤ **integrability** *n,* **integrable** *adj,* **integrative** *adj,* **integrator** *n.*

integrated circuit *n* an electronic circuit formed in or on a single tiny piece of semiconductor material, e.g. silicon.

integrated services digital network *n* a telecommunications network that allows both voice and computer data to be transmitted as digital signals.

integration *n* **1** the act or an instance of integrating or being integrated. **2** the bringing together of peoples or groups who were formerly segregated to form a single community.

integrationist *n* an advocate of social, *esp* racial, integration.

integrity *n* **1** uncompromising adherence to a code of *esp* moral or artistic values. **2** the quality or state of being complete or undivided. **3** *formal* an unimpaired condition; wholeness.

integument *n* a skin, membrane, husk, or other covering or enclosure, *esp* of an animal or plant.

intellect *n* **1** the capacity for intelligent thought, *esp* when highly developed. **2** *informal* a highly intelligent person.

intellectual[1] *adj* **1a** of the intellect. **b** developed or chiefly guided by the intellect rather than by emotion or experience. **2** given to or requiring the use of the intellect. ➤➤ **intellectuality** *n,* **intellectually** *adv.*

intellectual[2] *n* an intellectual person.

intellectualise *v* see INTELLECTUALIZE.

intellectualism *n* devotion to the exercise of intellect or to intellectual pursuits, *esp* excessively and to the detriment of the emotions. ➤➤ **intellectualist** *n.*

intellectualize *or* **-ise** *v* **1** to make (something) intellectual or more intellectual. **2** to consider (something) in a intellectual way. **3** to think or reason.

intellectual property *n* in law, property that is the product of the creative imagination and cannot therefore be touched but may still be owned, such as a copyright.

intelligence *n* **1** the ability to learn, apply knowledge, or think abstractly. **2a** information concerning an enemy, or an organization or group with the task of gathering such information. **b** news or information of any kind. **3** an intelligent being.

intelligence quotient *n* a number expressing the ratio of somebody's intelligence as determined by a test to the average for his or her age.

intelligent *adj* **1** having or indicating intelligence, *esp* high intelligence. **2** of electronic equipment: able to respond to change and to initiate action based on that response. ➤➤ **intelligently** *adv.*

intelligentsia *n* (*used as sing. or pl*) the intellectuals who form an artistic, social, or political class or vanguard.

intelligible *adj* capable of being understood. ➤➤ **intelligibility** *n,* **intelligibly** *adv.*

intemperate *adj* **1** going beyond the bounds of reasonable behaviour; unrestrained. **2** marked by lack of moderation; excessive. ➤➤ **intemperance** *n,* **intemperately** *adv.*

intend *v* **1a** to have in mind as a purpose or goal. **b** to design for a specified use or future. **2** to mean or signify. ➤➤ **intender** *n.*

intended[1] *adj* planned; future.

intended[2] *n informal* somebody's future spouse.

intense *adj* **1a** feeling emotion deeply, *esp* by nature or temperament. **b** of an emotion: deeply felt. **2** highly concentrated; intensive. **3** existing or occurring in an extreme degree: *intense heat.* ➤➤ **intensely** *adv,* **intenseness** *n.*

intensifier *n* **1** a word or form, e.g. *very*, that gives force or emphasis. **2** in photography, a chemical used to improve the clarity of image of a negative.

intensify *v* (**-ies, -ied**) to make or become intense. ➤➤ **intensification** *n.*

intensity *n* (*pl* **-ies**) **1** extreme degree of strength, force, or energy. **2** the magnitude of force or energy per unit, e.g. of surface, charge, or mass. **3** the purity of a colour.

intensive *adj* **1** highly concentrated. **2** dealing very thoroughly with a subject and at a fast pace: *intensive training.* **3** (*usu in combination*) using a specified factor of production to a greater extent than others: *labour-intensive.* **4** constituting or relating to a method designed to increase productivity by the expenditure of more capital and labour rather than by increase in the land or raw materials used: *intensive farming.* ➤➤ **intensively** *adv,* **intensiveness** *n.*

intensive care *n* the continuous care and treatment of a seriously ill patient.

intent[1] *n* **1 a** the fact of intending; intention. **b** the state of mind with which an act is done. **2** meaning or significance. ✱ **to all intents and purposes** in every practical or important respect.

intent[2] *adj* **1** (+ on/upon) having the mind, attention, or will concentrated on something or some end or purpose. **2** directed with strained or eager attention; concentrated. ➤➤ **intently** *adv,* **intentness** *n.*

intention *n* **1** what somebody intends to do or bring about; an aim. **2** a determination to act in a certain way; a resolve. **3** (*in pl*) purpose with respect to proposal of marriage.

intentional *adj* done by intention or design; deliberate. ➤➤ **intentionally** *adv.*

inter *v* (**interred, interring**) to place (a dead body) in the earth or a tomb.

inter- *prefix* **1** between; among: *intercity; interstellar.* **2** reciprocally: *intermarry.*

interact *v* to act upon each other. ➤➤ **interactant** *n,* **interaction** *n.*

interactive *adj* characterized by interaction; *specif* involving the exchange of information between a computer and user while a program is being run. ➤➤ **interactively** *adv,* **interactivity** *n.*

inter alia *adv* among other things.

interbreed *v* (*past tense and past part.* **interbred**) **1** to crossbreed or cause (*esp* animals) to crossbreed. **2** to breed within a single family or other closed population.

intercalary *adj* of a day or month: inserted in a calendar to resynchronize it with some objective time-measure, e.g. the solar year, as is February 29 in the Gregorian calendar.

intercede *v* to beg or plead on behalf of another person with a view to reconciling differences.

intercellular *adj* occurring between cells.

intercept[1] *v* to stop, seize, or interrupt (something or somebody) in progress, course, or movement, *esp* from one place to another. ➤➤ **interception** *n,* **interceptor** *n.*

intercept[2] *n* **1** an interception, *esp* the interception of a missile. **2** the distance from the origin to a point where a graph crosses a coordinate axis, or the point itself.

intercession *n* the act or an instance of interceding, *esp* by prayer. ➤➤ **intercessor** *n,* **intercessory** *adj.*

interchange[1] *v* **1** to put each of (two things) in the place of the other. **2** to give (one thing in return for another), to exchange. ➤➤ **interchangeability** *n,* **interchangeable** *adj,* **interchangeably** *adv.*

interchange[2] *n* **1** a junction of two or more roads having a system of separate levels that permit traffic to pass from one to another without the crossing of traffic streams. **2** the act or an instance of interchanging.

intercity *adj* existing or travelling between cities.

intercom *n* an internal communication system, e.g. in a building, with a microphone and loudspeaker at each station.

intercommunicate *v* **1** of rooms: to have free passage from one to another. **2** to hold a conversation or exchange information. ➤➤ **intercommunication** *n.*

interconnect *v* to connect with one another. ➤➤ **interconnection** *n.*

intercontinental *adj* extending among continents, carried on between continents, or capable of travelling between continents.

intercostal[1] *adj* of a body part: situated between the ribs.

intercostal[2] *n* an intercostal muscle.

intercourse *n* **1** = SEXUAL INTERCOURSE. **2** *formal* communication or dealings between people or groups.

intercrop *v* (**intercropped, intercropping**) to grow (a crop) in between rows, plots, etc of another crop.

intercut *v* (**intercutting,** *past tense and past part.* **intercut**) to insert shots from (one cinematic scene) alternately with shots from a contrasting scene.

interdenominational *adj* occurring between or involving different religious denominations.

interdepartmental *adj* carried on between or involving different departments.

interdependent *adj* depending one on the other. ➤➤ **interdependence** *n.*

interdict[1] *n* **1** a prohibition, *esp* a court order forbidding something. **2** a Roman Catholic disciplinary measure withdrawing most sacraments and Christian burial from a person or district.

interdict[2] *v* to forbid in a formal or authoritative manner. ➤➤ **interdiction** *n.*

interdisciplinary *adj* involving two or more disciplines or fields of study.

interest[1] *n* **1a** readiness to be concerned with or have one's attention attracted by something; curiosity. **b** the quality in a thing that arouses interest, or the thing itself. **2** a charge for borrowed money, generally a percentage of the amount borrowed. **3** benefit or advantage to somebody. **4** a right, title, or legal share in something. **5** a person or group with a financial stake. **6** a business in which somebody has a financial stake.

interest[2] *v* **1** to engage the attention or arouse the interest of. **2** to induce or persuade (somebody) to have or do something.

interested *adj* **1** having the interest aroused or attention engaged. **2** affected or involved; not impartial. ➤➤ **interestedly** *adv.*

interesting *adj* holding the attention. ➤➤ **interestingly** *adv,* **interestingness** *n.*

interface[1] *n* **1** the place at which independent systems meet and act on or communicate with each other, *esp* a piece of computer hardware or software that allows a user to communicate with a computer. **2** a surface forming a common boundary between two bodies, regions, or phases.

interface[2] *v* **1** to connect (things) by means of an interface. **2** to serve as an interface for. **3** to interact.

interfacing *n* stiffening material attached between two layers of fabric.

interfaith *adj* involving people of different religious faiths.

interfere *v* **1** (+ with) to get in the way or be a hindrance. **2** (*often* + in) to enter into or take a part in matters that do not concern one. **3** of sound, light, etc waves: to act so as to augment, diminish, or otherwise affect one another. **4** *informal* (+ with) to carry out a sexual assault, *esp* one that falls short of rape.

interference *n* **1** the act or an instance of interfering. **2** something that produces the confusion of received radio signals by unwanted signals or noise, or the signals or noises themselves. **3** the phenomenon resulting from the meeting of two successions of waves, e.g. of light or sound, with an increase in intensity at some points and a decrease at others. ➤➤ **interferential** *adj.*

interferon *n* a protein that inhibits the development of viruses and is produced by cells in response to infection by a virus.

interfuse *v* to blend or cause (two or more things) to blend. ➤➤ **interfusion** *n.*

intergalactic *adj* existing, carried on, or operating between galaxies.

interglacial[1] *adj* occurring or formed between two periods of glacial activity when much of the earth was covered by ice sheets.

interglacial[2] *n* an interglacial period of relatively mild climate marked by a temporary retreat or shrinking of the ice.

intergovernmental *adj* existing or occurring between two or more governments.

interim[1] *n* an intervening time.

interim[2] *adj* temporary or provisional.

interior[1] *adj* **1** lying, occurring, or functioning within or inside something. **2** away from the border or shore. **3** relating to the domestic affairs of a country; internal. **4** of the mind or soul. ⋙ **interiority** *n*, **interiorly** *adv*.

interior[2] *n* **1** the internal or inner part of a thing. **2** the part of a country that lies away from the border or the shore. **3** the internal affairs of a country. **4** a representation of the interior of a building or room.

interior decoration *n* the decorating and furnishing of the interiors of rooms.

interior design *n* = INTERIOR DECORATION.

interiorize *or* **-ise** *v* to make (something) interior, *esp* to make (something) into a part of one's own inner being or personality.

interior monologue *n* a literary device presenting a character's thoughts and feelings in the form of a monologue.

interject *v* to throw in (e.g. a remark) abruptly among or between other things.

interjection *n* an abruptly uttered word or phrase that expresses emotion; an exclamation.

interlace *v* **1** to join (things) by lacing them together; to interweave. **2** to intersperse (something) with other things.

interlard *v* to intersperse (something) with something else, *esp* with something very different or irrelevant.

interleave *v* **1** to supply (a book) with blank pages for notes or with sheets to protect colour plates, etc. **2** to insert between layers.

interline *v* to provide (a garment) with an interlining.

interlinear *adj* inserted between lines already written or printed.

interlining *n* a lining sewn between the ordinary lining and the outside fabric of a garment, curtain, etc to give additional warmth or bulk.

interlock[1] *v* to become firmly connected or related to each other, usu by parts designed to fit together.

interlock[2] *n* **1** a mechanism for synchronizing or coordinating the operation of other parts. **2** a fabric knitted with interlocking stitches.

interlocutor *n formal* somebody who takes part in dialogue or conversation. ⋙ **interlocution** *n*.

interlocutory *adj* **1** of a judgment, etc: pronounced during a legal action and having only provisional status. **2** relating to or consisting of a dialogue.

interlope *v* **1** to be an interloper. **2** to intrude or interfere. **3** to encroach on the rights of others.

interloper *n* somebody who interferes or encroaches; an intruder.

interlude *n* **1** an intervening period, space, or event, *esp* of a contrasting character; an interval. **2** a break between parts of a play or other performance. **3** a musical composition inserted between the parts of a longer composition, a drama, or a religious service.

intermarriage *n* **1** marriage between members of different families, peoples, etc. **2** marriage between close relations; endogamy.

intermarry *v* (**-ies, -ied**) **1** to marry somebody from the same group. **2** to become connected by marriage with another group.

intermediary[1] *n* (*pl* **-ies**) somebody or something acting as a mediator or go-between.

intermediary[2] *adj* **1** intermediate. **2** acting as a mediator.

intermediate[1] *adj* being or occurring at the middle place, level, or degree or between two others or extremes. ⋙ **intermediacy** *n*.

intermediate[2] *n* somebody or something intermediate.

intermediate[3] *v* to act as an intermediary; to mediate or intervene. ⋙ **intermediation** *n*.

interment *n* the placing of a corpse in a grave; burial.

intermezzo /intə'metsoh/ *n* (*pl* **intermezzi** *or* **intermezzos**) **1** a movement that comes between the major sections of an extended musical work, e.g. an opera. **2** a short independent instrumental composition.

interminable *adj* having or seeming to have no end, *esp* wearisomely long. ⋙ **interminably** *adv*.

intermingle *v* to mix or mingle (things) together or combine (something) with something else.

intermission *n* **1** a break between acts of a performance. **2** a pause or respite.

intermittent *adj* coming and going at intervals; not continuous. ⋙ **intermittence** *n*, **intermittently** *adv*.

intermix *v* to mix together or cause (diverse things) to mix together. ⋙ **intermixture** *n*.

intermolecular *adj* existing or acting between molecules.

intern[1] *v* to confine (somebody) e.g. in prison or a concentration camp, *esp* during a war. ⋙ **internment** *n*.

intern[2] *or* **interne** *n* a graduate who is receiving practical training in the workplace. ⋙ **internship** *n*.

internal *adj* **1** existing or situated within the limits or surface of something; inside. **2** present within the body or an organism. **3** within a state; domestic. **4** of or existing within the mind. ⋙ **internality** *n*, **internally** *adv*.

internal-combustion engine *n* an engine in which the combustion that generates the heat energy takes place inside the engine, e.g. in a cylinder, as opposed to in a separate furnace.

internalize *or* **-ise** *v* to incorporate (e.g. learned values) within the self and use them as guiding principles. ⋙ **internalization** *n*.

internal market *n* **1** a system in which different departments within an organization, *esp* a local council or other public body, purchase goods and services from each other. **2** the market for labour, capital, goods, and services existing between countries of the European Union.

international[1] *adj* **1** affecting or involving two or more nations. **2** known, recognized, or renowned in more than one country. **3** open to all nations; not belonging to a particular country. ⋙ **internationality** *n*, **internationally** *adv*.

international[2] *n* **1** a sporting or other contest between two national teams. **2** a player who has taken part in such a contest. **3** (*often* **International** *or* **Internationale**) any of several socialist or communist organizations of international scope.

International Date Line *n* an arbitrary line approximately along the 180th meridian, east and west of which the date differs by one calendar day.

Internationale *n* **1** (**the Internationale**) a socialist revolutionary song widely adopted as an anthem by socialist organizations. **2** see INTERNATIONAL[2] (3).

internationalise *v* see INTERNATIONALIZE.

internationalism *n* **1** international character, interests, or outlook. **2** cooperation among nations, or support for such cooperation. ➤➤ **internationalist** *n.*

internationalize *or* **-ise** *v* to become or make international. ➤➤ **internationalization** *n.*

international law *n* a body of rules accepted as governing relations between nations.

interne *n* see INTERN².

internecine *adj* **1** of or involving conflict within a group. **2** mutually destructive.

internee *n* an interned person; a prisoner.

Internet *n* (**the Internet**) the worldwide computer network that can link all smaller networks via telephone lines and satellite links.

internist *n NAm* a doctor who specializes in the treatment of internal diseases and disorders.

interpenetrate *v* to penetrate mutually. ➤➤ **interpenetration** *n,* **interpenetrative** *adj.*

interpersonal *adj* involving or dealing with relations between people. ➤➤ **interpersonally** *adv.*

interplanetary *adj* existing, carried on, or operating between planets.

interplay *n* the effect that two or more things have on each other; interaction.

Interpol *n* an international police organization for liaison between national police forces.

interpolate *v* **1** to insert (something) between other things or parts, *esp* to insert (words) into a text or conversation. **2** to alter or corrupt (e.g. a text) by inserting new, false, or misleading matter. **3** in mathematics, to estimate values of (a function) between two known values. ➤➤ **interpolation** *n,* **interpolator** *n.*

interpose *v* **1** to place (something) between two things or in an intervening position. **2** to introduce (something) by way of interference or intervention. **3** to interrupt with (words) during a conversation or argument. **4** to be or come in an intervening position. ➤➤ **interposition** *n.*

interpret *v* (**interpreted, interpreting**) **1** to understand the meaning of (something), often in the light of one's beliefs, judgments, or circumstances. **2** to explain the meaning of. **3** to give an oral translation of somebody's words. **4** to represent (something) by means of art, bringing to realization one's understanding of it or one's feelings about it. ➤➤ **interpretable** *adj,* **interpretative** *adj,* **interpretive** *adj.*

interpretation *n* **1a** the act or an instance of interpreting. **b** the result of interpreting. **2** the act or an instance of artistic interpreting in performance or adaptation. ➤➤ **interpretational** *adj.*

interpreter *n* **1** somebody who translates orally for people speaking in different languages. **2** a computer program that translates another program into machine language for immediate execution.

interracial *adj* of or involving members of different races. ➤➤ **interracially** *adv.*

interregnum *n* (*pl* **interregnums** *or* **interregna**) the time during which a throne is vacant between reigns or the normal functions of government are suspended.

interrelate *v* to be in a relationship where each one person or thing depends upon or is acting upon another. ➤➤ **interrelatedness** *n,* **interrelation** *n,* **interrelationship** *n.*

interrogate *v* **1** to question formally, exhaustively, or aggressively. **2** to give or send out a signal to (e.g. a computer) to trigger a response. ➤➤ **interrogation** *n,* **interrogator** *n.*

interrogative¹ *adj* **1** questioning. **2** used in a question. ➤➤ **interrogatively** *adv.*

interrogative² *n* a word, *esp* a pronoun, used in asking questions.

interrogatory *adj* = INTERROGATIVE¹.

interrupt *v* **1** to break the flow or action of (a speaker or speech). **2** to break the uniformity or continuity of (something). ➤➤ **interruptible** *adj,* **interruption** *n,* **interruptive** *adj.*

interrupter *or* **interruptor** *n* **1** somebody or something that interrupts. **2** an automatic device for periodically interrupting or breaking an electric current.

intersect *v* **1** to pierce or divide (e.g. a line or area) by passing through or across it. **2** of lines, roads, etc: to meet and cross at a point.

intersection *n* **1** the act or an instance of intersecting. **2** a place where two or more things, e.g. streets, roads, etc, intersect. ➤➤ **intersectional** *adj.*

intersex *n* an intersexual individual or its intersexual nature.

intersexual *adj* **1** intermediate in sexual character between a typical male and a typical female. **2** existing between the sexes. ➤➤ **intersexuality** *n.*

interspace¹ *v* to separate (e.g. printed letters) by spaces.

interspace² *n* an intervening space; an interval.

intersperse *v* **1** to insert (things) at intervals among other things. **2** (+ with) to diversify or vary (something) with scattered things. ➤➤ **interspersion** *n.*

interstadial *n* an interglacial period, typically one that is short or not extensive. ➤➤ **interstadial** *adj.*

interstate¹ *adj* between two or more states, *esp* of the USA or of Australia.

interstate² *n NAm* a wide road allowing for fast travel between states.

interstate³ *adv Aus* to or in another state.

interstellar *adj* existing or operating between the stars.

interstice *n formal* a small space between adjacent things.

interstitial *adj* of or situated in interstices. ➤➤ **interstitially** *adv.*

intertextuality *n* in literary criticism, reference made in one text to a different text.

intertwine *v* to twist together or join (things) by wrapping or twisting them round each other.

interval *n* **1** an intervening space, e.g. a time between events or states; a pause. **2** the difference in pitch between two notes. **3** *Brit* a break in the presentation of an entertainment, e.g. a play. ➤➤ **intervallic** *adj.*

intervene *v* **1** to occur or come between two things, *esp* points of time or events. **2** to come in or between things so as to hinder or modify them. ➤➤ **intervener** *n,* **intervenor** *n.*

intervention *n* **1** the act or an instance of intervening. **2** action taken when intervening, *esp*: **a** government influence brought to bear on the economy, usu for political reasons. **b** medical treatment. ➤➤ **interventional** *adj.*

interventionism *n* **1** action taken by a government to influence the domestic economy, usu in order to bring about a political objective. **2** interference in the political affairs of another country. ➤➤ **interventionist** *n and adj.*

interview¹ *n* **1** a formal consultation usu to evaluate qualifications, e.g. of a prospective student or employee. **2** a meeting at which information is obtained from somebody. ➤➤ **interviewee** *n,* **interviewer** *n.*

interview[2] *v* to invite or subject (somebody) to an interview.

interwar *adj* occurring or falling between wars, *esp* World War I and World War II.

interweave *v* (*past tense* **interwove,** *past part.* **interwoven**) **1** to weave (things) together. **2** to become woven together.

intestate[1] *adj* having made no valid will. ➤➤ **intestacy** *n.*

intestate[2] *n* somebody who dies intestate.

intestine *n* (*also in pl*) the tubular part of the alimentary canal that extends from the stomach to the anus. ➤➤ **intestinal** *adj.*

intifada /inti'fahdə/ *n* a resistance movement, originating in the late 1980s, among Palestinian Arabs of the West Bank and the Gaza Strip against Israeli occupation.

intimacy *n* (*pl* **-ies**) **1** the state of being intimate; familiarity. **2** an intimate remark.

intimate[1] *adj* **1** belonging to or characterizing one's deepest nature: *He shared his intimate thoughts.* **2a** marked by a warm friendship developing through long association. **b** suggesting informal warmth or privacy: *an intimate atmosphere.* **3** of a very personal or private nature: *an intimate diary.* **4** marked by very close association, contact, or familiarity: *an intimate knowledge of the law.* **5** *euphem* involved in a sexual relationship, *esp* engaging in an act of sexual intercourse. ➤➤ **intimately** *adv.*

intimate[2] *v* **1** to make (something) known, e.g. by announcing it formally. **2** to hint at or imply. ➤➤ **intimation** *n.*

intimate[3] *n* a close friend or confidant.

intimidate *v* **1** to frighten or unnerve. **2** to compel or deter with threats. ➤➤ **intimidation** *n,* **intimidator** *n,* **intimidatory** *adj.*

into *prep* **1a** so as to be inside: *Come into the house.* **b** so as to be: *One day she'll grow into a woman.* **c** so as to be in (a state): *Don't get into trouble.* **d** so as to be expressed in: *Translate it into French.* **e** so as to be dressed in: *He changed into his uniform.* **f** so as to be engaged in: *He went into farming.* **2** used in division as the inverse of *by* or *divided by*: *Divide 35 into 70.* **3** used to indicate a partly elapsed period of time or a partly traversed extent of space: *far into the night; deep into the jungle.* **4** in the direction of: *Don't look into the sun.* **5** to a position of contact with; against: *The car ran into a wall.* **6** *informal* involved with: *They were into hard drugs.* **7** *informal* keen on: *Are you into meditation?*

intolerable *adj* too bad or unpleasant to endure; unbearable. ➤➤ **intolerably** *adv.*

intolerant *adj* **1** unwilling to grant or share social, professional, political, or religious rights; bigoted. **2** (+ of) unable or unwilling to endure. ➤➤ **intolerance** *n,* **intolerantly** *adv.*

intonation *n* **1** the rise and fall in pitch of the voice in speech. **2** performance of music with respect to correctness of pitch. **3** the act or manner of intoning something.

intone *v* to recite or say in a monotonous tone or in a monotone.

in toto *adv* totally or entirely.

intoxicant *n* something that intoxicates, *esp* an alcoholic drink.

intoxicate *v* **1a** to excite or stupefy with alcohol or drugs, *esp* to the point where physical and mental control is markedly diminished. **b** to cause to lose self-control through excitement or elation. **2** to poison. ➤➤ **intoxicating** *adj,* **intoxication** *n.*

intra- *prefix* inside; within: *intrauterine.*

intractable *adj* **1** not easily solved or dealt with. **2** not easily influenced or directed; stubborn. ➤➤ **intractability** *n,* **intractably** *adv.*

intramural *adj* within the limits of a community or institution, *esp* within a college or university.

intranet *n* an internal computer network that operates by using Internet protocols.

intransigent[1] *adj* refusing to compromise or to abandon a position or attitude, *esp* in politics; uncompromising. ➤➤ **intransigence** *n,* **intransigently** *adv.*

intransigent[2] *n* an intransigent person.

intransitive *adj* of a verb or a sense of a verb: not having a direct object. ➤➤ **intransitively** *adv,* **intransitivity** *n.*

intrauterine *adj* within the uterus.

intrauterine device *n* a contraceptive device inserted and left in the uterus, e.g. a coil.

intravenous *adj* situated in a vein, or entering by way of a vein. ➤➤ **intravenously** *adv.*

in tray *n* a receptacle for mail, memos, and other items yet to be dealt with.

intrench *v archaic* see ENTRENCH.

intrepid *adj* fearless, bold, and resolute. ➤➤ **intrepidity** *n,* **intrepidly** *adv.*

intricacy *n* (*pl* **-ies**) **1** the quality of being intricate. **2** something intricate.

intricate *adj* having many complexly interrelating parts or elements. ➤➤ **intricately** *adv.*

intrigue[1] *v* **1** to arouse the interest or curiosity of. **2** to develop or execute a secret scheme. ➤➤ **intriguer** *n.*

intrigue[2] *n* **1a** a secret scheme or plot. **b** the practice of engaging in or using scheming or underhand plots. **2** a clandestine love affair.

intriguing *adj* engaging the interest to a great degree; fascinating. ➤➤ **intriguingly** *adv.*

intrinsic *adj* belonging to the essential nature or constitution of something. ➤➤ **intrinsically** *adv.*

intro- *prefix* in or inwards: *introvert.*

introduce *v* **1** to bring in, *esp* for the first time. **2a** to bring into play. **b** to bring into practice or use; to institute. **3** to make (somebody) known, e.g.: **a** to cause (somebody or oneself) to be acquainted with another person. **b** to present (somebody) formally, e.g. at court or into society. **c** to make preliminary explanatory or laudatory remarks about (e.g. a speaker). **4** to announce (something, e.g. a piece of legislation) formally or by an official reading. **5** to place or insert somewhere. **6** to present (a radio or television programme). ➤➤ **introducer** *n.*

introduction *n* **1a** the act or an instance of introducing or being introduced. **b** a formal presentation of one person to another. **2** something that introduces, e.g.: **a** a part of a book, lecture, etc that is preliminary to the main part. **b** a book or course of study that gives a basic grounding in a subject. **3** something introduced; *specif* a plant or animal new to an area.

introductory *adj* of or being a first step that sets something going or puts it into proper perspective; preliminary.

introit *or* **Introit** *n* the antiphon or psalm sung as the priest approaches the altar to celebrate Mass or Holy Communion.

intromission *n technical* the insertion of the penis in the vagina in intercourse.

introspection *n* the examining of one's own mind or its contents reflectively. ➤➤ **introspective** *adj,* **introspectively** *adv.*

introvert *n* **1** somebody whose attention and interests are directed towards his or her own mental life: compare EXTROVERT. **2** somebody who is uneasy in company; a shy person: compare EXTROVERT. ➤➤ **introversion** *n,* **introvert** *adj,* **introverted** *adj.*

intrude *v* **1** to thrust oneself into a situation or a place without invitation or welcome. **2** to force (something) in or on something, *esp* without permission or suitable reason. **3** to enter as a geological intrusion. **4** to cause (e.g. rock) to intrude.

intruder *n* somebody who intrudes, *esp* a burglar.

intrusion *n* **1** the act or an instance of intruding or an action that intrudes. **2a** something that intrudes. **b** rock or magma forced while molten into or between other rock formations, or its forcible entry.

intrusive *adj* **1** constituting an intrusion, or tending to intrude. **2** of a rock: being an intrusion. ➤➤ **intrusively** *adv,* **intrusiveness** *n.*

intrust *v* see ENTRUST.

intubate *v* to introduce a tube into a hollow organ, e.g. the windpipe. ➤➤ **intubation** *n.*

intuit *v* (**intuited, intuiting**) to apprehend by intuition.

intuition *n* **1** quick and ready insight. **2a** the power of attaining direct knowledge without evident rational thought or the drawing of conclusions from evidence available. **b** knowledge gained by this power.

intuitive *adj* **1** known or perceived by intuition; directly apprehended. **2** possessing or given to intuition or insight. ➤➤ **intuitively** *adv,* **intuitiveness** *n.*

Inuit *n* (*pl* **Inuits** *or* **Inuit**) **1** a member of the indigenous peoples inhabiting N Canada, Alaska, and Greenland. **2** the language spoken by these peoples. ➤➤ **Inuit** *adj.*

Usage note

Inuit *or* **Eskimo**? The indigenous peoples of the Arctic prefer to be known as the *Inuit* rather than *Eskimos.* The term *Eskimo* is still sometimes used, but *Inuit* should be preferred.

inundate *v* **1** to cover or overwhelm (an area) with water; to flood. **2** to overwhelm (somebody) with demands, offers, etc. ➤➤ **inundation** *n.*

inure *or* **enure** *v* (+ to) to accustom (somebody) to something undesirable.

in utero *adv and adj* in the uterus.

invade *v* **1** to enter (e.g. a country) for hostile purposes. **2** to encroach on (something). **3a** to spread over or into (something) as if invading it. **b** to affect (a part of the body) injuriously and progressively. ➤➤ **invader** *n.*

invaginate *v* **1** to fold in (something) so that an outer surface becomes an inner surface. **2** to enclose or sheathe. ➤➤ **invagination** *n.*

invalid[1] *n* somebody who is unwell or disabled. ➤➤ **invalidity** *n.*

invalid[2] *adj* **1** without legal force. **2** logically inconsistent. ➤➤ **invalidity** *n,* **invalidly** *adv.*

invalid[3] *v* (*usu* + out) to remove (somebody) from active duty by reason of sickness or disability.

invalidate *v* to make invalid, *esp* to weaken or destroy the convincingness of (e.g. an argument or claim). ➤➤ **invalidation** *n.*

invaluable *adj* very useful. ➤➤ **invaluably** *adv.*

invariable[1] *adj* not changing; constant. ➤➤ **invariability** *n,* **invariably** *adv.*

invariable[2] *n* an invariable quantity or thing; a constant.

invariant[1] *adj* unchanging; *specif* unaffected by a particular mathematical operation. ➤➤ **invariance** *n.*

invariant[2] *n* something that remains constant and unchanging.

invasion *n* **1** a hostile attack on a foreign territory by an army. **2** the incoming or spread of something harmful, e.g. a tumour. ➤➤ **invasive** *adj.*

invective *n* abusive or insulting language.

inveigh *v* (+ against) to speak or protest bitterly or vehemently.

Usage note

inveigh *or* **inveigle**? These two words are sometimes confused. *Inveigh* is always followed by the preposition *against.* To *inveigh against* someone or something is to speak or write about them in a very bitter, hostile and condemnatory way: *inveighed against the enemies of the working class. Inveigle* is followed by a direct object and means 'to use cunning or deceitful methods in order to get someone to do something': *inveigled her into parting with most of her savings.*

inveigle *v* (*usu* + into) to win (somebody or something) over by ingenuity or flattery. ➤➤ **inveiglement** *n.*

Usage note

inveigle *or* **inveigh**? See note at INVEIGH.

invent *v* **1** to produce (e.g. a device or machine) for the first time. **2** to think up, *esp* in order to deceive. ➤➤ **inventor** *n.*

invention *n* **1** something invented. **2** something thought up, *esp* to deceive. **3** productive imagination; inventiveness. **4** the act or an instance of inventing.

inventive *adj* showing evidence of original thought or ingenuity; creative. ➤➤ **inventively** *adv,* **inventiveness** *n.*

inventory[1] *n* (*pl* **-ies**) **1** an itemized list, e.g. of the contents of a building or stock in a warehouse. **2** *NAm* the quantity of goods, components, or raw materials on hand; stock.

inventory[2] *v* (**-ies, -ied**) to make an inventory of (things); to catalogue.

inverse[1] *adj* **1** opposite in order, direction, nature, or effect. **2a** of a mathematical function: expressing the same relationship as another function but from the opposite viewpoint. **b** relating to an inverse function. ➤➤ **inversely** *adv.*

inverse[2] *n* **1** a direct opposite. **2** in mathematics: **a** an inverse function or operation. **b** a reciprocal.

inverse proportion *n* the relation between two quantities, one of which increases proportionally as the other decreases.

inversion *n* **1** the act or an instance of inverting something. **2** a reversal of position, order, form, or relationship. **3** (*also* **temperature inversion**) a reversal of the normal atmospheric temperature gradient, in which the layer of air nearest the earth is cooler than the layer above it. ➤➤ **inversive** *adj.*

invert *v* **1** to turn (something) inside out or upside down. **2** to reverse the position, order, or relationship of (things). ➤➤ **inverter** *n,* **invertible** *adj.*

invertebrate *n* an animal that does not have a spinal column, such as an insect, mollusc or worm. ➤➤ **invertebrate** *adj.*

inverted comma *n* = QUOTATION MARK.

inverted snob *n* somebody who sneers indiscriminately at people and things associated with wealth and high social status.

invert sugar *n* a mixture of glucose and fructose found in fruits or produced artificially from sucrose.

invest[1] *v* **1** (*often* + in) to commit money to a particular use in order to earn a financial return. **2** (*often* + in) to devote (e.g. time or effort) to something for future advantages. ➤➤ **investable** *adj*, **investor** *n*.

invest[2] *v* **1** (+ in) to confer authority, office, or rank on (somebody), *esp* ceremonially. **2** (+ with) to endow (something) with something: *The whole affair was invested with an air of mystery.*

investigate *v* **1** to make a systematic examination or study of (something or somebody). **2** to conduct an official enquiry into (something or somebody). ➤➤ **investigation** *n*, **investigator** *n*, **investigatory** *adj*.

investigative *adj* **1** having the duty to investigate or the function of investigating. **2** of journalism: enquiring searchingly into issues and uncovering wrongdoings, anomalies, etc.

investiture *n* a formal ceremony conferring an office or honour on somebody.

investment *n* **1** a sum of money invested for income or profit. **2** an asset, e.g. property, purchased. **3** the act or an instance of investing something other than money, e.g. time or effort.

investment trust *n* an investment company that purchases securities on behalf of its investors.

inveterate *adj* **1** firmly, obstinately, and persistently established: *He had an inveterate tendency to back off from arguments.* **2** confirmed in a habit; habitual: *an inveterate liar.* ➤➤ **inveteracy** *n*, **inveterately** *adv*.

invidious *adj* **1** tending to cause discontent, ill will, or envy. **2** of a comparison: objectionable because of discriminating unfairly. ➤➤ **invidiously** *adv*, **invidiousness** *n*.

invigilate *v Brit* to supervise candidates at an examination. ➤➤ **invigilation** *n*, **invigilator** *n*.

invigorate *v* to give fresh life and energy to (somebody or something). ➤➤ **invigorating** *adj*, **invigoration** *n*.

invincible *adj* incapable of being overcome. ➤➤ **invincibility** *n*, **invincibly** *adv*.

inviolable *adj* that cannot or must not be violated or degraded. ➤➤ **inviolability** *n*, **inviolably** *adv*.

inviolate *adj* not violated or profaned.

invisible *adj* **1** incapable of being seen, whether by nature or because of concealment. **2a** not appearing in published financial statements: *invisible assets.* **b** not reflected in statistics: *invisible earnings.* **c** of or being trade in services, e.g. insurance or tourism, rather than goods. **3** too small or unobtrusive to be seen or noticed; inconspicuous. ➤➤ **invisibility** *n*, **invisibly** *adv*.

invitation *n* **1** the act or an instance of inviting, *esp* an often formal request to be present or participate. **2** something that incites or induces somebody to behave in a particular way.

invite[1] *v* **1** to request (something), or the presence of (somebody), *esp* formally or politely. **2** to increase the likelihood of (something), often unintentionally. ➤➤ **invitee** *n*, **inviter** *n*.

invite[2] *n informal* an invitation.

inviting *adj* attractive or tempting. ➤➤ **invitingly** *adv*.

in vitro *adv and adj* outside the living body and in an artificial environment such as a test tube.

in vivo *adv and adj* in the living body of a plant or animal.

invocation *n* **1** the act or an instance of petitioning somebody for help or support. **2** an incantation or prayer asking a deity or spirits for help or support. ➤➤ **invocatory** *adj*.

invoice[1] *n* an itemized list of goods or services provided, together with a note of the sum of money the recipient owes.

invoice[2] *v* **1** to submit an invoice to. **2** to submit an invoice for (goods or services provided).

invoke *v* **1a** to petition (e.g. a deity) for help or support. **b** to appeal to (an arbitrator or other authority) for help, a judgment, etc. **2** to call forth (e.g. a spirit) by uttering a spell or magical formula. **3** to make an earnest request for. **4** to put into effect: *They invoked economic sanctions.* ➤➤ **invoker** *n*.

involuntary *adj* **1** not subject to conscious control; reflex. **2** done contrary to or without choice. ➤➤ **involuntarily** *adv*, **involuntariness** *n*.

involute *adj* **1** *technical* **a** of a shell: curled spirally. **b** of a leaf: curled or curved inwards, *esp* at the edge. **2** *formal* very intricate or complex; convoluted.

involution *n* **1** in medicine, a shrinking or return to a former size, e.g. of the uterus following pregnancy. **2** *formal* the complicated nature of something.

involve *v* **1a** to cause (somebody) to be associated or take part. **b** to occupy (oneself) absorbingly or to commit (oneself) emotionally. **2** to require (something) as a necessary accompaniment. **3** to relate (something) closely. ➤➤ **involvement** *n*.

involved *adj* **1** complex, *esp* needlessly or excessively so. **2a** taking part. **b** connected with something, *esp* emotionally.

invulnerable *adj* **1** incapable of being injured or harmed. **2** immune to or protected against attack. ➤➤ **invulnerability** *n*, **invulnerably** *adv*.

inward[1] *adj* **1** situated within or directed towards the inside; interior. **2** of or relating to the mind or spirit; inner. **3** of investment: coming into a country or region from outside it. ➤➤ **inwardly** *adv*, **inwardness** *n*.

inward[2] *adv NAm* see INWARDS.

inwards (*NAm* **inward**) *adv* **1** towards the inside, centre, or interior. **2** towards the inner being.

inwrap *v* see ENWRAP.

in-your-face *adj informal* consciously aggressive or controversial.

i/o *abbr* input/output.

iodide *n* a compound of iodine with an element or radical, *esp* a salt or ester of hydriodic acid.

iodine *n* **1** a blackish grey non-metallic chemical element of the halogen group, used in various compounds in medicine and photography. **2** a solution of iodine in alcohol, used as an antiseptic.

IOM *abbr* Isle of Man.

ion *n* **1** an atom or group of atoms that carries a positive or negative electric charge as a result of having lost or gained one or more electrons. **2** a free electron or other charged subatomic particle.

-ion *suffix* forming nouns, denoting: **1a** the act or process of: *validation.* **b** the result of a specified act or process: *regulation.* **2** the quality or condition of: *ambition.*

ion exchange *n* a reversible reaction, used *esp* for softening or removing dissolved substances from water, in which one kind of ion is interchanged with another of similar charge.

Ionian *n* **1** a member of an ancient people formerly inhabiting Attica and the Aegean islands. **2** a native or inhabitant of the Ionian Islands.

Ionic *adj* relating to or denoting one of the three Greek orders of architecture, characterized *esp* by fluted columns and a scroll-shaped CAPITAL[3] (upper part of a column): compare CORINTHIAN, DORIC[1].

ionic *adj* **1** of, existing as, or characterized by ions. **2** functioning by means of ions. ➤➤ **ionically** *adv*.

ionize *or* **-ise** *v* to convert or become converted wholly or partly into ions. ⪢ **ionizable** *adj*, **ionization** *n*, **ionizer** *n*.

ionosphere *n* the layer of the earth's atmosphere that extends from an altitude of about 60km (about 40mi), to at least 480km (about 300mi) and consists of several distinct regions containing free ions, atoms, and electrons. ⪢ **ionospheric** *adj*.

iota *n* **1** the ninth letter of the Greek alphabet (Ι, ι), equivalent to roman i. **2** an infinitesimal amount; a bit.

IOU *n* a written acknowledgment of a debt.

IOW *abbr* Isle of Wight.

IP *abbr* Internet Protocol.

IPA *abbr* International Phonetic Alphabet.

ipecacuanha /ˌipikakyooˈahnə/ *n* the underground stem and root of a S American plant, formerly used dried as a purgative and emetic.

ipsilateral *adj* situated on or affecting the same side of the body.

ipso facto *adv* by that very fact, or by the very nature of the case.

IQ *abbr* intelligence quotient.

Ir *abbr* the chemical symbol for iridium.

ir- *prefix* see IN-[1], IN-[2].

IRA *abbr* Irish Republican Army.

Iranian *n* a native or inhabitant of Iran. ⪢ **Iranian** *adj*.

Iraqi *n* (*pl* **Iraqis**) **1** a native or inhabitant of Iraq. **2** the dialect of Arabic spoken in Iraq. ⪢ **Iraqi** *adj*.

irascible *adj* having an easily provoked temper; irritable. ⪢ **irascibility** *n*, **irascibly** *adv*.

irate *adj* extremely angry. ⪢ **irately** *adv*.

ire *n literary* intense and usu openly displayed anger.

irenic *or* **eirenic** *or* **irenical** *or* **eirenical** *adj* conducive to or operating towards peace or conciliation. ⪢ **irenically** *adv*.

iridaceous *adj* relating or belonging to the iris family.

irides *n* pl of IRIS.

iridescent *adj* displaying a shimmering shift of colours. ⪢ **iridescence** *n*, **iridescently** *adv*.

iridium *n* a silver-white metallic chemical element of the platinum group.

iris *n* **1** (*pl* **irises** *or* **irides**) the opaque contractile diaphragm perforated by the pupil that forms the coloured portion of the eye. **2** (*pl* **irises** *or* **iris**) a plant with long straight leaves and large showy flowers.

Irish[1] *adj* **1** of Ireland, the people of Ireland, or the Celtic language of Ireland. **2** *offensive* amusingly illogical. ⪢ **Irishman** *n*, **Irishness** *n*, **Irishwoman** *n*.

Irish[2] *n* **1** (*used as pl*) the people of Ireland. **2** (*also* **Irish Gaelic**) the Celtic language of the people of Ireland.

Irish coffee *n* hot sugared coffee with Irish whiskey and whipped cream.

Irish moss *n* = CARRAGEEN.

Irish setter *n* a gundog of a chestnut-brown or mahogany-red breed with a long silky coat.

Irish stew *n* a stew consisting chiefly of mutton, potatoes, and onions in a thick gravy.

Irish wolfhound *n* a hound of a very large tall breed with a shaggy coat.

irk *v* to make irritated or angry.

irksome *adj* troublesome or annoying. ⪢ **irksomely** *adv*, **irksomeness** *n*.

iron[1] *n* **1** a silver-white magnetic metallic chemical element that is heavy and malleable, readily rusts in moist air, occurs in most igneous rocks, and is vital to biological processes. **2** a metal implement with a smooth flat typically triangular base that is heated and used to smooth or press clothing. **3** a heated metal implement used for branding, cauterizing, or soldering. **4** (*usu in pl*) a device, *esp* fetters, used to bind or restrain. **5** any of a series of golf clubs with metal heads of varying angles. **6** any of various tools, implements, or devices made of iron. ✱ **iron in the fire** a prospective course of action, or a plan not yet realized [from the days when smoothing irons for pressing clothes were heated in the fire; as one cooled with use another would be in the fire heating up].

iron[2] *adj* **1** made of iron. **2** resembling iron, e.g. in appearance, strength, solidity, or durability.

iron[3] *v* to smooth (e.g. a garment) with a heated iron.

Iron Age *n* (**the Iron Age**) the period of human culture characterized by the widespread use of iron for making tools and weapons and dating from before 1000 BC.

ironclad *adj esp* of warships: sheathed in iron or steel armour.

Iron Curtain *n* (**the Iron Curtain**) a political and ideological barrier between the Communist countries of E Europe and the non-Communist countries of W Europe and those friendly to them.

iron hand *n* stern or rigorous control: compare VELVET GLOVE.

ironic *adj* **1** containing or constituting irony. **2** tending to use irony. ⪢ **ironical** *adj*, **ironically** *adv*.

ironing *n* clothes and other items of laundry that are ironed or are to be ironed.

ironing board *n* a narrow flat board on which clothes, etc are ironed, mounted on collapsible legs.

ironist /ˈierənist/ *n* somebody who uses irony.

iron lung *n* a device, formerly used for artificial respiration, in the form of a rigid metal case that fits over the patient's chest and forces air into and out of the lungs.

iron maiden *n* a medieval instrument of torture consisting of a box lined with iron spikes.

iron man *n* **1** a man of outstanding strength or athletic prowess. **2** any of various sporting contests that demand such qualities.

ironmonger *n Brit* a dealer in hardware. ⪢ **ironmongery** *n*.

iron out *v* to put right or correct (e.g. a problem or defect).

iron pyrites *n* iron disulphide occurring as a lustrous pale brass-yellow mineral.

iron rations *pl n* emergency food rations, *esp* for a soldier.

ironstone *n* **1** a hard sedimentary iron ore. **2** a type of hard dense stoneware.

ironwork *n* **1** articles made of iron. **2** (*in pl, used as sing. or pl*) a place where iron or steel is smelted or heavy iron or steel products are made.

irony /ˈierəni/ *n* (*pl* **-ies**) **1** the use of words to express a meaning other than the literal meaning, *esp* the opposite of it, usu for humorous effect. **2a** incongruity between actual circumstances and the appropriate or expected result. **b** an event or situation showing such incongruity.

Iroquois /ˈirəkwoy(z)/ *n* (*pl* **Iroquois**) **1** (*in pl*) a confederation of Native American tribes of the western USA. **2** a member of any of these tribes. **3** any of the languages of these tribes. ⋙ **Iroquoian** *adj*, **Iroquois** *adj*.

irradiate *v* **1** to expose (food) to electromagnetic radiation in order to kill bacteria and prolong its shelf life. **2** to cast rays of light on. **3** to emit (something resembling rays of light). ⋙ **irradiance** *n*, **irradiant** *adj*, **irradiation** *n*, **irradiative** *adj*, **irradiator** *n*.

irrational *adj* **1a** not governed by or according to reason; illogical. **b** not capable of reasoning. **2** of a number: having a value that cannot be expressed exactly as the result of dividing one integer by another: compare RATIONAL, SURD². ⋙ **irrationalism** *n*, **irrationalist** *n*, **irrationality** *n*, **irrationally** *adv*.

irreconcilable *adj* impossible to reconcile; incompatible. ⋙ **irreconcilably** *adv*.

irrecoverable *adj* not capable of being recovered or put right. ⋙ **irrecoverably** *adv*.

irredeemable *adj* **1** too bad to be saved or improved; beyond remedy. **2** of bonds, etc: without a specified date for repayment. ⋙ **irredeemably** *adv*.

irredentism *n* advocacy of the restoration of territories to the countries to which they are historically or ethnically related. ⋙ **irredentist** *n and adj*.

irreducible *adj* impossible to be brought into a desired or simpler state. ⋙ **irreducibly** *adv*.

irrefutable *adj* not able to be denied or disproved; incontrovertible. ⋙ **irrefutability** *n*, **irrefutably** *adv*.

irregardless *adj and adv* regardless.

Usage note

Irregardless is a non-standard word that was probably formed from *irrespective* and *regardless*.

irregular¹ *adj* **1** lacking continuity or regularity, *esp* of occurrence or activity. **2** lacking symmetry or evenness. **3** contrary to rules, customs, or moral principles. **4** of a word: not inflected in the normal manner. **5** of troops: not belonging to the regular army organization. ⋙ **irregularity** *n*, **irregularly** *adv*.

irregular² *n* an irregular soldier.

irrelevant *adj* not relevant; inapplicable. ⋙ **irrelevance** *n*, **irrelevancy** *n*, **irrelevantly** *adv*.

irreligion *n* hostility to or disregard of religion. ⋙ **irreligionist** *n*, **irreligious** *adj*, **irreligiously** *adv*.

irremediable *adj* impossible to remedy; incurable. ⋙ **irremediably** *adv*.

irremovable *adj* not able to be removed.

irreparable *adj* not able to be restored to a previous condition. ⋙ **irreparably** *adv*.

irreplaceable *adj* having no adequate substitute. ⋙ **irreplaceably** *adv*.

irrepressible *adj* impossible to restrain or control. ⋙ **irrepressibility** *n*, **irrepressibly** *adv*.

irreproachable *adj* beyond criticism, blame, or reproach. ⋙ **irreproachability** *n*, **irreproachably** *adv*.

irresistible *adj* too attractive or enticing to resist. ⋙ **irresistibility** *n*, **irresistibly** *adv*.

irresolute *adj* lacking decisiveness or a firm purpose. ⋙ **irresolutely** *adv*, **irresolution** *n*.

irrespective *adv* regardless. ✱ **irrespective of** without regard or reference to; in spite of. ⋙ **irrespectively** *adv*.

irresponsible *adj* **1** showing no regard for the consequences of one's actions; reckless. **2** unable to bear responsibility. ⋙ **irresponsibility** *n*, **irresponsibly** *adv*.

irretrievable *adj* not retrievable or recoverable. ⋙ **irretrievably** *adv*.

irreverence *n* lack of respect, or something done or said that shows a lack of respect. ⋙ **irreverent** *adj*, **irreverently** *adv*.

irreversible *adj* unable to be changed back into a previous state or condition. ⋙ **irreversibility** *n*, **irreversibly** *adv*.

irrevocable *adj* incapable of being revoked or altered. ⋙ **irrevocability** *n*, **irrevocably** *adv*.

irrigate *v* **1** to supply (land) with water by artificial means, e.g. canals or channels. **2** to flush (e.g. an eye or wound) with a stream of liquid. ⋙ **irrigable** *adj*, **irrigation** *n*, **irrigator** *n*.

irritable *adj* **1** easily angered or exasperated. **2** abnormally sensitive to stimuli. ⋙ **irritability** *n*, **irritableness** *n*, **irritably** *adv*.

irritable bowel syndrome *n* any of various abnormal conditions of the intestines that are accompanied by discomfort and pain and have no apparent organic cause.

irritant¹ *n* something that irritates.

irritant² *adj* causing irritation. ⋙ **irritancy** *n*.

irritate *v* **1** to make impatient or angry. **2** to cause (a part of the body) to become sore or inflamed. **3** in biology, to stimulate (a cell, etc) so that it produces a response. ⋙ **irritating** *adj*, **irritatingly** *adv*, **irritation** *n*, **irritative** *adj*.

irrupt *v* to rush in forcibly or violently. ⋙ **irruption** *n*, **irruptive** *adj*, **irruptively** *adv*.

is *v* third person sing. present tense of BE.

is- *or* **iso-** *comb. form* equal or uniform: *isomorphic*.

ISA /'iesə/ *n* an individual savings account, a tax-free savings scheme.

ISBN *abbr* International Standard Book Number.

ischaemia (*NAm* **ischemia**) /is'keemi·ə/ *n* deficiency of blood in a part of the body, *esp* the heart, due to decreased arterial flow. ⋙ **ischaemic** *adj*.

ischium /'iski·əm/ *n* (*pl* **ischia**) the rearmost and lowest of the three principal bones composing either half of the pelvis. ⋙ **ischial** *adj*.

ISDN *abbr* integrated services digital network.

-ise *suffix* see -IZE.

-ish *suffix* **1** forming adjectives, denoting: **a** a particular quality or aptitude: *childish*; *bookish*. **b** a nationality: *Finnish*. **2** forming adjectives, meaning: **a** slightly; somewhat: *purplish*; *biggish*. **b** approximately: *fortyish*.

isinglass *n* **1** a very pure gelatin prepared from the air bladders of fish and used *esp* in jellies and glue. **2** *chiefly NAm* mica or a similar substance.

Islam *n* **1** the religious faith of Muslims including belief in Allah as the sole deity and in Muhammad as his prophet. **2** the civilization based on Islam. ⋙ **Islamic** *adj*, **Islamist** *n*.

Islamise *v* see ISLAMIZE.

Islamize *or* **-ise** *v* **1** to make Islamic. **2** to convert to Islam. ⋙ **Islamization** *n*.

island *n* **1** an area of land surrounded by water and smaller than a continent. **2** something that is isolated or surrounded. **3** = TRAFFIC ISLAND. ⋙ **islander** *n*.

isle *n* an island, *esp* a small one.

islet *n* **1** a little island. **2** in anatomy, a small isolated mass of one type of tissue.

islets of Langerhans *pl n* any of the groups of endocrine cells in the pancreas that secrete insulin.

ism *n often derog* a distinctive doctrine, cause, theory, or practice.

-ism *suffix* forming nouns, denoting: **1** an act or practice: *plagiarism; cannibalism.* **2a** a state or property: *magnetism.* **b** a pathological state or condition: *alcoholism; gigantism.* **3a** a doctrine or cult: *Buddhism; stoicism.* **b** prejudice: *sexism.* **4** a characteristic or peculiar feature of language: *colloquialism; anglicism.*

Ismaili *n* (*pl* **Ismailis**) a member of the branch of Shiite Islam believing that Ismail, the eldest son of the sixth imam, was the rightful seventh imam.

isn't *contr* is not.

ISO *abbr* **1** Imperial Service Order. **2a** International Organization for Standardization. **b** in photography, used in classifications of film speeds.

iso- *comb. form* see IS-.

isobar *n* a line on a chart connecting places where the atmospheric pressure is the same. ➤➤ **isobaric** *adj.*

isochronal *adj* **1** having equal duration. **2** recurring at regular intervals. **3** occurring simultaneously. ➤➤ **isochronally** *adv,* **isochronism** *n.*

isochronous *adj* = ISOCHRONAL.

isogenic *adj* characterized by essentially identical genes.

isogloss *n* a line on a chart dividing places or regions that differ in a particular linguistic feature. ➤➤ **isoglossal** *adj.*

isogonal *adj* = ISOGONIC.

isogonic *adj* of or having equal angles.

isohyet /iesoh'hie·ət/ *n* a line on a chart connecting areas of equal rainfall. ➤➤ **isohyetal** *adj.*

isolate[1] *v* **1** to set apart from others. **2** to quarantine in order to prevent the spread of infection. **3** to separate (a substance) from another substance so as to obtain in a pure form. **4** to break the electrical connection between (an appliance) and a supply or network. ➤➤ **isolable** *adj,* **isolation** *n,* **isolator** *n.*

isolate[2] *n* somebody or something that has become isolated or separated.

isolated *adj* **1** separate or cut off from others. **2** single or exceptional: *an isolated example.*

isolationism *n* a policy of refraining from engaging in international relations. ➤➤ **isolationist** *n and adj.*

isoleucine *n* an amino acid found in most proteins and an essential constituent of the human diet.

isomer *n* **1** a chemical compound that has the same chemical formula as another or others but has different properties and a different arrangement of atoms. **2** an atom that has the same mass number and atomic number as another or others but different energy states and rates of radioactive decay. ➤➤ **isomeric** *adj,* **isomerism** *n.*

isomerize *or* **-ise** *v* to change into an isomer. ➤➤ **isomerization** *n.*

isometric *adj* **1** having equal dimensions or measurements. **2** of or involving isometrics. **3** denoting a representation of an object in which three mutually perpendicular axes are equally inclined to the drawing surface. ➤➤ **isometrically** *adv.*

isometrics *pl n* (*used as sing. or pl*) physical exercise in which opposing muscles are contracted to increase the tone of the muscle fibres.

isomorphic *adj* having structural similarity or identity. ➤➤ **isomorph** *n,* **isomorphism** *n,* **isomorphous** *adj.*

isosceles /ie'sosəleez/ *adj* of a triangle: having two equal sides.

isotherm *n* a line on a chart connecting points having the same temperature. ➤➤ **isothermal** *adj.*

isotonic *adj* **1** having the same concentration as a surrounding medium or a liquid under comparison: compare HYPERTONIC, HYPOTONIC. **2** of a drink: containing minerals and essential salts designed to replace those lost as a result of strenuous exercise. **3** relating to the contraction of muscles under fairly constant tension. ➤➤ **isotonicity** *n.*

isotope *n* any of two or more forms of a chemical element that have the same atomic number and similar chemical behaviour but differ in atomic mass or mass number and physical properties. ➤➤ **isotopic** *adj,* **isotopy** *n.*

isotropic *adj* having physical properties with the same values in all directions. ➤➤ **isotropy** *n.*

ISP *abbr* an Internet service provider, a commercial company providing individual users with an Internet connection and related services.

I-spy *n* a children's game in which a visible object is guessed from the initial letter of its name.

Israeli *n* (*pl* **Israelis**) a native or inhabitant of modern Israel. ➤➤ **Israeli** *adj.*

Israelite *n* **1** a member of any of the twelve tribes descended from the Hebrew patriarch Jacob's sons. **2** a native or inhabitant of the ancient kingdom of Israel. **3** a Jew. ➤➤ **Israelite** *adj.*

ISSN *abbr* International Standard Serial Number.

issue[1] *n* **1** a matter or topic, *esp* one that is in dispute. **2a** the whole quantity of things published or distributed at one time. **b** the act or an instance of issuing something. **3** *formal* the action of going or flowing out. **4** *formal* offspring. ✱ **at issue** under discussion or consideration; in dispute. ➤➤ **issueless** *adj.*

issue[2] *v* **1** to send (e.g. a newspaper) out for sale or circulation. **2** to give (e.g. a statement) out officially. **3** to go, come, or flow out. ➤➤ **issuance** *n,* **issuer** *n.*

-ist[1] *suffix* forming nouns, denoting: **1** somebody who does, produces, or uses something: *cyclist; novelist.* **2** somebody who specializes in or practises something: *geologist; ventriloquist.* **3** somebody who adheres to or advocates a doctrine or code of behaviour: *socialist; hedonist.* **4** somebody who is prejudiced: *sexist.*

-ist[2] *suffix* forming adjectives, with the meanings: **1** relating to, or characteristic of: *obscurantist.* **2** showing prejudice on grounds of: *racist.*

isthmus *n* a narrow strip of land connecting two larger land areas. ➤➤ **isthmian** *adj.*

IT *abbr* **1** Information Technology. **2** Intermediate Technology.

it *pron* **1** used as subject or object: **a** that thing, animal, etc. **b** the person in question: *Who is it?* **2** used as subject of an impersonal verb: *It's raining.* **3** used as anticipatory subject or object of a verb: *I take it that you refuse.* **4** used to refer to a state of affairs: *How's it going?* **5** the important or appropriate thing.

Italian *n* **1** a native or inhabitant of Italy. **2** the language of Italy. ➤➤ **Italian** *adj,* **Italianate** *adj.*

italic[1] *n* a printed character that slants upwards to the right, as the labels *n, adj,* etc do in this dictionary, or a typeface comprising such characters.

italic[2] *adj* of a printed character: in italic.

italicize *or* **-ise** *v* to print (something) in italics. ➤➤ **italicization** *n.*

ITC *abbr* Independent Television Commission.

itch[1] *v* **1** to have or produce an itch. **2** *informal* to have a restless desire.

itch[2] *n* **1** an irritating sensation in the skin that makes one want to scratch. **2** *informal* a restless desire.

itchy *adj* (**-ier, -iest**) **1** affected by an itch. **2** causing an itch. ➤➤ **itchiness** *n.*

itchy feet *pl n informal* a restless desire for travel or change of circumstances.

it'd *contr* it had or it would.

-ite[1] *suffix* forming nouns, denoting: **1** somebody who belongs to the specified place, group, etc: *Israelite; socialite.* **2** an adherent or follower: *Pre-Raphaelite.* **3** a product of something: *metabolite.* **4** a commercially manufactured product: *ebonite.* **5** a fossil: *ammonite.* **6** a mineral: *bauxite.* ➤➤ **-itic** *suffix.*

-ite[2] *suffix* forming adjectives relating to nouns ending in -ITE[1].

-ite[3] *suffix* forming nouns, denoting: salt or ester of a specified acid with a name ending in *-ous*: *sulphite.*

item[1] *n* **1** a separate piece of news or information. **2** a separate article or unit in a series. **3** (**an item**) *informal* two people in a romantic or sexual relationship.

item[2] *adv archaic* and in addition, used to introduce each article in a list.

itemize *or* **-ise** *v* to set down in the form of a list of individual elements. ➤➤ **itemization** *n.*

iterate *v* to say, do, or use again or repetitively. ➤➤ **iteration** *n.*

iterative *adj* **1** iterating or involving iteration. **2** relating to successive repetition of a mathematical process, using the result of one stage as the input for the next.

itinerant[1] *adj* travelling from place to place.

itinerant[2] *n* somebody who moves from place to place.

itinerary *n* (*pl* **-ies**) the proposed route of a journey, sometimes including a list of stops to be made on the way.

itinerate *v* to travel from place to place, *esp* on a preaching or judicial circuit. ➤➤ **itineration** *n.*

-itious *suffix* forming adjectives, with the meaning: relating to or having the characteristics of: *fictitious.*

-itis *suffix* forming nouns, denoting: disease or inflammation: *bronchitis.* ➤➤ **-itic** *suffix.*

it'll *contr* it will or it shall.

ITN *abbr* Independent Television News.

its *adj* belonging to or associated with a thing, animal, etc already mentioned.

Usage note

its *or* it's? *Its* is the possessive form of *it* and has no apostrophe; *it's* is a shortened form of *it is* or *it has.*

it's *contr* it is or it has.

Usage note

it's *or* its? See note at ITS.

itself *pron* used reflexively or for emphasis to refer to a thing, animal, etc that is the subject of the clause. ✱ **in itself** intrinsically considered.

itsy-bitsy *or* **itty-bitty** *adj informal* tiny.

ITV *abbr* Independent Television.

-ity *suffix* forming nouns, denoting: **1** a quality or state: *authority; obscenity.* **2** an amount or degree: *humidity.*

IUD *abbr* intrauterine device.

-ium *suffix* (*pl* **-iums** *or* **-ia**) forming nouns, denoting: **1** a chemical element: *sodium.* **2** a biological part: *epithelium.*

IV *abbr* **1** intravenous. **2** intravenously.

I've *contr* I have.

-ive[1] *suffix* forming adjectives, with the meaning: tending to do or doing something: *corrective; descriptive.*

-ive[2] *suffix* forming nouns, denoting: **1** a person or thing that does something: *sedative; detective.* **2** somebody who is in or affected by a specified state or condition: *captive.*

IVF *abbr* in vitro fertilization.

ivied *adj literary* overgrown with ivy.

Ivorian *n* a native or inhabitant of Côte d'Ivoire. ➤➤ **Ivorian** *adj.*

ivory *n* (*pl* **-ies**) **1** the hard creamy-white substance of which the tusks of elephants and other mammals are made. **2** a creamy white colour. **3** *informal* (*in pl*) things, e.g. piano keys or teeth, made of ivory or something resembling ivory. ➤➤ **ivory** *adj.*

ivory tower *n* **1** remoteness from everyday life or practical concerns. **2** a place encouraging such an attitude or position.

ivy *n* a common Eurasian woody climbing plant with evergreen leaves, small yellowish flowers, and black berries.

Ivy League *n* a group of long-established prestigious eastern US colleges and universities.

-ize *or* **-ise** *suffix* forming verbs, with the meanings: **1** to become or become like, or to cause to be or resemble: *liquidize; Americanize.* **2** to subject to: *criticize; hospitalize.* **3a** to impregnate, treat, or combine with: *oxidize.* **b** to treat like or make into: *lionize; prioritize.* **4** to engage in: *philosophize.*

Usage note

-ize *or* -ise? Either spelling is correct, in British English, for most verbs: *criticize* or *criticise*; *organize* or *organise*; *privatise* or *privatize.* There are, however, a number of verbs which must end in *-ise*, e.g. *advertise, advise, chastise, comprise, compromise, despise, devise, enfranchise, excise, exercise, franchise, improvise, merchandise, revise, supervise, surmise, surprise,* and *televise.*

j

J[1] *or* **j** *n* (*pl* **J's** *or* **Js** *or* **j's**) the tenth letter of the English alphabet.

J[2] *abbr* **1** in card games, jack. **2** joule.

jab[1] *v* (**jabbed, jabbing**) **1** to pierce or poke quickly or suddenly with or as if with a sharp object. **2** to strike with a short straight blow.

jab[2] *n* **1** an act of jabbing. **2** *informal* a hypodermic injection, *esp* a vaccination.

jabber *v* to talk rapidly and unintelligibly. ➤➤ **jabber** *n*, **jabberer** *n*.

jabiru /'jabirooh/ *n* **1** a large stork found in Central and S America, with white plumage, a dark-coloured naked head, and a dark bill. **2** a large Australian stork with black and white colouring.

jabot /'zhaboh/ *n* a decorative lace or cloth frill extending from the neckpiece down the centre of a blouse or shirt.

jacaranda *n* a tropical American tree with showy blue flowers.

jacinth /'jasinth/ *n* a reddish orange transparent variety of zircon used as a gem.

jack[1] *n* **1** a portable mechanism for exerting pressure or lifting a heavy object a short distance. **2** a playing card marked with the figure of a soldier or servant and ranking usu below the queen. **3a** = JACK PLUG. **b** = JACK SOCKET. **4** a small target ball in the game of bowls. **5a** (*in pl, used as sing.*) a game in which players toss and pick up small objects in between throws of a ball. **b** an object used in this game, *esp* a small six-pointed metal object. **6** a male donkey or ass. **7** a small national flag flown at the bow of a ship. **8a** a tropical seafish similar to a perch. **b** a young pike. ✱ **every man jack** everybody.

jack[2] *v* **1** (*usu* + up) to move or lift with a jack. **2** (+ up) to raise the level or quality of.

jackal *n* a wild dog of Africa, Asia, and Europe that is smaller than a wolf and scavenges or hunts in packs.

jackanapes *n* **1a** an impudent or conceited person. **b** a mischievous child. **2** *archaic* a monkey or ape.

jackaroo *or* **jackeroo** *n Aus* a young inexperienced worker on a cattle or sheep station.

jackass *n* **1** a male ass. **2** a stupid person; a fool.

jackboot *n* a leather military boot reaching to the knee. ➤➤ **jackbooted** *adj.*

jackdaw *n* a common black and grey Eurasian bird that is related to but smaller than the common crow.

jackeroo *n* see JACKAROO.

jacket[1] *n* **1** an outer garment for the upper body opening down the full length of the centre front. **2** a thermally insulating cover, e.g. for a hot-water tank. **3** = DUST JACKET. **4** the skin of a baked potato.

jacket[2] *v* (**jacketed, jacketing**) to put a jacket on (something or somebody); to enclose in or with a jacket.

jacket potato *n* (*pl* **jacket potatoes**) *Brit* a potato baked and served with the skin on.

Jack Frost *n* frost or frosty weather personified.

jackfruit *n* the immense fruit of a tropical tree related to the breadfruit, containing edible pulp and nutritious seeds.

jackhammer *n NAm* = PNEUMATIC DRILL.

jack in *v informal* to give up or abandon.

jack-in-the-box *n* a toy consisting of a small box out of which a figure springs when the lid is raised.

jackknife[1] *n* (*pl* **jackknives**) **1** a large pocket knife with a folding blade. **2** a dive in which the diver bends from the waist, touches the ankles with straight knees, and straightens out before hitting the water.

jackknife[2] *v* **1a** to double up like a jackknife. **b** to cause to jackknife. **2** of an articulated lorry: to go out of control so that the trailer swings round to form a V-shape. **3** of a diver: to perform a jackknife.

jack-of-all-trades *n* (*pl* **jacks-of-all-trades**) a handy versatile person.

jack-o'-lantern *n* **1** a lantern made from a hollowed-out pumpkin with holes cut in it to look like a human face. **2** = WILL-O'-THE-WISP.

jack plane *n* a plane used in the first stages of smoothing wood.

jack plug *n* a single-pronged electrical plug that can be inserted into a jack socket.

jackpot *n* a large prize, e.g. in a lottery. ✱ **hit the jackpot** *informal* to have a big success or a piece of good fortune.

jackrabbit *n* a large hare of western N America with long ears and long hind legs.

Jack Russell terrier *n* a terrier of a small pugnacious breed orig used to hunt rats.

jacksie *or* **jacksy** *n* (*pl* **-ies**) *Brit, informal* a person's bottom.

jack socket *n* an electrical socket that is designed to receive a jack plug.

jackstone *n* = JACK[1] (5B).

jacksy *n* see JACKSIE.

jack tar *n informal* a sailor.

Jack the lad *n* a brashly self-confident, stylish, and mischievous young man.

jack up *v* **1** = JACK[2]. **2** *slang* to inject oneself with a drug.

Jacobean *adj* of the reign of James I of England (1603–25).

Jacobin *n* **1** a member of a radical democratic political group during the French Revolution that seized power from moderate Republicans and instituted the Reign of Terror. **2** an extremist radical. ➤➤ **Jacobinism** *n.*

Word history

French *Jacobin,* orig in the sense 'Dominican'. The group was formed in the Dominican convent in the rue St-Jacques in Paris.

Jacobite *n* a supporter of James II of England or of the Stuarts after 1688. ➤➤ **Jacobitism** *n.*

Jacob's ladder *n* a plant of the phlox family that has bell-shaped white or blue flowers.

jacquard *n* **1** an apparatus for a loom using punched cards that enable decorated and patterned fabrics to be woven. **2** a fabric with an intricate variegated weave or pattern.

jacquerie /'zhakəri/ *n* a peasants' revolt.

jactitation *n* a tossing to and fro or jerking and twitching of the body.

Jacuzzi /jə'koohzi/ *n trademark* a large bath fitted with a system of underwater jets that massage the body.

jade[1] *n* **1** a hard typically green mineral used as a stone. **2** a light bluish green colour. ➤➤ **jade** *adj.*

jade[2] *n* **1** *archaic* a disreputable woman. **2** a worn-out old horse.

jaded *adj* **1** fatigued or bored, *esp* by a surfeit of something or by overwork. **2** lacking freshness. **3** overused.

jadeite *n* a green or white mineral, the more valuable variety of jade.

j'adoube /zha'doohb/ *interj* used in chess to indicate that one is touching a piece merely to adjust it rather than to move it.

jaeger /'yaygə/ *n* = SKUA.

Jaffa *n* a large thick-skinned orange grown *esp* in Israel.

jag[1] *v* (**jagged, jagging**) **1** to cut or tear unevenly or raggedly. **2** to stab or prick.

jag[2] *n* **1** a sharp projecting part. **2** *Scot* **a** a prick. **b** an injection.

jag[3] *n informal* a period of indulgence in an activity.

jagged *adj* having a sharply indented or uneven edge or surface. ➤➤ **jaggedly** *adv,* **jaggedness** *n.*

jaggy *adj* (**-ier, -iest**) **1** jagged or notched. **2** *Scot* prickly.

jaguar *n* a large wild animal of the cat family found in Central and S America that has a brownish yellow coat with black spots.

Jah *n* the Rastafarian name for God.

jail[1] *or* **gaol** *n* = PRISON.

jail[2] *or* **gaol** *v* to confine (somebody) in a jail.

jailbait *n informal* a girl below the age of consent.

jailbird *n* a person who is or has frequently been confined in jail.

jailbreak *n* an escape from jail.

jailer *or* **gaoler** *n* a person in charge of the prisoners in a jail.

jailhouse *n NAm* a prison.

Jain *n* an adherent of Jainism.

Jainism *n* a religion originating in India in the sixth cent. BC teaching liberation of the soul by self-denial and non-violence.

jake *adj NAm, Aus, informal* all right or satisfactory.

jalapeño /halə'paynyoh/ *n* (*pl* **jalapeños**) a short thick green chilli, often used in Mexican cooking.

jalopy *n* (*pl* **-ies**) *informal* a dilapidated old vehicle or aircraft.

jalousie /'zhaləzi, 'zhaloozee/ *n* a blind with adjustable horizontal slats for admitting light and air while excluding sun and rain.

jam[1] *v* (**jammed, jamming**) **1** to cause (e.g. a door or part of a machine) to become stuck so that it does not work or move properly. **2** to fill (e.g. a street) so that passage along it is blocked. **3a** to squeeze or pack (something) into a close or tight position. **b** to fill (something), sometimes to excess. **4** to send out interfering signals in order to make (a radio signal) unintelligible. **5** (+ on) to apply (e.g. brakes) suddenly and violently. **6** to become blocked, wedged, or stuck. **7** *informal* to take part in a jam session.

jam[2] *n* **1a** a crowded mass that impedes or blocks something. **b** the pressure or congestion of a crowd. **2** an instance of jamming and becoming inoperable. **3** *informal* a difficult or awkward situation. **4** = JAM SESSION.

jam[3] *n* a preserve made by boiling fruit and sugar to a thick consistency.

Jamaican *n* a native or inhabitant of Jamaica. ➤➤ **Jamaican** *adj.*

jamb *n* a straight vertical post or surface forming the side of an opening for a door, window, etc.

jambalaya /jambə'lie·ə/ *n* a dish of rice typically cooked with ham, chicken, shrimps, etc and seasoned with herbs.

jamboree *n* **1** a large festive gathering. **2** a large gathering of scouts or guides in a camp.

jammy *adj* (**-ier, -iest**) **1** *Brit, informal* lucky. **2** covered or filled with jam.

jam-packed *adj* full to overflowing.

jam session *n* an impromptu jazz performance that features group improvisation.

Jan. *abbr* January.

jangle *v* **1** to make or cause to make a harsh or discordant ringing noise. **2** of the nerves: to be in a state of tense irritation. ➤➤ **jangle** *n,* **jangly** *adj.*

janissary *or* **janizary** *n* (*pl* **-ies**) **1** a soldier of an elite corps of Turkish troops of the 14th to 19th cent. **2** a loyal or subservient official or supporter.

janitor *n NAm, Scot* a caretaker, *esp* of a school. ➤➤ **janitorial** *adj.*

janizary *n* see JANISSARY.

jankers *pl n Brit, slang* (*used as sing.*) punishment, *esp* confinement, for military offences.

Jansenism *n* a 17th- and 18th-cent. Roman Catholic movement based on the doctrine that those whom God had chosen for salvation would be saved. ➤➤ **Jansenist** *n and adj.*

January *n* the first month of the year.

Jap *n offensive* a Japanese person. ➤➤ **Jap** *adj.*

japan[1] *n* a black varnish giving a hard brilliant finish.

japan[2] *v* (**japanned, japanning**) to cover with a coat of japan.

Japanese *n* (*pl* **Japanese**) **1** a native or inhabitant of Japan. **2** the language of Japan. ➤➤ **Japanese** *adj.*

jape[1] *n* a jest or joke.

jape[2] *v* to jest or joke. ⋙ **japery** *n.*

japonica *n* a hardy ornamental shrub of the rose family with clusters of scarlet, white, or pink flowers.

jar[1] *n* **1** a cylindrical short-necked and wide-mouthed container, made *esp* of glass. **2** *informal* a glass of beer.

jar[2] *v* (**jarred, jarring**) **1** to have a disagreeable or incongruous effect. **2** to make a harsh or discordant noise. **3** to jolt or vibrate. **4** to give (something) a shock, shake, or jolt. ⋙ **jarringly** *adv.*

jar[3] *n* **1a** a sudden or unexpected jolt or shake. **b** an unsettling shock (e.g. to nerves or feelings). **2** a jarring noise.

jardinière /zhahdi'nyeə/ *n* **1** an ornamental stand or large pot for plants or flowers. **2** a garnish consisting of several vegetables arranged in groups.

jargon *n* the terminology or idiom of a particular activity or group. ⋙ **jargonistic** *adj.*

jasmine *n* a shrub or climbing plant that usu has extremely fragrant yellow or white flowers.

jasper *n* an opaque quartz that is usu reddish brown, yellow, or dark green, used as a gemstone.

jasperware *n* a fine-grained unglazed stoneware developed by Josiah Wedgwood, usu decorated with raised white classical motifs on a coloured ground.

jaundice *n* **1** an abnormal condition marked by yellowing of the skin, tissues, etc caused by the deposition of bile pigments. **2** a state of bitterness, envy, or resentment. ⋙ **jaundiced** *adj.*

jaunt[1] *n* a short journey for pleasure.

jaunt[2] *v* to go on a jaunt.

jaunty *adj* (**-ier, -iest**) **1** having or showing airy self-confidence. **2** smart or stylish. ⋙ **jauntily** *adv,* **jauntiness** *n.*

Java *n trademark* a computer programming language used to add interactivity to web pages.

Javanese *n* (*pl* **Javanese**) **1** a member of an Indonesian people inhabiting the island of Java. **2** the language of this people. ⋙ **Javanese** *adj.*

javelin *n* a light spear thrown in an athletic field event or as a weapon.

jaw[1] *n* **1a** either of two cartilaginous or bony structures that in most vertebrates form a framework above and below the mouth in which the teeth are set. **b** a similar structure in an invertebrate. **2** (*in pl*) the two parts of a machine, tool, etc between which something may be clamped or crushed. **3** (*in pl*) the imminent prospect of something unpleasant: *the jaws of death.* **4** *informal* **a** continual talk. **b** a friendly chat.

jaw[2] *v informal* to talk or gossip for a long time.

jawbone *n* the bone of a jaw, *esp* the lower jaw.

jawline *n* the outline of the lower jaw.

jay *n* a bird of the crow family with strongly patterned plumage.

jaywalk *v* to cross a street carelessly so that one is endangered by traffic. ⋙ **jaywalker** *n.*

jazz *n* music developed *esp* from ragtime and blues and characterized by syncopated rhythms and improvisation. ✱ **and all that jazz** *informal* and other similar things.

jazz up *v informal* to make more lively, interesting, or attractive.

jazzy *adj* (**-ier, -iest**) **1** having the characteristics of jazz. **2** *informal* colourful, garish, or showy. ⋙ **jazzily** *adv,* **jazziness** *n.*

JCB *n trademark* a type of mechanical earth-mover with a shovel at the front end and a digging bucket on an extendable arm at the rear.

JCR *abbr* Junior Common Room.

jealous *adj* **1** apprehensive and suspicious of rivalry, *esp* in sexual love. **2** resentful and envious of an advantage that somebody else is believed to enjoy. **3** vigilant in guarding a possession, right, etc. **4** intolerant of rivalry or unfaithfulness. ⋙ **jealously** *adv,* **jealousy** *n.*

jean *n* a durable twilled cotton cloth used *esp* for work clothes.

jeans *pl n* casual usu close-fitting trousers, made *esp* of blue denim.

jeep *n trademark* a small rugged general-purpose motor vehicle with four-wheel drive, used *esp* by the armed forces.

jeepers *or* **jeepers creepers** *interj chiefly NAm, informal* used to express surprise.

jeer[1] *v* to laugh mockingly or make rude and mocking comments. ⋙ **jeerer** *n,* **jeeringly** *adv.*

jeer[2] *n* a jeering remark; a taunt.

jehad /ji'hahd/ *n* = JIHAD.

Jehovah *n* = GOD[1] (1).

Jehovah's Witness *n* a member of a fundamentalist sect practising personal evangelism and preaching that the end of the present world is imminent.

jejune *adj* **1** lacking maturity; puerile. **2** lacking interest or significance. ⋙ **jejuneness** *n.*

jejunum *n* the section of the small intestine between the duodenum and the ileum. ⋙ **jejunal** *adj.*

Jekyll and Hyde *n* a person having a split personality, one side of which is good and the other evil. ⋙ **Jekyll-and-Hyde** *adj.*

jell *v chiefly NAm* see GEL[2] (2), (3).

jellaba *n* see DJELLABA.

jello *n NAm* a fruit jelly made from a commercially manufactured powder.

jelly[1] *n* (*pl* **-ies**) **1** a soft fruit-flavoured transparent dessert set with gelatin. **2** a savoury food product or other substance resembling jelly in consistency.

jelly[2] *v* (**-ies, -ied**) **1** to set like a jelly. **2** to set (something) in a jelly.

jelly[3] *n Brit, informal* = GELIGNITE.

jelly baby *n* (*pl* **-ies**) a small soft gelatinous sweet in the shape of a baby.

jelly bean *n* a small bean-shaped sweet with a hard sugar coating and a gelatinous filling.

jellyfish *n* (*pl* **jellyfishes** *or* **jellyfish**) a free-swimming invertebrate sea animal that has a nearly transparent saucer-shaped body and stinging tentacles.

jelly shoe *n* a light plastic sandal for beach or casual wear.

jemmy[1] (*NAm* **jimmy**) *n* (*pl* **-ies**) a short steel crowbar, used *esp* by burglars.

jemmy[2] (*NAm* **jimmy**) *v* (**-ies, -ied**) to force open (e.g. a door or window) with a jemmy.

je ne sais quoi /,zhə nə say 'kwah/ *n* a quality that cannot be adequately described or expressed.

jenny *n* (*pl* **-ies**) **1** a female donkey or ass. **2** = SPINNING JENNY.

jeon /jun/ *n* (*pl* **jeon**) a unit of currency in South Korea, worth 100th of a won.

jeopardize *or* **-ise** *v* to put in danger.

jeopardy *n* risk of death, loss, injury, etc; danger.

jerboa *n* a nocturnal mouselike African and Eurasian desert rodent with long back legs adapted for jumping.

jeremiad /jerə'mie·əd/ *n* a prolonged lamentation or complaint.

Jeremiah *n* somebody who is mournfully pessimistic.

jerk[1] *v* **1** to move (something) with a short sudden pull, push, twist, or jolt. **2** to make a sudden spasmodic motion. ⋙ **jerker** *n.*

jerk[2] *n* **1** a single quick, forceful motion. **2** an involuntary spasmodic muscular movement due to reflex action. **3** in weightlifting, the pushing of a weight from shoulder height to a position above the head. **4** *chiefly NAm, informal* a foolish person.

jerk[3] *v* to preserve (meat) by cutting it into long slices or strips and drying it in the sun.

jerk[4] *n* = JERKY[2].

jerk around *v NAm, informal* to treat (somebody) badly or without consideration.

jerkin *n* a close-fitting hip-length sleeveless jacket.

jerk off *v chiefly NAm, coarse slang* to masturbate.

jerky[1] *adj* (**-ier, -iest**) **1** marked by irregular or spasmodic movements. **2** marked by abrupt or awkward changes. ⋙ **jerkily** *adv,* **jerkiness** *n.*

jerky[2] *n* raw meat cut into strips and dried in the sun; jerked meat.

jeroboam /jerə'boh·əm/ *n* a wine bottle holding four times the amount of a normal bottle.

jerrican *n* see JERRY CAN.

Jerry *n* (*pl* **-ies**) *chiefly Brit, dated* a German, *esp* a German soldier in World War II, or the Germans collectively.

jerry-build *v* (*past tense and past part.* **jerry-built**) to build (e.g. houses) cheaply and flimsily. ⋙ **jerry-builder** *n,* **jerry-built** *adj.*

jerry can *or* **jerrican** *n* a narrow flat-sided container for carrying liquids, *esp* petrol or water.

jersey *n* **1** a knitted garment usu with sleeves that is worn on the upper body; a jumper. **2** a shirt worn by a footballer or other sports player. **3** a plain knitted fabric made of cotton, wool, etc and used *esp* for clothing. **4** (*often* **Jersey**) an animal of a small short-horned breed of cattle noted for their rich milk.

Jerusalem artichoke *n* the edible sweet-tasting tubers of a perennial N American sunflower.

Word history

This vegetable has nothing to do with Jerusalem, nor is it closely related to the artichoke. The plant was apparently imported to Britain from Italy, and *girasole* is the Italian word for a sunflower. Folk etymology changed *girasole* to *Jerusalem*, while a supposed similarity of flavour to the artichoke produced the second part of the name.

jess *n* a short strap secured to the leg of a hawk with a ring on the other end for attaching a leash.

jessamine *n* = JASMINE.

jessie *n Brit, derog* an effeminate man.

jest[1] *n* **1** an amusing or mocking act or utterance; a joke. **2** a way of behaving, speaking, etc that is not intended to be taken seriously: *I said it in jest.*

jest[2] *v* **1** to speak or act without seriousness. **2** to make a witty remark.

jester *n* a clown formerly employed in great households to provide casual amusement.

Jesuit /'jezyoo·it/ *n* a member of the Society of Jesus, a Roman Catholic order founded by St Ignatius Loyola in 1534.

jesuitical *adj* **1** (*often* **Jesuitical**) relating to the Jesuits. **2** *derog* given to subtle, hair-splitting argumentation or deception. ⋙ **jesuitically** *adv.*

Jesus[1] *or* **Jesus Christ** *n* the Jewish religious teacher whose life, death, and resurrection as reported in the New Testament are the basis of Christianity.

Jesus[2] *or* **Jesus Christ** *interj informal* used to express surprise, dismay, annoyance, etc.

jet[1] *n* **1** a stream of fluid forced out under pressure from a narrow opening or a nozzle. **2a** = JET ENGINE. **b** an aircraft powered by one or more jet engines.

jet[2] *v* (**jetted, jetting**) **1** to spurt out. **2** to travel by jet aircraft.

jet[3] *n* **1** a hard black form of coal that is polished and used for jewellery. **2** an intense black colour.

jet-black *adj* of an intense black colour.

jeté /zhə'tay/ *n* a high arching leap in ballet with one leg stretched forwards and the other backwards.

jet engine *n* an engine that produces motion by discharging a jet of fluid in the opposite direction, *esp* an aircraft engine discharging hot gases produced by burning fuel.

jet lag *n* a temporary disruption of a person's normal bodily rhythms after a long flight, *esp* due to differences in local time. ⋙ **jet-lagged** *adj.*

jet-propelled *adj* moving by jet propulsion.

jet propulsion *n* propulsion of a body produced by the discharge of a jet of fluid, as in a jet engine.

jetsam *n* goods thrown overboard from a ship and washed up on shore: compare FLOTSAM.

jet set *n* (*used as sing. or pl*) wealthy people who frequently travel by air to fashionable resorts anywhere in the world. ⋙ **jet-set** *adj,* **jetsetter** *n,* **jetsetting** *n.*

jet-ski[1] *n* a small motorized vessel, consisting of a platform with a steering column and handlebars, which is ridden as a form of water sport.

jet-ski[2] *v* (**jet-skied, jet-skiing**) to ride over water on a jet-ski.

jet stream *n* a current of strong winds high in the atmosphere usu blowing from a westerly direction.

jettison *v* **1** to cast off as superfluous; to abandon. **2a** to throw (e.g. goods) overboard to lighten the load of a ship. **b** to drop (e.g. unwanted material) from an aircraft or spacecraft in flight.

jetty *n* (*pl* **-ies**) **1** a small landing pier. **2** a structure extending into a body of water to influence the current or tide or to protect a harbour.

jeu d'esprit /,zhuh de'spree/ *n* (*pl* **jeux d'esprit** /,zhuh de'spree/) a witty comment or composition.

jeunesse dorée /zhuh,nes daw'ray/ *n* young people of wealth and fashion.

jeux d'esprit *n* pl of JEU D'ESPRIT.

Jew *n* **1** a member of a Semitic people orig existing as a nation in Palestine and now living throughout the world. **2** a person whose religion is Judaism.

jewel *n* **1** a precious stone, such as a diamond, ruby, or emerald. **2** a piece of jewellery. **3** a bearing for a watch or compass made of crystal, precious stone, or glass. **4** a highly valued person or thing. ⋙ **jewelled** *adj.*

jeweller (*NAm* **jeweler**) *n* somebody who deals in, makes, or repairs jewellery.

jeweller's rouge *n* a fine powder of ferric oxide used as a metal polish.

jewellery (*NAm* **jewelry**) *n* personal ornaments such as rings and necklaces, made of precious stones or precious metals.

Jewess *n dated or offensive* a Jewish woman or girl.

Jewish *adj* of or denoting Jews or Judaism. ➤➤ **Jewishness** *n.*

Jewry *n* **1** the Jewish people collectively. **2** a Jewish quarter of a town.

Jew's harp *n* a small lyre-shaped musical instrument that is placed between the teeth and sounded by striking a metal tongue with the finger.

Jezebel *n* a shameless or immoral woman.

jiao /jow/ *n* a unit of currency in China, worth a tenth of a yuan.

jib[1] *n* a triangular sail set on a stay extending from the top of the foremast to the bow or the bowsprit.

jib[2] *v* (**jibbed, jibbing**) of a horse: to refuse to proceed further. ✱ **jib at** to take fright or balk at. ➤➤ **jibber** *n.*

jib[3] *n* the projecting arm of a crane.

jibe[1] *or* **gibe** *v* to make scornful, taunting, or insulting remarks.

jibe[2] *or* **gibe** *n* a scornful, taunting, or insulting remark.

jibe[3] *v NAm, informal* to be in accord; to agree.

jiffy *or* **jiff** *n informal* a moment or instant.

jig[1] *n* **1** a lively springy dance in triple time. **2** a device used to hold a piece of work in position, e.g. during machining or assembly, and to guide the tools working on it.

jig[2] *v* (**jigged, jigging**) **1** to move up and down in a rapid and jerky fashion. **2** to dance a jig. **3** to machine (something) using a jig to guide the cutting or drilling tool.

jigger[1] *n* **1** a variable measure of spirits used *esp* in preparing mixed drinks. **2** a small sail set at the stern of a boat. **3** a mechanical device or part of a mechanism that operates with a jerky movement. **4** a person who dances a jig.

jigger[2] *n* = CHIGOE.

jiggered *adj Brit, informal* damaged, broken, or exhausted. ✱ **I'll be jiggered** *informal* used to express astonishment.

jiggery-pokery *n Brit, informal* dishonest underhand dealings or scheming.

jiggle *v informal* to move or cause to move with quick short jerks. ➤➤ **jiggle** *n.*

jigsaw *n* **1** a puzzle consisting of small irregularly cut pieces, *esp* of wood or card, that are fitted together to form a picture. **2** a power-driven fretsaw.

jigsaw puzzle *n* = JIGSAW (1).

jihad /ji'had/ *n* a holy war waged on behalf of Islam as a religious duty or a personal striving against evil.

jilt *v* to break off a romantic relationship with (somebody) suddenly.

Jim Crow *n NAm* **1** (*used before a noun*) racial discrimination, *esp* against black Americans. **2** *offensive* a black person.

jimjams[1] *pl n informal* a state of extreme nervousness.

jimjams[2] *pl n informal* = PYJAMAS.

jingle[1] *v* to make or cause to make a light clinking or tinkling sound.

jingle[2] *n* **1** a light metallic clinking or tinkling sound. **2** a short catchy song or rhyme characterized by repetition of phrases and used *esp* in advertising. ➤➤ **jingly** *adj.*

jingo *n* (*pl* **-oes**) *dated* a belligerently patriotic person, a jingoist. ✱ **by jingo** used to express surprise or add emphasis.

jingoism *n* belligerent patriotism; chauvinism. ➤➤ **jingoist** *n,* **jingoistic** *adj.*

jink[1] *n* a quick turn or sidestep while running, *esp* to avoid being caught.

jink[2] *v* to move quickly with sudden turns and shifts.

jinn *or* **djinn** *or* **djin** *n* (*pl* **jinns** *or* **jinn**) a spirit that according to Muslim demonology inhabits the earth, assuming various forms, and exercises supernatural power.

jinx[1] *n informal* something or somebody that brings bad luck.

jinx[2] *v* to put a jinx on or bring bad luck to.

jitney *n* (*pl* **-eys**) *NAm, informal* **1** a small bus that carries passengers over a regular route according to a flexible timetable. **2** = NICKEL[1] (2).

jitter[1] *n* **1** (**the jitters**) panic or extreme nervousness. **2** an irregular random movement. ➤➤ **jittery** *adj.*

jitter[2] *v* **1** to be nervous or act nervously. **2** to make continuous fast repetitive movements.

jitterbug[1] *n* a lively dance popular in the 1940s, a jazz variation of the two-step in which couples swing and twirl.

jitterbug[2] *v* (**jitterbugged, jitterbugging**) to dance the jitterbug.

jiu-jitsu *n* = JU-JITSU.

jive[1] *n* **1** a style of energetic dancing, popular from the 1940s to the early 1960s, performed to fast jazz or swing music and later to rock and roll. **2** *NAm* **a** a type of slang used *esp* by black Americans. **b** glib or deceptive talk.

jive[2] *v* **1** to dance the jive. **2** *NAm* to deceive or mislead. **3** *NAm* to cajole or tease.

jnr *abbr* junior.

joanna *n Brit, informal* a piano.

job[1] *n* **1** a regular paid position or occupation. **2** a piece of work. **3** a task. **4** a specific duty, role, or function. **5** *informal* a crime, *esp* a robbery. **6** *informal* a piece of plastic surgery to improve one's appearance: *a nose job.* ✱ **a good job** a fortunate state of affairs. **jobs for the boys** *Brit* lucrative employment for friends, associates, etc, or a system involving this. **just the job** exactly what is needed. **on the job 1** engaged in doing something; at work. **2** *coarse slang* having sexual intercourse. ➤➤ **jobless** *adj.*

job[2] *v* (**jobbed, jobbing**) **1** to do occasional work, usu at a stated rate. **2a** to carry on the business of a middleman or wholesaler. **b** to work as a stockjobber. **3** to buy and sell (e.g. shares) for profit. ➤➤ **jobber** *n.*

jobbery *n* the use of a public office for personal gain; corruption.

jobbing *adj* doing casual or occasional work.

jobcentre *n* a government office where unemployed people can look at job vacancies on display and arrange interviews with prospective employers.

job lot *n* a miscellaneous collection of goods sold as one item.

Job's comforter /johbz/ *n* somebody whose attempts to encourage or comfort a sufferer have the opposite effect.

job share[1] *n* an arrangement by which the work and responsibilities of a full-time employee are divided between two or more part-time workers.

job share[2] *v* to work part-time in a job share. ➤➤ **jobsharer** *n,* **jobsharing** *n.*

jobsworth *n Brit, informal* a minor official who follows procedures rigidly and is unhelpful to the public. ➤➤ **jobsworth** *adj.*

Jock *n Brit, informal* a Scotsman.

jock[1] *n NAm, informal* **1** a male athlete. **2** = JOCKSTRAP.

jock[2] *n informal* = DISC JOCKEY.

jockey[1] *n* **1** somebody who rides a horse in races, *esp* as a professional. **2** *NAm* somebody who operates a specified vehicle, device, or object.

jockey[2] *v* (**-eys, -eyed**) **1** to ride as a jockey. **2** to manipulate by adroit or devious means. **3** to manoeuvre for advantage.

jockstrap *n* a support for the genitals worn by men taking part in strenuous *esp* sporting activities.

jocose *adj formal* playfully humorous. ➤➤ **jocosely** *adv*, **jocoseness** *n*, **jocosity** *n.*

jocular *adj* jolly or joking. ➤➤ **jocularity** *n*, **jocularly** *adv.*

jocund *adj literary* cheerful and good-humoured. ➤➤ **jocundity** *n*, **jocundly** *adv.*

jodhpurs *pl n* (*pl* **jodhpurs**) riding trousers cut full at the hips and close-fitting from knee to ankle.

joey *n* (*pl* **-eys**) *Aus* **1** a young kangaroo. **2** any young animal or a young child.

jog[1] *v* (**jogged, jogging**) **1** to give a slight shake or push to. **2** to prompt (the memory). **3** to run at a slow steady pace, *esp* to keep fit. **4** of a horse or rider: to move or ride at a slow trot. **5** to go or progress at a slow or monotonous pace.

jog[2] *n* **1** a slight nudge or shake. **2** a period of jogging. **3** a jogging pace.

jogger *n* somebody who jogs to keep fit.

joggle *v informal* to move or shake slightly. ➤➤ **joggle** *n.*

jog trot *n* a slow regular trot, e.g. of a horse.

john *n* **1** *NAm, informal* = TOILET (I). **2** *chiefly NAm, informal* a prostitute's client.

John Bull *n* **1** the English nation personified. **2** a typical Englishman.

John Doe *n* **1** a person involved in legal proceedings or a crime whose true name is unknown or withheld. **2** *chiefly NAm* an average man.

John Dory *n* (*pl* **John Dories** *or* **John Dory**) a common European food fish with an oval compressed body, long spines on its back, and a dark spot on each side.

johnny *n* (*pl* **-ies**) *Brit, informal* **1** a fellow or guy. **2** a condom.

Johnny-come-lately *n* (*pl* **-ies**) a late or recent arrival; a newcomer.

joie de vivre /,zhwah də 'veev/ *n* keen enjoyment of life.

join[1] *v* **1a** to put (two or more things) together so that they form a unit, or to come together in this way. **b** to connect, meet, or merge with. **2a** to enter into the company of. **b** (*usu* + in) to associate oneself with (another or others) in doing something. **c** to become a member or employee of (a club, organization, etc). **3** (+ in) to take part in a collective activity. ✱ **join battle** to engage in battle or conflict. **join forces** to form an alliance or combine efforts. ➤➤ **joinable** *adj.*

join[2] *n* a place where two parts are joined.

joiner *n* **1** somebody who constructs or repairs wooden articles, *esp* furniture or fittings. **2** *informal* a gregarious person who joins many organizations.

joinery *n* **1** the craft or trade of a joiner. **2** woodwork done or made by a joiner.

joint[1] *n* **1** a place where two parts are joined. **2** a point of contact between two or more bones together with the parts that surround and support it. **3** a large piece of meat cut suitable for roasting. **4** a point on a plant stem at which a leaf or branch emerges. **5** *informal* a place of entertainment, café, etc. **6** *slang* a cannabis cigarette. ✱ **out of joint 1** said of a bone: dislocated. **2** disordered or disorganized.

joint[2] *adj* **1** united or combined. **2** common to, held or shared by, or involving two or more: *a joint account.* **3** sharing with another: *joint heirs.* ➤➤ **jointly** *adv.*

joint[3] *v* **1** to provide or fit together with a joint or joints. **2** to prepare (e.g. a board) for joining by planing the edge. **3** to cut (e.g. meat) into joints. ➤➤ **jointer** *n.*

joint and several *adj* of a legal obligation: involving two or more people, each of whom is individually liable for the whole.

jointure *n* property settled on a wife as provision for her widowhood.

join up *v* **1** to enlist in an armed service. **2** to come together or link with something else.

joist *n* any of the parallel timbers or metal beams that support a floor or ceiling.

jojoba /hə'hohbə/ *n* a N American shrub with edible seeds that yield a valuable oil used in cosmetics.

joke[1] *n* **1a** a brief story told to provoke laughter. **b** = PRACTICAL JOKE. **c** something said or done in fun. **2a** something of little difficulty or seriousness. **b** something that is ridiculously unsuitable or inadequate. ➤➤ **jokey** *adj*, **joky** *adj.*

joke[2] *v* **1** to make jokes. **2** to speak facetiously. ➤➤ **jokingly** *adv.*

joker *n* **1** somebody given to joking. **2** a playing card with a picture of a jester, added to a pack usu as a wild card. **3** *chiefly NAm* an unsuspected or misunderstood clause in a document that greatly alters it. **4** *informal* an insignificant or incompetent person. ✱ **the joker in the pack** an unpredictable person or factor.

jolie laide /,zholi 'led/ *n* (*pl* **jolies laides** /,zholi 'led(z)/) a woman whose conventionally unattractive looks enhance her fascination and charm.

jollification *n* merrymaking or a celebration.

jollity *n* the quality or state of being jolly; merriment.

jolly[1] *adj* (**-ier, -iest**) **1** cheerful, lively, and good-humoured. **2** expressing or inspiring gaiety. ➤➤ **jolliness** *n.*

jolly[2] *adv informal* very.

jolly[3] *v* (**-ies, -ied**) (+ along) to put in good humour, *esp* to gain an end.

jolly[4] *n* (*pl* **-ies**) *chiefly Brit* a good time; a jollification.

jolly boat *n* a ship's boat of medium size used for general work.

Jolly Roger *n* a pirate's black flag with a white skull and crossbones.

jolt[1] *v* **1** to move or cause to move with a jerky motion. **2** to give a sudden knock to. **3** to disturb abruptly the composure of (somebody).

jolt[2] *n* an unsettling blow, movement, or shock. ➤➤ **jolty** *adj.*

jonquil *n* a plant of the narcissus family with yellow or white fragrant flowers.

Jordanian *n* a native or inhabitant of Jordan. ➤➤ **Jordanian** *adj.*

josh[1] *v* **1** to make fun of; to tease. **2** to engage in banter; to joke. ➤➤ **josher** *n.*

josh[2] *n chiefly NAm* a good-humoured joke.

Joshua tree *n* a tall yucca tree of the SW USA with sword-shaped leaves and clusters of greenish white flowers.

joss stick *n* a slender stick of incense.

jostle *v* **1** to push and shove roughly. **2** to vie or compete with other people. ➤➤ **jostle** *n*.

jot[1] *n* the least bit.

jot[2] *v* (**jotted, jotting**) (*usu* + down) to write briefly or hurriedly.

jotter *n* a small notebook or pad.

jotting *n* a brief note.

joule *n* the SI unit of work or energy equal to the work done when a force of one newton moves its point of application through a distance of one metre.

jounce *v* to jolt or bounce. ➤➤ **jounce** *n*.

journal *n* **1** a periodical dealing *esp* with a specialist subject. **2a** a daily record of business transactions. **b** a private diary. **c** a record of the transactions of a public body, learned society, etc. **3** the part of a rotating shaft or axle that turns in a bearing.

journalese *n* a style of cliché-ridden writing supposed to be characteristic of newspapers.

journalism *n* the profession or activity of collecting and editing material of current interest for presentation through news media.

journalist *n* a person who works in journalism, *esp* one working for a newspaper or magazine. ➤➤ **journalistic** *adj*.

journey[1] *n* (*pl* **-eys**) **1** an act of travelling from one place to another. **2** the distance involved in a journey, or the time taken to cover it.

journey[2] *v* (**-eys, -eyed**) to make a journey; to travel. ➤➤ **journeyer** *n*.

journeyman *n* (*pl* **journeymen**) **1** a skilled worker who is employed by another person, usu by the day. **2** an experienced and reliable worker or performer, as distinguished from one who is outstanding.

journo *n* (*pl* **-os**) *informal* a journalist.

joust[1] *n* a combat on horseback between two knights armed with lances.

joust[2] *v* **1** to fight in a joust or tournament. **2** (*often* + with) to engage in a contest or argument with somebody. ➤➤ **jouster** *n*.

Jove ✱ **by Jove** used to express surprise or strong agreement.

jovial *adj* good-humoured and cheerful. ➤➤ **joviality** *n*, **jovially** *adj*.

Jovian *adj* of the god or planet Jupiter.

jowl[1] *n* **1** the jaw; *esp* the lower jaw. **2** either of the cheeks.

jowl[2] *n* **1** (*also in pl*) usu slack and drooping flesh associated with the lower jaw or throat. **2** the dewlap of an animal or the wattle of a bird.

joy *n* **1** a feeling of great happiness or pleasure. **2** a cause of delight. **3** *Brit, informal* success or satisfaction: *We had no joy at the local shops.* ➤➤ **joyless** *adj*, **joylessness** *n*.

joyful *adj* filled with, causing, or expressing joy. ➤➤ **joyfully** *adv*, **joyfulness** *n*.

joyous *adj literary* joyful. ➤➤ **joyously** *adv*, **joyousness** *n*.

joypad *n* a device with buttons used to control the screen image in computer games.

joyride *n* a ride taken for pleasure in a car, *esp* one in a stolen car involving reckless driving. ➤➤ **joyrider** *n*, **joyriding** *n*.

joystick *n* **1** a hand-operated lever used to control an aircraft. **2** a lever for controlling the image on a computer screen, *esp* in games.

JP *abbr* Justice of the Peace.

Jr *abbr* Junior.

jubilant *adj* filled with or expressing great joy. ➤➤ **jubilance** *n*, **jubilantly** *adv*.

jubilation *n* great joy and satisfaction; rejoicing.

jubilee *n* **1** a special anniversary of an event such as a sovereign's accession, *esp* a 25th, 50th, or 60th anniversary. **2** (*often* **Jubilee**) a year of emancipation and restoration provided by ancient Hebrew law to be kept every 50 years.

Judaean *or* **Judean** *n* a native or inhabitant of Judaea, the ancient kingdom and Roman province forming the southern part of Palestine. ➤➤ **Judaean** *adj*.

Judaeo- (*NAm* **Judeo-**) *comb. form* **1** Jewish. **2** Jewish and: *Judaeo-Christian.*

Judaic *adj* of Jews or Judaism.

Judaise *v* see JUDAIZE.

Judaism *n* **1** the religious faith developed among the ancient Jews and characterized by belief in one transcendent God. **2** the cultural, social, and religious beliefs and practices of the Jews. ➤➤ **Judaist** *n*.

Judaize *or* **-ise** *v* **1** to adopt the customs, beliefs, etc of the Jews. **2** to convert to Judaism. ➤➤ **Judaization** *n*.

Judas *n* somebody who betrays, *esp* under the guise of friendship.

judas *n* a peephole in a door.

judas hole *n* = JUDAS.

Judas tree *n* a Eurasian tree with purplish pink flowers that open before the leaves.

judder[1] *v chiefly Brit* to vibrate jerkily.

judder[2] *n* a sharp vibration or jerky movement.

Judean *n* see JUDAEAN.

Judeo- *comb. form NAm* see JUDAEO-.

judge[1] *v* **1** to form or express an opinion about, *esp* after deliberation. **2** to sit in judgment on (somebody). **3** to decide the result of (a competition or contest). **4** to consider (something) to be the case.

judge[2] *n* **1** a public official authorized to decide questions brought before a court. **2** somebody appointed to decide the winner of a competition or contest. **3** somebody who is qualified to give an opinion. ➤➤ **judgeship** *n*.

judgement *n* see JUDGMENT.

judgemental *adj* see JUDGMENTAL.

judgment *or* **judgement** *n* **1** the capacity for forming considered opinions or making wise decisions. **2** an opinion or evaluation based on examining and comparing. **3** a formal decision by a court or judge. **4** a calamity held to be sent by God as a punishment. ✱ **against one's better judgment** in spite of one's feeling that something is unwise.

judgmental *or* **judgemental** *adj* **1** given to making moral judgments about other people's behaviour. **2** relating to the use of judgment.

Judgment Day *n* the day of God's judgment of humankind at the end of the world.

judicature *n* **1** the administration of justice. **2** = JUDICIARY (2). ➤➤ **judicatory** *adj*.

judicial *adj* **1** of or ordered by a judge or a court of law. **2** relating to justice. **3** of or expressing judgment. ➤➤ **judicially** *adv*.

Usage note

judicial *or* **judicious**? These two words are sometimes confused. A *judicial* decision is one made by a court of law or by a judge; a *judicious* decision is one that shows wisdom and good judgment. A person can be described as *judicious* but not as *judicial*. *Judicial* is typically used in phrases such as *a judicial enquiry, judicial proceedings*, and *the British judicial system*.

judiciary *n* (*pl* **-ies**) **1** the branch of government concerned with the administration of justice. **2** the judges collectively who preside over a country's courts. **3** a system of courts of law. ⋙ **judiciary** *adj*.

judicious *adj* having, exercising, or characterized by sound judgment. ⋙ **judiciously** *adv*, **judiciousness** *n*.

Usage note

judicious *or* judicial? See note at JUDICIAL.

judo *n* a martial art developed from ju-jitsu using quick movement and leverage to throw an opponent.

jug[1] *n* **1** *chiefly Brit* a vessel for holding and pouring liquids that typically has a handle and a lip or spout. **2** *chiefly NAm* a large deep container for liquids that usu has a handle and a narrow mouth. **3** *informal* prison. **4** *coarse slang* (*in pl*) a woman's breasts. ⋙ **jugful** *n*.

jug[2] *v* (**jugged, jugging**) to stew (e.g. a hare) in a covered vessel.

juggernaut *n* **1** *chiefly Brit* a very large, usu articulated, lorry. **2** an inexorable force or object that crushes anything in its path.

Word history

Hindi *Jagannāth*, title of the God Vishnu, literally 'lord of the world'. It was formerly believed that devotees of Vishnu threw themselves beneath the wheels of a cart bearing his image in procession.

juggle[1] *v* **1** to keep several objects in motion in the air at the same time by alternately tossing and catching them. **2** to deal with (several activities) at the same time through skilful organization. **3** to manipulate (e.g. facts or figures), *esp* in order to achieve a desired end. ⋙ **juggler** *n*, **jugglery** *n*.

juggle[2] *n* an act of juggling.

Jugoslav *n archaic* = YUGOSLAV.

jugular[1] *adj* relating to the throat or neck.

jugular[2] *n* = JUGULAR VEIN.

jugular vein *n* any of several veins of each side of the neck that return blood from the head.

juice[1] *n* **1a** the liquid contained in something, *esp* a fruit or vegetable. **b** a drink made from fruit juice. **2** (*in pl*) the natural fluids of an animal body. **3** *informal* a source of power, such as electricity or petrol. ⋙ **juiceless** *adj*.

juice[2] *v* to extract the juice from (e.g. a fruit).

juice fasting *n* a form of diet restricted to liquidized fruit and vegetables.

juicer *n* an appliance for extracting juice from fruit or vegetables.

juice up *v NAm, informal* to liven up.

juicy *adj* (**-ier, -iest**) **1** succulent; full of juice. **2** *informal* rich in interest, *esp* because of titillating content. **3** *informal* financially rewarding or profitable. ⋙ **juicily** *adv*, **juiciness** *n*.

ju-jitsu *or* **jiu-jitsu** /jooh 'jitsooh/ *n* a martial art employing holds, throws, and paralysing blows to subdue or disable an opponent.

juju *n* **1** a charm or fetish used by some W African peoples. **2** the magic attributed to jujus.

jujube *n* **1** the dark red edible berry-like fruit of a tree of the buckthorn family. **2** a fruit-flavoured gum or lozenge.

jukebox *n* a coin-operated machine that automatically plays records or CDs chosen from a list.

Jul. *abbr* July.

julep *n chiefly NAm* a drink consisting of a spirit and sugar poured over crushed ice and garnished with mint.

Julian calendar *n* a calendar introduced in Rome in 46 BC establishing the twelve-month year of 365 days with an extra day every fourth year: compare GREGORIAN CALENDAR.

julienne /joohli'en/ *n* vegetables cut into long thin strips used as a garnish or in soup.

July *n* the seventh month of the year.

jumble[1] *v* (*often* + up) to mix up in a confused or disordered mass.

jumble[2] *n* **1** a mass of things mingled together without order or plan. **2** *Brit* articles for a jumble sale.

jumble sale *n Brit* a sale of donated secondhand articles, usu to raise money for charity.

jumbo *n* (*pl* **-os**) **1** a very large specimen of its kind. **2** a jumbo jet. ⋙ **jumbo** *adj*.

jumbo jet *n* a large jet aeroplane capable of carrying several hundred passengers.

jump[1] *v* **1a** to spring into the air, *esp* using the muscular power of feet and legs. **b** to pass over (e.g. an obstacle) by jumping. **2** to move quickly or energetically. **3** to move suddenly or involuntarily from shock, surprise, etc. **4a** to pass rapidly or abruptly from one point or state to another. **b** to undergo a sudden sharp increase. **c** to pass over (something intervening); to skip or bypass. **5** (+ on/upon) to make a sudden verbal or physical attack. **6** to bustle with activity. **7a** to act, move, or begin before (e.g. a signal). **b** to fail to stop at (a traffic light). **8** *NAm, coarse slang* to have sexual intercourse with. ✱ **jump at** to accept (e.g. a chance) eagerly. **jump down somebody's throat** to reply to somebody in a very angry or hostile way. **jump ship** of a crew member: to leave a ship in violation of one's contract of employment. **jump the queue 1** to move in front of others in a queue. **2** to obtain an unfair advantage over others who have been waiting longer. **jump to it 1** to make an enthusiastic start. **2** to hurry.

jump[2] *n* **1a** an act of jumping; a leap. **b** a height or distance cleared by a jump. **2** an obstacle to be jumped over, e.g. in a horse race. **3** a sudden involuntary movement; a start. **4** a descent by parachute from an aircraft. **5** a sudden sharp increase. ✱ **be one jump ahead of somebody** to have advanced to a further stage or reached an objective before somebody. **get the jump on somebody** to get somebody at a disadvantage by acting quickly.

jumped-up *adj derog* recently risen in wealth, rank, or status.

jumper[1] *n* **1** *Brit* a usu knitted garment worn on the upper body. **2** *NAm* = PINAFORE (2).

jumper[2] *n* a jumping animal, *esp* a horse trained to jump obstacles.

jumping bean *n* a seed of a Mexican shrub that tumbles about because of the movements of a larva inside it.

jump-jet *n chiefly Brit* a jet aircraft able to take off and land vertically.

jump leads *pl n* two lengths of thick cable used to start a motor vehicle with a flat battery by connecting it to another battery.

jump-off *n* the final round, *esp* an extra deciding round, of a showjumping competition.

jump seat *n* a folding seat for temporary use in a vehicle or aircraft.

jump-start *v* to start (a motor vehicle) with jump leads. ➤➤ **jump start** *n.*

jumpsuit *n* a one-piece garment combining top and trousers or shorts.

jumpy *adj* (**-ier, -iest**) **1** nervous or jittery. **2** having jumps or sudden variations. ➤➤ **jumpiness** *n.*

Jun. *abbr* June.

jun *n* (*pl* **jun**) a unit of currency in North Korea, worth 100th of a won.

junction *n* **1** the act of joining or being joined. **2** an intersection of roads or railway lines. **3** a place where things meet or join. **4** a point of contact or interface between dissimilar metals or semiconductor regions.

junction box *n* a box containing connections between separate electric circuits.

juncture *n* **1** a point of time, *esp* a critical one. **2** an instance or place of joining.

June *n* the sixth month of the year.

Jungian /'yoongi·ən/ *adj* relating to the psychoanalytical psychology of Carl Jung (d.1961). ➤➤ **Jungian** *n.*

jungle *n* **1** an area overgrown with trees and other vegetation, *esp* in the tropics. **2a** a confused or complex mass. **b** a place of ruthless struggle for survival. **3** a type of fast electronic dance music popular in the 1990s. ➤➤ **jungly** *adj.*

jungle fever *n* a severe malarial fever.

jungle fowl *n* an Asian wild bird from which the domestic fowl has prob descended.

junior[1] *n* **1** a person who is younger than another: *She is three years my junior.* **2a** a person holding a lower or subordinate rank. **b** a member of a junior school, team, etc. **3** *NAm* a student in the penultimate year before graduating. **4** *NAm, informal* a male child; a son.

junior[2] *adj* **1** used, *esp* in the USA, to distinguish a son with the same name as his father. **2** lower in standing or rank. **3** comprising younger pupils, players, etc. **4** of or for juniors.

junior college *n* a US college that offers studies corresponding to the first two years of a four-year college course.

Junior Common Room *n* a common room for students, pupils, etc.

junior school *n* a primary school for children aged *esp* from seven to eleven.

junior technician *n* a member of the Royal Air Force ranking below a corporal.

juniper *n* an evergreen shrub or tree with small purple cones resembling berries that are used to flavour gin and in cooking.

junk[1] *n* **1a** secondhand or discarded articles or material; rubbish. **b** something of little value or inferior quality. **2** *slang* narcotics, *esp* heroin. ➤➤ **junky** *adj.*

junk[2] *v informal* to get rid of (something) as worthless.

junk[3] *n* a sailing ship used in the Far East with a high poop and overhanging stem.

junk bond *n* a high-yield speculative security, *esp* one issued to finance an intended takeover.

junket[1] *n* **1** a dessert of sweetened flavoured milk curdled with rennet. **2** *chiefly informal* a trip made by a person or group at public or a firm's expense.

junket[2] *v* (**junketed, junketing**) *informal* to go on a junket.

junk food *n* processed food that typically has a high carbohydrate content but overall low nutritional value.

junkie *or* **junky** *n* (*pl* **-ies**) *informal* a drug addict.

junk mail *n* unsolicited mail, e.g. advertising circulars.

junk shop *n* a shop selling secondhand articles or inferior antique goods.

junky *n* see JUNKIE.

Junoesque *adj* of a woman: tall, stately, and imposing in appearance.

junta *n* (*used as sing. or pl*) a political council or committee, *esp* a group controlling a government after a revolution.

Jurassic *adj* of the second period of the Mesozoic era, lasting from about 208 million to about 146 million years ago, and marked by the dominance of large reptiles and the first appearance of birds. ➤➤ **Jurassic** *n.*

juridical *adj* relating to justice, jurisprudence, or legal proceedings. ➤➤ **juridically** *adv.*

jurisdiction *n* **1** the power, right, or authority to apply the law. **2** the authority of a sovereign power. **3** the limits within which authority may be exercised. ➤➤ **jurisdictional** *adj,* **jurisdictionally** *adv.*

jurisprudence *n* **1** the science or philosophy of the law. **2** a branch or body of law. ➤➤ **jurisprudential** *adj.*

jurist *n* **1** somebody with a thorough knowledge of law. **2** *NAm* a lawyer or a judge. ➤➤ **juristic** *adj.*

juror *n* **1** a member of a jury. **2** a person who takes an oath.

jury[1] *n* (*pl* **-ies**) **1** a body of usu twelve people who are sworn to give an honest verdict based on evidence heard in court. **2** a committee for judging a contest or exhibition. ✱ **the jury is still out (on something)** a decision has not yet been reached.

jury[2] *adj* improvised for temporary use, *esp* in an emergency.

jury-rigged *adj* **1** improvised for temporary use. **2** of a ship: with an improvised mast, spars, and tackle.

just[1] *adj* **1** in conformity with what is morally upright or equitable; fair. **2a** being what is merited; appropriate. **b** legally correct. **3** conforming to fact or reason; well-founded. ➤➤ **justly** *adv,* **justness** *n.*

just[2] *adv* **1** exactly or precisely. **2** at or nearly at the moment in question. **3** by a very small margin; barely. **4** only or simply. **5** perhaps or possibly: *It might just work.* **6** *informal* very or completely. ✱ **just about 1** almost. **2** not more than. **just in case** as a precaution. **just so 1** tidily arranged. **2** used to express agreement.

justice *n* **1a** the quality of being just, impartial, or fair. **b** just dealing or right action. **2** the administration of law in accordance with established principles. **3** a judge or magistrate. ✱ **bring to justice** to arrest somebody and try them in a court of law. **do justice to 1** to treat fairly or adequately. **2** to show due appreciation for. **3** to represent in the best light.

justice of the peace *n* a lay magistrate empowered to hear minor cases.

justiciable *adj* **1** liable to trial. **2** able to be decided legally. ➤➤ **justiciability** *n.*

justiciary[1] *n* (*pl* **-ies**) **1** an administrator of justice. **2** the administration of justice.

justiciary[2] *adj* relating to the administration of justice.

justifiable *adj* capable of being justified; defensible. ➤➤ **justifiability** *n,* **justifiably** *adv.*

justify *v* (**-ies, -ied**) **1** to prove or show to be just, right, or reasonable. **2** to space out (e.g. a line of printed text) so that it is flush with a margin. ➤➤ **justification** *n,* **justificatory** *adj,* **justifier** *n.*

jut[1] *v* (**jutted, jutting**) (*often* + out) to extend out, over, up, or forwards; to project or protrude.

jut[2] *n* something that juts out.

Jute *n* a member of a Germanic people that invaded S England in the fifth cent. AD. ⋙ **Jutish** *adj.*

jute *n* the glossy fibre of an E Indian plant used chiefly for sacking and twine.

juvenile[1] *adj* **1** characteristic of or suitable for children or young people. **2** physiologically immature or undeveloped. ⋙ **juvenilely** *adv,* **juvenility** *n.*

juvenile[2] *n* **1** a young person, *esp* one under the age of 18. **2** a young bird, animal, etc.

juvenile court *n* a court with special jurisdiction over delinquent and dependent young people.

juvenile delinquent *n* a child or young person who has committed a criminal offence. ⋙ **juvenile delinquency** *n.*

juvenilia *pl n* artistic or literary works produced in an artist's or author's youth.

juxtapose *v* to place side by side. ⋙ **juxtaposition** *n.*

K

K[1] *or* **k** *n* (*pl* **K's** *or* **Ks** *or* **k's**) the eleventh letter of the English alphabet.

K[2] *abbr* **1** kelvin. **2** kilobyte. **3** in chess or card games, king. **4** Köchel (number). **5** *informal* thousand.

K[3] *abbr* the chemical symbol for potassium.

k *abbr* kilo-.

kabbala *or* **kabbalah** *n* see CABALA.

Kabinett *n* a high-quality German wine with no added sugar, usu a light dry white table wine.

kabuki /kə'boohki/ *n* traditional Japanese popular drama with singing and dancing performed in a highly stylized manner by males only.

Kaddish *n* a Jewish prayer recited in the daily ritual of the synagogue and by mourners after the death of a close relative.

Kaffir *n chiefly SAfr, derog, offensive* a black S African.

kaffir corn *n* a variety of sorghum grown in southern Africa for its grain and as fodder.

Kaffir lily *n* a plant with fleshy strap-shaped leaves and showy funnel-shaped flowers.

kaffiyeh *n* see KEFFIYEH.

Kafkaesque *adj* suggestive of the writings of Franz Kafka (d.1924), *esp* in expressing the anxieties of 20th-cent. people and their sense of isolation and unreality.

kaftan *or* **caftan** *n* a loose ankle-length garment with long sleeves, traditionally worn in Arab countries.

kagoul *n* see CAGOULE.

kai *n NZ* food.

kail *n* see KALE.

kaiser /'kiezə/ *n* **1** an emperor of Germany during the period from 1871 to 1918. **2** in former times, the emperor of Austria or the head of the Holy Roman Empire.

kaka /'kahkə/ *n* an olive brown New Zealand parrot with grey and red markings.

kakapo /'kahkəpoh/ *n* (*pl* **-os**) a chiefly nocturnal burrowing New Zealand parrot with green and brown plumage.

kakemono /kaki'mohnoh/ *n* (*pl* **-os**) a Japanese painting or inscription on a silk or paper scroll designed to be hung on a wall.

kala-azar /ˌkahlə ə'zah, ˌkalə/ *n* a severe infectious disease, chiefly of Asia, marked by enlargement of the spleen and liver and transmitted by sand flies.

kalanchoe /kalən'koh·i/ *n* a tropical succulent plant with clusters of small brightly coloured tubular flowers.

Kalashnikov *n* a type of automatic rifle made in Russia.

kale *or* **kail** *n* a hardy cabbage with curled often finely cut leaves that do not form a dense head.

kaleidoscope *n* **1** a tubular instrument containing loose chips of coloured glass between flat plates and mirrors so placed that an endless variety of symmetrical patterns is produced as the instrument is rotated. **2** something that is continually changing. ➤➤ **kaleidoscopic** *adj*, **kaleidoscopically** *adv*.

kalends *pl n* see CALENDS.

Kalmuck *or* **Kalmyk** *n* (*pl* **Kalmucks** *or* **Kalmuck** *or* **Kalmyks** *or* **Kalmyk**) **1** a member of a group of Mongolian peoples inhabiting a region stretching from W China to the Caspian Sea. **2** the language of these peoples.

Kamasutra /kahmə'soohtrə/ *n* (**the Kamasutra**) an ancient treatise on erotic love and sexual technique.

kameez *n* a long-sleeved tunic or long shirt traditionally worn above trousers by women of the Indian subcontinent.

kamikaze[1] /kami'kahzi/ *n* **1** in World War II, a member of the Japanese air force who volunteered to crash an aircraft laden with explosives suicidally on a target. **2** an aircraft used in such an attack.

Word history

Japanese *kamikaze*, literally 'divine wind'. The word *kamikaze* was originally applied to a providential storm that destroyed a Mongol fleet attacking Japan in 1281; the name was revived in 1944 when Japan resorted to desperate measures to hold off the advancing US fleet.

kamikaze[2] *adj* extremely reckless or foolhardy; self-defeating or self-destructive.

kampong *n* a hamlet or village in a Malay-speaking country.

Kampuchean *n and adj* = CAMBODIAN.

kana *n* a set of characters representing the syllables of the Japanese language.

kanga *or* **khanga** *n* a woman's dress of African origin, consisting of a length of cloth wound round the body and usu printed with colourful patterns.

kangaroo *n* (*pl* **kangaroos**) a plant-eating marsupial mammal of Australia that hops on its long powerful hind legs and has a long thick tail.

kangaroo court *n* an unofficial or irregular court, *esp* one in which justice is disregarded or perverted.

kangaroo paw *n* an Australian plant with long thin leaves and tubular hairy flowers.

kangaroo rat *n* a pouched nocturnal burrowing rodent of NW America that hops on its well-developed hind legs.

kangaroo vine *n* an Australian evergreen vine with glossy green leaves, widely grown as a house plant.

kanji *n* a set of characters derived from Chinese writing used to represent the syllables of the Japanese language.

Kantian *adj* relating to Immanuel Kant (d.1804) or his philosophy. ⋙ **Kantianism** *n.*

kaolin *n* a fine usu white clay used *esp* in ceramics and medicine.

kapellmeister /ka'pelmiestə/ *n* the director of a choir or orchestra, *esp* in German-speaking royal households of the 18th cent.

kapok *n* a mass of silky fibres that surround the seeds of a tropical tree and are used *esp* as a soft filling for cushions, sleeping bags, soft toys, etc.

Kaposi's sarcoma *n* a cancer of the skin and connective tissue that is characterized by brown or purple patches, *esp* on the feet and hands, and often occurs in people affected by Aids.

kappa *n* the tenth letter of the Greek alphabet (Κ, κ), equivalent to roman k.

kaput *adj informal* broken or useless.

karabiner *or* **carabiner** *n* an oblong ring with an openable side that is used in mountaineering to hold freely running rope.

karakul *or* **caracul** *n* **1** a sheep of a hardy breed from Bukhara. **2** the tightly curled glossy black coat of karakul lambs, valued as fur.

karaoke /karə'ohki/ *n* **1** a machine designed to play recorded music that a singer can use as accompaniment. **2** the practice of singing to such an accompaniment, *esp* as a form of social recreation or entertainment.

karat *n NAm* see CARAT (2).

karate /kə'rahti/ *n* a martial art in which the hands and feet are used to deliver crippling blows.

Karen *n* (*pl* **Karens** *or* **Karen**) **1** a member of a group of peoples of E and S Myanmar (formerly Burma). **2** a group of languages spoken by these peoples.

karma *n* **1** the force generated by a person's actions that is believed in Hinduism and Buddhism to influence their destiny. **2** fate or destiny. **3** an aura or spirit felt to emanate from a person, place, or thing. ⋙ **karmic** *adj.*

karri *n* (*pl* **karris**) an Australian eucalyptus tree with hard dark red wood.

karst *n* an irregular limestone region with underground streams, caverns, and potholes. ⋙ **karstic** *adj.*

kart *n* = GO-KART.

karting *n* the sport of racing go-karts.

karyotype *n* the specific characteristics, e.g. number, size, and shape, of the chromosomes of a cell. ⋙ **karyotypic** *adj.*

kasbah *or* **casbah** *n* **1** the older Arab section of a N African city. **2** a market in such a N African city.

Kashmiri *n* (*pl* **Kashmiris** *or* **Kashmiri**) **1** a native or inhabitant of Kashmir. **2** the language of Kashmir. ⋙ **Kashmiri** *adj.*

kat *or* **khat** /kaht, kat/ *n* the leaves and buds of a shrub cultivated by the Arabs that have addictive stimulant properties when chewed or used as a tea.

katabolism *n* see CATABOLISM.

Kathakali /kahthə'kahli/ *n* a form of S Indian classical drama, using stylized and elaborate costumes and make-up, in which stories from Hindu mythology are enacted in mime and dance.

Katharevusa /kahthə'revəsah/ *n* modern Greek conforming to classical Greek usage.

katydid *n* a large green long-horned grasshopper of N America, the males of which have organs on the forewings that produce a loud shrill sound when rubbed together.

kauri /'kowri/ *n* (*pl* **kauris**) a tall coniferous timber tree of New Zealand that yields fine white straight-grained wood and a brown resin used in varnishes and linoleum.

kava *n* an intoxicating beverage made from the crushed root of an Australasian pepper plant.

kayak /'kie(y)ak/ *n* **1** an Eskimo canoe made of a frame covered with skins except for a small opening in the centre and propelled by a double-bladed paddle. **2** a similar canvas-covered or fibreglass boat used chiefly for sport or recreation. ⋙ **kayaking** *n.*

kayo[1] *n* (*pl* **-os**) *informal* = KNOCKOUT (1B).

kayo[2] *v* (**kayoes** *or* **kayos, kayoed, kayoing**) *informal* to knock out (a boxing opponent).

Kazakh *n* **1** a member of a people of Kazakhstan. **2** the language of Kazakhstan. ⋙ **Kazakh** *adj.*

kazoo *n* (*pl* **kazoos**) a musical instrument consisting of a tube into which the player hums to vibrate a membrane covering a hole, which adds a buzzing or nasal quality to the sound.

KB *abbr* kilobyte.

KBE *abbr Brit* Knight Commander of the Order of the British Empire.

KC *abbr* King's Counsel.

kcal *abbr* kilocalorie.

KCB *abbr Brit* Knight Commander of the Order of the Bath.

KCMG *abbr Brit* Knight Commander of the Order of St Michael and St George.

KCVO *abbr Brit* Knight Commander of the Royal Victorian Order.

kea /'kee·ə/ *n* a large green New Zealand parrot that normally eats insects but sometimes kills sheep.

kebab *n* **1** cubes of meat, vegetables, etc, grilled on a skewer. **2** = DONER KEBAB.

kecks *pl n N Eng, informal* trousers.

kedge[1] *v* to pull (a boat or ship) along by means of a line attached to an anchor.

kedge[2] *n* a small anchor used *esp* in kedging.

kedgeree *n* a dish containing rice, flaked smoked fish, and chopped hard-boiled eggs.

keel[1] *n* **1** a structure that runs lengthways along the centre of the bottom of a ship or boat and that often projects downward to improve stability. **2** a projection or ridge suggesting a keel, e.g. the breastbone of a bird.

keel[2] *v* **1** (*usu* + over) to turn over; to capsize. **2** *informal* (+ over) to fall over in or as if in a faint.

keelhaul *v* **1** to drag under the keel of a ship as punishment. **2** to rebuke severely.

keelson *or* **kelson** *n* a structural beam fastened to the keel of a ship for strength and to support the flooring.

keen¹ *adj* **1a** enthusiastic; eager. **b** of emotion or feeling: intense. **2** sharp: *a keen blade.* **3** intellectually alert or shrewdly astute. **4** *Brit* of prices: low in order to be competitive. ✱ **keen on** interested in, attracted to, or fond of. ➤➤ **keenly** *adv,* **keenness** *n.*

keen² *v* to utter a loud wailing lamentation, *esp* for the dead. ➤➤ **keener** *n.*

keen³ *n* a lamentation for the dead uttered in a loud wailing voice, *esp* at Irish funerals.

keep¹ *v* (*past tense and past part.* **kept**) **1** to retain possession or control of. **2a** to cause to remain in a specified place or condition. **b** to store habitually for use. **c** to have (goods) customarily in stock for sale. **d** to record (accounts, events, etc) by entries in a book. **3a** to defend or guard: *Keep us from harm.* **b** to take care of, *esp* as an owner. **c** to support or provide for. **d** to continue to maintain (order, etc). **e** to manage or run (a shop, household, etc). **4** to obey or honour (a law, promise, etc). **5a** to delay or detain (somebody). **b** to save or reserve (something). **c** to refrain from revealing (something secret). **6a** to maintain a specified course. **b** to continue or persist in doing something: *Just keep talking.* **7a** to stay or remain in a specified usu desirable place, situation, or condition: *We must keep calm.* **b** *esp* of food: to remain in good condition. ✱ **keep from** to refrain from (doing something). **keep oneself to oneself** to remain solitary or apart from other people. **keep to 1** to stay in or on (a place, path, etc). **2** not to deviate from (a schedule, promise, etc).

keep² *n* **1** a castle, fortress, or fortified tower. **2** the essentials of living, *esp* food. ✱ **for keeps** permanently.

keep back *v* **1** to prevent from moving forward or making progress. **2a** to conceal or refuse to disclose (information). **b** to keep (some of something) in one's possession.

keeper *n* **1a** a protector, guardian, or custodian. **b** somebody who looks after animals, *esp* in a zoo. **c** a goalkeeper or wicketkeeper. **2** any of various devices for keeping something in position. **3** = ARMATURE (2).

keep fit *n* physical exercises designed to keep one's body healthy and supple.

keeping *n* **1** custody; care. **2** conformity or accordance with something implied or specified: *The new building is out of keeping.*

keepnet *n* a large net suspended in the water in which an angler keeps caught fish alive.

keep on *v* **1** to continue to do something. **2** to continue to employ (somebody). **3** to continue to use (something).

keepsake *n* something kept as a memento, *esp* of the giver.

keep up *v* **1** to persist or persevere in (an activity). **2** to preserve (something) from decline. **3** (*often* + with) to maintain an equal pace or level of activity, progress, etc.

kef *n* see KIF.

keffiyeh *or* **kaffiyeh** /kə'fee(y)ə/ *n* a cotton head covering worn by Arabs.

keg *n Brit* a small barrel having a capacity of 10gall (about 45.5l) or less; *specif* a metal barrel from which beer is pumped by pressurized gas.

kelim *n* see KILIM.

keloid *n* a thick scar resulting from excessive growth of fibrous tissue at the point of injury.

kelp *n* **1** a large brown seaweed. **2** the ashes of seaweed used *esp* as a source of iodine.

kelpie¹ *n* a water sprite of Scottish folklore, usu in the form of a horse.

kelpie² *n* a dog bred in Australia from British collies and used there as a sheepdog.

kelson *n* see KEELSON.

Kelt *n* see CELT.

kelt *n* a salmon or sea trout after spawning.

Keltic *adj and n* see CELTIC¹, CELTIC².

Kelvin *adj* of or being a scale of temperature on which absolute zero is at 0° and water freezes at 273.16° under standard conditions.

kelvin *n* the SI unit of temperature defined by the Kelvin scale.

kempt *adj* neatly kept; trim or tidy.

ken¹ *v* (**kenned** *or* **kent, kenning**) *chiefly Scot* to know or recognize.

ken² *n* range of perception, understanding, or knowledge.

kendo *n* a Japanese martial art of fencing with bamboo sticks.

kennel¹ *n* **1** a shelter for a dog. **2** (*also in pl*) an establishment for the breeding or boarding of dogs.

kennel² *v* (**kennelled, kennelling,** *NAm* **kenneled, kenneling**) to put or keep (a dog) in a kennel.

kent *v* past tense and past part. of KEN¹.

Kenyan *n* a native or inhabitant of Kenya. ➤➤ **Kenyan** *adj.*

kepi /'kaypee/ *n* a round French military cap with a flat top and a horizontal peak.

kept¹ *v* past tense and past part. of KEEP¹.

kept² ✱ **a kept man/woman** a lover or mistress who is supported financially by somebody.

kerat- *or* **kerato-** *comb. form* **1** denoting the cornea: *keratitis.* **2** horny: *keratin.*

keratin *n* a fibrous protein that forms the chemical basis of nails, claws, hooves, horns, feathers, and hair. ➤➤ **keratinous** *adj.*

keratitis *n* inflammation of the cornea of the eye.

kerato- *comb. form* see KERAT-.

keratoplasty *n* surgery carried out on the cornea.

kerb (*NAm* **curb**) *n* an edging, *esp* of stone or concrete, to a pavement, path, etc. ➤➤ **kerbing** *n.*

kerb crawling *n* the act of driving slowly close to a pavement with the intention of enticing a potential sexual partner into the car. ➤➤ **kerb crawler** *n.*

kerb drill *n Brit* a sequence of actions, *esp* looking to right and left, performed before crossing a road.

kerbstone *n* a block of stone or concrete forming a kerb.

kerchief *n* (*pl* **kerchiefs** *or* **kerchieves**) **1** a square or triangle of cloth worn on the head or around the neck. **2** = HANDKERCHIEF.

kerf *n* a slit or notch made *esp* by a saw.

kerfuffle *n chiefly Brit, informal* a fuss or commotion.

kermes /'kuhmiz/ *n* the dried bodies of insects that are found on the kermes oak, used as a red dyestuff.

kermes oak *n* a dwarf often shrubby Mediterranean oak tree.

kern¹ *n* a part of a letter that overhangs the piece of type on which it is cast.

kern² *v* **1** to provide (a printed character) with a kern. **2** to adjust the space between (printed characters).

kern³ *n* **1** a lightly-armed medieval Irish foot soldier. **2** *archaic* a peasant or yokel.

kernel *n* **1** the inner, softer, and often edible part of a seed, fruit stone, or nut. **2** a whole seed of a cereal. **3** a central or essential part; the core of something.

kerosene *or* **kerosine** *n chiefly NAm, Aus, NZ* = PARAFFIN.

kersey *n* a heavy compact ribbed woollen cloth with a short nap.

kestrel *n* a small falcon that is noted for its habit of hovering in the air against the wind.

ketamine /'keetəmeen/ *n* a synthetic chemical compound used as an anaesthetic and analgesic drug and sometimes illegally to induce hallucinations.

ketch *n* a sailing vessel with two masts, the forward mast being taller than the after mast, which is located ahead of the rudder.

ketchup (*NAm* **catchup**) *n* a sauce made from tomatoes, vinegar, and seasonings.

ketone *n* an organic compound, e.g. acetone, with a carbonyl group attached to two carbon atoms.

kettle *n* a metal or plastic vessel used for boiling water, usu having a lid, handle, and spout and heated on a hob or by an internal electric element. ✱ **a different/another kettle of fish** *informal* an altogether different matter. **a pretty/fine kettle of fish** *informal* a muddled or awkward state of affairs.

kettledrum *n* a percussion instrument that consists of a hollow metal hemisphere with a covering stretched across it, the tension of which can be changed to vary the pitch.

key[1] *n* **1a** a metal instrument by which the bolt of a lock is turned. **b** something having a similar form or function, e.g. a device used to wind a clock. **2** a small button on a keyboard, e.g. of a computer or typewriter, that is pushed down to work the machine. **3** any of the levers of a musical instrument that is pressed to produce notes by operating a mechanism controlling an air hole, etc. **4** a small switch for opening or closing an electric circuit. **5a** a means of gaining or preventing entrance, possession, or control. **b** an instrumental or deciding factor. **6** something that gives an explanation, e.g. of symbols used on a chart, or provides a solution, e.g. to a puzzle or code. **7** in music, a system of seven notes based on their relationship to the first and lowest note. **8** a characteristic style or tone. **9** a dry usu single-seeded fruit, e.g. of an ash or elm tree. **10** the roughness or roughening of a surface to improve adhesion of plaster, paint, glue, etc. ➤➤ **keyed** *adj*, **keyless** *adj*.

key[2] *v* **1** (*often* + in) to enter (e.g. data, a number, or text) by means of a keyboard or keypad. **2** to roughen (a surface) to improve adhesion of plaster, paint, etc. **3** to bring into harmony or conformity. **4** to provide with an explanatory key. ✱ **be keyed up** to be nervous, tense, or excited. ➤➤ **keyer** *n*.

key[3] *adj* of great importance; fundamental.

key[4] *n* a low island or reef, *esp* in the Caribbean.

keyboard[1] *n* **1a** a set of keys on a piano, organ, or similar musical instrument. **b** (*also in pl*) a musical instrument having such a keyboard, *esp* an electronic instrument. **2** a set of systematically arranged keys by which a machine, e.g. a computer or typewriter, is operated.

keyboard[2] *v* to enter or typeset (e.g. data or text) by means of a keyboard. ➤➤ **keyboarder** *n*.

key card *n* a plastic card containing a magnetic strip encoded with information that can be read by an electronic locking device on a door.

key grip *n* the person in charge of the handling and manoeuvring of cameras in a film or television studio.

keyhole *n* a hole in a lock into which the key is put.

keyhole surgery *n* surgery performed through a very small incision.

key money *n* a payment made by a tenant to secure occupancy of a rented property.

Keynesianism /'kaynzi·əniz(ə)m/ *n* the economic theories of J M Keynes (d.1946); *specif* the theory that the monetary and taxation policies of a government directly affect actual demand, inflation, and employment. ➤➤ **Keynesian** *adj and n*.

keynote *n* **1a** the fundamental or central principle, idea, or mood. **b** (*used before a noun*) of a speech: presenting the issues of primary interest to an assembly. **2** the first note of a musical scale considered as the base note.

keypad *n* a small keyboard or set of buttons for operating something, e.g. a telephone, calculator, or security system.

keypunch *n* a machine with a keyboard used to transfer data by cutting holes or notches in punched cards.

key signature *n* the sharps or flats placed on a musical staff to indicate the key.

keystone *n* **1** the wedge-shaped piece at the highest point of an arch that locks the other pieces in place. **2** something on which associated things depend for support.

keystroke *n* a single instance of pressing down a key on a keyboard.

KG *abbr Brit* Knight of the Order of the Garter.

kg *abbr* kilogram.

KGB *n* the secret police of the former USSR.

khaki *n* **1** a dull yellowish brown colour. **2** a khaki-coloured cloth made usu of cotton or wool and used *esp* for military uniforms. ➤➤ **khaki** *adj*.

Khalsa /'kalsə, 'kulsə/ *n* an order of orthodox Sikhs.

khamsin *n* a hot southerly Egyptian wind coming from the Sahara.

khan /kahn/ *n* **1** a medieval supreme ruler over the Turkish, Tartar, and Mongol peoples. **2** a local chieftain or person of rank in some countries of Central Asia. ➤➤ **khanate** *n*.

khanga *n* see KANGA.

khat *n* see KAT.

khazi /'kahzi/ *n* (*pl* **-ies**) *Brit, informal* a toilet.

Khmer *n* (*pl* **Khmer** *or* **Khmers**) **1** a member of the majority ethnic group of Cambodia. **2** the language of Cambodia. ➤➤ **Khmer** *adj*.

Khoikhoi *n* **1** a member of a people of southern Africa. **2** the language of this people. Also called NAMA. ➤➤ **Khoikhoi** *adj*.

khoum /khoom/ *n* a unit of currency in Mauritania, worth one fifth of an ouguiya.

kHz *abbr* kilohertz.

kia ora *interj NZ* used as a greeting or to express good wishes.

kibble *v* to grind (e.g. grain) coarsely.

kibbutz /ki'boots/ *n* (*pl* **kibbutzim**) a farm or settlement in Israel run as a cooperative.

kibbutznik *n* a member of a kibbutz.

kiblah *n* the direction of Mecca, to which Muslims turn when praying.

kibosh *or* **kybosh** ✱ **put the kibosh on** to ruin or put an end to (a plan, etc).

kick[1] *v* **1a** to strike (something or somebody) forcefully with the foot. **b** to strike out with the foot or feet. **2** *informal* to free oneself of (a habit or addiction). **3** to show opposition; to rebel. **4** of a gun: to recoil when fired. ✱ **kick oneself** to reprove oneself, *esp* with hindsight. **kick one's heels 1** to be kept waiting. **2** to be idle. **kick over the traces** to cast off restraint or control. **kick the bucket** *informal, humorous* to die. **kick upstairs** to promote to a higher but less influential position. ➤➤ **kicker** *n.*

kick² *n* **1a** a blow or sudden forceful thrust with the foot. **b** a repeated motion of the legs used in swimming. **2** the recoil of a gun. **3** power or strength to resist. **4a** a stimulating effect. **b** (*also in pl*) a pleasurable experience or feeling. **c** an absorbing or obsessive new interest. ✱ **kick in the teeth** *informal* a sharp rebuff or harsh disappointment.

kick about *v* = KICK AROUND.

kick around *v informal* **1** to treat (somebody) inconsiderately or high-handedly. **2** to consider or discuss (an idea, problem, etc) in a casual or desultory way. **3** to lie unused or unwanted.

kick-ass *adj chiefly NAm, informal* forceful and aggressive.

kickback *n* **1** a sharp violent reaction. **2** money received, often secretly or illicitly, because of help or favours given.

kickboxing *n* a martial art in which contestants punch with gloved hands and kick with bare feet. ➤➤ **kickboxer** *n.*

kickdown *n* a method of changing gear by pressing the accelerator down to the floor in a vehicle with automatic transmission.

kick in *v* **1** to start functioning. **2** to begin to take effect.

kickoff *n* a kick that puts the ball into play in football, rugby, etc, *esp* at the beginning of a game.

kick off *v* **1** in ball games, to start or resume play with a kickoff. **2** *informal* to begin proceedings.

kick out *v informal* to dismiss or eject forcefully or unceremoniously.

kick pleat *n* a short inverted pleat, *esp* at the lower edge of a narrow skirt, to allow freedom of movement.

kickshaw *n archaic* **1** a fancy dish; a delicacy. **2** a bauble or trinket of little value.

kickstand *n* a swivelling stand attached to a bicycle or motorcycle that can be kicked into position to hold it upright when stationary.

kick-start *v* **1** to start (an engine or motorcycle) by kicking down a lever. **2** to cause (something) to start, restart, or become more active or productive, *esp* by sudden or forceful action. ➤➤ **kick-start** *n,* **kick-starter** *n.*

kick up *v informal* to stir up (a row, a fuss, trouble, etc).

kid¹ *n* **1** the young of a goat or related animal. **2** = KIDSKIN. **3a** *informal* a child or young person. **b** (*used before a noun*) younger: *my kid sister.* ✱ **with kid gloves** with great care.

kid² *v* (**kidded, kidding**) of a goat: to give birth to young.

kid³ *v* (**kidded, kidding**) *informal* **1a** to deceive as a joke. **b** to convince (oneself) of something untrue or improbable. **2** to tease or make fun of in a playful manner. ➤➤ **kidder** *n.*

kiddie *or* **kiddy** *n* (*pl* **-ies**) *informal* a small child.

kidnap *v* (**kidnapped, kidnapping,** *NAm* **kidnaped, kidnaping**) to seize and detain (a person) by force and often for ransom. ➤➤ **kidnap** *n,* **kidnapper** *n.*

kidney *n* (*pl* **-eys**) **1** either of a pair of organs situated near the spinal column that excrete urine. **2** the kidney of an animal eaten as food. **3** sort, kind, or type, *esp* with regard to temperament.

kidney bean *n* the dark red kidney-shaped mature seed of the French bean.

kidney machine *n* a machine that artificially purifies the blood of somebody whose kidneys do not function properly.

kidney stone *n* **1** a hard stony mass that forms abnormally in the kidney. **2** = NEPHRITE.

kidology *n chiefly Brit, informal* playful deception or teasing.

kidskin *n* a soft pliant leather made from the skin of a young goat or related animal.

kids' stuff (*NAm* **kid stuff**) *n informal* something extremely simple or easy.

kieselguhr *or* **kieselgur** /'keezlgooə/ *n* loose or porous silica-containing material used for polishing, filtering, and in the manufacture of dynamite.

kif *or* **kef** *n* **1** a state of drowsy tranquillity. **2** a substance, e.g. marijuana, that is smoked to produce such a state.

Kikuyu /ki'kooh·yooh/ *n* (*pl* **Kikuyus** *or* **Kikuyu**) **1** a member of a people of Kenya. **2** the language of this people. ➤➤ **Kikuyu** *adj.*

kilim *or* **kelim** *n* a pileless woven rug from Turkey or Iran.

kill¹ *v* **1** to deprive of life. **2** to put an end to. **3** to destroy or neutralize the effect of. **4** to pass or occupy (time), e.g. while waiting. **5** *informal* **a** to cause (e.g. an engine) to stop. **b** to turn off (e.g. lights). **6** *informal* **a** to cause extreme pain to. **b** to exhaust almost to the point of collapse. **c** to overwhelm. ✱ **kill two birds with one stone** to deal with two matters simultaneously by the same means.

kill² *n* **1** an act or the moment of killing. **2** something killed, *esp* as game or prey. **3** an enemy aircraft, submarine, etc destroyed by military action. ✱ **in at the kill** present at the triumphant or successful conclusion of an undertaking.

killdeer *n* (*pl* **killdeers** *or* **killdeer**) a plover of temperate N America with a mournful penetrating cry.

killer *n* **1** a person or thing that kills. **2** *informal* something that is extremely arduous or exhausting. **3** *informal* a highly amusing joke.

killer cell *n* a white blood cell that can destroy foreign or infected cells.

killer whale *n* a flesh-eating black-and-white toothed whale.

killifish *n* (*pl* **killifishes** *or* **killifish**) a small fish used as bait and to control mosquitoes, whose larvae they eat.

killing¹ *n* **1** an act of causing death. **2** *informal* a sudden notable gain or profit.

killing² *adj* **1** causing death. **2** *informal* **a** extremely exhausting or difficult to endure. **b** highly amusing. ➤➤ **killingly** *adv.*

killing field *n* a place where a large number of people have been killed or massacred.

killjoy *n* somebody who spoils the pleasure of others.

kill off *v* to destroy totally or in large numbers.

kiln *n* an oven, furnace, or heated enclosure used for burning, firing, or drying a substance, e.g. clay.

kilo /'keeloh/ *n* (*pl* **kilos**) **1** a kilogram. **2** a kilometre.

kilo- *comb. form* **1** denoting a thousand: *kilometre.* **2** in some computing contexts, 1024: *kilobyte.*

kilobyte *n* in computing, a unit of memory or information equal to 1024 bytes.

kilocalorie *n* = CALORIE (2).

kilogram *n* the basic metric SI unit of mass approximately equal to the weight of one litre of water (about 2.205lb).

kilohertz *n* a unit of frequency equal to 1000 hertz.

kilojoule *n* a unit of work or energy equal to 1000 joules.

kilolitre (*NAm* **kiloliter**) *n* a metric unit of volume equal to 1000 litres (about 220gall).

kilometre (*NAm* **kilometer**) *n* a metric unit of length equal to 1000m (about 0.62mi).

kiloton *n* a unit of explosive force equivalent to that of 1000 tons of TNT.

kilovolt *n* a unit of potential difference equal to 1000 volts.

kilowatt *n* a unit of electrical power equal to 1000 watts.

kilowatt-hour *n* a unit of work or energy equal to that expended by one kilowatt in one hour.

kilt[1] *n* a tartan skirt traditionally worn by Scotsmen that is pleated at the back and sides and wrapped round the body, fastening at the front.

kilt[2] *v* **1** to pleat (fabric or a garment). **2** (*often* + up) to tuck up (e.g. a skirt).

kilter ✱ **out of kilter** not in proper working order or balance.

kimberlite *n* a coarse-grained igneous rock that is found chiefly in South Africa and often contains diamonds.

kimono *n* (*pl* **-os**) a loose robe with wide sleeves and a broad sash traditionally worn by the Japanese.

kin[1] *n* (*used as sing. or pl*) one's relatives.

kin[2] *adj* kindred; related.

-kin *suffix* forming nouns, denoting: a small kind of something: *manikin*.

kina /ˈkeenə/ *n* the basic monetary unit of Papua New Guinea.

kinaesthesia (*NAm* **kinesthesia**) *n* the sense of the position and movement of the parts of the body. ➤➤ **kinaesthetic** *adj.*

kind[1] *n* **1** fundamental nature or quality. **2a** a group united by common features. **b** a member of a category. ✱ **in kind 1** in goods, services, etc as distinguished from money. **2** in a similar way. **kind of 1** to a moderate degree; somewhat. **2** roughly or approximately. **of a kind 1** of the same type, having the same interests, etc: *We're two of a kind.* **2** barely worthy of the name: *They offer accommodation of a kind.* **one of a kind** unique.

kind[2] *adj* **1** having or showing a considerate or compassionate nature. **2** helpful, benevolent, or generous.

kindergarten /ˈkindəgahtn/ *n* a school or class for young children.

kindle[1] *v* **1** to cause to start burning. **2** to arouse (e.g. an emotion). ➤➤ **kindler** *n.*

kindle[2] *v* of a hare or rabbit: to give birth.

kindling *n* material, e.g. dry wood and leaves, for starting a fire.

kindly[1] *adj* (**-ier, -iest**) sympathetic; generous. ➤➤ **kindliness** *n.*

kindly[2] *adv* **1a** in a kind manner. **b** in an appreciative manner. **2** used to add politeness to a request or emphasis to a command. ✱ **not take kindly to** to react with displeasure to (e.g. a request or suggestion).

kindness *n* **1** the quality of being kind. **2** a kind deed or kind behaviour.

kindred[1] *n* **1** (*used as sing. or pl*) one's relatives. **2** family relationship.

kindred[2] *adj* **1** similar in nature or character. **2** related.

kindred spirit *n* somebody with interests, opinions, etc that are similar to one's own.

kine *pl n archaic* cows; cattle.

kinematics *pl n* (*used as sing. or pl*) a branch of physics that deals with aspects of motion without consideration of mass or force. ➤➤ **kinematic** *adj,* **kinematically** *adv.*

kinesis *n* (*pl* **kineses**) a movement made by an organism in response to the intensity rather than the direction of a stimulus.

-kinesis *comb. form* (*pl* **-kineses**) forming nouns, denoting: movement: *telekinesis.*

kinet- *or* **kineto-** *comb. form* denoting movement or motion: *kinetoscope.*

kinetic *adj* relating to motion. ➤➤ **kinetically** *adv.*

kinetic art *n* art, e.g. sculpture, depending for its effect on the movement of surfaces or parts.

kinetic energy *n* energy that a body or system has by virtue of its motion.

kinetics *pl n* (*used as sing. or pl*) a branch of science that deals with the effects of forces on the motions of bodies or with changes in a physical or chemical system.

kinetic theory *n* a theory in physics based on the fact that constituent particles of a substance are in vigorous motion.

kineto- *comb. form* see KINET-.

kinfolk *pl n chiefly NAm* = KINSFOLK.

king[1] *n* **1** a male monarch of a state, country, etc, *esp* one who inherits his position and rules for life. **2** the holder of a preeminent position within a particular sphere: *the king of jazz.* **3** in chess, the principal piece of each colour, which can move one square in any direction and must be protected against check. **4** a playing card marked with the figure of a king and ranking usu below the ace. **5** in draughts, a piece that has reached the opposite side of the board and can therefore move both forwards and backwards. ✱ **a king's ransom** a large amount of money. ➤➤ **kinghood** *n,* **kingliness** *n,* **kingly** *adj,* **kingship** *n.*

king[2] ✱ **king it** to behave in an overbearing or arrogant manner.

kingbolt *n* a large or major bolt.

King Charles spaniel *n* a spaniel of a small breed with a short turned-up nose.

king cobra *n* a large brownish venomous cobra of SE Asia.

kingcup *n* = MARSH MARIGOLD.

kingdom *n* **1** a territorial unit with a monarchical form of government. **2** an area or sphere in which somebody or something holds a preeminent position. **3** the eternal kingship of God. **4** any of the primary divisions into which natural objects are commonly classified.

kingdom come *n informal* **1** the next world. **2** the end of the world.

kingfisher *n* a small brightly-coloured fish-eating bird with a large head and a long stout sharp bill.

King James Version *n* = AUTHORIZED VERSION.

kinglet *n* **1** *chiefly derog* a weak or insignificant king, *esp* one who rules over a small territory. **2** *chiefly NAm* a small bird related to the warblers, e.g. the goldcrest or firecrest.

kingmaker *n* somebody having influence over the choice of candidates for office.

king of arms *n* in heraldry, an officer of arms of the highest rank; a chief herald.

King of Kings *n* in the Christian church, God.

king penguin *n* a large Antarctic penguin.

kingpin *n* **1** the key person or thing in a group or undertaking. **2a** = KINGBOLT. **b** a pin connecting two pivoting parts, e.g. on a hinge joint.

king post *n* a centrally placed vertical post rising to the apex of a triangular framework supporting a roof or other structure.

king prawn *n* a large prawn found in Australian waters.

King's Bench *n* used when the British monarch is a king: = QUEEN'S BENCH.

King's Counsel *n* used when the British monarch is a king: = QUEEN'S COUNSEL.

King's English *n* used when the British monarch is a king: = QUEEN'S ENGLISH.

King's evidence *n* used when the British monarch is a king: = QUEEN'S EVIDENCE.

King's Guide *n* used when the British monarch is a king: = QUEEN'S GUIDE.

King's highway *n* used when the British monarch is a king: = QUEEN'S HIGHWAY.

king-size *or* **king-sized** *adj* larger or longer than the regular or standard size.

King's Scout *n* used when the British monarch is a king: = QUEEN'S SCOUT.

King's speech *n* used when the British monarch is a king: = QUEEN'S SPEECH.

kink[1] *n* **1** a short twist or curl. **2** an eccentricity or quirk, *esp* in sexual behaviour or preferences. **3** an imperfection likely to cause difficulties.

kink[2] *v* to make or become twisted, curled, or bent.

kinkajou *n* a slender nocturnal tree-dwelling mammal of Central and South America that has a long prehensile tail and large lustrous eyes.

kinky *adj* (**-ier, -iest**) **1** twisted or curled. **2** *informal* **a** sexually perverted or deviant. **b** idiosyncratic, unusual, or bizarre. ➤➤ **kinkily** *adv,* **kinkiness** *n.*

-kins *suffix* forming nouns, denoting: a small kind of something, *esp* to express endearment: *bunnikins.*

kinsfolk *pl n* one's relatives.

kinship *n* **1** blood relationship. **2** similarity.

kinsman *n* (*pl* **kinsmen**) a male relative.

kinswoman *n* (*pl* **kinswomen**) a female relative.

kiosk *n* **1** a small stall or stand used *esp* for the sale of newspapers, cigarettes, and sweets. **2** *Brit* a public telephone box.

kip[1] *n chiefly Brit, informal* **1** a period of sleep. **2** a place to sleep.

kip[2] *v* (**kipped, kipping**) *chiefly Brit, informal* to sleep.

kip[3] *n* (*pl* **kip** *or* **kips**) the basic monetary unit of Laos.

kipper[1] *n* a fish, *esp* a herring, that has been split open, salted, and dried, usu in smoke.

kipper[2] *v* to cure (a fish) by salting and drying, usu in smoke.

kipper tie *n* a very wide tie worn *esp* during the 1960s.

kir /kiə/ *n* a drink consisting of white wine mixed with blackcurrant liqueur.

Kirghiz *n* see KYRGYZ.

kirk *n* **1** *chiefly Scot* a church. **2** (**the Kirk**) the national Church of Scotland.

Kirk session *n* the ruling body of a Church of Scotland congregation, consisting of the minister and the elders.

kirsch /kiəsh/ *n* a dry colourless spirit distilled from the fermented juice of the black morello cherry.

kismet *n* fate or destiny.

kiss[1] *v* **1** to touch with the lips, *esp* as a mark of affection or greeting. **2** to touch gently or lightly. ➤➤ **kissable** *adj.*

kiss[2] *n* an act of kissing.

kissagram *or* **kissogram** *n* a surprise greeting, usu on a special occasion, accompanied by a kiss from the person employed to deliver it.

kiss-and-tell *adj* of a book, article, etc: revealing intimate secrets about former associates or famous people.

kiss-curl *n* a small curl of hair falling on the forehead or cheek.

kisser *n* **1** somebody who kisses, *esp* in the specified way. **2** *informal* the mouth or face.

kissing gate *n Brit* a gate swinging in a V- or U-shaped enclosure so that only one person can pass through at a time.

kiss of death *n informal* an act bound to cause ruin or failure.

kiss of life *n* **1** artificial respiration in which the rescuer blows air into the victim's lungs by mouth-to-mouth contact. **2** an action that restores or revitalizes something.

kiss of peace *n* a ceremonial kiss, embrace, or handclasping used in Christian services of worship, *esp* the Eucharist.

kissogram *n* see KISSAGRAM.

kist *n chiefly SAfr* a large chest or trunk, *esp* one used for storing a bride's trousseau.

Kiswahili *n* = SWAHILI (2).

kit[1] *n* **1a** a set of tools or implements. **b** a set of clothes, equipment, supplies, etc for use in a particular situation or activity. **2** a set of parts ready to be assembled. ✱ **get one's kit off** *informal* to undress.

kit[2] *v* (**kitted, kitting**) *chiefly Brit* (+ out/up) to equip or clothe (somebody) for a particular situation or activity.

kit[3] *n* = KITTEN[1].

kitbag *n* a large cylindrical bag carried over the shoulder and used by soldiers, travellers, etc to carry their possessions.

kitchen *n* a room where food is prepared and cooked.

kitchen cabinet *n* an informal group of advisers to the head of a government, often considered to have more influence than the official cabinet.

kitchenette *n* a small kitchen or part of a room containing cooking facilities.

kitchen garden *n* a garden in which vegetables are grown.

kitchen midden *n* a domestic refuse heap, *esp* one marking the site of a prehistoric settlement.

kitchen paper *n* absorbent paper used chiefly in the kitchen, e.g. for draining food cooked in fat.

kitchen-sink *adj Brit* of drama: portraying modern daily life in a realistic and often sordid manner.

kitchen tea *n Aus, NZ* a party at which a bride-to-be receives presents of kitchen equipment.

kitchenware *n* utensils and equipment for use in a kitchen.

kite[1] *n* **1** a light frame covered with thin material that is flown in the air at the end of a long string. **2** a hawk with long narrow wings, a deeply forked tail, and feet adapted for taking insects and small reptiles as prey. **3** *informal* an aircraft. **4** *informal* a fraudulent worthless cheque or bill of exchange. **5** a quadrilateral with two pairs of equal adjacent sides.

kite[2] *v* **1** to move or cause to move or rise rapidly. **2** *chiefly NAm, informal* to write, issue, or use (a fraudulent cheque or bill of exchange).

kith ✱ **kith and kin** one's friends and relations.

kitsch *n* artistic or literary material that is pretentious or inferior and is usu designed to appeal to popular or sentimental taste. ➤➤ **kitsch** *adj*, **kitschy** *adj.*

kitten[1] *n* the young of a cat or any of various other small mammals, e.g. the beaver. ✱ **have kittens** *Brit, informal* to be extremely worried or upset.

kitten[2] *v* to give birth to kittens.

kittenish *adj* coyly playful or flirtatious. ➤➤ **kittenishly** *adj*, **kittenishness** *n.*

kittiwake *n* a gull with mainly white plumage and black-tipped wings.

kitty[1] *n* (*pl* **-ies**) used chiefly as a pet name: a cat or kitten.

kitty[2] *n* (*pl* **-ies**) **1** a jointly held fund of money, e.g. for household expenses. **2** a fund in a card game. **3** in bowls, the jack.

kitty-cornered *adj* = CATERCORNER.

kiwi *n* (*pl* **kiwis**) **1** a flightless New Zealand bird with stout legs, a long bill, and greyish brown hair-like plumage. **2** (**Kiwi**) *chiefly informal* a New Zealander. **3** = KIWI FRUIT.

kiwi fruit *n* the edible oval fruit of an Asian climbing plant, which has a brown hairy skin, green flesh, and black seeds.

kJ *abbr* kilojoule.

KKK *abbr* Ku Klux Klan.

kl *abbr* kilolitre.

Klan *n* = KU KLUX KLAN. ➤➤ **Klansman** *n*, **Klanswoman** *n.*

Kleenex *n trademark* a paper handkerchief.

Klein bottle /klien/ *n* a one-sided surface that is formed by passing the narrow end of a tapered tube through the side of the tube and flaring it out to join the other end.

kleptomania *n* an irresistible and recurrent desire to steal, *esp* when not accompanied by economic or other motives. ➤➤ **kleptomaniac** *n.*

klieg light /kleeg/ *n* a powerful arc lamp used in film studios.

klutz *n chiefly NAm, informal* a foolish, clumsy, or awkward person. ➤➤ **klutzy** *adj.*

km *abbr* kilometre.

kn. *abbr* knot.

knack *n* **1** a special capacity or skill that enables something difficult to be done with ease. **2** a tendency or aptitude.

knacker[1] *n Brit* somebody who buys and slaughters worn-out horses and other animals.

knacker[2] *v chiefly Brit, informal* to exhaust (somebody).

knacker[3] *n coarse slang* a testicle.

knacker's yard *n* **1** *Brit* a slaughterhouse, *esp* for horses. **2** *informal* a place for somebody or something discarded as no longer useful.

knap *v* (**knapped, knapping**) to hit or break (stone, *esp* flint) with quick sharp blows in order to make tools or building material. ➤➤ **knapper** *n.*

knapsack *n* a bag strapped on the back and used by soldiers, hikers, etc for carrying supplies or personal belongings.

knapweed *n* a European plant with a tough wiry stem and purple thistle-like flowers.

knave *n* **1** *archaic* a wicked or unprincipled man; a scoundrel. **2** = JACK[1] (2). ➤➤ **knavery** *n*, **knavish** *adj*, **knavishly** *adv.*

knead *v* **1** to work and press (something soft, e.g. dough) with the hands. **2** to manipulate by or as if by kneading. ➤➤ **kneader** *n.*

knee[1] *n* **1a** a joint in the middle part of the human leg between the thighbone and the shinbone. **b** the part of the leg that includes this joint. **c** the upper surface of the thigh of a seated person; the lap. **2** the part of an article of clothing that covers the knees. **3** something shaped like a bent knee. ✱ **bend/bow the knee** to submit. **bring (somebody) to their knees** to cause (somebody) to submit or accept defeat or failure.

knee[2] *v* to strike with the knee.

kneecap[1] *n* a thick flat triangular movable bone that protects the front of the knee joint. Also called PATELLA.

kneecap[2] *v* (**kneecapped, kneecapping**) to smash or shoot the kneecap of (somebody) as a punishment or torture.

knee-deep *adj* **1** = KNEE-HIGH. **2a** immersed up to the knees. **b** deeply engaged or occupied.

knee-high *adj* high or deep enough to reach up to the knees.

knee jerk *n* an involuntary forward kick produced by a light blow on the tendon below the kneecap

knee-jerk *adj* occurring as a conditioned response; automatic.

kneel *v* (*past tense and past part.* **knelt** *or* **kneeled**) to fall or rest on the knee or knees.

kneeler *n* **1** somebody who kneels. **2** something for kneeling on, e.g. a cushion or a low stool.

knees-up *n* (*pl* **knees-ups**) *chiefly Brit, informal* a boisterous celebration, usu with dancing.

knee-trembler *n Brit, informal* an act of sexual intercourse between two standing people.

knell[1] *v* of a bell: to ring, *esp* for a death, funeral, etc.

knell[2] *n* **1** the sound of a bell rung slowly, e.g. for a funeral or disaster. **2** an indication of the end or failure of something.

knelt *v* past tense and past part. of KNEEL.

Knesset /'knesit/ *n* the legislative assembly of Israel.

knew *v* past tense of KNOW[1].

Knickerbocker *n* a descendant of the early Dutch settlers of New York.

knickerbocker glory *n* an elaborate dessert consisting of layers of fruit, jelly, ice cream, and cream served in a tall glass.

knickerbockers *pl n* short baggy trousers gathered on a band at the knee.

knickers *pl n* **1** *Brit* women's or girls' pants. **2** *NAm* = KNICKERBOCKERS. ✱ **get one's knickers in a twist** *Brit, informal* to become agitated or angry.

knick-knack *or* **nicknack** *n informal* a small trivial ornament or trinket.

knife[1] *n* (*pl* **knives**) **1** a cutting implement consisting of a blade fastened to a handle. **2** a sharp cutting blade or tool in a machine. ✱ **have/get one's knife into** to behave in a hostile way towards. ➤➤ **knifelike** *adj.*

knife[2] *v* to cut, slash, or stab with a knife.

knife-edge *n* **1** the cutting edge of a knife. **2** an uncertain or precarious position or condition. **3** something sharp and narrow, e.g. a ridge of rock. **4** a sharp wedge of steel used as a fulcrum or pivot in a pair of scales, a pendulum, etc.

knife pleat *n* a narrow flat pleat, *esp* any of a series of such pleats on a skirt.

knifepoint ✱ **at knifepoint** under a threat of death or injury by being knifed.

knight[1] *n* **1** in medieval times, a mounted armed soldier serving a feudal superior. **2** in Britain, a man honoured by a sovereign for merit, bearing the title 'Sir'. **3** in chess, either of two pieces of each colour, usu in the shape of a horse's head, that move diagonally from one corner to another of a rectangle of three by two squares. ⋙ **knighthood** *n*, **knightly** *adj.*

knight[2] *v* to make a knight of (somebody).

knight-errant *n* (*pl* **knights-errant**) a knight travelling in search of chivalrous adventures. ⋙ **knight-errantry** *n.*

knight of the road *n informal* **1** a tramp. **2a** a commercial traveller. **b** a truck driver. **3** a courteous driver of a motor vehicle.

Knight Templar *n* (*pl* **Knights Templars** *or* **Knights Templar**) = TEMPLAR.

kniphofia /ni'fohfi·ə/ *n* = RED-HOT POKER.

knit[1] *v* (**knitted** *or* **knit, knitting**) **1a** to form (a fabric or garment) by working yarn into a series of interlocking loops using knitting needles or a knitting machine. **b** to work (a specified number of stitches or rows) in this way, *specif* using knit stitch. **2** to link or unite firmly or closely. **3** to contract (one's brow) into wrinkles. **4** of bone: to grow together. ⋙ **knitter** *n.*

knit[2] *n* **1** a basic knitting stitch that produces a raised pattern on the front of the work. **2** a fabric or garment made by knitting.

knit stitch *n* = KNIT[2] (1).

knitting *n* **1** work that has been or is being knitted. **2a** the action or process of producing this. **b** (*used before a noun*) of or used to produce knitting: *a knitting machine.*

knitting needle *n* either of a pair of long thin pointed rods, usu of metal or plastic, around which yarn is looped in knitting.

knitwear *n* knitted clothing, *esp* jumpers and cardigans.

knives *n* pl of KNIFE[1].

knob *n* **1a** a rounded protuberance or ornament. **b** a small rounded handle or control for pushing, pulling, or turning. **2** a small piece or lump. **3** *chiefly NAm* a rounded usu isolated hill. **4** *Brit, coarse slang* the penis. ⋙ **knobbed** *adj,* **knobby** *adj.*

knobble *n* a small knob or lump. ⋙ **knobbly** *adj.*

knobkerrie *n* a short wooden club with a knobbed head used *esp* by S African tribesmen.

knock[1] *v* **1a** to strike (a surface) sharply with the knuckles or a hard object. **b** to strike a door with a sharp audible blow seeking admittance. **2** to drive, make, or remove by striking. **3** to collide or cause to collide. **4** *informal* to find fault with; to criticize. **5** *informal* to have sexual intercourse with. **6** of an internal-combustion engine: to make a metallic rapping noise because of a mechanical defect. ✱ **be knocking on** *informal* to be growing old. **knock on the head** *informal* to put an end to or prevent the development of (an idea, plan, etc). **knock spots off** *informal* to surpass or outdo with ease. **knock together** to make or assemble hurriedly or in a makeshift way.

knock[2] *n* **1a** a sharp blow or collision. **b** the sound made by a sharp blow on a hard surface. **c** the sound of knocking in an internal-combustion engine. **2** a piece of bad luck or misfortune. **3** a harsh and often petty criticism.

knockabout *adj* boisterous or characterized by boisterous antics.

knock about *v* **1** *informal* to treat roughly or violently. **2** to be present by chance. **3a** to travel or wander about. **b** to associate or keep company.

knock around *v* = KNOCK ABOUT.

knock back *v informal* **1** *chiefly Brit* to drink (*esp* an alcoholic drink) rapidly. **2** to surprise or disconcert.

knock-back *n* a setback or refusal.

knockdown *adj* **1** of furniture: easily assembled or dismantled. **2** of a price: very low or substantially reduced.

knock down *v* **1** to strike to the ground. **2** to dispose of (an item for sale at an auction). **3** *informal* **a** to make a reduction in (a price). **b** to cause (somebody) to make such a reduction.

knocker *n* **1** a metal object hinged to a door for use in knocking. **2** *informal* somebody who finds fault; a critic. ✱ **on the knocker** *informal* promptly or immediately.

knockers *pl n coarse slang* a woman's breasts.

knock-for-knock *adj* denoting an agreement between insurance companies whereby each company indemnifies its own policyholder regardless of legal liability.

knocking shop *n Brit, coarse slang* a brothel.

knock-knees *pl n* a condition in which the legs curve inward at the knees. ⋙ **knock-kneed** *adj.*

knock off *v* **1** to stop doing something, *esp* work. **2** to do or produce hurriedly or routinely. **3** to deduct (an amount). **4** *informal* to murder. **5** *informal* to steal. ✱ **knock it off** to stop doing something.

knock-on effect *n* any or all of a series of events, actions, etc, each caused by the preceding one.

knockout *n* **1a** knocking out or being knocked out. **b** in boxing, a blow that knocks an opponent down for longer than a specified time and ends the match. **2** a competition with successive rounds in which losing competitors are eliminated. **3** *informal* a sensationally striking or attractive person or thing.

knock out *v* **1a** to make unconscious. **b** to defeat (a boxing opponent) by a knockout. **2** to eliminate (an opponent) from a knockout competition. **3** *informal* to overwhelm with amazement, admiration, or pleasure. **4** to make or produce quickly or hastily.

knockout drops *pl n* drops of a liquid drug put into a drink to produce unconsciousness or stupefaction.

knock up *v* **1** to make or arrange hastily or in a makeshift way. **2** *chiefly NAm, informal* to make (a woman) pregnant. **3** to achieve a total of (the specified amount or number). **4** to practise a racket game informally before a match.

knock-up *n* a period of informal practice before a match in tennis, badminton, squash, etc.

knoll *n* a small round hill; a mound.

knot[1] *n* **1a** a looping or interlacing of string, thread, etc pulled tight to form a fastening or lump. **b** a tangled mass, e.g. of hair. **c** a sense of tight constriction, *esp* in the stomach. **2** a protuberant lump or swelling in tissue. **3** the base of a woody branch enclosed in the stem from which it arises, or the cross-section of this appearing as a rounded area in timber. **4** a cluster of people or things. **5** a unit of speed equal to one nautical mile per hour. ✱ **at a rate of knots** *informal* very fast. **get knotted** *informal* used in angry or contemptuous dismissal. **tie in knots** to confuse utterly; to bewilder. **tie the knot** to get married. ⋙ **knotless** *adj.*

knot[2] *v* (**knotted, knotting**) **1** to tie in or with a knot. **2** to cause (e.g. hair) to become tangled. **3** to cause (e.g. muscles) to become tense or constricted. ⋙ **knotter** *n.*

knot[3] *n* (*pl* **knots** *or* **knot**) a sandpiper with grey plumage that breeds in the Arctic and winters in temperate or warm parts of the world.

knot garden *n* a formal garden with plants arranged to form intricate knot-like patterns.

knotgrass *n* a widely occurring plant with jointed stems and minute green flowers.

knothole *n* a hole in a board or tree trunk where a knot or branch has come out.

knotty *adj* (**-ier, -iest**) **1** full of knots. **2** complicated or difficult to solve. ➤➤ **knottiness** *n.*

knout /nowt/ *n* a whip formerly used in Russia for flogging criminals.

know[1] *v* (*past tense* **knew,** *past part.* **known**) **1** to be aware of or have information about. **2a** to be convinced or certain of. **b** to have a practical understanding of (how to do something). **3a** to recognize or identify. **b** to be acquainted or familiar with. **c** to have experience of. **4** *archaic* to have sexual intercourse with. ✱ **be known as** to be called, e.g. as a nickname. **know no bounds** to be unlimited or unconfined. **know what's what** to be competent, experienced, or knowledgeable. **you know** used for adding emphasis to a statement. ➤➤ **knowable** *adj,* **knower** *n.*

know[2] ✱ **in the know** in possession of confidential or otherwise exclusive knowledge or information.

know-all *n* somebody who behaves as if they know everything.

know-how *n* expertise in a particular field.

knowing[1] *adj* **1** implying knowledge of a secret: *a knowing look.* **2** shrewd or astute. **3** deliberate or conscious. ➤➤ **knowingly** *adv,* **knowingness** *n.*

knowing[2] *n* the fact or condition of being aware of or understanding something: *There's no knowing what will happen.*

know-it-all *n* = KNOW-ALL.

knowledge *n* **1** information, understanding, or skills acquired through learning or experience. **2** the total body of known facts, or those associated with a particular subject. **3** awareness of something. ✱ **to one's knowledge** as far as one knows.

knowledgeable *adj* having or exhibiting knowledge or intelligence; well-informed. ➤➤ **knowledgeably** *adv.*

known[1] *v* past part. of KNOW[1].

known[2] *adj* **1** generally recognized. **2** identified: *a known thief.*

knuckle[1] *n* **1** the rounded prominence formed by any of the joints between the hand and the fingers or the bones of the fingers. **2** a cut of meat consisting of the lowest leg joint of a pig, sheep, etc with the adjoining flesh. ✱ **near the knuckle** almost improper or indecent.

knuckle[2] *v* to hit, press, or rub with the knuckles.

knuckle down *v* to apply oneself earnestly.

knuckle-duster *n* a metal device worn over the front of the doubled fist for use as a weapon.

knucklehead *n informal* a stupid person. ➤➤ **knuckleheaded** *adj.*

knuckle sandwich *n informal* a punch in the face with the fist.

knuckle under *v* to give in; to submit.

knurl *n* a small knob or protuberance, *esp* any of a series of small ridges on a surface to aid in gripping. ➤➤ **knurled** *adj.*

KO[1] *n* (*pl* **KOs**) *informal* = KNOCKOUT (1B).

KO[2] *v* (**KO's, KO'ing, KO'd**) *informal* to knock out (a boxing opponent).

koala /koh'ahlə/ *n* an Australian tree-dwelling marsupial mammal that has large hairy ears, grey fur, and sharp claws and feeds on eucalyptus leaves.

koala bear *n* = KOALA.

koan /'koh·ahn/ *n* a paradox to be meditated upon, used by Zen Buddhist monks to gain enlightenment.

kobo *n* (*pl* **kobo**) a unit of currency in Nigeria, worth 100th of a naira.

Köchel number /'kuhkh(ə)l/ *n* any of a group of numbers used as a cataloguing system for Mozart's works.

kodiak bear *n* a brown bear of Alaska.

kofta *n* an Indian dish of minced meat or vegetables formed into small balls and fried.

kohl *n* a black powder, or a cosmetic preparation made from it, used to darken the eyelids.

kohlrabi /kohl'rahbi/ *n* (*pl* **kohlrabies**) a cabbage with a greatly enlarged fleshy edible stem resembling a turnip.

koi *n* a common carp of a colourful breed that originated in Japan, often kept as an aquarium or pond fish.

kola *n* see COLA.

kola nut *or* **cola nut** *n* the bitter caffeine-containing seed of a tree of the cocoa family that is chewed *esp* as a stimulant and used in beverages.

kolkhoz /kol'hawz, kol'khoz, 'kolkoz/ *n* (*pl* **kolkhozy** *or* **kolkhozes**) a collective farm of the former USSR.

Kol Nidre /,kol 'nidray/ *n* in Judaism, a formula for the annulment of private vows chanted in the synagogue on the eve of Yom Kippur.

komodo dragon *n* a very large Indonesian monitor lizard that can reach 3m (10ft) in length.

kook *n NAm, informal* an eccentric or crazy person. ➤➤ **kookiness** *n,* **kooky** *adj.*

kookaburra *n* a large Australian kingfisher that has a call resembling loud laughter.

kop *n* **1** *Brit* a bank of terracing at a football ground, or the supporters who stand or sit there. **2** *SAfr* a prominent peak or hill.

kopeck *or* **copeck** *or* **kopek** /'kohpek/ *n* a unit of currency in Russia, Tajikistan, and Belarus, worth 100th of a rouble.

kopiyka /ko'piekə/ *n* a unit of currency in Ukraine, worth 100th of a hryvna.

kora *n* a lute-shaped stringed musical instrument of West Africa that has 21 strings and is played like a harp.

Koran /kaw'rahn, kə'rahn/ *or* **Qur'an** /koo'rahn/ *n* the sacred book of Islam, composed of writings accepted by Muslims as revelations made to Muhammad by Allah. ➤➤ **Koranic** *adj.*

Korean *n and adj* **1** a native or inhabitant of North or South Korea. **2** the language of the Koreans. ➤➤ **Korean** *adj.*

korma *n* an Indian dish of meat, fish, or vegetables braised in water, stock, yogurt, or cream.

koruna *n* (*pl* **koruny** *or* **korunas**) the basic monetary unit of the Czech Republic and Slovakia.

kosher[1] /'kohshə/ *adj* **1** of food: prepared according to Jewish law. **2** *informal* **a** proper or legitimate. **b** genuine or authentic.

kosher[2] *v* to prepare (food) according to Jewish law.

Kosovar *n* a native or inhabitant of Kosovo. ➤➤ **Kosovan** *adj.*

koto *n* (*pl* **-os**) a Japanese plucked stringed musical instrument with a long rectangular wooden body and 13 silk strings.

koumiss *or* **kumiss** *n* an alcoholic drink of fermented mare's milk made orig by the nomadic peoples of central Asia.

kowhai /'kohwie/ *n* a golden-flowered shrub or small tree found in Australasia and Chile.

kowtow[1] *n* a former Chinese gesture of deep respect in which one kneels and touches the ground with one's forehead.

kowtow² *v* **1** to make a kowtow. **2** to show obsequious deference.

kph *abbr* kilometres per hour.

Kr *abbr* the chemical symbol for krypton.

kraal¹ *n* **1** a village in southern Africa, often enclosed by a fence. **2** an enclosure for domestic animals in southern Africa.

kraal² *v* to pen (animals) in a kraal.

kraft *n* a strong paper made from wood pulp boiled in an alkaline solution.

krait /kriet/ *n* a brightly coloured extremely venomous E Asian snake that is active at night.

kraken /'krahkən/ *n* a mythical Scandinavian sea monster.

Kraut *n offensive* a German.

Krebs cycle *n* a sequence of respiratory reactions in the living cell that releases energy for storage.

kremlin *n* **1** a citadel within a Russian town or city. **2a** (**the Kremlin**) the building in Moscow that houses the national government offices. **b** the government of Russia.

krill *pl n* small marine invertebrate animals that resemble shrimps and constitute the principal food of many sea animals, e.g. whalebone whales.

kris *n* a Malay or Indonesian dagger with a scalloped blade.

Krishna *n* a god of Hinduism worshipped as an incarnation of Vishnu. ➤➤ **Krishnaism** *n.*

krona *n* (*pl* **kronor**) the basic monetary unit of Sweden.

króna *n* (*pl* **krónur**) the basic monetary unit of Iceland.

krone /'krohnə/ *n* (*pl* **kroner**) the basic monetary unit of Denmark and Norway.

kronor *n* pl of KRONA.

krónur *n* pl of KRÓNA.

kroon *n* (*pl* **kroon** *or* **kroons**) the basic monetary unit of Estonia.

Krugerrand *n* a gold coin of S Africa weighing one ounce (28.35g).

krummhorn *or* **crumhorn** *n* a Renaissance woodwind musical instrument with a double reed and a hooked tube.

krypton *n* a colourless gaseous element found in very small amounts in air and used *esp* in fluorescent lights.

KS *abbr* Kansas (US postal abbreviation).

Kshatriya /'kshatri·ə/ *n* a Hindu of an upper caste traditionally assigned to military occupations: compare BRAHMAN, SUDRA, VAISYA.

KStJ *abbr Brit* Knight of the Order of St John.

KT *abbr* **1** *Brit* Knight of the Order of the Thistle. **2** Knight Templar.

Kt *abbr* knight.

kt *abbr* knot.

kudos /'kyoohdos/ *n* renown and prestige, *esp* resulting from an act or achievement.

kudu /'koohdooh/ *n* (*pl* **kudus** *or* **kudu**) a greyish brown African antelope with large spirally twisted horns.

Ku Klux Klan *n* a secret political organization in the USA that is hostile to black people.

kukri /'kookri/ *n* (*pl* **kukris**) a short curved knife used *esp* by Gurkhas.

kulak /'koohlak/ *n* a prosperous peasant farmer in prerevolutionary Russia.

kulfi *n* an Indian dessert resembling ice cream that is flavoured with nuts and usu cone-shaped.

kumara *n NZ* = SWEET POTATO.

kumiss *n* see KOUMISS.

kumkum *n* a red powder used by Hindu women to make a small mark on the forehead.

kümmel /'kooml/ *n* a colourless aromatic liqueur flavoured with caraway seeds.

kumquat *or* **cumquat** *n* a small orange citrus fruit with sweet spongy rind and rather acid pulp.

kuna /'koohnə/ *n* the basic monetary unit of Croatia.

kung fu *n* a Chinese martial art resembling karate.

Kurd *n* a member of a pastoral and agricultural people who chiefly inhabit adjoining parts of Turkey, Iran, and Iraq. ➤➤ **Kurdish** *adj.*

Kurdish *n* the language of the Kurds. ➤➤ **Kurdish** *adj.*

kurgan *n* a prehistoric burial mound found in E Europe, *esp* in S Russia.

kurrajong *n* an Australian tree or shrub yielding strong woody fibre.

kurta *n* a loose-fitting collarless shirt worn by Hindu men and women.

kuru *n* a fatal disease of the nervous system that occurs among tribespeople of eastern New Guinea.

kurus /koo'roohsh/ *n* (*pl* **kurus**) a unit of currency in Turkey, worth 100th of a lira.

Kuwaiti *n* a native or inhabitant of Kuwait. ➤➤ **Kuwaiti** *adj.*

kV *abbr* kilovolt.

kvetch *v NAm, informal* to complain persistently.

kW *abbr* kilowatt.

kwacha *n* (*pl* **kwacha**) the basic monetary unit of Zambia and Malawi.

kwanza *n* (*pl* **kwanza** *or* **kwanzas**) the basic monetary unit of Angola.

Kwanzaa *n NAm* an African-American cultural festival observed between 26 December and 1 January.

kwashiorkor *n* severe malnutrition in babies and children that is caused by a diet high in carbohydrate and low in protein.

kWh *abbr* kilowatt-hour.

KY *abbr* Kentucky (US postal abbreviation).

kyat /ki'aht/ *n* (*pl* **kyat** *or* **kyats**) the basic monetary unit of Myanmar (formerly Burma).

kybosh *n* see KIBOSH.

kyle *n Scot* often in place names: a narrow sea channel.

kylie *n Aus* a type of boomerang.

kyphosis *n* an abnormal curvature of the spine resulting in a humped back: compare LORDOSIS, SCOLIOSIS.

Kyrgyz /'kiəgiz, kiə'geez/ *or* **Kirghiz** *n* (*pl* **Kyrgyz** *or* **Kirghiz**) **1** a member of a Mongolian people inhabiting chiefly the Central Asian steppes. **2** the language of this people. ➤➤ **Kyrgyz** *adj.*

Kyrie *n* a short prayer that begins with or consists of the words 'Kyrie eleison' or their English translation 'Lord, have mercy'.

Kyrie eleison *n* = KYRIE.

L

L[1] *or* **l** *n* (*pl* **L's** *or* **Ls** *or* **l's**) **1** the twelfth letter of the English alphabet. **2** the Roman numeral for 50.

L[2] *abbr* **1** Large (clothing size). **2** *Brit* learner driver. **3** lost (used in tables of match results).

l *abbr* **1** lake. **2** left. **3** length(s). **4** line. **5** litre(s). **6** *archaic* pound(s).

LA *abbr* **1** Los Angeles. **2** Louisiana (US postal abbreviation).

La *abbr* the chemical symbol for lanthanum.

la *or* **lah** *n* in music, the sixth note of a major scale in the tonic sol-fa system.

laager[1] *n SAfr* **1** formerly, an encampment protected by a circle of wagons. **2** an entrenched position or point of view.

laager[2] *v SAfr* formerly, to arrange (wagons) in a laager.

lab *n informal* a laboratory.

label[1] *n* **1** a slip, e.g. of paper or cloth, attached to something to give information about it. **2** a brand name, *esp* the name of a fashion house or a record company. **3** a descriptive or identifying word or phrase. **4** in chemistry or biology, a radioactive ISOTOPE (form in which an atom can occur), a fluorescent dye, or an enzyme used to follow through a chemical reaction or biological process. **5** in computing, a number or word that identifies a location within a computer program.

label[2] *v* (**labelled, labelling,** *NAm* **labeled, labeling**) **1** to fasten a label to (an item). **2** to describe or categorize (somebody or something), *esp* unfairly or sweepingly. **3** to make (a chemical compound, atom, cell, etc) traceable using a label.

labia *n* pl of LABIUM.

labial *adj* relating to or in the region of the lips or labia.

labiate *adj* belonging or relating to the family of plants that have petals or sepals that project one over the other like lips, e.g. mint, thyme, and sage.

labile *adj* **1** in chemistry, liable to break down; unstable. **2** *technical* apt to change.

labium *n* (*pl* **labia**) **1** a lower mouthpart of an insect. **2** (*in pl*) the outer and inner folds of the vulva.

labor[1] *n NAm, Aus* see LABOUR[1].

labor[2] *v NAm, Aus* see LABOUR[2].

laboratory *n* (*pl* **-ies**) **1** a place equipped for scientific experiment, testing, or analysis. **2** a place where chemicals and chemical products are developed.

labored *adj NAm* see LABOURED.

laborer *n NAm* see LABOURER.

laborious *adj* **1** requiring a lot of time or effort. **2** of writing: lacking ease of expression; laboured. ➤➤ **laboriously** *adv*, **laboriousness** *n*.

laborite *n NAm* see LABOURITE.

labour[1] (*NAm, Aus* **labor**) *n* **1** work, *esp* when difficult or done for wages; toil. **2** workers collectively. **3** (**Labour**) (*used as sing. or pl*) the Labour Party. **4** the process of childbirth.

labour[2] (*NAm, Aus* **labor**) *v* **1a** to work hard. **b** to do unskilled manual work. **2** to struggle to do something difficult. **3** to move with difficulty. **4** (+ under) to be misled by (something). **5** to deal with or explain in laborious detail.

labour camp *n* a prison camp in which inmates are forced to work.

Labour Day *n* a public holiday in recognition of working people, held in some countries on 1 May, and in the USA and Canada on the first Monday in September.

laboured (*NAm* **labored**) *adj* **1** showing signs of effort; lacking natural grace or easy fluency. **2** performed with great effort.

labourer (*NAm* **laborer**) *n* a person who does unskilled manual work, *esp* outdoors.

labour-intensive *adj* using a high proportion of labour in the process of production.

labourite (*NAm* **laborite**) *n* (*often* **Labourite**) a member or supporter of a Labour party.

labour of love *n* a task performed for the pleasure it yields rather than for personal gain.

Labour Party *n* in Britain, a political party founded in 1900 to represent working people, based on socialist principles.

labour-saving *adj* designed to replace or decrease manual labour.

labra *n* pl of LABRUM.

Labrador *n* a retriever of a gold-coloured or black breed originating in Newfoundland.

labradorite *n* a mineral that is a variety of feldspar occurring in igneous rocks.

Labrador retriever *n* = LABRADOR.

labrum *n* (*pl* **labra**) an upper or front mouthpart of a crustacean, insect, or other arthropod.

laburnum *n* a shrub or tree of the pea family with bright yellow flowers that hang in clusters and pods of poisonous seeds.

labyrinth *n* **1** a place that is a network of intricate passageways, tunnels, blind alleys, etc. **2** something perplexingly complex or tortuous in structure or arrangement. **3** in anatomy, the complex network of twisting bony cavities that forms the inner ear. ➤➤ **labyrinthine** *adj.*

lac[1] *n* a resinous substance secreted by a scale insect and used to make varnishes, including shellac.

lac[2] *n* see LAKH.

laccolith *n* a mass of igneous rock that is forced up between beds of existing rock and produces domed bulging of the overlying strata.

lace[1] *n* **1** a fine decorative cotton or silk fabric made by twisting or looping thread in symmetrical patterns and figures. **2** a cord or string used for drawing together two edges, e.g. of a garment or shoe.

lace[2] *v* **1** to fasten (something, e.g. a shoe) by means of a lace. **2** to entwine or interlace (*esp* the fingers). **3** to add a dash of an alcoholic drink to (*esp* another drink).

lacerate *v* to tear or cut (skin or flesh) roughly. ➤➤ **laceration** *n.*

lacewing *n* an insect that has wings with a fine network of veins, long antennae, and very bright eyes.

lachrymal *or* **lacrimal** *or* **lacrymal** *adj* **1** *formal or literary* causing tears to be shed or marked by the shedding of tears. **2** (**lacrimal**) relating to or in the region of the glands that produce tears.

lachrymatory *or* **lacrimatory** *adj* **1** *literary* prompting tears. **2** in medicine, relating to tears or the shedding of tears.

lachrymose *adj formal or literary* **1** tearful. **2** sad or mournful.

lacing *n* **1** a laced fastening. **2** a dash of spirits added to food or drink.

lack[1] *v* **1** to suffer from the absence or deficiency of. **2** (*often* + in) to be deficient in something. **3** (*usu* + for) to be short of or have need of something.

lack[2] *n* an absence or shortage of something.

lackadaisical *adj* **1** lacking enthusiasm or zest. **2** reprehensibly casual or negligent; lax. ➤➤ **lackadaisically** *adv.*

lackey *n* (*pl* **-eys**) **1** a servant, *esp* a liveried footman. **2** a servile follower; a toady.

lacklustre (*NAm* **lackluster**) *adj* **1** lacking in vitality or enthusiasm; uninspired. **2** lacking in sheen or radiance; dull.

laconic *adj* using a minimum of words; terse or concise. ➤➤ **laconically** *adv.*

lacquer[1] *n* **1** a clear or coloured varnish obtained by dissolving a substance, e.g. shellac, in a solvent, e.g. alcohol. **2** the sap of the lacquer tree, used as a wood varnish. **3** *Brit* a substance sprayed onto the hair to fix it in place. **4** decorative wooden articles that have been coated with lacquer.

lacquer[2] *v* to coat or spray with lacquer.

lacquer tree *n* an E Asian tree with a sap from which a hard-wearing varnish is obtained.

lacrimal *adj* see LACHRYMAL.

lacrimatory *adj* see LACHRYMATORY.

lacrosse *n* a game played between teams of ten players who try to throw a ball into the opposing side's goal with a long-handled stick that has a triangular head with a loose mesh pouch.

lacrymal *adj* see LACHRYMAL.

lactate[1] *v* of a female mammal: to produce or secrete milk.

lactate[2] *n* a chemical salt or ester formed by combination between lactic acid and a metal atom, an alcohol, or another chemical group.

lactation *n* **1** the production of milk by the mammary glands. **2** the period during which milk is produced and the young are suckled.

lacteal[1] *adj* conveying or containing a milky fluid.

lacteal[2] *n* any of the lymphatic vessels that convey CHYLE (type of lymph) to the thoracic duct.

lactic *adj* relating to or obtained from milk.

lactic acid *n* an organic acid formed in the muscles during strenuous exercise and found in sour milk.

lactose *n* a sugar that is present in milk and consists of glucose and galactose.

lacto-vegetarian *n* a vegetarian who eats dairy products such as milk and cheese, sometimes including eggs.

lacuna *n* (*pl* **lacunae** *or* **lacunas**) **1** a blank space or a missing part. **2** in anatomy, a small cavity in a bone or other body part. ➤➤ **lacunar** *adj.*

lacustrine *adj technical or literary* of or occurring in lakes.

lacy *adj* (**-ier, -iest**) resembling or consisting of lace.

lad *n* **1** *informal* a boy or young man. **2** *chiefly Brit, informal* a man with whom other men socialize. **3** *Brit, informal* a boisterous or macho man.

ladder[1] *n* **1** a structure for climbing up or down that has two long sidepieces of metal, wood, rope, etc joined at intervals by crosspieces on which one steps. **2** a hierarchy seen as having steps or stages allowing for advancement. **3** *Brit* a vertical line in hosiery or knitting caused by stitches becoming unravelled.

ladder[2] *v Brit* to cause a ladder to develop in (e.g. tights), or to become damaged by a ladder.

ladder-back *n* a chair with a back consisting of two upright posts connected by horizontal slats.

ladder stitch *n* an embroidery stitch consisting of transverse bars worked between raised lines.

laddie *n chiefly Scot, informal* a boy or young man.

laddish *adj* characteristic of some young men, *esp* irritatingly rowdy or macho. ➤➤ **laddishness** *n.*

lade *v* (*past tense* **laded,** *past part.* **laden**) *archaic* to put a load on or in (a ship); to load.

laden *adj* carrying a heavy load.

ladette *n informal* a young woman who has an independent, liberated lifestyle and is seen as flouting the conventional ideas of femininity.

la-di-da *or* **lah-di-dah** *adj informal* affectedly refined, *esp* in voice and pronunciation.

ladies *pl n Brit* (*used as sing.*) a public lavatory for women.

ladies' fingers *pl n* see LADY'S FINGERS.

ladies' man *or* **lady's man** *n informal* a man who enjoys flirting with women.

Ladino /lə'deenoh/ *n* (*pl* **-os**) **1** a language spoken by some Sephardic Jews, a descendant of medieval Spanish. **2** a Spanish-American of mixed descent.

ladle[1] *n* a deep-bowled long-handled spoon. ➤➤ **ladleful** (*pl* **ladlefuls**) *n.*

ladle[2] *v* to serve with a ladle.

ladle out *v* to distribute lavishly or effusively.

lady *n* (*pl* **-ies**) **1** a woman of refinement or superior social position. **2** used in courteous or formal reference: a woman. **3** (**Lady**) a title given to a marchioness, countess, viscountess, baroness, or to the wife of a knight, baronet, or member of the peerage. ✱ **My Lady** used as a form of address to women judges and noblewomen.

ladybird *n* a small beetle of temperate and tropical regions, *esp* one that has red wing cases with black spots.

ladybug *n NAm* a ladybird.

lady chapel *n* (*often* **Lady Chapel**) a chapel dedicated to the Virgin Mary that is usu part of a larger church.

Lady Day *n* the feast of the Annunciation, observed on 25 March.

lady-in-waiting *n* (*pl* **ladies-in-waiting**) a woman appointed to wait on a queen or princess.

lady-killer *n informal* a man who captivates women.

ladylike *adj* resembling or befitting a well-bred woman or girl; refined and dignified.

lady's bedstraw *n* a common Eurasian plant that is a variety of bedstraw and has bright yellow flowers.

lady's fingers *or* **ladies' fingers** *pl n Brit* = OKRA.

ladyship *n* (*usu* **Your/Her Ladyship**) a title used to women with the rank of Lady.

lady's man *n* see LADIES' MAN.

lady's mantle *n* a perennial plant with broad flat leaves and clusters of delicate greenish flowers.

lady's slipper *n* an orchid with flowers that have a shape that suggests a slipper.

laevulose (*NAm* **levulose**) *n* = FRUCTOSE.

lag[1] *v* (**lagged, lagging**) (*often* + behind) to stay or fall behind, *esp* to fail to keep pace.

lag[2] *n* an interval between two events; a time lag or delay.

lag[3] *v* (**lagged, lagging**) to cover or provide (e.g. pipes) with lagging.

lag[4] *n Brit, informal* a convict or ex-convict.

lager *n* a light beer brewed by slow fermentation and usu served chilled.

lager lout *n Brit, informal* a drunken hooligan.

laggard[1] *n* a person who lags or lingers. ➤➤ **laggardly** *adv and adj.*

laggard[2] *adj* slow or reluctant.

lagging *n* material for thermal insulation, e.g. wrapped round pipes.

lagoon *n* **1** a shallow channel or pool usu separated from a larger body of water by a sand bank, reef, etc. **2** *NAm, Aus, NZ* a freshwater lake near a larger body of water.

lah *n* see LA.

lah-di-dah *adj* see LA-DI-DA.

laicize *or* **-ise** *v formal* to remove the religious or ecclesiastical element from; to secularize. ➤➤ **laicism** *n,* **laicization** *n.*

laid *v* past tense and past part. of LAY[1].

laid back *adj informal* relaxed or casual.

lain *v* past part. of LIE[1].

lair *n* **1** the resting or living place of a wild animal. **2** a refuge or place for hiding; a den.

laird *n Scot* a person who owns a large country estate.

laissez-faire *or* **laisser-faire** /ˌlesay ˈfeə/ *n* **1** a doctrine opposing government interference in economic affairs. **2** a deliberate refraining from interfering in the freedom and choices of others.

laity *n* (**the laity**) (*usu used as pl*) lay people.

lake[1] *n* a large inland body of water.

lake[2] *n* **1** a deep purplish red pigment orig prepared from lac or cochineal. **2** a vivid red colour; carmine.

lakh *or* **lac** *n* in India, the number 100,000.

Lallans *n* a literary form of the Scottish dialect spoken in the Lowlands of Scotland.

lam *v* (**lammed, lamming**) *informal* **1** to hit (somebody) hard. **2** (*usu* + into) to strike something with great force.

lama *n* **1** a title given to a Tibetan Buddhist spiritual leader. **2** a Tibetan or Mongolian Buddhist monk.

Lamarckism *n* a theory of evolution asserting that changes in the environment cause changes that are transmitted to offspring. ➤➤ **Lamarckian** *n and adj.*

lamasery *n* (*pl* **-ies**) a monastery of lamas.

lamb[1] *n* **1** a young sheep. **2** a meek or innocent person.

lamb[2] *v* **1** of a ewe: to give birth to lambs. **2** to tend (ewes) at lambing time. ➤➤ **lambing** *n.*

lambada /lamˈbahdə/ *n* a fast ballroom dance of Brazilian origin.

lambaste *or* **lambast** *v* to attack verbally; to censure.

lambda *n* the eleventh letter of the Greek alphabet (Λ, λ), equivalent to roman l.

lambent *adj literary* **1** playing lightly on or over a surface; flickering. **2** softly bright or radiant.

Lamb of God *n* (**the Lamb of God**) a title given to Jesus Christ.

Lambrusco *n* a variety of grape grown in N Italy, or the slightly sparkling wine produced from it.

lamb's lettuce *n* a plant of the valerian family with small green leaves that are eaten raw in salads.

lamb's tails *pl n Brit* the catkins that grow on a hazel tree.

lame[1] *adj* **1** having a leg or foot so disabled as to impair freedom of movement. **2** of a story or excuse: weak and unconvincing. **3** *informal* socially inept and lacking in street credibility. ➤➤ **lamely** *adv,* **lameness** *n.*

lame[2] *v* to make (a person or animal) lame.

lamé *n* a brocaded clothing fabric interwoven with metallic gold or silver threads.

lamebrain *n informal* a dull-witted person. ➤➤ **lamebrained** *adj.*

lame duck *n* **1** a weak or incapable person or thing. **2** *NAm* an elected officer or group continuing to hold office in the period before the inauguration of a successor.

lamella *n* (*pl* **lamellae** *or* **lamellas**) a thin flat scale, membrane, or part. ➤➤ **lamellar** *adj,* **lamellate** *adj.*

lamellibranch *n* a bivalve.

lament[1] *n* **1** an expression of grief; a wail. **2** a song or poem expressing grief.

lament[2] *v* **1** to feel or express grief or sorrow for (a person's loss or death); to mourn. **2** (+ for/over) to express regret, disappointment, or sorrow over something. ➤➤ **lamentation** *n.*

lamentable *adj* **1** that is to be regretted; regrettable. **2** woefully bad or inadequate; deplorable. ➤➤ **lamentably** *adv.*

lamina *n* (*pl* **laminae** *or* **laminas**) *technical* a thin plate, scale, layer, or flake. ➤➤ **laminar** *adj.*

laminar flow *n* a smooth nonturbulent flow of gases or liquids passing over or near a solid usu streamlined surface.

laminate[1] *v* **1** to overlay (something) with a thin sheet or sheets of material, e.g. metal or plastic. **2** to make (e.g. a building material) by uniting superimposed layers of one or more materials. **3** to separate (a substance) into layers. **4** to roll or compress (e.g. metal) into a thin plate or plates. ➤➤ **lamination** *n,* **laminator** *n.*

laminate[2] *n* a product made by laminating.

laminate[3] *adj* covered with or consisting of a lamina or laminae.

lamington *n* a cake made by dipping a cube of sponge cake in chocolate and coconut.

Lammas *or* **Lammas Day** *n* 1 August, formerly celebrated in England as a harvest festival.

lammergeier *or* **lammergeyer** *n* a large vulture that lives in mountain regions from the Pyrenees to northern China.

lamp *n* **1** a container filled with an inflammable substance, e.g. oil or gas, that is burned to give out artificial light. **2** a usu portable electric device containing a light bulb. **3** any of various light-emitting devices, e.g. a sunlamp, that produce electromagnetic radiation, e.g. heat radiation.

lampblack *n* a pigment made from finely powdered black soot.

lampoon[1] *v* to make (somebody or something) the subject of a satire; to ridicule.

lampoon[2] *n* a satirical attack on a person, literary work, etc.

lamprey *n* (*pl* **-eys**) an eel-like aquatic vertebrate that has a large sucking mouth with no jaws.

LAN *abbr* local area network.

Lancashire hotpot *n* a meat and vegetable stew with a topping of sliced potatoes.

Lancastrian *n* **1** a native or inhabitant of Lancashire or Lancaster. **2** an adherent of the English royal house of Lancaster that ruled from 1399 to 1461. ➤➤ **Lancastrian** *adj.*

lance[1] *n* **1** a weapon with a long shaft and a sharp steel head, carried by horsemen for use when charging. **2** a metal pipe or tube through which oxygen is directed, e.g. to pierce a hot metal surface.

lance[2] *v* **1** to open (e.g. a boil) with a lancet or other sharp instrument. **2** to pierce with a lance or other sharp weapon or instrument.

lance corporal *n* a non-commissioned officer of the lowest rank in the British army, Royal Marines, and US Marines.

lancelet *n* a small translucent marine animal that lives buried in sand.

lanceolate *adj technical* tapering to a point at the apex and sometimes at the base.

lancer *n* **1** a soldier who carries a lance. **2** (**Lancer**) a member of a regiment armed with lances. **3** (*in pl, used as sing.*) a set of five quadrilles each danced to music in a different time.

lancet *n* a sharp-pointed and usu two-edged surgical instrument used to make small incisions.

lancet window *n* a high window composed of one or more narrow pointed openings.

Lancs *abbr* Lancashire.

Land /land/ *n* (*pl* **Länder** /'lendə/) any of the provinces of Germany or Austria.

land[1] *n* **1** the solid part of the earth's surface, as distinct from seas, lakes, rivers, etc. **2** ground owned as property or attached to a building. **3** a particular country, region, or state. ✱ **how the land lies** how things are in a particular situation. **in the land of the living** alive; conscious. ➤➤ **landless** *adj.*

land[2] *v* **1** to bring (e.g. an aeroplane) to a surface from the air. **2** of an aircraft, bird, etc: to alight on a surface. **3** to set or put (somebody or something) on shore from a ship. **4** to go ashore from a ship; to disembark. **5** of a boat, ship, etc: to come to shore. **6** to arrive in a ship, aircraft, etc. **7** *informal* to gain or secure. **8** to catch and bring in (a fish). **9** *informal* (+ in) to put (somebody) in a specified place, position, or condition. **10** *informal* to cause (a blow) to hit somebody. **11** *informal* (+ with) to present or burden (somebody) with something unwanted. **12** to strike or come to rest on a surface, e.g. after a fall.

land agent *n* **1** *Brit* the manager of a large country estate. **2** a person who buys and sells land on behalf of clients.

landau *n* a four-wheeled carriage with a folding top divided into two sections.

land bridge *n* a piece of land connecting two areas of land, e.g. continents, that are now separate.

land crab *n* a crab that lives mostly on land and breeds in the sea.

landed *adj* **1** owning land, *esp* through inheritance. **2** consisting of or including land.

Länder /'lendə/ *n* pl of LAND.

lander *n* a space vehicle that is designed to land on the moon, a planet, etc.

landfall *n* **1** the act or an instance of sighting or reaching land after a voyage or flight. **2** the collapse of a mass of land, *esp* one that causes a route to be blocked.

landfill *n* **1** the disposal of rubbish by burying it in a pit or natural depression and then covering it with earth. **2** rubbish that is disposed of in this way.

landform *n* a natural feature of the earth's surface, e.g. a mountain.

landgirl *n Brit* a member of the Women's Land Army during the two World Wars.

landgrave *n* a title given to certain German princes.

landholder *n* the owner or occupier of an area of land.

landing *n* **1** the act of coming or bringing something to land. **2** a place for discharging and taking on passengers and cargo. **3** a level space at the end of a flight of stairs or between two flights of stairs.

landing craft *n* a naval craft designed for putting troops and equipment ashore.

landing gear *n* the undercarriage of an aircraft.

landing stage *n* a platform for landing passengers or cargo from a ship.

landlady *n* (*pl* **-ies**) **1** a woman who owns land, buildings, or accommodation for lease or rent. **2** a woman who keeps a guesthouse, lodging house, or pub.

land-line *n* a telecommunications link using cables as opposed to radio transmission.

landlocked *adj* completely or almost completely enclosed by land.

landlord *n* **1** a person, usu a man, who owns land, buildings, or accommodation for lease or rent. **2** a person, usu a man, who keeps a guesthouse, lodging house, or pub.

landlubber *n informal* a person unacquainted with the sea or seamanship.

landmark *n* **1** a conspicuous object that can be used to identify a locality. **2** an event that marks a turning point or new development.

landmass *n* a continent or other large mass of land.

landmine *n* an explosive mine hidden just below the surface of the ground.

landowner *n* a person who owns large areas of land. ➤➤ **landownership** *n,* **landowning** *adj and n.*

land rail *n* a corncrake.

landscape[1] *n* **1** an expanse of natural inland scenery. **2** a picture, drawing, etc of a landscape. **3** the distinctive features of a situation or area of intellectual activity. **4** (*used before a noun*) denoting a printed format in which the object or text is wider than it is high: compare PORTRAIT.

landscape[2] *v* to improve (a natural landscape). ⋙ **landscaper** *n.*

landscape architect *n* a person who designs the features of the outdoor environment in a particular area of land. ⋙ **landscape architecture** *n.*

landscape gardener *n* a person who designs and arranges the layout of gardens and grounds. ⋙ **landscape gardening** *n.*

landslide *n* **1** a usu rapid movement of rock, earth, etc down a slope, or the moving mass of rock, earth, etc itself. **2** an overwhelming victory in an election.

landslip *n chiefly Brit* a small landslide.

landsman *n* (*pl* **landsmen**) a person who knows little of the sea or seamanship.

land up *v* to end up at or in a place or situation.

landward[1] *or* **landwards** *adv* to or towards the land.

landward[2] *adj* lying or being towards the land or on the side towards the land.

landwards *adv* see LANDWARD[1].

lane *n* **1** a narrow passageway or road, *esp* between fences or hedges. **2** a strip of road for a single line of vehicles, e.g. on a motorway. **3** any of several marked parallel courses to which a competitor must keep during a race, e.g. in running or swimming. **4** a fixed route used by ships or aircraft.

langlauf /'lang·lowf/ *n* cross-country running or racing on skis.

langouste /'longgoohst/ *n* a spiny lobster, *esp* when cooked.

langoustine /'longgoosteen/ *n* a Norway lobster.

language *n* **1a** the ability to make and use audible, articulate, and meaningful sound by the action of the vocal organs. **b** a systematic means of communicating ideas or feelings by the use of conventionalized signs, sounds, gestures, or marks that have understood meanings. **2a** the words, their pronunciation, and the methods of combining them that are used and understood by a particular community. **b** the specialized vocabulary and phraseology belonging to a particular group or profession. **c** a formal system of signs and symbols, e.g. for use in programming a computer, together with rules for their use. **3** a particular form or manner of verbal expression; *specif* style. ✱ **speak the same language** to have the same interests, ideas, etc.

language laboratory *n* a room, usu divided into booths equipped with tape recorders, where foreign languages are learned by listening and speaking.

langue de chat /longg də 'shah/ *n* a long thin finger-shaped piece of chocolate or crisp biscuit.

languid *adj* **1** without energy; spiritless or apathetic. **2** drooping or flagging from fatigue or exhaustion; weak. ⋙ **languidly** *adv,* **languidness** *n.*

languish *v* **1** to be or become feeble. **2** to suffer hardship or neglect. **3** *archaic* (*often* + for) to become dispirited or depressed; to pine.

languor *n* **1** weakness or weariness of body or mind. **2** a feeling or mood of wistfulness or dreaminess. **3** heavy or soporific stillness of the air. ⋙ **languorous** *adj,* **languorously** *adv.*

langur *n* a slender long-tailed monkey native to Asia, with a very loud cry.

laniard *n* see LANYARD.

lank *adj* **1** of hair: straight and limp. **2** thin and unhealthy-looking; gaunt.

lanky *adj* (**-ier, -iest**) tall, thin, and ungraceful. ⋙ **lankily** *adv,* **lankiness** *n.*

lanolin *or* **lanoline** *n* wool grease, *esp* when refined for use in ointments and cosmetics.

lantern *n* **1** a portable protective case with transparent windows that houses a light, e.g. a candle. **2** the chamber in a lighthouse containing the light. **3** a structure above an opening in a roof which has glazed or open sides for light or ventilation.

lantern fish *n* a small deep-sea fish that has rows of luminous spots on its body.

lantern jaw *n* a long narrow lower jaw that projects beyond the upper jaw, *esp* one that gives the cheeks and face a hollow appearance. ⋙ **lantern-jawed** *adj.*

lantern slide *n* a transparency, *esp* of glass, formerly used for projecting pictures with a magic lantern.

lanthanide *n* any one of a series of chemical elements of increasing atomic numbers beginning with lanthanum and ending with lutetium.

lanthanum *n* a silver-white metallic chemical element of the rare-earth group that is soft and malleable, and is used in alloys.

lanyard *or* **laniard** *n* **1** a piece of rope or line for fastening something on board ship or for extending or tightening rigging. **2** a cord worn round the neck as a decoration or to hold something, e.g. a whistle.

Laodicean *adj archaic* lukewarm or indifferent, *esp* with regard to religion or politics.

Laotian *n* a native or inhabitant of Laos. ⋙ **Laotian** *adj.*

lap[1] *n* the front part of the lower trunk and thighs of a seated person. ✱ **drop/fall into somebody's lap** to come to somebody easily or effortlessly. **drop something in somebody's lap** to cause something to become somebody's responsibility. **in the lap of luxury** in an environment of great ease, comfort, and wealth. **in the lap of the gods** beyond human influence or control. ⋙ **lapful** (*pl* **lapfuls**) *n.*

lap[2] *n* **1** one circuit round a closed course or track. **2** one stage of a journey. **3** a part of an object that overlaps another. **4** one complete turn, e.g. of a rope round a drum.

lap[3] *v* (**lapped, lapping**) **1** to overtake and thereby lead or increase the lead over (another contestant in a race) by a full circuit of a track. **2** *literary* (+ in) to hold or wrap (somebody or something) protectively in something. **3** to overlap or project beyond something.

lap[4] *v* (**lapped, lapping**) **1** of an animal: to take in (liquid) with the tongue. **2** of water: to flow or splash against (something) in little waves.

lap[5] *n* the act or sound of lapping.

laparoscopy *n* (*pl* **-ies**) a surgical procedure in which a fine fibre-optic tube is inserted into the abdomen or other bodily cavity to allow direct observation of the contents. ⋙ **laparoscope** *n,* **laparoscopic** *adj.*

laparotomy *n* (*pl* **-ies**) a surgical incision through the abdominal wall.

lap dancing *n* erotic dancing performed by a dancer who circulates among members of the audience, dancing closely to each in turn. ⋙ **lap dancer** *n.*

lapdog *n* **1** a small pet dog, *esp* one that is docile. **2** somebody who is completely controlled by or under the influence of somebody else.

lapel *n* a fold of the top front edge of a coat or jacket that is continuous with the collar.

lapidary[1] *adj* **1** of or relating to the cutting, polishing, and engraving of stones and gems. **2** of a literary style: elegant and dignified.

lapidary[2] *n* (*pl* **-ies**) a person who cuts, polishes, or engraves stones and gems.

lapis lazuli *n* **1** a rich blue semiprecious stone, used in making jewellery. **2** = ULTRAMARINE (1).

lap joint *n* a joint made by overlapping two ends or edges and fastening them together.

Laplander *n* a native or inhabitant of Lapland.

lap of honour *n Brit* a celebratory circuit of a track performed by a winning runner, driver, etc.

Lapp *n* **1** a member of a nomadic people of Lapland, a region of N Europe that covers N Scandinavia and the Kola peninsula of N Russia. **2** the language of the people of Lapland. ⋙ **Lapp** *adj.*

lappet *n* **1** a flat overlapping or hanging piece, *esp* of flesh or membrane, e.g. the wattle of a bird. **2** a fold or flap on a garment or headdress.

Lappish *n* = LAPP (2).

lapse[1] *n* **1** a slight error, e.g. of memory or in manners. **2** a fall or decline, *esp* a moral fall or decline. **3** a continuous passage or elapsed period; an interval. **4** in law, the termination of a right or privilege through failure to exercise it.

lapse[2] *v* **1** to go out of existence or use; to cease. **2** to become invalid, e.g. because of omission or negligence. **3** to abandon a religion or doctrine. **4a** to fall from a high level, e.g. of morals or manners, to one much lower. **b** (+ into) to return to a particular state, way of behaving, etc. **5** of time: to run its course; to pass.

laptop *n* a portable computer with an integral keyboard and a flat screen that folds down to form a lid.

lap up *v* **1** to drink (a liquid). **2** to take in eagerly or uncritically; to enjoy.

lapwing *n* a crested plover that is native to Europe, Africa, and Asia, noted for its shrill wailing cry.

larboard *n archaic* the left side of a boat or ship; port.

larceny *n* (*pl* **-ies**) *dated* theft of personal property.

larch *n* a tree of the pine family with short deciduous needles and tough wood.

lard[1] *n* a soft white solid fat obtained by rendering the abdominal fat of a pig, used in cooking. ⋙ **lardy** *adj.*

lard[2] *v* **1** to dress (e.g. meat) for cooking by inserting or covering with fat, bacon, etc. **2** (+ with) to intersperse or embellish (speech or writing) with something.

larder *n* a room or cupboard where food is stored; a pantry.

lardon *or* **lardoon** *n* a strip, e.g. of pork fat or bacon, with which meat is larded.

lardy cake *n Brit* a sweet cake made with yeast dough, dried fruit, and lard.

large[1] *adj* **1** great or relatively great in size, quantity, extent, etc. **2** dealing in great numbers or quantities or operating on an extensive scale. **3** having more than usual power, capacity, or scope; comprehensive. ⋙ **largeness** *n,* **largish** *adj.*

large[2] ✱ **at large 1** not imprisoned or restrained; at liberty. **2** as a whole.

large calorie *n* = CALORIE (2).

large intestine *n* the rear division of the vertebrate intestine that is divided into the caecum, colon, and rectum.

largely *adv* to a large extent; mostly.

large-scale *adj* involving great numbers or quantities.

largesse *or* **largess** *n* **1** generosity, *esp* to people regarded as occupying an inferior position. **2** something, e.g. money, given generously.

largo *adj and adv* of a piece of music: to be performed in a very slow and broad manner.

lari /'lahri/ *n* (*pl* **lari** *or* **laris**) **1** the basic monetary unit of Georgia. **2** a unit of currency in the Maldives, worth 100th of a rufiyaa.

lariat *n* a rope used as a lasso or for tethering animals.

lark[1] *n* a brown singing bird mostly of Europe, Asia, and northern Africa, e.g. a skylark.

lark[2] *n informal* **1** a prank or light-hearted adventure. **2** *Brit* a type of activity, *esp* one regarded as misguided or foolish. ⋙ **larky** *adj.*

lark[3] *v informal* (+ about/around) to have fun in a playful or mischievous way.

larkspur *n* a plant related to the delphinium, *esp* a cultivated annual delphinium grown for its bright irregular flowers.

larrikin *n Aus, NZ* **1** a hooligan or lout. **2** a maverick.

larva *n* (*pl* **larvae**) **1** the immature, wingless, and often wormlike feeding form that hatches from the egg of many insects and is transformed into a pupa or chrysalis from which the adult emerges. **2** the early form of an animal that undergoes metamorphosis before becoming an adult, e.g. a tadpole. ⋙ **larval** *adj.*

laryngeal *adj* relating to or in the region of the larynx.

larynges *n* pl of LARYNX.

laryngitis *n* inflammation of the larynx.

larynx *n* (*pl* **larynges** *or* **larynxes**) the upper part of the trachea of air-breathing vertebrates.

lasagne /lə'zanyə/ *n* **1** pasta in the form of broad flat sheets. **2** a baked dish of minced meat or vegetables in tomato sauce layered with lasagne, white sauce, and cheese.

lascivious *adj* showing or expressing an unseemly or offensive sexual interest. ⋙ **lasciviously** *adv,* **lasciviousness** *n.*

laser *n* a device that generates an intense narrow beam of light or other electromagnetic radiation of a single wavelength by using the natural oscillations of atoms or molecules.

laserdisc *n* a multimedia storage medium that looks like a large compact disc.

laser printer *n* a high-quality computer printer in which a laser writes a pattern of electrostatically charged dots that transfer a powdered pigment called toner onto paper.

lash[1] *v* **1** to strike (something or somebody) with a whip or similar object. **2** to beat hard against. **3** of an animal: to flick (the tail) quickly or sharply. **4** of rain: to beat against something. ⋙ **lasher** *n.*

lash[2] *n* **1** a stroke or blow with a whip. **2** the flexible part of a whip. **3** an eyelash.

lash[3] *v* to bind or fasten with a cord, rope, etc. ⋙ **lasher** *n.*

lashing[1] *n* a physical or verbal beating.

lashing[2] *n* a cord used for binding, wrapping, or fastening.

lashings *pl n Brit, informal* (+ of) an abundance of something.

lash out *v* **1** to make a sudden violent or physical attack; to hit out. **2** *Brit, informal* to spend money freely or recklessly.

lash-up *n chiefly Brit, informal* something improvised or makeshift.

lass *n chiefly Scot, N Eng* a girl or young woman.

Lassa fever *n* an acute severe virus disease of tropical countries that is often fatal.

lassi *n* a refreshing Indian drink made from natural yogurt blended with fruit or herbs.

lassie *n* = LASS.

lassitude *n* physical or mental fatigue; weariness.

lasso[1] *n* (*pl* **-os** *or* **-oes**) a rope or long thong of leather with a running noose that is used *esp* in N America for catching horses and cattle.

lasso[2] *v* (**lassoes** *or* **lassos, lassoed, lassoing**) to catch with a lasso. ➤➤ **lassoer** *n.*

last[1] *adj* **1** following all the rest; final in time or place. **2** least suitable or likely. **3** most up-to-date; latest. **4** next before the present. **5** being the only remaining. ✱ **on one's last legs** near the end of one's resources; on the verge of failure, exhaustion, etc.

last[2] *adv* **1** on the most recent occasion. **2** after all others; at the end. **3** (*used in combinations*) denoting the last or latest thing: *the last-born child.* **4** in conclusion; lastly.

last[3] *n* (*pl* **last**) **1** somebody or something that is last. **2** (**the last**) the final moments of something, *esp* of somebody's life. ✱ **at last/at long last** after everything; after much delay. **the last of** the remaining part, amount, etc of something.

last[4] *v* **1** to continue in time; to go on. **2** to continue to live. **3** to remain in good or adequate condition, use, or effectiveness; to endure. **4** to continue to be available or unexhausted; to be sufficient or enough. **5** to be enough for the needs of (somebody) during a length of time.

last[5] *n* a shoemaker's metal model of the human foot, over which a shoe is shaped or repaired.

last-ditch *adj* made as a final effort, *esp* to avert disaster.

last-gasp *adj informal* done at the very last moment.

lasting *adj* existing or continuing for a long while; enduring. ➤➤ **lastingly** *adv,* **lastingness** *n.*

Last Judgment *n* the final judgment of humankind before God at the end of the world.

lastly *adv* at the end; last.

last minute *n* the moment just before a climactic, decisive, or disastrous event.

last name *n* a surname.

last out *v* **1** to be sufficient. **2** to survive.

last post *n* **1** the second of two bugle calls sounded at the hour for retiring in a military camp. **2** a bugle call sounded at a military funeral or tattoo.

last rites *pl n* rites performed by a Roman Catholic priest for somebody who is about to die.

Last Supper *n* the supper eaten by Jesus and his disciples on the night of his betrayal.

last thing *adv* as the final action, *esp* before going to bed.

last word *n* **1** the definitive statement or treatment of something. **2** the most up-to-date or fashionable example of its kind. **3** the final remark in a verbal exchange.

lat *n* (*pl* **lati** *or* **lats**) the basic monetary unit of Latvia.

lat. *abbr* latitude.

latch[1] *n* **1** a fastener, e.g. for a gate, with a pivoted bar that falls into a notch on the gatepost. **2** a fastener, e.g. for a door, in which a spring slides a bolt into a hole.

latch[2] *v* to fasten (e.g. a door) with a latch.

latchkey *n* a key to an outside door, *esp* the front door of a house.

latchkey child *n* a child whose parents are still at work when he or she comes home from school.

latch on *v* **1** to understand something. **2** to take up something enthusiastically. **3** to attach oneself to somebody or something.

late[1] *adj* **1** occurring or arriving after the expected time. **2** happening or belonging far on in a particular time or period. **3** far on in the day or night. **4a** recently deceased. **b** former. **5** very recent. ✱ **late in the day** at a late stage. ➤➤ **lateness** *n.*

late[2] *adv* **1** after the usual or proper time. **2** at or near the end of a period of time or of a process. **3** far on in the day or night. **4** (+ of) until lately. ✱ **of late** in the period shortly or immediately before; recently.

latecomer *n* somebody who arrives late.

lateen *adj* denoting a rig characterized by a triangular sail hung from a long spar set at an angle on a low mast.

lately *adv* recently; of late.

latent *adj* present but not manifest or active. ➤➤ **latency** *n,* **latently** *adv.*

latent heat *n* heat given off or absorbed in a change of phase, e.g. from a solid to a liquid, without a change in temperature.

latent image *n* the invisible image first produced on photographic film, paper, etc by a reaction with light which is then made visible, usu by chemical developers.

latent period *n* the incubation period of a disease.

later *adv* **1** afterwards. **2** at a time in the future.

lateral[1] *adj* situated on, directed towards, or coming from the side. ➤➤ **laterally** *adv.*

lateral[2] *n* a lateral part of something, e.g. a side branch or root.

lateral thinking *n chiefly Brit* thinking that concentrates on unexpected aspects of a problem or that proceeds by seemingly illogical methods.

laterite *n* a usu red clay formed from rock decay and consisting *esp* of iron oxides and aluminium hydroxides.

latest *n* the most recent news or style. ✱ **at the latest** no later than the specified time.

latex *n* (*pl* **latices** *or* **latexes**) **1** a milky usu white fluid that is produced by various flowering plants and is the source of rubber and chewing gum. **2** a water emulsion of a synthetic rubber or plastic, used in paints and other liquid preparations.

lath *n* a thin narrow strip of wood, *esp* for nailing to woodwork, e.g. rafters or studding, as a support for tiles or plaster.

lathe *n* a machine for shaping wood or metal. The work is rotated about a horizontal axis and shaped by a fixed tool.

lather[1] *n* **1** a foam or froth formed when a detergent, e.g. soap, is agitated in water. **2** foam or froth on a horse's skin from profuse sweating. **3** *informal* an agitated or overwrought state.

lather[2] *v* **1** to form a lather or cause (soap) to form a lather. **2** to rub (something) until a lather is produced. **3** (+ with) to spread something with (a substance). **4** *informal* to beat or defeat (somebody); to thrash.

lathi /'lahti/ *n* a heavy stick often of bamboo bound with iron used in India as a weapon, *esp* by police.

latices *n* pl of LATEX.

Latin[1] *n* **1** the Italic language of ancient Rome and the Roman Empire. **2** a member of any of the peoples whose language developed from Latin. **3** *chiefly NAm* a native or inhabitant of Latin America.

Latin[2] *adj* **1** of or relating to Latin. **2** of the peoples or countries using Romance languages. **3** *chiefly NAm* of the peoples or countries of Latin America. **4** relating to those branches of the Christian Church that use a Latin liturgy; *specif* Roman Catholic.

Latina /la'teenə/ *n NAm* a girl or woman of Latin American or Spanish American descent.

Latin American *n* a native or inhabitant of a part of the American continent where Spanish or Portuguese is spoken. ⪢ **Latin American** *adj.*

Latinate *adj* of, resembling, or derived from Latin.

Latin cross *n* a plain cross consisting of a long upright bar crossed near the top by a shorter transverse bar.

latinise *v* see LATINIZE.

Latinism *n* **1** a characteristic feature of Latin occurring in another language. **2** a Latin quality, character, or mode of thought.

latinize *or* **-ise** *v* **1** to give a Latin form to (a word). **2** to make (something) Latin in doctrine, ideas, or traits; *specif* to cause (something) to conform to the Roman Catholic Church. ⪢ **latinization** *n.*

Latino /la'teenoh/ *n* (*pl* **-os**) *NAm* a person of Latin American or Spanish American descent.

latitude *n* **1** the angular distance of a point on the surface of the earth measured North or South from the equator. **2** (*in pl*) regions as marked by their latitude. **3** freedom of action or choice. ⪢ **latitudinal** *adj*, **latitudinally** *adv.*

latitudinarian *adj* liberal in standards of religious belief and conduct. ⪢ **latitudinarian** *n*, **latitudinarianism** *n.*

latke *n* in Jewish cookery, a fried pancake, *esp* one made from grated potato.

latrine *n* a small pit used as a toilet, *esp* in a military camp or barracks.

latte /'lahtay/ *n* a caffè latte.

latter[1] *adj* **1** near the end; later. **2** recent or present. **3** second of two things mentioned or understood.

latter[2] *n* (*pl* **latter**) the second mentioned.

Usage note

latter *and* **former**. See note at FORMER[2].

latter-day *adj* of present or recent times, *esp* referring to somebody resembling somebody in the past.

Latter-Day Saint *n* a Mormon.

latterly *adv* **1** recently. **2** towards the end or latter part of a period.

lattice *n* **1** a framework or structure of crossed wooden or metal strips with open spaces between. **2** a network or design like a lattice. **3** a regular geometrical arrangement of points or objects over an area or in space. ⪢ **latticed** *adj.*

lattice window *n* a window with very small panes fitted in leaded, diamond-shaped panels.

latticework *n* a design or structure made of lattices.

Latvian *n* **1** a native or inhabitant of Latvia. **2** the language of the people of Latvia. ⪢ **Latvian** *adj.*

laud *v formal* to praise (somebody or something) enthusiastically or generously. ⪢ **laudation** *n.*

laudable *adj* worthy of praise; commendable. ⪢ **laudably** *adv.*

laudanum *n* any of various preparations of opium formerly used in medicine, *esp* as painkillers.

laudatory *adj* expressing praise.

lauds *pl n* a religious service usu immediately following matins.

laugh[1] *v* **1** to make the explosive vocal sounds characteristically expressing amusement, mirth, joy, or derision. **2** (+ at) to ridicule (somebody or something); to make fun of. ✱ **be laughing** *informal* to be successful or fortunate. **laugh on the other side of one's face** to be embarrassed after feeling confident or proud. **laugh up one's sleeve** to be secretly amused. ⪢ **laugher** *n.*

laugh[2] *n* **1** the act or an instance of laughing. **2** (*also in pl*) a means of entertainment; a diversion. **3** *informal* a cause for derision or merriment; a joke. ✱ **have the last laugh** to be proved right, successful, etc.

laughable *adj* provoking laughter or derision; ridiculous. ⪢ **laughably** *adv.*

laughing gas *n* = NITROUS OXIDE.

laughing jackass *n Aus* the kookaburra.

laughing stock *n* an object of ridicule.

laugh off *v* to minimize or dismiss (something) by treating it as amusingly trivial.

laughter *n* **1** the sound of laughing. **2** the action of laughing.

launch[1] *v* **1** to set (a boat or ship) afloat. **2** to release or send off (e.g. a rocket). **3** to start or set (something or somebody) in motion, e.g. on a course or career. **4** to introduce (a new product) onto the market. **5** to throw (oneself) forward. **6** (+ into) to begin to do something energetically and with commitment.

launch[2] *n* an act or an instance of launching something.

launch[3] *n* **1** a large motorboat. **2** formerly, the largest boat carried by a warship.

launcher *n* a device for launching rockets, missiles, etc.

launder *v* **1** to make (clothes) ready for use again by washing and ironing. **2** *informal* to pass (money obtained illegally) through a bank or legal business. ⪢ **launderer** *n.*

launderette *or* **laundrette** *n* a self-service laundry providing coin-operated machines.

laundress *n* a woman who launders clothes and linen as a job.

laundrette *n* see LAUNDERETTE.

laundry *n* (*pl* **-ies**) **1** clothes and linen that have been or are to be washed and dried. **2** a place where laundering is done, *esp* a commercial laundering establishment.

laureate[1] *n* **1** a person specially honoured for achievement in an art or science. **2** a Poet Laureate. ⪢ **laureateship** *n.*

laureate[2] *adj literary* crowned with laurel as a token of preeminence or honour.

laurel *n* **1** an evergreen tree or shrub that has smooth shiny leaves, small flowers, and oval-shaped berries. **2a** (*in pl*) a crown of laurel awarded as a token of victory or preeminence. **b** distinction or honour. ✱ **look to one's laurels** to take care that one's position is not lost to a rival. **rest on one's laurels** to become complacent in the wake of previous successes or achievements.

lava *n* molten rock that flows from a volcano or from a crack in the earth's surface.

lavage *n* the medical washing out of an organ, e.g. the colon.

lava lamp *n* an electric lamp containing a viscous liquid in which a lump of a coloured waxy substance stretches and forms blobs as the lamp warms up.

lavatorial *adj* **1** relating to lavatories. **2** characterized by excessive reference to lavatories and bodily functions.

lavatory *n* (*pl* **-ies**) a toilet or a room containing one or more toilets.

lave *v literary* to wash or bathe (somebody or something).

lavender *n* **1** a Mediterranean plant of the mint family widely cultivated for its narrow aromatic leaves and spikes of lilac or purple flowers which are traditionally dried and used in perfume sachets. **2** a pale purple colour. ➤➤ **lavender** *adj.*

lavender water *n* a perfume consisting of lavender oils and alcohol.

laver *n* an edible reddish purple seaweed.

lavish[1] *adj* **1** spent, given, or produced in abundance. **2** giving or spending profusely. ➤➤ **lavishly** *adv,* **lavishness** *n.*

lavish[2] *v* to spend or give with profusion.

law *n* **1a** a rule of conduct formally recognized as binding or enforced by authority. **b** the whole body of such rules, comprising common law, civil law, and statute law. **2** the science or philosophy of law; jurisprudence. **3** control or authority. **4** (**the law**) *informal* the police. **5a** a statement of an order or relation of natural phenomena. **b** a necessary relation between mathematical or logical expressions. **6** a rule of action or procedure in a sport. ✱ **be a law unto oneself** to be unconventional. **lay down the law** to give orders or express one's opinions with great force. **take the law into one's own hands** to do something, e.g. as an act of revenge, that is not strictly legal or can by law only be done by the police or other authorized people.

law-abiding *adj* abiding by or obedient to the law.

law agent *n* in Scotland, a solicitor.

lawbreaker *n* somebody who violates the law.

law centre *n* in Britain, a publicly funded centre dispensing free legal advice to members of the public.

lawful *adj* constituted, authorized, or allowed by law; rightful or legal. ➤➤ **lawfully** *adv,* **lawfulness** *n.*

lawgiver *n* a person who makes or gives laws.

lawless *adj* **1** not regulated by or based on law. **2** not restrained or controlled by law; unruly. ➤➤ **lawlessly** *adv,* **lawlessness** *n.*

Law Lord *n* in Britain, a member of the House of Lords qualified to take part in its judicial proceedings.

lawmaker *n* a legislator.

lawman *n* (*pl* **lawmen**) in the USA, a law-enforcement officer, e.g. a sheriff or police officer.

lawn[1] *n* an area of ground that is covered with mown grass.

lawn[2] *n* a fine sheer linen or cotton fabric.

lawn mower *n* a machine for cutting grass on lawns.

lawn tennis *n dated or formal* tennis played on a grass court.

law of averages *n* the principle that one extreme will always be cancelled out by its opposite at some future time, and the balance redressed.

law officer *n* a British attorney general or solicitor general.

lawrencium *n* a radioactive metallic chemical element that is short-lived and artificially produced.

lawsuit *n* a non-criminal case in a court of law.

lawyer *n* a person whose profession is to conduct lawsuits or to advise on legal matters.

lax *adj* **1** not strict or stringent; negligent. **2** not tense, firm, or rigid; relaxed or slack. ➤➤ **laxity** *n,* **laxly** *adv,* **laxness** *n.*

laxative *n* a medicinal preparation that loosens or relaxes the bowels to relieve constipation. ➤➤ **laxative** *adj.*

lay[1] *v* (*past tense and past part.* **laid**) **1** to put or set down on a surface. **2a** to spread (something) over or on a surface. **b** to set (something) in order or position for use: *to lay a table; to lay a fire.* **3** to impose as a duty or burden. **4a** to advance (a charge or accusation). **b** to assign (blame, emphasis, etc). **5** of a bird: to produce (an egg). **6** to place (a bet). **7** to exorcize (a ghost). **8** *coarse slang* to have sexual intercourse with. ✱ **lay about one** to lash out violently. **lay before** to present for consideration. **lay claim to** to claim as a right. **lay hands on 1** to seize forcibly. **2** to find. **lay into** *informal* to attack or criticize fiercely. **lay open** to explain or make known. **lay open to** to expose (somebody) to a risk. **lay to rest 1** to dispel (a fear or anxiety). **2** to bury (a body) in a grave.

lay[2] *n* **1** the position or situation in which something lies or has been laid. **2** *coarse slang* an act of sexual intercourse or a sexual partner.

lay[3] *v* past tense of LIE[1].

lay[4] *adj* **1** not belonging to the clergy; not ecclesiastical. **2** denoting domestic or manual workers in a religious community: *a lay brother.* **3** not belonging to a particular profession.

lay[5] *n* **1** a simple narrative poem intended to be sung; a ballad. **2** *literary* a song.

layabout *n* a lazy shiftless person.

lay aside *v* to dismiss or postpone.

lay by *v* to reserve for future use.

lay-by *n* (*pl* **lay-bys**) an area at the side of a road to allow vehicles to stop without obstructing traffic.

lay down *v* **1** to formulate (e.g. a rule). **2** to store (wine) in a cellar. **3** to sacrifice (one's life). **4** to begin to build (a ship or railway).

layer[1] *n* **1** a single thickness of some substance spread or lying over or under another. **2** a branch or shoot of a plant tied or staked so as to induce rooting while still attached to the parent plant. **3** somebody or something that lays.

layer[2] *v* **1** to arrange in layers. **2** to cut (hair) in layers. **3** to propagate (a plant) by means of layers.

layette *n* a complete outfit of clothing and equipment for a newborn baby.

lay in *v* to accumulate a supply for future use.

layman *n* (*pl* **laymen**) a male layperson.

layoff *n* **1** the laying off of an employee or workforce. **2** a period of unemployment, inactivity, or idleness.

lay off *v* **1** to cease to employ (a worker) because of a shortage of work. **2** *informal* **a** to avoid or give up: *lay off the beer.* **b** to stop doing something annoying. **c** to leave (somebody) alone.

lay on *v* to supply or organize.

layout *n* **1** the plan, design, or arrangement of something laid out, e.g. rooms in a building or material to be printed. **2** something laid out.

lay out *v* **1** to arrange or construct (something on the ground) according to a plan. **2** *informal* to make (somebody) unconscious. **3** *informal* to spend (an amount of money). **4** to prepare (a body) for burial.

layover *n NAm* a stop at an intermediate point in a journey.

layperson *n* (*pl* **laypeople**) **1** a person who is not a member of the clergy. **2** a person without special, e.g. professional, knowledge of some field.

lay reader *n* in the Anglican Church, a layperson authorized to conduct parts of church services but not to celebrate the Eucharist.

lay up *v* **1** to put into storage. **2** to take (a vehicle, etc) out of service. ✱ **be laid up** to be incapacitated by an illness or injury.

laywoman *n* (*pl* **laywomen**) a female layperson.

laze[1] *v* to act or rest lazily; to idle.

laze[2] *n* an instance of being lazy or idling.

lazy *adj* (**-ier, -iest**) **1** disinclined or averse to activity; indolent. **2** not energetic or vigorous. **3** encouraging inactivity or indolence: *a lazy afternoon.* ⋙ **lazily** *adv*, **laziness** *n.*

lazybones *n* (*pl* **lazybones**) *informal* a lazy person.

lazy eye *n* an eye with impaired vision, *esp* in a person with a squint.

lb *abbr* pound.

lbw *abbr* in cricket, leg before wicket.

l.c. *abbr* **1** Latin *loco citato*: in the place cited. **2** in printing, lower case.

LCD *abbr* **1** liquid crystal display. **2** (*also* **lcd**) lowest (or least) common denominator.

LCM *abbr* (*also* **lcm**) lowest (or least) common multiple.

LEA *abbr Brit* Local Education Authority.

lea *n chiefly literary* an area of grassland or pasture.

leach *v* to separate the soluble components from (e.g. soil or other mixed material) by the action of a liquid, *esp* water, passing through it.

lead[1] *v* (*past tense and past part.* **led**) **1a** to guide (a person or an animal) along a way, *esp* by going in front. **b** to cause (somebody) to go with one, *esp* under duress. **c** to direct or guide (somebody) on a course or to a state or condition; to influence. **2a** to be first or ahead. **b** to go or be at the head of. **c** to act as or be a leader in or of. **d** to direct the operations, activity, or performance of; to have charge of. **e** to be ahead of (a rival or rivals). **3** to have or go through (a specified kind of life); to live. **4** in card games, to begin play with (a card). **5** to serve as an entrance or passage. **6** to tend or be directed towards a specified result. ✱ **lead somebody astray** to encourage somebody to behave badly. **lead somebody a merry dance** to cause somebody a lot of trouble. **lead up to** to prepare the way for (something), *esp* by using a gradual or indirect approach.

lead[2] *n* **1a** a position at the front or ahead. **b** a margin or position of advantage or superiority. **c** guidance, direction, or example. **d** an indication or clue. **2** the act or privilege of leading in cards, or the card or suit led. **3** a principal role in a dramatic production, or an actor who plays a principal role. **4** a news story of chief importance. **5** *Brit* a line or strap for leading or restraining a dog. **6** an insulated wire or cable that conducts an electrical current.

lead[3] *n* **1** a bluish white metallic chemical element that is heavy and soft, and is used in pipes, batteries, shields against radioactivity, etc. **2** a thin stick of graphite or crayon in or for a pencil. **3a** the lead weight on a sounding line. **b** (*in pl*) lead framing for panes in windows. **c** in printing, a space between lines of type, or a thin strip of metal used to create this. **d** bullets or similar projectiles. **e** *Brit* (*in pl*) a flat roof covered with thin lead sheets, or the lead sheets themselves.

lead crystal *n* = LEAD GLASS.

leaded *adj* **1** of windows: made up of small panes fixed in position with leads. **2** of petrol: containing tetraethyl lead. **3** covered or weighted with lead.

leaden *adj* **1a** oppressively heavy. **b** lacking spirit or animation; sluggish. **2a** *archaic* made of lead. **b** dull grey. ⋙ **leadenly** *adv.*

leader *n* **1a** somebody or something that ranks first, precedes others, or holds a principal position. **b** somebody who has commanding authority or influence. **c** the principal officer of a political party, trade union, etc. **d** *Brit* either of two government ministers in charge of initiating business in Parliament. **e** somebody who guides or inspires others. **2** the principal first violinist of an orchestra. **3** *Brit* a newspaper editorial; a leading article. **4** a blank section at the beginning or end of a reel of film or recording tape. ⋙ **leaderless** *adj*, **leadership** *n.*

leader board *n* a board or other display that shows the scores of the leading competitors, e.g. in a golf tournament.

lead glass *n* glass containing lead monoxide, *esp* a tough brilliant high-quality glass containing 30% or more lead monoxide.

lead-in *n* introductory matter.

leading *adj* coming or ranking first; foremost.

leading aircraftman *or* **leading aircraftwoman** *n* a member of the Royal Air Force ranking below a senior aircraftman or senior aircraftwoman.

leading article *n Brit* a newspaper editorial.

leading edge *n* **1** the foremost edge of an aerofoil, e.g. a wing or propeller blade. **2** the most advanced position or group in a particular field of activity, *esp* technology.

leading lady *n* a female actor who plays a principal role in a film, play, etc.

leading light *n* a prominent and influential person in a particular sphere.

leading man *n* a male actor who plays a principal role in a film, play, etc.

leading question *n* a question so phrased as to suggest the desired answer.

leading seaman *n* a member of the Royal Navy ranking below a petty officer.

lead on *v* to cause (somebody) to believe that one is attracted to them.

lead time *n* the period between the initiation and the completion of a new production process.

leaf[1] *n* (*pl* **leaves**) **1a** a flat, usu green, and typically broad-bladed outgrowth from the stem of a plant that functions primarily in food manufacture by photosynthesis. **b** foliage, or the state of having foliage. **2a** a part of a book or folded sheet of paper containing a page on each side. **b** a part of a window shutter, folding door, or table that slides or is hinged. **c** a section that can be inserted into a tabletop to extend it. **d** metal, e.g. gold or silver, in sheets that are usu thinner than foil. ✱ **take a leaf out of somebody's book** to copy or imitate somebody's behaviour. **turn over a new leaf** to make a change for the better, *esp* in one's way of living. ⋙ **leafless** *adj.*

leaf[2] *v* of a plant: to produce leaves. ✱ **leaf through** to turn over the pages of (a book, magazine, etc) quickly while only glancing at the contents.

leafage *n* foliage.

leaflet[1] *n* **1** a single sheet of paper or small pamphlet containing printed matter, e.g. an advertisement or public information. **2a** a small or young foliage leaf. **b** any of the divisions of a compound leaf.

leaflet[2] *v* (**leafleted, leafleting**) to distribute leaflets to (people).

leaf mould *n* a compost or soil layer composed chiefly of decayed vegetable matter.

leaf spring *n* a spring made of superimposed metal strips.

leafy *adj* (**-ier, -iest**) **1** having abundant trees or foliage. **2** consisting chiefly of leaves. ⋙ **leafiness** *n.*

league[1] *n* **1a** an association of nations, groups, or people for a common purpose or to promote a common interest. **b** an association of people or sports clubs that organizes a competition for an overall title, in which each person or team plays all the others at least once. **2** a class or category. ✱ **in league** in alliance or conspiracy.

league² *v* to be formed or to form (nations, groups, or people) into a league.

league³ *n* a former unit of distance equal to about 3mi (5km).

league table *n* **1** a table showing the relative positions of competitors in a league. **2** a list in order of merit.

leak¹ *v* **1a** of a liquid, gas, etc: to enter or escape through a crack or hole, usu accidentally. **b** of a container: to let something enter or escape in this way. **2** (*often* + out) of information: to become known despite efforts at concealment. **3** to give out (information) surreptitiously. ⋙ **leakage** *n*, **leaker** *n*.

leak² *n* **1a** a crack or hole through which something, e.g. a liquid or gas, enters or escapes, usu accidentally. **b** a means by which information becomes known despite efforts at concealment. **2** an instance of leaking or something that leaks out. **3** *informal* an act of urinating. ✱ **spring a leak** of a vessel or container: to develop a leak.

leaky *adj* (**-ier, -iest**) permitting something to leak in or out; not watertight.

lean¹ *v* (*past tense and past part.* **leaned** *or* **leant**) **1a** to incline or bend from a vertical position. **b** (+ on/against) to rest supported on or against something. **2** (+ on/upon) to rely on somebody for support or inspiration. **3** (+ towards) to incline in a particular direction in opinion, taste, etc. **4** *informal* (+ on) to exert pressure on somebody to do something. **5** (+ on/against) to place (something) on or against something for support.

lean² *n* an instance or degree of leaning.

lean³ *adj* **1a** of a person or animal: lacking or deficient in flesh or bulk; thin. **b** of meat: containing little or no fat. **2** lacking richness, sufficiency, or value. **3a** deficient in an essential or important quality or ingredient. **b** of a fuel mixture: low in the combustible component. ⋙ **leanly** *adv*, **leanness** *n*.

lean⁴ *n* the part of meat that consists principally of fat-free muscular tissue.

lean-burn *adj* of an internal-combustion engine: using a reduced proportion of fuel in the fuel-air mixture, thus lessening fuel consumption and pollution from exhaust fumes.

leaning *n* an attraction, tendency, or partiality.

leant *v* past tense and past part. of LEAN¹.

lean-to *n* (*pl* **-os**) a small building with a roof that rests on the side of a larger building or wall.

leap¹ *v* (*past tense and past part.* **leaped** *or* **leapt**) **1** to jump in or through the air. **2a** to move or pass abruptly from one state, topic, etc to another, *esp* to rise quickly. **b** (+ at) to seize an opportunity, offer, etc eagerly. **3** to pass over (something) by leaping. ⋙ **leaper** *n*.

leap² *n* **1** a jump, or the distance covered by it. **2** a sudden transition, *esp* a rise or increase. ✱ **a leap in the dark** an action undertaken in uncertainty of the outcome. **by/in leaps and bounds** very rapidly.

leapfrog¹ *n* a game in which one player bends down and another leaps over them with legs apart.

leapfrog² *v* (**leapfrogged, leapfrogging**) **1** to leap over (somebody or something) in leapfrog. **2** to progress rapidly by passing over (rivals, obstacles, etc).

leapt *v* past tense and past part. of LEAP¹.

leap year *n* a year with an extra day added to make it coincide with the solar year, *esp* a year in the Gregorian calendar with 29 February as the 366th day.

learn *v* (*past tense and past part.* **learned** *or* **learnt**) **1a** to gain knowledge of or skill in. **b** to memorize. **c** to come to be able (to do something). **d** to come to realize or know. **2** *non-standard* to teach (somebody). ⋙ **learnable** *adj*, **learner** *n*.

Usage note

Learn is not used in standard English to mean 'teach'. It never takes a personal pronoun or a person's name as a direct object: *I learned my acting skills from her; she taught me to act.*

learned *adj* characterized by or associated with learning; erudite. ⋙ **learnedly** *adv*, **learnedness** *n*.

learning *n* acquired knowledge or skill, *esp* knowledge acquired by study or education.

learning curve *n* the rate at which somebody learns something, e.g. a new job or procedure, or the rate at which new knowledge has to be assimilated.

learning difficulties *pl n* difficulties in learning basic skills at the same rate as people of the same age, often caused by mental handicap.

learnt *v* past tense and past part. of LEARN.

lease¹ *n* a contract putting the land or property of one party at the disposal of another, usu for a stated period and rent. ✱ **new lease of life** a renewed period of healthy activity or usefulness.

lease² *v* **1** to grant (property) by lease. **2** to hold (property) under a lease. ⋙ **leasable** *adj*.

leaseback *n* an arrangement by which one party sells or gives something to another but continues to have the use of it in return for rent or hire.

leasehold *n* **1** tenure by lease. **2** property held by lease. ⋙ **leaseholder** *n*.

leash¹ *n* a line or strap for leading or restraining a dog.

leash² *v* to put (a dog) on a leash.

least¹ *adj* **1a** smallest in quantity or extent. **b** used in the names of plants and animals: of a kind distinguished by small size: *the least bittern*. **c** smallest possible; slightest: *I haven't the least idea.* **2** lowest in rank, degree, or importance.

least² *n* **1** the smallest number or amount. **2** somebody or something that is lowest in importance. ✱ **at least 1** as a minimum; if not more. **2** if nothing else; at any rate. **not in the least** not at all.

least³ *adv* to the smallest degree or extent. ✱ **least of all** especially not. **not least** especially.

leastways *adv chiefly dialect* at least; at any rate.

leastwise *adv* = LEASTWAYS.

leat *n Brit* a trench or ditch taking water to a watermill.

leather¹ *n* **1a** animal skin dressed for use. **b** (*used before a noun*) made of leather. **2 a** a piece of chamois or similar material used for polishing metal or glass. **b** (*in pl*) leather clothing, *esp* a motorcyclist's jacket and trousers.

leather² *v* **1** to cover with leather. **2** *informal* to beat (a person or animal) with a strap.

leatherback *n* the largest existing sea turtle, which has a flexible carapace composed of a mosaic of small bones embedded in a thick leathery skin.

leatherette *n* an imitation leather.

leatherjacket *n Brit* the tough-skinned larva of the crane fly.

leathern *adj archaic* made of leather.

leathery *adj* resembling leather in appearance or consistency, *esp* tough.

leave[1] *v* (*past tense and past part.* **left**) **1a** to go away from (a place). **b** to desert or abandon (somebody). **c** to withdraw from (an organization, institution, etc). **2** to put, station, deposit, or deliver (something), *esp* before departing: *The postman left a package for you; Leave your name with the receptionist.* **3a** to cause or allow (something or somebody) to be or remain in a specified or unaltered condition: *His manner left me cold; Leave the washing-up for tomorrow.* **b** (*also* + off/out) to fail to include, use, or take: *She left her notes at home; They left his name off the list.* **c** to permit (something) to be or remain subject to the action or control of a specified person or thing: *Just leave everything to me; We left nothing to chance.* **d** to allow (somebody) to do or continue something without interference. **4** to bequeath (property). **5** to have (members of one's family) remaining after one's death. **6** to have (a quantity) remaining or as a remainder: *Ten from twelve leaves two.* ✱ **leave alone/be** *informal* to stop or refrain from interfering with, annoying, disturbing, or interrupting (somebody or something). **leave a lot to be desired** to be less than satisfactory. **leave go** *informal* to stop holding (something). **leave off** to stop or cease (doing something). **leave somebody standing** to surpass somebody spectacularly. ➤➤ **leaver** *n.*

leave[2] *n* **1** authorized absence, e.g. from employment. **2** *formal* permission to do something. ✱ **take one's leave** (*often* + of) to say farewell; to leave.

leaven[1] *n* **1** a substance, e.g. yeast, used to produce fermentation or a gas in dough, batter, etc to lighten it and make it rise. **2** something that modifies or lightens something.

leaven[2] *v* **1** to produce fermentation in (dough, batter, etc) and make it rise by adding leaven. **2** to mingle or permeate (something) with a modifying or enlivening element.

leaves *n* pl of LEAF[1].

leave-taking *n* a departure or farewell.

leavings *pl n* remains or residue.

Lebanese *n* (*pl* **Lebanese**) a native or inhabitant of the Lebanon. ➤➤ **Lebanese** *adj.*

Lebensraum /'layb(ə)nzrowm/ *n* territory believed to be necessary for national existence or self-sufficiency.

lech[1] *n informal, derog* **1** a lecherous man. **2** a lascivious act or urge.

lech[2] *v informal, derog* (*usu* + after) to behave lasciviously towards somebody; to lust after them.

lecher *n* a lecherous man.

lechery *n* inordinate sexual desire or indulgence in sexual activity; debauchery or lasciviousness. ➤➤ **lecherous** *adj,* **lecherously** *adv.*

lecithin *n* a substance found in animals and plants, e.g. in nerve tissue and egg yolk, that is used in the manufacture of margarine, chocolate, etc to stabilize oil and water mixtures and retard the deterioration of fats and oils.

lectern *n* a reading desk, *esp* one from which the Bible is read in church.

lecture[1] *n* **1** a discourse given to an audience, *esp* for instruction. **2** a reproof delivered at length; a reprimand.

lecture[2] *v* **1** to deliver a lecture or series of lectures. **2** to reprove (somebody) at length or severely.

lecturer *n* **1** somebody who lectures. **2** a British university or college teacher below professorial rank.

lectureship *n* the office or position of an academic lecturer.

LED *abbr* light-emitting diode, a small semiconductor diode that emits light when an electric current is passed through it and that is used on display screens, instrument panels, etc.

led *v* past tense and past part. of LEAD[1].

lederhosen /'laydəhohz(ə)n/ *pl n* traditional leather shorts worn by men in Austria, Bavaria, etc.

ledge *n* **1** a narrow horizontal surface that projects from a vertical or steep surface, e.g. a wall or rock face. **2** an underwater ridge or reef.

ledger *n* a book containing the complete record of a company's accounts.

ledger line *or* **leger line** *n* in music, a short line added above or below a stave to extend its range.

lee *n* **1** protecting shelter. **2** the side, e.g. of a ship, that is sheltered from the wind or that faces the direction towards which the wind is blowing.

leech[1] *n* **1** a flesh-eating or bloodsucking freshwater worm having a flattened segmented body with a sucker at each end. **2** a person who leeches on another. **3** *archaic* a physician or surgeon.

leech[2] *v* (*often* + on/off) to gain or seek to gain profit or advantage from another person, *esp* by clinging persistently.

leek *n* the stalk and bulb of a plant that is related to the onion and garlic, used as a vegetable.

leer[1] *v* to give a lascivious or sly look.

leer[2] *n* a lascivious or sly look.

leery *adj* (**-ier, -iest**) (*often* + of) suspicious or wary. ➤➤ **leeriness** *n.*

lees *pl n* the sediment of a liquor, e.g. wine, during fermentation and ageing.

lee shore *n* a shore lying off a ship's lee side.

leeward[1] *adj and adv* in or facing the direction towards which the wind is blowing: compare WINDWARD[1].

leeward[2] *n* the side or direction towards which the wind is blowing: compare WINDWARD[2].

leeway *n* **1a** an allowable margin of freedom or variation; tolerance. **b** *Brit* a margin of shortcoming in performance, *esp* due to lost or wasted time. **2** off-course sideways movement of a ship in the direction of the wind.

left[1] *adj* **1a** of, on, or being the side of somebody or something that is nearer the west when the front faces north. **b** of, on, or being the side of something that is closer to the left hand of an observer positioned directly in front. **c** located on the left side when facing downstream. **2** (*often* **Left**) of the left or left wing in politics.

left[2] *adv* on or towards the left.

left[3] *n* **1a** the part on the left side. **b** the location or direction of the left side. **c** the left hand, or a blow struck with it. **2** (*often* **the Left**) (*used as sing. or pl*). **a** those professing socialist or radical political views. **b** = LEFT WING (1).

left[4] *v* past tense and past part. of LEAVE[1].

left-back *n* in football, hockey, etc, a defensive player on the left wing.

left-field *adj* unorthodox; not conforming to mainstream opinion, taste, etc.

left-hand *adj* **1** situated on the left. **2** of, designed for, or done with the left hand.

left-handed[1] *adj* **1** using the left hand habitually or more easily than the right. **2** of, designed for, or done with the left hand. **3** of a rotary motion or spiral curve: anticlockwise. **4** ambiguous or double-edged.

left-handed[2] *adv* using the left hand.

left-hander *n* **1** a left-handed person. **2** a blow struck with the left hand.

leftism *n* (*often* **Leftism**) left-wing principles and policy, or advocacy of these. ⋙ **leftist** *n and adj.*

left-luggage *n Brit* a room, e.g. at a railway station, where passengers' luggage may be left temporarily.

leftover *n* (*also in pl*) an unused or unconsumed residue, *esp* of food. ⋙ **leftover** *adj.*

leftward *adj* towards or on the left.

left wing *n* **1** (*often* **Left Wing**) the more socialist division of a group or party. **2** in sport, the left side of the field when facing towards the opposing team, or the players positioned on this side. ⋙ **left-wing** *adj*, **left-winger** *n.*

lefty *n* (*pl* **-ies**) **1** *informal* a left-wing person. **2** a left-handed person.

leg *n* **1** a limb of a person or animal used for supporting the body and for walking. **2** a pole or bar serving as a support or prop, e.g. for a tripod or a table. **3a** a portion of a trip; a stage. **b** the part of a relay race run by one competitor. **c** a round of a competition, or one of two or more events or games constituting a round. **4a** = LEG SIDE. **b** in cricket, a fielding position on the leg side of the pitch. ✱ **not have a leg to stand on** not to have the least support or basis for one's position, *esp* in a controversy.

legacy *n* (*pl* **-ies**) **1** a gift of money or property by will; a bequest. **2** something passed on by an ancestor or predecessor or remaining from the past.

legal *adj* **1** of law. **2** permitted by law. **3** established by or deriving authority from law. ⋙ **legally** *adv.*

legal aid *n* money from public funds to pay for legal advice or representation for those who cannot afford it.

legalese *n* the specialized language or jargon of the legal profession.

legalise *v* see LEGALIZE.

legalism *n* strict or excessive conformity to the law or to a moral code. ⋙ **legalist** *n and adj*, **legalistic** *adj.*

legality *n* (*pl* **-ies**) **1** the state of being legal; lawfulness. **2** (*in pl*) the requirements and procedures of the law.

legalize *or* **-ise** *v* to make legal. ⋙ **legalization** *n.*

legal tender *n* currency that a creditor is bound by law to accept as payment of a debt.

legate *n* **1** an official delegate or messenger. **2** a representative of the pope.

legatee *n* a person to whom a legacy is bequeathed.

legation *n* **1** a diplomatic mission, *esp* one in a foreign country headed by a minister. **2** the official residence of a diplomat on such a mission.

legato /li'gahtoh/ *adj and adv* of a piece of music: to be performed in a smooth and connected manner.

leg before wicket *adj* of a batsman in cricket: out because of having obstructed with a part of the body, *esp* the legs, a ball that would otherwise have hit the wicket.

leg break *n* in cricket, a slow bowled ball that turns from the leg side towards the off side when it bounces.

legend *n* **1** a story coming down from the past, *esp* one popularly regarded as historical although not verifiable. **2** a person, act, or thing that inspires legends. **3a** an inscription or title on an object, e.g. a coin. **b** a caption. **c** the key to a map, chart, etc.

legendary *adj* **1** of, described in, or characteristic of legend. **2** celebrated as if in legend; very famous.

legerdemain *n* **1** manual skill or dexterity in conjuring; sleight of hand. **2** a display of artful skill, trickery, or adroitness.

leger line *n* see LEDGER LINE.

leggings *pl n* **1** very close-fitting stretchy trousers worn by women or children. **2** close-fitting usu protective garments, e.g. of leather, that reach from the ankles to the knees or thighs.

leggy *adj* (**-ier, -iest**) **1** having disproportionately long legs. **2** of a plant: having unnaturally long thin stems; spindly.

legible *adj* capable of being read or deciphered. ⋙ **legibility** *n*, **legibly** *adv.*

legion[1] *n* **1** the principal unit of the ancient Roman army comprising 3000–6000 foot soldiers and cavalry. **2** (*also in pl*) a very large number; a multitude.

legion[2] *adj* many or numerous.

legionary[1] *adj* of or being a legion.

legionary[2] *n* (*pl* **-ies**) a member of a Roman legion.

legionnaire *n* a member of a foreign legion or an ex-servicemen's association.

legionnaire's disease *n* a serious infectious disease resembling pneumonia that is caused by a bacterium and often affects groups of people associated in one place.

leg iron *n* a metal band or chain around the ankle of a prisoner.

legislate *v* **1** to make or enact laws. **2** to bring about by legislation.

legislation *n* laws or the making of laws.

legislative *adj* **1** having the power or performing the function of legislating. **2** of or created by a legislature or legislation. ⋙ **legislatively** *adv.*

legislator *n* a maker of laws, *esp* a member of a legislative body.

legislature *n* a body of people having the power to legislate.

leg it *v* (**legged it, legging it**) *informal* **1** to walk. **2** to run away.

legitimate[1] *adj* **1a** in accordance with law. **b** ruling by or based on the strict principle of hereditary right. **2** neither spurious nor false; genuine. **3** recognized as lawful offspring; born in wedlock. **4** conforming to recognized principles or accepted rules and standards. **5** in accordance with reason or logic. ⋙ **legitimacy** *n*, **legitimately** *adv.*

legitimate[2] *v* **1** to give legal status to. **2** to justify. ⋙ **legitimation** *n.*

legitimatize *or* **-ise** *v* = LEGITIMATE[2].

legitimize *or* **-ise** *v* = LEGITIMATE[2]. ⋙ **legitimization** *n.*

legless *adj* **1** *chiefly Brit, informal* very drunk. **2** having no legs.

Lego *n trademark* a toy construction kit.

leg-of-mutton *or* **leg-o'-mutton** *adj* of a sleeve: having an approximately triangular shape.

legroom *n* space in which to extend the legs while seated.

leg side *n* the side of a cricket field away from which the receiving batsman's or batswoman's feet are turned: compare OFF SIDE.

legume *n* **1** any of a large family of plants, shrubs, and trees having pods containing seeds and root nodules containing nitrogen-fixing bacteria and including important food and forage plants, e.g. peas, beans, or clovers. **2** the usu edible pod or seed of such a plant. ⋙ **leguminous** *adj.*

leg-up *n informal* **1** assistance in mounting a horse, climbing a wall, etc. **2** a helping hand; a boost.

leg-warmers *pl n* knitted leg coverings resembling long footless socks.

legwork *n* work involving physical activity and usu forming the basis of more creative or mentally exacting work.

lei[1] /lay/ *n* a Polynesian wreath or necklace of flowers or leaves.

lei[2] /lay/ *n* pl of LEU.

Leicester *n* an orange-red cheese with a mild flavour and a firm texture.

Leics *abbr* Leicestershire.

leishmaniasis *n* a disease caused by any of a genus of parasitic protozoans (single-celled organisms; see PROTOZOAN).

leisure *n* freedom provided by the cessation of activities, *esp* time free from work or duties. ✱ **at leisure/at one's leisure 1** at an unhurried pace. **2** at one's convenience. ➤➤ **leisured** *adj.*

leisure centre *n* a public building offering facilities such as a swimming pool, gym, and function rooms.

leisurely[1] *adj* characterized by leisure; unhurried. ➤➤ **leisureliness** *n.*

leisurely[2] *adv* without haste; deliberately.

leisurewear *n* casual clothes suitable for sport or relaxation.

leitmotiv *or* **leitmotif** /'lietmohteef/ *n* **1** a musical phrase that signals an idea, person, or situation, *esp* in the operas of Wagner. **2** a recurring theme, *esp* in a literary work.

lek[1] *n* the basic monetary unit of Albania.

lek[2] *n* an area where black grouse or other social birds congregate to carry on display and courtship behaviour.

lemming *n* **1** a small furry volelike rodent with a short tail, *esp* one of a species living in northern mountains that periodically undergoes mass migrations resulting in the death of many through drowning in the sea. **2** a member of a group mindlessly pursuing a course of action that will lead to mass destruction.

lemon *n* **1** an oval yellow citrus fruit with a thick rind and acid flesh. **2** a pale yellow colour. **3** *informal* a feeble or useless person or thing. ➤➤ **lemony** *adj.*

lemonade *n* a soft drink, often carbonated, made or flavoured with lemon.

lemon balm *n* a bushy plant of the mint family that has white or pinkish flowers and fragrant lemon-scented leaves.

lemon curd *n* a conserve made from lemons, sugar, eggs, and butter.

lemongrass *n* a robust grass that grows in tropical regions and is the source of an essential oil with an odour of lemon or verbena.

lemon sole *n* a brown flatfish of N Atlantic and European waters that is highly valued for food.

lempira /'lempirə/ *n* the basic monetary unit of Honduras.

lemur *n* a tree-dwelling mammal of Madagascar that typically has a pointed muzzle, large eyes, and a long furry tail.

lend *v* (*past tense and past part.* **lent**) **1a** to give (something) to somebody for temporary use on condition that it be returned. **b** to give (money) to somebody for temporary use on condition of repayment, usu with interest. **2a** to give the assistance or support of; to add or contribute: *His scholarly manner lent force to his criticisms.* **b** (*usu* + to) to adapt or apply (oneself or itself) to something: *The topic lends itself to class discussion.* ➤➤ **lender** *n.*

Usage note

lend, loan, *and* **borrow.** These words are sometimes confused. To *lend* means 'to allow somebody to take and use something that is yours': *they lent me their lawn mower.* To *borrow* means 'to take and use something that belongs to somebody else': *I borrowed their lawn mower.* To *loan* means the same as to *lend* and is mainly used with reference to money: *The bank loaned them £100,000.*

lending library *n chiefly Brit* the lending department of a public library.

length *n* **1** the quality or state of being long. **2a** the longer or longest dimension of an object. **b** the extent from end to end. **c** the full extent of something. **3a** duration or extent in time. **b** extent from beginning to end. **4** the length of something taken as a unit of measure. **5** (*also in pl, used as sing.*) the degree to which something, e.g. a course of action, is carried; a limit or extreme. **6a** a long expanse or stretch. **b** a piece of something long and narrow. ✱ **at length 1** fully; comprehensively. **2** for a long time. **3** finally; at last.

lengthen *v* to become or make longer.

lengthways *adv and adj* in the direction of the length.

lengthwise *adv and adj* = LENGTHWAYS.

lengthy *adj* (**-ier, -iest**) **1** of great or unusual length; long. **2** excessively or tediously protracted. ➤➤ **lengthily** *adv,* **lengthiness** *n.*

lenient *adj* having or showing a merciful or tolerant nature; not severe. ➤➤ **lenience** *n,* **leniency** *n,* **leniently** *adv.*

Leninism *n* the communist principles and policies advocated by the Russian political leader Vladimir Ilyich Lenin (d.1924). ➤➤ **Leninist** *n and adj.*

lens *n* **1a** a piece of glass or other transparent material with two opposite regular surfaces, at least one of which is curved, that is used to form an image by focusing rays of light. **b** a combination of two or more lenses, e.g. in a camera or microscope. **2** a transparent lens-shaped or nearly spherical body in the eye that focuses light rays on the retina. ➤➤ **lensed** *adj.*

Lent *n* the 40 weekdays from Ash Wednesday to Easter Saturday observed by Christians as a time of penitence and fasting. ➤➤ **Lenten** *adj.*

lent *v* past tense and past part. of LEND.

lenticular *adj* **1** having the shape of a lens with both sides convex. **2** of a lens.

lentil *n* a small flattish seed of a plant of the pea family. It is typically yellow or orange and rich in protein, and is used as a vegetable.

lento *adj and adv* of a piece of music: to be performed in a slow manner.

Leo *n* **1** in astronomy, a constellation (the Lion) depicted as a lion. **2** in astrology, the fifth sign of the zodiac, or a person born under this sign. ➤➤ **Leonian** *adj and n.*

leone /li'ohni/ *n* the basic monetary unit of Sierra Leone.

leonine *adj* of or resembling a lion.

leopard *or* **leopardess** *n* a big cat of S Asia and Africa that has a tawny or buff coat with black spots arranged in broken rings or rosettes.

leotard *n* a close-fitting stretchy one-piece garment worn for dance, gymnastics, and other exercise.

leper *n* **1** a person suffering from leprosy. **2** a person shunned for moral or social reasons; an outcast.

lepidopteran *n* any of a large order of insects comprising the butterflies and moths that are caterpillars in the larval stage and have four wings covered with minute overlapping scales when adult. ≫ **lepidopteran** *adj,* **lepidopterous** *adj.*

lepidopterist *n* a person who collects or studies butterflies and moths.

leprechaun *n* a mischievous elf of Irish folklore.

leprosy *n* a bacterial disease characterized by the formation of lumps or patches on the skin that enlarge and spread, loss of sensation with eventual paralysis, and a wasting of muscle.

leprous *adj* of, resembling, or suffering from leprosy.

lepta *n* pl of LEPTON[1].

leptin *n* a protein that regulates the storage of fat in the body.

lepton[1] *n* (*pl* **lepta**) a unit of currency in Greece, worth 100th of a drachma.

lepton[2] *n* any of a group of elementary particles, e.g. an electron or muon, that take part in weak interactions with other elementary particles.

lesbian *n* a homosexual woman. ≫ **lesbian** *adj,* **lesbianism** *n.*

lese majesty /leez/ *n* **1** a crime, e.g. treason, committed against a sovereign power. **2** an offence violating the dignity of a ruler.

lesion *n* an abnormal change in the structure of an organ or tissue due to injury or disease, *esp* a well-defined area or patch of structural change.

less[1] *adj* **1a** smaller in quantity or extent. **b** *informal* fewer. **2** lower in rank, degree, or importance.

Usage note

less *or* fewer? See note at FEWER.

less[2] *adv* to a smaller degree or extent.

less[3] *prep* diminished by (something); minus.

less[4] *n* a smaller portion or quantity.

-less *suffix* **1** forming adjectives from nouns, with the meanings: **a** destitute of; not having: *childless.* **b** free from: *painless.* **2** forming adjectives from verbs, with the meaning: unable to so act or be acted on: *tireless.*

lessee *n* somebody who holds property under a lease.

lessen *v* **1** to reduce (something) in size, extent, etc. **2** to diminish or decrease.

lesser *adj and adv* less in size, quality, or significance.

lesser celandine *n* = CELANDINE (I).

lesson *n* **1** a period of instruction. **2a** an instructive or warning example. **b** something, *esp* a piece of wisdom, learned by study or experience. **3** a passage from sacred writings read in a service of worship.

lessor *n* somebody who grants property by lease.

lest *conj* **1** so that not; in case. **2** used after an expression of fear, anxiety, etc: that.

Usage note

Lest should be followed by a verb in the subjunctive or by a verb formed with *should*: *lest it rain before we are finished; lest there should be any doubt about the seriousness of the situation.*

let[1] *v* (**letting,** *past tense and past part.* **let**) **1** to allow or provide with an opportunity to do something, either by positive action or by not preventing it. **2** to allow to move in a specified direction: *Please let us through.* **3** to cause (something) to happen: *let it be known.* **4** used in the imperative to introduce request or proposal: *Let's go now.* **5** used to introduce a mathematical proposition: *Let x equal y.* **6** to allow somebody the use of (accommodation) for rent or lease. ✱ **let alone** to refrain from disturbing. **let fly** to act violently or lose one's temper. **let go** see GO[1]. **let oneself go 1** to behave with abandonment. **2** to allow one's appearance or habits to deteriorate.

let[2] *n Brit* an act or period of letting premises, e.g. a flat.

let[3] *n* **1** a serve, shot, or rally in tennis, squash, etc that does not count, e.g. because of obstruction or dispute, and must be replayed. **2** *formal* something that impedes; an obstruction: *without let or hindrance.*

-let *suffix* forming nouns, with the meanings: **1** a smaller or lesser person or thing: *starlet.* **2** an article worn on a specified part of the body: *anklet.*

letdown *n informal* a disappointment or disillusionment.

let down *v* **1** to fail in one's support or loyalty to (somebody). **2** to deflate (e.g. a tyre).

lethal *adj* **1** relating to or capable of causing death. **2** gravely damaging or destructive; devastating. ≫ **lethality** *n,* **lethally** *adv.*

lethargy *n* **1** lack of energy or interest. **2** abnormal drowsiness. ≫ **lethargic** *adj,* **lethargically** *adv.*

let in *v* to allow (a person or animal) to enter a building or room. ✱ **let in for** to involve (somebody) in something dangerous or undesirable. **let in on** to allow (somebody) to share confidential information.

let off *v* **1** to excuse from punishment or a responsibility. **2** to cause (a gun, bomb, or firework) to explode.

let on *v* **1** to pretend. **2** to reveal or admit confidential information.

let out *v* **1** to allow (a person or animal) to leave or escape. **2** to reveal (confidential information). **3** to utter (a sound or cry). **4** to make (a piece of clothing) wider or looser.

let's *contr* let us.

letter[1] *n* **1** a symbol, usu written or printed, representing a speech sound and constituting a unit of an alphabet. **2** a written or printed message addressed to a person or organization and usu sent through the post. **3** (*in pl, used as sing. or pl*) literature. **4** (**the letter**) the precise wording; the strict or literal meaning. ✱ **to the letter** precisely or literally.

letter[2] *v* **1** to set down in letters. **2** to mark with letters.

letter bomb *n* an explosive device concealed in an envelope or package.

letter box *n Brit* a hole in a door or a box outside a house to receive material delivered by post.

letterhead *n* a printed heading on a sheet of writing paper showing the name, address, etc of a person or organization.

lettering *n* the letters used in an inscription, *esp* as regards their style or quality.

letter of credit *n* a letter issued by a bank authorizing the bearer to draw on the issuing bank or on its agent in another country up to a certain sum.

letterpress *n* a method of printing from an inked raised surface, or matter produced by this method.

letters of administration *pl n* a legal document giving authority to administer the estate of a person who dies without making a valid will.

letters patent *pl n* a formal open document, e.g. from a sovereign, conferring on somebody a right or privilege, *esp* the sole right to exploit their invention.

lettuce *n* **1** a common garden plant with succulent edible leaves that are eaten raw in salads. **2** any of various similar or related plants, e.g. lamb's lettuce.

letup *n informal* a cessation or lessening of effort, activity, or intensity.

let up *v* **1** to diminish or become less intense. **2** to relax one's efforts. ✱ **let up on** to become less severe towards (somebody).

leu /'layooh/ *n* (*pl* **lei** /lay/) **1** the basic monetary unit of Romania. **2** the basic monetary unit of Moldova.

leucine *n* an amino acid found in most proteins and an essential constituent of the human diet.

leucocyte (*NAm* **leukocyte**) *n* any of the white or colourless blood cells that have nuclei, do not contain haemoglobin, and are concerned with body defence mechanisms and repair; a white blood cell. ≫ **leucocytic** *adj.*

leucotomy *n* (*pl* **-ies**) = LOBOTOMY.

leukaemia (*NAm* **leukemia**) *n* a type of cancer that is characterized by an abnormal increase in the number of white blood cells in the body tissues, *esp* the blood. ≫ **leukaemic** *adj.*

leukocyte *n NAm* see LEUCOCYTE.

lev *n* (*pl* **leva**) the basic monetary unit of Bulgaria.

Levant *n* (**the Levant**) *archaic* the countries of the eastern Mediterranean.

levanter *n* a strong easterly Mediterranean wind.

levee[1] *n* a reception, usu in honour of a particular person.

levee[2] *n chiefly NAm* **1a** an embankment constructed to prevent flooding. **b** the natural embankment of silt deposited by a river. **2** a river landing place.

level[1] *n* **1a** a horizontal line, plane, or surface. **b** a horizontal state or condition. **c** the equilibrium of a fluid marked by a horizontal surface of even altitude. **2a** a position of height, *esp* in relation to the ground. **b** a layer or tier in a vertical structure, e.g. a floor in a building. **3** a position or place in a scale or rank, e.g. of value or importance. **4** a device, e.g. a spirit level, for establishing a horizontal line or plane. **5** (*also in pl*) a practically horizontal or flat area, *esp* of land. ✱ **on the level** *informal* honest; genuine.

level[2] *adj* **1a** having no part higher than another. **b** parallel with the plane of the horizon. **c** (*often* + with) of or at the same height. **2a** even or unvarying in magnitude. **b** equal in advantage, progression, or standing. **c** steady or unwavering. **3** distributed evenly; uniform. ✱ **a level playing field** a situation in which nobody has an unfair advantage. ≫ **levelly** *adv,* **levelness** *n.*

level[3] *v* (**levelled, levelling,** *NAm* **leveled, leveling**) **1** (*also* + off) to make (a line or surface) horizontal. **2a** (*often* + at) to bring (e.g. a weapon) to a horizontal aiming position. **b** (+ at/against) to aim or direct (criticism, an accusation, etc) at somebody. **3** to bring (people or things) to a common level, plane, or standard; to equalize. **4** to lay (a building, village, etc) level with the ground; to raze. **5** (+ out/off) to attain or come to a level; to become level. **6** *informal* (+ with) to deal frankly and openly with somebody.

level crossing *n Brit* the crossing of a railway and a road on the same level.

leveler *n NAm* see LEVELLER.

levelheaded *adj* having sound judgment; sensible. ≫ **levelheadedly** *adv,* **levelheadedness** *n.*

leveller (*NAm* **leveler**) *n* **1** something that tends to reduce differences between people. **2** (**Leveller**) a member of a radical group during the English Civil War who advocated legal equality and religious tolerance.

level pegging *adj Brit* (*used after a noun*) of two contestants: equal.

lever[1] *n* **1** a bar used for prising up or dislodging something. **2a** a rigid bar used to exert a pressure or sustain a weight at one end by applying force at the other and pivoting it on a support. **b** a projecting part by which a mechanism is operated or adjusted.

lever[2] *v* to prise, raise, or move with a lever, or as if with a lever.

leverage[1] *n* **1** the action of a lever or the mechanical advantage gained by it. **2** power or influence.

leverage[2] *v* to finance (a buyout or other speculative business deal) largely by borrowing, in the expectation that interest repayments on the loan can be paid out of the profits of the deal.

leveret *n* a hare in its first year.

leviathan *n* **1** (*often* **Leviathan**) a biblical sea monster. **2** something very large or powerful.

levitate *v* to rise or float in the air, *esp* in apparent defiance of gravity, or to cause (something or somebody) to do this. ≫ **levitation** *n.*

levity *n* lack of seriousness, *esp* excessive or unseemly frivolity.

levulose *n NAm* see LAEVULOSE.

levy[1] *n* (*pl* **-ies**) **1a** the imposing or collection of a tax, fine, etc. **b** an amount levied. **2** *archaic* **a** the enlistment or conscription of men for military service. **b** (*used as sing. or pl*) troops raised by levy.

levy[2] *v* (**-ies, -ied**) **1** to impose, collect, or demand (something, e.g. a tax) by legal authority. **2** *archaic* to enlist or conscript for military service. **3** *archaic* (*often* + on/upon) to prepare for and make (war).

lewd *adj* sexually coarse or suggestive. ≫ **lewdly** *adv,* **lewdness** *n.*

lexical *adj* **1** of words or the vocabulary of a language as distinguished from its grammar and construction. **2** of a lexicon. ≫ **lexically** *adv.*

lexicography *n* the compiling of dictionaries. ≫ **lexicographer** *n,* **lexicographic** *adj.*

lexicon *n* **1** the vocabulary of a language, individual, or subject. **2** a dictionary.

lexis *n* the complete vocabulary of a language.

ley[1] *n* arable land used temporarily for hay or grazing.

ley[2] *n* an alignment of landmarks held to mark the course of a prehistoric trackway and associated by some people with paranormal phenomena.

Leyden jar *n* an early form of CAPACITOR (device for storing electrical energy) consisting of a glass jar coated inside and outside with metal foil and having the inner coating connected to a conducting rod passed through the insulating stopper.

Leyland cypress *n* = LEYLANDII.

leylandii *n* (*pl* **leylandii**) a fast-growing hybrid conifer that is widely cultivated for screening.

ley line *n* = LEY².

LF *abbr* low frequency.

LGV *abbr* large goods vehicle.

Li *abbr* the chemical symbol for lithium.

liability *n* (*pl* **-ies**) **1** being liable. **2** something for which one is liable, *esp* a debt. **3** a hindrance or drawback.

liable *adj* **1** legally responsible. **2** (+ to) exposed or subject to something. **3** habitually likely to do something.

liaise *v* **1** (*often* + with) to establish a connection and cooperate. **2** to maintain communication, e.g. between departments of an organization.

liaison *n* **1** communication, e.g. between departments of an organization. **2a** a close bond or connection. **b** an illicit sexual relationship.

Usage note
Liaison is often misspelt. It has two *i*'s and one *a*.

liana *or* **liane** *n* a climbing plant, *esp* of tropical rain forests, that roots in the ground.

liar *n* a person who tells lies, *esp* habitually.

Lias *n* a geological epoch, the first epoch of the Jurassic period, lasting from about 208 million to 178 million years ago. ➤➤ **Liassic** *adj.*

lib *n* (*often* **Lib**) *informal* liberation. ➤➤ **libber** *n.*

libation *n* **1** a liquid used in a sacrifice to a god, or an act of pouring such a liquid. **2** *humorous* an alcoholic drink.

Lib Dem *n informal* a Liberal Democrat.

libel[1] *n* **1** defamation of somebody by published writing or pictorial representation as distinguished from spoken words or gestures: compare SLANDER[1]. **2** a false defamatory written statement. ➤➤ **libellous** *adj.*

libel[2] *v* (**libelled, libelling,** *NAm* **libeled, libeling**) to make or publish a libel about (somebody).

liberal[1] *adj* **1a** broad-minded or tolerant, *esp* not bound by authoritarianism, orthodoxy, or tradition. **b** advocating or favouring individual rights and freedom. **2a** (*often* **Liberal**) based on or advocating political liberalism. **b** (**Liberal**) in Britain, of, belonging to, or supporting the Liberal Democrats. **3** of education, studies, etc: intended to provide general knowledge and develop intellectual capacities rather than professional or vocational skills. **4a** generous or openhanded. **b** abundant or ample. **5** not literal; loose. ➤➤ **liberalism** *n,* **liberality** *n,* **liberally** *adv.*

liberal[2] *n* **1** a person who is not strict in the observance of orthodox ways, e.g. in religion; somebody with liberal views. **2** (**Liberal**) in Britain, a Liberal Democrat.

liberal arts *pl n chiefly NAm* the cultural branches of learning, e.g. language, literature, history, etc, as opposed to science and technology.

Liberal Democrat *n* a member or supporter of a British political party created in 1988 from the former Liberal and Social Democratic parties.

liberalize *or* **-ise** *v* to become or cause to become liberal. ➤➤ **liberalization** *n.*

liberate *v* **1** to set free; *specif* to free (a country) from foreign domination. **2** to free from social conventions, injustices, or discrimination. ➤➤ **liberated** *adj,* **liberation** *n,* **liberationist** *n,* **liberator** *n.*

liberation theology *n* a theory or movement holding that theology involves a political commitment to change society by liberating humankind from social and political injustice.

Liberian *n* a native or inhabitant of Liberia. ➤➤ **Liberian** *adj.*

libertarian *n* **1** an advocate of liberty. **2** a believer in free will. ➤➤ **libertarianism** *n.*

libertine *n* a person who is unrestrained by convention or morality; *specif* a person who leads a dissolute life. ➤➤ **libertinism** *n.*

liberty *n* (*pl* **-ies**) **1a** the power to do as one pleases. **b** freedom from physical restraint or dictatorial control. **c** the enjoyment of various rights and privileges. **d** the power of choice. **2** a right or immunity awarded or granted; a privilege. **3** *informal* (*also in pl*) a breach of etiquette or propriety.

Liberty Hall *n informal* a place where one can do as one likes.

libidinous *adj* having or marked by strong sexual desire; lascivious.

libido *n* (*pl* **-os**) sexual drive. ➤➤ **libidinal** *adj.*

Libra *n* **1** in astronomy, a constellation (the Scales) depicted as a pair of scales. **2** in astroloy, the seventh sign of the zodiac, or a person born under this sign. ➤➤ **Libran** *n and adj.*

librarian *n* a person who manages or assists in a library. ➤➤ **librarianship** *n.*

library *n* (*pl* **-ies**) **1** a room, building, or other place in which books, periodicals, CDs, videos, etc are kept for reference or for borrowing by the public. **2** a collection resembling or suggesting a library. **3** a series of related books issued by a publisher.

libretto *n* (*pl* **libretti** *or* **librettos**) the text of a work that is both theatrical and musical, e.g. an opera. ➤➤ **librettist** *n.*

Libyan *n* a native or inhabitant of Libya. ➤➤ **Libyan** *adj.*

lice *n* pl of LOUSE.

licence (*NAm* **license**) *n* **1a** permission granted by authority to engage in a particular business, e.g. selling alcoholic drink, or activity, e.g. driving a vehicle, that would otherwise be unlawful. **b** a document giving evidence of such permission. **2** freedom of action. **3** freedom claimed by an artist or writer to alter facts or deviate from rules, *esp* for the sake of the effect gained.

license *v* **1** to give official permission to (somebody) to do something, e.g. to drive a vehicle. **2** to give official permission for (something, e.g. the sale of alcoholic drink). ➤➤ **licensable** *adj,* **licensor** *n.*

licensee *n* the holder of a licence, *esp* a licence to sell alcoholic drink.

license plate *n NAm* a numberplate.

licentiate *n* **1** a person licensed to practise a profession. **2** an academic degree awarded by some European universities. ➤➤ **licentiateship** *n.*

licentious *adj* behaving in a sexually unrestrained manner. ➤➤ **licentiously** *adv,* **licentiousness** *n.*

lichen *n* a complex plant made up of an alga and a fungus growing in symbiotic association on a solid surface, e.g. a rock or tree trunk. ➤➤ **lichened** *adj,* **lichenous** *adj.*

lich-gate *n* see LYCH-GATE.

licit *adj* not forbidden by law; permissible.

lick[1] *v* **1** to pass the tongue over (something), *esp* in order to taste, moisten, or clean it. **2** to dart like a tongue. **3** *informal* to defeat (somebody), *esp* decisively or thoroughly. ✱ **lick into shape** to put (something or somebody) into proper form or condition. **lick one's wounds** to recover after defeat or humiliation. **lick somebody's boots** *informal* to behave sycophantically towards somebody.

lick[2] *n* **1a** an act of licking. **b** *informal* a small amount; a touch. **2** *informal* an improvised piece of jazz or pop music usu added into a written composition. ✱ **a lick and a promise** *informal* a quick wash. **at a lick** *informal* at a fast speed or pace.

lickerish *or* **liquorish** *adj* lecherous. ➤➤ **lickerishly** *adv.*

lickspittle *n* an obsequious subordinate; a toady.

licorice *n NAm* see LIQUORICE.

lid *n* **1** a hinged or detachable cover for a receptacle. **2** an eyelid. ➤➤ **lidded** *adj,* **lidless** *adj.*

lido *n* (*pl* **-os**) **1** a public open-air swimming pool. **2** a fashionable beach resort.

lie[1] *v* (**lying,** *past tense* **lay,** *past part.* **lain**) **1a** to be or to stay at rest in a horizontal position; to rest or recline. **b** (*often* + down) to assume a horizontal position. **c** to be or remain in a specified state or condition: *The machinery was lying idle.* **2** of something inanimate: to be or remain in a flat or horizontal position on a surface: *Books were lying on the table.* **3** to have as a direction; to lead: *The route lay* *to the west.* **4** to occupy a specified place or position: *The responsibility lies with us.* ✱ **lie low** to stay in hiding; to strive to avoid notice.

lie[2] *n* **1** the way, position, or situation in which something lies. **2** a place frequented by an animal or bird.

lie[3] *n* **1** an untrue or false statement, *esp* when made with intent to deceive. **2** something that misleads or deceives. ✱ **give the lie to** to show to be false or untrue.

lie[4] *v* (**lies, lied, lying**) **1** to make an untrue statement with intent to deceive; to speak falsely. **2** to create a false or misleading impression.

Liebfraumilch /'leebfrowmilsh/ *n* a white wine made in the Rhine valley.

Liechtensteiner *n* a native or inhabitant of Liechtenstein.

lied /leed, leet/ *n* (*pl* **lieder**) a German song, *esp* a 19th-cent. setting of a lyrical poem with piano accompaniment.

lie detector *n* an instrument for detecting physical evidence, e.g. a change in pulse or breathing rate, of the mental tension that accompanies telling lies.

lie-down *n chiefly Brit* a brief rest, *esp* on a bed.

lief *adv archaic* soon; gladly.

liege[1] *adj* **1** of a lord: entitled to feudal allegiance. **2** of a vassal: owing feudal allegiance.

liege[2] *n* **1** a feudal superior. **2a** a feudal vassal. **b** a loyal subject.

liege lord *n* = LIEGE[2] (1).

lie in *v chiefly Brit* to stay in bed later than usual in the morning.

lie-in *n chiefly Brit* an instance of staying in bed later than usual.

lien *n* the legal right to hold another's property until a debt is paid.

lierne *n* a nonstructural rib in a vaulted ceiling that passes from one main rib to another.

lieu ✱ **in lieu** in substitution; instead.

lieutenant *n* **1** an official empowered to act for a higher official; a deputy or representative. **2a** an officer in the Royal Navy and US navy ranking below a lieutenant commander. **b** an officer in the British army and Royal Marines ranking below a captain. ➤➤ **lieutenancy** *n*.

lieutenant colonel *n* an officer ranking below a colonel in the British and US armies, US air force, Royal Marines, and US Marines.

lieutenant commander *n* an officer in the Royal Navy and US navy ranking below a commander.

lieutenant general *n* an officer ranking below a general in the British army, the Royal Marines, and the US army, air force, and marines.

life *n* (*pl* **lives**) **1** the quality that distinguishes a living and functional being from a dead body or inanimate object. **2a** the sequence of physical and mental experiences that make up the existence of an individual. **b** an aspect of the process of living: *the sex life of the frog.* **c** a state or condition of existence: *life after death.* **d** *informal* a sentence of life imprisonment. **3** a way or manner of living: *a holy life.* **4a** a person. **b** living beings, e.g. of a specified kind or environment: *forest life.* **5** (*used before a noun*) using a living model: *a life class.* **6** the period of usefulness, effectiveness, or functioning of something inanimate. **7** the active part of human existence, *esp* in a wide range of circumstances or experiences. **8** any of several chances to participate given to a contestant in some games, one of which is forfeited each time they lose. ✱ **for the life of me** *informal* no matter how hard I try. **get a life** *informal* (*usu in imperative*) to have a bit of sense, relax, and get more out of life. **not on your life** *informal* certainly not.

life assurance *n chiefly Brit* = LIFE INSURANCE.

lifebelt *n chiefly Brit* a buoyant ring for keeping a person afloat.

lifeblood *n* **1** *literary* the blood necessary to life. **2** a vital or life-giving force.

lifeboat *n* **1** a shore-based boat for use in saving lives at sea. **2** a boat carried by a ship for use in an emergency.

lifebuoy *n chiefly Brit* a buoyant float to which a person may cling in the water.

life cycle *n* the series of stages in form and functional activity through which an organism passes during its lifetime.

life expectancy *n* the expected length of somebody's life, based on statistical evidence.

lifeguard *n* an expert swimmer employed to safeguard others at a swimming pool or beach.

life imprisonment *n* a sentence of imprisonment for a long time, given in Britain for murder and other very serious crimes.

life insurance *n* insurance providing for payment of a stipulated sum to a beneficiary on the death of the insured person or to the insured person at the end of a fixed period.

life jacket *n* an inflatable or buoyant device that is designed to keep a person afloat.

lifeless *adj* **1a** dead. **b** inanimate. **2** having no living beings. **3** lacking qualities expressive of life and vigour; dull. ➤➤ **lifelessly** *adv*, **lifelessness** *n*.

lifelike *adj* accurately representing or imitating real life.

lifeline *n* **1** a rope or line for saving or safeguarding life, e.g. one stretched along the deck of a ship for use in rough weather or one for lowering or raising a person to safety. **2** something, *esp* a sole means of communication, regarded as indispensable for the maintenance or protection of life. **3** a line on the palm of the hand, taken by palmists as an indication of the length of a person's life.

lifelong *adj* lasting or continuing throughout life.

life peer *or* **life peeress** *n* a British peer whose title is not hereditary.

life preserver *n* a life jacket, lifebuoy, etc.

lifer *n informal* a person sentenced to life imprisonment.

life raft *n* a usu inflatable raft for use in an emergency at sea.

lifesaver *n* **1** somebody or something that saves life, or prevents or relieves distress or difficulty. **2** *Aus* a lifeguard, *esp* on a surfing beach.

life science *n* a branch of science, e.g. biology, medicine, anthropology, or sociology, that deals with living organisms and life processes.

life span *n* **1** the duration of existence of an individual. **2** the average length of life of a kind of organism or of a material object, *esp* in a particular environment or in specified circumstances.

lifestyle *n* an individual's way of life, or the activities, possessions, etc associated with this.

life-support system *n* a system that provides all or some of the items necessary for maintaining the life of a person.

lifetime *n* **1** the length of time for which a living being exists. **2** the length of time for which a thing remains useful, valid, etc.

lift[1] *v* **1a** to raise or be raised from a lower to a higher position. **b** to raise in rank, condition, intensity, etc. **c** to pick (something or somebody) up in order to move them. **2** to put an end to (a blockade or siege) by withdrawing the surrounding forces. **3** to revoke or rescind. **4** *informal* to steal (something). ➤➤ **liftable** *adj,* **lifter** *n.*

lift[2] *n* **1** *Brit* a device for conveying people or objects from one level to another, *esp* in a building. **2** the act or an instance of lifting. **3** a free ride as a passenger in a motor vehicle. **4** the distance or extent to which something rises or is lifted. **5** a feeling of cheerfulness or encouragement, usu a temporary one. **6** the component of the aerodynamic force acting on an aircraft or wing that is perpendicular to the relative wind and usu constitutes the upward force opposing the pull of gravity.

lift off *v* of an aircraft, spacecraft, or missile: to take off vertically.

lift-off *n* a vertical takeoff by an aircraft, spacecraft, or missile.

lig[1] *v* (**ligged, ligging**) *Brit, informal* to obtain refreshment or entertainment at another's expense; to freeload. ➤➤ **ligger** *n.*

lig[2] *n Brit, informal* a party or other function at which free refreshment or entertainment is provided.

ligament *n* a tough band of tissue connecting two or more bones or cartilages or supporting an organ and keeping it in place. ➤➤ **ligamentous** *adj.*

ligand *n* an ion, molecule, etc joined by many bonds to a central atom in a complex chemical compound.

ligate *v* to tie (something, e.g. an artery) with a ligature.

ligature *n* **1a** something that is used to bind; *specif* a thread used in surgery. **b** something that unites or connects. **2** in music, a slur or tie. **3** in printing, a character consisting of two or more letters or characters joined together, e.g. ﬁ.

light[1] *n* **1a** something that makes vision possible by stimulating the sense of sight. **b** electromagnetic radiation in the wavelength that is visible to the human eye. **2** a source of light, e.g. a lamp or a candle. **3** daylight. **4** a flame or spark for lighting something, e.g. a cigarette. **5** (*also in pl*) a traffic light. **6a** spiritual illumination. **b** understanding or knowledge. **7** enlightening information or explanation. **8** a particular aspect or appearance in which something is viewed. **9** a medium, e.g. a window, through which light is admitted. **10** a specified expression perceived as being in somebody's eyes. **11** (*in pl*) a set of principles, standards, or opinions. ✱ **bring to light** to disclose or reveal. **come to light** to be revealed or disclosed. **in the light of** with the insight provided by. **see the light 1** to understand suddenly; to gain insight. **2** to undergo conversion. **see the light of day 1** to be born or come into existence. **2** to be published or come to public attention. ➤➤ **lightless** *adj.*

light[2] *adj* **1** having plenty of light; bright. **2** pale in colour or colouring. ➤➤ **lightness** *n.*

light[3] *v* (*past tense* **lit,** *past part.* **lit** *or* **lighted**) **1** to become illuminated. **2** to catch fire. **3** to set fire to. **4** to provide light in (a place).

light[4] *adj* **1a** having little weight; not heavy. **b** designed to carry a comparatively small load. **c** having relatively little weight in proportion to bulk. **d** carrying little or no cargo. **2** not abundant or intense. **3a** of sleep or a sleeper: easily disturbed. **b** exerting a minimum of force or pressure; gentle or soft: *a light touch.* **c** resulting from very slight pressure; faint: *light print.* **4** requiring little effort: *light work.* **5** graceful, deft, or nimble. **6a** lacking seriousness; frivolous. **b** of little importance; trivial. **7** free from care; cheerful. **8** intended chiefly to entertain: *light reading.* **9** of industry: requiring relatively small investment and usu producing small consumer goods. ➤➤ **lightish** *adj,* **lightly** *adv,* **lightness** *n.*

light[5] *adv* **1** lightly. **2** with the minimum of luggage.

light[6] *v* (*past tense and past part.* **lit** *or* **lighted**) **1** (+ on/upon) to settle or alight. **2** (+ on/upon) to arrive by chance; to happen.

light box *n* a box containing an electric light and having a translucent lid, used for viewing photographic transparencies, etc.

light bulb *n* a glass bulb containing a filament or gas that gives off light when heated by electricity.

light-emitting diode *n* see LED.

lighten[1] *v* **1** to make or become lighter or less burdensome. **2** to make or become less serious or more cheerful.

lighten[2] *v* **1** to make (a place) light or bright; to illuminate. **2** to make (a colour, hair, etc) lighter or paler. **3** to grow lighter; to brighten.

lighter[1] *n* a device for lighting a cigarette, cigar, etc.

lighter[2] *n* a large flat-bottomed barge used in unloading or loading ships.

light-fingered *adj* expert at or given to stealing, *esp* by picking pockets.

light-flyweight *n* the lightest weight in amateur boxing or wrestling.

light-footed *adj* moving gracefully and nimbly.

light-headed *adj* **1** faint or dizzy. **2** frivolous.

light-hearted *adj* **1** free from care or worry; cheerful. **2** not serious; playful or amusing. ➤➤ **light-heartedly** *adv.*

light-heavyweight *n* a weight in boxing and wrestling between heavyweight and middleweight.

lighthouse *n* a tower, mast, etc equipped with a powerful light to warn or guide shipping at sea.

lighting *n* **1** an artificial supply of light, or the apparatus providing it. **2** the arrangement of lights, *esp* to produce a particular effect.

lighting-up time *n Brit* the time when motorists are required by law to have the lights of their vehicles on.

light meter *n* a small device for measuring the degree of illumination, *esp* an exposure meter.

light-middleweight *n* a weight in amateur boxing between middleweight and welterweight.

lightning *n* **1** the flashing of light produced by a discharge of atmospheric electricity between two clouds or between a cloud and the earth. **2** (*used before a noun*) very quick, short, or sudden: *a lightning strike.*

lightning conductor (*NAm* **lightning rod**) *n* a metal rod fixed to the highest point of a building or mast and connected to the earth or water below as a protection against damage by lightning.

light pen *n* **1** a pen-shaped photoelectric device that is pointed at or moved over a VDU screen to communicate with a computer. **2** a hand-held pen-shaped device used to read bar codes.

light pollution *n* excessive artificial light, e.g. from street lamps, causing the night sky to be unnaturally bright and obscuring faint stars.

lights *pl n* the lungs of a slaughtered sheep, pig, etc, used *esp* as food for pets.

lightship *n* a moored vessel equipped with a powerful light to warn or guide shipping at sea.

light up *v* **1a** to become illuminated or illuminate, *esp* in a sudden or conspicuous manner. **b** to make or become more animated or cheerful. **2** to start smoking a cigarette, pipe, etc.

lightweight[1] *n* **1** a weight in boxing and wrestling between welterweight and featherweight. **2** *informal* somebody of little ability or importance.

lightweight[2] *adj* **1** having less than average weight. **2** *informal* lacking in seriousness or profundity; inconsequential.

light-welterweight *n* a weight in amateur boxing between welterweight and lightweight.

light-year *n* in astronomy, a unit of length equal to the distance that light travels in one year in a vacuum, approximately 9460 thousand million km (about 5878 thousand million mi).

ligneous *adj* of or resembling wood; woody.

lignin *n* a substance that together with cellulose forms the woody cell walls of plants and the cementing material between them.

lignite *n* a brownish black coal that is harder than peat but usu retains the texture of the original wood.

lignocaine *n* a synthetic local anaesthetic.

likable *or* **likeable** *adj* pleasant or agreeable. ➤➤ **likably** *adv.*

like[1] *prep* **1a** having the characteristics of (something or somebody); similar to: *His house is like a palace.* **b** typical of (somebody or something). **2a** in the manner of (somebody or something); similarly to: *Don't act like a fool.* **b** to the same degree as (something): *This dress fits like a glove.* **3** appearing to be, threaten, or promise (something): *It looks like rain.* **4a** of the class of (something): *a subject like physics.* **b** used to introduce an example: such as: *foods that are high in fibre, like wholemeal bread.*

Usage note

like *and* **such as**. Sometimes the use of *like* can be ambiguous: *a boy like you* could mean either 'a boy, for example, you' or 'a boy who resembles you'. The ambiguity can be avoided if *like* is used to introduce a comparison and *such as* is used to introduce an example. However in the latter case, the use of *such as* is normally restricted to more formal contexts.

like[2] *conj informal* **1** in the same way as: *if she can sing like she can dance.* **2** as if: *He acts like he knows what he's doing.*

like[3] *n* somebody or something that is similar or equal to another, *esp* in excellence, magnitude, etc; a counterpart. ✱ **the like** similar things.

like[4] *adj* similar in appearance, character, or quantity.

like[5] *adv* **1** likely or probably. **2** *informal* so to speak.

like[6] *v* **1** to find (something or somebody) agreeable, acceptable, or pleasant. **2** to wish or choose (to have, be, or do something); to want.

like[7] *n* a liking or preference.

-like *comb. form* forming adjectives from nouns, with the meaning: resembling or characteristic of: *bell-like; ladylike.*

likeable *adj* see LIKABLE.

likelihood *n* probability.

likely[1] *adj* (**-ier, -iest**) **1** having a high probability of being or occurring. **2a** reliable or credible. **b** used ironically: incredible: *A likely story!* **3** promising: *a likely candidate.*

likely[2] *adv* probably: *He will most likely give up.* ✱ **as likely as not** very probably.

like-minded *adj* having a similar outlook or disposition.

liken *v* (+ to) to discover or point out the resemblance of (somebody or something) to another; to compare.

likeness *n* **1** resemblance. **2** a copy or portrait. **3** an appearance or semblance.

likewise *adv* **1** moreover; in addition. **2** similarly.

liking *n* **1** favourable regard. **2** taste or fondness.

likuta /li'koohtə/ *n* (*pl* **makuta**) a former unit of currency in Zaïre (now the Democratic Republic of Congo), worth 100th of a zaïre.

lilac *n* **1** a European shrub of the olive family with heart-shaped leaves and large clusters of fragrant white or pale pinkish purple flowers. **2** a pale pinkish purple colour.

lilangeni /leelang'gayni/ *n* (*pl* **emalangeni**) the basic monetary unit of Swaziland.

Lilliputian *n* somebody or something that is remarkably small. ➤➤ **Lilliputian** *adj.*

Li-Lo *n* (*pl* **-os**) *trademark* an airbed.

lilt[1] *v* to sing or speak rhythmically and with varying pitch. ➤➤ **lilting** *adj,* **liltingly** *adv.*

lilt[2] *n* a rhythmic swing, flow, or rising and falling inflection in music or speech.

lily *n* (*pl* **-ies**) a plant that grows from bulbs and has variously coloured showy flowers.

lily-livered *adj* lacking courage.

lily of the valley *n* (*pl* **lilies of the valley**) a low perennial plant of the lily family that has large leaves and fragrant bell-shaped white flowers.

lily pad *n* a large flat floating leaf of a water lily.

lily-white *adj* **1** pure white. **2** irreproachable or pure.

lima bean *n* a seed of a bean plant of tropical American origin, used as a vegetable.

limb[1] *n* **1** a leg or arm of a human being. **2** a large primary branch of a tree. **3** an extension or branch; *specif* any of the four branches or arms of a cross. ✱ **out on a limb** in an exposed and unsupported position. ➤➤ **limbless** *adj.*

limb[2] *n* the outer edge of the apparent disc of a celestial body.

limber[1] *adj* supple in body or mind; flexible.

limber[2] *n* the detachable front part of a gun carriage consisting of a frame supporting two wheels and an ammunition box used as a seat.

limber up *v* to prepare for physical action by gentle exercise.

limbic *adj* of or being a group of structures in the brain, including the hypothalamus and hippocampus, that are concerned with emotion and motivation.

limbo[1] *n* **1** in Roman Catholic theology, an abode of the souls of those who died before receiving Christian baptism and are barred from heaven. **2** an intermediate or transitional place or state.

limbo[2] *n* (*pl* **-os**) a W Indian acrobatic dance that involves bending over backwards and passing under a low horizontal pole.

limbo[3] *v* (**limbos, limboed, limboing**) to dance the limbo.

lime[1] *n* **1a** a caustic solid consisting of calcium oxide and some magnesium oxide, obtained by heating calcium carbonate, e.g. in the form of shells or limestone, to a high temperature, and used in building and in agriculture. **b** calcium hydroxide, occurring as a dry white powder, made by treating caustic lime with water. **c** = CALCIUM. **2** *archaic* birdlime. ➤➤ **limy** *adj.*

lime[2] *v* to treat or cover (e.g. soil) with lime.

lime[3] *n* a tree with heart-shaped leaves, clusters of yellow flowers, and light fine-grained wood.

lime[4] *n* **1** a small green citrus fruit with acid juicy pulp used as a flavouring and as a source of vitamin C. **2** a soft drink made from sweetened lime juice. **3** a bright greenish yellow colour.

limeade *n* a soft drink consisting of sweetened lime juice mixed with plain or carbonated water.

limekiln *n* a kiln or furnace for reducing calcium-containing material, e.g. limestone or shells, to lime for burning.

limelight *n* **1** (**the limelight**) the centre of public attention. **2** an intense white light formerly used for stage lighting, produced by directing a flame on a cylinder of lime.

limerick *n* a humorous verse form of five lines with a rhyme scheme of aabba.

Word history

named after *Limerick*, a city and county in Eire. It is thought that a refrain, 'Will you come up to Limerick?', was once added between the verses of a limerick at a party.

limestone *n* a widely-occurring rock consisting mainly of calcium carbonate.

limewash *n* a mixture of lime and water used as a coating, e.g. for walls.

limey *n* (*pl* **-eys**) (*often* **Limey**) *NAm, Aus, informal, derog* a British person.

liminal *adj technical* **1** of the point at which a physiological or psychological effect begins to be produced. **2** barely perceptible. ⋙ **liminality** *n*.

limit[1] *n* **1a** a line or point that cannot or should not be passed. **b** (*in pl*) the place enclosed within a boundary. **2a** something that bounds, restrains, or confines. **b** the furthest point or extreme degree of something. **c** a prescribed maximum or minimum amount, quantity, or number. ✻ **to be the limit** *informal* to be exasperating or intolerable. ⋙ **limitless** *adj*, **limitlessly** *adv*, **limitlessness** *n*.

limit[2] *v* (**limited, limiting**) **1** to restrict (somebody or something) to specific bounds or limits. **2** to curtail or reduce in quantity or extent; to curb. ⋙ **limiter** *n*.

limitation *n* **1 a** a restriction or curb. **b** a defect, undesirable quality, or weak point. **2** the act or an instance of limiting. **3** in law, a period defined by statute after which a claimant is barred from bringing a legal action.

limited *adj* **1** confined within limits; restricted. **2** of a monarchy or government: restricted as to the scope of powers. **3** lacking the ability to grow or do better. **4** *Brit* being a limited company.

limited company *n* a company in which the responsibility of an individual shareholder for the company's debts is limited according to the amount of the company's capital that he or she contributed.

limited liability *n Brit* liability, e.g. of a shareholder or shipowner, limited by law or contract.

limn *v archaic or literary* to represent (something) by drawing or painting it, or to describe it in words. ⋙ **limner** /'limnə/ *n*.

limo *n* (*pl* **-os**) *informal* = LIMOUSINE.

limonene *n* a chemical compound that occurs in essential oils, e.g. of oranges or lemons, and is used in the manufacture of resins and as a solvent.

limousine *n* a large luxurious motor car.

limp[1] *v* **1** to walk with an uneven step to avoid putting the full weight of the body on an injured leg. **2** to proceed slowly or with difficulty.

limp[2] *n* a limping movement or gait.

limp[3] *adj* **1** lacking firmness and stiffness; drooping or shapeless. **2** lacking energy. ⋙ **limply** *adv*, **limpness** *n*.

limpet *n* a marine mollusc that has a low conical shell with a broad opening beneath for its large suction foot, that enables it to cling very tightly to rock when disturbed.

limpet mine *n* an adhesive or magnetic explosive device; *esp* one designed to cling to the hull of a ship.

limpid *adj* **1** transparent or clear. **2** clear and simple in style. ⋙ **limpidity** *n*, **limpidly** *adv*.

limp-wristed *adj informal, offensive* of a man, *esp* a homosexual: = EFFEMINATE.

linage *n* the number of lines in a piece of printed or written matter.

linchpin *or* **lynchpin** *n* **1** a locking pin inserted crosswise, e.g. through the end of an axle or shaft. **2** somebody or something regarded as a vital or coordinating factor.

Lincs *abbr* Lincolnshire.

linctus *n* a syrupy usu medicated liquid used to relieve throat irritation and coughing.

lindane *n* an insecticide and weedkiller, now often restricted in use because it persists in the environment.

linden *n* = LIME[3].

line[1] *n* **1** a long narrow mark across a surface. **2a** something, e.g. a ridge or seam, that is distinct, elongated, and narrow. **b** a narrow crease, e.g. on the face; a wrinkle. **3** a real or imaginary straight line oriented in terms of stable points of reference. **4a** a boundary demarcating an area, or separating it from another one; a border. **b** a mark, e.g. on a map, indicating the position of a boundary or the outline of an area, or connecting points of e.g. equal height or depth. **5** a railway track. **6** a defining outline; an edge or contour. **7** a rank of objects of one kind; a row. **8** a horizontal row of written or printed characters. **9a** a short sequence of words spoken by an actor playing a particular role. **b** (*in pl*) all of the text making up a particular role. **10** *Brit* (*in pl*) a specified number of lines of writing to be copied as a school punishment. **11** a related series of people or things coming one after the other in time; a family. **12** an arrangement of operations in industry permitting various stages of manufacture to take place in sequence. **13a** a thread, string, cord, or rope. **b** a device for catching fish that consists of a cord with hooks and is attached to a rod or other fishing gear. **14a** a conducting wire or cable conveying electrical power through a circuit or system or carrying a telecommunications signal. **b** a telephone connection. **15** a particular type of merchandise, product, or service. **16a** a course of conduct, action, or thought; a policy. **b** a field of activity, interest, or business. **17** (*in pl*) a general plan; a model. **18** a group of vehicles, ships, etc carrying passengers or goods regularly over a route. **19** a linked series of trenches and fortifications, *esp* facing the enemy. ✻ **draw the line** to set a limit, *esp* as regards what is or is not acceptable. **fall in/into line** to conform. **hold the line 1** to remain connected and wait while making a telephone call. **2** to resist an attack without retreating or making concessions. **in line for** in the right position for; likely to get. **in line with** conforming to. **lay it on the line** to speak bluntly or make the situation absolutely clear. **on the line** at risk. **out of line** *informal* behaving in an unacceptable fashion, *esp* rudely and disrespectfully. **the end of the line** the point at which something stops, or beyond which no further progress is possible.

line[2] *v* **1** to form a line along (something). **2** to form (something) into a line or lines; to line up. **3** to mark or cover with a line or lines.

line[3] *v* **1** to cover the inner surface of. **2** to serve as the lining of.

lineage *n* **1** a line of descent from a common ancestor or source. **2** in biology, a group of organisms belonging to the same line of descent.

lineal *adj* **1** consisting of, or being in, a direct line of ancestry or descent. **2** composed of or arranged in lines. ➤➤ **lineally** *adv.*

lineament *n* **1** (*also in pl*) a distinctive outline, feature, or contour of a body or figure, *esp* a face. **2** in geology, a linear feature, e.g. of the earth or a planet.

linear *adj* **1a** arranged in or resembling a line. **b** consisting of or relating to lines. **2a** involving a single dimension. **b** of an equation, function, etc: containing any number of variables, all of the first degree, and, in the case of two variables, represented graphically by a straight line. ➤➤ **linearity** *n,* **linearly** *adv.*

lineation *n* **1** the action of marking with lines. **2** an arrangement of lines.

linebacker *n* in American football, a defensive player positioned close behind the linemen.

line dancing *n* a type of dancing to country and western music, performed by people in rows executing a sequence of steps simultaneously. ➤➤ **line dancer** *n.*

line drawing *n* a drawing composed only of lines, e.g. drawn with a pen or pencil.

line feed *n* in computing, a control character that moves a printer or a screen onto the next line.

lineman *n* (*pl* **linemen**) **1** *Brit* somebody who lays railway tracks. **2** *NAm* somebody who repairs and installs telephone or power lines.

line manager *n* a person in an organization who has immediate authority over employees on the next level down in the hierarchy. ➤➤ **line management** *n.*

linen *n* **1** a hard-wearing cloth or yarn made from flax. **2** household articles, e.g. sheets and tablecloths, made typically, *esp* formerly, of linen.

line of fire *n* the path or expected path of a missile, bullet etc.

line-out *n* in Rugby Union, a method of returning the ball to play after it has crossed a touchline which involves throwing it in between two lines of forwards from each team.

line printer *n* a high-speed printing device that prints each line as a unit rather than character by character.

liner[1] *n* **1** a passenger ship belonging to a shipping company and usu sailing scheduled routes. **2** somebody or something that makes, draws, or uses lines.

liner[2] *n* something used to line an item of clothing or a container.

linesman *n* (*pl* **linesmen**) **1** an official who assists the referee or umpire in various games, *esp* in determining if a ball or player is out of the prescribed playing area. **2** *chiefly Brit* somebody who sets up or repairs telephone lines, electric power cables, etc.

line up *v* **1** to assume an orderly arrangement in a line. **2** to put (people or things) into alignment. **3** to assemble or organize (people or things).

line-up *n* **1** a line of people arranged for inspection or as a means of identifying a suspect. **2** a group of people or items assembled for a particular purpose.

ling[1] *n* a large long-bodied food fish of the cod family, found in shallow seas off Greenland and Europe.

ling[2] *n* = HEATHER .

-ling *suffix* forming nouns, denoting: **1** somebody connected with: *sibling*. **2** a young, small, or lesser kind of: *duckling*. **3** somebody having (a specified quality or attribute): *darling*.

linga *or* **lingam** *n* a phallus symbolic of the divine generative power and of the Hindu god Siva.

linger *v* **1a** to delay going, *esp* because of reluctance to leave; to tarry. **b** to be protracted or slow in disappearing. **2a** (+ over/on/upon) to spend a long time doing, dealing with, or looking at something, usu because it gives pleasure. **b** to be slow to act; to procrastinate. **3** (*often* + on) to continue in a failing or moribund state. ➤➤ **lingerer** *n,* **lingering** *adj.*

lingerie *n* women's underwear and nightclothes.

lingo *n* (*pl* **-oes** *or* **-os**) *informal* **1** a foreign language. **2** the special vocabulary of a particular subject; jargon.

lingua franca *n* (*pl* **lingua francas** *or* **linguae francae**) a language used as a common or commercial tongue among people not speaking the same native language.

lingual *adj* **1** relating to or in the region of the tongue. **2** = LINGUISTIC. ➤➤ **lingually** *adv.*

linguini *or* **linguine** /ling'gweeni/ *pl n* (*used as sing. or pl*) pasta in the form of flat strands.

linguist *n* **1** somebody accomplished in languages. **2** somebody who studies linguistics.

linguistic *adj* relating to language or linguistics. ➤➤ **linguistically** *adv.*

linguistics *pl n* (*used as sing.*) the scientific study of human language with regard to its nature, structure, and use. ➤➤ **linguistician** *n.*

liniment *n* a liquid preparation that is applied to the skin, *esp* to allay pain or irritation.

lining *n* a protective or decorative layer of a different material used to cover the inside of something, e.g. a garment.

link[1] *n* **1** a connecting element, e.g. a single ring or division of a chain. **2** a connection, relationship, or correspondence between people or things. **3a** a system or connection that enables people, machines, etc to communicate with each other. **b** a means of transportation between one place and another. ➤➤ **linker** *n.*

link[2] *v* **1** to join or connect (two or more things or people). **2** to suggest that (people or things) are significantly associated or have a relationship with each other. **3** (*often* + up) to become connected by a link.

linkage *n* **1** the act or an instance of linking or being linked. **2** a system of links.

linkman *n* (*pl* **linkmen**) a broadcaster whose function is to link and introduce separate items, *esp* in a news programme.

links *pl n* **1** = GOLF LINKS. **2** *Scot* sand hills, *esp* along the seashore.

linkup *n* **1** the establishment of a physical or nonphysical connection or contact. **2a** something that serves as a linking device or factor. **b** a means of communication between people, machines, or places.

Linnaean *or* **Linnean** *adj* following or relating to the systematic methods of the Swedish botanist Linnaeus (d.1778) who established the system of binomial nomenclature for all living things.

linnet *n* a common small African and Eurasian finch with brown plumage, the male having a red breast and forehead.

lino *n* (*pl* **-os**) *chiefly Brit, informal* = LINOLEUM.

linocut *n* a design cut in relief on a piece of linoleum.

linoleate *n* a salt or ester of linoleic acid.

linoleic acid *n* a liquid polyunsaturated fatty acid found in oils obtained from plants, e.g. linseed or peanut oil, and essential for mammalian nutrition.

linoleum *n* a floor covering with a canvas back and a coloured or patterned surface of hardened linseed oil and a filler, e.g. cork dust.

linseed *n* the seed of flax used as a source of linseed oil, as a medicine, or as animal feed.

linseed oil *n* a yellowish oil obtained from flaxseed and used in paint, varnish, printing ink, and linoleum.

linsey-woolsey *n* a coarse sturdy fabric of wool and linen or cotton.

lint *n* **1** a soft absorbent material with a fleecy surface that is made from linen and is used chiefly for surgical dressings. **2** the fibrous coat of thick hairs that covers cotton seeds. **3** fluff or shreds of fibre from cloth. ➤➤ **linty** *adj.*

lintel *n* a horizontal architectural member spanning and usu carrying the load above an opening.

lion *or* **lioness** *n* **1** a flesh-eating big cat of open or rocky areas of Africa and formerly southern Asia that has a tawny body with a tufted tail and in the male a shaggy blackish or dark brown mane. **2** a courageous or ferocious person.

lionhearted *adj* courageous and brave.

lionize *or* **-ise** *v* to treat (somebody) as an object of great interest or importance. ➤➤ **lionization** *n.*

lion's share *n* the largest or best portion.

lip[1] *n* **1** either of the two fleshy folds that surround the mouth. **2** = LABIUM. **3** the edge of a hollow vessel or cavity; *esp* one shaped to make pouring easy. **4** *informal* impudent or insolent talk, *esp* in reply. ✱ **pass one's lips** to be eaten, drunk, or spoken. ➤➤ **lipless** *adj.*

lip[2] *v* (**lipped, lipping**) of water: to lap against (something).

lipa /'leepə/ *n* (*pl* **lipa** *or* **lipas**) a unit of currency in Croatia, worth 100th of a kuna.

lipase *n* an enzyme that accelerates the HYDROLYSIS (chemical breakdown) or synthesis of fats or the breakdown of lipoproteins.

lip gloss *n* a cosmetic for giving a gloss to the lips.

lipid *n* any of various substances that with proteins and carbohydrates form the principal structural components of living cells, and that include fats, waxes, and related and derived compounds.

lipoprotein *n* a protein that has a lipid molecule attached to it and carries lipids in the bloodstream.

liposome *n* a microscopic sphere composed of layers of fatty tissue, which occurs naturally in cells or is manufactured artificially for medical research.

liposuction *n* a technique in plastic surgery for the removal of excess body fat in which the fat is drawn out through a metal tube by vacuum suction.

lippy *adj* (**-ier, -iest**) *informal* cheeky or impudent.

lip-read *v* (*past tense and past part.* **lip-read**) to understand speech by watching the movements of a person's lips. ➤➤ **lip-reader** *n.*

lipsalve *n* an ointment for sore or chapped lips.

lip service *n* support expressed in words but not in actions.

lipstick *n* **1** a waxy solid cosmetic for colouring the lips. **2** a stick of this, with its case.

lip-synch[1] *or* **lip-sync** *n* the exact synchronization of lip movement with recorded speech or song.

lip-synch[2] *v* to move the lips in lip-synch with a recording.

liquefy *or* **liquify** *v* (**-ies, -ied**) to become liquid or reduce to a liquid state. ➤➤ **liquefaction** *n,* **liquefiable** *adj,* **liquefier** *n.*

liquescent *adj* being or tending to become liquid.

liqueur *n* a strong usu sweet alcoholic drink flavoured, e.g. with fruit or aromatics.

liquid[1] *adj* **1** flowing freely like water. **2** neither solid nor gaseous; in a state where the constituent molecules can move freely among themselves but do not tend to separate like those of gases: *liquid mercury.* **3a** shining and clear: *large liquid eyes.* **b** smooth and unconstrained in movement. **4** of sounds: flowing, pure, and free of harshness. **5** of assets: consisting of or capable of ready conversion into cash. ➤➤ **liquidly** *adv,* **liquidness** *n.*

liquid[2] *n* a substance that is liquid, *esp* one that is liquid at normal temperatures.

liquidate *v* **1a** to settle (a debt), *esp* by payment. **b** to bring the commercial activities of (e.g. a business) to an end and use the assets towards paying off the debts. **2** to convert (assets) into cash. **3** *informal* to kill (somebody). ➤➤ **liquidation** *n,* **liquidator** *n.*

liquid crystal *n* a liquid having certain physical, *esp* optical, properties shown by crystalline solids but not by ordinary liquids.

liquid crystal display *n* a display of numbers or symbols, e.g. in a digital watch or calculator, produced by applying an electric field to liquid crystal cells in order to change the amount of light they reflect.

liquidise *v* see LIQUIDIZE.

liquidiser *n* see LIQUIDIZER.

liquidity *n* **1** the state of being liquid. **2** the liquid assets of a company.

liquidize *or* **-ise** *v* to mash or process (e.g. fruit or vegetables) into a liquid.

liquidizer *or* **liquidiser** *n chiefly Brit* a domestic electric appliance for grinding, pureeing, liquidizing, or blending foods.

liquid measure *n* a unit or series of units for measuring liquid capacity.

liquid paraffin *n* a colourless oily mixture of chemical compounds obtained from petroleum, used as a laxative.

liquify *v* see LIQUEFY.

liquor *n* **1** alcoholic drink, *esp* spirits. **2** any liquid substance, *esp* water in which food has been cooked. **3** a solution of a drug in water.

liquorice (*NAm* **licorice**) *n* the pungent black dried root of a plant of the pea family, extracts of which are used in brewing, confectionery, and as a laxative.

liquorish *adj* see LICKERISH.

lira /'liərə/ *n* (*pl* **lire** *or* **liras**) the basic monetary unit of Italy, San Marino, Malta, and Turkey.

lisente /li'sente/ *n* pl of SENTE.

lisle *n* a smooth tightly twisted thread usu made of long-staple cotton.

lisp[1] *v* **1** to pronounce /s/ and /z/ imperfectly, *esp* by giving them the sounds of /th/ and /dh/. **2** to speak with a lisp. ➤➤ **lisper** *n.*

lisp[2] *n* a speech defect or affectation characterized by lisping.

lissom *or* **lissome** *adj* flexible, lithe, or supple. ➤➤ **lissomness** *n.*

list[1] *n* a series or catalogue of words or numbers, e.g. representing people or objects of a particular kind, usu arranged in order so as to be easily found.

list[2] *v* **1** to make a list of (things or people). **2** to include (something or somebody) on a list. **3** *archaic* to recruit (somebody).

list[3] *v* to lean to one side.

list[4] *n* a sideways tilt, *esp* of a ship's hull.

list[5] *n* **1** (*in pl*) **a** the enclosed area for a tournament, or the fence surrounding this. **b** a scene of competition. **2** a band or strip of material; *esp* a selvage.

list[6] *v* **1** *archaic* to please; to suit. **2** *archaic or literary* to wish or choose.

list[7] *n archaic* a desire.

listed *adj* **1** *Brit* of a building: protected by being included in an official list as being historically or architecturally important. **2** of a company: having shares that are quoted on the main market of the London Stock Exchange.

listen[1] *v* **1** to pay attention to sound. **2** to hear or consider with thoughtful attention; to heed. **3** to be alert to catch an expected sound. ➤➤ **listenable** *adj*, **listener** *n*.

listen[2] *n informal* an act of listening.

listen in *v* **1** to tune in to or monitor a broadcast. **2** to listen to a conversation, *esp* surreptitiously.

listening post *n* **1** an advanced position used by troops to gather information about the enemy's movements. **2** a place where information, e.g. about another country or area, is received and monitored.

listeria *n* a rod-shaped bacterium that causes listeriosis in humans and many species of wild and domesticated animals.

listeriosis *n* an often fatal food poisoning, caused by infection with listeria, usu characterized by flu-like symptoms, septicaemia, and meningitis and, in pregnant women, miscarriages.

listing *n* **1** an entry in a list. **2** a list or catalogue.

listless *adj* characterized by indifference, lack of energy, and disinclination for exertion. ➤➤ **listlessly** *adv*, **listlessness** *n*.

list price *n* the basic price of an item as published in a catalogue, price list, or advertisement.

lit *v* past tense and past part. of LIGHT[3], LIGHT[6].

litany *n* (*pl* **-ies**) **1** a prayer consisting of a series of petitions by the leader, each of which is followed by a response, usu the same response, from the congregation. **2** any repetitive recital.

litas /'leetas/ *n* (*pl* **litas**) the basic monetary unit of Lithuania.

litchi *n* see LYCHEE.

-lite *comb. form* forming nouns, denoting: minerals, rocks, and fossils: *graptolite*.

liter *n NAm* see LITRE.

literacy *n* **1** the ability to read and write. **2** skill in or knowledge of a particular subject: *computer literacy*.

literal[1] *adj* **1** denoting the factual or primary meaning of a word or expression, as opposed to a figurative one. **2a** keeping strictly to the basic and straightforward meaning of a written text. **b** reproduced word for word; exact or verbatim. **3** relating to or expressed in letters. **4** characterized by a lack of imagination; prosaic. ➤➤ **literality** *n*, **literalness** *n*.

literal[2] *n Brit* in printing, a misprint involving a single letter.

literalism *n* adherence to the literal meanings of words or texts. ➤➤ **literalist** *n*, **literalistic** *adj*.

literally *adv* **1** in the literal sense; without metaphor or exaggeration. **2** with exact equivalence; verbatim. **3** *informal* used to intensify a metaphorical expression.

literary *adj* **1** constituting, concerning, or producing literature. **2** characteristic of literature; formal or picturesque. ➤➤ **literarily** *adv*, **literariness** *n*.

literate[1] *adj* **1** able to read and write. **2** educated or cultured. **3** possessing knowledge or skill in a particular field of activity: *computer literate*. ➤➤ **literately** *adv*.

literate[2] *n* a literate person.

literati /litə'rahtee/ *pl n* the educated or cultured class; the intelligentsia.

literature *n* **1** writings in prose or verse, *esp* those having artistic value or merit. **2** the body of writings on a particular subject. **3** printed matter, e.g. leaflets or circulars.

lith- *comb. form* see LITHO-.

-lith *comb. form* forming nouns, denoting: stone or rock: *megalith*.

lithe *adj* flexible or supple. ➤➤ **lithely** *adv*, **litheness** *n*.

-lithic *comb. form* forming adjectives, denoting: a specified stage in human beings' use of stone implements: *Neolithic*.

lithium *n* **1** a light soft silver-white metallic element that is used in alloys. **2** a lithium salt used in the treatment of manic-depressive conditions.

litho /'liethoh/ *n* (*pl* **-os**) **1** = LITHOGRAPH[1]. **2** = LITHOGRAPHY.

litho- *or* **lith-** *comb. form* denoting stone: *lithotomy*.

lithograph[1] /'lithəgrahf, -graf/ *n* a print made by lithography. ➤➤ **lithographic** *adj*, **lithographically** *adv*.

lithograph[2] *v* to produce or copy by lithography.

lithography *n* the process of printing from a stone or metal surface on which the image to be printed is ink-receptive and the blank area ink-repellent. ➤➤ **lithographer** *n*.

lithology *n* the study of the composition, shape, etc of rocks and rock formations. ➤➤ **lithological** *adj*.

lithophyte *n* a plant that grows on rock.

lithosphere *n* the solid rocky crust of the earth.

lithotomy *n* (*pl* **-ies**) the surgical removal of a stone, *esp* from the urinary system.

Lithuanian *n* **1** a native or inhabitant of Lithuania. **2** the language of Lithuania. ➤➤ **Lithuanian** *adj*.

litigant *n* a person engaged in a lawsuit. ➤➤ **litigant** *adj*.

litigate *v* **1** to carry on a lawsuit. **2** to contest (an issue) at law. ➤➤ **litigable** *adj*, **litigation** *n*, **litigator** *n*.

litigious *adj* **1** inclined to engage in lawsuits. **2** subject to litigation. ➤➤ **litigiously** *adv*, **litigiousness** *n*.

litmus *n* a colouring matter from lichens that turns red in acid solutions and blue in alkaline solutions.

litmus paper *n* absorbent paper coloured with litmus and used as an indicator of acidity or alkalinity.

litotes /lie'tohteez/ *n* (*pl* **litotes**) understatement in which an affirmative is expressed by the negative of its opposite (e.g. in *not a bad singer*).

litre (*NAm* **liter**) *n* a metric unit of capacity equal to one cubic decimetre (about 1.75 pints).

LittD *abbr* Doctor of Letters.

litter[1] *n* **1a** rubbish or waste products, *esp* in a public place. **b** an untidy accumulation of things. **2** a group of animal offspring born at one birth. **3a** absorbent material placed in a location where a domestic animal, *esp* a cat, urinates and defecates. **b** straw or similar material used as bedding for animals. **c** the uppermost slightly decayed layer of organic matter on the forest floor. **4a** a covered and curtained couch carried by people or animals. **b** a device for carrying a sick or injured person.

litter[2] *v* to strew (an area) with litter.

litterbug *or* **litter lout** *n informal* a person who carelessly drops rubbish in public places.

little[1] *adj* **1** small in size or extent. **2** of a person: young or younger. **3** small in importance or interest; trivial. **4** amounting to only a small quantity;

not much. **5** short in duration; brief. **6** (**a little**) at least some but not much. ➤➤ **littleness** *n.*

little[2] *adv* (**less, least**) **1** (**a little**) to a small extent or degree. **2** (*usu in combination*) not much: *little-known.* **3** hardly or not at all.

little[3] *n* **1a** only a small quantity; not much. **b** (**a little**) a small amount or portion. **2** (**a little**) a short time or distance.

little by little *adv* by small degrees or amounts; gradually.

little end *n* the smaller end of a connecting rod in an engine operated by pistons.

Little Englander *n* an opponent of British involvement in international affairs, *esp* in the 19th cent.

little finger *n* the smallest finger of the hand.

little people *pl n* the imaginary beings, e.g. fairies, elves, etc, of folklore.

littoral[1] *adj* of or on the shore of a sea or lake.

littoral[2] *n* a coastal region; *esp* the intertidal zone.

liturgical *adj* of or having the characteristics of liturgy. ➤➤ **liturgically** *adv.*

liturgy *n* (*pl* **-ies**) **1** the form of service used in the celebration of Communion, *esp* in the Orthodox Church. **2** a prescribed form of public worship. ➤➤ **liturgist** *n.*

livable *or* **liveable** *adj* **1a** suitable for living in. **b** (+ with) pleasant to live with. **2** possible to continue or cope with; endurable. ➤➤ **livability** *n,* **livableness** *n.*

live[1] *v* **1** to be alive; to have the life of an animal or plant. **2** to continue alive. **3** to pass (an amount of time). **4** to maintain oneself; to subsist: *She lives by writing.* **5** to have a home: *They live in the country.* ✱ **live it up** *informal* to enjoy an exciting social life. **live off** to rely on for subsistence. **live through** to survive (a dangerous or unpleasant experience). **live together** of two people: to share a home and have a sexual relationship without being married. **live up to** to achieve (a certain standard or example).

live[2] *adj* **1** having life. **2** containing living organisms: *live yogurt.* **3 a** glowing: *live coals.* **b** connected to a source of electric power. **c** unexploded or unfired: *live ammunition.* **4** of continuing or current interest. **5** performed, performing, or recorded in the presence of an audience. **6** broadcast as it happens.

live[3] *adv* **1** in person and in front of an audience. **2** simultaneously as it happens.

liveable *adj* see LIVABLE.

live action *n* in films, etc, action involving real people or animals, as opposed to animation.

lived-in *adj* **1** showing agreeable signs of having been used and occupied; comfortable and homely. **2** of a person's face: lined or wrinkled.

live down *v* to cause (a mistake or offence) to be forgotten by future good behaviour.

live in *v* to live at one's place of work.

live-in *adj* **1** living at one's place of employment. **2** living with somebody else in his or her home.

livelihood *n* something, *esp* a job, that provides a person with the means to support themselves.

livelong /'livlong/ *adj chiefly literary* whole or entire: *the livelong day.*

lively *adj* (**-ier, -iest**) **1a** active and energetic. **b** done with energy or vigour. **2** full of life, movement, or incident. **3** intellectually active or perceptive. **4** having a striking or stimulating effect on the mind or senses. ➤➤ **livelily** *adv,* **liveliness** *n.*

liven *v* (*often* + up) to make or become more lively.

live out *v* **1** to live to the end of (a period of time). **2** to carry out (something imagined) in real life.

liver[1] *n* **1** a large glandular organ of vertebrates that secretes bile and causes changes in the blood. **2** the liver of an animal eaten as food.

liver[2] *n* a person who lives, *esp* in a specified way.

liver fluke *n* a worm that invades and damages the liver of a sheep or other mammal.

liverish *adj* **1** suffering from liver disorder; bilious. **2** peevish or irascible. ➤➤ **liverishness** *n.*

Liverpudlian *n* **1** a native or inhabitant of Liverpool. **2** the dialect or accent of the people of Liverpool. ➤➤ **Liverpudlian** *adj.*

liver salts *pl n* mineral salts taken in water as a cure for indigestion.

liver sausage *n* a sausage consisting chiefly of cooked minced liver, often with pork trimmings.

liver spot *n* a brown mark on the skin that frequently occurs in older people.

liverwort *n* a plant of a class related to and resembling the mosses but differing in reproduction and development.

livery *n* (*pl* **-ies**) **1a** the distinctive clothing worn by a member of a livery company. **b** a distinctive uniform worn by servants, employees, officials, etc. **c** a distinctive colour scheme, e.g. on a vehicle, distinguishing an organization. **2** = LIVERY STABLE. ➤➤ **liveried** *adj.*

Word history

Middle English via Old French *livrer* to dispense, deliver, from Latin *liberare* to free. The word originally denoted the provision of food and clothing to one's retainers, or the food or clothing supplied, hence distinctive clothing or uniform.

livery company *n* any of various London craft or trade associations that are descended from medieval guilds.

liveryman *n* (*pl* **liverymen**) a freeman of the City of London who is a member of a livery company.

livery stable *n* **1** an establishment where horses are stabled and fed for their owners. **2** an establishment that hires out horses.

lives *n* pl of LIFE.

livestock *n* farm animals kept for use and profit.

live wire *n informal* an alert or active person.

livid *adj* **1** *informal* very angry. **2** discoloured by bruising. **3** ashen or pallid. ➤➤ **lividity** *n,* **lividly** *adv,* **lividness** *n.*

living[1] *adj* **1a** alive; not dead. **b** still in use, *esp* still spoken. **2** true to life; exact. ✱ **in living memory** in a time that people who are alive now can remember.

living[2] *n* **1a** means of subsistence; a livelihood. **b** *Brit* = BENEFICE. **2** the condition of being alive. **3** a way of life.

living room *n* a room in a home used for everyday activities.

living wage *n* a wage sufficient to provide an acceptable standard of living.

living will *n* a document detailing a person's wishes with regard to medical treatment in a situation where they are unable to give informed consent.

lizard *n* a reptile having usu two pairs of functional limbs, a long body and tail, and eyes with movable lids.

LJ *abbr* Lord Justice.

ll. *abbr* lines.

'll *contr* will or shall.

llama *n* a usu domesticated S American ruminant mammal with a woolly fleece that is related to but smaller than the camel.

llano /'l(y)ahnoh/ *n* (*pl* **-os**) an open grassy plain, *esp* in Spanish America.

LLB *abbr* Bachelor of Laws.

LLD *abbr* Doctor of Laws.

LLM *abbr* Master of Laws.

Lloyd's *n* an association of London underwriters specializing in marine insurance and shipping news and insuring against losses of almost every kind.

lm *abbr* lumen.

LMS *abbr* local management of schools.

LNB *abbr* low noise blocker, a device used to select the required signal from a transmission received by a satellite dish.

LNG *abbr* liquefied natural gas.

lo *interj archaic* used to call attention or to express wonder. ✱ **lo and behold** *usu humorous* used to greet a surprise appearance or to introduce a surprising event in a story.

loach *n* a small freshwater fish with a long slender body and spines round the mouth.

load[1] *n* **1a** an amount, *esp* a large or heavy one, that is carried or supported. **b** (*often in combinations*) a quantity carried at one time by a specified means: *a boatload of tourists.* **2** the forces to which a structure is subjected. **3** a burden of responsibility, anxiety, etc. **4** the amount of power delivered by a generator, circuit, etc. **5** the amount of work to be performed by a person, machine, etc. **6** *informal* (*also in pl*) a large quantity; a lot. ✱ **get a load of** *informal* to pay attention to (something surprising) or impressive.

load[2] *v* **1a** to put a load in or on (e.g. a vehicle) or ship. **b** to place (a load) in or on a vehicle or ship. **2a** to weight or shape (dice) to make them fall in a particular way. **b** to make (something) subject to prejudicial influences; to bias. **3a** to put bullets, ammunition, etc into (a gun). **b** to insert (e.g. a film or tape) in a device or piece of equipment. ✱ **load the dice** (*often* + against/in favour of) to prearrange all the elements of a situation, *esp* to somebody's advantage or disadvantage. ➤➤ **loader** *n*.

loaded *adj* **1** carrying a load. **2** of a question, argument, etc: misleading or biased. **3** of a dice: weighted so that it falls in a particular way. **4** having hidden implications. **5** *informal* having a large amount of money. **6** *informal* drunk or intoxicated.

loading *n* **1** a cargo, weight, or stress placed on something. **2** an amount added to an insurance premium to represent extra risks. **3** *Aus* a weighting added to a wage or salary.

load line *n* = PLIMSOLL LINE.

loadstar *n* see LODESTAR.

loadstone *n* see LODESTONE.

loaf[1] *n* (*pl* **loaves**) **1** a mass of baked bread usu having a regular shape. **2** a shaped mass of other food, e.g. sugar. **3** *Brit, informal* the head or brains: *Use your loaf!*

loaf[2] *v* to spend time in idleness.

loafer *n* **1** an idler or slacker. **2** *trademark* a low leather shoe similar to a moccasin but with a broad flat heel.

loam *n* **1** rich crumbly soil consisting of a mixture of clay, silt, and sand. **2** a mixture of clay, sand, and other materials used e.g. for plastering. ➤➤ **loaminess** *n*, **loamy** *adj*.

loan[1] *n* **1** something lent, *esp* money lent at interest. **2** the act of lending or permission to borrow. **3** a loanword. ✱ **on loan** being temporarily used by a borrower.

loan[2] *v* to lend. ➤➤ **loanable** *adj*, **loaner** *n*.

Usage note

See note at LEND.

loan shark *n informal* a person who lends money at exorbitant rates of interest.

loanword *n* a word taken from another language and at least partly naturalized.

loath *or* **loth** *adj* (*usu* + to) unwilling to do something; reluctant.

loathe *v* to dislike intensely, often with a feeling of disgust. ➤➤ **loather** *n*.

loathing *n* extreme dislike or disgust.

loathsome *adj* hateful or disgusting. ➤➤ **loathsomely** *adv*, **loathsomeness** *n*.

loaves *n* pl of LOAF[1].

lob[1] *v* (**lobbed, lobbing**) to throw or hit (e.g. a ball) in a high arc.

lob[2] *n* in sports, a ball or shot that is lobbed.

lobar *adj* relating to or affecting a lobe, e.g. the lobe of a lung.

lobate *adj* having or resembling a lobe or lobes.

lobby[1] *n* (*pl* **-ies**) **1a** a porch or small entrance hall. **b** a large entrance hall serving as a foyer. **2** an anteroom of a legislative chamber, *esp* one to which members of either of the Houses of Parliament go to vote during a division. **3** (*used as sing. or pl*) a group of people engaged in lobbying as representatives of a particular interest group.

lobby[2] *v* (**-ies, -ied**) **1** to try to influence members of a legislative body in favour of or against a policy or course of action. **2** to try to influence (a legislator) with respect to a particular issue. ➤➤ **lobbyer** *n*, **lobbyist** *n*.

lobe *n* a curved or rounded projection or division, e.g. of a bodily organ. ➤➤ **lobed** *adj*.

lobelia *n* a widely distributed and cultivated herbaceous plant with clusters of small showy blue or red flowers.

lobotomize *or* **-ise** *v* to perform a lobotomy on.

lobotomy *n* (*pl* **-ies**) a brain operation used, *esp* formerly, in the treatment of some mental disorders, in which nerve fibres in the cerebral cortex are cut.

lobster *n* (*pl* **lobsters** *or* **lobster**) a large edible ten-legged marine crustacean with stalked eyes, a pair of large claws, and a long abdomen.

lobster pot *n* a basket used as a trap for catching lobsters.

lobster thermidor *n* a dish of lobster cooked in a cream sauce and served in its shell with a grilled cheese topping.

lobworm *n* a large earthworm used as bait by anglers.

local[1] *adj* **1** of a particular place; not general or widespread. **2** primarily serving the needs of a particular limited district. **3** involving or affecting only a restricted part of a living organism. **4** relating to position in space. ➤➤ **locally** *adv*.

local[2] *n* **1** a local person or thing. **2** *Brit, informal* the neighbourhood pub.

local anaesthetic *n* an anaesthetic that causes loss of sensation in a specific area of the body only.

local area network *n* a communications system linking together computer terminals in an office building, manufacturing plant, etc.

local authority *n Brit* the body of people who have political and administrative power in a British city, district, etc.

locale /loh'kahl/ *n* a place or locality, *esp* when viewed in relation to a particular event or characteristic.

local government *n* the government of subdivisions of a major political unit.

localise *v* see LOCALIZE.

locality *n* (*pl* **-ies**) **1** a particular place or neighbourhood. **2** a position in space or time.

localize *or* **-ise** *v* **1** to restrict or assign to a particular place. **2** to give local characteristics to. ➤➤ **localizable** *adj*, **localization** *n*.

local time *n* the actual time in a particular place, as contrasted with that in a different time zone.

locate *v* **1** to determine or indicate the position of. **2** to set or establish in a particular spot. **3** *NAm* to establish oneself or one's business in a particular place; to settle. ➤➤ **locatable** *adj*, **locater** *n*.

location *n* **1** a particular place or position. **2** a place outside a studio where a broadcast or film is made. **3** the act of locating. ➤➤ **locational** *adj*.

locative *adj* denoting a grammatical case expressing the idea of location in or movement towards a particular place.

loc. cit. *abbr* in the place cited.

loch /lokh/ *n* a lake or nearly landlocked arm of the sea in Scotland.

loci *n* pl of LOCUS.

lock[1] *n* **1** a fastening that can be opened and often closed only by means of a particular key or combination. **2** an enclosed section of a river or canal that has gates at each end and in which the water level can be raised or lowered as boats pass through. **3** in wrestling, etc, a hold secured on a usu specified body part. **4** *chiefly Brit* the extent to which the front wheels of a vehicle are turned to change the direction of travel. **5** = LOCK FORWARD. **6** *archaic* a gunlock.

lock[2] *v* **1a** to fasten or make secure with or as if with a lock. **b** to be fitted and fastenable with a lock. **2** to shut in or make inaccessible by locking a door, lid, etc. **3** to make or become fixed or jammed immovably. **4a** to hold in a close embrace or grapple in combat. **b** to engage in a discussion, conflict, etc. ✱ **lock horns** to engage in an argument or dispute. ➤➤ **lockable** *adj*.

lock[3] *n* **1a** a curl, tuft, etc of hair. **b** *literary (in pl)* the hair of the head. **2** a tuft or bunch of wool, cotton, etc.

locker *n* **1** a cupboard or compartment that may be closed with a lock. **2** a storage compartment on a boat or ship.

locker room *n* a changing room for participants in sporting activities, usu having lockers for personal possessions.

locket *n* a small gold or silver case that has space for a memento and is usu worn on a chain round the neck.

lock forward *n* in rugby, either of two players positioned inside the second row of the scrum.

lockjaw *n* **1** an early symptom of tetanus characterized by spasm of the jaw muscles and inability to open the jaws. **2** = TETANUS.

locknut *n* **1** a nut screwed hard up against another to prevent it from moving. **2** a nut so constructed that it locks itself when screwed up tight.

lock on *v* (*often* + to) to sight and follow (a target) automatically by means of a radar beam or sensor.

lockout *n* a temporary closing of a workplace by an employer in order to gain concessions from or resist demands of employees.

lock out *v* **1** to prevent (somebody) from entering a place by locking the door, gate, etc. **2** to subject (a body of employees) to a lockout.

locksmith *n* somebody who makes or mends locks as an occupation.

lock, stock, and barrel *adv* wholly or completely.

lockup *n* **1** a prison, *esp* a small or temporary one. **2** *Brit* a shop or garage that can be locked up. **3** an investment that is meant to be held over a long term.

lock up *v* **1** to lock all the doors of a building. **2** to put in prison. **3** to invest (capital) in such a way that it cannot easily be converted into ready money.

loco[1] *n* (*pl* **-os**) *informal* a locomotive.

loco[2] *adj informal* out of one's mind.

locomotion *n* the act or power of moving from place to place.

locomotive[1] *n* an engine that moves under its own power, *esp* one that moves railway carriages and wagons.

locomotive[2] *adj* of or assisting movement from place to place.

locomotor *adj* of or involving the locomotive organs of the body.

locum *n informal* a doctor or cleric temporarily taking the place of another.

locum tenens *n* (*pl* **locum tenentes** /te'nenteez, -tiz/) *formal* = LOCUM.

locus /'lohkəs, 'lokəs/ *n* (*pl* **loci** /'lohsie, 'lohkie/) **1** a place or position. **2** in mathematics, the set of all points whose location is determined by a stated condition or conditions.

locust *n* **1** a migratory grasshopper that often travels in vast swarms through tropical areas, stripping them of all vegetation. **2** any of various hardwooded trees, e.g. the carob.

locust tree *n* = LOCUST (2).

locution *n* **1** a word or expression characteristic of a region or group. **2** a style or manner of speaking.

lode *n* an ore deposit.

loden *n* **1** a thick woollen waterproof cloth used for making coats. **2** a dull greyish green colour typical of this cloth.

lodestar *or* **loadstar** *n* a star that guides, *esp* the pole star.

lodestone *or* **loadstone** *n* a piece of magnetized mineral, *esp* magnetite.

lodge[1] *n* **1** a house lived in during a particular season, e.g. the hunting season. **2a** a small house orig for the use of a gamekeeper, gardener, or other employee of an estate. **b** a porter's room, e.g. at the entrance to a college, block of flats, etc. **3a** the meeting place of a branch of a fraternal organization. **b** a particular branch of such an organization, or its members collectively. **4** a den or lair of beavers or otters. **5** a Native American tent or dwelling.

lodge[2] *v* **1a** to provide temporary, *esp* rented, accommodation for. **b** to reside temporarily as a lodger. **2** to fix or become fixed firmly in place. **3** to lay (e.g. a complaint) before an authority. **4** to deposit (e.g. money) for safekeeping. ➤➤ **lodgement** *n*.

lodger *n* somebody who occupies a rented room in somebody else's house.

lodging *n* **1** a temporary place to live. **2** (*in pl*) a rented room or rooms for residing in, usu in a private house.

lodging house *n* a house where lodgings are provided and let.

loess /'loh·is, les/ *n* a yellowish brown loamy deposit believed to be carried by the wind.

loft[1] *n* **1** = ATTIC. **2a** a gallery in a church or hall. **b** (*often in combination*) an upper floor in a barn or warehouse used for storage: *a hayloft*. **c** a shed or coop for pigeons. **3a** in golf, the backward slant of the face of a club head. **b** a stroke or shot using this. **4** the thickness of padding or insulation.

loft[2] *v* to propel (e.g. a ball) high up into the air.

lofty *adj* (**-ier, -iest**) **1** impressively high. **2** elevated in character and spirit; noble. **3** having a haughty overbearing manner; supercilious. ⋙ **loftily** *adv,* **loftiness** *n.*

log[1] *n* **1** a piece or length of unshaped timber ready for sawing or for use as firewood. **2** the full record of a ship's voyage or an aircraft's flight. **3** an apparatus for measuring the rate of a ship's motion through the water. **4** any of various records of performance.

log[2] *v* (**logged, logging**) **1** to enter in a log. **2a** to attain (e.g. an indicated distance, speed, or time) as noted in or measured by a log. **b** (*often* + up) to achieve or have (something) to one's credit. **3** to cut trees or logs for timber. ⋙ **logging** *n.*

log[3] *n* = LOGARITHM.

-log *comb. form NAm* see -LOGUE.

loganberry *n* (*pl* **-ies**) a sweet red edible berry, a hybrid of a raspberry and a dewberry.

logarithm *n* the exponent that indicates the power to which a number is raised to produce a given number. ⋙ **logarithmic** *adj,* **logarithmically** *adv.*

logbook *n* **1** a book used to record the details of a ship's voyage or an aircraft's flight. **2** *Brit* = REGISTRATION DOCUMENT.

loge /lohzh/ *n* a private box in a theatre.

logger *n NAm* a lumberjack.

loggerhead *n* **1** a very large flesh-eating turtle of the W Atlantic. **2** *archaic* a fool or dunce. ✱ **at loggerheads** in quarrelsome disagreement.

loggia /'loj(i)ə/ *n* (*pl* **loggias** *or* **loggie**) a roofed open gallery behind a colonnade or arcade.

logic *n* **1** a science that deals with the formal principles and structure of thought and reasoning and assesses arguments on the basis of their validity. **2** rationality or a rationally discernible sequence in thought or argument. **3** an inevitable progression of cause and effect following a particular event, set of circumstances, etc. **4** the fundamental principles and the connection of circuit elements for performing operations in a computer. ⋙ **logician** *n.*

logical *adj* **1** of or conforming with logic. **2** capable of reasoning or of using reason in an orderly fashion. ⋙ **logicality** *n,* **logically** *adv.*

logical positivism *n* a philosophical movement of the 20th cent. stressing linguistic analysis and rejecting metaphysical theories. ⋙ **logical positivist** *n.*

logic bomb *n* a computer virus designed to become active in specific circumstances.

log in *v* = LOG ON.

logistics *pl n* (*used as sing. or pl*) the work of planning and organizing the details of a large and complex operation. ⋙ **logistic** *adj,* **logistically** *adv.*

logjam *n* **1** a deadlock or impasse. **2** a mass of logs jammed together in a river, causing a blockage.

logo *n* (*pl* **-os**) an identifying symbol used by a company.

logo- *comb. form* forming words, denoting: thought or speech: *logogram.*

log off *v* to end a session at a computer terminal by performing a fixed set of operations.

logogram *n* a character or sign used, e.g. in shorthand, to represent an entire word.

log on *v* to begin a session at a computer terminal by performing a fixed set of operations.

logorrhoea (*NAm* **logorrhea**) *n* excessive and often incoherent talkativeness or wordiness.

logotype *n* **1** a single block or piece of type that prints a whole word. **2** = LOGO.

log out *v* = LOG OFF.

logrolling *n NAm* the trading of votes by members of a legislature to secure favourable action on projects of mutual interest.

-logue (*NAm* **-log**) *comb. form* forming nouns, denoting: conversation or talk: *duologue.*

-logy *or* **-ology** *comb. form* forming nouns, denoting: **1** a doctrine, theory, or science: *ethnology.* **2** oral or written expression: *phraseology.* **3** writings of a specified kind or on a specified subject: *trilogy.* ⋙ **-logic** *comb. form,* **-logical** *comb. form,* **-logist** *comb. form.*

loin *n* **1a** the part of the body on each side of the spinal column between the hipbone and the lower ribs. **b** a cut of meat comprising this part of a carcass with the adjoining half of the vertebrae included. **2** (*in pl*) **a** the upper and lower abdominal regions and the region about the hips. **b** the genitals.

loincloth *n* a cloth worn about the hips and covering the genitals.

loiter *v* **1** to remain in an area for no obvious reason; to hang about. **2** to make frequent pauses while travelling; to dawdle. ⋙ **loiterer** *n.*

loll *v* **1** to recline or move in a lazy or relaxed manner; to lounge. **2** to hang down loosely.

Lollard *n* a follower of the English religious reformer John Wycliffe (d.1384).

lollipop *n* **1** a large round sweet of boiled sugar on the end of a stick. **2** *Brit* an ice lolly.

lollipop man *or* **lollipop lady** *n* (*pl* **lollipop men** *or* **lollipop ladies**) *Brit, informal* somebody controlling traffic to allow children to cross busy roads, *esp* near a school.

lollop *v* (**lolloped, lolloping**) to move or proceed with an ungainly loping motion.

lollo rosso *n* a variety of lettuce with curly reddish leaves and a slightly bitter taste.

lolly *n* (*pl* **-ies**) **1** a lollipop or ice lolly. **2** *Brit, informal* = MONEY.

Lombard *n* **1** a member of a Teutonic people who invaded Italy in the sixth cent. **2** a native or inhabitant of Lombardy in N Italy. **3** the dialect of Lombardy. ⋙ **Lombardic** *adj.*

Lombardy poplar *n* a tall narrow European poplar with upward-sloping branches.

Londoner *n* a native or inhabitant of London.

London pride *n* a plant of the saxifrage family with small pinkish white flowers growing out of a rosette of leaves.

lone *adj* **1** only or sole. **2** situated alone or separately; isolated. **3** *formal* having no company; solitary.

lonely *adj* (**-ier, -iest**) **1** sad from being alone or without friends. **2** cut off from others; solitary. **3** not frequented by people; desolate. ⋙ **loneliness** *n.*

lonely hearts *pl n* lonely people seeking companions or spouses, *esp* by advertising in a newspaper.

loner *n* a person who prefers solitude.

lonesome[1] *adj chiefly NAm* = LONELY. ⋙ **lonesomeness** *n.*

lonesome[2] ✱ **on/by one's lonesome** *informal* by oneself; alone.

lone wolf *n* a person who prefers to work, act, or live alone.

long[1] *adj* **1a** extending for a considerable distance. **b** having greater length than usual. **2** having a specified length. **3** extending over a considerable or specified time. **4** containing a large or specified number of items or units: *a long list.* **5** of a speech sound or syllable: of relatively long duration. **6** of a ball, etc: hit for a considerable distance. **7a** of betting odds: greatly differing in the amounts wagered on each side. **b** subject to great odds; unlikely. ✱ **be long** *informal* to take a long time. **in the long run** in the course of prolonged time, trial, or experience. **long in the tooth** past one's best days; old. **long on** *informal* having a large amount of, or being well endowed with. **not by a long chalk** see CHALK[1]. ⋙ **longish** *adj.*

long[2] *adv* (**longer, longest**) **1** for a long time. **2** throughout a specified period: *all night long.* **3** of the act of striking a ball: over a long distance or past the target. ✱ **no longer 1** not now, though usu previously. **2** not for a greater length of time. **so/as long as 1** during and up to the end of the time that; while. **2** = PROVIDING. **so long** *informal* goodbye.

long[3] *n* a long period of time. ✱ **the long and (the) short** the gist; the outline.

long[4] *v* (*often* + for) to feel a strong desire or craving.

long. *abbr* longitude.

long ago *n* the distant past.

longboat *n* the largest boat carried by a sailing vessel.

longbow *n* **1** a medieval English bow of about 2m (6ft) in length. **2** a similar bow used in archery.

long-distance[1] *adj* covering or operating over a long distance.

long-distance[2] *adv* between points a long distance apart.

long division *n* arithmetical division in which the calculations corresponding to parts of the operation are written out.

long-drawn *adj* = LONG-DRAWN-OUT.

long-drawn-out *adj* prolonged or protracted.

long drink *n* a cool refreshing drink containing a comparatively large quantity of liquid but little or no alcohol.

longevity /lon'jeviti, long-/ *n* great length of life.

long face *n* a facial expression of sadness or melancholy.

longhand *n* ordinary writing; handwriting.

long haul *n* **1** a lengthy usu difficult task or period of time. **2** the transport of goods or passengers over long distances.

long-headed *adj dated* having unusual foresight or wisdom. ⋙ **long-headedness** *n.*

long hop *n* in cricket, an easily hit short-pitched delivery of a ball.

longhorn *n* an animal of a long-horned breed of cattle of Spanish derivation.

longing *n* a strong desire, *esp* for something difficult to attain. ⋙ **longing** *adj,* **longingly** *adv.*

longitude *n* the angular distance of a point on the surface of the earth measured E or W from a prime meridian, e.g. that of Greenwich.

longitudinal *adj* **1** relating to length or the lengthways dimension. **2** relating to longitude. ⋙ **longitudinally** *adv.*

long johns *pl n informal* underpants with legs extending usu down to the ankles.

long jump *n* an athletic field event consisting of a jump for distance from a running start. ⋙ **long jumper** *n.*

long leg *n* in cricket, a fielding position near the boundary behind the batsman on the leg side of the pitch.

long-life *adj* of a commercial product: processed so as to be long-lasting.

long-lived *adj* **1** characterized by long life. **2** long-lasting or enduring. ⋙ **long-livedness** *n.*

long off *n* in cricket, a fielding position near the boundary behind the bowler on the off side of the pitch.

long on *n* in cricket, a fielding position near the boundary behind the bowler on the leg side of the pitch.

long-range *adj* **1** of or fit for long distances. **2** involving a long period of time.

longship *n* a long open Viking warship propelled by oars and a sail.

longshore *adj* on, along, or of the shore.

longshore drift *n* a process by which material is moved along a shore by a current flowing approximately parallel to the shore-line.

longshoreman *n* (*pl* **longshoremen**) *NAm* = DOCKER.

long shot *n* a venture that involves considerable risk and has little chance of success. ✱ **by a long shot** by a great deal.

longsighted *or* **long-sighted** *adj* unable to see things that are close to the eyes clearly. ⋙ **longsightedness** *n.*

long-standing *adj* of long duration.

long stop *n* in cricket, a fielding position directly, and some distance, behind the wicketkeeper.

long-suffering *adj* patiently enduring pain, difficulty, or provocation. ⋙ **long-sufferingly** *adv.*

long suit *n* **1** in card games, the suit of which one has the greatest number of cards in one's hand. **2** the activity or quality in which a person excels: *Diplomacy wasn't exactly her long suit.*

long-term *adj* occurring over or involving a relatively long period of time.

longueur /long'guh/ *n* a dull and tedious part or period.

long vacation *n* the long summer holiday of British law courts and universities.

long wave *n* a band of radio waves typically used for sound broadcasting and covering wavelengths of 1000m or more.

longways *adv* = LENGTHWAYS.

long-winded *adj* tediously long in speaking or writing. ⋙ **long-windedly** *adv,* **long-windedness** *n.*

longwise *adv chiefly NAm* = LENGTHWAYS.

loo[1] *n Brit, informal* = TOILET.

loo[2] *n* an old card game in which the winner of each trick takes a portion of the pool while losing players have to contribute to the next pool.

loofah *n* a dried seed pod of a plant of the cucumber family that is used as a bath sponge.

look[1] *v* **1a** to use one's eyes to see. **b** to direct one's sight in a specified direction: *Look over there.* **2** to appear or seem: *You look tired.* **3** to have a specified outlook: *The house looks east.* ✱ **look after** to take care of. **look back** to think about the past. **look down on** to regard (somebody) as inferior. **look for** to try to find. **look here** used to attract somebody's attention. **look into** to investigate. **look like** *informal* to be likely: *It looks like they're not coming.* **look sharp** to be quick; to hurry. **not look back** to continue to enjoy great success.

look[2] *n* **1** an act of looking; a glance. **2a** a facial expression. **b** (*in pl*) physical appearance, *esp* when pleasing. **c** the general appearance of somebody or something. **3** a style or fashion.

look[3] *interj* used to attract attention or to show annoyance.

lookalike *n* somebody or something that looks like another; a double.

looker *n* **1** (*often in combination*) a person having an appearance of a specified kind. **2** *informal* an attractive person.

look in *v* to pay a short visit.

look-in *n informal* **1** a chance to take part. **2** a chance of success.

looking glass *n* = MIRROR[1].

look on *v* to be a spectator at an event.

lookout *n* **1** a place or structure affording a wide view for observation. **2a** somebody engaged in keeping watch. **b** a careful watch. **3** *Brit, informal* a matter of care or concern: *It's your lookout if you do such a silly thing.*

look out *v* **1** to keep watching. **2** to take care.

look over *v* to check or examine.

look-see *n informal* a relatively quick assessment or investigation.

look to *v* **1** (*often* + for) to rely on (somebody or something) to do or provide something. **2** to pay careful attention to.

look up *v* **1** to improve in prospects: *Business is looking up.* **2** to search for in a source of reference. ✱ **look up to** to have much respect for (somebody).

loom[1] *n* a frame or machine for weaving yarn or thread into cloth.

loom[2] *v* **1** to come into sight indistinctly, often in menacing form. **2a** to appear in an impressively great or exaggerated form. **b** to take shape as an impending occurrence.

loon[1] *n informal* a mad or silly person.

loon[2] *n NAm* = DIVER (3).

loon[3] *v Brit, informal* to behave in a crazy or excited manner.

loony[1] *adj* (**-ier, -iest**) *informal* crazy or foolish. ➤➤ **looniness** *n.*

loony[2] *n* (*pl* **-ies**) a crazy or foolish person.

loony bin *n informal, derog* a hospital or home for people who are mentally ill.

loop[1] *n* **1** a figure that has a curved outline surrounding a central opening. **2a** something shaped like or in the form of a loop. **b** a manoeuvre in which an aircraft flies in a vertical circle. **3** a piece of film or magnetic tape whose ends are spliced together so as to reproduce the same material continuously. **4** a series of instructions, e.g. for a computer, that is repeated until a terminating condition is reached. **5** a closed electric circuit. **6** = LOOP LINE.

loop[2] *v* **1** to form or move in a loop or loops. **2** to execute a loop in an aircraft. **3** to make a loop in or around. **4** to put into a loop of film, tape, computer instructions, etc. ✱ **loop the loop** to perform a loop in an aircraft.

looper *n* a small hairless caterpillar that moves in a series of loops by arching its body. Also called INCHWORM.

loophole *n* **1** an ambiguity or omission in a text through which its intent may be evaded. **2** a small opening through which missiles may be discharged or light and air admitted.

loop line *n* a railway line that leaves and later rejoins a main line.

loopy *adj* (**-ier, -iest**) *informal* slightly crazy or foolish. ➤➤ **loopiness** *n.*

loose[1] *adj* **1a** not tightly fastened or securely attached. **b** not tight-fitting. **2a** free from a state of confinement or restraint. **b** not kept together in a bundle, container, etc. **3** not dense or compact in structure or arrangement. **4** not tightly drawn or stretched; slack. **5** lacking in precision or exactness. **6** *dated* **a** careless or irresponsible. **b** dissolute or promiscuous. ➤➤ **loosely** *adv,* **looseness** *n.*

Usage note

loose *or* **lose**? The spelling of these two words can cause problems. *Loose,* spelt with *-oo-* and pronounced with a soft *s* to rhyme with *goose* is mainly used as an adjective meaning 'not tight': *a loose-fitting dress; the knot has worked loose. Lose* with one *o* and pronounced to rhyme with *whose* is a verb meaning 'to be unable to find': *I'm always losing my spectacles.*

loose[2] *v* **1** to free from restraint; to release. **2** to unfasten or detach. **3** to make less tight; to relax or loosen. **4** (*often* + off) to fire or discharge (e.g. a bullet or a volley).

loose[3] *adv* in a loose manner; loosely.

loose[4] ✱ **on the loose** free from restraint or confinement, *esp* having escaped.

loose box *n Brit* an individual enclosure within a barn or stable in which an animal may move about freely.

loose cannon *n* somebody who acts independently and disruptively in an organization or group.

loose cover *n Brit* a removable cloth cover for an article of furniture.

loose end *n* an incomplete or unexplained detail. ✱ **at a loose end** bored or unoccupied.

loose-leaf *adj* of an album or book: bound so that individual leaves can be detached or inserted.

loosen *v* to make or become loose or looser. ➤➤ **loosener** *n.*

loosen up *v* **1** to become more relaxed. **2** to warm up one's muscles before exercising.

loosestrife *n* **1** a plant of the primrose family with leafy stems and yellow or white flowers. **2** a plant of the henna family with showy spikes of purple flowers.

loot[1] *n* **1** goods, usu of considerable value, taken in war or illegally by force or deception. **2** *informal* money.

loot[2] *v* to seize and carry away goods from a place by force or illegally, *esp* in war or public disturbance. ➤➤ **looter** *n.*

lop[1] *v* (**lopped, lopping**) **1a** to cut off (a branch, limb, etc). **b** to cut off branches or twigs from (a tree). **2** (+ off/away) to remove (something unnecessary or undesirable). ➤➤ **lopper** *n.*

lop[2] *n* small branches and twigs cut from a tree.

lope[1] *n* an easy bounding gait.

lope[2] *v* to move at a lope.

lop-eared *adj* of an animal: having ears that droop.

lopsided *adj* **1** having one side heavier or lower than the other. **2** lacking in balance, symmetry, or proportion. ➤➤ **lopsidedly** *adv,* **lopsidedness** *n.*

loquacious *adj formal* = TALKATIVE. ➤➤ **loquaciously** *adv,* **loquaciousness** *n,* **loquacity** *n.*

loquat *n* the small yellow edible plumlike fruit of an Asian evergreen tree.

Lord[1] *n* **1a** God. **b** Jesus Christ. **2** (**the Lords**) the House of Lords. **3** used as the title of a lord or as a prefix to some official titles. ✱ **My Lord** used as a form of address to judges, bishops, and noblemen.

Lord[2] *interj* used to express surprise or dismay.

lord[1] *n* **1** a man of rank or high position, *esp* a British nobleman. **2** a ruler by hereditary right, to whom service and obedience are due. **3** somebody who exercises leadership or great power in some area.

lord[2] ✻ **lord it over** to behave domineeringly towards.

Lord Advocate *n* the chief law officer of the Crown in Scotland.

Lord Chamberlain *n* the chief officer of the British royal household.

Lord Chancellor *n* an officer of state who presides over the House of Lords and serves as head of the judiciary.

Lord Chief Justice *n* the president of the Queen's Bench Division of the High Court.

Lord Justice *n* (*pl* **Lords Justices**) a judge of the Court of Appeal.

Lord Lieutenant *n* (*pl* **Lords Lieutenant** *or* **Lord Lieutenants**) an official representative of a sovereign in a British county.

lordly *adj* (**-ier, -iest**) **1** of or having the characteristics of a lord; dignified or noble. **2** disdainful and arrogant. ➤➤ **lordliness** *n.*

Lord Mayor *n* the mayor of the City of London and other large British cities.

lordosis *n* an abnormal forward curvature of the spine: compare KYPHOSIS, SCOLIOSIS.

Lord President of the Council *n* (*pl* **Lord Presidents of the Council**) the president of the Privy Council.

Lord Privy Seal *n* a member of the British Cabinet with no departmental duties.

Lord Provost *n* the provost of a Scottish district council.

lords and ladies *n* = CUCKOOPINT.

Lord's Day *n* (*usu* **the Lord's Day**) = SUNDAY.

lordship *n* **1** the authority or power of a lord; dominion. **2** (**Lordship**) used as a title to address or refer to a bishop, a High Court Judge, or a peer.

Lord's Prayer *n* (**the Lord's Prayer**) the prayer taught by Jesus beginning 'Our Father'.

Lords Spiritual *pl n* the archbishops and senior bishops in the House of Lords.

Lords Temporal *pl n* the peers in the House of Lords who are not bishops.

lore *n* a specified body of knowledge or tradition.

lorgnette /law'nyet/ *n* (*also in pl*) a pair of glasses or opera glasses with a handle.

lorikeet *n* a small tree-dwelling Australasian parrot with bright-coloured plumage.

loris *n* a small nocturnal slow-moving tree-dwelling primate of S and SE Asia.

lorry *n* (*pl* **-ies**) *Brit* a large motor vehicle for carrying loads by road.

lory *n* (*pl* **-ies**) a small Australasian or Indonesian parrot with long slender protuberances on the tongue that are used for extracting nectar from flowers.

lose *v* (*past tense and past part.* **lost**) **1** to miss from one's possession and fail to find. **2** to suffer deprivation of; to cease to have. **3** to suffer loss through the death of. **4a** to fail to win (a contest or something competed for). **b** to suffer a defeat. **5** to fail to use (e.g. an opportunity). **6** to get rid of. **7** to fail to keep or maintain (e.g. one's balance). **8** *informal* to escape from or shake off (a pursuer). **9** to withdraw (oneself) from immediate reality. **10** (*usu in passive*) to cause the destruction or death of. **11** of a watch or clock: to run slow by (a specified amount). **12** to make a financial loss. ✻ **lose face** to lose one's dignity or reputation. **lose heart** to become dispirited. **lose it** *informal* to lose control of oneself. **lose one's way 1** to be unable to find the correct direction to go in; to get lost. **2** to go astray intellectually or morally.

Usage note
lose *or* **loose**? See note at LOOSE[1].

lose out *v* **1** (*often* + on) to make a loss. **2** to be the loser, *esp* unluckily.

loser *n* **1** somebody who loses a contest. **2** somebody who loses consistently; a failure.

loss *n* **1a** the act or an instance of losing possession. **b** the harm or privation resulting from loss. **2** a person, thing, or amount lost. **3** failure to gain, win, or use something. **4** an amount by which cost exceeds revenue. ✻ **at a loss 1** uncertain or puzzled. **2** not making enough money to cover costs.

loss adjuster *n* somebody who investigates insurance claims and decides how much compensation to award.

loss leader *n* an article sold at a loss in order to draw customers.

lost[1] *adj* **1a** unable to find the way. **b** bewildered or helpless. **2** (*usu* + in) rapt or absorbed. ✻ **be lost for words** to be unable to think what to say, e.g. because of shock. **be lost on** to be unnoticed or unappreciated by. **get lost** *informal* (*usu in imperative*) to go away.

lost[2] *v* past tense and past part. of LOSE.

lost cause *n* a cause that has lost all prospect of success.

lost generation *n* a generation considered socially and emotionally disadvantaged; *specif* the generation reaching adulthood during World War I.

lot[1] *n* **1** *informal* (*also in pl*) a considerable amount or number. **2** (**the lot**) *chiefly Brit* the whole amount or number. **3** *informal* (*used as sing. or pl*) a number of associated people or things; a set. **4** an article or a number of articles offered as one item in an auction sale. **5a** an object used to decide a question by chance. **b** the use of lots as a means of making a choice. **6a** something that falls to somebody by lot; a share. **b** one's way of life or worldly fate; fortune. **7** a portion of land. ✻ **a lot 1** *informal* much, considerably, or to a great extent. **2** *informal* often or frequently. **draw/cast lots** to decide an issue by random selection of objects. **throw in one's lot with** to join forces or ally oneself with.

lot[2] *v* (**lotted, lotting**) to form or divide into lots.

loth *adj* see LOATH.

Lothario /lə'thahrioh/ *n* (*pl* **-os**) a man whose chief interest is seducing women.

loti /'lohti/ *n* (*pl* **maloti** /ma'lohti/) the basic monetary unit of Lesotho.

lotion *n* a medicinal or cosmetic liquid for external use.

lottery *n* (*pl* **-ies**) **1** a way of raising money by selling tickets bearing numbers, some of which are later randomly selected to entitle the holder to a prize. **2** an event or affair whose outcome is decided or apparently decided by chance.

lotto *n* **1** a children's game similar to bingo. **2** *NAm, Aus* = LOTTERY.

lotus *n* **1** a water lily. **2** a fruit considered in Greek legend to cause indolence and dreamy contentment.

lotus-eater *n* somebody who lives in dreamy indolence.

lotus position *n* a yoga position in which one sits with legs folded, the feet resting on the thighs.

louche /loohsh/ *adj* morally dubious; disreputable or seedy.

loud[1] *adj* **1** marked by or producing a high volume of sound. **2** obtrusive in appearance; flashy. ➤➤ **loudly** *adv,* **loudness** *n.*

loud[2] *adv* in a loud manner. ✱ **out loud** aloud.

louden *v* to make or become loud or louder.

loud-hailer *n chiefly Brit* = MEGAPHONE.

loudmouth *n informal* a person who frequently talks in a loud offensive way. ➤➤ **loudmouthed** *adj.*

loudspeaker *n* a device that converts electrical energy into acoustic energy and that is used to reproduce sounds.

lough /lokh/ *n* a loch in Ireland.

lounge[1] *v* to act or move idly or lazily; to loll.

lounge[2] *n* **1** a sitting room in a private house. **2** a room in a public building providing comfortable seating. **3** a waiting room, e.g. at an airport.

lounge bar *n Brit* = SALOON (1A).

lounger *n* **1** a comfortable chair, *esp* an extended one. **2** somebody who lounges.

lounge suit *n Brit* a man's suit for wear during the day.

lour[1] *or* **lower** /'lowə/ *v* **1** to scowl or look sullen. **2** of the sky or weather: to become dark and threatening. ➤➤ **louring** *adj,* **louringly** *adv.*

lour[2] *or* **lower** *n* a sullen expression.

louse *n* (*pl* **lice**) **1a** a small wingless insect parasitic on warm-blooded animals. **b** (*usu in combination*) a small insect or related animal that lives on fish, plants, etc. **2** (*pl* **louses**) *informal* a contemptible person.

louse up *v informal* to spoil or make a mess of.

lousy *adj* (**-ier, -iest**) **1** *informal* very bad, unpleasant, useless, etc. **2** *informal* very mean; despicable. **3** *informal* (+ with) having large numbers of; teeming with. **4** infested with lice. ➤➤ **lousily** *adv,* **lousiness** *n.*

lout *n* a rough ill-mannered person, usu a man or youth. ➤➤ **loutish** *adj.*

louvre (*NAm* **louver**) /'loohvə/ *n* **1** any of a set of slanted strips of metal, wood, glass, etc fitted across an opening to allow the air, light, or sound to enter while providing privacy. **2** a roof lantern or turret with slatted apertures to let smoke out or light in. ➤➤ **louvred** *adj.*

lovable *or* **loveable** *adj* having qualities that inspire love or affection; sweet, charming, or amiable. ➤➤ **lovableness** *n,* **lovably** *adv.*

lovage *n* an aromatic perennial plant sometimes cultivated as a herb or flavouring agent.

love[1] *n* **1** a strong feeling of attachment, tenderness, and protectiveness for another person. **2** attraction or devotion based on sexual desire. **3** warm interest in and enjoyment of something. **4** the object of love. **5** a score of zero in tennis, squash, etc. **6** *Brit, informal* used as a friendly or affectionate form of address. ✱ **make love** to have sexual intercourse. ➤➤ **loveless** *adj.*

love[2] *v* **1** to feel love for. **2** to have a great liking or enthusiasm for. ➤➤ **loving** *adj,* **lovingly** *adv.*

loveable *adj* see LOVABLE.

love affair *n* **1** a sexual liaison or romantic attachment between people, *esp* a temporary one. **2** a lively enthusiasm.

lovebird *n* a small usu grey or green parrot that shows great affection for its mate.

lovebite *n* a temporary red mark produced by biting or sucking an area of the skin in sexual play.

love child *n euphem* an illegitimate child.

love feast *n* a meal eaten together by a Christian congregation in token of brotherly love.

love-in-a-mist *n* a European garden plant with pale blue or white flowers enveloped in numerous very fine leaves.

love-lies-bleeding *n* a plant with drooping clusters of small usu scarlet or purple flowers.

lovelorn *adj* sad because of unrequited love.

lovely[1] *adj* (**-ier, -iest**) **1** delicately or delightfully beautiful. **2** very pleasing; fine. ➤➤ **loveliness** *n.*

lovely[2] *n* (*pl* **-ies**) *informal* a beautiful woman.

lovemaking *n* **1** sexual activity; *esp* sexual intercourse. **2** *archaic* courtship.

love nest *n informal* a secret place used for conducting a usu illicit sexual relationship.

lover *n* **1** a person with whom somebody has a sexual relationship, *esp* outside marriage. **2** somebody who is keen on something: *an opera lover.*

love seat *n* an S-shaped double chair or settee that allows two people to sit side by side though facing each other.

lovesick *adj* languishing with love. ➤➤ **lovesickness** *n.*

lovey-dovey *adj informal* excessively loving or romantic.

loving cup *n* a large ornamental drinking vessel with two or more handles that is passed among a group of people for all to drink from.

low[1] *adj* **1a** not measuring much from the base to the top; not high. **b** situated or rising only a little above the ground or some other reference point. **c** situated below the normal level. **2** of less than the usual degree, size, amount, or value. **3** considered comparatively unimportant. **4a** of sound: not loud; soft. **b** of a note: depressed in pitch. **5** lacking strength or spirit; weak or depressed. **6** morally reprehensible or vulgar. **7** unfavourable or disparaging. **8** humble in character or status. **9** of a gear: designed for slow speed. ➤➤ **lowness** *n.*

low[2] *n* **1** a relatively or unusually small amount or depressed level. **2** a region of low atmospheric pressure.

low[3] *adv* at or to a low place or degree.

low[4] *v* to make the deep sustained throat sound characteristic of a cow. ➤➤ **low** *n.*

lowboy *n NAm* a low chest or side table.

lowbrow *adj informal, derog* catering for or having unsophisticated or unintellectual tastes. ➤➤ **lowbrow** *n.*

Low Church *adj* tending to minimize emphasis on the priesthood, sacraments, and ceremonial in the Anglican Church. ➤➤ **Low Churchman** *n.*

lowdown *n* (**the lowdown**) *informal* useful information.

low-down *adj informal* underhand or despicable.

lower[1] *adj* **1** relatively low in position, rank, or order. **2** less advanced in the scale of evolutionary development. **3** denoting an earlier division of the named geological period or series. **4** denoting the southern part of a specified area.

lower[2] *v* **1a** to cause to descend; to move down. **b** to reduce the height of. **2a** to reduce in value, amount, degree, pitch, etc. **b** to degrade.

lower[3] *v* see LOUR[1].

lower[4] *n* see LOUR[2].

lower case *n* letters belonging to the series typically used elsewhere than at the beginning of sentences or proper names, e.g. a, b, c rather than A, B, C. ➤➤ **lower-case** *adj.*

lower chamber *n* = LOWER HOUSE.

lower class *n* (*used as sing. or pl*) a social class occupying a position below the middle class. ➤➤ **lower-class** *adj.*

lower house *n* the larger legislative house in a parliament that has two chambers, usu made up of elected members.

lowest common denominator *n* **1** the lowest common multiple of two or more denominators. **2** *derog* something that is common, acceptable, or comprehensible to all or the greatest possible number of people.

lowest common multiple *n* the smallest number that is a multiple of each of two or more numbers.

low frequency *n* a radio frequency in the range between 30 and 300kHz.

Low German *n* the German dialects of N Germany.

low-impact *adj* **1** of physical exercise: making no stressful demands on the body. **2** causing little environmental harm.

low-key *adj* of low intensity; restrained.

lowland *n* **1** (*also in pl*) low or level country. **2** (**the Lowlands**) the central and E part of Scotland lying S of the Highlands. ➤➤ **lowlander** *n.*

low-level *adj* **1** occurring, done, or placed at a low level. **2** being of low importance or rank. **3** of a computer language: in which each word, symbol, etc is equivalent to one machine code instruction.

lowlife *n* (*pl* **lowlifes**) *informal* a criminal or immoral person.

low-loader *n* a truck or railway carriage with a low load-carrying platform.

lowly[1] *adj* (**-ier, -iest**) **1** humble and modest in manner or spirit. **2** low in the scale of biological or cultural evolution. **3** ranking low in a social or economic hierarchy. ➤➤ **lowliness** *n.*

lowly[2] *adv* **1** in a humble or meek manner. **2** in a low position, manner, or degree.

low-lying *adj* lying below the normal level or at a low altitude.

low profile *n* a mode of operation or behaviour intended to attract little attention. ➤➤ **low-profile** *adj.*

low relief *n* sculpture with forms barely projecting from the background; bas-relief.

low-rise *adj* of a building: constructed with relatively few storeys.

low season *n* a time of low profitability, *esp* a period when the number of holidaymakers is low.

low-spirited *adj* dejected or depressed.

Low Sunday *n* the Sunday following Easter.

low-tech *adj* using low technology.

low technology *n* technology that is simple and unsophisticated.

low tide *n* **1** the tide when the water reaches its lowest level. **2** the time when this occurs.

low water *n* = LOW TIDE.

lox[1] *n* liquid oxygen.

lox[2] *n* smoked salmon.

loyal *adj* having or showing unswerving support for or allegiance to a person, country, or cause; faithful. ➤➤ **loyally** *adv.*

loyalist *n* somebody loyal to a government or sovereign, *esp* in time of revolt. ➤➤ **loyalism** *n.*

loyalty *n* (*pl* **-ies**) **1** being loyal. **2** a feeling of allegiance or duty.

loyalty card *n Brit* a card issued by a retailer, e.g. a supermarket, to reward regular customers by giving them points towards discounts on future purchases.

lozenge *n* **1** a small often medicated sweet. **2** a figure with four equal sides and two acute and two obtuse angles; a diamond or rhombus.

LP *n* a gramophone record designed to be played at 33 revolutions per minute and typically having a diameter of 30.5cm (12in.).

LPG *abbr* liquefied petroleum gas.

L-plate *n Brit* a sign bearing a letter L fixed to a motor vehicle to show that the driver is not yet qualified.

Lr *abbr* the chemical symbol for lawrencium.

LRP *abbr* lead replacement petrol.

LSD *n* lysergic acid diethylamide, a drug taken illegally for its potent action in producing hallucinations and altered perceptions.

LSE *abbr* London School of Economics.

Lt. *abbr* Lieutenant.

Ltd *abbr Brit* Limited.

Lu *abbr* the chemical symbol for lutetium.

lubber *n* a big clumsy person. ➤➤ **lubberly** *adj and adv.*

lubber line *n* a fixed line on the compass of a ship or aircraft that is aligned with the fore-and-aft line of the craft.

lubricant *n* a substance, e.g. grease or oil, capable of reducing friction and wear by forming a film between solid surfaces. ➤➤ **lubricant** *adj.*

lubricate *v* **1** to make smooth or slippery. **2** to apply a lubricant to or act as a lubricant on. ➤➤ **lubrication** *n,* **lubricator** *n.*

lubricious *or* **lubricous** *adj formal* **1** lecherous or salacious. **2** slippery or smooth. ➤➤ **lubriciously** *adv,* **lubricity** *n.*

lucent *adj literary* **1** glowing with light; luminous. **2** clear or translucent. ➤➤ **lucency** *n,* **lucently** *adv.*

lucerne *n* = ALFALFA.

lucid *adj* **1** clear to the understanding; plain. **2** having full use of one's faculties; sane. ➤➤ **lucidity** *n,* **lucidly** *adv,* **lucidness** *n.*

Lucifer *n* **1** the devil. **2** the planet Venus when appearing as the morning star.

luck *n* **1** whatever good or bad events happen to a person by chance. **2** the tendency for a person to be consistently fortunate or unfortunate. **3** success as a result of good fortune. ✱ **hard/tough/worse luck!** *informal* used to express commiseration. **no such luck** *informal* unfortunately not. **try one's luck** attempt to do something that may or may not succeed.

luckless *adj* unlucky or unfortunate. ➤➤ **lucklessly** *adv,* **lucklessness** *n.*

luck out *v NAm* to prosper or succeed, *esp* through chance or good fortune.

lucky *adj* (**-ier, -iest**) having, resulting from, or bringing good luck. ➤➤ **luckily** *adv,* **luckiness** *n.*

lucky dip *n Brit* an attraction, e.g. at a fair, in which small prizes can be drawn unseen from a receptacle.

lucrative *adj* producing wealth; profitable. ➤➤ **lucratively** *adv,* **lucrativeness** *n.*

lucre *n* money, wealth, or profit.

lucubrate *v formal* to study or write, *esp* at night.

lucubration *n formal* **1** laborious study or meditation, *esp* at night. **2** studied or pretentious expression in speech or writing.

lud *n* (*usu* **m'lud**) *Brit* used to address a judge in court.

Luddite *n* **1** a member of a group of early 19th-cent. English workmen who destroyed labour-saving machinery as a protest against unemployment. **2**

somebody opposed to technological progress. ➤➤ **Luddism** *n.*

ludicrous *adj* amusingly absurd. ➤➤ **ludicrously** *adv,* **ludicrousness** *n.*

ludo *n* a simple board game played on a square board with counters and dice.

luff[1] *n* the forward edge of a fore-and-aft sail.

luff[2] *v* **1** (*often* + up) to sail nearer the wind. **2** to raise or lower (a jib on a crane).

Luftwaffe /ˈlooftvahfə, ˈlooftwahfə/ *n* the German Air Force, *esp* during World War II.

lug[1] *v* (**lugged, lugging**) to drag, pull, or carry (something) with great effort.

lug[2] *n* = LUGSAIL.

lug[3] *n* **1** something, e.g. a handle, that projects like an ear. **2** *Brit, dialect or humorous* an ear. **3** a clumsy man.

luge[1] /loohzh/ *n* a small toboggan that is ridden in a supine position and used in racing.

luge[2] *v* to ride on a luge.

luggage *n* cases, bags, etc containing a traveller's belongings.

lugger *n* a small boat with one or more lugsails.

lughole *n Brit, dialect or humorous* an ear.

lugsail *n* a four-sided fore-and-aft sail attached to an obliquely hanging yard.

lugubrious *adj* mournful, *esp* exaggeratedly or affectedly so. ➤➤ **lugubriously** *adv,* **lugubriousness** *n.*

lugworm *n* a marine worm that burrows in sand and is used for bait.

lukewarm *adj* **1** moderately warm; tepid. **2** lacking enthusiasm; indifferent. ➤➤ **lukewarmly** *adv,* **lukewarmness** *n.*

lull[1] *v* **1** to cause to sleep or rest with soothing sounds, motion, etc. **2** to cause to relax vigilance, *esp* by deception. **3** to become less in intensity or strength.

lull[2] *n* a temporary pause or decline in activity.

lullaby *n* (*pl* **-ies**) a song used to lull children to sleep.

lulu *n informal* a remarkable or wonderful person or thing.

lum *n chiefly Scot* a chimney.

luma *n* (*pl* **luma** *or* **lumas**) a unit of currency in Armenia, worth 100th of a dram.

lumbago *n* muscular pain in the lower back.

lumbar *adj* relating to or in the region of the loins or the lower back.

lumbar puncture *n* a medical procedure in which a hollow needle is inserted into the spinal cord, e.g. to withdraw cerebrospinal fluid for diagnosis.

lumber[1] *v* to move heavily or clumsily.

lumber[2] *n* **1** surplus or disused articles, e.g. furniture, that are stored away. **2** *NAm* timber or logs.

lumber[3] *v* **1** *Brit, informal* to encumber or saddle (somebody) with something. **2** *NAm* to cut down and saw timber. ➤➤ **lumberer** *n.*

lumberjack *n* a person engaged in logging.

lumberjacket *n* a heavy usu brightly checked woollen jacket that is fastened up to the neck.

lumen *n* (*pl* **lumina** *or* **lumens**) the SI unit of luminous flux equal to the amount of light emitted in a solid angle of one steradian by a point source of light with an intensity of one candela.

luminance *n* the luminous intensity of a surface in a given direction per unit of projected area.

luminary *n* (*pl* **-ies**) **1** a person brilliantly outstanding in some respect. **2** a natural body that gives light, e.g. the sun or moon.

luminesce *v* to exhibit luminescence.

luminescence *n* an emission of light that occurs at low temperatures and that is produced by physiological processes, chemical action, friction, or electrical action. ➤➤ **luminescent** *adj.*

luminosity *n* (*pl* **-ies**) **1** being luminous. **2** the relative quantity of light or brightness.

luminous *adj* **1** emitting or full of light; bright. **2** relating to light. ➤➤ **luminously** *adv,* **luminousness** *n.*

lummox *n informal* a clumsy or stupid person.

lump[1] *n* **1** a compact mass of indefinite size and shape. **2** an abnormal swelling. **3** *informal* a heavy thickset person; *specif* one who is stupid or dull. **4** (**the lump**) *Brit, informal* the whole group of casual non-union building workers. ✱ **a lump in one's throat** a dry feeling in the throat caused by emotion.

lump[2] *v* **1** (*usu* + together) to group without discrimination. **2** (*usu* + along) to move in a heavy way.

lump[3] *v informal* to put up with: *If you don't like it you can lump it.*

lumpectomy *n* (*pl* **-ies**) the surgical removal of a tumour, *esp* in breast cancer.

lumpen *adj informal* stupid or unenlightened.

lumpenproletariat *n* (*used as sing. or pl*) in Marxist theory, the poorest people in society, regarded as unenlightened and not interested in revolution.

lumpfish *n* (*pl* **lumpfishes** *or* **lumpfish**) = LUMPSUCKER.

lumpish *adj* **1** dull or sluggish. **2** heavy or awkward. ➤➤ **lumpishly** *adv,* **lumpishness** *n.*

lumpsucker *n* a sea fish of the N Atlantic with a large rounded body and pelvic fins that are modified into a sucker.

lump sum *n* a large sum of money given in a single payment.

lumpy *adj* (**-ier, -iest**) **1** filled or covered with lumps. **2** of water: characterized by choppy waves. ➤➤ **lumpily** *adv,* **lumpiness** *n.*

lunacy *n* (*pl* **-ies**) **1** wild foolishness; extravagant folly. **2** *no longer in technical use* insanity.

lunar *adj* **1** of the moon. **2** measured by the motion of the moon: *a lunar day.*

lunar eclipse *n* an eclipse in which the moon passes through the earth's shadow.

lunar month *n* the period of time, averaging 29 days, between two successive new moons.

lunar year *n* a period of twelve lunar months.

lunate *adj* shaped like a crescent.

lunatic *n* **1** *no longer in technical use* a mentally ill person. **2** a foolish or foolhardy person. ➤➤ **lunatic** *adj.*

lunatic fringe *n* the extremist or fanatical members of a political or social movement.

lunation *n* in astronomy, a lunar month.

lunch[1] *n* a midday meal. ✱ **out to lunch** *informal* crazy or out of touch with reality.

lunch[2] *v* to eat lunch. ➤➤ **luncher** *n.*

luncheon *n formal* = LUNCH[1].

luncheon meat *n* a precooked mixture of pork and cereal shaped in a loaf and usu canned.

luncheon voucher *n Brit* a voucher given to an employee as a benefit and exchangeable for food in some restaurants and shops.

lunette *n* **1** a semicircular window opening in a wall or dome. **2** a semicircular section of wall that is partly surrounded by a vault, often filled by a mural or sculpture. **3** a temporary fortification consisting of two walls forming a projecting angle. **4** a case used to hold the consecrated host in the Roman Catholic Church. **5** a towing ring on a vehicle.

lung *n* either of the paired respiratory organs in the chest of air-breathing vertebrates. ➤➤ **lungful** *n.*

lunge[1] *v* to make a sudden forward movement or thrust, e.g. with a weapon.

lunge[2] *n* the act or an instance of lunging.

lunge[3] *n* a long rein used to hold and guide a horse in training.

lungfish *n* (*pl* **lungfishes** *or* **lungfish**) a fish that breathes by a modified air bladder as well as gills.

lungi *n* (*pl* **lungis**) a usu cotton cloth worn variously as a loincloth, turban, or sash.

lungwort *n* **1** a European plant with white-spotted leaves covered in rough hairs, and blue or pink flowers. **2** a lichen formerly used in the treatment of lung disease.

lupin *or* **lupine** /'loohpin/ *n* a plant cultivated *esp* for its long spikes of flowers.

lupine /'loohpien/ *adj* relating to or resembling a wolf.

lupus *n* any of several diseases characterized by ulcers or scaly patches on the skin, *esp* tuberculosis of the skin.

lupus erythematosus *n* a progressive disease marked by reddish skin lesions, arthritic changes, and wasting.

lurch[1] *n* an abrupt, uncontrolled, and jerky movement.

lurch[2] *v* **1** to move in an abrupt, uncontrolled, and jerky manner. **2** to stagger and sway.

lurch[3] ✱ **in the lurch** in a vulnerable and unsupported position; deserted: *He left me in the lurch.*

lurcher *n* a swift-running dog that is a cross between a greyhound or whippet and another breed, e.g. the collie or terrier.

lure[1] *n* **1a** somebody or something used to entice or decoy. **b** a bait for attracting animals, birds, or fish so that they can be caught. **2** a bunch of feathers and often meat attached to a long cord and used by a falconer to recall a bird. **3** the power to appeal or attract.

lure[2] *v* to attract with something that promises pleasure, food, or gain.

lurgy *n* (*pl* **-ies**) *Brit, humorous* an illness, *esp* a widespread minor infection.

lurid *adj* **1** unnaturally or unattractively bright in colour; gaudy. **2** sensational or shocking. ➤➤ **luridly** *adv,* **luridness** *n.*

lurk[1] *v* **1** to lie hidden in wait, *esp* with evil intent. **2** to be present but undetected; *esp* to be a hidden threat. ➤➤ **lurker** *n.*

lurk[2] *n Aus, informal* a ruse or stratagem; a racket.

luscious *adj* **1** having a delicious taste or smell. **2** *esp* of a woman: extremely attractive. **3** richly luxurious or appealing to the senses. ➤➤ **lusciously** *adv,* **lusciousness** *n.*

lush[1] *adj* **1** producing or covered by luxuriant growth. **2** opulent or sumptuous. **3** *informal* sexually attractive or voluptuous. ➤➤ **lushly** *adv,* **lushness** *n.*

lush[2] *n chiefly NAm, informal* a heavy drinker; an alcoholic.

lust[1] *n* **1** strong sexual desire, *esp* as opposed to love. **2** an intense longing; a craving. ➤➤ **lustful** *adj,* **lustfully** *adv,* **lustfulness** *n.*

lust[2] *v* (*usu* + for/after) to have an intense desire or craving, *esp* a sexual desire.

lustra *n* pl of LUSTRUM.

lustral *adj* relating to a ceremony of religious purification.

lustrate *v* to purify ceremonially. ➤➤ **lustration** *n.*

lustre (*NAm* **luster**) *n* **1** a glow of reflected light; a sheen. **2** glory or distinction. **3** a glass pendant used *esp* to ornament a chandelier. **4** a lustrous fabric. **5** an iridescent glaze used to decorate pottery or porcelain. ➤➤ **lustred** *adj,* **lustreless** *adj.*

lustreware (*NAm* **lusterware**) *n* ceramic ware decorated with an iridescent glaze.

lustrous *adj* softly and evenly shining. ➤➤ **lustrously** *adv,* **lustrousness** *n.*

lustrum *n* (*pl* **lustrums** *or* **lustra**) a period of five years.

lusty *adj* (**-ier, -iest**) full of vitality; healthy and vigorous. ➤➤ **lustily** *adv,* **lustiness** *n.*

lutanist *n* see LUTENIST.

lute[1] *n* a stringed musical instrument with a large pear-shaped body, a long neck, and pairs of strings played by plucking.

lute[2] *n* a substance, e.g. cement or clay, used for sealing or packing joints or for coating a porous surface to make it impervious.

lute[3] *v* to seal or coat with lute.

lutecium *n* see LUTETIUM.

lutenist *or* **lutanist** *n* a lute player.

lutetium *or* **lutecium** *n* a silver-white metallic element found in ytterbium alloys.

Lutheran[1] *n* a member of a Lutheran church.

Lutheran[2] *adj* relating to religious doctrines, e.g. justification by faith alone, or Protestant churches derived from Martin Luther (d.1546) or his followers. ➤➤ **Lutheranism** *n.*

luting *n* = LUTE[2].

lutz *n* in ice-skating, a jump from one skate with a complete turn in the air and a return to the other skate.

luvvie *or* **luvvy** *n* (*pl* **-ies**) *Brit, informal or humorous* an actor, *esp* seen as affected.

lux *n* (*pl* **lux**) the SI unit of illumination, equal to one lumen per square metre.

luxate *v* to dislocate (a part of the body). ➤➤ **luxation** *n.*

luxe *n* = LUXURY.

Luxembourger *n* a native or inhabitant of Luxembourg.

luxuriant *adj* characterized by abundant growth: *luxuriant vegetation.* ➤➤ **luxuriance** *n,* **luxuriantly** *adv.*

Usage note

luxuriant *or* **luxurious**? These two words are sometimes confused. *Luxuriant* means 'growing thickly and abundantly': *luxuriant vegetation. Luxurious* is the adjective connected with the ordinary sense of *luxury*: *the sort of luxurious accommodation you would expect from a five-star hotel.*

luxuriate *v* (*often* + in) to enjoy oneself consciously; to revel.

luxurious *adj* **1** extremely comfortable and usu furnished with articles of high quality: *luxurious accommodation.* **2** *literary* fond of luxury or self-indulgence. ➤➤ **luxuriously** *adv,* **luxuriousness** *n.*

Usage note
luxurious *or* **luxuriant?** See note at LUXURIANT.

luxury *n* (*pl* **-ies**) **1** great ease or comfort based on habitual or liberal use of expensive items. **2a** something desirable but costly or difficult to obtain. **b** something relatively expensive adding to pleasure or comfort but not essential.

LV *abbr Brit* luncheon voucher.

LW *abbr* **1** long wave. **2** low water.

lwei /lə'way/ *n* (*pl* **lwei** *or* **lweis**) a unit of currency in Angola, worth 100th of a kwanza.

lx *abbr* lux.

-ly[1] *suffix* forming adjectives, with the meanings: **1** having the characteristics of: *fatherly.* **2** recurring regularly at intervals of; every: *hourly.*

-ly[2] *suffix* forming adverbs, with the meaning: in such a manner: *slowly.*

lycanthrope *n literary* = WEREWOLF.

lycanthropy *n* the supernatural transformation of a human being into a wolf. ➤➤ **lycanthropic** *adj.*

lycée /'leesay/ *n* a French secondary school.

lyceum *n* **1** (*often* **Lyceum**) a public building, cinema, theatre, etc. **2** *NAm, archaic* a hall for public lectures or discussions.

lychee *or* **litchi** *n* a small oval fruit with a scaly outer covering and a hard seed surrounded by edible soft white fragrant pulp.

lych-gate *or* **lich-gate** *n* a roofed gate at the entrance to a churchyard orig used as a resting place for a coffin.

Lycra *n trademark* a synthetic stretchy yarn made from polyurethane and used chiefly in tight-fitting sportswear and swimwear.

lye *n* **1** a strong alkaline liquid rich in potassium carbonate used in making soap. **2** a strong alkaline solution, e.g. of sodium hydroxide or potassium hydroxide.

lying[1] *v* present part. of LIE[1].

lying[2] *v* present part. of LIE[4].

lykewake *n Brit* a watch held over a dead body.

Lyme disease *n* an infectious disease characterized by fever, joint pain, chronic lethargy, and a rash, caused by a tick-borne bacterium.

lymph *n* a pale fluid resembling blood plasma containing white blood cells that circulates in the lymphatic vessels and bathes the cells of the body.

lymph- *or* **lympho-** *comb. form* denoting lymph or lymphatic tissue.

lymphatic[1] *adj* **1** of or produced by lymph, lymphoid tissue, or lymphocytes. **2** conveying lymph. **3** lacking physical or mental energy; sluggish.

lymphatic[2] *n* a vessel that contains or conveys lymph.

lymphatic system *n* the network of vessels that transport lymph to the bloodstream.

lymph gland *n* = LYMPH NODE.

lymph node *n* any of the rounded masses of lymphoid tissue in the lymphatic system where lymphocytes are formed.

lympho- *comb. form* see LYMPH-.

lymphocyte *n* a white blood cell that is present in large numbers in lymph and blood and defends the body, e.g. by producing antibodies. ➤➤ **lymphocytic** *adj.*

lymphoid *adj* of or constituting the tissue characteristic of the lymph nodes.

lymphoma *n* (*pl* **lymphomas** *or* **lymphomata**) cancer of the lymph nodes.

lynch *v* to put (an alleged offender) to death illegally by mob action. ➤➤ **lyncher** *n.*

lynchet *n Brit* a terrace formed on a hillside by prehistoric cultivation.

lynchpin *n* see LINCHPIN.

lynx *n* (*pl* **lynxes** *or* **lynx**) a wildcat with relatively long legs, a short stubby tail, a mottled coat, and often tufted ears.

lynx-eyed *adj* having keen eyesight.

lyrate *adj* shaped like a lyre.

lyre *n* a stringed musical instrument of the harp family with a U-shaped frame and strings stretched from a crossbar to the base, used by the ancient Greeks.

lyrebird *n* an Australian songbird the male of which displays tail feathers in the shape of a lyre during courtship.

lyric[1] *n* **1** (*in pl*) the words of a popular song. **2** a lyric poem.

lyric[2] *adj* **1** of poetry: expressing direct personal emotion, or suitable for being set to music and sung. **2** of a singer: having a light voice and a melodic style.

lyrical *adj* **1** having a beautiful or songlike quality. **2** full of admiration or enthusiasm. **3** = LYRIC[2] (I). ➤➤ **lyrically** *adv.*

lyricism *n* **1a** a pleasantly melodious and songlike quality, *esp* in music. **b** a directly personal style in art, literature, etc. **2** great enthusiasm or exuberance.

lyricist *n* a writer of lyrics.

lyrist /'lie·ərist/ *n* **1** somebody who plays the lyre. **2** /'lirist/ = LYRICIST.

lysergic acid *n* an acid obtained from alkaloids that occur in the fungus ergot, and from which the drug LSD is obtained.

lysergic acid diethylamide *n* = LSD.

lyses *n* pl of LYSIS.

lysin *n* a substance capable of causing lysis; *esp* an antibody capable of causing disintegration of red blood cells or micro-organisms.

lysine *n* a basic amino acid found in most proteins and an essential constituent of the human diet.

lysis *n* (*pl* **lyses** /'lieseez/) **1** a process of disintegration or dissolution of cells. **2** the gradual decline of a disease process, e.g. fever. ➤➤ **lytic** *adj,* **lytically** *adv.*

-lysis *comb. form* forming nouns, denoting: decomposition, disintegration, or breaking down: *electrolysis.* ➤➤ **-lytic** *comb. form.*

M

M[1] *or* **m** *n* (*pl* **M's** *or* **Ms** *or* **m's**) **1** the 13th letter of the English alphabet. **2** the Roman numeral for 1000.

M[2] *abbr* **1** mark. **2** mega-. **3** Monsieur. **4** motorway.

m *abbr* **1** male. **2** married. **3** masculine. **4** mass. **5** metre. **6** mile. **7** milli-. **8** million. **9** minute. **10** month.

'm *contr* am.

MA *abbr* **1** Massachusetts (US postal abbreviation). **2** Master of Arts.

ma *n informal* one's mother.

ma'am /mam, mahm; *unstressed* məm/ *n* used *esp* in Britain when addressing the Queen: madam.

Maasai *n* see MASAI.

mac *or* **mack** *n Brit, informal* a raincoat.

macabre /mə'kahb(r)ə/ *adj* **1** ghastly; gruesome. **2** relating to or depicting the grimmer or uglier aspects of death.

macadam *n* small broken stones compacted into a solid mass, bound together with tar or asphalt, and used in making a road surface: compare TARMACADAM.

macadamia *n* the edible waxy round nut of an Australian evergreen tree.

macaque /mə'kahk/ *n* a short-tailed monkey of S Asia and the E Indies, with cheek pouches in which food is stored.

macaroni *pl n* (*used as sing. or pl*) pasta shaped in hollow tubes.

macaronic *adj* denoting a type of burlesque verse characterized by a mixture of Latin and vernacular words.

macaroon *n* a small cake or biscuit composed chiefly of egg whites, sugar, and ground almonds or coconut.

macaw *n* a large long-tailed parrot of S and Central America with showy plumage.

McCarthyism *n* a fanatical campaign against alleged Communists in the US senate and in public life, carried on by Senator Joseph McCarthy (d.1957) in the early 1950s. ➤➤ **McCarthyist** *n and adj*, **McCarthyite** *n and adj.*

McCoy ✱ **the real McCoy** *informal* something that is neither imitation nor substitute; the genuine article.

mace[1] *n* **1** a heavy medieval spiked staff or club. **2** an ornamental staff used as a symbol of authority.

mace[2] *n* an aromatic spice consisting of the dried external covering of a nutmeg.

macédoine /masə'dwahn, 'masədoyn/ *n* a mixture of fruits or vegetables served sometimes in jelly as a salad, cocktail, or garnish.

Macedonian *n* **1** a native or inhabitant of the ancient kingdom of Macedonia in SE Europe, the modern republic of Macedonia in the Balkans, or the region of Macedonia in Greece. **2** the language of modern Macedonia. ➤➤ **Macedonian** *adj.*

macerate *v* to cause (food) to become soft or separated into constituent elements by steeping in liquid. ➤➤ **maceration** *n.*

McGuffin *n* an incident or device in a book or film that precipitates the action, important to the main characters but overlooked by the reader or audience.

Mach /mak, mahk/ *n* = MACH NUMBER.

machair /'makhə/ *n* in W Scotland, a flat strip of sandy grass-grown land close to the shore, used for grazing.

machete /mə'sheti/ *n* a large heavy knife used for cutting vegetation and as a weapon.

Machiavellian *adj* cunning, opportunist, and deceitful. ➤➤ **Machiavellian** *n.*

Machiavellianism *n* the political theory of the Italian statesman Machiavelli (d.1527); *esp* the view that any means, however unscrupulous, can justifiably be used in securing or retaining political power.

machicolation *n* an opening between the corbels of a projecting parapet or in the roof of a portal for discharging missiles upon assailants below. ➤➤ **machicolated** *adj.*

machinate *v* (*often* + against) to scheme or plot, *esp* to do harm. ➤➤ **machinator** *n.*

machination *n* a scheming move intended to accomplish some usu discreditable end.

machine[1] *n* **1a** an apparatus having a combination of mechanically, electrically, or electronically operated parts for performing a task. **b** an instrument, e.g. a lever or pulley, designed to transmit power, force, or motion. **2** a person or organization that operates with mechanical efficiency.

machine[2] *v* to make or operate on (something) with a machine. ➤➤ **machinability** *n,* **machinable** *adj,* **machineable** *adj.*

machine code *n* a system of symbols and rules for coding information in a form usable by a computer or other machine.

machine gun *n* an automatic gun for rapid continuous fire.

machine language *n* = MACHINE CODE.

machine-readable *adj* directly usable by a computer.

machinery *n* **1a** machines in general or as a functioning unit. **b** the working parts of a machine. **2** the system or organization by which an activity or process is controlled.

machine tool *n* a usu power-driven machine designed for cutting or shaping wood, metal, etc.

machinist *n* **1** a person who operates a machine. **2** a person who makes or repairs machinery.

machismo /mə'kizmoh, mə'chizmoh/ *n* an exaggerated awareness and assertion of masculinity.

Mach number /mak, mahk/ *n* a number representing the ratio of the speed of a body to the speed of sound in the surrounding atmosphere.

macho /'machoh/ *adj* toughly or aggressively virile.

macintosh *n* see MACKINTOSH.

mack *n Brit, informal* see MAC.

mackerel *n* (*pl* **mackerels** *or* **mackerel**) an important food fish of the N Atlantic that has a green back with dark blue bars and a silvery belly.

mackerel sky *n* a sky covered with rows of small white clouds, resembling the patterns on a mackerel's back.

mackintosh *or* **macintosh** *n chiefly Brit* a raincoat.

macr- *comb. form* see MACRO-.

macramé /mə'krahmi/ *n* the art of tying threads or cords in patterns to make decorative articles.

macro *n* (*pl* **-os**) a single computer instruction that stands for a complete sequence of operations.

macro- *or* **macr-** *comb. form* **1** long in duration or size: *macrobiotic*. **2** large or abnormally large: *macrocosm*.

macrobiotic *adj* denoting a restricted diet, *esp* one consisting chiefly of whole grains and vegetables, that is intended to promote health and prolong life.

macrocarpa *n* a Californian cypress grown in New Zealand and elsewhere to provide hedging or windbreaks.

macroclimate *n* the predominant or normal climate of a large region.

macrocosm *n* **1** the universe. **2** a complex that is a large-scale reproduction of one of its constituents. ⋙ **macrocosmic** *adj*.

macroeconomics *pl n* (*used as sing. or pl*) a study of large-scale economics, e.g. of a nation. ⋙ **macroeconomic** *adj*.

macroinstruction *n* = MACRO.

macro lens *n* a lens with which subjects can be photographed at very close range.

macromolecule *n* a large molecule, e.g. of a protein or rubber, built up from smaller chemical structures. ⋙ **macromolecular** *adj*.

macron *n* a mark (¯) placed over a vowel or syllable to show a long or stressed sound.

macroscopic *adj* **1** large enough to be observed by the naked eye. **2** considered in terms of large units or elements. ⋙ **macroscopically** *adv*.

macula *n* (*pl* **maculae** /-lee/ *or* **maculas**) **1** = MACULE. **2** = MACULA LUTEA. ⋙ **macular** *adj*.

macula lutea /'loohti·ə/ *n* (*pl* **maculae luteae** /'loohti·ee/) a small yellowish area lying near the centre of the retina that constitutes the region of best vision.

maculation *n* the arrangement of spots and markings on an animal or plant.

macule *n* a discoloured spot on the skin that is not raised above the surface.

macumba *n* a Brazilian religious cult combining features of voodoo and of Christianity.

mad *adj* (**madder, maddest**) **1** mentally disordered; insane. **2** utterly foolish; senseless. **3** very angry. **4** carried away by enthusiasm or desire. **5** of a dog: affected with rabies. **6** intensely excited or distraught; frantic. **7** characterized by intense and often chaotic activity. ✱ **like mad** *informal* very hard, fast, loud, etc. ⋙ **madly** *adv*, **madness** *n*.

Madagascan *n* a native or inhabitant of the island of Madagascar. ⋙ **Madagascan** *adj*.

madam *n* **1** used as a form of respectful address to a woman. **2** the female head of a brothel. **3** *Brit, informal* a conceited or petulant young lady or girl.

madame /'madəm/ *n* (*pl* **mesdames** /'maydam, may'dam/) used as a title equivalent to *Mrs* before the name of a married French-speaking woman or as a form of address equivalent to *madam*.

madcap *adj* impulsive or reckless.

mad cow disease *n informal* BSE (bovine spongiform encephalopathy).

madden *v* **1** to drive mad. **2** to exasperate or enrage. ⋙ **maddeningly** *adv*.

madder *n* a red dye prepared from the root of a Eurasian plant.

madding *adj archaic or literary* acting as if mad; frenzied.

made *v* past tense and past part. of MAKE[1]. ✱ **have it made** *informal* to be certain of success; to be in a fortunate situation.

Madeira *n* a fortified wine from Madeira.

Madeira cake *n Brit* a very rich sponge cake.

madeleine *n* a small rich sponge cake baked in a small mould and often decorated with jam and coconut.

mademoiselle /,madmwə'zel/ *n* (*pl* **mademoiselles** *or* **mesdemoiselles** /,maydmwə'zel/) used as a title or form of address equivalent to *Miss* for an unmarried French-speaking girl or woman.

made-to-measure *adj* of a garment: made according to an individual's measurements in order to achieve a good fit.

made-up *adj* **1** wearing make-up. **2** fictional, invented, or untrue. **3** of a road: covered in tarmac.

madhouse *n* **1** *dated* an institution for the insane. **2** *informal* a place of uproar or confusion.

madman *n* (*pl* **madmen**) **1** a man who is insane. **2** a crazy or reckless man.

Madonna *n* (**the Madonna**) the Virgin Mary.

madras *n* **1** a fine cotton plain-woven fabric, usu in brightly coloured checked or striped designs. **2** a spicy curry.

madrigal *n* **1** an unaccompanied and often complex secular song for several voices. **2** a short medieval love poem. ⋙ **madrigalist** *n*.

madwoman *n* (*pl* **madwomen**) **1** a woman who is insane. **2** a crazy or reckless woman.

maelstrom /'maylstrohm, 'maylstrəm/ *n* **1** a powerful whirlpool. **2** something resembling a maelstrom in turbulence and violence.

maenad /'meenad/ *n* **1** a female participant in ancient Greek ritual orgies in honour of Dionysus. **2** a frenzied woman. ⋙ **maenadic** *adj*.

maestro /'miestroh/ *n* (*pl* **maestros** *or* **maestri** /'miestree/) a master in an art; *esp* an eminent composer, conductor, or teacher of music.

MAFF *abbr Brit* Ministry of Agriculture, Fisheries, and Food.

Mafia *n* **1** (**the Mafia**) (*used as sing. or pl*) a secret criminal organization originating in Sicily and prevalent *esp* in the USA, chiefly concerned with the financial control of illicit activities. **2** (*often* **mafia**) an excessively influential coterie of a usu specified kind: *the mental health mafia.*

mafioso /mafi'ohsoh/ *n* (*pl* **mafiosi** /-see/) a member of the Mafia.

magazine *n* **1a** an illustrated periodical containing miscellaneous pieces by different authors. **b** a television or radio programme containing a number of usu topical items. **2** a holder from which cartridges can be fed into a gun chamber automatically. **3** a storeroom for arms, ammunition, or explosives.

Word history

early French *magazine* via Old Provençal from Arabic *makhāzin*, pl of *makhzan* storehouse. From its original meaning 'storehouse' the word was used in book titles in the 17th cent. to suggest a store of information, giving rise in the 18th cent. to its chief current meaning of a periodical.

magenta[1] *adj* **1** of a deep purplish red colour. **2** in photography and colour printing, of a pinkish red colour.

magenta[2] *n* **1** a deep purplish red colour. **2** a brilliant bluish red dye.

maggot *n* a soft-bodied legless grub that is the larva of a fly. ⋙ **maggoty** *adj.*

magi /'mayjie/ *n* pl of MAGUS.

magic[1] *n* **1** the use of charms, spells, or other means believed to have supernatural power over natural forces. **2** the art of producing illusions by sleight of hand. **3** an extraordinary power or influence producing surprising results and defying explanation.

magic[2] *adj* **1** relating to magic. **2** having seemingly supernatural qualities. **3** *informal* very good; marvellous. ⋙ **magical** *adj,* **magically** *adv.*

magic[3] *v* (**magicked, magicking**) *informal* to create, transform, or move by or as if by magic.

magician *n* **1** somebody skilled in magic. **2** a conjurer. **3** a person extraordinarily skilled at something; a wonder-worker.

magic lantern *n* an early device for the projection of still pictures from slides.

magic mushroom *n informal* a fungus that has hallucinogenic properties.

magic realism *n* the depiction in art and literature of fantastic, surrealistic, and mythical elements in a style of scrupulous realism. ⋙ **magic realist** *n and adj.*

magic square *n* a square array of numbers in which the sum of each vertical, horizontal, or diagonal row is the same.

magisterial *adj* **1a** assuming authority, *esp* inappropriately; high-handed or dictatorial. **b** authoritative, definitive, or masterly. **2** relating to the office of a magistrate. ⋙ **magisterially** *adv.*

magistracy *n* (*pl* **-ies**) **1** the office or power of a magistrate. **2** magistrates considered as a group.

magistrate *n* a paid or unpaid local judicial officer who presides in a magistrates' court. ⋙ **magistrature** *n.*

magistrates' court *n* a court of summary jurisdiction for minor criminal cases and preliminary hearings.

maglev *n* a railway system in which an electrically driven train is raised and held above the track by powerful magnets.

magma *n* molten rock material within the earth from which an igneous rock results by cooling. ⋙ **magmatic** *adj.*

Magna Carta *n* a charter of liberties to which the English barons forced King John to assent in 1215.

magna cum laude *adv chiefly NAm* used in reference to the gaining of degrees, etc: with distinction.

magnanimous *adj* showing nobility of feeling and generosity of mind; not subject to petty feelings. ⋙ **magnanimity** *n,* **magnanimously** *adv.*

magna opera *n* pl of MAGNUM OPUS.

magnate *n* **1** a prominent and wealthy industrialist or businessman; a tycoon. **2** *archaic* a person of wealth or influence.

magnesia *n* **1** a white oxide of magnesium used *esp* in making cements, insulation, fertilizers, and rubber. **2** magnesium oxide or hydrated magnesium carbonate used in medicine as an antacid and mild laxative.

magnesium *n* a light silver-white metallic element which burns with an intense white light and is used in making light alloys.

magnet *n* **1** a body that has the property of attracting iron and producing a magnetic field outside itself, *esp* a mass of iron, steel, etc that has this property artificially imparted. **2** something that attracts.

magnet- *or* **magneto-** *comb. form* denoting magnetic force or magnetism: *magnetometer.*

magnetic *adj* **1a** relating to magnetism or a magnet. **b** capable of being magnetized. **c** working by magnetic attraction. **2** possessing an extraordinary power or ability to attract or charm. ⋙ **magnetically** *adv.*

magnetic dip *n* the angle formed with the horizon by a magnetic needle free to rotate in the vertical plane.

magnetic equator *n* an imaginary line on the earth's surface, roughly parallel to the geographical equator and connecting all points at which the magnetic dip is zero.

magnetic field *n* a region of space near a body possessing magnetism or carrying an electric current in which magnetic forces can be detected.

magnetic inclination *n* = MAGNETIC DIP.

magnetic needle *n* a slender bar of magnetized iron, steel, etc that when freely suspended indicates the direction of a magnetic field in which it is placed, and that is the essential part of a magnetic compass.

magnetic north *n* the northerly direction in the earth's magnetic field as indicated by a horizontal magnetic needle.

magnetic pole *n* **1** either of two small regions in the N and S geographical polar areas of the earth towards which a magnetic needle points. **2** either of the regions of a magnet at which the magnetic forces are strongest.

magnetic resonance *n* the resonant vibration of electrons, atoms, molecules, or nuclei when in a magnetic field in response to radio waves at particular frequencies.

magnetic resonance imaging *n* in medicine, the use of magnetic resonance to create a scanned image of a part of the body.

magnetic storm *n* a marked local disturbance of the earth's magnetic field.

magnetic tape *n* a ribbon of thin paper or plastic with a magnetizable coating for use in recording sound or video signals and in computing.

magnetise *v* see MAGNETIZE.

magnetism *n* **1** a physical phenomenon that is associated with moving particles having electric charge and includes the attraction for iron observed in magnets. **2** an ability to attract or charm.

magnetite *n* iron oxide occurring as a black mineral strongly attracted by a magnet.

magnetize *or* **-ise** *v* to cause to become magnetic. ➤➤ **magnetizable** *adj,* **magnetization** *n,* **magnetizer** *n.*

magneto /mag'neetoh/ *n* (*pl* **-os**) an alternator with permanent magnets formerly used to generate a high voltage for the ignition in an internal-combustion engine.

magneto- *comb. form* see MAGNET-.

magnetohydrodynamic *adj* relating to or denoting phenomena arising from the motion of electrically conducting fluids in the presence of electric and magnetic fields. ➤➤ **magnetohydrodynamics** *pl n.*

magnetometer *n* an instrument for measuring magnetic intensity, *esp* of the earth's magnetic field. ➤➤ **magnetometry** *n.*

magnetosphere *n* a region surrounding a celestial body, *specif* the earth, in which charged particles are trapped by its magnetic field.

magnetron *n* an electronic valve that in the presence of an externally applied magnetic field is used as a high-power microwave source, e.g. for a radar transmitter.

Magnificat *n* **1** the canticle of the Virgin Mary in Luke 1:46–55. **2** a musical setting of this.

magnification *n* **1** the process of magnifying or being magnified. **2a** the degree to which something is magnified. **b** a measure of the magnifying power of an optical instrument or lens.

magnificent *adj* **1a** sumptuous in structure and adornment. **b** strikingly beautiful or impressive. **2** exceptionally fine or excellent. ➤➤ **magnificence** *n,* **magnificently** *adv.*

magnifico *n* (*pl* **-oes**) *informal* a person of high position or distinguished appearance and manner.

magnify *v* (**-ies, -ied**) **1** of a lens, optical instrument, etc: to enlarge in appearance. **2** to increase or exaggerate the significance of. **3** *archaic* to glorify (God). ➤➤ **magnifier** *n.*

magnifying glass *n* a single optical lens for magnifying.

magniloquent *adj* speaking in a high-flown, often bombastic, style or manner; grandiloquent. ➤➤ **magniloquence** *n,* **magniloquently** *adv.*

magnitude *n* **1a** size or extent. **b** a numerical quantity or value. **2** importance or significance. **3** the brightness of a star measured on a logarithmic scale.

magnolia[1] *n* **1** a shrub or tree with large white, yellow, rose, or purple flowers. **2** a very pale creamy white colour.

magnolia[2] *adj* of a very pale creamy white colour.

magnox *n* an alloy of magnesium that is used to enclose rods of uranium fuel in some nuclear reactors.

magnum *n* (*pl* **magnums**) **1** a wine bottle holding twice the usual amount (about 1.5l). **2** a firearm using cartridges of standard size with an extra-powerful charge.

magnum opus *n* (*pl* **magnum opuses** *or* **magna opera**) the greatest achievement of an artist, writer, etc.

magpie *n* **1** a bird of the crow family with a very long tail and black-and-white plumage. **2** a bird resembling or related to the magpie; *esp* an Australian bird with black-and-white plumage. **3** a person who chatters noisily. **4** a person who collects objects in a random fashion.

maguey /'magway/ *n* a Mexican fleshy-leaved agave used to make the alcoholic drink pulque.

magus /'maygəs/ *n* (*pl* **magi** /'mayjie/) **1a** a member of a Zoroastrian hereditary priestly class in ancient Persia. **b** (*often* **Magus**) any of the three wise men from the East who traditionally paid homage to the infant Jesus. **2** a magician or sorcerer.

Magyar *n* **1** a member of the Finno-Ugric people of Hungary. **2** a language spoken in Hungary, Romania, and other countries; = HUNGARIAN (2). ➤➤ **Magyar** *adj.*

maharajah *or* **maharaja** *n* a Hindu Indian prince ranking above a rajah.

maharani *or* **maharanee** *n* **1** the wife of a maharaja. **2** a Hindu Indian princess ranking above a rani.

maharishi *n* a Hindu teacher of mystical knowledge.

mahatma *n* used as a title of honour, *esp* by Hindus: a person revered for outstanding moral and spiritual qualities.

Mahayana *n* a branch of Buddhism prevalent in Tibet, China, and Japan that includes ritual and devotional practices: compare THERAVADA.

Mahdi *n* **1** the expected messiah of Muslim tradition. **2** a leader claiming to be this messiah.

Mahican *n* (*pl* **Mahicans** *or* **Mahican**) **1** a member of a Native American people formerly living in the environs of the Hudson river. **2** the language spoken by this people. ➤➤ **Mahican** *adj.*

mah-jong *or* **mah-jongg** *n* a game of Chinese origin usu played by four people with 144 tiles.

mahogany *n* **1** the dark-coloured hard and heavy wood of a tropical tree, used for cabinetwork. **2** a reddish brown colour. ➤➤ **mahogany** *adj.*

mahonia *n* an evergreen shrub with spiny leaves and clusters of small yellow flowers.

mahout /mə'howt/ *n* a keeper and driver of an elephant.

maid *n* **1** a female servant. **2** *archaic or literary* an unmarried girl or woman.

maiden[1] *n* **1** *archaic or literary* **a** an unmarried girl or woman. **b** a virgin. **2** in cricket, an over in which no runs are credited to the batsman. ➤➤ **maidenhood** *n,* **maidenly** *adj.*

maiden[2] *adj* **1** *esp* of an older woman: not married. **2** denoting the first venture of somebody or something untried.

maidenhair fern *n* a fern with fronds that have delicate spreading branches.

maidenhead *n* **1** *archaic* a woman's virginity. **2** = HYMEN.

maiden name *n* the surname of a woman prior to marriage.

maiden over *n* = MAIDEN[1] (2).

maid of honour *n* (*pl* **maids of honour**) **1** *NAm* a bride's principal unmarried wedding attendant. **2** an unmarried noblewoman attending a queen or princess. **3** a puff pastry tartlet filled with custard.

maidservant *n dated* a female servant.

mail[1] *n* **1** letters, parcels, etc that are conveyed by the postal system. **2** the postal system. **3** = E-MAIL[1] (2).

mail[2] *v* **1** to send (e.g. a letter) by post. **2** = E-MAIL[2]. ➤➤ **mailable** *adj.*

mail[3] *n* armour made of interlocking metal rings or plates.

mailbag *n* **1** a bag used to carry mail. **2** = POSTBAG (2).

mailbox *n* **1** *NAm* a letter box. **2** in computing, a file where e-mail messages are stored.

mailer *n* **1** *chiefly NAm* the sender of mail. **2** in computing, a program for sending e-mail.

mailing list *n* an organization's list of the names and addresses to which it regularly sends information.

maillot /'mieyoh/ *n* **1** tights for dancers, acrobats, or gymnasts. **2** a tight-fitting top or jersey, e.g. one worn for cycling. **3** *NAm* a woman's one-piece usu strapless swimsuit.

mailman *n* (*pl* **mailmen**) *NAm* a postman.

mail merge *n* in computing, the automatic merging of names and addresses with a template to create personalized letters.

mail order *n* a system by which goods are ordered by post or telephone and delivered to a person's house. ⋙ **mail order** *adj*

mailshot *n* an advertising or information leaflet posted to many people at one time.

maim *v* to mutilate or wound seriously; to cripple.

main[1] *adj* chief or principal. ✱ **by main force** using sheer strength.

main[2] *n* **1** a principal pipe or cable carrying gas, electricity, or water. **2** (**the mains**) the central source of water, gas, or electricity supplied to an area for use by a large number of consumers. **3** (**the main**) *literary or archaic* the open sea. ✱ **in/for the main** on the whole. **with all one's might and main** with all one's strength.

mainbrace *n* the brace attached to the main yard of a sailing ship.

mainframe *n* a large computer that can run several independent programs simultaneously or is connected to other smaller computers.

mainland *n* the largest land area of a continent, country, etc, considered in relation to smaller offshore islands. ⋙ **mainlander** *n.*

mainline *v slang* to inject (a drug) into a vein.

main line *n* **1** a principal railway line. **2** *slang* a major vein into which drugs can be injected.

mainly *adv* in most cases or for the most part; chiefly.

main man *n* **1** a leading figure on whom others rely, e.g. in a team or organization. **2** *informal* a close and trusted companion.

mainmast *n* a sailing vessel's principal mast.

mainsail *n* the principal fore-and-aft sail, or the lowest square sail, on the mainmast of a sailing vessel.

mainspring *n* **1** the chief spring, *esp* of a watch or clock. **2** the chief motive, agent, or cause of something.

mainstay *n* **1** the chief support or main part of something. **2** a rope or wire stretching forward from the head of the mainmast of a sailing ship and providing its chief support.

mainstream *n* (**the mainstream**) the prevailing influences, values, and activities of a group or society. ⋙ **mainstream** *adj.*

maintain *v* **1** to keep (something) in its required state of operation or repair. **2** to sustain against opposition or danger; to defend. **3** to continue or keep up (something). **4** to support, sustain, or provide for (e.g. dependants). **5** to affirm in argument; to assert. ⋙ **maintainable** *adj,* **maintainer** *n.*

maintained school *n* a school provided, controlled, or aided by a British local education authority.

maintenance *n* **1** the work of maintaining or the state of being maintained. **2** *chiefly Brit* payments for the support of one spouse by another following legal separation or divorce.

maiolica /mə'yolikə/ *n* see MAJOLICA.

maisonette *n* a part of a house, usu on two floors, let or sold separately.

maître d'hôtel /,metrə doh'tel/ *n* (*pl* **maîtres d'hôtel** /,metrə/) **1** the manager or owner of a hotel or restaurant. **2** a head waiter.

maize *n* a tall cereal grass bearing seeds on elongated ears.

majestic *adj* **1** having or showing great grandeur or dignity; noble. **2** having an impressive bearing or aspect; magnificent. ⋙ **majestically** *adv.*

majesty *n* (*pl* **-ies**) **1a** impressive bearing or aspect. **b** greatness or splendour of quality or character. **2** sovereign power. **3** (**Majesty**) used in addressing or referring to a king or queen.

majolica /mə'jolikə, mə'yol-/ *or* **maiolica** /mə'yol-/ *n* a type of early Italian tin-glazed earthenware.

major[1] *adj* **1** notable in effect or scope; considerable. **2** involving serious risk to life. **3** greater in importance, size, rank, or degree. **4a** of a musical scale: having semitones between the third and fourth and the seventh and eighth steps. **b** of or based on a major scale.

major[2] *n* **1** an officer in the British army, and some other armed forces, ranking below a lieutenant colonel. **2** a major musical scale, key, etc. **3** *chiefly NAm* **a** a main subject of academic study. **b** a student specializing in a specified subject.

major[3] *v chiefly NAm* (+ in) to take courses in one's main subject.

Majorcan *n* a native or inhabitant of Majorca. ⋙ **Majorcan** *adj.*

major-domo *n* (*pl* **major-domos**) a man, e.g. a head steward, who has charge of a large household.

majorette *n* a baton-twirling girl or woman who marches with or ahead of a procession usu accompanying a band.

major general *n* an officer in the British army and some other armed forces ranking below a lieutenant general.

majority *n* (*pl* **-ies**) **1a** a number greater than half of a total. **b** the amount by which such a greater number exceeds the remaining smaller number. **2** the greatest in number of two or more groups constituting a whole. **3** the number by which the votes cast for the winning party exceed those for its nearest rival or those for the remaining parties. **4** the age, usu 18 or 21, at which full legal rights and responsibilities are acquired. ✱ **be in the majority** to constitute the larger group.

major league *n* a league of highest classification in US professional sport, *esp* baseball.

major planet *n* = PLANET .

majuscule *n* a letter in a style of handwriting employing only capital or uncial letters. ⋙ **majuscular** *adj,* **majuscule** *adj.*

make[1] *v* (*past tense and past part.* **made**) **1** to form or put together from ingredients or components. **2** to produce or bring about by work or effort: *to make peace.* **3** to perform or carry out: *to make a speech.* **4** to cause to be in a particular state: *The journey made us tired.* **5** (+ into) to change (something) so that it becomes something different: *They have made the story into a film.* **6** to have as a possible function; to serve as: *The box makes a good table.* **7a** to cause to act in a certain way: *The sun makes the flowers grow.* **b** to compel (somebody) to do something: *I made them stay and help.* **8a** to gain or receive (money) as income. **b** to achieve or reach. **9** to estimate as an amount or total: *I make that twenty pounds.* **10** to arrange the sheets and blankets tidily on (a bed) ready for use. **11** to attempt to move in a particular direction: *They were making for the coast.* ✱ **make away with** to take or steal. **make believe** to pretend. **make do** to manage with the limited resources available. **make it** *informal* to be successful. **make something of 1** to attribute significance to. **2** to understand. **make way** to give room or allow somebody to pass. ➤➤ **maker** *n.*

make² *n* a manufacturer or brand. ✱ **on the make 1** *informal* rising or attempting to rise to a higher social or financial status. **2** *informal* in search of a sexual partner.

make-believe *n* **1** the activity of pretending or imagining. **2** something imaginary or pretended. ➤➤ **make-believe** *adj.*

make off *v* to leave in haste. ✱ **make off with** to take or steal.

make out *v* **1** to manage to perceive or understand, often with difficulty. **2** to claim or pretend. **3** to write out (a document, etc). **4** *informal* to fare or manage.

makeover *n* **1** the refurbishing of a garment, piece of furniture, room, etc. **2** the remodelling of somebody's appearance with a different hairstyle, clothes, and make-up.

make over *v* **1** to transfer the title of (property). **2a** to give (somebody) a new look with a different hairstyle, new clothes, etc. **b** to refurbish (a building or room).

Maker *n* (**the/our/one's Maker**) God.

makeshift *adj* being a crude and temporary expedient. ➤➤ **makeshift** *n.*

make up *v* **1** to invent (a story or excuse), *esp* in order to deceive. **2a** to assemble from parts. **b** of parts: to constitute (a whole). **3** to settle a disagreement or be reconciled. **4** (+ for) to compensate for a disappointment or loss. **5** to apply cosmetics. ✱ **make it up to** to compensate for a disappointment or unfairness.

make-up *n* **1** cosmetics applied to the face to give colour or emphasis. **2a** the way in which the parts of something are put together. **b** physical and mental constitution. **3** the arrangement of typeset matter, illustrations, etc on a page.

makeweight *n* **1** something added to bring a weight to a desired value. **2** something of little intrinsic value thrown in to fill a gap.

making *n* **1** the process of producing or developing something. **2** (*in pl*) the ingredients or qualities needed to make or become something: *She has the makings of a great artist.* ✱ **be the making of** to bring about the advancement or success of. **in the making** in the process of becoming, forming, or developing.

mako *n* (*pl* **-os**) an Australian shark that is a notable sport fish.

makuta *n* pl of LIKUTA.

mal- *comb. form* **1a** bad or badly: *malpractice.* **b** faulty or faultily: *malfunction.* **2** abnormal or abnormally: *malformed.* **3** not: *malcontent.*

malabsorption *n* the deficient absorption of food substances, vitamins, etc from the stomach and intestines.

malacca *n* a type of cane, often of mottled appearance, from an Asiatic rattan palm, or a walking stick made from this.

malachite *n* hydrated copper carbonate occurring as a green mineral and used for ornaments.

maladjusted *adj* manifesting behavioural difficulties through failure to cope with one's social environment and conditions of life. ➤➤ **maladjustment** *n.*

maladminister *v formal* to administer (something) incompetently or corruptly. ➤➤ **maladministration** *n.*

maladroit *adj* clumsy or inept. ➤➤ **maladroitly** *adv,* **maladroitness** *n.*

malady *n* (*pl* **-ies**) a disease or disorder.

Malagasy *n* (*pl* **Malagasies** *or* **Malagasy**) **1** a native or inhabitant of the Malagasy Republic (Madagascar). **2** the language of Madagascar. ➤➤ **Malagasy** *adj.*

malaise *n* **1** an indeterminate feeling of debility or ill health. **2** a vague sense of mental or moral unease. **3** social or economic disquiet.

malapropism *n* an incongruous misapplication of a word, as in 'polo bears'.

Word history

named after Mrs *Malaprop,* a character often misusing words in *The Rivals,* a comedy by R B Sheridan d.1816, Irish dramatist. The many gaffes made by Mrs Malaprop include the observation: 'As headstrong as an allegory [alligator] on the banks of the Nile'.

malaria *n* a disease caused by blood parasites transmitted by the bite of mosquitoes and characterized by periodic attacks of chills and fever. ➤➤ **malarial** *adj.*

malarkey *n informal* nonsense.

malathion /malə'thieon, -ən/ *n* an insecticide used against household flies and greenfly.

Malawian *n* a native or inhabitant of Malawi. ➤➤ **Malawian** *adj.*

Malay *n* **1** a member of a people of the Malay peninsula and adjacent islands. **2** the language of the Malay peninsula. ➤➤ **Malay** *adj.*

Malayalam *n* a language of SW India. ➤➤ **Malayalam** *adj.*

Malayan *n* = MALAY.

Malaysian *n* a native or inhabitant of Malaysia. ➤➤ **Malaysian** *n.*

malcontent *n* a discontented person; *esp* somebody violently opposed to a government or regime.

mal de mer *n* seasickness.

Maldivian *n* **1** a native or inhabitant of the Maldives. **2** the language of the Maldives. ➤➤ **Maldivian** *adj.*

male¹ *adj* **1** of or denoting the sex that fertilizes or inseminates the female to produce offspring. **2** of a plant or flower: having stamens but no ovaries. **3** relating to or characteristic of the male sex. **4** made up of male individuals. **5** designed for fitting into a corresponding hollow part. ➤➤ **maleness** *n.*

Usage note

male *or* **masculine?** *Male* is used to describe the sex that does not bear offspring; *masculine* is used to describe qualities that are characteristic of or traditionally ascribed to male human beings, and also to classify nouns, adjectives, and pronouns in some languages.

male² *n* a male person, animal, or plant.

male chauvinist *n* a man who believes in the inherent superiority of men over women and is excessively loyal to his own sex. ➤➤ **male chauvinism** *n.*

malediction *n literary* a curse. ➤➤ **maledictory** *adj.*

malefactor *n* **1** *formal or literary* a person who commits a crime. **2** a wrongdoer.

malefic *adj literary* harmful or malicious. ➤➤ **maleficence** *n,* **maleficent** *adj.*

malevolent *adj* intending or wishing harm; full of hate. ➤➤ **malevolence** *n,* **malevolently** *adv.*

malfeasance *n* in law, misconduct or wrongdoing, *esp* by a public official.

malformation *n* abnormal formation or structure. ⋙ **malformed** *adj.*

malfunction *v* to fail to operate in the normal manner. ⋙ **malfunction** *n.*

Malian /'mahli·ən/ *n* a native or inhabitant of Mali. ⋙ **Malian** *adj.*

malic acid *n* an acid found in the juices of certain fruits, e.g. apples, and other plants.

malice *n* a conscious desire to do harm; spite.

malice aforethought *n* in law, predetermination to commit a violent crime, which must be proved in a murder case.

malicious *adj* **1** motivated by malice. **2** intended to cause harm. ⋙ **maliciously** *adv,* **maliciousness** *n.*

malign[1] *adj* evil in nature or effect. ⋙ **malignity** /mə'ligniti/ *n,* **malignly** *adv.*

malign[2] *v* to speak ill of, *esp* spitefully or unfairly.

malignancy *n* (*pl* **-ies**) **1a** a malignant tumour. **b** the presence of a malignant tumour or disease. **c** the degree to which a growth, etc is malignant. **2** malevolence; malignity.

malignant *adj* **1** harmful; malevolent. **2** of a tumour or disease: tending to infiltrate and spread. ⋙ **malignantly** *adv.*

malinger *v* to pretend illness or incapacity so as to avoid duty or work. ⋙ **malingerer** *n.*

mall *n* **1** a large covered shopping precinct, usu with associated parking space. **2** a public promenade, often bordered by trees.

mallard *n* a common large wild duck that is the ancestor of the domestic ducks.

malleable *adj* **1** of metals or other materials: capable of being beaten or rolled into a desired shape. **2** easily shaped by outside forces or influences. ⋙ **malleability** *n.*

mallee *n* a low-growing shrubby Australian eucalyptus.

mallet *n* **1** a hammer with a large usu wooden head, used e.g. for hitting a chisel. **2** a long-handled implement with a large usu cylindrical wooden head for striking the ball in croquet or polo.

mallow *n* a plant with deeply cut lobed leaves and showy pink, purple, or white flowers.

malmsey /'mahmzi/ *n* the sweetest variety of Madeira wine.

malnourished *adj* suffering from malnutrition.

malnutrition *n* faulty or inadequate nutrition.

malocclusion *n* a defect in the meeting and alignment of the upper and lower teeth when the jaws are brought together.

malodorous *adj formal* smelling bad.

maloti *n* pl of LOTI.

malpractice *n* failure to exercise due professional skill or care.

malt[1] *n* **1** grain softened in water, allowed to germinate, then roasted and used in brewing and distilling. **2** unblended malt whisky produced in a particular area. ⋙ **maltiness** *n,* **malty** *adj.*

malt[2] *v* **1** to convert (grain) into malt. **2** to make or mix with malt or malt extract.

maltase *n* an enzyme that accelerates the breakdown of maltose to glucose, is found in plants, bacteria, and yeasts, and is secreted by the intestines during digestion.

Maltese *n* (*pl* **Maltese**) **1** a native or inhabitant of Malta. **2** the language of Malta. ⋙ **Maltese** *adj.*

Maltese cross *n* a cross consisting of four equal arms that broaden from the centre and have their ends indented by a shallow V.

malt extract *n* a sweet light-brown syrup prepared from an infusion of malt and water.

Malthusian *adj* relating to Thomas Malthus (d.1834) or his theory that population tends to increase faster than its means of subsistence unless its growth is checked. ⋙ **Malthusian** *n,* **Malthusianism** *n.*

malt liquor *n* a fermented alcoholic drink, e.g. beer or ale, made with malt.

maltose *n* a sugar formed by the breakdown of starch.

maltreat *v* to treat cruelly or roughly. ⋙ **maltreatment** *n.*

maltster *n* a person who makes or deals in malt.

malt whisky *n* whisky distilled from malted barley.

malversation *n formal* corruption in office.

mama *or* **mamma** *n informal* one's mother.

mamba *n* a tropical African venomous snake related to the cobra but with no hood.

mambo *n* (*pl* **-os**) a ballroom dance of Haitian origin that resembles the rumba.

mamilla *or* **mammilla** *n* (*pl* **mamillae** *or* **mammillae**) **1** a nipple. **2** a nipple-shaped part, structure, or protuberance.

mamma *n* see MAMA.

mammal *n* any of a class of higher vertebrates comprising humans and all other animals that have mammary glands and nourish their young with milk. ⋙ **mammalian** *adj.*

mammary *adj* relating to or in the region of the mammary glands or breasts.

mammary gland *n* the milk-producing gland in female mammals, e.g. the breast in women.

mammilla *n* see MAMILLA.

mammography *n* the examination of the breasts by taking X-ray photographs, e.g. for early detection of cancer. ⋙ **mammogram** *n.*

Mammon *n* material wealth or possessions, *esp* considered as an evil.

mammoth[1] *n* an extinct hairy elephant of the Pleistocene epoch with a long tail and long tusks.

mammoth[2] *adj* of very great size.

mammy *n* (*pl* **-ies**) **1** *Brit, informal* one's mother. **2** *NAm, offensive* a black nanny of white children, *esp* formerly in the southern USA.

man[1] *n* (*pl* **men**) **1** an adult human male. **2** an individual or person. **3** the human race. **4** (*usu used in combinations*) a man belonging to a usu specified category, e.g. by birth or occupation: *a businessman.* **5a** a husband. **b** a male sexual partner. **6** (*in pl*) **a** the ranks of a military force. **b** the working force, as distinguished from the employer or management. **c** the members of a team. **7** any of the pieces moved by each player in a board game. ✱ **man and boy** from childhood. **to a man** without exception. ⋙ **manless** *adj,* **manlike** *adj.*

Usage note

Man should not be used unthinkingly in any context to mean 'men and women' or 'the human race'. Substitutes are *humanity, human beings, the human race, people,* etc. Many compounds with 'man' can be altered to gender-inclusive forms: *man-made* to *artificial* or *synthetic; fireman* to *firefighter,* etc.

man[2] *v* (**manned, manning**) to provide (e.g. a machine or a place) with the necessary people.

man[3] *interj informal* used to express intensity of feeling.

mana /'mahnə/ *n* in Polynesia and Melanesia, the power of elemental forces embodied in an object or person.

man about town *n* a worldly and socially active man.

manacle[1] *n* (*usu in pl*) a shackle or handcuff.

manacle[2] *v* **1** to confine with manacles. **2** to subject to a restraint.

manage *v* **1** to conduct the running of (e.g. a business). **2** to control or supervise (a person or an animal). **3** to guide or have charge of (a sports team, entertainer, etc). **4** to use (e.g. money) economically. **5** to succeed in handling or accomplishing (something cumbersome or difficult). **6** to be able to fit in (e.g. an appointment). **7** to be able to cope with a difficult situation. ➤➤ **manageable** *adj.*

management *n* **1** the activity, work, or art of managing. **2** (*used as sing. or pl*) the collective body of those who manage or direct a business, etc.

manager *n* **1** a person who manages a business, etc, or controls a group of personnel. **2** a person who manages a sports team, entertainer, etc. **3** in computing, a program that organizes a resource or process. ➤➤ **manageress** *n,* **managerial** *adj,* **managership** *n.*

managing *adj* denoting a post bearing executive responsibility.

mañana /man'yahnə/ *adv* at an indefinite time in the future.

manat *n* (*pl* **manat**) the basic monetary unit of Azerbaijan or Turkmenistan.

man-at-arms *n* (*pl* **men-at-arms**) in former times, a heavily armed and usu mounted soldier.

manatee *n* a tropical aquatic plant-eating mammal with a broad tail.

Manchester *n Aus, NZ* linen goods, e.g. sheets.

manciple *n archaic* a steward or caterer, *esp* in a college or monastery.

Mancunian *n* a native or inhabitant of Manchester. ➤➤ **Mancunian** *adj.*

-mancy *comb. form* forming nouns, denoting: divination: *necromancy.*

mandala *n* a Hindu or Buddhist symbol in the form of a circle enclosing a square with a deity on each of its four sides used to represent the universe.

mandamus /man'dayməs/ *n* (*pl* **mandamuses**) a judicial writ requiring something to be carried out.

mandarin *n* **1** (**Mandarin**) **a** the dialect of Chinese used by the court and officials under the Empire. **b** the chief dialect of modern Chinese. **2** a public official in the Chinese Empire. **3** a person of position and influence, *esp* in literary or bureaucratic circles. **4** a yellow to orange loose-skinned citrus fruit.

mandarin collar *n* a narrow stand-up collar.

mandarin duck *n* a brightly marked crested Asian duck.

mandate[1] *n* **1** an authoritative command from a superior. **2** an authorization to act on behalf of another. **3** the authority to act on behalf of the electorate perceived as given to the winner of an election. **4** formerly, an order granted by the League of Nations to a member nation for the establishment of a responsible government over a conquered territory.

mandate[2] *v* **1** to give a mandate to. **2** to make mandatory. **3** to administer or assign (e.g. a territory) under a mandate.

mandatory *adj* **1** containing or constituting a command. **2** compulsory or obligatory. ➤➤ **mandatorily** *adv.*

mandible *n* **1a** the jaw. **b** the lower jaw together with its surrounding soft parts. **c** the upper or lower part of a bird's bill. **2** any of various mouth parts in insects or other invertebrates for holding or biting food. ➤➤ **mandibular** *adj.*

mandolin *or* **mandoline** *n* **1** a stringed musical instrument of the lute family with four pairs of strings and a fretted neck. **2** a utensil with adjustable blades set in a frame, for slicing vegetables.

mandragora /man'dragərə/ *n* = MANDRAKE.

mandrake *n* a Mediterranean plant with whitish or purple flowers and a large forked root traditionally thought to resemble the human form and formerly used to promote conception, as a laxative, or to induce sleep or hypnosis.

mandrel *or* **mandril** *n* **1** an axle or spindle inserted into a hole in a workpiece to support it during machining. **2** a metal bar round which material, e.g. metal, may be cast, shaped, etc.

mandrill *n* a large gregarious W African baboon, the male of which has red and blue striped cheeks and hindquarters.

mane *n* **1** long thick hair growing on the neck of a horse, male lion, etc. **2** long thick hair on a person's head.

manège /ma'nezh/ *n* **1** a school for training horses and teaching horsemanship. **2** the movements or paces of a trained horse.

manes /'mahnayz/ *pl n* the spirits of the ancient Roman dead to which graveside sacrifices were made.

man Friday *n* a trustworthy male assistant.

manful *adj* showing courage and resolution. ➤➤ **manfully** *adv,* **manfulness** *n.*

manga *n* a Japanese cartoon genre found in comic books and animated films, characteristically on science-fiction or fantasy themes.

mangabey *n* a long-tailed African monkey.

manganese *n* a greyish white brittle metallic element, used mainly in alloys.

mange *n* a contagious skin disease chiefly affecting domestic animals, characterized by inflammation and loss of hair and caused by a minute parasitic mite.

mangel-wurzel *n* a large yellow to orange type of beet grown as food for livestock.

manger *n* a trough or open box in a stable for holding feed.

mangetout /'monzhtooh/ *n* (*pl* **mangetouts** *or* **mangetout**) a variety of garden pea with thin flat edible pods.

mangey *adj* see MANGY.

mangle[1] *v* **1** to hack or crush. **2** to spoil by inept rendering.

mangle[2] *n* a machine with rollers for squeezing water from laundry.

mangle[3] *v* to squeeze (laundry) with a mangle.

mango *n* (*pl* **-oes** *or* **-os**) a yellowish red tropical fruit with a firm skin, large stone, and juicy edible pulp.

mangold *n* = MANGEL-WURZEL.

mangonel *n* a military engine formerly used to throw rocks, stones, etc.

mangosteen *n* a dark reddish brown tropical fruit with thick rind and edible flesh.

mangrove *n* a tropical maritime tree or shrub with roots that grow above ground and form dense masses.

mangy *or* **mangey** *adj* (**-ier, -iest**) **1** suffering or resulting from mange. **2** having many worn or bare spots; shabby. ➤➤ **manginess** *n.*

manhandle *v* **1** to move (a large, heavy, or cumbersome object) by human force. **2** to handle (somebody or something) roughly.

manhole *n* a covered opening in a floor, pavement, etc, giving access to an underground system, *esp* a sewer.

manhood *n* **1** the condition of being an adult male as distinguished from a child or a female. **2** *literary* (*used as sing. or pl*) the adult males of a country, etc collectively. **3** manly qualities, such as physical strength and sexual prowess.

mania *n* **1** abnormal excitement and euphoria marked by mental and physical hyperactivity and disorganization of behaviour. **2** an excessive or unreasonable enthusiasm or obsession.

-mania *comb. form* forming nouns, denoting: **1** abnormal obsession or desire: *megalomania.* **2** excessive enthusiasm: *bibliomania.*

maniac[1] *n* **1** a person who behaves in a wild, violent, or uncontrolled way. **2** a person who has an inordinate enthusiasm for something. **3** *archaic* an insane person; a lunatic.

maniac[2] *adj* = MANIACAL.

maniacal /mə'nie·əkl/ *adj* **1** affected with or suggestive of madness. **2** characterized by ungovernable frenzy. ➤➤ **maniacally** *adv.*

manic[1] *adj* of or affected by mania. ➤➤ **manically** *adv.*

manic[2] *n* a person suffering from mania.

manic depression *n* a mental disorder characterized by alternating mania and extreme depression. ➤➤ **manic-depressive** *adj and n.*

Manichaean *or* **Manichean** /mani'kee·ən/ *n* a believer in a religious dualism originating in Persia in the third cent. AD and teaching the release of the spirit from matter through austere living. ➤➤ **Manichaean** *adj,* **Manichaeanism** *n,* **Manichaeism** *n.*

manicure[1] *n* a treatment for the care of the hands and fingernails.

manicure[2] *v* **1** to give a manicure to. **2** to trim (e.g. a lawn) closely and evenly. ➤➤ **manicurist** *n.*

manifest[1] *adj* readily perceived by the sight or mind; obvious. ➤➤ **manifestly** *adv.*

manifest[2] *v* **1** to make (e.g. a quality) evident or certain; to show or display. **2** of a spirit, ghost, etc: to appear in visible form.

manifest[3] *n* a list of passengers or an invoice of cargo, *esp* for a ship.

manifestation *n* **1** the process or an instance of manifesting or of being manifested. **2** something that provides evidence or proof. **3** a sign, e.g. materialization, of the presence of a spirit.

manifesto *n* (*pl* **-os** *or* **-oes**) a public declaration of intentions, *esp* by a political party before an election.

manifold[1] *adj* many and varied.

manifold[2] *n* a hollow fitting, e.g. connecting the cylinders of an internal combustion engine with the exhaust pipe, that has several outlets or inlets for connecting one pipe with other pipes.

manikin *or* **mannikin** *n* **1** a little man. **2** an anatomical model of the body for use in medical or art instruction. **3** = MANNEQUIN.

Manila *or* **Manilla** *n* **1** a fibre obtained from the leafstalk of a banana plant. **2** a strong paper of a brownish or buff colour with a smooth finish, made orig from this fibre. **3** a cigar made in the city of Manila.

Manila hemp *n* = MANILA (1).

Manila paper *n* = MANILA (2).

Manilla *n* see MANILA.

man in the street *n* an average or typical person.

manioc *n* = CASSAVA.

maniple *n* a subdivision of the ancient Roman legion consisting of either 120 or 60 men.

manipulate *v* **1** to handle or operate, *esp* skilfully. **2** to control, exploit, or influence by artful, unfair, or insidious means, *esp* to one's own advantage. **3** to examine and treat (a fracture, sprain, etc) by moving bones into the proper position manually. ➤➤ **manipulable** *adj,* **manipulation** *n,* **manipulative** *adj,* **manipulator** *n.*

manitou *n* a supernatural force held by the Algonquians of N America to pervade the natural world.

mankind *n* (*used as sing. or pl*) **1** the human race. **2** men as distinguished from women.

manky *adj* (**-ier, -iest**) *Brit, informal* nasty or dirty.

manly *adj* (**-ier, -iest**) having or denoting the qualities traditionally thought to befit a man, e.g. courage or strength. ➤➤ **manliness** *n.*

man-made *adj* **1** made or produced by human beings rather than nature. **2** synthetic or artificial.

manna *n* **1** in the Bible, food miraculously supplied to the Israelites in their journey through the wilderness. **2** a usu sudden and unexpected source of benefit. **3** a sweet substance exuded from plants that yields mannitol and acts as a mild laxative.

manned *adj* **1** equipped with people. **2** of a spacecraft: carrying a human crew.

mannequin *n* a model of the human figure used by an artist, dressmaker, etc or for displaying clothes in a shop.

manner *n* **1** the way in which something is done. **2** a style of artistic execution or presentation. **3** *chiefly literary* a kind or sort. **4** a characteristic or distinctive bearing or air. **5** (*in pl*) **a** rules of conduct in accordance with customs. **b** polite social behaviour. ✱ **in a manner of speaking** in one sense; in a way. **to the manner born** accustomed from birth or as if from birth. ➤➤ **mannerless** *adj.*

mannered *adj* **1** (*used in combinations*) having manners of the kind specified: *well-mannered.* **2** having an artificial or stilted character.

mannerism *n* **1** a characteristic gesture or trait; an idiosyncrasy. **2a** exaggerated or affected adherence to a particular style in art or literature. **b** (**Mannerism**) a style of art in Italy and elsewhere in Europe between about 1520 and 1610, characterized by elongation or distortion of the human figure. ➤➤ **mannerist** *n and adj.*

mannerly *adj* showing or having good manners; polite. ➤➤ **mannerliness** *n.*

mannikin *n* see MANIKIN.

mannish *adj* of a woman, her appearance, or her manner: resembling, befitting, or typical of a man. ➤➤ **mannishly** *adv,* **mannishness** *n.*

mannitol *n* a sweet-tasting alcohol obtained from manna and seaweed and used e.g. in a test for kidney function.

manoeuvre[1] (*NAm* **maneuver**) *n* **1** a movement requiring skill and dexterity. **2** a strategic move adopted in a social or political situation. **3** (*in pl*) a large-scale training exercise for the armed forces.

manoeuvre[2] (*NAm* **maneuver**) *v* **1** to perform a manoeuvre. **2** to use stratagems. **3** to shift (something) into the desired position. **4** to edge (somebody) into a certain situation as part of a plan or scheme. ➤➤ **manoeuvrability** *n,* **manoeuvrable** *adj,* **manoeuvrer** *n.*

man of God *n* **1** a clergyman. **2** a godly man, e.g. a saint or prophet.

man of letters *n* **1** a scholar. **2** a reputable author.

man of straw *n* **1** a person of no moral stamina. **2** a financially unreliable person.

man of the cloth *n* a clergyman.

man-of-war *or* **man-o'-war** *n* (*pl* **men-of-war** *or* **men-o'-war**) a sailing ship used as a warship.

manometer *n* an instrument, typically consisting of a U-shaped tube filled with liquid, used for measuring the pressure of gases and vapours. ⋙ **manometric** *adj.*

manor *n* **1** a landed estate. **2** a medieval unit of territory under a lord who held a variety of rights over land and tenants. **3** a house owned or formerly owned by the lord of a manor. **4** *Brit, informal* one's territory or home ground. ⋙ **manorial** *adj.*

man-o'-war *n* see MAN-OF-WAR.

manpower *n* the total supply of people available for work or service.

manqué /'mongkay/ *adj* (*used after a noun*) that could have been but failed to be what is specified: *a poet manqué.*

mansard *or* **mansard roof** *n* a roof with a lower steeper slope and a higher shallower one on all four sides.

manse *n* the residence of a Presbyterian or Baptist clergyman.

manservant *n* (*pl* **menservants**) a male servant, *esp* a valet.

-manship *suffix* forming nouns, denoting: the art or skill of somebody who practises an activity: *horsemanship.*

mansion *n* a large imposing residence.

manslaughter *n* the unlawful killing of somebody without malicious intent, e.g. by avoidable negligence or in the course of an unlawful act: compare MURDER[1].

manta *or* **manta ray** *n* an extremely large flat ray of warm seas.

mantel *or* **mantle** *n* a mantelpiece or mantelshelf.

mantelpiece *or* **mantlepiece** *n* **1** an ornamental structure round a fireplace. **2** a mantelshelf.

mantelshelf *or* **mantleshelf** *n* a shelf forming part of or above a mantelpiece.

mantes /'manteez/ *n* pl of MANTIS.

manticore *n archaic or literary* a mythical beast having a lion's body, a man's face, and usu a scorpion's tail.

mantilla *n* a light scarf worn over the head and shoulders, *esp* by Spanish and Latin-American women.

mantis *n* (*pl* **mantises** *or* **mantes** /'manteez/) an insect that feeds on other insects and clasps its prey in forelimbs held as if in prayer.

mantle[1] *n* **1** a loose sleeveless garment worn over other clothes; a cloak. **2** something that covers or conceals. **3** a role or persona that one adopts or takes over from somebody else. **4** a lacy hood or sheath that when placed over the flame of a gas or oil lamp increases the amount of light given off. **5** the part of the earth that lies between the crust and the central core.

mantle[2] *v* to cover with or as if with a mantle.

mantle[3] *n* see MANTEL.

mantlepiece *n* see MANTELPIECE.

mantleshelf *n* see MANTELSHELF.

mantra *n* **1** orig in Hinduism or Buddhism, a word or sound used to focus the mind and help concentration, e.g. as a preliminary to meditation. **2** a Vedic hymn.

mantrap *n* a trap for catching trespassers or poachers.

manual[1] *adj* **1** of or involving the hands. **2** requiring or using physical skill and energy. **3** worked or done by hand rather than by machine or automatically. ⋙ **manually** *adv.*

manual[2] *n* **1** a book of instructions; a handbook. **2** a keyboard of an organ played with the hands.

manufactory *n* (*pl* **-ies**) *archaic* a factory.

manufacture[1] *n* **1** the large-scale making of wares by hand or by machinery. **2** the act or process of producing something.

manufacture[2] *v* **1** to make (wares) from raw materials by hand or by machinery, *esp* on a large scale. **2** to invent or fabricate. **3** to produce as if by manufacturing. ⋙ **manufacturer** *n,* **manufacturing** *n.*

manuka /'mahnookə/ *n* an evergreen New Zealand shrub that forms large areas of scrub.

manumit *v* (**manumitted, manumitting**) to give (slaves) their freedom. ⋙ **manumission** *n.*

manure[1] *n* material that fertilizes land; *esp* the faeces of domestic animals.

manure[2] *v* to enrich (land) by the application of manure.

manuscript *n* a composition or document written by hand or typed as distinguished from a printed or published copy.

Manx *n* the Celtic language of the people of the Isle of Man, now rarely used. ⋙ **Manx** *adj.*

Manx cat *n* a cat of a short-haired tailless domestic breed associated with the Isle of Man.

Manxman *n* (*pl* **Manxmen**) a male native or inhabitant of the Isle of Man.

Manxwoman *n* (*pl* **Manxwomen**) a female native or inhabitant of the Isle of Man.

many[1] *adj* (**more, most**) amounting to a large but unspecified number. ✱ **a good/great many** numerous. **as many** the same in number.

many[2] *pron* (*used as pl*) a large number of people or things.

many[3] *n* (**the many**) *literary* the great majority.

manzanilla *n* a pale very dry sherry.

Maoism /'mowiz(ə)m/ *n* Marxism-Leninism as developed in China chiefly by Mao Zedong (d.1976). ⋙ **Maoist** *n and adj.*

Maori *n* (*pl* **Maoris** *or* **Maori**) **1** a member of the aboriginal people of New Zealand. **2** the language of this people.

map[1] *n* **1** a representation on a reduced scale and usu a flat surface of part of the earth's surface, showing geographical features, political divisions, towns, roads, etc. **2** a representation of something in a maplike form. ✱ **put something on the map** to make something well known. **wipe something off the map** to consign something to oblivion.

map[2] *v* (**mapped, mapping**) **1** to make a map of. **2** (*often* + out) to plan in detail. ⋙ **mappable** *adj,* **mapper** *n,* **mapping** *n.*

maple *n* a tree of the sycamore family that has broad leaves with pointed lobes, clusters of paired flat winged seeds, and hard light-coloured close-grained wood.

maple syrup *n* syrup made by concentrating the sap of sugar maple trees.

map reference *n* a pair of coordinates for finding a point on a map.

maquette *n* a small preliminary model of a sculpture, e.g. in wax or clay.

maquis /ma'kee/ *n* (*pl* **maquis**) **1** scrubland vegetation of Mediterranean coastal areas, consisting mainly of evergreen shrubs or small trees. **2** (**the Maquis**) the French Resistance movement during World War II.

Mar. *abbr* March.

mar *v* (**marred, marring**) to detract from the perfection or wholeness of; to spoil.

marabou *n* **1** a large grey and white African stork that has an inflatable pouch of pink skin at its throat and feeds on carrion. **2** a soft fluffy material prepared from marabou or turkey feathers and used for trimming hats or clothes.

marabout /'marəbooh/ *n* a Muslim holy man of N Africa.

maraca /mə'rakə/ *n* a dried gourd or gourd-shaped rattle that is used as a percussion instrument, usu one of a pair.

marae /mah'rie/ *n* the courtyard of a Maori meeting house as the central meeting ground of a village.

maraschino /marə'sheenoh, -'skeenoh/ *n* (*pl* **-os**) **1** a sweet liqueur distilled from the fermented juice of a bitter wild cherry. **2** a usu large cherry preserved in maraschino.

maraschino cherry *n* = MARASCHINO (2).

marasmus *n* severe malnutrition, *esp* in the very young, resulting in emaciation and growth retardation.

marathon *n* **1** a long-distance race; *specif* a foot race of 42.2km (about 26mi 385yd) that is contested on an open course in major athletics championships. **2** (*also used before a noun*) an event or activity characterized by great length or concentrated effort.

Word history

named after *Marathon* in Greece, site of a victory of Greeks over invading Persians in 490 BC, the news of which was carried to Athens by a long-distance runner. In the original account by the Greek historian Herodotus, the messenger Pheidippides ran from Athens to Sparta before the battle to ask for help.

maraud *v* **1** to roam about in search of plunder. **2** to raid or pillage (a place). ➤➤ **marauder** *n.*

marble[1] *n* **1** a form of limestone in which the original crystals have dissolved and recrystallized to form a hard rock with a veined or mottled appearance that can be polished to a very smooth finish. **2** a small glass ball used in various children's games. **3** (*in pl, used as sing.*) a game played with marbles. **4** *informal* (*in pl*) elements of common sense, *esp* sanity: *He seems to have lost his marbles.* ➤➤ **marbly** *adj.*

marble[2] *v* to give a veined or mottled appearance to (e.g. the edges of a book).

marbling *n* coloration or markings resembling or suggestive of marble.

marc *n* **1** the organic residue remaining after an extraction process, e.g. the pressing of grapes. **2** brandy made from the residue of grapes after pressing.

marcasite *n* **1** a white or pale yellow form of the mineral iron pyrites, used in jewellery. **2** polished steel or a similar white metal used for making jewellery.

March *n* the third month of the year.

march[1] *v* **1** to move along steadily, usu in step with others. **2a** to walk in a direct purposeful manner. **b** to make steady progress. **3** to participate in an organized march. **4** to cause (e.g. an army) to march. ➤➤ **marcher** *n.*

march[2] *n* **1a** the action of marching. **b** a regular measured stride or rhythmic step used in marching. **2** a musical composition that has a strongly accentuated beat and is designed or suitable to accompany marching. **3** a procession of people organized as a demonstration of support or protest. ✻ **on the march 1** marching. **2** moving steadily; advancing.

march[3] *n* (*often* **the Marches**) a border region; *esp* a tract of land between two countries whose ownership is disputed.

march[4] *v* (+ with) to have a common border with another territory or piece of land.

March hare *n* a brown hare in its breeding season, noted for eccentric behaviour such as boxing, leaping, and running round in circles.

marching orders *pl n* **1** official notice for troops to move. **2** notice of dismissal.

marchioness *n* **1** the wife or widow of a marquess. **2** a woman having in her own right the rank of a marquess.

marchpane *n archaic* marzipan.

Mardi Gras /,mahdi 'grah/ *n* a carnival period culminating on Shrove Tuesday often observed with parades and festivities.

mare[1] *n* the female of a horse or other equine animal, *esp* when fully mature.

mare[2] /'mahray/ *n* (*pl* **maria** /'mahri·ə/) a large dark area on the surface of the moon or Mars.

mare's nest *n* a false discovery, illusion, or deliberate hoax.

mare's tail *n* **1** a common aquatic plant having long shoots covered with narrow leaves. **2** a long streak of cirrus cloud.

margarine *n* a substitute for butter made usu from vegetable oils churned with skimmed milk to a smooth emulsion.

margarita *n* a cocktail consisting chiefly of tequila and lemon or lime juice, traditionally served in a salt-rimmed glass.

margay *n* a small American spotted cat resembling the ocelot.

marge[1] *n Brit, informal* margarine.

marge[2] *n literary* a margin or rim.

margin *n* **1** the part of a page outside the main body of printed or written matter. **2a** the outside limit of an area, etc; the edge. **b** a part adjoining an edge; a rim or border. **c** (*usu in pl*) the periphery of a community, movement, organization, etc. **3** a spare amount or measure allowed: *a margin of error.* **4** an extreme limit beyond which something becomes impossible or is no longer desirable. **5a** the difference between one amount and another. **b** the difference between net sales and the cost of merchandise sold, from which expenses are met or profit derived. ➤➤ **margined** *adj.*

marginal[1] *adj* **1** written or printed in the margin. **2** of or situated at or in a margin. **3** close to the lower limit of qualification, acceptability, etc. **4** denoting a constituency where the Member of Parliament was elected with only a small majority. **5** representing a slight difference. ➤➤ **marginality** *n,* **marginally** *adv.*

marginal[2] *n* a marginal constituency.

marginalia *pl n* marginal notes, e.g. in a book.

marginalize *or* **-ise** *v* to treat as peripheral or unimportant. ➤➤ **marginalization** *n.*

margrave *n* **1** the hereditary title of some princes of the Holy Roman Empire. **2** a member of the German nobility corresponding in rank to a British marquess.

marguerite *n* = OXEYE DAISY.

maria *n* pl of MARE[2].

mariachi /mari'ahchi/ *n* (*pl* **mariachis**) **1** a group of Mexican street musicians, or a member of such a group. **2** the folk music traditionally played by such musicians.

marigold *n* a plant of the daisy family with showy yellow or red flower heads.

marijuana *or* **marihuana** /mari'(h)wahnə/ *n* a usu mild form of cannabis that is smoked for its intoxicating effect.

marimba *n* a percussion instrument of Southern Africa and Central America that resembles a large xylophone, has a resonant tone, and is played with soft-headed hammers.

marina *n* a dock or basin providing secure moorings for motorboats, yachts, etc.

marinade[1] *n* a blend of oil, wine or vinegar, herbs, and spices in which meat, fish, etc is soaked before cooking to enrich its flavour or make it tender.

marinade[2] *v* to soak in a marinade.

marinara *adj* (*used after a noun*) cooked with a spicy tomato sauce containing onions and garlic.

marinate *v* = MARINADE[2].

marine[1] *adj* **1** of the sea. **2** relating to the navigation or commerce of the sea.

marine[2] *n* **1** any of a class of soldiers serving on shipboard or in close association with a naval force. **2** seagoing ships of a specified nationality or class.

mariner *n formal or literary* a sailor.

Mariolatry /meəri'olətri/ *n* excessive veneration of the Virgin Mary.

marionette *n* a small-scale figure with jointed limbs that is moved from above by strings or wires.

marital *adj* relating to marriage or to the relationship between husband and wife. ⋙ **maritally** *adv.*

maritime *adj* **1** relating to navigation or commerce on the sea. **2** associated with or found near the sea. **3** of a climate: having small variations in seasonal temperatures because of the influence of the sea.

marjoram *n* **1** a fragrant and aromatic plant of the mint family with small pale purple or pink flowers and leaves that are used as a herb. **2** = OREGANO.

mark[1] *n* **1** a spot, scratch, etc on the surface of something. **2** a line, notch, etc designed to record position. **3a** a symbol used for identification or indication of ownership. **b** a distinguishing characteristic. **c** a written or printed symbol. **4** a sign or token. **5** a point or level reached or achieved. **6** a symbol or figure indicating an assessment of merit, e.g. of a student's work. **7** (**Mark**) used with a number to specify a particular model of a vehicle, weapon, machine, etc. **8** a goal or target, e.g. the jack in a game of bowls. **9** the starting line or position in a track event. ✱ **be quick/slow off the mark** to react or respond smartly or sluggishly. **close to/near the mark** not far off the truth. **make one's mark** to make one's name or leave behind a record of one's achievement. **off/wide of the mark** not accurate or appropriate. **of mark** *literary* of distinction. **on your marks** used as a command to competitors in a race to take their starting positions. **up to the mark** (*usu with a negative*) reaching the desired standard.

mark[2] *v* **1** to make or leave a mark on. **2a** to evaluate or give a mark to (a piece of written work). **b** to add appropriate symbols, characters, or other marks to (e.g. a text). **c** to indicate or identify by a mark or symbol. **3** to register or record. **4a** to characterize or distinguish. **b** to be a sign of. **c** to be the occasion of (something notable). **5** (*usu* + off) to set apart or delineate by or as if by a line or boundary. **6** to observe or take notice of. **7** in a team sport, to stay close to (an opponent), *esp* to prevent the opponent from getting or passing the ball. ✱ **mark time 1** to keep the time of a marching step by moving the feet alternately without advancing. **2** to pass time unproductively while waiting.

mark[3] *n* the basic monetary unit of Germany.

mark down *v* **1** to put a lower price on (an item for sale). **2** to reduce the number of marks awarded to (a candidate). **3** (+ as) to characterize somebody in a certain way, *esp* unfavourably.

marked *adj* **1a** having natural marks. **b** made identifiable by marking. **2** having a distinctive or emphasized character. **3** being an object of attack, suspicion, or vengeance. ⋙ **markedly** /'mahkidli/ *adv.*

marker *n* **1** something used to mark a position, place, direction, etc. **2** a felt-tip pen with a broad tip. **3** a person who marks something. **4** in a team game, a player who marks an opponent.

market[1] *n* **1a** a meeting together of people for the purpose of trade, by private purchase and sale. **b** a place where provisions, livestock, etc are sold. **2a** a geographical area or section of the community offering opportunities for the sale of products. **b** an opportunity for selling. **c** commercial activity. **d** the area of economic activity in which the forces of supply and demand affect prices. ✱ **on the market** available for purchase.

market[2] *v* (**marketed, marketing**) to sell or offer for sale. ⋙ **marketable** *adj.*

marketeer *n* **1** a person who trades in a market. **2** a person who supports a particular type of market: *a free marketeer.*

market forces *pl n* the mechanism of supply and demand operating within a system of free enterprise.

market garden *n* a plot in which vegetables are grown for market. ⋙ **market gardening** *n,* **market gardener** *n.*

marketing *n* the skills and functions, including packaging, promotion, and distribution, involved in selling goods.

market-maker *n* a wholesale dealer in securities who is prepared to buy and sell specified securities at all times.

marketplace *n* **1** an open place in a town where markets are held. **2** an opportunity for selling.

market research *n* the collection and analysis of information about consumer preferences, used to ascertain the demand for a particular product. ⋙ **market researcher** *n.*

market value *n* the value of an asset if sold in a free market: compare BOOK VALUE.

markhor *n* a large Himalayan wild goat with long spiralled horns.

marking *n* **1** a mark or marks. **2** an arrangement, pattern, or disposition of marks.

markka *n* (*pl* **markkaa** *or* **markkas**) the basic monetary unit of Finland.

marksman *or* **markswoman** *n* (*pl* **marksmen** *or* **markswomen**) a person skilled in hitting a mark or target. ⋙ **marksmanship** *n.*

markup *n* an amount added to the price of something to guarantee the seller a profit.

mark up *v* to set a higher price on.

markup language *n* in desktop publishing and typesetting, a set of codes in a text that determines type styles, format, etc.

marl *n* a crumbly earthy deposit, e.g. of silt or clay, which contains calcium carbonate and is used as a fertilizer for lime-deficient soils.

marlin *n* a large oceanic game fish that has a spear-shaped projection extending from the snout.

marlinspike *or* **marlinespike** *n* a pointed steel tool used to separate strands of rope or wire.

marmalade *n* a clear sweetened preserve made from citrus fruit, *esp* oranges.

Marmite *n trademark* a concentrated yeast extract used as a savoury spread.

marmoreal *adj literary* made of or resembling marble.

marmoset *n* a small S and Central American monkey with a long tail and silky fur.

marmot *n* a burrowing rodent with short legs and coarse fur.

Maronite *n* a member of a Syrian Christian Church now existing chiefly in the Lebanon.

maroon[1] *v* **1** (*usu as past part.*) to abandon (somebody) on a desolate island or coast. **2** (*usu as past part.*) to isolate (somebody) in a helpless state.

maroon[2] *adj* of a dark brownish red colour. ⋙ **maroon** *n.*

maroon[3] *n* an explosive rocket used as a distress signal.

marque *n* a make of vehicle, as distinct from a particular model.

marquee *n* **1** a large tent, e.g. for an outdoor party or exhibition. **2** *NAm* a permanent canopy projecting over an entrance, e.g. of a hotel or theatre.

marquess *n* a member of the British peerage ranking below a duke and above an earl.

marquetry *or* **marqueterie** *n* decorative work consisting of pieces of wood, ivory, etc inlaid in a wood veneer that is then applied to a surface, e.g. of a piece of furniture.

marquis *n* **1** a nobleman in Europe ranking above a count and below a duke. **2** a marquess.

marquise *n* **1** a marchioness. **2** a gem or ring setting shaped like an oval with pointed ends.

marram grass *n* a strong wiry grass that grows on sandy shores and prevents erosion.

marriage *n* **1a** the state of being husband and wife or the mutual relation it represents. **b** the institution whereby a man and a woman are joined in a special kind of social and legal dependence. **2** an act or the rite of marrying; *esp* the wedding ceremony. **3** an intimate or close union. ⋙ **marriageable** *adj.*

marriage of convenience *n* a marriage contracted for advantage rather than for love.

married[1] *adj* joined in marriage.

married[2] *n* (*pl* **marrieds**) a married person.

marrons glacés /,maronh 'glasay/ *pl n* chestnuts candied or preserved in syrup.

marrow *n* **1** a fruit of a plant of the gourd family, used as a vegetable. **2** a soft tissue that fills the cavities and porous part of most bones and in which red blood cells and certain white blood cells are produced. ✱ **to the marrow** through and through.

marrowbone *n* a bone rich in marrow.

marrowfat *n* any of several types of large pea.

marry[1] *v* (**-ies, -ied**) **1a** to take as a spouse. **b** to perform the ceremony of marriage for (a couple). **2** to bring (two or more things) together closely, harmoniously, and usu permanently. ✱ **marry into** to become a member of (a family) or obtain (something) by marriage: *She married into money.*

marry[2] *interj archaic* used for emphasis, *esp* in assertion or concurrence.

Marsala *n* a sweet fortified wine from Sicily.

marsh *n* an area of soft wet land usu covered with sedges, rushes, etc. ⋙ **marshy** *adj.*

marshal[1] *n* **1** an officer of the highest military rank. **2** a chief officer in the USA responsible for court processes in a district. **3a** a person who arranges and directs a ceremony. **b** a person who arranges the procedure at races. **4** an official in Britain who assists a circuit judge.

marshal[2] *v* (**marshalled, marshalling,** *NAm* **marshaled, marshaling**) **1** to place (e.g. soldiers) in proper rank or position. **2** to bring together and order (e.g. facts) in an effective way. **3** to lead (a group of people) ceremoniously or solicitously; to usher.

marshalling yard *n* a place where railway vehicles are shunted and assembled into trains.

marshal of the Royal Air Force *n* an officer of the highest rank in the Royal Air Force.

marsh gas *n* methane.

marshmallow *n* **1** a pink-flowered Eurasian marsh plant of the mallow family. **2** a light spongy confection made from sugar, albumen, and gelatin.

marsh marigold *n* a European and N American marsh plant of the buttercup family with large bright yellow flowers. Also called KINGCUP.

marsupial *n* a mammal such as a kangaroo, wombat, or opossum, the females of which have a pouch on the abdomen for carrying young, and do not develop a placenta.

mart *n* a place of trade, e.g. an auction room or market.

Martello *n* a circular masonry fort or blockhouse formerly used, e.g. in Britain, for coastal defence.

Martello tower *n* = MARTELLO.

marten *n* (*pl* **martens** *or* **marten**) a tree-dwelling mammal with a slender body.

martial *adj* relating to war; warlike. ⋙ **martially** *adv.*

martial art *n* an Oriental art of combat, e.g. judo or karate, practised as a sport.

martial law *n* the law administered by military forces in occupied territory or in an emergency.

Martian[1] *adj* relating to or coming from the planet Mars.

Martian[2] *n* a supposed inhabitant of Mars.

martin *n* **1** = HOUSE MARTIN. **2** = SAND MARTIN.

martinet *n* a strict disciplinarian.

Word history

named after Jean *Martinet* d.1672, French army officer. The Marquis de Martinet served in Louis XIV's own regiment of infantry and introduced a system of drill to train and discipline new recruits. He died at the siege of Duisburg.

martingale *n* **1** one or more straps fastened to the girth of a horse's harness for checking the upward movement of the horse's head. **2** in betting, any of several systems in which the stake is doubled every time a bet is lost.

Martiniquan *or* **Martinican** *n* a native or inhabitant of Martinique. ⋙ **Martiniquan** *adj.*

martyr[1] *n* **1** a person who is put to death because of their religious beliefs. **2** any person who suffers for any cause or set of beliefs. **3** a person who behaves unnecessarily, even pointedly, in a self-sacrificing manner. ⋙ **martyrdom** *n.*

martyr[2] *v* **1** to put to death as a martyr. **2** to inflict agonizing pain on.

martyrology *n* that part of ecclesiastical history concerned with the lives and sufferings of martyrs.

marvel[1] *n* something or somebody amazing.

marvel[2] *v* (**marvelled, marvelling,** *NAm* **marveled, marveling**) (+ at) to be filled with wonder or amazed curiosity.

marvellous (*NAm* **marvelous**) *adj* **1** causing wonder. **2** of the highest kind or quality. ➤➤ **marvellously** *adv.*

Marxism *n* the principles and policies advocated by the German political philosopher and economist Karl Marx (d.1883), which stress the importance of human labour in determining economic value, the struggle between classes as an instrument of social change, and dictatorship of the proletariat. ➤➤ **Marxist** *n and adj.*

Marxism-Leninism *n* a theory and practice of communism developed by the Russian political leader Lenin (d.1924) from the doctrines of Marx.

marzipan *n* a paste made from ground almonds, sugar, and egg whites, used for coating cakes or shaped into small sweets.

Masai *or* **Maasai** /'masie/ *n* (*pl* **Masais** *or* **Masai**) a member of a pastoral and hunting people of Kenya and Tanzania.

masala /mə'sahlə/ *n* a mixture of spices ground into a powder or paste, used in Indian cooking.

mascara *n* a cosmetic for colouring, *esp* darkening, the eyelashes.

mascarpone /maskə'pohni/ *n* a soft rich Italian cream cheese.

mascot *n* a person, animal, or object adopted as a good luck symbol.

masculine *adj* **1a** male. **b** having qualities appropriate to a man. **2** in grammar, of, belonging to, or being the gender that normally includes most words or grammatical forms referring to males. ➤➤ **masculinity** *n.*

Usage note

masculine *or* **male**? See note at MALE[1].

maser *n* a device that works like a laser for amplifying or generating microwave radiation.

mash[1] *n* **1** crushed malt or grain meal steeped and stirred in hot water to ferment. **2** a mixture of bran or similar feeds and usu hot water for livestock. **3** a soft pulpy mass. **4** *Brit, informal* mashed potatoes.

mash[2] *v* **1** to crush or pound to a soft pulpy state. **2** to heat and stir (e.g. crushed malt) in water as part of the process of brewing beer. **3** *Brit, dialect* to brew (tea). ➤➤ **masher** *n.*

mask[1] *n* **1a** a covering or partial covering for the face used for disguise or protection. **b** a grotesque false face worn at carnivals or in rituals. **c** a copy of a face made by sculpting or by means of a mould. **2** a device covering the mouth and nose, used: **a** to promote breathing, e.g. by connection to an oxygen supply. **b** to remove noxious gases from the air. **c** to prevent the spread of infective material breathed out, e.g. by a surgeon. **3** a face pack.

mask[2] *v* **1** to provide, cover, or conceal with a mask. **2** to disguise or conceal from view. **3** to make (e.g. a flavour) indistinct or imperceptible. **4** to cover for protection. ➤➤ **masked** *adj.*

masked ball *n* a ball at which the participants wear masks.

masking tape *n* an adhesive tape used to cover a surface and keep it free from paint when painting an adjacent area.

masochism *n* the act or an instance of obtaining pleasure or gratification, *esp* sexual pleasure, by being physically or mentally abused. ➤➤ **masochist** *n,* **masochistic** *adj.*

mason *n* **1** a skilled worker with stone. **2** (**Mason**) a freemason.

Masonic *adj* relating to Freemasons or Freemasonry.

masonry *n* **1** stonework. **2** (**Masonry**) Freemasonry.

masque *n* a short allegorical dramatic entertainment of the 16th and 17th cents performed by masked actors.

masquerade[1] *n* **1** a social gathering of people wearing masks and often fantastic costumes. **2** something that is merely show; pretence.

masquerade[2] *v* **1** to disguise oneself or to wear a disguise. **2** (+ as) to assume the appearance of something that one is not.

mass[1] *n* **1** (**Mass**) the liturgy or a celebration of the Eucharist, *esp* in Roman Catholic and Anglo-Catholic churches. **2** a musical setting for the parts of the Mass that do not vary.

mass[2] *n* **1** a quantity of matter or the form of matter that holds or clings together in one body. **2** in physics, the property of a body that is a measure of its resistance to having its speed or position changed when a force is applied to it, causes it to have weight in a gravitational field, and is commonly taken as a measure of the amount of material it contains. **3** the principal part or main body. **4** *informal* (*in pl*) a large quantity, amount, or number. **5** a large body of people in a compact group. **6** (**the masses**) (*in pl*) the body of ordinary people as contrasted with the elite.

mass[3] *v* to assemble (usu homogeneous elements) into a mass.

mass[4] *adj* **1** relating to or intended for the mass of the people: *a mass market.* **2** participated in by or affecting a large number of individuals: *mass murder.* **3** large-scale: *mass production.*

massacre[1] *v* **1** to kill (people) deliberately and violently; to slaughter. **2** *informal* to defeat (an opponent or opposing team) severely.

massacre[2] *n* **1** the ruthless and indiscriminate killing of large numbers of people. **2** *informal* a complete defeat.

massage[1] *n* the kneading, rubbing, etc of the body in order to relieve aches, give relaxation, etc.

massage[2] *v* **1** to perform massage on (somebody). **2** (+ in/into) to rub a substance, e.g. oil, into (the skin or the scalp). **3** to adjust (data) so as to present a particular appearance. ✱ **massage somebody's ego** to flatter somebody and make them feel good about themselves.

masseur /ma'suh/ *or* **masseuse** /ma'suhz/ *n* a man or woman who practises massage and physiotherapy.

massif /'maseef, ma'seef/ *n* a principal mountain mass that gives rise to a number of peaks towards its summit.

massive *adj* **1a** large, solid, or heavy. **b** large in comparison to what is typical. **c** extensive and severe. **2a** of a mineral: not obviously crystalline. **b** of a rock: fairly uniform in appearance; homogeneous. ➤➤ **massively** *adv,* **massiveness** *n.*

mass-market *adj* of a product: designed for or aimed at a wide range of people.

mass noun *n* a noun, e.g. *sand* or *justice*, that characteristically denotes a substance or concept and not an individual item, that does not form a plural, and that cannot be used with the indefinite article: compare COUNT NOUN.

mass number *n* in physics, the number of protons and neutrons in the nucleus that expresses the mass of an isotope.

mass-produce *v* to produce (goods) in large quantities by standardized mechanical processes. ➤➤ **mass-produced** *adj.*

mast[1] *n* **1** a tall pole or structure rising from the keel or deck of a ship, *esp* for carrying sails. **2** a vertical pole or lattice supporting a radio or television aerial.

mast[2] *n* beechnuts, acorns, etc accumulated on the forest floor and often serving as food for animals, e.g. pigs.

mastectomy *n* (*pl* **-ies**) the excision or amputation of a breast.

master[1] *n* **1a** a person having control or authority over another; a ruler or governor. **b** an owner, *esp* of a slave or animal. **c** a male teacher. **d** the head of a college. **2** (**Master**) used as a title for a youth or boy too young to be called *Mr.* **3** a person holding an academic degree higher than a bachelor's but lower than a doctor's. **4** an artist, performer, player, exponent of something, etc who is extremely skilled or accomplished. **5** an original film, recording, etc from which copies can be made.

master[2] *v* **1a** to become skilled or proficient in the use of (a device, etc). **b** to gain a thorough understanding of (a subject). **2** to become master of (somebody or something).

master[3] *adj* **1** controlling: *a master switch.* **2** principal or main: *the master bedroom.* **3** qualified to teach apprentices: *a master carpenter.*

master-at-arms *n* (*pl* **masters-at-arms**) a petty officer responsible for maintaining discipline aboard ship.

master class *n* a class in which an eminent musician, actor, etc advises and corrects advanced pupils.

masterful *adj* **1** inclined to take control and dominate. **2** having or showing the technical, artistic, or intellectual skill of a master. ➤➤ **masterfully** *adv.*

Usage note

masterful *or* **masterly**? Both these words can be used to mean 'having or showing the skill of a master', but *masterly* should be preferred in this sense: *a masterly performance.* The main sense of *masterful* is 'showing strength or dominance': *a masterful type who took charge in any situation.* In modern usage *masterly* cannot be used in this sense.

master key *n* a key designed to open several different locks.

masterly *adj* demonstrating exceptional expertise.

Usage note

masterly *or* **masterful**? See note at MASTERFUL.

mastermind[1] *n* **1** a person who masterminds a project. **2** a person of outstanding intellect.

mastermind[2] *v* to be the intellectual force behind (a project).

master of ceremonies *n* **1** a person who determines the procedure to be observed on a state or public occasion. **2** a person who acts as host, *esp* by introducing speakers, performers, etc, at an event.

Master of the Rolls *n* the presiding judge of the Court of Appeal in England and Wales.

masterpiece *n* a work done with extraordinary skill.

mastery *n* **1a** the authority of a master. **b** the upper hand in a contest or competition. **2** skill or knowledge that makes one master of a subject.

masthead *n* **1** the top of a mast. **2** the name of a newspaper displayed on the top of the first page.

mastic *n* **1** an aromatic resin that exudes from a S European evergreen tree and is used in varnishes. **2** a substance like putty used as a protective coating or cement.

masticate *v* to grind or crush (food) before swallowing; to chew. ➤➤ **mastication** *n.*

mastiff *n* a very large smooth-coated dog of a breed used chiefly as guard dogs.

mastitis *n* inflammation of the breast or udder, usu caused by infection.

mastodon *n* an extinct mammal similar to the related mammoths and elephants but with a different form of molar teeth.

mastoid *n* **1** the mastoid process. **2** = MASTOIDITIS.

mastoiditis *n* inflammation of the mastoid process.

mastoid process *n* a somewhat conical prominent or projecting part of the temporal bone behind the ear.

masturbate *v* to practise masturbation on oneself. ➤➤ **masturbator** *n,* **masturbatory** *adj.*

masturbation *n* stimulation of the genitals accomplished by any means except sexual intercourse.

mat[1] *n* **1** a piece of thick fabric used as a covering for an area of floor, e.g. a doormat or a bathmat. **2** a relatively thin usu decorative piece of material used to protect a surface, e.g. from heat, moisture, or scratches. **3** a large thick pad or cushion used as a surface for wrestling and gymnastics. **4** a mass of intertwined or tangled strands. ✱ **on the mat** *informal* in trouble; due to be punished.

mat[2] *v* (**matted, matting**) of fibres, hair, etc: to become tangled or intertwined.

matador *n* a bullfighter who has the principal role and who kills the bull in a bullfight.

match[1] *n* **1** a contest between two or more teams or individuals. **2** a person or thing that is the equal of another. **3a** one thing that corresponds exactly to another. **b** a pair of things that correspond exactly. **4a** a prospective partner in marriage. **b** a marriage union. ✱ **meet one's match** to meet one's equal.

match[2] *v* **1a** to correspond or cause (two things) to correspond. **b** to be the exact counterpart or equal of (something). **2a** to be equal to (something or somebody). **b** to pit (a person or thing) in competition or opposition.

match[3] *n* **1** a short slender piece of wood, cardboard, etc tipped with a mixture that ignites when subjected to friction. **2** formerly, a chemically prepared wick or cord used in firing firearms or powder.

matchboard *n* a board with a groove cut along one edge and a tongue along the other so as to fit snugly with the edges of similarly cut boards.

matchless *adj* having no equal; peerless.

matchlock *n* a musket equipped with a mechanism by which a slow-burning cord is lowered over a hole in the breech to ignite the charge.

matchmaker *n* a person who arranges marriages or speculatively introduces one party to another.

match play *n* a golf competition scored by number of holes won rather than strokes played.

match point *n* a situation in tennis in which a player will win the match by winning the next point.

matchstick *n* **1** the wooden stem of a match. **2** (*used before a noun*) denoting a figure drawn with single straight lines.

matchwood *n* wood splinters.

mate[1] *n* **1a** *Brit, Aus* used as a familiar form of address between men: a friend. **b** (*often in combination*) an associate or companion. **c** an assistant to a more skilled workman. **2** an officer on a merchant ship ranking below the captain. **3a** a marriage partner. **b** either member of a breeding pair of animals.

mate[2] *v* **1** of animals: to come together to breed. **2** to join or fit (two parts) together.

mate[3] *v* in chess, to checkmate (an opponent).

mate[4] *n* in chess, checkmate.

maté /'matay, 'mahtay/ *n* a tealike aromatic beverage made from the leaves of a S American holly.

matelot *n Brit, informal* a sailor.

materfamilias *n* (*pl* **matresfamilias**) a female head of a household.

material[1] *n* **1** the elements, constituents, or substances of which something is composed or can be made. **2** cloth; fabric. **3** (*in pl*) apparatus necessary for doing or making something.

material[2] *adj* **1a** important or significant. **b** (+ to) relevant. **2** of or concerned with physical rather than spiritual things. ➤➤ **materiality** *n*, **materially** *adv.*

materialise *v* see MATERIALIZE.

materialism *n* **1** a preoccupation with or stress on material rather than spiritual things. **2** a theory that only physical matter is real and that all processes and phenomena can be explained by reference to matter. ➤➤ **materialist** *n and adj*, **materialistic** *adj.*

materialize *or* **-ise** *v* **1** of a ghost or spirit: to assume bodily form. **2** to become reality; to become tangible. ➤➤ **materialization** *n.*

materiel *n* equipment and supplies used by the armed forces.

maternal *adj* **1** relating to or characteristic of a mother. **2** related through one's mother. ➤➤ **maternally** *adv.*

maternity *n* **1** motherhood. **2** (*used before a noun*) relating to pregnancy or pregnant women: *a maternity dress.*

matey *or* **maty** *adj* (**matier, matiest**) *informal* friendly. ➤➤ **mateyness** *n*, **matily** *adv*, **matiness** *n.*

math *n NAm* mathematics.

mathematics *pl n* (*used as sing. or pl*) the science of numbers and their operations, interrelations, and combinations and of space configurations and their structure, measurement, etc. ➤➤ **mathematical** *adj*, **mathematically** *adv*, **mathematician** *n.*

maths *pl n Brit* (*used as sing. or pl*) mathematics.

matinée *n* a musical or dramatic performance during the day, *esp* the afternoon.

matinée coat *n* = MATINÉE JACKET.

matinée jacket *n Brit* a cardigan worn by babies.

matins *pl n* (*used as sing. or pl*) a morning prayer service, *esp* a daily morning office of the Anglican Church.

matresfamilias *n* pl of MATERFAMILIAS.

matriarch *n* a woman who rules a family, group, or state; *specif* a mother who is the head of her family. ➤➤ **matriarchal** *adj.*

matriarchy *n* (*pl* **-ies**) a system of social organization in which the female is the head of the family, and descent and inheritance are traced through the female line.

matrices *n* pl of MATRIX.

matricide *n* **1** the act of murdering one's mother. **2** a person who commits matricide. ➤➤ **matricidal** *adj.*

matriculate *v* to be admitted or admit (somebody) as a member of a college or university. ➤➤ **matriculation** *n.*

matrilineal *adj* relating to or tracing descent through the maternal line. ➤➤ **matrilineally** *adv.*

matrimony *n* marriage. ➤➤ **matrimonial** *adj.*

matrix *n* (*pl* **matrices** *or* **matrixes**) **1** a substance, environment, etc within which something else originates or develops. **2** a mould in which something is cast. **3** the natural material in which something, e.g. a fossil, gem, or specimen for study, is embedded. **4** a rectangular array of mathematical elements treated as a unit and subject to special algebraic laws. **5** something resembling a mathematical matrix, *esp* in rectangular arrangement of elements into rows and columns.

matron *n* **1** a woman in charge of living arrangements in a school, residential home, etc. **2** *Brit* a woman in charge of the nursing in a hospital; a senior nursing officer. **3** a married woman, *esp* one who is dignified and mature. **4** *NAm* a female prison warden. ➤➤ **matronly** *adj.*

matron of honour *n* a bride's principal married wedding attendant.

matt[1] *or* **matte** *adj* lacking lustre or gloss; not shiny.

matt[2] *or* **matte** *n* **1** a roughened or dull finish, e.g. on gilt or paint. **2** a border round a picture acting as a frame or as a contrast between picture and frame.

matte *n* a crude mixture of sulphides formed in smelting copper, lead, etc sulphide ores.

matter[1] *n* **1a** the substance of which a physical object is composed. **b** a physical substance occupying space and having mass. **2** (**the matter**) a source of disquiet. **3** a subject of interest or concern. **4a** that part of a legal case which deals with facts rather than principles of law. **b** something to be proved in a court of law. **5** something written or printed. ✱ **a matter of** a period of time reckoned merely in (minutes, hours, days, etc). **as a matter of fact** in truth; actually. **for that matter** so far as that is concerned. **in the matter of** concerning (something or somebody). **no matter 1** that is of no importance. **2** regardless or irrespective of a certain thing.

matter[2] *v* to be of importance.

matter of course *n* something routine or to be expected as a natural consequence.

matter-of-fact *adj* keeping to or concerned with fact; *esp* not fanciful or imaginative.

matting *n* material, e.g. hemp, for mats.

mattock *n* a digging tool with a head like that of a pick and often a blade like that of an axe or adze.

mattress *n* a fabric case filled with resilient material, e.g. feathers, foam rubber, or an arrangement of coiled springs, used as, or on, a bed.

maturation *n* **1** the process of becoming mature. **2** the formation of pus in a boil or abscess; suppuration.

mature[1] *adj* **1** characteristic of or being in a condition of full or adult development; full-grown. **2** physically, emotionally, or mentally advanced. **3a** having completed natural growth and development; ripe. **b** having attained a final or desired state: *mature wine.* **4** based on slow careful consideration: *a mature judgment.* **5** due for payment: *a mature loan.* ➤➤ **maturely** *adv.*

mature[2] *v* **1** to become mature. **2** to become due for payment.

maturity *n* **1** the quality or state of being mature; *esp* full development. **2** the date when a bond, note, insurance policy, etc becomes due.

matutinal *adj literary* of or occurring in the morning.

maty *adj* see MATEY.

matzo *or* **matzoh** /'matsoh/ *n* (*pl* **matzoth** /'matsoht, 'matsohth/ *or* **matzos**) a wafer of unleavened bread eaten during Passover.

maudlin *adj* weakly and effusively sentimental; tearful.

maul[1] *v* **1** of an animal: to attack and tear the flesh of (an animal or person). **2** to handle (somebody or something) roughly.

maul[2] *n* **1** in Rugby Union, a situation in which one or more players from each team close round the player carrying the ball. **2** a heavy two-handed hammer.

maulstick *n* a stick used by painters to support and steady the hand while working.

maunder *v* **1** to act or wander idly. **2** to speak in a rambling or indistinct manner.

Maundy *n* the distribution of Maundy money.

Maundy money *n* specially minted coins given to selected poor people by the British Sovereign in a ceremony on Maundy Thursday.

Maundy Thursday *n* the Thursday before Easter observed in commemoration of the Last Supper.

Mauritanian *n* a native or inhabitant of Mauritania. ➤➤ **Mauritanian** *adj.*

Mauritian *n* a native or inhabitant of Mauritius. ➤➤ **Mauritian** *adj.*

mausoleum *n* (*pl* **mausoleums** *or* **mausolea**) a large and elaborate tomb; *esp* a stone building with places for entombment of the dead above ground.

mauve *adj* of a pinkish purple to bluish purple colour. ➤➤ **mauve** *n.*

maven *n chiefly NAm* an expert or enthusiast.

maverick *n* **1** an independent and nonconformist individual. **2** *NAm* an unbranded range animal; *esp* a motherless calf.

Word history

named after Samuel A *Maverick* d.1870, US pioneer who did not brand his calves. The practice soon arose of calling unbranded cattle *mavericks* and the term was then extended to independent-minded or masterless people.

maw *n* the throat, gullet, or jaws, *esp* of a voracious flesh-eating animal.

mawkish *adj* **1** sickly or feebly sentimental. **2** *archaic or dialect* having an insipid often unpleasant taste.

max. *abbr* maximum.

maxi *n* (*pl* **maxis**) a floor-length coat, skirt, etc.

maxilla *n* (*pl* **maxillae** *or* **maxillas**) **1** either of two bones of the upper jaw of a human or other higher vertebrate. **2** any of the one or two pairs of mouthparts behind the mandibles in insects and other arthropods. ➤➤ **maxillary** *adj.*

maxim *n* a succinct expression of a general truth, fundamental principle, or rule of conduct.

maxima *n* pl of MAXIMUM[1].

maximize *or* **-ise** *v* to increase (something) to a maximum or to the highest possible degree. ➤➤ **maximization** *n.*

maximum[1] *n* (*pl* **maxima** *or* **maximums**) the greatest amount, number, intensity, level, or extent possible or recorded. ➤➤ **maximal** *adj.*

maximum[2] *adj* of or being a maximum.

maxwell *n* the unit of magnetic flux in the centimetre-gram-second system.

May *n* the fifth month of the year.

may[1] *v aux* (*third person sing. present tense* **may,** *past tense* **might**) **1** used to express permission or opportunity: *You may go now.* **2** used to express possibility: *They may be right.* **3** used to express a wish or hope: *Long may the good weather last.* ✱ **be that as it may** whether that is true or not; in spite of that.

may[2] *n* hawthorn or hawthorn blossom.

Maya *n* (*pl* **Mayas** *or* **Maya**) a member of a group of Native American peoples inhabiting the Yucatán peninsula. ➤➤ **Mayan** *adj and n.*

maybe *adv* perhaps.

Mayday *n* used as an international radio distress signal.

May Day *n* 1 May, celebrated as a springtime festival and in many countries as a public holiday in honour of working people.

mayflower *n* any of various plants that bloom in the spring.

mayfly *n* (*pl* **-ies**) an insect with an aquatic nymph and a short-lived fragile adult with membranous wings.

mayhem *n* a state of great confusion or disorder.

mayn't *contr* may not.

mayonnaise *n* a thick dressing made with egg yolks, vegetable oil, and vinegar or lemon juice.

mayor *n* the chief executive or nominal head of a city or borough. ➤➤ **mayoral** *adj,* **mayorship** *n.*

mayoralty *n* (*pl* **-ies**) the office or term of office of a mayor.

mayoress *n* **1** the wife of a mayor. **2** a woman who is a mayor.

maypole *n* a tall ribbon-wreathed pole forming a centre for dances, *esp* on May Day.

mayweed *n* **1** a foul-smelling Eurasian plant with white flowers like daisies. **2** a similar related plant that is scentless.

maze *n* **1** a network of paths designed to confuse and puzzle those who attempt to walk through it. **2** something intricately or confusingly complicated.

mazel tov /'maz(ə)l tof, tov/ *interj* used by Jews: congratulations.

mazurka *n* a Polish folk dance in moderate triple time.

MB *abbr* Bachelor of Medicine.

Mb *abbr* megabyte(s).

MBA *abbr* Master of Business Administration.

MBE *abbr* Member of the Order of the British Empire.

MBM *abbr* meat and bone meal.

MBO *abbr* management buyout.

MC *abbr* **1** Master of Ceremonies. **2** *NAm* Member of Congress. **3** *Brit* Military Cross.

MCC *abbr* Marylebone Cricket Club.

MD *abbr* **1** Doctor of Medicine. **2** *Brit* Managing Director. **3** Maryland (US postal abbreviation).

Md *abbr* the chemical symbol for mendelevium.

MDF *abbr* medium density fibreboard.

MDMA *abbr* methylenedioxymethamphetamine (the drug Ecstasy).

ME *abbr* **1** myalgic encephalomyelitis. **2** Maine (US postal abbreviation).

me[1] *pron* used as the objective case: I.

me[2] *n* something suitable for me: *That dress isn't really me.*

me[3] *n* see MI[1].

mea culpa /ˌmayah 'koolpah, 'kulpə/ *n* a formal or humorous acknowledgment of personal fault.

mead[1] *n* a fermented alcoholic drink made of water and honey.

mead[2] *n archaic or literary* a meadow.

meadow *n* an area of moist low-lying usu level grassland.

meadowlark *n* a N American songbird, typically brown and buff with a yellow breast marked with a black crescent.

meadow saffron *n* a lilac-flowered European crocus.

meadowsweet *n* a tall Eurasian plant of the rose family with creamy-white fragrant flowers.

meagre (*NAm* **meager**) *adj* **1** deficient in quality or quantity. **2** having little flesh. ⪢ **meagrely** *adv*, **meagreness** *n*.

meal[1] *n* **1** the portion of food taken or provided at one time to satisfy appetite. **2** the time of eating a meal. ✱ **make a meal of something** *informal* to carry something out in an unduly laborious way.

meal[2] *n* **1** the usu coarsely ground seeds of a cereal grass or pulse. **2** a product resembling this, *esp* in texture.

mealie *n SAfr* an ear of maize.

meal ticket *n informal* somebody or something that can be milked as a source of income.

mealworm *n* the larva of the meal beetle that is often raised as food for insect-eating animals, bait for fishing, etc.

mealy *adj* (**-ier, -iest**) **1** soft, dry, and crumbly. **2** containing meal. **3** pallid or blanched.

mealybug *n* a scale insect with a white powdery covering that is a pest, *esp* of fruit trees.

mealy-mouthed *adj* hypocritically unwilling to speak plainly or directly, e.g. for fear of incurring odium.

mean[1] *adj* **1** not generous; stingy. **2** characterized by petty malice; spiteful or nasty. **3** particularly bad-tempered, unpleasant, or disagreeable. **4** of poor shabby inferior quality or status. **5** lacking distinction or eminence; merely ordinary. **6** *informal* excellent or impressive. ⪢ **meanly** *adj*, **meanness** *n*.

mean[2] *v* (*past tense and past part.* **meant**) **1** to have in mind as a purpose; to intend. **2** to serve or intend to convey, produce, or indicate; to signify. **3** to intend for a particular use or purpose: *These pills are meant to relieve the pain.* **4** (*usu* + to) to have significance or importance: *The remark meant nothing to me.* ✱ **mean well** to have good intentions.

mean[3] *n* **1** a middle point between extremes. **2** a value that lies within a range of values and is estimated according to a prescribed law.

mean[4] *adj* **1** occupying a position about midway between extremes; average. **2** occupying a middle position; intermediate.

meander[1] *v* **1** of a river or road: to follow a winding or intricate course. **2** to wander aimlessly or casually without definite direction.

meander[2] *n* **1** a turn or winding of a stream. **2** a winding path, course, or pattern.

meaning[1] *n* **1** that which is conveyed or which one intends to convey, *esp* by language. **2** significant quality; value. **3** sense or significance.

meaning[2] *adj* significant or expressive.

meaningful *adj* **1** having meaning; significant. **2** having a hidden or special significance; expressive. **3** having a purpose; worthwhile. ⪢ **meaningfully** *adv*, **meaningfulness** *n*.

meaningless *adj* **1** devoid of meaning. **2** having no purpose; futile. ⪢ **meaninglessly** *adv*, **meaninglessness** *n*.

means *pl n* **1** (*used as sing. or pl*) **a** that which enables a desired purpose to be achieved. **b** the method used to attain an end. **2** (*used as pl*) resources available for disposal; *esp* wealth. ✱ **by all means** of course; certainly. **by means of** with the help or use of. **by no means** not at all; in no way.

means test *n* an examination into somebody's financial state to determine their eligibility for public assistance, for a student grant, etc.

means-test *v* to subject (somebody) to, or make (something) conditional on, a means test.

meant *v* past tense and past part. of MEAN[2].

meantime[1] *n* the intervening time.

meantime[2] *adv* meanwhile.

meanwhile[1] *adv* **1** during the intervening time. **2** during the same period.

meanwhile[2] *n* the meantime.

measles *pl n* (*used as sing.*) an infectious viral disease marked by a rash of distinct red circular spots and high fever.

measly *adj* (**-ier, -iest**) *informal* contemptibly small or few; worthless or insignificant.

measure[1] *v* **1** to ascertain the size, amount, or degree of (something) in terms of a standard unit or in comparison with something else. **2** to have (a specified measurement). **3** (+ out) to take or allot in measured amounts. ⪢ **measurable** *adj*, **measurably** *adv*.

measure[2] *n* **1a** a step planned or taken to achieve an end. **b** a proposed legislative act or bill. **2** a standard or unit of measurement. **3** an instrument or utensil for measuring. **4a** an appropriate or due portion. **b** a moderate extent, amount, or degree. **5a** poetic rhythm measured by quantity or accent; metre. **b** a metrical unit; a foot. **6** (*in pl*) rock strata. ✱ **for good measure** in addition to the main item or to what is strictly necessary. **get the measure of** to get to know the character or abilities of (somebody) or the nature or requirements of (something).

measured *adj* **1** rhythmical; *esp* slow and regular. **2** carefully controlled or thought out.

measureless *adj* having no observable limit; immeasurable.

measurement *n* **1** the act or an instance of measuring. **2** a figure, extent, or amount obtained by measuring. **3** a system of standard measuring units.

measure up *v* to have the necessary ability, skill, or qualities; to be adequate.

meat *n* **1** animal flesh used as food. **2** the core or essence of something. ✱ **easy meat** *informal* an easy prey.

meatball *n* a small ball-shaped mass of minced meat, usu beef, for cooking.

meatloaf *n* a dish consisting of minced meat, usu with flavourings, made into the shape of a loaf and baked.

meatus *n* (*pl* **meatuses** *or* **meatus**) the opening to the outside of a natural body passage.

meaty *adj* (**-ier, -iest**) **1** consisting of, tasting like, or with a similar texture to meat. **2** fleshy or heavily built. **3** rich in ideas or points to think about or discuss. ⪢ **meatiness** *n*.

Mecca *n* a place regarded as a goal by a specified group of people.

mechanic *n* a skilled worker who repairs or maintains machinery.

mechanical *adj* **1** operated by or relating to machinery or machines. **2** done as if by machine; lacking in spontaneity. **3** of, dealing with, or in accordance with the principles of mechanics. ⪢ **mechanically** *adv*.

mechanical advantage *n* the ratio of the force that performs the useful work of a machine to the force that is applied to the machine.

mechanical drawing *n* a drawing done with the aid of instruments.

mechanical engineering *n* the branch of engineering concerned with the design, construction, and operation of machines.

mechanics *pl n* **1** (*used as sing. or pl*) the branch of science that deals with energy and forces, and their effect on moving and stationary bodies. **2** (*used as pl*) the working parts of something. **3** (*used as pl*) the functional details of something.

mechanise *v* see MECHANIZE.

mechanism *n* **1** a set of moving parts designed to perform a particular function, *esp* inside a piece of machinery. **2** a process or technique for achieving a result.

mechanistic *adj* relating to the theory that all natural phenomena are mechanically determined and can be explained by the laws of physics and chemistry.

mechanize *or* **-ise** *v* **1a** to equip (e.g. a factory) with machinery. **b** to equip (a force) with armed and armoured motor vehicles. **2** to make mechanical, automatic, or monotonous. ⋙ **mechanization** *n.*

meconium *n* a dark greenish mass that accumulates in the bowels during foetal life and is discharged shortly after birth.

med. *abbr* **1** medical. **2** medium.

medal *n* a piece of metal with a stamped design, emblem, inscription, etc that commemorates a person or event or is awarded for excellence or achievement.

medalist *n NAm* see MEDALLIST.

medallion *n* **1** a pendant in the shape of a medal. **2** a decorative tablet, panel, etc, often bearing a figure or portrait in relief.

medallist (*NAm* **medalist**) *n* a person who has received a medal as an award, *esp* for sporting achievement.

meddle *v* (*usu* + in/with) to interest oneself in what is not one's concern. ⋙ **meddler** *n,* **meddlesome** *adj.*

Mede *n* a native or inhabitant of ancient Media in Persia.

media *n* **1** pl of MEDIUM[1]. **2** the means of communication, such as the press and television, supplying news and information to the general public.

Usage note

Media is a plural form, the plural of *medium*: *Television is a medium; Television and radio are media.* The form *a media* is grammatically incorrect. The form *the media* meaning 'all the various institutions that spread news and information' should be followed by a plural verb: *The media have shown little interest in this event.*

mediaeval *adj* see MEDIEVAL.

medial *adj* being, occurring in, or extending towards the middle. ⋙ **medially** *adv.*

median[1] *adj* **1** *technical* lying in the plane that divides an animal into right and left halves. **2** of or constituting a statistical median.

median[2] *n* **1** a statistical value in an ordered set of values below and above which there is an equal number of values, or which is the arithmetic mean of the two middle values if there is no one middle value. **2** a line from a point of intersection of two sides of a triangle to the midpoint of the opposite side.

mediate *v* **1** to intervene between parties in order to reconcile them. **2** *technical* to transmit or effect (something) by acting as an intermediate mechanism or agency. ⋙ **mediation** *n,* **mediator** *n.*

medic *n informal* a medical doctor or student.

medical[1] *adj* relating to physicians or the science or practice of medicine. ⋙ **medically** *adv.*

medical[2] *n* an examination to determine a person's physical fitness.

medical officer *n* a doctor who is responsible for health services in an organization, local authority, etc.

medicament *n* a medicine.

medicate *v* **1** to treat (a patient, wound, etc) medicinally. **2** to impregnate (something) with a medicinal substance.

medication *n* **1** a medicine, drug, or remedy. **2** treatment with drugs.

Medicean *adj* of or relating to the Medici family, rulers of Florence from the 15th cent. until 1737.

medicinal *adj* **1** used to cure disease or relieve pain. **2** relating to or involving medicines or drugs. ⋙ **medicinally** *adv.*

medicine *n* **1** the science and art of the maintenance of health and the prevention and treatment of disease. **2** a substance or preparation used in treating or preventing disease. ✱ **give somebody a taste/dose of their own medicine** to treat somebody in the same unpleasant way that they have treated somebody else.

medicine ball *n* a heavy ball used for throwing and catching as a form of exercise.

medicine man *n* among Native Americans and some other peoples, a healer or sorcerer believed to have supernatural powers; a shaman.

medico *n* (*pl* **-os**) *informal* a medical doctor or student.

medieval *or* **mediaeval** *adj* **1** dating from or typical of the Middle Ages. **2** *informal* extremely old-fashioned or out of date. ⋙ **medievally** *adv.*

medievalist *n* a specialist in or devotee of medieval history, culture, or languages.

mediocre *adj* of ordinary or average quality.

mediocrity *n* (*pl* **-ies**) **1** the quality or state of being mediocre. **2** a mediocre person.

meditate *v* **1** to empty the mind of thoughts and fix the attention on one matter, *esp* as a religious or spiritual exercise. **2** (*often* + on/upon) to focus one's attention on; to consider or plan in the mind. ⋙ **meditative** *adj,* **meditatively** *adv,* **meditator** *n.*

meditation *n* **1** the act or an instance of meditating. **2** a written or spoken communication of the results of extended study of a topic.

Mediterranean *adj* **1** of or characteristic of the Mediterranean Sea or the region around it. **2** of a climate: characterized by hot dry summers and relatively warm but wet winters.

medium[1] *n* (*pl* **media** *or* **mediums**) **1a** a means of doing something; a vehicle. **b** a channel or means of communication, *esp* one designed to reach large numbers of people. **2** a material or technical means of artistic expression. **3** a substance regarded as the means of transmission of a force or effect. **4** a disk, tape, etc on which the output of a computer can be stored. **5** a liquid, e.g. oil or water, with which dry colouring material can be mixed. **6** (*pl* **mediums**) a person through whom others seek to communicate with the spirits of the dead. **7** a middle position or state.

medium[2] *adj* intermediate or average in amount, quality, position, or degree.

medium frequency *n* a radio frequency in the range between 300 and 3000 kilohertz.

medium wave *n chiefly Brit* a band of radio waves, typically used for sound broadcasting, covering wavelengths between about 180m and 600m.

medlar *n* a small brown fruit like a crab apple that is used in preserves.

medley *n* (*pl* **-eys**) **1** a mixture, *esp* a confused mixture. **2** a musical composition made up of a series of songs or short musical pieces.

Médoc /'medok, may'dok/ *n* (*pl* **Médoc**) a red wine produced in the Médoc district of SW France.

medulla *n* (*pl* **medullae** *or* **medullas**) **1** the inner region of an organ or tissue in the body, e.g. the kidney. **2** the internal tissue of a plant; the pith.

medulla oblongata *n* (*pl* **medulla oblongatas** *or* **medullae oblongatae**) the pyramid-shaped part of the brainstem of vertebrates that merges into the spinal cord.

medusa *n* (*pl* **medusae** *or* **medusas**) the umbrella-shaped free-swimming form of a class of animals related to the jellyfish that produces sperm and eggs for sexual reproduction.

meed *n archaic* just reward or compensation.

meek *adj* lacking spirit and courage; timid or submissive. ➤➤ **meekly** *adv*, **meekness** *n*.

meerkat *n* a small flesh-eating S African mammal related to the mongoose.

meerschaum *n* **1** a fine light white clayey mineral that is a form of magnesium silicate. **2** a tobacco pipe with a bowl made of meerschaum.

meet[1] *v* (*past tense and past part.* **met**) **1a** to come into the presence of (somebody) by accident or design. **b** to become acquainted with (somebody). **2** (*often* + with) to encounter or experience (something). **3** to come into contact or conjunction with (something); to join. **4** to conform to (something), *esp* exactly and precisely; to satisfy.

meet[2] *n* **1** the assembling of participants for a hunt or for competitive sports. **2** an athletics meeting.

meet[3] *adj archaic* suitable or proper.

meeting *n* **1** an assembly of people for a common purpose, *esp* for a formal discussion. **2** a coming together, *esp* of two or more people.

mega *adj informal* very big, famous, prestigious, or important.

mega- *comb. form* **1** great or large: *megalith.* **2** one million (10^6): *megawatt.* **3** in computing, 2^{20}: *megabyte.*

megabit *n* a unit of computer information equal to one million bits or, strictly, 2^{20} bits.

megabucks *pl n informal* a large amount of money.

megabyte *n* a unit of computer storage equal to one million bytes or, strictly, 2^{20} bytes.

megaflop *n* a unit of processing speed for computers, equal to one million, or, strictly, 2^{20} floating-point operations per second.

megahertz *n* (*pl* **megahertz**) a unit of frequency equal to one million hertz.

megalith *n* a huge undecorated block of stone; *esp* one used in prehistoric monuments. ➤➤ **megalithic** *adj.*

megalomania *n* **1** an obsessive craving for power or unhealthy delight in wielding it over other people. **2** a mental disorder characterized by delusory feelings of personal omnipotence and grandeur. ➤➤ **megalomaniac** *adj and n.*

megaphone *n* a hand-held funnel-shaped device used to amplify or direct the voice.

megapode *n* a large bird found in Australia, New Guinea, and nearby islands, that lives on the ground and lays its eggs in a large mound of earth and decaying vegetable matter so that they incubate by natural heat.

megastar *n informal* a superstar.

megaton *n* an explosive force produced by an atom or hydrogen bomb equivalent to that of one million tons of TNT.

megavolt *n* a unit of electromotive force equal to one million volts.

megawatt *n* a unit of power equal to one million watts.

meiosis *n* (*pl* **meioses**) **1** a process of division in gamete-producing cells by which one of each pair of chromosomes passes to each resulting gametic cell which thus has half the number of chromosomes of the original cell and is usually genetically unique: compare MITOSIS. **2** = LITOTES. ➤➤ **meiotic** *adj.*

Meistersinger /'miestəzingə/ *n* (*pl* **Meistersinger** *or* **Meistersingers**) a member of any of various German guilds formed chiefly in the 15th and 16th cents for the cultivation of poetry and music.

meitnerium *n* an unstable radioactive chemical element made artificially by high-energy ion bombardment.

melamine *n* a plastic used for coatings.

melancholia *n* melancholy.

melancholy[1] *n* a feeling or state of deep sadness or depression. ➤➤ **melancholic** *adj.*

melancholy[2] *adj* **1** depressed in spirits; dejected. **2** causing sadness; depressing.

Melanesian *n* a native or inhabitant of Melanesia. ➤➤ **Melanesian** *adj.*

melange /'maylonhzh, may'lonhzh/ *n* a mixture of incongruous elements.

melanin *n* a dark brown or black pigment in the hair and skin, responsible for tanning when the skin is exposed to sunlight.

melanoma *n* (*pl* **melanomas** *or* **melanomata**) a tumour of the cells in the skin and retina that produce melanin, which may be malignant and can be caused by exposure to sunlight.

Melba toast *n* very thin crisp toast.

meld *v* to combine or blend (two or more different substances or things) together to form a single substance or thing.

melee *n* a confused or riotous struggle; *esp* a general hand-to-hand fight.

mellifluous *adj* of a sound or voice: sounding sweet and flowing smoothly. ➤➤ **mellifluously** *adv*, **mellifluousness** *n.*

mellow[1] *adj* **1** rich and soft. **2a** made gentle by age or experience. **b** relaxed or genial, *esp* because of intoxication.

mellow[2] *v* **1** to become mellow, *esp* to become more genial. **2** to make (somebody or something) mellow.

melodeon *or* **melodion** *n* **1** a type of small accordion used in folk music. **2** a small organ similar to the harmonium.

melodic *adj* **1** relating to or having melody. **2** melodious. ➤➤ **melodically** *adv.*

melodion *n* see MELODEON.

melodious *adj* having a pleasant sound or tune.

melodrama *n* **1** a film or play characterized by crude emotional appeal and by the predominance of plot and action over characterization. **2** sensational or sensationalized events, language, or behaviour. ➤➤ **melodramatic** *adj*, **melodramatically** *adv.*

melody *n* (*pl* **-ies**) **1** a rhythmic succession of single notes organized as an aesthetic whole; a tune. **2** the principal part in a harmonic composition.

melon *n* a large round or oval fruit with a hard rind, sweet juicy edible flesh and a central cavity packed with many seeds.

melt *v* **1** to become altered from a solid to a liquid state by heating. **2** to reduce (a substance) from a solid to a liquid state by heating. **3** to dissolve or disintegrate. **4** to disappear as if by dissolving. **5** to be, become, or make tender or gentle.

meltdown *n* **1** the overheating to melting point of the uranium fuel in the core of a nuclear reactor, so that it burns through its container and allows dangerous radioactivity to escape. **2** a catastrophic collapse, e.g. of an economy or market. **3** *informal* a state of furious rage or of mental breakdown.

melting point *n* the temperature at which a solid melts.

melting pot *n* **1** a place or situation in which diverse peoples, traditions, etc come together and mix. **2** an uncertain situation; a state of flux.

member *n* **1** an individual or unit belonging to or forming part of a group or organization. **2** a constituent part of a whole, e.g. an element of a mathematical set. **3** *archaic* a part of the human body, *esp* a limb. ➤➤ **membership** *n.*

membrane *n* **1** a thin pliable sheet or layer covering, lining, or connecting organs or cells in animals and plants. **2** a thin pliable sheet of material. ➤➤ **membraneous** *adj,* **membranous** *adj.*

meme *n* a behavioural or cultural trait that is passed on by other than genetic means, e.g. by imitation. ➤➤ **memetic** *adj.*

memento *n* (*pl* **-os** *or* **-oes**) something that serves as a reminder of past events.

memento mori /'mawri/ *n* (*pl* **memento mori**) a reminder of mortality, *esp* a human skull.

memo *n* (*pl* **-os**) *informal* a memorandum.

memoir *n* **1** a narrative or biography written from personal experience. **2** (*in pl*) an autobiography, *esp* one written by a public figure.

memorabilia *pl n* objects valued because of their connection with memorable people or events.

memorable *adj* **1** worth remembering; notable. **2** easy to remember. ➤➤ **memorably** *adv.*

memorandum *n* (*pl* **memorandums** *or* **memoranda**) **1** a usu brief communication for internal circulation, e.g. within an office. **2** an often unsigned informal record or communication; a written reminder.

memorial[1] *n* something, *esp* a monument, that commemorates a person or event.

memorial[2] *adj* serving to commemorate a person or event.

memorialize *or* **-ise** *v* to remember or commemorate.

memorize *or* **-ise** *v* to commit (facts or information) to memory; to learn by heart.

memory *n* (*pl* **-ies**) **1** the brain's or an individual's ability to remember experience in general or to recall particular experiences. **2** the store of things learned and retained from an individual's experience. **3** an image or impression of somebody or something stored in the brain. **4** the time within which past events can be or are remembered. **5a** a device, *esp* in a computer, into which data can be inserted for storage, and from which it may be extracted when wanted. **b** the capacity of a device for storing information.

men *n* pl of MAN[1].

menace[1] *n* **1** a person or thing that is threatening, dangerous, or annoying. **2** a threatening atmosphere or tone.

menace[2] *v* to threaten or show intent to harm (somebody or something). ➤➤ **menacing** *adj.*

ménage à trois /me'nahzh ah 'trwah/ *n* (*pl* **ménages à trois** /ah 'trwah/) a sexual relationship involving three people, *esp* a situation in which a third person lives with a married couple.

menagerie *n* a place where animals are kept, *esp* for exhibition.

ménages à trois *n* pl of MÉNAGE À TROIS.

menaquinone *n* a vitamin found in putrefying organic matter and synthesized by bacteria in the intestines; vitamin K_2.

menarche *n* the first menstrual period; the onset of menstruation.

mend[1] *v* **1** to restore to a sound condition or working order; to repair. **2** to improve or rectify. **3** to improve in health; to heal. ➤➤ **mendable** *adj,* **mender** *n.*

mend[2] *n* a mended place or part; a repair. ✱ **on the mend** improving, *esp* in health.

mendacious *adj* given to deception or falsehood. ➤➤ **mendaciously** *adv,* **mendacity** *n.*

mendelevium *n* a radioactive metallic chemical element that is artificially produced.

Mendelian *adj* relating to or according with the principles of heredity put forward by the Austrian botanist Gregor Mendel (d.1884). ➤➤ **Mendelism** *n.*

mendicant[1] *n* **1** a beggar. **2** (*often* **Mendicant**) a friar living off alms.

mendicant[2] *adj* **1** given to begging. **2** of a member of a religious order: dependent on begging.

menfolk *pl n* the men of a family or community.

menhir *n* a single upright roughly shaped monolith, usu of prehistoric origin.

menial[1] *adj* of work: lacking in interest or status and involving little skill.

menial[2] *n* somebody with a menial job.

meningeal *adj* relating to or in the region of the meninges.

meninges *n* pl of MENINX.

meningitis *n* inflammation of the meninges (membranes enveloping the brain and spinal cord; see MENINX), usu caused by bacterial, fungal, or viral infection.

meninx *n* (*pl* **meninges**) any of the three membranes that envelop the brain and spinal cord.

meniscus *n* (*pl* **menisci** *or* **meniscuses**) **1** the curved concave or convex upper surface of a column of liquid. **2** a lens that is concave on one side and convex on the other.

menopause *n* the natural cessation of menstruation occurring usu between the ages of 45 and 50, or the time in a woman's life at which this occurs. ➤➤ **menopausal** *adj.*

menorah *n* a candelabrum, usu with seven branches, that is a symbol of Judaism.

menses *pl n* **1** (*also used as sing.*) the menstrual flow. **2** (*used as sing.*) the time of menstruation.

menstrual *adj* of or relating to menstruation.

menstruate *v* of a woman or other female primate: to discharge blood, secretions, and tissue debris from the uterus at intervals of approximately 28 days. ➤➤ **menstruation** *n.*

mensuration *n* **1** measurement. **2** geometry applied to the computation of lengths, areas, or volumes from given dimensions or angles.

-ment *suffix* forming nouns from verbs, denoting: **1** the concrete result, object, or agent of the action specified: *embankment; entanglement.* **2** an action or process: *encirclement; development.* **3** the place of a specified action: *encampment.*

mental *adj* **1** relating to the mind or its activity. **2** performed or experienced in the mind: *mental arithmetic.* **3a** of or relating to a psychiatric disorder. **b** intended for the care of people suffering from a psychiatric disorder. **4** *informal* mad. ➤➤ **mentally** *adv.*

mental age *n* a measure used in psychological testing that expresses an individual's mental attainment in terms of the number of years it takes an average child to reach the same level.

mental block *n* a temporary inability to remember something or to carry out a mental task.

mental handicap *n dated, sometimes offensive* an impairment of a person's intellectual abilities, through brain damage or underdevelopment, that renders him or her unable to live a fully independent life. ➤➤ **mentally handicapped** *adj.*

mentality *n* (*pl* **-ies**) **1** a mode of thought; mental disposition or outlook. **2** mental power or capacity; intelligence.

menthol *n* an alcohol that occurs *esp* in mint oils and has the smell and cooling properties of peppermint. ➤➤ **mentholated** *adj.*

mention[1] *n* **1** a brief reference to somebody or something; a passing remark. **2** a formal citation for outstanding achievement.

mention[2] *v* **1** to refer to (somebody or something) briefly in speech or writing. **2** to cite (somebody or something) for outstanding achievement.

mentor[1] *n* **1** a wise and trusted adviser. **2** an experienced member of an organization or institution entrusted with training and advising younger or less experienced members.

mentor[2] *v* to act as a mentor to (somebody).

menu *n* (*pl* **menus**) **1a** a list of the dishes that may be ordered, e.g. in a restaurant. **b** the dishes to be served at a meal. **2** a list of available programs, functions, commands, etc, displayed on a computer screen, from which the user can select a particular option.

meow *v* see MIAOW.

MEP *abbr* Member of the European Parliament.

Mephistophelian *or* **Mephistophelean** *adj* in the manner of Mephistopheles, a devil in medieval mythology to whom Faust sold his soul; fiendish or sardonic.

mephitic *adj* of a gas or vapour: foul-smelling or noxious.

mercantile *adj* relating to merchants or trading.

mercantilism *n* an economic system that was intended to increase the power and wealth of a nation by strict governmental regulation of the national economy. ➤➤ **mercantilist** *n and adj.*

Mercator's projection *or* **Mercator projection** *n* a map projection showing the lines of longitude as parallel evenly spaced straight lines and the lines of latitude as parallel straight lines whose distance from each other increases with their distance from the equator.

mercenary[1] *n* (*pl* **-ies**) a soldier who is hired to fight for a foreign country.

mercenary[2] *adj* acting primarily for financial reward.

mercer *n Brit esp* formerly, a dealer in fine textile fabrics, e.g. silk.

mercerize *or* **-ise** *v* to give (e.g. cotton thread or fabrics) lustre and strength by chemical treatment under tension with an alkali, e.g. caustic soda.

merchandise[1] *n* **1** goods for sale, e.g. in a shop. **2** products developed and sold to promote a film, band, etc.

merchandise[2] *or* **-ize** *v* to promote the sale of (goods) through skilful packaging and presentation. ➤➤ **merchandiser** *n.*

merchant *n* **1a** a wholesaler. **b** *chiefly NAm* a shopkeeper. **2** *informal, derog* a person who indulges in a specified activity: *a doom merchant.* **3** (*used before a noun*) of or used in commerce: *merchant ships.*

merchantable *adj* of commercially acceptable quality.

merchant bank *n chiefly Brit* a firm of private bankers that handles bills of exchange and guarantees new issues of securities. ➤➤ **merchant banker** *n.*

merchantman *n* (*pl* **merchantmen**) a ship used in commerce.

merchant marine *n chiefly NAm* = MERCHANT NAVY.

merchant navy *n chiefly Brit* the privately or publicly owned commercial ships of a nation.

merciful *adj* **1** showing mercy. **2** constituting a benefit or blessing, *esp* a relief from suffering. ➤➤ **mercifully** *adv.*

merciless *adj* having no mercy; pitiless. ➤➤ **mercilessly** *adv,* **mercilessness** *n.*

mercurial *adj* **1** characterized by rapid and unpredictable changes of mood. **2** of or containing mercury.

mercury *n* a silver-white heavy poisonous metallic chemical element that is liquid at ordinary temperatures, and is used in thermometers and barometers. ➤➤ **mercuric** *adj,* **mercurous** *adj.*

mercy[1] *n* (*pl* **-ies**) **1** compassion or forbearance shown *esp* to an offender or an enemy. **2** a fortunate circumstance. **3** (*used before a noun*) giving or bringing help and relief to people in distress: *a mercy mission.* ✱ **at the mercy of** wholly in the power of (somebody or something).

mercy[2] *interj archaic* used to express surprise.

mere[1] *adj* **1** being what is specified and nothing else: *a mere child.* **2** (**the merest**) the slightest.

mere[2] *n literary* a lake.

merely *adv* only; simply.

meretricious *adj* attractive in a showy or tawdry way.

merganser *n* a usu crested fish-eating and diving sawbill duck.

merge *v* **1** to combine or unite. **2** to blend or come together gradually without abrupt change. **3** to cause (two or more things) to combine or blend.

merger *n* a combining or combination, *esp* of two organizations, e.g. business concerns.

meridian *n* **1** a circle on the surface of the earth or other celestial body passing through both poles, or the representation of this on a map or globe. **2** in astronomy, a circle passing through the poles of the CELESTIAL SPHERE (imaginary circle against which stars and planets appear to be placed) and the zenith of a given place. **3** in acupuncture, one of the pathways in the body along which vital energy is said to flow.

meridional *adj* **1** relating to or situated in the south, *esp* of France; southern. **2** relating to a meridian.

meringue *n* **1** a mixture of stiffly beaten egg whites and sugar baked until crisp. **2** a small cake or other confection made with meringue.

merino *n* (*pl* **-os**) **1** a sheep of a fine-woolled white breed originating in Spain. **2** a soft wool or wool and cotton clothing fabric resembling cashmere.

meristem *n* a plant tissue that is the major area of growth and is made up of small cells capable of dividing indefinitely.

merit[1] *n* **1** worth or excellence. **2** (*usu in pl*) a good or praiseworthy quality; a virtue.

merit[2] *v* (**merited, meriting**) to be worthy of (something); to deserve.

meritocracy *n* (*pl* **-ies**) **1** government by people chosen on the basis of their ability. **2** a society in which talented people hold power. ⋙ **meritocratic** *adj.*

meritorious *adj* deserving of reward or honour.

merlin *n* a small N American and European falcon with pointed wings.

Merlot /'meəloh, meə'loh/ *n* a variety of grape often blended with Cabernet Sauvignon grapes, or a red wine produced from it.

mermaid *n* a mythical sea creature usu represented with a woman's head and trunk and a fish's tail.

mermaid's purse *n* the leathery egg case of a skate, ray, or related fish.

merman *n* (*pl* **mermen**) a mythical sea creature usu represented with a man's head and trunk and a fish's tail.

Merovingian *adj* of the Frankish dynasty that ruled in Gaul and Germany from about AD 500 to AD 751. ⋙ **Merovingian** *n.*

merriment *n* light-hearted gaiety or fun.

merry *adj* (**-ier, -iest**) **1** cheerful and lively; jolly. **2** *Brit, informal* slightly drunk; tipsy. ✱ **make merry** *literary* to celebrate or indulge in jollity. ⋙ **merrily** *adv,* **merriness** *n.*

merry-go-round *n* **1** a revolving fairground machine with model horses or vehicles that people ride on. **2** a busy round of activity.

merrymaking *n* happy, festive activity; fun.

mes- *or* **meso-** *comb. form* **1** middle: *Mesolithic.* **2** intermediate: *meson.*

mesa /'maysə/ *n* an isolated hill with steeply sloping sides and a level top.

mésalliance /me'zali·əns/ *n* a marriage to somebody of inferior social position.

mescal *n* **1** a colourless Mexican spirit distilled from the sap of an agave. **2** = PEYOTE (I).

mescaline *or* **mescalin** *n* a hallucinogenic drug obtained from peyote cacti.

Mesdames /may'dahm/ *n* pl of MRS.

mesdames /may'dam/ *n* pl of MADAME.

mesdemoiselles /,maydəmwah'zel/ *n* pl of MADEMOISELLE.

mesembryanthemum *n* (*pl* **mesembryanthemums**) a fleshy leaved herbaceous plant with bright flowers.

mesh[1] *n* **1** the cords, wires, etc that make up a net; a network. **2** an open space in a net, network, etc. **3** an interlocking or intertwining arrangement or construction. **4** in computing, a network of connections having two or more connections between each pair of items. **5** in computing, a set of finite elements that represent a geometric object to be modelled or analysed.

mesh[2] *v* **1** of the teeth of a gearwheel: to be in or come into mesh. **2** to become entangled. **3** to fit together properly; to coordinate or harmonize.

mesmeric *adj* exerting a hypnotic influence or having a hypnotic effect; completely absorbing. ⋙ **mesmerically** *adv.*

mesmerise *v* see MESMERIZE.

mesmerism *n* hypnotism, *esp* as formerly practised and expounded by the Austrian physician Franz Mesmer (d.1815) and his disciples. ⋙ **mesmerist** *n.*

mesmerize *or* **-ise** *v* to fascinate; to rivet.

meso- *comb. form* see MES-.

mesoderm *n* **1** the middle of the three primary germ layers of an embryo that is the source of bone, muscle, connective tissue, and the inner layer of the skin in the adult. **2** the tissue that derives from this germ layer. ⋙ **mesodermal** *adj.*

Mesolithic *adj* of a transitional period of the Stone Age between the Palaeolithic and the Neolithic, extending from about 12,000 to 3000 BC, following the withdrawal of ice sheets and marked by a rising temperature that allowed new types of vegetation to grow.

mesomorph *n* a person with a compact body shape and muscular build: compare ECTOMORPH, ENDOMORPH. ⋙ **mesomorphic** *adj.*

meson *n* any of a group of unstable elementary particles that are bosons and have a mass between that of an electron and a proton.

Mesopotamian *n* a native or inhabitant of Mesopotamia. ⋙ **Mesopotamian** *adj.*

mesosphere *n* a layer of the upper atmosphere which extends from the top of the stratosphere (50km; 30mi) to an altitude of about 85km (about 50mi).

mesotrophic *adj* of a body of water: having a moderate amount of dissolved nutrients, e.g. chemical compounds or food: compare EUTROPHIC, OLIGOTROPHIC.

Mesozoic *adj* of the geological era between the Palaeozoic and Cenozoic eras, lasting from about 245 million to about 65 million years ago, and marked by the appearance of dinosaurs, reptiles, and evergreen trees. ⋙ **Mesozoic** *n.*

mesquite *n* a spiny tree or shrub that forms extensive thickets in the SW USA and Mexico and bears sugar-rich pods used as a livestock feed.

mess[1] *n* **1** an untidy, disordered, dirty, or generally unpleasant state or condition. **2** *euphem* the excrement of a domestic animal. **3** a prepared dish of soft or liquid food. **4** a disorganized situation. **5** a place where servicemen or women eat their meals.

mess[2] *v* **1a** to make a mess. **b** *euphem* of a domestic animal: to defecate. **2a** (*usu* + with) to handle or play with something, *esp* carelessly. **b** *informal* (*usu* + with) to interfere or meddle with something or somebody. **3** to take meals in a mess. **4** to make (something or somebody) look untidy.

mess about *v* to waste time, *esp* by behaving in a silly way.

message[1] *n* **1** a communication in writing, in speech, or by signals. **2** a central theme or idea intended to inspire, urge, warn, enlighten, advise, etc. ✱ **be on/off message** *informal* chiefly in politics, to make statements that accord or do not accord with officially approved policy. **get the message** *informal* to understand what somebody is saying.

message[2] *v* to send (somebody) a message, *esp* an e-mail.

mess around *v* = MESS ABOUT.

messeigneurs /mese'nyuh/ *n* pl of MONSEIGNEUR.

messenger *n* a person who carries a message.

messenger RNA *n* an RNA that carries the code for a particular protein from the cell's DNA to the RIBOSOME (the specialized structure in a cell) and there acts as a template for the formation of the protein.

messiah *n* **1** (**the Messiah**) **a** the expected king and deliverer of the Jews. **b** Jesus, regarded by

Christians as fulfilling this role. **2** a professed leader of a cause.

messianic *adj* **1** associated with a messiah or the Messiah. **2** marked by idealistic enthusiasm for a cherished cause. ➤➤ **messianism** *n.*

messieurs /me'syuh, mə'syuhz/ *n* pl of MONSIEUR.

Messrs *n* pl of MR.

messy *adj* (**-ier, -iest**) **1** disorderly or dirty. **2** unpleasantly or tryingly difficult to deal with. ➤➤ **messily** *adv,* **messiness** *n.*

mestiza /me'steezə/ *n* a woman of mixed European and Native American ancestry.

mestizo /me'steezoh/ *n* (*pl* **-os**) a man of mixed European and Native American ancestry.

met *v* past tense and past part. of MEET[1].

meta- *or* **met-** *prefix* **1a** a position behind or beyond: *metacarpus.* **b** a later or more highly organized or specialized form: *metazoan.* **2** a change or transformation: *metamorphosis.* **3** something more comprehensive or of a higher or second order: *metalanguage.*

metabolise *v* see METABOLIZE.

metabolism *n* the chemical changes in living cells by which energy is provided and new material is assimilated. ➤➤ **metabolic** *adj.*

metabolite *n* **1** a product of metabolism. **2** a substance essential to the metabolism of a particular organism or to a particular metabolic process.

metabolize *or* **-ise** *v* to process (a substance) by, or to undergo the processes of, metabolism.

metacarpus *n* (*pl* **metacarpi**) the group of five long bones in the hand between the wrist and fingers. ➤➤ **metacarpal** *adj and n.*

metal *n* **1** a usu hard and shiny substance that is ductile and capable of being melted and fused, and is a good conductor of electricity and heat. **2** broken stones used in making and repairing roads or ballasting railways; road metal.

metalanguage *n* the language and terminology used to talk analytically about language itself.

metal detector *n* an electronic device that gives an audible or visual signal when it detects the presence of metal objects.

metaled *adj NAm* see METALLED.

metalize *v NAm* see METALLIZE.

metalled (*NAm* **metaled**) *adj* **1** of a road: covered with a surface of broken stones. **2** coated with metal.

metallic *adj* **1** of, containing, like, or being metal. **2** of a sound: sharp and ringing, like metal striking metal. **3** bitter or acrid in taste. ➤➤ **metallically** *adv.*

metalliferous *adj* yielding or containing metal.

metallize *or* **-ise** (*NAm* **metalize**) *v* **1** to treat, combine, or coat with a metal. **2** to make metallic.

metallography *n* the study of the microscopic structure of metals. ➤➤ **metallographic** *adj.*

metallurgy *n* the branch of science concerned with the properties of metals and their extraction, production and refining. ➤➤ **metallurgical** *adj,* **metallurgist** *n.*

metalwork *n* **1** the craft of shaping things out of metal. **2** products made from metal.

metamorphic *adj* of rock: having undergone metamorphism.

metamorphism *n* a change in rock effected *esp* by heat and pressure and resulting in a more compact and crystalline structure.

metamorphose *v* **1** of an insect or amphibian: to undergo metamorphosis. **2** to transform or be transformed. **3** to cause (rock) to undergo metamorphism.

metamorphosis *n* (*pl* **metamorphoses**) **1** a marked abrupt change in the form or structure of an insect or amphibian occurring in the course of development, e.g. the change from a tadpole to a frog. **2a** change of form, structure, or substance, *esp* by supernatural means. **b** a striking alteration, e.g. in appearance or character.

metaphor *n* **1** a figure of speech in which a word or phrase literally denoting one kind of object or idea is applied to another to suggest a likeness or analogy between them, e.g. in *the ship ploughs the sea.* **2** an object, activity, or idea treated as a metaphor. ➤➤ **metaphoric** *adj,* **metaphorical** *adj,* **metaphorically** *adv.*

metaphysic *n* a particular system of metaphysics.

metaphysical *adj* **1** of or relating to metaphysics. **2** beyond nature or what is physical; supernatural. **3** (*often* **Metaphysical**) of or being English poetry, *esp* of the early 17th cent., that is marked by ingenious witty imagery expressing subtleties of thought and emotion. ➤➤ **metaphysically** *adv.*

metaphysics *pl n* (*used as sing. or pl*) **1** a division of philosophy concerned with ultimate causes and the underlying nature of things; *esp* ontology. **2** *informal* abstract and impractical theorizing. ➤➤ **metaphysician** *n.*

metastable *adj* **1** of a state of equilibrium: stable as long as it is subject only to a small degree of disturbance. **2** of a substance or particle: unstable in theory but lasting long enough for practical purposes.

metastasis *n* (*pl* **metastases**) a secondary growth of a malignant tumour at a site distant from the primary growth.

metatarsus *n* (*pl* **metatarsi**) the bones in the foot between the ankle and toes. ➤➤ **metatarsal** *adj and n.*

metathesis *n* (*pl* **metatheses**) the transposition of two phonemes in a word, e.g. in Old English *bridd,* Modern English *bird.*

metazoan *n* any member of a kingdom or subkingdom of animals comprising all those with multicellular bodies differentiated into tissues, except sponges and protozoans.

mete *v* (+ out) to distribute, allot, or inflict.

metempsychosis *n* (*pl* **metempsychoses**) the passing of the soul at death into another body; reincarnation.

meteor *n* a small particle of matter from space, observable directly only when it falls into the earth's atmosphere and is heated by friction so that it glows.

meteoric *adj* **1** associated with a meteor or meteorite. **2** resembling a meteor in speed or in sudden and temporary brilliance.

meteorite *n* a rock from interplanetary space that reaches the surface of the earth.

meteoroid *n* an object in orbit round the sun that becomes a meteor or meteorite when it meets the earth's atmosphere.

meteorology *n* the science of the atmosphere and its phenomena, *esp* weather and weather forecasting. ➤➤ **meteorological** *adj,* **meteorologist** *n.*

meter[1] *n* an instrument for measuring and recording the amount of something, e.g. gas, electricity, or parking time used.

meter[2] *v* to measure by means of a meter.

meter[3] *n NAm* see METRE[1], METRE[2].

-meter[1] *comb. form* forming nouns, denoting: a measure or unit of metrical verse: *pentameter.*

-meter[2] *comb. form* forming nouns, denoting: an instrument or means for measuring: *barometer.*

methadone *n* a synthetic narcotic drug used as a substitute narcotic in the treatment of heroin addiction and as a painkiller.

methamphetamine *n* an amphetamine drug, used illegally as a stimulant.

methane *n* a colourless, odourless flammable gas that is a product of decomposition of plant or animal matter in marshes and mines, and is used as a fuel.

methanol *n* a volatile flammable poisonous liquid alcohol that is added to ethyl alcohol to make it unfit to drink and is used as a solvent.

methinks *v* (*past tense* **methought**) *archaic* it seems to me.

methionine *n* a sulphur-containing amino acid that is found in most proteins and is an essential constituent of human diet.

method *n* **1** a systematic procedure for doing something, or the regular way in which something is done. **2a** an orderly arrangement or system. **b** the habitual practice of orderliness and regularity. **3** (**the Method**) a dramatic technique by which an actor seeks to identify closely with the inner personality of the character being portrayed.

methodical *adj* characterized by or performed with method or order; systematic. ➤➤ **methodic** *adj*, **methodically** *adv.*

Methodist *n* a member of any of the denominations deriving from the Wesleyan revival in the Church of England, having an evangelical character and stressing personal and social morality. ➤➤ **Methodism** *n*, **Methodist** *adj.*

methodology *n* (*pl* **-ies**) the body of methods and rules employed by a science or discipline. ➤➤ **methodological** *adj*, **methodologist** *n.*

methought *v* past tense of METHINKS.

meths *n Brit, informal* methylated spirits.

Methuselah *n* **1** a person who has lived to a great age. **2** a champagne bottle holding eight times the usual amount.

methyl *n* a chemical group, CH_3, derived from the gas methane by removing one hydrogen atom.

methyl alcohol *n* = METHANOL.

methylate *v* **1** to impregnate or mix with methanol or methylated spirits. **2** to introduce the methyl group into (something, e.g. a compound). ➤➤ **methylated** *adj*, **methylation** *n.*

methylated spirits *or* **methylated spirit** *n* alcohol mixed with an adulterant, *esp* methanol, to make it undrinkable and therefore exempt from duty.

metical /meti'kal/ *n* (*pl* **meticais** /meti'kiesh/) the basic monetary unit of Mozambique.

meticulous *adj* marked by extreme or excessive care over detail. ➤➤ **meticulously** *adv*, **meticulousness** *n.*

métier /'maytyay/ *n* **1** one's trade. **2** something, e.g. an activity, in which one is expert or successful.

metonym *n* a word used in metonymy. ➤➤ **metonymic** *adj.*

metonymy *n* (*pl* **-ies**) a figure of speech in which the word for a part, aspect, or attribute of a thing is used to mean the thing itself, e.g. *the White House* used to mean the US president and executive or *wheels* used to mean a car.

metope *n* the space between two triglyphs (square projections; see TRIGLYPH) of a Doric frieze, often adorned with carvings.

metre[1] (*NAm* **meter**) *n* the basic metric SI unit of length equal to 100 centimetres (about 39.37in.).

metre[2] (*NAm* **meter**) *n* **1** the rhythm of verse, determined by the number and type of feet in a line. **2** the basic recurrent rhythmical pattern of accents and beats per bar in a piece of music.

metric *adj* using decimal units of measure based on the metre, litre, and kilogram as standards.

metrical[1] *adj* relating to or composed in poetic metre. ➤➤ **metrically** *adv.*

metrical[2] *adj* to do with measurement. ➤➤ **metrically** *adv.*

metricate *v* to change (measurements) into the metric system. ➤➤ **metrication** *n.*

metric system *n* a decimal system of weights and measures based on the metre, the litre, and the kilogram.

metric ton *or* **metric tonne** *n* a tonne.

metro *n* (*pl* **-os**) an underground railway system in a city, *esp* Paris.

metronome *n* a device designed to help musicians by marking the speed of a beat with a regularly repeated tick. ➤➤ **metronomic** *adj.*

metropolis *n* the chief or capital city of a country, state, or region.

metropolitan[1] *adj* **1** relating to a metropolis. **2** of or constituting a parent state, as opposed to an overseas colony or dependency. **3** relating to a metropolitan or the see of a metropolitan.

metropolitan[2] *n* **1a** in the Eastern Churches, the head of an ecclesiastical province, ranking above an archbishop and below a patriarch. **b** in the Church of England or Roman Catholic Church, an archbishop or chief bishop of a province. **2** a person who lives in a metropolis.

metropolitan county *n* any of the six areas in England, each centred on a large city, that formed an administrative unit for purposes of local government between 1974 and 1986.

mettle *n* **1** strength of spirit or temperament. **2** staying quality; stamina. ✱ **on one's mettle** ready to do one's best.

meunière /muh'nyeə/ *adj* with a sauce of melted butter, parsley, and lemon juice: *sole meunière.*

MeV *abbr* million electron volts.

mew[1] *v* to utter the high-pitched, plaintive sound characteristic of a cat or a gull. ➤➤ **mew** *n.*

mew[2] *n* a cage or building used to keep trained falcons in, *esp* when they are moulting.

mew[3] *v* **1** (*often* + up) to shut (somebody) up in something; to confine. **2** to keep (a moulting hawk) in a mew. **3** of a trained falcon: to moult.

mewl *v* **1** to cry weakly; to whimper. **2** to mew.

mews *n* (*pl* **mews**) *Brit* a street or row of houses converted from former stables, or built in this style.

Mexican *n* a native or inhabitant of Mexico. ➤➤ **Mexican** *adj.*

Mexican wave *n* a wavelike movement made by a large number of seated people, *esp* spectators in a sports stadium, in which several adjacent files of people in unison stand up, raise their arms, and then sit down again.

meze /'mayzay/ *n* (*pl* **meze** *or* **mezes**) an assortment of simple snacks served as appetizers, e.g. in Middle Eastern countries.

mezuzah /mə'zoohzə/ *n* (*pl* **mezuzahs** *or* **mezuzoth**) a small oblong case containing a parchment inscribed with religious texts, fixed to the doorpost by some Jewish families as a sign of their faith.

mezzanine *n* **1** a low-ceilinged storey between two main storeys of a building; *esp* an intermediate storey that projects in the form of a balcony. **2** *NAm* the lowest balcony in a theatre.

mezzo /'metsoh/ *n* (*pl* **-os**) = MEZZO-SOPRANO.

mezzo-soprano *n* (*pl* **-os**) a female singer having a voice between soprano and contralto.

mezzotint *n* **1** a method of engraving on copper or steel by scraping or burnishing a roughened surface to produce light and shade. **2** a print produced by this method.

MF *abbr* medium frequency.

Mg *abbr* the chemical symbol for magnesium.

mg *abbr* milligram(s).

Mgr *abbr* **1** Monseigneur. **2** Monsignor.

mgr *abbr* manager.

MHz *abbr* megahertz.

MI *abbr* Michigan (US postal abbreviation).

mi[1] *or* **me** *n* in music, the third note of a major scale in the tonic sol-fa system.

mi[2] *abbr* mile(s).

MI5 *n no longer in official use* the British government agency responsible for internal security and counter-intelligence.

MI6 *n no longer in official use* the British government agency responsible for counterintelligence and security overseas.

miaow *or* **meow** *v* to make the characteristic cry of a cat. ➤➤ **meow** *n*, **miaow** *n*.

miasma *n* (*pl* **miasmas** *or* **miasmata**) *literary* **1** a heavy or foul-smelling vapour. **2** a pervasive influence or atmosphere that tends to weaken or corrupt.

mica *n* any of various coloured or transparent silicate materials occurring as crystals that readily separate into very thin flexible leaves.

mice *n* pl of MOUSE[1].

Michaelmas *n* the Christian feast of St Michael the Archangel (29 September).

Michaelmas daisy *n* an aster with daisy-like flowers that bloom in the autumn.

Michaelmas term *n* *Brit* the university term beginning in October.

mickey ✱ **take the mickey** *chiefly Brit, informal* to make fun of, tease, or ridicule. ➤➤ **mickey-taking** *n*.

Mickey Finn *n* *informal* an alcoholic drink doctored with a drug.

Word history

perhaps from the name *Mickey Finnish*. The term is said to come from a notorious figure in 19th-cent. Chicago.

Mickey Mouse *adj informal* trivial or petty.

mickle[1] *adj Scot, N Eng, or archaic* great or much. ➤➤ **mickle** *adv*.

mickle[2] *n Scot, N Eng, or archaic* a great amount.

Micmac *or* **Mi'kmaq** *n* (*pl* **Micmacs** *or* **Mi'kmaqs** *or* **Micmac** *or* **Mi'kmaq**) a member of a Native American people of E Canada.

micr- *comb. form* see MICRO-.

micra *n* pl of MICRON.

micro[1] *adj* very small or microscopic.

micro[2] *n* (*pl* **-os**) **1** a microcomputer. **2** a microprocessor.

micro- *or* **micr-** *comb. form* **1** smallness or a reduced size: *microdot*. **2** a reduced concept or scope: *microclimate*. **3** a factor of one millionth (10^{-6}): *microsecond*.

microanalysis *n* chemical analysis on a small scale that usu requires special techniques or very sensitive apparatus.

microbe *n* a micro-organism, *esp* a bacterium that causes disease. ➤➤ **microbial** *adj*.

microbiology *n* the biology of viruses, bacteria and other microscopic biological organisms.

microchip *n* = CHIP[1] (5).

microcircuit *n* a compact electronic circuit, *esp* an integrated circuit.

microclimate *n* a climate restricted to a small area or habitat and different from that of the surrounding region.

microcomputer *n* a small self-contained computer that is based on one or more microprocessors.

microcosm *n* **1** something, e.g. a community or situation, regarded as having the characteristics of a larger whole. **2** human life or human nature regarded as an epitome of the universe. ➤➤ **microcosmic** *adj*.

microdot *n* **1** a photographic reproduction of printed matter reduced to the size of a single dot for security or ease of transmission. **2** a small tablet containing a hallucinogenic drug.

microeconomics *pl n* (*used as sing. or pl*) a study of economics in terms of individual areas of activity, e.g. a firm, household, or prices.

microelectronics *pl n* (*used as sing. or pl*) a branch of electronics that deals with or produces miniaturized electronic circuits and components.

microfiche *n* a sheet of microfilm containing rows of very small images of pages of printed matter.

microfilm *n* a photographic film on which graphic matter, e.g. printing, can be recorded in miniaturized form.

microgram *n* a metric unit of mass equal to one millionth of a gram.

micrograph *n* a photograph or graphic reproduction of an object as seen through a microscope.

microgravity *n* an environment in which conditions of near weightlessness are experienced, e.g. by an astronaut in an orbiting spacecraft.

microinstruction *n* a very low-level instruction, sequences of which are stored within a computer processor and correspond to a single machine operation.

microlight *n chiefly Brit* a very small light aircraft for one or two people.

microliter *n NAm* see MICROLITRE.

microlitre *n* (*NAm* **microliter**) a metric unit of capacity equal to one millionth of a litre.

micrometer *n* an instrument for measuring distances between objects seen through a microscope or telescope.

micrometre (*NAm* **micrometer**) *n* a metric unit of length equal to one millionth of a metre.

micron *n* (*pl* **microns** *or* **micra**) *no longer in technical use* one millionth part of a metre.

Micronesian *n* a native or inhabitant of Micronesia. ➤➤ **Micronesian** *adj*.

micronutrient *n* a nutrient, e.g. a trace element, required in small quantities.

micro-organism *n* an organism of microscopic size or smaller, e.g. a bacterium.

microphone *n* a device that converts sounds into electrical signals, *esp* for transmission or recording.

microphotograph *n* a reduced photograph that must be magnified for viewing.

microprocessor *n* an integrated circuit forming the central processing unit of a small computer.

micro scooter /'miekroh ,skoohtə/ *n* a folding aluminium scooter popular with children but also used by adults for quick and easy movement over short distances about town, etc.

microscope *n* an optical instrument consisting of a lens or combination of lenses mounted above a base plate and used to magnify minute objects.

microscopic *adj* **1** invisible or indistinguishable without the use of a microscope. **2** *informal* very small. **3** of or conducted with the microscope or microscopy. ➤➤ **microscopically** *adv.*

microscopy *n* the use of a microscope.

microsecond *n* one millionth of a second.

microstructure *n* the structure of a mineral, alloy, living cell, etc, which can be seen through a microscope.

microsurgery *n* minute surgical dissection or manipulation of living tissue, usu under a microscope, e.g. in eye surgery.

microwave[1] *n* **1** a band of very short electromagnetic waves of between 0.001m and 0.3m in wavelength. **2** a microwave oven.

microwave[2] *v* to cook or heat (food) in a microwave oven. ➤➤ **microwavable** *adj,* **microwaveable** *adj.*

microwave oven *n* an oven in which food is cooked by the heat produced as a result of the interaction between penetrating microwaves and the substance of the food.

micturate *v formal* to urinate. ➤➤ **micturition** *n.*

mid[1] *adj* **1** being the part in the middle or midst. **2** occupying a middle position.

mid[2] *prep literary* amid.

mid- *comb. form* forming words, denoting: the middle part or point of something: *in mid-sentence.*

Midas touch *n* the talent for making wealth out of any activity one turns one's hand to.

midbrain *n* the middle of the three primary divisions of the vertebrate brain in both its fully developed and embryonic forms.

midday *n* the middle part of the day; noon.

midden *n* **1** a dunghill. **2** = KITCHEN MIDDEN.

middle[1] *adj* **1** equally distant from the extremes of something; central. **2** intermediate, e.g. in rank or quality.

middle[2] *n* **1** a middle part, point, or position. **2** *informal* the waist and abdomen.

middle age *n* the period of life from about 40 to about 60. ➤➤ **middle-aged** *adj.*

Middle Ages *pl n* (*usu* **the Middle Ages**) the period of European history from about AD 1000 to about 1500, or more technically, from the deposition of the last Roman emperor in the West in AD 476 to the fall of Constantinople in 1453.

Middle America *n* **1** the middle classes of the USA. **2** the midwestern states of the USA.

middlebrow *adj informal, derog* having a quite easily accessible intellectual content and conventional form.

middle C *n* in music, the note designated by the first ledger line below the treble staff and the first above the bass staff.

middle class *n* (*also in pl, used as sing. or pl*) a class occupying a position between upper and lower, consisting of business and professional people. ➤➤ **middle-class** *adj.*

middle distance *n* the part of a picture or view between the foreground and the background.

middle-distance *adj* in athletics, denoting a race over a distance between 400m and 1500m (or between 440yd and 1mi).

middle ear *n* a cavity through which sound waves are transmitted by a chain of tiny bones from the eardrum to the inner ear.

Middle East *n* the countries of SW Asia and N Africa, usu taken to include Turkey, Libya, Egypt, Lebanon, Syria, Israel, Jordan, the states of the Arabian Peninsula, Iran, and Iraq. ➤➤ **Middle Eastern** *adj.*

Middle England *n* a collective term for middle-class, middle-income people living in small towns or suburban or rural areas.

Middle English *n* English from about 1150 to 1500.

middle ground *n* a standpoint midway between extremes.

middleman *n* (*pl* **middlemen**) an intermediary between two parties; *esp* a dealer intermediate between the producer of goods and the retailer or consumer.

middle name *n* a person's name between the first name and the surname.

middle-of-the-road *adj* **1** conforming to the majority in taste, attitude, or conduct. **2** moderate in political conviction.

middle school *n* in Britain, a school for pupils aged 8–12 or 9–13.

middle-sized *adj* neither large nor small; of medium size.

middleweight *n* a weight in boxing and wrestling between light-heavyweight and welterweight.

middling *adj* of middle or moderate size, degree, or quality. ➤➤ **middling** *adv.*

Middx *abbr* Middlesex.

midfield *n* **1** the part of a pitch or playing field midway between the goals. **2** the group of players in a football team who act as a link between the defenders and strikers. ➤➤ **midfielder** *n.*

midge *n* **1** a small two-winged fly often found near water, some of which feed on blood. **2** *informal* a small person.

midget *n* **1** a very small person; a dwarf. **2** (*used before a noun*) of a much smaller size than usual: *a midget submarine.*

MIDI *n* (*often used before a noun*) a standard specification for linking up electronic musical instruments to a computer.

midi *n* (*pl* **midis**) a woman's skirt, dress, or coat that extends to the mid-calf.

midi system *n Brit* a compact unit consisting of parts making up a hi-fi system.

midland *n* the central region of a country. ➤➤ **midland** *adj.*

Midlands *n* (**the Midlands**) part of the central area of England, usually taken as comprising Leicestershire, Nottinghamshire, Derbyshire, Staffordshire, the West Midlands metropolitan district, and the E parts of Herefordshire and Worcestershire. ➤➤ **Midlander** *n.*

midnight *n* the middle of the night; *specif* twelve o'clock at night.

midnight sun *n* the sun visible at midnight in the arctic or antarctic summer.

mid-off *n* in cricket, a fielding position near the bowler on the off side of the pitch.

mid-on *n* in cricket, a fielding position near the bowler on the leg side of the pitch.

midpoint *n* a point midway between the beginning and end of something.

midrib *n* the large central vein of a leaf.

midriff *n* the middle part of the human torso.

midship *n* the middle section of a ship or boat.

midshipman *n* (*pl* **midshipmen**) **1** a person training to become a naval officer in the Royal Navy. **2** a cadet in the US navy.

midships *adv and adj* amidships.

midst[1] *n archaic or literary* the inner or central part or point of something. ✱ **in somebody's midst** among a group of people, or within a group or organization: *It was clear that we had an informer in our midst.*

midst[2] *prep archaic or literary* amid.

midstream *n* the part of a stream towards the middle. ✱ **in midstream** in the middle of a process or activity.

midsummer *n* **1** the period around the middle of summer. **2** the summer solstice.

Midsummer Day *or* **Midsummer's Day** *n* 24 June.

midterm *n* the period around the midpoint of an academic term, a term of office, or a pregnancy.

midway *adv and adj* halfway.

midweek *n* the middle of the week. ⪢ **midweek** *adj and adv.*

Midwest *n* the N central part of the USA, including the states of Ohio, Illinois, Michigan, Indiana, Wisconsin, Minnesota, Iowa, Missouri, Nebraska, and Kansas. ⪢ **Midwestern** *adj.*

mid-wicket *n* in cricket, a fielding position on the leg side equidistant from each wicket.

midwife *n* (*pl* **midwives**) a nurse trained to assist women in childbirth. ⪢ **midwifery** *n.*

midwinter *n* **1** the period around the middle of winter. **2** the winter solstice.

mien *n* a person's air or bearing, *esp* as expressive of mood or personality.

miff *v informal* to make (somebody) cross or peeved.

might[1] *v* the past tense of MAY[1] used to express: **1** permission or possibility: *He asked whether he might come.* **2** a past or present possibility that is unfulfilled: *I might well have been killed.* **3** expectation or obligation: *You might at least apologize.* **4** a polite or ironic question: *Who might you be?*

might[2] *n* great power or strength. ✱ **with might and main** with all the strength or power that one has.

mightn't *contr* might not.

mighty *adj* (**-ier, -iest**) **1** powerful or strong. **2** *informal* very large or loud. ⪢ **mightily** *adv,* **mightiness** *n.*

mignonette /minyə'net/ *n* an annual garden plant with fragrant greenish yellow flowers.

migraine *n* a recurrent severe headache usu associated with disturbances of vision, sensation, and movement often on only one side of the body.

migrant *n* **1** an animal that moves from one habitat to another for feeding or breeding. **2** a person who moves regularly in order to find seasonal work. ⪢ **migrant** *adj.*

migrate *v* **1** of an animal: to pass seasonally from one region or climate to another for feeding or breeding. **2** of a person: to move from one country or locality to another. **3** in computing, to change from one hardware or software system to another. ⪢ **migration** *n,* **migratory** *adj.*

mihrab /'meerab, 'meerəb/ *n* a niche in the wall of a mosque that indicates the direction towards Mecca.

mikado /mi'kahdoh/ *n* (*pl* **-os**) a title formerly used for the emperor of Japan.

mike *n informal* a microphone.

Mi'kmaq *n* see MICMAC.

mil[1] *n* a unit of length equal to 1000th of an inch (about 0.0254mm).

mil[2] *abbr informal* millions.

milady *n* (*pl* **-ies**) formerly used as a term of address to an Englishwoman of noble or gentle birth.

milage *n* see MILEAGE.

milch *adj* of a domestic animal: bred or used primarily for milk production.

milch cow *n* a source of easily acquired gain.

mild[1] *adj* **1** gentle in nature or manner. **2** not severe. **3** not strong in flavour or effect. **4** not extreme, *esp* not acutely felt or strongly expressed. **5** of the weather: quite warm. ⪢ **mildly** *adv,* **mildness** *n.*

mild[2] *n Brit* a dark-coloured beer not flavoured with hops.

mildew[1] *n* a usu whitish growth on the surface of organic matter, e.g. paper or leather, or living plants, caused by fungi.

mildew[2] *v* to affect with mildew.

mild steel *n* a type of strong steel that is easily worked, containing a low proportion of carbon.

mile *n* **1a** (*also* **statute mile**) a unit of distance equal to 1760yd (about 1.61km). **b** = NAUTICAL MILE. **2** (*often in pl*) a large distance or amount: *We travelled miles.* ✱ **be miles away** to be inattentive.

mileage *or* **milage** *n* **1a** a total length, distance, or distance covered, in miles. **b** the number of miles travelled over a period of time. **2** *informal* the benefit derived from something or the amount of service it has given.

mileometer *or* **milometer** *n Brit* an instrument fitted in a car or other vehicle to record the number of miles it travels.

milepost *n* **1** *chiefly NAm, Aus* a post indicating the distance in miles from or to a given point. **2** a post indicating one mile from the end of a race.

miler *n* a person or horse that competes in mile races.

miles *adv informal* very much: *He's miles happier in that new job.*

milestone *n* **1** a stone serving as a milepost. **2** a crucial stage in something's development.

milfoil *n* **1** yarrow. **2** a water plant with submerged leaves divided into very narrow segments.

miliary *adj* of a disease: characterized by many small projections, blisters, or nodules resembling millet seed.

milieu /'meelyuh, meel'yuh/ *n* (*pl* **milieus** *or* **milieux**) a person's environment or setting.

militant *adj* aggressively active, e.g. in a cause; combative. ⪢ **militancy** *n,* **militant** *n,* **militantly** *adv.*

militarise *v* see MILITARIZE.

militarism *n* a policy of aggressive military preparedness. ⪢ **militarist** *n,* **militaristic** *adj.*

militarize *or* **-ise** *v* **1** to equip (somebody or something) with military forces and defences. **2** to give a military character to (something).

military[1] *adj* relating to or characteristic of soldiers, arms, or war. ⪢ **militarily** *adv.*

military[2] *n* (**the military**) a country's armed forces.

Military Cross *n* a medal for meritorious conduct and distinguished service that could be awarded to commissioned officers below the rank of major, or to warrant officers.

military police *n* (*used as pl*) a branch of an army that carries out police functions within it.

militate *v* (*usu* + against) to have significant weight or effect against something.

Usage note

militate *or* **mitigate**? These two words are sometimes confused. *Militate* is related in form and meaning to *militant* and *military,* and its earliest meaning is 'to serve as a soldier' or 'to fight'. It is usually followed by *against* and in modern English means 'to exert a powerful influence against' or 'make very difficult or unlikely': *Present circumstances militate against an early resumption of peace talks. Mitigate* is followed by a direct object and means 'to make less severe': *measures intended to mitigate the harshness of prison life.*

militia *n* (*used as sing. or pl*) a body of citizens with some military training who are called on to fight only in an emergency. ➤➤ **militiaman** *n.*

milk[1] *n* **1a** a white or creamy liquid secreted by the mammary glands of female mammals for the nourishment of their young. **b** the milk of cows, goats and similar animals used as food for humans. **2** a liquid similar to milk, e.g. the latex of a plant or the juice of a coconut.

milk[2] *v* **1** to draw milk from (a cow, goat, etc). **2a** to draw all possible advantage from (a situation or person). **b** to extract money from (somebody) over a period of time.

milk-and-water *adj* weak or insipid.

milk bar *n Brit* a snack bar that sells milk drinks, particularly milk shakes.

milk chocolate *n* solid chocolate made with the addition of milk.

milk fever *n* a disease of cows, sheep, goats, etc that have recently given birth.

milk float *n Brit* a light usu electrically propelled vehicle for carrying milk for domestic delivery.

milkmaid *n archaic* a girl or woman who works in a dairy.

milkman *n* (*pl* **milkmen**) a man who sells or delivers milk.

milk pudding *n Brit* a pudding consisting of rice, tapioca, sago, etc boiled or baked in sweetened milk.

milk round *n* **1** *Brit* a regular route for delivering milk. **2** a series of visits to universities made by representatives of large firms in the hope of recruiting people who are about to graduate.

milk run *n* a regular journey, e.g. by an aircraft.

milk shake *n* a beverage made of milk and a flavouring syrup, thoroughly shaken or blended.

milksop *n* a weak and timid person.

milk tooth *n* a tooth of a mammal, *esp* a child, that is replaced later in life.

milky *adj* (**-ier, -iest**) **1** containing milk. **2** resembling milk in colour or consistency. **3** cloudy or semi-opaque. ➤➤ **milkily** *adv,* **milkiness** *n.*

Milky Way *n* a broad irregular band of faint light that stretches completely round the celestial sphere and is caused by the light of the many stars forming the galaxy of which the sun and the solar system are a part.

mill[1] *n* **1** a building provided with machinery for grinding grain into flour. **2** a machine or apparatus for grinding grain. **3** a machine or hand-operated device for crushing or grinding a solid substance, e.g. coffee beans or peppercorns. **4** a building or collection of buildings with machinery for manufacturing. ✱ **go/be put through the mill** to undergo an unpleasant or trying experience.

mill[2] *v* **1** to grind (grain or a similar substance) into flour, meal, or powder. **2** to shape or dress (metal) by means of a rotary cutter. **3** to give a raised rim or a ridged edge to (a coin). **4** (+ about/around) to move in a confused swirling mass.

millboard *n* strong cardboard suitable for book covers and for panelling in furniture.

millefeuille /'meelfœi/ *n* a small cake made of layers of puff pastry with jam and cream in between.

millenarian *adj* relating to or believing in the imminent Second Coming of Christ. ➤➤ **millenarian** *n.*

millenarianism *n* the belief that a 1000-year period of blessedness will immediately follow or precede the Second Coming of Christ. ➤➤ **millenarianist** *adj and n.*

millenary[1] *n* (*pl* **-ies**) **1** a period of a thousand years. **2** a thousandth anniversary.

millenary[2] *adj* relating to or consisting of a thousand.

millennia *n* pl of MILLENNIUM.

millennialism *n* = MILLENARIANISM. ➤➤ **millennialist** *adj and n.*

millennium *n* (*pl* **millennia** *or* **millenniums**) **1a** a period of a thousand years, *esp* measured from the traditional date of the birth of Christ. **b** a thousandth anniversary. **2** the date on which one period of a thousand years ends and another begins. **3** the thousand years mentioned in the Bible (Rev. 20) during which holiness is to prevail and Christ is to reign on earth. ➤➤ **millennial** *adj.*

Usage note

Millennium is spelt with two *l's* and two *n's*, separated by an *e.*

miller *n* a person who owns or works a mill, *esp* for corn.

millesimal *adj* relating to division into thousandths.

millet *n* a small-seeded annual cereal and forage grass cultivated for grain and used as food.

milli- *comb. form* 1000th part of a specified unit: *milligram.*

millibar *n* a unit of pressure equal to 1000th of a bar.

millieme /mil'yem/ *n* a unit of currency in Egypt, worth 1000th of a pound.

milligram *or* **milligramme** *n* one thousandth of a gram.

millilitre (*NAm* **milliliter**) *n* one thousandth of a litre (0.002 pints).

millim *n* a unit of currency in Tunis, worth 1000th of a dinar.

millimetre (*NAm* **millimeter**) *n* one thousandth of a metre (about 0.039in.).

milliner *n* a person who makes or sells women's hats. ➤➤ **millinery** *n.*

million *n* (*pl* **millions** *or* **million**) **1** the number 1,000,000 (10^6). **2** *informal* (*also in pl*) an indefinitely large number. ➤➤ **million** *adj,* **millionth** *adj and n.*

millionaire *or* **millionairess** *n* a man or woman whose wealth is estimated at a million or more money units.

millipede *n* an invertebrate animal related to the centipedes, usu with a cylindrical segmented body and two pairs of legs on each segment.

millisecond *n* one thousandth of a second.

millpond *n* a pond produced by damming a stream to produce a head of water for operating a mill.

millrace *n* a channel in which water flows to and from a mill wheel, or the usu swift-flowing current in such a channel.

millstone *n* **1** either of a pair of circular stones that rotate against each other and are used for grinding grain. **2** a heavy or crushing burden.

millstream *n* a stream flowing past a mill and used to turn a mill wheel.

mill wheel *n* a waterwheel that drives a mill.

milo *n* a small usu early-growing drought-resistant variety of sorghum with compact heads of large seeds.

milometer *n* see MILEOMETER.

milord *n* formerly used as a term of address to an Englishman of noble or gentle birth.

milt *n* the male reproductive glands of fishes when filled with secretion, or the secretion of these glands.

Miltonian *adj* of or characteristic of the English poet John Milton (d.1674).

Miltonic *adj* = MILTONIAN.

mime[1] *n* **1** the art of portraying a character or telling a story by gesture and body movement. **2** a performance of mime. **3** a performer of mime.

mime[2] *v* **1** to act a part with gesture and body movement rather than words. **2** to act or express (something) using mime. **3** to pretend to sing or play a musical instrument, *esp* during a prerecorded performance.

Mimeograph *n trademark* a duplicating machine for making copies from a stencil through which ink is pressed.

mimesis *n* **1** in art or literature, the imitative representation of reality. **2** in biology or sociology, imitation or mimicry.

mimetic *adj* **1** imitative. **2** relating to, characterized by, or exhibiting mimicry.

mimic[1] *v* (**mimicked, mimicking**) **1** to imitate (somebody or something, e.g. their voice or mannerisms); to ape. **2** to ridicule (somebody or something) by imitation. **3** to simulate (something). **4** in biology, to resemble (something) by mimicry.

mimic[2] *n* somebody or something that mimics another or others.

mimicry *n* **1** the act or an instance of mimicking. **2** in biology, resemblance of one organism to another that secures it an advantage, e.g. protection from predators.

mimosa *n* **1** a tree or shrub that has globular heads of small yellow flowers and leaves that droop or close in response to light, touch, etc. **2** an acacia tree with sweetly scented yellow flowers in compact globular clusters.

mimsy *adj* prim; prudish.

min. *abbr* **1** minimum. **2** minute (unit of time).

mina *n* see MYNAH.

minaret *n* a slender tower attached to a mosque and surrounded by one or more projecting balconies from which the summons to prayer is made.

minatory *adj formal* menacing; threatening.

mince[1] *v* **1** to cut or chop (meat, etc) into very small pieces. **2** to walk with short steps in an affected manner. ✻ **not mince matters/one's words** to speak honestly and frankly. ➤➤ **mincer** *n.*

mince[2] *n chiefly Brit* minced meat.

mincemeat *n* a mixture of raisins, finely chopped apples, suet, spices, etc, used *esp* to fill pies. ✻ **make mincemeat of** to defeat soundly and conclusively.

mince pie *n* a small round pie filled with mincemeat.

mincing *adj* affectedly dainty or delicate. ➤➤ **mincingly** *adv.*

mind[1] *n* **1** the organized conscious and unconscious mental processes of an organism that result in reasoning, thinking, perceiving, etc. **2** recollection; memory. **3a** an intention or desire. **b** an opinion or view: *of the same mind.* **4** a person considered as an intellectual being. **5** the intellect and rational faculties as contrasted with the emotions. ✻ **a piece of one's mind** a severe scolding. **bear/keep in mind** to think of (something), *esp* at the appropriate time. **bring to mind** to cause (something) to be recalled. **change one's mind** to alter a decision or adopt a different plan. **on one's mind** occupying or troubling one's thoughts. **out of one's mind** insane. **put somebody in mind of something** to remind somebody of something.

mind[2] *v* **1a** to be concerned or care about (something). **b** to object to (something). **2** to attend to (something) closely. **3** to pay attention to or follow (advice, instructions, or orders). **4a** to be careful or sure to do (something). **b** to be cautious about (something). **5** to give protective care to (somebody or something). **6** (*often* + out) to be attentive or wary. ✻ **mind you** take this fact into account; notice this.

mind-bending *adj informal* **1** at the limits of understanding or credibility. **2** = MIND-BLOWING.

mind-blowing *adj informal* **1** of or causing a psychic state similar to that produced by a psychedelic drug. **2** mentally or emotionally exhilarating.

mind-boggling *adj informal* causing great surprise or wonder.

minded *adj* inclined; disposed: *He was not minded to report his losses.*

minder *n* **1** a person who looks after somebody or something. **2** *chiefly Brit, informal* a bodyguard.

mindful *adj* (*often* + of) keeping something in mind; aware of something.

mindless *adj* **1** devoid of thought or intelligence; senseless. **2** involving or requiring little thought or concentration. **3** (+ of) inattentive to or heedless of something. ➤➤ **mindlessly** *adv,* **mindlessness** *n.*

mind-numbing *adj* extremely dull or boring.

mindset *n* a habitual attitude of mind.

mind's eye *n* the faculty of visual memory or imagination.

mine[1] *pron* the one or ones that belong to or are associated with me. ✻ **of mine** belonging to or associated with me: *friends of mine.*

mine[2] *adj archaic* used before a vowel or *h* or after a noun: my: *mine host.*

mine[3] *n* **1** an excavation from which mineral substances are taken. **2** a rich source of something. **3** an encased explosive designed to destroy enemy personnel, vehicles, or ships. **4** an underground passage beneath an enemy position.

mine[4] *v* **1a** to obtain (ore, coal, etc) from a mine. **b** to dig into (the earth) for ore, coal, etc. **2** to place military mines in, on, or under. ➤➤ **miner** *n.*

minefield *n* **1** an area of land or water where explosive mines have been laid as a defence. **2** something that is full of hidden dangers or difficulties.

mineral *n* **1a** a solid homogeneous crystalline inorganic substance. **b** any of various naturally occurring substances, e.g. stone, coal, or petroleum, obtained by drilling, mining, etc. **2** something that is neither animal nor plant. **3** *Brit* (*usu in pl*) an effervescent non-alcoholic drink.

mineralize *or* **-ise** *v* **1** to convert (organic matter) into a mineral or inorganic compound. **2** to impregnate (water, etc) with a mineral. ➤➤ **mineralization** *n.*

mineralogy *n* a branch of geology dealing with the structure, properties, and classification of minerals. ➤➤ **mineralogical** *adj,* **mineralogist** *n.*

mineral oil *n* an oil of mineral origin, e.g. petroleum, as opposed to one derived from plants.

mineral water *n* water naturally or artificially impregnated with mineral salts or gases, e.g. carbon dioxide.

minestrone /mini'strohni/ *n* a rich thick vegetable soup usu containing pasta.

minesweeper *n* a ship designed for removing or neutralizing explosive mines.

Ming *n* **1** a Chinese dynasty dating from 1368 to 1644. **2** (*used before a noun*) of or being Chinese porcelain produced during this dynasty.

mingle *v* **1** to bring or mix (things) together. **2** to mix with or go among a group of people.

mingy *adj* (**-ier, -iest**) *informal* mean or miserly.

mini[1] *n* (*pl* **minis**) = MINISKIRT.

mini[2] *adj* small of its kind; miniature.

mini- *comb. form* miniature; small of its kind: *minicomputer.*

miniature[1] *n* **1a** a copy or representation on a much reduced scale. **b** something that is small of its kind. **2** a very small painting, e.g. a portrait on ivory or metal. **3** a painting in an illuminated manuscript. ➤➤ **miniaturist** *n.*

miniature[2] *adj* much smaller than the standard size.

miniaturize *or* **-ise** *v* **1** to design or construct as a small copy. **2** to reduce in scale.

minibar *n* a selection of drinks in a small refrigerator for the use of guests in a hotel room.

minibus *n* a small bus for carrying about ten passengers.

minicab *n* a taxi that can be hired by telephone but that cannot cruise in search of passengers.

minicomputer *n* a type of small and relatively inexpensive computer.

MiniDisc *n trademark* a small CD on which it is possible to record sound or data.

minim *n* **1** in music, a note with the time value of two crotchets or half a semibreve. **2** a unit of capacity equal to one sixtieth of a fluid drachm, approximately one drop of liquid.

minima *n* pl of MINIMUM[1].

minimal *adj* of or being a minimum; constituting the least possible. ➤➤ **minimally** *adv.*

minimal art *n* abstract art, *esp* sculpture, consisting of simple geometric forms and plain colours.

minimalism *n* **1a** a type of design characterized by simplicity of form and arrangement. **b** a type of music characterized by the repetition of simple elements. **c** = MINIMAL ART. **2** advocacy of moderating or restricting the powers of a political organization. ➤➤ **minimalist** *n and adj.*

minimize *or* **-ise** *v* **1** to reduce to a minimum. **2** to represent at less than true value; to play down. ➤➤ **minimization** *n,* **minimizer** *n.*

minimum[1] *n* (*pl* **minima** *or* **minimums**) **1** the least quantity or value assignable, admissible, or possible. **2** the lowest degree or amount reached or recorded.

minimum[2] *adj* of or being a minimum.

minimum wage *n* a wage fixed by law or contract as the least that may be paid to employees.

minion *n* **1** a servile attendant. **2** *derog* a minor official.

minipill *n* an oral contraceptive in the form of a pill taken daily by a woman and containing only progesterone.

miniseries *n* (*pl* **miniseries**) a television drama screened in a small number of episodes.

miniskirt *n* a woman's skirt with the hemline several inches above the knee.

minister[1] *n* **1** a member of the clergy, *esp* in a Protestant or nonconformist Church. **2** a high officer of state managing a division of government. **3** a diplomatic representative accredited to a foreign state. **4** *archaic* somebody or something that produces an effect; a cause or instrument. ➤➤ **ministerial** *adj,* **ministerially** *adv.*

minister[2] *v* **1** (+ to) to give assistance, care, or service to people who are sick or in need. **2** *archaic* to provide or supply.

Minister of State *n* a government minister ranking below a Secretary of State.

Minister of the Crown *n* in Britain and Canada, a member of the cabinet.

minister without portfolio *n* a government minister with no specific departmental responsibilities.

ministration *n* **1** *formal or humorous* (*also in pl*) an act of assistance, care, or service. **2** ministering, *esp* in religious matters. ➤➤ **ministrant** *n.*

ministry *n* (*pl* **-ies**) **1** a government department presided over by a minister. **2** the period of service or office of a minister of religion or government. **3** the office, duties, or functions of a minister of religion or government.

minivan *n* a small van with removable seats.

miniver *n* a white fur used chiefly for lining or trimming robes of state.

mink *n* (*pl* **minks** *or* **mink**) a semiaquatic flesh-eating mammal having partially webbed feet and a thick coat of soft fur which varies in colour from white to dark reddish brown.

minke whale /'mingkə, 'mingki/ *n* a small RORQUAL (whalebone whale) of northern seas.

minneola *n* a citrus fruit with a thin reddish orange skin that is a cross between a tangerine and a grapefruit.

minnesinger *n* a member of a class of German lyric poets and musicians of the 12th to the 14th cent.

minnow *n* (*pl* **minnows** *or* **minnow**) **1** a small dark-coloured freshwater fish, related to the carp, that is found in the upper parts of rivers. **2** something small or insignificant of its kind.

Minoan *adj* of or being a highly developed Bronze Age culture of Crete from around 3000 to 1100 BC. ➤➤ **Minoan** *n.*

minor[1] *adj* **1a** inferior in importance, size, rank, or degree. **b** not serious or involving risk to life. **2a** *esp* of a musical scale: having semitones between the second and third, fifth and sixth, and sometimes seventh and eighth steps. **b** being or based on a minor scale. **c** being a musical interval less by a semitone than a corresponding major interval. **d** of a chord: having an interval of a minor third between the root and the next note above it.

minor[2] *n* **1** a person who has not attained majority. **2** a minor musical interval, scale, key, etc. **3** *NAm* a student's subsidiary subject.

minor[3] *v NAm* (+ in) to study something as a subsidiary subject.

Minorcan *n* a native or inhabitant of the island of Minorca. ➤➤ **Minorcan** *adj.*

minor canon *n* a canon in the Church of England who assists in services but has no vote in the chapter.

minority *n* (*pl* **-ies**) **1a** the period before attainment of the age of majority. **b** the state of being a legal minor. **2** (*used as sing. or pl*) the smaller of two groups constituting a whole; *specif* a group with less than the number of votes necessary for control. **3** (*used as sing. or pl*) a group of people who share common characteristics or interests differing from those of the majority of a population.

minor league *n NAm* a league of lower classification than the major league in US professional sport, *esp* baseball.

minor planet *n* an asteroid.

Minotaur *n* in Greek mythology, a monster with the body of a man and the head of a bull, kept by Minos in a labyrinth on Crete and ultimately killed by Theseus.

minster *n* a large or important church often having cathedral status.

minstrel *n* a medieval singer, poet, or musical entertainer.

minstrelsy *n* the singing and playing of a minstrel.

mint[1] *n* **1a** a plant that has whorled leaves with a characteristic strong taste and smell, used *esp* as a flavouring. **b** the flavour of mint. **2** a sweet, chocolate, etc flavoured with peppermint. ➤➤ **minty** *adj.*

Word history

Old English *minte*; related to Old High German *minza*, ultimately from Latin *mentha* mint. The plant is said to be so called from Minthe, a nymph who was loved by Pluto and who was then turned by Pluto's jealous wife Proserpina into the plant named after her.

mint[2] *n* **1** a place where coins, medals, etc are made. **2** *informal* a vast sum or amount of money.

Word history

Old English *mynet* coin, money, related to Old High German *munizza* coin, ultimately from Latin *moneta* mint, coin, from *Moneta*, epithet of Juno. The connection with the Roman goddess Juno arises from the fact that the Romans coined money in the temple of Juno Moneta.

mint[3] *v* **1** to make (coins, etc) by stamping metal. **2** to fabricate or invent (a new word, etc).

mint[4] *adj* unspoilt, as if fresh from a mint.

mint julep *n* = JULEP.

minuet *n* a slow graceful dance in triple time.

minus[1] *prep* **1** diminished by. **2** *informal* without.

minus[2] *n* (*pl* **minuses**) **1** = MINUS SIGN. **2** a negative quantity. **3** a deficiency or defect.

minus[3] *adj* **1** less than zero; negative. **2** having negative qualities, *esp* involving a disadvantage. **3** used after a grade: falling lower than the specified grade. **4** of or having a negative electric charge.

minuscule *adj* **1** very small. **2** of, in, or being a lower-case letter or letters.

Usage note

Minuscule meaning 'tiny' is spelt with one *i* and two *u*'s. It can never be spelt *miniscule*.

minus sign *n* the symbol (–), denoting subtraction or a negative quantity, e.g. in *8 – 6 = 2* or *–10°*.

minute[1] *n* **1a** a unit of time equal to one sixtieth of an hour. **b** a unit of angular measurement equal to one sixtieth of a degree. **2** *informal* a short space of time; a moment. **3a** a short note or memorandum. **b** (*in pl*) the official record of the proceedings of a meeting.

minute[2] *v* **1** to make notes or a brief summary of (a meeting). **2** to send (somebody) a minute.

minute[3] *adj* **1** extremely small. **2** marked by painstaking attention to detail. ➤➤ **minutely** *adv,* **minuteness** *n.*

minute steak *n* a small thin steak that can be quickly cooked.

minutia *n* (*pl* **minutiae**) (*usu in pl*) a small or precise detail.

minx *n* a flirtatious or cunning girl or young woman.

Miocene *adj* of the fourth geological epoch of the Tertiary period, lasting from about 23.5 million to 5.2 million years ago, and marked by the first appearance of apes. ➤➤ **Miocene** *n.*

mips *abbr* million instructions per second (measure of computing speed).

miracle *n* **1** an extraordinary and welcome event that manifests or is attributed to divine intervention in human affairs. **2** an astonishing and wonderful event, thing, or accomplishment. **3** somebody or something that is a remarkable example or instance of the specified thing.

miracle play *n* a medieval drama based on episodes from the Bible or the life of a saint.

miraculous *adj* **1** of the nature of a miracle; supernatural. **2** evoking wonder like a miracle; marvellous. ➤➤ **miraculously** *adv.*

mirage *n* **1** an optical illusion appearing *esp* as a pool of water or as the reflection of distant objects and caused by the reflection of rays of light by a layer of heated air. **2** something illusory and unattainable.

mire[1] *n* **1** a tract of soft waterlogged ground; a marsh or bog. **2** a situation of great difficulty, complexity, or involvement. ➤➤ **miry** *adj.*

mire[2] *v* **1** to cause (somebody or something) to sink or stick fast in a mire. **2** to cover or soil (somebody or something) with mire. **3** to be in a difficult or complex situation.

mirepoix /miə'pwah/ *n* (*pl* **mirepoix**) a mixture of diced vegetables sautéed and used in sauces or as a bed on which to braise meat.

mirk *n* see MURK.

mirky *adj* = MURKY (1).

mirror[1] *n* **1** a smooth or polished surface, e.g. of metal or silvered glass, that forms images by reflection. **2** something that gives a true representation.

mirror[2] *v* **1** to reflect (somebody or something) in a mirror, or as if in a mirror. **2** to copy, represent, or correspond to (something) exactly.

mirror ball *n* a large sphere covered with squares of reflective glass that is hung from the ceiling and revolves to create a decorative lighting effect.

mirror image *n* something that has its parts reversely arranged in comparison with an otherwise identical thing.

mirror site *n* a replica of a web site, created to allow faster access.

mirth *n* happiness or amusement accompanied with laughter. ➤➤ **mirthful** *adj.*

MIRV *n* multiple independently targeted re-entry vehicle, an intercontinental missile having multiple warheads that may be directed to separate targets.

mis- *prefix* **1 a** badly; wrongly; unfavourably: *misjudge; misbehave.* **b** not: *misunderstand.* **2 a** bad; wrong: *misdeed.* **b** opposite or lack of: *mistrust.* **c** suspicious; apprehensive: *misgiving.*

misadventure *n* **1** a misfortune or mishap. **2** (*also* **death by misadventure**) in law, death due to an action not intended to cause harm.

misalliance *n* an improper or unsuitable alliance, *esp* a mésalliance.

misandry *n* hatred of men.

misanthrope *n* a person who hates or distrusts other people or humankind in general. ➤➤ **misanthropic** *adj,* **misanthropy** *n.*

misanthropist *n* = MISANTHROPE.

misapprehend *v* to misunderstand (something). ⋙ **misapprehension** *n.*

misappropriate *v* to appropriate or take wrongly, e.g. by theft or embezzlement. ⋙ **misappropriation** *n.*

misbegotten *adj* **1** having a disreputable or improper origin; ill-conceived. **2** wretched; contemptible. **3** *archaic* illegitimate.

misbehave *v* to behave badly. ⋙ **misbehaviour** *n.*

misbelief *n* a false belief.

miscalculate *v* to calculate or assess wrongly. ⋙ **miscalculation** *n.*

miscarriage *n* **1** the expulsion of a human foetus before it is capable of survival outside the womb, *esp* between the 12th and 20th weeks of pregnancy. **2** a failure in administration: *a miscarriage of justice.*

miscarry *v* (**-ies, -ied**) **1** to suffer miscarriage of a foetus. **2** to fail to achieve an intended purpose; to go wrong.

miscast *v* (*past tense and past part.* **miscast**) to cast (an actor) in an unsuitable role.

miscegenation *n* interbreeding of races, *esp* between people of different skin colour.

miscellanea *pl n* a miscellaneous collection, *esp* of literary works.

miscellaneous *adj* **1** consisting of diverse items or members. **2** having various characteristics or capabilities. ⋙ **miscellaneously** *adv.*

miscellany *n* (*pl* **-ies**) a collection or mixture of various things.

mischance *n* bad luck.

mischief *n* **1** playful action that annoys or irritates, usu without causing or intending serious harm. **2** somebody or something that causes harm or annoyance. **3** a specific injury or damage from a particular agent.

mischievous *adj* **1a** disruptively playful. **b** playfully provocative; arch. **2** able or tending to cause annoyance or minor injury. ⋙ **mischievously** *adv,* **mischievousness** *n.*

miscible *adj* of a liquid: capable of being mixed; *specif* capable of being mixed with another liquid in any proportion without separating.

misconceive *v* to interpret wrongly; to misunderstand.

misconceived *adj* badly judged, planned, or conceived.

misconception *n* a false or mistaken idea, opinion, or attitude.

misconduct[1] *n* **1** intentional wrongdoing; *specif* deliberate violation of a law or standard. **2** bad or improper behaviour.

misconduct[2] *v formal* to conduct (oneself) badly or improperly.

misconstrue *v* (**misconstrues, misconstrued, misconstruing**) to construe wrongly; to misinterpret. ⋙ **misconstruction** *n.*

miscreant[1] *n* **1** a person who behaves criminally or maliciously. **2** *archaic* a heretic or unbeliever.

miscreant[2] *adj* behaving criminally or maliciously.

miscue[1] *n* in billiards or snooker, a faulty stroke in which the cue slips.

miscue[2] *v* (**miscues, miscued, miscueing** *or* **miscuing**) to make a miscue.

misdeed *n* a wrong deed; an offence.

misdemeanour (*NAm* **misdemeanor**) *n* **1** a minor crime, *esp* one formerly technically distinguished from a felony. **2** a minor offence or wrongdoing.

misdiagnose *v* to diagnose wrongly.

misdirect *v* **1** to give a wrong direction or instruction to (somebody). **2** to direct (effort, etc) wrongly or inappropriately. **3** to address (mail) incorrectly. ⋙ **misdirection** *n.*

mise-en-scène /,meez onh 'sen/ *n* **1** the arrangement of actors, props, and scenery on a stage in a theatrical production. **2** the environment or setting in which something takes place.

miser *n* a mean grasping person, *esp* one who lives miserably in order to hoard wealth.

miserable *adj* **1a** in a pitiable state of distress or unhappiness. **b** habitually gloomy or morose. **2a** wretchedly inadequate or meagre. **b** causing or characterized by extreme discomfort or unhappiness. **3** shameful; contemptible. ⋙ **miserableness** *n,* **miserably** *adv.*

miserere /mizə'reəri/ *n* **1** (**Miserere**) the 51st Psalm. **2** a plea or lament, *esp* a cry for mercy

misericord *n* a ledge on the underside of the hinged seat of a choir stall to support the occupant in a standing position when the seat is turned up.

miserly *adj* **1** of or characteristic of a miser; mean. **2** of an amount: small and inadequate. ⋙ **miserliness** *n.*

misery *n* (*pl* **-ies**) **1** physical or mental suffering or discomfort; great unhappiness or distress. **2** a cause of great suffering or distress. **3** *chiefly Brit, informal* a morose or querulous person.

misfire *v* **1** of a motor vehicle, engine, etc: to have the explosive or propulsive charge fail to ignite at the proper time. **2** of a firearm: to fail to fire. **3** to fail to have an intended effect.

misfit *n* **1** a person who is poorly adjusted to their environment. **2** something that fits badly.

misfortune *n* **1** bad luck. **2** a distressing or unfortunate incident or event.

misgiving *n* a feeling of doubt, suspicion, or apprehension.

misgovern *v* to govern (a nation, etc) badly.

misguided *adj* directed by mistaken ideas, principles, or motives.

mishandle *v* **1** to treat (somebody or something) roughly; to maltreat. **2** to mismanage (a situation, crisis, etc).

mishap *n* an unfortunate accident.

mishear *v* (*past tense and past part.* **misheard**) to hear wrongly.

mishit *v* (**mishitting,** *past tense and past part.* **mishit**) to hit (a ball or stroke) in a faulty manner.

mishmash *n informal* a hotchpotch or jumble.

Mishnah *or* **Mishna** *n* the collection of Jewish traditions chiefly concerned with the law that was compiled about AD 200 and forms the basis of the Talmud.

misinform *v* to give untrue or misleading information to. ⋙ **misinformation** *n.*

misinterpret *v* (**misinterpreted, misinterpreting**) to understand or explain wrongly. ⋙ **misinterpretation** *n.*

misjudge *v* **1** to estimate wrongly. **2** to judge (somebody) wrongly, *esp* to have an unjustly bad opinion of (somebody). ⋙ **misjudgment** *n.*

mislay *v* (*past tense and past part.* **mislaid**) to put or leave (something) in a place that is subsequently forgotten; to lose temporarily.

mislead *v* (*past tense and past part.* **misled**) to lead (somebody) into a mistaken action or belief. ⋙ **misleading** *adj.*

mismanage *v* to manage (a situation, finances, etc) wrongly or incompetently. ⯮ **mismanagement** *n.*

mismatch[1] *v* to match (people or things) incorrectly or unsuitably, e.g. in marriage.

mismatch[2] *n* a poor or unsuitable match.

misnomer *n* **1** an incorrect or inappropriate name or designation. **2** the use of such a name or designation.

miso /'meesoh/ *n* a thick brown salty paste made from fermented soya beans, used to flavour savoury dishes.

misogyny *n* hatred of women. ⯮ **misogynist** *n,* **misogynistic** *adj.*

misplace *v* to put in the wrong place.

misplaced *adj* **1** directed towards the wrong or an unsuitable object or outcome. **2** used at the wrong or an inappropriate time or place.

misprint[1] *n* a printing error.

misprint[2] *v* to print (something) incorrectly.

mispronounce *v* to pronounce (a word or name) wrongly. ⯮ **mispronunciation** *n.*

misquote *v* **1** to quote incorrectly. **2** to repeat or report incorrectly what was said by (somebody). ⯮ **misquotation** *n.*

misread *v* (*past tense and past part.* **misread**) to read or interpret incorrectly.

misrepresent *v* to represent (something) falsely; to give an untrue or misleading account of (something). ⯮ **misrepresentation** *n.*

misrule[1] *v* to rule (a nation, etc) incompetently; to misgovern.

misrule[2] *n* **1** misruling or being misruled. **2** disorder; anarchy.

miss[1] *v* **1** to fail to hit, reach, meet, catch, or attain. **2** to discover or feel the absence of (something), *esp* with regret. **3** to escape or avoid (something). **4** (*often* + out) to leave out; to omit. **5** to fail to understand, sense, or experience. **6** to fail to attend (work, school, an appointment, etc). **7** to fail to watch, listen to, or take part in (a show, party, etc). **8** to fail to take advantage of (an opportunity, etc). ✱ **miss out on** to fail to have or experience (something desirable). **miss the boat** *informal* to fail to take advantage of an opportunity.

miss[2] *n* **1** a failure to hit something. **2** a failure to attain a desired result. ✱ **give (something) a miss** *chiefly Brit, informal* to avoid, bypass, or omit (something) deliberately.

miss[3] *n* **1** (**Miss**) **a** used as a title preceding the name of an unmarried woman or a girl. **b** used as a term of address to a female schoolteacher. **2** *derog or humorous* a young unmarried woman or a girl.

missal *n* a book containing all that is said or sung at mass for the whole year.

missel thrush *n* see MISTLE THRUSH.

misshape *v* (*past tense* **misshaped,** *past part.* **misshaped** *or* **misshapen**) *archaic* to shape (something or somebody) badly; to deform. ⯮ **misshapen** *adj.*

missile *n* **1** an object thrown or projected, usu so as to strike something at a distance. **2** a self-propelled weapon that travels through the air; a ballistic missile or guided missile.

missing *adj* **1** absent or lost. **2** not confirmed as either alive or dead.

missing link *n* a hypothetical intermediate form between human beings and their anthropoid ancestors.

mission *n* **1** a specific task with which a person or group is charged. **2** (*used as sing. or pl*) a body of people sent to perform a service or carry on an activity, e.g.: **a** a group sent to a foreign country to negotiate, advise, etc. **b** a permanent embassy or legation. **3** a definite military, naval, or aerospace task. **4a** a ministry commissioned by a religious organization to propagate its faith or carry on humanitarian work, usu abroad. **b** a mission establishment. **5** a calling or vocation.

missionary[1] *n* (*pl* **-ies**) a person in charge of a religious mission.

missionary[2] *adj* **1** relating to, engaged in, or devoted to missions. **2** characteristic of a missionary.

missionary position *n* a position for sexual intercourse in which the woman lies underneath and face to face with the man, regarded as the conventional position.

mission statement *n* a formal statement of the policies, aims, values, etc of a company or other organization.

missis *n* see MISSUS.

missive *n formal or humorous* a letter.

misspell *v* (*past tense* **misspelt,** *past part.* **misspelt** *or* **misspelled**) to spell incorrectly. ⯮ **misspelling** *n.*

misspend *v* (*past tense and past part.* **misspent**) to spend (money, time, etc) wrongly or foolishly; to squander.

misstate *v* to state incorrectly. ⯮ **misstatement** *n.*

misstep *n* **1** a wrong step. **2** a blunder.

missus *or* **missis** *n* (*pl* **missuses** *or* **missises**) **1** *informal or humorous* somebody's wife. **2** *informal* used as a term of address to a married woman.

missy *n* (*pl* **-ies**) *informal* used as a term of address to a young girl.

mist[1] *n* **1** water in the form of diffuse particles in the atmosphere, *esp* near the earth's surface. **2** condensed water vapour on a surface, *esp* on glass.

mist[2] *v* **1** (*often* + up/over) to be or become covered with or obscured by mist. **2** to cover with mist, or as if with mist.

mistake[1] *v* (*past tense* **mistook,** *past part.* **mistaken**) **1a** to misunderstand the meaning, intention, or significance of (something or somebody). **b** to estimate wrongly. **2a** to identify (somebody or something) wrongly. **b** to confuse (somebody or something) with another.

mistake[2] *n* **1** a wrong action or statement arising from faulty judgment, inadequate knowledge, or carelessness. **2** a misunderstanding of the meaning or significance of something.

mistaken *adj* **1** of an action, idea, etc: based on wrong thinking; incorrect. **2** of a person: wrong in opinion. ⯮ **mistakenly** *adv.*

mister *n* **1** (**Mister**) = MR. **2** (*often* **Mister**) used as a generalized informal term of address to a man; sir.

mistime *v* to time badly; to do or say at the wrong or inappropriate time.

mistle thrush *or* **missel thrush** *n* a large Eurasian thrush with greyish brown upper parts and larger spots on its underparts than the song thrush.

mistletoe *n* a European shrub that grows as a parasite on the branches of trees and has thick leaves, small yellowish flowers, and waxy white glutinous berries.

mistook *v* past tense of MISTAKE[1].

mistral *n* a strong cold dry northerly wind of S France.

mistreat *v* to treat (somebody or something) badly. ⯮ **mistreatment** *n.*

mistress *n* **1** a woman in a position of power, authority, possession, or control. **2** a woman who has achieved mastery of a subject or skill. **3** a woman with whom a man has a continuing sexual relationship outside marriage. **4** *chiefly Brit* a female schoolteacher. **5** *archaic* a sweetheart. **6** (**Mistress**) *archaic* used as a title preceding the name of a woman and now superseded by *Mrs, Miss,* and *Ms.*

mistrial *n* a trial declared void because of some error in the proceedings.

mistrust[1] *v* **1** to have little trust in (somebody or something); to be suspicious of. **2** to doubt the reliability or effectiveness of.

mistrust[2] *n* a lack of trust; distrust. ➤➤ **mistrustful** *adj.*

misty *adj* (**-ier, -iest**) **1a** covered with or obscured by mist. **b** consisting of or marked by mist. **2** not clear; indistinct, blurred or vague. ➤➤ **mistily** *adv,* **mistiness** *n.*

misunderstand *v* (*past tense and past part.* **misunderstood**) **1** to fail to understand (something or somebody). **2** to interpret incorrectly.

misunderstanding *n* **1** a failure to understand; a misinterpretation. **2** *euphem* a disagreement; a dispute.

misunderstood *v* past tense and past part. of MISUNDERSTAND.

misuse[1] *v* **1** to put to wrong or improper use. **2** to abuse or maltreat (somebody or something).

Usage note
misuse *or* abuse? See note at ABUSE[1].

misuse[2] *n* **1** incorrect or improper use. **2** maltreatment; abuse.

MIT *abbr* Massachusetts Institute of Technology.

mite *n* **1** any of a large order of small to minute invertebrate animals related to the spiders and ticks. **2a** a very small child or animal. **b** a very small amount or particle. ✱ **a mite** *informal* to a small extent; somewhat.

miter[1] *n NAm* see MITRE[1].

miter[2] *v NAm* see MITRE[2].

mither *v chiefly N Eng dialect* to make a fuss or pester somebody.

mitigate *v* **1** to make less harsh or hostile. **2a** to make less severe or painful; to alleviate. **b** to lessen the seriousness of. ➤➤ **mitigable** *adj,* **mitigation** *n,* **mitigator** *n,* **mitigatory** *adj.*

Usage note
mitigate *or* militate? See note at MILITATE.

mitochondrion /mietoh'kondri·ən/ *n* (*pl* **mitochondria**) in biology, a specialized part of a cell found outside the nucleus, that produces energy through cellular respiration. ➤➤ **mitochondrial** *adj,* **mitochondrially** *adv.*

mitosis *n* (*pl* **mitoses**) the formation during cell division of two new nuclei from a dividing nucleus, each having the same number of chromosomes as the original nucleus: compare MEIOSIS (I). ➤➤ **mitotic** *adj.*

mitral *adj* denoting the heart valve situated between the upper and lower chambers on the left-hand side.

mitre[1] (*NAm* **miter**) *n* **1** a tall pointed divided ceremonial hat, worn by bishops and abbots. **2** a joint made by cutting the ends of two pieces of wood or other material obliquely so that they form a right angle when fitted together.

mitre[2] (*NAm* **miter**) *v* **1** to cut (e.g. the ends of pieces of wood) obliquely to make a mitre. **2** to join (pieces) in a mitre.

mitt *n* **1a** a glove that leaves the fingers or the ends of the fingers uncovered. **b** = MITTEN (I). **c** a baseball catcher's protective glove. **2** *informal* a hand.

mitten *n* **1** a covering for the hand and wrist that has one section for all four fingers and another for the thumb. **2** = MITT (IA).

mix[1] *v* **1a** to combine or blend into one mass. **b** to combine (one ingredient) with another or others. **c** to prepare (something) by mixing ingredients. **d** to be capable of mixing. **2** to control the balance of (various sounds), *esp* during the recording of a film, broadcast, record, etc: compare DUB[2]. **3** to seek or enjoy the company of other people. ✱ **mix it** *informal* to start an argument or fight.

mix[2] *n* **1** a product of mixing; *specif* a commercially prepared mixture of food ingredients. **2** a combination. **3** the proportion in which elements are mixed or combined. **4** a version of a musical recording that has been mixed to produce a different type of sound from the original.

mixed *adj* **1** combining diverse elements. **2** made up of or involving people of different sexes, races, religions, etc. **3** including or accompanied by conflicting or dissimilar elements.

mixed bag *n* a miscellaneous collection; an assortment.

mixed blessing *n* something with both advantages and disadvantages, e.g. a desirable situation or occurrence that also has undesirable elements.

mixed economy *n* an economic system in which private enterprise and nationalized industries coexist.

mixed farming *n* the growing of crops and rearing of livestock on the same farm.

mixed grill *n Brit* a dish of several meats and vegetables grilled and served together.

mixed marriage *n* a marriage between people of different races or religions.

mixed metaphor *n* a combination of incongruous metaphors, e.g. in *iron out bottlenecks.*

mixed-up *adj informal* in perplexity or disorder; confused.

mixer *n* **1** a device or machine for mixing something, e.g. food or concrete. **2** a person considered with respect to their sociability. **3** a non-alcoholic drink intended to be mixed with an alcoholic drink. **4a** an electronic device used to combine *esp* sound signals from a number of sources for recording, broadcasting, etc. **b** a person who operates such a device.

mixer tap *n* a tap that supplies hot water, cold water, or a mixture of the two in variable proportions through a single outlet.

mixture *n* **1** the act or an instance of mixing. **2a** a product of mixing; a combination or blend. **b** a combination of two or more components in varying proportions that retain their own properties. **3** the relative proportions of the constituents of a mixture; *specif* the proportion of fuel to air produced in a carburettor.

mix up *v* **1** to mistake or confuse (somebody or something) for another. **2** to make untidy or disordered. ✱ **be/get mixed up in** to be or become involved in an illegal or suspect activity.

mix-up *n informal* a state or instance of confusion.

mizzen *or* **mizen** *n* **1** the mast behind the mainmast in a sailing vessel. **2** the principal fore-and-aft sail on a mizzenmast.

mizzenmast *n* = MIZZEN (I).

mizzle[1] *v chiefly dialect* = DRIZZLE[1].

mizzle[2] *n* = DRIZZLE[2]. ➤➤ **mizzly** *adj.*

Mk *abbr* mark (unit of currency or numbered model).

ml *abbr* **1** mile. **2** millilitre.

MLA *abbr* Member of the Legislative Assembly.

MLitt *abbr* Master of Letters.

Mlle *abbr* Mademoiselle.

Mlles *abbr* Mesdemoiselles.

MM *abbr* **1** Messieurs. **2** *Brit* Military Medal.

mm *abbr* millimetre.

Mme *abbr* Madame.

Mmes *abbr* Mesdames.

MMR *abbr* measles, mumps, and rubella (vaccination).

MN *abbr* **1** *Brit* Merchant Navy. **2** Minnesota (US postal abbreviation).

Mn *abbr* the chemical symbol for manganese.

mnemonic[1] *adj* **1** assisting or intended to assist the memory. **2** of memory or mnemonics. ➤➤ **mnemonically** *adv.*

mnemonic[2] *n* a mnemonic device or code.

mnemonics *pl n* (*used as sing. or pl*) the art of or a system for improving the memory.

MO *abbr* **1** Medical Officer. **2** Missouri (US postal abbreviation). **3** modus operandi. **4** money order.

Mo *abbr* the chemical symbol for molybdenum.

mo *or* **mo'** *n chiefly Brit, informal* a very short space of time; a moment.

moa *n* a very large extinct flightless bird of New Zealand.

moan[1] *n* **1a** a low prolonged sound usu of pain or grief. **b** a sound resembling this, *esp* a mournful sound made by the wind. **2** *informal* a complaint.

moan[2] *v* **1** to produce a moan. **2** *informal* to complain or grumble. ➤➤ **moaner** *n,* **moanful** *adj.*

moat *n* a deep wide trench, usu filled with water, constructed round a castle or other fortified place. ➤➤ **moated** *adj.*

mob[1] *n* **1** (*also before a noun*) a large, disorderly, or riotous crowd. **2a** a large group. **b** *chiefly Brit, informal* a particular group of people. **3** (**the mob**) the masses; the populace. **4** (*usu* **the Mob**) *chiefly NAm* the Mafia or a similarly organized criminal gang. **5** *chiefly Aus* a flock, drove, or herd of animals.

mob[2] *v* (**mobbed, mobbing**) **1** to attack (somebody) in a large crowd or group. **2** to crowd round (somebody), *esp* out of curiosity or admiration.

mob cap *n* a woman's full soft cap with a frill round the edge, worn indoors *esp* in the 18th cent.

mobile[1] *adj* **1** capable of moving or being moved. **2a** of a library, shop, etc: set up in a vehicle and able to move from place to place. **b** *informal* having the use of a vehicle for transport. **3** of people: able and willing to move into a different job, home, social class, etc. **4** of a face or features: readily changing to express different moods.

mobile[2] *n* **1** a decorative structure with suspended parts that are moved by air currents. **2** = MOBILE PHONE.

mobile home *n* a caravan, *esp* one used as permanent accommodation.

mobile phone *n* a portable telephone for use in a cellular radio system.

mobility allowance *n* a state benefit to provide means of transport for disabled people.

mobilize *or* **-ise** *v* **1a** to assemble and make ready (troops) for active service. **b** to marshal (resources) for action. **2a** to put into movement or circulation. **b** to release (something stored in the body) for use in an organism. ➤➤ **mobilizable** *adj,* **mobilization** *n.*

Möbius strip *n* a one-sided surface that is constructed from a rectangle by holding one end, rotating the opposite end through 180°, and joining it to the first end.

mobster *n informal* a member of a criminal gang.

moccasin *n* **1** a soft leather heelless shoe with the sole brought up the sides of the foot and joined with a puckered seam to a U-shaped top piece. **2** = WATER MOCCASIN.

mocha *n* **1** a coffee of superior quality; *specif* one grown on the Arabian peninsula. **2** a flavouring obtained from strong coffee or from coffee mixed with cocoa or chocolate. **3** a pliable suede-finished glove leather made from African sheepskin.

mock[1] *v* **1** to treat with contempt or ridicule; to deride. **2** to disappoint or frustrate. **3** to copy or mimic in fun or derision. ➤➤ **mocker** *n,* **mocking** *adj,* **mockingly** *adv.*

mock[2] *n* (*also in pl*) a school examination used as practice for an official one.

mock[3] *adj* **1** not real; imitation. **2** of a battle, examination, etc: simulated for purposes of practice or training.

mockers ✱ **put the mockers on 1** *Brit, informal* to ruin or put an end to. **2** *Brit, informal* to bring misfortune to.

mockery *n* (*pl* **-ies**) **1** jeering or contemptuous behaviour or words. **2** an object of derision or ridicule. **3** a deceitful or contemptible imitation; a travesty. ✱ **make a mockery of something** to undermine it or render it pointless.

mock-heroic *adj* using heroic style, character, or action for satirical effect in the treatment of an unheroic subject.

mockingbird *n* a songbird of the USA that imitates the calls of other birds.

mock orange *n* an ornamental shrub of the saxifrage family with showy fragrant white flowers.

mock turtle soup *n* a soup made from a calf's head in imitation of turtle soup.

mock-up *n* a full-sized model or representation, e.g. for study, testing, or display.

MOD *abbr Brit* Ministry of Defence.

mod *n* (*often* **Mod**) a member of a group of young people in Britain, *esp* in the 1960s, noted for their neat appearance and stylish clothing: compare ROCKER (2).

mod. *abbr* **1** moderate. **2** moderato. **3** modern.

modal *adj* **1** of general form or structure, as opposed to particular substance or content. **2** denoting a grammatical form or category indicating mood. **3** of or being in a musical mode rather than a major or minor key. ➤➤ **modally** *adv.*

modal auxiliary verb *n* in grammar, a verb such as *will, shall, should, would, may, might,* that helps another verb to form tenses, voices, and moods that cannot be indicated by inflection.

modality *n* (*pl* **-ies**) a modal quality or attribute; a form.

mod cons *pl n Brit, informal* modern conveniences, *esp* household fittings or devices designed to increase comfort or save time.

mode *n* **1** a way of doing something. **2** a particular functional arrangement or condition. **3** a prevailing fashion or style, e.g. of dress or behaviour. **4** an arrangement of the eight notes of a musical scale within an octave in any of several fixed schemes that use different patterns of tones and semitones between successive notes. **5** in statistics, the most frequently occurring value in a set of data.

model[1] *n* **1a** a replica of something in three dimensions. **b** a representation of something to be constructed. **2a** an example used for reproducing or copying. **b** an outstanding example worthy of imitation or emulation. **c** (*used before a noun*) exemplary **3a** a person who poses for an artist or photographer. **b** a person who is employed to wear clothing in order to display it. **4** a type or design of an article or product, e.g. a garment or car. **5** a system of postulates, data, and inferences presented as a mathematical description of an entity or state of affairs, often stored in a computer.

model[2] *v* (**modelled, modelling,** *NAm* **modeled, modeling**) **1a** to shape in a mouldable material. **b** to produce a model of. **2** (*often* + on) to plan, construct, or fashion (something) in imitation of something else. **3a** to display, *esp* by wearing. **b** to work as a model, *esp* a fashion model. ⋙ **modeller** *n.*

modem *n* an electronic device that converts digital data from a computer into an audio signal that can be transmitted via a telephone line.

moderate[1] *adj* **1a** avoiding extremes. **b** calm, mild, or temperate. **c** avoiding extreme political or social measures; not radical. **2** being average or somewhat less than average in quality, amount, degree, or extent. ⋙ **moderately** *adv.*

moderate[2] *v* **1** to decrease in violence, severity, intensity, or extremeness. **2** to preside over (a meeting or debate). **3** to ensure consistency of grading in (examination papers or results). **4** in physics, to slow down (neutrons) with a moderator.

moderate[3] *n* a person who holds moderate views or favours a moderate course.

moderation *n* **1** the process of moderating or of being moderated. **2** the avoidance of extremes, *esp* in personal behaviour; restraint; self-control. ✱ **in moderation** within reasonable limits.

moderator *n* **1** a person who arbitrates; a mediator. **2** a person who presides over an assembly, meeting, debate, etc, e.g. the presiding officer of a Presbyterian governing body. **3** a person who moderates examination papers or results. **4** in physics, a substance used for slowing down neutrons in a nuclear reactor. ⋙ **moderatorship** *n.*

modern[1] *adj* **1** characteristic of the present or the immediate past; contemporary. **2** involving recent techniques, styles, or ideas. **3** (**Modern**) constituting the present or most recent period of a language. ⋙ **modernity** *n,* **modernness** *n.*

modern[2] *n* a person of modern times or having modern views.

modernise *v* see MODERNIZE.

modernism *n* **1** methods, practices, or styles characteristic of modern times. **2** a new direction in art, literature, theology, etc, emphasizing contemporary ideas and involving a deliberate break with the past. ⋙ **modernist** *n and adj,* **modernistic** *adj.*

modernize *or* **-ise** *v* **1** to adapt to modern needs, style, or standards. **2** to adopt modern views, habits, or techniques. ⋙ **modernization** *n,* **modernizer** *n.*

modern pentathlon *n* a contest in which all participants compete in a 300m freestyle swimming race, a 4000m cross-country run, a 5000m 30-jump equestrian steeplechase, épée fencing, and target shooting at 25m.

modest *adj* **1** showing a moderate estimate of one's abilities or worth; not boastful or self-assertive. **2** small or limited in size, amount, or aim. **3** carefully observant of proprieties of dress and behaviour; decent. ⋙ **modestly** *adv,* **modesty** *n.*

modicum *n* a small or limited amount.

modification *n* **1a** a small or limited change made to something. **b** the making of such a change. **2** the limiting of a statement; a qualification. ⋙ **modificatory** *adj.*

modifier *n* **1** a word or word group that qualifies or limits the meaning of another, e.g. *horror* in *horror film.* **2** somebody or something that modifies.

modify *v* (**-ies, -ied**) **1a** to make minor changes in. **b** to make basic changes in (something), often for a specific purpose. **2** in grammar, to limit (a word or phrase) in meaning. ⋙ **modifiable** *adj.*

modi operandi *n* pl of MODUS OPERANDI.

modish *adj* fashionable; stylish. ⋙ **modishly** *adv,* **modishness** *n.*

modiste *n dated* a person who makes and sells fashionable women's clothing, *esp* dresses and hats.

modi vivendi *n* pl of MODUS VIVENDI.

modular *adj* **1** of or based on a module or modulus. **2** consisting of or constructed from modules. ⋙ **modularity** *n.*

modulate *v* **1** to vary (one's voice, etc) in tone, pitch, etc. **2** to keep in proper measure or proportion; to temper or regulate. **3** to vary the amplitude, frequency, or phase of (a wave) to match the variations of another, *esp* in combining a radio wave with a sound or vision signal. **4** in music, to pass from one key or tonality into another. ⋙ **modulation** *n,* **modulator** *n.*

module *n* **1** any of a set of standardized units for use together in construction, e.g. of buildings, computers, or furniture. **2** a unit of an educational course, treating a specific subject or topic. **3** an independent unit that is part of the total structure of a space vehicle.

modulus *n* (*pl* **moduli**) **1** a number or quantity that expresses the degree in which a physical property is possessed by a substance or body. **2** the positive square root of the sum of the squares of the real and imaginary parts of a complex number.

modus operandi /,mohdəs opə'randi, -'randie/ *n* (*pl* **modi operandi** /,mohdee, ,mohdie/) a method or procedure.

modus vivendi /vi'vendee, -die/ *n* (*pl* **modi vivendi** /,mohdee, ,mohdie/) **1** a practical compromise, *esp* between opposed or quarrelling parties. **2** a manner of living; a way of life.

moggie *or* **moggy** *n* (*pl* **-ies**) *Brit, informal* a cat.

mogul *n* **1** (**Mogul, Moghul**) a member of a Muslim dynasty that ruled India from the 16th to the 18th cent. **2** *informal* a great, wealthy, or powerful person; a magnate.

MOH *abbr* Medical Officer of Health.

mohair *n* **1** the long silky hair of the Angora goat. **2** a fabric or yarn made wholly or partly from this hair.

Mohammedan *adj* see MUHAMMADAN.

Mohawk *n* (*pl* **Mohawks** *or* **Mohawk**) **1a** a member of a Native N American people of the Mohawk river valley in New York State. **b** the Iroquoian language of this people. **2** (*often* **mohawk**) *NAm* = MOHICAN (2). ⋙ **Mohawk** *adj.*

Mohegan *n* (*pl* **Mohegans** *or* **Mohegan**) a member of a Native American people formerly inhabiting Connecticut and Massachussetts.

Mohican *n* **1** see MAHICAN. **2** (*often* **mohican**) a punk hairstyle in which the head is shaved except for a strip of erect hair running from front to back.

Moho *n* (**the Moho**) the zone beneath the earth's surface that represents a distinct boundary separating the earth's crust from the underlying mantle.

moidore *n* a former Portuguese gold coin.

moiety *n* (*pl* **-ies**) either of two equal or approximately equal parts; a half.

moil[1] *v archaic, dialect* **1** to work hard; to drudge. **2** to be in a state of continuous agitation; to churn or swirl. ⋙ **moiler** *n.*

moil[2] *n* **1** laborious work; drudgery. **2** confusion or turmoil.

moiré *or* **moire** *n* **1** an irregular wavy finish on a fabric. **2** a fabric having a wavy watered appearance. ⯮ **moiré** *adj.*

moist *adj* **1** slightly wet; damp. **2** of or having high humidity. ⯮ **moistly** *adv,* **moistness** *n.*

moisten *v* to make or become moist.

moisture *n* liquid diffused as vapour or condensed as tiny droplets.

moisturize *or* **-ise** *v* to add or restore moisture to (the skin, etc). ⯮ **moisturizer** *n.*

mojo *n* (*pl* **-os**) *chiefly NAm* **1** a magic spell or charm. **2** magic.

moke *n informal Brit* a donkey.

mol *n* see MOLE[5].

molar[1] *n* a grinding tooth with a rounded or flattened surface towards the back of the jaw.

molar[2] *adj* **1** of or containing one mole of a substance. **2** of a solution: containing one mole of solute per litre of solution.

molasses *n* **1** the darkest most viscous syrup remaining after the refining of raw sugar. **2** *NAm* treacle or golden syrup.

mold[1] *n NAm* see MOULD[1].

mold[2] *v NAm* see MOULD[2].

mold[3] *n NAm* see MOULD[3].

mold[4] *n NAm* see MOULD[4].

Moldavian *n* **1** a native or inhabitant of Moldavia. **2** = MOLDOVAN. ⯮ **Moldavian** *adj.*

molder *v NAm* see MOULDER.

molding *n NAm* see MOULDING.

Moldovan *n* a native or inhabitant of Moldova. ⯮ **Moldovan** *adj.*

moldy *adj NAm* see MOULDY.

mole[1] *n* **1** a small burrowing insect-eating mammal with tiny eyes, concealed ears, and soft fur. **2a** a spy operating from a well-established position of trust *esp* within the security organization of a government. **b** a person who leaks secret information about an organization in which they are involved.

mole[2] *n* a dark-coloured permanent spot or small lump on the human body.

mole[3] *n* **1** a structure formed of masonry, large stones, etc laid in the sea as a pier or breakwater. **2** a harbour formed by a mole.

mole[4] *n* an abnormal mass in the womb, *esp* one containing foetal tissues.

mole[5] *or* **mol** *n* the basic SI unit of amount of substance equal to the amount of a substance that contains the same number of atoms, molecules, ions, etc as there are atoms in 0.012kg of carbon-12.

mole[6] /'mohlay/ *n* a spicy Mexican sauce made with chillis and chocolate.

molecular *adj* of, produced by, or consisting of molecules. ⯮ **molecularity** *n,* **molecularly** *adv.*

molecular biology *n* a branch of biology dealing with the structure, organization, and functioning of the molecules of living matter.

molecule *n* the smallest unit of a substance that retains its characteristic properties, usu consisting of two or more atoms of the same or different chemical elements bonded together.

molehill *n* a mound of earth thrown up by a burrowing mole. ✱ **make a mountain out of a molehill** to overdramatize a minor problem.

moleskin *n* **1** the skin of the mole used as fur. **2** a heavy durable cotton fabric with a short thick velvety nap on one side. **3** (*in pl*) clothes, *esp* trousers or overalls, made of moleskin.

molest *v* to annoy, disturb, or attack; *specif* to abuse or attack sexually. ⯮ **molestation** *n,* **molester** *n.*

moll *n informal* **1** a gangster's female friend or companion. **2** a prostitute.

mollie *or* **molly** *n* (*pl* **-ies**) a small black or brightly coloured aquarium fish.

mollify *v* (**-ies, -ied**) **1** to lessen the anger or hostility of. **2** to reduce in intensity or severity. ⯮ **mollification** *n,* **mollifier** *n.*

mollusc (*NAm* **mollusk**) *n* any of a large phylum of invertebrate animals including the snails, shellfish, and squids, that have a soft unsegmented body often enclosed in a shell. ⯮ **molluscan** *adj.*

molly *n* (*pl* **-ies**) see MOLLIE.

mollycoddle[1] *v* to treat with excessive indulgence, attention, or protection.

mollycoddle[2] *n* a spoilt or effeminate man or boy.

Molotov cocktail *n* a crude hand grenade made from a bottle filled with inflammable liquid with a wick, usu a saturated rag, that is ignited just before it is thrown.

molt[1] *v NAm* see MOULT[1].

molt[2] *n NAm* see MOULT[2].

molten *adj* liquefied by heat; melted.

molto *adv* used in music: much; very.

molybdenum *n* a hard silver-white metallic chemical element, used *esp* in strengthening and hardening steel.

mom *n NAm, informal* = MUM[1].

moment *n* **1a** a very brief interval of time. **b** a specific point in time. **2a** present time. **b** a time of excellence or prominence. **3** *formal* importance. **4a** a tendency to produce motion, *esp* rotational motion. **b** a measure of this tendency, equal to the product of a force and its perpendicular distance from a particular axis or point.

momenta *n* pl of MOMENTUM.

momentarily *adv* **1** for a very short time. **2** *chiefly NAm* very soon or immediately.

momentary *adj* lasting a very short time; transitory. ⯮ **momentariness** *n.*

moment of truth *n* **1** a moment of testing or crisis on the outcome of which everything depends. **2** the moment of the final sword thrust in a bullfight.

momentous *adj* of great consequence or significance. ⯮ **momentously** *adv,* **momentousness** *n.*

momentum *n* (*pl* **momenta**) **1** the ability or tendency to continue onwards possessed by an object in motion or an operation in progress. **2** in physics, a property of a moving body that resists slowing down, measured by multiplying the mass of the body by its velocity.

momma *n* **1** *NAm, informal* = MOM. **2** a buxom mature woman.

mommy *n* (*pl* **-ies**) = MOM.

Mon. *abbr* Monday.

mon- *or* **mono-** *comb. form* **1** one; single; alone: *monaural*; *monoplane*. **2** containing one specified atom, radical, or group: *monoxide*.

monad *n* a fundamental unit or entity; one. ⯮ **monadic** *adj.*

monarch *n* **1** a person who reigns over a kingdom or empire. **2** a large migratory N American butterfly with orange-brown wings. ⯮ **monarchal** *adj,* **monarchic** *adj,* **monarchical** *adj.*

monarchism *n* the principle of government by monarchy, or support for this principle. ⯮ **monarchist** *n and adj,* **monarchistic** *adj.*

monarchy *n* (*pl* **-ies**) **1** a state in which sovereignty is actually or nominally held by a monarch. **2** the institution represented by the sovereign and the royal family.

monastery *n* (*pl* **-ies**) a residence occupied by a religious community, *esp* of monks, or the community itself.

monastic[1] *adj* **1** of monasteries, monks, or nuns. **2** resembling, e.g. in seclusion or austerity, life in a monastery. ⋙ **monastically** *adv*, **monasticism** *n*.

monastic[2] *n* a monk, nun, or other person with a monastic way of life.

monaural *adj* **1** of or involving only one ear. **2** using only one channel to record or reproduce sound; monophonic. ⋙ **monaurally** *adv*.

Monday *n* the day of the week following Sunday.

monecious *adj NAm* see MONOECIOUS.

Monégasque *n* a native or inhabitant of the Mediterranean principality of Monaco. ⋙ **Monégasque** *adj*.

monetarism *n* an economic theory that the most effective way of controlling the economy is by controlling only the supply of money. ⋙ **monetarist** *n and adj*.

monetary *adj* of money or its circulation in the economy. ⋙ **monetarily** *adv*.

monetize *or* **-ise** *v* **1** to convert into money. **2** to establish as legal tender. ⋙ **monetization** *n*.

money *n* (*pl* **-eys** *or* **-ies**) **1** something generally accepted as a measure of value or means of payment, *esp* coins or paper currency. **2a** payment. **b** wealth reckoned in terms of money. **3** (*in pl*) a sum or sums of money. ✱ **for one's money** in one's opinion. **in the money** *informal* having a lot of money, *esp* money gained suddenly as winnings, profits, etc.

moneybags *n* (*pl* **moneybags**) *informal* a wealthy person.

moneyed *or* **monied** *adj* having much money; wealthy.

money-grubbing *adj informal* greedily bent on accumulating money, *esp* by sordid or unscrupulous means. ⋙ **money-grubber** *n*.

money market *n* the institutions dealing with, or the trade in, short-term loans and foreign exchange.

money of account *n* a denomination used in keeping accounts that does not necessarily correspond to any actual coin or note in circulation.

money order *n* a postal order, or similar printed form ordering payment of a specified amount issued by a bank.

money spider *n* a small spider supposed to bring luck to the person on whom it crawls.

money-spinner *n chiefly Brit, informal* a highly successful money-making product or enterprise. ⋙ **money-spinning** *adj and n*.

-monger *comb. form* forming nouns, denoting: **1** a trader or dealer: *fishmonger*. **2** a person who attempts to stir up or spread something that is usu petty or discreditable: *gossipmonger*.

mongo *n* (*pl* **mongo** *or* **mongos**) a unit of currency in Mongolia, worth 100th of a tugrik.

Mongol *n* **1** a member of any of the Mongoloid peoples of Mongolia, north China, and central Asia. **2** = MONGOLIAN. **3** (**mongol**) *offensive* a person who is affected with Down's syndrome. ⋙ **Mongol** *adj*.

Mongolian *n* **1** a native or inhabitant of Mongolia. **2** any of a group of Altaic languages of central Asia, Mongolia, and northern China. ⋙ **Mongolian** *adj*.

mongolism *n offensive* = DOWN'S SYNDROME.

Mongoloid[1] *adj* **1** of a major racial grouping including peoples of N and E Asia, Malaysians, Inuit, and some Native Americans. **2** (**mongoloid**) *offensive* affected with Down's syndrome.

Mongoloid[2] *n* a member of a Mongoloid people.

mongoose *n* (*pl* **mongooses**) a ferret-sized agile mammal of Asia, Africa, and S Europe with grey-brown fur, short legs, and a long furry tail.

mongrel *n* **1** a dog of unknown ancestry, resulting from interbreeding. **2** a cross between different types of person, animal, plant, or thing. ⋙ **mongrelism** *n*, **mongrelly** *adj*.

monicker *n* see MONIKER.

monied *adj* see MONEYED.

monies *n* pl of MONEY.

moniker *or* **monicker** *n informal* a name or nickname.

monism *n* a doctrine asserting that a complex entity is basically simple and undifferentiated, *esp* that mind and matter are not separate. ⋙ **monist** *n*, **monistic** *adj*.

monitor[1] *n* **1** a pupil appointed to help a teacher, e.g. by performing a specific task. **2** somebody or something that monitors, e.g. a device for observing a biological condition or function. **3a** a receiver used to view the picture being picked up by a television camera. **b** a screen displaying information from a computer. **4** a large lizard of tropical Asia, Africa, and Australia, closely related to the iguana. ⋙ **monitorial** *adj*, **monitorship** *n*.

monitor[2] *v* to observe, inspect, listen to, or record, *esp* for a special purpose over a period of time.

monitor lizard *n* = MONITOR[1] (4).

monk *n* a male member of a religious order who lives usu in a monastery under vows of poverty, chastity, etc. ⋙ **monkhood** *n*.

monkey[1] *n* **1** any of the smaller longer-tailed primates usu living in trees in tropical countries, *esp* as contrasted with the apes. **2** *informal* a mischievous child; a scamp. **3** *Brit, informal* the sum of £500. ✱ **have a monkey on one's back** *slang* to be addicted to or dependent on drugs. **make a monkey of** to make appear ridiculous. **not give a monkey's** *slang* not to care at all.

monkey[2] *v informal* **1** (*often* + about/around) to act in an absurd or mischievous manner. **2** to meddle or tamper with something.

monkey business *n informal* mischievous or underhand activity.

monkey nut *n Brit* a peanut.

monkey-puzzle *n* a S American evergreen conifer tree that has a network of intertwined branches covered with spirals of stiff sharp needlelike leaves.

monkey shines *pl n NAm* = MONKEY TRICKS.

monkey suit *n informal* a dinner suit.

monkey tricks *pl n informal* mischievous or underhand acts.

monkey wrench *n* a large spanner with one fixed and one adjustable jaw.

monkfish *n* (*pl* **monkfishes** *or* **monkfish**) **1** an edible fish with a flattened body with large winglike pectoral fins, that is closely related to the sharks and rays. **2** = ANGLERFISH.

monkshood *n* a very poisonous Eurasian plant with showy spikes of white or purplish flowers.

mono[1] *adj* **1** = MONOPHONIC. **2** = MONOCHROME[2].

mono[2] *n* **1** monophonic sound reproduction. **2** reproduction in monochrome.

mono- *comb. form* see MON-.

monoamine *n* an amine that has one carbon-containing chemical group attached to the nitrogen atom; *specif* one that functions as a neurotransmitter.

monobasic *adj* of an acid: having only one replaceable hydrogen atom in each molecule.

monochromatic *adj* **1** having one colour or hue. **2** of light or other radiation: of a single wavelength. ➤➤ **monochromatically** *adv.*

monochrome[1] *n* reproduction or execution in shades of one colour, black and white, or shades of grey. ➤➤ **monochromic** *adj.*

monochrome[2] *adj* **1** executed in shades of a single colour. **2** reproducing or transmitting visual images in black, white, and tones of grey; black-and-white. **3** lacking in variety or interest; dull.

monocle *n* a device to improve vision consisting of a single lens for one eye, held in position by the facial muscles. ➤➤ **monocled** *adj.*

monoclonal *adj* denoting or involving cells cloned from a single cell or individual.

monocoque *n* **1** a type of construction, e.g. of a fuselage, in which the outer skin carries all or nearly all the stresses. **2** a type of vehicle construction in which the body is integral with the chassis.

monocotyledon *n* a flowering plant with a single cotyledon and typically long narrow leaves with parallel veins, of a class that includes the grasses, orchids, and lilies. ➤➤ **monocotyledonous** *adj.*

monocular *adj* of, involving, or suitable for use with only one eye. ➤➤ **monocularly** *adv.*

monoculture *n* the cultivation of a single agricultural product to the exclusion of other uses of the land.

monocycle *n* = UNICYCLE.

monody *n* (*pl* **-ies**) **1** an ode sung by one voice, *esp* in a Greek tragedy. **2** a style of music that has one melody with little or no accompaniment. ➤➤ **monodic** *adj,* **monodist** *n.*

monoecious (*NAm* **monecious**) *adj* **1** having separate female and male flowers on the same plant: compare DIOECIOUS. **2** having male and female reproductive organs in the same organism; hermaphrodite.

monogamy *n* the practice of being married to one person, or having only one sexual partner, at a time. ➤➤ **monogamist** *n,* **monogamous** *adj,* **monogamously** *adv.*

monoglot *adj* speaking only one language. ➤➤ **monoglot** *n.*

monogram *n* a design usu formed of the interwoven initials of a name. ➤➤ **monogrammatic** *adj,* **monogrammed** *adj.*

monograph *n* **1** a treatise on a small area of learning. **2** a written account of a single thing. ➤➤ **monographic** *adj.*

monohull *n* a boat with a single hull, e.g. as opposed to a catamaran.

monokini *n* a one-piece swimming costume, *esp* a topless bikini.

monolingual *adj* knowing or using only one language.

monolith *n* **1** a single large block of stone, often in the form of an obelisk or column. **2** a massive structure. **3** a complex structure or organization in which individual parts function together as a single powerful whole.

monolithic *adj* **1** formed of a single large block of stone. **2** constituting a massive uniform whole.

monologue *n* **1a** a long speech by an actor alone or as if alone on stage. **b** a dramatic sketch performed by one actor. **2** a long usu tedious speech that monopolizes a conversation. ➤➤ **monologist** *n,* **monologuist** *n.*

monomania *n* obsessional preoccupation with or concentration on a single object or idea. ➤➤ **monomaniac** *n and adj,* **monomaniacal** *adj.*

monomer *n* any of the identical units that combine to form a polymer. ➤➤ **monomeric** *adj.*

monomial *n* a mathematical expression consisting of a single term, e.g. $3xy^2$. ➤➤ **monomial** *adj.*

monomorphic *adj* **1** of a species: showing little variation, e.g. in appearance, between members or sexes. **2** of an organism: showing little structural change during the life cycle.

monophonic *adj* denoting a system for sound recording or reproduction that uses only one channel between the source of the signal and its final point of use: compare STEREOPHONIC. ➤➤ **monophonically** *adv.*

monophthong *n* a simple vowel sound, e.g. /i/ in *bid.* ➤➤ **monophthongal** *adj.*

monoplane *n* an aeroplane with only one main pair of wings.

monopole *n* **1** a hypothetical single concentrated electric charge or magnetic pole, or a hypothetical particle having such a pole. **2** a radio aerial consisting of a single straight radiating element.

monopolise *v* see MONOPOLIZE.

monopolist *n* a person who has or favours a monopoly. ➤➤ **monopolistic** *adj.*

monopolize *or* **-ise** *v* **1** to assume exclusive possession, control, or use of. **2** to obtain or exploit a monopoly of. ➤➤ **monopolization** *n,* **monopolizer** *n.*

monopoly *n* (*pl* **-ies**) **1a** exclusive ownership or control, e.g. of a commodity or market. **b** a person or group having a monopoly. **c** something, *esp* a commodity, controlled by a monopoly. **2** exclusive possession, control, or use of something. **3** (**Monopoly**) *trademark* a board game in which players buy, sell, rent and mortgage properties with the aim of bankrupting their opponents.

monopsony *n* (*pl* **-ies**) a market consisting of one single buyer.

monorail *n* a single rail serving as a track for a wheeled vehicle.

monosaccharide *n* a sugar, e.g. glucose, that cannot be broken down to simpler sugars.

monoski *n* a wide ski attached to both feet of the skier. ➤➤ **monoskier** *n,* **monoskiing** *n.*

monosodium glutamate *n* a white chemical compound added to foods to intensify their natural flavour.

monosyllabic *adj* **1** consisting of one syllable or of monosyllables. **2** using or speaking only monosyllables. **3** pointedly brief in answering or commenting; terse. ➤➤ **monosyllabically** *adv.*

monosyllable *n* a word of one syllable, *esp* one used as a complete utterance.

monotheism *n* the doctrine or belief that there is only one God. ➤➤ **monotheist** *n,* **monotheistic** *adj,* **monotheistically** *adv.*

monotone *n* **1** a succession of speech sounds in one unvarying pitch. **2** a single unvaried musical note. **3** a tedious sameness or repetition. ➤➤ **monotone** *adj.*

monotonous *adj* **1** tediously uniform or repetitive. **2** uttered or sounded in one unvarying tone. ➤➤ **monotonously** *adv,* **monotonousness** *n,* **monotony** *n.*

monotreme *n* any of an order of egg-laying mammals including the platypus and echidna. ➤➤ **monotrematous** *adj.*

monounsaturated *adj* of a fat or oil: having only one double or triple chemical bond.

monoxide *n* an oxide containing one atom of oxygen.

monseigneur /monse'nyuh/ *n* (*pl* **messeigneurs** /mayse'nyuh/) (*often* **Monseigneur**) used as a title for a French dignitary, e.g. a prince or bishop.

monsieur /mə'syuh/ *n* (*pl* **messieurs** /mə'syuh, mə'syuhz/) (*often* **Monsieur**) used by or to a French-speaking man as a title equivalent to *Mr* or as a term of direct address equivalent to *sir*.

monsignor /mon'seenyə, monsee'nyaw/ *n* (*pl* **monsignori** /-'nyawree/) (*often* **Monsignor**) used as a title for certain high-ranking Roman Catholic priests, e.g. prelates and officers of the papal court.

monsoon *n* **1** a seasonal wind of S Asia blowing from the SW in summer and the NE in winter. **2** the season of the SW monsoon, marked by very heavy rains. ➤➤ **monsoonal** *adj.*

mons pubis /,monz 'pyoohbis/ *n* (*pl* **montes pubis** /,monteez/) a rounded raised mass of fatty tissue over the pubic bone.

monster *n* **1** an imaginary animal of incredible shape or form that is usu dangerous or horrifying. **2** an animal or plant of grotesquely abnormal form. **3a** something exceptionally large for its kind. **b** *informal* (*used before a noun*) exceptionally large. **4** a person of appalling ugliness, wickedness, or cruelty.

monstera *n* any of a genus of tropical American evergreen climbing plants that includes the Swiss cheese plant.

monstrance *n* in the Roman Catholic Church, a vessel in which the consecrated Host is exposed for veneration.

monstrosity *n* (*pl* **-ies**) **1** something deviating wildly from the normal; a monster or freak. **2** an excessively bad or shocking example; a hideous thing.

monstrous *adj* **1a** having the qualities or appearance of a monster. **b** extraordinarily large. **c** extraordinarily ugly or vicious. **2a** outrageously wrong or ridiculous. **b** shocking; appalling. ➤➤ **monstrously** *adv,* **monstrousness** *n.*

mons veneris /,monz 'venəris/ *n* (*pl* **montes veneris** /,monteez/) the mons pubis of a woman or girl.

montage /monh'tahzh/ *n* **1** a picture made by combining or overlapping several separate pictures. **2a** a method of film editing in which the chronological sequence of events is interrupted by juxtaposed or rapidly succeeding shots. **b** a film sequence using montage.

montane *adj* of or found in mountainous areas, *esp* the relatively moist cool slopes just below the tree line.

montbretia /mon(t)'breeshə/ *n* a widely grown hybrid plant of the iris family with bright yellow or orange flowers.

Montenegrin *n* **1** a native or inhabitant of Montenegro in the Balkans. **2** the Serbo-Croatian language as spoken in Montenegro. ➤➤ **Montenegrin** *adj.*

montes pubis *n* pl of MONS PUBIS.

Montessori *adj* of or being a system of teaching young children through play.

montes veneris *n* pl of MONS VENERIS.

month *n* **1a** any of the twelve named periods, between 28 and 31 days in duration, into which the year is divided. **b** a period of four weeks. **c** the interval between the same date in adjacent months. **2** (*in pl*) an indefinite, usu protracted, period of time. **3** one ninth of the typical duration of human pregnancy. ✱ **a month of Sundays** *informal* a very long period of time.

monthly[1] *adj* **1** payable or reckoned by the month. **2** done, occurring, or published every month.

monthly[2] *adv* every month, once a month, or by the month.

monthly[3] *n* (*pl* **-ies**) **1** a monthly periodical. **2** *dated, informal* (*in pl*) a menstrual period.

monument *n* **1** a memorial stone, sculpture, or structure erected to commemorate a person or event. **2** a structure or site of historical or archaeological importance. **3** a lasting evidence or reminder of somebody or something notable or influential.

monumental *adj* **1a** serving as a monument. **b** occurring or used on a monument. **2a** very great in degree. **b** imposing or outstanding. ➤➤ **monumentally** *adv.*

moo[1] *v* to make the deep characteristic noise of a cow.

moo[2] *n* a mooing sound.

mooch *v informal* **1** (+ around/about/along) to wander aimlessly or disconsolately. **2** *NAm* to sponge or cadge. ➤➤ **moocher** *n.*

mood[1] *n* **1a** a predominant emotion, feeling, or frame of mind. **b** the right frame of mind. **c** the evocation of mood in art, literature, music, etc. **2** a fit of often silent anger or bad temper.

mood[2] *n* a distinct form of a verb used to express whether the action or state it denotes is considered a fact, a possibility, or a wish, or whether a sentence is a statement, a command, or a question.

moody *adj* (**-ier, -iest**) **1** sullen or gloomy. **2** subject to sharply fluctuating moods; temperamental. ➤➤ **moodily** *adv,* **moodiness** *n.*

moola *or* **moolah** *n informal* money.

mooli *n* a type of radish with a large white root. Also called DAIKON.

moon[1] *n* **1a** (**the Moon**) the earth's natural satellite that shines by reflecting the sun's light. **b** a satellite of a planet. **2** *literary* a month. ✱ **over the moon** *informal* absolutely delighted. ➤➤ **moonless** *adj,* **moonlike** *adj.*

moon[2] *v* **1** *informal* (*often* + around/about) to move about listlessly. **2** *informal* (*often* + around/about) to spend time in idle gazing or daydreaming. **3** *informal* to expose one's buttocks to somebody as a joke or insult.

moon boot *n* a warm padded boot with a plastic or fabric outer cover.

mooncalf *n* (*pl* **mooncalves**) a fool or simpleton.

moon-faced *adj* having a very round face.

Moonie *n informal* a member of the Unification Church, a religious sect founded in 1954 by Sun Myung Moon.

moonlight[1] *n* the light of the moon.

moonlight[2] *v* (*past tense and past part.* **moonlighted**) *informal* to hold a second job, *esp* a secret or illegal one done at night, in addition to one's regular work. ➤➤ **moonlighter** *n.*

moonlight flit *n Brit, informal* an act of leaving a place in secret, *esp* at night, to avoid paying rent or other money that is owed.

moonscape *n* **1** the surface of the moon as seen or as depicted. **2** a similarly barren or devastated landscape.

moonshine *n* **1** empty talk; nonsense. **2** *chiefly NAm, informal* illegally distilled or smuggled spirits, *esp* whisky.

moon shot *n informal* the launching of a spacecraft to the moon or its vicinity.

moonstone *n* a transparent or milky-white translucent variety of feldspar with a pearly lustre, used as a gem.

moonstruck *adj* mentally unbalanced or romantically sentimental.

moony *adj* (**-ier, -iest**) *informal* inanely dreamy.

Moor *n* a member of the mixed Arab and Berber people that conquered Spain in the eighth cent. AD. ➤➤ **Moorish** *adj.*

moor[1] *n chiefly Brit* an expanse of open uncultivated peaty upland that is typically overgrown by heathers, grasses, etc.

moor[2] *v* **1** to secure (a boat or buoy) in position with cables, an anchor, etc. **2** to become secured in this way.

moorhen *n* a common blackish bird of the rail family that nests in reeds and bushes near fresh water.

mooring *n* **1** (*also in pl*) a place where or an object to which a ship, boat, etc can be made fast. **2** (*usu in pl*) a line, chain, etc used to moor a vessel.

moose *n* (*pl* **moose**) **1** a large N American deer that belongs to the same species as the European elk and has very large flattened antlers. **2** *NAm* the European elk.

moot[1] *n* **1** an early English local assembly held for debate, administration, and legal matters. **2** a mock court in which law students argue hypothetical cases.

moot[2] *v* to put (an idea) forward for discussion.

moot[3] *adj* open to question; debatable.

mop[1] *n* **1** an implement consisting of a head made of absorbent material fastened to a long handle and used *esp* for cleaning floors. **2** something that resembles a mop, *esp* a shock of untidy hair.

mop[2] *v* (**mopped, mopping**) **1** to clean or wipe with or as if with a mop. **2** (*often* + up) to soak up (water or other liquid) with or as if with a mop. ➤➤ **mopper** *n.*

mope *v* to give oneself up to brooding; to become listless or dejected. ➤➤ **moper** *n,* **mopy** *adj.*

moped *n* a low-powered motorcycle; *specif* one with an engine capacity of 50cc or under.

moppet *n informal* an endearing young child, *esp* a sweet little girl.

mop up *v* **1** to absorb or deal with (*esp* a remnant or remainder). **2** to eliminate (remaining resistance, enemy forces, etc) after a battle by killing or taking prisoners.

moquette *n* a carpet or upholstery fabric with a velvety pile.

MOR *abbr* middle-of-the-road (said of music).

mor *n* a humus usu found in forests that forms a distinct layer above the underlying soil.

moraine *n* an accumulation of earth and stones carried and deposited by a glacier. ➤➤ **morainal** *adj,* **morainic** *adj.*

moral[1] *adj* **1** relating to the principles of right and wrong in human behaviour; ethical. **2** expressing or teaching a conception of right behaviour. **3** conforming to a standard of right behaviour or to the dictates of one's conscience. ➤➤ **morally** *adv.*

moral[2] *n* **1** the moral significance of or practical lesson to be learned from a story, event, experience, etc. **2** (*in pl*) moral practices or teachings; standards of behaviour.

morale *n* the mental and emotional condition, e.g. of enthusiasm or loyalty, of an individual or group, *esp* at a particular time or with regard to the task at hand.

moralise *v* see MORALIZE.

moralist *n* **1** a person who is concerned with moral principles and problems. **2** *often derog* a person who is concerned with regulating the morals of others. ➤➤ **moralistic** *adj,* **moralistically** *adv.*

morality *n* (*pl* **-ies**) **1a** right behaviour or moral correctness. **b** degree of conformity to moral standards. **2** a system or sphere of moral values or principles.

morality play *n* a form of allegorical drama popular *esp* in the 15th and 16th cents, in which the characters personify moral or abstract qualities such as pride or youth.

moralize *or* **-ise** *v* **1** to talk about matters of morality, in particular the moral lapses of other people, *esp* tediously or sanctimoniously. **2** to interpret from a moral perspective, or draw a moral from. **3** to make moral or morally better. ➤➤ **moralization** *n,* **moralizer** *n.*

moral majority *n* **1** the reputedly major part of a society who uphold traditional moral values. **2** (**the Moral Majority**) a right-wing political and social movement in the USA grounded in Protestant fundamentalist beliefs.

moral philosophy *n* the branch of philosophy dealing with ethics.

moral support *n* encouragement, approval, or other assistance that has a psychological rather than a physical or tangible effect.

moral victory *n* a situation involving apparent defeat, but from which some form of ethical consolation can be taken.

morass *n* **1** a marsh or swamp. **2** a confused and disorganized situation.

moratorium *n* (*pl* **moratoriums** *or* **moratoria**) **1** (*often* + on) a suspension of activity, *esp* a temporary one agreed between all involved. **2** a legally authorized delay in the performance of an obligation or the payment of a debt.

Moravian *n* **1** a native or inhabitant of Moravia, the region forming the eastern part of the Czech Republic. **2** a member of the Moravian Church, a Protestant denomination derived from the Hussite movement for religious reform in Bohemia and Moravia. ➤➤ **Moravian** *adj.*

moray *n* any of numerous species of large often brightly coloured predatory eels that live in warm seas.

moray eel *n* = MORAY.

morbid *adj* **1** characterized by gloomy feelings, *esp* having an unnatural preoccupation with death. **2** showing an unhealthy interest in grisly and gruesome things, *esp* death and disease. **3** indicative of or relating to disease or things that are diseased. ➤➤ **morbidity** *n,* **morbidly** *adv,* **morbidness** *n.*

mordant[1] *adj* **1** caustic or sharply critical in thought, manner, or style. **2** acting as a mordant. ➤➤ **mordancy** *n,* **mordantly** *adv.*

mordant[2] *n* **1** a chemical that fixes a dye by combining with it to form an insoluble compound. **2** a corroding substance used in etching.

more[1] *adj* **1** greater in quality, quantity, or number. **2** additional; further.

more[2] *adv* **1a** as an additional amount. **b** again: *once more.* **2** to a greater degree, extent, or amount. **3** used with an adjective or adverb to form the comparative. ✱ **more and more** to a progressively increasing degree; with increasing frequency. **more often than not** at most times; usually. **more or less** **1** to some extent or degree; somewhat. **2** almost. **3** approximately. **more than** very: *more* *than grateful for your help.* **no more 1** nothing further. **2** never again. **3** dead.

more[3] *n* **1** a greater or additional quantity, amount, or part. **2** additional ones. ✱ **more of** nearer to being (something specified) than something else: *It's more of a sofa than a bed.*

moreish *or* **morish** *or* **more-ish** *adj Brit, informal* so tasty as to cause a desire for more.

morel *n* a large edible fungus with a light yellowish brown cap.

morello *n* (*pl* **-os**) a cultivated sour cherry with a dark-red skin, used *esp* in jams.

moreover *adv* in addition to what has been said.

mores *pl n* the customs or conventions of a particular group.

morganatic *adj* denoting a marriage between people of different rank in which the rank of the inferior partner remains unchanged and the children do not succeed to the titles or property of the parent of higher rank. ➤➤ **morganatically** *adv.*

morgue *n* **1a** a mortuary. **b** *informal* a gloomy, dispiriting, or deserted place. **2** a collection of reference works and files in a newspaper office, used *esp* in compiling information for obituaries.

moribund *adj* **1** dying. **2** having almost completely lost former vigour, vitality, or drive; nearing the end of existence. ➤➤ **moribundity** *n.*

morish *adj* see MOREISH.

Mormon *n* a member of the Church of Jesus Christ of Latter-Day Saints, founded in 1830 in the USA by Joseph Smith. ➤➤ **Mormon** *adj,* **Mormonism** *n.*

morn *n literary* morning.

mornay *or* **Mornay** *adj* denoting or served with a rich creamy cheese sauce.

morning *n* **1a** the time from midnight to noon or sunrise to noon. **b** the dawn. **2** the beginning or an early period, e.g. of time or life. ✱ **in the morning 1** during the morning. **2** tomorrow morning. **the morning after** the morning after a night of excessive drinking, etc, or the unpleasant aftereffects often felt then.

morning-after pill *n* an oral contraceptive that blocks implantation of a fertilized egg in the human womb and so prevents conception.

morning coat *n* a man's tailcoat worn on formal occasions during the day.

morning dress *n* men's dress for formal occasions during the day usu consisting of a black morning coat and striped trousers.

morning glory *n* a twining plant of the bindweed family with showy trumpet-shaped flowers.

mornings *adv chiefly NAm, informal* in the morning; on any morning.

morning sickness *n* nausea and vomiting occurring, *esp* in the morning, during the earlier months of a woman's pregnancy.

morning star *n* a bright planet, *esp* Venus, seen in the eastern sky before or at sunrise.

Moroccan *n* a native or inhabitant of Morocco. ➤➤ **Moroccan** *adj.*

morocco *n* (*pl* **-os**) a fine leather made from goatskin tanned with sumach.

moron *n informal* a very stupid person. ➤➤ **moronic** *adj,* **moronically** *adv,* **moronism** *n,* **moronity** *n.*

morose *adj* **1** marked by or expressive of gloom. **2** having a gloomy disposition. ➤➤ **morosely** *adv,* **moroseness** *n.*

morph *v* in cinematography, to change by MORPHING.

-morph *comb. form* forming nouns, denoting: a person or thing having a specified form: *endomorph.* ➤➤ **-morphic** *comb. form,* **-morphous** *comb. form,* **-morphy** *comb. form.*

morpheme *n* the smallest indivisible unit of language that has a meaning, e.g. 'cat' or the various elements of a word such as 'lovingly', which is composed of three morphemes, 'love', '-ing', and '-ly'. ➤➤ **morphemic** *adj,* **morphemically** *adv.*

morphia *n dated* morphine.

-morphic *comb. form* see -MORPH.

morphine *n* the principal alkaloid of opium that is an addictive narcotic drug and is medicinally used as a powerful painkiller. ➤➤ **morphinic** *adj,* **morphinism** *n.*

morphing *n* in cinematography, the smooth and gradual changing of one image into another by means of a computer program.

morphology *n* **1** the form and structure of animals and plants, or the scientific study concerned with this. **2** the study and description of the forms of words. ➤➤ **morphologic** *adj,* **morphological** *adj,* **morphologically** *adv,* **morphologist** *n.*

-morphous *comb. form* see -MORPH.

-morphy *comb. form* see -MORPH.

morris dance *n* any of several traditional English dances that are performed by groups of people, usu men, wearing costumes to which small bells are attached and carrying handkerchiefs or small sticks. ➤➤ **morris dancer** *n,* **morris dancing** *n,* **morris man** *n.*

morrow *n* (*usu* **the morrow**) *archaic or literary* the next day.

Morse *n* a signalling code in which letters of the alphabet are represented by combinations of dots and dashes, which are transmitted as short and long sounds or flashes of light.

Morse code *n* = MORSE.

morsel *n* **1** a small piece of food. **2** a small quantity; a scrap.

mortadella *n* a large smooth-textured steamed Italian sausage made from spiced pork or beef, usu served cold.

mortal[1] *adj* **1a** not living for ever; subject to death. **b** of human existence. **2** causing death; fatal. **3** marked by relentless hostility: *mortal enemy.* **4** very great, intense, or severe: *mortal terror.* **5** *informal* **a** humanly conceivable: *every mortal thing.* **b** very tedious and prolonged. ➤➤ **mortally** *adv.*

mortal[2] *n* a human being.

mortality *n* (*pl* **-ies**) **1** the state of being mortal. **2** the death of large numbers of people, animals, etc. **3** the human race. **4a** the number of deaths in a given time or place. **b** the ratio of deaths in a given time to population.

mortal sin *n* in Christian theology, a sin, e.g. murder, of such gravity that it totally debars the soul from divine grace: compare VENIAL SIN. ➤➤ **mortal sinner** *n.*

mortar[1] *n* **1** a bowl-shaped vessel in which substances are pounded or ground with a pestle. **2** a light usu muzzle-loading artillery gun, used by infantry for firing shells at high angles over short distances.

mortar[2] *n* a mixture of cement, lime, gypsum plaster, etc with sand and water, used to join bricks, stones, etc or for plastering.

mortar[3] *v* to plaster, fix, or join with mortar.

mortarboard *n* **1** a square board with a handle underneath, used by bricklayers for holding mortar; = HAWK[1] (2). **2** an academic cap consisting of a close-fitting crown with a stiff flat square attached on top.

mortgage[1] *n* **1** an agreement by which a person borrows money pledging a piece of real property, usu a house that he or she is buying, as security. **2a** the loan received through such an agreement. **b** the sum paid, usu monthly, towards repayment of the loan.

mortgage[2] *v* **1** to transfer the ownership of (property) by a mortgage. **2** to make (*esp* oneself) subject to a claim or obligation. ➤➤ **mortgageable** *adj.*

mortgagee *n* the lender in a mortgage, usu a bank or building society.

mortgagor *or* **mortgager** *n* the borrower in a mortgage, usu a person buying a house.

mortice[1] *n* see MORTISE[1].

mortice[2] *v* see MORTISE[2].

mortician *n chiefly NAm* an undertaker.

mortify *v* (**-ies, -ied**) **1** to subject to feelings of shame or acute embarrassment. **2** to subdue (e.g. bodily needs and desires), *esp* by abstinence or self-inflicted suffering. **3** of flesh: to become necrotic or gangrenous. ➤➤ **mortification** *n,* **mortifying** *adj,* **mortifyingly** *adv.*

mortise[1] *or* **mortice** *n* a usu rectangular cavity cut into a piece of material, e.g. wood, to receive a protrusion, *esp* a tenon, of another piece.

mortise[2] *or* **mortice** *v* **1** to join or fasten securely, *specif* by a mortise and tenon joint. **2** to cut or make a mortise in.

mortise lock *n* a lock that is designed to be fitted into a mortise in the edge of a door.

mortuary[1] *n* (*pl* **-ies**) a room or building in which dead bodies are kept before burial or cremation.

mortuary[2] *adj* of death or the burial of the dead.

morwong *n* (*pl* **morwongs** *or* **morwong**) a large brightly coloured edible fish with a tapering body, thick lips, and a long dorsal fin, found around the coasts of Australasia.

Mosaic *adj* of Moses, the biblical prophet and lawgiver.

mosaic *n* **1** decorative work made from small pieces of different coloured material, e.g. glass or stone, inlaid to form pictures or patterns. **2** a picture or pattern produced from this. ➤➤ **mosaicist** *n.*

Moselle *or* **Mosel** *n* a typically light-bodied white table wine made in the valley of the Moselle.

Moses basket *n* a baby's wicker cot, usu with handles for portability.

mosey[1] *v* (**-eys, -eyed**) *informal* (*usu* + along/around/off) to go in a leisurely, unhurried, or aimless way; to wander or saunter.

mosey[2] *n informal* a casual and unhurried walk.

mosh *v Brit, informal* to dance in an energetic bouncing way, often deliberately colliding with other dancers, usu to heavy metal, thrash, or punk music. ➤➤ **mosher** *n.*

Moslem *n* see MUSLIM.

mosque *n* a building used for public worship by Muslims.

mosquito *n* (*pl* **-oes** *or* **-os**) any of various species of small two-winged flies, the females of which suck the blood of animals and humans, often transmitting diseases such as malaria and yellow fever to them.

mosquito net *n* a net or screen hung across a door or window or round a bed to keep out mosquitoes.

moss *n* **1a** any of a phylum of primitive plants with small leafy stems bearing sex organs at the tip. **b** many of these plants growing together and covering a surface. **2** *chiefly Scot* a peat bog. ➤➤ **mossiness** *n,* **mosslike** *adj,* **mossy** *adj.*

moss agate *n* an agate containing brown, black, or green mosslike markings.

mossie *or* **mozzie** *n chiefly Aus, informal* = MOSQUITO.

moss stitch *n* a knitting stitch made up of alternate plain and purl stitches.

most[1] *adj* **1** the majority of. **2** greatest in quantity or extent. ✱ **for the most part** in most cases or respects; mainly.

most[2] *adv* **1** (*often* **the most**) to the greatest degree or extent. **2** used with an adjective or adverb to form the superlative. **3** very.

most[3] *n* the greatest quantity, number, or amount. ✱ **at most/at the most** as a maximum limit. **make the most of** to use (something) or present (oneself) to the best advantage or with the best effect.

most[4] *adv archaic, dialect, or NAm* almost.

-most *suffix* forming adjectives, with the meanings: **1** most; to the highest possible degree: *innermost; utmost.* **2** nearest to (a specified place or part): *rearmost; topmost.*

Most Honourable *adj* a title given to marquesses, marchionesses, members of the Privy Council, and holders of the Order of the Bath.

mostly *adv* **1** for the greatest part; mainly. **2** in most cases; usually.

Most Reverend *adj* a title given to Anglican archbishops and Irish Roman Catholic bishops.

MOT[1] *or* **MoT** *n* **1** in the UK, a compulsory annual roadworthiness test for motor vehicles older than a certain age. **2** a certificate to show that a vehicle has passed such a test.

MOT[2] *or* **MoT** *v* (**MOTs, MOTing, MOTed** *or* **MOT'd**) **1** (*usu in passive*) to put (a vehicle) through an MOT test. **2** to carry out an MOT test on (a vehicle).

mote *n* a small particle, *esp* a particle of dust suspended in the air.

motel *n* a roadside hotel, usu with the rooms arranged around a parking area, catering *esp* for passing motorists.

motet *n* a choral composition on a sacred text.

moth *n* **1** any of numerous species of flying insects similar to butterflies. **2** = CLOTHES MOTH.

mothball[1] *n* a ball of naphthalene or, formerly, camphor, used to keep moths from clothing, linen, etc. ✱ **in/into mothballs 1** in or into a state of temporary suspension; on hold. **2** in or into a state of indefinitely long protective storage.

mothball[2] *v* **1** to protect (clothes) with mothballs. **2** to take out of use, but preserve for possible reuse later. **3** to set aside or postpone indefinitely.

moth-eaten *adj* **1** damaged by moths or moth larvae. **2a** very worn-out or shabby in appearance. **b** antiquated; outmoded.

mother[1] *n* **1a** a female parent of a child or offspring. **b** a female acting as the parent of a child or offspring. **2a** a woman considered as the originator, inventor, or founder of something. **b** a source, origin, or producer of something. **3** (*often used as a term of address*) a mother superior. **4** *informal, sometimes considered offensive* a very big, good, bad, or otherwise notable or extreme example of something. **5** *taboo* = MOTHERFUCKER. ➤➤ **motherhood** *n,* **motherless** *adj,* **motherlessness** *n.*

mother[2] *v often derog* to care for or protect (a person, animal, etc) like a mother, sometimes to an excessive or unnecessary degree. ⋙ **mothering** *n.*

motherboard *n* a printed circuit board that contains the main electronic components of a computer.

mother country *n* **1** one's native country. **2** a country from which settlers or colonists emigrate.

motherfucker *n taboo* **1** a contemptible or offensive person or thing. **2** an exceptional, formidable, or impressive person or thing. ⋙ **motherfucking** *adj.*

Mothering Sunday *n Brit, dated* = MOTHER'S DAY.

mother-in-law *n* (*pl* **mothers-in-law**) the mother of one's husband or wife.

motherland *n* one's native country.

mother lode *n* the major vein of ore, e.g. in an area.

motherly *adj* **1** characteristic of a mother. **2** showing the characteristics associated with a mother, e.g. care and kindness. ⋙ **motherliness** *n.*

mother-of-pearl *n* the hard pearly iridescent substance forming the inner layer of the shells of certain molluscs, *esp* abalones and oysters. Also called NACRE.

mother's boy *n* a boy or man regarded as depending too much on his mother.

Mother's Day *n* a day set aside for the honouring of mothers, the second Sunday in May in the USA, Canada, and Australia, and the fourth Sunday of Lent in Britain. Also called MOTHERING SUNDAY.

mother ship *n* **1** a spaceship which acts as a service and supply base for one or more smaller craft. **2** a ship that provides supplies and facilities for a number of smaller craft.

mother superior *or* **Mother Superior** *n* the head of a religious community of women.

mother tongue *n* **1** one's native language. **2** a language from which another language derives.

motif *n* **1** a recurring element forming a theme in a work of art, music, or literature. **2a** a repeated design or colour. **b** a single decoration, such as a logo, e.g. on an item of clothing.

motile *adj* of a cell, sperm, protozoan, etc: exhibiting or capable of movement. ⋙ **motility** *n.*

motion[1] *n* **1a** the act or an instance of changing position; a movement. **b** the way in which somebody or something moves. **c** the ability to move. **2** a gesture. **3** a moving part or mechanism. **4** a proposal for action, *esp* a formal proposal made in a deliberative assembly. **5a** (*also in pl*) an evacuation of the bowels. **b** the matter evacuated from the bowels at one time; a stool. ✱ **go through the motions** to carry out an activity half-heartedly or mechanically. **set in motion** to get (something) started. ⋙ **motional** *adj,* **motionless** *adj,* **motionlessly** *adv,* **motionlessness** *n.*

motion[2] *v* to direct by a gesture.

motion picture *n chiefly NAm* a cinema film.

motivate *v* to provide with a motive or incentive to do something. ⋙ **motivator** *n.*

motivation *n* **1** the act or an instance of motivating or being motivated. **2** a motivating force or incentive that directs one's action towards achieving a desired goal; a motive. **3** enthusiasm or drive. ⋙ **motivational** *adj,* **motivationally** *adv.*

motive[1] *n* **1** a need, desire, etc that causes somebody to act. **2** = MOTIF. ⋙ **motiveless** *adj,* **motivelessly** *adv,* **motivelessness** *n.*

motive[2] *adj* **1** moving or tending to move to action; motivating. **2** of or causing motion.

motive power *n* **1** something such as water or steam whose energy is used to impart motion to machinery. **2** the energy itself.

mot juste /ˌmoh 'zhoohst/ *n* (*pl* **mots justes**) the exactly right or most appropriate word or phrasing.

motley[1] *adj* (**-ier, -iest**) **1** composed of varied, often disreputable or unsightly, elements. **2** multicoloured.

motley[2] *n* **1a** a woollen fabric of mixed colours. **b** the characteristic clothing of a jester, made of motley. **2** a haphazard mixture of often incompatible elements.

motocross *n* the sport of racing motorcycles across country on a rugged usu hilly course.

motor[1] *n* **1** any of various machines or devices that transform energy into motion, e.g. an internal-combustion engine. **2** *chiefly Brit* **a** *informal* a motor vehicle, *esp* a car. **b** for motor vehicles. **3a** somebody or something that imparts motion. **b** (*used before a noun*) causing or imparting motion. **c** (*used before a noun*) of a nerve: conveying impulses from the brain, spinal cord, or a nerve centre to a muscle, gland, etc. **d** (*used before a noun*) of or involving muscles or muscular movement. ⋙ **motorless** *adj.*

motor[2] *v* **1** to travel by car. **2** *informal* to make rapid progress. ⋙ **motorable** *adj.*

motor bike *n informal* a motorcycle.

motorboat *or* **motor boat** *n* a usu small boat propelled by a motor.

motorcade *n* a procession of motor vehicles.

motor car *n Brit* = CAR (1).

motorcycle[1] *n* a two-wheeled motor vehicle that can carry one or two people astride the engine.

motorcycle[2] *v* to travel by motorcycle. ⋙ **motorcyclist** *n.*

motorise *v* see MOTORIZE.

motorist *n* somebody who drives a car.

motorize *or* **-ise** *v* **1** to equip (e.g. a vehicle) with a motor. **2** to provide (e.g. troops) with motor-driven equipment, e.g. for transport. ⋙ **motorization** *n.*

motorman *n* (*pl* **motormen**) a driver of a motor-driven vehicle, e.g. a bus or underground train.

motormouth *n informal* a brashly talkative person.

motor neuron *n* a nerve cell in a pathway conveying impulses from the brain or spinal cord to a muscle or gland.

motor neuron disease *n* a degenerative disease affecting the motor neurons that causes wasting of the muscles.

motor racing *n* the sport of racing in cars that are specially designed for speed.

motor scooter *n* a light motorcycle with the driver's seat placed in front rather than on top of the enclosed engine.

motor vehicle *n* a road vehicle powered by a motor, *esp* an internal-combustion engine.

motorway *n Brit* a major road, designed for high-speed traffic, that has separate carriageways each with several lanes.

motte *n* a specially constructed mound of earth on which a fortified wooden tower was built.

mottle[1] *n* **1** an irregular pattern of spots or blotches on a surface. **2** a coloured spot or blotch.

mottle[2] *v* to mark with mottles. ⋙ **mottled** *adj.*

motto *n* (*pl* **-oes** *or* **-os**) **1** a short expression of a guiding principle; a maxim. **2** a usu humorous or sentimental saying, *esp* found in party crackers.

moue *n* a little grimace; a pout.

mouflon *or* **moufflon** *n* (*pl* **mouflons** *or* **mouflon**) a small wild reddish brown sheep of the mountains of Corsica and Sardinia.

mould[1] (*NAm* **mold**) *n* **1** a cavity, dish, or form in which a substance, e.g. a jelly or a metal casting, is shaped. **2** something formed in a mould; a moulding. **3** a fixed pattern or form. **4** distinctive character or type. ✱ **break the mould 1** to bring about fundamental changes in an established system. **2** to produce somebody or something unique.

mould[2] (*NAm* **mold**) *v* **1** to give shape to. **2** to form in a mould. **3** to exert a steady formative influence on (a person, opinions, etc). **4** to fit closely to the contours of (a person's body, etc). ➤➤ **mouldable** *adj,* **moulder** *n.*

mould[3] (*NAm* **mold**) *n* **1** an often woolly growth on the surface of damp or decaying organic matter. **2** the fungus that produces this.

mould[4] (*NAm* **mold**) *n* crumbling soft soil suited to plant growth, *esp* soil rich in humus.

mouldboard *n* a curved plate on a ploughshare for lifting and turning the soil.

moulder (*NAm* **molder**) *v* (*often* + away) to crumble into dust or decayed fragments.

moulding (*NAm* **molding**) *n* a decorative band or strip used for ornamentation or finishing, e.g. on a cornice.

mouldy (*NAm* **moldy**) *adj* (**-ier, -iest**) **1** covered with mould. **2** old and mouldering; fusty, crumbling. **3** *informal* **a** miserable or nasty. **b** stingy. **c** bad.

moules marinière /,mool marin'yiə/ *pl n* (*also* **moules à la marinière**) mussels cooked in a white wine sauce and served in their shells.

moult[1] (*NAm* **molt**) *v* of birds, animals, etc: to shed (hair, feathers, shell, horns, or an outer layer) periodically.

moult[2] (*NAm* **molt**) *n* an instance or the process or time of moulting.

mound[1] *n* **1a** a heap or pile. **b** a large quantity. **2** a small hill. **3** an artificial bank or hill of earth or stone, e.g. for defence or as a place of burial. **4** in baseball, the slightly elevated ground on which a pitcher stands to deliver the ball.

mound[2] *v* to form into a mound.

mount[1] *v* **1a** to go up or climb. **b** to get up onto something above ground level, *esp* to seat oneself on a horse, etc to ride it. **2** (*often* + up) to increase in amount or degree. **3a** to attach to a support. **b** to fix to a backing, *esp* for display. **4a** to initiate and carry out (e.g. an attack, a campaign). **b** to organize and present (e.g. a show).

mount[2] *n* **1** something on which something is mounted for display or use, e.g. the backing material for a picture, a jewellery setting, or a slide for a specimen in microscopy. **2** a horse for riding.

mount[3] *n* **1** *literary* a hill. **2** used in hill or mountain names.

mountain *n* **1** a landmass that projects conspicuously above its surroundings and is higher than a hill. **2a** (*also in pl*) a vast amount or quantity. **b** a supply, *esp* of a specified usu agricultural commodity, in excess of demand.

mountain ash *n* a tree of the rose family usu with small red fruits; ROWAN.

mountain bike *n* a wide-tyred heavy-duty bicycle with a large number of gears, orig designed to cope with rugged terrain. ➤➤ **mountain biker** *n,* **mountain biking** *n.*

mountaineer *n* a person who climbs mountains.

mountaineering *n* the pastime or technique of climbing mountains and rock faces.

mountain goat *n* any goat or goatlike animal that inhabits mountainous regions, noted proverbially for its agility and sure-footedness.

mountain lion *n* = PUMA.

mountainous *adj* **1** of a region: containing many mountains. **2** resembling a mountain; huge. ➤➤ **mountainously** *adv.*

mountebank *n* **1** a swindler or charlatan. **2** formerly, somebody who sold quack medicines to the public, e.g. from a bench or stall. ➤➤ **mountebankery** *n.*

mounted *adj* **1a** riding on a horse, etc. **b** operating on horseback. **2** of a photograph, stamp, etc: on a mounting.

Mountie *or* **Mounty** *n* (*pl* **-ies**) *informal* a member of the Royal Canadian Mounted Police.

mounting *n* = MOUNT[2].

Mounty *n* see MOUNTIE.

mourn *v* to feel or express grief or sorrow, *esp* for a death. ➤➤ **mourner** *n.*

mournful *adj* **1** gloomy or sad. **2** expressing, causing, or filled with sorrow. ➤➤ **mournfully** *adv,* **mournfulness** *n.*

mourning *n* **1** the act or state of somebody who is mourning. **2a** an outward sign, e.g. black clothes or a black armband, of grief for a person's death. **b** a period of time during which signs of grief are shown.

mousaka *n* see MOUSSAKA.

mouse[1] *n* (*pl* **mice**) **1** a small rodent with a pointed snout, grey to brown fur, and a long slender almost hairless tail. **2** (*pl also* **mouses**) in computing, a small movable box connected to a computer, that, when moved across a desk or mat, causes a cursor to move across a VDU screen, and has click buttons enabling the operator to execute commands or change data. **3** a timid person; *esp* a shy or very quiet girl or woman. **4** *informal* = BLACK EYE.

mouse[2] *v* to hunt for or catch mice. ➤➤ **mouser** *n.*

mousetrap *n* **1** a trap for mice. **2** *Brit, informal* low-quality cheese.

mousey *adj* see MOUSY.

moussaka *or* **mousaka** *n* a Greek dish consisting of layers of minced lamb or other meat, aubergine, tomato, and cheese with a cheese or savoury custard topping.

mousse[1] *n* **1** a light sweet or savoury cold dish usu containing cream, gelatin, and whipped egg whites. **2** a frothy cosmetic preparation applied to the hair to hold it in a desired style.

mousse[2] *v* to put mousse on (hair) in order to style.

mousseline /'moohsleen/ *n* **1** a fine sheer fabric (e.g. of rayon) that resembles muslin. **2** a frothy sauce, e.g. a hollandaise sauce that has whipped cream or beaten eggs added to it.

moustache (*NAm* **mustache**) *n* the hair growing on somebody's upper lip. ➤➤ **moustached** *adj.*

mousy *or* **mousey** *adj* (**-ier, -iest**) **1** of or resembling a mouse, e.g.: **a** quiet or stealthy. **b** timid; lacking personality. **2** of hair: light greyish brown. ➤➤ **mousily** *adv,* **mousiness** *n.*

mouth[1] *n* (*pl* **mouths**) **1a** the opening through which food passes into a person's or animal's body and through which speech, etc flows. **b** the cavity in the head bounded externally by the lips and enclosing the tongue, gums, and teeth. **2 a** the place where a river enters a sea, lake, etc. **b** the opening of a cave, volcano, harbour, etc. **c** the opening of a container. **3** an individual requiring food. **4** *informal* **a** a tendency to talk too much, *esp* boastfully; boastful talk, *esp* if not followed by action. **b** impertinent language. ✱ **down in the**

mouth/at mouth sad or dejected. **keep one's mouth shut** to remain silent. ⋙ **mouthed** *adj,* **mouthless** *adj.*

mouth² *v* **1** to say, *esp* insincerely or pompously. **2** to form (words) soundlessly with the lips. **3** to take into the mouth, or move around in the mouth.

mouthbrooder *n* a fish that protects its eggs or young by carrying them inside its mouth.

mouthful *n* (*pl* **mouthfuls**) **1** the amount, e.g. of food, put into the mouth at one time. **2a** a word or phrase that is very long or difficult to pronounce. **b** *Brit, informal* a rude or angry answer or remark.

mouth off *v informal* **1** to express opinions or complaints loudly and forcefully. **2** to talk impertinently or abusively.

mouth organ *n* a harmonica.

mouthpart *n* a structure or appendage near or forming part of the mouth of an insect or other arthropod.

mouthpiece *n* **1** a part of e.g. a musical instrument or a telephone that goes in or is put next to the mouth. **2** somebody or something that expresses or interprets another's views.

mouth-to-mouth *adj* denoting a method of artificial respiration in which the rescuer blows air directly into the victim's lungs by placing his or her mouth over the victim's mouth.

mouthwash *n* a liquid medical preparation for cleansing and freshening the mouth and breath.

mouth-watering *adj* **1** stimulating or appealing to the appetite; appetizing. **2** extremely attractive. ⋙ **mouth-wateringly** *adv.*

mouthy *adj* (**-ier, -iest**) inclined to talk too much, *esp* impudently or boastfully.

movable¹ *or* **moveable** *adj* **1** capable of being moved. **2** of a church festival, etc: changing date from year to year. **3** *esp* in law, denoting personal property that can be moved, e.g. the furniture in a house that has been sold. ⋙ **movability** *n,* **movableness** *n,* **movably** *adv.*

movable² *or* **moveable** *n* (*usu in pl*) *esp* in law, an item of movable personal property, as distinguished from buildings, land, etc.

move¹ *v* **1** to go or cause to go or progress in a particular direction. **2** to change or cause to change position or shape. **3a** to change one's residence or place of work. **b** to take (one's possessions) from one place of residence to another. **4** to change to a new activity, topic, etc. **5** to take action or prompt (somebody) to take action. **6** to spend one's time in a particular social environment: *to move in fashionable circles.* **7** to affect (somebody) emotionally: *They were moved to tears.* **8** to propose formally for discussion or consideration. **9** of the bowels: to discharge faeces. ⋙ **mover** *n.*

move² *n* **1** a movement; a change of position, posture, etc. **2** a step taken so as to gain an objective; a manoeuvre. **3** a change of residence or location. **4a** the act or an instance of moving a piece, e.g. in chess. **b** the turn of a player to move. ✱ **get a move on** to hurry up. **make a move on** to make advances towards (somebody), *esp* of a sexual nature. **on the move 1** moving about from place to place. **2** moving ahead or making progress. **3** very busy.

moveable¹ *adj* see MOVABLE¹.

moveable² *n* see MOVABLE².

move in *v* to take up residence.

movement *n* **1a** the act or process of moving, *esp* a change of place, position, or posture. **b** a particular instance or manner of moving. **c** (*in pl*) the activities of a person, *esp* during a specified time. **2** an organized effort to achieve a goal or the body of people involved in it. **3** a trend, *esp* in prices. **4** the moving parts of a mechanism that transmit motion. **5** in music, a unit or division forming a separate part of an extended musical composition. **6a** an act of emptying the bowels. **b** the faeces evacuated.

move on *v* to change to a new location, job, etc.

move out *v* to leave a residence or place of work.

move over *v* **1** to move along a seat to make more room. **2** (*often* + to) to change allegiance or loyalty.

movers and shakers *pl n* people of power and influence, who can introduce or back new developments.

move up *v* **1** to move along a seat to make more room. **2** to be promoted.

movie *n* **1** a cinema film. **2** (**the movies**) **a** cinema films collectively. **b** the cinema industry.

moving *adj* **1** marked by or capable of movement. **2** evoking a deep emotional response. ⋙ **movingly** *adv.*

mow *v* (*past tense* **mowed,** *past part.* **mowed** *or* **mown**) **1** to cut down (a crop, *esp* hay or corn); to cut (grass). **2** to cut down the grass, etc of (e.g. a field). ⋙ **mower** *n,* **mowings** *pl n.*

mow down *v* to kill or knock down (somebody or something), *esp* in great numbers or mercilessly.

mown *v* past part. of MOW.

moxa *n* a downy material obtained from the dried leaves of a plant, e.g. wormwood, used in MOXIBUSTION.

moxibustion *n* the burning of moxa on or near the skin in Eastern medicine to produce surface irritation and relieve deeper-seated pain.

Mozambican *n* a native or inhabitant of Mozambique in SE Africa. ⋙ **Mozambican** *adj.*

Mozartian *or* **Mozartean** *adj* relating to Wolfgang Amadeus Mozart d.1791, Austrian composer, or characteristic of his music.

mozzarella *n* a moist white unsalted unripened curd cheese.

mozzie *n* see MOSSIE.

MP *abbr* **1** Member of Parliament. **2** Military Police. **3** Military Policeman or -woman.

mpg *abbr* miles per gallon.

mph *abbr* miles per hour.

MPhil *abbr* Master of Philosophy.

MPV *abbr* multipurpose vehicle.

Mr *n* (*pl* **Messrs**) **1** used as a conventional title of courtesy before a man's surname. **2** used in direct address before a man's title of office.

MRI *abbr* magnetic resonance imaging.

MRP *abbr* manufacturer's recommended price.

Mrs *n* (*pl* **Mesdames**) **1** used as a conventional title of courtesy before a married woman's surname. **2** (*often* **the/my Mrs**) *informal* a person's wife.

MS *abbr* **1** manuscript. **2** Mississippi (US postal abbreviation). **3** multiple sclerosis.

Ms *n* used instead of Mrs or Miss, *esp* when the woman's marital status is unknown or irrelevant.

ms *abbr* **1** millisecond. **2** manuscript.

MSc *abbr* Master of Science.

MS-DOS *abbr trademark* Microsoft disk operating system.

Msgr *abbr* **1** Monseigneur. **2** Monsignor.

MSP *abbr* Member of the Scottish Parliament.

MSS *or* **mss** *abbr* manuscripts.

MT *abbr* Montana (US postal abbreviation).

Mt¹ *abbr* Mount.

Mt² *abbr* the chemical symbol for meitnerium.

MTB *abbr* **1** motor torpedo boat. **2** mountain bike.

mu *n* the twelfth letter of the Greek alphabet (M, μ), equivalent to roman m.

much[1] *adj* (**more, most**) **1** *chiefly formal* great in quantity or extent. **2** used with a negative word to suggest or emphasize smallness of quantity or extent: *not much money.* **3** used in questions about quantity or extent: *How much milk is there?*

much[2] *adv* **1a** to a great degree or extent; considerably: *much happier.* **b** by far: *much the fatter of the two.* **c** frequently, often: *a much married man.* **2** used with a negative word to suggest or emphasize smallness of degree or extent. **3** used in questions about degree or extent. ✱ **much as 1** (*also* **as much as**) however much; even though. **2** to a similar extent or degree, or in a similar way. **much less** and certainly not.

much[3] *n* **1** a great quantity, amount, or part: *So little done, so much to do* — Cecil Rhodes. **2** used with a negative word to suggest or emphasize smallness of amount or extent: *He's not much of a help.* **3** used to ask questions about amount or extent. ✱ **a bit much** *informal* rather excessive or unreasonable. **as much 1** the same quantity. **2** that; so. **make much of** to treat as of great importance or significance. **not up to much** not very good. **too much** terrible; awful. **too much for 1** more than a match for. **2** beyond the endurance of.

muchness ✱ **much of a muchness** *Brit* of two or more things, etc: very similar; having little to differentiate them in quality, etc.

mucilage *n* **1** a thick gelatinous substance produced by plants and obtained *esp* from seaweeds, used in pharmaceutical products. **2** a thick sticky solution, e.g. of a gum, used *esp* as an adhesive. ➤➤ **mucilaginous** *adj.*

muck *n* **1** soft moist manure. **2** dirt or filth, *esp* if moist or slimy. **3** mire or mud. **4** *informal* coarse or disgusting speech or writing. ➤➤ **muckily** *adv,* **muckiness** *n,* **mucky** *adj.*

muck about *v chiefly Brit, informal* **1** to engage in aimless or silly activity; to waste time. **2** (+ with) to interfere with or spoil. **3** *chiefly Brit, informal* to treat discourteously or inconsiderately.

muck around *v* = MUCK ABOUT.

mucker *n Brit, informal* a friend or pal.

muck in *v Brit, informal* **1** to share or join in a task. **2** to share sleeping accommodation.

muckle *adj and n* = MICKLE[1], MICKLE[2].

muck out *v* to remove manure or filth, *esp* from an animal's quarters.

muckrake *v* to search out and publicly expose real or apparent misconduct of prominent individuals. ➤➤ **muckraker** *n,* **muckraking** *n.*

muck up *v informal* **1** to bungle or spoil. **2** *chiefly Brit* to make dirty or messy.

mucosa *n* (*pl* **mucosae** *or* **mucosas**) = MUCOUS MEMBRANE. ➤➤ **mucosal** *adj.*

mucous *adj* **1** of mucus. **2** secreting or covered with mucus.

mucous membrane *n* a membrane, rich in glands secreting mucus, that lines body passages and cavities with openings to the exterior.

mucus *n* a thick slippery secretion produced by mucous membranes, e.g. in the nose, which it moistens and protects.

mud *n* **1** soft wet earth or any sticky mixture of a solid and a liquid resembling this. **2** abusive or malicious remarks or charges. ✱ **here's mud in your eye** an informal and humorous drinking toast. **sling/throw mud at** to make abusive or malicious remarks about. **somebody's name is mud** *informal* the person concerned is in disgrace or very unpopular.

mudbank *n* a bank of mud in a river or the sea.

mudbath *n* **1** a bath in heated mud, e.g. at a spa, for the relief of rheumatism, arthritis, etc. **2** a place with a lot of mud.

muddle[1] *v* **1** to confuse. **2** (*often* + up) to confuse (two or more people or things) in one's mind; to mix up. **3** (*often* + up) to get (things) out of the required arrangement and into a confused mess, etc. **4** (+ along/on) to proceed or get along in a confused aimless way. ➤➤ **muddled** *adj,* **muddler** *n,* **muddling** *n and adj,* **muddlingly** *adv,* **muddly** *adj.*

muddle[2] *n* **1** a state of confusion. **2** a confused mess. **3** a mix-up or mistake.

muddleheaded *adj* **1** mentally confused. **2** inept or bungling. ➤➤ **muddleheadedly** *adv,* **muddleheadedness** *n.*

muddle through *v* to succeed in spite of incompetence or lack of understanding or planning.

muddy[1] *adj* (**-ier, -iest**) **1a** full of or covered with mud. **b** like mud. **2a** lacking in clarity or brightness. **b** obscure in meaning; muddled, confused. ➤➤ **muddily** *adv,* **muddiness** *n.*

muddy[2] *v* (**-ies, -ied**) to make muddy, cloudy, dull, or confused.

mudflap *n* a flap suspended behind the wheel of a vehicle to prevent mud, splashes, etc being thrown up.

mudflat *n* (*also in pl*) a muddy area of ground exposed at low tide but covered at high tide.

mudguard *n* a metal or plastic guard over the wheel of a bicycle, motorcycle, etc to deflect or catch mud.

mudlark *n* somebody, *esp* a destitute Victorian child, who tries to find useful or saleable objects in river mud.

mudpack *n* a face-pack containing fuller's earth.

mudskipper *n* a small Asian fish of the goby family with fleshy modified front fins that enable it to leave the water and move about on mud.

mudslinging *n* directing abuse, invective, and scandalous allegations against a political opponent, competitor, etc. ➤➤ **mudslinger** *n.*

mudstone *n* a hardened shale produced by the consolidation of mud.

muesli *n* (*pl* **mueslis**) a dish of Swiss origin, usu eaten at breakfast, consisting of rolled oats, dried fruit, nuts, grated apple, etc.

muezzin *n* in Islam, a mosque official who calls the faithful to prayer at fixed daily times, usu from a minaret: compare IMAM.

muff[1] *n* **1** a warm cylindrical wrap in which both hands are placed. **2** *coarse slang* a woman's genitalia.

muff[2] *v* to handle awkwardly; to bungle (an attempt, etc).

muff[3] *n* **1** a failure to hold a ball in attempting a catch. **2** any bungled or failed attempt.

muffin *n* **1** in Britain, a light round yeast-leavened bun usu split into two, toasted and buttered. **2** in the USA and Canada, a round sweet individual-sized cake.

muffle *v* **1** (*often* + up) to wrap up so as to conceal, protect, or keep warm. **2** to deaden the sound of (a gun, drum, hammer, etc).

muffler *n* **1** a warm scarf worn round the neck. **2** a device for deadening sound, e.g. on a drum, piano, bell, etc. **3** *NAm* a silencer for a motor vehicle.

mufti[1] *n* (*pl* **muftis**) a professional Muslim jurist.

mufti[2] *n* civilian or ordinary clothes worn by somebody who is usually in uniform, *esp* a member of the armed forces or the police force.

mug[1] *n* **1** a large usu cylindrical drinking cup. **2** *informal* the face or mouth of somebody. **3** *Brit, informal* somebody who is easily deceived; a sucker.

mug[2] *v* (**mugged, mugging**) to assault and rob, *esp* in the street or some other public place. ➤➤ **mugger** *n*, **mugging** *n*.

muggins *n* (*pl* **mugginses** *or* **muggins**) *informal* a stupid or gullible person, *esp* used when referring to oneself.

muggy *adj* (**-ier, -iest**) of the weather: warm, damp, and close. ➤➤ **muggily** *adv*, **mugginess** *n*.

Mughal /'moogahl/ *n* = MOGUL (I).

mug's game *n chiefly Brit, informal* an activity that is liable to involve loss, failure, or danger.

mug shot *n informal* a photograph of a person's face, *esp* one used by police for identification purposes.

mug up *v Brit, informal* (*often* + on) to study something hard, e.g. before an exam.

mugwort *n* a tall Eurasian plant with small brownish flower heads common on waste ground and in hedgerows.

mugwump *n chiefly NAm* a person who remains aloof or apart, *esp* an independent in politics.

Muhammadan *or* **Mohammedan** *adj dated, now usu considered offensive* of Muhammad or Islam; = MUSLIM. ➤➤ **Muhammadan** *n*, **Muhammadanism** *n*.

mujahedin *or* **mujaheddin** *or* **mujahideen** *pl n* Islamic resistance fighters, *esp* opposing the Soviet-backed government in Afghanistan in the 1980s. ➤➤ **mujahedin** *adj*.

mukluk *n* a boot, usu made of sealskin or reindeer skin, traditionally worn by North American Inuits.

mulatto *n* (*pl* **-oes** *or* **-os**) a person who has one parent who is black and one who is white. ➤➤ **mulatto** *adj*.

mulberry *n* (*pl* **-ies**) **1a** an edible red, purple, or white fruit resembling a raspberry. **b** a tree of the fig family that bears this fruit. **2** a dark purple or purplish black colour. ➤➤ **mulberry** *adj*.

mulch[1] *n* a protective covering, e.g. of compost, spread on the ground to control weeds, enrich the soil, etc.

mulch[2] *v* **1** to put mulch on or round (e.g. a plant). **2** to treat (ground or soil) with mulch.

mulct[1] *n formal* a fine or penalty.

mulct[2] *v formal* **1** to punish by a fine. **2a** to swindle. **b** to obtain by swindling.

mule[1] *n* **1a** the sterile offspring of a mating between a female horse and an ass: compare HINNY. **b** a sterile hybrid animal or plant. **2** a very stubborn person. **3** a machine for producing yarn or thread and winding it onto spindles. **4** *informal* a courier transporting illegal drugs.

mule[2] *n* a backless shoe or slipper.

muleteer *n* somebody who drives mules.

mulga *n* (*pl* **mulgas** *or* **mulga**) **1** a shrubby plant widespread in the drier parts of Australia and often used as fodder. **2** (**the mulga**) *Aus, informal* the outback.

muliebrity *n chiefly literary* **1** the quality or status of being a woman; femininity. **2** womanhood.

mulish *adj* unreasonably and inflexibly obstinate. ➤➤ **mulishly** *adv*, **mulishness** *n*.

mull[1] *v* to heat, sweeten, and flavour (e.g. wine or beer) with spices.

mull[2] *n* used *esp* in place names: a headland or peninsula in Scotland.

mull[3] *n* crumbly soil humus forming a layer on top of mineral soil.

mull[4] *n* a soft fine sheer fabric of cotton, silk, or rayon.

mullah *n* a Muslim of a quasi-clerical class trained in traditional Islamic law and doctrine. ➤➤ **mullahism** *n*.

mullein *or* **mullen** *n* a plant of the figwort family with woolly leaves and spikes of usu yellow flowers.

muller *n* a pestle usu for grinding substances, e.g. artists' pigments, on a slab.

mullet *n* (*pl* **mullets** *or* **mullet**) any of several species of red, golden, or grey food fishes, many of which have two barbels on the chin.

mulligatawny *n* a rich meat soup of Indian origin seasoned with curry.

mullion[1] *n* a slender vertical bar placed *esp* between panes or panels of a window or door.

mullion[2] *v* to fit a mullion or mullions in (a window, etc).

mullock *n* **1** *Aus, NZ* mining refuse. **2** *Brit dialect, Aus, NZ* rubbish; nonsense.

mull over *v* to consider (something) at length.

mulloway *n* (*pl* **mulloways** *or* **mulloway**) a large predatory edible marine fish of Australian coastal waters.

multi- *comb. form* many; multiple; much: *multistorey*.

multiaccess *adj* of a computer system: allowing two or more users simultaneous access and use.

multicast[1] *v* (*past tense and past part.* **multicast**) to transmit (data) via a computer network to several users simultaneously.

multicast[2] *n* a set of multicast data.

multicolour (*NAm* **multicolor**) *adj* = MULTICOLOURED.

multicoloured (*NAm* **multicolored**) *adj* having or composed of various colours.

multicultural *adj* relating to or composed of a combination of several distinct cultures. ➤➤ **multiculturalism** *n*, **multiculturalist** *n*, **multiculturally** *adv*.

multifaceted *adj* having several distinct facets or aspects.

multifarious *adj* having or occurring in great variety; diverse. ➤➤ **multifariously** *adv*, **multifariousness** *n*.

multiflora *n* an orig Chinese and Japanese variety of rose growing as a shrub, with clusters of small white or pink flowers.

multiform *adj* having many forms or appearances. ➤➤ **multiformity** *n*.

multigym *n* an exercise apparatus with a variety of weights and levers, used for toning the muscles of the body.

multilateral *adj* **1** participated in by more than two parties. **2** having many sides. ➤➤ **multilaterally** *adv*.

multilingual *adj* **1** written or spoken in several languages. **2** using or able to use several languages. ➤➤ **multilingualism** *n*, **multilingually** *adv*.

multimedia *n* (*used before a noun*) **1** the use of several different means of expression or communication, e.g. in education, marketing, or art. **2** the handling of various media, such as text, graphics, and sound, by a computer.

multimillionaire *n* somebody whose wealth is estimated at many millions of money units.

multinational[1] *adj* **1** involving more than two nations. **2** operating or having branches, etc in more than two countries.

multinational[2] *n* a multinational company.

multipack *n* a pack containing several items of the same type, e.g. bottles, sold as a single unit.

multiparty *adj* of or involving more than two political parties.

multiphase *adj* = MULTIPHASIC.

multiphasic *adj* having various phases or elements.

multiple[1] *adj* **1** consisting of or involving more than one part or element. **2** many and varied. **3** of a disease: affecting several different parts of the body.

multiple[2] *n* **1** the product of a quantity by an integer. **2** *chiefly Brit* = MULTIPLE STORE.

multiple-choice *adj* having several answers from which one is to be chosen.

multiple sclerosis *n* a chronic condition characterized by progressive paralysis and jerking muscle tremor resulting from the formation of patches of hardened tissue in nerves of the brain and spinal cord.

multiple store *n chiefly Brit* a chain store.

multiple unit *n* a train that has one or more carriages containing motors for propulsion.

multiplex[1] *adj* **1** manifold; multiple. **2** of a cinema building: having several auditoriums. **3** denoting a communications system allowing several messages to be transmitted simultaneously by the same circuit or channel.

multiplex[2] *n* **1** a cinema building with several auditoriums screening various films. **2** a multiplex communications system.

multiplex[3] *v* to send (messages or signals) by a multiplex system. ➤➤ **multiplexer** *or* **multiplexor** *n.*

multiplicand *n* a number that is to be multiplied by another (the multiplier).

multiplication *n* **1** the process of multiplying or being multiplied. **2** a mathematical operation that at its simplest is an abbreviated process of adding an integer to itself a specified number of times (e.g. $2 \times 3 = 2 + 2 + 2$). ➤➤ **multiplicative** *adj,* **multiplicatively** *adv.*

multiplication sign *n* the symbol (×) denoting that the quantities on either side of it are to be multiplied together.

multiplication table *n* any of a number of tables that show the results of multiplying two numbers together.

multiplicity *n* (*pl* **-ies**) **1** the state of being multiple or various. **2** a great number.

multiplier *n* **1** a number by which another number (the multiplicand) is multiplied. **2** an instrument or device for multiplying or intensifying some effect.

multiply[1] /'multiplie/ *v* (**-ies, -ied**) **1** to increase in number, *esp* greatly. **2** to combine (numbers) by multiplication. **3** to breed or propagate. ➤➤ **multipliable** *adj.*

multiply[2] /'multipli/ *adv* in a multiple manner; in several ways.

multiprocessing *n* the processing of several computer programs at the same time.

multiprocessor *n* a computer system consisting of several processors sharing a single memory, so allowing MULTIPROCESSING.

multiprogramming *n* a technique for executing several independent computer programs simultaneously, e.g. by sequentially taking one instruction from each program.

multipurpose *adj* serving several purposes.

multiracial *adj* composed of, involving, or representing various races. ➤➤ **multiracialism** *n.*

multistage *adj* **1** having successive operating stages, *esp* having propulsion units that operate in turn. **2** conducted in stages.

multistorey[1] *adj* of a building: having several storeys.

multistorey[2] *n* (*pl* **-eys**) a multistorey car park.

multitasking *n* the execution of a number of tasks simultaneously by a computer.

multitrack *adj* of or involving several separately recorded sound tracks.

multitude *n* **1** a great number. **2** a crowd. **3** (**the multitude**) ordinary people; the masses.

multitudinous *adj formal* **1** composed of a multitude of individuals. **2** very numerous. ➤➤ **multitudinously** *adv,* **multitudinousness** *n.*

multivalent *adj* **1** = POLYVALENT. **2** having many values, meanings, or appeals. ➤➤ **multivalence** *n,* **multivalency** *n.*

mum[1] *n chiefly Brit, informal* = MOTHER[1].

mum[2] *adj* silent; not divulging information. ✱ **mum's the word** do not tell anyone about this.

mum[3] *v* (**mummed, mumming**) to take part in mumming.

mumble[1] *v* to speak or say in a low and indistinct voice. ➤➤ **mumbler** *n,* **mumbling** *adj and n,* **mumblingly** *adv.*

mumble[2] *n* something that is difficult to understand because it is said in a low and indistinct voice.

mumbo jumbo *n* elaborate but meaningless activity or language that obscures and confuses.

mummer *n* **1** a person who takes part in mumming. **2** *chiefly archaic, derog or humorous* an actor in the theatre.

mummery *n* (*pl* **-ies**) **1** a performance of mumming. **2** an absurd or pretentious ceremony or performance.

mummify *v* (**-ies, -ied**) **1** to embalm and dry (a dead body). **2** to preserve (something) outdated or in an outdated form. ➤➤ **mummification** *n.*

mumming *n* the practice of performing in traditional English folk-plays.

mummy[1] *n* (*pl* **-ies**) *chiefly Brit, informal* an affectionate name for one's mother.

mummy[2] *n* (*pl* **-ies**) a body embalmed and wrapped for burial in the manner of the ancient Egyptians.

mumps *pl n* (*used as sing. or pl*) an infectious viral disease marked by swelling of the parotid glands and mainly affecting children.

mumsy *adj* (**-ier, -iest**) *Brit, informal* **1** warm and sympathetic; motherly. **2** dowdy and old-fashioned.

mun. *abbr* municipal.

munch *v* to chew (food) with a crunching sound and visible movement of the jaws. ➤➤ **muncher** *n.*

Munchausen's syndrome *n* a psychiatric disorder in which sufferers pretend to have various serious illnesses in order to get medical treatment, often in hospital. ✱ **Munchausen's syndrome by proxy** a similar psychiatric disorder in which sufferers harm other people, usu children, to attract medical attention.

munchies *pl n* **1** (*usu* **the munchies**) *informal* a craving for food. **2** snacks of various kinds.

mundane *adj* **1** practical and ordinary, *esp* to the point of dull familiarity. **2** of this world, e.g. in contrast to heaven. ➤➤ **mundanely** *adv,* **mundaneness** *n,* **mundanity** *n.*

mung bean *n* **1** a small edible green or yellow bean grown in tropical climates. **2** the erect bushy plant that bears this bean, grown *esp* as the chief source of bean sprouts.

municipal *adj* **1** of a municipality. **2** relating to or having local self-government. ➤➤ **municipally** *adv.*

municipality *n* (*pl* **-ies**) a political unit, such as a town, city, or district, having corporate status and some self-government.

munificent *adj formal* characterized by great generosity. ➤➤ **munificence** *n,* **munificently** *adv.*

muniments *pl n* in law, documents kept as evidence of title or privilege.

munitions *pl n* armaments, ammunition, military equipment, stores, etc.

Munro *n* (*pl* **-os**) a British mountain over 3000 feet (914.4 metres) in height.

muntjac *or* **muntjak** *n* a small deer of SE Asia, India, and China, with a brown coat, short horns, and a cry like a dog's bark.

muon *n* an unstable elementary particle similar to but heavier than the electron, that occurs *esp* in cosmic rays. ➤➤ **muonic** *adj.*

mural[1] *n* a work of art, e.g. a painting, applied directly onto a wall. ➤➤ **muralist** *n.*

mural[2] *adj* of, resembling, or applied to a wall.

murder[1] *n* **1** the crime of unlawfully and intentionally killing somebody: compare MANSLAUGHTER. **2** *informal* something that is very difficult, dangerous, or disagreeable. ✱ **get away with murder** *informal* to do whatever one likes without being punished or having to face the consequences. **scream/yell/cry blue/bloody murder** *informal* to make a huge fuss or a loud protest.

murder[2] *v* **1** to kill unlawfully and intentionally. **2a** *informal* to mutilate, mangle, or ruin. **b** *informal* to beat comprehensively. **c** *informal* to eat or drink (something) with enthusiasm. ➤➤ **murderer** *n,* **murderess** *n.*

murderous *adj* **1a** having the purpose or capability of murder. **b** causing murder or bloodshed. **2** *informal* **a** extremely difficult or unpleasant. **b** dangerous. ➤➤ **murderously** *adv,* **murderousness** *n.*

murex *n* (*pl* **murices** *or* **murexes**) a spiny-shelled tropical marine gastropod mollusc that yields a purple dye.

murices *n* pl of MUREX.

murine *adj* of mice, rats, and similar rodents.

murk *or* **mirk** *n* **1** gloom; darkness. **2** fog.

murky *adj* (**-ier, -iest**) **1a** dark and gloomy. **b** of water: cloudy, muddy, or dirty. **2** obscure or unknown, *esp* deliberately so in order to conceal something dishonest, immoral, etc. ➤➤ **murkily** *adv,* **murkiness** *n.*

murmur[1] *n* **1a** a low indistinct continuous sound. **b** a subdued or gentle utterance. **c** a half-suppressed or muttered complaint. **2** an atypical sound of the heart indicating an abnormality. ✱ **without a murmur** without complaining.

murmur[2] *v* **1** to say in a murmur. **2** to make a murmur. **3** to complain or grumble. ➤➤ **murmurer** *n,* **murmuring** *adj and n,* **murmuringly** *adv,* **murmurous** *adj.*

Murphy's law *n informal* a facetious principle that states that, if it is possible for something to go wrong or turn out badly, then it will do just that. Also called SOD'S LAW.

murrain *n* **1** any of various highly infectious diseases, e.g. red water and anthrax, that affect cattle and other domestic animals. **2** *archaic* a plague, *esp* one affecting domestic animals or plants.

muscadel *n* see MUSCATEL.

Muscadet *n* a variety of grape used in the production of very dry white wine, or the wine itself.

muscat *n* **1** a cultivated grape used in the production of sweet white wine and raisins. **2** = MUSCATEL (1).

muscatel *or* **muscadel** *n* **1** a sweet white wine produced from muscat grapes. **2** a raisin made from muscat grapes.

muscle *n* **1a** a tissue made of modified elongated cells that contract and relax when stimulated to produce motion. **b** an organ consisting of this tissue that moves a part of the body. **2a** muscular strength; brawn. **b** power or force. ➤➤ **muscled** *adj,* **muscly** *adj.*

muscle-bound *adj* **1** having enlarged muscles with impaired elasticity, often as a result of excessive exercise. **2** lacking flexibility; rigid.

muscle in *v informal* (*often* + on) to interfere or take a share in something forcibly.

muscleman *n* (*pl* **musclemen**) **1** a strong muscular man; a body-builder. **2** a man hired to give physical protection or intimidate opponents.

muscovado *n* unrefined sugar obtained from sugarcane.

Muscovite *n* **1** a native or inhabitant of Moscow. **2** *archaic* a Russian. **3** (**muscovite**) a form of mica. ➤➤ **Muscovite** *adj.*

Muscovy *n archaic* Russia.

Muscovy duck *n* a widely domesticated large S American crested duck with green, grey, or white feathers.

muscular *adj* **1a** of or affecting muscle or the muscles. **b** having well-developed musculature. **2** having strength of expression or character; vigorous. ➤➤ **muscularity** *n,* **muscularly** *adv.*

muscular dystrophy *n* progressive wasting of muscles occurring as a hereditary disease: compare DYSTROPHY.

musculature *n* the system of muscles of the body or part of the body.

musculoskeletal *adj* relating to or affecting both the muscular and skeletal systems of the body.

muse[1] *v* **1** to become absorbed in thought; to engage in daydreaming. **2** to think or say reflectively. ➤➤ **muser** *n.*

muse[2] *n* **1** (**Muse**) any of the nine sister goddesses in Greek mythology who were the patrons of the arts and sciences. **2** a woman who is a source of inspiration to a creative artist, *esp* a poet.

museum *n* an institution devoted to the acquiring and display of objects of historical, artistic, cultural, or scientific value.

museum piece *n Brit, informal* somebody or something regarded as being absurdly old-fashioned.

mush[1] *n* **1** a soft mass of semiliquid material. **2** mawkish sentimentality.

mush[2] *v* to reduce (something) to a mush.

mush[3] *interj* a command to sledge dogs to start pulling or to travel more quickly.

mush[4] /moosh/ *Brit, informal* **1** a person's face or mouth. **2** used *esp* to address somebody: a person.

mushroom[1] *n* **1** the enlarged, *esp* edible, fleshy fruiting body of a class of fungus, consisting typically of a stem bearing a flattened or domed cap. **2** (*used before a noun*) of growth, development, expansion, etc: happening rapidly and often suddenly. **3** a pale brownish pink colour.

mushroom[2] *v* to spring up suddenly or multiply or grow rapidly.

mushroom cloud *n* the mushroom-shaped cloud of dust, etc that forms above a nuclear explosion.

mushy *adj* (**-ier, -iest**) **1** having the consistency of mush. **2** mawkishly sentimental. ➤➤ **mushily** *adv,* **mushiness** *n.*

music *n* **1** vocal, instrumental, or mechanical sounds that have rhythm, melody, or harmony. **2a** the science or art of writing music. **b** a musical accompaniment. **c** the score of a musical composition set down on paper. ✱ **music to one's ears** something that one is very pleased to hear or learn.

musical[1] *adj* **1** having the pleasing harmonious qualities of music. **2** having an interest in or talent for music. **3** set to or accompanied by music. **4** of music, musicians, or music lovers. ➤➤ **musicality** *n,* **musically** *adv.*

musical[2] *n* a film or theatrical production that consists of songs, dances, and dialogue based on a unifying plot.

musical box *n* a container enclosing an apparatus that reproduces music mechanically when activated.

musical chairs *pl n* **1** (*used as sing.*) a children's game in which players march round a row of chairs numbering one less than the players and scramble for seats when the music stops. **2** any situation involving people making frequent changes of position.

musical comedy *n* a musical, *esp* one of a sentimental or humorous nature.

music centre *n Brit, dated* a usu stereophonic unit housing a record player, a radio, and a cassette tape recorder.

music hall *n* **1** entertainment consisting of a variety of unrelated acts, e.g. acrobats, comedians, singers, and dancers. **2** *esp* formerly, a theatre where such entertainments are performed.

musician *n* a composer, conductor, or performer of music, *esp* an instrumentalist. ➤➤ **musicianly** *adj,* **musicianship** *n.*

musicology *n* the study of music as a branch of knowledge or field of research. ➤➤ **musicological** *adj,* **musicologist** *n.*

musique concrète *n* a montage of recorded natural sounds, e.g. voices, traffic noise, and bird calls, arbitrarily modified and arranged.

musk *n* **1** a substance with a penetrating persistent smell that is obtained from a gland of the male musk deer and used as a perfume fixative. **2** any of various plants with musky smells. ➤➤ **muskiness** *n,* **musky** *adj.*

musk deer *n* a small heavy-limbed hornless deer of central Asia, the male of which produces musk.

muskeg *n* a sphagnum bog of northern N America, often with tussocks.

musket *n* a long-barrelled gun with a smooth bore, fired from the shoulder.

musketeer *n* **1** a soldier armed with a musket. **2** a soldier of the household guard of the French monarch in the 17th and 18th cents.

musketry *n* **1** muskets collectively or troops armed with muskets. **2** musket fire. **3** the art or technique of using a musket or other small firearms.

muskmelon *n* a melon that has orange coloured flesh with a musky flavour and a rind with raised netlike markings.

musk ox *n* a thickset shaggy-coated wild ox of Greenland and northern N America that gives off a strong musky odour.

muskrat *n* (*pl* **muskrats** *or* **muskrat**) **1** an aquatic rodent of N America with thick brown fur, a long scaly tail, webbed hind feet, and musk glands at the base of the tail. **2** the fur of this animal.

Muslim *or* **Moslem** *n* an adherent of Islam. ➤➤ **Muslim** *adj.*

muslin *n* a delicate plain-woven cotton fabric.

muso *n* (*pl* **-os**) *Brit, informal* **1** *chiefly derog* a musician, *esp* one who plays pop music and is more concerned with technique than with content or expression. **2** a person who has a strong interest in or vast knowledge of music, *esp* pop music.

musquash *n archaic* = MUSKRAT.

muss[1] *n NAm, informal* a state of disorder; mess. ➤➤ **mussy** *adj.*

muss[2] *v NAm, informal* (*often* + up) to make untidy; to disarrange or dishevel.

mussel *n* **1** a marine bivalve mollusc with a dark elongated shell. **2** a freshwater bivalve mollusc which sometimes produces pearls.

Mussulman *n* (*pl* **Mussulmen** *or* **Mussulmans**) *archaic* a Muslim.

must[1] *v aux* (*third person sing. present tense* **must,** *past tense in reported speech* **must**) **1** to have to; to be obliged to. **2** to be required or necessary. **3** to be supposed or likely. **4** used to express insistence.

must[2] *n* an essential or prerequisite.

must[3] *n* grape juice before and during fermentation.

must[4] *n* mould or mustiness.

must[5] *n* see MUSTH.

mustache *n* see MOUSTACHE.

mustachio *n* (*pl* **-os**) (*also in pl*) a moustache, *esp* a large or elaborate one. ➤➤ **mustachioed** *adj.*

mustang *n* the small hardy feral or semi-wild horse of the western plains of the USA.

mustard *n* **1** a pungent yellow or brownish paste or powder used *esp* with meat as a condiment, ground from the seeds of a plant of the cabbage family. **2** a brownish yellow colour. ➤➤ **mustard** *adj,* **mustardy** *adj.*

mustard gas *n* an irritant and blister-inducing oily liquid used as a poison gas, *esp* in chemical warfare.

mustelid *n technical* any of a family of predatory mammals such as a weasel, ferret, badger, skunk, marten, or otter. ➤➤ **musteline** *adj.*

muster[1] *v* **1a** to assemble or convene (e.g. troops). **b** *esp* of troops: to come together; to congregate. **2** (*often* + up) to summon (*esp* courage, nerve) in response to a need.

muster[2] *n* **1** an instance of assembling, e.g. for military inspection, duty, etc. **2** *Aus, NZ* the act or process of rounding up livestock. ✱ **pass muster** to be acceptable; to be of a satisfactory standard.

musth *or* **must** *n* a periodic state of frenzy in certain large male mammals, e.g. elephants and camels, usu connected with the rutting season.

mustn't *contr* must not.

musty *adj* (**-ier, -iest**) **1a** affected by mould, damp, or mildew. **b** tasting or smelling of damp and decay. **2a** trite or stale. **b** antiquated. **c** out of date. ➤➤ **mustily** *adv,* **mustiness** *n.*

mutable *adj* capable of or liable to change or alteration. ➤➤ **mutability** *n,* **mutableness** *n,* **mutably** *adv.*

mutagen *n* something that causes genetic mutation or increases its frequency. ➤➤ **mutagenesis**

n, **mutagenic** *adj,* **mutagenically** *adv,* **mutagenicity** *n.*

mutant[1] *n* an animal, organism, cell, etc that has undergone mutation.

mutant[2] *adj* relating to, affected by, showing, etc mutation.

mutate *v* to undergo or cause to undergo mutation. ⋙ **mutator** *n.*

mutation *n* **1a** the act or an instance of changing; alteration. **b** an alteration, *esp* a significant and fundamental one. **2a** a relatively permanent change in an organism's hereditary material. **b** an individual or strain differing from others of its type and resulting from such a change. ⋙ **mutational** *adj,* **mutationally** *adv.*

mutatis mutandis *adv* with the necessary changes having been made.

mute[1] *adj* **1a** not speaking. **b** unable to speak; dumb. **2a** felt but not expressed. **b** in law, refusing to plead. **3** of a letter: appearing in the spelling of a word but not pronounced. ⋙ **mutely** *adv,* **muteness** *n.*

mute[2] *n* **1** a person who cannot or does not speak. **2** a device attached to a musical instrument to reduce, soften, or muffle its tone. **3** in law, a person who refuses to plead. **4** formerly, a hired mourner.

mute[3] *v* **1** to muffle or reduce the sound of (e.g. a musical instrument). **2** to tone down (a colour, etc).

muted *adj* subdued. ⋙ **mutedly** *adv.*

mute swan *n* the common white swan of Europe and W Asia, so called because it produces no loud notes.

mutilate *v* **1** to injure or damage (somebody, something, or a body part) severely. **2** to damage or deface (e.g. a text). ⋙ **mutilation** *n,* **mutilator** *n.*

mutineer *n* somebody who mutinies.

mutinous *adj* tending to mutiny; rebellious. ⋙ **mutinously** *adv,* **mutinousness** *n.*

mutiny[1] *n* (*pl* **-ies**) open resistance to authority, *esp* concerted revolt of e.g. soldiers or a naval crew against discipline or a superior officer.

mutiny[2] *v* (**-ies, -ied**) to take part in a mutiny; to rebel against authority, a command, etc.

mutism *n* speechlessness caused by psychological reasons rather than by physiological damage.

mutt *n informal* **1** *often humorous or derog* a dog, *esp* a mongrel. **2** a dull or stupid person.

mutter[1] *v* **1** to utter sounds or words in a low or indistinct voice. **2** to utter muffled threats or complaints. ⋙ **mutterer** *n.*

mutter[2] *n* muttered sounds or words.

mutton *n* the flesh of a mature sheep used as food. ✱ **mutton dressed as lamb** *Brit, informal, derog* a middle-aged or elderly woman dressed in clothing more suited to a younger person. ⋙ **muttony** *adj.*

muttonchops *pl n* side-whiskers that are narrow at the temple and broad by the lower jaws.

muttonchop whiskers *pl n* = MUTTONCHOPS.

muttonhead *n informal, dated* a slow-witted or stupid person; a blockhead. ⋙ **muttonheaded** *adj.*

mutual *adj* **1a** directed by each towards the other. **b** of two or more people, groups, etc: having the same specified feeling for each other. **2** shared by two or more people, groups, etc; in common. **3** denoting a building society, insurance company, etc owned by its members who share its profits and expenses, there being no other shareholders. ⋙ **mutuality** *n,* **mutually** *adv.*

Usage note

mutual, reciprocal, *or* **common?** *Mutual* and *reciprocal* can both mean 'directed towards each other'. Two people share *a mutual* or *reciprocal hatred,* if they hate each other. They also, however, might share *a common hatred* if both independently hate some other person or thing. Because *common* has several other meanings apart from 'shared', *mutual* is sometimes used where the strictly correct word would be *common.* The best-known example is *our mutual friend,* meaning 'your friend as well as mine', a phrase reinforced by the title of Dickens' novel and now generally accepted in modern English.

mutual induction *n* the production of an electromotive force in a circuit by a change of current in another circuit linked to it by a magnetic field.

mutuel *n NAm* = PARI-MUTUEL (system for betting).

muumuu *n* a brightly coloured loose, often long, dress of a type traditionally worn by women in Hawaii.

Muzak *n trademark* recorded background music played in public places.

muzzle[1] *n* **1a** the projecting jaws and nose of a dog or other animal. **b** a covering for the mouth of an animal used to prevent biting, barking, etc. **2** the discharging end of a pistol, rifle, etc.

muzzle[2] *v* **1** to fit (e.g. a dog) with a muzzle. **2** to restrain from free expression; to gag. ⋙ **muzzler** *n.*

muzzy *adj* (**-ier, -iest**) **1** of a person, recollection, etc: mentally confused; befuddled. **2a** of an image: blurred; unclear. **b** of a sound: indistinct. ⋙ **muzzily** *adv,* **muzziness** *n.*

MV *abbr* motor vessel.

MVO *abbr* Member of the Royal Victorian Order.

MW *abbr* **1** medium wave. **2** megawatt.

MY *abbr* motor yacht.

my[1] *adj* **1** belonging to or associated with me. **2** used in expressions of surprise, horror, disbelief, etc.

my[2] *interj* (*also reduplicated*) used to express surprise, distress, pleasure, etc.

myalgia *n* pain in one or more muscles. ⋙ **myalgic** *adj.*

myalgic encephalomyelitis *n dated* = CHRONIC FATIGUE SYNDROME.

myall *n* **1** an Australian acacia tree with hard fragrant wood. **2** a member of an indigenous Australian people who lives in a traditional way.

myasthenia *n* muscular weakness. ⋙ **myasthenic** *adj.*

myasthenia gravis *n* a disease characterized by progressive weakness and exhaustibility of voluntary muscles without wasting.

mycelium *n* (*pl* **mycelia**) the mass of interwoven hyphae (threadlike filaments; see HYPHA) that forms the body of a fungus. ⋙ **mycelial** *adj.*

Mycenaean *or* **Mycenian** *adj* relating to a late Bronze Age culture that flourished at Mycenae, a city of ancient Greece, and whose influence spread to other Peloponnesian cities. ⋙ **Mycenaean** *n.*

mycology *n* the scientific study of fungal life or fungi. ⋙ **mycologic** *adj,* **mycological** *adj,* **mycologically** *adv,* **mycologist** *n.*

mycotoxin *n* a toxic substance produced by a fungus, *esp* a mould.

myelin *n* a soft white fatty material that forms a thick sheath about the cytoplasmic core of nerve cells adapted for fast conduction of nervous impulses. ⋙ **myelinic** *adj.*

myelitis *n* inflammation of the spinal cord or the bone marrow.

myeloid *adj* **1** relating to or in the region of the spinal cord. **2** relating to or resembling bone marrow.

myeloma *n* (*pl* **myelomas** *or* **myelomata**) a tumour of the bone marrow, usu one that is malignant. ⋙ **myelomatous** *adj.*

mynah *or* **myna** *or* **mina** *n* any of various Asian starlings, *esp* a largely black one that can easily be taught to pronounce words.

myocardium *n* (*pl* **myocardia**) the middle muscular layer of the heart wall. ⋙ **myocardial** *adj,* **myocarditis** *n.*

myopia *n* **1** defective vision of distant objects resulting from the visual images being focused in front of the retina; shortsightedness: compare HYPERMETROPIA. **2** a lack of foresight, imagination, or intellectual objectivity. ⋙ **myopic** *adj,* **myopically** *adv.*

myosin *n* a fibrous protein that reacts with actin to form the principal contractile element of muscles.

myositis *n* inflammation and soreness of the muscles.

myosotis *n* any of a genus of plants of the borage family including the forget-me-not.

myriad[1] *n* **1** (*also in pl*) an indefinitely large number. **2** *archaic* ten thousand.

myriad[2] *adj* innumerable; countless.

myriapod *or* **myriopod** *n* a millipede, centipede, or related arthropod with a body made up of numerous similar segments bearing jointed legs.

myrmidon *n* a subordinate who carries out orders unquestioningly.

myrrh *n* an aromatic gum resin obtained from various African and Asian trees, used e.g. in perfumes, medicines, and incense.

myrtle *n* an evergreen S European bushy shrub with shiny leaves, fragrant white or rosy flowers, and black berries.

myself *pron* used reflexively or for emphasis to refer to the person speaking or writing: *I have hurt myself; I myself have said it.* ✱ **be myself** to be fit or healthy as normal.

mysterious *adj* **1** difficult to comprehend. **2** containing, suggesting, or implying mystery. ⋙ **mysteriously** *adv,* **mysteriousness** *n.*

mystery[1] *n* (*pl* **-ies**) **1a** something or somebody not understood or beyond understanding; an enigma. **b** something that cannot be explained. **c** a profound, enigmatic, or secretive quality or character. **2** a fictional work dealing usu with the solution of a mysterious crime. **3a** a religious truth disclosed by revelation alone and not fully understandable. **b** any of the 15 events, e.g. the Nativity, the Crucifixion, or the Assumption, serving as a subject for meditation during the saying of the rosary. **c** (*also in pl*) a secret religious rite believed, e.g. in certain ancient religions, to impart enduring bliss.

mystery[2] *n* (*pl* **mysteries**) *archaic* a trade or craft, or the body of people engaged in it.

mystery play *n* a medieval religious drama based on episodes from the Scriptures or the lives of the saints.

mystery tour *n Brit* a pleasure trip, *esp* by coach, to a destination that is not made known to those taking part when they set out.

mystic[1] *n* a person who believes that God or ultimate reality can be apprehended by direct personal experience.

mystic[2] *adj* = MYSTICAL.

mystical *adj* **1** having a sacred or spiritual meaning not given by normal modes of thought or feeling. **2** of or resulting from direct experience of communion with God or ultimate reality. **3a** mysterious or incomprehensible. **b** obscure or esoteric. **c** arousing awe and wonder. ⋙ **mystically** *adv.*

mysticism *n* **1** the belief that direct knowledge of God, spiritual truth, or ultimate reality can be attained through subjective experience, e.g. intuition or insight. **2** vague speculation; a belief without sound basis.

mystify *v* (**-ies, -ied**) **1** to perplex or bewilder. **2** to make mysterious or obscure. ⋙ **mystification** *n,* **mystifier** *n,* **mystifyingly** *adv.*

mystique *n* **1** a reverential atmosphere or quality associated with a person or thing. **2** an aura of secrecy and esoteric skill surrounding an activity regarded by outsiders as intriguing or puzzling.

myth *n* **1a** a traditional story that embodies popular beliefs or explains a practice, belief, or natural phenomenon. **b** = MYTHOLOGY. **2a** a fictitious person or thing. **b** a belief subscribed to uncritically by some groups.

mythical *adj* **1** based on or described in a myth. **2** invented or imagined. ⋙ **mythically** *adv.*

mythological *adj* **1** relating to or dealt with in mythology or myths. **2** lacking factual or historical basis. ⋙ **mythologically** *adv.*

mythologize *or* **-ise** *v* to build a myth round (a person, thing, event, etc). ⋙ **mythologizer** *n.*

mythology *n* (*pl* **-ies**) **1** a body of myths, *esp* those dealing with the gods and heroes of a particular people. **2** a study of myths. **3** a body of beliefs, usu with little factual foundation, lending glamour or mystique to somebody or something. ⋙ **mythologist** *n.*

mythomania *n* an excessive tendency to tell lies or exaggerate. ⋙ **mythomaniac** *n and adj.*

mythopoeia *n* the composition or making of a myth or myths. ⋙ **mythopoeic** *adj.*

myxomatosis *n* a severe and usu fatal viral disease of rabbits characterized by swelling of the mucous membranes and the formation of tumour-like tissue below the skin.

N[1] *or* **n** *n* (*pl* **N's** *or* **Ns** *or* **n's**) the 14th letter of the English alphabet.

N[2] *abbr* **1** (*also* **Kt**) in chess, knight. **2** used on electric plugs: neutral. **3** in place names, New. **4** in physics, newton or newtons. **5** North. **6** Northern.

N[3] *abbr* the chemical symbol for nitrogen.

n[1] *abbr* **1** name. **2** (*usu used in combinations*) in physics, etc, nano-. **3** in grammar: **a** neuter. **b** nominative. **c** noun.

n[2] *adj* **1** in mathematics, etc, a symbol for an indefinite number. **2** *informal* a vast number.

'n' *or* **'n** *conj informal* and.

-n *suffix* see -EN[1], -EN[2], -EN[3].

Na *abbr* the chemical symbol for sodium.

n/a *abbr* **1** not applicable. **2** not available.

NAAFI *or* **Naafi** *n* **1** the organization which runs shops and canteens in British military establishments. **2** any of these shops or canteens.

naan *n* see NAN[2].

nab *v* (**nabbed, nabbing**) *informal* **1** to arrest or apprehend. **2** to catch hold of or grab.

Nabataean *or* **Nabatean** *n* **1** a member of an ancient Arab trading people whose capital was at Petra. **2** the now extinct form of Aramaic spoken by this people. ➤➤ **Nabataean** *adj.*

nabob *n* **1** (*also* **nawab**) a provincial governor of the Mogul empire in India. **2** orig of an Englishman grown rich in India: a man of great wealth. ➤➤ **nabobess** *n.*

nacelle *n* a housing for an aircraft engine.

nacho *n* (*pl* **nachos**) a Mexican savoury consisting of a piece of tortilla covered with melted cheese, chopped peppers, etc.

nacre *n* mother-of-pearl. ➤➤ **nacred** *adj,* **nacreous** *adj.*

nadir *n* **1** in astronomy, the point of the celestial sphere directly opposite the ZENITH and vertically downward from the observer. **2** a person's or thing's lowest or worst point.

naevus (*NAm* **nevus**) *n* (*pl* **naevi**) a congenital pigmented area on the skin; a birthmark.

naff *adj Brit, informal* lacking sophistication, coolness, or style; crassly stupid. ➤➤ **naffness** *n.*

naff off *v Brit, informal* (*usu in imperative*) used in contemptuous dismissal of somebody, their opinions, etc.

nafka *n* the basic monetary unit of Eritrea, divided into 100 cents.

NAFTA *or* **Nafta** *abbr* North American Free Trade Agreement.

nag[1] *n* a horse, *esp* one that is old or in poor condition.

nag[2] *v* (**nagged, nagging**) **1** (*often* + at) **a** to find fault incessantly. **b** to subject to constant scolding or urging. **2** of a pain or worry: to be a persistent source of annoyance or discomfort. ➤➤ **nagger** *n,* **nagging** *adj,* **naggingly** *adv.*

nag[3] *n* **1** a person, *esp* a woman, who nags habitually. **2** a nagging feeling.

Nahuatl *n* (*pl* **Nahuatls** *or* **Nahuatl**) **1** a group of Native American peoples of S Mexico and Central America. **2** a Uto-Aztecan language of central Mexico.

naiad *n* (*pl* **naiads** *or* **naiades**) **1** (*often* **Naiad**) a water nymph in classical mythology living in springs, rivers, etc. **2** the aquatic larva of a mayfly, dragonfly, damselfly, etc.

naif[1] *or* **naïf** /nah'eef/ *adj* = NAIVE.

naif[2] *or* **naïf** *n* a naive person.

nail[1] *n* **1** a slender pointed and headed spike designed to be hammered or driven into a surface. **2** a horny sheath protecting the upper end of each finger and toe of human beings and other primates. ✱ **a nail in the coffin of** a step towards the destruction, extinction, or disappearance of. **hit the nail on the head** to speak appositely. **on the nail** of payment: immediate. ➤➤ **-nailed** *comb. form,* **nailless** *adj.*

nail[2] *v* **1** (*often* + down/together) to fasten with or as if with a nail or nails. **2** *informal* to trap, catch, or arrest (a criminal, etc). **3** *informal* to detect or expose (a lie or liar).

nail-biting *adj informal* characterized by or causing emotional tension or anxiety.

nail bomb *n* an explosive device containing nails, used typically by terrorists in crowded areas, with the intention of causing mutilation.

nail down *v* **1** to define, identify, or establish clearly. **2** to secure a definite promise or decision from.

nail file *n* a small metal file or emery board for shaping the fingernails.

nail polish *n* coloured or clear varnish applied to the fingernails or toenails for adornment.

nail varnish *n chiefly Brit* = NAIL POLISH.

nainsook *n* a soft lightweight cotton cloth.

naira *n* (*pl* **naira**) the basic monetary unit of Nigeria.

naive *or* **naïve** *adj* **1** ingenuous or unsophisticated. **2** lacking in worldly wisdom or informed judgment; credulous. **3** of art or artists: either self-taught or untutored, or rejecting Western sophistication in favour of a stronger, simpler African or Pacific style; = PRIMITIVE[1]. ⋙ **naively** *adv,* **naiveness** *n.*

naivety *or* **naïvety** *or* **naiveté** *n* (*pl* **naiveties** *or* **naïveties** *or* **naivetés**) **1** naive behaviour; lack of sophistication or worldliness. **2** a naive remark or action.

naked *adj* **1** having no clothes on. **2a** of a tree, plant, animal, or bird: without foliage, or without fur, hair, or feathers. **b** of a light: not shaded. **3** open and undisguised: *naked greed.* **4** *literary* unarmed or defenceless; vulnerable to attack. ✱ **the naked eye** one's eyesight unaided by a magnifying glass, microscope, or telescope. ⋙ **nakedly** *adv,* **nakedness** *n.*

Nam *or* **'Nam** *n NAm, informal* Vietnam, *esp* with reference to the Vietnam War.

Nama *n* (*pl* **Namas** *or* **Nama**) **1** a member of one of the Khoikhoi peoples of Namibia. **2** the Khoisan language spoken by these peoples. Also called KHOIKHOI. ⋙ **Nama** *adj.*

namaskar *n* a traditional Indian gesture of greeting, performed by joining the palms in front of the face or chest and bowing. Also called NAMASTE[2].

namaste[1] *interj* a traditional Indian word of greeting.

namaste[2] *n* = NAMASKAR.

namby-pamby[1] *adj* **1** insipidly sentimental. **2** lacking resolution or firmness; soft. ⋙ **namby-pambyism** *n.*

namby-pamby[2] *n* (*pl* **-ies**) a namby-pamby person.

name[1] *n* **1** a word or phrase identifying a person, place or thing, by which they are known, referred to, or addressed. **2** a famous or important person, company, etc. **3** one's reputation. **4** *Brit* in insurance, an underwriter with Lloyd's. ✱ **call somebody names** to insult verbally. **in all but name** effectively though not officially. **in name only** officially, or in outward form, but not in reality. **in/under the name of 1** reserved, etc, for (so-and-so). **2** for the sake of (a cause, etc). **make a name for oneself** to become well-known. **the name of the game** *informal* the main point to note or recognize in relation to some activity. **to one's name** (*usu in negative contexts*) in one's possession.

name[2] *v* **1** to give a name to. **2** to identify or mention by name. **3** to appoint or nominate. **4** to specify (a sum, date, etc). ✱ **name after** (*NAm* **name for**) to give (somebody or something) the same name as somebody or something else. **name names** to mention specific people, *esp* in distributing blame. **name the day** to decide on a date for one's wedding. ⋙ **nameable** *adj,* **namer** *n.*

namecheck[1] *n* the public mention of somebody or something specifically by name, e.g. in a broadcast programme.

namecheck[2] *v* to refer to (somebody) specifically by name.

name day *n* the feast day of the saint after whom one is named.

name-dropping *n* the practice of trying to impress others by the apparently casual mention of prominent people as acquaintances or contacts. ⋙ **name-drop** *v.*

nameless *adj* **1a** having no name; without a name. **b** not named; anonymous. **2** obscure, undistinguished, or forgotten. **3a** hard to define. **b** too terrible to describe. ⋙ **namelessly** *adv,* **namelessness** *n.*

namely *adv* that is to say.

namesake *n* somebody or something with the same name as the person or thing in question.

nametape *n* a piece of tape attached to a garment, etc that bears the owner's name.

Namibian *n* a native or inhabitant of Namibia. ⋙ **Namibian** *adj.*

nan[1] *n Brit, informal* used by children: one's grandmother.

nan[2] *or* **naan** *n* a traditional Indian type of leavened bread, usu formed into large flat leaf-shaped pieces.

nana[1] *or* **nanna** /'nanə/ *n Brit, informal* used by children: one's grandmother.

nana[2] /'nahnə/ *n Brit, informal* a silly idiot; a fool.

nan bread *n* = NAN[2].

nancy *or* **nance** *n* (*pl* **-ies**) *offensive* an effeminate or homosexual man.

nancy boy *n* = NANCY.

nandrolone *n* an anabolic steroid, similar to testosterone, which is an illegal substance for athletes.

nankeen *n esp* formerly, a durable brownish yellow cotton fabric orig made in China.

nanna *n* see NANA[1].

nanny[1] *or* **nannie** *n* (*pl* **-ies**) *chiefly Brit* a child's nurse; a nursemaid.

nanny[2] *v* (**-ies, -ied**) **1** to look after (children) as a nanny. **2** to treat (people) with an interfering overprotectiveness.

nanny goat *n informal* a female domestic goat.

nanny state *n* a state with a government that decides what is best for people and interferes to an unwarrantable extent in their lives.

nano- *comb. form* forming words, denoting: a one-thousand-millionth (10^{-9}) part of a unit, etc.

nanometre (*NAm* **nanometer**) *n* one thousand-millionth of a metre.

nanosecond *n* one thousand-millionth of a second.

nanotechnology *n* the technology of manufacturing and measuring objects of microscopically small size, *esp* between 0.1 and 100 nanometres.

nap[1] *v* (**napped, napping**) to take a short sleep, *esp* during the day. ✱ **catch somebody napping** to catch somebody when they are unprepared or inattentive.

nap[2] *n* a short sleep, *esp* during the day.

nap[3] *n* a hairy or downy surface, e.g. on a woven fabric; a pile. ⋙ **napless** *adj,* **napped** *adj.*

nap[4] *n* **1** = NAPOLEON. **2** *Brit* in horse-racing: **a** betting all one's money on a single potential winner. **b** a tipster's selection for such a bet. ✱ **go nap 1** to try to take all five tricks in the game of napoleon. **2** to risk all in a single venture.

nap[5] *v* (**napped, napping**) *Brit* in horse racing, to recommend (a horse) as a possible winner.

napalm *n* **1** a thickener consisting of a mixture of aluminium soaps. **2** petrol jellied with napalm and used *esp* in incendiary bombs and flamethrowers.

nape *n* the back of the neck.

napery *n* household linen; *esp* table linen.

nap hand *n* **1** in the game of napoleon, a hand of cards on which a player would be justified in going nap. **2** *informal* a series of five successes, victories, or winning points, in a sport, game, etc.

naphtha *n* **1** petroleum. **2** any of various liquid hydrocarbon mixtures used chiefly as solvents.

naphthalene *n* a hydrocarbon usu obtained by distillation of coal tar and used *esp* in mothballs, and the synthesis of organic chemicals. ➤➤ **naphthalenic** *adj.*

napkin *n* **1** a square piece of material, e.g. linen or paper, used at table to wipe the lips or fingers and protect the clothes. **2** *chiefly Brit, formal* a baby's nappy. **3** *chiefly NAm* = SANITARY TOWEL.

napoleon *n* a card game resembling whist played with hands of five cards in which players bid to name the numbers of tricks they will take.

Napoleonic *adj* relating to or resembling Napoleon I.

napper *n Brit, informal* a person's head.

nappy *n* (*pl* **-ies**) *chiefly Brit* a shaped pad or a square piece of towelling worn around the waist and between the legs by babies to absorb and retain urine and faeces.

nappy rash *n* a skin rash concentrated round a baby's genital and anal area, caused by irritation from the ammonia in a urine-soaked nappy.

narcissi *n* pl of NARCISSUS.

narcissism *n* **1** abnormal interest in or admiration for oneself or one's appearance. **2** sensual pleasure derived from contemplating one's own body. ➤➤ **narcissist** *n and adj,* **narcissistic** *adj.*

narcissus *n* (*pl* **narcissi** *or* **narcissuses**) a daffodil with pale outer petals and a shallow orange or bright yellow central crown.

narcolepsy *n* an abnormal tendency to brief spells of deep sleep. ➤➤ **narcoleptic** *n and adj.*

narcosis *n* drowsiness, stupor, or unconsciousness produced by narcotics or other chemicals.

narcotic[1] *n* **1** a drug that induces drowsiness, stupor, or unconsciousness, and relieves pain. **2** any drug, *esp* an illegal or addictive one, that affects mood and behaviour and is taken for recreational rather than medical purposes.

narcotic[2] *adj* **1** inducing mental lethargy; soporific. **2** relating to narcotics or to addiction to narcotics. ➤➤ **narcotically** *adv.*

narghile *or* **nargileh** /'nahgili/ *n* a WATER PIPE (oriental smoking apparatus), *esp* with several flexible tubes: compare HOOKAH.

nark[1] *n informal* **1** *Brit, Aus, NZ* a police informer. **2** *Aus, NZ* an annoying person or thing.

nark[2] *v* **1** *Brit, Aus, NZ, informal* (*often* + on) to spy or inform on people, *esp* for the police. **2** *informal* (*usu in passive*) to offend or affront (somebody).

narky *adj* (**-ier, -iest**) *Brit, informal* easily annoyed; irritable.

Narraganset *n* (*pl* **Narragansets** *or* **Narraganset**) **1** a member of a Native American people of Rhode Island. **2** the extinct Algonquian language of this people. ➤➤ **Narraganset** *adj.*

narrate *v* **1** to relate or tell (a story). **2** to give a spoken commentary in accompaniment to (a film, etc). ➤➤ **narration** *n,* **narrator** *n.*

narrative[1] *n* **1** something that is related or narrated; a story. **2** the narrated parts of a novel or other literary work, as distinct from the dialogue. **3** the art or practice of narration.

narrative[2] *adj* of or relating to narration. ➤➤ **narratively** *adv,* **narrativity** *n.*

narrow[1] *adj* **1** of little width, *esp* in comparison with height or length. **2** limited in size or scope; restricted. **3** inflexible in attitudes or beliefs. **4** only just sufficient or successful. ➤➤ **narrowness** *n.*

narrow[2] *n* (*in pl*) a narrow sea passage; = STRAIT[2].

narrow[3] *v* **1** to make or become narrow or narrower. **2** (*often* + down) to restrict the scope or sphere of (research, an enquiry, etc).

narrowboat *n* a canal barge with a width of 2.1m (7ft) or less.

narrowcast[1] *v* (*past tense and past part.* **narrowcast**) to transmit (a programme) to a restricted region or audience, e.g. by cable television.

narrowcast[2] *n* a narrowcast transmission.

narrow gauge *n* a railway gauge narrower than the standard gauge of 1.435m (4ft 8$^1/_2$ inches).

narrowly *adv* **1** by a narrow margin; only just. **2** with close concentration.

narrow-minded *adj* lacking tolerance or breadth of vision; bigoted. ➤➤ **narrow-mindedly** *adv,* **narrow-mindedness** *n.*

narthex *n* **1** the western portico or inner porch of an early church. **2** in modern churches, a vestibule at the west end.

narwhal *or* **narwal** *n* a small arctic whale, the male of which has a long twisted ivory tusk.

NASA *abbr NAm* National Aeronautics and Space Administration.

nasal[1] *adj* **1** relating to the nose. **2** of speech sounds: uttered through the nose with the mouth passage closed, e.g. *m, n, ng.* **3** of somebody's speech, of a language, etc: characterized by resonance produced through the nose. ➤➤ **nasality** *n,* **nasally** *adv.*

nasal[2] *n* a nasal speech sound.

nasalize *or* **nasalise** *v* to utter (speech sounds) with resonance through the nose. ➤➤ **nasalization** *n.*

nascent *adj formal* in the process of being born; just beginning to develop. ➤➤ **nascence** *n,* **nascency** *n.*

nasturtium *n* a widely cultivated plant with circular leaves and bright orange, red, or yellow flowers, and pungent seeds.

nasty[1] *adj* (**-ier, -iest**) **1** unpleasant, repugnant, or disgusting. **2** of people or their behaviour: spiteful. **3** uncharitable. **4** harmful or dangerous. ✱ **turn nasty** to become violent or vicious if provoked, etc. ➤➤ **nastily** *adv,* **nastiness** *n.*

nasty[2] *n* (*pl* **-ies**) *informal* a nasty or offensive person or thing.

nat. *abbr* **1** national. **2** nationalist. **3** natural.

natal *adj* related to or associated with one's birth.

natality *n* the birthrate.

natch *adv informal* often used as an interjection: naturally.

nates *pl n* the buttocks.

nation *n* (*used as sing. or pl*) **1** a people with a common origin, tradition, and language. **2** a community of people possessing a more or less defined territory and government.

national[1] *adj* **1** relating to or belonging to a nation. **2** of an industry, etc: belonging to or maintained by the central government. ➤➤ **nationally** *adv.*

national[2] *n* **1** a citizen of a specified nation. **2** a national newspaper in contrast to a local one.

national curriculum *n* in England and Wales since 1989, a curriculum designed to operate throughout the state-maintained school system, with set attainment targets and assessment of pupils at four stages.

national debt *n* the amount of money owed by the government of a country.

National Diploma *n Brit* an advanced qualification, usu in a technical or applied subject, obtained at either of two levels typically by part-time or sandwich-course study.

national grid *n* **1** in Britain, a country-wide network of high-voltage cables between major power stations. **2** in Britain, the system of coordinates used for map reference by the Ordnance Survey.

National Guard *n* a militia force recruited by each state of the USA and equipped by the federal government, available for service to either.

National Health *n* = NATIONAL HEALTH SERVICE.

National Health Service *n* the British system of medical care, started in 1948, by which every person is entitled to medical treatment paid for mainly by taxation.

national hunt *or* **National Hunt** *n* in Britain, the sport of horse-racing over jumps; steeplechasing.

national insurance *or* **National Insurance** *n Brit* a compulsory social-security scheme funded by contributions from employers, employees, and the government, which insures the individual against sickness, retirement, and unemployment.

nationalise *v* see NATIONALIZE.

nationalism *n* **1** loyalty and devotion to one's nation; *esp* the exalting of one's nation above all others. **2** the pursuit of political independence for one's country or nation. ➤➤ **nationalist** *n and adj*, **nationalistic** *adj*.

nationality *n* (*pl* **-ies**) **1** the fact or status of belonging to a particular nation. **2** an ethnic group within a larger unit.

nationalize *or* **nationalise** *v* to transfer control or ownership of (an industry or other major concern) to the state government. ➤➤ **nationalization** *n*, **nationalizer** *n*.

national park *n* an area of special scenic, historical, or environmental importance, preserved and maintained by the government for public enjoyment or the preservation of wildlife, etc.

national service *n* a statutory period of compulsory service in one's country's armed forces. ➤➤ **national serviceman** *n*, **national servicewoman** *n*.

National Socialism *n* the policies of the Nazis, including anti-Semitism, territorial expansion, state control of the economy, etc. ➤➤ **National Socialist** *n and adj*.

nation-state *n* a sovereign state inhabited by a relatively homogeneous people as opposed to several nationalities.

nationwide *adj and adv* throughout the whole country.

native[1] *adj* **1** relating to or being the place of one's birth. **2** belonging to a particular place by birth. **3** of a plant, etc: living or growing naturally in a particular region; indigenous. **4** characteristic of or produced by a particular locality or its indigenous population. **5** inborn; innate. ✱ **go native** *derog* said of a person living abroad: to adopt the way of life of the local population. ➤➤ **natively** *adv*, **nativeness** *n*.

native[2] *n* **1** a person born or reared in a particular place. **2** *dated, offensive* an original or indigenous inhabitant, *esp* of a country colonized by Europeans. **3** a plant, animal, etc living or growing in a particular locality. **4** *chiefly humorous* a local resident.

Usage note

There are few problems with *native* used as an adjective: *native land, native language,* and *native Yorkshireman* are all unexceptionable. The noun *native*, however, is extremely offensive if used to mean simply 'a non-white person' or 'an original (and by implication usually uncivilized) inhabitant of a country'. The only currently safe use of the noun *native* is in the meaning 'a person who was born in a particular place': *I am a native of Hertfordshire.* See also note at NATIVE AMERICAN.

Native American *n* **1** a member of any of the indigenous races of N America. **2** more generally, a member of any of the indigenous races of N, S, or Central America; = AMERICAN INDIAN.

Usage note

This is now generally accepted as the correct term to use for a person whose ancestors lived in America before the arrival of Europeans. The term *Red Indian* for a Native (North) American should be avoided. See also note at AMERICAN INDIAN.

native speaker *n* a person who speaks the language in question as their native language.

nativity *n* (*pl* **-ies**) **1** one's birth. **2a** (**the Nativity**) the birth of Jesus Christ. **b** the festival celebrating this; Christmas. **c** a painting or other artistic representation of this.

NATO *or* **Nato** *abbr* North Atlantic Treaty Organization.

natron *n* hydrated sodium carbonate occurring as a mineral and used in ancient times in embalming.

natter[1] *v chiefly Brit, informal* to chatter or gossip.

natter[2] *n* the act or an instance of nattering.

natterjack *n* a common brownish yellow W European toad with short hind legs, which runs rather than hops.

natty *adj* (**-ier, -iest**) *informal* **1** of clothes or their wearer: neat and trim; spruce. **2** of a gadget, contrivance, etc: clever, neat, or apt. ➤➤ **nattily** *adv*, **nattiness** *n*.

natural[1] *adj* **1** existing in or produced by nature without human intervention. **2** relating to nature or the physical world as an object of study and research. **3a** happening in accordance with the ordinary course of nature. **b** normal; expected. **c** following from the nature of the case; warranted by the facts. **4a** innate; inherent. **b** having a specific character or attribute by nature. **5** not affected or forced; easy and relaxed. **6a** related by blood rather than adoption. **b** *archaic* illegitimate. **7** of musical notes: neither sharp nor flat. **8a** of fabric: unbleached or undyed. **b** off-white or creamy beige in colour.

natural[2] *n* **1** *informal* a person having natural skills, talents, or abilities. **2a** a sign (♮) placed on the musical stave to indicate that the following note or notes are not sharp or flat. **b** a note to which the natural sign applies. **3** *Brit, informal* one's life.

natural-born *adj* equipped by nature to be the specified thing.

natural childbirth *n* the management of labour by the mother, through special breathing and relaxation techniques, so that the use of drugs is kept to a minimum.

natural gas *n* a combustible mixture of methane and other hydrocarbons, occurring naturally underground and used chiefly as a fuel.

natural history *n* the usu amateur study of natural objects, e.g. plants and animals, often in a particular area.

naturalise *v* see NATURALIZE.

naturalism *n* realism in art or literature, *esp* when emphasizing scientific observation of life without idealization of the ugly. ➤➤ **naturalistic** *adj*, **naturalistically** *adv*.

naturalist *n* **1** a follower or advocate of naturalism. **2** a student of natural history. ➤➤ **naturalist** *adj*.

naturalize *or* **naturalise** *v* **1** to admit (a foreigner) to the citizenship of a country. **2** (*in passive*) **a** of a plant or animal: to become established in the wild in an area where it is not indigenous. **b** of an originally foreign word, e.g. shampoo: to develop the phonology and grammatical features of a native word.

natural law *n* **1a** the set of moral principles that are understood to govern human conduct. **b** any one of these principles. **2** a law of nature that is an observed pattern operating in relation to natural phenomena.

natural logarithm *n* a logarithm with *e* as base.

naturally *adv* **1** by nature. **2** as might be expected; of course. **3** in a natural manner.

natural number *n* the number 1 or any positive whole number, e.g. 3, 12, 432.

natural philosophy *n archaic* natural or physical science, *esp* physics.

natural resources *pl n* industrial materials and capacities, e.g. mineral deposits and waterpower, supplied by nature.

natural science *n* any of the sciences dealing with the physical world and its phenomena, including physics, chemistry, biology, and geology. ⯮ **natural scientist** *n.*

natural selection *n* a natural process of evolution that tends to result in the survival of organisms best adapted to their environment.

nature *n* **1** the physical world in terms of landscape, plants, and animals, as distinct from human creations. **2** the inherent character or constitution of a person or thing; essence. **3** disposition or temperament. **4** an individual's inborn or inherited characteristics, as distinct from those attributable to nurture. **5** a kind or class of thing. ✱ **in the nature of things** inevitable or inevitably.

nature reserve *n* an area of great botanical or zoological interest protected from exploitation by human beings.

nature trail *n* a walk, e.g. in a nature reserve, planned to indicate points of interest to the observer of nature.

naturism *n* = NUDISM. ⯮ **naturist** *adj and n.*

naturopathy *n* treatment of disease emphasizing stimulation of the natural healing processes, including the use of herbal medicines, diet control, exercise, and massage. ⯮ **naturopath** *n,* **naturopathic** *adj.*

naught *n* **1** *archaic or literary* nothing. **2** *NAm* the arithmetical symbol 0; nought.

naughty *adj* (**-ier, -iest**) **1** of a child: badly behaved; disobedient. **2** *euphem or humorous* slightly improper. ⯮ **naughtily** *adv,* **naughtiness** *n.*

nausea *n* **1** a feeling of discomfort in the stomach accompanied by a distaste for food and an urge to vomit. **2** extreme disgust.

nauseate *v* to affect with nausea or disgust. ⯮ **nauseating** *adj,* **nauseatingly** *adv.*

nauseous *adj* **1** affected with nausea or disgust. **2** disgusting. ⯮ **nauseously** *adv,* **nauseousness** *n.*

nautical *adj* relating to or associated with seamen, navigation, or ships. ⯮ **nautically** *adv.*

nautical mile *n* a unit of distance used for sea and air navigation, *esp* a former British unit equal to 6080ft (about 1853.18m), replaced in 1970 by an international unit equal to 1852m (about 6076.17ft).

nautilus *n* (*pl* **nautiluses** *or* **nautili**) a mollusc with a light spiral shell, upright during swimming, that inhabits the Pacific and Indian Oceans.

Navajo *or* **Navaho** *n* (*pl* **Navajos** *or* **Navahos** *or* **Navajo** *or* **Navaho**) **1** a member of a Native American people of New Mexico, Utah, and Arizona. **2** the language of this people.

naval *adj* relating to a navy.

navarin *n* a mutton or lamb casserole cooked with root vegetables.

nave[1] *n* the main long central space of a church lying to the west of the chancel and usu flanked by aisles.

nave[2] *n* the hub of a wheel.

navel *n* the depression in the middle of the abdomen marking the point of former attachment of the umbilical cord.

navel-gazing *n humorous* **1** unproductive self-analysis. **2** obsession with a single narrow issue.

navel orange *n* a seedless orange with a pit at the top enclosing a small secondary fruit.

navigable *adj* **1** of a river, channel, etc: suitable for ships to pass through or along. **2** of a vessel or craft: capable of being steered. ⯮ **navigability** *n.*

navigate *v* **1** to plan or direct the course of a ship or aircraft, *esp* with the aid of maps and instruments. **2** to sail through (seas) or travel across (terrain). **3** in computing, to explore (the Internet) using hypertext links. **4** of a car passenger: to read the map and advise the driver about the route.

navigation *n* **1** the activity of navigating. **2** the science of determining position, course, distance travelled, and the best course to be steered in a ship or aircraft. **3** traffic on any stretch of water; the passage of vessels. ⯮ **navigational** *adj.*

navigation lights *pl n* the set of lights displayed at night by a ship or aircraft to indicate position and direction.

navigator *n* **1** the person in charge of navigating a ship, aircraft, etc. **2** formerly, an explorer by sea. **3** (**Navigator**) *trademark* a computer program for browsing on the Internet.

navvy *n* (*pl* **-ies**) *Brit* an unskilled labourer.

navy *n* (*pl* **-ies**) **1** (*often* **Navy**) (*used as sing. or pl*) the branch of a country's armed services supplying the crews and the supporting personnel for ships of war and support vessels. **2** = NAVY BLUE.

navy blue *adj* of a deep dark blue colour. ⯮ **navy blue** *n.*

nawab /nə'wahb/ *n* **1** = NABOB (1). **2** a Muslim of high or noble status.

nay[1] *adv* **1** *literary* not merely this but even: *She was happy, nay, ecstatic.* **2** *N Eng or archaic* no.

nay[2] *n* a denial or refusal.

Nazarene *n* **1** a native or inhabitant of Nazareth in Galilee (now N Israel). **2** (**the Nazarene**) Jesus Christ. **3** a member of a Jewish sect of early Christians.

Nazi /'nahtsi/ *n* (*pl* **Nazis**) **1** a member of the National Socialist German Workers' Party, which controlled Germany from 1933 to 1945. **2** *derog* a person with fascist, authoritarian, or racist attitudes. ⯮ **Nazi** *adj,* **Nazism** *n.*

NB *abbr* **1** New Brunswick (US postal abbreviation). **2** (Latin) nota bene: note well.

Nb *abbr* the chemical symbol for niobium.

nb *abbr* in cricket, no ball.

NC *abbr* **1** network computer. **2** North Carolina (US postal abbreviation).

NCO *abbr* non-commissioned officer.

ND *abbr* North Dakota (US postal abbreviation).

Nd *abbr* the chemical symbol for neodymium.

Ndebele /əndə'beeli, -'bayli/ *n* (*pl* **Ndebeles** *or* **Ndebele**) a member of a people of Zimbabwe and NE South Africa. ⯮ **Ndebele** *adj.*

NE *abbr* **1** Nebraska (US postal abbreviation). **2** Northeast. **3** Northeastern.

Ne *abbr* the chemical symbol for neon.

né /nay/ *adj* the masculine of NÉE: originally called: *David Swinton, né Schwitzer.*

Neanderthal *n* **1** an extinct Palaeolithic species of human that inhabited Europe widely between 120,000 and 35,000 years ago, characterized by a receding forehead and prominent brow ridges, and producing flints worked on one side only. **2** *informal* a man who is primitive in behaviour or attitudes.

Neanderthal man *n* = NEANDERTHAL.

neap *n* a tide just after the first and third quarters of the moon, when the difference between high and low tide is at its smallest.

Neapolitan *adj* **1** of or relating to the city of Naples. **2** of ice cream: having different-coloured layers. ➤➤ **Neapolitan** *n.*

neap tide *n* = NEAP.

near[1] *adv* **1** (*often* + to) at or to only a short distance away. **2** (*used before an adjective*) almost: *with near-disastrous results.*

near[2] *prep* near to: *near the edge.*

near[3] *adj* **1** close in place, time, or connection. **2** almost but not quite a certain thing: *a near disaster.* **3** denoting the side of a vehicle nearest the kerb. ➤➤ **nearness** *n.*

near[4] *v* to approach (a place or point).

nearby *adv and adj* close at hand.

Near East *n* the countries of SW Asia between the Mediterranean coast and India.

nearly *adv* **1** almost but not quite. **2** closely. ✱ **not nearly** by no means.

near miss *n* **1** something one does not quite achieve. **2** a near-collision between vehicles, *esp* aircraft.

nearside *n Brit* the left-hand side of a vehicle or the road: compare OFF SIDE.

nearsighted *adj* able to see near things more clearly than distant ones; myopic.

neat *adj* **1** tidy or orderly. **2** entirely satisfactory; well-defined or precise. **3** *NAm, informal* excellent. **4** of spirits: without addition or dilution; straight. ➤➤ **neatly** *adv,* **neatness** *n.*

neaten *v* to make neat or neater.

neath *or* **'neath** *prep literary* beneath.

neat's-foot oil *n* a pale yellow oil made by boiling the feet of cattle, used as a leather dressing.

neb *n archaic or dialect* **1** the nose. **2** an animal's snout or bird's beak.

nebuchadnezzar *n* a very large champagne bottle that holds 20 times the normal amount (about 16 litres).

nebula *n* (*pl* **nebulas** *or* **nebulae**) any of many immense bodies of highly rarefied gas or dust in interstellar space. ➤➤ **nebular** *adj.*

nebulise *v* see NEBULIZE.

nebuliser *n* see NEBULIZER.

nebulize *or* **-ise** *v* to reduce (a liquid) to a fine spray or atomize (a liquid).

nebulizer *or* **nebuliser** *n* a device for discharging a liquid, *esp* a medicine for inhaling, in the form of a fine spray; = ATOMIZER.

nebulous *adj* **1** of ideas, etc: indistinct or vague. **2** relating to or resembling a nebula; nebular. **3** hazy; misty. ➤➤ **nebulosity** *n.*

necessarily *adv* as a necessary consequence; inevitably.

necessary[1] *adj* **1** essential; indispensable. **2** inevitable; inescapable. **3** logically unavoidable: *a necessary conclusion.*

necessary[2] *n* (*pl* **-ies**) **1** an indispensable item; an essential. **2** (**the necessary**) **a** *informal* the action required; the needful. **b** *Brit, informal* money.

necessitate *v* to make necessary or unavoidable.

necessitous *adj formal* lacking life's necessities; needy.

necessity *n* (*pl* **-ies**) **1** the quality of being necessary, indispensable, or unavoidable. **2** impossibility of a contrary order or condition, *esp* in a specified sphere: *physical necessity.* **3** pressing need or desire. **4** something necessary or indispensable. ✱ **of necessity** necessarily.

neck[1] *n* **1** the part of a person or animal that connects the head with the body. **2** a relatively narrow part shaped like a neck, e.g.: **a** the constricted end of a bottle. **b** the part of a stringed musical instrument extending from the body and supporting the fingerboard and strings. **3** *Brit, informal* insolent boldness; cheek. ✱ **breathe down somebody's neck** see BREATHE. **by a neck** by a narrow margin. **catch/get it in the neck** *informal* to be severely rebuked or punished. **neck and neck** keeping abreast in a race. **neck of the woods** *usu humorous* a district or locality, *esp* if undistinguished. **save one's neck** to make good one's escape from a compromising situation, etc. **up to one's neck in** deeply involved in (some business). ➤➤ **neckless** *adj.*

neck[2] *v informal* to kiss and caress in sexual play.

neckband *n* a band of fabric forming the neck piece of a garment.

neckcloth *n* a large cravat.

neckerchief *n* a square of fabric folded and worn round the neck.

necklace[1] *n* a string of jewels, beads, etc worn round the neck as an ornament.

necklace[2] *v* to kill (somebody) by placing a petrol-soaked tyre round their neck and setting it alight.

necklet *n* a rigid, close-fitting ornament for wearing round the neck.

neckline *n* the upper edge of a garment that forms the opening for the neck and head.

necromancy *n* **1** the conjuring up of the spirits of the dead in order to predict or influence the future. **2** magic or sorcery generally. ➤➤ **necromancer** *n,* **necromantic** *adj.*

necrophilia *n* obsession with, erotic interest in, or sexual intercourse with corpses. ➤➤ **necrophiliac** *adj and n.*

necrophobia *n* an irrational fear of death or corpses.

necropolis *n* (*pl* **necropolises** *or* **necropoleis**) a cemetery, *esp* a large elaborate cemetery of an ancient city.

necropsy *n* (*pl* **-ies**) examination of a body after death.

necrosis *n* (*pl* **necroses**) the death of living tissue through disease, injury, or interruption of the blood supply. ➤➤ **necrotic** *adj.*

necrotize *or* **-ise** *v* **1** to undergo necrosis. **2** to cause necrosis in (cells or tissues).

nectar *n* **1** a sweet liquid secreted by the flowers of many plants that is collected and made into honey by bees. **2** in classical mythology, the drink of the gods.

nectarine *n* a type of peach with a smooth thin downless skin and firm flesh.

nectary *n* (*pl* **-ies**) a plant gland found in flowers or leaves that secretes nectar.

née *or* **nee** /nay/ *adj* used to identify a married woman by her maiden name: born as: *Mary Thomson, née Wilkinson.*

need[1] *v* **1** to be in need of or require. **2** to be constrained or required to do something: *We need to discuss this urgently.* ➤ *v aux* (*third person sing. present tense* **need**) (*chiefly in questions or with neg-atives*) to be under necessity or obligation to do something: *She need not decide straight away; Need you shout?*

need[2] *n* **1** obligation. **2** sufficient reason; grounds. **3** (*also in pl*) something one requires. **4** a condition requiring supply or relief. **5** poverty; want.

needful *adj* **1** necessary or requisite. **2** *archaic* needy. ✱ **the needful** *informal* what is needed, *esp* money.

needle[1] *n* **1** a small slender usu steel instrument with an eye for thread at one end and a sharp point at the other, used for sewing. **2** any of various similar larger instruments without an eye that are used, e.g. in crocheting or knitting. **3** a slender hollow pointed end of a hypodermic syringe. **4** a slender pointed indicator on a dial, e.g. the magnetic needle of a compass. **5** a stylus for playing records. **6** a needle-shaped leaf, *esp* of a conifer. **7** *Brit, informal* ill feeling; hostility.

needle[2] *v* **1** *literary* to sew or pierce with a needle, or as if with a needle. **2** *informal* to provoke by persistent teasing or gibes.

needlecord *n* a fine corduroy with close ribs and a flattish pile.

needlepoint *n* **1** (*also* **needlelace**) lace worked with a needle over a paper or parchment pattern. **2** embroidery worked on canvas usu in a simple even stitch, e.g. cross-stitch or tent stitch.

needless *adj* not needed; unnecessary. ✱ **needless to say** naturally; of course. ➤➤ **needlessly** *adv.*

needlewoman *n* (*pl* **needlewomen**) a woman who does needlework, *esp* skilfully.

needlework *n* sewing or embroidery.

needn't *contr* need not.

needy *adj* (**-ier, -iest**) in want; impoverished. ➤➤ **neediness** *n.*

neem *or* **nim** *n* a SE Asian tree from which wood, insecticide, gum, and medicinal products are obtained.

neep *n Scot and N Eng* a turnip.

ne'er *adv literary* never.

ne'er-do-well *n* an idle worthless person.

nefarious *adj* iniquitous; criminal.

negate *v* **1** to nullify or make ineffective or invalid. **2** to deny the existence or truth of. **3** in grammar or logic, to make (a statement, clause, etc) negative.

negation *n* **1** a denial or contradiction of something. **2** something that represents the absence or opposite of something actual or positive.

negative[1] *adj* **1** indicating or expressing denial, prohibition, or refusal. **2** denoting the absence or the contradiction of something. **3** expressing negation. **4** lacking positive qualities. **5** of a number: less than zero. **6** being, relating to, or charged with electricity of which the electron is the elementary unit. **7** gaining electrons. **8** having lower electric potential and constituting the part towards which the current flows from the external circuit. **9** of a test result: not affirming the presence of the organism or condition in question. **10** of a photographic image: having the light and dark parts of the subject reversed. ➤➤ **negatively** *adv,* **negativity** *n.*

negative[2] *n* **1** in grammar, etc, a word such as *no, not,* or *never* that expresses negation, denial, or refusal, or a statement employing such an expression. **2** in logic, etc, something that is the opposite or negation of the thing in question. **3** a minus number. **4** a photographic image, usu on transparent film, used for printing positive pictures, with the light and dark of the original reversed.

negative[3] *v* **1** to reject, veto, or refuse to accept or approve (a proposal, etc). **2** to contradict, disprove, or demonstrate the falsity of (a statement, claim, argument, etc). **3** to nullify or render ineffective.

negative equity *n* a situation placing the owner of a mortgaged property potentially in debt when the market value of the property falls below the amount of mortgage left to be repaid.

negative pole *n* that pole of a magnet which turns southwards when the magnet swings freely.

negative sign *n* = MINUS SIGN.

neglect[1] *v* **1** to fail to give (a person, animal, or thing) proper care and attention. **2** to fail (to do something required of one). **3** to disregard, or fail to act in accordance with (one's duties, somebody's advice, etc).

neglect[2] *n* **1** failure to give, or the resulting lack of, proper care and attention. **2** the act of neglecting something.

neglectful *adj* (*often* + of) careless, heedless, or forgetful.

negligee *or* **negligé** /'neglizhay/ *n* a woman's light decorative dressing gown.

negligence *n* **1** carelessness or forgetfulness. **2** in law, the offence of failing to take due care, when this is judged to have contributed to or caused the damage in question. ➤➤ **negligent** *adj.*

negligible *adj* so slight or insignificant as to be not worth considering; trifling. ➤➤ **negligibly** *adv.*

negotiable *adj* **1** transferable to another person. **2** of a road, route, passage, etc: capable of being passed along or through. **3** capable of being dealt with or settled through discussion. ➤➤ **negotiability** *n.*

negotiate *v* **1** to confer with others affected by a disputed issue, with the aim of reaching agreement over it. **2** to achieve (a settlement, etc) by discussion with others. **3** to pass or deal with (an obstacle en route). **4** to transfer (a cheque or bill of exchange) to somebody else's legal possession. ➤➤ **negotiator** *n,* **negotiation** *n.*

Negress *n now offensive* a woman or girl of black African race.

negritude *n* **1** the fact or quality of being of black African race. **2** conscious pride in the African heritage.

Negro *n* (*pl* **-oes**) *now offensive* a member or descendant of any of a group of black peoples native to Africa south of the Sahara Desert. ➤➤ **Negro** *adj.*

Usage note

Negro, black, *and* coloured. See note at BLACK[2].

Negroid *adj sometimes offensive* belonging to one of the divisions of humankind represented by the indigenous races of central and S Africa.

Negrophobia *n* an irrational fear or dislike of black people. ➤➤ **Negrophobe** *n.*

neigh *v* to make the characteristic cry of a horse. ➤➤ **neigh** *n.*

neighbour[1] (*NAm* **neighbor**) *n* **1** a person who lives next door, or very close, to one. **2** a person next to one, or a country, etc next to one's own. ➤➤ **neighbourly** *adj.*

neighbour[2] (*NAm* **neighbor**) *v literary or archaic* to adjoin or lie near to (a place).

neighbourhood (*NAm* **neighborhood**) *n* **1** the area surrounding one's own home. **2** the area around the thing specified. **3** a particular place or location. ✱ **in the neighbourhood of** approximately (a certain amount).

neighbourhood watch *n* a scheme organized within a local community, by which members take joint responsibility for keeping a watch on each other's property.

neither[1] *adj* not the one or the other of two; not either: *neither hand.*

neither[2] *pron* not the one or the other of two: *neither of us.*

Usage note

Neither should be followed by a verb in the singular when it is the subject of a sentence: *Neither of them was caught.* If two or more particular things or people are being mentioned, *neither* is followed by *nor,* not by *or*: *Neither Janet nor her sister is coming* (see NEITHER[3]). Both pronunciations ('niedhə or 'needhə) are acceptable: British English tends to prefer the former and American English the latter.

neither[3] *conj* used with NOR[1]: not either: *neither here nor there.*

neither[4] *adv* **1** similarly not; also not; = NOR[2]: *'I can't understand it.' 'Neither can I'.* **2** *archaic or dialect* either: *I saw Mark Antony offer him a crown – yet 'twas not a crown neither – 'twas one of these coronets* — Shakespeare.

nekton *n* a collective term for aquatic animals, such as whales or squid, that swim freely independent of water currents, as distinct from plankton. ➤➤ **nektonic** *adj.*

nelly ✱ **not on your nelly** *informal* certainly not; not on your life.

nelson *n* a wrestling hold in which leverage is applied against one's opponent's head, neck, and arm.

nematode *n* an elongated cylindrical worm of a group that are parasitic in animals or plants or living freely in soil or water, including the threadworms, roundworms, and eelworms.

nemesis *n* (*pl* **nemeses**) **1** retribution or vengeance. **2** a person or thing that is the agent of this.

neo- *comb. form* **1** new; recent: *neonate.* **2** in a revived form: *neoclassicism.*

neoclassic *adj* = NEOCLASSICAL.

neoclassical *adj* relating to or constituting a revival or adaptation of the classical, *esp* in literature, music, art, or architecture. ➤➤ **neoclassicism** *n,* **neoclassicist** *n and adj.*

neocortex *n* (*pl* **neocortices**) the back part of the CORTEX (area of brain controlling higher-thought ability) that is unique to mammals, considered the most recently evolved part of the cortex and responsible for sight and hearing. ➤➤ **neocortical** *adj.*

neodymium *n* a silver-grey metallic chemical element of the rare-earth group that is used in colouring glass.

neo-Impressionism *n* a late 19th-cent. development of Impressionism in France, whose chief exponents were Seurat, Signac, and Camille Pissarro, their work being characterized by formal composition and the use of pointillism. ➤➤ **neo-Impressionist** *adj and n.*

Neolithic *adj* of the last period of the Stone Age, a geological period characterized by polished stone implements. ➤➤ **Neolithic** *n.*

neologism *n* a new word, usage, or expression.

neon *n* **1** a gaseous chemical element of the noble gas group, used in fluorescent signs and lighting. **2** fluorescent signs and lighting using neon. **3** (*used before a noun*) of or relating to neon: *a neon sign.*

neonate *n technical* a newborn child less than a month old. ➤➤ **neonatal** *adj,* **neonatology** *n.*

neon tetra *n* a small tropical fish with a glowing blue-green band along each side and a red band on the tail, sought after for aquariums.

neophobia *n* irrational dislike or fear of anything new and unfamiliar. ➤➤ **neophobic** *adj.*

neophyte *n* **1** a new convert to a religious faith. **2** a recently ordained priest or a novice in a religious order. **3** a beginner in a subject, skill, etc.

neoplasm *n* an abnormal growth of tissue; a tumour. ➤➤ **neoplastic** *adj.*

Neoplatonism *n* a modified form of the philosophy of Plato developed in the third cent. AD, incorporating Pythagorean and Aristotelian features, along with elements of oriental mysticism. ➤➤ **Neoplatonic** *adj,* **Neoplatonist** *n.*

neoprene *n* a synthetic rubber resistant to oils.

neoteny *n* **1** in zoology, the retention of some larval or immature characters in adulthood. **2** in zoology, the attainment of sexual maturity during the larval stage, e.g. in the axolotl. ➤➤ **neotenic** *adj,* **neotenous** *adj.*

Nepalese *n and adj* (*pl* **Nepalese**) see NEPALI.

Nepali *n* (*pl* **Nepalis** *or* **Nepali**) **1** a native or inhabitant of Nepal. **2** the official language of Nepal. ➤➤ **Nepali** *adj.*

nephew *n* the son of one's brother or sister or of one's brother-in-law or sister-in-law.

nephridium *n* (*pl* **nephridia**) a tubular glandular organ for excreting waste matter, characteristic of various invertebrate animals, e.g. earthworms.

nephrite *n* a green, white, or black variety of jade.

nephritic *adj* **1** relating to the kidneys; = RENAL. **2** relating to or affected with nephritis.

nephritis *n* inflammation of the kidneys.

nephrosis *n* degenerative, as distinct from inflammatory, kidney disease.

nepotism *n* favouritism shown to a relative, e.g. by appointment to office. ➤➤ **nepotistic** *adj.*

Word history

French *népotisme* from Italian *nepotismo,* from *nepote* nephew, from Latin *nepot-, nepos* grandson, nephew. The reference is to the 'nephews' of some popes (in many cases their illegitimate sons) who were given privileges and career advancement.

neptunium *n* a silvery radioactive metallic chemical element artificially produced by bombarding uranium with neutrons.

nerd *or* **nurd** *n informal* **1** a boring or socially inept person. **2** a person obsessed with computing; a computer freak. ➤➤ **nerdish** *adj,* **nerdy** *adj.*

neroli *n* a fragrant pale yellow essential oil obtained from the flowers of the orange tree and used in cologne and as a flavouring.

nerve[1] *n* **1** a threadlike band of nervous tissue that connects parts of the nervous system with the other organs and conducts nervous impulses. **2** a combination of courage, self-discipline, adventurous spirit, and tenacity. **3** *informal* cheek; audacity. **4** (*in pl*) feelings of acute nervousness or anxiety. ✱ **hit/touch a nerve** to mention a subject that causes one's hearer particular distress.

nerve[2] *v* (*also* + up/for) to prepare (oneself) psychologically for a challenge.

nerve cell *n* = NEURON.

nerve centre *n* **1** a group of connected nerve cells associated with a particular bodily function. **2** the control centre or headquarters of an operation.

nerve fibre *n* the AXON (thread of nerve tissue) leading from a NEURON (nerve cell).

nerve gas *n* a deadly gas, *esp* an organophosphate, that interferes with nerve transmission and disrupts the vital functions, e.g. respiration.

nerveless *adj* **1** lacking strength or vigour; inert. **2** not agitated or afraid; cool. **3** without nerves or nervures.

nerve-racking *or* **nerve-wracking** *adj* placing a great strain on the nerves; hair-raising.

nervous *adj* **1** relating to the nerves. **2** anxious or apprehensive. **3** constitutionally anxious or easily upset. **4** of an ailment such as a headache: caused by anxious anticipation. ⋙ **nervously** *adv*, **nervousness** *n*.

nervous breakdown *n* a mental and emotional disorder in which worrying, depression, severe tiredness, etc prevent one from coping with one's responsibilities.

nervous system *n* the brain, spinal cord, or other nerves and nervous tissue together forming a system for interpreting stimuli from the sense organs and transmitting impulses to muscles, glands, etc.

nervous wreck *n informal* a description of somebody in a severely stressed condition.

nervure *n* **1** in an insect, any of the ribs supporting the wings. **2** any of the veins, *esp* the principal vein, of a leaf.

nervy *adj* (**-ier, -iest**) **1** *chiefly Brit* suffering from nervousness or anxiety. **2** *NAm, informal* brash or imprudent. ⋙ **nervily** *adv*, **nerviness** *n*.

nescience *n literary* ignorance; lack of knowledge. ⋙ **nescient** *adj*.

ness *n archaic* found in place names: a cape or headland.

-ness *suffix* forming nouns, denoting: a state or quality, or an instance of it: *goodness; a kindness*.

nest[1] *n* **1** a structure built by a bird for laying eggs in, and for sheltering its young. **2** a place or structure where other creatures, e.g. insects, breed or shelter. **3** a den or haunt. **4** a set of things in a range of sizes, that fit one inside the other.

nest[2] *v* **1** of birds: to construct or occupy a nest ready for rearing young. **2** to fit (a set of tables, etc) one inside the other.

nest box *n* a specially constructed box provided for a bird to nest in.

nest egg *n* **1** a real or artificial egg left in a nest to induce a fowl to continue to lay there. **2** an amount of money saved up as a reserve.

nesting box *n* = NEST BOX.

nestle *v* **1** to settle snugly or comfortably. **2** of a place: to lie in a sheltered position.

nestling *n* a young bird that has not abandoned the nest.

net[1] *n* **1** an open meshed fabric of any of various degrees of coarseness or fineness, twisted, knotted, or woven together at regular intervals. **2** a device made of net for catching fish, birds, or insects. **3** a net barricade which divides a tennis, badminton, etc court in half. **4** a football, hockey, etc goal. **5** (*usu in pl*) a practice cricket pitch surrounded by nets. **6** arrangements made for trapping or ensnaring somebody. **7 a** a group of communications or broadcasting stations under unified control. **b** an interlinked series of computers. **c** (**the Net**) the Internet. ✱ **fall/slip through the net** to escape the elaborate system set up to entrap one.

net[2] *v* (**netted, netting**) **1** to cover or enclose with a net, or as if with a net. **2** to catch (a fish, etc) in a net, or as if in a net. **3a** to hit (a ball) into the net for the loss of a point in a game in tennis, badminton, etc. **b** to hit or kick (a ball or puck) into the goal for a score in hockey, football, etc.

net[3] *or Brit* **nett** *adj* **1** free from all charges or deductions, e.g.: **a** remaining after all deductions, e.g. for taxes, outlay, or loss: compare GROSS[1] (2A). **b** excluding all TARE[2] (deduction for weight of container). **2** final; ultimate.

net[4] *or Brit* **nett** *v* (**netted, netting**) **1** to make (a sum) by way of profit; to clear. **2** to get possession of (something) for oneself.

netball *n* a game played between teams of seven players who try to score goals by tossing an inflated ball through a high horizontal ring on a post at each end of a hard court.

nether *adj formal* lower or under. ⋙ **nethermost** *adj*.

nether regions *pl n* **1** the world of the dead; the underworld; Hades. **2** Hell. **3** *euphem* a person's bottom and genital area.

Netizen *n* an Internet user, especially one who actively contributes to the development of the Net.

net profit *n* the gross profit of an operation or transaction minus expenses such as operating costs, employees' wages, overheads, and depreciation.

netsuke /'netsooki, 'nets(ə)ki/ *n* (*pl* **netsuke** *or* **netsukes**) a small and often intricately carved toggle, e.g. of ivory, used to fasten a pouch to a kimono sash.

nett *adj and v* see NET[3], NET[4].

netting *n* a fabric or other material made of net.

nettle[1] *n* a widely distributed plant with greenish flowers and jagged leaves covered with stinging hairs. ✱ **grasp the nettle** to tackle a problem with bold determination.

nettle[2] *v* of a remark, etc: to goad or sting (somebody).

nettle rash *n* a raised itchy skin rash caused by allergy; = URTICARIA.

net-top box *n* a device that makes it possible to access the Internet via a television set.

network[1] *n* **1** a structure of crisscrossing cords, wires, etc, secured at the intersections, e.g. by knots. **2** any system of intersecting horizontal and vertical lines. **3** a system of interconnected railways, roads, etc. **4** a group of broadcasting stations linked together for a simultaneous broadcast. **5** a set of interconnected computers or terminals.

network[2] *v* **1** *Brit* to broadcast (a programme) on a network. **2** to link up (computers or terminals) so as to interact with each other. **3** to create useful contacts for oneself by talking and interacting with others. ⋙ **networker** *n*.

neur- *or* **neuro-** *comb. form* nerve; nervous system: *neural*.

neural *adj* relating to a nerve or the nervous system. ⋙ **neurally** *adv*.

neuralgia *n* intense paroxysms of pain radiating along the course of a nerve, *esp* in the head or face. ⋙ **neuralgic** *adj*.

neuritis *n* inflammation of a nerve or nerves, causing pain, sensory disturbances due to impaired function, etc.

neuro- *comb. form* see NEUR-.

neurogenic *adj* arising in or controlled by the nervous system.

neuroleptic *adj* of a drug: having a tranquillizing effect.

neurology *n* the study of the nervous system, its structure, and its function. ⋙ **neurological** *adj*, **neurologist** *n*.

neuron *or* **neurone** *n* any of the many specialized cells that form the functional units of the nervous system.

neuropathology *n* the study of the diseases of the nervous system. ⋙ **neuropathological** *adj*, **neuropathologist** *n*.

neuropathy *n* any dysfunctional state of the nerves or nervous system. ⋙ **neuropathic** *adj*.

neurophysiology *n* the physiology of the nervous system. ⋙ **neurophysiological** *adj*, **neurophysiologist** *n*.

neurosis *n* (*pl* **neuroses**) a nervous disorder, unaccompanied by disease of the nervous system, in which phobias, compulsions, anxiety, and obsessions make normal life difficult.

neurosurgery *n* surgery to a part of the nervous system. ⋙ **neurosurgeon** *n*, **neurosurgical** *adj*.

neurotic *adj* **1** relating to or caused by a neurosis. **2** affected by a neurosis; hypersensitive or obsessive about something. **3** *informal* unduly anxious. ⋙ **neurotic** *n*, **neurotically** *adv*, **neuroticism** *n*.

neurotoxin *n* any poison that acts on the nervous system, *esp* a poisonous protein such as that in snake venom.

neurotransmitter *n* a substance, e.g. acetylcholine, that is released at a nerve ending and transmits nerve impulses across the SYNAPSE (gap between nerve cells). ⋙ **neurotransmission** *n*.

neuter[1] *adj* **1** in grammar, denoting or belonging to the gender of nouns that is neither masculine nor feminine. **2** of an animal: **a** lacking generative organs, or having non-functioning ones. **b** castrated or spayed. **3** of a flower or plant: without pistils or stamens.

neuter[2] *n* in grammar, a neuter noun or other neuter form.

neuter[3] *v* **1** to spay or castrate (a domestic animal). **2** to render feeble or ineffective.

neutral[1] *adj* **1** of a country or a person: not engaged on either side of a war, dispute, etc. **2** impartial or unbiased. **3** of indefinite character; having no strongly distinctive characteristics. **4** denoting a colour that is any shade of beige or grey. **5** denoting chemical substances having a pH value of about 7, so neither acid nor alkaline. **6** not electrically charged, or neither positive nor negative; not live, as the blue-covered wire in an electric plug. ⋙ **neutralism** *n*, **neutralist** *n*, **neutrality** *n*, **neutrally** *adv*.

neutral[2] *n* **1** a neutral person or state. **2** a neutral colour or shade, *esp* beige. **3** the gear position in which no gear is engaged. **4** an electrically neutral or non-live terminal, etc.

neutralize *or* **-ise** *v* **1** to nullify or render ineffective by having the opposite effect. **2** to make (a substance) chemically neutral. **3** to disarm (a bomb). **4** *euphem* to kill (somebody). ⋙ **neutralization** *n*.

neutrino *n* (*pl* **-os**) either of two forms of an uncharged elementary particle that is created in the process of particle decay, e.g. inside a star, is believed to be massless, and interacts only slightly with other matter.

neutron *n* an uncharged elementary particle with a mass about that of the proton, present in the nuclei of all atoms except those of normal hydrogen.

neutron bomb *n* a nuclear bomb that produces relatively large amounts of radiation in the form of neutrons and a relatively small blast, being designed to destroy life while leaving buildings, etc intact.

neutron star *n* any of various very dense celestial bodies that consist mainly of closely packed neutrons thought to be the remainder of a much larger star the core of which collapsed under its own gravity.

névé /'nevay/ *n* partly compacted granular snow, *esp* forming the surface part of the upper end of a glacier.

never *adv* **1** not ever; at no time. **2** used emphatically for *not*. **3** surely not. ✱ **Well, I never!** used to express incredulity.

nevermore *adv literary* never again.

never-never *or* **the never-never** *n informal Brit* = HIRE PURCHASE.

never-never land *n* an ideal or imaginary place.

nevertheless *adv* in spite of that; yet; however.

nevus *n* (*pl* **nevi**) *NAm* see NAEVUS.

new[1] *adj* **1** recently bought, made, built, etc. **2** just invented or discovered. **3** fresh; unused. **4** doing something for the first time: *new parents*. **5** replacing the previous one. **6** fresh; unfamiliar; different. **7** refreshed; regenerated. ⋙ **newness** *n*.

new[2] *adv* (*used in combinations*) newly or recently: *new-mown grass*.

New Age *n* a cultural movement of the late 1980s, characterized by popular enthusiasm for alternative beliefs and disciplines, including astrology, mysticism, meditation, and holistic medicine.

newborn[1] *n* (*pl* **newborn** *or* **newborns**) a recently born child or animal.

newborn[2] *adj* **1** just born. **2** of hope, zeal, etc: reborn; regenerated.

newcomer *n* **1** a recent arrival. **2** a beginner or novice.

newel *n* **1** an upright post about which the steps of a spiral staircase wind. **2** a principal post supporting either end of a staircase handrail.

newel post *n* = NEWEL (2).

newfangled *adj derog* modern and unnecessarily complicated or gimmicky.

Newfoundland *n* a large intelligent dog of a breed with coarse dense hair.

New Guinean *n* a native or inhabitant of New Guinea. ⋙ **New Guinean** *adj*.

newly *adv* **1** lately; recently. **2** anew.

newlywed *n* a recently married person.

new man *n* a man who rather than adopting an aggressively male social role participates in activities traditionally regarded as more appropriate to women.

new maths (*NAm* **new math**) *pl n* (*used as sing. or pl*) mathematics that is based on set theory, *esp* as taught in primary and secondary schools.

new moon *n* **1** the phase of the moon when its dark side is towards the earth. **2** the thin crescent moon seen a few days after this.

news *pl n* (*used as sing.*) **1** information about something that has recently happened. **2** information about recent events in the world, reported in the newspapers, or on radio and television. **3** (**the news**) a broadcast report of such events.

news agency *n* (*pl* **-ies**) an organization that collects news items for distribution to newspapers.

newsagent *n chiefly Brit* a retailer of newspapers and magazines.

newscast *n* a broadcast news report. ⋙ **newscaster** *n*.

news conference *n* a press conference.

newsflash *n* a brief broadcast reporting an important item of news, *esp* one that interrupts a programme.

newsgroup *n* a forum of Internet users or e-mail correspondents who exchange news and views about topics of mutual interest.

newsletter *n* a publication containing news and articles relevant to a particular group, association, etc, for circulation to its members.

newsman *n* (*pl* **newsmen**) a reporter or correspondent.

newspaper *n* a printed daily or weekly publication consisting of folded sheets and containing news reports, articles, and advertising.

newspeak *or* **Newspeak** *n* propagandistic language marked by euphemism and the inversion of customary meanings.

newsprint *n* cheap paper made chiefly from wood pulp and used mostly for newspapers.

newsreader *n* a broadcaster who reads the news.

newsreel *n* a short film dealing with current events.

newsroom *n* a place, e.g. an office, where news is prepared for publication or broadcast.

newsstand *n* a stall where newspapers and periodicals are sold.

New Stone Age *n* (**the New Stone Age**) the Neolithic period.

New Style *adj* the method of dating based on the Gregorian calendar.

news wire *n* an up-to-the-minute news service accessible via the Internet.

newsworthy *adj* (**-ier, -iest**) sufficiently interesting to warrant reporting.

newsy *adj* (**-ier, -iest**) of a letter, etc: full of news, *esp* personal news.

newt *n* a small amphibian of the salamander type, with a long slender body and tail and short legs.

New Testament *n* the second part of the Christian Bible, comprising the canonical Gospels and Epistles, the books of Acts, and the book of Revelation.

newton *n* the SI unit of force equal to the force that would impart an acceleration of one metre per second per second to a free mass of one kilogram.

Newtonian *adj* relating to, following, or agreeing with the English mathematician and scientist Sir Isaac Newton (d.1727) or his discoveries.

new town *n* in Britain, any of several towns planned and built as a unit since 1946.

new wave *n* **1** (*often* **New Wave**) a cinematic movement characterized by improvisation, abstraction, and the frequent use of experimental photographic techniques. **2** a style of rock music that developed from punk rock.

New World *n* (**the New World**) the W hemisphere, *esp* the continental landmass of N and S America.

New Year *n* **1** the first day or days of a calendar year. **2** the festive period around 31 December and 1 January.

New Year's Day *n* 1 January.

New Year's Eve *n* 31 December.

New Yorker *n* a native or inhabitant of the US city or state of New York.

New Zealander *n* a native or inhabitant of New Zealand.

next[1] *adj* **1** immediately adjacent or following, e.g. in place or order: *the next house.* **2** immediately after the present or a specified time: *next week.*

next[2] *adv* **1** in the time, place, or order nearest or immediately succeeding: *the next-closest school.* **2** on the following occasion or the first occasion to come: *when next we meet.* ✱ **next but one** not the next one but the one after.

next[3] *n* a person or thing that is next: *laughing one minute and crying the next.*

next door *adv* in or to the next building, room, etc.

next-door *adj* situated or living in the next building, room, etc.

next of kin *n* (*pl* **next of kin**) the person most closely related to oneself.

next to[1] *prep* immediately following or adjacent to.

next to[2] *adv* very nearly; almost.

nexus *n* (*pl* **nexuses** *or* **nexus**) **1** a connection or link. **2** a connected group or series. **3** the focus or nub of something.

Nez Percé /,nez 'puhs/ *n* (*pl* **Nez Percé** *or* **Percés**) a member of a Native American people of Idaho, Washington, and Oregon.

NF *abbr* **1** National Front. **2** Newfoundland (US postal abbreviation).

NFL *abbr NAm* National Football League.

ngaio /'nieoh/ *n* (*pl* **-os**) a small tree of New Zealand with white wood and edible fruit.

ngultrum /en'gooltrəm, eng-/ *n* (*pl* **ngultrum**) the basic monetary unit of Bhutan.

ngwee /(ə)ng'gwee/ *n* (*pl* **ngwee**) a unit of currency in Zambia, worth 100th of a kwacha.

NH *abbr* New Hampshire (US postal abbreviation).

NHS *abbr Brit* National Health Service.

NI *abbr* **1** *Brit* National Insurance. **2** Northern Ireland.

Ni *abbr* the chemical symbol for nickel.

niacin *n* = NICOTINIC ACID.

nib *n* **1** the writing point of a pen, from which the ink is distributed. **2** (*in pl*) shelled and crushed coffee or cocoa beans, nuts, etc.

nibble[1] *v* **1a** to bite (something) cautiously, gently, or playfully. **b** to eat or chew (something) in small bites. **2** to produce (a hole, etc) by repeated small bites. **3** to show cautious or qualified interest.

nibble[2] *n* **1** an act of nibbling. **2** a very small amount, e.g. of food. **3** *informal* (*in pl*) savoury morsels served at a reception, etc.

nibs ✱ **his nibs** *informal* an important or self-important man or one who demands a lot of attention.

Nicam *or* **NICAM** *n* in British television transmission, a digital system by means of which standard video signals are provided with high-quality stereo sound.

Nicaraguan *n* a native or inhabitant of Nicaragua. ➤➤ **Nicaraguan** *adj.*

NICE /nies/ *abbr* National Institute for Clinical Excellence.

nice *adj* **1** pleasant or agreeable. **2** of a person: kind, considerate, or accommodating. **3** socially respectable. **4** satisfactorily performed, competent, or skilful. **5** *ironic* fine: *She's a nice one to complain.* **6** subtle. **7** *archaic* fastidious or precise. ✱ **nice and** pleasantly; agreeably: *nice and warm.* ➤➤ **nicely** *adv,* **niceness** *n.*

nicety *n* (*pl* **-ies**) **1** a fine point or distinction. **2** subtlety or precision. **3** a point of etiquette or protocol. ✱ **to a nicety** to the point at which the thing in question is at its best: *roasted to a nicety.*

niche *n* **1** a recess in a wall, *esp* for a statue. **2** a place or activity for which a person is best suited. **3** the ecological role of an organism in a community, *esp* in regard to food consumption. **4** (*often used before a noun*) a specialized but rewarding retailing opportunity: *niche marketing.*

nick[1] *n* **1** a small cut, notch, or groove. **2** the point at which the back or side wall of a squash court meets the floor. **3** (**the nick**) *Brit, informal* a prison or police station. ✱ **in good/bad nick** *Brit, informal* in good or bad condition. **in the nick of time** at the final critical moment; just before it would be too late.

nick² *v* **1** to make a nick in. **2** to cut (a part of the body, etc) slightly. **3** *Brit, informal* to steal. **4** *Brit, informal* to arrest (somebody).

nickel¹ *n* **1** a silver-white metallic chemical element that is hard and malleable, with similar magnetic properties to iron, capable of a high polish and resistant to corrosion, occurs naturally in various ores, and is used in coins and in alloys. **2** a US coin worth five cents.

nickel² *v* (**nickelled, nickelling,** *NAm* **nickeled, nickeling**) to coat (a metal) with nickel.

nickel-and-dime *adj NAm, informal* unimportant; small-time.

nickel brass *n* an alloy of copper and zinc with a small amount of nickel.

nickel silver *n* a silver-white alloy of copper, zinc, and nickel.

nickel steel *n* stainless steel strengthened by the addition of chromium and nickel.

nicker¹ *n* (*pl* **nicker**) *Brit, informal* the sum of £1.

nicker² *v* of a horse: to whinny.

nicknack *n* see KNICK-KNACK.

nickname¹ *n* a familiar or humorous name used in place of or in addition to a proper name.

nickname² *v* to give (a person or thing) a nickname.

Niçois /nee'swah/ *or* **Niçoise** /nee'swahz/ *adj* (*usu after a noun*) denoting dishes garnished with tomatoes, anchovies, and capers: *salade Niçoise.*

nicotiana *n* a plant related to the tobacco plant, with fragrant tubular flowers.

nicotine *n* a poisonous chemical compound, the alkaloid that occurs in tobacco, used as an agricultural insecticide, causing disorders of the respiratory system, dizziness, increased blood pressure, and disturbances of hearing and vision.

nicotine patch *n* a skin patch impregnated with nicotine, worn to control the craving for tobacco.

nicotinic acid *n* a vitamin of the vitamin B complex that is found widely in animals and plants, deficiency in which results in PELLAGRA (skin disease).

nictate *v technical* to blink. ➤➤ **nictation** *n.*

nictitate *v* = NICTATE.

nictitating membrane *n* in birds, reptiles, and some mammals, e.g. cats, a thin membrane capable of extending across the eyeball under the eyelids.

nidi *n* pl of NIDUS.

nidification *n* the act, process, or technique of building a nest.

nidus *n* (*pl* **nidi** *or* **niduses**) **1** a nest or breeding place, *esp* a place in an animal or plant where bacteria or other organisms lodge and multiply. **2** a place where something originates, develops, or is found.

niece *n* a daughter of one's brother or sister or of one's brother-in-law or sister-in-law.

niello *n* **1** a black enamel-like compound of sulphur with silver, copper, and lead, used for filling in incised designs on silver or other metals. **2** decorated work of this kind.

Nietzschean /'neetshi·ən/ *adj* relating to the teachings of the German philosopher Friedrich Nietzsche (d.1900), *esp* his doctrine of the superman.

niff¹ *n Brit, informal* an unpleasant smell. ➤➤ **niffy** *adj.*

niff² *v Brit, informal* to smell unpleasant; to stink.

nifty *adj* (**-ier, -iest**) *informal* **1** very good or effective. **2** cleverly conceived or executed. ➤➤ **niftily** *adv.*

nigella *n* a plant with finely segmented leaves and white, blue, or yellow flowers, *esp* love-in-a-mist.

Niger-Congo *n* a large language family of sub-Saharan Africa which includes the Bantu, Kwa, and Mande languages. ➤➤ **Niger-Congo** *adj.*

Nigerian *n* a native or inhabitant of Nigeria. ➤➤ **Nigerian** *adj.*

niggard *n* a mean or stingy person.

niggardly *adj* **1** grudgingly mean; miserly. **2** provided in meagre amounts.

nigger *n offensive or derog* a black person, *esp* one of African race.

niggle *v* **1** of a pain or worry: to cause minor but persistent discomfort or anxiety. **2** to find fault constantly in a petty way. ➤➤ **niggle** *n,* **niggly** *adj.*

nigh *adv, adj, and prep archaic* near.

night *n* **1** the period of darkness from dusk to dawn caused by the earth's daily rotation. **2** an evening characterized by a specified event or activity: *bingo night; opening night.* **3** darkness; nightfall.

nightbird *n* = NIGHT OWL.

night blindness *n* reduced vision in dim light, *esp* at night.

nightcap *n* **1** formerly, a cloth cap worn in bed. **2** a drink taken at bedtime.

nightclothes *or* **night clothes** *pl n* clothes worn for sleeping in.

nightclub *n* a place of entertainment open at night that usu has a disco and a bar.

nightdress *n* a woman's or girl's nightgown.

nightfall *n* dusk.

nightgown *n* a loose garment for sleeping in.

nightie *or* **nighty** *n* (*pl* **-ies**) *informal* a nightdress.

nightingale *n* a small migratory thrush with brown plumage and a red-brown tail, noted for the sweet song of the male, typically heard at night.

nightjar *n* an insect-eating bird with large eyes and greyish brown plumage that is active at night and has a characteristic discordant call.

nightlife *n* late evening entertainment or social life.

night light *n* a dim light kept burning all night long, *esp* in the bedroom.

nightly¹ *adj* **1** happening at night. **2** happening every night.

nightly² *adv* every night.

nightmare *n* **1** a frightening or distressing dream. **2** an experience or situation that causes anxiety or terror or seems beyond one's control. ➤➤ **nightmarish** *adj.*

night owl *n informal* somebody who tends to be most active at night.

nights *adv informal* regularly every night.

night safe *n* a safe accessible from the exterior wall of a bank, used for depositing money when the bank is closed.

night school *n* classes, often in subjects leading to a qualification, held in the evening.

nightshirt *n* a long loose shirt for sleeping in.

nightside *n* the side of a planet or moon that is not in daylight.

night soil *n* human excrement collected for fertilizing the soil.

nightstick *n NAm* a club carried by a policeman.

night watchman *n* **1** a person who keeps watch, e.g. over a building, by night. **2** in cricket, a relatively inexpert batsman who is sent in to bat towards the end of a day's play.

nighty *n* (*pl* **-ies**) see NIGHTIE.

nigrescent *adj literary* blackish; dusky. ⯮ **nigrescence** *n.*

nigritude *n formal* blackness.

nihilism *n* **1** a view that rejects all values and beliefs as meaningless or unfounded. **2** the philosophical view that nothing has real existence; extreme scepticism. ⯮ **nihilist** *n,* **nihilistic** *adj.*

-nik *suffix* forming nouns, denoting: a person who is associated with a particular activity or cause: *refusenik.*

Nikkei average /'nikay/ *n* = NIKKEI INDEX.

Nikkei index *n* a figure indicating the average closing price of 225 representative stocks on the Tokyo Stock Exchange.

nil *n* nothing, zero. ⯮ **nil** *adj.*

Nilotic *adj* **1** denoting or belonging to the Nile or Nile region, or its people or languages. **2** denoting a group of languages spoken in Sudan and E Africa.

nim *n* see NEEM.

nimbi *n* pl of NIMBUS.

nimble *adj* **1** quick, light, and easy in movement. **2** quick and clever in thought and understanding. ⯮ **nimbly** *adv.*

nimbostratus *n* a cloud formation consisting of a dark rainy cloud layer, occurring at medium altitude.

nimbus *n* (*pl* **nimbi** *or* **nimbuses**) **1** a heavy grey rain-bearing cloud. **2** a luminous vapour, cloud, or atmosphere surrounding a god or goddess. **3** a luminous circle about the head of a representation of a god, saint, or sovereign: compare AUREOLE.

Nimby *n* (*pl* **Nimbys** *or* **Nimbies**) a person who, while not objecting in principle to a specified kind of development, etc, is averse to its occurring in their immediate neighbourhood.

niminy-piminy *adj* affectedly dainty or delicate.

Nimrod *or* **nimrod** *n literary* a huntsman.

nincompoop *n* a silly or foolish person.

nine *n* the number 9. ✱ **dressed to/up to the nines** *informal* dressed very smartly or elaborately. ⯮ **nine** *adj,* **ninefold** *adj and adv.*

nine days' wonder *n* something that creates a short-lived sensation.

ninepins *pl n* **1** (*used as sing.*) the games of skittles. **2** (*in sing.*) a skittle. ✱ **go down/drop/fall like ninepins** to fall over, fall ill, or die, in large numbers.

nineteen *adj and n* the number 19. ✱ **talk nineteen to the dozen** *informal* to talk or converse volubly. ⯮ **nineteenth** *adj and n.*

nineteenth hole *n humorous* the bar of a golf club.

ninety *adj and n* (*pl* **-ies**) **1** the number 90. **2** (*in pl*) the numbers 90 to 99. ⯮ **ninetieth** *adj and n.*

ninja *n* (*pl* **ninja** *or* **ninjas**) a person skilled in ninjutsu.

ninjutsu /nin'jootsooh/ *n* the Japanese martial art of espionage and camouflage.

ninny *n* (*pl* **-ies**) *informal* a silly or foolish person.

ninth *adj and n* **1** having the position in a sequence corresponding to the number nine. **2** one of nine equal parts of something. **3** in music, an interval of nine degrees of a diatonic scale, or the combination of two notes at such an interval. ⯮ **ninthly** *adv.*

niobium *n* a silver-grey metallic chemical element that is ductile, occurs naturally in columbite and tantalite, and is used in superconductive alloys.

Nip *n derog* a Japanese.

nip[1] *v* (**nipped, nipping**) **1** to catch hold of (something) and squeeze or pinch it sharply. **2** to give a small, sharp bite to (somebody or something). **3** of cold or frost: to injure (e.g. a plant) or numb (a part of the body). **4** *chiefly Brit, informal* to go quickly or briefly; to hurry. ✱ **nip something in the bud** to prevent the growth, development, or success of something at an early stage.

nip[2] *n* **1** a sharp stinging cold. **2** a sharp squeeze, *esp* between finger and thumb; a pinch. **3** a small, sharp bite. ✱ **nip and tuck 1** *chiefly NAm* neck and neck. **2** a piece of cosmetic surgery.

nip[3] *n* a small measure or drink of spirits.

nipper *n* **1** (*in pl*) any of various devices, e.g. pincers or pliers, for gripping or cutting. **2** *chiefly Brit, informal* a child.

nipple *n* **1** the small protuberance of a mammary gland, e.g. a breast, from which milk is drawn in the female. **2** an artificial teat through which a bottle-fed infant feeds. **3** a device with a hole through which the discharge of a liquid can be regulated. **4** a small projection through which oil or grease is injected into machinery.

nipplewort *n* a plant of the daisy family with small yellow flower heads, growing in woodland and wasteland.

nippy *adj* (**-ier, -iest**) **1** nimble and lively. **2** of the weather: chilly.

nirvana /nuh'vahnə/ *n* **1** (*often* **Nirvana**) a Hindu and Buddhist state of final bliss and freedom from the cycle of rebirth, attainable through the extinction of desire and individual consciousness. **2** a place or state of peaceful relief from pain or anxiety.

Nissen hut *n* a prefabricated shelter with a semicircular arching roof of corrugated iron and a concrete floor.

nit[1] *n* the egg or larva of a louse or other parasitic insect.

nit[2] *n chiefly Brit, informal* a nitwit.

nit[3] *or* **nepit** *n* a unit of information equal to 1.44 bits.

niterie *n* (*pl* **-ies**) *informal* a nightclub.

nitpick *v* to criticize in a petty and often unjustified way. ⯮ **nitpicker** *n.*

nit-picking *n* petty and often unjustified criticism.

nitr- *or* **nitro-** *comb. form* denoting a chemical compound that contains nitric acid, nitrogen, or nitrates: *nitrocellulose.*

nitrate[1] *n* a salt or ester of nitric acid.

nitrate[2] *v* to treat or combine (a substance) with nitric acid. ⯮ **nitration** *n.*

nitric acid *n* a corrosive inorganic liquid acid, used as an oxidizing agent and in making fertilizers, dyes, etc.

nitric oxide *n* a colourless poisonous gas that is obtained from nitrogen or ammonia and reacts in air to produce brown fumes of nitrogen dioxide gas.

nitride *n* a compound of nitrogen with one other element.

nitrify *v* (**-ies, -ied**) to combine or impregnate (a substance) with nitrogen or one of its compounds. ⯮ **nitrification** *n.*

nitrile *n* an organic compound containing the cyanide group.

nitrite *n* a salt or ester of nitrous acid.

nitro *n* (*pl* **-os**) nitroglycerine.

nitro- *comb. form* see NITR-.

nitrobenzene *n* an oily liquid with an almond smell, used as a solvent and in making aniline.

nitrocellulose *n* a chemical compound formed by the action of nitric acid on cellulose and used for making explosives, plastics, rayon, and varnishes.

nitrogen *n* a trivalent gaseous chemical element that constitutes about 78% by volume of the atmosphere and is found in combined form as a constituent of all living things. ➤➤ **nitrogenous** *adj.*

nitrogen dioxide *n* a red-brown highly poisonous gas that is formed by the combination of nitric oxide with oxygen and is used in the manufacture of nitric acid and in rocket fuel to provide oxygen needed for combustion.

nitrogen narcosis *n* a state of euphoria and exhilaration that occurs, *esp* in deep-water diving, when nitrogen in normal air is breathed at a higher than normal pressure.

nitroglycerine *or* **nitroglycerin** *n* an oily explosive liquid used chiefly in making dynamite.

nitrous *adj* relating to or containing nitrogen, *esp* with a relatively low valency.

nitrous acid *n* an unstable acid containing less oxygen than nitric acid and occurring only in solution or in the form of its salts.

nitrous oxide *n* a gas used as a general anaesthetic, *esp* in obstetrics and dentistry.

nitty-gritty *n informal* the important basic realities.

nitwit *n informal* a scatterbrained or stupid person.

nix[1] *n informal* nothing.

nix[2] *interj NAm, informal* no.

nix[3] *v NAm, informal* to veto, forbid, or cancel (a suggestion, deal, etc).

nix[4] *or* **nixie** *n* a water sprite of Germanic folklore.

Nizari /ni'zahri/ *n* (*pl* **Nizaris**) a member of an Ismaili Muslim sect now living mainly in India under the leadership of the Aga Khan.

NJ *abbr* New Jersey (US postal abbreviation).

NM *abbr* New Mexico (US postal abbreviation).

nm *abbr* **1** nanometre. **2** nautical mile.

NMR *abbr* nuclear magnetic resonance.

NNE *abbr* north-northeast.

NNW *abbr* north-northwest.

No[1] *abbr* the chemical symbol for nobelium.

No[2] *or* **Noh** *n* (*pl* **No** *or* **Noh**) classic Japanese dance-drama.

no[1] *interj* **1** used in answers expressing negation, dissent, denial, or refusal; contrasted with yes. **2** used like a question tag, demanding assent to the preceding statement. **3** used as an interjection to express incredulity. ✻ **not take no for an answer** to be persistent in trying to persuade somebody.

no[2] *adv* **1** used to mean 'not' in negating an alternative choice: *whether his mother would let him or no.* **2** (*in comparisons*) not in any respect or degree: *no better than before.* **3** *chiefly Scot* not: *It's no right.* ✻ **no longer/more** not any more; not as formerly.

no[3] *adj* **1** not any. **2** hardly any; very little. **3** not a; quite other than a: *He's no expert.* **4** used before a noun phrase to give force to an opposite meaning: *in no uncertain terms.* ✻ **no place** *NAm* nowhere. **no through road** used in signs: passage blocked or not allowed. **no two ways about it** there's no doubt about it; it's quite clear. **no way** *informal* used in emphatic refusal or denial: certainly not!

no[4] *n* (*pl* **noes**) a negative reply or vote.

no. *abbr* **1** in cricket, not out. **2** number.

Noachian *adj* relating to the Biblical patriarch Noah.

nob[1] *n informal* a person's head.

nob[2] *n chiefly Brit, informal* a wealthy or influential person. ➤➤ **nobby** *adj.*

no-ball *n and interj* an illegal delivery of the ball in cricket which cannot take a wicket and counts one run to the batsman's side if the batsman does not score a run off it.

nobble *v informal* **1** to incapacitate (a racehorse), *esp* by drugging. **2** to win over to one's side, *esp* by dishonest means. **3** to get hold of (something), *esp* dishonestly. **4** to swindle or cheat.

nobelium *n* a radioactive metallic chemical element that is artificially produced.

Nobel prize *n* any of various annual prizes established by the will of Alfred Nobel (d.1896) for the encouragement of people who work for the interests of humanity, e.g. in the fields of peace, literature, medicine, and physics.

nobility *n* (*pl* **-ies**) **1** the quality of being noble. **2** (*used as sing. or pl*) the people making up a noble class.

noble[1] *adj* **1** gracious and dignified in character or bearing. **2** of or relating to high birth or exalted rank. **3** imposing; stately. **4** having or showing a magnanimous character or high ideals. **5** chemically inert or unreactive: compare BASE[3]. ✻ **the noble art/science** *archaic or literary* boxing. ➤➤ **nobly** *adv.*

noble[2] *n* **1** a person of noble rank or birth. **2** a former English gold coin worth 6s 8d.

noble gas *n* any of a group of gaseous elements that react only slightly with other elements and include helium, neon, argon, krypton, xenon, and radon.

nobleman *n* (*pl* **noblemen**) a man of noble rank.

noble metal *n* a metal, *esp* gold, silver, or platinum, that is unreactive, is unaffected by acids, and does not corrode.

noble rot *n* a mould that grows on over-ripe grapes and is deliberately cultivated to give certain wines their distinctive flavour.

noble savage *n* the idealized concept of primitive man popularized by Romantic literature.

noblesse *n* (*used as sing. or pl*) the members of a country's nobility.

noblesse oblige *phrase* rank brings its responsibilities.

noblewoman *n* (*pl* **noblewomen**) a woman of noble rank.

nobody[1] *pron* no person; not anybody.

nobody[2] *n* (*pl* **-ies**) a person of no influence or consequence.

no-brainer *n informal* something easy or straightforward.

nock[1] *n* **1** a notch cut at the end of an archer's bow to hold the string. **2** a notch in the arrow into which the bowstring fits.

nock[2] *v* to fit (an arrow) to a bowstring.

no-claim bonus *or* **no-claims bonus** *n Brit* a discount allowed in an insurance premium when no claim has been made under the policy in previous years.

noctambulist *n* a sleepwalker; = SOMNAMBULIST. ➤➤ **noctambulism** *n.*

noctuid *n* a nocturnal moth of a large family, typically with pale or coloured hindwings, whose larvae, including the cutworms, are in many cases destructive agricultural pests.

noctule *n* a large reddish brown insect-eating bat with rounded ears.

nocturn *n* a principal division of MATINS (first of the daily services in the Catholic Church), orig said at night.

nocturnal *adj* **1** relating to or occurring in the night. **2** of an animal: active at night. ⋙ **nocturnally** *adv.*

nocturnal emission *n* an ejaculation of semen that takes place during sleep.

nocturne *n* a work of art dealing with evening or night; *esp* a dreamy pensive composition for the piano.

nod[1] *v* (**nodded, nodding**) **1** to make a short downward movement of the head, e.g. in assent, understanding, or greeting. **2** to make repeated down-and-up movements with the head. **3** of flowers or trees: to bend or sway gently downwards or forwards. **4** to become drowsy or sleepy. **5** to make a slip or error in a moment of inattention. ✱ **a nodding acquaintance** a slight acquaintance. **be on nodding terms with** to know (somebody) slightly. **nod something through** to approve something with a nod, as distinct from a formal vote, etc.

nod[2] *n* an act of nodding. ✱ **give somebody/something the nod** to choose or approve the choice of. **go through on the nod** of a proposal, etc: to be accepted by informal general consent. **Land of Nod** the world of slumbers; sleep.

noddy *n* (*pl* **-ies**) a stout-bodied tern of tropical seas.

node *n* **1** in anatomy or pathology, any normal or abnormal knot, thickness, or swelling. **2** in a plant, the point on a stem at which one or more leaves are attached. **3** in mathematics, the point where a curve intersects itself. **4** in physics: **a** a point, line, etc of a vibrating body at which the vibration is at a minimum. **b** a point where current or voltage is zero. **5** in computing: **a** a point in a network where lines cross or branch. **b** a computer terminal or peripheral attached to a network.

nod off *v* to fall asleep, *esp* unintentionally while in a sitting position.

nodose *adj technical* having protuberances, *esp* if conspicuous. ⋙ **nodosity** *n.*

nodule *n* **1** any small hardish rounded mass, e.g. an abnormal aggregation of cells in the body. **2** a small rounded lump of a mineral or mineral aggregate. **3** a swelling on the root of a leguminous plant, e.g. clover, containing symbiotic bacteria that convert atmospheric nitrogen into a form in which it can be used by the plant. ⋙ **nodular** *adj.*

Noel *or* **Noël** *n* Christmas.

noes *n* pl of NO[4].

noetic *adj* relating to or based on the intellect.

noggin *n* **1** a small measure of spirits, usu 0.142 litres (pt). **2** *informal* a person's head.

no-go *adj* denoting an area of prohibited or restricted access.

Noh *n* see NO[2].

no-hit game *n* = NO-HITTER.

no-hitter *n* in baseball, a game in which no hits are scored off the pitcher's throws.

no-hoper *n informal* a person who has no chance of success.

nohow *adv* **1** *NAm, informal* used emphatically with a negative. **2** *archaic* in poor shape.

noise *n* **1** loud confused discordant sound, e.g. of shouting; din. **2** a sound, *esp* if sudden or harsh. **3** unwanted signals or fluctuations in an electrical circuit. **4** irrelevant or meaningless information occurring with desired information in the output of a computer. **5** (*usu in pl*) remarks intended to convey an attitude or response. ✱ **noises off 1** sounds made offstage for the benefit of the audience. **2** unwanted background noise. ⋙ **noiseless** *adj,* **noiselessly** *adv.*

noisette /nwah'zet/ *n* **1** a small round thick boneless slice of lamb or other meat. **2** a chocolate containing hazelnuts.

noisome *adj literary* repellent; offensive.

noisy *adj* (**-ier, -iest**) **1** making a lot of noise. **2** full of noise. ⋙ **noisily** *adv,* **noisiness** *n.*

nomad *n* **1** a member of a people that wanders from place to place, usu seasonally and within a well-defined territory. **2** a person who wanders aimlessly from place to place. ⋙ **nomadic** *adj,* **nomadically** *adv,* **nomadism** *n.*

no-man's-land *n* **1** an area of waste or unclaimed land. **2** an unoccupied area between opposing armies.

nom de guerre /ˌnom də 'geə/ *n* (*pl* **noms de guerre**) an assumed name; a pseudonym.

nom de plume /ˌnom de 'ploohm/ *n* (*pl* **noms de plume**) a pseudonym under which an author writes.

nomen *n* (*pl* **nomina**) an ancient Roman's family name, usu the second of three names, e.g. *Julius* in *Caius Julius Caesar*.

nomenclature *n* **1** a name or designation. **2** the activity or an instance of selecting names for things, *esp* within a particular system. **3** a system of terms used in a particular science, discipline, or art. ⋙ **nomenclatural** *adj.*

nomina *n* pl of NOMEN.

nominal *adj* **1** of the status of somebody or something: being so in name only. **2** of a sum of money: very small. **3** of a quantity or measurement: not necessarily corresponding to that specified. **4** in grammar, having the function of a noun. ⋙ **nominally** *adv.*

nominalise *v* see NOMINALIZE.

nominalism *n* a theory that abstract things and general ideas are mere names and have no independent reality inside or outside the mind. ⋙ **nominalist** *n.*

nominalize *or* **-ise** *v* to form a noun from (a verb or adjective), as, *upkeep* from *keep up*, or *warmth* from *warm*. ⋙ **nominalization** *n.*

nominal value *n* **1** the value stated on a cheque, share certificate, etc. **2** the value stated on a coin or note; = FACE VALUE.

nominate *v* **1** to appoint or recommend for appointment. **2** to propose for an honour, award, or candidature. **3** *literary* to designate or specify by name. ⋙ **nomination** *n,* **nominator** *n.*

nominative[1] *adj* **1** denoting a grammatical case expressing the subject of a verb. **2** of an office-bearer, etc: appointed by nomination as distinct from election.

nominative[2] *n* the nominative case or a word in this case.

nominee *n* **1** a person who is nominated as a candidate or nominated to an office. **2** (*often used before a noun*) a person or company nominated to act on behalf of somebody else, or to hold stock on their behalf: *a nominee shareholder*.

-nomy *comb. form* forming nouns, denoting: a system of laws or principles governing a specified field; the science of something: *agronomy*.

non- *prefix* **1** not of the class or category specified: *non-alcoholic*. **2** the reverse or absence of the thing specified: *nonconformity*. **3** designed not to have a typical tendency: *non-stick*.

nona- *or* **non-** *comb. form* nine: *nonagon.*

nonage *n* a period or state of youth or immaturity.

nonagenarian *n* a person between 90 and 99 years old.

nonagon *n* a polygon with nine angles and nine sides. ⋙ **nonagonal** *adj.*

non-alcoholic *adj* of a drink: containing no alcohol.

non-aligned *adj* of a state or country, *esp* during the cold war: not allied with any of the superpowers. ⋙ **non-alignment** *n.*

non-allergenic *adj* of skin preparations, etc: specially formulated so as not to cause an allergic reaction.

non-allergic *adj* = NON-ALLERGENIC.

nonce[1] *adj* of words, expressions etc: occurring only once; devised for one specific occasion.

nonce[2] ✱ **for the nonce** *literary* for the present; for the time being.

nonce[3] *n Brit, slang* a sexual deviant, *esp* one convicted of an offence such as child molestation.

nonchalant *adj* giving an impression of easy unconcern or indifference. ⋙ **nonchalance** *n,* **nonchalantly** *adv.*

non-com *n informal* = NON-COMMISSIONED OFFICER.

non-combatant *n* in wartime, a civilian, army chaplain, etc who does not engage in combat.

non-commissioned officer *n* a subordinate officer, e.g. a sergeant, in the armed forces appointed from among the personnel who do not hold a commission.

non-committal *adj* giving no clear indication of attitude or feeling. ⋙ **non-committally** *adv.*

non-conductor *n* a substance that conducts heat, electricity, etc only very slightly under normal conditions.

nonconformist *n* **1** a person who does not conform to a generally accepted pattern of thought or behaviour. **2** (*often* **Nonconformist**) a person who does not conform to an established Church; *specif* a member of a Protestant body separated from the Church of England. ⋙ **Nonconformism** *n,* **nonconformism** *n,* **Nonconformist** *adj,* **nonconformist** *adj,* **nonconformity** *n.*

non-content *n* a member of the House of Lords who votes against a particular motion.

non-contributory *adj* of a pension: paid for by regular contributions from the employer only, and not requiring contributions from the employee.

non-cooperation *n* refusal to cooperate, *esp* as a form of protest.

non-delivery *n esp* in legal contexts, the failure to provide or deliver goods.

non-denominational *adj* of a religious foundation, system of religious instruction, etc: not attached or specific to any particular Christian denomination.

nondescript *adj* lacking distinctive or interesting qualities; dull.

non-destructive *adj* of scientific testing procedures: not involving harm to or destruction of the specimen.

none[1] *pron* (*used as sing. or pl when referring to a pl n or pronoun*) **1** not any. **2** *literary* nobody: *None lament/laments his departure.* **3** not any such thing or person: *Stale bread is better than none.* ✱ **none but** only: *none but her closest friends.* **none other than** used in identifying somebody or something surprising: *The culprit was none other than the common cold virus.*

Usage note

None can be used with a singular or a plural verb, depending on the meaning. If you want to emphasize the individuals in a group, you use the singular, and *none* is equivalent to 'not one': *None of them is a professional actor.* When you want to emphasize a group or collection of people or things, the plural is more usual and *none* is equivalent to the plural meaning of 'not any': *None of them are professional actors.* When *none* is used of non-countable things, it is treated as singular and is equivalent to the singular meaning of 'not any': *None of the cheese is left.*

none[2] *adv* (*used with a compar*) not in the least; not at all: *none the worse for her adventure.*

none[3] *or* **nones** *or* **None** *or* **Nones** *n* in the Roman Catholic Church, the fifth of the times set for divine service, orig fixed for 3 p.m.

nonentity *n* (*pl* **-ies**) **1** somebody or something of little importance or interest. **2** non-existence.

nones *pl n* (*used as sing. or pl*) **1** in the ancient Roman calendar, the ninth day before the ides, that is the fifth of the month, but the seventh of March, May, July, and October: compare CALENDS, IDES. **2** see NONE[3].

non-essential *adj* not indispensable; not absolutely required. ⋙ **non-essential** *n.*

nonesuch *or* **nonsuch** *n literary, chiefly archaic* a person or thing without an equal; a paragon.

nonet *n* **1** a piece of music for nine voices or instruments. **2** a group of nine singers or instrumentalists.

nonetheless *or* **none the less** *adv* nevertheless.

non-event *n* an event that hardly deserves the name, having turned out to be dull or inconsequential.

non-existent *adj* **1** not real; existing only in the imagination. **2** totally absent.

nonfeasance *n* failure to act according to a legal requirement.

non-ferrous *adj* relating to or denoting a metal other than iron, or not containing iron.

non-fiction *n* prose writing based directly on fact; literature other than novels and stories. ⋙ **non-fictional** *adj.*

non-flammable *adj* difficult or impossible to set alight.

non-fulfilment *n* failure to fulfil something such as a contract, requirement, or condition.

non-functional *adj* **1** having no function, or not having its standard function. **2** not in working order; not operational.

non-governmental *adj* **1** denoting an organization, typically a large one, such as a cultural body, a charity, or a professional body, having recognized official status but independent of the government. **2** not relating to the affairs of government.

non-inflammable *adj* = NON-FLAMMABLE.

non-interference *n* abstention from interfering, *esp* the policy or practice of not interfering in the internal affairs of another state.

non-intervention *n* the policy of not intervening, *esp* in the affairs of another state. ⋙ **non-interventionist** *n and adj.*

non-invasive *adj* **1** of medical or surgical procedures: not involving a large incision or the introduction of instruments into the body. **2** of a tumour, etc: not spreading dangerously or transferring to other parts of the body. **3** of a plant: not inclined to upset ecological balance by taking over the habitat of established plants.

nonjuror *n* **1** a person refusing to take an oath. **2** (*usu* **Nonjuror**) a member of the clergy in Britain who refused to take an oath of allegiance to William and Mary after 1688.

non-linear *adj* **1** not arranged in, or involving, a straight line. **2** not following a linear progression or sequence; random. **3** of a mathematical equation: including terms not of the first degree, that is, terms representing squares or cubes.

non-member *n* a person, state, etc, that is not a member of the body in question.

non-metal *n* a chemical element, e.g. boron or carbon, that is not a metal. ➤➤ **non-metallic** *adj.*

non-natural *adj* not involving natural processes.

non-negotiable *adj* **1** of a decision, etc: final; not open to discussion or alteration. **2** of a document such as a cheque, voucher, etc: not transferable to the ownership of another person.

no-no *n* (*pl* **-os**) *informal* something to be avoided; something quite unacceptable.

no-nonsense *adj* **1** serious; businesslike. **2** without trifles or frills.

non-operational *adj* **1** not working; not in use. **2** not actively functioning as such.

nonpareil /'nonpərel, nonpə'rayl/ *n literary, chiefly archaic* somebody or something having no equal. ➤➤ **nonpareil** *adj.*

non-person *n* (*pl* **non-persons**) **1** a person who usu for political or ideological reasons is removed from official recognition or consideration. **2** a person regarded as of no interest or significance.

nonplus *v* (**nonplussed, nonplussing,** *NAm* **nonplused, nonplusing**) (*often as past part.*) **1** to perplex or disconcert (somebody) or put them at a loss. **2** *chiefly NAm* used in the opposite sense through misapprehension of *non-* as NON-: to fail to perturb or upset.

non-prescription *adj* of medicines, etc: available for purchase without a prescription.

non-productive *adj* failing to produce or yield.

non-profit *adj NAm* = NON-PROFITMAKING.

non-profitmaking *adj* of an organization: not constituted or run with the intention of making a profit.

non-proliferation *n* stoppage of the proliferation of something, *esp* nuclear weapons.

non-resident *adj* **1** not living in the place, country, etc in question. **2** of a job or academic course: not requiring residence in the place of work or study. **3** of computer software: not kept permanently in the memory. ➤➤ **non-resident** *n.*

nonsense *n* **1** meaningless words or language. **2** foolish or absurd language, conduct, or thought. **3** frivolous or insolent behaviour. **4** used interjectionally to express forceful disagreement. ➤➤ **nonsensical** *adj,* **nonsensically** *adv.*

non sequitur *n* **1** a conclusion that does not follow from the premises. **2** a statement that does not follow logically from anything previously said.

non-specific urethritis *n* infection of the URETHRA (canal carrying urine from the bladder) that is sexually transmitted but caused by bacteria other than those causing gonorrhoea.

non-standard *adj* **1** not conforming to a required norm or standard. **2** of language: not conforming in pronunciation, grammatical construction, idiom, or word choice to accepted usage.

non-starter *n* **1** somebody or something that is sure to fail. **2** a competitor, racehorse, etc that fails to take part in a race.

non-stick *adj* **1** of a pan surface: treated so that food does not stick to it during cooking. **2** of a pan: having such a surface.

non-stop *adj* **1** continuous. **2** of a journey: with no intermediate stops. ➤➤ **non-stop** *adv.*

nonsuch *n* see NONESUCH.

non-U *adj* of words, social conduct, etc: not characteristic of the upper classes.

non-uniform *adj* **1** subject to variation; not uniform. **2** not involving the wearing of uniform.

non-verbal *adj* not involving words or speech.

non-violence *n* **1** abstention from violence on moral grounds. **2** passive resistance or peaceful demonstration for political ends. ➤➤ **non-violent** *adj.*

non-white *n* a person not of mainly Caucasian or European descent, *esp* one of black African descent. ➤➤ **non-white** *adj.*

noodle[1] *n humorous* **1** a silly or foolish person. **2** *NAm* the head.

noodle[2] *n* (*usu in pl*) a narrow flat ribbon of pasta made with egg.

nook *n* a small secluded or sheltered place; a corner or recess. ✱ **every nook and cranny** everywhere possible.

nooky *or* **nookie** *n informal* lovemaking; sexual intercourse.

noon *n* twelve o'clock in the day; midday.

noonday *n literary* (*often used before a noun*) the middle of the day; noon: *in the noonday heat.*

no one *or* **no-one** *pron* nobody.

noontide *n literary* the middle of the day; noon.

noontime *n NAm* = NOONTIDE.

noose[1] *n* a loop with a running knot that tightens as the rope is pulled. ✱ **put one's head in a noose** to put oneself into a vulnerable position or bring about one's own downfall.

noose[2] *v* to secure (a quarry) by a noose.

nootropic *n* a drug used to enhance memory or sharpen other mental functions. ➤➤ **nootropic** *adj.*

NOR *n* in electronics, denoting a gate or circuit that has an output only if there is no signal on any of the input connections.

nor[1] *conj* **1** used with NEITHER[3]: and not; and not either: *neither she nor I; She neither knew nor cared.* **2** *archaic or literary* neither: *Nor heaven nor earth have been at peace tonight* — Shakespeare. **3** *dialect, chiefly archaic* than: *I know better nor you* — George Eliot.

nor[2] *adv and conj* and not; neither: *'I don't approve.' 'Nor do I'; It didn't seem hard, nor was it.*

nor' *n* (*used in combinations*) north: *nor'easter.*

noradrenalin *or* **noradrenaline** *n* a compound from which adrenalin is formed in the body and which is the major NEUROTRANSMITTER (medium transmitting nerve impulses) released from the nerve endings of the sympathetic nervous system.

Nordic[1] *adj* **1** relating to or belonging to a tall, fair, longheaded, blue-eyed physical type characteristic of the Germanic peoples of N Europe, *esp* Scandinavia. **2** of competitive ski events: consisting of ski jumping and cross-country racing: compare ALPINE[2] (4).

Nordic[2] *n* a person of Nordic physical type or of a supposed Nordic division of the Caucasian race; *esp* one from N Europe.

Norfolk jacket *n esp* formerly, a man's semifitted belted single-breasted jacket with box pleats.

norm *n* **1** an authoritative standard; a model. **2** a set standard of development or achievement, usu derived from the average achievement of a large group.

normal[1] *adj* **1** conforming to or constituting a norm, rule, or principle. **2** in geometry, of a line or plane: intersecting another at right angles; perpendicular. ⋙ **normalcy** *n*, **normality** *n*, **normally** *adv.*

normal[2] *n* **1** somebody or something that is normal. **2** in geometry, a line or plane intersecting another at right angles.

normal distribution *n* in statistics, a frequency distribution whose graph is a standard symmetrical bell-shaped curve.

normalize *or* **-ise** *v* to make (something abnormal or irregular) normal. ⋙ **normalization** *n.*

normal school *n* in N America, *esp* formerly, a teacher-training college.

Norman *n* **1** a member of a people of mixed Frankish and Scandinavian stock who settled in Normandy in the tenth cent. **2** any of the Norman-French conquerors of England in 1066, or their descendants. **3** the northern form of Old French spoken by the medieval Normans. **4** a style of architecture characterized, *esp* in its English form, by semicircular arches and heavy pillars. ⋙ **Norman** *adj.*

Norman French *n* = NORMAN (3).

normative *adj* serving as or prescribing a norm.

normotensive *adj* having normal blood pressure for one's age, etc.

Norse[1] *n* **1** (**the Norse**) (*used as pl*) the Norwegians, or generally, the Scandinavians, *esp* of the medieval period. **2** = OLD NORSE.

Norse[2] *adj* Scandinavian; *esp* of ancient or medieval Scandinavia or Norway.

Norseman *n* (*pl* **Norsemen**) a native or inhabitant of ancient or medieval Scandinavia.

north[1] *n* **1** the direction in which a compass needle normally points, 90° anticlockwise from east. **2** regions or countries lying to the north. ⋙ **northbound** *adj and adv.*

north[2] *adj and adv* **1** at, towards, or coming from the north. **2** of the wind: blowing from the north. ✱ **north by east/west** in a position or direction between north and north-northeast (or north-north-west).

North American *n* a native or inhabitant of North America, *esp* of the USA or Canada. ⋙ **North American** *adj.*

Northants *abbr* Northamptonshire.

northeast[1] *n* **1** the direction midway between north and east. **2** regions or countries lying to the northeast. ⋙ **northeastern** *adj*, **northeastward** *adj and adv*, **northeastwards** *adv.*

northeast[2] *adj and adv* **1** at, towards, or coming from the northeast. **2** of the wind: blowing from the northeast.

northeaster *n* a wind blowing from the northeast.

northeasterly[1] *adj and adv* **1** in a northeastern position or direction. **2** of the wind: blowing from the northeast.

northeasterly[2] *n* (*pl* **-ies**) a wind blowing from the northeast.

northerly[1] *adj and adv* **1** in a northern position or direction. **2** of the wind: blowing from the north.

northerly[2] *n* (*pl* **-ies**) a wind blowing from the north.

northern *adj* in or towards the north; inhabiting the north. ⋙ **northernmost** *adj.*

Northerner *n* a native or inhabitant of the North.

northern lights *pl n* = AURORA BOREALIS.

northernmost *adj* found or situated furthest north.

northing *n* **1** distance due north in latitude from the preceding point of measurement. **2** northerly progress.

North Korean *n* a native or inhabitant of North Korea. ⋙ **North Korean** *adj.*

northland *or* **northlands** *or* **Northland** *or* **Northlands** *n literary* land in the north; the north of a country.

north light *n* strong natural light without direct sunlight, traditionally preferred by artists as the dominant illumination for a studio.

north-northeast *n* the direction midway between north and northeast. ⋙ **north-northeast** *adj and adv.*

north-northwest *n* the direction midway between north and northwest. ⋙ **north-northwest** *adj and adv.*

North Star *n* = POLE STAR.

Northumb. *abbr* Northumberland.

northward *adj and adv* towards the north; in a direction going north. ⋙ **northwards** *adv.*

northwest[1] *n* **1** the direction midway between north and west. **2** regions or countries lying to the northwest. ⋙ **northwestern** *adj*, **northwestward** *adj and adv*, **northwestwards** *adv.*

northwest[2] *adj and adv* **1** at, towards, or coming from the northwest. **2** of the wind: blowing from the northwest.

northwester *n* a wind blowing from the northwest.

northwesterly[1] *adj and adv* **1** in a northwestern position or direction. **2** of the wind: blowing from the northwest.

northwesterly[2] *n* (*pl* **-ies**) a wind blowing from the northwest.

Norwegian *n* **1** a native or inhabitant of Norway. **2** the language of Norway. ⋙ **Norwegian** *adj.*

nose[1] *n* **1** the projecting part above the mouth on the face of a person or animal, containing the nostrils and used for breathing and smelling. **2** the sense of smell. **3** the aroma or bouquet of wine. **4** an instinct for detecting a certain thing. **5** *informal* an act of investigating. **6** the front end of a vehicle. ✱ **by a nose** used in reference to a win: by a narrow margin. **cut off one's nose to spite one's face** to damage one's own interests in one's eagerness to take revenge on another. **follow one's nose** see FOLLOW. **get up somebody's nose** *informal* to annoy somebody. **keep one's nose clean** *informal* to stay out of trouble. **keep one's nose out of** *informal* to refrain from interfering in (e.g. somebody else's business). **look down one's nose at** *informal* to show or express disdain for (a person or thing). **nose to tail** of vehicles: in a long slowly-moving queue. **on the nose 1** *informal* of betting on a horse: to win, as distinct from being placed. **2** *NAm* precisely. **pay through the nose** *informal* to pay exorbitantly. **put somebody's nose out of joint** *informal* to offend or affront somebody. **rub somebody's nose in it** *informal* to remind somebody mischievously of a painful failure or mistake. **turn one's nose up at** *informal* to show or express disdain for (a person or thing).

nose[2] *v* **1** of an animal: to push its nose into or against (a person or thing). **2** to sniff investigatively. **3** *literary* to scent (something) or detect it using one's sense of smell. **4** (*often* + about/around) to pry. **5** of a vehicle or driver: to pull slowly forward.

nose bag *n* a bag for feeding a horse or other animal, that covers the muzzle and is fastened on top of the head.

noseband *n* the part of a bridle that passes over a horse's nose.

nosebleed *n* an attack of bleeding from the nose.

nose dive *n* **1** a downward nose-first plunge of an aircraft or other flying object. **2** a sudden dramatic drop.

nose-dive *v* to make a nose dive.

nosegay *n* a small bunch of flowers; a posy.

nose job *n informal* a surgical operation to improve the shape of the nose.

nosey *adj* see NOSY.

nosh[1] *v informal* to eat.

nosh[2] *n informal* food; a meal.

no-show *n informal* a person who has made a reservation or appointment but fails to attend or cancel.

nosh-up *n Brit, informal* a large meal.

nosocomial *adj* of a disease: having originated in hospital.

nosology *n* a branch of medical science that deals with the classification of diseases.

nostalgia *n* **1** a wistful or excessively sentimental yearning for something past or irrecoverable. **2** the evocation of or indulgence in such sentiment. ➤➤ **nostalgic** *adj,* **nostalgically** *adv.*

nostril *n* either of the two external openings of the nose.

nostrum *n* (*pl* **nostrums**) **1** a medicine of secret composition recommended by its preparer usu without proof of its effectiveness. **2** a facile or questionable remedy.

nosy *or* **nosey** *adj* (**-ier, -iest**) *informal* inquisitive; prying. ➤➤ **nosily** *adv,* **nosiness** *n.*

nosy parker *n Brit, informal* a busybody.

NOT *n* in electronics, denoting a gate or circuit that has an output signal only if there is no input signal.

not *adv* **1** (*also, as suffix* **-n't**) used to form negatives. **2** used as substitute for a whole negative clause: *whether we agree or not.* **3** used to negate other words: *George III, not George II.* **4** less than (a surprisingly small amount): *not five minutes later.*

nota bene /,nohtə 'benay/ *interj* used to call attention to something important.

notability *n* (*pl* **-ies**) **1** a prominent person. **2** being notable.

notable[1] *adj* **1** worthy of note; remarkable. **2** distinguished; prominent.

Usage note

notable *or* **noticeable**? These two words are close in meaning but there is nevertheless a clear distinction between them. *Notable* means 'worthy of notice' and thus, often, 'important' or 'remarkable': *a notable achievement. Noticeable,* on the other hand, means 'visible' or 'perceptible': *a noticeable improvement in quality.* A *notable difference* between two things would generally be a large as well as significant one, whereas a *noticeable* difference might only be very small.

notable[2] *n* a prominent person.

notably *adv* **1** remarkably. **2** in particular.

notarize *or* **-ise** *v chiefly NAm* (*often as past part.*) to validate (a document, etc) as a notary public.

notary *n* (*pl* **-ies**) a public officer appointed to administer oaths and draw up and authenticate documents. ➤➤ **notarial** *adj.*

notary public *n* (*pl* **notaries public** *or* **notary publics**) = NOTARY.

notate *v* to put (e.g. music in aural form) into notation.

notation *n* **1** a system or set of marks, signs, symbols, figures, characters, or abbreviated expressions used to present e.g. mathematical, musical, or choreographical elements. **2** *chiefly NAm* an annotation or note. ➤➤ **notational** *adj.*

notch[1] *n* **1** a V-shaped indentation. **2** a slit or cut in a surface. **3** a degree or point on a scale.

notch[2] *v* **1** to make a notch in. **2** (+ up) to score or achieve (e.g. a success).

note[1] *n* **1** (*also in pl*) a memorandum; a condensed or informal record. **2** a brief comment or explanation. **3** a short informal letter. **4** a piece of paper money. **5** a sound having a definite pitch, *esp* made by a musical instrument or the human voice. **6** a call or sound; *esp* the musical call of a bird. **7** a written symbol used to indicate the duration and pitch of a tone by its shape and position on the musical stave. **8** an element in a flavour, taste, smell, etc. **9** a feeling or element of something: *a note of sadness in her voice.* ✱ **hit/strike the right/wrong/a false note** to act appropriately or inappropriately. **of note 1** distinguished. **2** significant. **take note** (*often* + of) to pay attention.

note[2] *v* **1** to pay due attention to (information being presented to one). **2** to notice or observe. **3** (*often* + down) to record (information) in writing. **4** to make special mention of (a fact).

notebook *n* **1** a book for notes or memoranda. **2** a small portable computer.

noted *adj* well-known; famous.

notelet *n* a folded sheet of paper bearing a printed design on the front, for a brief informal letter.

notepad *n* **1** a pad of paper for writing notes on. **2** a small hand-held computer with which a stylus is used for inputting data.

notepaper *n* paper for letter-writing.

noteworthy *adj* worthy of or attracting attention; notable.

nothing *pron and n* **1** not anything; no thing. **2** a thing of no consequence or significance. **3** in calculating, nought. ✱ **for nothing 1** without pay or without paying. **2** to no purpose. **nothing but** only. **nothing doing 1** *informal* used to refuse cooperation. **2** *informal* no progress. **sweet nothings** *humorous* affectionate exchanges between lovers. **think nothing of it** used as a deprecatory response to thanks, etc.

nothingness *n* **1** nonexistence. **2** utter insignificance. **3** a void; emptiness.

notice[1] *n* **1** attention or observation. **2** advance warning. **3** formal notification of one's intention to terminate an agreement, typically relating to employment or tenancy. **4** a placard or poster displaying information. **5** a brief announcement in a newspaper, etc. **6** a short critical account or review of a production, etc. ✱ **at a moment's/at short notice** with little or no warning. **put somebody on notice/serve notice on somebody** to warn somebody of an imminent occurrence. **take no notice of** to disregard or pay no heed to (somebody or something). **take notice of** to observe or treat (somebody or something) with special attention.

notice[2] *v* **1** to take notice of or become aware of. **2** to attract comment; to become well-known: *He is beginning to be noticed.* **3** *archaic* to comment upon or refer to (something).

noticeable *adj* **1** deserving notice; significant. **2** capable of being noticed; perceptible. ➤➤ **noticeably** *adv.*

Usage note

noticeable *or* **notable**? See note at NOTABLE[1].

notifiable *adj* of a disease: required by law to be reported to official health authorities.

notify *v* (**-ies, -ied**) (*also* + of) to give, *esp* formal or official, notice to (somebody). ➤➤ **notification** *n.*

notion *n* **1** a broad general concept. **2** (*usu in negative contexts*) a conception or impression. **3** a whim or fancy. **4** an intention.

notional *adj* **1** theoretical; speculative; adduced for the purpose of forward planning. **2** existing only in the mind; imaginary. ➤➤ **notionally** *adv.*

notochord *n* a cartilaginous rod that forms the longitudinal support of the body in the lancelet, lamprey, etc and in the embryos of higher vertebrates.

notorious *adj* well-known for something bad or unfavourable; infamous. ➤➤ **notoriety** *n,* **notoriously** *adv.*

Notts *abbr* Nottinghamshire.

notwithstanding[1] *prep* (*also after the noun*) in spite of (something).

notwithstanding[2] *adv* nevertheless.

notwithstanding[3] *conj* (*usu* + that) although.

nougat *n* a sweet consisting of nuts or fruit pieces in a semisolid sugar paste.

nougatine *n* chocolate-covered nougat.

nought *n and pron* **1** the arithmetical symbol 0; zero. **2** = NAUGHT (1).

noughts and crosses *pl n* (*usu used as sing.*) a game in which two players alternately put noughts and crosses in nine square spaces arranged in a grid in an attempt to get a row of three noughts or three crosses.

noumenon *n* (*pl* **noumena**) in Kantian philosophy, a thing in itself, as distinct from a thing as apprehended by the senses. ➤➤ **noumenal** *adj.*

noun *n* a word that is: **a** a term for a person, thing, animal, place, quality, or state. **b** a name identifying a person, thing, animal, or place.

noun phrase *n* in grammar, a group of words such as, e.g. *a general practitioner,* that can function like a noun as the subject of a sentence, or as an object after a verb or preposition.

nourish *v* **1** to nurture or rear (e.g. a child or animal). **2** to provide (e.g. soil or a plant) with nutriment; to feed. **3** to cherish or entertain (an idea, feeling, etc). ➤➤ **nourishing** *adj.*

nourishment *n* **1** food or nutriment. **2** the process of nourishing or of being nourished.

nous *n* **1** the mind, reason, or intellect. **2** *chiefly Brit* practical common sense; gumption.

nouveau riche /ˌnoohvoh ˈreesh/ *n* (*pl* **nouveaux riches**) a person who has recently become rich, *esp* one who displays their wealth unsubtly. ➤➤ **nouveau riche** *adj.*

nouvelle cuisine /noohˈvel kwiˈzeen/ *n* a style of cooking that uses high quality ingredients and emphasizes the natural flavours and textures of the food.

nouvelle vague /noohˈvel ˈvahg/ *or* **Nouvelle Vague** *n* = NEW WAVE (1).

Nov. *abbr* November.

nova *n* (*pl* **novas** *or* **novae**) a double star system that becomes suddenly much brighter as a result of a thermonuclear explosion and then fades away to its former obscurity over months or years.

novation *n* in law, the substitution of a new obligation for an old one, e.g. by substituting a new contract, creditor, or debtor for a previous one.

novel[1] *n* an invented prose narrative that is usu long and complex and deals *esp* with human experience and social behaviour.

novel[2] *adj* **1** new and unlike anything previously known. **2** original and striking, *esp* in conception or style.

novelette *n* a short novel or long short story, often of a sentimental nature.

novelise *v* see NOVELIZE.

novelist *n* a writer of novels.

novelistic *adj* relating to or typical of novels.

novelize *or* **-ise** *v* (*often as past part*) to convert (a story) from another form, e.g. a play or cinema film, into a novel. ➤➤ **novelization** *n.*

novella *n* (*pl* **novellas** *or* **novelle**) a short novel or substantial short story.

novelty *n* (*pl* **-ies**) **1** something new and unusual. **2** the quality or state of being novel. **3** a small manufactured often cheap article for personal or household adornment. **4** (*used before a noun*) denoting an article designed to amuse by virtue of its unusualness: *novelty socks.*

November *n* the eleventh month of the year.

novena *n* (*pl* **novenas** *or* **novenae**) in the Roman Catholic Church, nine days' devotion of prayers for the intercession of a particular saint for a special purpose.

novice *n* **1** a person admitted to probationary membership of a religious community. **2** a new or inexperienced person in a job, etc; a beginner. **3** a racehorse that has yet to win a certain number of races.

novitiate *or* **noviciate** *n* **1** the state of being a novice, or the duration of this. **2** a house where novices are trained. **3** a novice, *esp* in a religious order.

now[1] *adv* **1a** at the present time. **b** immediately. **c** as things have turned out; in the light of recent developments: *It doesn't matter now; A spring election is now certain.* **d** used in narrative to refer to the time in question: *It was now snowing heavily.* **2** used in conversation or discourse: **a** to mark a transition, emphasize a point, etc: *Now then, let's deal with this other matter; Let me see now, how old is she?* **b** to comfort, exhort, admonish, or respond quizzically: *Now, now, don't cry; There now, it's OK; 'Mum, I need some money.' 'Do you now?'.* ✱ **now and/every now and again/then** occasionally.

now[2] *conj* (*often* + that) as a result of the circumstance that; since.

nowadays *adv* in these modern times, in contrast to the past.

nowhere *adv and pron* not anywhere. ✱ **get/go nowhere/nowhere fast** to make no progress. **nowhere near** not nearly.

nowise *adv archaic* in no way whatever.

nowt *n N Eng* nothing.

noxious *adj* **1** harmful to living things. **2** *literary* morally harmful; unwholesome.

nozzle *n* a projecting part with an opening that usu serves as an outlet.

NP *abbr* Notary Public.

Np *abbr* the chemical symbol for neptunium.

NRA *abbr* **1** *NAm* National Rifle Association. **2** *Brit* National Rivers Authority.

NS *abbr* **1** in dates, New Style. **2** Nova Scotia (US postal abbreviation).

ns *abbr* nanosecond.

NSPCC *abbr Brit* National Society for the Prevention of Cruelty to Children.

NSU *abbr* non-specific urethritis.

NSW *abbr* New South Wales.

NT *abbr* **1** National Trust. **2** New Testament. **3** Northern Territory. **4** Northwest Territories.

-n't *contr and suffix* used with auxiliary verbs, modal auxiliary verbs, and 'be' and 'have' as ordinary verbs: not: *isn't; won't.*

nth *adj* **1** denoting an unspecified member of an ordinally numbered series. **2** *informal* denoting the last in a long series of instances.

nu *n* the 13th letter of the Greek alphabet (N, ν), equivalent to roman n.

nuance *n* a subtly distinct gradation in colour, meaning, or tone; a shade. ➤➤ **nuanced** *adj.*

nub *n* **1** a knob, lump, or protuberance. **2** (**the nub**) the gist or crux of a matter.

nubbin *n* a small lump or protuberance.

Nubian *adj* **1** a native or inhabitant of the region of N Sudan and S Egypt corresponding to ancient Nubia. **2** a group of languages of Sudan and S Egypt. **3** a goat of a short-haired breed with long legs and drooping ears, orig from Africa. ➤➤ **Nubian** *adj*

nubile *adj* of a girl: **a** of marriageable age. **b** young and sexually attractive. ➤➤ **nubility** *n.*

nubuck *n* cowhide rubbed on the flesh side to give a soft suede-like finish.

nucha *n* (*pl* **nuchae**) the nape of the neck. ➤➤ **nuchal** *adj.*

nuciferous *adj* of a tree: producing nuts.

nuclear *adj* **1** relating to or constituting a nucleus. **2** relating to the atomic nucleus, atomic energy, the atom bomb, or atomic power.

nuclear family *n* a family unit that consists of husband, wife, and children.

nuclear fuel *n* a fuel that consists of a substance that can sustain a fission chain reaction and is therefore usable as a source of nuclear energy.

nuclear magnetic resonance *n* a technique for finding the MAGNETIC RESONANCE (absorption of electromagnetic radiation) of an atomic nucleus, used e.g. in body-scanning to determine structure.

nuclear medicine *n* the branch of medicine specializing in the use of radioactive nuclides in the diagnosis and treatment of disease.

nuclear physics *n* (*used as sing.*) the branch of physics concerned with atomic nuclei, their behaviour and interactions, *esp* as a source of energy.

nuclear power *n* power produced by a nuclear reactor, *esp* if electric or motive.

nuclear reactor *n* an apparatus in which a self-sustaining reaction occurs, involving the breakdown of the nuclei of atoms of uranium, plutonium, etc with the release of large amounts of energy.

nuclear waste *n* radioactive waste, *esp* from the use or reprocessing of nuclear fuel.

nuclear winter *n* a state of darkness and extreme cold on earth, caused by clouds of dust and smoke blocking sunlight, which some scientists consider a likely consequence of a nuclear war.

nuclease *n* any of various enzymes that promote the breakdown of nucleic acids.

nucleate[1] *v* **1** to form a nucleus. **2** of villages or settlements: to cluster round a centre. ➤➤ **nucleation** *n.*

nucleate[2] *adj* having a nucleus or nuclei.

nucleated *adj* = NUCLEATE[2].

nuclei *n* pl of NUCLEUS.

nucleic acid *n* RNA, DNA, or another complex organic substance present in living cells, composed of a chain of nucleotide molecules linked to each other.

nucleon *n* either of two elementary particles, that is, a proton or a neutron, that are found *esp* in an atomic nucleus.

nucleoside *n* any of several compounds, e.g. adenosine, consisting of a purine or pyrimidine base combined with deoxyribose or ribose and occurring *esp* as a constituent of nucleotides.

nucleotide *n* any of several compounds that form the structural units of RNA and DNA and consist of a nucleoside combined with a phosphate group.

nucleus *n* (*pl* **nuclei** *or* **nucleuses**) **1** a small bright and dense part of a galaxy or head of a comet. **2** a central point, mass, etc about which gathering, concentration, etc takes place: e.g. **a** a usu round ORGANELLE (specialized structure within a cell) containing the chromosomes and surrounded by a membrane. **b** a discrete mass of nerve cells in the brain or spinal cord. **c** the positively charged central part of an atom that accounts for nearly all of the atomic mass and consists of protons and usu neutrons.

nude[1] *adj* without clothing; naked. ➤➤ **nudity** *n.*

nude[2] *n* **1** a representation, e.g. in painting or sculpture, of a nude human figure. **2** a nude person.

nudge[1] *v* **1** to poke (somebody) gently with one's elbow, *esp* to draw their attention to something. **2** to push gently. **3** to move (something) slightly in a certain direction. **4** to encourage (somebody) gently to do something by hints and reminders.

nudge[2] *n* **1** the act of nudging or pushing gently. **2** a gentle hint or reminder.

nudibranch *n* a shell-less marine mollusc of an order that have external gills and strikingly coloured bodies; the sea-slugs.

nudism *n* the cult or practice of going nude as much as possible. ➤➤ **nudist** *n.*

nugatory *adj formal* **1** trifling; inconsequential. **2** of a law, etc: invalid or inoperative.

nugget *n* **1** a solid lump, *esp* of a precious metal in its natural state. **2** a useful fact.

nuisance *n* a circumstance, person or thing that is a source of trouble, annoyance, or inconvenience.

nuke[1] *n informal* a nuclear weapon.

nuke[2] *v informal* to attack (a population) with nuclear weapons.

null[1] *adj* **1** having no force in law; invalid. **2** amounting to nothing; nil. **3** without character or distinction.

null[2] *n* **1** zero on a scale. **2** a minimum or zero value of an electric current or of a radio signal. **3** a meaningless group of letters or characters included in a coded message to hinder interpretation by unauthorized people.

nulla *n* = NULLA-NULLA.

nulla-nulla *n* a hardwood club used by Australian aboriginals.

null hypothesis *n* a statistical hypothesis to be tested and accepted or rejected in favour of an alternative; *specif* the hypothesis that an observed difference, e.g. between the means of two samples, is due to chance alone.

nullify *v* (**-ies, -ied**) **1** to make legally null and void. **2** to render ineffective or cancel out. ➤➤ **nullification** *n.*

nullity *n* (*pl* **-ies**) **1** in law, something that is legally null and void. **2** the state of being legally null and void; invalidity.

numb[1] *adj* devoid of sensation, *esp* as a result of cold or anaesthesia. ➤➤ **numbly** *adv,* **numbness** *n.*

numb[2] *v* **1** to make (a person or a bodily part) numb. **2** to reduce the sharpness of (a pain).

numbat *n* a small Australian marsupial with a long snout, bushy tail, and black-and-white-striped back, that feeds on termites.

number[1] *n* **1** a word, numeral, digit or other symbol that is used in counting or calculating quantities, and in referring to things by their position in a series. **2** several. **3** in grammar, singular and plural, or the inflections and word forms that distinguish them. **4** a numeral or set of digits used to identify or designate somebody or something: *a telephone number.* **5** a member of a group or sequence designated by *esp* consecutive numbers. **6** a single act in a variety show or a single issue of a periodical, singled out from a group. **7** a piece of pop or jazz music. **8** an article of *esp* women's clothing: *a chic little black number.* ✻ **by numbers** following instructions of the simplest kind, *esp* where each step is indicated by a number. **have somebody's number** to understand somebody's real motives or game. **somebody's number is up** *informal* somebody is doomed. **without number** innumerable.

Usage note

number of. The phrase *a number of* meaning 'some' or 'several' should be used with a verb in the plural: *There are a number of things to discuss; A number of you, I know, disagree.* When *number* means 'the overall quantity' in *the number of* it is used with a singular verb: *The number of meningitis cases is increasing.*

number[2] *v* **1** to amount to (a certain total). **2** to enumerate and assign numbers to (things in a series). **3** (*usu* + among) to regard (a person or thing) as being included in a certain group. ✻ **somebody's days are numbered** somebody is likely to die, fall from power, etc, very soon.

number-cruncher *n* **1** a powerful computer or program that processes large amounts of numerical data very quickly. **2** *derog* a statistician.

numbered account *n* a bank account identified by a number as distinct from a personal name, *esp* in a Swiss bank.

numberless *adj* innumerable; countless.

number one *n* **1** something that is first in rank, order, or importance. **2** *informal* oneself and one's interests, as deserving prior consideration.

numberplate *n chiefly Brit* a rectangular identifying plate fastened to a vehicle and bearing the vehicle's registration number.

numbers game *n* **1** *derog* the manipulation of statistics for one's own purposes. **2** *NAm* an illegal lottery based on unpredictable combinations of numbers in published figures.

number two *n* a second-in-command.

numbskull *n* see NUMSKULL.

numen *n* (*pl* **numina**) a divine force associated with a place or natural object.

numerable *adj* capable of being counted.

numeral[1] *n* a conventional symbol that represents a natural number or zero.

numeral[2] *adj* relating to or expressing numbers.

numerate *adj* understanding basic mathematics; able to use numbers in calculation. ➤➤ **numeracy** *n.*

numeration *n* **1** counting. **2** designating by a number. **3** a system of numbering or counting.

numerator *n* the part of a fraction that is above the line and signifies the number of parts of the denominator that is shown by the fraction.

numerical *adj* relating to, expressed in, or involving numbers or a number system. ➤➤ **numerically** *adv.*

numerology *n* the study of the occult significance of numbers. ➤➤ **numerological** *adj,* **numerologist** *n.*

numerous *adj* consisting of many units or individuals. ➤➤ **numerously** *adv.*

numina *n* pl of NUMEN.

numinous *adj* **1** awe-inspiring or mysterious. **2** filled with a sense of the presence of divinity.

numismatics *pl n* (*used as sing.*) the study or collection of coins, medals, tokens, etc. ➤➤ **numismatist** *n.*

numskull *or* **numbskull** *n* a dull or stupid person.

nun *n* **1** a female member of a religious order living in a convent under vows of chastity, poverty, etc and often engaged in educational or nursing work. **2** a pigeon with a crest on its head reminiscent of a nun's hood.

nunatak *n* an isolated pointed rock mass projecting above the surface of an inland snow or ice field.

Nunc Dimittis *n* a canticle based on the prayer of Simeon in the Bible, Luke 2, 29–32.

nuncio *n* (*pl* **-os**) a papal ambassador to a civil government.

nunnery *n* (*pl* **-ies**) a convent of nuns.

nuptial[1] *adj* **1** relating to marriage. **2** in zoology, characteristic of or occurring in the breeding season.

nuptial[2] *n* (*usu in pl*) a wedding.

nurd *n* see NERD.

nurse[1] *n* a person skilled or trained in caring for the sick or infirm.

nurse[2] *v* **1** to tend (e.g. a sick person). **2** to suckle (a baby). **3** to attempt to cure (e.g. an illness or injury) by appropriate treatment. **4** to hold (e.g. a baby) lovingly or caressingly. **5** to hold or handle (something) carefully. **6** to harbour (a feeling) in one's mind. **7** of a baby: to suck at the breast.

nurse[3] *n* a grey shark of Australia, found in shallow coastal waters.

nursemaid *n* a girl or woman employed to look after children.

nursery *n* (*pl* **-ies**) **1** a child's bedroom or playroom. **2** = NURSERY SCHOOL. **3** an area where plants, trees, etc are grown for propagation, sale, or transplanting.

nurseryman *n* (*pl* **nurserymen**) a person whose occupation is the cultivation of plants, usu for sale.

nursery nurse *n* a person trained to look after babies and young children in nurseries and crèches.

nursery rhyme *n* a short traditional story in rhyme for children.

nursery school *n* a school for children aged usu from three to five.

nursery slope *n* a usu gentle ski slope for beginners.

nurse shark *n* a shark with barbels round the nose.

nursing home *n* a usu private hospital or home, where care is provided for the aged, chronically ill, etc.

nurture[1] *n* **1** training; upbringing. **2** the provision of food and nourishment. **3** the environmental, educational, etc factors that influence the inherent genetic make-up or nature of an individual.

nurture[2] *v* **1** to give care and nourishment to (a child). **2** to rear or bring up (a child). **3** to encourage and develop (an interest, talent, etc). **4** to cherish (a hope, ambition, etc).

nut[1] *n* **1** a dry fruit or seed consisting of a hard separable rind or shell and often edible kernel; the kernel itself. **2** a typically hexagonal usu metal block that has a central hole with an internal screw thread cut on it, and can be screwed onto a piece, *esp* a bolt, with an external thread to tighten or secure something. **3** a small piece or lump: *a nut of butter.* **4** *informal* a person's head. **5** *informal* **a** an insane or wildly eccentric person. **b** an ardent enthusiast: *a tennis nut.* **6** *coarse slang* (*in pl*) a man's testicles. ✱ **a tough/hard nut (to crack)** a person or problem that is difficult to deal with. **do one's nut** *informal* to get very angry. **nuts and bolts** the basic practical issues. ➤➤ **nutty** *adj.*

nut² *v* (**nutted, nutting**) *informal* to butt (somebody) with one's head.

nutation *n* **1** a slight nodding of the earth's axis superimposed on its normal PRECESSION (motion like that of a spinning top). **2** a spontaneous usu irregular spiral movement of a growing stem, tendril, root, etc.

nutcase *n informal* a mad person.

nutcracker *n* (*also in pl*) an implement for cracking nuts, usu consisting of two hinged metal arms between which the nut is held and compressed.

nuthatch *n* a Eurasian tree-climbing bird with bluish grey upper parts and a black stripe through the eye region.

nut loaf *n* a vegetarian dish consisting of chopped or ground nuts, vegetables, and herbs shaped into a loaf for baking and slicing.

nutmeg *n* the round hard aromatic seed of an Indonesian tree, used as a spice.

nutria *n* **1** a coypu. **2** the fur of the coypu.

nutrient *n* something that provides nourishment.

nutriment *n* something that nourishes or promotes growth; nourishment.

nutrition *n* **1** all the processes by which an organism takes in and uses food. **2** the branch of science concerned with nutrients and their assimilation. ➤➤ **nutritional** *adj,* **nutritionally** *adv,* **nutritionist** *n.*

nutritious *adj* nourishing. ➤➤ **nutritiously** *adv.*

nutritive *adj* **1** relating to nutrition. **2** nourishing.

nuts *adj informal* crazy; mad.

nutshell *n* the hard outside covering enclosing the kernel of a nut. ✱ **in a nutshell** in brief; in essence.

nutter *n chiefly Brit, informal* a crazy fool; a lunatic.

nux vomica *n* (*pl* **nux vomica**) a S Asian tree that bears poisonous seeds containing strychnine and other alkaloids.

nuzzle *v* to rub (something or somebody) affectionately with the nose or face.

NV *abbr* Nevada (US postal abbreviation).

NVQ *abbr Brit* National Vocational Qualification.

NW *abbr* **1** Northwest. **2** Northwestern.

NY *abbr* New York (US postal abbreviation).

nyala *n* (*pl* **nyalas** *or* **nyala**) a S African antelope with a crest of white hair along its length.

NYC *abbr* New York City.

nyctalopia *n* = NIGHT BLINDNESS.

nyctophobia *n* intense, *esp* irrational, fear of the night or of darkness.

nylon *n* **1** a strong tough elastic synthetic polyamide material fashioned into fibres, sheets, etc and used *esp* in textiles and plastics. **2** nylon fabric or yarn. **3** (*in pl*) stockings made of nylon.

nymph *n* **1** a minor female spirit of nature in classical mythology. **2** *literary* a girl, *esp* a beautiful one. **3** an immature insect; *esp* a larva of a dragonfly or other insect with incomplete metamorphosis. ➤➤ **nymphal** *adj.*

nymphet *or* **nymphette** *n* a sexually desirable girl in early adolescence.

nympho *n* (*pl* **-os**) *informal* a nymphomaniac.

nympholepsy *n literary* a frenzy of emotion inspired by something unattainable. ➤➤ **nympholeptic** *adj.*

nymphomania *n* excessive sexual desire in a female. ➤➤ **nymphomaniac** *n.*

nystagmus *n* a rapid involuntary oscillation of the eyeballs, e.g. from dizziness.

O o

O[1] *or* **o** *n* (*pl* **O's** *or* **Os** *or* **o's**) **1** the 15th letter of the English alphabet. **2** a representation in speech of zero. **3** in the ABO system of human blood classification, a type lacking the A and B antigens.

O[2] *interj* = OH[1], used *esp* in addressing somebody or expressing a wish.

O[3] *abbr* the chemical symbol for oxygen.

oaf *n* a clumsy slow-witted person. ➤➤ **oafish** *adj.*

oak *n* (*pl* **oaks** *or* **oak**) a tree or shrub of the beech family, with a tough hard wood and lobed leaves, and producing acorns. ➤➤ **oaken** *adj.*

oak apple *n* a large round gall produced on oak stems or leaves by a gall wasp.

oakum *n* hemp or jute fibre obtained by untwisting old rope impregnated with tar or a tar derivative and used in packing joints and stopping up gaps between the planks of a ship.

OAP *abbr Brit* old age pensioner.

oar *n* a long usu wooden shaft with a broad blade at one end used for propelling or steering a boat. ✱ **put/stick one's oar in** to interfere.

oarsman *or* **oarswoman** *n* (*pl* **oarsmen** *or* **oarswomen**) somebody who rows a boat.

OAS *abbr* Organization of American States.

oases *n* pl of OASIS.

oasis *n* (*pl* **oases**) **1** a fertile area in a desert or other dry region. **2** a place or time affording relaxation or relief.

oast *n* a kiln for drying hops or malt.

oast house *n* a usu circular building housing an oast.

oat *n* (*usu in pl*) a widely cultivated cereal grass with a loosely branched flower head, producing grain that is used mainly as a livestock feed. ✱ **get one's oats** *Brit, informal* to have sex. **sow one's wild oats** see SOW[2]. ➤➤ **oaty** *adj.*

oatcake *n* a usu crisp savoury biscuit made of oatmeal.

oath *n* (*pl* **oaths**) **1a** a solemn calling upon God or a revered person or thing to witness to the true or binding nature of a declaration. **b** something, e.g. a promise, formally confirmed by an oath. **2a** an irreverent or offensive use of a sacred name. **b** any swearword. ✱ **on/under oath** bound by a solemn promise to tell the truth.

oatmeal *n* meal made from oats, used *esp* in porridge and oatcakes.

ob- *or* **oc-** *or* **of-** *or* **op-** *or* **os-** *prefix* forming words, with the meanings: **1** out or forth: *obtrude.* **2** exposed: *obverse.* **3** so as to involve compliance: *observe.* **4** against or in opposition to: *opponent.* **5** resisting: *obstinate.* **6** in the way of; hindering: *obstacle.* **7** hidden or concealed: *occult.*

obbligato *or* **obligato** /obli'gahtoh/ *n* (*pl* **obbligatos** *or* **obligatos** *or* **obbligati** *or* **obligati**) an elaborate, *esp* melodic, accompaniment usu played by a single instrument and not to be omitted from the piece.

obdurate *adj* **1** stubbornly refusing to change opinions, decisions, etc. **2** not inclined to feel sympathy; hardhearted. ➤➤ **obduracy** *n,* **obdurately** *adv,* **obdurateness** *n.*

OBE *abbr* Officer of the Order of the British Empire.

obeah /'ohbi·ə/ *n* **1** sorcery of a kind practised by some people in the West Indies. **2** a charm used in obeah.

obedient *adj* submissive to the will or authority of a superior. ➤➤ **obedience** *n,* **obediently** *adv.*

obeisance /oh'bay(i)səns/ *n* **1** a movement or gesture made as a sign of respect or submission. **2** deference or homage. ➤➤ **obeisant** *adj,* **obeisantly** *adv.*

obeli *n* pl of OBELUS.

obelisk *n* **1** an upright four-sided pillar that gradually tapers towards the top. **2** = DAGGER (2).

obelus *n* (*pl* **obeli**) **1** a symbol (– or ÷) used in ancient manuscripts to mark a passage of doubtful authenticity. **2** = DAGGER (2).

obese *adj* very overweight, *esp* unhealthily so. ➤➤ **obesity** *n.*

obey *v* **1** to submit to the commands or authority of. **2** to comply with (instructions).

obfuscate *v* to make obscure or difficult to understand. ➤➤ **obfuscation** *n,* **obfuscatory** *adj.*

obi *n* a broad sash worn with a Japanese kimono.

obit *n informal* an obituary.

obiter dictum *n* (*pl* **obiter dicta**) **1** an incidental observation made by a judge which is not material to the judgment and therefore not binding. **2** an incidental remark.

obituary *n* (*pl* **-ies**) a notice of a person's death printed in a newspaper, etc, usu with a short biography. ➤➤ **obituarist** *n.*

object[1] *n* **1a** something that is capable of being seen and touched. **b** something that is being considered or examined. **2** something or somebody that arouses an emotion or provokes a reaction or response. **3** an end towards which effort, action, etc is directed; a goal. **4** a noun or noun equivalent following a preposition or representing the recipient of the action of a verb. **5** in computing, a component of a software system. ✱ **no object** not a problem or obstacle; not something that will restrict one's actions: *If money's no object.* ⋙ **objectless** *adj.*

object[2] *v* **1** (*often* + to) to oppose something with words or arguments. **2** (*often* + to) to feel dislike or disapproval. ⋙ **objector** *n.*

objectify *v* (**-ies, -ied**) **1** to represent (something abstract) as a concrete thing. **2** to reduce to the status of a mere object. ⋙ **objectification** *n.*

objection *n* **1** a reason or argument presented in opposition. **2** a feeling or statement of dislike, disapproval, or opposition.

objectionable *adj* unpleasant or offensive. ⋙ **objectionableness** *n,* **objectionably** *adv.*

objective[1] *adj* **1** dealing with facts without distortion by personal feelings or prejudices. **2 a** existing independently of the mind. **b** belonging to the external world and observable or verifiable. **3** denoting a grammatical case that follows a preposition or a transitive verb. ⋙ **objectively** *adv,* **objectiveness** *n,* **objectivity** *n.*

objective[2] *n* **1** something towards which efforts are directed; a goal. **2** the lens or system of lenses nearest to the object being viewed in a telescope, microscope, etc.

objectivism *n* **1** emphasis on what is real or objective, rather than on thoughts or feelings, e.g. in art and literature. **2** in philosophy, the theory that objective reality exists and is not simply created by our apparent perception of it. ⋙ **objectivist** *n,* **objectivistic** *adj.*

object lesson *n* something that serves as a concrete illustration of a principle.

objet d'art /ˌobzhay 'dah/ *n* (*pl* **objets d'art** /ˌobzhay/) a usu small article of some artistic value.

objet trouvé /'troohvay/ *n* (*pl* **objets trouvé** /'troohvay/) a natural or manufactured object displayed as having artistic value.

objurgate *v formal* to denounce or reproach harshly; to castigate. ⋙ **objurgation** *n.*

oblate[1] *adj* of a spheroid: flattened or depressed at the poles: compare PROLATE. ⋙ **oblateness** *n.*

oblate[2] *n* a member of a Roman Catholic community whose life is devoted to religious service but who has not taken monastic vows.

oblation *n* **1** (**Oblation**) the act of offering to God the bread and wine used at Communion. **2** an offering made for religious purposes. ⋙ **oblational** *adj,* **oblatory** *adj.*

obligate *v* to compel legally or morally. ⋙ **obligator** *n.*

obligati /obli'gahtee/ *n* pl of OBLIGATO.

obligation *n* **1** something one is bound to do; a duty. **2** indebtedness for a service or favour. **3** something, e.g. a contract or promise, that binds somebody to a course of action.

obligato /obli'gahtoh/ *n* see OBBLIGATO.

obligatory *adj* **1** compulsory. **2** binding in law or conscience. **3** of or enforcing an obligation. ⋙ **obligatorily** *adv.*

oblige *v* **1** to compel by force or circumstance. **2a** (*usu in passive*) to put in one's debt by a favour or service. **b** to do a favour for.

obliging *adj* eager to help; accommodating. ⋙ **obligingly** *adv,* **obligingness** *n.*

oblique[1] *adj* **1a** neither perpendicular nor parallel; sloping. **b** of a cone, cylinder, etc: having the axis not perpendicular to the base. **c** of a triangle: having no right angle. **2** not straightforward or explicit; indirect. ⋙ **obliquely** *adv,* **obliqueness** *n,* **obliquity** *n.*

oblique[2] *n* = SOLIDUS .

obliterate *v* **1** to destroy all trace of. **2** to make illegible or imperceptible. ⋙ **obliteration** *n,* **obliterator** *n.*

oblivion *n* **1** the state of forgetting or being oblivious. **2a** the state of being forgotten. **b** the state of no longer existing; extinction.

oblivious *adj* (+ of/to) lacking conscious knowledge; completely unaware. ⋙ **obliviously** *adv,* **obliviousness** *n.*

oblong[1] *adj* rectangular with adjacent sides of unequal length.

oblong[2] *n* something that is oblong in shape.

obloquy *n* (*pl* **-ies**) **1** strongly worded condemnation. **2** discredit or disgrace.

obnoxious *adj* highly offensive or repugnant. ⋙ **obnoxiously** *adv,* **obnoxiousness** *n.*

oboe *n* a woodwind musical instrument with a double reed and a conical tube. ⋙ **oboist** *n.*

obol *n* an ancient Greek coin worth one sixth of a drachma.

obscene *adj* **1** offending standards of propriety or decency; *specif* inciting sexual depravity. **2** morally repugnant. ⋙ **obscenely** *adv.*

obscenity *n* (*pl* **-ies**) **1** the quality or state of being obscene. **2** an obscene act or utterance.

obscurantism *n* opposition to the advancement of knowledge or the revealing of facts. ⋙ **obscurant** *n,* **obscurantist** *n and adj.*

obscure[1] *adj* **1** hard to understand, *esp* because not clearly expressed; abstruse. **2** not well-known or widely acclaimed. **3** difficult to see or identify; indistinct. ⋙ **obscurely** *adv,* **obscureness** *n,* **obscurity** *n.*

obscure[2] *v* **1** to prevent from being seen, identified, or discovered; to conceal. **2** to make indistinct or unintelligible. ⋙ **obscuration** *n.*

obsequies /'obsikwiz/ *pl n formal* a funeral ceremony; funeral rites.

obsequious *adj* showing a servile willingness to oblige or admire; fawning. ⋙ **obsequiously** *adv,* **obsequiousness** *n.*

observance *n* **1** (*usu in pl*) a customary practice, rite, or ceremony. **2** the act or an instance of complying with a custom, rule, or law.

observant *adj* **1** quick to notice; alert. **2** paying close attention; watchful. **3** (+ of) careful to observe rules, etc; mindful. ⋙ **observantly** *adv.*

observation *n* **1a** the act or an instance of observing. **b** the faculty of observing. **2** the gathering of information by noting facts or occurrences. **3** a remark or comment. **4** the condition of somebody or something that is observed: *under observation.* ⋙ **observational** *adj.*

observatory *n* (*pl* **-ies**) a building or institution for the observation and interpretation of astronomical or other natural phenomena.

observe *v* **1** to perceive or take note of, *esp* by concentrated attention. **2a** to act in due conformity with (e.g. a law). **b** to celebrate or perform (e.g. a ceremony or festival) according to a prescribed or traditional form. **3** to utter as a comment. **4** to make a medical or scientific observation of. ⋙ **observable** *adj.*

observer *n* **1** somebody who observes or makes an observation. **2** somebody sent to observe but not participate officially in something.

obsess *v* **1** (*usu in passive*) to preoccupy intensely or abnormally. **2** (*usu* + on/over) to be obsessed by something; to brood over it obsessively. ⋙ **obsessed** *adj.*

obsession *n* **1** the state of being obsessed; *specif* a persistent preoccupation with an unreasonable idea, associated with a psychiatric disorder. **2** something that preoccupies somebody. ⋙ **obsessional** *adj,* **obsessionally** *adv.*

obsessive *adj* **1** of or suffering from obsession. **2** excessive to the point of abnormality. ⋙ **obsessively** *adj,* **obsessiveness** *n.*

obsessive-compulsive *adj* denoting a disorder in which a particular type of behaviour is frequently repeated as a means of keeping fears or other unwelcome thoughts at bay.

obsidian *n* a usu black volcanic glass-like rock that splits to give a convex surface.

obsolescent *adj* going out of use; becoming obsolete. ⋙ **obsolesce** *v,* **obsolescence** *n.*

obsolete *adj* **1** no longer in use. **2** no longer in vogue; outmoded. **3** in biology, e.g. of an organ or body part: rudimentary or vestigial. ⋙ **obsoleteness** *n.*

obstacle *n* something that hinders or obstructs.

obstacle course *n* **1** an area of land containing obstacles, e.g. walls and ditches, to be surmounted, *esp* by soldiers undergoing training. **2** an activity containing a series of obstacles or difficulties.

obstacle race *n* a race in which the runners must negotiate contrived obstacles.

obstetrics *pl n* (*used as sing. or pl*) a branch of medicine dealing with the care and treatment of women before, during, and after childbirth. ⋙ **obstetric** *adj,* **obstetrician** *n.*

obstinate *adj* **1** clinging stubbornly to an opinion, decision, or course of action; unyielding. **2** not easily remedied or removed. ⋙ **obstinacy** *n,* **obstinately** *adv.*

obstreperous *adj* **1** aggressively resistant to control or authority; unruly. **2** noisy and boisterous. ⋙ **obstreperously** *adv,* **obstreperousness** *n.*

obstruct *v* **1** to block or close with an obstacle. **2** to impede the progress of; to hinder. ⋙ **obstructive** *adj,* **obstructively** *adv,* **obstructiveness** *n,* **obstructor** *n.*

obstruction *n* **1** something that obstructs. **2** a condition of being clogged or blocked. **3** an attempted delay of business in a deliberative body. **4** a foul, e.g. in football or hockey, in which a player gets between an opponent and the ball.

obstructionism *n* the deliberate hindering or delaying of business, e.g. the business of a legislative body. ⋙ **obstructionist** *n and adj,* **obstructionistic** *adj.*

obtain *v* **1** to gain by effort or request; to acquire. **2** *formal* to be generally accepted or practised; to be in existence. ⋙ **obtainable** *adj,* **obtainer** *n,* **obtainment** *n.*

obtrude *v* **1** to thrust oneself or itself forward with unwarranted or unwelcome assertiveness. **2** to thrust out. **3** to assert without the right or without being asked. **4** to push (oneself) forward obtrusively. ⋙ **obtruder** *n,* **obtrusion** *n.*

obtrusive *adj* **1** unduly, irritatingly, or disturbingly noticeable. **2** forward in manner; pushy. ⋙ **obtrusively** *adv,* **obtrusiveness** *n.*

obtuse *adj* **1** lacking sensitivity or mental alertness. **2a** of an angle: greater than 90° but less than 180°. **b** not pointed or acute. ⋙ **obtusely** *adv,* **obtuseness** *n.*

obverse[1] *adj* **1** facing the observer or opponent. **2** constituting a counterpart or complement. ⋙ **obversely** *adv.*

obverse[2] *n* **1** the side of a coin, medal, etc that bears the principal design and lettering and is regarded as the front: compare REVERSE[3]. **2** a counterpart to a fact or truth.

obviate *v* **1** to anticipate and dispose of (a difficulty, etc) in advance. **2** to make unnecessary. ⋙ **obviation** *n.*

obvious *adj* **1** evident to the senses or understanding; clear. **2** lacking subtlety. ⋙ **obviously** *adv,* **obviousness** *n.*

OC *abbr Brit* Officer Commanding.

oc- *prefix* see OB-.

ocarina *n* a simple wind instrument with an elongated egg-shaped body, a projecting mouthpiece, and usu eight finger holes and two thumb holes.

Occam's razor *or* **Ockham's razor** *n* a scientific principle that explanations should include as little reference as possible to things that are not known for certain.

occasion[1] *n* **1** a time at which something occurs. **2** a suitable opportunity or circumstance. **3** *formal* a state of affairs that provides a reason or grounds. **4** a special event or ceremony. ✱ **on occasion** from time to time. **rise to the occasion** to perform well when a situation demands it.

occasion[2] *v formal* to bring about; to cause.

occasional *adj* **1** occurring at irregular or infrequent intervals. **2** acting in a specified capacity from time to time. **3** designed for use as the occasion demands. **4** composed for a particular occasion. ⋙ **occasionally** *adv.*

Occident /'oksid(ə)nt/ *n* (**the Occident**) *formal or literary* the countries of the West, as distinct from the Orient.

Occidental *n* a member of any of the indigenous peoples of the Occident.

occidental *or* **Occidental** *adj* of or situated in the Occident.

occiput /'oksipət/ *n* (*pl* **occiputs** *or* **occipita** /ok'sipitə/) the back part of the head. ⋙ **occipital** *adj.*

Occitan /'ositən/ *n* the language of the people of Languedoc in southern France, including medieval literary Provençal. ⋙ **Occitan** *adj.*

occlude *v* **1** to stop up or block (a passage or opening). **2** to obstruct or hinder. **3** to take up and hold (e.g. a gas) by absorption or adsorption. **4** of teeth: to fit together with the opposing teeth when the mouth is closed. ⋙ **occlusive** *adj.*

occluded front *n* = OCCLUSION (2).

occlusion *n* **1** the act or an instance of occluding or being occluded. **2** a weather front formed by a cold front overtaking a warm front and lifting the warm air above the earth's surface.

occult[1] *n* (**the occult**) matters involving the action or influence of supernatural agencies or some secret knowledge of them. ⋙ **occultism** *n,* **occultist** *n.*

occult[2] *adj* **1** involving supernatural powers. **2** known only to the initiated few; esoteric. **3** not easily understood; abstruse. **4** in medicine, not manifest or detectable by the unaided eye. ⋙ **occultly** *adv.*

occult[3] *v* **1** to hide from view, *esp* by putting something else in front. **2** to conceal or become concealed by occultation.

occultation *n* the eclipsing of one celestial body by another, usu much larger, one.

occupancy *n* (*pl* **-ies**) **1** the act or an instance of occupying land, a property, etc. **2** the state of being an occupant. **3** the state of being occupied. **4** a period of occupation. **5** the proportion of a building, e.g. a hotel, that is occupied.

occupant *n* **1** somebody who occupies a particular building, *esp* a resident. **2** somebody who occupies a particular position.

occupation *n* **1a** an activity by which one earns a living. **b** an activity in which one engages. **2** the occupancy of land. **3a** the act of taking possession or control of a place, *esp* by a foreign military force. **b** the period of time for which a place is occupied.

occupational *adj* of or resulting from a particular occupation: *occupational hazards.* ➤➤ **occupationally** *adv.*

occupational psychology *n* the branch of psychology that deals with behaviour in the workplace.

occupational therapy *n* creative activity used as therapy for promoting recovery or rehabilitation. ➤➤ **occupational therapist** *n.*

occupy *v* (**-ies, -ied**) **1** to engage the attention or energies of. **2** to fill up (a portion of space or time). **3** to take or maintain possession of (e.g. land). **4** to reside in or use (a building) as an owner or tenant. **5** to hold (a particular job or position). ➤➤ **occupier** *n.*

occur *v* (**occurred, occurring**) **1** to happen. **2** to be found; to exist. **3** (+ to) to come to mind.

occurrence *n* **1** something that takes place; an event. **2** the act or an instance of occurring.

ocean *n* **1a** any or all of the large expanses of salt water that cover much of the earth's surface. **b** *literary* the sea. **2** *informal* (*in pl*) a huge amount. ➤➤ **oceanic** /ohshi'anik/ *adj.*

oceanarium *n* (*pl* **oceanariums** *or* **oceanaria**) a large marine aquarium.

Oceanian *n* a native or inhabitant of Oceania, islands in the central and southern Pacific Ocean. ➤➤ **Oceanian** *adj.*

oceanography *n* the science dealing with oceans and their form, biology, and resources. ➤➤ **oceanographer** *n,* **oceanographic** *adj.*

oceanology *n* oceanography, *esp* the applied technological aspects of oceanography. ➤➤ **oceanological** *adj,* **oceanologist** *n.*

ocelot *n* a medium-sized wildcat of Central and S America with a yellow or greyish coat dotted and striped with black.

och /okh/ *interj Scot, Irish* an expression of surprise, impatience, or regret.

oche /'oki/ *n* the line behind which a player must stand when throwing darts at a dartboard.

ochre (*NAm* **ocher**) *n* **1** a brownish yellow colour. **2** an earthy usu red or yellow pigment made from impure iron ore. ➤➤ **ochreous** *adj.*

ocker *or* **Ocker** *n Aus, NZ, informal* an Australian, *esp* one regarded as uncultivated or loutish.

Ockham's razor *n* see OCCAM'S RAZOR.

o'clock *adv* used in specifying the exact hour when telling the time.

OCR *abbr* **1** optical character reader. **2** optical character recognition.

Oct. *abbr* October.

octa- *or* **octo-** *or* **oct-** *comb. form* eight: *octagon.*

octad *n* a group or series of eight.

octagon *n* a polygon with eight angles and eight sides. ➤➤ **octagonal** *adj,* **octagonally** *adv.*

octahedron *n* (*pl* **octahedrons** *or* **octahedra**) a polyhedron with eight faces. ➤➤ **octahedral** *adj.*

octal *adj* of a number system having eight as its base.

octameter *n* a line of verse consisting of eight metrical feet.

octane *n* a colourless liquid that is an organic chemical compound occurring *esp* in petroleum.

octane number *n* a number that indicates the antiknock properties of a liquid motor fuel.

octane rating *n* = OCTANE NUMBER.

octant *n* **1** any of the eight parts into which a space is divided by three coordinate planes. **2** an eighth part of a circle.

octave *n* **1a** a musical interval of eight notes on the diatonic scale. **b** the whole series of notes within this interval. **c** a note separated from a lower note by this interval. **2** a group of eight lines of verse.

octavo /ok'tayvoh/ *n* (*pl* **-os**) a size of book page that is created when a standard sheet is folded into 8 leaves or 16 pages, approximately 16 × 23cm or 6 × 9in.

octennial *adj* **1** taking place every eight years. **2** lasting for eight years.

octet *n* **1** a group of eight instruments, voices, or performers. **2** a musical composition for an octet. **3** = OCTAVE (2).

octo- *comb. form* see OCTA-.

October *n* the tenth month of the year.

octogenarian *n* a person between 80 and 89 years old. ➤➤ **octogenarian** *adj.*

octopus *n* (*pl* **octopuses**) a mollusc related to the squid and cuttlefish that has eight muscular arms equipped with two rows of suckers.

octoroon *n archaic* a person of one eighth black ancestry.

octroi /'oktrwah/ *n* in France and some other European countries, a tax levied on goods brought into some towns.

octuple[1] *adj* eight times as many or as much.

octuple[2] *v* to increase by eight times.

octuple[3] *n* a quantity eight times larger than another.

ocul- *or* **oculo-** *comb. form* denoting the eye: *oculist.*

ocular[1] *adj* **1** performed or perceived with the eyes. **2** of the eye.

ocular[2] *n* an eyepiece.

ocularist *n* somebody who makes artificial eyes.

oculist *n* an ophthalmologist or optician.

oculo- *comb. form* see OCUL-.

OD[1] *n* an overdose of a drug.

OD[2] *v* (**OD's, OD'd, OD'ing**) to take an overdose of a drug.

odalisque *n* a female slave or concubine in a harem.

odd *adj* **1** different from the usual or conventional; strange. **2a** left over when others are paired or grouped. **b** not matching. **3** of a number: not divisible by two without leaving a remainder. **4** casual or occasional; spare: *at odd moments.* **5** (*in combination*) somewhat more than the specified number: *300-odd pages.* ➤➤ **oddly** *adv,* **oddness** *n.*

oddball *n informal* an eccentric or peculiar person.

oddity *n* (*pl* **-ies**) **1** an odd person, thing, event, or trait. **2** oddness or strangeness.

odd jobs *pl n* various nonspecialized household jobs, *esp* miscellaneous repairs or manual work. ➤➤ **odd-job man** *n.*

odd man out *n* somebody or something that differs in some respect from all the others in a set or group.

oddment *n* **1** something left over; a remnant. **2** (*in pl*) miscellaneous things; odds and ends.

odd one out *n* = ODD MAN OUT.

odds *pl n* **1** the probability, often expressed as a ratio, that one thing will happen rather than another. **2** the ratio between the amount to be paid for a winning bet and the amount of the bet. **3a** an amount by which one thing exceeds or falls short of another in terms of strength, support, etc. **b** a difference in terms of advantage or disadvantage: *It makes no odds.* ✱ **at odds** in disagreement or at variance. **give/lay odds** to offer a bet in which the odds are favourable to the other person. **over the odds** *Brit* more than is right, fair, or acceptable. **take odds** to offer a bet in which the odds are favourable to oneself.

odds and ends *pl n* miscellaneous items or remnants.

odds-on *adj* **1** viewed as having a better than even chance to win. **2** likely to succeed, happen, etc.

ode *n* a poem expressing intense emotion, often addressed to a particular person or thing, marked by an exalted tone and varying metre.

odious *adj* arousing hatred or revulsion. ➤➤ **odiously** *adv,* **odiousness** *n.*

odium *n formal* general condemnation or disgrace associated with a despicable act.

odometer *n* an instrument for measuring the distance travelled by a vehicle.

odontology *n* the science dealing with the structure, development, and diseases of the teeth. ➤➤ **odontological** *adj,* **odontologist** *n.*

odorant *n* an odorous substance added to a product.

odoriferous *adj* giving off an odour, *esp* a pleasant odour.

odorous *adj* having a characteristic scent or odour.

odour (*NAm* **odor**) *n* **1** the quality of something that stimulates the sense of smell; a scent. **2** *chiefly derog* a characteristic quality. **3** *formal* repute or favour: *in bad odour.* ➤➤ **odourless** *adj.*

odyssey *n* (*pl* **-eys**) a long and wandering journey or quest.

OECD *abbr* Organization for Economic Cooperation and Development.

OED *abbr* Oxford English Dictionary.

oedema (*NAm* **edema**) *n* abnormal swelling caused by an accumulation of liquid in the spaces between tissue cells.

Oedipus complex *n* in Freudian psychology, an adult personality disorder resulting from the sexual attraction developed by a child towards the parent of the opposite sex: compare ELECTRA COMPLEX. ➤➤ **Oedipal** *adj.*

OEM *abbr* own or original equipment manufacturer, a company that builds computers to individual customers' specifications using components manufactured by others.

oenology (*NAm* **enology**) *n* the science of wine and winemaking. ➤➤ **oenological** *adj,* **oenologist** *n.*

oenophile (*NAm* **enophile**) *n* a wine connoisseur.

o'er *adv and prep literary* over.

oesophagus /ee'sofəgəs/ *n* (*pl* **oesophagi** /-gie/) the muscular tube leading from the back of the mouth to the stomach; the gullet. ➤➤ **oesophageal** /-'jee·əl/ *adj.*

oestr- *or* **oestro-** (*NAm* **estr-** *or* **estro-**) *comb. form* denoting oestrus: *oestrogen.*

oestradiol (*NAm* **estradiol**) *n* the major oestrogenic steroid sex hormone in human females.

oestro- *comb. form* see OESTR-.

oestrogen (*NAm* **estrogen**) *n* a steroid hormone that stimulates the development of secondary sex characteristics in female vertebrates and promotes oestrus in lower mammals. ➤➤ **oestrogenic** *adj.*

oestrus (*NAm* **estrus**) *n* a regularly recurrent state of sexual excitability in the female of most lower mammals when she will copulate with the male; heat. ➤➤ **oestral** *adj,* **oestrous** *adj.*

oeuvre /'uhvrə/ *n* the total work produced by a writer, artist, or composer.

of *prep* **1** used to indicate origin or derivation. **2a** composed or made from. **b** containing. **3** from among. **4a** belonging or related to. **b** possessing or characterized by. **c** connected with. **5a** in respect to. **b** directed towards. **6** used to indicate apposition. **7** *NAm* to a specified hour; to.

Usage note

Of must not be confused with the weak form of *have* following *could, should, would,* or *must,* as in *I should've told you.*

of- *prefix* see OB-.

of course *adv* **1** as might be expected; naturally. **2** used in reply to express agreement or permission.

off[1] *adv* **1** from a place or position. **2a** away in space or ahead in time. **b** from a course; aside. **c** into sleep or unconsciousness. **3a** so as not to be in contact or attached. **b** so as to be divided. **4a** to or in a state of discontinuance or suspension. **b** so as to be no longer existent. **c** in or into a decayed state. **5** away from an activity or function.

off[2] *prep* **1a** used to indicate physical separation or distance from. **b** lying or turning aside from. **c** away from. **2a** not occupied in. **b** no longer interested in or using. **c** below the usual standard or level of.

off[3] *adj* **1a** started on the way. **b** cancelled. **c** of a dish on a menu: no longer being served. **2a** not up to standard. **b** not busy; slack. **3** no longer fresh and beginning to decay. **4** provided: *How are you off for socks?* **5** situated to one side; adjoining. **6** *informal* of behaviour: not what one has a right to expect.

off[4] *v NAm, slang* to kill (somebody).

off[5] *n* **1** the start or outset. **2** in cricket, = OFF SIDE (1).

offal *n* **1** the liver, heart, kidney, etc of a butchered animal used as food. **2** refuse.

off and on *adv* at irregular intervals; from time to time.

offbeat[1] *n* an unaccented beat of a musical bar.

offbeat[2] *adj informal* unusual or unconventional.

off-break *n* a slow bowled ball in cricket that turns from the off side towards the leg side when it bounces.

off chance *n* a remote possibility. ✱ **on the off chance** just in case.

off-colour *adj* **1** unwell. **2** *chiefly NAm* somewhat indecent; risqué.

offcut *n* a piece, e.g. of paper or wood, that is left after the original piece required has been cut.

offence (*NAm* **offense**) *n* **1** something that provokes a sense of outrage. **2** a feeling of displeasure or resentment. **3a** a misdeed. **b** a crime. **4** a military attack; an assault. **5** *chiefly NAm* the attacking team in a sport. ✱ **take offence** to be offended.

offend *v* **1** to cause to feel indignation or disgust. **2** to cause pain or displeasure to; to hurt. **3** to commit a crime or wrongdoing. ➤➤ **offender** *n.*

offensive[1] *adj* **1** causing indignation or outrage. **2** arousing physical disgust; repellent. **3a** aggressive or attacking. **b** of or designed for attack. ➤➤ **offensively** *adv,* **offensiveness** *n.*

offensive[2] *n* **1** the position or attitude of an attacking party. **2** a military attack on a large scale.

offer[1] *v* **1** to present for acceptance, rejection, or consideration. **2** to make available; to provide. **3** to declare one's willingness (to do something). **4** to display (a quality). **5** (*often* + up) to present (e.g. a prayer or sacrifice) in an act of worship or devotion. ➤➤ **offerer** *n.*

offer[2] *n* **1** an undertaking to do or give something. **2** a price named by a prospective buyer. **3** *archaic* a proposal, *specif* a proposal of marriage. ✱ **on offer 1** for sale at a reduced price. **2** available to use or buy.

offering *n* something offered or presented, e.g. a sacrifice or donation.

offertory *n* (*pl* **-ies**) **1** the offering of the Communion bread and wine to God before consecration. **2** the collection of money from the congregation at public worship.

offhand[1] *or* **offhanded** *adj* **1** without proper respect, courtesy, or warmth; curt. **2** informal or casual. ➤➤ **offhandedly** *adv,* **offhandedness** *n.*

offhand[2] *adv* without forethought or preparation.

office *n* **1a** a room in which administrative or clerical work is performed. **b** a group of people sharing such a room. **c** a building where the business of a particular organization is carried out. **d** *chiefly Brit* (*in pl*) the rooms, buildings, or outhouses in which the activities attached to the service of a house are carried on. **2** (**Office**) a major administrative unit in some governments. **3** a position giving authority or having special responsibilities. **4a** *formal* a service carried out for another. **b** (*usu in pl*) a minor duty or task. **5** a prescribed form or service of worship.

office boy *n* a young man employed to run errands in an office.

office girl *n* a young woman employed to run errands in an office.

officer *n* **1a** somebody who holds a position of authority or command in the armed forces; *specif* a commissioned officer. **b** a member of a police force. **2** somebody who holds a position with special duties or responsibilities, e.g. in a government or business.

office rage *n* angry, violent, or aggressive behaviour directed at office colleagues, caused by work-related stress, etc but often occasioned by minor irritations.

official[1] *adj* **1** prescribed or sanctioned by an authority; authorized. **2** of or holding a position of authority. **3** suitable for or characteristic of people in positions of authority; formal. ➤➤ **officially** *adv.*

Usage note

official *or* **officious**? A letter, a document, or an announcement can be *official* ('written or made by someone in authority'). Only a person or their words or behaviour can be *officious* in its ordinary meaning. It is an uncomplimentary word meaning 'bossy and interfering'.

official[2] *n* somebody who holds a position of authority, *esp* in a public organization or institution. ➤➤ **officialdom** *n.*

officialese *n* the characteristic language of official statements, typically wordy, pompous, or obscure.

Official Receiver *n* a public official appointed to administer a bankrupt's property.

official secret *n* a piece of information that must be kept from the general public for the purposes of national security.

officiant *n* a priest who officiates at a religious ceremony.

officiate *v* **1** to perform an *esp* religious ceremony, function, or duty. **2** to act as an official. ➤➤ **officiation** *n,* **officiator** *n.*

officinal *adj* medicinal. ➤➤ **officinally** *adv.*

officious *adj* given to or marked by overzealousness in exercising authority or carrying out duties. ➤➤ **officiously** *adv,* **officiousness** *n.*

Usage note

officious *or* **official**? See note at OFFICIAL[1].

offing *n* the part of the deep sea visible from the shore. ✱ **in the offing** likely to happen in the near future.

offish *adj informal* inclined to be aloof or distant. ➤➤ **offishness** *n.*

off-key *adj and adv* varying in pitch from the proper tone of a melody.

off-licence *n Brit* a shop licensed to sell alcoholic drinks to be consumed off the premises.

off limits *adv and adj* not to be entered; out-of-bounds.

off-line[1] *adj* **1** not currently connected to a computer or network. **2** not controlled directly by a computer.

off-line[2] *adv* while not connected to or controlled by a computer.

off-load *v* **1** to unload (cargo). **2** to get rid of (something unwanted).

off-message *adj* inappropriate, unacceptable, or not in conformity with an official position.

off-peak *adj and adv* at a time of less than the maximum demand or activity.

off-piste *adj and adv* away from regular skiing runs, on unprepared slopes.

offprint *n* a separately printed excerpt, e.g. an article from a magazine.

off-putting *adj chiefly Brit, informal* disagreeable or disconcerting.

off-road *adj and adv* for or on rough terrain rather than prepared road surfaces.

off-roader *n* an off-road vehicle.

offscreen *adv and adj* out of sight of the film or television viewer.

off season *n* a time of suspended or reduced activity in business or trade. ➤➤ **off-season** *adv and adj.*

offset[1] *v* (**offsetting,** *past tense and past part.* **offset**) **1** to balance or compensate for. **2** to print (e.g. a book) using the offset process. **3** to place to one side.

offset[2] *n* **1** something that serves to balance or compensate for something else. **2** a printing process in which an inked impression from a plate is first made on a rubber surface and then transferred to paper. **3** a short shoot growing out to the side from the base of a plant. **4** the amount or condition of being placed or turned out of line.

offshoot *n* **1** a branch of a plant's main stem. **2** something that develops out of something else.

offshore *adj and adv* **1** away from the shore. **2** at a distance from the shore. **3** located or operating abroad.

offside *adv and adj* illegally in advance of the ball or puck in a team game.

off side *n* **1** the side of a cricket field that the batsman's or batswoman's body faces when they are receiving: compare LEG SIDE. **2** *chiefly Brit* the right side of a vehicle, furthest from the kerb: compare NEARSIDE.

offspin *n* spin that causes a cricket ball bowled at slow speed to turn from the off side towards the leg side when it bounces. ➤➤ **off-spinner** *n.*

offspring *n* (*pl* **offspring**) the progeny of a person, animal, or plant; young.

offstage *adv and adj* not visible to the audience in a theatre.

off-the-cuff *adj informal* not prepared in advance; impromptu.

off-the-peg *adj chiefly Brit* of clothes: ready-made in standard sizes, rather than made to measure.

off-the-record *adj* given or made unofficially or in confidence.

off-the-shelf *adj* available as a stock item, not specially designed or custom-made.

off-the-wall *adj informal* strikingly eccentric; crazy.

off-white *adj* of a yellowish or greyish white colour. ⋙ **off-white** *n.*

Ofsted *abbr* Office for Standards in Education.

OFT *abbr Brit* Office of Fair Trading.

oft *adv literary* often.

often *adv* **1** at many times. **2** in many cases.

ogam *n* see OGHAM.

ogee *n* **1** a moulding in the form of a shallow S-shaped curve. **2** a pointed arch with shallow S-shaped sides.

ogham *or* **ogam** *n* a 20-character alphabet used in ancient Celtic and Pictish inscriptions, with lines meeting at or crossing a straight line.

ogive *n* **1** a pointed arch. **2** a diagonal rib across a Gothic vault. ⋙ **ogival** *adj.*

ogle¹ *v* to glance or stare at with sexual interest, *esp* obviously and offensively. ⋙ **ogler** *n.*

ogle² *n* lecherous glance or stare.

ogre *or* **ogress** *n* **1** a hideous giant of folklore believed to feed on human beings. **2** a dreaded person or thing. ⋙ **ogreish** *adj.*

OH *abbr* Ohio (US postal abbreviation).

oh¹ *interj* **1** an expression of surprise, pain, disappointment, etc. **2** used to introduce a remark when addressing somebody. **3** used to acknowledge something said.

oh² *or* **O** *n* zero.

ohm *n* the SI unit of electrical resistance equal to the resistance between two points of a conductor when a constant potential difference of one volt applied to these points produces a current of one ampere.

OHMS *abbr* On His/Her Majesty's Service.

Ohm's law *n* the principle that the flow of electric current through a conductor is directly proportional to the potential difference and inversely proportional to the resistance.

OHP *abbr* overhead projector.

OHT *abbr* overhead transparency.

oi *interj informal* used to attract somebody's attention.

-oid *suffix* **1** forming nouns, denoting: something resembling a specified object or having a specified quality: *asteroid.* **2** forming adjectives, with the meaning: having the form or appearance of: *anthropoid.*

OIEO *abbr* offers in excess of.

oik *n slang* a vulgar, loud, or otherwise obnoxious person.

oil¹ *n* **1** a smooth greasy liquid substance obtained from plants or animals that burns readily and is not soluble in water. **2a** = PETROLEUM. **b** a substance derived from petroleum, used for fuel, lubrication, etc. **c** *Brit* = PARAFFIN. **d** (*used before a noun*) of or fuelled by petroleum, a petroleum derivative, or paraffin: *an oil lamp.* **3** a substance of oily consistency, used cosmetically, in cooking, in medicine, etc. **4** = OIL PAINT.

oil² *v* to apply oil to, *esp* for lubrication.

oil cake *n* the solid residue of an oil-bearing crop such as linseed after the oil has been extracted, used mainly as an animal feed.

oilcan *n* a container with a long nozzle designed to release oil in a controlled flow, e.g. for lubricating machinery.

oilcloth *n* cotton cloth treated with oil and used e.g. for table coverings.

oilfield *n* a region rich in petroleum deposits, *esp* one producing petroleum in commercial quantities.

oil-fired *adj* of a heating system, etc: fuelled by oil.

oil of turpentine *n* = TURPENTINE (2).

oil paint *n* paint consisting of ground pigment mixed with oil, used by artists. ⋙ **oil painting** *n.*

oil palm *n* an African palm tree with fruit that yields palm oil.

oil rig *n* the equipment for drilling an oil well, with or without the platform that supports it.

oilseed *n* a seed or crop, e.g. rape, grown largely for oil.

oil shale *n* shale from which oil can be distilled.

oilskin *n* **1** an oiled waterproof cloth used for coverings and garments. **2a** an outer garment made of oilskin or other waterproof material. **b** (*in pl*) a set of such garments.

oil slick *n* a film of oil floating on an expanse of water.

oilstone *n* a sharpening stone used with a surface coating of oil.

oil well *n* a well drilled in the earth from which petroleum is obtained.

oily *adj* (**-ier, -iest**) **1** resembling, containing, or covered with oil. **2** too eager to please or flatter; ingratiating. ⋙ **oiliness** *n.*

oink *v* of a pig: to make a characteristic grunting noise. ⋙ **oink** *n.*

ointment *n* a soothing or healing oily cream applied to the skin.

OIRO *abbr* offers in the region of.

Ojibwa *n* (*pl* **Ojibwas** *or* **Ojibwa**) **1** a member of a Native American people orig from north of Lake Huron. **2** a language spoken in north central USA and Ontario.

OK¹ *or* **okay** *interj* an expression of agreement or permission.

Word history

perhaps abbr of *oll korrect,* humorous alteration of *all correct.* It was taken up and used as a slogan during the presidential campaign of 1840 by supporters of the Democratic candidate Martin Van Buren, whose nickname 'Old Kinderhook' (from his birthplace, Kinderhook) coincidentally had the initials 'OK'.

OK² *or* **okay** *adv and adj* quite good or well, but not outstandingly so.

OK³ *or* **okay** *v* (**OK's, OK'd, OK'ing** *or* **okays, okayed, okaying**) to give approval or authorization to.

OK⁴ *or* **okay** *n* (*pl* **OK's** *or* **okays**) an approval or endorsement.

OK⁵ *abbr* Oklahoma (US postal abbreviation).

okapi /oh'kahpi/ *n* (*pl* **okapis** *or* **okapi**) an African mammal closely related to the giraffe but with a shorter neck and black and cream rings on the upper parts of the legs.

okay *interj, adv and adj, v, and n* see OK¹, OK², OK³, OK⁴.

okeydoke *or* **okeydokey** *interj informal* an expression of agreement or permission.

okra *n* the long green pods of a plant of the mallow family, used as a vegetable, *esp* in soups and stews.

-ol *suffix* forming nouns, denoting: a chemical compound containing a hydroxyl group; an alcohol: *glycerol.*

old[1] *adj* **1** advanced in years or age. **2** having existed for a specified period of time: *three years old.* **3a** dating from the past, *esp* the remote past. **b** persisting from an earlier time. **c** of long standing. **4** former. **5a** worn with time or use. **b** no longer in use; discarded. **6** used to express affection or in various informal forms of address. ➤➤ **oldish** *adj,* **oldness** *n.*

Usage note
older *or* elder? See note at ELDER[1]

old[2] *n* **1** used in combinations to denote a person or animal of a specified age: *a three-year-old.* **2** an old or earlier time: *men of old.*

old age *n* the final stage of the normal life span.

old age pension *n* a retirement pension. ➤➤ **old age pensioner** *n.*

Old Bill *n* = BILL.

old boy *n chiefly Brit* **1** a former pupil of a particular school. **2** used as an informal term of address for a man. **3** *informal* an old man, *esp* one who is sprightly or resilient.

old boy network *n chiefly Brit* the system of favouritism operating among people of a similar privileged background, *esp* among former pupils of public schools.

old country *n* (**the old country**) an immigrant's country of origin.

olden *adj literary* of a bygone era.

Old English *n* the earliest form of the English language, dating from around the seventh to the eleventh cents; Anglo-Saxon.

Old English sheepdog *n* a sheepdog of an English breed with a very long shaggy coat.

olde-worlde *adj* belonging to a past age, or quaintly imitating earlier styles.

old-fashioned *adj* **1** belonging to or characteristic of a past era; outdated. **2** clinging to the customs, tastes, or fashions of a past era. ➤➤ **old-fashionedly** *adv.*

Old French *n* the earliest form of the French language, dating from the 9th to the 14th cents.

old girl *n chiefly Brit* **1** a former pupil of a particular school. **2** used as an informal term of address to a woman. **3** *informal* an old woman, *esp* one who is sprightly or resilient.

Old Glory *n* the flag of the USA.

old gold *adj* of a dull brownish yellow colour. ➤➤ **old gold** *n.*

old guard *n* (*used as sing. or pl*) the conservative members of a group or party, often the founding members.

old hand *n* somebody with a great deal of experience; a veteran.

old hat *adj* **1** tediously familiar or overused; hackneyed. **2** laughably old-fashioned.

oldie *n* an old person or thing.

old lady *n* **1** an elderly woman. **2** *informal* somebody's wife or mother.

old maid *n* **1** *derog* a single woman of advanced age; a spinster. **2** *informal* a prim fussy person. **3** a simple card game in which each player tries to avoid holding a designated unpaired card at the end.

old man *n informal* **1** an elderly man. **2** somebody's husband or father.

old-man's beard *n* **1** a clematis with long grey feathery flower parts. **2** a greenish grey lichen that grows in long hair-like strands on trees.

old master *n* **1** a distinguished European painter of the 16th to early 18th cents. **2** a painting produced by an old master.

Old Nick *n informal* the devil.

Old Norse *n* the early forms of the North Germanic language as used in Scandinavia and Iceland.

old school *n* (**the old school**) adherents of traditional ideas and practices.

old school tie *n* (**the old school tie**) the conservatism and upper-class solidarity traditionally attributed to former members of British public schools.

old stager *n* somebody with years of experience and service; an old hand.

oldster *n chiefly NAm, informal* an elderly person.

Old Stone Age *n* the Palaeolithic period.

Old Style *n* the former method of reckoning dates, according to the Julian calendar.

Old Testament *n* a collection of writings forming the Jewish canon of Scripture and the first part of the Christian Bible.

old-time *adj* belonging to or characteristic of a period in the recent past.

old-timer *n* somebody with years of experience and service; a veteran.

old wives' tale *n* a traditional superstitious notion.

old woman *n informal* **1** an elderly woman. **2** somebody's wife or mother. **3** *informal, derog* a timid, prim, or fussy person, *esp* a man. ➤➤ **oldwomanish** *adj.*

Old World *n* (**the Old World**) Europe, Asia, and Africa, the parts of the world known to Europeans before the discovery of America.

olé /oh'lay/ *interj* a cry of approval or success, *esp* at bullfights.

ole- *or* **oleo-** *comb. form* denoting oil: *oleaginous.*

oleaginous *adj* **1** resembling, containing, or producing oil; oily. **2** obsequious or unctuous in manner. ➤➤ **oleaginously** *adv,* **oleaginousness** *n.*

oleander *n* a poisonous evergreen shrub with fragrant white, pink, or red flowers.

olefin *or* **olefine** *n* = ALKENE.

oleic acid *n* an unsaturated fatty acid found as glycerides in natural fats and oils.

oleo- *comb. form* see OLE-.

oleograph *n* a picture printed on cloth to resemble an oil painting. ➤➤ **oleographic** *adj,* **oleography** *n.*

O level *n* **1** a former secondary school examination in England and Wales, replaced by the GCSE. **2** a pass at O level.

olfaction *n formal or technical* the sense of smell. ➤➤ **olfactive** *adj,* **olfactory** *adj.*

olig- *or* **oligo-** *comb. form* few: *oligarchy.*

oligarchy *n* (*pl* **oligarchies**) **1** government by a small group. **2** a state or organization in which a small group exercises control. **3** a small group governing or exercising control. ➤➤ **oligarch** *n,* **oligarchic** *adj,* **oligarchical** *adj.*

oligo- *comb. form* see OLIG-.

Oligocene *adj* of the third geological epoch of the Tertiary period, lasting from about 35.5 million to about 23.5 million years ago, and marked by extensive movements of the earth's crust and the appearance of the first primates. ➤➤ **Oligocene** *n.*

oligopoly *n* a market situation in which a few producers affect the market without any one of them having control over it. ➤➤ **oligopolist** *n*, **oligopolistic** *adj*.

oligopsony *n* a market situation in which a few buyers exert a disproportionate influence on the market.

oligotrophic *adj* of a body of water: deficient in plant nutrients and having abundant dissolved oxygen: compare EUTROPHIC, MESOTROPHIC.

olio *n* (*pl* **olios**) **1** a highly spiced stew of Spanish origin. **2** a miscellaneous collection of items.

olivaceous *adj* of an olive-green colour.

olive *n* **1** a small green or purplish black stone fruit used as a food and a source of oil. **2** the small evergreen tree that bears this fruit, grown *esp* in the Mediterranean. **3** a dull greyish green colour resembling that of an unripe olive. ➤➤ **olive** *adj*.

olive branch *n* an offer or gesture of conciliation or goodwill.

Word history

with reference to the biblical story of Noah, in which a dove released from the Ark returned carrying an olive twig, showing that the flood had receded and that God and man were reconciled (Genesis 8:11).

olive drab *n* **1** a greyish green colour. **2** a fabric of this colour, or a uniform made from it.

olive-green *adj* = OLIVE (3). ➤➤ **olive green** *n*.

olive oil *n* an oil obtained from ripe olives and used in cooking and salad dressings.

olivine *n* a usu greenish mineral that is a silicate of magnesium and iron.

Olmec *n* (*pl* **Olmecs** *or* **Olmec**) a member of an ancient indigenous people of Central and South America. ➤➤ **Olmec** *adj*.

-ology *comb. form* = -LOGY.

oloroso *n* (*pl* **-os**) a golden-coloured, full-bodied, sweet sherry.

Olympiad *n* **1** any of the four-year intervals between Olympian games by which time was reckoned in ancient Greece. **2** a holding of the modern Olympic Games.

Olympian[1] *adj* **1** of the ancient Greek region of Olympia. **2** of the Olympic Games. **3a** characteristic of or befitting a god. **b** supremely aloof or detached.

Olympian[2] *n* **1** an inhabitant of the ancient Greek region of Olympia. **2** any of the ancient Greek deities dwelling on Olympus. **3** a loftily detached or superior person. **4** a participant in the Olympic Games.

Olympic *adj* **1** of ancient Olympia. **2** of the Olympic Games.

Olympic Games *pl n* (*used as sing. or pl*) **1** an international sports meeting held once every four years in a different host country. **2** an ancient Greek festival held every four years at Olympia, with athletic, literary, and musical contests.

Olympics *pl n* (**the Olympics**) (*used as sing. or pl*) the modern Olympic Games.

OM *abbr Brit* Order of Merit.

om *n* a sacred word used in Hindu and Buddhist meditation and devotion.

-oma *suffix* (*pl* **-omas** *or* **-omata**) forming nouns, denoting: a tumour: *adenoma*.

Omani *n* (*pl* **Omanis**) a native or inhabitant of Oman. ➤➤ **Omani** *adj*.

ombre (*NAm* **omber**) /'ombə/ *n* a card game for three players using a pack of 40 cards, popular in Europe in the 17th and 18th cents.

ombré /'ombray/ *adj* of fabrics: graduated in colour from light to dark.

ombudsman *n* (*pl* **ombudsmen**) a government official appointed to investigate complaints made by individuals against government or public bodies.

omega *n* **1** the 24th and last letter of the Greek alphabet (Ω, ω), equivalent to roman ō. **2** the last one in a series, order, etc.

omelette (*NAm* **omelet**) *n* a mixture of beaten eggs cooked until set in a shallow pan and often served folded in half over a filling.

omen *n* an event or phenomenon believed to be a sign of some future occurrence.

omertà /ohmə'tah/ *n* the code of silence about the Mafia's activities observed by its members and associates.

omicron *n* the 15th letter of the Greek alphabet (Ο, ο), equivalent to roman o.

ominous *adj* suggesting or signalling future disaster or evil. ➤➤ **ominously** *adv*, **ominousness** *n*.

omission *n* **1** the act or an instance of omitting or being omitted. **2** something neglected or left undone.

omit *v* (**omitted, omitting**) **1** to leave out or unmentioned. **2** to fail to do. ➤➤ **omissible** *adj*.

omni- *comb. form* all or universally: *omnidirectional*.

omnibus *n* **1a** a book containing reprints of a number of works, usu by one author. **b** a television or radio programme consisting of two or more episodes of a series, orig broadcast separately. **c** (*used before a noun*) being an omnibus. **2** *formal, dated* a bus.

omnicompetent *adj* **1** competent in all matters. **2** competent to legislate or make judgments on all matters. ➤➤ **omnicompetence** *n*.

omnidirectional *adj* receiving or transmitting radio waves equally well in all directions.

omnifarious *adj* of all varieties, forms, or kinds.

omnipotent *adj* having unlimited or very great power or influence. ➤➤ **omnipotence** *n*.

omnipresent *adj* **1** present in all places at all times. **2** ubiquitous. ➤➤ **omnipresence** *n*.

omniscient *adj* **1** having infinite awareness or understanding. **2** possessed of complete knowledge; all-knowing. ➤➤ **omniscience** *n*, **omnisciently** *adv*.

omnium-gatherum *n* (*pl* **omnium-gatherums**) a miscellaneous collection of things or people.

omnivorous *adj* **1** feeding on both animal and vegetable substances. **2** avidly taking in, *esp* reading, everything. ➤➤ **omnivore** *n*, **omnivorously** *adv*, **omnivorousness** *n*.

omophagous *adj* feeding on raw flesh. ➤➤ **omophagy** *n*.

ON *abbr* **1** Old Norse. **2** Ontario.

on[1] *prep* **1** in contact with or supported from below by. **2** attached or fastened to. **3** carried on the person of. **4** very near to, *esp* along an edge or border. **5a** within the limits of. **b** in the direction of. **c** with regard to; concerning. **d** carrying out a specified action or activity. **e** working for, supporting, or belonging to. **6** at the expense of; paid for by. **7a** in the specified state, process, manner, etc. **b** using by way of transport. **c** regularly taking. **8a** at the time of or on the occasion of. **b** immediately after and usu in consequence of. **c** in the course of.

on[2] *adv* **1** so as to be supported from below. **2** so as to be worn. **3** so as to be attached. **4a** ahead or forwards in space or time. **b** with the specified part forward. **c** without interruption. **d** in continuance or succession. **5a** in or into operation. **b** in or into an activity or function.

on[3] *adj* **1a** taking place. **b** performing or broadcasting. **c** intended or planned. **d** worn as clothing. **2** *chiefly Brit (usu in negative contexts)* possible or practicable. **3a** *chiefly Brit, informal* nagging: *She's always on at him about his hair.* **b** *informal* talking dully, excessively, or incomprehensibly: *What are you on about?* **4** in cricket, on or towards the side of the field that is opposite to the side that the batsman's or batswoman's body faces when they are receiving.

-on[1] *suffix* forming nouns, denoting: a chemical compound: *interferon.*

-on[2] *suffix* forming nouns, denoting: an inert gas: *neon.*

onager /'onəjə/ *n* a small Asian wild ass with a broad stripe on its back.

on and off *adv* at irregular intervals; from time to time.

onanism *n* **1** = COITUS INTERRUPTUS. **2** masturbation. ⯮ **onanistic** *adj.*

once[1] *adv* **1** one time and no more. **2** at some indefinite time in the past; formerly. **3** by one degree of relationship: *second cousin once removed.* **4** even one time; ever. ✱ **once again/more 1** now again as before. **2** for one more time. **once and for all/once for all** for the final or only time; conclusively. **once in a while** occasionally. **once or twice** a few times. **once upon a time** used as a traditional formula to begin a children's story: at some time in the past.

once[2] *n* one single time. ✱ **all at once 1** all at the same time. **2** without warning; suddenly. **at once 1** simultaneously. **2** immediately. **for once** on this occasion only, or at least.

once[3] *conj* from the moment when; as soon as.

once-over *n informal* a swift appraising glance.

oncogene *n* a gene, e.g. in some viruses, that causes cancer.

oncogenic *adj* of or causing the formation of tumours.

oncology *n* the study and treatment of cancer and malignant tumours. ⯮ **oncological** *adj,* **oncologist** *n.*

oncoming *adj* **1** approaching from the front. **2** coming nearer in time or space; advancing.

oncost *n* = OVERHEAD[3].

one[1] *adj* **1a** being a single unit or thing. **b** being the first: *on page one.* **2** being a particular but unspecified instance. **3** the same; identical. **4** being in a state of agreement; united. **5** being some unspecified future time. **6** being a particular object or person.

one[2] *pron* (*pl* **ones**) **1** an indefinitely indicated person; anybody at all. **2** used to refer to a noun or noun phrase previously mentioned or understood.

one[3] *n* **1** the number 1. **2** the first in a set or series. **3a** a single person or thing. **b** a unified entity: *They rose as one.* **c** a particular example or instance. ✱ **at one** in agreement or harmony. **for one** not to mention others. **one after another/the other** in succession. **one and all** everybody. **one by one** singly or successively. **one or other** either; any. **one or two** a few.

one another *pron* (*not used as the subject of a verb*) each of two or more in reciprocal action or relationship.

one-armed bandit *n* a fruit machine that is operated by a lever on one side of the machine.

one-dimensional *adj* lacking depth; superficial.

one-horse *adj* **1** pulled by one horse. **2** *informal* of little importance or interest: *a one-horse town.* **3** with only one contender: *a one-horse race.*

Oneida *n* (*pl* **Oneidas** *or* **Oneida**) a member of a Native American people of New York State.

oneiric /oh'nierik/ *adj* of dreams; dreamy.

one-liner *n* a short funny remark.

one-man band *n* **1** a street entertainer who has a number of musical instruments attached to his or her body in such a way that they can be played at the same time. **2** somebody who runs a business single-handedly, or the business run by such a person.

oneness *n* **1** the state of being only one in number; singleness. **2** the state of being whole, identical, or in agreement.

one-night stand *n* **1** a sexual relationship lasting only one night. **2** a performance given only once in any particular place.

one-off[1] *adj chiefly Brit* made or intended as a single and unrepeated item or occurrence.

one-off[2] *n* a unique person or thing.

one-on-one *adj* = ONE-TO-ONE (2).

onerous *adj* representing or involving a burden. ⯮ **onerousness** *n.*

oneself *pron* used reflexively or for emphasis to refer to an indefinitely indicated person or to people in general: *One might hurt oneself; One must learn to do it oneself.*

one-sided *adj* **1** giving advantage or favour unfairly to one party in a dispute, contest, etc; biased or uneven. **2** having or occurring on one side only. ⯮ **one-sidedly** *adv,* **one-sidedness** *n.*

one-step *n* a ballroom dance marked by quick walking steps.

one-time *adj* former.

one-to-one *adj* **1** pairing each element of a set uniquely with an element of another set. **2** involving contact between two people only, e.g. a teacher and one pupil.

one-track *adj* interested or absorbed in one thing only: *a one-track mind.*

one-two *n* **1** a combination of two quick blows in boxing, usu with different hands and in rapid succession. **2** a pass in football whereby one player kicks the ball to another and runs forward immediately to receive the return.

one up *adj* in a position of advantage.

one-upmanship *n* the art of gaining a psychological advantage over others by professing superiority.

one-way *adj* **1** moving or allowing movement in only one direction. **2** involving no collaboration or reciprocation; unilateral.

ongoing *adj* **1** actually in progress. **2** growing or developing.

onion *n* a pungent smelling, strong tasting edible bulb that is used as a vegetable. ✱ **know one's onions** *Brit, informal* to be very knowledgeable about something.

on-line[1] *adj* **1** currently connected to a computer or network. **2** controlled directly by a computer. **3** in operation or production.

on-line[2] *adv* **1** while connected to or controlled by a computer or network. **2** into operation or production.

onlooker *n* a passive spectator. ⯮ **onlooking** *adj.*

only[1] *adj* **1** alone in its class or kind; sole. **2** without a brother or sister.

only[2] *adv* **1a** nothing more than; merely. **b** solely or exclusively. **2** by a very small amount or margin: *We only just caught the bus.* **3a** in the final outcome. **b** with nevertheless the final result. **4** no earlier than. ✱ **only too** very much, sometimes regrettably so.

only[3] *conj informal* **1** but or however. **2** were it not for the fact that.

o.n.o. *abbr* used with prices of goods for sale: or nearest offer.

onomastics *pl n* (*used as sing. or pl*) the science or study of proper names. ⋙ **onomastic** *adj.*

onomatopoeia *n* the formation or use of words intended to be a vocal imitation of the sound associated with the thing or action designated, e.g. *buzz, cuckoo.* ⋙ **onomatopoeic** *adj,* **onomatopoeically** *adv.*

Onondaga *n* (*pl* **Onondagas** *or* **Onondaga**) a member of a Native American people of New York State.

onrush *n* a forceful rushing forwards.

onset *n* **1** a time or point at which something begins. **2** an attack or assault.

onshore *adj and adv* **1** towards the shore. **2** on or near the shore.

onside *adv and adj* **1** in a position permitted by the rules of the game; not offside. **2** in or into a position of agreement or support.

onslaught *n* a fierce attack.

on stream *adj and adv* in or into production.

ont- *or* **onto-** *comb. form* **1** denoting being or existence: *ontology.* **2** denoting an organism: *ontogenesis.*

-ont *comb. form* forming nouns, denoting: a cell or organism: *symbiont.*

onto *or* **on to** *prep* **1** to a position on. **2** in or into a state of awareness about. **3** *chiefly Brit* in or into contact with.

Usage note

There is no objection to spelling *onto* as a single word when it means 'to a position on': *The book fell onto the floor.* However, *onto* should not be used when the word *on* is an adverb attached to the preceding verb, as in *We walked on to the end of the lane.*

onto- *comb. form* see ONT-.

ontogenesis *n* (*pl* **ontogeneses**) the entire set of processes involved in the development of an individual organism. ⋙ **ontogenetic** *adj,* **ontogenetically** *adv.*

ontogeny *n* = ONTOGENESIS.

ontology *n* a branch of philosophy concerned with the nature of being. ⋙ **ontological** *adj,* **ontologist** *n.*

onus *n* **1** a duty or responsibility. **2** the burden of proof in a legal case.

onward[1] *adj* directed or moving onwards; forward.

onward[2] *adv* = ONWARDS.

onwards *adv* towards or at a point lying ahead in space or time; forwards.

-onym *comb. form* forming nouns, denoting: **1** a name: *pseudonym.* **2** a word: *antonym.*

onyx *n* **1** a translucent variety of quartz with layers of different colours. **2** a translucent or semitranslucent calcium carbonate mineral, usu calcite, with marble-like bands of colour.

oocyte /'oh·əsiet/ *n* a cell that becomes an ovum after it has divided.

oodles *pl n informal* a great quantity; a lot.

oogenesis /oh·ə'jenəsis/ *n* the formation and maturation of eggs or ova. ⋙ **oogenetic** *adj.*

ooh *interj* an expression of amazement or pleased surprise.

oolite /'oh·əliet/ *n* limestone consisting of small round grains, *esp* of calcium carbonate. ⋙ **oolitic** *adj.*

oolith /'oh·əlith/ *n* any of the small round grains that make up oolite.

oology /oh'oləji/ *n* the study or collecting of birds' eggs. ⋙ **oological** *adj,* **oologist** *n.*

oolong *n* a dark China tea that is partially fermented before drying.

oompah *n* the deep rhythmical sound of a tuba, euphonium, or similar brass band instrument.

oomph *n informal* **1** vitality or enthusiasm. **2** sexual attractiveness.

oops *interj* an expression of apology or surprise, *esp* when causing an accident or making a mistake.

ooze[1] *v* **1a** to pass or emit slowly through small openings. **b** to diminish gradually. **2** to exude moisture. **3** to display (a quality) in abundance.

ooze[2] *n* **1** an infusion of vegetable material, e.g. bark, used for tanning leather. **2** the act of oozing or something that oozes. ⋙ **oozy** *adj.*

ooze[3] *n* **1** a soft deposit of mud, slime, debris, etc on the bottom of a body of water. **2** a marsh or bog, or its muddy ground. ⋙ **oozy** *adj.*

OP *abbr* **1** observation post. **2** Order of Preachers, i.e. the Dominicans. **3** organophosphate. **4** out of print.

op *n informal* a military or surgical operation.

op. *abbr* opus.

op- *prefix* see OB-.

opacity *n* **1** the quality of being opaque. **2** obscurity of meaning; unintelligibility.

opah *n* a large brilliantly coloured marine fish with rich oily red flesh.

opal *n* a transparent to translucent mineral used in its opalescent forms as a gem.

opalescent *adj* reflecting a milky iridescent light. ⋙ **opalescence** *n.*

opal glass *n* glass to which fluorides have been added to give it a milky translucent quality.

opaline[1] *adj* resembling opal; opalescent.

opaline[2] *n* = OPAL GLASS.

opaque[1] *adj* **1** not able to be seen through; not transparent or translucent. **2** hard to understand; unintelligible. ⋙ **opaquely** *adv,* **opaqueness** *n.*

opaque[2] *n* an opaque paint for blocking out portions of a photographic negative or print.

op art *n* a style of art characterized by the repeated use of geometric shapes and patterns designed to create optical illusions.

op. cit. *abbr* (Latin) opere citato = in the work cited.

OPEC *abbr* Organization of Petroleum Exporting Countries.

open[1] *adj* **1a** allowing access or passage; not shut or locked. **b** having no enclosing or confining barrier. **c** presenting no obstacle to passage or view. **d** having the parts or surfaces spread out or unfolded. **2a** not fastened or sealed. **b** not covered or protected. **3** in operation, *esp* ready for business or use. **4a** exposed to general view or knowledge; public. **b** vulnerable to attack or question; liable. **5a** available or remaining available. **b** not finally decided or settled. **c** not restricted to a particular category of participants. **6a** willing to receive and consider: *open to suggestions.* **b** candid or frank. **c** willing to consider new ideas; unprejudiced: *an open mind.* **7** free from checks or restraints. **8** containing many small openings or spaces. **9** of a string on a musical instrument: not stopped by the finger. **10** of a vowel: articulated with the tongue low in the mouth. ✻ **with open arms** in a welcoming or enthusiastic manner. ⋙ **openness** *n.*

open[2] *v* **1** to change or cause to change from a closed position. **2a** to gain access to the contents of (a package, etc). **b** to unfold or spread out. **3a** to start or cause to start operating for business. **b** to begin an activity. **4** to declare to be available for use, especially in a ceremony. **5** (+ into/onto) to give access: *The door opens onto a terrace.*

open[3] *n* **1** (**the open**) a large outdoor space, *esp* in the countryside. **2** (*often* **Open**) a contest in which anybody can compete. ✻ **be in/bring into the open** to be, or cause to be, generally known.

open air *n* (**the open air**) a large outdoor space; outdoors. ⋙ **open-air** *adj.*

open-and-shut *adj* easily settled.

opencast *adj* of a mine or mining: worked from or carried out on the earth's surface by removing material covering the mineral.

open circuit *n* an incomplete circuit of electrical components through which current cannot flow.

open court *n* a court or trial to which the public are admitted.

open day *n* a day on which an institution is open to the public.

open door *n* **1** a policy of equal commercial relations with all nations. **2** a policy of unrestricted access. ⋙ **open-door** *adj.*

open-ended *adj* without any definite limits or restrictions set in advance. ⋙ **open-endedness** *n.*

opener *n* **1a** a device that opens something. **b** somebody who begins something; *specif* an opening batsman or batswoman. **2** the first item or event in a series. ✻ **for openers** *informal* to start with.

open-faced *adj* with a facial expression that suggests frankness and lack of duplicity.

openhanded *adj* generous in giving.

openhearted *adj* **1** kind, generous, or affectionate. **2** candidly straightforward.

open-hearth process *n* a process of making steel from pig iron in a reverberatory furnace.

open-heart surgery *n* surgery in which the heart is actually exposed and blood circulation performed by machine.

open house ✻ **keep open house** to be ready to receive visitors at all times.

opening[1] *n* **1** a space through which something can pass; a gap. **2a** a standard series of moves made at the beginning of a game of chess or draughts. **b** a first performance. **c** a beginning or first part. **3a** a favourable opportunity; a chance. **b** an opportunity for employment; a vacancy.

opening[2] *adj* coming at or marking the beginning of something.

open letter *n* a letter, *esp* of protest, appeal, or explanation, usu addressed to an individual but intended for the general public and published in a newspaper, periodical, etc.

openly *adv* in an open and frank manner.

open market *n* a market based on free competition and an unrestricted flow of goods, e.g. between countries.

open marriage *n* a marriage in which both partners, by mutual consent, are free to have sexual relations with others.

open-minded *adj* receptive to new arguments or ideas. ⋙ **open-mindedness** *n.*

open out *v* to speak freely.

open-plan *adj* having no or few internal dividing walls.

open prison *n* a prison with less restrictive security, to which criminals considered unlikely to attempt escape may be sent.

open question *n* a matter that has yet to be decided or resolved.

open-reel *adj* = REEL-TO-REEL.

open sandwich *n* a sandwich without a top slice of bread.

open season *n* a period during which it is legal to kill or catch game or fish protected at other times by law.

open secret *n* a supposed secret that is in fact widely known.

open shop *n* a place of work in which employment is not dependent on membership of a trade union: compare CLOSED SHOP.

open up *v* **1** to allow access to a building. **2** to start to speak more freely. **3** to start firing weapons. **4** of an activity: to become more interesting.

open verdict *n* a verdict at an inquest that records a death but does not state its cause.

openwork *n* ornamental work (e.g. in fabric or metal) that is perforated or pierced.

opera[1] *n* **1** a drama set to music and made up of vocal pieces and orchestral music. **2** the branch of the arts concerned with such works. **3** a company performing operas or a theatre where they are performed.

opera[2] *n* pl of OPUS.

operable *adj* **1** suitable for surgical treatment. **2** fit, possible, or desirable to use; practicable. **3** able to be operated.

opéra bouffe /ˌop(ə)rə 'boohf/ *n* (*pl* **opéras bouffes** /ˌop(ə)rə 'boohf/) = OPERA BUFFA.

opera buffa /'boohfə/ *n* (*pl* **opera buffas**) a farcical or satirical opera, *esp* of a form popular in the 18th cent.

opéra comique /ko'meek/ *n* (*pl* **opéras comiques** /ˌop(ə)rə ko'meek/) = COMIC OPERA.

opera glasses *pl n* small binoculars suitable for use at the opera or theatre.

opera hat *n* a man's collapsible top hat.

opera house *n* a theatre designed for the performance of opera.

operand *n* a quantity on which an operation is performed in mathematics.

operant[1] *adj* effective or functioning.

operant[2] *n* a type of behaviour, e.g. the pressing of a lever by a rat to obtain food, that operates on the environment to produce rewarding effects.

opera seria *n* (*pl* **opera serias**) an 18th-cent. opera with a heroic or legendary subject.

operate *v* **1** to function or cause (e.g. a machine) to function; to work. **2** to exert power or influence; to act or produce a desired effect. **3** to be in effect. **4** to be in action; *specif* to carry out trade or business. **5** (*often* + on) to perform surgery. **6** to carry on a military or naval action or mission.

operatic *adj* **1** of opera. **2** overtly theatrical in behaviour; flamboyant. ⋙ **operatically** *adv.*

operatics *pl n* (*used as sing. or pl*) the performance of operas.

operating system *n* the computer software that supports and controls the running of a computer and its associated equipment.

operating table *n* a high table on which a patient lies while undergoing surgery.

operating theatre *n Brit* a room in a hospital where surgical operations are carried out.

operation *n* **1a** the act or an instance of operating or being operated. **b** something done or to be done; an activity. **2** the state of being functional or operative. **3** a surgical procedure carried out on a living body with special instruments, usu for the repair of damage or the restoration of health. **4** a mathematical or logical process carried out to derive one expression from others according to a rule. **5** a usu military action, mission, or manoeuvre and its planning. **6** a single step performed by a computer in the execution of a program.

operational *adj* **1** of, based on, or involved in operations. **2** currently functioning or in a state in which functioning is possible. ⋙ **operationally** *adv.*

operations room *n* a room from which military or other operations are controlled.

operative[1] *adj* **1** in force or operation. **2a** significant or relevant. **b** producing an appropriate effect; efficacious. **3** of or using a surgical operation. ⋙ **operatively** *adv,* **operativeness** *n.*

operative[2] *n* **1** a worker. **2** a secret agent. **3** *NAm* a private detective.

operator *n* **1a** somebody who operates a machine or device. **b** somebody who owns or runs a business, organization, etc. **c** somebody who works at a telephone switchboard. **2** a mathematical or logical symbol denoting an operation to be performed. **3** *informal* a shrewd and skilful manipulator.

operculum *n* (*pl* **opercula** *or* **operculums**) **1** a lid or covering flap, e.g. of the gills of a fish. **2** a hard plate at the end of the foot in many gastropod molluscs that closes the shell. ⋙ **opercular** *adj.*

operetta *n* a less formal or serious opera, usu on a romantic or humorous theme, that includes dancing and spoken dialogue. ⋙ **operettist** *n.*

ophidian *adj* of or resembling snakes.

ophthalm- *or* **ophthalmo-** *comb. form* denoting the eye or eyeball: *ophthalmology.*

ophthalmia *n* inflammation of the conjunctiva or the eyeball.

ophthalmic *adj* of the eye.

ophthalmic optician *n* an optician qualified to test eyesight and prescribe correctional lenses.

ophthalmo- *comb. form* see OPHTHALM-.

ophthalmology *n* the branch of medical science dealing with the structure, functions, and diseases of the eye. ⋙ **ophthalmological** *adj,* **ophthalmologically** *adv,* **ophthalmologist** *n.*

ophthalmoscope *n* an instrument used to view the retina and other structures inside the eye. ⋙ **ophthalmoscopic** *adj,* **ophthalmoscopy** *n.*

-opia *comb. form* forming nouns, denoting: the condition of having a specified visual defect: *myopia.*

opiate[1] *adj* **1** of or containing opium. **2** inducing sleep; narcotic.

opiate[2] *n* **1** a preparation or derivative of opium; a narcotic. **2** something that induces inaction or calm.

opine *v formal* to state as an opinion.

opinion *n* **1** a view or judgment formed about a particular matter. **2a** a belief that is not supported by positive knowledge. **b** a generally held view. **3** a formal expression by an expert of his or her professional judgment or advice. ✱ **matter of opinion** something that cannot be decided objectively or proved conclusively one way or the other.

opinionated *adj* having strong opinions and always ready to express them.

opinion poll *n* a survey conducted by questioning people selected at random or by quota in order to establish public opinion on some matter.

opium *n* **1** an addictive drug derived from the juice of poppy seeds, containing morphine and other narcotic alkaloids. **2** something that has an addictive effect, *esp* something that inhibits thought or action.

opossum *n* (*pl* **opossums** *or* **opossum**) **1** an American tree-dwelling marsupial with a prehensile tail. **2** = POSSUM (2).

opponent *n* **1** somebody who takes the opposite side in a contest, conflict, etc. **2** somebody who opposes something, e.g. a plan or proposal.

opportune *adj* **1** suitable or convenient for a particular occurrence or action. **2** occurring at an appropriate time. ⋙ **opportunely** *adv,* **opportuneness** *n.*

opportunism *n* the taking advantage of opportunities or circumstances, *esp* with little regard for principles or consequences. ⋙ **opportunist** *n.*

opportunistic *adj* **1** tending to seize opportunities with little regard for principles or consequences. **2** of a disease: affecting only those whose immune systems have been weakened in some way.

opportunity *n* (*pl* **-ies**) **1** a favourable set of circumstances. **2** a chance for advancement or progress.

opposable *adj* **1** capable of being opposed or resisted. **2** of a thumb or other digit: capable of being placed opposite and against the remaining digits.

oppose *v* **1a** to be hostile to or against; to resist. **b** to fight or compete with. **2** to place opposite or against something else, e.g. as a contrast or counterbalance. ⋙ **opposer** *n,* **opposing** *adj.*

opposed *adj* set in opposition; contrary.

opposite[1] *adj* **1a** in a position with regard to somebody or something else that is on the other side. **b** of angles: on opposite sides of a point where two lines intersect. **2a** occupying an opposing position. **b** diametrically different; contrary. **3** being the other of a matching or contrasting pair: *the opposite sex.* ⋙ **oppositely** *adv,* **oppositeness** *n.*

opposite[2] *prep* **1** across from and usu facing. **2** in a role complementary to.

opposite[3] *adv* on or to an opposite side.

opposite[4] *n* **1** an opposite person or thing. **2** an antonym. **3** something that is contrary.

opposite number *n* a counterpart.

opposition *n* **1** the act or an instance of opposing or the state of being opposite. **2** hostility or resistance. **3** (*used as sing. or pl*) **a** the body of people opposing something. **b** (*often* **Opposition**) the main political party opposing the party in power. **4** in astronomy, an opposite position of the sun and another celestial body in which their longitude differs by 180°. ⋙ **oppositional** *adj.*

oppress *v* **1** to crush (e.g. a people) by harsh or authoritarian rule. **2** to weigh heavily on the mind or spirit of. ⋙ **oppression** *n,* **oppressor** *n.*

oppressive *adj* **1** unreasonably harsh or severe; authoritarian. **2** causing a sense of being mentally weighed down. **3** of the weather: stiflingly warm and windless; close. ⋙ **oppressively** *adv,* **oppressiveness** *n.*

opprobrious *adj formal* sharply critical, scornful, or abusive. ⋙ **opprobriously** *adv.*

opprobrium *n formal* the public disgrace or contempt that results from shameful behaviour.

oppugn *v formal* to cast doubt on.

ops *pl n* operations, *esp* military operations.

-opsy *comb. form* forming nouns, denoting: an examination: *autopsy.*

opt *v* to make a choice in favour of or against something.

optative *adj* of or belonging to a grammatical mood, e.g. in Greek, expressing wish or desire.

optic[1] *adj* of vision or the eye.

optic[2] *n* **1** any of the lenses, prisms, or mirrors of an optical instrument. **2** *Brit* a device that delivers a measure of alcoholic spirit when fitted to the neck of an inverted bottle.

optical *adj* **1** of optics. **2** of or designed to aid vision. **3** of or using light. ➤➤ **optically** *adv.*

optical art *n formal* = OP ART.

optical character reader *n* an electronic device that can read documents, books, tables, or other data by measuring the variation in the light reflected from the paper.

optical character recognition *n* a process whereby handwritten or printed material is scanned electronically for inputting to a computer system.

optical fibre *n* a very thin glass or plastic fibre used in fibre optics to transmit light.

optical glass *n* a high-quality glass used *esp* for making lenses.

optical illusion *n* something that deceives the observer into believing that they are seeing something they are not.

optician *n* somebody who prescribes correctional lenses for eye defects or supplies spectacles on prescription.

optics *pl n* **1** (*used as sing. or pl*) the science of the nature, properties, and uses of light. **2** optical properties or components.

optima *n* pl of OPTIMUM[2].

optimal *adj* most satisfactory; optimum. ➤➤ **optimally** *adv.*

optimise *v* see OPTIMIZE.

optimism *n* **1** a tendency to emphasize favourable aspects of situations or events or to expect the best possible outcome; hopefulness. **2** the doctrine that this world is the best possible world. ➤➤ **optimist** *n,* **optimistic** *adj,* **optimistically** *adv.*

optimize *or* **-ise** *v* to make (something) as effective or advantageous as possible. ➤➤ **optimization** *n.*

optimum[1] *adj* most favourable or desirable.

optimum[2] *n* (*pl* **optima** *or* **optimums**) something that is most favourable to a particular end.

option *n* **1a** an alternative course of action; a choice. **b** an item offered in addition to or in place of standard equipment. **2** the right to choose. **3** a right to buy or sell something at a specified price during a stipulated period. ✱ **keep/leave one's options open** to not commit oneself by opting for something.

optional *adj* available as a choice; not compulsory. ➤➤ **optionally** *adv.*

optometry *n* the art or profession of examining the eye for defects and prescribing correctional lenses or exercises but not drugs or surgery. ➤➤ **optometric** *adj,* **optometrist** *n.*

opt out *v* **1** to choose not to participate in something. **2** *Brit* e.g. of a school: to choose to withdraw from local authority control and manage financial and administrative affairs independently.

opulent *adj* having or showing evidence of great wealth; rich or luxurious. ➤➤ **opulence** *n,* **opulently** *adv.*

opuntia *n* any of a genus of cacti that includes the prickly pears.

opus *n* (*pl* **opera** *or* **opuses**) **1** a musical composition or set of compositions, usu numbered in the order of issue. **2** an artistic work of any kind.

opus Dei /'day·ee/ *n* **1** in the Christian Church, worship that follows the prescribed forms, regarded as the Christian duty to God. **2** (**Opus Dei**) a Roman Catholic organization whose members are dedicated to promoting Christian principles.

OR *abbr* Oregon (US postal abbreviation).

or[1] *conj* **1** used to join two words or sentence elements to indicate that what immediately follows is another alternative. **2** used to introduce a word or phrase mentioned by way of definition or explanation of a preceding word or phrase. **3** used to indicate the result of rejecting a preceding choice. **4** used to introduce an afterthought.

or[2] *n* in heraldry, a yellow or gold tincture.

-or[1] *suffix* forming nouns, denoting: somebody or something that performs a specified action: *vendor.*

-or[2] *suffix* forming nouns, denoting: a quality, condition, or state, or an instance of one: *error.*

orache *or* **orach** /'orich/ *n* a plant with green, white, or red leaves, sometimes cultivated and eaten like spinach.

oracle *n* **1a** an often cryptic answer to some question, usu regarding the future, purporting to come from a deity. **b** a priest or priestess of ancient Greece or Rome who delivered oracles. **2** a source of authoritative decisions or information.

oracular *adj* **1** of or denoting an oracle. **2** resembling an oracle in authority or obscurity of expression.

oracy *n* the ability to understand and express oneself intelligibly in speech.

oral[1] *adj* **1a** uttered in words; spoken. **b** involving speech rather than writing. **2a** of, given or taken through, or affecting the mouth. **b** in psychoanalysis, of or relating to the first stage of sexual development in which gratification is derived from eating, sucking, and biting: compare ANAL, GENITAL. ➤➤ **orality** *n,* **orally** *adv.*

Usage note

oral *or* **aural**? See note at AURAL.

oral[2] *n* an oral examination.

oral history *n* history based on traditions handed down in a community or personal memories recorded orally, e.g. on tape, rather than in written documents.

oral sex *n* sexual activity in which the genitals of one person are stimulated by the mouth of another.

Orange *adj* of Orangemen. ➤➤ **Orangeism** *n.*

orange *n* **1** a spherical fruit with a reddish yellow leathery rind and sweet juicy edible pulp. **2** the colour of oranges, between red and yellow in the spectrum. **3** a drink made from oranges. ➤➤ **orange** *adj,* **orangey** *adj,* **orangy** *adj.*

orangeade *n* a beverage of sweetened orange juice mixed with carbonated water.

orange flower water *n* a solution of NEROLI (extract of orange flowers) in water, used as a food flavouring and formerly as a toilet water.

Orangeman *n* (*pl* **Orangemen**) a member of a Protestant loyalist society in Northern Ireland and elsewhere.

Word history

named after William III of England d.1702, Prince of *Orange,* city in France, Protestant ruler who deposed the Roman Catholic James II.

orange pekoe *n* a black tea made from the tiny leaf and bud at the end of the stalk.

orangery *n* (*pl* **-ies**) a protected place, e.g. a greenhouse, for growing oranges in cool climates.

orangestick *n* a thin stick with a pointed end used in manicuring.

orang-utan *or* **orang-utang** *n* a tree-dwelling anthropoid ape of Borneo and Sumatra with orange-brown skin and hair and very long arms.

orate *v* to speak in an elevated and often pompous manner.

oration *n* a speech delivered in a formal and dignified manner.

orator *n* a skilled public speaker.

oratorio *n* (*pl* **-os**) a large-scale choral work usu with orchestral accompaniment and based on a religious subject.

oratory[1] *n* (*pl* **-ies**) a place of prayer, *esp* a private or institutional chapel.

oratory[2] *n* **1** the art of public speaking. **2** public speaking characterized by impressive or excessive eloquence. ➤➤ **oratorical** *adj.*

orb *n* **1** a golden globe surmounted by a cross, symbolizing royal power and justice. **2** a spherical object.

orbicular *adj* **1** spherical. **2** circular. ➤➤ **orbicularity** *n.*

orbit[1] *n* **1a** a path followed by one celestial body in its revolution round another, or by a spacecraft, satellite, etc round a celestial body. **b** the path of an electron around the nucleus of an atom. **2** a sphere of activity or influence. **3** in anatomy, the bony socket of the eye. ➤➤ **orbital** *adj.*

orbit[2] *v* (**orbited, orbiting**) to revolve in an orbit round (e.g. a celestial body).

orbital *adj* **1** relating to the orbit of a celestial body or an object in space. **2** of a road: bypassing and circling a major city.

orbiter *n* a spacecraft designed to orbit a celestial body without landing on its surface.

orc *n* a fairytale monster of varying description, most commonly a human-like creature.

orca *n* = KILLER WHALE.

Orcadian *n* a native or inhabitant of the Orkney Islands. ➤➤ **Orcadian** *adj.*

orchard *n* a usu enclosed area in which fruit trees are planted.

orchestra *n* **1** a large group of musicians, *esp* one comprising string, woodwind, brass, and percussion sections. **2** = ORCHESTRA PIT. **3** *NAm* the stalls in a theatre. **4** the circular space used by the chorus in front of the stage in an ancient Greek theatre. ➤➤ **orchestral** *adj,* **orchestrally** *adv.*

orchestra pit *n* in a theatre, the space in front of the stage where the members of the orchestra sit.

orchestrate *v* **1** to compose or arrange (music) for an orchestra. **2** to provide (e.g. a performance) with orchestral music. **3** to arrange or control (something) cleverly to achieve the desired outcome. ➤➤ **orchestration** *n,* **orchestrator** *n.*

orchid *n* a plant related to the grasses and lilies having striking three-petalled flowers with an enlarged liplike middle petal. ➤➤ **orchidaceous** *adj.*

orchitis *n* inflammation of the testicles.

ordain *v* **1** to invest officially with the authority of a priest or minister. **2a** to order by decree or law; to command. **b** to make destined to happen; to foreordain. ➤➤ **ordainment** *n.*

ordeal *n* **1** a severe or testing experience. **2** a method formerly used to determine guilt or innocence by submitting the accused to dangerous or painful tests whose outcome was believed to depend on divine or supernatural intervention.

order[1] *n* **1a** a specific command or authoritative direction. **b** the rule of law or proper authority. **2** a request for goods to be supplied, food to be served, work to be done, etc. **3** a proper, orderly, or functioning condition. **4** regular, correct, or harmonious arrangement. **5a** customary procedure, *esp* in debate. **b** a prescribed form of a religious service. **6a** a religious body or community living under a specific rule. **b** any of the several grades of the Christian ministry. **c** (*in pl*) the office of a person in the Christian ministry. **7a** a rank or group in a community. **b** a category in the classification of living things ranking above the family and below the class. **8** any rank or level. **9a** a category or kind. **b** the arrangement of objects, people, or events according to sequence in space, time, value, importance, etc. **10** a style of building, *esp* any of the classical styles of architecture. **11** a military or other decoration. ✻ **in/of the order of** about as much or as many as; approximately. **in order that** so that. **in order to** for the purpose of. **on order** having been ordered. **out of order 1** not in the correct sequence. **2** not in working condition. **3** not following correct procedure; not allowed by the rules. **4** *informal* not acceptable or appropriate. **to order** according to the specifications of an order.

order[2] *v* **1** to put in order; to arrange. **2a** to give an order to; to command. **b** to place an order for (e.g. goods). **c** to command or prescribe (an action, etc).

ordered *adj* **1** marked by regularity or self-discipline. **2** with elements arranged in a regular or harmonious order.

Order in Council *n* an order made by the British sovereign on the advice of the privy council, giving the force of law to administrative regulations.

orderly[1] *adj* **1a** arranged in order; neat. **b** liking or exhibiting order; methodical. **2** well behaved or peaceful. ➤➤ **orderliness** *n.*

orderly[2] *n* (*pl* **-ies**) **1** a soldier assigned to carry messages, relay orders, etc for a superior officer. **2** a hospital attendant who does routine or heavy work.

orderly room *n* the administration office of a military unit.

order of magnitude *n* a range of magnitude extending from a particular value to ten times that value.

order of the day *n* **1a** an agenda, e.g. of business to be attended to. **b** a proclamation or instructions issued by a commanding officer. **2** the characteristic or dominant feature or activity. **3** *informal* the only option available.

order paper *n* a programme of the day's business in a legislative assembly.

ordinal[1] *n* **1** = ORDINAL NUMBER. **2** (**Ordinal**) the forms of religious service for ordination, or a book containing them.

ordinal[2] *adj* **1** of a specified order or rank in a series. **2** in biology, relating to an order in taxonomy.

ordinal number *n* a number designating the place, e.g. first, second, or third, occupied by an item in an ordered set: compare CARDINAL NUMBER.

ordinance *n* **1** an authoritative order or regulation. **2** a prescribed usage, practice, or ceremony.

ordinand *n* a candidate for ordination; a trainee priest or minister.

ordinary[1] *adj* **1** routine or usual; customary. **2** not exceptional; commonplace. ➤➤ **ordinarily** *adv,* **ordinariness** *n.*

ordinary[2] *n* (*pl* **-ies**) **1** (*often* **Ordinary**) the invariable parts of the Roman Catholic mass. **2** any of the simplest heraldic charges used in coats of arms. **3** a bishop or judge having jurisdiction over a specified territory or group in his own right, not by delegation. ✱ **out of the ordinary** not usual or customary.

Ordinary level *n* = O LEVEL.

ordinary seaman *n* the lowest rank in the Royal Navy, below able seaman.

ordinary share *n* a share entitling the holder to dividends or assets only after the claims of debenture holders and preference shares have been met: compare PREFERENCE SHARE.

ordinate *n* in mathematics, the coordinate of a point obtained by measuring the distance from the x-axis parallel to the y-axis: compare ABSCISSA.

ordination *n* the act or an instance of ordaining somebody as a priest or minister.

ordnance *n* **1a** military supplies. **b** a government department dealing with military supplies. **2** heavy artillery.

ordnance datum *n* a standard mean sea level used by the Ordnance Survey.

Ordnance Survey *n* a government organization that produces a survey of Great Britain and Ireland published as a series of detailed maps.

Ordovician *adj* of the second geological period of the Palaeozoic era, lasting from about 510 million to about 439 million years ago, and marked by the first appearance of vertebrates in the sea. ➤➤ **Ordovician** *n.*

ordure *n formal* excrement.

ore *n* a mineral containing a metal or other valuable constituent for which it is mined.

öre /'uhrə/ *n* (*pl* **öre**) a unit of currency in Sweden, worth 100th of a krona.

øre /'uhrə/ *n* (*pl* **øre**) a unit of currency in Denmark and Norway, worth 100th of a krone.

oread /'awreead/ *n* in Greek and Roman mythology, a mountain nymph.

oregano /ori'gahnoh, ə'regənoh/ *n* a bushy plant of the mint family whose leaves are used as a herb in cooking.

orfe *n* (*pl* **orfes**) a golden-yellow European freshwater fish that is a popular pond and aquarium fish.

organ *n* **1a** a musical instrument consisting of sets of pipes activated by compressed air and controlled by keyboards. **b** an electronic keyboard instrument producing a similar sound. **2** a specialized biological structure, e.g. the heart or a leaf, performing some specific function in an organism. **3** a subordinate organization that performs specialized functions. **4** *formal* a newspaper or periodical. **5** *informal* a penis. ➤➤ **organist** *n.*

organ- *or* **organo-** *comb. form* organic: *organophosphate.*

organdie *or* **organdy** *n* a very fine transparent muslin with a stiff finish.

organelle *n* a part of a cell that has a specialized structure and usu a specific function.

organ-grinder *n* an itinerant street musician who operates a barrel organ.

organic *adj* **1a** of or derived from living organisms. **b** of food, farming, etc: produced or carried out without the aid of chemical fertilizers, pesticides, etc. **2a** of or arising in a bodily organ. **b** affecting the structure of the organism. **3a** forming an integral element of a whole. **b** having systematic coordination of parts. **c** resembling or developing in the manner of an organism. **4** containing carbon compounds, *esp* those occurring in living organisms, or denoting the branch of chemistry dealing with these. ➤➤ **organically** *adv.*

organisation *n* see ORGANIZATION.

organise *v* see ORGANIZE.

organism *n* **1** an individual member of a biological species; a being. **2** a complex structure of interdependent and subordinate elements.

organization *or* **-isation** *n* **1a** the act or an instance of organizing. **b** the state or manner of being organized. **2a** an association or society. **b** an administrative and functional body, e.g. a business or a political party. ➤➤ **organizational** *adj.*

organize *or* **-ise** *v* **1** to arrange or form (elements) into a complete or functioning whole. **2** to arrange by systematic planning and effort. **3** to persuade (people) to associate in an organization, *esp* a trade union. ➤➤ **organizer** *n.*

organo- *comb. form* see ORGAN-.

organophosphate *n* an organic compound, *esp* a pesticide, containing phosphorus.

organza *n* a sheer dress fabric resembling organdie, usu made of silk, rayon, or nylon.

orgasm *n* **1** the climax of sexual excitement. **2** any intensely pleasurable sensation. ➤➤ **orgasmic** *adj,* **orgastic** *adj.*

orgy *n* (*pl* **-ies**) **1a** a wild party characterized by sexual promiscuity. **b** drunken revelry. **2** an excessive indulgence in a specified activity. ➤➤ **orgiastic** *adj.*

oriel window *n* a bay window projecting from an upper storey and supported by a corbel or bracket.

orient[1] *n* (**the Orient**) *dated* the countries of eastern Asia, *esp* China, Japan, and their neighbours.

orient[2] *v* = ORIENTATE.

orient[3] *adj archaic* oriental.

Oriental *n offensive* a member of any of the indigenous peoples of the Orient.

oriental *adj* (*often* **Oriental**) of, from, or characteristic of the Orient.

orientalism *or* **Orientalism** *n* **1** a characteristic feature of the peoples or culture of the Orient. **2** scholarship or learning in oriental subjects. ➤➤ **orientalist** *n.*

orientate *v chiefly Brit* **1** to ascertain the position or bearings of (oneself) in unfamiliar surroundings. **2** to set in a definite position, *esp* in relation to the points of the compass. **3** to adjust or tailor to a particular environment or situation.

orientation *n* **1a** the act or an instance of orientating or being orientated. **b** an arrangement, alignment, or relative position. **2** a lasting tendency of thought, inclination, or interest. ➤➤ **orientational** *adj.*

orientation course *n chiefly NAm* a course that is designed to introduce people to a new situation or organization.

orienteering *n* a sport in which contestants have to cross difficult unfamiliar country on foot using a map and compass to navigate their way between checkpoints. ➤➤ **orienteer** *v and n.*

orifice *n* an opening through which something may pass, *esp* one in the body.

oriflamme *n* a banner, symbol, or ideal inspiring devotion or courage.

origami /ori'gahmi/ *n* the Japanese art of folding paper into complex shapes.

origin *n* **1** a source or starting-point. **2** ancestry or parentage. **3** in mathematics, the point of intersection of axes, e.g. on a graph, where the value of the variables is zero.

original[1] *adj* **1** initial or earliest. **2a** not secondary, derivative, or imitative. **b** being the source of a copy, reproduction, or translation. **3** inventive or creative. ➤➤ **originally** *adv.*

original[2] *n* **1** something from which a copy, reproduction, or translation is made. **2** an eccentric person.

originality *n* **1** freshness or novelty, e.g. in design or style. **2** the power of imaginative and independent thought or creation. **3** the quality or state of being original.

original sin *n* in Christianity, the innate sinfulness of all human beings that is supposed to have resulted from Adam's disobedience of God.

originate *v* **1** to begin or come into existence. **2** to bring into existence; to initiate. ➤➤ **origination** *n,* **originator** *n.*

oriole *n* **1** a brightly coloured songbird of Africa, Europe, and Asia. **2** an American songbird with black and orange or yellow plumage.

orison *n archaic* a prayer.

-orium *suffix* (*pl* **-oriums** *or* **-oria**) forming nouns, denoting: a place for a particular function: *crematorium.*

ormolu *n* gilded brass or bronze used to decorate furniture, ornaments, etc.

ornament[1] *n* **1a** something that adds beauty to a person or thing. **b** a small decorative object. **c** decoration or embellishment. **2** in music, an embellishing note or notes not belonging to the essential harmony or melody.

ornament[2] *v* to decorate or embellish. ➤➤ **ornamentation** *n.*

ornamental[1] *adj* **1** used or intended as an ornament; decorative. **2** of a plant: cultivated for its beauty. ➤➤ **ornamentally** *adv.*

ornamental[2] *n* a plant cultivated for its beauty.

ornate *adj* **1** elaborately or excessively decorated. **2** affectedly elaborate or florid in style. ➤➤ **ornately** *adv,* **ornateness** *n.*

ornery *adj NAm, informal* bad-tempered or cantankerous.

ornith- *or* **ornitho-** *comb. form* denoting a bird or birds: *ornithology.*

ornithischian *n* a dinosaur with a pelvic structure similar to that of a bird: compare SAURISCHIAN. ➤➤ **ornithischian** *adj.*

ornitho- *comb. form* see ORNITH-.

ornithology *n* a branch of zoology dealing with birds. ➤➤ **ornithological** *adj,* **ornithologist** *n.*

oro- *comb. form* denoting a mountain: *orogeny.*

orogenesis *n* = OROGENY.

orogeny *n* the process of mountain formation, *esp* by folding of the earth's crust. ➤➤ **orogenic** *adj.*

orography *n* a branch of physical geography that deals with mountains. ➤➤ **orographic** *adj,* **orographical** *adj.*

orotund *adj* **1** of the voice: marked by fullness of sound; sonorous or resonant. **2** of writing or speech: pompous or bombastic. ➤➤ **orotundity** *n.*

orphan[1] *n* a child whose parents are dead.

orphan[2] *v* to make (somebody) an orphan.

orphanage *n* an institution for the care of orphans.

orpiment *n* an orange to yellow mineral consisting of arsenic trisulphide and formerly used as a pigment.

orrery *n* (*pl* **-ies**) a clockwork apparatus showing the relative positions and motions of celestial bodies in the solar system.

orris *n* the fragrant rhizome of an iris, prepared for use in perfumery.

orrisroot *n* = ORRIS.

orth- *or* **ortho-** *comb. form* forming words, with the meanings: **1** straight, vertical, or perpendicular: *orthogonal.* **2** correct or corrective: *orthoptics.*

orthoclase *n* a common feldspar mineral, usu white or pink in colour, consisting of potassium aluminium silicate.

orthodontics *pl n* (*used as sing. or pl*) a branch of dentistry dealing with the correction of irregularities of the teeth. ➤➤ **orthodontic** *adj,* **orthodontist** *n.*

orthodox *adj* **1a** conforming to established, dominant, or official doctrine, e.g. in religion. **b** in accordance with proper practice; conventional. **2a** (**Orthodox**) of or denoting any of the Eastern Churches headed by the patriarch of Constantinople that separated from the Western Church in the eleventh cent.. **b** (*usu* **Orthodox**) of or denoting Judaism that keeps to strict and traditional interpretation of Jewish scripture and authoritative rabbinic tradition. ➤➤ **orthodoxly** *adv.*

orthodoxy *n* (*pl* **-ies**) **1** being orthodox. **2** an orthodox belief or practice.

orthogonal *adj* of lines, planes, axes, etc: perpendicular to one another. ➤➤ **orthogonally** *adv.*

orthography *n* (*pl* **-ies**) **1** correct spelling. **2** the spelling system of a language. ➤➤ **orthographer** *n,* **orthographic** *adj,* **orthographically** *adv.*

orthopaedics (*NAm* **orthopedics**) *pl n* (*used as sing. or pl*) a branch of medicine dealing with the correction or prevention of skeletal and muscular deformities, *esp* by surgery. ➤➤ **orthopaedic** *adj,* **orthopaedist** *n.*

orthoptics *pl n* (*used as sing. or pl*) the study of disorders of vision, *esp* those caused by weak eye muscles, and the use of exercises and other non-surgical methods to correct them. ➤➤ **orthoptic** *adj,* **orthoptist** *n.*

orthorexia /ˌawthohˈreksiə/ *n* an obsessive concern with eating only health-giving food. ➤➤ **orthorexic** *n and adj.*

ortolan *n* a small brown and greyish green European bunting that is eaten as a delicacy, *esp* in France.

Orwellian *adj* characteristic of the novels of George Orwell (d.1950), *esp* in depicting the way in which people are manipulated by an authoritarian state.

-ory[1] *suffix* forming nouns, denoting: **1** a place for a particular function: *observatory.* **2** something that serves a particular function: *directory.*

-ory[2] *suffix* forming adjectives, with the meanings: **1** of or involving: *compulsory.* **2** serving for or producing: *justificatory.*

oryx *n* (*pl* **oryxes** *or* **oryx**) a large African antelope with long straight horns.

OS *abbr* **1** operating system. **2** ordinary seaman. **3** Ordnance Survey. **4** outsize.

Os *abbr* the chemical symbol for osmium.

os- *prefix* see OB-.

Oscar *n* a gold statuette awarded annually by the American Academy of Motion Picture Arts and Sciences for outstanding achievement in the cinema. Also called ACADEMY AWARD.

oscillate *v* **1a** to swing backward and forward like a pendulum. **b** to move or travel back and forth between two points. **2** to vary between opposing beliefs, feelings, courses of action, etc. **3** in physics, to undergo or cause to undergo a regular change from maximum to minimum, *esp* in a flow of electricity periodically changing direction. ⋙ **oscillation** *n,* **oscillator** *n,* **oscillatory** *adj.*

oscilloscope *n* an instrument in which electrical oscillations register as a temporary visible wave form on the fluorescent screen of a cathode-ray tube. ⋙ **oscilloscopic** *adj.*

oscula *n* pl of OSCULUM.

oscular *adj* **1** relating to the mouth or to kissing. **2** relating to an osculum.

osculate *v humorous or formal* to kiss (somebody). ⋙ **osculation** *n,* **osculatory** *adj.*

osculum *n* (*pl* **oscula**) in zoology, an opening in a living sponge from which water flows out.

-ose[1] *suffix* forming adjectives, with the meanings: **1** full of or possessing the quality of: *verbose.* **2** having, consisting of, or resembling: *ramose.* ⋙ **-osity** *suffix.*

-ose[2] *suffix* forming nouns, denoting: a carbohydrate, *esp* a sugar: *fructose.*

osier *n* a willow with pliable twigs that are used for furniture and basketry.

-osis *suffix* (*pl* **-oses** *or* **-osises**) forming nouns, denoting: **1a** an action, process, or state: *hypnosis.* **b** an abnormal or pathological condition: *thrombosis.* **2** the increase or formation of something: *fibrosis.* ⋙ **-otic** *suffix.*

-osity *suffix* see -OSE[1], -OUS.

osmium *n* a hard brittle blue-grey metallic element that is the heaviest metal known, occurs naturally in platinum ores, and is used in alloys.

osmoregulation *n* the automatic regulation of osmotic pressure or water content, *esp* in the body of an organism.

osmose *v* to pass by osmosis.

osmosis *n* **1** movement of a solvent through a membrane into a solution of higher concentration, which tends to equalize the concentrations on the two sides of the membrane. **2** a process suggestive of osmosis, e.g. the assimilation of knowledge. ⋙ **osmotic** *adj,* **osmotically** *adv.*

osmotic pressure *n* pressure associated with osmosis and dependent on concentration and temperature, *esp* the pressure that must be applied to a solution to prevent osmosis.

osprey *n* (*pl* **ospreys**) a large fish-eating hawk with dark brown and white plumage.

osseous *adj technical* consisting of bone; bony.

ossicle *n* a small bone or bony structure, *esp* one in the middle ear.

ossify *v* (**-ies, -ied**) **1** to become or change into bone. **2** to become inflexible in habit or attitude. ⋙ **ossification** *n.*

osso bucco /ˌosoh 'boohkoh/ *n* an Italian dish made from sliced shin of veal including marrowbone braised with tomatoes and white wine.

ossuary *n* (*pl* **-ies**) a place or container for the bones of the dead.

oste- *or* **osteo-** *comb. form* denoting bone: *osteopathy.*

ostensible *adj* seeming to be so, but not necessarily true or real. ⋙ **ostensibly** *adv.*

ostentation *n* unnecessary display of wealth, knowledge, etc designed to impress or attract attention. ⋙ **ostentatious** *adj,* **ostentatiously** *adv.*

osteo- *comb. form* see OSTE-.

osteoarthritis *n* a degenerative form of arthritis usu associated with increasing age. ⋙ **osteoarthritic** *adj.*

osteology *n* a branch of anatomy dealing with the bones. ⋙ **osteological** *adj,* **osteologist** *n and adj.*

osteoma *n* (*pl* **osteomas** *or* **osteomata**) a benign tumour composed of bone tissue.

osteomyelitis *n* an infectious inflammatory disease of bone or bone marrow.

osteopathy *n* a system of treatment of disease based on the manipulation of bones or other parts of the body. ⋙ **osteopath** *n,* **osteopathic** *adj.*

osteoporosis *n* a disease that causes enlargement of the internal cavities in the bones and makes them thin, brittle, and porous. Also called BRITTLE BONE DISEASE.

ostinato *n* (*pl* **-os**) a musical figure repeated persistently at the same pitch throughout a composition.

ostler (*NAm* **hostler**) *n* in former times, a groom or stableman at an inn.

ostracize *or* **-ise** *v* to exclude (somebody) by general consent from a group or society. ⋙ **ostracism** *n.*

ostrich *n* **1** a large swift-running flightless bird of N Africa that has dark plumage, a naked head, long legs, and two toes on each foot. **2** a person who refuses to face up to unpleasant realities.

Word history

(sense 2) from the belief that the ostrich when pursued hides its head in the sand and believes itself to be unseen.

Ostrogoth *n* a member of the E division of the Goths. ⋙ **Ostrogothic** *adj.*

OT *abbr* **1** occupational therapy. **2** occupational therapist. **3** Old Testament. **4** overtime.

ot- *or* **oto-** *comb. form* denoting the ear: *otitis.*

OTC *abbr* **1** Officers' Training Corps. **2** over-the-counter.

OTE *abbr* on target earnings, the projected remuneration of a sales representative or other person on commission.

other[1] *adj* **1a** being the remaining one or ones of two or more. **b** being one or ones distinct from that or those previously mentioned. **c** second; alternate: *every other Tuesday.* **2a** not the same; different. **b** far or opposite. **3** additional or further. **4** recently past: *the other day.*

other[2] *pron* **1** the remaining or opposite one. **2** a different or additional one. ✱ **no other** *archaic* nothing else.

otherness *n* the state of being other or different.

other ranks *pl n chiefly Brit* military persons not holding commissioned rank.

otherwise[1] *adv* **1** in different circumstances. **2** in other respects. **3** in a different way. **4** if not; or else. **5** used to express the opposite: *guilty unless proved otherwise.*

otherwise[2] *adj* of a different kind or in a different state.

other woman *n* the female lover of a married man.

other world *n* the spirit world or the afterlife.

otherworldly *adj* concerned with spiritual or intellectual matters rather than the material world. ⋙ **otherworldliness** *n.*

otic *adj* relating to or in the region of the ear.

-otic *suffix* see -OSIS.

otiose *adj formal* futile or pointless; lacking use or effect.

otitis *n* inflammation of the ear.

oto- *comb. form* see OT-.

otoscope *n* a medical instrument for examining the eardrum and outer ear.

OTT *abbr* over-the-top.

otter *n* (*pl* **otters** *or* **otter**) an aquatic fish-eating mammal with webbed and clawed feet, a long streamlined body, and dark brown fur.

Ottoman *adj* **1** of the Turks or Turkey; Turkish. **2** of the Ottoman Empire, a former Turkish sultanate in SE Europe, W Asia, and N Africa, founded around 1300 and dissolved after World War I.

ottoman *n* (*pl* **ottomans**) **1** (**Ottoman**) a Turk, *esp* of the Ottoman Empire. **2** an upholstered box or seat without a back or arms.

OU *abbr* Open University.

ouabain /wah'bah·in, 'wahbah·een/ *n* a poisonous chemical compound obtained from several African shrubs or trees and used in medicine as a heart stimulant.

oubliette /oohbli'et/ *n* a dungeon with an opening only at the top.

ouch *interj* used to express sudden sharp pain.

ought *v aux* (*third person sing. present tense* **ought,** *past tense in reported speech* **ought**) **1** used to express moral obligation. **2** used to express what is advisable or recommended. **3** used to express probability or expectation.

Usage note

The negative form of *ought* is *ought not*, which can be shortened to *oughtn't*. The form *didn't ought* is not standard English.

oughtn't *contr* ought not.

ouguiya /ooh'gee·ə/ *n* the basic monetary unit of Mauritania.

Ouija board /'weejə, 'weeji/ *n trademark* a board with letters, numbers, and other signs around the edge and a moving pointer that is used to produce messages, answers to questions, etc in spiritualistic seances.

ounce[1] *n* **1a** a unit of weight equal to one sixteenth of a pound (about 28.35g). **b** a unit of troy weight or apothecaries' weight equal to one twelfth of a pound or 480 grains (about 31g). **2** (*usu with a negative*) the least amount.

ounce[2] *n* = SNOW LEOPARD.

our *adj* **1** belonging to or associated with me and one or more other people. **2** belonging to or associated with people in general. **3** used by writers and monarchs as a formal word for *my*.

-our *suffix* = -OR[2].

Our Father *n* the Lord's Prayer.

Our Lord *n* **1** God. **2** Jesus.

ours *pron* the one or ones that belong to or are associated with us. ✱ **of ours** belonging to or associated with us: *friends of ours.*

ourself *pron* used instead of *myself* when *we* is used instead of *I*, e.g. by a monarch.

ourselves *pron* used reflexively or for emphasis to refer to the people speaking or to a person speaking and associated people: *We have hurt ourselves; We ourselves said it.*

-ous *suffix* forming adjectives, with the meanings: **1** full of or characterized by: *envious.* **2** in chemistry, having a valency relatively lower than in compounds or ions named with an adjective ending in *-ic*: *ferrous.* ➤➤ **-osity** *suffix,* **-ously** *suffix.*

ousel *n* see OUZEL.

-ously *suffix* see -OUS.

oust *v* **1** to take the place of or supplant (somebody). **2** to deprive (somebody) of possession, *esp* of land.

out[1] *adv* **1a** away from the inside or centre. **b** from among other things. **c** away from the shore, the city, etc. **d** away from one's home or business. **e** clearly in or into view. **2** inaccurate in reckoning. **3** no longer in vogue or fashion. **4a** to or in a state of extinction. **b** to the fullest extent or degree; completely. **c** in or into a state of determined effort: *out to fight pollution.* **5a** aloud. **b** in or into public knowledge or circulation. **6** so as to be eliminated, *esp* from a game. **7** in or into a state of unconsciousness. **8** used on a two-way radio to indicate that a message is complete and no reply is expected. ✱ **have it out** *informal* to settle a matter of contention by discussion or a fight. **out of 1a** from within to the outside of. **b** beyond the range or limits of. **c** away from. **2a** used to indicate a change in quality, state, or form. **b** used to indicate a position or state that is not correct or desirable: *out of alignment.* **3a** used to indicate origin or cause. **b** using the specified material. **4** used to indicate exclusion from or deprivation of. **5** from among. **out of it** not part of a group, activity, or fashion.

out[2] *v* **1** to expel or eject; to put or throw out. **2** *informal* to reveal that (somebody) is homosexual.

out[3] *adj* **1** directed or serving to direct outwards. **2** not permissible, possible, or worth considering. **3a** in cricket, baseball, etc, not allowed to continue batting. **b** of a ball, shot, etc: landing outside the prescribed area. **4** *informal* open about one's homosexuality.

out[4] *prep non-standard or NAm* out of.

out[5] *n* a way of escaping from an embarrassing or difficult situation.

out- *prefix* **1** forth: *outburst.* **2** denoting a result or product: *output.* **3** in a manner that goes beyond, surpasses, or excels: *outstrip.* **4** located outside; external: *outbuilding.*

outage *n* a period of nonoperation, e.g. of a power supply.

out-and-out *adj* utter; absolute: *an out-and-out liar.*

outback *n* remote rural country, *esp* in Australia.

outbalance *v* to exceed in value or importance.

outbid *v* (**outbidding,** *past tense and past part.* **outbid**) to make a higher bid than.

outboard[1] *adv and adj* in a lateral direction from the hull of a ship or the fuselage of an aircraft.

outboard[2] *n* **1** an outboard motor. **2** a boat with an outboard motor.

outboard motor *n* a motor, propeller, and rudder attached as a unit to the stern of a small boat.

outbound *adj* outward-bound.

outbreak *n* a sudden or violent breaking out or occurrence.

outbuilding *n* a smaller building separate from but belonging to a main building.

outburst *n* **1** a violent expression of feeling. **2** a surge of activity or growth.

outcast *n* a person who is cast out by society. ➤➤ **outcast** *adj.*

outclass *v* to excel or surpass in quality, skill, etc.

outcome *n* a result or consequence.

outcrop[1] *n* the part of a rock formation that appears at the surface of the ground.

outcrop[2] *v* (**outcropped, outcropping**) to project as an outcrop.

outcry *n* (*pl* **-ies**) a public expression of anger or disapproval.

outdated *adj* old-fashioned or obsolete; outmoded.

outdid *v* past tense of OUTDO.

outdistance *v* to go far ahead of (somebody), e.g. in a race.

outdo *v* (**outdoes,** *past tense* **outdid,** *past part.* **outdone**) to surpass (somebody) in action or performance.

outdoor *adj* **1** of or performed outdoors. **2** not enclosed; without a roof.

outdoors[1] *adv* outside a building; in or into the open air.

outdoors[2] *n* a place or the whole area outside buildings; the open air.

outer[1] *adj* **1** of or situated on the outside; external. **2** away from a centre; situated farther out. ⋙ **outermost** *adj.*

outer[2] *n* the ring on a shooting target that is outermost and worth the least score, or a shot that hits this ring.

outer bar *n* (**the outer bar**) in Britain, junior barristers who are not Queen's Counsels or King's Counsels.

outer space *n* space outside the earth's atmosphere.

outface *v* **1** to confront (somebody) unflinchingly. **2** to cause (somebody) to waver or submit by staring at them.

outfall *n* the outlet for a river, lake, drain, sewer, etc.

outfield *n* **1** the part of a cricket field beyond the prepared section on which the wickets are laid out. **2** the part of a baseball field outside a line connecting the bases. ⋙ **outfielder** *n.*

outfit[1] *n* **1a** a set of garments worn together, often for a specified occasion or activity. **b** a complete set of equipment needed for a particular purpose. **2** *informal* (*used as sing. or pl*) a group that works as a team.

outfit[2] *v* (**outfitted, outfitting**) to provide (somebody) with an outfit. ⋙ **outfitter** *n.*

outflank *v* **1** to go round the flank of and outmanoeuvre (an opposing force). **2** to gain an advantage over (somebody) by doing something unexpected.

outflow *n* **1** the act or process of flowing out. **2** something that flows out.

outfox *v* to get the better of by cunning.

outgoing[1] *adj* **1a** retiring or withdrawing from a position: *the outgoing president.* **b** going away; departing. **2** friendly or sociable.

outgoing[2] *n* **1** the act or an instance of going out. **2** (*in pl*) expenditure, *esp* overheads.

outgrow *v* (*past tense* **outgrew,** *past part.* **outgrown**) **1** to grow or increase faster than. **2** to grow too large for (e.g. clothes). **3** to lose or leave behind (e.g. a habit) as one grows older.

outgrowth *n* **1** something that grows out of something else. **2** the process of growing out. **3** a consequence or by-product.

outgun *v* (**outgunned, outgunning**) to surpass in firepower, weaponry, or shooting; *broadly* to defeat.

outhouse *n* an outbuilding.

outing *n* **1** a short pleasure trip. **2** *informal* the act of revealing somebody's homosexuality against their will.

outlandish *adj* strikingly unusual; bizarre. ⋙ **outlandishly** *adv.*

outlast *v* to last longer than.

outlaw[1] *n* **1** a fugitive from the law. **2** somebody excluded from the protection of the law.

outlaw[2] *v* **1** to make illegal; to ban. **2** to deprive of the protection of the law. ⋙ **outlawry** *n.*

outlay *n* expenditure or payment.

outlet *n* **1a** a place or opening through which something is let out; an exit or vent. **b** a means of release or satisfaction for an emotion or drive. **2** a shop or other agency through which a product is sold. **3** *chiefly NAm* an electric socket.

outlier *n* **1** something separated or lying away from a main or related body. **2** a formation of younger rocks surrounded by older ones.

outline[1] *n* **1** a line bounding the outer limits of something or indicating its shape. **2** a drawing with no shading or detail. **3** a summary of a written work. **4** a preliminary plan or draft showing the main features only.

outline[2] *v* **1** to draw the outline of. **2** to summarize or indicate the principal features of.

outlive *v* **1** to live longer than. **2** to survive the effects of.

outlook *n* **1** a view from a particular place. **2** an attitude or point of view. **3** a prospect for the future.

outlying *adj* remote from a centre or main point.

outmanoeuvre (*NAm* **outmaneuver**) *v* to defeat by more skilful manoeuvring.

outmatch *v* to prove superior to.

outmoded *adj* **1** no longer in fashion. **2** no longer acceptable; obsolete.

outnumber *v* to exceed in number.

out-of-body experience *n* a feeling of being separate from one's body and so able to observe oneself as if from a distance.

out-of-bounds *adv and adj* outside the prescribed boundaries or limits.

out-of-court *adj* of a settlement: agreed between disputing parties without the intervention of a court of law.

out-of-date *adj* **1** old-fashioned or obsolete; outmoded. **2** no longer valid or usable.

out-of-the-way *adj* **1** off the beaten track; remote. **2** unusual.

outpace *v* to surpass in speed, growth, development, etc.

outpatient *n* a patient who visits a hospital for diagnosis or treatment but does not stay there overnight.

outperform *v* to do better than in performance or achievement.

outplacement *n* advice and assistance in finding new jobs for redundant employees.

outplay *v* to play better than and defeat in a game.

outpost *n* **1** a post or detachment established at a distance from a main body of troops. **2a** an outlying or frontier settlement. **b** an outlying branch of a main organization or body.

outpouring *n* **1** (*usu in pl*) an outburst of powerful emotion. **2a** the act of pouring out. **b** something that pours out.

output[1] *n* **1a** the amount produced by somebody in a given time. **b** the act or process of producing. **2** something produced, e.g. in industry, by a writer or artist, or from a computer. **3a** power or energy produced by a machine or system. **b** the terminal for the output on an electrical device.

output[2] *v* (**outputting,** *past tense and past part.* **output**) to produce as output.

outrage[1] *n* **1** the anger and resentment aroused by injury or insult. **2** an act that violates accepted standards of behaviour or taste. **3** an act of violence or brutality.

outrage[2] *v* **1** to arouse intense anger or resentment in. **2** to violate the standards or principles of.

outrageous *adj* **1** going beyond all standards of propriety, decency, or taste; shocking or offensive. **2** not conventional or moderate; extravagant. ⋙ **outrageously** *adv,* **outrageousness** *n.*

outran *v* past tense of OUTRUN.

outrank *v* **1** to rank higher than. **2** to exceed in importance.

outré /'oohtray/ *adj* violating convention or propriety; bizarre.

outreach[1] *v* to reach further than.

outreach[2] *n* **1** involvement with and education of people in the community. **2** the act or extent of reaching out.

outrider *n* a mounted attendant or motorcyclist who rides ahead of or beside a carriage or car as an escort or guard.

outrigger *n* **1** a spar, beam, or framework projecting from a ship's side. **2** a projecting framework by which a float is attached beside a canoe to give it greater stability, or a canoe so equipped.

outright[1] *adv* **1** completely; altogether. **2** instantaneously; on the spot. **3** without reservation; directly. **4** without restrictions.

outright[2] *adj* **1** utter; complete. **2** without reservation; direct. **3** without restrictions.

outrun *v* (**outrunning,** *past tense* **outran,** *past part.* **outrun**) **1** to run faster than. **2** to exceed or surpass.

outsell *v* (*past tense and past part.* **outsold**) to exceed in numbers sold.

outset *n* (**the outset**) the beginning or start.

outshine *v* (*past tense and past part.* **outshone**) **1** to shine brighter than. **2** to outdo or surpass.

outside[1] *n* **1** the outer side or surface of something. **2** an outer manifestation; an appearance. **3** the part surrounding or beyond the boundaries of something. **4a** the side of a pavement that is nearer the traffic. **b** the side of a curve or bend that has the longer edge. **c** in sport, the section of a playing area towards the sidelines. ✱ **at the outside** at the most.

outside[2] *adj* **1** of, on, or near the outside. **2a** originating elsewhere. **b** not belonging to one's regular occupation or duties: *outside interests.* **3** maximum. **4** barely possible; remote: *an outside chance.*

outside[3] *adv* **1** on or to the outside. **2** outdoors. ✱ **outside of 1** *chiefly NAm* beyond the limits of. **2** *chiefly NAm* except for or apart from.

outside[4] *prep* **1** on or to the outside of. **2** beyond the limits of. **3** except or besides.

outside broadcast *n* a television or radio broadcast recorded or filmed on location, not in a studio.

outsider *n* **1** somebody who does not belong to a particular group. **2** a competitor who has only a remote chance of winning.

outsize *adj* of an exceptionally large or larger than standard size.

outskirts *pl n* the parts of a town or city that are farthest from the centre.

outsmart *v* to get the better of by superior cleverness; to outwit.

outsold *v* past tense and past part. of OUTSELL.

outsource *v* to obtain (components, services, etc) from outside suppliers.

outspoken *adj* direct and open in speech or expression; frank. ➤➤ **outspokenly** *adv,* **outspokenness** *n.*

outspread *adj* spread or stretched out; fully extended.

outstanding *adj* **1a** marked by excellence or distinction. **b** standing out from a group; conspicuous. **2a** unpaid. **b** continuing or unresolved. ➤➤ **outstandingly** *adv.*

outstare *v* to stare at (somebody) for longer than they can stare back.

outstation *n* a remote or outlying station.

outstay *v* to stay beyond the time or limits of: *He outstayed his welcome.*

outstretch *v* **1** to stretch out or extend (e.g. one's arms). **2** to go beyond the limits of.

outstrip *v* (**outstripped, outstripping**) **1** to go faster or farther than; to leave behind. **2** to do better than. **3** to be greater than or grow faster than.

out-take *n* a section of film, recording, etc that is cut out during editing.

out tray *n* a tray on a desk for papers, letters, etc that have been dealt with.

outturn *n* **1** a quantity produced; output. **2** a result or outcome.

outvote *v* to defeat by a majority of votes.

outward[1] *adj* **1a** situated on or directed towards the outside. **b** being or going away from home. **2** relating to external appearances; superficial. ➤➤ **outwardly** *adv.*

outward[2] *adv* = OUTWARDS.

outward-bound *adj* going in an outward direction, e.g. away from a home port.

outwards *adv* towards the outside; away from the centre.

outweigh *v* to exceed in weight, value, or importance.

outwit *v* (**outwitted, outwitting**) to get the better of by superior cleverness.

outwith *prep Scot* outside.

outwork *n* **1** a minor defensive position constructed outside a fortified area. **2** work done for a business or organization off its premises usu by employees based at home. ➤➤ **outworker** *n.*

outworn *adj* no longer useful or acceptable; outmoded.

ouzel *or* **ousel** /'oohzl/ *n* **1** = RING OUZEL. **2** = DIPPER (2).

ouzo /'oohzoh/ *n* an unsweetened Greek spirit flavoured with aniseed that is usu drunk with water.

ov- *or* **ovi-** *or* **ovo-** *comb. form* denoting an egg or ovum.

ova *n* pl of OVUM.

oval[1] *adj* having the shape of an egg or ellipse.

oval[2] *n* **1** an oval figure or object. **2a** an oval sports field or track. **b** *Aus* a ground for Australian Rules football.

ovariectomy *n* (*pl* **-ies**) the surgical removal of an ovary.

ovary *n* (*pl* **-ies**) **1** either of the pair of female reproductive organs that produce eggs and female sex hormones in human beings and other animals. **2** the hollow rounded part at the base of the female reproductive organ of a flowering plant that contains one or more ovules. ➤➤ **ovarian** *adj.*

ovate *adj* shaped like an egg.

ovation *n* an expression of popular acclaim, *esp* sustained and enthusiastic applause.

oven *n* an enclosed compartment or chamber used for baking, heating, or drying, *esp* one used in a kitchen for cooking food.

oven glove *n Brit* a cloth pad or mitten used for handling hot cooking pots and dishes.

ovenproof *adj* sufficiently heat-resistant for use in an oven.

oven-ready *adj* of food: sold ready to be cooked without further preparation.

ovenware *n* heat-resistant dishes in which food can be cooked in an oven.

over[1] *adv* **1a** across a barrier or intervening space. **b** to a particular place. **c** downwards from an upright position. **d** so as to be inverted or reversed. **2** beyond some quantity or limit. **3** in excess; remaining. **4** so as to cover the whole surface. **5a** at an end. **b** used on a two-way radio to indicate that a reply is expected. **6a** used to show repetition. **b** *chiefly NAm* once more. ✻ **over with** finished or completed.

over[2] *prep* **1a** higher than. **b** vertically above but not touching. **c** used to indicate downward movement. **d** from one side of (a barrier or intervening space) to the other; across. **e** so as to cover. **2** used to indicate authority, power, superiority or preference. **3** more than. **4** by means of (a medium or channel of communication). **5** during. **6** used to indicate an object of care, reference, occupation, or activity. ✻ **over against** as opposed to; in contrast with. **over and above** besides; in addition to.

over[3] *n* in cricket, any of the divisions of an innings during which one bowler bowls six balls from the same end of the pitch.

over- *comb. form* **1** upper or higher: *overlord.* **2** outer or covering: *overcoat.* **3** excessive or excessively: *overcapacity; overambitious.* **4** above: *overarch.* **5** downwards: *overthrow.*

overabundance *n* an excess or surfeit. ➤➤ **overabundant** *adj.*

overact *v* to perform (a part) with undue exaggeration.

overall[1] *adv* **1** as a whole. **2** from end to end.

overall[2] *n* **1** (*in pl*) a protective garment resembling a boiler suit or dungarees. **2** *chiefly Brit* a usu loose-fitting protective coat worn over other clothing.

overall[3] *adj* including everything.

overambitious *adj* excessively ambitious and therefore unlikely to be realized.

overarch *v* to form an arch over.

overarching *adj* **1** forming an arch overhead. **2** dominating or embracing everything else.

overarm *adj and adv* with the hand and arm brought forward and down from above shoulder level.

overate *v* past tense of OVEREAT.

overawe *v* to fill with respect or fear.

overbalance *v* **1a** to lose balance and fall. **b** to cause to overbalance. **2** to outweigh (something).

overbearing *adj* harshly masterful or domineering. ➤➤ **overbearingly** *adv.*

overbid *v* (**overbidding,** *past tense and past part.* **overbid**) **1** in an auction, to bid in excess of value or in excess of (another person's bid). **2** in bridge, to bid more than the scoring capacity of one's hand. ➤➤ **overbid** *n.*

overbite *n* in dentistry, the projection of the upper front teeth over the lower when the jaws are in contact.

overblown[1] *adj* inflated or pretentious.

overblown[2] *adj* past the prime of bloom.

overboard *adv* over the side of a ship or boat into the water. ✻ **go overboard 1** to be very enthusiastic. **2** to go to extremes.

overbook *v* to take bookings for (e.g. a hotel or flight) in excess of the space available.

overburden *v* to place an excessive burden on.

overcame *v* past tense of OVERCOME.

overcapacity *n* an excess of capacity for production.

overcast[1] *adj* **1** of the sky or weather: cloudy. **2** sewn with long stitches passing over a raw edge to prevent fraying.

overcast[2] *v* (*past tense and past part.* **overcast**) **1** to darken or overshadow. **2** to sew over (a raw edge), *esp* with long slanting widely spaced stitches, to prevent fraying.

overcharge *v* **1** to charge (a customer) too much. **2** to charge (a battery) too much.

overcloud *v* **1** to cover with clouds. **2** to make dim or dark.

overcoat *n* **1** a warm coat for wearing outdoors over other clothing. **2** a protective coat of paint or varnish.

overcome *v* (*past tense* **overcame,** *past part.* **overcome**) **1** to deal with (a problem, handicap, etc) successfully. **2** to overpower or overwhelm. **3** to defeat.

overcompensate *v* to try to make up for a weakness or failing by exaggerating some other trait. ➤➤ **overcompensation** *n.*

overcook *v* to cook too much or for too long.

overcrowd *v* to cause (a place) to be too crowded.

overdo *v* (**overdoes,** *past tense* **overdid,** *past part.* **overdone**) **1a** to do or use to excess. **b** to exaggerate. **2** to cook (food) too much. ✻ **overdo it/things** to exhaust oneself, *esp* through overwork.

overdose[1] *n* a dangerously excessive dose of drugs, medicine, etc.

overdose[2] *v* **1** to take an overdose. **2** to give (somebody) an overdose. ➤➤ **overdosage** *n.*

overdraft *n* **1** an act of overdrawing a bank account or the state of being overdrawn. **2** the sum overdrawn. **3** permission to overdraw a bank account.

overdraw *v* (*past tense* **overdrew,** *past part.* **overdrawn**) to withdraw more money from (a bank account) than the balance, with or without authorization.

overdrawn *adj* **1** of a bank account: in deficit. **2** of a person: having an overdrawn account.

overdress[1] *v* to dress too elaborately or formally.

overdress[2] *n* a dress worn over another dress or over a jumper, blouse, etc.

overdrew *v* past tense of OVERDRAW.

overdrive[1] *n* a transmission gear in a motor vehicle that provides a ratio higher than the normal top gear and is used at high speeds. ✻ **go into overdrive** to be extremely active.

overdrive[2] *v* (*past tense* **overdrove,** *past part.* **overdriven**) to overwork or overuse.

overdub[1] *v* (**overdubbed, overdubbing**) to record (new sounds) on top of an existing recording.

overdub[2] *n* an instance of overdubbing.

overdue *adj* **1** unpaid when due. **2** delayed beyond the proper or appointed time.

overeat *v* (*past tense* **overate,** *past part.* **overeaten**) to eat to excess.

over-egg ✻ **over-egg the pudding** to make something more elaborate than is necessary.

overestimate *v* **1** to estimate as being more than the actual amount or size. **2** to place too high a value on; to overrate. ➤➤ **overestimate** *n,* **overestimation** *n.*

overexpose *v* **1** to expose excessively. **2** to expose (photographic film) to too much light. ➤➤ **overexposure** *n.*

overextend *v* **1** to extend beyond a safe or reasonable point. **2** to impose an excessive burden of work, financial commitment, etc on.

overfall *n* **1** a place where water overflows, e.g. from a dam. **2** a patch of turbulent water, e.g. where currents meet or pass over a ridge below the surface.

overfeed *v* (*past tense and past part.* **overfed**) to feed to excess.

overfish *v* to deplete (a fishing ground or stock of fish) by fishing excessively.

overflew *v* past tense of OVERFLY.

overflow[1] *v* **1** to flow over or beyond a brim, edge, or limit. **2** to be filled with something.

overflow[2] *n* **1** a flowing over, *esp* of liquid. **2** an excess of people, things, etc that cannot be accommodated. **3** an outlet or receptacle for surplus liquid.

overfly *v* (**overflies,** *past tense* **overflew,** *past part.* **overflown**) to fly over (a place), *esp* in an aircraft.

overground *adj and adv* on the surface; not underground.

overgrown *adj* **1** grown over or choked with vegetation. **2** grown too large. ➤➤ **overgrowth** *n.*

overhand *adj and adv* with the hand brought forward and down from above shoulder level.

overhang[1] *v* (*past tense and past part.* **overhung**) to project over or beyond.

overhang[2] *n* something that overhangs, or the extent by which something overhangs.

overhaul *v* **1** to examine (e.g. a machine) thoroughly and carry out any necessary repairs. **2** to overtake. ➤➤ **overhaul** *n.*

overhead[1] *adv* above one's head.

overhead[2] *adj* operating, situated, or coming from above.

overhead[3] *n* **1** (*also in pl*) a business expense, e.g. rent, insurance, or heating, that is not chargeable to a particular part of the work or product: compare FIXED COSTS, VARIABLE COST. **2** (*used before a noun*) denoting such an expense.

overhead projector *n* a device that projects a magnified image of a horizontal transparency onto a screen via a mirror.

overhear *v* (*past tense and past part.* **overheard**) to hear (somebody speaking or something said) without the speaker's knowledge or intention.

overheat *v* **1** to heat to excess or become excessively hot. **2** of an economy: to undergo rapid inflation caused by excessive demand.

overhung *v* past tense of OVERHANG[1].

overindulge *v* **1** to indulge in something to an excessive degree. **2** to indulge (somebody) to an excessive degree. ➤➤ **overindulgence** *n,* **overindulgent** *adj.*

overissue *v* (**overissues, overissued, overissuing**) to issue (shares, banknotes, etc) in excess of the limit of capital, credit, or authority. ➤➤ **overissue** *n.*

overjoyed *adj* extremely pleased; elated.

overkill *n* **1** the capability of destroying an enemy or target with a force, *esp* of nuclear weapons, that is larger than required. **2** an excess of something beyond what is required or suitable for a particular purpose.

overlaid *v* past tense and past part. of OVERLAY[1].

overlain *v* past part. of OVERLIE.

overland[1] *adv and adj* by land rather than sea or air.

overland[2] *v Aus* **1** in former times, to drive (livestock) overland for long distances. **2** to travel a long distance overland. ➤➤ **overlander** *n.*

overlap *v* (**overlapped, overlapping**) **1** to extend over and cover a part of. **2** of two or more things: to overlap each other. **3** to coincide partly; to have something in common. ➤➤ **overlap** *n.*

overlay[1] *v* (*past tense and past part.* **overlaid**) **1** to lay or spread over something; to superimpose. **2** (+ with) to cover or decorate (a surface) with something laid or spread over it.

overlay[2] *n* **1** something laid or spread over something else; a covering. **2a** a transparent sheet of drawings, details, etc to be superimposed on another sheet. **b** a decorative veneer.

overlay[3] *v* past tense of OVERLIE.

overleaf *adv* on the other side of the page.

overlie *v* (*past tense* **overlay,** *past part.* **overlain**) to lie or be situated on top of.

overload *v* to load to excess. ➤➤ **overload** *n.*

overlocking *n* the act or process of oversewing a raw edge of fabric using a small machine stitch to prevent unravelling. ➤➤ **overlocker** *n.*

overlong *adj and adv* too long.

overlook[1] *v* **1a** to fail to notice; to miss. **b** to ignore or excuse. **2** to have or provide a view of from above.

overlook[2] *n NAm* a high place commanding a good view.

overlord *n* **1** a lord who is superior to other lords. **2** an absolute or supreme ruler. ➤➤ **overlordship** *n.*

overly *adv* to an excessive degree.

overman[1] *v* (**overmanned, overmanning**) to provide with too many workers.

overman[2] *n* (*pl* **overmen**) a foreman or overseer.

overmantel *n* an ornamental often shelved structure above a mantelpiece.

overmaster *v* to overpower or subdue.

overmatch *v chiefly NAm* to be stronger, more skilful, etc than (an opponent).

overmuch *adj and adv and n* too much.

overnight[1] *adv* **1** during or throughout the night. **2** for a single night. **3** suddenly.

overnight[2] *adj* **1** done, occurring, operating, or used during the night. **2** lasting for a single night. **3** sudden.

overpaid *v* past tense and past part. of OVERPAY.

overpass *n* = FLYOVER (1).

overpay *v* (*past tense and past part.* **overpaid**) to pay (somebody) too much.

overplay *v* **1** to exaggerate (e.g. a dramatic role). **2** to give too much emphasis to (something). ✱ **overplay one's hand** to overestimate one's capacities.

overplus *n* a surplus.

overpopulation *n* the condition of having a population so dense as to cause environmental deterioration or impaired quality of life. ➤➤ **overpopulated** *adj.*

overpower *v* **1** to defeat or overcome by superior force. **2** to be so strong or intense as to overwhelm. ➤➤ **overpowering** *adj,* **overpoweringly** *adv.*

overprice *v* to price too high.

overprint *v* to print over with something additional.

overproduce *v* to produce an excess of. ➤➤ **overproduction** *n.*

overproof *adj* containing more alcohol than proof spirit does.

overprotect *v* to protect (e.g. a child) excessively or unduly. ➤➤ **overprotection** *n,* **overprotective** *adj.*

overqualified *adj* having more education, training, or experience than a job calls for.

overran *v* past tense of OVERRUN.

overrate *v* to rate too highly.

overreach *v* **1** to defeat (oneself) by trying to do or gain too much. **2** to get the better of (somebody), typically by unscrupulous or crafty methods.

overreact *v* to show an excessive or exaggerated reaction. ⯮ **overreaction** *n.*

override[1] *v* (*past tense* **overrode,** *past part.* **overridden**) **1** to prevail over; to dominate. **2a** to set aside or annul (e.g. a decision) by superior authority. **b** to take manual control of (e.g. an automatic control). **3** to overlap.

override[2] *n* a device or system used to override a control.

overriding *adj* more important than any other.

overripe *adj* having passed beyond maturity or ripeness towards decay.

overrode *v* past tense of OVERRIDE[1].

overrule *v* **1** to reject or disallow (a decision, judgment, objection, etc) by superior authority. **2** to overrule the decision, argument, objection, etc of (somebody).

overrun *v* (**overrunning,** *past tense* **overran,** *past part.* **overrun**) **1a** to swarm or spread over (a place). **b** to invade and occupy (a place) in large numbers. **2a** to run or go beyond or past. **b** to exceed (e.g. an allowed cost or time). **c** to exceed a desired or expected limit in time or space. ⯮ **overrun** *n.*

oversaw *v* past tense of OVERSEE.

overseas[1] *adv* beyond or across the sea; abroad.

overseas[2] *adj* of, from, to, or in places across the sea; foreign.

overseas[3] *n* a place or places across the sea; a foreign country or foreign countries.

oversee *v* (*past tense* **oversaw,** *past part.* **overseen**) to watch and direct (a task, operation, etc). ⯮ **overseer** *n.*

oversell *v* (*past tense and past part.* **oversold**) **1** to sell more of (something) than is available. **2** to make excessive claims for; to praise too highly.

oversensitive *adj* unduly or extremely sensitive. ⯮ **oversensitivity** *n.*

oversew *v* (*past part.* **oversewn,** *or* **oversewed**) to sew over (an edge or two edges placed together) with small closely worked stitches.

oversexed *adj* having an abnormally strong sexual drive.

overshadow *v* **1** to cast a shadow over. **2** to exceed in importance; to outweigh.

overshoe *n* a shoe worn over another as protection.

overshoot *v* (*past tense and past part.* **overshot**) **1** to shoot or pass over or beyond (e.g. a target) and miss it. **2** of an aircraft: to fly or taxi beyond the end of a runway. ⯮ **overshoot** *n.*

oversight *n* **1** an inadvertent omission or error. **2** supervision.

oversimplify *v* (**-ies, -ied**) to simplify to such an extent as to cause distortion, misunderstanding, or error. ⯮ **oversimplification** *n.*

oversized *or* **oversize** *adj* of above average or normal size.

overskirt *n* a skirt worn over another skirt or over a dress.

oversleep *v* (*past tense and past part.* **overslept**) to sleep beyond the intended time for waking.

oversold *v* past tense and past part. of OVERSELL.

overspend[1] *v* (*past tense and past part.* **overspent**) **1** to spend more than (an allotted amount). **2** to spend beyond one's means.

overspend[2] *n* an amount spent that exceeds the available budget.

overspent *v* past tense and past part. of OVERSPEND[1].

overspill *n chiefly Brit* the movement of excess urban population into less crowded areas, e.g. new towns, or the excess population itself.

overstaff *v* to provide with too many staff.

overstate *v* to state in too strong terms; to exaggerate. ⯮ **overstatement** *n.*

overstay *v* to stay beyond the time or limits of: *She overstayed her welcome.*

oversteer *v* of a motor vehicle: to steer into a sharper turn than the driver intends. ⯮ **oversteer** *n.*

overstep *v* (**overstepped, overstepping**) to exceed or transgress. ✱ **overstep the mark** to go beyond what is acceptable.

overstrung *adj* **1** too highly strung; too sensitive. **2** of a piano: having strings in sets that cross each other at an oblique angle.

overstuff *v* to cover (e.g. a chair) completely and thickly with upholstery.

oversubscribe *v* (*usu in passive*) to subscribe or apply for more of (something) than is available or offered for sale. ⯮ **oversubscription** *n.*

overt *adj* open to view; not concealed. ⯮ **overtly** *adv,* **overtness** *n.*

overtake *v* (*past tense* **overtook,** *past part.* **overtaken**) **1** to catch up with and move past (e.g. a vehicle going in the same direction). **2** to catch up with and do better than. **3** to come upon (somebody) suddenly.

overtax *v* **1** to tax too heavily. **2** to put too great a burden or strain on.

over-the-counter *adj* of a drug or medicine: able to be sold lawfully without prescription.

overthrow[1] *v* (*past tense* **overthrew,** *past part.* **overthrown**) **1** to cause the downfall of; to remove from power. **2** to overturn or upset. **3** to throw (a ball) further than intended.

overthrow[2] *n* **1** the act or an instance of overthrowing. **2** in cricket, a return of the ball from a fielder that passes beyond the fielders near the wickets, or a further run scored from this.

overtime *n* **1** time in excess of a set limit, *esp* working time in excess of a standard working day or week. **2** the wage paid for overtime. **3** *NAm* = EXTRA TIME. ⯮ **overtime** *adv.*

overtone *n* **1a** in music, any of the higher tones produced simultaneously with the principal note of a harmonic series. **b** = HARMONIC[2]. **2** (*also in pl*) a secondary effect, quality, or meaning; a suggestion or connotation.

overtook *v* past tense of OVERTAKE.

overtop *v* (**overtopped, overtopping**) **1** to rise above the top of. **2** to surpass.

overtrousers *pl n* waterproof or protective trousers worn over other trousers.

overture *n* **1a** the orchestral introduction to a musical dramatic work. **b** an orchestral concert piece written as a single movement. **2** (*also in pl*) **a** an initiative towards an agreement, negotiation, or relationship. **b** something introductory; a prelude.

overturn *v* **1a** to cause to turn over; to upset or invert. **b** to turn over. **2** to overthrow or destroy. **3** to cancel or reverse (e.g. a decision). ⯮ **overturn** *n.*

overuse[1] *n* excessive use.

overuse[2] *v* to use excessively.

overview *n* a usu brief general survey.

overweening *adj* **1** arrogant or presumptuous. **2** immoderate or exaggerated.

overweight *adj* exceeding the expected, normal, or proper weight.

overwhelm *v* **1** to defeat or overcome (e.g. an army) by superior force or numbers. **2** to affect with intense emotion. **3** to cover over completely; to submerge. ➤➤ **overwhelming** *adj*, **overwhelmingly** *adv.*

overwind *v* (*past tense and past part.* **overwound**) to wind (e.g. a watch) too much.

overwinter *v* to survive or spend the winter.

overwork *v* **1** to work or cause to work too hard or too long. **2** to make excessive use of (something). ➤➤ **overwork** *n.*

overwound *v* past tense and past part. of OVERWIND.

overwrite *v* (*past tense* **overwrote**, *past part.* **overwritten**) **1** to write in an inflated or pretentious style. **2a** to write on top of (existing writing). **b** to destroy (existing data) in a computer file by replacing it with new data.

overwrought *adj* **1** extremely excited or agitated. **2** too elaborate in construction or design.

ovi- *comb. form* see OV-.

oviduct *n* the tube through which eggs pass from an ovary.

oviform *adj* egg-shaped.

ovine *adj* of or resembling sheep.

oviparous *adj* producing eggs that hatch outside the mother's body: compare VIVIPAROUS. ➤➤ **oviparity** *n.*

ovipositor *n* a specialized organ, *esp* of an insect, for laying eggs.

ovo- *comb. form* see OV-.

ovoid *adj* shaped like an egg. ➤➤ **ovoid** *n.*

ovoidal *adj* = OVOID.

ovoviviparous *adj* producing eggs that develop and hatch within the mother's body. ➤➤ **ovoviviparity** *n.*

ovulate *v* to produce eggs or discharge them from an ovary. ➤➤ **ovulation** *n*, **ovulatory** *adj.*

ovule *n* **1** a reproductive structure within the ovary of a seed plant that develops into a seed after fertilization of the egg cell it contains. **2** a small egg, *esp* one in an early stage of growth. ➤➤ **ovular** *adj.*

ovum *n* (*pl* **ova**) a female reproductive cell in animals that when fertilized can develop into a new individual.

ow *interj* used to express sudden mild pain.

owe *v* **1a** to be under obligation to pay (money) to somebody. **b** to be under obligation to give or show (an explanation, respect, etc) to somebody. **2** (*usu* + to) to have or enjoy (something) as a result of the action or existence of something or somebody else: *He owes his success to luck.*

owing *adj* unpaid; due. ✱ **owing to** because of.

Usage note

owing to *or* **due to**? See note at DUE[1].

owl *n* a nocturnal bird of prey with a large head, a short neck, large eyes, and a short hooked bill.

owlet *n* a small or young owl.

owlish *adj* **1** having a round face or a wide-eyed stare. **2** solemn or wise. ➤➤ **owlishly** *adv.*

own[1] *adj* used after a possessive: belonging to, relating to, or done by oneself or itself.

own[2] *v* **1** to have or hold as property; to possess. **2** to acknowledge or admit. ➤➤ **owner** *n*, **ownership** *n.*

own[3] *pron* used after a possessive: one or ones belonging to oneself or itself: *a country with oil of its own.* ✱ **on one's own 1** in solitude; alone. **2** without assistance or control.

own-brand *adj* denoting goods offered for sale under the label or trade name of the retail distributor, e.g. a chain store.

owner-occupier *n* somebody who owns the house they live in.

own goal *n* **1** a goal, *esp* in football, accidentally scored by a player against his or her own team. **2** an action that brings unfortunate results to the person who took it.

own up *v* to confess a fault or wrongdoing frankly.

owt *pron N Eng* anything.

ox *n* (*pl* **oxen** *or* **ox**) **1** a domestic bovine mammal. **2** an adult castrated male ox.

oxalic acid *n* a poisonous strong acid that occurs in various plants and is used *esp* as a bleach.

oxalis *n* a wood sorrel or related plant having leaves that contain oxalic acid and usu white, pink, or yellow flowers.

oxbow *n* **1** a U-shaped collar round a draught ox's neck for supporting the yoke. **2a** a U-shaped river bend. **b** a curved lake formed from such a bend in a meandering river.

oxbow lake *n* = OXBOW (2B).

Oxbridge *n* the universities of Oxford and Cambridge.

oxen *n* pl of OX.

oxeye daisy *n* a leafy-stemmed European plant with long white ray flowers.

Oxford *n* a low shoe laced or tied over the instep.

Oxford bags *pl n* wide-legged trousers.

oxidant *n* = OXIDIZING AGENT.

oxidation *n* **1** the act or process of oxidizing. **2** the state or result of being oxidized. ➤➤ **oxidative** *adj.*

oxide *n* a compound of oxygen with a chemical element or group.

oxidize *or* **-ise** *v* **1** to combine with oxygen. **2** to remove hydrogen atoms from. **3** to cause (e.g. an atom, ion, or molecule) to lose one or more electrons. **4** to undergo a loss of hydrogen atoms or electrons. ➤➤ **oxidizable** *adj*, **oxidizer** *n.*

oxidizing agent *n* a substance that oxidizes something by gaining electrons: compare REDUCING AGENT.

oxlip *n* a Eurasian primula similar to the cowslip but unscented and having larger flowers.

Oxon. *abbr* **1** Oxfordshire. **2** used with academic awards: of Oxford University.

Oxonian *n* **1** a native or inhabitant of Oxford. **2** a student or graduate of Oxford University. ➤➤ **Oxonian** *adj.*

oxpecker *n* an African bird that perches on large animals and feeds on ticks.

oxtail *n* the tail of an ox, used *esp* in making soup.

oxter *n chiefly Scot, Irish, N Eng* the armpit or the crook of the arm.

oxy-[1] *comb. form* denoting sharpness: *oxytocin.*

oxy-[2] *comb. form* containing or using oxygen: *oxyhaemoglobin.*

oxyacetylene *adj* of or using a mixture of oxygen and acetylene, *esp* to produce a hot flame for cutting or welding.

oxygen *n* a colourless odourless gaseous element that forms about 21% of the atmosphere and is essential for the life of most organisms.

oxygenate *v* to impregnate, combine, or supply (e.g. blood) with oxygen. ➤➤ **oxygenation** *n*, **oxygenator** *n.*

oxyhaemoglobin *n* haemoglobin loosely combined with oxygen that it releases to the tissues.

oxymoron *n* (*pl* **oxymora**) a combination of contradictory or incongruous words, e.g. *cruel kindness*.

oxytocin *n* a hormone secreted by the pituitary gland that stimulates contractions of the muscular wall of the womb, *esp* during childbirth, and assists the release of milk.

oyez /oh'yay, oh'yes/ *interj* uttered by a court official or public crier to gain attention.

oyster *n* **1** an edible marine invertebrate animal with a rough irregular hinged shell that is found in coastal waters or estuaries. **2** a pinkish white colour, sometimes with a greyish tone. **3** a small mass of meat contained in a hollow of the pelvic bone on each side of the back of a fowl.

oystercatcher *n* a wading bird with stout legs, black or black and white plumage, and a heavy wedge-shaped orange beak adapted for opening shellfish.

oyster mushroom *n* an edible mushroom with a soft grey cap that is shaped like an oyster.

Oz *n informal* Australia.

oz. *abbr* ounce.

ozone *n* **1** a form of oxygen with three atoms in each molecule that is a bluish gas with a pungent smell, formed naturally in the upper atmosphere by the action of ultraviolet solar radiation on oxygen or generated commercially for use as a sterilizing, purifying, bleaching, or oxidizing agent. **2** *informal* pure and refreshing air.

ozone-friendly *adj* not harmful to the ozone layer; *specif* not using or containing chlorofluorocarbons.

ozone layer *n* an atmospheric layer at heights of approximately 30–50km (20–30mi) that has a high ozone content and protects the earth by absorbing ultraviolet radiation from the sun.

ozonosphere *n* = OZONE LAYER.

P p

P[1] *or* **p** *n* (*pl* **P's** *or* **Ps** *or* **p's**) the 16th letter of the English alphabet.

P[2] *abbr* **1** parking. **2** in chess, pawn.

P[3] *abbr* the chemical symbol for phosphorus.

p *abbr* **1** page. **2** pence. **3** penny. **4** in music, piano.

P2P *abbr* peer-to-peer, denoting a system that allows computers to communicate directly with each other through the Internet without a central server.

PA *abbr* **1** Pennsylvania (US postal abbreviation). **2** personal assistant. **3** public address.

Pa[1] *abbr* pascal.

Pa[2] *abbr* the chemical symbol for protactinium.

pa *n informal* one's father.

p.a. *abbr* per annum.

paan *or* **pan** *n* a betel leaf filled with spices and chewed as a stimulant, *esp* by Indians.

pa'anga /pah'ang(g)ə/ *n* (*pl* **pa'anga**) the basic monetary unit of Tonga.

pabulum *n* bland or unsatisfying intellectual matter or entertainment.

paca *n* a large edible rodent of S America that has a brown coat spotted with white and a hide used for leather.

pace[1] *n* **1a** a step in walking. **b** the distance covered by a single step. **2a** a gait of a horse, *esp* a gait in which a horse has been trained to move. **b** a fast two-beat gait in which the horse moves its two left legs and its two right legs in unison alternately. **3** rate or speed of moving, working, developing, etc. ✱ **keep pace with** to move, change, or progress at the same speed as. **off the pace** behind the leader or leaders in a race or contest. **put somebody through their paces** to test somebody by making them demonstrate their abilities. **set the pace** to control the speed at which a race is run or an activity progresses. **stand/stay the pace** to be able to maintain the same speed as others.

pace[2] *v* **1** to walk or traverse with a slow or measured tread. **2** of a horse: to go at a pace. **3** (*often* + out/off) to measure (a distance) by pacing. **4a** to set or regulate the pace of (e.g. a race); *specif* to go ahead of (e.g. a runner) as a pacemaker. **b** to set (oneself) a steady rate of doing something, e.g. working, or to hold (oneself) back to such a pace.

pace[3] /'paysi/ *prep* used when contradicting or disagreeing with somebody: with due respect to: *This, pace the bishop, is not a religious issue.*

pacemaker *n* **1a** somebody or something that sets the pace, e.g. in a race. **b** somebody who takes the lead or sets an example. **2a** an electronic device implanted in the body to stimulate or steady the heartbeat. **b** the area of tissue in the heart that serves to establish and maintain its rhythm. ➤➤ **pacemaking** *n.*

pacesetter *n* = PACEMAKER (I). ➤➤ **pacesetting** *n and adj.*

pacey *adj* see PACY.

pacha *n* see PASHA.

pachyderm *n* an elephant, rhinoceros, or other thick-skinned hoofed mammal.

pacific *adj* **1** having a peaceable nature or tending to bring about peace. **2** (**Pacific**) of or found near the Pacific Ocean. ➤➤ **pacifically** *adv.*

pacifier *n* **1** somebody or something that pacifies. **2** *NAm* a baby's dummy.

pacifism *n* opposition to war as a means of settling disputes. ➤➤ **pacifist** *n and adj.*

pacify *v* (**-ies, -ied**) **1** to allay the anger or agitation of. **2** to restore (a country) to a peaceful state or subdue.

pack[1] *n* **1** a light, non-rigid paper or cardboard container for goods. **2** a knapsack or rucksack. **3** a set of playing cards. **4** a set or collection of things, *esp* related documents in a folder. **5** (*used as sing. or pl*) a number of animals, kept together or naturally grouping together, *esp* for hunting. **6** (*used as sing. or pl*) **a** a troop of Cub Scouts or Brownie Guides. **b** the forwards in a rugby team, *esp* when acting together. **c** the main group of competitors in a race when bunched together behind the leaders. **7** a compact manufactured article designed to perform a specific function. **8** a concentrated mass of snow or ice. **9** a pad of wet absorbent material for application to the body for therapeutic purposes.

pack[2] *v* **1** to place inside a container, *esp* for transportation or storage. **2** to cover or surround with packing material for protection. **3** (*often* + away) to be foldable or collapsible, for easy storage or transport. **4** (*often* + with) to fill with a large amount of material or a large number of things. **5a** (+ in/into) to fit (a large number of people) into a relatively small space. **b** *informal* (+ in) to attract a large number of (people). **6** (+ down) of rugby forwards: to gather into a tight formation ready for a scrum. **7** *chiefly NAm, informal* to carry or wear (a gun). ✱ **pack a punch 1** to be capable of hitting hard. **2** to be very strong or effective. ➤➤ **packable** *adj,* **packer** *n.*

pack[3] *v* to influence the composition of (a jury) so as to bring about a desired result.

package[1] *n* **1** an object or number of objects wrapped or packed up together. **2 a** a group of contract benefits gained through collective bargaining between management and union. **b** a set of computer programs for carrying out a relatively generalized operation, sold as a self-contained product. **c** = PACKAGE DEAL. **d** = PACKAGE HOLIDAY.

package[2] *v* **1** to enclose in a package or covering. **2** to group (various items) together for sale as a whole. **3** to present in a way that will appeal to an audience. **4** to organize the writing and illustration of (a book) on behalf of a publisher. ⋙ **packaged** *adj*, **packager** *n*.

package deal *n* an offer or agreement involving a number of related items, acceptance of one being dependent on the acceptance of all.

package holiday *or* **package tour** *n* a holiday organized by a travel agent who arranges all the transport and accommodation for an inclusive price.

packaging *n* **1** material used for packing. **2** the promotion of the image of a product or person via the media.

pack animal *n* an animal used for carrying packs.

pack drill *n* a military punishment consisting of marching up and down in full kit.

packet[1] *n* **1a** a small paper or cardboard container. **b** = PARCEL[1] (1). **2** in computing, a unit of data sent as part of a message from one user to another through a packet-switching network. **3** (**a packet**) *Brit, informal* a large sum of money.

packet[2] *v* (**packeted, packeting**) to wrap in a packet.

packetize *or* **-ise** *n* in computing, to divide (data) into packets for transmission through a packet-switching network.

packet-switching network *n* a digital communications system in which messages are transmitted as many separate packets of data which are reassembled in the correct order by the receiving equipment.

pack ice *n* sea ice crushed together into a large floating mass.

packing *n* material used to pack goods.

pack off *v informal* to send (somebody) away abruptly or unceremoniously.

packsack *n NAm* a rucksack.

packsaddle *n* a saddle designed to support a pack on an animal's back.

pack up *v informal* to cease to function.

pact *n* an agreement or treaty.

pacy *or* **pacey** *adj* (**-ier, -iest**) *Brit* fast or speedy.

pad[1] *n* **1 a** padding used to shape an article of clothing or worn to shield body parts against impact. **b** a piece of absorbent material used as a surgical dressing or protective covering. **2** the cushioned thickening of the underside of the toes of animals. **3** a number of sheets of paper fastened together at one edge. **4** a flat surface for a vertical takeoff or landing. **5** *informal* living quarters.

pad[2] *v* (**padded, padding**) **1** to provide with a pad or padding. **2** (*often* + out) to fill out (speech or writing) with superfluous matter.

pad[3] *v* (**padded, padding**) to walk with a muffled step. ⋙ **pad** *n*.

padding *n* material with which something is padded.

paddle[1] *n* **1a** a wooden implement similar to but smaller than an oar, used to propel a small craft. **b** an implement with a short handle and broad flat blade used for stirring and mixing. **2** any of the broad boards at the circumference of a paddle wheel or waterwheel. **3** a flattened limb or flipper of a bird or mammal that swims.

paddle[2] *v* **1** to propel (a craft) by a paddle. **2** to swim with short strokes as an animal does. ✻ **paddle one's own canoe** to be independent and self-reliant. ⋙ **paddler** *n*.

paddle[3] *v* to walk or wade in shallow water. ⋙ **paddle** *n*, **paddler** *n*.

paddle wheel *n* a power-driven wheel with paddles round its circumference used to propel a boat.

paddock *n* **1** a small enclosed field for pasturing or exercising animals. **2** a field where racehorses are paraded before a race. **3** an area at a motor-racing track where cars are worked on before a race.

Paddy *n* (*pl* **-ies**) *derog, offensive* an Irish person.

paddy[1] *n* (*pl* **-ies**) **1** = PADDYFIELD. **2** threshed unmilled rice.

paddy[2] *n* (*pl* **-ies**) *Brit, informal* a temper tantrum.

paddyfield *n* a field of wet land in which rice is grown.

padlock[1] *n* a portable lock with a shackle that can be passed through a link and then secured.

padlock[2] *v* to secure using a padlock.

padre *n informal* a military chaplain.

pad saw *n* a narrow pointed fine-toothed saw used for cutting tight curves.

paean *n* a joyously exultant song of praise or tribute.

paederast *n* see PEDERAST.

paederasty *n* see PEDERASTY.

paediatrician *n* a specialist in paediatrics.

paediatrics (*NAm* **pediatrics**) *pl n* (*used as sing. or pl*) medicine dealing with the care and diseases of children. ⋙ **paediatric** *adj*.

paedo- (*NAm* **pedo-**) *comb. form* forming words, denoting: child.

paedophile (*NAm* **pedophile**) *n* a person affected with paedophilia.

paedophilia (*NAm* **pedophilia**) *n* sexual desire directed towards children.

paella /pie'ela/ *n* a saffron-flavoured Spanish dish containing rice, meat, seafood, and vegetables.

paeony *n* (*pl* **-ies**) see PEONY.

pagan *n* **1** a follower of a polytheistic religion. **2** an irreligious person. ⋙ **pagan** *adj*, **paganish** *adj*, **paganism** *n*.

page[1] *n* **1** a leaf of a book or periodical, or a single side of a leaf. **2** an event worth being recorded in writing: *an exciting page in Germany's history.* **3** a sizable subdivision of computer memory used for convenience of reference in programming. **4** an electronic document published on the World Wide Web.

page[2] *v* **1** to paginate (a book). **2** (*often* + through) to turn pages in a haphazard manner.

page[3] *n* **1** a boy serving as an honorary attendant at a wedding. **2** somebody employed to deliver messages or run errands. **3** a boy being trained for the medieval rank of knight and in the personal service of a knight. **4** a young man or boy attending on a person of rank.

page[4] *v* to summon over a public-address system or by a coded signal emitted by a short-range radio transmitter.

pageant *n* **1** a colourful spectacle with dramatic presentations or a procession expressing a common theme. **2** an ostentatious display.

pageantry *n* colourful or splendid display.

page boy *n* **1** a boy serving as a page. **2** a woman's hairstyle in which the ends of the hair are turned under.

pager *n* a small electronic device that can be used to communicate with somebody by emitting an audible tone or sending a text message.

page-three *adj Brit* pictured on page three of a tabloid newspaper where photographs of topless young women are regularly featured.

page-turner *n informal* a compulsively readable book.

paginate *v* to number the sides of the leaves of (a book or periodical) in a sequence: compare FOLIATE². ⪢ **pagination** *n.*

pagoda *n* a Buddhist temple or memorial in the Far East with many storeys, with upturned projecting roofs at the division of each storey.

paid *v* past and past part. of PAY¹. ✱ **put paid to** to bring to an abrupt end.

paid-up *adj* **1** having paid the necessary fees to be a full member of an organization. **2** showing the characteristic attitudes of a specified group: *a fully paid-up member of the awkward squad.*

pail *n* a bucket. ⪢ **pailful** *n.*

paillasse *n* see PALLIASSE.

pain¹ *n* **1** a bodily sensation induced by a harmful stimulus or physical disorder and characterized by pricking or aching. **2** mental or emotional distress. **3** *informal* somebody or something that is a nuisance. **4** (*in pl*) the trouble involved or care taken in doing something. ✱ **on/under pain of** subject to penalty of. **pain in the neck** *informal* a nuisance.

pain² *v* to cause distress to or hurt (somebody).

pained *adj* showing pain or distress.

painful *adj* **1** causing or feeling pain or distress. **2** proceeding slowly and involving great effort. **3** *informal* very bad; awful. ⪢ **painfully** *adv,* **painfulness** *n.*

painkiller *n* a drug that relieves pain.

painless *adj* **1** not causing any pain. **2** easy or effortless. ⪢ **painlessly** *adv,* **painlessness** *n.*

painstaking *adj* showing diligence and effort. ⪢ **painstakingly** *adv,* **painstakingness** *n.*

paint¹ *v* **1a** to apply paint or cosmetics to. **b** to apply with a movement resembling that used in painting. **2** to represent (a subject) in colours on a surface by applying paint. **3** to describe or evoke as if by painting: *Her novel paints glowing pictures of rural life.* ✱ **paint the town red** *informal* to go out and celebrate.

paint² *n* **1** a mixture of a pigment and a suitable liquid which forms a closely adherent coating when spread on a surface. **2** *informal* make-up. ⪢ **painty** *adj.*

paintball *n* a war game involving contestants equipped with special guns that fire dye-filled pellets.

paintbox *n* a metal box containing small blocks of water-colour pigment.

paintbrush *n* a brush for applying paint.

Painte *n* (*pl* **Paintes** *or* **Painte**) **1** a member of a Native American people of Utah, Arizona, Nevada, and California. **2** the language of this people.

painted lady *n* a migratory butterfly with wings mottled in brown, orange, red, and white.

painter¹ *n* **1** an artist who paints. **2** somebody who applies paint to buildings as an occupation.

painter² *n* a line used for securing or towing a boat.

painterly *adj* **1** relating to or typical of a painter. **2** denoting a style of painting that emphasizes colour, tone, and texture. ⪢ **painterliness** *n.*

painting *n* **1** a painted work of art. **2** the art or occupation of painting.

paint shop *n* the part of a factory where the products are painted.

paintwork *n* a painted surface.

pair¹ *n* **1** two corresponding things used together. **2** a single thing made up of two connected corresponding pieces: *a pair of trousers.* **3** two people in a marriage or other partnership. **4** two mated animals. **5** two playing cards of the same value in a hand. **6** two members from opposite sides of a deliberative body who agree that neither will vote if either is absent so that the balance between the two sides is maintained.

pair² *v* (*often* + up) to arrange in pairs.

pair off *v* to form a couple or a group of two.

pair up *v* **1** to organize in pairs. **2** = PAIR OFF.

paisa *n* (*pl* **paise**) **1** a unit of currency in India, Nepal, and Pakistan, worth 100th of a rupee. **2** a unit of currency in Bangladesh worth 100th of a taka.

paisley *n* a pattern of colourful abstract teardrop-shaped figures.

pakamac *n* a very thin plastic raincoat that folds up very small.

pak choi (*NAm* **bok choy**) *n* a Chinese cabbage with long dark green leaves and succulent white stems.

pakeha *n* (*pl* **pakehas** *or collectively* **pakeha**) *NZ* a white New Zealander.

Paki *n Brit, informal, offensive* = PAKISTANI.

Pakistani *n* a native or inhabitant of Pakistan. ⪢ **Pakistani** *adj.*

pakora *n* an Indian savoury snack consisting of diced vegetables or meat fried in batter.

PAL *abbr* phase alternation line (a system of transmitting colour television programmes).

pal *n informal* a close friend.

palace *n* **1** a large stately house or public building. **2** the official residence of a sovereign or bishop.

palace coup *n* the relatively nonviolent overthrow of a ruler by members of the ruling group.

paladin *n* **1** a knight renowned for chivalry and valour. **2** one of the twelve legendary peers of Charlemagne.

palae- *or* **palaeo-** (*NAm* **pale-, paleo-**) *comb. form* forming words, with the meanings: **1** involving or dealing with ancient forms or conditions. **2** early, primitive, or archaic.

Palaearctic (*NAm* **Palearctic**) *adj* of a biogeographic region that includes Europe and N Asia, Arabia, and Africa.

Palaeocene (*NAm* **Paleocene**) *adj* of the first geological epoch of the Tertiary period, lasting from about 65 million to about 56.5 million years ago and marked by the emergence of mammals. ⪢ **Palaeocene** *n.*

palaeography (*NAm* **paleography**) *n* the study of ancient writings and inscriptions. ⪢ **palaeographer** *n,* **palaeographical** *adj,* **palaeographically** *adv.*

Palaeolithic (*NAm* **Paleolithic**) *adj* of the earliest geological period of the Stone Age, lasting from about 750,000 to about 15,000 years ago, and marked by the development and use of crude, chipped stone implements. ⪢ **Palaeolithic** *n.*

palaeontology (*NAm* **paleontology**) *n* a science dealing with the life of past geological periods as discovered from fossil remains. ➤➤ **palaeontological** *adj*, **palaeontologist** *n*.

Palaeozoic (*NAm* **Paleozoic**) *adj* of the geological era before the Mesozoic era, lasting from about 570 million to about 245 million years ago, and marked by the appearance of fish, land plants, amphibians, and reptiles. ➤➤ **Palaeozoic** *n*.

palais *n Brit* a public dance hall.

palanquin *or* **palankeen** *n* a litter formerly used in eastern Asia to carry one person.

palatable *adj* **1** pleasant to the taste. **2** = ACCEPTABLE. ➤➤ **palatability** *n*, **palatably** *adv*.

palatal *adj* **1** relating to or in the region of the palate. **2** of a speech sound: formed with the front of the tongue near or touching the hard palate. ➤➤ **palatally** *adv*.

palatalize *or* **-ise** *v* to pronounce (a sound) as a palatal sound. ➤➤ **palatalization** *n*.

palate *n* **1** the roof of the mouth, separating it from the nasal cavity. **2a** the sense of taste. **b** an intellectual taste or liking. **3** flavour, *esp* the flavour of wine.

palatial *adj* **1** magnificent and luxurious. **2** relating to a palace. ➤➤ **palatially** *adv*.

palatinate *n* the territory of a palatine.

palatine[1] *n* a feudal lord with sovereign power.

palatine[2] *adj* of a feudal lord in the Middle Ages: possessing sovereign authority within a particular territory.

palaver[1] *n* **1** a tediously involved procedure; fuss or bother. **2** unnecessary or time-consuming talk.

palaver[2] *v* to talk in an idle or tedious way.

palazzo *n* (*pl* **palazzi**) a large imposing building in Italy.

palazzo pants *pl n* loose wide-legged trousers for women.

pale[1] *adj* **1** deficient in colour or intensity of colour. **2** not bright or brilliant. **3** feeble or faint. **4** of a colour: light and whitish. ➤➤ **palely** *adv*, **paleness** *n*, **palish** *adj*.

pale[2] *v* **1** to become pale. **2** to seem inferior or less important: *He was so worried about the children that everything else seemed to pale into insignificance.*

pale[3] *n* **1** an upright post forming part of a fence. **2** formerly, a district within certain bounds or under a particular jurisdiction. **3** a broad vertical band down the centre of a heraldic shield. ✱ **beyond the pale** in violation of social convention.

pale- *comb. form NAm* see PALAE-.

paleface *n derog* a white person, as distinguished from a Native American.

paleo- *comb. form NAm* see PALAE-.

Palestinian *n* a native or inhabitant of Palestine. ➤➤ **Palestinian** *adj*.

palette *n* **1** a thin board held by a painter for mixing pigments. **2a** the set of colours put on the palette. **b** a particular range or use of colour. **c** a comparable range or use of available elements in music. **d** the range of colours a computer is able to display on a VDU.

palette knife *n* a knife with a flexible steel blade and no cutting edge, used for mixing and applying paints or in cooking.

palfrey *n* (*pl* **-eys**) *archaic* a saddle horse other than a war-horse, *esp* for a woman.

palimony *n informal* an allowance paid by one member of an unmarried couple formerly living together to the other.

palimpsest *n* a parchment or tablet, reused after earlier writing has been erased.

palindrome *n* a word or sentence, etc that reads the same backwards or forwards.

paling *n* a fence made of stakes, or a stake used in such a fence.

palisade *n* **1** a fence of stakes for defence. **2** *NAm* (*in pl*) a line of steep cliffs.

pall[1] *n* **1** something heavy or dark, such as smoke or dust, that covers or conceals: *a pall of thick black smoke.* **2a** a square of linen used to cover the chalice containing the wine used at Communion. **b** a heavy cloth draped over a coffin or tomb. **3** = PALLIUM (2).

pall[2] *v* to cease to be interesting or attractive.

Palladian *adj* denoting a classical style of architecture based on the examples and principles of Andrea Palladio (d.1580). ➤➤ **Palladianism** *n*.

palladium *n* a silver-white metallic chemical element that occurs naturally in various ores, and is used *esp* in electrical contacts and as a catalyst.

pallbearer *n* a person who helps to carry the coffin at a funeral or is part of its immediate escort.

pallet[1] *n* **1** a portable platform intended for storing or moving materials and packages. **2** a flat-bladed wooden tool used by potters for shaping clay. **3** a lever or surface in a timepiece that receives an impulse from the escapement wheel and imparts motion to a balance or pendulum.

pallet[2] *n* **1** a straw-filled mattress. **2** a small hard makeshift bed.

palletize *or* **-ise** *v* to transport or store on pallets. ➤➤ **palletization** *n*.

pallia *n* pl of PALLIUM.

palliasse *or* **paillasse** *n* a thin straw mattress.

palliate *v* **1** to lessen the unpleasantness of (a disease) without removing the cause. **2** to moderate the intensity or gravity of (something). ➤➤ **palliation** *n*, **palliator** *n*.

palliative *n* something, e.g. a drug, that palliates. ➤➤ **palliative** *adj*, **palliatively** *adv*.

pallid *adj* **1** lacking colour; wan. **2** lacking sparkle or liveliness. ➤➤ **pallidly** *adv*, **pallidness** *n*.

pallium *n* (*pl* **pallia** *or* **palliums**) **1** a white woollen band in the shape of two Y's that meet on the shoulders, worn by a pope or archbishop. **2** a draped rectangular cloth worn as a cloak by men of ancient Rome. ➤➤ **pallial** *adj*.

pallor *n* facial paleness.

pally *adj* (**-ier, -iest**) *informal* = FRIENDLY[1] (1).

palm[1] *n* **1** a tropical or subtropical tree having a simple stem and a crown of large leaves. **2** a leaf of the palm as a symbol of victory or distinction.

palm[2] *n* **1** the concave part of the human hand between the bases of the fingers and the wrist. **2** a unit of measurement based on the length or breadth of the human hand. ✱ **in the palm of one's hand** entirely under one's control. ➤➤ **palmar** /ˈpalmə/ *adj*.

palm[3] *v* **1** to conceal (e.g. a playing card) in the hand. **2** to pick up (something) stealthily.

palmate *adj* **1** resembling a hand with the fingers spread. **2** having lobes radiating from a common point. **3** of an aquatic bird: having the front toes webbed.

palmcorder *n* a video camera and recorder that is small enough to be held in the palm of the hand.

palmer *n* a pilgrim wearing two crossed palm leaves as a sign of a visit to the Holy Land.

palmetto *n* (*pl* **-os** *or* **-oes**) a low-growing fan-leaved palm of the USA.

palmier /ˈpalmiay/ *n* a pastry in the shape of a palm leaf.

palmistry *n* the art of reading a person's character or future from markings on the palms. ➤➤ **palmist** *n.*

palm off *v* **1** (*often* + on) to get rid of (something unwanted) by deceiving somebody into taking it. **2** *informal* (+ with) to trick into believing something untrue.

Palm Sunday *n* the Sunday before Easter celebrated as a festival in the Christian Church commemorating Christ's triumphal entry into Jerusalem.

palmtop *n* a small computer that can be held in the palm of the hand.

palmy *adj* (**-ier, -iest**) marked by prosperity; flourishing: *palmy days*.

palomino *n* (*pl* **-os**) a light tan or cream-coloured slender-legged horse.

palp *n* a segmented feeler on the mouthparts of an arthropod. ➤➤ **palpal** *adj.*

palpable *adj* **1** capable of being touched or felt. **2** easily perceptible by the mind; obvious. ➤➤ **palpability** *n,* **palpably** *adv.*

palpate *v* to examine (a part of the body), *esp* medically, by touch. ➤➤ **palpation** *n.*

palpi *n* pl of PALPUS.

palpitant *adj* marked by trembling or throbbing.

palpitate *v* **1** to beat rapidly and strongly. **2** to tremble or flutter. ➤➤ **palpitation** *n.*

palpus *n* (*pl* **palpi**) = PALP.

palsy[1] *n* (*pl* **palsies**) *dated* uncontrollable tremor of the body.

palsy[2] *v* (**-ies, -ied**) to affect (a part of the body) with palsy.

palter *v archaic* **1** to act insincerely or deceitfully. **2** (+ with) = HAGGLE. ➤➤ **palterer** *n.*

paltry *adj* (**-ier, -iest**) **1** extremely or insultingly small. **2** mean and petty. ➤➤ **paltriness** *n.*

palynology *n* a branch of botany dealing with pollen and spores. ➤➤ **palynological** *adj,* **palynologist** *n.*

pampas *n* (*used as sing. or pl*) an extensive grass-covered plain of temperate S America.

pampas grass *n* a tall S American grass with large silky flower heads frequently cultivated as an ornamental plant.

pamper *v* to treat with excessive care and attention.

pamphlet[1] *n* a small unbound printed publication with a paper cover, often dealing with topical matters.

pamphlet[2] *v* (**pamphleted, pamphleting**) to hand out pamphlets to.

pamphleteer[1] *n* a writer of pamphlets, *esp* political ones.

pamphleteer[2] *v* to write and publish pamphlets.

pan[1] *n* **1** a round metal container, usu with a long handle, used for cooking food on the hob of a cooker. **2** a broad, shallow, open receptacle for domestic use, e.g. a dustpan or a bedpan. **3** either of the receptacles in a pair of scales. **4** a round shallow metal container for separating gold from waste by washing. **5** *Brit* the bowl of a toilet. **6** the part of the gunlock in old guns that holds a small charge of powder directly ignited by the spark from the flint to set off the main charge. **7** a hollow in land, e.g. a saltpan. **8** a drum in a steel band.

pan[2] *v* (**panned, panning**) **1** to wash earth or gravel in a pan in search of gold. **2** *informal* to subject to damning criticism.

pan[3] *v* (**panned, panning**) to rotate (a film or television camera) horizontally so as to keep a moving object in view or obtain a panoramic effect. ➤➤ **pan** *n.*

pan[4] *n* see PAAN.

pan- *comb. form* all or completely: *Pan-American.*

panacea *n* a remedy for all maladies.

panache *n* dash or flamboyance in style and action.

panama *or* **Panama** *n* a lightweight hat of plaited straw.

Panamanian *n* a native or inhabitant of Panama in central America. ➤➤ **Panamanian** *adj.*

Pan-American *adj* relating to all the people of North, South, and Central America. ➤➤ **Pan-Americanism** *n.*

panatella *n* a long slender cigar.

pancake[1] *n* **1** a flat cake made from thin batter and cooked on both sides in a frying pan. **2** make-up compressed into a flat cake or stick form.

pancake[2] *v* **1** of an aircraft: to make a pancake landing. **2** *informal* to make or become flattened.

Pancake Day *n* Shrove Tuesday, marked by the eating of pancakes.

pancake landing *n* a landing in which an aircraft descends in an approximately horizontal position with little forward motion.

pancake race *n* a race in which contestants must toss a pancake while running.

pancetta *n* belly of pork that has been cured and spiced, used in Italian cooking.

panchromatic *adj* of photographic film: sensitive to light of all colours in the visible spectrum.

pancreas *n* a large compound gland that secretes digestive enzymes into the intestines. ➤➤ **pancreatic** *adj.*

pancreatitis *n* inflammation of the pancreas.

panda *n* **1** a large black-and-white mammal of western China resembling a bear but related to the raccoons. Also called GIANT PANDA. **2** a long-tailed Himalayan mammal resembling the American raccoon and having long chestnut fur.

panda car *n Brit* a small car used by police patrols.

pandanus *n* (*pl* **pandanuses**) a tropical tree or shrub with slender stems and swordlike leaves that yield fibre.

pandemic[1] *adj* of a disease: occurring over a wide area and affecting an exceptionally high proportion of the population.

pandemic[2] *n* an outbreak of a pandemic disease.

pandemonium *n* a scene of wild and noisy confusion; uproar.

pander[1] *v* (+ to) to provide gratification for the desires of.

pander[2] *n dated* a pimp.

pandit *n* often used as an honorary title: a scholarly expert in Hindu religion and philosophy.

P & O *abbr* Peninsular and Oriental (Steamship Company).

Pandora's box *n* a prolific source of troubles.

p & p *abbr Brit* postage and packing.

pane *n* **1** a framed sheet of glass in a window or door. **2** any of the sections into which a sheet of postage stamps is cut for distribution.

paneer *n* a type of curd cheese used in Asian cooking.

panegyric *n* a speech or piece of writing in praise of somebody or something. ➤➤ **panegyrical** *adj,* **panegyrist** *n.*

panegyrize *or* **-ise** *v archaic* to eulogize.

panel[1] *n* **1 a** a thin rectangular section of a door or other surface. **b** a piece of fabric forming a vertical section of a garment. **2** a usu vertical mounting for controls on the dashboard of a car or aircraft. **3** a flat insulated support for computer machinery or parts of an electrical device with controls on one face. **4a** a group of people selected to serve as a committee of investigation or arbitration. **b** a group of people who take part in a discussion or quiz show on radio or television. **5** a list of people summoned for service as jurors. **6** *Brit* a list of doctors in a particular area available for consultation by National Health Service patients.

panel[2] *v* (**panelled, panelling,** *NAm* **paneled, paneling**) to furnish or decorate with panels.

panel beater *n* a person whose job is to repair the metal bodywork of motor vehicles by beating out dents.

panel game *n* a quiz played on television or radio by a panel of people.

panelling (*NAm* **paneling**) *n* decorative wood panels joined to line a room.

panellist (*NAm* **panelist**) *n* a member of a panel, *esp* in a radio or television show.

panel pin *n* a short slender nail used for woodwork.

panel saw *n* a fine saw for cutting thin wood.

panettone /pani'tohnay, -ni/ *n* (*pl* **panettoni**) a rich Italian fruitcake, traditionally eaten at Christmas.

pan-fry *v* (**-ies, -ied**) to fry in a pan in a small amount of oil or fat.

pang *n* **1** a brief piercing spasm of pain. **2** a sharp attack of mental anguish.

panga *n* a large broad-bladed African knife.

Pangloss *n* a person who is blindly optimistic. ➤➤ **Panglossian** *adj.*

pangolin *n* an insect-eating mammal that has a body covered with large overlapping horny scales.

panhandle *n NAm* a narrow strip of land projecting from one territory or state into another.

panic[1] *n* a sudden overpowering feeling of fear. ➤➤ **panicky** *adj.*

panic[2] *v* (**panicked, panicking**) to feel or cause to feel panic.

panic attack *n* a sudden disabling feeling of extreme anxiety.

panic button *n* an emergency control or signalling device used to activate an alarm or summon help. ✱ **press the panic button** *informal* to panic or to cause other people to react with alarm.

panicle *n* **1** a flower head in which the main stem branches and the flowers are borne on short stalks. **2** a loosely branched flower cluster in the shape of a pyramid. ➤➤ **panicled** *adj.*

panic stations *n Brit, informal* a state of confused anxiety caused by a sudden emergency.

Panjabi *n and adj* see PUNJABI.

panjandrum *n humorous* a powerful personage or self-important official.

pannage *n* the mainly historical right to feed animals, e.g. pigs, in a wood.

panne *n* a silk or rayon velvet with lustrous pile flattened in one direction.

pannier *n* **1** either of a pair of large baskets carried on the back of an animal. **2** either of a pair of bags or boxes fixed on either side of the rear wheel of a bicycle or motorcycle. **3** a hoop petticoat or looped-up overskirt, formerly worn to give extra width to the sides of a skirt at hip level.

pannikin *n Brit* a small metal pan or cup.

panoply *n* **1** a magnificent or impressive array. **2** a full suit of armour. ➤➤ **panoplied** *adj.*

panoptic *adj* showing a whole view at a time.

panorama *n* **1a** an unobstructed or complete view of a landscape or area. **b** a comprehensive presentation or survey of a series of events. **2** a large pictorial representation encircling the spectator. ➤➤ **panoramic** *adj,* **panoramically** *adv.*

pan out *v* to turn out as specified; *esp* to succeed.

panpipes *pl n* a wind instrument consisting of a graduated series of short vertical pipes bound together with the mouthpieces in an even row.

pansexual *adj* omnisexual.

panstick *n* make-up compressed into stick form.

pansy *n* (*pl* **-ies**) **1** a garden plant derived from wild pansies and violets, with flowers that have rounded velvety petals. **2** *informal, derog* an effeminate man or male homosexual.

pant *v* **1** to breathe quickly or in a laboured manner. **2** to long eagerly; to yearn. ➤➤ **pant** *n.*

pant- *or* **panto-** *comb. form* all: *pantisocracy; pantomime.*

Pantagruelian *adj literary* huge.

pantalettes (*NAm* **pantalets**) *pl n* a trouser-like undergarment with a ruffle at the bottom of each leg, worn by women and children in the early 19th cent.

pantaloons *pl n* **1** loose-fitting trousers worn by women, gathered at the ankle. **2** tight-fitting trousers formerly worn by men, fastened under the instep with straps.

pantechnicon *n Brit* a large van for transporting household possessions and furniture.

pantheism *n* **1** a doctrine that equates God with the forces and laws of nature. **2** the worship of all the gods of different religions and cults. ➤➤ **pantheist** *n,* **pantheistic** *adj.*

pantheon *n* **1** the gods of a people collectively. **2** a building containing memorials to famous dead. **3** a group of illustrious persons.

panther *n* (*pl* **panthers** *or* **panther**) **1** a leopard, *esp* of the black colour phase. **2** *NAm* = PUMA.

pantie girdle *n* see PANTY GIRDLE.

panties *pl n* pants for women or children.

pantihose *pl n* see PANTYHOSE.

pantile *n* a roofing tile whose transverse section is a flattened S-shape. ➤➤ **pantiled** *adj.*

panto *n* (*pl* **-os**) *Brit, informal* = PANTOMIME.

panto- *comb. form* see PANT-.

pantograph *n* **1** an instrument for copying something, e.g. a map, on a predetermined scale consisting of four light rigid bars jointed in parallelogram form. **2** a collapsible framework mounted on an electric vehicle, e.g. a railway locomotive, for collecting current from an overhead wire. ➤➤ **pantographic** *adj.*

pantomime *n* **1** a British theatrical and musical entertainment of the Christmas season based on a nursery tale with stock roles and topical jokes. **2** communication of a story by bodily or facial movements in drama or dance. **3** something absurd or meaningless.

pantothenic acid *n* a vitamin of the vitamin B complex, which is found in all living tissues and is essential for cell growth.

pantry *n* (*pl* **-ies**) a room or cupboard used for storing provisions or tableware.

pants[1] *pl n* **1** *Brit* an undergarment that covers the crotch and hips and that may extend to the waist and partly down each leg. **2** *NAm* trousers. ✱ **bore/scare the pants off somebody** *informal* to bore/scare somebody very much. **by the seat of one's pants** *informal* by instinct rather than by logic or using mechanical aids. **catch somebody with their pants down** *informal* to take somebody by surprise and at a disadvantage.

pants[2] *adj Brit, informal* of very poor quality; terrible.

pantsuit *or* **pants suit** *n NAm* = TROUSER SUIT.

panty girdle *or* **pantie girdle** *n* a woman's girdle shaped like pants.

pantyhose *or* **pantihose** *pl n NAm* = TIGHTS.

panzer *n* a German tank of World War II.

pap[1] *n* **1** soft food for infants or invalids. **2** something, e.g. a novel, lacking solid value or substance.

pap[2] *n chiefly dialect* a nipple or teat.

papa *n informal* an affectionate name for one's father.

papacy *n* (*pl* **-ies**) the office of pope, or period of his reign.

papain *n* an enzyme in the juice of unripe papaya, used to tenderize meat.

papal *adj* relating to a pope or the papacy. ➤➤ **papally** *adv.*

paparazzo *n* (*pl* **paparazzi**) a freelance photographer who specializes in taking sensational photographs of famous people.

papaw *n* see PAWPAW.

papaya *n* a large oval tropical fruit with a yellow skin, orange flesh, and a central cavity filled with round black seeds.

paper[1] *n* **1** a material for writing, printing on, etc made from compacted vegetable fibres, e.g. wood, in the form of thin sheets. **2a** (*also in pl*) a written or printed document, *esp* one showing proof of identity or ownership. **b** (*in pl*) an individual's personal documents and records, diaries, etc. **3** = NEWSPAPER. **4a** a written composition designed for publication or to be read aloud. **b** a government report or discussion document. **5a** a set of questions to be answered during a single examination. **b** a set of answers to examination questions written by a candidate. **6** = WALLPAPER[1]. **7** (*used before a noun*) existing only in theory. ✱ **on paper 1** in writing. **2** in theory.

paper[2] *v* **1** to cover with paper; *esp* to apply wallpaper to (a wall). **2** *informal* to give out free tickets for (a performance). ➤➤ **paperer** *n.*

paperback *n* a book with a flexible paper binding.

paperboy *n* a boy who delivers newspapers.

paper chase *n* a type of cross-country race in which some of the runners scatter bits of paper as a trail which others follow to find and catch them.

paper clip *n* a small clip made from two loops of wire, used for holding sheets of paper together.

papergirl *n* a girl who delivers newspapers.

paperknife *n* (*pl* **paperknives**) a blunt ornamental knife for slitting envelopes.

paper money *n* bank notes.

paper over *v* **1** to gloss over or patch up (major differences) in order to maintain a semblance of unity. **2** to hide or conceal (a crack) with wallpaper.

paper round *n* a job of delivering newspapers to people's houses.

paper-thin *adj* extremely thin or insubstantial.

paper tiger *n* a person or power represented as strong or threatening, but actually ineffectual.

paper trail *n chiefly NAm* documentary evidence of somebody's activities.

paperweight *n* a small heavy object used to hold down loose papers on a desk.

paperwork *n* routine clerical or record-keeping work.

papery *adj* resembling paper in thinness or consistency.

papier-mâché *n* a light strong moulding material made of paper pulped with glue, used for making boxes, trays, etc.

papilla *n* (*pl* **papillae**) **1** a small projecting nipple-shaped body part. **2** a piece of connective tissue extending into and nourishing the root of a hair, feather, etc. ➤➤ **papillary** *adj,* **papillate** *adj,* **papillose** *adj.*

papilloma *n* (*pl* **papillomas** *or* **papillomata**) a benign tumour, e.g. a wart.

papillon *n* a small slender toy spaniel with large butterfly-shaped ears.

papist *or* **Papist** *n derog* = ROMAN CATHOLIC[1]. ➤➤ **papism** *n,* **papist** *adj,* **papistry** *n.*

papoose *n* **1** a young Native American child. **2** a bag worn on the back, used for carrying a baby.

pappardelle /papar'delay/ *pl n* (*used as sing. or pl*) pasta in broad flat ribbons.

pappus *n* (*pl* **pappi**) a tuft of hairy appendages crowning the ovary or fruit in various plants, e.g. the dandelion. ➤➤ **pappose** *adj.*

pappy *adj* of or resembling pap.

paprika *n* a red condiment consisting of the finely ground dried pods of sweet peppers: compare CAYENNE PEPPER, CHILLI.

Pap smear *or* **Pap test** *n* a method for the early detection of cancer in which cells from mucous membrane in the cervix are scraped off and examined under the microscope.

Papuan *n* **1** a native or inhabitant of Papua or Papua New Guinea. **2** the group of languages spoken in New Guinea and nearby islands. ➤➤ **Papuan** *adj.*

papule *or* **papula** *n* (*pl* **papules** *or* **papulae**) a small solid conical projection from the skin. ➤➤ **papular** *adj.*

papyri *n* pl of PAPYRUS.

papyrus *n* (*pl* **papyruses** *or* **papyri**) **1** a tall sedge of the Nile valley. **2** the pith of the papyrus plant made into a material for writing on. **3** an ancient manuscript written on papyrus.

par[1] *n* **1** in golf, the standard score of a good player for each hole of a golf course. **2a** an amount taken as an average or norm. **b** a usual standard of physical condition or health. **3** the money value assigned to each share of stock in the charter of a company. ✱ **on a par with** equal to. **par for the course** what is to be expected in a particular situation.

par[2] *v* (**parred, parring**) to score par on (a hole in golf).

par- *prefix* see PARA-.

para[1] *n* (*pl* **paras**) *informal* **1** a paratrooper. **2** = PARAGRAPH.

para[2] *n* (*pl* **paras** *or* **para**) a unit of currency in parts of Yugoslavia, worth 100th of a dinar.

para- *or* **par-** *prefix* **1a** beside or alongside: *parathyroid; parallel.* **b** beyond: *paranormal; paradox.* **2a** associated in a subsidiary or auxiliary capacity: *paramedical.* **b** closely resembling or related to: *paratyphoid.*

parable *n* a short story illustrating a moral or religious principle.

parabola *n* a symmetrical curve of the kind generated when a cone is intersected by a plane parallel to its side: compare ELLIPSE, HYPERBOLA.

parabolic *adj* **1** of or having the form of a parabola. **2** expressed by or being a parable. ➤➤ **parabolical** *adj*, **parabolically** *adv.*

paraboloid *n* a surface some plane sections of which are parabolas: compare ELLIPSOID, HYPERBOLOID. ➤➤ **paraboloidal** *adj.*

paracetamol *n* a chemical compound that is widely used as a painkiller and in the synthesis of other chemical compounds.

parachute[1] *n* a folding expanse of light fabric attached by lines to a harness, that opens out into an umbrella shape to ensure a safe descent of a person or object through the air from a great height, e.g. from an aeroplane. ➤➤ **parachutist** *n.*

parachute[2] *v* to descend or drop by means of a parachute.

Paraclete *n* = HOLY SPIRIT.

parade[1] *n* **1** a public procession. **2** a formal assembly or march past by a body of troops before a superior officer. **3** a succession of things or people on display. **4** an ostentatious display or demonstration of something. **5** *chiefly Brit* a row of shops. **6** a place for strolling; a promenade.

parade[2] *v* **1** to march in a procession. **2** to walk up and down, *esp* in a vain or eye-catching manner. **3** (+ as) = MASQUERADE[2] (2). **4** to cause to manoeuvre or march. **5** to exhibit ostentatiously. ➤➤ **parader** *n.*

paradiddle *n* a pattern in drumming, consisting of four beats played with alternate sticks, either left, right, left, left, or right, left, right, right.

paradigm *n* **1** an outstandingly clear or typical example. **2** in grammar, an example of a conjugation or declension showing a word in all its inflectional forms. **3** a model used in science as a framework for ideas. ➤➤ **paradigmatic** *adj.*

paradigm shift *n* a complete change in approach.

paradise *n* **1a** (*often* **Paradise**) = HEAVEN. **b** (*often* **Paradise**) the Garden of Eden. **2** an intermediate place or state where the righteous dead await resurrection and judgment. **3** an idyllic place or state. ➤➤ **paradisaical** *adj*, **paradisal** *adj*, **paradisiacal** *adj*, **paradisical** *adj.*

parador /'paradawr/ *n* (*pl* **paradors** *or* **paradores** /para'dawrayz/) a country hotel in Spain or Latin America that is run by the government.

paradox *n* **1** a statement that is apparently contradictory or absurd and yet might be true. **2** a person, condition, or act, with seemingly contradictory qualities or phases. ➤➤ **paradoxical** *adj*, **paradoxically** *adv.*

paraffin *n* **1** a waxy inflammable mixture of hydrocarbons obtained from distillates of coal, petroleum, etc and used in candles, chemical synthesis, and cosmetics. **2** *Brit* an inflammable liquid hydrocarbon obtained by distillation of petroleum and used as a fuel. **3** *no longer in technical use* = ALKANE.

paragliding *n* the sport of travelling through the air by means of a rectangular parachute after being released at a height. ➤➤ **paraglider** *n.*

paragon *n* a model of excellence or of a particular quality.

paragraph *n* **1** a usu indented division of a written composition that develops a single point or idea. **2** a sign, e.g. (¶), used as a reference mark or to indicate the beginning of a paragraph.

Paraguayan *n* a native or inhabitant of Paraguay in S America. ➤➤ **Paraguayan** *adj.*

parakeet *or* **parrakeet** *n* a small slender long-tailed parrot.

paralegal[1] *n chiefly NAm* a person with specialized training who assists an lawyer.

paralegal[2] *adj chiefly NAm* of or being a paralegal.

paralipsis *n* a rhetorical device in which the speaker uses a formula, e.g. 'not to mention . . . ' or 'to say nothing of . . . ', that suggests that something is not going to be spoken of, but in fact gives it greater emphasis.

parallax *n* **1** the apparent displacement or the difference in apparent direction of an object as seen from two different points not on the same straight line. **2** in astronomy, the difference in direction of a celestial body as measured from two points on the earth or on the earth's orbit round the sun. ➤➤ **parallactic** *adj.*

parallel[1] *adj* **1** extending in the same direction and always the same distance apart. **2** in computing, performing several operations simultaneously. **3** denoting an electrical circuit having a number of conductors in parallel. **4** analogous or comparable. ➤➤ **parallelism** *n.*

parallel[2] *n* **1** somebody or something equal or similar to another. **2** a comparison that shows a resemblance. **3a** a parallel line, curve, or surface, *esp* a line representing any of the imaginary circles on the surface of the earth parallel to the equator. **b** in printing, a sign || used as a reference mark. **4** a method of connecting electric components or circuits separately to a power source so that they receive the same voltage.

parallel[3] *v* (**paralleled, paralleling**) **1** to run parallel to (something else). **2a** to equal or match (something): *No one has paralleled my success in business.* **b** to follow a similar course to (something); to correspond to (it): *Her career paralleled mine.*

parallel bars *pl n* a pair of bars supported horizontally by a common base, used in a gymnastic event.

parallelepiped *n* a polyhedron with faces that are parallelograms.

parallel import *n* an imported item that undercuts the price of a locally manufactured article.

parallelogram *n* a quadrilateral with opposite sides parallel and equal.

parallel processing *n* the processing by a computer of a number of items of data simultaneously.

Paralympics *pl n* (*used as sing. or pl*) an international sports contest for disabled athletes. ➤➤ **Paralympic** *adj.*

paralyse (*NAm* **paralyze**) *v* **1** to affect with paralysis. **2** to make powerless or ineffective. **3** to make immobile or to transfix.

paralysis *n* (*pl* **paralyses**) **1** loss or partial loss of motion or sensation in a part of the body. **2** loss of the ability to move or to act.

paralytic *adj* **1** of paralysis. **2** *chiefly Brit, informal* very drunk. ➤➤ **paralytically** *adv.*

paramagnetic *adj* relating to a substance that in a magnetic field is slightly attracted towards points of higher field intensity. ➤➤ **paramagnetism** *n.*

paramecium *n* (*pl* **paramecia** *or* **parameciums**) a single-celled animal that has an elongated body covered with cilia and a funnel-shaped groove at the tip.

paramedic *n* **1** a member of an ambulance crew who is trained to carry out emergency medical procedures. **2** a person whose job supports the job of doctors in a hospital, e.g. a laboratory technician. ➤➤ **paramedical** *adj.*

parameter *n* **1** an arbitrary constant whose value characterizes a member of a system. **2** a quantity that describes a statistical population. **3** any of a set of physical properties whose values determine the characteristics or behaviour of something. **4** *informal* a limiting factor or characteristic. ⋙ **parametric** *adj*, **parametrically** *adv*.

paramilitary[1] *adj* formed on a military pattern.

paramilitary[2] *n* (*pl* **-ies**) a member of a paramilitary force.

paramount *adj* superior to all others. ⋙ **paramountcy** *n*.

paramour *n archaic* an illicit lover.

paranoia *n* **1** a mental disorder characterized by delusions of persecution. **2** a tendency towards irrational suspiciousness and distrustfulness of others. ⋙ **paranoiac** *adj and n*, **paranoid** *adj and n*.

paranormal *adj* not scientifically explainable; supernatural. ⋙ **paranormally** *adv*.

parapenting *n* the sport of paragliding down the side of a mountain from a high point. ⋙ **parapenter** *n*.

parapet *n* **1** a wall, rampart, or mound of earth to protect soldiers. **2** a low wall to protect the edge of a platform, roof, or bridge.

paraphernalia *n* (*used as sing. or pl*) all the trappings associated with any particular pursuit or production.

paraphrase[1] *n* a restatement of a text, passage, or work giving the meaning in another form.

paraphrase[2] *v* to make a paraphrase of.

paraplegia *n* paralysis of the lower half of the body, resulting from injury or disease. ⋙ **paraplegic** *adj and n*.

parapsychology *n* the investigation of evidence for the occurrence of psychic phenomena. ⋙ **parapsychological** *adj*, **parapsychologist** *n*.

paraquat *n* a very poisonous herbicide used as a weedkiller.

parasail[1] *v* to take part in the sport of parasailing.

parasail[2] *n* a parachute used in the sport of parasailing.

parasailing *n* the sport of rising into the air and parachuting down while wearing a parachute and being towed by a motor boat.

parascend *v* to take part in the sport of parascending.

parascending *n* the sport of rising into the air and parachuting down while wearing a parachute and being towed by a motor vehicle or a boat. ⋙ **parascender** *n*.

parasite *n* **1** an organism living in or on another organism and drawing its nourishment directly from it. **2** a person who depends on somebody else for existence or support without making a useful or adequate return. ⋙ **parasitic** *adj*, **parasitical** *adj*, **parasitically** *adv*.

parasitize *or* **-ise** *v* to infest or live on (an organism) as a parasite. ⋙ **parasitization** *n*.

parasitoid *n* an insect, *esp* a wasp, that develops within the body of another insect and eventually kills it.

parasol *n* a lightweight umbrella used as a protection from the sun.

parastatal *adj* of a business: owned or controlled by the government.

parasympathetic *adj* relating to the part of the autonomic nervous system that contains nerves that induce secretion, increase the tone and contractility of smooth muscle, and cause the dilation of blood vessels.

paratha *n* a flat type of Indian unleavened bread.

parathion *n* a very poisonous insecticide used in farming.

parathyroid *n* a small endocrine gland near the thyroid gland that produces a hormone.

paratroops *pl n* troops equipped to parachute into combat areas from an aeroplane. ⋙ **paratrooper** *n*.

paratyphoid *n* a disease that resembles typhoid fever and is commonly contracted by eating contaminated food.

par avion *adv* used on mail: by airmail.

parboil *v* to boil (vegetables) briefly as a preliminary or incomplete cooking procedure.

parcel[1] *n* **1** an object wrapped in paper for sending by post. **2** a plot of land. **3** a collection or group of people, animals, or things.

parcel[2] *v* (**parcelled, parcelling,** *NAm* **parceled, parceling**) **1** (*often* + up) to make up into a parcel. **2** (+ out) to divide into parts; to distribute. **3** to cover (a rope) with strips of canvas.

parch *v* **1** to make or become dry or scorched. **2** to roast (peas) slightly in a dry heat.

parched *adj* **1** *informal* of a person: extremely thirsty. **2** of land: dry because of lack of rainfall.

parchment *n* **1** the skin of a sheep or goat, prepared as material for writing on. **2** strong paper made to resemble parchment. **3** a parchment manuscript.

pard *n archaic or literary* a leopard.

pardon[1] *n* **1** excuse or forgiveness for a fault or offence. **2** a release from legal penalties. **3** in the Christian Church, formerly, an indulgence.

pardon[2] *v* **1** to absolve from the consequences of a fault or crime. **2** to allow (an offence) to pass without punishment. ✱ **pardon my French** see FRENCH[2]. **pardon me** used in courteous denial or apology. ⋙ **pardonable** *adj*, **pardonably** *adv*.

pardoner *n* a medieval preacher delegated to raise money by granting indulgences.

pare *v* **1a** to cut or shave off the outer surface of; to peel. **b** to trim off the outer edges of (*esp* the nails). **2** (*often* + down/away) to diminish gradually as if by paring. ⋙ **parer** *n*.

paregoric *n* a camphorated tincture of opium, formerly used to relieve pain and coughing.

parenchyma *n* **1** a fleshy tissue of the fruits, stems, etc of higher plants that consists of thin-walled living cells. **2** the essential and distinctive tissue of an organ, as distinguished from its supportive framework. ⋙ **parenchymatous** *adj*.

parent[1] *n* **1** a father or mother. **2** an animal or plant regarded in relation to its offspring. **3** the material or source from which something is derived. **4** *archaic* an ancestor. ⋙ **parental** *adj*, **parentally** *adv*, **parenthood** *n*.

parent[2] *v* to be or act as the parent of.

parentage *n* descent from parents or ancestors.

parent company *n* a company that owns other subsidiary companies.

parenteral *adj* **1** situated or occurring outside the intestine. **2** of a drug: introduced into the body other than through the intestines, e.g. by injection. ⋙ **parenterally** *adv*.

parenthesis *n* (*pl* **parentheses**) **1a** an amplifying or explanatory word or phrase inserted in a passage and set off, in writing, by punctuation. **b** either or both of the curved marks (or) used in writing and printing to enclose a parenthesis. Also called BRACKET[1] (I). **2** an interlude or interval. ⋙ **parenthetic** *adj*, **parenthetical** *adj*, **parenthetically** *adv*.

parergon *n* (*pl* **parerga**) supplementary or subsidiary work.

paresis *n* (*pl* **pareses**) **1** slight or partial paralysis. **2** insanity and paralysis resulting from syphilis. ➤➤ **paretic** *adj.*

par excellence *adj* (*used after a noun*) being the best example of a kind: *the fashionable shopping city par excellence.*

parfait *n* a frozen flavoured dessert that contains whipped cream and eggs.

parget[1] *v* (**pargeted, pargeting**) to coat (a wall) with ornamental plaster.

parget[2] *n* plasterwork, *esp* in raised ornamental figures on walls.

pargeting *n* = PARGET[2].

pariah *n* **1** = OUTCAST. **2** formerly, a member of a low caste of S India and Burma (now Union of Myanmar).

pariah dog *n* = PYE-DOG.

parietal *adj* **1** relating to or in the region of the walls of an anatomical part or cavity, *esp* the upper rear wall of the skull. **2** of a developing seed or its support: attached to the main wall of the ovary. **3** *NAm* concerning life or regulations within a college.

parietal bone *n* either of a pair of bones of the top and side of the skull.

parietal lobe *n* the middle lobe of each cerebral hemisphere.

pari-mutuel *n* **1** a betting pool in which those who bet on the winners of the first three places share the total amount bet, minus a percentage for the management. **2** *NAm* = TOTALIZATOR (1).

paring *n* **1** the act of cutting away an edge or surface. **2** something pared off.

parish *n* **1** a subdivision of a diocese served by a single church or clergyman. **2** a unit of local government in rural England.

parishioner *n* a member or inhabitant of a parish.

parish-pump *adj Brit* having a restricted outlook or limited interest.

parish register *n* a book containing records of baptisms, marriages, and burials in a parish.

Parisian *n* a native or inhabitant of Paris. ➤➤ **Parisian** *adj.*

parity[1] *n* **1** the state of being equal or equivalent. **2** equivalence of a commodity price expressed in one currency to its price expressed in another. **3** the property of an integer with respect to being odd or even.

parity[2] *n* **1** the state or fact of having borne offspring. **2** the number of children previously borne.

parity check *n* a check made on computer data by which errors are detected.

park[1] *n* **1a** an area of land for recreation in a city or town. **b** an area maintained in its natural state as a public property. **2** an enclosed area of lawns, woodland, etc attached to a country house and used as a game reserve or for recreation. **3** a site for a number of buildings housing establishments of a similar type: *a science park.* **4** (*usu in combination*) an area set aside for vehicles to be parked in. **5a** (**the park**) *Brit, informal* a football pitch. **b** *NAm* an arena or stadium used for ball games.

park[2] *v* **1** to leave or place (a vehicle) for a time. **2** *informal* to leave (somebody or something) temporarily.

parka *n* **1** a weatherproof thigh-length jacket with a hood. **2** a similar hooded garment made of animal hide worn by Arctic peoples.

park-and-ride *n* an urban transport system in which public transport takes passengers into the centre of a town from large car parks situated on the outskirts.

parkin *n* a thick heavy ginger cake made with oatmeal and treacle.

parking lot *n NAm* an outdoor car park.

parking meter *n* a coin-operated device which registers the payment and displays the time allowed for parking a motor vehicle.

Parkinson's disease *or* **Parkinsonism** *n* a long-lasting progressive nervous disease, marked by tremor, weakness of resting muscles, and a peculiar gait. ➤➤ **parkinsonian** *adj.*

Parkinson's Law *n* an observation in office organization that work expands so as to fill the time available for its completion.

parkland *n* land with clumps of trees and shrubs in cultivated condition.

parkway *n NAm* a broad landscaped road or highway.

parky *adj* (**-ier, -iest**) *Brit, informal* = CHILLY (1).

parlance *n* a manner of speech and choice of words.

parlay[1] *v NAm* to bet (a sum of money) in a parlay.

parlay[2] *n NAm* an accumulator bet.

parley[1] *v* to discuss terms with an enemy.

parley[2] *n* (*pl* **-eys**) a conference under truce to discuss terms with an enemy.

parliament *n* **1** the supreme legislative body of the UK that consists of the House of Commons and the House of Lords and is called together and dissolved by the sovereign. **2** a similar body in another nation or state.

parliamentarian *n* **1** *Brit* a Member of Parliament who is an expert in parliamentary rules and practice. **2** (*often* **Parliamentarian**) an adherent of the parliament during the English Civil War. ➤➤ **parliamentarian** *adj.*

parliamentary *adj* **1** of, appropriate to, or enacted by a parliament. **2** supporting the parliament during the English Civil War.

parliamentary private secretary *n* a Member of Parliament in the UK who assists a government minister.

parlour (*NAm* **parlor**) *n* **1a** *dated* a room in a private house for the entertainment of guests. **b** a room in an inn, hotel, or club for conversation or semiprivate uses. **2** a shop or business: *a funeral parlour; a beauty parlour.* **3** a place for milking cows.

parlour game *n* an indoor word game, board game, etc.

parlourmaid *n* a maid who waits at table.

parlous *adj often humorous* giving cause for concern or alarm. ➤➤ **parlously** *adv.*

Parma ham *n* Italian cured ham, eaten uncooked in thin slices.

Parmesan *n* a very hard strongly flavoured Italian cheese that is often used grated.

parmigiana /parmi'jahnə/ *adj* (*after noun*) made or topped with Parmesan cheese: *veal parmigiana.*

parochial *adj* **1** relating to a church parish. **2** limited or provincial in outlook; concerned only with local affairs. ➤➤ **parochially** *adv.*

parochialism *n* selfish pettiness or narrowness.

parody[1] *n* (*pl* **-ies**) **1** a literary or musical work in which the style of an author is imitated for comic or satirical effect. **2** a feeble or ridiculous imitation. ➤➤ **parodic** *adj,* **parodist** *n.*

parody[2] *v* (**-ies, -ied**) to imitate for comic or satirical effect.

parole[1] *n* **1** a conditional release of a prisoner. **2** formerly, the promise of a prisoner of war to fulfil stated conditions in consideration of release or the granting of privileges.

parole[2] *v* to put (a prisoner) on parole. ⋙ **parolee** *n.*

paronomasia *n* a play on words; a pun.

parotid gland *n* either of a pair of large salivary glands below and in front of the ear. ⋙ **parotid** *adj.*

parotitis *n* inflammation of the parotid glands; *esp* mumps.

paroxysm *n* **1** a fit, attack, or sudden increase of disease symptoms; a convulsion. **2** a sudden violent emotion. ⋙ **paroxysmal** *adj.*

parquet *n* **1** a floor or flooring made of blocks of wood laid in geometrical patterns. **2** *NAm* the stalls in a theatre.

parquetry *n* work in the form of geometrically patterned wood laid or inlaid, *esp* for floors.

parr *n* (*pl* **parrs** *or* **parr**) a young salmon actively feeding in fresh water.

parrakeet *n* see PARAKEET.

parricide *n* **1** the act of murdering one's father or mother. **2** a person who commits parricide. ⋙ **parricidal** *adj.*

parrot[1] *n* a large tropical bird with brightly coloured plumage, a curved hooked beak, and in some cases the ability to mimic speech.

parrot[2] *v* (**parroted, parroting**) to repeat or imitate (another's words) without understanding or thought.

parrot-fashion *adv* without regard for meaning.

parrot fish *n* a spiny-finned sea fish with teeth like a beak.

parry[1] *v* (**-ies, -ied**) **1** to ward off (a blow). **2** to evade (e.g. an accusation) *esp* by an adroit answer.

parry[2] *n* (*pl* **-ies**) **1** an act of parrying a blow. **2** an evasive reply.

parse *v* to resolve (a sentence) into component parts of speech and describe them grammatically.

parsec *n* a unit of distance used in astronomy equal to about 3.25 light years; the distance at which the radius of the earth's orbit subtends an angle of one second of arc.

Parsi *or* **Parsee** *n* a Zoroastrian descended from Persian refugees settled principally in Bombay.

parsimonious *adj* spending as little money as possible; frugal. ⋙ **parsimoniously** *adv,* **parsimoniousness** *n.*

parsimony *n* the quality of being careful with money.

parsley *n* a plant of the carrot family cultivated for its leaves, which are used as a herb or garnish in cooking.

parsnip *n* a plant of the carrot family used as a vegetable.

parson *n* **1** the clergyman in charge of an Anglican parish. **2** any clergyman.

parsonage *n* the house provided by a church for its parson.

parson's nose *n* the fatty extension of the rump of a cooked fowl.

part[1] *n* **1** any of the subdivisions into which something is divided. **2** a certain amount or a contributing factor but not the whole. **3** a separable piece in a machine; a component. **4** an organ, member, or other constituent element of a plant or animal body. **5** any of the opposing sides in a conflict or dispute. **6** a division of a literary work. **7** a vocal or instrumental line in music arranged for more than one voice or instrument, or the written music for a particular voice or instrument. **8** an actor's role in a play. **9** somebody's contribution to an action or event. **10** (*in pl*) an unspecified territorial area. **11** *dated* (*in pl*) personal abilities; talents: *a man of parts.* ✱ **for one's part** as far as one is concerned. **in part** in some degree; partially. **look the part** to have a physical appearance appropriate to one's role or function. **on the part of** by or on behalf of. **take part** (*often* + in) to join in. **take something in good part** to accept (a joke or critical remark) without offence.

part[2] *v* **1** to separate from or cause to separate from somebody. **2** to become separated into parts. **3** to separate or become separated into parts. **4** (+ with) to relinquish possession of, *esp* reluctantly.

part[3] *adv* = PARTLY.

partake *v* (*past* **partook,** *past part.* **partaken**) *formal* (+ in/of) to participate. ⋙ **partaker** *n.*

part and parcel *n* an essential part or element.

parterre *n* **1** an ornamental garden with paths between the beds. **2** *NAm* a theatre pit.

part-exchange *n Brit* a method of paying for something whereby part of the payment takes the form of goods, the balance being made up in money.

parthenogenesis *n* reproduction by development of an unfertilized gamete that occurs among lower plants and invertebrate animals. ⋙ **parthenogenetic** *adj.*

Parthian shot *n* = PARTING SHOT.

partial *adj* **1** of a part rather than the whole; not total. **2** inclined to favour one party more than the other. **3** (+ to) markedly fond of. ⋙ **partially** *adv.*

Usage note

partially *or* **partly**? Do not confuse these two words. *Partly* means 'as regards one part': *The building is constructed partly of brick and partly of stone. Partially* means 'to a limited extent; incompletely': *partially sighted. Partly* is used to introduce an explanatory clause or phrase: *Partly because of the weather and partly because of the weak economy, profits were down last year.*

partiality *n* (*pl* **-ies**) **1** unfair preference for somebody or something. **2** a special taste or liking.

participate *v* to join with others in doing something. ⋙ **participant** *n,* **participation** *n,* **participator** *n,* **participatory** *adj.*

participle *n* a verbal form, e.g. *singing* or *sung,* that has the function of an adjective and can also be used in compound verb forms. ⋙ **participial** *adj,* **participially** *adv.*

particle *n* **1** a minute quantity or fragment of a physical substance. **2** a minute subdivision of matter, *esp* at subatomic level, e.g. an electron or proton. **3** a minor unit of speech including all uninflected words or all words except nouns and verbs.

particle board *n* a board made of very small pieces of wood bonded together.

particle physics *n* a branch of physics dealing with the constitution, properties, and interactions of elementary particles.

parti-coloured *or* **particoloured** (*NAm* **parti-colored** *or* **particolored**) *adj* showing different colours or tints.

particular[1] *adj* **1** relating to a single person or thing; specific. **2** worthy of notice; special, unusual. **3** detailed or exact. **4a** attentive to details; meticulous. **b** hard to please; exacting.

particular[2] *n* an individual fact, point, or detail. ✱ **in particular** specifically or especially.

particularise *v* see PARTICULARIZE.

particularity *n* (*pl* **-ies**) **1a** (*usu in pl*) a minute detail; a particular. **b** an individual characteristic; a peculiarity. **2** the quality of being particular as opposed to universal. **3** the quality or state of being fastidious.

particularize *or* **-ise** *v* **1** *formal* to state in detail; to specify. **2** *formal* to go into details. ⋙ **particularization** *n.*

particularly *adv* **1** to an unusual degree. **2** in detail; specifically.

particulate *n* a substance consisting of minute separate particles. ⋙ **particulate** *adj.*

parting *n* **1** the act or an instance of parting from somebody. **2** *Brit* the line where the hair is parted. **3** a place where a division or separation occurs.

parting shot *n* a pointed remark made when leaving.

parti pris *n* (*pl* **partis pris**) a preconceived opinion; a prejudice.

partisan *n* **1** a firm adherent to a party, cause, or person; *esp* one exhibiting blind allegiance. **2** a member of a guerrilla band operating behind enemy lines. ⋙ **partisan** *adj,* **partisanship** *n.*

partis pris *n* pl of PARTI PRIS.

partita *n* (*pl* **partitas** *or* **partite**) a musical suite.

partition[1] *n* **1a** division into parts. **b** a part or section of a whole. **2** a light interior dividing wall. ⋙ **partitioner** *n,* **partitionist** *n.*

partition[2] *v* **1** to divide (e.g. a country) into parts or shares. **2a** to divide (e.g. a room) by a partition. **b** (*usu* + off) to separate (an area) off from a larger one with a partition.

partitive[1] *adj* in grammar, of a part of a whole. ⋙ **partitively** *adv.*

partitive[2] *n* in grammar, a noun or pronoun indicating a partitive construction.

partly *adv* not completely; to some extent or degree.

Usage note

partly *or* partially? See note at PARTIAL.

partner[1] *n* **1a** a member of a partnership. **b** an associate in a joint venture. **2a** either of a couple who dance together. **b** somebody who plays with one or more others in a game against an opposing side. **c** a spouse, lover, etc.

partner[2] *v* to act as a partner to.

partnership *n* **1** the state of being a partner; association. **2** two or more joint principals in a business. **3** an association involving close cooperation.

part of speech *n* a class of words distinguished according to the kind of idea denoted and the function performed in a sentence.

partook *v* past of PARTAKE.

partridge *n* (*pl* **partridges** *or* **partridge**) a medium-sized game bird with variegated plumage.

part song *n* an unaccompanied song consisting of two or more voice parts.

part-time[1] *adj* involving or working less than the customary or standard hours. ⋙ **part-timer** *n.*

part-time[2] *adv* for part of the time.

partway *adv* to some extent; partially or partly.

part work *n Brit* a series of magazines devoted to one subject that is designed to be bound together in book form.

party[1] *n* (*pl* **-ies**) **1** a social gathering. **2** a group of people holding broadly similar views, organized to take part in politics. **3** a group of people organized to carry out an activity together. **4** a person or group taking one side of a dispute or contest. **5** a person or group participating in a legal action; a participant. **6** *informal* a particular individual.

party[2] *v* (**-ies, -ied**) *informal* to celebrate.

party line *n* **1** the official principles of a political party. **2** a single telephone line shared by two or more subscribers.

party-pooper *n informal* somebody who spoils a party by refusing to join in the fun.

party wall *n* a wall that divides two adjoining properties and in which each owner has a joint interest.

parvenu *n* a person of low social position who has recently acquired wealth or power. ⋙ **parvenu** *adj.*

parvovirus *n* any of a family of very small viruses that contain DNA, found *esp* in rodents and dogs.

pas *n* (*pl* **pas**) a dance step or combination of steps.

Pascal *n* a high-level computer language based on Algol that is used as a teaching language in computer studies and for business and commercial applications.

pascal *n* the SI unit of pressure equal to the pressure produced by a force of one newton applied uniformly over an area of one square metre.

Pascal's triangle *n* a set of numbers arranged in a triangle, each of which is obtained by adding together the numbers above it, and which is used to determine the coefficients of the terms in an expansion made using the binomial theorem.

paschal *adj* relating to the Jewish Passover or to Easter.

pas de deux *n* (*pl* **pas de deux**) a dance or set of dance steps for two performers.

pasha *or* **pacha** *n* a man of high rank or office in Turkey or N Africa.

pashmina *n* **1** a fine woollen fabric made from the hair of goats. **2** a shawl made of this fabric.

Pashto *n* the Indo-Iranian language of the Pathan.

paso doble *n* a ballroom dance with two beats to the bar, based on a Latin American march step.

pasqueflower *n* a plant of the buttercup family with large white or purple flowers.

pass[1] *v* **1** to move or proceed past or in a specified direction. **2** to transfer (something) to another person. **3** to go past (another vehicle) in the same direction. **4a** of time: to elapse. **b** of a situation or event, *esp* an unwelcome one: to complete its course and cease: *The troubles soon passed.* **c** of a right, office, etc: to be transferred to another person: *The throne passed to the king's daughter.* **5** to spend (time). **6** to go from one quality or state to another. **7a** to be successful in (an examination or test). **b** to judge (a candidate) to be successful or declare (something) to be satisfactory. **8** to cause (a law or proposal) to be enacted or approved. **9** in a team game, to hit, throw, or kick (the ball) to another player. **10** to pronounce (a judgment or sentence). **11a** to utter (a remark). **b** of a remark: to be said. **12** to decline an opportunity or offer. **13** to discharge (urine or faeces) from the body. ✱ **pass as/for** resemble or qualify as.

pass[2] *n* **1** the act of passing. **2a** a written permission for somebody to go somewhere or to be absent from a military post. **b** a ticket allowing free travel or admission. **3** the passing of an examination. **4** *informal* a sexual approach. **5** a single complete mechanical operation, e.g. in data processing. **6** in sport, an act of passing a ball or puck to a teammate. **7** in card games, an announcement of a decision not to bid or play.

pass[3] *n* a narrow passage in a mountain range.

passable *adj* **1** barely good enough; tolerable. **2** capable of being passed or travelled on. ⋙ **passably** *adv.*

passage *n* **1** the action or process of passing from one place or condition to another. **2a** a way through or along which one can move. **b** a corridor or lobby. **3a** an act of travelling, *esp* by sea or air. **b** a right or permission to pass. **4** a brief portion of a written work or a musical composition.

passageway *n* = CORRIDOR (1).

passata *n* a thick tomato purée, used in Italian cooking.

pass away *v* to die.

passband *n* a band of frequencies, e.g. in an electronic circuit, that is transmitted with maximum efficiency.

passbook *n* a building society account-holder's book in which deposits and withdrawals are recorded.

pass by *v* **1** to go past. **2** to escape the notice of.

passé *adj* **1** no longer fashionable or current; outmoded. **2** past one's prime.

passenger *n* **1** somebody who travels in, but does not operate, a public or private conveyance. **2** a member of a group who contributes little to the functioning of the group.

passe-partout *n* **1** a strong paper gummed on one side and used for mounting pictures. **2** *archaic* a master key.

passer-by *n* (*pl* **passers-by**) a person who happens by chance to pass by a particular place.

passerine *adj* belonging to the largest order of birds that consists chiefly of perching songbirds.

passim *adv* used to refer to the occurrence of an item in a piece of text: at various points throughout the text.

passing[1] *adj* **1** having a brief duration: *a passing whim.* **2** carried out quickly or casually.

passing[2] *n euphem* a death.

passing note *n* a melodic but discordant note interposed between essential notes of adjacent chords.

passion *n* **1a** intense or uncontrollable feeling. **b** an outbreak of anger. **2a** ardent affection; love. **b** a strong liking or interest. **c** strong sexual desire. **3** (*usu* **Passion**) the sufferings of Christ between the night of the Last Supper and his death. ➤➤ **passional** *adj*, **passionless** *adj*.

passionate *adj* **1** capable of or expressing love, hatred, or anger. **2** extremely enthusiastic; keen. ➤➤ **passionately** *adv*, **passionateness** *n*.

passionflower *n* a tropical plant with showy flowers and pulpy berries.

passionfruit *n* a fruit from a passionflower; *esp* a granadilla.

passion play *n* a dramatic representation of the passion and crucifixion of Christ.

passive[1] *adj* **1** lacking in energy or initiative. **2** offering no resistance; submissive. **3** acted on or influenced by external forces or impressions. **4** in grammar, of a verb form or voice: expressing an action that is done to the grammatical subject of a sentence, e.g. *was hit* in *the ball was hit.* **5** of an electronic device: using no electrical power for amplifying or controlling an electrical signal. **6** in a state of chemical inactivity, *esp* resistant to corrosion. ➤➤ **passively** *adv*, **passiveness** *n*, **passivity** *n*.

passive[2] *n* a passive verb form or voice.

passive resistance *n* resistance characterized by nonviolent non-cooperation.

passive smoking *n* the involuntary inhalation of tobacco smoke from other people's cigarettes, pipes, etc.

passkey *n* = MASTER KEY.

pass off *v* **1** (+ off) to represent (somebody or something) falsely in order to deceive. **2** to take place and cease, usually in a satisfactory way: *His stay in France passed off smoothly.*

pass out *v* **1** to lose consciousness. **2** *chiefly Brit* to complete a period of military training satisfactorily.

Passover *n* the Jewish festival celebrating the liberation of the Israelites from slavery in Egypt.

pass over *v* **1** to ignore or avoid (a remark, topic, etc) and continue. **2** to dismiss the claims of (somebody) to advancement.

passport *n* an official document issued by a government as proof of identity and nationality to one of its citizens for use when leaving or reentering the country.

pass up *v* to decline or reject (an opportunity).

password *n* **1** a word or phrase that must be spoken by a person before being allowed into a place. **2** a combination of letters and numbers used to gain access to part of a computer system.

past[1] *adj* **1a** just gone or elapsed: *for the past few months.* **b** having gone by; earlier: *past generations.* **2** finished or ended: *Winter is past.* **3** of the verb tense that expresses action or state in time gone by. **4** preceding or former.

Usage note

past *or* passed? See note at PASS[1].

past[2] *prep* **1a** beyond the age of or for. **b** subsequent to. **2a** at the farther side of (something). **b** up to and then beyond. **3** beyond the capacity, range, or sphere of. ✱ **not put it past somebody** *informal* to believe somebody to be perfectly capable of. **past it** *informal* no longer in one's prime.

past[3] *n* **1** time gone by. **2** in language, a verb form expressing past events. **3** a past life, *esp* one that is kept secret.

past[4] *adv* so as to pass by the speaker.

pasta *n* dough formed into various shapes and used fresh or dried, e.g. as spaghetti.

paste[1] *n* **1 a** a preparation of starch and water used as an adhesive. **b** a clay mixture used in making pottery or porcelain. **2** a smooth preparation of meat, fish, etc used as a spread. **3** a brilliant glass used in making imitation gems.

paste[2] *v* **1** to stick (something) with paste. **2** in computing, to insert (a piece of text) into a document. **3** *informal* to thrash or defeat (somebody).

pasteboard *n* board made by pasting together sheets of paper.

pastel[1] *n* **1** a paste of powdered pigment mixed with gum, or a crayon made of this. **2** a drawing in pastel. **3** a pale colour. ➤➤ **pastelist** *n*, **pastellist** *n*.

pastel[2] *adj* pale in colour.

pastern *n* a part of a horse's foot or other animal's from the fetlock to the hoof.

paste-up *n* a piece of copy for photographic reproduction consisting of text and artwork in the proper positions.

pasteurisation *n* see PASTEURIZATION.

pasteurise *v* see PASTEURIZE.

pasteurization *or* **-isation** *n* partial sterilization of a substance, *esp* milk, by heating for a short period.

pasteurize *or* **-ise** *v* to subject (e.g. milk) to pasteurization. ➤➤ **pasteurizer** *n*.

pastiche *n* an artistic or musical work that imitates the style of a previous work.

pastille *or* **pastil** *n* **1** an aromatic or medicated lozenge. **2** a small cone of aromatic paste, burned to scent a room.

pastime *n* an enjoyable hobby, game, etc.

pastis *n* (*pl* **pastis**) an alcoholic drink flavoured with aniseed.

past master *n* somebody who is expert in a particular activity.

pastor *n* the minister in charge of a congregation. ➤➤ **pastorate** *n*, **pastorship** *n*.

pastoral[1] *adj* **1a** used for livestock rearing. **b** of or relating to the countryside. **c** peaceful and innocent; idyllic. **2a** providing spiritual care or guidance for a church congregation. **b** providing personal guidance and care for pupils or students. ➤➤ **pastoralism** *n*, **pastorally** *adv*.

pastoral[2] *n* **1** a pastoral literary work. **2** an idealized depiction of country life.

pastoralist *n Aus* a farmer who keeps cattle or sheep.

past participle *n* a participle, e.g. finished, expressing a past event.

pastrami *n* a highly seasoned smoked beef.

pastry *n* (*pl* **-ies**) **1** a fat-enriched dough that is used to make pies, flans, and tarts. **2** a sweet tart or small cake.

pasturage *n* = PASTURE[1].

pasture[1] *n* **1** land used for grazing. **2** the feeding of livestock.

pasture[2] *v* **1** to feed (animals) on pasture. **2** of animals: to graze on pasture.

pasty[1] *n* (*pl* **-ies**) a small savoury pastry case with a filling.

pasty[2] *adj* (**-ier, -iest**) pallid and unhealthy in appearance. ➤➤ **pastiness** *n*.

pat[1] *n* **1** a light tap with the hand or a flat instrument. **2** a light tapping sound. **3** a small mass of butter. ✱ **a pat on the back** an expression of congratulation or praise.

pat[2] *v* (**patted, patting**) **1** to strike lightly with the open hand or some other flat surface. **2** to flatten or put into place or shape with light blows.

pat[3] *adj* **1** prompt or immediate. **2** suspiciously appropriate; contrived.

pat[4] *adv* aptly or promptly. ✱ **have something off pat** to have memorized something so that one can say it without hesitation.

pataca *n* the basic monetary unit of Macao.

Patagonian *n* a native or inhabitant of Patagonia in S America. ➤➤ **Patagonian** *adj*.

patch[1] *n* **1** a piece of material used to mend a hole or reinforce a weak spot. **2** a shield worn over an injured eye. **3a** a small area distinct from its surroundings. **b** a small piece of land used for growing vegetables. **4** a piece of adhesive plaster impregnated with a drug, which is worn on the skin to allow the drug to be absorbed. **5** a temporary connection in a communications system. **6** a small file supplied to correct a fault in a computer program. **7** *chiefly Brit, informal* a specified period. **8** *chiefly Brit* an area for which a particular individual or unit, e.g. of police, has responsibility. ✱ **not a patch on** *Brit, informal* not nearly as good as.

patch[2] *v* **1** to mend (a hole or weak spot) with a patch. **2** *informal* (*often* + up/together) to mend in a hasty or shabby fashion. **3** *informal* (+ up) to bring (a quarrel, etc) to an end. **4** to make a patch in (a computer program). **5** to connect (circuits) by a patch cord. ➤➤ **patcher** *n*.

patchouli *or* **patchouly** *n* a plant of the mint family that yields a fragrant essential oil.

patch pocket *n* a flat pocket attached to the outside of a garment.

patch test *n* a test for allergies in which small amounts of various substances are applied to the skin.

patchwork *n* **1** work consisting of pieces of cloth of various colours and shapes sewn together. **2** something composed of miscellaneous or incongruous parts.

patchy *adj* (**-ier, -iest**) **1** uneven in quality. **2** of certain types of weather: appearing in patches. ➤➤ **patchily** *adv*, **patchiness** *n*.

pate *n archaic or humorous* the head.

pâté *n* a rich savoury paste of seasoned and spiced meat, fish, etc.

pâté de foie gras /ˌpatay də ˌfwah 'grah/ *n* pâté made from the liver of a specially fattened goose.

patella *n* (*pl* **patellae**) = KNEECAP[1]. ➤➤ **patellar** *adj*.

paten *n* a plate holding the bread used at Communion.

patent[1] *n* a formal document giving an inventor the exclusive right to make, use, or sell an invention for a specified period.

patent[2] *adj* **1** readily visible or intelligible; perfectly obvious. **2** protected by or made under a patent. ➤➤ **patency** *n*, **patently** *adv*.

patent[3] *v* to obtain a patent for (an invention). ➤➤ **patentable** *adj*.

patentee *n* somebody to whom a grant is made or a privilege secured by patent.

patent leather *n* a leather with a hard smooth glossy surface, used for shoes.

patent medicine *n* a medicine that is made and marketed under a patent or trademark.

pater *n Brit, dated, informal* an affectionate name for one's father.

paterfamilias *n* (*pl* **patresfamilias**) the male head of a household.

paternal *adj* **1** typical of or appropriate to a father. **2** related through one's father. ➤➤ **paternally** *adv*.

paternalism *n* a system under which a government or organization deals with its subjects or employees in an authoritarian but benevolent way. ➤➤ **paternalist** *n and adj*, **paternalistic** *adj*, **paternalistically** *adv*.

paternity *n* **1** being a father. **2** origin or descent from a father.

paternity suit *n chiefly NAm* a lawsuit brought to establish the paternity of a child.

paternity test *n* the comparison of the genetic attributes of a mother, a child, and a man to determine whether the man could be the child's father.

paternoster *n* (*often* **Paternoster**) the Lord's Prayer, *esp* in Latin, or the recital of this in the Roman Catholic Church.

path *n* **1** a track made for walking on or worn by walking. **2** a course or route: *the path of a planet.* **3** in computing, the route taken by an operating system when searching through directories to locate a file. ➤➤ **pathless** *adj*.

path- *or* **patho-** *comb. form* denoting pathological state or disease: *pathogen.*

-path *comb. form* **1** a practitioner of the system of medicine specified: *naturopath.* **2** a sufferer from a disorder affecting a particular part: *psychopath.*

Pathan *n* a member of a people of NW Pakistan and SE Afghanistan.

path-breaking *adj* introducing new methods or ideas; pioneering.

pathetic *adj* **1a** arousing pity; pitiful. **b** *informal* contemptible or inadequate. **2** *archaic* of the emotions. ➤➤ **pathetically** *adv*.

pathetic fallacy *n* the attribution of human characteristics or feelings to animals or inanimate nature, e.g. in *the cruel sea.*

pathfinder *n* **1** somebody who travels through unexplored regions to mark out a new route. **2** somebody who makes a discovery, e.g. in a field of knowledge.

pathname *n* in computing, the full description of the location of a file in a hierarchical filing system.

patho- *comb. form* see PATH-.

pathogen *n* a bacterium, virus, or other disease-causing agent. ➤➤ **pathogenic** *adj,* **pathogenicity** *n.*

pathological (*NAm* **pathologic**) *adj* **1** altered or caused by disease. **2** *informal* irrationally habitual. **3** of pathology. ➤➤ **pathologically** *adv.*

pathology *n* **1** the study of the essential nature of diseases, *esp* their causes and the changes that they produce. **2** the anatomical and physiological abnormalities that characterize a particular disease. ➤➤ **pathologist** *n.*

pathos *n* **1** a quality in artistic representation, etc evoking pity or compassion. **2** an emotion of sympathetic pity.

pathway *n* **1** a path, course, or progression. **2** a sequence of biochemical reactions occurring in a living cell.

-pathy *comb. form* **1** feeling or being acted upon: *empathy; telepathy.* **2** a disorder of a particular part or system: *neuropathy.* **3** a system of medicine based on a particular factor: *osteopathy.*

patience *n* **1** the capacity to bear pains or trials without complaint. **2** *chiefly Brit* a card game played by one person that involves the arranging of cards into a prescribed pattern.

patient[1] *adj* calm and forbearing. ➤➤ **patiently** *adv.*

patient[2] *n* a person awaiting or receiving medical care.

patina *n* **1** a green or brown film formed on copper and bronze by weathering or simulated weathering and valued as aesthetically pleasing. **2** a surface appearance of polished wood that has grown more beautiful with age.

patio *n* (*pl* **-os**) **1** a paved area adjoining a dwelling. **2** an open inner court characteristic of dwellings in Spain or Latin America.

patio door *n* (*usu in pl*) a glass door leading to a patio or balcony.

patisserie *n* **1** an establishment where pastries and cakes are sold. **2** pastries and cakes.

Patna rice *n* a long-grained rice suitable for use in savoury dishes.

patois *n* (*pl* **patois**) **1** a provincial dialect other than the standard or literary dialect. **2** the jargon of a particular group.

patr- *or* **patro-** *comb. form* father: *patronymic.*

patresfamilias *n* pl of PATERFAMILIAS.

patriarch *n* **1a** a man who is head of a patriarchy. **b** any of the biblical fathers of the human race or of the Hebrew people. **c** a venerable old man. **2a** a bishop in various Orthodox and Eastern churches. **b** a Roman Catholic bishop next in rank to the pope. ➤➤ **patriarchal** *adj.*

patriarchate *n* the office or jurisdiction of a patriarch.

patriarchy *n* (*pl* **-ies**) **1** a system of social organization marked by the supremacy of the father in the clan or family and the reckoning of descent in the male line. **2** a society governed by men.

patrician *n* **1** a person of high birth; an aristocrat. **2** a member of any of the original citizen families of ancient Rome. ➤➤ **patrician** *adj.*

patricide *n* **1** the act of killing one's father. **2** somebody who commits patricide. ➤➤ **patricidal** *adj.*

patrilineal *adj* relating to or tracing descent through the paternal line.

patrimony *n* (*pl* **-ies**) **1** property inherited from one's father or male ancestor. **2** something derived from one's ancestors; heritage. ➤➤ **patrimonial** *adj.*

patriot *n* a person who zealously supports their country. ➤➤ **patriotic** *adj,* **patriotically** *adv,* **patriotism** *n.*

patristic *or* **patristical** *adj* of the fathers of the early Christian Church, or their writings.

patro- *comb. form* see PATR-.

patrol[1] *n* **1** a person or group sent to move around a district, garrison, etc for observation or the maintenance of security. **2** the action of patrolling a district, etc. **3** a reconnaissance, security, or combat mission, or the people employed on such a mission. **4** a subdivision of a Scout troop or Guide company that has six to eight members.

patrol[2] *v* (**patrolled, patrolling**) to carry out a patrol of (an area). ➤➤ **patroller** *n.*

patrolman *n* (*pl* **patrolmen**) *NAm* a police officer assigned to a beat.

patrol wagon *n NAm, Aus, NZ* an enclosed van used by police to carry prisoners.

patron *n* **1** a person who uses wealth or influence to help an individual, institution, or cause. **2** a regular customer of a pub, restaurant, etc.

patronage *n* **1** the support or influence of a patron. **2** the power to control appointments to government jobs or the right to privileges. **3** the granting of favours in a condescending way. **4** the business that the patrons of an establishment or service provide.

patroness *n* **1** a woman who uses wealth or influence to help an individual, institution, or cause. **2** a woman who is chosen, named, or honoured as a special guardian, protector, or supporter.

patronize *or* **-ise** *v* **1** to adopt an air of condescension towards (somebody). **2** to be a patron of. ➤➤ **patronizer** *n,* **patronizing** *adj,* **patronizingly** *adv.*

patron saint *n* a saint regarded as protecting a particular person, group, etc.

patronymic *n* a name derived from that of the bearer's father or paternal ancestor, usu by the addition of an affix.

patsy *n* (*pl* **-ies**) *chiefly NAm, informal* a person who is duped or victimized.

patten *n* a sandal or overshoe set on a wooden sole or metal device to elevate the foot, worn formerly to keep one's feet out of the mud.

patter[1] *v* **1** to strike or tap rapidly and repeatedly. **2** to run with quick light steps.

patter[2] *n* a quick succession of taps or pats.

patter[3] *n* **1** rapid glib talk, as used by an entertainer or street hawker. **2** the jargon of a profession or group, *esp* criminal jargon.

patter[4] *v* to talk glibly and volubly.

pattern[1] *n* **1** a repeated decorative design. **2** a natural or chance arrangement or sequence. **3** a design, model, or set of instructions for making things. **4** a model for making a mould into which molten metal is poured to form a casting. **5** a model proposed for imitation; an example. **6** a specimen, e.g. of wallpaper.

pattern[2] *v* **1** to decorate with a design. **2** (+ on/after) to make or model (something) according to a pattern.

patty *n* (*pl* **-ies**) **1** a small flat cake of chopped food. **2** a little pie or pasty.

paua *n* **1** a shellfish with a rainbow-coloured shell. **2** a fishhook made from a paua shell.

paucity *n* smallness of number or quantity.

paunch *n* a large or protruding belly. ⋙ **paunchiness** *n*, **paunchy** *adj*.

pauper *n* **1** a very poor person. **2** formerly, somebody supported by charity or from public funds. ⋙ **pauperism** *n*.

pauperize *or* **-ise** *v* to reduce to poverty or destitution. ⋙ **pauperization** *n*.

pause[1] *n* **1** a temporary stop or inaction. **2** the sign denoting the lengthening of a musical note or rest. **3** a mechanism on a video or tape recorder that causes the tape to stop for a short time during playing or recording. ✱ **give one pause** to make one hesitate.

pause[2] *v* **1** to stop or cause to stop temporarily. **2** to linger for a time.

pavane *or* **pavan** *n* a stately court dance introduced into England in the 16th cent.

pave *v* to cover (a piece of ground) with stone or concrete, to form a firm level surface for walking or travelling on. ✱ **pave the way for** to prepare a smooth easy way for. ⋙ **paver** *n*, **paving** *n*.

pavement *n* **1** *Brit* a surfaced raised walk for pedestrians at the side of a road. **2** *NAm* the artificially covered surface of a road. **3** in geology, a level area of bare rock.

pavement artist *n Brit* a person who draws coloured pictures on the pavement in the hope of getting money from passers-by.

pavilion *n* **1** *Brit* a permanent building on a sports ground containing changing rooms and seats for spectators. **2a** a light ornamental structure in a garden or park. **b** a temporary structure for an individual exhibitor at an exhibition. **c** a large sumptuous tent.

pavlova *n* a dessert made of meringue topped with cream and fruit.

Pavlovian *adj* of a reaction: produced automatically in response to a stimulus.

paw[1] *n* **1** the clawed, padded foot of a lion, dog, or other animal. **2** *informal* a human hand.

paw[2] *v* **1** *informal* to touch (somebody) clumsily or indecently. **2** to touch, scrape, or strike at (something) with a paw or hoof.

pawky *adj* (**-ier, -iest**) *chiefly Scot, N Eng* having a dry wit; sardonic. ⋙ **pawkily** *adv*, **pawkiness** *n*.

pawl *n* a pivoted tongue or sliding bolt on one part of a machine that is adapted to fall into notches on another part so as to permit motion in only one direction.

pawn[1] *n* **1** in chess, any of eight pieces of each colour of least value. **2** somebody who can be used to further the purposes of somebody else.

pawn[2] *v* to deposit (something) with a pawnbroker as security.

pawn[3] *n* the state of being pledged.

pawnbroker *n* a person who lends money on the security of personal property pledged, which can be sold if the money is not repaid. ⋙ **pawnbroking** *n*.

Pawnee *n* (*pl* **Pawnee**) a member of a Native American people formerly living in Nebraska, but now mainly in Oklahoma.

pawnshop *n* a pawnbroker's shop.

pawpaw *or* **papaw** *n* **1** = PAPAYA. **2** a yellow edible fruit.

pax *n* = KISS OF PEACE.

pay[1] *v* (*past and past part.* **paid**) **1** to give money due to (somebody) for goods or services received. **2a** to give (wages or a salary) in return for goods or services. **b** to discharge a debt or obligation for (a bill or account). **3** to give or forfeit (something) in reparation or retribution. **4** to give or offer (attention, one's respects, etc). **5** to make (a visit). **6** to make amends or be punished. ✱ **pay court to** to flatter. **pay through the nose** see NOSE[1]. ⋙ **payee** *n*, **payer** *n*.

pay[2] *n* money paid as a salary or wage. ✱ **in the pay of** employed by.

pay back *v* **1** to repay (money owed). **2** to get revenge on.

paybed *n* in Britain, a hospital bed in a National Health Service hospital which is paid for by the occupant.

pay channel *n* a television channel paid for separately by the viewer.

PAYE *abbr Brit* pay as you earn, a system of deducting income tax from pay before an employee receives it.

payee *n* a person receiving payment, e.g. somebody to whom a cheque is made out.

paying guest *n* a lodger.

payload *n* **1** the revenue-producing load that a vehicle can carry. **2** the explosive charge carried in the warhead of a missile. **3** the load carried in a spacecraft that relates directly to the purpose of the flight.

paymaster *n* **1** an officer or agent whose duty it is to pay salaries or wages. **2** a person or organization employing and controlling somebody.

paymaster general *n* (*pl* **paymasters general** *or* **paymaster generals**) (*often* **Paymaster General**) a British government minister, orig in charge of payments, who is often made a member of the cabinet and entrusted with special functions.

payment *n* **1** the act of paying. **2** something that is paid. **3** a reward or punishment.

payoff *n informal* **1** a profit or reward, *esp* received by a player in a game. **2** a decisive factor resolving a situation or bringing about a definitive conclusion. **3** the denouement of a narrative.

pay off *v* **1** to give all that is due to (somebody), *esp* when discharging an employee. **2** to pay (a debt or a creditor) in full. **3** to bribe (somebody). **4** *informal* to be successful or profitable.

payola *n chiefly NAm* an undercover or indirect payment for unofficial promotion of a commercial product.

pay out *v* **1** to give out or disburse (money). **2** to slacken (a rope) and allow it to run out gradually.

pay-per-view *n* a service offered by cable or satellite television companies by which subscribers pay an additional fee to watch a particular programme.

payphone *n* a public telephone that is operated by coins or a phonecard.

payroll *n* a list of those entitled to be paid by a company and of the amounts due to each.

pay TV *n* a television broadcasting system in which viewers pay a subscription to watch a particular channel.

pay up *v* to pay (money owed) in full or on demand.

PB *abbr* in athletics, personal best.

Pb *abbr* the chemical symbol for lead.

pb *abbr* paperback.

PBS *abbr NAm* Public Broadcasting Service.

PC *abbr* **1** personal computer. **2** police constable. **3** political correctness. **4** politically correct.

pc *abbr* **1** per cent. **2** postcard.

PCB *abbr* **1** polychlorinated biphenyl. **2** printed circuit board.

PCP *abbr* **1** phencyclidine. **2** pneumocystis carinii pneumonia.

PCV *abbr Brit* passenger-carrying vehicle.

PD *abbr NAm* police department.

Pd *abbr* the chemical symbol for palladium.

PDQ *adv informal* immediately.

PDSA *abbr Brit* People's Dispensary for Sick Animals.

PDT *abbr* Pacific daylight time.

PE *abbr* physical education.

pea *n* **1** the rounded green seed of a leguminous climbing plant used as a vegetable. **2** (*in pl*) the immature pods of the pea with their seeds.

pea-brain *n informal* a stupid person. ➤➤ **pea-brained** *adj.*

peace *n* **1 a** freedom from civil disturbance. **b** public order and security maintained by law or custom. **2a** mutual concord between countries. **b** an agreement to end hostilities. **3** freedom from disquieting thoughts or emotions. **4** harmony in personal relations. ✱ **at peace 1** in a state of concord or tranquillity. **2** *euphem* dead. **hold one's peace** to remain silent in spite of having something to say. **keep the peace** to avoid or prevent discord.

peaceable *adj* **1** not inclined to dispute or quarrel. **2** free from strife or disorder. ➤➤ **peaceableness** *n,* **peaceably** *adv.*

peace corps *n* a body of trained volunteer personnel sent by the US government to assist developing nations.

peace dividend *n* the money saved on armaments that is available for other purposes when a nation reduces its military capacity.

peaceful *adj* **1** untroubled by conflict or commotion; tranquil. **2** devoid of violence or force. **3** not inclined to dispute or quarrel. ➤➤ **peacefully** *adv,* **peacefulness** *n.*

peacekeeping *n* the preserving of peace; *esp* international enforcement of a truce between hostile states or communities. ➤➤ **peacekeeper** *n.*

peacenik *n informal* a pacifist, *esp* one who is a political activist.

peace offering *n* **1** something given or done to produce peace or reconciliation. **2** in the Bible, an offering to God.

peace pipe *n* = CALUMET.

peace sign *n* a sign made by holding the palm outwards and forming a V with the index and middle fingers, used to indicate the desire for peace.

peacetime *n* **1** a time when a nation is not at war. **2** (*used before a noun*) relating to a time of peace.

peach[1] *n* **1** a fruit with downy skin and sweet yellow flesh. **2** a light yellowish pink colour. **3** *informal* a particularly excellent person or thing. ✱ **peaches and cream** of a complexion: clear and pale, with pink cheeks. ➤➤ **peach** *adj,* **peachy** *adj.*

peach[2] *v informal* to turn informer.

peach Melba *n* a dish of peaches topped with ice cream and raspberry purée.

peacock *n* **1** a male peafowl with very large tail feathers with eyelike spots that can be erected and spread in a fan. **2** a peafowl.

peacock blue *adj* of a lustrous greenish blue colour. ➤➤ **peacock blue** *n.*

peacock butterfly *n* a butterfly with large eyespots on the wings.

peafowl *n* a very large ornamental pheasant.

pea green *adj* of a light yellowish green colour. ➤➤ **pea green** *n.*

peahen *n* a female peafowl.

pea jacket *n* a heavy woollen double-breasted jacket formerly worn by sailors.

peak[1] *n* **1** the top of a mountain ending in a point, or a mountain with a pointed top. **2** a projecting part on the front of a cap. **3a** a high point in a course of development. **b** the highest level or greatest degree. ➤➤ **peaked** *adj.*

peak[2] *v* to reach a maximum or high point.

peak load *n* maximum demand or density, e.g. of electricity or traffic.

peak time *n* the time of greatest demand for a service, e.g. television programmes.

peaky *or* **peaked** *adj* (**-ier, -iest**) looking pale and wan.

peal[1] *n* **1** the loud ringing of bells. **2** a set of bells tuned to the notes of the major scale for change ringing. **3** a loud prolonged sound.

peal[2] *v* **1** of bells: to ring loudly. **2** of laughter or thunder: to sound in a peal. **3** to utter or sound (something) sonorously.

peanut *n* **1** the pod or oily edible seed of a leguminous plant. **2** *informal* (*in pl*) a trifling amount of money.

peanut butter *n* a spread made from ground peanuts.

pear *n* a yellowish brown fruit, which widens at the end furthest from the stalk.

pearl[1] *n* **1a** a milky-white, lustrous mass of mother-of-pearl layers, formed in the shell of some molluscs, *esp* oysters, and used as a gem. **b** an artificial imitation of this. **c** = MOTHER-OF-PEARL. **2** something very rare or precious. **3** a slightly bluish grey or white colour. ➤➤ **pearl** *adj.*

pearl[2] *v* **1** to set or adorn with pearls. **2** *literary* to form drops or beads like pearls. **3** to fish or search for pearls.

pearl[3] *n Brit* = PICOT.

pearl barley *n* barley that has been ground into medium-sized grains.

pearlescent *adj* having a pearly finish.

pearlized *or* **-ised** *adj* given a pearly surface or finish.

pearl onion *n* a very small white onion often eaten pickled.

pearly[1] *adj* (**-ier, -iest**) resembling or decorated with pearls or mother-of-pearl. ➤➤ **pearliness** *n.*

pearly[2] *n* (*pl* **-ies**) *Brit* **1** (*in pl*) the clothes worn by a pearly king or queen, or the buttons used to decorate these clothes. **2** *informal* (*in pl*) teeth.

Pearly Gates *pl n informal* the gates of heaven.

pearly king *or* **pearly queen** *n* a man or woman who is a member of a family of London costermongers who traditionally wear clothes covered with pearl buttons on ceremonial occasions.

pearmain *n* a pear-shaped eating apple.

pear-shaped *adj* having a figure with wide hips and a narrow upper part. ✱ **go pear-shaped** *Brit, informal* to go wrong.

peasant *n* **1** a small landowner or farm labourer. **2** *informal* an uneducated or rude person. ➤➤ **peasantry** *n.*

pease *n archaic* a pea.

pease pudding *n chiefly Brit* a puree of boiled split peas.

peashooter *n* a toy blowpipe for shooting peas.

pea-souper *n Brit, informal* a heavy yellowish fog.

peat *n* partially carbonized vegetable tissue formed by partial decomposition in water of plants found in large bogs, which is used as a fuel and a fertilizer. ⋙ **peaty** *adj.*

peat moss *n* **1** = SPHAGNUM. **2** a peat bog.

peau-de-soie /pohdəswah/ *n* a smooth silk or rayon fabric with a finely ribbed surface.

pebble *n* **1** a small rounded stone, worn smooth by the action of water or sand. **2** = ROCK CRYSTAL. **3** *informal* (*used before a noun*) very thick: *pebble lenses.* ⋙ **pebbly** *adj.*

pebbledash *n chiefly Brit* a finish for exterior walls consisting of small pebbles embedded in a stucco base. ⋙ **pebbledashed** *adj.*

pec *n informal* (*usu in pl*) a pectoral muscle.

pecan *n* a smooth oblong edible nut.

peccadillo *n* (*pl* **-oes** *or* **-os**) a slight or trifling offence.

peccant *adj archaic* **1** guilty or sinning. **2** producing disease. ⋙ **peccancy** *n.*

peccary *n* (*pl* **-ies**) a mammal resembling the related pigs.

peck[1] *v* **1** to strike or pierce (something) with the beak or a pointed tool. **2** to make (a hole) by pecking. **3** to kiss (somebody) perfunctorily. **4** *informal* to eat reluctantly and in small bites.

peck[2] *n* **1** an impression or hole made by pecking. **2** a quick sharp stroke. **3** a light kiss.

peck[3] *n* **1** a unit of volume or capacity equal to 2gall (9.092l). **2** *archaic* a large quantity: *a peck of troubles.*

pecker *n NAm, coarse slang* a penis. ✱ **keep one's pecker up** *Brit, informal* to stay cheerful in the face of adversity [from an earlier meaning 'courage'].

pecking order *n* **1** the natural hierarchy within a flock of birds, *esp* poultry, in which each bird pecks another lower in the scale without fear of retaliation. **2** a social hierarchy.

peckish *adj chiefly Brit, informal* slightly hungry.

pecorino *n* an Italian cheese made from sheep's milk.

pecten *n* (*pl* **pectines** *or* **pectens**) **1** a body part that resembles a comb. **2** a scallop.

pectin *n* a water-soluble substance that binds adjacent cell walls in plant tissues and yields a gel that acts as a setting agent in jams and jellies. ⋙ **pectic** *adj.*

pectines *n* pl of PECTEN.

pectoral[1] *adj* relating to or in the region of the chest.

pectoral[2] *n* **1** a pectoral muscle. **2** a breastplate worn on the chest.

pectoral muscle *n* any of the muscles connecting the front walls of the chest with the bones of the upper arm and shoulder.

peculiar[1] *adj* **1** different from the usual or normal; strange. **2** (+ to) belonging exclusively to. **3** *formal* special or distinctive. ⋙ **peculiarly** *adv.*

peculiar[2] *n chiefly Brit* a church or parish independent of the diocese in which it is situated.

peculiarity *n* (*pl* **-ies**) **1** a distinguishing characteristic. **2** the state of being peculiar.

pecuniary *adj formal* of or measured in money. ⋙ **pecuniarily** *adv.*

-ped *or* **-pede** *comb. form* forming nouns, denoting: a foot or feet: *quadruped.*

pedagogics *pl n dated* (*used as sing. or pl*) pedagogy. ⋙ **pedagogic** *adj,* **pedagogical** *adj,* **pedagogically** *adv.*

pedagogue *n formal or humorous* a teacher.

pedagogy *n* (*pl* **-ies**) the science, profession, or theory of teaching.

pedal[1] *n* **1** a lever operated by the foot, *esp* on a bicycle or in a motor vehicle. **2** a lever pressed by the foot in playing a musical instrument. **3** = PEDAL-NOTE (2).

pedal[2] *v* (**pedalled, pedalling,** *NAm* **pedaled, pedaling**) to work the pedals of (a bicycle, piano, etc). ⋙ **pedaller** *n.*

pedal[3] *adj* relating to or in the region of the foot or feet.

pedal-note *n* **1** any of the lowest notes that can be sounded on a brass instrument. **2** a single note that is normally sustained in the bass and sounds against changing harmonies in the other parts.

pedalo *n* (*pl* **-os** *or* **-oes**) *Brit* a small pleasure boat that is propelled by paddles turned by pedals.

pedal pushers *pl n* calf-length trousers worn by women and girls.

pedant *n* a person who is unnecessarily concerned with detail, *esp* in the presentation or use of knowledge. ⋙ **pedantic** *adj,* **pedantically** *adv,* **pedantry** *n.*

peddle *v* **1a** to sell (goods) as a pedlar. **b** to sell (illegal drugs). **2** *derog* to seek to disseminate (ideas or opinions).

peddler *n* a person who peddles something.

-pede *comb. form* see -PED.

pederast *or* **paederast** *n* a man who has sexual intercourse with a boy. ⋙ **pederastic** *adj.*

pederasty *or* **paederasty** *n* sexual intercourse between a man and a boy.

pedestal *n* **1a** a base supporting a column. **b** the base of a statue. **2** a supporting column of a washbasin or a toilet. **3** a position of esteem or idealized respect: *He put his wife on a pedestal.*

pedestrian[1] *n* a person going on foot.

pedestrian[2] *adj* commonplace. ⋙ **pedestrianly** *adv.*

pedestrianize *or* **-ise** *v* to convert (a street or an area) to a paved area for pedestrians only. ⋙ **pedestrianization** *n.*

pedicel *n* **1** a plant stalk that supports a fruiting or spore-bearing organ. **2** the narrow stalk joining a spider's abdomen to the rest of its body. ⋙ **pedicellate** *adj.*

pedicle *n* **1** = PEDICEL. **2** part of a skin graft that is still attached to its original site.

pedicure *n* a treatment for the care of the feet and toenails.

pedigree *n* **1** the recorded purity of breed of an animal. **2** a person's ancestral line, *esp* a distinguished one. **3** the origin and history of something. **4** (*used before a noun*) of or producing pedigree animals: *a pedigree dog.* ⋙ **pedigreed** *adj.*

pediment *n* the triangular piece of wall in the angle formed by the two slopes of a roof in classical architecture. ⋙ **pedimental** *adj,* **pedimented** *adj.*

pedlar (*NAm* **peddler**) *n* a person who travels about offering small wares for sale.

pedo- *comb. form NAm* see PAEDO-.

pedometer *n* an instrument that records the distance a walker covers by responding to body motion at each step.

peduncle *n* **1** a stalk bearing a flower or fruit. **2** a narrow stalklike part by which some larger part or the whole body of an organism is attached. ⋙ **peduncular** *adj,* **pedunculate** *adj.*

pee[1] *v informal* to urinate.

pee[2] *n informal* **1** an act of urinating. **2** urine.

peek[1] *v* **1** to take a brief look. **2** to stick up or out, so as to be just visible.

peek[2] *n* a brief or furtive look; a glance.

peekaboo[1] *or* **peek-a-boo** *n* a game for amusing a baby in which one repeatedly hides and comes back into view.

peekaboo[2] *adj* **1** of a garment: trimmed with eyelet embroidery or made from sheer fabric. **2** of a hairstyle: having a fringe that covers one eye.

peel[1] *v* **1** to strip off an outer layer of (e.g. a fruit or vegetable). **2** to remove (something) by stripping it. **3** to lose an outer layer, e.g. of skin.

peel[2] *n* the skin or rind of a fruit or vegetable.

peel[3] *or* **pele** *n* a small fortified tower built in the 16th cent. along the Scottish–English border.

peeler[1] *n* a knife or other utensil for peeling fruit or vegetables.

peeler[2] *n Brit, informal, archaic* a policeman.

peeling *n* (*usu in pl*) a strip of skin, rind, etc that has been stripped off a vegetable or fruit.

peel off *v* **1** to remove (something) or come off by peeling. **2** *Brit* to take off one's clothes. **3** to break away from a group or formation, e.g. of marchers or aircraft.

peen[1] *or* **pein** *n* the hemispherical or wedge-shaped end of the head of a hammer that is opposite the face.

peen[2] *or* **pein** *v* to hammer (something) with a peen.

peep[1] *v* **1** to look cautiously or slyly. **2** (*often* + out) to begin to emerge from concealment.

peep[2] *n* **1** a brief or furtive look. **2** the first faint appearance of something.

peep[3] *v* **1** to make a feeble shrill sound. **2** to utter the slightest sound. ➤➤ **peep** *n.*

peeper *n* **1** somebody who peeps. **2** *informal* (*usu in pl*) an eye.

peephole *n* a hole in a door through which callers can be observed.

Peeping Tom *n* a voyeur.

peep show *n* an erotic or pornographic film or object, e.g. a small painting, viewed through a small opening or a magnifying glass.

peepul *n* see PIPAL.

peer[1] *v* **1** to look searchingly at something difficult to discern. **2** to be partially visible.

peer[2] *n* **1** a duke, marquess, earl, viscount, or baron of the British peerage. **2** a person who belongs to the same group in society as another, as determined by age, grade, or status. ✱ **without peer** unequalled.

peerage *n* **1** the rank or title of a peer. **2** (**the peerage**) (*used as sing. or pl*) the body of peers.

peeress *n* **1** a woman having the rank of a peer. **2** the wife or widow of a peer.

peer group *n* a group of people of approximately the same age or status.

peerless *adj* matchless or incomparable. ➤➤ **peerlessly** *adv.*

peeve[1] *v informal* to make peevish or resentful; to annoy.

peeve[2] *n informal* a grievance or grudge.

peevish *adj* querulous or fretful. ➤➤ **peevishly** *adv,* **peevishness** *n.*

peewee *n* see PEWEE.

peewit *or* **pewit** *n Brit* the lapwing.

peg[1] *n* **1** a small pointed or tapered piece of wood, metal, or plastic used to pin down or fasten things. **2** *Brit* a clothes peg. **3** a projecting piece used to hold or support something: *He hung his hat on the peg in the hall.* **4** a predetermined level at which something, e.g. a price, is fixed. **5** *informal* a person's leg. **6** *Brit* a drink, *esp* of spirits. ✱ **off the peg** *chiefly Brit* of clothes: ready-made. **square peg in a round hole** see SQUARE[2]. **take somebody down a peg or two** to reduce somebody's sense of self-importance.

peg[2] *v* (**pegged, pegging**) **1** to fix or mark with pegs. **2** to fix or hold (prices, etc) at a predetermined level.

peg away *v informal* (*often* + at) to work hard and steadily at something.

pegboard *n* a board with holes into which hooks or pegs may be inserted for the storage or display of articles.

peg leg *n informal* an artificial leg.

pegmatite *n* a coarse granite occurring as dykes or veins.

peg out *v chiefly Brit, informal* to die.

peignoir *n* a woman's loose negligee.

pein[1] *n* see PEEN[1].

pein[2] *v* see PEEN[2].

pejorative *adj* expressing criticism; disparaging. ➤➤ **pejoratively** *adv.*

peke *n* (*often* **Peke**) *informal* = PEKINGESE (1).

Pekinese *n* see PEKINGESE.

Peking duck *n* a Chinese dish of crispy roast duck usu served with thin pancakes, spring onions, and plum sauce.

Pekingese *or* **Pekinese** *n* (*pl* **Pekingese** *or* **Pekinese**) **1** a dog of a breed with a broad flat face and a long thick soft coat. **2a** a native or inhabitant of Beijing (formerly Peking). **b** the dialect of Mandarin Chinese spoken in Beijing. ➤➤ **Pekingese** *adj.*

pekoe *n* a black tea of superior quality.

pelage *n* the hairy covering of a mammal.

pelagic *adj* **1** of the open sea. **2** of fish: living at or above moderate depths in the sea: compare DEMERSAL.

pelargonium *n* a plant of the geranium family with showy red, pink, or white flowers.

pele *n* see PEEL[3].

pelf *n archaic* money or riches.

pelican *n* a bird with a very large bill containing a pouch that can be distended for catching and keeping fish.

pelican crossing *n* in Britain, a crossing at which the movement of vehicles and pedestrians is controlled by pedestrian-operated traffic lights.

pelisse *n* **1** an early 19th-cent. full-length frock-coat for women. **2** a long cloak lined or trimmed with fur; *esp* one formerly part of a hussar's uniform.

pellagra *n* a disease associated with a deficiency of nicotinic acid in the diet, marked by inflammation and flaking of the skin, diarrhoea, and disorders of the central nervous system.

pellet[1] *n* **1** a small rounded body of food or medicine. **2** a piece of small shot. **3** a mass of undigested food regurgitated by a bird of prey.

pellet[2] *v* (**pelleting, pelleted**) **1** to form or compact (something) into pellets. **2** to strike with pellets, or as if with pellets.

pellicle *n technical* a thin skin or film, e.g. the outer layer of a single-celled organism, or a growth of bacteria on the surface of a liquid culture.

pell-mell *adv and adj* in confusion or disorder.

pellucid *adj* **1** clear or transparent. **2** easy to understand.

Pelmanism *n* **1** a system of memory training. **2** (*often* **pelmanism**) a card game in which players try to turn up pairs of playing cards spread at random face down on a table.

pelmet *n* a length of board or fabric placed above a window to conceal curtain fixtures.

pelota *n* a Spanish or Latin-American court game.

peloton *n* the main group of riders in a cycle race.

pelt[1] *v* **1** to strike with or to throw missiles. **2** of rain, etc: to fall heavily and continuously. **3** to run fast.

pelt[2] *n archaic* speed or force. ✱ **(at) full pelt** with great speed.

pelt[3] *n* **1** an undressed animal skin with its hair, wool, or fur. **2** an animal skin stripped of hair or wool before tanning.

peltate *adj* of a leaf: shaped like a shield.

peltry *n* animal pelts.

pelves *n* pl of PELVIS.

pelvic *adj* relating to or in the region of the pelvis.

pelvic girdle *n* the bony or cartilaginous arch that supports the hind limbs of a vertebrate.

pelvic inflammatory disease *n* inflammation of the female reproductive organs, characterized by lower abdominal pain and high fever.

pelvis *n* (*pl* **pelvises** *or* **pelves**) **1** a basin-shaped structure in the skeleton that is formed by the pelvic girdle and adjoining bones of the spine. **2** the funnel-shaped cavity of the kidney into which urine is discharged.

pemmican *or* **pemican** *n* a concentrated food of dried pounded meat mixed with melted fat traditionally made by Native Americans.

pemphigus *n* a disease characterized by large blisters on the skin.

pen[1] *n* **1** an implement for writing or drawing with. **2** (**the pen**) writing as an occupation. **3** an electronic device used with a computer, e.g. to enter data. **4** the horny feather-shaped internal shell of a squid.

pen[2] *v* (**penned, penning**) to write (something).

pen[3] *n* **1** a small enclosure for farm animals. **2** a small place of confinement or storage. **3** a heavily fortified dock for a submarine.

pen[4] *v* (**penned, penning**) to shut in a pen.

pen[5] *n* a female swan.

penal *adj* **1** relating to or prescribing punishment. **2** of an offence: liable to punishment. **3** harsh. ➤➤ **penally** *adv.*

penal code *n* a code of laws concerning crimes and their punishment.

penalize *or* **-ise** *v* **1** to inflict a penalty on. **2** to put at a serious disadvantage. **3** to declare (an act) punishable by law. ➤➤ **penalization** *n.*

penal servitude *n* a sentence of imprisonment with hard labour.

penalty *n* (*pl* **-ies**) **1** a punishment legally imposed for committing a crime. **2** a disadvantage imposed for violation of the rules of a sport. **3** a penalty kick. **4** disadvantage, loss, or suffering due to some action.

penalty area *or* **penalty box** *n* a rectangular area 40m (44yd) wide and 16m (18yd) deep in front of each goal on a football pitch.

penalty kick *n* a free kick at goal in football or rugby.

penalty shoot-out *n* in football, a method of deciding the winner of a drawn match, in which players from each team alternately try to score a goal with a penalty kick.

penalty spot *n* a spot 11m (12yd) in front of the goal on a football pitch, from which penalty kicks are taken.

penance *n* **1** an act of self-abasement performed to show repentance for sin. **2** a sacramental rite of the Roman Catholic, Orthodox, and some Anglican Churches involving confession and a penance directed by the confessor.

pence *n* pl of PENNY.

penchant *n* (*often* + for) a strong liking.

pencil[1] *n* **1** an implement for writing or drawing consisting of a slender strip of graphite. **2** a small medicated or cosmetic roll or stick for local applications.

pencil[2] *v* (**pencilled, pencilling,** *NAm* **penciled, penciling**) to draw or write (something) with a pencil. ✱ **pencil something in** to include an appointment, etc provisionally. ➤➤ **penciller** *n.*

pencil skirt *n* a narrow straight skirt.

pendant[1] *n* **1** an ornament hanging from a chain worn round the neck. **2** an electric light fitting suspended from the ceiling.

pendant[2] *adj* = PENDENT.

pendent *adj* **1** supported from above; suspended. **2** remaining undetermined; pending. ➤➤ **pendency** *n.*

pending[1] *prep* while awaiting; until.

pending[2] *adj* **1** not yet decided or dealt with. **2** imminent or impending.

pendulous *adj* suspended or hanging downwards.

pendulum *n* **1** a body suspended from a fixed point so as to swing freely, used to regulate movements, e.g. of clockwork. **2** something that changes regularly, *esp* going from one extreme to another.

peneplain *or* **peneplane** *n* an almost flat land surface shaped by erosion.

penes *n* pl of PENIS.

penetralia *pl n* the innermost or hidden parts of a place or thing.

penetrant *n* a substance that increases the penetration of a liquid, e.g. into porous material.

penetrate *v* **1a** to pass into or through. **b** to enter (an organization or a market), *esp* by overcoming resistance. **c** to insert the penis into the vagina or anus of (a sexual partner). **2a** to see into or through. **b** to discover the inner contents or meaning of. **3** to diffuse through or into. **4** to be understood. ➤➤ **penetrability** *n,* **penetrable** *adj,* **penetrator** *n.*

penetrating *adj* **1** having the power of entering or pervading. **2** acute or discerning. ➤➤ **penetratingly** *adv.*

penetration *n* **1** the act of penetrating. **2** the depth to which something penetrates. **3** the ability to discern deeply and acutely.

penetrative *adj* **1** able to pass into or through something. **2** of sexual activity: involving insertion of the penis into the vagina or anus of a partner.

penetrometer *n* an instrument for measuring firmness or consistency, e.g. of soil.

pen-friend *n chiefly Brit* a person with whom a friendship is made through correspondence.

penguin *n* a flightless aquatic bird of the southern hemisphere, with a dark back and white or pale belly, wings resembling flippers, and webbed feet.

penicillin *n* an antibiotic orig obtained from moulds, that is active against a wide range of bacteria.

penile *adj* relating to or in the region of the penis.

peninsula *n* a piece of land almost surrounded by water. ➤➤ **peninsular** *adj.*

penis *n* (*pl* **penises** *or* **penes**) the male organ of copulation by which semen is introduced into the female during coïtus, also used for urination.

penitent[1] *adj* feeling sorrow for sins or offences. ➤➤ **penitence** *n*, **penitently** *adv*.

penitent[2] *n* **1** somebody who repents of sin. **2** in the Roman Catholic Church, somebody under church censure but admitted to penance, *esp* under the direction of a confessor.

penitential *adj* of penitence or penance. ➤➤ **penitentially** *adv*.

penitentiary *n* (*pl* **-ies**) **1** *NAm* a prison for people convicted of the more serious crimes. **2** an officer in some Roman Catholic dioceses vested with power from the bishop to absolve in certain special cases.

penknife *n* (*pl* **penknives**) a small pocketknife.

penlight *n* a small electric torch resembling a fountain pen.

penman *n* (*pl* **penmen**) **1** a professional copyist or scribe. **2** *dated* somebody with a specified quality or style of handwriting: *a poor penman*. **3** an author. ➤➤ **penmanship** *n*.

pen name *n* an author's pseudonym.

pennant *n* **1** any of various nautical flags used for identification or signalling. **2** a flag that tapers to a point or has a swallowtail.

penne *pl n* (*used as sing. or pl*) pasta in short tubes with diagonally cut ends.

penni /'peni/ *n* (*pl* **penniä** *or* **pennis**) a unit of currency in Finland, worth 100th of a markka.

penniless *adj* lacking money; poor. ➤➤ **pennilessness** *n*.

pennon *n* a long triangular or swallow-tailed streamer attached to the head of a lance as a knight's personal flag.

penny *n* (*pl* **-ies** *or* **pence**) **1a** a unit of currency in Britain and many other countries, worth 100th of a pound. **b** a bronze coin representing a former British monetary unit worth 240th of a pound. **2** *NAm, informal* a cent. **3** (*in negative contexts*) the least amount of money: *He didn't have a penny*. ✱ **the penny drops** *chiefly Brit, informal* the true meaning finally dawns [refers to coin-operated machines which worked only when a penny was put in and had dropped].

penny black *n* the first adhesive postage stamp, issued in Britain in 1840.

penny dreadful *n* formerly, a novel of violent adventure or crime orig costing a penny.

penny-farthing *n Brit* an early type of bicycle having a small rear wheel and a large front wheel.

penny-pinching *adj* mean or stingy. ➤➤ **penny-pincher** *n*, **penny-pinching** *n*.

pennyroyal *n* a mint with aromatic leaves.

pennyweight *n* a unit of troy weight equal to one twentieth of an ounce troy (about 1.56g).

penny whistle *n* a simple musical pipe with a whistle mouthpiece and finger holes.

pennywort *n* **1** a plant that grows on rocks and walls and has long spikes of flowers. **2** a marsh plant with small flowers and shiny round leaves.

pennyworth *n* **1** a penny's worth. **2** a small quantity; a modicum. ✱ **put in one's pennyworth** *Brit* to contribute to a discussion.

penology *n* a branch of criminology dealing with prison management and the treatment of offenders. ➤➤ **penological** *adj*, **penologist** *n*.

pen pal *n* a pen-friend.

pen pusher *n informal* a clerk.

pensile *adj* pendent or hanging.

pension[1] *n* **1** a fixed sum paid regularly to a person, e.g. following retirement or as compensation for a wage-earner's death. **2** a regular payment made, *esp* formerly, to somebody as patronage or as a reward for service. ➤➤ **pensionless** *adj*.

pension[2] *v* to pay a pension to. ➤➤ **pensionable** *adj*.

pension[3] /'ponhsyonh/ *n* a hotel or boarding house, *esp* in continental Europe.

pensioner *n* a person who receives a pension, *esp* an old-age pension.

pension off *v* to retire (somebody) from service with a pension.

pensive *adj* deeply thoughtful. ➤➤ **pensively** *adv*, **pensiveness** *n*.

penstemon *n* see PENTSTEMON.

penstock *n* **1** a sluice or gate for regulating a flow of water. **2** a conduit or pipe for conducting water to a hydroelectric station.

penta- *or* **pent-** *comb. form* **1** five: *pentahedron; pentode*. **2** containing five atoms, groups, or chemical equivalents in the molecular structure.

pentacle *n* a pentagram.

pentad *n* a group or series of five.

Pentagon *n* (**the Pentagon**) the US military establishment.

pentagon *n* a polygon with five angles and five sides. ➤➤ **pentagonal** *adj*.

pentagram *n* a five-pointed star used as a magical symbol.

pentahedron *n* (*pl* **pentahedrons** *or* **pentahedra**) a polyhedron of five faces. ➤➤ **pentahedral** *adj*.

pentameter *n* a line of verse consisting of five metrical feet.

pentane *n* a volatile liquid that is a member of the alkane series of organic chemical compounds and is obtained from petroleum.

pentangle *n* a pentagram.

pentaprism *n* a five-sided prism that gives a constant deviation of 90° to light from any direction.

Pentateuch *n* the first five books of the Old Testament: Genesis, Exodus, Leviticus, Numbers, and Deuteronomy.

pentathlete *n* an athlete who competes in the pentathlon.

pentathlon *n* **1** = MODERN PENTATHLON. **2** a women's athletic contest in which all contestants compete in the 100m hurdles, shot put, high jump, long jump, and 200m sprint.

pentatonic *adj* of or being a musical scale consisting of five tones.

Pentecost *n* **1** a Christian festival commemorating the descent of the Holy Spirit on the apostles observed on the seventh Sunday after Easter. **2** the Jewish festival of Shabuoth, observed on the 50th day after the second day of Passover.

Pentecostal *adj* **1** of evangelical Christian bodies that lay particular emphasis on the gifts of the Holy Spirit, e.g. speaking in tongues and healing. **2** of Pentecost. ➤➤ **Pentecostalism** *n*, **Pentecostalist** *adj and n*.

penthouse *n* **1** a dwelling on the roof or in the uppermost part of a building. **2** *archaic* a structure attached to and sloping from a wall or building.

pentimento /penti'mentoh/ *n* (*pl* **pentimenti** /-tee/) a reappearance in a painting of underlying work that has been painted over.

pentose *n* any of various monosaccharides, e.g. ribose, that contain five carbon atoms in the molecule.

pentstemon *or* **penstemon** *n* a plant with showy blue, purple, red, yellow, or white flowers.

pent-up *adj* confined or held in check.

penult *n* the next to the last syllable of a word.

penultimate[1] *adj* next to the last.

penultimate[2] *n* a penult.

penumbra *n* (*pl* **penumbrae** *or* **penumbras**) **1** a region of partial darkness, e.g. in an eclipse, in a shadow surrounding the umbra. **2** a less dark region surrounding the dark centre of a sunspot. ➤➤ **penumbral** *adj*.

penurious *adj formal* **1** very poor. **2** frugal. ➤➤ **penuriously** *adv*.

penury *n* severe poverty.

peon *n* **1** (*pl* **peones**) an agricultural labourer in Spanish America. **2** an Indian or Sri Lankan infantryman, orderly, or other worker.

peony *or* **paeony** *n* (*pl* **-ies** *or* **-ies**) a plant with very large showy red, pink, or white flowers.

people[1] *pl n* **1** human beings in general. **2** (*used with a possessive adjective*) the members of a family or kinship. **3** (**the people**) the mass of a community. **4** (**the people**) the citizens of a state who are qualified to vote. **5** (*used as sing. or pl*) a body of persons that are united by a common culture and that often constitute a politically organized group.

Usage note

people *or* **persons**? *People* is generally used as the plural of *person*: *one person*; *two people*. The form *persons* is reserved for formal or legal contexts: *committed by a person or persons unknown*.

people[2] *v* **1** to fill (a place) with people. **2** (*usu in passive*) to dwell in or inhabit (a place).

people carrier *n* a large motor car with three rows of seats.

people mover *n* a means of transporting people over short distances, e.g. a moving pavement in an airport.

pep[1] *n informal* energy or high spirits.

pep[2] *v* (**pepped, pepping**) (*usu* + up) to fill (somebody or something) with energy or enthusiasm.

peperoni *n* see PEPPERONI.

peplum *n* a short flounce attached to the waistline of a blouse, jacket, or dress.

pepper[1] *n* **1** a climbing shrub with aromatic leaves; *esp* one with berries from which black pepper and white pepper are prepared. **2** the ground black or white powder obtained from the peppercorns of this shrub. **3** a hot pepper or sweet pepper. ➤➤ **peppery** *adj*.

pepper[2] *v* **1** to season (food) with pepper. **2** to cover extensively with many instances of a thing. **3** to shower (somebody or something) with shot or other missiles.

pepper-and-salt *adj* of hair: having streaks of grey.

peppercorn *n* a dried berry of the pepper plant, used as a spice or ground as powder.

peppercorn rent *n Brit* a very small amount of money paid as a nominal rent.

peppermint *n* **1a** a mint with dark green tapering leaves and whorls of small pink flowers. **b** an aromatic essential oil obtained from this. **2** a sweet flavoured with peppermint oil. ➤➤ **pepperminty** *adj*.

pepperoni *or* **peperoni** *n* a spicy Italian beef and pork sausage.

pep pill *n informal* a tablet of a stimulant drug.

pepsin *n* an enzyme of the stomach that breaks down most proteins in an acid environment.

pep talk *n informal* a talk designed to encourage somebody.

peptic *adj* of or promoting digestion.

peptic ulcer *n* an ulcer caused by the action of pepsin and stomach acid on the mucous membranes of the digestive tract.

peptide *n* a short chain of two or more joined amino acids.

per *prep* **1** for each. **2** *archaic* by the means or agency of; through. ✱ **as per usual** *informal* as usual.

per- *prefix* **1a** through or throughout: *perambulate*; *pervade*. **b** thoroughly or very: *perfervid*; *perfect*. **2** containing a large proportion of a specified chemical element or group: *peroxide*.

peradventure[1] *adv archaic* perhaps or possibly.

peradventure[2] *n archaic* doubt or chance.

perambulate *v* **1** *formal* to travel through (a place) on foot. **2** *Brit* formerly, to walk round (e.g. a parish) to establish the boundaries. ➤➤ **perambulation** *n*, **perambulatory** *adj*.

per annum *adv* in or for each year.

percale *n* a closely woven cotton cloth used for clothing, sheeting, and industrial uses.

per capita *or* **per caput** *adv and adj* per unit of population; for each person.

perceive *v* **1** to become aware of (something) through the senses. **2** to regard as something specified. ➤➤ **perceivable** *adj*, **perceivably** *adv*, **perceiver** *n*.

per cent[1] *adv* in or for each hundred.

per cent[2] *n* (*pl* **per cent**) **1** one part in a hundred. **2** a percentage.

percentage *n* **1** a proportion expressed as per cent of a whole. **2** a share of winnings or profits. **3** any proportion of a whole.

percentile *n* **1** in statistics, any of 99 values in a FREQUENCY DISTRIBUTION that divides it into 100 parts, each containing 1% of the individuals or, items under consideration. **2** any of the 100 groups of individuals, items, etc comprising such a part or interval.

percept *n* a mental impression of a perceived object.

perceptible *adj* capable of being perceived by the senses. ➤➤ **perceptibility** *n*, **perceptibly** *adv*.

perception *n* **1** an awareness of one's surroundings that is produced by the operation of the senses. **2** a result of perceiving; an observation. **3** intuitive discernment; insight. ➤➤ **perceptional** *adj*.

perceptive *adj* exhibiting keen perception; observant or discerning. ➤➤ **perceptively** *adv*, **perceptiveness** *n*.

perceptual *adj* of perception, *esp* in relation to immediate sensory experience. ➤➤ **perceptually** *adv*.

perch[1] *n* **1** a roost for a bird. **2** a resting place or vantage point; a seat.

perch[2] *v* **1** to alight or settle, *esp* briefly or precariously. **2** to place on a perch, height, or precarious spot.

perch[3] *n* (*pl* **perches** *or* **perch**) a freshwater fish with vertical stripes and spiny fins.

perch[4] *n chiefly Brit* **1** a former unit of length equal to one quarter of a chain (about 5.029m). **2** a former unit of area equal to one hundred and sixtieth of an acre (about 25.29 square m).

perchance *adv archaic or literary* perhaps or possibly.

Percheron *n* a powerful draught horse of a breed that originated in the Perche region of France.

percipient[1] *adj* perceptive or discerning. ➤➤ **percipience** *n*, **percipiently** *adv*.

percipient[2] *n* somebody who is able to perceive things, *esp* somebody who is telepathic.

percolate *v* **1** of a liquid or gas: to pass through a porous substance, so that a soluble constituent is extracted. **2** to spread gradually through a group or area; to diffuse. **3** to prepare (coffee) in a percolator. **4** of coffee: to be prepared in a percolator. ➤➤ **percolation** *n*.

percolator *n* a coffee pot in which boiling water is deflected downward through a perforated basket containing ground coffee beans.

percuss *v* in medicine, to perform percussion on (a body part).

percussion *n* **1a** the beating or striking of a musical instrument. **b** percussion instruments that form a section of a band or orchestra. **2** in medicine, the tapping of the surface of a body part to learn the condition of the parts beneath by the resultant sound. ➤➤ **percussive** *adj*.

percussion cap *n* a small container containing an explosive charge, e.g. for a toy gun.

percussionist *n* a person who plays percussion instruments.

percutaneous *adj* in medicine, done or performed through the skin. ➤➤ **percutaneously** *adv*.

per diem *adj and adv* by the day or for each day.

perdition *n* in Christianity, eternal damnation; Hell.

père *n* used after the surname of a father to distinguish him from a son of the same name: *Clark père was an idler with a taste for expensive yachts* — Geoffrey Hulton.

peregrinate *v archaic or humorous* to walk.

peregrination *n archaic or humorous* a long and wandering journey. ➤➤ **peregrinator** *n*.

peregrine *or* **peregrine falcon** *n* a falcon with dark grey wings and back.

peremptory *adj* **1** characterized by imperious self-assurance. **2** expressive of urgency or command. **3** in law, admitting no contradiction. ➤➤ **peremptorily** *adv*, **peremptoriness** *n*.

perennial[1] *adj* **1** lasting throughout the year or for several years. **2** of a plant: living for several years, usu with new herbaceous growth each year: compare ANNUAL[1], BIENNIAL. **3** lasting for a long time or forever; constant. ➤➤ **perennially** *adv*.

perennial[2] *n* a plant living for more than two years.

perestroika *n* the restructuring of a system or organization; *esp* the political and social reform of the communist system of the former Soviet Union.

perfect[1] *adj* **1a** entirely without fault or defect; flawless. **b** satisfactory in every respect. **2** lacking in no essential detail; complete. **3** absolute or utter. **4** in grammar, of a verb tense or form that expresses an action or state completed at the time of speaking or at a time spoken of. **5** in mathematics, of an integer: equal to the sum of all the integers by which it can be divided without leaving a remainder, including 1 but excluding itself, e.g. 6 or 28. ➤➤ **perfectness** *n*.

perfect[2] *v* **1** to make perfect. **2** to bring to final form. ➤➤ **perfecter** *n*, **perfectibility** *n*, **perfectible** *adj*.

perfection *n* **1** making or being perfect. **2** unsurpassable accuracy or excellence, or an example of this.

perfectionism *n* **1** a disposition to regard anything short of perfection, *esp* in one's own work, as unacceptable. **2** the doctrine that a state of perfection is attainable. ➤➤ **perfectionist** *adj and n*.

perfectly *adv* **1** in a perfect manner. **2** to an adequate extent; quite.

perfect pitch *n* = ABSOLUTE PITCH (2).

perfervid *adj literary* particularly fervid; ardent.

perfidious *adj* faithless or disloyal; treacherous. ➤➤ **perfidiously** *adv*, **perfidiousness** *n*.

perfidy *n literary* faithlessness or disloyalty; treachery.

perforate *v* **1** to make a hole through (something). **2** to make a line of holes in or between (rows of postage stamps in a sheet, etc) to make separation easier. ➤➤ **perforated** *adj*, **perforation** *n*, **perforator** *n*.

perforce *adv formal* by force of circumstances; unavoidably.

perform *v* **1** to do or carry out. **2** to give a rendering of (a dramatic or musical piece). ➤➤ **performable** *adj*, **performer** *n*.

performance *n* **1** the act or an instance of performing. **2** a presentation to an audience of a play, a piece of music, etc. **3** the ability of a machine to work or operate. **4** *informal* **a** a lengthy or troublesome process. **b** a display of bad behaviour. ➤➤ **performatory** *adj*.

performance art *n* art which combines an element of theatre with visual or auditory elements. ➤➤ **performance artist** *n*.

performing arts *pl n* arts, e.g. music and drama, that are performed to an audience.

perfume[1] *n* **1** a pleasant-smelling liquid preparation worn on the skin. **2** a sweet or pleasant smell.

perfume[2] *v* **1** to imbue with a sweet smell. **2** to apply perfume to.

perfumery *n* (*pl* **-ies**) **1** the manufacture of perfumes. **2** a place where perfumes are made or sold. ➤➤ **perfumer** *n*.

perfunctory *adj* mechanical or cursory. ➤➤ **perfunctorily** *adv*.

perfuse *v* **1** to suffuse with a colour, liquid, etc. **2** in medicine, to force a fluid through (an organ or tissue), *esp* by way of the blood vessels. ➤➤ **perfusion** *n*, **perfusionist** *n*.

pergola *n* an arbour made by training plants over a trellis, or the trellis itself.

perhaps *adv* **1** possibly but not certainly; maybe. **2** used in polite requests: *Perhaps you would open the window.*

peri- *prefix* **1** round or about: *periscope*; *peripatetic*. **2** near: *perihelion*; *perigee*. **3** enclosing or surrounding: *perimeter*, *peritoneum*.

perianth *n* the external envelope of a flower.

pericardium *n* (*pl* **pericardia**) the membranous sac that surrounds the heart. ➤➤ **pericardial** *adj*.

pericarp *n* the structure that surrounds the seeds of a fruit and consists of the ripened and modified wall of a plant ovary.

peridot *n* a deep yellowish green transparent gem consisting of silicates of iron and magnesium.

perigee *n* the point nearest the earth reached by the moon or a satellite in its orbit: compare APOGEE (1).

perihelion *n* (*pl* **perihelia**) the point in the path of a planet, comet, etc that is nearest to the sun: compare APHELION.

peril *n* exposure to the risk of being injured, destroyed, or lost; danger. ➤➤ **perilous** *adj*, **perilously** *adv*, **perilousness** *n*.

perimeter *n* **1** the boundary of a closed plane figure. **2** the outer edge or limits of something. **3** an instrument used to measure field of vision. ⯮ **perimetric** *adj.*

perinatal *adj* relating to the time immediately before and after childbirth. ⯮ **perinatally** *adv.*

perineum *n* (*pl* **perinea**) the area between the anus and the back part of the genitals. ⯮ **perineal** *adj.*

period *n* **1** a portion of time. **2** a chronological division; a stage of history. **3** (*used before a noun*) of a particular historical period: *period costume*. **4** a division of geological time longer than an epoch and included in an era. **5** any of the divisions of the school day. **6** a single occurrence of menstruation. **7** *chiefly NAm* a full stop. **8** in physics, the interval of time that elapses before a phenomenon begins to repeat itself.

periodic *adj* **1** recurring at regular intervals. **2** consisting of or containing a series of repeated stages. ⯮ **periodicity** *n.*

periodical[1] *adj* **1** recurring at regular intervals. **2** of a magazine or journal: published at fixed intervals, e.g. weekly or quarterly. ⯮ **periodically** *adv.*

periodical[2] *n* a periodical publication.

periodic table *n* an arrangement of chemical elements in the order of their atomic numbers that shows a periodic variation in their properties.

period piece *n* a piece of furniture or work of art, the special value of which lies in its evocation of a historical period.

perioperative *adj* at the time of a surgical operation.

peripatetic *adj* **1** travelling or itinerant. **2** of a teacher, e.g. a music teacher: teaching in various schools. ⯮ **peripatetically** *adv.*

peripheral[1] *adj* **1** of or forming a periphery. **2** of minor significance. **3a** relating to or situated near the surface of the body. **b** supplying the part of the nervous system other than the brain and the spinal cord. **4** auxiliary or supplementary. ⯮ **peripherally** *adv.*

peripheral[2] *n* a device, e.g. a printer or disk drive, connected to a computer and able to exchange signals with it.

periphery *n* (*pl* **-ies**) **1** the outer limits or edge of something. **2** a less important or central position.

periphrasis *n* (*pl* **periphrases**) the use of circumlocution or roundabout phrasing. ⯮ **periphrastic** *adj.*

periscope *n* a tubular optical instrument containing mirrors or prisms for seeing objects not in the direct line of sight. ⯮ **periscopic** *adj.*

perish *v* **1** to die, *esp* in a terrible way. **2** to be ruined or destroyed. **3** to deteriorate or rot. **4** of cold or exposure: to weaken or numb (somebody). ✱ **perish the thought** *informal* used as an exclamation to express horror at an idea.

perishable[1] *adj* liable to rot or decay. ⯮ **perishability** *n.*

perishable[2] *n* (*in pl*) items of food that are liable to rot or decay.

perisher *n Brit, informal* an annoying person; *esp* a mischievous child.

perishing *adj* **1** *Brit, informal* freezingly cold. **2** *dated* damnable or confounded. ⯮ **perishingly** *adv.*

peristalsis *n* successive waves of involuntary contraction passing along the walls of a hollow muscular structure, *esp* the intestine, and forcing the contents onward. ⯮ **peristaltic** *adj.*

peristyle *n* a colonnade surrounding a building or court.

peritoneum *n* (*pl* **peritoneums** *or* **peritonea**) the smooth transparent membrane that lines the cavity of the abdomen and is folded inwards over the organs of the abdomen. ⯮ **peritoneal** *adj.*

peritonitis *n* inflammation of the peritoneum, causing severe abdominal pain.

periwig *n* = PERUKE.

periwinkle[1] *n* a trailing evergreen plant with blue or white flowers.

periwinkle[2] *n* a marine snail with a spiral shell.

perjure *v* to make (oneself) guilty of perjury. ⯮ **perjurer** *n.*

perjury *n* (*pl* **-ies**) the voluntary violation of an oath by a witness in a court of law. ⯮ **perjurious** *adj.*

perk[1] *n informal* a privilege or profit incidental to regular salary or wages.

perk[2] *v informal* of coffee: to percolate.

perk up *v* to recover or cause to recover one's vigour or cheerfulness.

perky *adj* (**-ier, -iest**) **1** lively; jaunty. **2** briskly self-assured; cocky. ⯮ **perkily** *adv,* **perkiness** *n.*

perlite *n* a greyish volcanic glass that has a concentric structure and appears as if composed of small globular bodies.

perm[1] *n* a long-lasting wave set in the hair by chemicals.

perm[2] *v* to give a perm to (the hair).

perm[3] *n Brit, informal* a permutation; *specif* any of the possible combinations of teams that can be chosen in the football pools.

perm[4] *v Brit, informal* to permute (something); *specif* to pick out and combine (a specified number of teams in the football pools) in all the possible permutations.

permaculture *n* an agricultural system using renewable natural resources, producing a self-sustaining ecosystem.

permafrost *n* a layer of permanently frozen ground in very cold regions.

permanent *adj* lasting or stable. ⯮ **permanence** *n,* **permanency** *n,* **permanently** *adv.*

permanent magnet *n* a magnet that retains its magnetism after removal of the magnetizing force.

permanent wave *n* = PERM[1].

permanent way *n Brit* the rails, sleepers, and ballast that make up the track of a railway system.

permanganate *n* a dark purple salt containing manganese.

permeable *adj* capable of being permeated; *esp* having pores or openings that permit liquids or gases to pass through. ⯮ **permeability** *n.*

permeate *v* **1** to spread or diffuse throughout (something). **2** to pass through the pores, gaps, cracks, etc of. ⯮ **permeation** *n.*

Permian *adj* of the last geological period of the Palaeozoic era, lasting from about 290 million to about 245 million years ago, and marked by the expansion of reptiles. ⯮ **Permian** *n.*

permissible *adj* allowable. ⯮ **permissibility** *n,* **permissibly** *adv.*

permission *n* formal consent; authorization.

permissive *adj* **1** tolerant; *esp* accepting a relaxed social or sexual morality. **2** allowing but not enforcing; optional. ⯮ **permissively** *adv,* **permissiveness** *n.*

permit[1] *v* (**permitted, permitting**) **1** to give (somebody) leave or authorization to do something. **2** to consent to (something). **3** *formal* (+ of) to allow for. ⯮ **permitter** *n.*

permit[2] *n* a written warrant allowing the holder to do or keep something.

permittivity *n* the ability of a DIELECTRIC[2] (substance that does not contain an electric current) to store electrical potential energy when placed in an electric field.

permutation *n* **1** any of the various possible ordered arrangements of a set of objects, numbers, etc, or the changing from one to another of these: compare COMBINATION. **2** *Brit* a combination of teams that can be chosen in the football pools. ➤➤ **permutational** *adj.*

permute *v* to change the order or arrangement of (objects, numbers, etc).

pernicious *adj* highly injurious or destructive; deadly. ➤➤ **perniciously** *adv*, **perniciousness** *n.*

pernicious anaemia *n* anaemia marked by a decrease in the number of red blood cells, which is caused by a reduced ability to absorb vitamin B_{12}.

pernickety *adj chiefly Brit, informal* **1** fussy about small details; fastidious. **2** requiring precision and care.

Pernod *n trademark* a French aperitif with a strong aniseed flavour.

perorate *v formal* **1** to deliver a long or pompous oration. **2** to conclude a speech.

peroration *n* the concluding part of a discourse, in which the main points are summed up.

peroxide[1] *n* **1** an oxide containing a high proportion of oxygen. **2** *not in technical use* hydrogen peroxide.

peroxide[2] *v* to bleach (hair) with hydrogen peroxide.

perpendicular[1] *adj* **1** being or standing at right angles to the plane of the horizon or a given line or plane. **2** extremely steep; precipitous. **3** (**Perpendicular**) of or built in a style of Gothic architecture prevalent in England from the late 14th to the 16th cent. characterized by large windows and fan vaults. ➤➤ **perpendicularity** *n*, **perpendicularly** *adv.*

perpendicular[2] *n* a line, plane, or surface at right angles to the plane of the horizon or to another line or surface.

perpetrate *v* to be guilty of performing or doing (something wrong). ➤➤ **perpetration** *n*, **perpetrator** *n.*

perpetual *adj* **1** continuing or valid forever; everlasting. **2** occurring continually; constant. **3** of a plant: blooming continuously throughout the season. ➤➤ **perpetually** *adv.*

perpetual motion *n* the hypothetical continuous operation of an isolated machine without the introduction of energy from an external force.

perpetuate *v* to cause to last indefinitely. ➤➤ **perpetuation** *n*, **perpetuator** *n.*

perpetuity *n* (*pl* **-ies**) **1** the quality or state of being perpetual; eternity. **2** an investment, e.g. a bond, with no fixed maturity date.

perplex *v* to puzzle or confuse. ➤➤ **perplexity** *n.*

per pro *prep* used to indicate that a person is signing a letter or document on behalf of somebody else.

perquisite *n* **1** *formal* a perk. **2** formerly, something held or claimed as a special or exclusive right or possession.

Usage note

perquisite *or* **prerequisite**? *Perquisite* is the full and formal form of *perk*: the *perquisites of an office* are the additional or fringe benefits somebody acquires by being in office over and above the position and the salary. *Prerequisite* is usually followed by *for* and means 'a necessary condition or attribute': *The presentation of a passport or a birth certificate is a prerequisite for the issuing of a marriage licence.*

perry *n* (*pl* **-ies**) an alcoholic drink made from fermented pear juice.

per se *adv* in itself; intrinsically.

persecute *v* **1** to harass (somebody) in a manner designed to injure or afflict them, *esp* because of their religion, political beliefs, etc. **2** to annoy (somebody) with persistent approaches, pleas, etc; to pester. ➤➤ **persecution** *n*, **persecutor** *n.*

persecution complex *n* a strong and irrational belief that one is hated and being persecuted by other people.

persevere *v* (*often* + in/with) to persist in an undertaking in spite of adverse influences or discouragement. ➤➤ **perseverance** *n.*

Persian *n* **1** a native or inhabitant of ancient Persia or modern Iran. **2** the Indo-Iranian language of ancient Persia and modern Iran. **3** = PERSIAN CAT. ➤➤ **Persian** *adj.*

Persian carpet *n* a carpet or rug made, *esp* in medieval Persia or modern Iran, to a traditional pattern by knotting yarn by hand onto a woven backing.

Persian cat *n* a short-nosed domestic cat with long silky fur.

Persian lamb *n* the pelt of the karakul lamb, characterized by very silky, tightly curled fur.

persiflage *n formal* frivolous bantering talk.

persimmon *n* a round yellow, orange, or red fruit with flesh that is extremely astringent when unripe but edible when fully ripened.

persist *v* **1** (*often* + in/with) to go on resolutely or stubbornly in spite of opposition or warning. **2** (*often* + with) to be insistent in the repetition or pressing of a question, opinion, etc. **3** to continue to exist, *esp* past a usual, expected, or normal time.

persistent *adj* **1a** persisting or inclined to persist in a course of action, etc. **b** continuing or recurring. **c** continuing to exist in spite of interference or treatment. **2** remaining beyond the usual period. **3a** remaining without change in function or structure. **b** of a structure characteristic of a young or larval stage: remaining in the adult. ➤➤ **persistence** *n*, **persistently** *adv.*

persistent vegetative state *n* a medical condition resulting from brain damage or brain degeneration in which a patient is unconscious and shows no signs of thought, feeling, or responsiveness to stimuli.

persnickety *adj NAm* = PERNICKETY.

person *n* (*pl* **people** *or formal* **persons**) **1** a human being considered as having a character of their own, or as being different from all others. **2** a living human body or its outward appearance. **3** any of three forms of verb or pronoun that indicate reference to the speaker, to somebody or something spoken to, or to somebody or something spoken of: compare FIRST PERSON, SECOND PERSON, THIRD PERSON. **4** (*usu* **Person**) any of the three modes of being in the Trinity as understood by Christians. ✱ **in person** in one's own bodily presence.

Usage note

persons *or* **people**? See note at PEOPLE[1].

-person *comb. form* forming nouns, denoting: a person who performs a role or function: *chairperson.*

persona *n* **1** (*pl* **personas** *or* **personae**) a role or character adopted by a person. **2** (*pl* **personas**) an individual's social facade, which, *esp* in Jungian psychology, reflects the role that the individual is playing in life: compare ANIMA.

personable *adj* pleasing in person; attractive. ⯮ **personably** *adv.*

personae *n* pl of PERSONA.

personage *n* a person, *esp* somebody of rank, note, or distinction.

personal *adj* **1** of or affecting a person; private. **2a** done in person without the intervention of another; proceeding from a single person: *She's making a personal appearance.* **b** carried on between individuals directly: *a personal interview with the manager.* **3** of the person or body: *personal hygiene.* **4a** of the private affairs of an individual. **b** referring to the character, conduct, motives, or private affairs of an individual, often in an offensive manner: *personal remarks.* **5** existing as a person: *I don't believe in a personal God.* **6** denoting grammatical person.

personal assistant *n* a person performing administrative and secretarial duties as assistant to a business executive, etc.

personal column *n* a section of a newspaper containing personal messages, notices, and advertisements.

personal computer *n* a microcomputer for personal or business use.

personal equity plan *n* in Britain, an investment scheme whereby individuals are permitted to invest a limited annual sum in British shares without paying tax on capital gains or dividend income.

personal identification number *n* = PIN NUMBER.

personalise *v* see PERSONALIZE.

personality *n* (*pl* **-ies**) **1** the totality of an individual's behavioural and emotional tendencies; a distinguishing complex of individual or group characteristics. **2a** distinction or excellence of personal and social traits. **b** a person who has distinction or excellence of personal or social traits. **c** a person of importance, prominence, renown, or notoriety.

personalize *or* **-ise** *v* **1a** to mark (something) as the property of a particular person. **b** to design or make (something) so as to fit in with a particular person's wishes or needs. **2** to focus (an argument, etc) on personalities rather than issues. **3** to personify (a quality, etc). ⯮ **personalization** *n.*

personally *adv* **1** in person. **2** for oneself; as far as oneself is concerned. **3** as directed against oneself in a personal way.

personal organizer *n* **1** a loose-leaf file holding a diary, address book, and notebook. **2** a small computerized device offering similar facilities.

personal pronoun *n* a pronoun, e.g. *I, you,* or *they,* that expresses a distinction of person.

personal property *n* in law, all property other than freehold estates and interests in land.

personal stereo *n* a very small cassette player or CD player which is listened to through earphones.

personalty *n* in law, personal property: compare REALTY.

persona non grata /puh,sohnə non 'grahtə/ *n* (*pl* **personae non gratae** /puh,sohnee non 'grahtee/) a person who is personally unacceptable or unwelcome to another person, etc.

personate *v formal* **1** to impersonate or represent. **2** to assume (some character or capacity) with fraudulent intent. ⯮ **personation** *n.*

personify *v* (**-ies, -ied**) **1** to conceive of or represent (an inanimate object, abstract quality, etc) as having human qualities or human form. **2** to be the embodiment of (some quality) in human form. ⯮ **personification** *n.*

personnel *n* (*used as sing. or pl*) a body of people employed, e.g. in a factory, office, or organization, or engaged on a project.

perspective *n* **1a** the aspect of an object of thought from a particular standpoint. **b** the true relationship or relative importance of things, or the capacity to discern this. **2a** the way in which the relationship of solid objects to each other in space appears to the eye, or the technique of accurately representing this on a flat or curved surface. **b** linear perspective; the representation of space in art by converging parallel lines. **c** a picture or view giving a distinctive impression of distance; a vista.

Perspex *n trademark* a transparent acrylic plastic.

perspicacious *adj* of acute mental vision or discernment. ⯮ **perspicaciously** *adv,* **perspicacity** *n.*

perspicuous *adj* plain to the understanding, *esp* because of clarity and precision of presentation. ⯮ **perspicuity** *n,* **perspicuously** *adv.*

perspiration *n* **1** sweating. **2** sweat.

perspire *v* to sweat.

persuade *v* **1** to move (somebody) by argument, reasoning, evidence, or entreaty to a belief, position, or course of action. **2** (*often* + of) to cause (somebody) to think or feel certain about something; to convince. ⯮ **persuadable** *adj,* **persuader** *n.*

persuasion *n* **1** persuading or being persuaded. **2a** an opinion held with complete assurance. **b** a particular system of religious beliefs, or a group adhering to it.

persuasive *adj* tending or able to persuade. ⯮ **persuasively** *adv,* **persuasiveness** *n.*

pert *adj* **1** impudent and forward; saucy. **2** trim and chic; jaunty: *a pert little hat.* ⯮ **pertly** *adv,* **pertness** *n.*

pertain *v* **1a** to belong to somebody or something or exist as a part, attribute, feature, function, or right. **b** to be appropriate. **2** *formal* (+ to) to have reference to something.

pertinacious *adj formal* clinging resolutely to an opinion or purpose often to the point of stubbornness. ⯮ **pertinaciously** *adv,* **pertinacity** *n.*

pertinent *adj* clearly relevant to the matter in hand. ⯮ **pertinence** *n,* **pertinently** *adv.*

perturb *v* **1** (*usu in passive*) to disturb (somebody) greatly in mind; to trouble. **2** to throw into confusion or disorder. **3** to cause (a moving object, celestial body, etc) to deviate from a theoretically regular motion such as a regular path of orbit. ⯮ **perturbation** *n.*

pertussis *n* = WHOOPING COUGH.

peruke *n* a long curly wig worn by men in the 17th and 18th cent.

peruse *v formal* to examine or consider (a document, etc) with attention and in detail; to study. ⯮ **perusal** *n,* **peruser** *n.*

Peruvian *n* a native or inhabitant of Peru. ⯮ **Peruvian** *adj.*

perv *or* **perve** *n informal* **1** a sexual pervert. **2** *Aus, NZ* a lustful or lecherous look. ⯮ **pervy** *adj.*

pervade *v* to be or become diffused throughout every part of (something). ⯮ **pervasion** *n,* **pervasive** *adj,* **pervasively** *adv,* **pervasiveness** *n.*

perve *n* see PERV.

perverse *adj* **1a** obstinate in opposing what is right, reasonable, or accepted; wrongheaded. **b** arising from or indicative of stubbornness or obstinacy. **2** unreasonably opposed to the wishes of others; uncooperative, contrary. ⯮ **perversely** *adv,* **perverseness** *n,* **perversity** *n.*

perversion *n* **1** the act or an instance of perverting. **2** something perverted, *esp* abnormal sexual behaviour.

pervert[1] *v* **1** to cause (somebody) to turn aside or away from what is good, true, or morally right; to corrupt. **2a** to divert (something) to a wrong use or purpose; to misuse. **b** to twist the meaning or sense of (something); to misinterpret.

pervert[2] *n* a person given to some form of sexual perversion.

perverted *adj* marked by perversion, *esp* sexual perversion. ➤➤ **pervertedly** *adv.*

pervious *adj* permeable.

peseta /pə'saytə/ *n* the basic monetary unit of Spain, also used in Andorra.

pesewa /pi'saywah/ *n* a unit of currency in Ghana, worth 100th of a cedi.

pesky *adj* (**-ier, -iest**) *informal* troublesome or annoying.

peso /'paysoh/ *n* (*pl* **-os**) the basic monetary unit of certain Spanish-speaking Latin American countries, e.g. Argentina, Chile, Mexico, Uruguay, and the Philippines.

pessary *n* (*pl* **-ies**) **1** a vaginal suppository. **2** a device worn in the vagina to support the uterus or prevent conception.

pessimism *n* **1** a tendency to stress the adverse aspects of a situation or event or to expect the worst possible outcome. **2** in philosophy, the doctrine that this is the worst of all possible worlds. ➤➤ **pessimist** *n,* **pessimistic** *adj,* **pessimistically** *adv.*

pest *n* **1** somebody or something that pesters or annoys; a nuisance. **2** a plant or animal capable of causing damage or carrying disease.

pester *v* to harass or annoy with petty irritations and demands.

pesticide *n* a chemical used to destroy insects and other pests of crops, domestic animals, etc.

pestiferous *adj* **1** *humorous* annoying. **2** *literary* carrying or propagating infection.

pestilence *n* a virulent and devastating epidemic disease; *specif* bubonic plague.

pestilent *adj* = PESTILENTIAL.

pestilential *adj* **1** destructive of life; deadly. **2** morally harmful; pernicious. **3** *archaic* causing displeasure or annoyance; irritating.

pestle *n* a club-shaped implement for pounding substances in a mortar.

pesto *n* a paste made from crushed basil leaves, garlic, pine nuts, olive oil, and Parmesan cheese.

pet[1] *n* **1** an animal, bird, etc kept for companionship, amusement, etc. **2** somebody who is treated with unusual kindness or consideration; a favourite. **3** *chiefly Brit* used as an affectionate form of address: darling.

pet[2] *adj* **1a** kept or treated as a pet. **b** for pet animals. **2** expressing fondness or endearment: *a pet name.* **3** favourite. **4** strongest; particular.

pet[3] *v* (**petted, petting**) **1** to stroke (an animal, etc) in a gentle or loving manner. **2** to engage in amorous embracing, caressing, etc.

pet[4] *n* a fit of sulkiness or anger.

peta- *comb. form* forming words, denoting: thousand billion (10^{15}).

petal *n* any of the modified, often brightly coloured, leaves of the COROLLA (flower) of a flowering plant.

pétanque /pay'tongk/ *n* = BOULE.

petard *n* formerly, a case containing an explosive for military demolitions. ✱ **be hoist with one's own petard** to be the victim of one's own scheming or trickery.

peterman *n* (*pl* **petermen**) *archaic* a safebreaker.

peter out *v* to diminish gradually and come to an end; to give out.

Peter Pan *n* **1** a man who seems never to age. **2** an immature man.

Peter principle *n* (**the Peter principle**) the proposition that members of a hierarchical organization tend to be promoted until they reach a position that is beyond their capabilities.

petersham *n* a heavy corded ribbon used for belts and put round hats.

Peters' projection *n* a PROJECTION (representation of latitude and longitude on flat surface) in which regions and countries of the world are shown in their correct relative sizes but therefore with distorted shapes.

pethidine *n* a synthetic narcotic drug often used to relieve labour pains.

pétillant /'payteeyonh/ *adj* of a wine: mildly effervescent.

petiole *n* the stalk by which a leaf is attached to a stem.

petit bourgeois *or* **petty bourgeois** /'peti 'booəzh·wah/ *n* (*pl* **petits bourgeois** /,peti 'booəzh·wah/) a member of the petite bourgeoisie, *esp* a conventional and conservative person. ➤➤ **petit bourgeois** *adj.*

petite *adj* of a woman: having a small trim figure.

petite bourgeoisie /booəzh·wah'zee/ *or* **petty bourgeoisie** *n* (*used as sing. or pl*) the lower middle class, *esp* as considered conventional and conservative in attitudes and behaviour.

petit four /'faw/ *n* (*pl* **petits fours** *or* **petit fours** /,peti 'fawz/) a small fancy cake or biscuit, usu iced.

petition[1] *n* **1** a formal written request made to somebody in authority, e.g. a government, *esp* one made by a large number of people. **2** an earnest request; an entreaty. **3** a formal request for legal action addressed to a court.

petition[2] *v* **1** to present a petition to. **2** (*usu* + for) to make a request by petition for something to be done. ➤➤ **petitioner** *n.*

petit mal /'mal/ *n* mild epilepsy, or a mild epileptic attack lasting only a short time: compare GRAND MAL.

petit point /'poynt/ *n* needlepoint embroidery worked on canvas across single threads in tent stitch.

petit pois /'pwah, pətee/ *n* (*pl* **petits pois**) (*usu in pl*) a small young sweet green pea.

petits bourgeois /,peti 'booəzh·wah/ *n* pl of PETIT BOURGEOIS.

petits fours /,peti 'fawz/ *n* pl of PETIT FOUR.

petits pois /,peti 'pwah(z)/ *n* pl of PETIT POIS.

petrel *n* a seabird with thick plumage, webbed feet, a hooked bill, and distinctive tubular nostrils, which characteristically flies far from land, and comes ashore only to breed.

petri dish *or* **Petri dish** *n* a small shallow glass or plastic dish with a loose cover, used *esp* for cultures of micro-organisms.

petrify *v* (**-ies, -ied**) **1** (*usu in passive*) to paralyse with fear, amazement, or awe; to make very afraid. **2** to convert (something) into stone or a hard or stony substance. **3** to make (somebody or something) lifeless or inactive; to deaden. ➤➤ **petrifaction** *n,* **petrification** *n.*

petrochemical[1] *n* a chemical obtained from petroleum or natural gas.

petrochemical[2] *adj* **1** relating to petrochemicals or the properties and processing of petroleum and natural gas. **2** obtained from petrochemicals.

petrodollar *n* a unit of foreign exchange obtained by a petroleum-exporting country by sales abroad.

petroglyph *n* an ancient or prehistoric carving, painting, or inscription on a rock.

petrography *n* the description and systematic classification of rocks. ➤➤ **petrographer** *n*, **petrographic** *adj*.

petrol *n chiefly Brit* a volatile inflammable liquid hydrocarbon mixture refined from petroleum and used as a fuel for internal-combustion engines.

petrolatum *n* = PETROLEUM JELLY.

petrol bomb *n* a simple hand-thrown bomb consisting of a bottle filled with petrol and having a piece of rag to act as a fuse.

petroleum *n* a dark oily inflammable liquid composed of a mixture of hydrocarbons, widely occurring in the upper strata of the earth, and refined for use as petrol, naphtha, etc.

petroleum jelly *n* a semisolid mixture of hydrocarbons obtained from petroleum, used as an ointment.

petrology *n* a science that deals with the origin, structure, composition, etc of rocks. ➤➤ **petrological** *adj*, **petrologist** *n*.

petticoat *n* **1** a woman's light undergarment hanging from the waist or shoulders. **2** *humorous or derog* (*used before a noun*) characteristic of or exercised by women: *a petticoat government.*

pettifog *v* (**pettifogged, pettifogging**) *archaic* **1** to quibble over insignificant details. **2** to engage in legal chicanery. ➤➤ **pettifogger** *n*, **pettifoggery** *n*, **pettifogging** *adj*.

pettish *adj* peevish or petulant. ➤➤ **pettishly** *adv*, **pettishness** *n*.

petty *adj* (**-ier, -iest**) **1** trivial. **2** having secondary rank or importance. **3** small-minded. **4** in law, of a crime, etc: minor. ➤➤ **pettily** *adv*, **pettiness** *n*.

petty bourgeois *n* see PETIT BOURGEOIS. ➤➤ **petty bourgeoisie** *n*.

petty cash *n* cash kept on hand for payment of minor items.

petty officer *n* a rank of non-commissioned officer in the navy.

petulant *adj* characterized by expressions or bouts of childish bad temper; peevish. ➤➤ **petulance** *n*, **petulantly** *adv*.

petunia *n* a plant of the nightshade family with large brightly coloured funnel-shaped flowers.

pew *n* **1** a bench fixed in a row for the use of the congregation in a church. **2** *Brit, informal* a seat.

pewee *or* **peewee** *n* a small olive grey N American flycatcher.

pewit *n* see PEEWIT.

pewter *n* any of various alloys containing tin, *esp* one of tin and lead used formerly, or a modern alloy containing copper and antimony.

peyote /pay'ohti, pi-/ *n* **1** a small cactus with rounded stems covered with small jointed protuberances that contain mescaline and are chewed by some Native Americans for their hallucinogenic effect. **2** = MESCALINE.

pf *abbr* pfennig.

pfennig /'(p)fenig, '(p)fenikh/ *n* (*pl* **pfennigs** *or* **pfennige**) a unit of currency in Germany, worth 100th of a mark.

PFI *abbr* Private Finance Initiative.

PG *adj* in Britain, a classification of cinema films for which parental guidance is recommended because some scenes may be considered unsuitable for children.

pH *n* a figure used to express the acidity or alkalinity of a solution on a scale of 0 to 14 with 7 representing neutrality.

phaeton *n* a light open four-wheeled carriage.

phage *n* any of various viruses that attack and destroy bacteria.

phagocyte *n* a body cell that characteristically engulfs foreign material, e.g. bacteria, and consumes debris, e.g. from tissue injury. ➤➤ **phagocytic** *adj*.

phalange *n* = PHALANX (3).

phalangeal *adj* relating to or in the region of a phalanx or the phalanges.

phalanger *n* a small marsupial of the Australian region that lives in trees and has thick fur and a long tail.

phalanges *n* pl of PHALANX (3).

phalanx *n* **1** (*pl* **phalanxes**) **a** (*used as sing. or pl*) a closely massed arrangement of people, animals, or things. **b** a body of people organized for a common purpose. **2** (*pl* **phalanxes**) (*used as sing. or pl*) a body of troops in close array behind a wall of shields. **3** (*pl* **phalanges**) any of the digital bones of the hand or foot of a vertebrate.

phalarope *n* (*pl* **phalaropes** *or* **phalarope**) a small wading bird that has lobed toes and is a good swimmer.

phalli *n* pl of PHALLUS.

phallic *adj* of or resembling a phallus. ➤➤ **phallically** *adv*.

phallicism *n* the worship of generative power as symbolized by the phallus.

phallocentric *adj* **1** centred on the phallus. **2** of or holding a belief in maleness as the norm and in the supremacy of men over women. ➤➤ **phallocentrism** *n*.

phallus *n* (*pl* **phalli** *or* **phalluses**) the penis, or a symbol or representation of the penis, *esp* an erect penis, as a symbol of generative power or male dominance.

phantasm *n literary* **1** an illusion. **2a** a ghost or spectre. **b** a figment of the imagination; a fantasy. ➤➤ **phantasmal** *adj*, **phantasmic** *adj*.

phantasmagoria *n* a constantly shifting, confused succession of things seen or imagined, e.g. in a dreaming or feverish state. ➤➤ **phantasmagoric** *adj*, **phantasmagorical** *adj*.

phantom[1] *n* **1a** something, e.g. a ghost, apparent to the senses but with no substantial existence. **b** something existing only in the imagination. **2** something existing in appearance only; a form without substance.

phantom[2] *adj* fictitious, dummy, or non-existent: *phantom voters.*

phantom limb *n* the feeling that a person may have that an amputated limb is still present and attached to the body.

phantom pregnancy *n* a physiological state resembling pregnancy.

pharaoh *n* (*often* **Pharaoh**) a ruler of ancient Egypt. ➤➤ **pharaonic** *adj*.

pharisaic *adj* **1** (**Pharisaic**) of the Pharisees. **2** marked by hypocritical self-righteousness.

pharisaical *adj* = PHARISAIC.

pharisee *n* **1** (**Pharisee**) a member of a Jewish party noted for strict adherence to the Torah. **2** a pharisaic person.

pharmaceutical[1] *adj* of or engaged in pharmacy or in the manufacture of medicinal substances. ➤➤ **pharmaceutically** *adv.*

pharmaceutical[2] *n* a medicinal drug.

pharmacology *n* **1** the science of drugs and their effect on living things. **2** the properties and effects of a particular drug. ➤➤ **pharmacologic** *adj,* **pharmacological** *adj,* **pharmacologist** *n.*

pharmacopoeia (*NAm* **pharmacopeia**) *n* **1** a book describing drugs, chemicals, and medicinal preparations. **2** a stock of drugs.

pharmacy *n* (*pl* **-ies**) **1a** a place where medicines are compounded or dispensed. **b** a chemist's shop. **2** the preparation and dispensing of medicinal drugs. ➤➤ **pharmacist** *n.*

pharyngeal *adj* relating to or in the region of the pharynx.

pharynges *n* pl of PHARYNX.

pharyngitis *n* inflammation of the pharynx.

pharynx *n* (*pl* **pharynges** *or* **pharynxes**) in vertebrates, the part of the alimentary canal between the mouth cavity and the oesophagus.

phase[1] *n* **1** a discernible part or stage in a course, development, or cycle. **2** a particular appearance or state in a regularly recurring cycle of changes: *the phases of the moon.* **3** in physics, a particular stage of progress reached in a regularly recurring motion or cyclic process with respect to a standard or reference position or assumed starting point. **4** a homogeneous, physically distinct, and mechanically separable portion of matter present in a complex mixture the constituents of which have different physical states. ✱ **in phase** synchronized or correlated. **out of phase** not synchronized or correlated.

phase[2] *v* (*usu in passive*) to conduct or carry out (a project, etc) by planned phases.

phase in *v* to introduce the practice, production, or use of (something) in gradual stages.

phase modulation *n* a modulation of the phase of a wave, *esp* a radio carrier wave by the characteristics of the signal carried, or a method of transmitting using this: compare AMPLITUDE MODULATION, FREQUENCY MODULATION.

phase out *v* to discontinue the practice, production, or use of (something) in gradual stages.

phasic *adj* of a phase or phases, occurring in phases.

phatic *adj* of speech: expressing feelings or establishing an atmosphere of sociability rather than communicating ideas.

PhD *abbr* Doctor of Philosophy.

pheasant *n* (*pl* **pheasants** *or* **pheasant**) a large long-tailed and brightly coloured bird reared as an ornamental or game bird.

phencyclidine *n* a synthetic drug used in veterinary medicine as an anaesthetic and illegally as a hallucinogenic.

phenix *n NAm* see PHOENIX.

phenobarbital *n NAm* = PHENOBARBITONE.

phenobarbitone *n* a barbiturate used as a sedative and anticonvulsant in the treatment of epilepsy.

phenol *n* **1** a caustic poisonous acidic chemical compound present in coal tar, used in dilute solution as a disinfectant. **2** any of various acidic chemical compounds analogous to phenol. ➤➤ **phenolic** *adj.*

phenology *n* the study of the relations between climate and periodic biological phenomena, e.g. bird migration or plant flowering. ➤➤ **phenological** *adj.*

phenolphthalein *n* a synthetic compound used in medicine as a purgative and in chemical analysis as an indicator of alkalinity.

phenomena *n* pl of PHENOMENON.

phenomenal *adj* **1** extraordinary or remarkable. **2** known through the senses rather than through thought or intuition. ➤➤ **phenomenally** *adv.*

phenomenology *n* **1** the description of the formal structure of what is directly experienced and of consciousness, in abstraction from any consideration of causal connections between what is experienced and the external world. **2a** the description of a related group of phenomena. **b** an analysis produced by phenomenological investigation. ➤➤ **phenomenological** *adj,* **phenomenologist** *n.*

phenomenon *n* (*pl* **phenomena**) **1** an observable fact or event. **2** an object of sense perception rather than of thought or intuition. **3** (*pl usu* **phenomenons**) an exceptional, unusual, or abnormal person, thing, or event; a prodigy.

Usage note

phenomenon *and* **phenomena**. *Phenomenon* is a singular noun. *Phenomena* is its plural and should never be used as if it were singular: *a strange phenomenon that occurs during an eclipse; the strange phenomena that occur during eclipses.*

phenotype *n* the visible characteristics of an organism that are produced by the interaction of the organism's genes and the environment: compare GENOTYPE.

phenyl *n* (*often used in combinations*) a univalent radical $-C_6H_5$ that is derived from benzene by removal of one hydrogen atom.

phenylalanine *n* an amino acid found in most proteins that is essential for human development and health.

pheromone *n* a chemical substance that is produced by an animal and stimulates one or more behavioural responses in other individuals of the same species.

phi /fie/ *n* the 21st letter of the Greek alphabet (Φ, φ), equivalent to roman ph.

phial *n* a small closed or closable vessel, *esp* for holding liquid medicine.

phil- *or* **philo-** *comb. form* loving, or having an affinity for: *philanthropy; philoprogenitive.*

-phil *comb. form* see -PHILE.

philadelphus *n* (*pl* **philadelphuses**) an ornamental shrub of the hydrangea family with white cup-shaped flowers with a scent like orange blossom, *esp* MOCK ORANGE.

philander *v* of a man: to have many casual love affairs. ➤➤ **philanderer** *n.*

philanthropy *n* goodwill to one's fellow human beings, *esp* active effort to promote the welfare of others. ➤➤ **philanthrope** *n,* **philanthropic** *adj,* **philanthropically** *adv,* **philanthropist** *n.*

philately *n* the study and collection of postage stamps. ➤➤ **philatelic** *adj,* **philatelist** *n.*

-phile *or* **-phil** *comb. form* forming nouns, with the meaning: a person or thing having an affinity or liking for: *Francophile.* ➤➤ **-phile** *comb. form.*

philharmonic *adj* used *esp* in the names of choirs, orchestras, etc: devoted to music.

philhellene *n* an admirer or supporter of Greece or the Greeks. ➤➤ **philhellenic** *adj,* **philhellenism** *n.*

-philia *or* **-phily** *comb. form* forming nouns, denoting: a liking for or interest in, *esp* an abnormal appetite or liking for: *Francophilia; necrophilia.*

▶▶ **-philiac** *comb. form,* **-philic** *comb. form,* **-philous** *comb. form.*

philippic *n literary* a speech or declamation full of bitter invective.

Philippine *adj* of or relating to the Republic of the Philippines.

philistine *n* **1** (**Philistine**) a native or inhabitant of ancient Philistia. **2** a person who professes indifference or opposition to intellectual or aesthetic values. ▶▶ **philistinism** *n.*

Phillips screw *n trademark* a screw with a cross-shaped slot in the head.

Phillips screwdriver *n trademark* a screwdriver with a cross-shaped tip.

phillumenist *n* a person who collects books of matches or matchbox labels.

philo- *comb. form* see PHIL-.

philodendron *n* (*pl* **philodendrons** *or* **philodendra**) a plant of the arum family cultivated for its showy foliage.

philology *n* **1** the study of the historical development of a language or the comparison of different languages. **2** the study of ancient texts. **3** the study of texts as a field of study that sheds light on cultural history. ▶▶ **philological** *adj,* **philologist** *n.*

philoprogenitive *adj formal* **1** producing many offspring; prolific. **2** of love of one's offspring.

philosopher *n* **1** a specialist in philosophy. **2** a scholar or thinker.

philosopher's stone *n* a substance believed by alchemists to have the power of transmuting base metals into gold.

philosophic *adj* = PHILOSOPHICAL.

philosophical *adj* **1** of philosophers or philosophy. **2** calm in the face of trouble. ▶▶ **philosophically** *adv.*

philosophize *or* **-ise** *v* to engage in philosophical reasoning.

philosophy *n* (*pl* **-ies**) **1a** the study of the nature of knowledge and existence and the principles of moral and aesthetic value. **b** the philosophical principles or teachings of a specified individual, group, period, or field of study. **2** the sum of beliefs and attitudes of a specified individual, group, or period.

philtre (*NAm* **philter**) *n* a potion or drug reputed to have the power to arouse sexual passion or desire.

-phily *comb. form* see -PHILIA.

phiz *n* = PHIZOG.

phizog *n Brit, informal* a person's face or expression.

phlebitis *n* inflammation of a vein.

phlebotomy *n* (*pl* **-ies**) the letting or taking of blood in the treatment or diagnosis of disease. ▶▶ **phlebotomist** *n.*

phlegm *n* **1** thick mucus secreted in abnormal quantities in the respiratory passages. **2a** intrepid coolness; composure. **b** dull or apathetic coldness or indifference. **3** one of the four humours in medieval physiology, considered to be cold and moist and to cause sluggishness. ▶▶ **phlegmy** *adj.*

phlegmatic *adj* having or showing a slow and stolid temperament. ▶▶ **phlegmatically** *adv.*

phloem *n* a complex vascular tissue of higher plants that functions chiefly in the conduction of soluble food substances, e.g. sugars.

phlox *n* (*pl* **phloxes** *or* **phlox**) an American plant with red, purple, white, or variegated flowers.

-phobe *comb. form* forming nouns, denoting: a person afraid of or averse to: *Francophobe.*

phobia *n* an exaggerated and illogical fear of something. ▶▶ **phobic** *adj and n.*

-phobia *comb. form* forming nouns, denoting: abnormal fear or dislike of: *claustrophobia.* ▶▶ **-phobic** *comb. form.*

Phoenician *n* a native or inhabitant of ancient Phoenicia in SW Asia. ▶▶ **Phoenician** *adj.*

phoenix (*NAm* **phenix**) *n* a mythical bird believed to live for 500 years, burn itself on a pyre, and rise alive from the ashes to live another cycle.

phon- *or* **phono-** *comb. form* sound; voice; speech: *phonograph.*

phone¹ *n* **1** = TELEPHONE¹. **2** *informal* (*also in pl*) = EARPHONE.

phone² *v* = TELEPHONE².

-phone *comb. form* **1** sound: *homophone; xylophone.* **2** speaker of: *Anglophone.*

phone book *n* a telephone directory.

phonecard *n* a plastic card that can be used to make prepaid telephone calls from a public telephone.

phone-in *n* a broadcast programme in which viewers or listeners can participate by telephone.

phoneme *n* the smallest unit of speech that can be used to differentiate words, e.g. /b/, /p/, and /f/, which differentiate the words *bin, pin,* and *fin.* ▶▶ **phonemic** *adj,* **phonemically** *adv.*

phonetic *adj* **1a** of spoken language or speech sounds. **b** of the study of phonetics. **2** representing speech sounds by symbols that each have one value only. ▶▶ **phonetically** *adv.*

phonetics *pl n* (*used as sing. or pl*) the study and classification of speech sounds.

phoney¹ *or* **phony** *adj* (**-ier, -iest**) *informal* **1** not genuine or real. **2** of a person: pretentious. ▶▶ **phonily** *adv.*

phoney² *or* **phony** *n* (*pl* **-eys** *or* **-ies**) somebody or something that is phoney.

phonic *adj* **1** of or producing sound; acoustic. **2a** of speech sounds. **b** of phonics. ▶▶ **phonically** *adv.*

phonics *pl n* (*used as sing. or pl*) a method of teaching reading and pronunciation through the phonetic value of letters, syllables, etc.

phono *adj* of a plug used in audio and video equipment: in which the central prong of the plug is one conductor and the outer cylinder is the other conductor.

phono- *comb. form* see PHON-.

phonograph *n* **1** an early device for recording or reproducing sound in which a stylus cuts or follows a groove on a cylinder. **2** *NAm* a record player. ▶▶ **phonographic** *adj.*

phonology *n* (*pl* **-ies**) **1** the study of the sound system of a language or languages. **2** the phonemic system of a language. ▶▶ **phonological** *adj,* **phonologically** *adv.*

phony¹ *adj* (**-ier, -iest**) see PHONEY¹.

phony² *n* (*pl* **-ies**) see PHONY².

phooey *interj informal* used to express scorn or incredulity.

phormium *n* (*pl* **phormiums**) a plant of the agave family having long dark green lance-shaped leaves that are a source of a fibre used in ropes, mats, etc.

phosgene *n* a very poisonous colourless gas that is a severe respiratory irritant and was formerly used in warfare.

phosphate *n* a salt or ester of a phosphoric acid.

phosphine *n* a colourless, extremely poisonous, inflammable gas, a compound of phosphorus and hydrogen that has a smell of decaying fish.

phospholipid *n* any LIPID (fatty compound) containing a PHOSPHATE (compound of phosphoric acid), found in all living cells, *esp* in membranes.

phosphor *n* a substance showing phosphorescence.

phosphoresce *v* to exhibit phosphorescence.

phosphorescence *n* **1** light emission that is caused by the absorption of radiation and continues for a noticeable time after the radiation has stopped. **2** lasting emission of light without noticeable heat. **3** emitted light. ➤➤ **phosphorescent** *adj.*

phosphoric *adj* of or containing phosphorus, *esp* in its higher valency.

phosphoric acid *n* any of several forms of acid used in preparing phosphates, e.g. for fertilizers, in rustproofing metals, and as a flavouring in soft drinks.

phosphorus *n* a non-metallic chemical element of the nitrogen family that occurs widely, *esp* as phosphates. ➤➤ **phosphorous** *adj.*

phot- *or* **photo-** *comb. form* **1** light; radiant energy: *photic*; *photography.* **2** photograph or photographic: *photoengraving.* **3** photoelectric: *photocell.*

photic *adj* **1** of or involving light, *esp* in its effect on living organisms. **2** of a layer or level of the sea, etc: penetrated by the sun's light sufficiently to allow photosynthesis and plant growth.

photo *n* (*pl* **photos**) = PHOTOGRAPH[1].

photo- *comb. form* see PHOT-.

photocall *n* a session at which a person is photographed, typically for the purpose of publicity.

photo CD *n* a compact disc that can be used to store images which can be displayed from it onto a video or television screen.

photocell *n* = PHOTOELECTRIC CELL.

photochemistry *n* the effect of radiant energy in producing chemical changes, or the branch of chemistry that deals with this. ➤➤ **photochemical** *adj.*

photochromic *adj* of a substance that is capable of changing colour on exposure to radiant energy, e.g. light, or using such a substance.

photocopy[1] *n* (*pl* **-ies**) a reproduction of written or printed text, photographs, etc by a process involving photography.

photocopy[2] *v* (**-ies, -ied**) to make a photocopy of. ➤➤ **photocopiable** *adj,* **photocopier** *n.*

photoelectric *adj* involving or using any of various electrical effects caused by the interaction of radiation, e.g. light, with matter, *esp* involving or using the release of electrons due to such interaction.

photoelectric cell *n* a device with electrical properties that are modified by the action of light, used in burglar alarms, exposure meters, etc.

photoengraving *n* a process for making line and halftone blocks by photographing an image on a metal plate and then etching, or a plate made by this process.

photo finish *n* a race finish so close that the winner is only revealed by a photograph of the contestants as they cross the finishing line.

photofit *n* (*often* **Photofit**) a likeness of a person's face constructed from photographs, *esp* for identification.

photogenic *adj* **1** looking attractive in photographs. **2** producing or generating light; luminescent.

photograph[1] *n* a picture or likeness obtained by photography.

photograph[2] *v* to take a photograph of. ➤➤ **photographer** *n,* **photographic** *adj.*

photographic memory *n* an ability to retain visual images in perfect detail.

photography *n* the art or process of producing images on a sensitized surface, e.g. a film, by the action of radiant energy, *esp* light.

photogravure *n* a process for making prints from an intaglio plate prepared by photographic methods, or a picture produced in this way.

photojournalism *n* journalism which places more emphasis on photographs than on written material. ➤➤ **photojournalist** *n.*

photolysis *n* chemical decomposition by the action of radiant energy, *esp* light.

photometer *n* an instrument for measuring light intensity, illumination, or brightness. ➤➤ **photometric** *adj,* **photometry** *n.*

photomicrograph *n* a photograph of an object magnified under a microscope.

photomontage *n* a picture made up of several juxtaposed, overlapping, or superimposed photographs.

photon *n* a QUANTUM (very small quantity) of electromagnetic radiation. ➤➤ **photonic** *adj.*

photo opportunity *n* a photocall.

photophobia *n* painful sensitiveness to strong light. ➤➤ **photophobic** *adj.*

photorealism *n* extremely realistic representation of detail as an artistic style, *esp* in painting or sculpture. ➤➤ **photorealist** *n and adj,* **photorealistic** *adj.*

photoreceptor *n* a receptor for light stimuli; a light-sensitive organ or cell.

photosensitive *adj* sensitive or sensitized to radiant energy, *esp* light. ➤➤ **photosensitivity** *n.*

photosphere *n* the luminous surface layer of the sun or another star.

Photostat *n* **1** *trademark* a device for making a photographic copy of written, printed, or graphic material. **2** (*also* **photostat**) a copy made in this way.

photostat *v* (**photostatted, photostatting**) to copy on a Photostat or similar device.

photosynthesis *n* the synthesis of organic chemical compounds from carbon dioxide using radiant energy, *esp* light; *specif* the formation of carbohydrates in the chlorophyll-containing tissues of plants exposed to light. ➤➤ **photosynthetic** *adj.*

photosynthesize *or* **-ise** *v* to produce by means of photosynthesis.

phototropism *n* the turning or curving of an organism, *esp* a plant, or of one of its parts, towards or away from light. ➤➤ **phototropic** *adj.*

photovoltaic *adj* of or using the generation of an electromotive force when radiant energy such as light falls on the boundary between dissimilar substances in close contact.

phrasal verb *n* a compound verb consisting of a simple verb plus an adverb, a preposition, or both, *esp* one in which the meaning cannot be deduced from the meanings of the words from which it is formed, e.g. *put up with* or *fall out.*

phrase[1] *n* **1** a group of two or more grammatically related words that do not form a clause, e.g. a preposition with the words it governs. **2** a brief idiomatic or pithy expression; a catchphrase. **3** a group of musical notes forming a natural unit of melody that is usu three or four bars in length. ➤➤ **phrasal** *adj.*

phrase[2] *v* to express in words or in appropriate or telling terms.

phrase book *n* a book containing words and idiomatic expressions of a foreign language and their translation.

phraseology *n* (*pl* **-ies**) **1** the phrases used by a particular group, or the way in which they are used. **2** a manner of putting words and phrases together; a style.

phrasing *n* **1** a style of expression; phraseology. **2** the grouping of notes into musical phrases.

phrenology *n* the formerly popular study of the shape of the skull as a supposed indicator of mental faculties and character. ➤➤ **phrenological** *adj*, **phrenologist** *n*.

Phrygian *n* a native or inhabitant of ancient Phrygia in Asia Minor. ➤➤ **Phrygian** *adj*.

phthisis *n* (*pl* **phthises**) a progressive wasting condition, *esp* lung tuberculosis.

phut *n* a dull sound as of something bursting.

phyla *n* pl of PHYLUM.

phylactery *n* (*pl* **-ies**) either of two small square leather boxes containing passages from scripture, traditionally worn on the left arm and forehead by Jewish men during morning weekday prayers.

phyllo /'feeloh/ *n* see FILO.

phylloquinone *n* a naturally occurring vitamin found *esp* in green plants; vitamin K_1.

phylloxera *n* a plant louse that is destructive to many plants such as grapevines.

phylogeny *n* (*pl* **-ies**) the evolution of a genetically related group of organisms, e.g. a race or species, or the history of this.

phylum *n* (*pl* **phyla**) a major group of related species in the classification of plants and animals.

physalis *n* a plant with bell-shaped flowers and a balloon-like CALYX (outer part of flower head).

physic *n archaic* **1** a medicinal preparation, e.g. a drug, *esp* a purgative. **2** medical treatment.

physical[1] *adj* **1a** having material existence; perceptible, *esp* through the senses, and subject to the laws of nature. **b** of material things: *the physical world*. **2a** of the body: *a physical examination*. **b** concerned or preoccupied with the body and its needs, as opposed to spiritual matters. **c** involving bodily contact: *physical sports*. **3a** of sciences such as physics, chemistry, and astronomy. **b** of or involving physics. ➤➤ **physicality** *n*, **physically** *adv*.

physical[2] *n* a medical examination of a person's body to determine their health and fitness.

physical chemistry *n* the branch of chemistry concerned with the relationship between the chemical structure of substances and their physical properties.

physical education *n* instruction in sports, athletic games, and gymnastics.

physical geography *n* geography that deals with the exterior physical features and changes of the earth rather than political boundaries, etc.

physical science *n* the natural sciences, such as physics, astronomy, or chemistry, that deal primarily with nonliving materials, or any one of these.

physical therapy *n NAm* = PHYSIOTHERAPY.

physician *n* a person skilled in the art of healing; *specif* a doctor of medicine.

physicist *n* an expert or specialist in physics.

physics *pl n* **1** (*used as sing. or pl*) a science that deals with matter and energy and their properties and interactions in such fields as mechanics, heat, electricity, magnetism, atomic structure, etc. **2** (*used as pl*) the physical properties and phenomena of a particular system.

physio *n* (*pl* **-os**) *Brit, informal* **1** a physiotherapist. **2** physiotherapy.

physiognomy *n* (*pl* **-ies**) the facial features, *esp* when revealing qualities of mind or character.

physiology *n* **1** the branch of biology that deals with the functions and activities of life or of living matter, e.g. organs, tissues, or cells, and the physical and chemical phenomena involved. **2** the physiological activities of an organism, or part of one, or a particular bodily function. ➤➤ **physiological** *adj*, **physiologist** *n*.

physiotherapy *n* the treatment of disease, injury, etc by physical and mechanical means, e.g. massage and regulated exercise. ➤➤ **physiotherapist** *n*.

physique *n* the form or structure of a person's body.

phytoplankton *n* planktonic plant life.

PI *abbr* private investigator.

pi *n* (*pl* **pis**) **1** the 16th letter of the Greek alphabet (Π, π), equivalent to roman p. **2a** the ratio of the circumference of a circle to its diameter with a value, to eight decimal places, of 3.14159265. **b** the symbol (π) denoting this ratio.

pia mater /,pie-ə 'mahtə, ,pee-ə, 'maytə/ *n* the thin innermost membrane that envelops the brain and spinal cord.

pianism *n* the art or technique of piano playing, or skill in playing the piano.

pianissimo *adj and adv* of a piece of music: to be performed very softly.

pianist *n* a person who plays the piano, *esp* a skilled or professional performer.

pianistic *adj* **1** of or characteristic of the piano. **2** skilled in or well adapted to piano playing.

piano[1] *n* (*pl* **-os**) a keyboard instrument with a wooden case containing strings that are stretched across a frame and struck by hammers when keys are pressed. ➤➤ **pianist** *n*.

piano[2] *adj and adv* of a piece of music: to be performed in a soft or quiet manner.

piano accordion *n* an accordion with a small piano-like keyboard for the right hand.

pianoforte /pi,anoh'fawti/ *n formal* a piano.

Pianola *n trademark* a mechanical piano operated by the pressure of air through perforations in a paper roll.

piastre (*NAm* **piaster**) /pi'astə/ *n* a unit of currency in certain Middle Eastern countries, e.g. Egypt and Syria, worth 100th of the basic monetary unit.

piazza /pi'atsə/ *n* an open square, *esp* in an Italian town.

pibroch *n* music for the Scottish Highland bagpipes in the form of a set of martial or mournful variations.

pic *n* (*pl* **pics** *or* **pix**) *informal* a photograph.

pica *n* **1** a unit of one sixth of an inch (4.23mm) or 12 points used in measuring typographical material. **2** a size of typewriter type providing 10 characters to the linear inch. **3** a former size of printing type equal to 12 point.

picador *n* (*pl* **picadors** *or* **picadores**) a horseman who in a bullfight prods the bull with a lance to weaken its neck and shoulder muscles.

picaninny *n* (*pl* **-ies**) *NAm* see PICCANINNY.

picaresque *adj* of a type of fiction narrating in loosely linked episodes the adventures of a rogue.

picayune *n* a five-cent piece or other small coin.

piccalilli *n* (*pl* **piccalillies** *or* **piccalillis**) a hot relish of chopped vegetables, mustard, and spices.

piccaninny (*NAm* **picaninny** *or* **pickaninny**) *n* (*pl* **-ies**) *offensive* a small black child.

piccolo *n* (*pl* **-os**) a small flute with a range an octave higher than that of an ordinary flute.

pick[1] *v* **1** to choose or select from a number of choices or possibilities. **2** to remove (a fruit or flower) by pulling it from a tree or plant. **3a** to remove (unwanted matter) from the nose or teeth with a finger or pointed instrument. **b** to make (a hole) by digging at a surface. **4** to steal from (a person's pocket). **5** to provoke (a quarrel or fight). **6a** to unlock (a lock) with a wire or other device other than the key. **b** to loosen or pull apart with a sharp point. ✱ **pick and choose** to choose the best of something. **pick at** to eat (food) sparingly and with little appetite. **pick holes in** to find fault or weaknesses in. **pick on** to single out for unpleasant treatment. **pick one's way** to go forward carefully or with difficulty. **pick somebody's brains** to get ideas from somebody who is well informed. **pick through/over** to sort (a number of items). **pick to pieces** to criticize harshly.

pick[2] *n* **1** the act or privilege of choosing or selecting; a choice. **2** (*used as sing. or pl*) the best or choicest.

pick[3] *n* **1** a heavy iron or steel tool with a long wooden handle and a head that is pointed at one or both ends. **2** *informal* a plectrum.

pickaninny *n* (*pl* **-ies**) *NAm* see PICCANINNY.

pickaxe (*NAm* **pickax**) *n* = PICK[3] (1).

picket[1] *n* **1** a person or group of people posted by a trade union at a place of work affected by a strike to try to persuade workers not to go in or to prevent them doing so. **2** (*used as sing. or pl*) a small body of troops detached to guard an army from surprise attack. **3** a pointed or sharpened stake or post.

picket[2] *v* (**picketed, picketing**) to walk or stand in front of (a place of work, etc) as a picket.

pickings *pl n* **1** gleanable or eatable fragments; scraps. **2** yield or return for effort expended; *esp* rewards obtained by dishonest or dubious means.

pickle[1] *n* **1a** a brine or vinegar solution in which foods are preserved. **b** food, e.g. a mixture of chopped vegetables, preserved in a brine or vinegar solution. **c** (*also in pl*) a vegetable that has been preserved in a brine or vinegar solution, *esp* a cucumber. **2** *informal* a difficult or confused situation; a mess.

pickle[2] *v* to preserve in pickle.

pickled *adj informal* drunk.

pick-me-up *n informal* something that stimulates or restores; a tonic.

pick off *v* to aim at and shoot at (a target in a group).

pick out *v* **1** to select or distinguish (one person or thing) in a group. **2** to play the notes of (a tune) by ear or one by one.

pickpocket *n* a person who steals from pockets or bags.

pickup *n* **1** the act or an instance of picking up. **2** a light motor truck having an open body with low sides and tailboard. **3a** a device on a record player that converts mechanical movements into electrical signals, or this device and the slender arm to which it is attached. **b** a device on a guitar that converts the vibrations of the strings into electrical signals.

pick up *v* **1** to take hold of and lift. **2a** to collect or take (passengers or goods) in a vehicle. **b** to collect or buy on one's way. **c** to acquire or learn casually or by chance. **3** to begin a casual relationship with (somebody). **4a** to receive (a radio signal). **b** to become aware of (another person's feeling, etc). **5** to return to (a previous topic). **6** to recover or improve. ✱ **pick up on** to question or criticize (somebody) who has just spoken. **pick up speed** to go faster. **pick up the bill** to accept the cost of or responsibility for.

pickup truck *n* = PICKUP (2).

picky *adj* (**-ier, -iest**) fussy or choosy.

picnic[1] *n* **1** an informal meal eaten in the open, or an outing including such a meal. **2** *informal* a pleasant or amusingly carefree experience. **3** *informal* an easily accomplished task or feat.

picnic[2] *v* (**picnicked, picnicking**) to have or go on a picnic. ➤➤ **picnicker** *n.*

pico- *comb. form* forming words, denoting: million millionth (10^{-12}).

picot *n* a small ornamental loop on ribbon or lace.

picric acid *n* a strong toxic yellow acid used in powerful explosives, as a dye, and as an antiseptic.

Pict *n* a member of the Celtic people who once occupied northern Britain and later became amalgamated with the Scots in AD 843.

pictogram *n* = PICTOGRAPH.

pictograph *n* **1** an ancient or prehistoric drawing or painting, often on a rock wall. **2** any of the symbols used in a system of picture writing such as Chinese or Egyptian hieroglyphics. **3** a diagram representing statistical data by pictorial forms. ➤➤ **pictographic** *adj.*

pictorial[1] *adj* consisting of or illustrated by pictures. ➤➤ **pictorially** *adv.*

pictorial[2] *n* a newspaper or magazine with many pictures in it.

picture[1] *n* **1** a design or representation made by painting, drawing, photography, etc. **2** a description so vivid or graphic as to suggest a mental image or give an accurate idea of something. **3a** a transitory visible image or reproduction, e.g. on a television screen. **b** a cinema film. **c** *chiefly Brit, informal (in pl)* the cinema. ✱ **in the picture** *informal* fully informed and up to date.

picture[2] *v* **1** to paint, draw, or photograph a representation, image, or visual conception of (somebody or something); to depict. **2** to describe graphically in words. **3** to form a mental image of; to imagine.

picture postcard *n* a postcard with a picture on one side.

picture-postcard *adj* picturesque.

picturesque *adj* **1** quaintly or charmingly attractive. **2** evoking striking mental images; vivid. ➤➤ **picturesquely** *adv,* **picturesqueness** *n.*

picture window *n* a large single-paned window usu facing an attractive view.

PID *abbr* pelvic inflammatory disease.

piddle *v informal* **1** (*usu* + about/around) to act or work in an idle or trifling manner. **2** to urinate.

piddling *adj informal* trivial or paltry.

pidgin *n* a language based on two or more languages and used for purposes of communication, *esp* for trade, between people with different native languages: compare CREOLE.

pi-dog *n* see PYE-DOG.

pie *n* a dish consisting of a sweet or savoury filling covered or encased by pastry and baked in a container. ✱ **pie in the sky** *informal* an illusory hope or prospect of future happiness.

piebald[1] *adj* of a horse: spotted or blotched with different colours, *esp* black and white.

piebald[2] *n* a piebald horse.

piece[1] *n* **1a** a part of a whole, *esp* a part detached, cut, or broken from a whole, or one of the elements from which something is made. **b** a distinct separate bit or item of something. **2** a literary, artistic, dramatic, or musical work. **3** a coin, *esp* of a specified value. **4** a small object of some shape used in playing a board game. **5a** a gun. **b** *chiefly NAm, slang* a firearm. ✱ **go to pieces** to suffer a mental breakdown; to lose control of oneself, e.g. because of stress, shock, or anger. **in one piece** unharmed; without being damaged. **of a piece** alike; consistent. **piece by piece** by one piece after another; in small stages. **tear/pull something to pieces** to criticize something severely; to show the faults or flaws in it. **tear somebody to pieces** to criticize somebody harshly. **to pieces** into fragments.

piece[2] *v* **1** (*often* + together) to join (parts of something) into a whole. **2** (*often* + up) to repair, renew, or complete by adding pieces; to patch.

pièce de résistance /ˌpyes də rəˈzistanhs/ *n* (*pl* **pièces de résistance**) an outstanding item; a showpiece.

piecemeal[1] *adv* **1** one piece at a time; gradually. **2** in pieces or fragments; apart.

piecemeal[2] *adj* done, made, or accomplished piece by piece or in a fragmentary or unsystematic way.

piece of cake *n informal* something easily accomplished.

piece of eight *n* (*pl* **pieces of eight**) a former Spanish coin worth eight reals.

piece of work *n informal* a person.

piece rate *n* a system whereby wages are calculated according to a set rate per unit produced.

pièces de résistance /ˌpyes də ˈrəzistanhs/ *n* pl of PIÈCE DE RÉSISTANCE.

piecework *n* work that is paid for at a set rate per unit.

pie chart *n* a graphical means of showing the composition of a whole, each component being represented by a sector of a circle.

pied *adj* having patches of two or more colours.

pied-à-terre /ˌpyay dah ˈteə/ *n* (*pl* **pieds-à-terre**) a temporary or second lodging, e.g. a flat in a city kept by somebody who lives in the country.

pie-dog *n* see PYE-DOG.

pied piper *n* (*often* **Pied Piper**) a person who offers strong but delusive enticement.

Word history

named after *The Pied Piper of Hamelin,* title and hero of a poem by Robert Browning d.1889, English poet. The poem recounts a German folk tale about a piper who first rids the town of Hamelin (Hameln, near Hanover) of rats, and then, when payment for this service is refused, leads away the children of the town to a nearby hill, where they disappear through a door never to be seen again.

pieds-à-terre /ˌpyay dah ˈteə/ *n* pl of PIED-À-TERRE.

pie-eyed *adj informal* drunk.

pier *n* **1** a structure extending into navigable water for use as a landing place, promenade, etc. **2** an intermediate support for the adjacent ends of two bridge spans. **3a** a vertical structural support, e.g. for a wall. **b** a short section of wall between two openings.

pierce *v* **1** to make a hole in or through; to perforate. **2** to force or make a way into or through. ➤➤ **piercer** *n.*

piercing *adj* **1** penetratingly loud or shrill. **2** bright and seeming to be able to see through or into things clearly. **3** penetratingly cold. **4** strongly unkind and hurtful. **5** perceptive.

Pierrot /ˈpiəroh/ *n* a stock comic character of old French pantomime usu having a whitened face, baggy white clothing, and a pointed hat.

pietà /peeayˈtah, pyayˈtah/ *n* (*often* **Pietà**) a representation of the Virgin Mary mourning over the dead body of Christ.

piety *n* (*pl* **-ies**) **1** the quality or state of being pious; religious devotion. **2** a conventional belief adhered to unthinkingly.

piezoelectricity *n* **1** electricity or electric polarity due to pressure, *esp* in a crystalline substance such as quartz. **2** the creation of pressure in such a crystalline substance due to electricity. ➤➤ **piezoelectric** *adj.*

piffle *n informal* trivial nonsense.

piffling *adj informal* trivial or derisory.

pig[1] *n* **1** a stout-bodied short-legged omnivorous mammal with a thick bristly skin and a long mobile snout, *esp* a domesticated variety. **2** *informal* a person who is like or suggestive of a pig in habits or behaviour, e.g. in dirtiness, greed, or selfishness. **3** *slang, derog* a police officer. **4** a shaped mass of cast crude metal, *esp* iron. ✱ **a pig in a poke** something offered in such a way as to obscure its value, lack of value, or real nature [from the practice of putting a cat in a poke (bag) to fool a customer into thinking they were buying a sucking pig]. **make a pig's ear of something** *informal* to make a mess of something; to do or handle it badly. ➤➤ **piglet** *n.*

pig[2] *v* (**pigged, pigging**) *informal* **1** to eat (food) greedily. **2** to overindulge (oneself).

pigeon *n* a bird with a stout body and smooth and compact plumage.

pigeon breast *n* a deformity of the chest marked by a sharply projecting breastbone. ➤➤ **pigeon-breasted** *adj.*

pigeon chest *n* = PIGEON BREAST.

pigeonhole[1] *n* **1** a small open compartment, e.g. in a desk or cabinet, for letters or documents. **2** a neat category which usu fails to reflect actual complexities. **3** a hole for a pigeon to nest in.

pigeonhole[2] *v* to assign (somebody or something) to a category, *esp* in an overly restrictive way.

pigeon-toed *adj* having the toes turned in.

piggery *n* (*pl* **-ies**) **1** a place where pigs are kept. **2** dirty, greedy, or nasty behaviour.

piggish *adj* of or resembling a pig, *esp* in being dirty, greedy, bad-mannered etc.

piggy[1] *n* (*pl* **-ies**) used by or to children: a pig. ✱ **piggy in the middle 1** a children's game in which two people throw a ball to one another while a person standing between them tries to intercept it. **2** *informal* a person who is caught in an awkward or harmful situation between two others who are in disagreement or conflict.

piggy[2] *adj* (**-ier, -iest**) **1** of or resembling a pig. **2** like a pig in being dirty, greedy, bad-mannered, etc; = PIGGISH.

piggyback[1] *adv* up on the back and shoulders.

piggyback[2] *n* a ride on somebody's back and shoulders.

piggy bank *n* a box to keep money in, often in the shape of a pig.

pigheaded *adj* obstinate; stubborn.

pig iron *n* crude iron from the blast furnace, before refining.

pigment[1] *n* **1** a substance that colours other materials, *esp* a powdered substance that is mixed with a liquid in which it is relatively insoluble and is used to colour paints, inks, plastics, etc. **2** any of various colouring matters in animals and plants. ➤➤ **pigmentary** *adj,* **pigmentation** *n.*

pigment[2] *v* to colour with pigment, or as if with pigment.

pigmy *n* (*pl* **-ies**) see PYGMY.

pigskin *n* the skin of a pig, or leather made from the skin of a pig.

pigsty *n* (*pl* **-ies**) **1** an enclosure with a covered shed for pigs. **2** a dirty, untidy, or neglected place.

pigswill *n* waste food fed to pigs.

pigtail *n* a tight plait of hair, *esp* when worn singly at the back of the head. ➤➤ **pigtailed** *adj.*

pika *n* a small tailless mammal related to the rabbits, found mostly in mountainous regions in Asia, E Europe, and western N America.

pike[1] *n* (*pl* **pikes** *or* **pike**) a large long-snouted bony fish widely distributed in cooler parts of the N hemisphere and valued for food and as a game fish.

pike[2] *n* a weapon consisting of a long wooden shaft with a pointed steel head that was used by foot soldiers.

pike[3] *n* a body position, e.g. in diving, in which the hands touch the toes or clasp the legs at the knees, the hips are bent forward, and the knees are straight.

pikelet *n Brit, dialect* a crumpet.

pikestaff *n* the staff of a foot soldier's pike.

pilaf *or* **pilaff** /'peelaf, 'pilaf/ *or* **pilau** /'peelow, pi'low/ *or* **pulao** *n* a dish of seasoned rice or wheat, with meat, vegetables, etc.

pilaster *n* a shallow pier or a flat representation of a usu classical column in shallow relief projecting slightly from a wall.

pilau /'peelow, pi'low/ *n* see PILAF.

pilchard *n* a food fish of the herring family that occurs in large schools along the coasts of Europe.

pile[1] *n* **1a** a quantity of things heaped together. **b** (*also in pl*) a large quantity, number, or amount. **2** a great amount of money; a fortune. **3** a large building.

pile[2] *v* **1** (*often* + up) to lay or place (things) in a pile. **2** to put or heap (things) in large quantities. **3** (+ into/out of) to get into or out of a vehicle in a confused rush. ✱ **pile into** of a vehicle: to crash into (something). **pile it on** *informal* to exaggerate.

pile[3] *n* a soft raised surface on a fabric or carpet, consisting of cut threads or loops.

pile[4] *n* a beam of timber, steel, reinforced concrete, etc driven into the ground to carry a vertical load.

pile-driver *n* a machine for driving piles into the ground.

piles *pl n* haemorrhoids.

pile up *v* to accumulate.

pile-up *n informal* a collision involving usu several motor vehicles and causing damage or injury.

pileus *n* (*pl* **pilei**) the cap of many fungi, e.g. mushrooms.

pilfer *v* to steal (items of little value). ➤➤ **pilferage** *n.*

pilgrim *n* **1** a person making a pilgrimage. **2** *archaic or literary* a traveller.

pilgrimage *n* a journey to a shrine or sacred place as an act of devotion, in order to acquire spiritual merit, or as a penance.

pill[1] *n* **1** a small solid mass of medicine to be swallowed whole. **2** (**the Pill**) an oral contraceptive in the form of a pill.

pill[2] *v* of a fabric: to become rough with or mat into little balls of fibre.

pillage[1] *n* the act or an instance of looting or plundering.

pillage[2] *v* **1** to plunder (a place) ruthlessly; to loot. **2** to take as plunder. ➤➤ **pillager** *n.*

pillar *n* **1a** a firm upright support for a superstructure. **b** an ornamental column or shaft. **c** anything like a pillar in shape. **2** a person perceived as a prop or mainstay of their class, group, etc. ✱ **from pillar to post** from one place or one situation to another. ➤➤ **pillared** *adj.*

pillar box *n* a red pillar-shaped public postbox.

pillbox *n* **1** a box for pills. **2** a small low concrete weapon emplacement. **3** a small round brimless hat with a flat crown and straight sides, worn *esp* by women.

pillion[1] *n* a seat for a passenger on a motorcycle or motor scooter.

pillion[2] *adv* on a pillion, or as if on a pillion.

pillock *n Brit, informal* a stupid or objectionable person.

pillory[1] *n* (*pl* **-ies**) a device for publicly punishing offenders, consisting of a wooden frame with holes to hold the head and hands.

pillory[2] *v* (**-ies, -ied**) **1** to put in a pillory. **2** to expose to public contempt, ridicule, or scorn.

pillow[1] *n* a usu rectangular cloth container filled with soft material such as feathers or synthetic fibre and used to support the head of a reclining or sleeping person. ➤➤ **pillowy** *adj.*

pillow[2] *v* to rest or lay (something) on a pillow, or as if on a pillow.

pillowcase *n* a removable washable cover for a pillow.

pillow talk *n* intimate conversation in bed between lovers.

pilot[1] *n* **1** a person who handles or is qualified to handle the controls of an aircraft or spacecraft. **2** a person who is qualified and usu licensed to conduct a ship into and out of a port or in specified waters. **3** a trial run of a project or a trial programme on radio or television, e.g. to test public opinion or reaction.

pilot[2] *v* (**piloted, piloting**) **1** to act as a pilot of (an aircraft, ship, etc). **2** to test (a product, programme idea, etc) by means of a pilot.

pilotage *n* **1** the piloting of a ship, aircraft, spacecraft, etc. **2** the fee paid to a ship's pilot. **3** the navigation of an aircraft by direct observation of landmarks and use of charts.

pilot fish *n* a small oceanic fish of warm and tropical seas that is marked with distinctive dark-coloured vertical bands and often swims in the company of a large fish, *esp* a shark.

pilot light *n* **1** an indicator light showing whether power is on or where a switch or circuit breaker is located. **2** a small permanent flame used to ignite gas at a burner, e.g. on a gas cooker or a central-heating boiler.

pilot officer *n* an officer of the lowest rank in the Royal Air Force.

pilot whale *n* a toothed whale with a bulbous head.

Pilsner *or* **Pilsener** *n* a light beer with a strong flavour of hops.

pimento *n* (*pl* **-os**) **1** see PIMIENTO. **2** = ALLSPICE.

pimiento *or* **pimento** *n* (*pl* **-os**) any of various sweet peppers with a mild sweet flavour.

pimp[1] *n* a man who solicits clients for a prostitute or brothel and takes some of their earnings.

pimp[2] *v* to act as a pimp.

pimpernel *n* a plant of the primrose family, such as the scarlet pimpernel.

pimple *n* a small solid inflamed elevation of the skin, usu containing pus. ➤➤ **pimpled** *adj,* **pimply** *adj.*

PIN *abbr* = PIN NUMBER.

pin[1] *n* **1a** a small thin pointed piece of metal with a head used for fastening cloth, paper, etc. **b** an ornament or badge fastened to clothing with a pin. **2** a relatively long and slender piece of solid material, e.g. wood or metal, used for fastening separate articles together, as a safety catch, or as a support. **3a** any of the bottle-shaped wooden pieces constituting the target in various games, e.g. skittles and tenpin bowling. **b** the staff of the flag marking a hole on a golf course. **4** a projecting metal bar on a plug that is inserted into a socket. **5** *informal (usu in pl)* a leg.

pin[2] *v* (**pinned, pinning**) **1** to fasten or attach with a pin or pins. **2** to hold (somebody or something) firmly so they cannot move. ✱ **pin one's hopes on** to rely on completely. **pin something on** to assign the blame or responsibility for something on (somebody or something).

pina colada /ˌpeenə kəˈlahdə/ *n* a drink made from rum, coconut milk, and pineapple juice.

pinafore *n Brit* **1** an apron, usu with a bib. **2** a sleeveless dress designed to be worn over a blouse or sweater.

pinafore dress *n* = PINAFORE (2).

pinball *n* a game in which a ball is propelled across a sloping surface at pins and targets that score points if hit.

pince-nez /ˈpans nay, ˈpins/ *n* (*pl* **pince-nez**) glasses clipped to the nose by a spring.

pincer *n* **1a** (*in pl*) an instrument having two short handles and two grasping jaws working on a pivot and used for gripping things. **b** the front claw of a lobster, crab, etc, resembling a pair of pincers. **2** either part of a two-pronged attack aiming to surround an enemy position.

pinch[1] *v* **1a** to squeeze tightly and usu painfully between the finger and thumb or between the jaws of an instrument. **b** to squeeze or compress painfully. **2** *informal* to steal (something). **3** *slang* of the police: to arrest. **4a** to cause physical or mental pain to. **b** (*usu in passive*) to cause (somebody, *esp* their face) to appear thin or shrunken. **5** to be frugal.

pinch[2] *n* **1a** an act of pinching; a squeeze. **b** as much as may be taken between the finger and thumb. **2** (**the pinch**) hardship; privation: *After a year of sanctions, they began to feel the pinch.* ✱ **at a pinch** in an emergency.

pinchbeck[1] *n* an alloy of copper and zinc used to imitate gold in jewellery.

pinchbeck[2] *adj* sham, counterfeit, or imitative.

pincushion *n* a small cushion in which pins are stuck ready for use.

pin down *v* **1** to force (somebody) to be decisive or explicit about their intentions. **2** to define or categorize clearly. **3** to restrict the movement of (an enemy or fugitive) by surrounding them or firing on them.

pine[1] *n* a coniferous evergreen tree which has long slender needles and straight-grained white or yellow wood.

pine[2] *v* **1** (*often* + away) to lose vigour or health, e.g. through grief; to languish. **2** (+ for) to yearn intensely and persistently, *esp* for something unattainable; to long for it.

pineal body *n* a small appendage of the brain of most vertebrates that has the structure of an eye in a few reptiles and that secretes melatonin and other hormones.

pineal gland *n* = PINEAL BODY.

pineapple *n* a large oval prickly fruit with succulent yellow flesh.

pinecone *n* a cone of a pine tree.

pine marten *n* a slender Eurasian marten with a yellowish patch on the chest and throat.

pine nut *n* the edible seed of any of various chiefly western N American pine trees.

ping *v* to make or cause to make a sharp ringing sound. ➤➤ **ping** *n,* **pinger** *n.*

pingin /ˈping·gin/ *n* (*pl* **pingin**) a unit of currency in Ireland, worth 100th of a punt.

Ping-Pong *n trademark* = TABLE TENNIS.

pinguid *adj* fat and greasy.

pinhead *n* **1** the head of a pin. **2** *informal* a stupid person.

pinhole *n* a very small hole.

pinhole camera *n* a photographic camera with a minute aperture and no lens.

pinion[1] *n* the section of a bird's wing where the flight feathers grow.

pinion[2] *v* **1** to disable or restrain (somebody) by holding or binding their arms. **2** to restrain (a bird) from flight, *esp* by cutting off the pinion of a wing.

pinion[3] *n* a gear with a small number of teeth designed to mesh with a larger gear wheel or rack.

pink[1] *adj* **1** of a colour midway between red and white. **2** of a person or their political views: slightly left of centre. **3** relating to homosexuals or homosexuality: *the pink pound.* ➤➤ **pinkish** *adj.*

pink[2] *n* any of various shades of colour midway between red and white. ✱ **in the pink 1** of a business, economy, etc: flourishing or prospering. **2** in the very best of condition, health, etc.

pink[3] *n* a plant related to the carnation and widely grown for its attractive and sometimes scented flowers.

pink[4] *v* to cut a zigzag pattern on the edge of (fabric) to prevent fraying.

pink[5] *v* of an internal-combustion engine: to make a series of popping or rattling noises as an indication that the combustion of the fuel-air mixture in the cylinders is faulty.

pink gin *n* a drink consisting of gin flavoured with angostura bitters which give the drink a pale pink colour.

pinkie *or* **pinky** *n* (*pl* **-ies**) *informal* the little finger.

pinking shears *pl n* shears or scissors with a saw-toothed inner edge on the blades, used to give a zigzag edge on cloth.

pinko *n* (*pl* **-os** *or* **-oes**) *informal, derog* somebody who holds political views that are left of centre.

pinky *n* (*pl* **-ies**) see PINKIE.

pin money *n* extra money earned or given for casual spending.

pinna *n* (*pl* **pinnae** *or* **pinnas**) the largely cartilaginous projecting portion of the outer ear in humans and other mammals.

pinnacle *n* **1** the highest or most successful point of development or achievement. **2** a mountain peak or similar towering structure. **3** an architectural ornament resembling a small spire and used *esp* to crown a buttress.

pinnae *n* pl of PINNA.

pinnate *adj* of a leaf: resembling a feather, *esp* in having similar parts arranged on opposite sides of an axis like the barbs on the shaft of a feather.

PIN number *n* a four-digit number known only to the holder of a plastic card, that is used as a security check when the card is used, e.g. to withdraw money from a cash dispenser.

pinny *n* (*pl* **-ies**) *informal* = PINAFORE (1).

Pinot /ˈpeenoh/ *n* a variety of grape, related to Chardonnay, or the wine produced from it.

pinpoint[1] *v* to fix, determine, or identify (the site of something) with precision.

pinpoint[2] *adj* extremely precise.

pinpoint[3] *n* a very small point or area.

pinprick *n* a small puncture made by a pin.

pins and needles *pl n* (*used as sing. or pl*) a pricking tingling sensation in a limb or the fingers or toes when they are recovering from numbness.

pinstripe *n* **1** a very thin stripe, *esp* on a fabric. **2** (*usu in pl*) a suit or trousers with pinstripes. ➤➤ **pinstriped** *adj.*

pint *n* **1** a unit of capacity equal to one eighth of a gallon (0.568l in Britain or 0.473l in the USA for liquid measure; 0.551l in Britain and the USA for dry measure). **2** *Brit, informal* a pint of beer.

pintail *n* (*pl* **pintails** *or* **pintail**) a slender grey and white dabbling duck with an upwardly pointing tail.

pintle *n* a usu upright pivot on which another part, *esp* a rudder, turns.

pinto *n* (*pl* **-os** *or* **-oes**) *NAm* a piebald or blotched horse or pony.

pinto bean *n* a mottled bean that resembles the kidney bean in size and shape.

pint-size *adj* very small, *esp* smaller than normal.

pint-sized *adj* = PINT-SIZE.

pin tuck *n* a very narrow tuck in a garment, *esp* a shirt front or dress bodice.

pin-up *n* a picture or poster of a sexually attractive person, usu either a famous celebrity or somebody seductively or scantily clothed.

pinwheel *n* **1** = CATHERINE WHEEL. **2** a type of cogwheel that has pins projecting radially or axially from its rim.

Pinyin *n* the standard modern spelling system for transliterating Chinese characters into the roman alphabet.

pion *n* in physics, any of several positive, negative, or neutral unstable elementary particles of the meson family responsible for the force between nucleons.

pioneer[1] *n* **1a** a person or group that originates or helps open up a new line of thought or activity or a new method or technical development. **b** any of the first people to settle in a territory. **2** a member of a military unit engaging in light construction and defensive works.

pioneer[2] *v* to originate or take part in the development of (something).

pious *adj* **1** devout; deeply religious. **2** dutiful; reverential. **3** marked by sham or hypocritical virtue; sanctimonious. ➤➤ **piously** *adv,* **piousness** *n.*

pip[1] *n* a small fruit seed of an apple, orange, etc.

pip[2] *n* (*usu in pl*) a short high-pitched tone, *esp* one of a series given as a time signal in a radio broadcast or as an indication on a payphone that the caller should insert more money.

pip[3] *v* (**pipped, pipping**) of a hatching bird: to crack open (its eggshell).

pip[4] *n* **1a** any of the dots on dice and dominoes that indicate numerical value. **b** any of the symbols on a set of playing cards that indicate suit and rank. **2** a star worn, *esp* on the shoulder, to indicate an army officer's rank.

pip[5] *n* a disease of poultry marked by the formation of a scale or crust on the bird's tongue and the presence of thick mucus in its throat.

pip[6] *v* (**pipped, pipping**) *informal* to beat (somebody or something) by a narrow margin. ✱ **pip at the post** to beat at the very last minute, *esp* in a race or competition.

pipal *or* **peepul** *n* a large long-lived Indian fig tree.

pipe[1] *n* **1** a long tube or hollow body for conducting a liquid, gas, etc. **2** a wood, clay, etc tube with a mouthpiece at one end, and at the other a small bowl in which tobacco is burned for smoking. **3a** a simple musical instrument consisting of a tube with holes in it, the holes being covered by the fingers in varying configurations to produce different notes when air is blown into the tube. **b** (**the pipes**) bagpipes. **c** any cylindrical tube that produces music, e.g. on an organ. **4** a high-pitched noise, *esp* a shrill birdsong. ✱ **put that in one's pipe and smoke it** *informal* to be forced to accept a situation or fact despite one's objections or its disadvantages.

pipe[2] *v* **1** to convey (a fluid substance, *esp* water, gas, or oil) along a pipe. **2** to transmit (a radio or television broadcast, music, or an electrical signal) along wires or cables. **3** to put (a decoration or message) on a cake, etc in icing or cream using a bag with a nozzle. **4** to trim (clothing, soft furnishings, etc) with decorative cord, etc. **5** to say or sing in a shrill voice. **6** to play (a tune) on a pipe.

pipe clay *n* a fine white clay used *esp* for making tobacco pipes and for whitening leather and other materials.

pipe cleaner *n* a piece of flexible wire covered with tufted fabric which is used to clean the stem of a tobacco pipe.

piped music *n* recorded background music played through loudspeakers in public places.

pipe down *v informal* to stop talking or making noise.

pipe dream *n* an unattainable or fantastic plan or hope.

pipeline[1] *n* **1** a line of pipe with pumps, valves, and control devices for conveying liquids, gases, etc. **2** in computing, a method of increasing processing speed by performing a task in stages that work in parallel. ✱ **in the pipeline** in the process of being done, completed, developed, or delivered.

pipeline[2] *v* **1** to convey (a fluid substance) along a pipeline. **2** in computing, to carry out (instructions) using a pipeline.

pipe organ *n* = ORGAN (1A).

piper *n* somebody who plays a pipe or bagpipes.

pipette (*NAm* **pipet**) *n* a narrow tube that has a small-bore aperture at the lower end and usu widens into a bulb in the middle, into which a liquid is drawn by suction and retained by closing the upper end, used for measuring or transferring quantities of liquid.

pipe up *v* to begin to play, sing, or speak, *esp* unexpectedly.

piping *n* **1** a quantity or system of pipes. **2a** a narrow cord trimming used to decorate upholstery, garments, etc. **b** a thin cordlike line of icing or cream used to decorate cakes, etc.

piping hot *adj* very hot.

pipistrelle *n* a small insect-eating bat.

pipit *n* a small songbird with brown plumage streaked with darker brown or black.

pippin *n* an eating apple with a yellow skin strongly flushed with red.

pipsqueak *n informal* a small or insignificant person.

piquant *adj* **1** having an agreeably stimulating taste; savoury. **2** pleasantly stimulating to the mind. ➤➤ **piquancy** *n,* **piquantly** *adv.*

pique[1] *n* resentment resulting from wounded pride, or the bad temper that results from this.

pique[2] *v* (**piques, piqued, piquing**) **1** to arouse anger or resentment in (somebody), *esp* by offending or insulting them. **2** to arouse or provoke (curiosity or interest).

piqué *or* **pique** /'peekay/ *n* a durable ribbed fabric made from cotton, rayon, or silk.

piquet *n* **1** a card game for two players played with a 32-card pack. **2** = PICKET[1] (3).

piracy *n* **1** the act of committing robbery or illegal violence on the high seas. **2** the infringement of a copyright, patent, etc.

piranha /pi'rahn(y)ə/ *n* a small S American freshwater fish with strong jaws and sharp teeth which it uses for ripping flesh from its prey.

pirate[1] *n* **1** somebody who commits piracy. **2** (*used before a noun*) relating to something that has been obtained without the owner's permission: *pirate videos*. **3** (*used before a noun*) denoting or relating to an unauthorized radio station. ⋙ **piratic** *adj*.

pirate[2] *v* to reproduce (somebody else's work, ideas, etc) without authorization.

pirogue *n* a long narrow canoe made from a hollowed-out tree trunk and used mainly in the Caribbean and the waters round Central America.

pirouette[1] *n* in ballet and skating, a fast spin of the body, *esp* one performed on the toes or ball of one foot while the other foot is raised.

pirouette[2] *v* to perform a pirouette.

pis *n* pl of PI.

piscatorial *adj* = PISCATORY.

piscatory *adj* relating to fish or fishing.

Pisces *n* **1** in astronomy, a constellation (the Fish or Fishes) depicted as two fishes joined at the tails. **2** in astrology, the twelfth sign of the zodiac or a person born under this sign. ⋙ **Piscean** *adj and n*.

pisciculture *n* the breeding and rearing of fish under artificial or controlled conditions.

piscina /pi'seenə/ *n* (*pl* **piscinas** *or* **piscinae**) in the Roman Catholic Church, a stone basin with a drain where water used in the Mass can be poured away.

piscine *adj* relating to fish.

piscivorous *adj* of an animal: feeding only or mainly on fish. ⋙ **piscivore** *n*.

piss[1] *v coarse slang* to urinate.

piss[2] *n coarse slang* **1** urine. **2** an instance of urinating. ✻ **take the piss** *Brit, coarse slang* to make fun of, tease, or mock somebody or something.

piss about *v chiefly Brit, coarse slang* to waste time doing something that has no value.

piss around *v* = PISS ABOUT.

pissed *adj* **1** *Brit, coarse slang* drunk. **2** *NAm, slang* very angry or upset.

piss off *v* **1** *Brit, coarse slang* to go away. **2** *coarse slang* to cause (somebody) to be annoyed or fed up.

pissoir *n* a public urinal, *esp* in the street in some European countries.

piss-up *n chiefly Brit, coarse slang* a heavy drinking session.

pistachio *n* (*pl* **-os**) a pale green or yellowish edible nut, often roasted and salted or used to flavour confectionery, *esp* ice cream.

piste /peest/ *n* a prepared slope for skiing.

pistil *n* in botany, the female parts of a flowering plant, comprising the OVARY (the part where the seeds develop), the STYLE[1] (an extension of the ovary), and the STIGMA (the top of the style where pollen is deposited).

pistol *n* a short firearm intended to be aimed and fired with one hand.

pistol-whip *v* (**pistol-whipped, pistol-whipping**) to beat with the butt or barrel of a pistol.

piston *n* **1** a sliding disc or short cylinder fitting within a cylinder in which it moves back and forth or up and down by or against fluid pressure. In an internal-combustion engine, it turns a crankshaft to produce motion. **2** a sliding valve in a cylinder in a brass instrument, which, when depressed, alters a note's pitch.

pit[1] *n* **1a** a hole, shaft, or cavity in the ground. **b** a mine where coal or minerals are excavated. **2** (*often* **the pits**) an area at the side of a motor-racing track for servicing, refuelling, and tyre changing. **3a** a natural hollow in the surface of the body. **b** the bottom of an anatomical part: *the pit of the stomach*. **4** a sunken area in a garage, workshop, etc where a mechanic can work on the underside of vehicles. **5** the area on the floor of a stock exchange where specified commodities are traded. **6** *archaic* an enclosed area where animals, *esp* bears, are made to fight each other. **7a** (**the Pit**) *literary* = HELL. **b** (**the pits**) *informal* the worst imaginable. **8** = ORCHESTRA PIT.

pit[2] *v* (**pitted, pitting**) **1** to make small holes or indentations in the surface of. **2** (+ against) to set (a person or oneself) in competition with another person.

pita *n NAm* see PITTA.

pita bread *n NAm* see PITTA BREAD.

pit-a-pat[1] *or* **pitapat** *n* a series of light tapping sounds.

pit-a-pat[2] *or* **pitapat** *adv and adj* with light tapping sounds.

pit bull *n* = PIT BULL TERRIER.

pit bull terrier *n* a US breed of short-haired terrier with a powerful stocky muscular body, orig bred for fighting.

pitch[1] *n* **1** *chiefly Brit* a piece of ground with boundaries and other areas marked on it, used for playing a team sport. **2** the distinctive quality that a sound has according to the frequency of the vibrations produced at the sound's source, with fast vibrations producing a higher pitch than slow ones. **3** an erratic heaving motion, *esp* an up-and-down movement of a ship, aircraft, or vehicle. **4** a slope, *esp* of a roof, or the degree of this. **5** a level or degree, *esp* an abnormally high one. **6** *informal* **a** a speech given for a specified purpose. **b** a way of talking, *esp* one that uses persuasive language. **7** *chiefly Brit* **a** a place where a street vendor's stall is regularly situated. **b** a place where a street performer regularly does his or her act. ✻ **make a pitch for 1** to put forward a case for (something). **2** to bid for or try to obtain (a contract, business deal, etc).

pitch[2] *v* **1a** to throw in a careless, rough, or casual way; to toss. **b** to move or fall heavily, *esp* forwards or downwards. **c** of a ship, aircraft, or vehicle: to move with or be affected by a heaving or rocking motion. **2a** to set at a specified level: *Don't pitch your hopes of getting the job too high*. **b** in music, to set (a piece of music, one's voice, or an instrument) at a particular pitch. **c** to express (a speech, piece of writing, etc) at a specified level or to adapt it for a particular audience: *He pitched his lecture at a level that was accessible to all*. **d** to set (a price) at a specified level. **3** to erect (a tent, etc) temporarily. **4** to give (a roof) a specified downward incline from the ridge.

pitch[3] *n* **1** a black or dark viscous substance obtained as a residue in the distillation of organic materials, *esp* tars, or any of various similar substances. **2** resin obtained from various conifers.

pitch-black *adj* completely black or dark.

pitchblende *n* a radium-containing uranium oxide occurring as a brown to black lustrous mineral.

pitch-dark *adj* completely dark.

pitched battle *n* **1** a battle between armies fought on previously chosen ground, rather than a chance encounter. **2** a fierce conflict.

pitcher[1] *n* a large jug.

pitcher[2] *n* the player who pitches the ball in a baseball game.

pitcher plant *n* an insectivorous plant having specially modified leaves that form fluid-filled basins in which insects become trapped.

pitchfork[1] *n* a long-handled fork with two or three long curved prongs used for lifting and tossing hay.

pitchfork[2] *v* **1** to lift and toss (hay, straw, etc) with a pitchfork. **2** to thrust (somebody) into a position, office, etc, *esp* suddenly or without preparation.

pitch in *v* to contribute to or cooperate in something.

pitch pine *n* a N American pine tree grown commercially for timber, which is used in the construction of buildings and in the manufacture of furniture, and as a source of turpentine.

pitch up *v informal* to arrive; to turn up.

pitchy *adj* (**-ier, -iest**) very dark in colour.

piteous *adj* causing or deserving pity or compassion. ➤➤ **piteously** *adv,* **piteousness** *n.*

pitfall *n* **1** a hidden or not easily recognized danger or difficulty. **2** a trap or snare, *esp* a camouflaged pit used to capture animals.

pith *n* **1a** the white tissue surrounding the flesh and directly below the skin of a citrus fruit. **b** the spongy cellular tissue in the stems of most vascular plants. **2a** the essential part of something. **b** meaning or substance.

pithead *n* the top of a mining pit and the ground and buildings around it.

pith helmet *n* a hat made from the pith of any of various Indian swamp plants and worn in tropical regions to protect the head and the back of the neck from the sun.

pithos *n* (*pl* **pithoi**) a large earthenware or ceramic jar used in classical times for storing oil or grain.

pithy *adj* (**-ier, -iest**) **1** of language, a speech, etc: full of meaning or substance and concisely expressed. **2** of a plant or plant part: resembling pith or having a great deal of pith. ➤➤ **pithily** *adv,* **pithiness** *n.*

pitiable *adj* **1** deserving or arousing pity. **2** contemptibly inadequate. ➤➤ **pitiably** *adv.*

pitiful *adj* **1** deserving or arousing pity or commiseration. **2** woefully small or inadequate. ➤➤ **pitifully** *adv,* **pitifulness** *n.*

pitiless *adj* showing little or no pity; merciless. ➤➤ **pitilessly** *adv,* **pitilessness** *n.*

piton *n* a spike or peg that is driven into a rock or ice surface as a support, *esp* for a rope, in mountaineering.

pitot /'peetoh/ *n* a tube with a short right-angled bend that is used with a manometer to measure the velocity of fluid flow.

pitot tube *n* = PITOT.

pit stop *n* in motor racing, a stop at the pits (see PIT[1] (2)) for refuelling, changing tyres, or servicing.

pitta (*NAm* **pita**) *n* slightly leavened bread, typically flat and oval in shape, that is often split open to hold a savoury filling.

pitta bread (*NAm* **pita bread**) *n* = PITTA.

pittance *n* a small amount or allowance, *esp* a meagre wage or inadequate remuneration.

pitter-patter[1] *n* a rapid succession of light tapping sounds.

pitter-patter[2] *adj and adv* with a succession of light tapping sounds.

pituitary *n* (*pl* **-ies**) a small two-lobed endocrine organ attached to the brain which secretes many important hormones controlling growth, metabolism, the function of other endocrine glands, etc.

pituitary body *n* = PITUITARY.

pituitary gland *n* = PITUITARY.

pity[1] *n* (*pl* **-ies**) **1** sympathetic sorrow or compassion for the suffering, distress, or unhappiness of another. **2** something to be regretted; a source of disappointment. ✱ **for pity's sake** used to express exasperation or as an urgent appeal. **more's the pity** used to express regret or disappointment.

pity[2] *v* (**-ies, -ied**) to feel pity for (somebody or something).

pivot[1] *n* **1** a shaft or pin on which something, *esp* a mechanized part, turns. **2** a person or thing that has a major or central role or function.

pivot[2] *v* (**pivoted, pivoting**) **1** to turn on a pivot, or as if on a pivot. **2** (*usu* + on) to depend on (something or somebody). ➤➤ **pivotable** *adj.*

pivotal *adj* **1** vitally important; crucial. **2** relating to or constituting a pivot.

pix[1] *n* pl of PIC.

pix[2] *n* see PYX.

pixel *n* one of thousands of tiny spots on a computer display screen that together can be manipulated to form an image or character.

pixelate *or* **pixellate** *or* **pixilate** *v* to break down (an image on a screen) into pixels. ➤➤ **pixelation** *n.*

pixie *or* **pixy** *n* (*pl* **-ies**) a fairy or elf, *esp* one typically depicted in folklore as a small human with large pointed ears and wearing a pointed hat. ➤➤ **pixieish** *adj.*

pixilate *v* see PIXELATE.

pixilated *or* **pixillated** *adj* confused or crazy. ➤➤ **pixilation** *n.*

pixy *n* (*pl* **-ies**) see PIXIE.

pizazz *n* see PIZZAZZ.

pizza *n* a round base of baked bread dough spread with a mixture of tomatoes, cheese, herbs, etc.

pizzazz *or* **pizazz** *or* **pzazz** *n* an attractive and often flamboyant combination of spirited vitality and glamorous style.

pizzeria /peetsə'riə/ *n* a place where pizzas are made or sold.

pizzicato /pitsi'kahtoh/ *adj and adv* of a piece of music for stringed instruments: to be performed by plucking instead of bowing. ➤➤ **pizzicato** *n.*

pizzle *n archaic* an animal's penis, *esp* a bull's.

Pl *abbr* used in street names: Place.

pl. *abbr* plural.

placable *adj archaic* easily calmed or appeased.

placard[1] *n* a sign or notice for display, placed on a wall or carried as part of a demonstration.

placard[2] *v* to cover with placards.

placate *v* to soothe or mollify, *esp* by concessions; to appease. ➤➤ **placatory** *adj.*

place[1] *n* **1** a position or point in space. **2** a city, town, or other geographical location. **3** a building, house, room, etc that is occupied by a specified person. **4** a space occupied by or assigned to somebody or something. **5a** the correct, usual, or expected position: *This book isn't in its alphabetical place; I feel out of place among all these younger people.* **b** a role, right, or duty: *It's not my place to tell you what to do.* **c** a suitable setting or an appropriate occasion: *There's no place for that kind of language here.* **6a** a position held or won by something or somebody in sequence with another or others, *esp* in a competition or race. **b** in mathematics, a position that a figure has in a series of others, *esp* a figure that follows the point in decimal notation. **7** (*often* **Place**) a short, usu residential street or a town square with houses or offices. ✱ **go places 1** to travel widely. **2** to succeed. **in place of** as an alternative to or substitute for (somebody or something). **know one's place** to be aware of and accept one's position or status, *esp* when it is an inferior or humble one. **put somebody in their place** to humiliate somebody or prove them wrong, *esp* when they have shown arrogance, conceit, presumptuousness, etc. **take one's place** to go into one's assigned, usual, or correct position. **take place** to happen. **take the place of** to be or act as a substitute for (somebody or something).

place[2] *v* **1a** to put in a specified position: *He placed the ornament back on the shelf.* **b** to put into a specified order, relation, or condition: *She placed the books in alphabetical order.* **c** to assign (something or somebody), *esp* to an authority: *I placed my trust in the justice system; He places great emphasis on accuracy.* **d** to cause (somebody, oneself, or something) to be in a specified position, condition, or situation. **2** to set or estimate: *He placed the value at around £200.* **3** to identify, classify, or rank: *I couldn't place his face; The selectors have placed her among the top five runners in the country.* **4** to find employment or a home for. **5a** to put (an advertisement or notice) in a newspaper, etc. **b** to put on (a bet). **c** to submit, arrange, or apply for: *John placed an order for a new car.*

placebo *n* (*pl* **-os**) **1** a medication or treatment regime that has no physiological effect and is prescribed for the patient's psychological benefit. **2** a substance that has no effects and which is used as a control against another substance, *esp* a drug, which is known to have or is being tested for a specific effect.

placed *adj* of a competitor at the end of a race, etc: in a leading place, *esp* second or third.

placekick *n* in American football, rugby, and Association Football, a kick at a ball placed or held in a stationary position on the ground.

place-kick *v* of a player: to take a placekick. ➤➤ **place-kicker** *n.*

placeman *n* (*pl* **placemen**) a political appointee to a public office, *esp* one who is given the post in recognition of previous political support and who is expected to continue giving allegiance.

placement *n* **1** the act or an instance of putting somebody or something in a specified place, or the result or effect of doing this. **2** the act or an instance of finding work or a school for somebody or of finding a home for a person or animal. **3** a temporary spell of work, *esp* one that allows a student to gain practical experience.

place name *n* the name of a geographical locality, such as a town, or a geographical feature, such as a mountain, lake, etc.

placenta *n* (*pl* **placentas** *or* **placentae**) a large rounded vascular organ that develops in the uterus during pregnancy in most higher mammals. It is linked to the foetus by the umbilical cord and provides the foetus with oxygen and nourishment. ➤➤ **placental** *adj.*

placer *n* (*often used before a noun*) an alluvial or glacial deposit containing particles of valuable minerals, *esp* gold: *placer deposits.*

placid *adj* not easily upset or excited; calm. ➤➤ **placidity** *n,* **placidly** *adv.*

placing *n* **1** the act or an instance of placing or being placed. **2** (*in pl*) the positions or rankings given to competitors during or following a race or other competition.

placket *n* **1** a slit in a garment, *esp* a skirt, for a fastening or pocket. **2** a flap of fabric covering this.

plagiarize *or* **-ise** *v* to appropriate and pass off (the ideas or words of another) as one's own. ➤➤ **plagiarism** *n,* **plagiarist** *n,* **plagiarizer** *n.*

plague[1] *n* **1** any of several epidemic virulent diseases that cause many deaths, *esp* a fever caused by a bacterium carried by rat fleas and transmitted to humans via their bite: compare BUBONIC PLAGUE. **2** a large destructive influx of insects or animals that cause widespread damage.

plague[2] *v* (**plagues, plagued, plaguing**) **1** to annoy or harass continually. **2** to infest or afflict (a people, area, etc) with disease, calamity, etc.

plaice *n* (*pl* **plaice**) a large edible N Atlantic European flatfish with a brown skin flecked with orange that is valued commercially.

plaid *n* a usu twilled woollen fabric with a tartan pattern.

Plaid Cymru /,plied 'kumri/ *n* the Welsh Nationalist Party.

plain[1] *adj* **1a** not fancy or decorated. **b** of a fabric: without a pattern. **c** consisting of a single colour. **d** flat or smooth. **2** free of added substances; pure. **3** unobstructed. **4** obvious; easy to understand; unambiguous. **5** free from deceitfulness or subtlety; candid. **6** lacking special distinction or affectation; ordinary. **7a** characterized by simplicity; not complicated. **b** not rich or elaborately prepared or decorated. **8** of a person: not particularly attractive. **9** of knitting: done in rows of knit stitches. **10** used for emphasis: utter; absolute. ➤➤ **plainly** *adv,* **plainness** *n.*

plain[2] *n* **1** an extensive area of level or rolling treeless country. **2** a broad unbroken expanse of land.

plain[3] *adv* **1** in a plain manner; clearly or simply. **2** totally; utterly.

plainchant *n* = PLAINSONG.

plain chocolate *n Brit* chocolate that has no milk added to it, making it darker and more bitter than milk chocolate.

plain clothes *pl n* ordinary civilian dress as opposed to uniform, *esp* a police uniform.

plain flour *n Brit* flour that has no raising agent added to it, used in making biscuits, pastry, etc.

plain sailing *n* easy or uninterrupted progress.

plainsong *n* unaccompanied vocal music of the medieval church.

plain-spoken *adj* candid or blunt in what one says.

plaint *n* **1** *Brit* a legal document in which the grounds of a complaint are recorded for submission to a court of law. **2** *archaic* a protest.

plaintext *n* computer-generated text in its non-encrypted or decrypted form.

plaintiff *n* somebody who brings a civil legal action against another in a court of law: compare DEFENDANT.

plaintive *adj* expressing sorrow or sounding very sad; mournful. ➤➤ **plaintively** *adv,* **plaintiveness** *n.*

plain weave *n* a simple weave in which the weft yarns pass alternatively over and under the warp yarns.

plait[1] *n* a length of plaited material, *esp* hair or rope, made up of three or more interwoven strands.

plait[2] *v* to interweave the strands of (hair, rope, etc) to form a plait or plaits.

plan[1] *n* **1** a detailed account or proposal of how something can be done or achieved. **2** (*also in pl*) a proposed or intended course of action. **3** a financial arrangement, *esp* one that is designed to give security in the future. **4a** a detailed map of an area, usu on a large scale. **b** a diagram or outline of something. **c** a technical drawing in the horizontal plane of the structure of something, *esp* a building or a single floor of a building.

plan[2] *v* (**planned, planning**) **1** to arrange in advance. **2** (+ to/on) to intend (to do something). **3** to design (something). ⯮ **planner** *n.*

planar *adj* of, being, or lying in a mathematical plane.

planchette *n* a small board on castors with a pencil attached to it, used at séances and spiritualist meetings in the belief that it will spell out telepathic messages when touched lightly with the fingers.

plane[1] *n* **1a** in mathematics, a surface on which any two included points can be joined by a straight line lying wholly within the surface. **b** a flat or level physical surface. **2** a level of existence, consciousness, or development. **3** *informal* an aeroplane.

plane[2] *adj* **1** having no elevations or depressions; flat. **2a** of or dealing with geometric planes. **b** lying in a plane.

plane[3] *v* **1a** of a bird: to fly with the wings motionless. **b** of something airborne: to glide. **2** of a speedboat, surfboard, etc: to skim across the surface of the water.

plane[4] *n* a tool with a sharp blade protruding from the base of a flat metal or wooden stock for smoothing or shaping a wooden surface by removing thin shavings.

plane[5] *v* to make (a surface, *esp* a wooden one) flat or even with a plane. ⯮ **planer** *n.*

plane[6] *n* a large deciduous tree with deeply cut lobed leaves and thin bark that is shed in flakes.

planet *n* **1** any of the nine celestial bodies that move round our sun in various elliptical orbits. **2** (**the planet**) the earth. **3** any celestial body which orbits a star and which is of substantial size but is not massive enough to become a star itself. ⯮ **planetary** *adj.*

planetarium *n* (*pl* **planetariums** *or* **planetaria**) **1** an optical projector for showing images of celestial bodies and effects as seen in the night sky. **2** a domed building or room where these images are shown.

planetary nebula *n* a bright ring-shaped expanding nebula of fluorescent gas around a star.

planetesimal *n* any of numerous small solid celestial bodies that may aggregate to form larger planets. ⯮ **planetesimal** *adj.*

planetoid *n* = ASTEROID.

plangent *adj literary* **1** of a sound: loudly reverberating. **2** of a sound: having an expressive, *esp* plaintive, quality. ⯮ **plangency** *n,* **plangently** *adv.*

planimeter *n* an instrument for measuring the area of a plane figure by tracing its boundary line. ⯮ **planimetric** *adj,* **planimetry** *n.*

planisphere *n* a polar projection of the celestial sphere and the stars on a plane to show the relative positions of the constellations at any given time. ⯮ **planispheric** *adj.*

plank *n* **1** a long thick piece of wood, *esp* a piece of sawn timber used in constructing floors, roofs, and walls. **2** a major article in an official programme, *esp* a policy that is fundamental to the declared aims of a political party. ✻ **walk the plank** to be made to walk off the end of a plank jutting out from a ship, *esp* by pirates. ⯮ **planked** *adj,* **planking** *n.*

plankton *n* the minute animals and plants, mainly microscopic diatoms and protozoans, but also tiny crustaceans, fish eggs, and larvae, that float near the surface of seas and lakes. ⯮ **planktonic** *adj.*

planned economy *n* an economy in which a nation's central government sets and controls the levels of investment, production, prices, and incomes.

planning permission *n Brit* formal permission given by a local authority for the erection or alteration of buildings or other structures.

plant[1] *n* **1** any of various living but immobile multicellular organisms such as trees and flowers that typically have cellulose cell walls, root systems for absorbing water and inorganic substances, and leaves that manufacture nutrients. **2a** a building or collection of buildings where large-scale manufacturing or processing takes place. **b** machinery and equipment necessary for a large-scale manufacturing or processing operation to function. **3a** a person who secretly infiltrates an organization in order to spy, gain information, or cause trouble. **b** something that has surreptitiously been put in a person's belongings, home, etc with the intention of incriminating them.

plant[2] *v* **1** to put (a seed, plant, bulb, etc) in a place with the right conditions to encourage germination or growth. **2** to put or settle (something, somebody, or oneself) firmly in a specified place. **3** to send (somebody) to infiltrate an organization to spy, gain information, or cause trouble. **4** to place or hide (an explosive device). **5** to establish (an idea, etc) in somebody's mind. **6** to put (something incriminating) surreptitiously in somebody's belongings, home, etc.

Plantagenet *adj* of the English royal house that ruled from 1154 to 1485. ⯮ **Plantaganet** *n.*

plantain[1] *n* a short-stemmed plant with dense spikes of minute greenish or brownish flowers and usu a rosette of oval or sword-shaped leaves, typically found growing on wasteland or road verges.

plantain[2] *n* a green-skinned fruit, resembling a banana but more angular in form, that is a staple food in many tropical regions.

plantar *adj* relating to the sole of the foot.

plantation *n* **1** a large estate where commercial crops, such as coffee, tea, tobacco, and rubber, are grown, *esp* in tropical areas. **2** an area where trees are grown for commercial purposes.

planter *n* **1** somebody who owns or manages a plantation. **2** a container in which ornamental plants are grown.

plantigrade *adj* of humans and certain mammals, such as bears: walking on the sole with the heel touching the ground: compare DIGITIGRADE.

plant out *v* to transplant (e.g. seedlings or a house plant) from a pot, seed tray, etc to open ground.

plaque *n* **1** a commemorative or decorative inscribed tablet, *esp* one fixed to a wall. **2a** a film of mucus on teeth where bacteria multiply. **b** a localized abnormal patch in a body part or on the surface of a body part, often the result of injury or a build-up of mineral deposits.

plash[1] *n* **1** *literary* a shallow or muddy pool. **2** a splashing noise. ⯮ **plashy** *adj.*

plash[2] *v literary* **1** to break the surface of (water) with a splash. **2** to cause a splashing or spattering effect.

plasm *n* = PLASMA (2).

plasma *n* **1a** the fluid part of blood, lymph, or milk in which material such as corpuscles, fat globules, and other cells are suspended. **b** a sterilized preparation made from the plasma of donated blood and used in transfusions. **2** protoplasm or cytoplasm. **3** a highly ionized gas containing approximately equal numbers of positive ions and electrons. **4** a green variety of chalcedony used as a semiprecious gemstone. ⋙ **plasmatic** *adj*, **plasmic** *adj*.

plaster[1] *n* **1** a paste-like mixture, e.g. of lime, water, and sand, that hardens on drying and is used *esp* for coating walls, ceilings, and partitions. **2** an adhesive strip, often with a small pad in the middle, used for covering and protecting small cuts, blisters, etc. **3** a rigid dressing made from plaster of Paris and used for immobilizing a broken bone, *esp* in a limb, to allow it to heal in the correct position.

plaster[2] *v* **1** to coat (a wall, ceiling, etc) with plaster. **2** to apply plaster to (a wall, ceiling, etc). **3a** to coat or cover thickly with a specified substance: *She plastered her face with make-up.* **b** to cause to lie flat or stick to another surface: *He plastered his hair down; The heavy rain plastered his shirt to his body.* ⋙ **plasterer** *n*.

plasterboard *n* a board with a plaster core used *esp* as a substitute for plaster on interior walls.

plaster cast *n* = PLASTER[1] (3).

plastered *adj informal* drunk.

plaster of Paris *n* a white powder made from gypsum that forms a quick-setting paste when mixed with water, and which is chiefly used for making casts for broken limbs, etc and moulds, *esp* in sculpture.

plasterwork *n* plaster on interior walls, *esp* when it has a decorative effect.

plastic[1] *n* **1** a synthetic organic polymer that, while soft, can be moulded, cast, etc into shapes and then set to have a rigid or slightly elastic form. **2** *informal* = PLASTIC MONEY.

plastic[2] *adj* **1** made of plastic. **2** capable of being moulded; soft and pliable. **3** of an art form: involving moulding or modelling to create three-dimensional objects. **4** *derog* artificial. ⋙ **plastically** *adv*, **plasticity** *n*.

plastic bullet *n* a bullet made from PVC or other plastic material for use in riot control and crowd dispersal, causing less damage than a conventional bullet.

plastic explosive *n* a pliable doughlike explosive substance that can be moulded by hand to fit and adhere to a surface.

Plasticine *n trademark* a soft pliable coloured substance used for modelling.

plasticise *v* see PLASTICIZE.

plasticiser *n* see PLASTICIZER.

plasticize *or* **-ise** *v* **1** to treat with a plastic. **2** to make plastic. ⋙ **plasticization** *n*.

plasticizer *or* **plasticiser** *n* a chemical added *esp* to rubbers and plastics to give or increase flexibility.

plasticky *adj* made of or resembling plastic, *esp* in being artificial or of poor quality.

plastic money *n informal* a credit card, or credit cards collectively.

plastic surgery *n* surgery concerned with the repair, restoration, or cosmetic improvement of parts of the body chiefly by the grafting of tissue. ⋙ **plastic surgeon** *n*.

plastron *n* **1** a quilted pad worn in fencing to protect the chest, waist, and sides. **2** the underside of the shell of a tortoise or turtle. **3a** the starched front of a man's evening or dress shirt. **b** the front part of a type of dress bodice popular during the 19th cent.

plat du jour /ˌplah doo ˈzhooə/ *n* (*pl* **plats du jour** /ˌplah/) a dish featured by a restaurant on a particular day in addition to those offered on the regular menu.

plate[1] *n* **1** a flat and usu circular dish from which food is eaten or served. **2a** a flat sheet or strip of metal, *esp* one that is rolled or hammered to become very thin and used to coat another metal. **b** metal or metal objects coated in this. **c** tableware and other household articles made of gold or silver. **3** a thin piece of metal or plastic with an inscription on it. **4** a piece of metal or other material used for strengthening or joining purposes. **5a** a flat piece of a naturally occurring material, often one of several fused together to form an organic structure such as the outer covering of an animal's body or the shell of a turtle, tortoise, etc. **b** any of the rigid but mobile blocks that together form the earth's crust. **6a** a sheet of metal or other material with text or an image on it, used for printing multiple copies of the text or image. **b** an impression taken from this type of sheet or from a woodcut. **c** a full-page book illustration, *esp* one produced on high-quality paper. **d** a sheet coated with a light-sensitive film used in early cameras to capture an image. **7** in architecture, a horizontal supporting member, *esp* in a wood-frame construction. ✱ **on a plate** without having to make any great effort. **on one's plate** to be dealt with.

plate[2] *v* to coat (a surface, *esp* a metallic one, or a metal object) with a thin layer of rolled or hammered metal, usu gold, silver, or steel. ⋙ **plater** *n*.

plate armour *n* armour constructed from flat pieces of metal that overlap and articulate with each other.

plateau[1] *n* (*pl* **plateaus** *or* **plateaux**) **1** a wide, fairly flat area of ground that is much higher than the land around it. **2** a state of stability or a lack of change, *esp* after a period of activity.

plateau[2] *v* (**plateaus, plateaued, plateauing**) to reach a stage where there is little or no change, *esp* after a period of activity.

plate glass *n* (*often used before a noun*) rolled, ground, and polished sheet glass, used *esp* in shop and office windows.

platelet *n* any of the minute discs in the blood of vertebrates that assist in blood clotting.

platen *n* **1** a flat plate that exerts pressure, *esp* in a printing press where it holds the paper against the type. **2** the roller of a typewriter against which the paper is held.

plate tectonics *pl n* (*used as sing.*) the study of the formation of the major structures of the earth's surface, *esp* in the context of the theory that the LITHOSPHERE (earth's crust) is composed of rigid plates that can interact with each other at their boundaries because of the molten nature of the mantle below them.

platform *n* **1a** a raised area where a speaker or performer can be seen by the audience. **b** a level horizontal surface that is raised above the area around it. **c** a raised area by the track at a railway station where passengers can wait for and board or leave trains. **2** a raised structure housing the equipment used for drilling for oil and gas. **3** in computing, the combination of a particular type of CPU and operating system, which determines what programs can be run. **4** an official policy, *esp* a declared political one that distinguishes one party or group from the others and is used as a means of attracting support. **5** an opportunity, means, or place where opinions can be expressed; a forum. **6** (*usu in pl*) a shoe with a built-up sole.

platform game *n* a type of computer game in which a player's object is to manipulate a character through various obstacles and so progress from one level or platform to the next.

platinize *or* **-ise** *v* to coat (something, *esp* another metal) with platinum. ⋙ **platinization** *n*.

platinoid *n* an alloy of copper, nickel, and zinc having a high degree of resistance to the passage of an electric current.

platinum *n* **1** a greyish white precious metallic chemical element that is heavy and does not corrode, occurs naturally in copper and nickel ores, and is used as a catalyst and in making jewellery. **2** (*used before a noun*) silvery in colour.

platinum blonde *or* **platinum blond** *adj* of hair: having a pale silvery-blonde colour.

platinum disc *n* a music award in the form of a framed platinum record given to an artist, group, etc in Britain for selling 300,000 copies of an album.

platitude *n* a trite remark stating the self-evident, typically made for the sake of something to say. ➤➤ **platitudinous** *adj.*

platitudinize *or* **-ise** *v* to utter platitudes.

platonic *adj* **1** (**Platonic**) characteristic of or relating to the Greek philosopher Plato (d.349 BC) or to Platonism. **2** of a friendship or love: close but not sexual. ➤➤ **platonically** *adv.*

Platonism *n* the philosophy of Plato, according to which actual things, such as cats and beds, and ideas, such as truth or beauty, are copies of transcendent ideas which are the objects of true knowledge. ➤➤ **Platonist** *n,* **Platonistic** *adj.*

platoon *n* (*used as sing. or pl*) a subdivision of a military company normally consisting of two or more sections or squads, each composed of ten to twelve soldiers.

plats du jour /ˌplah doo ˈzhooə/ *n* pl of PLAT DU JOUR.

platter *n* **1** a large often oval plate used *esp* for serving meat. **2** an aluminium disc used in a hard drive. ✱ **on a (silver) platter** *informal* used to indicate something that is given or achieved easily or effortlessly.

platypus *n* (*pl* **platypuses**) a small aquatic Australian and Tasmanian primitive egg-laying mammal that has a fleshy bill resembling that of a duck, webbed feet, and a broad flattened tail. Also called DUCK-BILLED PLATYPUS.

plaudit *n* (*usu in pl*) an expression of enthusiastic approval.

plausible *adj* **1** apparently fair, reasonable, or valid but often specious. **2** of a person: persuasive or believable, but deceptive. ➤➤ **plausibility** *n,* **plausibly** *adv.*

play[1] *v* **1a** to take part in activities for enjoyment or recreation. **b** (+ with) to use something for amusement or fun. **2a** to take part in (a sport or game). **b** to take (a specified position) in a game. **c** to compete with (an opponent) in a game. **3** to move (a piece) or lay (a card, etc) at one's turn in a game. **4a** to perform music on (a musical instrument). **b** to produce (music) or perform (a piece of music). **5** to make (a radio, etc) produce music or sounds. **6** to perform (a role) in a drama, film, etc. **7** *informal* to cooperate. **8** to feature intermittently or briefly: *The lights played on the water.* ✱ **play ball** *informal* to cooperate. **play fast and loose** to act irresponsibly. **play for time** to concoct delays in order to gain an advantage. **play hard to get** *informal* to be indifferent to personal advances. **play into the hands of** act in a way that unintentionally gives somebody an advantage over one. **play it by ear** to act by instinct and adapt to circumstances. **play one's cards right** to act correctly or successfully. **play the game** to behave fairly. **play with** to treat frivolously or unfairly.

play[2] *n* **1** activity that is done for fun, recreation, or amusement. **2** a piece of dramatic literature meant to be acted out on stage or broadcast on television or radio. **3** conduct of a specified nature, *esp* in sports or games, or in dealing with other people: *fair play.* **4** in a sport or game, a move or the action. **5a** ease or freedom of movement, *esp* of a machine part. **b** freedom or scope. **c** brief, intermittent, or free motion: *the play of snowflakes against the window.* ✱ **in/into play 1** in/into condition or position to be legitimately played. **2** in/into operation or consideration. **make a play for** to take deliberate action to try to obtain (somebody or something). **out of play** not in play.

play about *v* **1** to behave irresponsibly. **2** *informal* to have a sexual affair.

play-act *v* **1** to pretend or make believe. **2** to behave in a misleading, insincere, or histrionic manner.

play along *v* **1** to pretend to cooperate. **2** to give a musical accompaniment or join in with music being played.

playback *n* the act or an instance of reproducing previously recorded images or sound.

play back *v* to reproduce (sound or pictures) from a recorded medium.

playboy *n* a wealthy man who devotes himself to luxury and enjoyment.

play down *v* to minimize or conceal the importance of.

player *n* **1** a person who takes part in a sport or game. **2** a person who plays a musical instrument. **3** a device for playing back music, videos, etc. **4** a person or group taking part in some activity or working in a specified way or at a specified level: *The appointee must be an excellent team player.*

player-manager *n* somebody who manages a sports team and who also plays for it.

playful *adj* **1** full of fun; high-spirited. **2** humorously light-hearted or good-natured. ➤➤ **playfully** *adv,* **playfulness** *n.*

playground *n* a piece of land for children to play on.

playgroup *n chiefly Brit* a supervised group of children below school age who play together regularly.

playhouse *n* **1** a theatre. **2** a toy house for children to play in.

playing card *n* any of a set of usu 52 thin rectangular pieces of cardboard etc, used in playing numerous card games.

playing field *n* (*also in pl*) a field used for playing organized games.

playlist *n* a list of the songs or musical pieces chosen to be broadcast on a radio programme.

playmaker *n* a player in a team sport who creates attacking moves and scoring opportunities.

playmate *n* a friend with whom a child regularly plays.

play off *v* **1** to bring (other people) into conflict for one's own advantage. **2** of two teams or players: to take part in a play-off.

play-off *n* a final contest or an extra match played to determine a winner.

play on words *n* a pun.

play out *v* to use up (a person's energy, etc).

playpen *n* a portable usu collapsible enclosure in which a baby or young child may play safely.

playschool *n* a place where preschool children meet for sessions of supervised play, storytelling, singing, etc.

plaything *n* **1** a toy. **2** a person regarded or treated dismissively.

play up *v* **1** to emphasize the importance of. **2** *Brit, informal* **a** to cause distress to. **b** to be troublesome or mischievous. **c** to be not working properly. ✻ **play up to** to flatter or behave obsequiously towards.

playwright *n* somebody who writes plays.

plaza *n* **1** a public square in a city or town. **2** *NAm* a shopping complex with extensive facilities.

plc *abbr* (*also* **PLC**) public limited company.

plea *n* **1** an earnest request or appeal, *esp* one made in an urgent or emotional way. **2** an accused person's answer to an indictment. **3** something offered by way of excuse or justification. **4** an allegation made by a party in support of his or her case.

plea bargaining *n* the act or process of pleading guilty to a lesser charge in order to avoid standing trial for a more serious one.

pleach *v* to interlace (twigs or branches) to form a hedge or canopy.

plead *v* (*past tense and past part.* **pleaded** *or* **plead** *or NAm, Scot* **pled**) **1** to make an impassioned or earnest request or appeal. **2** to give or offer (a specified condition) as an excuse or reason: *to plead ignorance*. **3** of an accused person in a court of law: to answer an accusation in a specified way: *She pleaded not guilty*. **4** of a lawyer: to argue (a case) on behalf of an accused party. **5** of an accused person: to put forward (a reason) or invoke (a point of law), *esp* as a form of defence. ➤➤ **pleadable** *adj*, **pleader** *n*.

pleading[1] *n* **1** the advocacy of a case in a court. **2** any of the formal usu written allegations made alternately by the parties in a legal action. **3** the act or an instance of making an impassioned or earnest request or appeal.

pleading[2] *adj* of a look, etc: imploring. ➤➤ **pleadingly** *adv*.

pleasance *n* a secluded garden or landscaped area laid out with trees and walks, *esp* one attached to a large house.

pleasant *adj* **1** having qualities that tend to give pleasure; agreeable. **2** of a person: likable; friendly and helpful or thoughtful. ➤➤ **pleasantly** *adv*, **pleasantness** *n*.

pleasantry *n* (*pl* **-ies**) a polite but trivial remark.

please[1] *v* **1** to give a feeling of satisfaction, pleasure, or contentment to. **2** *formal* to be the wish or will of (somebody or something): *If it please the court, I'll call my next witness*. ✻ **if you please 1** used to indicate surprise or indignation. **2** if you want to. **please oneself** to do as one likes. ➤➤ **pleasing** *adj*, **pleasingly** *adv*.

please[2] *adv* **1** used in a polite request or an urgent appeal. **2** (*also* **yes please**) used as a polite or enthusiastic affirmative reply.

pleased *adj* **1** satisfied or contented. **2** glad or willing (to do something). **3** (+ with) happy about or contented with something. ✻ **pleased with oneself** smugly satisfied.

pleasurable *adj* pleasant; enjoyable. ➤➤ **pleasurably** *adv*.

pleasure[1] *n* **1a** a feeling of satisfaction or contentment. **b** a source of enjoyment and delight. **c** enjoyment or recreation, *esp* in contrast to necessity. **2** sensual gratification or indulgence. ✻ **at His/Her Majesty's pleasure** *Brit* detained in prison.

pleasure[2] *v archaic* to give sexual pleasure to.

pleat[1] *n* a fold in cloth made by doubling material over on itself and stitching or pressing it in place.

pleat[2] *v* to make a pleat or pleats in.

pleb *n chiefly Brit, informal, derog* = PLEBEIAN[1]. ➤➤ **plebby** *adj*.

plebeian[1] *n* **1** a member of the common people in ancient Rome. **2** a member of a lower class in any society.

plebeian[2] *adj* **1** of plebeians. **2** crude or coarse in manner or style; common.

plebiscite *n* a vote by the people of an entire country or district for or against a proposal, *esp* on an important issue such as choosing a new government or ruler. ➤➤ **plebiscitary** *adj*.

plectrum *n* (*pl* **plectra** *or* **plectrums**) a small thin piece of plastic, metal, etc used to pluck the strings of a stringed instrument, *esp* a guitar.

pled *v NAm, Scot* past tense and past part. of PLEAD.

pledge[1] *n* **1** a solemn and binding promise or undertaking. **2** something given as a token of love, remembrance, loyalty, etc. **3** something handed over to an authority as security, redeemable only on the fulfilment of a promise, discharge of a debt, etc. **4** (**the pledge**) an undertaking to abstain from drinking alcohol. **5** *archaic* a toast or drink to a person's health.

pledge[2] *v* **1** to promise (something or to do something). **2** to deposit as security. **3** *archaic* to drink the health of.

Pleistocene *adj* of the first geological epoch of the Quaternary period, lasting from about 1.64 million to about 10,000 years ago, and marked by glaciation and the first appearance of human beings. ➤➤ **Pleistocene** *n*.

plenary[1] *adj* **1** absolute; unqualified. **2** of a meeting, lecture, etc: attended by all entitled to be present.

plenary[2] *n* (*pl* **-ies**) a plenary meeting or session.

plenipotentiary[1] *n* (*pl* **-ies**) somebody, *esp* a diplomat, invested with full power to transact business.

plenipotentiary[2] *adj* **1** *esp* of a diplomat: having or invested with full power. **2** giving a person full power.

plenitude *n formal* **1** an abundance. **2** the condition of being ample, full, or complete.

plenteous *adj literary* plentiful.

plentiful *adj* **1** characterized by, constituting, or existing in plenty. **2** containing or yielding plenty. ➤➤ **plentifully** *adv*.

plenty[1] *n* (*pl* **-ies**) **1a** (*used as sing. or pl*) a full or more than adequate amount or supply. **b** a large number or amount. **2** ample supplies.

plenty[2] *adv informal* quite or abundantly.

plenum *n* (*pl* **plenums** *or* **plena**) **1** an assembly or meeting at which all the people eligible to attend are present. **2** in physics, a space that is completely filled with matter.

pleonasm *n* the use of more words than are necessary to convey an intended sense. ➤➤ **pleonastic** *adj*.

plesiosaur *n* a Mesozoic marine reptile with a flattened body, a long neck, and limbs flattened into paddles.

plessor *n* see PLEXOR.

plethora *n* a large, and *esp* excessive, quantity: *a plethora of regulations*.

pleura *n* (*pl* **pleurae** *or* **pleuras**) the delicate membrane that lines each half of the thorax of mammals and surrounds the lung of the same side. ➤➤ **pleural** *adj*.

pleurisy *n* inflammation of the pleura, usu with fever and painful breathing. ➤➤ **pleuritic** *adj*.

Plexiglas *n NAm, trademark* a type of transparent plastic used as a substitute for glass.

plexor *or* **plessor** *n* a small rubber-headed hammer used for testing body reflexes.

plexus *n* (*pl* **plexus** *or* **plexuses**) **1** a network of interconnected blood vessels or nerves. **2** a network of parts or elements in a structure or system. ⯮ **plexiform** *adj.*

pliable *adj* **1** easily bent without breaking; flexible. **2** yielding readily to others; compliant. ⯮ **pliability** *n.*

pliant *adj* = PLIABLE.

plié /'pleeay/ *n* (*pl* **pliés**) the action in ballet of bending the knees outwards while holding the back straight.

pliers *pl n* a tool with a pair of pincers with jaws for holding small objects or for bending and cutting wire.

plight[1] *n* a condition of extreme hardship, difficulty, or danger.

plight[2] *v archaic* to promise (something) solemnly.

plimsoll *n Brit* a shoe with a rubber sole and canvas top worn for sports.

Plimsoll line *n* a marking indicating the level to which a vessel may legally be loaded in various seasons and waters.

plink *v* to make a quick sharp tinkling noise. ⯮ **plink** *n,* **plinky** *adj.*

plinth *n* **1** a usu square block serving as a base for a pedestal, column, statue, etc. **2** a part of a structure forming a continuous foundation or base.

Pliocene *adj* of the last geological epoch of the Tertiary period, lasting from about 5.2 million to about 1.64 million years ago, and marked by the appearance of many modern mammals. ⯮ **Pliocene** *n.*

pliosaur *n* any of various marine reptiles of the Mesozoic era, plesiosaurs with short necks, large heads, and powerful jaws.

PLO *abbr* Palestine Liberation Organization.

plod[1] *v* (**plodded, plodding**) **1a** (*often* + along/on) to walk heavily or slowly; to trudge. **b** (*often* + along) to proceed slowly or tediously. **2** to work laboriously and monotonously. ⯮ **plodder** *n.*

plod[2] *n* **1** a slow trudging walk. **2** (*also* **PC Plod/Mr Plod**) *Brit, informal* a policeman.

plonk[1] *v* to put (something or oneself) down heavily, clumsily, or carelessly. ⯮ **plonk** *n.*

plonk[2] *n chiefly Brit, informal* cheap or inferior wine.

plonker *n informal* a stupid or useless person.

plop *v* (**plopped, plopping**) to drop or move suddenly with a sound suggestive of something dropping into water. ⯮ **plop** *n.*

plosive[1] *n* a consonant such as *b, p,* or *d* that is articulated by blocking the outward flow of air through the mouth, e.g. with the lips or tongue, and then allowing air to escape in a sharp burst.

plosive[2] *adj* relating to a plosive.

plot[1] *n* **1** a secret plan to do something illegal, harmful, or dishonest. **2** the sequence of events or main story of a literary work, film, etc. **3** a small piece of land, *esp* one used or designated for a specific purpose. **4** a chart or other graphic representation. ⯮ **plotless** *adj.*

plot[2] *v* (**plotted, plotting**) **1** to plan or contrive (something), *esp* secretly. **2** to invent or devise the plot of (a literary work, film, etc). **3** to mark or note on a map or chart. **4a** to assign a position to (a point) by means of coordinates. **b** to draw (a curve) by means of plotted points. ⯮ **plotter** *n.*

plough[1] (*NAm* **plow**) *n* **1** any of various devices used to cut, lift, and turn over soil, *esp* in preparing ground for sowing. **2** (**the Plough**) a formation of seven stars in the northern sky.

plough[2] (*NAm* **plow**) *v* **1** to turn, break up, or work (earth or land) with a plough. **2** (*often* + into) to force a way, *esp* violently. **3** (*often* + through) to proceed steadily and laboriously; to plod. **4** (*often* + in/into) to invest (money or resources). ⯮ **ploughable** *adj.*

plough back *v* to reinvest (profits) in an industry.

ploughman's lunch *n Brit* a cold lunch of bread, cheese, and usu pickles.

ploughshare (*NAm* **plowshare**) *n* the part of a plough that cuts the furrow.

plover *n* (*pl* **plovers** *or* **plover**) a wading bird with a short beak and usu a stout compact build.

plow[1] *n NAm* see PLOUGH[1].

plow[2] *v NAm* see PLOUGH[2].

plowshare *n NAm* see PLOUGHSHARE.

ploy *n* a cunningly devised or contrived plan or act.

pluck[1] *v* **1a** to take a firm hold of (something) and remove it. **b** to pick (a flower, fruit, etc). **2a** to pull out (feathers) from a chicken, etc. **b** to remove the feathers from (a bird's carcass). **3a** to pull out (hairs), *esp* from the eyebrows. **b** to neaten (the eyebrows) by pulling some of the hairs out. **4a** to produce sounds from (a stringed musical instrument) using the fingers or a plectrum. **b** to use the fingers or a plectrum on (the strings of a musical instrument). **5** (+ at) to tug.

pluck[2] *n* **1** courage and determination. **2** the heart, liver, and lungs of a slaughtered animal, *esp* as food.

pluck up *v* to summon up or muster (the necessary courage, etc) to do something difficult or frightening.

plucky *adj* (**-ier, -iest**) showing spirited courage and determination, *esp* when faced with a difficulty or danger. ⯮ **pluckily** *adv,* **pluckiness** *n.*

plug[1] *n* **1** something used to seal a hole, often tightly enough to prevent anything escaping; a stopper. **2a** an insulated device with metal prongs that connects an electrical appliance to an electricity supply at a socket. **b** *not in technical use* an electric socket. **3** *informal* a publicity boost, *esp* one given on a television or radio programme. **4** a small piece of tobacco taken from a compressed cake, used for chewing rather than smoking.

plug[2] *v* (**plugged, plugging**) **1** to block, close, or secure (a hole or gap) with a plug. **2** *informal* to publicize (a book, film, etc), *esp* by media promotion. **3** *informal* to shoot (somebody or something). **4** (*usu* + away) to work doggedly and persistently. ⯮ **plugger** *n.*

plughole *n Brit* a hole in a sink, basin, bath, or shower tray where the water drains away and which can often be temporarily sealed with a rubber plug.

plug in *v* to attach or connect (an electrical appliance) to a power point.

plug-in *n* a computer module or software program designed to be added to a system to enhance or upgrade an existing feature or function.

plum *n* **1** an edible globular to oval smooth-skinned fruit with yellow, purple, red, or green skin and an oblong seed. **2** *informal* (*used before a noun*) denoting an excellent or superior opportunity, etc: *a plum job.* **3** a dark reddish purple colour.

plumage *n* a bird's feathers.

plumb[1] *n* a lead weight attached to a cord and used to determine the depth of water or to gauge the verticality of a surface, line, or edge.

plumb[2] *adv informal* exactly; precisely.

plumb[3] *v* **1** to measure (the depth of water) with a plumb. **2** to examine (something) minutely and critically, *esp* in order to understand it. **3** to adjust or test (the trueness or verticality of a surface, line, or edge) by a plumb line.

plumb[4] *adj* exactly vertical or true.

plumbago *n* (*pl* **-os**) **1** a plant of the thrift family with spikes of attractive blue, grey, or red flowers. **2** *archaic* = GRAPHITE.

plumb bob *n* a metal bob or weight of a plumb line.

plumber *n* somebody who installs, repairs, and maintains water piping and fittings, central heating systems, etc.

plumb in *v* to connect (a bath, shower, toilet, etc, or an appliance, *esp* a washing machine) to a water supply.

plumbing *n* **1** a plumber's occupation or trade. **2** the system of pipes, tanks, and fixtures installed or required in supplying the water, sanitation, and heating in a house or building.

plumbism *n* chronic or acute lead poisoning.

plumb line *n* a line that has a weight at one end and is used to determine verticality.

plume[1] *n* **1** a bird's feather, *esp* a long attractive and brightly coloured one used for display. **2** a feather or cluster of feathers worn e.g. in a hat, as a decoration. **3** something resembling a feather in shape, appearance, or lightness. **4** a column of molten material rising from the earth's mantle. ⋙ **plumed** *adj.*

plume[2] *v* to provide or decorate with plumes.

plummet[1] *v* (**plummeted, plummeting**) to fall sharply and abruptly.

plummet[2] *n* **1** a fall or drop, *esp* one that is rapid or unexpected. **2** a plumb or plumb line.

plummy *adj* (**-ier, -iest**) **1** of somebody's voice or accent: characteristic of or resembling that of the English upper classes, often in an affected or exaggerated way. **2** *informal* sought after or desirable: *a plummy role in the film.* **3** resembling plums.

plump[1] *adj* having a full rounded form; slightly fat. ⋙ **plumpish** *adj,* **plumpness** *n.*

plump[2] *v* (*also* + up) to make or become rounder or fatter.

plump[3] *v* **1** (*usu* + down/into) to drop or sink suddenly or heavily. **2** to drop, throw, or place (something or oneself) suddenly or heavily. **3** (+ for) to decide on something out of several choices or courses of action.

plump[4] *adv informal* with a sudden or heavy drop.

plum pudding *n* a rich boiled or steamed pudding containing dried fruit and spices.

plum tomato *n* a type of oval tomato that is often tinned and used in making sauces, etc.

plumule *n* **1** a rudimentary bud in an embryonic plant which will develop into a shoot during germination. **2** a bird's down feather.

plumy *adj* (**-ier, -iest**) **1** of or resembling a feather or feathers. **2** consisting of or decorated with feathers.

plunder[1] *v* **1** to pillage or sack (a town, etc). **2a** to take (goods) by force, *esp* in a war, riot, or disturbance. **b** to take goods forcibly from (somewhere). ⋙ **plunderer** *n.*

plunder[2] *n* **1** something taken by force, theft, or fraud; loot. **2** the act or an instance of plundering or pillaging.

plunge[1] *v* **1** to fall or move rapidly, suddenly, or unexpectedly. **2** (*usu* + into) to jump or dive, *esp* in water. **3** to cause (a place) to be in a usu dangerous or unwelcome condition: *A power cut plunged the building into darkness.* **4** to immerse (something, *esp* a food) in a liquid.

plunge[2] *n* **1** a dive or swim. **2** a sudden downward movement; a sharp fall, *esp* in value. ✻ **take the plunge** *informal* to decide to do something, *esp* after considering the potential risks.

plunge pool *n* a small but relatively deep pool, usu of cold water, that people jump into between or after sauna sessions.

plunger *n* **1** a device, such as a piston in a pump, that acts with a plunging or thrusting motion. **2** a rubber suction cup on a handle used for clearing blocked pipes, drains, etc.

plunk *v* **1** to play (a keyboard instrument) so as to produce a hollow, metallic, or harsh sound. **2** *informal* (*also* + down) to set (something or oneself) down suddenly. ⋙ **plunk** *n.*

pluperfect *n* the pluperfect tense, or a verb in this tense.

plural[1] *adj* **1** in grammar, of a word or word form: denoting more than one, or in some languages more than two or three, persons, things, or instances. **2** consisting of or containing more than one kind, thing, or class. ⋙ **plurally** *adv.*

plural[2] *n* in grammar, the plural number, the inflectional form denoting it, or a word in that form.

pluralise *v* see PLURALIZE.

pluralism *n* **1** a state of society in which members of diverse social groups develop their traditional cultures or special interests within a common civilization. **2** the holding of two or more offices or positions, *esp* benefices, at the same time. ⋙ **pluralist** *adj and n,* **pluralistic** *adj.*

plurality *n* (*pl* **-ies**) **1a** the state of being plural or numerous. **b** a large number or quantity. **2** a benefice or other position or office held by pluralism. **3** *NAm* an excess of votes over those cast for an opposing candidate in an election.

pluralize *or* **-ise** *v* **1** to make more numerous. **2** to put (a word) into its plural form. ⋙ **pluralization** *n.*

plus[1] *prep* **1** increased by; with the addition of. **2** and also.

plus[2] *n* (*pl* **pluses** *or* **plusses**) **1** a positive factor, quantity, or quality. **2** = PLUS SIGN.

plus[3] *adj* **1** arithmetically or electrically positive. **2** additional and welcome: *a plus factor.* **3** of an academic grade: slightly higher than that specified: *He got a B plus.*

plus[4] *conj* and moreover.

plus ça change /plooh sa 'shonzh/ *phrase* used to express the opinion or acknowledge the fact that things never really change.

plus fours *pl n* loose wide trousers gathered on a band and finishing just below the knee.

plush[1] *n* a fabric with an even pile that is longer and less dense than the pile of velvet.

plush[2] *adj* **1** made of or resembling plush. **2** luxurious, expensive, or lavish. ⋙ **plushy** *adj.*

plus sign *n* a sign (+) denoting addition or a positive quantity.

plutocracy *n* (*pl* **-ies**) **1** government by a controlling class of wealthy people. **2** a state that is governed by wealthy people. **3** a class of wealthy people who govern a state. ⋙ **plutocratic** *adj.*

plutocrat *n often derog* a person whose status or power is based on or dependent on their wealth.

Plutonian *adj* relating to the planet Pluto.

plutonic *adj* **1** of igneous rock: formed by solidification of a molten magma deep within the earth. **2** (**Plutonic**) relating to the underworld or the Greek god Pluto.

plutonium *n* a silvery radioactive metallic chemical element similar to uranium that is formed in atomic reactors, and is used in weapons and as a fuel for atomic reactors.

pluvial *adj* **1** of or caused by rain. **2** characterized by abundant rainfall.

ply[1] *n* (*pl* **-ies**) **1** a strand in a yarn, wool, etc. **2** any of several layers of cloth usu sewn together or sheets of wood laminated together.

ply[2] *v* (**-ies, -ied**) **1a** to use (a tool, etc) steadily and diligently. **b** to practise or perform (an occupation) steadily and diligently. **2a** to keep furnishing or supplying something to (somebody). **b** to keep asking (somebody) questions. **3** of a ship, taxi, etc: to go or travel over or on (a specified route) regularly. **4** of a boatman, taxi driver, etc: to wait regularly in a particular place for custom.

plywood *n* a light structural material consisting of thin sheets of wood glued or cemented together with the grains of adjacent layers arranged crosswise.

PM *abbr* **1** postmortem. **2** Prime Minister.

Pm *abbr* the chemical symbol for promethium.

p.m. *abbr* post meridiem, used to indicate the time after midday.

PMS *abbr* premenstrual syndrome.

PMT *abbr* premenstrual tension.

pneumatic *adj* operated by or containing gas or air under pressure or by a vacuum. ➤➤ **pneumatically** *adv.*

pneumatic drill *n* a large mechanical drill, operated by compressed air, and used *esp* for breaking up a road surface.

pneumatics *pl n* (*used as sing. or pl*) the branch of science that deals with the mechanical properties of gases.

pneumococcus *n* (*pl* **pneumococci**) a bacterium that causes acute pneumonia. ➤➤ **pneumococcal** *adj,* **pneumococcic** *adj.*

pneumoconiosis *n* a crippling disease of the lungs, *esp* of miners, caused by the habitual inhalation of irritant mineral or metallic particles.

pneumonia *n* a lung infection that causes the air sacs to fill with pus, so that the lungs change from a soft spongy consistency to become quite solid. ➤➤ **pneumonic** *adj.*

PO *abbr* **1** Petty Officer. **2** Pilot Officer. **3** postal order. **4** Post Office.

Po *abbr* the chemical symbol for polonium.

po *n* (*pl* **pos**) *Brit, informal* = CHAMBER POT.

poach[1] *v* to cook (e.g. fish or an egg) in a simmering liquid, *esp* milk, water, or stock.

poach[2] *v* **1** to take (game or fish) illegally by hunting or fishing in an area without the owner's permission. **2** to take (an idea, work, etc belonging to somebody else) and use it to one's own advantage. **3** to entice (an employee working for another company) to come and work for one. ➤➤ **poacher** *n.*

POB *abbr* Post Office box.

pochard *n* (*pl* **pochards** *or* **pochard**) a diving duck, the males of which have reddish brown heads.

pock *n* **1** a pustule in an eruptive disease, *esp* smallpox. **2** = POCKMARK. ➤➤ **pocky** *adj.*

pocket[1] *n* **1** a small bag sewn or inserted in a garment and open at the top or side. **2** a supply of money; financial resources. **3** a pouchlike compartment for storage. **4** any of several openings at the corners or sides of a billiard or snooker table into which balls are propelled. **5** a small isolated area or group. ✱ **in pocket** having made a profit. **in somebody's pocket** under that person's control or influence. **line one's pocket** to make money, *esp* by dishonest means. **out of pocket** having suffered a financial loss. **put one's hand in one's pocket** to spend one's own money. ➤➤ **pocketful** (*pl* **pocketfuls**) *n.*

pocket[2] *v* **1a** to put in one's pocket. **b** to appropriate for one's own use; to steal. **2** to drive (a ball) into a pocket of a billiard or snooker table.

pocket[3] *adj* **1** small enough to be carried in the pocket. **2** small; miniature.

pocketbook *n* **1** *Brit* a small notebook. **2** *NAm* a wallet or small money bag.

pocket borough *n* an English parliamentary constituency which, before reform in 1832, was under the control of one person or family.

pocketknife *n* a knife with blades that fold into the handle, making it safe and small enough to be carried in the pocket.

pocket money *n* money for small personal expenses, *esp* a weekly sum given to a child.

pocket-size *or* **pocket-sized** *adj* = POCKET[3] (1).

pocket watch *n* a watch usu on the end of a chain, designed to be carried in a person's jacket or waistcoat pocket.

pockmark *n* a mark or pit in the skin left by smallpox, chickenpox, etc. ➤➤ **pockmarked** *adj.*

poco /'pohkoh/ *adv* used in music: somewhat.

pod[1] *n* **1** a long seed capsule or fruit, *esp* of the pea, bean, or other leguminous plant, and the seeds contained inside it. **2** a streamlined compartment under the wings or fuselage of an aircraft, used as a container for fuel, etc. **3** a detachable compartment on a spacecraft or aircraft.

pod[2] *v* (**podded, podding**) **1** of a plant: to produce pods. **2** to remove (peas, beans, etc) from a pod.

pod[3] *n* a small group of animals, *esp* whales, seals, or other marine animals, swimming or living close together.

podagra *n* gout of the foot, *esp* the big toe. ➤➤ **podagral** *adj.*

podge *n* **1** *chiefly Brit, informal* a fat person. **2** excess fat.

podgy *adj* (**-ier, -iest**) short and plump; chubby.

podia *n* pl of PODIUM.

podiatry *n chiefly NAm* = CHIROPODY. ➤➤ **podiatric** *adj,* **podiatrist** *n.*

podium *n* (*pl* **podiums** *or* **podia**) **1** a small raised platform for an orchestral conductor, lecturer, public speaker, nightclub dancer, etc. **2** *NAm* a lectern.

podzol *or* **podsol** *n* a soil, typical of coniferous forests, with a grey upper layer from which humus and compounds of iron and aluminium have leached to the layer below. ➤➤ **podzolic** *adj,* **podzolization** *n.*

poem *n* **1** a literary composition in verse, often with rhyme, following a set rhythm and using words for their sound as well as meaning. **2** a creation, experience, or object suggesting a poem.

poesy *n archaic or literary* poetry.

poet *n* **1** somebody who writes poetry. **2** a very imaginative or sensitive person with considerable powers of expression.

poetaster *n* an inferior poet.

poetess *n dated* a woman who writes poetry.

poetic *adj* **1a** relating to or characteristic of poets or poetry. **b** having qualities associated with poetry, such as grace, beauty, or nobility. **2** written in verse. ➤➤ **poetically** *adv,* **poeticism** *n.*

poetical *adj* = POETIC.

poeticize *or* **-ise** *v* to give (something) a poetic quality or form.

poetic justice *n* an outcome in which vice is punished and virtue rewarded in a manner that is particularly or ironically appropriate.

poetic licence *n* **1** allowable departure from the normal rules of grammar, factual accuracy, etc for a particular literary effect. **2** *informal* liberties taken with rules or conventions of any kind.

poetics *pl n* (*used as sing. or pl*) the study of poetry and the techniques used by poets.

poet laureate *n* (*pl* **poets laureate** *or* **poet laureates**) (*often* **Poet Laureate**) in Britain, a poet appointed for life by the sovereign as a member of the royal household and expected to compose poems for state occasions.

poetry *n* **1a** literary writing in the form of a poem or poems. **b** the art of writing poetry. **2** a quality of beauty, grace, and great feeling.

po-faced *adj Brit, informal* having a foolishly solemn, humourless, or disapproving expression.

pogo *v* (**-oes, -oed**) to jump or dance up and down in a jerky uncontrolled way, *esp* to punk music.

pogo stick *n* a pole with a spring at the bottom and two footrests on which somebody can jump up and down or move along.

pogrom *n* an organized massacre of people from a particular ethnic group, *esp* of Jews in eastern Europe and Russia.

poignant *adj* of memories, experiences, etc: causing pangs of distress or pity; painfully sad. ➤➤ **poignance** *n*, **poignancy** *n*, **poignantly** *adv.*

poikilotherm *n* a living organism, e.g. a frog, with a variable body temperature that is usu slightly higher than the temperature of its environment. ➤➤ **poikilothermal** *adj*, **poikilothermic** *adj*, **poikilothermy** *n.*

poinciana *n* an ornamental tropical tree or shrub with bright orange or red flowers.

poinsettia *n* a small shrub of the spurge family bearing delicate yellow flower clusters surrounded by bright red, showy bracts.

point[1] *n* **1** the sharp, tapering, or narrow and rounded end of something; a tip. **2a** a very small mark; a dot. **b** a full stop. **c** a decimal point. **3a** a precisely indicated position. **b** an exact moment. **4a** an end or object to be achieved; a purpose. **b** (*often* **the point**) the most important element of a discussion or matter. **5** an individual detail; an item. **6** a unit of counting, e.g. in scoring a game or quoting stock market prices. **7** any of the 32 evenly spaced compass directions, or the interval between any two adjoining compass points. **8** a projecting and usu tapering piece of land. **9** *Brit* (*in pl*) a device with two movable rails that joins two railway lines and enables a train to move from one to the other. **10** in printing, a unit of measurement equal to 0.351 mm (about 1/72in). **11a** *Brit* an electric socket. **b** a contact in the distributor of a motor vehicle. **12** in cricket, a fielding position on the off side, close to the batsman and more or less in line with the stumps. **13** (*in pl*) in ballet, the tips of the toes. ✱ **beside the point** irrelevant. **make a point of** to take particular care to. **on the point of** just about to. **to the point** relevant. **up to a point** to a certain extent.

point[2] *v* **1** to indicate the position or direction of something, *esp* by directing a finger. **2** to cause to be turned or aimed in a particular direction. **3** to face or be turned in a particular direction: *The ship was pointing north.* **4** (+ to) to indicate the fact or probability of: *The evidence pointed to an accident.* **5** to provide with a point or sharp tip. **6** to scratch out the old mortar from the joints of (brickwork) and fill it with new mortar.

point-blank *adv* **1** from very close range. **2** directly and without explanation. ➤➤ **point-blank** *adj.*

point duty *n* traffic control carried out by a police officer, etc stationed at a particular point, *esp* a road junction.

pointe /pwant/ *n* a ballet position in which the body is balanced on the extreme tip of the toe.

pointed *adj* **1** having a point. **2** *esp* of a critical remark: clearly aimed at a particular person or group. **3** conspicuous. ➤➤ **pointedly** *adv*, **pointedness** *n.*

pointer *n* **1a** a rod used to point at things on maps, charts, etc. **b** a needle that indicates a reading on a dial or other scale. **2** a useful suggestion or hint; a tip. **3** a large strong gundog of a smooth-haired breed that indicates the presence of game by pointing its head and body towards it.

pointillism *n* in art, the technique of applying small strokes or dots of pure colour to a surface so that from a distance they blend together. ➤➤ **pointillist** *n and adj*

pointing *n* mortar or cement used to fill joints in brickwork.

pointless *adj* devoid of meaning, relevance, or purpose; senseless. ➤➤ **pointlessly** *adv*, **pointlessness** *n.*

point of order *n* (*pl* **points of order**) a question relating to procedure in an official meeting.

point of view *n* (*pl* **points of view**) **1** a position from which something or somebody is observed, considered, or evaluated. **2** an opinion or attitude.

point out *v* to direct somebody's attention to.

point-to-point *n* a cross-country steeplechase for amateur riders on hunting horses. ➤➤ **point-to-pointer** *n.*

point up *v* to emphasize or show the importance of.

poise[1] *n* **1a** easy self-possessed assurance of manner; composure or dignity. **b** a particular way of carrying oneself, *esp* with grace or elegance. **2** a stable balanced state; equilibrium.

poise[2] *v* **1** to hold or carry in equilibrium; to balance. **2** to hold (something) supported or suspended without motion in a steady position. **3** to be poised.

poise[3] *n* a unit of dynamic viscosity; the viscosity of a liquid or gas that would require a force of one dyne per square centimetre to move either of two parallel layers one centimetre apart with a velocity of one centimetre per second relative to the other layer.

poised *adj* **1a** marked by composure or dignity; self-possessed. **b** balanced. **2** in a state or position of readiness: *poised to jump.*

poisha *n* a monetary unit of Bangladesh, worth 100th of a taka.

poison[1] *n* **1** a substance that through its chemical action kills or harms a living organism. **2** something that destroys or corrupts.

poison[2] *v* **1a** to harm or kill with poison. **b** to taint or contaminate with poison. **2** to exert a harmful influence on; to corrupt. ➤➤ **poisoner** *n*, **poisoning** *n.*

poison[3] *adj* poisoned or poisonous.

poisoned chalice *n* something given or awarded, e.g. a task or responsibility, that is likely to bring misfortune or unpopularity to the receiver.

poison ivy *n* a N American climbing plant with greenish flowers and white berries that produces an oil that causes an intensely itching skin rash.

poisonous *adj* **1** having the properties or effects of poison. **2** malicious. ➤➤ **poisonously** *adv.*

poison-pen letter *n* a letter written, usu anonymously, with malicious intent to frighten or offend.

poison pill *n* in business, a strategy employed by a company to make a takeover bid unattractive or impracticable.

poke[1] *v* **1a** to hit with a fingertip or something sharp; to prod. **b** to produce (e.g. a hole) by piercing, stabbing, or jabbing. **2** to protrude or cause to protrude. **3** to stir the coals or logs of (a fire) so as to promote burning. **4** (+ about/around) to look about or through something in a random manner; to rummage. **5** *informal* to punch (somebody). **6** *coarse slang* of a man: to have sexual intercourse with (a woman). ✱ **poke one's nose into** to meddle in or interfere with (*esp* something that does not concern one).

poke[2] *n* **1** a prod or jab. **2** *informal* a punch. **3** *coarse slang* an act of sexual intercourse. **4** a women's bonnet with a projecting brim at the front, worn *esp* in the 18th and 19th cents.

poke[3] *n NAm, Scot* a bag or sack.

poke bonnet *n* = POKE[2] (4).

poker[1] *n* a metal rod for poking a fire.

poker[2] *n* a card game in which a player bets that the value of his or her hand is greater than that of the hands held by others, who must equal or raise the bet or drop out.

poker face *n* an inscrutable face that reveals no hint of a person's thoughts or feelings. ➤➤ **poker-faced** *adj.*

pokerwork *n* decorative designs burned into wood or other material using a heated metal rod.

pokey *n NAm, informal* a jail.

poky *or* **pokey** *adj* (**-ier, -iest**) **1** *informal* small and cramped. **2** *NAm* annoyingly slow. ➤➤ **pokily** *adv,* **pokiness** *n.*

Polack *n NAm, offensive* a Polish person.

polar *adj* **1** of or in the region round a geographical pole. **2** of the poles of a magnet. **3** in chemistry, exhibiting polarity, *esp* having groups with opposing properties at opposite ends. **4** completely opposite in nature, tendency, or action.

polar bear *n* a large white bear native to arctic regions.

polar circle *n* either the Arctic or Antarctic Circle.

polarise *v* see POLARIZE.

polarity *n* (*pl* **-ies**) **1** the quality or condition of a body that has opposite properties or powers in opposite directions. **2** magnetic attraction towards a particular object or in a specific direction. **3** the state of having either a positive or negative electrical charge. **4** the state of being diametrically opposed.

polarize *or* **-ise** *v* **1a** to cause (e.g. light waves) to vibrate in a definite or restricted pattern or direction. **b** to give (something) electrical or magnetic polarity. **2** to divide (e.g. people or their opinions) into two opposing factions or categories. ➤➤ **polarizable** *adj,* **polarization** *n,* **polarizer** *n.*

Polaroid *n* **1** *trademark* **a** a light-polarizing material used in sunglasses to prevent glare. **b** (*in pl*) sunglasses with lenses made from this material. **2a** a camera that produces a finished print soon after the photograph has been taken. **b** a photographic print from such a camera.

polder *n* an area of low land reclaimed from a body of water, *esp* in the Netherlands.

Pole *n* a native or inhabitant of Poland. ➤➤ **Polish** *adj.*

pole[1] *n* **1a** a long thin usu cylindrical piece of wood, metal, etc. **b** a shaft that extends from the front axle of a wagon between the horses or other animals pulling it. **2** = ROD (4). **3** = POLE POSITION. ✱ **up the pole 1** *chiefly Brit, informal* slightly mad; crazy. **2** *chiefly Brit, informal* misguided or mistaken.

pole[2] *n* **1** either extremity of an axis of a sphere or of a body, *esp* the earth, resembling a sphere. **2a** either of the two terminals of an electric cell, battery, or dynamo. **b** any of two or more regions in a magnetized body at which the magnetism is concentrated. **3** either of two related opposites. ✱ **poles apart** having nothing in common; totally unrelated.

poleaxe[1] (*NAm* **poleax**) *n* **1** a battle-axe with a short handle and often a hook or spike opposite the blade. **2** an axe used, *esp* formerly, in slaughtering cattle.

poleaxe[2] (*NAm* **poleax**) *v* **1** to attack, strike, or fell with a poleaxe. **2** *informal* to give (somebody) a great shock.

polecat *n* (*pl* **polecats** *or* **polecat**) **1** a carnivorous mammal with dark brown fur, related to the weasel, native to Europe, Asia, and N Africa, and noted for its unpleasant smell. **2** *NAm* = SKUNK .

polemic *n* **1** an aggressive attack on or refutation of somebody's opinions or principles. **2** (*in pl, used as sing. or pl*) the art or practice of disputation or controversy. ➤➤ **polemic** *adj,* **polemical** *adj,* **polemically** *adv,* **polemicist** *n.*

polenta *n* **1** fine maize flour used in Italian cooking. **2** cooked polenta served as a thick paste with fish, meat, etc or sliced and fried.

pole position *n* in motor racing, the best position, on the inside of the front row of the starting grid, at the start of a race.

Pole Star *n* a star in the constellation Ursa Minor that lies very close to the N celestial pole.

pole vault *n* an athletic field event consisting of a jump over a high crossbar with the aid of a long flexible pole. ➤➤ **pole-vault** *v,* **pole-vaulter** *n.*

police[1] *n* **1** (*used as sing. or pl*) a body of trained people entrusted by a government with maintenance of public order and enforcement of laws. **2** (*used as pl*) members of this body; police officers.

police[2] *v* **1** to control (an area, event, etc) by use of police. **2** to supervise the operation or administration of (e.g. an industry or election), *esp* to prevent violation of rules.

policeman *or* **policewoman** *n* (*pl* **policemen** *or* **policewomen**) a man or woman who is a member of the police.

police officer *n* a member of the police.

police state *n* a country or state characterized by repressive governmental control of political, economic, and social life, usu enforced by secret police.

police station *n* the headquarters of a local police force.

policewoman *n* see POLICEMAN.

policy[1] *n* (*pl* **-ies**) **1a** a definite course of action selected from among alternatives, *esp* in the light of given conditions. **b** an overall plan intended to guide and determine decisions. **2** wise or sensible procedure.

policy[2] *n* (*pl* **-ies**) a contract of insurance.

polio *n* = POLIOMYELITIS.

poliomyelitis *n* an infectious viral disease, *esp* of children, characterized by inflammation of the nerve cells of the spinal cord, paralysis, and wasting of skeletal muscles.

Polish *n* the Slavonic language of Poland in E Europe. ➤➤ **Polish** *adj.*

polish[1] *v* **1** to make smooth and glossy, usu by rubbing. **2** to make more refined. **3** (*often* + up) to bring (e.g. a skill) to a highly developed or finished state; to improve or perfect. ➤➤ **polisher** *n.*

polish[2] *n* **1** a preparation rubbed onto a surface to shine and protect it. **2** the act of polishing. **3** a smooth glossy surface. **4** refinement, elegance, or social grace.

polish off *v* to consume or dispose of rapidly or completely.

politburo *n* (*pl* **-os**) the principal policy-making and executive committee of a communist party.

polite *adj* (**politer, politest**) **1** characterized by consideration and deference towards others; courteous. **2** characterized by correct social usage; refined. ➤➤ **politely** *adv,* **politeness** *n.*

politesse *n* formal politeness; decorousness.

politic *adj* **1** wise or expedient. **2** shrewd in managing or dealing with people and situations.

political *adj* **1** relating to government or public affairs. **2a** relating to politics, *esp* party politics. **b** active in or sensitive to politics. **3** involving or charged with acts against a government. **4** concerned with relationships of power within an organization rather than matters of practicality or principle. ➤➤ **politically** *adv.*

political correctness *n* the quality of being politically correct, or adherence to politically correct forms and conventions.

politically correct *adj* sensitive to the risk of offending particular groups of people and therefore careful to avoid judgmental or discriminatory words or actions. ➤➤ **politically incorrect** *adj.*

political prisoner *n* somebody imprisoned for their political beliefs, affiliations, or activities.

political science *n* a social science concerned chiefly with political institutions and processes. ➤➤ **political scientist** *n.*

politician *n* **1** a person experienced or engaged in politics, *esp* a political representative voted into office. **2** *NAm, derog* somebody who uses underhand methods for personal advancement.

politicize *or* **-ise** *v* **1** to give a political tone or character to. **2** to make aware of political issues or politically active. **3** to discuss or engage in politics. ➤➤ **politicization** *n.*

politicking *n chiefly derog* political activity, *esp* insincere or opportunistic attempts to win votes or support.

politico *n* (*pl* **-os**) *informal, chiefly derog* a politician or political person.

politics *pl n* **1** (*used as sing. or pl*) **a** the art or science of government. **b** = POLITICAL SCIENCE. **2** (*used as sing. or pl*) **a** the activities associated with government; political affairs. **b** political life as a profession. **3** a person's political sympathies. **4** (*used as sing. or pl*) the complex of relations between human beings in society or within an organization.

polity *n* (*pl* **-ies**) **1** a country or state regarded as a politically organized unit. **2** a form of government or social organization.

polka *n* a lively dance of Bohemian origin with two beats to the bar. ➤➤ **polka** *v.*

polka dot *n* any of many regularly distributed dots in a textile design. ➤➤ **polka-dot** *adj,* **polka-dotted** *adj.*

poll[1] *n* **1a** the casting or recording of votes. **b** (*in pl*) the place where votes are cast. **c** the number of votes recorded. **2** a survey conducted by questioning people selected at random or by quota. **3** the head or scalp.

poll[2] *v* **1** to receive (a usu specified number of votes). **2** to receive and record the votes of (e.g. a constituency or an electorate). **3** to question (people) in a poll. **4** in computing, to ascertain the status of (a device), *esp* in a regular status check. **5** to cut off or cut short the hair or horns of (e.g. domestic livestock). ➤➤ **pollee** *n,* **poller** *n.*

pollack *or* **pollock** *n* (*pl* **pollacks** *or* **pollocks** *or* **pollack** *or* **pollock**) a N Atlantic food fish resembling the cod but darker and with a more obviously protruding lower jaw.

pollard[1] *n* a tree cut back to the main stem to promote the growth of a dense head of foliage.

pollard[2] *v* to make a pollard of (a tree).

pollen *n* the minute granules that are discharged as a fine dust from the male reproductive organ of a flower and serve to fertilize the ovules. ➤➤ **pollinic** *adj.*

pollen count *n* a figure representing the amount of pollen in the air, available as a warning to people affected by hay fever or other allergic conditions.

pollinate *v* to place pollen on the female reproductive organ and so fertilize (a flower or plant). ➤➤ **pollination** *n,* **pollinator** *n.*

polliwog *or* **pollywog** *n dialect, NAm* a tadpole.

pollock *n* see POLLACK.

pollster *n* somebody who conducts a poll or compiles data obtained by a poll.

poll tax *n* any tax of a fixed amount per person levied on adults.

pollute *v* **1** to contaminate, *esp* with toxic substances. **2** to make morally impure; to corrupt or defile. ➤➤ **pollutant** *n,* **polluter** *n.*

pollution *n* **1** the act of polluting or the state of being polluted. **2** material that pollutes.

Pollyanna *n* an irrepressible optimist. ➤➤ **Pollyannaish** *adj.*

pollywog *n* see POLLIWOG.

polo *n* a game of Eastern origin played by teams of usu four players on horseback using long mallets to drive a wooden ball into the opponents' goal.

polonaise *n* a stately Polish processional dance in moderate time with three beats to the bar.

polo neck *n chiefly Brit* a very high closely fitting collar worn folded over, or a jumper with such a collar.

polonium *n* a radioactive metallic chemical element that occurs naturally in uranium ores.

polony *n* = BOLOGNA.

polo shirt *n* a casual knitted cotton shirt with a soft collar and buttons at the neck.

poltergeist *n* a mischievous ghost said to be responsible for unexplained noises and throwing objects about.

poltroon *n archaic* a complete coward.

poly *n* (*pl* **polys**) *Brit, informal* a polytechnic.

poly- *comb. form* **1** many or much: *polyphonic; polygyny.* **2** polymer of: *polyurethane.*

polyamide *n* a chemical compound characterized by more than one amide group or a synthetic fibre made from this, e.g. nylon.

polyandry *n* the fact of having more than one husband or male mate at a time: compare POLYGAMY, POLYGYNY. ➤➤ **polyandrous** *adj.*

polyanthus *n* (*pl* **polyanthuses** *or* **polyanthi**) a flowering plant that is a hybrid between the wild primrose and primula.

poly bag *n Brit, informal* a small bag made of thin usu transparent polythene; a plastic bag.

polycarbonate *n* a tough transparent plastic characterized by high impact strength and high softening temperature.

polychlorinated biphenyl *n* a chemical compound produced when the hydrogen atoms in biphenyl are replaced with chlorine, that is a poisonous environmental pollutant.

polychromatic *adj* showing a variety or a change of colours; multicoloured. ⯮ **polychromatism** *n.*

polychrome *adj* relating to, made with, or decorated in several colours. ⯮ **polychromy** *n.*

polycotton *n* a fabric that is blend of polyester and cotton. ⯮ **polycotton** *adj.*

polyester *n* **1** a polymer containing ester groups used *esp* in making fibres or plastics. **2** a synthetic fibre made from polyester.

polyethylene *n* = POLYTHENE.

polygamy *n* the practice or condition of being married to more than one person at a time, *esp* marriage in which a husband has more than one wife: compare POLYANDRY, POLYGYNY. ⯮ **polygamist** *n,* **polygamous** *adj,* **polygamously** *adv.*

polyglot[1] *adj* **1** speaking several languages; multilingual. **2** containing text in several languages.

polyglot[2] *n* somebody who speaks several languages.

polygon *n* a two-dimensional geometric figure, usu closed, with three or more straight sides. ⯮ **polygonal** *adj.*

polygraph *n* an instrument for recording variations of the pulse rate, blood pressure, etc simultaneously, *esp* one used as a lie detector. ⯮ **polygraphic** *adj.*

polygyny *n* the fact of having more than one wife or female mate at a time: compare POLYANDRY, POLYGAMY. ⯮ **polygynous** *adj.*

polyhedron *n* (*pl* **polyhedrons** *or* **polyhedra**) a solid geometric figure with four or more plane faces. ⯮ **polyhedral** *adj.*

polymath *n* somebody who has a wide range of learning or accomplishments. ⯮ **polymathic** *adj,* **polymathy** *n.*

polymer *n* a chemical compound consisting essentially of repeating structural units and formed by chemical combination of many small molecules. ⯮ **polymeric** *adj,* **polymerize** *v.*

polymerase *n* an enzyme that speeds up the formation of polymers; *specif* any of several enzymes that take part in the formation of DNA or RNA.

polymorphic *adj* having, assuming, or occurring in various forms, characters, or styles. ⯮ **polymorph** *n,* **polymorphism** *n,* **polymorphous** *adj.*

Polynesian *n* **1** a native or inhabitant of Polynesia, islands in the central and southern Pacific. **2** a group of Austronesian languages, including Maori and Samoan. ⯮ **Polynesian** *adj.*

polynomial *n* in mathematics, a sum of two or more algebraic terms each of which consists of a constant multiplied by one or more variables raised to a power.

polyp *n* **1** a sea anemone, coral, or related organism with a hollow cylindrical body that is attached at one end and has a central mouth surrounded by tentacles at the other. **2** a small abnormal tissue growth projecting from the surface of a mucous membrane. ⯮ **polypoid** *adj,* **polypous** *adj.*

polypeptide *n* a long chain of amino acids joined by peptide bonds.

polyphonic *adj* **1** of music: consisting of several different parts played or sung simultaneously. **2** having several different sounds or voices. ⯮ **polyphonically** *adv,* **polyphony** *n.*

polyploid[1] *adj* having three or more homologous sets of chromosomes: compare DIPLOID, HAPLOID. ⯮ **polyploidy** *n.*

polyploid[2] *n* a polyploid cell or organism.

polypropylene *n* any of various plastics or fibres that are polymers of propylene.

polyrhythm *n* in music, the simultaneous combination of contrasting rhythms. ⯮ **polyrhythmic** *adj.*

polysaccharide *n* a carbohydrate, e.g. cellulose or starch, consisting of chains of monosaccharide molecules.

polysemous *adj* said of a word or phrase: having many meanings. ⯮ **polysemy** *n.*

polystyrene *n* a rigid transparent polymer of styrene with good insulating properties used *esp* in moulded products, foams, and sheet materials.

polysyllabic *adj* **1** having two or more syllables. **2** characterized by polysyllabic words. ⯮ **polysyllabically** *adv.*

polytechnic *n* in Britain, *esp* formerly, a higher-education institution offering courses for qualifications up to degree level with a bias towards the vocational.

polytheism *n* belief in or worship of two or more gods. ⯮ **polytheist** *n,* **polytheistic** *adj.*

polythene *n* a lightweight plastic that is a polymer of ethylene, used *esp* for packaging and making moulded articles, e.g. bowls, buckets, etc.

polytunnel *n* a tunnel-shaped garden frame covered with polythene.

polyunsaturated *adj* of a fat or oil: rich in double and triple chemical bonds.

polyurethane *n* any of various polymers used *esp* in foams, paints, and resins.

polyvalent *adj* **1a** in chemistry, having a valency greater than two. **b** in chemistry, having more than one valency. **2** of a vaccine, antibody, etc: effective against more than one toxic substance, antigen, etc. ⯮ **polyvalence** *n.*

polyvinyl acetate *n* a colourless synthetic resin made from vinyl acetate and used *esp* in paints, adhesives, and sealants.

polyvinyl chloride *n* = PVC.

pom *n informal* **1** (*often* **Pom**) = POMERANIAN. **2** (*often* **Pom**) = POMMY.

pomace *n* a pulpy residue, *esp* of apples crushed to extract juice for cider-making.

pomade[1] *n* a perfumed ointment for the hair or scalp.

pomade[2] *v* to apply pomade to (the hair or scalp).

pomander *n* a mixture of aromatic substances enclosed in a perforated bag or other container, used to scent clothes, perfume a room, or, in former times, guard against infection.

pome *n* in botany, a fruit consisting of an outer thickened fleshy layer and a central core with the seeds enclosed in a capsule, e.g. an apple.

pomegranate *n* a thick-skinned reddish fruit about the size of an orange that contains many seeds surrounded by edible crimson pulp.

pomelo *n* (*pl* **pomelos**) **1** = SHADDOCK. **2** *chiefly NAm* = GRAPEFRUIT.

Pomeranian *n* a small dog of a breed with long straight hair, pointed ears and muzzle, and a curling tail.

pomiculture *n* the growing of fruit.

pommel[1] *n* **1** the raised part at the front and top of a saddle. **2** a knob on the hilt of a sword. **3** either of the handles on a pommel horse.

pommel[2] *v* (**pommelled, pommelling,** *NAm* **pommeled, pommeling**) = PUMMEL.

pommel horse *n* a vaulting horse with two handles on the top, used for swinging and balancing exercises.

Pommy *or* **Pommie** *n* (*pl* **-ies**) *Aus, NZ, informal, chiefly derog* a British person.

pomp *n* **1** a stately or ceremonial display; splendour. **2** ostentatious boastful display.

pompadour *n* **1** a woman's hairstyle in which the hair is turned back into a loose full roll from the forehead. **2** *NAm* a man's hairstyle in which the hair is combed straight back from the forehead without a parting.

pompano *n* (*pl* **pompanos** *or* **pompano**) a N American food fish of the butterfish family found in coastal Pacific waters.

pom-pom[1] *or* **pompom** *n* **1** an ornamental ball or tuft used *esp* on clothing, hats, etc. **2** = POMPON (1).

pom-pom[2] *or* **pompom** *n* an automatic gun mounted on ships and used against aircraft in World War II.

pompon *n* **1** a chrysanthemum or dahlia with small rounded flower heads. **2** = POM-POM[1] (1).

pompous *adj* **1** self-important or pretentious. **2** excessively elevated or ornate. **3** *archaic* characterized by pomp; magnificent or splendid. ➤➤ **pomposity** *n*, **pompously** *adv*, **pompousness** *n*.

ponce[1] *n Brit, informal* **1** = PIMP[1]. **2** *derog* a man who behaves in an effeminate manner. ➤➤ **poncey** *adj*, **poncy** *adj*.

ponce[2] *v Brit, informal* **1** = PIMP[2]. **2** (+ around/about) to act in a frivolous, showy, or effeminate manner.

poncho *n* (*pl* **ponchos**) a cloak resembling a blanket with a slit in the middle for the head, orig worn in S America.

pond *n* **1** a relatively small body of fresh water. **2** (**the Pond**) *informal* the Atlantic Ocean.

ponder *v* **1** to give careful and often lengthy thought or consideration to. **2** (*often* + over) to think or consider, *esp* quietly, soberly, and deeply. ➤➤ **ponderer** *n*.

ponderable *adj* capable of being weighed or appraised; appreciable.

ponderosa pine *n* a tall N American pine tree with long needles and reddish wood.

ponderous *adj* **1** unwieldy or clumsy because of weight and size. **2** oppressively dull. ➤➤ **ponderosity** *n*, **ponderously** *adv*, **ponderousness** *n*.

pond skater *n* any of numerous species of long-legged insects that move about on the surface of water.

pondweed *n* an aquatic plant with a jointed stem, floating or submerged leaves, and spikes of greenish flowers.

pong[1] *v Brit, informal* to emit an unpleasant smell; to stink.

pong[2] *n* an unpleasant smell; a stink.

ponga *or* **punga** *n* a tall tree fern native to New Zealand.

pongee *n* **1** a thin soft fabric of Chinese origin woven from raw silk and usu left unbleached and undyed. **2** an imitation of this fabric in cotton or rayon.

poniard *n* a small slender dagger.

pons /ponz/ *n* (*pl* **pontes** /'ponteez/) a broad mass of nerve fibres on the lower front surface of the brain.

Pontefract cake *n* a small flat circular liquorice sweet.

pontes *n* pl of PONS.

pontiff *n* the pope.

pontifical *adj* **1** of the pope; papal. **2** pretentiously dogmatic. ➤➤ **pontifically** *adv*.

pontifical mass *n* the solemn celebration of the Roman Catholic Mass by a bishop or cardinal.

pontificate[1] *v* **1** to speak or express opinions in a pompous or dogmatic way. **2** to officiate at a pontifical mass. ➤➤ **pontification** *n*, **pontificator** *n*.

pontificate[2] *n* the office or term of office of the pope.

pontoon[1] *n* **1** a flat-bottomed boat or portable float used in building a temporary bridge or in salvage work. **2** a floating landing stage, e.g. in a marina.

pontoon[2] *n* a gambling card game in which the object is to be dealt cards scoring more than those of the dealer up to but not exceeding 21.

pony *n* (*pl* **-ies**) **1** a small horse, *esp* a member of any of several breeds of stocky horses under 14.2 hands in height. **2** *Brit, informal* a sum of £25.

ponytail *n* a hairstyle in which the hair is drawn back tightly and tied at the back of the head.

pony trekking *n* the pastime of riding ponies long distances cross-country in a group, usu at a leisurely pace.

poo[1] *n informal* faeces.

poo[2] *v* (**poos, pooed, pooing**) *informal* to defecate.

pooch *n informal* a dog.

poodle *n* **1** a dog of an active intelligent breed with a thick curly coat that is often clipped and shaved in a distinctive way. **2** a servile person.

poof *or* **pouf** *or* **poofter** *n Brit, informal, offensive* **1** an effeminate man. **2** a homosexual man.

pooh[1] *interj* used to express contempt, disapproval, or distaste at an unpleasant smell.

pooh[2] *n* = POO[1].

pooh[3] *v* = POO[2].

pooh-bah *or* **Pooh-Bah** *n* a person holding many public or private offices.

pooh-pooh *v* to express contempt for; to disparage or dismiss.

pool[1] *n* **1** a small body of standing water or other liquid; a puddle. **2** a small and relatively deep body of still or slow-moving water in a stream or river. **3** = SWIMMING POOL.

pool[2] *n* **1a** the combined stakes of the players of a gambling game. **b** (*in pl*) a form of organized gambling based on forecasting football results, winnings being paid from the pool of entry money. **2** any of various games played on a billiard table with six pockets and usu 15 numbered balls: compare BILLIARDS, SNOOKER[1]. **3** a collective supply of things, e.g. vehicles or funds, or people for common use. **4** an association or agreement between business organizations for the purpose of gaining control of a market by driving out competition.

pool[3] *v* to combine (e.g. resources or effort) in a common stock or for a common purpose.

poop[1] *n* a raised structure or deck at the stern of a ship above the main deck.

poop[2] *v* **1** *chiefly NAm, informal* (*usu in passive, often* + out) to exhaust; to tire out. **2** *NAm, informal* (+ out) to withdraw or fail through exhaustion, loss of courage, etc.

poop[3] *n informal* faeces.

poop[4] *v informal* to defecate.

pooper-scooper *n* a portable device for removing dog faeces dropped in public places.

poop-scoop *n* = POOPER-SCOOPER.

poor *adj* **1** lacking sufficient money or material possessions for an adequate standard of living. **2a** less than adequate; meagre. **b** (+ in) lacking in something specified. **3** inferior in quality, value, skill, etc. **4** inspiring pity. ➤➤ **poorness** *n*.

poorhouse *n* = WORKHOUSE (1).

poorly[1] *adv* in a poor, inadequate, or inferior manner.

poorly[2] *adj* somewhat ill; unwell.

poor relation *n* **1** a family member with little money. **2** an inferior counterpart to or derivative from something.

poor white *n chiefly derog* a member of an inferior or underprivileged white social group, *esp* in the southern USA.

pootle *v Brit, informal* to go in a leisurely fashion.

pop[1] *v* (**popped, popping**) **1a** to make or burst with a sharp explosive sound. **b** to cause to explode or burst open. **2** *informal* **a** to go or come suddenly or quickly. **b** to put quickly or for a short time. **3** of eyes: to appear to protrude from the sockets, e.g. in amazement. **4** *informal* to take (drugs) orally or by injection. **5** *Brit, informal* to pawn. ✻ **pop one's clogs** *Brit, informal* to die. **pop the question** *informal* to propose marriage.

pop[2] *n* **1** a popping sound. **2** a flavoured carbonated soft drink.

pop[3] *adv informal* with or as if with a popping sound; suddenly.

pop[4] *n chiefly NAm, informal* an affectionate name for one's father.

pop[5] *adj* **1** of pop music. **2** denoting a mass culture widely disseminated through the media.

pop[6] *n* = POP MUSIC.

popadom *n* = POPPADOM.

pop art *n* art that incorporates items from popular culture and the mass media, e.g. comic strips. ➤➤ **pop artist** *n.*

popcorn *n* **1** maize kernels that swell and burst when heated to form a white starchy mass. **2** the swollen and burst kernels eaten as a snack.

pope *n* (*often* **Pope**) the bishop of Rome as head of the Roman Catholic Church.

popery *n derog* Roman Catholicism.

pop-eyed *adj* having staring or bulging eyes, e.g. as a result of surprise or excitement.

popgun *n* **1** a toy gun that shoots a cork or pellet and produces a popping sound. **2** *informal* an inadequate or inefficient firearm.

popinjay *n archaic* a conceited or supercilious person.

popish *adj derog* Roman Catholic. ➤➤ **popishly** *adv.*

poplar *n* a slender quick-growing tree of the willow family.

poplin *n* a strong usu cotton fabric in plain weave with fine crosswise ribs.

popliteal *adj* in anatomy, of the back part of the leg behind the knee joint.

pop music *n* modern commercially promoted popular music that is usu simple in form and has a strong beat.

pop off *v informal* **1** to leave suddenly. **2** to die unexpectedly.

poppa *n NAm, informal* an affectionate name for one's father.

poppadom *or* **poppadum** *n* a crisp wafer-thin pancake of deep-fried dough eaten chiefly with Indian food.

popper *n* **1** *Brit, informal* = PRESS-STUD. **2** *informal* a capsule of amyl nitrite that is crushed and inhaled.

poppet *n chiefly Brit, informal* a lovable or enchanting person or animal.

popping crease *n* either of the lines drawn across a cricket pitch 4ft (about 1.22m) in front of each wicket, behind which the batsman must have a foot or the bat on the ground to avoid being run out or stumped.

poppy *n* (*pl* **-ies**) **1** a plant with showy red, orange, or yellow flowers and a large seed case, that often grows wild in cornfields and has species that produce opium. **2** an artificial red poppy worn in the period leading up to Remembrance Sunday.

poppycock *n informal* empty talk; nonsense.

Poppy Day *n Brit, informal* = REMEMBRANCE SUNDAY.

pop socks *pl n* calf-length nylon stockings worn under long skirts or trousers.

popsy *n* (*pl* **-ies**) *Brit, informal, dated* a girlfriend, or any attractive young woman.

populace *n* (*used as sing. or pl*) the general public; the masses.

popular *adj* **1a** generally liked or admired. **b** liked or favoured by a particular person or group. **2** suited to the needs, means, tastes, or understanding of the general public. **3** of or used by the general public. **4** widespread or prevalent. ➤➤ **popularity** *n,* **popularly** *adv.*

popular front *n* a coalition of left-wing political parties organized against a common opponent.

popularize *or* **popularise** *v* **1** to make popular. **2** to present in a generally understandable or interesting form. ➤➤ **popularization** *n,* **popularizer** *n.*

populate *v* **1** to occupy or inhabit (a place). **2** to provide (a place) with inhabitants.

population *n* **1** (*used as sing. or pl*) the whole number of people living in a place. **2** (*used as sing. or pl*) a body of people with something in common. **3** a set of individuals or items from which samples are taken for statistical measurement. **4** a group of organisms of a particular species inhabiting a particular area. **5** the act of populating a place.

populist *n* **1** a member of a political party claiming to represent ordinary people. **2** somebody who has or cultivates an appeal to ordinary people. ➤➤ **populism** *n,* **populist** *adj,* **populistic** *adj.*

populous *adj* having many inhabitants; densely populated. ➤➤ **populously** *adv,* **populousness** *n.*

pop-up *adj* **1** denoting a device that causes its contents to spring up or stand out in relief. **2** denoting a computer facility, e.g. a menu, that can be brought up onto the screen during the running of a program to provide the user with a set of options, instructions, etc.

porbeagle *n* a shark of the N Atlantic and Pacific oceans with a pointed nose and crescent-shaped tail.

porcelain *n* **1** a hard nonporous translucent white ceramic material. **2** objects made of porcelain. ➤➤ **porcellaneous** *adj,* **porcellanous** *adj.*

porch *n* **1** a covered entrance to a building, *esp* one that projects from the doorway. **2** *NAm* = VERANDA.

porcine *adj* of or resembling a pig or pigs.

porcupine *n* a relatively large rodent with stiff sharp bristles mingled with its hair that it can raise to protect itself from attack.

pore[1] *n* a minute opening, *esp* one in the skin, through which liquids or gases pass.

pore[2] *v* **1** (*usu* + over) to study something closely or attentively. **2** (+ on/over/upon) to reflect or meditate on something.

pork *n* the flesh of a pig used as food.

pork barrel *n chiefly NAm, informal* a government project yielding rich benefits for a particular constituency, usu introduced to gain political support. ➤➤ **pork-barrelling** *n.*

porker *n* **1** a young pig fattened for food. **2** *informal, offensive* a person who is overweight.

pork pie *n* a pie filled with minced pork that has a raised crust and is usu served cold.

porkpie hat *n* a man's hat with a low crown, a flat top, and usu a turned-up brim.

porky[1] *adj* (**-ier, -iest**) **1** of or resembling pork. **2** *informal* rather overweight.

porky[2] *n* (*pl* **-ies**) *Brit, slang* (*usu in pl*) a lie, *esp* a trivial one.

porn[1] *n informal* pornography.

porn[2] *or* **porno** *adj informal* pornographic.

pornography *n* books, photographs, films, etc containing erotic material intended to cause sexual excitement. ➤➤ **pornographer** *n,* **pornographic** *adj,* **pornographically** *adv.*

porous *adj* **1** permeable to liquids and gases. **2** having pores or spaces. ➤➤ **porosity** *n,* **porously** *adv,* **porousness** *n.*

porphyria *n* a rare hereditary metabolic disorder characterized *esp* by discoloured urine, extreme sensitivity to light, and phases of mental derangement.

porphyry *n* **1** a rock consisting of crystals of the mineral feldspar embedded in a compact dark red or purple mass of surrounding rock. **2** any igneous rock having distinct crystals in a relatively fine-grained base. ➤➤ **porphyritic** *adj.*

porpoise *n* (*pl* **porpoises** *or* **porpoise**) a small gregarious whale with a blunt snout that resembles a dolphin and is about 2m (6ft) long.

porridge *n* **1** a soft food made by boiling oatmeal or another cereal in milk or water until thick. **2** *Brit, informal* time spent in prison.

porringer *n* a small bowl from which soft or liquid foods, e.g. soup or porridge, are eaten.

port[1] *n* **1** a town or city with a harbour where ships may take on and discharge cargo and passengers. **2** = HARBOUR[1].

port[2] *n* the left side of a ship or aircraft looking forward: compare STARBOARD[1]. ➤➤ **port** *adj.*

port[3] *v* to turn (the helm of a ship or boat) to the left.

port[4] *n* a fortified sweet wine of rich taste and aroma made in Portugal.

port[5] *n* **1** an opening, e.g. in machinery, allowing liquid or gas to enter or escape. **2** a socket or circuit by which a computer communicates with a printer, disk drive, etc. **3a** an opening in a ship's side for loading and unloading cargo. **b** = PORTHOLE (1). **4** a hole in an armoured vehicle or fortification through which guns may be fired.

port[6] *v* **1** to carry (a military weapon) diagonally in front of the body with a muzzle pointing upwards to the left. **2** in computing, to transfer (software) from one type of system to another.

port[7] *n Aus, informal* a bag or case, *esp* one used by travellers.

portable[1] *adj* **1** capable of being carried or moved about, *esp* because small or light. **2** of computer software: able to be ported without modification. **3** of e.g. a pension: able to be transferred. ➤➤ **portability** *n,* **portably** *adv.*

portable[2] *n* something, e.g. a television or typewriter, that is portable.

portage[1] *n* **1** the carrying of boats or their cargo overland from one body of navigable water to another. **2** a place where such a transfer is necessary.

portage[2] *v* to carry (a boat or its cargo) from one body of water to another.

Portakabin *n trademark* a portable prefabricated hut, e.g. for use on building sites.

portal *n* **1** a door, gateway, or entrance, *esp* one that is grand or imposing. **2** in computing, an Internet site providing numerous links to other sites and other information.

portal vein *n* a vein that transfers blood from one part of the body to another without passing through the heart, *esp* the vein carrying blood from the digestive organs and spleen to the liver.

portamento /pawtə'mentoh/ *n* (*pl* **portamenti** /-tee/) in music, a continuous gliding movement from one note to another by the voice, a trombone, or a bowed stringed instrument.

portcullis *n* a usu iron or wood grating that can be lowered between grooves to prevent passage through the gateway of a fortified place.

portend *v* to be an omen, warning, or sign of (something unpleasant or momentous to come).

portent *n* **1** something foreshadowing a coming event; an omen. **2** *archaic* a marvel or prodigy.

portentous *adj* **1** of or being a portent; ominous. **2** self-consciously important or solemn; pompous. ➤➤ **portentously** *adv,* **portentousness** *n.*

porter[1] *n chiefly Brit* a gatekeeper or doorkeeper, *esp* of a large building, who usu regulates entry and answers enquiries.

porter[2] *n* **1** somebody employed to carry luggage, e.g. in a hotel or railway station. **2** somebody employed to move patients or equipment in a hospital. **3** *NAm* a sleeping-car attendant. **4** a heavy dark brown beer brewed from partly browned malt. ➤➤ **porterage** *n.*

porterhouse *n* **1** a large steak cut from the back end of the sirloin above the ribs and containing part of the fillet. **2** in former times, an establishment where porter and sometimes steaks were served.

portfolio *n* (*pl* **-os**) **1** a hinged cover or flexible case for carrying loose papers, pictures, etc. **2** a set of drawings, photographs, etc assembled and presented as evidence of creative talent. **3** the office or responsibilities of a government minister or member of a cabinet. **4** the securities held by an investor.

porthole *n* **1** a small window in the side of a ship or aircraft. **2** = PORT[5] (4).

portico *n* (*pl* **-oes** *or* **-os**) a roof supported by columns and attached to a building, usu as a porch at the entrance.

portiere *n* a curtain hanging across a doorway.

portion[1] *n* **1** a part or share of something, e.g.: **a** a helping of food. **b** a share of an estate received by gift or inheritance. **c** *archaic* a dowry. **2** *archaic* an individual's lot or fate.

portion[2] *v* **1** (*usu* + out) to divide (something) into portions and distribute it. **2** to give (somebody) a portion.

Portland cement *n* a cement capable of setting underwater.

Portland stone *n* a type of limestone widely used in building.

portly *adj* (**-ier, -iest**) rather overweight; stout. ➤➤ **portliness** *n.*

portmanteau *n* (*pl* **portmanteaus** *or* **portmanteaux**) **1** a large bag or case for a traveller's belongings that opens into two equal parts. **2** (*used before a noun*) denoting something that combines two or more uses or qualities.

portmanteau word *n* = BLEND[2].

portmanteaux *n* pl of PORTMANTEAU.

port of call *n* **1** a port where ships customarily stop during a voyage. **2** a stop included in an itinerary.

portrait *n* **1** a pictorial likeness of a person. **2** any portrayal or representation, e.g. in a novel, film, etc. **3** (*used before a noun*) denoting a printed format in which the body of text, illustration, etc is higher than it is wide: compare LANDSCAPE[1]. ➤➤ **portraitist** *n,* **portraiture** *n.*

portray *v* **1** to make a picture of. **2a** to describe or depict, *esp* in words. **b** to represent in a particular way. **3** to play the role of in a film, play, etc. ➤➤ **portrayal** *n,* **portrayer** *n.*

Portuguese *n* (*pl* **Portuguese**) **1** a native or inhabitant of Portugal. **2** the Romance language of the people of Portugal, Brazil, and some other countries. ➤➤ **Portuguese** *adj.*

Portuguese man-of-war *n* a coelenterate that resembles the jellyfish, has very long stinging tentacles, and floats on the surface of the sea.

pose[1] *v* **1** to assume a position, or to place (e.g. a model) in a particular position or attitude, *esp* for artistic purposes. **2** to constitute (e.g. a problem or threat). **3** to present (e.g. a question) for attention or consideration. **4** (+ as) to pretend to be. **5** *Brit, informal* to behave or dress in a self-consciously stylish way to impress others.

pose[2] *n* **1** a sustained posture assumed for artistic purposes, e.g. in acting or modelling. **2** an assumed attitude or mode of behaviour intended to impress or deceive others.

poser[1] *n* a puzzling or baffling question.

poser[2] *n* **1** somebody who poses. **2** = POSEUR .

poseur *n* somebody who is affected, insincere, or adopts a distinctive style of dress or behaviour simply to impress.

posey *or* **posy** *adj* (**-ier, -iest**) *informal* pretentious.

posh[1] *adj informal* **1** very fine; splendid. **2** socially exclusive or fashionable, *esp* upper-class.

posh[2] *adv informal* in a posh way, *esp* in an educated or upper-class accent.

posit *v* (**posited, positing**) **1** to assume or put forward as fact, *esp* for the purposes of an argument; to postulate. **2** to place in position.

position[1] *n* **1a** the place occupied by somebody or something. **b** the proper place for something. **c** a place occupied by troops for strategic reasons. **d** the part of a field or playing area in which a member of a sports team generally operates. **2** the way in which somebody or something is disposed or arranged. **3a** a condition or situation. **b** social or official rank or status. **4** *formal* a post or job. **5** an opinion. ➤➤ **positional** *adj.*

position[2] *v* to put in a proper or specified position.

positive[1] *adj* **1a** concentrating on what is good or beneficial; optimistic. **b** capable of being constructively applied; helpful. **2** marked by or indicating acceptance, approval, or affirmation. **3** showing the presence of something sought or suspected to be present. **4** fully assured; confident or certain: *I'm positive that he is right.* **5** utter: *a positive disgrace.* **6** numerically greater than zero. **7** of a photographic image: having the light and dark parts corresponding to those of the original subject. **8** having higher electric potential and constituting the part from which the current flows to the external circuit. **9** in grammar, denoting the simple form of an adjective or adverb that expresses no degree of comparison. ➤➤ **positively** *adv,* **positiveness** *n,* **positivity** *n.*

positive[2] *n* **1** something positive, e.g. something about which an affirmation can be made. **2** a positive photograph or a print from a negative.

positive discrimination *n* a bias in favour of members of a group that is discriminated against or inadequately represented in a particular situation.

positive vetting *n* investigation into the character of a candidate for the civil service that makes use of any secret information gathered by the security services.

positivism *n* **1** a theory rejecting theology and metaphysics in favour of knowledge based on the scientific observation of natural phenomena. **2** = LOGICAL POSITIVISM. ➤➤ **positivist** *adj and n,* **positivistic** *adj.*

positron *n* a positively charged elementary particle that has the same mass and magnitude of electrical charge as the electron and is its ANTIPARTICLE.

posse *n* **1** (*used as sing. or pl*) in former times, a body of people summoned by a sheriff to assist in enforcing the law or preserving the public peace, usu in an emergency. **2** a large group, often with a common interest.

possess *v* **1a** to have and hold as property; to own. **b** to have as an attribute, knowledge, or skill. **2a** to influence (somebody) so strongly as to direct their actions. **b** of a demon, evil spirit, etc: to enter into and control (somebody). ✱ **what possessed you?** why were you so foolish or imprudent (as to)? ➤➤ **possessor** *n.*

possessed *adj* influenced or controlled by something, e.g. an evil spirit or a passion.

possession *n* **1a** the state of having or owning something. **b** in law, control or occupancy, e.g. of property, without regard to ownership. **c** in sport, control of the ball by a player or team. **2a** something owned or controlled. **b** (*in pl*) wealth or property. **3** domination by something, e.g. an evil spirit or a passion.

possessive[1] *adj* **1** insisting on undivided love or attention. **2** reluctant to share or give up possessions. **3** denoting a grammatical case expressing ownership or a relation corresponding to ownership. ➤➤ **possessively** *adv,* **possessiveness** *n.*

possessive[2] *n* the possessive case or a word in this case.

posset *n* a comforting hot beverage of sweetened and spiced milk curdled with ale or wine, formerly used as a remedy for colds.

possibility *n* (*pl* **-ies**) **1** the condition or fact of being possible. **2a** something possible. **b** a person or thing worth considering for selection, etc. **3** (*usu in pl*) potential or prospective value.

possible[1] *adj* **1** within the limits of ability, capacity, or realization. **2** that may or may not occur.

possible[2] *n* **1** something possible. **2** somebody or something that may be selected for a specified role, task, etc.

possibly *adv* **1** it is possible that; maybe. **2** used as an intensifier with *can* or *could.*

possum *n* **1** = OPOSSUM (I). **2** *Aus, NZ* = PHALANGER. ✱ **play possum** *informal* to pretend to be ignorant, asleep, or dead in order to deceive somebody.

post[1] *n* **1** a piece of timber, metal, etc fixed firmly in an upright position, *esp* as a stay or support. **2** a pole marking the starting or finishing point of a race, *esp* a horse race. ✱ **first past the post** see FIRST[3].

post[2] *v* **1** (*often* + up) to fasten (e.g. a notice) to a wall, board, etc in a public place. **2** to publish, announce, or advertise. **3** to record or achieve (e.g. a score).

post[3] *n chiefly Brit* **1** the letters, parcels, etc handled by a postal system; mail. **2** a single collection or delivery of post. **3** a postal system.

post[4] *v* **1** to send by post. **2** to enter (an item) in a ledger. **3** *archaic* to ride or travel with haste; to hurry. ✱ **keep somebody posted** to provide somebody with news of the latest developments.

post[5] *n* **1** the place at which somebody, e.g. a sentry, is stationed. **2** an office or position to which a person is appointed; a job.

post[6] *v* **1** to station (e.g. a sentry or body of troops) somewhere. **2** *chiefly Brit* to send (somebody) to work in a different unit or location.

post- *prefix* after, subsequent, or later: *postdate; postscript.*

postage *n* the fee for sending something by post.

postage stamp *n* an adhesive or printed stamp used as evidence of prepayment of postage.

postal *adj* **1** relating to a system for the conveyance of letters, parcels, etc between a large number of users. **2** conducted by post. ➤➤ **postally** *adv.*

postal card *n NAm* = POSTCARD.

postal code *n* = POSTCODE.

postal order *n Brit* an order issued by a post office for payment of a specified sum of money usu at another post office.

postbag *n* **1** *Brit* = MAILBAG. **2** a single batch of mail delivered to one address, *esp* letters from the general public to a person or organization.

postbox *n* **1** a secure receptacle for the posting of outgoing mail, *esp* a public box erected in the street. **2** = LETTER BOX .

postcard *n* a card on which a message can be written and sent by post without an envelope.

post chaise *n* a four-wheeled horse-drawn carriage, used in former times for the rapid transporting of mail and passengers.

postcode *n* a combination of letters and numbers that is used in the postal address of a place in Britain to assist sorting: compare ZIP CODE.

postcode lottery *n Brit* disparities in the medical treatment or social care provided by different authorities, so making the level of service a person receives dependent on where they live.

post-coital *adj* occurring or done during the period immediately following sexual intercourse.

postdate *v* **1a** to mark (e.g. a cheque) with a future date. **b** to assign to (an event) a later date than that of actual occurrence. **2** to follow (something) in time.

postdoctoral *adj* of or engaged in advanced academic or professional work beyond a doctor's degree.

poster *n* **1** a large advertisement displayed in a public place. **2** a large printed picture hung on a wall for decoration.

poste restante /,pohst 'restont/ *n chiefly Brit* a service in which mail is kept for a limited period of time at a post office for collection by the person to whom it is addressed.

posterior[1] *adj* **1** later in time or order. **2** situated behind or towards the back, *esp* towards the back of the body: compare ANTERIOR. ➤➤ **posteriority** *n,* **posteriorly** *adv.*

posterior[2] *n informal* the buttocks.

posterity *n* all future generations.

postern *n* a lesser door or gate of a castle or other large building.

poster paint *n* an opaque watercolour paint containing gum.

post-feminist *adj* denoting feminist ideas that are a development or moderation of those of the original feminist movement. ➤➤ **post-feminism** *n,* **post-feminist** *n.*

postgraduate *n* **1** a student continuing higher education after completing a first degree. **2** (*used before a noun*) of or being such a student or their studies.

posthaste *adv* with all possible speed.

post horn *n* a simple brass or copper wind instrument without valves, used *esp* by guards of mail coaches in the 18th and 19th cents.

posthumous *adj* occurring, published, awarded, etc after a person's death. ➤➤ **posthumously** *adv.*

postilion *or* **postillion** *n* a person who rides on the nearside leading horse of a team drawing a coach to guide them in the absence of a coachman.

postimpressionism *n* a movement in art in the late 19th cent. that reacted against impressionism, stressing the formal or subjective elements in painting. ➤➤ **postimpressionist** *adj and n,* **postimpressionistic** *adj.*

post-industrial *adj* denoting a period characterized by the decline of heavy industry and the emergence of other forms of economic activity, e.g. those based on information technology.

posting *n* an appointment to a post or command.

postman *or* **postwoman** *n* (*pl* **postmen** *or* **postwomen**) a man or woman who delivers the post.

postman's knock *n* a children's game in which a kiss is the reward for the pretended delivery of a letter.

postmark[1] *n* a cancellation mark showing the date and place of posting of a piece of mail.

postmark[2] *v* to mark with a postmark.

postmaster *or* **postmistress** *n* a man or woman in charge of a post office.

postmaster general *n* (*pl* **postmasters general**) an official in charge of a national post office.

postmillennialism *n* the belief that Christ will return only after the MILLENNIUM (thousand-year period mentioned in the Bible). ➤➤ **postmillennialist** *n.*

postmistress *n* see POSTMASTER.

postmodernism *n* in the arts, any movement that reacts against the ideas of a previous movement considered modernist, often advocating a reinterpretation of classical ideas, forms, and practices. ➤➤ **postmodern** *adj,* **postmodernist** *n and adj.*

postmortem[1] *n* **1** an examination of a body after death to determine the cause of death. **2** an analysis or discussion of an event after it is over, *esp* after it has failed.

postmortem[2] *adj* **1** occurring after death. **2** following the event.

postnatal *adj* relating to the period following childbirth. ➤➤ **postnatally** *adv.*

post office *n* **1** a national organization that runs a postal system. **2** a local branch of a national post office. **3** *NAm* = POSTMAN'S KNOCK.

post office box *n* a numbered box in a post office where mail is kept for collection by the person or organization renting it.

post-operative *adj* following a surgical operation.

postpaid *adv* with the postage paid.

postpartum *adj* relating to the period following birth.

postpone *v* to move to a later time; to defer. ➤➤ **postponable** *adj,* **postponement** *n,* **postponer** *n.*

postpositive *adj* of a word: placed after or at the end of another word. ➤➤ **postpositively** *adv.*

postprandial *adj formal or humorous* following a meal.

postscript *n* a note added at the end of a letter, completed article, etc.

post-structuralism *n* a mode of literary criticism derived from structuralism, that centres on the notion that there is no absolute meaning in language and an indeterminate number of interpretations of any text are possible. ➤➤ **post-structural** *adj,* **post-structuralist** *n and adj.*

post-traumatic stress disorder *n* a condition in which stress resulting from trauma persists long after the event and causes symptoms such as emotional withdrawal, depression, and anxiety.

postulant *n* a person seeking admission to a religious order. ➤➤ **postulancy** *n.*

postulate[1] *v* **1** to assume or claim that (something) is true or that it exists, *esp* for the purposes of an argument. **2** to put forward (a candidate for ecclesiastical office) for the approval of a higher authority. ➤➤ **postulation** *n,* **postulator** *n.*

postulate[2] *n* **1** a hypothesis advanced as a premise in a train of reasoning. **2** a statement, e.g. in logic or mathematics, that is accepted without proof.

posture[1] *n* **1** a position in which the body or a part of it is held. **2** a state or condition, *esp* in relation to other people or things. **3** a frame of mind; an attitude. ➤➤ **postural** *adj.*

posture[2] *v* **1** to assume an affected posture that is designed to attract attention and impress others. **2** to assume an artificial or insincere attitude; to attitudinize. ➤➤ **posturer** *n.*

postviral syndrome *n* = CHRONIC FATIGUE SYNDROME.

postwar *adj* of or being the period after a war, *esp* World War I or II.

postwoman *n* see POSTMAN.

posy[1] *n* (*pl* **-ies**) a small bouquet of flowers.

posy[2] *adj* see POSEY.

pot[1] *n* **1** a usu rounded container (e.g. of metal, glass, or earthenware) used for holding liquids or solids. **2** = FLOWERPOT. **3** = POTTY[2]. **4** *Brit* a shot in billiards or snooker in which a ball goes into a pocket. **5a** the total of the bets at stake at one time in a gambling game. **b** *chiefly NAm* the common fund of a group. **6** *informal* (*usu in pl*) a large amount, *esp* of money. ✱ **go to pot** *informal* to deteriorate or collapse. **keep the pot boiling** to maintain an activity, *esp* at a vigorous level. ➤➤ **potful** (*pl* **potfuls**) *n.*

pot[2] *v* (**potted, potting**) **1a** to preserve (food) in a sealed pot, jar, or can. **b** to plant (e.g. a seedling) in a flowerpot. **2a** to shoot (an animal) for food. **b** to take a potshot at (somebody or something). **3** in billiards or snooker, to send (a ball) into a pocket. **4** to make pottery.

pot[3] *n slang* cannabis.

potable *adj* of water: suitable for drinking. ➤➤ **potability** *n.*

potage /po'tahzh/ *n* thick soup.

potash *n* **1a** = POTASSIUM CARBONATE. **b** = POTASSIUM HYDROXIDE. **2** potassium or a potassium compound, *esp* as used in agriculture or industry.

potassium *n* a silver-white metallic chemical element of the alkali metal group that is soft and light.

potassium carbonate *n* a strongly alkaline chemical compound used in making glass and soap. Also called POTASH.

potassium hydroxide *n* a caustic alkaline chemical compound used chiefly in making liquid soaps and detergents. Also called POTASH.

potation *n formal or humorous* **1** the act of drinking. **2** an alcoholic drink.

potato *n* (*pl* **-oes**) the starchy edible tuber of a plant of the nightshade family, widely used as a vegetable.

potbelly *n* (*pl* **-ies**) a protruding abdomen. ➤➤ **potbellied** *adj.*

potboiler *n* a novel, painting, etc of little artistic merit and usu in a calculatedly popular style, produced to make a living.

pot-bound *adj* of a potted plant: having roots that fill the available space in the pot, allowing no room for further growth.

poteen *or* **potheen** /po'cheen, po'teen/ *n* Irish whiskey illicitly distilled, or any distilled alcoholic drink made at home.

potent *adj* **1** strong and powerful; *esp* producing a powerful reaction or effect, often unexpectedly. **2** of a man: able to have sexual intercourse, *esp* able to achieve erection. ➤➤ **potence** *n,* **potency** *n,* **potently** *adv.*

potentate *n* somebody who wields great power; a ruler.

potential[1] *adj* existing in possibility; capable of coming into being or developing further. ➤➤ **potentiality** *n,* **potentially** *adv.*

potential[2] *n* **1a** capacity to develop or turn out in a particular way. **b** qualities that seem to promise future achievements or benefits. **2** the work required to move a unit of positive electrical charge from a reference point, e.g. infinity to a specified point in an electric field.

potential difference *n* the voltage difference between two points that represents the work involved in the transfer of a unit quantity of electricity from one point to another.

potential energy *n* the energy that something has because of its position in a magnetic, electrical, or gravitational field, or because of the arrangement of parts.

potentiate *v* to make (two drugs or their action) more effective by administering them together. ➤➤ **potentiation** *n,* **potentiator** *n.*

potentilla *n* a shrub of the rose family that has usu yellow flowers with five petals.

potentiometer *n* **1** an instrument for measuring ELECTROMOTIVE FORCE. **2** a device used to provide variable resistances in an electronic circuit, e.g. to control volume in a radio. ➤➤ **potentiometric** *adj,* **potentiometry** *n.*

potheen *n* = POTEEN.

pother *n* **1** a noisy disturbance; a commotion. **2** needless agitation over a trivial matter; fuss.

pothole[1] *n* **1** an unwanted hole in a road surface caused by wear, weathering, etc. **2** a natural vertically descending hole in the ground or in the floor of a cave, or a system of these. ➤➤ **potholed** *adj.*

pothole[2] *v* to explore underground pothole systems as a leisure activity. ➤➤ **potholer** *n,* **potholing** *n.*

potion *n* a dose of medicine, poison, etc in liquid form.

potlatch *n* a ceremonial Native American feast marked by the lavish distribution of gifts as a display of wealth and prestige.

pot-luck *n* whatever luck or chance may bring. ✱ **take pot-luck** to share in whatever may be available to make a meal.

potoroo *n* (*pl* **potoroos**) = RAT KANGAROO.

potpourri *n* **1** a mixture of dried flowers, herbs, and spices, usu kept in a bowl for its fragrance. **2** a miscellaneous collection; a medley.

pot-roast *v* to cook (a joint of meat) slowly by braising in a covered pot. ⋙ **pot roast** *n*.

potsherd *n* a fragment of pottery.

potshot *n* **1** a shot taken in a casual manner or at an easy target. **2** a critical remark made at random.

pottage *n* a thick soup or stew of vegetables and meat.

potted *adj* **1** planted or grown in a flowerpot. **2** preserved in a sealed pot. **3** *chiefly Brit* abridged or summarized, usu in a simplified or popular form.

potter[1] *n* somebody who makes pottery.

potter[2] *v* **1** (*often* + around/about) to spend time in aimless or leisurely activity. **2** to move or travel in a leisurely or random fashion.

potter's wheel *n* a horizontal disc revolving on a vertical spindle, on which clay is shaped by a potter.

pottery *n* (*pl* **-ies**) **1** articles made of baked clay, *esp* earthenware. **2a** the art or craft of a potter. **b** the manufacture of pottery. **3** a place where ceramic ware is made and fired.

potting shed *n* a garden shed used for potting seedlings, storing tools, etc.

potty[1] *adj* (**-ier, -iest**) *Brit, informal* **1** slightly crazy. **2** foolish or silly. **3** (*usu* + about) having a great interest in or liking for something or somebody. ⋙ **pottiness** *n*.

potty[2] *n* (*pl* **-ies**) a bowl-shaped receptacle used by a small child for urination and defecation.

pouch[1] *n* **1** a small bag made of flexible material, for storing or transporting goods. **2** an anatomical part resembling a pouch, *esp* a pocket of skin in the abdomen of marsupials for carrying their young or in the cheeks of some rodents for storing food. ⋙ **pouched** *adj*, **pouchy** *adj*.

pouch[2] *v* **1** to put into a pouch. **2** to form into a pouch or a pouch-like shape.

pouf *n* see POOF.

pouffe *or* **pouf** *n* **1** a large firmly stuffed cushion that serves as a low seat or footrest. **2** a bouffant arrangement of the hair.

poult *n* a young turkey or other domestic fowl.

poulterer *n* somebody who deals in poultry or game.

poultice *n* a soft moist mass of clay, bread, mustard, etc spread on cloth and applied to inflamed or injured parts of the body.

poultry *n* chickens, ducks, and other domestic fowl kept for eggs or meat.

pounce[1] *v* **1** to spring forward or swoop down suddenly to seize something. **2** (*often* + on) to act or react swiftly to take advantage of something, e.g. a mistake.

pounce[2] *n* the act or an instance of pouncing.

pounce[3] *n* **1** a fine powder used in former times to prevent ink from running. **2** a fine powder for making stencilled patterns.

pound[1] *n* (*pl* **pounds** *or* **pound**) **1a** an avoirdupois unit of weight equal to 16oz (about 0.454kg). **b** a troy unit of weight equal to 12oz (about 0.373kg). **2** the basic monetary unit of Britain, several Middle Eastern countries, and Cyprus. **3** a monetary unit of the Sudan, worth one-tenth of a dinar.

pound[2] *v* **1** to reduce to powder or pulp by beating or crushing. **2** to strike heavily or repeatedly. **3** to move along with heavy steps. **4** to beat or throb with a heavy rhythm.

pound[3] *n* **1** an enclosure for animals, *esp* stray or unlicensed animals. **2** a place where items of personal property, *esp* illegally parked vehicles, are held until redeemed by the owner. **3** a trap or prison.

poundage *n* **1a** a fee, tax, or charge of so much per pound sterling. **b** the proportion of the takings of a business paid in wages. **2** weight expressed in pounds.

pound cake *n* a rich cake, traditionally made with a pound each of butter, flour, sugar, and eggs.

pound out *v informal* to produce (e.g. a rhythm) by the forceful or heavy-handed use of some instrument or implement.

pour *v* **1** to flow, or cause (a liquid or powder) to flow, in a stream. **2** to dispense (a drink) into a container. **3** to supply or produce freely or copiously. **4** to move, come, or go with a continuous flow and in large quantities. **5** (*often* + down) to rain hard. ✱ **pour cold water on** to be critical of or unenthusiastic about (something). **pour oil on troubled waters** to calm or defuse a heated situation. ⋙ **pourable** *adj*, **pourer** *n*.

pour out *v* to speak or express (e.g. feelings) volubly or at length.

poussin *n* a chicken that has been killed young for food.

pout[1] *v* to thrust out one's lips to show displeasure or in a sexually provocative way. ⋙ **poutingly** *adv*.

pout[2] *n* **1** an act or an instance of pouting. **2a** a sullen expression. **b** (*usu* **the pouts**) a fit of pique.

pouter *n* a domestic pigeon of a breed having a crop that can be inflated to an immense size.

poverty *n* **1** the lack of sufficient money or material possessions for a life of moderate comfort. **2** *formal* **a** a scarcity. **b** the condition of lacking desirable elements; deficiency.

poverty line *n* an income below which an individual or family is officially regarded as living in poverty.

poverty-stricken *adj* very poor; destitute.

poverty trap *n* a situation in which somebody's total income fails to increase with earnings because of the resultant loss of state benefits.

POW *abbr* prisoner of war.

powder[1] *n* **1** a solid substance that has been reduced to dry loose particles, e.g. by crushing or grinding. **2a** a substance, *esp* a cosmetic or a medicine, produced in the form of fine particles. **b** fine dry light snow. **3** gunpowder. ✱ **keep one's powder dry** to remain alert and ready for action. **take a powder** *NAm, informal* to leave in a hurry, *esp* from a difficult situation. ⋙ **powdery** *adj*.

powder[2] *v* **1** to sprinkle or cover with powder. **2** to reduce or convert to powder. ✱ **powder one's nose** *euphem* of a woman: to go to the lavatory. ⋙ **powderer** *n*.

powder blue *adj and n* pale blue.

powder keg *n* **1** a small usu metal cask for holding gunpowder or blasting powder. **2** a place or situation with the potential to erupt into violence or produce a major disaster.

powder monkey *n* **1** somebody who works with explosives, e.g. in blasting operations. **2** a boy who in former times carried gunpowder from the magazine to the gunners on board a warship.

powder puff *n* a small fluffy pad for applying cosmetic powder to the skin.

powder room *n* a public toilet for women in a hotel, department store, etc.

power[1] *n* **1a** the ability to do something or to produce an effect. **b** legal or official authority, capacity, or right. **2** the possession of control or authority over others and the ability to determine the course of events. **3** the position of being the ruler or government of a country or of exercising supreme political control. **4a** somebody or something that possesses great authority or influence. **b** a sovereign state, especially from the point of view of its international influence and military strength. **5a** physical strength. **b** mental or moral incisiveness and effectiveness; vigour. **6a** the energy supplied to a system or a machine to make it operate, *esp* electricity. **b** the energy or driving force generated by a motor or a similar machine. **7** in physics, the amount of work done or energy emitted or transferred per unit of time. **8** the number of times a given number is to be multiplied by itself. ✱ **do somebody a power of good** to do somebody a great deal of good. **the powers that be** established authority or any controlling group [from Romans 13:1 'the powers that be are ordained by God'].

power² *v* **1** to supply (a machine, vehicle, etc) with *esp* motive power. **2** (*often* + down/up) to switch an electrical device off or on. **3** to move in a powerful and vigorous manner.

power base *n* an area or group that provides the main support for a politician.

powerboat *n* a motorboat, *esp* a fast motorboat designed for racing. ➤➤ **powerboating** *n.*

power broker *n* somebody who exerts a strong but usu covert political influence, e.g. on the choice of candidates for office. ➤➤ **power-broking** *n.*

power cut *n* a failure in or reduction of the supply of electric power to an area.

power dressing *n* a smart or formal style of dressing by women intended to enhance their business and professional status.

powerful *adj* **1** having great power, prestige, or influence. **2a** very strong or forceful. **b** extremely effective. ➤➤ **powerfully** *adv.*

powerhouse *n informal* a person or thing characterized by great physical or mental energy and force.

powerless *adj* **1** devoid of strength or resources; helpless. **2** lacking the authority or capacity to act. ➤➤ **powerlessly** *adv,* **powerlessness** *n.*

power of attorney *n* the legal authority to act for another person in various legal or financial matters.

power pack *n* **1** a unit for converting a power supply to a voltage suitable for an electronic circuit. **2** a compact unit that stores electrical power and supplies it to a machine.

power plant *n* **1** = POWER STATION. **2** the engine and related equipment that supply power to a vehicle or a machine.

power play *n* **1** a tactic in which a display of strength or the threat of force is used to gain an advantage. **2** in team sports, an attacking manoeuvre that concentrates a large number of players in one particular area.

power station *n* an electricity generating station.

power steering *n* a form of steering in which power from the engine reinforces the effort applied by the driver to the steering wheel.

powertrain *n* the system of gears and shafts by which power is transmitted from an engine to e.g. the axles of a vehicle.

powwow¹ *n* **1** *informal* a meeting for discussion. **2** a traditional Native American ceremony with feasting and dancing.

powwow² *v* to hold a powwow.

pox *n* (*pl* **pox** *or* **poxes**) **1** a virus disease, e.g. chickenpox, characterized by the formation of spots on the skin that may leave pockmarks after healing. **2a** *informal* syphilis. **b** *archaic* smallpox. ✱ **a pox on somebody/something** *archaic* used to express extreme annoyance with somebody or something.

poxy *adj* (**-ier, -iest**) *chiefly Brit, informal* used to express annoyance or disgust with something: awful or worthless.

pp *abbr* **1** pages. **2** Latin *per procurationem*: used to indicate that a person is signing on behalf of somebody else. In 'Smith pp Jones', Smith is the writer of the document and Jones is signing on behalf of Smith. **3** pianissimo.

PPE *abbr* Philosophy, Politics, and Economics.

ppm *abbr* **1** in computing, pages per minute. **2** parts per million.

PPS *abbr* **1** Parliamentary Private Secretary. **2** Latin *post postscriptum*: used to introduce a second or further postscript.

PPV *abbr* pay-per-view.

PR *abbr* **1** proportional representation. **2** public relations.

Pr *abbr* the chemical symbol for praseodymium.

practicable *adj* **1** capable of being carried out; feasible. **2** usable. ➤➤ **practicability** *n,* **practicableness** *n,* **practicably** *adv.*

Usage note

practicable *or* **practical**? See note at PRACTICAL¹.

practical¹ *adj* **1** relating to the actual performance and real-life experience rather than to theory. **2a** able to be put to use or put into effect in real situations. **b** adapted or suitable for a particular use. **3** realistic and down-to-earth dealing with problems or situations. **4** good at carrying out ordinary, *esp* manual tasks. **5** very nearly as described, or as described in practice or effect if not in name; virtual: *a practical certainty.* ✱ **for practical purposes** in real terms or situations; effectively; virtually. ➤➤ **practicalness** *n.*

Usage note

practical *or* **practicable**? A *practical* plan or suggestion is one that is useful, realistic, and effective: the *practical* applications of a theory. A *practicable* plan is, simply, one that it is possible to carry out. A person can be described as *practical* ('good at ordinary tasks' or 'down-to-earth'), but not as *practicable.*

practical² *n* a practical examination or lesson.

practicality *n* (*pl* **-ies**) **1** the practical nature of something or somebody, *esp* the ability of something to be put into practice. **2** (*in pl*) the practical aspects of a situation or question.

practical joke *n* a trick or prank played on somebody to make them appear foolish. ➤➤ **practical joker** *n.*

practically *adv* **1** almost; nearly. **2** in a practical manner.

practice *n* **1a** regular or repeated exercise to acquire skill in an activity. **b** a session devoted to improving one's skills. **2** the actual carrying out of tasks, use of objects, etc as opposed to theory. **3a** a habit. **b** the usual way something is done. **4a** work in a profession, *esp* law or medicine. **b** the business or business premises of a professional person, e.g. a doctor. ✱ **in practice 1** in real situations. **2** currently able to do something well. **3** working in a profession. **out of practice** currently unable to do something well.

Usage note

In British English *practice* is the correct spelling for the noun in all its senses: *piano practice; theory and practice; veterinary practice.* The spelling for all senses of the verb is *practise*: *to practise the piano,* etc. In American English, the spelling *practice* is used for both the noun and the verb.

practiced *adj NAm* see PRACTISED.

practise (*NAm* **practice**) *v* **1** to perform (an activity) repeatedly so as to become proficient in it. **2** to carry out or apply (something) in fact or in real situations, as opposed to talking or theorizing about it. **3** to be a committed follower of (a particular religion). **4** to be professionally engaged in (a particular type of work). **5** *formal* (+ on/upon) to take advantage of (someone or something). ⋙ **practiser** *n.*

Usage note

practise *or* practice? See note at PRACTICE.

practised (*NAm* **practiced**) *adj* **1** experienced or skilled. **2** *often derog* learned by practice.

practitioner *n* **1** somebody who practises a profession, *esp* law or medicine. **2** somebody who practises a skill or art.

praesidium *n* see PRESIDIUM.

praetor (*NAm also* **pretor**) *n* an ancient Roman magistrate ranking below a consul. ⋙ **praetorial** *adj,* **praetorship** *n.*

Praetorian Guard *n* the Roman imperial bodyguard.

pragmatic *adj* **1** concerned with practicalities or expediency rather than theory or dogma; realistic. **2** relating to philosophical pragmatism. ⋙ **pragmatically** *adv.*

pragmatism *n* **1** a practical approach to problems and affairs. **2** a US philosophical movement asserting that the meaning or truth of a concept depends on its practical consequences. ⋙ **pragmatist** *adj and n,* **pragmatistic** *adj.*

prairie *n* an extensive area of level or rolling and practically treeless grassland, *esp* in N America.

prairie chicken *n* a large grouse of the N American prairie, the male of which has an orange air sac on each side of its throat.

prairie dog *n* a yellow-brown burrowing rodent related to the marmots, that has a sharp barklike call and lives in colonies in the N American prairie.

prairie oyster *n* a raw egg yolk or egg beaten with seasonings and swallowed whole, *esp* as a remedy for a hangover.

prairie schooner *n* a horse-drawn covered wagon of the type used by the pioneers who settled the American West.

praise[1] *v* **1** to express approval or admiration of. **2** to glorify or extol (e.g. God or a god). ⋙ **praiser** *n.*

praise[2] *n* **1** admiration and approval, or words expressing this. **2** worship.

praiseworthy *adj* deserving praise; commendable. ⋙ **praiseworthily** *adv,* **praiseworthiness** *n.*

praline *n* a sweet substance made from nuts, *esp* almonds, caramelized in boiling sugar, or a chocolate with a filling of this substance.

pram *n chiefly Brit* a small four-wheeled carriage for a baby, pushed by a person on foot.

prance *v* **1** to walk with high dancing steps in a lively and carefree or a silly and affected manner. **2** of a horse: to move with a springy high-stepping gait. ⋙ **prance** *n,* **prancer** *n,* **prancingly** *adv.*

prandial *adj literary* relating to a meal.

prang[1] *v Brit, informal* to crash or damage (a vehicle or aircraft).

prang[2] *n Brit, informal* a crash involving a vehicle, aircraft, etc.

prank *n* a mildly mischievous act; a trick.

prankster *n* somebody who plays pranks.

prase *n* a translucent light-green form of CHALCEDONY.

praseodymium *n* a soft silver-white metallic chemical element of the rare-earth group, used chiefly in making special alloys and colouring glass.

prat *n Brit, slang* a foolish or contemptible person.

prate *v* (*often* + about) to talk foolishly and excessively; to chatter. ⋙ **prater** *n,* **pratingly** *adv.*

pratfall *n informal* **1** a fall on the buttocks. **2** a humiliating mishap or blunder.

prattle[1] *v* to chatter in an artless, childish, or inconsequential manner. ⋙ **prattler** *n,* **prattlingly** *adv.*

prattle[2] *n* idle or childish talk.

prawn *n* a widely distributed edible ten-legged crustacean that resembles a large shrimp.

praxis *n* (*pl* **praxes**) **1** the practice of an art, science, or skill, as opposed to theory. **2** *formal* customary practice or conduct.

pray[1] *v* **1** (*often* + for/to) to speak to God or a god aloud or in thought, e.g. making a request or confession. **2** (*usu* + for) to wish or hope fervently.

pray[2] *adv formal* used as a polite, or ironically polite, formula inserted into a question, request, or plea: *Pray tell me.*

prayer *n* **1** a personal request, confession, or expression of praise or thanksgiving, addressed to God or a god. **2** the action or practice of praying to God or a god. **3** (*in pl*) a religious service consisting chiefly of prayers. **4** an earnest request or devout wish. **5** something prayed or earnestly wished for. ✱ **not have a prayer** to have no chance of success.

prayerful *adj* **1** inclined to prayers; devout. **2** characterized by prayer. ⋙ **prayerfully** *adv,* **prayerfulness** *n.*

prayer wheel *n* a revolving cylinder to which written prayers may be attached, used by Tibetan Buddhists.

praying mantis *n* = MANTIS.

pre- *prefix* **1a** earlier than: *prehistoric.* **b** in advance: *prefabricate.* **2** situated in front of: *premolar.*

preach *v* **1** to deliver a sermon in the course of a religious service. **2** to explain or proclaim (a religious idea or system) in public. **3** (*often* + at) to give advice or warnings in a tiresome or highly moral manner. **4** to advocate (something) earnestly. ⋙ **preacher** *n.*

preachify *v* (**-ies, -ied**) *informal* to preach, *esp* to give advice or moralize in a long-winded and boring way.

preachy *adj* (**-ier, -iest**) *informal* characterized by or prone to moralizing. ⋙ **preachily** *adv,* **preachiness** *n.*

preamble *n* an introductory statement; *specif* that of a constitution or statute.

preamp *n informal* = PREAMPLIFIER.

preamplifier *n* an amplifier used to amplify a relatively weak signal, e.g. from a microphone, before feeding it to the main amplifier.

prearrange *v* to arrange beforehand. ⋙ **prearrangement** *n.*

prebend *n* **1** a stipend provided by a cathedral or collegiate church to a member of its chapter. **2** a clergyman who receives a prebend. ⋙ **prebendal** *adj.*

prebendary *n* (*pl* **-ies**) **1** a canon in a cathedral chapter who receives a prebend. **2** an honorary canon in the Church of England.

Precambrian *adj* the earliest aeon of geological history ending about 570 million years ago, during which the earth's crust solidified and the earliest life forms appeared. ⋙ **Precambrian** *n.*

precancerous *adj* of a cell or a medical condition: likely to become cancerous if not treated.

precarious *adj* **1** characterized by a lack of security or stability, *esp* by the danger of falling. **2** dependent on chance or uncertain circumstances. ⋙ **precariously** *adv,* **precariousness** *n.*

precast *adj esp* of objects made of concrete: cast in the form required before being placed in position.

precaution *n* **1** a measure taken beforehand to avoid possible undesirable consequences. **2** *informal* (*in pl*) contraceptive measures. ⋙ **precautionary** *adj.*

precede *v* **1** to be, go, or come before or in front of. **2** (*usu* + with) to introduce or preface. ⋙ **preceding** *adj.*

Usage note

precede *or* **proceed**? These two words are sometimes confused. To *precede* is to 'go before': *She preceded me into the room; The meeting had been held on the Tuesday preceding the Easter weekend.* To *proceed* means to 'go forward': *I was proceeding along the High Street; The work is proceeding well.* Only *proceed* can be followed by *to* and another verb: *She then proceeded to read the paragraph in question.*

precedence *n* **1** greater importance or priority in being dealt with. **2** the right to be treated as ranking above others on a ceremonial or formal occasion.

precedent[1] /'presid(ə)nt/ *n* **1** an earlier similar occurrence of something under consideration. **2** something done or said that may influence or justify a subsequent act or statement; *specif* a judicial decision that serves as a rule for similar cases.

precedent[2] /pri'seed(ə)nt, 'presid(ə)nt/ *adj* prior in time, order, arrangement, or significance.

precentor *n* **1** a leader of the singing of a choir or congregation. **2** a clergyman, *esp* in a cathedral, who directs choral services. ⋙ **precentorial** *adj,* **precentorship** *n.*

precept *n* a command or principle intended as a general rule of conduct. ⋙ **preceptive** *adj.*

preceptor *n* a teacher or tutor. ⋙ **preceptorial** *adj.*

precession *n* a slow movement of the axis of rotation of a spinning body about another line intersecting it. ⋙ **precessional** *adj.*

precession of the equinoxes *n* the slow westward motion of the equinoctial points along the ecliptic causing the earlier occurrence of the equinoxes in each successive sidereal year.

precinct *n* **1** (*in pl*) the region immediately surrounding a place; environs. **2** (*also in pl*) **a** an enclosure bounded by the walls surrounding a building. **b** a boundary. **3** an area of a town not allowing access to traffic and usu with a specific function. **4** *NAm* an administrative district for election purposes or police control.

preciosity *n* (*pl* **-ies**) exaggerated delicacy and excessive refinement, e.g. in choice or use of language.

precious[1] *adj* **1** of great value or high price. **2** highly esteemed or cherished; dear. **3** excessively refined; affected. **4** used as an intensifier: highly valued but worthless: *Keep your precious lawnmower, I'll buy a goat!* ⋙ **preciously** *adv,* **preciousness** *n.*

precious[2] *adv* very; extremely: *precious little.*

precious[3] *n* a dear one; a darling.

precious metal *n* gold, silver, or platinum.

precious stone *n* a stone such as a diamond, ruby, or emerald, that has great value and is used as a jewel.

precipice *n* **1** a very steep or perpendicular slope, *esp* a sheer rockface or cliff. **2** disaster, or the brink of disaster.

precipitant[1] *adj* unduly hasty or sudden; precipitate. ⋙ **precipitance** *n,* **precipitancy** *n,* **precipitantly** *adv.*

precipitant[2] *n* **1** a chemical agent that causes the formation of a precipitate. **2** a causative factor that precipitates something.

precipitate[1] *v* **1** to throw violently; to hurl. **2** to bring (an event or action) about suddenly or unexpectedly. **3a** to separate out, or cause (a substance) to separate out, from a solution or suspension. **b** to cause (vapour) to condense and fall as rain, snow, etc. ⋙ **precipitable** *adj,* **precipitative** *adj,* **precipitator** *n.*

precipitate[2] *n* a substance separated from a solution or suspension by chemical or physical change.

precipitate[3] *adj* acting or carried out very suddenly or with undue haste; rash. ⋙ **precipitately** *adv,* **precipitateness** *n.*

precipitation *n* **1** rainfall, snowfall, hail, dew or condensed moisture from the atmosphere in any other form, or the amount of it that falls. **2** the process of precipitating something. **3** acting precipitately.

precipitous *adj* **1a** dangerously steep or high. **b** extremely sudden and very severe or calamitous in effect. **2** = PRECIPITATE[3] . ⋙ **precipitously** *adv,* **precipitousness** *n.*

precis[1] /'praysee/ *n* (*pl* **precis**) a concise summary of the essential points, facts, etc of something.

precis[2] *v* (**precising, precised**) to make a precis of.

precise *adj* **1** accurate and specific or detailed with regard to the nature or facts of something. **2** carried out with great attention to accuracy. **3** particular; very: *at that precise moment.* **4** strictly conforming to a rule, standard, convention, etc; punctilious. ⋙ **precisely** *adv,* **preciseness** *n,* **precision** *n.*

precision *adj* **1** adapted for extremely accurate measurement or operation. **2** marked by precision of execution.

preclude *v* to make it impossible in advance for (something) to happen or (somebody) to do something. ⋙ **preclusion** *n,* **preclusive** *adj.*

precocious *adj* **1a** showing mature qualities at an unusually early age. **b** *derog* of a child: behaving in an affectedly adult way. **2** occurring or developing at an exceptionally early time. ⋙ **precociously** *adv,* **precociousness** *n,* **precocity** *n.*

precognition *n* the apparent ability to foresee future events; clairvoyance. ⋙ **precognitive** *adj.*

pre-Columbian *adj esp* of a culture or historical artefact: dating from a time before the arrival of Columbus in America.

preconceive *v* to form (e.g. an opinion) prior to actual knowledge or experience.

preconception *n* **1** a preconceived idea. **2** a prejudice.

precondition[1] *n* something that must happen or be in existence to enable something else to happen or exist.

precondition[2] *v* **1** to put into an appropriate condition for a process that is about to take place. **2** to accustom (somebody) in advance to react to particular situations in a particular way. ⋙ **preconditioning** *n.*

precursor *n* somebody or something that precedes and prepares the way for somebody or something else; a forerunner. ⋙ **precursory** *adj.*

predacious *or* **predaceous** *adj* living by preying on other animals; predatory.

predate *v* to exist at or date from a time before (something or somebody).

predation *n* **1** the mode of life of a predator. **2** the act of preying or plundering; depredation.

predator *n* **1** an animal that lives by hunting, killing, and eating other animals. **2a** somebody who exploits other people for personal gain. **b** a company that is actively seeking to take over other companies.

predatory *adj* **1** of an animal: living by hunting, killing, and eating other animals. **2** of a person: likely to rob or exploit others for his or her own gain. ➤➤ **predatorily** *adv.*

predecease *v* to die before (another person). ➤➤ **predecease** *n.*

predecessor *n* **1** the previous occupant of a position to which another person has succeeded. **2** a person or thing that has been replaced or superseded by something else.

predestinarian *n* a person who believes in predestination. ➤➤ **predestinarian** *adj,* **predestinarianism** *n.*

predestination *n* **1a** the religious doctrine that God foreordains all events. **b** a religious doctrine, associated with Calvinism, stating that God has irrevocably destined some people for salvation and some for damnation. **2** the act of predestining or the fact of being predestined.

predestine *v* to decide the fate of (somebody or something) irrevocably in advance.

predetermine *v* **1** to decide on or arrange beforehand. **2** to impose a direction or tendency on beforehand. ➤➤ **predetermination** *n.*

predeterminer *n* in grammar, an adjective or adverb (e.g. *both* or *twice*) that can occur before a DETERMINER (e.g. *the* or *her*) in a noun phrase such as *both her hands*.

predicable *adj* capable of being asserted.

predicament *n* a difficult, perplexing, or trying situation.

predicate[1] *n* **1** the part of a sentence or clause that contains the verb and says something about the subject. **2** something that is stated or denied of the subject in a logical proposition.

predicate[2] *v formal* **1** to base or found on something else. **2** (*usu* + of) to assert (something) to be a quality or property of something or somebody.

predicative *adj* **1** of a modifying word: contained in the predicate of a sentence, e.g. *red* in *the dress is red*: compare ATTRIBUTIVE. **2** relating to a predicate. ➤➤ **predicatively** *adv.*

predict *v* to declare in advance that (something) will happen; *esp* on the basis of observation, experience, or scientific reason. ➤➤ **predictor** *n.*

predictable *adj* **1** capable of being predicted. **2** *derog* irritatingly obvious and easy to foresee, or always acting in an easily foreseeable way. ➤➤ **predictability** *n,* **predictably** *adv.*

prediction *n* **1** a statement of what will or is likely to happen in the future. **2** the act of predicting. ➤➤ **predictive** *adj,* **predictively** *adv.*

predigest *v* **1** to treat (food) so as to make it easier to digest. **2** to prepare (a book or text) in simplified form to make it easier to understand. ➤➤ **predigested** *adj,* **predigestion** *n.*

predilection *n* a liking or preference.

predispose *v* **1** to make more likely or more willing to do something. **2** (+ to) to make susceptible to something. ➤➤ **predisposition** *n.*

predominant *adj* **1** constituting the largest part of or element in something; main. **2** having greater strength, influence, or authority than others. ➤➤ **predominance** *n,* **predominantly** *adv.*

predominate *v* **1** to be greater in numbers or quantity or more common than any other. **2** to exert a controlling power or influence. ➤➤ **predomination** *n.*

preeclampsia *n* a serious abnormal condition that develops in late pregnancy and is characterized by a sudden rise in blood pressure and fluid retention.

preembryo *n* (*pl* **preembryos**) a fertilized ovum in the period before implantation in the womb.

preeminent *adj* superior to all others, *esp* in a particular field of activity. ➤➤ **preeminence** *n,* **preeminently** *adv.*

preempt *v* **1** to render (somebody else's action or intention) ineffective by acting first. **2** to take (something) over *esp* to prevent others having it. ➤➤ **preemptive** *adj,* **preemptor** *n.*

preemption *n* **1** acting first in order to forestall others. **2** a prior seizure or appropriation. **3a** the right of purchasing before others. **b** a purchase under this right.

preen *v* **1** of a bird: to clean and smooth its feathers with its beak. **2** to make oneself look smart or attractive in an ostentatious way. **3** *usu derog* to pride or congratulate (oneself) on something, *esp* some imagined good quality. ➤➤ **preener** *n.*

preexist *v* to exist in a former state or at a previous time. ➤➤ **preexistence** *n,* **preexistent** *adj.*

prefab *n* a prefabricated structure or building. ➤➤ **prefab** *adj.*

prefabricate *v* to make or manufacture the parts of (e.g. a building) at a factory ready for assembly elsewhere. ➤➤ **prefabrication** *n,* **prefabricator** *n.*

preface[1] *n* **1** an introduction to a book, speech, etc. **2** something that precedes or heralds; a preliminary.

preface[2] *v* **1** (*usu* + by/with) to provide a preface or introduction to (something said, written, or done). **2** to be a preliminary or preface to (something). ➤➤ **prefacer** *n,* **prefatory** *adj.*

prefect *n* **1** *Brit, Aus, NZ* a senior student in a secondary school who is appointed to have some authority over other students. **2** in France, Italy, etc, the chief administrative officer of a department or region.

prefecture *n* **1** the office or official residence of a prefect. **2** the district governed by a prefect. ➤➤ **prefectural** *adj.*

prefer *v* (**preferred, preferring**) **1** (*often* + to) to like better than something or somebody else. **2** *formal* to bring (a charge) against somebody. **3** *archaic* to give promotion or advancement to. ➤➤ **preferrer** *n.*

preferable *adj* that is preferred; more desirable. ➤➤ **preferability** *n.*

preferably *adv* as the best or most desirable option.

preference *n* **1** (*usu* + for) greater liking for one thing rather than another. **2** a person, thing, or option preferred; a first choice. **3** special favour or consideration given to some over others.

preference share *n* a share guaranteed priority over ordinary shares in the payment of dividends: compare ORDINARY SHARE.

preferential *adj* **1** showing special or undue favour and consideration. **2** intended to give a special advantage to certain countries in trade relations. ➤➤ **preferentially** *adv.*

preferment *n* advancement or promotion to a higher rank or office, *esp* in the Church.

prefigure *v* **1** to represent or suggest in advance; to foreshadow. **2** to picture or imagine beforehand. ➤➤ **prefiguration** *n,* **prefigurative** *adj,* **prefigurement** *n.*

prefix[1] *n* **1** an affix, e.g. *un* in *unhappy*, placed at the beginning of a word or before a word root: compare SUFFIX[1]. **2** a title used before a person's name. ➤➤ **prefixal** *adj,* **prefixally** *adv.*

prefix[2] *v* **1** to attach (something) as a prefix to a word. **2** to add (something) to the beginning.

preggers *adj Brit, informal* = PREGNANT (1).

pregnancy *n* (*pl* **-ies**) the state or period of carrying an unborn child or young in the womb.

pregnant *adj* **1** of a woman or female animal: having an unborn child or unborn young in the womb. **2** rich in significance or implication. ➤➤ **pregnantly** *adv.*

preheat *v* to heat before use, *esp* to heat (an oven) to the temperature required for cooking.

prehensile *adj* adapted for seizing or grasping, *esp* by wrapping round. ➤➤ **prehensility** *n.*

prehistoric *adj* **1** dating from the period of human history before written records were made. **2** *informal* extremely old-fashioned or out of date. ➤➤ **prehistorically** *adv,* **prehistory** *n.*

preignition *n* the detonation of the fuel-air mixture in an internal-combustion engine too early for the engine to operate effectively.

preindustrial *adj* prior to the development of large-scale industry.

prejudge *v* to pass judgment on prematurely or before a full and proper examination. ➤➤ **prejudger** *n,* **prejudgment** *n.*

prejudice[1] *n* **1a** a preconceived opinion, *esp* a biased and unfavourable one formed without sufficient reason or knowledge. **b** preconceived or biased judgments generally. **2** an irrational attitude of hostility directed against an individual or group. **3** in law, disadvantage resulting from some judgment or action of another. ✱ **without prejudice to** without affecting any legal right or claim.

prejudice[2] *v* **1** to cause to have an unreasonable bias. **2** to cause harm to or put at a disadvantage. ➤➤ **prejudiced** *adj.*

prejudicial *adj* **1** detrimental. **2** leading to prejudiced judgments. ➤➤ **prejudicially** *adv.*

prelapsarian *adj* relating to the time or state before the Fall of Man.

prelate *n* a clergyman of high rank, e.g. a bishop or abbot.

preliminary[1] *n* (*pl* **-ies**) **1** something that precedes or is introductory or preparatory to something else. **2** a preliminary round in a sports contest.

preliminary[2] *adj* preceding and preparing for what is to follow; introductory. ➤➤ **preliminarily** *adv.*

preliterate *adj* denoting a society or culture that has not yet developed the use of writing. ➤➤ **preliterate** *n.*

prelude[1] *n* **1** an introductory or preliminary performance, action, or event. **2a** a musical section or movement serving as an introduction, e.g. to an opera. **b** the introductory section of a literary work. ➤➤ **preludial** *adj.*

prelude[2] *v* to serve as prelude to. ➤➤ **preluder** *n.*

premarital *adj* occurring before marriage.

premature *adj* **1** happening or performed before the proper or usual time. **2** of a human baby: born three or more weeks before the end of the normal gestation period. **3** hasty or impulsive. ➤➤ **prematurely** *adv,* **prematureness** *n,* **prematurity** *n.*

premed *n informal* **1** = PREMEDICATION. **2** a premedical student.

premedical *adj* preceding or preparing for the professional study of medicine.

premedication *n* the drugs that prepare a patient awaiting surgery to receive a general anaesthetic.

premeditate *v* to think over and plan beforehand. ➤➤ **premeditated** *adj,* **premeditation** *n,* **premeditative** *adj,* **premeditator** *n.*

premenstrual *adj* occurring in the period just before menstruation. ➤➤ **premenstrually** *adv.*

premenstrual syndrome *n* a condition experienced by some women just before menstruation, involving emotional tension, mood swings, headaches, fluid retention, etc.

premier[1] *adj* first in position, rank, or importance; principal.

premier[2] *n* **1** = PRIME MINISTER. **2** in Canada and Australia, the head of government in a province or state. ➤➤ **premiership** *n.*

premiere[1] *n* a first public performance of a play, film, opera, etc.

premiere[2] *v* to give a first public performance of (a play, film, etc).

premiership *n* **1** the position or office of a premier. **2** (**the Premiership**) the top division of the league competition for professional Association Football clubs in England.

premise[1] *or* **premiss** *n* **1** a proposition stated or assumed as a basis of argument or inference. **2** something assumed or taken for granted.

premise[2] *v* **1** to presuppose or postulate. **2** to state as a premise or introduction to what follows.

premises *pl n* **1** a piece of land with the buildings on it. **2** a building or part of a building, *esp* as occupied and used for commercial purposes.

premiss *n* see PREMISE[1].

premium[1] *n* **1** the sum paid in order to obtain insurance for something or somebody. **2** a sum added to the standard price, wage, etc, paid chiefly as an incentive. **3** a high value or a value in excess of that normally expected. ✱ **at a premium** valuable because rare or difficult to obtain.

premium[2] *adj chiefly NAm* of exceptional quality or amount.

Premium Bond *n* a British government bond that is issued in units of £1 and which instead of earning interest is entered into a monthly draw for money prizes.

premolar *n* a tooth situated in front of the true molar teeth. ➤➤ **premolar** *adj.*

premonition *n* a strong feeling or intuition that something is going to happen. ➤➤ **premonitory** *adj.*

prenatal *adj* occurring or being in a stage before birth. ➤➤ **prenatally** *adv.*

prenuptial *adj* occurring or made before marriage.

prenuptial agreement *n* a contract made between a couple before they marry in which they set down how their assets are to be divided in the event of a divorce.

preoccupation *n* **1** (*often* + with) complete mental absorption. **2** something that absorbs all one's attention.

preoccupied *adj* (*often* + with) devoting all one's thoughts and attention to something.

preoccupy *v* (**-ies, -ied**) to engage or engross the attention to the exclusion of other things.

preordain *v* to decree or decide in advance. ➤➤ **preordainment** *n,* **preordination** *n.*

prep *n* **1** *Brit* homework done at or away from school. **2** a period devoted to doing homework.

prepackage *v* to package (e.g. food) before offering it for sale to the consumer.

prepaid *v* past tense and past part. of PREPAY.

preparation *n* **1** the activity of preparing for something. **2** (*usu in pl*) a preparatory act or measure. **3** something prepared, *esp* a medicine.

preparative[1] *n* something that prepares the way for something else.

preparative[2] *adj* = PREPARATORY.

preparatory *adj* **1** preparing or intended to prepare for something. **2** (+ to) in preparation for something. ⋙ **preparatorily** *adv.*

preparatory school *n* **1** *Brit* a private school preparing pupils for entrance to a public school. **2** *NAm* a private school preparing pupils for college.

prepare *v* **1a** to make ready beforehand for some purpose, use, or activity. **b** to put into a suitable frame of mind for something. **2** to work out the details of. **3a** to put together from various ingredients. **b** to draw up (something) in written form. ✱ **to be prepared to do something** to be willing to do something. ⋙ **preparer** *n.*

preparedness *n* a state of readiness to act or react, *esp* of having made adequate preparations for war.

prepay *v* (*past tense and past part.* **prepaid**) to pay for in advance. ⋙ **prepayment** *n.*

preponderant *adj* **1** occurring in greater number or quantity. **2** having superior weight, force, or influence; predominant. ⋙ **preponderance** *n,* **preponderantly** *adv.*

preponderate *v* (*often* + over) to be preponderant. ⋙ **preponderation** *n.*

preposition *n* a word or group of words, e.g. *by, on, from,* or *on account of,* that combines with a noun or pronoun to link it to another part of the sentence, as in 'Put it *on* the floor' and 'Where did they come *from*?'. ⋙ **prepositional** *adj,* **prepositionally** *adv.*

prepossessing *adj* tending to create a favourable impression; attractive. ⋙ **prepossessingly** *adv,* **prepossessingness** *n.*

preposterous *adj* absurd, *esp* ridiculous and absurd. ⋙ **preposterously** *adv,* **preposterousness** *n.*

preppy[1] *or* **preppie** *adj* (**-ier, -iest**) *chiefly NAm* **1** typical of somebody educated at a preparatory school in the USA. **2** of clothes or a person's way of dressing: neat, smart, and stylishly understated.

preppy[2] *or* **preppie** *n chiefly NAm* a typical product of private secondary education.

preprandial *adj* suitable for or occurring in the time just before a meal.

prep school *n* = PREPARATORY SCHOOL.

prepubescent *adj* in or typical of the period just before puberty.

prepuce *n* the foreskin, or a similar fold surrounding the clitoris. ⋙ **preputial** *adj.*

prequel *n* a book, film, etc that portrays the events that lead up to those described in an already existing work.

Pre-Raphaelite[1] *n* a member of a group of 19th-cent. English artists (the Pre-Raphaelite Brotherhood) who aimed to restore the artistic principles of the early Renaissance and whose work is characterized by intense richness of colour and detail.

Pre-Raphaelite[2] *adj* **1** typical of the Pre-Raphaelites and their style. **2** of a woman: having a pale skin and auburn hair in abundance, like the Pre-Raphaelites' favourite female models.

prerecord *v* to record (material for broadcasting) in advance of presentation or use.

prerequisite *n* a requirement that must be satisfied in advance. ⋙ **prerequisite** *adj.*

Usage note

prerequisite *or* **perquisite**? See note at PERQUISITE.

prerogative *n* **1** an exclusive right or privilege belonging *esp* to a person or group of people by virtue of rank or status. **2** the discretionary power possessed by the Crown.

presage[1] *n* **1** an omen. **2** a presentiment. ⋙ **presageful** *adj.*

presage[2] *v* **1** to give an omen or warning of; to portend. **2** to have a presentiment of.

presbyter *n* **1** a member of the governing body of an early Christian Church. **2** = ELDER[2] (3). ⋙ **presbyterate** *n,* **presbyterial** *adj.*

Presbyterian[1] *adj* denoting a Christian Church governed by elected representative bodies and traditionally Calvinistic in doctrine. ⋙ **Presbyterianism** *n.*

Presbyterian[2] *n* a member of a Presbyterian Church.

presbytery *n* (*pl* **-ies**) **1** a local ruling body in Presbyterian churches. **2** the house of a Roman Catholic parish priest. **3** the part of a church, e.g. the east end of the chancel, reserved for the officiating clergy.

preschool *adj* relating to the period from infancy to first attendance at a primary school. ⋙ **preschooler** *n.*

prescience *n* foreknowledge of events; foresight. ⋙ **prescient** *adj,* **presciently** *adv.*

prescribe *v* **1a** of a doctor: to order or recommend (a drug, medicine, or treatment) as a remedy for an illness. **b** to recommend (something) to somebody as beneficial. **2** to give specific and authoritative instructions regarding. ⋙ **prescriber** *n.*

Usage note

prescribe *or* **proscribe**? To *prescribe* is what doctors do – they specify a particular medicine for a patient. It means 'to lay down or order' positively that something should be done: *in the form prescribed by law.* To *proscribe* is a much rarer word and it has the opposite meaning - 'to forbid' or 'to ban': *Such practices were considered immoral and were proscribed by law.*

prescription *n* **1** a written direction for the preparation and use of a medicine, or the medicine prescribed. **2a** the action of laying down authoritative rules or directions. **b** an authoritative ruling. **3** the establishment of a claim to something by use and enjoyment of it over a long period.

prescriptive *adj* **1** giving instructions or laying down rules, e.g. regarding the correct use of language. **2** established by prescription or long-standing custom. ⋙ **prescriptively** *adv.*

presence *n* **1** the fact or condition of being present. **2** the immediate proximity of a person, *esp* a person of importance. **3** something non-physical that is felt to be present, such as a spirit. **4** a body of people from one country playing an influential role in another. **5a** personal distinction or magnetism that enables *esp* a performer to impress others. **b** a dignified bearing or appearance. ✱ **make one's presence felt** to compel attention and exert an influence on a situation.

presence of mind *n* the ability to retain one's self-possession and act calmly in emergencies or difficult situations.

present[1] *n* something presented; a gift.

present[2] *v* **1a** to give or award *esp* formally or ceremonially. **b** (+ with) to allow (somebody) to gain something without effort. **2** to introduce (somebody) formally, *esp* to a person of higher rank. **3a** to bring (e.g. a play or performer) before the public. **b** to act as a presenter of (e.g. a television or radio programme). **4** to offer (a particular type of appearance) to the view of others; to show or exhibit. **5** to submit (something written) for approval or consideration. **6** (*often* + to) to describe or explain (e.g. a plan, idea, or policy) in a particular way. **7** (*often* + to) to constitute or pose (a problem or difficulty). **8** (*usu* + with) to come forward for medical examination, *esp* showing particular symptoms. ✻ **present arms** to hold a weapon, *esp* a rifle, upright in front of the body as a salute. **present itself** to arise; to come about. **present oneself** to be present; to appear.

present[3] *adj* **1a** in or at a usu specified place. **b** existing in something mentioned or understood. **2a** now existing or in progress. **b** currently doing something or being discussed, dealt with, or considered. **3** denoting a verb tense that expresses present time or the time of speaking. ⋙ **presentness** *n.*

present[4] *n* **1** (**the present**) the present time. **2** in language, a verb form describing a current event or state. ✻ **at present** now. **for the present** now and for some time in the future; for the time being.

presentable *adj* **1** fit to be seen or inspected. **2** fit in dress or manners to appear in company. ⋙ **presentability** *n,* **presentableness** *n,* **presentably** *adv.*

presentation *n* **1a** the manner in which something is set forth or presented. **b** the act or process of presenting something. **2** an occasion on which something, e.g. a gift or an award, is presented. **3** an informative talk or lecture on a subject, often with illustrative material. **4** the position in which the foetus lies in the uterus in labour. ⋙ **presentational** *adj.*

present-day *adj* now existing or occurring; current or modern.

presenter *n* a broadcaster who introduces and provides comments on broadcast material during a programme.

presentiment *n* a feeling that something is about to happen; a premonition. ⋙ **presentimental** *adj.*

presently *adv* **1** before long; soon. **2** at the present time; now.

present participle *n* a participle, e.g. *dancing, being,* expressing a current event or state.

preservationist *n* a conservationist.

preservative *n* something that has the power to preserve, *specif* a substance used to protect foodstuffs against decay. ⋙ **preservative** *adj.*

preserve[1] *v* **1a** to keep (something) in its original or present condition, in good condition, or free from decay. **b** to keep in existence. **2** to maintain (an appearance or type of behaviour) in spite of adverse circumstances or provocation. **3** to keep safe from injury, harm, or destruction. **4a** to can, pickle, or similarly prepare (a perishable food) to keep it for future use. **b** to make a preserve of (fruit). ⋙ **preservable** *adj,* **preservation** *n,* **preserver** *n.*

preserve[2] *n* **1** a preparation, e.g. a jam or jelly, consisting of fruit preserved by cooking whole or in pieces with sugar. **2** an area restricted for the preservation of natural resources, e.g. animals or trees, *esp* one used for regulated hunting or fishing. **3** something, e.g. a sphere of activity, reserved for certain people.

preset *v* (**presetting,** *past tense and past part.* **preset**) to set beforehand, *esp* to set a timing device on (an appliance) so that it switches itself on or off at a particular time. ⋙ **preset** *adj,* **presettable** *adj.*

preshrunk *adj* of a material: subjected to a process during manufacture designed to reduce later shrinking.

preside *v* **1** to occupy the place of authority, e.g. in a meeting or court. **2** (+ over) to exercise guidance, authority, or control. ⋙ **presider** *n.*

presidency *n* (*pl* **-ies**) **1** the office of president. **2** the term during which a president holds office.

president *n* **1** (*often* **President**) an elected head of state in a republic. **2** *chiefly NAm* the chief officer of an organization, e.g. a business corporation or university. **3** an official chosen to preside over a meeting or assembly. ⋙ **presidential** *adj,* **presidentially** *adv.*

presidium *or* **praesidium** *n* (*pl* **presidia** *or* **presidiums**) a permanent executive committee in a Communist country.

pre-Socratic *adj* denoting or relating to Greek philosophers or philosophy before Socrates. ⋙ **pre-Socratic** *n.*

press[1] *v* **1a** to push firmly and steadily against (something), e.g. in order to operate it. **b** to move (something) in this way. **2a** to flatten or mould to a particular shape by pressing. **b** to iron (clothes). **3a** to squeeze. **b** to squeeze out the juice or oil from (a fruit, vegetable, etc). **4a** to try hard to persuade or compel (somebody) to do something. **b** (+ for) to make vigorous efforts to obtain or bring about something. **c** to put forward (e.g. a claim) forcefully. **5** (*often* + ahead/forward) to make one's way determinedly. **6** of time: to be short. ✻ **be pressed for** to have little (of something) at one's disposal. **be pressed to do** to have difficulty in doing. ⋙ **presser** *n.*

press[2] *n* **1** an apparatus or machine by which pressure is applied, e.g. for shaping material, extracting liquid, or compressing something. **2a** = PRINTING PRESS. **b** a publishing house or printing firm, or its premises. **3** (**the press**) (*used as sing. or pl*). **a** newspapers and magazines collectively. **b** journalists collectively. **4** comment or notice in newspapers and magazines. **5** a crowd of people; a throng. **6** a cupboard, *esp* one for books or clothes. ✻ **go to press** to be printed.

press[3] *v* in former times, to force into military service, *esp* in an army or navy. ✻ **press into service** to take and force (something or somebody) into any, usu temporary, service.

press conference *n* an interview given by a public figure to journalists by appointment.

press cutting *n Brit* a paragraph or article cut from a newspaper or magazine.

press gang *n* (*used as sing. or pl*) a detachment empowered to press men into military or naval service.

press-gang *v* **1** to force (somebody) into service by a press gang. **2** to force (somebody) to do something unwillingly.

pressie *n* see PREZZIE.

pressing[1] *adj* **1** very important or demanding immediate action or attention; urgent. **2** earnest or insistent. ⋙ **pressingly** *adv.*

pressing[2] *n* one or more records or other objects produced from a single mould or matrix.

pressman *or* **presswoman** *n* (*pl* **pressmen** *or* **presswomen**) *Brit* a newspaper reporter.

press on *v* **1** to continue on one's way. **2** to proceed in an urgent or resolute manner.

press release *n* a prepared statement released to the news media.

press-stud *n Brit* a metal fastener consisting of two parts joined by pressing.

press-up *n* an exercise performed in a prone position by raising and lowering the body with the arms while supporting it only on the hands and toes.

pressure[1] *n* **1** the application of force to something by something else in direct contact with it; the force exerted by pressing or squeezing. **2** influence or compulsion directed towards achieving a particular end. **3** demands made by people or circumstances that necessitate a quick response or a sustained effort. **4** distress or difficulty resulting from domestic, social, or economic factors. **5** in physics, the force or thrust exerted over a surface divided by its area.

pressure[2] *v* **1** to try to persuade or force (somebody) to do something. **2** *chiefly NAm* = PRESSURIZE.

pressure cooker *n* a metal vessel with an airtight lid used to cook food quickly in superheated steam. ⋙ **pressure-cook** *v.*

pressure group *n* an interest group organized to influence government policy or public opinion.

pressure point *n* a point where a blood vessel may be compressed against a bone, e.g. to check bleeding.

pressure suit *n* an inflatable suit to protect the body from low pressure.

pressurize *or* **pressurise** *v* **1** to maintain near-normal atmospheric pressure in (e.g. an aircraft cabin). **2** to subject to strong persuasion or coercion. **3** to design to withstand pressure. ⋙ **pressurization** *n,* **pressurizer** *n.*

prestidigitation *n* conjuring or sleight of hand. ⋙ **prestidigitator** *n.*

prestige *n* **1** high standing or esteem, based on achievement or success. **2** an aura of glamour and desirability resulting from associations of social rank or material success. ⋙ **prestigious** *adj.*

prestissimo *adj and adv* of a piece of music: to be performed at a very fast tempo.

presto[1] *adj and adv* of a piece of music: to be performed at a fast tempo.

presto[2] *interj* = HEY PRESTO.

prestress *v* to introduce internal stresses into (e.g. a structural beam) to counteract stresses that will result from an applied load. ⋙ **prestress** *n.*

presumably *adv* it is reasonable to assume that; as one may reasonably assume.

presume *v* **1a** to suppose or assume, *esp* with some degree of certainty. **b** to take for granted. **2** to undertake to do something without leave or justification; to dare to do something. **3** (+ on/upon) to take advantage, *esp* in an unscrupulous manner. ⋙ **presumable** *adj,* **presumer** *n.*

presumption *n* **1** a presumptuous attitude or presumptuous conduct; effrontery. **2a** an attitude or belief based on reasonable evidence or grounds; an assumption. **b** a ground or reason for presuming something. **3** a legal inference as to the existence or truth of a fact.

presumptive *adj* based on probability or presumption. ⋙ **presumptively** *adv.*

presumptuous *adj* going beyond the limit of what is appropriate or acceptable; overconfident or forward. ⋙ **presumptuously** *adv,* **presumptuousness** *n.*

presuppose *v* **1** to suppose beforehand, usu without proof or justification. **2** to require (something) to exist or be the case in order that something else may exist or be true or valid. ⋙ **presupposition** *n.*

prêt-à-porter *adj* = OFF-THE-PEG.

pretence (*NAm* **pretense**) *n* **1** the act of pretending. **2** an outward and often insincere or inadequate display of something. **3** (+ to) a claim made or implied, *esp* one not supported by fact.

pretend[1] *v* **1** to act as if one were not who or what one is or as if things were different from the way they really are, *esp* in play. **2** to claim or make it appear that one has, thinks, or feels (something that one does not); to simulate (something). **3a** (+ to) to claim to have. **b** (+ to) to be ambitious for or suggest one has a right to.

pretend[2] *adj* make-believe.

pretender *n* somebody who lays claim to something; *specif* a claimant, *esp* a false claimant, to a throne.

pretense *n NAm* see PRETENCE.

pretension *n* **1a** a claim, *esp* an unjustified one. **b** an ambition or aspiration. **2** vanity; pretentiousness.

pretentious *adj* trying to appear impressive by an exaggerated and false display of importance or some otherwise admirable quality. ⋙ **pretentiously** *adv,* **pretentiousness** *n.*

preterite (*NAm* **preterit**) *adj* denoting a verb tense that expresses action in the past. ⋙ **preterite** *n.*

preterm *adj* occurring, born, or giving birth before the full time of a normal pregnancy has elapsed.

preternatural *adj formal* **1** extraordinary. **2** supernatural. ⋙ **preternaturally** *adv,* **preternaturalness** *n.*

pretext *n* a false reason given to disguise the real one; an excuse.

pretor *n NAm* see PRAETOR.

prettify *v* (**-ies, -ied**) to make pretty or to depict prettily, *esp* in an inappropriate way. ⋙ **prettification** *n.*

pretty[1] *adj* (**-ier, -iest**) **1** attractive or aesthetically pleasing, *esp* in delicate or graceful ways, but less than beautiful. **2** used ironically: dreadful or terrible. ✻ **a pretty penny** *informal* a considerable amount of money. ⋙ **prettily** *adv,* **prettiness** *n,* **prettyish** *adj.*

pretty[2] *adv* **1a** to some degree; moderately. **b** very. **2** *informal* in a pretty manner; prettily. ✻ **be sitting pretty** to be in a strong position; to be well placed financially or in other respects. **pretty much/nearly/well** *informal* almost; very nearly.

pretty[3] *v* (**-ies, -ied**) *informal* (*usu* + up) to make pretty.

pretty[4] *n* (*pl* **-ies**) *archaic* a pretty person or thing, *esp* a dear or pretty child or young woman.

pretty-pretty *adj* pretty in an insipid or inappropriate way.

pretzel *n* a brittle glazed and salted biscuit typically having the form of a loose knot.

prevail *v* **1** (*often* + against/over) to gain a victory or the ascendancy through strength or superiority. **2** (+ on/upon/with) to persuade successfully. **3** to be frequent; to predominate.

prevailing *adj* **1** most frequently occurring. **2** currently widespread or predominant. ⋙ **prevailingly** *adv.*

prevalent *adj* generally or widely occurring or existing; widespread. ⋙ **prevalence** *n,* **prevalently** *adv.*

prevaricate *v* to speak or act evasively so as to hide the truth. ⋙ **prevarication** *n,* **prevaricator** *n.*

prevent *v* **1** to stop from happening or existing. **2** (*often* + from) to hold or keep (somebody or something) back; to stop (them). ⯮ **preventability** *n,* **preventable** *adj,* **preventer** *n,* **preventible** *adj,* **prevention** *n.*

preventative[1] *adj* = PREVENTIVE[1].

preventative[2] *n* = PREVENTIVE[2].

preventive[1] *adj* **1** intended to prevent something. **2** undertaken to forestall an anticipated hostile action. ⯮ **preventively** *adv,* **preventiveness** *n.*

preventive[2] *n* something that prevents, *esp* a drug or treatment that prevents disease.

preview[1] *v* **1** to view or show (e.g. a film or play) in advance of public presentation. **2** to describe or report on (events, films, programmes, etc) that are to be presented in the near future.

preview[2] *n* **1** an advance showing or performance, e.g. of a film or play. **2** a description of coming events or entertainments. **3** *chiefly NAm* a film or television trailer.

previous *adj* **1** going before in time or order. **2** *informal* acting too soon; premature. ✱ **previous to** before; prior to. ⯮ **previously** *adv,* **previousness** *n.*

prey[1] *n* **1** an animal taken by a predator as food. **2** somebody or something that is helpless or unable to resist attack; a victim.

prey[2] *v* **1a** (*often* + on/upon) to seize and devour prey. **b** (*often* + on/upon) to live by extortion, deceit, or exerting undue influence. **2** (+ on/upon) to have a continuously oppressive or distressing effect. ⯮ **preyer** *n.*

prezzie *or* **pressie** *n informal* a present.

priapic *adj* = PHALLIC.

priapism *n* continuous, abnormal, and often painful erection of the penis.

price[1] *n* **1** the amount of money demanded by a seller of something or paid by a buyer. **2** the cost at which something is done or obtained. **3** the odds in betting. ✱ **at any price** whatever the cost, effort, etc required. **at a price** paying a high price or at a heavy cost. **what price ... ? 1** what are the chances of ... ? **2** what has become of ... ?

price[2] *v* **1** to set a price on. **2** to find out the price of. ✱ **price oneself out of the market** to sell things at a higher price than most buyers are willing to pay. ⯮ **pricer** *n.*

priceless *adj* **1** having a value that is too great to be calculated. **2** *informal* particularly amusing or absurd.

price tag *n* **1** a label on merchandise showing the price at which it is offered for sale. **2** price or cost.

price war *n* a period of commercial competition characterized by the repeated cutting of prices below those of competitors.

pricey *or* **pricy** *adj* (**-ier, -iest**) *chiefly Brit, informal* expensive.

prick[1] *v* **1** to pierce slightly with a sharp point. **2** to puncture. **3** to feel or cause discomfort as if from being pricked. **4** (*often* + up) of an animal: to raise (its ears) so that they stand erect. **5** (*usu* + out) to transplant (seedlings) from the place where they germinate to a more permanent position. ✱ **prick up one's ears** to start to listen intently. ⯮ **pricker** *n.*

prick[2] *n* **1** the act of pricking something or the sensation of being pricked. **2** a mark or shallow hole made by a pointed instrument. **3** *coarse slang* the penis. **4** *coarse slang* a disagreeable person. ✱ **kick against the pricks** to harm oneself in a vain attempt to oppose or resist something.

prickle[1] *n* **1** a small sharp pointed spike sticking out from the leaf or stem of a plant or the skin of an animal. **2** a prickling sensation.

prickle[2] *v* to cause or feel a prickling or stinging sensation; to tingle.

prickly *adj* (**-ier, -iest**) **1** full of or covered with prickles. **2** marked by prickling; stinging. **3** easily irritated. ⯮ **prickliness** *n.*

prickly heat *n* a rash of red spots on the skin producing intense itching and tingling, experienced during hot and humid weather.

prickly pear *n* a cactus with yellow flowers that produces a prickly oval fruit.

pricy *adj* see PRICEY.

pride[1] *n* **1** a feeling of delight or satisfaction arising from some action, achievement or possession. **2a** a consciousness of one's own worth and dignity; self-respect. **b** an excessive sense of one's own importance; conceit. **3a** a source of pride. **b** (*used as sing. or pl*) the best in a group or class. **4** (*used as sing. or pl*) a group of lions. ✱ **pride of place** the highest or first position.

pride[2] *v* (+ on/upon) to take pride in (oneself) for something.

prie-dieu /'pree dyuh/ *n* (*pl* **prie-dieux**) a kneeling bench with a raised shelf, designed for use by a person at prayer.

priest *n* a person authorized to perform the sacred rites of a religion, *specif* a clergyman ranking below a bishop and above a deacon. ⯮ **priesthood** *n,* **priestliness** *n,* **priestly** *adj.*

priestess *n* a female priest of a non-Christian religion.

priest hole *n* a secret room or place of concealment for a priest, e.g. in an English house during the persecution of Roman Catholic priests.

prig *n* somebody who is excessively self-righteous. ⯮ **priggery** *n,* **priggish** *adj,* **priggishly** *adv,* **priggishness** *n.*

prim *adj* (**primmer, primmest**) **1** stiffly formal and proper; decorous. **2** prudish. ⯮ **primly** *adv,* **primness** *n.*

prima ballerina *n* (*pl* **prima ballerinas**) the principal female dancer in a ballet company.

primacy *n formal* the state of being first, e.g. in importance, order, or rank; preeminence.

prima donna *n* (*pl* **prima donnas**) **1** a principal female singer, e.g. in an opera company. **2** an extremely sensitive or temperamental person.

primaeval *adj chiefly Brit* see PRIMEVAL.

prima facie[1] *adv* at first view; on the first appearance.

prima facie[2] *adj* valid or sufficient at first impression; apparent.

primal *adj* **1** original or primitive. **2** first in importance; fundamental. ⯮ **primality** *n.*

primarily *adv* **1** for the most part; chiefly. **2** in the first place; originally.

primary[1] *adj* **1a** first in rank, importance, or value; principal. **b** basic or fundamental. **2** first in order of time or development; primitive. **3a** preparatory to something else in a continuing process. **b** denoting or relating to the education of children aged between about five and eleven. **4** denoting an industry that produces raw materials: compare SECONDARY, TERTIARY[1].

primary[2] *n* (*pl* **-ies**) **1** in the USA, an election in which qualified voters express a preference for a particular candidate for political office, choose party officials, or select delegates for a party convention. **2** = PRIMARY SCHOOL.

primary care *n* the first level of health care provided in the community by general medical practitioners and specialist clinics.

primary colour *n* any of the three coloured pigments red, yellow, and blue that cannot be matched by mixing other pigments.

primary school *n* a school usu for pupils aged from about five to about eleven.

primate[1] *n* any of an order of mammals that includes human beings, the apes, monkeys, and lemurs, that have hands or feet adapted for grasping and a relatively large brain.

primate[2] *n* a bishop who has precedence in a province or nation. ➤➤ **primateship** *n*.

primatology *n* the branch of zoology dealing with primates. ➤➤ **primatological** *adj*, **primatologist** *n*.

prime[1] *n* **1a** the most active or successful stage or period, *esp* of one's life. **b** *archaic or literary* the earliest period. **2** = PRIME NUMBER. **3** the symbol (′) used in mathematics as a distinguishing mark or as a symbol for feet or minutes. **4** (*often* **Prime**) the second of the traditional daily services of the Roman Catholic Church, orig fixed for 6 a.m.

prime[2] *adj* **1** first in importance or authority; principal. **2a** first-rate or excellent. **b** of the highest grade or best quality. **3** not deriving from something else; primary. ➤➤ **primely** *adv*, **primeness** *n*.

prime[3] *v* **1** to put (*esp* a pump) into working order by filling or charging it with something. **2** to apply a first coat to (a surface), *esp* in preparation for painting. **3** to give (somebody) instructions or a warning beforehand. **4** to prepare (a firearm or charge) for firing by supplying with priming or a primer.

prime minister *n* **1** the chief executive of a parliamentary government. **2** the chief minister of a ruler or state. ➤➤ **prime ministership** *n*.

prime mover *n* **1** an initial source of motive power, e.g. a windmill, water wheel, or internal-combustion engine. **2** the originator of a development or undertaking. **3** God.

prime number *n* any positive whole number that can only be divided by itself and 1, e.g. 3, 5, 17.

primer[1] *n* a book that provides a basic introduction to a subject.

primer[2] *n* material used in priming a surface, *esp* a type of paint used as a first coat on plaster, wood, etc.

prime time *n* the peak television viewing time, for which the highest rates are charged to advertisers.

primeval *or* **primaeval** *adj* dating from or relating to the earliest age or ages. ➤➤ **primevally** *adv*.

priming *n* the explosive used for igniting a charge.

primitive[1] *adj* **1a** characteristic of an early stage of development; crude or rudimentary. **b** characteristic of a relatively simple, *esp* non-industrial or preliterate people or culture. **2** *usu derog* **a** of accommodation or facilities: not up to the usual modern standards of comfort and hygiene. **b** of people's behaviour: lacking in good manners or sophistication; crude or boorish. **3a** not having received any formal training in an art or craft; self-taught. **b** denoting a style of painting typical of or deliberately imitating the productions of artists without formal training. ➤➤ **primitively** *adv*, **primitiveness** *n*.

primitive[2] *n* **1** a member of a people with an undeveloped preindustrial way of life. **2a** an artist, *esp* a self-taught artist, whose work is marked by directness and naiveté. **b** a primitive work of art.

primitivism *n* **1** belief in the superiority of a simple way of life close to nature. **2** the style of art of primitive artists. ➤➤ **primitivist** *n and adj*, **primitivistic** *adj*.

primogeniture *n* **1** the fact of being the firstborn of the children of the same parents. **2** the principle by which right of inheritance belongs to the eldest son.

primordial *adj* **1** existing from or at the beginning of time; primeval. **2** earliest formed in the development of an individual or structure. ➤➤ **primordially** *adv*.

primordial soup *n* the liquid mixture of chemical molecules, e.g. amino acids, fats, and sugars, from which life on earth is thought to have originated.

primp *v chiefly NAm* to arrange (e.g. one's dress, hair) in a careful or fastidious manner.

primrose *n* **1** a small early-flowering perennial plant with pale yellow flowers. **2** pale yellow.

primula *n* any of a genus of plants that includes the primrose, oxlip, cowslip, and polyanthus.

Primus *n trademark* a portable oil-burning stove used chiefly for cooking when camping.

primus inter pares *n* first among equals.

prince *n* **1** the son or grandson of a monarch. **2** a sovereign ruler, *esp* of a principality. **3** a title borne by noblemen of varying rank and status in various countries. ➤➤ **princedom** *n*, **princeship** *n*.

prince charming *n* an ideal suitor.

prince consort *n* (*pl* **princes consort**) the husband of a reigning female sovereign.

princeling *n* a petty or insignificant prince.

princely *adj* **1** relating to or befitting a prince. **2a** magnificent or lavish. **b** *usu used ironically* of a sum of money: large, generous. ➤➤ **princeliness** *n*, **princely** *adv*.

Prince of Darkness *n* = SATAN.

princess *n* **1** a daughter or granddaughter of a sovereign. **2** the wife or widow of a prince. **3** a woman who has the rank of a prince in her own right.

princess royal *n* the eldest daughter of a reigning king or queen.

principal[1] *adj* **1** most important, consequential, or influential; chief. **2** denoting a capital sum placed at interest, due as a debt, or used as a fund. ➤➤ **principally** *adv*.

Usage note

principal *or* **principle**? These two words, which are pronounced the same, are often confused. *Principle* is only ever a noun and has the basic sense of 'a fundamental truth or standard': *it's the principle of the thing; I object to that on principle*. *Principal* is most often used as an adjective meaning 'main': *their principal aim in life*. As a noun, *principal* means the 'head of an educational establishment' (it is the American English word for a 'head teacher') or 'a leading actor or performer' (see PRINCIPAL[2]).

principal[2] *n* **1** a person with controlling authority or a leading position within an organization. **2a** the head of an educational institution. **b** *NAm* a headteacher. **3** somebody who employs somebody else to act for him or her. **4** a leading performer in e.g. a play or opera. **5** a capital sum placed at interest, due as a debt, or used as a fund. ➤➤ **principalship** *n*.

principal boy *n* the role of the hero in British pantomime, traditionally played by a woman.

principality *n* (*pl* **-ies**) the office or territory of a prince.

principle *n* **1** a universal and fundamental law or doctrine. **2a** a rule or code of conduct. **b** devotion to the rules of right conduct and morality; integrity. **3** the essence of or basic idea behind something. **4** a law or fact of nature underlying the working of a natural phenomenon or an artificial system. **5** an ingredient, e.g. a chemical, that exhibits or imparts a characteristic quality. ✱ **in principle** in theory. **on principle** on the basis of one's beliefs or moral code.

Usage note
principle *or* **principal**? See note at PRINCIPAL[1].

principled *adj* exhibiting, based on, or characterized by principle.

prink *v* to dress or groom (oneself) carefully. ➤➤ **prinker** *n.*

print[1] *n* **1** a mark made by pressure; an impression. **2** printed state or form. **3** printed matter or letters. **4** a copy made by printing, e.g.: **a** a photograph produced from a negative or transparency. **b** a reproduction of an original work of art, e.g. a painting. **5a** cloth or clothing with a pattern applied by printing. **b** a pattern of this kind. **6** (*usu in pl*) = FINGERPRINT[1]. ✱ **in print** of a book: obtainable from the publisher. **out of print** of a book: no longer obtainable from the publisher.

print[2] *v* **1** to stamp or impress with a mark, design, etc. **2a** to make a copy of by transferring ink to paper automatically, e.g. in a printing press or computer printer. **b** to publish (e.g. a book or newspaper). **3** to make (a positive image) from a negative or transparency. **4** to write with each letter produced separately, not joined together. ➤➤ **printability** *n,* **printable** *adj.*

printed circuit *n* an electronic circuit with the components connected by conductive material deposited in thin continuous paths on an insulating surface.

printer *n* **1** somebody whose work is producing printed matter. **2** a machine that produces printed matter, e.g. computer printout.

printing *n* **1** reproduction in printed form. **2** = IMPRESSION (7C). **3** handwriting with unjoined letters.

printing press *n* a machine that produces printed matter, *esp* by pressing paper against an inked surface.

printmaker *n* somebody, *esp* an artist, who designs and produces prints from blocks or plates. ➤➤ **printmaking** *n.*

printout *n* a printed record produced automatically, *esp* by a computer.

prion *n* an infectious particle composed solely of protein thought to be responsible for brain diseases such as BSE and CJD.

prior[1] *adj* **1** earlier in time or order. **2** taking precedence, e.g. in importance. ✱ **prior to** before in time.

prior[2] *n NAm, informal* a previous conviction for a criminal offence.

prior[3] *n* **1** the deputy head of a monastery ranking next below the abbot. **2** the head of a house of any of various religious communities. ➤➤ **priorate** *n,* **priorship** *n.*

prioress *n* a nun corresponding in rank to a prior.

prioritize *or* **prioritise** *v* **1** to give priority to. **2** to arrange in order of priority. ➤➤ **prioritization** *n.*

priority *n* (*pl* **-ies**) **1a** the fact of being considered more important. **b** the right to go first, e.g. at road junctions. **2a** something meriting prior attention. **b** (*in pl*) the relative importance attached to each of a number of things.

priory *n* (*pl* **-ies**) a religious house under a prior or prioress.

prise *or* **prize** *v* **1** to press or force open or apart, e.g. with a lever. **2** to obtain or remove with difficulty.

prism *n* **1** a POLYHEDRON (three-dimensional figure) whose ends are similar, equal, and parallel polygons and whose sides are parallelograms. **2** a transparent prism, *esp* one with triangular ends, that is used to deviate or disperse a beam of light.

prismatic *adj* **1** of or like a prism. **2** formed, dispersed, or refracted by or as if by a prism. ➤➤ **prismatically** *adv.*

prison *n* a place of enforced confinement, *esp* a building in which people are confined while awaiting trial or for punishment after conviction.

prisoner *n* **1** somebody kept in enforced confinement, *esp* somebody awaiting trial or convicted of an offence. **2** somebody who is trapped by a particular set of circumstances. ✱ **take no prisoners** to be ruthlessly determined in achieving a goal.

prisoner of conscience *n* a person imprisoned for his or her political or religious beliefs.

prisoner of state *n* (*pl* **prisoners of state**) a political prisoner.

prisoner of war *n* somebody captured in war.

prissy *adj* (**-ier, -iest**) prim and prudish, *esp* in a fussy way. ➤➤ **prissily** *adv,* **prissiness** *n.*

pristine *adj* **1** in its original unspoilt state. **2** free from impurity or decay; fresh and clean as if new. ➤➤ **pristinely** *adv.*

prithee *interj archaic* please.

privacy *n* **1** a state of being apart from the company or observation of others; seclusion. **2** freedom from undesirable intrusions, *esp* avoidance of publicity.

private[1] *adj* **1** restricted to the use of a particular person or group. **2** owned or run by an independent individual or company, not by the state. **3a** not intended to be known about by others. **b** not confiding in or seeking the company of other people. **4a** of a person, citizen: not holding public office or employment. **b** not related to one's job or position; personal. **5** of a place: where one is likely to be alone or undisturbed. **6** of a soldier: having the rank of private.

private[2] *n* **1** somebody of the lowest rank in the British and US armies and the US marines. **2** *informal* (*in pl*) = PRIVATE PARTS.

private company *n* a company whose shares cannot be offered for sale to the general public.

private detective *n* a person employed by an individual or organization other than the state to investigate somebody's activities, e.g. in divorce cases.

private enterprise *n* **1** business undertaken by private individuals or privately owned companies. **2** = FREE ENTERPRISE.

privateer *n* a privately owned armed ship that can be commissioned by a government for use against an enemy in wartime. ➤➤ **privateering** *n.*

private eye *n informal* = PRIVATE DETECTIVE.

private income *n* income arising from investments or capital rather than from wages or a salary.

private investigator *n* = PRIVATE DETECTIVE.

private life *n* the personal relationships, activities, etc of somebody, as distinct from their public or professional life.

private means *n* = PRIVATE INCOME.

private member *n* a Member of Parliament who does not hold a government appointment.

private parts *pl n euphem* a person's genitalia.

private practice *n* in Britain, a medical practice that is outside the National Health Service.

private school *n Brit* a school that is supported by the fee-paying parents of pupils, not by the government.

private secretary *n* **1** a secretary employed to assist with a person's individual and confidential business matters. **2** a civil servant who assists and advises a senior government official.

private sector *n* the part of the economy that is not owned or directly controlled by the state.

private view *n* an opportunity to see an art exhibition before it opens to the general public.

privation *n* the condition of being deprived, *esp* in lacking the necessities of life.

privatise *v* see PRIVATIZE.

privatize *or* **-ise** *v* to transfer (a state-owned business, industry, etc) to private ownership. ➤➤ **privatization** *n.*

privet *n* an ornamental shrub with evergreen leaves and small white flowers widely used as hedging.

privilege *n* **1a** a right or advantage granted exclusively to a particular person, class, or group. **b** the possession of privileges, *esp* those conferred by rank or wealth. **2** immunity from normal legal sanctions, enjoyed e.g. by MPs.

privileged *adj* **1** having one or more privileges. **2** not subject to disclosure in court.

privy[1] *adj* **1** (+ to) sharing in the knowledge of something secret. **2** *archaic* secret; private. ➤➤ **privily** *adv.*

privy[2] *n* (*pl* **-ies**) a small building containing a toilet.

Privy Council *n* an advisory council nominally chosen by the British monarch and usu functioning through its committees. ➤➤ **Privy Councillor** *n,* **Privy Counsellor** *n.*

privy purse *n* (*often* **Privy Purse**) in Britain, an allowance for the monarch's private expenses paid out of public revenues.

privy seal *n* in Britain, a seal attached to certain state documents authorized by the monarch.

prize[1] *n* **1a** something offered as a reward for success in a competition, game of chance, etc. **b** (*used before a noun*) denoting a competition, game of chance, etc in which a prize is offered. **c** (*used before a noun*) having received or worthy of receiving a prize. **2a** something exceptionally desirable or precious. **b** (*used before a noun*) highly valued. **c** *often used ironically* (*used before a noun*) excellent or outstanding; complete.

prize[2] *v* to value highly; to esteem.

prize[3] *v* see PRISE.

prizefight *n* a boxing match, *esp* an unlicensed one in which there is a prize, usu of money. ➤➤ **prizefighter** *n,* **prizefighting** *n.*

PRO *abbr* **1** Public Records Office. **2** public relations officer.

pro[1] *n* (*pl* **pros**) **1** (*usu in pl*) an argument or piece of evidence in favour of a particular proposition or view: compare CON[4]. **2** a supporter of a particular proposition or view.

pro[2] *adv* in favour or affirmation: compare CON[5].

pro[3] *prep* for; in favour of.

pro[4] *n* (*pl* **pros**) *informal* = PROFESSIONAL[2].

pro[5] *adj* = PROFESSIONAL[1].

pro[6] *n* (*pl* **pros**) *informal* = PROSTITUTE[1].

pro-[1] *prefix* **1** before in time, place, order, etc: *prologue.* **2** projecting: *prognathous.*

pro-[2] *prefix* **1** favouring; supporting: *pro-American.* **2** taking the place of; substituting for: *pronoun.* **3** onward; forward: *progress.*

proactive *adj* tending to take the initiative or to act in anticipation of events.

pro-am *n* a competition, *esp* in golf, in which amateurs play professionals. ➤➤ **pro-am** *adj.*

probabilistic *adj* of or based on probability.

probability *n* (*pl* **-ies**) **1** the state of being probable. **2** something, e.g. an occurrence or circumstance, that is probable. **3** *esp* in statistics, the likelihood that a given event will occur or a measure of this.

probable[1] *adj* **1** supported by strong evidence but not certain. **2** likely to be or become true or real. ➤➤ **probably** *adv.*

probable[2] *n* a person who will probably be selected for something.

probable cause *n NAm* in law, reasonable grounds or sufficient evidence e.g. for a person to be arrested.

probate *n* **1** the judicial determination of the validity of a will. **2** an official copy of a will certified as valid.

probation *n* **1** subjection of an individual to a period of testing to ascertain suitability, e.g. for a job. **2** a method of dealing with offenders by which sentence is suspended subject to good behaviour and regular supervision by a probation officer. ➤➤ **probational** *adj,* **probationary** *adj.*

probationer *n* **1** somebody whose suitability for a job is being tested during a trial period. **2** an offender on probation.

probation officer *n* an officer appointed to supervise the conduct of offenders on probation.

probe[1] *n* **1** a slender surgical instrument for examining a cavity. **2a** a slender pointed metal conductor, e.g. of electricity or sound, temporarily inserted in something to be monitored or measured. **b** an unmanned spacecraft used to explore and send back information from space. **3** a penetrating or critical investigation, *esp* one carried out by a newspaper into corruption; an enquiry.

probe[2] *v* **1** to examine with or as if with a probe. **2** to investigate thoroughly. ➤➤ **prober** *n,* **probing** *adj,* **probingly** *adv.*

probiotic /,prohbie'otik/ *n* a preparation containing bacteria beneficial to health, especially to the healthy functioning of the gut. ➤➤ **probiotic** *adj.*

probity *n formal* honesty or integrity.

problem *n* **1a** a situation or question that is difficult to understand or resolve. **b** something or somebody that causes trouble or harm and is difficult to deal with. **2** a proposition in mathematics or physics for which a solution has to be found or from which a principle, etc can be demonstrated.

problematic *adj* **1** presenting a problem or problems. **2** open to question or debate; questionable. ➤➤ **problematical** *adj,* **problematically** *adv.*

pro bono publico *adv and adj* **1** for the public good. **2** (*usu* **pro bono**) of legal services: free to the client.

proboscides *n* pl of PROBOSCIS.

proboscis /prə'bosis/ *n* (*pl* **proboscises** /-seez/ *or* **proboscides** /-deez/) **1** a long flexible snout, e.g. the trunk of an elephant. **2** an elongated or extendable tubular mouthpart of an invertebrate animal, e.g. an insect, used *esp* for sucking.

proboscis monkey *n* a large monkey of Borneo with a long fleshy nose.

procaryote *n* see PROKARYOTE.

procedure *n* **1** a particular way of acting or accomplishing something. **2** a series of ordered steps. **3** an established method of doing things. ➤➤ **procedural** *adj*, **procedurally** *adv*.

proceed *v* **1a** to begin and carry on an action or movement. **b** to begin and carry on a legal action. **2a** to move along a course; to advance. **b** to continue after a pause or interruption. **3** to arise from a source; originate.

Usage note

proceed *or* precede? See note at PRECEDE.

proceedings *pl n* **1** a series of events, *esp* the events involved in an established procedure. **2** legal action. **3** an official record of things said or done.

proceeds *pl n* **1** the total amount brought in. **2** the net amount received.

process[1] *n* **1a** a series of actions or operations designed to achieve an end, e.g. in manufacturing. **b** a natural phenomenon marked gradual changes that produce a particular result: *the process of growth*. **2** in law, a summons or writ. **3** a projecting part of a living organism or anatomical structure. ✱ **in the process of 1** currently engaged in doing or undergoing something. **2a** while. **b** during.

process[2] *v* **1** to subject (e.g. food, photographic film, etc) to a special process or treatment. **2** to take appropriate action on. **3** in computing, to operate on (data). ➤➤ **processable** *adj*.

process[3] *v chiefly Brit* to move in a procession.

procession *n* **1a** a group of people, vehicles, etc, moving along in an orderly way. **b** the act or action of moving along in this way. **2** a succession or sequence.

processional[1] *n* a book containing hymns, prayers, or other compositions used in or intended for a religious procession.

processional[2] *adj* **1** of or moving in a procession. **2** used, intended, or suitable for a procession.

processor *n* **1** a person or device that processes something. **2** in computing, = CENTRAL PROCESSING UNIT.

pro-choice *adj* of a person, pressure group, etc: advocating or in favour of legally available abortion.

proclaim *v* **1** to declare publicly and usu officially; to announce. **2** to give clear outward indication of. **3** to declare (somebody) to be something or to have a specified quality: *The press proclaimed him a racist liar*. ➤➤ **proclamation** *n*.

proclivity *n* (*pl* **-ies**) an inclination or predisposition towards something, *esp* something reprehensible.

proconsul *n* **1** a governor or military commander of an ancient Roman province. **2** an administrator in a modern dependency or occupied area.

procrastinate *v formal* to put off doing something until a later time. ➤➤ **procrastination** *n*, **procrastinator** *n*.

procreate *v formal* to conceive or produce offspring; to reproduce. ➤➤ **procreation** *n*, **procreative** *adj*, **procreator** *n*.

Procrustean *adj* seeking to enforce or establish conformity, e.g. to a policy or doctrine, by arbitrary and often violent means.

proctology *n* the branch of medicine that deals with the structure and diseases of the anus, rectum, and lower part of the large intestine. ➤➤ **proctological** *adj*, **proctologist** *n*.

proctor *n* an officer at certain universities, *esp* one appointed to maintain student discipline.

procumbent *adj* **1** of a stem: trailing along the ground without rooting. **2** of a plant: having or producing such stems.

procuracy *n* (*pl* **-ies**) the office or position of a procurator.

procurator *n* **1** an agent or attorney. **2** an administrator of the Roman Empire entrusted with the financial management of a province.

procurator fiscal *n* (*pl* **procurators fiscal** *or* **procurator fiscals**) a local coroner and public prosecutor in Scotland.

procure *v* **1** to obtain (something), *esp* by particular care and effort. **2** to obtain (somebody) to act as a prostitute, *esp* on behalf of somebody else. **3** *formal* to achieve; to bring about. ➤➤ **procurable** *adj*, **procurement** *n*.

procurer *or* **procuress** *n* a man or a woman who obtains prostitutes for other people.

Prod *n* (*also* **Proddy, Proddie**) *informal, derog* a Protestant, *esp* in Ireland.

prod[1] *v* (**prodded, prodding**) **1** to poke or jab (somebody or something) with a finger, pointed instrument, etc. **2** to incite (somebody) to action; to stir or stimulate.

prod[2] *n* **1** a pointed instrument. **2** a prodding action; a jab. **3** an incitement to act; a stimulus.

Proddy *or* **Proddie** *n* (*pl* **-ies**) see PROD.

prodigal[1] *adj* **1** recklessly extravagant or wasteful. **2** yielding abundantly; lavish. ➤➤ **prodigality** *n*, **prodigally** *adv*.

prodigal[2] *n* **1** somebody who is recklessly extravagant or wasteful. **2** a repentant sinner or reformed spendthrift.

prodigious *adj* **1** causing amazement or wonder. **2** remarkable in bulk, quantity, or degree; enormous. ➤➤ **prodigiously** *adv*.

prodigy *n* (*pl* **-ies**) **1** somebody, *esp* a child, with extraordinary talents. **2a** something extraordinary, inexplicable, or marvellous. **b** (+ of) an exceptional and wonderful example of a specified quality: *a prodigy of patience*.

produce[1] *v* **1** to give being, form, or shape to (something); to make or manufacture. **2** to give birth or rise to (something). **3** to offer (something) to view or notice: *She produced her passport*. **4** to act as a producer of (e.g. a film, play, piece of recorded music, etc). ➤➤ **producer** *n*, **producible** *adj*.

produce[2] *n* **1** agricultural products, *esp* fresh fruit and vegetables. **2** anything that is produced; a product or products.

product *n* **1** a saleable or marketable commodity. **2a** something produced by a natural or artificial process. **b** a result of a combination of incidental causes or conditions. **3** the result of multiplying two or more numbers or expressions together.

production *n* **1** the act or process of producing. **2** total output, *esp* of a commodity or an industry. **3a** something produced; a product. **b** a literary or artistic work. **c** a work presented in the theatre or cinema or television or radio.

production line *n* = ASSEMBLY LINE.

productive *adj* **1** having the quality or power of producing, *esp* in abundance. **2** yielding significant results or benefits. **3** (+ of) effective in bringing about or causing something. ➤➤ **productively** *adv*, **productiveness** *n*.

productivity *n* **1** the state or quality of being productive. **2** the relationship between the output of goods and services and the input used to produce them, *esp* the effectiveness of labour in terms of industrial output.

product placement *n* a form of advertising in which companies pay to have their products featured in films, television programmes, etc.

profane[1] *adj* **1** not concerned with religion or religious purposes. **2a** debasing or defiling what is holy; irreverent. **b** indecent, obscene, or blasphemous.

profane[2] *v* **1** to treat (something sacred) with abuse, irreverence, or contempt; to desecrate. **2** to debase (something) by an unworthy or improper use. ➤➤ **profanation** *n.*

profanity *n* (*pl* **-ies**) **1a** profane language. **b** a profane utterance; a swear word. **2** the state or quality of being profane.

profess *v* **1a** to declare or admit openly or freely; to affirm. **b** to declare falsely; to claim or pretend. **2** to confess one's faith in or allegiance to (e.g. a religion).

professed *adj* **1** openly and freely admitted or declared: *a professed atheist.* **2** claiming to be qualified: *a professed solicitor.* **3** pretended or false: *professed misery.* ➤➤ **professedly** *adv.*

profession *n* **1a** an occupation requiring specialized knowledge and often long and intensive academic preparation. **b** (*used as sing. or pl*) the whole body of people engaged in such an occupation. **2a** an act of openly declaring or claiming a faith, opinion, etc. **b** a protestation, declaration, or claim. **3** an avowed religious faith.

professional[1] *adj* **1a** relating or belonging to or engaged in a profession. **b** characterized by or conforming to the technical or ethical standards of a profession. **c** characterized by conscientious workmanship. **2** of a person: taking part in an activity, *esp* a sport, as a paid occupation, as distinct from being an amateur. ➤➤ **professionally** *adv.*

professional[2] *n* **1** somebody who engages in an occupation or activity professionally. **2** somebody with sufficient experience or skill in an occupation or activity to resemble a professional.

professional foul *n* in sport, *esp* football, an intentional foul that prevents a member of the opposing side from gaining an advantage or scoring.

professionalism *n* the conduct, aims, or qualities, usu of a high and consistent standard, that characterize a profession or a professional person.

professor *n* **1a** a staff member of the highest academic rank at a university; *esp* the head of a university department. **b** *NAm* a teacher at a university. **2** somebody who professes or declares something, e.g. a faith or opinion. ➤➤ **professorial** *adj,* **professorship** *n.*

proffer *v* to present for acceptance; to tender or offer.

proficient *adj* competent or expert in an art, skill, branch of knowledge, etc. ➤➤ **proficiency** *n,* **proficiently** *adv.*

profile[1] *n* **1** a side view, *esp* of the human face. **2** an outline seen or represented in sharp relief; a contour. **3a** a concise biographical or descriptive outline. **b** the extent to which somebody or something features in the media or attracts public attention. ✱ **in profile** as seen from one side; appearing side on. **keep a low profile** to take up or remain in a position that does not attract attention.

profile[2] *v* **1** to produce a profile of (somebody or something), e.g. by drawing or writing. **2** to shape the outline of (something), *esp* by using a template. ➤➤ **profiler** *n.*

profiling *n* **1** an analysis of a person's DNA to determine their physical characteristics. **2** an analysis of a person's psychological make-up, *esp* to determine their suitability for a particular job or to see if they fit a known type of criminal offender.

profit[1] *n* **1** a gain or benefit. **2** the excess of revenue over expenditure, *esp* in business. ➤➤ **profitless** *adj.*

profit[2] *v* (**profited, profiting**) **1** (*often* + from/by) to derive benefit; to gain: *She profited greatly from these lessons.* **2** to be of service to; to benefit: *It will not profit you to start an argument.*

profitable *adj* producing an advantage or financial or other gains. ➤➤ **profitability** *n,* **profitably** *adv.*

profit and loss account *n* a summary account used at the end of an accounting period to show income and expenditure and the resulting net profit or loss.

profiteer[1] *v* to make an unreasonable profit, *esp* on the sale of scarce and essential goods. ➤➤ **profiteering** *n.*

profiteer[2] *n* somebody who profiteers.

profiterole *n* a small hollow ball of cooked choux pastry filled with whipped cream and covered with a chocolate sauce.

profit margin *n* the amount by which a business's net income exceeds its outgoings or the difference between the selling price of a product and its cost price.

profit-sharing *n* a system or process under which employees receive a part of the profits of an industrial or commercial enterprise.

profligate[1] *adj* **1** utterly dissolute; immoral. **2** wildly extravagant; prodigal. ➤➤ **profligacy** *n.*

profligate[2] *n* a profligate person.

pro forma[1] *adj* **1** made or carried out in a perfunctory manner or as a formality. **2** provided in advance to prescribe form or describe items.

pro forma[2] *adv* as a formality; as a matter of convention or politeness.

pro forma[3] *n* a standard form or document.

profound *adj* **1a** having intellectual depth and insight. **b** difficult to fathom or understand. **2a** extending far below a surface. **b** coming from, reaching to, or situated at a depth; deep-seated. **3** characterized by intensity of feeling or quality. ➤➤ **profoundly** *adv,* **profoundness** *n,* **profundity** *n.*

profuse *adj* **1** liberal; extravagant. **2** greatly abundant; bountiful. ➤➤ **profusely** *adv,* **profuseness** *n,* **profusion** *n.*

progenitive *adj* capable of reproducing.

progenitor *n* **1a** a direct ancestor; a forefather. **b** a biologically ancestral form. **2** a precursor or originator. ➤➤ **progenitorial** *adj.*

progeniture *n* the act of producing offspring.

progeny *n* **1** (*used as sing. or pl*) descendants or children. **2** (*used as sing. or pl*) offspring of animals or plants.

progesterone *n* a steroid hormone that is secreted by the CORPUS LUTEUM (tissue forming in the ovary after ovulation) and causes changes in the uterus in preparation for pregnancy.

progestogen *n* any of several steroid hormones involved in pregnancy and the prevention of ovulation.

prognathous *adj* having the lower jaw projecting beyond the upper part of the face.

prognosis *n* (*pl* **prognoses**) **1** the prospect of recovery as anticipated from the usual course of disease or peculiarities of a particular case. **2** *formal* a forecast or prediction.

prognostic *adj* used to make a prognosis.

prognosticate *v formal* to foretell from signs or symptoms; to predict. ➤➤ **prognostication** *n,* **prognosticator** *n.*

program[1] *n* **1** a sequence of coded instructions that can be stored in a mechanism, e.g. a computer, enabling it to perform a specific operation. **2** *chiefly NAm* see PROGRAMME[1].

Usage note

program *or* programme? British English has adopted the spelling *program* as standard in computer contexts: *a computer program; to program a computer.* In all other contexts the correct British English spelling is *programme,* while the correct American English spelling is *program.*

program[2] *v* (**programmed, programming,** *NAm* **programed, programing**) **1a** to provide (a computer) with a program. **b** to prepare or arrange (instructions, data, etc) for use by a computer or other mechanism. **2** *chiefly NAm* see PROGRAMME[2]. ➤➤ **programmable** *adj,* **programmer** *n.*

programmatic *adj* **1** of programme music. **2** of, resembling, or having a programme. ➤➤ **programmatically** *adv.*

programme[1] (*NAm* **program**) *n* **1a** a brief usu printed list of the features to be presented, the people participating, etc, in a public performance. **b** a radio or television broadcast usu characterized by some theme or purpose giving it coherence and continuity. **2** a systematic plan of action. **3** a curriculum, prospectus, or syllabus.

Usage note

programme *or* program? See note at PROGRAM[1].

programme[2] (*NAm* **program**) *v* (**programmed, programming,** *NAm* **programed, programing**) **1a** to arrange or provide a programme of or for (something). **b** to enter (something) in a programme; to schedule (something) as part of a programme. **2** to cause (something or somebody) to conform to a pattern, e.g. of thought or behaviour; to condition (something or somebody). ➤➤ **programmable** *adj,* **programming** *n.*

programme music *n* music intended to suggest a sequence of images or incidents.

progress[1] *n* **1** forward or onward movement, e.g. towards a destination, objective, or goal; advance. **2** gradual improvement, *esp* a continuous development towards an improved, more modern, or more complete state. **3** *archaic* a ceremonial journey, *esp* a monarch's tour.

progress[2] *v* **1** to move forward; to proceed. **2** to develop to a higher, better, or more advanced stage.

progression *n* **1** the act or an instance of progressing; advance. **2a** a continuous and connected series; a sequence. **b** a sequence of numbers in which each term is related to its predecessor by a uniform law. **3** a succession of musical notes or chords. ➤➤ **progressional** *adj.*

progressive[1] *adj* **1a** of or characterized by progress or progression. **b** making use of or interested in new ideas, findings, or opportunities. **2** moving forward continuously or in stages; advancing. **3** increasing in extent or severity: *a progressive disease.* **4** increasing in rate as the base increases: *a progressive tax.* **5** of a dance, card game, etc: involving successive changes of partner. ➤➤ **progressively** *adv,* **progressiveness** *n.*

progressive[2] *n* **1** somebody who advocates progressive ideas, e.g. in education. **2** somebody believing in moderate political change, *esp* social improvement.

prohibit *v* (**prohibited, prohibiting**) **1** to forbid (something) by authority. **2a** to prevent (somebody) from doing something. **b** to prevent (something) from happening.

prohibition *n* **1** the act or an instance of prohibiting something. **2** an order that forbids or prevents something. **3** (*often* **Prohibition**) the legal ban on the manufacture and sale of alcohol from 1920 to 1933 in the USA. ➤➤ **prohibitionist** *n.*

prohibitive *adj* **1** tending to prohibit or restrain. **2** of a cost, charge, etc: tending to prevent or discourage the use or acquisition of something. ➤➤ **prohibitively** *adv.*

prohibitory *adj* = PROHIBITIVE.

project[1] *n* **1** a specific plan or design; a scheme. **2** a planned undertaking, e.g.: **a** a piece of research with a definite plan. **b** a task or problem engaged in usu by a group of pupils. **3** *NAm* a group of houses for rent, usu with government subsidies.

project[2] *v* **1a** to devise in the mind; to design. **b** to plan, calculate, or estimate (something future) on the basis of known data or present trends. **c** to present (something) or transport (somebody) in imagination. **2** to throw (something or somebody) forward or upward, *esp* by mechanical means. **3** to cause (light or an image) to fall on a surface. **4** to protrude or cause to protrude. **5a** to cause (one's voice) to be heard at a distance. **b** to communicate (something) vividly, *esp* to an audience. **c** to present or express (oneself) in a manner that wins approval. **6** to reproduce (e.g. a point, line, or area) on a surface by motion in a prescribed direction. **7** to attribute (something in one's own mind) to a person, group, or object.

projectile[1] *n* **1** a body projected by external force and continuing in motion by its own inertia, *esp* a missile fired from a weapon. **2** a self-propelling weapon, e.g. a rocket.

projectile[2] *adj* **1** propelled with great force. **2** being or capable of being thrust forward.

projection *n* **1** an estimate of future possibilities based on present trends. **2** the act of projecting something or somebody. **3** a part that juts out. **4** the display of films or slides by projecting an image onto a screen. **5a** a systematic representation on a flat surface of latitude and longitude from the curved surface of the earth, the celestial sphere, etc. **b** the process of reproducing a spatial object on a surface by projecting its points or a reproduction formed by this process. **6** the act or an instance of perceiving a subjective mental image as objective. **7** the attribution of one's own ideas, feelings, or attitudes to other people. ➤➤ **projective** *adj.*

projectionist *n* the operator of a film projector.

projector *n* an apparatus for projecting films or slides onto a surface.

prokaryote *or* **procaryote** *n* a minute organism, e.g. a bacterium, that does not have a distinct nucleus: compare EUKARYOTE. ➤➤ **prokaryotic** *adj.*

prolactin *n* a protein hormone produced by the front lobe of the pituitary gland that is important in the reproduction of mammals and that stimulates milk production.

prolapse[1] *n* the falling down or slipping forward of a body part, e.g. the uterus, from its usual position.

prolapse[2] *v* of a body part: to fall down or slip forward from its usual position.

prolate *adj* of a spheroid: elongated in the direction of a line joining the poles: compare OBLATE[1].

prole *n and adj informal, derog* = PROLETARIAN.

prolegomenon *n* (*pl* **prolegomena**) an introductory section to a learned work. ➤➤ **prolegomenous** *adj.*

prolepsis *n* (*pl* **prolepses**) **1** *formal* anticipation, *esp* the representation of a future act or development as if it already exists or has already been accomplished. **2** in rhetoric, the answering of anticipated objections.

proletarian *n* a member of the proletariat. ➤➤ **proletarian** *adj.*

proletariat *n (used as sing. or pl)* **1** the lowest social or economic class of a community. **2** in ancient Rome, the lowest class of citizens.

pro-life *adj* of a person, pressure group, etc: opposed to legally available abortion. ➤➤ **pro-lifer** *n.*

proliferate *v* **1** to grow or reproduce by rapid production of new parts, cells, buds, or offspring. **2** to increase rapidly in number or quantity. ➤➤ **proliferation** *n,* **proliferative** *adj.*

prolific *adj* **1** producing offspring, fruit, etc freely. **2** marked by abundant inventiveness or productivity. ➤➤ **prolifically** *adv.*

proline *n* an amino acid that forms part of many proteins and that can be synthesized by animals.

prolix *adj* **1** unduly or tediously prolonged or repetitious. **2** given to using more words than are needed in speaking or writing; long-winded. ➤➤ **prolixity** *n,* **prolixly** *adv.*

prologue (*NAm* **prolog**) *n* **1** the preface or introduction to a literary, cinematic, or musical work. **2** a speech, often in verse, addressed to the audience at the beginning of a play. **3** an introductory or preceding event or development.

prolong *v* **1** to lengthen (something) in time. **2** to lengthen (something) in space. ➤➤ **prolongation** *n,* **prolonged** *adj.*

PROM *abbr* programmable read-only memory.

prom *n* **1** (*often* **Prom**) = PROMENADE CONCERT. **2** *Brit* = PROMENADE[1] . **3** *NAm* a formal dance given for a high-school or college class, *esp* at the end of an academic year.

promenade[1] *n* a place for strolling, *esp* a paved walk along the seafront at a resort.

promenade[2] *v* to take a leisurely stroll or ride.

promenade concert *n* a concert of classical music at which some of the audience stand or walk about.

promenade deck *n* an upper deck of a passenger ship where people can take a stroll.

promenader *n* somebody attending a promenade concert, *esp* a member of the audience in the area without seating.

Promethean *adj* daringly original or creative.

promethium *n* a metallic chemical element of the rare-earth group obtained from the radioactive decay of uranium.

prominence *n* **1** the state or quality of being prominent or conspicuous. **2** something prominent; a projection.

prominent *adj* **1a** widely and popularly known; famously eminent. **b** readily noticeable; conspicuous. **2** projecting beyond a surface or line; protuberant. ➤➤ **prominently** *adv.*

promiscuous *adj* **1** indulging in or characterized by numerous casual and short-lived sexual relationships. **2** not restricted to one class or person; indiscriminate. **3** casual; irregular. ➤➤ **promiscuity** *n,* **promiscuously** *adv.*

promise[1] *n* **1** a declaration that one will or will not do something specified. **2** grounds for expectation usu of success, improvement, or excellence.

promise[2] *v* **1** to make a promise. **2** to suggest beforehand; to indicate: *dark clouds promising rain.* **3** to give grounds for expectation, *esp* of something good.

promised land *n* **1** (**the Promised Land**) the land of Canaan, which God promised Abraham that his descendants would possess (Genesis 12:7). **2** a place or condition believed to promise final satisfaction or realization of hopes.

promisee *n* in law, a person to whom a promise is made.

promising *adj* full of promise; likely to succeed or to yield good results. ➤➤ **promisingly** *adv.*

promisor *n* a person who makes a legally binding promise.

promissory *adj* containing or conveying a promise.

promissory note *n* a written signed promise to pay a sum of money to a specified individual or to the bearer.

promo *n* (*pl* **-os**) *informal* an advertising promotion, *esp* a video or film.

promontory *n* (*pl* **-ies**) **1** a high point of land or rock projecting into a body of water; a headland. **2** a prominence or projection on a part of the body.

promote *v* **1a** to contribute to the growth or prosperity of; to further. **b** to help bring (e.g. an enterprise) into being; to launch. **c** to present (e.g. merchandise) for public acceptance through advertising and publicity. **d** to contribute to (something) in a beneficial way. **2a** to cause (somebody) to advance in position, rank, or status. **b** to assign (a team) to a higher division of a sporting competition, e.g. a football league. ➤➤ **promoter** *n.*

promotion *n* **1a** the act or fact of being raised in position or rank. **b** the act or fact of being assigned to a higher division of a sporting competition. **2a** the act of furthering the growth or development of something, *esp* sales or public awareness. **b** something, e.g. a price reduction or free sample, intended to promote something or increase sales. ➤➤ **promotional** *adj.*

prompt[1] *v* **1** to move (somebody) to action; to incite. **2** to serve as the inciting cause of; to urge. **3** to assist (somebody acting or speaking) by saying the next words of something forgotten or imperfectly learned.

prompt[2] *adj* **1** performed readily or immediately. **2a** ready and quick to act as occasion demands. **b** happening or arriving on time; punctual. ➤➤ **promptly** *adv,* **promptness** *n.*

prompt[3] *n* **1a** the act or an instance of prompting. **b** somebody or something that prompts or reminds somebody. **2** in computing, any of various symbols on a VDU screen that indicate to the user the place where a command should go.

prompt[4] *adv informal* exactly; punctually: *The lecture will start at seven o'clock prompt.*

prompter *n* a person who is positioned offstage during a performance of a play and who prompts actors when they forget their lines.

prompt note *n* a reminder of a limit of time given for payment.

promulgate *v* **1** to make known by open declaration; to proclaim. **2** to put (a law, decree, etc) into action or force, *esp* by official proclamation. **3** to promote publicly. ➤➤ **promulgation** *n,* **promulgator** *n.*

pronate *v* to rotate (the hand or foot) so that the palm or sole faces downward or backward: compare SUPINATE. ➤➤ **pronation** *n.*

pronator *n* a muscle that is involved in pronating a hand or foot.

prone *adj* **1** (+ to) having a tendency or inclination to something. **2a** having the front or lower surface downward. **b** lying flat on the ground. **3** (*used in combinations*) liable to suffer: *accident-prone; strike-prone*. **4** *archaic* sloping downward. ➤➤ **proneness** *n*.

prong[1] *n* **1** any of the slender sharp-pointed parts of a fork or similar instrument. **2** a subdivision of an argument, attacking force, etc. ➤➤ **pronged** *adj*.

prong[2] *v* to stab, pierce, or spear with a prong.

pronghorn *n* (*pl* **pronghorns** *or* **pronghorn**) a cud-chewing mammal of treeless parts of western N America that resembles an antelope.

pronominal *adj* of, resembling, or constituting a pronoun. ➤➤ **pronominally** *adv*.

pronoun *n* a word used as a substitute for a noun or noun phrase and referring to a previously named or an already understood person or thing, e.g. *I, he, that*.

pronounce *v* **1** to utter the sound or sounds of (a letter, syllable, word, etc), *esp* to say it correctly. **2** to declare (somebody or something) as being officially or ceremoniously in a specified state: *The priest pronounced them man and wife*. **3** to declare (somebody or something) as being authoritatively the case or as being an opinion: *The doctor pronounced him fit to work*. ➤➤ **pronounceable** *adj*, **pronouncement** *n*, **pronouncer** *n*.

pronounced *adj* strongly marked or very conspicuous.

pronto *adv informal* without delay; quickly.

pronunciation *n* the act or manner of pronouncing a letter, syllable, word, etc.

proof[1] *n* **1a** evidence that compels acceptance of a truth or a fact. **b** the process of establishing the truth or validity of a statement. **c** an act, effort, or operation designed to establish or discover a fact or the truth; a test. **2a** a sample printing of a piece of text, an engraving, etc, made for examination or correction. **b** a test photographic print. **3** a test of the quality of an article or substance. **4** the alcoholic content of a beverage compared with the standard for proof spirit. **5** in Scots law, a trial before a judge without a jury.

proof[2] *adj* (*often used in combinations*) designed for or successful in resisting or repelling; impervious: *soundproof*.

proof[3] *v* **1** to make or take a proof of (a typeset text, etc). **2** to make waterproof. **3** = PROOFREAD. ➤➤ **proofer** *n*.

proofread *v* to read and mark corrections on (a proof). ➤➤ **proofreader** *n*.

proof spirit *n* a mixture of alcohol and water containing a standard amount of alcohol, in Britain 57.1% by volume.

prop[1] *n* **1** a rigid usu auxiliary vertical support, e.g. a pole. **2** a source of strength or support. **3** = PROP FORWARD.

prop[2] *v* (**propped, propping**) **1** to support (something or somebody) by placing something under or against them. **2** to support (something or somebody) by placing them against something.

prop[3] *n* any article or object used in a play or film other than painted scenery or costumes.

prop[4] *n informal* a propeller.

propaganda *n* **1** the usu organized spreading of ideas, information, or rumours designed to promote or damage an institution, movement, etc. **2** the ideas, information, etc so spread.

propagandize *or* **-ise** *v* to spread propaganda. ➤➤ **propagandist** *n and adj*.

propagate *v* **1** to cause (something, e.g. a plant) to reproduce or multiply by natural or artificial processes. **2** to pass down (e.g. a characteristic) to offspring. **3a** to cause (something) to spread out and affect a greater number or area. **b** to publicize. **c** to transmit (*esp* energy) in the form of a wave. ➤➤ **propagation** *n*.

propagator *n* **1** a box in which germinating plants, young seedlings, and cuttings are kept until they have established root systems. **2** a person who spreads ideas, beliefs, etc to others.

propane *n* a heavy inflammable gas that is found in crude petroleum and natural gas and is used as a fuel.

propel *v* (**propelled, propelling**) **1** to drive (something) forward by means of a force that imparts motion. **2** to urge (somebody) on; to motivate.

propellant *n* **1** a gas in a pressurized container for expelling the contents when the pressure is released. **2** an explosive for propelling projectiles. **3** fuel plus oxidizer used by a rocket engine to provide thrust.

propellent *or* **propellant** *adj* capable of propelling.

propeller *n* a device, consisting of a central hub with radiating twisted blades, that is used to propel a ship or aircraft.

propeller shaft *n* a shaft that transmits mechanical power, *esp* from an engine to the wheels of a vehicle or the propeller of a ship or aircraft.

propelling pencil *n Brit* a usu metal or plastic pencil with a thin replaceable lead that can be moved forward as it wears down.

propensity *n* (*pl* **-ies**) *formal* a natural inclination or tendency.

proper[1] *adj* **1** suitable; appropriate. **2a** strictly accurate; correct. **b** strictly decorous; genteel. **3** (*often used after a noun*) being strictly so-called: *not part of the city proper*. **4** (+ to) belonging characteristically to a species or individual; peculiar to something or somebody: *ailments proper to tropical climates*. **5** *chiefly Brit, informal* thorough; complete: *a proper idiot*. **6** (*often used after a noun*) of a representation of something in heraldry: appearing in its natural colour.

proper[2] *adv informal or dialect* in a thorough manner; completely.

proper fraction *n* a fraction in which the NUMERATOR (number above the line) is less than the DENOMINATOR (number below the line).

properly *adv* **1** in a fit manner; suitably. **2** in the required or appropriate way; correctly. **3** strictly in accordance with fact. **4** *chiefly Brit, informal* to the full extent; completely.

proper name *n* = PROPER NOUN.

proper noun *n* a noun that designates a particular person, place, or thing and is usu capitalized, e.g. *Janet, London*.

propertied *adj* of a person, class, etc: possessing property, *esp* land.

property *n* (*pl* **-ies**) **1a** something owned or possessed. **b** ownership. **c** something to which somebody has a legal title. **2** a piece of land and the building or buildings on it. **3a** a quality, attribute, or power inherent in something. **b** an attribute common to all members of a class.

prop forward *n* in rugby, either of the two players on either side of the hooker in the front row of the scrum.

prophecy *n* (*pl* **-ies**) **1** a prediction of an event. **2a** an inspired declaration of divine will and purpose. **b** the function or vocation of a prophet; the capacity to utter prophecies.

prophesy *v* (**-ies, -ied**) **1** to predict with assurance or on the basis of mystic knowledge. **2** to utter by divine inspiration.

prophet *or* **prophetess** *n* **1** a man or woman who utters divinely inspired revelations. **2** somebody who foretells future events; a predictor. **3** a spokesperson for a doctrine, movement, etc.

prophetic *adj* **1** of or characteristic of a prophet or prophecy. **2** foretelling events; predictive. ⋙ **prophetical** *adj*, **prophetically** *adv.*

prophylactic[1] *adj* guarding against, protecting from, or preventing disease.

prophylactic[2] *n* **1** a prophylactic drug. **2** *chiefly NAm* a condom.

prophylaxis *n* (*pl* **prophylaxes**) action taken to prevent the spread of disease.

propinquity *n formal* **1** nearness in place or time; proximity. **2** nearness of relationship; kinship.

propitiate *v* to gain or regain the favour or goodwill of; to appease. ⋙ **propitiation** *n*, **propitiatory** *adj.*

propitious *adj* **1** boding well; auspicious. **2** tending to favour; opportune. **3** *archaic* favourably disposed; benevolent. ⋙ **propitiously** *adv*, **propitiousness** *n.*

propjet *n* = TURBOPROP.

propolis *n* a brownish resinous material of waxy consistency collected by bees from the buds of trees and used as a glue in constructing and strengthening the hive.

proponent *n* somebody who argues in favour of something; an advocate.

proportion[1] *n* **1** the relation of one part to another or to the whole with respect to magnitude, quantity, or degree. **2** harmonious relation of parts to each other or to the whole; balance. **3** a relationship of constant ratio. **4a** a proper or equal share. **b** a fraction or percentage. **5** (*in pl*) size; dimensions. ✱ **in proportion** having the correct or desirable relationship between constituent parts. **out of proportion** lacking the correct or desirable relationship between constituent parts. **sense of proportion** an ability to assess the relative importance or significance of things.

proportion[2] *v* **1** to adjust (a part or thing) in proportion to other parts or things. **2** to make the parts of (something) harmonious or symmetrical.

proportional *adj* (*often* + to) being in a corresponding or appropriate relation with respect to size, shape, etc. ⋙ **proportionality** *n*, **proportionally** *adv.*

proportional representation *n* an electoral system in which each political group gains a number of seats in a legislative assembly that is in proportion to the number of votes it wins.

proportionate *adj* being in due proportion. ⋙ **proportionately** *adv.*

proposal *n* **1a** a proposed idea or plan of action; a suggestion. **b** an offer of marriage. **2** the act or an instance of putting something forward for consideration.

propose *v* **1a** to present (an idea, a plan, etc) for consideration or adoption. **b** to establish as an aim or intention. **2a** to recommend (somebody) to fill a place or vacancy; to nominate. **b** to announce (a toast). **3** to make an offer of marriage. ⋙ **proposer** *n.*

proposition[1] *n* **1a** something offered for consideration or acceptance. **b** *informal* a proposal of sexual intercourse. **c** a formal mathematical statement to be proved. **2** somebody or something to be dealt with. ⋙ **propositional** *adj.*

proposition[2] *v* to make a proposal to (somebody); *specif* to propose sexual intercourse to (somebody).

propound *v formal* to offer for discussion or consideration. ⋙ **propounder** *n.*

proprietary *adj* **1** of or characteristic of a proprietor. **2** made and marketed under a patent, trademark, etc. **3** privately owned and managed.

proprietary name *n* a name that is registered as a trademark.

proprietor *or* **proprietress** *n* **1** a man or woman having the legal right or exclusive title to something; an owner. **2** somebody having an interest less than absolute right, e.g. control or present use. ⋙ **proprietorial** *adj*, **proprietorially** *adv.*

propriety *n* (*pl* **-ies**) **1** the quality or state of being proper; fitness. **2** the standard of what is socially or morally acceptable in conduct or speech; decorum. **3** (*in pl*) the conventions and manners of polite society.

propulsion *n* the action or process of propelling. ⋙ **propulsive** *adj.*

prop up *v* to give e.g. moral or financial support to (something or somebody).

propyl *n* a chemical group with a valency of one that is derived from propane.

propylene *n* an inflammable gas obtained from petroleum and used chiefly in the synthesis of other chemical compounds.

pro rata[1] /ˌproh ˈrahtə/ *adj* proportional.

pro rata[2] *adv* proportionally; in proportion.

prorogue *v* (**prorogues, prorogued, proroguing**) to terminate a session of (e.g. a parliament) without dissolving it. ⋙ **prorogation** *n.*

prosaic *adj* **1** characteristic of prose as distinguished from poetry. **2** belonging to the everyday world; dull or commonplace. ⋙ **prosaically** *adv.*

proscenium *n* (*pl* **proscenia** *or* **prosceniums**) **1** the stage of an ancient Greek or Roman theatre. **2** the part of a stage in front of the curtain in a modern theatre.

proscenium arch *n* the arch in a conventional theatre through which the spectator sees the stage.

prosciutto /prəˈshootoh/ *n* raw cured Italian ham, usu served in very thin slices.

proscribe *v* **1** to condemn or forbid (*esp* something considered harmful); to prohibit. **2** to outlaw or exile. ⋙ **proscription** *n*, **proscriptive** *adj.*

Usage note

proscribe *or* prescribe? See note at PRESCRIBE.

prose[1] *n* ordinary language without metrical structure.

prose[2] *v* to write or speak in a dull prosaic manner.

prosecute *v* **1a** to institute and pursue criminal proceedings against (somebody). **b** to institute legal proceedings with reference to (something): *prosecute a claim.* **2** *formal* to follow (something) through, to pursue: *determined to prosecute the investigation.* **3** *formal* to engage in (e.g. a trade). ⋙ **prosecutable** *adj.*

prosecution *n* **1** the act or an instance of prosecuting; *specif* the formal institution and pursuit of a criminal charge. **2** (*used as sing. or pl*) the party that institutes or conducts criminal proceedings. **3** the act or an instance of doing something, *esp* until it is completed.

prosecutor *n* somebody who institutes or conducts an official prosecution.

proselyte *n* **1** a person who has been newly converted to a religion, political party, different way of thinking, etc. **2** a Gentile who has converted to Judaism. ⋙ **proselytism** *n.*

proselytize *or* **-ise** *v* to convert (somebody), *esp* to a new religion. ⋙ **proselytizer** *n.*

prosody *n* **1a** the patterns of rhythm, metre, rhyme, and versification used in poetry. **b** the study of versification, *esp* of metrical structure. **2** the stress and intonation patterns in language. ⋙ **prosodic** *adj,* **prosodist** *n.*

prospect[1] *n* **1a** a mental picture of something to come. **b** expectation; possibility. **c** (*in pl*) financial and social expectations. **d** (*in pl*) chances, *esp* of success. **2** a potential client, candidate, etc. **3** an extensive view; a scene.

prospect[2] *v* to explore (an area), *esp* for mineral deposits. ⋙ **prospector** *n.*

prospective *adj* **1** likely to come about; expected. **2** likely to be or become. ⋙ **prospectively** *adv.*

prospectus *n* (*pl* **prospectuses**) a printed statement or brochure describing an organization or enterprise, and distributed to prospective students, customers, participants, etc.

prosper *v* to succeed or thrive; *specif* to achieve economic success.

prosperity *n* the condition of being successful or thriving, *esp* economic well-being.

prosperous *adj* marked by success, *esp* financial success. ⋙ **prosperously** *adv.*

prostaglandin *n* any of a group of compounds derived from fatty acids that occur widely in body tissues and act locally to control various processes, e.g. the induction of labour and abortion.

prostate *n* in male mammals, a small mass of muscular and glandular tissue that is situated around the neck of the bladder and secretes an alkaline liquid constituting most of the volume of semen. ⋙ **prostatic** *adj.*

prosthesis *n* (*pl* **prostheses**) an artificial device to replace a missing part of the body. ⋙ **prosthetic** *adj.*

prosthetics *pl n* **1** (*used as sing.*) the branch of surgery concerned with the replacement of missing or damaged body parts with artificial devices. **2** artificial body parts. ⋙ **prosthetist** *n.*

prostitute[1] *n* a person, *esp* a woman, who engages in sexual activities for money.

prostitute[2] *v* **1** to make a prostitute of (oneself or somebody else). **2** to devote (something) to corrupt or unworthy purposes; to debase. ⋙ **prostitution** *n.*

prostrate[1] *adj* **1a** lying full-length face downwards, *esp* in adoration or submission. **b** extended in a horizontal position; flat. **2** physically or emotionally weak or exhausted; overcome. **3** of a plant: trailing on the ground.

prostrate[2] *v* **1** to throw or put (*esp* oneself) into a prostrate position. **2** to put (oneself) in a humble and submissive posture or state. **3** to reduce (somebody) to submission, helplessness, or exhaustion; to overcome. ⋙ **prostration** *n.*

prosy *adj* (**-ier, -iest**) of speech or writing: dull or tedious.

prot- *or* **proto-** *comb. form* **1** first in time; earliest; original: *prototype.* **2** first-formed; primary: *protozoan.*

protactinium *n* a shiny metallic radioactive chemical element of relatively short life.

protagonist *n* **1** somebody who takes the leading part in a drama, novel, film, or story. **2** a leader or notable supporter of a cause.

protea *n* an evergreen shrub of the southern hemisphere grown for its dense flower heads surrounded by attractive coloured bracts (modified leaves; see BRACT).

protean *adj* **1** readily assuming different shapes or roles. **2** displaying great diversity or variety.

protect *v* **1a** to cover or shield (something or somebody) from injury or destruction. **b** to guard or defend (something or somebody) against attack, harm, danger, etc. **c** to take measures to save (an endangered species) from extinction. **2** to shield or foster (a home industry) by an import tariff. **3** to provide funds to guarantee payment of (e.g. a bill of exchange).

protection *n* **1** the act or an instance of protecting or being protected. **2** something that protects. **3a** immunity from threatened violence, often purchased under duress. **b** money extorted by racketeers for such immunity.

protectionism *n* the shielding of the producers of a country from foreign competition by import tariffs. ⋙ **protectionist** *adj and n.*

protective *adj* **1** providing or able to provide protection. **2** of or being an import tariff intended to protect domestic producers rather than to yield revenue. ⋙ **protectively** *adv,* **protectiveness** *n.*

protective custody *n* detention of somebody for their own safety.

protector *n* **1** somebody or something that protects. **2** (*often* **Protector**) somebody in charge of a kingdom during the minority or absence of the sovereign; a regent.

protectorate *n* **1** a state that is partly controlled by and dependent on the protection of another more powerful state, without being fully annexed. **2** (**Protectorate**) the government of the Commonwealth of England, Scotland, and Ireland from 1653 to 1659.

protectress *n* a female protector.

protégé *or* **protégée** /'protizhay/ *n* somebody under the protection, guidance, or patronage of a more experienced or influential person.

protein *n* any of numerous naturally occurring extremely complex organic chemical compounds that are essential constituents of all living cells and form an important part of the diet of human beings and other animals.

pro tem *adv and adj* for the time being.

Proterozoic *adj* of the latter part of the Precambrian aeon, preceding the Palaeozoic era, lasting from about 2,500 to 570 million years ago, and marked by rocks containing a few fossils of algae and soft-bodied invertebrate animals. ⋙ **Proterozoic** *n.*

protest[1] *v* **1** to express usu strong disagreement or objection. **2** to engage in an organized public demonstration of disapproval. **3** to make a formal or solemn declaration or affirmation of (something): *He protested his innocence.* ⋙ **protester** *n,* **protestor** *n.*

protest[2] *n* **1** a formal or solemn declaration of disapproval, disagreement, or objection. **2** an organized public demonstration of disapproval.

Protestant *n* an adherent of any of those Western Christian Churches that separated from the Roman Catholic Church at the Reformation or subsequently. ⋙ **Protestant** *adj,* **Protestantism** *n.*

Protestant ethic *n* a belief that working hard and being thrifty is a person's duty and that living this way brings enough reward in itself.

Protestant work ethic *n* = PROTESTANT ETHIC.

protestation *n* **1** the act or an instance of protesting. **2** a solemn declaration or avowal.

prothalamion *or* **prothalamium** *n* (*pl* **prothalamia**) a song or poem in celebration of a forthcoming marriage.

protist *n* a single-celled organism of a group including protozoans, single-celled algae, and simple fungi.

protium *n* the ordinary, most common, and lightest isotope of hydrogen containing one proton in the atomic nucleus.

proto- *comb. form* see PROT-.

protocol *n* **1** a code of conduct, etiquette, and procedure, *esp* for official or ceremonial occasions. **2a** an original draft of a diplomatic document, e.g. a treaty. **b** a signed record of agreement made at a diplomatic conference, internation negotiations, etc. **3** in computing, a set of rules relating to the form in which data must be presented, e.g. for transmission between computers. **4** the plan or a record of a scientific experiment or medical treatment.

proton *n* an elementary particle that carries a single positive electrical charge and forms part of the nucleus of all known atoms, with the exception of the hydrogen atom of which it forms the entire nucleus.

protoplasm *n* **1** the living material of a cell and its nucleus consisting of a complex of organic and inorganic substances, e.g. proteins and salts in solution. **2** the cytoplasm of a cell. ⋙ **protoplasmic** *adj.*

prototype *n* **1** an original model on which something is based or from which it derives. **2** a first full-scale and usu operational form of a new type or design of a construction, e.g. an aeroplane. **3** somebody or something that exemplifies the essential features of a type. ⋙ **prototypical** *adj.*

protozoan *or* **protozoon** *n* (*pl* **protozoans** *or* **protozoa**) a minute single-celled animal of a group that vary in structure and physiology, occur in almost every kind of habitat, and include some serious parasites of human beings and domestic animals. ⋙ **protozoan** *adj.*

protract *v* **1** to prolong in time or space. **2** of a muscle: to extend (a part of the body) forward or outward. ⋙ **protracted** *adj,* **protraction** *n.*

protractor *n* a usu flat semicircular instrument marked with degrees that is used for drawing or measuring angles.

protrude *v* to project from or extend beyond the surrounding surface or place. ⋙ **protrusion** *n.*

protuberant *adj* projecting from a surrounding or adjacent surface, often as a rounded mass; prominent or bulging. ⋙ **protuberance** *n.*

proud *adj* **1** very pleased or satisfied, e.g. with some achievement or possession. **2a** having or displaying excessive self-esteem. **b** having proper self-respect. **3a** stately; magnificent. **b** giving reason for pride; glorious. **4** projecting slightly from a surrounding surface. ✱ **do somebody proud 1** to treat somebody very well, *esp* to entertain them lavishly. **2** to give somebody cause for pride or gratification. ⋙ **proudly** *adv.*

prove *v* (*past part.* **proved** *or* **proven**) **1** to establish the truth or validity of (something) by evidence or demonstration. **2** to test the quality of; to try out: *The exception proves the rule.* **3** in law, to obtain probate of (a will). **4** to show (oneself) to have the required abilities, qualities, etc. **5** to turn out, *esp* after trial: *The new drug proved to be effective.* **6** of bread dough: to rise and become aerated through the action of yeast. ⋙ **provable** *adj.*

provenance *n* a place of origin or record of ownership, e.g. of a work of art.

Provençal /provonh'sahl/ *n* **1** a native or inhabitant of Provence. **2** the language of the people of Provence. ⋙ **Provençal** *adj.*

provençale /prohvonh'sahl/ *adj* (*used after a noun*) of food: cooked in a way that is typical of the French region of Provence, *esp* in a sauce made from tomatoes, garlic, and olive oil.

provender *n* **1** dry food for domestic animals. **2** *humorous* food; provisions.

proverb *n* a brief pithy saying embodying a truth, a widely held belief, or a piece of advice.

proverbial *adj* **1** of or resembling a proverb. **2** characteristic, stereotypical, or well-known. ⋙ **proverbially** *adv.*

provide *v* **1** to supply what is needed for sustenance and support: *She has to provide for a large family.* **2** to furnish or equip (somebody with something): *They provided us with a picnic lunch.* **3** to supply or afford: *Curtains provide privacy.* **4** to make adequate provision; to take precautions: *You must provide against future loss.* **5** to make a proviso or stipulation: *The constitution provides for an elected president.* ⋙ **provider** *n.*

provided *conj* = PROVIDING.

providence *n* **1** (**Providence**) God or nature conceived as the power sustaining and guiding human destiny. **2** adequate preparation or proper precautions taken in anticipation of future events.

provident *adj* **1** showing foresight in providing for the future; prudent. **2** thrifty. ⋙ **providently** *adv.*

providential *adj* of or determined by providence, or as if by providence; lucky. ⋙ **providentially** *adv.*

providing *conj* on condition; if and only if.

province *n* **1a** an administrative district or division of a country. **b** (**the provinces**) all of a country except the capital, *esp* when regarded as lacking sophistication. **2a** somebody's proper business, function, or activity. **b** a field or sphere of knowledge or activity.

provincial[1] *adj* **1** of or coming from a province or the provinces. **2a** limited in outlook; narrow-minded. **b** lacking the sophistication or refinement associated with urban society. ⋙ **provincialism** *n,* **provinciality** *n,* **provincially** *adv.*

provincial[2] *n* somebody living in or coming from a province or provinces.

proving ground *n* **1** a place designed for or used in testing equipment or scientific experimentation. **2** a place where something new is tried out.

provision[1] *n* **1a** the act or an instance of providing something. **b** a measure taken beforehand; a preparation or precaution. **2** (*in pl*) a stock of food or other necessary supplies. **3** a proviso or stipulation, e.g. in a legal document.

provision[2] *v* to supply (somebody or something) with provisions.

Provisional *n* a member of the unofficial wing of the IRA or of Sinn Fein.

provisional *adj* **1a** serving for the time being; *specif* requiring later confirmation. **b** *Brit* of a driving licence: allowing the holder to drive under supervision until they have passed their driving test and a full licence has been issued. **2** (**Provisional**) relating to or denoting the unofficial wing of the IRA or of Sinn Fein. ⋙ **provisionally** *adv.*

proviso *n* (*pl* **-os** *or* **-oes**) **1** a clause in an unofficial document, contract, etc that introduces a condition. **2** a conditional stipulation.

provisory *adj* **1** conditional. **2** provisional.

provitamin *n* a substance that can be converted in the body into a specific vitamin.

Provo *n* (*pl* **-os**) *informal* = PROVISIONAL.

provocation *n* **1** the act or an instance of provoking; incitement. **2** something that provokes, usu to anger or irritation.

provocative *adj* serving or tending to provoke or arouse to indignation, interest, sexual desire, etc. ⋙ **provocatively** *adv*, **provocativeness** *n*.

provoke *v* **1** to incite (a person or animal) to anger; to incense. **2** to cause (somebody or something) to behave in a specified way. **3** to stir up or evoke. **4** to provide the needed stimulus for.

provolone *n* a lightly smoked Italian soft cheese.

provost *n* **1** the head of certain university colleges, public schools, etc. **2** the head of certain Scottish district councils. **3** the head of the CHAPTER (assembly of canons) in a cathedral or other church.

provost marshal *n* an officer who supervises military police.

prow *n* the bow of a ship or boat.

prowess *n* **1** outstanding ability. **2** military valour and skill.

prowl[1] *v* to move about or roam over a place in a stealthy or predatory manner.

prowl[2] *n* the act or an instance of prowling. ⋙ **prowler** *n*.

proximal *adj* of an anatomical part: next to or nearest the point of attachment or origin: compare DISTAL. ⋙ **proximally** *adv*.

proximate *adj formal* **1a** very near; close. **b** coming soon; imminent. **2** next preceding or following. **3** approximate. ⋙ **proximately** *adv*.

proximity *n* nearness in space, time, or association.

proxy *n* (*pl* **-ies**) **1** a deputy authorized to act as a substitute for another. **2** authority to act or vote for another.

Prozac *n trademark* a drug taken as an antidepressant.

prude *n* a person who shows or affects extreme modesty or propriety, *esp* in sexual matters. ⋙ **prudish** *adj*, **prudery** *n*.

prudence *n* **1** discretion or shrewdness in the management of affairs. **2** skill and good judgment in the use of resources; frugality. **3** caution or circumspection with regard to danger or risk. ⋙ **prudent** *adj*, **prudently** *adv*.

prudential *adj* **1** of or proceeding from prudence. **2** exercising prudence, *esp* in business matters. ⋙ **prudentially** *adv*.

prune[1] *n* a dried plum.

prune[2] *v* **1** to cut off the dead or unwanted parts of (a woody plant or shrub). **2a** to reduce (text, etc) by eliminating superfluous matter. **b** to remove (something) as superfluous.

prurient *adj* inclined to, having, or arousing an excessive or unhealthy interest in sexual matters. ⋙ **prurience** *n*, **pruriently** *adv*.

pruritic *adj* of or marked by itching.

pruritus *n* an intense sensation of itching, or any of various disorders, *esp* of the skin, that cause this.

Prussian *n* a native or inhabitant of Prussia. ⋙ **Prussian** *adj*.

Prussian blue *n* any of numerous blue pigments consisting of iron cyanides.

prussic acid *n* = HYDROCYANIC ACID.

pry *v* (**-ies, -ied**) (*usu* + into) to enquire in an over-inquisitive or impertinent manner. ⋙ **prying** *adj*.

PS *abbr* **1** Police Sergeant. **2** (*also* **ps**) postscript. **3** Private Secretary.

psalm *n* a sacred song or poem used in worship, *esp* any of the biblical hymns attributed to King David of Israel and others and collected in the Book of Psalms. ⋙ **psalmist** *n*.

psalmody *n* the practice or art of singing psalms in worship. ⋙ **psalmodic** *adj*, **psalmodist** *n*.

Psalter *n* a book containing a collection of biblical Psalms for liturgical or devotional use.

psaltery *n* (*pl* **-ies**) an ancient stringed musical instrument similar to a dulcimer but plucked.

p's and q's *pl n informal* something, *esp* manners or language, that one should be mindful of.

PSBR *abbr* public sector borrowing requirement.

psephology *n* the scientific study of elections. ⋙ **psephologist** *n*.

pseud *n informal* an intellectually or socially pretentious person.

pseud- *or* **pseudo-** *comb. form* **1** false; spurious: *pseudonym*. **2** resembling closely; imitating: *pseudo-intellectual*.

pseudo[1] *adj* **1** apparent rather than actual; spurious. **2** *informal* false; pretentious.

pseudo[2] *n* (*pl* **-os**) somebody who is pretentious or not genuine.

pseudo- *comb. form* see PSEUD-.

pseudonym *n* a fictitious name, *esp* one used by an author. ⋙ **pseudonymity** *n*, **pseudonymous** *adj*, **pseudonymously** *adv*.

psf *abbr* pounds per square foot.

psi[1] /sie, psie/ *n* **1** the 23rd letter of the Greek alphabet (Ψ, ψ), equivalent to roman ps. **2** psychic or paranormal phenomena or abilities.

psi[2] *abbr* pounds per square inch.

psilocybin *n* a hallucinogenic organic compound obtained from various mushrooms.

psittacine[1] *adj* of the parrot family; like a parrot.

psittacine[2] *n* a bird of the parrot family.

psittacosis *n* a severe infectious disease of parrots and other birds that is caused by a parasitic micro-organism and that causes a serious form of pneumonia when transmitted to human beings.

psoriasis *n* a chronic skin condition characterized by distinct red patches covered by white scales. ⋙ **psoriatic** *adj*.

PST *abbr* Pacific standard time.

PSV *abbr Brit* public service vehicle.

psych *or* **psyche** *v informal NAm* to psychoanalyse (somebody).

psych- *or* **psycho-** *comb. form* **1a** mind; mental processes: *psychology*. **b** mental and: *psychosomatic*. **2** psyche: *psychic*.

psyche[1] *n* **1** the soul or self. **2** the mind. **3** the spirit; the underlying principle affecting a group's attitudes, etc.

psyche[2] *v* see PSYCH.

psychedelia *n* art, music, etc, associated with psychedelic drugs.

psychedelic *adj* **1a** of drugs: capable of producing altered states of consciousness that involve changed mental and sensory awareness, hallucinations, etc. **b** produced by or associated with the use of psychedelic drugs. **2a** imitating or reproducing effects, e.g. bright colours, or distorted or bizarre images or sounds associated with or resembling those produced by psychedelic drugs. **b** having colours and a swirling pattern. ⋙ **psychedelically** *adv*.

psychiatry *n* a branch of medicine that deals with mental, emotional, or behavioural disorders. ⋙ **psychiatric** *adj*, **psychiatrically** *adv*, **psychiatrist** *n*.

psychic[1] *adj* **1** lying outside the sphere of physical science or knowledge; involving telepathy, clairvoyance, or psychokinesis. **2** of a person: **a** sensitive to nonphysical or supernatural forces or influences. **b** having a mysterious sensitivity, perception, or understanding; telepathic. **3** of or originating in the mind, soul, or spirit. ➤➤ **psychical** *adj*, **psychically** *adv*.

psychic² *n* **1** a psychic person. **2** a person through whom some people believe it is possible to communicate with the spirits of the dead.

psycho *n* (*pl* **-os**) *informal* a psychopath or psychotic person. ➤➤ **psycho** *adj*.

psycho- *comb. form* see PSYCH-.

psychoactive *adj* of drugs: affecting the mind or behaviour.

psychoanalyse (*NAm* **psychoanalyze**) *v* to examine (somebody or something) or treat (somebody) by means of psychoanalysis.

psychoanalysis *n* a method of analysing unconscious mental processes and treating mental disorders, *esp* by allowing the patient to talk freely about early childhood experiences, dreams, etc. ➤➤ **psychoanalyst** *n*, **psychoanalytic** *adj*.

psychoanalyze *v NAm* see PSYCHOANALYSE.

psychobabble *n informal* popularized psychological jargon used in a loose, trendy, or pretentious way to describe human feelings and relationships.

psychodrama *n* **1a** the playing of roles as a technique of psychotherapy or education. **b** an improvised dramatization of events from a patient's life designed to afford insight into and resolution of personal conflicts. **2** a drama in which the main interest is in the psychological behaviour and development of the characters.

psychokinesis *n* movement in physical objects produced by the power of the mind without physical contact. ➤➤ **psychokinetic** *adj*.

psycholinguistics *pl n* (*used as sing. or pl*) the study of the interrelation between linguistic behaviour and the minds of speaker and hearer, e.g. in the production and comprehension of speech, language acquisition by children, and speech and language disorders. ➤➤ **psycholinguist** *n*, **psycholinguistic** *adj*.

psychological *adj* **1a** of or relating to psychology. **b** mental; of the mind. **2** directed towards or intended to affect the will, morale, or mind. ➤➤ **psychologically** *adv*.

psychology *n* **1** the science or study of mind and behaviour. **2** the mental or behavioural characteristics of an individual or group. ➤➤ **psychologist** *n*.

psychometrics *pl n* (*used as sing. or pl*) the branch of psychology concerned with the measurement of mental capacities and attributes, *esp* by the use of psychological tests, such as intelligence tests.

psychometry *n* **1** divination of facts concerning an object or its owner through physical contact with the object or proximity to it. **2** = PSYCHOMETRICS. ➤➤ **psychometric** *adj*, **psychometrist** *n*.

psychopath *n* a person suffering from a severe emotional and behavioural disorder characterized by antisocial tendencies and usu the pursuit of immediate gratification through often violent acts. ➤➤ **psychopathic** *adj*, **psychopathy** *n*.

psychopathology *n* psychological and behavioural aberrations occurring in mental disorder, or the study of such aberrations. ➤➤ **psychopathological** *adj*, **psychopathologist** *n*.

psychoses *n* pl of PSYCHOSIS.

psychosexual *adj* of the emotional, mental, or behavioural aspects of sex. ➤➤ **psychosexually** *adv*.

psychosis *n* (*pl* **psychoses**) severe mental derangement, e.g. schizophrenia, that results in the impairment or loss of contact with reality. ➤➤ **psychotic** *adj and n*, **psychotically** *adv*.

psychosocial *adj* **1** relating social conditions to mental health. **2** of or involving matters that are both psychological and social. ➤➤ **psychosocially** *adv*.

psychosomatic *adj* of or resulting from the interaction of psychological and somatic factors, *esp* the production of physical symptoms or disorders by mental processes or psychological factors such as stress. ➤➤ **psychosomatically** *adv*.

psychosurgery *n* brain surgery used to treat mental disorder. ➤➤ **psychosurgical** *adj*.

psychotherapy *n* treatment by psychological methods for mental, emotional, or psychosomatic disorders. ➤➤ **psychotherapeutic** *adj*, **psychotherapist** *n*.

psychotic *adj and n* see PSYCHOSIS.

psychotropic *adj* = PSYCHOACTIVE.

psych out *v* to intimidate or scare (somebody) by psychological means.

psychrometer *n* a HYGROMETER (instrument for measuring humidity) consisting of two similar thermometers with the bulb of one being kept wet so that the resulting cooling provides a measure of the dryness of the atmosphere.

psych up *v informal* to make (oneself) psychologically ready for doing something.

PT *abbr* physical training.

Pt *abbr* the chemical symbol for platinum.

pt *abbr* **1** part. **2** pint. **3** point. **4** port.

PTA *abbr* **1** Parent-Teacher Association. **2** *Brit* Passenger Transport Authority.

ptarmigan *n* (*pl* **ptarmigans** *or* **ptarmigan**) a grouse of northern regions whose plumage turns white in winter.

Pte *abbr* Private.

pteranodon *n* a pterosaur of the late Cretaceous period that had large toothless jaws, a hornlike crest, a small body, and very large membranous wings.

pterodactyl *n* a pterosaur of the Jurassic and Cretaceous periods that had toothed jaws and membranous wings.

pterosaur *n* an extinct flying reptile of the Jurassic and Cretaceous periods, having membranous wings that extended from the side of the body along the arm to the end of the greatly enlarged fourth digit.

PTFE *abbr* polytetrafluoroethylene.

PTO *or* **pto** *abbr* please turn over.

Ptolemaic /toli'mayik/ *adj* **1** of Ptolemy, second-cent. Egyptian astronomer, mathematician, and geographer. **2** of the Graeco-Egyptian Ptolemies who ruled Egypt from 323 BC to 30 BC.

Ptolemaic system *n* the theoretical system of planetary movements according to which the sun, moon, and planets revolve round a stationary earth: compare COPERNICAN SYSTEM.

ptomaine *n* any of various sometimes poisonous organic compounds formed by the action of putrefactive bacteria on nitrogen-containing matter.

PTSD *abbr* post-traumatic stress disorder.

Pu *abbr* the chemical symbol for plutonium.

pub *n* **1** *chiefly Brit* an establishment where alcoholic beverages are sold and consumed. **2** *Aus, NZ* a hotel.

pub crawl *n chiefly Brit, informal* a visit to a series of pubs, involving at least one drink at each.

puberty *n* the period during which adolescents become capable of reproducing sexually. ➤➤ **pubertal** *adj*.

pubes *n* (*pl* **pubes**) **1** the pubic region. **2** *informal* pubic hair. **3** pl of PUBIS.

pubescent *adj* **1** arriving at or having reached puberty. **2** covered with fine soft short hairs. ⋙ **pubescence** *n.*

pubic *adj* relating to or in the region of the pubis, the external genital organs, or the pubic hair.

pubic hair *n* the hair that appears at puberty round the genitals.

pubis *n* (*pl* **pubes**) the bottom front of the three principal bones that form either half of the pelvis.

public[1] *adj* **1a** of or affecting all the people or the whole area of a nation or state. **b** of or being in the service of the community. **2** general or popular. **3** of national or community concerns as opposed to private affairs; social. **4** accessible to or shared by all members of the community. **5a** exposed to general view; open. **b** known to people in general. **c** prominent; celebrated. ✱ **go public 1** to become a public company. **2** to reveal information to the public. ⋙ **publicly** *adv.*

public[2] *n* **1** (**the public**) people as a whole; the populace. **2** audience; fans: *He said he owed it to his public not to call off the show.* ✱ **in public** in the presence, sight, or hearing of strangers.

public-address system *n* an apparatus including a microphone and loudspeakers used to address a large audience.

publican *n* **1a** *chiefly Brit* the licensee of a public house. **b** *Aus, NZ* a person who keeps a hotel. **2** a private individual acting as a tax or revenue collector for the ancient Romans.

publication *n* **1** the act or process of publishing. **2** a published work.

public bar *n Brit* a plainly furnished and often relatively cheap bar in a public house.

public company *n* a company whose shares may be offered to the general public and apply for listing on the stock exchange.

public convenience *n Brit* public toilet facilities.

public domain *n* the status in law of property rights that are unprotected by copyright or patent and are subject to appropriation by anybody.

public enemy *n* a person, *esp* a notorious wanted criminal, who is a danger to the public.

public health *n* the protection and improvement of community health, *esp* sanitation, by government regulation and community effort.

public house *n chiefly Brit* an establishment where alcoholic beverages are sold to be drunk on the premises.

publicise *v* see PUBLICIZE.

publicist *n* a person whose job is to publicize something such as a book or organization; a press agent.

publicity *n* **1a** information with news value issued as a means of gaining public attention or support. **b** paid advertising. **c** the dissemination of information or promotional material. **2** public attention or acclaim.

publicize *or* **-ise** *v* to give publicity to (an event, organization, product, etc).

public lending right *n* the right of authors to a royalty on issues of their books from public libraries.

public limited company *n* in Britain, a company whose shareholders have only a limited liability for any debts or losses created by the company.

public nuisance *n* **1** an illegal act that is harmful to the safety, comfort, or rights of the general public as a whole rather than of a particular individual. **2** *informal* a disruptive or dangerous person or group.

public prosecutor *n* an official who conducts criminal prosecutions on behalf of the state.

public relations *pl n* the business of inducing the public to have understanding for and goodwill towards a famous person, organization, or institution.

public school *n* **1** in Britain, an endowed independent, often single-sex, school, typically a large boarding school preparing pupils for higher education. **2** in N America and, *esp* formerly, in Scotland, a state school.

public sector *n* the part of the economy owned or controlled by the national government or local authorities.

public servant *n* a person who works for a government, state, local authority, etc.

public-spirited *adj* motivated by concern for the general welfare.

public utility *n* a business organization providing a public amenity, e.g. supplying water, gas, or electricity, and subject to special governmental regulation.

publish *v* **1a** to produce (a book, newspaper, etc) or release (it) for sale or distribution to the public. **b** to print (information, an article, a letter, etc) in a book, newspaper, etc. **2** to announce publicly. **3** to communicate (something libellous or defamatory about somebody) to another person. ⋙ **publishable** *adj,* **publishing** *n.*

publisher *n* a person or company whose business is publishing books, etc.

puce *adj* of a brownish purple colour. ⋙ **puce** *n.*

puck[1] *n* a vulcanized rubber disc used in ice hockey.

puck[2] *n* a mischievous sprite.

pucker[1] *v* **1** to become wrinkled or irregularly creased. **2** to cause (material, etc) to pucker.

pucker[2] *n* a crease or wrinkle in a normally even surface.

puckish *adj* impish; whimsical.

pud *n Brit, informal* a pudding.

pudding *n* **1a** any of various sweet or savoury dishes of a soft to spongy or fairly firm consistency that are made from rice, tapioca, flour, etc and are cooked by boiling, steaming, or baking. **b** dessert. **2** a sausage-like food, e.g. black pudding. **3** *informal* a small podgy person. ✱ **in the pudding club** *informal* pregnant. ⋙ **puddingy** *adj.*

puddle[1] *n* **1** a small pool of liquid, *esp* one of rainwater. **2** a mixture, e.g. of clay, sand, and gravel, used as a waterproof covering.

puddle[2] *v* **1** to work (a wet mixture of earth or concrete) into a dense impervious mass. **2** to subject (iron) to puddling. ⋙ **puddler** *n.*

puddling *n* the conversion of pig iron into wrought iron by heating and stirring with oxidizing substances.

pudendum *n* (*pl* **pudenda**) (*usu in pl*) the external genital organs of a human being, *esp* of a female.

pudgy *adj* (**-ier, -iest**) = PODGY.

pueblo /'pwebloh, poo'ebloh/ *n* (*pl* **-os**) **1a** a Native American village of Arizona, New Mexico, and adjacent areas, consisting of contiguous flat-roofed stone or clay houses in groups sometimes several storeys high. **b** (**Pueblo** *pl* **Pueblos** *or* **Pueblo**) a member of any of the Native American peoples inhabiting such villages. **2** a small town or village in Spain or Spanish America. ⋙ **Pueblo** *adj.*

puerile *adj* **1** not befitting an adult; childish. **2** juvenile. ⋙ **puerility** *n.*

puerperal fever *n* an often serious and sometimes fatal infection of the female reproductive organs following childbirth or abortion, causing blood poisoning and inflammation.

Puerto Rican *n* a native or inhabitant of Puerto Rico. ➤➤ **Puerto Rican** *adj.*

puff[1] *v* **1a** to exhale or blow forcibly. **b** to breathe hard and quickly; to pant. **c** to emit small whiffs or clouds, e.g. of smoke or steam. **d** to move while emitting puffs of smoke, etc. **2** (*usu* + out/up) to become distended; to swell. **3** (*usu* + out/up) to distend (something) with air or gas, or as if with air or gas; to inflate. **4** to draw on (a pipe, cigarette, etc) with intermittent exhalations of smoke. **5** to praise (somebody or something) extravagantly and usu exaggeratedly, or to advertise (somebody or something) by this means. ➤➤ **puffer** *n.*

puff[2] *n* **1a** the act or an instance of puffing. **b** a slight explosive sound accompanying a puff. **c** a small cloud, e.g. of smoke, emitted in a puff. **d** a draw on a pipe or cigarette; a smoke. **2** a light round hollow pastry made of puff pastry. **3** *chiefly Brit, informal* one's breath. **4** a highly favourable notice or review, *esp* one that publicizes something or somebody.

puff adder *n* a large venomous African viper that inflates its body and hisses loudly when disturbed.

puffa jacket *n Brit* a type of padded waterproof jacket with or without sleeves.

puffball *n* any of various spherical and often edible fungi that discharge a cloud of ripe spores when pressed or struck.

puffed *adj chiefly Brit, informal* out of breath.

puffed out *adj* = PUFFED.

puffed sleeve *n* = PUFF SLEEVE.

puffer fish *n* = GLOBEFISH.

puffin *n* (*pl* **puffins** *or* **puffin**) a seabird of the auk family that has a short neck and a deep grooved multicoloured bill.

puff pastry *n* a type of light flaky pastry made with a rich dough containing a large quantity of butter.

puff sleeve *n* a short full sleeve gathered at the upper and lower edges.

puffy *adj* (**-ier, -iest**) *esp* of the eyes or cheeks: swollen. ➤➤ **puffiness** *n.*

pug *n* a dog of a breed with a small sturdy compact body, a tightly curled tail, and a broad wrinkled face.

pugilism *n formal* boxing. ➤➤ **pugilist** *n,* **pugilistic** *adj.*

pugnacious *adj* inclined to fight or quarrel; belligerent. ➤➤ **pugnacity** *n.*

pug nose *n* a nose having a slightly concave bridge and flattened nostrils. ➤➤ **pug-nosed** *adj.*

puisne /'pyoohni/ *adj* of a judge: lower in rank.

puissance /'pyooh·is(ə)ns, 'pwees(ə)ns/ *n* **1** a show-jumping competition which tests the horse's power to jump high obstacles. **2** *archaic or literary* strength or power. ➤➤ **puissant** *adj.*

puja /'poohjah/ *n* in Hinduism, an act of worship or an offering given as part of a religious ceremony.

puke[1] *v informal* (*often* + up) to vomit.

puke[2] *n informal* vomit. ➤➤ **pukey** *adj.*

pukka *adj* **1** *informal* **a** genuine or authentic. **b** first-class or excellent. **2** *chiefly Brit* stiffly formal or proper.

pul /poohl/ *n* (*pl* **puls** *or* **puli**) a unit of currency in Afghanistan, worth 100th of an afghani.

pula /'poolə/ *n* the basic monetary unit of Botswana.

pulao /pi'low/ *n* see PILAF.

pulchritude *n formal* physical beauty. ➤➤ **pulchritudinous** *adj.*

pule *v literary* to whine or whimper. ➤➤ **puling** *adj.*

puli /'poohli, 'poohlee/ *n* pl of PUL.

pull[1] *v* **1a** to exert a force on (somebody or something) so as to make it move towards oneself or the source of the force. **b** to move (something) in this way. **2a** to make something come apart by force. **b** to remove or detach (something) by pulling it. **3** to strain (a muscle, tendon, etc). **4** to bring out (a weapon) ready for use. **5** to hold back (a horse) from winning a race. **6** to move steadily: *A car pulled out in front of us.* **7** to commit (a crime). **8** *informal* to attract (somebody) sexually. **9** to withdraw or remove (support). ✱ **pull a face** to grimace. **pull a fast one** *informal* to perpetrate a trick or fraud. **pull oneself together** to regain one's self-control. **pull one's punches** to use less force or aggression than one could. **pull one's weight** to do one's full share of work. **pull rank on** to assert one's authority over (somebody) to persuade them to do something. **pull somebody's leg** to deceive or tease somebody playfully. **pull strings** to use one's influence to achieve something. **pull the plug on** *informal* to bring (an undertaking) to an end or prevent it starting.

pull[2] *n* **1a** the act or an instance of pulling. **b** a force that attracts, compels, or influences; an attraction. **2a** a deep draught of liquid. **b** an inhalation of smoke, e.g. from a cigarette. ✱ **on the pull** *informal* trying to find a sexual partner.

pull apart *v* **1** to separate into pieces. **2** to criticize harshly.

pull back *v* **1** to withdraw or retreat. **2** to improve one's position in a competitive sport.

pull down *v* to demolish or destroy.

pullet *n* a young female domestic fowl less than a year old.

pulley *n* (*pl* **-eys**) **1** a wheel with a grooved rim that is used with a rope or chain to change the direction and point of application of a pulling force. **2** a wheel used to transmit power or motion by means of a belt, rope, or chain.

pull in *v* **1** of a vehicle: to stop by the side of the road. **2** *informal* to attract (a crowd, etc). **3** to acquire (a sum of money) as payment or profit. **4** *informal* to arrest.

Pullman *n* (*pl* **Pullmans**) a luxurious railway passenger carriage.

pull off *v* to achieve (something difficult or unexpected).

pullout *n* a removable section of a magazine, newspaper, or book.

pull out *v* **1** of a vehicle: to move out into a stream of traffic. **2** to withdraw from an undertaking or agreement. ✱ **pull out all the stops** to do everything possible to achieve something.

pullover *n* a sweater put on by being pulled over the head.

pullulate *v* **1a** of plants: to germinate or sprout. **b** to breed or produce rapidly and abundantly. **2** *formal* to swarm or teem.

pull up *v* **1** to come to a stop. **2** to reprimand or rebuke. ✱ **pull one's socks up** to make an effort to improve one's behaviour.

pulmonary *adj* relating to or in the region of the lungs.

pulp[1] *n* **1a** the soft juicy or fleshy part of a fruit or vegetable. **b** a soft mass of vegetable matter from which most of the water has been pressed. **c** a material prepared by chemical or mechanical means from rags, wood, etc that is used in making paper. **2** a soft shapeless mass, *esp* one produced by crushing or beating. **3** (*used before a noun*) cheap and sensational: *pulp fiction.* ⋙ **pulpy** *adj.*

pulp[2] *v* **1** to reduce to pulp. **2** to produce or reproduce (written matter) in pulp form. ⋙ **pulper** *n.*

pulpit *n* a raised platform or high reading desk in church from which a sermon is preached.

pulque /'poolkay, 'poolki/ *n* a Mexican alcoholic drink made from the fermented juice of maguey plants.

pulsar *n* a celestial source, prob a rotating neutron star, of frequent intermittent bursts of radio waves.

pulsate *v* **1** to beat with a pulse. **2** to throb or move rhythmically; to vibrate. **3** in physics and astronomy, to vary in brightness, magnitude, etc. ⋙ **pulsation** *n.*

pulsator *n* a device that works with a throbbing movement.

pulse[1] *n* **1a** a regular throbbing caused in the arteries by the contractions of the heart, palpable through the skin of the wrist or the neck. **b** the number of times a pulse beats in a specific period of time. **2a** underlying sentiment or opinion, or an indication of this. **b** a feeling of liveliness; vitality. **3a** rhythmical vibrating or sounding. **b** a single beat or throb. **4a** a short-lived variation of electrical current, voltage, etc whose value is normally constant. **b** an electromagnetic wave or sound wave of brief duration.

pulse[2] *v* **1** to pulsate or throb. **2** to produce or modulate (electromagnetic waves, etc) in the form of pulses.

pulse[3] *n* the edible seeds of any of various leguminous crops, e.g. peas, beans, or lentils.

pulverize *or* **-ise** *v* **1** to reduce to very small particles, e.g. by crushing or grinding. **2** *informal* to annihilate or defeat (somebody) utterly. ⋙ **pulverizer** *n.*

puma *n* (*pl* **pumas** *or* **puma**) a powerful tawny big cat formerly widespread in the Americas but now extinct in many areas.

pumice *n* a light porous volcanic rock used *esp* as an abrasive and for polishing.

pummel *v* (**pummelled, pummelling,** *NAm* **pummeled, pummeling**) to pound or strike (somebody or something) repeatedly, *esp* with the fists.

pump[1] *n* **1** a device that raises, transfers, or compresses fluids or that reduces the density of gases, *esp* by suction or pressure or both. **2** a mechanism for transporting atoms, ions, or molecules across cell membranes.

pump[2] *v* **1a** to move (air, water, etc) with a pump. **b** to raise (water, etc) with a pump. **c** (*often* + out) to draw a gas or liquid out of (a container, etc) with a pump. **2a** (*usu* + up) to inflate (a tyre, etc) by means of a pump or bellows. **b** to supply (an organ, etc) with air by means of a pump or bellows. **3a** to give or inject (something) in large quantities or with force or enthusiasm. **b** to fire (bullets) repeatedly into somebody or something. **c** *informal* to question persistently and exhaustively. **4** to move (something) rapidly up and down, as if working a pump handle. ✻ **pump iron** *informal* to exercise using weights.

pump[3] *n* **1** a flat shoe without fastenings. **2** *chiefly N Eng* a plimsoll.

pumpernickel *n* a dark, coarse, slightly sour-tasting bread made from wholemeal rye.

pumpkin *n* the large usu round orange or yellow fruit of a prickly plant of the gourd family, used as a vegetable.

pump priming *n* government investment expenditure designed to induce a self-sustaining expansion of economic activity.

pun[1] *n* a humorous use of a word with more than one meaning or of words with the same or a similar sound but different meanings.

pun[2] *v* (**punned, punning**) to make puns. ⋙ **punster** *n.*

Punch *n* (*often* **Mr Punch**) a hook-nosed, hump backed, deceitful, and brutal man, the chief male character in a Punch-and-Judy puppet show.

punch[1] *v* **1a** to hit (somebody or something), *esp* with a hard and quick thrust of the fist. **b** to hit or push (something, e.g. a button or key). **2** *NAm* to drive or herd cattle. ⋙ **puncher** *n.*

punch[2] *n* **1** a blow with the fist. **2** *informal* effective energy or forcefulness.

punch[3] *n* **1** a tool, usu in the form of a short steel rod, used *esp* for perforating, embossing, cutting, or driving the heads of nails below a surface, or a machine incorporating such a tool. **2** a device for cutting holes or notches in paper or cardboard.

punch[4] *v* **1** to emboss, cut, perforate, or make (a hole or pattern) with a punch, or as if with a punch. **2** to make a hole in or pattern on (something) with a punch, or as if with a punch.

punch[5] *n* a drink made from wine or spirits mixed with fruit, spices, water, and occasionally tea.

punchbag *n* an inflated or stuffed bag punched with the fists as a form of exercise or training, *esp* in boxing.

punchball *n* an inflated or stuffed ball on a flexible support that is punched with the fists as a form of exercise or training, *esp* in boxing.

punch bowl *n* **1** a large bowl in which punch is mixed and served. **2** *chiefly Brit* a bowl-shaped hollow among hills.

punch card *n* = PUNCHED CARD.

punch-drunk *adj* **1** suffering brain damage as a result of repeated punches or blows to the head. **2** behaving as if punch-drunk; dazed.

punched card *n* a card formerly used in data processing in which a pattern of holes or notches was cut to represent information or instructions.

puncheon *n* **1** a short upright timber for a frame, *esp* to carry a load, e.g. a roof. **2** a PUNCH[3] (tool for embossing, perforating, etc), *esp* a die used by goldsmiths, cutlers, and engravers.

punch line *n* a sentence or phrase that forms the climax to a joke, story, etc.

punch-up *n chiefly Brit, informal* a fight, *esp* with the bare fists.

punchy *adj* (**-ier, -iest**) having punch; forceful.

punctilio *n* (*pl* **-os**) **1** a minute and often petty detail of ceremony or observance. **2** careful observance of forms, e.g. in social conduct.

punctilious *adj* **1** strict or precise in observing codes of conduct or conventions. **2** paying or showing careful attention to detail. ⋙ **punctiliously** *adv,* **punctiliousness** *n.*

punctual *adj* **1** arriving, happening, performing, etc at the exact or agreed time. **2** having the habit of arriving, etc at agreed times. ⋙ **punctuality** *n,* **punctually** *adv.*

punctuate *v* **1** to mark or divide (a text) with punctuation marks. **2** to break into or interrupt (something) at intervals.

punctuation *n* **1** the dividing of writing with marks such as commas, colons, and full stops, in order to clarify meaning. **2** a system of punctuation, or the symbols used.

punctuation mark *n* a standardized mark or sign such as a comma, colon, or full stop, used in punctuation.

puncture[1] *n* a hole or narrow wound made by piercing by or with a pointed object, *esp* a small hole made accidentally in a pneumatic tyre.

puncture[2] *v* **1** to pierce (the skin, a tyre, etc) with a pointed object. **2** to cause a puncture in (a tyre, etc). **3** to destroy (somebody's confidence, overconfidence, etc).

pundit *n* **1** a person who gives opinions in an authoritative manner. **2** = PANDIT. ➤➤ **punditry** *n.*

punga *n* see PONGA.

pungent *adj* **1** having a strong sharp smell or taste; acrid. **2a** marked by a sharp incisive quality. **b** to the point; highly expressive. ➤➤ **pungency** *n,* **pungently** *adv.*

Punic[1] *adj* of or relating to Carthage.

Punic[2] *n* the language of ancient Carthage.

punish *v* **1a** to impose a penalty on (an offender). **b** to impose a penalty for (an offence). **2** *informal* to treat (something) roughly or damagingly. ➤➤ **punishable** *adj.*

punishing *adj* very demanding or exhausting.

punishment *n* **1a** the act or an instance of punishing. **b** something done in order to punish; a judicial penalty. **2** *informal* rough or damaging treatment.

punitive *adj* **1** inflicting or intended to inflict punishment. **2** punishing. ➤➤ **punitively** *adv.*

Punjabi /pun'jahbi, poon-/ *or* **Panjabi** *n* **1** a native or inhabitant of the Punjab of NW India and NE Pakistan. **2** the language of the Punjab. ➤➤ **Punjabi** *adj.*

punk[1] *n* **1** = PUNK ROCK. **2** somebody who wears aggressively outlandish clothes and hairstyles and listens to or plays punk rock. ➤➤ **punkish** *adj,* **punky** *adj.*

punk[2] *adj* **1** *NAm, informal* of very poor quality; inferior; worthless. **2** of the punk movement or punk rock.

punkah *or* **punka** *n* a fan used *esp* formerly in India, consisting of a cloth-covered frame suspended from the ceiling and swung to and fro by means of a cord.

punk rock *n* a style of rock music originating in the late 1970s, characterized by a driving tempo, crude or obscene lyrics, and an aggressive delivery. ➤➤ **punk rocker** *n.*

punnet *n Brit* a small basket of wood, plastic, etc, *esp* for soft fruit or vegetables.

punt[1] *n* a long narrow flat-bottomed boat with square ends, usu propelled with a pole.

punt[2] *v* **1** to transport (somebody or something) by punt. **2** to propel a punt; to go punting.

punt[3] *v* **1** to play against the banker at a gambling game. **2** *Brit, informal* to bet or gamble.

punt[4] *n Brit, informal* a bet.

punt[5] *v* **1** in rugby, etc, to kick (a football) with the top or tip of the foot after the ball is dropped from the hands and before it hits the ground. **2** to give (a ball) a long high kick.

punt[6] *n* the act or an instance of punting a football.

punt[7] /poont/ *n* the Irish pound, the basic monetary unit of the Republic of Ireland.

punter *n informal* **1** a person who gambles, *esp* somebody who bets against a bookmaker. **2** *Brit* a client, customer, or patron.

puny *adj* (**-ier, -iest**) **1** slight or inferior in power, size, or importance; weak. **2** small in quantity. ➤➤ **puniness** *n.*

pup[1] *n* **1** a young dog. **2** a young seal, rat, etc. ✱ **sell somebody a pup** *Brit, informal* to cheat somebody by selling them something worthless.

pup[2] *v* (**pupped, pupping**) to give birth to a pup or pups.

pupa *n* (*pl* **pupae** *or* **pupas**) the intermediate, usu inactive, form of an insect that undergoes metamorphism, e.g. a bee, moth, or beetle, that occurs between the larva, e.g. caterpillar, and the IMAGO (adult) stages. ➤➤ **pupal** *adj.*

pupate *v* of an insect: to become a pupa. ➤➤ **pupation** *n.*

pupil[1] *n* **1** a child or young person at school or receiving tuition. **2** a person who is training to become a barrister.

pupil[2] *n* the round dark opening in the iris of the eye that varies in size to regulate the amount of light that passes to the retina.

pupillage *or* **pupilage** *n* **1** the state or period of being a pupil. **2** apprenticeship to a barrister.

puppet *n* **1** a small-scale toy figure, e.g. of a person or animal, that is moved by strings, wires, or rods attached to the head, body, and limbs, or by movements of the hand and fingers inside the body. **2** a person whose acts are controlled by an outside force or influence. ➤➤ **puppeteer** *n,* **puppetry** *n.*

puppy *n* (*pl* **-ies**) a young dog, *esp* one that is less than a year old. ➤➤ **puppyish** *adj.*

puppy fat *n* temporary plumpness in children and adolescents.

puppy love *n* short-lived romantic affection between adolescents.

purblind *adj* **1** partly blind. **2** lacking in vision or insight; obtuse.

purchase[1] *v* to obtain by paying money or its equivalent; to buy. ➤➤ **purchasable** *adj,* **purchaser** *n.*

purchase[2] *n* **1a** something obtained by payment of money or its equivalent. **b** the act or an instance of purchasing something. **2** a mechanical hold or advantage, *esp* one applied through a pulley or lever. **3** a firm grip or contact, e.g. in climbing.

purdah *n* the seclusion of women from public view among some Muslims and some Hindus, *esp* in India.

pure *adj* **1a** unmixed with any other matter. **b** free from anything that vitiates or weakens. **2** free from contamination. **3a** free from moral fault. **b** chaste. **4** sheer or unmitigated: *pure folly.* **5** abstract or theoretical, as opposed to applied or practical: *pure mathematics.* **6** of a musical sound: being in tune and free from harshness. ➤➤ **purely** *adv.*

purebred *adj* of an animal: bred over many generations from members of a recognized breed or variety without mixture of other blood.

puree[1] *or* **purée** /'pyooəray/ *n* a thick pulp, e.g. of fruit or vegetables, produced by blending in a liquidizer or rubbing through a sieve.

puree[2] *or* **purée** *v* (**purees** *or* **purées, pureed** *or* **puréed, pureeing** *or* **puréeing**) to reduce (fruit, vegetables, etc) to a puree.

purgation *n* the act or result of purging.

purgative[1] *adj* causing evacuation of the bowels.

purgative[2] *n* a purgative substance or medicine.

purgatory *n* (*pl* **-ies**) **1** a place or state of punishment in which, according to Roman Catholic doctrine, the souls of those who die in God's grace may make amends for past sins and so become fit for heaven. **2** *informal* a place or state of temporary suffering or misery. ➤➤ **purgatorial** *adj.*

purge[1] *v* **1** to rid of impurities. **2a** to rid (a nation, party, etc) of unwanted or undesirable members, often summarily or by force. **b** to get rid of (undesirable people) by means of a purge. **3** in law, to relieve oneself of (a legal offence, e.g. contempt of court, or the sentence for it) by some appropriate action. **4a** to cause evacuation of faeces from (the bowels). **b** to cause evacuation of faeces from the bowels of (somebody).

purge[2] *n* the act or an instance of purging, *esp* of purging people from a group.

puri /'pooəri/ *n* (*pl* **puris**) a deep-fried wheaten cake eaten *esp* with Indian curries.

purify *v* (**-ies, -ied**) **1** to free (somebody) of guilt or moral impurity or imperfection. **2** to free (something) from undesirable elements. ⋙ **purification** *n*, **purifier** *n*.

purist *n* a person who keeps strictly and often excessively to established or traditional usage, *esp* in language. ⋙ **purism** *n*.

puritan *n* **1** (**Puritan**) a member of a 16th- and 17th-cent., mainly Calvinist, Protestant group in England and New England which wished to purify the Church of England of all very ceremonial worship. **2** a person who practises or preaches a rigorous or severe moral code. ⋙ **Puritan** *adj*, **puritan** *adj*, **puritanical** *adj*, **Puritanism** *n*, **puritanism** *n*.

purity *n* pureness.

purl[1] *n* a basic knitting stitch made by inserting the needle into the back of a stitch that produces a raised pattern on the back of the work.

purl[2] *v* to knit (a stitch) in purl.

purl[3] *v* of a stream, brook, etc: to flow in eddies with a soft murmuring sound.

purler *n Brit, informal* a heavy headlong fall.

purlieu *n* (*pl* **purlieus**) **1** (*in pl*) environs or neighbourhood; **2** land once part of, but later separated from, an English royal forest.

purlin *or* **purline** *n* a horizontal beam in a roof bracing the rafters.

purloin *v formal* to take dishonestly; to steal.

purple[1] *n* **1a** the colour between red and blue in hue. **b** a pigment or dye that colours purple. **2a** a purple robe worn as an emblem of rank or authority. **b** the red robes of a cardinal.

purple[2] *adj* **1** of the colour about midway between red and blue in hue. **2** of writing: highly rhetorical; ornate. ⋙ **purplish** *adj*, **purply** *adj*.

purple heart *n* **1** (**Purple Heart**) a US military decoration awarded to any member of the armed forces wounded in action. **2** *Brit, slang* a purplish blue heart-shaped tablet containing the drug phenobarbitone, formerly prescribed as a hypnotic or sedative and often abused by addicts.

purple passage *n* = PURPLE PATCH (1).

purple patch *n* **1** a piece of obtrusively ornate writing. **2** *informal* a period of good luck or success.

purport[1] *n formal* **1** professed or implied meaning; import. **2** purpose; intention.

purport[2] *v* to claim (to be something); to seem, *esp* to be intended to seem (to be something): *The book purports to be an objective analysis but is nothing more than a string of prejudices.* ⋙ **purported** *adj*, **purportedly** *adv*.

purpose[1] *n* **1** the object for which something exists or is done. **2** the reason or intention underlying some action. **3** resolution or determination. **4** use, value, or advantage. ✱ **on purpose** intentionally. ⋙ **purposeless** *adj*.

purpose[2] *v formal* to have as one's intention.

purposeful *adj* **1** full of determination. **2** having a purpose or aim. ⋙ **purposefully** *adv*, **purposefulness** *n*.

purposely *adv* with a deliberate or express purpose.

purposive *adj formal* **1** serving or effecting a useful function though not necessarily as a result of deliberate intention. **2** having or tending to fulfil a conscious purpose; purposeful. ⋙ **purposively** *adv*, **purposiveness** *n*.

purr *v* **1** of a cat: to make a low vibratory murmur. **2** to make a sound resembling a purr. ⋙ **purr** *n*.

purse[1] *n* **1a** a small flattish bag for money, or a wallet with a compartment for holding change. **b** *NAm* a handbag. **2a** resources; funds. **b** a sum of money offered as a prize or present, or the total amount of money offered in prizes for a given event.

purse[2] *v* to pucker or knit (the lips).

purser *n* an officer on a ship who is responsible for documents and accounts.

purse seine *n* a large net that can be closed, designed to be set round a school of fish by two boats.

purse strings *pl n* control over expenditure.

purslane *n* a fleshy-leaved trailing plant with tiny yellow flowers, sometimes eaten in salads.

pursuance *n formal* a carrying out of a plan or order.

pursuant to *prep formal* in carrying out; according to.

pursue *v* (**pursues, pursued, pursuing**) **1** to follow (a fugitive, etc) in order to overtake, capture, kill, or defeat them. **2** to find or employ measures to obtain or accomplish (a goal). **3** to follow (a plan, etc). **4a** to engage in (some activity). **b** to follow up (an argument). ⋙ **pursuer** *n*.

pursuit *n* **1** the act or an instance of pursuing. **2** an activity that one regularly engages in as a pastime or profession.

pursuivant *n* an officer of the College of Arms ranking below a herald.

purulent *adj* **1** of or containing pus. **2** accompanied by suppuration. ⋙ **purulence** *n*.

purvey *v* to supply (provisions, etc), *esp* in the course of business. ⋙ **purveyor** *n*.

purview *n formal* **1** the range or limit of authority, responsibility, or concern. **2** the range of vision or understanding.

pus *n* thick opaque yellowish or greenish white fluid matter formed by suppuration, e.g. in an abscess.

push[1] *v* **1a** to exert a force on (somebody or something) so as to make it move away from oneself or the source of the force. **b** to move (somebody or something) forward or into something in this way. **2** to urge (somebody or oneself) to do something or make greater efforts. **3a** to develop or promote (an idea or argument). **b** to make strong efforts to sell (a product, etc). **c** *informal* to engage in the illicit sale of (drugs). **4** to approach in age or number: *He is pushing 80.* **5** to press forward energetically. ✱ **be pushed** *informal* have too little time. **push for** to demand strenuously. **push one's luck** *informal* to risk having continuing luck after initial success. ⋙ **pusher** *n*.

push[2] *n* **1** the act or an instance of pushing. **2** a vigorous effort to attain an end; a drive. **3** vigorous enterprise or energy. ✱ **at a push** *chiefly Brit, informal* if really necessary, although with some difficulty. **get the push** *Brit, informal* to be dismissed, dropped, etc. **give somebody the push** *Brit, informal* to dismiss or drop somebody. **if/when push comes to shove** if or when a necessity arises, a difficulty must be faced, etc.

push ahead *v* to continue in a determined way with an undertaking.

push along *v Brit, informal* to leave.

push around *v* to bully or intimidate.

push-bike *n Brit, informal* a pedal cycle.

pushcart *n* a cart that is pushed or pulled by hand.

pushchair *n Brit* a light folding chair on wheels in which a young child may be pushed.

push in *v* to force one's way into a queue.

pushing *adv informal esp* of ages: almost: *He is pushing 60.*

push off *v Brit, informal* to leave hastily.

push on *v* to continue doggedly with something difficult.

pushover *n informal* **1** an opponent who is easy to defeat or a victim who is incapable of effective resistance. **2** something accomplished without difficulty.

push through *v* to force acceptance of (a proposal, etc).

pushy *adj* (**-ier, -iest**) self-assertive, often to an objectionable degree. ➤➤ **pushiness** *n.*

pusillanimous *adj* lacking courage and resolution; contemptibly timid. ➤➤ **pusillanimity** *n.*

puss *n informal* **1** used in addressing or calling to a cat: a cat. **2** a girl.

pussy[1] *n* (*pl* **-ies**) *informal* used chiefly by or to young children: a cat.

pussy[2] *n* (*pl* **-ies**) *coarse slang* **1** the vulva. **2** sexual intercourse with a woman. **3** women or a woman regarded sexually.

pussycat *n* = PUSSY[1].

pussyfoot *v* **1** to tread or move warily or stealthily. **2** to avoid committing oneself to a course of action.

pussy willow *n* any of various willows having grey silky catkins.

pustule *n* **1** a small raised spot on the skin having an inflamed base and containing pus. **2** a small raised area like a blister or pimple. ➤➤ **pustular** *adj.*

put[1] *v* (**putting,** *past tense and past part.* **put**) **1** to place or move to a specified position. **2** to bring into a specified condition: *The new rules put them in a state of alarm.* **3** to devote or apply to some purpose: *The money was put to good use.* **4** to assign to do something: *Put them to work.* **5** to estimate or set a value on: *I'd put her age at about 40.* **6** to present (an idea or proposal) for consideration. **7** to throw (a shot or weight) in athletics. **8** of a ship: to take a specified course.

put[2] *n* a throw made with an overhand pushing motion; *specif* the act or an instance of putting the shot.

put about *v* **1** to spread (a false story, etc). **2** of a ship: to change direction.

put across *v* to convey (a fact or meaning) effectively.

put aside *v* **1** to save for a later time. **2** to ignore or pay no attention to.

putative *adj formal* **1** commonly accepted or supposed. **2** assumed to exist or to have existed. ➤➤ **putatively** *adv.*

put away *v* **1** to store or keep for future use. **2** *informal* to confine in a prison or institution. **3** *informal* to eat or drink in large quantities.

put back *v* **1** to return (something) to its former place after using it. **2** to set (a clock or watch) to an earlier time. **3** to postpone or delay (an event).

put by *v* to save (money) for future use.

put down *v* **1** to suppress or bring to an end. **2** to kill (a sick or injured animal) painlessly. **3a** to write down. **b** to enter (a name, etc) on a list. **4** to pay (a sum of money) as a deposit. **5** *informal* to disparage or belittle (somebody) publicly. ✻ **put down to 1** to attribute to: *I put it down to his inexperience.* **2** of an aircraft: to land.

put-down *n informal* a humiliating remark.

put forth *v formal or literary* **1** to assert or propose. **2** of a ship: to leave port.

put forward *v* **1** to propose. **2** to set (a clock or watch) to a later time.

put in *v* **1** to submit (a claim, request, offer, etc). **2** to spend (time) in an activity. **3** of a ship: to enter a port or harbour.

put off *v* **1a** to disconcert or distract (somebody). **b** to dissuade or discourage (somebody). **2** to postpone. **3** to get rid of (somebody) with excuses. **4** to switch off (an electric light or devise).

put on *v* **1** to dress oneself in (an item of clothing). **2** to assume (an attitude or feeling). **3** to increase in weight by a specified amount. **4** to switch on (an electric light or device). **5** to present (a performance). ✻ **put on to** to inform (somebody) about (something).

put out *v* **1a** to annoy or irritate. **b** to inconvenience: *She'll always put herself out for you.* **2** to extinguish (a fire). **3** to dislocate (a part of the body). **4** to publish or broadcast. **5** of a ship: to set out from shore.

put-put[1] *n* a repeated popping sound made by a small motor.

put-put[2] *v* (**put-putted, put-putting**) **1** said of e.g. a motor: to make a repeated popping sound. **2** to move while put-putting.

putrefy *v* (**-ies, -ied**) to become rotten or putrid. ➤➤ **putrefaction** *n.*

putrescent *adj* becoming rotten or putrid. ➤➤ **putrescence** *n.*

putrid *adj* **1** of organic matter: in a state of decomposition; decaying; rotten. **2** foul-smelling or corrupt as a result of putrefaction.

putsch /pooch/ *n* a secretly plotted and suddenly executed attempt to overthrow a government.

putt[1] *n* a gentle golf stroke made to roll the ball towards or into the hole.

putt[2] *v* to hit (a golf ball) towards or into the hole with a gentle stroke. ➤➤ **putting** *n.*

puttee *n* a long cloth strip wrapped spirally round the leg from ankle to knee, *esp* as part of an army uniform.

putter[1] *n* a golf club used for putting.

putter[2] *n* a rapidly repeated popping sound made by a small motor.

putter[3] *v* **1** of a motor: to make a rapidly repeated popping sound. **2** to move along while puttering.

putti /'pootee/ *n* pl of PUTTO.

putting green *n* **1** a smooth grassy area at the end of a golf fairway containing the hole into which the ball must be played. **2** an area of smooth grass laid out with a number of holes for putting as a game.

putto /'pootoh/ *n* (*pl* **putti**) *esp* in Renaissance painting, a figure of a naked little boy, often with wings; a cherub or cupid.

putty *n* (*pl* **-ies**) a doughlike cement, usu made of WHITING[2] (ground chalk) and linseed oil, used *esp* for fastening glass into windows and filling crevices in woodwork.

put up *v* **1** to build or erect. **2** to accommodate for a short time. **3** to stay or take shelter: *We'll put up here for the night.* **4** to nominate for election. **5** to offer or present: *to put up a struggle.* ✻ **put up or shut up** *informal* to take action or stop talking about it. **put up to** to encourage (somebody) to do (something wrong or unwise). **put up with** to tolerate.

put-up *adj informal* contrived secretly beforehand: *a put-up job.*

put upon *v* to exploit the good nature of (somebody).

puzzle[1] *v* **1** to offer or represent to (a person or their mind) a problem that is difficult to solve or a situation that is difficult to understand or resolve; to confuse or perplex. **2** to exert (oneself or one's mind) over a problem or situation; to make (oneself) think hard. **3** (*usu* + about/over) to be uncertain as to action, choice, or meaning. ➤➤ **puzzled** *adj*, **puzzlement** *n*, **puzzling** *adj*.

puzzle[2] *n* **1** somebody or something that puzzles. **2** a problem, toy, etc designed for testing one's ingenuity. ➤➤ **puzzler** *n*.

PVA *abbr* polyvinyl acetate, a colourless synthetic resin used in paints and adhesives.

PVC *abbr* polyvinyl chloride, a colourless plastic vinyl used as a rubber substitute, e.g. in raincoats and wire covering.

PVS *abbr* persistent vegetative state.

PW *abbr* policewoman.

pw *abbr* per week.

PWA *abbr* person with Aids.

PWR *abbr* pressurized water reactor.

pya *n* a unit of currency in Myanmar, worth 100th of a kyat.

pyaemia (*NAm* **pyemia**) *n* blood poisoning accompanied by multiple abscesses.

pye-dog *or* **pie-dog** *or* **pi-dog** *n* a half-wild dog common in and around Asian villages.

pyemia *n NAm* see PYAEMIA.

pygmy *or* **pigmy** *n* (*pl* **-ies**) **1** (**Pygmy**) a member of a people of equatorial Africa under 1.5m (about 5ft) in height. **2a** *derog* a very short person; a dwarf. **b** something that is a small example of its kind. **c** (*used before a noun*) being a small variety of something. **3** a person who is insignificant or inferior in a specified sphere or manner: *a political pygmy.*

pyjamas (*NAm* **pajamas**) *pl n* **1** a suit of loose lightweight jacket or top and trousers for sleeping in. **2** loose lightweight trousers traditionally worn in the East.

pylon *n* **1** a tower for supporting either end of a wire, *esp* electricity power cables, over a long span. **2** either of two towers with sloping sides flanking the entrance to an ancient Egyptian temple.

pylorus *n* (*pl* **pylori**) the opening from the vertebrate stomach into the intestine. ➤➤ **pyloric** *adj*.

pyr- *or* **pyro-** *comb. form* **1** fire; heat: *pyromania.* **2** produced by or as if by the action of heat: *pyroelectricity.*

pyracantha *n* a Eurasian thorny shrub of the rose family with white or cream-coloured flowers and red, orange, or yellow berries.

pyramid *n* **1a** a massive structure typically having a square ground plan, smooth or stepped outside walls in the form of four triangles that meet in a point at the top, and inner burial chambers, *esp* any of a number of such structures found in Egypt and enclosing the burial chambers of the pharaohs. **b** any structure or object of a similar form. **2** in geometry, a polyhedron having a base that is a polygon and other faces that are triangles with a common vertex. ➤➤ **pyramidal** *adj*.

pyramid selling *n* a system whereby agents for the sale of a product buy stock which they then recruit further agents to sell.

pyre *n* a heap of combustible material, *esp* one used for burning a dead body as part of a funeral rite.

pyrethrum *n* **1** a flower of the daisy family with finely divided aromatic leaves and bright flowers. **2** an insecticide made from the dried heads of some of these chrysanthemums.

pyretic *adj* of or relating to fever.

Pyrex *n trademark* glass or glassware that is resistant to heat.

pyrexia *n technical* fever.

pyridoxine *n* a vitamin of the vitamin B complex, found *esp* in cereal foods and convertible in the body into phosphate compounds that are important coenzymes; vitamin B_6.

pyrite *n* = IRON PYRITES.

pyrites *n* (*pl* **pyrites**) any of various metallic-looking sulphide minerals, *esp* IRON PYRITES.

pyro- *comb. form* see PYR-.

pyroclastic *adj* formed from rock fragments or ash resulting from volcanic action, *esp* occurring as a fast-moving hot dense cloud.

pyroelectricity *n* a state of electrical polarization produced, e.g. in crystals, by a change of temperature.

pyrogenic *adj* **1** producing or produced by heat or fever. **2** of a rock: = IGNEOUS.

pyrography *n* the art of burning decorative designs into wood.

pyromania *n* a compulsive urge to start fires. ➤➤ **pyromaniac** *n*.

pyrotechnics *pl n* **1** fireworks. **2** the art of making fireworks. **3** a brilliant or spectacular display. ➤➤ **pyrotechnic** *adj*, **pyrotechnical** *adj*.

Pyrrhic victory *n* a victory won at such great cost as to be barely a victory.

Pythagoras' theorem *n* a theorem in geometry, according to which the square of the length of the hypotenuse of a right-angled triangle equals the sum of the squares of the lengths of the other two sides.

Pythagorean *adj* of or relating to the Greek philosopher and mathematician Pythagoras (d.c.500 BC) and his followers. ➤➤ **Pythagorean** *n*.

python *n* a non-venomous snake found in Africa, Asia, and Australia, that kills its prey by constriction.

pyx *or* **pix** *n* a container in which the bread used at Communion is kept, *esp* one used for carrying the Eucharist to the sick.

pzazz *n* see PIZZAZZ.

Q[1] *or* **q** *n* (*pl* **Q's** *or* **Qs** *or* **q's**) the 17th letter of the English alphabet.

Q[2] *abbr* **1** in chess and card games, queen. **2** question.

Qatari *n* a native or inhabitant of Qatar. ▶▶ **Qatari** *adj.*

QB *abbr* Queen's Bench.

QC *abbr* Queen's Counsel.

QED *abbr* (Latin) quod erat demonstrandum = which was to be demonstrated, used at the conclusion of a proof.

qi *n* see CHI[2].

qindar /kin'dah/ *or* **qintar** /kin'tah/ *n* (*pl* **qindarka** *or* **qintars**) a unit of currency in Albania, worth 100th of a lek.

QPM *abbr* Queen's Police Medal.

qt *abbr* quart.

q.t. ✱ **on the q.t.** *informal* secretly.

qua *prep* in the capacity or character of (somebody or something).

quack[1] *v* to make the cry of a duck. ▶▶ **quack** *n.*

quack[2] *n* **1** somebody who pretends to have medical skills or qualifications. **2** *informal* a doctor. ▶▶ **quackery** *n.*

quad[1] *n* a quadrangle.

quad[2] *n* a quadruplet.

quad[3] *adj* quadraphonic.

quad bike *n* a vehicle resembling a motorcycle with four large wheels, designed for off-road use.

quadr- *comb. form* see QUADRI-.

quadragenarian *n* a person between 40 and 49 years old. ▶▶ **quadragenarian** *adj.*

Quadragesima *n* the first Sunday in Lent.

quadrangle *n* **1** = QUADRILATERAL[1]. **2** a rectangular enclosure, *esp* a courtyard, with buildings on all four sides. ▶▶ **quadrangular** *adj.*

quadrant *n* **1a** a quarter of the circumference of a circle. **b** the area of one quarter of a circle that is bounded by an arc containing an angle of 90°. **2** any of the four quarters into which something is divided by two real or imaginary lines that intersect each other at right angles. **3** an instrument for measuring angles, usu consisting of a graduated arc of 90°.

quadraphonic *or* **quadrophonic** *adj* of or being a system for recording or reproducing sound that uses four electrical channels. ▶▶ **quadraphony** *n.*

quadrate *adj* square or approximately square.

quadratic *adj* in mathematics, relating to the power of two, or involving one or more terms of this but no higher power.

quadrennial *adj* **1** consisting of or lasting for four years. **2** occurring every four years.

quadri- *or* **quadr-** *or* **quadru-** *comb. form* four: *quadrilateral.*

quadriceps *n* (*pl* **quadriceps**) the large muscle at the front of the thigh that acts to extend and straighten the leg at the knee joint.

quadrilateral[1] *n* a polygon having four sides.

quadrilateral[2] *adj* having four sides.

quadrille *n* **1** a square dance for four couples made up of five or six figures. **2** a card game for four players, a variant of ombre, popular *esp* in the 18th cent.

quadrillion *n* **1** *Brit* a million million million millions, the number one followed by 24 zeros (10^{24}). **2** *NAm* a thousand million millions, the number one followed by 15 zeros (10^{15}). ▶▶ **quadrillion** *adj,* **quadrillionth** *adj and n.*

quadripartite *adj* **1** consisting of or divided into four parts. **2** shared by or involving four parties or people.

quadriplegia *n* paralysis of both arms and both legs. ▶▶ **quadriplegic** *adj and n.*

quadroon *n* a person of one-quarter black ancestry.

quadrophonic *adj* see QUADRAPHONIC.

quadru- *comb. form* see QUADRI-.

quadruped *n* an animal that walks on four legs or feet. ▶▶ **quadrupedal** *adj.*

quadruple[1] *adj* **1** having four units or members. **2** being four times as great or as many. **3** in music, marked by four beats per bar.

quadruple[2] *v* to become or make four times as great or as many.

quadruple[3] *n* a number or amount four times as great as another.

quadruplet *n* any of four offspring born at one birth.

quadruplicate[1] *adj* consisting of or existing in four corresponding or identical parts or examples.

quadruplicate[2] *v* **1** to make four times as great or as many; to multiply by four. **2** to prepare (e.g. a document) in quadruplicate.

quadruplicate[3] ✱ **in quadruplicate** in the form of four identical copies.

quaff *v chiefly literary* to drink (something), *esp* in long draughts or large amounts. ⋙ **quaffable** *adj*, **quaffer** *n*.

quag *n archaic* a marsh or bog. ⋙ **quaggy** *adj*.

quagga *n* a recently extinct wild zebra of southern Africa with a brown back and striped head, neck, and forequarters.

quagmire *n* **1** an area of soft boggy land that yields under the foot. **2** a predicament from which it is difficult to extricate oneself.

quail[1] *n* (*pl* **quails** *or* **quail**) a game bird of Europe and Asia with a rounded body and short tail that is related to but smaller than the partridge.

quail[2] *v* to shrink back in fear; to cower.

quaint *adj* **1** pleasingly or strikingly old-fashioned or unusual. **2** unfamiliar or different in character or appearance; odd. ⋙ **quaintly** *adv*, **quaintness** *n*.

quake[1] *v* **1** to shake or vibrate, usu from shock or instability. **2** to tremble or shudder, *esp* inwardly from fear.

quake[2] *n informal* an earthquake.

Quaker *n* a member of a pacifist Christian sect founded by George Fox (d.1691) that stresses divine influence guiding the soul and rejects sacraments and a formal ministry. ⋙ **Quakerism** *n*.

Word history

QUAKE[1] + -ER[2]. Often said to come from the exhortation of its founder, George Fox, to his followers to 'tremble at the word of the Lord', but the term had been used earlier in a similar meaning. The sect is properly called the Society of Friends.

qualification *n* **1** an official record that a person has completed a course or passed an examination. **2** a quality or skill that makes a person suitable for a particular task or appointment. **3** a condition that must be complied with, e.g. for the attainment of a privilege. **4** a restriction in meaning or application; a limiting modification. **5** the act of qualifying.

qualifier *n* **1** somebody or something that satisfies requirements or meets a specified standard. **2** in grammar, a word that restricts the meaning of another; a modifier. **3** a preliminary heat or contest; a qualifying round.

qualify *v* (**-ies, -ied**) **1** to be fit for an office or position: *He qualifies for the job by virtue of his greater experience*. **2** to reach an accredited level of competence: *She has just qualified as a lawyer*. **3** to exhibit a required degree of ability or achievement in a preliminary contest. **4a** to make (somebody or something) suitable by training, skill, etc for a particular purpose. **b** to render (somebody) legally capable or entitled. **5a** to reduce (something) from a general to a particular or restricted form: *He subsequently qualified the statement to exclude single parents*. **b** to make less harsh or strict; to moderate. **c** in grammar, to have a subordinate relation to (a word or phrase); to modify. **6** (*often* + as) to characterize or describe (something).

qualitative *adj* relating to or involving quality or kind. ⋙ **qualitatively** *adv*.

qualitative analysis *n* chemical analysis designed to identify the components of a substance or mixture.

quality *n* (*pl* **-ies**) **1a** degree of excellence; grade. **b** superiority in kind; high standard. **c** *archaic* high social position. **2a** peculiar and essential character; nature. **b** an inherent feature; a property. **3** a distinguishing attribute; a characteristic.

quality control *n* a system of ensuring adequate quality, *esp* in manufactured products, involving design analysis and the sampling of output with inspection for defects.

quality time *n* time in which one's attention is given entirely to a personal relationship.

qualm *n* **1** a scruple or feeling of uneasiness, *esp* about a point of conscience or honour. **2** *archaic* a sudden and brief attack of faintness or nausea.

quandary *n* (*pl* **-ies**) a state of perplexity or doubt; a dilemma.

quango *n* (*pl* **-os**) *Brit* an autonomous body set up by the government and having statutory powers in a specific field.

quant *n* a long pole used for propelling a punt or barge.

quanta *n* pl of QUANTUM.

quantifier *n* in grammar, a word or phrase expressing quantity, *esp* one other than a number, e.g. *many, several, lots of*.

quantify *v* (**-ies, -ied**) to determine, express, or measure the quantity of. ⋙ **quantifiable** *adj*, **quantification** *n*.

quantise *v* see QUANTIZE.

quantitative *adj* **1** relating to or involving the measurement of quantity or amount. **2** expressed or expressible in terms of quantity. ⋙ **quantitatively** *adv*.

quantitative analysis *n* chemical analysis designed to determine the amounts or proportions of the components of a substance.

quantitive *adj* = QUANTITATIVE. ⋙ **quantitively** *adv*.

quantity *n* (*pl* **-ies**) **1** a specified or unspecified amount or number. **2** (*also in pl*) a considerable amount or number. **3** the aspect in which something is measurable in terms of magnitude.

quantity surveyor *n* somebody who estimates or measures quantities of materials and labour needed for a building project.

quantize *or* **-ise** *v* **1** to subdivide (e.g. energy) into quanta. **2** to restrict (something) to a set of fixed values. ⋙ **quantization** *n*.

quantum *n* (*pl* **quanta**) **1** in physics, any of the discrete quantities that form the smallest units into which energy can be subdivided or by which it can increase or decrease. **2** *formal* **a** a quantity, *esp* a total specified amount. **b** a portion or part.

quantum jump *n* = QUANTUM LEAP.

quantum leap *n* a sudden large increase or major advance.

quantum mechanics *pl n* (*used as sing. or pl*) a branch of mechanics based on quantum theory that deals with the physical behaviour of atoms and particles of matter, e.g. their interactions with other particles or radiation, for which the laws of classical mechanics are inapplicable.

quantum theory *n* a theory in physics based on the concept of the subdivision of energy into quanta.

quarantine[1] *n* a state or period of isolation imposed on people or animals, designed to prevent the spread of disease.

quarantine[2] *v* to put (a person or animal) into quarantine.

quark[1] *n* in physics, a hypothetical particle that carries a fractional electric charge and is held to be a constituent of known elementary particles, e.g. the proton or neutron.

quark[2] *n* a type of low-fat soft cheese made from skimmed milk curd.

quarrel[1] *n* **1** a usu verbal conflict between people; an argument. **2** a reason for dispute or complaint.

quarrel[2] *v* (**quarrelled, quarrelling,** *NAm* **quarreled, quarreling**) **1** to have a quarrel; to argue. **2** (+ with) to find fault with something.

quarrel[3] *n* a short heavy arrow or bolt with a square head, *esp* for a crossbow.

quarrelsome *adj* inclined or quick to quarrel, *esp* in a petty manner.

quarry[1] *n* (*pl* **-ies**) an open excavation from which building materials are obtained.

quarry[2] *v* (**-ies, -ied**) **1** to obtain (e.g. stone) from a quarry. **2** to make a quarry in (e.g. land). ➤➤ **quarrier** *n.*

quarry[3] *n* (*pl* **-ies**) **1** the prey or game of a predator or hunter. **2** somebody or something pursued or sought.

quarry tile *n* a hardwearing unglazed floor tile.

quart *n* a unit of liquid capacity equal to 2 pints (about 1.136l in Britain), (about 0.946l in the USA).

quarter[1] *n* **1** any of four equal parts into which something is divisible or divided. **2** a quarter of a pound or hundredweight. **3a** any of four three-month divisions of a year. **b** a period of 15 minutes or a point of time marking this, *esp* before or after the hour: *at a quarter past four.* **4** a quarter of a US or Canadian dollar, or a coin of this value. **5** a limb of an animal or carcass together with the adjacent parts, *esp* a hindquarter. **6a** a compass point or the region around it. **b** a person, group, direction, or place not specifically identified: *We had financial help from many quarters.* **7** a division or district of a town or city: *the Chinese quarter.* **8a** (*usu in pl*) an assigned station or post. **b** (*in pl*) living accommodation or lodgings, e.g. for military personnel or domestic staff. **9** merciful consideration of an opponent; *specif* sparing the life of a defeated enemy: *The champion gave him no quarter.*

quarter[2] *v* **1** to divide (something) into four equal or approximately equal parts. **2** to provide (somebody) with lodgings or shelter, *esp* to assign (a member of the armed forces) to accommodation. **3** to lodge or dwell. **4** *esp* of a gundog: to crisscross (an area) in all directions in search of game, or in order to pick up an animal's scent. **5** to arrange or bear (e.g. different coats of arms) in heraldic quarters on one shield. **6** in former times, to divide (a criminal's body) into four parts, usu after hanging, as a form of capital punishment.

quarterback *n* in American football, a player usu positioned behind the centre who directs the attacking play of the team.

quarter day *n* a day that begins a quarter of the year and on which a quarterly payment often falls due.

quarterdeck *n* the stern area of a ship's upper deck, traditionally used for official or ceremonial purposes.

quarterfinal *n* any of four matches in a knockout competition, the winners of which go through to the semifinals.

quarter-hour *n* = QUARTER[1] (3B).

quarter light *n Brit* a small often triangular panel in the side window of a motor vehicle that can usu be opened for ventilation.

quarterly[1] *n* (*pl* **-ies**) a periodical published at three-monthly intervals.

quarterly[2] *adj* **1** payable at three-monthly intervals. **2** recurring, issued, or spaced at three-monthly intervals.

quarterly[3] *adv* at three-monthly intervals.

quartermaster *n* **1** an army officer who provides supplies and quarters for a body of troops. **2** a petty officer or seaman who attends to a ship's compass, steering, and signals.

quarter sessions *pl n* in former times, a local court in England and Wales with limited criminal and civil jurisdiction, held quarterly.

quarterstaff *n* (*pl* **quarterstaves**) a long stout staff formerly used as a weapon.

quarter tone *n* in music, an interval of half a semitone.

quartet *or* **quartette** *n* **1a** (*used as sing. or pl*) in music, a group of four instruments, voices, or performers. **b** a musical composition for such a group. **2** (*used as sing. or pl*) a group or set of four.

quartic *adj* in mathematics, relating to the power of four, or involving one or more terms of this but no higher power.

quartile *n* in statistics, any of three numbers that divide a frequency distribution into four groups with equal frequencies, or any of the groups of individuals, items, etc so formed.

quarto *n* (*pl* **-os**) **1** a book format in which a folded sheet forms four leaves. **2** a book in this format. **3** a size of paper corresponding to a leaf of such a book, usu 10 × 8in. (about 25 × 20cm).

quartz[1] *n* a crystalline mineral consisting of silicon dioxide that is a major constituent of many rocks, e.g. granite and sandstone, and occurs in colourless and coloured forms.

quartz[2] *adj* of a clock or watch: controlled by the oscillations of a quartz crystal.

quartzite *n* a compact granular quartz rock derived from sandstone.

quasar *n* any of various unusually luminous very distant compact celestial objects thought to be supermassive black holes accreting matter in the centre of galaxies.

quash *v* **1a** to annul (e.g. a law or judgment). **b** to reject (a legal document) as invalid. **2** to suppress or crush (e.g. a rumour or rebellion).

quasi- *comb. form* **1** to some degree; partly: *quasi-officially.* **2** seemingly: *quasi-stellar object.*

quasi-stellar object *n* a quasar or similar astronomical body.

quassia *n* a bitter substance obtained from the heartwood of various tropical trees, used medicinally and as an insecticide.

quatercentenary *n* (*pl* **-ies**) a 400th anniversary.

quaternary *adj* **1a** of or based on the number four. **b** fourth in a series. **2** (**Quaternary**) of the second geological period of the Cenozoic era, lasting from about 1.64 million years ago to the present day, and marked by the first appearance of humans. ➤➤ **Quaternary** *n.*

quatrain *n* a stanza of four lines.

quatrefoil *n* a stylized figure or ornament in the form of a four-lobed leaf or flower.

quattrocento /kwatroh'chentoh/ *n* (*often* **Quattrocento**) the 15th cent., *esp* in Italian art.

quaver[1] *v esp* of the voice: to tremble or shake. ➤➤ **quavery** *adj.*

quaver[2] *n* **1** a musical note with the time value of half a crotchet or a quarter of a minim. **2** a tremulous sound.

quay *n* a landing place built beside navigable water for loading and unloading ships.

quayside *n* a quay or the land bordering a quay.

queasy *adj* (**-ier, -iest**) **1** causing or suffering from nausea. **2** causing or feeling anxiety or uneasiness. ➤➤ **queasily** *adv,* **queasiness** *n.*

Quechua /'kechwə/ *n* (*pl* **Quechuas** *or* **Quechua**) **1** a member of a Native American people of central Peru. **2** the language of the Quechua people and of the Inca Empire, spoken in Peru, Bolivia, and Ecuador. ➤➤ **Quechuan** *adj and n.*

queen[1] *n* **1** a female monarch. **2** the wife or widow of a king. **3** a woman, or something personified as a woman, that is preeminent in a specified respect. **4** in chess, the most powerful piece of each colour, which has the power to move any number of squares in any direction. **5** a playing card marked with a stylized figure of a queen and ranking usu below the king. **6** the fertile fully developed female in a colony of bees, wasps, ants, or termites. **7** *informal* an effeminate male homosexual. ➤➤ **queenly** *adj.*

queen[2] *v* to promote (a pawn) to a queen in chess. ✱ **queen it** of a woman: to behave in a domineering or arrogant manner.

Queen Anne *adj* of the reign of Queen Anne (1702–14).

queen bee *n* **1** the reproductive female bee in a hive. **2** *informal* the dominant woman in a group or organization.

queen dowager *n* the widow of a king.

queen mother *n* a woman who is the widow of a king and the mother of the reigning sovereign.

queen post *n* either of two vertical posts connecting the sides of a triangular framework supporting a roof or other structure with the base.

Queen's Bench *n* used when the British monarch is a queen: a division of the High Court hearing both civil and criminal cases.

Queensberry rules *pl n* the basic rules of boxing.

Queen's Counsel *n* used when the British monarch is a queen: a senior barrister who has been appointed counsel to the Crown as a mark of professional distinction.

Queen's English *n* used when the British monarch is a queen: standard or correct British English in speech or writing.

Queen's evidence *n* used when the British monarch is a queen: evidence given for the Crown by an accomplice in a crime against the other people charged with that crime.

Queen's Guide *n* used when the British monarch is a queen: a Guide who has reached the highest level of proficiency.

Queen's highway *n* used when the British monarch is a queen: any public road.

queen-size *adj esp* of a bed: larger or longer than the regular or standard size but smaller than king-size.

queen-sized *adj* = QUEEN-SIZE.

Queen's Scout *n* used when the British monarch is a queen: a Scout who has reached the highest level of proficiency.

Queen's speech *n* used when the British monarch is a queen: a speech read by the sovereign at the opening of a new session of parliament, giving details of the government's proposed legislative programme.

queer[1] *adj* **1a** odd or strange. **b** eccentric or mildly insane. **2** questionable or suspicious. **3** *informal* slightly unwell; faint or queasy. **4** *informal, derog* homosexual. ➤➤ **queerish** *adj,* **queerly** *adv.*

queer[2] *v informal* to spoil or thwart. ✱ **queer somebody's pitch** to prejudice or ruin somebody's chances in advance.

queer[3] *n informal, derog* a male homosexual.

quell *v* **1** to overwhelm (e.g. a rebellion) thoroughly; to suppress or subdue. **2** to overcome or alleviate.

quench *v* **1** to relieve or satisfy (thirst) with liquid. **2** to bring (something) to an end, *esp* by satisfying, damping, or decreasing it. **3a** to put out (e.g. a fire); to extinguish. **b** to cool (e.g. hot metal) suddenly by immersion in oil, water, etc. ➤➤ **quencher** *n.*

quenelle *n* a small ball of a seasoned meat or fish mixture.

quern *n* a simple hand mill for grinding grain.

querulous *adj* complaining, *esp* habitually; fretful or peevish. ➤➤ **querulously** *adv,* **querulousness** *n.*

query[1] *n* (*pl* **-ies**) **1** a question, *esp* one expressing doubt or uncertainty. **2** = QUESTION MARK.

query[2] *v* (**-ies, -ied**) **1** to question the accuracy of (e.g. a statement). **2** to express doubt or uncertainty about (something).

query language *n* a computer language designed for easy access and retrieval of information from a database.

quest[1] *n* **1** the act or an instance of seeking; a pursuit or search. **2** an adventurous journey undertaken by a knight in medieval romance.

quest[2] *v literary* to seek or search for something.

question[1] *n* **1** a word, phrase, or sentence used to elicit information or test knowledge. **2** the act or an instance of asking; an enquiry. **3a** a subject or concern that is in dispute or at issue. **b** a matter. **c** a problem to be resolved. **4a** doubt or objection. **b** chance or possibility. ✱ **in question** under discussion. **out of the question** preposterous or impossible.

question[2] *v* **1** to ask (somebody) a question or a series of questions. **2** to doubt or dispute (something). ➤➤ **questioner** *n.*

questionable *adj* **1** open to doubt or challenge; not certain or exact. **2** of doubtful morality or propriety; shady. ➤➤ **questionably** *adv.*

question mark *n* a punctuation mark (?) used at the end of a sentence to indicate a direct question.

question-master *n* the person who asks the questions during a quiz.

questionnaire *n* a set of questions, usu on a form, to be asked of a number of people to obtain statistically useful information.

question time *n* a period during which members of a parliamentary body may put questions to a minister.

quetzal *n* (*pl* **quetzals** *or* **quetzales**) **1** a Central American bird that has brilliant blue, green, red, and gold plumage, a rounded hairlike crest on the head, and, in the male, very long upper tail feathers. **2** the basic monetary unit of Guatemala.

queue[1] *n* **1** a waiting line, *esp* of people or vehicles. **2** in computing, a list where items are inserted at one end and accessed or deleted at the other.

queue[2] *v* (**queues, queued, queuing** *or* **queueing**) **1** to line up or wait in a queue. **2** in computing, to arrange (items) in a queue so that they can be accessed in order.

queue-jump *v* to join a queue at a point in front of those already waiting.

quibble[1] *n* **1** a minor objection or criticism, *esp* used as an equivocation. **2** *archaic* a pun.

quibble[2] *v* **1** to make minor or trivial objections. **2** to engage in petty argument; to bicker.

quiche *n* a pastry shell filled with a rich savoury egg and cream custard and other ingredients such as ham, cheese, or vegetables.

quick[1] *adj* **1a** fast in development or occurrence. **b** done with rapidity. **c** lasting a short time; brief. **d** marked by speed, readiness, or promptness of physical movement. **e** inclined to hastiness, e.g. in action or response: *quick to find fault.* **2a** fast in understanding, thinking, or learning; mentally agile. **b** reacting with speed and keen sensitivity. **c** aroused immediately and intensely: *a quick temper.* **3** *archaic* alive. ✱ **quick with child** *archaic* pregnant. ➤➤ **quickly** *adv,* **quickness** *n.*

quick[2] *adv informal* in a quick manner; quickly.

quick[3] *n* **1** painfully sensitive flesh, *esp* under a fingernail or toenail. **2** the very centre of something; the heart. **3** (**the quick**) *archaic* (*used as pl*) living people. ✱ **cut to the quick** to make (somebody) feel deeply hurt or upset.

quicken *v* **1** to become or make more rapid; to accelerate. **2** to enliven or stimulate (something). **3** to come to life. **4a** of a pregnant woman: to reach the stage of pregnancy at which foetal motion is felt. **b** of a foetus: to begin to show signs of life.

quickfire *adj* coming or operating quickly, *esp* in quick succession.

quickie *n informal* **1a** a brief act of sexual intercourse. **b** (*used before a noun*) done or made quickly: *a quickie divorce.* **2** an alcoholic drink consumed rapidly or in haste.

quicklime *n* = LIME[1] (1A).

quick march *n* a military march in quick time.

quicksand *n* a deep mass of loose wet sand into which heavy objects readily sink.

quickset *n chiefly Brit* plant cuttings, *esp* hawthorn, set in the ground to grow into a hedge.

quicksilver[1] *n* = MERCURY.

quicksilver[2] *adj* changeable in mood or rapid in movement.

quickstep *n* a ballroom dance that is a fast foxtrot characterized by a combination of short rapid steps.

quick-tempered *adj* easily angered; irascible.

quickthorn *n* = HAWTHORN.

quick time *n* a rate of marching of about 120 steps per minute.

quick-witted *adj* quick in understanding or response; mentally alert.

quid[1] *n* (*pl* **quid**) *Brit, informal* a pound sterling. ✱ **quids in** *Brit, informal* in the state of having made a usu large profit.

quid[2] *n* a wad of something, *esp* tobacco, for chewing.

quiddity *n* (*pl* **-ies**) *formal* **1** that which makes something what it is; essence. **2** a quibble.

quidnunc *n archaic or literary* somebody who wants to know all the latest news or gossip.

quid pro quo *n* (*pl* **quid pro quos**) something given or received in exchange for something else.

quiescent *adj* **1** causing no trouble. **2** at rest; inactive. ➤➤ **quiescence** *n,* **quiescently** *adv.*

quiet[1] *adj* (**quieter, quietest**) **1a** making little or no noise. **b** free from noise or uproar; peaceful. **c** marked by little or no motion, activity, or excitement; calm. **d** informal and usu involving small numbers of people: *a quiet wedding.* **2a** gentle or reserved. **b** unobtrusive or conservative: *quiet clothes.* **3** private or discreet: *a quiet word.* ➤➤ **quietly** *adv,* **quietness** *n.*

quiet[2] *n* being quiet; tranquillity or silence. ✱ **on the quiet** without telling anyone; discreetly or secretly.

quiet[3] *adv* in a quiet manner.

quieten *v chiefly Brit* to become or make quiet.

quietism *n* **1** a system of religious mysticism teaching that perfection and spiritual peace are attained by annihilation of the will and passive absorption in contemplation of God and divine things. **2** a passive withdrawn attitude or policy towards the world or worldly affairs. ➤➤ **quietist** *adj and n.*

quietude *n formal* being quiet; repose.

quietus *n* (*pl* **quietuses**) *literary* death as a release from life.

quiff *n Brit* a lock of hair brushed so that it stands up over the forehead.

quill *n* **1a** the hollow horny barrel of a feather. **b** any of the large stiff feathers of a bird's wing or tail. **c** any of the hollow sharp spines of a porcupine, hedgehog, etc. **2** a bird's feather fashioned into a writing pen.

quilling *n* the craft of shaping paper into rounded ridges or fluted folds.

quilt[1] *n* **1** a thick warm top cover for a bed consisting of padding held in place between two layers of cloth by usu crisscross lines of stitching. **2** a thin usu decorative top cover for a bed; a bedspread.

quilt[2] *v* to stitch or sew (fabric) together in layers with padding in between. ➤➤ **quilter** *n,* **quilting** *n.*

quim *n coarse slang* the female genitals.

quin *n Brit* a quintuplet.

quince *n* a round or pear-shaped fruit with hard acid flesh, used for marmalade, jelly, and preserves.

quincentenary *n* (*pl* **-ies**) a 500th anniversary. ➤➤ **quincentennial** *adj and n.*

quincunx *n* an arrangement of five things, e.g. marks on a playing card, with one at each corner of a square or rectangle and one in the middle. ➤➤ **quincuncial** *adj.*

quinine *n* a bitter-tasting chemical compound that is obtained from cinchona bark, is an ingredient of tonic water, and was formerly used in the treatment of malaria.

quinone *n* **1** a chemical compound that is a derivative of benzene and is used in photography. **2** any of various related compounds including several that are biologically important as in energy-producing reactions inside cells.

quinqu- *comb. form* see QUINQUE-.

quinquagenarian *n* a person between 50 and 59 years old. ➤➤ **quinquagenarian** *adj.*

Quinquagesima *n* the Sunday before Lent.

quinque- *or* **quinqu-** *comb. form* five: *quinquennium.*

quinquennia *n* pl of QUINQUENNIUM.

quinquennial *adj* **1** consisting of or lasting for five years. **2** occurring or being done every five years. ➤➤ **quinquennially** *adv.*

quinquennium *n* (*pl* **quinquenniums** *or* **quinquennia**) a period of five years.

quinquereme *n* an ancient Roman or Greek galley with five banks of oars.

quinsy *n* a severe inflammation of the tonsils, throat, or adjacent parts with swelling and fever.

quintal *n* **1** a unit of weight equal to 112lb (about 50.8kg) or 100lb (about 45.4kg); a hundredweight. **2** a metric unit of weight equal to 100kg (about 220.5lb).

quintessence *n* **1** the pure and concentrated essence of something. **2** the most typical example or perfect embodiment, e.g. of a quality or class. ➤➤ **quintessential** *adj,* **quintessentially** *adv.*

quintet *or* **quintette** *n* **1a** (*used as sing. or pl*) in music, a group of five instruments, voices, or performers. **b** a musical composition for such a group. **2** (*used as sing. or pl*) a group or set of five.

quintillion *n* **1** *Brit* the number one followed by 30 zeros (10^{30}). **2** *NAm* the number one followed by

18 zeros (10^{18}). ⋙ **quintillion** *adj*, **quintillionth** *adj and n.*

quintuple[1] *adj* **1** having five units or members. **2** being five times as great or as many.

quintuple[2] *v* to become or make five times as great or as many.

quintuple[3] *n* a number or amount five times as great as another.

quintuplet *n* any of five offspring born at one birth.

quintuplicate *adj* consisting of or existing in five corresponding or identical parts or examples.

quip[1] *n* a clever, witty, or sarcastic observation or response. ⋙ **quipster** *n.*

quip[2] *v* (**quipped, quipping**) to make a quip.

quire *n* **1** 24 or 25 sheets of paper of the same size and quality; one twentieth of a ream. **2** a set of folded sheets of paper, e.g. leaves or pages of a book, fitting one within another; *specif* four sheets of paper folded to form eight leaves or sixteen pages.

quirk *n* **1** an odd or peculiar trait; an idiosyncrasy. **2** an accident or vagary. **3** an abrupt twist or curve, e.g. in drawing or writing. ⋙ **quirkiness** *n*, **quirky** *adj.*

quirt *n* a riding whip with a short handle and a leather lash.

quisling *n* a traitor who collaborates with invaders.

quit[1] *v* (**quitting,** *past tense and past part.* **quitted** *or* **quit**) **1** to leave or depart from (a person or place). **2** to relinquish (e.g. a way of thinking or acting); to stop. **3** to give up (e.g. an activity or employment). **4** *archaic* to conduct (oneself) in a usu specified way. **5** *informal* to admit defeat; to give up.

quit[2] *adj* (+ of) released or free from obligation, charge, or penalty.

quitch *n* = COUCH GRASS.

quite *adv and adj* **1a** wholly or completely: *I'm quite sure.* **b** positively or certainly: *It's quite the best I've seen.* **2** more than usually; rather: *It took quite a while.* **3** *chiefly Brit* to only a moderate degree: *quite good but not perfect.* ✻ **quite so** used to express agreement.

quits *adj* on even terms as a result of repaying a debt or retaliating for an injury. ✻ **call it quits 1** to acknowledge that terms are now even or that neither side now has an advantage. **2** to call a halt to an activity.

quittance *n archaic or literary* discharge or release from a debt or obligation.

quitter *n informal* a person who gives up too easily; a defeatist.

quiver[1] *n* a case for carrying or holding arrows.

quiver[2] *v* to shake or move with a slight rapid trembling motion. ⋙ **quivery** *adj.*

quiver[3] *n* the act or an instance of quivering; a tremor.

qui vive /ˌkee 'veev/ ✻ **on the qui vive** on the alert or lookout.

quixotic *adj* idealistic or chivalrous in a rash or impractical way. ⋙ **quixotically** *adv.*

quiz[1] *n* (*pl* **quizzes**) **1** a public test of knowledge, *esp* as a form of entertainment. **2** a set of usu short quick questions. **3** *archaic* an eccentric or quizzical person. **4** *archaic* a practical joke or hoax.

quiz[2] *v* (**quizzes, quizzed, quizzing**) **1** to question (somebody) closely. **2** *archaic* to look quizzically at (somebody), *esp* through an eyeglass.

quizmaster *n Brit* the person who asks the questions during a quiz.

quizzical *adj* indicating a state of puzzlement; questioning. ⋙ **quizzicality** *n*, **quizzically** *adv.*

quoin *n* **1** a solid exterior corner of a building. **2** a block used to form a quoin, usu distinguished visually from the adjoining surfaces.

quoit *n* **1** a ring of rubber or iron used in a throwing game. **2** (*in pl, used as sing.*) a game in which quoits are thrown at an upright pin.

quokka *n* a small short-tailed wallaby of W Australia.

quoll *n* = DASYURE.

quondam *adj formal* former; sometime.

quorate *adj formal* having a quorum.

Quorn *n trademark* a form of vegetable protein derived from fungi.

quorum *n* (*pl* **quorums**) the minimum number of members of a body that must be assembled for proceedings to be constitutionally valid.

quota *n* **1** a proportional part or share, *esp* the share or proportion to be either contributed or received by an individual or body. **2** the number or amount constituting a proportional share. **3** a numerical limit set on a class of people or things.

quotable *adj* fit for or worth quoting. ⋙ **quotability** *n.*

quotation *n* **1** something quoted, *esp* a passage or phrase quoted from literature. **2** the act of quoting. **3** a statement of the expected cost of a service or commodity; an estimate. **4a** the naming or publishing of current bids and offers for or prices of shares, securities, commodities, etc. **b** the current buying or selling price of a commodity, stock, share, etc.

quotation mark *n* (*usu in pl*) either of a pair of punctuation marks (“ ” or ‘ ’) used to indicate the beginning and end of a direct quotation or to enclose a word or phrase, e.g. a title or definition.

quote[1] *v* **1a** to repeat (a passage or phrase previously said or written, *esp* by another) in writing or speech. **b** to repeat a passage or phrase from (a writer or work). **2a** to make an estimate of or give exact information on (the price of a commodity or service). **b** to give a quotation for a service or commodity. **3a** to name the current buying or selling price of (a commodity, stock, share, etc). **b** to quote the shares of (a company) on a stock exchange.

quote[2] *n informal* **1** = QUOTATION (1), (3). **2** = QUOTATION MARK.

quoth *v archaic* (*used only in first and third person sing.*) said.

quotidian *adj* **1** occurring or recurring every day. **2** commonplace or ordinary.

quotient *n* **1** the result of dividing one number by another. **2** the ratio, usu multiplied by 100, between a test score and a measurement on which that score might be expected largely to depend.

Qur'an /kə'rahn/ *n* see KORAN.

qursh /kooəsh/ *n* (*pl* **qursh**) a unit of currency in Saudi Arabia, worth 20th of a rial.

q.v. *abbr* (Latin) quod vide = which see, used to indicate a cross-reference.

qwerty *adj* of computer and typewriter keyboards: having the conventional arrangement of keys for English, with *q,w,e,r,t,y* on the left side of the top row of letters.

R[1] *or* **r** *n* (*pl* **R's** *or* **Rs** *or* **r's**) the eighteenth letter of the alphabet.

R[2] *abbr* **1** rand. **2** Regina. **3** registered (as a trademark). **4** reverse (gear). **5** Rex. **6** river. **7** röntgen. **8** in chess, rook. **9** rouble. **10** rupee.

r *abbr* **1** radius. **2** right. **3** in cricket, runs.

-r[1] *suffix* forming the comparative degree of adjectives and adverbs that end in *e*.

-r[2] *suffix* forming nouns from words that end in *e*, denoting: a person who does a particular activity or is associated with something in particular: *teenager; diner.*

RA *abbr* **1** Royal Academician. **2** Royal Academy. **3** Royal Artillery.

Ra *abbr* the chemical symbol for radium.

RAAF *abbr* Royal Australian Air Force.

rabbet[1] *n chiefly NAm* = REBATE[3].

rabbet[2] *v* (**rabbeted, rabbeting**) *chiefly NAm* = REBATE[4].

rabbi *n* (*pl* **rabbis**) **1** a Jewish scholar qualified to teach and give advice on Jewish law. **2** the official leader of a Jewish congregation.

rabbinate *n* **1** the office or tenure of a rabbi. **2** the whole body of rabbis.

rabbinic *adj* **1** of rabbis or their writings. **2** of Jewish law or teaching. ➤➤ **rabbinical** *adj.*

rabbit[1] *n* (*pl* **rabbits** *or* **rabbit**) **1a** a small long-eared short-tailed mammal related to the hare that lives in a burrow. **b** the soft fur of a rabbit. **c** *NAm* a hare. **2** *informal* an unskilful player, e.g. in golf, cricket, or tennis. **3** *Brit, informal* a chat. ➤➤ **rabbity** *adj.*

rabbit[2] *v* (**rabbited, rabbiting**) **1** to hunt rabbits. **2** *Brit, informal* (*often* + on) to talk aimlessly or inconsequentially.

rabbit punch *n* a short chopping blow delivered to the back of the neck.

rabble *n* **1** a disorderly crowd of people; a mob. **2** (**the rabble**) the lowest class of society; the common people.

rabble-rouser *n* somebody who stirs up anger or violence in a crowd; a demagogue. ➤➤ **rabble-rousing** *adj and n.*

Rabelaisian *adj* marked by the robust humour or extravagant caricature characteristic of the writings of François Rabelais (d.1553).

rabid *adj* **1** unreasoning or fanatical. **2** of or affected with rabies. ➤➤ **rabidity** *n,* **rabidly** *adv,* **rabidness** *n.*

rabies *n* a usu fatal viral disease of the nervous system of mammals, transmitted through the bite of an affected animal and characterized by extreme fear of water and convulsions.

RAC *abbr Brit* **1** Royal Armoured Corps. **2** Royal Automobile Club.

raccoon *or* **racoon** *n* (*pl* **raccoons** *or* **racoons** *or* **raccoon** *or* **racoon**) a small carnivorous mammal of N America that has a bushy ringed tail and lives in trees.

race[1] *n* **1a** a contest of speed, e.g. in running or riding. **b** (*in pl*) a meeting in which several races, *esp* for horses, are run. **c** a contest or rivalry for an ultimate prize or position. **2** a track or channel in which something rolls or slides; *specif* a groove for the balls in a ball bearing. **3a** a strong or rapid current of water in the sea, a river, etc. **b** a watercourse used industrially, e.g. to turn the wheel of a mill.

race[2] *v* **1a** to compete in a race. **b** to have a race with (somebody). **c** to enter (e.g. a horse or vehicle) in a race. **2** to go or move at top speed or out of control. **3** of a motor, engine, etc: to run at a very high speed.

race[3] *n* **1a** a division of humankind having physical characteristics that are transmissible by descent, e.g. skin colour. **b** the division of humankind into races; racial origin. **c** an ethnic group. **d** a group of people having a common ancestor. **2** an interbreeding group within a species of plants or animals; a subspecies.

racecard *n* the programme of events at a horse race meeting.

racecourse *n* a place or track where races, *esp* horse races, are held.

racehorse *n* a horse bred or kept for racing.

raceme *n* a simple stalk of flowers in which the flowers are borne on short side-stalks of about equal length along a tall main stem: compare CYME. ➤➤ **racemose** *adj.*

race meeting *n Brit* an individual fixture for horse racing at a particular racecourse.

racer *n* a person, animal, vehicle, etc that races or is used for racing.

race relations *pl n* relations between members of a country's different racial communities.

racetrack *n* a closed track on which races, e.g. between cars or runners, are held.

rachitis *n* = RICKETS. ➤➤ **rachitic** *adj.*

Rachmanism *n Brit* the unscrupulous exploitation of poor tenants by corrupt landlords.

Word history
named after Peter *Rachman* d.1962, English landlord. Rachman used intimidation to make tenants paying controlled rents leave so that he could let the properties for higher rents.

racial *adj* **1** of or based on a race. **2** existing or occurring between people of different races. **3** directed towards a particular race or based on distinctions of race. ➤➤ **racially** *adv.*

racialism *n* = RACISM. ➤➤ **racialist** *n and adj.*

racing *n* the sport of competing in or organizing races, *esp* horse races.

racing car *n* a car designed for use in motor racing.

racing driver *n* a driver who takes part in motor racing.

racism *n* **1** the belief that race is the primary determinant of human traits and capacities. **2** hostility towards or discrimination against people of races other than one's own. ➤➤ **racist** *n and adj.*

rack[1] *n* **1** a framework, stand, or grating on which articles are placed. **2** a bar with teeth on one face for meshing with a pinion or worm gear. **3** (**the rack**) an instrument of torture formerly used to stretch the victim's body. **4a** a triangular frame used for arranging pool balls at the beginning of the game. **b** a single game of pool.

rack[2] *v* **1** to cause to suffer torture, pain, or anguish. **2** to place (an object) in a rack.

rack[3] *n* the front rib section of lamb used for chops or as a roast.

rack[4] ✱ **rack and ruin/wrack and ruin** a state of destruction or extreme neglect.

rack[5] *v* to draw off (wine or beer) from the lees or sediment.

rack[6] *or* **wrack** *n* a wind-driven mass of high, often broken clouds.

rack-and-pinion *adj* denoting a mechanism, *esp* a steering system, in which a toothed wheel engages with a notched bar or other shaft to convert linear into rotary motion or vice versa.

racket[1] *or* **racquet** *n* **1** a lightweight bat consisting of netting stretched across an open frame with a handle attached, used in tennis, squash, badminton, etc. **2** (*in pl, used as sing.*) a game similar to squash for two or four players, played with a hard ball and rackets on a four-walled court.

racket[2] *n* **1** a loud and confused noise; a din. **2** *informal* **a** a fraudulent enterprise operated for profit. **b** an easy and lucrative means of earning a living. **c** a usu specified occupation or business.

racket[3] *v* (**racketed, racketing**) to move with or make a racket.

racketeer *n* a person who is involved in fraudulent schemes. ➤➤ **racketeering** *n.*

rackety *adj* noisy or rowdy.

rack railway *n* a railway with a rack between its running rails that meshes with a gear wheel or pinion on a locomotive.

rack rent *n* an excessive or unreasonably high rent.

rack up *v* to accumulate (a score or amount).

raclette *n* a dish of French or Swiss origin in which slices of potato are cooked with cheese or other toppings, traditionally over a fire but now usually under a grill.

raconteur *or* **raconteuse** *n* a man or woman who is very good at telling anecdotes.

racoon *n* see RACCOON.

racquet *n* see RACKET[1].

racy *adj* (**-ier, -iest**) **1** slightly indecent; risqué. **2** full of zest or vigour. ➤➤ **racily** *adv,* **raciness** *n.*

rad[1] *n* a unit of absorbed dose of ionizing radiation equal to an energy of 100 ergs per gram of irradiated material.

rad[2] *adj chiefly NAm, informal* excellent or admirable.

rad. *abbr* **1** radian. **2** radiator. **3** radius.

RADA /'rahdə/ *abbr Brit* Royal Academy of Dramatic Art.

radar *n* an electronic system that detects the presence, course, and speed of nearby ships, aircraft, etc by generating high-frequency radio waves and analysing those reflected back from the objects they strike.

radar gun *n* a hand-held electronic device that uses radar technology to measure the speed of a moving object, *esp* a motor vehicle.

radar trap *n* a stretch of road at which police officers regularly monitor drivers' speed using radar guns.

raddled *adj* haggard with age or the effects of a dissipated lifestyle.

radi- *comb. form* see RADIO-.

radial[1] *adj* **1** arranged like rays or radii from a central point or axis, or having parts that are arranged in this way. **2** of a tyre: having the cords of its fabric running at right angles to the circumference of the tyre. ➤➤ **radially** *adv.*

radial[2] *n* **1** a radial tyre. **2** any line in a system of radial lines.

radial engine *n* an internal-combustion engine with cylinders arranged radially round the crankshaft.

radial-ply *adj* = RADIAL[1] (2).

radial symmetry *n* a pattern of symmetry, e.g. in the starfish, in which similar parts are arranged around a central axis.

radian *n* a unit of angular measurement that is equal to the angle at the centre of a circle subtended by a part of the circumference equal in length to the radius, taken as 57.3°.

radiant[1] *adj* **1a** vividly bright and shining; glowing. **b** expressing love or happiness, health, etc. **2a** emitted or transmitted by radiation. **b** of or emitting radiant heat or radiant energy. ➤➤ **radiance** *n,* **radiantly** *adv.*

radiant[2] *n* a point or object from which light or heat emanates; *specif* the part of a gas or electric heater that becomes incandescent.

radiant energy *n* energy in the form of electromagnetic waves, e.g. heat, light, or radio waves.

radiant heat *n* heat transmitted by radiation rather than by conduction or convection.

radiate *v* **1a** to send (energy) out in rays or waves. **b** to be given out in the form of rays or waves. **2** to show or display (a quality, feeling, etc) clearly. **3** to proceed in a direct line from or towards a centre. ➤➤ **radiative** *adj.*

radiation *n* **1** the process of emitting radiant energy in the form of waves or particles. **2** energy radiated in the form of waves or particles, *esp* emission from radioactive sources. ➤➤ **radiational** *adj.*

radiation sickness *n* sickness that results from overexposure to radiation from X-rays, radioactive material, etc.

radiator *n* **1** a room heater with a large surface area for radiating heat; *specif* one through which hot water or steam circulates as part of a central heating system. **2** a device with a large surface area used for cooling an internal-combustion engine by means of water circulating through it.

radical[1] *adj* **1a** affecting or involving the basic nature or composition of something; fundamental. **b** marked by a considerable departure from the usual or traditional; innovative. **2** of surgery: designed to remove the root of a disease or all diseased tissue. **3a** favouring or making extreme changes in existing views, habits, conditions, or institutions. **b** of or denoting a political group associated with views, practices, and policies of extreme change. **4** of a mathematical or linguistic root. **5** of or growing from the root or the base of a stem. **6** *chiefly NAm, informal* excellent or admirable. ⋙ **radicalism** *n,* **radically** *adj,* **radicalness** *n.*

radical[2] *n* **1** a person who is a member of a radical political party or who holds radical views. **2a** in chemistry, a group of atoms that is replaceable in a molecule by a single atom and is capable of remaining unchanged during a series of reactions. **b** = FREE RADICAL.

radical chic *n derog* fashionable and usu superficial left-wing radicalism.

radicalize *or* **-ise** *v* to make radical, *esp* in politics. ⋙ **radicalization** *n.*

radical sign *n* the sign √ placed before a number to denote its square root, or some other root corresponding to an index number placed over the sign.

radicchio /ra'dikioh/ *n* (*pl* **-os**) a variety of chicory with red cabbage-like leaves, used *esp* in salads.

radices /'raydiseez/ *n* pl of RADIX.

radicle *n* the lower part of a plant embryo or seedling that includes the embryonic root.

radii *n* pl of RADIUS[1].

radio[1] *n* (*pl* **-os**) **1** the transmission and reception of signals by means of electromagnetic waves. **2** a system that transmits and receives signals in this way, *esp* for the purposes of sound broadcasting or two-way communication. **3a** a device designed to receive sound broadcasts. **b** a device designed to allow two-way communication by radio. **4a** a radio broadcasting organization or station. **b** the radio broadcasting industry.

radio[2] *v* (**radios, radioed, radioing**) **1** to send (a message) by radio. **2** to send a radio message to (somebody).

radio- *or* **radi-** *comb. form* **1** denoting radio: *radiotelegraphy.* **2a** denoting radiation or radioactivity: *radiotherapy.* **b** denoting radioactive isotopes of (a specified element): *radiocarbon.*

radioactive *adj* of, caused by, or exhibiting radioactivity. ⋙ **radioactively** *adv.*

radioactivity *n* the property possessed by some elements, e.g. uranium, of spontaneously emitting alpha, beta, or gamma rays by the disintegration of the nuclei of atoms.

radio astronomy *n* a branch of astronomy dealing with radio waves received from outside the earth's atmosphere.

radiobiology *n* a branch of biology dealing with the effects of radiation on living organisms or the use of radioactive materials in biological and medical investigation. ⋙ **radiobiological** *adj,* **radiobiologist** *n.*

radiocarbon *n* any of various radioactive isotopes of carbon, *esp* carbon-14, used as a tracer element and in carbon dating.

radio-controlled *adj* remotely controlled by means of a handset that makes use of radio technology.

radioelement *n* a chemical element that is naturally radioactive.

radiogram *n* **1** *Brit* a combined radio and record player. **2** = RADIOGRAPH.

radiograph *n* a picture produced on a sensitive surface by a form of radiation other than light; *specif* an X-ray. ⋙ **radiographer** *n,* **radiographic** *adj,* **radiography** *n.*

radioisotope *n* a radioactive isotope. ⋙ **radioisotopic** *adj.*

radiology *n* the study and use of radioactive substances and high-energy radiation, *esp* the use of X-rays and gamma rays in the diagnosis and treatment of disease. ⋙ **radiological** *adj,* **radiologist** *n.*

radiometer *n* an instrument for measuring the intensity of radiant or sound energy. ⋙ **radiometric** *adj,* **radiometry** *n.*

radionics *pl n* (*used as sing. or pl*) a technique in complementary medicine that is based on the theory that all living things give off radiation.

radio-opaque *adj* = RADIOPAQUE.

radiopaque *adj* opaque to various forms of radiation, e.g. X-rays. ⋙ **radiopacity** *n.*

radiophonic *adj* denoting or creating sounds that are electronically produced. ⋙ **radiophonically** *adv.*

radioscopy *n* observation of objects opaque to light, *esp* by means of X-rays. ⋙ **radioscopic** *adj.*

radiotelephone *n* an apparatus for enabling telephone messages to be sent by radio, e.g. from a moving vehicle. ⋙ **radiotelephonic** *adj,* **radiotelephony** *n.*

radio telescope *n* a radio receiver connected to a large aerial for recording and measuring radio waves from celestial bodies.

radiotherapy *n* the treatment of disease, e.g. cancer, by means of X-rays or radiation from radioactive substances. ⋙ **radiotherapeutic** *adj,* **radiotherapist** *n.*

radio wave *n* an electromagnetic wave of radio frequency.

radish *n* the pungent fleshy dark red root of a plant of the mustard family, eaten raw as a salad vegetable.

radium *n* an intensely radioactive metallic element that occurs in minute quantities in pitchblende and is used chiefly in luminous materials and in the treatment of cancer.

radius[1] *n* (*pl* **radii** *or* **radiuses**) **1** a straight line extending from the centre of a circle or sphere to the circumference or surface, or the length of this line. **2** a radial part, e.g. a spoke of a wheel. **3** the circular area defined by a stated radius: *all police cars within a two-mile radius.* **4** the bone on the thumb side of the human forearm, or a corresponding part in other animals: compare ULNA.

radius[2] *v* (**radiused, radiusing**) to give a rounded edge to (e.g. a machine part).

radix *n* (*pl* **radices** /-seez/ *or* **radixes**) **1** the base of a number system. **2** a root or rootlike part.

radome *n* a housing sheltering a radar antenna, *esp* on an aircraft.

radon *n* a radioactive gaseous element that is used in radiotherapy.

RAF *abbr Brit* Royal Air Force.

raffia *or* **raphia** *n* fibre from the leaves of a Madagascan palm tree used *esp* for making baskets, hats, and table mats.

raffish *adj* marked by careless unconventionality; rakish. ⋙ **raffishly** *adv,* **raffishness** *n.*

raffle[1] *n* a lottery in which the prizes are usually goods.

raffle² *v* (*often* + off) to give (something) away as a prize in a raffle.

raft¹ *n* **1a** a simple flat boat made by tying together a number of logs. **b** a flat usu wooden structure designed to float on water and used as a platform or vessel. **2** a floating cohesive mass, e.g. of seaweed or insect eggs.

raft² *v* to travel or transport by or as if by raft. ➤➤ **rafting** *n.*

raft³ *n* a large collection or quantity.

rafter¹ *n* any of the parallel beams that form the framework of a roof.

rafter² *n* somebody who travels on a raft.

rag¹ *n* **1a** a piece of old worn cloth. **b** (*in pl*) clothes that are in poor or ragged condition. **2** something resembling a rag, e.g. an unevenly shaped fragment. **3** *informal* a newspaper, *esp* one that is sensational or poorly written. ✱ **lose one's rag** *informal* to lose one's temper.

rag² *v* (**ragged, ragging**) to apply paint to (e.g. a wall) using a rag to create a marbled effect.

rag³ *n* **1** a series of processions and stunts organized by students to raise money for charity. **2** *Brit, informal, dated* an outburst of boisterous fun; a prank.

rag⁴ *v* (**ragging, ragged**) **1** *Brit* to tease. **2** to scold.

rag⁵ *n* ragtime music, or a ragtime tune.

rag⁶ *n* a hard rock used in building.

raga /'rahgə/ *n* **1** any of the ancient traditional melodic patterns or modes in Indian music. **2** a musical composition based on one of these traditional patterns.

ragamuffin *or* **raggamuffin** *n* **1** a ragged often disreputable person, *esp* a child. **2** = RAGGA. **3** somebody who performs or listens to ragga.

rag-and-bone man *n Brit* a usu itinerant dealer in old clothes, furniture, etc.

ragbag *n* **1** a bag in which scraps of fabric are stored. **2** a miscellaneous collection.

rag doll *n* a stuffed cloth doll.

rage¹ *n* **1a** violent and uncontrolled anger. **b** (*used in combinations*) anger caused by a particular situation: *road rage.* **2** an intense feeling; a passion. **3** a fashionable and temporary enthusiasm, or the object of it. **4** *Aus, NZ, informal* a lively party with dancing.

rage² *v* **1** to be in a rage. **2** to be violently stirred up or in tumult. **3** to be unchecked in violence or effect: *The controversy still rages.* **4** *Aus, NZ, informal* to have an enjoyable time.

ragga *n chiefly Brit* a style of reggae dance music with rap monologues.

raggamuffin *n* see RAGAMUFFIN.

ragged /'ragid/ *adj* **1a** of clothes: torn or worn to tatters. **b** wearing tattered clothes. **2a** having an irregular edge or outline; jagged. **b** executed or performed in an irregular, faulty, or uneven manner. ✱ **run somebody ragged** to exhaust somebody. ➤➤ **raggedly** *adv,* **raggedness** *n.*

ragged robin *n* a perennial Eurasian plant of the pink family with ragged pink or white flowers.

raggle-taggle *adj* unkempt or ragged.

raging *adj* **1** causing great pain or distress. **2** violent or wild. **3** *informal* extraordinary or tremendous.

raglan sleeve *n* a sleeve that extends to the neckline with slanted seams from the underarm to the neck.

ragout /ra'gooh/ *n* a thick well-seasoned stew, *esp* of meat and vegetables.

rag-rolling *n* a technique of interior decorating in which a final coat of paint is textured by rubbing it with a cloth.

ragtag *adj* **1** scruffy. **2** consisting of a varied or odd mixture: *ragtag civilian militias.*

ragtime *n* music with a rhythm characterized by strong syncopation in the melody and a regularly accented accompaniment, developed in America in about 1900 and usu played on the piano.

rag trade *n informal* the clothing trade.

ragworm *n* a marine segmented worm having pairs of bristly flat appendages and used as bait by sea anglers.

ragwort *n* a yellow-flowered plant of the daisy family that has deeply cut leaves and is toxic to livestock.

rai /rie/ *n* a style of popular music that originated in Algeria and was influenced by traditional Bedouin music.

raid¹ *n* **1a** a usu hostile incursion made in order to seize somebody or something. **b** a surprise attack by a small force. **2** a sudden invasion by the police, e.g. in search of criminals or stolen goods. **3** an act of robbery.

raid² *v* **1** to make a raid on. **2** to take or steal something from (a place). ➤➤ **raider** *n.*

rail¹ *n* **1** a horizontal bar, usu supported by posts or attached to a wall, that serves as a barrier or from which something may be hung. **2** any of a number of vertical metal or wooden posts that form a fence or railing. **3a** either of a pair of lengths of steel forming a guide and running surface for trains or other wheeled vehicles. **b** the railway. **4** (*usu in pl*) either of the fences on each side of a horse-racing track. ✱ **be/go off the rails 1** *informal* to be or become mentally unbalanced; to behave strangely. **2** *informal* to be or become misguided or mistaken.

rail² *v* **1** (*often* + off) to enclose or separate (an area) with a rail or rails. **2** to transport (goods) by train.

rail³ *n* (*pl* **rails** *or* **rail**) a wading bird of small or medium size with very long toes that enable it to run on soft wet ground.

rail⁴ *v* (*often* + against/at) to utter angry complaints or abuse. ➤➤ **railer** *n.*

railcar *n Brit* a railway carriage fitted with its own engine.

railcard *n Brit* a card that entitles the holder to rail fares at reduced rates.

railhead *n* **1** a point at which a railway meets important roads and other transport routes. **2** the farthest point reached by a railway; the terminal.

railing *n* **1** a fence or similar barrier comprising a series of vertical posts or rails. **2** any of the posts in such a fence or barrier.

raillery *n* good-humoured teasing.

railroad¹ *n NAm* a railway.

railroad² *v informal* **1a** to hustle into taking action or making a decision. **b** to push (e.g. a proposal) through hastily or without due consideration. **2** *NAm* to transport (people or things) by rail.

railway *n chiefly Brit* **1a** a track usu having two parallel rails on which trains run. **b** such a track and its assets, e.g. rolling stock and buildings, constituting a single property. **2** a railway network or the organization that runs it.

raiment *n archaic or literary* clothing; dress.

rain¹ *n* **1a** water falling in drops condensed from vapour in the atmosphere. **b** water that has fallen as rain; rainwater. **2** rainy weather. **3** (*in pl*) the rainy season, *esp* in tropical or sub-tropical climates. **4** a dense flow or fall of something.

rain² *v* **1** of rain: to fall in drops from the clouds. **2** to fall or bestow in profusion. ✱ **rain cats and dogs** to rain heavily. ➤➤ **rainless** *adj.*

rainbow *n* **1** an arch in the sky coloured red, orange, yellow, green, blue, indigo, and violet, and formed by the refraction, reflection, and interference of the sun's rays in raindrops, spray, etc. **2** an array of bright colours. **3** a wide range of things of any kind.

rainbow coalition *n* an alliance of numerous small political groups, often formed temporarily to address a particular issue.

rainbow trout *n* a large stout-bodied reddish trout of Europe and western N America.

rain check *n NAm* **1** the stub of a ticket for an outdoor event giving free admission at a later date if the event is interrupted by rain. **2** an assurance that an offer that cannot at present be accepted will remain open: *I'll take a rain check on that.*

raincoat *n* a coat made from waterproof or water-resistant material.

raindrop *n* a single drop of rain.

rainfall *n* **1** a fall of rain. **2** the amount of rain that has fallen in a given area during a given time.

rainforest *n* a dense tropical woodland with a heavy annual rainfall and containing tall broad-leaved evergreen trees.

rainmaker *n* **1** somebody who attempts to produce rain. **2** *NAm, informal* a highly successful professional person. ➤➤ **rainmaking** *n.*

rain off *v* (*usu in passive*) to interrupt or prevent (e.g. a sporting fixture) by rain.

rain shadow *n* an area of relatively light rainfall in the lee of a mountain range.

rainwater *n* water that has fallen as rain and is therefore usu soft.

rainy *adj* (**-ier, -iest**) having or characterized by heavy rainfall. ➤➤ **raininess** *n.*

rainy day *n* a future period when money or other things may be in short supply: *I'll keep it for a rainy day.*

raise¹ *v* **1a** to lift to a higher position. **b** to bring to an upright position. **2** to build or erect. **3a** to increase the strength, intensity, degree, or pitch of. **b** to cause to rise in level or amount. **c** to place higher in rank or dignity; to elevate. **4** to multiply (a quantity) by itself a number of times so as to produce a specified power. **5** to bet more than (a previous better). **6** to bring up (a subject) for consideration or debate. **7a** to bring (people) together for a purpose. **b** to collect (e.g. money). **8** to cause to occur or appear. **9a** to rear (a child or an animal). **b** to grow or cultivate (crops or other plants). **10a** to awaken. **b** to recall from death. **11** to end or suspend the operation of (e.g. a siege). **12** to cause (hunted game) to come out from concealment. **13** *Brit, informal* to establish radio or telephone communication with (a person or place). ✱ **raise an eyebrow/one's eyebrows** to show surprise, doubt, or disapproval. **raise Cain** *informal* to create a disturbance. **raise hell 1** *informal* to create a disturbance. **2** *informal* to complain angrily about something. **raise the roof** *informal* to make a loud noise, *esp* by cheering. ➤➤ **raisable** *adj,* **raiser** *n.*

raise² *n chiefly NAm* an increase in salary; a rise.

raisin *n* a dried grape. ➤➤ **raisiny** *adj.*

raising agent *n* any substance, e.g. yeast, that causes dough to rise.

raison d'être /,rayzon(h) 'detrə/ *n* (*pl* **raisons d'être** /,rayzon(h) 'detrə/) the main reason that something exists; its reason for being.

raita /'rietə/ *n* an Indian side dish consisting of a chopped vegetable, e.g. onion or cucumber, mixed with yoghurt and served cold.

Raj *n* (**the Raj**) British rule in India before it gained independence in 1947.

rajah *or* **raja** *n* **1** an Indian or Malayan prince or chief. **2** a person bearing a Hindu title of nobility.

Rajput *or* **Rajpoot** /'rahjpoot/ *n* a member of a land-owning military caste of N India.

rake¹ *n* **1** a long-handled implement with a row of prongs on the head for gathering hay, grass, etc or for loosening or levelling the surface of the ground. **2** any similar implement, e.g. a tool used to draw together the money or chips on a gaming table.

rake² *v* **1** to gather, loosen, or level with or as if with a rake. **2** to scrape, e.g. in passing. **3** to sweep the length of, e.g. with gunfire. **4** to pull or drag through something. **5** (+ through) to search through. ➤➤ **raker** *n.*

rake³ *n* **1** inclination from the perpendicular, or the angle of inclination. **2** the angle of the cutting surface of a tool.

rake⁴ *v* to incline or cause to incline from the perpendicular.

rake⁵ *n* a dissolute man, *esp* in fashionable society.

rake in *v informal* to earn or gain (money) rapidly or in abundance.

rake-off *n informal* a share of profits, *esp* those gained dishonestly.

rake over *v* = RAKE UP (1).

rake up *v* **1** to revive (something long forgotten). **2** to find or collect, *esp* with difficulty.

raki /'rahki/ *n* a strong grain-based spirit from Turkey and other parts of the Middle East.

rakish *adj* **1** of a car, boat, etc: having a smart stylish appearance suggestive of speed. **2** stylish or suggestive of a lively personality; dashing: *She wore her hat at a rakish angle.* ➤➤ **rakishly** *adv,* **rakishness** *n.*

rallentando *adj and adv* of a piece of music: to be performed with a gradual decrease in tempo.

rally¹ *v* (**-ies, -ied**) **1** to bring or come together for a common cause. **2** to summon (personal qualities) in preparation for action. **3** to come or bring together again to renew an effort. **4** to recover from illness, a state of depression, etc. **5** to drive in a rally. ✱ **rally round** to gather for the purpose of pooling practical or emotional support for somebody or something. ➤➤ **rallier** *n.*

rally² *n* (*pl* **-ies**) **1** a mass meeting of people sharing a common interest or supporting a common cause. **2** an event at which vehicles of a particular type are displayed. **3** a motor race over public roads or countryside tracks, designed to test both driving and navigational skills. **4** a recovery of strength or courage. **5** a series of strokes interchanged between players, e.g. in tennis, before a point is won.

rally³ *v* (**-ies, -ied**) *archaic* to ridicule or tease in a good-humoured way.

RAM *abbr* random access memory.

ram¹ *n* **1** an uncastrated male sheep. **2** a battering ram. **3** the weight that strikes the blow in a pile driver. **4** a heavy beak on the prow of a warship, formerly used for piercing enemy vessels.

ram² *v* (**rammed, ramming**) **1** to force down or in by driving, pressing, or pushing. **2** to strike against (something) violently and usu head-on. ✱ **ram something down somebody's throat** to force somebody to accept or listen to something, *esp* by constant repetition. ➤➤ **rammer** *n.*

Ramadan *or* **Ramadhan** *n* the ninth month of the Muslim year, during which fasting is practised daily from dawn to sunset.

ramble[1] *v* **1** to walk for pleasure in the countryside. **2** to talk or write in a disconnected long-winded fashion. **3** to grow or extend irregularly.

ramble[2] *n* a leisurely walk taken for pleasure in the countryside.

rambler *n* **1** a climbing rose with small flowers in large clusters. **2** somebody who regularly rambles in the countryside.

Rambo *n* (*pl* **-os**) a tough aggressive man who attempts to solve all problems by force or violence. ⋙ **Ramboesque** *adj.*

rambunctious *adj chiefly NAm, informal* full of youthful energy and boisterousness; rumbustious. ⋙ **rambunctiously** *adv,* **rambunctiousness** *n.*

rambutan /ram'boohtn/ *n* the bright red spiny tropical fruit of a Malaysian tree.

ramekin *or* **ramequin** *n* an individual baking and serving dish.

ramie /'raymee, 'ramee/ *n* a strong shiny flexible flaxlike fibre obtained from the stem of an Asian plant.

ramification *n* **1** (*usu in pl*) a wide-reaching and complex consequence. **2a** the act or process of branching out. **b** the arrangement of branches, e.g. on a plant. **3** a branch or subdivision of anything.

ramify *v* (**-ies, -ied**) to separate into branches, divisions, or constituent parts.

ramjet *n* a jet engine that uses the flow of compressed air produced by the forward movement of the aeroplane, rocket, etc to burn the fuel.

ramp[1] *n* **1** a slope leading from one level to another. **2** a stairway for entering or leaving an aircraft. **3** *Brit* a speedbump. **4** a point at which ongoing roadworks cause a sharp rise or fall in the level of the road.

ramp[2] *v* **1** to add a ramp to. **2** (*often* + up) to increase. **3** of a plant: to climb or spread vigorously. **4** *archaic* of an animal: to stand or advance menacingly, with forelegs or arms raised.

rampage[1] *v* to rush about wildly or violently. ⋙ **rampager** *n.*

rampage[2] *n* violent or uncontrolled behaviour. ✱ **on the rampage** behaving in a wild or violent way, *esp* carrying out a series of violent attacks.

rampant *adj* **1a** characterized by wildness or absence of restraint. **b** spreading or growing unchecked. **2** (*usu used after a noun*) of a heraldic animal: rearing up on one hind leg with forelegs extended. ⋙ **rampancy** *n,* **rampantly** *adv.*

rampart *n* a broad embankment or wall built as a fortification, e.g. around a castle or city, and usu surmounted by a parapet.

ram raid *n* a robbery in which entrance is gained to a building, e.g. a shop or bank, by driving a vehicle at speed through the front window. ⋙ **ram-raider** *n,* **ram-raiding** *n.*

ramrod *n* a rod for ramming home the charge in a muzzle-loading firearm.

ramshackle *adj* badly constructed or needing repair; rickety.

RAN *abbr* Royal Australian Navy.

ran *v* past tense of RUN[1].

ranch[1] *n* **1** a large farm for raising livestock, *esp* in N America and Australia. **2** *NAm* a ranch house.

ranch[2] *v* to own, work, or live on a ranch. ⋙ **rancher** *n.*

ranch house *n NAm* a large single-storey house, usu with a low-pitched roof and an open-plan interior.

rancid *adj* of food: smelling or tasting unpleasantly sour as a result of no longer being fresh. ⋙ **rancidity** *n,* **rancidness** *n.*

rancour (*NAm* **rancor**) *n* bitter and deep-seated ill will or hatred. ⋙ **rancorous** *adj,* **rancorously** *adv.*

rand *n* (*pl* **rand**) the basic monetary unit of S Africa.

R & B *abbr* rhythm and blues.

R & D *abbr* research and development.

random[1] *adj* **1** lacking a definite plan, purpose, or pattern. **2a** of or denoting statistical elements or events with an ungoverned or unpredictable outcome, but with definite probability of occurrence. **b** of or denoting a statistical sample drawn from a population each member of which has equal probability of occurring in the sample. ⋙ **randomly** *adv,* **randomness** *n.*

random[2] ✱ **at random** without a definite aim, direction, rule, or method.

random access memory *n* the working memory of a computer, where programs are loaded before they can be used and in which data can be accessed directly and changed: compare READ-ONLY MEMORY.

randomize *or* **-ise** *v* in statistics, to arrange (e.g. samples) so as to simulate a chance distribution and yield unbiased statistical data.

R and R *abbr* **1** rest and recreation. **2** rescue and resuscitation.

randy *adj* (**-ier, -iest**) *chiefly Brit, informal* sexually aroused; lustful. ⋙ **randily** *adv,* **randiness** *n.*

rang *v* past tense of RING[3].

rangatira *n NZ* a Maori chief or noble.

range[1] *n* **1** a sequence, series, or scale between limits. **2a** a number of individual people or objects forming a distinct class or series. **b** a variety or cross-section. **3** the space or extent included, covered, or used; scope. **4** the extent of pitch within the capacity of a voice or instrument. **5a** the distance between a weapon and target, a camera and subject, etc. **b** the distance within which something functions. **6** a series of things in a line, *esp* a large connected group of mountains. **7a** an open region over which livestock may roam and feed, *esp* in N America. **b** the region throughout which a kind of living organism or community naturally lives or occurs. **8a** a place where shooting is practised. **b** a place where golf drives are practised. **9** a large cooking stove, usu fired by solid fuel, that has one or more ovens and a flat metal top for heating pans.

range[2] *v* **1** to change or differ within limits. **2** to travel or roam at large or freely. **3** to extend in a usu specified direction. **4** to include a large number of topics. **5** to set in a row, in the proper order, or in a specified position.

rangefinder *n* a device for indicating or measuring range, e.g. between a gun and a target.

ranger *n* **1** a keeper of a park or forest. **2a** a law-enforcement officer in N America who patrols a usu specified region. **b** a soldier in the US army specially trained in close-range fighting and raiding tactics. **3** (**Ranger**) *Brit* a senior member of the Guide movement aged from 14 to 19.

Ranger Guide *n* = RANGER (3).

rangy *adj* (**-ier, -iest**) **1** of a person: tall and slender. **2** of an animal: long-limbed and long-bodied. ⋙ **ranginess** *n.*

rani *n* (*pl* **ranis**) a Hindu queen or princess, *esp* the wife of a rajah.

rank[1] *n* **1a** a degree or position in a hierarchy or order, *esp* in the armed forces. **b** high social position. **2** a row or series of people or things, *esp* a line of soldiers standing side by side. **3** (**the ranks**) the ordinary members of an armed force as distinguished from the officers. **4** (*in pl*) the people belonging to a group or class. **5** any of the eight rows of squares that extend across a chessboard parallel to the players' sides: compare FILE[3] (2). **6** *Brit* a place where taxis wait to pick up passengers.

rank[2] *v* **1** to have a position in relation to others. **2** to arrange in lines or in a regular formation. **3** to determine the relative position of; to rate. **4** *NAm* to outrank.

rank[3] *adj* **1** offensive in odour or flavour. **2** offensively gross or coarse. **3a** shockingly conspicuous; flagrant. **b** absolute or complete. **4** of vegetation: excessively vigorous and often coarse in growth. ➤➤ **rankly** *adv*, **rankness** *n*.

rank and file *n* (*used as sing. or pl*) **1** = RANK[1] (3). **2** the ordinary members of an organization, society, or nation as distinguished from the leading or principal members.

ranker *n* **1** a person who serves in the ranks. **2** a commissioned officer promoted from the ranks.

ranking *n* a position in a hierarchy or on a scale.

rankle *v* to cause continuing anger, irritation, or bitterness.

ransack *v* **1** to go through (a place) randomly stealing things and causing general chaos and destruction. **2** to search thoroughly.

ransom[1] *n* a price paid or demanded for the release of a captured or kidnapped person. ✱ **hold somebody to ransom 1** to kidnap somebody and demand money for their release. **2** to try to make somebody do something by threatening to cause harm.

ransom[2] *v* **1** to free from captivity by paying a ransom. **2** to demand a ransom for.

rant[1] *v* to talk in a wild or declamatory manner. ➤➤ **ranter** *n*.

rant[2] *n* a loud, impassioned, or bombastic speech.

ranunculus *n* (*pl* **ranunculuses** *or* **ranunculi**) a buttercup, crowfoot, or related plant that typically has yellow flowers with five petals.

rap[1] *n* **1** a sharp blow or knock, or the sound made by it. **2** a sharp rebuke or criticism. **3** *informal* the responsibility for or adverse consequences of an action: *I ended up taking the rap.* **4** *chiefly NAm, informal* a criminal charge. ✱ **a rap on/over the knuckles** *informal* a scolding.

rap[2] *v* (**rapped, rapping**) **1** to strike with a sharp blow. **2** to strike against something hard. **3** (+ out) to utter (e.g. a command) abruptly and forcibly. **4** *informal* to criticize sharply.

rap[3] *n* **1** *chiefly NAm, informal* talk or conversation. **2** a type of pop music of black American origin characterized by rapidly chanted lyrics accompanied by electronic music with a heavy beat.

rap[4] *v* (**rapped, rapping**) **1** *chiefly NAm, informal* to talk freely and frankly. **2** to chant the lyrics to rap music. ➤➤ **rapper** *n*.

rapacious *adj* **1** excessively grasping or covetous. **2** of an animal: living on prey. ➤➤ **rapaciously** *adv*, **rapaciousness** *n*, **rapacity** *n*.

rape[1] *n* **1a** the crime of forcing somebody to have sexual intercourse against his or her will. **b** an instance of this crime. **2** the act or an instance of despoiling: *the rape of the countryside.*

rape[2] *v* **1** of a man: to commit rape on. **2** to treat in a violent or destructive way; to despoil.

rape[3] *n* a European plant of the mustard family that has bright yellow flowers and is widely grown as a forage crop and for its oil-rich seeds.

rapeseed *n* the seeds of the rape plant, used for making oil.

raphia *n* see RAFFIA.

rapid[1] *adj* moving, acting, or occurring with speed; swift. ➤➤ **rapidity** *n*, **rapidly** *adv*, **rapidness** *n*.

rapid[2] *n* (*usu in pl*) a part of a river where the water flows swiftly over a steep usu rocky slope in the river bed.

rapid eye movement *n* rapid movement of the eyes that occurs during the phases of sleep when dreaming is taking place.

rapier *n* a straight two-edged sword with a narrow pointed blade.

rapine *n literary* the forcible seizing and destroying of other people's property; pillage.

rapist *n* a man who commits rape.

rappel[1] *v* (**rappelled, rappelling**) to abseil.

rappel[2] *n* an act of abseiling.

rappen *n* (*pl* **rappen**) a unit of currency in German-speaking parts of Switzerland and in Liechtenstein, worth 100th of a Swiss franc.

rapport /ra'paw/ *n* a sympathetic or harmonious relationship.

rapporteur /rapaw'tuh/ *n* a person responsible for preparing and presenting reports, e.g. from a committee to a higher body.

rapprochement /ra'proshmonh/ *n* the reestablishment of cordial relations, *esp* between nations.

rapscallion *n archaic* a rascal.

rapt *adj* **1** completely engrossed. **2** blissfully happy or joyful; enraptured. **3** *Aus, informal* = WRAPPED. ➤➤ **raptly** *adv*, **raptness** *n*.

raptor *n* a bird of prey. ➤➤ **raptorial** *adj*.

rapture *n* **1** a state of overwhelming emotion, *esp* joyous ecstasy. **2** (*usu in pl*) an expression of extreme happiness or enthusiasm: *She went into raptures over the new car.* **3** a mystical experience in which the spirit is exalted to a knowledge of divine things. ➤➤ **rapturous** *adj*, **rapturously** *adv*, **rapturousness** *n*.

rara avis /,rahrə 'ayvis, ,reərə/ *n* (*pl* **rara avises** *or* **rarae aves** /,rahri 'ayveez, ,reəri/) a rare or unusual person or thing.

rare[1] *adj* **1** seldom occurring or found. **2** marked by unusual quality, merit, or appeal. ➤➤ **rareness** *n*.

rare[2] *adj* of red meat: cooked lightly so that the inside is still red.

rarebit *n* = WELSH RAREBIT.

rare earth *n* any of a series of metallic elements that includes the elements with atomic numbers from 58 to 71, usu lanthanum, and sometimes yttrium and scandium.

raree show *n archaic* a side show or peep show.

rarefied *adj* **1** of air or the atmosphere: of a density that is lower than normal; thin. **2** very high or exalted, e.g. in rank. **3** intended for an elite or for the initiated only; esoteric or abstruse.

rarefy *v* (**-ies, -ied**) **1** to make (e.g. air or the atmosphere) less dense. **2** to make more spiritual, refined, or abstruse. ➤➤ **rarefaction** *n*.

rare gas *n* = NOBLE GAS.

rarely *adv* **1** not often; seldom. **2** in an extreme or exceptional manner.

raring *adj informal* full of enthusiasm or eagerness: *The horses were raring to go.*

rarity *n* (*pl* **-ies**) **1** the quality or state of being rare. **2** a rare person or thing.

rascal *n* **1** a mischievous person or animal. **2** an unprincipled or dishonest person. ⋙ **rascality** *n,* **rascally** *adj and adv.*

rase *v* see RAZE.

rash[1] *adj* acting with or resulting from undue haste or impetuosity. ⋙ **rashly** *adv,* **rashness** *n.*

rash[2] *n* **1** an outbreak of reddening or spots on the body. **2** a large number of instances of a specified thing during a short period.

rasher *n* a thin slice of bacon or ham.

rasp[1] *v* **1** to file with a rasp. **2** to utter in a grating tone. **3** to make a grating sound.

rasp[2] *n* **1** a coarse file with rows of cutting teeth. **2** a grating sound.

raspberry *n* (*pl* **-ies**) **1** a reddish pink edible berry that grows in clusters. **2** *informal* a rude sound made by sticking the tongue out and blowing noisily.

Rasta *n and adj informal* = RASTAFARIAN.

Rastafarian *n* a member of a religious and political movement among black W Indians that takes the former Emperor of Ethiopia, Haile Selassie, to be God. ⋙ **Rastafarian** *adj,* **Rastafarianism** *n.*

raster *n* a pattern of parallel lines, the intensity of which is controlled to form an image on a television screen or computer monitor.

rat[1] *n* **1** a rodent that resembles but is considerably larger than a mouse and is widely regarded as a pest. **2** *informal* a contemptible person; *specif* somebody who betrays or deserts friends or associates. **3** *NAm, informal* a person who spends a lot of time in a specified place. ⋙ **ratlike** *adj.*

rat[2] *v* (**ratted, ratting**) **1** to catch or hunt rats. **2** *informal* to desert one's party or cause. **3** *informal* (+ on) to betray or inform on one's associates. **4** *informal* (+ on) to default on an agreement. ⋙ **ratter** *n,* **ratting** *n.*

rata /'rahtə/ *n* a New Zealand tree that bears bright red flowers and yields a hard dark red wood.

ratable *adj* see RATEABLE.

ratafia /ratə'fiə/ *n* **1** a liqueur flavoured with almonds or fruit. **2** a small sweet almond-flavoured biscuit.

rat-arsed *adj Brit, coarse slang* very drunk.

rat-a-tat *or* **rat-a-tat-tat** *n* a sharp repeated knocking or tapping sound.

ratatouille /ratə'tooh·i/ *n* a dish containing tomatoes, onions, and other vegetables, typically aubergines, courgettes, and peppers, stewed slowly.

ratbag *n Brit, informal* an unpleasant or disagreeable person.

ratchet *n* **1** a mechanism that consists of a bar or wheel with angled teeth into which a cog, etc drops so that motion is allowed in one direction only. **2** a toothed wheel held in position or turned by a notched sliding bolt.

ratchet wheel *n* = RATCHET (2).

rate[1] *n* **1** a quantity or degree of something measured per unit of something else. **2** a charge, payment, or price fixed according to a ratio, scale, or standard. **3** speed of movement, change, development, etc. **4** (*usu in pl*) a tax levied by a British local authority, based on property values. ✱ **at any rate** in any case; anyway. **at a rate of knots** *Brit, informal* very fast.

rate[2] *v* **1** to assign a relative rank or class to. **2** to assign a rate to (e.g. a job or property). **3** to consider to be of a particular standard. **4** to be worthy of; to deserve. **5** *informal* to think highly of.

rate[3] *v archaic* to scold angrily; to berate.

-rate *comb. form* forming adjectives, with the meaning: of the level of quality specified: *fifth-rate.*

rateable *or* **ratable** *adj* capable of being rated, estimated, or apportioned.

rateable value *n* the estimated value of a British commercial property on which annual rate payments are calculated.

ratel /'raytl, 'raytel/ *n* an African or Asiatic nocturnal carnivorous mammal resembling the badger.

rate of exchange *n* = EXCHANGE RATE.

ratepayer *n* in Britain, an ordinary citizen regarded as somebody to whom local or national governments are accountable.

rather[1] *adv* **1** more readily or willingly; sooner: *I'd rather not go.* **2** to some degree; somewhat. **3** somewhat excessively. **4** more properly, reasonably, or truly. **5** on the contrary; instead.

rather[2] *interj Brit, dated* used to express enthusiastic approval or acceptance.

rathskeller /'rahtskelə/ *n NAm* a basement restaurant or beer cellar.

ratify *v* (**-ies, -ied**) to approve or confirm (e.g. a treaty) formally, so that it can come into force. ⋙ **ratification** *n,* **ratifier** *n.*

rating *n* **1** a classification according to grade. **2** a relative estimate or evaluation; standing. **3** (*in pl*) any of various indexes that list television programmes, new records, etc in order of popularity. **4** *Brit* a noncommissioned sailor, *esp* an ordinary seaman.

ratio *n* (*pl* **-os**) **1** the relationship in quantity or degree between one thing and another; proportion. **2** the indicated division of one mathematical expression by another.

ratiocinate *v formal* to reason logically or formally. ⋙ **ratiocination** *n,* **ratiocinative** *adj.*

ration[1] *n* **1** a share or amount, e.g. of food in short supply, that somebody is allowed. **2** (*in pl*) regular supplies of food given to troops in wartime. **3** (*in pl*) food supplies generally; provisions.

ration[2] *v* **1** to limit (a person or commodity) to a fixed ration. **2** to use sparingly.

rational *adj* **1** based on or compatible with reason; reasonable. **2** endowed with the ability to think logically. **3** of a number: having a value that can be expressed as the result of dividing one integer by another: compare IRRATIONAL, SURD[2]. ⋙ **rationality** *n,* **rationally** *adv.*

rationale /rashə'nahl/ *n* a logical basis for or explanation of beliefs, actions, or phenomena.

rationalise *v* see RATIONALIZE.

rationalism *n* **1** the belief that reason, not emotion, intuition, religion, etc, should govern the actions that people take. **2** a theory that reason is a source of knowledge superior to and independent of sense perception. ⋙ **rationalist** *adj and n,* **rationalistic** *adj.*

rationalize *or* **-ise** *v* **1** to attribute (e.g. one's actions) to rational and creditable motives in order to provide plausible reasons for conduct. **2** to increase the efficiency of (e.g. an industry) by more effective organization, usu entailing reductions in the workforce. ⋙ **rationalization** *n,* **rationalizer** *n.*

rat kangaroo *n* a small ratlike Australian marsupial with long hind legs resembling those of the kangaroo. Also called POTOROO.

ratline *n* any of the short transverse ropes attached to the shrouds of a ship to form rungs.

ratpack *n informal* journalists and photographers who aggressively pursue the subjects of their stories, often as a group.

rat race *n informal* a fiercely competitive and wearisome activity, *esp* the struggle to maintain one's position in a career or survive the pressures of modern urban life.

rat run *n Brit, informal* a minor road used by drivers to avoid congestion in the rush hour.

rat's tail *n* (*usu in pl*) something resembling the tail of a rat, *esp* lank or greasy hair.

rattan *n* a tropical climbing palm tree with very long tough stems used for walking sticks and wickerwork.

ratted *adj Brit, informal* drunk.

rattle[1] *v* **1** to make or cause to make a rapid succession of short sharp clinking, knocking, or jangling sounds, usu as a result of being shaken. **2** to move with a rattling sound. **3** (*often* + on) to chatter incessantly and aimlessly. **4** (+ about/around) to live in or occupy a house, building, etc that is too large. **5** *informal* to upset (somebody) to the point of loss of poise and composure. **6** (+ off) to say or perform in a brisk lively fashion.

rattle[2] *n* **1** a rattling sound. **2** a device that produces a rattling sound, *esp* a child's toy. **3** the sound-producing organ on a rattlesnake's tail. **4** a throat noise caused by air passing through mucus and heard *esp* at the approach of death. ➤➤ **rattly** *adj.*

rattler *n* **1** something that rattles. **2** *NAm, informal* a rattlesnake.

rattlesnake *n* an American poisonous snake with horny interlocking joints at the end of the tail that rattle when shaken.

rattletrap *n informal* a noisy old vehicle, *esp* a car.

rattling *adj* **1** making a rattle. **2** *informal, dated* quite fast; brisk. **3** *informal, dated* extremely good; excellent.

ratty *adj* (**-ier, -iest**) **1** *Brit, informal* irritable. **2** *informal* in a state of very poor repair; dilapidated or shabby. **3** resembling a rat. **4** infested with rats. ➤➤ **rattily** *adv,* **rattiness** *n.*

raucous *adj* disagreeably harsh or strident; noisy. ➤➤ **raucously** *adv,* **raucousness** *n.*

raunch *n informal* sexual suggestiveness; earthiness.

raunchy *adj* (**-ier, -iest**) *informal* energetic and sexually suggestive. ➤➤ **raunchily** *adv,* **raunchiness** *n.*

ravage[1] *v* to wreak havoc on; to devastate. ➤➤ **ravager** *n.*

ravage[2] *n* (*usu in pl*) damage resulting from ravaging.

rave[1] *v* **1** to talk irrationally, *esp* in delirium. **2** to talk or write with extreme or passionate enthusiasm. **3** *chiefly Brit, informal* to attend a rave.

rave[2] *n* **1** *informal* an extravagantly favourable review of somebody or something. **2** a very popular person or thing. **3** *chiefly Brit, informal* a very large organized party with dancing to loud electronic music.

ravel[1] *v* (**ravelled, ravelling,** *NAm* **raveled, raveling**) **1** (+ out) to unravel or disentangle. **2** (*often* + up) to entangle or confuse.

ravel[2] *n* **1** a tangle or tangled mass. **2** a loose thread.

raven[1] *n* a very large glossy black bird of the crow family.

raven[2] *adj* of a glossy black colour.

raven[3] /'rav(ə)n/ *v archaic* **1** to devour greedily. **2** to hunt for prey. ➤➤ **ravening** *adj.*

ravenous *adj* **1** extremely hungry; famished. **2** voracious or insatiable. ➤➤ **ravenously** *adv,* **ravenousness** *n.*

raver *n* **1** *informal* an energetic and uninhibited person who enjoys a wild social life. **2** *chiefly Brit, informal* somebody who often goes to raves. **3** somebody who raves, e.g. in delirium.

rave-up *n Brit, informal* a wild party.

ravine *n* a narrow steep-sided valley smaller than a canyon.

raving[1] *n* (*usu in pl*) a burst of speech that is irrational, incoherent, or wild.

raving[2] *adj and adv informal* used as an intensifier: great or greatly.

ravioli /ravi'ohli/ *pl n* (*used as sing. or pl*) pasta in the form of little cases containing meat, cheese, etc.

ravish *v archaic or literary* **1** to fill with joy, delight, etc. **2** to take (somebody) away by force. **3** to rape. ➤➤ **ravisher** *n,* **ravishment** *n.*

ravishing *adj* exceptionally attractive or pleasing. ➤➤ **ravishingly** *adv.*

raw[1] *adj* **1** not cooked. **2** not processed or purified and therefore still in its natural state. **3** not analysed or modified: *raw data.* **4** not having a hem: *a raw edge.* **5** having the surface abraded or chafed. **6** sensitive. **7** not refined or disguised in the least; crude: *raw emotion.* **8** lacking experience, training, etc; new. **9** disagreeably damp or cold. ➤➤ **rawly** *adv,* **rawness** *n.*

raw[2] *n* (**the raw**) a sensitive place or state. ✱ **in the raw 1** in the natural or crude state. **2** *informal* naked.

rawboned *adj* having a heavy or clumsy frame that seems inadequately covered with flesh.

raw deal *n* an instance of unfair treatment.

rawhide *n* **1** untanned leather. **2** *NAm* a strip of rawhide used as a whip.

raw material *n* material that can be converted by manufacture, treatment, etc into a new and useful product.

ray[1] *n* **1a** any of the lines of light that appear to radiate from a bright object. **b** a narrow beam of radiant energy, e.g. light or X-rays. **c** a stream of particles, *esp* radioactive particles, travelling in the same line. **2** any of a group of lines diverging from a common centre. **3** a slight manifestation or trace: *a ray of hope.* **4** any of the strap-shaped florets forming the outer ring of the head of a composite plant, e.g. an aster or daisy. **5a** any of the bony rods that support the fin of a fish. **b** any of the radiating parts of the body of a radially symmetrical animal, e.g. a starfish. ➤➤ **rayed** *adj,* **rayless** *adj.*

ray[2] *n* a fish with a flat body, large pectoral fins that look like wings, and a long narrow tail.

ray[3] *n* in music, the second note of a major scale in the tonic sol-fa system.

ray gun *n* in science fiction, any of various weapons that stun or kill an enemy by directing at them a beam of energy.

rayon *n* a textile fibre produced by forcing and drawing cellulose through minute holes, or a fabric made from this fibre.

raze *or* **rase** *v* to destroy (e.g. a town or building) completely.

razor[1] *n* a sharp-edged cutting implement for shaving hair.

razor[2] *v* to cut or shave with a razor.

razorback *n* **1** = RORQUAL. **2** a semiwild pig of the USA, with a narrow body and a ridged back.

razorbill *n* a black and white N Atlantic auk with a flat sharp-edged bill.

razor-shell *n* a marine bivalve mollusc with a long narrow curved thin shell.

razor wire *n* fencing wire fitted at intervals with sharp-edged rectangular metal projections resembling razor blades.

razz *v chiefly NAm, informal* **1** to tease. **2** to heckle or deride.

razzamatazz *n* see RAZZMATAZZ.

razzle ✱ **on the razzle** *informal* enjoying a spell of partying or drinking.

razzle-dazzle *n* = RAZZMATAZZ.

razzmatazz *or* **razzamatazz** *n informal* a noisy, colourful, and showy atmosphere or activity.

Rb *abbr* the chemical symbol for rubidium.

RC *abbr* **1** Red Cross. **2** Roman Catholic.

Rd *abbr* in street names, road.

RDA *abbr* recommended daily allowance (of a food or drug).

RDF *abbr* radio direction-finder.

RE *abbr* **1** religious education. **2** *Brit* Royal Engineers.

Re *abbr* the chemical symbol for rhenium.

re[1] *prep* with regard to or in the matter of; concerning.

re[2] *n* = RAY[3].

re- *prefix* **1** again or anew: *reprint.* **2** again in a new, altered, or improved way: *rewrite.* **3** back or backwards: *recall.* **4** away or down: *recede.*

're *contr informal* are.

reach[1] *v* **1a** (+ out) to stretch out (a part of the body). **b** to make a stretch with or as if with one's hand. **2** to touch or grasp by extending a part of the body. **3** to extend to. **4** to achieve or arrive at. **5** to contact or communicate with. **6** to make an impression or have an effect on. ➤➤ **reachable** *adj.*

reach[2] *n* **1** the distance or extent of somebody's ability to reach: *out of my reach.* **2** range, e.g. of somebody's comprehension. **3** the action or an act of reaching. **4** (*usu in pl*) a continuous stretch or expanse, *esp* a straight portion of a river. **5** the tack sailed by a sailing vessel with the wind blowing more or less from the side.

reach-me-down *n Brit, informal, dated* a second-hand garment; a cast-off.

react *v* **1** to respond to something in a particular way. **2** (+ against) to act in opposition to a force or influence. **3** to have a particular physiological response, e.g. to a drug. **4** to undergo chemical reaction or physical change.

reactance *n* the part of the impedance of an alternating-current circuit that is due to capacitance or inductance or both, expressed in ohms.

reactant *n* a substance that is altered in the course of reacting chemically with another.

reaction *n* **1** the act or an instance of reacting. **2** a mental or emotional response to circumstances. **3** a bodily response to a stimulus. **4** tendency towards a former and usu outmoded political or social order. **5a** a chemical transformation or change; *specif* an action between atoms, molecules, etc to form one or more new substances. **b** a process involving change in atomic nuclei resulting from interaction with a particle or another nucleus. **6** in physics, the force that something subjected to the action of a force exerts equally in the opposite direction.

reactionary[1] *adj* opposing radical social or political change or favouring a return to a former order.

reactionary[2] *n* (*pl* **-ies**) a reactionary person.

reactivate *v* to make (something) active again. ➤➤ **reactivation** *n.*

reactive *adj* **1** of reaction or reactance. **2** tending to react chemically. **3** tending to react passively to situations, instead of initiating or controlling them. **4** of an illness, etc: caused by a reaction to a drug or other treatment. ➤➤ **reactivity** *n.*

reactor *n* **1** an apparatus in which a chain reaction of fissile material, e.g. uranium or plutonium, takes place, *esp* for the production of nuclear power; a nuclear reactor. **2** a vat in which an industrial chemical reaction takes place. **3** somebody who reacts, e.g. to a drug.

read[1] *v* (*past tense and past part.* **read**) **1a** to look at and understand (e.g. words). **b** to utter aloud (printed or written words). **c** to read the words of (a sign, book, etc). **2a** to read works of (an author or type of literature). **b** to read (a particular newspaper, magazine, etc) regularly. **3** to learn or find out from written or printed matter. **4** to attribute a meaning to; to interpret. **5** to learn or understand the nature of (something or somebody) by observing outward expression or signs: *I can read him like a book.* **6** to proofread. **7** to grant a reading to (a legislative bill). **8a** to look at the measurement shown on (e.g. a dial or gauge). **b** to indicate (a specified measurement). **9** *chiefly Brit* to study (a subject), *esp* for a degree. **10a** of a computer: to sense the meaning of (coded information recorded or stored). **b** of a computer: to take (information) from a storage medium, e.g. a CD-ROM. **11** to receive and understand (a message) by radio. ✱ **read between the lines** to work out the implicit meaning of something, rather than what is actually written. **take something as read** to accept something as agreed; to assume it.

read[2] *n* **1** *informal* something to read considered in terms of the interest, enjoyment, etc it provides: *a good read.* **2** *chiefly Brit* a period or act of reading.

readable *adj* **1** legible. **2** pleasurable or interesting to read. ➤➤ **readability** *n,* **readably** *adv.*

reader *n* **1a** a person who reads. **b** a proofreader. **c** somebody who evaluates manuscripts. **2** (**Reader**) a member of a British university staff between the ranks of lecturer and professor. **3** a usu instructive and introductory book or anthology. **4** a device that reads or displays coded information on a tape, microfilm, etc.

readership *n* **1** (*used as sing. or pl*) the readers of a particular publication or author. **2** (**Readership**) the position or duties of a university Reader.

readily *adv* **1** without hesitating; willingly. **2** without much difficulty; easily.

reading *n* **1a** an event at which something is read to an audience. **b** an act of formally reading a bill that constitutes one of the stages of approval by a legislature. **2** material read or intended for reading: *It makes interesting reading.* **3** a particular interpretation. **4** the value indicated or data produced by an instrument.

reading age *n* a child's reading ability expressed as the age of the average child with the same ability.

readjust *v* **1** to adapt to new or changing circumstances. **2** to adjust (e.g. a control) to a new setting. ➤➤ **readjustment** *n.*

read-only memory *n* a memory in a computer system that is used for permanent storage of data and allows the user only to read the data and not to change it: compare RANDOM ACCESS MEMORY.

readout *n* **1** the retrieval of information from a computer storage medium, e.g. computer memory or a CD-ROM. **2** the information retrieved from storage.

read up *v* (*often* + on) to learn about something by reading.

read-write head *n* in a computer, an electromagnetic device that allows data to be both read from and copied onto a disk or tape.

ready[1] *adj* (**-ier, -iest**) **1a** prepared for an experience or action. **b** prepared or available for immediate use. **2** willingly disposed. **3** likely or about to do the specified thing. **4** spontaneously prompt. ✱ **make ready** to prepare. ➤➤ **readiness** *n.*

ready[2] *v* (**-ies, -ied**) to make ready.

ready[3] *n* (*pl* **-ies**) (*also* **the ready**) *Brit, informal* (*in pl*) available money. ✱ **at/to the ready** available for immediate use.

ready cash *n* = READY MONEY.

ready-made *adj* **1** made beforehand, *esp* for general sale or use rather than to individual specifications. **2** lacking originality or individuality. **3** readily available.

ready-mixed *adj* of concrete, food, etc: having ingredients already mixed.

ready money *n* **1** immediately available cash **2** payment on the spot.

ready reckoner *n Brit* an arithmetical table or set of tables used as an aid in calculating.

ready-to-wear *adj* of a garment: made in a standard size for general sale, rather than to an individual's measurements; off-the-peg.

reafforest *v chiefly Brit* = REFOREST. ➤➤ **reafforestation** *n.*

reagent *n* a substance that takes part in or brings about a particular chemical reaction.

real[1] *adj* **1** not artificial, fraudulent, illusory, or fictional; actual, genuine, or authentic. **2** made or served according to traditional methods: *real ale.* **3** significant. **4** used chiefly for emphasis: complete or great: *Her visit was a real surprise.* **5** measured by purchasing power rather than the paper value of money: *real income.* **6** of an image: formed by light rays converging at a point: compare VIRTUAL. **7** of or belonging to the set of real numbers. ➤➤ **realness** *n.*

real[2] *n* (**the real**) that which is real; reality. ✱ **for real** *informal* in earnest; genuinely.

real[3] *adv chiefly NAm, Scot, informal* very.

real[4] /ray'ahl/ *n* (*pl* **reals** *or* **reales**) **1** the basic monetary unit of Brazil. **2** a former monetary unit of Spain and Spanish colonies.

real estate *n chiefly NAm* property in buildings and land.

realign *v* **1** to align again or in a different way. **2** to change one's affiliations and become part of a different group, *esp* a political party or faction. ➤➤ **realignment** *n.*

realise *v* see REALIZE.

realism *n* **1** concern for fact or reality and rejection of things regarded as impractical or visionary. **2** representation of things in art and literature in a way that is true to nature. **3** in philosophy, the belief or doctrine that objects of sense perception, or classes and universals, exist independently of the mind. ➤➤ **realist** *adj and n.*

realistic *adj* **1** basing aims or opinions on known facts or reasonable expectations, rather than on ideals. **2** depicting things in a way that seems real. **3** of realism in philosophy. ➤➤ **realistically** *adv.*

reality *n* (*pl* **-ies**) **1** the state of being real. **2a** a real entity or state of affairs. **b** the totality of real things and events. **3** in philosophy, something that exists independently of our perception or awareness of it. ✱ **in reality** in actual fact.

realize *or* **-ise** *v* **1** to be or become fully aware of. **2** to cause to become a reality; to accomplish. **3a** to convert (property, assets, etc) into actual money. **b** to earn (money) by sale, investment, or effort. ➤➤ **realizable** *adj,* **realization** *n,* **realizer** *n.*

really[1] *adv* **1** in reality; actually. **2** without question; thoroughly. **3** more correctly.

really[2] *interj* used as an expression of surprise or indignation.

realm *n* **1** a kingdom. **2** (*also in pl*) a domain or sphere.

real number *n* a number that does not include a part that is a multiple of the square root of minus one.

realpolitik /ray'ahlpoliteek, ray'al-/ *n* politics based on practical factors rather than on moral or ethical objectives.

real property *n* property in buildings and land.

real tennis *n* an early form of tennis, played with a racket and a solid ball in an irregularly-shaped indoor court divided by a net.

real-time *adj* of a computer system: being constrained by the timing of events in the outside world, or collecting data from an external source, e.g. an air traffic control system.

realtor *n NAm* an estate agent.

realty *n* real property: compare PERSONALTY.

ream[1] *n* **1** a quantity of paper equal to 20 quires or variously 480, 500, or 516 sheets. **2** (*usu in pl*) a great amount, e.g. of something written or printed.

ream[2] *v* **1** to enlarge (a hole) with a reamer. **2** to remove by reaming.

reamer *n* a rotating finishing tool with cutting edges used to enlarge a hole.

reap *v* **1** to cut or harvest (a crop). **2** to obtain or win, *esp* as the reward for effort.

reaper *n* a person or machine that harvests crops. ✱ **the reaper/grim reaper** death, or the personification of death as a skeleton wielding a scythe.

reappear *v* to appear again after being absent for a while. ➤➤ **reappearance** *n.*

reappoint *v* to appoint again to the same position. ➤➤ **reappointment** *n.*

reappraise *v* to assess again, and usu form a different opinion. ➤➤ **reappraisal** *n.*

rear[1] *n* **1a** the back part of something. **b** *informal* the buttocks. **2** the space or position at the back. ✱ **bring up the rear** to be the last in a group, series, order, etc.

rear[2] *adj* at the back.

rear[3] *v* **1a** to breed (an animal) or grow (e.g. a crop) for use or sale. **b** to bring up (a child). **2** to raise into an upright position. **3** (*often* + up) *esp* of a horse: to rise up on the hind legs. **4** (+ up) to react with anger, indignation, or resentment. **5** *literary* (*usu* + up/over) to rise to a height. ➤➤ **rearer** *n.*

rear admiral *n* a naval officer ranking above a commodore and below a vice admiral.

rear end *n informal* the buttocks.

rear guard *n* **1** a military detachment for guarding the rear of a main body or force, *esp* during a retreat. **2** the most conservative or reactionary faction within a group, *esp* a political party.

rearguard action *n* vigorous resistance, *esp* in the face of defeat.

rearm *v* **1** to arm (e.g. a nation or military force) again, *esp* with new or better weapons. **2** to become armed again. ➤➤ **rearmament** *n.*

rearmost *adj* farthest in the rear; last.

rearrange *v* to arrange (something) differently. ➤➤ **rearrangement** *n.*

rearview mirror *n* a mirror in a motor vehicle that gives a view of the road and traffic behind the vehicle.

rearward[1] *adj* located at or directed towards the rear.

rearward[2] *adv* = REARWARDS.

rearwards *adv* at or towards the rear; backwards.

rear-wheel drive *n* a transmission system in a motor vehicle that sends power to the rear wheels.

reason[1] *n* **1a** an explanation or justification. **b** a rational ground or motive. **c** a cause. **2** the power of comprehending, inferring, or thinking, *esp* in orderly rational ways. **3** sanity. ✻ **it stands to reason** it is obvious, logical, or reasonable. **listen to reason** to be willing to accept advice to act sensibly. **within reason** within reasonable limits.

reason[2] *v* **1** to use the faculty of reason to arrive at conclusions. **2** (+ with) to talk or argue with another person so as to influence or persuade them. **3** (*often* + out) to formulate, assume, analyse, or conclude (something) by the use of reason. ⋙ **reasoner** *n*, **reasoning** *n*.

reasonable *adj* **1a** moderate or fair. **b** not extreme or excessive. **c** in accord with reason; logical. **2a** sensible. **b** *archaic* having the faculty of reason; rational. ⋙ **reasonableness** *n*, **reasonably** *adv*.

reassemble *v* **1** to put back together. **2** of a group of people: to come together again.

reassess *v* to assess again or in a different way. ⋙ **reassessment** *n*.

reassure *v* to restore confidence to; to calm. ⋙ **reassurance** *n*, **reassuring** *adj*, **reassuringly** *adv*.

rebarbative *adj formal* repellent or unattractive.

rebate[1] *n* **1** a return of part of a payment. **2** a deduction from a sum before payment; a discount.

rebate[2] *v* **1** to give a rebate to. **2** to make a rebate of. ⋙ **rebatable** *adj*.

rebate[3] *n* a groove or step cut into the edge of a piece of wood to which another piece is to be joined by means of a corresponding groove or step.

rebate[4] *v* **1** to cut a rebate in (an edge). **2** to join (pieces) by means of a rebate.

rebec *or* **rebeck** *n* a medieval pear-shaped musical instrument, usu with three strings, played with a bow.

rebel[1] *n* somebody who rebels against a government, authority, convention, etc.

rebel[2] *v* (**rebelled, rebelling**) **1a** to oppose or disobey authority or control. **b** to carry out armed resistance to a government. **2a** to act in or show opposition. **b** to feel or exhibit anger or revulsion.

rebellion *n* **1** opposition to authority or dominance. **2** open armed resistance to an established government, or an instance of such resistance.

rebellious *adj* **1** given to or engaged in rebellion. **2** tending to oppose or defy authority or dominance. ⋙ **rebelliously** *adv*, **rebelliousness** *n*.

rebirth *n* **1a** a new or second birth. **b** spiritual regeneration. **2** a renaissance or revival.

reboot *v* to start up (a computer system) again.

rebore[1] *v* to enlarge and renew the bore of (a cylinder in an internal-combustion engine).

rebore[2] *n* **1** the process of reboring a cylinder. **2** an engine that has rebored cylinders.

reborn *adj* **1** brought back to life; born again. **2** regenerated or spiritually renewed.

rebound[1] *v* **1** to spring back on collision or impact with another body. **2** to return to an original strong or healthy state after a setback, illness, etc. **3** (*often* + on) to return with an adverse effect.

rebound[2] *n* **1a** an instance of rebounding. **b** a recovery. **2** a shot, e.g. in basketball or football, that rebounds. ✻ **on the rebound** while in an unsettled or emotional state resulting from a setback, the end of a relationship, etc.

rebrand *v* **1** to change the brand name of (a product). **2** to update the image of (a company).

rebuff[1] *v* to reject or refuse sharply; to snub.

rebuff[2] *n* a curt rejection or refusal.

rebuild *v* (*past tense and past part.* **rebuilt**) **1** to build again, *esp* after severe damage to or destruction of the original. **2** to make extensive changes to; to remodel.

rebuke[1] *v* to criticize severely; to reprimand.

rebuke[2] *n* a reprimand.

rebus *n* a representation of words or syllables by pictures that suggest the same sound, or a riddle that makes use of such representations.

rebut *v* (**rebutted, rebutting**) to disprove or expose the falsity of (e.g. a claim). ⋙ **rebuttal** *n*.

recalcitrant[1] *adj* **1** obstinately defiant of authority or restraint. **2** difficult to handle or control. ⋙ **recalcitrance** *n*, **recalcitrantly** *adv*.

recalcitrant[2] *n* somebody who is recalcitrant.

recall[1] *v* **1a** to bring back to mind; to remember. **b** to make somebody think of; to remind them of. **2a** to summon (somebody) back officially. **b** to request the return of (a faulty product) to the manufacturer. **3** to retrieve (stored material) in an information retrieval system. ⋙ **recallable** *adj*.

recall[2] *n* **1** a summons to return or a request to return something. **2** remembrance of what has been learned or experienced; recollection. **3** the ability (e.g. of an information retrieval system) to retrieve stored material.

recant *v* **1** to withdraw or renounce (a statement or belief) formally and publicly. **2** to make an open confession of error, *esp* to disavow a religious or political opinion or belief. ⋙ **recantation** *n*, **recanter** *n*.

recap[1] *v* (**recapped, recapping**) *informal* = RECAPITULATE.

recap[2] *n informal* = RECAPITULATION.

recapitulate *v* to repeat the principal points of (an argument, discourse, etc); to sum up. ⋙ **recapitulatory** *adj*.

recapitulation *n* **1** the act or an instance of recapitulating. **2** in music, a modified repetition of the main themes forming the third section of a movement written in sonata form.

recapture *v* **1** to capture again. **2** to recreate or experience again. ⋙ **recapture** *n*.

recast *v* (*past tense and past part.* **recast**) **1** to cast again. **2** to remodel or refashion.

recce[1] *n chiefly Brit, informal* a reconnaissance.

recce[2] *v* (**recced** *or* **recceed, recceing**) *chiefly Brit, informal* to reconnoitre.

recede *v* **1a** to move back or away; to withdraw. **b** to slant backwards: *a receding chin.* **c** of hair or a hairline: to stop growing around the temples and above the forehead. **2** to grow less, smaller, or more distant; to diminish.

receipt *n* **1** a written or printed acknowledgment of having received goods or money. **2** the act of receiving. **3** (*usu in pl*) something, *esp* money, received.

receivable *adj* **1** capable of being received. **2** liable for payment.

receivables *pl n* amounts of money owed to a company and thus part of its assets.

receive *v* **1a** to acquire or be given. **b** to take delivery of. **c** *chiefly Brit, informal* to buy and sell (stolen goods). **2** to convert (an incoming signal, *esp* radio waves) into a form suitable for human perception.

3a to act in response to. **b** to elicit (a particular response). **4** to assimilate (e.g. ideas or impressions) through the mind or senses. **5** in tennis, squash, etc, to be the player who returns (the service of an opponent). **6** to suffer or be forced to experience. **7** to act as a receptacle or container for. **8** to accept as authoritative or true: *received wisdom*. **9a** to welcome, greet, or entertain formally. **b** to have a visit from. **c** to permit to enter; to admit.

Received Pronunciation *n* the form of British English pronunciation used by many educated people in southeastern England and widely regarded as the standard pronunciation.

receiver *n* **1a** a radio, television, or other part of a communications system that receives the signal. **b** the part of a telephone that contains the mouthpiece and earpiece. **2** a person appointed to administer the affairs of a business that is being wound up. **3** somebody who or something that receives.

receivership *n* **1** the office or function of a receiver. **2** the state of being in the hands of a receiver.

recension *n* **1** the critical revision of a text. **2** a revised text.

recent *adj* **1a** of a time not long past. **b** having lately come into existence. **2** (**Recent**) = HOLOCENE. ⋙ **recency** *n*, **recently** *adv*, **recentness** *n*.

receptacle *n* **1** an object that receives and contains something. **2** the end of the flower stalk of a flowering plant which bears the petals and stamens.

reception *n* **1** the action or process of receiving somebody or something. **2** a formal social gathering during which guests are received. **3** an office or desk where visitors or clients are received on arrival. **4** *Brit* a class for the youngest children in a primary school. **5** a response or reaction. **6** the receiving of a radio or television broadcast, or the quality of the signal received.

receptionist *n* a person employed to greet and assist callers or clients, e.g. at an office or hotel.

reception room *n* **1** a room in a private residence where guests may be entertained. **2** a room used for banquets and receptions in a hotel.

receptive *adj* able or inclined to receive, *esp* open and responsive to ideas, impressions, or suggestions. ⋙ **receptively** *adv*, **receptiveness** *n*, **receptivity** *n*.

receptor *n* a cell or group of cells that receives stimuli which are then transmitted as nerve impulses, e.g. a sense organ that receives information about temperature, light, sound, etc from the environment.

recess[1] *n* **1a** an alcove or niche. **b** an indentation or cleft. **2** (*in pl*) hidden, secret, or secluded places. **3a** a suspension of business or activity, e.g. of a legislative body or law court, usu for a period of rest. **b** *chiefly NAm* a break between school classes.

recess[2] *v* **1** (*usu in passive*) to put or install in a recess. **2** to make a recess in (e.g. a wall). **3** *chiefly NAm* to interrupt (e.g. a meeting) for a recess.

recession *n* **1** a period of reduced economic activity and prosperity. **2** *formal* the act or an instance of receding; a withdrawal. ⋙ **recessionary** *adj*.

recessional[1] *n* a hymn or musical piece sung or played while the clergy and choir withdraw at the conclusion of a church service.

recessional[2] *adj* **1** of a recession. **2** of a parliamentary recess.

recessive[1] *adj* **1** receding or tending to recede. **2** denoting the one of a pair of contrasting inherited characteristics that is suppressed if a dominant gene is present, or the gene that determines the characteristic: compare DOMINANT[1] (3).

recessive[2] *n* a recessive gene or inherited characteristic.

recharge *v* **1** to charge (*esp* a battery) again. **2** to renew (one's energies or strength). ⋙ **rechargeable** *adj*, **recharger** *n*.

recherché /rə'sheəshay/ *adj* **1** obscure or rare. **2** pretentious or affected.

recidivist *n* somebody who relapses, *esp* into criminal behaviour. ⋙ **recidivism** *n*, **recidivist** *adj*, **recidivistic** *adj*.

recipe /'resipi/ *n* **1** a list of ingredients and instructions for making a food dish. **2** a procedure likely to result in the specified thing: *a recipe for success*.

recipient *n* somebody who or something that receives. ⋙ **recipient** *adj*.

reciprocal[1] *adj* **1** felt or shown by both sides; mutual. **2** given, shown, felt, or done in return. **3** marked by or based on reciprocity. ⋙ **reciprocally** *adv*.

Usage note

reciprocal, mutual, *or* **common?** See note at MUTUAL.

reciprocal[2] *n* a quantity that when multiplied by a given quantity gives a product of one.

reciprocal pronoun *n* a pronoun, e.g. *each other*, used to denote mutual action or relationship.

reciprocate *v* **1** to give and take (something) mutually. **2** to return (something) in kind or degree. **3** to move forwards and backwards alternately. ⋙ **reciprocation** *n*.

reciprocating engine *n* an engine in which the to-and-fro motion of a piston is transformed into circular motion of the crankshaft.

reciprocity *n* **1** mutual dependence, action, or influence. **2** a mutual exchange of privileges, *esp* between countries or institutions.

recital *n* **1** a concert or public performance given by a musician or a small group of musicians. **2a** the act or an instance of reciting. **b** a detailed account. ⋙ **recitalist** *n*.

recitative *n* a rhythmically free style of singing used in opera and oratorio for dialogue and narration.

recite *v* **1** to repeat from memory or read aloud, *esp* before an audience. **2** to relate in detail; to enumerate. ⋙ **recitation** *n*, **reciter** *n*.

reck *v archaic* **1** to take account of. **2** to matter to; to concern.

reckless *adj* marked by lack of proper caution; careless of consequences. ⋙ **recklessly** *adv*, **recklessness** *n*.

reckon *v* **1a** to estimate or calculate. **b** to determine by reference to a fixed basis. **2** to consider or think of in a specified way. **3** *informal* to suppose or think. **4** (+ on) to place reliance on somebody or something. ✱ **reckon with** to take into account. **reckon without** to fail to consider or take into account; to ignore.

reckoning *n* **1** the act or an instance of reckoning. **2** a summing up; an appraisal. **3a** a calculation. **b** *archaic* an account or bill. **4** events regarded as retribution for earlier behaviour.

reclaim[1] *v* **1** to claim back; to recover. **2** to make (land) available for human use by changing natural conditions. **3** to obtain (a useful substance) from a waste product. **4** *literary* to rescue or convert (somebody) from an undesirable state; to reform. ⋙ **reclaimable** *adj*, **reclaimer** *n*, **reclamation** *n*.

reclaim[2] *n* **1** the act of reclaiming something. **2** the condition of being fit to be reclaimed: *beyond reclaim*.

recline *v* **1** to lean backwards or cause to lean backwards. **2** to be in or place in a relaxed position. ⋙ **reclinable** *adj.*

recliner *n* **1** a comfortable chair with a back that can be lowered to various angles for extra comfort. **2** a person who reclines.

recluse *n* somebody who leads a secluded or solitary life. ⋙ **reclusion** *n,* **reclusive** *adj.*

recognisance *n* see RECOGNIZANCE.

recognise *v* see RECOGNIZE.

recognition *n* the act of recognizing something or somebody, or the fact of being recognized.

recognizance *or* **-isance** *n* in law, a bond entered into before a court or magistrate that requires a person to do something, e.g. pay a debt or appear in court at a later date.

recognize *or* **-ise** *v* **1** to perceive (a thing or a person) to be something or somebody previously known or encountered. **2a** to acknowledge the status or validity of. **b** to acknowledge the existence or independence of (e.g. a government or state). **c** to admit that (something) is a fact. **3** to show appreciation of, e.g. by praise or reward. **4** e.g. of a computer: to be able to identify correctly and deal with (e.g. a printed character). ⋙ **recognizable** *adj.*

recoil[1] *v* **1** to shrink back physically or emotionally, e.g. in horror, fear, or disgust. **2** of a firearm: to move backwards sharply when fired. **3** to spring back or rebound. **4** (+ on/upon) to return with an adverse effect to a source or starting point.

recoil[2] *n* the act or an instance of recoiling, *esp* the backwards movement of a gun on firing.

recollect *v* **1** to bring back to the level of conscious awareness; to remember. **2** to bring (oneself) back to a state of composure or concentration. ⋙ **recollection** *n.*

recombinant *adj* denoting DNA formed by combining pieces of DNA from different organisms.

recombination *n* **1** the act or process of combining again. **2** the formation in offspring of new combinations of genes that did not occur in the parents, by processes whereby sections of the chromosomes become interchanged.

recommend *v* **1a** to endorse as fit, worthy, or competent. **b** to declare to be worth accepting or trying. **2** to advise (a course of action). **3** to make acceptable or desirable: *The school has other things to recommend it.* ⋙ **recommendable** *adj,* **recommendation** *n,* **recommendatory** *adj.*

recompense[1] *v* **1** to give something to (somebody) by way of compensation or payment, e.g. for a service rendered or damage incurred. **2** to amount to compensation for (something).

recompense[2] *n* an equivalent or a return for something done, suffered, or given.

reconcile *v* **1a** to restore (e.g. opposing factions) to friendship or harmony. **b** to settle or resolve (e.g. differences of opinion). **2** (+ with) to make (something) consistent or congruous with something else. **3** (+ to) to cause (somebody) to submit to or accept something. ⋙ **reconcilable** *adj,* **reconciliation** *n.*

recondite *adj* known only by a few people; obscure.

recondition *v Brit* to restore to good working condition, e.g. by replacing parts.

reconnaissance /ri'konəs(ə)ns/ *n* **1** an exploratory military survey of enemy territory or positions. **2** any preliminary or exploratory survey.

reconnoitre (*NAm* **reconnoiter**) /rekə'noytə/ *v* (**reconnoitres, reconnoitred, reconnoitring,** *NAm* **reconnoiters, reconnoitered, reconnoitering**) to make an exploratory military survey of (e.g. an enemy position or a region of land).

reconsider *v* to consider again with a view to change or revocation. ⋙ **reconsideration** *n.*

reconstitute *v* **1** to build or constitute again or differently. **2** to restore (food, etc) to its natural state by adding water, *esp* to dried ingredients. ⋙ **reconstitution** *n.*

reconstruct *v* **1** to restore to a previous condition; to rebuild. **2** to reorganize or reestablish. **3** to build up a mental image or physical representation of (e.g. a crime or a battle) from the available evidence. ⋙ **reconstruction** *n,* **reconstructive** *adj.*

reconvert *v* to cause to undergo conversion back to a former state. ⋙ **reconversion** *n.*

record[1] *v* **1a** to commit (something) to writing, film, etc so as to supply evidence of it. **b** to state or indicate for or as if for a record. **2a** to register by mechanical or other means. **b** to indicate (a measurement on a scale). **3** to give evidence of (something); to show (it). **4** to convert (e.g. sound) into a permanent form fit for reproduction. ⋙ **recordable** *adj.*

record[2] *n* **1a** a permanent account of something that serves as evidence of it. **b** something that recalls, relates, or commemorates past events or feats. **2** a body of known or recorded facts regarding something or somebody. **3** a list of previous criminal convictions. **4** a performance, occurrence, or condition that goes beyond others of its kind; *specif* the best recorded performance in a competitive sport. **5** a flat plastic disc with a spiral groove whose undulations encode musical or other sounds for reproduction on a record player. **6** a unit making up a computer file. ✱ **for the record** to be reported as official. **off the record** not for publication. **on record** in or into the status of being known, published, or documented. **put/set the record straight** to correct a mistake or misapprehension.

record-breaking *adj* bettering all previous attempts or surpassing all previous totals. ⋙ **record-breaker** *n.*

recorded delivery *n* a postal service available in Britain in which the delivery of a posted item is recorded.

recorder *n* **1** something that records. **2** a person who keeps official records. **3** (*often* **Recorder**) a barrister or solicitor who sits as a circuit judge or a part-time judge in the crown court. **4** a simple woodwind instrument consisting of a tube with usu eight finger holes and a mouthpiece. ⋙ **recordership** *n.*

recording *n* something, e.g. sound or a television programme, that has been recorded.

recordist *n* a person who makes recordings, *esp* sound recordings.

record player *n* an apparatus for playing records, consisting of a turntable, stylus, and amplifying equipment.

recount[1] *v* to relate in detail.

recount[2] *v* to count again.

recount[3] *n* a second or fresh counting, *esp* of votes.

recoup *v* to regain or make up for (something lost). ⋙ **recoupable** *adj,* **recoupment** *n.*

recourse *n* **1** a source of help or strength; a resort. **2** the use of somebody or something for help or protection: *to have recourse to the law.*

recover *v* **1** to regain possession or use of. **2** to regain a normal or stable position or condition, e.g. of health. **3a** to make up for (e.g. losses). **b** to obtain (e.g. costs) by legal action. **4** to obtain from an ore, waste product, etc. ⋙ **recoverable** *adj*, **recoverer** *n*.

re-cover *v* to provide (e.g. a chair) with a new cover.

recovery *n* (*pl* **-ies**) **1a** a return to normal health. **b** a regaining of balance or control, e.g. after a stumble or mistake. **c** an economic upturn, e.g. after a depression. **2** the recovering of something, e.g. a vehicle that has broken down.

recovery position *n Brit* a position in which an unconscious person is placed to prevent choking, with the body lying face down and to the side.

recreant *adj archaic* **1** cowardly. **2** unfaithful to duty or allegiance. ⋙ **recreancy** *n*, **recreant** *n*.

recreate *v* **1** to reproduce exactly. **2** to visualize or create (something that exists or has existed) in the imagination.

recreation *n* a pleasurable activity engaged in for relaxation or enjoyment.

re-creation *n* the act or an instance of recreating.

recreational *adj* **1** of or for recreation. **2** of drugs or their use: taken for pleasure. ⋙ **recreationally** *adv*.

recreation ground *n Brit* an open space on which games can be played, usu provided by the local council for public use.

recriminate *v* to make recriminations. ⋙ **recriminative** *adj*, **recriminatory** *adj*.

recrimination *n* (*usu in pl*) an accusation of wrongdoing made against somebody who has made a similar accusation.

recrudesce *v formal* of something undesirable, *esp* a disease: to break out or become active again. ⋙ **recrudescence** *n*, **recrudescent** *adj*.

recruit[1] *n* a newcomer to a field, occupation, or activity; *specif* a newly enlisted member of the armed forces.

recruit[2] *v* **1** to enlist (a person) as a recruit. **2** to enrol (a person) as a member of a group. **3** to secure the services of; to employ. **4** to obtain the help of. ⋙ **recruiter** *n*, **recruitment** *n*.

recta *n* pl of RECTUM.

rectal *adj* relating to or in the region of the rectum. ⋙ **rectally** *adv*.

rectangle *n* a polygon with four right angles and four sides, *esp* one with adjacent sides of different lengths. ⋙ **rectangular** *adj*.

rectifier *n* a device for converting alternating current into direct current.

rectify *v* (**-ies, -ied**) **1** to put right; to remedy or correct. **2** to convert (alternating current) to direct current. **3** to purify (e.g. alcohol), *esp* by repeated or fractional distillation. ⋙ **rectifiable** *adj*, **rectification** *n*.

rectilineal *adj* = RECTILINEAR.

rectilinear *adj* **1** moving in or forming a straight line. **2** characterized by straight lines.

rectitude *n formal* **1** moral integrity. **2** correctness in judgment or procedure.

recto *n* (*pl* **-os**) a right-hand page: compare VERSO.

rector *n* **1a** a person in charge of a parish; *specif* one in a Church of England parish where the tithes were formerly paid to the incumbent. **b** a Roman Catholic priest directing a church with no pastor or one whose pastor has other duties. **2** the head of a university or college. **3** a student elected to serve on a Scottish university's governing body. ⋙ **rectorate** *adj*, **rectorial** *adj*, **rectorship** *n*.

rectory *n* (*pl* **-ies**) **1** a rector's residence. **2** a benefice held by a rector.

rectum *n* (*pl* **rectums** *or* **recta**) the last part of the intestine, ending at the anus.

recumbent *adj* **1** lying down or reclining. **2** of a plant: growing close to the ground. **3** of a bodily organ: resting against another organ. ⋙ **recumbency** *n*, **recumbently** *adv*.

recuperate *v* **1** to regain a former healthy state or condition; to recover. **2** to regain (something lost). ⋙ **recuperable** *adj*, **recuperation** *n*, **recuperative** *adj*.

recur *v* (**recurred, recurring**) **1** to occur again, *esp* repeatedly or after an interval. **2** to come back to one's mind. ⋙ **recurrence** *n*, **recurring** *adj*.

recurrent *adj* returning or happening repeatedly or periodically. ⋙ **recurrently** *adv*.

recurring decimal *n* a decimal in which a particular digit or sequence of digits repeats itself indefinitely at some stage after the decimal point.

recursion *n* **1** *formal* a return. **2** in mathematics, the repeated application of a particular procedure to the previous result, e.g. to determine a sequence of numbers.

recursive *adj* **1** of or involving mathematical recursion. **2** denoting a computer program that calls itself into operation or calls other programs which in turn recall the original. ⋙ **recursively** *adv*.

recusant *n* **1** a person who refuses to accept or obey established authority. **2** formerly, a Roman Catholic refusing to attend services of the Church of England. ⋙ **recusance** *n*, **recusancy** *n*, **recusant** *adj*.

recycle *v* **1** to process (sewage, waste paper, glass, etc) for conversion back into a useful product. **2** to reclaim or re-use. ⋙ **recyclable** *adj*, **recycler** *n*.

red[1] *adj* (**redder, reddest**) **1** of the colour of blood or a ruby, at the end of the spectrum next to orange. **2** of hair or fur: in the colour range between orange and brown. **3** of the face: flushed, *esp* with anger or embarrassment. **4** of wine: made from dark grapes and coloured by their skins. **5** failing to show a profit: compare BLACK[1] (7). **6** *informal, derog* communist or socialist: compare WHITE[1] (10). **7** *archaic or literary* involving force, violence, or bloodshed. ⋙ **reddish** *adj*, **redly** *adv*, **redness** *n*.

red[2] *n* **1** a red colour. **2** *informal, derog* a communist or socialist. ✱ **in the red** financially not in credit; insolvent; not making a profit. **see red** *informal* to become angry suddenly.

redact *v* to prepare for publication; to edit. ⋙ **redaction** *n*, **redactor** *n*.

red admiral *n* a common N American and European butterfly that has broad orange-red bands on the forewings.

redback *n* a poisonous Australian spider that has a broad red stripe on its back.

red blood cell *n* any of the haemoglobin-containing cells that carry oxygen to the tissues and are responsible for the red colour of vertebrate blood; an erythrocyte: compare WHITE BLOOD CELL.

red-blooded *adj* full of vigour; virile.

redbreast *n chiefly Brit, informal* a robin.

redbrick *adj* denoting a British university founded between 1840 and World War II, as distinct from the ancient British universities.

redcap *n* **1** *Brit, informal* a military police officer. **2** *NAm* a railway porter.

red card *n* a red card held up by a football referee to indicate the sending-off of a player: compare YELLOW CARD. ⋙ **red-card** *v*.

red carpet *n* a long piece of red carpet laid down for an important guest to walk on.

red cell *n* = RED BLOOD CELL.

red cent *n NAm* **1** a one-cent coin. **2** a trivial amount.

redcoat *n* **1** a British soldier at a former time when scarlet jackets were worn. **2** in Britain, a person who works as an entertainer at a Butlin's holiday camp.

Red Crescent *n* the Red Cross as it exists in Muslim countries, with the sign of a crescent in place of the cross.

Red Cross *n* an international humanitarian organization that has as its emblem a red cross on a white background.

redcurrant *n* a small red edible berry.

red deer *n* a large common deer of temperate Europe and Asia that has a reddish brown coat in summer.

Red Delicious *n* a variety of eating apple with a red skin and soft sweet flesh.

redden *v* **1** to make or become red or reddish. **2** to blush.

reddle *n* = RED OCHRE.

red dwarf *n* a star with a low surface temperature and a mass about one tenth of that of the sun.

redeem *v* **1a** to offset the bad effect of. **b** to atone for (a mistake, error of judgment, etc). **c** to make worthwhile; to retrieve. **2a** to release from blame or debt; to clear. **b** to free from the consequences of sin or evil. **c** to make up for an earlier poor performance or wrongdoing by (oneself). **3a** to get, win, or buy back, e.g. by repaying a loan or debt. **b** to remove the obligation of (e.g. a bond) by making a stipulated payment. **c** to convert (trading stamps, tokens, etc) into money or goods. **4** to fulfil (e.g. a promise). ⋙ **redeemable** *adj*, **redeeming** *adj*.

Redeemer *n* **1** (**the Redeemer**) Jesus Christ regarded as the saviour of humankind. **2** (**redeemer**) a person who redeems somebody or something.

redemption *n* **1** the act of redeeming or the fact of being redeemed. **2** something that redeems somebody from sin or makes up for past offences. ⋙ **redemptive** *adj*.

red ensign *n* a red flag with a Union Jack in the upper corner flown by British merchant ships and pleasure boats.

redeploy *v* to transfer (e.g. troops or workers) from one area or activity to another. ⋙ **redeployment** *n*.

redevelop *v* to design, develop, or build (something, e.g. a deteriorating or depressed area) again. ⋙ **redeveloper** *n*, **redevelopment** *n*.

red-eye *n* **1** in photography, an effect that makes people seem to have red eyes, caused by the flash being too close to the lens of the camera. **2** *chiefly NAm, informal* a passenger aircraft making a long-distance overnight flight. **3** *NAm, informal* cheap whisky.

red-faced *adj* embarrassed, or flushed with embarrassment.

red flag *n* **1** an international symbol of danger. **2** the symbol of communism or socialism.

red giant *n* a star that has a low surface temperature and a large diameter relative to the sun.

red grouse *n* a dark reddish brown grouse that is an important game bird and is found on the moors of N England and Scotland.

red-handed *adj* in the act of committing a crime or misdeed.

redhead *n* a person with red hair. ⋙ **redheaded** *adj*.

red heat *n* the temperature at which a substance is red-hot.

red herring *n* **1** a herring cured by salting and smoking to a dark brown colour. **2** something irrelevant that distracts attention from the real issue.

Word history

(sense 2) from the practice of drawing a red herring across a trail to confuse hunting dogs.

red-hot *adj* **1** glowing red with heat; extremely hot. **2** arousing enthusiasm; very popular. **3** marked by intense emotion; ardent.

red-hot poker *n* a S African plant of the lily family with tall erect spikes of yellow flowers changing to bright red towards the top.

redid *v* past tense of REDO.

Red Indian *n dated, offensive* a Native American.

redingote *n* **1** an overcoat with a large collar worn, *esp* by men, in the 18th and 19th cents. **2** a woman's lightweight coat with a cut-away front below the waist.

redirect *v* **1** to change the course or direction of. **2** to send (post) to a different address. ⋙ **redirection** *n*.

redistribution *n* the distribution of something, e.g. wealth, in different and usu more appropriate or fair proportions.

red lead *n* a red lead oxide formerly used in glass and ceramics, as a paint pigment, etc.

Red Leicester *n* = LEICESTER.

red-letter day *n* a day of special significance, *esp* a particularly happy occasion.

Word history

from the practice of marking holy days in red letters in church calendars.

red light *n* a red warning light commanding traffic to stop.

red-light district *n* a district that has many brothels.

redline *v chiefly NAm, informal* **1** to refuse to lend money or to provide insurance cover to (somebody living in a high-risk area). **2** to drive (a vehicle) at its maximum rpm.

red meat *n* dark-coloured meat, e.g. beef or lamb: compare WHITE MEAT.

red mullet *n* a food fish with reddish skin and long barbels on its chin, found throughout the Mediterranean.

redneck *n NAm, informal, derog* **1** a white member of the rural labouring class of the southern USA. **2** a bigoted reactionary.

redo *v* (*third person sing. present tense* **redoes,** *past tense* **redid,** *past part.* **redone**) **1** to do again or differently. **2** *informal* to decorate (a room or interior of a building) anew.

red ochre *n* a red earthy mineral containing iron oxide, used as a pigment.

redolent *adj* **1** (+ of/with) suggesting a particular quality; evocative. **2** (+ of/with) full of a specified fragrance. **3** *archaic or literary* having a pleasant smell. ⋙ **redolence** *n*, **redolently** *adv*.

redone *v* past part. of REDO.

redouble *v* to make or become greater, more numerous, or more intense.

redoubt *n* **1** a small usu temporary enclosed defensive fortified structure. **2** a secure place; a stronghold.

redoubtable *adj* **1** causing fear or alarm; formidable. **2** inspiring or worthy of awe or reverence. ⋙ **redoubtably** *adv*.

redound *v formal* **1** (+ to) to lead or contribute to something. **2** *archaic* (+ on/upon) to rebound on or upon somebody.

redox *n* (*used before a noun*) of or involving both oxidation and reduction.

red panda *n* = PANDA (2).

red pepper *n* the ripe red fruit of the capsicum or sweet pepper.

redpoll *n* a small finch that resembles and is closely related to the linnet.

red poll *n* an animal of a large red hornless breed of dairy and beef cattle.

redress[1] *v* **1** to set right; to remedy. **2** to adjust evenly, making it stable or equal again: *to redress the balance.* ⋙ **redressable** *adj*, **redresser** *n*.

redress[2] *n* **1** compensation for wrong or loss. **2** the putting right of what is wrong, or the possibility of putting it right.

re-dress *v* to dress (e.g. a wound) again.

red rose *n* **1** an emblem of the House of Lancaster. **2** a symbol of the Labour Party in Britain.

red salmon *n* = SOCKEYE.

red setter *n* = IRISH SETTER.

redshank *n* a wading bird with pale red legs and feet, found throughout Europe and Asia.

red shift *n* a shift in the wavelengths of the light emitted by a celestial body when seen from a distant point, e.g. the earth, from their normal positions in the spectrum towards longer wavelengths.

redskin *n dated, offensive* a Native American.

red snapper *n* a reddish food fish found in warm seas.

red spider *n* a small mite that attacks crop plants.

red squirrel *n* a reddish brown Eurasian squirrel native to British woodlands.

redstart *n* **1** a small songbird with a chestnut tail and underparts, native to Europe. **2** an American warbler with conspicuous red or orange markings.

red tape *n* excessively complex bureaucratic routine that results in delay.

reduce *v* **1** to make or become less in size, amount, degree, or value. **2** to make or become more concentrated, e.g. by boiling. **3** to lower the price of. **4** to lower in grade, rank, condition, or status. **5** to bring or force to a specified state or condition: *reduced to tears.* **6** to change to a simpler or more basic form. **7** *archaic* to force (e.g. a city) to capitulate. **8a** to cause (a chemical compound) to lose oxygen atoms. **b** to combine (a chemical substance) with hydrogen; to add hydrogen atoms to. **c** to add one or more electrons to (e.g. an atom, molecule, or ion). **9** to correct (e.g. a fracture of a bone) by bringing the displaced or broken parts back into their normal positions. **10** *chiefly NAm* to lose weight by dieting. ⋙ **reducer** *n*, **reducible** *adj*.

reducing agent *n* a substance that reduces a chemical compound, usu by donating electrons: compare OXIDIZING AGENT.

reductant *n* = REDUCING AGENT.

reductio ad absurdum *n* proof of the falsity of a proposition by revealing the absurdity of its logical consequences.

reduction *n* **1** the act or an instance of reducing. **2** the amount by which something is reduced. **3** a reproduction, e.g. of a picture, in a smaller size. **4** a liquid, e.g. a sauce, that has been reduced.

reductionism *n* a procedure or theory that reduces complex data or phenomena to simple terms, *esp* oversimplification. ⋙ **reductionist** *n and adj*.

reductive *adj* **1** tending to reduce complex data or phenomena to simplified or oversimplified terms. **2** of chemical reduction.

redundancy *n* (*pl* **-ies**) **1** being redundant. **2** the part of a message that can be eliminated without loss of essential information. **3** *chiefly Brit* the act or an instance of dismissing a redundant employee.

redundant *adj* **1a** no longer useful or necessary; superfluous. **b** characterized by or containing an excess; *specif* excessively verbose. **2** *chiefly Brit* no longer required for a job. ⋙ **redundantly** *adv*.

reduplicate *v* **1** to make or perform (something) again; to copy or repeat (it). **2** to form (a word) by reduplication. ⋙ **reduplicate** *adj*.

reduplication *n* **1** the act or an instance of reduplicating. **2** the doubling of a word, or part of a word, with or without partial modification, e.g. in *hocus pocus* or *dilly-dally*. ⋙ **reduplicative** *adj*.

redwing *n* a Eurasian thrush with red patches beneath its wings.

redwood *n* a Californian timber tree of the pine family with durable reddish wood that often reaches a height of 100m (about 300ft).

reebok *n* see RHEBOK.

re-echo *v* (**re-echoes, re-echoed, re-echoing**) **1** to repeat or return an echo. **2** to repeat (something said).

reed *n* **1** a tall grass that grows in wet or marshy areas, having thin, often prominently jointed stems. **2a** reeds used for thatching. **b** the stem of a reed. **3** a thin tongue or flattened tube of cane, metal, or plastic, fastened over an air opening in a musical instrument, e.g. an organ, oboe, or clarinet, which produces a sound by vibration. **4** a person or thing too weak to rely on.

reeding *n* **1** a narrow semicircular convex moulding that is usu one of several set parallel as architectural decoration. **2** architectural decoration consisting of a series of reedings.

reedmace *n* a tall reedy marsh plant with brown furry fruiting spikes.

reed organ *n* a keyboard instrument in which the wind acts on a set of freely vibrating reeds.

re-educate *v* to cause to think or behave in a different way. ⋙ **re-education** *n*.

reedy *adj* (**-ier, -iest**) **1** full of, covered with, or made of reeds. **2** slender or frail. **3** of a voice: having the tonal quality of a reed instrument, *esp* thin and high. ⋙ **reediness** *n*.

reef[1] *n* **1** a ridge of rocks, sand, or coral at or near the surface of water. **2** a vein of ore; a lode.

reef[2] *n* a part of a sail taken in or let out to regulate the area exposed to the wind.

reef[3] *v* to reduce the area of (a sail) exposed to the wind by rolling up or taking in a portion.

reefer[1] *n* a close-fitting usu double-breasted jacket of thick cloth.

reefer[2] *n informal* a cannabis cigarette.

reefer[3] *n* somebody who reefs a sail.

reefer jacket *n* = REEFER[1].

reef knot *n* a symmetrical knot made of two half-knots tied in opposite directions.

reek[1] *v* **1a** to have a strong or offensive smell. **b** (+ of/with) to give a strong impression of some usu undesirable quality or feature. **2** *archaic* to give off smoke or vapour.

reek[2] *n* **1** a strong or disagreeable smell. **2** *chiefly Scot, N Eng* smoke or vapour. ⋙ **reeky** *adj*.

reel[1] *n* **1** a spool for thread, film, tape, cable, etc. **2** a quantity of something wound on a reel. **3** a small wheel at the butt of a fishing rod for winding the line. **4** a part of a film.

reel[2] *v* **1** to wind on or as if on a reel. **2** (+ in) to draw (a fish) out of the water by reeling a line. **3** (+ in) to entice (somebody) slowly and steadily.

reel[3] *v* **1** to be giddy or bewildered. **2** to waver or fall back, e.g. from a blow. **3** to walk or move unsteadily, e.g. from intoxication.

reel[4] *n* a lively Scottish or Irish dance in which two or more couples perform a series of circular figures and winding movements.

reel off *v* to say or repeat readily and without pause.

reel-to-reel *adj* denoting or using magnetic tape passing between two reels that are not in a cassette or cartridge.

re-entrant *adj* of an angle, point, etc: directed or pointing inwards.

re-entry *n* (*pl* **-ies**) **1** the return to and entry of the earth's atmosphere by a space vehicle. **2** a second or new entry, e.g. to a country.

reeve[1] *n* **1** the local administrative agent of an Anglo-Saxon king. **2** a medieval English manor officer with the job of ensuring that feudal obligations were discharged.

reeve[2] *v* (*past tense and past part.* **rove** *or* **reeved**) **1** to pass (e.g. a rope) through a hole or opening. **2** to fasten by passing through a hole or round something.

reeve[3] *n* a Eurasian bird, the female of the ruff.

re-export[1] *v* to export (something that has been imported), e.g. after further processing. ⪢ **re-exportation** *n,* **re-exporter** *n.*

re-export[2] *n* the act of re-exporting, or something re-exported.

ref *n informal* the referee of a football match or other sporting contest.

ref. *abbr* **1** reference. **2** referred.

refection *n literary* a light meal, or the taking of one.

refectory *n* (*pl* **-ies**) a dining hall in an institution, e.g. a monastery or college.

refectory table *n* a long narrow dining table with heavy legs.

refer *v* (**referred, referring**) **1** (+ to) to direct attention to something by mentioning or alluding to it. **2** (+ to) to have recourse to something, e.g. for information; to consult it. **3** to send or direct (somebody) for treatment, aid, information, testimony, etc. **4** to explain (something) in terms of a general cause. **5** to fail (somebody taking an examination). ✱ **refer to drawer** *Brit* used to inform the payee of a cheque that payment has been suspended. ⪢ **referable** *adj,* **referral** *n,* **referrer** *n.*

referee[1] *n* **1** an official who supervises the play and enforces the rules in a sport, e.g. football or boxing. **2a** a person to whom a legal matter is referred for investigation or settlement. **b** a person who reviews an academic paper before publication. **c** a person who gives a professional or character reference to a candidate's prospective employer.

referee[2] *v* (**referees, refereed, refereeing**) to act as a referee for.

reference[1] *n* **1** the act of referring to or consulting something or somebody for information, guidance, etc. **2** bearing on or connection with a matter. **3a** an allusion or mention. **b** something that refers somebody to another source of information. **c** a source of information to which somebody is referred. **4** a statement of the character, ability, or qualifications of a person seeking employment or appointment. **5** a standard for measuring, evaluating, etc. ⪢ **referential** *adj.*

reference[2] *v* to provide (e.g. a book) with references to authorities and sources of information.

reference library *n* a library in which books and other materials are for consultation only, not for loan.

referendum *n* (*pl* **referendums** *or* **referenda**) a vote by the whole electorate on a single question or measure proposed by a legislative body or by popular initiative.

referent *n* in linguistics, the thing that a symbol, e.g. a word or sign, stands for.

referred pain *n* pain that is not felt at the actual source but in another part of the body.

refill[1] *n* **1** a fresh supply of a drink in the same cup or glass. **2** a replacement for a container of a consumable substance, e.g. ink in a pen.

refill[2] *v* to make or become full again. ⪢ **refillable** *adj.*

refinance *v* to renew or reorganize the financing of (something), e.g. at a lower rate of interest.

refine *v* **1** to free (a raw material) from impurities. **2** to improve or perfect (e.g. a method) by pruning or polishing. ⪢ **refiner** *n.*

refined *adj* **1a** without crudeness or vulgarity; elegant, fastidious, or cultivated. **b** subtle and sophisticated. **2** processed industrially to remove impurities.

refinement *n* **1** refining or being refined. **2a** a subtle feature, method, or distinction. **b** a contrivance or device intended to improve or perfect.

refinery *n* (*pl* **-ies**) a plant where raw materials, e.g. oil or sugar, are refined.

refit[1] *v* (**refitted, refitting**) to fit out (e.g. a ship) again with new fixtures and equipment.

refit[2] *n* a repair or replacement of parts, fittings, etc.

reflate *v* to expand the volume of available money and credit or economic activity of (an economy), *esp* as a result of government policy. ⪢ **reflation** *n,* **reflationary** *adj.*

reflect *v* **1** to send or throw (light, sound, etc) back or at an angle. **2** to show as an image or likeness; to mirror. **3** to make (something) manifest or apparent. **4** to think quietly and calmly. **5** (+ on) to tend to bring about a specified appearance or impression: *The results reflect unfavourably on the department.*

reflectance *n* a measure of the ability of a surface to reflect light or other radiant energy, equal to the ratio of the rate of flow of reflected energy to that of energy falling on the surface.

reflecting telescope *n* a telescope using a mirror that reflects light rays as its principal focusing element rather than a lens.

reflection *n* **1** the reflecting of light, sound, etc. **2** an image given back by or as if by a reflecting surface. **3** (*usu* + on) an often obscure or indirect criticism. **4** consideration, or a thought formed by consideration. ⪢ **reflectional** *adj.*

reflective *adj* **1** capable of reflecting light, images, or sound waves. **2** thoughtful or deliberative. **3** relating to or caused by reflection. ⪢ **reflectively** *adv,* **reflectiveness** *n,* **reflectivity** *n.*

reflector *n* **1** something intended to reflect light, radio waves, etc. **2** = REFLECTING TELESCOPE.

reflex[1] *n* **1a** an action that takes place automatically in response to a stimulus and involves no conscious thought. **b** (*in pl*) the power of acting or responding in this way. **2** a reproduction or reflection that corresponds to some usu specified original. **3** *archaic* reflected heat, light, or colour.

reflex[2] *adj* **1** of an action: produced by a reflex without intervention of consciousness. **2** of an angle: greater than 180° but less than 360°. **3** *archaic* of light: reflected. **4** bent, turned, or directed back. ⪢ **reflexly** *adv.*

reflex camera *n* a camera in which the image formed by the lens is reflected onto a ground-glass screen or is seen through the viewfinder for focusing and composition.

reflexion *n archaic* = REFLECTION.

reflexive *adj* **1a** denoting a pronoun, e.g. *himself*, that refers back to the subject of a clause or sentence. **b** denoting a verb whose action is directed back on the grammatical subject, e.g. *to perjure oneself*. **2** relating to a physiological reflex. ➤➤ **reflexively** *adv*, **reflexiveness** *n*, **reflexivity** *n*.

reflexology *n* a therapy used in alternative medicine that involves massaging nerve endings in the feet to relieve tension or to treat disorders in specific parts of the body. ➤➤ **reflexologist** *n*.

reflux[1] *n* **1** in chemistry, the process of heating a liquid to form vapours that cool, condense, and return to be heated again. **2** *technical* a flowing back; an ebb.

reflux[2] *v* **1** in chemistry, to undergo reflux. **2** *technical* to flow back or return.

refocus *v* (**refocused** *or* **refocussed, refocusing** *or* **refocussing**) **1** to focus (a lens or the eyes) again. **2** to change the emphasis or direction of.

reforest *v* to renew the forest cover of (an area) by seeding or planting. ➤➤ **reforestation** *n*.

reform[1] *v* **1** to change for the better. **2** to induce or cause (somebody) to adopt a more virtuous, healthier, etc way of life. ➤➤ **reformable** *adj*, **reformative** *adj*, **reformatory** *adj*.

reform[2] *n* the act or an instance of reforming or being reformed.

re-form *v* to form again.

reformat *v* (**reformatted, reformatting**) to arrange in or put into a new format.

reformation *n* **1** reforming or being reformed. **2** (**the Reformation**) a 16th-cent. religious movement marked ultimately by the rejection of papal authority and the establishment of the Protestant Churches. ➤➤ **reformational** *adj*.

reformatory *n* (*pl* **-ies**) *NAm, dated* a penal institution to which young or first offenders are sent for reform.

Reformed *adj* Protestant; *specif* of the Calvinist Protestant Churches.

reformer *n* **1** somebody who works for or urges reform. **2** (**Reformer**) a leader of the Protestant Reformation.

reformism *n* a doctrine, policy, or movement of reform. ➤➤ **reformist** *n and adj*.

Reform Judaism *n* a liberalizing and modernizing branch of Judaism.

reform school *n* an institution to which young offenders were formerly sent, instead of prison.

refract *v* to deflect (e.g. light) by refraction.

refracting telescope *n* a telescope using a lens that concentrates light rays as its principal focusing element rather than a mirror.

refraction *n* the deflection or deviation of a wave, e.g. a beam of light, from one straight path to another when passing at an angle from one medium into another, e.g. from glass into air.

refractive *adj* **1** of a substance, lens, etc: having power to cause refraction. **2** of or due to refraction. ➤➤ **refractively** *adv*, **refractivity** *n*.

refractive index *n* the ratio of the velocity of light or other radiation in two adjacent mediums.

refractor *n* **1** something that causes refraction, e.g. a lens. **2** = REFRACTING TELESCOPE.

refractory *adj* **1** *formal* resisting control or authority; stubborn or unmanageable. **2** resistant to treatment or cure. **3** difficult to fuse, corrode, or draw out; *esp* capable of enduring high temperatures. ➤➤ **refractoriness** *n*.

refrain[1] *v* (+ from) to keep oneself from doing, feeling, or indulging in something.

refrain[2] *n* a regularly recurring phrase or verse, *esp* at the end of each division of a poem or song; a chorus.

refrangible *adj* capable of being refracted. ➤➤ **refrangibility** *n*.

refresh *v* **1a** to restore strength or vigour to, e.g. by food or rest. **b** to restore freshness or colour to (something stale or faded). **2** to restore or maintain by a fresh supply; to replenish. **3** to arouse or stimulate (e.g. the memory). **4** in computing, to update the data in (a file, Web page, etc).

refresher *n* **1** something, e.g. a drink, that refreshes. **2** a course of instruction designed to keep one abreast of developments in one's professional field. **3** an extra fee paid to a lawyer in a protracted case.

refresher course *n* = REFRESHER (2).

refreshing *adj* **1** providing refreshment. **2** agreeably stimulating because of freshness or newness. ➤➤ **refreshingly** *adv*.

refreshment *n* **1** refreshing or being refreshed. **2a** something, e.g. food or drink, that refreshes. **b** (*in pl*) assorted food and drink, *esp* for a light snack.

refried beans *n* dried beans that have been boiled, mashed, and fried with seasonings, *esp* in Mexican cookery.

refrigerant[1] *n* a substance used in refrigeration.

refrigerant[2] *adj* causing cooling or freezing.

refrigerate *v* to make or keep (something) cold or cool; *specif* to freeze or chill (e.g. food) for preservation. ➤➤ **refrigeration** *n*, **refrigeratory** *adj*.

refrigerator *n* an insulated appliance for keeping food, drink, etc cool.

refringent *adj* refractive or refracting. ➤➤ **refringence** *n*.

refuel *v* (**refuelled, refuelling,** *NAm* **refueled, refueling**) to provide with or take on additional fuel.

refuge *n* **1** a place that provides shelter or protection from danger or distress. **2** a person, thing, or course of action that is resorted to in difficulties: *Patriotism is the last refuge of a scoundrel* — Dr Johnson.

refugee *n* somebody who flees to a foreign country to escape danger or persecution.

refulgence *n formal or literary* radiance or brilliance. ➤➤ **refulgent** *adj*, **refulgently** *adv*.

refund[1] *v* **1** to return (money) to somebody, e.g. a dissatisfied customer. **2** to pay (somebody) back. ➤➤ **refundable** *adj*.

refund[2] *n* **1** the act or an instance of refunding. **2** a sum refunded.

refurbish *v* to repair, redecorate, and usu re-equip (e.g. a house). ➤➤ **refurbishment** *n*.

refusal *n* **1** the act or an instance of refusing. **2** the right or option of refusing or accepting something before others.

refuse[1] *v* **1** to show or express unwillingness to accept or do (something). **2** to be unwilling to allow or grant (something) to (somebody). **3** to withhold acceptance, compliance, or permission. **4** of a horse: to decline to jump over (e.g. a fence). ➤➤ **refuser** *n*.

refuse[2] *n* worthless or useless stuff that has been thrown away; rubbish.

refusenik *n* **1** formerly, a Soviet Jew who was refused permission to emigrate, *esp* to Israel. **2**

somebody who refuses to accept a situation or proposal; a dissenter.

refute *v* **1** to prove wrong by argument or evidence. **2** to deny the truth or accuracy of (e.g. a claim). ⋙ **refutable** *adj,* **refutation** *n,* **refuter** *n.*

Usage note

To *refute* statements, accusations, or people is properly to prove them wrong by producing evidence or arguments against them, not merely to assert that they are wrong.

regain *v* to gain or reach again; to recover.

regal *adj* **1** of or suitable for a king or queen. **2** stately or splendid. ⋙ **regality** *n,* **regally** *adv.*

regale *v* **1** to entertain sumptuously. **2** to give pleasure or amusement to.

regalia *pl n* (*used as sing. or pl*) **1** the ceremonial emblems or symbols indicative of royalty. **2** special dress, *esp* official finery.

regard[1] *n* **1** attention or consideration. **2** a protective interest; care. **3** a feeling of respect and affection; esteem. **4** (*in pl*) friendly greetings. **5** an aspect to be taken into consideration; a respect: *We were fortunate in that regard.* **6** a gaze or look. ✱ **in/with regard to** with respect to; concerning.

regard[2] *v* **1** (*usu* + as/with) to think of or feel about in a specified way; to consider. **2** to look steadily at. **3** to relate to; to concern. **4** to pay attention to; to take into consideration or account. ✱ **as regards** in so far as it concerns.

regardful *adj formal* (+ of) heedful or observant.

regarding *prep* about; on the subject of.

regardless[1] *adj* (+ of) heedless or careless. ⋙ **regardlessly** *adv,* **regardlessness** *n.*

regardless[2] *adv* despite everything.

regardless of *prep* in spite of.

regatta *n* a series of boat races.

Regency *adj* of or resembling the styles, e.g. of furniture or dress, prevalent during the time of the Prince Regent (1811–20).

regency *n* (*pl* **-ies**) **1** the office, period of rule, or government of a regent. **2** (*used as sing. or pl*) a body of regents.

regenerate[1] *v* **1a** to replace (a body part or tissue) by new growth. **b** to produce (something) from a derivative or modified form, *esp* by chemical treatment. **2a** to change radically and for the better. **b** to subject to spiritual or moral renewal or revival. ⋙ **regeneration** *n,* **regenerative** *adj,* **regenerator** *n.*

regenerate[2] *adj* spiritually reborn or converted.

regent *n* somebody who governs a kingdom in the minority, absence, or disability of the sovereign. ⋙ **regent** *adj.*

reggae /'regay/ *n* popular music of West Indian origin, combining elements of rock, soul, and calypso, that is characterized by a strong accent on the usu unaccented beats in a bar.

regicide *n* **1** the act of murdering a king. **2** a person who commits regicide. ⋙ **regicidal** *adj.*

regime *or* **régime** /ray'zheem/ *n* **1a** a form of management or government. **b** a government in power. **2a** = REGIMEN. **b** a regular pattern of occurrence or action, e.g. of seasonal rainfall.

regimen *n* a systematic plan, e.g. of diet, exercise, or medical treatment, adopted to achieve some end.

regiment[1] *n* **1** a permanent military unit consisting of a number of companies, troops, batteries, or battalions. **2** a large number or group. **3** *archaic* governmental rule. ⋙ **regimental** *adj,* **regimentally** *adv.*

regiment[2] *v* to subject (people or things) to strict and stultifying organization or control. ⋙ **regimentation** *n.*

regimentals *pl n* formal military uniform or dress, *esp* that of a particular regiment.

Regina /ri'jienə/ *n* **1** a title given to a reigning queen and used after the first name. **2** used in legal cases, when the British monarch is a queen, to denote the Crown as a party to the action.

region *n* **1a** an indefinite area of the world or universe. **b** a broadly uniform geographical or ecological area. **2** an administrative area. **3** an indefinite area surrounding a specified body part. ✱ **in the region of** approximately.

regional *adj* **1** of or characteristic of a region. **2** affecting a particular region; localized. ⋙ **regionally** *adv.*

regionalise *v* see REGIONALIZE.

regionalism *n* **1** development of an administrative system based on areas. **2** a characteristic feature of a geographical area, e.g. a dialect word or phrase. ⋙ **regionalist** *n and adj.*

regionalize *or* **-ise** *v* to arrange (e.g. a country) in administrative regions. ⋙ **regionalization** *n.*

register[1] *n* **1** a written record containing official entries of items, names, transactions, etc. **2a** a record of pupils' attendance at school. **b** a list of qualified or available individuals. **3a** a part of the range of a human voice or musical instrument. **b** an organ stop. **4** the language style and vocabulary appropriate to particular circumstances. **5** a condition of correct alignment or proper relative position, e.g. of the plates used in colour printing. **6** a device, e.g. in a computer, for temporarily storing and working on small amounts of data.

register[2] *v* **1a** to enter (information) officially in a register. **b** to put one's name in a register. **c** to enrol formally. **d** to record automatically; to indicate. **2a** to show (an emotion) through facial expression or body language. **b** of an emotion: to be shown in this way. **3a** to become aware of; to perceive. **b** to make a mental note of. **4** to make or convey an impression. **5** to correspond exactly. ⋙ **registrable** *adj,* **registrant** *n.*

register office *n Brit* a place where births, marriages, and deaths are recorded and civil marriages are conducted.

registrar *n* **1a** an official recorder or keeper of records. **b** a senior administrative officer of a university. **c** a court official who deals with administrative matters and acts as a subordinate judge. **2** *Brit* a senior hospital doctor ranking below a consultant.

registration *n* **1** the act or an instance of registering or being registered. **2** = REGISTRATION NUMBER.

registration document *n Brit* an official document relating to a motor vehicle that gives the registration number, make, engine size, etc and details of the current ownership.

registration mark *n* = REGISTRATION NUMBER.

registration number *n Brit* an identifying combination of letters and numbers assigned to a motor vehicle.

registry *n* (*pl* **-ies**) **1** a place of registration; *specif* a register office. **2** registering or being registered.

registry office *n* = REGISTER OFFICE.

Regius professor /'reejəs/ *n* a holder of a professorship founded by royal subsidy at a British university.

regnal *adj* of a reign; *specif* calculated from a monarch's accession: *in his eighth regnal year.*

regnant *adj* reigning, usu as opposed to being a royal consort.

regress[1] *n* = REGRESSION.

regress[2] *v* **1** to undergo or exhibit regression, *esp* to an earlier state or condition. **2** to induce, *esp* by hypnosis, a state of psychological regression in. ⋙ **regressor** *n.*

regression *n* **1** the act or an instance of declining or moving backwards. **2a** a trend or shift towards a lower, less perfect, or earlier state. **b** reversion to an earlier mental or behavioural level, *esp* of childhood or a supposed previous life.

regressive *adj* **1** tending to regress or produce regression. **2** characterized by or showing regression. **3** of a tax: decreasing in rate as the amount taxed increases. ⋙ **regressively** *adv,* **regressiveness** *n.*

regret[1] *v* (**regretted, regretting**) **1** to be very sorry about. **2** to mourn the loss or death of.

regret[2] *n* **1** grief or sorrow tinged with disappointment, longing, or remorse. **2** (*in pl*) a conventional expression of disappointment or apology, *esp* on declining an invitation. ⋙ **regretful** *adj,* **regretfulness** *n.*

regretfully *adv* **1** in a regretful manner. **2** *nonstandard* regrettably.

regrettable *adj* other than as one would wish; unwelcome.

regrettably *adv* **1** in a regrettable manner; to a regrettable extent. **2** it is regrettable that.

regroup *v* to reorganize or become reorganized, e.g. after a setback or defeat, for renewed activity.

regular[1] *adj* **1** formed or arranged according to some rule, pattern, or type. **2** of a polygon: having sides of equal length and angles of equal size. **3a** steady or uniform in course, practice, or occurrence; habitual, usual, or constant. **b** recurring or functioning at fixed or uniform intervals. **4** constituted or done in conformity with established or prescribed usages, rules, etc. **5** in grammar, of a word, *esp* a verb: conforming to the normal pattern of inflection. **6** complete or absolute. **7** *NAm* standard or medium. **8a** belonging to a religious order. **b** denoting or belonging to a permanent standing army. ⋙ **regularity** *n,* **regularly** *adv.*

regular[2] *n* **1** somebody who is usu present or participating, *esp* a habitual customer. **2a** a member of the regular clergy. **b** a soldier in a regular army.

regularize *or* **-ise** *v* to make regular. ⋙ **regularization** *n.*

regulate *v* **1** to control or direct according to rules. **2** to bring order, method, or uniformity to. **3** to fix or adjust the time, amount, degree, or rate of. ⋙ **regulative** *adj,* **regulator** *n,* **regulatory** *adj.*

regulation *n* **1** the act or an instance of regulating or being regulated. **2a** an authoritative rule dealing with details or procedure. **b** a rule or order having the force of law. **3** (*used before a noun*) conforming to regulations; official.

regulo *n Brit* the temperature in a gas oven expressed as a specified number.

regurgitate *v* **1** to bring (incompletely digested food) back from the stomach to the mouth. **2** to reproduce in speech or writing with little or no alteration. ⋙ **regurgitation** *n.*

rehab *n informal* rehabilitation.

rehabilitate *v* **1a** to restore (somebody) to a condition of health or useful activity, e.g. after illness or imprisonment. **b** to restore (something) to a former capacity or state, e.g. of efficiency or soundness. **2** to reestablish the good name of. ⋙ **rehabilitation** *n,* **rehabilitative** *adj.*

rehash[1] *v* to present or use again in another form without substantial change or improvement.

rehash[2] *n* something rehashed.

rehearsal *n* **1** a practice session, *esp* of a play, concert, etc preparatory to a public performance. **2** the act or an instance of rehearsing.

rehearse *v* **1a** to hold a rehearsal of (a play, piece of music, etc). **b** to engage in a rehearsal. **2a** to present an account of (something) again. **b** to recount (points) in order. ⋙ **rehearser** *n.*

reheat[1] *v* to heat (e.g. cooked food) again. ⋙ **reheater** *n.*

reheat[2] *n* the injection of fuel into the tailpipe of a turbojet engine to obtain extra thrust by combustion with uncombined air in the exhaust gases.

rehoboam /ree·ə'boh·əm/ *n* a wine bottle, *esp* for champagne, that contains six times the amount of a standard bottle.

rehouse *v* to establish in new or better-quality housing.

rehydrate *v* to restore fluid lost in dehydration to (something or somebody). ⋙ **rehydration** *n.*

Reich /riekh/ *n* the German empire.

reify *v* (**-ies, -ied**) to regard (something abstract) as a material thing. ⋙ **reification** *n.*

reign[1] *n* **1** the time during which somebody or something reigns. **2a** royal authority; sovereignty. **b** the dominion or influence of somebody likened to a monarch.

reign[2] *v* **1** to possess or exercise sovereign power; to rule. **2** to be predominant or prevalent. **3** to be the current holder of a trophy or title, *esp* in a sports event: *the reigning champion.*

reiki /'rayki/ *n* a treatment for pain and stress using healing energy that is channelled from the therapist to the patient.

reimburse *v* to pay back (money) to (somebody). ⋙ **reimbursable** *adj,* **reimbursement** *n.*

reimport[1] *v* to import (products made from raw materials that were exported). ⋙ **reimportation** *n.*

reimport[2] *n* the act of reimporting, or something reimported.

rein[1] *n* **1** (*usu in pl*) a long line fastened to a bit, by which a rider or driver controls an animal. **2** (*in pl*) controlling or guiding power. ✱ **give free rein to** to allow to proceed or function freely.

rein[2] *v* **1** (*often* + in) to check or stop (a horse) by pulling on the reins. **2** (*often* + in) to restrain or stop.

reincarnate *v* (*usu in passive*) to cause (a person or his or her soul) to be reborn in another body after death. ⋙ **reincarnate** *adj,* **reincarnation** *n.*

reindeer *n* (*pl* **reindeers** *or* **reindeer**) a deer with large antlers that inhabits N Europe, Asia, and America and is often domesticated.

reinforce *v* **1** to strengthen with additional material or support. **2** to strengthen or increase (e.g. an army) with additional forces. **3** to encourage (a response) with a reward. ⋙ **reinforcement** *n,* **reinforcer** *n.*

reinforced concrete *n* concrete in which metal is embedded for strengthening.

reinstate *v* to restore to a former position or state. ⋙ **reinstatement** *n.*

reinsure *v* of an insurance company: to transfer (all or part of a risk) to another insurance company. ⋙ **reinsurance** *n,* **reinsurer** *n.*

reintegrate *v* **1** (*often* + into) to restore (something or somebody) to their place as part of a whole. **2** to restore to a state of wholeness or unity. ⋙ **reintegration** *n.*

reintroduce *v* **1** to introduce again. **2** to bring (an animal or plant species) back to a former habitat. ⋙ **reintroduction** *n.*

reinvent *v* to remake or redo completely. ✱ **reinvent the wheel** to waste time and effort making or devising something that already exists. ➤➤ **reinvention** *n.*

reinvest *v* to invest (e.g. earnings or investment income) rather than take or distribute the surplus as dividends or profits. ➤➤ **reinvestment** *n.*

reissue *v* (**reissues, reissued, reissuing**) to issue (something) again; *esp* to cause (a product) to become available again. ➤➤ **reissue** *n.*

reiterate *v* to say or do (something) again or repeatedly. ➤➤ **reiteration** *n.*

reive /reev/ *v chiefly Scot* to go raiding for the purpose of obtaining plunder. ➤➤ **reiver** *n.*

reject[1] *v* **1a** to refuse to accept, consider, submit to, or use (something). **b** to refuse to accept or admit (somebody). **2** to fail to accept (e.g. a skin graft or transplanted organ) because of immunological differences. ➤➤ **rejection** *n.*

reject[2] *n* a rejected person or thing; *esp* a substandard article of merchandise.

rejig *v* (**rejigged, rejigging**) to rearrange or reorganize.

rejoice *v* **1** to feel or express joy or great delight. **2** (+ in) to have or enjoy (something noteworthy).

rejoin[1] *v* to say in response, *esp* in a sharp or critical way.

rejoin[2] *v* **1** to return to. **2** to join (two things) together again.

rejoinder *n* **1** a reply, *esp* a sharp or critical answer. **2** *dated* in law, the answer made by the defendant to the plaintiff's first reply.

rejuvenate *v* **1** to make young or youthful again. **2** to restore to an original or more vigorous state. ➤➤ **rejuvenation** *n,* **rejuvenator** *n.*

rekindle *v* **1** to arouse (e.g. an emotion) again. **2** to light (a fire) again.

relaid *v* past tense and past part. of RELAY[3].

relapse[1] *n* a recurrence of symptoms of a disease after a period of improvement.

relapse[2] *v* **1** to slip or fall back into a former worse state. **2** to sink or subside.

relate *v* **1** to give an account of; to tell. **2** to show or establish logical or causal connection between (two or more things). **3** (*often* + to) to have reference or connection. **4** (+ to) to have or establish a relationship. **5** (+ to) to respond, *esp* favourably, to somebody or something. ➤➤ **relater** *n,* **relator** *n.*

related *adj* **1** belonging to the same group or type. **2** connected by common ancestry or sometimes by marriage. ➤➤ **relatedness** *n.*

relation *n* **1a** a person connected by blood, marriage, or adoption. **b** relationship by blood, marriage, or adoption; kinship. **2** (*in pl*) **a** the attitude or behaviour which two or more people or groups show towards one another. **b** dealings or communication. **c** *euphem* sexual intercourse. **3a** an aspect or quality that connects two or more things and enables them to be considered together. **b** reference, respect, or connection. **4** the act of telling a story. ✱ **in/with relation to** with regard to; concerning. ➤➤ **relational** *adj.*

relationship *n* **1** the state of being related or interrelated. **2** the way in which people or things are related. **3** a state of affairs existing between those having relations or dealings. **4** a close friendship or love affair.

relative[1] *n* **1** = RELATION (1A). **2** an animal or plant related to another by common descent.

relative[2] *adj* **1a** assessed or considered by comparison with something else; not absolute. **b** existing only in connection with or measurable only by reference to something else. **2a** of a pronoun, adverb, etc: introducing a subordinate clause qualifying an expressed or implied antecedent. **b** of a clause: introduced in this way. ✱ **relative to 1** with regard to. **2** relating or relevant to. ➤➤ **relatively** *adv,* **relativeness** *n.*

relative atomic mass *n* the ratio of the average mass of an atom of an element to the mass of an atom of the most abundantly occurring isotope of carbon.

relative density *n* the ratio of the density of a substance to the density of another substance taken as a standard.

relative humidity *n* the ratio of the actual water vapour present in the air to that when the air is saturated with water vapour at the same temperature.

relativism *n* a theory that knowledge and moral principles are relative and have no objective standard. ➤➤ **relativist** *n.*

relativistic *adj* **1** of or characterized by relativity or relativism. **2** in physics, denoting or moving at a velocity that causes a significant change in properties in accordance with the theory of relativity. ➤➤ **relativistically** *adv.*

relativity *n* **1** the quality or state of being relative. **2** the state of being dependent on or determined by a relation to something else. **3** a theory based on the postulates that the speed of light in a vacuum is constant and independent of the source or observer and that the laws of physics are the same in all systems, leading to the assertion that mass, dimension, and time will change with increased velocity.

relaunch *v* to start (something) again, *esp* in a new form. ➤➤ **relaunch** *n.*

relax *v* **1** to make or become less tense or rigid. **2** to refrain from work or other activity and rest or enjoy leisure or recreation. **3** to cast off inhibition, nervous tension, or anxiety. **4** to make (e.g. a rule) less severe or stringent. ➤➤ **relaxer** *n.*

relaxant *n* a substance, *esp* a drug, that produces relaxation or relieves muscular tension. ➤➤ **relaxant** *adj.*

relaxation *n* **1** the act or an instance of relaxing or the state of being relaxed. **2** a relaxing or recreational activity or pastime.

relaxed *adj* **1** friendly and informal in manner or atmosphere. **2** feeling at rest or at ease. **3** not strict or demanding.

relay[1] *n* **1** a number of people or animals that relieve others in some work. **2** a race between teams in which each team member covers a set portion of the course and then is replaced by another. **3a** a device set in operation by variation in an electric circuit and operating other devices in turn. **b** a device that receives and retransmits a signal. **4** the act of passing something along by stages.

relay[2] *v* **1** to pass (e.g. information) along by relay. **2a** to retransmit (a radio or television signal) by means of a relay. **b** to broadcast (a radio or television transmission), *esp* from a specified place.

relay[3] *v* (*past tense and past part.* **relaid**) to lay again.

release[1] *v* **1a** to set free from restraint or confinement. **b** to free from an obligation or responsibility. **2a** to give permission for the publication, performance, or sale of. **b** to publish or issue. **3a** to move (e.g. a handle or catch) in order to allow a mechanism free movement. **b** to allow free movement to (a mechanism) in this way. **4** of a cell, tissue, etc: to allow (e.g. a hormone) to pass from its place of origin or storage into the bloodstream, digestive tract, etc. **5** in law, to give up (a right, claim, etc) in favour of somebody else. ➤➤ **releasable** *adj,* **releaser** *n.*

release[2] *n* **1** the act or an instance of releasing or being released. **2** relief or deliverance from sorrow, suffering, or trouble. **3** relinquishment or conveyance of a legal right or claim, or a document effecting this. **4** a device used to release a mechanism. **5** a newly issued film, CD, etc.

relegate *v* **1** to assign or move to an inferior or insignificant place or status. **2** *Brit* to demote (a team) to a lower division of a sporting competition, e.g. a football league. ➤➤ **relegation** *n.*

relent *v* **1** to become less severe, harsh, or strict. **2** to become less intense or violent.

relentless *adj* **1** of a person: showing no sign of stopping or becoming less determined. **2** remaining constant at the same demanding level: *a relentless pace.* ➤➤ **relentlessly** *adv,* **relentlessness** *n.*

relevant *adj* **1** having a significant and demonstrable bearing on the matter at hand. **2** having practical application, *esp* to the real world. ➤➤ **relevance** *n,* **relevancy** *n,* **relevantly** *adv.*

reliable *adj* fit to be relied on; dependable. ➤➤ **reliability** *n,* **reliably** *adv.*

reliance *n* **1** the act of relying. **2** the condition or attitude of somebody who relies. ➤➤ **reliant** *adj.*

relic *n* **1** something left behind after decay, disintegration, or disappearance; a trace of something past. **2** an outmoded custom, belief, or practice. **3** a part of the body of a saint or martyr, or some object associated with them, that is preserved as an object of reverence.

relict *n* **1** a group of plants or animals that is a surviving remnant of an otherwise extinct form. **2** *archaic* a widow.

relied *v* past tense and past part. of RELY.

relief *n* **1** removal or lightening of something oppressive, painful, or distressing. **2** a feeling of happiness or comfort brought about by the removal of a burden. **3** a means of breaking or avoiding monotony or boredom. **4** aid in the form of money or necessities. **5** somebody who takes over the post or duty of another. **6** release from a post or from the performance of a duty. **7** the liberation of a besieged city, castle, etc. **8** a method of sculpture in which forms and figures stand out from a surrounding flat surface. **9** sharpness of outline due to contrast. **10** the differences in height of a land surface. ✱ **on relief** *NAm* of a person: receiving money or other aid from the government because of need.

relief map *n* a map representing relief graphically by shading, etc, or by means of a three-dimensional scale model.

relieve *v* **1** (*often* + of) **a** to free from a burden. **b** to set free from an obligation or restriction. **2a** to bring about the removal or alleviation of (e.g. pain). **b** (*usu in passive*) to remove or alleviate the anxiety or distress of: *I was relieved to hear that she was safe.* **3** to release (somebody) from a post or duty by taking their place or substituting somebody else. **4** to remove or lessen the monotony of. ✱ **relieve oneself** to urinate or defecate. ➤➤ **reliever** *n.*

religion *n* **1** the organized belief in and worship of a god, gods, or the supernatural. **2** a particular system of religious beliefs. **3** a cause, principle, etc held to with ardour and faith; something considered to be of supreme importance.

religiose *adj* excessively or sentimentally religious. ➤➤ **religiosity** *n.*

religious[1] *adj* **1** of or devoted to the beliefs or observances of a religion. **2** pious or devout. **3** scrupulously and conscientiously faithful. ➤➤ **religiously** *adv,* **religiousness** *n.*

religious[2] *n* (*pl* **religious**) a member of a monastic order.

relinquish *v* **1** to renounce or abandon; to give up. **2a** to stop holding physically. **b** to give over possession or control of. ➤➤ **relinquishment** *n.*

reliquary *n* (*pl* **-ies**) a container or shrine in which sacred relics are kept.

reliquiae *pl n* fossil remains of plants or animals.

relish[1] *n* **1** enjoyment of or delight in something. **2** a highly seasoned sauce, e.g. of pickles or mustard, eaten with plainer food. **3** *archaic* characteristic, pleasing, or piquant flavour or quality.

relish[2] *v* **1** to enjoy greatly. **2** to anticipate with pleasure. **3** *archaic* to add relish to (food).

relive *v* to experience again in the imagination.

relocate *v* to establish one's home or business in a new place. ➤➤ **relocation** *n.*

reluctant *adj* neither quick nor eager to do something; unwilling. ➤➤ **reluctance** *n,* **reluctantly** *adv.*

rely *v* (**-ies, -ied**) **1** (+ on/upon) to have confidence in; to trust. **2** to be dependent on.

REM *abbr* rapid eye movement.

rem *n* a unit of ionizing radiation equal to the dosage that will cause the same biological effect as one röntgen of X-ray or gamma-ray radiation.

remade *v* past tense and past part. of REMAKE[1].

remain *v* **1a** to be neither destroyed, taken, nor used up. **b** to be something yet to be shown, done, or treated. **2** to stay in the same place; to stay behind. **3** to continue to be.

remainder[1] *n* **1a** a remaining group, part, or trace. **b** the final undivided part left after division. **2** a book sold at a reduced price after sales have fallen off.

remainder[2] *v* to dispose of (copies of a book) as remainders.

remains *pl n* **1** a remaining part or trace. **2** a dead body.

remake[1] *v* (*past tense and past part.* **remade**) to make again or in a different form.

remake[2] *n* a new version of a film.

remand[1] *v* to place (a defendant or prisoner) in custody or on bail until they appear again in court.

remand[2] *n* the state of being remanded.

remark[1] *v* **1** to express as an observation or comment. **2** *formal* to take notice of; to observe.

remark[2] *n* **1** a casual expression of an opinion or judgment. **2** mention or notice.

remarkable *adj* striking or extraordinary. ➤➤ **remarkably** *adv.*

remaster *v* to make a new master audio recording of, *esp* digitally, to improve sound quality.

rematch *n* a second match between the same contestants or teams.

remedial *adj* **1** intended as a remedy. **2** of or denoting teaching methods or equipment designed to help people with learning difficulties. ➤➤ **remedially** *adv.*

remedy[1] *n* (*pl* **-ies**) **1** a medicine or treatment that relieves or cures a disease. **2** something that corrects or counteracts an evil or deficiency. **3** legal compensation or amends.

remedy[2] *v* (**-ies, -ied**) to provide or serve as a remedy for. ➤➤ **remediable** *adj.*

remember *v* **1** to bring to mind or think of again. **2** to retain in the memory. **3** to give or leave (somebody) a present, tip, legacy, etc. **4** to convey greetings from (somebody): *Please remember me to your mother.* **5** to record or commemorate. ⋙ **rememberer** *n.*

remembrance *n* **1** an act of recalling to mind. **2** a memory of a person, thing, or event, or something that serves as a reminder of them or it. **3** a commemoration or memorial.

Remembrance Day *n* = REMEMBRANCE SUNDAY.

Remembrance Sunday *n* the Sunday closest to 11 November, dedicated to the commemoration of the dead of both World Wars and of the end of hostilities in 1918 and 1945.

remind *v* **1** to cause (somebody) to remember something. **2** (+ of) to appear to (somebody) to be like somebody or something else.

reminder *n* **1** a thing that helps somebody to remember something. **2** a letter reminding somebody to pay a bill.

reminisce *v* to think, talk, or write about events or people from one's past.

reminiscence *n* **1** the process of reminiscing. **2a** a remembered experience. **b** (*usu in pl*) an account of a memorable experience. **3** something that recalls or is suggestive of something else.

reminiscent *adj* **1** tending to remind one of something seen or known before. **2** of or given to reminiscence. ⋙ **reminiscently** *adv.*

remiss *adj* negligent in the performance of work or duty.

remission *n* **1** the act or an instance of remitting. **2** a state or period during which something, e.g. a disease, is remitted. **3** *Brit* reduction of a prison sentence, *esp* because of good behaviour.

remit[1] *v* (**remitted, remitting**) **1a** to refrain from inflicting or exacting (e.g. a debt or punishment). **b** to pardon (a sin). **2** to send (money) in payment. **3** to refer (something) for consideration or judgment. **4** to lessen in force or intensity; to moderate. ⋙ **remittal** *n,* **remitter** *n.*

remit[2] *n* **1** something remitted to another person or authority for consideration or judgment. **2** the area of responsibility or concern assigned to a person or organization.

remittance *n* **1** a sum of money remitted. **2** the act of remitting money.

remittent *adj* of a disease: marked by alternating periods of abatement and increase of symptoms.

remix[1] *v* to change the balance of sounds of (a recording).

remix[2] *n* a musical recording that has been remixed.

remnant *n* **1** a usu small part or trace remaining. **2** an unsold or unused end of fabric.

remodel *v* (**remodelled, remodelling,** *NAm* **remodeled, remodeling**) to reconstruct or alter the structure of.

remonstrance *n* an act or instance of remonstrating.

remonstrate *v* (*usu* + with) to make one's objections or opposition to somebody's conduct, opinions, etc known forcefully. ⋙ **remonstration** *n,* **remonstrative** *adj,* **remonstrator** *n.*

remora *n* a fish with a sucking disc on the head by means of which it clings to other fishes and to ships.

remorse *n* a deep and bitter distress arising from a sense of guilt for past wrongdoing. ⋙ **remorseful** *adj,* **remorsefully** *adv.*

remorseless *adj* **1** having no remorse; merciless. **2** persistent or indefatigable. ⋙ **remorselessly** *adv,* **remorselessness** *n.*

remortgage *v* to take out another mortgage on (a property).

remote *adj* **1** far removed in space, time, or relation. **2** situated far away from the main centres of activity or population; out-of-the-way or secluded. **3a** involving an infrared or radio signal. **b** controlling something or being controlled indirectly or from a distance. **4** small in degree; slight. **5** distant in manner; aloof. ⋙ **remotely** *adv,* **remoteness** *n.*

remote control *n* **1** control over an operation, e.g. of a machine or weapon, exercised from a distance usu by means of an electrical circuit or radio waves. **2** a device by which this is carried out. ⋙ **remote-controlled** *adj.*

remote sensing *n* the act of studying the earth or another planet from space.

remoulade /'remoolahd/ *n* a mayonnaise sauce flavoured with mustard and herbs.

remould[1] (*NAm* **remold**) *v* **1** to mould again. **2** *Brit* to refashion the tread of (a worn tyre).

remould[2] (*NAm* **remold**) *n* a remoulded tyre.

remount *v* **1** to mount (e.g. a horse) again. **2** to put (e.g. a picture) in a new mount.

removal *n* **1** the act or an instance of removing. **2** *Brit* the moving of household goods from one residence to another.

remove[1] *v* **1** to move by lifting, pushing aside, or taking away or off. **2** to get rid of; to eliminate. **3** to dismiss from office. **4** *formal* to change location, station, or residence. ⋙ **removable** *adj,* **remover** *n.*

remove[2] *n* **1** a degree or stage of separation. **2** a form intermediate between two others in some British schools.

removed *adj* **1** of a younger or older generation: *my first cousin once removed.* **2** separate or remote in space, time, or character.

remunerate *v* to pay (somebody) for work done; to recompense. ⋙ **remuneration** *n,* **remunerative** *adj.*

renaissance *n* **1** (**Renaissance**) the humanistic revival of classical influence in Europe from the 14th to the 17th cent., expressed in a flowering of art, literature, etc and by the beginnings of modern science. **2** (*often* **Renaissance**) a movement or period of vigorous artistic and intellectual activity. **3** a rebirth or revival.

Renaissance man *n* a person of wide interests and expertise; *specif* a person equally at home in the arts and sciences.

renal *adj* relating to or in the region of the kidneys.

renascence *n* = RENAISSANCE.

renascent *adj formal* becoming active or vigorous again.

rend *v* (*past tense and past part.* **rent**) **1** to pull or tear apart or in pieces by violence. **2** to cause mental or emotional pain to. **3** to pierce (the silence or air) with sound.

render[1] *v* **1** to cause to be or become. **2a** to convey or to deliver. **b** to give up; to yield. **c** to submit (e.g. an opinion) for consideration, approval, etc. **3** to do (a service) for or give (assistance) to another. **4a** to reproduce or represent by artistic or verbal means; to depict. **b** to give a performance of (e.g. a piece of music). **c** to translate. **5a** to melt down (fat). **b** to extract e.g. fat from (meat) by melting. **6** to apply a coat of plaster or cement directly to (brickwork, stone, etc). ⋙ **renderer** *n.*

render[2] *n* a material made of cement, sand, etc applied to a wall for protection or decoration.

rendering *n* **1** = RENDITION. **2** plaster applied to a wall; render.

rendezvous[1] /'rondayvooh/ *n* (*pl* **rendezvous** /-vooh/) **1** a meeting at an appointed place and time. **2** a place appointed for assembling or meeting.

rendezvous[2] *v* (**rendezvouses** /-voohz/, **rendezvoused** /-voohd/, **rendezvousing** /-vooh·ing/) to come together at a rendezvous.

rendition *n* **1** a performance or interpretation. **2** a translation.

renegade *n* **1** a deserter from one faith, cause, or allegiance to another. **2** an individual who rejects lawful or conventional behaviour. ➤➤ **renegade** *adj.*

renege *or* **renegue** /ri'neeg, ri'nayg/ *v* (*usu* + on) to go back on a promise or commitment. ➤➤ **reneger** *n.*

renegotiate *v* to negotiate (something) again; *esp* to change (e.g. a price or terms) by negotiation. ➤➤ **renegotiable** *adj,* **renegotiation** *n.*

renegue *v* see RENEGE.

renew *v* **1** to begin (something) again; to resume. **2** to make (something) as if new; to restore to freshness, vigour, or perfection. **3** to grant or obtain an extension of (e.g. a subscription or licence). **4** to replace or replenish. ➤➤ **renewal** *n,* **renewer** *n.*

renewable *adj* capable of being renewed; *esp* capable of being replaced by natural processes. ➤➤ **renewability** *n.*

rennet *n* **1** the membrane lining the stomach of a young calf or related animal, or a prepared extract from this, used for curdling milk. **2** any preparation containing rennin or a substance having the action of rennin on milk.

rennin *n* an enzyme that coagulates milk and is used in making cheese, *esp* one from the mucous membrane of a calf's stomach.

renounce *v* **1** to give up, refuse, or resign, usu by formal declaration. **2** to refuse to follow, obey, or recognize any further. ➤➤ **renouncement** *n,* **renouncer** *n.*

renovate *v* to restore to a better state, e.g. by cleaning, repairing, or rebuilding. ➤➤ **renovation** *n,* **renovator** *n.*

renown *n* the state of being widely known and admired; fame.

renowned *adj* celebrated or famous.

rent[1] *n* **1** a usu fixed periodical payment made by a tenant of property to the owner. **2** a similar payment for the use of goods, equipment, etc.

rent[2] *v* **1** to take and hold (e.g. property or equipment) under an agreement to pay rent. **2** to grant the possession and use of (e.g. property or equipment) for rent. ➤➤ **rentable** *adj.*

rent[3] *n* an opening or split; a tear.

rent[4] *v* past tense and past part. of REND.

rental[1] *n* **1** an amount paid or collected as rent. **2** the act of renting. **3** *NAm* something, e.g. a house, that is rented.

rental[2] *adj* of rent or renting.

rent boy *n Brit, informal* a young male prostitute.

renter *n* **1** the lessee or tenant of property. **2** a distributor of cinema films. **3** something, e.g. a video cassette, that is rented.

rentier /'rontiay, 'ronh-/ *n* somebody who lives mainly on unearned income, e.g. from land or shares.

renumber *v* to number (something) again or differently.

renunciation *n* the act or practice of renouncing; *specif* self-denial practised for religious reasons.

reoffend *v* to commit another crime, *esp* after punishment. ➤➤ **reoffender** *n.*

reopen *v* to open again.

reorder *v* **1** to order again. **2** to arrange in a different way.

reorganize *or* **-ise** *v* to organize again or in a different way. ➤➤ **reorganization** *n,* **reorganizer** *n.*

rep[1] *n informal* a sales representative.

rep[2] *n informal* a repertory theatre or company.

rep[3] *or* **repp** *n* a plain-weave fabric with raised crosswise ribs.

repaid *v* past tense and past part. of REPAY.

repair[1] *v* **1** to restore to a sound or healthy state, e.g. by replacing a part or putting together what is torn or broken. **2** to make good; to remedy. ➤➤ **repairable** *adj,* **repairer** *n.*

repair[2] *n* **1a** the act or process of repairing. **b** an instance or result of repairing. **2** the relative condition of something with respect to soundness or need of repair: *in good repair.*

repair[3] *v formal* to go.

reparable *adj* capable of being repaired.

reparation *n* **1a** the act of making amends for a wrong or injury. **b** something done or given as amends. **2** (*usu in pl*) damages; *specif* compensation payable by a defeated nation for war damages. ➤➤ **reparative** *adj.*

repartee *n* conversation involving the exchange of amusing and witty remarks.

repast *n formal* a meal.

repatriate *v* to restore (somebody) to his or her country of origin. ➤➤ **repatriate** *n,* **repatriation** *n.*

repay *v* (*past tense and past part.* **repaid**) **1** to pay back. **2** to give or inflict in return or requital. **3** to compensate, requite, or reward. ➤➤ **repayable** *adj,* **repayment** *n.*

repayment mortgage *n* a mortgage in which a portion of the capital and interest is paid back in each instalment.

repeal *v* to revoke (a law). ➤➤ **repeal** *n,* **repealable** *adj.*

repeat[1] *v* **1a** to say or state again. **b** to say through from memory. **c** to say after somebody else. **2** to make, do, experience, etc again. **3a** to express (oneself) again in the same words. **b** to present (itself) again in the same form. **4** (*often* + on) of food: to continue to be tasted intermittently after being swallowed. ➤➤ **repeatability** *n,* **repeatable** *adj,* **repeated** *adj,* **repeatedly** *adv.*

repeat[2] *n* **1** the act of repeating. **2** something repeated; *specif* a television or radio programme that has previously been broadcast at least once. **3** a musical passage to be repeated in performance.

repel *v* (**repelled, repelling**) **1** to drive back or away. **2** to cause aversion in; to disgust. **3a** to be incapable of sticking to, mixing with, or absorbing another substance. **b** of a magnetic pole or electric field: to tend to force (e.g. another magnet) away by mutual action at a distance.

repellent[1] *or* **repellant** *adj* **1a** serving to drive away. **b** impervious to or not absorbing. **2** repulsive. ➤➤ **repellently** *adv.*

repellent[2] *or* **repellant** *n* something that repels, *esp* a substance used to prevent insect attacks.

repent *v* **1** to feel regret or contrition. **2** to feel sorrow, regret, or contrition for (something). ➤➤ **repentance** *n*, **repentant** *adj*, **repenter** *n*.

repercussion *n* a widespread, indirect, or unforeseen effect of an action or event. ➤➤ **repercussive** *adj*.

repertoire *n* **1** a list of dramas, operas, pieces, or parts that a company or person is prepared to perform. **2** a range of skills, techniques, etc.

repertory *n* (*pl* **-ies**) **1a** the presentation of several different plays, in alternation or for short periods, in one season at a theatre. **b** a theatre presenting plays in repertory. **c** = REPERTORY COMPANY. **2** = REPERTOIRE. **3** = REPOSITORY (1).

repertory company *n* a theatre company presenting plays in repertory.

repetition *n* **1** the act or an instance of repeating or being repeated. **2** a reproduction or copy. ➤➤ **repetitional** *adj*.

repetitious *adj* characterized or marked by repetition; *esp* tediously repeating. ➤➤ **repetitiously** *adv*, **repetitiousness** *n*.

repetitive *adj* = REPETITIOUS. ➤➤ **repetitively** *adv*, **repetitiveness** *n*.

repetitive strain injury *n* a medical condition characterized by pains in the wrists or arms, caused by making repeated awkward or jarring hand movements, and affecting mainly keyboard operators and musicians.

rephrase *v* to put in different words, *esp* to make the meaning clearer.

repine *v formal or literary* to feel dejection or discontent.

replace *v* **1** to restore to a former place or position. **2** to take the place of, *esp* as a substitute or successor. **3** (*often* + with) to put something new in the place of (something). ➤➤ **replaceable** *adj*, **replacer** *n*.

Usage note

replace *or* **substitute**? These two words differ somewhat in use. One *replaces* an old thing *with* a new thing, or one *substitutes* a new thing *for* an old thing. The meaning is essentially the same, but the prepositions are different (*replace ... with* (or *by*); *substitute ... for*), as is the order in which 'old thing' and 'new thing' follow the verb: *replace the House of Lords with an elected second chamber; substitute an elected second chamber for the House of Lords.*

replacement *n* **1** the process of replacing or being replaced. **2** something or somebody that replaces something or somebody else; a substitute.

replant *v* **1** to plant in a new place. **2** to provide (e.g. a garden) with new plants.

replay[1] *v* to play (something) again.

replay[2] *n* **1a** the act or an instance of replaying. **b** the playing of a tape, e.g. a videotape. **2** a repetition or reenactment. **3** a match played to resolve a tie in an earlier match.

replenish *v* to stock or fill up again. ➤➤ **replenisher** *n*, **replenishment** *n*.

replete *adj* **1** (+ with) fully or abundantly provided or filled. **2** abundantly fed; sated. ➤➤ **repleteness** *n*, **repletion** *n*.

replica *n* an accurate reproduction, copy, or model, *esp* on a smaller scale.

replicate[1] *v* **1** to duplicate or repeat, *esp* to repeat (an experiment or procedure) under the same conditions. **2a** to make an exact copy of . **b** of an organism or genetic material: to produce an exact copy of (itself). ➤➤ **replication** *n*.

replicate[2] *n* **1** an exact copy. **2** a repeat of an experiment or trial.

reply[1] *v* (**-ies, -ied**) **1** to respond in words or writing. **2** to do something in response.

reply[2] *n* (*pl* **-ies**) something said, written, or done in answer or response.

repo *n* (*pl* **-os**) *NAm, informal* a piece of property, e.g. a car, that has been repossessed.

report[1] *n* **1a** a usu detailed account or statement, *esp* of the results of an investigation or piece of research. **b** *Brit* a statement of a pupil's performance at school, sent to the pupil's parents or guardian. **2** a news item giving information about an event. **3** a loud explosive noise.

report[2] *v* **1a** (*often* + on) to make or submit a report. **b** to give news of or information about. **2** to make a formal complaint about, *esp* to the authorities. **3** to present oneself, *esp* on arrival somewhere or for a particular task. **4** *chiefly Brit* to be responsible to somebody superior. **5** of a parliamentary committee: to return (a bill) to Parliament with conclusions or recommendations. ➤➤ **reportable** *adj*.

reportage *n* **1** the act or process of reporting news. **2** writing intended to give a usu factual account of events.

reported speech *n* the words spoken by somebody grammatically adapted for inclusion in a sentence spoken or written by somebody else, as e.g. when John's saying *go home* becomes *John told us to go home*.

reporter *n* **1** a journalist who writes news stories. **2** somebody who gathers and broadcasts news.

report stage *n* the stage in the British legislative process before the third reading of a bill.

repose[1] *n* **1** the state of resting after exertion or strain; *esp* sleep. **2** composure of manner; poise. ➤➤ **reposeful** *adj*, **reposefully** *adv*.

repose[2] *v* **1** to be situated. **2** to lie resting.

repose[3] *v formal* (+ in) to place (e.g. confidence or trust) in someone or something specified.

reposition *v* to change the position of.

repository *n* (*pl* **-ies**) **1** a place or container where something is stored. **2** somebody or something that contains a nonmaterial thing, *esp* in large quantities.

repossess *v* to resume possession of (goods) in default of the payment of instalments due. ➤➤ **repossession** *n*, **repossessor** *n*.

repoussé[1] *adj* of sheet metal: decorated with patterns in relief made by hammering on the reverse side.

repoussé[2] *n* repoussé metalwork.

repp *n* see REP[3].

reprehend *v* to voice disapproval of; to censure.

reprehensible *adj* deserving censure; culpable. ➤➤ **reprehensibility** *n*, **reprehensibly** *adv*.

represent *v* **1a** to act for or in the place of. **b** to serve as the elected member of a legislative body for (a particular constituency or electorate). **2** to serve as a specimen, example, or instance of. **3** to serve as a sign or symbol of. **4** to have the nature or effect of; to constitute. **5** to portray or exhibit in art; to depict. **6** to attribute a specified character or identity to, *esp* falsely. **7** to act the part or role of. ➤➤ **representability** *n*, **representable** *adj*.

re-present *v* to present again or in a new way. ➤➤ **re-presentation** *n*.

representation *n* **1** somebody or something that represents something else, e.g. an artistic likeness or image. **2** the act or an instance of representing or being represented. **3a** (*in pl*) a statement made to influence opinion. **b** a usu formal protest.

representational *adj* **1** relating to representation. **2** in the graphic or plastic arts, involving realistic depiction of physical objects or appearances.

representative[1] *adj* **1a** serving as a typical or characteristic example. **b** containing typical examples. **2a** acting on behalf of somebody else, *esp* through delegated authority. **b** based on or involving representation of the people in government or lawmaking, usu by election. **3** serving to represent. ⋙ **representatively** *adv,* **representativeness** *n.*

representative[2] *n* **1a** somebody who represents a constituency, e.g. as a member of a parliament. **b** (*often* **Representative**) a member of the Australian or US House of Representatives or a US state legislature. **2a** an agent, deputy, substitute, or delegate. **b** somebody who represents a business organization, *esp* a sales representative. **3** a typical example of a group, class, or quality; a specimen.

repress *v* **1** to subdue by force. **2a** to prevent the natural or normal expression of (e.g. an emotion). **b** to exclude (e.g. a feeling) from consciousness by psychological repression: compare SUPPRESS. **3** to prevent the normal activity or development of; to hold in check; to curb. ⋙ **represser** *n,* **repressible** *adj.*

repression *n* **1** the act or an instance of repressing. **2** a psychological process by which unacceptable desires or impulses are excluded from conscious awareness.

repressive *adj* of a government or regime: unjustly or unduly restricting people's freedom. ⋙ **repressively** *adj,* **repressiveness** *n.*

reprieve[1] *v* **1** to delay or remit the punishment of (e.g. a condemned prisoner). **2** to remove the threat of an unpleasant fate, e.g. demolition, closure, etc, from temporarily.

reprieve[2] *n* **1** a suspension or remission of a sentence, *esp* a death sentence. **2** a temporary removal of a threat.

reprimand[1] *n* a severe and formal expression of disapproval.

reprimand[2] *v* to criticize sharply or formally, usu from a position of authority.

reprint[1] *n* **1** a subsequent impression of a book previously published in the same form. **2a** the act of reprinting (e.g. a book). **b** a reprinted copy of something.

reprint[2] *v* to print again.

reprisal *n* **1** a retaliatory act. **2** the seizure of goods or citizens of a foreign country in retaliation for an injury.

reprise[1] *n* a repetition of a musical passage, a musical number from a show, or a performance.

reprise[2] *v* to repeat (a passage of music, a musical number, or a performance).

reproach[1] *v* to express disappointment and displeasure with (somebody) for blameworthy conduct. ⋙ **reproachable** *adj,* **reproacher** *n,* **reproachingly** *adv.*

reproach[2] *n* **1** an expression of rebuke or disapproval. **2** discredit or disgrace. ⋙ **reproachful** *adj,* **reproachfully** *adv,* **reproachfulness** *n.*

reprobate[1] *n* somebody who is morally dissolute or unprincipled.

reprobate[2] *adj* morally dissolute; unprincipled.

reprocess *v* to treat or process again, so as to be suitable for reuse.

reproduce *v* **1** to repeat, copy, or emulate (something). **2** to make an image or copy of (something). **3** to translate (a recording) into sound or an image. **4** to produce offspring. ⋙ **reproducer** *n,* **reproducible** *adj,* **reproductive** *adj.*

reproduction *n* **1** the sexual or asexual process by which plants and animals give rise to offspring. **2a** something, e.g. a painting, that is reproduced; a copy. **b** (*used before a noun*) copied from an original or imitating the style of an earlier period. **3** the quality of sound or image produced by audio or video equipment.

reprogram *v* (**reprogrammed, reprogramming,** *NAm* **reprogramed, reprograming**) to alter the functioning of (e.g. a computer) by introducing a new program.

reprography *n* the science or practice of reproducing graphic matter, e.g. by photocopying. ⋙ **reprographer** *n,* **reprographic** *adj.*

reproof *n* criticism for a fault.

re-proof *v* **1** *Brit* to make (e.g. a garment) waterproof again. **2** to make a new proof of (e.g. a book).

reprove *v* to express disapproval of; to censure. ⋙ **reprover** *n,* **reproving** *adj,* **reprovingly** *adv.*

reptile *n* **1** any of a class of usu cold-blooded vertebrates, usu covered with scales or bony plates, that includes crocodiles, lizards, snakes, turtles, and extinct related forms, e.g. dinosaurs. **2** *informal* a grovelling or despicable person. ⋙ **reptilian** *adj.*

republic *n* a state whose head is not a monarch and in which supreme power resides in the people and is exercised by their elected representatives governing according to law.

republican[1] *adj* **1a** relating to or belonging to a republic. **b** advocating a republic. **2** (**Republican**) denoting a political party in the USA favouring a restricted governmental role in social and economic life. ⋙ **republicanism** *n.*

republican[2] *n* **1** somebody who favours republican government. **2** (**Republican**) a member of the US Republican party. **3** (**Republican**) a supporter of the union of Northern Ireland with the Irish Republic.

repudiate *v* **1** to refuse to have anything to do with; to disown. **2a** to refuse to accept; *esp* to reject as unauthorized or invalid. **b** to reject (e.g. a charge) as untrue or unjust. **3** to refuse to acknowledge or pay (e.g. a debt). **4** *archaic* to divorce or disown (a wife). ⋙ **repudiation** *n.*

repugnance *n* strong dislike, aversion, or antipathy.

repugnant *adj* **1** arousing strong dislike or aversion. **2** incompatible or inconsistent. ⋙ **repugnantly** *adv.*

repulse[1] *v* **1** to drive (attackers) back. **2** to repel by discourtesy, coldness, or denial. **3** to cause repulsion in.

repulse[2] *n* **1** a rebuff or rejection. **2** the act of repelling an assailant or being repelled.

repulsion *n* **1** a feeling of strong aversion. **2** in physics, a force, e.g. between like electric charges or like magnetic poles, tending to produce separation.

repulsive *adj* **1** arousing strong aversion or disgust. **2** serving or able to repulse. ⋙ **repulsively** *adv,* **repulsiveness** *n.*

reputable *adj* held in good repute; well regarded. ⋙ **reputably** *adv.*

reputation *n* **1** overall quality or character as seen or judged by others. **2** fame; celebrity. **3** recognition by other people of some characteristic or ability.

repute[1] *n* **1** the character or status commonly ascribed to somebody or something. **2** the state of being favourably known or spoken of.

repute[2] *v* (*usu in passive*) to believe or consider to be as specified.

reputed *adj* being such according to general or popular belief. ⋙ **reputedly** *adv.*

request[1] *n* **1** the act or an instance of asking for something, *esp* politely or formally. **2** something asked for. **3** the state of being sought after.

request[2] *v* **1** to make a request to or of (somebody). **2** to ask for (something), *esp* politely or formally.

request stop *n Brit* a point at which a public transport vehicle stops only by previous arrangement or when signalled.

requiem *n* **1** a mass for the dead. **2** (*often* **Requiem**) a musical setting of the mass for the dead.

require *v* **1a** to have to have (something) because it is necessary or essential. **b** to wish to have. **2** to call for as suitable or appropriate. **3** to regard as obligatory; to demand. **4** to impose an obligation on.

requirement *n* **1** something wanted or needed. **2** a necessary precondition for something.

requisite[1] *adj* necessary or required.

requisite[2] *n* **1** something that is required or necessary. **2** an article of the specified sort.

requisition[1] *n* **1** the act of compulsorily taking over goods or property for official use. **2** a formal and authoritative written demand or application. **3** the act of formally requesting somebody to perform an action.

requisition[2] *v* to demand the use or supply of formally or officially.

requite *v* **1** *formal* **a** to make suitable return for (a benefit or service). **b** to compensate sufficiently for (an injury). **2** to make retaliation for (e.g. a wrong). ⋙ **requital** *n.*

reran *v* past tense of RERUN.

reread *v* (*past tense and past part.* **reread**) to read (a piece of writing) again.

reredos *n* (*pl* **reredos**) a usu ornamental wood or stone screen or partition wall behind an altar.

rerun *v* (**rerunning,** *past tense* **reran,** *past part.* **rerun**) **1** to run (something, e.g. a race) again. **2** to show (e.g. a film or television programme) again. ⋙ **rerun** *n.*

resale price maintenance *n* the fixing by a manufacturer of a minimum price at which its goods may be sold to the public by a retailer, distributor, etc.

resat *v* past tense and past part. of RESIT.

reschedule *v* **1** to change the time that (an event) is to take place. **2** to set a new timetable for the repayment of (a debt).

rescind *v* **1** to cancel (e.g. an order). **2** to make (a law, contract, etc) void. ⋙ **rescindable** *adj,* **rescinder** *n,* **rescindment** *n.*

rescission *n* the act or an instance of rescinding.

rescue[1] *v* to free from confinement, danger, harm, or difficulty; to save. ⋙ **rescuer** *n.*

rescue[2] *n* the act or an instance of rescuing somebody or something.

research[1] *n* **1** scientific or scholarly investigation, *esp* aimed at making discoveries, establishing facts, or enabling new conclusions. **2** careful or systematic enquiry.

research[2] *v* **1** to engage in research on (a subject) or for (e.g. a book or television programme). **2** to search or investigate (something) thoroughly. ⋙ **researchable** *adj,* **researcher** *n.*

research and development *n* the work done by a commercial organization to investigate the possibility of developing new products or services.

resemblance *n* **1** the quality or state of resembling somebody or something else. **2** a point on which two people or things are similar. ⋙ **resemblant** *adj.*

resemble *v* to be similar to, *esp* in appearance or superficial qualities.

resent *v* to harbour or express ill will at (something considered wrong or unfair). ⋙ **resentful** *adj,* **resentfully** *adv,* **resentfulness** *n,* **resentment** *n.*

reservation *n* **1** the act or an instance of reserving something, e.g. a seat or hotel room, or a record of this. **2** (*usu in pl*) **a** a specific doubt or objection. **b** a limiting condition. **3** a strip of land separating carriageways on a major road. **4** an area of land set aside; *specif* one designated for the use of Native Americans by treaty. **5** *chiefly NAm* an area in which hunting is not permitted.

reserve[1] *v* **1** to retain for future use. **2** to arrange that (a seat, hotel room, etc) be kept for one's own or another's use at a specified future time. **3** to hold over until later; to defer. **4** to retain (e.g. a right).

reserve[2] *n* **1** a supply of something retained for future use or need. **2a** *chiefly Brit* an area, e.g. of public land, set apart for the conservation of natural resources or rare plants and animals. **b** = RESERVATION (4). **3** restraint, closeness, or caution in one's words and actions; reticence. **4** a qualification or doubt. **5** (*usu in pl*) a military force available as a support for regular forces when needed. **6a** in sport, a player or participant who has been selected to substitute for another if the need should arise, e.g. through injury. **b** (**the reserves**) a team made up of players who do not currently form part of the first team. **7** (*also in pl*) money, gold, foreign exchange, etc kept in hand usu to meet liabilities. ✱ **in reserve** held back ready for use if needed.

re-serve *v* to serve (somebody or something) again.

reserve bank *n* **1** a central bank that holds the reserves of other banks. **2** in the USA, a bank in the Federal Reserve System.

reserve currency *n* foreign currency that a country's central bank holds in reserve as a means of payment of international debt.

reserved *adj* restrained in speech and behaviour. ⋙ **reservedly** *adv,* **reservedness** *n.*

reserved occupation *n* an occupation that excuses a person from military service in time of war.

reserve price *n* a price announced at an auction as the lowest that will be considered.

reservist *n* a member of a military reserve.

reservoir *n* **1a** a natural or artificial lake where water is collected for use by a community. **b** a part of something, e.g. a machine, in which a liquid or gas is held. **c** a place in which fluid gathers, e.g. a cavity in the body or in rock. **2** an available extra source or supply.

reset *v* (**resetting,** *past tense and past part.* **reset**) **1** to set again or in a different way. **2** to change the reading of (e.g. a clock or meter); *specif* to restore (it) to zero. ⋙ **resettable** *adj.*

reshape *v* to give a new form or structure to.

reshuffle *v* **1** to rearrange (something) by altering the relative position or nature of its elements. **2** to reorganize (a group or team of people, *esp* government ministers) by a redistribution of roles. ⋙ **reshuffle** *n.*

reside *v* **1** to occupy a place as one's permanent home. **2a** (+ in) to lie in, or be associated or bound up with, a certain thing. **b** (+ in) to be vested as a right in a certain personage, etc.

residence *n* **1** the fact of living in a place. **2** a dwelling, *esp* a large and impressive house or the official home of a government minister or other dignitary. **3** = HALL OF RESIDENCE. ✻ **in residence** of a writer, artist, etc: serving in a regular capacity in a place, e.g. a college or gallery, and available to give instruction, advice, etc.

residency *n* (*pl* **-ies**) **1** = RESIDENCE (I). **2** a period of time spent as a writer or artist in residence, or the post itself. **3** *NAm* a period of advanced training as a medical specialist. **4** a regular engagement at the same venue for a singer, band, etc. **5** in former times, the official home of a diplomatic agent residing at a foreign court or seat of government.

resident[1] *adj* **1a** living in a place, *esp* for some length of time. **b** serving in a regular or full-time capacity. **c** living at one's place of work. **2** of an animal: not migratory.

resident[2] *n* **1a** somebody who lives in a place. **b** a guest staying for one or more nights at a hotel. **2** an animal that does not migrate. **3** *NAm* a doctor undergoing a residency. **4** in former times, a diplomatic agent residing at a foreign seat of government, *esp* a representative of the Crown in a British protectorate. ➤➤ **residentship** *n.*

residential *adj* **1** used as a residence or by residents. **2** relating to or involving residence. **3** given over to private housing as distinct from industry or commerce. ➤➤ **residentially** *adv.*

residua *n* pl of RESIDUUM.

residual[1] *adj* remaining as a residue, *esp* in a small quantity or for a short time. ➤➤ **residually** *adv.*

residual[2] *n* **1** something left over; a remainder. **2** (*also in pl*) a payment made to an actor, musician, etc when a film, television programme, or other work they were involved in is rerun after the first showing.

residue *n* **1** something that remains after a part, *esp* the greater part, has been taken away or used up. **2** the part of a deceased person's estate that remains after the payment of all debts and bequests. **3** a substance remaining after a chemical process, e.g. distillation or combustion.

residuum *n* (*pl* **residua**) a residue, *esp* the residual product of a chemical reaction or process.

resign *v* **1** to give up one's job or position. **2** to relinquish (e.g. a right or position) by a formal act. **3** (+ to) to reconcile (oneself) to an unpleasant fact, circumstance, etc. ➤➤ **resigner** *n.*

re-sign *v* to sign (e.g. a document) again.

resignation *n* **1a** a formal notification of resigning. **b** the act or an instance of resigning. **2** the state of being resigned to something.

resigned *adj* marked by submission to something unpleasant regarded as inevitable. ➤➤ **resignedly** *adv,* **resignedness** *n.*

resilient *adj* **1a** capable of withstanding shock without permanent deformation or rupture. **b** able to return to shape after bending, stretching, etc. **2** *esp* of a person: able to recover from or adjust to misfortune or change. ➤➤ **resilience** *n,* **resiliency** *n,* **resiliently** *adv.*

resin[1] *n* **1** a solid or semisolid yellowish to brown plant secretion that is insoluble in water and used *esp* in varnishes, inks, and plastics. **2** any of numerous synthetic substances that have the qualities of natural resin. ➤➤ **resinous** *adj.*

resin[2] *v* (**resined, resining**) to treat with resin.

resinate *v* to impregnate or flavour with a resin.

resist[1] *v* **1** to withstand the force or effect of. **2** to strive against or oppose. **3** to refrain from (something tempting). ➤➤ **resister** *n,* **resistibility** *n,* **resistible** *adj.*

resist[2] *n* a protective coating applied to a surface to cause it to resist the action of a particular agent, e.g. an acid or dye.

resistance *n* **1** the act or an instance of resisting. **2a** the ability to resist. **b** an organism's ability to withstand infection or the effects of drugs, etc. **3** an opposing or retarding force. **4a** in physics, the opposition offered to the passage of a steady electric current through a body, circuit, etc. **b** = RESISTOR. **5** (*often* **Resistance**) an underground organization operating against occupying forces in a country or against those in power.

resistant *adj* (*used in combinations*) capable of or offering resistance to a specified thing.

resistivity *n* **1** resistance. **2** the ability of a substance to resist the passage through it of an electric current. ➤➤ **resistive** *adj.*

resistor *n* a component included in an electrical circuit to provide resistance.

resit *v* (*past tense and past part.* **resat, resitting**) *Brit* to take (an examination) again after failing. ➤➤ **resit** *n.*

resize *v* in computing, to alter the size of (a window or image).

resoluble *adj* capable of being resolved.

re-soluble *adj* able to be dissolved a second or subsequent time.

resolute *adj* firmly resolved; determined. ➤➤ **resolutely** *adv,* **resoluteness** *n.*

resolution *n* **1a** the process of resolving, e.g. a problem or dispute. **b** the process of reducing something to a simpler form or separating it into its component parts. **2** courageous firmness of purpose; determination. **3a** a statement of firm intent. **b** a formal expression of opinion or intent voted by a body or group. **4a** the capability, e.g. of a television or computer screen, to produce a clear and detailed image, or the degree of clarity produced. **b** = RESOLVING POWER. **5** in music, the act of passing from a discordant to a concordant note or chord.

resolve[1] *v* **1a** to deal with (e.g. a dispute) successfully; to settle (it). **b** to find a solution to (a problem). **2a** to reach a firm decision to do something. **b** to declare or decide by a formal resolution and vote. **3** to break up or separate into constituent parts. **4** in music, to make (notes or chords) progress from dissonance to agreeable harmony. **5** to separate (adjacent parts of an image) and make them distinguishable and independently visible. **6** to change (itself) gradually into a different apparent form. ➤➤ **resolvability** *n,* **resolvable** *adj,* **resolved** *adj,* **resolvedly** *adv,* **resolver** *n.*

resolve[2] *n* **1a** the state of being determined or decided. **b** a firm decision. **2** a legal or official decision, *esp* a formal resolution.

resolving power *n* **1** the ability of an optical system to form distinct images of objects separated by small distances. **2** the ability of a photographic film to reproduce fine detail.

resonance *n* **1** the quality or state of being resonant. **2** the intensification and enrichment of a musical tone by supplementary vibration.

resonant *adj* **1a** continuing to sound; echoing. **b** intensified and enriched by resonance. **2** of a space, hollow object, etc: tending to intensify and enrich sound. **3** suggesting meanings or associations other than those that are immediately present. ➤➤ **resonantly** *adv.*

resonate *v* **1a** to produce or exhibit resonance. **b** to resound or reverberate. **2** to suggest meanings or associations beyond those that are immediately present. ➤➤ **resonator** *n.*

resorb *v* **1** to absorb again. **2** in physiology, to break down and incorporate (a previously differentiated tissue or structure) into the surrounding tissue. ➤➤ **resorbent** *adj,* **resorption** *n,* **resorptive** *adj.*

resort[1] *n* **1** a frequently visited place providing accommodation and recreation, *esp* for holiday-makers. **2a** somebody or something turned to for help or protection; a refuge or resource. **b** the act of resorting to somebody or something; recourse.

resort[2] *v* **1** (+ to) to turn to somebody or something or adopt a course of action to achieve an end. **2** *formal* to go, *esp* frequently or in large numbers. ⋙ **resorter** *n.*

resound *v* **1** to become filled with sound. **2** to produce a sonorous or echoing sound. **3** to become renowned.

resounding *adj* emphatic; unequivocal. ⋙ **resoundingly** *adv.*

resource[1] *n* **1a** (*usu in pl*) an available means of support or provision. **b** (*usu in pl*) a source of wealth or revenue, e.g. minerals. **c** a source of information or expertise. **d** something to which one has recourse in difficulty. **2** (*usu in pl*) the ability to deal with a difficult situation; resourcefulness.

resource[2] *v* to equip or supply (e.g. a school) with resources.

resourceful *adj* good at devising ways of dealing with difficult situations; enterprising. ⋙ **resourcefully** *adv,* **resourcefulness** *n.*

respect[1] *n* **1a** high or special regard; esteem. **b** polite regard or deference. **c** (*in pl*) expressions of respect or politeness. **2** an aspect or detail. **3** particular attention or consideration. ✱ **in respect of 1** in relation to; concerning. **2** in payment of. **with respect to** in relation to; concerning.

respect[2] *v* **1** to consider worthy of respect. **2** to refrain from violating or interfering with. **3** to recognize and abide by (e.g. a decision). ⋙ **respecter** *n.*

respectable *adj* **1** worthy of respect. **2** decent or conventional in character or conduct. **3a** acceptable in size or quantity. **b** fairly good; tolerable. **4** fit to be seen; presentable. ⋙ **respectability** *n,* **respectably** *adv.*

respectful *adj* showing respect or deference. ⋙ **respectfully** *adv,* **respectfulness** *n.*

respecting *prep* with regard to; concerning.

respective *adj* belonging or relating to each; particular and separate. ⋙ **respectiveness** *n.*

respectively *adv* **1** separately. **2** in the order given.

respell *v* (**respelt** *or* **respelled**) to spell (a word) again or in another way, *esp* according to a particular phonetic system.

respirate *v* to use artificial respiration to enable (somebody) to breathe.

respiration *n* **1a** the action of breathing. **b** a single act of breathing in and out. **2** the process by which most organisms supply their cells and tissues with the oxygen needed for life-supporting processes and remove the carbon dioxide formed in energy-producing reactions. ⋙ **respirational** *adj,* **respiratory** *adj.*

respirator *n* **1** a device worn over the mouth or nose to prevent the breathing of poisonous gases, harmful dusts, etc. **2** a device for maintaining artificial respiration, *esp* over a long period.

respiratory system *n* a system of organs carrying out the function of respiration that consists typically of the lungs and the channels by which these are connected with the outer air.

respire *v* **1** *formal* to breathe. **2** of a cell or tissue: to take up oxygen and produce carbon dioxide during respiration.

respite *n* **1** a period of temporary delay, *esp* a reprieve. **2** a period of rest or relief.

respite care *n* temporary care given to an elderly or disabled person so that their usual carer can have time off.

resplendent *adj* shining brilliantly; characterized by splendour. ⋙ **resplendence** *n,* **resplendency** *n,* **resplendently** *adv.*

respond *v* **1** to write or speak in reply; to answer. **2** to act in reply. ⋙ **responder** *n.*

respondent *n* **1** a defendant, *esp* in an appeal or divorce case. **2** a person who replies to a survey, advertisement, etc.

response *n* **1** an act of responding. **2** a reply or reaction. **3** a change in the activity of an organism or any of its parts resulting from stimulation.

responsibility *n* (*pl* **-ies**) **1** the state of being responsible. **2** something or somebody for which one is responsible, e.g.: **a** a moral or legal obligation. **b** a task assigned to one. **3** the opportunity to act independently, take decisions, be in control of people or things, etc.

responsible *adj* **1a** liable to be called to account as the person who did something. **b** constituting the reason or cause of something. **2a** (*usu* + for) having control or care of something or somebody. **b** involving important duties, decision-making, control of others, accountability, etc. **3** able to discriminate between right and wrong and therefore accountable for one's own actions. **4** trustworthy or reliable. **5** having or showing sound judgment; sensible. **6** (+ to) required to report or answer to the specified person or body. ⋙ **responsibleness** *n,* **responsibly** *adv.*

responsive *adj* **1** quick to respond appropriately or sympathetically. **2** giving or constituting a response. ⋙ **responsively** *adv,* **responsiveness** *n.*

respray *v* to spray (e.g. a car) with a fresh coat of paint. ⋙ **respray** *n.*

rest[1] *n* **1a** freedom or a break from activity or work. **b** a state of motionlessness or inactivity. **c** repose, relaxation, or sleep. **2** in music, a silence of a specified duration, or a symbol representing this. **3** something used for support. ✱ **at rest 1** resting or reposing, *esp* in sleep or death. **2** not moving.

rest[2] *v* **1** to relax the body or mind, e.g. by lying down or sleeping. **2** to stop working or exerting oneself. **3a** to be set or lie supported. **b** to place on a support. **4** (+ on) to be based or founded. **5** (+ with) to depend for action or accomplishment. **6** to be left without further attention. **7** to stop introducing evidence in a law case. ✱ **rest on one's laurels** see LAUREL. ⋙ **rester** *n.*

rest[3] *n* **1** (**the rest**) the part, amount, or number that remains. **2** (**the rest**) the other people or things.

rest[4] *v* to remain as specified.

restate *v* to state again or in a different way, e.g. more emphatically. ⋙ **restatement** *n.*

restaurant *n* a place where refreshments, *esp* meals, are sold usu to be eaten on the premises.

restaurant car *n* = DINING CAR.

restaurateur *n* the manager or proprietor of a restaurant.

restful *adj* **1** marked by or conducive to rest and repose. **2** quiet and peaceful. ⋙ **restfully** *adv,* **restfulness** *n.*

rest home *n* a residential home for elderly people who need a degree of medical or nursing care.

restitution *n* **1a** the returning of something, e.g. property, to its rightful owner. **b** compensation given for an injury or wrong. **2** restoration to a former or original state.

restive *adj* **1** stubbornly resisting authority or control. **2** restless and uneasy. ⋙ **restively** *adv,* **restiveness** *n.*

Usage note

restive *or* restless? These two words are difficult to keep apart. *Restive* means 'difficult to control or keep still': children and horses are commonly described as *restive,* as are people who get impatient with restrictions placed on them: *The military were growing restive and kept urging the government to act. Restless* is applied much more widely – not only to people, but also to movements and things: *restless pacing to and fro; a restless night.*

restless *adj* **1** characterized by inability to rest, *esp* due to mental agitation. **2** giving no rest. **3** continuously moving or active. **4** discontented with the present situation and anxious for change. ⋙ **restlessly** *adv,* **restlessness** *n*

Usage note

restless *or* restive? See note at RESTIVE.

restoration *n* **1a** the process of restoring something to its former or original state. **b** the repair and renovation e.g. of a ruined building. **2a** a reinstatement of somebody to a position previously held. **b** a handing back of something. **3** (**Restoration**) the reestablishment of the monarchy in England in 1660 under Charles II or the period that followed this.

restorative *adj* capable of restoring health or vigour. ⋙ **restorative** *n,* **restoratively** *adv.*

restore *v* **1** to bring back to its former or original state, e.g. by repairing damage. **2** to bring back into existence, force, or use. **3** *formal* to give back; to return. **4** *formal* to put (somebody) in possession of something again. ⋙ **restorable** *adj,* **restorer** *n.*

restrain *v* **1** to keep under control; to limit, repress, or check. **2** to prevent from doing something. **3a** to hold onto and physically prevent (a person or animal) from moving, attacking, etc. **b** to deprive of liberty, *esp* by placing under arrest. ⋙ **restrainable** *adj,* **restrainer** *n.*

restrained *adj* characterized by restraint, *esp* not extravagant or emotional. ⋙ **restrainedly** *adv.*

restraint *n* **1** moderation of one's behaviour; self-restraint. **2** the absence of extravagance or indulgence. **3a** the act of restraining. **b** a restraining force or influence. **c** a device that prevents freedom of movement.

restrict *v* **1** to prevent from moving or acting freely. **2** to confine within bounds; to limit. ⋙ **restrictive** *adj.*

restricted *adj* **1a** not general; limited. **b** available only to particular groups or for a particular purpose. **c** subject to control, *esp* by law. **d** not intended for general circulation. **2** narrow or confined. ⋙ **restrictedly** *adv,* **restrictedness** *n.*

restriction *n* **1** a regulation that restricts or restrains. **2** the act of restricting or the state of being restricted.

restrictive practice *n* **1** an anti-competitive trading agreement between companies that is against the public interest. **2** a practice by the members of a trade union that limits the freedom of action of other workers or management.

rest room *n NAm* public toilet facilities in a building, e.g. a restaurant.

restructure *v* to change the make-up or organization of (e.g. an institution or business).

result[1] *v* **1** to proceed or arise as an effect or conclusion, usu from something specified. **2** (+ in) to have the specified outcome or end.

result[2] *n* **1** something that happens as a consequence, effect, or conclusion. **2** something obtained by calculation, experiment, or investigation. **3a** the outcome or final score, mark, etc of a contest or examination. **b** *informal* a win in a sporting contest or successful conclusion to an operation.

resultant *adj* derived or resulting from something else. ⋙ **resultantly** *adv.*

resume *v* **1** to take or occupy (e.g. a position) again. **2** to continue or begin again after an interruption. ⋙ **resumable** *adj.*

résumé *n* **1** a summary. **2** *NAm* = CURRICULUM VITAE.

resumption *n* the act or an instance of resuming.

resurface *v* **1** to provide (e.g. a road) with a new or fresh surface. **2** to rise again to the surface *esp* of water. **3** to appear or show up again.

resurgence *n* a rising again into life, activity, or influence. ⋙ **resurgent** *adj.*

resurrect *v* **1** to bring back to life from the dead. **2** to bring back into use or into a position of prominence or popularity.

resurrection *n* **1a** (**the Resurrection**) the rising of Christ from the dead. **b** (*often* **the Resurrection**) in the Christian faith, the rising again to life of all the human dead before the Last Judgment. **2** a resurgence, revival, or restoration. ⋙ **resurrectional** *adj.*

resuscitate *v* **1** to revive from unconsciousness or apparent death. **2** to impart new energy or vigour to; to revitalize. ⋙ **resuscitation** *n,* **resuscitative** *adj,* **resuscitator** *n.*

ret *v* (**retted, retting**) to soak (e.g. flax) so that the fibres are loosened from the woody tissue.

retail[1] /'reetayl/ *v* **1a** to sell (goods) to final consumers who will not resell them. **b** to be sold or available for sale to final consumers. **2** /ri'tayl/ to relate or recount (e.g. gossip). ⋙ **retailer** *n.*

retail[2] *n* the sale of goods in small quantities to final consumers who will not resell them: compare WHOLESALE[1]. ⋙ **retail** *adj and adv.*

retail price index *n* an index based on the retail prices of a range of selected essential commodities, used to show monthly changes in the cost of living in Britain.

retail therapy *n* = SHOPPING THERAPY.

retain *v* **1a** to continue to have or hold. **b** to keep in one's pay or employment; *specif* to engage the services of (somebody) by paying them a retainer. **c** to keep in one's mind or memory. **2a** to have the ability to hold or contain. **b** to hold in place. ⋙ **retainable** *adj,* **retainment** *n.*

retainer *n* **1** a fee paid to a lawyer or professional adviser in return for access to their services whenever they are required. **2** a reduced rent paid to reserve accommodation during the tenant's absence. **3a** an old and trusted domestic servant. **b** in former times, somebody who served a person of high rank.

retaining wall *n* a wall built to hold back a mass of earth, water, etc.

retake[1] *v* (*past tense* **retook,** *past part.* **retaken**) **1** to recapture. **2** to film, photograph, or record again. **3** to sit (a test or examination) again.

retake[2] *n* **1** a second filming, photographing, or recording. **2** a retaken test or examination.

retaliate *v* to take action that repays somebody, usu in kind, for some wrong they have done. ⋙ **retaliation** *n,* **retaliative** *adj,* **retaliatory** *adj.*

retard *v* to slow down or delay, *esp* to hinder the progress, development, or accomplishment of something. ⋙ **retardation** *n,* **retarder** *n.*

retardant *adj* slowing down or preventing something, *esp* a chemical reaction. ⋙ **retardant** *n.*

retarded *adj* slow in intellectual or emotional development.

retch *v* to experience a vomiting spasm without actually vomiting anything. ⋙ **retch** *n.*

retell *v* (*past tense and past part.* **retold**) to tell (e.g. a story) again or in a different form.

retention *n* **1** the act of retaining or the state of being retained. **2** abnormal retaining within the body of something that should be eliminated, e.g. urine.

retentive *adj* able or tending to retain something, *esp* knowledge. ⋙ **retentively** *adv,* **retentiveness** *n.*

rethink *v* (*past tense and past part.* **rethought**) to reconsider (a plan, attitude, etc) with a view to changing it. ⋙ **rethink** *n.*

reticent *adj* inclined to be silent or reluctant to speak; reserved. ⋙ **reticence** *n,* **reticently** *adv.*

reticulated *adj* arranged in the form of a net or network, or with netlike markings.

reticulation *n* a reticulated structure or pattern.

reticule *n* a decorative drawstring bag used as a handbag by women in the 18th and 19th cents.

retina *n* (*pl* **retinas** *or* **retinae**) the light-sensitive membrane at the back of the eye that receives the image formed by the lens and is connected with the brain by the optic nerve. ⋙ **retinal** *adj.*

retinitis *n* inflammation of the retina often leading to blindness.

retinitis pigmentosa *n* a hereditary disease causing a gradual degeneration of the retina and subsequent loss of vision.

retinol *n* a yellow chemical compound occurring *esp* in egg yolk, vegetables, and fish liver oil and essential for growth and vision; vitamin A.

retinue *n* a group of attendants accompanying an important person, e.g. a head of state.

retire *v* **1a** to give up one's position or occupation permanently, *esp* at the end of one's working life. **b** to cause or force to retire from a position or occupation. **2** *formal* **a** to withdraw from a place. **b** to go to bed. **3** of troops: to fall back or retreat. **4** to withdraw from a sporting contest. **5** of a jury: to leave the court to consider their verdict. ⋙ **retired** *adj,* **retirer** *n.*

retirement *n* **1a** withdrawal from one's position or occupation, *esp* permanent withdrawal from active working life. **b** the age at which one normally retires from work. **c** the state of being retired. **2** *literary* a place of seclusion or privacy.

retiring *adj* tending to avoid contact with other people; shy. ⋙ **retiringly** *adv.*

retold *v* past tense and past part. of RETELL.

retook *v* past tense of RETAKE[1].

retool *v* **1** to equip (*esp* a factory) with new tools. **2** *chiefly NAm* to reorganize (something), *esp* with a view to improving efficiency.

retort[1] *v* to answer back sharply or tersely.

retort[2] *n* a terse, witty, angry, or cutting reply.

retort[3] *n* **1** *esp* formerly, a container with a long neck bent downward, used for distillation and other chemical processes. **2** a container for the large-scale production of metal, gas, etc by heating a substance, e.g. ore or coal.

retort[4] *v* to heat in a retort.

retouch *v* to restore or improve the appearance of (something) with small additions or changes. ⋙ **retouch** *n,* **retoucher** *n.*

retrace *v* **1** to go over (e.g. footsteps or a route) again, usu in the opposite direction. **2** to go back over (something) for the purposes of discovery or clarification.

retract *v* **1** to draw back or in. **2a** to withdraw (something said or written). **b** to refuse to abide by (e.g. a promise or agreement). ⋙ **retractable** *adj,* **retractive** *adj.*

retractile *adj* capable of being retracted. ⋙ **retractility** *n.*

retraction *n* the act or an instance of retracting; *specif* a statement that retracts an earlier one.

retractor *n* **1** a surgical instrument for holding back organs or tissues, *esp* at the edges of an incision. **2** a muscle that draws in a body part: compare PROTRACTOR.

retrain *v* to learn or teach new skills.

retread[1] *v* to renew the tread of (a worn tyre).

retread[2] *n* a tyre with a new tread.

retreat[1] *n* **1** the act or instance of withdrawing, *esp* from something difficult or dangerous; *specif* the forced withdrawal of troops after a battle from an advanced position. **2** a place of peace, privacy, or safety. **3** a period of withdrawal for prayer, meditation, and study.

retreat[2] *v* **1** to make a retreat; to withdraw. **2** *NAm* to slope backward; to recede. ⋙ **retreater** *n.*

retrench *v* **1a** to reduce (*esp* costs or expenses). **b** to make reductions; to economize. **2** *Aus* to make (a worker) redundant. ⋙ **retrenchment** *n.*

retrial *n* a second or subsequent legal trial.

retribution *n* punishment or retaliation for an insult or injury. ⋙ **retributive** *adj,* **retributively** *adv,* **retributory** *adj.*

retrieve *v* **1a** to get back again. **b** to rescue or save. **2** of a dog: to find and bring in (killed or wounded game). **3** to recover (e.g. data) from a computer memory. ⋙ **retrievability** *n,* **retrievable** *adj,* **retrieval** *n.*

retriever *n* a dog of a breed used to retrieve game in shooting.

retro[1] *adj* in the style of an earlier period, usu in the recent past.

retro[2] *n* objects, artworks, music, clothes, etc that imitate the style of an earlier period.

retro- *prefix* **1a** back towards the past: *retrograde.* **b** backward: *retroflex.* **2** situated behind: *retrochoir.*

retroactive *adj* extending in scope or effect to a prior time. ⋙ **retroaction** *n,* **retroactively** *adv,* **retroactivity** *n.*

retrochoir *n* the part of a large church or cathedral behind the high altar.

retrofit *v* (**retrofitted, retrofitting**) to provide (a manufactured article) with new parts or equipment not available at the time of manufacture. ⋙ **retrofit** *n.*

retroflex *adj esp* of a body or plant part: turned or curved backward. ⋙ **retroflection** *n,* **retroflexion** *n.*

retrograde[1] *adj* **1** resulting in a worse or less advanced state. **2** moving or directed backward. **3** ordered opposite to normal; reversed. **4** of orbital or rotational movement: in a direction contrary to normal or that of neighbouring celestial bodies. ⋙ **retrogradely** *adv.*

retrograde[2] *v* **1** to move backwards, *esp,* in astronomy, to show retrograde motion. **2** = RETROGRESS. ⋙ **retrogradation** *n.*

retrogress *v* to return to an earlier usu worse state. ⋙ **retrogressive** *adj,* **retrogressively** *adv.*

retrogression *n* a reversal in development, *esp* a return to a less advanced or specialized state during the development of an organism.

retro-rocket *n* a rocket on an aircraft, spacecraft, etc that produces thrust in a direction opposite to its motion in order to slow it down.

retrospect *n* a survey or review of past events. ✻ **in retrospect** when considering the past or a past event, *esp* in the light of present knowledge or experience; with hindsight. ⋙ **retrospection** *n.*

retrospective[1] *adj* **1** relating to or affecting things in the past; retroactive. **2** of an art exhibition: showing the evolution of an artist's work over a period of years. ⋙ **retrospectively** *adv.*

retrospective[2] *n* a retrospective exhibition.

retroussé /rə'troohsay/ *adj* of a nose: turned up at the end.

retroversion *n* **1** the process of turning back or regressing. **2** the bending backward of a body part or organ, *esp* the womb. ⋙ **retroverted** *adj.*

retrovirus *n* any of a family of RNA-containing viruses that can generate DNA from their RNA, many of which induce cancer and one of which causes Aids.

retsina *n* a white Greek wine flavoured with resin from pine trees.

retune *v* to tune (e.g. a musical instrument or television set) again or differently.

return[1] *v* **1a** to go back or come back. **b** (+ to) to go back to something in thought, conversation, or practice. **2** to put back in a former or proper place or state. **3** to give or send back, *esp* to its owner. **4** to elect (a candidate). **5** to state or present (a verdict). **6** to bring in (e.g. a profit). **7** to repay (e.g. a compliment or favour). **8** in sport, to play (a ball or shuttlecock) hit by an opponent. ⋙ **returnable** *adj,* **returner** *n.*

return[2] *n* **1** the act of coming back to or from a place or condition. **2a** the act of returning something, *esp* to a former place or owner. **b** (*also in pl*) something returned, e.g. an unsold newspaper or unwanted ticket returned for a refund. **3** *Brit* a ticket bought for a trip to a place and back again: compare SINGLE² (4). **4** (*also in pl*) the profit from work, investment, or business. **5a** a financial account or formal report. **b** (*usu in pl*) a declaration of the results of an election. **6** the continuation, usu at a right angle, of the facade of a building or of a moulding. ✻ **by return (of post)** by the next post to the sender of an item received. **in return** in compensation or repayment. **many happy returns (of the day)** a birthday greeting.

return[3] *adj* **1** relating to the act of returning. **2a** done or given in return. **b** of a game or match: played against the same opponent or opponents as before.

returnee *n* **1** somebody who returns, *esp* an exile or refugee returning from abroad. **2** a person who resumes a working life after a prolonged period of *esp* voluntary unemployment.

returning officer *n Brit* an official who presides over an election and declares the result.

reunify *v* (**-ies, -ied**) to restore the unity of (e.g. a previously divided country). ⋙ **reunification** *n.*

reunion *n* **1** a gathering of people, e.g. relatives or former associates, after a period of separation. **2** the act or an instance of reuniting.

reunite *v* to come or bring together again.

reuse *v* to use again, *esp* after reclaiming or reprocessing. ⋙ **reusable** *adj,* **reuse** *n,* **reuser** *n.*

Rev. *abbr* Reverend.

rev[1] *n informal* (*usu in pl*) a revolution per minute of an engine.

rev[2] *v* (**revved, revving**) *informal* (*often* + up) to increase the number of revolutions per minute of (an engine), *esp* while stationary.

revalue *v* **1** to change, *esp* to increase, the exchange value of (a currency). **2** to assess again, *esp* arriving at a different conclusion. ⋙ **revaluation** *n.*

revamp *v* to change and improve the appearance or structure of. ⋙ **revamp** *n.*

revanchism *n* a policy designed to recover lost territory or status. ⋙ **revanchist** *n and adj.*

rev counter *n* = TACHOMETER.

Revd *abbr* Reverend.

reveal[1] *v* **1** to make known (something secret or hidden). **2** to open (something) up to view. **3** to make known through divine inspiration. ⋙ **revealable** *adj,* **revealer** *n,* **revealment** *n.*

reveal[2] *n* the side of an opening in a wall for a door or window.

revealing *adj* **1** exposing something usu concealed from view. **2** providing significant or interesting information, often unintentionally.

reveille *n* a call or signal to get up in the morning; *specif* a military bugle call.

revel[1] *v* (**revelled, revelling,** *NAm* **reveled, reveling**) **1** (+ in) to derive intense satisfaction from something. **2** to enjoy oneself in a noisy and exuberant way. ⋙ **reveller** *n,* **revelry** *n.*

revel[2] *n* (*also in pl*) a riotous party or celebration.

revelation *n* **1a** the act or an instance of revealing something. **b** something revealed, *esp* a sudden and illuminating disclosure. **2** a truth believed to be revealed by God to man, or the communicating of it.

revelatory *adj* serving to reveal something.

revenant *n literary* somebody who returns, *esp* from the dead.

revenge[1] *n* **1a** the act of retaliating in order to get even for a wrong or injury. **b** a desire to retaliate in this way. **2** an opportunity for getting even. ⋙ **revengeful** *adj.*

revenge[2] *v* **1** to retaliate for (an insult, injury, etc), *esp* by inflicting something similar on the perpetrators. **2** to take revenge on behalf of (oneself or somebody else). ⋙ **revenger** *n.*

revenue *n* **1** the total income produced by a given source, e.g. an investment, or received by a business or other organization. **2** the income, e.g. taxes, that a government collects for public use.

reverberate *v* **1** of a sound: to be reflected, *esp* many times; to continue in a series of echoes. **2** to have a continuing and powerful effect. ⋙ **reverberant** *adj,* **reverberantly** *adv,* **reverberation** *n,* **reverberative** *adj,* **reverberator** *n,* **reverberatory** *adj.*

revere *v* to regard with deep and devoted respect.

reverence[1] *n* **1** honour or respect, *esp* profound respect accorded to something sacred. **2** a gesture, e.g. a bow, denoting respect. **3** (**Reverence**) used as a form of address to a member of the clergy.

reverence[2] *v* to regard or treat with reverence.

reverend[1] *adj* **1** worthy of reverence; revered. **2** (**Reverend**) used as a title for a member of the clergy.

reverend[2] *n informal* a member of the clergy.

Reverend Mother *n* the title of the Mother Superior of a convent.

reverent *adj* showing or characterized by reverence. ⋙ **reverently** *adv.*

reverential *adj* **1** expressing or having the quality of reverence. **2** inspiring reverence. ➤➤ **reverentially** *adv.*

reverie *n* **1** a daydream. **2** the condition of being lost in thought or dreamlike fantasy. **3** a musical composition suggesting a dreamy state.

revers /ri'viə/ *n* (*pl* **revers**) a wide turned-back part or applied facing along the front edges of a garment; *specif* a lapel.

reversal *n* the act or an instance of reversing, *esp* movement in an opposite direction, or the causing of such movement.

reverse[1] *adj* **1a** opposite or contrary to a previous or usual condition or direction. **b** having the front turned away from an observer. **2** causing backward movement. ➤➤ **reversely** *adv.*

reverse[2] *v* **1a** to move in the opposite direction. **b** to go or drive backward. **2a** to change to an opposite position or direction. **b** to turn upside down or inside out. **3a** to overthrow or annul (a legal judgment). **b** to change (e.g. a decision or policy) to the contrary. ✱ **reverse the charges** *Brit* to arrange for the recipient of a telephone call to pay for it. ➤➤ **reverser** *n.*

reverse[3] *n* **1** the opposite of something. **2a** the side of a coin, medal, etc that does not bear the principal design and lettering: compare OBVERSE[2]. **b** the back part of something, e.g. the back cover of a book. **3** a gear that causes backward motion or reverses the direction of operation. **4** a change for the worse; a setback or misfortune. ✱ **in reverse 1** backward. **2** in the opposite direction.

reverse engineering *n* the pirating or reproducing of a competitor's product after a detailed study of its workings.

reverse takeover *n* the purchase of a large company, usu a public company, by a smaller company.

reversible *adj* **1** capable of going through a sequence, e.g. of changes, in either direction. **2** of fabric or clothing: designed to be used with either side outward. **3** capable of being reversed. ➤➤ **reversibility** *n,* **reversibly** *adv.*

reversing light *n* a light on the rear of a vehicle that is switched on automatically when reverse gear is selected.

reversion *n* **1** the act of reverting, *esp* a return to an earlier inferior state. **2** a return to an ancestral type or reappearance of an ancestral characteristic. **3** the right to possess property at some future time, usu on the death of the present owner. **4** the sum to be paid on death in accordance with a life-insurance policy. ➤➤ **reversionary** *adj.*

revert *v* **1a** to return to an earlier state, *esp* one considered worse or more primitive. **b** to return to a former practice, belief, etc. **c** of an organism: to develop characteristics present in ancestors but not present in the species for some time. **2** of property: to return to the original owner, or to the heirs of the original owner. ➤➤ **reverter** *n,* **revertible** *adj.*

revetment *n* **1** a facing of stone, concrete, etc built to protect a wall or retain an embankment. **2** a barricade to provide shelter, e.g. against bomb splinters.

review[1] *n* **1** an act of inspecting or examining something, *esp* in order to decide if changes need to be made. **2a** a critical evaluation of a book, play, etc. **b** a magazine or newspaper, or part of one, devoted chiefly to critical articles. **3a** a general survey, e.g. of current affairs. **b** a retrospective view or survey, e.g. of somebody's life or work. **4** a formal military or naval inspection. **5** = REVUE.

review[2] *v* **1** to make, hold, write, etc a review of. **2** to examine or study again. ➤➤ **reviewer** *n.*

revile *v* to criticize very harshly or abusively. ➤➤ **revilement** *n,* **reviler** *n.*

revise[1] *v* **1** to make an amended, improved, or up-to-date version of (*esp* a text). **2** *Brit* to refresh one's knowledge of (e.g. a subject), *esp* before an examination. **3** to change (e.g. an opinion), *esp* in the light of further consideration or new information. ➤➤ **revisable** *adj,* **reviser** *n,* **revisory** *adj.*

revise[2] *n* a printing proof that incorporates changes marked in a previous proof.

revision *n* **1** the act of revising. **2** a revised version of something, *esp* a text. ➤➤ **revisionary** *adj.*

revisionism *n* **1** the desire to revise politics, attitudes, etc. **2** *chiefly derog* a movement in Marxist socialism favouring an evolutionary rather than a revolutionary transition to socialism. ➤➤ **revisionist** *adj and n.*

revitalize *or* **-ise** *v* to impart new life or vigour to. ➤➤ **revitalization** *n.*

revival *n* **1a** a return or bringing back to life, vigour, popularity, etc. **b** restoration of an earlier fashion, style, or practice. **2** a new presentation or production, e.g. of a play. **3** a period of renewed religious fervour.

revivalism *n* **1** the spirit or methods characteristic of religious revivals. **2** the desire or tendency to revive earlier fashions, styles, or practices. ➤➤ **revivalist** *n and adj,* **revivalistic** *adj.*

revive *v* **1** to return to a state of consciousness, health, or strength. **2** to bring back into an active state or current use. ➤➤ **revivable** *adj,* **reviver** *n.*

revivify *v* (**-ies, -ied**) to give new life or vigour to; to revitalize. ➤➤ **revivification** *n.*

revoke *v* to declare to be no longer valid or operative; to annul. ➤➤ **revocable** *adj,* **revocation** *n,* **revoker** *n.*

revolt[1] *v* **1** to reject the authority or control of a government, employer, etc; to rebel. **2** to cause to feel disgust or loathing; to nauseate. ➤➤ **revolter** *n.*

revolt[2] *n* **1** a rebellion, *esp* a determined and armed one. **2** a movement or expression of vigorous opposition.

revolting *adj* extremely offensive; nauseating. ➤➤ **revoltingly** *adv.*

revolution *n* **1a** a fundamental political change, *esp* the overthrow of one government and the substitution of another. **b** a sudden or far-reaching change. **2a** the movement of an object round a central point or axis; rotation. **b** one complete turn made in this way.

revolutionary[1] *adj* **1** completely new and different. **2a** of or being a revolution. **b** promoting or engaging in revolution.

revolutionary[2] *n* (*pl* **-ies**) somebody who advocates or is engaged in a revolution.

revolutionize *or* **-ise** *v* to change fundamentally or completely.

revolve[1] *v* **1** to move in a circular course or round a central point or axis. **2** (+ around) to be centred on a specified theme or main point. **3** *literary* to ponder. ➤➤ **revolvable** *adj,* **revolving** *adj.*

revolve[2] *n Brit* a device used on a stage to allow a set or piece of scenery to be rotated.

revolver *n* a handgun with revolving chambers each holding one cartridge and allowing several shots to be fired without reloading.

revolving door *n* a door with usu four sections that pivot on a central axis.

revue *n* a theatrical production consisting typically of brief often satirical sketches, songs, and dances.

revulsion *n* **1** a feeling of utter distaste or repugnance. **2** a sudden or violent reaction or change. ➤➤ **revulsive** *adj.*

reward[1] *v* **1** to give a reward to (somebody). **2** to give a reward to somebody for (something). ➤➤ **rewardable** *adj,* **rewarder** *n.*

reward[2] *n* **1** something offered or given for service, effort, or achievement. **2** a sum of money offered in return for the capture of a criminal or the recovery of lost or stolen property. **3** something that is justly received as a consequence of good or bad behaviour; deserts. ➤➤ **rewardless** *adj.*

rewarding *adj* yielding a reward; personally satisfying.

rewind *v* (*past tense and past part.* **rewound**) to wind (film, tape, etc) back to the beginning or to an earlier point. ➤➤ **rewind** *n.*

rewire *v* to provide (e.g. a house) with new electric wiring. ➤➤ **rewirable** *adj.*

reword *v* to alter the wording of; to restate in different words.

rework *v* **1** to revise or rewrite. **2** to reprocess (e.g. used material) for further use.

rewound *v* past tense and past part. of REWIND.

rewrite[1] *v* (*past tense* **rewrote,** *past part.* **rewritten**) to write again, *esp* differently. ➤➤ **rewriter** *n.*

rewrite[2] *n* **1** the act or an instance of rewriting. **2** something rewritten.

rewritten *v* past part. of REWRITE[1].

rewrote *v* past tense of REWRITE[1].

Rex *n* **1** a title given to a reigning king and used after the first name. **2** used in legal cases, when the British monarch is a king, to denote the Crown as a party to the action.

Rf *abbr* the chemical symbol for rutherfordium.

RFC *abbr* Rugby Football Club.

Rh[1] *abbr* rhesus (factor).

Rh[2] *abbr* the chemical symbol for rhodium.

rh *abbr* right hand.

RHA *abbr Brit* Regional Health Authority.

rhadamanthine *adj* (*often* **Rhadamanthine**) *literary* rigorously just or uncompromising.

rhapsodize *or* **-ise** *v* to speak or write with ardent enthusiasm or deep emotion. ➤➤ **rhapsodist** *n.*

rhapsody *n* (*pl* **-ies**) **1** a musical composition in one continuous movement, usu a free fantasy. **2a** an expression in speech or writing of ardent enthusiasm or deep emotion. **b** a state of rapture or ecstasy. **3** an epic poem short enough to be recited in a single sitting. ➤➤ **rhapsodic** *adj,* **rhapsodically** *adv.*

rhea *n* a large flightless S American bird similar to but smaller than the ostrich.

rhebok *or* **reebok** *n* a small antelope of S Africa with a woolly coat of brownish grey hair and short horns.

Rhenish *adj* of the river Rhine or the adjoining regions.

rhenium *n* a silver-grey metallic chemical element similar to manganese used *esp* in catalysts and thermocouples.

rheology *n* a branch of physics dealing with the deformation and flow of matter. ➤➤ **rheological** *adj,* **rheologist** *n.*

rheostat *n* a device that regulates an electric current by varying resistance. ➤➤ **rheostatic** *adj.*

rhesus baby *n* a baby born with a blood disease caused by the presence of antibodies in its mother's Rh-negative blood that act on and destroy the cells of its own Rh-positive blood.

rhesus factor *n* any of several substances present in red blood cells that are used to define blood groups and can provoke intense allergic reactions when incompatible blood types are mixed, e.g. during pregnancy or in blood transfusions.

rhesus monkey *n* a small pale brown monkey of S Asia that is a macaque.

rhesus negative *adj* lacking rhesus factor in the red blood cells.

rhesus positive *adj* having rhesus factor in the red blood cells.

rhetoric *n* **1** the art of speaking or writing effectively. **2** impressive language that is calculated to produce an effect but may be insincere or exaggerated.

rhetorical *adj* **1** relating to or involving rhetoric. **2** of language: impressive or used merely to impress. ➤➤ **rhetorically** *adv.*

rhetorical question *n* a question to which no answer is expected, used to make a statement with dramatic effect.

rhetorician *n* **1** an eloquent or pretentious writer or speaker. **2** an expert in or teacher of rhetoric.

rheum *n* a watery discharge from the eyes, nose, etc. ➤➤ **rheumy** *adj.*

rheumatic[1] *adj* relating to, suffering from, or affected by rheumatism. ➤➤ **rheumatically** *adv.*

rheumatic[2] *n* somebody suffering from rheumatism.

rheumatic fever *n* an acute disease that occurs chiefly in children and young adults and is characterized by fever, inflammation and pain in the joints.

rheumaticky *adj informal* rheumatic.

rheumatics *pl n informal* (*used as sing. or pl*) rheumatism.

rheumatism *n* **1** any of various conditions characterized by inflammation and pain in muscles, joints, or fibrous tissue. **2** = RHEUMATOID ARTHRITIS.

rheumatoid *adj* characteristic of or affected by rheumatism or rheumatoid arthritis.

rheumatoid arthritis *n* a progressively worsening disease of unknown cause that is characterized by painful inflammation and swelling of joint structures.

rheumatology *n* a branch of medicine dealing with rheumatic diseases. ➤➤ **rheumatological** *adj,* **rheumatologist** *n.*

rhinestone *n* a colourless artificial gemstone made of glass, paste, quartz, etc.

rhinitis *n* inflammation of the mucous membrane of the nose.

rhino *n* (*pl* **rhinos** *or* **rhino**) *informal* a rhinoceros.

rhinoceros *n* (*pl* **rhinoceroses** *or* **rhinoceros**) a large plant-eating hoofed mammal of Africa and Asia with a very thick skin and either one or two horns on the snout.

rhinoplasty *n* plastic surgery of the nose. ➤➤ **rhinoplastic** *adj.*

rhizome *n* a long thick horizontal underground plant stem distinguished from a true root in having buds and usu scalelike leaves. ➤➤ **rhizomatous** *adj.*

rho *n* the 17th letter of the Greek alphabet (Ρ, ρ), equivalent to roman rh.

Rhodesian *n* a native or inhabitant of Rhodesia (now Zimbabwe). ➤➤ **Rhodesian** *adj.*

Rhodes scholarship *n* any of numerous scholarships available at Oxford University to candidates from the Commonwealth and the USA. ➤➤ **Rhodes scholar** *n.*

rhodium *n* a white hard metallic chemical element of the platinum group used in alloys and to plate jewellery.

rhododendron *n* a shrub of the heather family with clusters of showy red, pink, purple, or white flowers and usu large leathery evergreen leaves.

rhombi *n* pl of RHOMBUS.

rhombohedron *n* (*pl* **rhombohedrons** *or* **rhombohedra**) a six-sided solid whose faces are rhombuses. ➤➤ **rhombohedral** *adj.*

rhomboid[1] *n* a parallelogram with adjacent sides of unequal length.

rhomboid[2] *adj* shaped like a rhombus or rhomboid.

rhomboidal *adj* = RHOMBOID[2].

rhombus *n* (*pl* **rhombuses** *or* **rhombi**) a parallelogram with equal sides but unequal angles; a diamond-shaped figure. ➤➤ **rhombic** *adj.*

rhubarb *n* **1** a plant of the dock family with large fleshy leaves and edible stalks, that are usu cooked with sugar and eaten as a dessert. **2** *Brit* a noise made by actors, traditionally by repeating the word *rhubarb* in a low voice, to suggest the sound of background conversation. **3** *chiefly Brit, informal* nonsense or rubbish.

rhumb *n* **1** any of the 32 points of the compass. **2** = RHUMB LINE.

rhumba *n* see RUMBA.

rhumb line *n* an imaginary line on the surface of the earth that crosses each meridian at the same oblique angle and is the course sailed by a ship following a single compass direction.

rhyme[1] *n* **1a** correspondence in the sound of words or their final syllables, *esp* those at the ends of consecutive or alternate lines of verse. **b** a word that corresponds with another in this way. **2** rhyming verse, or a poem written in such verse. ✱ **rhyme or reason** good sense, reasonableness, or logic. ➤➤ **rhymeless** *adj.*

rhyme[2] *v* **1a** of a word or syllable: to constitute a rhyme. **b** of a line of verse: to end with a rhyming word or syllable. **2** to compose rhymes. **3** to use (a word) as a rhyme. ➤➤ **rhymer** *n.*

rhymester *n* a poet, *esp* one regarded as inferior; a poetaster.

rhyming slang *n* slang in which a word is replaced by a rhyming phrase that is usu subsequently reduced to the first element, e.g. *head* becomes *loaf of bread* and then *loaf.*

rhyolite *n* a fine-grained acid volcanic rock similar to granite but formed from lava. ➤➤ **rhyolitic** *adj.*

rhythm *n* **1a** the pattern of strong and weak or long and short elements in the flow of sound, *esp* in speech. **b** the pattern of stresses on the words used in poetry; metre. **2a** in music, the regular recurrence of a pattern of stress and length of notes. **b** a characteristic pattern of this kind. **3** movement or fluctuation marked by a regular recurrence or pattern of elements.

rhythm and blues *n* popular music with elements of blues and jazz, developed by black American musicians.

rhythmic *adj* **1** of or involving rhythm. **2** moving or progressing with a pronounced or flowing rhythm. **3** regularly recurring. ➤➤ **rhythmical** *adj,* **rhythmically** *adv,* **rhythmicity** *n.*

rhythm method *n* a method of birth control that involves not having sexual intercourse on those days when conception is most likely to occur.

rhythm section *n* the group of instruments in a band that supply the rhythm, *esp* the drums and the bass.

RI *abbr* **1** religious instruction. **2** Rhode Island (US postal abbreviation).

ria *n* a narrow inlet caused by the submergence of a river valley, or part of one.

rial *n* **1** the basic monetary unit of Iran, Oman, and Yemen. **2** = RIYAL (I).

rib[1] *n* **1** any of the paired curved rods of bone or cartilage that stiffen the body walls of most vertebrate animals and protect the heart, lungs, etc. **2 a** a transverse member of the frame of a ship that runs from keel to deck. **b** a structural member of the wing of an aircraft that runs from the leading edge to the trailing edge. **c** any of the rods supporting the fabric of an umbrella. **d** an arched support or ornamental band in vaulting. **3** an elongated ridge, e.g.: **a** a vein of a leaf or an insect's wing. **b** any of a series of narrow ridges in a knitted or woven fabric.

rib[2] *v* (**ribbed, ribbing**) to form into ribs or ridges; *specif* to form a pattern of vertical ridges in (a piece of knitting) by alternating knit and purl stitches. ➤➤ **ribbed** *adj.*

rib[3] *v* (**ribbed, ribbing**) *informal* to tease (somebody). ➤➤ **ribbing** *n.*

ribald *adj* crudely or obscenely humorous. ➤➤ **ribaldry** *n.*

riband *n* a ribbon used *esp* as an award for achievement.

ribbing *n* **1** an arrangement of ribs. **2** a ribbed part of a piece of knitting.

ribbon *n* **1a** a narrow band of fabric used for decorative effect, e.g. in fastening the hair, tying parcels, etc. **b** a piece of usu multicoloured ribbon worn as a military decoration or in place of a medal. **2a** a long narrow ribbonlike strip. **b** a strip of inked material used in a typewriter or computer printer. **3** (*in pl*) tatters or shreds. ➤➤ **ribboned** *adj,* **ribbonlike** *adj.*

ribbon development *n* the development of a row of buildings, *esp* housing, along a main road.

ribcage *n* the enclosing wall of the chest consisting chiefly of the ribs and their connective tissue.

riboflavin *n* a yellow chemical compound of the vitamin B complex occurring *esp* in green vegetables, milk, eggs, and liver and often used as a colouring.

ribonucleic acid *n* = RNA.

ribose *n* a sugar with five carbon atoms in its molecule that occurs in riboflavin, RNA, etc.

ribosome *n* any of the minute granules containing RNA and protein that occur in cells and are the sites where proteins are synthesized. ➤➤ **ribosomal** *adj.*

rib-tickler *n* an amusing joke, story, etc. ➤➤ **rib-tickling** *adj.*

rice[1] *n* **1** a cereal grass widely cultivated in warm climates. **2** the grains of this plant used as food.

rice[2] *v* to press (soft food, e.g. cooked potato) through a ricer or similar utensil.

rice paper *n* **1** a very thin edible material resembling paper made from various plant sources and used *esp* to prevent small cakes or biscuits from sticking to the baking tin. **2** a very thin paper made from the pith of a Chinese tree or shrub, used *esp* for painting.

ricer *n* a kitchen utensil with perforations, through which soft foods, e.g. cooked potato, are pressed to produce particles about the size of rice grains.

rich *adj* **1a** having abundant possessions, *esp* material and financial wealth. **b** of a country or area: having abundant natural resources, successful industries, a strong economy, etc. **2a** having high worth, value, or quality. **b** impressively lavish;

sumptuous. **3** (*often* + in) well supplied or endowed. **4a** vivid and deep in colour. **b** full and mellow in tone or quality. **5** highly productive or remunerative; high-yielding. **6a** of soil: having abundant plant nutrients. **b** of food: highly seasoned, fatty, oily, or sweet. **c** of a fuel–air mixture, *esp* in an internal combustion engine: containing a higher proportion of fuel than normal. **7** *informal* highly amusing or irritating, *esp* because ironic or ridiculous. ⋙ **richness** *n.*

riches *pl n* great wealth.

richly *adv* **1** in a rich manner. **2** in full measure; amply.

Richter scale *n* a logarithmic scale for expressing the magnitude of a seismic disturbance, e.g. an earthquake.

ricin /'riesin, 'risin/ *n* a poisonous protein in the bean of the castor-oil plant.

rick[1] *n* a stack of hay, corn, etc in the open air, *esp* one constructed in a regular shape, often with a thatched top.

rick[2] *v chiefly Brit* to wrench or sprain (e.g. one's neck). ⋙ **rick** *n.*

rickets *pl n* (*used as sing.*) a disease, *esp* of children, characterized by softening and deformation of bones, usu due to a lack of sunlight or vitamin D.

rickety *adj* **1** likely to collapse, *esp* because badly made or old and worn; unsound. **2** suffering from rickets. ⋙ **ricketiness** *n.*

rickrack *or* **ricrac** *n* a flat braid woven to form zigzags and used *esp* as trimming on clothing.

rickshaw *or* **ricksha** *n* a small covered two-wheeled vehicle pulled by one or more people, used *esp* in SE Asia.

ricochet[1] *n* **1** the rebound of a projectile (e.g. a bullet) that strikes a hard or flat surface at an angle. **2** something that rebounds in this way.

ricochet[2] *v* (**ricocheted** *or* **ricochetted, ricocheting** *or* **ricochetting**) of e.g. a bullet: to rebound off one or more hard or flat surfaces.

ricotta *n* a soft white unsalted Italian cheese made from sheep's milk.

ricrac *n* see RICKRACK.

rictus *n* an unnatural gaping grin or grimace. ⋙ **rictal** *adj.*

rid *v* (**ridding,** *past tense and past part.* **rid** *or* **ridded**) to relieve of something unwanted. ✱ **get rid of** to free oneself of (something unwanted).

riddance *n* deliverance from something or somebody unwanted. ✱ **good riddance** an expression of relief at becoming free of something or somebody unwanted.

ridden *v* past part. of RIDE[1].

-ridden *comb. form* forming adjectives, with the meanings: **1** afflicted or excessively concerned with: *conscience-ridden.* **2** excessively full of or supplied with: *priest-ridden.*

riddle[1] *n* **1** a short and *esp* humorous verbal puzzle. **2** something or somebody difficult to understand.

riddle[2] *v* to speak in riddles. ⋙ **riddler** *n.*

riddle[3] *n* a large coarse sieve, e.g. for sifting grain or gravel.

riddle[4] *v* **1** to separate (e.g. grain from chaff) with a riddle. **2** to pierce with many holes. **3** to spread through (something), *esp* as an affliction: *The state ... was riddled with poverty* — Thomas Wood.

ride[1] *v* (*past tense* **rode,** *past part.* **ridden**) **1a** to travel mounted on and controlling an animal, bicycle, etc. **b** to travel in a vehicle. **c** to travel across or patrol (an area), *esp* on horseback. **2a** to be borne up or supported by. **b** of a ship: to be moored or anchored. **3** (*usu* + out) to survive (e.g. a storm) without great damage or loss. **4** (*usu* + up) of clothing: to work its way up the body as one moves. **5** to yield to (a punch) so as to soften the impact. **6a** (*usu in passive*) to obsess or oppress. **b** *NAm* to harass persistently. ✱ **be riding for a fall** to act in such a way as to make disaster seem inevitable. **ride high** to experience success. **ride on** to be dependent on.

ride[2] *n* **1** an outing or journey by horseback or by vehicle. **2** any of various mechanical devices, e.g. at a funfair, for riding on. **3** a usu straight road or path in a wood, forest, etc used for riding, for access, or as a firebreak. ✱ **take for a ride** *informal* to deceive or trick (somebody).

rider *n* **1** somebody who rides a horse, a bicycle, or a motorcycle. **2** something added by way of qualification or amendment, e.g. a clause appended to a legal document. ⋙ **riderless** *adj.*

ridge[1] *n* **1** a long narrow stretch of elevated land or mountain range. **2** the line along which two upward-sloping surfaces meet; *specif* the top of a roof at the intersection of two sloping sides. **3** an elongated part raised above a surrounding surface, e.g. the raised part between furrows on ploughed ground. **4** in meteorology, an elongated area of high pressure. ⋙ **ridgy** *adj.*

ridge[2] *v* to form into or mark with a ridge or ridges.

ridgepiece *n* a horizontal beam in a roof that supports the upper ends of the rafters.

ridgepole *n* the horizontal pole at the top of a tent.

ridge tent *n* a tent with a ridged roof usu supported on a ridgepole.

ridgeway *n Brit* a path or road along the ridge of a hill.

ridicule[1] *n* scornful or contemptuous words or actions; derision.

ridicule[2] *v* to treat with ridicule; to mock.

ridiculous *adj* arousing or deserving ridicule; absurd or preposterous. ⋙ **ridiculously** *adv,* **ridiculousness** *n.*

riding[1] *n* **1** the riding of horses as a sport or pastime. **2** a path used for horse riding; a bridle path.

riding[2] *n* **1** (*often* **Riding**) any of three former administrative jurisdictions of Yorkshire. **2** an administrative or electoral district of Canada.

riding crop *n* a short whip that a rider uses to urge a horse on.

riding light *n* a light indicating that a boat or ship is at anchor.

riel *n* the basic monetary unit of Cambodia.

riempie *n SAfr* a narrow leather thong used *esp* in furniture construction.

Riesling *n* a variety of grape grown *esp* in Germany, or the medium-dry white wine produced from it.

rife *adj* **1** occurring everywhere or to a great degree; prevalent. **2** (+ with) abundantly supplied with or full of something.

riff[1] *n* a constantly repeated phrase in jazz or rock music.

riff[2] *v* to play riffs.

riffle[1] *v* **1a** to leaf through (something) rapidly, *esp* by running a thumb over the edges of the leaves. **b** to shuffle (playing cards) by separating the deck into two parts and running the thumbs over the edges of the cards to interleave them. **2** to search through (something) rapidly.

riffle[2] *n* an instance of riffling.

riffraff *n* disreputable or worthless people; rabble.

rifle[1] *n* **1** a firearm, usu held at shoulder level, with a long barrel that has spiral grooves cut inside it to spin the bullet and produce a straight trajectory. **2** (*in pl*) a body of soldiers armed with rifles.

rifle[2] *v* **1** to cut spiral grooves inside the barrel of (a rifle, cannon, etc). **2** to propel (e.g. a ball) with great force or speed.

rifle[3] *v* **1** to search through (e.g. a drawer or safe), *esp* in order to find and steal something. **2** to steal. ➤➤ **rifler** *n.*

rifleman *n* (*pl* **riflemen**) a soldier armed with a rifle.

rifle range *n* a place for shooting practice with rifles.

rifling *n* a system of spiral grooves inside the barrel of a gun.

rift *n* **1** a fissure or crack, *esp* in the earth. **2** a disruption of friendly relations between individuals, nations, etc.

rift valley *n* a valley formed by the subsidence of the earth's crust between two or more parallel faults.

rig[1] *v* (**rigged, rigging**) **1a** to fit out (e.g. a ship) with rigging, sails, etc. **b** to prepare (sails, etc) for use. **2** (*usu* + out) to clothe or dress. **3** (*often* + out) to supply with equipment for a particular use. **4** (*often* + up) to assemble or erect, *esp* for temporary use.

rig[2] *n* **1** the distinctive arrangement of a ship's sails and masts. **2** an outfit of clothing worn for a particular occasion or activity. **3** equipment or machinery fitted for a usu specified purpose. **4** *chiefly NAm* a truck.

rig[3] *v* (**rigged, rigging**) to manipulate, influence, or control for dishonest purposes.

rigatoni *pl n* (*used as sing. or pl*) pasta in short, ridged, and sometimes curved tubes.

rigger *n* **1** (*used in combinations*) a ship of a specified rig. **2a** somebody who rigs boats, ships, etc. **b** somebody who works on an oil rig. **c** somebody skilled in operating cranes, erecting scaffolding, etc.

rigging *n* **1a** the ropes and chains used aboard a ship for controlling sails and supporting masts. **b** the ropes, wires, and struts used to support the structure of a biplane, hang-glider, etc. **2** any similar system used for support and manipulation, e.g. of theatrical scenery.

right[1] *adj* **1** in accordance with what is morally good, just, or proper. **2** conforming to facts or truth. **3** suitable or appropriate. **4** acting or judging in accordance with truth or fact; not mistaken. **5** in a correct, proper, or healthy state. **6a** denoting or located on the side of somebody or something that is nearer the east when the front faces north. **b** of, on, or being the side of something that is closer to the right hand of an observer positioned directly in front. **c** located on the right side when facing downstream. **7** (*often* **Right**) of the right or right wing in politics. **8** *chiefly Brit, informal* real or utter. ✱ **as right as rain** fine and healthy. **on the right side of 1** in favour with. **2** less than the specified age. ➤➤ **rightness** *n.*

right[2] *n* **1** qualities that together merit moral approval. **2a** a power, privilege, interest, etc to which one has a just claim. **b** (*in pl*) entitlement to publish, perform, film, etc a work. **3a** the part on the right side. **b** the location or direction of the right side. **c** the right hand, or a blow struck with it. **4** (*often* **the Right**) (*used as sing. or pl*) those professing conservative or reactionary political views. ✱ **by rights** with reason or justice; properly. **in one's own right** by virtue of one's own qualifications or attributes. **in the right** correct in what one says or does. **to rights** into proper order. ➤➤ **rightward** *adv,* **rightwards** *adv.*

right[3] *adv* **1** in a proper or correct manner. **2** in the exact location or position. **3** in a direct line or course; straight. **4** all the way; completely. **5** without delay; immediately. **6** on or towards the right.

right[4] *v* **1** to restore to the proper state or condition; to correct. **2** to bring or restore (e.g. a boat) to an upright position. **3** to compensate for or avenge (a wrong, an injustice, etc). ➤➤ **rightable** *adj,* **righter** *n.*

right[5] *interj informal* an expression of agreement or compliance.

right angle *n* an angle of 90°, e.g. at the corner of a square. ✱ **at right angles** forming a right angle. ➤➤ **right-angled** *adj.*

right ascension *n* in astronomy, the distance measured eastward along the celestial equator between the point where the sun crosses it in spring and the point where it is cut by a line drawn from the celestial pole through a given celestial object.

right away *adv* without delay or hesitation.

right-back *n* in football, hockey, etc, a defensive player on the right wing.

righteous *adj* **1** morally right or justified. **2** arising from an outraged sense of justice. ➤➤ **righteously** *adv,* **righteousness** *n.*

rightful *adj* **1** in accordance with notions of fairness; equitable. **2a** having a just claim; legitimate. **b** held by right; legal. **3** fitting or proper. ➤➤ **rightfully** *adv,* **rightfulness** *n.*

right hand *n* **1** the hand on the right side of the body. **2** a reliable or indispensable person. **3** a place of honour.

right-hand *adj* **1** situated on the right. **2** of, designed for, or done with the right hand.

right-handed[1] *adj* **1** using the right hand habitually or more easily than the left. **2** designed for or done with the right hand. **3** of a rotary motion or spiral curve: clockwise. ➤➤ **right-handedly** *adv,* **right-handedness** *n.*

right-handed[2] *adv* using the right hand.

right-hander *n* **1** a right-handed person. **2** a blow struck with the right hand.

right-hand man *n* somebody's most highly valued, trusted, and useful assistant.

Right Honourable *adj* used as a title for certain dignitaries, e.g. privy councillors and senior government ministers.

rightism *n* (*often* **Rightism**) right-wing principles and policy, or advocacy of these. ➤➤ **rightist** *n and adj.*

rightly *adv* **1** fairly or legitimately. **2** properly. **3** according to truth or fact; correctly.

right-minded *adj* thinking and acting by just or honest principles.

right off *adv informal* without delay or hesitation.

right of way *n* (*pl* **rights of way**) **1a** a legal right to pass over another person's property. **b** the course along which a right of way exists. **2** a precedence accorded to one vehicle, vessel, etc over another by custom or law.

right on *interj informal* an expression of agreement or approval.

right-on *adj informal* conforming to current trends in social or political thinking.

Right Reverend *adj* used as a title for high ecclesiastical officials.

rights issue *n* an issue of new shares available to existing shareholders only.

rightsize *v* to change the size of (a business company) in order to maximize efficiency, usu by cutting the workforce.

right-thinking *adj* = RIGHT-MINDED.

right-to-life *adj* = PRO-LIFE.

right whale *n* a large whalebone whale with no dorsal fin, very long whalebone plates instead of teeth, and a large head.

right wing *n* **1** (*often* **Right Wing**) the more conservative division of a group or party. **2** in sport, the right side of the field when facing towards the opposing team, or the players positioned on this side. ➤➤ **right-wing** *adj*, **right-winger** *n*.

rigid *adj* **1** unable to bend or be bent; stiff. **2** inflexibly set in opinions or habits. **3** strictly maintained; unable to be changed. ➤➤ **rigidity** *n*, **rigidly** *adv*, **rigidness** *n*.

rigidify *v* (**-ies, -ied**) to make or become rigid.

rigmarole *n* **1** an absurdly long and complex procedure. **2** a confused or nonsensical account or explanation.

rigor mortis *n* the temporary rigidity of muscles that occurs after death.

rigorous *adj* **1** exercising or favouring rigour; very strict. **2** harsh or severe. **3** scrupulously accurate; precise. ➤➤ **rigorously** *adv*.

rigour (*NAm* **rigor**) *n* **1** the quality of being unyielding or inflexible; strictness. **2** (*also in pl*) a condition that makes life difficult or unpleasant. **3** strict mathematical or logical precision.

rigout *n informal* a complete outfit of clothing.

rile *v* **1** to make angry or resentful. **2** *NAm* = ROIL (1).

rill *n* **1** a small brook. **2** a small channel formed in soil or rock.

rillettes /ree'yet/ *pl n* (*used as sing. or pl*) pork, goose, or other meat cooked in its own fat and potted as pâté.

rim[1] *n* **1** an outer edge or border, *esp* of something circular or curved. **2** the outer ring of a wheel not including the tyre. **3** an outer edge or boundary. ➤➤ **rimless** *adj*.

rim[2] *v* (**rimmed, rimming**) to serve as a rim for; to border. ➤➤ **rimmed** *adj*.

rime[1] *n* a thin coating of frost.

rime[2] *v* to cover with or as if with rime.

rime[3] *n archaic* = RHYME[1].

rime[4] *v archaic* = RHYME[2].

rimu *n* a large coniferous tree of New Zealand.

rind *n* **1** a hard or tough outer layer of fruit, cheese, bacon, etc. **2** the bark of a tree.

rinderpest *n* an infectious fever, *esp* of cattle.

ring[1] *n* **1a** a circular band usu of precious metal, worn on the finger for adornment, etc. **b** a circular band for holding, connecting, hanging, fastening, etc. **2** a circular line, figure, arrangement, or object. **3** an electric element or gas burner in the shape of a circle, set into the top of a cooker, etc. **4a** a space, often a circular one, for exhibitions or competitions, *esp* such a space at a circus. **b** a square enclosure in which boxing or wrestling matches are held. **5** = TREE RING. **6** (*used as sing. or pl*) an exclusive association of people, often for a corrupt purpose. **7** a closed chain of atoms in a molecule. ✱ **hold the ring** to act as a neutral monitor or umpire in a dispute. **run rings round somebody** *informal* to surpass or outdo somebody, *esp* in a way that makes them appear foolish.

ring[2] *v* (*past tense and past part.* **ringed**) **1** to place or form a ring round; to encircle. **2** to attach a ring to (a bird or animal). **3** to cut a ring in the bark around (a tree), usu in order to kill it. ➤➤ **ringed** *adj*.

ring[3] *v* (*past tense* **rang**, *past part.* **rung**) **1a** to make, or cause to make, a resonant sound like that of a bell. **b** (+ for) to sound a bell as a summons. **c** (*often* + in/out) to announce (something) by, or as if by, ringing. **2a** (*often* + with) to be filled with resonant sound; to resound. **b** of one's ears: to have the sensation of a continuous humming sound. **3** *chiefly Brit* (*often* + up) to telephone. ✱ **ring a bell** to sound familiar. **ring the changes** to vary the manner of doing or arranging something. **ring true** to appear to be true or authentic. **ring up/down the curtain 1** to raise the curtain at the start, or lower it at the end, of a theatrical show. **2** (*often* + on) to start, or finish, something.

ring[4] *n* **1a** the act or an instance of ringing. **b** *Brit, informal* a telephone call. **2** a clear resonant sound made by vibrating metal, or a similar sound. **3** a set of bells. **4** a sound or character suggestive of a particular quality or feeling: *This story has a familiar ring to it.*

ring binder *n* a loose-leaf binder in which split metal rings attached to a metal back hold perforated sheets of paper in place.

ringdove *n Brit* a woodpigeon.

ringer *n* **1** *informal* somebody or something that strongly resembles another. **2** *informal* a horse fraudulently entered in a race in place of another. **3** *slang* a stolen motor vehicle with a false numberplate, serial number, etc. **4** somebody who rings bells, e.g. at a church. **5** *Aus, NZ* **a** the shearer who has shorn the most sheep in a shed. **b** somebody who owns or works with livestock.

ring fence *n* **1** a fence that surrounds an area completely. **2** a prohibition against using money for any other purpose than the one specified.

ring-fence *v* **1** to surround (an area) with a ring fence. **2** to prohibit (money intended for a specific purpose) from being used for any other purpose.

ring finger *n* the third finger, *esp* of the left hand, on which the wedding ring is usu worn.

ringgit *n* (*pl* **ringgit** *or* **ringgits**) the basic monetary unit of Malaysia.

ringhals *n* see RINKHALS.

ringing *adj* **1** resounding. **2** vigorously unequivocal. ➤➤ **ringingly** *adv*.

ringleader *n* a leader of a group that engages in illegal or objectionable activities.

ringlet *n* a long lock of hair curled in a spiral.

ring main *n Brit* a domestic wiring circuit in which a number of power points are connected to cables which form a closed loop.

ringmaster *n* the person in charge of performances in a circus ring.

ringneck *n* a bird or animal with a ring of colour round its neck, e.g. the ring-necked pheasant.

ring off *v Brit* to terminate a telephone conversation.

ring out *v* to sound resonantly.

ring ouzel *n* an Old World thrush, the male of which is black with a broad white bar across the breast.

ring-pull *n* a built-in device for opening a tin consisting of a ring that removes a hermetically sealed tab.

ring road *n* a road round a town or town centre designed to relieve traffic congestion.

ringside *n* **1** the area surrounding a ring, *esp* providing a close view of a contest. **2** (*used before a noun*) **a** at the ringside. **b** giving a close view.

ring up *v* **1** to record (a sale) by means of a cash register. **2** to telephone.

ringworm *n* a contagious fungous disease in which ring-shaped discoloured patches form on the skin.

rink *n* **1a** a surface of ice for ice-skating, ice hockey, or curling. **b** an enclosure for roller-skating. **2** part of a bowling green being used for a match. **3** (*used as sing. or pl*) a team in bowls, curling, or quoits.

rinkhals *or* **ringhals** *n* (*pl* **rinkhalses** *or* **ringhalses** *or* **rinkhals** *or* **ringhals**) a venomous spitting cobra of southern Africa, with one or two white rings around its throat.

rinse[1] *v* **1** (*often* + out) to remove soap from (washed clothing) with clean water. **2** (*often* + out) to remove (dirt, impurities, or unwanted matter) by washing lightly. ⋙ **rinser** *n.*

rinse[2] *n* **1** the act or an instance of rinsing. **2a** liquid used for rinsing. **b** a solution that temporarily tints the hair.

Rioja *n* a dry red or white wine produced in La Rioja, N Spain.

riot[1] *n* **1** violent public disorder; *specif* a disturbance of the peace by three or more people. **2** a profuse and random display. **3** *informal* somebody or something wildly funny. ✱ **read the riot act** to give somebody a severe warning or reprimand. **run riot 1** to act wildly or without restraint. **2** to grow or occur in profusion.

riot[2] *v* (**rioted, rioting**) **1** to participate in a riot. **2** to behave in an unrestrained way. ⋙ **rioter** *n.*

riotous *adj* **1** wild and disorderly. **2** exciting; exuberant. **3** profuse; bright. ⋙ **riotously** *adv,* **riotousness** *n.*

RIP *abbr* may he/she/they rest in peace.

rip[1] *v* (**ripped, ripping**) **1a** to tear or become torn. **b** (+ out/off) to remove by force. **2** to rush along. ✱ **let rip** *informal* to do something without restraint. **rip into** to criticize (somebody) fiercely. ⋙ **ripper** *n.*

rip[2] *n* a tear or torn split.

rip[3] *n* a body of rough water formed by the meeting of opposing currents, winds, etc.

rip[4] *n informal, dated* **1a** a mischievous young person. **b** a debauched person. **2** a worn-out worthless horse.

riparian *adj* of or occurring on the bank of a river.

rip cord *n* a cord or wire for releasing a parachute from its pack.

ripe *adj* **1** of fruit or grain: fully grown and developed; mature. **2** of a cheese or wine: brought by ageing to full flavour or the best state; mellow. **3a** (+ for) fully prepared or ready for (something). **b** *often* + for) propitious. **4** (+ with) full of. ✱ **a ripe old age** a very great age. ⋙ **ripely** *adv,* **ripeness** *n.*

ripen *v* to make or become ripe.

rip off *v informal* **1** to defraud. **2a** to steal. **b** to rob.

rip-off *n informal* **1** an instance of financial exploitation, *esp* the charging of an exorbitant price. **2** an illegal or poor-quality imitation or copy, e.g. of a film or book. **3** the act or an instance of stealing.

riposte[1] *n* **1** a piece of retaliatory banter. **2** a fencer's quick return thrust following a parry.

riposte[2] *v* to make a riposte.

ripper *n* **1** somebody or something that rips, e.g. a murderer who kills and mutilates with a knife. **2** *chiefly Aus, informal* an excellent example or instance of something.

ripping *adj Brit, informal, dated* extremely good; excellent. ⋙ **rippingly** *adv.*

ripple[1] *n* **1** a small wave or a succession of small waves. **2a** a sound like that of rippling water. **b** a feeling or emotion that spreads through a person, place, etc. **3** a small periodic fluctuation or variation in an otherwise steady current or voltage. **4** ice cream with coloured and flavoured bands of syrup running through it. ⋙ **ripply** *adj.*

ripple[2] *v* **1a** to stir up small waves on (water). **b** to flow in small waves. **2** to spread irregularly outwards, *esp* from a central point. ⋙ **rippler** *n.*

rip-roaring *adj* noisily excited or exciting; exuberant.

ripsaw *n* a coarse-toothed saw designed to cut wood in the direction of the grain.

ripsnorter *n chiefly NAm, informal* somebody or something exceptionally powerful, unusual, or exciting. ⋙ **ripsnorting** *adj.*

riptide *n* **1** = RIP[3]. **2** a strong surface current flowing outwards from a shore.

RISC *abbr* reduced instruction set computer.

rise[1] *v* (*past tense* **rose**, *past part.* **risen**) **1a** to move upwards; to ascend. **b** to slope upwards. **2a** to assume an upright position, *esp* from lying, kneeling, or sitting. **b** to get up from sleep or from one's bed. **3** of the sun, moon, etc: to appear above the horizon. **4a** to increase in height or volume. **b** to increase in amount or number. **5** to attain a higher office or rank. **6** (+ to) to show oneself equal to a challenge. **7** (+ to) to respond to nasty words or behaviour, *esp* by annoyance or anger. **8** (*often* + up) to rebel; to take up arms. **9** *chiefly Brit* to end a session; to adjourn. **10** of a river: to have its source. **11** to return to life. ✱ **rise above** to overcome or not be affected by (difficulties, unworthy feelings, etc).

rise[2] *n* **1 a** a movement upwards. **b** emergence, e.g. of the sun, above the horizon. **2a** an upward slope or gradient. **b** a spot higher than surrounding ground. **3a** an increase, *esp* in amount, number, or intensity. **b** *Brit* an increase in pay. **4** the vertical height of something; *specif* the vertical height of a step. ✱ **get/take a rise out of** to provoke to annoyance by teasing. **give rise to** to be the origin or cause of.

riser *n* **1** somebody who rises in a specified manner: *an early riser.* **2** the upright part between two consecutive stair treads. **3** a vertical pipe conveying liquid or gas upwards.

risible *adj* arousing or provoking laughter. ⋙ **risibility** *n,* **risibly** *adv.*

rising[1] *adj* **1** approaching a specified age. **2** achieving a higher rank or greater influence.

rising[2] *n* an insurrection or uprising.

rising damp *n Brit* moisture that has entered the floor of a building and moved up a wall.

risk[1] *n* **1** a dangerous element or factor; a hazard. **2** possibility of loss, injury, or damage. **3a** the chance of loss or the dangers to that which is insured in an insurance contract. **b** somebody or something that is a specified hazard to an insurer. ✱ **at risk** (*often* + of) in danger. **at somebody's (own) risk** with the person concerned accepting responsibility for any possible harm or loss to themselves.

risk[2] *v* **1** to expose (e.g. one's life) to danger. **2** to incur the risk or danger of (something unpleasant happening).

risk capital *n* capital invested in a new enterprise.

risky *adj* (**-ier, -iest**) involving danger or the possibility of loss or failure. ⋙ **riskily** *adv,* **riskiness** *n.*

risotto *n* (*pl* **-os**) an Italian dish of rice cooked in stock and flavoured with vegetables, shellfish, etc.

risqué *adj* verging on impropriety or indecency.

rissole *n* a small fried cake or ball of cooked minced food, *esp* meat.

ritardando /ritah'dandoh/ *adj and adv* of a piece of music: to be performed with a gradual decrease in tempo. ⋙ **ritardando** *n.*

rite *n* **1** a ceremonial act or action, or a prescribed form of words or actions for this purpose. **2** the characteristic liturgy of a church or group of churches.

rite of passage *n* (*usu in pl*) a ritual associated with a change of status, e.g. assuming adult status and responsibilities, in the life of an individual.

ritual[1] *n* **1a** a solemn or religious ceremony involving a series of actions carried out in a set order. **b** such ceremonies collectively. **2** any series of actions habitually and usu solemnly carried out in a set order.

ritual[2] *adj* **1** of rites or a ritual; ceremonial. **2** according to religious law or social custom. ➤➤ **ritually** *adv.*

ritualise *v* see RITUALIZE.

ritualism *n* the use of ritual, or excessive devotion to it. ➤➤ **ritualist** *n,* **ritualistic** *adj,* **ritualistically** *adv.*

ritualize *or* **-ise** *v* to convert (an act) into a ritual. ➤➤ **ritualization** *n,* **ritualized** *adj.*

ritz ✱ **put on the ritz** *informal, dated* to put on a show of glamour and luxury.

ritzy *adj* (**-ier, -iest**) *informal* ostentatiously smart. ➤➤ **ritzily** *adv,* **ritziness** *n.*

rival[1] *n* **1a** any of two or more people competing for a single goal. **b** somebody who tries to compete with and be superior to another. **2** somebody or something that equals another in desirable qualities. ➤➤ **rivalry** *n.*

rival[2] *v* (**rivalled, rivalling,** *NAm* **rivaled, rivaling**) to possess qualities that approach or equal (those of another).

rive *v* (*past tense* **rived,** *past part.* **riven**) (*usu in passive*) to wrench open or tear apart or to pieces.

river *n* **1** a natural stream of water of considerable volume. **2a** a flow that matches a river in volume. **b** (*in pl*) a copious or overwhelming quantity. ✱ **sell down the river** to betray (somebody) or destroy their faith or expectations. ➤➤ **riverless** *adj.*

riverine *adj literary* **1** of or resembling a river. **2** living or situated on the banks of a river.

rivet[1] *n* a headed metal pin used to unite two or more pieces by passing the shank through a hole in each piece and then beating down the plain end to make a second head.

rivet[2] *v* (**riveted, riveting**) **1** to fasten with or as if with rivets. **2** (*usu in passive*) to attract and hold (the attention, etc) completely. ➤➤ **riveter** *n.*

riveting *adj* holding the attention; fascinating.

riviera *n* (*also* **Riviera**) a coastal region, usu with a mild climate, frequented as a resort.

rivulet *n* a small stream.

riyal *n* **1** the basic monetary unit of Qatar and of Saudi Arabia. **2** = RIAL (1).

RL *abbr* Rugby League.

RM *abbr Brit* Royal Marines.

RN *abbr Brit* Royal Navy.

Rn *abbr* the chemical symbol for radon.

RNA *n* a nucleic acid similar to DNA that contains ribose and uracil as structural components instead of deoxyribose and thymine, and is associated with the control of cellular chemical activities.

RNLI *abbr Brit* Royal National Lifeboat Institution.

RNZAF *abbr* Royal New Zealand Air Force.

RNZN *abbr* Royal New Zealand Navy.

roach[1] *n* (*pl* **roaches** *or* **roach**) a silver-white European freshwater fish of the carp family.

roach[2] *n informal* **1** *chiefly NAm* a cockroach. **2** the butt of a cannabis cigarette.

road *n* **1** an open way, usu a paved one, for the passage of vehicles, people, and animals. **2a** a route or path: *the road to ruin.* **b** space or room, *esp* for forward movement. **3** (*also in pl, used as sing.*) a relatively sheltered stretch of water near the shore where ships may ride at anchor. ✱ **one for the road** *informal* a last alcoholic drink before leaving. **on the road** travelling or touring, e.g. on business. ➤➤ **roadless** *adj.*

roadblock *n* a road barricade set up by an army, the police, etc.

road-fund licence *n* = TAX DISC.

road hog *n informal* a reckless driver of a motor vehicle who obstructs or intimidates others.

roadholding *n* the ability of a moving vehicle to remain stable, *esp* when cornering.

roadhouse *n* a pub or restaurant situated on a main road in a country area.

road hump *n* = SLEEPING POLICEMAN.

roadie *n informal* a person who looks after the transport and setting up of equipment of entertainers, *esp* a rock group.

road pricing *n* the practice of charging motorists for the use of certain busy roads, in order to relieve congestion.

road rage *n* violent and aggressive behaviour by a motorist towards another road user.

roadrunner *n* either of two species of fast-running American birds of the cuckoo family that rarely fly.

road show *n* **1** a group of touring entertainers, *esp* pop musicians, or a performance given by them. **2** a public-relations or government information unit that travels from place to place to give displays or demonstrations. **3** a radio or television programme broadcast from different locations.

roadstead *n* a sheltered stretch of water; = ROAD (3).

roadster *n* **1** an open sports car that seats two people. **2** a sturdy bicycle for ordinary use on common roads.

road tax *n* = VEHICLE EXCISE DUTY.

road test *n* **1** a test of a vehicle taken under practical operating conditions on the road. **2** a test of any piece of equipment in use. ➤➤ **road-test** *v.*

roadway *n* **1** a road. **2** the part of a road used by vehicles.

roadwork *n* **1** *Brit* (*in pl*) the repair or construction of roads, or the site of such work. **2** conditioning for an athletic contest, e.g. a boxing match, consisting mainly of long runs.

roadworthy *adj* of a vehicle: in a fit condition to be used on the roads. ➤➤ **roadworthiness** *n.*

roam *v* **1** to go aimlessly from place to place; to wander. **2** to range or wander over (an area). ➤➤ **roam** *n,* **roamer** *n.*

roan[1] *adj* of horses and cattle: having a coat of a reddish brown base colour lightened by some white hairs.

roan[2] *n* an animal, e.g. a horse, with a roan coat.

roar[1] *n* **1** the deep prolonged cry characteristic of a wild animal, e.g. a lion. **2** a loud cry, call, etc, e.g. of pain, anger, or laughter. **3** a loud continuous confused sound.

roar[2] *v* **1a** to give a roar. **b** to sing or shout with full force. **2a** to laugh loudly and deeply. **b** of a fire: to burn fiercely and noisily. **3** to happen or progress rapidly. ➤➤ **roarer** *n.*

roaring *adj informal* marked by energetic or successful activity. ➤➤ **roaringly** *adv.*

roaring forties *pl n* (**the roaring forties**) either of two areas of stormy westerly winds between latitudes 40° and 50° N and S.

roast[1] *v* **1a** to cook (food, *esp* meat) by exposing it to dry heat, e.g. in an oven. **b** to dry and brown slightly by exposure to heat. **2** to be excessively hot. **3** to criticize (somebody) severely. ➤➤ **roaster** *n.*

roast[2] *n* **1** a piece of meat roasted or suitable for roasting. **2** *NAm* a party at which food is roasted, *esp* in the open air.

roast[3] *adj* of food, *esp* meat: roasted.

roasting[1] *adj informal* extremely hot.

roasting[2] *n informal* a severe scolding.

rob *v* (**robbed, robbing**) **1** to steal something from (a person or place), *esp* by violence or threat. **2** (+ of) to deprive of something due, expected, or desired. **3** *informal* to overcharge. ➤➤ **robber** *n.*

robbery *n* (*pl* **-ies**) the act or an instance of robbing; *specif* theft accompanied by violence or threats.

robe[1] *n* **1** (*also in pl*) a long flowing outer garment, *esp* one used for ceremonial occasions or as a symbol of office or profession. **2** *NAm* a dressing gown.

robe[2] *v* **1** (*usu in passive*) to clothe or cover with or as if with a robe. **2** to put on a robe. ➤➤ **robed** *adj.*

robin *n* **1** a small brownish European bird of the thrush family with an orange-red throat and breast. **2** a large N American thrush with a dull reddish breast and underparts.

robot *n* **1** a machine programmed to carry out a sequence of actions automatically, e.g. on an assembly line. **2a** *esp* in science fiction, a machine, often in a roughly human shape and with near human intelligence, that carries out human functions. **b** a person who carries out tasks mechanically or, though efficient, lacks human warmth and sensitivity.

robotic *adj* **1** relating to or resembling a robot. **2** of a person: efficient or clever but lacking in human warmth or sensitivity.

robotics *pl n* (*used as sing. or pl*) a field of interest concerned with the construction, maintenance, and behaviour of robots.

robust *adj* **1a** exhibiting vigorous health or stamina. **b** strongly formed or constructed. **2a** forceful and determined. **b** straightforward and commonsensical. **3** of food and wine: substantial and strongly flavoured. ➤➤ **robustly** *adv,* **robustness** *n.*

robusta *n* a variety of coffee bean indigenous to Central Africa, or coffee prepared from such beans.

roc *n* a mythical bird of gigantic size.

rock[1] *n* **1a** hard solid mineral matter forming the earth's crust and in places exposed above its surface. **b** a particular form of this mineral matter, e.g. granite or limestone. **c** a large mass of rock forming an outcrop, cliff, etc. **d** a boulder. **e** *NAm* a stone. **2** *Brit* a coloured and flavoured sweet, usu produced as a hard and brittle cylindrical stick. **3** *informal* a gem, *esp* a diamond. ✱ **on the rocks 1** *informal* in difficulties and probably about to fail. **2** of a drink: served over ice cubes.

rock[2] *v* **1** to move gently back and forth or from side to side. **2a** to sway or cause to sway rapidly or violently back and forth, e.g. in an earthquake. **b** of a piece of news, etc: to disturb or upset. **3** to dance to or play rock music. **4** *informal* to be full of excitement and noise or of people enjoying themselves. ✱ **rock the boat** to disturb the equilibrium of a situation.

rock[3] *n* **1** = ROCK 'N' ROLL. **2** a style of popular music derived from rock and roll that is usu played on electronically amplified instruments and characterized by a persistent, heavily accented beat.

rockabilly *n* rock music with a strong country-and-western influence.

rock and roll *n* see ROCK 'N' ROLL.

rock bottom *n* the lowest or most fundamental part or level. ➤➤ **rock-bottom** *adj.*

rock cake *n* a small cake with a rough irregular surface, containing currants and sometimes spice.

rock crystal *n* transparent colourless quartz.

rocker *n* **1** a rock musician or fan. **2** *Brit* a member of a group of leather-jacketed young British motorcyclists in the 1960s who waged war on the mods: compare MOD. **3a** either of the two curved pieces of wood or metal on which an object, e.g. a cradle, rocks. **b** a rocking chair. **4** a device that works with a rocking motion. ✱ **off one's rocker** *informal* crazy, mad.

rockery *n* (*pl* **-ies**) a bank or mound of rocks and earth where rock plants are grown.

rocket[1] *n* **1a** a firework consisting of a long case filled with a combustible material fastened to a guiding stick and projected through the air. **b** such a device used as an incendiary weapon or as a propelling unit, e.g. for a lifesaving line. **2** a spacecraft, missile, etc propelled by a jet engine that carries with it everything necessary for its operation and is thus independent of the oxygen in the air. **3** *Brit, informal* a sharp reprimand.

rocket[2] *v* (**rocketed, rocketing**) **1** of prices, etc: to increase rapidly or spectacularly. **2** to travel with the speed of a rocket.

rocket[3] *n* a Mediterranean plant of the cabbage family, the larger leaves of which are used when young in salad.

rocketeer *n* somebody who designs or travels in space rockets.

rocketry *n* the study of or use of rockets.

rocket scientist *n chiefly NAm, informal* a highly intelligent person.

rock garden *n* **1** a garden containing one or more rockeries. **2** a rockery.

rockhopper *n* a medium-sized penguin with a stout bill and yellow crests on the side of the head.

rocking chair *n* a chair mounted on rockers.

rocking horse *n* a toy horse mounted on rockers.

rock music *n* = ROCK[3] (2).

rock 'n' roll *or* **rock and roll** *n* a style of popular music that originated in the 1950s, characterized by a heavy beat, much repetition of simple phrases, and often country, folk, and blues elements.

rock plant *n* a small plant, *esp* an alpine plant, that grows among rocks or in rockeries.

rock salmon *n Brit, not now used technically* a dogfish or wolffish when used as food.

rock salt *n* common salt occurring as a solid mineral.

rock solid *adj* **1** completely firm, fixed, or stable. **2** unwavering; committed.

rock wool *n* mineral wool made from limestone or siliceous rock.

rocky[1] *adj* (**-ier, -iest**) **1** full of or consisting of rocks. **2** filled with obstacles; difficult. ➤➤ **rockiness** *n.*

rocky[2] *adj* (**-ier, -iest**) unsteady; tottering. ➤➤ **rockily** *adv,* **rockiness** *n.*

rococo[1] *adj* **1a** of a style of architecture and decoration in 18th-cent. Europe characterized by elaborate sometimes asymmetrical curved forms and shell motifs. **b** of an 18th-cent. musical style marked by much light ornamentation. **2** excessively ornate or florid.

rococo[2] *n* rococo work or style.

rod *n* **1a** a slender bar, e.g. of wood or metal. **b** a pole with a line for fishing. **2** a straight slender stick. **3a** a stick or bundle of twigs used for corporal punishment. **b** (**the rod**) punishment with such a rod. **4** *chiefly Brit* formerly, a unit of length equal to about 5m (5yd). **5** any of the relatively long rod-shaped light receptors in the retina that are sensitive to faint light: compare CONE (6). **6** *NAm, slang* a pistol. ⋙ **rodless** *adj,* **rodlike** *adj.*

rode *v* past tense of RIDE[1].

rodent *n* any of an order of gnawing mammals including the mice, rats, squirrels, and beavers.

rodenticide *n* something, *esp* a poison, that kills rodents.

rodent ulcer *n* a malignant tumour that appears as an ulcer of exposed skin on the face and spreads slowly outwards.

rodeo *n* (*pl* **-os**) **1** a public performance featuring the riding skills of cowboys. **2** a roundup.

rodomontade *n* **1** a bragging speech. **2** vain boasting or bluster; bombast.

roe[1] *n* **1** the eggs of a female fish, *esp* when still enclosed in a membrane, or the corresponding part of a male fish. **2** the eggs or ovaries of an invertebrate, e.g. a lobster.

roe[2] *n* = ROE DEER.

roebuck *n* (*pl* **roebucks** *or* **roebuck**) a male roe deer.

roe deer *n* a small Eurasian deer with erect cylindrical antlers noted for its nimbleness and grace.

roentgen *n* see RÖNTGEN.

rogan josh *n* an Indian dish of curried meat, prawns, or vegetables, in a tomato and capsicum sauce.

Rogation Day *n* any of the days of prayer, *esp* for the harvest, observed on the three days before Ascension Day and, by Roman Catholics, also on 25 April.

roger[1] *interj* used in radio and signalling to indicate that a message has been received and understood.

roger[2] *v Brit, coarse slang* of a man: to have sexual intercourse with.

rogue *n* **1** a wilfully dishonest or corrupt person. **2** a mischievous person; a scamp. **3** a plant or an animal that displays a chance variation making it different to and sometimes inferior to others. **4** (*used before a noun*) of an animal: roaming alone and vicious and destructive.

roguery *n* (*pl* **-ies**) an act or behaviour characteristic of a rogue.

rogues' gallery *n informal* a collection of pictures of people arrested as criminals.

roguish *adj* **1** dishonest or corrupt. **2** mischievous. ⋙ **roguishly** *adv,* **roguishness** *n.*

roil *v* **1** to make (a liquid) muddy or opaque by stirring up the sediment in it. **2** of a liquid: to become turbulent or opaque with sediment.

roister *v* to engage in noisy revelry. ⋙ **roisterer** *n,* **roisterous** *adj.*

role *or* **rôle** *n* **1a** a part played by an actor. **b** a socially expected behaviour pattern, usu determined by an individual's status in a particular society. **2** a function.

role model *n* somebody who serves as an example to others of how to behave in a particular role.

role playing *n* behaving in a way typical of another or of a stereotype, often for therapeutic or educational purposes.

roll[1] *v* **1a** to move along by turning over and over. **b** of a vehicle: to move on wheels. **c** to rotate (the eyes) in their sockets. **2** to move steadily onward or pass in continuous succession: *as the years roll by.* **3** of a ship, aircraft, etc: to rock from side to side as it moves forward. **4** to begin operating, or to cause (a machine) to begin operating. **5a** (*often* + up) to wrap (something) round itself so that it forms a cylinder or ball. **b** (*often* + up) to curl or wind itself into a cylindrical shape. **6** to shape or flatten by rolling or pressing between rollers. **7** of thunder: to make a long reverberating sound. **8** to pronounce (the letter *r*) with a trill. ✱ **be rolling in it/in money** *informal* to be very wealthy. **roll with the punches** **1** of a boxer: to move back when a blow lands to lessen its impact. **2** to accept misfortunes and adapt to them.

roll[2] *n* **1** something rolled up to resemble a cylinder, e.g. a quantity of fabric or paper or any of various food preparations. **2** a small round or cylindrical loaf of bread, often eaten with a filling of meat, cheese, etc. **3a** a written document that may be rolled up; *specif* one bearing an official or formal record. **b** an official list of people's names, e.g. of members of a school or qualified voters. **4** *NAm, Aus* paper money folded or rolled into a wad.

roll[3] *n* **1** a rolling movement, e.g.: **a** a swaying movement in walking or dancing or of a ship. **b** a flight manoeuvre in which an aircraft turns completely over sideways while flying straight ahead. **2** a gymnastic manoeuvre in which the body is tucked up in a ball and rolled completely over forwards or backwards. **3a** a sound produced by rapid strokes on a drum. **b** a prolonged reverberating sound of thunder. ✱ **a roll in the hay/sack** *informal* an act of sexual intercourse. **on a roll** *informal* having a period of success.

roll back *v* to slow or reverse (a process).

roll bar *n* a metal bar above the body of a car that is designed to act as overhead protection if the car rolls over.

roll call *n* **1** the calling out of a list of names, e.g. for checking attendance. **2** a comprehensive survey.

rolled gold *n* metal, e.g. brass, coated with a thin layer of gold.

rolled oats *pl n* oats that have been husked and flattened.

roller[1] *n* **1** a revolving cylinder used to move, press, shape, or apply something. **2a** a hair curler. **b** a cylinder or rod on which something, e.g. a blind, is rolled up. **3** a long heavy wave.

roller[2] *n* a brightly coloured Old World bird noted for performing aerial rolls in its nuptial display.

rollerball *n* **1** a pen whose writing tip is a small movable ball. **2** a ball manipulated with the fingers to move the cursor around a computer screen.

roller bearing *n* a bearing in which the rotating part turns on rollers held in a cylindrical housing.

Rollerblade *n trademark* (*usu in pl*) an in-line skate (see IN-LINE SKATES).

rollerblade *v* to skate on Rollerblades. ⋙ **rollerblader** *n.*

roller coaster *n* **1** an elevated railway in a funfair, constructed with curves and inclines on which the cars roll. **2** a situation in which one experiences highs and lows. ⋙ **roller-coaster** *v.*

roller skate *n* a boot with a metal frame on its sole holding usu four small wheels that allows the wearer to glide over hard surfaces. ⋙ **roller-skate** *v,* **roller skater** *n,* **roller skating** *n.*

roller towel *n* a continuous towel hung from a roller.

rollick *v* to move or behave in a carefree boisterous manner; to frolic.

rollicking[1] *adj* boisterously carefree.

rollicking[2] *n Brit, informal* a severe scolding.

roll in *v informal* **1** to be received in large quantities. **2** to arrive casually, *esp* when late.

rolling *adj* **1** of landscape: gently undulating. **2** of e.g. a process: proceeding steadily in a succession of stages.

rolling mill *n* an establishment or machine in which metal is rolled into plates and bars.

rolling pin *n* a long cylinder for rolling out dough.

rolling stock *n* **1** the vehicles owned and used by a railway. **2** *NAm* the road vehicles owned and used by a haulage company.

rolling stone *n* somebody who leads a wandering or unsettled life.

rollmop *n* a herring fillet rolled up and pickled by being marinated in spiced vinegar or brine.

roll neck *n* a loose high collar, *esp* on a jumper, worn rolled over.

roll-on *n* a liquid preparation, e.g. deodorant, applied to the skin by means of a rolling ball in the neck of the container.

roll-on roll-off *adj* of a ferry: allowing vehicles to drive on or off.

rollout *n* the public introduction or unveiling of a new aircraft.

roll out *v* **1** to spread something out by unrolling it. **2** to introduce or unveil (a new product).

rollover *n* **1** the extension of a loan or debt for a longer period. **2** in a lottery, the carrying-over of unwon prize money to be added to prize money for the following draw.

roll over *v* **1a** to move by a rolling motion. **b** of a boat, etc: to capsize or overturn. **2** to negotiate new terms for (a financial contract), e.g. to allow (a loan) to continue to a later date than orig contracted. **3** to add (unwon prize money in a lottery) to the jackpot for the next draw. **4** to defeat overwhelmingly.

rolltop desk *n* a writing desk with a sliding cover often of parallel slats fastened to a flexible backing.

roll up *v* **1** to roll into a cylinder. **2** *informal* to arrive. ✱ **roll up one's sleeves** to get ready to work vigorously or fight.

roll-up *n informal* **1** *Brit* a hand-rolled cigarette. **2** *Aus* the people attending a meeting.

roly-poly[1] *n* (*pl* **-ies**) a pudding consisting of pastry spread with a filling, e.g. jam, rolled, and baked or steamed.

roly-poly[2] *adj informal* short and plump.

ROM *abbr* read-only memory.

romaine lettuce *n chiefly NAm* a cos lettuce.

Roman[1] *adj* **1** of Rome or the Romans. **2** (**roman**) of type: not slanted; perpendicular. **3** of the Roman Catholic Church.

Roman[2] *n* **1** a native or inhabitant of ancient or modern Rome. **2** (**roman**) roman letters or type.

roman à clef /ˌrohmonh a ˈklay/ *n* (*pl* **romans à clef**) a novel in which real people or actual events are fictionally disguised.

Roman alphabet *n* the alphabet used for writing most European languages, based on the alphabet developed in ancient Rome.

Roman candle *n* a cylindrical firework that discharges balls or stars of fire at intervals.

Roman Catholic[1] *n* a member of the Roman Catholic Church. ⯮ **Roman Catholicism** *n.*

Roman Catholic[2] *adj* relating or belonging to the Roman Catholic Church.

Roman Catholic Church *n* a Christian episcopal church headed by the pope, who is Bishop of Rome, and having a form of service centred on the Mass.

Romance *n* the family of languages that developed from Latin and that includes e.g. French, Spanish, and Italian. ⯮ **Romance** *adj.*

romance[1] *n* **1** romantic love, or the feelings and behaviour usually associated with it. **2** a love affair. **3** a story or film about romantic love. **4a** a medieval verse tale dealing with chivalric love and adventure. **b** a prose narrative dealing with imaginary characters involved in heroic, adventurous, or mysterious events. **5** an emotional aura attaching to an enthralling era, adventure, or pursuit.

romance[2] *v* **1a** of a couple: to behave in a romantic way together, e.g. dancing or kissing. **b** to court (somebody). **2** = ROMANTICIZE.

romancer *n* **1** somebody prone to romancing. **2** a writer of romance.

Roman Empire *n* (**the Roman Empire**) the empire ruled by the Roman emperors from 27 BC until AD 395.

Romanesque *n* a style of architecture developed in Italy and western Europe between c.AD 900–1200 and characterized by the use of the round arch and vault. ⯮ **Romanesque** *adj.*

roman-fleuve /ˌrohmonh ˈfluhv/ *n* (*pl* **romans-fleuves**) a novel or series of novels in the form of a long and leisurely chronicle of a family or community; = SAGA (1).

Roman holiday *n* an entertainment at the expense of others' suffering.

Romanian *or* **Rumanian** *n* **1** a native or inhabitant of Romania in E Europe. **2** the Romance language of Romania and Moldova. ⯮ **Romanian** *adj.*

Romanic *n and adj* = ROMANCE.

romanize *or* **-ise** *v* **1** (*often* **Romanize**) formerly, to make (a people or country) Roman; to Latinize. **2** to make Roman Catholic. **3** to write or print (text, etc) in the roman alphabet or in roman type. ⯮ **romanization** *n.*

roman law *n* (*also* **Roman law**) the legal system of the ancient Romans, which forms the basis of many modern legal codes.

Roman nose *n* a nose with a prominent, slightly aquiline bridge.

Roman numeral *n* a numeral in the ancient Roman system of numbering using the symbols i, v, x, l, c, d, m.

romans à clef *n* pl of ROMAN À CLEF.

Romansch *or* **Romansh** *n* a Romance language spoken in parts of southern Switzerland. ⯮ **Romansch** *adj.*

romans-fleuves *n* pl of ROMAN-FLEUVE.

Romansh *n* see ROMANSCH.

romantic[1] *adj* **1** involving sexual attraction accompanied by tender, loving feelings and elaborate courtship. **2** feeling, associated with, or conducive to romantic love. **3** impractical or overly idealistic; having no basis in real life. **4** (*often* **Romantic**) of or having the characteristics of romanticism. ⯮ **romantically** *adv.*

romantic[2] *n* **1** a romantic person. **2** (**Romantic**) a Romantic writer, artist, or composer.

romanticise *v* see ROMANTICIZE.

romanticism *n* (*also* **Romanticism**) a chiefly late 18th- and early 19th-cent. literary, artistic, and philosophical movement that emphasized individual aspirations, nature, the emotions, and the remote and exotic. ➤➤ **romanticist** *n.*

romanticize *or* **-ise** *v* **1** to present (a person or incident) in a misleadingly romantic way. **2** to hold romantic ideas. ➤➤ **romanticization** *n.*

Romany *n* (*pl* **-ies**) **1** the Indic language of the gypsies. **2** a gypsy. ➤➤ **Romany** *adj.*

Romeo *n* (*pl* **-os**) a romantic male lover.

Romish *adj chiefly derog* Roman Catholic.

romp[1] *v* **1** to play in a boisterous manner. **2** *informal* to engage in light-hearted sexual activity. ✻ **romp home** *informal* to win easily.

romp[2] *n* **1** boisterous or bawdy entertainment or play. **2** *informal* an effortless win. **3** *informal* a period of light-hearted sexual activity.

rompers *pl n* a one-piece child's garment combining a top or bib and short trousers.

romper suit *n* = ROMPERS.

rondeau /'rondoh/ *n* (*pl* **rondeaux** /'rondoh(z)/) a 13-line poem in three stanzas with only two rhymes, in which the opening words of the first line are used as a refrain to the second and third stanzas.

rondel *n* a rondeau usu consisting of 13 lines of eight or ten syllables, in which the first two lines are repeated as a refrain in the middle of the poem and the first line is again repeated as the last line.

rondo *n* (*pl* **-os**) an instrumental composition, often the last movement in a concerto or sonata, usu with an opening section that recurs in the form ABACADA.

röntgen *or* **roentgen** *n* a unit of ionizing radiation equal to the amount that produces ions of one sign carrying a charge of 2.58×10^{-4} coulomb in 1kg of air.

roo *n* (*pl* **roos** *or* **roo**) *Aus, informal* a kangaroo.

rood *n* **1** a cross or crucifix; *specif* a large crucifix on a beam or screen at the entrance to the chancel of a church. **2** *chiefly Brit* a former unit of land area equal to about $1011m^2$ (a quarter of an acre).

roof[1] *n* (*pl* **roofs**) **1a** the upper rigid cover of a building, vehicle, etc. **b** the vaulted or covering part of the mouth, skull, etc. **c** a ceiling. **2** the highest point or level. ✻ **go through the roof 1** of e.g. prices: to reach extraordinarily high levels. **2** hit the roof (see HIT[1]). ➤➤ **roofless** *adj.*

roof[2] *v* (*usu in passive*) to cover with or as if with a roof. ➤➤ **roofed** *adj,* **roofer** *n,* **roofing** *n.*

roof rack *n chiefly Brit* a metal frame fixed on top of a car roof, for carrying things.

rooftree *n* = RIDGEPIECE.

rooibos /'roybos/ *n* a S African evergreen shrub with red leaves, which are used to make a form of tea.

rook[1] *n* a common Old World bird with black plumage, similar to the related carrion crow but having a bare grey face.

rook[2] *v informal* to defraud, cheat, or overcharge.

rook[3] *n* in chess, either of two pieces of each colour that can move straight along the ranks or files across any number of squares; = CASTLE[1] (2).

rookery *n* (*pl* **-ies**) **1** the nests, usu built in the upper branches of trees, of a colony of rooks. **2** a breeding ground or haunt of a colony of penguins, seals, etc.

rookie *n informal* **1** a recruit, *esp* in the armed forces or the police force. **2** a novice.

room[1] *n* **1** an extent of space occupied by, or sufficient or available for, something. **2a** a partitioned part of the inside of a building. **b** (*also in pl*) a set of rooms used as a separate lodging. **3** opportunity for: *room for improvement.* ➤➤ **roomful** (*pl* **roomfuls**) *n.*

room[2] *v NAm* (*often* + with) to occupy a room or rooms, often paying rent; to share lodgings.

roomer *n NAm* a lodger.

rooming house *n chiefly NAm* a lodging house.

roommate *n* **1** any of two or more people sharing the same room, e.g. in a university hall of residence. **2** *NAm* a flatmate.

room service *n* the facility by which a hotel guest can have food, drinks, etc brought to their room.

roomy *adj* (**-ier, -iest**) having ample room; spacious. ➤➤ **roomily** *adv,* **roominess** *n.*

roost[1] *n* a support or place where birds roost.

roost[2] *v* of a bird or bat: to settle down for rest or sleep; to perch.

rooster *n chiefly NAm* the adult male of the domestic fowl; = COCK[1] (1).

root[1] *n* **1a** the underground part of a flowering plant that anchors and supports it and absorbs and stores food. **b** a fleshy and edible root, bulb, or tuber, e.g. a carrot or turnip. **2a** the end of a nerve nearest the brain and spinal cord. **b** the part of a tooth, hair, the tongue, etc by which it is attached to the body. **3a** something that is an underlying cause or basis, e.g. of a condition or quality. **b** (*in pl*) a feeling of belonging established through close familiarity or family ties with a particular place. **4** in grammar, the base element from which a word is derived. **5** in music, the lowest note of a chord. **6** a number which produces a given number when multiplied by itself an indicated number of times. ✻ **take root 1** of a plant: to become rooted. **2** to become fixed or established. ➤➤ **rootless** *adj,* **rootlet** *n,* **rootlike** *adj,* **rooty** *adj.*

root[2] *v* **1** to enable (a plant) to develop roots. **2** to fix or implant as if by roots. ✻ **be rooted in** to originate or have developed from. ➤➤ **rooted** *adj,* **rootedness** *n.*

root[3] *v* **1** of a pig: to dig with the snout. **2** (+ about/in) to poke or dig about in something; to search unsystematically for something.

root[4] *v informal* (+ for) to lend vociferous or enthusiastic support to. ➤➤ **rooter** *n.*

root and branch *adv* so as to leave no remnant; completely. ➤➤ **root-and-branch** *adj.*

root beer *n chiefly NAm* a sweetened effervescent drink flavoured with extracts of roots and herbs.

root canal *n* the part of the central cavity of a tooth, containing blood vessels and nerves, lying in the root of a tooth.

rootle *v Brit, informal* = ROOT[3].

root-mean-square *n* the square root of the arithmetic mean of the squares of a set of numbers.

root out *v* to get rid of or destroy (somebody or something) completely.

rootstock *n* **1** an underground plant part formed from several stems. **2a** a plant or plant part consisting of roots and lower trunk onto which a scion is grafted. **b** a plant from which cuttings are taken.

ropable *adj* see ROPEABLE.

rope[1] *n* **1** a strong thick cord composed of strands of fibres or wire twisted or braided together. **2** a row or string consisting of things united by or as if by braiding, twining, or threading. **3** (**the ropes**) methods or procedures. ✻ **on the ropes 1** in boxing, having been forced against the ropes that enclose the ring. **2** close to defeat.

rope² *v* **1a** to fasten or tie with a rope. **b** to catch (e.g. cattle) with a lasso. **2** (*usu* + off) to enclose or separate off with a rope. **3** to connect (a party of climbers) with a rope.

ropeable *or* **ropable** *adj* **1** able to be roped. **2** *Aus, informal* violently angry.

rope in *v* to enlist (somebody), *esp* somebody reluctant, in a group or activity.

rope ladder *n* a ladder having rope sides and rope, wood, or metal rungs.

ropy *or* **ropey** *adj* (**-ier, -iest**) **1** like rope in texture or appearance. **2** *Brit, informal* **a** of poor quality; shoddy. **b** somewhat unwell. ➤➤ **ropiness** *n.*

Roquefort *n trademark* a strong-flavoured crumbly French cheese with bluish green veins, made from ewes' milk.

ro-ro *adj* roll-on roll-off.

rorqual *n* a large whalebone whale with the skin of the throat marked with deep longitudinal furrows.

Rorschach test *n* a personality test based on the interpretation of a person's reactions to a set of standard inkblot designs.

rort¹ *n Aus, informal* **1** a fraud or swindle. **2** a boisterous social gathering.

rort² *v Aus, informal* **1** to swindle. **2** to roister. ➤➤ **rorter** *n.*

rosacea /roh'zayshi·ə/ *n* a disorder of the skin of the face in which blood vessels enlarge, so giving the face a flushed rosy appearance.

rosaceous *adj* of or belonging to the rose family.

rosary *n* (*pl* **-ies**) **1** a series of prayers in Roman Catholicism. **2** a string of beads used in counting the prayers of the rosary while they are being recited.

rose¹ *n* **1a** a widely cultivated prickly shrub with showy fragrant flowers. **b** a flower of this shrub. **2 a** a perforated outlet for water, e.g. from a shower or watering can. **b** a circular fitting that anchors the flex of a light bulb to a ceiling. **3** a pale to dark pinkish colour. ✱ **be coming up roses** to be turning out very favourably or successfully. **come out/up smelling of roses** to escape from a potentially compromising situation with one's reputation intact. ➤➤ **rose** *adj,* **roselike** *adj.*

rose² *v* past tense of RISE¹.

rosé *n* a light pink table wine made from red grapes by removing the skins after fermentation has begun.

roseate *adj* resembling a rose, *esp* in colour.

rosebay *n* **1** = ROSEBAY WILLOWHERB. **2** an azalea of N America.

rosebay willowherb *n* a tall Eurasian and N American plant of the evening primrose family with long spikes of pinkish purple flowers.

rosebud *n* **1** the bud of a rose. **2** *Brit, dated* a pretty girl or young woman.

rose-coloured *adj* of a pale to dark pinkish colour. ✱ **look/see/etc through rose-coloured glasses/spectacles** to view (a person, situation, etc) in an overoptimistic unrealistic light.

rosehip *n* see HIP².

rosella *n* a brightly coloured parakeet of Australia.

rosemary *n* a fragrant shrubby Eurasian plant the leaves of which are used as a cooking herb.

rose of Sharon *n* a Eurasian Saint-John's-wort often grown for its large yellow flowers.

roseola *n* a rash of pink spots occurring in German measles or a similar virus disease, *esp* of children. ➤➤ **roseolar** *adj.*

rose-tinted *adj* = ROSE-COLOURED.

rosette *n* **1** an ornament usu made of material gathered so as to resemble a rose and worn as a badge, trophy, or trimming. **2** a stylized carved or moulded rose used as a decorative motif in architecture. **3** a cluster of leaves in crowded circles or spirals, e.g. in the dandelion.

rose water *n* a solution of rose oils in water, used as a perfume.

rose window *n* a circular window filled with tracery radiating from its centre.

rosewood *n* the valuable dark red or purplish wood of a tropical tree, streaked and variegated with black.

Rosh Hashanah *or* **Rosh Hashana** *n* the Jewish New Year.

Rosicrucian *n* an adherent or member of any of various organizations derived from a 17th- and 18th-cent. movement devoted to occult or esoteric wisdom. ➤➤ **Rosicrucian** *adj,* **Rosicrucianism** *n.*

rosin¹ *n* a translucent resin that is the residue from the distillation of turpentine, used in making varnish and soldering flux and for rubbing on violin bows. ➤➤ **rosiny** *adj.*

rosin² *v* (**rosined, rosining**) to rub or treat (the bow of a violin, etc) with rosin.

RoSPA *abbr Brit* Royal Society for the Prevention of Accidents.

roster¹ *n* **1** a list or register giving the order in which personnel are to perform a duty, go on leave, etc. **2** an itemized list, *esp* of people available for a particular task or duty.

roster² *v* (*usu in passive*) to place on a roster.

rösti /'rosti, 'ruhsti/ *n* a Swiss dish of grated potato, and sometimes onion, formed into a cake and fried.

rostrum *n* (*pl* **rostra** *or* **rostrums**) **1a** a stage for public speaking. **b** a raised platform on a stage. **c** a platform supporting a film or television camera. **2** a body part, e.g. an insect's snout or beak, shaped like a bird's bill. ➤➤ **rostral** *adj.*

rosy *adj* (**-ier, -iest**) **1a** rose-pink. **b** (*often in combination*) having a rosy complexion. **2** characterized by or encouraging optimism. ➤➤ **rosily** *adv,* **rosiness** *n.*

rot¹ *v* (**rotted, rotting**) **1** to decompose, *esp* by the action of bacteria or fungi. **2a** to go to ruin. **b** to become morally corrupt.

rot² *n* **1a** the state of rotting or being rotten; decay. **b** something rotting or rotten. **c** = DRY ROT. **d** = WET ROT. **2** any of several plant or animal diseases, *esp* of sheep, that cause breakdown and death of tissues. **3** *informal* nonsense or rubbish.

rota *n chiefly Brit* a list specifying a fixed order of rotation, e.g. of people or duties.

Rotarian¹ *n* a member of a Rotary Club.

Rotarian² *adj* relating to Rotarians, Rotary Clubs, or Rotary International.

rotary¹ *adj* **1a** turning on an axis like a wheel. **b** proceeding about an axis. **2** having a principal part that turns on an axis. **3** characterized by rotation.

rotary² *n* (*pl* **-ies**) **1** a rotary machine. **2** *NAm* a traffic roundabout.

Rotary Club *n* a club belonging to Rotary International, an organization of business and professional men and women devoted to serving the community and advancing world peace.

rotate *v* **1** to turn about an axis or a centre; to revolve. **2** to take turns at performing an act or operation. **3a** to order (something) in a recurring sequence. **b** to cause (a crop or crops) to grow in rotation. **c** to exchange (individuals or units) with others. ➤➤ **rotatable** *adj,* **rotative** *adj,* **rotatory** *adj.*

rotation *n* **1a** movement on or around an axis or centre. **b** one complete turn. **2a** recurrence in a regular series. **b** the growing of different crops in succession in one field. ⋙ **rotational** *adj.*

rotator *n* something that rotates or causes rotation, *esp* a muscle that partially rotates a body part on its axis.

rotavator *or* **rotovator** *n trademark* an implement with blades or claws that revolve rapidly and till or break up the soil.

rote *n* the mechanical use of the memory.

rotgut *n informal* alcoholic spirits of low quality.

rotisserie *n* **1** a restaurant specializing in roast and barbecued meats. **2** an appliance fitted with a spit on which food is cooked.

rotogravure *n* a type of photogravure in which the impression is produced by a rotary press.

rotor *n* **1** a part that revolves in a machine, *esp* the rotating member of an electrical machine. **2** a complete system of more or less horizontal blades that supplies the force supporting a helicopter in flight.

rotovator *n* see ROTAVATOR.

rotten[1] *adj* **1** having rotted; putrid. **2** morally or politically corrupt. **3a** *informal* extremely unpleasant. **b** unhappy; ashamed. **c** inferior; useless; not good. ⋙ **rottenly** *adv,* **rottenness** *n.*

rotten[2] *adv informal* very much.

rotten borough *n esp* before 1832, an English election district with very few voters.

rotter *n informal, dated* a thoroughly objectionable person.

rottweiler *n* a tall strongly-built black-and-tan dog with short hair.

rotund *adj* **1** markedly plump. **2** rounded. ⋙ **rotundity** *n,* **rotundly** *adv.*

rotunda *n* (*pl* **rotundas**) a round building, *esp* one covered by a dome.

rouble *or* **ruble** *n* the basic monetary unit of Russia, Belarus, and Tajikistan.

roué *n* a debauched man, *esp* one past his prime.

rouge[1] *n* a red cosmetic, *esp* for the cheeks or lips.

rouge[2] *v* to apply rouge to (the cheeks or lips).

rough[1] *adj* **1a** having an irregular or uneven surface; not smooth. **b** covered with coarse hair. **c** of terrain: covered with bushes, boulders, etc and difficult to cross. **2** not gentle; harsh or violent. **3a** of the sea: moving violently, with large waves. **b** of the weather: unpleasant; stormy. **4** lacking finish or refinement, e.g.: **a** crudely made or executed hastily. **b** not thoroughly worked out; approximate. **5** of a voice: harsh-sounding. **6** *informal* difficult or unpleasant.

rough[2] *n* **1** *chiefly Brit, informal* a hooligan or ruffian. **2** (**the rough**) uneven ground covered with high grass, brush, and stones; *specif* such ground bordering a golf fairway. **3a** a quick preliminary drawing or layout. **b** a crude or preliminary state. **4** (**the rough**) the rugged or disagreeable side or aspect.

rough[3] *adv Brit* in want of material comforts; without proper lodging.

rough[4] *v* to roughen. ✻ **rough it** *informal* to live in uncomfortable or primitive conditions.

roughage *n* coarse bulky food, e.g. bran, that is relatively high in fibre and stimulates intestinal peristalsis.

rough-and-ready *adj* **1** of a method, etc: crudely or hastily constructed or conceived; makeshift. **2** of a person: uncouth or unsophisticated.

rough-and-tumble[1] *n* disorderly unrestrained fighting or physical play.

rough-and-tumble[2] *adj* **1** disorderly and unrestrained. **2** rough, rowdy, or disorganized.

roughcast[1] *n* a plaster of lime mixed with shells or pebbles used for covering buildings.

roughcast[2] *v* (*past tense and past part.* **roughcast**) to plaster with roughcast.

rough cut *n* a print of a film after only preliminary editing.

rough diamond *n* **1** an uncut diamond. **2** a person without social graces but of an upright or amiable nature.

roughen *v* to make or become rough.

rough-hew *v* (*past part.* **rough-hewed** *or* **rough-hewn**) to hew (timber or stone) coarsely without smoothing or finishing.

rough-hewn *adj* of a person: lacking refinement.

roughhouse[1] *n chiefly NAm, informal* an instance of brawling or excessively boisterous play.

roughhouse[2] *v* **1** to engage in a roughhouse. **2** *informal* to treat in a boisterously rough manner.

roughly *adv* **1a** with insolence or violence. **b** in primitive fashion; crudely. **2** approximately.

roughneck *n* **1** *informal* a tough. **2** a worker who handles the heavy drilling equipment of an oil rig.

rough out *v* to shape or plan in a preliminary way.

roughrider *n* a person who is accustomed to riding unbroken or little-trained horses.

roughshod ✻ **ride roughshod over** to treat (a person or their rights) without justice or consideration.

rough stuff *n informal* violent behaviour; violence.

rough trade *n informal* **1** male homosexual prostitution involving violence or brutality. **2** male homosexuals, *esp* prostitutes, who engage in such acts.

rough up *v informal* to beat up.

roulade /rooh'lahd/ *n* a roll of food, e.g. a rolled and cooked slice of stuffed meat.

roulette *n* a gambling game in which players bet on which compartment of a revolving wheel a small ball will come to rest in.

round[1] *adj* **1a** circular. **b** cylindrical. **c** spherical. **2a** shaped in a smooth curve. **b** well filled out; plump. **3** of a voice: richly resonant in tone. **4** of a number: **a** approximately correct; expressed as the nearest large unit: *in round figures.* **b** complete: *a round dozen.* **5** direct, frank, and usu unsparing: *berated him in round terms.* ⋙ **roundness** *n.*

round[2] *adv chiefly Brit* **1a** in a circular or curved path. **b** with revolving or rotating motion. **c** in circumference. **d** in, along, or through a circuitous or indirect route. **e** in an encircling position. **2a** in rotation or recurrence. **b** from beginning to end; through: *all year round.* **c** in or to the other or a specified direction: *Turn round.* **d** back to consciousness or awareness; = TO². **e** in the specified order or relationship: *the right way round.* **3** about, approximately: *round 1900.* **4** to a particular person or place: *invite somebody round.* ✻ **round about 1** approximately; more or less. **2** in a ring round; on all sides of.

round[3] *prep chiefly Brit* **1a** so as to revolve or progress about (a centre). **b** so as to encircle or enclose. **c** so as to avoid or get past. **d** in a position on the other side of: *round the corner.* **e** near to: *somewhere round here.* **2a** in all directions outwards from. **b** here and there in or throughout.

round[4] *n* **1** a circular piece or spherical mass. **2** (*often in pl*) a route regularly travelled, e.g. by a person making deliveries or a doctor visiting patients. **3** a recurring sequence of events or tasks: *the weekly* *round.* **4** an event or series of events constituting a single stage in a larger process, *esp*, in sport: **a** a division of a tournament. **b** a division of a boxing or wrestling match. **5** in music, an unaccompanied song for three or more voices in which each sings the same tune starting one after the other. **6** a set of drinks served at one time to each person in a group. **7** a unit of ammunition enabling a gun to fire one shot. **8** *Brit* **a** a single slice of bread or toast. **b** a sandwich made with two whole slices of bread. **c** a cut of beef between the rump and the lower leg. ✱ **go/make the rounds** to be passed from person to person. **in the round 1** of sculpture: free-standing and able to be viewed from all sides. **2** of theatre: on or with a central stage surrounded by the audience.

round[5] *v* **1** to go round (a bend or corner). **2** (*often* + off/up/down) to express (a figure) as a round number. **3** to make or become round or rounded. **4** (*often* + off/out) to bring to completion or perfection.

roundabout[1] *n* **1** a road junction formed round a central island about which traffic moves in one direction only. **2** *Brit* **a** a merry-go-round. **b** a rotatable platform that is an amusement in a children's playground.

roundabout[2] *adj* circuitous; indirect.

round dance *n* **1** a folk dance in which participants form a ring. **2** a ballroom dance in which couples progress round the room.

rounded *adj* **1** made round; smoothly curved. **2** fully developed in all respects; mature.

roundel *n* a round figure or object, e.g.: **a** a circular panel, window, etc. **b** a circular mark identifying the nationality of a warplane.

roundelay *n literary* a simple song with a refrain.

rounders *pl n* (*used as sing.*) a field game between two teams with bat and ball that resembles baseball, where players try to score 'rounders' by running round all four bases before the ball is fielded.

Roundhead *n* an adherent of Parliament in the English Civil War.

roundhouse *n* **1** a circular building for housing and repairing locomotives. **2** *informal* a blow in boxing delivered with a wide swing. **3** formerly, a cabin or apartment on the after part of a quarter-deck.

roundly *adv* **1a** in a blunt or severe manner. **b** thoroughly. **2** in a round or circular form or manner.

round on *v* to turn against (somebody) and attack them, *esp* to scold (somebody) suddenly.

round robin *n* **1** a tournament in which every contestant plays every other contestant in turn. **2** a written petition or protest, *esp* one on which the signatures are arranged in a circle so that no name heads the list.

round-shouldered *adj* having stooping or rounded shoulders.

roundsman *n* (*pl* **roundsmen**) **1** *Brit* somebody, e.g. a milkman, who sells or delivers goods on an assigned route. **2** *Aus, NZ* a journalist covering a particular subject.

round table *n* a meeting or conference of several people on equal terms. ➤➤ **round-table** *adj.*

round-the-clock *adj* lasting or continuing 24 hours a day; constant.

round trip *n* a trip to a place and back, usu over the same route.

roundup *n* **1** a gathering in of scattered people or things, *esp* of cattle by cowboys. **2** a summary of information, e.g. from news bulletins.

round up *v* to gather in or bring together (people or things) from various quarters.

roundworm *n* = NEMATODE.

rouse *v* **1** to wake up. **2a** to make active. **b** to stimulate or excite (e.g. one's curiosity).

rouseabout *n Aus, NZ* a handyman on a sheep farm; a labourer.

rousing *adj* giving rise to enthusiasm; stirring. ➤➤ **rousingly** *adv.*

roust *v* **1** to rouse, *esp* out of bed. **2** *NAm, informal* to treat roughly.

roustabout *n* an unskilled or semiskilled labourer, *esp* in an oilfield or refinery.

rout[1] *n* **1** a confused retreat; headlong flight. **2** a disastrous defeat.

rout[2] *v* to defeat (an army, team, etc) decisively or disastrously.

rout[3] *n archaic* **1** a disorderly crowd of people; a mob. **2** a fashionable social gathering.

rout[4] *v* **1** to gouge out or make a furrow in (a surface). **2** of a pig: to dig with the snout; = ROOT[3] (1).

route[1] *n* **1** a course planned or taken to get from a starting point to a destination. **2** *NAm* **a** a major highway. **b** = ROUND[4] (2).

route[2] *v* (**routeing** *or* **routing**) to send by a selected route.

route march *n* a long and tiring march, *esp* as military training.

router /'rowtə/ *n* **1** a plane for cutting a groove. **2** a machine with a revolving cutter for milling out the surface of wood or metal.

routine[1] *n* **1** a sequence of actions performed regularly or habitually in the same order and manner. **2** a fixed piece of entertainment often repeated. **3** a particular sequence of computer instructions for carrying out a given task.

routine[2] *adj* **1** of or in accordance with established procedure. **2** commonplace or repetitious in character. ➤➤ **routinely** *adv.*

rout out *v* = ROOT OUT.

roux /rooh/ *n* (*pl* **roux**) a cooked mixture of fat and flour used as a thickening agent in a sauce.

rove[1] *v* **1** to wander aimlessly or idly. **2** of the eyes: to stray and change direction without concentration.

rove[2] *v* past tense and past part. of REEVE[2].

rover[1] *n* a wanderer.

rover[2] *n archaic* a pirate.

roving commission *n Brit* authority given without rigidly defined terms.

roving eye *n* promiscuous sexual interests.

row[1] /roh/ *n* a number of objects or people arranged in a straight line. ✱ **in a row** *informal* one after another; successively.

row[2] /roh/ *v* **1** to propel a boat by means of oars. **2** to engage in the sport of rowing. ➤➤ **rower** *n.*

row[3] /roh/ *n* a period of rowing a boat.

row[4] /row/ *n informal* **1** *chiefly Brit* a noisy quarrel or stormy dispute. **2** *chiefly Brit* excessive or unpleasant noise. **3** *Brit* a reprimand.

row[5] /row/ *v chiefly Brit, informal* to engage in quarrelling.

rowan *n* a small Eurasian tree of the rose family with white flowers and red berries.

rowdy[1] *adj* (**-ier, -iest**) coarse or boisterous. ➤➤ **rowdily** *adv,* **rowdiness** *n.*

rowdy[2] *n* (*pl* **-ies**) a rowdy person; a tough. ➤➤ **rowdyism** *n.*

rowel *n* a revolving disc with sharp marginal points at the end of a spur.

rowing machine *n* an exercise machine that works all the major muscle groups by simulating rowing movements.

rowlock *n* a device for holding an oar in place and providing a fulcrum for its action.

royal[1] *adj* **1** relating, related, or belonging to a monarch. **2** suitable for royalty; regal or magnificent. **3** of superior size or quality. ➤➤ **royally** *adv.*

royal[2] *n informal* a member of a royal family.

Royal Assent *n* (**the Royal Assent**) formal ratification of a parliamentary bill by a British sovereign.

royal blue *n* rich purplish blue. ➤➤ **royal-blue** *adj.*

Royal Commission *n* in Britain, a committee of enquiry appointed by the Crown.

royal flush *n* in poker, a straight flush having an ace as the highest card.

royal icing *n chiefly Brit* icing made with beaten egg white, *esp* for covering fruit cakes.

royalist *n* (*also* **Royalist**) a supporter of a king or queen or of monarchical government, e.g. a Cavalier. ➤➤ **royalism** *n,* **royalist** *adj.*

royal jelly *n* a highly nutritious secretion of the honeybee that is fed to the very young larvae and to all larvae that will develop into queens.

royal tennis *n* = REAL TENNIS.

royalty *n* (*pl* **-ies**) **1** people of royal blood. **2** regal character or bearing. **3a** a payment made to an author, composer, or inventor for each copy or example of their work sold. **b** a share of the product or profit reserved by somebody who grants an oil or mining lease. **4** a monetary benefit received by a sovereign, e.g. a percentage of minerals.

royal warrant *n* a warrant authorizing a company to supply goods to a royal household.

rozzer *n Brit, informal* a police officer.

RP *abbr* Received Pronunciation.

RPI *abbr* retail price index.

rpm *abbr* **1** resale price maintenance. **2** revolutions per minute.

RPV *abbr* remotely piloted vehicle.

RRP *abbr Brit* recommended retail price.

RS *abbr Brit* Royal Society.

Rs *abbr* rupee.

RSA *abbr* **1** Republic of South Africa. **2** Royal Scottish Academician or Academy. **3** Royal Society of Arts.

RSC *abbr* Royal Shakespeare Company.

RSI *abbr* repetitive strain injury.

RSJ *abbr* rolled steel joist.

RSM *abbr Brit* Regimental Sergeant Major.

RSPB *abbr Brit* Royal Society for the Protection of Birds.

RSPCA *abbr Brit* Royal Society for the Prevention of Cruelty to Animals.

RSV *abbr* Revised Standard Version (of the Bible).

RSVP *abbr* please reply.

RTE *abbr* Irish Radio and Television.

RTF *abbr* rich text format.

Rt Hon. *abbr Brit* Right Honourable.

RU *abbr* Rugby Union.

Ru *abbr* the chemical symbol for ruthenium.

rub[1] *v* (**rubbed, rubbing**) **1** to subject to pressure and friction, *esp* with a back-and-forth motion. **2a** to move with pressure and friction along a surface. **b** to apply (a substance) to a surface by rubbing. ✱ **rub/rub up the wrong way** to irritate or displease. **rub shoulders** to associate closely; to mix socially. **rub somebody's nose in something** see NOSE[1].

rub[2] *n* **1** the act or an instance of rubbing. **2** a cream or ointment for rubbing on a painful body part. **3** (**the rub**) an obstacle or difficulty. **4** in bowls, an unevenness of the surface of the green, or the effect this has on the movement of a bowl.

rub along *v Brit, informal* **1** to continue coping in a difficult situation. **2** to remain on friendly terms.

rubato /roo'bahtoh/ *n* (*pl* **rubatos** *or* **rubati**) expressive fluctuation of speed within a musical phrase.

rubber[1] *n* **1** an elastic substance obtained by coagulating the milky juice of the rubber tree and used in car tyres, waterproof materials, etc. **2a** *Brit* a small piece of rubber or plastic used for rubbing out pencil marks on paper. **b** an instrument used in rubbing, polishing, or cleaning. **3 a** *NAm, informal* a condom. **b** *NAm* (*usu in pl*) a galosh. ➤➤ **rubbery** *adj.*

rubber[2] *n esp* in bridge or whist, a contest consisting of an odd number of games or matches won by the side that takes a majority.

rubber band *n* a continuous band of rubber used for holding small objects together.

rubber bullet *n* a solid rubber projectile that is designed to be fired from a special gun to control rioters.

rubberneck[1] *n informal* **1** an overinquisitive person. **2** a tourist or sightseer, *esp* one on a guided tour.

rubberneck[2] *v informal* **1** to show exaggerated curiosity. **2** to engage in sightseeing.

rubbernecker *n* = RUBBERNECK[1].

rubber plant *n* a plant that yields rubber, *esp* a tall Asian tree of the fig family with glossy leathery leaves, also grown as a houseplant.

rubber stamp *n* **1** a stamp of rubber for making imprints. **2** somebody who unthinkingly assents to the actions or policies of others. **3** a routine endorsement or approval.

rubber-stamp *v* **1** to imprint with a rubber stamp. **2** to approve (a plan, etc) as a matter of routine or at the dictate of somebody else.

rubber tree *n* a S American tree of the spurge family cultivated in plantations as the chief source of rubber.

rubbing *n* an image of a raised surface obtained by placing paper over it and rubbing the paper with charcoal, chalk, etc.

rubbish[1] *n* **1** *chiefly Brit* worthless or rejected articles; trash. **2** often used as an exclamation: something worthless; nonsense. ➤➤ **rubbishy** *adj.*

rubbish[2] *v Brit, informal* to condemn as rubbish.

rubbish[3] *adj* (*often* + at) worthless or very bad.

rubble *n* broken fragments of building material, e.g. brick, stone, etc, *esp* from a demolished building.

rub down *v* to clean, smooth, or dry (something) by rubbing it. ➤➤ **rubdown** *n.*

rube *n NAm, informal* an unsophisticated rustic; a bumpkin.

rubella *n* a virus disease that is milder than typical measles but is damaging to the foetus when occurring early in pregnancy; = GERMAN MEASLES.

Rubicon *n* a bounding or limiting line, *esp* one that when crossed commits somebody irrevocably.

rubicund *adj* ruddy. ➤➤ **rubicundity** *n.*

rubidium *n* a silver-white metallic chemical element of the alkali metal group, used in photocells.

Rubik's cube *or* **Rubik cube** *n* a puzzle consisting of a usu plastic cube having each face divided into nine small coloured square segments that must be rotated so that each face shows nine identical squares.

rub in ✱ **rub it in** *informal* to dwell on something unpleasant or embarrassing.

ruble *n* see ROUBLE.

rub off *v* **1** to remove by rubbing, or disappear as the result of rubbing. **2** (*often* + on) to exert an influence through contact or example.

rub out *v* **1** to remove or be removable with a rubber. **2** *chiefly NAm, slang* to kill or murder.

rubric *n* **1** a heading, e.g. in a book or manuscript, written or printed in a distinctive colour or style. **2a** a heading under which something is classed. **b** an authoritative rule, *esp* a rule for the conduct of church ceremonial. ⋙ **rubrical** *adj.*

ruby *n* (*pl* **-ies**) **1** a red corundum used as a precious gem. **2** the dark red colour of the ruby. **3** (*used before a noun*) of or marking a 40th anniversary.

RUC *abbr* Royal Ulster Constabulary.

ruche *n* a pleated or gathered strip of fabric used for trimming. ⋙ **ruched** *adj.*

ruching *n* = RUCHE.

ruck[1] *n* **1** a situation in Rugby Union in which players close round the ball when it is on the ground and try to kick it out to their own team. **2** in Australian Rules football, three players who do not have fixed positions. **3a** an indistinguishable mass of people or things. **b** (**the ruck**) the usual run of people or things.

ruck[2] *v* in Rugby Union or Australian Rules football, to be part of a ruck.

ruck[3] *v* (*often* + up) to wrinkle or crease.

ruck[4] *n* a wrinkle or crease.

ruck[5] *n Brit, informal* a fight.

rucksack *n* a lightweight bag carried on the back and fastened by straps over the shoulders, used *esp* by walkers and climbers.

ruckus *n* a row or disturbance.

ruction *n informal* **1** (*in pl*) a violent dispute. **2** a disturbance or uproar.

rudd *n* (*pl* **rudd**) a silver-coloured freshwater European fish of the carp family resembling the roach.

rudder *n* **1** a flat piece hinged vertically to a ship's stern for changing course with. **2** a movable auxiliary aerofoil attached to the fin that serves to control direction of flight of an aircraft in the horizontal plane.

rudderless *adj* **1** lacking a rudder. **2a** lacking direction. **b** lacking a strong leader.

ruddle *n* RED OCHRE, *esp* when used for marking sheep.

ruddy *adj* (**-ier, -iest**) **1** said of a complexion: having a healthy reddish colour. **2** red; reddish. **3** *Brit, euphem* = BLOODY[3]. ⋙ **ruddily** *adv,* **ruddiness** *n.*

rude *adj* **1** lacking refinement or propriety, e.g.: **a** discourteous. **b** vulgar; indecent. **c** ignorant; unlearned. **2** sudden and unpleasant; abrupt. **3** robust; vigorous. **4a** in a rough or unfinished state. **b** primitive; undeveloped. ⋙ **rudely** *adv,* **rudeness** *n,* **rudery** *n.*

rudiment *n* **1** (*usu in pl*) a basic principle or element, or a fundamental skill. **2a** (*usu in pl*) something as yet unformed or undeveloped. **b** a body part or organ in its earliest stage of development. ⋙ **rudimental** *adj.*

rudimentary *adj* **1** basic; fundamental. **2** of a primitive kind; crude. **3** very poorly developed or represented only by a vestige. ⋙ **rudimentarily** *adv.*

rue[1] *v* to feel penitence or bitter regret for (e.g. a past deed).

rue[2] *n archaic* **1** deep regret; bitter sorrow. **2** compassion; pity.

rue[3] *n* a strong-scented woody plant with bitter leaves formerly used in medicine.

rueful *adj* expressing sorrow or regret, often mixed with self-deprecating humour. ⋙ **ruefully** *adv,* **ruefulness** *n.*

ruff[1] *n* **1** a broad starched collar of fluted linen or muslin worn in the late 16th and early 17th cents. **2** a fringe of long hairs or feathers growing round the neck of a bird or other animal. **3** (*fem* **reeve**) a Eurasian sandpiper the male of which has a large ruff of erectable feathers during the breeding season. ⋙ **ruffed** *adj.*

ruff[2] *v* = TRUMP[2] (I).

ruff[3] *n* the act or an instance of trumping in cards.

ruffian *n* a brutal and lawless person. ⋙ **ruffianism** *n,* **ruffianly** *adj.*

ruffle[1] *v* **1a** to disturb the smoothness of. **b** to trouble or vex (somebody). **2** to make (fabric) into a ruffle. ⋙ **ruffled** *adj.*

ruffle[2] *n* a strip of fabric gathered or pleated on one edge.

rufiyaa *n* (*pl* **rufiyaa**) the basic monetary unit of the Maldives.

rufous *adj* of an animal: reddish brown.

rug *n* **1** a heavy mat, usu smaller than a carpet and with a thick pile, used as a floor covering. **2** *chiefly Brit* a woollen blanket used as a wrap, *esp* when travelling. **3** *chiefly NAm, informal* a wig or toupee.

rugby *or* **Rugby** *n* a football game played between two teams with an oval football, which features kicking, lateral hand-to-hand passing, and tackling.

Rugby League *n* a form of rugby originating in the north of England, played by teams of 13 players each, featuring a six-player scrum.

Rugby Union *n* a form of rugby played by teams of 15 players each and featuring an eight-player scrum, which was restricted to amateurs until 1995.

rugged *adj* **1** of terrain: having a rough uneven surface or outline. **2a** presenting a severe test of ability or stamina. **b** strongly built or constituted; sturdy. **3** of a man: having attractively strong masculine features. ⋙ **ruggedly** *adv,* **ruggedness** *n.*

ruggedized *or* **-ised** *adj* strengthened or reinforced for durability.

rugger *n Brit, informal* rugby.

rugose *adj* in biology, wrinkled or ridged. ⋙ **rugosely** *adv,* **rugosity** *n.*

rug rat *n NAm, informal* a very young child.

ruin[1] *n* **1a** a state of great dilapidation and decay. **b** (*often in pl*) the remains of something dilapidated or destroyed. **2a** a person's downfall, or the cause of it. **b** the total loss of one's money and other assets. **3** destruction or spoiling.

ruin[2] *v* **1a** to damage irreparably; to reduce to ruins. **b** to reduce to financial ruin. **c** *archaic* to ravish or deflower (a virgin). **2** to make thoroughly unpleasant or unenjoyable; to spoil.

ruination *n* the act or an instance of ruining or being ruined, or a cause of it.

ruinous *adj* **1** causing ruin or the likelihood of ruin. **2** dilapidated or ruined. ⋙ **ruinously** *adv,* **ruinousness** *n.*

rule[1] *n* **1** a statement that sets out what constitutes right conduct or action and that people are expected to obey. **2** the exercise of sovereign authority, or the period during which a particular ruler or government exercises it. **3** the regulations prescribed for the members of a religious order by its founder. **4** (**the rule**) what happens normally or customarily. **5** = RULER (2). **6** a printed or written line or dash. ✱ **as a rule** generally; for the most part.

rule² *v* **1** to have sovereign power over (a nation, people). **2a** to exercise control over. **b** to keep under control; to restrain. **3** to make a judicial decision. **4a** to draw (a line) with a ruler. **b** to mark (paper) with parallel lines. ✱ **rule the roost** to be in charge.

rule in *v* to consider as a possibility.

rule of thumb *n* a rough practical or commonsense method rather than a precise or technical one.

rule out *v* **1a** to exclude or eliminate. **b** to deny the possibility of. **2** to make impossible; to prevent.

ruler *n* **1** somebody, *specif* a sovereign, who rules. **2** a smooth-edged strip of metal, wood, plastic, etc that is marked off in units, e.g. centimetres, and is used for drawing straight lines, for measuring, or for marking off lengths. ⋙ **rulership** *n.*

ruling¹ *n* an official or authoritative decision.

ruling² *adj* **1** exerting power or authority. **2** chief; predominant.

rum¹ *n* an alcoholic spirit made by distilling a fermented cane product, e.g. molasses.

rum² *adj* (**rummer, rummest**) *Brit, informal, dated* peculiar; strange. ⋙ **rumly** *adv,* **rumness** *n.*

Rumanian *n and adj* see ROMANIAN.

rumba *or* **rhumba** *n* a ballroom dance of Cuban origin marked by steps with a delayed transfer of weight and pronounced hip movements.

rum baba *n* = BABA.

rumble¹ *v* **1** to make a low heavy rolling sound. **2** *NAm, informal* to engage in a street fight. **3** *Brit, informal* to discover the true character of. ⋙ **rumbler** *n,* **rumbling** *adj.*

rumble² *n* **1** a rumbling sound. **2** *NAm, informal* a street fight, *esp* between gangs.

rumble seat *n NAm* a folding seat at the rear of an open-topped car.

rumbustious *adj chiefly Brit, informal* irrepressibly or coarsely exuberant. ⋙ **rumbustiously** *adv,* **rumbustiousness** *n.*

ruminant¹ *adj* **1** denoting a group of hoofed mammals including the cattle, sheep, and camels that chew the cud and have a complex three- or four-chambered stomach. **2** meditative; contemplative.

ruminant² *n* a ruminant mammal.

ruminate *v* **1** to engage in deep thought. **2** of a ruminant: to chew the cud. ⋙ **rumination** *n,* **ruminative** *adj,* **ruminatively** *adv,* **ruminator** *n.*

rummage¹ *v* to engage in a haphazard search. ⋙ **rummager** *n.*

rummage² *n* **1** a thorough search, *esp* among a jumbled assortment of objects. **2** *chiefly NAm* = JUMBLE² (2).

rummage sale *n chiefly NAm* a jumble sale.

rummy *n* a card game in which each player tries to assemble combinations of related cards and to be the first to turn all their cards into such combinations.

rumour¹ (*NAm* **rumor**) *n* a statement or report circulated without confirmation of its truth.

rumour² (*NAm* **rumor**) *v* (*usu in passive*) to tell or spread by rumour.

rump *n* **1** the rear part of a quadruped mammal, bird, etc; the buttocks. **2** *humorous* a person's buttocks. **3** a cut of beef from between the loin and round. **4** a small or inferior remnant of a larger group, e.g. a parliament. ⋙ **rumpless** *adj.*

rumple¹ *v* (*usu in passive*) to make or become wrinkled, crumpled, or dishevelled. ⋙ **rumpled** *adj,* **rumply** *adj.*

rumple² *n* a fold or wrinkle.

rumpus *n* a noisy commotion.

rumpus room *n NAm* a room, usu in the basement of a house, that is used for recreation, e.g. hobbies and games.

rumpy-pumpy *n informal* sexual activity.

run¹ *v* (**running,** *past tense* **ran,** *past part.* **run**) **1** to go at a speed faster than a walk, with only one foot on the ground at any time. **2** to hasten or move quickly. *Run and fetch the doctor.* **3** of a bus or train: to operate on a regular route. **4** to take part in a race. **5** to be a candidate in an election. **6** to cause to move lightly or freely: *She ran a comb through her hair.* **7** to manage or carry on (a business, enterprise, etc). **8a** to operate (a vehicle, machine, etc). **b** of a machine: to function. **9** of an agreement etc: to continue in force: *the lease has two more years to run.* **10** (+ in) of a characteristic: to be prevalent: *Delinquency runs in the family.* **11** to convey (somebody) a short distance in a vehicle: *Can I run you home?* **12** to smuggle (goods). **13a** to cause (water, etc) to flow. **b** of a liquid: to flow. **c** of a colour: to spread or dissolve when wet. **14** to reach a specified level: *Profits are running high; Inflation is running at 4 per cent.* **15a** to publish (a story in a newspaper, etc). **b** of a story: to be published. **16** *chiefly NAm* of stockings or tights: to ladder. ✱ **run across** to meet with or discover by chance. **run after 1** to pursue or chase. **2** to seek the company of. **run a temperature** to be feverish. **run into 1** to encounter (somebody) by chance. **2** to collide with. **run short** to become insufficient. **run short of** to have little left of (a supply).

run² *n* **1** the act or an instance of running. **2a** a short excursion in a car. **b** the distance covered in a period of continuous journeying. **c** a regularly travelled course or route: *ships on the Far East run.* **d** freedom of movement in or access to a place: *He has the run of the house.* **3a** a continuous series or unbroken course, *esp* of identical or similar things: *a run of bad luck.* **b** a rapid passage up or down a musical scale. **c** an unbroken course of performances or showings. **d** a persistent and heavy commercial or financial demand: *a run on gilt-edged securities.* **e** three or more playing cards of the same suit in consecutive order of rank. **4** general tendency or direction: *You need to watch the run of the stock market.* **5** the average or prevailing kind or class: *the general run of students.* **6a** a way, track, etc frequented by animals. **b** an enclosure for domestic animals where they may feed or exercise. **7** an inclined course, e.g. for skiing. **8** in cricket, a unit of scoring made typically by each batsman running the full length of the wicket. **9** a ladder in tights or a stocking. **10** (**the runs**) *informal* diarrhoea. ✱ **give somebody a run for their money** to present a serious challenge to somebody. **on the run 1** in haste; without pausing. **2** in hiding or running away, *esp* from lawful authority.

runabout *n* a light motor car or aeroplane.

run along *v informal* to leave.

runaround *n* (**the runaround**) *informal* delaying action, *esp* in response to a request: *When I phoned to complain, they just gave me the runaround.*

run around *v* to have a series of sexual encounters. ✱ **run around with** to associate with.

runaway *n* **1** a fugitive. **2** (*used before a noun*) **a** running out of control: *a runaway train.* **b** won by a long lead; decisive: *a runaway victory.*

run away *v* **1** to flee or escape. **2** to avoid responsibilities. ✱ **to run away with 1** to go beyond the control of: *His imagination started to run away with him.* **2** to believe too easily: *Don't run away with the idea that you can stay.*

runcible spoon *n* a sharp-edged fork with three broad curved prongs.

rundown *n* an item-by-item report; a résumé.

run down *v* **1** to knock down with a vehicle. **2** to find by searching. **3** to criticize or disparage. **4a** to reduce or be reduced in size or strength. **b** to deteriorate.

run-down *adj* **1** in a state of disrepair. **2** in poor health.

rune *n* **1** any of the characters of an alphabet probably derived from Latin and Greek and used in medieval times, *esp* in carved inscriptions, by the Germanic peoples. **2** a magical or cryptic utterance or inscription. ⋙ **runic** *adj.*

rung[1] *n* **1a** any of the crosspieces of a ladder. **b** a rounded part placed as a crosspiece between the legs of a chair. **2** a level or stage in something that can be ascended.

rung[2] *v* past part. of RING[3].

run in *v* **1** to use (a vehicle) carefully when it is new. **2** *informal* to arrest (somebody).

run-in *n* **1** *informal* a quarrel. **2** the final part of a race or racetrack.

runnel *n* a small stream; a brook.

runner *n* **1** an entrant for a race that actually competes in it. **2a** a bank or stockbroker's messenger. **b** (*usu in combination*) somebody who smuggles or distributes illicit or contraband goods: *a gun-runner.* **3 a** a longitudinal piece on which a sledge or ice skate slides. **b** a groove or bar along which something, e.g. a drawer or sliding door, slides. **4** a horizontal stem from the base of a plant that buds to produce new plants. **5** a long narrow carpet, e.g. for a hall or staircase. ✱ **do a runner** *Brit, informal* to leave in haste, *esp* to avoid paying for something or to escape the scene of a crime.

runner bean *n chiefly Brit* the long green pod of a tropical American climbing bean with large bright red flowers, used as a vegetable.

runner-up *n* (*pl* **runners-up**) a competitor or team that comes second in a contest or race.

running[1] *n* **1** the act or an instance of running. **2** management; operation. ✱ **in/out of the running** having a good/poor chance of winning. **make the running** to set the pace.

running[2] *adj* **1** runny. **2a** having stages that follow in rapid succession: *a running battle.* **b** made during the course of a process or activity: *a running commentary.* **3** cursive; flowing.

running[3] *adv* in succession.

running board *n* a footboard, *esp* at the side of a motor car.

running head *n* a headline repeated on consecutive pages of a book.

running knot *n* a knot that slips along the rope or line round which it is tied.

running light *n* any of the lights carried by a moving ship, aeroplane, car, etc, *esp* at night.

running mate *n* a candidate standing for a subordinate place in a US election.

running repairs *pl n* repairs, usu minor or temporary ones, made to machinery that is in operation.

running stitch *n* a small even sewing stitch run in and out of cloth, e.g. for gathering.

runny *adj* (**-ier, -iest**) having a tendency to run.

runoff *n* **1** a final decisive race, contest, or election. **2** the portion of the rainfall that ultimately reaches streams.

run off *v* **1** to compose or produce quickly. **2** to decide a competition with an extra contest. ✱ **run off with** to run away with.

run-of-the-mill *adj* average; commonplace.

run on *v* to continue without interruption.

run out *v* to become used up. ✱ **run out of** to finish the available supply of. **run out on** *informal* to desert (somebody).

run over *v* **1** to injure or kill with a motor vehicle. **2** to read through quickly.

runt *n* an animal unusually small of its kind, *esp* the smallest of a litter of pigs. ⋙ **runty** *adj.*

run through *v* **1** to pierce with a weapon. **2** to read through quickly.

run-through *n* **1** a sequence of actions performed for practice. **2** a cursory reading, summary, or rehearsal.

run-time *n* **1** the time that a computer program takes to run. **2** the time when a computer program is being run by a user as opposed to when it is being created by a programmer.

run up *v* **1** to accumulate (debts). **2** to make or erect quickly. ✱ **run up against** to experience (an unexpected difficulty).

run-up *n* **1** a period that immediately precedes an action or event. **2** an approach run to provide momentum, e.g. for a jump or throw.

runway *n* **1** an artificially surfaced strip of ground on an airfield for the landing and takeoff of aeroplanes. **2** a narrow stage in the centre of a room on which fashion shows are held; = CATWALK (1). **3** a path made by or for animals.

rupee /rooh'pee/ *n* the basic monetary unit of various countries of the Indian subcontinent and the Indian Ocean, i.e. India, Mauritius, Nepal, Pakistan, the Seychelles, and Sri Lanka.

rupiah /rooh'pee·ə/ *n* the basic monetary unit of Indonesia.

rupture[1] *n* **1** the act or an instance of breaking apart or bursting. **2** a hernia.

rupture[2] *v* **1a** to part (something) by violence; to break or burst. **b** to create a breach of (a peaceful situation, etc). **2** to cause a rupture in (oneself or a body part).

rural *adj* of the country, country people or life, or agriculture. ⋙ **ruralism** *n,* **ruralist** *n,* **rurality** *n,* **rurally** *adv.*

rural dean *n chiefly Brit* a priest supervising one district of a diocese.

Ruritanian *adj* of or characteristic of an imaginary Central European country used as a setting for adventure stories of romance and intrigue.

ruse *n* a wily subterfuge.

rush[1] *v* **1** to move forward, progress, or act quickly or eagerly or without preparation. **2** to push or impel (somebody or something) forward with speed or violence. **3** to perform or finish in a short time or at high speed: *He rushed his breakfast.* **4** to urge (somebody) to an excessive speed. **5** to run against (somebody or something) in attack, often with an element of surprise; to charge.

rush[2] *n* **1a** a rapid and violent forward motion. **b** a sudden onset of emotion: *a quick rush of sympathy.* **2a** a surge of activity, or busy or hurried activity: *the bank holiday rush.* **b** a burst of productivity or speed. **c** a sudden demand for something. **3** a great movement of people, *esp* in search of wealth. **4** (*usu in pl*) the unedited print of a film scene processed directly after shooting. **5** an immediate brief pleasurable feeling, *esp* one resulting from an intravenous injection of a drug such as heroin.

rush[3] *n* a tufted marsh plant with cylindrical hollow leaves, used for the seats of chairs and for plaiting mats. ⋙ **rushy** *adj.*

rush hour *n* a period of the day when traffic is at a peak.

rushlight *n* formerly, a candle that consisted of the pith of a rush dipped in grease.

rusk *n* a piece of sliced bread baked again until dry and crisp, or a light dry biscuit similar to this.

russet[1] *n* **1** a reddish to yellowish brown colour. **2** a russet-coloured winter eating apple. **3** formerly, a coarse homespun reddish brown or grey fabric used for clothing.

russet[2] *adj* of a reddish to yellowish brown colour.

Russian *n* **1** a native or inhabitant of Russia. **2** the language of Russia. ⋙ **Russian** *adj.*

Russian doll *n* any of a series of progressively smaller, brightly painted dolls that fit inside each other.

Russian Orthodox Church *n* (**the Russian Orthodox Church**) the largest branch of the Orthodox Church, and the national church in Russia.

Russian roulette *n* an act of bravado consisting of spinning the cylinder of a revolver loaded with one cartridge, pointing the muzzle at one's own head, and pulling the trigger.

Russki *or* **Russky** *n* (*pl* **Russkis** *or* **Russkies**) *derog* a Russian.

rust[1] *n* **1a** brittle reddish hydrated ferric oxide that forms as a coating on iron, *esp* iron chemically attacked by moist air. **b** a comparable coating produced on another metal, or anything similar. **2** a destructive fungal disease of plants in which reddish brown pustular lesions form. **3** a reddish brown to orange colour. ⋙ **rustless** *adj.*

rust[2] *v* to form rust; to become oxidized.

rustbelt *n informal* an area of the northern USA marked by the prevalence of heavy industry which is now in decline.

rustic[1] *adj* **1** of or suitable for the country. **2** characteristic of the countryside, *esp* in being simple or unsophisticated. **3** of furniture: made of the rough branches of trees. ⋙ **rustically** *adv,* **rusticity** *n.*

rustic[2] *n often derog* an unsophisticated rural person.

rusticate *v* **1** *Brit* to suspend (a student) from college or university. **2** to bevel or cut a groove, channel, etc, in (the edges of stone blocks, etc) to make the joints conspicuous. ⋙ **rustication** *n.*

rustle[1] *v* **1a** to make or cause a rustle. **b** to move with a rustling sound. **2** to steal (cattle or horses). ⋙ **rustler** *n.*

rustle[2] *n* a quick succession or confusion of faint sounds.

rustle up *v informal* to produce (food, etc) adeptly or at short notice.

rustproof[1] *adj* able to resist rust.

rustproof[2] *v* to make (something) incapable of rusting.

rusty *adj* (**-ier, -iest**) **1** affected by rust, *esp* stiff with rust. **2** of the colour rust. **3a** slow or lacking skill through lack of practice or advanced age. **b** showing lack of practice. ⋙ **rustily** *adv,* **rustiness** *n.*

rut[1] *n* **1** a track worn by habitual passage, *esp* of wheels on soft or uneven ground. **2** an established practice, *esp* a tedious routine. ⋙ **rutted** *adj.*

rut[2] *n* **1** an annually recurrent state of readiness to copulate, in the male deer or other mammal. **2** (*often* **the rut**) the period during which rut normally occurs.

rut[3] *v* (**rutted, rutting**) to be in a state of rut.

rutabaga *n NAm* a swede.

ruth *n archaic* pity, compassion, or remorse.

ruthenium *n* a rare white metallic chemical element of the platinum group that occurs naturally in platinum ores, and is used in hardening platinum alloys and in catalysts.

rutherfordium *n* an artificially produced radioactive chemical element.

ruthless *adj* showing no pity or compassion. ⋙ **ruthlessly** *adv,* **ruthlessness** *n.*

ruttish *adj* lustful.

RV *abbr NAm* recreational vehicle.

Rwandan *or* **Rwandese** *n* a native or inhabitant of Rwanda. ⋙ **Rwandan** *adj,* **Rwandese** *adj.*

-ry *suffix* see -ERY.

rye *n* **1a** a hardy grass widely grown for grain. **b** the seeds of this grass, from which a wholemeal flour is made. **2** = RYE WHISKY. **3** = RYE BREAD.

rye bread *n* bread made wholly or in part of rye flour and usu containing caraway seeds.

ryegrass *n* any of several species of grasses used *esp* for pasture.

rye whisky *n* a whisky distilled from rye or from rye and malt.

S

S[1] *or* **s** *n* (*pl* **S's** *or* **Ss** *or* **s's**) the 19th letter of the English alphabet.

S[2] ***abbr*** **1** saint. **2** siemens. **3** small. **4** South. **5** Southern.

S[3] ***abbr*** the chemical symbol for sulphur.

s ***abbr*** **1** second. **2** shilling. **3** singular. **4** son.

's ***contr*** *informal* **1** is: *She's here.* **2** has: *He's seen them.* **3** used in questions: does: *What's he want?* **4** us: *Let's go.* See note at APOSTROPHE[1].

-s[1] ***suffix*** **1** forming the plural of most nouns that do not end in *s, z, sh, ch,* or *y* after a consonant: *cats.* **2** (*also* **-'s**) forming the plural of abbreviations, numbers, letters, and symbols used as nouns: *the 1940s.*

-s[2] ***suffix*** forming the third person sing. present of most verbs that do not end in *s, z, sh, ch,* or *y* after a consonant: *falls.*

-'s[1] ***suffix*** forming the possessive of singular nouns, plural nouns not ending in *s*, and some pronouns: *boy's.*

-'s[2] ***suffix*** see -s[1] (2).

SA ***abbr*** **1** Salvation Army. **2** South Africa. **3** South America. **4** South Australia.

saag ***n*** *Indian* spinach.

Sabbatarian ***n*** somebody who observes the sabbath, *esp* on Saturday, in strict conformity with the fourth commandment. ➤➤ **Sabbatarian** *adj,* **Sabbatarianism** *n.*

sabbath ***n*** **1** (*usu* **the Sabbath**) the seventh day of the week observed from Friday evening to Saturday evening as a day of rest and worship, *esp* by Jews. **2** (*often* **the Sabbath**) Sunday observed among Christians as a day of rest and worship. **3** a midnight assembly of witches.

sabbatical[1] ***n*** a period of leave, often with pay, granted usu every seventh year, e.g. to a university teacher.

sabbatical[2] ***adj*** **1** (*often* **Sabbatical**) *archaic* of the sabbath. **2** of or being a sabbatical.

saber ***n*** *NAm* see SABRE.

Sabine ***n*** a member of an ancient people of the Apennines in central Italy. ➤➤ **Sabine** *adj.*

sable[1] ***n*** (*pl* **sables** *or* **sable**) **1** a mammal related to the martens and weasels that is found in the forests of N Asia and feeds on small animals and eggs. **2** the valuable dark brown fur of the sable.

sable[2] ***adj*** **1** (*often used after a noun*) in heraldry, black. **2** *literary* black, dark, or gloomy.

sabot /'saboh/ ***n*** a wooden shoe worn in various European countries.

sabotage[1] ***n*** **1** destructive or obstructive action by enemy agents, discontented workers, etc that is intended to hinder military or industrial activity. **2** deliberate subversion, e.g. of a plan or project.

sabotage[2] ***v*** to destroy, obstruct, or subvert by sabotage.

saboteur ***n*** somebody who commits sabotage.

sabra ***n*** (*often* **Sabra**) a native-born Israeli Jew.

sabre (*NAm* **saber**) ***n*** **1** a heavy cavalry sword with a curved single-edged blade. **2** a light fencing or duelling sword with an arched guard that covers the back of the hand and a tapering flexible blade.

sabre-rattling ***n*** the display of military power, *esp* in an aggressively intimidating way.

sabre-toothed tiger ***n*** any of various extinct large members of the cat family with long curved upper canines.

sac ***n*** a pouch, often filled with fluid, within an animal or plant.

saccharide ***n*** a simple sugar or a combination of simple sugars.

saccharin ***n*** a chemical compound that is several hundred times sweeter than sugar and is used in low-calorie diets.

saccharine ***adj*** **1** of, like, or containing sugar. **2** excessively sweet; mawkish.

sacerdotal ***adj*** of priests or the priesthood.

sacerdotalism ***n*** a religious belief emphasizing the powers of priests as essential mediators between God and human beings.

sachem /'saych(ə)m, 'sach(ə)m/ ***n*** a Native American chief.

Sachertorte /'sakətohtə, 'zakə-/ ***n*** (*pl* **Sachertorten**) a rich dark chocolate cake with a filling of apricot jam.

sachet ***n*** a small sealed plastic or paper bag or packet usu holding just enough of something, e.g. shampoo or sugar, for use at one time.

sack[1] ***n*** **1** a usu rectangular large bag, e.g. of paper or canvas. **2** (**the sack**) *informal* dismissal from employment. **3** (**the sack**) *informal* bed. ✱ **hit the sack** *informal* to go to bed.

sack[2] ***v*** *informal* to dismiss (somebody) from a job. ➤➤ **sackable** *adj.*

sack[3] ***n*** any of various dry white wines formerly imported to Britain from S Europe.

sack[4] *n* the plundering of a place captured in war.

sack[5] *v* **1** to plunder (e.g. a town) after capture. **2** to strip (a place) of valuables.

sackbut *n* an early form of trombone used in the Renaissance.

sackcloth *n* a coarse fabric used as sacking. ✱ **sackcloth and ashes** a usu public display of mourning or penitence.

sacking *n* material for sacks, *esp* a coarse fabric such as hessian.

sack race *n* a race in which each contestant has their legs enclosed in a sack and progresses by jumping.

sacra *n* pl of SACRUM.

sacral[1] *adj* relating to or in the region of the sacrum.

sacral[2] *adj* relating to or used in sacred rites or symbols.

sacrament *n* **1** a formal religious act, e.g. baptism, regarded as conferring divine grace on the recipient. **2** (**the Sacrament**) the bread and wine used in the Eucharist; *specif* the consecrated bread. **3** something considered to have sacred or religious significance.

sacramental[1] *adj* of or having the character of a sacrament. ⪢ **sacramentally** *adv.*

sacramental[2] *n* a sacrament-like action or object of devotion in Roman Catholic practice.

sacramentalism *n* belief in or use of sacramental rites, acts, or objects; *specif* belief that the sacraments bring about and are necessary for salvation.

sacred *adj* **1a** dedicated or set apart for the service or worship of a god or gods. **b** dedicated as a memorial: *sacred to his memory.* **2a** worthy of religious veneration; holy. **b** commanding reverence and respect. **3** relating to, used in, or suitable for religion; not secular or profane: *sacred music.* ⪢ **sacredly** *adv,* **sacredness** *n.*

sacred cow *n* somebody or something granted unreasonable immunity from criticism.

sacrifice[1] *n* **1a** an act of making an offering to a deity, *esp* the killing of a victim on an altar. **b** something or somebody offered in sacrifice. **2a** the losing or surrender of one thing for the sake of a greater. **b** something forgone or done without.

sacrifice[2] *v* **1** to offer (something or somebody) as a sacrifice. **2** to give up or lose (something) for the sake of an ideal or end. ⪢ **sacrificial** *adj.*

sacrilege *n* **1** a violation of what is sacred, e.g. the improper or secular use of a sacred object. **2** gross irreverence towards somebody or something sacred. ⪢ **sacrilegious** *adj.*

sacristan *or* **sacrist** *n* somebody in charge of the sacristy and ceremonial equipment of a church.

sacristy *n* (*pl* **-ies**) a room in a church where sacred vessels and vestments are kept and where the clergy put on their vestments.

sacroiliac *adj* relating to or in the region of the sacrum and the ILIUM (part of the pelvis) or the joint between them.

sacrosanct *adj* accorded the highest reverence and respect. ⪢ **sacrosanctity** *n.*

sacrum *n* (*pl* **sacra**) the part of the spinal column that is directly connected with or forms part of the pelvis and in human beings consists of five fused vertebrae.

SAD *abbr* seasonal affective disorder.

sad *adj* (**sadder, saddest**) **1a** affected with or expressing unhappiness. **b** causing or associated with unhappiness. **c** deplorable; regrettable. **2** *informal* pathetic or contemptible. ⪢ **sadness** *n.*

sadden *v* to make sad.

saddhu /'sahdooh/ *n* see SADHU.

saddle[1] *n* **1** a usu padded and leather-covered seat secured to the back of a horse for the rider to sit on. **2** a seat on a bicycle or tractor. **3** something like a saddle in shape, position, or function, e.g. a marking on the back of an animal. **4** a ridge connecting two peaks. **5** a large cut of meat from a sheep, hare, rabbit, deer, etc consisting of both sides of the unsplit back including both loins. **6** the rear part of a male fowl's back extending to the tail. ✱ **in the saddle** in control.

saddle[2] *v* **1** to put a saddle on (a horse). **2** to burden or encumber (somebody).

saddleback *n* any of several animals with saddle-shaped markings on the back, *esp* a medium-sized black pig with a white band crossing the back. ⪢ **saddlebacked** *adj.*

saddlebag *n* a pouch or bag attached to the back of a saddle.

saddler *n* somebody who makes, repairs, or sells saddles and other leather equipment for horses.

saddlery *n* (*pl* **-ies**) **1** the usu leather equipment, e.g. saddles, bridles, etc, used for riding and controlling a horse. **2a** the making, repair, or sale of saddlery. **b** a saddler's place of work or trade.

saddle soap *n* a mild oily soap used for cleansing and conditioning leather.

saddle-stitched *adj* fastened by stitches or staples through the fold.

saddo *n* (*pl* **-os**) *Brit, informal* a pathetic or contemptible person.

Sadducee *n* a member of a Jewish aristocratic and priestly sect noted at the time of Jesus Christ for rejecting various beliefs of the Pharisees, e.g. resurrection and the existence of angels. ⪢ **Sadducean** *adj.*

sadhu *or* **saddhu** /'sahdooh/ *n* an Indian ascetic, usu a wandering holy man.

sadism *n* **1** the act or an instance of obtaining sexual pleasure or gratification by inflicting physical pain or emotional or mental torture, *esp* through humiliation, on another person. **2** an inclination towards sadism. ⪢ **sadist** *n,* **sadistic** *adj,* **sadistically** *adv.*

sadly *adv* **1** in a sad manner. **2** it is sad or regrettable that; unfortunately.

sadomasochism *n* **1** the act or an instance of obtaining sexual pleasure or gratification through sadism and masochism. **2** an inclination towards sadism and masochism. ⪢ **sadomasochist** *n,* **sadomasochistic** *adj.*

sae *abbr* stamped addressed envelope.

safari *n* (*pl* **safaris**) an overland expedition, *esp* in E Africa, to observe, hunt, or study wild animals in their natural habitat.

safari jacket *n* a jacket made of lightweight material, *esp* cotton, and typically having short sleeves, two breast pockets, and a belt.

safari park *n* a large tract of land where wild animals, e.g. lions, are kept so that visitors can drive through and observe them.

safari suit *n* a suit comprising a safari jacket and matching shorts, trousers, or skirt.

safe[1] *adj* **1** secure from threat of danger, harm, or loss. **2** free from harm or risk; no longer in danger. **3** providing protection or security from danger. **4a** not threatening or entailing danger: *Is your dog safe?* **b** unlikely to cause controversy: *a safe topic of conversation.* **5a** not liable to take risks. **b** trustworthy; reliable. ✱ **to be on the safe side** as a precaution. ⪢ **safely** *adv,* **safeness** *n.*

safe[2] *n* a reinforced usu fireproof room or cabinet, often with a complex lock or locking system, where money, valuables, etc are stored.

safe[3] *adv* in a safe manner or condition; safely.

safe-conduct *n* an official guarantee of protection given to a person, e.g. when passing through a military zone or occupied area.

safe-deposit *n* a place, e.g. the vault of a bank, for the safe storage of valuables.

safeguard[1] *n* a precautionary measure or stipulation.

safeguard[2] *v* to provide a safeguard for (something or somebody); to protect.

safe house *n* a place used for concealment and safety, e.g. a meeting place for spies or terrorists or a shelter for people threatened with violence.

safekeeping *n* protection or the state of being kept safe.

safe period *n* the time during a woman's menstrual cycle when conception is least likely to occur, usu just before or just after her period.

safe seat *n* a parliamentary seat that was won with a large majority by one party at an election and is likely to be retained by that party in a subsequent election.

safe sex *n* sexual activity in which precautions are taken to prevent the transmission of Aids and similar diseases, e.g. sexual intercourse with the protection of a condom.

safety *n* (*pl* **-ies**) **1** the condition of being safe from causing or suffering harm or loss. **2a** (*used before a noun*) designed to prevent injury, damage, or accidental use. **b** a safety device, *esp* a safety catch.

safety belt *n* = SEAT BELT.

safety catch *n* a device, e.g. on a gun or a machine, designed to prevent accidental use.

safety curtain *n* a fireproof curtain in a theatre that can isolate the stage from the auditorium in case of fire.

safety-deposit *n* = SAFE-DEPOSIT.

safety glass *n* glass that has been strengthened or laminated so that it will not shatter into dangerously sharp pieces.

safety match *n* a match capable of being ignited only on a specially prepared surface, usu the side of its own matchbox.

safety net *n* **1** a net designed to protect people working or performing in high places by catching them if they fall. **2** a measure intended to provide protection or assistance in times of hardship or difficulty: *the safety net of unemployment benefit.*

safety pin *n* a pin in the form of a clasp with a guard covering its point when fastened.

safety razor *n* a razor with a guard for the blade to prevent users from cutting their skin.

safety valve *n* **1** an automatic escape or pressure-relief valve, e.g. for a steam boiler. **2** an outlet for pent-up energy or emotion.

safflower *n* a widely grown SW Asian and N African plant of the daisy family with seeds rich in edible oil.

saffron *n* a deep gold aromatic pungent spice made from the dried stigmas (flower parts; see STIGMA) of a type of crocus and used to colour and flavour foods.

sag[1] *v* (**sagged, sagging**) **1** to droop, sink, or settle from weight, pressure, or loss of tautness. **2** to lose strength or vigour.

sag[2] *n* an instance or amount of sagging. ➤➤ **saggy** *adj.*

saga *n* **1** a medieval Icelandic or Norse narrative dealing with historic or legendary figures and events. **2** a long detailed account, often of a series of related events.

sagacious *adj* **1** having sound judgment or perception. **2** prompted by or indicating keen discernment or foresight. ➤➤ **sagaciously** *adv,* **sagacity** *n.*

sage[1] *n* somebody, e.g. a great philosopher, renowned or revered for wise teachings or sound judgment.

sage[2] *adj* having or showing great wisdom derived from reflection and experience. ➤➤ **sagely** *adv,* **sageness** *n.*

sage[3] *n* a plant of the mint family having greyish green aromatic leaves that are used as a herb.

sagebrush *n* an aromatic low-growing shrub of the daisy family that covers large areas of plains in the W USA.

sage green *adj* of a greyish green colour. ➤➤ **sage green** *n.*

Sagittarius *n* **1** in astronomy, a constellation (the Archer) depicted as a centaur shooting an arrow. **2** in astrology, the ninth sign of the zodiac, or a person born under this sign. ➤➤ **Sagittarian** *adj and n.*

sago *n* (*pl* **-os**) **1** a dry powdered starch prepared from the pith of a palm and used as a food, e.g. in a milk pudding. **2** a dessert made with sago.

saguaro *n* (*pl* **-os**) a huge treelike cactus of the southwestern US and Mexico that has upward curving branches, white flowers, and an edible fruit.

Saharan *n* of the Sahara desert.

sahib *n* a term of address used in India, *esp* among the indigenous population in colonial times, as a mark of respect to a European man.

said[1] *v* past tense and past part. of SAY[1].

said[2] *adj* aforementioned.

sail[1] *n* **1** an expanse of fabric that is spread to catch or deflect the wind as a means of propelling a ship, boat, etc. **2** something resembling a sail in function or form: *the sails of a windmill.* **3a** a voyage by ship or boat. **b** an excursion in a sailing vessel. ✱ **under sail** with sails set and not propelled by an engine.

sail[2] *v* **1a** to travel in a boat or ship. **b** to travel in or handle a sailing boat as a sporting or leisure activity. **2a** to travel on water, *esp* by the action of wind on sails. **b** to move without visible effort or in a stately manner. **3** to begin a journey by water. **4** to travel over (a body of water) in a ship or boat. **5** to direct or manage the operation of (a ship or boat). ✱ **sail close to the wind 1** to sail as close as possible to the direction from which the wind is blowing. **2** to be near to a point of danger or to a limit that it is unwise to cross. **sail through** to succeed in (something) with ease.

sailboard *n* a flat buoyant board with a mast and a sail, used in windsurfing. ➤➤ **sailboarder** *n,* **sailboarding** *n.*

sailcloth *n* **1** a heavy canvas used for sails, tents, or upholstery. **2** a lightweight canvas used for clothing.

sailfish *n* (*pl* **sailfishes** *or* **sailfish**) a large marine fish related to the swordfish but having a very large sail-like fin along the back that can be lowered to give increased speed.

sailing boat *n* a boat fitted with sails for propulsion.

sailing ship *n* a ship fitted with sails for propulsion.

sailor *n* **1a** somebody who sails a ship or boat; a mariner. **b** a member of a ship's crew, *esp* one below the rank of officer. **c** somebody who sails as a sporting or leisure activity. **2** a person who travels by water, *esp* one considered with reference to their susceptibility to seasickness.

sailor collar *n* a broad collar that has a square flap across the back and tapers to a V in the front.

sailplane *n* a glider designed for sustained soaring flights.

sainfoin *n* a Eurasian red- or pink-flowered plant widely grown for hay and pasture.

saint[1] *n* **1** a person officially recognized by the Christian Church, *esp* through canonization, as being outstandingly holy and so worthy of veneration. **2** any of the spirits of the dead in heaven. **3** a person of outstanding piety or virtue. ➤➤ **sainthood** *n*, **saintliness** *n*, **saintly** *adj*.

saint[2] *v* to recognize or designate as a saint; *specif* to canonize.

Saint Anthony's fire *n* any of several inflammations or gangrenous conditions of the skin, e.g. erysipelas or ergotism.

Saint Bernard *n* a large powerful dog of a breed originating in the Swiss Alps, having a thick shaggy coat and orig kept to rescue travellers who got into difficulty in the snow.

Saint Elmo's fire *n* a flamelike electrical discharge sometimes seen in stormy weather at prominent points, e.g. on an aeroplane, ship, or building.

Saint George's Cross *n* **1** a cross consisting of two intersecting bars that form the shape of a plus sign (+). **2** a red cross of this kind on a white background, e.g. on a flag, *esp* the national flag of England.

Saint John's wort *n* **1** a plant or shrub with attractive five-petalled yellow flowers. **2** a preparation made from this plant and used as a natural antidepressant.

Saint Lucian *n* a native or inhabitant of St Lucia. ➤➤ **Saint Lucian** *adj*.

saintpaulia *n* = AFRICAN VIOLET.

saint's day *n* a day in the calendar of the Christian Church on which a saint is commemorated.

Saint Swithin's Day *n* 15 July observed in honour of St Swithin and traditionally held to be a day on which, if it rains, it will continue to rain for the next 40 days.

saith *v* archaic third person sing. present of SAY[1].

saithe *n* (*pl* **saithes** *or* **saithe**) = COLEY.

sake[1] *n* benefit, purpose, or interest. ✱ **for God's/goodness/heaven's sake** used as an exclamation of protest, impatience, etc. **for old times' sake** because of or as an acknowledgment of a shared past; in memory of something in the past. **for the sake of 1** in order to help or please; for the benefit of: *We moved to the country for the sake of the children.* **2** for the purpose of; in the interest of: *OK, for the sake of peace, you can have the last of the ice cream.* **3** so as to get, keep, or improve: *You should relax more for the sake of your health.*

sake[2] *or* **saki** /'sahki/ *n* a Japanese alcoholic drink made from fermented rice.

Sakti *n* see SHAKTI.

salaam[1] *n* a ceremonial greeting or gesture of respect performed in Arab-speaking and Muslim countries by bowing low and placing the right palm on the forehead.

salaam[2] *v* to perform a salaam.

salable *adj* see SALEABLE.

salacious *adj* **1** arousing sexual desire; lewd. **2** lecherous; lustful. ➤➤ **salaciously** *adv*, **salaciousness** *n*.

salad *n* mixed raw vegetables, e.g. lettuce, cucumber, and tomato, served as a side dish or a main course.

salad cream *n Brit* a bottled dressing for salads.

salad days *pl n* a time of youthful inexperience or indiscretion.

salamander *n* **1** an amphibian that superficially resembles a lizard but is scaleless and covered with a soft moist skin. **2a** a mythical animal that lives in fire or that can withstand the effects of fire. **b** an elemental being said to inhabit fire. **3** a metal plate that is heated and held over food to brown the top. ➤➤ **salamandrine** *adj*.

salami /sə'lahmi/ *n* (*pl* **salamis**) a highly seasoned sausage that is usu thinly sliced and eaten cold.

salary *n* (*pl* **-ies**) a fixed usu monthly payment made to an employee, *esp* a professional or office worker. ➤➤ **salaried** *adj*.

salchow *n* in ice-skating, a jump from the inside backward edge of one skate to the outside backward edge of the other skate with one or more turns in the air.

sale *n* **1** the act or an instance of selling; *specif* the transfer of ownership of and title to property or goods from one person to another for a price. **2a** an event at which goods are offered for sale. **b** an opportunity to buy or a period of selling goods at bargain prices. **c** a public disposal of goods to the highest bidder; an auction. **3** (*in pl*) operations and activities involved in promoting and selling goods or services. ✱ **on/for sale** available for purchase.

saleable *or* **salable** *adj* capable of being or fit to be sold. ➤➤ **saleability** *n*.

sale or return *n* an arrangement by which a buyer, *esp* a retail outlet, pays only for the goods that are sold and may return what is unsold.

saleroom *n chiefly Brit* a place where goods are displayed for sale, *esp* by auction.

salesman *or* **saleswoman** *n* (*pl* **salesmen** *or* **saleswomen**) a salesperson. ➤➤ **salesmanship** *n*.

salesperson *n* (*pl* **salespersons** *or* **salespeople**) somebody employed to sell goods or services, e.g. in a shop or within an assigned territory.

salicylic acid *n* an acid used as a fungicide and to make chemical compounds, e.g. aspirin, that are used to relieve pain and fever and in the treatment of rheumatism.

salient[1] *adj* **1** most noticeable or important. **2** projecting beyond a line or level. **3** of an angle, point, etc: pointing upward or outward. ➤➤ **salience** *n*, **saliency** *n*, **saliently** *adv*.

salient[2] *n* something, e.g. a promontory, that projects outward or upward from its surroundings; *specif* an outwardly projecting part of a fortification, trench system, or line of defence.

saline[1] *adj* **1** of, containing, or resembling salt. **2** *esp* of a laxative: containing salts of potassium, sodium, or magnesium. ➤➤ **salinity** *n*.

saline[2] *n* a saline solution.

saliva *n* a slightly alkaline mixture of water, protein, salts, and often enzymes that is secreted into the mouth by glands, providing lubrication to make chewing food easier, often beginning the breakdown of starches. ➤➤ **salivary** *adj*.

salivate *v* **1** to have a flow of saliva, *esp* in anticipation of food. **2** to show great or excessive eagerness or excitement. ➤➤ **salivation** *n*.

sallow[1] *n* a Eurasian broad-leaved willow, some of which are important sources of charcoal.

sallow[2] *adj* of a sickly yellowish colour. ➤➤ **sallowish** *adj*, **sallowness** *n*.

sally[1] *n* (*pl* **-ies**) **1** a sortie of troops from a besieged position. **2** a witty remark or retort.

sally[2] *v* (**-ies, -ied**) (*usu* + forth) to set out, e.g. on a journey.

salmagundi *n* (*pl* **salmagundis**) **1** a dish of chopped meats, anchovies, eggs, and vegetables often arranged in rows. **2** a mixture composed of many usu unrelated elements.

salmon *n* (*pl* **salmons** *or* **salmon**) a large soft-finned game and food fish of the N Atlantic that is highly valued for its pink flesh.

salmonella *n* (*pl* **salmonellae**) **1** a bacterium that causes diseases, *esp* food poisoning, in human beings and other warm-blooded animals. **2** food poisoning caused by this. ➤➤ **salmonellosis** *n.*

salmon trout *n* = SEA TROUT.

salon *n* **1** a commercial establishment where hairdressers, beauticians, couturiers, etc see their clients. **2** an elegant reception room or living room. **3** formerly, a gathering of literary figures, artists, and the socially or politically prominent, held regularly in a fashionable home. **4** (**Salon**) an exhibition, *esp* in France, of works of art by living artists.

saloon *n* **1a** *Brit* a comfortable, well-furnished, and often relatively expensive bar in a public house. **b** *NAm* a room or establishment in which alcoholic beverages are sold and consumed. **2** a public room or hall, e.g. a ballroom, an exhibition room, or a lounge on a passenger ship. **3** *Brit* an enclosed car with two or four doors and a separate boot. **4** a well-appointed railway carriage with no compartments.

saloon car *n* = SALOON (3).

salopettes *pl n* high-waisted usu padded or quilted trousers with shoulder straps worn for skiing.

salsa *n* **1** a type of Latin American popular music of Cuban origin that is lively, rhythmic, and sensuous. **2** a spicy Mexican relish of chopped mixed vegetables, usu tomatoes and onions, with chillies.

salsify *n* (*pl* **-ies**) the long tapering root of a plant of the daisy family, used as a vegetable.

SALT *abbr* Strategic Arms Limitation Talks.

salt[1] *n* **1** (*also* **common salt**) sodium chloride occurring naturally, e.g. as a mineral deposit, and dissolved in sea water and used in the form of white powder or crystals for seasoning or preserving food. **2** any of numerous chemical compounds resulting from replacement of all or part of the hydrogen atoms of an acid by a metal atom or other chemical group. **3** an experienced sailor. ✱ **below the salt** in a socially disadvantageous position. **rub salt into the wound/somebody's wounds** to make something that is already painful, embarrassing, humiliating, etc even worse. **the salt of the earth** a person whose goodness, kindness, honesty, etc makes them worthy of respect and admiration. **with a pinch/grain of salt** with doubts or reservations as to the truth. **worth one's salt** competent or effective, *esp* in doing one's work [from the money paid to soldiers in Roman times to buy salt].

salt[2] *v* **1** to treat, season, or preserve with common salt or brine. **2** to give flavour or piquancy to (e.g. a story). **3** to sprinkle with salt; *specif* to sprinkle salt on (a road or path) to melt ice or snow.

salt[3] *adj* **1** containing or impregnated with salt; saline or salty. **2** containing, overflowed by, or growing in salt water. ➤➤ **saltness** *n.*

salt away *v* to put (*esp* money) by in reserve; to save or hoard.

saltbush *n* a shrubby plant of the goosefoot family that thrives in dry alkaline soil and is often an important grazing plant in dry regions.

saltcellar *n* a cruet for salt, *esp* a small open dish or a shaker with one or more holes in the top used for salt at table.

salt flat *n* (*usu in pl*) a salt-encrusted flat area resulting from evaporation of a former body of water.

saltimbocca *n* an Italian dish of veal rolled and stuffed with ham and sage.

salting *n chiefly Brit* (*usu in pl*) a marshy coastal area flooded regularly by tides.

saltire *n* a diagonal cross, one of the ordinaries (basic designs; see ORDINARY[2] (2)) used in heraldry.

salt lick *n* a place to which animals regularly go to lick a salt deposit, or a block of selected minerals provided for animals to lick.

salt marsh *n* flat land that is frequently flooded by seawater and supports a characteristic community of plants able to survive under these conditions.

saltpan *n* a natural or artificial basin where salt is produced by the evaporation of salt water.

saltpetre (*NAm* **saltpeter**) *n* **1** potassium nitrate. **2** sodium nitrate.

saltwater *adj* of, living in, or being salt water.

salty *adj* (**-ier, -iest**) **1** of, seasoned with, or containing salt. **2** having a usu strong taste of salt. **3a** piquant; witty. **b** earthy; coarse. ➤➤ **saltily** *adv,* **saltiness** *n.*

salubrious *adj* **1** favourable to or promoting health or well-being. **2** pleasant; respectable. ➤➤ **salubriously** *adv,* **salubriousness** *n,* **salubrity** *n.*

saluki /sə'loohki/ *n* (*pl* **salukis**) a dog of a breed originating in N Africa, having a smooth silky coat, long droopy ears, and fringed feet.

salutary *adj* **1a** having a beneficial or edifying effect. **b** *esp* of a bad experience: offering an opportunity to learn or improve. **2** *archaic* promoting health.

salutation *n* an expression of greeting or courtesy by word or gesture. ➤➤ **salutational** *adj,* **salutatory** *adj.*

salute[1] *v* **1** to address (somebody) with expressions of greeting, goodwill, or respect. **2a** to show respect and recognition to (e.g. a military superior) by assuming a prescribed position, *esp* by raising the hand to the side of the head. **b** to honour (somebody) by a conventional military or naval ceremony, *esp* by the firing of a gun or guns into the air. **c** to praise (something or somebody). ➤➤ **saluter** *n.*

salute[2] *n* **1** a greeting or salutation. **2** a sign or ceremony expressing goodwill or respect. **3** an act of saluting somebody, *esp* a military superior, or the prescribed position, gesture, etc for this. **4** a firing of guns into the air as a ceremonial sign of respect, honour, or celebration.

Salvadorean *or* **Salvadorian** *n* a native or inhabitant of El Salvador. ➤➤ **Salvadorean** *adj,* **Salvadorian** *adj.*

salvage[1] *n* **1a** the act or an instance of saving or rescuing a ship or its cargo from loss at sea. **b** the act or an instance of saving or rescuing property, e.g. from fire. **c** in law, payment made to somebody who saves or rescues something, *esp* a ship or its cargo, from loss or damage. **2** property saved or rescued from a calamity, e.g. a wreck or fire.

salvage[2] *v* **1** to save or rescue (something, e.g. a ship or its cargo) from loss or damage. **2** to extract or preserve (something of use or value) from destruction or failure. ➤➤ **salvageable** *adj,* **salvager** *n.*

salvation *n* **1** deliverance from danger, difficulty, or destruction. **2** (*often* **one's salvation**) somebody or something that brings about salvation. **3** in Christian theology, deliverance from the power and effects of sin brought about by faith in Christ.

Salvation Army *n* an international evangelical and charitable Christian group organized on military lines.

salvationism *n* religious teaching emphasizing the saving of the soul. ➤➤ **salvationist** *adj and n.*

Salvationist *n* a member of the Salvation Army.

salve[1] *n* **1** an ointment for soothing wounds or sores. **2** a soothing influence or agency.

salve[2] *v* to soothe or assuage: *salve a troubled conscience.*

salver *n* a tray, *esp* an ornamental silver one, on which food and drinks are served or letters and visiting cards are presented.

salvia *n* **1** any of various widely distributed plants or shrubs of the mint family, including sage. **2** an ornamental species of salvia grown for its scarlet or purple flowers.

salvo *n* (*pl* **-os** *or* **-oes**) **1** a simultaneous discharge of two or more guns or missiles in military or naval action or as a salute. **2** a sudden or emphatic burst, e.g. of criticism or applause.

sal volatile /,sal və'latili/ *n* an aromatic solution of ammonium carbonate in alcohol or aqueous ammonia used as smelling salts.

salwar /sul'wah, -'vah/ *or* **shalwar** *n* light trousers that are loose-fitting around the waist and hips, tapering to a close fit at the ankle, traditionally worn under a kameez by women from N India, Pakistan, and Bangladesh.

SAM *abbr* surface-to-air missile.

Samaritan *n* **1** a native or inhabitant of ancient Samaria. **2a** somebody who selflessly gives aid to those in distress. **b** (**the Samaritans**) *Brit* an organization that offers a telephone counselling service to people in despair. ➤➤ **Samaritan** *adj.*

samarium *n* a pale grey metallic chemical element of the lanthanide series, that is used in alloys that form permanent magnets.

samba[1] *n* a Brazilian dance of African origin characterized by a dip and spring upward at each beat of the music.

samba[2] *v* (**sambas, sambaed, sambaing**) to dance the samba.

Sam Browne belt *n* a leather belt supported by a light strap passing over the right shoulder and worn by certain military and police officers.

same[1] *adj* **1a** being one single thing, person, or group: *sitting at the same table.* **b** used as an intensive: *born in this very same house.* **2** being the specified one or ones: *make the same mistake as last time.* **3** identical in appearance, quantity, type, etc: *two women wearing the same dress.*

same[2] *pron* **1** the same thing, person, or group: *do the same for you.* **2** something previously mentioned: *He ordered a drink and refused to pay for same.* ✱ **all/just the same** nevertheless.

Usage note

The use of *same* as a pronoun (*To installing one electric shower and connecting and testing same: £170*) is a commercial or legal use. It should not be used in formal speech or writing.

same[3] *adv* (*usu* **the same**) in the same manner: *two words spelt the same.*

sameness *n* **1** identity or similarity. **2** monotonous uniformity.

samey *adj* (**samier, samiest**) *Brit, informal* lacking individuality or originality; boringly monotonous.

Sami *n* (*pl* **Samis** *or* **Sami**) a member of an indigenous people inhabiting Lapland. ➤➤ **Sami** *adj.*

samite *n* a rich medieval silk fabric interwoven with gold or silver.

samizdat *n* in the former USSR and some countries of eastern Europe, a system by which literature suppressed by the government was clandestinely printed and distributed.

Samoan *n* **1** a native or inhabitant of Samoa. **2** the language of the people of Samoa. ➤➤ **Samoan** *adj.*

samosa /sə'mohsə/ *n* (*pl* **samosas** *or* **samosa**) a small triangular pastry case filled with spiced minced meat, vegetables, etc and deep-fried.

samovar *n* a metal urn with a tap at its base and an interior heating tube that is used, *esp* in Russia, to boil water for tea.

Samoyed /samə'yed, sə'moy·ed/ *n* (*pl* **Samoyeds** *or* **Samoyed**) **1** a member of a group of indigenous, mainly nomadic, peoples inhabiting northeastern parts of European Russia and northwestern parts of Siberia. **2** a dog of a breed originating in Siberia, having a very thick whitish or creamish coat and used orig for pulling sledges. ➤➤ **Samoyed** *adj.*

sampan *n* a small flat-bottomed boat used in rivers and harbours in the Far East and usu propelled by an oar or oars at the stern.

samphire *n* a European rock plant of the carrot family that grows near the sea and has fleshy edible leaves.

sample[1] *n* **1** a part or item serving to show the character or quality of a larger whole or group. **2** a selection of items or individuals from a statistical population whose properties are studied to gain information about the whole. **3** a specimen, e.g. of blood, urine, etc, taken for scientific testing or analysis. **4a** a sound created by electronic sampling. **b** a piece of recorded music incorporated into another piece of usu electronic music by sampling.

sample[2] *v* **1** to take a sample of or from (something), e.g. for testing or analysis. **2** to experience or get a taste of. **3** to take an extract from (a recording) and mix it into a new recording.

sampler *n* **1** a decorative piece of needlework typically having letters or verses embroidered on it in various stitches as an example of skill. **2** a collection of representative specimens, extracts, or examples. **3** in recording, a piece of equipment used for sampling, *esp* a computer with special software.

sampling *n* **1** a statistical sample. **2** the act, process, or technique of selecting or taking a sample. **3** a technique in which recorded sounds or extracts are incorporated into a new recording.

samurai /'sam(y)oorie/ *n* (*pl* **samurai**) a member of the warrior aristocracy of feudal Japan.

San *n* (*pl* **San**) **1** a member of the Bushmen of southern Africa. **2** a group of languages spoken by these peoples.

sanatorium *n* (*pl* **sanatoriums** *or* **sanatoria**) **1** an establishment where people suffering or recovering from long-term illnesses receive medical treatment or care. **2** *Brit* a room, *esp* in a boarding school, where sick people are looked after.

sancta *n* pl of SANCTUM.

sanctify *v* (**-ies, -ied**) **1** to set apart for a sacred purpose or for religious use. **2** to free from sin. **3** to give moral, social, or religious sanction to. **4** to make or declare productive of holiness or piety. ➤➤ **sanctification** *n,* **sanctifier** *n.*

sanctimonious *adj* **1** making a show or pretence of piety. **2** assured of one's own rightness, virtue, or moral superiority; self-righteous. ➤➤ **sanctimoniously** *adv,* **sanctimoniousness** *n,* **sanctimony** *n.*

sanction[1] *n* **1** official permission or authoritative ratification. **2a** a penalty attached to an offence. **b** (*usu in pl*) an economic or military measure adopted to force a nation to change some policy or comply with international law.

sanction[2] *v* **1** to give authoritative approval or consent to. **2** to make valid or binding; to ratify. ➤➤ **sanctionable** *adj.*

sanctity *n* (*pl* **-ies**) **1** holiness of life and character. **2** the quality or state of being holy or inviolable. **3** (*usu in pl*) a sacred object, obligation, etc.

sanctuary *n* (*pl* **-ies**) **1** a consecrated place. **2** a place of refuge and protection. **3a** a refuge for wildlife where predators are controlled and hunting is illegal. **b** a refuge for animals that have been injured, neglected, ill-treated, etc. **4** the immunity from punishment by law formerly extended to somebody taking refuge in a church or other sacred building.

sanctum *n* (*pl* **sanctums** *or* **sancta**) **1** a sacred place. **2** a place of total privacy and security, e.g. a study.

Sanctus *n* in the Christian Church, a hymn of adoration sung or said before the prayer of consecration in the celebration of the Eucharist.

sand[1] *n* **1** loose granular particles smaller than gravel and coarser than silt that result from the disintegration of rock, *esp* quartz, forming the main constituent of beaches and the beds of seas and rivers. **2** (*usu in pl*) an area of sand, *esp* on the seashore.

sand[2] *v* **1** (*often* + down) to smooth or prepare (a surface, floor, etc) by grinding or rubbing with an abrasive, e.g. sandpaper. **2** to sprinkle (something, e.g. an icy road surface) with sand.

sandal *n* a light shoe typically consisting of a sole held on the foot by straps or thongs. ➤➤ **sandalled** *adj.*

sandalwood *n* the fragrant yellowish wood of an Indo-Malayan tree.

sandbag[1] *n* a bag filled with sand and used as ballast in a boat or balloon, as a means of preventing flood water entering a property, or as protection in a temporary fortification such as a trench.

sandbag[2] *v* (**sandbagged, sandbagging**) **1** to barricade, stop up, or weight with sandbags. **2** to hit or stun with a sandbag, or as if with a sandbag. ➤➤ **sandbagger** *n.*

sandbank *n* a large deposit of sand, *esp* one that becomes visible at low tide or forms a shallow area in a river or coastal waters.

sandbar *n* a ridge of sand built up by currents in a river or sea.

sandblast *v* to treat (a surface) with a high-speed jet of sand propelled by air or steam, e.g. in engraving or cleaning glass or stone. ➤➤ **sandblaster** *n.*

sandboy ✱ **happy as a sandboy** very happy or carefree.

sandcastle *n* a model of a castle or other structure made in damp sand.

sander *n* a power tool that smooths, polishes, or scours by means of abrasive material usu in the form of a disc or belt.

sanderling *n* a small plump sandpiper with largely grey-and-white plumage.

sandfly *n* (*pl* **-ies**) **1** any of various small biting flies that transmit disease. **2** *Aus, NZ* the blackfly.

Sandinista *n* a member of the Sandinista National Liberation Front, the ruling political group in Nicaragua from 1979 to 1990.

sandman *n* (**the sandman**) a mythical figure who supposedly sends children to sleep by sprinkling sand in their eyes.

sand martin *n* a small brown-and-white martin of the N hemisphere that usu nests in colonies in holes bored into banks of sand.

sandpaper[1] *n* paper that has a thin layer of sand glued to it, used in smoothing wood, etc. ➤➤ **sandpapery** *adj.*

sandpaper[2] *v* to rub or smooth (a surface) with sandpaper.

sandpiper *n* a small wading bird with long slender legs and a longer bill than the related plover.

sandpit *n* **1** an enclosure containing sand for children to play in. **2** a pit from which sand is extracted.

sandshoe *n* a light canvas shoe; a plimsoll.

sandstone *n* a sedimentary rock consisting of sand grains, usu of quartz, held together by silica, calcium carbonate, or other cement.

sandstorm *n* a strong wind driving clouds of sand, *esp* in a desert.

sandwich[1] *n* **1** two slices of usu buttered bread containing any of various fillings. **2** a sponge cake with jam, cream, etc between its two or more layers.

sandwich[2] *v* **1** (+ between) to insert (something) between two things of a different quality or character. **2** (+ together) to put (things) together in layers.

sandwich board *n* either of two boards hung in front of and behind the body by straps from a person's shoulders and used for advertising.

sandwich course *n Brit* a vocational course consisting of alternate periods of study and employment or practical experience.

sandy *adj* (**-ier, -iest**) **1** consisting of, containing, or sprinkled with sand. **2** of hair: having a yellowish brown or gingerish colour. ➤➤ **sandiness** *n.*

sane *adj* **1** mentally sound; able to anticipate and assess the effect of one's actions. **2** proceeding from a sound mind; rational. ➤➤ **sanely** *adv,* **saneness** *n.*

sang *v* past tense of SING.

sangfroid /song'frwah/ *n* self-possession or coolness, *esp* under strain.

Sangiovese /sanjoh'vayzi/ *n* a variety of grape used in the production of red wine, e.g. Chianti, or the wine produced from it.

sangria /sang'gree·ə/ *n* a Spanish drink made of red wine, fruit, and soda water or lemonade.

sanguinary *adj formal* **1** bloodthirsty; murderous. **2** causing or accompanied by bloodshed.

sanguine *adj* **1** confident; optimistic. **2** in medieval physiology, having blood as the predominating HUMOUR[1] (3) (body fluid believed to determine a person's disposition), marked by sturdiness, high colour, and cheerfulness.

Sanhedrin /san'heedrin, 'sanidrin/ *n* the supreme council and tribunal of the Jews before AD 70, having religious, civil, and criminal jurisdiction.

sanitarium *n* (*pl* **sanitariums** *or* **sanitaria**) *NAm* = SANATORIUM.

sanitary *adj* **1** of or promoting health. **2** free from dirt, germs, etc and so posing no danger to health; hygienic.

sanitary napkin *n NAm* = SANITARY TOWEL.

sanitary towel *n* a disposable absorbent pad worn externally during menstruation to absorb the flow of blood.

sanitary ware *n* bathroom plumbing fixtures, e.g. sinks, toilet bowls, baths, etc.

sanitation *n* facilities and measures that are involved in the promotion of hygiene and prevention of disease, *esp* the disposal of sewage and collection of rubbish.

sanitize *or* **-ise** *v* **1** to make sanitary by cleaning, sterilizing, etc. **2** to make more acceptable by removing offensive or undesirable features. ⋙ **sanitization** *n.*

sanity *n* **1** the state or quality of being sane; soundness or health of mind. **2** rational or sensible behaviour or judgment.

sank *v* past tense of SINK[1].

sans *prep archaic* without.

sans-culotte /sanzkyoo'lot/ *n* **1** an extreme radical republican of the French Revolution, *esp* one belonging to the lower classes. **2** a radical or revolutionary political extremist.

Sanskrit *n* the ancient Indic language of the people of India, now only used as a language of religion and scholarship. ⋙ **Sanskrit** *adj.*

sans serif *or* **sanserif** /,san 'serif/ *n* a letter or typeface with no serifs (short lines at upper and lower ends of strokes; see SERIF).

Santa Claus *or* **Santa** *n* = FATHER CHRISTMAS.

santim /'santeem/ *n* a unit of currency in Latvia, worth 100th of a lat.

sap[1] *n* **1a** a watery solution containing dissolved sugars, mineral salts, etc that circulates through the conducting system of a plant. **b** vitality; vigour. **2** *informal* a foolish or gullible person.

sap[2] *v* (**sapped, sapping**) to drain (something or somebody) of sap or vitality.

sap[3] *n* the extension of a trench to a point beneath or near an enemy's fortifications.

sap[4] *v* (**sapped, sapping**) **1** to dig a sap. **2** to destroy (something) by undermining, or as if by undermining. **3** to weaken or exhaust (somebody) gradually.

sapele /sə'peeli/ *n* a W African tree with hard cedar-scented reddish brown wood resembling mahogany.

sapid *adj* **1** having a usu strong pleasant flavour. **2** agreeable; engaging.

sapient *adj formal* possessing or expressing great wisdom or discernment.

sapling *n* **1** a young tree. **2** *literary* a youth.

sapodilla *n* **1** a round edible fruit with a brownish bristly skin and sweet yellowish brown flesh. **2** a large American evergreen tree with hard durable wood that bears this fruit and that also yields CHICLE (a substance used in chewing gum).

saponify *v* (**-ies, -ied**) to convert (fat, oil, etc) into soap by decomposition with an alkali. ⋙ **saponification** *n.*

sapper *n* **1** a soldier specializing in battlefield construction, e.g. digging trenches and laying mines. **2** in the British army, a soldier of the Royal Engineers.

sapphic *adj* **1** (**Sapphic**) characteristic of the ancient Greek lyric poetry of Sappho (d.6th cent. BC), *esp* in relation to her erotic descriptions of love between women. **2** lesbian.

sapphire *n* **1** any transparent or translucent variety of the mineral corundum of a colour other than red, *esp* a transparent rich blue variety used as a gem. **2** a deep brilliant blue colour. ⋙ **sapphire** *adj.*

sapphism *n* lesbianism. ⋙ **sapphist** *n.*

sappy *adj* (**-ier, -iest**) of a plant: containing a lot of sap.

saprophyte *n* a plant, fungus, or bacterium that lives on or obtains nourishment from dead or decaying plant and animal tissues. ⋙ **saprophytic** *adj.*

sapwood *n* the younger softer outer wood of a tree trunk or branch that lies between the bark and the heartwood and consists of living tissue.

saraband *or* **sarabande** *n* a stately court dance of the 17th and 18th cents resembling the minuet.

Saracen *n* **1** a member of a nomadic people of the desert area between Syria and Arabia, *esp* in classical Roman times. **2** a Muslim at the time of the Crusades. ⋙ **Saracen** *adj.*

sarcasm *n* the use of caustic and ironic language to express contempt or bitterness, *esp* towards an individual. ⋙ **sarcastic** *adj,* **sarcastically** *adv.*

sarcenet *or* **sarsenet** *n* a soft thin silk.

sarcoma *n* (*pl* **sarcomas** *or* **sarcomata**) a usu cancerous tumour arising *esp* in connective tissue.

sarcophagus *n* (*pl* **sarcophagi** *or* **sarcophaguses**) a stone coffin, *esp* one with a carved decoration or inscription.

Word history

Latin *sarcophagus lapis* limestone used for coffins, from Greek *lithos sarkophagos,* literally 'flesh-eating stone', from Greek *sark-, sarx* flesh + *phagein* to eat. The stone used to make a sarcophagus was believed to destroy the flesh of the corpse inside it.

sard *n* a deep orange-red variety of chalcedony used as a gemstone.

sardar /'suhdah, suh'dah/ *n* see SIRDAR.

sardine *n* (*pl* **sardines** *or* **sardine**) a small or immature fish of the herring family, *esp* the young of the European pilchard of a size suitable for preserving for food. ✱ **like sardines** very closely packed or crowded together.

Sardinian *n* **1** a native or inhabitant of Sardinia. **2** the language of the people of Sardinia. ⋙ **Sardinian** *adj.*

sardonic *adj* disdainfully or cynically humorous; derisively mocking. ⋙ **sardonically** *adv,* **sardonicism** *n.*

sardonyx *n* a quartz mineral consisting of parallel layers of orange-red sard and milky-white chalcedony, used as a gemstone.

saree /'sahri/ *n* see SARI.

sargasso *n* (*pl* **-os**) a large mass of floating vegetation, *esp* sargassum, in the sea.

sargassum *n* a brown seaweed that has small air bladders enabling it to float, often in large masses, on the surface of the water.

sarge *n informal* a sergeant.

sari *or* **saree** /'sahri/ *n* (*pl* **saris** *or* **sarees**) a garment that consists of a length of lightweight cloth draped so that one end forms a long skirt and the other a covering for the shoulder or head, traditionally worn by women from the Indian subcontinent.

sarky *adj* (**-ier, -iest**) *Brit, informal* sarcastic. ⋙ **sarkily** *adv,* **sarkiness** *n.*

sarnie *n Brit, informal* a sandwich.

sarong *n* a loose skirt made of a long strip of cloth wrapped round the body, traditionally worn by men and women in Malaysia and the Pacific islands.

sarsaparilla *n* **1** the dried roots of a tropical American plant, or an extract of these, used *esp* as a flavouring. **2** a sweetened nonalcoholic fizzy drink flavoured with sarsaparilla.

sarsen *n* a large mass of very hard siliceous sandstone left after the erosion of a continuous bed or layer and used in prehistoric monuments such as Stonehenge.

sarsenet *n* see SARCENET.

sartorial *adj* relating to tailoring or clothing, *esp* men's clothing. ⋙ **sartorially** *adv.*

SAS *abbr* Special Air Service.

sash[1] *n* a band of cloth worn round the waist or over one shoulder as part of a uniform or official dress, a symbol of rank, etc.

sash[2] *n* a frame in which panes of glass are set in a window or door.

sashimi /'sashimi/ *n* a Japanese dish consisting of thinly sliced raw fish served in bite-sized pieces with a spicy dip, usu of soy sauce.

sash window *n* a window having one or two sashes that slide vertically in a frame to open it.

Sasquatch *n* a hairy humanlike animal that is supposed to live in the mountain areas of W Canada where it is said to leave huge footprints. Also called BIGFOOT.

sassafras *n* the dried aromatic root bark of a N American tree, used for flavouring and as the source of a yellowish oil used in perfumery.

Sassenach *n Scot, Irish, derog* an English person. ➤➤ **Sassenach** *adj.*

SAT *abbr* standard assessment task.

Sat. *abbr* Saturday.

sat *v* past tense and past part. of SIT[1].

Satan *n* the adversary of God and lord of evil in Judaism and Christianity.

satang *n* (*pl* **satang** *or* **satangs**) a unit of currency in Thailand, worth 100th of a baht.

satanic *adj* of Satan or satanism. ➤➤ **satanically** *adv.*

satanism *n* the worship of Satan, typically marked by the travesty of Christian ceremonies. ➤➤ **satanist** *n and adj.*

satay *n* a dish of southeast Asia consisting of pieces of marinated spiced meat that are skewered, barbecued, and usu served with a peanut-flavoured sauce.

satchel *n* a usu stiff rectangular bag often with a shoulder strap, *esp* used for carrying schoolbooks, etc.

sate *v* **1** to satisfy (e.g. a thirst or appetite) by indulging it to the full. **2** to supply (somebody or something) with more than is needed or desired.

sateen *n* a smooth durable shiny linen or cotton fabric resembling satin.

satellite *n* **1a** a celestial body orbiting another of larger size. **b** an artificial device that orbits the earth, the moon, or another celestial body, *esp* one that collects astronomical or other scientific information or one that is used in transmitting and receiving communication or television signals. **2** somebody or something attendant, subordinate, or dependent, *esp* a country subject to another more powerful country.

satellite dish *n* a dish-shaped aerial used to transmit and receive signals in satellite communications, *esp* satellite television.

satellite television *n* a system of broadcasting television signals using satellites in space to transmit and receive signals.

satiate *v* = SATE. ➤➤ **satiation** *n.*

satiety *n* the feeling or state of being fed or gratified to or beyond capacity.

satin *n* **1** a fabric, orig made from silk, in which the warp threads predominate on the face to produce a smooth shiny front and a dull back. **2** (*used before a noun*) made of or resembling satin. ➤➤ **satiny** *adj.*

satin stitch *n* a long embroidery stitch nearly alike on both sides and worked in straight parallel lines so closely as to resemble satin.

satinwood *n* **1** a deciduous tree of the mahogany family that grows in India and Sri Lanka. **2** a related tree that grows in the islands of the Caribbean and in southern Florida. **3** the shiny yellowish brown wood of either of these trees, used in furniture making, marquetry, etc.

satire *n* **1a** a literary work that holds up human vices and follies to ridicule or scorn. **b** the genre of such literature. **2** biting wit, irony, or sarcasm intended to expose foolishness or vice. ➤➤ **satirist** *n.*

satirical *or* **satiric** *adj* **1** characterized by or involving the use of satire. **2** bitingly sarcastic or humorously critical. ➤➤ **satirically** *adv.*

satirize *or* **-ise** *v* to censure or ridicule (somebody or something) by means of satire.

satisfaction *n* **1** the fulfilment of something that is necessary, expected, or desired, or the good feeling that is experienced when this happens or is achieved. **2a** compensation for a loss, insult, or injury; atonement or restitution. **b** the discharge of a legal obligation or claim, e.g. by payment of a debt. **3** full assurance or certainty.

satisfactory *adj* **1** fulfilling a need, expectation, or desire; acceptable. **2** adequate, but not exceptionally good. ➤➤ **satisfactorily** *adv.*

satisfy *v* (**-ies, -ied**) **1** to fulfil the needs, expectations, or desires of (somebody or something). **2** to meet or comply with (the requirements of something or somebody). **3** to provide with reassurance, proof, etc; to convince. **4** to pay off (a debt or a creditor).

satisfying *adj* **1** of a job or activity: enjoyably fulfilling. **2** of food or a meal: filling and tasty.

satori /sə'tawri/ *n* a state of intuitive enlightenment achieved or sought in Zen Buddhism.

satrap *n* **1** a governor of a province in ancient Persia. **2** a subordinate ruler, *esp* a despotic one.

satsuma *n* a sweet seedless type of tangerine with a loose skin.

saturate[1] /'sachoorayt/ *v* **1a** to treat, provide, or fill (a substance) with another substance to the point where no more of it can be absorbed, dissolved, or retained. **b** to cause (two or more substances) to combine chemically until there is no further capability or tendency to combine. **2** to cause (something or somebody) to become thoroughly wet. **3a** to fill completely with a permeating or suffusing effect or substance. **b** to fill to capacity. **4** to supply (a market) with all the goods it will absorb. **5** to overwhelm (an area) with military forces or firepower.

saturate[2] *n* a saturated fat.

saturated *adj* **1a** of a solution containing a dissolved substance: not capable of absorbing or dissolving any more of that substance. **b** of a chemical compound: unable or not tending to form products by chemical addition or by uniting directly with another compound. **2** of a colour: free from dilution with white; bright and rich.

saturation *n* **1** the action of saturating or the state of being saturated. **2** (*used before a noun*) denoting maximum concentration: *saturation bombing.*

saturation point *n* the stage at which no more, e.g. of a substance, can be absorbed or tolerated.

Saturday *n* the day of the week following Friday.

Saturnalia *n* (*pl* **Saturnalias** *or* **Saturnalia**) **1** (*used as sing. or pl*) the festival of Saturn in ancient Rome, beginning on 17 December, a time of general and unrestrained merrymaking. **2** (*often* **saturnalia**) a wild party or an occasion when a great amount of alcohol is consumed; an orgy. ➤➤ **saturnalian** *adj.*

Saturnian *adj* of or influenced by the planet Saturn.

saturnine *adj* **1** of a person or their temperament: gloomy or sullen. **2** dark and brooding.

satyr *n* **1** (*also* **Satyr**) in classical mythology, a woodland god associated with drunken revelry and lustfulness, represented as a man with certain attributes of a horse or goat. **2** a lecherous man, *esp* one affected by satyriasis. ➤➤ **satyric** *adj.*

satyriasis *n* excessive sexual desire in a male.

sauce[1] *n* **1** a liquid or semiliquid used as a relish, dressing, or accompaniment to food. **2** *NAm* stewed fruit eaten as a dessert. **3** *chiefly Brit, informal* cheek or impudence.

sauce[2] *v* **1** to dress or prepare (food) with a sauce. **2** to make more interesting. **3** *informal* to be impudent to.

sauce boat *n* a shallow jug with a handle for serving sauce, gravy, etc at the table.

saucepan *n* a deep usu cylindrical cooking pan typically with a long handle and a lid.

saucer *n* a small usu circular shallow dish with a central depression in which a cup is set.

saucy *adj* (**-ier, -iest**) *informal chiefly Brit* mildly titillating or sexually suggestive, *esp* in a humorous way. ➤➤ **saucily** *adv,* **sauciness** *n.*

Saudi /'sowdi/ *n* (*pl* **Saudis**) **1** a native or inhabitant of Saudi Arabia. **2** a member of the ruling dynasty of Saudi Arabia. ➤➤ **Saudi** *adj.*

Saudi Arabian *n* a native or inhabitant of Saudi Arabia. ➤➤ **Saudi Arabian** *adj.*

sauerkraut /'sowəkrowt/ *n* finely chopped pickled cabbage.

sauna *n* a small room, usu timber-clad, where people go to invigorate their bodies in extremely hot dry air, which is periodically relieved by throwing water over hot stones to produce steam.

saunter[1] *v* to walk about in an idle or casual manner; to stroll.

saunter[2] *n* a casual stroll.

-saur *comb. form* forming nouns, denoting: the names of reptiles, *esp* extinct ones: *dinosaur.*

saurian *adj* relating to or resembling a lizard.

saurischian *n* a dinosaur with a pelvic structure with three branches, similar to that of a lizard: compare ORNITHISCHIAN. ➤➤ **saurischian** *adj.*

sauropod *n* a plant-eating dinosaur with a long neck and tail, a small head, and very large limbs, e.g. an apatosaurus.

-saurus *comb. form* forming nouns, denoting: the genus name of reptiles, *esp* extinct ones: *stegosaurus.*

sausage *n* **1** a food made from finely chopped raw meat, or a meat substitute, often mixed with cereal and seasonings, and put in a tubular casing, orig one made from animal intestines. **2** a similar food made from cooked or cured meat, often with the addition of spices, and often sold in thin slices to be eaten cold. ✱ **not a sausage** *Brit, informal* nothing at all or not a bit.

sausage dog *n Brit, informal* = DACHSHUND.

sausage meat *n* seasoned minced meat, usu pork, mixed with cereal, used to fill sausages and sausage rolls, and as a poultry stuffing.

sausage roll *n* a small roll or oblong of sausage meat wrapped in pastry.

sauté[1] /'sawtay, 'sohtay/ *v* (**sautés, sautéed** *or* **sautéd, sautéing**) to fry (*esp* potatoes) in a small amount of hot oil or fat.

sauté[2] *adj* fried quickly in shallow hot oil or fat.

sauté[3] *n* a dish of food that has been fried quickly in a small amount of hot oil or fat.

Sauternes /soh'tuhn/ *n* a sweet golden-coloured Bordeaux wine made in the commune of Sauternes in France.

Sauvignon /'sohvinyanh/ *n* a variety of grape used in the production of white wine, or a wine produced from it.

savage[1] *adj* **1** not domesticated or under human control; untamed. **2** of a person or their behaviour: **a** boorish; uncivilized. **b** wild; cruel; ferocious. **3** of a place or landscape: rugged and usu uncultivated. **4** *offensive* of a people: lacking a developed culture. ➤➤ **savagely** *adv,* **savagery** *n.*

savage[2] *n* **1** *offensive* a member of a society or people regarded as lacking a developed culture. **2** a brutal, rude, or unmannerly person.

savage[3] *v* **1** to attack or treat (somebody or something) brutally or ferociously. **2** to criticize (somebody or something) severely.

savanna *or* **savannah** *n* a tropical or subtropical grassland with scattered trees.

savant *or* **savante** /'sav(ə)nt/ *n* a man or woman who has exceptional knowledge of a particular field, *esp* science or literature.

save[1] *v* **1a** to keep (somebody or something) safe. **b** to rescue or deliver (somebody or something) from danger or harm. **c** to prevent (somebody) from dying. **d** to preserve or guard (somebody or something) from injury, destruction, or loss. **e** in Christianity, to preserve (somebody's soul) from damnation. **2a** to put aside for a particular use: *She saves her newspapers for recycling.* **b** to put aside as a store or reserve; to accumulate. **3** in computing, to preserve (e.g. a file) by copying and storing it in the computer's memory or on a disk. **4a** to economize in the use of (something); to conserve: *Driving like this saves petrol.* **b** to keep (something) from being spent, wasted, or lost: *Save money on a new car by buying it abroad.* **5** to make unnecessary; to avoid or obviate: *It saves an hour's waiting.* **6** to prevent an opponent from scoring or winning (e.g. a trick, goal, or point) or scoring with (a ball). ✱ **save face** to avoid being humiliated. **save one's breath** to refrain from saying something because it would be pointless. **save somebody's skin/neck/bacon** to rescue or help somebody in difficulty. **save the day/situation** to come up with a solution to a problem.

save[2] *n* **1** in sport, *esp* football and hockey, the act or an instance of preventing an opponent from scoring. **2** in computing, a command to copy material onto a disk.

save[3] *prep formal or literary* except or other than: *Nobody was home save Clio the cat.*

save[4] *conj formal or literary* were it not; only: *We would have protested save that he was a friend.*

saveloy *n Brit* a highly seasoned red cooked sausage made from smoked pork.

saver *n* **1** a person who regularly saves money, *esp* in a bank or through a saving scheme. **2** (*used in combinations*) something that helps to reduce the consumption of a commodity: *a great money-saver.*

saving[1] *n* **1** an economy or reduction, e.g. in money or time. **2** (*in pl*) money that has been saved, *esp* in a bank or through a saving scheme.

saving[2] *adj* (*used in combinations*) preventing waste or loss: *time-saving appliances.*

saving[3] *prep* **1** except. **2** *archaic* without disrespect to.

saving grace *n* **1** a redeeming or compensatory quality or feature. **2** God's redeeming grace.

savings account *n* a type of bank or building society account in which interest is earned on money that is saved.

savings and loan association *n NAm* an institution for saving money at interest and borrowing money for house purchases and other major expenses.

savings bank *n* a bank organized to receive savings accounts only.

Savings Bond *n Brit* = PREMIUM BOND.

saviour (*NAm* **savior**) *n* **1** (**the/our Saviour**) in Christianity, Jesus Christ or God. **2** a person who saves somebody or something from danger or destruction.

savoir faire /,savwah 'feə/ *n* the ability to behave appropriately in social situations.

savor¹ *v NAm* see SAVOUR¹.

savor² *n NAm* see SAVOUR².

savory¹ *n* (*pl* **-ies**) an aromatic plant of the mint family used as a herb.

savory² *adj NAm* see SAVOURY¹.

savory³ *n NAm* see SAVOURY².

savour¹ (*NAm* **savor**) *v* **1** to appreciate (something, *esp* the taste or smell of food or drink) with relish. **2a** to enjoy and appreciate to the full. **b** to enjoy the apprehension or experience of (something), *esp* at length. **3** (+ of) to have a specified smell or quality.

savour² (*NAm* **savor**) *n* **1** a characteristic taste, flavour, or smell. **2** a slight hint or trace.

savoury¹ (*NAm* **savory**) *adj* **1** of food: having a salty or spicy flavour, often in contrast to being sweet. **2** morally wholesome or respectable.

savoury² (*NAm* **savory**) *n* (*pl* **-ies**) *chiefly Brit* a salty or spicy snack or a savoury dish served as an appetizer or dessert.

savoy *n* a hardy cabbage with compact heads of wrinkled and curled leaves.

savvy¹ *v* (**-ies, -ied**) *informal* to know or understand (an idea or concept).

savvy² *n informal* practical know-how or shrewd judgment.

savvy³ *adj* (**-ier, -iest**) *informal* shrewd or knowledgeable.

saw¹ *v* past tense of SEE¹.

saw² *n* **1a** a hand tool with a toothed blade, used for cutting hard material by moving the blade backwards and forwards. **b** a power tool with a toothed disc or a band that rotates. **2** a serrated organ or body part.

saw³ *v* (*Brit past part.* **sawn,** *NAm* **sawed**) **1** to cut (wood, etc) with a saw. **2** to make or shape by cutting with a saw. **3** to cut through or sever with a saw, or as if with a saw. **4** to make sawing motions.

saw⁴ *n* a maxim or proverb.

sawdust *n* fine particles of wood produced in sawing.

sawed-off *adj NAm* see SAWN-OFF.

sawfish *n* (*pl* **sawfishes** *or* **sawfish**) a large elongated fish related to the ray, with a long flattened snout with large teeth on each side, giving a serrated effect.

sawfly *n* (*pl* **-ies**) an insect related to the wasp, the females of which lay their eggs in plant tissue that they penetrate by means of a pair of serrated blades in the egg-laying organ.

sawhorse *n* a rack on which wood is laid for sawing.

sawmill *n* a factory or machine in which wood is cut, e.g. into planks.

sawn *v* past part. of SAW³.

sawn-off (*NAm* **sawed-off**) *adj* **1** of a shotgun: having the end of the barrel shortened to make it easier to use or conceal. **2** *informal* of a garment, *esp* a skirt: shortened.

sawtooth *or* **sawtoothed** *adj* shaped or arranged like the teeth of a saw; serrated.

sawyer *n* a person who saws timber.

sax *n informal* a saxophone or saxophone player.

saxe *adj* of a light blue colour with a greenish or greyish tinge. ➤➤ **saxe** *n.*

saxhorn *n* a valved brass instrument of a family ranging from sopranino to bass usu played upright like a tuba and used *esp* in brass and military bands.

saxifrage *n* a low-growing plant with showy flowers and often tufted leaves.

Saxon *n* **1** a member of a Germanic people that invaded England along with the Angles and Jutes in the fifth and sixth cents AD. **2** a native or inhabitant of modern Saxony in Germany. **3** the language spoken by the ancient Saxons. **4** = OLD ENGLISH. ➤➤ **Saxon** *adj.*

saxophone *n* a brass instrument of a family played with a single reed like a clarinet but with a conical bore like an oboe and finger keys, used *esp* in jazz and popular music. ➤➤ **saxophonic** *adj,* **saxophonist** *n.*

say¹ *v* (*third person sing. present tense* **says,** *past tense and past part.* **said**) **1** to state in spoken words. **2** to utter or pronounce (a sound, word, sentence, etc). **3** to recite or repeat. **4a** to indicate or show: *The clock says half past twelve.* **b** to give expression to or communicate: *That look says it all.* **5** to allege: *The house is said to be 300 years old.* **6** to form an opinion about or remember: *I can't say when I met him.* **7** to assume for the purposes of discussion: *Say she's telling the truth; what then?* ✱ **go without saying** to be obvious. **how say you?** used in addressing the jury in a court of law to find out what verdict has been reached. **say the word** to give permission for something to go ahead. **say when** used to tell somebody when to stop, *esp* when a drink is being poured. **that is to say 1** in other words; in effect. **2** or at least. **there is no saying** it is impossible to know. **they say** it is proposed or rumoured. **when all is said and done** once everything has been taken into consideration. **wouldn't say boo to a goose** used to describe somebody who is very timid. ➤➤ **sayable** *adj,* **sayer** *n.*

say² *n* **1** an expression of opinion or a chance to speak. **2** a right or power to influence something.

say³ *adv* **1** at a rough estimate; about. **2** for example.

SAYE *abbr* save as you earn, a government-run saving scheme with tax benefits.

saying *n* a maxim or proverb.

say-so *n informal* **1** a person's unsupported assertion; a bare assurance. **2** the right of final decision.

Sb *abbr* the chemical symbol for antimony.

SBS *abbr* Special Boat Service.

SC *abbr* South Carolina (US postal abbreviation).

Sc *abbr* the chemical symbol for scandium.

sc. *abbr* scilicet.

scab¹ *n* **1** a crust of hardened blood and serum over a wound. **2** mange or scabies of domestic animals, *esp* mange of sheep caused by a parasitic mite. **3** any of various plant diseases characterized by crusted spots, or a spot itself. **4** *informal* **a** a contemptible person. **b** a strikebreaker or a person brought in to a factory, etc to work while the employees are on strike. ➤➤ **scabby** *adj.*

scab² *v* (**scabbed, scabbing**) **1** (*often* + over) of a cut or graze: to become covered with a scab. **2** of somebody during an industrial dispute: to act or work as a scab.

scabbard *n* a sheath for a sword, dagger, or bayonet.

scabies *n* a contagious skin disease caused by a parasitic mite that burrows in the skin, usu characterized by intense itchiness and inflammation.

scabious *n* a plant with blue, lilac, or violet flowers in dense heads at the end of usu long stalks.

scabrous *adj* **1** rough to the touch with scales, scabs, raised patches, etc. **2** dealing with indecent or offensive themes; salacious.

scaffold[1] *n* **1** a raised platform formerly used in public executions for hanging or beheading criminals. **2** a structure made from scaffolding.

scaffold[2] *v* to erect scaffolding around (a building). ⋙ **scaffolder** *n.*

scaffolding *n* **1** a temporary structure consisting of connected poles and planks, erected on the outside of a building that is being built or repaired. **2** the poles and planks used for a scaffold.

scag *n* see SKAG.

scalable *adj* **1** capable of being climbed. **2** able to be changed in size or scale. **3** *technical* able to be measured on a given scale. ⋙ **scalability** *n.*

scalar[1] *adj* of a quantity: having magnitude but not direction.

scalar[2] *n* **1** a real number rather than a vector. **2** a quantity that has magnitude but no direction.

scalawag *n NAm* see SCALLYWAG.

scald[1] *v* **1** to injure or burn (something or somebody) with hot liquid or steam. **2** to bring (a liquid, *esp* milk) almost to boiling point. **3** to subject to immersion in boiling water.

scald[2] *n* an injury or burn to the body caused by scalding.

scale[1] *n* **1** any of the numerous small overlapping plates that cover and protect the skin of fish, reptiles, etc. **2** a dry flake of dead skin. **3a** a white deposit of lime formed on the inside of a kettle, iron, hot water pipes, etc caused by the evaporation or constant passage of hard water. **b** a white deposit of tartar on teeth.

scale[2] *v* **1** to remove the scale or scales from (something), usu by scraping. **2** to separate and come off in scales; to peel or flake off.

scale[3] *n* **1** (*usu in pl*) any of various instruments or machines for weighing, orig one consisting of a simple balance, but now usu a device with an internal mechanism. **2** either pan or tray of a balance. ✱ **tip the scales 1** to register weight. **2** to shift the balance of power or influence; to be a deciding factor in something.

scale[4] *v* to have a specified weight on scales.

scale[5] *n* **1a** a graduated range of values used in measuring something. **b** a measuring instrument with such a range of values marked on it. **2** the relative size, degree, or extent of something. **3** the ratio between the size of an existing object and a model or representation of the object. **4** in music, a series of rising or falling notes with a regular pattern of intervals between them. ✱ **to scale** of a map, model, or representation of something: produced with a uniform size ratio between it and the original.

scale[6] *v* **1** to climb up or over, or reach the top of (something high). **2** to make a map, model, or representation of (something) using a uniform size ratio. **3** to measure using a specified scale. **4** to arrange in a graduated series. **5** to pattern, make, regulate, set, or estimate according to a rate or standard. **6** (*usu* + up) to increase (something). **7** (*usu* + down/back) to decrease (something).

scale insect *n* a small bug that attaches itself by its mouthparts to a plant and then produces a protective scale about its body.

scalene *adj* of a triangle: having sides of unequal length.

scallion *n* an onion, such as the spring onion, that has a small bulb and long leaves and is used *esp* in salads.

scallop[1] *n* **1** an edible bivalve marine mollusc that has a shell consisting of two wavy-edged halves each with a fan-shaped pattern of ridges, and that swims by opening and closing the halves of the shell. **2** any of a continuous series of rounded or angular projections forming a decorative border on material, clothes, linen, etc.

scallop[2] *v* (**scalloped, scalloping**) **1a** to shape, cut, or finish (an edge or border) in decorative scallops. **b** to form decorative scallops on (material, etc). **2** *NAm* to gather or dredge for scallops.

scally *n* (*pl* **-ies**) *NW English dialect, informal* a rogue or rascal.

scallywag (*NAm* **scalawag**) *n informal* a mischievous but likable person; a rascal.

scalp[1] *n* **1** the skin and underlying tissue at the top and back of the human head, usu including the hair. **2** a part of this with the hair attached, cut or torn from an enemy and taken as a battle trophy, *esp* formerly by Native American warriors.

scalp[2] *v* **1** to remove the scalp of (somebody, *esp* a dead enemy). **2** *informal* to punish or defeat. ⋙ **scalper** *n.*

scalpel *n* a small very sharp thin-bladed knife used in surgery.

scaly *adj* (**-ier, -iest**) **1** covered with or composed of scale or scales. **2** flaky.

scam[1] *n informal* a swindle or a scheme for obtaining money dishonestly.

scam[2] *v* (**scammed, scamming**) *informal* to swindle. ⋙ **scammer** *n.*

scamp *n* an impish or playful person, *esp* a child. ⋙ **scampish** *adj.*

scamper[1] *v* to run about nimbly and playfully.

scamper[2] *n* a dash or scurry.

scampi *n* (*used as sing. or pl*) Norway lobsters or large prawns, prepared and cooked, e.g. in batter or breadcrumbs.

scan[1] *v* (**scanned, scanning**) **1** to glance at (something, *esp* written matter) hastily, casually, or in search of a particular item. **2** to make a detailed examination of (part or all of the body) using any of various sensing devices. **3** to examine successive small portions of (an object) with a sensing device. **4a** to change (an image) into an electrical signal by moving an electron beam across it according to a predetermined pattern for television transmission. **b** to convert (data, graphics, an image, etc) into a digital format for electronic purposes. **5** to examine (an object or region) using a radar scanner. **6** to read or mark (a piece of text) in order to show metrical structure. **7** of verse: to conform to a metrical pattern. ⋙ **scannable** *adj.*

scan[2] *n* **1** the act or an instance of scanning. **2a** a medical examination of a part of the body using a scanner. **b** an image produced by a medical scanner. **3** a radar or television trace.

scandal *n* **1** an act or event that is generally regarded as morally or legally unacceptable or utterly disgraceful. **2** malicious or damaging rumour, or the gossip that arises from this. ⋙ **scandalous** *adj,* **scandalously** *adv.*

scandalize *or* **-ise** *v* to shock or offend by immoral or disgraceful behaviour.

Scandinavian *n* **1** a native or inhabitant of Scandinavia. **2** a group of languages comprising Swedish, Norwegian, Danish, Icelandic, and Faeroese. ➤➤ **Scandinavian** *adj.*

scandium *n* a rare silver-white metallic chemical element.

scanner *n* **1** a device used to scan the human body with X-rays, ultrasonic waves, etc. **2** a device that converts data, graphics, an image, etc into a digital format for electronic purposes.

scansion *n* **1** the analysis of verse to show its metre. **2** the way in which a particular piece of verse scans.

scant *adj* **1** barely sufficient; inadequate. **2a** falling short of or barely making up a specified amount, measurement, etc. **b** (*usu* + of) having an inadequate supply of something. ➤➤ **scantly** *adv*, **scantness** *n.*

scantling *n* **1** a small piece of timber, e.g. an upright piece in the framework of a house. **2** (*also in pl*) **a** the dimensions of timber and stone used in building. **b** the dimensions of a frame or STRAKE (band of hull planking or plates) used in shipbuilding.

scanty *adj* (**-ier, -iest**) **1** small or insufficient in quantity. **2** of clothing: skimpy and revealing. ➤➤ **scantily** *adv.*

scapegoat[1] *n* **1** a person who is made to take the blame for somebody else's wrongdoing or mistake. **2** in the Bible, a goat that was sent out into the wilderness after the chief priest of the Jews had symbolically placed the sins of the Israelites on it.

scapegoat[2] *v* to make a scapegoat of (somebody).

scapegrace *n archaic* an incorrigible rascal.

scapula *n* (*pl* **scapulae** *or* **scapulas**) a large flat triangular bone on each side of the vertebrate pectoral girdle; the shoulder blade in mammals.

scapular[1] *n* a long wide band of cloth with an opening for the head, worn front and back over the shoulders as part of a monastic habit.

scapular[2] *adj* relating to or in the region of the shoulder or the shoulder blade.

scar[1] *n* **1** a mark left on the skin or other body tissue by an injury, *esp* one that is healing. **2** a mark left on a plant stem, *esp* one where a leaf formerly grew. **3** a lasting ill effect, *esp* a psychological one caused by trauma.

scar[2] *v* (**scarred, scarring**) **1** to mark with a scar. **2** to do lasting injury or psychological damage to. **3** to form a scar. **4** to become scarred.

scar[3] *n* a steep rocky cliff on a mountainside.

scarab *n* **1** a large dung beetle that the ancient Egyptians held sacred. **2** a representation of this sacred beetle, e.g. carved on an amulet or formed from a gemstone, used as a talisman.

scarce *adj* **1** not plentiful or abundant, *esp* not plentiful enough to meet demand. **2** few in number; rare. ✱ **make oneself scarce** *informal* to leave a place, *esp* to avoid trouble, recriminations, etc. ➤➤ **scarcely** *adv*, **scarcity** *n.*

scare[1] *v* **1** to frighten (a person or animal) suddenly; to alarm. **2** (+ off/away) to drive (a person or animal) away by frightening them. **3** to become afraid.

scare[2] *n* **1** a sudden or unwarranted fright. **2** a widespread state of alarm or panic.

scarecrow *n* an object, usu suggesting a human figure, set up to frighten birds away from crops.

scared *adj* thrown into or living in a state of fear, fright, or panic; afraid.

scarf[1] *n* (*pl* **scarves** *or* **scarfs**) a strip or square of cloth worn round the shoulders or neck or over the head.

scarf[2] *n* (*pl* **scarfs**) a method of joining two pieces of timber to form one continuous straight piece without any variation in width, in which the ends of the two pieces are chamfered, notched, or halved to fit each other.

scarf[3] *v* to join the ends of (two pieces of wood) with a scarf joint.

scarify *v* (**-ies, -ied**) **1** to scrape (a lawn) in order to remove moss, dead leaves, and other debris. **2** to break up and loosen the surface of (e.g. soil or a road). **3** to make scratches or small cuts in (the skin or other tissue) as a medical treatment or in certain traditional forms of skin decoration. **4** to injure the feelings of (somebody), e.g. by harsh criticism. ➤➤ **scarification** *n*, **scarifier** *n.*

scarlatina *n* = SCARLET FEVER.

scarlet *adj* of a vivid red colour tinged with orange. ➤➤ **scarlet** *n.*

scarlet fever *n* an infectious fever caused by a bacterium that attacks the red blood cells, characterized by a red rash and inflammation of the nose, throat, and mouth.

scarlet woman *n euphem* a woman who is sexually promiscuous; *esp* a prostitute.

scarp[1] *n* a steep slope, *esp* a cliff face, produced by faulting or erosion; an escarpment.

scarp[2] *v* to cut down or erode to form a vertical or steep slope.

scarper *v Brit, informal* to run away.

Scart *n* (*also* **SCART**) a 21-pin socket used *esp* to connect different pieces of home entertainment equipment.

scarves *n* pl of SCARF[1].

scary *adj* (**-ier, -iest**) *informal* **1** causing fear or alarm. **2** weird; spooky. ➤➤ **scarily** *adv.*

scat[1] *v* (**scatted, scatting**) *informal* to depart rapidly.

scat[2] *n* jazz singing with improvised vocals that sound like a musical instrument rather than conventional lyrics.

scat[3] *v* (**scatted, scatting**) to sing using improvised vocal sounds.

scathing *adj* bitterly severe; scornful. ➤➤ **scathingly** *adv.*

scatology *n* an obsession or preoccupation with excrement or excretion. ➤➤ **scatological** *adj.*

scatter[1] *v* **1** to cause (a group or collection) to separate widely. **2** to distribute carelessly or at irregular intervals. **3** to sow (seed) by casting in all directions; to strew. **4a** to reflect (e.g. a beam of light particles) irregularly and diffusely. **b** to diffuse or disperse (a beam of radiation). **5** to separate and go in various directions.

scatter[2] *n* a small supply or number of things irregularly distributed.

scatterbrain *n* somebody who is disorganized or incapable of concentration. ➤➤ **scatterbrained** *adj.*

scattergun *n* (*used before a noun*) targeting or covering a wide, usu random, area: *a scattergun approach.*

scattering *n* a small number or quantity interspersed here and there.

scattershot *n* = SCATTERGUN.

scatty *adj* (**-ier, -iest**) *Brit, informal* forgetful or disorganized, *esp* in a slightly eccentric way.

scaup *n* (*pl* **scaups** *or* **scaup**) a diving duck, the male of which has a glossy greenish or purplish head.

scavenge *v* **1** to search for (something that could be of use), *esp* among rubbish or discarded items. **2** of certain animals, birds, and fish: to search for and feed on (carrion or refuse). **3a** to remove (an undesirable constituent) from a substance or region by chemical or physical means. **b** to clean and purify (molten metal) by combining with or causing the combination of impurities to form compounds that can be easily removed.

scavenger *n* **1** somebody who scavenges. **2** an animal that feeds habitually on refuse or carrion. **3** a chemical that removes something or makes an undesirable substance harmless.

SCE *abbr* Scottish Certificate of Education.

scenario *n* (*pl* **-os**) **1** an outline or synopsis of a dramatic work, novel, or film, including details of the plot, characters, and settings. **2** an account or synopsis of a projected course of action.

scene *n* **1** a place where something real or imaginary takes or took place. **2** a real or imaginary landscape or view. **3a** an episode or sequence in a play, film, etc. **b** a stage setting or the items of scenery in a play, opera, ballet, etc. **4** a public display of violent or unrestrained feeling. **5a** a sphere of activity or interest. **b** *informal* something in which a person is particularly interested or involved. ✱ **behind the scenes** out of the public view.

scenery *n* **1** the natural features of a landscape, *esp* when considered attractive. **2** the painted scenes or hangings and accessories used on a theatre stage or film set.

scenic *adj* **1** of or displaying natural scenery, *esp* when considered impressive or attractive. **2** of the stage, a stage setting, or stage representation. **3** of a picture: representing an action or event. ⋙ **scenically** *adv.*

scenic railway *n* a miniature railway with artificial scenery and sometimes natural landscape features along the way.

scent[1] *n* **1** a characteristic or particular smell, *esp* a pleasant one. **2** a light perfume worn on the skin. **3** a smell left by an animal on a surface that it has passed over, by which the animal may be traced.

scent[2] *v* **1** to impart or give a usu pleasant smell to. **2** to perceive by the sense of smell. **3** to get or have an inkling of: *I think I scent trouble.* ⋙ **scented** *adj.*

scent gland *n* a specially modified animal gland that secretes a PHEROMONE (chemical substance stimulating a response) or other strong-smelling substance, used for marking territory or for defence.

scepter *n NAm* see SCEPTRE.

sceptic (*NAm* **skeptic**) *n* **1** a person with a mistrustful attitude to accepted opinions. **2** a person who doubts basic religious principles, e.g. eternal life and divine guidance; an atheist. ⋙ **sceptical** *adj,* **sceptically** *adv,* **scepticism** *n.*

sceptre (*NAm* **scepter**) *n* a staff carried by a ruler as a symbol of sovereignty. ⋙ **sceptred** *adj.*

Schadenfreude /'shahdənfroydə/ *n* enjoyment obtained from the misfortunes of somebody else.

schedule[1] *n* **1** a plan of things to be done and the order in which to do them. **2** a timetable. **3** a statement of supplementary details appended to a legal or legislative document, often in the form of a list, table, or inventory. ✱ **on/to/according to schedule** as planned or on time.

schedule[2] *v* **1** to appoint or designate (something) to occur at a fixed time. **2** to include (somebody or something) in a schedule. **3** *Brit* to place (a property) on a list of the buildings or historical sites to be preserved or protected by law. ⋙ **scheduler** *n.*

scheduled *adj* **1** relating to or forming a schedule. **2** of an aeroplane or flight: operating or occurring as part of a regular timetable, as distinct from being specially chartered.

scheduled caste *n* in India, the official name for any of the inferior or untouchable classes: compare DALIT, UNTOUCHABLE[2].

schema *n* (*pl* **schemata** *or* **schemas**) a representation of something in the form of a diagram, plan, theory, or outline.

schematic *adj* **1** said of a diagram, plan, theory, or outline: crudely or simplistically representative. **2** of thinking, understanding, an idea, or response: unsophisticated or formulaic. ⋙ **schematically** *adv.*

schematize *or* **-ise** *v* **1** to express or depict schematically. **2** to form into a systematic arrangement.

scheme[1] *n* **1** a systematic plan or programme for a course of action or for putting an idea, project, etc into practice. **2** a systematic arrangement of parts or elements; a design. **3** a secret plan, *esp* one that involves something illegal or dishonest.

scheme[2] *v* **1** to make a plan to do something, *esp* something illegal or dishonest. **2** to plan (something) according to a scheme. ⋙ **schemer** *n.*

scheming *adj* shrewdly devious or cunning.

schemozzle *n* see SHEMOZZLE.

scherzo /'skeətsoh/ *n* (*pl* **scherzos** *or* **scherzi**) a lively instrumental musical composition or movement in quick, usu triple, time.

schilling *n* the basic monetary unit of Austria.

schism *n* **1** the separation of a group into opposing factions, *esp* because of different ideologies. **2** the formal division of a Church or religious body, either into two entities or with one faction ceasing to exist, usu caused by ideological or doctrinal differences.

schismatic[1] *adj* characteristic of or advocating schism.

schismatic[2] *n* a person who promotes schism, *esp* formerly in the Christian Church.

schist *n* a metamorphic crystalline rock composed of thin layers of different minerals, *esp* mica, and capable of being split into thin flaky planes.

schistosome *n* a parasitic blood fluke that infests snails, birds, and mammals, causing disease, e.g. bilharzia in humans.

schistosomiasis *n* a tropical disease caused by infestation by schistosomes, characterized by anaemia, inflammation of the blood vessels, and severe diarrhoea; bilharzia.

schizo *n* (*pl* **-os**) *informal, offensive* a schizophrenic person. ⋙ **schizo** *adj.*

schizoid[1] *adj* **1** in psychiatry, of a personality type: characterized by extreme shyness and an inability to cope in social situations. **2** *informal* resembling schizophrenia, *esp* in showing conflicting or contradictory attitudes. **3** *informal* mad or crazy.

schizoid[2] *n* somebody with a schizoid personality.

schizophrenia *n* any of several mental disorders characterized by loss of contact with reality and disintegration of personality, usu with hallucinations and disorder of feeling, behaviour, etc. ⋙ **schizophrenic** *adj and n.*

schloss /shlos/ *n* a German or Austrian castle.

schmaltz *or* **schmalz** *n* excessive sentimentalism, *esp* in music or art. ⋙ **schmaltzy** *adj.*

schnapps /shnaps/ *n* (*pl* **schnapps**) a strong alcoholic drink; *esp* strong gin as orig made in the Netherlands.

schnauzer /'shnowzə, 'shnowtsə/ *n* a dog of a German breed with a long head, wiry coat, and prominent whiskers.

schnitzel /'shnits(ə)l/ *n* a thin slice of meat, *esp* veal, coated in breadcrumbs and fried.

scholar *n* **1a** a person who specializes in or has knowledge of a particular subject, *esp* in arts, languages, etc. **b** *archaic or literary* a person of learning and academic interests. **2** a university student who holds a scholarship.

scholarly *adj* characteristic of or suitable for learned persons; academic.

scholarship *n* **1** the character, methods, or attainments of a scholar; learning. **2** a grant of money awarded to a student to pay for education, books, upkeep, etc while studying.

scholastic[1] *adj* **1** relating to education or schools. **2** (*often* **Scholastic**) relating to or denoting medieval Scholasticism.

scholastic[2] *n* (*often* **Scholastic**) an advocate or adherent of medieval Scholasticism.

scholasticism *n* (*often* **Scholasticism**) a philosophical movement dominant in W Christian civilization *esp* between the 12th and 14th cents, that combined religious dogma with the tradition of the writings of the authoritative early Christian writers, *esp* of St Augustine, and later with the philosophy of Aristotle.

school[1] *n* **1** a building or organization for educating children. **2** an establishment or organization dedicated to teaching a specified subject or skill: *a driving school.* **3a** a department or faculty in a British university, or its students, staff, and activities thought of collectively. **b** *informal* a N American university, or its students, staff, and activities thought of collectively. **4** a group of people who share the same approach to a subject or who adhere to the same doctrine, *esp* in the arts, philosophy, or theology. **5** *Brit* a group of people who gamble or drink together.

school[2] *v* **1** *NAm or formal* to educate in an institution of learning. **2** to train or drill (a person or animal) in a specified knowledge, skill, or ability.

school[3] *n* a large number of fish or aquatic animals of one kind swimming together.

school[4] *v* of fish or sea mammals: to form a school.

schoolhouse *n* **1** a building used as a school, *esp* a country primary school. **2** *Brit* a house attached to or near a school, where the teacher of the school lives.

schooling *n* **1** education or instruction received in school. **2** the training of a horse, *esp* in the formal techniques of show jumping, dressage, etc.

schoolmaster *n* a man who is a schoolteacher.

schoolmate *n informal* a companion at school.

schoolmistress *n* a woman who is a schoolteacher.

schoolteacher *n* a person who teaches in a school.

schooner *n* **1** a fore-and-aft rigged sailing vessel with two or more masts. **2a** *Brit* a large sherry glass. **b** *NAm, Aus, NZ* a tall beer glass.

schottische /sho'teesh/ *n* a round dance in duple time resembling a slow polka.

schtuck /shtook/ *n* see SHTOOK.

schtum /shtoom/ *adj* see SHTUM.

schuss[1] /shoos/ *v* to ski down a straight high-speed ski run.

schuss[2] *n* a straight high-speed ski run.

sciatic *adj* **1** relating to or in the region of the hip. **2** relating to, affected with, or caused by sciatica.

sciatica *n* pain in the back of the thigh, buttocks, and lower back caused by pressure on the sciatic nerve.

sciatic nerve *n* either of the two largest nerves in the body that run from the lower spine down the back of each thigh to the calf.

SCID *abbr* severe combined immune deficiency, a rare disorder of the immune system that manifests during the first three months of life, causing very low resistance to infections and diseases.

science *n* **1** the study, description, experimental investigation, and theoretical explanation of the nature and behaviour of phenomena in the physical and natural world. **2** a branch of systematized knowledge as an object of study.

science fiction *n* the genre of literature that involves the imaginative use of science and technology, usu set in the future.

science park *n* an area with a concentration of businesses involved in scientific and technological study, research, and manufacturing.

scientific *adj* **1** relating to, based on, or exhibiting the methods of science. **2** systematic. ➤➤ **scientifically** *adv.*

scientism *n* **1** methods and attitudes regarded as typical of scientists. **2** an exaggerated trust or belief in the power of scientific methods and knowledge, e.g. to explain psychological phenomena or solve pressing human problems.

scientist *n* a person who is an expert in or who studies one of the natural or physical sciences, or who puts scientific methods into practice.

Scientology *n trademark* a disputedly religious and psychotherapeutic movement that advocates self-knowledge as a means of spiritual fulfilment. ➤➤ **Scientologist** *n.*

sci-fi *n informal* = SCIENCE FICTION.

scilicet /'sieliset/ *adv* used to introduce a missing word or in clarifying something obscure: namely.

scilla *n* a bulbous plant of the lily family, similar to the bluebell, with clusters of pink, blue, or white flowers.

scimitar *n* a short sword with a curved blade that narrows towards the hilt, orig used in the Middle East.

scintilla *n* an iota or trace.

scintillate *v* **1** to emit sparks. **2** to sparkle or twinkle. ➤➤ **scintillation** *n.*

scintillating *adj* **1** shining, sparkling, or flashing. **2a** ingeniously witty. **b** captivatingly brilliant or vivacious in conversation.

scion *n* **1** a detached living part of a plant used in grafting and rooting. **2** a descendant or offspring, *esp* of a notable family.

scissor *v* **1** to cut (an object or shape) with scissors. **2** of the legs: to move like scissors.

scissors *pl n* **1** a cutting instrument with two blades pivoted so that their cutting edges slide past each other. **2** a gymnastic feat, e.g. on a horse or parallel bars, in which the leg movements suggest the opening and closing of scissors.

sclera *n* the opaque white outer coat that encloses the eyeball except for the part covered by the cornea. ➤➤ **scleral** *adj.*

scleroderma *n* chronic thickening and hardening of the lower tissue layers of the skin, affecting localized patches or the whole body.

sclerose *v* to undergo or cause (body tissue) to undergo sclerosis.

sclerosis *n* **1** abnormal hardening of tissue, *esp* from overgrowth of fibrous tissue. **2** a disease characterized by the hardening of tissue, *esp* multiple sclerosis.

sclerotic *adj* **1** relating to or in the region of the sclera. **2** relating to or affected with sclerosis.

scoff[1] *v* (*often* + at) to show contempt for something or speak contemptuously about it. ➤➤ **scoffer** *n.*

scoff[2] *n* an expression of scorn or contempt; a jeer.

scoff[3] *v chiefly Brit, informal* to eat (food) greedily, rapidly, or in an ill-mannered way.

scold[1] *v* to reprove or find fault with (somebody) angrily.

scold[2] *n archaic* a woman who habitually nags or quarrels.

scoliosis *n* (*pl* **scolioses**) an abnormal sideways curvature of the spine: compare KYPHOSIS, LORDOSIS. ➤➤ **scoliotic** *adj.*

sconce *n* a bracket attached to a wall, orig for holding a candle or gas light, but now also for a wall-mounted electric light.

scone *n* a small light cake made from a dough or batter and baked in a hot oven or on a griddle.

scoop[1] *n* **1a** a large ladle for taking up or skimming liquids. **b** a utensil with a handle and a small bowl used for spooning out soft food, *esp* ice cream. **2** a deep bucket forming part of a mechanical digger or dredger, used for lifting and moving building materials or corn. **3** *informal* a story or item of news secured for publication or broadcast, *esp* exclusively or ahead of rival journalists.

scoop[2] *v* **1** to take out or up with a scoop. **2** (*often* + out) to make (a hollow) with a scoop, or as if with a scoop. **3** to pick up as if with a scoop. **4** *informal* to report a news item in advance or to the exclusion of (a competitor). **5** *informal* to obtain (something, *esp* money) by swift action or sudden good fortune.

scoop neck *n* a low-cut rounded neckline on a woman's garment.

scoot *v informal* to go or move suddenly and swiftly; to dart.

scooter *n* **1** a child's toy consisting of a narrow board with usu one wheel at each end and an upright steering handle, propelled by rhythmically pressing one foot against the ground. **2** a type of light motorcycle.

scope[1] *n* **1** space or opportunity for unhampered action, thought, or development. **2** extent of treatment, activity, or influence: *That issue is beyond the scope of this enquiry.*

scope[2] *n informal* a periscope, telescope, oscilloscope, etc.

-scope *comb. form* forming nouns, denoting: an instrument for viewing or observing: *microscope.*

-scopic *comb. form* forming adjectives, with the meaning: relating to a viewing instrument: *microscopic.*

scopolamine *n* = HYOSCINE.

-scopy *comb. form* forming nouns, denoting: viewing or observation: *radioscopy.*

scorbutic *adj* relating to or affected with scurvy.

scorch[1] *v* **1** to burn or become burned in such a way that a change in colour or texture is produced. **2** to cause (something, *esp* land or vegetation) to become completely dried up because of the effects of intense heat; to parch. **3** *informal* to move or travel at great and usu excessive speed.

scorch[2] *n* a mark resulting from scorching.

scorched earth policy *n* a strategy during a military campaign in which anything that an invading army might use is deliberately destroyed.

scorcher *n* **1** *informal* a very hot day or a period of very hot weather. **2** *Brit, informal* something that is regarded as remarkable.

score[1] *n* **1** the number of points, goals, runs, etc a team or individual makes in an event. **2** (*pl* **score**) twenty or a group or set of twenty people or things. **3** an unspecified large number or quantity. **4** (**the score**) *informal.* **a** the way things are. **b** the current state of affairs; the latest news. **5** the handwritten notes of a musical composition, or the printed copy of this. **6** a line, scratch, or incision made with a sharp instrument. ✱ **pay/settle a/the score** to take revenge. ➤➤ **scoreless** *adj.*

score[2] *v* **1a** to gain (e.g. points) in a game, competition, etc. **b** to have (a specified number of points) as a value in a game or contest. **2** to keep score in a game or contest. **3** to mark (a surface) with lines, grooves, scratches, or notches. **4** (+ out/through) to delete or cancel something written or printed by putting a line through it. **5** to arrange (music) for an orchestra; to orchestrate. **6** *informal* to succeed in obtaining (something, *esp* illegal drugs). **7** *informal* to succeed in having sexual intercourse. ➤➤ **scorer** *n.*

scorecard *n* **1** a card for recording a score, *esp* in golf. **2** a card listing the names of the players in a game, *esp* in cricket.

scoreline *n* the result of a game or match.

scoria *n* (*pl* **scoriae**) **1** rough cindery lava; volcanic slag. **2** the refuse from smelting ores or melting metals. ➤➤ **scoriaceous** *adj.*

scorn[1] *n* vigorous contempt; disdain. ➤➤ **scornful** *adj,* **scornfully** *adv.*

scorn[2] *v* **1** to treat (something or somebody) with outspoken or angry contempt. **2** to refuse (something) out of scorn. ➤➤ **scorner** *n.*

Scorpio *n* in astrology, the eighth sign of the zodiac, or a person born under this sign. ➤➤ **Scorpian** *adj and n.*

scorpion *n* an arachnid that has an elongated body and a narrow tail bearing a venomous sting at the tip.

scorzonera *n* the black edible root of a European composite plant, used as a vegetable.

Scot *n* **1** a native or inhabitant of Scotland. **2** a member of a Gaelic people orig of N Ireland that settled in Scotland during the fifth cent. AD.

Scotch *n* = SCOTCH WHISKY.

scotch *v* **1** to put an end to; to crush or repudiate. **2** *archaic* to temporarily disable; to make harmless.

Scotch bonnet *n* a variety of very hot chilli pepper.

Scotch broth *n* soup made from beef or mutton, vegetables, and barley.

Scotch egg *n* a hard-boiled egg covered with sausage meat, coated with breadcrumbs and deep-fried, usu eaten cold.

Scotch mist *n* a heavy wet mist of the type that is characteristically found in the Scottish Highlands and Islands.

Scotch pancake *n* = DROP SCONE.

Scotch whisky *n* whisky distilled in Scotland, *esp* from malted barley.

scoter *n* (*pl* **scoters** *or* **scoter**) a sea duck with dark brown or black feathers, living mainly in northern regions.

scot-free *adj* without any penalty, payment, or injury.

Scotland Yard *n* (*used as sing. or pl*) the criminal investigation department of the London metropolitan police force.

scotoma *n* (*pl* **scotomas** *or* **scotomata**) a blind or dark spot in the visual field.

Scots[1] *adj* used *esp* of the people and language or in legal context: Scottish.

Scots[2] *n* the form of the English language spoken in Scotland.

Scots pine *n* a N European and Asian pine tree with spreading branches, bluish green needles, and hard yellow wood that provides valuable timber.

Scotticism *n* a characteristic feature of Scottish English.

Scottie *n informal* (*also* **Scottie dog**) = SCOTTISH TERRIER.

Scottish *n* (**the Scottish**) (*used as pl*) the people of Scotland. ➤➤ **Scottish** *adj*, **Scottishness** *n*.

Scottish Nationalist Party *n* the political party of Scotland that advocates complete independence for the country. ➤➤ **Scottish Nationalist** *n*.

Scottish terrier *n* a terrier of a Scottish breed having short legs and a very wiry coat of usu black hair.

scoundrel *n* an unscrupulous or dishonest person. ➤➤ **scoundrelly** *adj*.

scour[1] *v* **1** to clean by vigorous rubbing, *esp* with abrasive material. **2a** of running water or a glacier: to create an eroded channel in. **b** to erode (a channel or pool). ➤➤ **scourer** *n*.

scour[2] *n* **1** the act or process of scouring or the state of being scoured. **2** (*also in pl*) diarrhoea affecting livestock, *esp* cattle or pigs.

scour[3] *v* **1** to search (something) thoroughly in order to find something. **2** to hurry about, *esp* with the aim of finding something.

scourge[1] *n* **1** somebody or something that is the source or cause of trouble or distress. **2** a whip formerly used to inflict punishment.

scourge[2] *v* **1** to cause great distress to. **2** to flog with a scourge.

scours *n* see SCOUR[2] (2).

Scouse *n Brit, informal* **1** the dialect or accent of Liverpool. **2** (*also* **Scouser**) a native or inhabitant of Liverpool. ➤➤ **Scouse** *adj*.

scout[1] *n* **1** a person who is sent ahead to obtain information, *esp* a soldier sent out to survey land or assess an enemy's position or strength. **2** (**Scout**) a member of the Scout Association, a worldwide movement for young people that stresses qualities of leadership, responsibility, and helpfulness. **3** a talent scout. **4** the act or an instance of scouting.

scout[2] *v* **1** to make an advance survey, e.g. to obtain military information; to reconnoitre. **2** to act as a scout. **3** to observe or explore (a place) in order to obtain information. ➤➤ **scouter** *n*.

scow *n* a large flat-bottomed usu unpowered boat used chiefly for transporting ore, sand, refuse, etc.

scowl[1] *v* to frown or wrinkle the brows in expression of anger or displeasure.

scowl[2] *n* a facial expression of annoyance or displeasure; an angry frown.

SCR *abbr Brit* senior common room.

Scrabble *n trademark* a board game of word-building from individual letters on small tiles.

scrabble[1] *v* **1** to scratch or scrape about, e.g. in an attempt to find or catch hold of something. **2** to scramble or clamber.

scrabble[2] *n* the act or an instance of scrabbling.

scrag[1] *n* **1** a thin or scrawny person or animal. **2** *informal, archaic* a person's neck.

scrag[2] *v* (**scragged, scragging**) *informal chiefly Brit* to seize and beat (somebody).

scrag-end *n Brit* the bony end nearest the head of a neck of mutton or veal.

scraggy *adj* (**-ier, -iest**) lean and lanky; scrawny.

scram *v* (**scrammed, scramming**) *informal* to go away at once.

scramble[1] *v* **1** to move or climb, e.g. up a steep slope or over uneven ground, using the hands as well as the feet. **2** to move with haste, urgency, or panic. **3** to compete eagerly or chaotically for possession of something. **4** to become or cause to become muddled or jumbled up. **5** *esp* of an aircraft or its crew: to take off quickly, e.g. in response to an alert. **6** to cause or order (an aircraft) to scramble. **7** to prepare (eggs) in a pan by stirring during cooking. **8** to make (a message, etc) unintelligible to those without the means to decode it, *esp* by using an electronic device.

scramble[2] *n* **1** the act or an instance of scrambling. **2** *Brit* a motorcycle race over very rough ground. **3** a disordered mess; a muddle or jumble.

scrambler *n* **1** an electronic device that makes telephone, television, or radio signals impossible to access without the relevant decoding equipment. **2** a motorcycle designed for scrambling.

scrap[1] *n* **1** a small detached fragment; a bit. **2** (*in pl*) discarded or leftover food. **3** manufactured articles or parts, *esp* of metal, rejected or discarded and useful only for reprocessing.

scrap[2] *v* (**scrapped, scrapping**) **1** to abandon, discard, or get rid of. **2** to convert into scrap.

scrap[3] *v* (**scrapped, scrapping**) *informal* **1** to fight or quarrel. **2** (*usu* + for) to struggle or compete. ➤➤ **scrapper** *n*.

scrap[4] *n informal* **1** a fight or quarrel. **2** a struggle.

scrapbook *n* a blank book in which miscellaneous items may be pasted.

scrape[1] *v* **1a** to grate harshly over or against. **b** to damage or injure by contact with a rough surface. **c** to draw (something) roughly or noisily over a surface. **2a** to remove (clinging matter) from a surface by usu repeated strokes of an edged instrument. **b** to make (a surface) smooth or clean with strokes of an edged or rough instrument. **3** to achieve (e.g. an exam grade or a pass) by a narrow margin. ✱ **scrape the (bottom of the) barrel** *informal* to resort to the weakest or worst resources at one's disposal. ➤➤ **scraper** *n*.

scrape[2] *n* **1a** an act or the sound of scraping. **b** an injury or mark caused by scraping. **2** *informal* an awkward or embarrassing predicament. **3** *archaic* a type of bow in which the foot is drawn back along the ground.

scrape by *v* to manage with meagre resources.

scrape together *v* to collect or procure (money or other resources) with difficulty.

scrape up *v* = SCRAPE TOGETHER.

scrap heap *n* a pile of discarded materials, *esp* metal. ✱ **on the scrapheap** of somebody or something: no longer wanted or useful.

scrapie *n* a usu fatal virus disease of sheep, characterized by twitching, intense itching, emaciation, and finally paralysis.

scrappy *adj* (**-ier, -iest**) disjointed or incomplete. ➤➤ **scrappily** *adv*, **scrappiness** *n*.

scrapyard *n Brit* a yard where scrap metal and other discarded materials are collected or processed.

scratch[1] *v* **1a** to mark or cut the surface of (something) with or on a sharp or jagged object. **b** to make a superficial wound on (somebody or something). **2** to scrape or rub (a body part), *esp* to relieve itching. **3** to manage to do (something), *esp* with great difficulty: *He scratched a living selling his stories.*

4a to cancel or erase with a drawn line, or as if with a line. **b** to withdraw or withdraw (an entry) from a competition. **c** to cancel (e.g. a project). **5** of a disc jockey: to move (a vinyl record) manually backwards and forwards on a rotating turntable to create percussive effects, *esp* in modern dance music. **6** of a bird or animal: to use the beak or claws, *esp* to dig around for food. ✱ **scratch the surface** to deal with something inadequately or superficially. ➤➤ **scratcher** *n.*

scratch[2] *n* **1** a mark or injury produced by scratching. **2** *informal* a slight wound. **3** an act of scratching. ✱ **from scratch** from the very beginning. **up to scratch** reaching a satisfactory or adequate standard or level.

scratch[3] *adj* arranged or put together haphazardly or hastily.

scratchcard *n* a small card with a coated section or sections on it, which are scratched off to reveal symbols which indicate whether a prize has been won.

scratch file *n* in computing, a temporary file used for storing data while a program is in use.

scratching *n* an effect in modern dance music achieved by manually interfering with the rotation of a vinyl record on a turntable.

scratchy *adj* (**-ier, -iest**) **1** tending to scratch or irritate. **2** making a scratching noise. **3** made with scratches, or as if with scratches.

scrawl[1] *v* to write or draw (something) awkwardly, hastily, or carelessly.

scrawl[2] *n* an untidy or careless piece of writing or drawing.

scrawny *adj* (**-ier, -iest**) exceptionally thin; bony.

scream[1] *v* **1** to make a sudden loud piercing cry, *esp* in alarm, fright, or pain. **2** to move with or make a shrill noise resembling a scream. **3** to say in a loud, shrill, or hysterical voice.

scream[2] *n* **1** a loud shrill cry or noise. **2** *informal* somebody or something that is very amusing.

screamer *n* **1** somebody or something that screams. **2** *informal* something that is regarded as remarkable, *esp* in terms of its speed.

screamingly *adv* extremely.

scree *n* loose stones on rocky debris or a hillside or mountain slope formed from or covered with an accumulation of stones or rocks.

screech[1] *v* **1** to utter a shrill piercing cry; to cry out, *esp* in terror or pain. **2** to make a sound like a screech: *The car screeched to a halt.* ➤➤ **screecher** *n,* **screechy** *adj.*

screech[2] *n* a shrill sound or cry.

screech owl *n Brit* = BARN OWL.

screed *n* **1** an overlong speech or piece of writing, *esp* one that is dull. **2** a mixture of cement applied to a floor to give it a level surface. ➤➤ **screeding** *n.*

screen[1] *n* **1** a fixed or movable partition or curtain used as a room divider or to give protection, concealment, or privacy. **2** something that shelters, protects, or conceals. **3** fine netting set in a frame and used in a window or door to keep insects out. **4a** the part of a television set, radar receiver, video display unit, etc on which images or data are displayed. **b** a blank surface on which photographic images, cinematic films, etc are projected or reflected. **5a** the medium of television. **b** the film industry: *a star of stage and screen.*

screen[2] *v* **1a** to give shelter or protection to (somebody or something) with a screen. **b** to guard (somebody or something) from injury, danger, or punishment. **c** (*also* + off) to separate or enclose (somebody or something) with a screen. **2a** to project (a film, slide, etc) on a screen. **b** to show or broadcast (a film or television programme). **3a** to test or check (somebody or something) systematically, *esp* in order to ascertain qualification or suitability. **b** to carry out a test on (somebody) for the presence of disease. **c** to test or check (somebody or something) for the presence of weapons. ➤➤ **screener** *n.*

screenplay *n* the script of a film including description of characters, details of scenes and settings, dialogue, and stage directions.

screen-print *v* to print (something) through silk or other material treated so as to make some areas impervious. ➤➤ **screen print** *n.*

screen saver *n* a computer program that generates a blank screen or moving screen images, to prevent damage to the screen that a static image can cause.

screen test *n* a short film sequence used to assess an actor's suitability for a film role.

screen-test *v* to subject (an actor) to a screen test.

screenwriter *n* a writer of screenplays. ➤➤ **screenwriting** *n.*

screw[1] *n* **1a** a sharp-pointed tapering metal pin with a raised spiral thread running round it and a head with any of various types of slots in it suitable for the insertion of a screwdriver, turned in order to make the pin join parts, *esp* wooden ones, together. **b** a cylinder with a raised spiral thread running round the outside of it; a male screw. **2** the propeller of a ship or aircraft. **3** *informal* a prison warder. **4** *coarse slang* an act of sexual intercourse. ✱ **have a screw loose** *informal* to be slightly mad or eccentric.

screw[2] *v* **1** to attach, fasten, or close (something) by means of a screw. **2** to unite (parts) by means of a screw or a twisting motion. **3a** to operate, tighten, or adjust by means of a screw. **b** to cause to rotate spirally about an axis. **4** *informal* to cheat or defraud. **5** *coarse slang* to have sexual intercourse with. ✱ **have one's head screwed on (the right way)** *informal* to have plenty of common sense or act in a sensible way.

screwdriver *n* **1** a tool for turning screws, usu with a tip that fits into the head of the screw. **2** a cocktail made from vodka and orange juice.

screw propeller *n* = PROPELLER.

screw up *v* **1** to crush or crumple. **2** *informal* to cause to become anxious, neurotic, or emotionally disturbed. **3** *informal* to cause to go badly wrong. **4** *informal* to bungle a task completely. **5** to summon up (one's courage).

scribble[1] *v* **1** to write or draw (something) hurriedly without regard for legibility or coherence. **2** to write novels, poetry, etc. ➤➤ **scribbler** *n.*

scribble[2] *n* an untidy drawing or piece of writing, *esp* one that has been hastily or carelessly done.

scribe[1] *n* **1** a person who copied manuscripts in ancient and medieval times. **2** *informal* an author, *esp* a journalist. **3a** a Jewish record-keeper and interpreter of the law in ancient Israel. **b** a professional Jewish theologian and jurist. **4** = SCRIBER. ➤➤ **scribal** *adj.*

scribe[2] *v* **1** to mark a line on (a surface) by scoring with a pointed instrument. **2** *literary* to work as a scribe; to write.

scriber *n* a sharp-pointed tool for making marks, *esp* for marking out material, e.g. metal, to be cut.

scrim *n* **1** a durable plain-woven usu cotton fabric used in upholstery, curtain lining, etc. **2** a transparent sheet of fabric used in theatre sets as a backcloth or screen.

scrimmage[1] *n* **1** a disorderly struggle or fight. **2** in American football, the interplay between two teams that begins with the passing back of the ball from the ground and continues until the ball is dead.

scrimmage[2] *v* in American football, to take part in a scrimmage.

scrimp *v* (*often* + on) to be frugal or sparing with something; to skimp. ✱ **scrimp and save** to economize wherever possible.

scrimshank *v Brit, informal esp* of somebody in the armed forces: to avoid duties or obligations. ➤➤ **scrimshanker** *n.*

scrimshaw[1] *n* carved or coloured work made from ivory or whalebone, *esp* by sailors.

scrimshaw[2] *v* to carve or engrave designs on (ivory, bones, shells, etc).

scrip *n* **1** any of various documents entitling the holder or bearer to receive something, such as an allotment of land. **2** a certificate entitling the holder to a particular number of shares, bonds, etc. **3** such certificates collectively.

script[1] *n* **1** the written text of a stage play, film, or broadcast, *esp* the one used in a production or performance. **2a** written characters; handwriting. **b** the characters used in writing a particular language; an alphabet. **3** *Brit* a person's written answers to an exam.

script[2] *v* to prepare a script for (something).

scripture *n* **1** (*also in pl*) the sacred writings of the Christian religion as contained in the Bible. **2** the sacred writings of another religion. ➤➤ **scriptural** *adj.*

scriptwriter *n* a person who writes a script for a film or play, or for a radio or television programme. ➤➤ **scriptwriting** *n.*

scrivener *n* formerly, a professional copyist, scribe, or notary.

scrofula *n no longer in technical use* tuberculosis of the lymph glands, *esp* in the neck. ➤➤ **scrofulous** *adj.*

scroll[1] *n* **1** a roll of parchment, etc, usu with writing or a drawing on it. **2** a stylized ornamental design imitating the spiral curves of a scroll, e.g. on a column in classical architecture.

scroll[2] *v* in computing, to cause (text or graphics displayed on a screen) to move vertically or horizontally in such a way that one displayed line, etc is made to replace another. ➤➤ **scrollable** *adj,* **scroller** *n.*

scroll bar *n* a narrow panel at the side of a computer screen that allows a user to scroll through text or graphics using a mouse.

scrollwork *n* decoration made up of scroll-like patterns, *esp* spirals in wood.

Scrooge *n* a miserly person.

scrotum *n* (*pl* **scrota** *or* **scrotums**) the external pouch of skin that contains the testes. ➤➤ **scrotal** *adj.*

scrounge[1] *v informal* to try to obtain (something) for free or at another person's expense. ➤➤ **scrounger** *n.*

scrounge[2] *n informal* an act of scrounging.

scrub[1] *v* (**scrubbed, scrubbing**) **1** to clean by hard rubbing, *esp* with a stiff brush. **2** *informal* to cancel or abandon. **3** (*also* + up) of a surgeon: to spend time thoroughly washing the hands and forearms before performing an operation.

scrub[2] *n* **1** an act of scrubbing. **2** a gently abrasive skin cream. **3** (*in pl*) sterile clothing worn by staff in an operating theatre.

scrub[3] *n* **1** vegetation consisting chiefly of stunted trees or shrubs. **2** (*also in pl*) an area covered with such vegetation. ➤➤ **scrubby** *adj.*

scrubber *n* **1** a person or thing that scrubs. **2** an apparatus for removing impurities, *esp* from gases. **3** *chiefly Brit, informal* a promiscuous woman or a prostitute.

scruff[1] *n* the back of the neck; the nape.

scruff[2] *n Brit, informal* an untidily dressed or grubby person.

scruffy *adj* (**-ier, -iest**) slovenly and untidy, *esp* in appearance. ➤➤ **scruffily** *adv,* **scruffiness** *n.*

scrum[1] *n* **1** in rugby, a set piece in which the forwards of each side crouch in a tight formation with the two front rows of each team meeting shoulder to shoulder so that the ball can be put in play between them. **2** *Brit, informal* a disorderly struggle; a jostle.

scrum[2] *v* (**scrummed, scrumming**) to take part in a rugby scrum.

scrummage[1] *n* = SCRUM[1].

scrummage[2] *v* = SCRUM[2].

scrummy *adj* (**-ier, -iest**) *informal* delicious.

scrump *v Brit, informal* to steal (fruit, *esp* apples) from an orchard.

scrumptious *adj informal* delicious or delightful.

scrumpy *n Brit* dry rough cider, *esp* as traditionally brewed in the English West Country.

scrunch[1] *v* **1** to crunch, crush, or crumple. **2** to move with or make a crunching sound.

scrunch[2] *n* a crunching sound.

scrunchie *or* **scrunchy** *n* (*pl* **-ies**) *chiefly Brit* a loop of elastic, loosely covered in fabric, used for tying hair up or back.

scruple[1] *n* **1a** a moral consideration that raises a doubt or discourages an action. **b** an uneasy feeling that arises from having a conscious awareness about the morality of something. **2** a unit of weight equal to 20 grains (1.296 grams), formerly used by apothecaries.

scruple[2] *v* to hesitate or be reluctant to do something on grounds of conscience.

scrupulous *adj* **1** painstakingly exact. **2** having a strong desire to avoid doing anything wrong or immoral. ➤➤ **scrupulosity** *n,* **scrupulously** *adv,* **scrupulousness** *n.*

scrutineer *n* **1** a person who examines or observes something. **2** *Brit* a person who takes or counts votes at an election.

scrutinize *or* **-ise** *v* to examine painstakingly or in minute detail.

scrutiny *n* (*pl* **-ies**) **1** a searching study, enquiry, or inspection. **2** surveillance.

scry *v* (**-ies, -ied**) to predict events, etc by crystal gazing.

SCSI *abbr* small computer systems interface, a system for connecting a computer to a peripheral device.

scuba *n* an aqualung.

scuba-diving *n* underwater swimming with a scuba.

scud[1] *v* (**scudded, scudding**) to move or run swiftly, *esp* as if being swept along.

scud[2] *n* **1** ocean spray driven swiftly by the wind. **2** torn masses of cloud driven rapidly by the wind beneath the main cloud layer. **3** the act of scudding.

scuff[1] *v* **1** to scratch, chip, or damage the surface of (something, *esp* shoes). **2** to drag or shuffle (the feet) along while walking or back and forth while standing.

scuff[2] *n* a mark or damage caused by scuffing.

scuffle[1] *n* a confused impromptu usu brief fight.

scuffle[2] *v* **1** to struggle or fight at close quarters, often in a confused way. **2** to move in a quick but shuffling way.

scull[1] *n* **1a** an oar worked to and fro over the stern of a boat as a means of propulsion. **b** either of a pair of light oars used by a single rower. **2** a narrow light racing boat propelled by a scull or sculls.

scull[2] *v* to propel a boat by a scull or sculls. ➤➤ **sculler** *n.*

scullery *n* (*pl* **-ies**) a small kitchen or a room where kitchen work such as preparing vegetables is done.

scullion *n archaic* a kitchen servant who does the dirty or most menial jobs.

sculpt *v* to create by sculpture.

sculptor *n* an artist who creates sculptures.

sculptress *n* a female sculptor.

sculpture[1] *n* **1** the art of creating three-dimensional works of art out of mouldable or hard materials by carving, modelling, casting, etc. **2** a piece of work produced by sculpture. ➤➤ **sculptural** *adj.*

sculpture[2] *v* **1a** to form an image or representation of (something) from solid material, e.g. wood or stone. **b** to form (e.g. wood or stone) into a three-dimensional work of art. **2** to shape by carving or moulding, or as if by carving or moulding.

scum[1] *n* **1** pollutants or impurities risen to or collected on the surface of a liquid. **2** *informal* an utterly corrupt or despicable person, or a group of such people. ➤➤ **scummy** *adj.*

scum[2] *v* (**scummed, scumming**) to become covered with or cause to become covered with scum.

scumbag *n informal* a despicable or obnoxious person.

scumble[1] *v* **1** to soften the lines or colours of (a drawing or painting) by light rubbing or by applying a thin coat of opaque colouring or paint. **2** to produce an effect of broken colour on (a painted surface) by exposing some of the lower layers of paint.

scumble[2] *n* a coat of paint or layer of colouring applied in scumbling.

scupper[1] *n* an opening in a ship's side for draining water from the deck.

scupper[2] *v* **1** *chiefly Brit, informal* to prevent (something) from working, happening, etc. **2** to sink (a ship) deliberately.

scurf *n* thin dry scales flaking from the skin, e.g. dandruff. ➤➤ **scurfy** *adj.*

scurrilous *adj* of a person, report, etc: making defamatory remarks, *esp* with the intention of damaging somebody's reputation. ➤➤ **scurrility** *n.*

scurry[1] *v* (**-ies, -ied**) to move with short hurried steps; to scamper.

scurry[2] *n* (*pl* **-ies**) **1** an act or the sound of scurrying. **2** a flurry of snow.

scurvy[1] *n* a disease caused by a lack of vitamin C and marked by spongy gums, loosening of the teeth, and bleeding under the skin.

scurvy[2] *adj* (**-ier, -iest**) *archaic* disgustingly mean or contemptible.

scut *n* a short erect tail, *esp* that of a rabbit, hare, or deer.

scutter[1] *v chiefly Brit* to move with small quick steps or actions; to scurry or scamper.

scutter[2] *n chiefly Brit* an act or the sound of scuttering.

scuttle[1] *n* **1** a container used for carrying or storing coal indoors. **2** *Brit* the top part of the body of a car in front of the two front doors, to which the windscreen and instrument panel are attached.

scuttle[2] *v* to scurry or scamper.

scuttle[3] *n* **1** a quick shuffling pace. **2** a short dash, *esp* a quick departure.

scuttle[4] *v* **1** to sink (one's own ship) deliberately, e.g. by making holes in the hull, *esp* in order to avoid capture. **2** to destroy or wreck.

scuttle[5] *n* a small opening or hatchway with a movable lid on the deck of a ship.

scythe[1] *n* a long curving blade fastened at an angle to a long handle, for cutting crops, *esp* grass or corn.

scythe[2] *v* **1** to cut (grass, corn, etc) with a scythe. **2** to move rapidly and devastatingly through something.

Scythian *n* a member of an ancient nomadic people inhabiting Scythia, a region north of the Black Sea, now part of the Ukraine. ➤➤ **Scythian** *adj.*

SD *abbr* South Dakota (US postal abbreviation).

SDI *abbr NAm* Strategic Defense Initiative.

SDLP *abbr* in Northern Ireland, Social Democratic and Labour Party.

SDP *abbr Brit* Social Democratic Party.

SE *abbr* **1** Southeast. **2** Southeastern.

Se *abbr* the chemical symbol for selenium.

sea *n* **1a** the great body of salty water that covers much of the earth. **b** a large more or less landlocked body of salt water: *the Mediterranean Sea.* **2** something vast or overwhelming likened to the sea: *a sea of mud; a sea of faces.* ✻ **at sea 1** on the sea; *specif* on a sea voyage. **2** lost or bewildered.

sea anchor *n* a device, typically a canvas bag, thrown overboard to slow the drifting of a ship or seaplane and to keep its head to the wind.

sea anemone *n* a solitary and brightly coloured polyp with a cluster of tentacles superficially resembling a flower.

sea bass *n* a marine fish of American coastal waters.

seabed *n* the floor of the sea.

seabird *n* a bird, such as a gull or albatross, that lives on the sea or coast.

seaborgium *n* a radioactive transuranic chemical element that is artificially produced.

sea bream *n* a marine spiny-finned food fish.

sea breeze *n* a cool breeze blowing inland from the sea.

sea change *n* a complete transformation.

sea cow *n* either of two aquatic plant-eating mammals, the dugong or the manatee.

sea cucumber *n* a sea animal with a long flexible muscular body, some species of which are used as food.

sea dog *n informal* a veteran sailor.

seafarer *n* **1** a sailor. **2** a person who travels by sea.

seafaring[1] *n* travel by sea, *esp* the occupation of a sailor.

seafaring[2] *adj* frequently travelling by sea, *esp* while working as a sailor.

seafood *n* edible marine fish, shellfish, crustaceans, etc.

seafront *n* the part of a seaside town immediately beside the sea.

seagoing *adj* of or designed for travel on the sea.

sea-green *adj* of a light bluish green colour. ➤➤ **sea green** *n.*

sea gull *n* = GULL[1].

sea horse *n* a small fish with a head and body shaped like the head and neck of a horse.

sea kale *n* **1** a fleshy European plant of the mustard family used as a herb in cooking. **2** = CHARD.

seal[1] *n* **1a** a closure that must be broken in order to give access, and so when unbroken guarantees that the item so closed has not been opened or tampered with. **b** a tight and effective closure, e.g. against the passage of air, water, etc. **2a** something that confirms, ratifies, or makes secure; a guarantee or assurance. **b** an emblem or word impressed or stamped on a document as a mark of authenticity. **c** a device used to impress such a word or emblem, e.g. on wax or moist clay. ✻ **set/put one's seal on/to something 1** to seal something with one's personal seal. **2** to give one's approval and endorsement to something. **set/put the/a seal on something** to conclude a deal, confirm an arrangement or fact, etc.

seal[2] *v* **1a** to close (something) so as to prevent anything getting in or out, *esp* to make it airtight or watertight. **b** to close (a document, envelope, bottle, etc), with or without a seal, e.g. to prevent anybody opening it or tampering with the contents. **c** to cover (something porous, e.g. a plaster wall) with a coating of a nonporous substance. **2** to confirm (an arrangement, etc) or make it secure: *The agreement was sealed with a public handshake.* **3a** to set or affix an authenticating seal to (e.g. a document). **b** to authenticate or ratify. **c** to mark with a stamp or seal, e.g. as evidence of size, weight, capacity, or quality. **4** to determine irrevocably: *Her answer sealed our fate.* ✻ **my lips are sealed** I can be trusted to keep my mouth shut. ➤➤ **sealable** *adj.*

seal[3] *n* (*pl* **seals** *or* **seal**) a marine carnivorous mammal chiefly of cold regions with limbs modified into webbed flippers for swimming.

seal[4] *v* to hunt seal.

sealant *n* a sealing agent for closing, waterproofing, etc.

sea legs *pl n* bodily adjustment to the motion of a ship, indicated by ability to walk steadily and by freedom from seasickness.

sealer[1] *n* a coat, e.g. of size, applied to prevent subsequent coats of paint, varnish, or wallpaper paste from being too readily absorbed.

sealer[2] *n* a person or ship engaged in hunting seals.

sea level *n* the mean level of the surface of the sea midway between high and low tide.

sealing wax *n* a resinous composition that becomes soft when heated and is used for sealing letters, parcels, etc.

sea lion *n* a large seal found in the Pacific Ocean that has visible external ears, short coarse fur, and large flippers by means of which it can move around on land.

seal off *v* to close or surround securely, *esp* in order to prevent movement in or out.

Sea Lord *n* either of two senior naval officers who are members of the Admiralty Board of the Ministry of Defence.

Sealyham terrier *n* a terrier of a breed having a wiry, usu white, coat and short legs.

seam[1] *n* **1** a line of stitching joining two pieces of fabric, *esp* along their edges. **2a** a line, groove, or ridge formed at the meeting of two edges. **b** a layer or stratum of coal, rock, etc.

seam[2] *v* to join with a seam.

seaman *n* (*pl* **seamen**) a sailor or mariner. ➤➤ **seamanlike** *adj,* **seamanship** *n.*

seam bowling *n* in cricket, fast bowling in which the ball is made to bounce on its seam and thereby deviate from a straight line. ➤➤ **seam bowler** *n.*

sea mile *n* a unit of length that is the length of one MINUTE[1] (angular distance) of a GREAT CIRCLE (theoretical circle on surface of earth). The length varies from about 1842m at the equator to 1861m at the North and South Poles.

seamless *adj* **1** without seams. **2** without breaks, gaps, or discontinuities.

seamstress *n* a woman whose occupation is sewing.

seamy *adj* (**-ier, -iest**) unpleasant; sordid.

Seanad Éireann /ˌshanəd 'eərən, ˌshanədh/ *n* the upper house of parliament in the Republic of Ireland: compare DÁIL.

séance *or* **seance** /'sayons, 'sayonhs/ *n* a meeting at which people attempt to communicate with the dead.

seaplane *n* an aeroplane designed to take off from and land on the water, with floats or skis in place of wheels.

seaport *n* a port, harbour, or town accessible to seagoing ships.

sear[1] *v* **1** to burn or scorch (somebody or something) with a sudden application of intense heat. **2** to brown the surface of (meat) by frying it quickly in hot fat.

sear[2] *adj* see SERE.

search[1] *v* **1** (*usu* + for) to look or enquire carefully or thoroughly. **2a** (*often* + for) to look through or over carefully or thoroughly in order to find or discover something. **b** to examine (a person) for concealed articles, e.g. weapons or drugs. **c** to investigate (a computer file, database, etc) to find certain information. ✻ **search me!** *informal* used to express ignorance of the answer to a question. ➤➤ **searchable** *adj,* **searcher** *n.*

search[2] *n* the act or an instance of searching, *esp* an organized act of searching.

search engine *n* software that searches the Internet for information.

searching *adj* trying to find information, e.g. about somebody's opinions, feelings, etc.

searchlight *n* an apparatus for projecting a movable beam of light.

search party *n* a group of people organized to search for a missing person, etc.

search warrant *n* a warrant authorizing a search of premises by police officers.

searing *adj* **1** very hot. **2** very strong, angry, forceful, etc.

seascape *n* a picture representing a view of the sea.

sea shanty *n* = SHANTY[2].

seashell *n* the empty shell of a sea mollusc.

seashore *n* **1** land next to the sea. **2** in law, land between the high- and low-water marks.

seasick *adj* suffering from the motion sickness associated with travelling by ship, boat, or hovercraft. ➤➤ **seasickness** *n.*

seaside *n* land bordering the sea, *esp* a holiday resort or beach beside the sea.

sea slug *n* a shell-less marine gastropod mollusc.

season[1] *n* **1a** any of the four parts, often quarters, into which the year is commonly divided according to the prevailing weather conditions, etc. **b** a period characterized by a particular kind of weather: *the dry season.* **c** a period of the year characterized by or associated with a particular activity or phenomenon: *the holiday season.* **d** a time when an animal, bird, or fish may, or may not, legally be caught or killed. **2** *archaic* an appropriate time. ✻ **in season 1** of food: readily available and in the best condition for eating. **2** of game: legally available to be hunted or caught. **3** of a female animal: on heat; ready to mate and produce offspring.

season[2] *v* **1a** to give (food) more flavour by adding seasoning. **b** to enliven: *conversation seasoned with wit.* **2a** to treat or expose (timber) over a period so as to prepare it for use. **b** to make (somebody) fit or expert by experience: *a seasoned veteran.*

seasonable *adj* **1** suitable to the season or circumstances. **2** *archaic* occurring in good or proper time; opportune.

seasonal *adj* **1** of, occurring, or produced at a particular season. **2** determined by seasonal need or availability. ➤➤ **seasonality** *n,* **seasonally** *adv.*

seasonal affective disorder *n* a tendency to depression and lethargy during the winter months, apparently brought on by biochemical changes caused by lack of sunlight.

seasoning *n* something such as salt, pepper, a spice, or a herb, added to food.

season ticket *n Brit* a ticket sold, usu at a reduced price, for an unlimited number of trips over the same route during a limited period, admittance to a series of events, etc.

sea squill *n* = SQUILL (1A).

sea squirt *n* a small primitive sea animal that exists as a free-swimming tadpole-like larva but as an adult is a potato-shaped creature with a tough outer membrane and is permanently attached to a surface, such as a rock.

sea stack *n* = STACK[1] (6).

seat[1] *n* **1a** a piece of furniture, e.g. a chair, stool, or bench, for sitting in or on. **b** the part of something on which one rests when sitting. **c** the buttocks. **d** a place for sitting. **e** a unit of seating accommodation, or a ticket for this. **2a** a right of sitting, e.g. in parliament or on an elected committee. **b** *Brit* a parliamentary constituency. **3a** a place where something is established or practised: *a seat of learning.* **b** a place from which authority is exercised: *the seat of government.* **4** a large country mansion. **5a** a part at or forming the base of something. **b** a part or surface on or in which another part or surface rests: *a valve seat.* **6** posture in or a way of sitting on horseback.

seat[2] *v* **1a** to cause (somebody) to sit or assist (somebody) in finding a seat. **b** to provide seats for (a number of people). **c** to put (oneself or another person) in a sitting position. **2** (*usu in passive*) to place or settle (something) somewhere. ➤➤ **seating** *n.*

seat belt *n* an arrangement of straps designed to secure a person in a seat in an aeroplane, vehicle, etc.

sea trout *n* a European and N African fish related to the salmon that migrates into fresh water to spawn.

sea urchin *n* an ECHINODERM (sea creatures including starfish) usu with a thin spherical shell covered with movable spines.

seawall *n* a wall or embankment to protect the shore from erosion or to act as a breakwater.

seaway *n* **1** the sea as a route for travel. **2** a deep inland waterway that admits ocean shipping.

seaweed *n* an alga growing in the sea, typically having thick slimy fronds.

seaworthy *adj* of a ship: fit or safe for a sea voyage. ➤➤ **seaworthiness** *n.*

sebaceous *adj* of or secreting sebum or other fatty material.

sebaceous gland *n* a gland in the skin that secretes sebum.

sebum *n* fatty lubricant matter secreted by the sebaceous glands of the skin.

sec[1] *n Brit, informal* a second or moment.

sec[2] *adj* of wine: not sweet; dry.

sec. *abbr* secant.

secant *n* **1** a straight line cutting a curve at two or more points. **2** the trigonometric function that is the reciprocal of the cosine.

secateurs *pl n chiefly Brit* small pruning shears.

secede *v* to withdraw from an organization, federation, etc. ➤➤ **seceder** *n.*

secession *n* the act or an instance of seceding. ➤➤ **secessionism** *n,* **secessionist** *n.*

seclude *v* to remove or separate (oneself or another person) from contact with others.

secluded *adj* **1** screened or hidden from view. **2** living in seclusion.

seclusion *n* the act or an instance of secluding or being secluded.

second[1] *adj* **1a** denoting a person or thing having the position in a sequence corresponding to the number two. **b** next to the first in value, quality, or degree. **c** (+ to) inferior; subordinate: *As a musician, he was second to none.* **d** standing next below the top in authority or importance: *second mate.* **2** alternate; other: *The city elects a mayor every second year.* **3** another; one more: *Would you like a second cup?*

second[2] *n* **1a** somebody or something that is next after the first in rank, order, time, position, authority, or precedence. **b** a Cub Scout or Brownie Guide second in rank to a sixer. **2** a person who aids, supports, or stands in for another, *esp* the assistant of a duellist or boxer. **3** in Britain, a second-class honours degree. **4** the second forward gear of a motor vehicle. **5** (*usu in pl*) a slightly flawed or inferior article, e.g. of merchandise. **6** *informal* (*in pl*) a second helping of food or second course of a meal. **7** in music, an interval of two degrees of a diatonic scale, or the combination of two notes at such an interval.

second[3] *adv* = SECONDLY.

second[4] *n* **1** a 60th part of a minute of time or of a minute of angular measure. **2** a moment.

second[5] *v* **1** to give support or encouragement to. **2** to endorse (a motion or nomination). ➤➤ **seconder** *n.*

second[6] *v chiefly Brit* to release (a teacher, businessman, etc) from a regularly assigned position for temporary duty with another organization or at another post. ➤➤ **secondee** *n,* **secondment** *n.*

secondary *adj* **1** of second rank or importance. **2** immediately derived from something primary or basic; derivative: *secondary sources.* **3a** not first in order of occurrence or development. **b** of the second order or stage in a series or sequence. **4** of a level of education between primary and tertiary. **5** of or being a manufacturing industry: compare PRIMARY[1], TERTIARY[1]. ➤➤ **secondarily** *adv.*

secondary modern *n* formerly in Britain, a secondary school providing a practical rather than academic type of education.

secondary picketing *n chiefly Brit* picketing by members of a trade union and others at a place where there is an industrial dispute in which they are not directly involved.

secondary school *n* a school usu for pupils aged from about 11 to about 18.

secondary sexual characteristic *n* a physical or mental attribute characteristic of a particular sex, e.g. the breasts of a female mammal, that appears at puberty or in the breeding season, and is not directly concerned with reproduction.

second best *n* somebody or something that comes after the best in quality or worth. ➤➤ **second-best** *adj.*

second chamber *n* the upper chamber of a legislative assembly that has two chambers, such as the British Parliament or the US Congress.

second class *n* the second and next to highest group in a classification.

second-class[1] *adj* **1** of a second class. **2** inferior or mediocre. **3** of mail in the UK: handled less quickly than first-class mail but more cheaply.

second-class[2] *adv* **1** in accommodation, next below the best. **2** by second-class mail.

Second Coming *n* (**the Second Coming**) in Christianity, the return of Christ to judge the world on the last day.

second cousin *n* a child of a first cousin of either of one's parents.

second-degree burn *n* a burn characterized by blistering and surface destruction of the skin.

second fiddle *n* a secondary or subordinate role or function.

second-generation *adj* **1** denoting the children of immigrants to a particular country. **2** *esp* in computer science, relating to a second stage of technical development in which improvements are made to earlier models.

second-guess *v* **1** to try to guess the actions of (somebody else). **2** to foretell or predict.

secondhand[1] *adj* **1a** acquired after being owned by another. **b** dealing in secondhand goods. **2a** received from or through an intermediary. **b** not original; derivative.

secondhand[2] *adv* **1** from a dealer in secondhand goods; from among things that have been previously owned. **2** through an intermediary; indirectly.

second hand *n* the hand marking seconds on the face of a watch or clock.

second-in-command *n* an officer who is immediately subordinate to a commander.

second lieutenant *n* the lowest rank of commissioned officer in some armed forces.

secondly *adv* used to introduce a second point; second.

second nature *n* an action or ability that practice has made instinctive.

second person *n* a grammatical category referring to the person or thing addressed or any of the verb-forms or pronouns belonging to this category, e.g. *are* or *you*: compare FIRST PERSON, PERSON, THIRD PERSON.

second-rate *adj* of inferior quality or value. ➤➤ **second-rater** *n.*

second reading *n* a stage in the legislative process providing for debate on the principal features of a bill.

second sight *n* the ability to see future events, things happening elsewhere, etc.

second string *n chiefly NAm* a substitute player or team, e.g. in football.

second thoughts *pl n* a reconsideration of a previous decision.

second wind *n* renewed energy or endurance after a period of severe exertion.

Second World *n* the countries of the former communist bloc, including those of the former Soviet Union and many Eastern European countries, e.g. Poland and Romania: compare FIRST WORLD, THIRD WORLD (1).

secret[1] *adj* **1a** kept or hidden from knowledge or view. **b** marked by the practice of discretion; secretive. **c** conducted or operating in secret. **2** retired or secluded. **3** revealed only to the initiated; esoteric. ➤➤ **secrecy** *n,* **secretly** *adv.*

secret[2] *n* **1a** something kept hidden or unexplained. **b** a fact concealed from others or shared confidentially with a few. **2** something taken to be the means of attaining a desired end: *the secret of longevity.* **3** something that is not understood; a mystery.

secret agent *n* a spy.

secretaire *n* a writing desk with a top section for books.

secretariat *n* a government administrative department or its staff.

secretary *n* (*pl* **-ies**) **1** a person who is employed to handle correspondence and manage routine administrative work for an individual or organization. **2** an officebearer of an organization or society responsible for its records and correspondence. **3** in Britain, a senior civil servant who acts as assistant to a minister or ambassador. ➤➤ **secretarial** *adj.*

secretary bird *n* a large long-legged African bird of prey that feeds largely on reptiles.

secretary-general *n* (*pl* **secretaries-general**) a principal administrative officer, e.g. of the United Nations.

secretary of state *n* **1** in Britain, a member of the government who is the head of any of various government departments. **2** in the USA, the head of the government department responsible for foreign affairs.

secrete[1] *v* to form and give off (a secretion). ➤➤ **secretor** *n,* **secretory** *adj.*

secrete[2] *v* to deposit in a hidden place.

secretion *n* **1** the bodily process of making and releasing some material either functionally specialized, e.g. a hormone, saliva, latex, or resin, or isolated for excretion, e.g. urine. **2** a product formed by this process.

secretive *adj* inclined to secrecy; not open or outgoing in speech or behaviour. ➤➤ **secretively** *adv,* **secretiveness** *n.*

secret police *n* a police organization operating largely in secrecy, *esp* for the political purposes of a government.

secret service *n* **1** a governmental agency concerned with national security, operating largely in secrecy. **2** (**Secret Service**) a British government intelligence department.

secret society *n* a society whose members keep their activities secret from others.

sect *n* **1a** *usu derog* a dissenting or schismatic religious body, *esp* if smaller in numbers than established denominations and regarded by them as heretical or extreme. **b** *derog* a denomination. **2a** a group maintaining strict allegiance to a doctrine or leader. **b** a party or faction.

sectarian[1] *n* an adherent of a sect, *esp* if fanatical or intolerant of others.

sectarian[2] *adj* **1** of or characteristic of a sect or sectarian. **2** limited in character or scope; parochial. ➤➤ **sectarianism** *n.*

section[1] *n* **1a** a part of something considered in isolation. **b** a distinct part or portion of something written, *esp* a subdivision of a chapter or a part of a newspaper, etc dealing with one particular topic. **c** any of several component parts that may be separated and reassembled. **2a** a distinct part of a community or group of people. **b** a group having a distinct status or pursuing a special interest within an organization such as a political party. **3** the action or an instance of cutting or separating by cutting; *esp* the action of dividing tissues, etc surgically. **4a** a part removed or separated by or as if by cutting. **b** a very thin slice, e.g. of tissue, suitable for examination under a microscope. **5a** a shape or area as it would appear if a solid form were cut through by one plane. **b** the plane figure resulting from the cutting through of a solid form by one plane.

section[2] *v* **1** to cut or separate into sections. **2** to represent in sections, e.g. by a drawing. **3** to cut (a specimen, etc) so as to show a section of it. **4** *Brit* to confine to a psychiatric institution in accordance with a section of a mental health act. ➤➤ **sectional** *adj.*

sectionalism *n* an excessive concern for the interests of a region or group. ➤➤ **sectionalist** *adj and n.*

sector *n* **1a** a part of a field of activity, *esp* of business, trade, etc. **b** a portion of a military area of operation. **2** a part of a circle consisting of two radii and the portion of the circumference between them. **3** in computing, a section of a storage device such as a floppy disk that forms the smallest unit of storage. **4** a mathematical measuring device with two graduated arms hinged at one end. ➤➤ **sectoral** *adj.*

secular[1] *adj* **1a** of this world rather than the heavenly or spiritual. **b** not overtly or specifically religious or concerned with religion. **2** of clergy not belonging to a particular religious order. **3a** taking place once in an age or a century. **b** surviving or recurring through ages or centuries. **c** occurring very slowly over a long period of time. ➤➤ **secularity** *n,* **secularly** *adv.*

secular[2] *n* a member of the secular clergy.

secularise *v* see SECULARIZE.

secularism *n* disregard for or rejection or exclusion of religious beliefs and practices, e.g. in ethics, politics, or education. ➤➤ **secularist** *n.*

secularize *or* **-ise** *v* **1** to convert (somebody or something) to secularism. **2** to change (something) from a religious to a secular function or form. **3** to transfer (property, etc) from ecclesiastical to civil use. **4** to release from monastic vows.

secure[1] *adj* **1a** free from danger. **b** free from risk of loss. **c** affording safety. **d** firm; dependable. **e** firmly fixed or fastened. **f** free from risk of escape. **2a** calm in mind. **b** confident in opinion or hope. **3** assured or certain. ➤➤ **securely** *adv,* **secureness** *n.*

secure[2] *v* **1** to fix or fasten firmly; to shut tightly. **2** to make (something or somebody) safe from risk or danger; to protect (somebody or something) against intrusion or disturbance. **3** to guarantee (something) against loss or denial. **4a** to guarantee payment to (a creditor). **b** to guarantee payment of (a debt). **5** to obtain (something), *esp* as the result of effort. ➤➤ **securable** *adj,* **securement** *n.*

securitize *or* **-ise** *v* to make (a debt, e.g. a mortgage, or an asset, e.g. land) marketable in the form of securities. ➤➤ **securitization** *n.*

security *n* (*pl* **-ies**) **1a** freedom from danger, fear, anxiety, destitution, etc. **b** stability or dependability. **2** protection. **3** something pledged to guarantee the fulfilment of an obligation. **4** an evidence of debt or of ownership, e.g. a stock certificate.

security blanket *n* **1** a blanket or anything similar to which a young child becomes attached as a source of comfort and security. **2** *Brit* a withholding or suppression of information by those in authority for the sake of security.

sedan *n* **1** *NAm, Aus, NZ* = SALOON (3). **2** = SEDAN CHAIR.

sedan chair *n* a portable enclosed chair, *esp* of the 17th and 18th cents, designed to seat one person and be carried on poles by two people.

sedate[1] *adj* calm and even in temper or pace. ➤➤ **sedately** *adv,* **sedateness** *n.*

sedate[2] *v* to give a sedative to (a person or animal).

sedation *n* **1** the induction, *esp* with a sedative, of a relaxed easy state. **2** the condition of being in such a state.

sedative[1] *adj* tending to calm or to tranquillize nervousness or excitement.

sedative[2] *n* a sedative drug.

sedentary *adj* **1** doing or involving much sitting. **2** *esp* of birds: not migratory. **3** of animals: permanently attached to a surface, e.g. a rock.

sedge *n* a marsh plant differing from grasses *esp* in having a solid stem, usu triangular in cross-section.

sedge warbler *n* a small European songbird that breeds in marshy places and has streaked brown upper parts, a reddish brown rump, and a pale stripe above the eye.

sediment *n* **1** the matter that settles to the bottom of a liquid. **2** material deposited by water, wind, or glaciers.

sedimentary *adj* **1** of or containing sediment. **2** of rock: formed by or from deposits of sediment.

sedimentation *n* the forming or depositing of sediment.

sedition *n* incitement to defy or rise up against the government. ➤➤ **seditious** *adj,* **seditiously** *adv.*

seduce *v* **1** to persuade (somebody) to have sexual intercourse. **2** to lead astray, *esp* by false promises. **3** to incite to disobedience or disloyalty. ➤➤ **seducer** *n,* **seducible** *adj,* **seduction** *n.*

seductive *adj* tending to seduce; alluring; attractive. ➤➤ **seductively** *adv,* **seductiveness** *n.*

seductress *n* a female seducer.

sedulous *adj formal* **1** involving or accomplished with steady perseverance. **2** diligent in application or pursuit. ➤➤ **sedulity** *n,* **sedulously** *adv,* **sedulousness** *n.*

sedum *n* a fleshy-leaved plant of a widely distributed group that includes the stonecrops.

see[1] *v* (*past tense* **saw**, *past part.* **seen**) **1** to perceive with the eyes. **2** to watch or look at. **3** to experience or be aware of. **4** to perceive or deduce using reasoning or information: *I see you were right.* **5** to imagine or envisage: *I can't see them agreeing.* **6** to determine or decide: *I'll see if I can come.* **7** to make sure of: *See that you finish it.* **8** to give an audience to. **9a** to call on or visit. **b** to consult professionally: *He needs to see a doctor.* **10** to keep company with. **11** to escort (somebody) to a specified place: *I'll see you to the door.* ✱ **see about** to deal with or consider (a matter). **see one's way to** to feel able to undertake. **see somebody right** *informal* to look after or reward (somebody). **see the back of** to be rid of (somebody or something). **see through 1** to undergo or endure to the end: *We'll just have to see it through.* **2** to realize the true nature of (a deception). **see to** to attend to (something) or take care of (somebody).

see[2] *n* a bishopric.

seed[1] *n* (*pl* **seeds** *or* **seed**) **1** the grains or ripened fertilized ovules of plants used for sowing. **2** the fertilized ripened ovule of a flowering plant or conifer that contains an embryo and is capable of germination to produce a new plant. **3** a source of development or growth. **4** a competitor who has been seeded in a tournament. **5** something, e.g. a tiny particle, that resembles a seed in shape or size. **6** *archaic or literary* **a** semen. **b** offspring; progeny. ✱ **go/run to seed 1** of a plant: to develop seed. **2a** to decay. **b** to become unattractive by being shabby or careless about appearance. ➤➤ **seedless** *adj.*

seed[2] *v* **1** of a plant: to produce or shed seeds. **2a** to plant seeds in (a field, plot, etc). **b** to sow (seeds).

3 to extract the seeds from (raisins, etc). **4a** to schedule (tournament players or teams) so that superior ones will not meet in early rounds. **b** to rank (a contestant) relative to others on the basis of previous record. **5** to treat (a solution, etc) with solid particles to stimulate crystallization, condensation, etc.

seedbed *n* a bed of fine soil prepared for planting seed and growing young plants.

seedcake *n* a sweet cake containing aromatic seeds, e.g. caraway seeds.

seed capital *n* money required to set up an enterprise, fund preliminary research, etc.

seed corn *n* **1** corn of good quality that is used for sowing. **2** *Brit* an invaluable resource for future development.

seeder *n* an implement for sowing or planting seeds.

seed leaf *n* = COTYLEDON.

seedling *n* a plant grown from seed rather than from a cutting.

seed money *n* = SEED CAPITAL.

seed pearl *n* a very small often imperfect pearl.

seedsman *n* (*pl* **seedsmen**) a person who sows or deals in seeds.

seedy *adj* (**-ier, -iest**) **1** shabby or grubby. **2** somewhat disreputable; run-down. ➤➤ **seedily** *adv,* **seediness** *n.*

see in *v* to celebrate the beginning of (the New Year).

seeing *conj* (*often* + that) in view of the fact; since.

seek *v* (*past tense and past part.* **sought**) **1a** (*often* + out) to go in search of (something or somebody). **b** to try to discover: *They are seeking a solution to the problem.* **2** to ask for (advice, etc). **3** to try to acquire or gain: *He set out to seek fame and fortune.* **4** to make an effort (to do something): *We seek to cater for every taste.* ➤➤ **seeker** *n.*

seem *v* to give the impression, whether true or false, of being or doing something: *It seemed a long wait; You seem to be undecided; The noise seemed to come from the cupboard.* ✱ **not seem** used for 'seem not': *He doesn't seem to understand.* **would seem** used ironically for 'seem': *It would seem to be raining.*

seeming *adj* apparent rather than real.

seemingly *adv* **1** so far as can be seen or judged. **2** to outward appearance only.

seemly *adj* (**-ier, -iest**) in accord with good taste or propriety. ➤➤ **seemliness** *n.*

seen *v* past part. of SEE[1].

see off *v* **1** to be present at the departure of (somebody). **2** *informal* to chase away.

see out *v* **1** to escort (somebody) to the outside of a room or building. **2** to last until the end of (a period of time).

see over *v* to go round (a place) to view or inspect it.

seep *v* to pass slowly through fine pores or small openings. ➤➤ **seepage** *n.*

seer *n* a person who predicts future events.

seersucker *n* a light, slightly puckered fabric of linen, cotton, or rayon.

seesaw[1] *n* **1** a plank balanced in the middle so that one end goes up as the other goes down, or any similar device. **2a** an alternating up-and-down or backward-and-forward movement. **b** anything, e.g. a process or movement, that alternates.

seesaw[2] *v* **1** to move backward and forward or up and down. **2a** to alternate. **b** to vacillate.

seethe *v* **1a** to be in a state of agitated confused movement. **b** to churn or foam as if boiling. **2** to feel or express violent emotion.

seething *adj* **1** intensely hot. **2** constantly moving or active. **3** very angry.

see-through *adj esp* of clothing: transparent or almost so.

segment[1] *n* **1a** a separate piece of something. **b** any of the constituent parts into which a body, entity, or quantity is divided or marked off. **2** in mathematics, a portion cut off from a geometrical figure by one or more points, lines, or planes, e.g.: **a** a part of a circular area bounded by a chord of that circle and the arc subtended by it. **b** a part of a sphere cut off by a plane or included between two parallel planes. **c** the part of a line between two points in the line. ➤➤ **segmental** *adj,* **segmentary** *adj.*

segment[2] *v* to separate or divide (something) into segments.

segmentation *n* **1** the act or process of segmenting. **2** the formation of many cells from a single cell, e.g. in a developing egg. **3** the condition of having a body or body part made up of a series of similarly structured segments, or the form this takes.

segregate *v* **1** to separate (somebody or something) from others; to set apart. **2a** to cause or force separation of (a racial group, etc) from the rest of a community. **b** to cause or force separation, *esp* of racial groups, within (a community, etc).

segregated *adj* **1** set apart from others of the same kind. **2** administered separately for different groups or races.

segregation *n* **1** the separation or isolation of a race, class, or ethnic group. **2** the separation for special treatment or observation of individuals or items from a larger group. ➤➤ **segregational** *adj,* **segregationist** *n and adj.*

segue[1] /'segway, 'saygway/ *v* (**segues, segued, segueing**) to proceed without pause from one musical number or theme to another.

segue[2] *n* a request to join one musical number or theme to another without a break.

seicento /say'chentoh/ *n* the 17th cent. in Italy, *esp* with reference to its literature and art.

seigneur /say'nyuh/ *or* **seignior** /'saynjə/ *n* a feudal lord. ➤➤ **seigneurial** *adj,* **seigniorial** *adj.*

seine[1] *n* a large net with weights on one edge and floats on the other that hangs vertically in the water and is used to enclose fish when its ends are pulled together or drawn ashore.

seine[2] *v* **1** to fish with a seine. **2** to catch (fish) with a seine. ➤➤ **seiner** *n.*

seismic *adj* of or caused by an earth vibration, *esp* an earthquake. ➤➤ **seismical** *adj,* **seismically** *adv,* **seismicity** *n.*

seismogram *n* a record made by a seismograph.

seismograph *n* an apparatus to measure and record earth tremors. ➤➤ **seismographic** *adj.*

seismology *n* the science that deals with earth vibrations, *esp* earthquakes. ➤➤ **seismological** *adj,* **seismologist** *n.*

seismometer *n* a seismograph.

seize *v* **1** to take hold of (somebody or something) abruptly or eagerly. **2** to take possession of (something or somebody) by force. **3** to confiscate, *esp* by legal authority. **4** (+ on/upon) to lay hold of something suddenly, forcibly, or eagerly. **5a** (*often* + up) of brakes, pistons, etc: to become jammed through excessive pressure, temperature, or friction. **b** (*often* + up) of an engine: to fail to operate owing to the seizing of a part. ➤➤ **seizable** *adj.*

seizure *n* **1** the taking possession of somebody or something by legal process. **2** a sudden attack, e.g. of disease.

seldom *adv* in few instances; rarely or infrequently.

select[1] *adj* **1** picked out in preference to others. **2a** of special value or quality. **b** exclusively or fastidiously chosen, *esp* on the basis of social characteristics. ➤➤ **selectness** *n.*

select[2] *v* to take according to preference from among a number; to pick out or choose.

select committee *n* a temporary committee of a legislative body, established to examine one particular matter.

selection *n* **1** the act or an instance of selecting. **2a** somebody or something selected. **b** a collection of selected items. **3** a range of things from which to choose. **4** a process that results in the survival and propagation only of organisms with desired or suitable attributes so that their heritable characteristics only are perpetuated in succeeding generations.

selective *adj* **1** of or characterized by selection. **2** selecting or tending to select. ➤➤ **selectively** *adv,* **selectiveness** *n,* **selectivity** *n.*

selector *n Brit* a person who chooses the members of a sports team.

selenite *n* calcium sulphate occurring in transparent crystals or crystalline masses.

selenium *n* a grey non-metallic chemical element chemically resembling sulphur and tellurium that occurs naturally in various sulphide ores, and is used in electronic devices such as solar cells.

self[1] *n* (*pl* **selves**) **1** the entire being of an individual. **2** a person's individual character, or one part or aspect of it. **3** the body, emotions, thoughts, sensations, etc that constitute the individuality and identity of a person.

self[2] *pron* myself; himself; herself.

self[3] *adj* identical throughout, e.g. in colour or material.

self- *comb. form* **1a** oneself; itself: *self-supporting.* **b** of oneself or itself: *self-abuse.* **c** by oneself or itself: *self-propelled; self-starter.* **2a** to, with, for, or in oneself or itself: *self-confident; self-addressed.* **b** of or in oneself or itself inherently: *self-evident; self-explanatory.*

self-abandonment *n* **1** a surrender of selfish interests or desires. **2** a lack of self-restraint.

self-absorbed *adj* preoccupied with one's own thoughts, activities, or welfare. ➤➤ **self-absorption** *n.*

self-abuse *n* **1** the act of blaming or censuring oneself. **2** misuse of one's talents and abilities. **3** *euphem* masturbation.

self-addressed *adj* addressed for return to the sender.

self-adjusting *adj* adjusting automatically by itself.

self-appointed *adj* assuming a position of authority not ratified by others.

self-assembly *n* the putting together of furniture, etc by oneself from a set of components bought in a shop.

self-assertion *n* the act or an instance of firmly asserting oneself or one's own rights, claims, or opinions. ➤➤ **self-assertive** *adj.*

self-assurance *n* = SELF-CONFIDENCE. ➤➤ **self-assured** *adj.*

self-catering *adj* provided with lodging and kitchen facilities but not meals.

self-centred *adj* concerned excessively with one's own desires or needs. ➤➤ **self-centredly** *adv,* **self-centredness** *n.*

self-certification *n* in Britain, the system by which an employee who has been absent from work for no more than six days because of illness or incapacitation can fill in a form stating the reason for their absence rather than having to produce a certificate signed by a doctor.

self-coloured *adj* **1** of a single colour. **2** in its natural colour; not dyed.

self-confessed *adj* openly acknowledged.

self-confidence *n* confidence in oneself and one's powers and abilities. ➤➤ **self-confident** *adj,* **self-confidently** *adv.*

self-congratulation *n* a complacent acknowledgment of one's own superiority or good fortune. ➤➤ **self-congratulatory** *adj.*

self-conscious *adj* **1** uncomfortably conscious of oneself as an object of notice; ill at ease. **2a** conscious of oneself as a possessor of mental states and originator of actions. **b** intensely aware of oneself. ➤➤ **self-consciously** *adv,* **self-consciousness** *n.*

self-consistent *adj* having each element logically consistent with the rest; internally consistent. ➤➤ **self-consistency** *n.*

self-contained *adj* **1** complete in itself. **2** of accommodation: including within itself a kitchen, bathroom, etc, and usu a separate front door; not sharing facilities.

self-contradiction *n* a statement that contains two contradictory elements or ideas.

self-control *n* restraint of one's own impulses or emotions. ➤➤ **self-controlled** *adj.*

self-deception *n* the act of deceiving oneself, or the state of being deceived by oneself, e.g. about one's character or motives.

self-defeating *adj* of a plan or action: having the effect of preventing its own success.

self-defence *n* **1** the act of defending or justifying oneself. **2** the legal right to defend oneself with reasonable force. ➤➤ **self-defensive** *adj.*

self-denial *n* the restraint or limitation of one's desires or their gratification. ➤➤ **self-denying** *adj.*

self-deprecating *adj* given to self-depreciation. ➤➤ **self-deprecation** *n.*

self-depreciation *n* disparagement or understatement of oneself. ➤➤ **self-depreciating** *adj,* **self-depreciatory** *adj.*

self-destruct *v* to destroy oneself or itself. ➤➤ **self-destruction** *n,* **self-destructive** *adj.*

self-determination *n* **1** free choice of one's own actions or states without outside influence. **2** determination by the people of a place of its own political status; the right to choose one's own government, etc.

self-discipline *n* the power to discipline one's thoughts and actions, usu for the sake of improvement. ➤➤ **self-disciplined** *adj.*

self-doubt *n* a lack of confidence in oneself; diffidence.

self-drive *adj chiefly Brit* of a hired vehicle: intended to be driven by the hirer.

self-educated *adj* having taught oneself rather than having followed a course of education in school, college, etc or with a tutor.

self-effacement *n* the act of making oneself inconspicuous, *esp* because of modesty; humility. ➤➤ **self-effacing** *adj.*

self-employed *adj* earning income directly from one's own business, trade, or profession rather than as salary or wages from an employer. ⋙ **self-employment** *n.*

self-esteem *n* confidence and satisfaction in oneself; self-respect.

self-evident *adj* requiring no proof; obvious.

self-examination *n* **1** the analysis of one's conduct, motives, etc. **2** the examination of one's body in order to detect early signs of disease.

self-explanatory *adj* capable of being understood without explanation.

self-expression *n* the expression of one's individual characteristics, e.g. through painting or poetry.

self-fertilization *or* **self-fertilisation** *n* fertilization by the union of ova with pollen or sperm from the same individual.

self-fulfilling *adj* coming true, or likely to do so, because the fact that it has been asserted or assumed causes actions or behaviour that are bound to make it come true.

self-governed *adj* not influenced or controlled by others; *specif* having control of one's own political affairs. ⋙ **self-governing** *adj,* **self-government** *n.*

self-heal *n* a small violet-flowered plant of the mint family held to possess healing properties.

self-help *n* the bettering or helping of oneself without dependence on others.

selfhood *n* the state of existing as a unique individual.

self-image *n* one's conception of oneself or of one's role.

self-importance *n* an exaggerated sense of one's own importance. ⋙ **self-important** *adj.*

self-induced *adj* induced by oneself or itself.

self-indulgence *n* excessive or unrestrained gratification of one's own appetites, desires, or whims. ⋙ **self-indulgent** *adj.*

self-interest *n* a concern for one's own advantage and well-being. ⋙ **self-interested** *adj.*

selfish *adj* concerned with or directed towards one's own advantage, pleasure, or well-being without regard for others. ⋙ **selfishly** *adv,* **selfishness** *n.*

selfless *adj* having no concern for self; unselfish. ⋙ **selflessly** *adv,* **selflessness** *n.*

self-love *n* an *esp* selfish concern for one's own happiness or advantage.

self-made *adj* **1** having risen from poverty or obscurity by one's own efforts. **2** made by oneself.

self-motivated *adj* driven by one's own internal impetus; self-starting. ⋙ **self-motivation** *n.*

self-opinionated *adj* **1** conceited. **2** stubbornly holding to one's own opinion; opinionated.

self-perpetuating *adj* continuing or renewing oneself or itself indefinitely.

self-pity *n* a self-indulgent dwelling on one's own sorrows or misfortunes. ⋙ **self-pitying** *adj.*

self-pollination *n* the transfer of pollen from the anther of a flower to the stigma of the same or a genetically identical flower.

self-portrait *n* a portrait of an artist done by himself or herself.

self-possessed *adj* having or showing self-possession; composed in mind or manner; calm. ⋙ **self-possession** *n.*

self-preservation *n* an instinctive tendency to act so as to safeguard one's own existence.

self-proclaimed *adj* = SELF-STYLED.

self-propelled *adj* propelled by one's or its own power; *specif* containing within itself the means for its own propulsion. ⋙ **self-propelling** *adj.*

self-raising flour (*NAm* **self-rising flour**) *n* a commercially prepared mixture of flour containing a raising agent.

self-realization *or* **self-realisation** *n* fulfilment by oneself of the possibilities inherent in one's nature.

self-regard *n* **1** concern or consideration for oneself or one's own interests. **2** = SELF-RESPECT. ⋙ **self-regarding** *adj.*

self-regulating *adj* **1** regulating itself, *esp* automatically. **2** regulating its own activities without interference from outside bodies or the law. ⋙ **self-regulation** *n,* **self-regulatory** *adj.*

self-reliance *n* reliance on one's own efforts and abilities; independence. ⋙ **self-reliant** *adj.*

self-respect *n* a proper respect for one's human dignity. ⋙ **self-respecting** *adj.*

self-restraint *n* restraint imposed on oneself, *esp* on the expression of one's feelings.

self-righteous *adj* sure of one's own righteousness, *esp* in contrast with the actions and beliefs of others; narrow-mindedly moralistic. ⋙ **self-righteously** *adv,* **self-righteousness** *n.*

self-righting *adj* of a boat: capable of righting itself when capsized.

self-rising flour *n NAm* see SELF-RAISING FLOUR.

self-rule *n* control of one's own political affairs.

self-sacrifice *n* sacrifice of oneself or one's well-being for the sake of an ideal or for the benefit of others. ⋙ **self-sacrificing** *adj.*

selfsame *adj* precisely the same; identical: *He left the selfsame day.*

self-satisfaction *n* a smug satisfaction with oneself or one's position or achievements. ⋙ **self-satisfied** *adj.*

self-seeded *adj* of a plant: self-sowing.

self-seeking *adj* seeking only to safeguard or further one's own interests; selfish. ⋙ **self-seeker** *n.*

self-service *adj* of a shop, cafeteria, etc: where customers serve themselves.

self-serving *adj* serving one's own interests, *esp* at the expense of honesty or the welfare of others.

self-sow *v* (*past tense* **self-sowed,** *past part.* **self-sown** *or* **self-sowed**) of a plant: to grow from seeds spread naturally, e.g. by wind or water.

self-starter *n* a person with initiative, *esp* one who is able to work without supervision.

self-styled *adj* called by oneself, *esp* without justification: *a self-styled fashion expert.*

self-sufficient *adj* **1** able to maintain oneself or itself without outside aid; capable of providing for one's own needs. **2** having unwarranted assurance of one's own ability or worth. ⋙ **self-sufficiency** *n.*

self-supporting *adj* **1** meeting one's needs by one's own labour or income. **2** of a wall: supporting itself or its own weight.

self-sustaining *adj* **1** maintaining or able to maintain oneself by independent effort. **2** maintaining or able to maintain itself once started. ⋙ **self-sustained** *adj.*

self-tapping screw *n* a screw made of hard metal which cuts its own thread when driven in.

self-taught *adj* having knowledge or skills acquired by one's own efforts.

self-timer *n* a device on a camera that delays the operation of the shutter, so allowing the photographer to move to a position where they can be included in the photograph.

self-willed *adj* stubbornly or wilfully adhering to one's own desires or ideas; obstinate.

self-worth *n* = SELF-ESTEEM.

sell *v* (*past tense and past part.* **sold**) **1a** to give (goods or property) in exchange for money. **b** to deal in (a commodity or service). **c** to cause or promote the sale of. **d** to achieve a sale of (a certain number). **2** to give up (something worthwhile) dishonourably: *You sold the firm's good name for the sake of quick profits.* **3a** to persuade somebody about (an idea, etc). **b** *informal* (+ on) to persuade (somebody) to accept or enjoy something: *The purpose of the project is to sell children on reading.* **4** to be sold or achieve sales. **5** (+ at/for) to have a specified price. ✱ **sell short** to belittle or disparage. ➤➤ **sellable** *adj.*

sell-by date *n* **1** a date after which a perishable food product must not be offered for sale. **2** *informal* the time beyond which somebody or something begins to deteriorate or decline.

seller *n* **1** a person who sells something. **2** a product offered for sale and selling in a specified manner.

seller's market *n* a market in which demand exceeds supply: compare BUYER'S MARKET.

selling point *n* a particularly good or notable aspect or detail of something that is emphasized, e.g. in selling or promoting it.

sell off *v* to dispose of (something) completely by selling it until all stock is gone, *esp* at a reduced price. ➤➤ **sell-off** *n.*

Sellotape *n trademark* adhesive tape.

sellotape *v* to fix with Sellotape or any similar tape.

sell out *v* **1** to dispose of (something) entirely by sale. **2** to betray or be unfaithful to (e.g. one's cause or associates), *esp* for profit. **3** = SELL UP.

sell-out *n* **1** an event for which all tickets or seats are sold. **2** *informal* a betrayal.

sell up *v chiefly Brit* to sell a business or property completely.

selvage *or* **selvedge** *n* the edge on either side of a woven fabric, so finished as to prevent unravelling.

selves *n* pl of SELF[1].

semantic *adj* **1** of semantics. **2** of meaning in language. ➤➤ **semantically** *adv.*

semantics *pl n* **1** (*used as sing. or pl*) the branch of linguistics concerned with meaning. **2** (*used as sing.*) the meaning of a sentence, word, etc, or the interpretation of it. ➤➤ **semanticist** *n.*

semaphore[1] *n* **1** an apparatus for conveying information by visual signals, e.g. by the position of one or more pivoted arms. **2** a system of visual signalling by two flags held one in each hand.

semaphore[2] *v* to convey (information) by semaphore.

semblance *n* outward and often deceptive appearance; a show.

semen *n* a suspension of spermatozoa (male reproductive cells: see SPERMATOZOON) in the secretions of various glands, produced by the male reproductive glands and conveyed to the female reproductive tract during coitus.

semester *n* an academic term lasting half a year, *esp* in N America and Germany.

semi *n* (*pl* **semis**) *informal* **1** *Brit* a semidetached house. **2** a semifinal.

semi- *prefix* **1** half: *semicircle.* **2** to some extent or partly: *semiconscious; semidarkness.* **3** having some of the characteristics of: *semimetal.*

semiautomatic *adj* **1** operated partly automatically and partly by hand. **2** of a firearm: using gas pressure or force of recoil and mechanical spring action to eject the empty cartridge case after each first shot and to load the next cartridge from the magazine, but requiring release and another press of the trigger for each successive shot.

semibreve *n* a musical note with the time value of two minims or four crotchets.

semicircle *n* a half circle, or an object or arrangement in the form of a half circle. ➤➤ **semicircular** *adj.*

semicircular canal *n* any of the three loop-shaped tubular parts of the inner ear that together constitute a sensory organ associated with the maintenance of bodily equilibrium.

semicolon *n* a punctuation mark (;) used chiefly to mark a break or pause between sentence elements, such as clauses, that is greater than the break or pause indicated by a comma and less than that indicated by a full stop.

semiconductor *n* a substance, e.g. silicon or germanium, whose electrical conductivity at room temperature is between that of a conductor and that of an insulator, and whose conductivity increases with a rise in temperature or the presence of certain impurities. ➤➤ **semiconducting** *adj.*

semiconscious *adj* not fully aware or responsive.

semidarkness *n* partial darkness; shade.

semidetached *adj* forming one of a pair of residences joined by a common wall.

semifinal *n* a match or round that is next to the last in a knockout competition. ➤➤ **semifinalist** *n.*

semifluid[1] *adj* having qualities intermediate between those of a liquid and a solid; viscous.

semifluid[2] *n* a semifluid substance.

semiliquid[1] *adj* = SEMIFLUID[1].

semiliquid[2] *n* = SEMIFLUID[2].

Sémillon /saymi'yonh/ *n* a variety of grape used in the production of white wine, e.g. Sauternes, or a wine produced from it.

semilunar *adj* crescent-shaped.

semimetal *n* an element such as arsenic that has some metallic properties.

seminal *adj* **1a** original and influential. **b** containing or contributing the seeds of future development. **c** in a rudimentary, uncompleted form. **2** of, storing, or conveying seed or semen. ➤➤ **seminally** *adv.*

seminar *n* **1** a group of students studying with a university or college teacher, or a meeting of such a group. **2** a meeting for exchanging and discussing information.

seminary *n* (*pl* **-ies**) an institution for the training of the clergy, *esp* Roman Catholic priests and rabbis. ➤➤ **seminarian** *n,* **seminarist** *n.*

Seminole /'seminohl/ *n* (*pl* **Seminole** *or* **Seminoles**) a member of a Native American people of Florida.

semiology *n* the study of signs, *esp* semiotics. ➤➤ **semiological** *adj,* **semiologist** *n.*

semiotics *pl n* (*used as sing. or pl*) the study and general theory of signs and symbols in artificial and natural languages with regard to their relationship to the things they represent, to each other, and to their use. ➤➤ **semiotic** *adj,* **semiotician** *n.*

semipermeable *adj esp* of a membrane: permeable to small molecules but not to larger ones.

semiprecious *adj* of a gemstone: of less commercial value than a precious stone.

semiquaver *n* a musical note with the time value of half a quaver or a quarter of a crotchet.

semiskilled *adj* of, being, or requiring workers who have less training than skilled workers and more than unskilled workers.

semiskimmed *adj* of milk: with some of its cream removed.

semisolid *adj* having the qualities of both a solid and a liquid; highly viscous.

Semite *n* a member of any of a group of peoples of SW Asia chiefly represented now by the Jews and Arabs.

Semitic[1] *adj* **1** of the Semites, *esp* the Arabs and Jews; *specif* Jewish. **2** of a branch of the language family that includes Hebrew, Aramaic, Arabic, and Amharic.

Semitic[2] *n* the Semitic languages.

semitone *n* the smallest interval between two notes in European classical music; half a tone.

semolina *n* the purified hard parts left after milling of wheat, used to make pasta and in milk puddings.

sempiternal *adj chiefly literary* everlasting; eternal. ➤➤ **sempiternally** *adv.*

sempre /'sempri, 'sempray/ *adv* in music, always.

sempstress *n* = SEAMSTRESS.

Semtex *n trademark* a plastic explosive.

sen *n* (*pl* **sen**) **1** a former unit of currency in Japan, worth 100th of a yen. **2** a unit of currency in Cambodia, worth 100th of a new riel. **3** a unit of currency in Indonesia, worth 100th of a rupiah. **4** a unit of currency in Malaysia, worth 100th of a ringgit. **5** a unit of currency in Brunei, worth 100th of a dollar.

senate *n* (*used as sing. or pl*) **1a** the upper chamber in some legislatures that consist of two houses. **b** the supreme council of the ancient Roman republic and empire. **2** the governing body of some universities.

senator *n* a member of a senate. ➤➤ **senatorial** *adj,* **senatorship** *n.*

send *v* (*past tense and past part.* **sent**) **1** to cause or direct (somebody or something) to go to a place. **2** to cause to go or move quickly or violently: *The blow sent him half across the room.* **3** to cause (a message or communication) to be delivered or transmitted. **4** (*often* + out) to emit or discharge: *The kitchen sent out delicious aromas.* **5** to cause (somebody) to be in a specified state: *The remark sent him into a rage.* **6** *informal* to delight or move. **7** (*usu* + for) to summon or order somebody or something: *We had better send for a doctor.* ✱ **send packing** to dismiss (somebody) roughly or in disgrace. ➤➤ **sender** *n.*

send down *v* **1** *Brit* to suspend or expel (a student) from a university. **2** *informal* to send (a convicted person) to prison.

send off *v* of a referee: to order (a player) to leave the playing field because of a misdemeanour.

send-off *n* an enthusiastic demonstration of goodwill at the beginning of a trip, etc.

send up *v chiefly Brit* to mock or ridicule (somebody or something).

send-up *n informal* a satirical imitation, *esp* on stage or television.

sene /'saynay/ *n* a unit of currency in Western Samoa, worth 100th of a tala.

Seneca /'senikə/ *n* (*pl* **Seneca** *or* **Senecas**) a member of a Native American people of W New York.

Senegalese *n* (*pl* **Senegalese**) a native or inhabitant of Senegal. ➤➤ **Senegalese** *adj.*

senescence *n* the condition or process of being or becoming old or withered. ➤➤ **senescent** *adj.*

seneschal *n* formerly, the agent or bailiff of a feudal lord's estate.

senile *adj* of, exhibiting, or characteristic of old age, or the mental or physical weakness associated with it. ➤➤ **senility** *n.*

senile dementia *n* progressive deterioration of mental faculties occurring in old age.

senior[1] *adj* **1** higher in standing or rank. **2a** older. **b** relating to old age and older people. **3a** *Brit* relating to students in the upper years of secondary school. **b** *NAm* relating to students in the final year preceding graduation from secondary or higher education. **4** used to distinguish a father with the same name as his son; elder. ➤➤ **seniority** *n.*

senior[2] *n* **1** a person who is older than another specified person. **2** in sporting competitions, etc, an adult as opposed to a junior, or a more advanced player as opposed to a less advanced one. **3** an elderly person. **4a** *Brit* a student in the upper years of secondary school. **b** *NAm* a student in the final year preceding graduation from secondary or higher education. **c** a person of higher standing or rank.

senior aircraftman *or* **senior aircraftwoman** *n* a rank of the Royal Air Force below junior technician, approximately equivalent to the rank of private in the army.

senior citizen *n* an elderly person, *esp* an old age pensioner.

senior common room *n* a common room for teachers, lecturers, etc.

senior nursing officer *n Brit* a person who is in charge of the nursing staff in a hospital.

senior registrar *n Brit* a doctor holding the grade of hospital doctor senior to registrar.

Senior Service *n* (**the Senior Service**) *Brit* the Royal Navy.

seniti /'seniti/ *n* (*pl* **seniti**) a unit of currency in Tonga, worth 100th of a pa'anga.

senna *n* **1** a leguminous plant, shrub, or tree of warm regions. **2** the dried leaflets or pods of certain of these plants, used as a laxative.

senor *or* **señor** /se'nyaw/ *n* (*pl* **senors** *or* **señores**) in Spanish-speaking countries, a title equivalent to *Mr,* also used as a generalized term of direct address to a man.

senora *or* **señora** /se'nyawrə/ *n* in Spanish-speaking countries, a title equivalent to *Mrs,* also used as a generalized term of direct address to a married woman.

señores *n* pl of SENOR.

senorita *or* **señorita** /senyə'reetə/ *n* in Spanish-speaking countries, a title equivalent to *Miss,* also used as a generalized term of direct address to a girl or an unmarried woman.

sensate *adj* **1** endowed with bodily senses. **2** relating to or apprehended through the senses.

sensation *n* **1a** a mental process, e.g. seeing or hearing, resulting from stimulation of a sense organ. **b** a state of awareness of a specified type resulting from internal bodily conditions or external factors; a feeling or sense. **2a** a surge of intense interest or excitement. **b** a cause of such excitement, *esp* somebody or something that is in some respect remarkable or outstanding.

sensational *adj* **1** arousing an immediate, intense, and usu superficial interest or emotional reaction. **2** *informal* exceptionally excellent or impressive. ➤➤ **sensationally** *adv.*

sensationalise *v* see SENSATIONALIZE.

sensationalism *n* the use of sensational subject matter or style, or the sensational material itself. ➤➤ **sensationalist** *n and adj,* **sensationalistic** *adj.*

sensationalize *or* **-ise** *v* to report (a story, etc) in sensationalist terms.

sense[1] *n* **1** a meaning conveyed or intended, *esp* any of a range of meanings a word or phrase may bear. **2a** the faculty of perceiving the external world or internal bodily conditions by means of feeling, hearing, sight, smell, taste, etc. **b** any of these individual faculties of perception. **3a** an ability to use the senses for a specified purpose: *a good sense of balance.* **b** a definite but often vague awareness or impression: *a sense of insecurity.* **c** an awareness that motivates action or judgment: *It was done out of a sense of justice.* **d** a capacity for discernment and appreciation: *a sense of humour.* **4** (*usu in pl, used as sing.*) soundness of mind or judgment. **5** an ability to put the mind to effective use; practical intelligence. **6** point or reason. ✱ **make sense 1** to be understandable. **2** to seem reasonable.

sense[2] *v* **1a** to perceive (something) by the senses. **b** to be or become conscious of. **2** to grasp or comprehend. **3** to detect (a symbol, radiation, etc) automatically.

senseless *adj* **1** unconscious. **2** foolish or stupid. **3** meaningless; purposeless. ⋙ **senselessly** *adv,* **senselessness** *n.*

sense organ *n* a bodily structure that responds to a stimulus, e.g. heat or sound waves, by initiating impulses in nerves that convey them to the central nervous system where they are interpreted as sensations.

sensibility *n* (*pl* **-ies**) (*usu in pl*) **1** refined or exaggerated sensitiveness in feelings and tastes. **2** feelings, *esp* moral feelings or scruples. **3** the ability to discern and respond freely to something, e.g. emotion in another person.

sensible *adj* **1a** having, containing, or indicative of good sense or sound reason. **b** plain and practical: *sensible shoes.* **2** (+ of/to) capable of sensing something: *sensible to pain.* **3** (+ of) aware or conscious of something. ⋙ **sensibleness** *n,* **sensibly** *adv.*

sensitise *v* see SENSITIZE.

sensitive *adj* **1** (+ to) capable of being stimulated or excited by external agents such as light, gravity, or contact. **2** (*often* + to) **a** easily provoked or hurt emotionally. **b** finely aware of the attitudes and feelings of others or of the subtleties of a work of art. **c** abnormally sensitive; allergic. **d** capable of registering minute differences; delicate. **3a** needing careful or tactful handling; tricky. **b** concerned with highly classified information. ⋙ **sensitively** *adv,* **sensitiveness** *n,* **sensitivity** *n.*

sensitive plant *n* a mimosa with leaves that fold or droop when touched.

sensitize *or* **-ise** *v* to make (somebody or something) sensitive or abnormally sensitive. ⋙ **sensitization** *n,* **sensitizer** *n.*

sensor *n* a device that responds to heat, light, sound, pressure, magnetism, etc and transmits a resulting impulse, e.g. for measurement or operating a control.

sensory *adj* of sensation or the senses. ⋙ **sensorily** *adv.*

sensual *adj* relating to or consisting in the gratification of the senses or the indulgence of appetites. ⋙ **sensualist** *n,* **sensuality** *n,* **sensually** *adv.*

Usage note

sensual *or* **sensuous**? *Sensual* is the more common word and the one that frequently carries overtones of sexual desire or pleasure: *pouting sensual lips; sensual pleasures. Sensuous* is the more neutral word: it also means 'appealing to the senses' but without the feeling of self-indulgence or sexiness associated with *sensual*: *the artist's sensuous use of colour and texture.*

sensuous *adj* **1a** providing or characterized by gratification of the senses; appealing strongly to the senses. **b** suggesting or producing rich imagery or sense impressions. **2** of the senses or objects perceived by the senses. **3** readily influenced by sense perception. ⋙ **sensuously** *adv,* **sensuousness** *n.*

Usage note

sensuous *or* **sensual**? See note at SENSUAL.

sent[1] *v* past tense and past part. of SEND.

sent[2] *n* (*pl* **sentee**) a unit of currency in Estonia, worth 100th of a kroon.

sente /'senti/ *n* (*pl* **lisente**) a unit of currency in Lesotho, worth 100th of a loti.

sentee *n* pl of SENT[2].

sentence[1] *n* **1** a grammatically self-contained speech unit that expresses an assertion, a question, a command, a wish, or an exclamation. **2a** a judgment formally pronounced by a court and specifying a punishment. **b** the punishment so imposed.

sentence[2] *v* (*often* + to) to impose a judicial sentence on (a criminal).

sentence adverb *n* in grammar, an adverbial expression such as *frankly* or *by the way,* which stands outside the construction.

sententious *adj* given to pompous moralizing. ⋙ **sententiously** *adv,* **sententiousness** *n.*

sentient *adj* **1** capable of perceiving through the senses; conscious. **2** keenly sensitive in perception or feeling. ⋙ **sentience** *n,* **sentiently** *adv.*

sentiment *n* **1a** emotion or sentimentality, or an attitude, thought, or judgment prompted or coloured by feeling or emotion. **b** (*usu in pl*) a specific view or opinion. **c** a feeling or attitude. **2a** sensitive feeling; refined sensibility, *esp* as expressed in a work of art. **b** indulgently romantic or nostalgic feeling.

sentimental *adj* **1** appealing to or resulting from feeling rather than reason. **2** having an excess of superficial sentiment. ⋙ **sentimentalism** *n,* **sentimentalist** *n,* **sentimentality** *n,* **sentimentally** *adv.*

sentimentalize *or* **-ise** *v* **1** to indulge in sentiment. **2** to make (somebody or something) an object of usu superficial sentiment; to romanticize.

sentinel[1] *n* somebody that keeps guard; a sentry.

sentinel[2] *v* (**sentinelled, sentinelling,** *NAm* **sentineled, sentineling**) to watch over (somebody or something) as a sentinel.

sentry *n* (*pl* **-ies**) a guard or watch, *esp* a soldier standing guard at a gate, door, etc.

sentry box *n* a shelter for a standing sentry.

sepal *n* any of the modified leaves comprising the CALYX (green outer part) of a flower.

separable *adj* capable of being separated or dissociated. ⋙ **separability** *n.*

separate[1] *v* **1** to become divided or detached; to move or come apart. **2** to cease to live together as husband and wife, *esp* by formal arrangement. **3a** to set or keep apart (two or more people or things); to divide or stand between. **b** (*often* + from) to make a distinction between (two or more people or things); to distinguish: *It is sometimes hard to separate religion from magic.* **c** to disperse (people or things) in space or time; to scatter: *The population lived in widely separated hamlets.* **d** to detach (somebody or something) from a larger group: *The wolves tried to separate a calf from the herd.* **e** to sever. **4a** (*often* + out) to isolate (something) from a mixture or compound: *This process separates the cream from the milk.* **b** (*often* + out) to divide (something) into constituent parts or types. ✱ **separate the wheat**

from the chaff to separate or distinguish what is useful from what is worthless. ➤➤ **separative** *adj.*

separate[2] *adj* **1** set or kept apart; detached or separated. **2** not shared with another; individual. **3a** existing independently; autonomous. **b** unconnected. **c** different in kind; distinct. ➤➤ **separately** *adv,* **separateness** *n.*

separates *pl n* garments, e.g. skirts, blouses, and trousers, that are designed to be worn together to form an interchangeable outfit.

separation *n* **1** the act or an instance of separating. **2** cessation of cohabitation between husband and wife by mutual agreement or judicial decree.

separatism *n* a belief or movement advocating separation, e.g. schism, secession, or racial segregation. ➤➤ **separatist** *n and adj.*

separator *n* a device for separating liquids of different specific gravities, e.g. cream from milk, or liquids from solids.

Sephardi *n* (*pl* **Sephardim**) a member or descendant of the non-Yiddish-speaking branch of European Jews that settled in Spain and Portugal: compare ASHKENAZI. ➤➤ **Sephardic** *adj.*

sepia *n* **1** the inky secretion of cuttlefishes, or a brown pigment obtained from this. **2** a rich dark brown, as seen in early photographic prints. ➤➤ **sepia** *adj.*

sepoy *n* an Indian soldier employed by a European power, *esp* Britain.

seppuku /se'poohkooh/ *n* = HARA-KIRI.

sepsis *n* (*pl* **sepses**) the spread of bacteria from a focus of infection, *esp* septicaemia.

Sept. *abbr* September.

sept- *comb. form* see SEPTI-.

septa *n* pl of SEPTUM.

September *n* the ninth month of the year.

septennial *adj* **1** consisting of or lasting for seven years. **2** occurring or performed every seven years.

septet *n* (*used as sing. or pl*) a group or set of seven, *esp* the performers of a septet.

septi- *or* **sept-** *comb. form* seven: *septuple; septillion.*

septic *adj* **1** putrefactive. **2** relating to, involving, or characteristic of sepsis. ➤➤ **septically** *adv,* **septicity** *n.*

septicaemia (*NAm* **septicemia**) *n* invasion of the bloodstream by micro-organisms from a focus of infection, with chills, fever, etc; blood poisoning.

septic tank *n* a tank in which the solid matter of continuously flowing sewage is disintegrated by bacteria.

septillion *n* **1** *Brit* the number one followed by 42 zeros (10^{42}). **2** *NAm* the number one followed by 24 zeros (10^{24}). ➤➤ **septillionth** *n and adj.*

septuagenarian *n* a person between 70 and 79 years old.

Septuagesima *n* the third Sunday before Lent.

Septuagint *n* a pre-Christian Greek version of the Jewish Scriptures arranged and edited by Jewish scholars about 300 BC.

septum *n* (*pl* **septa**) a dividing wall or membrane, *esp* between bodily spaces or masses of soft tissue. ➤➤ **septal** *adj.*

septuple[1] *adj* **1** having seven units or members. **2** seven times as great or as many.

septuple[2] *v* to become or make seven times as much or as many.

septuplet *n* **1** any of seven offspring born at one birth. **2** a combination of seven of a kind.

sepulcher *n NAm* see SEPULCHRE.

sepulchral *adj* **1** suited to or suggestive of a tomb; sombre or dismal; funereal. **2** relating to the burial of the dead. ➤➤ **sepulchrally** *adv.*

sepulchre (*NAm* **sepulcher**) *n* a place of burial; a tomb.

seq. *abbr* (*pl* **seqq.**) the following.

sequel *n* **1a** a play, film, or literary work continuing the course of a narrative begun in a preceding one. **b** subsequent development or course of events. **2** a consequence or result.

sequela *n* (*pl* **sequelae**) an aftereffect of disease or injury.

sequence[1] *n* **1** a continuous or connected series. **2** a continuous progression. **3** the order of succession of things, events, etc. **4** in music, a succession of not necessarily exact repetitions. **5a** a succession of related shots or scenes developing a single subject or phase of a film story. **b** an episode, *esp* in a film.

sequence[2] *v* to place (people, things, etc) in ordered sequence.

sequencer *n* any of various devices for arranging things into a sequence or for separating things in a sequence.

sequential *adj* **1** of or arranged in a sequence; serial. **2** following in sequence. ➤➤ **sequentiality** *n,* **sequentially** *adv.*

sequential access *n* in computing, a method of accessing data from a file by reading through the file from the beginning: compare DIRECT ACCESS.

sequester *v* **1** *chiefly literary* (*usu in passive or reflexive*) to segregate (somebody) from the company of others. **2a** in law, to seize (a person's property) and hold it temporarily until a debt is paid or a dispute is settled. **b** in international law, to seize (the property of an enemy).

sequestrate *v* **1** in law, = SEQUESTER (2A). **2** in Scots law, to declare (somebody) bankrupt, or to hand over (a bankrupt's property) to pay a debt. ➤➤ **sequestration** *n,* **sequestrator** *n.*

sequin *n* a very small disc of shining metal or plastic used for ornamentation, *esp* on clothing.

sequoia *n* a huge coniferous Californian tree.

sera *n* pl of SERUM.

seraglio /se'rahlioh, -lyoh/ *n* (*pl* **-os**) **1** = HAREM. **2** a sultan's palace.

serai /se'rie/ *n* = CARAVANSERAI.

serape /sə'rahpi/ *n* a brightly coloured woollen shawl worn over the shoulders, *esp* by Mexican men.

seraph *n* (*pl* **seraphim** *or* **seraphs**) any of the six-winged angels standing in the presence of God. ➤➤ **seraphic** *adj.*

Serb *n* a native or inhabitant of Serbia. ➤➤ **Serb** *adj.*

Serbian *n* **1** = SERB. **2** = SERBO-CROATIAN. ➤➤ **Serbian** *adj.*

Serbo-Croat *n* = SERBO-CROATIAN.

Serbo-Croatian *n* the language of the Serbs, Croats, Bosnians, and Montenegrins. ➤➤ **Serbo-Croatian** *adj.*

sere *or* **sear** *adj archaic or literary* shrivelled; withered.

serenade[1] *n* a complimentary vocal or instrumental performance, *esp* one given outdoors at night by a man for a woman who is the object of his desire.

serenade[2] *v* to perform a serenade in honour of (somebody). ➤➤ **serenader** *n.*

serendipity *n* the faculty of discovering pleasing or valuable things by chance. ➤➤ **serendipitous** *adj.*

serene *adj* **1** having or showing tranquillity and peace of mind. **2** free of storms or adverse changes; clear or fine. ➤➤ **serenely** *adv*, **serenity** *n*.

serf *n* a member of a class of agricultural labourers in a feudal society, bound in service to a lord. ➤➤ **serfdom** *n*.

serge *n* a durable twilled fabric with a pronounced diagonal rib on the front and the back.

sergeant *or* **serjeant** *n* **1** a police officer ranking in Britain between constable and inspector and in the USA below a lieutenant. **2** a non-commissioned officer in the army, air force, or marines, ranking above a corporal.

sergeant-at-arms *or* **serjeant-at-arms** *n* (*pl* **sergeants-at-arms** *or* **serjeants-at-arms**) an officer attending the British Speaker or Lord Chancellor, or a similar officer in other legislatures.

sergeant major *n* (*pl* **sergeant majors**) a warrant officer in the British army or Royal Marines.

serial[1] *n* **1** a work appearing, e.g. in a magazine or on television, in parts, usu at regular intervals. **2** a publication issued as one of a consecutively numbered continuing series.

Usage note

serial *or* cereal? See note at CEREAL.

serial[2] *adj* **1** of, in, or constituting a series, rank, or row. **2** appearing in successive instalments. **3** in computing, transferring data one bit at a time. ➤➤ **serially** *adv*.

Usage note

serial *or* cereal? See note at CEREAL.

serialise *v* see SERIALIZE.

serialism *n* the theory or practice of composing music based on a series of notes in an arbitrary but fixed order without regard for traditional tonality.

serialist *n* a person who writes serials or who composes serial music.

serialize *or* **-ise** *v* to arrange or publish (a story) in serial form. ➤➤ **serialization** *n*.

serial killer *n* a person who kills a number of people over a period of time, *esp* if using the same method of killing or involving a given category of victim.

serial number *n* a number used as a means of identification that indicates position in a series.

sericulture *n* the production of raw silk by breeding silkworms.

series *n* (*pl* **series**) **1** a number of things or events of the same kind following one another in spatial or temporal succession. **2** any group of systematically related items. **3** a number of radio or television programmes involving the same characters or with the same topic and/or presenters. **4** an arrangement of devices in an electrical circuit in which the whole current passes through each device. **5** a usu infinite mathematical sequence whose terms are to be added together. **6** a division of rock formations that is smaller than a system and comprises rocks deposited during an epoch.

serif *n* a tiny decorative line added at the tip of the stroke of a printed letter.

serine *n* an amino acid found in most proteins.

seriocomic *adj* containing a mixture of the serious and the comic.

serious *adj* **1** grave or thoughtful in appearance or manner; sober. **2a** sincere and in earnest; not joking or pretending. **b** deeply interested or committed. **3a** having or possibly leading to important or dangerous consequences; severe. **b** *informal* substantial in size or quantity: *earning serious money*. **4a** involving or requiring careful attention and concentration. **b** relating to a weighty or important matter. ➤➤ **seriousness** *n*.

seriously *adv* **1a** in a sincere or purposeful manner; earnestly. **b** to speak in a serious way. **2a** to a serious extent; severely. **b** *informal* extremely.

serjeant *n* see SERGEANT.

serjeant-at-arms *n* (*pl* **serjeants-at-arms**) see SERGEANT-AT-ARMS.

serjeant-at-law *n* (*pl* **serjeants-at-law**) a member of a former class of barristers of the highest rank.

sermon *n* **1** a religious discourse delivered in public, usu by a clergyman as a part of a religious service. **2** a speech on conduct or duty, *esp* one that is unduly long or tedious.

sermonize *or* **-ise** *v* to give moral advice in an officious or dogmatic manner.

serology *n* the medical study of the reactions and properties of serum, *esp* blood serum. ➤➤ **serological** *adj*, **serologist** *n*.

seronegative *adj* giving a negative result in serological tests; *specif* not having a significant level of serum antibodies, thus indicating no previous exposure to the infectious agent being tested.

seropositive *adj* giving a positive result in serological tests; *specif* having a significant level of serum antibodies, thus indicating previous exposure to the infectious agent being tested.

serotonin *n* a chemical compound that causes constriction of small blood vessels and occurs in blood platelets and as a neurotransmitter in the brain.

serous *adj* relating to, producing, or resembling serum.

serpent *n* **1** *literary* a large snake. **2** a wily treacherous person. **3** an obsolete bass woodwind instrument with an S-shaped barrel.

serpentine[1] *adj* **1** winding or turning first one way and then another. **2** relating to or like a serpent, e.g. in form or movement. **3** subtly tempting; wily or artful.

serpentine[2] *n* a usu dull green mottled mineral consisting mainly of hydrated magnesium silicate.

SERPS *abbr Brit* state earnings-related pension scheme.

serrated *adj* having projections like the teeth of a saw; jagged.

serration *n* **1** any of the teeth of a serrated edge. **2** a row of projections resembling the teeth of a saw.

serried *adj* crowded or pressed together; compact.

serum *n* (*pl* **serums** *or* **sera**) **1** the watery part of a body fluid remaining after clotting or curdling, *esp* the protein-rich fluid constituent of blood. **2** blood serum obtained from inoculated animals and containing specific antibodies.

servant *n* somebody who or something that serves others; *specif* somebody employed to perform personal or domestic duties for somebody else.

serve[1] *v* **1a** to hold a post or office or to discharge a duty for. **b** (*often* + as) to work in a particular capacity or hold office for (a period of time). **c** to be employed or spend time as a member of the armed forces of (a country). **2** to be imprisoned for (a period of time). **3** to attend to (a customer) in a shop, bar, etc. **4a** to distribute (food or drinks) during a meal. **b** to wait on (somebody) at table. **5** to act as a servant. **6a** (*often* + as/for) to fulfil a particular purpose or have a particular effect. **b** to be adequate or satisfactory: *This will serve for now*. **7** *formal* to be favourable, opportune, or convenient. **8** in tennis and other games, to begin a period of play by hitting the ball or shuttlecock. **9** to help or benefit; to be available to. **10** to act as a servant to. **11**

(*often* + on) to deliver or execute (a legal writ or summons). **12** of a male animal: to copulate with (a female). **13** *formal* to behave towards or treat (somebody) in a specified way: *They have served you ill.*

serve² *n* the act of serving in a game such as volleyball, badminton, or tennis.

server *n* **1** the player who serves, e.g. in tennis. **2a** something used in serving food or drink. **b** somebody who serves food or drink. **3** a computer or program that connects users in a network to a centralized resource or store of data.

servery *n* (*pl* **-ies**) a room, counter, or hatch from which food is served.

service¹ *n* **1** work or duty carried out for a person, organization, country, etc, *esp* when considered as contributing to the welfare of others rather than being for personal gain. **2** an operation, system, or facility designed to meet a public need: *a bus service.* **3a** the work of attending to and assisting customers in a shop, bar, hotel, etc, or the manner in which this work is done. **b** employment as a servant. **4** a helpful action; a favour. **5** a religious ceremony, *esp* in a Christian church, or a meeting for worship. **6** a routine operation carried out to repair and maintain a machine or motor vehicle. **7** a set of matching tableware for serving a specified meal, food, or drink: *a 24-piece dinner service.* **8** an administrative division, e.g. of a government or business: *the consular service.* **9a** (*usu in pl*) any of a nation's military forces, e.g. the army or navy. **b** *chiefly Brit* (*in pl, also used as sing.*) facilities, e.g. restaurants, toilets, and petrol stations, provided for the users of a motorway. **c** (*in pl*) utilities, e.g. gas, water, sewage, or electricity, available or connected to a building. **10** a serve in tennis, badminton, etc. ✱ **be at somebody's service** to be available, whenever required, to help somebody or to be used by them. **be of service to somebody** to help, benefit, or be of use to somebody. **in service 1** of a machine or vehicle: currently being used or operated. **2** of a person: working as a domestic servant. **out of service** not currently being used or operated.

service² *v* **1** to provide a service or services to (somebody or something). **2** to carry out routine repairs and maintenance on (a machine or vehicle). **3** to meet interest payments on and provide for the eventual repayment of the capital of (a debt). **4** of a male animal: to copulate with (a female).

serviceable *adj* **1** fit and ready to use; in working order. **2** giving good service; durable. ⋙ **serviceability** *n.*

service area *n chiefly Brit* an area at the side of a motorway or other road where there are facilities for travellers.

service charge *n* a proportion of a bill added on to the total bill to pay for service, usu instead of a tip.

service flat *n Brit* a flat with a charge for certain services, e.g. cleaning, included in its rent.

service industry *n* an industry that does work or provides goods or materials for other industries, but does not manufacture anything.

serviceman *n* (*pl* **servicemen**) a male member of the armed forces.

service provider *n* a company that provides computer users with access to the Internet.

service road *n* a small road that usu runs parallel to a major road and provides access to the houses, shops, etc that line it.

service station *n* a commercial establishment at the roadside that sells petrol and oil and sometimes carries out maintenance and repair work on vehicles.

servicewoman *n* (*pl* **servicewomen**) a female member of the armed forces.

serviette *n chiefly Brit* a table napkin.

servile *adj* **1** slavishly or unctuously submissive; abject or obsequious. **2** characteristic of or befitting a slave or a menial. ⋙ **servilely** *adv,* **servility** *n.*

serving *n* a single portion of food or drink; a helping.

servitor *n archaic or formal* a servant.

servitude *n* the state of being a slave or completely subject to somebody or something else.

servo *n* (*pl* **-os**) a servomotor or servomechanism.

servomechanism *n* an automatic device that enables a large power output to be controlled by relatively small power input, as in the power-assisted steering and braking systems of vehicles.

servomotor *n* a motor that provides the power in a servomechanism.

sesame *n* a plant grown in tropical Asia that produces small flattish seeds used as a source of oil and as a flavouring agent.

sesqui- *comb. form* one and a half times: *sesquicentennial.*

sesquicentenary *n* (*pl* **-ies**) = SESQUICENTENNIAL.

sesquicentennial *n* a 150th anniversary, or its celebration. ⋙ **sesquicentennial** *adj.*

sesquipedalian *adj* **1** many-syllabled. **2** fond of or characterized by the use of long words, usu to excess.

sessile *adj* **1** attached directly by the base without a stalk. **2** permanently attached or established and not free to move about.

session *n* **1** a period devoted to a particular activity, *esp* by a group of people. **2** a meeting or series of meetings of a body such as a court or council for the transaction of business; a sitting. **3** the period of the day or year during which a school conducts classes. ⋙ **sessional** *adj.*

sestet *n* a group of six lines of verse, *esp* the last six lines of a sonnet.

set¹ *v* (**setting,** *past tense and past part.* **set**) **1** to put (something) in a particular position, *esp* to place it deliberately and carefully. **2** to put (something or somebody) in a specified condition: *That will set his mind at rest.* **3** to decide on and fix (an amount, etc). **4** to create or provide: *You ought to set an example.* **5** to give somebody (a task) to perform. **6** to prepare or adjust (a device) ready for use. **7** to prepare (a table) ready for use at a meal. **8** to describe (an event, story, etc) as taking place at a particular place and time. **9** to provide music for (a text). **10** to arrange (type) for printing. **11** to fix (wet hair) in the right style after washing. **12** to put (a dislocated or fractured bone or limb) into its normal position for healing. **13** to fix (a gem) in a border of metal. **14** to become solid or thickened: *The cement sets quickly.* **15** of the sun, moon, etc: to go down below the horizon. **16** of a tide or wind: to take a specified course. **17** of fruit or seeds: to develop as a result of pollination. **18** of a gun dog: to indicate the position of game by crouching or pointing. ✱ **set on** to attack (somebody) suddenly and violently. **set sail** to begin a voyage by sea. **set the pace** to determine the speed or rate for others to follow. **set to work** to start to do something.

set² *adj* **1** arranged or laid down in advance, or fixed by authority; prescribed or specified: *set books.* **2** (*usu* + on/upon) resolutely intending to do something; determined: *She's set on going.* **3** unchanging and immovable or rigid: *a set frown.* **4** ready: *We're all set.* **5** conventional or stereotyped: *set phrases.*

set[3] *n* **1** a number of things, usu of the same kind, that belong or are used together or that form a unit. **2** (*used as sing. or pl*) a group of people associated by common interests. **3** (*used as sing. or pl*) a group of pupils of roughly equal ability in a particular subject who are taught together: compare STREAM[1] (5), BAND[1] (6). **4** an apparatus made up of electronic components assembled so as to function as a unit. **5** a collection of mathematical elements, e.g. numbers or points. **6** in tennis and similar sports, a division of a match won by the side that wins at least six games with a two-game advantage, or that wins a tie breaker. **7** the artificial scenery used for a particular play or scene in a play. **8** a session of jazz or rock music, usu followed by an intermission, or the music played during such a session. **9a** a young plant or rooted cutting ready for transplanting. **b** a small bulb, corm, or tuber used for propagation. **10** the manner in which something is positioned; bearing or posture. **11** = SETT. ✱ **make a dead set at** *Brit* to try very hard to win the attention and affection of (somebody).

set about *v* **1** to start doing something with determination. **2** to attack (somebody) physically or verbally.

set apart *v* to make (somebody or something) noticeable: *His height sets him apart.*

set aside *v* **1** to put to one side; to discard. **2** to override (a verdict or decision).

set-aside *n* **1** an agricultural policy whereby farmers are paid to take some of their land out of production, thus reducing agricultural surpluses. **2** the land so left unused.

setback *n* something that causes problems or delays and holds up the progress of something or somebody.

set back *v* **1** to prevent or hinder the progress of. **2** *informal* to cost (somebody) a specified amount.

set down *v* **1** to record in writing. **2** to allow (a passenger) to alight from a vehicle.

set forth *v* **1** to start on a journey. **2** to give an account of.

SETI *abbr* search for extraterrestrial intelligence.

set in *v* of something unwanted: to become established.

set off *v* **1** to start on a journey. **2** to cause (somebody) to start doing something. **3** to cause (a bomb) to explode. **4** to adorn or embellish.

set out *v* **1** to start on a journey or career. **2** to state or describe at length or in detail.

set piece *n* **1** a work of art, literature, etc, or part of one, that has a formal pattern or style. **2** any of various moves in football or rugby, e.g. a corner kick or free kick, by which the ball is put back into play after a stoppage.

set point *n* in tennis etc, a point that, if won, will enable one player to win the set, or a situation where one player can win the set by winning the next point.

set square *n chiefly Brit* a flat triangular instrument with one right angle and two other precisely known angles, used to mark out or test angles.

sett *n* **1** the burrow of a badger. **2** a usu rectangular block of stone formerly used for paving streets.

settee *n* a long often upholstered seat with a back and usu arms for seating more than one person; a sofa.

setter *n* a large gundog trained to point on finding game.

set theory *n* a branch of mathematics or of symbolic logic that deals with the nature and relations of sets.

setting *n* **1a** the background or surroundings to an object or event. **b** the time and place in which the action of a literary, dramatic, or cinematic work is supposed to occur. **2** the way in which something is set. **3** the music composed for a text, e.g. a poem. **4** a set of cutlery, glasses, etc arranged on a table for the use of one person. **5** the frame in which a gem is mounted.

settle[1] *v* **1** to find or produce an acceptable answer to (a question) or solution to (a problem). **2a** (*often* + down) to become calm or orderly. **b** (*usu* + down) to adopt an ordered or stable lifestyle. **3** to place or arrange (somebody, something, or oneself) firmly or comfortably. **4a** to become established in a particular place, or as a permanent condition: *His mood settled into apathy.* **b** to establish a home or a colony: *They settled in Canada.* **5** to become or make less anxious, agitated, or uncomfortable. **6a** to come to rest. **b** to descend gradually to the ground or onto a surface. **7** of a building, the ground, etc: to sink slowly to a lower level; to subside. **8** of a liquid: to become clearer by depositing sediment or scum. **9** to pay (an account, debt, etc). **10a** (+ on) to make a decision or choice regarding something. **b** (+ for) to be content with or accept something less than one originally hoped for. **11** (+ on) to bestow (property or money) on somebody for their lifetime by means of a legal document. ✱ **settle down to** to begin to do (something) in a concentrated and purposeful way.

settle[2] *n* a wooden bench with arms, a high solid back, and often an enclosed base which can be used as a chest.

settle in *v* to become comfortably established.

settlement *n* **1** the act or process of settling or of settling something. **2** an agreement resolving differences. **3** a place or region where a new community has been recently established. **4a** the act of bestowing property, money, etc on somebody, by means of a deed or will. **b** the sum, property, or income secured to a person by such a settlement.

settler *n* somebody who settles in an area that was previously uninhabited or sparsely inhabited.

settlor *n* somebody who makes a legal settlement, *esp* of property.

set-to *n* (*pl* **-os**) *informal* a usu brief and vigorous conflict.

set up *v* **1** to raise into position. **2** to assemble or erect. **3** to establish or found (a business, enterprise, etc). **4** to establish (somebody) in a certain role. **5** to produce or give voice to (a loud noise). ✱ **set up house** to live together as a household. **set up shop** to establish a business.

set-up *n informal* **1** the way in which something is organized or arranged. **2** a particular arrangement of apparatus required to perform a task. **3** an attempt to incriminate or deceive somebody.

seven *n* the number 7. ➤➤ **seven** *adj*, **sevenfold** *adj and adv.*

seven seas *pl n* all the oceans of the world.

seventeen *adj and n* the number 17. ➤➤ **seventeenth** *adj and n.*

seventh *adj and n* **1** having the position in a sequence corresponding to the number seven. **2** one of seven equal parts of something. **3** in music, an interval of seven degrees of a diatonic scale, or the combination of two notes at such an interval. ➤➤ **seventhly** *adv.*

Seventh-Day Adventist *n* a member of a group of Adventist Christians who advocate or observe Saturday as the Christian Sabbath.

seventh heaven *n* a state of supreme rapture or bliss.

seventy *adj and n* (*pl* **-ies**) **1** the number 70. **2** (*in pl*) the numbers 70 to 79. ⋙ **seventieth** *adj and n.*

seventy-eight *n* a gramophone record that plays at 78 revolutions per minute.

Seven Wonders of the World *pl n* the seven structures considered by ancient and medieval writers to be the most magnificent of the ancient world.

seven-year itch *n* marital discontent allegedly leading to infidelity after about seven years of marriage.

sever *v* **1** to divide (something) by cutting it. **2** to put or keep apart (two or more things or people); to separate. **3** to break off; to terminate. ⋙ **severable** *adj.*

several[1] *adj* **1** more than two or a few, but fewer than many. **2** *formal* separate or distinct from one another; respective.

several[2] *pron* (*used as pl*) an indefinite number more than two and fewer than many.

severally *adv formal* each in turn; separately or singly.

severance *n* **1a** the act of separating something by cutting or of cutting something off. **b** the state of being separated from something or somebody. **2** the act of putting an end to a connection or relationship with somebody.

severance pay *n* an amount payable to an employee on termination of employment.

severe *adj* **1** having a stern expression or character; austere. **2** rigorous in judgment, requirements, or punishment; stringent. **3** sober or restrained in decoration or manner; plain. **4** marked by harsh or extreme conditions. **5** requiring much effort; arduous. **6** having a powerful and dangerous effect; serious; grave. ⋙ **severely** *adv,* **severity** *n.*

Seville orange *n* a reddish orange fruit with a bitter rind and sour flesh, used for making marmalade.

Sèvres /'sevrə/ *n* an elaborately decorated fine porcelain.

sew *v* (*past tense* **sewed,** *past part.* **sewn** *or* **sewed**) **1** to unite, fasten, or attach by stitches made with a needle and thread. **2** to make or mend by sewing.

sewage *n* waste matter carried off by sewers.

sewage farm *n* a place where sewage is treated, *esp* to be made into fertilizer.

sewer[1] *n* an artificial usu underground drain or pipe used to carry off waste matter, *esp* excrement, from houses, schools, towns, etc and surface water from roads and paved areas.

sewer[2] *n* somebody who sews.

sewerage *n* **1** a system of sewers. **2** the removal and disposal of surface water by sewers. **3** sewage.

sewn *v* past part. of SEW.

sew up *v informal* to bring (something) to a successful or satisfactory conclusion.

sex[1] *n* **1** either of two categories, male or female, into which organisms are divided on the basis of their reproductive role, notably the type of gamete produced. **2** the structural, functional, and behavioural characteristics that are involved in reproduction and that distinguish males and females. **3a** = SEXUAL INTERCOURSE. **b** sexual activity in general.

Usage note

sex *and* gender See note at GENDER.

sex[2] *v* to identify the sex of (a young animal).

sex- *or* **sexi-** *comb. form* six: *sextuplet.*

sexagenarian *n* a person between 60 and 69 years old.

Sexagesima *n* the second Sunday before Lent.

sexagesimal *adj* relating to or based on the number 60.

sex appeal *n* sexual attractiveness.

sex chromosome *n* a chromosome concerned directly with the inheritance of male or female sex.

sexed *adj* having sex, sex appeal, or sexual instincts, *esp* to a specified degree: *under sexed.*

sex hormone *n* a hormone that affects the growth or function of the reproductive organs or the development of secondary sex characteristics, e.g. facial hair in men.

sexi- *comb. form* see SEX-.

sexism *n* **1** a belief that sex determines intrinsic capacities and role in society and that sexual differences produce an inherent superiority of one sex, usu the male. **2** discrimination on the basis of sex; *esp* prejudice against women on the part of men. ⋙ **sexist** *adj and n.*

sexless *adj* **1** lacking sexuality or sexual intercourse. **2** lacking sex appeal or the sexual urge.

sex life *n* a person's sexual activity and relationships.

sex object *n* a person regarded exclusively as a means of sexual satisfaction.

sexology *n* the study of human sexual behaviour. ⋙ **sexological** *adj,* **sexologist** *n.*

sexploitation *n* the use of sex for commercial gain, *esp* in films and publications.

sexpot *n informal* an extremely sexy person.

sex shop *n* a shop that sells objects that contribute to sexual arousal or pleasure, pornographic books and magazines, etc.

sex symbol *n* a person who famously embodies male or female sex appeal.

sext *n* the fourth of the daily religious services making up the Divine Office, orig fixed for twelve noon.

sextant *n* an instrument for measuring angles that is used, *esp* in navigation, to observe the altitudes of celestial bodies and so determine the observer's position on the earth's surface.

sextet *n* **1a** a group of six instruments, voices, or performers. **b** a musical composition for such a group. **2** (*used as sing. or pl*) a group or set of six.

sextillion *n* (*pl* **sextillions** *or* **sextillion**) **1** *Brit* the number one followed by 36 zeros (10^{36}). **2** *NAm* the number one followed by 21 zeros (10^{21}).

sexton *n* a church officer who takes care of the church property and is often also the gravedigger.

sex tourism *n* tourism that specifically aims to take advantage of less stringent laws or rules regarding sexual behaviour in foreign countries.

sextuple *adj* **1** being six times as great or as many. **2** having six units or members.

sextuplet *n* **1** any of six offspring born at one birth. **2** a group of six equal musical notes performed in the time ordinarily given to four of the same value.

sexual *adj* **1** relating to or involving the physical attraction and contacts between individuals ultimately associated with the desire to reproduce. **2** associated with being a member of one or the other sex or with relations between the two sexes. **3** of reproduction: involving the fusion of male and female gametes (reproductive cells; see GAMETE). ⋙ **sexually** *adv.*

sexual harassment *n* repeated unwelcome physical contact or sexual suggestions and remarks directed at somebody, *esp* in the workplace.

sexual intercourse *n* sexual activity with genital contact involving penetration, *esp* the penetration of the vagina by the penis.

sexualise *v* see SEXUALIZE.

sexuality *n* (*pl* **-ies**) **1** the condition of having a sexual nature and experiencing sexual desires. **2** a person's sexual orientation, as a heterosexual or a homosexual, or sexual preferences.

sexualize *or* **-ise** *v* to make (something) sexual; to endow (something) with a sexual character or significance.

sexually transmitted disease *n* any disease that is transmitted through sexual intercourse, e.g. syphilis or gonorrhoea.

sex worker *n euphem* = PROSTITUTE[1].

sexy *adj* (**-ier, -iest**) **1a** sexually attractive. **b** sexually suggestive or stimulating; erotic. **2** sexually aroused. **3a** capable of arousing interest and excitement; enjoyable. **b** trendy or fashionable. ➤➤ **sexily** *adv,* **sexiness** *n.*

Seychellois *n* a native or inhabitant of the Seychelles. ➤➤ **Seychellois** *adj.*

SF *abbr* science fiction.

sforzando /sfawt'sandoh/ *adj and adv* of a note or chord in music: to be performed with a heavy stress or accent.

SFX *abbr* special effects.

SG *abbr* specific gravity.

Sg *abbr* the chemical symbol for seaborgium.

SGML *abbr* standard generalized mark-up language; an international standard method used in publishing for representing texts in electronic form.

shabby *adj* (**-ier, -iest**) **1a** threadbare or faded from wear. **b** dilapidated; run-down. **2** dressed in worn or grubby clothes; seedy. **3** shameful or despicable. ➤➤ **shabbily** *adv,* **shabbiness** *n.*

shack *n* a small crudely built dwelling or shelter.

shackle[1] *n* **1** a pair of metal rings joined by a chain used to fasten a prisoner's hands or legs. **2** (*usu in pl*) something that restricts or prevents free action or expression. **3** a U-shaped piece of metal with a pin or bolt to close the opening.

shackle[2] *v* **1a** to bind with shackles; to fetter. **b** to make (somebody or something) fast with shackles. **2** to deprive (a person, group, organization, etc) of freedom of thought or action by means of restrictions or handicaps.

shack up *v informal* (*usu* + together/with) to live with and have a sexual relationship with somebody.

shad *n* (*pl* **shads** *or* **shad**) a fish of the herring family that swims up rivers from the sea to breed.

shaddock *n* a very large usu pear-shaped citrus fruit closely related to the grapefruit but often with coarse dry pulp. Also called POMELO.

shade[1] *n* **1a** partial darkness caused when something stands in the path of rays of light. **b** a place sheltered, e.g. by foliage, from the direct heat and glare of the sun. **2** (*usu* **the shade**) relative obscurity or insignificance. **3** a lampshade. **4** *informal* (*in pl*) sunglasses. **5** a particular variety of a colour, usu with respect to its darkness or lightness. **6** a minute difference or amount. **7** = GHOST[1] (I). ✻ **a shade** a tiny bit; somewhat. **shades of** used to indicate that one is reminded of or struck by a resemblance to a specified person or thing: *And – shades of Robin Hood – he only did it to help the poor!*

shade[2] *v* **1a** to shelter or screen (somebody or something) by intercepting radiated light or heat. **b** to cover with a shade. **2** to darken or obscure with a shadow, or as if with a shadow. **3a** to represent the effect of shade on. **b** to mark (a picture or drawing) with shading or gradations of colour. **4** to change (something) by gradual transition. **5** (+ into/off into) to pass by slight changes or imperceptible degrees.

shading *n* lines, dots, or colour used to suggest three-dimensionality, shadow, or degrees of light and dark in a picture.

shadow[1] *n* **1** a dark shape made upon a surface by an object positioned between it and a source of light. **2** partial darkness caused when an opaque object cuts off the light from a light source. **3** a small degree or portion; a trace. **4** a much reduced and weakened form of somebody or something; a vestige. **5** a source of gloom or disquiet. **6a** an inseparable companion or follower. **b** someone, e.g. a spy or detective, who follows and observes somebody else closely. **7** (*used before a noun*) denoting the leaders of a parliamentary opposition who constitute the probable membership of the cabinet when their party is returned to power and who act as opposition spokespersons on major issues.

shadow[2] *v* **1** to cast a shadow over (something or somebody). **2** to follow (somebody) secretly; to keep under surveillance. **3** to follow and observe (an experienced worker) in order to learn how to do a job.

shadow-box *v* to box with an imaginary opponent as a form of training.

shadowy *adj* (**-ier, -iest**) **1a** of the nature of or resembling a shadow; insubstantial. **b** scarcely perceptible; indistinct. **2** lying in or obscured by shadow. ➤➤ **shadowiness** *n.*

shady *adj* (**-ier, -iest**) **1** producing or giving shade. **2** sheltered from the direct heat or light of the sun. **3** *informal* **a** of questionable merit; unreliable. **b** of doubtful integrity; disreputable. ➤➤ **shadiness** *n.*

shaft[1] *n* **1a** the long handle of a spear, lance, or similar weapon. **b** the handle of a tool or implement, e.g. a hammer or golf club. **2** a usu cylindrical bar used to support rotating pieces in a machine or to transmit power or motion by rotation. **3a** a man-made vertical or inclined opening leading underground to a mine, well, etc. **b** a vertical opening or passage through the floors of a building. **4** a sharply delineated beam of light shining from an opening. **5** the cylindrical pillar between the capital and the base of a column. **6** either of two poles between which a horse is hitched to a vehicle. **7** a scornful, satirical, or pithily critical remark; a barb.

shaft[2] *v* **1** *informal* to treat unfairly or harshly. **2** *Brit, coarse slang* to have sexual intercourse with.

shag[1] *n* **1a** an unkempt or uneven tangled mass or covering, e.g. of hair. **b** long coarse or matted fibre or nap. **2** a strong coarse tobacco cut into fine shreds. **3** a European bird related and similar to but smaller than the cormorant.

shag[2] *v* (**shagged, shagging**) **1** *Brit, coarse slang* to have sexual intercourse with. **2** *Brit, slang* (+ out) to make utterly exhausted.

shag[3] *n Brit, coarse slang* an act of sexual intercourse.

shaggy *adj* (**-ier, -iest**) **1** covered with or consisting of long, coarse, or matted hair. **2** unkempt. ➤➤ **shaggily** *adv,* **shagginess** *n.*

shaggy-dog story *n* a protracted and inconsequential funny story whose humour lies in the pointlessness or irrelevance of the conclusion.

shagreen *n* **1** an untanned leather covered with small round granulations and usu dyed green. **2** the rough skin of various sharks and rays.

shah *n* a sovereign of Iran.

shake[1] *v* (*past tense* **shook,** *past part.* **shaken**) **1** to move back and forth or up and down with short rapid movements. **2** to tremble as a result of physical or emotional disturbance. **3** to brandish threateningly: *He shook his fist.* **4** to put in a specified state by quick jerky movements: *She shook herself free.* **5** to dislodge with jerky movements. **6** to shock or upset: *The news shook us.* **7** to weaken (somebody's confidence). ✱ **shake a leg** *informal* to hurry up. **shake hands** to clasp hands in greeting or farewell or to indicate agreement. **shake on** to shake hands as a sign of agreement to (something). **shake one's head** to move one's head from side to side to express refusal, disagreement, or disapproval.

shake² *n* **1** an act of shaking. **2** (*usu* **the shakes**) a condition of trembling, e.g. from chill or fever; *specif* DELIRIUM TREMENS. **3** = MILK SHAKE. ✱ **no great shakes** *informal* not very good or proficient.

shake down *v* **1** to become comfortably established somewhere. **2** to settle for the night, *esp* in a makeshift bed.

shake off *v* **1** to free oneself from (something unwelcome). **2** to escape from (a pursuer).

shaker *n* **1** a container or utensil used to sprinkle or mix a substance by shaking. **2** (**Shaker**) a member of an American sect practising celibacy and a self-denying communal life. **3** (**Shaker**) (*used before a noun*) denoting a simple, functional style of furniture orig produced by Shakers. ▶▶ **Shaker** *adj*, **Shakerism** *n*.

Shakespearean *or* **Shakespearian** *adj* characteristic of the plays and poetry of the English dramatist and poet William Shakespeare (d.1616). ▶▶ **Shakespearean** *n*, **Shakespearian** *n*.

shake up *v* **1** to mix by shaking. **2** to shock or upset. **3** to rouse from inactivity or complacency. **4** *informal* to reorganize drastically.

shake-up *n informal* an extensive and often drastic reorganization, e.g. of a company.

shako *n* (*pl* **-os** *or* **-oes**) a stiff military hat with a high crown and plume.

Shakti *or* **Sakti** *n* the dynamic energy of a Hindu god personified as his female consort; *broadly* cosmic energy as conceived in Hindu thought.

shaky *adj* (**-ier, -iest**) **1** not firm, still, or stable; shaking or likely to wobble or shake. **2a** unlikely to withstand pressure, opposition, etc; precarious. **b** of beliefs or principles: not held with great conviction or commitment. ▶▶ **shakily** *adv*, **shakiness** *n*.

shale *n* a finely stratified or laminated rock formed by the consolidation of clay, mud, or silt.

shall *v aux* (*third person sing. present tense* **shall,** *past tense* **should**) **1** used in the first person to express an action or state in the future: *We shall try to be there; At what time shall I expect you?* **2** used to express determination or insistence: *They shall not prevent us.* **3** used to express a polite request or suggestion: *Shall I open a window?* **4** *formal* used to express a requirement or command: *It shall be unlawful to carry firearms.*

Usage note

shall *or* will? Traditionally *shall* was used to form the future tense for the first person singular and plural (*I shall go tomorrow*) and to state a firm intention if used with any other personal pronoun (*You* shall *go to the ball*. Conversely *will* formed the future tense for the second and third person (*You will know soon enough*) and expressed a firm intention if used with *I* or *we* (*I* will *not put up with this*). This distinction has largely died out, with *I will* or *we will* being used in informal usage and the general use of the contraction *'ll*, e.g. *I'll, we'll*. See also note at SHOULD.

shallot *n* the small edible onion-like bulb of a perennial plant resembling the onion.

shallow¹ *adj* **1** having little depth. **2** superficial in knowledge, thought, or feeling. **3** not marked or accentuated. ▶▶ **shallowly** *adv*, **shallowness** *n*.

shallow² *n* (*usu in pl*) a shallow place in a body of water.

shalom /shə'lohm, shə'lom/ *interj* used as a Jewish greeting and farewell.

shalt *v* archaic second person sing. present tense of SHALL.

shalwar /shul'wah, -'vah/ *n* see SALWAR.

sham¹ *n* **1a** an imitation or counterfeit object purporting to be genuine. **b** a person who shams. **2** cheap falseness or hypocrisy.

sham² *adj* **1** not genuine; imitation. **2** pretended or feigned.

sham³ *v* (**shammed, shamming**) to pretend, or pretend to have or feel (something): *I shammed a headache.*

shaman *n* (*pl* **shamans**) a priest believed to exercise magic power, e.g. for healing and divination, *esp* through ecstatic trances. ▶▶ **shamanic** *adj*, **shamanism** *n*, **shamanist** *n*.

shamateur *n derog* a sports player who is officially classed as amateur but who takes payment.

shamble¹ *v* to walk awkwardly with dragging feet; to shuffle.

shamble² *n* a shambling gait.

shambles *n* (*pl* **shambles**) **1** a scene or a state of great destruction, chaos, or confusion; a mess. **2** *archaic* a slaughterhouse.

shambolic *adj Brit, informal* utterly chaotic or confused.

shame¹ *n* **1** a painful emotion caused by consciousness of guilt, impropriety, or disgrace. **2a** humiliating disgrace or disrepute; ignominy. **b** a cause of disgrace. **3** a cause of regret; a pity. ✱ **put to shame 1** to cause to feel ashamed. **2** to show (something) to be considerably inferior. **shame on you** you ought to feel ashamed.

shame² *v* **1** to bring shame to; to disgrace. **2** (*usu* + into) to compel (somebody) to do something by causing them to feel guilty.

shamefaced *adj* showing shame; ashamed. ▶▶ **shamefacedly** *adv*, **shamefacedness** *n*.

shameful *adj* **1** bringing disrepute or ignominy; disgraceful. **2** arousing the feeling of shame. ▶▶ **shamefully** *adv*, **shamefulness** *n*.

shameless *adj* **1** not feeling shame, *esp* in situations where other people would; brazen. **2** done with a complete disregard for the usual proprieties. ▶▶ **shamelessly** *adv*, **shamelessness** *n*.

shammy *n* (*pl* **-ies**) *informal* = CHAMOIS (2).

shampoo¹ *n* (*pl* **shampoos**) **1a** a usu foaming soap, detergent, etc used for washing and cleaning the hair. **b** a similar cleaning agent used on a carpet, car, etc. **2** an act of washing with shampoo.

shampoo² *v* (**shampoos, shampooed, shampooing**) to clean or wash with shampoo.

shamrock *n* a type of clover whose leaves consist of three leaflets, used as the national emblem of Ireland.

shandy *n* (*pl* **-ies**) a drink consisting of beer mixed with lemonade or ginger beer.

shanghai *v* (**shanghais, shanghaied, shanghaiing**) **1** to compel (somebody) to join a ship's crew, *esp* with the help of drink or drugs. **2** *informal* to trick or force (somebody) into doing something.

Shangri-la *n* a remote imaginary place where life approaches perfection.

shank *n* **1a** a leg; *specif* the part of the leg between the knee and the ankle. **b** a cut of beef, veal, mutton, or lamb from the upper or the lower part of the leg. **2** a straight narrow part of an object, e.g. the straight part of a nail or pin, or the part of a key between the handle and the bit. **3** a part of an object by which it can be attached to something else, e.g. a projection on the back of a solid button. **4** the band of a ring.

shanks's pony *n* one's own feet or legs considered as a means of transport.

shan't *contr* shall not.

shantung *n* a silk fabric in plain weave with a slightly irregular surface.

shanty[1] *n* (*pl* **-ies**) a small crudely built or dilapidated dwelling or shelter; a shack.

shanty[2] *n* (*pl* **-ies**) a song sung by sailors in rhythm with their work.

shantytown *n* a town, or area of a town, consisting mainly of shanties.

shape[1] *v* **1** to give a particular form or shape to. **2** to adapt the form or outline of (something) so as to fit neatly and closely. **3** to determine the nature or course of (e.g. events or a person's life). **4** (*often* + up) to develop or proceed. ⋙ **shaper** *n.*

shape[2] *n* **1a** the visible or tactile form of a particular thing or kind of thing. **b** spatial form: *All solids have shape.* **2** the contour of the body, *esp* of the trunk; the figure. **3a** a circle, square, or other standard geometrical form. **b** a piece of paper or any other material cut or made into a particular *esp* geometrical form. **4** an appearance adopted or assumed by somebody or something; a guise: *The devil appeared to Eve in the shape of a serpent.* **5** definite form, whether physical, structural, verbal, or mental. **6a** the condition of a person or thing, *esp* at a particular time: *He's in excellent shape for his age.* **b** a satisfactory condition. ✻ **in shape** in good condition, *esp* physically. **in the shape of** by way of. **lick/knock/whip into shape** to bring (somebody or something) into a satisfactory condition. **out of shape** in poor condition, *esp* physically. **take shape** to take on a definite or distinctive form. ⋙ **shaped** *adj.*

shapeless *adj* **1** having no definite shape. **2** deprived of its usual or proper shape; misshapen. ⋙ **shapelessly** *adv,* **shapelessness** *n.*

shapely *adj* (**-ier, -iest**) having a pleasing shape; well-proportioned. ⋙ **shapeliness** *n.*

shape up *v* **1** to proceed satisfactorily. **2** of a person: to become physically fit. **3** to develop in a certain way.

shard *n* a piece or fragment of something brittle, e.g. earthenware.

share[1] *n* **1** a portion belonging to, due to, or contributed by an individual. **2a** the part allotted or belonging to any member of a group owning property or interest together. **b** any of the equal portions into which the invested capital of a company is divided.

share[2] *v* **1** to partake of, use, experience, or enjoy (something) with others. **2** (+ out) to divide and distribute in shares; to apportion. ⋙ **sharable** *adj,* **shareable** *adj,* **sharer** *n.*

share[3] *n* a ploughshare.

sharecropper *n NAm* a tenant farmer who gives the landlord an agreed share of the crop as rent.

shareholder *n* the holder or owner of a share in the capital of a company. ⋙ **shareholding** *n.*

share option *n* a scheme that enables employees of a company to buy shares in it at a fixed price at some date in the future.

shareware *n* computer software which is made available free or at a token cost to any user.

sharia *or* **sheria** /shə'ree·ə/ *n* the body of divine law in Islam that governs the religious and secular life of Muslims.

shark[1] *n* (*pl* **sharks** *or* **shark**) a large, typically grey marine fish that is an active and voracious predator and has gill slits at the sides and a mouth on the under part of the body.

shark[2] *n* a greedy unscrupulous person who exploits others by usury, extortion, or trickery.

sharkskin *n* **1** leather made from the hide of a shark. **2** a smooth stiff durable fabric in twill or basket weave with small woven designs.

sharon fruit *n* a persimmon, *esp* a variety with a tough bright orange skin, no seeds, and sweet pulpy orange flesh.

sharp[1] *adj* **1** well adapted to cutting or piercing, usu by having a thin keen edge or fine point. **2a** characterized by hard lines and angles: *sharp features.* **b** involving an abrupt change in direction: *a sharp turn.* **3a** clear in outline or detail; distinct: *a sharp image.* **b** conspicuously clear; marked: *sharp contrast.* **4a** sudden and vigorous or violent: *a sharp tap.* **b** capable of acting or reacting quickly: *sharp reflexes.* **5a** of the senses: able to perceive clearly and distinctly. **b** intellectually alert and penetrating. **6a** causing intense usu sudden anguish. **b** cutting in language or implication. **7a** affecting the senses or sense organs intensely, e.g. pungent, tart, or acid, *esp* in flavour. **b** of a sound: shrill or piercing. **8** bitingly cold; icy. **9a** of a musical note: raised one semitone in pitch. **b** slightly higher than the true or desired pitch. **10** *informal* stylish or dressy. **11** paying shrewd usu selfish attention to personal gain. ⋙ **sharply** *adv,* **sharpness** *n.*

sharp[2] *adv* **1** in an abrupt manner. **2** exactly or precisely. **3** above the proper musical pitch.

sharp[3] *n* **1a** a musical note one semitone higher than the note shown at that position on the staff. **b** the character (#) on the musical staff that indicates a raising in pitch of one semitone. **2** a relatively long needle with a sharp point and a small rounded eye for use in general sewing.

sharpen *v* to make or become sharp or sharper. ⋙ **sharpener** *n.*

sharper *n* a cheat or swindler; *esp* a gambler who habitually cheats.

sharpish[1] *adv Brit, informal* with haste.

sharpish[2] *adj* fairly sharp.

sharp practice *n* dealing in which advantage is taken or sought unscrupulously.

sharpshooter *n* a good marksman.

sharp-tongued *adj* cutting or sarcastic in speech; quick to rebuke.

sharp-witted *adj* having or showing mental alertness or acute perceptions and intelligence.

shashlik *or* **shashlick** *n* a lamb kebab.

shat *v* past tense of SHIT[1].

shatter *v* **1** to break apart suddenly; to disintegrate. **2a** to break (something) into pieces, e.g. by a sudden blow. **b** to cause (something) to break down; to impair or disable. **3** to have a forceful or violent effect on the feelings of (somebody). **4** *informal* to cause (somebody) to be utterly exhausted. ⋙ **shattered** *adj.*

shave[1] *v* (*past tense* **shaved,** *past part.* **shaved** *or* **shaven**) **1** to cut off hair or beard close to the skin. **2** to remove the hair from (somebody or something) by cutting close to the roots. **3** to cut or trim closely. **4a** (*often* + off) to remove in thin layers or shreds. **b** to cut off thin layers or slices from. **5** to reduce (e.g. a price or record) by a small amount. **6** to come very close to or brush against in passing.

shave[2] *n* **1** the act or process of shaving. **2** a tool or machine for shaving.

shaven *v* past part. of SHAVE[1].

shaver *n* an electric-powered razor.

Shavian *adj* characteristic of the plays and writings of the Irish-born author and socialist George Bernard Shaw (d.1950).

shaving *n* **1** (*usu in pl*) something shaved off. **2** (*used before a noun*) used in the process of shaving one's face, legs, etc: *shaving cream.*

shawl *n* a usu decorative square, oblong, or triangular piece of fabric that is worn to cover the head or shoulders.

shawl collar *n* a collar that is rolled back and follows a continuous line round the neck and down the front edges of a garment.

shawm *n* an early woodwind musical instrument with a double reed, a precursor of the oboe.

Shawnee *n* (*pl* **Shawnees** *or* **Shawnee**) a member of a Native American people orig of the central Ohio valley.

she[1] *pron* **1** used to refer to a female person or creature, previously mentioned, who is neither the speaker nor hearer. **2** used to refer to something regarded as feminine, e.g. by personification.

she[2] *n* (*also in combination*) a female person or creature.

sheaf[1] *n* (*pl* **sheaves**) **1** a quantity of plant material, *esp* the stalks and ears of a cereal grass, bound together. **2** a collection of items laid or tied together.

sheaf[2] *v* to tie or bind into a sheaf or sheaves.

shear[1] *v* (*past tense* **sheared,** *past part.* **sheared** *or* **shorn**) **1** to cut off the wool, fleece, etc from (an animal). **2a** to cut with shears, or as if with shears. **b** (*often* + off) to cut or break (something) off something else. **3** to subject to a shear force. **4** to become divided or separated under the action of a shear force. ✱ **be shorn of** to be deprived of. ➤➤ **shearer** *n.*

shear[2] *n* **1** (*in pl*) a cutting implement similar to a pair of scissors but typically larger. **2** a force that causes or tends to cause two adjacent layers in a body to slide on each other in a direction parallel to their plane of contact.

shearwater *n* a long-winged, dark-coloured seabird that usu skims close to the waves in flight.

sheath *n* (*pl* **sheaths**) **1** a case or cover for a blade, e.g. of a knife or sword. **2** a cover or case of a plant or animal body, or part of one. **3** a cover or support applied like the sheath of a blade. **4** a condom. **5** a woman's very closely fitting dress.

sheathe *v* **1** to insert (a sword, dagger, etc) into its sheath. **2** of an animal, *esp* a cat: to retract (its claws). **3** to cover or encase as if in a sheath.

sheathing *n* material used to sheathe something.

sheath knife *n* a knife that has a fixed blade and is carried in a sheath.

sheave[1] *n* a grooved wheel, e.g. in a pulley block.

sheave[2] *v* to gather and bind (*esp* corn) into a sheaf.

sheaves *n* pl of SHEAF[1].

shebeen *n esp* in Ireland, Scotland, or South Africa, an unlicensed or illegally operated drinking establishment.

shed[1] *v* (**shedding,** *past tense and past part.* **shed**) **1a** to cast off or let fall (a natural covering such as leaves, hair, or a skin). **b** to take off (an item of clothing). **2** to get rid of (something or somebody). **3a** to cause (blood) to flow by wounding or killing. **b** to let (tears) flow. **c** to cast, spread, or diffuse (light, brightness, etc). **4** to drop (a load) accidentally. **5** to be incapable of holding or absorbing (a liquid); to repel. ✱ **shed light on something** to help to clarify something. ➤➤ **shedder** *n.*

shed[2] *n* **1** a usu single-storeyed building for shelter, storage, etc, *esp* with one or more sides open. **2** a large roofed structure, usu open on all sides, for storing or repairing vehicles, machinery, etc.

she'd *contr* **1** she had. **2** she would.

she-devil *n* an extremely cruel or malicious woman.

shedload *n informal* (*also in pl*) a large amount.

sheen *n* **1** a bright or shining quality or condition; brightness or lustre. **2** a subdued shininess or glitter of a surface. ➤➤ **sheeny** *adj.*

sheep *n* (*pl* **sheep**) **1** a ruminant mammal with a thick woolly coat; *specif* one domesticated for its flesh and wool. **2** an inane or docile person; *esp* one easily influenced or led. ✱ **separate the sheep from the goats** to identify and distinguish between those members of a group that are superior and those that are inferior.

sheep-dip *n* a liquid preparation into which sheep are plunged, *esp* to destroy parasites.

sheepdog *n* a dog used to tend, drive, or guard sheep; *esp* a Border collie.

sheepish *adj* embarrassed by consciousness of a fault. ➤➤ **sheepishly** *adv,* **sheepishness** *n.*

sheep's eyes *pl n* wistful amorous glances.

sheepshank *n* a knot for shortening a rope.

sheepskin *n* **1** the skin of a sheep, or leather made from it. **2** the skin of a sheep dressed with the wool on.

sheer[1] *adj* **1** not mixed or mingled with anything else; utter: *sheer ignorance.* **2** forming a vertical or almost vertical and unbroken surface to or from a great height; precipitous. **3** transparently fine; diaphanous. ➤➤ **sheerly** *adv,* **sheerness** *n.*

sheer[2] *adv* **1** altogether or completely. **2** straight up or down without a break.

sheer[3] *v* to deviate or cause to deviate from a course.

sheet[1] *n* **1** a broad piece of cloth; *specif* a rectangle of cloth, e.g. of linen or cotton, used as an article of bed linen. **2** a usu rectangular piece of paper. **3** a broad usu flat expanse. **4** a suspended or moving expanse: *a sheet of flame.* **5** a piece of something that is thin in comparison to its length and breadth.

sheet[2] *v* **1** to form into, provide with, or cover with a sheet or sheets. **2** to come down in sheets.

sheet[3] *n* **1** a rope that regulates the angle at which a sail is set in relation to the wind. **2** (*in pl*) the spaces at either end of an open boat.

sheet anchor *n* **1** an emergency anchor formerly carried in the broadest part of a ship. **2** a principal support or thing to be depended on, *esp* in danger; a mainstay.

sheeting *n* material in the form of sheets or suitable for making into sheets.

sheet lightning *n* lightning in diffused or sheet form due to reflection and diffusion by clouds.

sheet metal *n* metal in the form of a thin sheet.

sheet music *n* **1** music in its printed form. **2** a printed copy of a piece of music.

sheikh *or* **sheik** /shayk, sheek/ *n* **1** an Arab leader, *esp* the head of a clan or community. **2** a Muslim religious or community leader. ➤➤ **sheikhdom** *n.*

shekel /'shekl/ *n* **1** the basic monetary unit of Israel. **2** *informal* (*in pl*) money.

shelduck *n* (*pl* **shelducks** *or* **shelduck**) a common mostly black and white duck slightly larger than the mallard.

shelf *n* (*pl* **shelves**) **1** a thin flat usu long and narrow piece of a solid material fastened horizontally at a distance from the floor to hold objects. **2 a** a partially submerged sandbank or ledge of rocks. **b**

a flat projecting layer of rock. ✱ **off the shelf** available from stock, not made to order. **on the shelf 1** in a state of inactivity or uselessness. **2** considered unlikely to marry, *esp* because of being too old.

shelf-life *n* the length of time for which a product may be stored or displayed without serious deterioration.

shell[1] *n* **1a** a hard rigid often largely calcium-containing covering of an animal, e.g. a turtle, oyster, or beetle. **b** the hard or tough outer covering of an egg, *esp* a bird's egg. **2** a seashell. **3** the covering or outside part of a fruit or seed, *esp* when hard or fibrous. **4 a** a framework or exterior structure; *esp* the outer frame of a building that is unfinished or has been destroyed, or of the bodywork of a vehicle. **b** an edible case for holding a filling. **5a** a projectile for a large gun containing an explosive bursting charge. **b** a metal or paper case which holds the charge in cartridges, fireworks, etc. **6** *NAm* a cartridge. **7** a narrow light racing rowing boat. ✱ **come out of one's shell** to become less shy and reserved and more communicative. ➤➤ **shelly** *adj.*

shell[2] *v* **1** to take (something) out of its natural enclosing cover, e.g. a shell, husk, pod, or capsule. **2** to fire shells at, on, or into (a target).

she'll *contr* **1** she will. **2** she shall.

shellac[1] *n* **1** the purified form of a resin produced by various insects, usu obtained as yellow or orange flakes. **2** a solution of this in alcohol used in making varnish.

shellac[2] *v* (**shellacked, shellacking**) to treat or coat with shellac.

shell company *n* a company with no assets or trading operations of its own that is used as a means of controlling other companies or conducting various financial operations.

shellfire *n* the firing of large guns or the shells discharged from them.

shellfish *n* an aquatic invertebrate animal with a shell or carapace, *esp* an edible mollusc or crustacean.

shell out *v informal* to pay (money).

shell pink *adj* of a light yellowish pink colour. ➤➤ **shell pink** *n.*

shell program *n* a computer program that provides a basic framework within which users can run or develop their own programs.

shell shock *n* a mental disorder characterized by neurotic and often hysterical symptoms that occurs under conditions that cause intense stress, such as wartime combat.

shell suit *n* a lightweight tracksuit with a warm cotton lining and a typically shiny nylon covering.

Shelta *n* a secret language based on Gaelic and English used by some travelling people in the British Isles.

shelter[1] *n* **1** something, *esp* a structure, affording cover or protection. **2** the state of being covered and protected; refuge.

shelter[2] *v* **1** to serve as a shelter for; to protect. **2** to keep (somebody or something) concealed or protected. **3** to take shelter.

sheltered *adj* **1** protected from hardship or unpleasant realities. **2** of accommodation: designed for elderly or disabled people to live safely and as independently as possible, under the care of a resident warden.

shelve *v* **1** to provide (a space or piece of furniture) with shelves. **2** to place on a shelf. **3** to put (something) off or aside. **4** to slope gently.

shelves *n* pl of SHELF.

shelving *n* shelves, or material for constructing shelves.

shemozzle *or* **schemozzle** *n informal* a scene of confusion, dispute, or uproar.

shenanigan *n informal* (*usu in pl*) **1** deliberate deception; trickery. **2** boisterous mischief; high jinks.

Sheol *n* the abode of the dead in early Hebrew thought.

shepherd[1] *n* **1** somebody who tends sheep. **2** a pastor.

shepherd[2] *v* **1** to tend (sheep) as a shepherd. **2** to guide, marshal, or conduct (people) like sheep.

shepherdess *n* a woman or girl who tends sheep, *esp* as depicted in stories or paintings.

shepherd's pie *n* a hot dish of minced meat, *esp* lamb, with a mashed potato topping.

shepherd's purse *n* a white-flowered annual plant of the mustard family that has small flat heart-shaped seed pods and is a common weed.

Sheraton *adj* denoting a style of furniture that originated in England around 1800 and is characterized by straight lines and graceful proportions.

sherbet *n* **1a** a sweet powder that effervesces in liquid and is eaten dry or used to make fizzy drinks. **b** a drink made with this powder. **2** *NAm* a water ice or sorbet. **3** a Middle Eastern cold drink of sweetened and diluted fruit juice.

sherd *n* = POTSHERD.

sheria /shə'ree·ə/ *n* see SHARIA.

sheriff *n* **1** the honorary chief executive officer of the Crown in each English county who has mainly judicial and ceremonial duties. **2** the chief judge of a Scottish county or district. **3** a county law enforcement officer in the USA.

sheriff court *n* the main inferior court in Scotland, dealing with both civil and criminal cases.

Sherpa *n* (*pl* **Sherpa** *or* **Sherpas**) a member of a Tibetan people living on the high southern slopes of the Himalayas. ➤➤ **Sherpa** *adj.*

sherry *n* (*pl* **-ies**) a blended fortified wine from S Spain.

she's *contr* **1** she is. **2** she has.

Shetland pony *n* an animal of a breed of small stocky shaggy ponies that originated in the Shetland Islands.

shew *v Brit, archaic* = SHOW[1].

Shia /'shee·ə/ *n* (*pl* **Shias** *or* **Shia**) **1** the branch of Islam deriving authority from Muhammad's cousin and son-in-law Ali and his appointed successors, the Imams: compare SUNNI. **2** a member of this branch of Islam.

shiatsu *n* = ACUPRESSURE.

shibboleth *n* a custom, belief, or particular use of language that characterizes the members of a particular group.

Word history

Hebrew *shibbōleth* stream; from the use of this word as a test to distinguish Gileadites from Ephraimites, who pronounced it *sibbōleth*. In the biblical account (Judges 12:4–6) of a battle between the Ephraimites and Gileadites, the Ephraimites were defeated, and those of their forces who escaped the battlefield tried to pass themselves off as Gileadites and cross the river Jordan to safety. To identify them, everyone crossing the river was asked to pronounce the word *shibboleth*. The Ephraimites, who spoke a different dialect, could not cope with the /sh/ sound but could only pronounce it as /s/; thus they were found out, and 42,000 of them were killed. The metaphorical senses of the word entered English in the mid-17th cent.

shield[1] *n* **1** a piece of armour carried on the arm or in the hand and used *esp* for warding off blows. **2** somebody or something that protects or defends; a defence. **3** something designed to protect people from injury from moving parts of machinery, live electrical conductors, etc. **4** a defined area, the surface of which constitutes a heraldic field, on which heraldic arms are displayed. **5** an armoured screen protecting an otherwise exposed gun. **6 a** a trophy awarded in recognition of achievement, e.g. in a sporting event. **b** a decorative or identifying emblem, *esp* a US police officer's official badge.

shield[2] *v* **1** to protect (something or somebody) with a shield, or as if with a shield. **2** to prevent (somebody or something) from being seen. **3** to prevent radiation in the form of light, sound, etc escaping from (something).

shift[1] *v* **1** to change the place, position, or direction of (something or somebody); to move. **2** to change place, position, or direction. **3** *Brit, informal* to move fast. **4** *Brit* to remove (e.g. a stain) by cleaning, rubbing, etc. **5** *informal* to sell or dispose of (something), *esp* quickly or in large quantities. **6** *NAm* to change gear in a motor vehicle. ✱ **shift for oneself** to assume responsibility for providing for oneself. **shift oneself** *Brit, informal* to start moving fast; to hurry up. ➤➤ **shifter** *n.*

shift[2] *n* **1a** a change in direction. **b** a change in emphasis, judgment, or attitude. **2a** (*used as sing. or pl*) a group who work, e.g. in a factory, in alternation with other groups. **b** a scheduled period of work or duty. **3** a change in place or position. **4a** *archaic* a deceitful or underhand scheme or method. **b** (*usu in pl*) an expedient tried in difficult circumstances. **5** a loose unfitted slip or dress. **6** *NAm* the gear change in a motor vehicle.

shift key *n* a key on a keyboard that when held down permits a different set of characters, *esp* the capitals, to be printed.

shiftless *adj* lacking ambition or motivation; lazy. ➤➤ **shiftlessness** *n.*

shifty *adj* (**-ier, -iest**) **1** given to deception, evasion, or fraud; slippery. **2** indicative of a furtive or devious nature. ➤➤ **shiftily** *adv,* **shiftiness** *n.*

shigella *n* (*pl* **shigellae** *or* **shigellas**) a bacterium of a genus that causes dysentery in animals, *esp* human beings.

shih-tzu /shee'tsooh/ *n* a small dog of an old Chinese breed with short muscular legs and massive amounts of long dense hair.

shiitake /shi'tahkay/ *n* a large brown mushroom used in Oriental cookery.

Shiite /'sheeiet/ *n* an adherent of Islam as taught by the Shia. ➤➤ **Shiism** *n,* **Shiite** *adj.*

shiksa *or* **shikse** *n derog* a non-Jewish girl.

shillelagh *n* an Irish cudgel.

shilling *n* **1** a former monetary unit in Britain and various Commonwealth countries, worth one 20th of a pound or twelve old pence. **2** the basic monetary unit of Kenya, Somalia, Tanzania, and Uganda.

shilly-shally *v* (**-ies, -ied**) to show hesitation or lack of decisiveness. ➤➤ **shilly-shally** *n.*

shim[1] *n* a thin piece of wood, metal, etc used to fill in the space between things, e.g. for support or adjustment of fit.

shim[2] *v* (**shimmed, shimming**) to fill out or level up by the use of one or more shims.

shimmer[1] *v* to shine with a softly tremulous or wavering light; to glimmer.

shimmer[2] *n* a shimmering light. ➤➤ **shimmery** *adj.*

shimmy[1] *n* (*pl* **-ies**) a jazz dance characterized by a shaking of the body from the shoulders downwards.

shimmy[2] *v* (**-ies, -ied**) **1** to dance the shimmy. **2** to shake, quiver, or tremble.

shin[1] *n* **1** the front part of the leg of a vertebrate animal below the knee. **2** a cut of meat from this part.

shin[2] *v* (**shinned, shinning**) (*usu* + up/down) to climb by gripping with the hands or arms and the legs and hauling oneself up or lowering oneself down.

shinbone *n* = TIBIA .

shindig *n informal* a usu boisterous social gathering.

shindy *n* (*pl* **-ies**) *informal* a quarrel or brawl.

shine[1] *v* (*past tense and past part.* **shone**) **1** to emit light. **2** to be bright with reflected light. **3** to be outstanding or distinguished. **4** to have a radiant or lively appearance. **5** to direct the light of (e.g. a lamp or torch). **6** (*past tense and past part.* **shined**) to make bright by polishing.

shine[2] *n* **1** brightness caused by the emission or reflection of light. **2** brilliance or splendour. **3** an act of polishing. ✱ **take a shine to** *informal* to like or fancy (somebody or something) immediately.

shiner *n informal* = BLACK EYE.

shingle[1] *n* **1** a small thin piece of building material, usu wood, for laying in overlapping rows as a covering for the roof or sides of a building. **2** *NAm* a small signboard, *esp* indicating the office of a doctor, lawyer, etc.

shingle[2] *v* to cover (a roof, etc) with shingles.

shingle[3] *n* small rounded pebbles, or an area, *esp* on the seashore, that is covered with them. ➤➤ **shingly** *adj.*

shingles *pl n* (*used as sing.*) severe short-lasting inflammation of certain ganglia of the nerves that leave the brain and spinal cord, caused by a virus and associated with a rash of blisters and often intense neuralgic pain.

shin pad *n* a pad worn inside a sock to protect the shin when playing games such as football or hockey.

shinsplints *pl n* (*used as sing.*) a painful muscular swelling of the lower leg that is a common injury in athletes who regularly run on hard surfaces.

Shinto *n* the indigenous animistic religion of Japan, including the veneration of the Emperor as a descendant of the sun goddess. ➤➤ **Shintoism** *n,* **Shintoist** *n.*

shinty *n* a variation of hurling played in Scotland.

shiny *adj* (**-ier, -iest**) **1** bright or glossy in appearance; lustrous or polished. **2** of material, clothes, etc: rubbed or worn to a smooth surface that reflects light. ➤➤ **shininess** *n.*

ship[1] *n* **1a** a floating vessel, propelled by an engine or sails, for travelling over water, *esp* a large seagoing one. **b** a square-rigged sailing vessel having a bowsprit and usu three masts. **2** an airship, aircraft, or spacecraft. ✱ **when one's ship comes in** when one becomes rich.

ship[2] *v* (**shipped, shipping**) **1a** to transport (e.g. goods) on board a ship. **b** to transport (e.g. goods) by another means, such as by road or rail. **2** *informal* (*often* + off) to cause (somebody or something) to be sent somewhere. **3** to put (a piece of equipment) in place on a boat ready for use. **4** to take (something) into a ship or boat. **5** of a boat or ship: to take in (water) over the side. **6** to go or travel by ship. **7** to engage to serve on shipboard. ➤➤ **shipper** *n.*

-ship *suffix* forming nouns, denoting: **1** the state, condition, or quality of: *friendship*. **2** the office, status, or profession of: *professorship*. **3** the art or skill of: *horsemanship; scholarship*. **4** (*used as sing. or pl*) the whole group or body sharing the state specified: *readership; membership*. **5** somebody entitled to the rank, title, or appellation specified: *his Lordship*.

shipboard[1] ✱ **on shipboard** on board a ship.

shipboard[2] *adj* existing or taking place on board a ship.

shipbuilder *n* a person or company that designs or constructs ships. ⋙ **shipbuilding** *n*.

ship canal *n* a canal large enough to allow the passage of sea-going vessels.

shipmate *n* a fellow sailor.

shipment *n* **1** the act or process of shipping. **2** a consignment or quantity of goods shipped.

ship money *n* a tax levied at various times in England until 1640, to provide ships for the national defence.

ship of the line *n* a ship of war large enough to have a place in the line of battle.

shipping *n* **1** ships, *esp* those sailing in a particular area or belonging to one port or country. **2** the activity or business of a shipper.

ship's biscuit *n chiefly Brit* a type of hard biscuit orig for eating on board ship.

shipshape *adj* trim; tidy.

shipway *n* the structure on which a ship is built and from which it is launched.

shipworm *n* an elongated marine clam that resembles a worm and burrows in submerged wood.

shipwreck[1] *n* **1** a wrecked ship or its remains. **2** the destruction or loss of a ship.

shipwreck[2] *v* to cause (somebody or a ship) to undergo shipwreck.

shipwright *n* a carpenter skilled in ship construction and repair.

shipyard *n* a yard, place, or enclosure where ships are built or repaired.

Shiraz *n* a variety of grape used in the production of dark full-bodied red wine, or the wine produced from it.

shire *n* **1** an English county, *esp* one with a name ending in *-shire*. **2** (*usu* **the Shires**) an English district consisting chiefly of Leicestershire and Northamptonshire.

shire horse *n* an animal of a British breed of large heavy draught horses.

shirk *v* to evade or dodge (a duty, responsibility, etc). ⋙ **shirker** *n*.

shirr *v* (**shirred, shirring**) to gather (e.g. cloth) by drawing up the material along two or more parallel lines of stitching or by stitching in rows of elastic thread or an elastic webbing.

shirt *n* a garment for the upper body, usu one that opens the full length of the centre front and has sleeves and a collar. ✱ **have/take the shirt off somebody's back** *informal* to take somebody's last remaining possessions. **keep one's shirt on** *informal* to remain calm. **lose one's shirt** *informal* to lose a large amount of money, *esp* by losing a bet. **put one's shirt on** *Brit, informal* to bet all the money one has on (something).

shirtsleeve *n* the sleeve of a shirt. ✱ **in shirtsleeves** of a man: not wearing a jacket over his shirt. ⋙ **shirt-sleeved** *adj*.

shirtwaister (*NAm* **shirtwaist**) *n* a fitted dress that fastens down the centre front to just below the waist or to the hem.

shirty *adj* (**-ier, -iest**) *informal* bad-tempered; fractious. ⋙ **shirtily** *adv*, **shirtiness** *n*.

shish kebab *n* a kebab cooked on a skewer.

shit[1] *v* (**shitting,** *past tense and past part.* **shitted** *or* **shit** *or* **shat**) *coarse slang* to defecate. ✱ **shit oneself** *coarse slang* to be extremely frightened.

shit[2] *n coarse slang* **1** faeces. **2a** nonsense or foolishness. **b** a despicable person. ✱ **be up shit creek (without a paddle)** *coarse slang* to be in a very difficult situation. **not to give a shit** *coarse slang* to be totally unconcerned. **when the shit hits the fan** *coarse slang* when the really serious trouble begins.

shit[3] *interj coarse slang* used to express annoyance or impatience.

shite *noun and interj Brit, coarse slang* = SHIT[2], SHIT[3].

shit-hot *adj coarse slang* really good or brilliant.

shitless ✱ **be scared shitless** *coarse slang* to be extremely scared.

shitty *adj* (**-ier, -iest**) *coarse slang* **1** nasty or unpleasant. **2** covered in excrement.

shiver[1] *v* to tremble, *esp* with cold or fever.

shiver[2] *n* **1** an instance of shivering; a tremor. **2** (**the shivers**) a fit of shivering. ⋙ **shivery** *adj*.

shiver[3] *n* any of the small pieces that result from the shattering of something brittle.

shiver[4] *v* to break or cause to break into many small fragments.

Shoah *n* used by Jews: the Holocaust.

shoal[1] *n* **1** an underwater sandbank, *esp* one exposed at low tide. **2** an area of shallow water.

shoal[2] *v* of water: to become shallow or less deep.

shoal[3] *n* a large group, *esp* of fish.

shock[1] *n* **1a** a sudden or violent disturbance of a person's thoughts or emotions. **b** something that causes a disturbance of this kind. **2** a state in which most bodily functions temporarily cease to operate as normal, caused usu by severe injuries, bleeding, burns, or psychological trauma. **3** sudden stimulation of the nerves and convulsive contraction of the muscles caused by the passage of electricity through the body. **4a** a violent impact or collision. **b** a violent shaking or jarring.

shock[2] *v* **1a** to cause (somebody) to feel sudden surprise, terror, horror, or offence. **b** to cause (somebody) to undergo a physical or nervous shock. **2** to cause (e.g. an animal) to experience an electric shock. ⋙ **shockable** *adj*, **shockproof** *adj*.

shock[3] *n* a pile of sheaves of grain or stalks of maize set upright in a field.

shock[4] *n* a thick bushy mass, usu of hair.

shock absorber *n* a device for absorbing the energy of sudden jolts or shocks, *esp* fitted to a motor vehicle to give a smoother ride.

shocker *n informal* **1** something horrifying or offensive, e.g. a sensational work of fiction or drama. **2** an incorrigible or naughty person.

shock-headed *adj* having a thick bushy mass of hair.

shocking *adj* **1** giving cause for indignation or offence. **2** *Brit, informal* very bad. ⋙ **shockingly** *adv*.

shocking pink *adj* of a striking, vivid, or intense pink colour. ⋙ **shocking pink** *n*.

shock therapy *n* a treatment for some serious mental disorders that involves artificially inducing a coma or convulsions.

shock treatment *n* = SHOCK THERAPY.

shock troops *pl n* troops trained and selected for assault.

shock wave *n* **1** = BLAST[1] (IB). **2** a compressional wave formed whenever the speed of a body, e.g. an aircraft, relative to a medium, e.g. the air, exceeds that at which the medium can transmit sound.

shod *v* past tense and past part. of SHOE[2].

shoddy[1] *adj* (**-ier, -iest**) **1** hastily or poorly done; inferior. **2** discreditable or despicable. ⋙ **shoddily** *adv*, **shoddiness** *n*.

shoddy[2] *n* a fabric, often of inferior quality, manufactured wholly or partly from reclaimed wool.

shoe[1] *n* **1a** an outer covering for the foot that does not extend above the ankle and has a thick or stiff sole and often an attached heel. **b** a metal plate or rim for the hoof of an animal. **2** something resembling a shoe in shape or function. **3** the part of a vehicle braking system that presses on the brake drum. ✱ **be in somebody's shoes** to be in somebody else's situation or position. **dead men's shoes** a situation in which a job, position, or property can only be obtained through the death or voluntary withdrawal of somebody else.

shoe[2] *v* (**shoes, shoed, shoeing,** *past tense and past part.* **shod**) **1** to fit (e.g. a horse) with a shoe. **2** to protect or reinforce with a usu metal shoe. **3** (*usu in passive*) to equip with shoes.

shoehorn *n* a curved piece of metal, plastic, etc used to ease the heel into the back of a shoe.

shoe-horn *v* to force into a limited space.

shoelace *n* a lace or string for fastening a shoe.

shoemaker *n* somebody whose occupation is making or repairing footwear.

shoestring *n* **1** *NAm* = SHOELACE. **2** *informal* an amount of money inadequate or barely adequate to meet one's needs.

shoetree *n* a foot-shaped device inserted in a shoe to keep it in shape when not being worn.

shogun /'shohgən/ *n* any of a line of Japanese military governors who effectively ruled the country before the revolution of 1867–68. ⋙ **shogunate** *n*.

Shona /'shohnə/ *n* (*pl* **Shonas** *or* **Shona**) a member of a group of peoples inhabiting parts of southern Africa. ⋙ **Shona** *adj*.

shone *v* past tense and past part. of SHINE[1].

shook *v* past tense of SHAKE[1].

shoot[1] *v* (*past tense and past part.* **shot**) **1a** to strike and wound or kill (a person or an animal) with a bullet from a gun, arrow from a bow, or similar missile. **b** to fire (a gun) or release an arrow from (a bow). **2** to move or cause to move suddenly or swiftly forward. **3** to drive (e.g. a ball or puck) *esp* towards a goal or hole, by striking it. **4a** to utter (e.g. words or sounds) rapidly, suddenly, or violently. **b** to direct (e.g. a glance) at somebody with suddenness or intensity. **5** to photograph or film (somebody or something). **6** to push or slide (e.g. the bolt of a door or lock) into or out of a fastening. **7a** of a boat: to pass swiftly by, over, or along (a bridge, waterfall, or rapids). **b** *informal* of a vehicle or driver: to pass through (a road junction or traffic lights) without slowing down or stopping. **8** to produce a piercing sensation that moves rapidly through part of the body: *Pain shot up his arm.* **9** to grow or sprout by putting out shoots. ✱ **shoot a line** *informal* to lie about something, or to embroider an account of it in romantic or boastful detail. **shoot one's cuffs** to pull one's shirt cuffs down. **shoot oneself in the foot** to act inadvertently to one's own detriment. **shoot one's mouth off** *informal* to talk foolishly or indiscreetly. **shoot the breeze** *NAm, informal* to chat. **the whole shooting match** *informal* everything.

shoot[2] *n* **1** a stem or branch with its leaves, buds, etc, *esp* when not yet mature. **2a** a shooting trip or party. **b** land over which somebody holds the right to shoot game. **c** a shooting match. **3** = CHUTE. **4** a session during which a photographer takes photographs or a film or video is shot.

shoot down *v* **1** to kill or wound (somebody) by shooting them, *esp* callously. **2** to bring down (an aircraft or missile) by shooting.

shooter *n* **1** a person empowered to score goals in netball. **2** (*usu in combination*) a repeating pistol. **3** somebody who uses a gun.

shooting box *n Brit* a small country house used by a shooting party.

shooting gallery *n* a usu covered range equipped with targets for practice in shooting with firearms.

shooting star *n* a meteor appearing as a temporary streak of light in the night sky.

shooting stick *n* a spiked stick with a handle that opens out into a seat.

shoot-out *n informal* a usu decisive battle fought with handguns or rifles.

shoot up *v informal* to inject a narcotic drug into a vein.

shop[1] *n* **1** a building or room for the retail sale of merchandise or for the sale of services. **2** a place or part of a factory where a particular manufacturing or repair process takes place. ✱ **talk shop** to talk about one's business or profession, *esp* outside working hours.

shop[2] *v* (**shopped, shopping**) **1** to visit a shop in order to purchase goods. **2** *informal* to inform on; to betray. ⋙ **shopping** *n*.

shopaholic *n informal* somebody who shops obsessively.

shop around *v* to investigate a market or situation in search of the best buy.

shop assistant *n Brit* somebody employed to sell goods in a retail shop.

shopfitter *n* somebody who equips a shop with fittings, e.g. shelves.

shopfloor *n* **1** *Brit* the area in which machinery or workbenches are located in a factory or mill, *esp* considered as a place of work. **2** (*used as sing. or pl*) the workers in an establishment as distinct from the management.

shopfront *n* the front side of a shop facing the street.

shopkeeper *n* somebody who runs a retail shop.

shoplift *v* to steal from a shop. ⋙ **shoplifter** *n*, **shoplifting** *n*.

shopper *n* **1** somebody who is shopping. **2** *Brit* a bag used for shopping, *esp* a square bag on wheels that can be pulled along. **3** a bicycle that has small wheels and a basket.

shopping centre *n* a group of retail shops and service establishments of different types.

shopping mall *n* a large enclosed shopping centre, usu with space for car parking.

shopping rage *n* = SHOP RAGE.

shopping therapy *n* shopping undertaken as a release from and antidote to the stresses and strains of everyday life.

shop rage *n* violent or aggressive behaviour by shoppers, arising from various forms of frustration.

shopsoiled *adj chiefly Brit* soiled, faded, or in less than perfect condition through excessive handling or display in a shop.

shop steward *n* a union member elected to represent usu manual workers.

shopwalker *n Brit* somebody employed in a large shop to oversee the shop assistants and aid customers.

shopwindow *n* **1** a usu large window in which a shop displays merchandise. **2** a place where something or somebody can be exhibited to best advantage; a showcase.

shore[1] *n* **1** the land bordering the sea or another large body of water. **2** land as distinguished from the sea. ⋙ **shorewards** *adv.*

shore[2] *v* to support (something) with a beam or prop, *esp* to prevent it sinking or sagging.

shore[3] *n* a beam or prop used to shore something. ⋙ **shoring** *n.*

shore leave *n* time granted to members of a ship's crew to go ashore.

shoreline *n* the line where a body of water and the shore meet.

shorn *v* past part. of SHEAR[1].

short[1] *adj* **1** having little or insufficient length or height. **2** not extended in time; brief. **3** limited in distance. **4** seeming to pass quickly: *She made great progress in just a few short years.* **5a** not coming up to a measure or requirement: *in short supply.* **b** not reaching far enough: *The throw was short by five metres.* **c** (*often* + of) insufficiently supplied: *short of cash.* **6a** not lengthy or protracted; concise. **b** made briefer; abbreviated: *Sue is short for Susan.* **7a** abrupt or curt. **b** quickly provoked. **8a** of a speech sound: having a relatively short duration. **b** of one of a pair of similarly spelt vowel sounds: shorter in duration than the other. **9** of odds in betting: almost even. **10** of pastry: crisp and easily broken owing to the presence of fat; crumbly. ✱ **get/have somebody by the short and curlies** *informal* to have somebody totally at one's mercy. **in the short run** for the immediate future. **make short work of something** to get through something quickly. **short for** an abbreviation for. **short on** not having much of. ⋙ **shortish** *adj,* **shortness** *n.*

short[2] *adv* **1** in an abrupt manner; suddenly: *The car stopped short.* **2** before reaching a specified or intended point or target: *The shells fell short.* ✱ **be taken/caught short** *Brit, informal* to feel a sudden embarrassing need to defecate or urinate. **bring/pull somebody up short** to make somebody stop or pause suddenly. **short of 1** less than. **2** before reaching (an extreme).

short[3] *n* **1** *Brit, informal* a drink of spirits; *esp* such a drink as opposed to beer. **2** a brief film, often a documentary or educational film. **3** = SHORT CIRCUIT. ✱ **for short** as an abbreviation. **in short** by way of summary; briefly.

short[4] *v* to short-circuit or cause to short-circuit.

shortage *n* a lack or deficit.

short back and sides *n Brit* a hairstyle in which the hair round the ears and at the neck is cut very short.

shortbread *n* a thick crumbly biscuit made from flour, sugar, and fat.

shortcake *n* **1** = SHORTBREAD. **2** a thick short cake resembling biscuit that is usu sandwiched with a layer of fruit and cream and eaten as a dessert.

shortchange *v* **1** to give less than the correct amount of change to. **2** *informal* to cheat (somebody).

short circuit *n* the accidental or deliberate joining of two parts of an electric circuit by a conductor of less resistance that allows an excessive current to flow, usu blowing a fuse.

short-circuit *v* (**short-circuited, short-circuiting**) **1** to apply a short circuit to or cause a short circuit in (something) so as to render it inoperative. **2** to bypass or circumvent.

shortcoming *n* a deficiency or defect.

shortcrust pastry *n* a basic pastry used for pies, flans, and tarts and made with half as much fat as flour.

shortcut *n* a route or procedure quicker and more direct than one customarily followed.

short-dated *adj* of a stock or bond: having a short time to run before redemption.

short division *n* arithmetic division in which the successive steps can be worked out mentally.

shorten *v* **1** to make or become short or shorter. **2** to reduce the area or amount of (sail that is set).

shortening *n* an edible fat, e.g. butter or lard, used to shorten pastry, biscuits, etc.

shortfall *n* = DEFICIT.

shorthand *n* **1** a method of rapid writing that substitutes symbols and abbreviations for letters, words, or phrases. **2** a system or instance of rapid or abbreviated communication.

shorthanded *adj* short of the usual or requisite number of staff; understaffed.

short haul *n* the transport of goods or passengers over relatively short distances.

short head *n* in horse racing, a distance less than the length of a horse's head.

shorthold *adj* in English law, of or being a tenancy for a fixed period of between one and five years.

shorthorn *n* an animal of a breed of beef cattle with short horns.

shortie *n* see SHORTY.

short list *n Brit* a list of selected candidates, e.g. for a job, from whom a final choice must be made.

short-list *v Brit* to place on a short list.

short-lived *adj* not living or lasting long.

shortly *adv* **1a** in a short time. **b** at a short interval. **2a** in a few words; briefly. **b** in an abrupt manner.

short measure *n* a measured quantity, e.g. of alcohol, that is smaller than the amount paid for.

short-order *adj NAm* denoting or to do with food that can be quickly cooked.

short-range *adj* **1** relating to, suitable for, or capable of travelling only short distances. **2** involving a relatively short period of time.

shorts *pl n* **1** knee-length or less than knee-length trousers. **2** *NAm* men's underpants.

short shrift *n* summary or inconsiderate treatment.

short sight *n* = MYOPIA.

short-sighted *adj* **1** able to see near objects more clearly than distant objects; myopic. **2** lacking foresight. ⋙ **short-sightedly** *adv,* **short-sightedness** *n.*

short-staffed *adj* having fewer than the usual number of workers.

shortstop *n* in baseball, the fielder defending the area between second and third base.

short story *n* a short piece of prose fiction usu dealing with only a few characters and incidents.

short-tempered *adj* quickly or easily made angry.

short-term *adj* **1** involving a relatively short period of time. **2** involving a financial operation or obligation lasting for a brief period, *esp* one of less than a year.

short-termism *n* a tendency to concentrate on immediate results or prospects, and to neglect long-term strategy.

short time *n* reduced working hours because of a lack of work.

short-waisted *adj* of a garment: with an unusually high waist.

short wave *n* a band of radio waves having wavelengths between about 10m and 100m and typically used for amateur transmissions or long-range broadcasting.

short-winded *adj* affected with or characterized by shortness of breath.

shorty *or* **shortie** *n* (*pl* **-ies**) *informal* a short person or thing, *esp* a nightdress.

Shoshone /shə'shohni/ *n* (*pl* **Shoshones** *or* **Shoshone**) a member of a group of Native American peoples, orig ranging through California, Colorado, Idaho, Utah, and Wyoming.

shot[1] *n* **1** the act of firing a gun, bow, etc, or of discharging a bullet, arrow, etc at a target. **2** somebody who shoots, *esp* with regard to their ability. **3a** a stroke or throw in a game, e.g. tennis, billiards, or basketball. **b** a kick aimed at the goal in football. **4** *informal* an attempt or try. **5** a wild guess or conjecture. **6a** (*pl* **shot**) something propelled by shooting; *esp* small lead or steel pellets forming a charge for a shotgun. **b** (*pl* **shot**) a single non-explosive projectile for a gun or cannon. **7** a metal sphere that is thrown for distance as an athletic field event. **8a** a single photographic exposure; *esp* a snapshot. **b** a single sequence of a film or a television programme taken by one camera without interruption. **9a** a hypodermic injection of a drug or vaccine. **b** *informal* a single drink of spirits. **10** the launch of a rocket into space: *a moon shot.* ✱ **a shot in the arm** *informal* a stimulus or boost. **a shot in the dark** a wild guess. **give it/something one's best shot** to try to do something as well as one possibly can. **like a shot** *informal* very rapidly.

shot[2] *adj* **1** of a fabric: having colour effects which change with the light; iridescent. **2** (+ with) infused or permeated with a quality or element: *shot through with wit.* **3** *informal* utterly exhausted or ruined. ✱ **be/get shot of somebody/something** *chiefly Brit, informal* to be or get rid of somebody or something.

shot[3] *v* past tense and past part. of SHOOT[1].

shot-blast *v* to clean (*esp* metal) by directing a stream of shot at it.

shotgun *n* **1** an often double-barrelled smoothbore shoulder weapon for firing quantities of metal shot at short ranges. **2** (*used before a noun*) denoting something that is enforced or done in a hurry: *a shotgun merger.*

shotgun wedding *n informal* a wedding that is forced or required, *esp* because of the bride's pregnancy.

shot put *n* an athletic field event involving the throwing of a SHOT[1] (7) (heavy metal sphere). ➤➤ **shot-putter** *n*, **shot-putting** *n*.

should *v aux* the past tense of SHALL, used: **1** to introduce a possibility or presumption: *I should be surprised if he wrote.* **2** to introduce a fact that is the object of comment: *It's odd that you should mention that.* **3** to express obligation or recommendation: *You should take a bus to Marble Arch.* **4** in reported speech to express an action or state in the future: *She banged on the door and said we should be late.* **5** to express probability or expectation: *They should be here by noon.* **6** to express a polite form of direct statement: *I should have thought it was colder than that.*

Usage note

should *or* **would**? Traditionally, *should* and *would* were used in reported speech in the same way as *shall* and *will* were used in direct speech: *I said I should be there; She told me she would be there.* This distinction is now made more rarely, and *would* is generally used instead of *should.* In spoken and informal contexts any distinction between *should* and *would* is hidden by the use of the contraction *'d; I'd; we'd,* etc. Note, however, that only *should* is used with the meaning 'ought to' as in: *I should go, but I don't particularly want to.* See also note at SHALL.

shoulder[1] *n* **1** the part of the human body that connects the arm to the trunk. **2** a cut of meat including the upper joint of the foreleg and adjacent parts. **3** an area adjacent to a higher, more prominent, or more important part, e.g. the slope of a mountain near the top. ✱ **put one's shoulder to the wheel** to make an effort, *esp* a cooperative effort. **shoulder to shoulder** side by side or united.

shoulder[2] *v* **1a** to place or carry on one's shoulder or shoulders. **b** to assume the burden or responsibility of. **2** to push or thrust with one's shoulder. **3** to push (one's way) aggressively.

shoulder bag *n* a bag that has a strap attached at each side of sufficient length for the bag to be hung over the shoulder.

shoulder blade *n* = SCAPULA.

shoulder pad *n* a shaped pad sewn into the shoulder of a garment.

shoulder strap *n* a strap that passes across the shoulder and holds up a garment or supports a bag.

shoulder surfing *n* watching a person keying in a PIN number, etc, in order to memorize the number and make use of it for the fraudulent purchasing of goods and services: compare IDENTITY THEFT.

shouldn't *contr* should not.

shout[1] *v* **1** to utter a sudden loud cry. **2** to utter in a loud voice. ➤➤ **shouter** *n*.

shout[2] *n* **1** a loud cry or call. **2** *Brit, informal* a round of drinks, or one's turn to buy a round.

shout down *v* to drown the words of (a speaker) by shouting.

shove[1] *v* **1** to push along with steady force. **2** to push or put in a rough, careless, or hasty manner.

shove[2] *n* a hard push.

shove-halfpenny *n* a game played on a special flat board on which players shove discs, e.g. coins, into marked scoring areas.

shovel[1] *n* an implement consisting of a broad scoop or a dished blade with a handle, used to lift and throw loose material.

shovel[2] *v* (**shovelled, shovelling,** *NAm* **shoveled, shoveling**) **1** to dig, clear, or shift (e.g. snow) with a shovel. **2** to convey clumsily or in a mass as if with a shovel.

shoveler *n* see SHOVELLER.

shovel hat *n* a shallow-crowned hat with a wide brim turned up at the sides, formerly often worn by clergymen.

shoveller *or* **shoveler** *n* a dabbling duck that has a large and very broad beak.

shove off *v informal* to go away; to leave.

shove up *v informal* to move so that there is room for another person.

show[1] *v* (*past part.* **shown** *or* **showed**) **1a** to cause or permit to be seen. **b** to be visible. **2** to exhibit or put on display. **3** to present (a film or television programme) for people to watch. **4a** to display (a feeling or characteristic). **b** to treat (somebody) in a specified way: *They showed the prisoners little mercy.* **5** to indicate or point out: *I showed her where I lived.* **6** to explain: *Show me how to do it.* **7** to establish or prove. **8** to conduct or usher (somebody) to a specified place: *I'll show you to the door.* **9** *informal* to arrive or put in an appearance. ✱ **show one's face** to let oneself be seen; to appear. **show one's hand** to reveal one's intentions. **show one's teeth** to show one has power or authority. **show one's true colours** to reveal one's real nature or attitudes. **show somebody the door** to ask somebody to leave.

show² *n* **1a** a false appearance or demonstration of something; a pretence. **b** a true appearance or demonstration of something; a sign or display. **2a** a theatrical presentation. **b** a radio or television programme. **3** a large display or exhibition, e.g. to arouse interest or stimulate sales. **4** a competitive exhibition of animals, plants, etc. **5** *informal* an enterprise or affair: *Who's running this show?* ✱ **for show** simply in order to impress or attract attention. **on show 1** on display in an exhibition. **2** noticeable or being shown, e.g. in somebody's behaviour. **show of hands** a vote where people raise their hands to indicate assent or dissent, etc.

show biz *n informal* = SHOW BUSINESS. ⋙ **showbizzy** *adj.*

showboat *n* a paddle-wheel river steamship containing a theatre and carrying a troupe of actors who present plays for riverside communities.

show business *n* the arts, occupations, and businesses that comprise the entertainment industry.

showcase¹ *n* **1** a box or cabinet with a glass front or top used for displaying and protecting articles in a shop or museum. **2** a setting for exhibiting something to best advantage.

showcase² *v* to exhibit.

showdown *n* **1** the final settlement of a contested issue or the confrontation by which it is settled. **2** in poker, the placing of hands face up on the table to determine the winner of a round.

shower¹ *n* **1** a fall of rain, snow, etc of short duration. **2** something falling like a shower: *a shower of sparks.* **3a** an apparatus that provides a spray of water for washing the body. **b** an act of washing oneself in this way. **4** *chiefly NAm* a party for a bride-to-be or expectant mother, when gifts are given. **5** *Brit, informal* a motley or inferior collection of people. ⋙ **showery** *adj.*

shower² *v* **1** to fall or cause to fall in or as if in a shower. **2** to take a shower. **3** to cover or spray with or as if with a shower. **4** to present (somebody) with something in abundance.

showerproof *adj* of a fabric or garment: treated so as to give protection from light rain.

showgirl *n* a young woman who dances or sings in the chorus of a theatrical production.

show home *n* = SHOW HOUSE.

show house *n* a decorated and furnished house shown to prospective buyers of new houses on a development.

showing *n* **1** a display, exhibition, or presentation. **2** a performance in competition: *He made a good showing in the finals.*

showjumping *n* the competitive riding of horses one at a time over a set course of obstacles. ⋙ **showjumper** *n.*

showman *n* (*pl* **showmen**) **1a** somebody who presents a theatrical show. **b** the manager of a circus or fairground. **2** a person with a flair for dramatically effective presentation. ⋙ **showmanship** *n.*

shown *v* past part. of SHOW¹.

show off *v* **1** to behave boastfully or ostentatiously. **2** to display proudly.

show-off *n* somebody who shows off; an exhibitionist.

showpiece *n* a prime or outstanding example used for exhibition.

showplace *n* a place, e.g. an estate or building, regarded as an example of beauty or excellence.

showroom *n* a room where goods for sale are displayed.

show-stopper *n* an act, song, or performer that wins applause so prolonged as to interrupt a performance. ⋙ **show-stopping** *adj.*

show trial *n* a trial conducted by a state to make an impression at home or abroad.

show up *v* **1** to be evident or conspicuous. **2** *informal* to arrive, *esp* unexpectedly. **3** to reveal the shortcomings of (something) by comparison. **4** *informal* to embarrass.

showy *adj* (**-ier, -iest**) **1** making an attractive show: *showy flowers.* **2** given to or marked by pretentious display. ⋙ **showily** *adv,* **showiness** *n.*

shrank *v* past tense of SHRINK¹.

shrapnel *n* **1** bomb, mine, or shell fragments thrown out during explosion. **2** a hollow projectile containing bullets or pieces of metal that explodes to produce a shower of shrapnel.

shred¹ *n* **1** a narrow strip cut or torn off. **2** a fragment or scrap.

shred² *v* (**shredded, shredding**) to cut or tear into shreds.

shredder *n* a machine for shredding paper.

shrew *n* **1** a small usu nocturnal mammal with a long pointed snout, very small eyes, and velvety fur. **2** an ill-tempered nagging woman; a scold.

shrewd *adj* **1** marked by keen discernment and hardheaded practicality. **2** wily or artful. ⋙ **shrewdly** *adv,* **shrewdness** *n.*

shrewish *adj* bad-tempered, aggressive, or nagging. ⋙ **shrewishly** *adv,* **shrewishness** *n.*

shriek *v* **1** to make a shrill piercing cry; to screech. **2** to utter sharply and shrilly. ⋙ **shriek** *n,* **shrieker** *n.*

shrift *n archaic* the act of shriving; confession or absolution.

shrike *n* a grey or brownish songbird that often impales its prey on thorns.

shrill¹ *adj* **1** making or denoting a sharp high-pitched sound; piercing. **2** of complaints or protests: made in a loud, insistent way. ⋙ **shrillness** *n,* **shrilly** *adv.*

shrill² *v* to utter or emit a shrill sound.

shrimp¹ *n* (*pl* **shrimps** *or* **shrimp**) **1** a small usu marine edible crustacean with a long slender body and ten long legs. **2** *informal, humorous* a very small or puny person.

shrimp² *v* to fish for or catch shrimps. ⋙ **shrimper** *n.*

shrine¹ *n* **1a** a place in which devotion is paid to a saint or deity. **b** a receptacle for sacred relics. **c** a niche containing a religious image. **2** a place or object hallowed by its history or associations: *Oxford is a shrine of learning.*

shrine² *v literary* to enshrine.

shrink¹ *v* (*past tense* **shrank,** *past part.* **shrunk** *or* **shrunken**) **1a** to contract to a smaller volume or extent, e.g. as a result of heat or moisture. **b** to cause to shrink. **2** to draw back or cower away, e.g. from something painful or horrible. **3** (*usu* + from) to show reluctance, e.g. before an unpleasant duty; to recoil. ⋙ **shrinkable** *adj,* **shrinker** *n.*

shrink² *n informal* a psychiatrist.

shrinkage *n* **1** the act, process, or degree of shrinking. **2** loss of merchandise from a shop by shoplifting.

shrinking violet *n informal* a meek or very shy person.

shrink wrap *n* tough clear plastic film that is wrapped around an object and then shrunk to make a tight-fitting, sealed package. ➤➤ **shrink-wrap** *v.*

shrive *v* (*past tense* **shrove,** *past part.* **shriven**) **1** *archaic* of a priest: to hear the confession of (somebody) and absolve them. **2** to present (oneself) to be shrived.

shrivel *v* (**shrivelled, shrivelling,** *NAm* **shriveled, shriveling**) to contract and become dry and wrinkled, *esp* through loss of moisture.

shriven *v* past part. of SHRIVE.

shroud[1] *n* **1** a burial garment, e.g. a winding-sheet. **2** something that covers or conceals. **3** any of the ropes or wires giving support, usu in pairs, to a ship's mast. **4** a protective cover or guard.

shroud[2] *v* **1a** to envelop and conceal. **b** to obscure or disguise. **2** to dress (a body) for burial.

shrove *v* past tense of SHRIVE.

Shrove Tuesday *n* the Tuesday before Ash Wednesday.

shrub[1] *n* a low-growing woody plant that usu has several stems. ➤➤ **shrubby** *adj.*

shrub[2] *n* a drink made of sweetened fruit juice and spirits, *esp* rum.

shrubbery *n* (*pl* **-ies**) a planting or growth of shrubs.

shrug[1] *v* (**shrugged, shrugging**) to lift and contract (one's shoulders) as an expression of uncertainty, unconcern, or resignation.

shrug[2] *n* **1** an act of shrugging the shoulders. **2** a short frontless cardigan covering the arms, shoulders, and back.

shrug off *v* to brush aside; to disregard or belittle.

shrunk *v* past part. of SHRINK[1].

shrunken *v* past part. of SHRINK[1].

shtick *n informal* an entertainer's routine or gimmick; a turn.

shtook *or* **schtuck** /shtook/ *n informal* a bad or awkward situation; trouble: *I'm in shtook.*

shtum *or* **schtum** /shtoom/ *adj informal* silent or dumb: *Keep shtum!*

shubunkin /shə'bungkin/ *n* a goldfish that is mottled, *esp* with blue, and is often kept in an aquarium.

shuck[1] *n NAm* **1** a pod or husk, e.g. the outer covering of maize. **2** the shell of an oyster or clam. **3** *informal* (*in pl*) used as an interjection to express disappointment, surprise, or self-deprecation.

shuck[2] *v NAm* **1** to strip of shucks. **2** (*often* + off) to remove or dispose of like a shuck. ➤➤ **shucker** *n.*

shudder *v* **1** to tremble with a sudden brief convulsive movement. **2** to quiver or vibrate. ➤➤ **shudder** *n,* **shuddery** *adj.*

shuffle[1] *v* **1a** to move (the feet) along, or back and forth, without lifting them. **b** to walk or dance in this way. **2a** to rearrange (e.g. playing cards or dominoes) to produce a random order. **b** to move (things or people) about between various different positions or locations. **3** to behave in an evasive or underhand way. **4** (*usu* + off) to avoid or get rid of (e.g. responsibility). ➤➤ **shuffler** *n.*

shuffle[2] *n* **1** a shuffling, e.g. of cards. **2** a rearrangement of things or people; a reshuffle. **3a** a dragging sliding movement of the feet. **b** a dance characterized by such movement.

shuffleboard *n* a game in which players use long-handled cues to shove wooden discs into scoring areas of a diagram marked on a smooth surface.

shufti *n* (*pl* **shuftis**) *Brit, informal* a look or glance.

shun *v* (**shunned, shunning**) to avoid (somebody or something) deliberately, *esp* habitually.

shunt[1] *v* **1a** to move (e.g. a train) from one track to another. **b** *Brit* to move (railway vehicles) to different positions on the same track. **2a** (*often* + off/onto) to avoid (e.g. a task or responsibility) by transferring it to somebody else. **b** to move (something or somebody) to a less important position. **3** to travel back and forth. ➤➤ **shunter** *n.*

shunt[2] *n* **1** an act of shunting. **2** a conductor joining two points in an electrical circuit so as to form a parallel path through which a portion of the current may pass. **3** *informal* a minor motor accident, *esp* one in which one vehicle runs into the back of another.

shush *interj* used to demand silence.

shut[1] *v* (**shutting,** *past tense and past part.* **shut**) **1** to place or move into a position to close an opening. **2** to fasten with a lock or bolt. **3** to close by bringing parts together. **4** to prevent entrance to (a building or street). **5** to confine in a space. **6** to suspend operation, or cause to do this.

shut[2] *adj* **1** in the closed position. **2** not open for business.

shut away *v* to remove or isolate.

shutdown *n* the cessation or suspension of an activity, e.g. work in a factory.

shut down *v* to suspend operation, or cause to do this.

shut-eye *n informal* sleep.

shut off *v* **1** to cut off the flow of. **2** to stop the operation of. **3** to isolate.

shut out *v* **1** to exclude. **2** to prevent (an opponent) from scoring in a game.

shut-out *n chiefly NAm* **1** a sporting contest in which one side fails to score any goals, points, etc. **2** the act of preventing an opposing side from scoring.

shutter[1] *n* **1** a usu hinged outside cover for a window. **2** a device that opens and closes the lens aperture of a camera. **3** the movable slots in the box enclosing the swell part of an organ, which are opened to increase the volume of the sound.

shutter[2] *v* to provide or close with shutters.

shuttle[1] *n* **1a** a usu spindle-shaped device that holds a bobbin and is used in weaving for passing the thread of the weft between the threads of the warp. **b** a sliding thread holder that carries the lower thread in a sewing machine through a loop of the upper thread to make a stitch. **2a** a vehicle that regularly travels back and forth over a usu short route. **b** a reusable space vehicle; a space shuttle. **3** = SHUTTLECOCK.

shuttle[2] *v* **1** to travel to and fro rapidly or frequently. **2** to transport in or as if in a shuttle.

shuttlecock *n* the object hit back and forth between players in badminton, orig consisting of a cork with feathers stuck in it, now usu made of plastic.

shuttle diplomacy *n* diplomacy carried out by an intermediary who travels frequently between the countries concerned.

shut up *v* **1** to lock and prevent access to. **2** to imprison or confine. **3** *informal* to stop talking.

shy[1] *adj* (**-er, -est**) **1** easily alarmed; timid. **2** reserved or retiring; bashful. **3** (*often used in combinations*) tending to avoid a person or thing: *camera-shy.* **4** (*often* + of) wary of committing oneself; circumspect or reluctant. **5** *chiefly NAm, informal* lacking or short. ➤➤ **shyly** *adv,* **shyness** *n.*

shy[2] *v* (**-ies, -ied**) **1** *esp* of a horse: to start suddenly aside in fright or alarm. **2** (*usu* + away/away from) to avoid facing or committing oneself to something, *esp* through nervousness.

shy[3] *v* (**-ies, -ied**) *dated* to throw (e.g. a stone) with a jerking movement.

shy[4] *n* (*pl* **-ies**) the act of shying; a toss or throw.

shyster *n chiefly NAm, informal* somebody, *esp* a lawyer, who is professionally unscrupulous.

SI *abbr* **1** Statutory Instrument. **2** Système International (d'Unités), a system of units based on the metre, kilogram, second, ampere, kelvin, candela, and mole.

Si *abbr* the chemical symbol for silicon.

Siamese *n* (*pl* **Siamese**) **1** *dated* a native or inhabitant of Siam (now Thailand). **2** *dated* the Thai language. **3** = SIAMESE CAT. ⋙ **Siamese** *adj.*

Siamese cat *n* a cat of a domestic breed of oriental origin, having blue eyes, short hair, and a pale body with darker ears, paws, tail, and face.

Siamese twin *n* either of a pair of congenitally joined twins.

sib *n* **1** a blood relation. **2** a brother or sister considered irrespective of sex; a sibling.

Siberian *n* a native or inhabitant of Siberia. ⋙ **Siberian** *adj.*

sibilant[1] *adj* having, containing, or producing a hissing sound, e.g. /sh, zh, s, z/. ⋙ **sibilance** *n.*

sibilant[2] *n* in phonetics, a sibilant speech sound.

sibling *n* any of two or more individuals having one or both parents in common; a brother or sister.

sibyl *n* a female prophet of the ancient world; *broadly* any female prophet. ⋙ **sibylline** *adj.*

sic *adv* used after a printed word or passage to indicate that it is intended exactly as printed or that it exactly reproduces an original: intentionally so written.

Usage note

Sic is used when quoting someone else's words exactly to show that a mistake or oddity in them comes from the person quoted, not from the person quoting.

sick[1] *adj* **1** affected by a disease or medical condition; ill or ailing. **2** (*often used in combinations*) likely to vomit; queasy or nauseated. **3a** (+ of) having a strong aversion because of surfeit; satiated. **b** filled with disgust or chagrin. **4** *informal* disappointed or upset. **5a** mentally or emotionally disturbed. **b** of humour: macabre, morbid, or sadistic. ✱ **be sick 1** *chiefly Brit* to vomit. **2** to be ill. ⋙ **sickish** *adj.*

sick[2] *n Brit, informal* vomit.

sick[3] *v Brit, informal* (*usu* + up) to vomit.

sickbay *n* a place where sick people are treated, e.g. in a school or ship.

sickbed *n* the bed on which somebody lies sick.

sick building syndrome *n* a condition affecting workers in buildings with air-conditioning or humidification systems, characterized by headache, flu-like symptoms, etc.

sicken *v* **1** to drive to the point of disgust or loathing. **2** to become ill. **3** (+ for) to begin to show signs of illness.

sickening *adj* **1** causing a feeling of nausea. **2** *informal* very irritating or annoying. ⋙ **sickeningly** *adv.*

sick headache *n* a headache accompanied by a feeling of nausea, *esp* a migraine.

sickie *n informal* a day's absence from work claimed as sick leave.

sickle *n* an agricultural implement for cutting plants or hedges, consisting of a curved metal blade with a short handle.

sick leave *n* absence from work because of illness.

sickle-cell anaemia *n* a hereditary anaemia in which most of the red blood cells become crescent-shaped, causing recurrent short periods of fever and pain.

sickly *adj* (**-ier, -iest**) **1a** susceptible to illness and often unwell. **b** feeble or weak. **2** associated with or producing sickness or disease. **3a** tending to produce nausea or feelings of repugnance. **b** mawkish or saccharine. ⋙ **sickliness** *n.*

sickness *n* **1** ill health. **2** a specific disease. **3** nausea or queasiness.

sicko *n* (*pl* **-os**) *informal* somebody who is mentally ill or perverted.

sickroom *n* a room set aside for or occupied by sick people.

side[1] *n* **1a** a surface forming a face of an object, *esp* one that is not the front, back, top, or bottom. **b** either surface of a thin object. **c** a boundary line of a geometrical figure. **2a** a position to the right or left of something, somebody, or a reference point. **b** a region or direction considered in relation to a centre or line of division. **3** the right or left part of the body. **4a** a sports team. **b** a person or group in competition or dispute with another. **c** the attitude, opinions, or part of such a person or group: *He took my side in the argument.* **5** an aspect or part of something or somebody. **6** a line of descent traced through a parent. **7** *Brit, informal* a television channel. ✱ **on the side 1** in addition to a principal occupation; *specif* as an illicit secondary activity. **2** *chiefly NAm* in addition to the main dish and served separately. **take sides** to give one's support to one of the people or parties in a dispute.

side[2] *adj* **1** of, forming, or situated on a side. **2** directed towards or from the side. **3** accompanying the main dish but served separately. **4** incidental or subordinate: *a side issue.*

side[3] *v* (+ with/against) to support or oppose in a dispute.

side[4] *n Brit, informal* a self-important manner; arrogance or pretentiousness.

side arm *n* a weapon, e.g. a sword or revolver, worn at the side or in the belt.

sidebar *n chiefly NAm* an additional newspaper article dealing with a particular aspect of a main article.

sideboard *n* **1** a flat-topped piece of dining room furniture with cupboards and drawers. **2** *Brit* (*in pl*) = SIDEBURNS.

sideburns *pl n* hair on the side of the face that extends from the hairline to below the ears.

Word history

alteration of earlier *burnsides,* named after Ambrose *Burnside* d.1881, US general, who wore them.

side by side *adv* beside one another.

sidecar *n* a small vehicle with a single wheel, attached to the side of a motorcycle to carry passengers.

side drum *n* a small double-headed drum with one or more snares stretched across its lower head.

side effect *n* a secondary and usu adverse effect, e.g. of a drug.

sidekick *n informal* somebody closely associated with another, *esp* as a subordinate.

sidelight *n* **1a** a light at the side of the headlight on a motor vehicle. **b** the red port light or the green starboard light carried by ships travelling at night. **2** a window at the side of a door or a larger window.

sideline[1] *n* **1** a business or activity pursued in addition to a principal occupation. **2** a line at right angles to an end line and marking a side of a court or field of play. **3** (**the sidelines**) the standpoint of people not immediately participating.

sideline[2] *v* to remove (somebody) from action, participation, etc.

sidelong *adj and adv* directed to or from one side; oblique or obliquely.

sideman *n* (*pl* **sidemen**) a member of a band or orchestra, *esp* a jazz orchestra, other than the leader or featured performer.

side-on *adv* **1** with one side facing in a given direction. **2** in profile.

sidereal /sie'diəri·əl/ *adj* of, or expressed in relation to, stars or constellations.

sidereal day *n* the interval between two successive transits of the March equinox over the upper meridian of a particular place, approximately four minutes shorter than a solar day.

sidereal time *n* time based on the sidereal day.

sidesaddle[1] *n* a saddle for women riders in skirts in which the rider sits with both legs on the same side of the horse.

sidesaddle[2] *adv* on or as if on a sidesaddle.

sideshow *n* **1a** a minor show offered in addition to a main exhibition, e.g. of a circus. **b** a fairground game of luck or skill. **2** an incidental diversion.

sidesman *n* (*pl* **sidesmen**) a person who assists the churchwardens in an Anglican church, *esp* in taking the collection in services.

sidespin *n* sideways spin imparted to a ball.

sidesplitting *adj informal* extremely funny.

sidestep *v* (**sidestepped, sidestepping**) **1** to move quickly out of the way of by stepping to one side. **2** to evade (e.g. an issue or question).

side street *n* a minor street branching off a main thoroughfare.

sidestroke *n* a swimming stroke executed while lying on one's side.

sideswipe[1] *n* **1** an incidental deprecatory remark. **2** *chiefly NAm* a glancing blow.

sideswipe[2] *v chiefly NAm* to strike with a glancing blow along the side.

sidetrack[1] *v* to divert (somebody) from a course or purpose.

sidetrack[2] *n* **1** an unimportant line of thinking that is followed instead of a more important one. **2** *NAm* = SIDING (1).

sidewalk *n NAm* = PAVEMENT.

sidewall *n* the part of a tyre between the tread and the rim.

sideways (*NAm* **sideway**) *adv and adj* **1** to or from the side. **2** with one side forward.

side whiskers *pl n* long sideburns.

sidewinder *n* a rattlesnake of N America that moves over sand by looping its body into S-shaped curves.

sidewise *adv and adj* = SIDEWAYS.

siding *n* **1** a short length of railway track connected with a main track. **2** *NAm* material used to surface the outside walls of wooden-framed buildings.

sidle *v* **1** to move obliquely; to edge along. **2** (+ up) to walk timidly or furtively.

SIDS *abbr* sudden infant death syndrome.

siege *n* **1** a military operation in which a city or fortified place is surrounded and blockaded to compel it to surrender. **2** a similar operation, e.g. by a police force, to force somebody to surrender. ✱ **lay siege to** to besiege (e.g. a city) militarily.

siege mentality *n* a state of mind in which a person thinks that he or she is being attacked.

siemens *n* (*pl* **siemens**) the SI unit of conductance.

sienna *n* an earthy substance containing oxides of iron that is used as a brownish yellow or reddish brown pigment.

sierra *n* a range of mountains, *esp* with a serrated or irregular outline.

Sierra Leonean *n* a native or inhabitant of Sierra Leone. ➤➤ **Sierra Leonean** *adj.*

siesta *n* an afternoon nap or rest.

sieve[1] *n* a device with a meshed or perforated bottom that will allow the passage of liquids or fine solids while retaining coarser material or solids.

sieve[2] *v* = SIFT (1), (2), (3).

sievert *n* a unit of ionizing radiation equal to the dose equivalent of one joule per kilogram.

sift *v* **1** to put (e.g. flour) through a sieve to remove lumps or coarse particles. **2** (*often* + out) to separate or remove from a mixture using a sieve. **3a** to study or investigate thoroughly. **b** (*often* + through) to study or examine so as to pick out the best or most valuable things or parts; to screen. **4** to move or fall like the fine powder produced by a sieve. ➤➤ **sifter** *n.*

sigh[1] *v* **1** to take a long deep audible breath, e.g. in relief, weariness, or grief. **2** (+ for) to grieve or yearn.

sigh[2] *n* **1** an act of sighing. **2** a sound of or resembling sighing.

sight[1] *n* **1** the process or power of seeing. **2** the perception of an object by the eye; a view or glimpse. **3** the range of vision; the distance or area one can see. **4** something seen, *esp* a spectacle. **5a** (*in pl*) the things regarded as worth seeing in a particular place. **b** *informal* something ridiculous or displeasing in appearance. **6** a device for guiding the eye, e.g. in aiming a firearm or bomb. **7** an observation, e.g. by a navigator, to determine direction or position. **8** *informal* a great deal; a lot: *She earns a sight more than you.* ✱ **at first sight** when viewed without proper investigation. **at/on sight** as soon as seen. **in sight 1** able to be seen, within visual range, or under observation. **2** able to be reached or achieved in a relatively short time. **lose sight of 1** to be no longer able to see. **2** to be no longer aware of or paying attention to. **out of sight 1** hidden or too far away to see; not visible. **2** *chiefly NAm, informal, dated* marvellous or wonderful. **raise/lower one's sights** to become more/less ambitious. **set one's sights on** to aim to achieve; to have as one's goal or ambition. **sight for sore eyes** *informal* somebody or something whose appearance or arrival is an occasion for joy or relief. ➤➤ **sightless** *adj.*

sight[2] *v* **1** to see, *esp* briefly. **2** to look at through or as if through a sight. **3** to aim (e.g. a weapon) by means of sights. **4** to adjust the sights of (e.g. a gun). **5** to take aim, e.g. in shooting. ➤➤ **sighter** *n.*

sighted *adj* (*usu used in combinations*) having sight, *esp* of a specified kind: *short-sighted.*

sighting *n* **1** a view or glimpse. **2** an observation made with a sight, e.g. of a gun.

sightline *n* a line of sight, e.g. from a member of a theatre audience to some part of the stage.

sightly *adj* (**-ier, -iest**) pleasing to the eye; attractive. ➤➤ **sightliness** *n.*

sight-read *v* (*past tense and past part.* **sight-read**) to read and perform (music) without previous preparation or study. ➤➤ **sight-reader** *n.*

sight screen *n* in cricket, a screen placed on the boundary behind the bowler to improve the batsman's view of the ball.

sightsee *v* to make a tour of interesting or attractive sights. ➤➤ **sightseeing** *n,* **sightseer** *n.*

sight unseen *adv* without previous inspection or appraisal.

sigma *n* the 18th letter of the Greek alphabet (Σ, σ, or at the end of a word ς), equivalent to roman s.

sign[1] *n* **1a** something serving to indicate the presence or existence of something. **b** a presage or portent. **2** a board or notice giving warning, information, direction, etc. **3a** a motion or gesture by which a thought, command, or wish is made known; a signal. **b** a mark with a conventional meaning, e.g. in music or mathematics. **4** any of the twelve divisions of the zodiac.

sign[2] *v* **1a** to put a signature to (e.g. a letter, cheque, or work of art). **b** to write (one's name). **c** (*often* + over) to assign formally. **2** to engage or hire by securing a signature on a contract of employment. **3** to indicate, represent, or express by a sign. **4** to make a sign or signal. **5** to use sign language. ➤➤ **signer** *n.*

signage *n chiefly NAm* signs collectively.

signal[1] *n* **1a** an action, gesture, word, etc that has an agreed meaning, e.g. to begin a concerted action. **b** anything that prompts a particular action or event to take place. **2** a conventional sign, sound, etc that conveys information or gives a warning or command. **3** a sign, e.g. a set of coloured lights, that regulates the flow of traffic, *esp* on a railway line. **4** the sound or image conveyed by telephone, radio, radar, or television.

signal[2] *v* (**signalled, signalling,** *NAm* **signaled, signaling**) **1** to make or send a signal. **2** to warn, order, or request (somebody) to do something by a signal. **3** to communicate (something) by signals. **4** to be a sign of; to mark. ➤➤ **signaller** *n.*

signal[3] *adj* markedly different from the ordinary; conspicuous or outstanding. ➤➤ **signally** *adv.*

signal box *n Brit* a raised building above a railway line from which signals and points are worked.

signalize *or* **-ise** *v* **1** *chiefly NAm* to point out carefully or distinctly; to draw attention to. **2** to make noteworthy; to distinguish. ➤➤ **signalization** *n.*

signalman *n* (*pl* **signalmen**) somebody employed to operate signals, e.g. for a railway.

signal-to-noise ratio *n* the ratio of a wanted signal to that of unwanted random interference, usu expressed in decibels.

signatory *n* (*pl* **-ies**) somebody who signs a document along with another or others.

signature *n* **1a** the name of a person written with his or her own hand, usu in a distinctive way, to serve as a means of identification or authorization. **b** the act of signing one's name. **2a** = KEY SIGNATURE. **b** = TIME SIGNATURE. **3** a distinguishing or identifying mark, feature, or quality.

signature tune *n* a melody or song used to identify a programme, entertainer, etc.

signboard *n* a sign on a board, e.g. to advertise a product.

signet *n* a personal seal, often in a finger ring, used officially in lieu of signature.

signet ring *n* a finger ring engraved with a signet, seal, or monogram.

significance *n* **1** something conveyed as a meaning, often latently or indirectly. **2** the quality of being significant; importance or consequence.

significant *adj* **1** having meaning. **2** suggesting or containing a veiled or special meaning. **3** having or likely to have influence or effect; important. ➤➤ **significantly** *adv.*

significant figures *pl n* the specified number of digits in a number that are considered to give correct or sufficient information on its accuracy.

signification *n* **1** signifying by symbolic means, e.g. signs. **2** the meaning that a term, symbol, or character normally conveys or is intended to convey.

signify *v* (**-ies, -ied**) **1a** to mean or denote. **b** to be an indication of or imply. **2** to show (something), e.g. by a word, signal, or gesture. **3** to be important; to matter.

signing *n* **1** somebody who is signed, e.g. by a football club. **2** sign language. **3** an event at which an author signs copies of his or her book to generate publicity and boost sales.

sign language *n* a system of hand gestures and other signs used for communication, e.g. by the deaf.

sign off *v* **1** to end a letter, message, programme, or broadcast. **2** of a doctor: to declare (somebody) unfit for work because of illness.

sign on *v* **1** to commit oneself to a job by signature or agreement. **2** *Brit* to register as unemployed.

signor /'seenyaw, see'nyaw/ *n* (*pl* **signors** *or* **signori** /-ree/) used of or to an Italian-speaking man as a title equivalent to *Mr.*

signora /seen'yawrə/ *n* (*pl* **signoras** *or* **signore** /-ray/) used of or to an Italian-speaking married woman as a title equivalent to *Mrs* or as a generalized term of direct address.

signore /seen'yawray/ *n* (*pl* **signori** /-ree/) used to an Italian-speaking man as a generalized term of direct address equivalent to *sir.*

signorina /seenyaw'reenə/ *n* (*pl* **signorinas** *or* **signorine** /-nay/) used of or to an unmarried Italian-speaking girl or woman as a title equivalent to *Miss*, or as a generalized term of direct address.

sign out *v* **1** to indicate one's departure by signing in a register. **2** to record or approve the release or withdrawal of.

signpost[1] *n* a post, e.g. at a road junction, with signs on it to direct travellers.

signpost[2] *v* **1a** to provide (an area) with signposts. **b** to indicate the presence or direction of (e.g. a road or town) with a signpost. **2** to indicate or mark.

sign up *v* to join an organization or accept an obligation by signing a contract.

signwriter *n* somebody who designs and paints signs, *esp* for commercial premises. ➤➤ **signwriting** *n.*

sika /'seekə/ *n* (*pl* **sikas** *or* **sika**) a small reddish brown deer introduced into Britain from Japan.

Sikh /seek/ *n* an adherent of Sikhism. ➤➤ **Sikh** *adj.*

Sikhism *n* a monotheistic religion of India, founded by the Guru Nanak (1469–1539).

silage *n* fodder converted, *esp* in a silo, into succulent feed for livestock.

sild *n* (*pl* **silds** *or* **sild**) a young herring, *esp* one that is canned.

silence[1] *n* **1** absence of sound or noise. **2** a state of not speaking.

silence[2] *v* **1** to make silent or much quieter. **2** to prevent (somebody) from speaking, writing, or expressing an opinion.

silencer *n* a silencing device, *esp* for a firearm or the exhaust system of an internal-combustion engine.

silent *adj* **1** free from sound or noise. **2a** saying nothing. **b** not talkative. **3** conveyed by refraining from reaction or comment; tacit: *silent assent.* **4** of a letter: not pronounced, e.g. the *b* in *doubt.* **5** of a film: without spoken dialogue. ➤➤ **silently** *adv.*

silent majority *n* (*used as sing. or pl*) a majority who do not assert their views, which are believed to be moderate.

silhouette[1] *n* **1** the shape of somebody or something as it appears against a lighter background. **2**

a portrait in profile cut from dark material and mounted on a light background.

silhouette² *v* to cause to appear in silhouette.

silica *n* silicon dioxide occurring in many rocks and minerals, e.g. quartz, opal, and sand.

silica gel *n* silica resembling coarse white sand but possessing many fine pores and therefore extremely adsorbent.

silicate *n* an insoluble compound that contains silicon and oxygen and is a mineral used in cement, glass, etc.

siliceous *adj* of or containing silica or a silicate.

silicic *adj* derived from or containing silica or silicon.

silicon *n* a grey non-metallic element that is used in alloys, as a semiconductor, and in the manufacture of glass.

silicon carbide *n* a very hard dark compound of silicon and carbon that is used as an abrasive, as a heat-resisting material, and in electrical resistors.

silicon chip *n* = CHIP¹ (5).

silicone *n* an organic silicon compound obtained as an oil or plastic and used for lubricants, varnishes, electrical insulators, etc.

silicosis *n* a disease of the lungs marked by hardening of the tissue and shortness of breath and caused by prolonged inhalation of silica dusts.

silk *n* **1** a lustrous tough elastic fibre produced by silkworms and used for textiles. **2** thread or fabric made from silk filaments. **3** *Brit, informal* a King's or Queen's Counsel. **4** (*in pl*) the cap and shirt of a jockey made in the registered racing colour of his or her stable. **5** a silky material or filament, or silky fibres. ✱ **take silk** *Brit* to become a Queen's or King's Counsel.

silken *adj* **1** made of silk. **2** = SILKY (1A).

silk moth *n* a large Asiatic moth whose rough wrinkled hairless yellowish caterpillar produces the silk used commercially.

silk screen *n* a prepared silk or organdie screen used in screen-printing.

silk-screen *v* to produce (e.g. a print) using a silk screen.

silkworm *n* the larva of a silk moth, which spins a large amount of strong silk in constructing its cocoon.

silky *adj* (**-ier, -iest**) **1a** resembling silk, *esp* in softness or lustre. **b** consisting of silk. **2** of a voice: suave or ingratiating. ➤➤ **silkily** *adv,* **silkiness** *n.*

sill *n* **1a** a horizontal piece of wood, metal, etc that forms the lowest member of a framework or supporting structure, e.g. a window frame or door frame. **b** a narrow shelf projecting from the base of a window frame. **2** in geology, a horizontal sheet of intrusive igneous rock running between strata of other rocks.

silly¹ *adj* (**-ier, -iest**) **1a** showing a lack of common sense or sound judgment. **b** trifling or frivolous. **2** stunned or dazed. **3** in cricket, denoting or occupying a fielding position in front of and dangerously near the batsman. ➤➤ **sillily** *adv,* **silliness** *n.*

silly² *n* (*pl* **-ies**) *informal* a silly person.

silly season *n chiefly Brit* a period when newspapers resort to reporting trivial or frivolous matters through lack of important news.

silo *n* (*pl* **-os**) **1** a trench, pit, or tall cylinder, e.g. of wood or concrete, usu sealed to exclude air and used for making and storing silage. **2** an underground structure for housing a guided missile.

silt¹ *n* a deposit of sediment, e.g. at the bottom of a river. ➤➤ **silty** *adj.*

silt² *v* (*often* + up) to become or to cause to become choked or obstructed with silt. ➤➤ **siltation** *n.*

siltstone *n* a rock composed chiefly of hardened silt.

Silurian *adj* of the third geological period of the Palaeozoic era, lasting from about 439 million to about 409 million years ago, and marked by the first appearance of land plants. ➤➤ **Silurian** *n.*

silvan *adj* see SYLVAN.

silver¹ *n* **1a** a white metallic element that is ductile and malleable, takes a very high degree of polish, and is used in jewellery, ornaments, etc. **b** (*used before a noun*) made of or plated with silver. **2a** coins made of silver or cupro-nickel. **b** articles, *esp* tableware, made of or plated with silver. **c** cutlery made of any metal. **3** a whitish grey colour, *esp* with a lustrous sheen. ✱ **be born with a silver spoon in one's mouth** to be born into a wealthy, *esp* upper-class, family.

silver² *adj* **1** resembling silver, *esp* in having a whitish grey colour or lustrous sheen. **2a** giving a soft, clear, ringing sound. **b** eloquently persuasive: *a silver tongue.* **3** marking a 25th anniversary.

silver³ *v* **1** to cover or coat with silver or a substance resembling silver. **2** to become or cause to become silver, grey, or white in colour.

silver birch *n* a common Eurasian birch tree with silvery-white peeling bark.

silver fern *n* **1** = PONGA. **2** a silver fern leaf used as an emblem of New Zealand.

silverfish *n* (*pl* **silverfishes** *or* **silverfish**) a small wingless insect found in houses that is sometimes injurious to paper or fabrics.

silver fox *n* a colour phase of the common red fox in which the pelt is black tipped with white.

silver jubilee *n* the 25th anniversary of a special event, e.g. the accession of a sovereign.

silver medal *n* a medal of silver awarded to somebody who comes second in a competition. ➤➤ **silver medallist** *n.*

silver plate *n* **1** a plating of silver. **2** tableware and cutlery of silver or a silver-plated metal.

silver-plate *v* to coat (e.g. metal) with a thin layer of silver.

silver screen *n* (**the silver screen**) the film industry.

silver service *n* a style of serving food to diners in a restaurant or hotel, using a silver spoon and fork.

silverside *n Brit* a cut of beef from the outer part of the top of the leg.

silversmith *n* somebody who makes objects in silver.

silver-tongued *adj* eloquent or persuasive.

silverware *n* tableware and cutlery of silver or a silver-plated metal.

silvery *adj* **1** having the lustre or colour of silver. **2** containing or consisting of silver. **3** having a soft clear musical tone. ➤➤ **silveriness** *n.*

silviculture *n* the development and care of forests. ➤➤ **silvicultural** *adj,* **silviculturist** *n.*

sim *n informal* a computer or video game that involves simulating an activity.

simian¹ *adj* of or resembling a monkey or ape.

simian² *n* a monkey or ape.

similar *adj* **1** marked by correspondence or resemblance, *esp* of a general kind. **2** of geometric figures: having the same angles, and sides in the same ratio, so that they have the same shape but differ in size. ➤➤ **similarity** *n,* **similarly** *adv.*

simile /'simili/ *n* a figure of speech explicitly comparing two things of different kinds, e.g. in *cheeks like roses*.

similitude *n* correspondence in kind, quality, or appearance.

simmer *v* **1a** of a liquid: to bubble gently below or just at the boiling point. **b** to cook in a simmering liquid. **2** to be agitated by suppressed emotion. ⯮ **simmer** *n*.

simmer down *v* to become calm or less excited.

simnel cake *n Brit* a rich fruit cake with a layer of almond paste traditionally baked for mid-Lent and Easter.

simony /'siməni, 'sie-/ *n* the buying or selling of a church office or ecclesiastical promotion. ⯮ **simoniac** *adj and n*, **simoniacal** *adj*.

Word history

late Latin *simonia*, named after *Simon* Magus first cent. AD, Samaritan sorcerer, who tried to buy the gift of healing from the Apostle Peter (Acts 8:9–24).

simoom *or* **simoon** *n* a hot dry dust-laden wind blowing from an Asian or African desert.

simpatico *adj* **1** congenial or likeable. **2** having similar interests; compatible.

simper[1] *v* to smile in a foolish self-conscious manner. ⯮ **simpering** *adj*, **simperingly** *adv*.

simper[2] *n* a foolish self-conscious smile.

simple[1] *adj* **1** easily understood or performed. **2a** lacking ornamentation; basic or plain. **b** free from showiness; unpretentious. **3** lacking experience or sophistication; naive. **4** lacking intelligence; feeble-minded. **5** of humble birth or lowly position. **6** comprising a single unit; not compound or subdivided. ⯮ **simpleness** *n*.

simple[2] *n archaic* a medicinal plant.

simple eye *n* an eye, e.g. of an insect, with only one lens.

simple fracture *n* a bone fracture in which the surrounding skin and tissue remains undamaged.

simple-hearted *adj* having a sincere and unassuming nature; artless.

simple interest *n* interest paid or calculated only on the original capital sum of a loan.

simple-minded *adj* **1** lacking in intelligence or judgment; stupid or foolish. **2** devoid of subtlety; unsophisticated. ⯮ **simple-mindedly** *adv*, **simple-mindedness** *n*.

simple time *n* in music, time in which there are two, three, or four beats to a bar, each beat divisible by two, four, etc.

simpleton *n* somebody who is mentally deficient or who lacks common sense or intelligence.

simplex *adj* **1** consisting of a single part or structure; simple. **2** allowing telecommunication in only one direction at a time.

simplicity *n* the state or quality of being simple.

simplify *v* (**-ies, -ied**) to make simple or simpler. ⯮ **simplification** *n*.

simplistic *adj* deliberately or naively uncomplicated, *esp* where a more complex approach is appropriate; oversimplified. ⯮ **simplistically** *adv*.

simply *adv* **1a** without ambiguity; clearly. **b** without ornamentation or show. **2a** solely or merely. **b** without any question.

simulacrum /simyoo'laykrəm/ *n* (*pl* **simulacra** *or* **simulacrums**) *formal* **1** an image or representation of something or somebody. **2** a vague or superficial likeness or an imperfect imitation.

simulate *v* **1** to assume the outward qualities or appearance of, usu with the intent to deceive. **2** to make a functioning model of (a system, device, or process). ⯮ **simulation** *n*, **simulative** *adj*.

simulator *n* a device that simulates various conditions or the mechanisms involved in operating a system, e.g. for training or research.

simulcast *n* a simultaneous broadcast on television and radio, or on two or more channels or networks.

simultaneous *adj* existing, occurring, or functioning at the same time. ⯮ **simultaneity** *n*, **simultaneously** *adv*, **simultaneousness** *n*.

simultaneous equations *pl n* a set of equations that are satisfied by the same values of the variables.

sin[1] *n* **1** an offence against moral or religious law or divine commandments. **2** an action considered highly reprehensible. ✱ **live in sin** to cohabit. ⯮ **sinless** *adj*.

sin[2] *v* (**sinned, sinning**) to commit a sin. ⯮ **sinner** *n*.

sin[3] *abbr* sine.

sin bin *n* **1** *informal* an enclosure occupied by a player, e.g. in ice hockey, who has been temporarily sent off. **2** *Brit* a place where an offender, e.g. a persistently disruptive pupil in a school, is segregated.

since[1] *adv* **1** continuously from then until now. **2** before now; ago. **3** between then and now; subsequently.

since[2] *prep* **1** in the period between (a specified past time) and now. **2** from (a specified past time) until now.

since[3] *conj* **1** between now and the past time when. **2** continuously from the past time when. **3** in view of the fact that; because.

sincere *adj* free from deceit or hypocrisy; honest or genuine. ⯮ **sincereness** *n*, **sincerity** *n*.

sincerely *adv* in a sincere way. ✱ **yours sincerely** used to end a formal letter when the writer has addressed the recipient by name.

sine *n* in mathematics, the trigonometric function that for an acute angle in a right-angled triangle is the ratio between the side opposite the angle and the hypotenuse: compare COSINE, TANGENT[1].

sinecure /'sinikyooə, 'sie-/ *n* an office or position that provides an income while requiring little or no work.

sine curve *n* the continuous S-shaped graph of the equation $y = a\sin bx$ where a and b are constants.

sine die /,sieni 'deeay, 'die, ,sini/ *adv* without any future date being designated, e.g. for resumption.

sine qua non /,sini kwah 'non/ *n* an absolutely indispensable or essential thing.

sinew *n* **1** = TENDON. **2** (*usu in pl*) the chief means of support; mainstay.

sine wave *n* a wave form that represents periodic oscillations in which the amount of vertical displacement at each point is proportional to the sine of the horizontal distance from a reference point.

sinewy *adj* **1** having or resembling sinews. **2** possessing great muscular strength, usu in a lean and supple body.

sinfonia /sin'fohni·ə/ *n* (*pl* **sinfonie** /-neeay/ *or* **sinfonias**) **1** = SYMPHONY. **2a** an orchestral composition used as an introduction to vocal works, e.g. opera. **b** an instrumental interlude in baroque opera. **3** a symphony orchestra.

sinful *adj* marked by or full of sin; wicked. ⯮ **sinfully** *adv*, **sinfulness** *n*.

sing *v* (*past tense* **sang**, *past part.* **sung**) **1a** to produce musical sounds by means of the voice. **b** to utter words in musical notes. **c** to utter or perform (e.g. a song) by singing. **d** (+ along) to join in and accompany somebody else who is singing. **2** to make a shrill whining or whistling sound. **3** *esp* of a bird: to produce musical or melodious sounds. **4** (*usu* + out) to make a loud clear utterance. **5a** to relate or celebrate in verse. **b** to express vividly or enthusiastically: *They sang his praises.* ➤➤ **singable** *adj*, **singer** *n*, **singing** *n*.

singalong *n informal* = SINGSONG (2).

Singaporean *n* a native or inhabitant of Singapore. ➤➤ **Singaporean** *adj*.

singe[1] *v* (**singed, singeing**) **1** to burn superficially or slightly; to scorch. **2** to remove the hair, down, or nap from (something) by brief exposure to a flame.

singe[2] *n* a superficial burn; a scorch.

Singhalese *n* see SINHALESE.

single[1] *adj* **1** not accompanied by others; one, solitary, or sole. **2** consisting of a separate unique whole; individual or distinct: *every single child.* **3a** of, suitable for, or involving only one person. **b** consisting of or having only one part. **c** having only one aspect; uniform: *a single standard.* **4** (*in negative contexts*) even one. **5** not married. **6** of a plant or flower: having one set or whorl of petals: compare DOUBLE[1] (7). **7** of combat: involving only two people. ➤➤ **singleness** *n*, **singly** *adv*.

single[2] *n* **1** a CD or gramophone record, *esp* of popular music, with one short track on each side. **2** a single thing or amount. **3** in cricket, a single run scored. **4** *Brit* a ticket bought for a trip to a place but not back again: compare RETURN[2] (3). **5** (*usu in pl*) an unmarried adult.

single[3] *v* (+ out) to select or distinguish from a number or group.

single-action *adj* of a firearm: that requires the hammer to be cocked before firing.

single-blind *adj* denoting an experimental procedure in which the experimenters, but not the subjects, know the make-up of the test group and control group during the actual course of the experiments: compare DOUBLE-BLIND.

single bond *n* a chemical bond between two atoms in a molecule involving one shared pair of electrons.

single-breasted *adj* of a coat or jacket: having a centre fastening with one row of buttons: compare DOUBLE-BREASTED.

single cream *n Brit* cream that is thinner and lighter than double cream and is suitable for pouring: compare DOUBLE CREAM.

single file *n* a line, e.g. of people, moving one behind the other.

single-handed *adj* **1** performed or achieved by one person alone or unassisted by others. **2** using or requiring the use of only one hand. ➤➤ **single-handed** *adv*, **single-handedly** *adv*.

single-lens reflex *n* a camera in which the image is viewed using a mirror behind the lens and a five-sided prism in front of the eyepiece.

single malt *n* a high quality unblended Scottish malt whisky.

single market *n* a market in which there are no restrictions on trade between member countries.

single-minded *adj* having a single overriding purpose. ➤➤ **single-mindedly** *adv*, **single-mindedness** *n*.

single parent *n* a man or woman who is bringing up a child or children without a permanent partner.

singles *n* (*pl* **singles**) a game, e.g. of tennis, with one player on each side.

singlet *n chiefly Brit* a vest, or a similar garment worn by athletes.

single ticket *n* = SINGLE[2] (4).

singleton *n* **1** a card that is the only one of its suit in a dealt hand. **2** an individual as opposed to a pair or group; *specif* an offspring born singly.

single transferable vote *n* a system of voting in which candidates are listed in order of preference and votes are redistributed until enough members have been chosen.

singsong *n* **1** a voice delivery characterized by a monotonous rhythm or rising and falling inflection. **2** *Brit* a session of group singing. ➤➤ **singsong** *adj*.

singular[1] *adj* **1** superior; exceptional. **2** very unusual or strange; peculiar. **3** of a word or word form: denoting one person, thing, or instance. **4** single or unique. ➤➤ **singularly** *adv*.

singular[2] *n* in grammar, the singular number or form.

singularity *n* (*pl* **-ies**) **1** something singular, e.g. a peculiarity. **2** the state or quality of being singular. **3** in astronomy, a point of infinite density at the centre of a black hole.

sinh *abbr* hyperbolic sine.

Sinhalese *or* **Singhalese** *or* **Sinhala** *n* (*pl* **Sinhalese** *or* **Singhalese** *or* **Sinhala**) **1** a member of a people that inhabit Sri Lanka and form the major part of its population. **2** the language of this people. ➤➤ **Sinhalese** *adj*.

sinister *adj* **1** darkly or insidiously evil. **2** threatening evil or ill fortune; ominous. **3** of or on the left-hand side of a heraldic shield from the bearer's point of view: compare DEXTER. ➤➤ **sinisterly** *adv*, **sinisterness** *n*.

sinistral[1] *adj* **1** of or inclined to the left. **2** left-handed. ➤➤ **sinistrality** *n*, **sinistrally** *adv*.

sinistral[2] *n* somebody who is left-handed.

Sinitic *adj* of the Chinese, their language, or their culture.

sink[1] *v* (*past tense* **sank**, *past part.* **sunk**) **1a** to go down below the surface of liquid or a soft substance. **b** to fall or cause to fall to the bottom of a body of water. **c** (*usu* + in/into) to penetrate or cause to penetrate a solid through the surface. **d** to dig or bore (a well or shaft) in the earth. **2a** to fall or drop to a lower place or level. **b** to disappear from view. **3** to pass into a specified state: *He sank into a doze.* **4** to go downwards in quality, condition, amount, or worth. **5** to deteriorate physically. **6** (*usu in passive*) to overwhelm or defeat. **7** to invest (money or energy) in something. ✱ **sink or swim** to succeed or fail through one's own efforts. ➤➤ **sinkable** *adj*, **sinkage** *n*.

sink[2] *n* **1** a basin connected to a drain and a water supply and used for washing. **2** = SINK HOLE. **3** *technical* a body or process that stores or dissipates something, e.g. energy. **4** (*used before a noun*) of a school or a housing estate: located in a deprived area.

sinker *n* a weight for sinking a fishing line, sounding line, etc.

sink hole *n* a hollow, *esp* in a limestone region, through which surface water disappears into a connecting underground cavern or passage.

sink in *v* of information etc: to enter the mind or understanding.

sinking feeling *n* an uncomfortable feeling in the stomach, caused by hunger, fear, etc.

sinking fund *n* a fund built up by regular deposits for paying off the original capital sum of a debt when it falls due.

Sino- *comb. form* **1** denoting the Chinese nation, people, or culture: *sinology.* **2** Chinese and: *Sino-Tibetan.*

sinology *n* the study of the Chinese and their language, literature, history, and culture. ➤➤ **sinological** *adj*, **sinologist** *n*.

sinter[1] *n* **1** a deposit containing silica or calcium, formed by the evaporation of hot spring water. **2** material that has been sintered.

sinter[2] *v* to make (metal powders) into a coherent mass by heating and usu compressing them.

sinuous *adj* **1a** having a serpentine or wavy form; winding. **b** lithe; supple. **2** intricate or tortuous. ➤➤ **sinuosity** *n*, **sinuously** *adv*.

sinus *n* **1** a cavity in the bones of the skull that communicates with the nostrils. **2** any of various other bodily cavities or passages.

sinusitis *n* inflammation of a nasal sinus.

Sion *n* see ZION.

Sioux *n* (*pl* **Sioux**) **1** a member of a group of Native American peoples. **2** any of the languages of these peoples.

sip[1] *v* (**sipped, sipping**) to drink (something) delicately or a little at a time. ➤➤ **sipper** *n*.

sip[2] *n* a small quantity of a drink taken by sipping.

siphon[1] *or* **syphon** *n* **1** a tube by which a liquid can be transferred up over the side of a container then down to a lower level by using atmospheric pressure. **2** a bottle containing aerated water that is driven out through a tube by the pressure of the gas when a valve is opened. ➤➤ **siphonal** *adj*, **siphonic** *adj*.

siphon[2] *or* **syphon** *v* **1** (*also* + off) to convey or draw off (liquid) by a siphon. **2** (*also* + off) to draw off (money) gradually from a fund.

sir *n* **1a** used as a form of respectful or polite address to a man. **b** (**Sir**) used with *Dear* as a conventional form of address at the beginning of a letter. **2** (**Sir**) used as a title before the forename of a knight or baronet.

sirdar *or* **sardar** *n* **1** a person of high rank or authority, *esp* in India. **2** a Sikh.

sire[1] *n* **1** the male parent of a domestic animal. **2a** a father. **b** a male ancestor. **3** *archaic* used as a title and form of address to a man of rank or authority, *esp* a king.

sire[2] *v esp* of a male domestic animal: to beget (offspring).

siren *n* **1** an electrically operated device for producing a penetrating warning sound. **2** (*often* **Siren**) in Greek mythology, any of a group of women or winged creatures that lured sailors to destruction by their singing. **3** a dangerously alluring or seductive woman; a temptress.

sirenian *n* any of an order of aquatic plant-eating mammals including the manatee and dugong. ➤➤ **sirenian** *adj*.

sirloin *n* a cut of beef from the upper part of the hind loin just in front of the rump.

sirocco *n* (*pl* **-os**) a hot dust-laden wind from the N African deserts that blows onto the Mediterranean coast of S Europe.

sirrah *or* **sirra** *n archaic* used as a form of address to an inferior.

SIS *abbr* Secret Intelligence Service.

sis *n informal* used *esp* in direct address: sister.

sisal *n* a strong durable white fibre obtained from the leaves of a Mexican plant, used for ropes, matting, etc.

siskin *n* a small greenish yellow finch of temperate Europe and Asia.

sissy[1] *n* see CISSY[1].

sissy[2] *adj* see CISSY[2].

sister *n* **1** a female having the same parents as another person. **2a** (*often* **Sister**) a member of a women's religious order. **b** a fellow female member of a Christian Church. **3** a woman who shares a common tie or interest. **4** (*often* **Sister**) *Brit* a female nurse in charge of a hospital ward: compare CHARGE NURSE. **5** (*used before a noun*) related as if by sisterhood; of the same class, type, etc: *sister ships*. ➤➤ **sisterly** *adj*.

sisterhood *n* **1** the state of being sisters. **2a** a society or community of women bound by religious vows. **b** a group of women bound by a common tie or interest.

sister-in-law *n* (*pl* **sisters-in-law**) **1** the sister of one's husband or wife. **2** the wife of one's brother.

Sisyphean /sisi'fee·ən/ *adj* both endless and fruitless.

Word history

named after *Sisyphus*, mythical king condemned in Hades to roll uphill a heavy stone that constantly rolled down again.

sit[1] *v* (**sitting,** *past tense and past part.* **sat**) **1a** to rest or cause to rest in a position supported by the buttocks and with the back upright. **b** to rest with its body close to the ground. **2** to occupy a place as a member of an official body. **3** of a political body, etc: to be in session for official business. **4** of an object: to lie or stand in a particular position: *a kettle sitting on the stove*. **5** of a bird: to cover eggs for hatching. **6** to pose as a model for an artist or photographer. **7** *Brit* to be a candidate in (an examination). **8** of a table or room: to have enough seats for (a specified number). ✱ **sit on 1** to delay action on. **2** *informal* to repress or squash (somebody). **sit tight** *informal* to maintain one's position.

sit[2] *n* an act or period of sitting.

sitar *n* an Indian lute with a long neck, movable frets, and a varying number of strings. ➤➤ **sitarist** *n*.

sit back *v* to relax or reduce one's efforts.

sitcom *n informal* = SITUATION COMEDY.

sit down *v* to get into a sitting position.

sit-down *n* **1a** = SIT-DOWN STRIKE. **b** a form of protest in which people sit down in a public place and refuse to move. **2** *informal* a period of sitting, *esp* for rest. **3** (*used before a noun*) denoting a meal eaten while seated at a table.

sit-down strike *n* a strike in which workers continue to occupy their place of employment.

site[1] *n* **1a** an area of ground that was, is, or will be occupied by a building, town, etc. **b** a place for or scene of some specified activity: *a caravan site*. **2** the place or point of something. **3** = WEB SITE.

site[2] *v* to place (e.g. a building) on a site or in position; to locate.

sit in *v* **1** to participate as a visitor or observer. **2** to be a substitute.

sit-in *n* a continuous occupation of a building by a body of people as a protest.

Sitka spruce *n* a tall spruce tree native to N America with reddish brown bark, thin needles, and strong lightweight wood.

sit out *v* **1** to remain until the end of. **2** to refrain from taking part in.

sitter *n* **1** a person who sits, e.g. as an artist's model. **2** *NAm* a baby-sitter. **3** *informal* in sport, an easy shot, catch, etc.

sitting[1] *n* **1a** a single period of continuous sitting, e.g. for a portrait. **b** a period, *esp* one of two or more, in which a group of people are served a meal. **2** a session, *esp* of an official body.

sitting[2] *adj* **1** that is sitting. **2** in office or actual possession.

sitting duck *n informal* an easy or defenceless target for attack, criticism, etc.

sitting room *n chiefly Brit* a room, *esp* in a private house, used for recreation and relaxation.

sitting target *n informal* = SITTING DUCK.

sitting tenant *n Brit* a tenant who is at the present time in occupation, e.g. of a house or flat.

situate *v* to place in a location, situation, context, or category.

situated *adj* **1** located. **2** supplied to the specified extent with money or possessions: *comfortably situated*. **3** being in the specified circumstances.

situation *n* **1** the way in which something is placed in relation to its surroundings; location. **2** position with respect to conditions and circumstances. **3** the circumstances at a particular moment. **4** a position of employment; a post. ➤➤ **situational** *adj.*

situation comedy *n* a television or radio comedy series that involves the same basic cast of characters in a succession of connected or unconnected episodes.

sit up *v* **1** to rise from a reclining to a sitting position. **2** to sit with the back straight. **3** *informal* to start to take an interest.

sit-up *n* the movement of raising the upper body into a sitting position from a position lying flat on the back, performed repeatedly as an exercise to improve physical fitness.

sitz bath *n* a bath in which one remains in a sitting posture, immersed only up to the hips.

six *n* **1** the number 6. **2** a group of six Cub Scouts or Brownie Guides, the smallest unit in a pack. **3** a shot in cricket that crosses the boundary before it bounces and scores six runs. ✱ **at sixes and sevens** in disorder, confused, or in a muddle. **for six** *Brit, informal* so as to be totally overwhelmed, defeated, etc: *The virus knocked me for six.* **six of one and half a dozen of the other** a situation in which a choice must be made between alternatives that are almost or effectively the same. ➤➤ **six** *adj,* **sixfold** *adj and adv.*

sixer *n* the leader of a six in a pack of Cub Scouts or Brownie Guides.

six-pack *n* **1** a pack of six bottles or cans, *esp* of beer, bought together. **2** *informal* highly developed abdominal muscles.

sixpence *n* a small silver-coloured coin worth six old pence (2.5p).

six-shooter *n* a six-chambered revolver.

sixteen *adj and n* the number 16. ➤➤ **sixteenth** *adj and n.*

sixteenth note *n chiefly NAm* = SEMIQUAVER.

sixth *adj and n* **1** having the position in a sequence corresponding to the number six. **2** one of six equal parts of something. **3** in music, an interval of six degrees of a diatonic scale, or the combination of two notes at such an interval. ➤➤ **sixthly** *adv.*

sixth form *n* in England and Wales, the highest classes of a secondary school in which pupils study for A levels. ➤➤ **sixth-former** *n.*

sixth-form college *n* in England and Wales, a state school for pupils beyond GCSE level.

sixth sense *n* a keen intuitive power viewed as analogous to the five physical senses.

sixty *adj and n* (*pl* **-ies**) **1** the number 60. **2** (*in pl*) the numbers 60 to 69. ➤➤ **sixtieth** *adj and n.*

sixty-fourth note *n NAm* = HEMIDEMISEMIQUAVER.

sizable *or* **sizeable** *adj* fairly large; considerable. ➤➤ **sizably** *adv.*

size[1] *n* **1a** physical magnitude or extent; overall dimensions. **b** bigness. **2** any of a series of graduated measures, *esp* of clothing, conventionally identified by numbers or letters. ✱ **that's (about) the size of it** *informal* that is the actual state of affairs.

size[2] *v* **1** to arrange or grade according to size. **2** to make in a particular size. ➤➤ **sized** *adj,* **sizer** *n.*

size[3] *n* a thick sticky material, used for filling the pores in surfaces, e.g. of paper, textiles, or plaster.

size[4] *v* to cover, stiffen, or glaze with or as if with size.

sizeable *adj* see SIZABLE.

size up *v* **1** to form an opinion of. **2** to estimate the size of. **3** to conform to requirements or specifications.

sizzle[1] *v* **1** to make the hissing sound of frying food. **2** *informal* to be very hot. ➤➤ **sizzler** *n,* **sizzling** *adj.*

sizzle[2] *n* a sizzling sound.

sjambok /'shambok/ *n* in S Africa, a whip of rhinoceros hide.

SK *abbr* Saskatchewan (US postal abbreviation).

ska *n* popular music of W Indian origin that is a forerunner of reggae.

skag *or* **scag** *n slang* heroin.

skate[1] *n* an ice skate or a roller skate. ✱ **get/put one's skates on** *informal* to hurry up.

skate[2] *v* **1** to glide along on skates by sliding the feet forward alternately. **2** to glide or slide as if on skates. ✱ **skate over/round** to avoid dealing with (problems, controversial issues, etc). **skate through** to accomplish rapidly or easily. ➤➤ **skater** *n,* **skating** *n.*

skate[3] *n* (*pl* **skates** *or* **skate**) a food fish of the ray family with large flat pectoral fins.

skateboard[1] *n* a narrow board mounted on roller-skate wheels and ridden, usu standing up, for recreation.

skateboard[2] *v* to ride on a skateboard. ➤➤ **skateboarder** *n,* **skateboarding** *n.*

skean dhu /,skee·ən 'dhooh/ *n* a dagger worn in the stocking by Scottish Highlanders in full dress.

skedaddle *v informal* to run away; to depart in haste.

skeet *n* a form of clay-pigeon shooting in which targets are hurled across the shooting range from traps on either side.

skeg *n* a small fin fixed to the rear end of a yacht's keel or a surfboard.

skein *n* **1** a loosely coiled length of yarn or thread; a hank. **2** a flock of wildfowl, e.g. geese, in flight.

skeletal *adj* of, forming, attached to, or resembling a skeleton. ➤➤ **skeletally** *adv.*

skeleton *n* **1** a supportive or protective rigid framework of an organism, *esp* the bony internal framework of a vertebrate animal. **2** something reduced to its bare essentials. **3** an emaciated person or animal. **4** a basic structural framework. **5** (*used before a noun*) reduced to the bare minimum: *a skeleton staff.* ✱ **skeleton in the cupboard** a secret cause of shame, *esp* in a family.

skeletonize *or* **-ise** *v* to reduce to or produce in skeleton form.

skeleton key *n* a key, *esp* one with most or all of the serrations absent, that is able to open many simple locks.

skep *n* **1** a farm basket used *esp* in mucking out stables. **2** a domed beehive made of twisted straw.

skeptic *n NAm* see SCEPTIC.

skerry *n* (*pl* **-ies**) *chiefly Scot* a rocky island; a reef.

sketch[1] *n* **1** a preliminary study or draft, *esp* a rough drawing. **2** a brief description or outline. **3** a short theatrical piece having a single scene, *esp* a comic act.

sketch[2] *v* **1** to make a sketch of. **2** (*often* + out) to describe briefly; to outline. ⋙ **sketcher** *n.*

sketchbook *n* a book of sheets of plain paper used for sketching.

sketchy *adj* (**-ier, -iest**) lacking completeness or substance; superficial or scanty. ⋙ **sketchily** *adv,* **sketchiness** *n.*

skew[1] *adj* placed or running obliquely. ⋙ **skewness** *n.*

skew[2] *n* **1** obliqueness or slant. **2** distortion or bias.

skew[3] *v* **1** to take an oblique course; to twist or swerve. **2a** to distort or bias. **b** to cause (e.g. statistical data) to deviate from a true or expected value.

skewbald[1] *adj* of a horse: marked with spots and patches of white and another colour, *esp* not black.

skewbald[2] *n* a skewbald horse.

skewer[1] *n* a long pin of wood or metal used to hold food together while cooking.

skewer[2] *v* to fasten or pierce with or as if with a skewer.

skew-whiff *adj chiefly Brit, informal* not straight; askew.

ski[1] *n* (*pl* **skis**) **1a** either of a pair of long narrow strips of wood, metal, or plastic attached to the feet for gliding over snow. **b** = WATER SKI. **2** a runner shaped like a ski attached to the bottom of a vehicle, aircraft, etc.

ski[2] *v* (**skis, skied, skiing** *or* **ski-ing**) to glide on skis as a way of travelling, for recreation, or as a sport. ⋙ **skiable** *adj,* **skier** *n,* **skiing** *n.*

skid[1] *v* (**skidded, skidding**) **1** of a vehicle: to slide sideways out of the driver's control. **2** to slip or slide.

skid[2] *n* **1** the act or an instance of skidding. **2** a runner used as part of the landing gear of an aircraft. **3** a device placed under a wheel to act as a brake, e.g. on a hill. **4** (**the skids**) *informal* the road to defeat or downfall.

skidpan *n* a slippery surface on which vehicle drivers may practise the control of skids.

skid row *n chiefly NAm, informal* a district frequented by down-and-outs and alcoholics.

skiff *n* a light rowing or sailing boat.

skiffle *n* a style of popular music of the 1950s played by a group on guitars accompanied by improvised instruments, e.g. washboards.

ski jump *n* **1** a steep high ramp overhanging a slope, used for competitive ski jumping. **2** a jump made by a skier from such a ramp. ⋙ **ski-jump** *v,* **ski jumper** *n,* **ski jumping** *n.*

skilful (*NAm* **skillful**) *adj* possessing or displaying skill; expert. ⋙ **skilfully** *adv.*

ski lift *n* a power-driven conveyor consisting of a series of seats suspended from an overhead cable and used for transporting skiers up and down a mountainside.

skill *n* **1** special ability in a particular field, *esp* acquired by learning and practice. **2** a task, technique, trade, etc requiring skill.

skilled *adj* **1** having skill. **2** requiring workers with training in a particular field.

skillet *n* **1** a small frying pan. **2** *chiefly Brit* a small saucepan with three or four legs, used in former times for cooking on the hearth.

skim[1] *v* (**skimmed, skimming**) **1a** to clear (a liquid) of floating matter. **b** to remove (e.g. fat or scum) from the surface of a liquid. **2** to pass swiftly or lightly over (a surface). **3** to throw (a flat stone) so that it bounces along the surface of water. **4** to read (something) cursorily and rapidly for the most important points. **5** (*usu* + through/over) to give something a cursory glance or consideration. ⋙ **skimmer** *n.*

skim[2] *n* **1** a thin layer, coating, or film. **2** the act or an instance of skimming.

ski mask *n* a knitted protective covering for the head and face, worn *esp* by skiers.

skimmed milk *n* milk with the cream removed.

skimp *v* (*usu* + on) to spend too little on, use less than enough of, or give insufficient attention to something.

skimpy *adj* (**-ier, -iest**) inadequate in quality, size, etc; scanty. ⋙ **skimpily** *adv,* **skimpiness** *n.*

skin[1] *n* **1a** the external layer of the body of a person or animal. **b** any of various outer layers, e.g. the rind of a fruit or vegetable or the casing of a sausage. **2** the external covering of an animal separated from the body and prepared for use, e.g. in a garment. **3** a covering or casing forming the outside surface of a ship, aircraft, etc. **4** a film that forms on the surface of some liquids. **5** *Brit, informal* = SKINHEAD. ✱ **by the skin of one's teeth** by a very narrow margin. **get under somebody's skin** *informal* to irritate or interest somebody intensely. **no skin off somebody's nose** *informal* no disadvantage to somebody. **skin and bone** very thin; emaciated. ⋙ **skinless** *adj.*

skin[2] *v* (**skinned, skinning**) **1a** to scrape or peel away the skin of. **b** to scrape or graze the surface of (a part of the body). **2** to cover with or as if with skin.

skin-deep *adj* **1** as deep as the skin. **2** superficial.

skin diving *n* swimming under water with a face mask, flippers, and sometimes an aqualung. ⋙ **skin diver** *n.*

skinflint *n informal* a miser or niggardly person.

skinful *n Brit, informal* a large amount, *esp* of alcoholic drink.

skinhead *n* any of a group of young people with extremely short hair, a distinctive way of dressing, and often an aggressive racist attitude.

skink *n* a small lizard of tropical Africa and Asia that has smooth scales.

skinner *n* a person who deals in skins, pelts, or hides.

skinny *adj* (**-ier, -iest**) *informal* very thin. ⋙ **skinniness** *n.*

skinny-dipping *n chiefly NAm, informal* swimming in the nude. ⋙ **skinny-dipper** *n.*

skint *adj Brit, informal* having no money; penniless.

skin test *n* a test in which a substance is applied to or introduced beneath the skin, used in detecting allergies or immunity to disease.

skintight *adj* fitting extremely closely to the body.

skip[1] *v* (**skipped, skipping**) **1a** to move with light leaps and bounds. **b** to proceed by hopping on alternate feet. **2** to jump repeatedly over a rope swung round the body over the head and under the feet. **3** to pass over or omit (e.g. a section or step). **4** (+ through) to deal with something in a hasty or cursory manner. **5** to fail to attend; to miss.

skip[2] *n* a skipping movement.

skip[3] *n* **1** a large open container for waste or rubble. **2** a bucket or cage for raising or lowering workers and materials, e.g. in mining or quarrying.

ski pants *pl n* trousers made of stretchy fabric with a strap under the foot, worn by women for skiing or leisure.

skipjack *n* a tuna with a striped body that is an important food fish.

skipper[1] *n informal* the captain of a ship, aircraft, or sports team.

skipper[2] *v* to act as skipper of.

skipper[3] *n* somebody or something that skips.

skirl *v* to emit the high shrill sound of the bagpipes. ➤➤ **skirl** *n.*

skirmish[1] *n* **1** a minor or irregular military engagement. **2a** a brief clash or fight. **b** any minor or petty dispute.

skirmish[2] *v* to engage in a skirmish. ➤➤ **skirmisher** *n.*

skirt[1] *n* **1a** a garment worn by women and girls that hangs from and fits closely round the waist. **b** a free-hanging part of a dress or coat, extending from the waist down. **c** a part resembling a skirt in form or function. **2** *Brit* a membranous gristly cut of beef from the flank. **3** (*also in pl*) the borders or outer edge of an area or group. ✱ **bit of skirt** *informal* a woman regarded as a sex object. ➤➤ **skirted** *adj.*

skirt[2] *v* **1** to avoid through fear of difficulty, danger, or dispute. **2** to extend along or form the border or edge of. **3** (*often* + along/around) to lie or move along an edge, border, or margin.

skirting *n Brit* = SKIRTING BOARD.

skirting board *n Brit* a board, often with decorative moulding, that is fixed along the base of an interior wall.

skit *n* a satirical or humorous sketch or story.

skite *v chiefly Scot* to slip or slide obliquely.

skitter *v* **1** to glide or skip lightly or swiftly. **2** to skim along a surface.

skittish *adj* **1** easily frightened; restive. **2a** lively or frisky in behaviour. **b** variable or fickle. ➤➤ **skittishly** *adv,* **skittishness** *n.*

skittle *n* **1** (*in pl, used as sing.*) a bowling game played by rolling a wooden ball at a standing group of nine pins in order to knock over as many as possible. **2** a pin used in skittles.

skive *v Brit, informal* (*often* + off) to evade work or duty, *esp* out of laziness; to shirk. ➤➤ **skiver** *n.*

skivvy[1] *n* (*pl* **-ies**) *Brit, informal* a female domestic servant who performs menial tasks.

skivvy[2] *v* (**-ies, -ied**) *informal* to act as a skivvy.

skua *n* a large dark-coloured seabird that forces weaker birds to drop or disgorge the fish they have caught.

skulduggery *or* **skullduggery** *n* devious trickery, *esp* underhand or unscrupulous behaviour.

skulk *v* **1** to move in a stealthy or furtive manner. **2** to conceal oneself, *esp* for a sinister purpose; to lurk. ➤➤ **skulker** *n.*

skull *n* **1** a bony or cartilaginous case forming the skeleton of the head of a vertebrate animal. **2** *informal* the brain.

skull and crossbones *n* a representation of a human skull over two crossed thigh bones, usu used as a warning of danger to life and formerly displayed on pirate flags.

skullcap *n* a light brimless cap fitting closely over the crown of the head.

skullduggery *n* see SKULDUGGERY.

skunk *n* a common black-and-white American mammal of the weasel family with a pair of anal glands from which a foul-smelling secretion is ejected.

sky[1] *n* (*pl* **-ies**) **1** the upper atmosphere as seen from the earth; the heavens. **2** *literary* heaven. ✱ **praise to the skies** to praise very highly. **the sky's the limit** *informal* there is no limit to what can be achieved, won, etc.

sky[2] *v* (**-ies, -ied**) *informal* to throw or hit (a ball) high in the air.

sky blue *adj* of the light blue colour of the sky on a clear day. ➤➤ **sky blue** *n.*

skydiving *n* the sport of jumping from an aircraft and executing body manoeuvres in the air before opening one's parachute. ➤➤ **skydive** *v,* **skydiver** *n.*

sky-high *adv and adj* **1** very high into the air. **2** to a very high level or degree.

skyjack *v* to hijack (an aircraft). ➤➤ **skyjack** *n,* **skyjacker** *n.*

skylark[1] *n* a common brown lark noted for its song, *esp* as uttered in vertical flight or while hovering.

skylark[2] *v* to act in a high-spirited or mischievous manner.

skylight *n* a window in a roof or ceiling.

skyline *n* **1** an outline, e.g. of buildings or mountains, against the background of the sky. **2** the apparent juncture of earth and sky; the horizon.

skyrocket[1] *n* = ROCKET[1] (1A).

skyrocket[2] *v* (**skyrocketed, skyrocketing**) to increase rapidly or abruptly.

skyscape *n* an expanse of sky, *esp* as depicted by an artist.

skyscraper *n* a very tall many-storeyed building, *esp* one containing offices.

skyward *adj and adv* towards the sky; upward.

skywards *adv* = SKYWARD.

skyway *n chiefly NAm* a route used by aircraft.

skywriting *n* writing in the sky by means of smoke emitted from an aircraft.

slab *n* **1** a large thick flat piece or slice, e.g. of stone or cake. **2** the rough outside piece cut from a log when squaring it. **3** *Brit, informal* a mortuary table.

slack[1] *adj* **1** not taut; loose. **2** characterized by slowness or indolence; sluggish. **3** negligent or lax. **4** lacking in activity; not busy. ➤➤ **slackly** *adv,* **slackness** *n.*

slack[2] *n* **1** a part of something, e.g. a rope, that is not taut. **2** (*in pl*) trousers, *esp* for casual wear. **3** *informal* a lull or decrease in activity; a quiet season or period.

slack[3] *v* **1a** to be sluggish or negligent in doing something. **b** *Brit, informal* to shirk or evade work or duty. **2a** (*often* + off) to release tension in; to loosen. **b** to lessen or moderate. **3** (+ off/up) to be or become slack. ➤➤ **slacker** *n.*

slack[4] *n* coal in very small pieces.

slacken *v* **1** (*often* + off) to make or become slack. **2** (*often* + off) to make or become less active, rapid, or intense.

slack water *n* the period around the turn of the tide when there is no apparent tidal motion.

slag[1] *n* **1** waste matter from the smelting of metal ores. **2** *Brit* waste material from coal mining. **3** *Brit, informal, derog* a promiscuous woman or girl.

slag[2] *v* (**slagged, slagging**) *Brit, informal* (*also* + off) to criticize or make abusive comments about.

slagheap *n Brit* a high mound of waste material, e.g. from coal mining.

slain *v* past part. of SLAY.

slainte /ˈslahnzhə/ *interj Irish, Scot* used as a drinking toast.

slake *v* **1** to satisfy or quench (one's thirst or desire). **2** to cause (caustic lime) to react with water to produce calcium hydroxide.

slaked lime *n* a dry white powder consisting of calcium hydroxide produced by treating caustic lime with water.

slalom *n* a skiing or canoeing race on a zigzag or winding course between obstacles.

slam[1] *v* (**slammed, slamming**) **1a** to shut (e.g. a door) forcibly and noisily. **b** to close with a banging noise. **2a** to put or throw down noisily and violently. **b** to force into sudden and violent action. **c** (*usu* + into) to strike or crash into something violently. **3** *informal* to criticize harshly. **4** *informal* to defeat easily.

slam[2] *n* a banging noise, *esp* one made by a door in closing.

slam[3] *n* in bridge, the winning of all tricks or all tricks but one.

slam-dance *v chiefly NAm* to dance to rock music in a style that involves intentionally bumping into other dancers. ➤➤ **slam-dancing** *n.*

slammer *n* (**the slammer**) *slang* a prison.

slander[1] *n* **1** false spoken charges that do damage to another's reputation, or the crime of uttering such charges: compare LIBEL[1]. **2** a false defamatory oral statement. ➤➤ **slanderous** *adj,* **slanderously** *adv.*

slander[2] *v* to utter slander about. ➤➤ **slanderer** *n.*

slang[1] *n* **1** informal vocabulary that is composed typically of new words or meanings, impolite or vulgar references, etc. **2** language peculiar to a particular group; argot or jargon. ➤➤ **slangy** *adj.*

slang[2] *v informal* to abuse with harsh or coarse language.

slanging match *n chiefly Brit, informal* an angry and abusive exchange between two or more people.

slant[1] *v* **1** to incline from a horizontal or vertical line or level; to slope. **2** to interpret or present (e.g. information) in a biased way or from a particular point of view.

slant[2] *n* **1** a slanting direction, line, or plane; a slope. **2a** a particular or personal point of view. **b** an unfair bias or distortion. ➤➤ **slantwise** *adv and adj.*

slant[3] *adj* sloping.

slap[1] *n* **1a** a quick sharp blow, *esp* with the open hand. **b** a noise that suggests a slap. **2** *informal* make-up. ✱ **slap in the face** a rebuff or insult. **slap on the back** an expression of congratulation. **slap on the wrist** a token punishment or reprimand.

slap[2] *v* (**slapped, slapping**) **1** to strike sharply with the open hand or a flat object. **2** (*usu* + on) to put or apply with careless haste or force. **3** (*usu* + against) to hit something with the sound of a slap.

slap[3] *adv informal* directly or with force.

slap and tickle *n Brit, informal* playful lovemaking.

slap-bang *adv informal* **1** in a highly abrupt or forceful manner. **2** precisely.

slapdash *adj and adv* done in a haphazard or slipshod manner.

slaphappy *adj informal* **1** irresponsibly casual. **2** buoyantly carefree; happy-go-lucky.

slaphead *n Brit, informal, derog* a bald man.

slapper *n Brit, informal, derog* a promiscuous or coarse woman.

slapstick *n* **1** a form of comedy characterized by farce and horseplay. **2** a device comprising two flat pieces of wood fastened at one end and making a loud noise when used, *esp* in former times, by an actor or clown to strike somebody.

slap-up *adj chiefly Brit, informal* of a meal: lavish or luxurious.

slash[1] *v* **1** to cut with violent sweeping strokes. **2** to cut slits in (e.g. a garment). **3** *informal* to reduce (e.g. a price) drastically. **4** to criticize cuttingly. **5** *archaic* to whip or scourge (somebody). ➤➤ **slasher** *n.*

slash[2] *n* **1** a cut or stroke made by or as if by slashing. **2** = SOLIDUS. **3** *Brit, informal* an act of urinating.

slash-and-burn *adj* of or denoting a method of agriculture involving the felling and burning of shrubs or trees to make land available for arable crops.

slat *n* a thin narrow flat strip, *esp* of wood or metal, e.g. a lath or louvre. ➤➤ **slatted** *adj.*

slate[1] *n* **1** a fine-grained metamorphic rock that is easily split into thin layers. **2** a piece of such rock used as roofing material. **3** a tablet of slate or similar material used for writing on, *esp* in former times. **4** a dark bluish grey or greenish grey colour. **5** a list of candidates for nomination or election. ✱ **on the slate** *Brit* on credit. ➤➤ **slate** *adj,* **slaty** *adj.*

slate[2] *v* **1** to cover (a roof) with slates. **2** *chiefly NAm* **a** to schedule for action. **b** to nominate for election or appointment. ➤➤ **slater** *n.*

slate[3] *v chiefly Brit, informal* to criticize severely.

slattern *n dated* an untidy slovenly woman or girl. ➤➤ **slatternly** *adj.*

slaughter[1] *n* **1** the butchering of livestock for market. **2** the killing of many people, e.g. in battle; carnage. ➤➤ **slaughterous** *adj.*

slaughter[2] *v* **1** to kill (animals) for food. **2** to kill (people) violently or in large numbers. **3** *informal* to defeat (opposing players) decisively. ➤➤ **slaughterer** *n.*

slaughterhouse *n* an establishment where animals are killed for food.

Slav *n* a member of any of the peoples, *esp* of E Europe, who speak a Slavonic language as their native tongue.

slave[1] *n* **1** a person held in servitude as the property of another. **2** a person who is dominated by a specified thing: *a slave to fashion.* **3** a drudge.

slave[2] *v* **1** to work very hard; to toil. **2** to traffic in slaves.

slave driver *n informal* a harsh taskmaster.

slave labour *n* hard work for little reward.

slaver[1] *n* **1** a person engaged in the slave trade. **2** a ship used in the slave trade.

slaver[2] /'slavə/ *v* **1** to drool or slobber. **2** (*usu* + over) to show great or excessive desire for something or somebody.

slaver[3] *n* saliva dribbling from the mouth.

slavery *n* **1a** the state of being a slave. **b** the practice of owning slaves. **2** drudgery; toil.

slave state *n* a state of the USA in which slavery was legal until the American Civil War.

slave trade *n* traffic in slaves, *esp* the transportation of black Africans to America for profit before the American Civil War. ➤➤ **slave trader** *n.*

Slavic *n* = SLAVONIC. ➤➤ **Slavic** *adj.*

slavish *adj* **1** obsequiously imitative; devoid of originality. **2** abjectly servile. ➤➤ **slavishly** *adv,* **slavishness** *n.*

Slavonic *n* a branch of the Indo-European language family including Bulgarian, Czech, Polish, Russian, and Serbo-Croatian. ➤➤ **Slavonic** *adj.*

slaw *n NAm* coleslaw.

slay *v* (*past tense* **slew,** *past part.* **slain**) **1** *archaic or literary* to kill violently or with great bloodshed. **2** *NAm* to murder. **3** *informal* to affect overpoweringly, e.g. with awe or delight. ⋙ **slayer** *n.*

sleaze *n informal* **1** a sleazy quality; sleaziness. **2** *chiefly NAm* a sleazy thing or person.

sleazy *adj* (**-ier, -iest**) **1** of a place: squalid and disreputable. **2** of behaviour: corrupt or immoral. ⋙ **sleazily** *adv,* **sleaziness** *n.*

sled[1] *n NAm* = SLEDGE[1].

sled[2] *v* (**sledded, sledding**) *NAm* = SLEDGE[2].

sledge[1] *n* **1** a vehicle with runners that is pulled by reindeer, dogs, etc over snow or ice. **2** *Brit* = TOBOGGAN[1].

sledge[2] *v* to ride or transport in a sledge.

sledge[3] *n* = SLEDGEHAMMER.

sledge[4] *v* of a fielder in cricket: to break the concentration of (an opposing batsman) by making provocative remarks.

sledgehammer *n* **1** a large heavy hammer that is wielded with both hands. **2** (*used before a noun*) clumsy or heavy-handed.

sleek[1] *adj* **1a** smooth and glossy. **b** having a smooth well-groomed look. **c** having a well-fed or flourishing appearance. **2** elegant, stylish, or streamlined. ⋙ **sleekly** *adv,* **sleekness** *n.*

sleek[2] *v* to make (the hair) sleek or smooth.

sleep[1] *n* **1** a natural periodic suspension of consciousness that is essential for physical and mental well-being. **2** a sleeplike state. **3** a period spent sleeping. **4** *informal* dried mucus that sometimes collects in the eye corners when sleeping. ✱ **go to sleep 1** to fall asleep. **2** to lose sensation; to become numb. **put to sleep** to kill (e.g. a sick animal) humanely.

sleep[2] *v* (*past tense and past part.* **slept**) **1** to rest in a state of sleep. **2** *informal* (+ with/together) to have sexual intercourse or a sexual relationship. **3** to provide sleeping accommodation for (a specified number of people). **4** (+ off) to get rid of or recover from by sleeping. ✱ **sleep on** to consider more fully, *esp* overnight, before making a decision. **sleep rough** to sleep out of doors, *esp* in uncomfortable conditions.

sleep around *v* to be sexually promiscuous.

sleeper *n* **1** = SLEEPING CAR. **2** somebody or something unpromising or unnoticed that suddenly attains prominence or value. **3** *Brit* a ring or stud worn in a pierced ear to keep the hole open. **4** a timber, concrete, or steel transverse support to which railway rails are fixed.

sleep in *v* to sleep late, either intentionally or accidentally.

sleeping bag *n* a long thick bag of warm material for sleeping in, *esp* when camping.

sleeping car *n* a railway carriage divided into compartments having berths for sleeping.

sleeping partner *n* a partner who takes no active part in the running of a firm's business.

sleeping pill *n* a drug in the form of a tablet or capsule that is taken to induce sleep.

sleeping policeman *n* a hump in a road designed to slow vehicles to a low speed.

sleeping sickness *n* **1** a tropical disease that is marked by protracted lethargy and is caused by a parasite transmitted by tsetse flies. **2** *NAm* = SLEEPY SICKNESS.

sleepless *adj* **1** not able to sleep. **2** marked by lack of sleep.

sleepover *n* an occasion of staying overnight as a guest at somebody's home.

sleepwalk *v* to walk in one's sleep. ⋙ **sleepwalker** *n.*

sleepy *adj* (**-ier, -iest**) **1** ready to fall asleep. **2** lacking alertness; sluggish or lethargic. **3** sleep-inducing; soporific. **4** having little activity; tranquil. ⋙ **sleepily** *adv,* **sleepiness** *n.*

sleepyhead *n informal* a sleepy person.

sleepy sickness *n* inflammation of the brain caused by a viral infection and characterized by extreme drowsiness.

sleet[1] *n* **1** partly frozen falling rain, or snow and rain falling together. **2** *chiefly NAm* a thin coating of ice. ⋙ **sleety** *adj.*

sleet[2] *v* to send down sleet.

sleeve *n* **1** a part of a garment covering the arm or upper arm. **2** a paper or cardboard covering that protects a gramophone record when not in use. **3** a tubular machine part designed to fit over another part, e.g. to form a connection. ✱ **have up one's sleeve** to have as an undeclared resource. ⋙ **sleeved** *adj,* **sleeveless** *adj.*

sleeving *n Brit* the covering of an insulated electric cable.

sleigh[1] *n* a large sledge drawn by horses or reindeer.

sleigh[2] *v* to travel in a sleigh.

sleigh bell *n* a bell attached to the harness of a horse drawing a sleigh.

sleight *n literary* **1** deceitful craftiness. **2** a stratagem.

sleight of hand *n* **1** manual skill and dexterity in conjuring or juggling. **2** adroitness in deception.

slender *adj* **1a** gracefully slim. **b** small in circumference or width in proportion to length or height. **2** flimsy, tenuous, or meagre. ⋙ **slenderly** *adv,* **slenderness** *n.*

slept *v* past tense and past part. of SLEEP[2].

sleuth[1] *n informal* a detective.

sleuth[2] *v informal* to act as a detective.

S level *n* **1** an examination in any of various subjects at a higher level than A level and usu taken at the same time. **2** a pass in this examination.

slew[1] *v* **1** to turn, twist, or swing about. **2** to skid.

slew[2] *n* a slewing movement.

slew[3] *v* past tense of SLAY.

slew[4] *or* **slue** *n chiefly NAm, informal* a large number or quantity.

slice[1] *n* **1** a thin broad flat piece cut from a larger whole. **2** a portion or share. **3** an implement with a broad blade used for lifting food. **4a** in golf, the flight of a ball that deviates from a straight course in the direction of the player's dominant hand: compare HOOK[1]. **b** a similar shot in other sports, e.g. tennis.

slice[2] *v* **1** to cut with or as if with a knife. **2** to cut into slices. **3** to hit (a ball) so that a slice results. **4** to move rapidly or effortlessly. ⋙ **slicer** *n.*

slick[1] *adj* **1** deft or skilful. **2** superficially plausible or impressive; glib. **3** smooth or slippery. ⋙ **slickly** *adv,* **slickness** *n.*

slick[2] *n* **1** = OIL SLICK. **2** a tyre with no tread used for motor racing on a dry track.

slick[3] *v* to make (e.g. hair) sleek or smooth.

slicker *n NAm* **1** a raincoat with a smooth surface. **2** *informal* **a** an artful crook; a swindler. **b** a city dweller, *esp* one with sophisticated mannerisms.

slide[1] *v* (*past tense and past part.* **slid**) **1a** to move or cause to move in continuous contact with a smooth surface. **b** to glide over a slippery surface, e.g. snow or ice. **2** to pass quietly and unobtrusively. **3** to move smoothly and easily. **4** to pass gradually to a lower level or worse state. **5** to place unobtrusively or stealthily. ➤➤ **slider** *n.*

slide² *n* **1a** a structure with a sloping smooth surface down which children slide in play. **b** a track or slope suitable for sliding or tobogganing. **2a** the act or an instance of sliding. **b** = PORTAMENTO. **c** a technique in guitar playing in which a tube-shaped device is moved over the frets to produce a gliding effect between notes. **3** a sliding part or mechanism, e.g. a U-shaped section of tube in the trombone that is moved to produce notes of different pitch. **4a** a flat piece of glass on which an object is mounted for examination under a microscope. **b** a photographic transparency suitably mounted for projection. **5** *Brit* = HAIR-SLIDE.

slide guitar *n* = SLIDE² (2C).

slide rule *n* a ruler having a central sliding strip with graduations that enable calculations to be made.

sliding scale *n* a flexible scale, e.g. of fees or subsidies, that can be adjusted according to variation in some other factor.

slight¹ *adj* **1** small in amount or degree. **2a** having a slim or frail build. **b** lacking strength or bulk; flimsy. **c** unimportant; trivial. **d** not serious; minor. ➤➤ **slightly** *adv,* **slightness** *n.*

slight² *v* to treat with disdain or indifference; to snub.

slight³ *n* a humiliating affront.

slily *adv* slyly.

slim¹ *adj* (**slimmer, slimmest**) **1** slender in build; attractively thin. **2** small in circumference or width in proportion to length or height. **3** scanty or slight: *a slim chance.* ➤➤ **slimly** *adv,* **slimness** *n.*

slim² *v* (**slimmed, slimming**) **1** to become thinner, *esp* by dieting. **2** (*often* + down) to reduce the workforce of (a company, organization, etc). ➤➤ **slimmer** *n,* **slimming** *n.*

slime¹ *n* **1** soft wet mud. **2** a thick slippery substance often forming an unpleasant layer on a surface.

slime² *v* to smear or cover with slime.

slimeball *n informal* an unpleasant obsequious person.

slimline *adj* **1** having a slim shape. **2** of food and drinks: low-calorie.

slimy *adj* (**-ier, -iest**) **1** of, resembling, or covered with slime. **2** *informal* characterized by obsequious flattery; offensively ingratiating. ➤➤ **sliminess** *n.*

sling¹ *n* **1a** a looped line used to hoist, lower, or carry something. **b** a bandage suspended from the neck to support an injured arm or hand. **2** a simple weapon for throwing stones, usu consisting of a short strap that is looped round the missile, whirled round, and then released at one end.

sling² *v* (*past tense and past part.* **slung**) **1** to cast with a careless motion; to fling. **2** to throw (a stone) with a sling. **3** to hoist, lower, or carry in or as if in a sling. **4** *Brit, informal* (+ out) to expel unceremoniously. ➤➤ **slinger** *n.*

sling³ *n* a drink made of gin with water or fruit juice and sugar.

slingback *n* a backless shoe that is held on at the heel by a strap passing round the back of the ankle.

sling off *v chiefly Aus, informal* (*often* + at) to jeer or mock.

slingshot *n NAm* = CATAPULT¹ (1).

slink *v* (*past tense and past part.* **slunk**) **1** to move in a graceful provocative manner. **2** to move stealthily or furtively. ➤➤ **slink** *n.*

slinky *adj* (**-ier, -iest**) *informal* sleek and flowing in movement or outline, *esp* following the lines of the body in a sensual manner.

slip¹ *v* (**slipped, slipping**) **1a** to slide out of place or away from one's grasp. **b** to slide on a slippery surface. **2** to decline from a standard or accustomed level by degrees. **3a** to move or cause to move smoothly; to slide. **b** to move quietly and cautiously; to steal. **c** to pass smoothly or imperceptibly from one state or condition into another. **4** of time: to elapse or pass. **5a** to free oneself from (a restraint). **b** to escape from (one's memory or notice). **6** (+ on/off) to put on or take off (a garment) quickly or easily. **7** to insert, place, or pass quietly or secretly. **8** in knitting, to transfer (a stitch) from one needle to another without working it. **9** to keep (the clutch of a vehicle) in partial engagement by resting a foot continuously on the pedal. ✱ **let slip 1** to say (something) casually or accidentally. **2** to fail to take (e.g. a chance). ➤➤ **slippage** *n.*

slip² *n* **1** the act or an instance of slipping. **2** a usu minor mistake: *a slip of the tongue.* **3** a woman's undergarment that resembles a light skirt or sleeveless dress. **4** in cricket, a fielding position close to the batsman and just to the off side of the wicketkeeper. **5** = SLIPWAY. ✱ **give somebody the slip** *informal* to elude or evade somebody in pursuit.

slip³ *n* **1** a small piece of paper, e.g. a printed form. **2** a young and slim person: *a mere slip of a girl.* **3** a small shoot or twig cut for planting or grafting.

slip⁴ *n* a semifluid mixture of clay and water used by potters for coating or decorating ceramic ware.

slipcase *n* a protective container with one open end for one or more books.

slipcover *n* **1** = LOOSE COVER. **2** = DUST JACKET.

slipknot *n* **1** a knot that can be untied by pulling. **2** = RUNNING KNOT.

slip-on *adj esp* of shoes: having no fastenings and therefore easily slipped on or off. ➤➤ **slip-on** *n.*

slipover *n* a sleeveless pullover.

slipped disc *n* a protrusion of one of the cartilage discs that separate the spinal vertebrae, producing pressure on nerves that causes intense back pain.

slipper *n* **1** a flat-heeled comfortable shoe that is worn while relaxing at home. **2** a light slip-on shoe, *esp* one worn for dancing. ➤➤ **slippered** *adj.*

slippery *adj* (**-ier, -iest**) **1a** tending to cause sliding, *esp* because icy, greasy, wet, or polished. **b** tending to slip from the grasp. **2** of a person: not to be trusted; shifty. **3** of a situation: not firmly fixed; unstable. ✱ **slippery slope** a course of action that is bound to lead to trouble. ➤➤ **slipperiness** *n.*

slippery elm *n* a N American elm with hard wood and a slimy inner bark that was formerly used medicinally.

slippy *adj* (**-ier, -iest**) *informal* slippery. ✱ **be/look slippy** *Brit, dated* to be quick; to hurry up. ➤➤ **slippiness** *n.*

slip road *n Brit* a short one-way road providing access to or exit from a major road, *esp* a motorway.

slipshod *adj* **1** careless or slovenly. **2** *archaic* down-at-heel.

slip stitch *n* **1** a concealed stitch for sewing folded edges, e.g. hems. **2** a knitting stitch that is transferred from one needle to another without working it.

slipstream¹ *n* **1** a stream of air or water driven backward by a propeller. **2** an area of reduced air pressure and forward suction immediately behind a rapidly moving vehicle. **3** something that sweeps one along in its course.

slipstream[2] *v* to drive or ride in a slipstream and so gain the advantage of reduced air resistance, e.g. in a race.

slip up *v* to make a mistake; to blunder.

slip-up *n informal* a mistake or oversight.

slipway *n* a sloping ramp extending out into the water to serve as a place for launching, landing, building, or repairing ships or boats.

slit[1] *v* (**slitting,** *past tense and past part.* **slit**) to make a slit in. ➤➤ **slitter** *n.*

slit[2] *n* a long narrow cut or opening.

slither *v* **1** to move smoothly with a sliding or snakelike motion. **2** to slide unsteadily, *esp* on a slippery surface. ➤➤ **slither** *n,* **slithery** *adj.*

sliver[1] *n* a small slender piece cut or broken off something; a splinter.

sliver[2] *v* to cut or break into slivers.

slivovitz *n* a dry colourless plum brandy.

Sloane Ranger *n Brit, informal* a young upper-class person of conventional outlook and dress, *esp* one who leads an active social life with friends of the same type. ➤➤ **Sloaney** *adj.*

slob *n informal* a slovenly or uncouth person. ➤➤ **slobbish** *adj.*

slobber[1] *v* **1** to let saliva dribble from the mouth; to drool. **2** (*often* + over) to express emotion effusively and excessively. ➤➤ **slobberer** *n.*

slobber[2] *n* **1** saliva dribbled from the mouth. **2** oversentimental language or conduct. ➤➤ **slobbery** *adj.*

sloe *n* **1** = BLACKTHORN. **2** the small spherical blue-black fruit of the blackthorn, which has an acid taste.

sloe-eyed *adj* having soft dark almond-shaped or slanted eyes.

sloe gin *n* a liqueur consisting of gin in which sloes have been steeped.

slog[1] *v* (**slogged, slogging**) **1** to walk, move, or travel slowly and laboriously. **2** to work laboriously; to toil. **3** to hit (e.g. a cricket ball or a boxing opponent) hard and often wildly. ✱ **slog it out** to compete fiercely for success. ➤➤ **slogger** *n.*

slog[2] *n* **1** persistent hard work. **2** an arduous march or tramp. **3** a hard and often wild blow.

slogan *n* **1** a phrase used to express and make public a particular view, position, or aim. **2** a brief catchy phrase used in advertising. **3** a war cry or rallying cry formerly used by a Scottish clan.

slo-mo *n* = SLOW MOTION.

sloop *n* a fore-and-aft rigged sailing vessel with one mast and a single foresail.

sloop of war *n* a small warship carrying guns on one deck only.

slop[1] *v* (**slopped, slopping**) **1a** to cause (a liquid) to spill over the side of a container. **b** of a liquid: to become spilt or splashed. **2** to serve (food or drink) messily. **3** (+ through) to tramp through mud or slush. **4** (+ around/about) to slouch around, *esp* in casual or disreputable clothes. **5** *chiefly NAm* to show mawkish sentiment; to gush.

slop[2] *n* **1a** (*usu in pl*) waste food or a thin gruel fed to animals. **b** (*usu in pl*) liquid household refuse, e.g. dirty water or urine. **2** (*usu in pl*) tasteless drink or liquid food. **3** *NAm* mawkish sentiment in speech or writing.

slop basin *n* a bowl for receiving the dregs left in tea or coffee cups at table.

slope[1] *v* **1** to lie at a slant; to incline. **2** to cause to incline or slant. ➤➤ **sloping** *adj.*

slope[2] *n* **1** inclination or slant; gradient. **2a** a piece of inclined ground. **b** (*usu in pl*) the side of a mountain or hill. **3** an inclined surface.

slope off *v informal* to go away, *esp* furtively; to sneak off.

slop out *v* of a prisoner: to empty the contents of a chamber pot.

sloppy *adj* (**-ier, -iest**) **1a** wet so as to splash. **b** disagreeably wet; watery. **2** slovenly or careless. **3** excessively or mawkishly sentimental. **4** of a garment: loose-fitting and casual. ➤➤ **sloppily** *adv,* **sloppiness** *n.*

slosh[1] *n* **1** the slap or splash of liquid. **2** *Brit, informal* a heavy blow. ➤➤ **sloshy** *adj.*

slosh[2] *v* **1** of liquid: to flow or move with a splashing motion or sound. **2** to flounder or splash through water, mud, etc. **3** to splash (something) about in liquid. **4** to splash (a liquid) on or into something. **5** *Brit, informal* to hit or beat (somebody). ➤➤ **sloshy** *adj.*

sloshed *adj informal* drunk.

slot[1] *n* **1** a narrow opening or slit, e.g. for inserting a coin. **2** a place or position in an organization, sequence, or schedule.

slot[2] *v* (**slotted, slotting**) **1** (*often* + in/into) to place in or assign to a slot. **2** (*often* + in/into) to be fitted by means of a slot or slots. **3** (*often* + in/into) to have or take a place in an organization, schedule, etc.

sloth *n* **1** disinclination to action or work; indolence. **2** a slow-moving mammal that inhabits tropical forests of S and Central America, hanging from the branches and feeding on leaves, shoots, and fruits. ➤➤ **slothful** *adj.*

slot machine *n* **1** *Brit* = VENDING MACHINE. **2** = FRUIT MACHINE.

slouch[1] *v* **1** to sit, stand, or walk with a slouch. **2** to hang down limply; to droop. **3** *dated* to turn down one side of the brim of (a hat). ➤➤ **sloucher** *n.*

slouch[2] *n* **1** a gait or posture characterized by stooping or excessive relaxation of body muscles. **2** *informal* a lazy, incompetent, or awkward person: *He's no slouch at DIY.* ➤➤ **slouchy** *adj.*

slouch hat *n* a soft felt hat with a wide flexible brim.

slough[1] /slow/ *n* **1** a swamp. **2** a state of dejection, hopelessness, or degradation. ➤➤ **sloughy** *adj.*

slough[2] /sluf/ *n* **1** the cast-off skin of a snake. **2** a mass of dead tissue separating from a wound, an ulcer, etc. ➤➤ **sloughy** *adj.*

slough[3] *v* **1** to cast off (e.g. a skin or shell). **2** (+ off) to get rid of or discard as irksome or objectionable.

Slovak *n* **1** a native or inhabitant of Slovakia. **2** the language of Slovakia. ➤➤ **Slovak** *adj,* **Slovakian** *adj and n.*

sloven *n dated* a person who is habitually negligent of neatness or cleanliness.

Slovene *n* **1** a native or inhabitant of Slovenia. **2** the language of Slovenia. ➤➤ **Slovene** *adj,* **Slovenian** *adj and n.*

slovenly *adj* **1** untidy or dirty, *esp* in personal appearance. **2** lazily slipshod; careless. ➤➤ **slovenliness** *n.*

slow[1] *adj* **1a** moving or proceeding with little or less than usual speed. **b** marked by lack of speed or haste. **2** requiring or taking a long time; gradual. **3** of a clock or watch: registering a time earlier than the correct one. **4a** lacking in intelligence; dull. **b** naturally inert or sluggish. **5a** lacking in interest; boring. **b** lacking in activity; slack. **6** lacking in readiness, promptness, or willingness. **7** of an oven: set at a low temperature. **8** in photography, requiring a relatively long period of exposure. ⋙ **slowly** *adv*, **slowness** *n*.

slow² *adv* in a slow manner; slowly.

slow³ *v* (*often* + down/up) to make or become slow or slower.

slowcoach *n Brit, informal* a person who moves or acts slowly.

slow cooker *n* a usu electrically heated pot in which food is cooked very slowly.

slow handclap *n* a slow rhythmic clapping used by an audience to express annoyance or impatience.

slow march *n* a slow marching pace of about 60 or 70 paces a minute.

slow motion *n* a technique that makes filmed or televised action appear unnaturally slow, e.g. by playing back a video recording at less than the standard speed. ⋙ **slow-motion** *adj*.

slowpoke *n NAm, informal* = SLOWCOACH.

slow puncture *n* a puncture that causes a tyre to deflate gradually.

slowworm *n* a legless European lizard with a greybrown snakelike body.

SLR *abbr* single-lens reflex.

slub *n* **1** a small thickened section in a yarn or thread. **2** fabric woven from yarn containing slubs. **3** (*used before a noun*) having a knobbly effect caused by slubs.

sludge *n* **1** mud or ooze. **2** a slimy or slushy mass or sediment. **3** precipitated solid matter produced by sewage treatment processes. **4** a precipitate from a mineral oil, e.g. in an internal-combustion engine. ⋙ **sludgy** *adj*.

slue¹ *v* (**slues, slued, sluing**) = SLEW¹.

slue² *n* = SLEW².

slue³ *n* see SLEW⁴.

slug¹ *n* a slimy elongated invertebrate animal with no shell that is related to the snail.

slug² *n* **1** a quantity of alcoholic drink, *esp* spirits, swallowed at a single gulp. **2** a bullet. **3** *NAm* a disc for insertion in a slot machine.

slug³ *v* (**slugged, slugging**) to swallow (an alcoholic drink) at a single gulp.

slug⁴ *v* (**slugged, slugging**) *chiefly NAm, informal* to hit hard, *esp* with the fist or a bat. ✱ **slug it out** to compete fiercely for success. ⋙ **slugger** *n*.

slug⁵ *n chiefly NAm, informal* a heavy blow.

sluggard *n* a habitually lazy person. ⋙ **sluggardly** *adj*.

sluggish *adj* **1** slow in movement, flow, or growth. **2a** averse to activity or exertion; indolent. **b** lacking energy or activity; torpid. ⋙ **sluggishly** *adv*, **sluggishness** *n*.

sluice¹ *n* **1** an artificial passage for water fitted with a valve or gate for stopping or regulating flow. **2** = SLUICE GATE. **3** a channel to drain or carry off surplus water. **4** an act of sluicing.

sluice² *v* **1** to wash with or in running water. **2** to drench with a sudden vigorous flow; to flush.

sluice gate *n* a small gate for emptying the chamber of a lock or regulating the amount of water passing through a channel.

sluiceway *n* an artificial channel into which water is let by a sluice.

slum¹ *n* **1** (*usu in pl*) a poor overcrowded run-down area, *esp* in a city. **2** a squalid disagreeable place to live. ⋙ **slummy** *adj*.

slum² *v* (**slummed, slumming**) to live in squalor or on very slender means. ✱ **slum it** *informal* to live temporarily in conditions inferior to those to which one is accustomed. ⋙ **slummer** *n*.

slumber¹ *v literary* to sleep. ⋙ **slumberer** *n*.

slumber² *n literary* sleep.

slumbrous *or* **slumberous** *adj literary* **1** heavy with sleep; sleepy. **2** inducing sleep; soporific.

slump¹ *v* **1a** to drop down suddenly and heavily; to collapse. **b** to fall or sink abruptly. **2** to go into a marked or sustained decline.

slump² *n* **1** the act or an instance of slumping. **2** a marked or sustained decline, *esp* in economic activity or prices.

slung *v* past tense and past part. of SLING².

slunk *v* past tense and past part. of SLINK.

slur¹ *v* (**slurred, slurring**) **1** (+ over) to pass over something without due mention, consideration, or emphasis. **2a** to run together, omit, or pronounce unclearly (words, sounds, etc). **b** to utter (speech) in this manner. **3** in music, to perform (successive notes of different pitch) in a smooth or connected manner.

slur² *n* **1** a slurred utterance or manner of speech. **2** in music, a curved line connecting notes to be slurred.

slur³ *v* (**slurred, slurring**) to cast aspersions on; to disparage.

slur⁴ *n* an insulting or disparaging remark.

slurp¹ *v* to eat or drink noisily or with a sucking sound.

slurp² *n* a slurping sound.

slurry *n* (*pl* **-ies**) a watery mixture of insoluble matter, e.g. mud, manure, or lime.

slush *n* **1** partly melted or watery snow. **2** liquid mud; mire. **3** *informal* excessively sentimental language, literature, etc. ⋙ **slushy** *adj*.

slush fund *n* a fund for bribing officials or financing other corrupt practices.

slut *n* a promiscuous or slovenly woman. ⋙ **sluttish** *adj*.

sly *adj* (**-er, -est**) **1a** clever in concealing one's intentions; furtive. **b** lacking in integrity; crafty. **2** humorously mischievous; roguish. ✱ **on the sly** in a manner intended to avoid notice; secretly. ⋙ **slyly** *adv*, **slyness** *n*.

SM *abbr* **1** sadomasochism. **2** Sergeant Major.

Sm *abbr* the chemical symbol for samarium.

smack¹ *n* **1a** a sharp blow, *esp* with the open hand; a slap. **b** the sound of such a blow. **2** a loud kiss. ✱ **smack in the eye** *informal* a setback or rebuff.

smack² *v* **1** to hit (somebody) smartly, *esp* with the open hand in punishment. **2a** to strike (something) sharply or with the sound of a smack. **b** to put (something) down forcefully or noisily. **3** to open (the lips) with a sudden sharp sound, *esp* in anticipation of food or drink.

smack³ *adv informal* squarely and with force; directly.

smack⁴ *v* **1** (+ of) to have the taste or smell of something. **2** (+ of) to have a trace or suggestion of something.

smack⁵ *n* **1** a characteristic taste or smell. **2** a slight trace or suggestion.

smack⁶ *n* a small coastal fishing vessel.

smack⁷ *n slang* heroin.

smacker *n informal* **1** a loud kiss. **2a** *Brit* a pound sterling. **b** *NAm* a dollar.

small¹ *adj* **1a** of less than normal, usual, or average size; not large. **b** immature or young. **2a** not great in quantity, value, etc. **b** made up of few individuals or units. **3a** operating on a limited scale. **b** minor in power, influence, etc. **4** of little consequence; trivial. **5a** mean or petty. **b** reduced to a humiliating position: *They made me feel small.* ⋙ **smallness** *n.*

small² *n* **1** the narrowest part of the back. **2** *Brit, informal* (*in pl*) small articles of underwear.

small³ *adv* **1** in or into small pieces. **2** in a small manner or size.

small arm *n* (*usu in pl*) a portable firearm.

small beer *n chiefly Brit* people or matters of small importance.

small-bore *adj* of a firearm: having a relatively small calibre, *esp* 5.6mm (0.22in).

small calorie *n* = CALORIE (1).

small change *n* **1** coins of low denomination. **2** something trifling or commonplace.

small-claims court *n* a special court intended to simplify and speed up the process of handling claims for small sums of money.

small fry *pl n* **1** small fish. **2** insignificant people or things; *specif* young children.

smallholding *n Brit* a small farm. ⋙ **smallholder** *n.*

small hours *pl n* (**the small hours**) the hours immediately following midnight.

small intestine *n* the part of the intestine that lies between the stomach and the colon.

small-minded *adj* **1** having narrow interests or outlook. **2** characterized by petty meanness. ⋙ **small-mindedness** *n.*

smallpox *n* an acute infectious viral disease characterized by fever and pustules that dry up and form scabs, eventually leaving permanent scars.

small print *n* a part of a document containing important but unattractive conditions that is often printed in small type.

small-scale *adj* relatively small in scope or extent.

small screen *n* (**the small screen**) television.

small talk *n* light or casual conversation; chitchat.

small-time *adj informal* insignificant in operation and status; petty. ⋙ **small-timer** *n.*

smarm *v* **1** to seek favour by servile behaviour; to ingratiate oneself. **2** to flatten or smooth (one's hair) with an oily or greasy substance.

smarmy *adj* (**-ier, -iest**) *informal* marked by flattery, obsequiousness, or smugness; unctuous. ⋙ **smarmily** *adv,* **smarminess** *n.*

smart¹ *adj* **1a** neat, stylish, or elegant in dress or appearance. **b** of a place: characteristic of or frequented by fashionable society. **2** *informal* **a** mentally alert; bright. **b** clever or shrewd. **3** of or using the most modern technology; *specif* operating in a way that emulates human intelligence, behaviour, etc. **4** brisk or spirited. **5** forceful or vigorous. ⋙ **smartly** *adv,* **smartness** *n.*

smart² *v* **1** to have or be the cause of a sharp stinging pain. **2** to feel or endure mental distress.

smart³ *adv archaic* in a smart manner; smartly.

smart⁴ *n* **1** *NAm, informal* (*in pl*) intelligence or shrewdness. **2** a smarting pain.

smart alec *or* **smart aleck** *n informal* an arrogant person with pretensions to knowledge or cleverness. ⋙ **smart-alecky** *adj.*

smart-arse *n slang* = SMART ALEC.

smart-ass *n NAm* = SMART-ARSE.

smart card *n* a plastic card with an inbuilt memory chip that keeps a record of transactions conducted with the card.

smarten *v* (*often* + up) to make or become smarter in appearance.

smartish *adv chiefly Brit, informal* in a rapid manner; quickly.

smart money *n* people with inside information or much experience, or money ventured by such people.

smash¹ *v* **1** to break to pieces by violence; to shatter. **2a** to drive, throw, or hit violently, *esp* causing breaking or shattering. **b** to hit (a ball or shuttlecock) downward with a forceful overhand stroke. **3** (*often* + up) to destroy utterly; to wreck. **4a** (+ into) to crash into; to collide with. **b** (*usu* + against/through) to strike something violently, *esp* causing breakage or damage.

smash² *n* **1** the action or sound of smashing. **2a** a violent blow or collision. **b** a wreck due to collision. **3** a forceful overhand downward stroke in tennis or badminton. **4** *informal* = SMASH HIT.

smash³ *adv* with a resounding crash.

smash-and-grab *adj* denoting a robbery committed by smashing a shop window and snatching the goods on display.

smashed *adj informal* extremely drunk.

smasher *n Brit, informal* a very impressive or attractive person or thing.

smash hit *n informal* an outstanding success.

smashing *adj chiefly Brit, informal* extremely good; excellent.

smatter *n* = SMATTERING.

smattering *n* **1** (*usu* + of) a limited or superficial knowledge of a subject. **2** a small amount.

smear¹ *v* **1a** to spread or mark with a sticky, greasy, or viscous substance; to daub. **b** to apply (a substance) in this way. **2** to blacken the reputation of. **3** to obscure or blur; to smudge. ⋙ **smeary** *adj.*

smear² *n* **1** a mark made by or as if by smearing a substance. **2** an unsubstantiated accusation. **3** material taken or prepared for microscopic examination by smearing on a slide.

smear test *n* = CERVICAL SMEAR.

smegma *n* the secretion of a sebaceous gland; *specif* the sebaceous matter that collects beneath the foreskin of the penis.

smell¹ *v* (*past tense and past part.* **smelt** *or* **smelled**) **1a** to perceive the odour of (something) by the sense of smell. **b** to sniff (something) in order to perceive its odour. **2** to detect or become aware of by instinct. **3** to have a specified smell. **4** (+ of) to be suggestive of something. **5** to have an offensive smell; to stink. ✱ **smell a rat** *informal* to have a suspicion of something wrong. ⋙ **smeller** *n.*

smell² *n* **1** the sense by which odours are perceived by the brain through sensitive areas in the nose. **2a** the quality of something as perceived by this sense; an odour. **b** an unpleasant odour. **3** a pervading quality; an aura. **4** the act or an instance of smelling.

smelling salts *pl n* (*used as sing. or pl*) a usu scented preparation of ammonium carbonate and aqueous ammonia sniffed as a stimulant to relieve faintness.

smelly *adj* (**-ier, -iest**) having a strong, often unpleasant smell.

smelt¹ *n* (*pl* **smelts** *or* **smelt**) a small fish that closely resembles the trout and has delicate oily flesh with a distinctive smell and taste.

smelt² *v* **1** to melt (ore) to separate the metal. **2** to separate (metal) by smelting ore. ⋙ **smelter** *n.*

smelt³ *v* past part. of SMELL¹.

smew *n* a duck of N Europe and Asia, the male of which is mostly white with black patches round the eyes.

smidgin *or* **smidgen** *n informal* a small amount; a bit.

smile[1] *v* **1** to have or assume a smile. **2** (*often* + on) to bestow approval or favour. ⋙ **smiler** *n,* **smilingly** *adv.*

smile[2] *n* a change of facial expression in which the corners of the mouth curve slightly upwards to express amusement, friendliness, pleasure, etc.

smiley[1] *adj* smiling.

smiley[2] *n* a symbol used to represent a smiling face, *esp* in e-mail.

smirch[1] *v* **1** to make dirty or stained, *esp* by smearing. **2** to bring discredit or disgrace on (e.g. somebody's reputation).

smirch[2] *n* **1** a dirty mark; a smear or stain. **2** a blemish or flaw.

smirk[1] *v* to smile in a fatuous, smug, or scornful manner. ⋙ **smirker** *n,* **smirkingly** *adv.*

smirk[2] *n* a fatuous, smug, or scornful smile.

smite *v* (*past tense* **smote,** *past part.* **smitten**) **1** *archaic or literary* **a** to strike sharply or heavily, *esp* with an implement held in the hand. **b** to kill, injure, or damage, *esp* with sharp or heavy blows. **2a** to attack, afflict, or affect suddenly and powerfully: *smitten with grief.* **b** to attract (somebody) strongly: *smitten by her beauty.* ⋙ **smiter** *n.*

smith *n* **1** a person who works in metal, *esp* a blacksmith. **2** (*used in combinations*) a person who works with a specified material or who produces a specified type of article: *goldsmith*; *songsmith.*

smithereens *pl n* small fragments; bits.

smithy *n* (*pl* **-ies**) a blacksmith's forge.

smitten *v* past part. of SMITE.

smock[1] *n* **1** a protective outer garment worn e.g. by artists. **2a** a garment resembling a long loose shirt or dress gathered into a yoke and decorated with smocking, formerly worn by farm labourers. **b** a similar garment worn *esp* by pregnant women.

smock[2] *v* to decorate (e.g. a garment) with smocking.

smocking *n* a decorative effect, *esp* on a garment, made by gathering cloth in regularly spaced tucks held in place with ornamental stitching that often forms a diamond or honeycomb effect.

smog *n* a fog made heavier and darker by smoke and chemical fumes. ⋙ **smoggy** *adj.*

smoke[1] *n* **1** the gaseous products of burning, made visible by the presence of small particles of carbon. **2** fumes or vapour resembling smoke. **3a** an act or spell of smoking, *esp* tobacco. **b** *informal* something, e.g. a cigarette, that is smoked. ✱ **go up in smoke** to come to nothing; to disappear.

smoke[2] *v* **1** to emit smoke. **2** to inhale and exhale the smoke of (e.g. a cigarette or drug). **3** to smoke cigarettes, cigars, a pipe, etc, *esp* habitually. **4** to cure (e.g. meat or fish) by exposure to smoke. **5** to colour or darken (e.g. glass) with or as if with smoke. ⋙ **smokable** *adj,* **smokeable** *adj,* **smoked** *adj,* **smoking** *n and adj.*

smokehouse *n* a building or room where meat, fish, etc is smoked.

smokeless *adj* producing little or no smoke.

smokeless zone *n Brit* a designated neighbourhood where the emission of smoke, *esp* from domestic coal fires, is forbidden or where only smokeless fuel may be used.

smoke out *v* to drive out or away by smoke.

smoker *n* **1** somebody who regularly smokes tobacco. **2** a railway carriage or compartment in which smoking is allowed. **3** an informal gathering for men only.

smoke screen *n* **1** a screen of smoke to hinder observation of a military force, area, or activity. **2** something said or done in order to conceal, confuse, or deceive.

smokestack *n* a chimney or funnel through which smoke and gases are discharged, e.g. from a locomotive, ship, or factory.

smoking jacket *n* a man's loosely fitting usu velvet jacket formerly worn while smoking, *esp* at home after a meal.

smoky *adj* (**-ier, -iest**) **1** emitting smoke, *esp* in large quantities. **2a** having the characteristics or appearance of smoke. **b** suggestive of smoke, *esp* in flavour, smell, or colour. **3** filled with smoke. ⋙ **smokily** *adv,* **smokiness** *n.*

smolt *n* (*pl* **smolts** *or* **smolt**) a young salmon or trout that is about two years old and is assuming a silvery colour before its first migration from fresh water to the sea.

smooch *v informal* **1** to kiss and cuddle. **2** *Brit* to dance slowly, holding one's partner in a close embrace. ⋙ **smooch** *n,* **smoocher** *n,* **smoochy** *adj.*

smoodge *or* **smooge** *v Aus, NZ, informal* **1** to kiss and cuddle. **2** to try to ingratiate oneself.

smooth[1] *adj* **1a** having a continuous even surface. **b** of liquid: of an even consistency; free from lumps. **2** free from difficulties or obstructions. **3** even and uninterrupted in movement or flow. **4a** urbane; courteous. **b** excessively and often artfully suave; ingratiating. **5** not sharp or acid. ⋙ **smoothly** *adv,* **smoothness** *n.*

smooth[2] *v* **1** to make or become smooth. **2** (*often* + out) to press flat. **3** (*often* + down) to cause (e.g. hair) to lie evenly and in order. **4** (*often* + away/over) to dispel or alleviate (e.g. enmity or perplexity). **5** to free from obstruction or difficulty.

smoothbore *adj* of a firearm: lacking spiral grooves in its barrel; not rifled.

smoothie *or* **smoothy** *n* (*pl* **-ies**) **1** *informal* a person who behaves with suave self-assurance, *esp* a man with an ingratiating manner. **2** a non-alcoholic drink made from fresh fruit purée mixed with milk, yoghurt, or ice cream.

smooth snake *n* a European nonpoisonous snake that is reddish brown in colour and has smooth scales.

smooth-talking *adj* ingratiating and persuasive in speech. ⋙ **smooth-talk** *v,* **smooth-talker** *n.*

smooth-tongued *adj* = SMOOTH-TALKING.

smoothy *n* see SMOOTHIE.

smorgasbord *n* **1** a variety of foods and dishes, e.g. hors d'oeuvres, hot and cold meat or fish, cheeses, salads, etc. **2** a meal or buffet at which this is served.

smorzando /smawt'sandoh/ *adj and adv* of a piece of music: to be performed with gradually decreasing intensity of tone, so that the sound dies away.

smote *v* past tense of SMITE.

smother[1] *v* **1a** to kill by covering the nose and mouth in order to cut off the supply of air. **b** to overcome or cause discomfort to (somebody) through or as if through lack of air. **c** to extinguish (a fire) by excluding oxygen. **2a** to suppress or conceal (e.g. a feeling or laughter). **b** to prevent the growth or development of. **c** to cause to feel overwhelmed or oppressed. **3** to cover thickly.

smother[2] *n* **1** a dense cloud of gas, smoke, dust, etc. **2** a confused mass of things.

smoulder[1] (*NAm* **smolder**) *v* **1** to burn feebly with little flame and often much smoke. **2** to exist in a state of suppressed ferment. **3** to show suppressed anger, hate, jealousy, etc.

smoulder[2] (*NAm* **smolder**) *n* a slow burning fire or thick smoke coming from it.

smudge[1] *v* **1a** to smear or daub. **b** to make (e.g. writing) indistinct; to blur. **2** to soil (something) with or as if with a smudge. **3** to become smudged.

smudge[2] *n* **1** a blurry spot or streak. **2** an indistinct mass; a blur. ⋙ **smudgy** *adj.*

smug *adj* (**smugger, smuggest**) excessively pleased with oneself or one's actions; self-satisfied and complacent. ⋙ **smugly** *adv,* **smugness** *n.*

smuggle *v* **1** to import or export (goods) secretly and illegally, *esp* in order to avoid paying duties. **2** to convey or introduce surreptitiously and illicitly. ⋙ **smuggler** *n,* **smuggling** *n.*

smut[1] *n* **1** a particle of soot or other matter that soils something. **2** a destructive fungal disease, *esp* of cereals, marked by a transformation of plant organs into dark masses of spores. **3** obscene language, writing, pictures, etc. ⋙ **smutty** *adj.*

smut[2] *v* (**smutted, smutting**) **1** to mark or taint with smuts. **2** to affect (a crop or plant) with smut.

Sn *abbr* the chemical symbol for tin.

snack[1] *n* a light meal; food eaten between regular meals.

snack[2] *v* to eat a snack.

snaffle[1] *n* a simple usu jointed bit for a bridle.

snaffle[2] *v informal* to take possession of, *esp* by devious means.

snafu[1] *n chiefly NAm, informal* a state of total confusion. ⋙ **snafu** *adj.*

snafu[2] *v* (**snafus, snafued, snafuing**) *chiefly NAm, informal* to bring into a state of total confusion.

snag[1] *n* **1** a concealed or unexpected difficulty or obstacle. **2** a sharp or jagged projecting part. **3** an irregular tear or flaw made by or as if by catching on a snag. ⋙ **snaggy** *adj.*

snag[2] *v* (**snagged, snagging**) **1** to catch on or as if on a snag. **2** *chiefly NAm* to halt or impede. **3** *chiefly NAm* to catch or obtain by quick action.

snag[3] *n Aus, informal* a sausage.

snaggle-toothed *adj* of a person or animal: having irregular, broken, or prominently projecting teeth.

snail *n* **1** an invertebrate animal that has a soft body enclosed by an external spiral shell. **2** a slow-moving or sluggish person or thing.

snail mail *n informal* the ordinary postal system as opposed to e-mail.

snail's pace *n* a very slow speed or rate of progress.

snake[1] *n* **1** a limbless scaly reptile having a long tapering body and often producing venom that is injected through grooved or tubular fangs. **2** a sly treacherous person. ✱ **snake in the grass** a secretly treacherous friend or associate.

snake[2] *v* to move or extend silently, secretly, or windingly.

snakebite *n* **1** the bite of a snake, *esp* a venomous snake. **2** a drink consisting of cider mixed with an equal quantity of lager.

snake charmer *n* an entertainer who controls venomous snakes supposedly by magic, usu using music and rhythmical movements.

snakeroot *n* any of numerous plants that have roots believed to cure snakebites.

snakes and ladders *pl n* (*used as sing.*) a board game in which players move counters along numbered squares on a chequered board, sometimes advancing rapidly up a ladder or being forced backward down a snake.

snaky *adj* (**-ier, -iest**) **1** resembling a snake or snakes. **2** slyly venomous or treacherous. **3** *Aus, NZ* bad-tempered or angry. ⋙ **snakily** *adv,* **snakiness** *n.*

snap[1] *v* (**snapped, snapping**) **1** to make a sudden closing of the jaws; to seize something sharply with the mouth. **2** to utter sharp biting words; to give an irritable retort. **3a** to make or cause to make a sharp or cracking sound. **b** to break or cause to break suddenly with such a sound. **c** to close or fit in place with an abrupt movement or sharp sound. **4** to collapse under strain or lose self-control, *esp* suddenly. **5** (+ up) to take possession or advantage of suddenly or eagerly. **6** to take a snapshot of; to photograph. ✱ **snap out of something** *informal* to free oneself from a mood, habit, etc by an effort of will. ⋙ **snappingly** *adv.*

snap[2] *n* **1** the act or an instance of snapping; a sudden bite or snatch. **2** a sound made by snapping. **3** a sudden spell of harsh weather. **4** a thin brittle biscuit. **5** a catch or fastening that closes with a click. **6** = SNAPSHOT. **7** vigour; energy. **8** a card game in which each player tries to be the first to shout '*snap*' when two cards of identical value are laid successively.

snap[3] *adv* with a snap or the sound of a snap.

snap[4] *adj* **1** performed suddenly, unexpectedly, or without deliberation. **2** shutting or fastening with a click.

snapdragon *n* a garden plant of the foxglove family with attractive white, red, or yellow two-lipped flowers.

snap fastener *n chiefly NAm* = PRESS-STUD.

snapper *n* (*pl* **snappers** *or* **snapper**) a flesh-eating fish of warm seas caught for food or sport.

snappish *adj* **1a** given to curt irritable speech. **b** arising from annoyance or irritability. **2** of a dog: inclined to snap or bite. ⋙ **snappishly** *adv,* **snappishness** *n.*

snappy *adj* (**-ier, -iest**) **1** = SNAPPISH. **2a** brisk, sharp, or concise: *a snappy slogan.* **b** stylish; smart: *a snappy dresser.* ✱ **make it snappy!** *informal* be quick!; hurry up! ⋙ **snappily** *adv,* **snappiness** *n.*

snapshot *n* a casual photograph taken quickly and without regard to technique.

snare[1] *n* **1a** a trap, often consisting of a noose that pulls tight, for catching birds or small animals. **b** something designed or intended to trap or deceive. **2** a catgut string or metal spiral placed over the skin of a snare drum to produce a rattling sound.

snare[2] *v* to capture with or as if with a snare. ⋙ **snarer** *n.*

snare drum *n* a small double-headed drum with one or more snares stretched across its lower head.

snarl[1] *n* **1** a tangle, *esp* of hair or thread; a knot. **2** a confused or complicated situation; a snarl-up.

snarl[2] *v* **1** (*often* + up) to make or become tangled, knotted, or intertwined. **2** (*often* + up) to make or become excessively confused or complicated.

snarl[3] *v* **1** to growl with bared teeth. **2** to speak in a vicious or bad-tempered manner. ⋙ **snarl** *n,* **snarler** *n,* **snarly** *adj.*

snarl-up *n* a state of confusion, disorder, or obstruction; *specif* a traffic jam.

snatch[1] *v* **1** (*often* + at) to attempt to seize something suddenly. **2** to seize or grab suddenly and usu forcibly, wrongfully, or with difficulty. **3** to take or grasp abruptly or hastily. ⋙ **snatcher** *n.*

snatch[2] *n* **1** an act of snatching. **2a** a brief period of time or activity. **b** a fragment, e.g. of music or conversation. **3** *informal* a robbery. **4** in weightlifting, a lift in which the weight is raised from the floor directly to an overhead position.

snazzy *adj* (**-ier, -iest**) *informal* stylishly or flashily attractive.

sneak[1] *v* (*past tense and past part.* **sneaked** *or NAm informal* **snuck**) **1** to go stealthily or furtively. **2** *Brit, informal* to tell somebody in authority of another's wrongdoing. **3** to put, bring, or take in a furtive or artful manner.

sneak[2] *n* **1** somebody who acts in a stealthy or furtive manner. **2** *Brit, informal* somebody, *esp* a schoolchild, who informs on others. **3** (*used before a noun*) done stealthily, furtively, or without warning. ⋙ **sneakily** *adv,* **sneakiness** *n,* **sneaky** *adj.*

sneaker *n chiefly NAm* (*usu in pl*) a soft casual or sports shoe; a trainer.

sneaking *adj* **1** not openly expressed; secret. **2** instinctively felt but unverified. ⋙ **sneakingly** *adv.*

sneak thief *n* a thief who steals opportunistically and without using violence or breaking into buildings.

sneer[1] *v* to smile or speak in a scornfully jeering manner. ⋙ **sneerer** *n,* **sneering** *adj,* **sneeringly** *adv.*

sneer[2] *n* a sneering expression or remark.

sneeze[1] *v* to make a sudden violent involuntary audible expiration of breath from the nose and mouth, *esp* as a result of irritation to the nasal passages. ✱ **sneeze at** to make light of: *The idea is not to be sneezed at.* ⋙ **sneezer** *n,* **sneezy** *adj.*

sneeze[2] *n* an act or sound of sneezing.

snick[1] *v* **1** to cut slightly; to nick. **2** in cricket, to hit (the ball) with the edge of the bat.

snick[2] *n* **1** a small cut; a nick. **2** in cricket, a blow with the edge of the bat or the resulting deflection of the ball.

snicker[1] *v* **1** to snigger. **2** of a horse: to whinny.

snicker[2] *n* **1** a snigger. **2** a whinny.

snide *adj* **1** slyly disparaging; insinuating. **2** *chiefly NAm* mean; low. **3** counterfeit; bogus. ⋙ **snidely** *adv,* **snideness** *n,* **snidey** *adj.*

sniff[1] *v* **1** to draw air audibly up the nose, *esp* for smelling or for clearing the nasal passages. **2** to smell or inhale through the nose. **3** (+ out) to detect by or as if by smelling. ✱ **sniff at** to regard or treat with contempt or disdain. ⋙ **sniffer** *n.*

sniff[2] *n* **1** an act or sound of sniffing. **2** *informal* a trace or hint.

sniffer dog *n* a police dog trained to detect drugs or explosives by smell.

sniffle[1] *v* to sniff repeatedly, e.g. when crying or when suffering from a cold. ⋙ **sniffler** *n.*

sniffle[2] *n* **1** an act or sound of sniffling. **2** (*also in pl*) a head cold marked by a runny discharge from the nose. ⋙ **sniffly** *adj.*

sniffy *adj* (**-ier, -iest**) *informal* having or expressing a haughty attitude; supercilious. ⋙ **sniffily** *adv,* **sniffiness** *n.*

snifter *n informal* a small drink of spirits.

snigger[1] *v* to laugh in a partly suppressed and often derisive manner.

snigger[2] *n* an act or sound of sniggering.

snip[1] *n* **1a** a small piece, *esp* one snipped off. **b** a cut made by snipping. **c** an act or sound of snipping. **2** *Brit, informal* a bargain. **3** *Brit, informal* something easy to do; a cinch. **4** (*in pl*) shears used *esp* for cutting sheet metal by hand.

snip[2] *v* (**snipped, snipping**) (*often* + off) to cut with shears or scissors, *esp* with short rapid strokes.

snipe[1] *n* (*pl* **snipes** *or* **snipe**) a wading bird with a long slender straight bill.

snipe[2] *v* **1** (*often* + at) to shoot at exposed individuals usu from a hiding place at long range. **2** (*usu* + at) to aim a snide or obliquely critical attack at somebody. ⋙ **sniper** *n.*

snippet *n* a small part, piece, or item, *esp* a fragment of writing or conversation.

snippy *adj* (**-ier, -iest**) *informal* abrupt, *esp* in a rude way. ⋙ **snippily** *adv,* **snippiness** *n.*

snit *n NAm, Aus, NZ, informal* a bad or sulky mood.

snitch[1] *v* **1** *informal* to inform on somebody. **2** *informal* to steal.

snitch[2] *n informal* an informer.

snivel *v* (**snivelled, snivelling,** *NAm* **sniveled, sniveling**) **1** to have a runny nose. **2** to sniff mucus up the nose audibly. **3** to complain in a whining way. ⋙ **snivel** *n,* **sniveller** *n.*

snob *n* **1** somebody who tends to patronize or avoid those regarded as social inferiors. **2** somebody who blatantly attempts to cultivate or imitate those admired as social superiors. **3** somebody who has an air of smug superiority in matters of knowledge or taste. ⋙ **snobbery** *n,* **snobbish** *adj,* **snobbishly** *adv,* **snobbism** *n,* **snobby** *adj.*

Word history

the word *snob* originally meant a shoemaker, later any member of the lower classes; hence somebody who despises their own class and aspires to membership of a higher one.

SNOBOL *n* a high-level computer language for handling strings of symbols.

snog[1] *v* (**snogged, snogging**) *Brit, informal* to kiss and cuddle.

snog[2] *n informal* an act or period of snogging.

snood *n* **1** a net or fabric bag worn at the back of a woman's head to hold the hair, *esp* in former times. **2** a broad tubular knitted garment worn as a hood or scarf.

snook *n* a gesture of derision made by putting the thumb to the nose and spreading the fingers out: *cock a snook.*

snooker[1] *n* **1** a game played on a billiard table in which players hit a white ball with a cue in order to send 21 coloured balls in a set order into the pockets around the table: compare BILLIARDS, POOL[2]. **2** a position of the balls in the game of snooker in which a direct shot would lose points.

snooker[2] *v* **1** to position the cue ball so as to prevent (an opponent) from making a direct shot in snooker. **2a** *informal* to present an obstacle to. **b** to put in a difficult or impossible position. ⋙ **snookered** *adj.*

snoop[1] *v* to look or pry in a sneaking or interfering manner. ⋙ **snooper** *n,* **snoopy** *adj.*

snoop[2] *n* **1** somebody who snoops. **2** an act of snooping.

snoot *n informal* a snout or nose.

snooty *adj* (**-ier, -iest**) *informal* **1** haughty; disdainful. **2** characterized by snobbish attitudes. ⋙ **snootily** *adv,* **snootiness** *n.*

snooze[1] *v informal* to sleep lightly for a short time; to take a nap. ⋙ **snoozer** *n.*

snooze[2] *n informal* a short light sleep; a nap. ⋙ **snoozy** *adj.*

snooze button *n* a device on an alarm clock that causes the alarm to sound again a few minutes after the set time.

snore[1] *v* to breathe with a rough hoarse noise during sleep. ⋙ **snorer** *n.*

snore[2] *n* an act or sound of snoring.

snorkel[1] *n* a J-shaped tube allowing a swimmer or diver to breathe while face down in the water.

snorkel[2] *v* (**snorkelled, snorkelling,** *NAm* **snorkeled, snorkeling**) to swim using a snorkel. ⋙ **snorkeller** *n.*

snort[1] *v* **1** to force air violently through the nose with a rough harsh sound. **2** to express scorn, anger, or surprise by a snort. **3** *informal* to inhale (a drug). ⋙ **snorter** *n.*

snort[2] *n* **1** an act or sound of snorting. **2** *informal* a small drink, usu of spirits. **3** *informal* an amount of a drug inhaled or to be inhaled.

snot *n informal* **1** mucus from the nose. **2** a contemptible or unpleasant person.

snotty *adj* (**-ier, -iest**) *informal* **1** soiled or covered with nasal mucus. **2** arrogantly or snobbishly unpleasant. **3** contemptible; despicable.

snout *n* **1** a long projecting nose, e.g. of a pig. **2** a forward prolongation of the head of various animals. **3** something resembling an animal's snout in position, function, or shape, e.g. a nozzle. **4** *informal* a cigarette or tobacco. **5** *informal* an informer. ⋙ **snouted** *adj,* **snouty** *adj.*

snow[1] *n* **1a** white flakes falling from the sky that consist of small ice crystals formed from vapour in the atmosphere. **b** fallen snow. **c** (*also in pl*) a fall of snow. **2** small transient light spots on a television or radar screen, usu caused by weakness or absence of a signal. ⋙ **snowless** *adj.*

snow[2] *v* **1** to send down snow. **2** to fall like snow. **3** (+ in/up) to cover, shut in, or block with snow.

snowball[1] *n* **1** a round mass of snow pressed together for throwing. **2** a cocktail drink made of advocaat with lemonade.

snowball[2] *v* **1** to throw snowballs at. **2** to increase or expand at a rapidly accelerating rate.

snow blindness *n* temporarily impaired vision caused by exposure of the eyes to ultraviolet rays reflected from snow or ice. ⋙ **snow-blind** *adj.*

snowboard *n* a board resembling a large skateboard or a short wide ski used to descend a snow-covered slope in a standing position. ⋙ **snowboarder** *n,* **snowboarding** *n.*

snowbound *adj* confined or surrounded by snow.

snowcap *n* a covering of snow on a mountain top. ⋙ **snowcapped** *adj.*

snowdrift *n* a bank of snow blown together by the wind.

snowdrop *n* a European plant of the daffodil family that bears nodding white flowers in late winter or very early spring.

snowfall *n* the amount of snow falling at one time or in a given period.

snowfield *n* a broad level expanse of snow, *esp* a permanent mass of snow.

snowflake *n* a flake or crystal of snow.

snow goose *n* a large white goose with black-tipped wings that breeds chiefly in N America.

snow job *n chiefly NAm, informal* an attempt to persuade or deceive somebody by overwhelming them with information or flattery.

snow leopard *n* a large mammal of the cat family of upland central Asia with fur that is irregularly blotched with brownish black in summer and almost pure white in winter. Also called OUNCE[2].

snow line *n* the level, e.g. height above sea level or line of latitude, beyond which land is permanently covered in snow.

snowman *n* (*pl* **snowmen**) a pile of snow shaped to resemble a human figure.

snowmobile *n* a motor-powered vehicle for travel on snow.

snowplough[1] (*NAm* **snowplow**) *n* **1** a vehicle or device used for clearing snow. **2** in skiing, an act of snowploughing.

snowplough[2] (*NAm* **snowplow**) *v* to force the heels of one's skis outward, keeping the tips together, in order to descend slowly, stop, or turn.

snowshoe *n* a light oval wooden frame strung with thongs that is attached to the foot to enable a person to walk on soft snow without sinking.

snowstorm *n* a storm of or with snow.

snow under *v* (*usu in passive*) to overwhelm with more than can be handled or absorbed: *I'm snowed under with work.*

snowy *adj* (**-ier, -iest**) **1** composed of, characterized by, or covered with snow. **2** resembling snow, *esp* in whiteness. ⋙ **snowily** *adv,* **snowiness** *n.*

snowy owl *n* a very large white arctic owl that is a winter visitor to Europe and N America.

snr *abbr* senior.

snub[1] *v* (**snubbed, snubbing**) to treat with contempt or deliberately ignore.

snub[2] *n* an act of snubbing; a slight.

snub[3] *adj* of a nose: short and slightly turned-up.

snuck *v NAm, informal* past tense and past part. of SNEAK[1].

snuff[1] *v* **1** to extinguish (a flame or candle). **2** (+ out) to put an end to, *esp* suddenly or unexpectedly. ✱ **snuff it** *informal* to die.

snuff[2] *n* the charred part of a candle wick.

snuff[3] *n* a preparation of powdered tobacco usu inhaled through the nostrils. ✱ **up to snuff 1** *informal* up to standard. **2** *informal* in good health or condition.

snuff[4] *v* **1** to inhale, smell, or sniff at. **2** to take snuff.

snuffbox *n* a small often ornate box for holding snuff.

snuffer *n* an implement consisting of a small hollow cone attached to a handle, used for extinguishing candles.

snuffle[1] *v* **1** to sniff, usu audibly and repeatedly. **2** to draw air noisily through an obstructed nose. ⋙ **snuffler** *n.*

snuffle[2] *n* **1** an act or sound of snuffling. **2** (**the snuffles**) a cold in the nose. ⋙ **snuffly** *adj.*

snuff movie *n informal* a pornographic film in which one of the participants is actually murdered during filming.

snug[1] *adj* (**snugger, snuggest**) **1** enjoying or giving warm secure comfort or shelter; cosy. **2** fitting closely. ⋙ **snugly** *adv,* **snugness** *n.*

snug[2] *n Brit* a small room or compartment in a pub.

snuggery *n* (*pl* **-ies**) **1** *chiefly Brit* a snug cosy place, *esp* a small private room. **2** = SNUG[2].

snuggle *v* **1** to curl up comfortably or cosily; to nestle. **2** to draw close, *esp* for comfort or in affection.

so[1] *adv* **1a** in this way; thus. **b** used as a substitute for a preceding word or word group: *Do you really think so?* **c** in the same way; also. **d** correspondingly. **e** used to introduce the idea of purpose: *He hid so as not to get caught.* **2a** to such an extreme degree. **b** very. **c** to a definite but unspecified extent or degree: *We can only do so much.* **d** most certainly; indeed. **3** therefore; consequently. ✱ **and so forth/and so on 1** and others or more of the same kind. **2** and further in the same manner. **3** and the rest. **so be it** used to express often resigned acceptance. **so much as** even: *I can't so much as remember his name now.*

so[2] *conj* **1** with the result that. **2** in order that. **3** for that reason; therefore. **4a** used as an introductory particle. **b** used to belittle a point under discussion. **c** used to indicate awareness of a discovery.

so[3] *adj* **1** conforming with actual facts; true. **2** disposed in a definite order.

so[4] *pron* such as has been specified or suggested; the same. ✱ **or so** used to indicate an approximation or conjecture.

so[5] *n* see SOH.

soak[1] *v* **1** to immerse or lie immersed in liquid for some time. **2** to make thoroughly wet. **3** (*usu* + in/into/through) to enter or pass through something by or as if by pores or small openings; to permeate. **4** (*often* + up) to draw in by or as if by absorption. **5** to immerse the mind and feelings of (oneself or somebody else). **6** *informal* to charge (somebody) an excessive amount of money. ⪢ **soaked** *adj*, **soaker** *n*, **soaking** *adj and n*.

soak[2] *n* **1** an act or period of soaking or being soaked. **2** *informal* a person who drinks alcohol to excess, *esp* habitually. **3** *Aus* a natural depression where rainwater collects.

soakaway *n Brit* a hole dug in the ground into which rain or waste water flows and naturally drains away.

so-and-so *n* (*pl* **so-and-sos**) **1** an unnamed or unspecified person or thing. **2** *euphem* a disliked or unpleasant person.

soap[1] *n* **1** a substance used to cleanse that lathers in water and consists essentially of sodium or potassium combined with fatty acids. **2** = SOAP OPERA. ⪢ **soapless** *adj*.

soap[2] *v* **1** to rub soap over or into. **2** *informal* (*often* + up) to flatter.

soapbox *n* **1** an improvised platform used by an informal orator. **2** any public forum that allows people to express their views, exchange ideas, etc.

soap opera *n* a serialized radio or television drama usu dealing with the domestic lives of a group of characters who live or work in the same place.

soapstone *n* a soft greyish green or brown stone having a soapy feel and composed mainly of talc.

soapy *adj* (**-ier, -iest**) **1a** covered with soap; lathered. **b** containing soap. **c** resembling soap. **2** suave; ingratiating. ⪢ **soapily** *adv*, **soapiness** *n*.

soar *v* **1a** to fly or rise high into the air. **b** to glide or hover in the air, often at a great height. **2** to rise rapidly or to a very high level. **3** to be of imposing height or stature; to tower. ⪢ **soar** *n*, **soarer** *n*, **soaring** *adj*.

sob[1] *v* (**sobbed, sobbing**) **1** to weep with convulsive catching of the breath. **2** to express or utter with sobs.

sob[2] *n* an act, bout, or sound of sobbing.

s.o.b. *abbr NAm, informal* son of a bitch.

sober[1] *adj* **1** not drunk. **2** gravely or earnestly thoughtful; serious. **3** calmly self-controlled; sedate. **4** subdued in tone or colour. ⪢ **soberly** *adv*, **soberness** *n*.

sober[2] *v* (*usu* + up) to make or become sober. ⪢ **sobering** *adj*.

sobriety *n formal* the state of being sober.

sobriquet /'sohbrikay/ *or* **soubriquet** /'sooh-, 'soh-/ *n* a nickname.

sob story *n informal* a sentimental story or account intended to elicit sympathy.

soca /'sohkə/ *n* a style of popular music, associated particularly with Trinidad, blending elements of soul and calypso.

so-called *adj* **1** commonly named; popularly so termed. **2** falsely or improperly so named.

soccer *n* = ASSOCIATION FOOTBALL.

sociable *adj* **1** inclined to seek or enjoy companionship; companionable. **2** marked by or conducive to friendliness or cordial social relations. ⪢ **sociability** *n*, **sociably** *adv*.

Usage note

sociable *or* **social**? See note at SOCIAL[1].

social[1] *adj* **1** of human society. **2** of or based on status in a particular society. **3** of, involving, or promoting companionship or friendly interaction with others. **4a** tending to form cooperative relationships; gregarious. **b** living and breeding in more or less organized communities. ⪢ **socially** *adv*.

Usage note

social *or* **sociable**? *Social*, as an adjective, is an all-purpose neutral word meaning 'connected with society': *social conditions; social work. Sociable* is a complimentary term used mainly to describe people meaning 'fond of company' or 'friendly': *She's feeling very sociable this evening.*

social[2] *n* a social gathering, usu connected with a church or club.

social climber *n derog* somebody who strives to gain a higher social position or acceptance in fashionable society. ⪢ **social climbing** *n*.

social compact *n* = SOCIAL CONTRACT.

social contract *n* an agreement among individuals forming an organized society that defines and limits the rights and duties of each, *esp* one under which certain individual freedoms are surrendered in return for state protection.

social democracy *n* a political movement advocating a gradual and peaceful transition from capitalism to socialism by democratic means. ⪢ **social democrat** *n*.

social fund *n* in the UK, a fund set up as part of the social security system from which people in need may receive money as a grant or loan for a specified purpose.

socialise *v* see SOCIALIZE.

socialism *n* **1** an economic and political theory advocating collective or state ownership and administration of the means of production and distribution of goods. **2** an economic or political system based on this. ⪢ **socialist** *adj and n*, **socialistic** *adj*.

socialite *n* somebody who is socially active or prominent, *esp* in fashionable society.

sociality *n* **1** the tendency to associate in or form social groups. **2** the state of being social.

socialize *or* **-ise** *v* **1** to behave or interact in a sociable manner. **2** to make (somebody) fit or prepared for life in society. **3** to adapt to social needs or uses. **4** to constitute on a socialist basis. ⪢ **socialization** *n*, **socializer** *n*.

social market *n* an economic system in which a free market operates with equality of opportunity and social responsibility, supplemented by state assistance for the old, the unemployed, etc.

social realism *n* the use of realism in art for the purpose of social or political comment.

social science *n* **1** the scientific study of human society and the relationships between its members. **2** a subject, e.g. economics or politics, dealing with a particular aspect of human society. ⪢ **social scientist** *n*.

social secretary *n* somebody who arranges and handles the social engagements of a person or group.

social security *n* **1** state provision, e.g. through pensions, unemployment benefit, sickness benefit, etc, for the economic security and social welfare of individuals. **2** a social security allowance made to help people to meet the basic costs of living.

social service *n* **1** activity or assistance designed to promote social welfare. **2** (*in pl*) organized services, e.g. education or housing, provided by the state for this purpose.

social studies *pl n* (*used as sing.*) a branch of study relating to social relationships and the functioning of human society.

social work *n* the activities of professional agencies concerned with the aid of underprivileged or disadvantaged members of society. ➤➤ **social worker** *n.*

society *n* (*pl* **-ies**) **1** the human race considered in terms of its structure of social institutions. **2** a community having common traditions, institutions, and collective interests. **3a** a class of wealthy or privileged people regarded as arbiters of fashion or manners. **b** (*used before a noun*) of this class of people. **4** an organized group working together or periodically meeting because of common interests, beliefs, etc. **5** companionship or association with others; company. **6** a natural group of plants or animals, usu of a single species. ➤➤ **societal** *adj.*

socio- *comb. form* **1** social: *sociolinguistics.* **2** social and: *socioeconomic.*

sociobiology *n* the scientific study of animal behaviour from the point of view that all behaviour has evolved by natural selection. ➤➤ **sociobiological** *adj,* **sociobiologist** *n.*

socioeconomic *adj* of or involving a combination of social and economic factors.

sociolinguistics *pl n* (*used as sing.*) the study of language as determined by social and cultural factors. ➤➤ **sociolinguist** *n,* **sociolinguistic** *adj.*

sociology *n* the scientific study of social institutions and relationships, *esp* the development and behaviour of organized human groups. ➤➤ **sociological** *adj,* **sociologist** *n.*

sociopath *n* somebody suffering from an emotional and behavioural disorder characterized by asocial or antisocial behaviour; *broadly* a psychopath. ➤➤ **sociopathic** *adj,* **sociopathy** *n.*

sock[1] *n* **1** a usu knitted covering for the foot extending above the ankle. **2** an insole for a shoe. ✱ **pull one's socks up** *informal* to make a determined effort to do better. **put a sock in it** *Brit, informal* to stop talking.

sock[2] *v informal* to hit forcefully. ✱ **sock it to** *informal, dated* to impress or astound by doing something very well or vigorously.

sock[3] *n informal* a vigorous or forceful blow; a punch.

socket[1] *n* **1** an opening or hollow that forms a holder for something or into which something fits. **2** a device in an electrical circuit into which a plug, bulb, etc can be fitted.

socket[2] *v* (**socketed, socketing**) to provide with or place in a socket.

sockeye *n* (*pl* **sockeyes** *or* **sockeye**) a small but commercially important N Pacific salmon.

socking *adv chiefly Brit, informal* extremely.

Socratic *adj* characteristic of the philosophy of Socrates (d.399 BC), *esp* in relation to his method of achieving knowledge through question-and-answer sessions and deliberately casting doubt on accepted beliefs.

sod[1] *n* **1** a clump of grass together with the roots and surrounding soil; a piece of turf. **2** *literary* the grass-covered surface of the ground.

sod[2] *n chiefly Brit* **1** *slang* an objectionable person. **2** *informal, chiefly humorous* a person. **3** *informal* something difficult, trying, or unpleasant. ✱ **sod all** *Brit, slang* nothing at all.

sod[3] *v* (**sodded, sodding**) *Brit, slang* usu used in the imperative as an oath: to damn.

soda *n* **1** any of several chemical compounds containing sodium, e.g. sodium carbonate, sodium bicarbonate, or sodium hydroxide. **2a** = SODA WATER. **b** *chiefly NAm* a sweet fizzy drink.

soda bread *n* a bread leavened with sodium bicarbonate and cream of tartar rather than yeast.

soda fountain *n* **1** *chiefly NAm* an apparatus for dispensing soda water. **2** *NAm* a shop or counter where sodas, ice cream, etc are served.

sodality *n* (*pl* **-ies**) **1** a brotherhood, fellowship, or organized society. **2** a devotional or charitable association of lay Roman Catholics.

soda siphon *n* = SIPHON[1] (2).

soda water *n* water containing carbon dioxide under pressure causing it to fizz.

sodden *adj* **1** full of moisture or water; saturated. **2** (*usu used in combinations*) having drunk an excessive amount of alcohol: *whisky-sodden.* ➤➤ **soddenly** *adv,* **soddenness** *n.*

sodding *adj and adv Brit, slang* used as an intensifier to express annoyance, exasperation, etc.

sodium *n* a soft silver-white metallic element that occurs abundantly in nature in combination with other chemical compounds.

sodium bicarbonate *n* a white weakly alkaline chemical compound used *esp* in baking powders and in medicine to neutralize stomach acidity. Also called BAKING SODA.

sodium chloride *n* a chemical compound used *esp* as a seasoning for food; common salt.

sodium hydroxide *n* a white caustic chemical compound used *esp* in making soap, rayon, and paper. Also called CAUSTIC SODA.

sodium lamp *n* = SODIUM-VAPOUR LAMP.

sodium-vapour lamp *n* an electric lamp used *esp* for street lighting in which the discharge takes place through sodium vapour causing a characteristic yellow-orange light.

sod off *v Brit, slang* to go away.

sodomise *v* see SODOMIZE.

sodomite *n* somebody who practises sodomy.

sodomize *or* **-ise** *v* to have anal intercourse with.

sodomy *n* the penetration of the penis into the anus of another male or a female; anal intercourse.

sod's law *or* **Sod's Law** *n* = MURPHY'S LAW.

-soever *comb. form* forming adverbs or conjunctions, with the meaning: of any kind; at all: *howsoever.*

sofa *n* a long upholstered seat with a back and two arms or raised ends that typically seats two to four people.

sofa bed *n* a sofa that can be converted into a bed, *esp* by unfolding the seat part.

soffit *n* the underside of an overhanging part of a building, a staircase, an arch, etc.

soft[1] *adj* **1a** yielding to physical pressure. **b** of a consistency that may be shaped, spread, or easily cut. **c** relatively lacking in hardness. **2a** pleasing or agreeable to the senses. **b** smooth or delicate in texture; not rough. **c** not bright or glaring; subdued. **d** quiet in pitch or volume; not harsh. **3** of water: deficient in or free from substances, e.g. chemical compounds containing calcium or magnesium, that prevent lathering of soap. **4a** gentle or mild. **b** of pornography: soft-core. **c** of a drug: not of the most addictive or harmful kind. **5a** marked by kindness, leniency, or moderation. **b** *informal* demanding little effort; easy. **6a** lacking resilience or strength, *esp* as a result of pampering or luxury. **b** not protected against attack; vulnerable: *a soft target*. **c** *informal* mentally deficient; foolish. **7** readily influenced or imposed upon; lacking firmness or strength of character. **8** not sharply outlined, *esp* having a slight intentional blurring: *soft focus*. **9** marked by a gradually declining trend. ✱ **have a soft spot for** to have a fondness or sentimental weakness for (somebody or something). **soft on 1** amorously attracted to. **2** taking a lenient or compassionate view of; reacting to or treating without severity. ➤➤ **softly** *adv,* **softness** *n.*

soft² *adv* **1** in a soft or gentle manner. **2** in a weak or foolish manner.

softback *n* = PAPERBACK.

softball *n* a game similar to baseball played on a smaller field with a larger softer ball.

soft-boiled *adj* of an egg: cooked to the point at which the white solidifies but the yolk remains liquid.

soft copy *n* information stored in a computer's memory or shown on a screen and not in physical form.

soft-core *adj* of pornography: mildly titillating; excluding highly explicit pictures or descriptions of sexual acts.

soft drink *n* a non-alcoholic drink that is usu served cold.

soften *v* **1** to make or become soft or softer. **2** (*often* + up) to impair the strength or resistance of. ➤➤ **softener** *n.*

soft fruit *n chiefly Brit* a small stoneless edible fruit, e.g. a strawberry, raspberry, or blackcurrant.

soft furnishings *pl n chiefly Brit* articles made of cloth, e.g. curtains or chair covers, that make a room or piece of furniture more attractive or comfortable.

soft-headed *adj* foolish; stupid. ➤➤ **soft-headedness** *n.*

soft-hearted *adj* kind; compassionate. ➤➤ **soft-heartedly** *adv,* **soft-heartedness** *n.*

softie *or* **softy** *n* (*pl* **-ies**) **1** *informal* a sentimental or soft-hearted person. **2** a weak or foolish person.

softly-softly *adj Brit* characterized by caution, patience, or guile.

soft palate *n* the fleshy part at the back of the roof of the mouth.

soft pedal *n* a foot pedal on a piano that reduces the volume of sound.

soft-pedal *v* (**soft-pedalled, soft-pedalling,** *NAm* **soft-pedaled, soft-pedaling**) to attempt to minimize the importance of; to play down.

soft sell *n* the use of suggestion or gentle persuasion in selling rather than aggressive pressure.

soft soap *n* **1** a semifluid soap. **2** *informal* flattery.

soft-soap *v informal* to persuade or mollify with flattery or smooth talk.

soft-top *n* a motor car with a top that can be folded back.

soft touch *n informal* a person who is easily imposed on or taken advantage of, *esp* somebody who is known to be willing to lend money.

software *n* the programs, procedures, etc used by a computer: compare HARDWARE (1).

softwood *n* the wood of a coniferous tree.

softy *n* see SOFTIE.

soggy *adj* (**-ier, -iest**) **1** waterlogged; soaked. **2** heavy, damp, or doughy because of imperfect cooking. ➤➤ **soggily** *adv,* **sogginess** *n.*

soh *or* **so** *n* in music, the fifth note of a major scale in the tonic sol-fa system.

soi-disant /swah 'deezonh/ *adj* self-styled; so-called.

soigné *or* **soignée** /'swahnyay/ *adj* of a man or woman: well-groomed; elegant.

soil¹ *n* **1** loose material composed of weathered rock fragments and usu decayed plant and animal matter that covers large parts of the land surface of the earth, *esp* the upper layer in which plants grow. **2** country; land. **3** (**the soil**) agricultural life or work. ➤➤ **soilless** *adj.*

soil² *v* **1a** to make or become dirty, *esp* superficially. **b** to defecate on or in. **2** to blacken or tarnish (e.g. somebody's reputation).

soil³ *n* **1** dirt or defilement. **2** refuse or sewage.

soiree *or* **soirée** /'swahray/ *n* (*pl* **soirees** *or* **soirées**) a party or reception held in the evening, *esp* in a private house.

sojourn¹ *n formal* a temporary stay.

sojourn² *v formal* to stay as a temporary resident. ➤➤ **sojourner** *n.*

sol¹ *n* = SOH.

sol² *n* (*pl* **soles** /'solez, 'sohlez/) the basic monetary unit of Peru.

sol³ *n* a colloidal solution composed of solid particles dispersed in a liquid medium.

solace¹ *n* consolation or comfort in grief or anxiety.

solace² *v* to give solace to; to console. ➤➤ **solacer** *n.*

solar *adj* **1** of or derived from the sun. **2** measured by the earth's course in relation to the sun: *solar time*. **3** produced or operated by the action of the sun's light or heat.

solar cell *n* a device that converts the energy of sunlight into electrical energy and is used as a power source.

solar day *n* the interval between two crossings of the meridian by the sun.

solar eclipse *n* an eclipse in which the moon wholly or partially obscures the sun.

solar energy *n* **1** radiant energy from the sun. **2** = SOLAR POWER.

solar flare *n* = FLARE² (4).

solarium *n* (*pl* **solaria** *or* **solariums**) **1** a room with extensive areas of glass allowing the warmth and light of the sun to stream in. **2** a bed, room, or establishment equipped with sunbeds, sunlamps, etc.

solar panel *n* **1** a large number of solar cells grouped together, e.g. on a spacecraft. **2** a panel, e.g. on the roof of a building, that is used to generate heat or electricity from sunlight.

solar plexus *n technical* an interlacing network of nerves in the abdomen behind the stomach.

solar power *n* power derived from solar energy, used to generate electricity, heat, etc.

solar system *n* the sun together with the planets and other celestial bodies that revolve round it.

solar wind *n* the continuous flow of electrically charged particles from the sun's surface into and through space.

solar year *n* the time taken by the earth to move once round the sun, about 365 solar days.

sold *v* past tense and past part. of SELL.

solder¹ *n* an alloy, *esp* of tin and lead, used when melted to join metallic surfaces.

solder[2] *v* to unite or repair by or as if by solder. ➤➤ **solderer** *n.*

soldering iron *n* a usu electrically heated device with a pointed or wedge-shaped end that is used for melting and applying solder.

soldier[1] *n* **1** a person who is engaged in military service, *esp* in the army. **2** an enlisted man or woman, as opposed to a commissioned officer. ➤➤ **soldierly** *adj,* **soldiership** *n.*

soldier[2] *v* **1** to serve as a soldier. **2** (+ on) to persevere in the face of difficulties etc.

soldier of fortune *n* a person who engages in military service for financial gain or for the love of adventure; a mercenary.

soldiery *n* (*pl* **-ies**) **1** (*used as sing, or pl*) a body of soldiers. **2** the profession of being a soldier.

sole[1] *n* **1a** the undersurface of a foot. **b** the part of an article of footwear that makes contact with the ground. **2** the usu flat bottom of something or the base on which something rests. ➤➤ **soled** *adj.*

sole[2] *v* to provide (a shoe) with a sole.

sole[3] *n* (*pl* **soles** *or* **sole**) a marine flatfish with small eyes placed close together, *esp* one valued as a food fish.

sole[4] *adj* **1** being the only one; only. **2** belonging or relating exclusively to one individual or group. ➤➤ **soleness** *n.*

solecism /'solisiz(ə)m/ *n* **1** a minor blunder in speech or writing, e.g. a grammatical error. **2** a breach of etiquette or decorum. ➤➤ **solecistic** *adj.*

solely *adv* **1** without another; singly. **2** to the exclusion of all else; only.

solemn *adj* **1** performed or uttered with sincerity, *esp* so as to be legally binding. **2** marked by the observance of established form or ceremony. **3a** marked by seriousness and sobriety. **b** sombre; gloomy. ➤➤ **solemnly** *adv,* **solemnness** *n.*

solemnise *v* see SOLEMNIZE.

solemnity *n* (*pl* **-ies**) **1** the state of being solemn. **2** formal or ceremonious observance of an occasion or event. **3** a solemn event or occasion.

solemnize *or* **-ise** *v* **1** to observe or honour with solemnity. **2** to perform (e.g. a marriage) with ceremony or religious rites. **3** to make solemn or serious; to dignify. ➤➤ **solemnization** *n.*

solenoid /'solənoyd/ *n* a cylindrical coil of wire that, when carrying a current, produces a magnetic field and draws in a movable usu iron rod. ➤➤ **solenoidal** *adj.*

soleplate *n* **1** the undersurface of an iron used for pressing cloth or clothing. **2** the lower horizontal part of a framework supporting a wall.

sol-fa *n* **1** the syllables *doh, ray, me,* etc used in singing the notes of the scale. **2** = TONIC SOL-FA.

soli *n* pl of SOLO[1].

solicit *v* (**solicited, soliciting**) **1a** to make a formal or earnest appeal or request to. **b** to try to obtain by urgent requests or pleas. **2** to accost somebody publicly with an offer of sex for money. ➤➤ **solicitation** *n.*

solicitor *n* **1** a qualified lawyer who advises clients, represents them in the lower courts, and prepares cases for barristers to try in the higher courts: compare BARRISTER. **2** in the USA, the chief law officer of a municipality, county, or government department. ➤➤ **solicitorship** *n.*

Solicitor General *n* (*pl* **Solicitors General**) a Crown law officer ranking below the Attorney General or, in Scotland, the Lord Advocate.

solicitous *adj* **1** showing concern or anxiety. **2** showing meticulous or excessive care, attention, or consideration. ➤➤ **solicitously** *adv,* **solicitousness** *n.*

solicitude *n* **1** the state of being solicitous. **2** (*also in pl*) a cause of care or concern.

solid[1] *adj* **1a** without an internal cavity. **b** having no opening or division. **c** composed of or having a single substance or character. **2** three-dimensional. **3a** neither liquid nor gas; retaining shape without needing external support. **b** hard, dense, or compact. **4** without break or interruption. **5** of good substantial quality or kind. **6** reliable or sound. **7** united or unanimous. ➤➤ **solidity** *n,* **solidly** *adv,* **solidness** *n.*

solid[2] *n* **1a** a solid substance. **b** (*in pl*) solid food. **2** a three-dimensional geometrical figure.

solidarity *n* unity based on shared interests, objectives, and standards.

solidi *n* pl of SOLIDUS.

solidify *v* (**-ies, -ied**) to make or become solid. ➤➤ **solidification** *n,* **solidifier** *n.*

solid-state *adj* **1** relating to the arrangement or behaviour of ions, molecules, nucleons, electrons, and holes in the crystals of a substance, e.g. a semiconductor. **2** using the electric, magnetic, or photic properties of solid materials; not using thermionic valves.

solidus *n* (*pl* **solidi**) a punctuation mark (/) used e.g. to separate alternatives, the terms of a fraction, or the components of a date.

soliloquize *or* **-ise** *v* **1** to talk to oneself. **2** to perform a soliloquy. ➤➤ **soliloquist** *n.*

soliloquy *n* (*pl* **-ies**) **1** the act of speaking one's thoughts aloud while alone. **2** a speech of this kind in a play, etc, used *esp* to let the audience know the thoughts and motivations of a character.

solipsism *n* the philosophical belief that the only thing that can be known to exist is the self. ➤➤ **solipsist** *n,* **solipsistic** *adj.*

solitaire *n* **1a** a game played by one person in which a number of pieces, e.g. pegs or balls, are removed from a cross-shaped pattern by jumping one over another, the aim being to leave a single piece on the board. **b** *chiefly NAm* = PATIENCE (card game). **2** a single gem, *esp* a diamond, set alone, usu in a ring.

solitary[1] *adj* **1a** fond of being alone. **b** lonely. **c** performed or spent without companions. **2** being the only one; sole. **3** unfrequented; remote. **4** of e.g. insects: living alone; not gregarious, colonial, or social. ➤➤ **solitarily** *adv,* **solitariness** *n.*

solitary[2] *n* (*pl* **-ies**) **1** somebody who habitually seeks solitude; a recluse or hermit. **2** *informal* = SOLITARY CONFINEMENT.

solitary confinement *n* the state of being confined in isolation, *esp* as a punishment for a prisoner.

solitude *n* **1** the state of being alone or remote from society; seclusion. **2** a lonely or unfrequented place.

solmization *or* **solmisation** *n* the act or system of using syllables, *esp* doh, ray, me, etc, to denote musical notes or the degrees of a musical scale.

solo[1] *n* (*pl* **solos** *or* **soli**) **1** a musical composition, song, or dance for a single performer. **2** a flight by one person alone in an aircraft. **3** any of various card games in which a player elects to play without a partner against the other players. ➤➤ **soloist** *n.*

solo[2] *adv* without a companion; alone.

solo[3] *adj* **1** done or performed alone; unaccompanied. **2** being a single parent.

solo[4] *v* (**soloes, soloed, soloing**) to perform by oneself, *esp* to fly solo in an aircraft.

Solomon's seal *n* **1** = STAR OF DAVID. **2** a plant of the lily family with drooping usu greenish white bell-shaped flowers and long smooth fleshy leaves.

so long *interj informal* used to express farewell.

solo whist *n* a game of whist in which one player attempts to win by a previously declared margin against the other players.

solstice *n* either of the two occasions each year when the sun is furthest from the celestial equator and highest or lowest in the sky at noon; 22 June or 22 December.

soluble *adj* **1** of a substance: capable of being dissolved in a liquid. **2** capable of being solved or explained. ⋙ **solubility** *n*, **solubly** *adv.*

solute *n* a dissolved substance.

solution *n* **1a** an answer to a problem. **b** the act or process of solving a problem. **2a** a mixture formed when a solid, liquid, or gas is uniformly distributed in a solvent. **b** the process of dissolving or the state of being dissolved.

solve *v* to find an answer to or explanation for (a problem, mystery, etc). ⋙ **solvable** *adj*, **solver** *n.*

solvent[1] *adj* **1** able to pay all debts, *esp* with money in hand. **2** of a substance, *esp* a liquid: able to dissolve other substances. ⋙ **solvency** *n*, **solvently** *adv.*

solvent[2] *n* a substance, *esp* a liquid, that is capable of dissolving or dispersing one or more other substances.

solvent abuse *n* the practice of inhaling the intoxicating fumes from solvents, cleaning fluids, glues, etc.

Som. *abbr* Somerset.

som *n* (*pl* **som**) the basic monetary unit of Kyrgystan and Uzbekistan.

soma[1] *n* an intoxicating plant juice used in ancient India as an offering to the gods.

soma[2] *n* **1** all of an organism except the reproductive cells. **2** the body of an organism.

Somali *n* (*pl* **Somalis** *or* **Somali**) **1** a member of an indigenous people inhabiting Somalia. **2** the Cushitic language spoken by this people, also spoken in parts of Ethiopia, Kenya, and Djibouti. ⋙ **Somali** *adj.*

Somalian *n* a native or inhabitant of Somalia. ⋙ **Somalian** *adj.*

somatic *adj* of the body, *esp* as distinguished from the mind. ⋙ **somatically** *adv.*

somatotrophic hormone *or* **somatotrophin** *or* **somatotropin** *n* = GROWTH HORMONE (I).

sombre (*NAm* **somber**) *adj* **1** dark; gloomy. **2** of a dull or dark colour. **3a** serious; grave. **b** depressing; melancholy. ⋙ **sombrely** *adv*, **sombreness** *n.*

sombrero *n* (*pl* **-os**) a hat of felt or straw with a very wide brim, worn *esp* in Mexico.

some[1] *adj* **1a** being an unknown, undetermined, or unspecified unit or thing: *some film or other.* **b** being an unspecified member of a group or part of a class: *Some birds cannot fly.* **2a** being of an unspecified amount or number: *some water.* **b** being of an appreciable or considerable amount or number: *It may take some time.* **3** *chiefly informal* **a** important, striking, or excellent: *That was some party!* **b** no kind of: *Some friend you are!*

some[2] *pron* **1** some part, amount, or number but not all. **2** *chiefly NAm* an indefinite additional amount: *and then some.*

some[3] *adv* **1** approximately; about. **2** *chiefly NAm, informal* somewhat.

-some[1] *suffix* forming adjectives, with the meaning: characterized by the thing, quality, state, or action specified: *burdensome; cuddlesome.*

-some[2] *suffix* forming nouns, denoting: a group with the number of members, *esp* people, specified: *foursome.*

somebody[1] *pron* some indefinite or unspecified person.

somebody[2] *n* (*pl* **-ies**) a person of position or importance.

some day *adv* at some unknown or unspecified future time; sometime.

somehow *adv* **1a** by some means not known or designated. **b** no matter how. **2** for some mysterious reason.

someone *pron* = SOMEBODY[1].

someplace *adv chiefly NAm* = SOMEWHERE[1].

somersault[1] *n* **1** a leaping or rolling movement in which a person turns forward or backward in a complete revolution bringing the feet over the head. **2** a complete reversal of policy or opinion, a U-turn.

somersault[2] *v* to perform a somersault.

something[1] *pron* **1a** some indeterminate or unspecified thing. **b** some part; a certain amount. **2a** a thing or person of consequence. **b** some truth or value. ✱ **something else** *informal* something or somebody that makes others pall in comparison. **something of a** a fairly notable.

something[2] *adv* **1a** in some degree; somewhat. **b** used to suggest approximation. **2** *informal* to an extreme degree.

-something *comb. form informal* forming nouns, denoting: somebody of an age within the specified decade: *thirty-something.*

sometime[1] *adv* at some unknown or unspecified time.

sometime[2] *adj* having been formerly.

sometimes *adv* at intervals; occasionally.

somewhat *adv* to some degree; slightly.

somewhere[1] *adv* **1** in, at, or to some unknown or unspecified place. **2** at an approximate or unspecified point. ✱ **get somewhere** to make progress.

somewhere[2] *n* an undetermined or unnamed place.

sommelier *n* a waiter in charge of serving wines, *esp* in a restaurant.

somnambulist *n* somebody who walks in their sleep. ⋙ **somnambulism** *n*, **somnambulistic** *adj*, **somnambulistically** *adv.*

somnolent *adj* **1** inclined to or heavy with sleep; drowsy. **2** tending to induce sleep. ⋙ **somnolence** *n*, **somnolency** *n*, **somnolently** *adv.*

son *n* **1a** a male offspring, *esp* of human beings. **b** a male adopted child. **c** (*also in pl*) a male descendant. **2** (**Son** *or* **the Son**) the second person of the Trinity; Christ. **3** somebody closely associated with or deriving from a specified background, place, etc. **4** an informal form of address used *esp* to a boy or a younger man. ⋙ **sonless** *adj*, **sonship** *n.*

sonar *n* a system or device for detecting the presence and location of a submerged object by means of reflected sound waves.

sonata *n* a musical composition typically for one instrument, often with piano accompaniment, and usu with three or four movements.

sonde *n* a device for testing, and usu transmitting information about, physical conditions, e.g. at high altitudes.

son et lumière *n* an entertainment held at night at a historical site, e.g. a cathedral or stately home, that uses lighting and recorded sound to present the place's history.

song *n* **1a** a set of words to be sung to a musical tune with or without accompaniment. **b** the act or art of singing. **2** the melodious sounds made by birds and some other animals. **3** *literary* **a** poetry. **b** a poem. ✻ **for a song** for very little money. **on song** *Brit, informal* performing well; on form.

song and dance *n informal* **1** *chiefly Brit* a fuss or commotion. **2** *NAm* an involved explanation designed to confuse or mislead.

songbird *n* a bird that utters a succession of musical tones.

song cycle *n* a group of related songs designed to form a musical entity.

songster *n* **1** a skilled singer. **2** a writer of songs or poetry. **3** a songbird.

songstress *n* a female songster.

song thrush *n* a common African and Eurasian thrush that has a brown back and wings and a pale breast with small dark spots.

songwriter *n* somebody who writes words or music for songs, *esp* popular songs. ➤➤ **songwriting** *n.*

sonic *adj* **1** using or relating to sound waves. **2** of or being the speed of sound in air at sea level, about 340 metres per second (741mph): compare HYPERSONIC. ➤➤ **sonically** *adv.*

sonic boom *n* a sound resembling an explosion produced when a shock wave formed at the nose of an aircraft travelling at supersonic speed reaches the ground.

sonics *pl n* (*used as sing.*) the scientific study of the properties of sound, *esp* the study of vibrations in matter.

son-in-law *n* (*pl* **sons-in-law**) the husband of one's daughter.

sonnet *n* a short poem with any of various rhyming schemes and consisting typically of 14 lines of ten syllables each.

sonneteer *n* a writer of sonnets.

sonny *n* an informal form of address used *esp* to a young boy.

son of a bitch *n* (*pl* **sons of bitches**) *informal* an offensive or disagreeable person, often used as a term of abuse.

sonogram *or* **sonograph** *n* **1** a visual representation of the qualities of a sound, e.g. its frequency and intensity. **2** a visual image resulting from an ultrasound examination.

sonorant *n* a letter or speech sound that can function as a consonant or a vowel.

sonorous *adj* **1** pleasantly loud, rich, or deep in sound. **2** impressive in effect or style. ➤➤ **sonority** *n,* **sonorously** *adv,* **sonorousness** *n.*

sool *v Aus, NZ* **1** (*often* + on) to incite or urge (a person or animal), *esp* to attack. **2** *esp* of a dog: to attack (e.g. another animal). ➤➤ **sooler** *n.*

soon *adv* **1** before long; without undue time lapse. **2** in a prompt manner; speedily. **3** used in comparisons: in preference; willingly: *I'd sooner walk than drive.* ✻ **no sooner ... than** at the very moment that or immediately after. **sooner or later** at some uncertain future time; eventually.

Usage note

When the phrase *no sooner* starts a sentence, the normal order of the verb and subject following it should be reversed: *No sooner had she said this, than the telephone rang.* Note that the correct word to use after *no sooner* is *than,* not *when.*

soot *n* a fine black powder or flaky substance formed by the incomplete burning of organic matter, e.g. coal.

sooth[1] *adj archaic* true or real.

sooth[2] *n archaic* truth, fact, or reality. ✻ **in sooth** *archaic* truly.

soothe *v* **1** to calm (somebody) by showing attention or concern. **2** to relieve or alleviate (e.g. pain). **3** to bring comfort or reassurance to (somebody). ➤➤ **soother** *n,* **soothing** *adj,* **soothingly** *adv.*

soothsayer *n* somebody who predicts the future; a prophet. ➤➤ **soothsaying** *n.*

sooty *adj* (**-ier, -iest**) **1** covered or soiled with soot. **2** of the colour of soot; black. ➤➤ **sootily** *adv,* **sootiness** *n.*

sop[1] *n* **1** a piece of food, *esp* bread, dipped or soaked in a liquid, e.g. soup. **2** something offered or done as a concession, appeasement, or bribe.

sop[2] *v* (**sopped, sopping**) (*usu* + up) to mop up (e.g. water) so as to leave a dry surface.

sophism *n* an argument that is apparently correct but actually false, *esp* such an argument used to deceive.

sophist *n* **1** an ancient Greek teacher of rhetoric or philosophy, noted for their subtle and often specious reasoning. **2** a false reasoner; a user of sophistry. ➤➤ **sophistic** *adj,* **sophistical** *adj,* **sophistically** *adv.*

sophisticate[1] *v* **1** to make (somebody) more cultured, knowledgeable, or worldly-wise. **2** to make (something) more highly developed, elaborate, or complex. ➤➤ **sophistication** *n.*

sophisticate[2] *n* a sophisticated person.

sophisticated *adj* **1** highly developed; complex. **2a** having refined tastes; cultured. **b** worldly-wise; knowing. **3** intellectually subtle or refined. ➤➤ **sophisticatedly** *adv.*

sophistry *n* (*pl* **-ies**) **1** seemingly true but unsound subtle reasoning or argument. **2** = SOPHISM.

sophomore *n NAm* a second-year student at university, college, or high school. ➤➤ **sophomoric** *adj.*

soporific[1] *adj* causing or tending to cause sleep.

soporific[2] *n* something that induces sleep, e.g. a drug.

sopping *adj* wet through; soaking.

sopping wet *adj* = SOPPING.

soppy *adj* (**-ier, -iest**) *informal* **1** weakly sentimental; mawkish. **2** *chiefly Brit, informal* silly; inane. ➤➤ **soppily** *adv,* **soppiness** *n.*

soprano *n* (*pl* **-os**) **1** a woman or boy singer with a voice in the highest range. **2** a musical instrument having the highest or second highest range.

sorbet *n* a water ice, *esp* one made with fruit juice and sometimes egg whites.

sorcerer *n* a man or woman who uses sorcery; a wizard or witch.

sorceress *n* a female sorcerer.

sorcery *n* the art and practice of using magical power, *esp* with the aid of evil spirits.

sordid *adj* **1** dirty; squalid. **2** base; vile. **3** meanly greedy; niggardly. ➤➤ **sordidly** *adv,* **sordidness** *n.*

sore[1] *adj* **1a** causing or suffering pain. **b** painfully sensitive; tender. **2** severe; urgent. **3** *chiefly NAm* angry; upset. ➤➤ **soreness** *n.*

sore[2] *n* **1** a localized sore spot on the body, *esp* one with the tissues ruptured and usu infected. **2** a source of pain or distress; an affliction.

sore[3] *adv archaic* greatly or extremely.

sorely *adv* **1** much; extremely. **2** painfully; grievously.

sore point *n* a cause of irritation or distress to somebody.

sorghum *n* a tropical grass similar to maize but with the seed-bearing spikes in pairs on a hairy stalk.

SORN *abbr Brit* Statutory Off Road Notification, the requirement that a vehicle owner intending to keep a vehicle off the road and unlicensed must inform the DVLA of this intention.

sororal *adj formal* relating to or involving sisters; sisterly.

sorority *n* (*pl* **-ies**) a social club of girls or women, *esp* at a N American university or college: compare FRATERNITY (1B).

sorrel[1] *n* **1** a brownish orange to light brown colour. **2** a sorrel-coloured animal, *esp* a horse. ➤➤ **sorrel** *adj.*

sorrel[2] *n* a plant of the dock family with acidic-flavoured leaves that are eaten in salads.

sorrow[1] *n* **1** deep distress and regret, e.g. over the loss of something precious. **2** a cause of grief or sadness. ➤➤ **sorrowful** *adj,* **sorrowfully** *adv,* **sorrowfulness** *n.*

sorrow[2] *v* to feel or express sorrow.

sorry[1] *adj* (**-ier, -iest**) **1** full of regret, penitence, or pity. **2** inspiring sorrow, pity, or scorn. **3** bad or regrettable. ➤➤ **sorrily** *adv,* **sorriness** *n.*

sorry[2] *interj* an exclamation used to apologize.

sort[1] *n* **1a** a group constituted on the basis of any common characteristic; a class or kind. **b** an instance of a kind. **2** *informal* a person; an individual. **3** in computing, a process of arranging data in a prescribed order. ✱ **of sorts/of a sort** of an inconsequential or mediocre quality. **out of sorts 1** somewhat ill. **2** grouchy; irritable. **sort of** *informal* to a moderate degree; somewhat; in a way.

sort[2] *v* **1** to put in groups according to kind, class, or quality. **2** to arrange in an orderly manner; to put in order. ➤➤ **sortable** *adj,* **sorter** *n.*

sorted *adj Brit, informal* **1** organized; ready for use. **2** supplied with illegal drugs. **3** emotionally stable or well-adjusted.

sortie[1] *n* **1** a sudden emergence of troops from a defensive position against the enemy. **2** a single mission or attack by one aircraft. **3** a brief trip, *esp* to a hostile or unfamiliar place.

sortie[2] *v* (**sorties, sortied, sortieing**) to make a sortie.

sort out *v* **1** to clarify or resolve (e.g. a problem), *esp* by thoughtful consideration. **2a** to separate (something) from a mass or group. **b** to clear up or tidy (something). **3** *chiefly Brit, informal* to punish or take vengeance on.

SOS *n* **1** an internationally recognized signal of distress. **2** a call or request for help or rescue.

so-so[1] *adj* neither very good nor very bad; middling.

so-so[2] *adv* moderately well; tolerably.

sostenuto *adj and adv* of a piece of music: to be performed in a sustained or prolonged manner. ➤➤ **sostenuto** *n.*

sot *n* a habitual drunkard. ➤➤ **sottish** *adj.*

sotto voce *adv and adj* in a quiet voice; in an undertone.

sou *n* (*pl* **sous**) **1** any of various former French coins of low value. **2** *informal* the smallest amount of money.

soubrette *n* in traditional stage comedy, the role of a coquettish maid or frivolous young woman.

soubriquet *n* see SOBRIQUET.

soufflé *n* a light fluffy baked dish made by carefully folding egg yolks and other ingredients into stiffly beaten egg whites.

sough /sow/ *v* of the wind, waves, etc: to make a soft moaning, sighing, or rustling sound.

sought *v* past tense and past part. of SEEK.

sought-after *adj* greatly desired or courted; much in demand.

souk *n* an open-air bazaar or market in a Muslim country.

soukous *n* a style of dance music originating in Central Africa and influenced by Latin American rhythms.

soul *n* **1** the immaterial and spiritual part of a human being, believed by many to be immortal. **2** the essential or animating principle of a person, group, or thing. **3a** a person's emotional or moral nature. **b** emotional sensitivity or depth. **4** a person: *a dear old soul.* **5** exemplification or personification: *the soul of tact.* **6a** music that originated in black American gospel singing, is closely related to rhythm and blues, and is characterized by intensity of feeling and earthiness. **b** (*used before a noun*) characteristic of black Americans or their culture. ➤➤ **souled** *adj.*

soul-destroying *adj esp* of a task, job, etc: giving no chance for the mind to work; very uninteresting.

soul food *n* food, e.g. chitterlings and ham hocks, traditionally eaten by black Americans, *esp* in the southern states.

soulful *adj* expressing intense or excessive feeling. ➤➤ **soulfully** *adv,* **soulfulness** *n.*

soulless *adj* **1** having no soul or no warmth of feeling; lacking sensitivity or compassion. **2** bleak or uninviting. ➤➤ **soullessly** *adv,* **soullessness** *n.*

soul mate *n* a person with whom one has a close affinity; a lover.

soul-searching *n* scrutiny of one's mind and conscience, *esp* with regard to aims and motives.

sound[1] *n* **1a** the sensation perceived by the sense of hearing, caused by vibrations travelling *esp* through the air. **b** a particular auditory impression or quality; a noise or tone. **2** hearing distance; earshot. **3** an impression conveyed, e.g. by a report. **4a** recorded sounds, e.g. on records or film soundtracks. **b** radio broadcasting as opposed to television. ➤➤ **soundless** *adj,* **soundlessly** *adv,* **soundlessness** *n.*

sound[2] *v* **1a** to make, or cause to make, a sound. **b** to resound. **2** to have a specified import when heard; to seem: *That sounds unlikely.* **3** to examine or test the condition of (e.g. the chest or lungs) by tapping.

sound[3] *adj* **1a** free from injury or disease; healthy. **b** free from defect or decay. **c** free from error or fallacy. **2** grounded in thorough knowledge and experience. **3** showing integrity and good judgment. **4** of sleep: deep and undisturbed. **5** thorough or severe. **6** *Brit, informal* very good. ➤➤ **soundly** *adv,* **soundness** *n.*

sound[4] *adv* fully or thoroughly.

sound[5] *n* **1** a long broad sea inlet. **2** a long passage of water connecting two larger bodies or separating a mainland and an island.

sound[6] *v* **1** to measure (the depth of water in something). **2** to explore or examine (a body cavity) with a probe. **3** of a fish or whale: to dive down suddenly.

sound[7] *n* a probe for exploring or sounding body cavities.

sound barrier *n* a sudden large increase in aerodynamic drag that occurs as an aircraft nears the speed of sound.

sound bite *n* a short excerpt from a speech or statement, *esp* one chosen for its aptness or pithiness.

soundboard *n* **1** a thin resonant board placed in a musical instrument to reinforce its sound by sympathetic vibration. **2** a structure behind or over a pulpit, rostrum, or platform to direct sound forwards.

sound box *n* the hollow resonating chamber in the body of a musical instrument, e.g. a violin.

sound card *n* a printed circuit board used in a personal computer to produce good quality sound.

sound effect *n* a sound, other than speech or music, used to create an effect in a play, radio programme, film, etc, e.g. the shaking of a metal sheet to sound like thunder.

sounding[1] *n* **1a** the act of ascertaining the depth of water in something. **b** a measurement taken by sounding. **2** (*also in pl*) a probe, test, or sampling of opinion or intention.

sounding[2] *adj* **1** *archaic* sonorous or resounding. **2** imposing or pompous.

sounding board *n* **1a** someone whose reaction serves as a test for new ideas. **b** a device or agency that helps spread opinions or ideas. **2** = SOUNDBOARD.

sounding line *n* a line or wire weighted at one end for sounding.

sound off *verb intrans informal* **1** to voice opinions freely and vigorously. **2** *chiefly NAm* to speak loudly.

sound out *v* to attempt to find out the views or intentions of.

soundproof[1] *adj* designed or intended to prevent or minimize sound penetration.

soundproof[2] *v* to make (e.g. a room) soundproof.

sound system *n* electronic equipment for reproducing and amplifying sound.

sound track *n* **1** the narrow strip at the edge of a film that carries the sound recording. **2** the dialogue, sounds, and *esp* the recorded music accompanying a film.

sound wave *n* a wave by which sound is propagated.

soup *n* a liquid food typically having a meat, fish, or vegetable stock as a base and often thickened and containing pieces of solid food. ✻ **in the soup** *informal* in an awkward or embarrassing predicament.

soupçon /'soohpson, 'soohpsonh/ *n* (*pl* **soupçons**) a small amount; a dash.

soup kitchen *n* an establishment where free food, e.g. soup and bread, is given to the needy or homeless.

soup up *v informal* **1** to increase the power of (an engine or car). **2** to make (something) more attractive, interesting, etc.

soupy *adj* (**-ier, -iest**) **1** having the consistency of soup. **2** *informal* sentimental or mawkish.

sour[1] *adj* **1** having an acid taste similar to that of vinegar, lemons, etc. **2** smelling or tasting of fermentation or decay; rancid or rotten. **3** disenchanted or embittered. ✻ **go/turn sour 1** to turn out wrong or badly. **2** to become unpleasant or less harmonious. ➤➤ **sourish** *adj,* **sourly** *adv,* **sourness** *n.*

sour[2] *n chiefly NAm* a cocktail made with a usu specified spirit, lemon or lime juice, sugar, and sometimes soda water.

sour[3] *v* to make or become sour.

source[1] *n* **1a** a place, person, or thing from which something is obtained. **b** an origin. **c** a cause. **2** a person, publication, etc that supplies information, *esp* at first hand. **3** the point of origin of a stream of water. ✻ **at source** at the point of origin or issue.

source[2] *v* **1** to obtain (materials or components) for a manufacturing process. **2** to trace to a source.

sour cream *n* cream that has been deliberately made sour by the addition of bacteria, for use in cooking, salads, etc.

sourdough *n* **1** bread dough in which the yeast is still active, that is reserved from one baking for use as a leaven in the next. **2** bread made from this.

sour grapes *pl n* (*used as sing.*) an attitude of disparagement towards something achieved or owned by another because one is unable to attain it oneself.

sourpuss *n informal* a gloomy, bitter, or bad-tempered person.

sousaphone *n* a large tuba that has a flared adjustable bell and is designed to encircle the player and rest on the left shoulder. ➤➤ **sousaphonist** *n.*

souse[1] *v* **1** to pickle. **2a** to plunge in liquid. **b** to drench or saturate. **3** *informal* to make drunk.

souse[2] *n* **1** brine or vinegar in which foods are preserved. **2** *informal* a drunkard.

soutane /sooh'tan/ *n* a cassock, *esp* one worn by a Roman Catholic priest.

south[1] *n* **1** the direction 90° clockwise from east. **2** (*often* **South**) regions or countries lying to the south. ➤➤ **southbound** *adj and adv.*

south[2] *adj and adv* **1** at, towards, or coming from the south. **2** of the wind: blowing from the south. ✻ **south by east/west** in a position or direction between south and south-southeast (or south-southwest).

South African *n* a native or inhabitant of the Republic of South Africa. ➤➤ **South African** *adj.*

South American *n* a native or inhabitant of South America. ➤➤ **South American** *adj.*

southeast[1] *n* **1** the direction between south and east. **2** regions or countries lying to the southeast. ➤➤ **southeastern** *adj,* **southeastward** *adj and adv,* **southeastwards** *adv.*

southeast[2] *adj and adv* **1** at, towards, or coming from the southeast. **2** of the wind: blowing from the southeast.

southeaster *n* a wind blowing from the southeast.

southeasterly[1] *adj and adv* **1** in a southeastern position or direction. **2** of a wind: blowing from the southeast.

southeasterly[2] *n* (*pl* **-ies**) a wind blowing from the southeast.

southerly[1] *adj and adv* **1** in a southern position or direction. **2** of a wind: blowing from the south.

southerly[2] *n* (*pl* **-ies**) a wind blowing from the south.

southern *adj* in or towards the south; inhabiting the south. ➤➤ **southernmost** *adj.*

Southerner *n* (*also* **southerner**) a native or inhabitant of the South.

Southern lights *pl n* = AURORA AUSTRALIS.

southing *n* **1** distance due south in latitude from the preceding point of measurement, used *esp* in navigation at sea. **2** southerly progress.

South Korean *n* a native or inhabitant of South Korea. ➤➤ **South Korean** *adj.*

southpaw *n* **1** a left-handed boxer who leads with the right hand and guards with the left. **2** *chiefly NAm* a left-handed person.

south-southeast *n* the direction midway between south and southeast. ⋙ **south-southeast** *adj and adv.*

south-southwest *n* the direction midway between south and southwest. ⋙ **south-southwest** *adj and adv.*

southward *adj and adv* towards the south; in a direction going south. ⋙ **southwards** *adv.*

southwest[1] *n* **1** the direction between south and west. **2** regions or countries lying to the southwest. ⋙ **southwestern** *adj,* **southwestward** *adj and adv,* **southwestwards** *adv.*

southwest[2] *adj and adv* **1** at, towards, or coming from the southwest. **2** of the wind: blowing from the southwest.

southwester *n* a wind blowing from the southwest.

southwesterly[1] *adj and adv* **1** in a southwestern position or direction. **2** of a wind: blowing from the southwest.

southwesterly[2] *n* (*pl* **-ies**) a wind blowing from the southwest.

souvenir *n* something that serves as a reminder, e.g. of a person, place, or past event; a memento.

sou'wester *n* a waterproof hat with a wide slanting brim longer at the back than in front.

sovereign[1] *n* **1** somebody possessing supreme power, *esp* a monarch. **2** a former British gold coin worth one pound.

sovereign[2] *adj* **1** possessing supreme power. **2** unlimited in extent; absolute. **3** enjoying political autonomy. ⋙ **sovereignly** *adv.*

sovereignty *n* (*pl* **-ies**) **1a** supreme power, *esp* over a politically organized body. **b** freedom from external influence or control; autonomy. **2** an autonomous state.

Soviet *adj* of or relating to the former USSR.

soviet *n* **1** an elected governmental or administrative council in the former USSR. **2** (**Soviets**) the people, *esp* the political and military leaders, of the former USSR. ⋙ **sovietize** *v.*

sow[1] /sow/ *n* **1** an adult female pig. **2** the adult female of various other animals, e.g. the grizzly bear.

sow[2] /soh/ *v* (*past tense* **sowed,** *past part.* **sown** *or* **sowed**) **1a** to scatter (seed) on the earth to enable plants to grow, or to scatter the seed of (a particular plant). **b** to strew (an area) with seed. **2** to implant or initiate. ✱ **sow one's wild oats** to indulge in the wildness and promiscuity of youth, before settling down to a steady life. ⋙ **sower** *n.*

soy *n* **1** a brown liquid sauce made by fermenting soya beans, used in oriental cookery. **2** = SOYA.

soya *n* **1** an Asian plant of the pea family widely grown for its seeds and for forage and soil improvement. **2** protein from the edible seed of this plant.

soya milk *n* a milk substitute made from soya bean flour.

soy sauce *n* = SOY (1).

sozzled *adj informal* very drunk.

SP *abbr* starting price.

spa *n* **1** a spring of mineral water. **2** a usu fashionable resort with mineral springs. **3** a commercial establishment providing health and beauty treatments. **4** a bathtub with an apparatus for producing a whirlpool effect with jets of aerated water.

spa bath *n* = SPA (4).

space[1] *n* **1** the limitless three-dimensional extent in which objects and events occur and have relative position and direction. **2** the region beyond the earth's atmosphere or beyond the solar system. **3a** continuous unoccupied distance, area, or volume. **b** an amount of room set apart or available for something. **4** freedom for personal development and fulfilment. **5** a period of time; or its duration. **6** a blank area on a page, e.g. separating words or lines.

space[2] *v* (*often* + out) to place (two or more things) at intervals or arrange (them) with space between. ⋙ **spacer** *n,* **spacing** *n.*

space age *n* (**the space age**) the era in which the exploration of space and space travel have become possible.

space-age *adj* suggestive of the technology of the space age; ultra-modern or futuristic.

space bar *n* the horizontal bar at the bottom of a typewriter or computer keyboard, which is pressed to make a space.

space capsule *n* a small spacecraft, or the part of a larger spacecraft containing the crew, that is designed to be returned to earth.

spacecraft *n* (*pl* **spacecraft**) a vehicle designed to travel beyond the earth's atmosphere.

spaced out *adj informal* dazed or stupefied, *esp* by a narcotic substance.

spaceman *or* **spacewoman** *n* (*pl* **spacemen** *or* **spacewomen**) **1** somebody who travels outside the earth's atmosphere. **2** a visitor to earth from outer space.

space probe *n* = PROBE[1] (2B).

spaceship *n* a manned spacecraft.

space shuttle *n* a vehicle designed to serve as a reusable transport between the earth and destinations in space, *esp* a US space vehicle launched by rocket but able to land like an aircraft.

space station *n* a manned artificial satellite designed for a fixed orbit about the earth and to serve as a base.

space suit *n* a suit equipped to make life in space possible for its wearer.

space-time *n* a system of one temporal and three spatial coordinates by which any physical object or event can be located.

space-time continuum *n* = SPACE-TIME.

space walk *n* a trip outside a spacecraft made by an astronaut in space.

spacey *or* **spacy** *adj* (**-ier, -iest**) *informal* of or in a spaced-out state.

spacial *adj* see SPATIAL.

spacious *adj* containing ample space; roomy. ⋙ **spaciously** *adv,* **spaciousness** *n.*

spacy *adj* see SPACEY.

spade[1] *n* a digging implement with a flat, usu rectangular, metal blade and a long handle. ✱ **call a spade a spade** to speak frankly and usu bluntly. ⋙ **spadeful** (*pl* **spadefuls**) *n.*

spade[2] *v* to dig up, shape, or work with a spade.

spade[3] *n* **1** a playing card marked with one or more black figures in the shape of a spearhead. **2** (*in pl*) the suit comprising these cards. ✱ **in spades** *informal* in the extreme.

spadework *n* the routine preparatory work for an undertaking.

spadix /'spaydiks/ *n* (*pl* **spadices** /-seez/) a spike of crowded flowers, e.g. in an arum, with a fleshy or succulent axis usu enclosed in a spathe.

spaghetti *pl n* (*used as sing. or pl*) pasta in the form of thin solid strings of varying widths.

spaghetti western *n informal* a western film made cheaply in Europe.

spake *v archaic* past tense of SPEAK.

spall[1] *n* a small splinter or chip, *esp* of stone.

spall[2] *v* **1** to break up (stone, ore, etc) into fragments. **2** to break off in fragments; to chip.

Spam *n trademark* a tinned pork luncheon meat.

spam[1] *n* messages, *esp* inappropriate or unsolicited ones, sent to a large number of users or newsgroups on the Internet.

spam[2] *v* (**spammed, spamming**) to send a message to (many people) on the Internet. ➤➤ **spammer** *n.*

span[1] *n* **1** an extent or distance between two limits, e.g.: **a** a limited stretch of time, *esp* an individual's lifetime. **b** the full reach or extent. **c** a part of a bridge between supports. **d** = WINGSPAN. **2a** the distance from the end of the thumb to the end of the little finger of a spread hand. **b** a former English unit of length equal to 9in. (about 0.23m).

span[2] *v* (**spanned, spanning**) to extend across (something) in space or time.

Spandex *n trademark* an elastic textile fibre made largely from polyurethane.

spandrel *n* the space between the right or left exterior curve of an arch and an enclosing right angle.

spangle[1] *n* **1** = SEQUIN. **2** a small glittering object or particle. ➤➤ **spangly** *adj.*

spangle[2] *v* to cover with or as if with spangles.

Spaniard *n* a native or inhabitant of Spain.

spaniel *n* a dog of a small or medium-sized breed with short legs, long wavy hair, and large drooping ears.

Spanish *n* the official Romance language of Spain and many Central and S American countries. ➤➤ **Spanish** *adj.*

Spanish American *n* a native or inhabitant of any of the Spanish-speaking countries of America, or a citizen of the USA of Spanish descent. ➤➤ **Spanish-American** *adj.*

Spanish fly *n* **1** a green blister beetle of S Europe. **2** a preparation of Spanish flies used as an aphrodisiac.

Spanish guitar *n* a guitar of the classical acoustic type, *esp* as distinct from an electric guitar.

Spanish omelette *n* an omelette containing cooked chopped vegetables, e.g. onions, potatoes, and green peppers.

Spanish onion *n* a large mild-flavoured onion.

spank[1] *v* to strike, *esp* on the buttocks, with the open hand or something flat.

spank[2] *n* a slap or a series of slaps.

spanking[1] *adj* **1** vigorous or brisk. **2** remarkable of its kind; striking.

spanking[2] *n* a series of spanks.

spanner *n chiefly Brit* a tool consisting of a flat metal bar with one or both ends shaped for holding or turning nuts or bolts. ✱ **spanner in the works** *informal* an obstruction or hindrance, e.g. to a plan or operation.

spar[1] *n* **1** a stout pole. **2** a mast, boom, gaff, yard, etc used to support or control a sail.

spar[2] *v* (**sparred, sparring**) **1** to box without putting full force into one's blows, *esp* in practice. **2** to argue or wrangle.

spar[3] *n* a sparring match or session.

spar[4] *n* any of various non-metallic minerals which usu split easily.

spare[1] *adj* **1** not in use; *esp* reserved for use in emergency. **2a** in excess of what is required; surplus. **b** not taken up with work or duties; free. **3** plain and unelaborate, uncluttered, or concise. **4** healthily lean; wiry. ✱ **go spare** *Brit, informal* to become extremely angry or distraught. ➤➤ **sparely** *adv,* **spareness** *n.*

spare[2] *v* **1** to make available for others' use, or give up as surplus to requirements. **2** to refrain from destroying, punishing, or harming. **3** to refrain from using. **4** to relieve of the necessity of doing or undergoing something. ✱ **spare no expense** to pay as much as is needed. **to spare** above and beyond what is needed; available; left.

spare[3] *n* **1** a spare or duplicate item or part; *specif* a spare part for a motor vehicle. **2** = SPARE TYRE.

sparerib *n* a pork rib with most of the surrounding meat removed for use as bacon.

spare tyre *n* **1** an extra tyre carried by a motor vehicle as a spare. **2** *informal* a roll of fat at the waist.

sparing *adj* **1** not wasteful; frugal. **2** meagre or scant. ➤➤ **sparingly** *adv,* **sparingness** *n.*

spark[1] *n* **1a** a small particle of a burning substance thrown out by something that is on fire or left among its ashes. **b** a hot glowing particle struck from a larger mass. **2a** a luminous disruptive electrical discharge of very short duration between two conductors of opposite high potential separated by a gas, e.g. air. **b** an electrical discharge of this kind produced by a spark plug in an internal-combustion engine. **3** a sparkle or flash. **4** something that sets off or stimulates an event, development, etc. **5** a trace, *esp* one which may develop; a germ.

spark[2] *v* **1** to produce or give off sparks; *specif* to produce a spark in an internal-combustion engine. **2** (+ off) to prompt or precipitate (something).

sparking plug *n* = SPARK PLUG.

sparkle[1] *v* **1** to give off or reflect glittering points of light. **2** to show brilliance or animation.

sparkle[2] *n* **1** a little spark; a flash of light. **2** vivacity or gaiety. ➤➤ **sparkly** *adj.*

sparkler *n* **1** a hand-held firework that throws off brilliant sparks on burning. **2** *informal* a cut and polished diamond or other gem.

sparkling wine *n* wine that is fizzy, either through natural processes of fermentation or by having gas added.

spark plug *n* a part that fits into the cylinder head of an internal-combustion engine, e.g. of a car, and produces the electric spark that ignites the air–fuel mixture.

sparring partner *n* **1** a boxer's opponent for practice during training. **2** a habitual opponent, e.g. in friendly argument.

sparrow *n* a small dull-coloured songbird related to the finches.

sparrowgrass *n chiefly dialect* = ASPARAGUS.

sparrow hawk *n* a small hawk with a long tail and short rounded wings that preys on smaller birds.

sparse *adj* consisting of few and scattered elements; *esp* not thickly grown or settled. ➤➤ **sparsely** *adv,* **sparseness** *n,* **sparsity** *n.*

Spartan *n* a native or inhabitant of ancient Sparta, a city in ancient Greece. ➤➤ **Spartan** *adj.*

spartan *adj* not offering or designed for ease and comfort; austere.

spasm *n* **1** an involuntary and abnormal muscular contraction. **2** a sudden violent and brief effort or emotion.

spasmodic *adj* **1** occurring at intervals and usu suddenly and unpredictably. **2a** resembling a spasm, *esp* in sudden violence. **b** relating to or characterized by spasms. ➤➤ **spasmodically** *adv.*

spastic[1] *adj* **1** of or characterized by spasm. **2** *dated, sometimes offensive* affected by cerebral palsy. **3** *informal, offensive* ineffectual or incompetent. ⋙ **spastically** *adv*, **spasticity** *n*.

spastic[2] *n* **1** *dated, sometimes offensive* somebody who has cerebral palsy. **2** *informal, offensive* a clumsy or ineffectual person.

spat[1] *v* past tense and past part. of SPIT[1].

spat[2] *n* a cloth or leather gaiter covering the instep and ankle.

spat[3] *n informal* a small-scale or petty argument.

spat[4] *v* (**spatted, spatting**) to quarrel pettily or briefly.

spatchcock[1] *v* **1** to cook (a fowl or small game bird) by splitting along the backbone and frying or grilling. **2** to insert or combine (words) in a forced or incongruous way.

spatchcock[2] *n* a fowl that is spatchcocked immediately after slaughter.

spate *n* **1** a large number or amount, *esp* occurring in a short space of time. **2** a state of flood.

spathe *n* a sheath consisting of a bract or pair of bracts enclosing the cluster of flowers on a plant.

spatial *or* **spacial** *adj* relating to or occurring in space. ⋙ **spatiality** *n*, **spatially** *adv*.

spatter[1] *v* (**spattered, spattering**) **1** to splash or sprinkle with drops of liquid. **2** to scatter by splashing or sprinkling. **3** to spurt out in scattered drops.

spatter[2] *n* **1** the sound of spattering. **2** a drop spattered on something or a stain due to spattering.

spatula *n* an implement with a flat, thin, blunt-edged blade and a short handle, used for spreading, mixing, etc soft substances or powders.

spatulate *adj* shaped like a spatula.

spavin *n* a bony enlargement or soft swelling of the hock of a horse associated with strain. ⋙ **spavined** *adj*.

spawn[1] *v* **1** of an aquatic animal: to produce or deposit (eggs). **2** to produce, *esp* abundantly. ⋙ **spawner** *n*.

spawn[2] *n* **1** the large number of eggs produced by frogs, oysters, fish, etc. **2** (*used as sing. or pl*) = OFFSPRING. **3** mycelium, *esp* for propagating mushrooms.

spay *v* to remove the ovaries of (a female animal).

speak *v* **1a** to utter words with the voice. **b** to express one's thoughts or feelings to, or have a conversation with. **c** (*often* + to) to greet and have normal or polite relations with somebody or each other: *They're not speaking because of the quarrel last night.* **d** to make a speech. **2** to use, or be able to use, (a language) for oral communication. **3** to act as a spokesperson for. **4** to express thoughts or feelings in writing. **5** to be indicative or suggestive of. **6** to appeal or convey special meaning and significance to. ✻ **so to speak** used, often apologetically, to qualify a form of words that is unusual or imprecise. **speak in tongues** to speak in unintelligible language when ecstatic during religious worship. **speak one's mind** to say frankly what one thinks. **speak volumes** to communicate, suggest, or reveal a great deal. **to speak of** (*usu in negative contexts*) worthy of mention or notice: *no talent to speak of.*

-speak *comb. form* forming nouns, denoting: language characteristic of a specified person, group, subject, etc, *esp* when considered to be clumsy or obscure: *computerspeak; teenspeak.*

speakeasy *n* (*pl* **-ies**) *informal* a place where alcoholic drinks were illegally sold during Prohibition in the USA.

speaker *n* **1a** somebody who speaks, *esp* at public functions. **b** somebody who speaks a specified language. **2** the presiding officer of a deliberative or legislative assembly. **3** = LOUDSPEAKER.

speaking *adj* **1a** capable of speech. **b** (*usu used in combinations*) containing chiefly native speakers of the language specified. **2** highly significant or expressive; eloquent. **3** able to speak a specified language.

speaking clock *n Brit* a recorded message giving the correct time to telephone callers.

speak out *v* **1** to speak loudly enough to be heard. **2** to express an opinion frankly.

speak up *v* **1** (*usu in imperative*) to speak more loudly. **2** to express an opinion boldly. **3** (+ for) to speak in defence of.

spear[1] *n* a thrusting or throwing weapon with a long shaft and sharp head or blade used by hunters or foot soldiers.

spear[2] *v* to pierce, strike, or take hold of with or as if with a spear.

spear[3] *n* a usu young blade, shoot, or sprout, e.g. of asparagus or broccoli.

speargun *n* a device used for firing a spear in underwater fishing.

spearhead[1] *n* **1** the sharp-pointed head of a spear. **2** a leading element or force in a development, course of action, etc.

spearhead[2] *v* to serve as the leader of or a leading force in (e.g. an attack).

spearmint *n* a common mint grown for its aromatic oil.

spear side *n* the male branch of a family.

spec[1] ✻ **on spec** *informal* in the hope of finding or obtaining something desired.

spec[2] *n informal* = SPECIFICATION.

special[1] *adj* **1** distinguished from others of the same category, *esp* because in some way superior. **2** held in particular esteem. **3** other than or in addition to the usual. **4** designed or undertaken for a particular end or need. **5** for the use or education of children who have learning difficulties, emotional difficulties, or a physical disability. ⋙ **specialness** *n*.

Usage note

specially *or* **especially**? See note at ESPECIALLY.

special[2] *n* **1** a special person or thing. **2** a dish in a restaurant that is not normally on the menu. **3** a special offer in a shop. **4** *Brit* = SPECIAL CONSTABLE.

Special Branch *n* in Britain, the branch of the police force concerned with political security.

special constable *n Brit* somebody employed as an extra policeman, e.g. in times of emergency.

special delivery *n Brit* a service that offers the delivery of a letter or parcel by a guaranteed time.

special effect *n* (*usu in pl*) an unusual visual or sound effect introduced into a film or prerecorded television production by special processing.

specialise *v* see SPECIALIZE.

specialised *adj* see SPECIALIZED.

specialism *n* = SPECIALITY.

specialist *n* somebody who specializes in a special occupation or branch of knowledge. ⋙ **specialist** *adj*.

speciality (*NAm* **specialty**) *n* (*pl* **-ies**) **1a** a special aptitude or skill. **b** a particular occupation or branch of knowledge. **c** (*usu* **specialty**) a branch of medicine. **2** a product, service, etc that a person, place, or establishment specializes in.

specialize *or* **-ise** *v* **1** (*often* + in) to concentrate one's efforts in a special or limited activity or field. **2** (+ in) to make a habit of doing something. **3** to change so as to adapt to a particular mode of life or environment, e.g. in the course of evolution. ➤➤ **specialization** *n.*

specialized *or* **specialised** *adj* intended or fitted for a specific purpose or occupation.

specially *adv* **1** for a particular purpose. **2** in a special way.

Usage note

specially *or* **especially**? See note at ESPECIALLY.

special needs *pl n* in education, special requirements that a pupil has because of a physical disability, emotional or behavioural problems, or a learning difficulty.

special pleading *n* an argument that ignores the damaging or unfavourable aspects of a case.

specialty *n* (*pl* **-ies**) **1** *chiefly NAm* see SPECIALITY. **2** the particular branch of medicine in which a doctor specializes.

speciation *n* the evolutionary development of new biological species; the process by which a new species is formed.

specie *n* money in coins rather than notes.

species *n* (*pl* **species**) **1a** a class of organisms having common attributes and designated by a common name. **b** (*used before a noun*) denoting a plant belonging to a biological species as distinct from a hybridized horticultural variety. **2** a kind or sort.

speciesism *n* human disregard of the needs of other animals. ➤➤ **speciesist** *adj and n.*

specific[1] *adj* **1** distinct from others, clearly and individually identified. **2** free from ambiguity; explicit or particular. **3a** (*usu* + to) confined to a particular individual, group, or circumstance. **b** having a particular rather than a general influence, e.g. on a body part, disease, or chemical reaction. **4** in biology, of or constituting a species, *esp* a biological species. ➤➤ **specifically** *adv,* **specificity** *n.*

specific[2] *n* (*in pl*) particulars.

specification *n* **1** the act or an instance of specifying. **2** (*usu in pl*) a detailed description of something, e.g. a building or car, *esp* in the form of a plan. **3** a standard required in the workmanship and materials used in making something.

specific gravity *n* the ratio of the density of any substance to the density of a substance taken as a standard, e.g. pure water or hydrogen; relative density.

specify *v* (**-ies, -ied**) **1a** to identify clearly and individually. **b** to state explicitly or in detail. **2** to include as an item in a specification. ➤➤ **specifiable** *adj,* **specifier** *n.*

specimen *n* **1a** an item or part typical of a group or whole; a sample. **b** a sample of urine, blood, tissue, etc taken for medical examination. **2a** a distinct individual within a particular category. **b** *informal* a person or individual.

specious *adj* **1** superficially persuasive or apparently sound but fallacious. **2** having a deceptive attraction or fascination. ➤➤ **speciously** *adv,* **speciousness** *n.*

speck[1] *n* **1** a small spot or blemish. **2** a small particle.

speck[2] *v* to mark with specks.

speckle[1] *n* a little speck, e.g. of colour.

speckle[2] *v* to mark with speckles. ➤➤ **speckled** *adj.*

specs *pl n informal* = SPECTACLES.

spectacle *n* a striking or dramatic public display or show. ✱ **make a spectacle of oneself** to attract attention by behaving, dressing, etc oddly.

spectacled *adj* **1** wearing a pair of spectacles. **2** having markings suggesting a pair of spectacles.

spectacles *pl n* a pair of lenses in a frame worn in front of the eyes to correct or improve one's vision; = GLASSES.

spectacular[1] *adj* extremely impressive, *esp* in being very large, colourful, exciting, and dramatic. ➤➤ **spectacularly** *adv.*

spectacular[2] *n* something, e.g. a stage show, that is spectacular.

spectate *v* to be present as a spectator, e.g. at a sports event.

spectator *n* **1** somebody who attends an event or activity in order to watch. **2** somebody who looks on without participating; an onlooker.

specter *n NAm* see SPECTRE.

spectra *n* pl of SPECTRUM.

spectral *adj* **1** of or suggesting a spectre. **2** of or made by a spectrum. ➤➤ **spectrally** *adv.*

spectre (*NAm* **specter**) *n* **1** a visible ghost. **2** something that haunts or perturbs the mind.

spectrogram *n* a photograph or diagram of a spectrum.

spectrograph *n* an instrument for dispersing light, sound waves, etc into a spectrum and recording or mapping it. ➤➤ **spectrographic** *adj,* **spectrographically** *adv,* **spectrography** *n.*

spectrometer *n* a spectroscope fitted for measurements of the spectra observed with it. ➤➤ **spectrometric** *adj,* **spectrometry** *n.*

spectroscope *n* an instrument for forming and examining optical spectra. ➤➤ **spectroscopic** *adj,* **spectroscopically** *adv,* **spectroscopist** *n,* **spectroscopy** *n.*

spectrum *n* (*pl* **spectra**) **1** the series of colours ranging from red to violet produced when a beam of white light is dispersed, e.g. by a prism. **2** the components of a beam of electromagnetic radiation arranged in the order of their wavelengths. **3** the entire range of wavelengths or frequencies of electromagnetic radiation or of any particular type of it. **4** an interrelated sequence or range.

specula *n* pl of SPECULUM.

speculate *v* **1** to form an opinion or theory about something in advance of the evidence to support it; to conjecture. **2** to assume a business risk in the hope of gain; *esp* to buy or sell in expectation of profiting from market fluctuations. ➤➤ **speculation** *n,* **speculator** *n.*

speculative *adj* **1** involving speculation; theoretical rather than demonstrable. **2** questioning or enquiring. ➤➤ **speculatively** *adv.*

speculum *n* (*pl* **specula** *or* **speculums**) an instrument inserted into a body passage for medical inspection or treatment.

sped *v* past tense and past part. of SPEED[2].

speech *n* **1** the communication or expression of thoughts in spoken words. **2** a public discourse; an address. **3a** a language or dialect. **b** an individual manner of speaking. **4** a unit of one or more lines to be spoken by a character in a play.

speech day *n Brit* an annual ceremonial day at some schools when prizes are presented.

speechify *v* (**-ies, -ied**) to speak or make a speech in a pompous manner. ➤➤ **speechifier** *n.*

speechless *adj* **1** unable to speak; dumb. **2** deprived of speech, e.g. through horror or rage. ➤➤ **speechlessly** *adv,* **speechlessness** *n.*

speech recognition *n* a computer system that converts speech into text.

speech therapy *n* therapy for people who have problems with speaking and language. ⋙ **speech therapist** *n.*

speed[1] *n* **1a** the act or state of moving swiftly; swiftness. **b** rate of motion. **2** rate of performance or execution. **3a** the sensitivity to light of a photographic film expressed numerically. **b** the power of a lens or optical system, e.g. in a camera, to admit more or less light. **c** the duration of a photographic exposure. **4** each of the gear ratios of a bicycle. **5** *slang* methamphetamine, or any of several chemically related stimulant amphetamine drugs. ✱ **at speed** while moving fast. **up to speed** having all the relevant information.

speed[2] *v* (*past tense and past part.* **sped** *or* **speeded**) **1** to move or go quickly. **2** to travel at excessive or illegal speed. **3** *archaic* to meet with success or prosperity. ⋙ **speeder** *n.*

speedball *n slang* cocaine mixed with heroin, usu taken by injection.

speedboat *n* a fast motorboat.

speedbump *n* a hump in a road designed to make vehicles travel at a slow speed.

speed camera *n* a camera placed at the side of a road to take photographs of vehicles that are speeding.

speed hump *n Brit* = SPEEDBUMP.

speed limit *n* the maximum speed permitted by law in a given area or under specified circumstances.

speedo *n* (*pl* **-os**) *informal* = SPEEDOMETER.

speedometer *n* an instrument for indicating a vehicle's speed.

speed up *v* to move or work, or cause to move or work, faster; to accelerate.

speedway *n* **1** a usu oval racecourse for motorcycles. **2** the sport of racing motorcycles. **3** *NAm* a fast road.

speedwell *n* a small creeping plant with slender stems and small blue or whitish flowers.

speedy *adj* (**-ier, -iest**) swift or quick. ⋙ **speedily** *adv,* **speediness** *n.*

speleology *n* **1** the scientific study of caves. **2** the sport of exploring caves; potholing. ⋙ **speleological** *adj,* **speleologist** *n.*

spell[1] *n* **1a** a spoken word or form of words held to have magic power. **b** a state of enchantment. **2** a compelling influence or attraction.

spell[2] *v* (*past tense and past part.* **spelt** *or* **spelled**) **1a** to name or write the letters of (a word) in order. **b** of letters: to form (a word). **2** to amount to or mean (something).

spell[3] *n* **1** a short or indefinite period or phase. **2** a sudden brief attack or fit of dizziness, shivering, coughing, etc. **3** *chiefly Aus* a period of rest from work, activity, or use.

spell[4] *v* (*past tense and past part.* **spelled**) **1** to give a brief rest to by relieving for a time. **2** *chiefly Aus* to rest from work or activity for a time.

spellbind *v* (*past tense and past part.* **spellbound**) to hold the attention of as if by a spell or charm; to bewitch. ⋙ **spellbinder** *n,* **spellbinding** *adj,* **spellbindingly** *adv.*

spellbound *adj* held as if by a spell.

spellcheck *v* to check the spelling in (a document) with a spellchecker.

spellchecker *n* a computer program used in word processing to check the spelling in a document by comparing each word with a dictionary held on disk.

speller *n* **1** somebody who spells words, *esp* in a specified way. **2** *chiefly NAm* a book with exercises for teaching spelling.

spelling *n* **1** the act of forming or the ability to form words from letters. **2** the sequence of letters that make up a particular word.

spell out *v* to explain (something) clearly and in detail.

spelt[1] *n* a primitive wheat whose ears contain two light red kernels.

spelt[2] *v* past tense and past part. of SPELL[2].

spencer *n* **1** a woman's thin woollen vest. **2** a short waist-length jacket.

spend[1] *v* (*past tense and past part.* **spent**) **1** to use up or pay out (money). **2** to wear out; to exhaust. **3** to cause or permit (time) to elapse; to pass (it). ✱ **spend a penny** *Brit, informal, euphem* to urinate. ⋙ **spendable** *adj,* **spender** *n.*

spend[2] *n informal* an amount of money spent.

spendthrift *n* somebody who spends carelessly or wastefully. ⋙ **spendthrift** *adj.*

spent *v* past tense and past part. of SPEND[1].

sperm *n* (*pl* **sperms** *or* **sperm**) **1** the male fertilizing fluid; semen. **2** a male gamete; = SPERMATOZOON.

spermaceti /spuhmə'seeti, -'seti/ *n* a waxy solid obtained from the oil of whales, *esp* sperm whales, and used in ointments, cosmetics, and candles.

spermatozoon /,spuhmətə'zoh·ən/ *n* (*pl* **spermatozoa**) a motile male gamete of an animal, usu with rounded or elongated head and a long tail-like flagellum. ⋙ **spermatozoal** *adj,* **spermatozoan** *adj.*

sperm bank *n* a place where semen for artificial insemination is stored.

sperm count *n* an indication of how fertile a man is, obtained by measuring the concentration of sperm in a given volume of seminal fluid.

spermicide *n* something that kills sperm, *esp* a substance, e.g. a cream or gel used as a contraceptive. ⋙ **spermicidal** *adj.*

sperm oil *n* a pale yellow oil obtained from the sperm whale.

sperm whale *n* a large toothed whale that has a vast blunt head with a cavity in the front part containing a fluid mixture of spermaceti and oil.

spew[1] *v* **1** to vomit. **2** to eject or be ejected with violence or in great quantity. ⋙ **spewer** *n.*

spew[2] *n* vomit.

SPF *abbr* sun protection factor.

sphagnum *n* any of a large genus of atypical mosses that grow only in wet acid areas, e.g. bogs, where their remains become compacted to form peat.

sphere *n* **1** a space or solid enclosed by a surface, all points of which are equidistant from the centre; a globe or ball. **2** any of the revolving spherical transparent shells in which, according to ancient astronomy, the celestial bodies are set. **3** the area covered by somebody's knowledge or expertise, or the milieu in which they exist or have influence. ⋙ **spheral** *adj,* **spheric** *adj,* **sphericity** *n.*

spherical *adj* **1** having the form of a sphere. **2** relating to a sphere or the properties of a sphere. ⋙ **spherically** *adv.*

spheroid *n* a figure resembling a sphere. ⋙ **spheroidal** *adj,* **spheroidicity** *n.*

spherule *n* a little sphere or spherical body.

sphincter *n* a muscular ring, surrounding and able to contract or close a bodily opening. ⋙ **sphincteral** *adj.*

sphinx *n* (*pl* **sphinxes** *or* **sphinges**) **1a** (**the Sphinx**) a female monster in Greek mythology, with a lion's body and a human head, that killed those who failed to answer a riddle it set them. **b** an enigmatic or mysterious person. **2** an ancient Egyptian image in the form of a recumbent lion, usu with a human head.

sphygmomanometer *n* an instrument for measuring arterial blood pressure. ⯮ **sphygmomanometry** *n.*

spic *n NAm, offensive* a Spanish-speaking Latin American person.

spic-and-span *adj* see SPICK-AND-SPAN.

spiccato *n* (*pl* **-os**) in music, a technique used by string players in which a short sound is produced by bouncing the bow on the string.

spice[1] *n* **1a** any of various aromatic vegetable products, e.g. pepper, ginger, or nutmeg, used to season or flavour foods. **b** such products collectively. **2** something that adds zest or relish.

spice[2] *v* **1** to season with spice. **2** (*often* + up) to add zest or relish to.

spick-and-span *or* **spic-and-span** *adj* spotlessly clean and tidy; spruce.

spicule *n* **1** a tiny pointed usu hard structure; *esp* any of the minute structures that support the tissue of various invertebrates, e.g. a sponge. **2** a jet of relatively cool gas rising through the lower atmosphere of the sun. ⯮ **spiculate** *adj.*

spicy *adj* (**-ier, -iest**) **1a** having the quality, flavour, or fragrance of spice. **b** strongly seasoned with spices. **2** somewhat scandalous or racy. ⯮ **spicily** *adv,* **spiciness** *n.*

spider *n* **1** any member of an order of usu small invertebrate animals with eight legs, and two or more pairs of specialized organs for spinning threads of silk that they use to make cocoons for their eggs, nests for themselves, or webs for entangling their prey. **2** *Brit* a bundle of elastic straps with hooks, used to attach a load to a bicycle or motor vehicle. **3** a support for a snooker cue that enables the player to hit the ball from above when other balls are in the way.

spider crab *n* any of numerous crabs with extremely long legs and nearly triangular bodies.

spider mite *n* a small mite that spins webs and often attacks crop plants.

spider monkey *n* a S American monkey with long slender limbs, a rudimentary or absent thumb, and a very long prehensile tail.

spider plant *n* any of various house plants with long narrow leaves, e.g. a tradescantia.

spidery *adj* **1** resembling a spider; *specif* long, thin, and sharply angular like the legs of a spider. **2** resembling a spider's web; esp composed of fine threads or lines in a weblike arrangement.

spiel[1] *n informal* a glib line of talk, usu designed to influence or persuade; patter.

spiel[2] *v* **1** *informal* to talk volubly or glibly. **2** *informal* (*usu* + off) to tell or describe glibly and at length. ⯮ **spieler** *n.*

spiffing *adj Brit, informal, dated* extremely good; excellent.

spiffy *adj* (**-ier, -iest**) *NAm, informal* smart or spruce.

spigot *n* **1** a small plug used to stop up the vent of a cask. **2** the part of a tap, *esp* on a barrel, which controls the flow. **3** a projection on the end of a piece of piping or guttering that fits into an adjoining piece.

spike[1] *n* **1** a pointed object or projection usu made of metal, e.g. on the top of a wall or fence. **2a** any of several metal projections set in the sole and heel of a running shoe to improve grip. **b** (*in pl*) track shoes. **3** an upright metal rod on which rejected copy is impaled in a newspaper office. **4** an unusually high and sharply defined maximum, e.g. on a graph.

spike[2] *v* **1** to pierce with or impale on a spike. **2a** to reject (newspaper copy). **b** to put an end to (e.g. a project). **3a** to add spirits to (a non-alcoholic drink). **b** to add something, e.g. a drug, to (food). ✱ **spike somebody's guns** to foil an opponent's plan. ⯮ **spiker** *n.*

spike[3] *n* **1** an elongated cluster of flowers growing directly without stalks, from a single main stem. **2** an ear of grain.

spikelet *n* in botany, any of the small spikes that make up the compound inflorescence of a grass or sedge.

spikenard *n* a fragrant ancient ointment believed to have been derived from an E Indian aromatic plant of the valerian family.

spiky *adj* (**-ier, -iest**) **1** having a sharp projecting point or points. **2** *informal* easily upset or annoyed.

spile *n* **1** a spigot or plug. **2** *NAm* a spout inserted in a tree to draw off sap.

spill[1] *v* (*past tense and past part.* **spilt** *or* **spilled**) **1** to cause or allow (usu liquid) to run out of a container so as to be lost or wasted, *esp* accidentally. **2** to cause (blood) to be shed. **3a** to flow or empty out of something. **b** to spread beyond a limit; to overflow. **4** *informal* to let (information) out; to divulge or disclose (it). ✱ **spill the beans** *informal* to divulge information, *esp* indiscreetly. ⯮ **spillage** *n,* **spiller** *n.*

spill[2] *n* **1** a quantity spilt. **2** a fall from a horse or vehicle.

spill[3] *n* a thin twist of paper or sliver of wood used for lighting a fire, pipe, etc.

spillikin *n* (*in pl, used as sing.*) a game in which a set of thin rods or straws is allowed to fall in a heap with each player in turn trying to remove them one at a time without disturbing the rest.

spillway *n* a passage for surplus water from a dam.

spilt *v* past tense and past part. of SPILL[1].

spin[1] *v* (**spinning,** *past tense and past part.* **spun**) **1a** to revolve rapidly; to whirl. **b** of wheels: to revolve rapidly without gripping, e.g. in mud or wet grass. **c** of a ball: to revolve in the air and deviate from a straight line on bouncing. **d** to have the sensation of spinning; to reel. **2a** to draw out and twist fibre into yarn or thread. **b** of a spider, silkworm, or insect: to form (e.g. a web) by extruding a sticky rapidly hardening liquid in threads. **3** to spin-dry (clothes). **4** to compose and tell (a usu long involved tale). **5** *informal* to present (information, news, etc) in a way that creates an impression favourable to a particular political party, politician, etc.

spin[2] *n* **1a** the act or an instance of spinning or twirling. **b** the whirling motion imparted, e.g. to a ball, by spinning. **2** a flight condition in which an aircraft stalls and plunges steeply downwards out of control rotating as it goes. **3** *informal* a particular interpretation or slant given to a proposal, policy, piece of information, etc; *esp* a favourable interpretation given by a spin doctor. **4** *informal* a short excursion, *esp* by motor vehicle. ✱ **in a spin** *informal* in a state of mental confusion; in a panic. ⯮ **spinning** *n and adj.*

spina bifida *n* a congenital defect in the formation of the spine allowing the membranes surrounding the spinal cord to protrude, usu associated with disorder of the nerves supplying the lower part of the body.

spinach *n* a plant of the goosefoot family cultivated for its large dark green edible leaves that are used as a vegetable.

spinach beet *n* a beet cultivated solely for its leaves that resemble spinach in flavour.

spinal *adj* relating to or in the region of the backbone. ➤➤ **spinally** *adv.*

spinal column *n* the elongated structure of bone running the length of the trunk and tail of a vertebrate, which consists of a jointed series of vertebrae and protects the spinal cord; the backbone.

spinal cord *n* the cord of nervous tissue that extends from the brain lengthways along the back, carries impulses to and from the brain, and serves as a centre for initiating and coordinating many reflex actions.

spinal tap *n NAm* a lumbar puncture.

spindle *n* **1** a round stick with tapered ends used to form and twist the yarn in hand spinning. **2a** a turned often decorative piece, e.g. in a baluster. **b** = NEWEL. **3** a pin or axis about which something turns.

spindleshanks *pl n informal, dated* **1** long thin legs. **2** (*used as sing.*) a person with long thin legs.

spindly *adj* (**-ier, -iest**) having an unnaturally tall or slender appearance, *esp* suggestive of physical weakness.

spin doctor *n informal* somebody who ensures that the media report political events and policies in a way favourable to a particular politician or party.

spin-drier *or* **spin-dryer** *n* a machine for spin-drying clothes.

spindrift *n* sea spray.

spin-dry *v* (**-ies, -ied**) to remove water by placing (wet laundry) in a rapidly rotating drum.

spin-dryer *n* see SPIN-DRIER.

spine *n* **1a** = SPINAL COLUMN. **b** something constituting a central axis or chief support. **c** the back of a book, usu lettered with the title and author's name. **2** a stiff pointed plant part. **3** a sharp rigid part of an animal or fish. ➤➤ **spined** *adj.*

spine-chiller *n* a book, film, etc that is terrifying in a sinister way.

spine-chilling *adj* causing fear or terror.

spinel *n* a colourless to ruby-red or black oxide of magnesium and aluminium used as a gem.

spineless *adj* **1a** having no spinal column; invertebrate. **b** lacking strength of character. **2** free from spines, thorns, or prickles. ➤➤ **spinelessly** *adv,* **spinelessness** *n.*

spinet *n* a small harpsichord that has the strings at an angle to the keyboard.

spine-tingling *adj informal* causing pleasurable nervous excitement; thrilling.

spinifex *n* an Australian grass with spiny seeds or stiff sharp leaves.

spinnaker *n* a large triangular sail set forward of a yacht's mast and used when running before the wind.

spinner *n* **1** somebody or something that spins. **2** a fisherman's lure that revolves when drawn through the water. **3** in cricket, a bowler who spins the ball, or a ball delivered with spin.

spinneret *n* **1** an organ, *esp* of a spider or caterpillar, for producing threads of silk from the secretion of silk glands. **2** a small metal plate or cap with fine holes through which a chemical solution, e.g. of cellulose, is forced in the spinning of man-made filaments.

spinney *n* (*pl* **-eys**) *Brit* a small wood with undergrowth.

spinning jenny *n* an early multiple-spindle machine for spinning wool or cotton.

spinning wheel *n* a small domestic machine for spinning yarn or thread by means of a spindle driven by a hand- or foot-operated wheel.

spin-off *n* **1** a by-product. **2** something which is a further development of some idea or product.

spin out *v* **1** to cause to last longer, *esp* by thrift. **2** to extend or prolong.

spinster *n* an unmarried woman, *esp* a woman who is past the usual age for marrying or who seems unlikely to marry. ➤➤ **spinsterhood** *n,* **spinsterish** *adj.*

spiny *adj* (**-ier, -iest**) **1** covered or armed with spines, prickles, or thorns. **2** *informal* full of difficulties or annoyances; puzzling. ➤➤ **spininess** *n.*

spiny anteater *n* = ECHIDNA.

spiracle *n* a breathing orifice, e.g. the blowhole of a whale or a tracheal opening in an insect. ➤➤ **spiracular** *adj.*

spiraea (*NAm* **spirea**) *n* a plant or shrub of the rose family with small white or pink flowers in dense clusters.

spiral[1] *adj* winding round a centre or pole in a continuous curve and either gradually approaching or receding, or remaining at a constant distance from it. ➤➤ **spirally** *adv.*

spiral[2] *n* **1a** a spiral curve, object, or pattern. **b** a single turn or coil in a spiral object. **2** a continuously expanding and accelerating increase or decrease.

spiral[3] *v* (**spiralled, spiralling,** *NAm* **spiraled, spiraling**) **1** to go, *esp* to rise, in a spiral course. **2** to increase or decrease at a continuously expanding and accelerating rate.

spiral binding *n* a book or notebook binding in which a continuous spiral wire or plastic strip is passed through holes along one edge. ➤➤ **spiral-bound** *adj.*

spire *n* a tall slim structure that tapers to a point on top of a tower. ➤➤ **spired** *adj,* **spiry** *adj.*

spirea *n NAm* see SPIRAEA.

spirit[1] *n* **1a** the immaterial intelligent or conscious part of a person. **b** the soul. **2a** a supernatural being. **b** a ghost. **c** (**the Spirit**) the Holy Spirit. **3** (*in pl*) temper or state of mind, *esp* when lively or excited. **4** liveliness, energy, or courage in a person or their actions. **5a** the prevailing character, attitude, or feeling in somebody or something. **b** the true meaning of something, e.g. a law, in contrast to a literal interpretation of it. **6a** (*also in pl*) distilled liquor of high alcoholic content, e.g. whisky or gin. **b** (*also in pl*) a readily vaporizing liquid obtained by distillation. ✱ **in spirit** sympathetically involved in an event or situation if not actually present. ➤➤ **spiritless** *adj.*

spirit[2] *v* (**spirited, spiriting**) (*often* + away) to carry off, *esp* secretly or mysteriously.

spirited *adj* **1** full of energy, animation, or courage. **2** (*usu used in combinations*) having the frame of mind specified: *low-spirited.* ➤➤ **spiritedly** *adv,* **spiritedness** *n.*

spirit gum *n* a solution, e.g. of gum arabic in ether, used by actors for attaching false hair to the skin.

spirit lamp *n* a lamp in which a vaporizing liquid fuel, e.g. methylated spirits, is burned.

spirit level *n* a device that uses the position of a bubble in a curved transparent tube of liquid to indicate whether a surface is level.

spiritous *adj* see SPIRITUOUS.

spiritual[1] *adj* **1** relating to the spirit and higher consciousness, as distinct from body and nature; non-corporeal. **2a** relating to religious matters or values. **b** ecclesiastical rather than lay or temporal. **3** based on or related through sympathy of thought or feeling. ⯮ **spiritualize** *v,* **spiritually** *adv.*

spiritual[2] *n* a usu emotional religious song of a kind developed among black Christians in the southern USA.

spiritualism *n* a belief that spirits of the dead communicate with the living, *esp* through a medium or at a séance. ⯮ **spiritualist** *n,* **spiritualistic** *adj.*

spirituality *n* **1** sensitivity or attachment to religious values. **2** a practice of personal devotion and prayer.

spirituous *or* **spiritous** *adj formal or archaic* containing or impregnated with alcohol obtained by distillation.

spirogyra *n* a freshwater green alga whose cells contain spiral chlorophyll bands.

spirometer *n* an instrument for measuring the air entering and leaving the lungs. ⯮ **spirometry** *n.*

spirt[1] *v* see SPURT[1].

spirt[2] *n* see SPURT[2].

spit[1] *v* (**spitting,** *past tense and past part.* **spat** *or* **spit**) **1a** to eject saliva from the mouth, often as an expression of aversion or contempt. **b** to eject (e.g. food) from the mouth. **2** of a cat: to make a characteristic rasping noise to show hostility. **3** to rain very lightly. **4** to sputter. **5** (*often* + out) to utter (words) or express (feelings) vehemently or with a spitting sound. ✱ **spit chips** *Aus, informal* to be very angry. **spit it out** (*usu in imperative*) to say what is on one's mind without further delay. ⯮ **spitter** *n.*

spit[2] *n* **1** spittle or saliva. **2** the act of spitting. **3** = SPITTING IMAGE.

spit[3] *n* **1** a slender pointed rod for holding meat over a source of heat, e.g. an open fire. **2** an elongated often hooked strip of sand or shingle extending from the coast.

spit[4] *v* (**spitted, spitting**) to fix (meat) on a spit; to impale.

spit and polish *n* extreme attention to cleanliness and orderliness.

spit-and-sawdust *adj Brit* of a pub: with very basic, unsmart, and usu old-fashioned facilities.

spite[1] *n* petty ill will or malice. ✱ **in spite of** regardless of; in defiance or contempt of. **in spite of oneself** in spite of one's intentions, wishes, character, etc. ⯮ **spiteful** *adj,* **spitefully** *adv,* **spitefulness** *n.*

spite[2] *v* to annoy or hinder out of spite.

spitfire *n* a quick-tempered or volatile person.

spitting cobra *n* either of two venomous African snakes that eject their venom towards the victim without striking.

spitting image *n* (**the spitting image**) the exact likeness.

spittle *n* **1** saliva ejected from the mouth. **2** a frothy secretion exuded by some insects.

spittoon *n* a receptacle for spit.

spit up *v informal esp* of a baby: to vomit.

spitz *n* a dog of a stocky heavy-coated breed with a pointed muzzle and ears.

spiv *n Brit, informal* a slick individual who lives by sharp practice or petty fraud; *specif* a black marketeer operating after World War II. ⯮ **spivvy** *adj.*

splash[1] *v* **1a** to fall into or move through a liquid causing it to fly up and scatter in drops. **b** to scatter (a liquid), or be scattered, in large drops or considerable quantities. **c** to make wet by splashing with a liquid. **2** to display prominently; *specif* to print (an item) in a conspicuous position in a newspaper or magazine. **3** *chiefly Brit* (*usu* + out) to spend money liberally.

splash[2] *n* **1** the action or sound of splashing. **2a** a spot or daub from splashed liquid. **b** a usu vivid patch of colour or of something coloured. **3** a small but usu significant amount of liquid; a dash. **4** *informal* a conspicuously featured item in a newspaper or magazine. ✱ **make a splash** to attract attention or make a vivid impression. ⯮ **splashy** *adj.*

splashback *n* a panel or screen, e.g. behind a sink or cooker, to protect the wall from splashes.

splash down *v* of a spacecraft: to land in the ocean. ⯮ **splashdown** *n.*

splat[1] *n* a single flat often ornamental piece of wood forming the centre of a chair back.

splat[2] *n* a splattering sound, as of the impact when something falls and is flattened. ⯮ **splat** *adv.*

splatter[1] *v* **1** to spatter heavy drops of. **2** to fall in heavy drops.

splatter[2] *n* a splash of something in heavy drops.

splatter movie *n informal* a film in which many people die in gruesome ways.

splay[1] *v* **1** to spread or open out, *esp* in a V or fan shape. **2** to make (e.g. the edges of an opening) slanting.

splay[2] *adj* turned outwards.

splay[3] *n* **1** a slope or bevel, *esp* of the sides of a door or window. **2** a spread or expansion.

splayfoot *n* a foot abnormally flattened and spread out. ⯮ **splayfoot** *adj,* **splayfooted** *adj.*

spleen *n* **1** a ductless organ near the stomach or intestine of most vertebrates that is concerned in the final destruction of blood cells, storage of blood, and production of lymphocytes. **2** bad temper; spite. ⯮ **spleenful** *adj.*

splendid *adj* **1a** magnificent or sumptuous. **b** shining or brilliant. **2** illustrious or distinguished. **3** of the best or most enjoyable kind; excellent. ⯮ **splendidly** *adv,* **splendidness** *n.*

splendiferous *adj informal, humorous* = SPLENDID. ⯮ **splendiferously** *adv,* **splendiferousness** *n.*

splendour (*NAm* **splendor**) *n* **1** great brightness or lustre; brilliance. **2** grandeur or pomp.

splenetic *adj* bad tempered or spiteful. ⯮ **splenetically** *adv.*

splenic *adj* relating to or in the region of the spleen.

splice[1] *v* **1a** to join (e.g. ropes) by interweaving the strands. **b** to unite (e.g. film, magnetic tape, or timber) by overlapping the ends or binding with adhesive tape. **2** *Brit, informal* (*usu in passive*) to unite (two people) in marriage. ✱ **splice the mainbrace** to serve rum on a ship. ⯮ **splicer** *n.*

splice[2] *n* **1** a joining or joint made by splicing. **2** a wedge-shaped projection on a cricket-bat handle that is fitted into the blade.

spliff *n slang* a marijuana cigarette; a joint.

spline *n* **1** a thin wood or metal strip used in building construction. **2** a piece or ridge that prevents a shaft from turning freely in a surrounding tubular part but usu allows lengthways motion. ⯮ **splined** *adj.*

splint[1] *n* **1** a device used to protect and immobilize a body part, e.g. a broken arm. **2** a thin strip of wood suitable for interweaving, e.g. into baskets. **3** a thin strip of wood used for lighting a fire.

splint² *v* to support and immobilize (e.g. a broken arm) with a splint.

splinter¹ *n* a sharp thin piece, *esp* of wood or glass, split or broken off lengthways. ⋙ **splintery** *adj.*

splinter² *v* **1** to split into long thin pieces; to shatter. **2** to split (e.g. a group or party) into parts or factions.

splinter group *n* a small group or faction broken away from a parent organization.

split¹ *v* (**splitting,** *past tense and past part.* **split**) **1** to divide lengthways, usu along a grain or seam or by layers; *broadly* to divide or separate. **2** to separate (constituent parts) by putting something in between. **3** to break apart; to burst or rupture. **4** to subject (an atom or atomic nucleus) to artificial disintegration, *esp* by fission. **5** to divide (something) between people; to share (it). **6** to divide (e.g. a political party) into opposing factions, parties, or groups. **7** (*often* + up) to sever relations or connections. **8** *informal* to leave, *esp* hurriedly or abruptly. **9** *Brit, informal* (*often* + on) to let out a secret; to act as an informer. ✻ **split hairs** to make oversubtle or trivial distinctions. **split one's sides** to laugh heartily. **split the difference** to compromise by taking the average of two amounts. ⋙ **splitter** *n.*

split² *n* **1** a narrow break made by splitting; a tear or crack. **2a** a division into divergent or antagonistic groups or elements; a breach. **b** the act or an instance of splitting. **3** (**the splits**) the act of lowering oneself to the floor or leaping into the air with the legs extended on each side at right angles to the trunk. **4** a sweet dish composed of a sliced fruit, *esp* a banana, filled with ice cream, syrup, etc. **5** a small bottle of wine, mineral water, tonic water, etc.

split end *n* (*usu in pl*) an end of a human hair that has split into two or more strands.

split infinitive *n* an infinitive with a word, usu an adverb, between *to* and the verb, as in *to fully agree.*

Usage note

To split an infinitive is to put a word or phrase, usually an adverb, between *to* and the verb: *to boldly go* or *to more than double.* This is not a grammatical error, but the practice is strongly disliked by many people and can be stylistically awkward. It is usually possible and preferable to place the adverb after the verb: *to travel hopefully.* There are, however, occasions when repositioning the adverb alters the sense. Compare *I really want you to try* with *I want you to really try.* In such cases it is better to split an infinitive than to misrepresent your sense or create an awkward sentence.

split-level *adj* **1** of a room, house, etc: divided so that the floor level in one part is less than a full storey higher than an adjoining part. **2** of a cooker: divided so that the hob and the oven are separate units. ⋙ **split-level** *n.*

split pea *n* a dried pea in which the cotyledons are usu split apart.

split personality *n* a personality with two or more internally consistent groups of behaviour tendencies each acting more or less independently of the other.

split pin *n* a strip of metal folded double that can be used as a fastener by inserting it through a hole and then bending back the ends.

split ring *n* a metal ring of two flat turns on which keys may be kept.

split screen *n* the display of two images simultaneously on a film, television, or computer screen.

split second *n* a fractional part of a second; a flash. ⋙ **split-second** *adj.*

splitting *adj* causing a piercing sensation: *a splitting headache.*

splodge¹ *n Brit, informal* a splotch or blot.

splodge² *v Brit, informal* to mark with a large irregular blot. ⋙ **splodgy** *adj.*

splosh¹ *v informal* to splash.

splosh² *n informal* = SPLASH².

splotch¹ *n informal* a large irregular spot or smear; a blotch. ⋙ **splotchy** *adj.*

splotch² *v informal* to mark with a splotch or splotches.

splurge¹ *n informal* **1a** a large amount of something used extravagantly or ostentatiously. **b** an ostentatious display of something. **2** an extravagant spending spree.

splurge² *v informal* **1** to make a splurge. **2** (*often* + on) to spend money extravagantly.

splutter¹ *v* **1** to spit out bits of food, saliva, etc noisily, e.g. when choking or laughing. **2** to speak hastily and confusedly. ⋙ **splutterer** *n,* **spluttering** *adj,* **spluttery** *adj.*

splutter² *n* a spluttering sound.

spoil¹ *v* (*past tense and past part.* **spoilt** *or* **spoiled**) **1a** to damage seriously; to ruin. **b** to impair the enjoyment of. **c** to fill in (e.g. a voting paper) wrongly so as to render invalid. **2a** to impair the character of (somebody) by overindulgence. **b** to treat (somebody) indulgently; to pamper (them). **3** to become unfit for use or consumption, usu as a result of decay. ✻ **be spoilt for choice** *Brit* to have so many choices that one cannot decide. **spoiling for a fight** having an eager desire for a fight. ⋙ **spoilage** *n.*

spoil² *n* **1** (*usu in pl*) plunder taken from an enemy in war or a victim in robbery; loot. **2** earth and rock excavated or dredged.

spoiler *n* **1** a long narrow plate along the upper surface of an aircraft wing that may be raised for reducing lift and increasing drag. **2** an air deflector at the front or rear of a motor vehicle to reduce the tendency to lift off the road at high speeds. **3** somebody or something that spoils, *esp* a story published in a newspaper to spoil another paper's sales.

spoilsport *n* somebody who spoils the fun of others.

spoilt *v* past tense and past part. of SPOIL¹.

spoke¹ *v* past tense of SPEAK.

spoke² *n* **1** any of the small radiating bars inserted in the hub of a wheel to support the rim. **2** any of the protruding knobs around the circumference of a ship's steering wheel. ✻ **put a spoke in somebody's wheel** to prevent somebody's plans from succeeding.

spoken¹ *adj* **1a** delivered by word of mouth; oral. **b** used in speaking or conversation; uttered. **2** (*used in combinations*) characterized by speaking in a specified manner.

spoken² *v* past part. of SPEAK.

spoken-for *adj* reserved or taken; *specif* engaged to be married.

spokeshave *n* a plane with a blade set between two handles, used for shaping curved surfaces.

spokesman *or* **spokeswoman** *n* (*pl* **spokesmen** *or* **spokeswomen**) somebody who speaks on behalf of somebody else or a group of people.

spokesperson *n* (*pl* **spokespersons** *or* **spokespeople**) a spokesman or spokeswoman.

spokeswoman *n* see SPOKESMAN.

spoliation *n* **1** the act of plundering. **2** the act of damaging or injuring, *esp* irreparably. ⋙ **spoliator** *n.*

spondee *n* a metrical foot consisting of two long or stressed syllables. ⋙ **spondaic** *adj.*

spondulicks *pl n Brit, informal* funds or money.

spondylitis *n* inflammation of the spinal vertebrae.

sponge[1] *n* **1** an elastic porous mass of interlacing horny fibres that forms the internal skeleton of various marine animals and is able when wetted to absorb water. **2a** a piece of sponge, e.g. for cleaning. **b** a porous rubber or cellulose product used as a sponge. **c** a piece of sponge used with spermicide as a barrier contraceptive. **3** an aquatic invertebrate animal that lives in colonies, permanently attached to underwater objects. **4** a sponge cake or sponge pudding. **5** *informal* a sponger.

sponge[2] *v* **1** (*often* + down/off) to clean, wipe, or moisten with a sponge. **2** (*often* + out) to erase or destroy with or as if with a sponge. **3** *informal* (*often* + on/off) to obtain *esp* money by exploiting people's natural generosity or organized welfare facilities. ➤➤ **spongeable** *adj.*

sponge bag *n Brit* a small waterproof bag for holding toilet articles.

sponge cake *n* a light sweet cake made with approximately equal quantities of sugar, flour, and eggs but no shortening.

sponge pudding *n Brit* a sweet steamed or baked pudding made with sugar, flour, and eggs.

sponger *n* somebody who lives off others, *esp* by exploiting their natural generosity.

spongiform *adj* resembling a sponge in appearance or texture.

spongy *adj* (**-ier, -iest**) resembling a sponge, *esp* in being soft, porous, absorbent, or moist. ➤➤ **sponginess** *n.*

sponsor[1] *n* **1** a person or organization that pays for a project or activity, e.g.: **a** somebody who pays towards the cost of a cultural or sporting event. **b** somebody who contributes to a charity by giving money for a participant's efforts in an organized fund-raising event. **c** *chiefly NAm* somebody who pays the cost of a radio or television programme, usu in return for limited advertising time during its course. **2** a person who presents a candidate for baptism; a godparent. **3** somebody who introduces and supports a bill, motion, etc in parliament. **4** somebody who assumes responsibility for some other person or thing. ➤➤ **sponsorial** *adj,* **sponsorship** *n.*

sponsor[2] *v* to be or stand as sponsor for.

spontaneous *adj* **1** proceeding from innate tendency, natural feeling or sudden impulse without external constraint. **2** by nature unconstrained or uninhibited. **3** developing without apparent external influence or cause. ➤➤ **spontaneity** *n,* **spontaneously** *adv,* **spontaneousness** *n.*

spontaneous combustion *n* self-ignition of combustible material through chemical action, e.g. oxidation, of its constituents.

spoof[1] *n informal* **1** a light, humorous, but usu telling parody. **2** a hoax or deception.

spoof[2] *v informal* **1** to make good-natured fun of. **2** to deceive or hoax.

spook[1] *n* **1** *informal* a ghost or spectre. **2** *chiefly NAm* = SPY[2].

spook[2] *v* to make frightened or frantic; *esp* to startle into violent activity.

spooky *adj* (**-ier, -iest**) *informal* causing irrational fear, *esp* because suggestive of supernatural presences; eerie. ➤➤ **spookily** *adv,* **spookiness** *n.*

spool[1] *n* a cylindrical device with a rim at each end on which thread, wire, tape, etc is wound.

spool[2] *v* **1** to wind (e.g. yarn or film) onto a spool. **2** to be wound onto or off a spool.

spool[3] *v* in computing, to transfer (data intended for a peripheral device) to an intermediate store, e.g. for output at a later time.

spoon[1] *n* an eating, cooking, or serving implement consisting of a small shallow bowl with a handle. ➤➤ **spoonful** *n.*

spoon[2] *v* **1** to take up and usu transfer (e.g. a liquid) in a spoon. **2** to propel (a ball) weakly upwards. **3** *dated, informal* to indulge in caressing and amorous talk.

spoonbill *n* a wading bird with a bill that is greatly expanded and flattened at the tip.

spoonerism *n* a transposition of the initial sounds or letters of two or more words, e.g. in *tons of soil* for *sons of toil*.

spoon-feed *v* **1** to feed by means of a spoon. **2** to present e.g. information or entertainment to (somebody) in an easily assimilable form that precludes independent thought or critical judgment.

spoor *n* a track, a trail, or droppings, *esp* of a wild animal.

sporadic *adj* occurring occasionally or in scattered instances. ➤➤ **sporadically** *adv.*

sporangium *n* (*pl* **sporangia**) a case or cell within which asexual spores are produced. ➤➤ **sporangial** *adj.*

spore *n* a primitive hardy reproductive body, usu with a single cell, produced by plants, algae, fungi, protozoans, bacteria, etc. ➤➤ **spored** *adj,* **sporiferous** *adj.*

sporran *n* a leather pouch worn hanging in front of the kilt with men's traditional Highland dress.

sport[1] *n* **1** (*often used in pl before another noun*) an activity or game requiring physical skill and having a set of rules, engaged in either individually or as a team for exercise or recreation or as a profession. **2** such activities collectively. **3** a person who is a good loser, generous-minded, and does not mind being laughed at. **4a** entertainment or pleasure, *esp* from a sport such as hunting. **b** *archaic* a source of pleasure or amusement. **5** *Aus, NZ, informal* used as a form of familiar address, chiefly to men. **6** a biological individual exhibiting a sudden deviation from type beyond the normal limits of variation, usu as a result of mutation; a freak of nature. ✱ **the sport of kings** horse racing. ➤➤ **sportful** *adj,* **sportfully** *adv,* **sportfulness** *n.*

sport[2] *v* **1** to wear (something, *esp* something distinctive). **2** *literary* to play about happily; to frolic. ➤➤ **sporter** *n.*

sporting *adj* **1** concerned with sport. **2** fond of or taking part in sports. **3** like a good sport; generous-minded. ✱ **a sporting chance** a reasonable chance of success, victory, or recovery. ➤➤ **sportingly** *adv.*

sportive *adj literary* frolicsome; playful. ➤➤ **sportively** *adv,* **sportiveness** *n.*

sports bar *n* a public bar where customers can watch non-stop televised sport.

sports car *n* a low fast motor car, usu having seats for two people.

sports coat *n NAm* = SPORTS JACKET.

sports jacket *n* a man's jacket for informal wear, usu made of tweed or other thick fabric.

sportsman *or* **sportswoman** *n* (*pl* **sportsmen** *or* **sportswomen**) **1** a man or woman who engages in sports. **2** a man or woman who is fair, a good loser, and a gracious winner. ➤➤ **sportsmanlike** *adj,* **sportsmanly** *adj,* **sportsmanship** *n.*

sportsperson *n* (*pl* **sportspeople** *or* **sportspersons**) a sportsman or sportswoman.

sportster *n* a sports car.

sportswear *n* clothes worn for sport or for casual wear, *esp* out of doors.

sportswoman *n* see SPORTSMAN.

sporty *adj* (**-ier, -iest**) **1** of a person: fond of sport and athletic activities. **2** of clothes: designed for sporting activities or casual wear. **3** of a car: like a sports car in appearance or performance. ➤➤ **sportily** *adv*, **sportiness** *n*.

sporule *n* a very small spore.

spot[1] *n* **1** a small roundish area different in colour or texture from the surrounding surface. **2** a dirty mark; a small stain. **3** a pimple or any small red blemish on the skin. **4** *chiefly Brit, informal* a small amount; a bit. **5** a place or area. **6** (*used before a noun*) denoting a system of trading in which goods are paid for and delivered immediately after sale. **7** a place allocated to a person on a broadcast programme or show; = SLOT[1] (2). **8** = SPOTLIGHT[1] (1). **9** (**the spot**) in football, = PENALTY SPOT. ✱ **change one's spots** (*usu in negative contexts*) to alter one's character for the better. **hit the spot** *esp* of food or drink: to be just what one requires. **in a spot/in a tight spot** *informal* in difficulties. **on the spot 1** immediately. **2** at the place of action. **3** in one place, without progressing. **put somebody on the spot** to place somebody in a situation where they must react appropriately without being fully prepared.

spot[2] *v* (**spotted, spotting**) **1** to notice or detect. **2** to single out or identify (somebody or something promising). **3** to watch for and record the sighting of (wildlife species, trains, etc). **4** to mark (a material, etc) with spots. **5** *chiefly Brit* (*with 'it' as subject*) to fall lightly in scattered drops. ➤➤ **spottable** *adj*, **spotted** *adj*.

spot check *n* a random check made to test overall quality, accuracy, etc.

spot-check *v* to sample or investigate on the spot and usu at random.

spot kick *n* in football, a penalty kick.

spotless *adj* **1** free from dirt or stains; immaculate. **2** pure or unblemished. ➤➤ **spotlessly** *adv*, **spotlessness** *n*.

spotlight[1] *n* **1** a lamp projecting a narrow intense beam of light focused on and brightly illuminating *esp* an actor on stage. **2** (**the spotlight**) full public attention.

spotlight[2] *v* (**spotlighting,** *past tense and past part.* **spotlighted** *or* **spotlit**) **1** to illuminate by focusing a spotlight on. **2** to direct public attention towards.

spot-on *or* **spot on** *adj Brit, informal* **1** absolutely correct or accurate. **2** exactly right. ➤➤ **spot on** *adv*.

spotted dick *n Brit* a steamed or boiled sweet suet pudding containing dried fruit, *esp* currants.

spotted dog *n* **1** = DALMATIAN (1). **2** = SPOTTED DICK.

spotted fever *n* a bacterial infection transmitted by ticks, accompanied by a fever and skin rash.

spotter *n* **1** (*used in combinations*) **a** a person who makes a hobby of watching for and recording the occurrence of things of a certain class. **b** a person on the lookout for a certain thing. **2** (*often used before a noun*) a pilot or aircraft detailed to spot enemy positions.

spotty *adj* (**-ier, -iest**) **1a** marked with spots. **b** of a person or a part of the body: having spots. **2** *chiefly NAm* lacking evenness or regularity, *esp* in quality. ➤➤ **spottily** *adv*, **spottiness** *n*.

spot-weld *v* to join together (metal parts) with small circular welds, executed at scattered points.

spousal *adj chiefly NAm or archaic or literary* relating to marriage or to a spouse. ➤➤ **spousally** *adv*.

spouse *n* a married person; a husband or wife.

spout[1] *v* **1** to eject (liquid, etc) or be forced out in a copious stream. **2** *informal* **a** to speak or utter (*esp* something platitudinous) in a strident or pompous manner. **b** to declaim or recite (poetry, etc). ➤➤ **spouter** *n*.

spout[2] *n* **1** a projecting tube, e.g. on a teapot or kettle, or lip, e.g. on a jug, to facilitate pouring. **2** a downpipe conveying water from a roof gutter. **3** a chute for conveying grain. **4** a forceful gush or jet of liquid. ✱ **up the spout 1** *informal* ruined; scuppered. **2** *informal* of a woman: pregnant. ➤➤ **spouted** *adj*, **spoutless** *adj*.

sprain[1] *v* to wrench or twist (a joint) violently so as to stretch or tear the ligaments and cause swelling and bruising.

sprain[2] *n* **1** the act or an instance of spraining a joint. **2** a sprained condition.

sprang *v* past tense of SPRING[1].

sprat *n* **1** a small sea fish of the herring family; = BRISLING. **2** *informal* any young or small fish, *esp* a herring. ✱ **a sprat to catch a mackerel** *Brit* a small outlay made, or minor risk taken, in the hope of attracting a major catch.

sprawl[1] *v* **1** to lie or sit with arms and legs spread out carelessly or awkwardly. **2** to spread or develop irregularly over a landscape, etc. ➤➤ **sprawling** *adj*, **sprawlingly** *adv*, **sprawly** *adj*.

sprawl[2] *n* **1** a sprawling position. **2** an irregular spreading mass or group.

spray[1] *v* **1** to discharge or apply (a fluid) as a spray. **2** to direct a spray of something onto (a surface) or throughout (a place). **3** of a male cat: to mark out its territory by urinating throughout (an area). ➤➤ **sprayer** *n*.

spray[2] *n* **1** fine droplets of water blown or falling through the air. **2** a jet of vapour or finely divided liquid. **3** a device, e.g. an aerosol or hose attachment, by which liquid is discharged or applied in a spray. **4** a substance, e.g. paint or insecticide, for spraying.

spray[3] *n* **1** a flowering branch or shoot of a plant. **2** a bouquet of cut flowers and foliage.

spray gun *n* an apparatus resembling a gun for dispensing a substance, e.g. paint or insecticide, in the form of a spray.

spread[1] *v* (**spreading,** *past tense and past part.* **spread**) **1** (*often* + out) to open or extend (something contracted or folded). **2a** to distribute (something) over an area. **b** to be distributed over, or cover, an ever-widening area. **3** (*often* + with) to cover (a surface) with an even layer of something. **4** (*often* + out) to divide out (work, etc) over a period or among a number of people. **5** to communicate (something), or be communicated, to an ever-widening group. ✱ **spread oneself too thin** to divide oneself between too many jobs or activities, so that one does nothing effectively. ➤➤ **spreadability** *n*, **spreadable** *adj*.

spread[2] *n* **1** the distribution or expansion of something, or the extent of this. **2a** the distance between two points; a gap or span. **b** a range of things. **3** the two facing pages forming an opening in a newspaper or magazine, or the matter occupying these pages, *esp* if continuous across the fold. **4** *NAm, dialect* a ranch. **5** a food product designed to be spread, e.g. on bread or biscuits. **6** *informal* a sumptuous meal; a feast.

spread betting *n* the laying of bets on the number of points, etc to be scored, rather than on the simple outcome of a contest, winnings being calculated according to the margin of difference between the spread of points quoted by the bookmaker and those represented in the result.

spread-eagle *v* to cause (somebody) to be stretched out with the arms and legs at an angle to the trunk.

spreader *n* any device for spreading something, e.g. a machine for distributing manure over an area, or for keeping things apart, e.g. a bar on which to space out the parallel wires of a multiwire antenna.

spreadsheet *n* a software system in which large groups of numerical data can be displayed on a VDU in a set format, e.g. in rows and columns, and rapid automatic calculations and adjustments can be made.

spree *n* (*used in combinations*) a bout of unrestrained indulgence in an activity.

sprezzatura *n* a deliberately cultivated appearance of well-bred insouciance or *esp*, in artistic or literary performance, of careless assurance.

sprig[1] *n* **1** a small shoot or twig. **2** an ornament in the form of a sprig, *esp* a moulded decoration for applying to a pot before firing. **3** a small headless nail. **4** *chiefly derog, informal* a young offspring; *specif* a youth. ➤➤ **spriggy** *adj.*

sprig[2] *v* (**sprigged, sprigging**) to decorate (pottery) with sprigs. ➤➤ **sprigger** *n.*

sprightly *or* **spritely** *adj* (**-ier, -iest**) usu of an elderly person: full of vitality and liveliness; spirited. ➤➤ **sprightliness** *n.*

spring[1] *v* (**springing,** *past tense* **sprang,** *past part.* **sprung**) **1** to move suddenly with a jumping action; to dart or bound. **2** to move by elastic force. **3** (*often* + up) of plants or buildings: to appear suddenly. **4** (*usu* + from) to appear suddenly or unexpectedly. **5** (*usu* + from) to originate or arise. **6** to cause (something with a spring mechanism) to operate. **7** (*usu in passive*) to provide (furniture, etc) with springs, or impart elasticity to (a wooden floor). **8** to cause (a game bird) to rise from cover. **9** *informal* to contrive the release or escape of (a prisoner). ✻ **spring something/a surprise on somebody** to amaze somebody with unexpected news.

spring[2] *n* **1** a source of supply; *esp* a source of water issuing from the ground. **2** the season of new growth between winter and summer, in the N hemisphere the months of March, April, and May. **3** a mechanical part, e.g. of bent or coiled metal, that recovers its original shape when released after deformation. **4** capacity for springing; resilience or bounce. **5** a jump or bound. ➤➤ **springless** *adj,* **springlike** *adj.*

spring balance *n* a device using a spiral spring for measuring weight or force.

springboard *n* **1** a flexible board on which a diver or gymnast springs to gain extra height before a dive or vault. **2** something that provides an initial stimulus or impetus.

springbok *n* (*pl* **springboks** *or* **springbok**) **1** a swift and graceful southern African gazelle noted for its habit of springing lightly and suddenly into the air. **2** (*often* **Springbok**) a sportsman or sportswoman representing S Africa in an international match.

spring chicken *n chiefly NAm* a young and tender chicken suitable for the table, orig only available in the spring. ✻ **be no spring chicken** *humorous* said of a person: to be no longer young.

spring-clean *v* to give a thorough cleaning to (a house or furnishings), typically in the springtime. ➤➤ **spring-clean** *n.*

springer *n* = SPRINGER SPANIEL.

springer spaniel *n* a small spaniel that was once used chiefly for finding and flushing small game.

spring fever *n* a feeling of restlessness, excitement, or desire for adventure and novelty, felt in spring.

spring greens *pl n* a young green cabbage that is picked before the heart has fully developed.

spring-loaded *adj* loaded or secured by means of spring tension or compression.

spring onion *n chiefly Brit* an onion with a small mild-flavoured thin-skinned bulb and long green shoots that is chiefly eaten raw in salads.

spring roll *n* in Chinese cuisine, a small thin pancake filled with bamboo shoots, prawns, meat, etc rolled into a cylinder and deep-fried.

spring tide *n* a tide of maximum height occurring at new and full moon.

springtime *n* **1** the season of spring. **2** *literary* one's youth.

springy *adj* (**-ier, -iest**) having an elastic or bouncy quality; resilient. ➤➤ **springily** *adv,* **springiness** *n.*

sprinkle[1] *v* **1** to scatter (a liquid) in fine drops or (a substance) in the form of a powder or fine particles. **2** to scatter a liquid or fine particles over (a surface); to wet (it) slightly. **3** (*usu in passive*) to dot (something) here and there.

sprinkle[2] *n* **1** an instance of sprinkling. **2** a light covering; = SPRINKLING.

sprinkler *n* **1** any of the series of nozzles in a SPRINKLER SYSTEM. **2** an apparatus for watering a lawn by spraying. ➤➤ **sprinklered** *adj.*

sprinkler system *n* a fire-extinguishing system consisting of a series of nozzles installed in the ceilings of a building that release water in response to the presence of smoke or a rise in temperature.

sprinkling *n* a small quantity or number, *esp* falling in scattered drops or particles or distributed randomly.

sprint[1] *v* **1** to run at top speed, *esp* over a short distance in competitive athletics. **2** *informal* to run; to dash. ➤➤ **sprinter** *n,* **sprinting** *n.*

sprint[2] *n* **1** the act or an instance of sprinting. **2** a running race of no more than 400m. **3a** a short fast swimming or cycling race. **b** a burst of speed.

sprit *n* a spar that crosses a four-cornered fore-and-aft sail diagonally to support the peak.

sprite *n* **1** a fairy or elf, *esp* one associated with water. **2** a computer graphic that can be manipulated as a unit on screen.

spritely *adj* see SPRIGHTLY.

spritsail *n* a sail extended by a sprit.

spritz[1] *v* to squirt or spray briefly.

spritz[2] *n* a brief spray or squirt of something.

spritzer *n* a long drink consisting of wine diluted with soda water, sparkling water, or lemonade.

sprocket *n* **1** a tooth or projection on the rim of a wheel, shaped so as to engage the links of a chain. **2** a wheel or cylinder having sprockets, e.g. to engage a bicycle chain.

sprog *n Brit informal* a baby.

sprout[1] *v* **1** of a shoot, etc: to grow or spring up. **2** of a plant: to send out shoots or new growth. **3** to develop or grow (something).

sprout[2] *n* **1** a shoot, e.g. from a seed or root. **2** = BRUSSELS SPROUT.

spruce[1] *n* any of numerous species of evergreen coniferous trees with a conical head of dense foliage and soft light wood.

spruce[2] *adj* neat or smart in dress or appearance; trim. ➤➤ **sprucely** *adv,* **spruceness** *n.*

spruce[3] *v* (+ up) to make (oneself or another person) spruce.

sprue[1] *n* a chronic disease suffered by visitors to the tropics, with diarrhoea, ulceration of the mouth, and other symptoms of food malabsorption and vitamin deficiency.

sprue[2] *n* **1** the hole through which molten metal or plastic enters a mould. **2** a piece of metal or plastic that has solidified in such a hole.

spruik *v Aus, informal* to give a public harangue, e.g. advertising a show. ⋙ **spruiker** *n.*

sprung[1] *v* past part. of SPRING[1].

sprung[2] *adj* fitted with springs, or possessed of springiness.

spry *adj* (**sprier** *or* **spryer, spriest** *or* **spryest**) vigorously active; nimble. ⋙ **spryly** *adv,* **spryness** *n.*

spud[1] *n* **1** *informal* a potato. **2** a small narrow spade.

spud[2] *v* (**spudded, spudding**) **1** to dig up or remove (weeds) with a spud. **2** to begin to drill (an oil well).

spud-bashing *n informal* the peeling of potatoes, *esp* when done as a punishment in a military camp.

spumante *n* any of various white Italian sparkling wines.

spume[1] *n literary* froth or foam. ⋙ **spumous** *adj,* **spumy** *adj.*

spume[2] *v* of a torrent, etc: to foam or froth.

spun *v* past tense and past part. of SPIN[1].

spun glass *n* fibreglass.

spunk *n* **1** *informal* spirit; pluck. **2** *Brit, coarse slang* semen. **3** *Aus, informal* a sexually attractive person. ⋙ **spunkily** *adv,* **spunky** *adj.*

spur[1] *n* **1** a pointed or wheel-shaped metal device secured to the heel of a rider's boot and used to prick the horse's flank in order to urge it on. **2** a goad to action; a stimulus or incentive. **3** something projecting like or suggesting a spur, e.g.: **a** a projecting root or branch of a tree. **b** a fruit-bearing side shoot. **c** a ridge that extends sideways from a mountain or range of mountains. **d** a short length of railway connecting with a major line. **e** a short road connecting with a major route, *esp* a motorway. ✻ **on the spur of the moment** suddenly; on impulse. **win one's spurs** to become recognized as competent in some activity. ⋙ **spurless** *adj.*

spur[2] *v* (**spurred, spurring**) **1** to urge (a horse) on with spurs. **2** (*often* + on) to incite or encourage to make a greater effort.

spurge *n* any of a genus of mostly shrubby plants with a bitter milky juice and greenish flowers.

spur gear *n* a gear wheel with teeth projecting parallel to its axis.

spurious *adj* **1** false; fake; invented. **2** of argument or reasoning: apparently sound but containing flaws.

spurn *v* to reject with disdain. ⋙ **spurner** *n.*

spurt[1] *or* **spirt** *v* **1** to gush out, or cause (a liquid) to gush out, in a jet. **2** to put on speed or increase effort.

spurt[2] *or* **spirt** *n* **1** a sudden forceful gush; a jet. **2** a sudden increase in effort or speed.

spur wheel *n* = SPUR GEAR.

sputa *n* pl of SPUTUM.

sputnik *n* any of a series of artificial satellites put into orbit by the former USSR, *esp* the first of all such satellites, launched in October 1957.

sputter[1] *v* **1** to make explosive popping sounds. **2** to speak in an explosive or incoherent manner. **3** to eject particles of food or saliva noisily from the mouth. ⋙ **sputterer** *n.*

sputter[2] *n* **1** confused and excited speech. **2** the act or an instance of sputtering, or the sound of sputtering.

sputum *n* (*pl* **sputa**) matter, made up of discharges from the respiratory passages and saliva, that is coughed up.

spy[1] *v* (**-ies, -ied**) **1** (*often* + for) to work for a government or other organization by secretly gathering data about enemies or rivals. **2** (+ on) to watch somebody secretly. **3** to catch sight of or spot. **4** (+ out) to find out by spying or observation. ✻ **spy out the land** to investigate how things stand before making any definite move.

spy[2] *n* (*pl* **-ies**) **1** a person who keeps secret watch on somebody or something. **2** a person who attempts to gain information in one country, company, etc and communicate it to another, usu hostile, one.

spyglass *n* a small telescope.

spyhole *n Brit* = PEEPHOLE.

sq. *abbr* square.

SQL *abbr* structured query language, a computer language used in database management and manipulation.

squab *n* **1** a fledgling bird, *esp* a pigeon. **2** *Brit* a thick upholstery cushion for a chair, car seat, etc. ⋙ **squabby** *adj.*

squabble[1] *v* to quarrel noisily, *esp* over trifles. ⋙ **squabbler** *n.*

squabble[2] *n* a noisy quarrel.

squad *n* (*used as sing. or pl*) **1** a small group of military personnel assembled for a purpose. **2** a small group working as a team. **3** a sports team.

squad car *n chiefly NAm* a police car having radio communication with headquarters.

squaddy *or* **squaddie** *n* (*pl* **-ies**) *Brit, informal* a private in the armed forces.

squadron *n* (*used as sing. or pl*) **1** a unit of an air force consisting usu of between 10 and 18 aircraft. **2** a unit of cavalry or of an armoured regiment, usu consisting of three or more troops. **3** a variable naval unit consisting of a number of warships on a particular operation.

squadron leader *n* an officer in the British air force senior in rank to a flight lieutenant, and junior to a wing commander.

squalid *adj* **1** filthy and degraded from neglect or poverty. **2** sordid; disreputable. ⋙ **squalidly** *adv,* **squalidness** *n.*

squall[1] *v* of a baby: to cry raucously; to scream. ⋙ **squaller** *n.*

squall[2] *n* a raucous cry; a scream.

squall[3] *n* **1** a sudden violent wind, often with rain or snow. **2** a short-lived commotion. ⋙ **squally** *adj.*

squalor *n* the quality or state of being squalid.

squamous *or* **squamose** *adj* **1** covered with or consisting of scales; scaly. **2** denoting a surface tissue consisting of a single layer of flat scalelike cells.

squander *v* to waste, dissipate, or misuse (something, e.g. money, time, or talents).

square[1] *n* **1** a plane figure with all four sides equal and four right angles. **2** an open usu four-sided space in a town, formed at the meeting of two or more streets, and often laid out with grass and trees. **3** the drilling area at a military barracks. **4** a closely trimmed area at the centre of a cricket ground, any oblong strip of which may be selected as the wicket. **5** a woman's headscarf. **6** any of the quadrilateral spaces marked out on a board, used for playing games. **7** a T-shaped or L-shaped instrument used to draw, measure, or test right angles. **8** the product of a number multiplied by itself. **9** *informal, dated* a person who is excessively conventional or conservative in tastes or outlook. ✱ **back to/at square one** back where one started without the least progress having been made.

square[2] *adj* **1** having four equal sides and four right angles, or approximating to this shape. **2a** forming a right angle. **b** at right angles. **c** level or parallel. **3** of a shape or build suggesting strength and solidity; broad in relation to length or height. **4** used before a unit of length: denoting an area equal to that of a square whose sides are of the specified unit. **5** placed after a length measurement: denoting the area of a square expanse or object whose sides are of the specified measurement: *ten foot square.* **6** (*usu* **all square**) leaving no balance; settled. **7** in a competition, even, tied. **8** *informal, dated* excessively conservative; dully conventional. ✱ **square peg in a round hole** a person in an environment incompatible with their personality or abilities. ➤➤ **squareness** *n,* **squarish** *adj.*

square[3] *v* **1** (*often* + off) to make square or rectangular. **2** (*often* + off) to mark off (a surface) into squares or rectangles. **3** to adjust (one's shoulders) so as to present a rectangular outline suggestive of resolution or determination. **4** to multiply (a number) by itself. **5** to be or to make compatible with a standard or principle. **6** to be in, or bring into agreement with. **7** to balance or settle (an account). **8** to even the score of (a contest). **9** *informal* to bribe (somebody) into acquiescence. ✱ **square the circle** to contrive something impossible [in reference to the hopeless mathematical task of constructing a square that is exactly equal in area to a given circle using only a ruler and compass]. ➤➤ **squarer** *n.*

square[4] *adv* **1** directly; precisely. **2** so as to face something directly. **3** transversely across a cricket pitch or football field.

square-bashing *n chiefly Brit* military drill, *esp* marching, on a barrack square.

square dance *n* a dance for four couples who form a hollow square. ➤➤ **square dancer** *n,* **square dancing** *n.*

square deal *n* an honest and fair arrangement or transaction.

square-eyed *adj humorous* having developed eyes the shape of a television screen, from too much viewing. ➤➤ **square eyes** *pl n.*

square leg *n* in cricket, a fielding position halfway to the boundary on the leg side, level with the batsman.

squarely *adv* directly, firmly, or unequivocally.

square meal *n* a nutritionally balanced and satisfying meal.

square measure *n* a system of units for measuring areas, or a unit in such a system.

square number *n* a number that is the product of another number multiplied by itself, e.g. 1, 4, 9, 16.

square rig *n* a sailing-ship rig in which the principal sails are set at right angles to the mast and keel. ➤➤ **square-rigged** *adj,* **square-rigger** *n.*

square root *n* the number which, when multiplied by itself, gives the number in question.

square up *v* **1** to settle a bill or pay somebody what one owes them. **2** of opponents: to face each other ready to fight. ✱ **square up to 1** to prepare oneself to meet (a challenge). **2** to assume a fighting stance towards (an opponent).

square wave *n* the rectangular wave form of a quantity that varies periodically and abruptly from one to the other of two constant values.

squash[1] *v* **1** to press or crush into a flat mass. **2** to squeeze or press oneself into a space. **3** to put down (a rebellion, etc); = QUASH. **4** to humiliate or reduce to silence, e.g. with a cutting remark. ➤➤ **squasher** *n,* **squashy** *adj.*

squash[2] *n* **1** the condition of being squashed, e.g. against other people in a crowd. **2** an indoor game played usu by two people in a four-walled court with light long-handled rackets and a small squashy rubber ball that can be played off any wall. **3** *Brit* a soft drink made from the sweetened and concentrated juice of citrus fruits, usu diluted for drinking.

squash[3] *n* (*pl* **squashes** *or* **squash**) any of various types of gourd whose flesh is cooked and eaten as a vegetable.

squash rackets *pl n* (*used as sing.*) = SQUASH[2] (2).

squat[1] *v* (**squatted, squatting**) **1** (*also* + down) to assume a position in which the body is supported on the feet and the knees are bent, so that the haunches rest on or near the heels. **2** to occupy property as a squatter.

squat[2] *n* **1** the posture of a person or animal that squats. **2a** an empty building occupied by or available to squatters. **b** the act or an instance of squatting in an uninhabited building.

squat[3] *adj* (**squatter, squattest**) disproportionately short or low and broad. ➤➤ **squatly** *adv,* **squatness** *n.*

squatter *n* **1** a person who occupies otherwise empty property without rights of ownership or payment of rent. **2** *Aus* a person who owns large tracts of grazing land.

squat thrust *n* a strenuous physical exercise in which one starts in a squatting position and thrusts one's legs out backward at full stretch.

squaw *n offensive* a Native N American woman or wife.

squawk[1] *v* **1** to utter a harsh abrupt scream. **2** *informal* to make a loud or vehement protest. ➤➤ **squawker** *n.*

squawk[2] *n* the act or an instance of squawking.

squawk box *n chiefly NAm, informal* a loudspeaker, *esp* as part of an intercom system.

squeak[1] *v* **1** to utter or make a squeak. **2** *informal* to turn informer; = SQUEAL[1]. **3** (+ through) to pass an examination or otherwise succeed, by the narrowest of margins. ➤➤ **squeaker** *n.*

squeak[2] *n* a short shrill cry or noise. ✱ **a narrow/near squeak** an escape barely managed. **not a squeak** not the slightest sound. ➤➤ **squeakily** *adv,* **squeakiness** *n,* **squeaky** *adj.*

squeaky-clean *adj informal* **1** orig of newly washed hair: so clean that it squeaks when rubbed. **2** absolutely clean. **3** morally unassailable; goody-goody.

squeal[1] *v* **1** to utter or make a squeal. **2** *informal* to turn informer. **3** *informal* to complain or protest. ➤➤ **squealer** *n.*

squeal[2] *n* a shrill sharp cry or noise.

squeamish *adj* **1** easily made to feel faint or nauseous, e.g. at the sight of blood. **2** easily shocked or offended. ➤➤ **squeamishly** *adv,* **squeamishness** *n.*

squeegee[1] *n* (*pl* **squeegees**) a tool with a rubber blade used for spreading liquid on or removing it from a surface, e.g. a window.

squeegee[2] *v* (**squeegees, squeegeed, squeegeeing**) to smooth, wipe, or treat (a surface, etc) with a squeegee.

squeeze[1] *v* **1** to compress *esp* by applying physical pressure to the sides. **2** to extract (liquid, etc) from something by pressure. **3** to force or cram (something, somebody, or oneself) into or through a restricted space. **4** to extract (money or information) from somebody, *esp* by threats or extortion. **5** to cause economic hardship to (a business, etc). **6** (+ in/into) to fit (a person or task) into a tight schedule. **7** (+ out) to force (somebody) out of their job, area of activity, etc. ⋙ **squeezability** *n*, **squeezable** *adj*, **squeezer** *n*.

squeeze[2] *n* **1** the act or an instance of squeezing; a compression. **2** a quick hug or embrace. **3** a quantity squeezed out from something. **4** *informal* a condition of being crowded together; a crush. **5** financial pressure caused by restricting credit, used *esp* by a government to reduce price inflation. **6** *NAm, informal* one's boyfriend or girlfriend. ✱ **put the squeeze on** *informal* to put pressure on (somebody), e.g. to part with money, information, etc.

squeeze-box *n informal* an accordion.

squeeze off *v informal* **1** to shoot (a round or shot) from a gun. **2** to take (a photograph).

squeezy *adj* (**-ier, -iest**) of a plastic container: flexible, so as to dispense its contents when squeezed.

squelch[1] *v* **1** to make the sucking sound typically produced by somebody walking through mud. **2** *informal* to crush or suppress (opposition, etc). ⋙ **squelcher** *n*, **squelchy** *adj*.

squelch[2] *n* a squelching sound.

squib *n* **1** a small firework that burns with a fizz and finishes with a small explosion. **2** a short witty or satirical speech or piece of writing.

squid *n* (*pl* **squids** *or* **squid**) any of numerous species of cephalopod molluscs that have eight arms, two long tentacles, a long tapered body and a tail fin on each side.

squidge *v informal* **1** to squash. **2** to squelch.

squidgy *adj* (**-ier, -iest**) *chiefly Brit, informal* soft and squashy.

squiffy *or* **squiffed** *adj* (**-ier, -iest**) *chiefly Brit, informal* slightly drunk; tipsy.

squiggle *n* a short wavy twist or line, *esp* in handwriting or drawing. ⋙ **squiggly** *adj*.

squill *n* **1a** a Mediterranean plant of the lily family with white flowers and broad leaves, that reproduces by bulbs. **b** (*also in pl, used as sing.*) an extract of this bulb, used medicinally, e.g. as an expectorant. **2** a plant resembling the hyacinth, with violet or blue-striped flowers.

squillion *n informal* an enormously high but unspecified quantity or number.

squinch[1] *n* an arch, lintel, etc placed across the interior corner of a square to support a dome.

squinch[2] *v chiefly NAm* to screw up (one's eyes or face).

squint[1] *v* **1** to have a squint in the eye. **2** to look or peer with eyes partly closed. ⋙ **squinter** *n*, **squintingly** *adv*.

squint[2] *n* **1** abnormal alignment of an eye, so that it turns permanently towards or away from the nose. **2** *informal* a quick glance. ⋙ **squinty** *adj*.

squirarchy *n* see SQUIREARCHY.

squire[1] *n* **1** formerly, the shield-bearer or armour-bearer of a knight, typically a young nobleman training for knighthood. **2** an owner of a country estate, *esp* the principal local landowner. **3** *Brit, informal* a form of address used by one man to another. ⋙ **squiredom** *n*, **squireship** *n*.

squire[2] *v* to escort (a woman).

squirearchy *or* **squirarchy** *n* (*pl* **-ies**) the gentry or landed-proprietor class. ⋙ **squirearch** *n*, **squirearchal** *adj*, **squirearchical** *adj*.

squirm[1] *v* **1** to twist about like a worm; to wriggle. **2** to feel or show acute discomfort at something embarrassing, shameful, or unpleasant. ⋙ **squirmer** *n*, **squirmy** *adj*.

squirm[2] *n* the act or an instance of squirming.

squirrel[1] *n* a tree-dwelling rodent with a long bushy tail and strong hind legs, that feeds chiefly on nuts and seeds.

squirrel[2] *v* (**squirrelled, squirrelling,** *NAm* **squirreled, squirreling**) (*usu* + away) to secrete somewhere or hoard for future use.

squirrelly *adj* **1** like a squirrel in appearance or habit. **2** *chiefly NAm* **a** restless; nervous. **b** eccentric or unpredictable.

squirrel monkey *n* a small soft-haired S American monkey with a long tail, that leaps from tree to tree.

squirt[1] *v* **1** to issue, or cause (a liquid) to issue, in a sudden forceful stream from a narrow opening. **2** to direct a jet or stream of liquid at. ⋙ **squirter** *n*.

squirt[2] *n* **1** a small rapid stream of liquid; a jet. **2** *informal* a small, insignificant, or impudent person.

squish[1] *v* **1** to make a slight squelching or sucking sound. **2** *informal* to squash.

squish[2] *n* the act or an instance of squishing.

squishy *adj* (**-ier, -iest**) soft and moist. ⋙ **squishiness** *n*.

squiz *n* (*pl* **squizzes**) *Aus, NZ, informal* a curious glance or look.

Sr[1] *abbr* **1** senior. **2** Señor. **3** Sir. **4** Sister.

Sr[2] *abbr* the chemical symbol for strontium.

sr *abbr* steradian or steradians.

Sra *abbr* Señora.

SRAM *abbr* static random-access memory.

Sri Lankan *n* a native or inhabitant of Sri Lanka. ⋙ **Sri Lankan** *adj*.

Srta *abbr* Señorita.

SS[1] *n* (*used as sing. or pl*) Adolf Hitler's bodyguard and special police force within the Nazi party.

SS[2] *abbr* **1** saints. **2** steamship.

SSE *abbr* south-southeast.

SSP *abbr Brit* statutory sick pay.

SSSI *abbr Brit* site of special scientific interest.

SSW *abbr* south-southwest.

St *abbr* **1** Saint. **2** in street names, street.

st. *abbr* **1** stone. **2** in cricket, stumped by.

stab[1] *n* **1** a wound produced by a pointed weapon. **2** a thrust with a pointed weapon or other pointed object. **3** a sharp spasm. **4** a pang of intense emotion. ✱ **a stab in the back** an act of treachery that causes somebody's downfall. **have/make a stab at** *informal* to make an attempt at (something).

stab[2] *v* (**stabbed, stabbing**) **1** to pierce or wound with or as if with a pointed weapon. **2** to thrust or jab (a pointed object) somewhere. ✱ **stab somebody in the back** to betray somebody. ⋙ **stabber** *n*, **stabbing** *n*.

stabbing *adj* of pain: sudden, sharp, intense and usu localized.

stabile *n* an abstract sculpture or construction similar to a mobile but stationary.

stabilise *v* see STABILIZE.

stabiliser *n* see STABILIZER.

stability *n* the quality of being stable.

stabilize *or* **-ise** *v* **1** to make or become stable or firm. **2** to limit fluctuations of (prices, etc). ⋙ **stabilization** *n*.

stabilizer *or* **stabiliser** *n* **1** a chemical substance added to prevent or retard an unwanted alteration of physical state. **2** a gyroscopic device to keep ships steady in a rough sea. **3** the horizontal tailplane of an aircraft. **4** (*in pl*) a pair of small wheels fitted either side of a child's bicycle to give support.

stable[1] *n* **1** (*also in pl*) a building in which domestic animals, *esp* horses, are sheltered and fed, usu with stalls or compartments. **2** (*used as sing. or pl*) **a** the racehorses or racing cars owned by one person or organization. **b** a group of sportspersons or performers under one management. **c** the team or organization behind a certain range of products, productions, etc. ➤➤ **stableful** *n*, **stableman** *n*.

stable[2] *v* to put or keep (a horse) in a stable.

stable[3] *adj* **1** likely to remain firmly upright; not likely to collapse, overturn, etc. **2** well-founded or securely established so as to endure and be dependable. **3a** not subject to change or fluctuation. **b** of a patient or their condition: not likely to deteriorate suddenly. **4** not subject to mental or emotional insecurity; sane, well-adjusted. **5** in physics, of such a nature as to return after disturbance to normal position, equilibrium, or steady motion. **6** able to resist alteration in chemical, physical, or biological properties. ➤➤ **stableness** *n*, **stably** *adv*.

stable boy *or* **stable girl** *or* **stable man** *n* an assistant employed in a stable.

stable companion *n* = STABLEMATE.

stable door *n* a door of the kind typical for a stable, horizontally divided so that the upper half may be opened leaving the lower half closed.

stable girl *n* see STABLE BOY.

stable lad *n Brit* a boy or man who works in a stable.

stable man *n* see STABLE BOY.

stablemate *n* **1** a horse stabled with the one in question. **2** a person or thing having the same source, work place, trainer, etc as the one specified.

stabling *n* indoor accommodation for animals.

staccato *adj and adv* **1** of a piece of music: to be performed with each note produced in a clear, abrupt, detached style. **2** of speech: with a jerky delivery rather than flowing smoothly. ➤➤ **staccato** *n*.

stack[1] *n* **1** a pile, *esp* an orderly one. **2** a cone-shaped, rectangular, or cylindrical pile of hay or straw, left standing in the field for storage. **3** a number of aircraft circling an airport at allocated altitudes, waiting their turn to land. **4** (*also in pl*) compact shelving for books at a library, not usu accessible to the public. **5** a chimney or vertical exhaust pipe. **6** *Brit* a pillar-shaped rocky islet near a cliffy shore that has been detached from the mainland by wave erosion. **7** *informal* (*also in pl*) a large quantity or number.

stack[2] *v* **1** to pile (things) into a stack. **2** to fill with stacks of things. **3** to assign (an aircraft) to a particular altitude and position within a stack. **4** to shuffle (a pack of cards) in such a way as to enable one to cheat. ✱ **be stacked against/in favour of** of conditions, etc: to be highly likely to produce an unfavourable/favourable result for. ➤➤ **stackable** *adj*, **stacker** *n*.

stacked *adj* **1** said of a heel: made from narrow layers of leather or wood glued together. **2** *informal* of a woman: having large breasts.

stack up *v NAm* **1** to accumulate into a queue or backlog. **2** *informal* (*often* + against) to measure up or compare. **3** *informal* (*usu in negative contexts*) to make sense or be plausible; to add up.

stadium *n* (*pl* **stadiums** *or* **stadia**) **1** a sports ground surrounded by tiers of seats for spectators. **2** in ancient Greece and Rome, a course for foot races or chariot races, surrounded by tiered seats.

staff[1] *n* **1** (*used as sing. or pl*) **a** the body of people who work for an institution, business, etc. **b** the body of teachers at a school or university. **c** a group of officers appointed to assist a commanding officer. **2** (*pl* **staves**) a long stick carried in the hand for support in walking or as a weapon. **3** a rod carried as a symbol of office or authority. **4** (*pl* **staves**) in music, the STAVE[1] (4). ✱ **the staff of life** *literary* bread or some other staple food.

staff[2] *v* to supply (an organization, etc) with a staff.

staff college *n* a college that trains military officers for staff appointments.

staffer *n chiefly NAm* a member of a staff, e.g. of a newspaper.

staff nurse *n Brit* a qualified nurse on the staff of a hospital who is next in rank below a sister or charge nurse.

staff officer *n* a commissioned officer assigned to a military commander's staff.

Staffordshire bull terrier *n* a terrier of a breed with a thickset muscular frame, broad head, and a short coat, usu white with markings.

staffroom *n* a common room for the use of teachers in a school or college.

Staffs *abbr* Staffordshire.

staff sergeant *n* a non-commissioned army officer of a rank senior to a sergeant and junior to a warrant officer.

stag[1] *n* **1** an adult male deer. **2** *chiefly NAm* an unaccompanied man at a social gathering. **3** (*used before a noun*) for men only. **4** *Brit* a person who buys newly issued shares in the hope of selling them to make a quick profit.

stag[2] *v* (**stagged, stagging**) to buy or apply for (shares in a new issue) with the intention of selling them immediately at a profit.

stag beetle *n* any of numerous large beetles the males of which have long and often branched mandibles suggesting the antlers of a stag.

stage[1] *n* **1a** a raised platform. **b** the raised platform or other area in a theatre where actors perform. **c** (**the stage**) the acting profession. **d** an arena of action or forum of discussion. **2** a distinguishable period or step in the progress or development of something. **3** a section of journey, race, or rally. **4** a propulsion section of a rocket, jettisoned when its fuel is exhausted. **5** a floor of a building. **6** a connected group of components performing a specific function, *esp* amplification, in an electrical circuit. **7** a range of rock strata corresponding to an age in geological time. **8** = STAGECOACH. ✱ **hold the stage** to be the centre of attention. **set the stage for** to provide the necessary conditions for the arrival, appearance, or occurrence of.

stage[2] *v* **1** to produce (a theatrical production) on a stage. **2** to produce and organize (a public event). **3** to contrive (something dramatic), *esp* with maximum publicity. ➤➤ **stageability** *n*, **stageable** *adj*.

stagecoach *n* formerly, a horse-drawn passenger and mail coach that ran on a regular schedule between established stops.

stagecraft *n* competence in writing or staging plays.

stage direction *n* an instruction, relating e.g. to sound effects or the movement or positioning of actors, provided in the text of a play.

stage door *n* the entrance to a theatre that is used by the people who work there.

stage fright *n* nervousness felt at appearing before an audience.

stagehand *n* a theatre worker who handles scenery, props, or lights.

stage-manage *v* **1** to be the stage manager of (a play, etc). **2** to arrange (an event, etc) so as to achieve a desired result. ⋙ **stage management** *n.*

stage manager *n* a person who is in charge of the stage during a performance and supervises related matters beforehand.

stage name *n* the name used professionally by an actor.

stagestruck *adj* **1** fascinated by the stage. **2** having an ardent desire to become an actor or actress.

stage whisper *n* **1** a loud whisper by an actor, audible to the audience, but supposedly inaudible to others on stage. **2** a whisper that is deliberately made audible.

stagey *adj* see STAGY.

stagflation *n* a state of affairs in which inflation in the economy is accompanied by zero growth in industrial production.

stagger[1] *v* **1** to reel from side to side, usu while moving; to totter. **2** to dumbfound or astonish. **3** to arrange (a set of things) so that they are not in line, start at different times, or partially overlap. ⋙ **staggerer** *n.*

stagger[2] *n* **1** (*in pl, used as sing.*) an abnormal condition of domestic animals and birds associated with damage to the brain and spinal cord, causing loss of muscular coordination and a staggering gait. **2** (**the staggers**) (*in pl, used as sing.*) an inability to stand or walk steadily. **3** a staggered arrangement, e.g. of runners on the track at the start of a distance race.

staggering *adj* astonishing or overwhelming. ⋙ **staggeringly** *adv.*

staging *n* **1a** a platform serving as a stage. **b** a set of temporary platforms supported by scaffolding. **2** *Brit* shelving in a greenhouse.

staging area *n* an assembly point or checkpoint for groups, *esp* military formations, en route for a destination.

staging post *n* a regular stopping place for vehicles, *esp* aircraft, between their point of departure and their destination.

stagnant *adj* **1** of an expanse of water: not flowing in a current or stream; motionless. **2** stale. **3** dull or inactive. ⋙ **stagnancy** *n,* **stagnantly** *adv.*

stagnate *v* to become or remain stagnant. ⋙ **stagnation** *n.*

stag night *n* an exclusively male celebration, *esp* one held for a man about to be married.

stag party *n* = STAG NIGHT.

stagy *or* **stagey** *adj* (**-ier, -iest**) of behaviour, speech, gestures, etc: artificially dramatic; consciously theatrical. ⋙ **stagily** *adv,* **staginess** *n.*

staid *adj* sedate; starchily old-fashioned in attitude. ⋙ **staidly** *adv,* **staidness** *n.*

stain[1] *v* **1** to mark, discolour, or soil. **2** *literary* to taint or dishonour (a person or their character, reputation, etc) through guilt, vice, corruption, etc. **3** to colour (wood or a biological specimen) by using processes or dyes affecting the material itself. ⋙ **stainability** *n,* **stainable** *adj,* **stainer** *n.*

stain[2] *n* **1** a soiled or discoloured spot. **2** a moral taint or blemish. **3a** a preparation, e.g. of dye or pigment, used in staining; *esp* one capable of penetrating the pores of wood. **b** a dye used in microscopy to make minute and transparent structures visible.

stained glass *n* glass coloured or stained, usu for use in leaded windows.

stainless *adj* **1** free from stain or stigma. **2** resistant to stain; rust-resistant. ⋙ **stainlessly** *adv,* **stainlessness** *n.*

stainless steel *n* steel containing chromium and highly resistant to rusting and corrosion.

stair *n* **1** (*usu in pl*) a flight of steps or a series of flights for passing from one level to another. **2** any step of a stairway.

staircase *n* **1** the structure or part of a building containing a stairway. **2** a flight of stairs with the supporting framework, casing, and balusters.

stairlift *n* a lift in the form of a chair, fitted at the edge of a domestic stair to carry an infirm or elderly person from one floor to the next.

stairway *n* one or more flights of stairs, usu with intermediate landings.

stairwell *n* a vertical shaft in which stairs are located.

staithe *n Brit* a wharf from which coal may be loaded on a vessel.

stake[1] *n* **1** a pointed wooden or iron post used for driving into the ground as a marker or support. **2a** a post to which a person, *esp* a religious heretic, was formerly bound for execution by burning. **b** (**the stake**) execution by this method.

stake[2] *v* **1a** (*often* + off/out) to mark out (an area) with stakes. **b** (*often* + off/out) to claim ownership of (a plot of land, etc) by this means. **2** to support (a plant) with a stake. ✻ **stake one's claim** to assert one's ownership of, or right to, something.

stake[3] *v* **1** to bet or hazard (a sum of money, one's reputation, etc). **2** *chiefly NAm* to back (a person or business concern) financially. ⋙ **staker** *n.*

stake[4] *n* **1** something, *esp* a sum of money, that is staked. **2** an interest or share in an undertaking, e.g. a commercial venture. **3** (*also in pl*) the prize in a contest, *esp* a horse race. **4** (*often* **Stakes**) (*in pl, used as pl or sing.*) a race in which all the owners of the competing horses contribute equally to the prize money. **5** (*in pl*) the competitive world of something. ✻ **at stake** at issue; in jeopardy.

stakeholder *n* **1** a usu neutral person who looks after the money wagered by betters. **2** a person with an interest in the welfare of an organization, e.g. any employee, shareholder, or customer of a company.

stakeholder pension *n* a low-cost flexible pension scheme intended especially to encourage people on low incomes to save for retirement.

stake out *v informal* to conduct a surveillance of (a suspected area, person, etc). ⋙ **stakeout** *n.*

stalactite *n* an icicle-like deposit of calcium carbonate hanging from the roof or sides of a cave.

stalagmite *n* a deposit of calcium carbonate like an inverted stalactite, growing upward from the floor of a cave, formed by drips from the ceiling.

stale[1] *adj* **1** of food: tasteless or unpalatable from age. **2** of air: musty or foul. **3a** of news: no longer fresh or interesting. **b** tedious from familiarity. **4** impaired in vigour or effectiveness, from overexertion or repetitiveness. ⋙ **stalely** *adv,* **staleness** *n.*

stale[2] *v* **1** to become stale. **2** to cause (something) to become stale.

stalemate *n* **1** a position in chess representing a draw, in which only the king can move and although not in check can move only into check. **2** any position of deadlock.

Stalinism *n* the theory and practice of communism developed by Stalin from Marxism-Leninism and characterized by rigid authoritarianism. ⋙ **Stalinist** *n and adj.*

stalk[1] *v* **1** to pursue (a prey or quarry) stealthily, so as eventually to effect a kill. **2** to follow and watch (a person, often a celebrity, with whom one has become obsessed), to the point of persecution. **3** *literary* of illness, death, or terror, etc: to sweep through (a population, etc). **4** to walk in a stiff haughty fashion. ⋙ **stalking** *n.*

stalk² *n* **1** the act or an instance of stalking quarry or prey. **2** a stiff or haughty walk.

stalk³ *n* **1a** the main stem of a herbaceous plant, often with its attached parts. **b** the stem of a leaf or fruit. **2** a slender upright supporting or connecting structure, *esp* in an animal. ⋙ **stalked** *adj,* **stalkless** *adj,* **stalklike** *adj,* **stalky** *adj.*

stalker *n* **1** a person who stalks game. **2** a person who, to the point of persecution, follows and watches somebody, often a celebrity, with whom they have become obsessed.

stalking-horse *n* **1** something used to mask a purpose. **2** in politics, a person who stands for the leadership of their party solely to bring about an election and allow a stronger and more likely contender to stand.

stall¹ *n* **1a** any of several compartments for domestic animals in a stable or barn. **b** (*in pl*) = STARTING STALLS. **2** a wholly or partly enclosed seat in the chancel of a church. **3a** a stand or counter at which articles are displayed or offered for sale, e.g. in a market place. **b** a sideshow at a fair, etc, where one can compete for prizes. **4** a small compartment. **5** *Brit* (*in pl*) the seats on the main floor of an auditorium, e.g. in a theatre. **6** a protective sheath for a finger or toe. **7a** the cutting-out of a vehicle engine. **b** the condition of an aircraft when airflow is so obstructed, e.g. from moving forward too slowly, that lift is lost.

stall² *v* **1** to put or keep (an animal) in a stall, e.g. to fatten it. **2** (*usu in passive*) to prevent the progress of (a transaction, etc). **3** of a vehicle, engine, driver, aircraft, or pilot: to suffer a stall.

stall³ *v* **1** to play for time; to delay. **2** to divert or delay (somebody), *esp* by evasion, prevarication, or deception.

stall⁴ *n* a delaying tactic; a ploy intended to divert or distract somebody.

stallholder *n* a person who runs a stall, *esp* in a market place.

stallion *n* an uncastrated male horse, *esp* one kept for breeding.

stalwart¹ *adj* **1** strong in body, mind, or spirit. **2** dependable; staunch. ⋙ **stalwartly** *adv,* **stalwartness** *n.*

stalwart² *n* a stalwart person, *esp* a staunch supporter.

stamen *n* the organ of a flower that produces the male reproductive cell enclosed in a pollen grain, and consists of an anther and a filament.

stamina *n* the capacity for sustained mental and physical effort.

stammer¹ *v* to speak or utter with involuntary stops and repetitions, *esp* of initial consonants; to stutter. ⋙ **stammerer** *n.*

stammer² *n* a tendency to stammer.

stamp¹ *v* **1a** to bring down (one's foot) forcibly, e.g. to show irritation, or to crush or compact something. **b** to walk with loud heavy steps. **2** to pound or crush (ore, etc) with a pestle or a heavy instrument. **3** to impress or imprint (words, etc) on something. **4** to leave (a permanent or indelible image) in someone's mind, etc. **5a** of a quality, etc: to characterize (something). **b** to leave (a characteristic mark) on something. **6** to attach a postage stamp to (an envelope, etc). **7** to cut out, bend, or form (something) using a stamp or die. **8** (+ on) to put a stop to something. ⋙ **stamper** *n.*

stamp² *n* **1** a device or instrument for stamping a mark, etc on a surface. **2** the impression or mark made by stamping. **3** a characteristic quality. **4** distinctive type. **5** a lasting mark. **6** the act of stamping the foot, or the noise made by this. **7** a printed adhesive piece of paper used as a token of credit, etc; = POSTAGE STAMP.

stamp duty *n* a tax on the legal recognition of certain documents.

stampede¹ *n* **1** a wild headlong rush or flight of frightened animals. **2** a sudden mass movement of people.

stampede² *v* **1** to run away or rush in panic or on impulse. **2** to panic (animals) into rushing headlong, or (people) into doing something precipitately.

stamping ground *n* one's favourite or habitual haunt.

stamp out *v* to eradicate or destroy.

stance *n* **1** a way of standing. **2** an intellectual or emotional attitude. **3** the position of body or feet from which a sportsperson, e.g. a batsman or golfer, plays. **4** *Scot* a site for a taxi rank or street stall.

stanch *v NAm* see STAUNCH¹.

stanchion *n* an upright bar, post, or support, e.g. for a roof. ⋙ **stanchioned** *adj.*

stand¹ *v* (*past tense and past part.* **stood**) **1a** to support oneself on one's feet in an upright position. **b** to rise to this position. **2** to rest upright on the ground or other surface. **3** to occupy a position or location. **4** to remain stationary: *A train was standing at the platform.* **5** to have a particular attitude or opinion: *Where do you stand on equal pay?* **6** to remain valid: *The agreement still stands.* **7** to be likely to receive or experience something: *She stands to inherit a fortune.* **8** (*usu in negative contexts or questions*) **a** to endure or tolerate (something unwelcome): *How can she stand the noise?* **b** to like: *I can't stand her husband.* **9** to withstand: *shoes that stand hard wear.* **10** to undergo: *to stand trial.* **11** to treat (somebody) to a meal or drink. **12** *Brit* to be a candidate in an election: *to stand for mayor.* ✻ **leave standing** to surpass spectacularly. **stand alone** to be unequalled. **stand by 1** to wait in readiness. **2** to support or remain loyal to. **stand for 1** to represent: *What does 'lb' stand for?* **2** (*usu in negative contexts*) to permit or tolerate. **stand on ceremony** to insist on correct procedure. **stand one's ground** to maintain one's position against opposition. **stand on one's own feet/two feet** to be self-reliant.

stand² *n* **1** a definite attitude taken towards something. **2** a determined effort to fight for or resist something. **3** in cricket, a partnership of two batsmen or batswomen. **4** (*also in pl*) a structure of tiered seats for spectators of a sport or spectacle. **5** a raised platform for a band, speaker, etc. **6** a small temporary outdoor stall selling food or other goods. **7** a usu temporary structure erected, e.g. at a trade exhibition, to display or demonstrate wares. **8** a place where taxis await hire. **9** a frame or rack on or in which to place things. **10** (**the stand**) *NAm* the witness-box. **11** a compact group of plants or trees.

stand-alone *adj* of a piece of computer hardware or software: operating independently of other software or hardware.

standard¹ *n* **1** a level of quality or achievement. **2** (*also in pl*) a requisite level of quality. **3** (*also in pl*) a norm used for comparison. **4** (*in pl*) principles of behaviour based on ideas of integrity or honour. **5** a flag or banner, *esp* that is personal to an individual or corporation and bears heraldic insignia. **6** a stanchion or support. **7a** a shrub or soft-stemmed plant grown with an erect main stalk so that it forms or resembles a tree. **b** a fruit tree grafted on a stock that does not induce dwarfing. **8** something standard, e.g.: **a** a musical composition, *esp* a popular song, that has become a part of the established repertoire. **b** a model of a car supplied without optional extras.

standard[2] *adj* **1** denoting the smallest size of a range of marketed products. **2** regularly and widely used, available, or supplied. **3** well established and very familiar. **4** recognized as authoritative and of lasting value. **5** of language: well established by usage in the speech and writing of educated people and widely accepted as a norm. ➤➤ **standardly** *adv.*

standard assessment tasks *pl n* in Britain, a series of standard tests given to schoolchildren at particular stages to assess their progress against the attainment targets specified for core subjects in the National Curriculum.

standard-bearer *n* **1** a person, e.g. a soldier, who carries a standard or banner. **2** a conspicuous figure at the forefront of an organization, movement, or party.

standard deviation *n* a measure of the extent to which values of a variable are scattered about the mean value in a frequency distribution.

standard gauge *n* a railway gauge of 4ft 8in. (1.435m), used on most railways. ➤➤ **standard-gauge** *adj.*

Standard Grade *n* in Scotland, an examination that is equivalent to English GCSE.

standardize *or* **-ise** *v* **1** to make (things) conform to a standard. **2** to test (a substance, etc) by comparison with a standard. **3** (+ on) to adopt a certain brand or make as standard equipment, etc. ➤➤ **standardization** *n.*

standard lamp *n* a lamp with a tall support that stands on the floor.

standard of living *n* a measure of the prosperity of an individual or community, shown *esp* by the level of consumption of necessities, comforts, and luxuries.

standard time *n* the officially established time, with reference to Greenwich Mean Time, of a region or country.

standby *n* (*pl* **standbys**) **1a** a person or thing that is held in reserve and can be relied on in case of necessity. **b** a state of readiness for duty or use. **c** (*used before a noun*) held in reserve and ready for use or duty. **2** (*used before a noun*) of tickets: unreserved and becoming available for sale shortly before e.g. a performance or the departure of a flight.

stand down *v Brit* to relinquish an office or position.

standee *n* (*pl* **standees**) a person standing when the norm is to be seated, e.g. as a passenger on a bus, audience member, spectator, etc.

stand in *v* to act as substitute for somebody.

stand-in *n* a substitute.

standing[1] *adj* **1** of timber or grain: not yet cut down or harvested. **2** of water: not flowing; stagnant. **3** of an offer, etc: permanently in force or available.

standing[2] *n* **1** status, position, or reputation. **2** length of existence or duration.

standing committee *n* a permanent committee appointed, *esp* by a legislative body such as Parliament, to consider a particular subject.

standing joke *n* something that is a regular source of amusement or target of derision.

standing jump *n* a jump performed from a stationary start, without a run-up.

standing order *n* **1** *Brit* **a** an order to a bank to pay a specified sum of money to another named account at specified times. **b** an instruction, e.g. to a supplier, in force until specifically changed. **2** (*in pl*) rules governing the procedure of an organization, which remain in force until specifically changed.

standing ovation *n* a prolonged burst of applause for a speaker or performer, during which the audience rise to their feet in enthusiasm.

standing start *n* the starting of a race from a stationary position.

standing stone *n* = MENHIR.

standing wave *n* a vibration of a body or physical system in which the amplitude varies from point to point but is constant at any particular point.

standoff *n* **1** a state of deadlock or stalemate between opponents. **2** = STAND-OFF HALF.

stand off *v* to keep a distance.

stand-off half *n* in rugby, the player positioned between the scrum-half and the three-quarter backs.

standoffish *adj derog* reserved; aloof. ➤➤ **standoffishly** *adv,* **standoffishness** *n.*

standout *n chiefly NAm, informal* a prominent, *esp* strikingly splendid, person or thing.

stand out *v* to be especially visible or noteworthy. ✱ **stand out for** to be stubborn in insisting on.

standpipe *n* a pipe fitted with a tap and used for an outdoor water supply.

standpoint *n* **1** the position from which one views a scene or object. **2** one's point of view with regard to some issue.

standstill *n* a state in which motion or progress is absent; a stop or impasse.

stand to *v* to take a position of readiness.

stand-to *n* the act or an instance of standing to.

stand up *v* **1** to rise to or maintain a standing position. **2** (*usu in negative contexts*) to bear close scrutiny: *That argument won't stand up.* **3** *informal* to fail to keep an appointment with (somebody). ✱ **stand up and be counted** to make one's views known. **stand up for** to defend against criticism. **stand up to 1** to confront or prepare to resist. **2** to withstand (wear, etc).

stand-up *adj* **1** of a comedian: performing solo in front of an audience. **2** designed so as to stand upright. **3** denoting a meal at a reception, etc, that is taken standing up. **4** of a fight, argument, etc: intense, passionate, and involving personal confrontation and sometimes violence.

stank *v* past tense of STINK[1].

Stanley knife *n trademark* a knife with a hollow handle and a short sharp replaceable blade, used for trimming carpets, hardboard, etc.

stannary *n* (*pl* **-ies**) (*also in pl*) *esp* formerly, a tin-mining region of Cornwall or Devon.

stanza *n* a division of a poem consisting of a series of lines arranged together in a recurring pattern of metre and rhyme; = VERSE. ➤➤ **stanza'd** *adj,* **stanzaed** *adj,* **stanzaic** *adj.*

staphylococcus *n* (*pl* **staphylococci**) any of various spherical bacteria that include parasites of skin and mucous membranes and cause boils, septic infections of wounds, etc. ➤➤ **staphylococcal** *adj,* **staphylococcic** *adj.*

staple[1] *n* **1** a small piece of wire with ends bent at right angles which can be driven through thin sheets of material, *esp* paper, and clinched to secure the items. **2** a U-shaped metal loop, both ends of which can be driven into a surface, e.g. to secure something to it.

staple[2] *v* to fasten (things) together, or (one thing) to another, with staples.

staple[3] *n* **1a** a food constituting the main nourishment of a community, etc. **b** the main constituent of something. **2** the main trading commodity or raw material of a region. **3** the fibre of cotton or wool graded for length and fineness.

staple[4] *adj* **1** denoting a leading commodity in the economy of a region. **2** main; principal; chief.

staple gun *n* a hand-held mechanical device that propels staples into a hard surface, used for fixing posters to walls, etc.

stapler *n* a small hand-operated device for inserting wire staples.

star[1] *n* **1** any of millions of gaseous bodies of great mass, heat, and light, such as the sun, that radiate energy and are visible as points of light in the night sky. **2** (*also in pl*) **a** in astrology, a configuration of the planets that is held to influence a person's destiny, character, etc. **b** (**the stars**) an astrological forecast; a horoscope. **3a** a stylized figure with five or more points that represents a star. **b** a star-shaped object or symbol used as a medal, badge of rank, mark of excellence, etc. **4a** any famous performer or celebrity of stage, screen, or television, or sports personality. **b** the leading performer of a group. **c** a person who stands out among their fellows. **d** *informal* a kind or generous person. **e** (*used before a noun*) denoting outstanding quality, etc. ✱ **see stars** *informal* to see dots and flashes before one's eyes, as when stunned or dazed. ➤➤ **starless** *adj*, **starlike** *adj*.

star[2] *v* (**starred, starring**) **1a** of a film, play, etc: to feature (a certain star) in a leading role. **b** to play a leading role in a production. **2** to mark (something) with a star or asterisk, for particular commendation or notice. **3** to spangle or adorn (a surface) with star-shaped decorations, etc.

star anise *n* a star-shaped fruit with a seed in each point, used unripened in Asian cuisine.

starboard[1] *n* the right side of a ship or aircraft looking forward: compare PORT[2]. ➤➤ **starboard** *adj*.

starboard[2] *v* to turn or put (a helm or rudder) to the right.

starburst *n* **1** a pattern of rays or lines radiating from a point or source of light. **2** an explosion that takes place with this effect. **3** a burst of star formation within a galaxy.

starch[1] *v* to stiffen (clothes or fabric) with starch. ➤➤ **starcher** *n*.

starch[2] *n* **1** an odourless tasteless complex carbohydrate that is an important foodstuff, being obtained chiefly from cereals and potatoes. **2** a material prepared from this, used in adhesives and sizes, and in the form of a powder or spray to stiffen fabric.

starchy *adj* (**-ier, -iest**) **1** of foods or other substances: containing a lot of starch. **2** of a social atmosphere, somebody's manner, etc: stiff and formal. ➤➤ **starchily** *adv*, **starchiness** *n*.

star-crossed *adj literary* ill-fated.

stardom *n* the status or position of a celebrity or star.

stardust *n* a cluster of far-distant stars apparently forming a bright cloud.

stare[1] *v* to look fixedly, often with wide-open eyes. ✱ **be staring death/defeat, etc in the face** to face imminent death, defeat, etc. **stare somebody in the face** of a solution, etc: to be only too obvious. ➤➤ **starer** *n*.

stare[2] *n* a staring look or expression.

stare down *v* = STARE OUT.

stare out *v* to cause (somebody) to look away by staring fixedly into their eyes.

starfish *n* (*pl* **starfishes** *or* **starfish**) a marine ECHINODERM that has a body consisting of a central disc surrounded by five equally spaced arms with tube feet on the underside, and feeds largely on molluscs, e.g. oysters.

starfruit *n* = CARAMBOLA.

stargazer *n informal* **1** an astrologer. **2** an astronomer.

stark *adj* **1** of a landscape, surroundings, etc: bleak or bare; desolate. **2** harshly clear or plain. **3** sheer; utter. ✱ **stark mad/stark staring mad** *informal* utterly mad. ➤➤ **starkly** *adv*, **starkness** *n*.

starkers *adj Brit, informal* completely naked.

stark-naked *adj* completely naked.

starlet *n* **1** a young film actress being coached for starring roles and given prominent billing. **2** a rising young female athlete.

starlight *n* the light of the stars. ➤➤ **starlit** *adj*.

starling *n* a gregarious European bird with dark brown, or in summer glossy greenish black, plumage.

star network *n* a type of computer network in which all nodes (terminals; see NODE) are individually connected to the central unit.

Star of David *n* a six-pointed star made from two superimposed equilateral triangles that is a symbol of Judaism and the State of Israel.

starry *adj* (**-ier, -iest**) **1** of the sky: adorned or studded with stars. **2** shining like stars; sparkling. **3** *informal* relating to the stars of the entertainment world.

starry-eyed *adj* given to thinking in a dreamy or overoptimistic manner.

Stars and Bars *pl n* (*usu used as sing.*) the first flag adopted by the Confederates at the time of the American Civil War.

Stars and Stripes *pl n* (**the Stars and Stripes**) (*used as sing.*) the flag of the USA.

star shell *n* a shell that on bursting releases a brilliant light for illumination and signalling.

starship *n* in science fiction, a large spaceship carrying personnel on interstellar journeys.

star sign *n* a sign of the zodiac.

star-spangled *adj literary* studded with stars.

star-struck *adj* fascinated by celebrities, *esp* film stars.

star-studded *adj* **1** covered with stars. **2** *informal* featuring a large number of well-known stars.

START *abbr* Strategic Arms Reduction Talks.

start[1] *v* **1** to come into operation or existence. **2** to begin functioning or moving, or to make (something) do this. **3** to begin (an activity or undertaking). **4** to cause (somebody) to do something: *That started us all laughing.* **5** to set (somebody) up in business. **6** to range from a specified amount: *Prices start from £300.* **7** to move suddenly or violently, *esp* as a result of shock or surprise. **8** of the eyes: to protrude or seem to protrude. **9** of timbers, rivets, etc: to become loosened or forced out of position. **10** to flush (game) out of a place of concealment. ✱ **start on 1** to embark on (a task, journey, etc). **2** *informal* to begin attacking (somebody) verbally. **to start with** as the first thing to be considered.

start[2] *n* **1** the beginning of a movement, activity, journey, etc. **2** a starting place, e.g. for a race. **3** a lead or handicap conceded to a competitor at the start of a race or competition. **4** an advantage or lead; a head start. **5** a sudden involuntary bodily movement or reaction, e.g. from surprise or alarm. ✱ **for a start** in the first place; to start with.

starter *n* **1** the person who gives the signal to start a race. **2** a runner or other competitor at the start of a race or competition. **3** a person who begins to engage in some activity, etc; a beginner. **4** an automatic device that activates machinery, *esp* a vehicle engine. **5** *chiefly Brit* (*also in pl*) the first course of a meal. ✱ **for starters** *chiefly Brit, informal* in the first place. **under starter's orders** of runners in a horse race, etc: awaiting the signal to start.

start in *v informal* to begin doing something, *esp* talking.

starting block *n* either of two angled supports mounted on a frame, against which a sprinter braces their feet when in a crouched position at the start of a race.

starting gate *n* a mechanically operated barrier raised at the start of a race, e.g. a horse race.

starting pistol *n* a pistol fired as the starting signal for a race.

starting price *n esp* in horse racing, the betting odds as they stand at the start of a race.

starting stalls *pl n* a line of stalls or traps in which horses or dogs are enclosed at the beginning of a race and from which they are released simultaneously.

startle *v* **1** to cause (somebody) to start in alarm, etc. **2** to alarm (somebody). ➤➤ **startled** *adj*, **startling** *adj*, **startlingly** *adv*.

start off *v* to begin talking, operating, etc, or to cause (somebody or something) to do this.

start out *v* to begin a journey or undertaking.

start over *v NAm* to begin again.

start up *v* to begin an undertaking.

star turn *n* the most prominently billed or impressive act in a show, etc.

starve *v* **1** to suffer severely from hunger or lack of nourishment. **2** to die of hunger. **3** to cause (a person or animal) to suffer from or to die of hunger. **4** *informal* to be ravenous. **5** (+ of) to deprive (a person or animal) of something. ➤➤ **starvation** *n*.

starveling *n archaic* a person or animal that is thin from or as if from lack of food.

stash[1] *v informal* (*often* + away) to store in a secret place for future use.

stash[2] *n informal* a secret store of drugs, weapons, etc.

stasis *n* (*pl* **stases**) **1** a slowing or stoppage of the normal flow of body fluids, e.g. slowing of the current of circulating blood. **2** a state of static balance or equilibrium; stagnation.

state[1] *n* **1** the condition or situation of somebody or something. **2a** a condition of nervous tension. **b** a squalid or confused condition. **3** formal dignity; pomp: *The coffin was borne in state to Westminster Abbey.* **4** (*often* **State**) (*used as sing. or pl*) a politically organized community usu occupying a definite territory; *esp* one that is sovereign. **5** the operations or concerns of the central government of a country. **6a** (*often* **State**) a constituent unit of a nation having a federal government. **b** (**the States**) the United States of America. ✱ **lie in state** of a deceased person, *esp* a head of state: to be placed on public view before burial so that people may pay their respects. **state of emergency** a situation involving national danger or extreme disaster, during which the government assumes special powers and suspends normal procedure. **state of affairs** (*also* **state of things**) a situation. **state of grace** the state of being free of sin, *esp* after spiritually administered forgiveness. **state of play 1** *Brit* the current score in a cricket or football match. **2** *Brit* the current situation. ➤➤ **statehood** *n*.

state[2] *v* to declare formally.

state capitalism *n* an economic system in which the state controls production and the deployment of capital.

statecraft *n* the art of conducting state affairs.

State Department *n* in the USA, the government department in charge of foreign affairs.

statehouse *n* **1** the building in which a US state legislature sits. **2** *NZ* a private house owned and rented out by the government.

stateless *adj* not recognized as a citizen of any country; having no nationality. ➤➤ **statelessness** *n*.

stately *adj* (**-ier, -iest**) **1** imposing; dignified. **2** impressive in size or proportions. ➤➤ **stateliness** *n*.

stately home *n Brit* a large country residence, usu of historical or architectural interest and open to the public.

statement *n* **1** the act or an instance of stating something orally or in writing. **2** something that is stated; a declaration. **3** a formal account or narration. **4** a summary of a financial account.

state-of-the-art *adj* using the most advanced technology available at the present time.

stateroom *n* **1** a large room in a palace or similar building for use on ceremonial occasions. **2** a private cabin in a ship.

state school *n* a British school that is publicly financed and provides compulsory free education.

state's evidence *n NAm* evidence for the prosecution in criminal proceedings, given by a participant or accomplice in the crime.

statesman *or* **stateswoman** *n* (*pl* **statesmen** *or* **stateswomen**) an experienced political leader, *esp* one who has come to be respected for shrewd judgment. ➤➤ **statesmanlike** *adj*, **statesmanship** *n*.

state socialism *n* a political system in which the government controls industry and services.

static[1] *adj* **1** characterized by a lack of movement, animation, or change. **2** of or relating to bodies at rest or forces in equilibrium: compare DYNAMIC[1] (1A). **3** relating to or producing stationary charges of electricity; electrostatic. **4** of computer memory: using devices that will preserve the stored information indefinitely without the need for any periodic attention or adjustment. ➤➤ **statically** *adv*.

static[2] *n* **1** electrical disturbances causing unwanted signals in a radio or television system; atmospherics. **2** = STATIC ELECTRICITY.

static electricity *n* a stationary electrical charge as distinct from a current, usu caused by friction, producing sparks or crackling, and attracting hair and dust.

statics *pl n* (*used as sing. or pl*) a branch of mechanics dealing with the relations of forces that produce equilibrium among solid bodies.

station[1] *n* **1** a regular or major stopping place for trains, with platforms for boarding and alighting, and buildings with passenger facilities. **2** the place or position in which something or somebody stands or is assigned to stand or remain. **3** a post or sphere of duty or occupation. **4** *Aus, NZ* a stock farm or ranch. **5** standing; rank. **6** a place for specialized observation and study of scientific phenomena. **7** a place established to provide a public service: *a petrol station*. **8** an establishment equipped for radio or television transmission or reception. **9** a radio or television channel. ✱ **stations of the cross** a series of representations in painting, sculpture, etc, of incidents in the progress of Christ as he carried his cross from Pilate's house to Calvary.

station[2] *v* to assign to a post or station.

stationary *adj* **1** having a fixed position; immobile: *a stationary vehicle.* **2** unchanging in condition; neither progressing nor deteriorating.

Usage note
stationary *or* stationery? These two words, which are pronounced the same, are often confused. *Stationary* is the adjective meaning 'standing still': *a stationary vehicle. Stationery* refers to the type of goods sold by a *stationer* (which is perhaps the easiest way of remembering the difference in spelling): paper, envelopes and the like.

stationer *n* a shopkeeper who deals in stationery.

stationery *n* **1** materials used for writing, typing, etc; office supplies. **2** paper and envelopes for letter writing.

Usage note
stationery *or* stationary? See note at STATIONARY.

station hand *n Aus, NZ* a worker on a large sheep farm or cattle ranch.

station house *n NAm* a police station or fire station.

stationmaster *n* an official in charge of a railway station.

statism *n* concentration of economic controls and planning in the hands of the state. ➤➤ **statist** *n and adj.*

statistic *n* **1** a single term or quantity in or computed from a collection of statistics. **2** a numerical value, e.g. the standard deviation or mean, used in describing and analysing data. ➤➤ **statistical** *adj,* **statistically** *adv.*

statistics *pl n* **1** (*used as sing. or pl*) a branch of mathematics dealing with the collection, analysis, interpretation, and presentation of masses of numerical data. **2** (*used as pl*) a collection of quantitative data. ➤➤ **statistician** *n.*

statoscope *n* an instrument for indicating small changes in the altitude of an aircraft.

stats *pl n informal* statistics.

statuary *n* statues collectively.

statue *n* a likeness, e.g. of a person or animal, sculptured, cast, or modelled in a solid material.

statuesque *adj* resembling a statue in dignity, formal beauty, or stately size or deportment. ➤➤ **statuesquely** *adv.*

statuette *n* a small statue.

stature *n* **1** the natural height of a person when standing upright. **2** standing or reputation. **3** status.

status *n* **1** the condition or standing of a person, territory, etc in the eyes of the law. **2** position or rank in relation to others in a hierarchy or social structure. **3** high social position; prestige. **4** a state of affairs; the situation in regard to something.

status quo *n* the existing state of affairs.

status symbol *n* a possession recognized as indicating high social status or wealth.

statute *n* **1** a law passed by a legislative body. **2** any of the permanent rules of an organization.

statute book *n* (**the statute book**) the whole body of legislation of a given jurisdiction.

statute law *n* enacted written law.

statute of limitations *n* a statute stipulating a time after which rights cannot be enforced or offences punished.

statutory *adj* **1** recognized by statute. **2** established, regulated, or imposed by or in conformity to statute. ➤➤ **statutorily** *adv.*

statutory instrument *n* an official document recording any law which has been made by a minister exercising their delegated legislative powers and which has not gone through parliament.

statutory rape *n* in US law, sexual intercourse with a girl who is below the statutory age of consent.

staunch[1] (*NAm* **stanch**) *v* **1** to stop the flow of (blood, etc). **2** to stop the flow of blood from (a wound).

staunch[2] *adj* **1** steadfast in loyalty or principle. **2** of a wall: sturdily constructed. **3** *archaic* of a ship: watertight. ➤➤ **staunchly** *adv,* **staunchness** *n.*

stave[1] *n* **1** an iron pole or wooden stick. **2** any of the narrow strips of wood or iron placed edge to edge to form a barrel, bucket, or other vessel or structure. **3** a verse or stanza of a poem. **4** a set of five horizontal spaced lines on and between which music is written.

stave[2] *v* (*past tense and past part.* **staved** *or* **stove**) (+ in) to crush or break (a hard casing, etc) inward.

stave off *v* to ward or fend off (a threatening ill), *esp* temporarily.

staves *n* pl of STAFF[1] (2), (4).

stay[1] *v* **1** to remain in a place and not move. **2** to remain in a particular state and not change. **3** to reside temporarily somewhere. **4** *Scot, SAfr* to dwell permanently somewhere. **5** to delay or prevent (a judicial procedure, such as an execution). ✱ **stay put** to stay where placed or left. **stay somebody's hand** *literary* to stop somebody acting. ➤➤ **stayer** *n.*

stay[2] *n* **1** a period of residing at a place. **2** the suspension of a judicial procedure.

stay[3] *n* a strong rope, now usu of wire, used to support a ship's mast or similar tall structure, e.g. a flagstaff.

stay[4] *v* to support (a mast, chimney, etc) with stays.

stay[5] *n* **1** *literary* somebody or something that serves as a prop; a support. **2** (*in pl*) formerly, a corset stiffened with bones.

stay[6] *v* to sustain or provide physical or moral support for.

staying power *n informal* stamina.

stay on *v* to remain in a place, *esp* after the expected time limit, or after others have left.

stay over *v* to stay for the night as a guest.

staysail *n* a FORE-AND-AFT sail (one aligned from bow to stern) hoisted on a stay.

stay stitching *n* a line of stitches sewn round an edge, e.g. a neckline, before making up a garment in order to prevent the cloth from stretching.

stay up *v* not to go to bed.

STD *abbr* **1** sexually transmitted disease. **2** subscriber trunk dialling.

stead *n* the place or function ordinarily or formerly occupied or carried out by somebody or something else: *A new chairman was appointed in his stead.* ✱ **stand somebody in good stead** to be an advantage to somebody.

steadfast *adj* **1** firmly fixed; steady or immovable. **2** of a person: loyal or unwavering. ➤➤ **steadfastly** *adv,* **steadfastness** *n.*

steading *n Scot, N Eng* a farmstead.

steady[1] *adj* (**-ier, -iest**) **1** firmly positioned or balanced; not shaking, rocking, etc. **2** direct or sure in movement; unfaltering. **3** showing or continuing with little variation or fluctuation; stable or uniform. **4** not easily moved or upset; calm. **5** constant and dependable; consistent, not erratic. ➤➤ **steadily** *adv,* **steadiness** *n.*

steady[2] *v* (**-ies, -ied**) to become or make steady or steadier. ➤➤ **steadier** *n.*

steady[3] *adv* used *esp* by sailors: in a steady manner; steadily. ✱ **go steady** *informal* to have a long-term relationship with a boyfriend or girlfriend. **steady on!** used to tell somebody to calm down.

steak *n* **1a** a slice of meat cut from a fleshy part, e.g. the rump, of a beef carcass and suitable for grilling or frying. **b** a poorer-quality, less tender beef cut, usu from the neck and shoulder, suitable for braising or stewing. **2** a thick slice of any meat, *esp* pork or gammon. **3** a cross-sectional slice from between the centre and tail of a large fish.

steak tartare *n* uncooked steak mince mixed with raw egg and onion and seasoned.

steal[1] *v* (*past tense* **stole,** *past part.* **stolen**) **1** to take (something) without permission or illegally, with no intention of returning it. **2** to take (a look, etc) surreptitiously. **3a** to gain (an advantage over a rival, etc) by getting the better of them. **b** in sport, to get (the ball or possession of it, a run, point, goal, etc) by catching one's opponent out. **4** to come or go stealthily or unobtrusively. ✱ **steal a march on** to gain an advantage over (somebody) by stealthy or underhand means. **steal somebody's thunder** to anticipate or preempt somebody's words or actions, thus lessening or destroying their effect. **steal the show** to make a bigger and better impression than other ostensibly more prominent participants. ➤➤ **stealer** *n.*

steal[2] *n informal* a bargain.

stealth *n* **1** caution and surreptitiousness in movement or activity on the part of somebody trying to avoid detection. **2** (*used before a noun*) denoting aircraft or missiles so designed technologically as to be able to avoid acoustic or radar detection: *stealth bombers.*

stealth wealth *n* the use of wealth in relatively unobtrusive ways, the opposite of conspicuous consumption.

stealthy *adj* (**-ier, -iest**) characterized by stealth. ➤➤ **stealthily** *adv,* **stealthiness** *n.*

steam[1] *n* **1** the vapour into which water is converted when heated to its boiling point. **2** the mist formed by the condensation of water vapour when cooled. **3** energy or power generated by steam under pressure. ✱ **gather/get up/pick up steam** of an activity: to gain speed and impetus. **have steam coming out of one's ears** *informal* to be absolutely furious. **let off/blow off steam** *informal* to release one's pent-up energy, emotional tension, etc. **under one's own steam** using one's own means of travel or transport; independently.

steam[2] *v* **1** to give off steam or vapour. **2** to move by means of steam power. **3** *informal* to move or progress quickly. **4** (+ up) of a glass surface: to become covered with condensed steam. **5** to cook (food) in steam from boiling water. **6** (+ off/open) to apply steam to (something stuck with gum, etc) in order to soften the adhesive and release its hold. **7** to expose (something, e.g. clothes for pressing) to steam. ✱ **get steamed up** *informal* to get angry or agitated.

steam bath *n* a room, e.g. at a fitness centre, that can be filled with hot steam to induce sweating and clean and refresh the body.

steamboat *n* a boat propelled by steam power, *esp* a US paddle-wheel river boat of the 19th cent.

steamed *adj* **1** of food: cooked by steaming. **2** *Brit, informal* helplessly drunk.

steam engine *n* a stationary or locomotive engine driven or worked by steam.

steamer *n* **1** a ship powered by steam. **2a** a saucepan for steaming food in. **b** a perforated metal device placed inside a saucepan for steaming food in.

steaming *adj* **1** giving off steam. **2** very hot or humid. **3** *Brit, informal* helplessly drunk. **4** *Brit, informal* furiously angry.

steam iron *n* an electric iron that emits steam through the soleplate onto the fabric being pressed.

steamroll *v* see STEAMROLLER[2].

steamroller[1] *n* a machine equipped with wide heavy rollers for compacting newly laid tarmacadam, etc.

steamroller[2] *or* **steamroll** *v* **1** of a legislative body, etc: to force acceptance of (a measure) by crushing opposition or curtailing discussion. **2** to force (somebody) into acquiescence or into doing something.

steam turbine *n* a turbine driven by the pressure of steam against the turbine blades.

steamy *adj* (**-ier, -iest**) **1** full of steam. **2** hot and humid. **3** *informal* of fiction, films, etc: portraying sexual activity. ➤➤ **steamily** *adv,* **steaminess** *n.*

stearic acid *n* a fatty acid that is obtained from hard fat, e.g. tallow, with salts that are used in soap manufacture.

stearin *or* **stearine** *n* **1** an ESTER (compound produced by reaction between acid and alcohol) of glycerol and stearic acid. **2** the solid portion of a fat.

steatite *n* the mineral talc in solid form; = SOAPSTONE.

steatopygia *n* a substantial development of fat on the buttocks, common among the Khoikhoi people, and other peoples of arid areas of S Africa. ➤➤ **steatopygous** *adj.*

steed *n archaic or literary* a swift or spirited horse.

steel[1] *n* **1** a bluish grey alloy of iron with carbon, notable for its strength and hardness, distinguished from cast iron by its malleability under certain conditions, and widely used in construction work. **2** cold hardness or unyielding strength: *a heart of steel; nerves of steel.* **3** a tool, e.g. a ridged rod with a handle, for sharpening knives. ➤➤ **steel** *adj.*

steel[2] *v* to nerve (oneself) to do something.

steel band *n* a band that plays steel drums.

steel drum *n* a drum-like percussion instrument, orig made in Trinidad, consisting of an oil drum with one end beaten into facets giving a range of notes.

steel pan *n* = STEEL DRUM.

steel wool *n* long fine loosely compacted steel fibres used for scouring and burnishing.

steelworks *pl n* (*used as sing. or pl*) a factory where steel is made.

steely *adj* (**-ier, -iest**) resembling steel in hardness, strength, colour, or brightness. ➤➤ **steeliness** *n.*

steelyard *n* a balance in which an object to be weighed is suspended from the shorter arm of a lever and the weight determined by moving a counterbalance along a graduated scale on the longer arm until equilibrium is attained.

steep[1] *adj* **1** sloping sharply, or nearly vertical. **2** of a rise or fall in an amount, level, etc: substantial and rapid. **3** *informal* of a price: unreasonably high. **4** *informal* **a** of a request, condition, etc: excessive; difficult to comply with. **b** of a story: difficult to credit; far-fetched. ➤➤ **steeply** *adv,* **steepness** *n.*

steep[2] *n chiefly literary* a steep mountain slope; a precipice.

steep[3] *v* **1** to soak or be soaked in a liquid, e.g. for softening, cleansing, bleaching, or extracting an essence. **2** (*usu in passive,* + in) to imbue (somebody) thoroughly with a subject, influence, etc.

steepen *v* to become or make steeper.

steeple *n* **1** a church tower with a spire. **2** a spire surmounting the tower of a church, or rising directly from its roof. ⯮ **steepled** *adj.*

steeplechase *n* **1** a horse race over a racecourse with hedges and ditches for jumping. **2** a middle-distance running race over obstacles. ⯮ **steeplechaser** *n,* **steeplechasing** *n.*

steeplejack *n* a person who climbs chimneys, towers, etc to paint, repair, or demolish them.

steer[1] *v* **1** to guide or control the course or direction of (a vehicle or ship). **2** to guide or channel (somebody or something) in a certain direction. ✱ **steer clear of** to keep well away from (somebody or something). ⯮ **steerable** *adj,* **steerer** *n,* **steering** *n.*

steer[2] *n informal* a piece of guidance or advice. ✱ **a bum steer** a misleading recommendation.

steer[3] *n* a bullock.

steerage *n* **1** *archaic or literary* the act or an instance of steering a ship. **2** formerly, a large section in a passenger ship for passengers paying the lowest fares.

steering column *n* the column that encloses the links between the steering wheel and the steering gear of a vehicle.

steering committee *n* a committee that determines the order in which business will be taken up, e.g. in Parliament.

steering group *n* = STEERING COMMITTEE.

steering wheel *n* a wheel that is turned by hand by a driver or helmsman to steer a motor vehicle, ship, etc.

steersman *n* (*pl* **steersmen**) a helmsman.

stegosaur *or* **stegosaurus** *n* (*pl* **stegosaurs** *or* **stegosauruses**) a dinosaur of the Jurassic and early Cretaceous periods, with a double row of strongly developed bony plates along the back.

stein /stien, shtien/ *n* a large earthenware beer mug.

stela *n* (*pl* **stelae**) = STELE.

stele *n* a usu carved or inscribed stone slab or pillar, sometimes used as a gravestone.

stellar *adj* **1** relating to a star or stars. **2** *informal* of profits, etc: enormous; astronomical.

stellate *or* **stellated** *adj* of a flower or its petals: having a radiating shape, like a stylized star.

stem[1] *n* **1** the main stalk or trunk of a plant or shrub, from which the leaves and flowers develop. **2** the slender stalk of a flower, leaf, or fruit. **3** the upright timber at the prow of a ship to which the sides are fixed. **4** the main unchanging part of a word to which inflectional endings or other formative affixes are added. **5** a vertical stroke of a letter or musical note. **6** the tube of a tobacco pipe. **7** the slender support between the base and bowl of a wineglass. ✱ **from stem to stern** with reference to a ship: from end to end.

stem[2] *v* (**stemmed, stemming**) **1** (+ from) to originate or arise from something. **2** to remove the stems from (fruit, etc). **3** of a ship: to make headway against (the tide or current).

stem[3] *v* (**stemmed, stemming**) **1** to stop (something flowing). **2** to stop (the onward progress of something). **3** to retard oneself by forcing the heel of one or both skis outward from the line of progress.

stem ginger *n* the underground part of the stem of a ginger plant, *esp* cut up and preserved in syrup or as crystallized pieces.

stem stitch *n* an embroidery stitch executed by overlapping stitches lengthways so as to form a narrow line.

stemware *n NAm* wine glasses or other glasses with a stem.

Sten *n* a lightweight British submachine gun.

stench *n* a stink.

stencil[1] *n* an impervious material, e.g. a sheet of paper or metal, perforated with a design or lettering through which a substance, e.g. ink or paint, is forced onto the surface below.

stencil[2] *v* (**stencilled, stencilling,** *NAm* **stenciled, stenciling**) **1** to produce (a design, etc) by means of a stencil. **2** to decorate (a surface) with a stencil.

stenography *n* the writing and transcription of shorthand. ⯮ **stenographer** *n,* **stenographic** *adj.*

stentorian *adj* of a person's voice or delivery: extremely loud.

step[1] *n* **1a** a movement made by raising one foot and bringing it down in front of the other in walking or running. **b** the space passed over in one step. **c** a short distance. **2a** (*also in pl*) a flat supporting surface for the foot in ascending or descending. **b** (*in pl*) a stepladder. **3a** a degree, grade, or rank in a scale. **b** a stage in the progress of something. **c** (*also in pl*) an action, proceeding, or measure. **4** in a yacht, etc, a socket designed to receive an upright spar; *esp* a block for supporting the base of a mast. ✱ **in step 1** (*often* + with) with each foot moving to the same time as the corresponding foot of others, or in time to music. **2** (*often* + with) in harmony or agreement. **out of step** (*often* + with) not in step. **watch/mind one's step** to behave or proceed with caution.

step[2] *v* (**stepped, stepping**) **1** to move by raising one foot and bringing it down in front of the other, or in another position. **2** to erect (a spar, mast, flagstaff, etc) by fixing the lower end into a socket. ✱ **step aside 1** to stand clear of something. **2** to resign from a position. **step back** to distance oneself from a situation in order to assess it more objectively. **step forward** to volunteer one's services. **step into somebody's shoes** to take over somebody's role or job. **step on it/the gas** *informal* to drive or move faster; to hurry up. **step out of line** to fail to conform. ⯮ **stepped** *adj.*

step- *comb. form* denoting a relationship by remarriage and not by blood: *stepfather.*

step aerobics *pl n* (*used as sing. or pl*) a kind of aerobics that involves stepping up onto and down from a portable plastic block.

stepbrother *n* a son of one's stepparent by a former marriage.

stepchild *n* (*pl* **stepchildren**) a child of one's wife or husband by a former marriage.

stepdaughter *n* a daughter of one's wife or husband by a former marriage.

step down *v* to retire or resign.

stepfamily *n* (*pl* **-ies**) a family that includes one or more stepchildren.

stepfather *n* the husband of one's mother by a subsequent marriage.

stephanotis *n* a climbing plant of Madagascar and Malaya, with fragrant waxy white flowers.

step in *v* **1** to intervene in an affair or dispute. **2** to take somebody's place in an emergency.

stepladder *n* a hinged ladder with flat rungs and often a platform.

stepmother *n* the wife of one's father by a subsequent marriage.

step out *v* **1** to begin to walk faster. **2** to leave a room for a short time.

stepparent *n* the husband or wife of one's parent by a subsequent marriage.

steppe *n* a vast grassy treeless plain, *esp* in SE Europe or Asia.

stepping-stone *n* **1** a stone on which to step, e.g. in crossing a stream, swampy or muddy patch, etc. **2** something regarded as a means of progress or advancement.

stepsister *n* a daughter of one's stepparent by a former marriage.

stepson *n* a son of one's wife or husband by a former marriage.

step up *v* to increase, augment, or advance (an operation, output, etc) by one or more steps.

stepwise *adj and adv* arranged in or proceeding in steps.

-ster *suffix* forming nouns, denoting: **1** a person who goes in for the activity specified: *songster; punster.* **2** a person characterized by being something: *youngster; oldster.*

steradian *n* the SI unit of solid angular measurement that is equal to the solid angle at the centre of a sphere subtended by an area on the surface of the sphere equal to the square of the radius of the sphere.

stereo[1] *n* (*pl* **-os**) **1** stereophonic sound. **2** a stereophonic record-player, etc.

stereo[2] *adj* **1** stereoscopic. **2** stereophonic.

stereography *n* the art, process, or technique of drawing solid bodies on a plane surface. ➤➤ **stereographic** *adj.*

stereophonic *adj* relating to or denoting sound reproduction or a system of sound reproduction in which the sound is split into and reproduced by two different channels to give spatial effect: compare MONOPHONIC. ➤➤ **stereophonically** *adv,* **stereophony** *n.*

stereoscope *n* an optical instrument with two eyepieces through which the observer views two pictures taken from points of view a little way apart to get the effect of a single three-dimensional picture. ➤➤ **stereoscopic** *adj.*

stereotype[1] *n* **1** a person or thing that conforms to a fixed or general pattern; a standardized simplistic image. **2** a relief printing plate made by making a cast from a mould of composed type. ➤➤ **stereotypic** *adj,* **stereotypical** *adj,* **stereotypically** *adv.*

stereotype[2] *v* to have a conventionalized mental image of, or represent (a person or thing) as a stereotype. ➤➤ **stereotypy** *n.*

sterile *adj* **1** of a person or animal: unable to produce young. **2** of a plant: unable to produce fruit or seeds. **3** of land: unable to produce crops; barren. **4** deficient in ideas or originality. **5** free from living organisms, *esp* micro-organisms. ➤➤ **sterilely** *adv,* **sterility** *n.*

sterilize *or* **-ise** *v* **1** to make (instruments, an environment, etc) sterile by destroying micro-organisms. **2** to make (a person or animal) unable to produce young by removing or blocking the organs of reproduction. ➤➤ **sterilization** *n.*

sterling[1] *n* British money.

sterling[2] *adj* of a person's character or efforts: of genuine worth or quality.

sterling silver *n* silver that is at least 92.25% pure.

stern[1] *adj* **1** harsh, strict, or severe, *esp* in imposing discipline or exercising authority. **2** tough; hard-hearted. **3** firm; uncompromising. ➤➤ **sternly** *adv,* **sternness** *n.*

stern[2] *n* the rear end of a ship. ➤➤ **sternmost** *adj,* **sternwards** *adv.*

sterna *n* pl of STERNUM.

sternpost *n* the principal supporting structure at the stern of a ship extending from keel to deck.

sternum *n* (*pl* **sternums** *or* **sterna**) a narrow flat vertical bone in the centre of the thorax, to which the collarbones and the upper seven ribs are attached. ➤➤ **sternal** *adj.*

sternutation *n formal* the action of sneezing.

steroid *n* any of numerous chemical compounds containing the ring of carbon atoms characteristic of the sterols and including the sterols and various hormones and glycosides which have important physiological effects. ➤➤ **steroidal** *adj.*

sterol *n* any of various solid CYCLIC (containing a ring of carbon atoms) alcohols, e.g. cholesterol, widely distributed in animal and plant fats.

stertorous *adj* of breathing: characterized by a harsh snoring or gasping sound. ➤➤ **stertorously** *adv.*

stet *v* (**stetted, stetting**) to direct retention of (a word or passage previously ordered to be deleted or omitted) by marking with a tick or the word *stet.*

stethoscope *n* an instrument used to detect and study sounds produced in the body, *esp* by the heart and lungs, consisting of a sound-transmitting disc connected by a pair of tubes to earpieces.

stetson *n NAm trademark* a broad-brimmed high-crowned felt hat.

stevedore *n* a person employed to load and unload ships.

stew[1] *n* **1** a dish of meat, vegetables, or both, cooked in liquid in a closed pan or casserole. **2** *informal* an agitated state; a panic. **3** *archaic* a public room providing steam baths.

stew[2] *v* **1** to cook (meat, fruit, etc) in liquid in a closed vessel. **2** of food: to cook slowly in a closed vessel. **3** of tea: to become over-strong and bitter from prolonged brewing. **4** *informal* to be in a state of agitation. ✱ **stew in one's own juice** *informal* to be left to suffer the consequences of one's own stupidity.

stew[3] *n Brit* **1** a fishtank. **2** an artificial oyster bed.

steward[1] *n* **1** a person who manages the provisioning of food and attends to the needs of passengers on an airliner, ship, or train. **2** a person who supervises the provision and distribution of food and drink in a club, college, etc. **3** an official in charge of arrangements and proceedings at a large public event, e.g. a race meeting. **4a** a person employed to manage a large house or estate. **b** *esp* formerly, an administrator of the Crown estates, attached to the British royal household. ➤➤ **stewardship** *n.*

steward[2] *v* to serve as steward of (an estate, etc) or manage (a public event, etc).

stewardess *n* a woman who attends to the needs of passengers aboard an airliner or ship.

stewed *adj* **1** of tea: bitter-tasting as a result of infusing for too long. **2** *informal* drunk.

stick[1] *n* **1** a twig or slender branch from a tree or shrub. **2** a long slender piece of wood specially fashioned for use, e.g.: **a** a club or staff used as a weapon; a stave. **b** a walking stick. **c** an implement used for striking or propelling a ball or other object in a game. **3** something prepared, e.g. by cutting, moulding, or rolling, in a long, slender, often cylindrical form: *a stick of rock.* **4a** a number of bombs arranged for release from a plane at intervals across a target. **b** a number of parachutists dropping together. **5** the threat of punishment as a means of obtaining compliance, often contrasted with a CARROT representing an inducement. **6** *informal* critical disapproving comment. **7** (**the sticks**) *informal, derog* remote or backward rural areas. ✱ **up sticks** *Brit, informal* to go and live elsewhere.

stick[2] *v* (*past tense and past part.* **stuck**) **1a** (*usu* + in/into/through) to thrust (a sharp or pointed object) into or through something. **b** to impale on a pointed object. **2** *informal* to poke (something) somewhere: *She stuck her head round the door.* **3** *informal* to put somewhere, *esp* temporarily: *Stick your bags in that corner.* **4** to attach (one thing) to another, or fix (several pieces) together. **5** *informal* (*in passive*) to become fixed or unable to move: *The wheels were stuck in the mud.* **6** *chiefly Brit, informal* (*usu in negative contexts*) to bear or stand (a person or thing): *I can't stick his voice.* **7** (*often* + into) of something sharp or pointed: to be fixed in something. **8** (+ out/out of/up) to protrude or project. **9** to become fixed or immovable. **10** (+ at) to persist at a task, etc. **11** (+ with) to persevere with something: *He decided to stick with science and train as a doctor.* **12** (+ to) not to deviate from something: *stick to the path.* **13** to become fixed or attached to a surface, etc: *The burrs stuck to her clothes.* ✱ **be stuck for** to lack or need (something). **be stuck on** *informal* to be infatuated with. **be stuck with 1** *informal* to be obliged to deal with (something). **2** *informal* to be unable to escape from (somebody or something). **get stuck in/into** *informal* to involve oneself wholeheartedly in a task, etc. **stick by 1** to continue to support (somebody). **2** to honour (a promise, etc). **stick one's neck out** *informal* to take an initiative or risk that leaves one vulnerable. **stick together** to continue to support each other; to remain united.

stick around *v informal* to linger somewhere.

sticker *n* an adhesive label or notice.

stick insect *n* an insect with a long thin body resembling a stick.

stick-in-the-mud *n* (*pl* **stick-in-the-muds**) *informal* a person who dislikes and avoids change.

stickleback *n* a small scaleless freshwater or coastal fish that has two or more spines in front of the dorsal fin.

stickler *n* a person who insists on exactness or completeness in the observance of something.

stick out *v* **1** to jut out; to project. **2** to be prominent or conspicuous; to stand out. ✱ **stick it out** *informal* to endure something unwelcome or arduous to the end. **stick out for** to insist on or persist in demanding (something).

stickpin *n NAm* a straight pin with an ornamental head, used to keep a necktie in place.

stick shift *n NAm* **1** a manually operated TRANSMISSION (gear-change) system in a motor vehicle. **2** a gear lever.

stick up *v* to stand upright or on end; to protrude. ✱ **stick up for** to defend against attack or criticism.

sticky *adj* (**-ier, -iest**) **1a** adhesive. **b** viscous; gluey. **c** coated with a sticky substance. **2a** of the weather: humid or muggy. **b** sweaty or clammy. **3a** awkward; stiff. **b** difficult; problematic. ✱ **come to a sticky end** *informal* to meet with ruin, disaster, a nasty death, etc, through one's own folly or wickedness. ➤➤ **stickily** *adv,* **stickiness** *n.*

sticky-fingered *adj informal* inclined to steal things.

sticky wicket *n* a cricket pitch drying after rain and therefore difficult to bat on. ✱ **on a sticky wicket** *informal* in a situation where one cannot be certain of one's ground.

stiction *n* the frictional force that is overcome to set one surface in motion when it is in contact with another.

stiff[1] *adj* **1** not easily bent; rigid. **2** of a handle, lever, lock, or other mechanism: hard to operate or turn. **3a** of the body or a part of it: not moving freely. **b** of the body or a part of it: painful to move as a result of intensive or unwonted exercise, or of strain. **4** of a mixture: thick. **5a** of social relations: formal; not relaxed and friendly. **b** lacking in ease or grace. **6a** of a contest: hard fought. **b** of a wind: strong. **c** of an alcoholic drink: strong. **d** of a punishment: harsh or severe. **e** of a physical challenge: arduous. **f** of a price: high. **7** *informal* used to intensify certain past participles used as adjectives: *scared stiff.* ✱ **a stiff upper lip** a stoical, dry-eyed self-control. **stiff with something** *informal* full of something: *The place was stiff with police.* ➤➤ **stiffly** *adv,* **stiffness** *n.*

stiff[2] *n informal* a corpse.

stiffen *v* to make or become stiff or stiffer. ➤➤ **stiffener** *n.*

stiff-necked *adj* haughty; stubborn; opinionated.

stifle[1] *v* **1** to suffocate (a person or animal) or prevent (a person or animal) from breathing freely. **2** to suppress (a yawn, a giggle, etc). **3** to curb or repress (something). ➤➤ **stifling** *adj,* **stiflingly** *adv.*

stifle[2] *n* the joint next above the hock in the hind leg of a horse or other four-legged animal corresponding to the knee in human beings.

stigma *n* (*pl* **stigmas** *or* **stigmata**) **1** a connotation of disgrace associated with certain things. **2** (*pl* **stigmata**) (*in pl*) in Christianity, marks resembling those left on Christ's body by the crucifixion appearing on the bodies, *esp* the palms, of saintly or particularly blessed people. **3** in medicine, a visible sign of a disease. **4** in flowers, the part of the PISTIL (female organ) that receives the pollen.

stigmatic[1] *adj* relating to a stigma, stigmas, or stigmata.

stigmatic[2] *or* **stigmatist** *n* a person marked with the stigmata of Christ.

stigmatize *or* **-ise** *v* **1** to describe or identify (somebody or something) in disapproving terms. **2** to mark (a person) with the stigmata of Christ. ➤➤ **stigmatization** *n.*

stile *n* a step or set of steps for climbing over a fence or wall.

stiletto *n* (*pl* **-os** *or* **-oes**) **1** a slender rodlike dagger. **2** a pointed instrument for piercing holes, e.g. for eyelets. **3** *Brit* an extremely narrow tapering high heel on a woman's shoe.

still[1] *adj* **1a** not moving. **b** calm or tranquil. **2** of drinks: not carbonated; not effervescent. ➤➤ **stillness** *n.*

still[2] *v* to make or become calm, quiet, or motionless.

still[3] *adv* **1** as before; even now or even then: *Drink it while it's still hot.* **2** in spite of that; nevertheless: *I still think it's immoral.* **3** (*used with comparatives*) even; yet: *I've thought of a still nicer idea.*

still[4] *n* **1** a still photograph, *esp* a photograph of actors or a scene from a film. **2** quiet; silence: *in the still of the night.*

still[5] *n* an apparatus used in distillation, *esp* of spirits.

stillbirth *n* the birth of a dead infant.

stillborn *adj* **1** of a baby: dead at birth. **2** of an idea, etc: failing from the start; abortive.

still life *n* (*pl* **still lifes**) a picture showing an arrangement of inanimate objects, e.g. fruit or flowers.

stilly[1] *adv* in a calm, still, or quiet manner.

stilly[2] *adj literary* still; quiet.

stilt *n* **1a** either of two poles each with a rest or strap for the foot, that enable the user to walk along above the ground. **b** any of a set of piles, posts, etc that support a building above ground or water level. **2** (*pl* **stilts** *or* **stilt**) a long-legged wading bird with three toes and mainly black and white plumage.

stilted *adj* of writing or speech: stiffly formal and unnatural. ➤➤ **stiltedly** *adv*, **stiltedness** *n*.

Stilton *n* either of two varieties of a white cheese enriched with cream: Blue Stilton, with blue veins, and White Stilton.

stimulant[1] *n* **1** a drug, etc that produces a temporary increase in the functional activity or efficiency of an organism. **2** anything that promotes interest or activity.

stimulant[2] *adj* having a stimulating effect.

stimulate *v* **1** to promote (a physiological process) or increase the activity of (an organ). **2** to give mental nourishment or encouragement to (a person, their mind, etc). ➤➤ **stimulation** *n*, **stimulator** *n*, **stimulatory** *adj*.

stimulus *n* (*pl* **stimuli**) **1** something, e.g. an environmental change, that directly influences the activity of living organisms, e.g. by exciting a sensory organ or evoking muscular contraction or glandular secretion. **2** something that rouses or incites to activity; an incentive.

sting[1] *v* (*past tense and past part.* **stung**) **1** *esp* of a plant, insect, or fish: to give an irritating or poisonous wound to (a person or animal). **2** of rain, wind, etc: to inflict pain on (somebody) as though by whipping or lashing. **3a** to cause a pang of bitterness or pain in. **b** (*usu* + into) to goad (somebody) into doing or feeling something. **4** *informal* to overcharge or cheat (somebody). **5** of a part of the body: to smart. ➤➤ **stinger** *n*.

sting[2] *n* **1a** a sharp organ, typically in certain plants, insects, or fish, that can wound by piercing and injecting a poisonous secretion. **b** a wound or pain caused by stinging. **2** a pang of emotional or mental pain, or the act or an instance of inflicting it. **3** *informal* **a** a confidence trick. **b** an elaborate deception mounted by law-enforcement officers to trap criminals. ✻ **a sting in the tail** a telling and unexpected climax to a story, etc.

stinging nettle *n* = NETTLE[1].

stingray *n* a ray with a whiplike tail bearing a long poisonous serrated spine capable of inflicting severe wounds.

stingy *adj* (**-ier, -iest**) *informal* **1** mean or ungenerous in giving or spending. **2** of an allotted share or portion: scanty or small. ➤➤ **stingily** *adv*, **stinginess** *n*.

stink[1] *v* (*past tense* **stank** *or* **stunk**, *past part.* **stunk**) **1** to give off a strong offensive smell. **2** *informal* **a** to be highly suspect, or suggestive of dishonest practice: *This appointment stinks of nepotism.* **b** to be contemptible: *Her proposal stinks.*

stink[2] *n* **1** a strong offensive smell; a stench. **2** *informal* a row or scandal. ✻ **like stink** *informal* very hard or intensively. ➤➤ **stinky** *adj*.

stink bomb *n* a small capsule which emits a foul smell when broken.

stinker *n informal* **1** an offensive or contemptible person. **2** something extremely difficult or unpleasant.

stinkhorn *n* a fungus noted for its foul smell.

stinking[1] *adj informal* **1** severe and unpleasant: *a stinking cold.* **2** having a strong offensive smell.

stinking[2] *adv informal* used as an intensifier expressing disapproval or contempt: *stinking rich.*

stint[1] *v* **1** to restrict (somebody, *esp* oneself) to a small share or allowance. **2** to be sparing with (a commodity). **3** (*often* + on) to be sparing or frugal.

stint[2] *n* **1** one's quota or round of duty or work. **2** restraint; limitation.

stint[3] *n* (*pl* **stints** *or* **stint**) a small sandpiper.

stipend *n* a fixed sum of money paid periodically as a salary or to meet expenses.

stipendiary *adj* **1** receiving a stipend, as distinct from working voluntarily. **2** relating to, or in the nature of, a stipend.

stipple[1] *v* **1** to dapple, speckle, or fleck (a surface). **2** to texture or roughen (a painted or cemented surface).

stipple[2] *n* a method of painting using small points, dots, dabs, or strokes to represent degrees of light, shade, and tone.

stipulate *v* **1** to specify as a condition or requirement of an agreement or offer: *The number of female members was stipulated in the constitution.* **2** to demand, promise, or agree (something) in making an agreement: *It was stipulated that weapons were to be handed in before peace negotiations commenced.* ➤➤ **stipulation** *n*.

stir[1] *v* (**stirred, stirring**) **1** to move (a liquid or semiliquid) around by means of repeated circular movement with a spoon or other implement, usu in order to blend the ingredients. **2** to make a slight movement or cause a slight movement in (something). **3** (*often* + up) to disturb or agitate (something lying still). **4** to move or exert (oneself). **5** to wake and begin to move. **6** to rouse (somebody) to activity. **7** to evoke (feelings, memories, etc). **8** *Brit, informal* to create trouble or ill-feeling between people by gossip, tale-bearing, etc. ➤➤ **stirrer** *n*.

stir[2] *n* **1** the act or an instance of stirring. **2** a sensation or commotion.

stir[3] *n informal* prison.

stir-fry *v* (**-ies, -ied**) to cook (small pieces of food) by stirring them together while rapidly frying them in hot oil.

stirring[1] *adj* rousing; inspiring. ➤➤ **stirringly** *adv*.

stirring[2] *n* **1** a slight movement. **2** the beginning of an emotion or feeling.

stirrup *n* **1** either of a pair of D-shaped metal frames or hoops in which a horse-rider's foot is placed, used to assist mounting and as a support while riding. **2** (*also* **lithotomy stirrup**) either of a pair of suspended supports for the ankles, used during childbirth, gynaecological examination, etc.

stirrup cup *n* a farewell alcoholic drink, formerly one taken by somebody already mounted.

stirrup pump *n* a portable hand pump held in position by a foot bracket and used in firefighting.

stitch[1] *n* **1** a loop of thread or yarn left in material or worked in fabric by a single in-and-out movement of the needle in sewing, embroidery, knitting, or crochet. **2** a method of stitching. **3** a local sharp and sudden pain in the side brought on by running or exercise. **4** *informal* (*usu in negative contexts*) the least scrap of clothing: *not wearing a stitch.* ✻ **in stitches** laughing uncontrollably.

stitch[2] *v* **1** to sew (fabric, a garment, etc). **2** to work on or decorate (fabric, etc) with stitches. ➤➤ **stitcher** *n*, **stitchery** *n*, **stitching** *n*.

stitch up *v Brit, informal* **1** to tamper with evidence, etc so as to incriminate (somebody). **2** to cheat or defraud (somebody). **3** to conclude (a deal, etc) to one's own advantage usu by dishonest manipulation.

stoa *n* (*pl* **stoas** *or* **stoae**) in classical Greek architecture, a portico, roofed colonnade, or colonnaded walk.

stoat *n* (*pl* **stoats** *or* **stoat**) a European weasel with a brown coat, turning white in winter in northern regions, and a long black-tipped tail.

stochastic *adj* **1** in statistics, relating to or denoting random sequential processes in which the probabilities at each step depend on the outcome of previous steps. **2** in statistics, random. ➤➤ **stochastically** *adv.*

stock[1] *n* **1a** a store or supply of raw materials or finished goods. **b** (*also in pl*) one's store or supply of anything. **c** (*used as sing. or pl*) farm animals kept for their milk or for slaughter; livestock. **2a** the capital raised by a company through the issue and subscription of shares. **b** (*also in pl*) the proportion of this capital held in the form of shares by an individual or company, entitling the holder to dividends, partial ownership, and voting rights. **c** (*in pl*) the shares of a particular company or type of company. **d** government securities issued at a fixed rate of interest in fixed units. **3a** the raw material from which something is made. **b** the liquid in which meat, fish, or vegetables have been simmered. **4a** the trunk or main stem of a plant, *esp* one into which a shoot (SCION) is inserted for grafting. **b** a plant or shrub of the cabbage family grown for its sweet-scented flowers. **5a** a person's line of descent; their family or lineage. **b** a breed or variety of a plant or animal, or the population representing it. **6** a neckband or cravat, usu white with flowing ends, worn by men. **7 a** (*in pl*) formerly, a device consisting of a wooden frame with holes in which the feet, or feet and hands, can be locked, in which petty criminals were held for public punishment. **b** the part to which the barrel and firing mechanism of a rifle or pistol are attached. ✱ **in stock** in the shop or warehouse and available for delivery. **out of stock** sold out; having none available for delivery. **put stock in** to attach importance to (something). **take stock** to review a situation.

stock[2] *v* **1** to supply (a place) with a stock of something. **2** to start or keep a stock of (something). ✱ **stock up** (*often* + on) to lay in a supply of something.

stock[3] *adj* **1a** kept in stock regularly: *clearance sale of stock goods.* **b** regularly and widely available or supplied: *dresses in all the stock sizes.* **2** *informal* commonly used or brought forward; standard: *the stock answer.*

stockade[1] *n* **1** a line of stout posts set vertically to form a defence. **2** an enclosure or pen made with posts and stakes.

stockade[2] *v* to fortify or surround (a homestead, encampment, etc) with a stockade.

stockbreeder *n* a person who breeds livestock.

stockbroker *n* a broker who buys and sells securities. ➤➤ **stockbroking** *n.*

stockbroker belt *n Brit* an area on the outskirts of a large town or city that is inhabited chiefly by wealthy middle-class people.

stock car *n* a racing car having the strengthened chassis of a commercially produced assembly-line model.

stock cube *n* a cube of compressed dehydrated meat, fish, or vegetable stock, used for flavouring stews, gravies, etc.

stock exchange *n* an association of people organized to provide an auction market among themselves for the purchase and sale of securities.

stockinet *or* **stockinette** *n* a soft elastic knitted fabric.

stocking *n* **1** a woman's closely fitting garment for the foot and leg, typically of fine knitted nylon and held up by suspenders or an elasticated strip. **2** *NAm or archaic* a man's long sock. **3** (*also* **Christmas stocking**) an ornamental stocking hung up by children on Christmas Eve, to be filled with presents. **4** a band of white extending up to a horse's knee or hock. ➤➤ **stockinged** *adj.*

stocking cap *n* a conical knitted cap tapering to a long point that hangs down.

stocking-filler *n Brit* a small inexpensive present for putting in somebody's Christmas stocking.

stocking stitch *n* a knitting stitch made by alternately knitting and purling rows of stitches to form a fabric with an even surface and uniform pattern.

stock-in-trade *n* **1** the equipment necessary to or used in a trade or business. **2** the range of skills typically on tap to a person in any particular line.

stockist *n Brit* a retailer who stocks goods, *esp* of a particular kind or brand.

stockman *n* (*pl* **stockmen**) *NAm, Aus* a person who owns or takes care of livestock.

stock market *n* a stock exchange or the transactions made on it.

stockpile[1] *n* an accumulated store, *esp* a reserve supply of something essential accumulated for use during a shortage.

stockpile[2] *v* to accumulate a stockpile of (an essential commodity, etc).

stockpot *n* a pot in which stock is prepared or kept as a basis for stews, soup, etc.

stock-still *adv* completely motionless.

stocktaking *n* the checking or taking of an inventory of goods or supplies held e.g. in a shop.

stocky *adj* (**-ier, -iest**) *esp* of a person: short, sturdy, and relatively thick in build. ➤➤ **stockily** *adv,* **stockiness** *n.*

stodge *n chiefly Brit, informal* **1** heavy filling starchy food, such as steamed pudding. **2** solid indigestible reading matter. ➤➤ **stodginess** *n,* **stodgy** *adj.*

stoep /stoohp/ *n SAfr* a raised veranda or open porch.

stoic[1] *n* **1** (**Stoic**) a member of an ancient Greek school of philosophy equating happiness with knowledge and holding that wisdom consists in self-mastery, submission to natural law, and indifference to pain, pleasure, and the caprices of fortune. **2** a person who bears pain, hardship, and sorrow without showing their feelings or complaining.

stoic[2] *adj* **1** (**Stoic**) relating to the Stoics or Stoicism. **2** = STOICAL.

stoical *adj* bearing pain, hardship, and sorrow without complaining or showing one's feelings. ➤➤ **stoically** *adv.*

stoicism *n* **1** (**Stoicism**) the philosophy of the Stoics. **2** stoical behaviour.

stoke *v* **1** to stir up or tend (a fire or furnace) and supply it with fuel. **2** to feed or encourage (an emotion). **3** *informal* (+ up) to eat plentifully in preparation for effort.

stoker *n* a person employed to tend a furnace, *esp* on a ship, and supply it with fuel.

STOL *abbr* short takeoff and landing.

stole[1] *v* past tense of STEAL[1].

stole[2] *n* **1** a large rectangular scarf or shawl worn by women across the shoulders, *esp* with evening dress. **2** an ecclesiastical vestment consisting of a long silk band worn over the shoulders.

stolen *v* past part. of STEAL[1].

stolid *adj* difficult to arouse emotionally or mentally; unemotional. ➤➤ **stolidity** *n,* **stolidly** *adv.*

stollen /'stolən/ *n* (*pl* **stollen** *or* **stollens**) a sweet spicy German yeast bread, containing fruit and nuts and coated with icing sugar.

stoma *n* (*pl* **stomas** *or* **stomata**) **1** any of various small simple bodily openings, *esp* in a lower animal. **2** any of the minute openings in the epidermis of a plant organ, e.g. a leaf, through which gases pass. **3** a permanent surgically made opening, e.g. through the abdominal wall into the bowel, or into the trachea.

stomach[1] *n* **1a** in a vertebrate, a saclike organ formed by a widening of the alimentary canal between the oesophagus at the top and the duodenum at the bottom, in which the first stages of digestion occur. **b** any of four such organs in ruminants (cattle, sheep, deer, etc; see RUMINANT[1]). **2** the part of the body that contains the stomach; the belly or abdomen. **3a** desire or capacity for food; appetite. **b** (*usu in negative contexts*) inclination or desire: *I had no stomach for an argument.* ✱ **a strong stomach** a lack of squeamishness.

stomach[2] *v* (*usu in negative contexts*) **1** to find (a specified food) palatable or digestible. **2** to bear (something irksome) without protest or resentment.

stomacher *n* a separate panel of fabric covering the chest and ending in a point at or below the waist, worn from the 15th cent. by men and women, and by women into the 18th cent.

stomach pump *n* a suction pump with a flexible tube for removing liquids from the stomach or injecting liquids into it.

stomata *n* pl of STOMA.

stomp *v informal* to walk or dance with a heavy step.

stomping ground *n NAm* = STAMPING GROUND.

stone[1] *n* **1** the hard compacted non-metallic earthy or mineral matter of which rock is composed. **2** a piece of rock; a pebble. **3** a gem. **4** (*used in combinations*) a piece of stone adapted to a particular function: *a paving stone; a gravestone.* **5** a greyish beige colour. **6** the hard seed in a peach, cherry, plum, etc. **7** (*pl usu* **stone**) *Brit* a unit of weight equal to 14 pounds (about 6.35 kilograms). ✱ **a stone's throw** no very great distance. **leave no stone unturned** to make every possible effort to find or obtain something.

stone[2] *v* **1** to hurl stones at (somebody), *esp* to kill (somebody) by this means. **2** to remove the stones or seeds of (a fruit). ✱ **stone me/stone the crows!** *Brit, informal* an exclamation of amazement.

stone[3] *adj* **1** made of stone. **2** of a greyish beige colour.

Stone Age *n* (**the Stone Age**) the first known period of prehistoric human culture characterized by the use of stone tools and weapons, covering about 2.5 million years and subdivided into the Palaeolithic, Mesolithic, and Neolithic periods.

stonechat *n* a common small thrush, the male of which has a black head and chestnut underparts.

stone circle *n* a circle of megaliths (large upright stones; see MEGALITH) of prehistoric, *esp* Bronze-Age, construction, having a presumed ritual function.

stone-cold *adj* absolutely cold. ✱ **stone-cold sober** utterly sober; not in the least drunk.

stonecrop *n* a plant with fleshy leaves that grows on rocks and walls.

stoned *adj informal* intoxicated by a drug, e.g. marijuana, or alcohol.

stone-dead *adj* completely dead.

stone-deaf *adj* completely deaf; having no residual hearing.

stonefish *n* (*pl* **stonefishes** *or* **stonefish**) a tropical fish of the Indian and Pacific Oceans with venomous dorsal spines.

stone-ground *adj* of flour: ground with millstones.

stonemason *n* a person who prepares stone for building.

stonewall *v* **1** to obstruct or delay parliamentary debate. **2** to be evasive or obstructive. **3** *chiefly Brit* to bat excessively defensively and cautiously in cricket.

stoneware *n* opaque ceramic ware that is fired at a high temperature and is nonporous: compare EARTHENWARE.

stonewashed *or* **stonewash** *adj* of *esp* denim clothing: washed with abrasive materials so as to produce a worn and faded appearance.

stonework *n* **1** masonry. **2** those parts of a building that are constructed of stone.

stonker *n informal* something or somebody that is pretty amazing. ➤➤ **stonking** *adj.*

stony *adj* (**-ier, -iest**) **1a** full of stones. **b** resembling stone. **2** cold or unresponsive; without compassion. ✱ **fall on stony ground** of good advice, etc: to go unheeded [in reference to Matthew 13:5]. ➤➤ **stonily** *adv.*

stony-broke *adj Brit, informal* completely without funds.

stood *v* past tense and past part. of STAND[1].

stooge[1] *n* **1** a person being used by somebody more powerful to do unpleasant or distasteful jobs. **2** the member of a comedy duo who speaks the feed lines and is the butt of the other's jokes.

stooge[2] *v* **1** (+ for) to act as stooge for a comedian. **2** *informal* (+ around/about) to move aimlessly to and fro.

stook[1] *n chiefly Brit* a group of sheaves of grain set upright against one another to dry.

stook[2] *v* to put (sheaves of grain) into stooks.

stool *n* **1** a seat usu without back or arms supported by three or four legs or a central pedestal. **2** *esp* in medicine, a discharge of faecal matter. **3** a tree stump or plant crown from which shoots grow out. **4** *NAm* a decoy bird used by hunters. ✱ **fall between two stools 1** to have elements of two categories and so belong satisfactorily to neither. **2** to fail to avail oneself of either of two possibilities.

stool pigeon *n* **1** a police informer. **2** a person acting as a decoy.

stoop[1] *v* **1a** to bend the body forward and downward, sometimes simultaneously bending the knees. **b** to stand or walk with a temporary or habitual forward inclination of the head, body, or shoulders. **2a** to condescend. **b** (*usu in negative contexts*) to lower oneself morally.

stoop[2] *n* a stooping position or posture.

stop[1] *v* (**stopped, stopping**) **1** to come or bring to an end. **2** to discontinue moving. **3** of a bus or train: to call at a place to take on or let off passengers. **4** to break a journey somewhere. **5a** to prevent from doing or continuing something. **b** to prevent from happening. **6a** to cease or discontinue (an activity). **b** to check or suppress. **c** to interrupt the functioning of (a mechanism). **7** to block or plug (a leak, opening, etc). **8a** to deduct or withhold (a sum due). **b** to instruct a bank not to give payment for (a cheque). **9** in music, to change the pitch of (a string) by pressing it with a finger. ✱ **stop at nothing** to be unscrupulous in achieving one's ends. **stop dead** to come to a sudden halt. ➤➤ **stoppable** *adj.*

stop² *n* **1a** the act or an instance of stopping. **b** a place where a train or bus halts to let passengers on or off. **2** a device or mechanism that prevents movement. **3a** a knob or lever on an organ or harpsichord that brings into play a set of organ pipes or strings of a particular tone quality and range of pitch. **b** a means of regulating the pitch of a musical instrument, e.g. any of the holes in a wind instrument. **4** in photography, the APERTURE (circular opening) of an optical system, e.g. a camera lens. ✱ **put a stop to something** to prevent something from continuing.

stop by *v chiefly NAm* to make a brief visit somewhere.

stopcock *n* a valve for stopping or regulating flow, e.g. of fluid through a pipe.

stopgap *n* a temporary expedient; a makeshift.

stop light *n* a red traffic signal.

stop-motion *n* the technique in cinematic animation of repeatedly stopping and restarting the camera, to create an illusion of movement in animated figures.

stop off *or* **stop over** *v* to break one's journey somewhere, *esp* overnight.

stoppage *n* **1** the act or an instance of stopping. **2** a blockage. **3** a concerted cessation of work by a group of employees that is usu more spontaneous and less serious than a strike. **4** *Brit* a deduction from pay by an employer for the payment of National Insurance, etc.

stoppage time *n* = INJURY TIME.

stopper¹ *n* **1** a plug or bung, *esp* one fitting into the neck of a bottle. **2** a person who stops something.

stopper² *v* to close or secure with a stopper.

stop press *n* late news added to a newspaper after printing has begun.

stop up *v* **1** to block (a hole, passage, etc). **2** *Brit, informal* to delay going to bed until late.

stopwatch *n* a watch with a hand that can be started and stopped at will for exact timing of races, etc.

storage *n* **1** the act or an instance of storing. **2a** the safekeeping of goods in a depository such as a warehouse. **b** the fee paid for warehousing property. **3** space available for storing things.

storage battery *n* a battery used for storing electrical energy.

storage cell *n* = STORAGE BATTERY.

storage heater *n Brit* an electric device that is used for storing heat when electricity is cheaply available, e.g. at night, and for radiating heat when electricity is expensive, e.g. in the daytime.

store¹ *v* **1** (*often* + up/away) to keep or accumulate (something) as a reserve supply. **2** to place (property, furniture, etc) in a warehouse, etc for later use or disposal. **3** to enter (data) in a computer memory, on a diskette, etc, for future access. **4** to have storage room for (goods, data, etc). ✱ **be stored with something** to have a rich supply of something.

store² *n* **1** a quantity of things kept for future use. **2** (*in pl*) in the armed forces, etc, a supply of food, equipment, ammunition, etc. **3** a collection or accumulation. **4** storage. **5** (*also* **department store**) a large shop selling a variety of goods. ✱ **in store** awaiting one in the future. **set store by something** to regard something as important and worthwhile.

storehouse *n* **1** a warehouse. **2** an abundant supply or source; a treasury.

storey (*NAm* **story**) *n* (*pl* **-eys** *or NAm* **-ies**) a horizontal division or level of a building.

storied *adj literary* celebrated in story or history.

stork *n* a large wading bird that has a long stout bill and typically black and white plumage.

storm¹ *n* **1** a violent disturbance of the weather marked by high winds and usu by rain, snow, hail, sleet, or thunder and lightning. **2** a violent shower of objects, e.g. missiles. **3** a tumultuous outburst. ✱ **go down a storm** *informal* of a performance, etc: to be rapturously received. **storm in a teacup** a disproportionate fuss about something relatively minor. **take by storm 1** of troops: to capture (a position, stronghold, etc) by a sudden violent attack. **2** to bowl over (an audience, etc).

storm² *v* **1** to shout angrily; to rage. **2** to rush furiously. **3** of troops: to move in a sudden assault or attack. **4** to attack or take (a fortified place, etc) by storm.

stormbound *adj* confined or delayed by a storm or its effects.

storm cloud *n* **1** a heavy dark cloud bringing rain or presaging a storm. **2** a build-up of circumstances likely to lead to trouble or conflict.

storm drain *n* a drain built to take away the extra water during a particularly heavy downfall.

stormer *n Brit, informal* something that is remarkably impressive.

storming *adj informal* usu of a sporting or musical performance: wonderfully fast and furious.

storm lantern *n chiefly Brit* = HURRICANE LAMP.

storm petrel *n* a small sooty black and white petrel whose appearance was formerly thought to presage bad weather.

storm sewer *n* = STORM DRAIN.

storm trooper *n* a member of a force of shock troops.

storm troops *pl n* = SHOCK TROOPS.

stormy *adj* (**-ier, -iest**) **1** wild, windy, characterized by thunderstorms, or in a state or of an appearance associated with storms. **2** full of turmoil or fury. ➤➤ **stormily** *adv,* **storminess** *n.*

story¹ *n* (*pl* **-ies**) **1** an account of incidents or events. **2** a statement of the facts of a situation in question. **3** the plot of a literary or dramatic work. **4** a rumour. **5** a lie. **6** a news article or broadcast.

story² *n* (*pl* **-ies**) *NAm* see STOREY.

storyboard *n* a series of drawings or photographs showing the shots planned for a television or cinema film.

storybook *n* **1** a book of children's stories, *esp* fairy tales. **2** (*used before a noun*) denoting romance of the kind associated with fairy tales.

storyline *n* the plot of a novel, play, film, etc.

stotin /sto'teen/ *n* a unit of currency in Slovenia, worth 100th of a tolar.

stotinka /sto'tingkə, stoh-/ *n* (*pl* **stotinki**) a unit of currency in Bulgaria, worth 100th of a lev.

stoup *n* a basin for holy water at the entrance of a church.

stour *n Scot* dust rising in a cloud or deposited in a thick layer. ➤➤ **stoury** *adj.*

stout¹ *adj* **1** heavily built; fat. **2** strong and thick; sturdily made. **3** bold and brave; not easily daunted. ➤➤ **stoutly** *adv,* **stoutness** *n.*

stout² *n* a dark sweet heavy-bodied beer brewed with roasted malt or barley.

stove¹ *n* **1** an enclosed appliance that burns fuel or uses electricity to provide heat chiefly for domestic purposes. **2** a cooker.

stove² *v* a past tense and past part. of STAVE².

stovepipe *n* metal piping used as a stove chimney or to connect a stove with a flue.

stovepipe hat *n* a tall silk hat of the mid-to-late 19th cent.

stovies *pl n Scot* a dish of stewed potatoes with onions.

stow *v* **1** to pack away in an orderly fashion in an enclosed space. **2** to fill (a ship's hold, etc) with cargo. ➤➤ **stowage** *n.*

stowaway *n* a person who stows away, *esp* on a ship.

stow away *v* to hide oneself aboard a vehicle, *esp* a ship, as a means of travelling without payment or escaping from a place undetected.

strabismus *n* the condition of having a squint.

straddle[1] *v* **1** to stand, sit, or be astride (something). **2** to be on land on either side of (something): *The village straddles the frontier.*

straddle[2] *n* a straddling stance or position.

Stradivarius *n* (*pl* **Stradivariuses**) a violin made by the Italian violin-maker Antonio Stradivari (d.1737) or his family or followers.

strafe[1] *v* to rake (ground troops, etc) with fire at close range, *esp* with machine-gun fire from low-flying aircraft.

strafe[2] *n* the act or an instance of strafing.

straggle[1] *v* **1** to lag behind or stray away from the main body, *esp* from a line of march. **2** to move or spread untidily away from the main body of something. ➤➤ **straggler** *n,* **straggly** *adj.*

straggle[2] *n* a straggling group, e.g. of people or objects.

straight[1] *adj* **1a** extending in one direction without bends or curves. **b** of hair: not wavy or curly. **c** of a course, route, aim, etc: going direct to its destination or target. **2a** level, upright, or symmetrically positioned; not skew. **b** in a proper or tidy state. **3a** honest or fair. **b** accurately sorted out; correct. **4a** clear, simple, or logical. **b** candid; frank; not evasive. **5** of successes: following consecutively or uninterruptedly. **6** of an alcoholic drink: unmixed; neat. **7a** in the theatre, denoting a conventional play as distinct from e.g. a farce or musical. **b** *informal* conventional in appearance, habits, opinions, etc; = SQUARE[2]. **c** *informal* heterosexual. ✻ **keep a straight face** to refrain from laughing. ➤➤ **straightly** *adv,* **straightness** *n.*

straight[2] *adv* **1** upright. **2** directly; in a straight line. **3** without delay or hesitation; immediately. ✻ **go straight** to leave one's life of crime and live honestly. **straight off/out** without hesitation. **straight up 1** *Brit, informal* honestly. **2** *NAm* neat; unmixed.

straight[3] *n* **1** a straight part or piece of something. **2** a poker hand containing five cards in sequence but not of the same suit. **3** *informal* **a** a conventional person. **b** a heterosexual. ✻ **the straight and narrow** a strictly honest or moral way of life [in reference to *Strait is the gate and narrow is the way which leadeth unto life* in Matthew 7:14].

straight angle *n* an angle of 180°.

straightaway *or* **straight away** *adv* immediately.

straightedge *n* a piece of wood, metal, etc with an accurate straight edge for testing surfaces, drawing straight lines, etc.

straighten *v* **1** (+ up) to sit or stand. **2** (+ up) of a vehicle, ship, etc: to stop turning and travel in a straight line. **3** (+ up) to set (something) straight. **4a** (*also* + out) to make (something) smooth or tidy. **b** (+ out) to sort out (a difficulty, etc).

straight fight *n chiefly Brit* a contest, *esp* an election contest, between two candidates only.

straight flush *n* a poker hand containing five cards of the same suit in sequence.

straightforward *adj* **1** of a person: truthful; easy to deal with. **2** free from evasiveness or ambiguity; direct. **3** presenting no hidden difficulties. ➤➤ **straightforwardly** *adv,* **straightforwardness** *n.*

straightjacket *n* see STRAITJACKET.

straightlaced *adj* see STRAITLACED.

straight man *n* a straight actor serving as foil to a clown or comedian.

strain[1] *v* **1a** to exert (a part of one's body) to the maximum. **b** to wrench or sprain (a part of one's body) through over-exertion. **2** to make great or excessive demands on (something). **3** to stretch (fabric, etc) to maximum extension and tautness. **4** to pass (a liquid) through a sieve or filter.

strain[2] *n* **1** a force being exerted on something. **2** in physics, the deformation of a material body subjected to stress, or the amount of such deformation. **3a** mental or emotional stress or tension, or something that causes this. **b** a wrench, sprain, or other bodily injury caused by excessive tension, effort, or use. **4** (*also in pl*) a tune, air, or passage of music.

strain[3] *n* **1a** a breed, race, or variety of an animal or plant. **b** a particular type of a bacterium or virus. **2** an inherited but not dominant characteristic, quality, or disposition.

strained *adj* **1** done or produced with excessive effort; not spontaneous: *a strained smile.* **2** tense; uneasy: *strained relations; a strained silence.* **3** showing the effects of strain: *a strained expression.*

strainer *n* a device, e.g. a sieve, to retain solid pieces while a liquid passes through.

strait[1] *adj archaic* narrow.

strait[2] *n* **1** (*also in pl*) a narrow channel connecting two large bodies of water. **2** (*in pl*) a situation of difficulty or distress.

straiten *v archaic* **1** (*usu in passive*) to subject (somebody) to severely restricting difficulties, *esp* of a financial kind. **2** to restrict in range or scope.

straitened *adj literary* denoting poverty-stricken circumstances in which severe economies must be made.

straitjacket *or* **straightjacket** *n* **1** a cover or outer garment of strong material used to bind the body and *esp* the arms closely, in restraining a violent prisoner or psychiatric patient. **2** something that restricts or confines like a straitjacket.

straitlaced *or* **straightlaced** *adj* excessively strict in manners or morals.

strake *n* **1** a continuous band of hull planking or plates running from stem to stern on a ship. **2** a projecting ridge added to an aircraft or other vehicle to increase stability.

stramash *n Scot* a row or commotion.

strand[1] *v* (*usu in passive*) **1** to run, drive, or cause (a ship) to drift onto a shore. **2** to leave (a person) in a strange or unfavourable place, *esp* without funds or means to depart.

strand[2] *n literary* a shore or beach.

strand[3] *n* **1** any of the threads, strings, or wires twisted or laid parallel to make a cord, rope, or cable. **2** any of the elements interwoven in a complex whole.

strange *adj* **1** not known, heard, seen, or visited before. **2** exciting wonder or surprise. **3** *archaic* (+ to) lacking experience or acquaintance of something; unaccustomed to it. ➤➤ **strangely** *adv.*

strangeness *n* **1** the state or fact of being strange. **2** in physics, the quantum property that explains the unexpectedly long lifetime possessed by certain elementary particles.

stranger *n* **1** a person who is unknown or with whom one is unacquainted. **2** a person unfamiliar in the place in question; a foreigner or alien. **3** (+ to) a person who is ignorant of or unacquainted with something.

strangle *v* **1** to choke (a person or animal), *esp* to death, by compressing their throat. **2** to suppress (a groan, cry, etc). **3** to hinder the development of (something). ➤➤ **strangler** *n.*

stranglehold *n* **1** a grip round the neck that can lead to strangulation. **2** a total control or monopoly of something.

strangulate *v* (*usu as past part.*) to constrict or compress (a blood vessel, loop of intestine, etc) in a way that interrupts the ability to act as a passage. ➤➤ **strangulation** *n.*

strap[1] *n* **1** a strip of leather, cloth, or other flexible material used for fastening, securing, holding together, or carrying, often with a buckle. **2** a band, plate, or loop of metal for binding objects together or for clamping an object in position. **3a** a strip of leather used for flogging, *esp* formerly in schools. **b** (**the strap**) punishment by this means. ➤➤ **strapless** *adj,* **strappy** *adj.*

strap[2] *v* (**strapped, strapping**) **1** to secure with or attach by means of a strap. **2** *Brit* (*also* + up) to support (a sprained joint, etc) with overlapping strips of adhesive plaster. **3** to beat with a strap.

strapline *n* a secondary heading or caption in a newspaper, etc.

strapped *adj informal* (*often* + for) short of money.

strapping[1] *adj* of a person: big, strong, and sturdy in build.

strapping[2] *n* **1** adhesive bandaging for wounds or injuries. **2** metal or leather straps collectively.

strata *n* pl of STRATUM.

stratagem *n* **1** an artifice or trick for deceiving and outwitting an opponent. **2** *archaic* cunning; guile.

strategic *adj* **1** relating to the long-term pursuit of objectives. **2** relating to military effectiveness. **3** of weapons, missiles, etc: designed to disrupt industry and communications in the enemy homeland, rather than for use on the battlefield: compare TACTICAL. ➤➤ **strategically** *adv.*

strategy *n* (*pl* **-ies**) **1a** the science and art of employing all the resources of a nation or group of nations to carry out agreed policies in peace or war. **b** the science and art of military command exercised to meet the enemy in combat under advantageous conditions: compare TACTICS. **2a** long-term planning in the pursuit of objectives, or the art of this. **b** a plan or method devised to meet a need. ➤➤ **strategist** *n.*

strath *n* a flat wide river valley, *esp* in Scotland.

strathspey *n* a slow Scottish dance that is similar to a reel.

strati *n* pl of STRATUS.

stratify *v* (**-ies, -ied**) **1** to form, deposit, or arrange (material, etc) in strata. **2** to divide (a population, etc) into status groups or social strata. ➤➤ **stratification** *n.*

stratigraphy *n* **1** the branch of geology concerned with the origin, distribution, and succession of rock strata. **2** the analysis of the chronological order of archaeological remains and deposits. ➤➤ **stratigrapher** *n,* **stratigraphic** *adj.*

stratocumulus *n* stratified cumulus consisting of large dark clouds often covering the whole sky.

stratosphere *n* **1** the layer of the earth's atmosphere between the troposphere and the mesosphere in which temperature increases with height. **2** *informal* the highest levels of something. ➤➤ **stratospheric** *adj.*

stratum *n* (*pl* **strata**) **1** a horizontal layer or series of layers of any homogeneous material, e.g. a sheet-like mass of rock or earth deposited between beds of other rock. **2** a socioeconomic level of society. ➤➤ **stratal** *adj.*

stratus *n* (*pl* **strati**) a cloud formation consisting of massive broad uniformly thick cloud.

straw *n* **1a** dry stalky plant residue, *esp* stalks of grain after threshing, used for bedding, thatching, fodder, etc. **b** a single stalk from such residue. **2** a tube of paper, plastic, etc for sucking up a drink. **3** a pale yellow colour. ✱ **catch/clutch/grasp at straws** to turn in desperation to any means of saving the situation. **draw the short straw** to be the person chosen to do something unpleasant. **straw in the wind** a hint that is an indication of a coming event.

strawberry *n* (*pl* **-ies**) **1** a small sweet red fruit covered with seeds. **2** a deep pinkish red colour.

strawberry blonde *n* a reddish blonde hair colour.

strawberry mark *n* a red elevated birthmark.

straw man *n* = MAN OF STRAW.

straw poll *n* an unofficial ballot carried out to test opinion on some issue.

straw vote *n NAm, NZ* = STRAW POLL.

stray[1] *v* **1** to wander away from the main group, or from the proper place or route. **2** *informal* to be unfaithful to one's spouse. **3** of an eye or hand: to move apparently casually in some direction.

stray[2] *n* a domestic animal wandering at large or lost.

stray[3] *adj* **1** of a domestic animal: having strayed; lost. **2** of hair: having escaped from an arrangement. **3** occurring at random or sporadically.

streak[1] *n* **1** a line or band of a different colour from the background. **2** an inherent quality, *esp* one that is only occasionally manifested: *a mean streak.* ✱ **on a winning streak** enjoying a series of successes or lucky breaks. **streak of lightning** a flash of lightning.

streak[2] *v* **1** (*usu in passive*) to make streaks on or in. **2** to move swiftly. **3** *informal* to run naked through a public place. ➤➤ **streaked** *adj,* **streaker** *n,* **streaking** *n.*

streaky *adj* (**-ier, -iest**) **1** marked with streaks. **2** of bacon: having lines of fat and lean. ➤➤ **streakily** *adv,* **streakiness** *n.*

stream[1] *n* **1** a body of running water, typically one narrower than a river. **2a** a body of flowing liquid or gas. **b** an unbroken flow, e.g. of gas or particles of matter. **3** a steady succession. **4** a continuous moving procession. **5** *Brit* any of a graded range of groups in a school to which pupils of the same age group are assigned according to their general academic ability: compare BAND[1] (6), SET[3] (3). ✱ **go with/against the stream** to conform to, or be opposed to, a general trend. **on/off stream** operational or available, or not so.

stream[2] *v* **1** to flow in a stream. **2** to flood or pour in great quantity. **3** to trail, or extend in a trail. **4** to run profusely with liquid. **5** *Brit* to divide (a school or an age group of pupils) into streams.

streamer *n* **1** a coiled strip of coloured paper for throwing at a party. **2** a pennant. **3** a banner headline in a newspaper.

streaming *adj* **1** of a cold: causing the eyes and nose to run uncontrollably. **2** denoting a tape drive on a computer for transferring data in bulk while the tape is running.

streamline *v* **1** to design or construct (a vehicle, etc) so as to minimize resistance to motion, e.g. through air. **2** to make (an organization) simpler or more efficient.

stream of consciousness *n* **1** in psychology, individual conscious experience considered as a continuous flow of reactions and experiences. **2** a literary technique used to convey this.

street *n* **1** a public thoroughfare in a city, town, or village. **2** (*used before a noun*) **a** homeless; living and sleeping in the streets: *street kids.* **b** relating to the culture of those adept at surviving in the urban environment: *street chic.* ✱ **on the street** homeless; vagrant. **on the streets** earning one's living as a prostitute. **streets ahead/better** *informal* immeasurably better. **up/down one's street** suited to one's abilities or tastes.

streetcar *n NAm* a tram.

street credibility *n* a convincing knowledge of what goes on in the urban subculture.

street value *n* the likely price that something, *esp* a quantity of drugs, could command if sold illegally on the street.

streetwalker *n* a prostitute who solicits in the streets.

streetwise *adj informal* **1** familiar with the life of city streets, *esp* with its disreputable or criminal underworld. **2** resourceful at surviving and prospering in modern urban conditions.

strelitzia *n* a S African plant with showy flowers, of a genus that includes the bird-of-paradise flower.

strength *n* **1** the physical power one has in one's body; muscle power. **2** in a material object, ability to withstand pressure, prolonged use, etc. **3** the intensity of something, or the degree to which it is present or exists. **4** used with reference to solutions, alcoholic drinks, etc: the amount contained of the effective ingredient. **5** force measured in membership, or members present: *below strength.* **6** a good point. ✱ **go from strength to strength** to become ever more successful. **on the strength of** on the basis of (something).

strengthen *v* to make or become stronger. ➤➤ **strengthener** *n.*

strenuous *adj* **1** vigorous and wholehearted. **2** requiring effort or stamina. ➤➤ **strenuously** *adv,* **strenuousness** *n.*

streptococcus *n* (*pl* **streptococci**) a bacterium of a genus that occurs in pairs or chains and includes some that cause diseases in human beings and domestic animals. ➤➤ **streptococcal** *adj.*

streptomycin *n* an antibiotic obtained from a soil bacterium and used in the treatment of tuberculosis.

stress[1] *n* **1** pressure exerted on a physical object. **2** mental or emotional tension; strain. **3** intensity of utterance given to a speech sound, syllable, or word so as to produce relative loudness; accent. ➤➤ **stressful** *adj.*

stress[2] *v* **1** to emphasize (a point, etc). **2** to accent or emphasize (a word, syllable, etc). **3** (*usu in passive, also* + out) to subject to emotional or mental stress.

stretch[1] *v* **1** to pull, extend, or expand (material) till it becomes taut. **2a** of material, garments, etc: to have an elastic quality. **b** of materials, garments, etc: to become permanently enlarged. **3a** (+ out) to lie at full length. **b** to extend one's body or limbs to full length to relieve muscle stiffness, etc. **4a** to enlarge (something) by force. **b** to provide adequate challenge for (a person or their mind). **c** to strain (some resource, etc): *Cash supplies were already stretched to their utmost.* **d** to supplement or expand (something) beyond normal limits: *I stretch my pay packet with a spot of overtime.* **5a** to extend in space; to reach or spread: *broad plains stretching to the sea.* **b** to extend over a period of time: *The summer holidays stretched ahead of her.* **6** to elongate oneself in trying to reach something; to reach out. ✱ **stretch a point** to distort the rules slightly so as to accommodate a need, etc. **stretch one's legs** to go for a walk. ➤➤ **stretchy** *adj.*

stretch[2] *n* **1** the act or an instance of stretching. **2** the quality of elasticity in a material, etc. **3** an extent or area: *a stretch of water; a fine stretch of coastline.* **4** a leg of a journey, course, track, etc: *the home stretch.* **5** a period of time: *She was left by herself for long stretches.* **6** *informal* a period in prison. ✱ **at a stretch 1** continuously. **2** with difficulty: *We can fit eight people round the table at a stretch.* **at full stretch** to full capacity. **not by any stretch of the imagination** not conceivably.

stretcher[1] *n* **1** a light portable bed for carrying a sick, injured, or dead person, typically consisting of a sheet of canvas or other fabric stretched between two poles. **2** in bricklaying, a brick or stone laid with its length parallel to the face of the wall. **3** a wooden frame over which a canvas for painting is stretched and fastened.

stretcher[2] *v* to carry (an injured or sick person) on a stretcher.

stretch limo *n informal* = STRETCH LIMOUSINE.

stretch limousine *n informal* a custom-built limousine that has been lengthened to provide extra seating.

stretch marks *pl n* permanent marks on the skin caused by significant, usu rapid, weight gain or loss, *esp* those on the abdomen resulting from pregnancy.

strew *v* (*past tense* **strewed,** *past part.* **strewn**) **1** to spread (something) by scattering. **2** (+ with) to cover (a place) with something scattered. **3** to become dispersed over (a place).

strewth *interj* see STRUTH.

stria *n* (*pl* **striae**) **1** a minute groove on the surface of a rock, crystal, etc. **2** a narrow groove, ridge, line of colours, etc, *esp* when one of a parallel series.

striate[1] *v* to mark with striae. ➤➤ **striation** *n.*

striate[2] *adj* = STRIATED.

striated *adj* marked with striae.

stricken[1] *adj* **1** of somebody's face or expression: horrified or distressed. **2a** (*often* + with/by) badly hurt or hit by illness. **b** (*used in combinations*) hit by the calamity, emotion, etc specified: *panic-stricken.*

stricken[2] *v NAm* past part. of STRIKE[1].

strict *adj* **1a** stringent in requirement or control. **b** severe in discipline. **2a** inflexibly maintained or adhered to; complete. **b** rigorously conforming to rules or standards. **3** narrowly construed; restricted. **4** exact or precise. ➤➤ **strictly** *adv,* **strictness** *n.*

stricture *n* **1** a restraint or restriction. **2** an adverse criticism; a censure. **3** an abnormal narrowing of a body passage.

stride[1] *v* (*past tense* **strode,** *past part.* **stridden**) **1** to walk with long steps, usu with energy or firmness of purpose. **2** to cross (an obstacle) with a single long step.

stride[2] *n* **1a** a long step. **b** the distance covered in a single stride. **2** a striding way of walking. **3a** the most effective natural pace. **b** a state of maximum competence or capability: *get into one's stride.* ✱ **make strides** to make good progress; to advance rapidly. **take something in one's stride** to confront or deal with something difficult or unpleasant calmly.

strident *adj* **1** loud and obtrusive. **2** expressing opinions, demands, etc loudly or urgently. ➤➤ **stridency** *n,* **stridently** *adv.*

stridulate *v esp* of crickets, grasshoppers, etc: to make a shrill creaking noise by rubbing together specialized body parts. ➤➤ **stridulation** *n.*

strife *n* **1** bitter conflict or dissension. **2** *Aus, NZ* trouble of any kind.

strike[1] *v* (*past tense* **struck,** *past part.* **struck** *or NAm* **stricken**) **1a** to hit (somebody or something) with one's hand, a weapon, etc. **b** to inflict: *She struck a blow for feminism.* **2** to afflict (somebody) suddenly: *He was stricken by a heart attack.* **3** to delete or cancel. **4a** to make a mental impact on: *They were struck by its speed.* **b** to occur suddenly to. **5** to make and ratify (a bargain). **6** to indicate (the time) by sounding. **7** to create (a particular mood, atmosphere, etc): *The speech struck a gloomy note.* **8** to send down or out: *Trees struck roots deep into the soil.* **9a** of light: to fall on. **b** of a sound: to become audible to. **10** to put (somebody) suddenly in a particular state: *The blow struck him unconscious.* **11a** to take down the tents of (a camp). **b** to dismantle (e.g. a stage set). **12a** to cause (a match) to ignite. **b** to produce (fire) by striking. **13** to produce (an object) by stamping. **14** to assume (a pose). **15** to arrive at (a balance). **16** to discover (something, *esp* minerals). **17** (+ off/out) to embark on a journey, *esp* in a particular direction: *They struck off across the field.* **18** to withdraw one's labour in protest against an employer.

strike[2] *n* **1** an act of hitting or colliding with something or somebody. **2** a stoppage of work, *esp* by members of a trade union, in order to make a protest or to force an employer to comply with demands. **3** a success in finding or hitting something, *esp* a discovery of a valuable mineral deposit. **4** a military air attack, *esp* an air attack on a target. **5** an act of striking a ball. **6** in tenpin bowling, the knocking down of all ten pins with the first bowl in a frame.

strikebreaker *n* somebody who works during a strike, *esp* somebody hired to replace a striking worker.

strike off *v* to forbid (somebody) to continue in professional practice usu because of misconduct or incompetence.

strike pay *n* an allowance paid by a trade union to its members on strike.

striker *n* **1** a player who strikes, *esp* a football player whose main role is to score goals. **2** a worker on strike.

strike rate *n* the number of goals or points scored by a player or team, *esp* an average number.

strike up *v* **1** to begin to sing or play. **2** to cause (something) to begin: *We struck up a conversation.*

striking *adj* attracting attention, *esp* because of unusual or impressive qualities. ➤➤ **strikingly** *adv.*

Strimmer *n trademark* a machine for trimming the edges of a lawn.

Strine *n informal* Australian English.

string[1] *n* **1** a narrow cord used *esp* to tie, hang, or fasten things. **2a** a length of gut, wire, etc used to produce notes in certain musical instruments, e.g. the violin and piano. **b** (*usu in pl*) a stringed instrument of an orchestra. **3a** a group of objects threaded on a string: *a string of beads.* **b** a set of things arranged in a sequence. **c** a succession or sequence: *the author of a string of bestsellers.* **d** in computing, a sequence of characters treated as a unit. **4** a plant fibre, e.g. a leaf vein. **5** any of the interwoven lengths of nylon, gut, etc stretched across the head of a sports racket. **6** (*in pl*) conditions or obligations attached to something: *a relationship with no strings attached.* ✱ **have two/several strings to one's bow** to have more than one resource to call on. ➤➤ **stringed** *adj.*

string[2] *v* (*past tense and past part.* **strung**) **1** to equip with strings. **2a** to thread (things) on a string, or as if on a string. **b** to tie, hang, or fasten with string. **3** (*often* + out) to extend or stretch (something) like a string.

string along *v informal* **1** to accompany somebody, *esp* reluctantly. **2** *informal* to deceive or fool (somebody), *esp* as a delaying tactic.

string bean *n* a bean with stringy fibres between the sides of the pods, *esp* a French bean or runner bean.

stringent *adj* **1** rigorous or strict, *esp* with regard to rules or standards. **2** of economic conditions: marked by money scarcity and credit strictness. ➤➤ **stringency** *n,* **stringently** *adv.*

stringer *n* **1** a horizontal structural support. **2** a longitudinal structural part, e.g. in an aircraft's fuselage or ship's hull. **3** a correspondent employed by a publication or news agency on a part-time or casual basis to provide reports from a particular place.

string quartet *n* a group of four musicians playing stringed instruments, usu comprising two violins, a viola, and a cello.

string up *v* to kill by hanging.

stringy *adj* (**-ier, -iest**) **1** containing or resembling fibrous matter or string. **2** slim and muscular; wiry. **3** of a liquid or sticky substance: capable of being drawn out to form a string.

stringybark *n* an Australian eucalyptus tree with thick fibrous bark.

strip[1] *v* (**stripped, stripping**) **1a** to remove clothing, covering, or surface material from (something or somebody). **b** to remove (wallpaper, paint, etc) from a surface. **c** to deprive of possessions, privileges, or rank. **2a** to remove furniture, equipment, or accessories from (e.g. a house or ship). **b** to dismantle (e.g. an engine). **3** to damage the thread or teeth of (a screw, cog, etc). **4** to sell off (a company's assets). **5** to undress.

strip[2] *n* the act or an instance of undressing, *esp* a striptease.

strip[3] *n* **1a** a long narrow piece of material. **b** a long narrow area of land or water. **2** *Brit* the distinctive clothes worn by a sports team.

strip cartoon *n* a series of drawings, e.g. in a magazine, forming a usu humorous narrative.

stripe[1] *n* **1** a line or narrow band differing in colour or texture from adjacent parts, *esp* any of a series of parallel bands of this type. **2** a bar, chevron, etc of braid or embroidery worn usu on the sleeve of a uniform to indicate rank or length of service.

stripe[2] *v* to mark stripes on. ➤➤ **striped** *adj.*

stripey *adj* see STRIPY.

strip light *n* a long tubular fluorescent lamp.

stripling *n archaic or humorous* an adolescent boy.

stripper *n* **1** somebody who performs a striptease. **2** a tool or solvent for removing something, *esp* paint.

strippergram *n* a message, e.g. birthday greetings, delivered by somebody hired to accompany it with a striptease.

strip poker *n* a poker game in which players pay their losses by removing articles of clothing.

strip-search *v* to undress and search (a person) for forbidden objects, e.g. drugs or weapons, concealed about the body.

striptease *n* an act or entertainment in which a performer undresses gradually in an erotic manner in front of the audience.

stripy *or* **stripey** *adj* (**-ier, -iest**) marked or coloured with stripes; striped.

strive *v* (*past tense* **strove** *or* **strived,** *past part.* **striven** *or* **strived**) **1** to endeavour; to try hard. **2** to struggle in opposition; to contend. ➤➤ **striver** *n.*

strobe *n* = STROBOSCOPE.

strobe lighting *n* flashing intermittent lights, e.g. at a disco, produced by a stroboscope.

stroboscope *n* an instrument for measuring or observing motion, *esp* rotation or vibration, by allowing successive views of very short duration so that the motion appears slowed or stopped, e.g. a lamp that flashes intermittently at varying frequencies. ➤➤ **stroboscopic** *adj.*

strode *v* past tense of STRIDE[1].

stroganoff *n* a dish of strips of meat, e.g. beef, cooked in a rich sauce with sour cream.

stroke[1] *v* to pass the hand over (something) gently in one direction.

stroke[2] *n* an act of stroking or caressing.

stroke[3] *n* **1** the act of striking, *esp* a blow with a weapon or implement. **2** a single unbroken movement, *esp* one that is repeated. **3** a striking of the ball in a game, e.g. cricket or tennis; *specif* a striking of the ball that constitutes the scoring unit in golf. **4a** an action by which something is done, produced, or achieved: *a stroke of genius.* **b** an unexpected occurrence: *a stroke of luck.* **5** a sudden reduction or loss of consciousness, sensation, and voluntary motion caused by rupture or obstruction of an artery of the brain. **6** a technique for propelling the body or a boat through water. **7** the slightest amount of effort or work: *She never does a stroke.* **8** the movement in either direction of a mechanical part, e.g. a piston rod, or the distance it travels. **9** the sound of a striking clock: *at the stroke of twelve.* **10a** a mark made by a single movement of a pen, brush, etc. **b** *Brit* = SOLIDUS. ✱ **at a stroke** by a single action. **off one's stroke** performing below one's usual standard.

stroke play *n* a golf competition scored by the total number of strokes.

stroll[1] *v* to walk in a leisurely manner.

stroll[2] *n* a leisurely walk.

stroller *n NAm* = PUSHCHAIR.

stroma *n* (*pl* **stromata**) **1** the supporting framework of some animal organs and cells. **2** a compact mass of fungal hyphae (threadlike filaments; see HYPHA) giving rise to a spore-producing body.

strong *adj* **1** having or marked by great physical power. **2** having moral or intellectual power. **3** having great resources of wealth, talent, etc. **4** of a specified number: *an army ten thousand strong.* **5a** striking or superior of its kind. **b** effective or efficient, *esp* in a specified area. **6** forceful or cogent. **7a** rich in some active agent, e.g. a flavour or extract; concentrated. **b** of a colour: intense. **8** moving with vigour or force. **9** full of passion or enthusiasm; ardent. **10** well established; firm. **11** not easily upset or nauseated. **12** having a pungent or offensive smell or flavour. **13** tending towards steady or higher prices. **14** in grammar, of or being a verb or verb conjugation that forms the past tense and past participle by internal vowel change, e.g. *drink, drank, drunk.* ✱ **come on strong** *informal* to behave in a forceful or aggressive manner. **(still) going strong** *informal* continuing to be active, effective, successful, etc. ➤➤ **strongly** *adv.*

strongarm *adj* using or involving undue force.

strongbox *n* a strongly made chest for money or valuables.

stronghold *n* **1** a fortified place. **2a** a place of refuge or survival. **b** a place dominated by a specified group: *a Tory stronghold.*

strong language *n* offensive language, *esp* swearing.

strong man *n* **1** a man who performs feats of muscular strength. **2** *informal* an autocratic leader.

strongpoint *n* a small fortified defensive position.

strong point *n* something in which one excels.

strong room *n* a room in which money and valuables are stored, typically a fireproof room that cannot be broken into.

strong suit *n* **1** in card games, a suit of which a player holds a number of cards of high value. **2** = STRONG POINT.

strontia *n* a white solid chemical compound resembling lime that is an oxide of strontium.

strontium *n* a silver-white metallic chemical element of the alkaline-earth group that occurs naturally in various minerals and is used to produce red flames in fireworks and flares.

strop[1] *n* **1** a strip of material, *esp* a leather band, used for sharpening a razor. **2** a band or loop of rope or metal used on a ship or boat to hold or lift heavy objects.

strop[2] *v* (**stropped, stropping**) to sharpen (a razor) on a strop.

strop[3] *n Brit, informal* an angry mood; a temper.

stroppy *adj* (**-ier, -iest**) *Brit, informal* quarrelsome or angrily uncooperative.

strove *v* past tense of STRIVE.

struck *v* past tense and past part. of STRIKE[1].

structural *adj* **1** of or affecting structure. **2** forming part of a structure. **3** used in or suitable for building structures. ➤➤ **structurally** *adv.*

structuralism *n* a method or approach used in anthropology, literary criticism, etc that seeks to analyse data in terms of the significance of underlying relationships and patterns of organization. ➤➤ **structuralist** *n and adj.*

structure[1] *n* **1** something that is constructed, e.g. a building. **2** the way in which something is constructed or organized. **3a** the arrangement of particles or parts in a substance or body. **b** arrangement or interrelation of elements.

structure[2] *v* to construct or organize in a particular way.

strudel *n* a pastry made from a thin sheet of dough rolled up with filling and baked.

struggle[1] *v* **1** to proceed with difficulty or great effort. **2** to make violent or strenuous efforts against opposition or confinement. **3** to compete. ➤➤ **struggler** *n.*

struggle[2] *n* **1** a violent effort or exertion. **2** a determined attempt in adverse circumstances. **3** a hard-fought contest. **4** a difficult task.

strum *v* (**strummed, strumming**) to play (a musical instrument, e.g. a guitar) by brushing the thumb, the fingertips, or a plectrum over the strings. ➤➤ **strum** *n.*

strumpet *n archaic or humorous* a prostitute or promiscuous woman.

strung *v* past tense and past part. of STRING[1].

strung-up *adj* extremely nervous or tense.

strut[1] *v* (**strutted, strutting**) **1** to walk with a proud or erect gait. **2** to provide, support, or stiffen with a strut.

strut² *n* **1** a structural piece designed to support or strengthen a framework by resisting pressure in the direction of its length. **2** a strutting step or walk.

struth *or* **strewth** *interj* an expression of surprise, alarm, or annoyance.

strychnine *n* a bitter poisonous chemical compound obtained from nux vomica and related plants.

Stuart *adj* relating or belonging to the royal house that ruled Scotland from 1371 to 1603 and Britain from 1603 to 1649 and from 1660 to 1714. ➤➤ **Stuart** *n.*

stub¹ *n* **1a** a small part of a page, e.g. of a chequebook, left on the spine as a record of the contents of the part torn away. **b** the part of a ticket returned to the user after inspection. **2** a short blunt part of a pencil, cigarette, etc left after a larger part has been used up or broken off. **3** something cut short, stunted, or blunted.

stub² *v* (**stubbed, stubbing**) **1** to strike (one's foot or toe) against a hard object or surface accidentally. **2** (+ out) to extinguish (e.g. a cigarette) by crushing the end.

stubble *n* **1** the stalky remnants of plants, *esp* cereal crops, that remain rooted in the soil after harvest. **2** a rough growth of short bristly hairs on a man's face. ➤➤ **stubbly** *adj.*

stubborn *adj* **1** unyielding or determined, *esp* unreasonably so. **2** difficult to get rid of. ➤➤ **stubbornly** *adv,* **stubbornness** *n.*

stubby *adj* (**-ier, -iest**) short and thick.

stucco¹ *n* (*pl* **-os** *or* **-oes**) a cement or fine plaster used to coat or decorate ceilings and interior and exterior walls.

stucco² *v* (**stuccoes** *or* **stuccos, stuccoed, stuccoing**) to coat or decorate (a wall or building) with stucco.

stuck *v* past tense and past part. of STICK¹.

stuck-up *adj informal* superciliously self-important or conceited.

stud¹ *n* **1a** a solid button with a shank or eye on the back inserted through an eyelet in a garment as a fastener or ornament. **b** a rivet or nail with a large head used for ornament or protection. **c** a small piece of jewellery for a pierced ear. **2** a projecting piece, e.g. on a boot or tyre, to increase grip.

stud² *v* (**studded, studding**) **1** to decorate, cover, or protect with studs. **2** to set (something) thickly with a number of prominent objects: *a sky studded with stars.*

stud³ *n* **1a** (*used as sing. or pl*) a group of animals, *esp* horses, kept primarily for breeding. **b** a place, e.g. a farm, where such animals are kept. **2a** a male animal, *esp* a stallion, kept for breeding. **b** *informal* a sexually active man.

student *n* **1a** somebody who undertakes a course of study, *esp* somebody who attends a college or university. **b** (*used before a noun*) denoting somebody training for a profession: *a student nurse.* **2** an attentive and systematic observer: *a student of human nature.* ➤➤ **studentship** *n.*

studhorse *n* a stallion kept for breeding.

studied *adj* **1** carefully considered or prepared. **2** produced or adopted for effect; deliberate: *studied indifference.*

studio *n* (*pl* **-os**) **1a** the workroom of a painter, sculptor, or photographer. **b** a place for the study of an art, e.g. dancing, singing, or acting. **2a** a place where films are made. **b** (*also in pl*) a film production company including its premises and employees. **3** a room equipped for the production of radio or television programmes.

studio flat *n* a small flat consisting typically of one main room with a small kitchen and bathroom.

studious *adj* **1** pursuing studies seriously and with commitment. **2a** marked by or suggesting serious thoughtfulness or diligence. **b** deliberate. ➤➤ **studiously** *adv,* **studiousness** *n.*

stud poker *n* a form of poker in which each player's first card is dealt face down and the next four face up, with a round of betting taking place after each of the last four rounds of dealing.

study¹ *n* (*pl* **-ies**) **1a** the application of the mind to acquiring knowledge, *esp* by reading. **b** a careful examination or analysis of a subject. **2** a room devoted to study, writing, reading, etc. **3** a literary or artistic work intended as a preliminary or experimental interpretation. **4** a musical composition intended for improvement of technique.

study² *v* (**-ies, -ied**) **1** to engage in study. **2** to engage in the study of (a subject). **3** to read, observe, or consider attentively or in detail. **4** to try to memorize.

stuff¹ *n* **1a** materials, supplies, or equipment used in various activities. **b** personal property; possessions. **2a** an unspecified material substance. **b** a group of miscellaneous objects. **3** subject matter or expertise: *a teacher who knows his stuff.* **4** the essence of a usu abstract thing: *the stuff of greatness.*

stuff² *v* **1a** to fill (something) by packing things in. **b** to gorge (oneself) with food. **c** to fill with stuffing. **d** to fill out the skin of (an animal) for mounting. **2** to force or thrust into a confined space. **3** (*usu* + up) to choke or block up (the nasal passages). **4** *Brit, informal* to defeat or thwart. ✱ **get stuffed!** *Brit, informal* a forceful expression of disagreement or anger.

stuffed shirt *n informal* a smug, pompous, and usu reactionary person.

stuffing *n* **1** material used to stuff something, *esp* upholstered furniture, soft toys, etc. **2** a seasoned mixture of ingredients used to stuff meat, vegetables, etc. ✱ **knock the stuffing out of somebody 1** to beat somebody severely. **2** to cause somebody to lose vigour or vitality.

stuffy *adj* (**-ier, -iest**) **1a** badly ventilated; close. **b** blocked or congested. **2** lacking interest or inspiration; dull. **3** narrowly conventional in behaviour; straitlaced. ➤➤ **stuffily** *adv,* **stuffiness** *n.*

stultify *v* (**-ies, -ied**) **1** to bore (somebody) by being tedious or repetitive. **2** to cause (something) to appear foolish or absurd. ➤➤ **stultification** *n,* **stultifying** *adj.*

stumble¹ *v* **1** to trip in walking or running. **2a** to walk unsteadily or clumsily. **b** to speak or act in a hesitant or faltering manner. **3** (+ upon/on/across) to find or discover something or somebody unexpectedly or by chance.

stumble² *n* an act of stumbling.

stumbling block *n* an obstacle to progress or understanding.

stump¹ *n* **1** the part of a tree remaining in the ground after the tree has been felled. **2** a remaining part; a stub. **3** any of the three upright wooden rods that together with the bails form the wicket in cricket. ✱ **on the stump** *informal* making a political speech as part of a campaign.

stump² *v* **1** *informal* (*usu in passive*) to baffle or bewilder. **2** of a wicketkeeper: to dismiss (a batsman who is out of the crease but not running) by breaking the wicket with the ball. **3** to walk heavily or noisily.

stumper *n informal* a puzzling question; a teaser.

stump up *v Brit, informal* to pay (what is due), *esp* unwillingly.

stumpy *adj* (**-ier, -iest**) short and thick; stubby.

stun *v* (**stunned, stunning**) **1** to make dazed or briefly unconscious, e.g. by a blow. **2** to overcome with astonishment or disbelief.

stung *v* past tense and past part. of STING[1].

stun gun *n* a weapon that discharges high-voltage electricity or missiles to immobilize a human target without inflicting lasting injury.

stunk *v* past tense and past part. of STINK[1].

stunner *n informal* an unusually attractive or impressive person or thing.

stunning *adj informal* strikingly attractive or impressive. ⋙ **stunningly** *adv.*

stunt[1] *v* to hinder or arrest the growth or development of (something or somebody).

stunt[2] *n* **1** an unusual or difficult feat, *esp* one displaying physical or acrobatic prowess. **2** something done purely as a way of attracting attention or publicity.

stuntman *or* **stuntwoman** *n* (*pl* **stuntmen** *or* **stuntwomen**) a man or woman employed, as a substitute for an actor, to perform dangerous feats.

stupa /'stoohpə/ *n* a Buddhist monument in the form of a dome- or bell-shaped building.

stupefy *v* (**-ies, -ied**) **1** to make groggy or insensible. **2** to astonish. ⋙ **stupefaction** *n.*

stupendous *adj* causing astonishment or wonder; marvellous. ⋙ **stupendously** *adv.*

stupid *adj* **1** lacking common sense or intelligence; slow-witted. **2** dulled in feeling or perception. **3** *informal* annoying or exasperating: *This stupid torch won't work.* ⋙ **stupidity** *n,* **stupidly** *adv.*

stupor *n* **1** a condition characterized by reduction or suspension of sense or feeling. **2** a state of extreme apathy or torpor. ⋙ **stuporous** *adj.*

sturdy *adj* (**-ier, -iest**) **1** strongly built or constructed. **2a** having physical strength or vigour; robust. **b** showing determination or firmness of purpose; resolute. ⋙ **sturdily** *adv,* **sturdiness** *n.*

sturgeon *n* a usu large edible fish whose roe is made into caviar.

Sturm und Drang /ˌstuhm ənt 'drang, ˌshtuhm oont/ *n* a German literary and artistic movement of the late 18th cent. characterized by high emotion and often dealing with the individual's revolt against society.

stutter[1] *v* **1** to speak with involuntary hesitation or disruption of speech, e.g. by spasmodic repetition or prolongation of vocal sounds. **2** to make a series of abrupt sounds or movements. ⋙ **stutterer** *n.*

stutter[2] *n* **1** the act or an instance of stuttering. **2** a speech disorder that produces stuttering.

sty[1] *n* (*pl* **-ies**) = PIGSTY.

sty[2] *or* **stye** *n* (*pl* **sties** *or* **styes**) an inflamed swelling of a sebaceous gland at the edge of an eyelid.

Stygian *adj formal or literary* extremely dark or gloomy.

style[1] *n* **1a** a distinctive or characteristic manner of doing something. **b** a fashionable or elegant way of living. **c** excellence, distinction, or grace in social behaviour, manner, or appearance. **2** a manner of expression in writing, painting, music, etc, *esp* when characteristic of an individual, period, etc. **3** a distinctive design, arrangement, or fashion. **4** a prolongation of a plant OVARY (seed-producing organ) bearing a STIGMA (pollen-receiving structure) at the top. **5** a mode of address; a title. ⋙ **styleless** *adj.*

style[2] *v* **1** to design or arrange in a particular style. **2** to designate (somebody or something) by an identifying term. ⋙ **styler** *n.*

styli *n* pl of STYLUS.

stylise *v* see STYLIZE.

stylish *adj* fashionably elegant. ⋙ **stylishly** *adv,* **stylishness** *n.*

stylist *n* **1** a hairdresser. **2** a writer who cultivates a fine literary style.

stylistic *adj* relating to style, *esp* literary or artistic style. ⋙ **stylistically** *adv.*

stylistics *pl n* (*used as sing. or pl*) the study of style, *esp* in literature.

stylize *or* **-ise** *v* to represent or design according to a conventional style or pattern rather than according to nature. ⋙ **stylization** *n.*

stylus *n* (*pl* **styli** *or* **styluses**) **1** a tiny piece of material, e.g. diamond, with a rounded tip used in a gramophone to follow the groove on a record and transmit the sound. **2** a pointed instrument used in ancient times for writing on clay or waxed tablets.

stymie *v* (**stymies, stymied, stymying**) to present an obstacle to (somebody or something); to thwart.

styptic *adj* tending to contract tissues, *esp* to check bleeding. ⋙ **styptic** *n.*

styrene *n* a colourless liquid chemical compound used chiefly in making rubber, plastics, etc.

Styrofoam *n NAm, trademark* an expanded plastic made from polystyrene.

suasion *n formal* the act of influencing or persuading.

suave *adj* **1** smoothly though often superficially charming and polite. **2** *esp* of men: elegant and sophisticated. ⋙ **suavely** *adv,* **suaveness** *n,* **suavity** *n.*

sub[1] *n informal* **1** a submarine. **2** a subscription. **3** a substitute, *esp* in a sport. **4** a subsistence allowance, an advance of money. **5** a subeditor.

sub[2] *v* (**subbed, subbing**) *informal* **1** to act as a substitute. **2** to lend or advance money to (somebody). **3** to subedit (a newspaper, etc).

sub- *or* **suc-** *or* **suf-** *or* **sug-** *or* **sup-** *or* **sur-** *or* **sus-** *prefix* **1** under, beneath, or below: *subsoil; submarine.* **2a** next in rank below; subordinate: *subdeacon.* **b** a repeated or further instance of a specified action or process: *subcontract; sublet.* **3** bearing an incomplete, partial, or inferior resemblance to; approximately: *subhuman.*

subalpine *adj* of or growing on high upland slopes below the treeline.

subaltern[1] *adj* low in rank or status; subordinate.

subaltern[2] *n* a commissioned officer in the British Army ranking below a captain.

subantarctic *adj* relating to or denoting a region just outside the Antarctic Circle.

sub-aqua *adj* relating to underwater sports or explorations, *esp* those requiring underwater breathing apparatus.

subaqueous *adj* existing, formed, or taking place in or under water.

subarctic *adj* relating to or denoting a region just outside the Arctic Circle.

subassembly *n* (*pl* **-ies**) an assembled unit designed to be incorporated with other units in a finished product.

subatomic *adj* **1** occurring within an atom. **2** smaller than an atom.

subcommittee *n* a subdivision of a committee usu organized for a specific purpose.

subconscious[1] *adj* **1** existing in the mind but not admitted to consciousness. **2** imperfectly or incompletely conscious. ⋙ **subconsciously** *adv,* **subconsciousness** *n.*

subconscious² *n* (**the subconscious**) the part of the mind in which mental activity takes place below the threshold of consciousness.

subcontinent *n* a vast discernible subdivision of a continent. ➤➤ **subcontinental** *adj.*

subcontract¹ *v* **1** to engage a third party to perform under a separate contract all or part of (work included in an original contract). **2** to undertake (work) under such a contract. ➤➤ **subcontractor** *n.*

subcontract² *n* a contract between a party to an original contract and a third party, *esp* one to provide all or a specified part of the work or materials required in the original contract.

subculture *n* a sector of society whose members have a shared pattern of behaviour and values distinguishable from the mainstream culture. ➤➤ **subcultural** *adj.*

subcutaneous *adj* being, situated, or applied under the skin. ➤➤ **subcutaneously** *adv.*

subdeacon *n* a cleric ranking below a deacon in some Christian Churches.

subdivide *v* to divide (something already divided, or one or more of its parts) into more and smaller parts.

subdivision *n* **1** any of the parts into which something is subdivided. **2** the act of subdividing.

subduction *n* the process by which one plate of the earth's crust sinks or is pushed under another, resulting in earthquakes and volcanic eruptions.

subdue *v* (**subdues, subdued, subduing**) **1** to reduce the intensity or degree of (e.g. light or colour). **2** to bring under control; to curb. **3** to conquer and bring (e.g. a people) into subjection.

subdued *adj* **1** lacking normal cheerfulness or liveliness; low-spirited. **2** reduced or lacking in force, intensity, or strength.

subedit *v* (**subedited, subediting**) *chiefly Brit* to edit (e.g. a newspaper article) in preparation for printing. ➤➤ **subeditor** *n.*

subfusc¹ *adj literary* drab or gloomy.

subfusc² *n* formal academic dress for members of a university, *esp* Oxford University.

subhead *or* **subheading** *n* a subordinate caption, title, or headline.

subhuman *adj* **1** below the level expected of or appropriate to normal human beings; debased. **2** of animals: lower than human beings in terms of evolutionary development, *esp* only slightly lower. ➤➤ **subhuman** *n.*

subject¹ *n* **1a** a branch of knowledge or learning, *esp* one taught or studied. **b** a person or thing concerning which something is said or done. **c** a matter dealt with in an article, speech, etc. **2a** somebody or something represented in a work of art. **b** an individual whose reactions are studied, e.g. in a psychological experiment. **3a** in grammar, the word or phrase in a sentence or clause denoting the person or thing about which something is stated or that performs the action of a verb. **b** a principal phrase of a musical composition or movement. **4** somebody owing obedience or allegiance to another, *esp* to a ruler or sovereign power. **5** in philosophy, the entity that sustains or assumes the form of thought or consciousness, e.g. the mind or ego.

subject² *adj* **1** (*often* + to) owing obedience or allegiance to another: *subject nations; They are subject to higher authority.* **2** (+ to) dependent or conditional on something: *The plan is subject to approval.* **3a** (+ to) liable or exposed to something: *subject to temptation.* **b** (+ to) having a tendency or inclination to something; prone to it: *subject to colds.*

subject³ *v* **1** (+ to) to cause (somebody or something) to undergo something. **2** (+ to) to make (somebody or something) liable to something. **3** (*often* + to) to bring (e.g. a people) under control or rule. ➤➤ **subjection** *n.*

subjective *adj* **1a** peculiar to a particular individual; personal. **b** relating to, determined by, or arising from the mind or self. **2** of a case of nouns and pronouns: relating to or denoting a grammatical subject. ➤➤ **subjectively** *adv,* **subjectivity** *n.*

subjectivism *n* a theory holding that all knowledge is subjective and that there is no objective reality. ➤➤ **subjectivist** *n and adj.*

subject matter *n* that which is represented or dealt with in speech, writing, or art.

subject to *prep* depending on (something): *Subject to your approval, I will go.*

sub judice /'joohdisi/ *adv* currently being considered by a court and therefore not open to discussion.

subjugate *v* to bring (somebody or something) under the control of another authority. ➤➤ **subjugation** *n.*

subjunctive¹ *adj* in grammar, of or being a verb mood that represents an act or state not as a fact but as a possibility or wish.

subjunctive² *n* a verb form expressing the subjunctive mood.

sublet¹ *v* (*past tense and past part.* **sublet, subletting**) of a tenant: to lease or rent (all or part of a property) to a subtenant.

sublet² *n* a property obtained by or available for subletting.

sublieutenant *n* a Royal Navy rank above midshipman and below lieutenant.

sublimate¹ *v* **1** in psychology, to divert the expression of (an instinctual desire or impulse) from a primitive form to a socially or culturally acceptable one. **2** = SUBLIME². **3** to make finer or of higher worth. ➤➤ **sublimation** *n.*

sublimate² *n* in chemistry, a solid obtained by sublimation.

sublime¹ *adj* **1** of the highest moral or spiritual worth; exalted. **2** astoundingly beautiful or grand. **3** outstanding or extreme. ➤➤ **sublimely** *adv,* **sublimity** *n.*

sublime² *v* in chemistry, to pass directly from the solid to the vapour state, without passing through the liquid state, and usu to pass directly back to the solid state.

subliminal *adj* **1** of a stimulus: inadequate to produce a conscious sensation or perception. **2** existing or functioning below the level of conscious awareness. ➤➤ **subliminally** *adv.*

sublunary *adj chiefly literary* belonging to the material world, *esp* as distinct from the spiritual world and subordinate to it; earthly.

submachine gun *n* an automatic or semiautomatic portable rapid-firing gun of limited range.

submarine¹ *n* a vessel designed for undersea operations, *esp* a warship armed with torpedoes or missiles. ➤➤ **submariner** *n.*

submarine² *adj* situated, occurring, or growing under water, *esp* in the sea.

submerge *v* **1** to go or put under water. **2** to cover with water; to flood. **3a** to cover completely; to obscure. **b** to bury or suppress (something, e.g. feelings). ➤➤ **submergence** *n.*

submerse *v technical* to submerge. ➤➤ **submersion** *n.*

submersible¹ *adj* capable of going or operating under water.

submersible[2] *n* a vessel used for undersea exploration and construction work.

submicroscopic *adj* too small to be seen using an ordinary microscope.

submission *n* **1** the act or an instance of submitting. **2** something submitted for consideration, inspection, etc.

submissive *adj* willing or tending to submit to others. ➤➤ **submissively** *adv*, **submissiveness** *n*.

submit *v* (**submitted, submitting**) **1a** to send or commit (something) to another person or authority for consideration, inspection, judgment, etc. **b** to put forward as an opinion; to suggest. **2a** to subject (something or somebody) to a process or practice. **b** to yield (something, somebody, or oneself) to the authority or will of another. **3** to allow oneself to be subjected to something.

subnormal *adj* **1** lower or smaller than normal. **2** having less of something, *esp* intelligence, than is normal. ➤➤ **subnormality** *n*, **subnormally** *adv*.

suborder *n* a category in the biological classification of living things below an order and above a family.

subordinate[1] *adj* **1** occupying a lower class, rank, or position; inferior. **2** of secondary importance. ➤➤ **subordinately** *adv*.

subordinate[2] *n* a subordinate person or thing, *esp* a person of lower rank.

subordinate[3] *v* **1** to place (somebody or something) in a subordinate position. **2** to make (e.g. a people) subject or subservient; to subdue. ➤➤ **subordination** *n*.

subordinate clause *n* a clause that functions as a noun, adjective, or adverb in a complex sentence and is dependent on the main clause, e.g. *when he heard* in *He laughed when he heard*.

suborn *v* to induce (somebody) to commit perjury or another illegal act, *esp* by bribery.

subplot *n* a subordinate plot in fiction or drama.

subpoena[1] *n* a writ commanding somebody to appear in court.

subpoena[2] *v* (**subpoenas, subpoenaed, subpoenaing**) to serve with a subpoena.

sub-post office *n* in Britain, a local post office offering a smaller range of services than a main post office.

subroutine *n* a sequence of computer instructions that can be used repeatedly in a program.

sub-Saharan *adj* relating or belonging to the regions of Africa that lie south of the Sahara desert.

subscribe *v* **1** (+ to) to pay regularly in order to receive a periodical or service. **2** (*usu* + for) to agree to purchase and pay for shares, *esp* of a new issue. **3** (+ to) to feel favourably disposed to something; to agree with it. **4** to give a written pledge to contribute (an amount of money). ➤➤ **subscriber** *n*.

subscriber trunk dialling *n Brit* the system by which a telephone user can dial direct to any telephone within the system.

subscript *adj* of a letter, number, or symbol: written or printed, usu in smaller type, below and to the right or left of another character. ➤➤ **subscript** *n*.

subscription *n* **1a** a purchase by prepayment of something, *esp* a certain number of issues of a periodical. **b** *Brit* membership fees paid regularly. **c** an application to purchase shares of a new issue. **2** a sum of money pledged. **3** *formal* a signature. **4** the act or an instance of subscribing to something.

subsection *n* a subdivision of a section.

subsequent *adj* following in time or order; succeeding. ➤➤ **subsequently** *adv*.

subserve *v formal* to serve as a means of furthering (e.g. a purpose or action).

subservient *adj* **1** obsequiously submissive; servile. **2** useful in an inferior capacity; subordinate. ➤➤ **subservience** *n*.

subset *n* a set contained within a larger set, *esp* a mathematical set of which all the elements are elements of a given set.

subside *v* **1** to become less forceful or intense; to abate. **2a** of ground: to cave in; to collapse. **b** to sink so as to form a depression. **c** to fall to a lower level or return to a normal level. **3** to sink or fall to the bottom; to settle.

subsidence *n* the act or an instance of subsiding, *esp* the slow sinking of an area of land.

subsidiarity *n* the principle that a central authority should control only those activities that cannot be satisfactorily controlled at a more immediate or local level.

subsidiary[1] *adj* **1** serving to assist or supplement; auxiliary. **2** of secondary importance.

subsidiary[2] *n* (*pl* **-ies**) a company that is wholly controlled by another.

subsidize *or* **-ise** *v* **1** to provide (somebody or something) with a subsidy, *esp* to aid or promote (e.g. a private enterprise) with public money. **2** to pay part of the cost of (a product or service), making it cheaper for those who buy or use it. ➤➤ **subsidization** *n*.

subsidy *n* (*pl* **-ies**) **1** a grant or gift of money, e.g. one made by a government to a person or organization to assist an enterprise deemed advantageous to the public. **2** in former times, a sum of money granted by Parliament to the Crown and raised by special taxation.

subsist *v* **1** to have only the basic necessities of life. **2** to continue to exist. **3** (+ in) to be present as an element or quality in something; to reside in it.

subsistence *n* **1** the state of subsisting. **2** the minimum, e.g. of food and shelter, necessary to support life.

subsistence level *n* a standard of living in which one has no more than the basic necessities of life.

subsoil *n* the layer of weathered material that lies under the surface soil.

subsonic *adj* being or travelling at a speed less than that of sound in air.

subspace *n* in mathematics, a subset of a space, *esp* one that has the properties, e.g. those of a vector space, of the including space.

subspecies *n* (*pl* **subspecies**) a category in the biological classification of living things that ranks immediately below a species.

substance *n* **1a** a physical material from which something is made or formed: *an oily substance*. **b** matter of particular or definite chemical constitution. **2a** the fundamental or essential part or import: *the substance of his argument*. **b** correspondence with reality: *The allegations were without substance*. **c** solid quality. **3** material possessions; property: *a man of substance*. **4** in philosophy, ultimate underlying reality. ✱ **in substance** essentially.

substandard *adj* of a quality lower than that expected or prescribed.

substantial *adj* **1** considerable in size or quantity; significantly large. **2** ample to satisfy and nourish. **3** firmly constructed; solid. **4** being largely but not wholly the specified thing. **5** having material existence; real. **6** well-to-do; prosperous. **7** relating to the fundamental substance or essence of something. ➤➤ **substantiality** *n*, **substantially** *adv*.

substantiate *v* to establish (e.g. a statement or claim) by proof or evidence; to verify. ⪢ **substantiation** *n.*

substantive[1] *adj* **1** having substance or significance; substantial. **2** being a totally independent entity. **3** defining rights and duties. ⪢ **substantively** *adv.*

substantive[2] *n* a noun.

substation *n* **1** an installation where the voltage of an electric current from a power station is transformed for distribution to consumers within a particular district. **2** a subsidiary station.

substituent *n* in chemistry, an atom or group that replaces another atom or group in a molecule.

substitute[1] *n* somebody or something that takes the place of another, e.g. a player who may replace another withdrawn from a game. ⪢ **substitutive** *adj.*

substitute[2] *v* **1** (*usu* + for) to put (one thing) in the place of another. **2** in sport, to introduce a substitute for. **3** to serve as a substitute. ⪢ **substitutable** *adj,* **substitution** *n.*

Usage note

substitute *or* replace? See note at REPLACE.

substrate *n* **1** = SUBSTRATUM (1). **2** the base on which an organism lives. **3** a substance acted on chemically, e.g. by an enzyme.

substratum *n* (*pl* **substrata**) **1** a layer of rock or soil that lies immediately below the surface. **2** a foundation or basis.

substructure *n* any structure that forms the foundation or framework on which something is constructed.

subsume *v* to include as a member of a group or type; to incorporate. ⪢ **subsumable** *adj.*

subtenant *n* somebody who rents all or part of a property from a tenant.

subtend *v* **1** to extend between the end points of the lines that converge to form (an angle). **2** to extend between the end points of (an arc).

subterfuge *n* **1** deception or trickery used as a means of concealment or evasion. **2** a trick or ruse.

subterranean *adj* existing, occurring, or operating under the surface of the earth.

subtext *n* the underlying meaning or theme of a text.

subtitle[1] *n* **1** (*also in pl*) a printed text, e.g. a translation or transcription of dialogue, that appears at the bottom of the screen during a film or television broadcast. **2** a secondary or explanatory title, e.g. of a book or article.

subtitle[2] *v* to provide a subtitle or subtitles for.

subtle *adj* **1a** pleasantly or tastefully delicate; understated. **b** difficult to understand, analyse, or distinguish. **2** showing keen insight and perception. **3** cleverly contrived; ingenious. ⪢ **subtly** *adv.*

subtlety *n* (*pl* **-ies**) **1** the quality of being subtle. **2** something subtle, *esp* a fine distinction.

subtotal *n* the sum of part of a series of figures to be added.

subtract *v* to take (one number) away from another in calculating the difference between them. ⪢ **subtraction** *n,* **subtractive** *adj.*

subtropics *pl n* subtropical regions. ⪢ **subtropical** *adj.*

subunit *n* a unit that forms a discrete part of a more comprehensive unit.

suburb *n* (*also in pl*) an outlying part of a city or large town, *esp* a residential district.

suburban *adj* **1** relating to or located in a suburb. **2** typical of suburbs or the people who live in them, *esp* limited and unadventurous in outlook. ⪢ **suburbanite** *n.*

suburbanize *or* **-ise** *v* **1** to make (an area) into a suburb. **2** to make (somebody or something) suburban.

suburbia *n* the suburbs of a city, or their inhabitants.

subvention *n* an endowment or subsidy, *esp* a government grant.

subversive[1] *adj* **1** tending to undermine the established system, e.g. of government. **2** engaging in subversive activities. ⪢ **subversively** *adv,* **subversiveness** *n.*

subversive[2] *n* a subversive person.

subvert *v* **1** to overthrow or undermine the power of (e.g. a government or institution). **2** to pervert or corrupt (somebody) by undermining their morals, allegiance, or faith. ⪢ **subversion** *n,* **subverter** *n.*

subway *n Brit* a passage under a street for pedestrians.

subwoofer *n* a loudspeaker that reproduces the lowest frequencies.

suc- *prefix* see SUB-.

succeed *v* **1a** to have a favourable result; to turn out well. **b** to achieve a desired object or end. **c** to attain wealth or fame. **2a** (+ to) to inherit something, *esp* sovereignty, rank, or title. **b** to follow after another in order. **3** to follow (something) in sequence. **4** to come after (somebody) as heir or successor.

success *n* **1a** a favourable outcome to an undertaking. **b** the achievement of a desired object or end. **c** the attainment of wealth or fame. **2** somebody or something that succeeds.

successful *adj* **1** resulting in success. **2** having succeeded. **3** having gained wealth, fame, professional or social standing, etc. ⪢ **successfully** *adv.*

succession *n* **1** the order or right of succeeding to a property, title, office, or throne. **2a** the act of following in order; sequence. **b** (*used as sing. or pl*) a number of people or things that follow each other in sequence. **3** the act or process of becoming entitled to a deceased person's property or title. **4** the change in the composition of an ecological community as the competing organisms respond to and modify the environment. ✱ **in succession** following one another without interruption. ⪢ **successional** *adj.*

successive *adj* following one after the other in succession. ⪢ **successively** *adv.*

successor *n* somebody or something that follows another, *esp* a person who succeeds to a throne, title, or office.

success story *n informal* somebody or something that is successful.

succinct *adj* clearly expressed in few words; concise. ⪢ **succinctly** *adv,* **succinctness** *n.*

succor[1] *n NAm* see SUCCOUR[1].

succor[2] *v NAm* see SUCCOUR[2].

succotash *n* a dish of beans, green maize, and other ingredients.

Succoth *n* see SUKKOTH.

succour[1] (*NAm* **succor**) *n* **1** relief from trouble, pain, etc. **2** assistance in time of difficulty.

succour[2] (*NAm* **succor**) *v* to go to the aid of (somebody in need or distress).

succubus *n* (*pl* **succubi**) a female demon believed to have sexual intercourse with men in their sleep: compare INCUBUS (1).

succulent[1] *adj* **1** of food: full of juice and flavour. **2** of a plant: having juicy fleshy tissues. ⋙ **succulence** *n*, **succulently** *adv.*

succulent[2] *n* a succulent plant, e.g. a cactus.

succumb *v* **1** (+ to) to yield or give in to something or somebody with superior strength or overpowering appeal. **2** to die from disease or injury.

such[1] *adj and adv* **1a** of the kind, quality, or extent: *His schedule is such that we rarely meet.* **b** used with *as* to introduce an example or comparison: *such trees as spruce or pine.* **c** of that or the same sort: *There's no such place.* **2** of so extreme a degree or extraordinary a nature: *ever such a lot of people; in such a hurry.* ✱ **such as 1** for example: *reptiles, such as lizards.* **2** the same kind as; like: *women such as my sister.* **3** used to suggest lack of merit, worth, quantity, etc: *We forced down the soup, such as it was.*

Usage note

such as *and* like See note at LIKE[1].

such[2] *pron* (*pl* **such**) **1** that thing, fact, or action: *Such was the result.* **2** (*in pl*) similar people or things: *tin and glass and such.* **3** (*in pl*) such people; those: *Such as wish to leave may do so.* ✱ **as such** in himself, herself, itself, or themselves; intrinsically: *As such the gift was worth little.*

such and such *adj informal* not named or specified.

suchlike[1] *adj* of the kind mentioned; similar.

suchlike[2] *pron* (*pl* **suchlike**) a similar person or thing.

suck[1] *v* **1a** to draw (e.g. liquid) into the mouth by creating a partial vacuum with the contracted lips and tongue. **b** to draw liquid from (something) in this way. **c** to eat (e.g. a sweet) by means of sucking movements of the lips and tongue. **2** to draw in or up by suction. **3** to draw (somebody) by irresistible force.

suck[2] *n* **1** the act of sucking. **2** a sucking movement, sound, or force. ✱ **give suck to** *archaic* to suckle (a baby or young animal).

sucker[1] *n* **1a** a cup-shaped device, *esp* of rubber, that can cling to a surface by suction. **b** a mouth, e.g. of a leech, or other animal organ adapted for sucking or clinging to a surface. **2** a shoot from the roots or stem of a plant that can grow into an independent plant if it becomes detached. **3** *informal* **a** a gullible person. **b** a person irresistibly attracted by something specified: *a sucker for chocolate.*

sucker[2] *v* of a plant: to send out suckers.

sucker punch *n informal* a devastating blow delivered unexpectedly.

suckle *v* to give milk to (a baby or young animal) from the breast or udder.

suckling *n* an unweaned baby or young animal.

sucks *interj informal* an expression of defiance or derision.

suck up *v informal* to act in an obsequious manner.

sucre /'soohkray/ *n* the basic monetary unit of Ecuador.

sucrose *n* the form of sugar obtained from sugarcane and sugar beet and occurring in most plants.

suction *n* **1** the act of exerting a force on a solid, liquid, or gaseous body that draws it in or causes adherence by means of reduced air pressure over part of its surface. **2** the force so exerted.

suction pump *n* a pump in which liquid is drawn by suction into the partial vacuum left when a piston is drawn out.

Sudanese *n* (*pl* **Sudanese**) a native or inhabitant of Sudan. ⋙ **Sudanese** *adj.*

sudden[1] *adj* **1a** happening or coming unexpectedly. **b** falling away sharply; steep. **2** marked by or showing haste; abrupt. ⋙ **suddenly** *adv*, **suddenness** *n.*

sudden[2] ✱ **all of a sudden** without warning; suddenly.

sudden adult death syndrome *or* **sudden death syndrome** *n* sudden fatal heart failure, especially in young adults.

sudden death *n* **1** an extra period of play to break a tie that ends the moment one player or side gains the lead. **2** unexpected death or death occurring within minutes, e.g. from a heart attack.

sudden infant death syndrome *n* = COT DEATH.

sudden wealth syndrome *n* psychological and other problems experienced by those who win large amounts of money in the National Lottery, on game shows, etc.

sudorific[1] *adj* causing sweating; diaphoretic.

sudorific[2] *n* a drug that induces sweating.

Sudra *n* a Hindu of the lowest caste traditionally restricted to menial occupations: compare BRAHMAN, KSHATRIYA, VAISYA.

suds *pl n* the lather on soapy water.

sudsy *adj* frothy or foamy.

sue *v* **1** to bring a legal action against (a person, institution, etc). **2** (*usu* + for/to) to make a formal request to (somebody) for something.

suede *n* leather with a velvety surface produced by rubbing the flesh side to make a soft nap of short fibres.

suet *n* the hard fat round the kidneys and loins in cattle or sheep, which yields tallow and is used in cooking.

suet pudding *n* a boiled or steamed pudding containing suet.

suf- *prefix* see SUB-.

suffer *v* **1** (*often* + from) to be affected by or be subject to (an illness or condition). **2** to experience or be forced to endure (something unpleasant). **3** to sustain loss or damage. **4** to be put at a disadvantage. **5** *archaic* **a** to allow (somebody to do something). **b** to tolerate. ⋙ **sufferer** *n.*

sufferance *n* **1** tolerance implied by a lack of objection rather than actual approval. **2** capacity to withstand; endurance.

suffice *v* **1** to meet a need; to be enough. **2** *archaic* to be enough for (somebody or something). ✱ **suffice (it) to say** used to indicate that further information has been withheld, e.g. for the sake of discretion.

sufficiency *n* (*pl* **-ies**) **1** a sufficient amount. **2** the quality of being sufficient; adequacy.

sufficient *adj* enough to meet the needs of a situation; adequate. ⋙ **sufficiently** *adv.*

suffix[1] *n* an affix, e.g. *-ness* in *happiness*, placed at the end of a word: compare PREFIX[1].

suffix[2] *v* to attach as a suffix. ⋙ **suffixation** *n.*

suffocate *v* **1** to die or cause to die from being unable to breathe. **2** to be or cause to be uncomfortable through lack of cool fresh air. ⋙ **suffocating** *adj*, **suffocation** *n.*

suffragan *n* a bishop assisting a diocesan bishop and having no right of succession.

suffrage *n* **1** the right to vote in political elections; franchise. **2** a short prayer of intercession, usu in a series.

suffragette *n* any of a group of militant women campaigning for the right to vote to be extended to women in Britain in the early 20th cent.

suffragist *n* somebody who advocates extending the right to vote, *esp* to women. ⋙ **suffragism** *n.*

suffuse *v* (*usu in passive*) to spread over or through (something). ⋙ **suffusion** *n,* **suffusive** *adj.*

Sufi *n* (*pl* **Sufis**) a Muslim mystic. ⋙ **Sufism** *n.*

sug- *prefix* see SUB-.

sugar[1] *n* **1a** a sweet crystalline substance that is obtained from sugarcane or sugar beet, is a source of dietary carbohydrate, and is used as a sweetener and preservative of other foods. **b** any of a class of water-soluble carbohydrates of varying sweetness, including glucose, ribose, and sucrose. **2** *chiefly NAm, informal* a term of endearment.

sugar[2] *v* **1** to sprinkle, coat, or sweeten with sugar. **2** to make palatable or attractive. ⋙ **sugared** *adj.*

sugar beet *n* a variety of beet grown for the sugar in its roots.

sugarcane *n* a tall grass with stout stems that is widely grown in warm regions as a source of sugar.

sugar-coated *adj* **1** covered with a hard coat of sugar. **2** superficially attractive.

sugar daddy *n informal* an elderly man who lavishes gifts and money on a young woman in return for sex or companionship.

sugarloaf *n* a moulded cone of refined sugar.

sugar maple *n* a N American maple tree with a sweet sap that is the chief source of maple syrup and maple sugar.

sugar snap pea *n* a variety of mangetout pea that has a thick rounded pod.

sugar soap *n* a substance consisting of soap and washing soda used for stripping paint or cleaning surfaces prior to painting.

sugary *adj* **1** containing or tasting of sugar. **2** exaggeratedly cute or sentimental.

suggest *v* **1** to put forward as a possibility or for consideration. **2** to call to mind by thought or association; to evoke. **3** to express indirectly; to imply.

suggestible *adj* easily influenced by suggestion. ⋙ **suggestibility** *n.*

suggestion *n* **1a** the act of suggesting. **b** something suggested. **2a** the natural association of ideas, used to evoke ideas or feelings. **b** the impressing of an idea, attitude, etc on the mind of another. **3** a slight indication; a trace.

suggestive *adj* **1a** (*often* + of) tending to suggest; indicative. **b** (*often* + of) stirring mental associations; evocative. **2** suggesting something improper or indecent; risqué. ⋙ **suggestively** *adv,* **suggestiveness** *n.*

suicide *n* **1a** the act of killing oneself intentionally. **b** the ruining of one's own interests: *political suicide.* **2** somebody who commits suicide. **3** (*used before a noun*) denoting action that will result in the death of the person undertaking it: *a suicide bombing.* ⋙ **suicidal** *adj,* **suicidally** *adv.*

suicide pact *n* an agreement between two or more people to commit suicide together.

sui generis *adj* unique.

suit[1] *n* **1a** an outer costume of two or more matching articles of clothing, *esp* a jacket and trousers or a skirt. **b** a costume to be worn for a specified purpose. **2** all the playing cards in a pack bearing the same symbol, i.e. hearts, clubs, diamonds, or spades. **3** a legal action; a lawsuit. **4** *informal* a business executive, *esp* one considered as faceless but influential. **5** *formal or archaic* **a** a petition or appeal. **b** courtship.

Usage note

suit *or* **suite**? A *suit* is a set of clothes or one of the four sets of playing cards making up a pack: *follow suit. Suit* can also mean 'a court action' or 'a request or appeal': *grant somebody's suit.* A *suite* is a set of matching furniture, of rooms, of related pieces of music, or of computer software.

suit[2] *v* **1** to please or be convenient to. **2a** to be becoming to or look right with. **b** to be good for the health or well-being of. **3** to adapt (something) to a particular situation, circumstance, etc. ✱ **suit somebody down to the ground** to suit somebody extremely well. ⋙ **suited** *adj.*

suitable *adj* appropriate for a particular person, situation, etc; fitting. ⋙ **suitability** *n,* **suitableness** *n,* **suitably** *adv.*

suitcase *n* a rectangular case with a hinged lid and a handle, used for carrying clothes and other personal items when travelling.

suite *n* **1** a group of rooms occupied as a unit. **2** a set of matching furniture, e.g. a settee and two armchairs. **3** a set of computer software. **4a** an instrumental musical form consisting of a series of dance-related pieces. **b** an orchestral arrangement of material drawn from a longer work, e.g. a ballet, in the form of a suite.

Usage note

suite *or* **suit**? See note at SUIT[1].

suiting *n* fabric suitable for making suits.

suitor *n* **1** *dated* somebody who courts a woman with a view to marriage. **2** somebody who is looking to buy or take over a business.

sukiyaki *n* a Japanese dish of thin slices of meat, soya-bean curd, and vegetables cooked in soy sauce, sake, and sugar.

Sukkoth *or* **Succoth** *n* a Jewish harvest festival celebrated in September or October.

sulfa drug *n NAm* see SULPHA DRUG.

sulfate *n NAm* see SULPHATE.

sulfide *n NAm* see SULPHIDE.

sulfite *n NAm* see SULPHITE.

sulfonamide *n NAm* see SULPHONAMIDE.

sulfonic *adj NAm* see SULPHONIC.

sulfur *n NAm* see SULPHUR.

sulfuric *adj NAm* see SULPHURIC.

sulfurous *adj NAm* see SULPHUROUS.

sulk[1] *v* to be moodily silent through resentment or disappointment.

sulk[2] *n* (*usu in pl*) a fit of sulking.

sulky *adj* (**-ier, -iest**) sulking or given to fits of sulking. ⋙ **sulkily** *adv,* **sulkiness** *n.*

sullen *adj* silently gloomy or resentful; unsociable. ⋙ **sullenly** *adv,* **sullenness** *n.*

sully *v* (**-ies, -ied**) to defile or tarnish.

sulpha drug (*NAm* **sulfa drug**) *n* any of various synthetic drugs chemically related to sulphanilamide that are used to kill or inhibit the growth of bacteria.

sulphate (*NAm* **sulfate**) *n* a salt or ester of sulphuric acid.

sulphide (*NAm* **sulfide**) *n* a compound containing sulphur and a less electronegative element.

sulphite (*NAm* **sulfite**) *n* a salt or ester of sulphurous acid.

sulphonamide (*NAm* **sulfonamide**) *n* any of a group of chemical compounds that are amides of a sulphonic acid, including sulpha drugs.

sulphonic (*NAm* **sulfonic**) *adj* of, being, or derived from the acid group $-SO_2OH$.

sulphur (*NAm* **sulfur**) *n* a non-metallic chemical element that occurs naturally *esp* as yellow crystals.

sulphur dioxide *n* a pungent toxic gas that is a major air pollutant.

sulphuric (*NAm* **sulfuric**) *adj* of or containing sulphur, *esp* high valency sulphur.

sulphuric acid *n* a heavy corrosive oily acid that is a vigorous oxidizing and dehydrating agent.

sulphurous (*NAm* **sulfurous**) *adj* **1** of or containing sulphur, *esp* low valency sulphur. **2** resembling or derived from sulphur.

sulphurous acid *n* a weak unstable acid used for bleaching and as a reducing agent.

sultan *n* a sovereign of a Muslim state, *esp* the former Ottoman Empire. ⋙ **sultanate** *n.*

sultana *n* **1** the light brown raisin of a pale yellow seedless grape. **2** a sultan's wife.

sultry *adj* (**-ier, -iest**) **1** oppressively hot and humid. **2** exciting strong sexual desire; sensual. ⋙ **sultrily** *adv,* **sultriness** *n.*

sum[1] *n* **1** an amount of money. **2** the result of adding numbers. **3** the whole amount of anything; the total. **4** numbers to be added, subtracted, multiplied, or divided; a simple arithmetical problem. ✱ **in sum** briefly.

sum[2] *v* (**summed, summing**) to calculate the sum of (several numbers or amounts).

sumach *or* **sumac** *n* a tree, shrub, or climbing plant with feathery leaves that turn to brilliant colours in the autumn and loose clusters of red or whitish berries.

Sumatran *n* a native or inhabitant of Sumatra. ⋙ **Sumatran** *adj.*

summa cum laude /ˌsoomə koom 'lowday/ *adv and adj* graduating with the highest class of university degree, *esp* from a N American university.

summarize *or* **-ise** *v* to reduce to a summary; to express in concise terms. ⋙ **summarization** *n,* **summarizer** *n.*

summary[1] *n* (*pl* **-ies**) a brief account covering the main points of something.

summary[2] *adj* **1a** done quickly without delay or formality. **b** tried or triable in a magistrates' court. **2** concise but comprehensive. ⋙ **summarily** *adv,* **summariness** *n.*

summary jurisdiction *n* the authority of a court to make an immediate judgment on a case.

summary offence *n* an offence that may be tried in a lower court without full legal proceedings.

summat *pron N Eng dialect* something.

summation *n* **1** the process of adding numbers. **2** a total. **3** cumulative action or effect. **4** the act of summing up. **5** a summary. ⋙ **summative** *adj.*

summer[1] *n* the season between spring and autumn. ⋙ **summery** *adj.*

summer[2] *adj* of crops: sown in the spring and harvested in the same year as sown: compare WINTER[2].

summer[3] *v* (+ in) to spend the summer in a particular place.

summerhouse *n* a small building in a garden designed to provide a shady place in summer.

summer pudding *n* a cold dessert consisting of soft fruits, e.g. raspberries and blackcurrants, encased by a basin-shaped mould of white bread.

summer school *n* a course of teaching held during the summer vacation, *esp* on university premises.

Summer Time *n* = BRITISH SUMMER TIME.

summertime *n* the season of summer.

summer-weight *adj* of clothing: lightweight and therefore suitable for summer.

summing-up *n* **1** a concluding summary. **2** a survey of the evidence in a case given by a judge to the jury before it considers its verdict.

summit *n* **1** the highest point of a hill or mountain. **2** the topmost level attainable. **3** a conference of heads of government.

summiteer *n* a person participating in a summit conference.

summon *v* **1** to order (somebody) to come. **2** to command (somebody) by a summons to appear in court. **3** (*often* + up) to call up or muster (a particular quality). **4** to call people to attend (a meeting).

summons[1] *n* (*pl* **summonses**) **1** a written notification ordering somebody to appear in court. **2** an official order to appear at a particular place or to attend to something.

summons[2] *v* to serve (somebody) with a summons.

sumo *n* Japanese wrestling between two contestants of immense build who lose if they are forced out of the contest area or if any part of their body other than the soles of their feet touches the ground.

sump *n* **1** *chiefly Brit* the lower section of the crankcase of an internal-combustion engine used as a reservoir for lubricating oil. **2** the lowest part of a mine shaft, into which water drains. **3** = CESSPOOL (1).

sumptuary *adj* designed to regulate personal expenditure and prevent extravagance.

sumptuous *adj* lavishly rich, costly, or luxurious. ⋙ **sumptuously** *adv,* **sumptuousness** *n.*

sum total *n* **1** a total arrived at through the counting of sums. **2** the whole amount; the totality.

sum up *v* **1** to summarize (something). **2** to express a concise appraisal of.

Sun. *abbr* Sunday.

sun[1] *n* **1a** (*often* **Sun**) the star nearest to the earth, round which the earth and other planets revolve. **b** a star or other celestial body that emits its own light. **2** the heat or light radiated from the sun. ✱ **under the sun** in the world: *He was the last person under the sun I expected to see.* ⋙ **sunless** *adj,* **sunward** *adj and adv,* **sunwards** *adv.*

sun[2] *v* (**sunned, sunning**) to expose (oneself) to the rays of the sun.

sunbaked *adj* dried or baked hard by exposure to sunshine.

sunbathe *v* to lie or sit in the sun in order to get a suntan. ⋙ **sunbather** *n.*

sunbeam *n* a ray of light from the sun.

sunbed *n* **1** a folding portable bed used for sunbathing, as a garden seat, etc. **2** a unit consisting of a couch and an array of sunlamps.

sunbelt *n* an area with a warm sunny climate.

sunblock *n* a cosmetic preparation that protects exposed skin from the ultraviolet rays in sunlight.

sunburn[1] *n* inflammation of the skin caused by overexposure to sunlight.

sunburn[2] *v* (**sunburned** *or* **sunburnt**) (*usu in passive*) to burn or cause to burn by exposure to sunlight.

sunburst *n* **1** a sudden and dazzling appearance of the sun from behind a cloud. **2** an ornament representing a sun surrounded by rays.

suncream *n* cream applied to protect the skin from the sun's ultraviolet rays.

sundae *n* a dish of ice cream served with a topping of fruit, nuts, syrup, etc.

sun dance *n* a Native N American religious ceremony held in honour of the sun.

Sunday *n* **1** the day of the week following Saturday. **2** a newspaper published on Sundays.

Sunday best *n informal* one's best clothes.

Sunday school *n* a class of religious instruction for children, held on Sundays.

sun deck *n* a deck of a ship that is not enclosed and can be used for sunbathing.

sunder *v archaic or literary* to break (something) apart or in two.

sundial *n* an instrument that shows the time of day by the shadow of a pointer on a graduated plate.

sundown *n chiefly NAm* = SUNSET.

sundowner *n* **1** *Brit, dated, informal* an alcoholic drink taken at sunset. **2** *Aus, informal* a homeless itinerant person; a tramp.

sundrenched *adj* of a place: where the sun almost always shines.

sundress *n* a lightweight dress designed for sunny weather, typically sleeveless and with shoulder straps.

sun-dried *adj* dried and preserved by exposure to sunlight.

sundries *pl n* miscellaneous small articles or items.

sundry[1] *adj* of various kinds; miscellaneous.

sundry[2] ✻ **all and sundry** everybody.

sunfish *n* (*pl* **sunfishes** *or* **sunfish**) a large marine fish with long pointed fins on its back.

sunflower *n* a tall plant of the daisy family with large yellow-rayed flowers.

sung *v* past part. of SING.

sunglasses *pl n* tinted glasses worn to protect the eyes from the sun.

sunhat *n* a large-brimmed hat worn to protect the head and face from the sun.

sunk *v* past part. of SINK[1].

sunken *adj* **1** submerged, *esp* lying at the bottom of a body of water. **2** lying or constructed below the surrounding or normal level. **3** hollow or recessed: *sunken cheeks*.

sunlamp *n* an electric lamp that emits *esp* ultraviolet light and is used for tanning the skin, muscular therapy, etc.

sunlight *n* light emitted by the sun; sunshine.

sunlit *adj* lit by the sun.

Sunna *n* the body of Islamic custom and practice based on Muhammad's words and deeds.

Sunni *n* (*pl* **Sunni** *or* **Sunnis**) **1** the major branch of Islam that keeps to the orthodox tradition and acknowledges the first four caliphs as rightful successors of Muhammad: compare SHIA. **2** a Sunnite. ➤➤ **Sunni** *adj.*

Sunnite *n* an adherent of the Sunni branch of Islam. ➤➤ **Sunnite** *adj.*

sunny *adj* (**-ier, -iest**) **1** bright with sunshine. **2** cheerful, optimistic. **3** exposed to or warmed by the sun. ➤➤ **sunnily** *adv*, **sunniness** *n.*

sunray pleats *pl n* a series of pleats in fabric, *esp* in a skirt, that are wider at the bottom than at the top.

sunrise *n* the rising of the topmost part of the sun above the horizon as a result of the rotation of the earth, or the time when this happens.

sunrise economy *n* an economy based on sunrise industries, or a country having such an economy.

sunrise industry *n* a comparatively new and expanding industry.

sunroof *n* an opening or removable panel in the roof of a car.

sunscreen *n* a substance used in sunblocks and suncreams to protect the skin from excessive ultraviolet radiation, or a preparation containing this.

sunset *n* **1** the descent of the topmost part of the sun below the horizon as a result of the rotation of the earth, or the time when this happens. **2** the period in which something declines.

sunshade *n* **1** a parasol. **2** an awning.

sunshine *n* **1** the sun's light or direct rays. **2** an informal and often ironic form of address. ➤➤ **sunshiny** *adj.*

sunspot *n* **1** a transient dark marking on the visible surface of the sun caused by a relatively cooler area. **2** *informal* a sunny holiday destination.

sunstroke *n* heatstroke caused by direct exposure to the sun.

suntan *n* a browning of the skin from exposure to the sun. ➤➤ **suntanned** *adj.*

suntrap *n* a sheltered place that receives a large amount of sunshine.

sunup *n chiefly NAm* = SUNRISE.

sun visor *n* a small hinged screen attached above a car's windscreen to provide protection against glare.

sup[1] *v* (**supped, supping**) *chiefly dialect* to drink (liquid) in small mouthfuls.

sup[2] *n chiefly dialect* a mouthful of liquid; a sip.

sup[3] *v* (**supped, supping**) *dated* to eat one's evening meal.

sup- *prefix* see SUB-.

super[1] *adj informal* a general term of approval.

super[2] *n informal* a superintendent or supervisor.

super- *prefix* **1** higher in quantity, quality, or degree than; more than: *superhuman*. **2a** in addition; extra: *supertax*. **b** to an excessive degree: *superabundant*. **c** surpassing others of its kind in size or power: *supertanker*. **3** situated or placed above something: *superscript*. **4** constituting a wider category: *superfamily*. **5** superior in status, title, or position: *superpower*.

superabundant *adj* more than ample; excessive. ➤➤ **superabundance** *n*, **superabundantly** *adv.*

superadd *v formal* to add (something) over and above something else. ➤➤ **superaddition** *n.*

superannuated *adj* **1** retired on a pension. **2** obsolete.

superannuation *n* **1** the regular contribution made by employees to their pension scheme, deducted from wages or salary. **2** a retirement pension funded in this way.

superb *adj* **1** of excellent quality. **2** grand or magnificent. ➤➤ **superbly** *adv*, **superbness** *n.*

superbug *n* a bacterium that has developed a resistance to antibiotics.

supercargo *n* (*pl* **-oes** *or* **-os**) an officer on a merchant ship in charge of the commercial concerns of the voyage.

supercharge *v* **1** to supply a charge to (an engine) at a pressure higher than that of the surrounding atmosphere. **2** to charge (a remark) with an excessive amount of energy or tension.

supercharger *n* a device supplying fuel or air to an internal-combustion engine at a pressure higher than normal for greater efficiency.

supercilious *adj* coolly disdainful; haughty. ➤➤ **superciliously** *adv*, **superciliousness** *n.*

supercomputer *n* a very powerful computer that is capable of performing at very fast rates and is used for repeated calculation cycles on vast amounts of data.

superconductivity *n* a complete disappearance of resistance to the passage of an electric current in various metals and alloys, usu at temperatures near absolute zero. ➤➤ **superconducting** *adj*, **superconductive** *adj.*

superconductor *n* a substance that exhibits superconductivity.

supercontinent *n* any of the large landmasses that are thought to have existed in the geological past and to have divided to form the present continents.

supercool *v* to cool (a liquid) below its freezing point without solidification or crystallization.

supercritical *adj* **1** in nuclear physics, having more than the critical mass. **2** of a flow of liquid: faster than the speed of waves in the liquid. **3** of an aerofoil: having supersonic airflow while travelling at subsonic speeds and therefore offering increased lift and speed.

super-duper *adj informal* of exceedingly great value or superiority.

superego *n* (*pl* **-os**) the part of the mind in psychoanalytic theory that is only partly conscious, reflects social rules, and functions as a conscience to reward and punish: compare EGO, ID.

supererogation *n* the act of performing more than is required by duty, obligation, or need. ➤➤ **supererogatory** *adj.*

superfamily *n* (*pl* **-ies**) a category in the biological classification of living things ranking next above a family.

superficial *adj* **1** lying on or affecting only the surface. **2** apparent rather than real. **3** of a person: not capable of serious thought; shallow. **4** not careful, thorough, or deep. **5** not significant; trivial. ➤➤ **superficiality** *n,* **superficially** *adv,* **superficialness** *n.*

superfine *adj* **1** of extremely fine size or texture. **2** of merchandise: of high quality or grade.

superfluid *n* a liquid that flows with negligible internal friction and carries heat extremely readily. ➤➤ **superfluid** *adj,* **superfluidity** *n.*

superfluity *n* (*pl* **-ies**) **1** an excess; a supply exceeding what is required. **2** something unnecessary or superfluous.

superfluous *adj* exceeding what is sufficient or necessary. ➤➤ **superfluously** *adv.*

supergiant *n* a rare type of star that may be five hundred times larger than the sun and thousands of times more luminous.

superglue *n* an adhesive that sets quickly to make a very strong bond.

supergrass *n Brit, informal* a police informer who gives information about a large number of criminals.

superheat *v* **1** to heat (a liquid) above its boiling point without conversion into vapour. **2** to heat (a vapour) so that it remains a gas without condensation. ➤➤ **superheater** *n.*

superhero *n* (*pl* **-oes**) a character in a cartoon, film, etc. who has extraordinary powers that he or she uses to fight crime or rescue people from danger.

superhighway *n NAm* a motorway.

superhuman *adj* **1** being above the human; divine. **2** exceeding normal human power or capability. ➤➤ **superhumanly** *adv.*

superimpose *v* to place (one thing) over or above something else. ➤➤ **superimposition** *n.*

superintend *v* to be in charge of; to supervise or direct. ➤➤ **superintendence** *n.*

superintendent *n* **1** a person who supervises or manages something. **2** a British police officer ranking next above a chief inspector. **3** the chief of a US police department. **4** *NAm* a caretaker.

superior[1] *adj* **1** of higher rank, quality, or importance. **2a** excellent of its kind; better. **b** greater in quantity or numbers. **3** situated higher up; upper. **4** in printing, denoting a letter or symbol written above the line; superscript. **5** serenely indifferent or unyielding to something painful or disheartening. **6** affecting an air of superiority; supercilious. ➤➤ **superiority** *n.*

superior[2] *n* **1** a person who is above another in rank or office; *esp* the head of a religious order. **2** somebody or something that surpasses another in quality or merit. **3** in printing, a letter or symbol printed above another.

superiority complex *n* an exaggeratedly high opinion of oneself.

superlative[1] *adj* **1** of the highest degree. **2** in grammar, denoting the degree of comparison expressing an extreme or unsurpassed level: compare COMPARATIVE[1] (3). ➤➤ **superlatively** *adv,* **superlativeness** *n.*

superlative[2] *n* **1** the superlative degree in a language. **2** an exaggerated expression of praise.

superlunary *adj literary* beyond the moon; celestial.

superman *n* (*pl* **supermen**) **1** in Nietzschean philosophy, a superior type of man that has learnt to renounce fleeting pleasures and attain fulfilment through the use of creative power. **2** *informal* a man of extraordinary power or achievements.

supermarket *n* a large self-service retail shop selling foods and household merchandise.

supermodel *n* a very successful fashion model who has become a celebrity.

supernal *adj* **1** *literary* heavenly. **2** located in or belonging to the sky. ➤➤ **supernally** *adv.*

supernatural[1] *adj* **1** departing from what is usual, so as to appear to transcend the laws of nature. **2** of an order of existence beyond the visible observable universe; *esp* of a god, spirit, or devil. **3** attributed to an invisible agent, e.g. a ghost or spirit. ➤➤ **supernaturally** *adv.*

supernatural[2] *n* (**the supernatural**) supernatural forces or beings.

supernormal *adj* exceeding the normal or average.

supernova *n* (*pl* **supernovae** *or* **supernovas**) a star that explodes, increasing in brightness by millions of times for a few weeks or months.

supernumerary[1] *adj* **1** exceeding the usual or stated number. **2** not listed among the regular components of a group, *esp* a military organization.

supernumerary[2] *n* (*pl* **-ies**) a person employed as an extra assistant or substitute.

superordinate[1] *adj* superior in rank or status.

superordinate[2] *n* **1** a superordinate thing in a system of classification. **2** a person who is superior in rank or status. **3** a word with a meaning that includes the meaning of words.

superpose *v* **1** to place (one thing) over or above something else. **2** to lay (a geometric figure) on another in such a way that all like parts coincide. ➤➤ **superposition** *n.*

superpower *n* any of a very few dominant nations in the world.

supersaturated *adj* **1** of a solution: containing more dissolved substance than a saturated solution. **2** of a vapour: containing more molecules than a saturated vapour. ➤➤ **supersaturation** *n.*

superscribe *v* **1** to write (an inscription) above or on the outside of something. **2** to write (e.g. a word) above existing text. ➤➤ **superscription** *n.*

superscript *adj* of a letter, number, or symbol: written or printed, usu in smaller type, above and to the right or left of another character. ➤➤ **superscript** *n.*

supersede *v* to take the place of (*esp* something inferior or outmoded).

Usage note

Supersede has no *c* in it and no double *e*. It comes from a Latin verb *supersedēre,* which literally means 'to sit above someone'.

supersonic *adj* **1** of or using speeds from one to five times the speed of sound in air. **2** to do with supersonic aircraft or missiles. **3** = ULTRASONIC. ➤➤ **supersonically** *adv.*

supersonics *pl n* (*used as sing. or pl*) = ULTRASONICS.

superstar *n* an extremely popular or successful entertainer or sportsperson. ➤➤ **superstardom** *n.*

superstate *n* a powerful state formed from a federation of nations.

superstition *n* **1** excessive belief in supernatural or irrational forces in human affairs. **2** a widely held belief that has no rational basis, *esp* one associated with supposedly supernatural influences. ➤➤ **superstitious** *adj,* **superstitiously** *adv.*

superstore *n* a very large supermarket, often situated on the outskirts of a town.

superstructure *n* **1a** the part of a building above the ground. **b** the structural part of a ship above the main deck. **2** a concept or complex based on a more fundamental one.

supertanker *n* a very large tanker.

supertax *n* a tax paid in addition to normal tax by people with high incomes.

supervene *v* to happen in a way that interrupts some plan or process. ➤➤ **supervenient** *adj,* **supervention** *n.*

supervise *v* to oversee (a task or workers). ➤➤ **supervision** *n,* **supervisor** *n,* **supervisory** *adj.*

superwoman *n* (*pl* **superwomen**) *informal* a woman of extraordinary power or achievements.

supinate *v* to rotate (the hand or foot) so that the palm or sole faces forwards or upwards: compare PRONATE. ➤➤ **supination** *n.*

supinator *n* a muscle that produces the motion of supination.

supine *adj* **1** lying on the back or with the face upwards. **2** mentally or morally weak. ➤➤ **supinely** *adv,* **supineness** *n.*

supper *n* **1** a light or informal evening meal. **2** a fund-raising social affair featuring a supper. ✱ **sing for one's supper** to do something in return for food, etc.

supplant *v* to take the place of. ➤➤ **supplanter** *n.*

supple *adj* **1a** capable of being bent or folded without cracks or breaks; pliant. **b** able to perform bending or twisting movements with ease and grace; lithe. **2** compliant to the point of submissiveness. ➤➤ **suppleness** *n.*

supplement[1] *n* **1** something that completes or makes an addition. **2** a part issued to extend a book or periodical. **3** an extra charge payable for something.

supplement[2] *v* to add a supplement to. ➤➤ **supplemental** *adj,* **supplementation** *n.*

supplementary *adj* added as a supplement; additional.

supplementary benefit *n Brit* a social security benefit formerly paid to those who did not qualify for unemployment benefit, replaced in 1988 by income support.

suppliant[1] *adj* humbly imploring or entreating.

suppliant[2] *n* = SUPPLICANT[1].

supplicant[1] *n* a person who supplicates.

supplicant[2] *adj* = SUPPLIANT[1].

supplicate *v* **1** to pray to God. **2** to ask humbly and earnestly for (something). ➤➤ **supplication** *n,* **supplicatory** *adj.*

supply[1] *v* (**-ies, -ied**) **1** to provide or furnish somebody with (something). **2** to provide for or satisfy (a need, etc). ➤➤ **supplier** *n.*

supply[2] *n* (*pl* **-ies**) **1a** the quantity of a commodity needed or available. **b** (*usu in pl*) provisions or stores. **2** the act of filling a want or need. **3** in economics, the quantities of goods and services offered for sale at specified prices at some period of time: compare DEMAND[1]. **4** (*used before a noun*) denoting a teacher who is on call to fill temporary vacancies in schools.

supply-side *adj* of an economic theory that reduced taxation stimulates economic activity by encouraging productivity and investment, so increasing tax revenues. ➤➤ **supply-sider** *n.*

support[1] *v* **1** to serve as a foundation or prop for (something). **2** to provide (somebody) with a home or provide a basis for their existence or subsistence. **3** to endure (something) bravely or quietly. **4** to help (somebody or something), e.g. with money. **5** to approve of or encourage (something). **6** to uphold or defend (something) as valid or right. **7** to substantiate or corroborate (something). **8a** to argue or vote for (a political party). **b** to be an enthusiastic or loyal follower of (e.g. a football team). **9a** to act with (a principal actor). **b** to perform before (the main act at a concert). **10** in computing, to work with (a program or device), or enable (it) to work. ➤➤ **supportable** *adj,* **supporter** *n,* **supporting** *adj.*

support[2] *n* **1** the act of supporting or the condition of being supported. **2** something that holds something up or serves as a prop. **3** somebody who offers help and encouragement. **4** a supporting act in a concert. **5** an appliance or garment worn to protect an injured part of the body.

supportive *adj* providing support; *esp* sustaining morale. ➤➤ **supportively** *adv,* **supportiveness** *n.*

suppose *v* **1a** to lay (something) down tentatively as a hypothesis or proposal: compare SUPPOSING. **b** to hold as an opinion; to believe. **c** to think (something) probable. **2** to assume or presuppose. ✱ **be supposed to do something** to be expected or allowed to do something.

supposed *adj* believed or imagined to be such. ➤➤ **supposedly** *adv.*

supposing *conj* if by way of hypothesis: compare SUPPOSE (1A): *Supposing they saw you … ?*

supposition *n* **1** the act of supposing. **2** something that is supposed; a hypothesis.

suppositious *adj* based on a supposition; hypothetical.

supposititious *adj* fraudulently substituted; spurious.

suppository *n* (*pl* **-ies**) a readily meltable cone or cylinder of medicated material for insertion into the rectum or vagina.

suppress *v* **1** to put an end to (something) by force. **2** to stop the publication or revelation of. **3** to hold back or restrain (something). **4** to deliberately exclude (a thought or feeling) from consciousness: compare REPRESS. ➤➤ **suppression** *n,* **suppressive** *adj,* **suppressor** *n.*

suppressant *n* a drug that tends to suppress rather than eliminate something undesirable.

suppurate *v* to form or discharge pus. ➤➤ **suppuration** *n,* **suppurative** *adj.*

supra- *prefix* **1** above or on top: *supraorbital.* **2** beyond or transcending: *supranational.*

supranational *adj* transcending national boundaries or interests.

supraorbital *adj* situated above the orbit of the eye.

supremacist *n* an advocate of group supremacy, *esp* somebody who believes in the superiority of one race over another. ⋙ **supremacist** *adj.*

supremacy *n* supreme authority, power, or position.

supreme *adj* **1** highest in rank or authority. **2** greatest, strongest, or most important. ⋙ **supremely** *adv.*

Supreme Being *n* (**the Supreme Being**) God.

Supreme Court *n* the highest judicial tribunal in a nation or state.

Supreme Soviet *n* the highest legislative body of the former Soviet Union or a former Soviet republic.

supremo *n* (*pl* **-os**) **1** *Brit, informal* a ruler or leader. **2** an administrator with a particular responsibility: *the marketing supremo.*

Supt *abbr* superintendent.

sur-[1] *prefix* above, over, or beyond: *surtax; surreal; surface.*

sur-[2] *prefix* see SUB-.

surcease[1] *v NAm or archaic* **1** to desist from (action). **2** to come to an end.

surcease[2] *n NAm or archaic* a temporary respite or end.

surcharge[1] *n* **1** an additional tax or cost. **2** an overprint on a stamp, *esp* one that alters the value.

surcharge[2] *v* **1** to subject (somebody) to a surcharge. **2** to mark a new value or a surcharge on (a stamp).

surcoat *n* a loose tunic formerly worn over armour.

surd[1] *adj* of a speech sound: uttered without vibration of the vocal chords; voiceless.

surd[2] *n* **1** an irrational root, e.g. $\sqrt{2}$, or an expression containing irrational roots: compare IRRATIONAL, RATIONAL. **2** a surd speech sound.

sure[1] *adj* **1** marked by or given to feelings of confident certainty. **2** (+ of) confident that something is true, will happen, etc. **3** certain: *She is sure to win.* **4** true and reliable. ✻ **for sure** as a certainty. **to be sure** it must be acknowledged; admittedly. ⋙ **sureness** *n.*

sure[2] *adv chiefly NAm, informal* surely or certainly.

sure enough *adv informal* as one might confidently expect.

sure-fire *adj informal* certain to succeed.

sure-footed *adj* **1** not liable to stumble or fall. **2** not liable to err.

surely *adv* **1** it is to be hoped or expected that: *Surely you like beer.* **2** without doubt; certainly. **3** without danger; safely. **4** *chiefly NAm, informal* willingly; of course.

sure thing *n informal* **1** something that is certain or guaranteed. **2** *chiefly NAm* certainly; of course.

surety *n* (*pl* **-ies**) **1** a person who assumes legal liability for the debt or failure in duty of somebody else. **2** a pledge given for the fulfilment of an undertaking; a guarantee. **3** the state of being certain or confident.

surf[1] *n* the foam and swell of waves breaking on the shore.

surf[2] *v* **1** to stand or lie on a surfboard and ride on the waves towards the shore. **2** to browse through (the Internet or TV channels) randomly. ⋙ **surfer** *n,* **surfing** *n.*

surface[1] *n* **1** the exterior or upper boundary or layer of something. **2** the area of a surface. **3** an external part or layer. **4** the uppermost level of a body of liquid. **5** the superficial aspect of something. ✻ **on the surface** to all outward appearances; superficially.

surface[2] *adj* **1** of or located on the surface of something. **2** situated or employed on the surface of the earth.

surface[3] *v* **1** to come or bring to the surface. **2** to become apparent. **3** to give a surface to. **4** *informal* to wake up or get out of bed.

surface-active *adj* capable of lowering the surface tension at the surface of contact between gas and liquid phases.

surface mail *n* mail sent by land or sea.

surface tension *n* a property of liquids that produces an effect such that the surface of the liquid in contact with air or another gas tends to have the smallest possible area.

surface-to-air missile *n* a missile launched from the ground against a target in the air.

surface-to-surface missile *n* a missile launched from the ground against a target on the ground.

surfactant *n* a surface-active substance, e.g. a detergent. ⋙ **surfactant** *adj.*

surfboard *n* a long narrow buoyant board used in surfing.

surfeit[1] *n* **1** an excessive amount. **2** *archaic* an illness caused by excessive indulgence in food, drink, etc.

surfeit[2] *v* **1** to feed or supply (somebody) to excess. **2** *archaic* to overindulge in something to the point of disgust or nausea.

surg. *abbr* **1** surgeon. **2** surgery. **3** surgical.

surge[1] *n* **1** the motion of swelling or sweeping forwards like that of a wave or series of waves. **2** a large wave or billow; a swell. **3** a sudden increase. **4** a short-lived sudden rise of current in an electrical circuit.

surge[2] *v* **1** to move with a surge or in surges. **2** to increase suddenly. **3** of an electrical current or voltage: to rise suddenly to an excessive or abnormal value.

surgeon *n* **1** a medical specialist who practises surgery. **2** a medical officer in the navy.

surgeon general *n* (*pl* **surgeons general**) the chief medical officer of a branch of the US armed services or of a US public health service.

surgery *n* (*pl* **-ies**) **1** the branch of medicine that deals with diseases and conditions by operative or manual procedures. **2a** the work done by a surgeon. **b** an operation. **3** *Brit* a place where a doctor or dentist treats patients. **4** *Brit* a session at which a lawyer, MP, or other professional person is available for consultation.

surgical *adj* **1** relating to surgeons or surgery. **2** used in surgery. **3** following or resulting from surgery. **4** involving precision bombing. ⋙ **surgically** *adv.*

surgical spirit *n Brit* a mixture consisting mainly of methylated spirits and used *esp* as a skin disinfectant.

surly *adj* (**-ier, -iest**) irritably sullen and bad-tempered. ⋙ **surlily** *adv,* **surliness** *n.*

surmise[1] *v* to imagine or infer on scanty evidence.

surmise[2] *n* a conjecture or guess.

surmount *v* **1** to overcome (a difficulty or obstacle). **2** to stand or lie on the top of. ⪢ **surmountable** *adj.*

surname *n* the name shared in common by members of a family.

surpass *v* **1** to go beyond (something) in quality, degree, or performance. **2** to transcend the reach, capacity, or powers of. ⪢ **surpassable** *adj.*

surpassing *adj archaic or literary* greatly exceeding others. ⪢ **surpassingly** *adv.*

surplice *n* a loose white outer ecclesiastical vestment, usu of knee length, with large open sleeves.

surplus *n* **1** an amount that remains over and above what is used or needed. **2** an excess of income over expenditure. **3** the excess of a company's net worth over the value of its capital stock. ⪢ **surplus** *adj.*

surprise[1] *n* **1** the feeling caused by an unexpected event; astonishment. **2** something unexpected or surprising. ✱ **take somebody by surprise 1** to come upon somebody without warning. **2** to capture somebody suddenly. **3** to astonish somebody.

surprise[2] *v* **1** to fill with wonder or amazement. **2** to take unawares. **3** to attack or capture unexpectedly. ⪢ **surprised** *adj.*

surprising *adj* causing surprise; unexpected. ⪢ **surprisingly** *adv.*

surreal *adj* **1** having a strange dreamlike irrational quality. **2** relating to surrealism.

surrealism *n* a movement in art, literature, and film dating from the 1920s which used the incongruous images formed by the unconscious to transcend reality as perceived by the conscious mind. ⪢ **surrealist** *n and adj.*

surrealistic *adj* **1** relating to surrealism. **2** = SURREAL (1). ⪢ **surrealistically** *adv.*

surrender[1] *v* **1** to give (oneself) up into the power of somebody else. **2** to hand over to the control or possession of somebody else, *esp* under compulsion. **3** to give up (something) completely. **4** to give (oneself) over to an influence or course of action.

surrender[2] *n* **1** the act of surrendering. **2** the voluntary cancellation of an insurance policy by the party insured in return for a payment.

surreptitious *adj* done by stealth; clandestine. ⪢ **surreptitiously** *adv,* **surreptitiousness** *n.*

surrey *n* (*pl* **-eys**) *NAm* a four-wheeled horse-drawn carriage with two seats, used for pleasure trips.

surrogacy *n* (*pl* **-ies**) the act or state of being a surrogate or a surrogate mother.

surrogate[1] *n* **1** a person appointed to act in place of another; a substitute. **2** a deputy appointed to act for a bishop in granting marriage licences.

surrogate[2] *adj* involving surrogate motherhood.

surrogate mother *n* a woman who carries and bears a child for a couple, who provide either a fertilized egg for implantation or semen for artificial insemination. ⪢ **surrogate motherhood** *n.*

surround[1] *v* **1** to enclose on all sides. **2** to be part of the environment of. **3** to cause to be encircled or enclosed by something.

surround[2] *n* **1** a border or edging. **2** (*in pl*) surroundings.

surroundings *pl n* the circumstances or objects by which one is surrounded; one's environment.

surtax *n* a graduated income tax formerly imposed in Britain in addition to the normal income tax for people whose net income exceeded a specified sum.

surtitle[1] *n* a translation of the dialogue of an opera or play which is projected onto a screen above the stage.

surtitle[2] *v* to provide surtitles for (an opera or play).

surveillance *n* close watch kept over somebody, e.g. by a detective.

survey[1] *v* **1** to look over and examine closely. **2** to contemplate (a subject) as a whole. **3** to determine and portray the form, extent, and position of (e.g. a tract of land). **4** *Brit* to examine the condition of and give a value for (a building). **5** to conduct a statistical survey on (a group of people).

survey[2] *n* **1** a description of something. **2** the examination of a building to determine its condition and value. **3** a statistical enquiry into the opinions or preferences of a group of people. **4** an act of surveying. **5** a report drawn up by a surveyor.

surveyor *n* **1** a person whose occupation is surveying land or buildings. **2** *Brit* a person who inspects buildings to determine their condition and value. ⪢ **surveyorship** *n.*

survival *n* **1** the fact of continuing to live or exist. **2** somebody or something that survives, *esp* after others of their kind have disappeared.

survivalism *n* the policy of ensuring one's own survival in the event of war or other catastrophe, e.g. by learning to handle weapons and live off the land. ⪢ **survivalist** *n and adj.*

survival of the fittest *n* = NATURAL SELECTION.

survive *v* **1** to continue to exist or live after (something). **2** to remain alive after the death of (somebody). ⪢ **survivable** *adj,* **survivor** *n.*

sus *n Brit, informal* suspicion of loitering with intent to commit a crime.

sus- *prefix* see SUB-.

susceptibility *n* (*pl* **-ies**) **1** being susceptible. **2** (*in pl*) feelings or sensibilities.

susceptible *adj* **1** open or unresistant to some influence or agency. **2** easily moved or emotionally affected; impressionable. **3** capable of submitting to an action or operation. ⪢ **susceptibly** *adv.*

sushi *n* a Japanese dish of balls or slices of cold boiled rice garnished with raw fish or other ingredients.

suspect[1] *v* **1** to imagine (something) to be true or probable. **2** to believe (somebody) to be guilty without conclusive proof. **3** to be suspicious of or distrust (something).

suspect[2] *n* somebody who is suspected, e.g. of a crime.

suspect[3] *adj* regarded with suspicion.

suspend *v* **1** to hang (something) so as to be free on all sides except at the point of support. **2** to keep (something) from falling or sinking by buoyancy. **3** to cause (something) to stop temporarily. **4** to set (something) aside. **5** to defer (a prison sentence) till later on particular conditions. **6** to hold (something) in an undecided state awaiting fuller information. **7** to debar (somebody) temporarily from an office or employment.

suspended animation *n* temporary suspension of the vital body functions, e.g. in people nearly drowned.

suspender *n* **1** *Brit* any of the fastening devices on a suspender belt or corset that holds up a woman's stockings. **2** *NAm* (*in pl*) = BRACES.

suspender belt *n Brit* a garment consisting of two pairs of short straps hanging from a belt or girdle with fastening devices for holding up a woman's stockings.

suspense *n* **1** a state of uncertain expectation as to a decision or outcome. **2** pleasant excitement. ⪢ **suspenseful** *adj.*

suspension *n* **1** suspending or being suspended. **2** the system of devices, e.g. springs, supporting the upper part of a vehicle on the axles. **3a** the state of a substance when it exists as particles mixed with but undissolved in a liquid, gas, or solid. **b** a substance in this state.

suspension bridge *n* a type of bridge that has its roadway suspended from cables.

suspicion *n* **1** the act or an instance of suspecting something wrong; mistrust. **2** a state of mental uneasiness and uncertainty; doubt. **3** a slight trace. ✱ **above suspicion** too honest or virtuous to be suspected of having done something wrong. **on suspicion** suspected. **under suspicion** suspected of having done something wrong.

suspicious *adj* **1** tending to arouse suspicion. **2** inclined to suspect; distrustful. ⯮ **suspiciously** *adv,* **suspiciousness** *n.*

suss[1] *v Brit, informal* to uncover the truth about; to realize.

suss[2] *n Brit, informal* knowledge or know-how.

sussed *adj Brit, informal* of a person: knowledgeable; aware.

suss out *v Brit, informal* **1** to realize; to work out. **2** to uncover the true nature of.

sustain *v* **1** to support the weight of. **2** to give support or relief to. **3** to cause (something) to continue; to prolong. **4** to suffer or undergo (something). **5** to support by adequate proof; to confirm. ⯮ **sustained** *adj,* **sustainer** *n,* **sustainment** *n.*

sustainable *adj* **1** able to be sustained. **2** able to be maintained at a fixed level without exhausting natural resources or damaging the environment. ⯮ **sustainability** *n,* **sustainably** *adv.*

sustenance *n* **1a** means of support or maintenance. **b** food or provisions; nourishment. **2** sustaining or being sustained.

susurration *or* **susurrus** *n literary* a whispering or rustling sound.

sutler *n* formerly, a person who sold provisions to an army.

sutra *n* **1** a Hindu sacred writing or saying, or a collection of these. **2** a discourse of the Buddha.

suttee *n* the former custom of a Hindu widow being cremated on the funeral pyre of her husband, as an indication of her devotion to him.

suture[1] *n* **1a** a strand or fibre used in the sewing together of parts of the living body. **b** a stitch made with a suture. **2** the solid join between two bones, e.g. of the skull.

suture[2] *v* to close or secure with sutures.

suzerain *n* **1** a dominant state controlling the foreign relations of an internally autonomous vassal state. **2** a feudal overlord. ⯮ **suzerainty** *n.*

Sv *abbr* sievert.

s.v. *abbr* used to indicate that a reference will be found under the word or heading given.

svelte *adj* slender in an elegant and attractive way.

Svengali *n* somebody who attempts, sometimes with sinister motives, to influence or mould another person.

S-VHS *abbr* super video home system.

SW *abbr* **1** short wave. **2** Southwest. **3** Southwestern.

swab[1] *or* **swob** *n* **1** a wad of absorbent material used for applying medication, cleaning wounds, taking bacterial specimens, etc. **2** a specimen taken with a swab. **3** a mop or sponge. **4** *archaic* a contemptible person.

swab[2] *or* **swob** *v* (**swabbed** *or* **swobbed, swabbing** *or* **swobbing**) **1** to clean (a wound) with a swab. **2** to apply medication to (a part of the body) with a swab. **3** (*often* + down) to clean (a deck) by washing, *esp* with a mop. ⯮ **swabber** *n.*

swaddle *v* **1** to wrap in swaddling clothes. **2** to swathe or envelop.

swaddling clothes *pl n* narrow strips of cloth formerly wrapped round a baby to restrict movement.

swag[1] *n* **1a** a suspended cluster, e.g. of flowers. **b** an arrangement of fabric hanging in a heavy curve or fold. **2** *informal* goods acquired by unlawful means; loot. **3** *Aus, NZ* a pack or roll of personal belongings.

swag[2] *v* (**swagged, swagging**) **1** to hang (tapestries or curtains) in heavy folds. **2** to hang heavily; to sag.

swagger[1] *v* to walk with an air of overbearing self-confidence or self-satisfaction. ⯮ **swaggerer** *n,* **swaggering** *adj.*

swagger[2] *n* **1** a self-confident or self-satisfied gait. **2** arrogant or conceitedly self-assured behaviour.

swagger stick *n* a short light stick carried *esp* by army officers.

swagman *n* (*pl* **swagmen**) *Aus, NZ* a tramp or itinerant worker who carries his possessions with him.

Swahili *n* (*pl* **Swahilis** *or* **Swahili**) **1** a member of a Bantu-speaking people of Zanzibar and the adjacent coast. **2** (*also* **Kiswahili**) a Bantu language used in trade and government in E Africa and the Congo region. ⯮ **Swahili** *adj.*

swain *n* **1** *archaic* a peasant. **2** *literary* a male admirer or suitor.

swallow[1] *n* a small long-winged bird with a forked tail that feeds on insects caught while flying.

swallow[2] *v* **1** to take (food or drink) through the mouth and oesophagus into the stomach. **2** to envelop or engulf. **3** to accept or believe without question. **4** to refrain from expressing or showing (an emotion). ⯮ **swallower** *n.*

swallow[3] *n* an act of swallowing.

swallow dive *n Brit* a forward dive executed with the back arched and arms spread sideways.

swallow hole *n* = SINK HOLE.

swallowtail *n* **1** a deeply forked and tapering tail. **2** a large butterfly with the hind wing lengthened to resemble a tail. ⯮ **swallow-tailed** *adj.*

swam *v* past tense of SWIM[1].

swami *n* (*pl* **swamis**) a Hindu ascetic or religious teacher.

swamp[1] *n* an area of wet spongy land; a marsh. ⯮ **swampy** *adj.*

swamp[2] *v* **1** to submerge or become submerged. **2** to overwhelm with too much of something.

swan[1] *n* a large long-necked mostly pure white aquatic bird. ⯮ **swanlike** *adj.*

swan[2] *v* (**swanned, swanning**) *Brit, informal* to go aimlessly or ostentatiously: *swanning round Europe.*

swan dive *n NAm* = SWALLOW DIVE.

swank[1] *v informal* to swagger; to show off.

swank[2] *n informal* ostentation of dress or manner.

swanky *adj* (**-ier, -iest**) *informal* **1** fashionably elegant; smart. **2** showy or ostentatious. **3** inclined to show off; conceited.

swannery *n* (*pl* **-ies**) *Brit* a place where swans are bred or kept.

swansdown *n* **1** the soft downy feathers of the swan used *esp* as trimming on clothing. **2** a heavy cotton flannel that has a thick nap on the face.

swan song *n* **1** a farewell appearance or final work. **2** a song said to be sung by a dying swan.

swan-upping *n Brit* the annual inspection and marking of royal swans on the River Thames.

swap[1] *or* **swop** *v* (**swapped** *or* **swopped, swapping** *or* **swopping**) **1** to give (something) in exchange. **2** to make an exchange.

swap[2] *or* **swop** *n* an exchange.

SWAPO *abbr* South-West Africa People's Organization.

sward *n* a surface of short grass, or a piece of ground covered with this.

swarf *n* metallic particles and abrasive fragments removed by a cutting or grinding tool.

swarm[1] *n* **1a** a large mass of flying insects. **b** a colony of honeybees, *esp* when emigrating from a hive with a queen bee to start a new colony elsewhere. **2** a group of things massing together.

swarm[2] *v* **1** of bees: to collect together and depart from a hive. **2** to move or assemble in a crowd. **3** (+ with) to teem with something. **4** (+ up) to climb rapidly by gripping with the hands and feet.

swart *adj archaic or literary* swarthy.

swarthy *adj* (**-ier, -iest**) of a dark complexion. ➤➤ **swarthiness** *n.*

swash[1] *v* **1** of water: to move with a splashing sound. **2** *archaic* to swagger.

swash[2] *n* a body of splashing water; *esp* seawater rushing up a beach.

swashbuckler *n* a swaggering adventurer or daredevil. ➤➤ **swashbuckling** *adj.*

swastika *n* **1** an ancient symbol in the shape of a cross with the ends of the arms extended at right angles in a clockwise or anticlockwise direction. **2** this symbol with arms extended clockwise as the emblem of the German Nazi Party.

swat[1] *v* (**swatted, swatting**) to hit (an insect) with a sharp slapping blow.

swat[2] *n* **1** a quick crushing blow. **2** a swatter.

swatch *n* **1** a sample piece of fabric or other material. **2** a collection of sample pieces bound together.

swath *n chiefly NAm* = SWATHE[1].

swathe[1] *n* **1** a row of cut grain or grass left by a scythe or mowing machine. **2** a long broad strip.

swathe[2] *v* **1** to wrap with a bandage or strip of material. **2** to envelop.

swathe[3] *n* **1** a band used in swathing. **2** something that envelops.

swatter *n* a flyswatter.

sway[1] *v* **1** to move or make (something) move slowly and rhythmically back and forth. **2** to walk in a swaying manner. **3** to move gently from an upright to a leaning position. **4** to change the opinions of (somebody), *esp* by eloquence or argument. **5** to fluctuate between one attitude and another. **6** *literary* to rule or govern.

sway[2] *n* **1** swaying or being swayed. **2a** controlling influence or power. **b** rule or dominion. ✱ **hold sway** to have influence or power.

Swazi *n* (*pl* **Swazis** *or* **Swazi**) **1** a native or inhabitant of Swaziland. **2** the Nguni language of the Swazis. ➤➤ **Swazi** *adj.*

swear *v* (*past tense* **swore,** *past part.* **sworn**) **1** to use profane or obscene language. **2** to utter or take (an oath) solemnly. **3** to promise emphatically or earnestly. **4** to bind (somebody) by an oath. ✱ **swear by** to place great confidence in. **swear off** *informal* to vow to abstain from. **swear to** to be positive about. ➤➤ **swearer** *n.*

swear in *v* to induct into office by administration of an oath.

swearword *n* a profane or obscene word.

sweat[1] *n* **1** the fluid excreted from the sweat glands of the skin; perspiration. **2** *informal* a state of anxiety or impatience. **3** *informal* hard work; drudgery. ✱ **in a cold sweat** *informal* in a state of anxiety. **no sweat** *informal* not a problem.

sweat[2] *v* (*past tense and past part.* **sweated** *or NAm* **sweat**) **1** to excrete (moisture) in visible quantities through the openings of the sweat glands; to perspire. **2** to emit or exude moisture. **3** to exert oneself; to work hard. **4** to undergo anxiety or tension. **5** to cook (vegetables) gently in melted fat until the juices run out. ✱ **sweat blood** *informal* to work or worry intensely.

sweatband *n* a band of material worn round the head or wrist to absorb sweat.

sweated *adj* of a sweatshop system: *sweated labour.*

sweater *n* = JUMPER[1] (1).

sweat gland *n* a tubular gland in the skin that secretes sweat through a minute pore on the surface of the skin.

sweat off *v* to lose (weight) by exercise or sweating.

sweat out *v* **1** to relieve (an illness) by sweating. **2** *informal* to endure (something unpleasant).

sweatpants *pl n* loose-fitting trousers worn by athletes or for leisure.

sweats *pl n chiefly NAm, informal* a sweatsuit or sweatpants.

sweatshirt *n* a loose collarless pullover of heavy cotton jersey.

sweatshop *n* a place of work in which workers are employed for long hours at low wages and under unhealthy conditions.

sweatsuit *n* a loose-fitting suit made up of a sweatshirt and sweatpants.

sweaty *adj* (**-ier, -iest**) **1** covered with or smelling of sweat. **2** causing sweat. ➤➤ **sweatily** *adv,* **sweatiness** *n.*

Swede *n* a native or inhabitant of Sweden.

swede *n* a plant with a bulbous yellow-fleshed root used as a vegetable.

Swedish *n* the language of Sweden and parts of Finland. ➤➤ **Swedish** *adj.*

sweep[1] *v* (*past tense and past part.* **swept**) **1** to clean by brushing. **2** to move or carry along with irresistible force. **3** to remove with a single forceful action. **4** to move through or along (a place) with overwhelming speed. **5** (+ away) to destroy (something) completely; to wipe (it) out. **6** to cover the entire range of. **7** to trace or describe the path or extent of (a line or circle). **8** *NAm* to win an overwhelming victory in (something). ✱ **sweep somebody off their feet** to cause somebody to fall in love with one. **sweep something under the carpet** to conceal something in the hope that it will be ignored. **sweep the board** to win everything in a contest.

sweep[2] *n* **1** an act of sweeping. **2** a chimney sweep. **3a** a curving course or line. **b** a broad extent. **c** the extent of a sweeping movement; scope. **4** *informal* a sweepstake. **5** *NAm* an overwhelming victory.

sweepback *n* the backward slant of an aircraft wing in which the outer portion of the wing is behind the inner portion.

sweeper *n* **1** a person or thing that sweeps. **2** in soccer, a defensive player who plays behind the backs as a last line of defence before the goalkeeper.

sweeping *adj* **1** extending in a wide curve or over a wide area. **2a** extensive; wide-ranging. **b** of a statement: marked by wholesale and indiscriminate inclusion. ➤➤ **sweepingly** *adv.*

sweepings *pl n* refuse or rubbish collected by sweeping.

sweepstake *n* (*also in pl*) **1** a race or contest in which the entire prize is awarded to the winner. **2** a lottery.

sweet[1] *adj* **1** inducing the one of the four basic taste sensations that is typically induced by sucrose. **2a** not sour, rancid, or stale. **b** not salt or salted; fresh. **c** fragrant. **3a** delightful or charming. **b** marked by gentle good humour or kindliness. **c** pleasing to the ear or eye. **4** much loved; dear. **5** working or moving smoothly. ✱ **keep somebody sweet** *informal* to keep somebody happy and cooperative. **sweet on somebody** *informal, dated* in love with somebody. ⋙ **sweetish** *adj,* **sweetly** *adv,* **sweetness** *n.*

sweet[2] *n* **1** *Brit* a small piece of confectionery prepared with chocolate or sugar. **2** *Brit* a dessert. **3** used as a form of address: a darling or sweetheart. **4** (*in pl*) pleasures; delights.

sweet-and-sour *adj* seasoned with a sauce containing sugar and vinegar or lemon juice.

sweetbread *n* the pancreas or thymus of a young animal used for food.

sweetbrier *or* **sweetbriar** *n* a wild rose with stout prickles and white to deep pink flowers.

sweet corn *n* maize with kernels that contain a high percentage of sugar, used as a vegetable.

sweeten *v* **1** to make or become sweet. **2** *informal* to soften the mood or attitude of. **3** to make less painful or trying.

sweetener *n* **1** a substance added to food or drink to sweeten it. **2** *chiefly Brit, informal* a bribe.

sweet Fanny Adams *n* see FANNY ADAMS.

sweetheart *n* **1** a person that one loves; a darling. **2** an affectionate form of address. **3** *informal* (*used before a noun*) relating to an agreement between two parties that has benefits for both but is disadvantageous to a third party.

sweetheart neckline *n* a low neckline on a woman's dress or top that has a heart-shaped effect.

sweetie *n informal* **1** *Brit* used by or to children: a sweet. **2** a term of endearment. **3** a pleasing or attractive person. **4** a grapefruit with a green skin and a sweet taste.

sweetie pie *n informal* **1** a term of endearment. **2** a pleasing or attractive person.

sweetmeal *adj Brit* made from sweetened wholemeal flour.

sweetmeat *n archaic* a sweet or delicacy rich in sugar.

sweet pea *n* a plant of the pea family with slender climbing stems and large fragrant flowers.

sweet pepper *n* a large mild thick-skinned capsicum fruit.

sweet potato *n* a plant of the bindweed family with a large sweet root used as a vegetable.

sweet talk *n informal* flattery.

sweet-talk *v informal* to persuade (somebody) to do something by flattering them.

sweet tooth *n* a fondness for sweet food.

sweet william *n* a plant of the pink family with small white to deep red flowers.

swell[1] *v* (*past tense* **swelled,** *past part.* **swollen, swelled**) **1a** to expand gradually beyond a normal or original limit. **b** to curve outwards or upwards; to bulge. **2** to increase the number, volume, or intensity of (something).

swell[2] *n* **1** a rounded protuberance or bulge. **2** the process of swelling. **3a** a gradual increase and decrease of the volume in music. **b** a device used in an organ for controlling volume of sound. **4** a surge of water, often continuing after its cause, e.g. a gale. **5** *informal, dated* a person of fashion or high social position.

swell[3] *adj* **1** *NAm, informal, dated* excellent. **2** *archaic* stylish or socially prominent.

swelling *n* **1** an abnormal bodily protuberance or enlargement. **2** the condition of being swollen.

swelter[1] *v* to suffer from heat.

swelter[2] *n* a state of oppressive heat.

sweltering *adj* oppressively hot.

swept *v* past tense and past part. of SWEEP[1].

swept-back *adj* of an aircraft wing: possessing sweepback.

swept-wing *adj* of an aircraft: having swept-back wings.

swerve[1] *v* to turn aside or make (something) turn aside abruptly from a straight course; to deviate.

swerve[2] *n* an instance of swerving.

swift[1] *adj* **1** moving or capable of moving at great speed. **2** occurring suddenly or within a very short time. ⋙ **swiftly** *adv,* **swiftness** *n.*

swift[2] *n* a dark-coloured bird noted for its fast darting flight in pursuit of insects.

swig[1] *n* a quantity drunk in one swallow.

swig[2] *v* (**swigged, swigging**) to drink in long draughts.

swill[1] *v* **1** *Brit* (*often* + out) to wash (something), *esp* by flushing with water. **2** *Brit, informal* to drink or eat greedily.

swill[2] *n* **1** a semiliquid food for pigs, composed of edible refuse mixed with water or milk. **2** *informal* a swig. **3** *informal* disgusting food or drink. **4** rubbish; waste.

swim[1] *v* (**swimming,** *past tense* **swam,** *past part.* **swum**) **1** to propel the body in water by bodily movements. **2** to float on a liquid. **3** to become immersed in or flooded with a liquid. **4** to have a floating or dizzy sensation: *Her head was swimming.* ✱ **swim against the tide** to move counter to the prevailing trend. ⋙ **swimmer** *n.*

swim[2] *n* **1** an act or period of swimming. **2** an area frequented by fish. ✱ **in the swim** involved in activities, current affairs, etc.

swim bladder *n* the air bladder of a fish that serves as a buoyancy mechanism.

swimming bath *n Brit* (*also in pl*) an indoor swimming pool.

swimming cap *n* a tight-fitting rubber cap worn when swimming.

swimming costume *n Brit* a close-fitting garment worn for swimming.

swimmingly *adv informal* very well; splendidly.

swimming pool *n* an artificial pool for people to swim in.

swimming trunks *pl n* shorts worn for swimming by men or boys.

swimsuit *n* = SWIMMING COSTUME.

swimwear *n* clothing suitable for swimming.

swindle[1] *v* to take money or property from (somebody) by fraud or deceit. ⋙ **swindler** *n.*

swindle[2] *n* an act of fraud or deceit.

swine *n* **1** (*pl* **swine**) *formal or NAm* a pig. **2** (*pl* **swine** *or* **swines**) *informal* a contemptible person. **3** *informal* something unpleasant. ⋙ **swinish** *adj.*

swine fever *n* a highly infectious viral disease of pigs.

swineherd *n* a person who tends pigs.

swing[1] *v* (*past tense and past part.* **swung**) **1a** to move or cause to move freely to and fro, *esp* when hanging from an overhead support. **b** to hang freely from a support. **2a** to move in or cause to move in a circle or arc. **b** to turn on or as if on a hinge or pivot. **3** to convey oneself by grasping a fixed support. **4** *informal* to die by hanging. **5** to throw (a punch) with a sweeping arm movement. **6** to fluctuate from one condition, position, or object of attention to another. **7** to influence (something) decisively. **8** *informal* to succeed in doing or having (something). **9** to play music or sing with a lively compelling rhythm. **10** *informal* to be lively and exciting. **11** *informal* to swap sexual partners. ✱ **swing the lead** *Brit, informal* to neglect one's work by inventing excuses; to malinger.

swing[2] *n* **1** a suspended seat on which one may swing to and fro. **2 a** a stroke or blow delivered with a sweeping arm movement. **b** a sweeping movement of the body or a body part. **c** the regular movement of a freely suspended object to and fro along an arc. **3** a shift from one condition, position, or object of attention to another. **4** jazz played with a steady lively rhythm, simple harmony, and a basic melody. ✱ **get into the swing of things** *informal* to accustom oneself to something. **go with a swing** *informal* to be enjoyable and successful. **in full swing** at the height of activity. **swings and roundabouts** *Brit* a situation where a loss made on one transaction is offset by a gain on another.

swingbin *n Brit* a rubbish bin that has a lid that swings shut.

swing bridge *n* a bridge that can be swung aside to let ships through.

swing door *n* a door that can be pushed open from either side and that swings closed when released.

swingeing *adj chiefly Brit* severe or drastic: *swingeing cuts in public expenditure.*

swinger *n informal, dated* a person who engages freely in swapping sexual partners.

swinging *adj informal* **1** lively and exciting. **2** sexually liberated.

swingle *n* a wooden instrument used for beating and cleaning flax.

swingletree *n chiefly Brit* the pivoted swinging bar to which the traces of a harness are attached and by which a vehicle or plough is drawn.

swingometer *n informal* a device for representing statistical movements by means of an adjustable pointer attached to a dial.

swing-wing *adj* of an aircraft: having movable wings giving the best angles of sweepback for both low and high speeds. ⋙ **swing-wing** *n.*

swipe[1] *v* **1** *informal* to strike or hit out with a sweeping motion. **2** *informal* to steal (something). **3** *informal* to pass (a swipe card) through a machine that can read it.

swipe[2] *n informal* **1** a strong sweeping blow. **2** an unexpected criticism.

swipe card *n* a plastic card containing a magnetic strip encoded with information which can be read when the card is passed through a special machine.

swirl[1] *n* **1** a whirling mass or motion. **2** a twisting shape or pattern. ⋙ **swirly** *adj.*

swirl[2] *v* to move or cause to move in eddies or whirls.

swish[1] *n* **1** a sharp hissing or brushing sound. **2** a swishing movement.

swish[2] *v* to move or cause to move with a swish.

swish[3] *adj Brit, informal* smart and fashionable.

Swiss *n* (*pl* **Swiss**) a native or inhabitant of Switzerland. ⋙ **Swiss** *adj.*

Swiss cheese plant *n* a plant of the arum family that has large dark green leaves with deep notches and many perforations.

Swiss roll *n Brit* a thin sheet of sponge cake spread with jam, cream, etc and rolled up.

switch[1] *n* **1** a device for making, breaking, or changing the connections in an electrical circuit. **2** a sudden shift or change. **3** a slender flexible twig or rod. **4** *NAm* a set of railway points. **5** a tress of hair attached to augment a hairstyle.

switch[2] *v* **1** to make a shift or change in (something). **2** to exchange (something). **3** *archaic* to beat with or as if with a switch. **4** to cause (an electric current) to flow, stop flowing, or change path by means of a switch. ⋙ **switchable** *adj,* **switcher** *n.*

switchback *n* **1** *Brit* a zigzag road or railway in a mountainous region. **2** a roller coaster.

switchblade *n chiefly NAm* a flick knife.

switchboard *n* a panel or frame on which switching devices are mounted for the manual switching of telephone calls.

switched-on *adj Brit, informal* alive to experience; responsive or alert.

switchgear *n* equipment used for the switching of electrical currents.

switch off *v* **1** to turn off (e.g. a light or machine) by operating an electrical switch. **2** *informal* to lose interest.

switch on *v* to turn on (e.g. a light or machine) by operating an electrical switch.

swivel[1] *n* a device joining two parts so that the moving part can pivot freely.

swivel[2] *v* (**swivelled, swivelling,** *NAm* **swiveled, swiveling**) to turn or cause to turn on or as if on a swivel.

swivel chair *n* a chair that swivels on its base.

swiz *n* (*pl* **swizzes**) *Brit, informal* something that does not live up to one's hopes or expectations.

swizzle[1] *n Brit, informal* a swiz.

swizzle[2] *n* an alcoholic cocktail.

swizzle[3] *v* to mix or stir (a drink) with a swizzle stick.

swizzle stick *n* a thin rod used to stir mixed drinks.

swob[1] *n* see SWAB[1].

swob[2] *v* see SWAB[2].

swollen *v* past part. of SWELL[1].

swoon[1] *v* to faint.

swoon[2] *n* a loss of consciousness.

swoop[1] *v* **1** to make a sudden attack or raid. **2** *informal* to carry off abruptly.

swoop[2] *n* an act of swooping. ✱ **at one fell swoop** see FELL[4].

swoosh[1] *n* a rushing or swirling sound.

swoosh[2] *v* to make or move with a rushing sound.

swop[1] *v* see SWAP[1].

swop[2] *n* see SWAP[2].

sword *n* **1** a cutting or thrusting weapon with a long sharp-pointed and sharp-edged blade. **2** (**the sword**) *literary* the use of force, e.g. in war. ✱ **cross swords** to fight or argue. **put somebody to the sword** to kill somebody with a sword.

sword-bearer *n* an official who carries a ceremonial sword on formal occasions.

sword dance *n* a Scottish-Highland solo dance performed in the angles formed by two swords crossed on the ground. ⋙ **sword dancer** *n.*

swordfish *n* (*pl* **swordfishes** *or* **swordfish**) a very large oceanic food fish that has a very long beak.

sword of Damocles *n* an impending disaster.

swordplay *n* the art or practice of wielding a sword.

swordsman *n* (*pl* **swordsmen**) a person skilled in swordplay. ▶▶ **swordsmanship** *n.*

swordstick *n* a walking stick in which a sword blade is concealed.

swore *v* past tense of SWEAR.

sworn[1] *v* past part. of SWEAR.

sworn[2] *adj* **1** made under oath, or as if under oath. **2** determined to remain a particular thing: *sworn enemies.*

swot[1] *n Brit, informal* a person who studies excessively.

swot[2] *v* (**swotted, swotting**) *Brit, informal* to study hard.

swum *v* past part. of SWIM[1].

swung *v* past tense and past part. of SWING[1].

swung dash *n* a character (~) used chiefly to represent part or all of a previously spelt-out word.

sybarite *n* somebody who likes to indulge in sensual pleasures. ▶▶ **sybaritic** *adj.*

sycamore *n* **1** a Eurasian maple widely planted as a shade tree. **2** *NAm* a very large spreading plane tree.

sycophant *n* a self-seeking flatterer; a toady. ▶▶ **sycophancy** *n,* **sycophantic** *adj.*

Sydenham's chorea *n* a nervous disorder mainly affecting children, marked by spasmodic movements and lack of coordination, associated with rheumatic fever.

syl- *prefix* see SYN-.

syllabary *n* (*pl* **-ies**) a set of written characters each one of which represents a syllable.

syllabi *n* pl of SYLLABUS.

syllabic *adj* **1** enunciated with separation of syllables. **2** of a consonant: constituting a syllable. ▶▶ **syllabically** *adv.*

syllabify *v* (**-ies, -ied**) to form or divide (words) into syllables. ▶▶ **syllabification** *n.*

syllable *n* a unit of spoken language that usu consists of one vowel sound either alone or with a consonant sound preceding or following.

syllabub *n* a cold dessert usu made by curdling sweetened cream with wine or other acidic liquid.

syllabus *n* (*pl* **syllabi** *or* **syllabuses**) a summary of a course of study or of examination requirements.

syllogism *n* a pattern of deductive reasoning consisting of two premises and a conclusion. ▶▶ **syllogistic** *adj.*

sylph *n* **1** a slender graceful woman or girl. **2** an imaginary being inhabiting the air. ▶▶ **sylphlike** *adj.*

sylvan *or* **silvan** *adj* **1** located in or characteristic of the woods or forest. **2** full of woods or trees.

sym- *prefix* see SYN-.

symbiont *n* an organism living in symbiosis.

symbiosis *n* (*pl* **symbioses**) the living together of two dissimilar organisms in intimate association, usu to the benefit of both. ▶▶ **symbiotic** *adj.*

symbol *n* **1** something that stands for or suggests something else by reason of association or convention; *esp* a visible sign of something invisible. **2** a sign used in writing or printing to represent operations, quantities, elements, etc in a particular field.

symbolic *adj* using or constituting a symbol or symbols. ▶▶ **symbolical** *adj,* **symbolically** *adv.*

symbolic logic *n* a method of developing and representing logical principles using a formalized system of symbols.

symbolise *v* see SYMBOLIZE.

symbolism *n* **1** the art or practice of representing things by symbols. **2** a system of symbols. **3** the literary and artistic mode of expression of the symbolists.

symbolist *n* **1** somebody who employs symbols or symbolism. **2** a writer or artist who uses symbols to convey a subjective view of reality and immaterial or intangible states or truths. ▶▶ **symbolist** *adj.*

symbolize *or* **-ise** *v* **1** to serve as a symbol of. **2** to represent or identify by means of symbols. ▶▶ **symbolization** *n.*

symbology *n* **1** the art of expression by symbols. **2** the study of symbols. **3** a system of symbols.

symmetrical *or* **symmetric** *adj* having the same proportions, shape, etc on both sides; *specif* capable of division by a longitudinal plane into similar halves. ▶▶ **symmetrically** *adv.*

symmetry *n* (*pl* **-ies**) **1** the property of being symmetrical. **2** balanced proportions, or beauty of form arising from balanced proportions.

sympathetic *adj* **1** given to or arising from compassion and sensitivity to others' feelings. **2** favourably inclined. **3** appropriate to one's mood or temperament; congenial. **4** existing or operating through an affinity or mutual association. **5** relating to or acting on the sympathetic nervous system. ▶▶ **sympathetically** *adv.*

sympathetic magic *n* magic in which an action performed in one place is thought to cause a similar event in another place.

sympathetic nervous system *n* the part of the autonomic nervous system that tends to depress secretion, decrease the tension and elasticity of smooth muscle, and cause the contraction of blood vessels.

sympathize *or* **-ise** *v* **1** to share in distress or suffering; to commiserate. **2** to agree with somebody or something. ▶▶ **sympathizer** *n.*

sympathy *n* (*pl* **-ies**) **1** the act or capacity of sharing the feelings or interests of another. **2a** inclination to think or feel alike. **b** (*also in pl*) a feeling of loyalty. **c** an affinity or relationship between people or things in which each is simultaneously affected in a similar way. **d** harmony in action or effect.

symphonic *adj* relating to or having the form of a symphony. ▶▶ **symphonically** *adv.*

symphonic poem *n* an extended orchestral composition, based on a legend, tale, etc.

symphonist *n* a composer of symphonies.

symphony *n* (*pl* **-ies**) **1** an extended piece for orchestra, classically in four contrasting movements. **2** something of great harmonious complexity.

symphony orchestra *n* a large orchestra comprising string, wind, brass, and percussion instruments.

symposium *n* (*pl* **symposia** *or* **symposiums**) **1** a formal meeting at which several specialists deliver short addresses on a topic. **2** a published collection of opinions on a subject.

symptom *n* **1** something giving indication of disease or physical disturbance. **2** something that indicates the existence of something else, *esp* something undesirable. ▶▶ **symptomless** *adj.*

symptomatic *adj* **1** being a symptom of a disease. **2** characteristic or indicative. ▶▶ **symptomatically** *adv.*

syn. *abbr* **1** synonym. **2** synonymous.

syn- *or* **syl-** *or* **sym-** *prefix* with, along with, or together: *sympathy*; *synthesis.*

synaesthesia (*NAm* **synesthesia**) *n* a sensation in one part of the body brought about by a stimulus in a different part. ➤➤ **synaesthetic** *adj.*

synagogue *n* the house of worship and communal centre of a Jewish congregation.

synapse *n* the point between two nerves across which a nervous impulse is transmitted. ➤➤ **synaptic** *adj.*

sync[1] *or* **synch** *n informal* synchronization.

sync[2] *or* **synch** *v informal* (*often* + up) to match (film and magnetic track) so that they run exactly in synchronization.

synchro *n* **1** synchronized swimming. **2** synchromesh.

synchromesh[1] *adj* designed to synchronize the speeds of the different moving parts involved in a gear change.

synchromesh[2] *n* a gear system using synchronized gear changing.

synchronic *adj* of or dealing with phenomena, *esp* of language, at one point in time, ignoring historical antecedents: compare DIACHRONIC. ➤➤ **synchronically** *adv.*

synchronicity *n* the coincidence in a person's life of two or more events which seem to be linked in significance but which have no causal connection.

synchronise *v* see SYNCHRONIZE.

synchronism *n* **1** the quality of being synchronous. **2** chronological arrangement of historical events so as to indicate coincidence or coexistence.

synchronize *or* **-ise** *v* **1** to happen or cause to happen at the same time. **2** to make (sound) exactly simultaneous with the action in a film or a television programme. ➤➤ **synchronization** *n,* **synchronizer** *n.*

synchronized swimming *n* exhibition or competitive swimming in which the movements of swimmers are synchronized with a musical accompaniment so as to form changing patterns.

synchronous *adj* **1** happening or arising at precisely the same time. **2** of an orbit: at a distance from the earth such that a satellite appears fixed. ➤➤ **synchronously** *adv.*

synchrony *n* synchronistic occurrence or treatment.

syncline *n* a trough of stratified rock in which the layers dip towards each other from either side: compare ANTICLINE. ➤➤ **synclinal** *adj.*

syncopate *v* to modify or affect (musical rhythm) by syncopation.

syncopation *n* a temporary displacement of the regular metrical accent in music caused by stressing a weak beat or omitting the strong beat.

syncope *n* **1** temporary loss of consciousness; fainting. **2** the dropping of sounds or letters in a word, e.g. in *fo'c'sle* for *forecastle.*

syncretise *v* see SYNCRETIZE.

syncretism *n* the combination of different forms of belief or practice. ➤➤ **syncretic** *adj,* **syncretist** *n and adj,* **syncretistic** *adj.*

syncretize *or* **-ise** *v* to attempt to reconcile (principles or sects). ➤➤ **syncretization** *n.*

syndic *n* **1** an agent who transacts business for a university or corporation. **2** a government administrator in some countries.

syndicalism *n* **1** a revolutionary doctrine according to which workers should seize control of the economy and the government by direct means. **2** a system of economic organization in which industries are owned and managed by the workers. ➤➤ **syndicalist** *adj and n.*

syndicate[1] *n* **1** (*used as sing. or pl*) a group of people or concerns who combine to carry out a particular transaction or to promote some common interest. **2** a business concern that supplies material for simultaneous publication in many newspapers or periodicals.

syndicate[2] *v* **1** to sell (e.g. a cartoon) to a syndicate for simultaneous publication in many newspapers or periodicals. **2** to manage by a syndicate. ➤➤ **syndication** *n.*

syndrome *n* **1** a group of signs and symptoms that occur together and characterize a particular medical abnormality. **2** a set of concurrent emotions or actions that form an identifiable pattern.

syne[1] *adv Scot* since then; ago.

syne[2] *conj and prep Scot* since.

synecdoche *n* a figure of speech in which a part is used to mean the whole, or the whole to mean a part.

synecology *n* a branch of ecology that deals with the structure and development of ecological communities. ➤➤ **synecological** *adj.*

synergic *adj* working together; cooperating.

synergism *n* cooperative action between two or more agencies whose combined effect is greater than the sum of their separate effects. ➤➤ **synergistic** *adj.*

synergist *n* something that enhances the effectiveness of an active agent.

synergy *n* **1** synergism. **2** cooperation between two organizations, which achieves more than both would achieve if they worked separately.

synesthesia *n NAm* see SYNAESTHESIA.

syngamy *n* sexual reproduction by union of gametes.

synod *n* **1a** the governing assembly of an Anglican province, diocese, or deanery. **b** a Presbyterian governing body ranking between the PRESBYTERY (ruling body) and the general assembly. **2** a formal meeting to decide ecclesiastical matters. ➤➤ **synodal** *adj.*

synodic *adj* relating to a conjunction or the period between two successive conjunctions of the same celestial bodies.

synodical *adj* **1** relating to a synod. **2** = SYNODIC.

synonym *n* any of two or more words in a language that are used with the same meaning.

synonymous *adj* **1** having the character of a synonym. **2** alike in meaning or significance. ➤➤ **synonymously** *adv,* **synonymy** *n.*

synopsis *n* (*pl* **synopses**) a condensed statement or outline.

synopsize *or* **-ise** *v* to make a synopsis of.

synoptic *adj* **1** affording a comprehensive view of a whole. **2** (**Synoptic**) of or being the first three Gospels of the New Testament. ➤➤ **synoptically** *adv.*

synovia *n* a transparent viscous lubricating fluid secreted by a joint or tendon membrane. ➤➤ **synovial** *adj.*

synovitis *n* inflammation of a synovial membrane.

syntactic *adj* of or conforming to the rules of syntax. ➤➤ **syntactical** *adj,* **syntactically** *adv.*

syntax *n* **1a** the way in which words are put together to form phrases, clauses, or sentences. **b** a set of rules for this. **2** in computing, the set of rules governing a programming language.

synth *n informal* = SYNTHESIZER.

synthesis *n* (*pl* **syntheses**) **1** the composition or combination of separate or diverse elements into a coherent whole: compare ANALYSIS. **2** the artificial production of a substance by chemical reaction. ➤➤ **synthesist** *n.*

synthesize *or* **-ise** *v* **1** to produce by synthesis. **2** to combine (things) to form a whole. **3** to produce (sound) electronically.

synthesizer *n* an electronic musical instrument that produces a sound that can be altered, e.g. to mimic other instruments, and is played by means of a keyboard.

synthetic[1] *adj* **1** produced by chemical reaction, *esp* as an imitation of something natural. **2** not genuine or sincere. ➤➤ **synthetically** *adv.*

synthetic[2] *n* a product of chemical synthesis, *esp* a textile fibre.

synthetize *or* **-ise** *v* = SYNTHESIZE.

syphilis *n* a sexually transmitted disease caused by a spirochaetal bacterium. ➤➤ **syphilitic** *adj and n.*

syphon[1] *n* see SIPHON[1].

syphon[2] *v* see SIPHON[2].

Syrah *n* = SHIRAZ.

Syrian *n* a native or inhabitant of Syria. ➤➤ **Syrian** *adj.*

syringe[1] *n* a device used to inject fluids into or withdraw them from the body; *esp* one that consists of a hollow barrel fitted with a plunger and a hollow needle.

syringe[2] *v* to irrigate or spray with a syringe.

syrinx *n* (*pl* **syringes** *or* **syrinxes**) **1** panpipes. **2** the vocal organ of birds.

syrup (*NAm* **sirup**) *n* **1a** a thick sticky solution of sugar and water, often flavoured or mixed with medicinal substances. **b** the concentrated juice of a fruit or plant, e.g. the sugar maple. **2** cloying sweetness or sentimentality. ➤➤ **syrupy** *adj.*

sysop *n* in computing, a system operator.

system *n* **1a** a regularly interacting or interdependent group of items forming a unified whole. **b** a group of devices or an organization forming a network. **2** a form of social, economic, or political organization. **3** an organized set of doctrines or principles, intended to explain the arrangement or working of a systematic whole. **4a** an organized or established procedure. **b** a manner of classifying, symbolizing, or formalizing things. **5** harmonious arrangement or pattern; order. **6** a major division of rocks including all those formed during a geological period or era. **7** the body considered as a functional unit. **8** (**the system**) an organized society or social situation regarded as stultifying. ✱ **get something out of one's system** *informal* to stop thinking about something.

systematic *adj* **1** relating to or presented as a system. **2** methodical in procedure or plan; thorough. ➤➤ **systematically** *adv.*

systematics *pl n* (*used as sing. or pl*) the branch of biology dealing with the classification and study of living things with regard to their natural relationships.

systematize *or* **-ise** *v* to arrange according to a set method; to order systematically. ➤➤ **systematization** *n.*

systemic *adj* **1** of or common to a system, e.g. affecting the body generally. **2** of an insecticide, pesticide, etc: making a plant toxic to a pest by entering the tissues. ➤➤ **systemically** *adv.*

systems analysis *n* the analysis of a complex task or procedure by computer in order to discover ways of accomplishing it more efficiently. ➤➤ **systems analyst** *n.*

systole *n* the contraction of the heart by which the blood is forced onwards and the circulation kept up: compare DIASTOLE. ➤➤ **systolic** *adj.*

syzygy *n* (*pl* **-ies**) **1** a configuration in which three celestial bodies, e.g. the sun, moon, and earth, lie in a straight line. **2** any pair of things.

T t

T[1] *or* **t** *n* (*pl* **T's** *or* **Ts** *or* **t's**) the twentieth letter of the English alphabet. ✱ **to a T** to perfection; exactly.

T[2] *abbr* **1** tera-. **2** tesla. **3** true.

T[3] *abbr* the chemical symbol for tritium.

t *abbr* ton.

't *pron archaic or literary* it.

TA *abbr* Territorial Army.

Ta *abbr* the chemical symbol for tantalum.

ta *interj Brit, informal* thanks.

tab[1] *n* **1** a flap or loop of material by which something can be held or lifted. **2** a projection from a card or file that gives information about its contents. **3** *chiefly NAm* a bill, *esp* for a meal or drinks. **4** *Brit* an insignia or marking on the collar of a military uniform that denotes a high-ranking officer. **5** *N Eng, informal* a cigarette. ✱ **keep tabs on** *informal* to keep under close surveillance. **pick up the tab** *informal* to pay a bill, e.g. in a restaurant.

tab[2] *v* (**tabbed, tabbing**) to provide with tabs.

tab[3] *n* = TABULATOR.

tab[4] *v* (**tabbed, tabbing**) to arrange (data) in tabular form; to tabulate.

tab[5] *n informal* a tablet, *esp* one containing an illegal drug.

tabard *n* **1** a short emblazoned tunic worn by a knight over his armour. **2** a herald's official coat emblazoned with the arms of his lord or sovereign. **3** a straight-hanging sleeveless outer garment with slits at the sides, worn by women.

Tabasco *n trademark* a hot pungent sauce made from capsicums.

tabbouleh *n* a Middle Eastern salad dish made from bulgur wheat mixed with tomatoes, olive oil, mint, and parsley.

tabby[1] *n* (*pl* **-ies**) **1a** a domestic cat with a brownish or grey coat striped with darker shades. **b** a female domestic cat. **2** *archaic* a plain silk taffeta fabric, *esp* with an irregular wavy finish.

tabby[2] *adj* of a cat: striped with darker colours.

tabernacle *n* **1a** (*often* **Tabernacle**) a tent sanctuary used by the Israelites during the Exodus. **b** the meeting place or church of Nonconformists or Mormons. **2** a receptacle for the consecrated bread and wine used at Communion. ➤➤ **tabernacular** *adj*.

tabla *n* a pair of small hand drums of different sizes used in Indian classical music.

tablature *n* an instrumental notation indicating the string, keys, or fingering to be used instead of the note to be sounded.

table[1] *n* **1** a piece of furniture consisting of a smooth flat slab of wood, etc fixed on legs or some other support. **2a** the food served at a meal: *He always keeps a good table.* **b** the act of assembling to eat; a meal. **3a** a systematically arranged list of figures, information, etc. **b** = MULTIPLICATION TABLE. ✱ **lay something on the table** to put something forward for discussion. **on the table** *chiefly Brit* put forward for discussion. **turn the tables** to bring about a reversal of the relative conditions or fortunes of two contending parties. **under the table** into a stupor: *She could drink the men under the table.*

table[2] *v* **1** to enter (information) in a table. **2a** *Brit* to place (a matter) on the agenda. **b** *NAm* to remove (a matter) from consideration indefinitely.

tableau *n* (*pl* **tableaux** *or* **tableaus**) **1** a graphic description or representation of a scene. **2** a dramatic or artistic grouping of figures. **3** a depiction of a scene presented on a stage by silent and motionless costumed participants.

tableau vivant *n* (*pl* **tableaux vivants**) = TABLEAU (3).

tablecloth *n* a cloth that is spread over a dining table before the places are set.

table d'hôte *n* (*pl* **tables d'hôte** *or* **table d'hôtes**) a meal consisting of a fixed number of courses with a limited choice, provided at a fixed price: compare À LA CARTE.

tableland *n* a broad level area of land elevated on all sides; a plateau.

table licence *n Brit* a licence that allows alcoholic drinks to be served in a restaurant only to patrons who are having a meal.

table manners *pl n* the conventional polite behaviour expected when one is eating a meal at table.

table mat *n* a small decorative mat placed under a hot dish to protect the surface of a table.

table salt *n* fine-grained salt suitable for use at the table.

tablespoon *n* a large spoon used for serving.

tablespoonful *n* (*pl* **tablespoonfuls**) **1** as much as a tablespoon can hold. **2** a unit of measure equal to about 15ml (about 0.5fl oz).

tablet *n* **1** a small solid shaped mass or capsule of medicinal material. **2** a flat slab or plaque suitable for an inscription. **3** a pad of paper for writing on.

table tennis *n* a game based on tennis and played with round wooden bats and a small hollow plastic ball on an indoor table.

tableware *n* glasses, dishes, plates, and cutlery, for serving and eating food at the table.

table wine *n* a relatively inexpensive wine considered suitable for drinking with food.

tabloid *n* **1** a newspaper having a relatively small page size and containing news stories in condensed form, often of a sensational nature. **2** (*used before a noun*) **a** relating to or characteristic of a tabloid. **b** dealing with material similar to that contained in tabloids.

taboo[1] *or* **tabu** *adj* **1** too sacred or evil to be touched, named, or used. **2** forbidden on grounds of morality, tradition, or social usage.

taboo[2] *or* **tabu** *n* (*pl* **taboos** *or* **tabus**) **1** a prohibition imposed by social custom. **2** an object, word, behaviour, etc that is prohibited.

taboo[3] *or* **tabu** *v* (**taboos** *or* **tabus, tabooed** *or* **tabued, tabooing** *or* **tabuing**) to set apart or ban as taboo.

tabor *or* **tabour** *n* a small drum with one head of soft calfskin used to accompany a pipe or fife.

tabu[1] *adj* see TABOO[1].

tabu[2] *n* see TABOO[2].

tabu[3] *v* see TABOO[3].

tabular *adj* **1** of data or statistics: arranged in a table. **2** having a broad flat surface.

tabula rasa *n* (*pl* **tabulae rasae**) **1** a person's mind, *esp* at birth, thought of as blank before receiving outside impressions. **2** the state of having no preconceived notions.

tabulate *v* to arrange (data) in tabular form. ➤➤ **tabulation** *n.*

tabulator *n* an attachment to a typewriter or software on a computer that is used for arranging data in columns.

tachism *or* **tachisme** *n* a form of action painting that originated in the 1940s in France and was seen as a way of expressing the unconscious. ➤➤ **tachist** *adj and n.*

tachistoscope *n* an apparatus for briefly exposing visual stimuli, used in the study of learning, attention, and perception.

tacho *n* (*pl* **-os**) *informal* **1** = TACHOGRAPH. **2** = TACHOMETER.

tachograph *n* a device for automatically recording the speed of a vehicle, *esp* a lorry.

tachometer *n* a device for indicating speed of rotation, e.g. of a vehicle engine.

tachycardia *n* relatively rapid heart action, often indicative of disease.

tachyon *n* a hypothetical elementary particle that travels faster than light.

tacit *adj* implied or understood but not actually expressed. ➤➤ **tacitly** *adv.*

taciturn *adj* not communicative or talkative. ➤➤ **taciturnity** *n,* **taciturnly** *adv.*

tack[1] *n* **1** a small short sharp-pointed nail with a broad flat head. **2** a long loose straight stitch used to hold two or more layers of fabric together temporarily. **3a** the direction of a sailing vessel with respect to the direction of the wind. **b** a change of course from one tack to another. **c** a course of action.

tack[2] *v* **1a** to fasten or attach with tacks. **b** to sew with long loose stitches, often temporarily. **2** (*often* + on) to add as a supplement. **3** to change the course of (a sailing vessel) from one tack to the other by turning the bow towards the wind. **4a** to follow a zigzag course. **b** to change one's policy or attitude abruptly. ➤➤ **tacker** *n.*

tack[3] *n* equipment used in horse riding.

tack[4] *n* cheap or worthless things or material.

tackle[1] *n* **1** a set of equipment used in a particular activity. **2a** a ship's rigging. **b** an assembly of ropes and pulleys arranged to gain mechanical advantage for hoisting and pulling. **3** an instance of tackling in sport. **4** *Brit, coarse slang* a man's genitals.

tackle[2] *v* **1a** to take hold of or grapple with (somebody) in an attempt to stop or restrain them. **b** to take or attempt to take the ball from (an opposing player) in hockey or football. **2a** to set about dealing with (a problem, etc). **b** to speak to (somebody) about a difficult matter. ➤➤ **tackler** *n.*

tacky[1] *adj* (**-ier, -iest**) slightly sticky to the touch. ➤➤ **tackiness** *n.*

tacky[2] *adj* (**-ier, -iest**) *informal* **1** shabby; shoddy. **2** in poor taste; vulgar. ➤➤ **tackily** *adv,* **tackiness** *n.*

taco *n* (*pl* **-os**) a tortilla that is filled, e.g. with meat, then rolled or folded and fried.

tact *n* a keen sense of how to handle people or affairs so as to avoid giving offence. ➤➤ **tactful** *adj,* **tactfully** *adv,* **tactfulness** *n,* **tactless** *adj,* **tactlessly** *adv,* **tactlessness** *n.*

tactic *n* **1** a method of employing forces in combat. **2** a device for achieving an end.

tactical *adj* **1 a** denoting small-scale actions serving a larger purpose: compare STRATEGIC. **b** made or carried out with only a limited or immediate end in view. **c** characterized by adroit planning or manoeuvring to accomplish a purpose. **d** of voting: made in favour of the candidate most likely to defeat the candidate one least wants to win rather than for the candidate one prefers but who has little chance of winning. **2 a** of combat tactics: involving operations of local importance or brief duration: compare STRATEGIC. **b** of nuclear weapons: of or designed for air attack in close support of ground forces: compare STRATEGIC. ➤➤ **tactically** *adv.*

tactician *n* somebody skilled in tactics.

tactics *pl n* (*used as sing. or pl*) **1a** the science and art of disposing and manoeuvring forces in combat: compare STRATEGY. **b** the art or skill of employing available means to accomplish an end. **2** a system or mode of procedure.

tactile *adj* **1** of or perceptible by the sense of touch. **2** of a person: in the habit of touching people in a friendly way. ➤➤ **tactility** *n.*

tad *n informal* a small amount. ✱ **a tad** somewhat, rather.

tadger *n Brit, informal* a penis.

tadpole *n* the larva of an amphibian, such as a frog or toad, having in the early stage a rounded body, a long tail, no legs, and external gills.

Tadzhik *n* see TAJIK.

tae kwon do *n* an Oriental system of self-defence, developed in Korea, that features kicking and punching.

taffeta *n* a crisp lustrous fabric used *esp* for women's clothing.

taffrail *n* a rail round the stern of a ship.

Taffy *n* (*pl* **-ies**) *Brit, chiefly derog* a Welshman.

taffy *n* (*pl* **-ies**) *NAm* a toffee-like sweet made from molasses or brown sugar.

tag[1] *n* **1a** a flap or loop on a garment by which to hang it up, or that carries information such as washing instructions. **b** a cardboard, plastic, etc marker used for identification or classification. **c** in computing, a label attached to data. **2** =

ELECTRONIC TAG. **3a** a saying or maxim; a trite quotation used for superficial effect. **b** a recurrent or characteristic verbal expression. **c** a final speech or line in a play or joke, *esp* one that serves to clarify a point, sum up a moral point, etc. **4** a rigid binding on an end of a shoelace. **5a** an identifying word or phrase accompanying or replacing a name. **b** a personal symbol, typically a pseudonym, sprayed in paint in a public place by a graffiti writer.

tag² *v* (**tagged, tagging**) **1 a** to supply with an identifying marker, price label, etc. **b** to label or brand as something: *He was tagged a chauvinist.* **c** to fit with an electronic tag. **2** (*often* + on) to attach as an addition; to append. **3** (*usu* + along/on) to go with somebody, keeping close to them.

tag³ *n* **1** a game in which one player chases others and tries to make one the next chaser by touching them. **2** the act of tagging (one's partner) in TAG WRESTLING.

tag⁴ *v* (**tagged, tagging**) to touch (somebody) in or as if in a game of tag.

tag end *n* **1** the last part. **2** a loose end of thread.

tagliatelle *pl n* (*used as sing. or pl*) pasta in the form of narrow ribbons.

tag line *n* = TAG¹ (3C).

tag question *n* an interrogative phrase attached to the end of a statement, usu to invite agreement with what has been said.

tag team *n* a team of two wrestlers in TAG WRESTLING.

tag wrestling *n* a form of wrestling involving two teams of two wrestlers, in which only one member of each team is in the ring at any one time.

tahini *n* a thick oily paste made from sesame seeds, used as a seasoning *esp* in Middle Eastern cookery.

Tahitian *n* **1** a native or inhabitant of Tahiti. **2** the language of the people of Tahiti. ➤➤ **Tahitian** *adj.*

t'ai chi *or* **t'ai chi ch'uan** *n* an Oriental system of physical exercise, based on a sequence of slow controlled movements.

taiga *n* moist coniferous forest that begins where the tundra ends and is dominated by spruces and firs.

tail¹ *n* **1** the rear end of the body of an animal, *esp* a flexible extension of the backbone of a vertebrate or the feathers at the rear end of a bird. **2a** the rear part of an aircraft consisting of horizontal and vertical stabilizing surfaces with attached control surfaces. **b** the luminous trail of gas and dust behind a comet. **3a** the lower or inferior part of something. **b** the bottom edge or margin of a printed page. **4** (*in pl*) **a** = COAT TAILS. **b** = TAILCOAT; *specif* formal evening dress for men including a tailcoat and a white bow tie. **5** (*in pl, used as sing. or pl*) the reverse of a coin. **6** *informal* a person who follows or keeps watch on somebody. ✱ **piece of tail** a woman regarded in terms of her sexual attractiveness. **turn tail** *informal* to reverse direction and run away. **with one's tail between one's legs** having been totally defeated or confounded. ➤➤ **tailed** *adj,* **tailless** *adj.*

tail² *v* **1** *informal* to follow (somebody) for purposes of surveillance. **2** to remove the stalk of (e.g. a gooseberry): compare TOP² (3). **3** (often + back) to form a long queue. **4** (+ off/away) to diminish gradually in strength, volume, etc.

tail³ *n* in law, = ENTAIL².

tailback *n* a long queue of motor vehicles, *esp* when caused by an obstruction that blocks the road.

tailboard *n* a hinged or removable board or gate at the rear of a vehicle.

tailcoat *n* a man's formal evening coat with two long tapering skirts at the back.

tail end *n* **1** the back or rear end. **2** the concluding period.

tail fin *n* **1** a fin at the rear end of a fish or other aquatic animal. **2** an ornamental finlike projection on each rear corner of a 1950s car.

tailgate¹ *n* **1** *esp NAm* = TAILBOARD. **2** a door at the rear of a car, *esp* one that opens upwards.

tailgate² *v* to drive dangerously close behind (another vehicle).

tail light *n* a red warning light mounted at the rear of a vehicle.

tailor¹ *n* somebody whose occupation is making or altering clothes, *esp* men's suits.

tailor² *v* **1** of a tailor: to make (a garment) for a particular customer. **2** (+ for/to) to make or adapt (something) to suit a special need or purpose.

tailored *adj* of clothing: **a** made by a tailor. **b** fashioned or fitted; cut so as to fit the figure well.

tailoring *n* **1** the business or occupation of a tailor. **2** the work or workmanship of a tailor.

tailor-made *adj* **1** of clothes: made by a tailor to fit a particular customer. **2** made or fitted for a particular use or purpose.

tailpiece *n* **1** a piece added at the end; an appendage. **2** an ornament placed below the text on a page, e.g. at the end of a chapter.

tailpipe *n* the exit pipe of the exhaust system of a motor vehicle's engine.

tailplane *n* the horizontal stabilizing projection of an aircraft's tail.

tailspin *n* **1** a spiralling dive by an aircraft. **2** *informal* a state of chaos or panic.

tailwind *n* a wind blowing in the same general direction as a vehicle, aircraft, or ship, is travelling.

taint¹ *v* **1** to affect with putrefaction; to spoil. **2** to contaminate morally; to corrupt.

taint² *n* **1** a defect or flaw. **2** a slight trace of contamination or of something undesirable. ➤➤ **taintless** *adj.*

taipan *n* an extremely venomous snake of Australia and New Guinea.

Taiwanese *n* (*pl* **Taiwanese**) a native or inhabitant of Taiwan. ➤➤ **Taiwanese** *adj.*

Tajik *or* **Tadzhik** *n* (*pl* **Tajiks** *or* **Tadzhiks** *or collectively* **Tajik** *or* **Tadzhik**) **1** a member of an indigenous people inhabiting Tajikistan, Afghanistan, Uzbekistan, and China. **2** (*also* **Tajiki, Tadzhiki**) the language spoken by this people. ➤➤ **Tadzhik** *adj,* **Tajik** *adj.*

taka *n* (*pl* **taka**) the basic monetary unit of Bangladesh.

takahe *n* a flightless New Zealand bird related to the rail.

take¹ *v* (*past tense* **took,** *past part.* **taken**) **1** to reach for and hold. **2** to grasp or grip: *He took her arm.* **3a** to get into one's possession or control. **b** to remove. **c** to acquire or use without right or authority. **4** to proceed to occupy: *to take a seat; to take office.* **5** to subtract (a number). **6** to choose: *I'll take the red one.* **7** to lead or carry to another place. **8** to use as a route or means of transport. **9** to bring to a particular state: *Her ability should take her far.* **10** to affect in a specified way: *The remark took us by surprise.* **11** to consume (food, drink, medicine, etc). **12a** to adopt or advance (a particular view). **b** to have recourse to: *to take measures.* **13** to be taught (a subject of study). **14** to claim as one's own: *They can't take all the credit.* **15** to hold or accommodate. **16** to need or call for: *It will take several days to finish.* **17** to consider: *Let us take each point in turn.* **18** to record or register: *The police took his fingerprints.* **19** to submit to or undergo: *We took a lot of criticism.* **20** to accept in payment: *The shop will take a credit card.* **21** to accept or make use of (a risk, opportunity, etc). **22a** to experience or feel (an emotion): *to take fright.* **b** to tolerate or endure. **23** to regard in a particular way: *He took it as a compliment.* **24** to work or mix well. **25** of a plant or seed: to begin to grow. **26** to win favour. ✱ **be taken ill/sick** to fall ill. **take after** to resemble (an older relative) in appearance or character. **take against** *chiefly Brit* to come to dislike. **take apart 1** to dismantle. **2** to analyse in detail. **3** *informal* to criticize or treat severely. **take it** to infer or assume: *I take it you're not coming.* **take to 1** to form a liking for. **2** to begin to do (something). **what it takes** the qualities or resources needed. ➤➤ **taker** *n.*

take² *n* **1a** the killing, capturing, or catching of something, e.g. game or fish. **b** the number or quantity, e.g. of animals, fish, or pelts, taken at one time; a catch or haul. **2a** the uninterrupted recording, filming, or televising of something. **b** the recording or scene produced by one take. **3a** the amount of money received from a business venture, sales, or admission charges; proceeds or takings. **b** a share or cut. **4** *chiefly NAm, informal* interpretation or slant. ✱ **on the take** *informal* taking bribes.

takeaway¹ *adj* **1** *Brit* of a meal: taken away from its place of sale rather than eaten on the premises. **2** of a shop or restaurant: that sells such food.

takeaway² *n Brit* **1** a cooked meal that is eaten away from the premises from which it was bought. **2** a shop or restaurant that sells takeaways.

take away¹ *v* **1** to remove. **2** to subtract. **3** to buy (food) for eating elsewhere. ✱ **take away from** to detract from.

take away² *prep* subtracting.

take back *v* **1** to retract (a statement). **2** to return (unsatisfactory goods) to the place where they were bought.

take down *v* **1** to remove or dismantle. **2** to write down on paper.

take-home pay *n* the part of gross salary or wages remaining after deductions, e.g. for income tax, insurance, etc.

take in *v* **1** to offer accommodation or shelter to. **2** *informal* to deceive or trick. **3** to make (a garment) smaller by alteration. **4** to include. **5** to comprehend or understand.

taken *v* past part. of TAKE¹.

takeoff *n* **1** a caricature or impersonation. **2** the launching of an aircraft or rocket.

take off *v* **1** to remove (clothing). **2** to deduct (an amount). **3** to spend (a period of time) as rest, holiday, etc. **4** to mimic (somebody). **5** of an aircraft: to become airborne. **6** *informal* to leave abruptly. **7** *informal* to be quickly successful.

take on *v* **1** to agree to (a task or undertaking). **2** to engage (staff, etc). **3** to assume (an appearance or quality). **4** *informal* to become emotional or distraught.

takeout *n NAm* = TAKEAWAY².

take out *v* **1** to extract or remove. **2** to obtain (authorization, insurance, etc). **3** to escort on a social occasion. ✱ **take it out of** to fatigue or exhaust. **take it out on** to vent one's anger or frustration on.

takeover *n* the act of taking over, *esp* the act of gaining control of a business company by buying a majority of the shares.

take over *v* **1** to assume control or possession of. **2** in printing, to move (text) to the following line. **3** to become dominant.

take up *v* **1** to pick up or lift. **2** to become engaged or interested in (an activity). **3** to occupy or require (space or time). **4** to shorten (a garment). **5** to resume or continue. **6** to discuss or pursue (a matter) further. ✱ **take somebody up on 1** to accept (an offer) from somebody. **2** to venture to disagree about (something). **take up with** to begin to associate with.

take-up *n* the act of claiming something, such as a grant or benefit.

taking *adj dated* attractive; captivating.

takings *pl n* the amount of money earned by a business during a specified period.

tala *n* the basic monetary unit of Western Samoa.

talc *n* **1** = TALCUM POWDER. **2** a soft mineral with a greasy feel, consisting of a magnesium silicate.

talcum¹ *n* = TALCUM POWDER.

talcum² *v* to put talcum powder on (something).

talcum powder *n* a preparation made from finely powdered talc, often perfumed, used for dusting the body.

tale *n* **1** a usu fictitious narrative; a story. **2** a lie; a falsehood.

talebearer *n dated* a person who spreads rumours, *esp* maliciously. ➤➤ **talebearing** *adj and n.*

talent *n* **1a** a special creative or artistic aptitude. **b** general ability or intelligence. **c** a person or people of talent in a field. **2** *informal* (*used as sing. or pl*) people considered in terms of their sexual attractiveness. **3** an ancient unit of weight or money. ➤➤ **talented** *adj,* **talentless** *adj.*

talent scout *n* a person engaged in discovering and recruiting people with talent in a specialized field of activity.

talent show *n* a show consisting of a series of individual performances by amateurs.

tali *n* pl of TALUS².

talisman *n* (*pl* **talismans**) **1** an engraved object believed to act as a charm to bring good fortune. **2** something believed to produce magical effects. ➤➤ **talismanic** *adj.*

talk¹ *v* **1** to produce or express (something) in speech. **2** to make (something) the subject of conversation; to discuss. **3** to be able to communicate in (a language). **4** to convey information or communicate with signs or sounds. **5** to reveal secret or confidential information. **6** (+ into/out of) to persuade (somebody) by talking: *I talked him out of driving home.* **7** to have influence: *Money talks.* ✱ **now you're talking** *informal* now at last you are saying something interesting. **talk about** *informal* used to introduce a wry or ironic comment about something. **you can talk 1** it is easy for you to say that as you are not involved. **2** (*also* **you can't talk**) you are just as bad yourself. ➤➤ **talker** *n.*

talk² *n* **1** a verbal exchange of thoughts or opinions; a conversation. **2a** bluster or empty threats: *He's all talk and no action.* **b** rumour; gossip. **3** (*also in pl*) a formal discussion or exchange of views. **4** an address or lecture.

talkative *adj* given to talking a lot. ➤➤ **talkatively** *adv,* **talkativeness** *n.*

talkback *n* **1** in radio and television broadcasting, a communication system that allows staff to talk to each other without what they are saying being broadcast. **2** *Aus, NZ* = PHONE-IN.

talk back *v* to answer impertinently.

talk down *v* **1** to silence (somebody) by argument or by loud talking. **2** to give radio instructions to (a pilot) to assist the landing of a plane when conditions are difficult. **3** (+ to) to speak in a condescending fashion to.

talkie *n* a cinema film with a synchronized sound track, as distinct from a silent one.

talking book *n* a recording of somebody reading a book aloud.

talking head *n* somebody talking directly to the audience on television, unsupported by film or other illustrative material.

talking picture *n* = TALKIE.

talking point *n* a subject of conversation or argument.

talking shop *n* **1** a place where matters are discussed, often with no useful outcome. **2** the people involved in this.

talking-to *n* (*pl* **talking-tos**) *informal* a reprimand or scolding.

talk out *v* to clarify or settle (a problem) by discussion.

talk over *v* to review or consider in conversation.

talk radio *n* **1** a radio broadcast in which the audience can phone in with their views on topical issues. **2** radio that concentrates on this type of broadcasting.

talk round *v* to persuade or convince at some length.

talk show *n* = CHAT SHOW.

tall *adj* **1a** of above average height. **b** of a specified height: *five feet tall.* **2** highly exaggerated; incredible: *a tall story.* ✱ **a tall order** an unreasonably difficult task or requirement. ➤➤ **tallish** *adj*, **tallness** *n.*

tallboy *n* a double chest of drawers with the upper section slightly smaller than the lower.

tallith *or* **tallis** *n* (*pl* **talliths** *or* **tallithim** *or* **tallisim**) a shawl with fringed corners traditionally worn over the head or shoulders by Jewish men during religious services.

tallow *n* the solid white rendered fat of cattle and sheep, used in soap and candles.

tall poppy syndrome *n Aus, informal* the tendency to disparage the achievements of successful people.

tall ship *n* a sailing ship with tall masts and square rig.

tally[1] *n* (*pl* **-ies**) **1a** a record of items or charges. **b** a record of the score in a game. **2** a device for visibly recording or accounting, *esp* a wooden stick notched with marks representing numbers and split so that each of two parties may have a record of a transaction.

tally[2] *v* (**-ies, -ied**) **1** to correspond or match: *Their stories tally.* **2** to make a count of. **3** to mark on a tally or tabulate as if on a tally.

tally-ho[1] *n* (*pl* **-os**) a call given by a huntsman to the hounds on sighting a fox.

tally-ho[2] *v* (**-os, -oed**) to shout tally-ho.

tallyman *or* **tallywoman** *n* (*pl* **tallymen** *or* **tallywomen**) **1** a person who keeps an account or record of the receipt of goods. **2** *Brit* a person who sells goods on credit, *esp* from door to door.

Talmud *n* the authoritative body of Jewish tradition. ➤➤ **Talmudic** *adj*, **Talmudist** *n.*

talon *n* **1** a claw, *esp* of a bird of prey. **2** an object or part of something shaped like a claw. ➤➤ **taloned** *adj.*

talus[1] *n* (*pl* **taluses**) a slope of rock debris at the base of a cliff or in a fortification.

talus[2] *n* (*pl* **tali**) *technical* the large bone in the ankle that articulates with the tibia, the fibula, and the calcaneus; the anklebone.

tam *n* = TAM-O'-SHANTER.

tamale *n* (*pl* **tamales**) a Mexican dish of minced meat seasoned with chilli, wrapped in maize husks, and steamed.

tamari *n* a rich soy sauce made in Japan from fermented soya beans.

tamarind *n* **1** a pod-like fruit eaten fresh or made into chutney. **2** the acidic sticky brown pulp of this fruit used as a flavouring and medicinally as a laxative.

tamarisk *n* a shrub or tree with tiny narrow leaves and masses of minute flowers.

tambala *n* (*pl* **tambala** *or* **tambalas**) a unit of currency in Malawi, worth 100th of a kwacha.

tambour *n* **1** a small drum. **2** in embroidery, a frame consisting of a set of two interlocking hoops between which cloth is stretched during stitching.

tamboura *or* **tambura** *n* an Asian stringed musical instrument used to produce a drone accompaniment to singing.

tambourine *n* a percussion instrument resembling a shallow one-headed drum with loose metallic discs at the sides, played by shaking or striking with the hand. ➤➤ **tambourinist** *n.*

tambura *n* see TAMBOURA.

tame[1] *adj* **1** of an animal: not afraid of human beings. **2** of a person: made docile and submissive. **3** lacking zest or interest. ➤➤ **tamely** *adv*, **tameness** *n.*

tame[2] *v* **1** to make or become tame. **2** to deprive (somebody) of spirit; to subdue (them). **3** to tone (something) down. ➤➤ **tamer** *n.*

Tamil *n* (*pl* **Tamils** *or* **Tamil**) **1** a member of an indigenous people inhabiting parts of southern India and Sri Lanka. **2** the language of this people. ➤➤ **Tamil** *adj.*

tammy *n* (*pl* **-ies**) = TAM-O'-SHANTER.

tam-o'-shanter *n* a round flat woollen or cloth cap of Scottish origin, with a pom-pom on top.

tamoxifen *n* a drug used to treat breast cancer and female infertility.

tamp *v* **1** (*often* + down) to pack (something) in or down by a succession of light or medium blows. **2** to fill up (a drill hole above a blasting charge) with material to confine the force of the explosion.

Tampax *n trademark* a tampon.

tamper *v* (+ with) to interfere or meddle without permission. ➤➤ **tamperer** *n*, **tamperproof** *adj.*

tampon *n* an absorbent plug put into the vagina to absorb menstrual bleeding.

tam-tam *n* = GONG[1].

tan[1] *v* (**tanned, tanning**) **1** to convert (animal skin) into leather by treatment with an infusion of tannin-rich bark or fish oil. **2a** to make (skin) take on a light-brown colour, *esp* by exposure to the sun. **b** to get tanned. **3** *informal* to thrash (somebody). ✱ **tan somebody's hide/tan the hide off somebody** *informal* to beat somebody severely. ➤➤ **tanner** *n*, **tanning** *n.*

tan[2] *n* **1** a brown colour given to the skin by exposure to sun. **2** a light yellowish brown. **3** = TANBARK. ➤➤ **tannish** *adj.*

tan[3] *adj* **1** of the colour tan. **2** *NAm* of a person, body part, or skin: tanned.

tan[4] *abbr* tangent.

tanager *n* a brightly coloured woodland bird.

tanbark *n* a bark, e.g. of an oak, rich in tannin, and used in tanning hides.

tandem[1] *n* **1** a bicycle having two seats one behind the other. **2** a carriage drawn by two horses harnessed one before the other. **3** any arrangement of two people one behind the other. ✱ **in tandem 1**

in partnership or conjunction. **2** arranged or harnessed one behind the other. ➤➤ **tandem** *adj.*

tandem² *adv* one behind the other.

tandoor *n* a large clay oven used in N Indian cooking.

tandoori *n* **1** a N Indian method of cooking meat in a tandoor. **2** (*used before a noun*) denoting a dish cooked in a tandoor.

tang *n* **1** a sharp distinctive flavour or smell. **2** a faint suggestion; a trace. **3** a projecting shank or tongue on a knife, file, or sword, that connects with a handle.

tanga *n* (*pl* **tangas**) a very brief undergarment for the lower part of the body in the form of two tiny triangles of material held together by strings at the sides.

tangelo *n* (*pl* **-os**) a citrus fruit that is a cross between a tangerine and a grapefruit.

tangent¹ *n* **1** in mathematics, the trigonometric function that, for an acute angle in a right-angled triangle, is the ratio between the shorter sides opposite and adjacent to the angle: compare SINE, COSINE. **2** a straight line touching a curve or surface at only one point. ✱ **fly/go off at a tangent** to change suddenly from one subject or course of action to another.

tangent² *adj* touching a curve or surface at only one point. ➤➤ **tangency** *n.*

tangential *adj* **1** of or like a tangent. **2** acting along or lying in a tangent. **3a** divergent; digressive. **b** incidental; barely relevant. ➤➤ **tangentially** *adv.*

tangerine *n* **1** a small loose-skinned citrus fruit with deep orange skin and pulp. **2** a bright reddish orange colour.

tangible¹ *adj* **1** capable of being perceived by the sense of touch. **2** substantially real; material. ➤➤ **tangibility** *n,* **tangibly** *adv.*

tangible² *n* a tangible asset.

tangle¹ *v* **1** to intertwine or become intertwined in disordered confusion. **2** to involve (somebody) so as to be trapped or hampered. **3** *informal* (*often* + with) to engage in conflict or argument. ➤➤ **tangled** *adj.*

tangle² *n* **1** a confused twisted mass. **2** a complicated state. ➤➤ **tangly** *adj.*

tango¹ *n* (*pl* **-os**) a ballroom dance of Latin-American origin in four time, characterized by long pauses and stylized body positions.

tango² *v* (**-oes, -oed**) to dance the tango.

tangram *n* a Chinese puzzle made by cutting a square into five triangles, a square, and a rhomboid which can be recombined in many different ways to form different figures.

tangy *adj* (**-ier, -iest**) having a sharp pungent taste or smell. ➤➤ **tanginess** *n.*

tanh *abbr* hyperbolic tangent.

tank¹ *n* **1a** a large receptacle for holding or transporting liquids or gas. **b** a container for fuel in a motor vehicle. **2** a clear-sided container in which to keep fish. **3** an enclosed heavily armoured combat vehicle that moves on caterpillar tracks. ➤➤ **tankful** (*pl* **tankfuls**) *n.*

tank² *v* **1** *informal* to inflict a heavy defeat on (an opponent). **2** *informal* to move very fast; to run.

tankard *n* a silver or pewter beer mug sometimes with a hinged lid.

tanked *adj informal* drunk.

tanked-up *adj* = TANKED.

tank engine *n* a steam locomotive that carries its own water and coal and does not have a tender.

tanker *n* a ship, aircraft, or road or rail vehicle designed to carry liquid in bulk.

tank top *n* a sleeveless pullover usu worn over a shirt or jumper.

tank up *v* to drink a large amount of alcohol.

tanner¹ *n* a person who tans animal hides.

tanner² *n Brit, informal* a coin worth six old pence.

tannery *n* (*pl* **-ies**) a place where tanning is carried out.

tannic *adj* of or derived from tanbark or a tannin.

tannic acid *n* = TANNIN.

tannin *n* a soluble astringent complex substance of plant origin used in tanning, dyeing, and making ink.

Tannoy *n trademark* a public address system that can broadcast throughout a large building.

tansy *n* (*pl* **-ies**) a plant with finely divided leaves and button-shaped yellow flowers.

tantalise *v* see TANTALIZE.

tantalize *or* **-ise** *v* to tease by presenting something desirable that is just out of reach or promising something and then withholding it. ➤➤ **tantalization** *n,* **tantalizing** *adj,* **tantalizingly** *adv.*

tantalum *n* a white metallic chemical element that is hard and acid-resistant.

tantalus *n* (*pl* **tantaluses**) a locked container for wine or spirits in which the contents are visible but not obtainable without a key.

tantamount *adj* (+ to) equivalent in value, significance, or effect to.

tantra *n* **1** any of a body of later Hindu and Buddhist scriptures marked by mysticism and magic. **2** the doctrine and cult deriving from the tantras. ➤➤ **tantric** *adj,* **tantrism** *n.*

tantrum *n* (*pl* **tantrums**) a fit of childish bad temper.

Tanzanian *n* a native or inhabitant of Tanzania. ➤➤ **Tanzanian** *adj.*

Tao *n* the principle of creative harmony which, in Taoism, is believed to underlie and govern the natural order of the universe.

Taoiseach *n* the prime minister of the Republic of Ireland.

Taoism *n* a Chinese philosophy traditionally founded by Lao-tzu in the sixth cent. BC that teaches action in conformity with nature rather than striving against it. ➤➤ **Taoist** *adj and n,* **Taoistic** *adj.*

tap¹ *n* **1a** a device consisting of a spout and valve attached to a pipe or bowl to control the flow of a fluid. **b** a plug designed to fit an opening in a barrel. **2** a tool for forming an internal screw thread. **3** a device that can be attached to a telephone to allow somebody to listen secretly to conversations. **4** = TAPROOM. **5** *Brit, informal* **a** an instance of asking for money from somebody. **b** the amount of money involved in this. ✱ **on tap 1** of beer, etc: on draught. **2** readily available.

tap² *v* (**tapped, tapping**) **1a** to pierce (a container, tree, etc) so as to let out or draw off a fluid. **b** to draw from (a source or supply). **c** to connect an electronic listening device to (a telephone or telegraph wire) in order to acquire secret information. **2** to form an internal screw thread in (a nut). **3** *informal* (*usu* + for) to ask for money from (somebody) as a loan or gift. ➤➤ **tapper** *n.*

tap³ *n* **1** a light blow, or the sound it makes. **2** any of several usu rapid drumbeats on a snare drum. **3a** a small piece of metal attached to the sole or heel of a tap-dancing shoe. **b** tap-dancing.

tap[4] *v* (**tapped, tapping**) **1** to strike lightly with a slight sound. **2** to give a light blow with (something). ⋙ **tapper** *n.*

tapas *pl n* light savoury snacks or appetizers, eaten *esp* with an alcoholic drink.

tap dance *n* a step dance tapped out audibly by means of shoes with soles and heels to which small pieces of metal have been fitted.

tap-dance *v* to perform a tap dance. ⋙ **tap-dancer** *n,* **tap-dancing** *n.*

tape[1] *n* **1** a narrow band of woven fabric. **2** the string stretched above the finishing line of a race. **3 a** = MAGNETIC TAPE. **b** = TAPE MEASURE. **c** adhesive tape, insulating tape, or masking tape. **4a** = TAPE RECORDING. **b** a cassette or videotape.

tape[2] *v* **1** to fasten or bind with tape. **2** to record on magnetic tape. ✱ **have something taped** to be in command or control of something.

tape deck *n* a mechanism or self-contained unit that causes magnetic tape to move past the heads of a magnetic recording device in order to make a recording.

tape measure *n* a narrow strip marked off in units for measuring.

tapenade *n* a paste or dip made from capers, black olives, anchovies, olive oil, and lemon juice.

taper[1] *n* **1a** a slender candle. **b** a long waxed wick for lighting candles, fires, etc. **2** a gradual narrowing in thickness, diameter, or width.

taper[2] *v* **1** to decrease or cause to decrease gradually in thickness, diameter, or width towards one end. **2** (*often* + off) to diminish gradually. ⋙ **tapering** *adj.*

tape-record *v* to make a tape recording of.

tape recorder *n* a device for recording sounds on magnetic tape and for subsequently reproducing them.

tape recording *n* a recording on magnetic tape of sounds, a television programme, etc, that can be reproduced on a tape recorder or video recorder.

tape streamer *n* in computing, a device for copying data from a hard disk onto magnetic tape.

tapestry *n* (*pl* **-ies**) **1** a heavy handwoven or machine-made textile used for hangings, curtains, and upholstery and characterized by complicated pictorial designs. **2** something that has great complexity or variety: *life's rich tapestry.* ⋙ **tapestried** *adj.*

tapeworm *n* a parasitic worm that has a long, ribbon-like body and lives in the intestine of human beings.

tapioca *n* **1** a granular preparation of cassava starch used *esp* in puddings. **2** a milk pudding made with this.

tapir *n* (*pl* **tapirs** *or* **tapir**) a hoofed mammal with an elongated flexible snout that is related to the horses and rhinoceroses.

tappet *n* a lever or projection moved by or moving some other piece, such as a cam.

taproom *n* a room in a hotel or pub where draught beer is served.

taproot *n* a main root of a plant that grows vertically downwards and gives off small side roots.

taps *pl n chiefly NAm* (*used as sing. or pl*) **1** the last bugle call at night, blown as a signal that lights are to be put out. **2** a similar call blown at military funerals and memorial services.

tar[1] *n* **1** a dark strong-smelling viscous liquid obtained by heating and distilling wood, coal, peat, etc. **2** a residue present in smoke from burning tobacco that contains resins, acids, and phenols.

tar[2] *v* (**tarred, tarring**) to cover or smear with tar. ✱ **tar and feather** to smear with tar and cover with feathers as a punishment or humiliation. **tarred with the same brush** of two or more people: having the same faults or assumed to have.

tar[3] *n informal, dated* a sailor.

taramasalata *n* a pinkish paste made from fish roe, olive oil, and seasoning, usu eaten as a starter.

tarantella *n* a vivacious folk dance of southern Italy in 6/8 time.

tarantula *n* (*pl* **tarantulas** *or* **tarantulae**) **1** a large hairy spider of tropical and subtropical America that can bite sharply. **2** a European wolf spider.

tarboosh *or* **tarbush** *n* a red hat similar to the fez worn by Muslim men.

tardy *adj* (**-ier, -iest**) **1** delayed; late. **2** moving or progressing slowly; sluggish. ⋙ **tardily** *adv,* **tardiness** *n.*

tare[1] *n* a vetch.

tare[2] *n* **1** a deduction from the gross weight of a substance and its container made in allowance for the weight of the container. **2** the weight of an unloaded goods vehicle without its fuel.

targe *n archaic* a light shield.

target[1] *n* **1a** an object to fire at in practice or competition, consisting of a series of concentric circles with a bull's-eye at the centre. **b** a person or object that is selected to be fired at or attacked. **2a** somebody or something that is the object of ridicule or criticism. **b** a goal or objective. ✱ **on/off target** **1** likely or unlikely to hit or achieve a target or objective. **2** succeeding or not succeeding in this.

target[2] *v* (**targeted, targeting**) **1** to make (somebody or something) a target. **2** to set as a goal.

target practice *n* the procedure of repeatedly shooting or firing arrows at a target to improve one's aim.

tariff[1] *n* **1** a schedule of duties, or a duty, imposed by a government on imported or exported goods. **2a** the rates of a business, e.g. a hotel, or public service, or a schedule of these rates. **b** *chiefly Brit* a menu. **3** a schedule of the sentences and damages that apply to different crimes.

tariff[2] *v* to price according to a tariff.

tarmac[1] *n* **1** = TARMACADAM. **2** a runway, apron, or road made of tarmac.

tarmac[2] *v* (**tarmacked, tarmacking**) to apply tarmac to (a road or path).

tarmacadam *n* a mixture of tar and aggregates used for surfacing roads: compare MACADAM.

tarn *n* a small mountain lake.

tarnation *n chiefly NAm, euphem* = DAMNATION[1].

tarnish[1] *v* **1** to dull the lustre of (something) by dirt, air, etc, or be dulled in this way. **2a** to spoil or be spoiled. **b** to bring discredit on or be discredited. ⋙ **tarnishable** *adj.*

tarnish[2] *n* a film of chemically altered material on the surface of a metal or mineral.

taro *n* (*pl* **taros**) a tropical plant of the arum family with a starchy tuberous rootstock, used as a vegetable.

tarot *n* **1** a set of 22 pictorial playing cards used for fortune-telling. **2** fortune-telling with these cards.

tarp *n informal* a tarpaulin.

tarpaulin *n* **1** heavy waterproof tarred canvas material used for protecting objects or ground exposed to the elements. **2** a piece or sheet of this.

tarpon *n* (*pl* **tarpons** *or* **tarpon**) a large silvery elongated edible marine fish.

tarragon *n* a plant of the daisy family, with pungent aromatic leaves, used as a flavouring.

tarry[1] *v* (**-ies, -ied**) *archaic or literary* **1** to stay in or at a place. **2** to delay or be slow in acting.

tarry[2] *adj* (**-ier, -iest**) like or covered with tar. ➤➤ **tarriness** *n.*

tarsal[1] *adj* relating to or in the region of the tarsus.

tarsal[2] *n* a bone or cartilage of the tarsus: compare TARSUS.

tarsi *n* pl of TARSUS.

tarsier *n* a small nocturnal tree-dwelling mammal related to the lemur.

tarsus *n* (*pl* **tarsi**) **1** the ankle, heel, and upper part of the foot: compare TARSAL[2]. **2** any of the bones in this part of the foot.

tart[1] *adj* **1** sharp or acid to the taste. **2** sarcastic or hurtful. ➤➤ **tartly** *adv,* **tartness** *n.*

tart[2] *n* a pastry shell containing a sweet or savoury filling.

tart[3] *n informal* **1** a female prostitute. **2** a sexually promiscuous woman.

tartan *n* **1** a textile design of Scottish origin consisting of checks and stripes of varying width and colour, usu patterned to designate a particular clan. **2** a fabric with a tartan design.

Tartar *n* **1** a member of a group of peoples of central Asia, including the Turks and the Mongols. **2** (**tartar**) a formidable or irascible person. ➤➤ **Tartar** *adj,* **Tartarian** *adj.*

tartar *n* **1** a substance consisting essentially of cream of tartar that is formed during the fermentation of grapes and is deposited in wine casks as a reddish crust or sediment. **2** an incrustation on the teeth consisting *esp* of calcium salts.

tartare *adj* of fish or meat: served raw, usu minced, seasoned, and formed into a patty. See also STEAK TARTARE.

tartare sauce *n* see TARTAR SAUCE.

tartaric acid *n* a strong carboxylic plant acid that is obtained from tartar and used in food and medicines.

tartar sauce *or* **tartare sauce** *n* mayonnaise with chopped pickles, olives, capers, and parsley, served *esp* with fish.

tartlet *n* a small tart with a sweet or savoury filling.

tartrate *n* a chemical salt or ester formed by combination between tartaric acid and a metal atom, an alcohol, or another chemical group.

tartrazine *n* a yellow dye used in foods and drugs, *esp* as an additive, and in dyeing.

tart up *v* **1** to dress (oneself) up, put on make-up, etc. **2** to do up (a place) *esp* somewhat cheaply or gaudily.

tarty *adj* (**-ier, -iest**) *informal* of or like a prostitute or a tarted-up woman. ➤➤ **tartily** *adv,* **tartiness** *n.*

Tarzan *n* a strong, well-built man who is also very agile.

task[1] *n* **1** an assigned piece of work; a duty. **2** something hard or unpleasant that has to be done; a chore. ✱ **take somebody to task** to rebuke somebody for a failure or mistake.

task[2] *v* **1** to assign a task to. **2** to subject to severe exertion.

task force *n* **1** a temporary military grouping under one leader for the purpose of accomplishing a definite objective. **2** a group of people that has been assigned a specific task, often with ongoing duties connected to it.

taskmaster *or* **taskmistress** *n* a man or woman who assigns tasks.

Tasmanian *n* a native or inhabitant of Tasmania. ➤➤ **Tasmanian** *adj.*

Tasmanian devil *n* a powerful Tasmanian marsupial that is about the size of a badger and has a black coat marked with white.

tassel[1] *n* a dangling ornament on a curtain, bedspread, or garment consisting of a bunch of cords or threads of even length fastened at one end.

tassel[2] *v* (**tasselled, tasselling,** *NAm* **tasseled, tasseling**) to decorate with tassels.

tassie *n Scot, archaic* a goblet or cup.

taste[1] *v* **1** to test the flavour of (food, drink, etc) by taking a little into the mouth. **2** to perceive or recognize (a substance, flavour, etc) by the sense of taste. **3** (*often* + of) to have a specified flavour. **4** to eat or drink (something) in small quantities. **5** to experience or undergo.

taste[2] *n* **1a** the one of the five basic physical senses by which the qualities of substances in contact with taste buds are interpreted by the brain as sweet, bitter, sour, or salt. **b** the quality of a substance as perceived by this sense. **2a** an instance of tasting. **b** a small amount tasted. **c** an instance of experiencing or undergoing something. **3** an individual preference; an inclination. **4** discernment in aesthetic or social matters, or a manner or quality indicative of this.

taste bud *n* any of the small organs on the surface of the tongue that receive and transmit the sensation of taste.

tasteful *adj* conforming to good judgment or acceptable behaviour. ➤➤ **tastefully** *adv,* **tastefulness** *n.*

tasteless *adj* **1** lacking flavour; insipid. **2** not conforming to good judgment or acceptable behaviour. ➤➤ **tastelessly** *adv,* **tastelessness** *n.*

taster *n* **1** somebody who tests food or drink by tasting. **2** a sample or specimen of something.

tasty *adj* (**-ier, -iest**) **1** having an appetizing flavour. **2** *informal* arousing interest. **3** *Brit, informal* sexually appealing. ➤➤ **tastily** *adv,* **tastiness** *n.*

tat[1] *n Brit, informal* low-quality or tasteless goods.

tat[2] *v* (**tatted, tatting**) **1** to work at tatting. **2** to make by tatting.

ta-ta *interj chiefly Brit, informal* goodbye.

tater *or* **tatie** *n dialect* = POTATO.

tatter *n* **1** an irregular torn shred of material. **2** (*in pl*) tattered clothing; rags. ✱ **in tatters 1** torn to pieces; ragged. **2** in a state of ruin or disarray.

tatterdemalion *n* a person dressed in ragged clothing.

tattered *adj* **1** of clothes, books, etc: old and torn. **2** run-down; dilapidated.

tattersall *n* a fabric with a pattern of coloured lines forming squares on a light background.

tattie *n dialect* = POTATO.

tatting *n* **1** a delicate handmade lace formed using a single cotton thread and a small shuttle. **2** the process or art of making such lace.

tattle[1] *v* **1** to chatter or gossip. **2** to disclose (secrets) by gossiping. ➤➤ **tattler** *n.*

tattle[2] *n* chatter; gossip.

tattletale *n chiefly NAm* a tattler; a TELLTALE.

tattoo[1] *n* (*pl* **-os**) an indelible mark or design on the skin made by tattooing.

tattoo[2] *v* (**tattooed, tattooing**) to mark (the body) by inserting pigments under the skin. ➤➤ **tattooer** *n,* **tattooist** *n.*

tattoo[3] *n* (*pl* **tattoos**) **1a** an evening drum or bugle call sounded as a call to soldiers to return to quarters. **b** an outdoor military display of marching, music, etc given by troops as an entertainment. **2** a rapid rhythmic beating or tapping.

tatty *adj* (**-ier, -iest**) *chiefly Brit, informal* shabby; dilapidated. ➤➤ **tattily** *adv*, **tattiness** *n*.

tau *n* the 19th letter of the Greek alphabet (Τ, τ), equivalent to roman t.

tau cross *n* a T-shaped cross.

taught *v* past tense and past part. of TEACH.

taunt[1] *v* to provoke or jeer at (somebody) in a mocking way. ➤➤ **taunter** *n*, **tauntingly** *adv*.

taunt[2] *n* a sarcastic provocation or insult.

taupe *adj* of a brownish grey colour. ➤➤ **taupe** *n*.

taurine *adj* of or resembling a bull.

Taurus *n* **1** in astronomy, a constellation (the Bull) depicted as the bull tamed by Jason. **2** in astrology, the second sign of the zodiac, or a person born under this sign. ➤➤ **Taurean** *adj and n*.

taut *adj* **1a** tightly drawn; tensely stretched. **b** showing anxiety; stressed. **2** of a ship: kept in good order. ➤➤ **tautly** *adv*, **tautness** *n*.

tauten *v* to make or become taut or more taut.

tautology *n* (*pl* **-ies**) the needless repetition of an idea, statement, or word, or an instance of this. ➤➤ **tautological** *adj*, **tautologous** *adj*.

tavern *n* **1** *Brit, humorous or archaic* a pub or inn. **2** *NAm and NZ* a place where alcoholic drinks are sold and served.

taverna *n* a Greek inn or restaurant.

TAVR *abbr* Territorial Army and Volunteer Reserve.

tawdry *adj* (**-ier, -iest**) **1** cheap and tastelessly ornate in appearance. **2** sordid or sleazy. ➤➤ **tawdrily** *adv*, **tawdriness** *n*.

tawny *adj* (**-ier, -iest**) of a warm sandy or brownish orange colour. ➤➤ **tawniness** *n*, **tawny** *n*.

tawny owl *n* a common brown European owl.

tawse *n chiefly Scot esp* formerly in schools, a leather strap used for beating children as a punishment.

tax[1] *v* **1** to levy a tax on (income, a person, etc). **2** to pay tax on (a vehicle). **3** to make strenuous demands on (somebody, a person's patience, etc). **4** (+ with) to charge (somebody) with a fault, or blame them for it. ➤➤ **taxable** *adj*.

tax[2] *n* **1** a charge, usu of money, imposed by a government on individuals, organizations, or property, *esp* to raise revenue. **2** a heavy demand or strain.

taxa *n* pl of TAXON.

taxation *n* **1** the action of taxing, *esp* the imposition of taxes. **2** revenue obtained from taxes. **3** a rate of tax or the amount assessed as a tax.

tax avoidance *n* the legal avoiding of paying taxes, by minimizing activities that make one liable for tax or by claiming for properly allowable deductions from income before tax.

tax-deductible *adj* legally permitted to be deducted from taxable income or capital.

tax disc *n* a circle of paper that must be displayed on the windscreen of a motor vehicle to show that its road tax has been paid.

tax evasion *n* deliberate failure to pay taxes.

tax exile *n* a person who lives abroad in order to avoid paying high taxes in their home country.

tax haven *n* a country with a relatively low level of taxation, *esp* on incomes.

taxi[1] *n* (*pl* **taxis**) a motor car that may be hired, together with its driver, to carry passengers.

taxi[2] *v* (**taxis** *or* **taxies, taxied, taxiing** *or* **taxying**) **1** to travel by taxi. **2** of an aircraft: to move at low speed along a runway before take-off or after landing.

taxicab *n* = TAXI[1].

taxidermy *n* the art of preparing, stuffing, and mounting the skins of animals to give a lifelike appearance. ➤➤ **taxidermic** *adj*, **taxidermist** *n*.

taximeter *n* a meter fitted in a taxi to calculate the charge for each journey, usu determined by the distance travelled.

taxing *adj* physically, mentally, or emotionally demanding.

taxi rank *n* a place where taxicabs park, usu to wait for customers.

taxiway *n* a usu paved strip for aircraft taxiing, e.g. from the terminal to a runway, at an airport.

taxman *n* (*pl* **taxmen**) *informal* an official who assesses and collects taxes, etc.

taxon *n* (*pl* **taxa**) a taxonomic group or entity.

taxonomy *n* (*pl* **-ies**) **1** classification, *esp* of plants and animals according to their presumed natural relationships. **2** the scientific study of the principles of classification. ➤➤ **taxonomic** *adj*, **taxonomical** *adj*, **taxonomist** *n*.

tax return *n* a formal statement, made to the Inland Revenue, of income and allowable deductions for tax assessment purposes.

tax year *n* the year that is taken as the basis for calculations of tax (in Britain generally from 6 April to 5 April).

tayberry *n* (*pl* **-ies**) a sweet dark red edible berry, a hybrid of a blackberry and raspberry.

TB *n* = TUBERCULOSIS.

Tb *abbr* the chemical symbol for terbium.

t.b.a. *abbr* to be announced.

T-bar *n* a T-shaped bar on a ski lift by which skiers are pulled up a slope.

T-bone *or* **T-bone steak** *n* a thick steak from the thin end of a beef sirloin containing a T-shaped bone.

tbs *or* **tbsp** *abbr* (*pl* **tbs** *or* **tbsp** *or* **tbsps**) **1** tablespoon. **2** tablespoonful.

Tc *abbr* the chemical symbol for technetium.

TCP/IP *abbr* in computing, transmission control protocol/Internet protocol, a protocol for communications between computers and the one that has become the standard for transmitting data over networks, including the Internet.

TD *abbr* (Irish Gaelic) Teachta Dála, member of the Dáil.

Te *abbr* the chemical symbol for tellurium.

te (*NAm* **ti**) /tee/ *n* in music, the seventh note of a major scale in the tonic sol-fa system.

tea *n* **1a** the leaves and leaf buds of a shrub of the camellia family, prepared and cured. **b** an aromatic refreshing drink prepared from tea leaves by steeping them in boiling water. **2** a drink made from the leaves, flowers, or fruit of various other plants. **3a** refreshments, usu including tea with sandwiches, cakes, or biscuits, served in the late afternoon. **b** a late-afternoon or early-evening meal.

tea bag *n* a cloth or paper bag holding enough tea for an individual serving when infused.

tea bread *n* any of various light often sweet breads or plain cakes.

tea break *n Brit* a short pause during the working day for refreshment, e.g. tea or coffee.

tea cake *n* a round yeast-leavened sweet bread bun that often contains currants and is usu eaten toasted with butter.

teach *v* (*past tense and past part.* **taught**) **1a** to cause (somebody or something) to know something or how to do something, *esp* by showing or instruction. **b** to impart the knowledge of (a subject, skill, etc). **2a** to instruct by precept, example, or experience. **b** to advocate. ⋙ **teachable** *adj*, **teaching** *n*.

teacher *n* a person whose occupation is teaching, *esp* in a school.

tea chest *n* a large square box used for exporting tea and also for storage, removals, etc.

teaching hospital *n* a hospital that is affiliated to a medical school and provides medical students with the opportunity of gaining practical experience.

tea cloth *n* = TEA TOWEL.

tea cosy *n* a thick or padded covering for a teapot, used to keep the tea warm.

teacup *n* a small cup used for tea.

tea dance *n* a dance held in the late afternoon.

teak *n* the hard yellowish brown wood of a tall tree native to India and SE Asia, used for furniture and shipbuilding.

teal *n* (*pl* **teals** *or* **teal**) **1** a small freshwater dabbling duck, the male of which often has distinctive bright patches of plumage. **2** (*also* **teal blue**) a greenish blue colour. ⋙ **teal** *adj*.

tea lady *n chiefly Brit* a woman who makes and/or serves tea, coffee, etc in a factory or office.

tea leaf *n* **1** (*usu in pl*) a fragment of a leaf of the tea plant, *esp* for or after infusion or soaking. **2** *Brit, informal* a thief.

team[1] *n* **1** (*used as sing. or pl*) **a** a group of players forming on one side in a sporting contest, debate, etc. **b** a group of two or more people who work together. **2** two or more draught animals harnessed together, *esp* for ploughing.

team[2] *v* **1** (*often* + up) to come together as a team. **2** (+ with) to combine (e.g. items of clothing) so as to form a harmonizing arrangement.

teammate *n* a fellow member of a team.

team player *n* a person who is good at playing or working as part of a team.

team spirit *n* willingness to work as part of a team and subordinate personal aims to group objectives.

teamster *n* **1** somebody who drives a team of horses. **2** *NAm* a lorry driver.

teamwork *n* mutual cooperation in a group enterprise.

teapot *n* a usu round pot with a lid, spout, and handle in which tea is brewed and from which it is served.

tear[1] *n* a drop of clear salty fluid secreted by the lachrymal gland that lubricates the eye and eyelids and is often released as a result of grief or other emotion. ✱ **in tears** crying; weeping. ⋙ **tearless** *adj*, **teary** *adj*.

tear[2] *v* (*past tense* **tore**, *past part.* **torn**) **1a** to pull apart by force; to damage in this way. **b** to wound (e.g. a muscle or ligament) by tearing. **2** to cause division or distress to (e.g. a person's mind): *She was torn between going and staying.* **3** (*often* + from) to remove (somebody or something) by force. **4** to make (a hole, pattern, etc) by tearing. **5** to move or act with violence, haste, or force: *The children went tearing down the street.* ✱ **tear a strip off** *informal* to rebuke (somebody) angrily. **tear into** to attack (somebody) physically or verbally without restraint or caution. **tear one's hair** to experience or express grief, rage, desperation, or anxiety. ⋙ **tearable** *adj*.

tear[3] *n* a hole, rip, or flaw made by tearing.

tearaway *n Brit, informal* an unruly and reckless young person.

tear away *v* to remove (oneself or somebody else) reluctantly.

tear down *v* to demolish.

teardrop *n* = TEAR[1].

tear duct *n* a tube which carries tears from the tear gland to the eye or from the eye to the nose.

tearful *adj* **1** causing tears. **2** crying or inclined to cry; sad. ⋙ **tearfully** *adv*, **tearfulness** *n*.

tear gas *n* a solid, liquid, or gaseous substance that on dispersion in the atmosphere blinds the eyes with tears and is used chiefly in dispelling crowds.

tear gland *n* a gland above the outer side of the eye where tears are formed.

tearing *adj informal* of a hurry: very great.

tearjerker *n informal* an excessively sentimental play, film, etc designed to provoke tears.

tearoom *n* a restaurant where light refreshments are served.

tea rose *n* a hybrid garden rose with abundant large pinkish or yellowish blossoms with a scent resembling that of tea.

tear sheet *n* a perforated sheet that can be torn from a publication, e.g. so that it can be sent somewhere or kept for future reference.

tear up *v* to tear into pieces.

tease[1] *v* **1a** to persistently and usu playfully irritate or make fun of. **b** to pretend to offer (somebody) something and then withhold it as a means of provoking anger or frustration. **c** to arouse (somebody) sexually with no intention of permitting sexual fulfilment. **2a** to disentangle and straighten (wool) by combing it. **b** to raise a nap on (cloth) with teasels.

tease[2] *n informal* **1** somebody or something that teases. **2** the act or an instance of teasing.

teasel *or* **teazel** *or* **teazle** *n* **1a** a tall European and N African plant of the scabious family with flower heads that are covered with stiff hooked bracts. **b** a flower head of a teasel, formerly used when dried to raise a nap on woollen cloth. **2** a wire substitute for this flower head.

tease out *v* to gain (information, the truth, etc) with difficulty, e.g. by working through a mass of data or by persuading somebody to speak.

teaser *n* **1** *informal* a frustratingly difficult question or problem. **2** somebody who derives malicious pleasure from teasing.

tea set *n* a matching set of usu china dishes for serving tea.

teaspoon *n* **1** a small spoon used for eating soft foods and for adding sugar, etc to hot drinks and stirring them. **2** = TEASPOONFUL.

teaspoonful *n* (*pl* **teaspoonfuls**) as much as a teaspoon will hold (about 5ml).

teat *n* **1** a nipple of the mammary gland of a female animal. **2** a rubber or plastic mouthpiece with one or more holes in it, attached to the top of a baby's feeding bottle.

tea towel *n* a cloth for drying dishes after they have been washed.

tea tree *n* a shrub or tree of the myrtle family found in Australia and New Zealand, with leaves that can be used as a substitute for tea and which yield an antiseptic oil used in cosmetics.

teazel *or* **teazle** *n* = TEASEL.

TEC *abbr Brit* Training and Enterprise Council.

tech *n Brit, informal* a technical school or college.

techie *n informal* somebody who is an expert in or an enthusiast for new technology, *esp* anything to do with electronic gadgetry, computing, the Internet, etc.

technetium *n* a radioactive metallic chemical element that is artificially produced as a product of fission in nuclear reactors and is used in radiotherapy.

technic *n* = TECHNICS.

technical *adj* **1** involving special and usu practical knowledge, *esp* of mechanical, industrial, or scientific subjects. **2a** marked by or characteristic of specialization. **b** relating to or used in a particular subject: *technical terms*. **c** complicated or difficult to understand. **3** marked by a strict legal interpretation or rigid application of the rules: *He had technical responsibility for all his subordinates*. **4** relating to technique. ▶▶ **technically** *adv.*

technical college *n* a further education college that offers courses in practical subjects.

technicality *n* (*pl* **-ies**) **1** the quality or state of being technical. **2a** a detail meaningful only to a specialist. **b** a detail arising from a strict or literal interpretation of a rule or law.

technical knockout *n* the termination of a boxing match when a boxer is declared by the referee to be unable to continue the fight, e.g. because of injuries.

technician *n* **1a** a specialist in the technical details of a subject or occupation. **b** somebody who has acquired the technique of an area of specialization, e.g. an art. **2** somebody employed to do practical work, e.g. in a laboratory.

Technicolor *n trademark* a process of colour photography in the cinema in which the three primary colours are recorded on separate films and then combined in a single print.

technicolour *n* vivid and often garish colour. ▶▶ **technicolour** *adj*, **technicoloured** *adj.*

technics *pl n* **1** (*used as sing.*) = TECHNOLOGY. **2** (*used as sing. or pl*) rules, procedures, technique, or technical details.

technique *n* **1** the manner in which an artist, performer, or athlete displays or manages the formal aspect of his or her skill. **2a** a body of technical methods, e.g. in a craft or in scientific research. **b** a method of accomplishing a desired aim; a knack.

techno *n* a form of fast electronically produced modern dance music with few, simple vocals.

technobabble *n informal* language that is full of complicated technical terms.

techno-clothing *n* clothing that incorporates items of modern technology, such as jackets equipped with mobile phones or small computers.

technocracy *n* (*pl* **-ies**) *chiefly derog* management of society by a body of technical experts. ▶▶ **technocrat** *n*, **technocratic** *adj.*

technology *n* (*pl* **-ies**) **1** the theory and practice of applied science as used in commerce and industry. **2** applied scientific methods. ▶▶ **technological** *adj*, **technologically** *adv*, **technologist** *n.*

technophilia *n* enthusiasm for new technology, such as computers. ▶▶ **technophile** *n*, **technophilic** *adj.*

technophobia *n* fear or distrust of new technology, *esp* of computers. ▶▶ **technophobe** *n*, **technophobic** *adj.*

technospeak *n informal* = TECHNOBABBLE.

techy *n* (*pl* **-ies**) = TECHIE.

tectonic *adj* **1** relating to or resulting from the deformation of the earth's crust, the forces involved in this, or the structures formed by it. **2** relating to or involved in building or construction. ▶▶ **tectonically** *adv.*

tectonics *pl n* (*used as sing. or pl*) in geology, structural features, *esp* those connected with folding and faulting.

teddy[1] *n* (*pl* **-ies**) = TEDDY BEAR.

teddy[2] *n* (*pl* **-ies**) a woman's one-piece undergarment that combines a camisole and French knickers.

teddy bear *n* a stuffed toy bear.

Teddy boy *n* a member of a cult of British youths, *esp* in the 1950s, who wore their hair in swept-up quiffs and were rock 'n' roll enthusiasts.

Te Deum /ˌtay 'dayəm, ˌtee 'dee·əm/ *n* (*pl* **Te Deums**) a liturgical Christian hymn of praise to God.

tedious *adj* **1** of a task, etc: tiresome through being both dull and interminable. **2** of people: boring; tiresome. ▶▶ **tediously** *adv*, **tediousness** *n.*

tedium *n* the state or quality of being tedious.

tee[1] *n* a mark aimed at in various games, e.g. curling.

tee[2] *n* **1** in golf, a peg or a small mound used to raise a golf ball into position for striking at the beginning of play on a hole. **2** the area from which a golf ball is struck at the beginning of play on a hole.

tee[3] *v* (*often* + up) to place (a golf ball) on a tee.

tee-hee[1] *n* a chuckle, suppressed giggle, or mocking laugh.

tee-hee[2] *v* to give a chuckle, suppressed giggle, or mocking laugh.

teem[1] *v* **1** (+ with) to abound. **2** to be present in large quantities.

teem[2] *v Brit* (*also* + down) to rain hard.

teen[1] *adj informal* = TEENAGE.

teen[2] *n informal* = TEENAGER.

-teen *comb. form* forming words for the numbers between 13 and 19.

teenage *adj* relating to, denoting, or suitable for a teenager or people in their teens. ▶▶ **teenaged** *adj.*

teenager *n* a person who is aged between 13 and 19.

teens *pl n* the years 13 to 19 in a lifetime.

teensy-weensy *adj* see TEENY-WEENY.

teeny *or* **teensy** *adj* (**-ier, -iest**) *informal* tiny.

teenybopper *n informal* a young teenager who zealously follows the latest trends in clothes, pop music, etc.

teeny-weeny *or* **teensy-weensy** *adj informal* tiny.

tee off *v* to drive a golf ball from a tee.

teepee *n* see TEPEE.

tee shirt *n* see T-SHIRT.

teeter *v* **1** to wobble or move unsteadily. **2** to waver or be unable to make up one's mind.

teeth *n* pl of TOOTH.

teethe *v* to cut one's milk teeth.

teething ring *n* a usu plastic ring for a teething infant to bite on.

teething troubles *pl n* temporary problems occurring with new machinery or during the initial stages of an activity.

teetotal *adj* practising complete abstinence from alcoholic drinks. ▶▶ **teetotalism** *n.*

teetotaller (*NAm* **teetotaler**) *n* somebody who is teetotal.

teetotum *n* (*pl* **teetotums**) a small top, usu inscribed with letters and used in games of chance.

TEFL *abbr* teaching English as a foreign language.

Teflon *n trademark* polytetrafluoroethylene, a tough plastic used *esp* for non-stick coatings and for insulation.

tein /'tay·in/ *n* (*pl* **teins** *or* **tein**) a unit of currency in Kazakhstan, worth 100th of a tenge.

tektite *n* a rounded dark glassy object believed to have been formed as a result of meteorite impact.

tel- *comb. form* see TELE-.

tele- *or* **tel-** *comb. form* **1** distant; at a distance; over a distance: *telegram; telepathy.* **2a** telegraph: *teleprinter.* **b** television: *telecast.*

telecast[1] *v* to televise. ➤➤ **telecaster** *n.*

telecast[2] *n* a televised broadcast.

telecommunication *n* **1** communication at a distance, e.g. by telegraph, telephone, television, etc. **2** (*usu in pl*) the science and technology of telecommunication.

telecommute *v* to work from home, using a personal computer, a modem, electronic mail, etc to communicate with clients and a central office. ➤➤ **telecommuter** *n.*

telecoms *or* **telecomms** *pl n* telecommunications.

teleconferencing *n* the process of holding a meeting involving people in different places who are linked by a telecommunication system, e.g. telephone or television. ➤➤ **teleconference** *n.*

telecottage *n* a building equipped with computers and telecommunications equipment that members of the community can use.

telegenic *adj* looking attractive or having a pleasant manner on television.

telegram *n* a message sent by telegraph and delivered as a written or typed note.

telegraph[1] *n* an apparatus or system for communicating at a distance, *esp* by making and breaking an electric circuit.

telegraph[2] *v* **1a** to send or communicate (a message) by telegraph. **b** to send a message to (somebody) by telegraph. **2** to make known by signs, *esp* unknowingly and in advance. ➤➤ **telegrapher** *n,* **telegraphist** *n,* **telegraphy** *n.*

telegraphese *n* the terse and abbreviated language characteristic of telegrams.

telegraphic *adj* **1** of the telegraph. **2** concise; terse. ➤➤ **telegraphically** *adv.*

telegraph pole *n* a pole erected to hold telephone or telegraph wires.

telekinesis *n* the supposed ability to move distant objects without physically touching them, *esp* just by concentrating the mind on them. ➤➤ **telekinetic** *adj.*

telemarketing *n* the practice of telephoning companies or individuals to try to sell them something. ➤➤ **telemarketer** *n.*

telematics *pl n* (*used as sing. or pl*) the combination of computers and telecommunication networks for the long-distance transmission of computerized information.

telemedicine *n* the use of the telephone, e-mail, video, etc for medical purposes, e.g. for consultations between doctors and patients.

Telemessage *n trademark* a message sent by telephone or telex and printed out for the recipient.

telemeter[1] *n* an electrical apparatus for measuring a quantity, e.g. pressure, speed, or temperature, and transmitting the result, e.g. by radio, to a distant place at which it is indicated or recorded. ➤➤ **telemetric** *adj,* **telemetry** *n.*

telemeter[2] *v* to obtain and transmit (a reading) by telemeter.

teleology *n* (*pl* **-ies**) **1** a doctrine explaining phenomena by reference to goals or purposes. **2** the character attributed to nature or natural processes of being directed towards an end or designed according to a purpose. ➤➤ **teleological** *adj.*

telepathy *n* communication that supposedly occurs directly from one mind to another without use of the known senses. ➤➤ **telepathic** *adj,* **telepathically** *adv.*

telephone[1] *n* **1** a device for reproducing sounds at a distance; *specif* one for converting sounds into electrical impulses for transmission to a particular receiver. **2** the system of communications that uses telephones. ➤➤ **telephonic** *adj,* **telephony** *n.*

telephone[2] *v* **1** to make a telephone call. **2** to speak or attempt to speak to (somebody) by telephone.

telephone box *n* a booth containing a public telephone.

telephone directory *n* a book giving the telephone numbers of subscribers.

telephone number *n* a number assigned to a particular telephone and used to call that telephone.

telephonist *n Brit* a telephone switchboard operator.

telephoto lens *n* a compound camera lens that has a longer focal length than a simple standard lens, to give a narrow field of vision and a magnified image.

teleport *v* in science fiction, to transport (something, somebody, or oneself) or to be transported across a considerable distance instantaneously, often with the use of machinery that causes dematerializing at the point of origin and rematerializing at the destination. ➤➤ **teleportation** *n.*

teleprinter *n* a typewriter keyboard that transmits telegraphic signals, a typewriting device activated by telegraphic signals, or a machine that combines both these functions, or any similar machine, e.g. one attached to a computer.

Teleprompter *n NAm, trademark* an Autocue.

telescope[1] *n* a usu tubular optical instrument for viewing distant objects by means of the refraction of light rays through a lens or the reflection of light rays by a concave mirror.

telescope[2] *v* **1** to slide one part within another like the cylindrical sections of a hand telescope. **2** to cause to telescope. **3** to condense or shorten. ➤➤ **telescopic** *adj,* **telescopically** *adv.*

Teletext *n trademark* an information service provided by a television network.

telethon *n* a long television programme designed to raise money for charity by getting viewers to phone in and pledge donations.

Teletype[1] *n* **1** *trademark* a teleprinter. **2** (*often* **teletype**) a message printed on a Teletype.

Teletype[2] *v trademark* to send (a message) by Teletype.

televangelist *n* a Christian evangelist, *esp* in the USA, who hosts television shows in which the church's message is preached and appeals are made to viewers for donations.

televise *v* to broadcast (a programme, event, or film) by television.

television *n* **1** an electronic system of transmitting changing images together with sound along a wire or through space by converting the images and sounds into electrical signals and then reconverting the received signals into images and sound. **2** a device with a screen and sound system for receiving and displaying television signals. **3** the television broadcasting industry. **4a** a television broadcasting organization or station. **b** the medium of television communication. **c** the programmes broadcast on television.

television set *n* = TELEVISION (2).

televisual *adj chiefly Brit* of or suitable for broadcast by television. ➤➤ **televisually** *adv.*

teleworking *n* telecommuting. ➤➤ **teleworker** *n.*

telex[1] *n* **1** a communications service involving teleprinters connected by wire through automatic exchanges. **2** a message sent by telex.

telex[2] *v* to send (a message) by telex.

tell *v* (*past tense and past part.* **told**) **1** to relate (facts) to. **2** to give information to. **3** to order or instruct (somebody) to do something: *Tell them to wait.* **4** to discern or ascertain. **5** to distinguish: *It's hard to tell one from the other.* **6** to decide definitely: *You can never quite tell.* **7** to have an effect: *The strain was beginning to tell.* **8** to play a part: *This will tell against you.* ✱ **tell on** *informal* to inform about (somebody). **tell tales 1** to be untruthful. **2** to reveal secrets or spread gossip. **tell the time** to read the information on a clock or watch. **you're telling me!** *informal* an expression of agreement with what somebody has said.

teller *n* **1** somebody who relates or communicates. **2a** somebody appointed to count votes. **b** a member of a bank's staff who deals directly with customers' transactions.

telling *adj* carrying great weight and producing a marked effect; significant. ➤➤ **tellingly** *adv.*

telling-off *n* (*pl* **tellings-off** *or* **telling-offs**) *informal* a harsh or severe reprimand.

tell off *v informal* to scold or reprimand.

telltale *n* **1** somebody who spreads gossip or rumours; an informer. **2** (*used before a noun*) revealing, betraying, or indicating something: *a telltale sign.*

telluric *adj formal* of the planet earth or soil.

telluride *n* a compound of tellurium.

tellurium *n* a silver-white semimetallic chemical element chemically related to selenium and sulphur, that occurs naturally in silver and gold ores, and is used in alloys.

telly *n* (*pl* **-ies**) *chiefly Brit, informal* = TELEVISION.

temazepam *n* a tranquillizing drug, used to treat insomnia and as a sedative.

temerity *n* unreasonable disregard for danger or opposition; excessive boldness.

temp[1] *n informal* a person, e.g. an office worker, employed temporarily, usu through an agency.

temp[2] *v informal* to work as a temp.

temper[1] *n* **1a** an uncontrolled and often disproportionate rage. **b** proneness to displays of such rages. **2** a characteristic cast of mind or state of feeling. **3** characteristic tone. **4** the state of a substance with respect to certain desired qualities, e.g. the degree of hardness or resilience given to steel by tempering. ✱ **keep one's temper** to keep one's anger under control. **lose one's temper** to show one's anger.

temper[2] *v* **1** (+ with) to moderate (something harsh) with the addition of something less severe. **2** to bring (*esp* steel) to the right degree of hardness by reheating and cooling it. ➤➤ **temperer** *n.*

tempera *n* **1** a method of painting using pigment ground and mixed with an emulsion, e.g. of egg yolk and water. **2** the emulsion used in this painting.

temperament *n* a person's own particular mental and emotional character, *esp* with regard to its effect on behaviour.

temperamental *adj* **1a** easily upset or irritated; liable to sudden changes of mood. **b** unpredictable in behaviour or operation; unreliable. **2** relating to or arising from individual character or constitution. ➤➤ **temperamentally** *adv.*

temperance *n* abstinence from alcohol.

temperate *adj* **1** moderate in the indulgence of appetites or desires; *esp* abstemious in the consumption of alcohol. **2a** having a moderate climate. **b** found in or associated with a temperate climate. ➤➤ **temperately** *adv.*

temperate zone *n* either of the two regions between a polar circle and the nearest tropic.

temperature *n* **1** degree of hotness or coldness as measured on a scale, e.g. in degrees Celsius. **2a** the degree of heat present in the body of a person or animal, either as a rule or at a particular time. **b** *informal* an abnormally high body heat.

temperature inversion *n* = INVERSION (3).

tempest *n* a violent storm.

tempestuous *adj* **1** characterized by passion, violence, and emotional turbulence. **2** characterized by storms and bad weather. ➤➤ **tempestuously** *adv,* **tempestuousness** *n.*

tempi *n* pl of TEMPO.

Templar *n* a knight of a religious military order, the Knights of the Temple of Solomon.

template *or* **templet** *n* **1** a pattern, mould, or stencil used as a guide to the shape of something that is being made or drawn. **2** a thing that serves as a model for other things.

temple[1] *n* a building dedicated to religious worship among any of various ancient civilizations and present-day non-Christian religions.

temple[2] *n* the flattened space on either side of the forehead.

templet *n* see TEMPLATE.

tempo *n* (*pl* **tempi** *or* **tempos**) **1** the speed of a musical piece or passage. **2** the speed or rate of motion or activity.

temporal[1] *adj* **1** relating to time as opposed to eternity or space; *esp* transitory. **2** relating to, dealing with, or having authority over lay or secular matters. ➤➤ **temporally** *adv.*

temporal[2] *adj* relating to or in the region of the temple.

temporal bone *n* either of two large bones, each of which forms a side and base of the human skull, is composed of four fused parts, and encloses the middle ear.

temporality *n* (*pl* **-ies**) the quality or state of being temporal.

temporal lobe *n* a large lobe at the side of each cerebral hemisphere that contains a sensory area associated with hearing and speech.

temporary[1] *adj* lasting only for a limited time. ➤➤ **temporarily** *adv,* **temporariness** *n.*

temporary[2] *n* (*pl* **-ies**) = TEMP[1].

temporize *or* **-ise** *v* to avoid coming to a decision or draw out negotiations so as to gain time.

Tempranillo /tempraneeyoh, -neelyoh/ *n* a variety of grape used in the production of Rioja wine, or the wine produced from it.

tempt *v* **1a** to make (somebody) feel strongly inclined to do something: *He was tempted to call it quits.* **b** to appeal to (somebody); to attract: *The idea tempts me.* **2** to try to persuade (somebody) to do something, *esp* something wicked or immoral, by the promise of pleasure or gain. **3** to risk provoking harm or retribution from (somebody or something): *You shouldn't tempt fate.* ➤➤ **tempter** *n.*

temptation *n* **1a** an urge to try, take, or enjoy something, *esp* something forbidden. **b** the state of being tempted, *esp* to do something evil or forbidden. **2** something tempting.

tempting *adj* arousing a strong desire to try, take, or enjoy; enticing.

temptress *n* a woman who tempts or entices; *specif* a woman who has very strong and obvious sex appeal.

tempura /tem'poōərə, 'tempərə/ *n* a Japanese dish of seafood or vegetables dipped in batter and fried.

ten *n* the number 10. ⋙ **ten** *adj*, **tenfold** *adj and adv.*

tenable *adj* **1a** capable of being defended or justified by rational argument or evidence. **b** capable of being held or defended against military attack. **2** (*usu* + for) of a position, award, etc: to be held for a specified period.

tenacious *adj* **1a** holding on very firmly. **b** tending to stick or cling, *esp* to another substance. **2** unwilling to desist or to give up on something; stubborn or persistent. ⋙ **tenaciously** *adv*, **tenacity** *n.*

tenancy *n* (*pl* **-ies**) temporary occupancy of land, a house, etc under a lease or rental agreement.

tenant[1] *n* **1** somebody who rents or leases a house or flat from a landlord. **2** in law, a holder of real estate by any kind of right.

tenant[2] *v* to live in or have the use of (a property) as a tenant.

tenant farmer *n* a farmer who works land owned by somebody else and pays rent.

tench *n* (*pl* **tenches** *or* **tench**) a Eurasian freshwater fish of the carp family with a greenish or blackish skin, noted for its ability to survive outside water.

Ten Commandments *pl n* the commandments given by God to Moses on Mount Sinai, recorded in Exodus 20:1–17.

tend[1] *v* **1a** to be likely or inclined to do something, or to have the habit of doing something: *She tends to exaggerate.* **b** (+ to/towards) to be likely to have or acquire a particular characteristic: *His style is plain and direct, tending sometimes to terseness.* **2** to move or direct one's course in a specified direction.

tend[2] *v* **1** to be in charge and take care of (somebody or something). **2** to provide care and treatment for (somebody or something).

tendency *n* (*pl* **-ies**) **1** an inclination or predisposition to do something, or to a particular characteristic. **2** a general trend or movement.

tendentious *adj* presenting a biased view, *esp* so as to promote a particular stance, ideology, etc. ⋙ **tendentiously** *adv*, **tendentiousness** *n.*

tender[1] *adj* (**tenderer, tenderest**) **1** showing or characterized by great gentleness and kindness. **2** showing or characterized by warmth of feeling, love, or affection. **3a** having a soft or yielding texture; easily broken, cut, or damaged. **b** of meat: easy to cut and chew. **4** easily hurt or made to feel pain; sensitive. **5** young and vulnerable. **6** demanding careful and sensitive handling; tricky. ✻ **tender mercies** ungentle, unkind, or positively brutal treatment. ⋙ **tenderly** *adv*, **tenderness** *n.*

tender[2] *n* **1** a boat or ship that carries supplies, passengers, etc to and from other ships. **2** a vehicle attached to a steam locomotive for carrying a supply of fuel and water. **3** a road vehicle that carries tools, equipment, or personnel, *esp* for use in an emergency.

tender[3] *v* **1** to present (something) formally for acceptance. **2** to offer (money) in payment. **3** (*often* + for) to present a bid in the hope of gaining a contract. ⋙ **tenderer** *n.*

tender[4] *n* a formal offer or bid.

tenderhearted *adj* easily moved to love, pity, or sorrow.

tenderize *or* **-ise** *v* to make (meat) tender by beating or using a substance that breaks down fibrous tissue. ⋙ **tenderizer** *n.*

tenderloin *n* a pork or beef fillet cut from between the sirloin and the ribs.

tendinitis *or* **tendonitis** *n* inflammation of a tendon.

tendon *n* a tough cord or band of dense white fibrous tissue that connects a muscle with a bone or other part and transmits the force exerted by the muscle.

tendonitis *n* see TENDINITIS.

tendril *n* a slender spirally coiling outgrowth that attaches a climbing plant to its support.

tenebrous *adj literary* in shadow or shut off from the light; dark; murky.

tenement *n* **1a** a large building constructed as or divided up into separate dwellings, *esp* one meeting minimum standards and typically found in the poorer parts of a large city in Scotland or the USA. **b** a flat in a tenement building. **2** in law, land or other property held by one person from another.

tenet *n* a principle, belief, or doctrine, *esp* one held in common by the members of an organization or group.

ten-gallon hat *n* a large hat with a broad brim and a very high crown, traditionally worn by cowboys.

tenge /'tengay/ *n* (*pl* **tenge** *or* **tenges**) **1** the basic monetary unit of Kazakhstan. **2** a unit of currency in Turkmenistan, worth 100th of a manat.

tenner *n Brit, informal* a £10 note.

tennis *n* **1** a game for two or four players that is played with rackets and a ball on a flat court divided by a low net. **2** = REAL TENNIS.

tennis elbow *n* inflammation and pain of the elbow, usu resulting from excessive twisting movements of the hand.

tennis shoe *n* a light shoe with a canvas or soft leather upper and a rubber sole.

tenon *n* a projecting part of a piece of material, e.g. wood, specially shaped for insertion into a matching slot or mortise.

tenon saw *n* a woodworking saw that has a reinforced blade and is used for making fine cuts.

tenor *n* **1** a male singer having a high voice. **2** a musical instrument having a range below that of alto. **3** the general meaning or implication of something spoken or written. **4** a continuance in a course or activity.

tenor clef *n* a C clef placed so as to designate the fourth line of the stave as middle C.

tenosynovitis *n* inflammation of the sheath covering a tendon.

tenpin *n* a bottle-shaped pin used in tenpin bowling.

tenpin bowling *n* an indoor bowling game using ten pins and a large ball.

tenrec *n* a small often spiny insect-eating mammal of Madagascar.

TENS *abbr* transcutaneous electrical nerve stimulation, used to control or relieve pain.

tense[1] *adj* **1a** feeling or showing nervousness and anxiety. **b** marked by strain or suspense. **2** stretched tight; taut. ⋙ **tensely** *adv*, **tenseness** *n.*

tense[2] *v* (*often* + up) to make or become tense.

tense[3] *n* a set of inflectional forms of a verb that express action taking place at a particular time.

tensile *adj* **1** able to be stretched or drawn out; ductile. **2** relating to or involving tension.

tensile strength *n* the greatest tension a substance can bear without breaking.

tension[1] *n* **1** the act or action of stretching or the condition or degree of being stretched to stiffness; tautness. **2a** mental or emotional unease; stress. **b** a feeling or state of nervous and excited anticipation or suspense. **3** a state of latent hostility or opposition between individuals or groups. **4** the strain caused by two forces pulling in opposite directions. **5** voltage or electrical potential, *esp* of a specified kind. **6** the degree of tightness or looseness of the stitches in knitting or sewing. ➤➤ **tensional** *adj.*

tension² *v* to tighten (something) and make it taut to a desired or appropriate degree.

tent¹ *n* a collapsible shelter made of canvas or similar material stretched and supported by poles. ➤➤ **tented** *adj.*

tent² *v* to cover (somebody or something) with a tent, or as if with a tent.

tentacle *n* an elongated flexible animal part, chiefly on the head or about the mouth, used for feeling, grasping, etc. ➤➤ **tentacled** *adj,* **tentacular** *adj.*

tentage *n* a collection of tents.

tentative *adj* **1** not fully worked out or developed; provisional. **2** hesitant or uncertain. ➤➤ **tentatively** *adv,* **tentativeness** *n.*

tenterhook ✻ **on tenterhooks** in a state of suspense or nervous anticipation.

tenth *adj and n* **1** having the position in a sequence corresponding to the number ten. **2** one of ten equal parts of something. **3** in music, an interval of ten degrees of a diatonic scale. ➤➤ **tenthly** *adv.*

tent stitch *n* a short diagonal stitch used in embroidery and canvas work.

tenuous *adj* **1** having little substance or strength; weak or flimsy. **2** not thick; fine. ➤➤ **tenuously** *adv,* **tenuousness** *n.*

tenure *n* **1** the holding of a position or an office. **2** the conditions under which a property is held or occupied. ➤➤ **tenurial** *adj.*

tepee *or* **teepee** *n* a Native American conical tent, usu made of skins.

tepid *adj* **1** moderately warm. **2** not enthusiastic. ➤➤ **tepidity** *n,* **tepidly** *adv.*

tequila /təˈkeelə/ *n* a strong Mexican alcoholic drink made by redistilling mescal.

tequila sunrise *n* a cocktail in which orange juice and grenadine are mixed with tequila.

ter- *comb. form* three times, threefold, or three: *tercentenary.*

tera- *comb. form* one million million (10^{12}): *terabyte.*

terabyte *n* a unit of information equal to one million million bytes.

teraflop *n* a unit of processing speed equal to one million million floating-point operations per second.

terai /təˈrie/ *n* a wide-brimmed felt sun hat worn *esp* in subtropical regions.

teratogen *n* something that causes developmental malformations in foetuses. ➤➤ **teratogenic** *adj.*

teratology *n* **1** the study of malformations in foetuses. **2** stories about mythical creatures and monsters. ➤➤ **teratological** *adj,* **teratologist** *n.*

terbium *n* a silvery metallic chemical element of the rare-earth group.

terce *n* the third daily religious service making up the Divine Office, observed at 9 a.m.

tercel *n* a male hawk, such as the male of the peregrine falcon or goshawk, *esp* when used in falconry: compare FALCON (2).

tercentenary *n* (*pl* **-ies**) a 300th anniversary. ➤➤ **tercentenary** *adj,* **tercentennial** *adj and n.*

terebinth *n* a small European tree of the sumach family that was formerly a source of turpentine.

teredo *n* (*pl* **teredos** *or* **teredines**) = SHIPWORM.

tergiversate *v formal* **1** to change sides or loyalties; to become a renegade. **2** to act evasively or equivocally. ➤➤ **tergiversation** *n.*

teriyaki /teriˈyahki/ *n* a Japanese dish consisting of pieces of meat or fish marinated in a mixture of soy sauce, sugar, and rice wine and grilled.

term¹ *n* **1a** a word or expression with a precise meaning, *esp* one used mainly in a particular field: *legal terms.* **b** (*in pl*) words or a mode of expression of a specified kind: *She spoke in flattering terms of my previous achievements.* **2** (*in pl*) provisions relating to an agreement: *terms of sale.* **3** a limited or definite extent of time; *esp* the time for which something lasts: *medium-term credit.* **4a** any of the usu three periods of instruction into which an academic year is divided. **b** any one of the periods of the year during which the courts are in session. **5a** an end or termination, *esp* a time fixed as the end of something or on which something falls due. **b** the time at which a pregnancy of normal length ends. **6a** a mathematical expression connected to another by a plus or minus sign. **b** an expression that forms part of a fraction or proportion or of a series or sequence. **7** a concept, word, or phrase appearing as subject or predicate in a logical proposition. ✻ **be on good/bad terms with** to have a friendly/unfriendly relationship with (somebody). **come to terms** (+ with) to accept or resign oneself to something sad or unpleasant. **in terms of** as expressed by; in relation to. **on terms** on an equal footing, *esp* having a same or nearly the same score in a game. ➤➤ **termly** *adj and adv.*

term² *v* to apply a particular term to (somebody or something).

termagant *n* an overbearing or nagging woman.

terminable *adj* capable of being terminated.

terminal¹ *adj* **1** forming an end, extremity, boundary, or terminus. **2** occurring during a term or each term in a school, college, etc. **3a** occurring at or causing the end of life. **b** relating to or suffering from a disease that is certain to cause death. **4** *informal* extreme or irredeemable. ➤➤ **terminally** *adv.*

terminal² *n* **1a** the end of a transport route, with its associated buildings and facilities. **b** a building at an airport with facilities for arriving and departing passengers. **2** a device attached to the end of a wire or cable or to an electrical apparatus for convenience in making connections. **3** a device through which a user can communicate with a computer. **4** an industrial installation where raw materials are stored and processed, *esp* an onshore installation receiving oil or gas through a pipeline.

terminal velocity *n* the constant maximum velocity attained by an object falling through a fluid under gravity when resistance prevents any further acceleration.

terminate *v* **1a** to bring to an end. **b** to take action to end (a pregnancy) prematurely. **2** to serve as an ending, limit, or boundary of. **3** *NAm, euphem* to kill or assassinate. **4** *NAm* to dismiss from employment. **5** to go or extend only as far as a particular point and then stop; *esp* to reach a terminus. **6** (*often* + in) to come to an end in time. ➤➤ **termination** *n,* **terminator** *n.*

terminator technology *n* a technique in genetic engineering that makes second-generation seed sterile, thereby preventing farmers from using seed harvested in one year's crop as seed for planting the next year, and so forcing them to buy fresh seed from the supplier each year.

termini *n* pl of TERMINUS.

terminology *n* (*pl* **-ies**) the technical terms used in a particular subject. ➤➤ **terminological** *adj.*

terminus *n* (*pl* **termini** *or* **terminuses**) **1** the end of a transport line or travel route, or the station or town at which it ends. **2** a finishing point; an end.

termite *n* an often destructive pale-coloured soft-bodied insect that lives in colonies and feeds on wood.

terms of reference *pl n* the precise definition of the scope or competence allowed to an individual or a body such as a committee.

terms of trade *pl n* the ratio of an index of export prices to the index of import prices.

tern *n* a water bird that has a black cap, a white body, and a forked tail.

ternary *adj* **1** made up of three parts. **2** using three as the base.

terpene *n* any of various hydrocarbons present in essential oils, e.g. from conifers, and used *esp* as solvents and in organic synthesis. ➤➤ **terpenoid** *adj and n.*

terpsichorean *adj* relating to dancing.

terrace[1] *n* **1** a relatively level paved or planted area adjoining a building. **2** a horizontal ridge cut, usu as one of a series, into a hillside and used for farming. **3** a level usu narrow and steep-fronted area bordering a river, sea, etc. **4** *chiefly Brit* a row of similar houses joined by common dividing walls. **5** *Brit* a series of shallow steps providing standing accommodation for spectators.

terrace[2] *v* **1** to cut terraces in (a slope). **2** to make (an area of ground) into a terrace.

terraced house *n Brit* a house in a continuous row of dwellings connected by common dividing walls.

terracotta *n* **1** an unglazed brownish red fired clay used for statuettes and vases and as a building material. **2** a brownish orange colour.

terra firma *n* dry land; solid ground.

terrain *n* an area of land, *esp* with respect to its physical features.

terra incognita /inkog'neetə, in'kognitə/ *n* unexplored territory.

terrapin *n* a small edible freshwater reptile similar to the tortoise but adapted for swimming.

terrarium *n* (*pl* **terraria** *or* **terrariums**) **1** an enclosure, *esp* a glass-fronted case, for small land-dwelling animals. **2** a transparent, often globe-shaped container in which plants are grown indoors.

terrazzo /te'rahtsoh/ *n* a mosaic flooring made by embedding and polishing small pieces of marble or granite in mortar.

terrene *adj* **1** relating to or living on dry land. **2** *formal* mundane or earthly.

terrestrial *adj* **1** relating to the planet earth or its inhabitants. **2a** relating to land as distinct from air or water. **b** of organisms: living on or in land or soil. **3** of a television system or service: not transmitting programmes via a satellite. ➤➤ **terrestrial** *n,* **terrestrially** *adv.*

terrible *adj* **1** *informal* **a** of very poor quality; awful. **b** highly unpleasant. **2** *informal* extreme or very great. **3** *informal* **a** very unwell. **b** very upset or guilty. **4** causing intense fear; terrifying. ➤➤ **terribleness** *n.*

terribly *adv informal* **1** very. **2** very badly.

terrier *n* a usu small dog belonging to any of various breeds, orig used by hunters to drive out small furred game from underground.

terrific *adj* **1** *informal* extraordinarily large or intense. **2** *informal* excellent, wonderful, or highly enjoyable. **3** arousing fear or awe. ➤➤ **terrifically** *adv.*

terrify *v* (**-ies, -ied**) to fill with terror or apprehension. ➤➤ **terrifying** *adj,* **terrifyingly** *adv.*

terrine *n* **1** an earthenware baking dish. **2** a food, *esp* pâté, cooked in a terrine.

Territorial *n* a member of the Territorial Army and Volunteer Reserve.

territorial *adj* **1a** relating to territory or land. **b** relating to private property. **2a** restricted to a particular area or district. **b** of an animal or bird: by nature disposed to mark out and defend its own territory. ➤➤ **territoriality** *n,* **territorially** *adv.*

Territorial Army and Volunteer Reserve *n* in Britain, a voluntary force organized to provide a trained army reserve for emergencies.

territorial waters *pl n* the waters under the sovereign jurisdiction of a nation.

territory *n* (*pl* **-ies**) **1a** a geographical area under the jurisdiction of a government. **b** an administrative subdivision of a country, *esp* a part of the USA not included within any state but with a separate legislature. **2a** an indeterminate geographical area, *esp* one having a specific characteristic. **b** a field of knowledge or interest. **3a** an assigned area; *esp* one in which an agent, sales representative, or distributor operates. **b** an area, often including a nesting site or den, occupied and defended by an animal or group of animals.

terror *n* **1** a state of intense fear. **2** somebody or something that inspires fear. **3** revolutionary violence, e.g. the planting of bombs. **4** *informal* an annoying or appalling person.

terrorise *v* see TERRORIZE.

terrorism *n* the systematic use of terror and violence for political ends. ➤➤ **terrorist** *adj and n.*

terrorize *or* **-ise** *v* to fill with terror or anxiety.

terry *n* (*pl* **-ies**) an absorbent fabric with uncut loops on both faces, used *esp* for towels. ➤➤ **terry** *adj.*

terse *adj* **1** using few words; concise. **2** brusque or curt. ➤➤ **tersely** *adv,* **terseness** *n.*

tertiary[1] *adj* **1** of third rank, importance, or value. **2a** *Brit* relating to higher education. **b** denoting or relating to service industries: compare PRIMARY[1], SECONDARY. **3** (**Tertiary**) of the first geological period of the Cenozoic era, lasting from about 65 million to about 1.6 million years ago, and marked by the dominance of mammals and the evolution of modern plants. **4** occurring in or being a third stage. ➤➤ **Tertiary** *n.*

tertiary[2] *n* (*pl* **-ies**) somebody belonging to a monastic third order.

Terylene *n trademark* a synthetic polyester textile fibre.

TESL *abbr* teaching English as a second language.

tesla *n* the SI unit of magnetic flux density.

TESOL *abbr* teaching English to speakers of other languages.

TESSA *abbr Brit* Tax-Exempt Special Savings Account, an interest-earning account, available from 1991 to 1999, that was free from tax.

tessellate *v* **1** to construct, pave, or decorate with mosaic. **2** of geometric shapes: to fit together exactly leaving no spaces. ➤➤ **tessellation** *n.*

tessera *n* (*pl* **tesserae**) **1** a small square piece of marble, glass, etc used in mosaic. **2** a piece of bone or wood used as a dice or token in ancient Greece and Rome.

tessitura *n* the part of the register in which most of the notes of a melody or voice part lie.

test[1] *n* **1** a means of assessing the quality, capabilities, reliability, or endurance of somebody or something. **2** a series of questions or exercises for measuring the knowledge, intelligence, ability, etc of an individual or group. **3** a real-life situation that reveals the worth or quality of something or somebody by subjecting them to stress or difficulties. **4** a chemical or physical procedure or reaction, or a chemical reagent, used to identify or test for the presence of a substance or constituent. **5** a basis for assessment; a criterion. **6** = TEST MATCH.

test[2] *v* **1** to ascertain the quality or capabilities of (something or somebody) by subjecting them to a test. **2** (*usu* + for) to use a chemical procedure to ascertain the presence of a substance in (something). **3** to subject (something) to severe strain: *His obtuseness tested my patience to the limit.* **4** (*usu* + for) to apply a test as a means of analysis or diagnosis: *We use this exercise to test for mechanical aptitude.* **5** (*usu* + for) to produce a result of a specified kind, usu positive or negative, in a medical or chemical test: *She tested negative for HIV.* ✱ **test the water** to find out what people's opinions or feelings about a matter are. ➤➤ **testable** *adj.*

test[3] *n* an external hard or firm covering of an invertebrate, e.g. the shell of a mollusc.

testa *n* (*pl* **testae**) the hard external coat of a seed.

testament *n* **1** (**Testament**) either of the two main divisions of the Bible. **2** a tangible proof of or tribute to something. **3** a will. **4** *archaic* a covenant between God and humanity. ➤➤ **testamentary** *adj.*

testate[1] *adj* having made a valid will.

testate[2] *n* a person who dies testate.

testator *n* a person who makes a will or leaves a valid will after his or her death.

test ban *n* a self-imposed ban on the testing of nuclear weapons.

test bed *n* a piece of equipment for testing a component separately from its intended working environment.

test card *n* a geometric pattern or fixed picture broadcast by a television transmitting station to facilitate the testing or adjustment of receivers.

test case *n* in law, a representative case whose outcome is likely to serve as a precedent.

test-drive *v* (*past tense* **test-drove,** *past part.* **test-driven**) to drive (a motor vehicle) before buying it in order to evaluate its suitability.

tester[1] *n* **1** a person or device that carries out tests. **2** a sample of a product, such as a cosmetic, for a prospective customer to try.

tester[2] *n* the canopy over a bed, pulpit, or altar.

testes *n* pl of TESTIS.

testicle *n* a testis, *esp* of a mammal and usu with its enclosing structures, e.g. the scrotum. ➤➤ **testicular** *adj.*

testify *v* (**-ies, -ied**) **1** to give evidence under oath as a witness in a court. **2** (*usu* + to) to serve as evidence or proof.

testimonial *n* **1** a letter of recommendation. **2** an expression of appreciation or esteem, e.g. in the form of a gift. **3** a sports match arranged in honour of and to raise money for a particular player.

testimony *n* (*pl* **-ies**) **1** a sworn statement or the evidence given by a witness in a court. **2** an outward sign; evidence.

testis *n* (*pl* **testes**) a male reproductive gland.

test match *n* any of a series of international matches, *esp* cricket matches.

testosterone *n* a male steroid hormone, produced by the testes or made synthetically, that induces and maintains male secondary sex characteristics.

test pilot *n* a pilot who specializes in putting new or experimental aircraft through manoeuvres designed to test them.

test tube *n* a thin glass tube closed at one end and used in chemistry, biology, etc.

test-tube baby *n* a baby conceived by artificial insemination taking place outside the mother's body.

testy *adj* (**-ier, -iest**) impatient or ill-humoured. ➤➤ **testily** *adv,* **testiness** *n.*

tetanic *adj* relating to or tending to produce tetanus or tetany.

tetanus *n* an infectious disease characterized by spasms of voluntary muscles, *esp* of the jaw.

tetany *n* muscle spasm usu associated with deficient secretion of parathyroid hormones.

tetchy *adj* (**-ier, -iest**) irritably or peevishly sensitive. ➤➤ **tetchily** *adv,* **tetchiness** *n.*

tête-à-tête[1] /,tet ah 'tet, ,tayt ah 'tayt/ *adv and adj* in private; private and intimate.

tête-à-tête[2] *n* a private conversation between two people.

tether[1] *n* a rope, chain, etc by which an animal is fastened so that it can move only within a set radius.

tether[2] *v* to fasten or restrain (an animal or person) by a tether.

tetra- *or* **tetr-** *comb. form* four or having four parts: *tetrahedron.*

tetrad *n* a group or arrangement of four cells, atoms, etc.

tetraethyl lead *n* a poisonous liquid formerly used as a petrol additive to prevent knocking in internal-combustion engines.

Tetragrammaton *n* the four Hebrew letters, usu transliterated YHWH or JHVH, used to refer to God in the Old Testament.

tetrahedron *n* (*pl* **tetrahedrons** *or* **tetrahedra**) a polyhedron with four faces. ➤➤ **tetrahedral** *adj.*

tetralogy *n* (*pl* **-ies**) a series of four closely related literary, cinematic, or musical works.

tetrameter *n* a line of verse consisting of four metrical feet.

tetraplegia *n* = QUADRIPLEGIA. ➤➤ **tetraplegic** *adj and n.*

tetrapod *n* **1** a vertebrate animal with two pairs of limbs or one in which these have been secondarily lost. **2** an object with four legs or supports.

tetrarch *n* in the Roman Empire, the governor of a quarter of a province or country.

tetrode *n* a thermionic valve that has four electrodes.

Teuton *n* **1** a member of an ancient Germanic people who lived in Jutland. **2** a German.

Teutonic *adj* **1** supposedly characteristic of the Germans. **2** relating to or characteristic of the Teutons.

Texan *n* a native or inhabitant of the US state of Texas. ➤➤ **Texan** *adj.*

Tex-Mex *adj* of food, music, etc: having a mixture of Mexican and Texan elements.

text[1] *n* **1a** printed or written words. **b** the main body of printed or written matter on a page or in a book, as opposed to illustrations, notes, etc. **2** the original written or printed words and form of a literary composition, as opposed to a revision or translation. **3** a literary or other work selected for special study. **4** a passage of Scripture chosen *esp* for the subject of a sermon or in authoritative support of a doctrine.

text[2] *v* to send a text message to.

Usage note
New means of communication sometimes bring in new ways – especially new space-and-money-saving ways – of writing English. The electric telegraph produced telegraphese (ARRIVED CREWE STOP DEPARTING STOCKPORT FRIDAY AM), and now e-mail and the text-message facility on mobile phones have engendered other abbreviated forms of expression. Formulas such as *4 sale* (= for sale) and *Y R U w8ing* (= why are you waiting?) have a practical space-saving value in the world of tiny hand-held devices, but they should not be used in place of ordinary full-length prose in normal writing.

textbook¹ *n* a book used in the study of a subject.

textbook² *adj* conforming to the principles or descriptions in textbooks; exemplary or typical: *This is a textbook case of insider dealing.*

textile *n* **1** cloth, *esp* a woven or knitted cloth. **2** (*used before a noun*) relating to fabrics or the making of cloth.

text message *n* a readable message sent from one mobile phone to another.

textual *adj* of or based on a text. ➤➤ **textually** *adv.*

textual criticism *n* **1** the study of a literary work that aims to establish the original text. **2** criticism of literature emphasizing a close reading and analysis of the text.

texture¹ *n* **1** the visual or tactile surface characteristics of something, *esp* fabric. **2a** the distinctive or identifying part or quality; character. **b** a pattern of musical sound created by notes or lines played or sung together. ➤➤ **textural** *adj.*

texture² *v* to give a particular texture to.

textured vegetable protein *n* a vegetable substance made from high-protein soya beans that is used as a meat substitute.

TGV *abbr train grande vitesse* (a high-speed train in France).

Th *abbr* the chemical symbol for thorium.

-th¹ *or* **-eth** *suffix* **1** forming ordinal numbers: *fortieth.* **2** forming nouns, denoting: fractions: *two hundredths.*

-th² *suffix* forming nouns, denoting: **1** the act or process of: *growth.* **2** the state or condition of: *filth.*

-th³ *suffix* see -ETH¹.

Thai /tie/ *n* (*pl* **Thai** *or* **Thais**) **1** a native or inhabitant of Thailand. **2** the national language of Thailand. ➤➤ **Thai** *adj.*

thalamus *n* (*pl* **thalami**) either of two egg-shaped masses in the base of the brain that together form a coordinating centre through which different nerve impulses are directed to appropriate parts of the brain cortex.

thalassaemia *n* a hereditary anaemia common in Mediterranean regions and characterized by abnormally small red blood cells.

thalassic *adj* relating to the sea.

thalassotherapy *n* a system of therapy using seawater.

thali /'taali/ *n* (*pl* **thalis**) in an Indian restaurant, a combination of dishes and side dishes served together.

thalidomide *n* a sedative and hypnotic drug found to cause malformation of infants born to mothers using it during pregnancy.

thalli *n* pl of THALLUS.

thallium *n* a white soft metallic chemical element chemically resembling lead that occurs naturally in some ores, and is used, in compounds, as a poison and in glass.

thallus *n* (*pl* **thalli** *or* **thalluses**) a body of a plant, alga, or fungus that is not differentiated into distinct tissues or parts, such as a stem or leaves.

than¹ *conj* **1** used with comparatives to introduce the second element in a comparison: *She is older than I am.* **2** used to introduce a rejected alternative to a particular course of action: *They would starve rather than beg.* **3** used after expressions such as *no sooner* to introduce what happened next: *No sooner had I sat down than the doorbell rang again.*

Usage note
My sister can run faster than I. This is the grammatically correct form – *than I* is short for *than I can*. However, the form that is considered correct by traditionalists sometimes sounds rather pedantic in speech: *My sister can run faster than I can* is correct, but *My sister can run faster than me* is more frequently used. Filling in the missing verb is often a good way of preserving grammar and avoiding awkwardness: *She spent far less time on it than he did.*

than² *prep* in comparison with: *Less than £10.*

thanatology *n* the study of medical, sociological, and psychological aspects and effects of death.

thane *n* **1** a free retainer of an Anglo-Saxon lord, *esp* one holding lands in exchange for military service. **2** a Scottish feudal lord.

thank *v* **1** to express gratitude to. **2** (*usu* + for) to hold responsible; to blame: *He had only himself to thank for his loss.* ✱ **thank God/goodness/heaven** used to express gratitude or relief for something. **thank one's lucky stars** to consider oneself very fortunate. **thank you** used as a conventional and polite formula for expressing gratitude.

thankful *adj* **1** conscious of having received a benefit; grateful. **2** feeling or expressing thanks. **3** pleased or glad. ➤➤ **thankfulness** *n.*

thankfully *adv* **1** in a thankful manner: *He sank down thankfully into the soft warm bed.* **2** it is a relief that: *But thankfully things have changed.*

thankless *adj* **1a** reaping neither profit nor appreciation. **b** futile. **2** not expressing or feeling gratitude.

thanks *pl n* **1** an expression of gratitude. **2** used as a somewhat informal but nonetheless courteous expression of gratitude. ✱ **no thanks to** not as a result of any action or goodwill on the part of. **thanks to 1** with the help of: *Thanks to modern medicine, life expectancy is increasing year by year.* **2** owing to: *Our arrival was delayed, thanks to the fog.*

thanksgiving *n* **1** an expression of gratefulness, *esp* to God. **2** (**Thanksgiving**) = THANKSGIVING DAY.

Thanksgiving Day *n* **1** the fourth Thursday in November observed as a public holiday in the USA. **2** the second Monday in October observed as a public holiday in Canada.

that¹ *pron* (*pl* **those**) **1** the thing or idea just mentioned: *That is a lie!* **2** a relatively distant person or thing introduced for observation or discussion: *Who is that?* **3** the kind or thing specified as follows: *The purest water is that produced by distillation.* **4** (*in pl*) the people; such: *There are those who think the time has already come.* **5** used to indicate emphatic agreement with or confirmation of an idea previously presented: *Is he a good worker? He is that.* ✱ **and (all) that** *informal* and everything connected with it. **like that 1** *informal* at once and without any apparent effort or difficulty. **2** *informal* apt to do that sort of thing or behave like that. **that is (to say)** used to introduce an explanation or clarification of what has just been said; in other words. **that's that** that concludes the matter.

that² *adj* (*pl* **those**) **1** denoting the person, thing, or idea specified, mentioned, or understood: *They've eaten all of that cake we bought.* **2** the one farther away or less immediately under observation: *This chair or that one?*

that³ *conj* **1** used to introduce a noun clause, e.g. as subject, object, or complement of a verb: *He said that he was afraid.* **2** used to introduce a subordinate clause expressing purpose, reason, or result: *She walked so fast that we couldn't keep up.* **3** used to introduce an exclamation, or to express a wish: *Oh, that he would come!*

that⁴ *pron* **1** used to introduce a restrictive relative clause that identifies or characterizes a particular person, thing, or group: *The book that you want is on the table.* **2** used as the object of a verb or of a following preposition: *the house that Jack built.* **3** at, in, on, by, with, for, or to which: *the reason that he came; the way that he spoke.*

that⁵ *adv* **1** to the extent indicated or understood: *a nail about that long.* **2** (*usu with the negative*) very; extremely: *It's not really that expensive.*

thatch¹ *v* to roof (a building) with thatch. ➤➤ **thatcher** *n.*

thatch² *n* **1** plant material such as straw or reeds used as a roof covering. **2** the hair on somebody's head.

Thatcherism *n* the political and economic policies associated with Margaret Thatcher, the former leader of the Conservative party in Britain and prime minister 1979–90. ➤➤ **Thatcherite** *adj and n.*

thaumaturge *n* a performer of miracles, *esp* a magician. ➤➤ **thaumaturgy** *n.*

thaw¹ *v* **1a** to go or cause to go from a frozen to a liquid state. **b** (*often* + out) to become less numb or stiff from cold as a result of exposure to warmth. **2** of the weather: to be warm enough to melt ice and snow. **3** to make or become less hostile. **4** to make or become less aloof, cold, or reserved.

thaw² *n* **1** the action, fact, or process of thawing. **2** a period of weather warm enough to thaw ice.

the¹ *definite article* **1a** used before nouns when the object or person in question has been previously referred to or is obvious from the circumstances: *Put the cat out.* **b** used to refer to somebody or something unique or universally recognized: *the pope.* **2** used before a noun to limit its application to that specified by what follows: *the University of London.* **3** used before the name of a familiar feature of daily life to indicate the person or thing in question is normally and readily available: *The postman is late today.* **4** used before a noun denoting a period of time to indicate the present one or the one under consideration: *book of the month.* **5** used before a singular noun to indicate generic use: *a history of the novel.* **6a** used before certain proper names: *the Rhine.* **b** used in the distinguishing titles given to some people, *esp* monarchs. **7** used in prepositional phrases to indicate that the following noun serves as a basis for computation: *sold by the kilo.* **8** used to transform an adjective or participle into a noun: *the British.*

the² *adv* **1** (*used with comparatives*) than before; than otherwise: *none the wiser.* **2** used with a pair of comparatives to indicate a relative relationship between them: *the sooner the better.* **3** used with superlatives: beyond all others: *I like this the best.*

theatre (*NAm* **theater**) *n* **1** a building specially constructed for the presentation of dramatic performances. **2a** dramatic literature or performances. **b** dramatic effectiveness or quality. **3** (**the theatre**) the world of actors, acting, and drama generally. **4** the place where significant events or actions take place. **5a** a room with rising tiers of seats, e.g. for lectures. **b** *Brit* = OPERATING THEATRE. **6** (*used before a noun*) in warfare, confined or appropriate to a limited sphere of operations.

theatrical *adj* **1** relating to the theatre or the presentation of plays. **2a** marked by exhibitionism; histrionic. **b** marked by artificiality, e.g. of emotion. ➤➤ **theatricality** *n,* **theatrically** *adv.*

theatricals *pl n* **1** the performance of plays. **2** theatrical behaviour.

theatrics *pl n* **1** the art of performing plays; theatrical technique. **2** showy or extravagant gestures, or theatrical behaviour.

thebe /'tebay/ *n* (*pl* **thebe**) a unit of currency in Botswana, worth 100th of a pula.

theca *n* (*pl* **thecae**) an enveloping sheath or case of an animal, or part of an animal's body.

thecodont *n* a reptile of the Triassic period believed to be an ancestor of the dinosaurs, birds, and crocodiles.

thee *pron* **1** *archaic or dialect* the objective case of THOU¹. **2** used by Quakers, *esp* among themselves: thou.

theft *n* the act or crime of stealing.

thegn *n* = THANE (1).

their *adj* **1a** belonging to or associated with them. **b** belonging to or associated with an indefinite singular person. **2** used in titles: *Their Royal Highnesses.*

Usage note

their, there, *or* **they're**? These three words, which are pronounced the same, are sometimes confused. *Their* is the possessive form of *they* (*It's their fault; They'll bring their own tools*). *There* is an adverb of place (*You'll find it over there*) and is used with the verb *to be* (*There is nothing I can do about it; Are there any more questions?*). *They're* is the shortened form of *they are*: *They're not quite ready yet.*

theirs *pron* the one or ones that belong to or are associated with them. ✱ **of theirs** belonging to or associated with them: *friends of theirs.*

theism *n* belief in the existence of a creator god immanent in the universe but transcending it. ➤➤ **theist** *n,* **theistic** *adj.*

them *pron* **1** used to refer to a previously mentioned group of people or things when the object of a verb or preposition. **2** used to refer to an indefinite singular person previously mentioned, when the object of a verb or preposition.

thematic *adj* relating to or constituting a theme. ➤➤ **thematically** *adv.*

theme¹ *n* **1** a subject or topic dealt with in a discursive or artistic work and usu forming a unifying thread running through it. **2a** a unifying concept in the planning or design of something. **b** (*used before a noun*) planned or designed around a single unifying concept: *a theme pub.* **3** a group of notes or melody forming the basis of a musical composition; a subject.

theme² *v* to design, create, or organize in accordance with a theme.

theme park *n* an amusement park in which the structures and settings are all based on a specific theme.

theme song *n* **1** a recurring melody in a musical play or in a film that characterizes the production or one of its characters. **2** a signature tune.

themself *pron* = THEMSELVES (2).

themselves *pron* **1** used reflexively or for emphasis to refer to the people, animals, or things that are the subject of the clause: *They were looking very pleased with themselves.* **2** used reflexively to refer to an indefinite singular person that is the subject of the clause: *We just prayed that nobody would hurt themselves.*

Usage note

themselves *and* **themself**. *Themselves* is the standard reflexive form of *they*: *I hope the children enjoyed themselves. Themself* is a 14th to 16th cent. form that has recently been revived for use as an equivalent to *they* meaning 'a person of either sex': *No one should blame themself for this tragedy.* This is a very controversial area of English usage where, in formal writing, it is often best to abide by what is universally approved or to take avoiding action: *Everyone ought to try it for himself or herself* or *Everyone ought to try it personally.* See also note at THEY.

---

then *adv* **1** at that time. **2a** soon after that; next. **b** besides or in addition. **3a** in that case: *Take it, then, if you want it so much.* **b** as may be inferred: *Your mind is made up, then?* **4** as a necessary consequence. **5** used after *but*: in fact; on the other hand. ✱ **then and there** at once; straight away.

thence *adv* **1** from there. **2** *formal* from that preceding fact or premise.

thenceforth *adv archaic or formal* from that time or point on.

thenceforward *adv* = THENCEFORTH.

theocentric *adj* having God as the central interest and ultimate concern.

theocracy *n* (*pl* **-ies**) government by immediate divine guidance or by officials regarded as divinely guided. ⯮⯮ **theocratic** *adj.*

theodicy *n* (*pl* **-ies**) the defence of the doctrines of God's goodness and omnipotence against arguments derived from the existence of evil.

theodolite *n* a surveyor's instrument for measuring horizontal and usu also vertical angles.

theogony *n* (*pl* **-ies**) an account of the origin and genealogy of the gods.

theologian *n* a specialist in theology.

theology *n* (*pl* **-ies**) **1** the study of God, *esp* by analysis of the origins and teachings of an organized religion. **2** a theological theory, system, or body of opinion. ⯮⯮ **theological** *adj,* **theologically** *adv,* **theologist** *n.*

theophany *n* (*pl* **-ies**) a visible manifestation of God or a god.

theorem *n* **1** a proposition in mathematics or logic deducible from other more basic propositions. **2** a rule or statement in algebra, geometry, etc expressed as a formula or equation.

theoretic *adj* = THEORETICAL.

theoretical *adj* **1a** relating to or having the character of theory; abstract. **b** confined to theory or speculation; speculative. **2** existing only in theory; hypothetical. ⯮⯮ **theoretically** *adv.*

theoretician *n* somebody who specializes in the theoretical aspects of a subject.

theorise *v* see THEORIZE.

theorist *n* = THEORETICIAN.

theorize *or* **-ise** *v* to form a theory; to speculate. ⯮⯮ **theorization** *n.*

theory *n* (*pl* **-ies**) **1** a belief, policy, or procedure forming the basis for action. **2a** the general or abstract principles of a subject. **b** a body of theorems presenting a concise systematic view of a subject. **3** a scientifically acceptable body of principles offered to explain a phenomenon. **4a** a hypothesis assumed for the sake of argument or investigation. **b** an unproved assumption; a conjecture. ✱ **in theory** on the basis of abstract principles or under ideal circumstances, but not necessarily in practice or reality.

theosophy *n* (*pl* **-ies**) a religious or philosophical system stressing the validity of mystical insight. ⯮⯮ **theosophical** *adj,* **theosophist** *n.*

therapeutic *adj* **1** relating to the treatment of disease or disorders by remedial agents or methods. **2** having a beneficial effect on a person's health. ⯮⯮ **therapeutically** *adv.*

therapeutics *pl n* (*used as sing.*) a branch of medicine dealing with the application of remedies to diseases.

therapsid *n* a reptile of the Permian and Triassic periods that is believed to be ancestral to the mammals.

therapy *n* (*pl* **-ies**) therapeutic treatment of bodily, mental, or social disorders, or a specific type of treatment. ⯮⯮ **therapist** *n.*

Theravada /therə'vaydə/ *n* a conservative and nontheistic branch of Buddhism viewing the original Pali scriptures alone as canonical: compare MAHAYANA.

there *adv* **1** in, at, or to that place. **2** on that point or in that particular respect. **3** used to draw attention to something. **4** used as an interjection to express satisfaction, approval, encouragement, or defiance. ✱ **so there** used to express defiance and emphasize a refusal. **there and then** at once.

Usage note

there, their, *or* **they're?** See note at THEIR.

---

thereabouts (*NAm also* **thereabout**) *adv* **1** in that vicinity. **2** near that time, number, degree, or quantity.

thereafter *adv formal* after that.

thereat *adv formal* **1** at that place. **2** because of or after that.

thereby *adv* by that means; as a result of which.

there'd *contr* **1** there had. **2** there would.

therefore *adv* **1** because of that; consequently. **2** as this proves.

therefrom *adv formal* from that or it.

therein *adv formal* in that; *esp* in that respect.

thereinafter *adv formal* in the following part of that document.

there'll *contr* **1** there will. **2** there shall.

thereof *adv formal* of that or it.

thereon *adv formal* on or onto that or it.

there's *contr* **1** there is. **2** there has.

thereto *adv formal* **1** to that place. **2** to that matter or document.

thereupon *adv formal* immediately after that.

therewith *adv* **1** *formal* with that or it. **2** *archaic* thereupon, forthwith.

therm *n* a quantity of heat equal to 100,000Btu (about 105,506MJ).

thermal[1] *adj* **1** relating to or caused by heat. **2** designed to prevent the dissipation of body heat. ⯮⯮ **thermally** *adv.*

thermal[2] *n* **1** a rising body of warm air. **2** (*in pl*) thermal underwear or clothing.

thermal capacity *n* the heat required to raise the temperature of a substance by unit temperature.

thermal imaging *n* a technique for detecting and producing a picture of an *esp* hidden heat source, used e.g. to find missing people or locate a target.

thermal spring *n* a hot spring.

thermic *adj* = THERMAL[1].

thermion *n* an electrically charged particle, *specif* an electron, emitted by an incandescent substance.

thermionic *adj* **1** relating to the emission of thermions. **2** denoting or relating to a device, e.g. a valve, that uses thermionic electrons as charge carriers.

thermionic tube *n* = THERMIONIC VALVE.

thermionic valve *n* an electron tube in which a regulated flow of electrons is produced by thermionic emission from a heated CATHODE (a conducting structure with a negative electric charge), used *esp* for controlling the flow of current in an electric circuit.

thermistor *n* a semiconducting electrical resistor whose resistance varies significantly with temperature.

thermobaric /,thuhmoh'barik/ *adj* denoting a weapon that destroys buildings and kills people by means of a massive wave of heat and pressure.

thermochromic *adj* able to change colour, reversibly, when heated or cooled.

thermocline *n* a layer of water in a lake, sea, etc that separates an upper warmer zone from a lower colder zone.

thermocouple *n* a combination of two conductors for producing a thermoelectric effect used in measuring temperature differences.

thermodynamics *pl n* (*used as sing. or pl*) the branch of physics dealing with the mechanical action of, or relations between, heat and other forms of energy. ➤➤ **thermodynamic** *adj*, **thermodynamically** *adv*.

thermoelectric *adj* producing electricity by means of differences in temperature.

thermogenesis *n* the production of heat by metabolic processes in the body. ➤➤ **thermogenic** *adj*.

thermogram *n* the record made by a thermograph.

thermograph *n* a temperature-measuring device that keeps a record of variations in temperature over a period or area. ➤➤ **thermographic** *adj*, **thermography** *n*.

thermoluminescence *n* phosphorescence developed in a previously irradiated substance when it is subsequently heated. ➤➤ **thermoluminescent** *adj*.

thermometer *n* an instrument for determining temperature, *esp* a glass bulb attached to a fine graduated tube of glass and containing a liquid, e.g. mercury, that rises and falls with changes of temperature.

thermonuclear *adj* relating to or making use of transformations occurring in the nucleus of low-atomic-weight atoms, e.g. hydrogen, at very high temperatures.

thermopile *n* a device that consists of a number of thermoelectric units combined so as to multiply their effect, used e.g. for measuring intensity of radiation or generating thermoelectric current.

thermoplastic *adj* capable of softening or melting when heated and of hardening again when cooled.

thermoregulation *n* the natural maintenance of the living body at a constant temperature.

Thermos *n trademark* a Thermos flask.

thermosetting *adj* capable of becoming permanently rigid when heated.

Thermos flask *n trademark* a cylindrical container with a vacuum between an inner and an outer wall used to keep material hot or cold.

thermosphere *n* the part of the earth's atmosphere above the mesosphere.

thermostat *n* an automatic device for regulating temperature. ➤➤ **thermostatic** *adj*, **thermostatically** *adv*.

theropod *n* a carnivorous dinosaur of a group that walked on two legs.

thesaurus *n* (*pl* **thesauri** *or* **thesauruses**) a book listing words and their synonyms.

these *pron* pl of THIS[1].

thesis *n* (*pl* **theses**) **1a** a proposition that a person offers to support and substantiate by argument. **b** a proposition to be proved or one advanced without proof; a hypothesis. **2** a dissertation embodying the results of original research; *specif* one submitted for a doctorate in Britain.

thespian[1] *adj* relating to acting, drama, or the theatre.

thespian[2] *n formal or humorous* an actor.

theta *n* the eighth letter of the Greek alphabet (Θ, θ), equivalent to roman th.

thew *n literary* (*usu in pl*) muscle or muscular power.

they *pron* **1a** used to refer to a previously mentioned group of people or things when the subject of a verb. **b** used to refer to an indefinite singular person previously mentioned, when the subject of a verb. **2a** used to refer to people in general. **b** used to refer to the authorities.

Usage note

The use of *they* as a singular pronoun meaning 'a person of either sex' has a very long history. It is no longer appropriate to use *he, him, his,* or *himself* after words like *everyone* or *no one,* but the forms *he or she, his or her* etc are undoubtedly often awkward to use. The use of *they, them* and *their* presents itself as an obvious and convenient solution – except that, traditionally, *they* is plural. A blanket objection to a singular *they* seems unreasonable. It is best perhaps to avoid it in formal writing and where the clash between singular and plural is very marked. *Everyone should do their best* is acceptable inasmuch as *everyone* is a plural concept if not a plural word. *A lawyer must respect their clients' confidence* is far less acceptable and could so easily be recast in unexceptionable form: *Lawyers must respect their clients' confidence.*

they'd *contr* **1** they had. **2** they would.

they'll *contr* **1** they will. **2** they shall.

they're *contr* they are.

Usage note

they're, their, *or* **there**? See note at THEIR.

they've *contr* they have.

thiamine *or* **thiamin** *n* a vitamin of the vitamin B complex, found *esp* in cereals and beans, that is essential to normal metabolism and nerve function and is widespread in plants and animals; vitamin B_1.

thick[1] *adj* **1a** having or being of relatively great depth or extent between opposite surfaces. **b** of comparatively large diameter in relation to length. **2a** containing closely-packed objects or material; dense. **b** great in number. **3a** not flowing or pouring easily; viscous. **b** not easy to see through, *esp* because foggy or misty. **4a** imperfectly articulated. **b** plainly apparent; marked. **5a** sluggish or dull. **b** *informal* obtuse or stupid. **6** *informal* on close terms; intimate. ✱ **a bit thick** *Brit, informal* unreasonable or unfair. **be as thick as thieves** *informal* to be very friendly or intimate with each other. **give somebody/get a thick ear** *Brit, informal* to give somebody/receive a blow on the ear as punishment. **lay it on thick 1** to overstate or exaggerate something. **2** to flatter somebody excessively. **thick and fast** in very quick succession. ➤➤ **thick** *adv*, **thickly** *adv*.

thick[2] *n* **1** the most crowded or active part. **2** the part of greatest thickness. ✱ **through thick and thin** in good times and bad times; in spite of every difficulty and obstacle.

thicken *v* **1** to make thick, compact, dense, or viscous. **2** to become thick or thicker. **3** to grow more complicated or intense: *The plot thickens.* ➤➤ **thickener** *n.*

thickening *n* **1** the act of making or becoming thick. **2** something used to thicken something else, e.g. flour to thicken gravy. **3** a thickened part or place.

thicket *n* a dense growth of shrubbery or small trees.

thickhead *n informal* a stupid person. ➤➤ **thick-headed** *adj.*

thickness *n* **1** the smallest of the three dimensions of a solid object, the distance through it as opposed to its length or height. **2** the thick part of something. **3** a layer or ply.

thickset *adj* **1** heavily built; burly. **2** placed close together, or growing thickly.

thick-skinned *adj* **1** callous or insensitive. **2** not easily provoked or upset.

thick-witted *adj* dull or stupid.

thief *n* (*pl* **thieves**) somebody who steals, *esp* secretly and without violence. ➤➤ **thievery** *n,* **thievish** *adj,* **thievishness** *n.*

thieve *v* to steal or rob.

thieves *n* pl of THIEF.

thigh *n* the part of the leg that extends from the hip to the knee and is supported by a single large bone.

thighbone *n* the femur.

thimble *n* a pitted metal or plastic cap or cover worn to protect the finger and to push the needle in sewing.

thimbleful *n* (*pl* **thimblefuls**) as much as a thimble will hold; a very small quantity.

thimblerig *n* a swindling trick in which a small ball or pea is quickly shifted from under one to another of three small cups to fool the spectator guessing its location. ➤➤ **thimblerigger** *n.*

thin[1] *adj* (**thinner, thinnest**) **1a** having little depth between opposite surfaces. **b** measuring little in cross section. **2** not dense or closely-packed. **3** without much flesh; lean. **4a** more rarefied than normal. **b** few in number. **5a** lacking substance or strength. **b** flimsy or unconvincing. **6a** somewhat feeble and lacking in resonance. **b** lacking in intensity or brilliance. **7** *informal* disappointingly poor or hard. ➤➤ **thin** *adv,* **thinly** *adv,* **thinness** *n.*

thin[2] *v* (**thinned, thinning**) **1** to make or become thin or thinner. **2** to reduce or diminish in strength, density, or number.

thine[1] *adj archaic* used *esp* before a vowel or h: thy.

thine[2] *pron* (*pl* **thine**) *archaic* the one or ones that belong to thee or are associated with thee.

thing *n* **1** an inanimate object as distinguished from a living being. **2a** a matter, affair, or concern. **b** an event or circumstance. **3a** an activity or action. **b** the aim of effort or activity. **4a** an object or entity not able to be precisely named. **b** (*in pl*) imaginary objects or entities. **5a** (*in pl*) possessions or effects. **b** (*in pl*) equipment or utensils, *esp* for a particular purpose. **6** an idea or notion. **7** used with an adjective expressing one's response, *esp* a sympathetic or envious one: an individual creature: *Poor thing!* **8** (*usu* **the thing**) the proper or fashionable way of behaving, talking, or dressing. **9** *informal* something, e.g. an activity, that offers special interest and satisfaction to the individual: *We let them do their own thing.*

thingamabob *n informal* = THINGAMAJIG.

thingamajig *or* **thingumajig** *n informal* something or somebody that is hard to classify or whose name is unknown or forgotten.

thingumajig *n* see THINGAMAJIG.

thingummy *n* (*pl* **-ies**) *informal* = THINGAMAJIG.

think[1] *v* (*past tense and past part.* **thought**) **1** to exercise one's mental powers; to create or work on ideas in the mind. **2** (+ of/about) to have in one's mind as the object of consideration or reflection. **3** (+ of) to hold a view, conception, or opinion: *He thinks of himself as a poet.* **4a** (+ of) to remember or call to mind. **b** (+ of) to have consideration for: *You must think first of your family.* **5** to expect or suspect: *Things turned out better than we thought possible.* **6** to have (something) as an opinion; to consider (that something is the case). **7** (*often* + over) to reflect on (something). **8** (+ up) to devise by thinking. **9** (+ out/through) to subject (something) to the processes of logical thought. ✱ **think better of** to decide on reflection to abandon (a plan). **think nothing of 1** to be entirely unconcerned about. **2** to disregard. **think twice** to consider very carefully. ➤➤ **thinkable** *adj,* **thinker** *n.*

think[2] *n informal* an act of thinking.

thinking[1] *n* opinion that is characteristic, e.g. of a period, group, or individual: *the current thinking on immigration.* ✱ **put/have on one's thinking cap** to ponder or reflect on something [from the cap formerly worn by judges while considering and announcing the sentence].

thinking[2] *adj* likely or able to give serious consideration to matters; intelligent or reflective.

think over *v* to ponder the advantages or disadvantages of; to consider.

think tank *n* (*used as sing. or pl*) a group of people formed as a consultative body to evolve new ideas and offer expert advice.

thinner *n* a solvent such as turpentine, *esp* one added to paint or varnish to thin it.

thin-skinned *adj* unduly susceptible to criticism or insult.

thiosulphate (*NAm* **thiosulfate**) *n* a salt or ester containing the group S_2O_3.

third *adj and n* **1** having the position in a sequence corresponding to the number three. **2** one of three equal parts of something. **3** the third forward gear of a motor vehicle. **4** in music, an interval of three degrees of a diatonic scale, or the combination of two notes at such an interval. **5** in Britain, a third-class honours degree. ➤➤ **thirdly** *adv.*

third age *n Brit* the later stages of human life, after middle age; old age.

third class *n* the third group in a classification.

third-class *adj* of a class or grade next below the second. ➤➤ **third-class** *adv.*

third degree *n* the subjection of a prisoner to torture to obtain information.

third-degree burn *n* a burn characterized by destruction of the skin and possibly the underlying tissues, loss of fluid, and sometimes shock.

third estate *n* the House of Commons.

third man *n* a fielding position in cricket lying near the boundary on the off side behind the slips.

third party *n* somebody other than the people principally involved in an action.

third-party *adj* of insurance: covering loss or damage sustained by somebody other than the insured.

third person *n* in grammar, any of the verb forms or pronouns that refer to somebody or something other than the speaker or writer of the utterance in which they occur or the one to whom that utterance is addressed: compare FIRST PERSON, PERSON, SECOND PERSON.

third rail *n* a rail for conducting current to an electric locomotive or train.

third-rate *adj* of extremely poor quality; mediocre.

third reading *n* **1** in the British parliament, the discussion of the committee's report on a bill. **2** the final stage of the consideration of a legislative bill before a vote.

third way *n* a policy or course of action between two extremes, *esp* a political programme that is neither of the right nor of the left, but aimed at reaching a consensus in the centre.

Third World *n* **1** (*used as sing. or pl*) a group of nations, *esp* in Africa, Asia, and Latin America, that were not formerly aligned with either the communist or the capitalist blocs: compare FIRST WORLD, SECOND WORLD. **2** the less industrialized nations of the world: compare FOURTH WORLD.

thirst[1] *n* **1** a desire or need to drink, or the sensation of dryness in the mouth and throat associated with this. **2** an ardent desire; a craving.

thirst[2] *v* **1** to feel thirsty. **2** to crave eagerly.

thirsty *adj* (**-ier, -iest**) **1a** feeling thirst. **b** causing thirst. **2** deficient in moisture; parched. **3** of a machine or engine: consuming large quantities of liquid fuel. **4** having a strong desire; avid. ➤➤ **thirstily** *adv*, **thirstiness** *n*.

thirteen *adj and n* the number 13. ➤➤ **thirteenth** *adj and n*.

thirty *adj and n* (*pl* **-ies**) **1** the number 30. **2** (*in pl*) the numbers 30 to 39. ➤➤ **thirtieth** *adj and n*.

this[1] *pron* (*pl* **these**) **1a** the thing or idea that has just been mentioned: *Who told you this?* **b** what is to be shown or stated: *Do it like this.* **2** a nearby person or thing introduced for observation or discussion: *This is iron and that is tin.*

this[2] *adj* (*pl* **these**) **1a** denoting the person, thing, or idea that is present or near in time or thought: *Who's this Mrs Fogg anyway?* **b** the nearer at hand or more immediately under observation: *this country.* **2a** constituting the immediate past or future period: *They have lived here these ten years.* **b** constituting what is to be shown or stated: *Have you heard this one?*

this[3] *adv* to the extent indicated or specified: *I've known her since she was this high.*

thistle *n* a prickly composite plant with dense heads of mostly tubular flowers, usu purple in colour.

thistledown *n* the fluffy hairs from the ripe flower head of a thistle.

thither *adv formal* to or towards that place.

thixotropy *n* the property of various gels of becoming fluid when disturbed, e.g. by shaking. ➤➤ **thixotropic** *adj*.

tho' *or* **tho** *adv or conj informal or literary* though.

thole *or* **tholepin** *n* a peg or pin; *esp* either of a pair of wooden pegs serving as rowlocks on a boat.

thong *n* **1** a narrow strip, *esp* of leather. **2** a skimpy bathing costume or piece of underwear resembling a G-string.

thoraces *n* pl of THORAX.

thoracic *adj* relating to or in the region of the thorax.

thorax *n* (*pl* **thoraxes** *or* **thoraces**) **1** the part of the mammalian body between the neck and the abdomen, or the cavity inside it in which the heart and lungs lie. **2** the division of the body of an insect, spider, etc corresponding to this.

thorium *n* a silver-white radioactive metallic chemical element that occurs naturally in various ores, and is used in alloys and as a source of nuclear energy.

thorn *n* **1** a short hard sharp-pointed plant part, usu projecting from a stem. **2** a woody plant, shrub, or tree with branches covered in thorns. **3** an orig runic letter þ used in Old and Middle English for either of the sounds /th/ or /dh/. ✱ **a thorn in somebody's flesh/side** a cause of great irritation.

thorny *adj* (**-ier, -iest**) **1** full of or covered in thorns. **2** full of difficulties or controversial points.

thorough *adj* **1** carried out with or showing great care, attention to detail, and a desire to leave nothing undone. **2** fully and without qualification as specified: *a thorough rogue.* ➤➤ **thoroughly** *adv*, **thoroughness** *n*.

thoroughbred[1] *adj* **1** bred from the best blood through a long line; purebred. **2** having the characteristics associated with good breeding or pedigree.

thoroughbred[2] *n* a purebred or pedigree animal.

thoroughfare *n* a public way, e.g. a road, street, or path.

thoroughgoing *adj* **1** extremely thorough or zealous. **2** absolute or utter: *a thoroughgoing villain.*

thorp *or* **thorpe** *n archaic* a village or hamlet.

those *pron and adj* pl of THAT[1] and THAT[2].

thou[1] *pron archaic or dialect* the one being addressed; you.

thou[2] *n* (*pl* **thou** *or* **thous**) **1** *informal* a thousand. **2** a unit of length equal to one thousandth of an inch (about 0.0254mm).

though[1] *adv* however; nevertheless.

though[2] *conj* **1** in spite of the fact that; while. **2** and yet; but.

thought[1] *v* past tense and past part. of THINK[1].

thought[2] *n* **1a** the act or process of thinking. **b** serious consideration. **2** an idea, opinion, concept, or intention. **3a** reasoning or conceptual power. **b** the intellectual product or the organized views of a period, place, group, or individual. **4** hope or expectation.

thoughtful *adj* **1a** having thoughts; absorbed in thought. **b** showing careful reasoned thinking. **2** showing concern for others. ➤➤ **thoughtfully** *adv*, **thoughtfulness** *n*.

thoughtless *adj* **1** lacking forethought; rash. **2** lacking concern for others. ➤➤ **thoughtlessly** *adv*, **thoughtlessness** *n*.

thousand *n* (*pl* **thousands** *or* **thousand**) **1** the number 1000. **2** an indefinitely large number. ➤➤ **thousand** *adj*, **thousandfold** *adj and adv*, **thousandth** *adj and n*.

Thousand Island dressing *n* a mayonnaise-based salad dressing flavoured with tomatoes, green peppers, and pimientos.

Thracian *n* a native or inhabitant of Thrace, an ancient country in SE Europe. ➤➤ **Thracian** *adj*.

thrall *n* a state of complete absorption or enslavement: *Her beauty held him in thrall.* ➤➤ **thraldom** (*NAm* **thralldom**) *n*.

thrash[1] *v* **1a** to beat soundly, *esp* with a stick or whip. **b** to defeat heavily or decisively. **2** (+ around/about) to move or stir about violently; to toss about.

thrash[2] *n* **1** an act of thrashing, *esp* in swimming. **2** *informal* a wild party. **3** = THRASH METAL.

thrash metal *n* a type of very loud, fast, and discordant rock music that combines features of punk and heavy metal.

thrash out *v* to discuss (e.g. a problem) exhaustively with a view to finding a solution.

thread[1] *n* **1** a filament, group of filaments twisted together, or continuous strand formed by spinning and twisting together short textile fibres. **2a** something, e.g. a thin stream of liquid, like a thread in length and narrowness. **b** a projecting spiral ridge, e.g. on a bolt or pipe, by which parts can be screwed together. **3** a pervasive recurring element: *a thread of melancholy marked all his writing.* **4** a series of linked messages replying to or commenting on each other on the Internet.

thread[2] *v* **1** to pass a thread through the eye of (a needle) or into position for use in (a machine). **2** to pass something into or through (something). **3** to string (things) together on a thread. **4** to form a screw thread on (e.g. a bolt) or in (e.g. a hole). **5** to make one's way cautiously. ⋙ **threader** *n.*

threadbare *adj* having the nap worn off so that the threads show; worn or shabby.

threadworm *n* a small usu parasitic nematode worm that infests the intestines of vertebrates.

thready *adj* (**-ier, -iest**) **1a** of threadlike appearance or substance; fibrous. **b** *esp* of a liquid: tending to form strands; viscid or stringy. **2** lacking in strength or vigour.

threat *n* **1** an indication of something unpleasant to come. **2** an expression of an intention to inflict punishment, injury, or damage. **3** something that is a source of imminent danger or harm.

threaten *v* **1** to utter threats against (somebody). **2a** to give ominous signs of (something). **b** to be a source of harm or danger to (somebody or something). ⋙ **threatening** *adj.*

three *n* the number 3. ⋙ **three** *adj,* **threefold** *adj and adv.*

three-dimensional *adj* **1** having three dimensions. **2** of an image or pictorial representation, *esp* when enhanced by stereoscopic means: giving the illusion of depth. **3** describing or being described in great depth; *esp* lifelike.

three-legged race *n* a race between pairs in which each contestant has one leg tied to one of his or her partner's legs.

three-line whip *n* an instruction from a party to its Members of Parliament that they must attend a debate and vote in the specified way.

threepence *n* the sum of three pence, *esp* three old British pence.

threepenny bit *n* a small twelve-sided coin worth three old pence.

three-piece *adj* consisting of or made in three, usu matching, pieces; *esp* denoting a suit of clothes consisting of a matching jacket, waistcoat, and trousers.

three-point turn *n* a method of turning a vehicle round in a narrow road by first turning obliquely forwards, then reversing, and finally turning forwards again.

three-quarter[1] *adj* **1** consisting of three fourths of the whole. **2** *esp* of a view of a rectangular object: including one side and one end.

three-quarter[2] *n* = THREE-QUARTER BACK.

three-quarter back *n* a player in rugby, positioned between the halfbacks and the fullback.

three-ring circus *n* **1** a circus with simultaneous performances in three rings. **2** something confusing.

three R's *pl n* the fundamentals taught in primary school; *esp* reading, writing, and arithmetic.

threescore *n and adj* sixty.

threesome *n* a group of three people or things.

threnody *n* (*pl* **-ies**) a song of lamentation, *esp* for the dead.

threonine *n* an amino acid found in most proteins and an essential constituent of the human diet.

thresh *v* **1** to separate the seeds from (a harvested plant) by beating it with a machine or flail. **2** = THRASH[1] (1).

thresher *n* **1** a person or machine that threshes. **2** a large shark reputed to thresh the water to round up fish on which it feeds using the greatly elongated curved upper lobe of its tail.

threshold *n* **1** the plank, stone, etc that lies under a door. **2a** the doorway or entrance to a building. **b** the point of entering or beginning. **3** a level, point, or value above which something is true or will take place.

threw *v* past tense of THROW[1].

thrice *adv archaic or literary* **1** three times. **2** (*usu in combination*) to a high degree: *thrice-blessed.*

thrift *n* **1** careful management, *esp* of money; frugality. **2** a tufted herbaceous plant, a sea-pink. ⋙ **thriftless** *adj.*

thrifty *adj* (**-ier, -iest**) showing careful management, *esp* of money. ⋙ **thriftily** *adv.*

thrill[1] *n* **1** a sudden feeling of pleasurable excitement. **2** something that causes such a feeling. **3** a sudden tremor of fear, nervousness, or emotion.

thrill[2] *v* **1** to experience or cause to experience a sudden tremor of excitement or emotion. **2** to tingle or throb. ⋙ **thrilling** *adj,* **thrillingly** *adv.*

thriller *n* a work of fiction or a film or drama characterized by a high degree of intrigue or suspense.

thrips *n* (*pl* **thrips**) a small sucking insect that feeds on and damages plants.

thrive *v* (*past tense* **throve** *or* **thrived,** *past part.* **thriven** *or* **thrived**) **1** to grow vigorously. **2** to gain in wealth or possessions. **3** (+ on) to enjoy or be stimulated by something. ⋙ **thriving** *adj.*

thro *or* **thro'** *prep, adv, and adj informal or literary* = THROUGH[1], THROUGH[2], and THROUGH[3].

throat *n* **1** the passage through the neck to the stomach and lungs. **2** the part of the neck in front of the spinal column. ✱ **at each other's throats** quarrelling violently.

throaty *adj* (**-ier, -iest**) uttered or produced low in the throat; hoarse or guttural. ⋙ **throatily** *adv,* **throatiness** *n.*

throb[1] *v* (**throbbed, throbbing**) **1** to pulsate with unusual force or rapidity. **2** of a pain: to come in waves that seem to beat or vibrate rhythmically.

throb[2] *n* a beat or pulse.

throe *n* **1** (*usu in pl*) a pang or spasm: *death throes; the throes of childbirth.* **2** (*in pl*) a hard or painful struggle: *The country is in the throes of revolutionary change.*

thrombi *n* pl of THROMBUS.

thrombosis *n* (*pl* **thromboses**) the formation or presence of a blood clot within a blood vessel. ⋙ **thrombotic** *adj.*

thrombus *n* (*pl* **thrombi**) a blood clot formed within a blood vessel and remaining attached to its place of origin.

throne[1] *n* **1** the chair of state of a sovereign or bishop. **2** (**the throne**) sovereignty.

throne[2] *v literary* to seat (somebody) on a throne.

throng[1] *n* a multitude of assembled people, *esp* when crowded together.

throng[2] *v* to crowd into (a place).

throstle *n Brit, archaic* = SONG THRUSH.

throttle[1] *n* **1** a valve for regulating the supply of a fluid, e.g. fuel, to an engine. **2** *archaic* **a** = THROAT. **b** = TRACHEA.

throttle[2] *v* **1a** to compress the throat of (somebody); to choke. **b** to kill by such action. **2a** to control the flow of (steam or fuel to an engine) by means of a valve. **b** (*usu* + back/down) to regulate, *esp* reduce the speed of (an engine), by such means.

through[1] *prep* **1** into at one side or point and out at the other. **2a** past a deceptive aspect of: *She saw through their deception.* **b** used to indicate passage into and out of during a treatment, handling, or process: *A thought flashed through my mind.* **3a** used to indicate means, agency, or intermediacy: by means of. **b** because of: *The plan failed through lack of preparation.* **4a** over or among the whole surface or extent of: *There are little farms scattered through the valley.* **b** used to indicate movement within a large expanse: *The ball flew through the air.* **c** used to indicate exposure to a set of conditions: *He put her through hell.* **5** (*usu* + all) during the entire period of; throughout. **6** used to indicate completion, exhaustion, or accomplishment.

through[2] *adv* **1** from one end or side to the other. **2a** all the way from beginning to end. **b** to a favourable or successful conclusion. **3** to the core; completely. **4** *chiefly Brit* in or into connection by telephone. ✱ **through and through** thoroughly; completely.

through[3] *adj* **1a** allowing a continuous journey from point of origin to destination without change or further payment: *a through train.* **b** starting at and destined for points outside a local zone: *through traffic.* **2** direct: *a through road.* **3** arrived at completion, cessation, or dismissal; finished: *I'm through with women.*

throughout[1] *adv* **1** in or to every part; everywhere: *Oddly, the house had been painted one colour throughout.* **2** during the whole time or action; from beginning to end: *His wife remained loyal throughout.*

throughout[2] *prep* **1** in or to every part of: *This is happening in cities throughout Europe.* **2** during the entire period of: *Backache troubled him throughout his life.*

throughput *n* the amount of material put through a process.

throve *v* past tense of THRIVE.

throw[1] *v* (*past tense* **threw,** *past part.* **thrown**) **1** to send with force through the air, *esp* by a forward motion of the hand and arm. **2** to cause (something or somebody) to move violently into or against something. **3a** to force (somebody) to fall to the ground. **b** of a horse: to unseat (its rider). **4** to put (somebody) in a specified position or condition, *esp* suddenly. **5a** (+ on/off) to put (clothing) on or off hurriedly. **b** to exert or apply (energy, effort, etc) to something. **6** to shape (a pot, etc) by hand on a potter's wheel. **7** to deliver (a punch). **8** to direct (light, a look, etc) in a certain direction. **9** to commit (oneself) for help, support, or protection. **10** to move (a lever or switch) so as to connect or disconnect parts of a mechanism. **11** to project (the voice) so that it seems to come from another source. **12** to give (a party). **13** to have (a tantrum or fit). **14** *informal* to confuse or disconcert (somebody). ✱ **be thrown back on** to have to rely on (something) when no other resources are available. **throw oneself into** to devote one's energy to (an activity). **throw one's weight about/around** *informal* to behave in a bullying or domineering manner. ⯮ **thrower** *n.*

throw[2] *n* **1a** the act or an instance of throwing. **b** a method of throwing an opponent in wrestling or judo. **2** a light cover, e.g. for a bed. **3** *informal* a chance, try, turn, etc.

throwaway *adj* **1** designed to be discarded after use; disposable. **2** of a remark: written or spoken with deliberate casualness.

throw away *v* **1** to get rid of as worthless or unwanted. **2a** to use in a foolish or wasteful manner. **b** to fail to take advantage of (an opportunity, etc).

throwback *n* reversion to an earlier genetic type or phase, or an individual exhibiting this.

throw in *v* **1** to add as a free item with other goods or services. **2** to introduce or interject (a remark, etc). ✱ **throw in the sponge/towel** to abandon a struggle or contest; to acknowledge defeat.

throw-in *n* in football, a throw made from the touchline to put the ball back in play after it has gone over the touchline.

thrown *v* past tense of THROW[1].

throw out *v* **1** to get rid of as worthless or unwanted. **2** to expel (somebody) abruptly from a room or building. **3** to dismiss or reject (a plan, proposal, etc).

throw over *v* to forsake or abandon (a lover, etc).

throw together *v* **1** to make or assemble hurriedly or in a makeshift way. **2** to cause (people) to meet casually or by chance.

throw up *v informal* to vomit.

thru *prep, adv, and adj NAm, informal* = THROUGH[1], THROUGH[2], and THROUGH[3].

thrum[1] *v* (**thrummed, thrumming**) **1** to make a monotonous hum. **2** to play (a stringed instrument, etc) in an idle or relaxed manner.

thrum[2] *n* a thrumming sound.

thrum[3] *n* a thread or fringe of threads, e.g. a fringe of warp threads left on a loom after the cloth has been removed.

thrush[1] *n* a small or medium-sized light-brown bird with a spotted breast, noted for its singing ability, e.g. a song thrush or mistle thrush.

thrush[2] *n* a whitish irritating fungal growth occurring on mucous membranes, *esp* in the mouth or vagina.

thrust[1] *v* (*past tense and past part.* **thrust**) **1** to push or drive (something or somebody) with force. **2** (*often* + into/through) to force an entrance or passage. **3** (+ on/upon) to press, force, or impose the acceptance of (something or somebody) on or upon somebody.

thrust[2] *n* **1a** a push or lunge with a pointed weapon. **b** a verbal attack. **c** a concerted military attack. **2** the salient or essential meaning. **3** a strong continued pressure, e.g.: **a** the force exerted by a propeller, jet engine, etc to give forward motion. **b** the sideways force of one part of a structure against another. **4** a forward or upward push. ⯮ **thruster** *n.*

thrusting *adj* aggressive or pushy.

thud *v* (**thudded, thudding**) to make a dull heavy sound. ⯮ **thud** *n.*

thug *n* **1** a violent person, *esp* a violent criminal. **2** (**Thug**) a member of a former religious sect in India given to robbery and murder. ⯮ **thuggery** *n,* **thuggish** *adj.*

thuggee *n* formerly, murder and robbery as practised by the Thugs of India.

thulium *n* a silver-grey metallic chemical element of the rare-earth group that occurs naturally in apatite, and is used in portable X-ray machines.

thumb[1] *n* the short thick digit of the hand that is next to the forefinger and is opposable to the other fingers. ✱ **under somebody's thumb** under somebody's control.

thumb[2] *v* **1a** to leaf through (pages) with the thumb. **b** to soil or wear (something) by repeated handling. **2** to request or obtain (a lift) in a passing vehicle by signalling with the thumb. ✱ **thumb one's nose at** *informal* to behave defiantly or contemptuously towards (somebody). ➤➤ **thumbed** *adj.*

thumb index *n* a series of notches cut in the unbound edge of a book for ease of reference.

thumbnail *n* **1** the nail of the thumb. **2** (*used before a noun*) brief; concise: *a thumbnail sketch.*

thumbscrew *n* an instrument of torture for squeezing the thumb.

thumbs-down *n informal* rejection, disapproval, or condemnation.

thumbs-up *n informal* approval; affirmation.

thumbtack *n NAm* = DRAWING PIN.

thump[1] *v* **1** to thrash or beat (somebody). **2** to strike or knock with a thump. **3** (+ out) to produce (music) mechanically or in a mechanical manner. **4a** to beat rapidly. **b** to make a thumping sound. ➤➤ **thumper** *n.*

thump[2] *n* a blow or knock with something blunt or heavy, or the sound of this.

thumping *adj* **1** *Brit, informal* impressively large or excellent. **2** throbbing: *a thumping headache.*

thunder[1] *n* **1** the low loud sound that follows a flash of lightning and is caused by sudden expansion of the air in the path of the electrical discharge. **2** a loud reverberating noise. ➤➤ **thundery** *adj.*

thunder[2] *v* **1a** (*usu impersonally*) to give forth thunder. **b** to make a sound like thunder. **2** to roar or shout.

thunderbolt *n* a single discharge of lightning with the accompanying thunder.

thunderclap *n* a clap of thunder.

thundercloud *n* a cloud charged with electricity and producing lightning and thunder.

thunderhead *n* a rounded mass of cumulonimbus cloud often appearing before a thunderstorm.

thundering *adj informal* very great, remarkable, or unusual.

thunderous *adj* **1** producing thunder. **2** making or accompanied by a noise like thunder. ➤➤ **thunderously** *adv.*

thunderstorm *n* a storm accompanied by lightning and thunder.

thunderstruck *adj* extremely surprised; astonished.

thurible *n* a censer.

Thurs. *abbr* Thursday.

Thursday *n* the day of the week following Wednesday.

thus *adv literary, formal* **1** because of this preceding fact or premise; consequently. **2** in the manner indicated; in this way. **3** to this degree or extent; so.

thwack[1] *v* to whack (somebody or something).

thwack[2] *n* a sharp blow; a whack.

thwart[1] *v* **1** to defeat the hopes or aspirations of. **2** to defeat (somebody's plans).

thwart[2] *n* a seat extending across a boat.

thy *adj archaic or dialect* of thee or thyself.

thyme *n* a plant of the mint family with small pungent aromatic leaves, *esp* a garden plant used in cooking as a seasoning.

thymi *n* pl of THYMUS.

thymine *n* a pyrimidine base that is one of the four bases whose order in the DNA chain codes genetic information: compare ADENINE, CYTOSINE, GUANINE, URACIL.

thymol *n* an antiseptic phenol made from thyme oil and used chiefly as a fungicide.

thymus *n* (*pl* **thymi**) a gland in the lower neck region that functions in the development of the body's immune system and in humans tends to atrophy after sexual maturity. ➤➤ **thymic** *adj.*

thyristor *n* a semiconductor device that acts as a switch or rectifier.

thyroid *n* (*also* **thyroid gland**) a large endocrine gland that lies at the base of the neck and produces hormones that increase the metabolic rate and influence growth and development.

thyroid-stimulating hormone *n* a hormone secreted by the front lobe of the pituitary gland that regulates the formation and secretion of thyroid hormones.

thyrotoxicosis *n* = HYPERTHYROIDISM.

thyrotrophin *or* **thyrotropin** *n* = THYROID-STIMULATING HORMONE.

thyroxine *or* **thyroxin** *n* the major hormone produced by the thyroid gland that is used to treat conditions in which the thyroid gland produces insufficient quantities of hormones.

thyself *pron archaic or dialect* that identical person that is thou; yourself.

Ti *abbr* the chemical symbol for titanium.

ti *n NAm* see TE.

tiara *n* **1** a decorative jewelled band worn on the head by women on formal occasions. **2** the three-tiered crown worn by the pope.

Tibetan *n* **1** a native or inhabitant of Tibet. **2** the language of Tibet. ➤➤ **Tibetan** *adj.*

tibia *n* (*pl* **tibiae** *or* **tibias**) the inner and usu larger of the two bones of the hind limb of higher vertebrates between the knee and ankle; the shinbone. ➤➤ **tibial** *adj.*

tic *n* a habitual spasmodic motion of particular muscles, *esp* of the face; a twitch.

tick[1] *n* **1** a small spot or mark, typically (√); *esp* one used to mark something as correct, to check an item on a list, etc. **2** a light rhythmic audible tap or beat, or a series of such sounds. **3** *Brit, informal* a moment or second.

tick[2] *v* **1** to mark with a written tick. **2** (*often* + off) to mark or count by ticks, or as if by ticks. **3** to make the sound of a tick. **4** *informal* to function or behave characteristically: *I'd like to know what makes him tick.*

tick[3] *n* **1** a bloodsucking arachnid that feeds on warm-blooded animals and often transmits infectious diseases. **2** *informal* a wingless bloodsucking insect, e.g. one that is parasitic on sheep.

tick[4] *n informal* credit; trust: *I bought it on tick.*

tick[5] *n* **1** a strong coarse fabric case of a mattress, pillow, or bolster. **2** = TICKING.

ticker *n* **1** *informal* **a** a watch. **b** the heart. **2** *NAm* a telegraphic receiving instrument that automatically prints out information on paper tape.

ticker tape *n* a paper tape on which a telegraphic receiving instrument prints out its information.

ticket[1] *n* **1** a printed card or piece of paper entitling its holder to the use of certain services, showing that a fare or admission has been paid, etc. **2** a tag or label. **3** an official notification issued to somebody who has violated a traffic regulation. **4** (**the ticket**) *informal* the correct, proper, or desirable thing.

ticket[2] *v* (**ticketed, ticketing**) to furnish or serve (somebody) with a ticket.

ticking *n* a strong linen or cotton fabric used for a case for a mattress or pillow.

tickle[1] *v* **1** to touch (a person or a body part) lightly and repeatedly so as to excite the surface nerves and cause uneasiness, laughter, or spasmodic movements. **2a** to excite (somebody) agreeably. **b** to provoke (somebody) to laughter. **3** to catch (a trout) in one's hands. **4** to have or cause a tingling or prickling sensation. ✱ **tickle pink** *informal* to amuse or delight. ➤➤ **tickler** *n*, **tickly** *adj.*

tickle[2] *n* **1** a tickling sensation. **2** the act or an instance of tickling.

ticklish *adj* **1** sensitive to tickling. **2** of a cough: causing irritation in the throat. **3** requiring delicate handling. **4** easily upset.

tick off *v Brit, informal* to scold or rebuke.

tick over *v* of an engine: to be turned on and running but with the transmission disengaged so that motion is impossible; to idle.

ticktacktoe *or* **tic-tac-toe** *n NAm* = NOUGHTS AND CROSSES.

tic tac man *n* in Britain, a bookmaker's assistant who signals changing odds at a race meeting by means of special hand signals.

tic-tac-toe *n* see TICKTACKTOE.

tidal *adj* of, caused by, or having tides. ➤➤ **tidally** *adv.*

tidal basin *n* a basin that only fills at high tide.

tidal bore *n* = BORE[5].

tidal wave *n* **1** an unusually high sea wave that sometimes follows an earthquake. **2** an unexpected, intense, and often widespread reaction.

tidbit *n NAm* see TITBIT.

tiddler *n Brit, informal* somebody or something small in comparison to others of the same kind, *esp* a small fish.

tiddly *adj* (**-ier, -iest**) *informal* **1** *chiefly Brit* slightly drunk. **2** *Brit* very small.

tiddlywinks *pl n* (*used as sing.*) a game in which the object is to flick small discs from a flat surface into a small container.

tide *n* **1** the periodic rise and fall of the surface of the sea that occurs twice a day and is caused by the gravitational attraction of the sun and moon. **2** something that fluctuates like the tides: *the tide of public opinion.* **3** (*in combination*) **a** a space of time; a period: *noontide.* **b** the season of an ecclesiastical anniversary or festival: *Whitsuntide.*

tideline *n* = TIDEMARK (1).

tidemark *n* **1** a mark left by or indicating the highest position of the tide. **2** *Brit* a mark left on a bath that shows the level reached by the water.

tide over *v* to enable (somebody) to surmount or withstand a difficulty, *esp* by giving them money.

tidewater *n* **1** water overflowing land at flood tide. **2** water affected by the ebb and flow of the tide.

tideway *n* a channel in which the tide runs.

tidings *pl n* a piece of news.

tidy[1] *adj* (**-ier, -iest**) **1a** neat and orderly in appearance or habits; well ordered and cared for. **b** methodical; precise. **2** *informal* large or substantial: *a tidy sum.* ➤➤ **tidily** *adv*, **tidiness** *n.*

tidy[2] *v* (**-ies, -ied**) to put in order; to make neat or tidy.

tidy[3] *n* (*pl* **-ies**) **1** the act or an instance of tidying. **2** a receptacle for odds and ends.

tidy away *v* to put away for the sake of tidiness.

tidy up *v* to make tidy or tidier. ➤➤ **tidy-up** *n.*

tie[1] *v* (**ties, tied, tying**) **1a** to fasten or attach with cord, string, etc. **b** to form a knot or bow in. **2** to make (something) by tying the constituent elements. **3** to make a bond or connection between (things or people). **4** (*often* + down) to restrict or limit the place or range of activity of (somebody). **5** to unite (people) in marriage. **6** to link (musical notes) with a tie. **7** to achieve an equal score in a game or contest.

tie[2] *n* **1** something that serves as a connecting link. **2** a narrow length of material designed to be worn round the neck and tied in a knot in the front. **3** a structural element, e.g. a rod or angle iron, holding two pieces together. **4** a curved line that joins two musical notes of the same pitch to denote a single sustained note with the time value of the two. **5a** *Brit* a match or game between two teams, players, etc. **b** a draw or dead heat in a contest.

tie-back *n* a decorative loop of fabric or cord used for draping a curtain to the side of a window.

tie break *n* a contest or game used to select a winner from among contestants with tied scores at the end of a previous contest or phase of a contest.

tie breaker *n* = TIE BREAK.

tied *adj* **1** *Brit* of a house: owned by an employer and reserved for occupancy by an employee. **2** of a public house: bound to sell only the products of the brewery that owns it or rents it out.

tie-dye *n* a hand method of producing patterns in textiles by tying portions of the fabric or yarn so that they will not absorb the dye.

tie in *v* **1** to bring (a thing) into harmony with another: *The illustrations are well tied in with the text.* **2** to be closely connected; to correspond: *That ties in with what I know already.*

tie-in *n* **1** something that ties in, relates, or connects. **2** a book published to coincide with a film or television production to which it is related in some way.

tiepin *n* a decorative pin used to hold a tie in place.

tier *n* **1** a row, rank, or layer of articles, *esp* any of two or more rows or ranks arranged one above another. **2** any of a series of levels, e.g. in an administration. ➤➤ **tiered** *adj.*

tierce *n* = TERCE.

tiercel *n* = TERCEL.

tie up *v* **1** to attach or fasten (somebody or something) securely. **2** to conclude (a matter) satisfactorily. **3** to invest (capital) in a way that leaves it unavailable for immediate use. **4** *informal* to keep (somebody) busy. **5** (+ with) to relate or correspond to something.

tie-up *n* a connection or association.

TIFF *abbr* in computing, tagged image file format.

tiff *n informal* a petty quarrel.

tiffin *n* in India, a meal or snack taken at midday or in the middle of the morning.

tig *n chiefly Brit* = TAG[3].

tiger *n* **1** a very large Asian cat having a tawny coat transversely striped with black. **2a** a country, *esp* in E Asia, with a dynamic economy. **b** (*used before a noun*) denoting such a dynamic economy.

tiger lily *n* an Asian lily commonly grown for its drooping orange-coloured flowers densely spotted with black.

tiger moth *n* a stout-bodied moth with broad striped or spotted wings.

tiger prawn *n* a large edible prawn of the Pacific and Indian oceans.

tiger shrimp *n* = TIGER PRAWN.

tight[1] *adj* **1a** fixed very firmly in place. **b** firmly stretched, drawn, or set. **c** of clothing: fitting closely or too closely. **2** (*often in combination*) so close or solid in structure as to prevent passage, e.g. of a liquid or gas. **3** firm in control, or characterized by such firmness. **4** packed, compressed, or condensed to the limit or near the limit. **5** set close together. **6** difficult to get through or out of. **7** evenly contested. **8a** scarce in proportion to demand: *tight money*. **b** characterized by such a scarcity: *a tight labour market*. **9** *informal* stingy or miserly. **10** *informal* intoxicated; drunk. **11** *informal* tense. **12** secretive. ✱ **run a tight ship** to keep strict control over an organization, etc. ➤➤ **tightly** *adv*, **tightness** *n*.

tight[2] *adv* **1** fast; tightly. **2** in a sound manner.

tighten *v* to make or become tight or tighter.

tightfisted *adj informal* reluctant to part with money.

tight-knit *adj* of a group of people: closely linked because of shared interests or affection.

tight-lipped *adj* **1** having the lips compressed, e.g. in determination. **2** reluctant to speak; taciturn.

tightrope *n* a rope or wire stretched taut for acrobats to perform on.

tights *pl n* a skintight garment covering each leg and foot and reaching to the waist.

tigress *n* a female tiger.

tike *n* see TYKE.

tikka *n* an Indian dish of pieces of meat or vegetables marinaded in spices and roasted on skewers.

tilapia *n* (*pl* **tilapias** *or* **tilapia**) an African freshwater fish used as food.

tilde /'tildə/ *n* a mark (˜) placed over the letter *n*, e.g. in Spanish *señor*, to denote the sound /ny/, or over vowels, e.g. in Portuguese *irmã*, to indicate nasality.

tile[1] *n* **1** a thin slab of fired clay, stone, or concrete shaped according to use, e.g. for roofs, floors, or walls. **2** a thin piece of resilient material, e.g. cork or linoleum, used for covering floors or walls. **3** a square or rectangular piece of plastic or other material, usu bearing special markings or figures, and used in mah-jong, Scrabble, etc. ✱ **on the tiles** *chiefly Brit* enjoying oneself socially.

tile[2] *v* **1** to cover (a surface) with tiles. **2** to arrange (windows) on a computer screen without overlapping. ➤➤ **tiler** *n*, **tiling** *n*.

till[1] *prep and conj* until.

Usage note

till *or* until? *Till* and *until* can be used interchangeably. *Until* is slightly more formal than *till* and in writing *until* is more commonly found than *till*.

till[2] *n* a cash register or drawer in which money is kept in a shop or bank.

till[3] *v* to work (land) by ploughing, sowing, and raising crops. ➤➤ **tillable** *adj*, **tillage** *n*, **tiller** *n*.

till[4] *n* glacial drift consisting of clay, sand, gravel, and boulders not deposited in distinct layers.

tiller *n* a lever used to turn the rudder of a boat from side to side.

tilt[1] *v* **1** to cause to slope or sit at an angle. **2** to shift so as to lean or incline. **3** formerly, to point or thrust (a lance) in a joust. **4a** *archaic* (+ with) to engage in combat with somebody using lances. **b** (+ at) to make an impetuous attack on something or somebody. ➤➤ **tilter** *n*.

tilt[2] *n* **1** the act or an instance of tilting, or the state of being tilted. **2** a sloping position or surface. **3a** formerly, a joust. **b** formerly, a thrust or charge with a lance or similar weapon. **4** (+ at) a written or verbal attack. ✱ **full tilt/at full tilt** with maximum speed.

tilth *n* **1** the state of being tilled. **2** the condition of tilled land.

timbale *n* a creamy mixture of meat, vegetables, etc baked in a cup-shaped mould.

timber *n* **1** wood suitable for carpentry or woodwork. **2** used interjectionally to warn of a falling tree. ➤➤ **timbered** *adj*.

timberline *n NAm* = TREE LINE.

timber wolf *n* a wolf formerly common over much of eastern N America.

timbre *n* the quality of tone distinctive of a particular singing voice or musical instrument.

timbrel *n archaic* a small hand drum or tambourine.

time[1] *n* **1a** the measurable period during which an action, process, or condition exists or continues. **b** a continuum in which events succeed one another. **2a** the point or period when something occurs. **b** the period required or taken for an action. **c** (**a time**) an indefinite period of time. **3a** a period set aside or suitable for an activity or event. **b** an appointed, fixed, or customary moment for something to happen, begin, or end. **c** *Brit* closing time in a public house as fixed by law. **4a** (*also in pl*) a historical period. **b** (*usu in pl*) conditions or circumstances prevalent during a period. **c** the expected moment of giving birth or dying. **d** the end or course of a future period. **5a** a period of apprenticeship. **b** *informal* a term of imprisonment. **6a** in music, a tempo. **b** in music, the grouping of the beats; the metre. **7** a moment, hour, day, or year as measured or indicated by a clock or calendar. **8a** any of a series of recurring instances or repeated actions. **b** (*in pl*) multiplied instances or fractional parts. **9** a person's specified experience, *esp* on a particular occasion: *We had a good time*. **10a** the hours or days occupied by one's work. **b** an hourly rate of pay. ✱ **behind the times** old-fashioned. **for the time being** for the present. **have no time for** to be unable or reluctant to spend time on (something or somebody). **have the time of one's life** to enjoy oneself very much. **in no time** very soon; very quickly. **in time 1** sufficiently early. **2** eventually. **3** in correct tempo. **make time** to find enough time to do something. **on time** at the appointed time. **time out of mind** from time immemorial.

time[2] *v* **1** to determine or record the time, duration, or speed of (something or somebody). **2** to arrange or set the time of. **3** to regulate the moment, speed, or duration of (something), *esp* to achieve the desired effect.

time and motion *adj* of or concerned with studying the efficiency of working methods, *esp* in industry.

time bomb *n* a bomb equipped with a timing device so that it will explode at a predetermined time.

time capsule *n* a capsule that has contemporary articles sealed in it and is then buried with the intention that people will open it in future years.

time-honoured *adj* sanctioned by custom or tradition.

time immemorial *n* time beyond living memory or historical record.

timekeeper *n* **1** somebody who records the time worked by employees, elapsed in a race, etc. **2a** an employee considered with regard to their record of conforming to the correct working hours. **b** a clock or watch considered in terms of its ability to keep time. ➤➤ **timekeeping** *n*.

time-lapse *adj* of or constituting a method of cinema photography in which a slow action is filmed in successive stages so as to appear speeded up on the screen.

timeless *adj* **1** not affected by time; ageless. **2** unending; eternal. ➤➤ **timelessly** *adv*, **timelessness** *n*.

time lock *n* a lock on a safe, etc with a timing mechanism that prevents it being opened before a certain time.

timely *adj* at an appropriate time. ⯮ **timeliness** *n.*

time machine *n* in science fiction, a machine that enables people to travel through time.

time out *v* of a computer or a program: to interrupt (an operation) automatically because a predetermined interval of time has elapsed.

time-out *n* in computing, the automatic interruption of an operation after a predetermined interval of time has elapsed.

timepiece *n* a clock, watch, etc.

timer[1] *n* **1** a device that can be set to give an indication, e.g. a sound when an interval of time has passed, or that starts or stops a device at predetermined times. **2** a timepiece, *esp* a stopwatch for timing races.

timer[2] *n* (*used in combinations*) somebody or something involved in something for the first, second, etc time: *a first-timer.*

times *prep* multiplied by.

time scale *n* the amount of time allotted for the completion of something.

timeserver *n* **1** somebody who fits behaviour and ideas to prevailing opinions or to their superiors' views. **2** somebody who makes little effort at work because they are just passing the time until they retire or leave.

timeshare *n* **1** = TIME-SHARING. **2** a share in a property under a time-sharing scheme.

time-sharing *n* a method of sharing holiday accommodation whereby people buy a share of a lease on a property, entitling them to spend a proportionate amount of time there each year.

time sheet *n* a sheet for recording the time spent working.

time signature *n* a sign placed on a musical staff or stave, being a fraction with the denominator indicating the kind of note taken as the unit for the beat and the numerator indicating the number of units per bar.

time switch *n* an electrical switch that operates automatically at a set time.

timetable[1] *n* a schedule showing a planned order or sequence of events.

timetable[2] *v* to arrange or provide for (something) in a timetable.

time travel *n* in science fiction, travel to another time, either in the past or in the future.

time trial *n* a race against the clock, *esp* in bicycle racing, in which competitors are successively timed over a set distance or in which distance travelled is measured for a set time.

time warp *n* an imaginary distortion of time in which the usual rules governing its progression do not apply.

timeworn *adj* **1** worn or impaired by time. **2** ancient; age-old.

timid *adj* (**timider, timidest**) lacking in courage, boldness, or self-confidence. ⯮ **timidity** *n,* **timidly** *adv,* **timidness** *n.*

timing *n* selection for maximum effect of the precise moment for doing something.

Timorese *n* (*pl* **Timorese**) a native or inhabitant of the island of Timor in the Malay Archipelago. ⯮ **Timorese** *adj.*

timorous *adj* timid or nervous. ⯮ **timorously** *adv,* **timorousness** *n.*

timothy *n* a European grass widely grown for hay.

timpani *or* **tympani** *pl n* a set of two or three kettledrums played by one performer, e.g. in an orchestra. ⯮ **timpanist** *n.*

tin[1] *n* **1** a silvery lustrous metallic element that is malleable and ductile at ordinary temperatures, occurs naturally in various ores, and is used for plating and in alloys. **2** *chiefly Brit* a hermetically sealed tinplate or aluminium container for preserving foods. **3** a tinplate or aluminium container in which food is cooked, *esp* in an oven. **4** (*used before a noun*) **a** made of tin or metal coated with tin. **b** made of corrugated iron: *a tin roof.* **c** made of lead or other metal: *a tin soldier.*

tin[2] *v* (**tinned, tinning**) **1** *chiefly Brit* to can (food). **2** to cover or plate with tin or a tin alloy. ⯮ **tinned** *adj.*

tinamou *n* (*pl* **tinamous** *or* **tinamou**) a small to medium-sized game bird of Central and S America.

tincture[1] *n* **1** a solution of a substance in alcohol for medicinal use. **2** a slight addition; a trace. **3** a heraldic metal, colour, or fur.

tincture[2] *v* (*usu in passive*) to tint or stain with a colour.

tinder *n* any combustible substance suitable for use as kindling.

tinderbox *n* formerly, a metal box for holding tinder and usu a flint and steel for striking a spark.

tine *n* **1** a prong, e.g. of a fork. **2** a pointed branch of an antler. ⯮ **tined** *adj.*

tinea *n* a fungal disease of the skin, *esp* ringworm.

tinfoil *n* a thin metal sheeting of tin, aluminium, or a tin alloy.

ting *v* to make a high-pitched sound like that made by a light tap on a crystal goblet. ⯮ **ting** *n.*

tinge[1] *v* (**tingeing** *or* **tinging**) **1** to colour (something) with a slight shade. **2** to impart a slight smell, taste, or other quality to.

tinge[2] *n* **1** a slight modifying quality; a trace. **2** a slight staining or suffusing colour.

tingle[1] *v* to feel or cause a stinging, prickling, or thrilling sensation. ⯮ **tingly** *adj.*

tingle[2] *n* a tingling sensation.

tin god *n* **1** a pompous and self-important person. **2** somebody who is unjustifiably esteemed or venerated.

tin hat *n chiefly Brit, informal* a metal military helmet.

tinker[1] *n* **1** an itinerant mender of household utensils. **2** *Brit, usu derog* a gypsy. **3** *Brit, informal* a mischievous child. **4** an act of tinkering.

tinker[2] *v* (+ with) to repair, adjust, or work with something in an unskilled or experimental manner. ⯮ **tinkerer** *n.*

tinker's cuss *or* **tinker's damn** ✱ **not give a tinker's cuss/damn** *informal* not to care at all.

tinkle[1] *v* **1** to make or cause to make a short light ringing sound. **2** *informal* to urinate. ⯮ **tinkly** *adj.*

tinkle[2] *n* **1** a tinkling sound. **2** *Brit, informal* a telephone call. **3** *informal* the act or an instance of urinating.

tinnitus *n* a ringing or roaring sensation in the ears that has no external cause.

tinny *adj* (**-ier, -iest**) **1** of, containing, or yielding tin. **2** having a thin metallic sound. **3a** not solid or durable; shoddy. **b** having the taste, smell, or appearance of tin. ⯮ **tinnily** *adv,* **tinniness** *n.*

tin opener *n Brit* a tool for opening tins.

tinplate *n* thin sheet iron or steel coated with tin.

tin-plate *v* to plate or coat (e.g. a metal sheet) with tin.

tin-pot *adj informal* paltry or inferior.

tinsel *n* **1** a thread, strip, or sheet of metal, plastic, or paper used to produce a glittering and sparkling effect, e.g. in decorations. **2** something superficial, showy, or glamorous. ➤➤ **tinselled** *adj.*

Tinseltown *n derog* Hollywood.

tinsmith *n* a person who works with sheet metal, e.g. tinplate.

tint[1] *n* **1a** a lighter or darker shade of a colour, *esp* one produced by adding white. **b** a usu slight or pale coloration; a hue. **2** hair dye. **3** a panel of light colour serving as background for printing on. **4** a small quantity or degree; a drop.

tint[2] *v* to apply a tint to; to colour.

tintinnabulation *n formal* **1** the ringing of bells. **2** a sound resembling that of bells.

tin whistle *n* = PENNY WHISTLE.

tiny[1] *adj* (**-ier, -iest**) very small or diminutive. ➤➤ **tinily** *adv,* **tininess** *n.*

tiny[2] *n* (*pl* **-ies**) *informal* a very young child.

tip[1] *n* **1** the pointed end of something. **2** a small piece or part serving as an end, cap, or point. ✱ **on the tip of one's tongue 1** about to be uttered. **2** not quite remembered.

tip[2] *v* (**tipped, tipping**) **1** to supply with a tip. **2** to cover or adorn the tip of. ➤➤ **tipped** *adj.*

tip[3] *v* (**tipped, tipping**) **1** (*often* + over) to overturn or upset. **2** (*often* + over) to topple. **3** to cant or tilt. **4** to lean or slant. **5** *Brit* to deposit or transfer (rubbish, etc) by tilting. ➤➤ **tipper** *n.*

tip[4] *n* **1** *Brit* a place for tipping something, e.g. rubbish; a dump. **2** *informal* a messy place.

tip[5] *n* a sum of money given in appreciation of a service performed.

tip[6] *v* (**tipped, tipping**) to give (somebody) a tip.

tip[7] *n* **1** a piece of useful or expert information. **2** a piece of inside information which, acted upon, may bring financial gain, e.g. by betting or investment.

tip[8] *v* (**tipped, tipping**) *Brit* to mention (somebody or something) as a prospective winner, success, or profitable investment.

tip off *v* to give a tip-off to.

tip-off *n informal* a tip given usu as a warning.

tipper *n* **1** a lorry, trailer, etc having a body that can be tipped on its chassis to empty the contents. **2** somebody who tips.

tippet *n* **1** a shoulder cape of fur or cloth often with hanging ends. **2** a long black scarf worn over the surplice by the clergy.

Tipp-Ex[1] *n Brit, trademark* correction fluid.

Tipp-Ex[2] *v* (*often* + out) to blot out (something typed or written) with correction fluid.

tipple[1] *v* to drink alcohol, *esp* continuously in small amounts. ➤➤ **tippler** *n.*

tipple[2] *n informal* an alcoholic drink.

tipstaff *n* an officer in certain law courts.

tipster *n* somebody who gives or sells tips, *esp* for gambling or speculation.

tipsy *adj* (**-ier, -iest**) slightly drunk. ➤➤ **tipsily** *adv,* **tipsiness** *n.*

tiptoe[1] *v* **1** to stand or walk on tiptoe. **2** to walk silently or stealthily with one's heels off the ground.

tiptoe[2] *n* the tip of a toe, or the ends of the toes: *walking on tiptoe.*

tip-top[1] *adj* excellent or first-rate.

tip-top[2] *n* the highest point or degree.

tirade *n* a long vehement speech or denunciation.

tiramisu /,tirəmi'sooh/ *n* an Italian dessert containing sponge cake, mascarpone cheese, and powdered chocolate.

tire[1] *v* **1** to become or cause to become tired. **2** (+ of) to become or cause to become bored or wearied.

tire[2] *n NAm* see TYRE.

tired *adj* **1** weary; fatigued. **2** (+ of) exasperated. **3a** trite; hackneyed. **b** lacking freshness. ➤➤ **tiredly** *adv,* **tiredness** *n.*

tireless *adj* indefatigable; untiring. ➤➤ **tirelessly** *adv,* **tirelessness** *n.*

tiresome *adj* wearisome; tedious. ➤➤ **tiresomely** *adv,* **tiresomeness** *n.*

tiro *n* (*pl* **-os**) see TYRO.

'tis *contr* it is.

tisane /ti'zan/ *n* an infusion of dried herbs used as a beverage or for medicinal effects.

tissue *n* **1** a cluster of cells, usu of a particular kind, together with their intercellular substance that form any of the structural materials of a plant or animal. **2** = TISSUE PAPER. **3** a paper handkerchief. **4a** a fine gauzy sheer fabric. **b** a web or network: *a tissue of lies.* ➤➤ **tissuey** *adj.*

tissue culture *n* the process or technique of growing fragments of body tissue in a sterile nourishing medium outside the organism.

tissue paper *n* a thin gauzy paper used for wrapping delicate objects.

tissue-typing *n* in organ transplantation, the identification of antigens in the donor and recipient to ensure that they are compatible.

tit[1] *n* a small tree-dwelling bird that lives on insects.

tit[2] *n* **1** *coarse slang* a woman's breast. **2** *Brit, informal* a stupid or despicable person.

titan *n* **1** somebody or something that is very large or strong. **2** somebody who is notable for outstanding achievement.

titanic *adj* colossal or gigantic. ➤➤ **titanically** *adv.*

titanium *n* a grey metallic chemical element that is light and strong, and is used in alloys and in aircraft manufacture etc.

titbit (*NAm* **tidbit**) *n* a choice or pleasing piece, e.g. of food or news.

titchy *adj* (**-ier, -iest**) *Brit, informal* small or short. ➤➤ **titch** *n.*

Word history

tich, titch small person or thing, from *Little Tich,* stage-name of Harry Ralph d.1928, English comedian, who was very small. Ralph got his nickname from his resemblance to Arthur Orton, known as *the Tichborne claimant,* who in 1866 claimed to be Roger Tichborne, heir to an English baronetcy, believed to have been lost at sea. Orton lost his case and was imprisoned for perjury.

titer *n NAm* see TITRE.

titfer *n Brit, informal* a hat.

tit for tat *n* an equivalent given in retaliation, e.g. for an injury or insult.

tithe[1] *n* **1** a tax or contribution of a tenth part of something, e.g. income, for the support of a religious establishment or other charitable work, *esp* such a tax formerly due in an English parish to support its church. **2** *archaic* a tenth.

tithe[2] *v* **1** to levy a tithe on. **2** to give a tithe of (one's income, etc).

tithe barn *n* a barn used to hold produce given in tithes.

titian *adj* (*also* **Titian**) *esp* of hair: reddish brown.

titillate *v* **1** to excite pleasurably; to arouse by stimulation. **2** *archaic* to tickle or caress. ➤➤ **titillating** *adj*, **titillation** *n*.

titivate *verb intrans or trans informal* to make smarter. ➤➤ **titivation** *n*.

title[1] *n* **1** the distinguishing name of a work of art, e.g. a book, film, or musical composition. **2** (*usu in pl*) written material introduced into a film or television programme to represent credits, dialogue, or fragments of narrative. **3** a descriptive name. **4** a hereditary or acquired appellation given to a person or family as a mark of rank, office, or attainment. **5** designation as champion. **6** legal ownership, or a document giving proof of this. **7a** something that justifies or substantiates a claim. **b** an alleged or recognized right.

title[2] *v* (*usu in passive*) **1** to provide a title for. **2** to designate or call by a title. ➤➤ **titled** *adj*.

title deed *n* the deed constituting evidence of ownership of property.

title role *n* the role in a film, play, etc that has the same name as the title of the production.

titmouse *n* (*pl* **titmice**) = TIT[1].

titrate *v* to subject (a substance) to titration.

titration *n* a method or the process of determining the strength of, or the concentration of a substance in, a solution by finding the amount of test liquid needed to bring about a complete reaction with a liquid of known concentration.

titre (*NAm* **titer**) *n* the strength of a solution or the concentration of a substance in solution as determined by titration.

titter[1] *v* to giggle or snigger.

titter[2] *n* a giggle or snigger.

tittle *n* a very small part.

tittle-tattle[1] *n* gossip.

tittle-tattle[2] *v* to gossip.

tittup *v* (**tittuped, tittuping**) *chiefly Brit* to move in a lively prancing manner.

titular *adj* **1** of or constituting a title. **2** in title only; nominal. ➤➤ **titularly** *adv*.

tiyin /tee'yin/ *n* (*pl* **tiyin** *or* **tiyins**) a unit of currency in Uzbekistan and Kyrgystan, worth 100th of a som.

tizzy *or* **tizz** *n* (*pl* **tizzies** *or* **tizzes**) *informal* a highly excited and confused state of mind.

T junction *or* **T-junction** *n* a junction formed by one road joining another at right angles.

TKO *abbr* in boxing, technical knockout.

Tl *abbr* the chemical symbol for thallium.

TLC *abbr informal* tender loving care.

TM *abbr* transcendental meditation.

Tm *abbr* the chemical symbol for thulium.

TN *abbr* Tennessee (US postal abbreviation).

TNT *n* trinitrotoluene, an inflammable derivative of toluene used as a high explosive.

to[1] *prep* **1** used to indicate a terminal point or destination: *a drive to the coast; the road to London.* **2** used to indicate a point in time before which a period is reckoned: *five minutes to five.* **3** used to indicate a purpose, result, or end: *It came to pieces; much to my surprise.* **4** used to indicate the one to which or for which something exists, is done, or directed: *She is kind to animals; a letter to my mother.* **5** used to indicate addition, connection, or possession: *Add 17 to 20; the key to the door.* **6** used to indicate accompaniment or response: *dancing to live music.* **7** used to indicate relationship or conformity: *next door to me; She won by 17 points to 11; true to type.* **8** used to introduce or stand for an infinite form of a verb: *She knows more than she used to.* **9** used to denote purpose: *He did it to annoy them.*

to[2] *adv* of a door or window: into contact, *esp* with the frame; shut. ✱ **to and fro** from one place to another; back and forth.

toad *n* **1** a tailless leaping amphibian that differs from the related frogs by living more on land and in having a shorter squatter body with a rough, dry, and warty skin. **2** a loathsome and contemptible person.

toadflax *n* a common Eurasian perennial plant typically having showy yellow and orange flowers.

toad-in-the-hole *n Brit* a dish of sausages baked in batter.

toadstool *n* a poisonous or inedible umbrella-shaped fungus.

toady[1] *n* (*pl* **-ies**) a sycophant.

toady[2] *v* (**-ies, -ied**) to behave as a toady; to be obsequious.

to-and-fro *v* (**toing-and-froing**) to move to and fro; to come and go.

toast[1] *n* **1** sliced bread browned on both sides by heat. **2a** the act or an instance of drinking in honour of somebody or something. **b** a highly popular or admired person.

toast[2] *v* **1** to make (bread, etc) crisp, hot, and brown by heat. **2** to warm (oneself, one's feet, etc) thoroughly, e.g. at a fire.

toast[3] *v* to drink to (somebody or something) as a toast.

toast[4] *v* of a DJ: to provide rap vocals over a pre-recorded music track, *esp* a reggae track.

toaster *n* an electrical appliance for toasting bread.

toastie *n Brit, informal* a toasted sandwich.

toasting fork *n* a long-handled fork on which bread is held for toasting in front of a fire.

toastmaster *or* **toastmistress** *n* a man or woman who presides at a banquet, proposes toasts, and introduces after-dinner speakers.

tobacco *n* (*pl* **-os**) the leaves of an American plant, prepared for use in smoking or chewing or as snuff.

tobacconist *n chiefly Brit* a person who sells tobacco.

to-be *adj* (*used after a noun, in combination*) future: *the bride-to-be.*

toboggan[1] *n* a long light sledge, usu curved up at the front and used for gliding downhill over snow or ice.

toboggan[2] *v* to ride on a toboggan. ➤➤ **tobogganist** *n*.

toby jug *n* a small jug or mug generally used for beer and shaped like a stout man with a cocked hat for the brim.

toccata /tə'kahtə/ *n* a musical composition in a free idiomatic style and characterized by rapid runs, usu for a keyboard instrument.

tocopherol *n* a fat-soluble compound found in leaves and oils made from seeds, the lack of which leads to infertility and the degeneration of muscle in many vertebrate animals; vitamin E.

tocsin *n archaic* an alarm bell rung as a warning.

tod ✱ **on one's tod** *Brit, informal* alone.

today[1] *adv* **1** on this day. **2** at the present time or age.

today[2] *n* **1** this day. **2** the present time or age.

toddle[1] *v* **1** of a very young child: to walk unsteadily. **2** *informal* to take a stroll; to saunter.

toddle[2] *n* the act or an instance of toddling.

toddler *n* a very young child who is just learning to walk.

toddy *n* (*pl* **-ies**) **1** a hot drink consisting of whisky or other spirits mixed with water, sugar, and spices. **2** the sap of certain palm trees, fermented into an alcoholic drink.

todger *n Brit, coarse slang* a penis.

to-do *n informal* bustle or fuss.

toe[1] *n* **1** any of the digits at the end of a human's or animal's foot. **2** a part like a toe in position or form. ✱ **on one's toes** alert; ready to act.

toe[2] *v* to touch, reach, or drive (somebody or something) with the toe. ✱ **toe the line** to conform rigorously to a rule or standard.

toea /ˈtoh·ə/ *n* (*pl* **toea**) a unit of currency in Papua New Guinea, worth 100th of a kina.

toe cap *n* a piece of steel or leather attached to the toe of a shoe or boot to reinforce or decorate it.

toehold *n* a hold or place of support for the toes, e.g. in climbing.

toenail *n* the nail of a toe.

toerag *n Brit, informal* a despicable person.

toff *n chiefly Brit, derog* a rich or upper-class person.

toffee *n* a sweet with a texture ranging from chewy to brittle, made by boiling sugar, water, and often butter.

toffee-apple *n* a toffee-covered apple held on a stick.

toffee-nosed *adj chiefly Brit, informal* stuck-up.

tofu *n* = BEAN CURD.

tog[1] *v* (**togged, togging**) *informal* (+ up/out) to dress (somebody), *esp* in fine clothing.

tog[2] *n Brit* a unit of thermal resistance used to measure the insulating properties of a quilt, a garment, etc.

toga *n* a loose outer garment worn in public by citizens of ancient Rome.

together[1] *adv* **1a** in or into one place, mass, collection, or group. **b** in joint agreement or cooperation; as a group. **2a** in or into contact, e.g. connection, collision, or union. **b** in or into association, relationship, or harmony: *colours that go well together.* **3a** at one time; simultaneously: *Everything happened together.* **b** in succession; without intermission: *She was depressed for days together.* **4** to or with each other: *His eyes are too close together.* ✱ **together with** with the addition of. ➤➤ **togetherness** *n.*

together[2] *adj informal* self-possessed and emotionally stable.

toggle[1] *n* **1** a piece or device for holding or securing, *esp* a crosspiece attached to a loop in a chain, rope, line, etc, to prevent slipping, to serve as a fastening, or as a grip for tightening. **2** in computing, a key or command for automatically alternating between operations.

toggle[2] *v* (+ between) in computing, to alternate automatically between operations using a toggle.

toggle switch *n* an electric switch that opens or closes a circuit by means of a projecting lever.

Togolese *n* (*pl* **Togolese**) a native or inhabitant of Togo. ➤➤ **Togolese** *adj.*

togs *pl n informal* clothes.

toil[1] *n* fatiguing labour.

toil[2] *v* **1** to work hard and long. **2** to proceed with laborious effort. ➤➤ **toiler** *n.*

toil[3] *n* (*usu in pl*) something by or with which one is held fast or inextricably involved: *He was caught in the toils of the law.*

toile /twahl/ *n* **1** a muslin model of a garment. **2** a plain or simple twill weave fabric, *esp* linen.

toilet *n* **1a** a fixture for receiving and disposing of faeces and urine. **b** a room or compartment containing a toilet and sometimes a washbasin. **2** *archaic or literary* the act or process of dressing and grooming oneself.

toiletry *n* (*pl* **-ies**) (*usu in pl*) an article or preparation used in washing, grooming, etc.

toilet-train *v* to give (a young child) toilet training.

toilet training *n* the process of training a young child to use the toilet.

toilet water *n* liquid containing a high percentage of alcohol, used as a light perfume.

toilsome *adj archaic or literary* involving fatiguing labour.

to-ing and fro-ing *n* (*pl* **to-ings and fro-ings**) bustling unproductive activity.

Tokay /tohˈkay/ *n* a sweet dark gold wine made near Tokaj in Hungary.

toke[1] *n informal* a puff on a cigarette or pipe containing marijuana.

toke[2] *v informal* to take a puff on a cigarette or pipe containing marijuana.

token[1] *n* **1** an outward sign or expression, e.g. of an emotion. **2a** *archaic* something given or shown as a guarantee, e.g. of authority, right, or identity. **b** a souvenir or keepsake. **3** a coinlike piece issued for use in place of money, e.g. for a bus fare. **4** a certified statement redeemable for a specified form of merchandise to the amount stated thereon. ✱ **by the same token** furthermore and for the same reason.

token[2] *adj* **1** done or given as a token, *esp* in partial fulfilment of an obligation or engagement. **2** done or given merely for show.

tokenism *n* the making of only a token effort. ➤➤ **tokenistic** *adj.*

tolar /ˈtolah/ *n* the basic monetary unit of Slovenia.

told *v* past tense and past part. of TELL.

tolerable *adj* **1** capable of being borne or endured. **2** moderately good or agreeable. ➤➤ **tolerability** *n,* **tolerably** *adv.*

tolerance *n* **1a** the act or fact of allowing something; toleration. **b** indulgence for beliefs or practices differing from one's own. **2** the ability to endure or adapt physiologically to the effects of a drug, virus, radiation, etc. **3** an allowable variation from a standard dimension.

tolerant *adj* **1** inclined to tolerate, *esp* marked by forbearance or endurance. **2** exhibiting tolerance, e.g. to a drug or environmental condition. ➤➤ **tolerantly** *adv.*

tolerate *v* **1** to endure or resist the action of (a drug, etc) without grave or lasting injury. **2** to allow or endure (something or somebody) without prohibition, hindrance, or contradiction. ➤➤ **toleration** *n.*

toll[1] *n* **1** a fee paid for some right or privilege, e.g. of passing over a highway or bridge, or for services rendered. **2** a grievous or ruinous price, *esp* cost in life or health.

toll[2] *v* **1** to sound (a bell) by pulling the rope. **2** to signal or announce by means of a tolled bell. **3** of a bell: to sound with slow measured strokes.

toll[3] *n* the sound of a tolling bell.

tollbooth *n* **1** a booth, e.g. on a bridge, where tolls are paid. **2** *Scot, archaic* a town hall. **3** *Scot, archaic* a jail.

tollgate *n* a barrier across a road to prevent passage until a toll is paid.

Toltec *n* a member of a Nahuatlan people of central and S Mexico. ➤➤ **Toltecan** *adj.*

toluene *n* a toxic inflammable hydrocarbon that is used as a solvent and in organic synthesis.

Tom, Dick, and Harry *or* **Tom, Dick, or Harry** *n* people taken at random.

tom *n* the male of various animals, *esp* a tomcat.

tomahawk *n* a light axe used by Native Americans as a throwing or hand weapon.

tomato *n* (*pl* **-oes**) a rounded red, yellow, or green pulpy fruit, used as a vegetable, *esp* in salads.

tomb *n* **1a** a chamber or vault for the dead, built either above or below ground and usu serving as a memorial. **b** an excavation in which a corpse is buried. **2** (**the tomb**) *literary* the state of being dead.

tombola *n Brit* a lottery in which people buy tickets which may entitle them to a prize.

tomboy *n* a girl who behaves in a manner conventionally thought of as typical of a boy. ➤➤ **tomboyish** *adj.*

tombstone *n* = GRAVESTONE.

tomcat *n* a male cat.

Tom Collins *n* a tall iced drink consisting of a gin base with lime, lemon juice, or soda and sugar.

tome *n formal* a book, *esp* a large scholarly one.

tomfoolery *n* foolish trifling; nonsense.

Tommy *n* (*pl* **-ies**) *informal* a British private soldier.

tommy gun *n* a submachine gun.

tomography *n* a diagnostic technique using X-ray photographs in which the shadows of structures in front of and behind the section under scrutiny do not show. ➤➤ **tomogram** *n.*

tomorrow[1] *adv* **1** on the day after today. **2** in the future.

tomorrow[2] *n* **1** the day after today. **2** the future.

tomtit *n* **1** any of various small active birds. **2** *Brit* a blue tit.

tom-tom *n* a long narrow drum commonly beaten with the hands.

-tomy *comb. form* forming nouns, denoting: incision; cutting: *laparotomy.*

ton *n* **1a** a unit of weight equal to 2240lb (about 1016kg); a long ton. **b** a metric ton. **c** a unit approximately equal to the volume of one long ton of seawater, used in reckoning the displacement of ships, and equal to 0.99 cubic m (35 cubic ft); a displacement ton. **2** *informal* (*also in pl*) a great quantity. **3** *chiefly Brit, informal* a group, score, or speed of 100.

tonal *adj* **1** of tone, tonality, or tonicity. **2** having tonality. ➤➤ **tonally** *adv.*

tonality *n* (*pl* **-ies**) **1** the organization of a musical composition in relation to its tonic key. **2** the arrangement or interrelation of the colours or shades of a picture.

tondo *n* (*pl* **tondi**) a circular painting or relief.

tone[1] *n* **1** a vocal or musical sound, *esp* one of a specified quality: *He spoke in low tones.* **2** an accent or inflection of the voice expressive of a mood or emotion. **3** style or manner of verbal expression: *It seemed wise to adopt a conciliatory tone.* **4a** a sound of a definite pitch. **b** a musical interval comprising two semitones. **5a** colour quality or value. **b** the colour that appreciably modifies a hue or white or black. **6** the general effect of light, shade, and colour in a picture. **7a** normal tension or responsiveness to stimuli. **b** the state of a living body in which the functions are healthy and performed with due vigour. **8** prevailing character, quality, or trend, e.g. of morals: *He lowered the tone of the discussion.* ➤➤ **toneless** *adj,* **tonelessly** *adv.*

tone[2] *v* **1** (*often* + up) to impart tone to (something or somebody). **2** (+ with) to blend or harmonize in colour with something. ➤➤ **toned** *adj.*

tone arm *n* the movable arm of a record player or deck that carries the pickup and permits tracking.

tone-deaf *adj* relatively insensitive to musical pitch.

tone down *v* to soften or reduce in colour, intensity, violence, loudness, or force.

tone poem *n* an extended orchestral composition based on a legend, tale, etc.

toner *n* **1** a cosmetic preparation applied to the skin to reduce oiliness. **2** a solution used to impart colour to a silver photographic image. **3** a substance used to develop a xerographic (dry-photocopied; see XEROGRAPHY) image.

tone-row *n* a series of chromatic notes within an octave placed in a fixed order that form the basis of a serial musical composition.

tong *n* a Chinese secret society or fraternal organization formerly notorious for gang warfare.

Tongan *n* **1** a native or inhabitant of the Tonga Islands in the S Pacific. **2** the language of the Tongans. ➤➤ **Tongan** *adj.*

tongs *pl n* any of various grasping devices consisting commonly of two pieces joined at one end by a pivot or hinged like scissors.

tongue[1] *n* **1** a fleshy muscular movable organ in the mouth that bears sensory end organs and small glands and functions in tasting and swallowing food and, in human beings, as a speech organ. **2** the tongue of an ox, sheep, etc used as food. **3a** manner or quality of utterance: *a sharp tongue.* **b** a language. **c** the ability to speak: *Have you lost your tongue?* **d** (*usu in pl*) ecstatic utterance, *esp* in Christian worship, of unintelligible sounds or of a language that the speaker does not know. **4** a long narrow strip of land projecting into a body of water. **5 a** the flap under the lacing or buckles on the front of a shoe or boot. **b** a piece of metal suspended inside a bell so as to strike against the sides as the bell is swung. **c** the reed of a musical instrument or organ pipe. **6** the rib on one edge of a board that fits into a corresponding groove in an edge of another board to make a flush joint. ✱ **hold one's tongue** to keep quiet; to say nothing. **with one's tongue hanging out** showing eagerness. **with one's tongue in one's cheek** in a tongue-in-cheek manner.

tongue[2] *v* (**tongues, tongued, tonguing**) **1** to articulate (notes) on a wind instrument by successively interrupting the stream of wind with the action of the tongue. **2** to touch or lick with the tongue.

tongue and groove *n* a joint made by a projecting rib on one edge of a board fitting into a corresponding groove on the edge of another board.

tongue-in-cheek *adj* characterized by irony or whimsical exaggeration. ➤➤ **tongue in cheek** *adv.*

tongue-lashing *n* a scolding or rebuke.

tongue-tied *adj* unable to speak freely, e.g. because of shyness.

tongue twister *n* a word or phrase difficult to articulate because of several similar consonantal sounds, e.g. 'She sells seashells on the seashore'.

tonic[1] *n* **1a** something, e.g. a medicine, that increases body tone. **b** something that invigorates, refreshes, or stimulates. **c** = TONIC WATER. **2** in music, the first note of a diatonic scale.

tonic[2] *adj* of or based on the first note of a scale.

tonicity *n* the property of possessing tone; *esp* healthy vigour of body or mind.

tonic sol-fa *n* a system of solmization that replaces the normal notation with sol-fa syllables.

tonic water *n* a carbonated slightly bitter-tasting mineral water flavoured with a small amount of quinine, lemon, and lime.

tonight[1] *adv* on this night or the night following today.

tonight[2] *n* this night or the night following today.

tonnage *n* **1** total weight in tons shipped, carried, or produced. **2** the size or carrying capacity of a ship in tons.

tonne *n* a metric unit of weight equal to 1000kg.

tonneau /'tonoh/ *n* (*pl* **tonneaus**) **1** the rear seating compartment of a motor car. **2** a cover used to protect the seats in an open-topped vehicle.

tons *adv Brit, informal* a great deal.

tonsil *n* either of a pair of small oval masses of lymphoid tissue that lie one on each side of the throat at the back of the mouth.

tonsil hockey *n informal* passionate kissing.

tonsillectomy *n* (*pl* **-ies**) the surgical removal of the tonsils.

tonsillitis *n* inflammation of the tonsils.

tonsorial *adj formal* of hairdressers or hairdressing.

tonsure[1] *n* the shaved patch on a monk's or other cleric's head.

tonsure[2] *v* to shave the head of (a monk or other cleric), *esp* to confer the tonsure on them.

ton-up *adj Brit, informal* denoting a person who has achieved a score or speed of 100.

Tony *n* (*pl* **Tonys**) in the USA, any of a number of awards given for notable achievement in the theatre.

too *adv* **1a** to a regrettable degree; excessively: *It's too large a house for us.* **b** to a higher degree than meets a standard: *She's too pretty for words.* **c** *informal* very: *You're too kind.* **2** also; in addition: *They sold the house and the furniture too.*

took *v* past tense of TAKE[1].

tool[1] *n* **1** an implement that is used to carry out work of a mechanical nature, e.g. cutting, levering, or digging. **2** something, e.g. an instrument or apparatus, used in performing an operation, or necessary for the practice of a vocation or profession. **3** somebody who is used or manipulated by another.

tool[2] *v* **1** (*usu in passive*) to work, shape, or finish (something) with a tool, *esp* to letter or ornament (leather, etc) by means of hand tools. **2** (*often* + up) to equip (a plant or industry) with tools, machines, and instruments for production. **3** *Brit, informal* (+ up) to be or become armed. **4** *informal* to drive or ride.

toolbar *n* a row or block of icons on a computer screen which can be clicked on to perform certain functions.

toolmaker *n* a skilled worker who makes, repairs, maintains, and calibrates the tools and instruments of a machine shop.

toot *v* **1** of a horn, etc: to produce a short blast or similar sound. **2** to cause (an instrument, etc) to produce a short blast. ⋙ **toot** *n.*

tooth *n* (*pl* **teeth**) **1a** any of the hard bony structures in the jaws of vertebrates that are used for biting and chewing food. **b** any of various hard and sharp projecting parts about the mouth of an invertebrate. **2** a taste or liking. **3a** a projection like the tooth of an animal. **b** any of the regular projections on the rim of a cogwheel. **4** (*in pl*) effective means of enforcement. ✻ **get one's teeth into something** *informal* to begin to understand and derive satisfaction from something. **in the teeth of** in direct opposition to. **set somebody's teeth on edge** to cause a jarringly unpleasant physical reaction in somebody. **sink one's teeth into something** *informal* to do something energetically and enthusiastically. **tooth and nail** with every available means: *She would fight tooth and nail to protect her child.* **to the teeth** *informal* to a great or the greatest extent: *Her bodyguards were armed to the teeth.* ⋙ **toothless** *adj.*

toothache *n* pain in a tooth.

toothbrush *n* a brush for cleaning the teeth.

toothcomb ✻ **with a fine toothcomb** *Brit* thoroughly.

toothed whale *n* a whale with numerous simple conical teeth.

tooth fairy *n* (**the tooth fairy**) a fairy said to remove children's milk teeth from under their pillow and leave money in its place.

toothpaste *n* a paste for cleaning the teeth.

toothpick *n* a pointed instrument for removing food particles lodged between the teeth.

toothsome *adj* **1** of food: delicious. **2** *informal* sexually attractive.

toothy *adj* (**-ier, -iest**) having or showing prominent teeth. ⋙ **toothily** *adv.*

tootle *v* **1** to toot gently or continuously. **2** *informal* to drive or move along in a leisurely manner. ⋙ **tootle** *n.*

tootsy *or* **tootsie** *n* (*pl* **-ies**) used chiefly to children: a foot or toe.

top[1] *n* **1a** the highest point, level, or part of something. **b** the upper end, edge, or surface. **2** a garment worn on the upper body. **3** a fitted or attached part serving as an upper piece, lid, or covering. **4a** the highest position, e.g. in rank or achievement. **b** somebody or something in the highest position. **5** (**the top**) the highest degree or pitch conceivable or attained; the acme or pinnacle. **6** a platform surrounding the head of a ship's mast. ✻ **off the top of one's head** without taking time to think about or research the matter; impromptu. **on top 1a** resting on the highest point or surface of something. **b** uppermost. **2** in a dominant position. **on top of 1** placed on or above the highest part of something. **2** in control of. **3** informed about. **4** in sudden and unexpected proximity to. **5** in addition to. **on top of the world** in high spirits. **over the top** exaggerated; *esp* excessively dramatic.

top[2] *v* (**topped, topping**) **1a** to be or become higher than. **b** to exceed or surpass. **c** to be superior to. **d** to gain ascendancy over. **2a** to cover with a top or on the top; to provide, form, or serve as a top for. **b** to supply with a decorative or protective finish or final touch. **3** to cut the top off (something). **4a** to rise to, reach, or be at the top of. **b** to go over the top of; to clear or surmount. **5** to strike (a ball) above the centre, thereby imparting topspin. **6** *informal* to kill (somebody), *esp* by hanging. ✻ **top and tail** *Brit* to cut the ends off (a fruit or vegetable).

top[3] *adj* **1** of or at the top. **2** foremost or leading. **3** of the highest quality, amount, or degree.

top[4] *n* a child's toy that has a tapering point on which it is made to spin.

topaz[1] *n* **1** a mineral that is predominantly a silicate of aluminium, usu occurs in variously coloured translucent or transparent crystals, and is used as a gem. **2a** a yellow sapphire. **b** a yellow quartz, e.g. cairngorm or citrine.

topaz[2] *adj* of a yellowish brown colour. ⋙ **topaz** *n.*

top boot *n* a high boot, often with an upper part of a different material or colour.

top brass *n* (*used as sing. or pl*) military officers or other officials of high rank.

topcoat *n* **1** a lightweight overcoat. **2** a final coat of paint.

top dog *n informal* a person in a position of authority, *esp* through victory in a hard-fought competition.

top drawer *n informal* the highest level, *esp* of society. ➤➤ **top-drawer** *adj.*

top-dress *v* to scatter fertilizer over (land) without working it in. ➤➤ **top-dressing** *n.*

tope[1] *v archaic or literary* to drink alcohol to excess. ➤➤ **toper** *n.*

tope[2] *n* a small shark with a liver very rich in vitamin A.

top-flight *adj* of the highest rank or quality; best.

topgallant *n* **1** the part of a ship's mast next above the topmast. **2** a sail set on a topgallant mast.

top hat *n* a man's tall-crowned hat with a flat top and vertical sides.

top-heavy *adj* having the top part too heavy for, or disproportionate to, the lower part.

Tophet *n* a place or state of misery; hell.

topiary *n* (*pl* **-ies**) **1** the practice or art of training, cutting, and trimming trees or shrubs into odd or ornamental shapes. **2** a tree or shrub cut in this way.

topic *n* a subject for discussion or consideration in writing or conversation.

topical *adj* **1** concerned with events and matters of current interest. **2** of or arranged by topics. **3** of medical drugs or treatments: designed to be applied externally to the affected part of the body. ➤➤ **topicality** *n,* **topically** *adv.*

topknot *n* **1** an arrangement or growth of hair or feathers on top of the head. **2** an ornament, e.g. of ribbons, worn as a headdress or as part of a hairstyle.

topless *adj and adv* **1** nude above the waist; *esp* having the breasts exposed. **2** of a garment: leaving the breasts exposed.

top-level *adj* **1** at the highest level of authority or importance. **2** made by or involving the most senior or important people.

top-line *adj* = TOP-LEVEL.

topmast *n* a mast fixed on top of the section of mast that rises from the deck.

topmost *adj* highest of all.

top-notch *adj informal* of the highest quality.

top off *v* to finish (something).

topography *n* **1a** the configuration of a land surface, including its relief and the position of its natural and man-made features. **b** the art or practice of making detailed maps or charts of a region. **2** the physical or natural features of an object or entity and their structural relationships. ➤➤ **topographer** *n,* **topographic** *adj,* **topographical** *adj.*

topology *n* **1** a branch of mathematics that deals with geometric properties which are unaltered by elastic deformation, e.g. stretching or twisting. **2** the way in which the various parts or features of something are interrelated. ➤➤ **topological** *adj,* **topologist** *n.*

toponym *n* a place name, or a name or word derived from a place name. ➤➤ **toponymic** *adj,* **toponymy** *n.*

top out *v* **1** to complete the basic structure of (a building) by putting on a cap or uppermost section. **2** to reach a peak or its highest level.

topper *n informal* = TOP HAT.

topping *n* something that forms a top; *esp* a garnish or edible decoration on top of a food.

topple *v* **1** to fall down or over, *esp* through being top-heavy. **2** to cause (something) to topple.

tops[1] *n* (*usu* **the tops**) *informal* somebody or something excellent or popular.

tops[2] *adv informal* at the most: *We were doing 40 tops when we skidded.*

topsail *n* **1** the sail next above the lowest sail on a mast in a square-rigged ship. **2** the sail set above and sometimes on the gaff in a fore-and-aft rigged ship.

top secret *adj* **1** demanding the greatest secrecy. **2** containing information whose unauthorized disclosure could result in exceptionally grave danger to the nation.

topside *n* **1** *Brit* a lean boneless cut of beef from the inner part of a round. **2** (*in pl*) the sides of a ship above the waterline.

topsoil *n* surface soil, usu including the organic layer in which plants form roots.

topspin *n* a rotary motion imparted to a ball that causes it to rotate forwards in the direction of its travel: compare BACKSPIN.

topsy-turvy *adj and adv* **1** upside down. **2** in utter confusion or disorder.

top up *v* **1** to make up to the full quantity, capacity, or amount; to replenish. **2** to increase (a money sum set aside for a specific purpose). **3** to replenish (a drink) or the drink of (somebody).

toque *n* **1** a woman's small soft brimless hat. **2** a tall white hat worn by a chef.

tor *n* a high rock or rocky mound.

Torah /'tawrə/ *n* **1** the Pentateuch. **2** Jewish Scripture and other sacred Jewish literature and oral tradition.

torc *or* **torque** *n* a twisted collar or neck chain, usu made of metal, worn by the ancient Gauls, Germans, and Britons.

torch[1] *n* **1** *Brit* a small portable electric lamp powered by batteries. **2** *esp* formerly, a burning stick of resinous wood or twist of tow used to give light. **3** something, e.g. wisdom or knowledge, that gives enlightenment or guidance. ✱ **carry a torch for** to be in love with (somebody who does not return one's love). **put to the torch/put a torch to** to destroy (something) by burning it.

torch[2] *v informal* to set fire to (something), *esp* as an act of arson.

torch song *n* a popular song of unrequited love.

tore *v* past tense of TEAR[1].

toreador /'tori·ədaw/ *n* a bullfighter, *esp* one on horseback.

torero /to'reəroh/ *n* (*pl* **-os**) a bullfighter, *esp* one on foot.

tori *n* pl of TORUS.

toric *adj* shaped like a torus or part of a torus.

torment[1] *n* **1** extreme pain or anguish of body or mind. **2** a source of vexation or pain.

torment[2] *v* **1** to cause severe usu persistent distress of body or mind to. **2** to tease unkindly. ➤➤ **tormentor** *n.*

torn *v* past part. of TEAR[1].

tornado *n* (*pl* **-oes** *or* **-os**) a violent or destructive whirlwind, usu progressing in a narrow path over the land and accompanied by a funnel-shaped cloud.

toroid *n* a doughnut-shaped figure; *specif* a surface or solid generated by a plane closed curve, e.g. an ellipse or circle, rotated about a line that lies in the same plane as the curve but does not intersect it. ⋙ **toroidal** *adj.*

torpedo[1] *n* (*pl* **-oes**) **1** a self-propelling cigar-shaped underwater explosive projectile used by submarines, aircraft, etc for attacking ships. **2** an electric ray.

torpedo[2] *v* (**torpedoes, torpedoed, torpedoing**) **1** to hit or destroy (e.g. a ship) by torpedo. **2** to destroy or nullify (e.g. a plan).

torpedo boat *n* a small fast warship armed primarily with torpedoes.

torpid *adj* **1** lacking energy or vigour, and slow and heavy when moving or functioning; sluggish. **2** of a hibernating animal: dormant. ⋙ **torpidity** *n,* **torpidly** *adv.*

torpor *n* **1** a state of sleepy inactivity or slow, heavy functioning; sluggishness. **2** a state of mental and motor inactivity with partial or total insensibility.

torque[1] *n* a force that produces or tends to produce rotation or torsion.

torque[2] *n* see TORC.

torque converter *n* a device for transmitting and amplifying torque, *esp* by hydraulic means.

torr *n* (*pl* **torr**) a unit of pressure equal to 133.32 pascals.

torrent *n* **1** a violent stream of water, lava, etc. **2** a raging tumultuous flow.

torrential *adj* of, caused by, or resembling a torrent. ⋙ **torrentially** *adv.*

torrid *adj* **1a** parched with heat, *esp* the heat of the sun. **b** giving off intense heat. **2** ardent or passionate. **3** very uncomfortable or unpleasant. ⋙ **torridly** *adv.*

torrid zone *n* the belt of the earth between the tropics.

torsi *n* pl of TORSO.

torsion *n* **1a** the act or process of twisting or turning something, *esp* by forces exerted on one end while the other is fixed or twisted in the opposite direction. **b** the state of being twisted. **2** the equal and opposite torque that an elastic solid exerts by reason of being under torsion. **3** the twisting of a body organ on its own axis. ⋙ **torsional** *adj.*

torsion bar *n* a steel bar that is part of the suspension of a vehicle and that acts as a torsional spring.

torso *n* (*pl* **torsos** *or* **torsi**) **1** the human trunk. **2** something, e.g. a piece of writing, that is mutilated or left unfinished.

tort *n* in law, a wrongful act, other than breach of contract, for which a civil action for damages may be brought.

torte /'tawtə/ *n* (*pl* **torten** *or* **tortes**) a gateau, *esp* a flat one topped with fruit, cream, etc.

tortellini /tawtə'leeni/ *pl n* (*used as sing. or pl*) pasta cut into small rounds, folded over a savoury filling, and boiled.

tortilla /taw'teeyə/ *n* a round thin maize pancake, usu eaten hot with a filling of meat or cheese.

tortious *adj* in law, implying or involving a tort.

tortoise *n* a land, freshwater, or marine reptile with a toothless horny beak and a bony shell which encloses the trunk and into which the head, limbs, and tail may be withdrawn.

tortoiseshell *n* **1** the mottled horny substance of the shell of some marine turtles used in inlaying and in making various ornamental articles. **2** a butterfly with striking orange, yellow, brown, and black coloration. **3** a cat of a breed with black, brown, and yellow markings.

tortuous *adj* **1** marked by repeated twists, bends, or turns. **2a** marked by devious or indirect tactics. **b** circuitous or involved. ⋙ **tortuosity** *n,* **tortuously** *adv,* **tortuousness** *n.*

torture[1] *n* **1** the infliction of intense physical or mental suffering as a means of punishment, coercion, or sadistic gratification. **2** anguish of body or mind, or something causing this.

torture[2] *v* to subject (a person or animal) to torture. ⋙ **torturer** *n.*

torturous *adj* of or involving torture. ⋙ **torturously** *adv.*

torus *n* (*pl* **tori** *or* **toruses**) **1** in geometry, a ring-shaped surface generated by a circle rotated about an axis in its plane that does not intersect the circle. **2** in architecture, a large convex semicircular moulding, *esp* on the base of a column, pedestal, etc. **3** something ring-shaped.

Tory *n* (*pl* **-ies**) **1a** a supporter of a Conservative party, *esp* the British Conservative Party. **b** a member of a major British political group of the 18th and early 19th cents favouring at first the Stuarts and later royal authority and the established Church and seeking to preserve the traditional political structure and defeat parliamentary reform: compare WHIG. **2** an American upholding the cause of the crown during the American Revolution. ⋙ **Tory** *adj,* **Toryism** *n.*

tosh *n Brit, informal* sheer nonsense.

toss[1] *v* **1a** to throw with a quick, light, or careless motion. **b** to throw (something or somebody) up in the air. **2** to move or move (something) repeatedly to and fro or up and down. **3** to shake or lift (one's head, hair, mane, etc) with a sudden jerking motion. **4** to mix (food) lightly with a tossing motion; *esp* to mix (a salad) lightly until well coated with a dressing. **5** to flip (a coin) to decide an issue according to which face lands uppermost.

toss[2] *n* an act or instance of tossing. ✱ **not give/care a toss** *Brit, informal* not to care at all; to be totally indifferent.

tosser *n Brit, coarse slang* an ineffective or despicable person.

toss off *v* **1** to accomplish, produce, or write (something) readily or easily. **2** to consume (a drink) quickly or in a single draught. **3** *Brit, coarse slang* to masturbate.

toss-up *n* **1** the tossing of a coin. **2** *informal* an even chance or choice.

tot[1] *n* **1** a small child; a toddler. **2** a small amount or allowance of alcoholic drink.

tot[2] *v* (**totted, totting**) **1** *chiefly Brit* (*usu* + up) to add (figures or amounts) together. **2** *chiefly Brit* (+ up) to increase by additions; to mount.

total[1] *adj* **1** comprising or constituting a whole; entire. **2** complete or absolute. ⋙ **totally** *adv.*

total[2] *n* **1** an amount that is the end product of adding two or more smaller amounts together. **2** an entire quantity.

total[3] *v* (**totalled, totalling,** *NAm* **totaled, totaling**) **1** to amount to (a figure). **2** to add (something) up. **3** *informal* to demolish completely.

total eclipse *n* an eclipse in which one celestial body is completely obscured by another.

totalisator *n* see TOTALIZATOR.

totalise *v* see TOTALIZE.

totaliser *n* see TOTALIZER.

totalitarian *adj* of or constituting a political regime based on subordination of the individual to the state and strict control over all aspects of the life and productive capacity of the nation. ⋙ **totalitarianism** *n.*

totality *n* **1** an entire amount; a whole. **2** a period during which one body is completely obscured by another during an eclipse.

totalizator *or* **totalisator** *n* **1** a machine for registering bets and calculating winnings in the tote betting system. **2** = TOTE².

totalize *or* **-ise** *v* **1** to add (something) up. **2** to express as a whole; to summarize. ⯮ **totalization** *n.*

totalizer *or* **totaliser** *n* a totalizator.

tote¹ *v informal* to carry by hand or on the person.

tote² *n* (*also* **the tote**) *informal* a betting system in which winners are paid a proportion of the total amount staked, less tax, based on the size of their stake, using a totalizator to calculate payouts.

tote bag *n* a large bag for carrying articles, e.g. shopping or personal possessions.

totem *n* **1a** a natural object serving as the emblem of a family or clan. **b** a carved or painted representation of this. **2** something that serves as an emblem or revered symbol. ⯮ **totemic** *adj.*

totem pole *n* a pole carved and painted with a series of totemic symbols erected by some Native American peoples.

totter¹ *v* **1a** to tremble or rock as if about to fall. **b** to become unstable; to threaten to collapse. **2** to move unsteadily; to stagger.

totter² *n* an unsteady gait. ⯮ **tottery** *adj.*

totting *n Brit, informal* the occupation of scavenging refuse for saleable goods, *esp* illicitly. ⯮ **totter** *n.*

totty *n* (*pl* **-ies**) *Brit, informal, offensive* women collectively, *esp* when viewed as sexual objects.

toucan *n* a fruit-eating bird of tropical America with brilliant colouring and a very large but light beak.

touch¹ *v* **1** to bring the hand or other part of the body in contact with. **2** to be in contact. **3** to come close; to verge. **4** to tap or push lightly. **5** to grasp or move in any way or degree. **6** (*usu in negative contexts*) to harm. **7** to cause (something) to be briefly in contact with something else. **8** to meet or adjoin (something) without overlapping or penetrating. **9** (*usu in negative contexts*) to use or accept. **10** to concern or affect. **11** to give a delicate tint or expression to. **12** to move (somebody) to sympathetic feeling. **13** *informal* (*usu in negative contexts*) to rival in ability or value. **14** *informal* to induce (somebody) to give or lend money. **15** (+ on/upon) to have a bearing; to relate. **16** (+ on/upon) to treat a topic in a brief or casual manner. **17** (+ at) of a ship: to make a brief or incidental stop at a port, etc. ✱ **touch wood** with luck [from the superstition that certain trees, usu the ash and oak, could give protection against evil]. ⯮ **touchable** *adj.*

touch² *n* **1** a light stroke, tap, or push. **2** the act or fact of touching. **3** the sense of feeling, *esp* as exercised deliberately with the hands, feet, or lips. **4** a specified sensation produced by touching something; a feel. **5** mental or moral sensitivity, responsiveness, or tact: *He has a wonderful touch in dealing with children.* **6a** a light attack: *a touch of fever.* **b** a small amount; a trace or dash: *a touch of spring in the air.* **c** (**a touch**) a bit; a little: *I aimed a touch too low and missed.* **7** an effective and appropriate detail; *esp* one used in creating or improving an artistic composition. **8** a distinctive or characteristic manner, trait, or quality. **9** the state or fact of being in contact or communication: *She had lost touch with her cousin; He is out of touch with modern times.* **10a** in football and hockey, the area outside the touchlines. **b** in rugby, the area outside and including the touchlines.

touch-and-go *adj* highly uncertain or precarious.

touchdown *n* **1** the moment when an aircraft or spacecraft makes contact with the ground in landing. **2** in rugby, the act of touching down a ball. **3** in American football, the act of receiving or having possession of the ball across the opponents' goal line.

touch down *v* **1** in rugby, to score by placing (the ball) on the ground over an opponent's goal line. **2** of an aircraft or spacecraft: to reach the ground in landing.

touché /tooh'shay/ *interj* used to acknowledge a hit in fencing or the success of an argument or witty point.

touched *adj* **1** emotionally moved, e.g. with gratitude. **2** *informal* slightly unbalanced mentally.

touching¹ *adj* capable of arousing tenderness or compassion. ⯮ **touchingly** *adv.*

touching² *prep formal* in reference to; concerning.

touch judge *n* in rugby, = LINESMAN.

touchline *n* in rugby and football, either of the lines that bound the sides of the field of play.

touch off *v* **1** to cause (something) to explode by touching it with a naked flame. **2** to release (something) with sudden intensity: *The incident touched off a storm of protest.*

touch pad *n* in computing, an input device used instead of a keyboard or to control a program; consisting of a plastic pad on which the user touches the area required.

touchpaper *n* paper impregnated with a substance, e.g. potassium nitrate, that burns slowly and is used for the ignition of fireworks or for firing gunpowder.

touch screen *n* in computing, a system which enables the operator to touch part of the screen physically instead of using a mouse to select menu items.

touchstone *n* **1** a black flintlike siliceous stone that when rubbed by gold or silver shows a streak of colour, formerly used to test the purity of these metals. **2** a test or criterion for determining the genuineness of something.

touch-tone *adj* of a telephone: having or using dialling buttons that generate a particular pitch when pressed.

touch-type *v* to type without looking at the keyboard, using a system that assigns a particular finger to each key.

touch up *v* **1** to improve or perfect by small alterations. **2** *Brit, informal* to make unwelcome physical or sexual contact with.

touchy *adj* (**-ier, -iest**) **1** ready to take offence on slight provocation. **2** calling for tact, care, or caution. ⯮ **touchily** *adv,* **touchiness** *n.*

touchy-feely *adj informal* showing emotion openly and readily, *esp* through physical contact or gestures and often in a way considered excessive; demonstrative.

tough¹ *adj* **1a** strong and flexible; not brittle or liable to cut, break, or tear easily. **b** of food: not easily chewed. **2** characterized by severity or uncompromising determination. **3** capable of enduring great hardship or exertion; hardy. **4** very hard to influence; stubborn. **5** extremely difficult or testing. **6** stubbornly fought. **7** aggressive or threatening in behaviour; unruly or rowdy. **8** without softness or sentimentality. **9** *informal* unfortunate or unpleasant. ⯮ **toughly** *adv,* **toughness** *n.*

tough² *n informal* a tough person, *esp* somebody aggressively violent.

tough³ *adv* in a tough manner: *He likes to talk tough.*

tough⁴ *v informal* (+ out) to endure (a difficult situation) without weakening.

toughen *v* to become or make tough.

tough love *n* a policy of helping somebody with a serious problem, e.g. drug addiction, by being strict rather than indulgent.

tough-minded *adj* unsentimental or realistic in disposition or outlook.

toupee *n* a wig or hairpiece worn to cover a bald spot.

tour[1] *n* **1a** a journey, e.g. for business or pleasure, in which one returns to the starting point. **b** a visit, e.g. to a historic site or factory, for pleasure or information. **c** a series of professional engagements involving travel. **2** (*also* **tour of duty**) a period during which an individual or unit is engaged on a specific duty, *esp* in one place.

tour[2] *v* to make a tour of (e.g. a building or place).

tour de force /ˌtooə də 'faws/ *n* (*pl* **tours de force**) an extremely impressive feat, performance, piece of work, etc.

tourer *n* a car or bicycle for touring.

Tourette's syndrome *n* a neurological disorder that causes the sufferer to make sudden involuntary movements and often obscene exclamations.

tourism *n* **1** the activity of visiting places, *esp* in foreign countries, for pleasure. **2** the organizing by commercial companies of travel, accommodation, etc for tourists.

tourist *n* **1** somebody who goes on a tour for pleasure, *esp* somebody who takes a holiday abroad. **2** a member of a sports team that is visiting another country to play. ⋙ **touristic** *adj.*

tourist class *n* the lowest class of accommodation, e.g. on a ship.

touristy *adj informal, derog* frequented by or appealing to tourists.

tourmaline *n* a variously coloured mineral consisting of a complex silicate of boron and aluminium, used in electrical and optical equipment and as a gem when transparent.

tournament *n* **1** a series of games or contests for a championship. **2** a contest between two parties of mounted medieval knights armed with usu blunted lances or swords.

tournedos *n* (*pl* **tournedos**) a small steak cut from the centre of a beef fillet and usu larded, tied, and held in shape with a skewer.

tourney[1] *n* (*pl* **-eys**) a tournament in the Middle Ages.

tourney[2] *v* (**-eys, -eyed**) to take part in a tournament in the Middle Ages.

tourniquet *n* a bandage or other device for applying pressure to check bleeding or blood flow.

tousle *v* (*usu in passive*) to make (something, *esp* somebody's hair) untidy.

tout[1] *v* **1a** to try to sell (something) by a very direct or insistent approach to potential customers. **b** *Brit* to sell (tickets in great demand) at exploitative prices. **2** to praise or publicize loudly or extravagantly.

tout[2] *n* (*also* **ticket tout**) *Brit* somebody who offers tickets for an event, e.g. a concert or football match, at vastly inflated prices.

tow[1] *v* to draw or pull along behind, *esp* by a rope or chain. ⋙ **towable** *adj.*

tow[2] *n* the act of towing or the state of being towed. ✱ **in tow 1** being towed. **2** in the position of a companion or follower.

tow[3] *n* short or broken fibre, e.g. of flax or hemp, prepared for spinning.

towage *n* the price paid for towing.

toward *adj archaic* happening at the moment; afoot.

towards *prep* **1** moving or situated in the direction of: *driving towards town.* **2a** along a course leading to: *a long stride towards disarmament.* **b** in relation to: *an attitude towards life.* **3** turned in the direction of: *His back was towards me.* **4** not long before: *towards the end of the afternoon.* **5** for the partial financing of: *I put the extra money towards a holiday.*

tow bar *n* a bar attached to the back of a vehicle so that a caravan or trailer can be towed.

towel[1] *n* **1** an absorbent cloth for wiping or drying something, e.g. crockery or the body, after washing. **2** a piece of absorbent paper used for drying the hands.

towel[2] *v* (**towelled, towelling,** *NAm* **toweled, toweling**) to rub or dry (e.g. the body) with a towel.

towelling (*NAm* **toweling**) *n* a cotton or linen fabric often used for making towels.

tower[1] *n* **1** a typically tall and narrow building or structure that may stand alone or be attached to a larger structure and that may be fully walled in or have a skeleton framework. **2** a citadel or fortress. **3** a tall unit for storage.

tower[2] *v* to reach or rise to a great height.

tower block *n Brit* a tall multi-storey building, usu containing flats or offices.

towering *adj* **1** impressively high or great. **2** reaching a high point of intensity. **3** going beyond proper bounds.

tower of strength *n* somebody who can be relied on as a source of sympathy and support.

towhead *n* somebody with a head of hair resembling tow, *esp* in being flaxen or tousled. ⋙ **towheaded** *adj.*

to wit *adv* that is to say.

towline *n* = TOWROPE.

town *n* **1a** a compactly settled area as distinguished from surrounding rural territory; *esp* one larger than a village but smaller than a city. **b** a large densely populated urban area; a city. **2** a neighbouring city, capital city, or metropolis. **3** the business centre of a large town or city. **4** the townspeople. ✱ **go to town** to deal with or exploit something enthusiastically or ostentatiously. **on the town** in pursuit of entertainment or amusement, e.g. city nightlife.

town clerk *n* **1** in the USA, a public officer charged with recording the official proceedings and statistics of a town. **2** in Britain until 1974, an official appointed to administer municipal affairs and to act as secretary to the town council.

town crier *n* somebody employed to make public proclamations.

townee *n* see TOWNIE.

town hall *n* the chief administrative building of a town.

town house *n* **1** a terrace house typically of three storeys. **2** the city residence of somebody who has a country seat.

townie *or* **townee** *n informal* somebody who lives in a town.

town planning *n* the study of the function of the various components of the urban environment and the planning of their arrangement and interrelationship for best results. ⋙ **town planner** *n.*

townscape *n* the overall visual aspect of a town.

townsfolk *pl n* = TOWNSPEOPLE.

township *n* **1** an urban area inhabited by non-white citizens in S Africa; *esp* one formerly designated as a black settlement. **2** in the USA and

Canada, a subdivision of a county, often with some powers of local government. **3** an ancient unit of administration in England identical in area with or being a division of a parish. **4** a small town or settlement in Australia or New Zealand.

townsman *or* **townswoman** *n* (*pl* **townsmen** *or* **townswomen**) a man or woman who is a native or resident of a town or city.

townspeople *pl n* the inhabitants of a town or city.

townswoman *n* see TOWNSMAN.

towpath *n* a path, e.g. along a canal, for use in towing boats.

towrope *n* a line used in towing a boat, car, etc.

toxaemia (*NAm* **toxemia**) *n* **1** an abnormal condition associated with the presence of toxic substances in the blood. **2** = PREECLAMPSIA.

toxic *adj* **1** = POISONOUS. **2** relating to or caused by a poison or toxin. ➤➤ **toxicity** *n.*

toxicant *n* a toxic substance; *esp* one used for insect control that kills rather than repels.

toxicology *n* a branch of biology that deals with poisons and their effects. ➤➤ **toxicological** *adj,* **toxicologist** *n.*

toxic shock syndrome *n* acute septicaemia that may be caused by toxins produced by certain bacteria and that has been linked with the use of tampons.

toxin *n* an often extremely poisonous protein produced by a living organism, e.g. a bacterium, *esp* in the body of a host.

toxocariasis *n* an infection in humans transmitted via domestic pets or soil contaminated by the larvae of a genus of roundworms.

toxophilite *n formal* a lover of or expert at archery.

toxoplasmosis *n* a disease caused by a genus of parasitic protozoans that is transmitted to humans, other mammals, and birds via infected soil or animal faeces.

toy[1] *n* **1a** something for a child to play with. **b** something designed for amusement or diversion rather than practical use. **2** (*used before a noun*) something tiny; *esp* an animal of a breed or variety of exceptionally small size: *a toy poodle.* ➤➤ **toylike** *adj.*

toy[2] *v* **1** (+ with) to touch or handle something in an absent-minded or nonchalant way. **2** (+ with) to consider something as a possibility but without committing oneself at all. **3** (+ with) to flirt.

toy boy *n Brit, informal* a young man taken as lover or companion by an older woman.

trace[1] *n* **1** a mark or line left by something that has passed. **2** something traced or drawn; *esp* the graphic record made by a seismograph or other recording instrument. **3** a minute and often barely detectable amount or indication. **4** a sign or evidence of some past thing; a vestige. **5** an attempt to find something or somebody.

trace[2] *v* **1a** to find by using signs, evidence, or remains. **b** to follow back or study in detail or step by step. **c** to follow the course or trail of. **2a** to copy (e.g. a drawing) by following the lines or letters as seen through a semitransparent superimposed sheet. **b** to delineate or sketch. ➤➤ **traceable** *adj.*

trace[3] *n* either of two straps, chains, or lines of a harness for attaching a vehicle to a horse.

trace element *n* a chemical element present in minute quantities; *esp* one essential to a living organism for proper growth and development.

tracer *n* **1** ammunition containing a chemical composition to mark the flight of projectiles by a trail of smoke or fire. **2** a substance, *esp* a labelled element or atom, used to trace the course of a chemical or biological process.

tracery *n* (*pl* **-ies**) **1** ornamental stone openwork in architecture, *esp* in the head of a Gothic window. **2** a decorative interlacing of lines, e.g. in a frost pattern or insect's wing. ➤➤ **traceried** *adj.*

trachea *n* (*pl* **tracheae** *or* **tracheas**) the main trunk of the system of tubes by which air passes to and from the lungs; the windpipe. ➤➤ **tracheal** *adj.*

tracheotomy *n* (*pl* **-ies**) the surgical operation of cutting into the trachea, *esp* through the skin, usu to relieve suffocation by inhaled matter.

trachoma *n* a chronic contagious eye disease that is caused by a minute organism and commonly results in blindness if left untreated.

tracing *n* **1** a copy, e.g. of a design or map, made on a superimposed semitransparent sheet. **2** a graphic record made by an instrument that monitors some movement.

track[1] *n* **1a** a path beaten by feet; a trail. **b** a roughly made path or road. **2** detectable evidence, e.g. a line of footprints or a wheel rut, that something has passed. **3** a specially laid-out course, *esp* for racing. **4a** the parallel rails of a railway. **b** a rail or length of railing along which something, *esp* a curtain, moves or is pulled. **5a** the course along which something moves. **b** the projection on the earth's surface of the path along which something, e.g. a missile or an aircraft, has flown. **6** either of two continuous usu metal belts on which a tracklaying vehicle travels. **7a** any of a series of parallel elongated regions on a magnetic tape on which a recording is made. **b** a more or less independent sequence of recording, e.g. a single movement or song, on a compact disc, record, or cassette. ✱ **keep/lose track of** to remain aware/no longer be aware of the development or whereabouts of something or somebody. **make tracks** *informal* to leave. **on the right/wrong track** likely/unlikely to achieve something by continuing one's present course of action. ➤➤ **trackless** *adj.*

track[2] *v* **1** to follow the tracks or traces of; to trail. **2** to follow the progress of. **3** to observe or plot the course of (e.g. a spacecraft or missile) instrumentally. **4a** to move a film or television camera towards, beside, or away from a subject while shooting a scene. **b** of a camera: to undergo tracking. ➤➤ **tracker** *n.*

trackball *n* in computing, a type of mouse consisting of a ball mounted in a box; the ball being rotated by the fingers or palm to control the cursor.

track down *v* to search for (somebody or something) until found.

track event *n* an athletic event that is a race.

track gauge spread *n* = TRACK SPREAD.

tracking *n* **1** the act or process of following the trail of a person or animal. **2** the alignment of a vehicle's wheels. **3** the process of finding the best quality video picture by aligning the heads with the tape. **4** in electrical engineering, the leaking of current between two insulated points because of moisture or dirt.

track record *n* a record of the past achievements or performance of an individual, organization, team, etc.

track spread *or* **track gauge spread** *n* the widening of a railway track due to the pressure exerted by trains passing along it.

tracksuit *n* a warm loose-fitting suit worn by athletes when training, or as casual wear.

tract[1] *n* a short practical treatise; *esp* a pamphlet of religious propaganda.

tract[2] *n* **1** a region or area of land of indefinite extent. **2** a system of body parts or organs that collectively serve some often specified purpose: *the digestive tract.*

tractable *adj* **1** of a person or animal: easily taught or controlled. **2** of a problem or situation: easy to deal with. ➤➤ **tractability** *n.*

tractate *n* a treatise or dissertation.

traction *n* **1a** pulling, being pulled, or the force exerted in pulling. **b** the use of motive power to pull a vehicle, or the motive power employed. **2** in medicine, a pulling force exerted on part of the body by means of a special device to treat fractures, cure deformities, etc. **3** the adhesive friction of a body on a surface on which it moves, e.g. a tyre on a road surface; grip.

traction engine *n* a large steam- or diesel-powered vehicle used to draw other vehicles or equipment over roads or fields and sometimes to provide power.

tractor *n* **1** a four-wheeled or tracklaying vehicle used for pulling or using farm machinery. **2** a truck with a short chassis and no body except a driver's cab, used to haul a large trailer or trailers.

trad[1] *adj informal* = TRADITIONAL.

trad[2] *n informal* traditional jazz.

trade[1] *n* **1** the business of buying and selling or bartering commodities. **2a** (*used as sing. or pl*) the people or group of firms engaged in a particular business or industry. **b** (*used as sing. or pl*) a firm's customers; a clientele. **3a** the business or work in which one engages regularly; an occupation. **b** an occupation requiring manual or mechanical skill; a craft. **4** = TRADE WIND.

trade[2] *v* **1** to engage in the exchange, purchase, or sale of goods. **2** (+ on) to exploit or take advantage of. **3** to give (something) in exchange for another commodity; to barter. ➤➤ **tradable** *adj,* **tradeable** *adj.*

trade deficit *n* = TRADE GAP.

trade gap *n* the amount by which the value of a country's imports exceeds that of its exports.

trade in *v* to give (a used item) as payment or part payment for a new item.

trademark[1] *n* **1** a name or distinctive symbol or device attached to goods produced by a particular firm or individual and legally reserved to the exclusive use of the owner of the mark as maker or seller. **2** a distinguishing feature firmly associated with somebody or something.

trademark[2] *v* to secure trademark rights for; to register the trademark of.

trade name *n* **1a** the name used for an article by the trade. **b** a name given by a manufacturer or seller to an article or service to distinguish it and protect it as a trademark. **2** the name under which a concern does business.

trade off *v* to give (something) up in return for something else.

trade-off *n* a giving up of one thing in return for another, *esp* as a compromise.

trade plates *pl n Brit* temporary number plates used on a vehicle before it is registered.

trade price *n* the price at which goods are sold to other people in the same trade or by a manufacturer or wholesaler to a retailer.

trader *n* **1** a retail or wholesale dealer. **2** somebody who buys and sells shares, commodities, etc in search of short-term profits. **3** a ship engaged in trade.

tradescantia *n* a commonly grown houseplant with usu blue or violet flowers and striped leaves.

tradesman *n* (*pl* **tradesmen**) **1** a shopkeeper. **2** a worker in a skilled trade.

trades union *n* = TRADE UNION.

trade surplus *n* the amount by which the value of a country's exports exceeds that of its imports.

trade union *n* an organization of workers formed for the purpose of advancing its members' interests. ➤➤ **trade unionism** *n,* **trade unionist** *n.*

trade wind *n* a mainly sea wind blowing almost continually towards the equator from the NE in the northern hemisphere and from the SE in the southern hemisphere roughly between latitudes 0 and 30.

trading estate *n Brit* an industrial estate.

trading post *n* a station of a trader or trading company established in a sparsely settled region where trade is carried on.

tradition *n* **1** the handing down of information, beliefs, and customs by word of mouth or by example from one generation to another. **2a** an inherited pattern of thought or action, e.g. a religious practice or a social custom. **b** a convention or set of conventions associated with or representative of an individual, group, or period. **3** cultural continuity in social attitudes and institutions.

traditional *adj* **1** of or handed down by tradition. **2** of or being a style of jazz orig played in New Orleans in the early 1900s. ➤➤ **traditionally** *adv.*

traditionalism *n* the doctrines or practices of those who follow or accept tradition. ➤➤ **traditionalist** *n and adj.*

traduce *v formal* to attempt to damage the reputation or standing of (somebody), *esp* by misrepresentation; to defame.

traffic[1] *n* **1a** the movement, e.g. of vehicles or pedestrians, through an area or along a route. **b** the vehicles, pedestrians, ships, or aircraft moving along a route. **c** the information or signals transmitted over a communications system. **2a** the passengers or cargo carried by a transport system. **b** the business of transporting passengers or freight. **3** trade, *esp* in illegal or disreputable merchandise.

traffic[2] *v* (**trafficked, trafficking**) to trade in something illegal or disreputable. ➤➤ **trafficker** *n.*

traffic calming *n* the use of deterrents to speed, e.g. the narrowing of a road or the installation of humps in it, in order to slow vehicles in an area.

traffic island *n* a paved or planted island in a road designed to guide the flow of traffic and provide refuge for pedestrians.

traffic jam *n* a line of vehicles that cannot move normally because of an obstruction.

traffic light *n* (*usu in pl*) an automatically operated signal with coloured lights for controlling traffic.

traffic warden *n Brit* an official who enforces parking regulations and helps in maintaining the traffic flow in urban areas.

tragedian *n* **1** an actor who plays tragic roles. **2** a writer of tragedies.

tragedienne *n* a female tragedian.

tragedy *n* (*pl* **-ies**) **1** a disastrous event; a calamity. **2** a serious drama in which destructive circumstances result in adversity for, and usu the deaths of, the main characters.

tragic *adj* **1a** deplorable or lamentable. **b** relating to sombre or disastrous events. **2** of, appropriate to, dealing with, or treated in literary tragedy. **3** expressive of woe. ➤➤ **tragical** *adj,* **tragically** *adv.*

tragicomedy *n* (*pl* **-ies**) a literary work in which tragic and comic elements are mixed in a usu ironic way. ➤➤ **tragicomic** *adj.*

trail[1] *n* **1a** a trace or mark left by somebody or something that has passed; a scent or track. **b** a marked path through a forest or mountainous region. **c** a route followed or to be followed for a particular purpose: *a campaign trail.* **2** something that follows or moves along as if being drawn behind; a train.

trail[2] *v* **1a** to hang down so as to sweep the ground. **b** to extend over a surface in a loose or straggling manner. **c** of a plant, branch, etc: to grow to such a length as to droop over towards the ground. **2a** to drag (something) loosely along a surface. **b** to carry or bring along as an addition, burden, or encumbrance. **c** to draw (something) along in one's wake. **3a** (*usu* + along) to walk or proceed heavily or wearily; to plod or trudge. **b** to lag behind; to do poorly in relation to others. **4** (*usu* + off/away) to become quieter or weaker; to dwindle. **5a** to follow the scent or trace of (e.g. an animal). **b** to follow behind or in the footsteps of. **c** to lag behind (e.g. a competitor). **6** to advertise (e.g. a film) with a trailer.

trail bike *n* a light motorcycle for cross-country or off-road riding.

trailblazer *n* **1** somebody who finds and marks a new route through wild country. **2** a pioneer; an innovator. ➤➤ **trailblazing** *adj.*

trailer *n* **1a** a wheeled vehicle designed to be towed, e.g. by a lorry or car. **b** *NAm* = CARAVAN. **c** the rear part of an articulated lorry. **2** a set of short excerpts from a film shown in advance for publicity purposes.

trailer park *n NAm* a caravan or mobile home site.

trailing edge *n* the rearmost edge of an aerofoil, e.g. a wing or propeller blade.

trail mix *n* a snack consisting of dried fruit and nuts.

train[1] *n* **1** a connected line of railway carriages or wagons with or without a locomotive. **2** a moving file of people, vehicles, or animals. **3** = RETINUE. **4** a connected series of ideas, actions, or events. **5** a part of a gown that trails behind the wearer.

train[2] *v* **1** to teach (a person or animal) to do something. **2** to undergo training. **3** to prepare (somebody), e.g. by exercise, for a test of skill. **4** to direct the growth of (a plant), usu by bending, pruning, and tying. **5** to aim (something) at an object or objective; to direct. ➤➤ **trainable** *adj,* **training** *n.*

trainee *n* somebody who is being trained for a job.

trainer *n* **1a** a person who trains the members of an athletic team. **b** a person who trains and prepares horses for racing. **2** *Brit* a sports shoe designed for running, jogging, etc.

training college *n Brit* a school offering specialized instruction.

training shoe *n* = TRAINER (2).

trainspotter *n* **1** *Brit* somebody whose hobby is to observe locomotives and trains and collect information about them. **2** *Brit, informal* somebody who is obsessed with any specialized hobby or interest, *esp* one that is regarded as boring. ➤➤ **trainspotting** *n.*

traipse[1] *v* to walk or trudge about, often to little purpose.

traipse[2] *n* a long or unpleasant walk.

trait *n* a distinguishing quality or characteristic.

traitor *n* **1** somebody who betrays another's trust. **2** somebody who commits treason. ➤➤ **traitorous** *adj.*

trajectory *n* (*pl* **-ies**) the curve that a planet, projectile, etc follows as it moves through space.

tram *n chiefly Brit* a passenger vehicle running on rails and typically operating on urban streets.

tramcar *n* = TRAM.

tramline *n* **1** *Brit* a track on which trams run. **2** (*in pl*) either of the two pairs of sidelines on a tennis or badminton court that mark off the area used in doubles play.

trammel[1] *n* **1** a net having three layers with the middle one finer-meshed and slack so that fish passing through carry some of the centre net through the coarser opposite net and are trapped. **2** *literary* (*in pl*) something that impedes freedom of action.

trammel[2] *v* (**trammelled, trammelling,** *NAm* **trammeled, trammeling**) to restrain or confine (somebody or something).

tramontana *n* a cold dry northerly wind blowing down the west coast of Italy.

tramp[1] *v* **1** to walk or tread, *esp* heavily. **2** to travel about on foot. ➤➤ **tramper** *n.*

tramp[2] *n* **1** a wandering homeless person who survives by taking the occasional job or by begging money and food. **2** a usu long and tiring walk. **3** the heavy rhythmic tread of feet. **4** a merchant vessel that does not work a regular route but carries general cargo to any port as required.

trample *v* **1** to press down, crush, or injure by treading, or as if by treading. **2** (*usu* + on/over/upon) to inflict injury with ruthlessness or contempt.

trampoline[1] *n* a resilient sheet or web supported by springs in a frame and used for bouncing up and down on and performing gymnastic tricks in the air. ➤➤ **trampolining** *n.*

trampoline[2] *v* to jump on a trampoline.

tramway *n Brit* a system of tracks, e.g. laid in the surface of urban streets, for trams.

trance *n* **1** a state of semiconsciousness or unconsciousness with reduced or absent sensitivity to external stimulation. **2** a usu self-induced state of altered consciousness or ecstasy in which religious or mystical visions may be experienced. **3** a state of profound abstraction or absorption. **4** a type of electronic dance music with a hypnotic beat.

tranche *n* a portion, *esp* a block of shares usu supplementary to an already existing issue.

tranny *or* **trannie** *n* (*pl* **-ies**) *informal* **1** *chiefly Brit* a transistor radio. **2** = TRANSVESTITE.

tranquil *adj* free from mental agitation or from disturbance or commotion; quiet or peaceful. ➤➤ **tranquillity** *n,* **tranquilly** *adv.*

tranquillize *or* **-ise** (*NAm* **tranquilize**) *v* to make (a person or animal) tranquil or calm; *esp* to relieve of mental tension and anxiety with drugs.

tranquillizer *or* **tranquilliser** (*NAm* **tranquilizer**) *n* a drug, e.g. diazepam, used to tranquillize.

trans- *prefix* **1** on or to the other side of, across, or beyond: *transatlantic.* **2** through: *transcutaneous.* **3** so or such as to change or transfer: *transliterate.*

transact *v* to perform (something); *esp* to conduct (business). ➤➤ **transactor** *n.*

transaction *n* **1** something transacted, *esp* an instance of buying and selling or a business deal. **2** the act of carrying out or conducting business. ➤➤ **transactional** *adj.*

transatlantic *adj* **1** crossing or extending across the Atlantic Ocean. **2** situated beyond the Atlantic Ocean. **3** relating to or characteristic of people or places situated beyond the Atlantic Ocean.

transceiver *n* a combined radio transmitter and receiver.

transcend *v* **1** to go beyond the limits of. **2** to surpass (somebody or something).

transcendent *adj* **1a** exceeding usual limits; surpassing. **b** beyond the limits of ordinary experience. **c** in the philosophy of Kant, beyond the limits of possible experience and knowledge. **2** transcending the universe or material existence: compare IMMANENT. ➤➤ **transcendence** *n*, **transcendently** *adv.*

transcendental *adj* **1** beyond the limits of ordinary experience; transcendent. **2** = SUPERNATURAL[1]. ➤➤ **transcendentally** *adv.*

transcendentalism *n* a philosophy that asserts the primacy of the spiritual over the material or that fundamental reality is transcendent. ➤➤ **transcendentalist** *adj and n.*

transcendental meditation *n* a method, derived from Hinduism, of relaxing and refreshing oneself by silently repeating a sacred word or sound.

transcontinental *adj* crossing or extending across a continent.

transcribe *v* **1a** to make a written copy or version of (e.g. something written or printed). **b** to write (something) in a different medium; to transliterate. **c** to write down or record. **2** to transfer (data) from one recording form to another. **3** to make a musical transcription of. ➤➤ **transcriber** *n.*

transcript *n* a written, printed, or typed copy; *esp* a usu typewritten copy of dictated or recorded material or shorthand notes.

transcriptase *n* an enzyme that catalyses the synthesis of RNA from DNA.

transcription *n* **1** the act or an instance of transcribing. **2** a copy or transcript, e.g. an often free arrangement of a musical composition for some instrument or voice other than the original.

transcutaneous *adj* passing or entering through the skin.

transdermal *adj* of medicine or drugs: taken into the body through the skin.

transducer *n* a device that transfers energy from one system to another; *esp* one that converts non-electrical energy into electrical energy or vice versa. ➤➤ **transduction** *n.*

transect[1] *v* to cut (something) transversely. ➤➤ **transection** *n.*

transect[2] *n* a sample area, e.g. of vegetation, usu in the form of a long continuous strip, that is used to study the composition of plant species, animal populations, etc.

transept *n* either of the projecting arms of the part of a cross-shaped church that crosses the E end of the nave at right angles.

transexual *n* see TRANSSEXUAL.

transfer[1] *v* (**transferred, transferring**) **1a** to carry or take (something) from one person, place, or situation to another. **b** to move or send to another location. **c** to move (a professional football player) to another football club. **d** to cause to pass from one person or thing to another; to transmit. **2** to make over the possession or control of (e.g. property). **3** to copy (e.g. a design) from one surface to another by contact. **4** to change from one vehicle or transport system to another. ➤➤ **transferable** *adj*, **transferral** *n.*

transfer[2] *n* **1** an act, process, or instance of transferring. **2** somebody or something that transfers or is transferred. **3** *Brit* a graphic image transferred by contact from one surface, e.g. specially prepared paper, to another.

transferee *n* **1** a person to whom a property is transferred. **2** somebody who is transferred.

transference *n* **1** the redirection of feelings and desires, *esp* those unconsciously retained from childhood, towards a new object, e.g. towards a psychoanalyst conducting therapy. **2** the action or process of transferring.

transfer fee *n* the fee paid by one professional football club to another for the transfer of a player.

transfer RNA *n* a relatively small RNA that transfers a particular amino acid to a growing polypeptide chain at the ribosome site for protein synthesis.

transfiguration *n* **1a** a change in form or appearance; a metamorphosis. **b** an exalting, glorifying, or spiritual change. **2** (**Transfiguration**) a festival of the Christian Church celebrated on 6 August commemorating the transfiguration of Christ (Matthew 17:2 and Mark 9:2–3).

transfigure *v* to transform (something) outwardly; *esp* to give (something) a more glorified form.

transfix *v* **1** to hold (a person or animal) motionless, *esp* with horror or shock. **2** to pierce through, e.g. with a pointed weapon.

transform *v* **1** to change or change (something) radically, e.g. in structure, appearance, or character. **2** to change (a current) in potential, e.g. from high voltage to low, or in type, e.g. from alternating to direct. ➤➤ **transformative** *adj.*

transformation *n* the act or an instance of transforming or being transformed. ➤➤ **transformational** *adj.*

transformer *n* an electrical device making use of the principle of mutual induction to convert variations of current in a primary circuit into variations of voltage and current in a secondary circuit.

transfuse *v* **1** to transfer (e.g. blood) into a vein or artery. **2** to diffuse into or through; to permeate. ➤➤ **transfusion** *n.*

transgender *adj* transsexual.

transgendered *adj* = TRANSGENDER.

transgenic *adj* having a gene or genes from another individual transplanted into the normal genetic material, e.g. to improve the qualities of the breed or confer disease resistance.

transgress *v* **1** to go beyond limits set or prescribed by (e.g. a principle). **2** to pass beyond or go over (a boundary). ➤➤ **transgressive** *adj*, **transgressor** *n.*

transgression *n* infringement or violation of a law, command, or duty.

tranship *v* see TRANSSHIP.

transhumance *n* the seasonal movement of livestock, *esp* sheep, between mountain and lowland pastures. ➤➤ **transhumant** *adj.*

transient[1] *adj* **1** passing quickly away; transitory. **2** making only a brief stay. ➤➤ **transience** *n*, **transiency** *n*, **transiently** *adv.*

transient[2] *n* a transient guest or worker.

transistor *n* **1** any of several semiconductor devices that have usu three electrodes and make use of a small current to control a larger one. **2** = TRANSISTOR RADIO.

transistorize *or* **-ise** *v* to equip (a device) with transistors.

transistor radio *n* a radio using transistorized circuitry.

transit[1] *n* the act or an instance of passing or conveying through or over; passage.

transit[2] *v* (**transited, transiting**) to pass over or through; to traverse.

transition *n* **1** the process of passing or developing from one state, stage, or form to another. **2** a change or transfer, e.g. from one point to the next, from one topic to another, etc. ⋙ **transitional** *adj*.

transition element *n* = TRANSITION METAL.

transition metal *n* any of various metallic elements, e.g. chromium, iron, or platinum, that have valency electrons in two shells instead of only one.

transitive *adj* in grammar, having or containing a direct object. ⋙ **transitively** *adv*, **transitivity** *n*.

transitory *adj* **1** tending to pass away. **2** of brief duration. ⋙ **transitorily** *adv*, **transitoriness** *n*.

translate *v* **1** to turn (text) into another language. **2** to express in different or more comprehensible terms; to explain or interpret. **3** to bear, remove, or change (somebody or something) from one place or condition to another; to transfer or transform. **4a** to practise translation or make a translation. **b** to be capable of or adaptable to translation. **5** to undergo a translation. ⋙ **translatable** *adj*.

translation *n* **1** the act of rendering from one language into another. **2** a version thus produced.

translator *n* **1** somebody who translates from one language into another. **2** a computer program used to convert from one computer language into another.

transliterate *v* to represent or spell (a letter or word) in the characters of another alphabet. ⋙ **transliteration** *n*.

translocate *v* to move (something) to another place. ⋙ **translocation** *n*.

translucent *adj* transmitting and diffusing light so that objects beyond cannot be seen clearly; semitransparent. ⋙ **translucence** *n*, **translucency** *n*.

transmigrate *v* of a soul: to pass at death from one body or being to another. ⋙ **transmigration** *n*.

transmission *n* **1** the act or an instance of transmitting. **2** something, e.g. a message or television programme, that is transmitted. **3** an assembly of parts by which the power is transmitted from a motor vehicle engine to an axle.

transmission line *n* a conductor that carries electrical signals from one place to another.

transmit *v* (**transmitted, transmitting**) **1** to send or transfer (something) from one person or place to another. **2a** to pass on (infection). **b** to convey by inheritance or heredity; to hand down. **3** to cause (e.g. force) to pass or be conveyed through a medium. **4a** to allow the passage of (e.g. energy); to conduct. **b** to send out (a signal) either by radio waves or over a wire. ⋙ **transmissible** *adj*, **transmittal** *n*.

transmitter *n* **1** the portion of a telegraphic or telephonic instrument that sends the signals. **2** a radio or television transmitting station or set.

transmogrify *v* (**-ies, -ied**) to transform (something), often with grotesque or humorous effect. ⋙ **transmogrification** *n*.

transmutation *n* **1** the act or an instance of transmuting or being transmuted. **2a** the conversion of one chemical element or type of atom into another, either naturally or artificially. **b** the conversion of base metals, e.g. iron and copper, into gold or silver.

transmute *v* **1** to change (something) in form, substance, or characteristics. **2** to subject (e.g. an element) to transmutation.

transnational *adj* extending beyond national boundaries.

transoceanic *adj* **1** situated beyond the ocean. **2** crossing or extending across the ocean.

transom *n* **1a** any of several crosswise timbers or beams secured to the sternpost of a boat. **b** the planking forming the stern of a square-ended boat. **2** a horizontal crossbar used to strengthen a structure, e.g. a lintel or a bar over a door.

transonic *or* **trans-sonic** *adj* **1** of or being a speed near the speed of sound in air. **2** moving, capable of moving, or using air currents moving, at a transonic speed.

transparency *n* (*pl* **-ies**) **1** being transparent. **2** a picture or design on glass, film, etc viewed by a light shining through it from behind; *esp* a photographic slide.

transparent *adj* **1a** transmitting light without appreciable scattering so that bodies lying beyond are entirely visible. **b** fine or sheer enough to be seen through. **2a** free from pretence or deceit. **b** easily detected or seen through. **c** readily understood. **d** open to public scrutiny; not clandestine. ⋙ **transparently** *adv*.

transpire *v* **1** to become known; to come to light. **2** to occur; to take place. **3** to give off or exude water vapour, *esp* from the surfaces of leaves. ⋙ **transpiration** *n*.

transplant[1] *v* **1** to lift and reset (a plant) in another soil or place. **2** to remove (something) from one place and settle or introduce it elsewhere. **3** to transfer (an organ or tissue) from one part or individual to another. ⋙ **transplantable** *adj*, **transplantation** *n*.

transplant[2] *n* **1** the act or an instance of transplanting, *esp* a surgical operation to transplant an organ. **2** something transplanted.

transponder *n* a radio or radar set that responds to a designated signal by emitting a radio signal of its own.

transport[1] *v* **1** to transfer or convey from one place to another. **2** to carry (somebody) away with strong and often pleasurable emotion. **3** to send (a convict) to a penal colony overseas. ⋙ **transportable** *adj*, **transportation** *n*.

transport[2] *n* **1** the conveying of goods or people from one place to another. **2a** a ship or aircraft for carrying soldiers or military equipment. **b** a lorry, aeroplane, etc used to transport people or goods. **3** a burst or experience of strong and usu pleasurable emotion.

transport café *n Brit* a roadside restaurant for long-distance lorry drivers.

transporter *n* a vehicle for transporting large or heavy loads.

transpose *v* **1** to change the relative position of (two or more things). **2** to transfer (something) from one place or period to another. **3** to write or perform (music) in a different key. ⋙ **transposable** *adj*, **transposition** *n*.

transputer *n* a powerful microprocessor chip capable of handling very large amounts of information very fast, which was developed as the building block for supercomputers.

transsexual *or* **transexual** *n* somebody physically of one sex with an urge to belong to or resemble the opposite sex. ⋙ **transsexual** *adj*, **transsexualism** *n*.

transship *or* **tranship** *v* (**transshipped, transshipping**) to transfer (cargo) from one ship or conveyance to another for further transportation. ⋙ **transshipment** *n*.

trans-sonic *adj* see TRANSONIC.

transubstantiation *n* the miraculous change by which, according to Roman Catholic and Eastern Orthodox dogma, bread and wine used at communion become the body and blood of Christ when they are consecrated.

transuranic *n* of an element: having an atomic number greater than that of uranium.

transverse *adj* lying or being across; set or made crosswise. ▸▸ **transversely** *adv.*

transvestite *n* somebody who adopts the dress of the opposite sex. ▸▸ **transvestism** *n.*

trap[1] *n* **1** a device for catching animals; *esp* one that holds them by springing shut suddenly. **2a** a plan or trick designed to catch a person unawares and put them at a disadvantage. **b** a situation from which it is difficult or impossible to escape. **3** a device for drains or sewers consisting of a bend or partitioned chamber in which the liquid forms a seal to prevent the passage of sewer gas. **4a** a device from which a greyhound is released at the start of a race. **b** a device for hurling clay pigeons into the air. **5** a golf bunker. **6** a light carriage with springs, pulled by a horse or pony. **7** *informal* the mouth.

trap[2] *v* (**trapped, trapping**) **1a** to catch or take (an animal) in a trap. **b** to trick (somebody) into doing something. **c** to place (something or somebody) in a restricted position; to confine. **2** to stop or retain (something).

trap[3] *n* any of various dark-coloured fine-grained igneous rocks, e.g. basalt, used *esp* in road making.

trapdoor *n* a lifting or sliding door covering an opening in a floor, ceiling, etc.

trapeze *n* a gymnastic or acrobatic apparatus consisting of a short horizontal bar suspended by two parallel ropes.

trapezium *n* (*pl* **trapeziums** *or* **trapezia**) **1** *Brit* a quadrilateral that has only two sides parallel. **2** *NAm* a quadrilateral that has no sides parallel.

trapezius *n* (*pl* **trapezii**) either of two large flat triangular muscles, one on each side of the upper part of the back, that serve chiefly to raise and rotate the shoulder blades.

trapezoid *n* **1** *Brit* a quadrilateral that has no sides parallel. **2** *NAm* a quadrilateral that has only two sides parallel. ▸▸ **trapezoidal** *adj.*

trapper *n* a person who traps wild animals for their skin or fur.

trappings *n* **1** outward signs and accessories. **2** ornamental coverings and harness for a horse.

Trappist *n* a member of a reformed branch of the Cistercian Order established in 1664 and noted for its vow of silence. ▸▸ **Trappist** *adj.*

traprock *n* = TRAP[3].

trash can *n NAm* = DUSTBIN.

trashy *adj* (**-ier, -iest**) of inferior quality or worth.

trattoria /tratə'ree·ə/ *n* (*pl* **trattorias** *or* **trattorie**) an Italian restaurant.

trauma *n* (*pl* **traumata** *or* **traumas**) **1a** a disordered mental or behavioural state resulting from mental or emotional stress or shock. **b** an injury, e.g. a wound. **2** an agent, force, or mechanism that causes trauma. ▸▸ **traumatic** *adj,* **traumatically** *adv.*

traumatize *or* **-ise** *v* to inflict a trauma on.

travail[1] *n* **1** *literary* (*also in pl*) physical or mental exertion, *esp* of a painful or laborious nature. **2** *archaic* labour pains.

travail[2] *v* **1** *literary* to labour hard. **2** *archaic* to suffer labour pains.

travel[1] *v* (**travelled, travelling,** *NAm* **traveled, traveling**) **1a** to go on a trip or tour. **b** to go as if by travelling; to pass: *The news travelled fast; My mind travelled back to our last meeting.* **2** to journey along (a road) or through or over (an area). **3** to move or be transmitted from one place to another: *The sound travelled in the still air.*

travel[2] *n* **1a** the act of travelling; passage. **b** (*in pl*) journeys, *esp* to distant or unfamiliar places. **2** (*used before a noun*) suitable for use when travelling, *esp* in being small and light: *a travel iron.* **3** the motion of a piece of machinery; *esp* alternate forward and backward motion.

travel agency *n* an agency that gives information on and arranges travel. ▸▸ **travel agent** *n.*

travelator *or* **travolator** *n* a moving walkway.

traveled *adj NAm* = TRAVELLED.

traveler *n NAm* = TRAVELLER.

traveler's check *n NAm* = TRAVELLER'S CHEQUE.

travelled (*NAm* **traveled**) *adj* **1** experienced in travel. **2** used by travellers.

traveller (*NAm* **traveler**) *n* **1** somebody who goes on a trip or journey; *esp* somebody who travels frequently. **2a** somebody who lives an alternative lifestyle, moving around from place to place in a van or other vehicle. **b** = GYPSY.

traveller's cheque (*NAm* **traveler's check**) *n* a cheque that is purchased from a bank or travel agency and that may be exchanged abroad for foreign currency.

traveller's joy *n* a wild clematis with white flowers and whitish grey feathery flower-parts.

travelling salesman *n* somebody who travels for a company, selling goods or gaining orders.

travelogue (*NAm* **travelog**) *n* **1** a film or illustrated talk or lecture on some usu exotic or remote place. **2** a narrated documentary film about travel.

traverse[1] *v* **1** to pass or travel across, over, or through (something). **2** to move to and fro over or along (something). **3** to move back and forth or from side to side. ▸▸ **traversable** *adj,* **traversal** *n.*

traverse[2] *n* **1** the act or an instance of traversing; crossing. **2** a sideways movement, or a device for imparting such movement. **3** something that crosses or lies across.

travertine *n* a mineral consisting of a limestone that is formed as a deposit from spring waters or hot springs.

travesty[1] *n* (*pl* **-ies**) **1** a crude or grotesque literary or artistic parody. **2** a debased, distorted, or grossly inferior imitation.

travesty[2] *v* (**-ies, -ied**) to make a travesty of; to parody or caricature.

travois /trə'voy/ *n* (*pl* **travois**) a primitive vehicle formerly used by Native Americans of the Great Plains region, consisting of two trailing poles serving as shafts for a dog or horse and bearing a platform or net for the load.

travolator *n* see TRAVELATOR.

trawl[1] *v* **1** to fish or catch (fish) with a trawl. **2** to search through a large number of things.

trawl[2] *n* **1** a large conical net dragged along the sea bottom to catch fish or other marine life. **2** an act of trawling.

trawler *n* a boat used in trawling.

tray *n* an open receptacle with a flat bottom and a low rim for holding or carrying articles.

treacherous *adj* **1** characterized by treachery; perfidious. **2a** of uncertain reliability. **b** providing insecure footing or support. **c** marked by hidden dangers or hazards. ▸▸ **treacherously** *adv,* **treacherousness** *n,* **treachery** *n.*

treacle *n* **1** *chiefly Brit* molasses. **2** golden syrup. ▸▸ **treacly** *adj.*

tread[1] *v* (*past tense* **trod,** *past part.* **trodden** *or* **trod**) **1** to move on foot; to walk. **2a** to set foot. **b** to put one's foot; to step. **3a** to step or walk on or over (something). **b** to walk along (e.g. a road); to follow. **4** to beat or press with the feet; to trample or crush. ✱ **tread on somebody's toes/corns** to give offence to or hurt somebody's feelings, *esp* by encroaching on their rights. **tread water 1** to keep the body nearly upright in the water and the head above water by a treading motion of the feet, usu aided by the hands. **2** to stay in the same position without making progress.

tread[2] *n* **1a** the action of treading. **b** an act of treading; a step. **c** the sound or manner of stepping or treading. **2** the upper horizontal part of a step. **3a** the part of a wheel or tyre that makes contact with a road or rail. **b** the pattern of ridges or grooves made or cut in the face of a tyre. **c** the part of a sole that touches the ground.

treadle[1] *n* a lever pressed by the foot to drive a machine, e.g. a sewing machine.

treadle[2] *v* to operate (a machine) using a treadle.

treadmill *n* **1a** a mill, used formerly to employ or punish prisoners, worked by people treading on steps inside a wide wheel with a horizontal axis. **b** a mill worked by an animal treading an endless belt. **2** an exercise machine that has a continuous moving belt on which to run or walk. **3** a wearisome or monotonous routine.

treason *n* **1** (*also* **high treason**) the offence of violating the duty of allegiance owed to one's crown or government. **2** the betrayal of a trust. ➤➤ **treasonable** *adj*, **treasonous** *adj*.

treasure[1] *n* **1** wealth, *esp* in a form which can be accumulated or hoarded. **2a** something of great worth or value. **b** *informal* somebody highly valued or prized.

treasure[2] *v* **1** to hold or preserve as precious; to cherish or prize. **2** to collect and store up (something valuable); to hoard.

treasure hunt *n* a game in which each player tries to be first to find whatever has been hidden.

treasurer *n* the financial officer of an organization, e.g. a society.

treasure trove *n* **1** under English law until 1996, hidden valuables, such as coins, articles of gold or silver, or jewellery, that are of unknown ownership and become the property of the Crown when found. **2** a valuable or productive discovery or source.

treasury *n* (*pl* **-ies**) **1a** a depository where the collected funds or revenues of a state, organization, society, or individual are deposited and kept, and from which drawings may be made, funds issued, etc. **b** the funds or revenues in such a depository. **2** (*often* **Treasury**) in certain countries, the government department in charge of finance and the economy. **3** a place where treasure is kept. **4** a source or collection of valuable or pleasing things.

Treasury bill *n* a bill of exchange issued by the treasury.

treat[1] *v* **1a** to behave towards (a person or animal) in a certain way. **b** to regard and deal with (something) in a specified manner: *I just treated the remark as a joke; Police are treating the incident as racially motivated.* **2** to present (a subject). **3** to care for or deal with (somebody or something) medically or surgically. **4** to apply a process or substance to: *The wood is treated with a preservative.* **5a** (+ to) to provide (somebody) with food, drink, or entertainment at one's own expense. **b** (+ to) to provide (oneself) with enjoyment or gratification. **6** *formal* (*usu* + with/for) to discuss terms with somebody; to negotiate. ➤➤ **treatable** *adj*, **treater** *n*.

treat[2] *n* **1** something that gives great pleasure. **2** (**one's treat**) an act of providing something for somebody else at one's own expense. ✱ **a treat** *Brit, informal* very well, successfully, or pleasurably: *The speech went down a treat.*

treatise *n* a formal written report on a subject, *esp* a systematic or technical one.

treatment *n* **1** the act, manner, or process of handling somebody or something. **2** the discussion or presentation of a subject, theme, etc, *esp* in the arts. **3** the medicine, therapy, surgery, etc involved in caring for or dealing with a patient or an injury or illness. **4** the use of a substance, etc to achieve a particular effect or to eliminate a specific condition.

treaty *n* (*pl* **-ies**) a formal agreement made by negotiation, *esp* between two or more states.

treble[1] *adj* **1** having three parts or uses; threefold. **2** being three times as great in number or as much in amount. **3a** relating to or having the range or part of a treble. **b** high-pitched or shrill.

treble[2] *n* **1** a singer having a high-pitched singing voice, *esp* a boy. **2** (*used before a noun*) a musical instrument having a relatively high range. **3** the higher portion of the audio frequency range considered *esp* in relation to its electronic reproduction.

treble[3] *v* to increase or cause to increase to three times as much or as many.

treble clef *n* in musical notation, a clef placing the G above middle C on the second lowest line of the stave.

trebly[1] *adj* of sound: having too much treble.

trebly[2] *adv* three times as much.

tree *n* **1** a tall woody plant having a single usu long and erect main stem, generally with few or no branches on its lower part. **2** a diagram or graph with a branching structure that shows the relationships or processes connecting the various elements plotted on it. **3** a piece of wood or a wooden structure. **4** *archaic or literary* the cross on which Jesus was crucified. ✱ **be barking up the wrong tree** *informal* to be taking useless action or acting misguidedly. ➤➤ **treeless** *adj*.

treecreeper *n* a small songbird with a slender curved beak used for pulling insects out of the bark of trees.

tree fern *n* a tree-like fern with a woody stem.

tree house *n* a structure built in the branches of a tree for children to play in.

tree-hugger *n* *informal* a person who is aware of environmental issues, *esp* somebody who campaigns against the development of the countryside for industrial, residential, or transport uses. ➤➤ **tree-hugging** *n*.

tree line *n* the upper limit of tree growth on a mountain or at a high northern or southern latitude.

treen *n* (*used as pl*) small domestic articles, *esp* antique tableware, made of wood.

tree of knowledge *n* according to the Bible, the tree in the Garden of Eden whose fruit Adam and Eve ate, thereby disobeying God (Genesis 3:22–4).

Tree of Life *n* according to the Bible, the tree in the Garden of Eden whose fruit gave anyone eating it eternal life (Genesis 2:9; 3:22).

tree ring *n* the layer of wood produced by a single year's growth of a tree.

tree surgeon *n* a person who specializes in treating and preserving diseased, damaged, and decaying trees. ➤➤ **tree surgery** *n*.

trefoil *n* **1** a wild plant with three-lobed leaves. **2** a stylized figure or ornament, *esp* in architectural tracery, in the form of a three-lobed leaf or flower.

trek[1] *n* a journey; *esp* a long or arduous one made on foot.

trek[2] *v* (**trekked, trekking**) to travel, *esp* by going on a long or arduous walk. ➤➤ **trekker** *n*.

Trekkie *n informal* an ardent fan of *Star Trek*, a US television science-fiction series.

trellis[1] *n* a frame of latticework used as a screen or as a support for climbing plants.

trellis[2] *v* (**trellised, trellising**) to provide or support with a trellis.

trematode *n* a parasitic flatworm of a class including the flukes.

tremble[1] *v* **1** to shake involuntarily, *esp* with fear or cold; to shiver. **2** to be affected by a quivering or vibratory motion. **3** to be affected with fear or apprehension.

tremble[2] *n* a fit or spell of involuntary shaking or quivering.

trembler *n Brit* a vibrating device that automatically makes or breaks an electric circuit.

trembly *adj* (**-ier, -iest**) *informal* shaking or quivering.

tremendous *adj* **1** very great in size, degree, amount, intensity, etc. **2** *informal* **a** highly impressive, unusual, or exciting. **b** great or extreme. ⋙ **tremendously** *adv,* **tremendousness** *n.*

tremolo *n* (*pl* **-os**) **1** in music, a very rapid repetition of a note or notes to produce a trembling effect. **2** a device on an electric guitar that produces a trembling effect.

tremolo arm *n* = TREMOLO (2).

tremor *n* **1** an involuntary trembling or shaking, usu because of physical weakness, emotional stress, or disease. **2** a slight quivering or vibratory motion; *esp* a distinct small movement of the earth that precedes or follows a major earthquake. **3** a sudden thrill or quiver of fear or excitement.

tremulous *adj* **1** characterized by or affected with trembling or tremors; shaking or quivering. **2** uncertain, timid, or fearful. ⋙ **tremulously** *adv,* **tremulousness** *n.*

trench[1] *n* **1** a long narrow ditch or excavation in the ground. **2** a deep ditch used for military defence, usu with the excavated earth banked up in front for protection. **3** a long, narrow, and usu steep-sided depression in the ocean floor.

trench[2] *v* to dig a trench or trenches in (a piece of ground).

trenchant *adj* **1** incisive and penetrating. **2** vigorously effective and articulate. **3** *archaic or literary* of a weapon or tool: sharp-edged. ⋙ **trenchancy** *n,* **trenchantly** *adv.*

trench coat *n* **1** a double-breasted raincoat with deep pockets, a belt, and epaulettes. **2** a waterproof overcoat designed to be worn by soldiers, *esp* in trenches.

trencher *n* a wooden platter formerly used for serving food.

trencherman *n* (*pl* **trenchermen**) a hearty eater or a person who enjoys good food.

trench fever *n* an infectious rickettsial disease that is transmitted by the body louse, causing fever and severe pains in the muscles, bones, and joints.

trench foot *n* a painful disorder of the foot, resembling frostbite, caused by prolonged immersion in cold water or mud.

trench warfare *n* a type of warfare in which the opposing forces fight from systems of trenches that face each other.

trend[1] *n* **1** a general or prevailing direction, tendency, or inclination. **2** a general movement or change. **3** a current style, fashion, or taste.

trend[2] *v esp* of a geographical feature: to extend or bend in a specified direction.

trendsetter *n* somebody who starts a new trend in fashion or popularizes an idea, theory, etc. ⋙ **trendsetting** *adj.*

trendy[1] *adj* (**-ier, -iest**) *informal* **1** very fashionable or up-to-date. **2** characterized by unthinking adherence to the latest fashions or progressive ideas. ⋙ **trendily** *adv,* **trendiness** *n.*

trendy[2] *n* (*pl* **-ies**) *informal* a person who follows the latest fashions or who accepts the most up-to-date ideas, etc.

trepan[1] *n* a primitive type of TREPHINE[1] (surgical instrument) used to remove circular pieces of tissue or bone, *esp* bone from the skull.

trepan[2] *v* (**trepanned, trepanning**) to remove a circular piece of bone from (a person's skull) using a surgical trepan. ⋙ **trepanation** *n.*

trephine[1] *n* a surgical instrument for cutting out circular sections, *esp* of bone or the cornea of the eye.

trephine[2] *v* to operate on (somebody's skull) using a trephine. ⋙ **trephination** *n.*

trepidation *n* a feeling of nervous agitation, apprehension, or fear, *esp* at the thought of something that is about to happen.

trespass[1] *v* **1** to enter somebody's land or property unlawfully or without permission. **2** (+ on/upon) to make an unwarranted or uninvited intrusion on or take unfair advantage of something. **3** *archaic or literary* (+ against) to commit an offence against a person or break a rule or law. ⋙ **trespasser** *n.*

trespass[2] *n* **1** entry to somebody's land or property that is unlawful or done without permission. **2** *archaic or literary* a moral violation; a sin.

tress *n* (*also in pl*) a long lock of hair.

trestle *n* **1** a framework consisting typically of a horizontal bar held at each end by two pairs of sloping legs, *esp* one designed to support something such as a table top. **2** a braced framework of timbers, piles, or girders for carrying a road or railway over a depression.

trestle table *n* a table consisting of a board or boards supported on trestles.

trestlework *n* = TRESTLE (2).

trews *pl n chiefly Brit* trousers.

tri- *comb. form* **1** three: *tripartite.* **2** having three elements or parts: *trigraph.* **3** into three: *trisect.*

triable *adj* of a criminal offence or a court case: liable or subject to trial.

triacetate *n* **1** a chemical compound containing three acetate groups in the molecular structure. **2** an artificial textile fibre made from a triacetate of cellulose.

triad *n* **1** a union or group of three related or associated people or things. **2** (*often* **Triad**) any of various Chinese secret societies, *esp* one engaged in organized crime, such as drug trafficking, extortion, and prostitution. ⋙ **triadic** *adj.*

triage *n* **1** the act or an instance of sorting or grouping things according to need or potential benefit. **2** the process of allocating treatment to patients according to a system of priorities based on assessing the urgency of their medical needs.

trial[1] *n* **1** a formal examination of the evidence in a civil or criminal court case in order to determine an accused person's guilt or innocence. **2** the act or process of testing something. **3a** a sports match in which the comparative skills of players are evaluated, *esp* in order to select team members. **b** (*in pl*) a competition in which the individual skills of a person or an animal are tested. **4** a test of faith, patience, or stamina, *esp* one that involves suffering or temptation. ✱ **on trial 1** of an accused person:

undergoing trial in a court of law. **2** of a new product: undergoing testing.

trial² *v* (**trialled, trialling,** *NAm* **trialed, trialing**) **1** to test (something) in order to assess its quality, durability, performance, etc. **2** of a sheepdog, horse, or sports player: to take part in trials.

trial and error *n* a process of trying out a number of methods in order to find the best way to achieve a desired result.

trialist (*Brit* **triallist**) *n* **1** a person who takes part in a sports trial or in a preliminary match for potential team or squad selection, etc. **2** a person who takes part in the trial of a new product.

trial run *n* an exercise to test the performance of something, *esp* a new product.

triangle *n* **1** a polygon with three angles and three sides. **2** something shaped like a triangle. **3** a percussion instrument consisting of a steel rod bent into the form of a triangle open at one angle and sounded by striking with a small metal rod. **4** a romantic or sexual relationship involving three people.

triangular *adj* **1a** relating to or having the form of a triangle. **b** having a triangular base or principal surface. **2** between or involving three elements, things, or people. ➤➤ **triangularity** *n,* **triangularly** *adv.*

triangulate *v* **1a** to divide (something, *esp* land) into triangles. **b** to survey or map (an area) by triangulation. **c** to calculate (a height, distance, etc) by triangulation. **2** to give triangular form to.

triangulation *n* the measurement of the angles and one side of a triangle to find an unknown position, distance, etc, *esp* the determination of the network of triangles into which any part of the earth's surface is divided in surveying, using this operation.

triangulation point *n* = TRIG POINT.

Triassic *adj* of the first geological period of the Mesozoic era, lasting from about 245 million to about 208 million years ago, and marked by an abundance of reptiles and the first appearance of dinosaurs. ➤➤ **Triassic** *n.*

triathlon *n* an athletic contest in which all contestants compete in three events, typically long-distance running, swimming, and cycling. ➤➤ **triathlete** *n.*

triatomic *adj* having three atoms in the molecule.

tribal¹ *adj* relating to or characteristic of a tribe or tribes. ➤➤ **tribally** *adv.*

tribal² *n* a member of a tribal group, *esp* in the Indian subcontinent.

tribalism *n* **1** the state of belonging to a tribe. **2** tribal consciousness and loyalty, *esp* exaltation of the tribe above other groups. ➤➤ **tribalist** *n.*

tribe *n* **1** a group of people, families, or clans with shared economic and social ties and usu a common culture, dialect, religion, and ancestry. **2** in ancient Rome, one of several (orig three) political divisions of the Roman people. **3** *derog* a group of people sharing a common occupation or interest, *esp* an insular social or political group. **4** *informal* (*also in pl*) large numbers of people or things. **5** a category in biological taxonomy ranking above a genus and below a family.

tribesman *or* **tribeswoman** *n* (*pl* **tribesmen** *or* **tribeswomen**) a man or woman who is a member of a tribe in a non-industrialized society.

tribology *n* the scientific study of the design, friction, wear, and lubrication of interacting surfaces in relative motion, e.g. in bearings or gears. ➤➤ **tribological** *adj,* **tribologist** *n.*

tribulation *n* **1** a state of great distress or suffering. **2** a source or cause of this.

tribunal *n* **1** *Brit* a board appointed to decide disputes of a specified kind. **2** a court or forum of justice.

tribune¹ *n* **1** an official of ancient Rome elected by and from the common people to protect their interests. **2** a person who defends the rights of the people. ➤➤ **tribunate** *n,* **tribuneship** *n.*

tribune² *n* **1** an apse in a basilica. **2** a dais or platform, *esp* one in a church.

tributary *n* (*pl* **-ies**) **1** a stream or river feeding a larger stream or river or a lake. **2** formerly, a ruler or state paying tribute to a conqueror.

tribute *n* **1** something, *esp* a gift or a formal statement, given or made as a demonstration of respect, gratitude, or affection. **2** evidence of the worth or effectiveness of something specified: *The vote was a tribute to their good sense.* **3** a payment by one ruler or nation formerly made to another, in acknowledgment of submission or as the price of protection.

trice ✱ **in a trice** very soon or immediately.

tricentenary *n* (*pl* **-ies**) = TERCENTENARY. ➤➤ **tricentennial** *adj and n.*

triceps *n* (*pl* **tricepses** *or* **triceps**) the large muscle along the back of the upper arm that extends the forearm from the elbow.

triceratops *n* a large plant-eating dinosaur of the Cretaceous period with three horns, a bony neck frill, and hoofed toes.

trichina *n* (*pl* **trichinae**) a small slender nematode worm that in the larval state is parasitic in the muscles of flesh-eating mammals, e.g. human beings and pigs.

trichinosis *n* infestation with or disease caused by trichinae and marked by muscular pain, fever, and oedema.

trichology *n* the scientific study of hair, hair growth, and disorders of the hair and scalp. ➤➤ **trichological** *adj,* **trichologist** *n.*

trichromatic *adj* **1** relating to, consisting of, or using three colours, *esp* the three primary ones. **2** relating to or having normal colour vision, in which the eye is sensitive to all three primary colours. ➤➤ **trichromatism** *n.*

trick¹ *n* **1a** a crafty action or plan, *esp* one intended to deceive, defraud, or outwit somebody. **b** a deceptive, dexterous, or ingenious feat designed to puzzle or amuse. **2a** a deceptive appearance; an illusion. **b** (*used before a noun*) relating to, denoting, or involving trickery or illusion: *trick photography.* **c** (*used before a noun*) causing confusion or mystery: *a trick question.* **3** a habitual peculiarity of behaviour or manner; a mannerism. **4** the cards played in one round of a card game, often used as a scoring unit. ✱ **do the trick** *informal* to produce the desired result. **tricks of the trade** the techniques that are used by experts in a particular profession or craft. **turn a trick** *informal* of a prostitute: to have a session with a client. **up to one's (old) tricks (again)** *informal* behaving in a characteristic, often undesirable, way. ➤➤ **trickery** *n.*

trick² *v* **1** to deceive, defraud, or outwit. **2** (+ into) to deceive (somebody) into doing something. **3** (+ out of) to cheat (somebody) out of something.

trickle¹ *v* **1** to flow in drops or a thin slow stream. **2a** to move or go gradually or one by one. **b** to dissipate slowly. **3** (+ down) of the wealth of large businesses and the rich: to benefit small businesses and poorer members of a society after a period of time.

trickle² *n* a thin slow stream or movement.

trick-or-treat *v* of a child: to take part in a Halloween custom that involves dressing up and going round houses to ask for treats, and threatening to play tricks on any householders who refuse.

trickster *n* a person who defrauds others by trickery.

tricksy *adj* (**-ier, -iest**) **1** full of tricks; mischievous or playful. **2** difficult to follow or make out; intricate or complicated.

tricky *adj* (**-ier, -iest**) **1** of a task, problem, situation, etc: requiring great skill, care, or tact. **2** full of unseen or concealed difficulties, hazards, or problems. **3** inclined to be sly, wily, or deceitful. ➤➤ **trickily** *adv,* **trickiness** *n.*

tricolour[1] (*NAm* **tricolor**) *n* a flag with three bands or blocks of different colours, *esp* the French national flag with its vertical bands of blue, white, and red.

tricolour[2] *or* **tricoloured** (*NAm* **tricolor** *or* **tricolored**) *adj* having three colours.

tricorn[1] *or* **tricorne** *adj* of a hat: having three horns or corners.

tricorn[2] *or* **tricorne** *n* a type of three-cornered hat worn by men, with an upturned brim.

tricot *n* a fine plain inelastic knitted fabric used in clothing, *esp* formerly for underwear.

tricuspid *adj* **1** of a tooth: having three cusps or points. **2** of an anatomical valve: having three segments or cusps.

tricycle *n* a three-wheeled pedal-driven vehicle.

tricyclic *adj* of a chemical compound: having a molecular structure containing three usu fused rings; *specif* belonging to a series of synthetic chemically related drugs used to treat depression. ➤➤ **tricyclic** *n.*

trident *n* a three-pronged spear.

tried *v* past tense and past part. of TRY[1].

triennia *n* pl of TRIENNIUM.

triennial *adj* **1** lasting for three years. **2** occurring every three years. ➤➤ **triennially** *adv.*

triennium *n* (*pl* **trienniums** *or* **triennia**) a period of three years.

trier *n* **1** somebody who perseveres with something. **2** a person who examines a judicial case.

trifid *adj esp* of a plant part or body part: deeply and narrowly cleft into three teeth, parts, or points.

trifle[1] *n* **1** *Brit* a type of cold dessert made from sponge cake, jelly, custard, and whipped cream. **2** something of little value or importance. **3** an insignificant amount of something.

trifle[2] *v* **1** (*often* + with) to behave frivolously, thoughtlessly, or disrespectfully towards somebody or something. **2** to talk in a jesting or mocking manner. ➤➤ **trifler** *n.*

trifling *adj* unimportant or frivolous. ➤➤ **triflingly** *adv.*

trifocal *adj* of glasses: having three focal lengths.

trifocals *pl n* glasses with three focal lengths.

trifoliate *adj* **1** of a compound leaf: having three leaflets. **2** of a plant: having three leaves.

triforium *n* (*pl* **triforia**) a gallery forming an upper storey to the aisle of a church and typically an arcaded storey above the arches of the nave and below the clerestory.

triform *adj technical* having three parts.

trifurcate[1] *v* to divide into three branches or forks. ➤➤ **trifurcation** *n.*

trifurcate[2] *adj* divided into three branches or forks.

trigger[1] *n* **1** a device that can be moved to release a catch or spring, activating a mechanism, *esp* the part of a gun that makes it fire. **2** something that causes an event or reaction.

trigger[2] *v* **1** to activate (a mechanism, *esp* that of a gun) by means of a trigger. **2** (*often* + off) to initiate, bring about, or set off (something, *esp* something unpleasant or unwanted).

trigger-happy *adj* inclined to resort to violence or guns too quickly, or to act or speak rashly and without considering the potential consequences.

triglyceride *n* an ester that is formed by the combination of one molecule of the alcohol glycerol and three organic acid molecules.

triglyph *n* in Doric architecture, a projecting rectangular tablet with three vertical grooves, used on ornamental friezes.

trigonometry *n* the branch of mathematics concerned with the properties of triangles and trigonometric functions and their applications. ➤➤ **trigonometric** *adj,* **trigonometrical** *adj.*

trig point *n Brit* a hilltop reference point, usu marked by a small tower, used by surveyors.

trigram *n* **1** in the Chinese system of divination, I Ching, any one of eight symbols, each composed of various combinations of three broken and unbroken lines, which, when paired, form the 64 hexagrams that are used as the basis for interpretations. **2** = TRIGRAPH.

trigraph *n* a combination of three letters representing a single speech sound, e.g. *eau* in *beau.*

trihedron *n* (*pl* **trihedra** *or* **trihedrons**) a geometrical figure with three faces formed by the intersection of three planes. ➤➤ **trihedral** *adj and n.*

trike *n informal* a tricycle.

trilateral[1] *adj* **1** of talks, an agreement, etc: involving three parties, states, etc. **2** of a geometric figure: having three sides.

trilateral[2] *n* a triangle.

trilby *n* (*pl* **-ies**) *chiefly Brit* a soft felt hat with an indented crown.

trilingual *adj* **1** using or able to use three languages with the fluency of a native speaker. **2** using or expressed in three languages. ➤➤ **trilingualism** *n.*

trill[1] *n* **1** in music, a rapid alternation of a main note and one above it. **2** a sound resembling a musical trill, e.g. one made by a bird.

trill[2] *v* to produce a warbling sound. ➤➤ **triller** *n.*

trillion *n* (*pl* **trillions** *or* **trillion**) **1** *Brit* a million million million or 1,000,000,000,000,000,000 (10^{18}). **2** *NAm* a million million or 1,000,000,000,000 (10^{12}). ➤➤ **trillion** *adj,* **trillionth** *adj and n.*

trilobite *n* an extinct Palaeozoic marine arthropod that had a three-lobed body.

trilogy *n* (*pl* **-ies**) a group of three closely related literary, cinematic, or musical works.

trim[1] *v* (**trimmed, trimming**) **1a** to make neater, shorter, or smaller by cutting or clipping. **b** (*often* + off/from) to remove (a specified length) from something by cutting or clipping. **2** to reduce the size of (something, *esp* expenditure) by eliminating any unnecessary or superfluous things. **3** to decorate with ribbons, lace, or ornaments. **4** to adjust (a sail on a sailing ship) to take advantage of the wind direction. **5** to change one's views, *esp* in the hope of achieving personal advancement. ✱ **trim one's sails (to the wind)** to alter one's way of life, *esp* in response to changed circumstances. ➤➤ **trimmer** *n.*

trim[2] *n* **1** the act or an instance of trimming. **2a** material used for decoration or trimming. **b** the upholstery, interior, and decorative accessories of a motor vehicle. ✱ **in trim 1** fit and healthy. **2** well-maintained.

trim[3] *adj* (**trimmer, trimmest**) in good order; neat and smart. ➤➤ **trimly** *adv*, **trimness** *n*.

trimaran *n* a yacht with three parallel hulls.

trimer *n* a large chemical molecule composed of three small identical molecules. ➤➤ **trimeric** *adj*.

trimester *n* **1** a period of three months, *esp* any of the three periods of about three months into which human pregnancy may be divided. **2** *NAm* any of the three divisions of the academic year. ➤➤ **trimestral** *adj*, **trimestrial** *adj*.

trimming *n* **1** (*in pl*) pieces cut off in trimming something. **2** ribbon, lace, or some other decoration added to clothing, upholstery, linen, etc. **3** *informal* (*in pl*) the traditional garnishes accompanying a dish or meal.

Trinidadian *n* a native or inhabitant of Trinidad. ➤➤ **Trinidadian** *adj*.

Trinitarian *n* an adherent of the doctrine of the Trinity. ➤➤ **Trinitarian** *adj*, **Trinitarianism** *n*.

trinitrotoluene *n* an inflammable derivative of toluene used as a high explosive and in chemical synthesis.

trinity *n* (*pl* **-ies**) **1** (**the Trinity**) according to Christian theology, the unity of Father, Son, and Holy Spirit as three persons in one Godhead. **2** a group of three closely related people or things.

trinket *n* a small ornament or piece of jewellery, *esp* one of little material value. ➤➤ **trinketry** *n*.

trinomial[1] *adj technical* consisting of three terms.

trinomial[2] *n* a trinomial expression or name.

trio *n* (*pl* **-os**) **1** a group or set of three people or things. **2** a group of three musicians or singers.

triode *n* **1** a thermionic valve with three electrodes. **2** a semiconductor rectifier with three connections.

trioxide *n* an oxide containing three atoms of oxygen per molecule.

trip[1] *v* (**tripped, tripping**) **1** (*also* + on/up/over) to catch the foot on or against something and stumble or fall. **2** (+ up) to make a mistake. **3** to dance, skip, or walk with light quick steps. **4** to cause (a device or mechanism) to start or stop operating, *esp* by releasing a catch or producing an electrical signal. **5** of machinery: to stop working, often as a result of an automatic safety mechanism being activated. **6** *informal* to experience the effects of a psychedelic drug, *esp* LSD. ✱ **trip the light fantastic** to dance.

trip[2] *n* **1** a journey or outing. **2** the act or an instance of catching the foot and stumbling or falling. **3** *informal* **a** a hallucinogenic experience induced by a psychedelic drug, *esp* LSD. **b** any highly charged, often distressing, emotional experience. **4** *informal* an obsessive, self-indulgent, self-serving, or absorbing course of action or frame of mind. **5** the act or an instance of releasing a catch or other device in order to activate, operate, or stop machinery or a mechanism.

tripartite *adj* **1** divided into or composed of three parts. **2** made between or involving three parties.

tripe *n* **1** the stomach tissue of an ox, cow, etc for use as food. **2** *informal* rubbish or nonsense.

trip-hammer *n* a large hammer raised by machinery and then tripped to drop on work below, used *esp* in forging metals.

triphthong *n* **1** a vowel sound, e.g. /ie·ə/ in *fire*, composed of three elements. **2** = TRIGRAPH.

triplane *n* an aeroplane with three main pairs of wings arranged one above the other.

triple[1] *adj* **1** having three units or members. **2** three times as much or as many. **3** repeated three times. ➤➤ **triply** *adv*.

triple[2] *n* **1** a triple sum, quantity, or number. **2** a combination, group, or series of three.

triple[3] *v* to increase or cause to increase by three times as much or as many.

triple bond *n* a chemical bond consisting of three pairs of electrons that are shared between two atoms in a molecule.

triple crown *n* **1** (*often* **Triple Crown**) the winning of three important sporting matches or horse races in a single season, or an award for this. **2** the pope's tiara.

triple jump *n* an athletic field event in which a competitor takes a running start and then performs a hop, a step, and a jump in succession, in an attempt to achieve a jump of the longest distance.

triplet *n* **1** one of three children or animals born at one birth. **2** a group of three musical notes performed in the time of two or four of the same value. **3** a unit of three lines of verse, *esp* lines that share the same end rhyme.

triple time *n* musical time with three beats to the bar.

triplex[1] *adj* threefold or triple.

triplex[2] *n NAm* a residential building that is divided into three separate apartments.

triplicate[1] *adj* consisting of or existing in three corresponding or identical parts or examples.

triplicate[2] *v* **1** to make three copies of (something, *esp* a document). **2** to multiply by three. ➤➤ **triplication** *n*, **triplicity** *n*.

triploid *adj* of a cell, nucleus, or organism: having or containing three times the basic number of chromosomes.

tripmeter *n* a device in a motor vehicle that measures distance, usu one that can be reset to record the mileage of individual journeys.

tripod *n* **1** a three-legged stand, *esp* one for supporting a camera or other piece of equipment. **2** *archaic* something, such as a stool, table, or cauldron, with three legs.

tripos *n* an honours examination for a BA degree at Cambridge University.

tripper *n Brit, informal* somebody who goes on a journey or outing, *esp* a short one taken for pleasure.

triptych *n* **1** a picture or carving covering three panels side by side, *esp* an altarpiece consisting of a central panel with two hinged flanking panels half its width that can be folded inwards to cover it completely. **2** a group of three related literary, cinematic, or musical works; a trilogy.

trip wire *n* a concealed wire placed near the ground that is used to trip up an intruder or to activate an explosive or warning device when pulled.

trireme *n* a galley with three banks of oars, *esp* one used by the ancient Greeks and Romans as a warship.

trisect *v* to divide (something) into three parts. ➤➤ **trisection** *n*.

trishaw *n* a passenger vehicle consisting of a tricycle with a rickshaw body over the rear wheels, used *esp* in Asian cities.

trisyllable *n* a word or metrical foot of three syllables. ➤➤ **trisyllabic** *adj*.

trite *adj* of a word, phrase, remark, idea, etc: lacking originality; hackneyed from overuse. ➤➤ **tritely** *adv*, **triteness** *n*.

triticale *n* a cereal grass, a hybrid between wheat and rye, that has a high yield and rich protein content, used as animal fodder.

tritium *n* a radioactive isotope of hydrogen with atoms of three times the mass of ordinary hydrogen atoms.

triturate *v technical* **1** to crush or grind (a substance) into a fine powder. **2** to chew (food) thoroughly before swallowing. ⋙ **trituration** *n.*

triumph[1] *n* **1a** a notable success, victory, or achievement. **b** the feeling of happiness, exultation, or satisfaction that such success, etc brings. **c** a highly successful or spectacular example of something. **2** in ancient Rome, a ceremonial procession that accompanied a victorious general as he returned to the city. ⋙ **triumphal** *adj.*

triumph[2] *v* **1** (*often* + over) to obtain victory. **2** to celebrate victory or success, *esp* boastfully or with too much exultation.

triumphalism *n* excessive or boastful exultation following a success or victory. ⋙ **triumphalist** *adj and n.*

triumphant *adj* **1** having won a battle, sports match, or contest; victorious. **2** rejoicing in or celebrating victory; jubilant. ⋙ **triumphantly** *adv.*

triumvir /trie'umvə/ *n* (*pl* **triumvirs** *or* **triumviri**) in ancient Rome, each of the three public officials who shared the responsibility of running any of the city's administrative departments. ⋙ **triumviral** *adj.*

triumvirate *n* **1** a group of three, *esp* a group of three powerful people or three notable things. **2** in ancient Rome, a group of three men jointly holding a public office.

triumviri /trie'umvrie/ *n* pl of TRIUMVIR.

triune *adj* three in one, *esp* in reference to or denoting the Trinity.

trivet *n* **1** a three-legged iron stand placed over an open fire to support a cooking pot or kettle. **2** a stand for putting a hot dish on at the table or on a worktop.

trivia *pl n* (*used as sing. or pl*) unimportant matters, details, or facts.

trivial *adj* of little worth or importance; insignificant. ⋙ **triviality** *n,* **trivially** *adv.*

trivialize *or* **-ise** *v* to treat (something) as being unimportant or less important than it is. ⋙ **trivialization** *n.*

-trix *suffix* (*pl* **-trices** *or* **-trixes**) forming nouns, with the meaning: a female agent, usu corresponding to masculine nouns ending in *-tor,* and now only current in legal contexts: *executrix.*

trochaic[1] *adj* of a poem, verse, or a line of poetry: featuring trochees or composed mainly of trochees.

trochaic[2] *n* a trochaic verse.

trochee *n* in prosody, a metrical foot consisting of one long or stressed syllable followed by one short or unstressed syllable, e.g. in *apple.*

trod *v* past tense and past part. of TREAD[1].

trodden *v* past part. of TREAD[1].

troglodyte *n* **1** a person who lives in a cave, *esp* in prehistoric times. **2** a person who deliberately shuns other people and the outside world. ⋙ **troglodytic** *adj.*

troika *n* **1a** a Russian vehicle pulled by three horses abreast. **b** the team of three horses pulling such a vehicle. **2** a group of three people, *esp* three managers, administrators, etc who work as a team.

troilism *n* any form of sexual activity that involves three people simultaneously.

Trojan *n* **1** a native or inhabitant of ancient Troy, a city in Asia Minor. **2** somebody who shows the qualities, e.g. pluck or endurance, attributed to the defenders of ancient Troy. ⋙ **Trojan** *adj.*

Trojan Horse *n* **1** somebody or something that undermines an organization from within it. **2** in computing, a program whose function is to cause some kind of damage to a system or to allow an unauthorized user to bypass a system's security, *esp* one that is disguised as ordinary software.

Word history

so called because of the large hollow wooden horse which, in Greek mythology, was left by the Greeks outside Troy, which they were besieging. The Trojans took the wooden horse into the city, whereupon soldiers hidden inside it let the Greek army in.

troll[1] *n* in Germanic and Scandinavian folklore, an ugly dwarf or giant that lives in caves or hills.

troll[2] *v* **1** to try to catch fish with a hook and line drawn through the water behind a moving boat. **2** *chiefly Brit* to stroll, saunter, or wander from place to place. ⋙ **troller** *n.*

troll[3] *n* **1** the action of trolling. **2** the bait or line used in trolling.

trolley *n* (*pl* **-eys**) **1** *Brit* **a** a large basket or a small cart on wheels, used for carrying things, e.g. shopping or luggage. **b** a shelved stand on wheels used for conveying something, *esp* food or drinks. **c** a hospital stretcher on wheels used for transporting patients. **2a** a device attached to a pole on the roof of an electrically powered vehicle, *esp* a tram, for collecting the current from an overhead wire. **b** = TROLLEYBUS. **c** *NAm* = TROLLEY CAR. ✱ **off one's trolley** *Brit, informal* crazy or stupid.

trolleybus *n* an electrically propelled bus running on a road and drawing power from two overhead wires via a trolley.

trolley car *n NAm* a tram that is powered by electricity collected from overhead wires.

trolley wheel *n* = TROLLEY (2A).

trombone *n* a brass musical instrument consisting of a long cylindrical metal tube with a movable slide to extend its length and thus vary the pitch. ⋙ **trombonist** *n.*

trompe l'oeil /,tromp 'luh·i/ *n* (*pl* **trompe l'oeils**) **1** a style of painting or decorating in which objects are depicted with three-dimensional reality. **2** a trompe l'oeil painting or effect.

troop[1] *n* **1** (*in pl*) soldiers or the army. **2a** a subdivision of a cavalry or tank regiment corresponding to an infantry platoon. **b** an artillery unit smaller than a battery. **3** a group of similar people, animals, etc. **4** a unit of at least three patrols of Scouts and their leader.

Usage note

troop *or* **troupe**? These two words are sometimes confused. A *troop* is a group of soldiers or Scouts, and the word is sometimes extended to mean simply any 'large group': *The visitors were beginning to arrive in troops.* A *troupe* is a group of actors or circus performers.

troop[2] *v* of a group of people: to move together, *esp* in a way that suggests regimentation. ✱ **troop the colour** to parade a regiment's flag along the ranks of its soldiers ceremonially.

troop carrier *n* a large aircraft or armoured vehicle for transporting military personnel.

trooper *n* **1** a cavalry soldier, *esp* a private in a cavalry or tank regiment. **2a** *NAm, Aus* a mounted police officer. **b** *NAm* a state police officer, *esp* one on a motorcycle or in a car. **3** *chiefly Brit* a troopship. ✱ **swear like a trooper** to be in the habit of using bad language.

troopship *n* a ship for transporting military personnel.

trope *n* a figurative use of a word or expression.

trophic *adj* **1** relating to or denoting nutrition or growth. **2** of a hormone or its effect: influencing the activity of a gland.

trophy *n* (*pl* **-ies**) **1** a cup, medal, plate, etc awarded to a person or team as a symbol of victory or success in a sports match or other contest. **2** something, such as a stuffed and mounted animal, that is a memento of a successful achievement, *esp* in sport or hunting.

tropic[1] *n* **1a** a parallel of latitude at about 23° north of the equator. **b** a parallel of latitude at about 23° south of the equator. **c** (**the tropics**) the region between these two parallels. **2** in astronomy, either of the two corresponding parallel celestial latitudes that are the apparent northern and southern limits of the passage of the sun.

tropic[2] *adj* tropical.

tropic[3] *adj* **1** of, relating to, or exhibiting tropism. **2** = TROPHIC (2).

tropical *adj* **1** of or relating to the tropics. **2** of the weather or a climate: very hot and usu humid. ➤➤ **tropically** *adv.*

tropical cyclone *n* a tropical storm.

tropical storm *n* a low-pressure weather system that originates over tropical oceans, bringing heavy rains and winds that can reach hurricane force.

tropic of Cancer *n* = TROPIC[1] (1A).

tropic of Capricorn *n* = TROPIC[1] (1B).

tropism *n* the turning or growing of an organism or part of an organism, *esp* a plant part, towards or away from an external stimulus, such as light, gravity, or heat.

troposphere *n* the lowest part of the earth's atmosphere, extending from the surface of the planet to the stratosphere. ➤➤ **tropospheric** *adj.*

troppo *adv* in music, too much; excessively.

Trot *n informal, derog* a Trotskyist or a person who holds extremely left-wing political views.

trot[1] *v* (**trotted, trotting**) **1** to progress or ride at a trot. **2** to run at a moderately fast pace. **3** *informal* to proceed briskly; to hurry.

trot[2] *n* **1** a moderately fast pace of a horse or other four-legged animal in which the legs move in diagonal pairs. **2** an act or period of trotting. **3** (**the trots**) *informal* diarrhoea. ✱ **on the trot 1** *Brit, informal* in succession. **2** *informal* busy, *esp* kept on one's feet for a long time.

troth *n* **1** *archaic or formal* **a** faith or loyalty. **b** a pledge to be faithful or loyal. **2** *archaic* truth. ✱ **pledge/plight one's troth** to make a solemn promise to be faithful or loyal, *esp* in marriage.

trot out *v informal* to produce or utter habitually or predictably.

Trotskyism *n* the political, economic, and social principles advocated by the Russian revolutionary Leon Trotsky (d.1940), *esp* the belief that continuing worldwide revolution was the only way to achieve a world where socialism was dominant. ➤➤ **Trotskyist** *n and adj,* **Trotskyite** *n and adj.*

trotter *n* **1** a horse trained for trotting races. **2** the foot of a pig, used as food.

trotting *n* a race at trotting speed between horses harnessed to two-wheeled carriages carrying drivers.

troubadour *n* a medieval poet musician of S France whose works were on the theme of courtly love.

trouble[1] *n* **1a** difficulty, problems, or danger. **b** an instance, cause, or source of this. **2** a problem, snag, or drawback. **3** (*also in pl*) public unrest or demonstrations of dissatisfaction. **4** effort or exertion taken over something. ✱ **ask for trouble** *informal* to do or say something that may lead to personal difficulty or problems. **in trouble** liable to be punished or suffer something unpleasant. **look for trouble** *informal* to do or say something that is deliberately provocative, *esp* in order to start a fight or argument.

trouble[2] *v* **1** to cause distress, anxiety, pain, or discomfort to. **2** to put (somebody) to some exertion or inconvenience. **3** (*often* + to) to make an effort or take the time to do or say something. **4** (+ about/over/with) to worry about somebody or something.

trouble and strife *n Brit, slang* a wife.

troubled *adj* **1** worried or anxious. **2** characterized by or experiencing difficulty or problems.

troublemaker *n* somebody who deliberately and habitually causes trouble, *esp* by making others discontented.

troubleshoot *v* **1** to identify the causes of disputes, e.g. in business or politics, and try to resolve them. **2** to locate faults and make repairs in machinery and technical equipment. ➤➤ **troubleshooter** *n.*

troublesome *adj* causing difficulty or problems. ➤➤ **troublesomeness** *n.*

trouble spot *n* a place where unrest, rioting, or conflict frequently or regularly occur.

troublous *adj archaic or literary* full of trouble.

trough *n* **1** a long shallow receptacle for the drinking water or feed of domestic animals. **2a** a drain or channel for water; *esp* a gutter along the eaves of a building. **b** a long narrow or shallow trench, e.g. between waves or ridges. **3** in meteorology, an elongated area of low atmospheric pressure. **4** any notably low point, e.g. in a trade cycle, on a statistical graph, or in activity or achievement.

trounce *v* **1** to defeat (a person, team, army, etc) decisively in a competition, contest, or battle. **2** to rebuke or punish severely.

troupe *n* a group of actors, dancers, or other performers, *esp* a touring theatrical company.

Usage note

troupe *or* **troop**? See note at TROOP[1].

trouper *n* **1** a member of a troupe, *esp* a veteran actor. **2** a loyal or dependable person.

trouser[1] *n* (*used before a noun*) relating to or designed for trousers or a pair of trousers: *a trouser pocket.*

trouser[2] *v Brit, informal* **1** to put (something) in one's trouser pocket. **2** to take for oneself, *esp* dishonestly, illegally, or without permission.

trousers *pl n* an outer garment extending from the waist to the ankle, with tube-like parts that cover each leg separately. ✱ **wear the trousers** *informal* to have the controlling authority or be the dominant person in a relationship. ➤➤ **trousered** *adj.*

trouser suit *n Brit* a woman's suit consisting of a matching jacket and trousers.

trousseau /'troohsoh/ *n* (*pl* **trousseaux** *or* **trousseaus**) the clothes, linen, and other items that a woman collects for her marriage.

trout *n* (*pl* **trouts** *or* **trout**) a fish related to the salmon, often having distinctive spotted markings. ✱ **old trout** *informal* an irritating, interfering, or bad-tempered person.

trove *n* a store of valuable things that have been discovered; a treasure trove.

trow *v archaic* to think or believe (something).

trowel[1] *n* **1** a small hand tool with a flat tapering blade used to apply, mix, and spread plaster, cement, etc. **2** a small hand tool with a scoop-shaped blade used for lifting small plants, turning earth, etc.

trowel[2] *v* (**trowelled, trowelling,** *NAm* **troweled, troweling**) to smooth, mix, and apply (plaster, etc) with a trowel, or as if with a trowel.

troy *n* a system of weights, used mainly for precious metals and gemstones, in which there are 12oz or 5760 grains to the pound: compare AVOIRDUPOIS.

troy weight *n* = TROY.

truant[1] *n* a pupil who stays away from school without good reason or permission. ✻ **play truant** to truant. ➤➤ **truancy** *n.*

truant[2] *v* to stay away from school without good reason or permission.

truant[3] *adj* straying or wandering.

truce *n* an agreement between enemies to stop fighting, often for a set period of time; a ceasefire.

truck[1] *n* **1** a lorry. **2** *Brit* a wagon for carrying goods by rail.

truck[2] *v informal* to walk or proceed at a leisurely pace.

truck[3] *n* **1** *archaic* **a** commercial dealings, *esp* bartering. **b** commodities for sale or barter, *esp* small household goods. **2** *NAm* fruit or vegetables grown for sale in a market garden. ✻ **have/want no truck with** to refuse to have anything to do with (somebody or something).

truck[4] *v archaic* to exchange or barter (goods).

trucker *n* a person who drives a truck, *esp* over long distances.

truckle *n* a small drum-shaped cheese, *esp* cheddar.

truckle bed *n chiefly Brit* a low bed on castors that can be stored under a higher bed and slid out when needed.

truck stop *n NAm* a transport café.

truculent *adj* aggressively defiant, sullen, or antagonistic. ➤➤ **truculence** *n,* **truculently** *adv.*

trudge[1] *v* to walk with slow, weary, or laborious steps; to plod.

trudge[2] *n* a long tiring walk.

true[1] *adj* (**truer, truest**) **1a** in accordance with fact or reality; not false, wrong, or made-up. **b** genuine or real. **c** properly or strictly so called. **d** basic or essential. **2a** accurate. **b** said of a musical note: properly in tune. **c** said of a compass bearing: determined or measured according to the earth's geographical poles, as distinct from its magnetic poles. **d** correctly or accurately fitted, adjusted, balanced, or formed. **e** upright or level. **3a** steadfast, loyal, or trusted. **b** (*usu* + to) consistent or conforming, e.g. to a standard or to expectations. **c** honest and trustworthy; truthful. ✻ **true to form/type** acting as expected. **true to life 1** accurately reflecting what goes on in real life. **2** realistic or lifelike. ➤➤ **trueness** *n.*

true[2] ✻ **in/out of (the) true** correctly, or incorrectly, aligned, *esp* in terms of being upright or level.

true[3] *v* (**trues, trued, truing** *or* **trueing**) to adjust or restore (e.g. a mechanical part) to the correct level, shape, or degree of accuracy.

true[4] *adv* **1** in accordance with fact or reality: *Her story rings true.* **2** without deviation: *The bullet flew straight and true.* ✻ **come true** to happen; to become real.

true-blue *adj* **1** *Brit* staunchly loyal to the Conservative Party. **2** *NAm* loyal or faithful.

true-born *adj* of a specified type through birth; genuine: *a true-born Englishman.*

true north *n* north as determined by the earth's axis, as distinct from magnetic north.

truffle[1] *n* **1** a dark rough-skinned European fungus that grows underground and is considered a great delicacy. **2** a rich chocolate sweet, often flavoured with alcohol, made into a rough ball shape and dusted with cocoa powder.

truffle[2] *v* to hunt for and dig up truffles.

trug *n Brit* a shallow rectangular wooden basket used for carrying fruit, flowers, and vegetables.

truism *n* an undoubted or self-evident truth, *esp* one too obvious or unimportant to be mentioned.

truly *adv* **1a** in agreement with fact or reality; truthfully. **b** accurately or exactly. **2** to a great or the greatest extent; absolutely or completely. **3** genuinely; sincerely. **4** used to express astonishment or doubt. ✻ **well and truly** totally; completely. **yours truly 1** (**Yours truly**) used as a formula to end a letter. **2** *humorous* used to refer to oneself.

trump[1] *n* **1a** (*in pl*) in various card games, the suit of cards that has been chosen, usu just for the duration of a single deal or hand, to have a higher value than the other three suits. **b** a card of the suit that is currently trumps. **2** something that can be used to gain an advantage. ✻ **come/turn up trumps** *chiefly Brit, informal* to do what is right, needed, or desirable, *esp* unexpectedly and at the last moment.

trump[2] *v* **1** to play a trump on (a card of another suit). **2** to beat or surpass (somebody) by doing or saying something better.

trump[3] *n archaic* a trumpet or a call made on one.

trumpery[1] *n* (*pl* **-ies**) something showy but useless or worthless.

trumpery[2] *adj* **1** worthless or useless. **2** cheap or tawdry.

trumpet[1] *n* **1** the highest-pitched of the brass musical instruments, with a cylindrical base that widens into a flared bell, and three finger-operated valves to vary the pitch. **2** something that resembles the flared shape of a trumpet, e.g. a daffodil's corona. **3** the loud penetrating cry of an elephant. ✻ **blow one's (own) trumpet** to boast about one's own abilities, achievements, virtues, etc.

trumpet[2] *v* (**trumpeted, trumpeting**) **1** to play a trumpet. **2** to make the characteristic sound of an elephant. **3** to proclaim (something) loudly or widely.

trumpeter *n* a trumpet player; *esp* somebody using a trumpet to give a fanfare, signal, etc.

trumpet major *n* the chief trumpet player of a cavalry regiment, often the regiment's principal musician.

trump up *v* to make up (a false charge, accusation, or excuse) with the intention of deceiving.

truncate *v* to shorten (something) by cutting off a part, *esp* by taking off a top or end part. ➤➤ **truncation** *n.*

truncheon *n chiefly Brit* a short thick stick carried and used as a weapon by police officers.

trundle[1] *v* to move or move (something) on wheels, or as if on wheels.

trundle[2] *n* an act of trundling.

trunk *n* **1** the main stem of a tree, as distinguished from branches and roots. **2** a person's or animal's body apart from the head, limbs, or other appendages; a torso. **3** the long flexible muscular nose of an elephant. **4** a large rigid box with a hinged lid, used for storing or transporting clothing and personal articles. **5** *NAm* the boot of a motor vehicle. **6** (*used before a noun*) relating to or denoting a main transport or communication route: *a trunk road.*

trunking *n* a system of shafts housing cables, wires, ventilation ducts, etc.

trunks *pl n* men's tight-fitting shorts worn for sports, *esp* swimming and boxing.

trunnion *n* a pin or pivot on which something can be rotated or tilted, *esp* either of two opposite projections on which a gun barrel can be tilted vertically.

truss[1] *n* **1** an arrangement of beams, rafters, girders, etc forming a rigid framework, e.g. in a roof or bridge. **2** a surgical appliance, often in the form of a padded belt tightly strapped to the body, used as a support for a hernia. **3** a large CORBEL[1] (stone or timber member projecting from a wall), *esp* one supporting a cornice. **4** *chiefly Brit* a bundle of hay or straw, *esp* formerly, one with a fixed weight of 56lb (25.4kg) for old hay, 60lb (27.2kg) for new hay, and 36lb (16.3kg) for straw. **5** a compact cluster of flowers or fruit growing on a single stalk, e.g. of a tomato plant.

truss[2] *v* **1** to tie up the wings or legs of (a chicken, turkey, etc) in preparation for cooking. **2** (*often* + up) to secure or bind tightly. **3** to support, strengthen, or stiffen (something, *esp* a hernia) with a truss.

trust[1] *n* **1a** confident belief in or reliance on the character, ability, strength, honesty, etc of somebody or something. **b** acceptance of the truth of something, *esp* without proof: *He took nothing on trust.* **2a** responsible charge or office: *I am putting you in a position of trust.* **b** care or custody: *The child was committed to his trust.* **3** an arrangement whereby money or other property is held by one person for the benefit of another. **4a** a body of trustees. **b** something managed by trustees. ✱ **in trust** in the care or possession of a trustee. ➤➤ **trustful** *adj*, **trustfully** *adv*, **trustfulness** *n*.

trust[2] *v* **1a** to rely on or believe in the truthfulness, accuracy, ability, etc of (somebody or something). **b** to place one's confidence in (somebody or something); to rely on. **2** to expect with confidence; to assume: *I trust you are well; We'll see you soon, I trust.* **3a** to place (somebody or something) in somebody's care or keeping; to entrust. **b** to be confident about allowing (somebody to do, have, or look after something). **4** (*often* + to/in) to place one's confidence or dependence in somebody or something. ➤➤ **trustable** *adj*, **trusted** *adj*.

trust company *n* a company that functions as a trustee for individuals or for companies and institutions.

trustee *n* **1** a person appointed to administer property in trust for a beneficiary, e.g. a person or a charitable organization. **2** any member of a board of people appointed to administer the affairs of a company, organization, or institution. **3** a state appointed by the United Nations to supervise a trust territory. ➤➤ **trusteeship** *n*.

trust fund *n* property, money, shares, or other assets held in trust.

trusting *adj* having or showing great trust, often to the extent of putting oneself in a position to be exploited or hurt. ➤➤ **trustingly** *adv*, **trustingness** *n*.

trust territory *n* a dependent territory placed under an administrative authority by the United Nations.

trustworthy *adj* known to be honest, truthful, and reliable. ➤➤ **trustworthiness** *n*.

trusty *adj* (**-ier, -iest**) *archaic or humorous* reliable; trustworthy.

truth *n* (*pl* **truths**) **1** the state or quality of being true. **2a** something that is true or is believed to be true, as distinct from a lie. **b** a statement, proposition, theory, etc that has been proved to be fact or that is generally accepted as true. ✱ **in truth** in fact; really. **to tell the truth/if truth be told/truth to tell** to speak openly and honestly.

truth drug *n* a substance administered in the belief that it has properties which will induce a person being questioned to tell the truth or talk freely.

truthful *adj* **1a** telling or expressing the truth. **b** inclined to tell the truth or be honest. **2** of a portrait, sculpture, or other representational work: realistic. ➤➤ **truthfully** *adv*, **truthfulness** *n*.

try[1] *v* (**-ies, -ied**) **1** to make an attempt to do (something). **2** to test or operate (something) to see if it is working or effective. **3a** to conduct the trial of (an accused person). **b** to investigate (a case) judicially. **4** to make severe demands on. ✱ **tried and tested** known to be reliable. **try and** *informal* to try to do something: *I'll try and finish quickly.* **try it on** *Brit, informal* to test somebody's credulity or patience. **try one's hand at** to attempt (something new).

try[2] *n* (*pl* **-ies**) **1** an attempt. **2** an experimental trial. **3** in rugby, a score made by touching down the ball behind the opponent's goal line, entitling the scoring side to attempt a kick at the goal for additional points.

trying *adj* **1** annoying or irritating. **2** uncomfortable, unpleasant, or tiring.

try on *v* to put on (a piece of clothing) to see if it is suitable.

try out *v* to test or investigate for suitability or effectiveness.

trypanosome *n* a parasitic PROTOZOAN (single-celled animal) that moves by means of whiplike structures and can infest the blood, causing sleeping sickness and other diseases.

trypanosomiasis *n* a disease caused by trypanosomes, *esp* sleeping sickness.

tryptophan *n* an essential amino acid, present in most proteins, that is necessary to vertebrates for growth and the synthesis of the vitamin niacin.

try square *n* an L-shaped instrument used for marking out right angles and testing whether work, *esp* brickwork or carpentry, is square.

tryst[1] *n literary* an agreement to meet, *esp* a secret agreement for a romantic meeting.

tryst[2] *v literary* to make or keep a tryst.

tsar *or* **czar** *or* **tzar** /zah, tsah/ *n* an emperor of Russia before 1917. ➤➤ **tsardom** *n*, **tsarism** *n*, **tsarist** *n and adj*.

tsarevitch *or* **tsarevich** *or* **czarevich** *or* **tzarevich** /'zahrəvich/ *n* a son of a Russian tsar, *esp* the eldest son.

tsarina *or* **czarina** *or* **tzarina** /zah'reenə/ *n* a Russian empress before 1917.

tsetse /'tetsi, 'tsetsi/ *n* a two-winged blood-sucking African fly that transmits diseases, *esp* sleeping sickness.

T-shirt *or* **tee shirt** *n* a collarless short-sleeved casual top, usu made from knitted cotton.

tsp *abbr* **1** teaspoon. **2** teaspoonful.

T square *n* a ruler with a crosspiece or head at one end used in making and testing parallel lines.

TSR *abbr* terminate-and-stay-resident, denoting a computer program that remains loaded in a computer's memory even when it is not running.

TSS *abbr* toxic shock syndrome.

tsunami /tsoo'nahmi/ *n* (*pl* **tsunami** *or* **tsunamis**) a huge sea wave that is produced by underwater earth movement or volcanic eruption, causing severe devastation if it reaches land.

TT *abbr* **1** teetotal or teetotaller. **2** Tourist Trophy.

TTL *abbr* **1** transistor transistor logic, denoting a widely used system of constructing integrated circuits. **2** through-the-lens, denoting a type of camera in which the same lens is used to form both the exposed image and the viewfinder image.

Tuareg /'twahreg/ *n* (*pl* **Tuaregs** *or* **Tuareg**) a member of a nomadic people inhabiting the western and central parts of the Sahara Desert. ➤➤ **Tuareg** *adj.*

tub *n* **1a** a low wide lidless container used for holding water, growing plants, etc. **b** a small plastic or cardboard container for food such as cream, ice cream, or margarine. **2** *informal* an old or slow boat, *esp* one that is awkward to sail.

tuba *n* the largest and lowest-pitched of the brass musical instruments, with a cylindrical bore that widens into a bell.

tubal *adj* relating to, denoting, or occurring in a tube, *esp* one in the body such as a Fallopian tube.

tubby *adj* (**-ier**, **-iest**) *informal* podgy or fat. ➤➤ **tubbiness** *n.*

tube[1] *n* **1** a hollow elongated flexible or rigid cylinder, *esp* one that conveys liquids or gases. **2** a slender channel within a plant or animal body; a duct. **3** a small cylindrical container of soft metal or plastic sealed at one end and fitted with a cap at the other from which a substance is dispensed by squeezing. **4** (**the tube**) *Brit, informal* the underground railway in London. **5a** an electron tube. **b** a cathode-ray tube, e.g. of a television set. ✱ **go down the tube/tubes** *informal* of a business, project, etc: to fail or be completely lost or wasted.

tube[2] *v* **1** to provide with a tube or a system of tubes. **2** to convey (liquid or gas) in a tube or through a system of tubes.

tubectomy *n* (*pl* **-ies**) surgical removal of the Fallopian tubes.

tuber *n* **1** a short fleshy usu underground stem, e.g. of a potato, that has buds which may develop into new plants and a food store for the plant or for any developing plants until they become established: compare BULB, CORM. **2** a fleshy root resembling this, e.g. that of the ginger plant.

tubercle *n* **1** a small rounded outgrowth or prominence, *esp* on a bone or on an outer part of a plant or animal. **2** a small abnormal lump in an organ or in the skin, *esp* a lesion in the lungs or on other tissue that is characteristic of tuberculosis.

tubercle bacillus *n* the bacterium that causes tuberculosis.

tubercular *adj* **1** relating to, characteristic of, or affected with tuberculosis. **2** having or covered with tubercles.

tuberculin *n* a sterile liquid extracted from the tubercle bacillus and used in the diagnosis of tuberculosis, *esp* in humans and cattle.

tuberculosis *n* a serious infectious disease caused by the tubercle bacillus and characterized by fever and the formation of abnormal lumps in the body, *esp* in the lungs.

tuberculous *adj* = TUBERCULAR.

tuberose[1] *n* a perennial Mexican plant cultivated for its fragrant white flowers and, formerly, for use as a flavouring, *esp* in making chocolate.

tuberose[2] *adj* = TUBEROUS.

tuberous *adj* **1** relating to, denoting, forming, or having a tuber or tubers. **2** characterized by or affected with rounded swellings.

tubifex *n* (*pl* **tubifexes** *or* **tubifex**) a slender reddish segmented worm that lives partly buried in tubes in fresh or slightly salt water and is widely used as food for aquarium fish.

tubing *n* a length or lengths of material in the form of a tube.

tub-thumping *adj* of a person, speech, etc: expressing opinions in an impassioned, ranting, or overzealous way. ➤➤ **tub-thumper** *n,* **tub-thumping** *n.*

tubular *adj* **1** cylindrical and hollow, like a tube. **2** made of or fitted with tubes or tube-shaped pieces.

tubular bells *pl n* a musical instrument consisting of a set of metal tubes tuned to different notes and suspended from a frame, played by striking the tubes with a mallet.

tubule *n* a small tube, *esp* a minute anatomical structure.

TUC *abbr Brit* Trades Union Congress.

tuck[1] *v* **1a** to push or fold into a confined or hidden place or between two surfaces. **b** to push (something or the loose or stray parts of something) into a more secure or tidy position or state. **2** (+ in/up) to settle (somebody or oneself) in a comfortable position, *esp* in bed. **3** to draw or gather (something, *esp* one's legs) into a folded position. **4** to stitch a flattened fold in (fabric or a garment), *esp* as a decorative finish or to improve the fit. ✱ **tuck into** to start eating (food) with enjoyment.

tuck[2] *n* **1** a fold stitched into fabric or a garment. **2** *Brit, informal* food eaten as a snack by schoolchildren.

tuck away *v* to store or hide (something or somebody) in a place that is difficult to find.

tucker *n* a piece of lace or cloth formerly worn in the neckline of a low-cut dress.

tuck in *v informal* to eat heartily.

-tude *suffix* forming nouns, denoting: a state or condition: *plenitude; altitude.*

Tudor *adj* of the English royal house that ruled from the accession of Henry VII in 1485 until the death of Elizabeth I in 1603. ➤➤ **Tudor** *n.*

Tudor rose *n* a stylized figure of a rose, combining the red rose of the House of Lancaster and the white rose of the House of York, that Henry VII adopted as the emblem of the royal House of Tudor.

Tue. *or* **Tues.** *abbr* Tuesday.

Tuesday *n* the day of the week following Monday.

tufa *n* a porous rock composed of calcium carbonate and formed as a deposit by mineral springs.

tuff *n* a light porous rock consisting of consolidated volcanic ash.

tuffet *n* **1** a tuft or clump, *esp* of grass. **2** a low seat or footstool.

tuft *n* a small cluster of long flexible hairs, feathers, grasses, etc attached or close together at the base. ➤➤ **tufted** *adj,* **tufty** *adj.*

tufted duck *n* a European freshwater diving duck, the male of which has a black tufted head and white flanks.

tug[1] *v* (**tugged, tugging**) to pull (something) hard or suddenly.

tug[2] *n* **1** a hard sudden pull or jerk. **2** a strongly built powerful boat used for towing larger boats and ships, *esp* in a harbour.

tugboat *n* = TUG[2] (2).

tug-of-war *n* (*pl* **tugs-of-war**) a contest in which teams pulling at opposite ends of a rope attempt to pull each other across a line marked between them.

tugrik /'toohgrik/ *n* (*pl* **tugrik** *or* **tugriks**) the basic monetary unit of Mongolia.

tuition *n* teaching or instruction, *esp* of small groups or individuals.

tulip *n* a bulbous plant of the lily family, with a single richly coloured cup-shaped flower at the top of a straight stem.

tulip tree *n* **1** a tall N American deciduous tree with large greenish yellow tulip-shaped flowers. **2** *informal* a magnolia.

tulle *n* a sheer, often silk, net used chiefly for veils and dresses.

tum *n informal* a person's stomach or the area around it.

tumble[1] *v* **1** to fall suddenly, helplessly, or awkwardly. **2** to perform acrobatic moves such as handstands, somersaults, back flips, etc. **3a** to roll over and over or to and fro. **b** to move hurriedly and confusedly. **4** of prices, etc: to decline suddenly and sharply. **5** *informal* (+ to) to realize, understand, or become aware of something suddenly. **6** to rumple or disarrange (*esp* hair or clothes).

tumble[2] *n* **1** an unexpected fall or drop. **2** a confused heap or an untidy state. **3** an acrobatic move such as a handstand, somersault, back flip, etc.

tumbledown *adj* of a building, etc: in a state of disrepair; dilapidated or ramshackle.

tumble-drier *n* see TUMBLE-DRYER.

tumble-dryer *or* **tumble-drier** *n* an electric machine that dries wet laundry by rotating it in hot air inside a metal drum. ⋙ **tumble-dry** *v.*

tumbler *n* **1** a large drinking glass without a handle. **2** an acrobat or gymnast. **3** a tumble-dryer. **4** a movable part of a lock, e.g. a lever, wheel, or pin, that must be adjusted to a particular position before the lock can be opened. **5** a tumbling barrel.

tumbleweed *n* a plant that grows in arid regions and becomes so light and dried out in late summer that it breaks off from its roots and is blown about in the wind.

tumbling barrel *n* a revolving device in which objects or materials, such as gemstones, are whirled about for cleaning, polishing, etc.

tumbrel *or* **tumbril** *n* **1** an open-ended farm cart that can be tipped up in order to empty out its contents. **2** a cart of this kind used for carrying political prisoners during the French Revolution to a place of execution.

tumefy *v* (**-ies, -ied**) to become swollen. ⋙ **tumefaction** *n.*

tumescent *adj* swollen or distended, or in the process of becoming so. ⋙ **tumescence** *n,* **tumescently** *adv.*

tumid *adj* **1** *esp* of a body part or tissue: marked by swelling or distension; bulging. **2** of speech, writing, etc: pompous, bombastic, or inflated. ⋙ **tumidity** *n,* **tumidly** *adv,* **tumidness** *n.*

tummy *n* (*pl* **-ies**) *informal* a person's stomach or the area around it.

tummy button *n informal* a person's navel.

tumor *n NAm* see TUMOUR.

tumour (*NAm* **tumor**) *n* a swelling on or in a part of the body, *esp* one involving an abnormal growth of tissue that may be benign or malignant. ⋙ **tumorous** *adj.*

tump *n chiefly English dialect* a small clump or a low rounded hill.

tumuli *n* pl of TUMULUS.

tumult *n* **1** a loud confused noise caused by a large number of people behaving boisterously; a commotion. **2** a state of violent mental or emotional agitation. **3** a confusion or disordered medley, e.g. of sounds or colours.

tumultuous *adj* **1** characterized by noise, disorder, commotion, or uproar. **2** marked by violent turbulence or upheaval. ⋙ **tumultuously** *adv,* **tumultuousness** *n.*

tumulus *n* (*pl* **tumuli**) an artificial mound, *esp* one over a grave.

tun *n* a large cask, *esp* for beer or wine.

tuna *n* (*pl* **tunas** *or* **tuna**) a large marine food fish of warm waters that is related to the mackerel.

tuna fish *n* = TUNA .

tundish *n Brit* **1** a reservoir in the top part of a mould into which molten metal is poured. **2** *dated* a funnel.

tundra *n* a vast level or undulating treeless plain characteristic of arctic and subarctic regions, that consists of a thin layer of black marshy soil overlying a permanently frozen subsoil.

tune[1] *n* a succession of musical notes; a melody. ✱ **call the tune** see CALL[1]. **change one's tune** *informal* to adopt a noticeably different attitude or point of view. **in/out of tune 1** of a musician, singer, musical instrument, etc: having or not having the correct musical pitch or intonation. **2** of a motor vehicle's engine: correctly or incorrectly adjusted. **3** of people: in or not in harmony or agreement. **to the tune of** *informal* to the amount of (a specified sum of money).

tune[2] *v* **1** to bring (a musical instrument) into tune, *esp* to a standard pitch. **2** (*often* + up) to adjust (the engine of a motor vehicle) for optimum performance. **3** to adjust (a radio or television receiver) to respond to waves of a particular frequency. **4** (+ into) to become aware of. **5** *informal* (+ out) to stop listening or paying attention. ⋙ **tuning** *n.*

tuneful *adj* having a pleasant tune; melodious. ⋙ **tunefully** *adv,* **tunefulness** *n.*

tune in *v* to switch on and listen to or watch radio or television, or a particular radio or television programme or channel.

tuneless *adj* not pleasant to listen to: unmelodious. ⋙ **tunelessly** *adv,* **tunelessness** *n.*

tuner *n* **1** a person who tunes musical instruments, *esp* pianos. **2** an electronic device for tuning something, e.g. a circuit that acts as a filter for radio and television broadcast signals by amplifying those required and rejecting others.

tunesmith *n informal* a composer of popular songs.

tune-up *n* a general adjustment to an engine to ensure operation at peak efficiency.

tungsten *n* a hard grey–white metallic chemical element that has a high melting point and is used for electrical purposes, *esp* as filaments in electric light bulbs.

tunic *n* **1** a simple loose sleeveless thigh-length or knee-length garment. **2** a close-fitting hip-length jacket worn as part of a uniform.

tunicate *n* a marine animal, such as the sea squirt, that has an unsegmented body protected by a tough or rubbery membranous outer layer.

tuning fork *n* a two-pronged metal implement that gives a fixed tone when struck and is useful for tuning musical instruments and setting pitches for singing.

tuning peg *n* a small peg at the end of the neck of a stringed musical instrument used to tune the instrument by adjusting the tension of the strings.

Tunisian *n* a native or inhabitant of Tunisia in N Africa. ⋙ **Tunisian** *adj.*

tunnel[1] *n* **1** an underground passage, *esp* one that allows people, vehicles, etc to pass through or under an obstruction such as a hill, river, or building. **2** a small underground passage excavated by a burrowing animal, e.g. a mole.

tunnel[2] *v* (**tunnelled, tunnelling,** *NAm* **tunneled, tunneling**) to construct an underground passage under or through an obstruction. ⋙ **tunneller** *n.*

tunnel vision *n* **1** an eye condition in which objects at the edges of the visual field are lost or can only be seen indistinctly. **2** *informal* extreme narrowness of viewpoint; narrow-mindedness.

tunny *n* (*pl* **tunnies** *or* **tunny**) a tuna.

tup[1] *n chiefly Brit* a ram.

tup[2] *v* (**tupped, tupping**) *chiefly Brit* of a ram: to copulate with (a ewe).

Tupi *n* (*pl* **Tupis** *or* **Tupi**) **1** a member of a group of indigenous peoples of Brazil. **2** any of the languages spoken by these peoples. ➤➤ **Tupi** *adj,* **Tupian** *adj.*

Tupi-Guarani *n* a group of S American languages spoken in parts of Brazil, Peru, and Paraguay, including Tupi and Guarani. ➤➤ **Tupi-Guarani** *adj,* **Tupi-Guaranian** *adj.*

tuppence *n Brit* see TWOPENCE.

tuppenny *adj Brit* see TWOPENNY.

Tupperware *n trademark* a range of kitchenware, *esp* sealable plastic containers for storing food.

turban *n* **1** a headdress worn *esp* by Muslim and Sikh men, consisting of a long cloth wound either round a cap or directly round the head. **2** a woman's hat or a headdress that resembles this. ➤➤ **turbaned** *adj,* **turbanned** *adj.*

turbid *adj* **1** of a liquid: cloudy, thick, or opaque, e.g. because of the effect of disturbed sediment. **2** characterized by or producing confusion, *esp* of the mind or emotions. ➤➤ **turbidity** *n,* **turbidly** *adv,* **turbidness** *n.*

turbine *n* a power-generating machine with a wheel or rotor, often fitted with vanes, that is driven by the pressure of water, steam, exhaust gases, etc.

turbo *n* (*pl* **-os**) **1** a turbine. **2** a turbocharger.

turbocharge *v* to fit (an internal-combustion engine) with a turbocharger in order to give an increase in power.

turbocharger *n* a compressor device, usu powered by a turbine driven by exhaust gas, that is used to supercharge an internal-combustion engine.

turbofan *n* a jet engine with a turbine-driven fan that forces air into the exhaust gases to increase thrust.

turbojet *n* a jet engine in which a compressor, driven by power from a turbine, supplies compressed air to the combustion chamber.

turboprop *n* a jet engine with a turbine-driven propeller.

turboshaft *n* a gas turbine engine in which the power is used to drive a shaft other than a propeller shaft, used *esp* in helicopter rotors and pumps.

turbot *n* (*pl* **turbots** *or* **turbot**) a large European flatfish with a brownish upper surface scattered with knobbly tubercles instead of scales, that is a highly valued food fish.

turbulence *n* **1** a commotion or a confused state; disorderliness. **2** irregular atmospheric motion, *esp* when characterized by strong currents of rising and falling air. **3** departure from a smooth flow in a gas or liquid.

turbulent *adj* **1** characterized by agitation or tumult; stormy. **2** relating to or denoting irregular atmospheric motion. **3** *technical* relating to or denoting departure from a smooth flow. ➤➤ **turbulently** *adv.*

turd *n coarse slang* **1** a piece of excrement. **2** a contemptuous term for a person one dislikes.

tureen *n* a deep bowl, often with a lid, from which food such as soup is served.

turf[1] *n* (*pl* **turfs** *or* **turves**) **1a** grass and the soil that is bound to its roots, forming a thick mat. **b** a piece of this that has been cut from the ground. **2** (**the turf**) the sport or business of horse racing. **3** *informal* **a** an area thought of as belonging to or being the domain of a particular person or group. **b** a person's sphere of interest, knowledge, or control. ➤➤ **turfy** *adj.*

turf[2] *v* to cover (an area) with turf.

turf accountant *n Brit, formal* a bookmaker.

turf out *v chiefly Brit, informal* **1** to force to leave. **2** to get rid of.

turgescent *adj technical* becoming or appearing to be swollen or distended. ➤➤ **turgescence** *n.*

turgid *adj* **1** swollen or distended. **2** of language, a speech, or a piece of writing, etc: pompous or bombastic and lacking any liveliness of style. ➤➤ **turgidity** *n,* **turgidly** *adv,* **turgidness** *n.*

Turk *n* **1** a native or inhabitant of Turkey. **2** a person who speaks any of the Turkic languages.

turkey *n* **1** a large domesticated game bird, orig native to N America, that has a heavy rounded body, lustrous black or bronze plumage, a bald head, and, in the male, distinctive red wattles. **2** *chiefly NAm, informal* something, *esp* a film or play, that is considered to be an utter failure. **3** an ineffectual or stupid person. ✱ **talk turkey** *NAm, informal* to have a frank and open discussion, *esp* one that relates to business.

turkey-cock *n* a male turkey.

turkey trot *n* a ragtime dance, popular during the 1920s, characterized by bouncy walking steps and shuddering up and down shoulder movements.

Turkic *n* the branch of the Altaic family of languages that includes Turkish, Azerbaijani, and Tatar. ➤➤ **Turkic** *adj.*

Turkish *n* the national language of the people of Turkey. ➤➤ **Turkish** *adj.*

Turkish bath *n* **1** a type of therapeutic or relaxing treatment involving sitting in hot steam followed by a rubdown, massage, and cold shower. **2** (*also in pl*) a room or building where this is available.

Turkish coffee *n* a strong usu sweetened coffee made from very finely ground beans.

Turkish delight *n* a jellylike confection, usu flavoured with flower essences, cut in cubes, and dusted with icing sugar.

Turkmen *n* (*pl* **Turkmens** *or* **Turkmen**) **1** a member of a group of peoples inhabiting parts of Turkmenistan and Afghanistan. **2** the Turkic language spoken by these peoples.

turmeric *n* **1** an Asian plant of the ginger family with a large rhizome. **2** a bright yellow aromatic powder obtained from the rhizome of this plant, used for flavouring and as a colouring agent, *esp* in Asian cookery.

turmoil *n* an extremely confused or agitated state.

turn[1] *v* **1** to move round or cause to move round on an axis, or so as to be facing the opposite direction. **2** to take or cause to take a different position, state, etc: *The weather has turned cold; She turned the dog loose; The fairy turned him into a frog.* **3** to change colour. **4** to pass or go round: *to turn a corner.* **5** to go beyond in space or time: *It has turned midnight.* **6** to affect or be affected with nausea or revulsion. **7** to make (a specified profit). **8** to sprain (an ankle). **9** to make or form using a lathe. **10** of milk: to become sour. ✱ **turn against** to become hostile towards. **turn to 1** to apply oneself to a task: *We must turn to and get the job done.* **2** to have recourse to (somebody) for help or support.

turn[2] *n* **1** an act of turning. **2** a bend or curve. **3** a turning. **4** in cricket, deviation of the ball after a bounce. **5** a single coil, e.g. of rope or wire wound round an object. **6** an alteration or change. **7** a point of change in time, *esp* at the beginning or end of a period: *the turn of the century.* **8** an opportunity or obligation to do something occurring in succession or rotation: *It's your turn to drive.* **9** a trip, *esp* a short walk or drive taken for pleasure. **10a** a spell or attack of illness, faintness, dizziness, etc. **b** *informal* a shock. **11** a usu short act or performance, e.g. in a variety show. ✱ **at every turn** on every occasion; constantly or continually. **by turns** alternately or successively. **do somebody a good turn** to do a favour for somebody. **in turn** in the correct order of succession. **on the turn** at the point of turning. **out of turn 1** not in the correct order of succession. **2** at a wrong time or place; imprudently or unwisely. **take turns/take it in turns** to do something alternatively or successively. **to a turn** perfectly. **turn and turn about** *chiefly Brit* one after another.

turnabout *n* a change or reversal of direction, trend, etc.

turnaround *n* **1** the process of unloading an aircraft, ship, lorry, etc, reloading it, and making it ready for its next trip. **2** the process of completing a task, or the time this takes.

turn around *v* = TURN ROUND.

turn away *v* **1** to reject or dismiss (somebody). **2** to start to leave or change direction.

turn back *v* **1** to return or go in the opposite direction. **2** to prevent from advancing.

turnbuckle *n* a device that connects and pulls together the ends of a wire, stay, etc to make it taut.

turncoat *n* a person who switches from one party, cause, etc to an opposing one.

turn down *v* **1** to reduce the strength or intensity of (volume level, etc) by using a control. **2** to decline to accept.

turned-on *adj informal* keenly aware of and responsive to what is new and fashionable.

turner *n* a person who forms articles on a lathe. ➤➤ **turnery** *n.*

turn in *v* **1** to hand (somebody) over to the authorities. **2** *informal* to go to bed for the night.

turning *n* **1a** a road, path, river, etc, that branches off another. **b** a place on a road, etc where it branches; a junction. **2a** the process or skill of using a lathe. **b** (*in pl*) waste parts formed in the process of using a lathe.

turning circle *n* the smallest circle in which a vehicle or vessel can turn without having to reverse.

turning point *n* a point at which a significant change occurs.

turnip *n* the large yellowish or white edible root of a plant of the cabbage family, used as a vegetable and livestock fodder.

turnkey[1] *n* (*pl* **turnkeys**) *archaic* a jailer; a prison warder.

turnkey[2] *adj* **1** of a product, service, etc: supplied, installed, built, etc complete and ready for immediate use. **2** of a contract: involving no subcontractors.

turn off *v* **1** to stop from working or flowing by operating a switch or tap. **2** to cause (somebody) to lose interest. **3** to leave one road and join another.

turn-off *n* **1a** a road, path, etc that branches off another. **b** a place on a road, etc where it branches; a junction. **2** *informal* somebody or something that a person finds repulsive or boring.

turn on *v* **1** to cause to start working or flowing by operating a switch or tap. **2** to make (somebody) interested or excited, *esp* sexually.

turn-on *n informal* somebody or something that a person finds attractive, exciting, or sexually stimulating.

turnout *n* the number of people attending or taking part in an event.

turn out *v* **1** to cause (an electric light) to stop working by operating a switch or tap. **2** to empty (a room, pocket, etc). **3** to produce (work, etc). **4** to prove ultimately to be in a specified condition: *The play turned out to be a success.*

turnover *n* **1a** the amount of money taken by a business in a particular period. **b** the amount of business transacted in a particular period. **c** the rate at which a business loses and replaces its staff. **d** the rate at which a business, *esp* a shop, sells and replaces stock. **2** an individual pie made by folding a circle of pastry in half and sealing it to enclose a filling.

turn over *v* **1** to put or be put the other way up; to invert. **2a** to cause (an engine) to revolve and fire. **b** of an engine: to revolve at low speed. **3** to do business to a specified amount. **4** to think about (a matter, problem, etc). **5** to search roughly through (a place). **6** to deliver or pass (somebody or something) to the proper authority. **7** of a person's stomach: to heave with nausea.

turnpike *n* **1** formerly: **a** a toll gate. **b** a road on which a toll was payable. **2** *NAm* a major road on which tolls are payable, *esp* an expressway.

turnround *n* = TURNAROUND.

turn round *v* **1** to complete the handling or processing of (goods or work) in a specified time. **2** to reform (a failing concern) so that it becomes successful.

turnstile *n* a gate with arms pivoted on the top that turns to admit one person at a time, used e.g. at sports grounds.

turnstone *n* a wading bird of the sandpiper family with a stubby wedge-shaped bill used for turning over pebbles on the shore to find the small crustaceans, insects, etc it feeds on.

turntable *n* **1** the platform on which a gramophone record is rotated while being played. **2** a circular platform for turning wheeled vehicles, *esp* railway engines.

turn up *v* **1** to appear unexpectedly, *esp* after being lost. **2** to arrive or occur. **3** to find or discover. **4** to increase the strength or intensity of (volume level, etc) by using a control.

turn-up *n Brit* **1** a hem, *esp* on a pair of trousers, that is folded up over itself on the outside. **2** *informal* an unexpected or surprising event or outcome.

turpentine *n* **1** a thick oily resinous secretion obtained from certain conifer trees and distilled to make rosin and oil of turpentine. Also called GUM TURPENTINE. **2** any of various colourless volatile oils distilled from this, used as solvents for paints and varnishes and as medicinal liniments. Also called OIL OF TURPENTINE.

turpitude *n formal* baseness, depravity, or wickedness.

turps *n informal* turpentine.

turquoise *n* **1** a blue, bluish green, or greenish grey mineral that takes a high polish and is valued as a semiprecious gemstone. **2** a light greenish blue colour. ➤➤ **turquoise** *adj.*

turret *n* **1** a little tower, often at the corner of a larger building, *esp* a castle. **2** an armoured structure, typically revolving, on warships, tanks, aircraft, etc in which guns are mounted. **3** a rotatable holder, e.g. for a tool or die, in a lathe, milling machine, etc. ➤➤ **turreted** *adj.*

turtle *n* **1** any of several species of marine and freshwater reptiles with a bony or leathery shell, resembling the related tortoises, but with limbs adapted for swimming. **2** in computer graphics, a small on-screen shape that acts as an easily manipulated drawing tool, used *esp* by children learning basic computing skills. ✱ **turn turtle** said *esp* of a boat: to capsize or overturn.

turtledove *n* a small wild dove with a distinctive soft cooing call, noted for being particularly affectionate towards its mate.

turtleneck *n* **1** *Brit* **a** a high, round, close-fitting neck on a garment. **b** a jumper, T-shirt, etc with a neck of this kind. **2** *NAm* = POLO NECK.

turves *n* pl of TURF¹.

Tuscan *n* **1** a native or inhabitant of Tuscany. **2** an order of classical architecture that is a modification of the Greek Doric but plainer in style. ➤➤ **Tuscan** *adj.*

Tuscarora *n* (*pl* **Tuscaroras** *or* **Tuscarora**) a member of a native N American people orig inhabiting North Carolina, and later New York State and Ontario.

tush¹ *interj archaic or humorous* used to express disapproval, irritation, contempt, etc.

tush² *n* a long pointed tooth, *esp* a canine tooth of a male horse.

tush³ *n chiefly NAm, informal* a person's buttocks.

tusk *n* a very long tapering tooth, *esp* one of a pair belonging to an elephant, walrus, boar, etc, that is clearly visible even when the animal's mouth is closed. ➤➤ **tusked** *adj.*

tusker *n* an animal, *esp* a male elephant or wild boar, with two prominent tusks.

tussle¹ *v* to struggle or fight roughly; to scuffle.

tussle² *n* **1** a physical contest or struggle; a scuffle. **2** a struggle, controversy, or argument.

tussock *n* a compact tuft of grass, sedge, etc. ➤➤ **tussocky** *adj.*

tussock grass *n* any of various grasses or sedges that typically grow in tussocks.

tussore *n* a type of coarse silk or silk fabric made from the silk produced by the larvae of various moths.

tut¹ *interj* used to express disapproval or impatience.

tut² *v* (**tutted, tutting**) to express disapproval or impatience by uttering 'tut' or 'tut-tut'.

tutee *n* somebody who is being tutored.

tutelage *n* **1** guardianship. **2** the state or period of being under a guardian or tutor. **3** instruction; tuition.

tutelary *adj* **1** having the guardianship of somebody or something. **2** relating to or denoting a guardian.

tutor¹ *n* **1** a person employed as a private teacher, *esp* one who teaches individuals or small groups, or who gives extra instruction or remedial help in addition to the education received at school, college, etc. **2** *Brit* a university or college teacher who teaches a small group, often also having responsibility for students' welfare. **3** *Brit* an instruction book. ➤➤ **tutorage** *n,* **tutorship** *n.*

tutor² *v* to act as a tutor to.

tutorial¹ *n* **1** a session of tuition given by a university or college tutor. **2** in computing, a teaching aid, often a series of on-screen interactive exercises, designed to familiarize a new user with a particular program, software, etc.

tutorial² *adj* relating to a tutor or the work of a tutor.

Tutsi *n* (*pl* **Tutsis** *or* **Tutsi**) a member of a Bantu-speaking people inhabiting Rwanda and Burundi where they are one of the minority ethnic groups: compare HUTU.

tutti *adj and adv* of a piece of music: to be performed by all the instruments of the orchestra or all the voices of the choir.

tutti-frutti *n* (*pl* **tutti-fruttis**) a type of ice cream or other confectionery containing a mixture of chopped, dried, or candied fruits.

tut-tut¹ *interj* = TUT¹.

tut-tut² *v* (**tut-tutted, tut-tutting**) = TUT².

tutu *n* a very short projecting stiff skirt worn by a ballerina.

Tuvaluan *n* **1** a native or inhabitant of Tuvalu, a country in the southwest Pacific comprising several coral islands. **2** the Austronesian language of the people of Tuvalu. ➤➤ **Tuvaluan** *adj.*

tu-whit tu-whoo *n* the conventional representation of an owl's cry.

tux *n chiefly NAm, informal* a tuxedo.

tuxedo *n* (*pl* **tuxedos** *or* **tuxedoes**) *chiefly NAm* **1** a man's formal tailless dinner jacket. **2** a formal evening suit with this type of jacket. ➤➤ **tuxedoed** *adj.*

TV *n* television.

TVP *abbr trademark* textured vegetable protein.

twaddle *n informal* trivial or nonsensical speech or writing; drivel.

twain *n archaic* two. ✱ **in twain** into two parts.

twang¹ *n* **1** a strong quick ringing sound like that of the string of a musical instrument being plucked or of a bowstring being released. **2** a distinctive nasal quality in the speech of a person or region. ➤➤ **twangy** *adj.*

twang² *v* to make, or cause (*esp* a musical instrument) to make a twang.

'twas *contr archaic or literary* it was.

twat *n coarse slang* **1** a woman's genitals. **2** a stupid, obnoxious, or contemptible person.

tweak¹ *v* **1** to pinch and pull with a sudden strong jerking or twisting movement. **2** *informal* to make fine adjustments to (*esp* a mechanical, electric, or electronic device).

tweak² *n* **1** an act of tweaking; a pinch. **2** *informal* a fine adjustment.

twee *adj* (**tweer, tweest**) *Brit* excessively or affectedly sentimental, pretty, cute, or coy. ➤➤ **tweely** *adv,* **tweeness** *n.*

tweed *n* **1** a rough woollen fabric, orig produced in Scotland, often of a brownish or greenish colour flecked with other colours, and used *esp* for suits and coats. **2** (*in pl*) tweed clothing, *esp* a tweed suit.

tweedy *adj* (**-ier, -iest**) **1** made of tweed. **2** *informal* of a person or group: enjoying country pursuits or holding staunchly conservative views. ➤➤ **tweedily** *adv,* **tweediness** *n.*

'tween *contr archaic or literary* between.

tweenager /'tweenayjə/ *n* a child who is not yet a teenager, especially one between the ages of eight and twelve.

tweeny *n* (*pl* **-ies**) *informal, archaic* a young female domestic servant.

tweet¹ *v* to make the characteristic chirping sound of a small bird.

tweet² *n* a tweeting sound.

tweeter *n* a small loudspeaker that mainly reproduces higher frequencies: compare WOOFER.

tweeze *v* to pluck, remove, or handle with or as if with tweezers.

tweezers *pl n* (*also* **pair of tweezers**) a small pincer-like device used for plucking out hairs and handling small or delicate objects.

twelfth *adj and n* **1** having the position in a sequence corresponding to the number twelve. **2** one of twelve equal parts of something. **3** in music, an interval of twelve degrees of a diatonic scale, or the combination of two notes at such an interval. **4** (**the (Glorious) Twelfth**) in Britain, 12 August, the day on which the grouse-shooting season begins.

twelfth man *n* the reserve member of a cricket team.

Twelfth Night *n* the evening of 5 January, traditionally the day when Christmas decorations are taken down.

twelve *n* the number 12. ➤➤ **twelve** *adj*, **twelvefold** *adj and adv.*

twelvemonth *n archaic* a year.

twelve-note *adj* relating to a system of composing music that treats the twelve chromatic notes of the octave equally, with no group of notes predominant as they are in the major/minor key system.

twelve-tone *adj* = TWELVE-NOTE.

twenty *adj and n* (*pl* **-ies**) **1** the number 20. **2** (*in pl*) the numbers 20 to 29. ➤➤ **twentieth** *adj and n.*

twenty-four-hour clock *n* a system of measuring time in hours using all 24 hours in a day, as distinct from measuring it in terms of two sets of twelve hours.

twenty-four-seven *or* **24–7** *or* **24/7** *adv chiefly NAm, informal* 24 hours a day, seven days a week; constantly.

twenty-one *n* the card game pontoon.

twenty-twenty *or* **20/20** *adj* said of a person's sight: of normal acuity; perfect.

'twere *contr archaic or literary* it were.

twerp *or* **twirp** *n informal* an absurd, stupid, or contemptible person.

twice *adv* **1** on two occasions. **2** two times; in doubled quantity or degree.

twiddle[1] *v* **1** (*often* + with) to play absentmindedly with something; to fiddle with it. **2** to rotate or twist (something) lightly or idly. ✱ **twiddle one's thumbs** to have nothing to do; to be bored or idle. ➤➤ **twiddler** *n.*

twiddle[2] *n* **1** an act or an instance of twiddling. **2** in music, a series of rapidly or intricately played notes. ➤➤ **twiddly** *adj.*

twig[1] *n* a small woody shoot or branch of a tree or bush, usu without its leaves. ➤➤ **twigged** *adj*, **twiggy** *adj.*

twig[2] *v* (**twigged, twigging**) *Brit, informal* to grasp or understand something; to catch on.

twilight *n* **1a** the soft shadowy or glowing light between sunset and the onset of the full darkness of the night. **b** the period between sunset and full night. **2** a period or state of obscurity or decline.

twilight sleep *n* a condition of semiconsciousness, usu lasting a few hours and induced by drugs, alcohol, epilepsy, or severe shock or trauma, in which some degree of awareness is retained, but memory of the period is often non-existent or distorted.

twilight zone *n* **1** any usu intermediate or border state or area characterized by ambiguity or decline. **2** a decaying urban area.

twilit *adj* lighted by or as if by twilight.

twill *n* **1** a weave that produces fabric with slightly raised parallel diagonal lines. **2** a fabric with this type of weave. ➤➤ **twilled** *adj.*

'twill *contr archaic or literary* it will.

twin[1] *n* **1** either of two children or offspring born to the same mother at the same birth. **2** either of two people or things closely related to or resembling each other.

twin[2] *v* (**twinned, twinning**) **1** (+ with) to link or join (one thing) with another. **2** *Brit* (+ with) to associate (a town in one country) officially with a town in another, *esp* in order to promote cultural, commercial, etc exchange. **3** to become paired or closely associated. **4** said of a crystal: to grow as or become a twin. ➤➤ **twinned** *adj*, **twinning** *n.*

twin[3] *adj* denoting either of two children who are twins, or either of two objects that match one another and, usu, function as a pair.

twine[1] *n* strong string, *esp* of a kind made from two or more strands twisted together.

twine[2] *v* **1** to twist (two or more things) together. **2** to form by twisting or weaving. **3** (*usu* + round/around) to coil or encircle. ➤➤ **twiner** *n.*

twinge[1] *n* **1** a sudden sharp stab of pain. **2** a moral or emotional pang.

twinge[2] *v* (**twingeing** *or* **twinging**) of a part of the body: to suffer or be affected by a twinge.

twinkle[1] *v* **1** of a star, light, precious stone, etc: to shine with a flickering or sparkling effect. **2** of a person's eyes: to have a bright sparkle, *esp* as a sign of amusement, mischief, etc. **3** to move or dart rapidly. ➤➤ **twinkler** *n.*

twinkle[2] *n* **1** an intermittent flickering or sparkling effect. **2** a rapid flashing movement. ➤➤ **twinkly** *adj.*

twinkletoed *adj informal* of a person, *esp* a dancer: very quick, nimble, and graceful. ➤➤ **twinkletoes** *n.*

twinkling *n* an instant. ✱ **in a/the twinkling of an eye** immediately or very quickly.

twin set *n chiefly Brit* a woman's jumper and cardigan designed to be worn together.

twin-to-twin syndrome *n* a disorder of twins in the womb, in which blood from one twin passes to the other twin via the placenta, one twin thereby coming to have too much blood and the other too little.

twin-tub *n* a type of washing machine with two separate top-loading drums, one for washing the laundry and the other for spinning it dry.

twirl[1] *v* to revolve, or cause to revolve, rapidly. ➤➤ **twirler** *n.*

twirl[2] *n* **1** an act of twirling. **2** a coiled or spiralling shape, *esp* a decorative one, e.g. an embellishment on a written letter or character. ➤➤ **twirly** *adj.*

twirp *n* see TWERP.

twist[1] *v* **1a** to cause to move with a rotating motion. **b** to turn to face in a different direction. **c** to twine or coil. **2a** to bend in a specified direction, *esp* out of true. **b** to follow a winding course. **c** to squirm or writhe. **3** to join (two or more things or parts) together by winding. **4** to wring or wrench (a joint) painfully. **5** to distort the meaning of. **6** *Brit, informal* to cheat. **7** to dance the twist. **8** in the card game pontoon, to request another card from the dealer. ✱ **twist somebody round one's little finger** see FINGER[1]. **twist somebody's arm** *informal* to persuade or force a person to do something.

twist[2] *n* **1** an act or an instance of twisting. **2a** something with a spiral or coiled shape. **b** a strong tightly twisted silk sewing thread. **c** a strip of citrus peel used to flavour a drink. **d** *Brit* a piece of paper twisted to form a small sachet, e.g. to hold salt. **e** a type of carpet with a tightly curled pile. **3** (**the twist**) a dance, first popular in the 1960s, featuring exaggerated twisting movements of the body, *esp* the hips and legs. **4** force causing twisting or turning applied to a body, e.g. a rod or shaft. **5** a turn, curve, or bend. **6a** an unexpected turn or development. **b** a different approach or method. ✱ **get one's knickers in a twist** see KNICKERS. **round the twist** *Brit, informal* completely mad. ⯮ **twisty** *adj.*

twister *n* **1** *Brit, informal* a dishonest person; a cheat or swindler. **2** *chiefly NAm* a tornado.

twit[1] *n chiefly Brit, informal* a silly or stupid person. ⯮ **twittish** *adj.*

twit[2] *v* (**twitted, twitting**) *informal* to tease or ridicule, *esp* light-heartedly.

twitch[1] *v* **1** to move with a sudden jerky motion. **2** to pull or tug lightly.

twitch[2] *n* **1** a twitching movement. **2** a physical or emotional pang; a twinge.

twitcher *n Brit, informal* a birdwatcher, *esp* one dedicated to finding rare birds.

twitchy *adj* (**-ier, -iest**) **1** *informal* nervous or anxious. **2** of a muscle, eye, etc: inclined to twitch.

twitter[1] *v* **1** of a bird: to make a series of quick tremulous or chirping sounds. **2** to talk quickly, *esp* in a nervous or giggling way or about trivial things. ⯮ **twitterer** *n.*

twitter[2] *n* **1** a twittering sound. **2** nervous, giggling, or trivial chatter. ✱ **all of/in a twitter** *informal* in a state of nervous agitation; quivering. ⯮ **twitterer** *n*, **twittery** *adj.*

'twixt *contr* betwixt.

twizzle[1] *v informal or dialect* to spin, or cause (something) to spin, round and round.

twizzle[2] *n* a twizzling movement.

two *n* the number 2. ✱ **put two and two together** to use the available evidence or information to draw a conclusion, *esp* an obvious one. **two by/and two** in pairs, *esp* also side by side. **two can play at that game** *informal* used to state forcibly that, if a person resorts to unfair tactics, etc, the speaker will do the same. ⯮ **two** *adj*, **twofold** *adj and adv.*

two-bit *adj NAm, informal* worthless, insignificant, or contemptible.

two-by-four *n* a length of trimmed timber that measures two inches by four inches in cross-section.

twoc *v* (**twocced, twoccing**) *Brit, slang* to steal (a car), *esp* for joyriding. ⯮ **twoccer** *n.*

two-dimensional *adj* **1** having two dimensions, *esp* length and breadth but no depth. **2** of a person, fictional character, etc: lacking depth; superficial. ⯮ **two-dimensionality** *n*, **two-dimensionally** *adv.*

two-edged *adj* = DOUBLE-EDGED.

two-faced *adj* insincere, double-dealing, or hypocritical.

two-handed *adj* **1** designed to be used with both hands. **2** requiring two people. **3** ambidextrous.

two-hander *n* a play with only two actors.

twopence *or* **tuppence** /'tup(ə)ns/ *n Brit* **1** the sum of two pence, *esp* before decimalization in 1971. **2** *informal* (*used with negatives*) a small amount; anything at all.

twopenn'orth /tooh'penəth/ *n* **1** an amount of two pence. **2** any small amount or value. ✱ **add/put in one's twopenn'orth** *informal* to have one's say; to make one's contribution to a discussion, etc.

twopenny *or* **tuppenny** *adj Brit* costing or worth two pence, *esp* before decimalization in 1971.

twopenny-halfpenny *adj Brit, informal* worthless or insignificant.

two-piece[1] *adj* of clothing: having two matching parts, usu top and bottom, that are designed to be worn together.

two-piece[2] *n* a two-piece garment, e.g. a swimming costume or suit.

two-ply *adj* consisting of two strands, layers, or thicknesses.

twosome *n* **1** a group of two people or things. **2** a sports match, *esp* in golf, played between two people.

two-step *n* a fast ballroom dance in duple time characterized by sliding steps.

two-stroke *adj* denoting an internal-combustion engine with a power cycle that is completed in a single up-and-down movement of a piston.

two-time *v informal* **1** to be unfaithful to (a partner or lover) by having a relationship with somebody else. **2** to cheat or double-cross. ⯮ **two-timer** *n.*

two-tone *adj* **1** having two colours or two shades of one colour. **2** having two sounds or tones.

'twould *contr archaic* it would.

two-up *n Aus, NZ* a game in which players bet on the fall of tossed coins.

two-up two-down *n Brit, informal* a house with two bedrooms upstairs, and two rooms, usu a living room and a dining room, downstairs.

two-way *adj* **1** involving movement, communication, etc that goes in two opposite directions. **2** involving two participants. ✱ **a two-way street** a situation that involves mutual responsibility or a reciprocal relationship.

two-way mirror *n* a piece of glass that reflects an image from one side and can be seen through from the other.

two-way switch *n* either of two electrical switches, e.g. at the top and bottom of a stairway, controlling a single device, *esp* a light.

TX *abbr* Texas (US postal abbreviation).

-ty[1] *suffix* forming words, denoting: the group of ten specified: *fifty.*

-ty[2] *suffix* forming nouns, denoting: a state, quality, or condition: *cruelty.*

tycoon *n* a person in business or industry who has exceptional wealth and power.

tying *v* present part. of TIE[1].

tyke *or* **tike** *n* **1** *informal* a small child, *esp* a cheeky or mischievous one. **2** a dog, *esp* a scruffy mongrel. **3** *Brit, informal* a person from Yorkshire.

tympana *n* pl of TYMPANUM.

tympani *n* see TIMPANI.

tympanic membrane *n* a thin membrane separating the outer ear from the middle ear; the eardrum.

tympanum *n* (*pl* **tympana** *or* **tympanums**) **1a** the cavity of the middle ear. **b** = TYMPANIC MEMBRANE. **2** in architecture: **a** the recessed triangular face of a pediment. **b** the space within an arch and above a lintel, e.g. in a medieval doorway. ⯮ **tympanic** *adj.*

Tynwald *n* the Parliament of the Isle of Man.

type[1] *n* **1a** a class or group of people, animals, or things that share similar characteristics. **b** a person or thing that is considered to be representative of a class or group. **c** *informal* a person who has a specified characteristic, nature, etc: *He's the quiet type.* **2a** a small metal block with a raised character or letter on its upper surface, used in printing. **b** a set of such blocks. **c** printed letters, characters, words, etc. **3** in theology, a person or event, e.g. in the Old

Testament, regarded as foreshadowing another, e.g. in the New Testament. ➤➤ **typal** *adj.*

type[2] *v* **1** to write using a typewriter or computer. **2** to determine the class of (*esp* blood or tissue). ➤➤ **typing** *n.*

typecast *v* (*past tense and past part.* **typecast**) **1** to cast (an actor) repeatedly in the same kind of role, *esp* because of previous successes in such roles. **2** to stereotype.

typeface *n* in printing, a particular style or design of type.

typescript *n* a typed copy of a text.

typeset *v* (**typesetting,** *past tense and past part.* **typeset**) to arrange the printing type for (a text). ➤➤ **typesetter** *n,* **typesetting** *n.*

type specimen *n* a single specimen or individual whose characteristics are used for the description of the characteristics of a biological species.

typewrite *v* (*past tense* **typewrote,** *past part.* **typewritten**) to write using a typewriter.

typewriter *n* a machine with a keyboard for writing in characters resembling type.

typewritten *v* past part. of TYPEWRITE.

typewrote *v* past tense of TYPEWRITE.

typhoid *n* a serious infectious bacterial disease characterized by fever, spots, diarrhoea, headache, and intestinal inflammation. ➤➤ **typhoidal** *adj.*

typhoid fever *n* = TYPHOID.

typhoon *n* a violent tropical storm, *esp* one occurring in the Indian or western Pacific oceans. ➤➤ **typhonic** *adj.*

typhus *n* an infectious disease marked by high fever, stupor alternating with delirium, intense headache, and a dark red rash. ➤➤ **typhous** *adj.*

typical *adj* **1** combining or exhibiting the essential characteristics of a type. **2** characteristic of somebody or something, *esp* showing the usual unfavourable trait. ➤➤ **typicality** *n,* **typically** *adv.*

typify *v* (**-ies, -ied**) to be typical of. ➤➤ **typification** *n,* **typifier** *n.*

typist *n* a person who uses a typewriter, *esp* as an occupation.

typo *n* (*pl* **typos**) *informal* a printing error.

typography *n* the style, arrangement, or appearance of typeset matter. ➤➤ **typographer** *n,* **typographic** *adj,* **typographical** *adj,* **typographically** *adv.*

typology *n* (*pl* **-ies**) **1** a classification according to general type, *esp* in the fields of archaeology, psychology, biology, and social science. **2** the study or analysis and classification of types, *esp* in theology. ➤➤ **typological** *adj,* **typologist** *n.*

tyrannical *adj* characterized by oppressive, unjust, or arbitrary behaviour or control. ➤➤ **tyrannic** *adj,* **tyrannically** *adv.*

tyrannicide *n* **1** the act of killing a tyrant. **2** a person who kills a tyrant. ➤➤ **tyrannicidal** *adj.*

tyrannize *or* **tyrannise** *v* to treat (an individual, people, etc) cruelly or oppressively. ➤➤ **tyrannizer** *n.*

tyrannosaur *or* **tyrannosaurus** *n* a very large flesh-eating dinosaur of the Cretaceous period with small forelegs and walking on its hind legs.

tyranny *n* (*pl* **-ies**) **1a** rule or government that is cruel or oppressive. **b** a state under such rule. **2** any form of cruel or oppressive treatment. ➤➤ **tyrannous** *adj,* **tyrannously** *adv.*

tyrant *n* **1** a cruel or oppressive ruler. **2** any person who exerts cruel or oppressive power or control. **3** a ruler who takes absolute power without any legal right, *esp* in ancient Greece.

tyre (*NAm* **tire**) *n* **1a** a continuous solid or inflated hollow rubber cushion fitted round a wheel to absorb shock and improve traction. **b** the external covering of a pneumatic tyre with an inner tube. **2** a metal hoop that forms a strengthening band around a wheel, *esp* of a horse-drawn wagon or a railway carriage.

tyro *or* **tiro** *n* (*pl* **tyros** *or* **tiros**) a beginner or novice.

Tyrolean *n* a native or inhabitant of the Alpine district of Tyrol, a region lying partly in western Austria and partly in northern Italy. ➤➤ **Tyrolean** *adj.*

Tyrolese *n* = TYROLEAN.

tyrosine *n* an amino acid found in most proteins and important in the synthesis of certain hormones.

tzar *n* see TSAR.

tzarevich *n* see TSAREVITCH.

tzarina *n* see TSARINA.

tzatziki *n* a dip or side dish that originated in Greece, made from yoghurt, cucumber, and garlic, often flavoured with mint.

tzigane *n* (*pl* **tziganes** *or collectively* **tzigane**) a Hungarian gypsy. ➤➤ **tzigane** *adj.*

U

U[1] *or* **u** *n* (*pl* **U's** *or* **Us** *or* **u's**) the 21st letter of the English alphabet.

U[2] *abbr* **1** United. **2** university.

U[3] *abbr* the chemical symbol for uranium.

U[4] *n* in Britain, a classification of cinema films suitable for all age groups.

U[5] *adj chiefly Brit, informal* of an accent, or language or behaviour, etc: characteristic of the upper classes.

UAE *abbr* United Arab Emirates.

UB40 *n* (*pl* **UB40's** *or* **UB40s**) in Britain, a card issued to somebody registered as unemployed.

U-bend *n* a U-shaped bend in a pipe, *esp* one in the waste pipe of a sink that prevents bad smells escaping.

Übermensch *n* (*pl* **Übermenschen**) in Nietzschean philosophy, an ideal human being of the future, who would use their passions creatively, ignoring Christian teachings, and would be able to formulate their own moral code.

ubiquitous *adj* existing or seeming to be everywhere at the same time; frequently encountered. ➤➤ **ubiquitously** *adv*, **ubiquitousness** *n*, **ubiquity** *n*.

U-boat *n* a German submarine, *esp* as used in World Wars I and II.

UBR *abbr* uniform business rate.

u.c. *abbr* upper case.

UCAS *abbr Brit* Universities and Colleges Admissions Service.

UDA *abbr* Ulster Defence Association.

udder *n* a large bag-like organ, e.g. of a cow, consisting of two or more mammary glands enclosed in a common structure and each having a single nipple.

UDI *abbr* unilateral declaration of independence.

UDR *abbr* Ulster Defence Regiment.

UEFA *abbr* Union of European Football Associations.

UFO *n* (*pl* **UFO's** *or* **UFOs**) an unidentified flying object, *esp* one popularly believed to be of extraterrestrial origin.

ufology *n* the study of unidentified flying objects. ➤➤ **ufologist** *n*.

Ugandan *n* a native or inhabitant of Uganda in E Africa. ➤➤ **Ugandan** *adj*.

ugh *interj informal* used to express disgust or horror.

Ugli *n* (*pl* **Uglis** *or* **Uglies**) *trademark* a large citrus fruit that is a cross between a grapefruit and a tangerine.

Ugli fruit *n* = UGLI.

uglify *v* (**-ies, -ied**) to make or become ugly or uglier. ➤➤ **uglification** *n*.

ugly *adj* (**-ier, -iest**) **1** offensive or displeasing to any of the senses, *esp* to the sight. **2a** ominous; threatening. **b** surly; quarrelsome. **c** frightful; horrible. ➤➤ **uglily** *adv*, **ugliness** *n*.

ugly duckling *n* somebody or something that appears unattractive or unpromising but turns out to be admirable or successful.

UHF *abbr* ultrahigh frequency.

uh-huh *interj* used to indicate affirmation or agreement.

uhlan *n* any of a body of European light cavalry, orig modelled on Tartar lancers.

UHT *abbr* said of milk or cream: ultraheat-treated.

uillean pipes *pl n* Irish bagpipes played by working bellows under the arm.

UK *abbr* United Kingdom.

ukase *n* **1** a proclamation by a Russian emperor or government having the force of law. **2** an arbitrary command or edict.

Ukrainian *n* **1** a native or inhabitant of Ukraine. **2** the Slavonic language of the people of Ukraine. ➤➤ **Ukrainian** *adj*.

ukulele *n* a small usu four-stringed guitar of Portuguese origin, popularized in light music and often conveying a Hawaiian atmosphere.

ulama *n* see ULEMA.

ulcer *n* **1** an open sore on the skin or a mucous membrane, often one that discharges pus and is slow to heal. **2** something that festers and corrupts. ➤➤ **ulcerous** *adj*.

ulcerate *v* **1** to develop into an ulcer. **2** to become affected with or as if with an ulcer. ➤➤ **ulceration** *n*, **ulcerative** *adj*.

-ule *suffix* forming nouns, denoting: a small kind of a specified thing: *granule*.

ulema *or* **ulama** *n* **1** (*used as sing. or pl*) a body of theologians and scholars who are experts in Islamic theology and sacred law. **2** a member of such a body.

-ulent *suffix* forming adjectives, with the meaning: full of the thing specified.

ullage *n* **1** the amount by which a container is less than full. **2a** loss of a liquid through evaporation, leakage, etc. **b** the amount of liquid lost through this.

ulna *n* (*pl* **ulnae** *or* **ulnas**) the bone of the human forearm on the side of the little finger: compare RADIUS[1] (4). ➤➤ **ulnar** *adj.*

ulster *n* a long loose overcoat made of heavy material, often with a belt or half belt and usu worn by men.

Ulsterman *or* **Ulsterwoman** *n* (*pl* **Ulstermen** *or* **Ulsterwomen**) a native or inhabitant of Northern Ireland or Ulster.

ulterior *adj* **1** underlying or going beyond what is openly said or shown; intentionally concealed. **2** further or future. ➤➤ **ulteriorly** *adv.*

ultimata *n* pl of ULTIMATUM.

ultimate[1] *adj* **1a** last in a progression or series. **b** eventual. **2** fundamental; basic. **3** maximum; best or greatest. ➤➤ **ultimately** *adv,* **ultimateness** *n.*

ultimate[2] *n* **1** (*usu* **the ultimate**) the most extreme, significant, important, etc of its kind. **2** a basic fact or principle.

ultima Thule *n* a remote and unknown region.

ultimatum *n* (*pl* **ultimatums** *or* **ultimata**) a final condition or demand, *esp* one whose rejection will end negotiations and cause a resort to direct action or retaliation.

ultra[1] *adj* going beyond others or beyond due limits; extreme.

ultra[2] *n* an extremist.

ultra- *prefix* **1** beyond in space; on the other side of: *ultramontane.* **2** beyond the range or limits of; transcending: *ultrasonic.* **3** excessively; extremely: *ultramodern.*

ultrahigh frequency *n* (*also* **UHF**) a radio frequency in the range between 300 megahertz and 3000 megahertz.

ultramarine *n* **1** a vivid deep blue pigment formerly made by powdering lapis lazuli. **2** the vivid deep blue colour of this. ➤➤ **ultramarine** *adj.*

ultramicroscope *n* an apparatus using scattered light to make visible particles that are too small to be perceived by the ordinary microscope.

ultramicroscopic *adj* **1** too small to be seen with an ordinary microscope. **2** relating to an ultramicroscope.

ultramodern *adj* having the very latest ideas, styles, etc. ➤➤ **ultramodernist** *n.*

ultramontane[1] *adj* **1** of countries or peoples beyond the Alps or other mountains. **2** favouring the supremacy of papal authority over national or diocesan authority in the Roman Catholic Church. ➤➤ **ultramontanism** *n.*

ultramontane[2] *n* a supporter or advocate of supreme papal authority.

ultrasonic *adj* of waves and vibrations: having a frequency above the range of the human ear, e.g. above about 20,000Hz. ➤➤ **ultrasonically** *adv.*

ultrasonics *pl n* (*used as sing.*) the scientific study or technology of ultrasonic waves or vibrations.

ultrasound *n* **1** ultrasonic waves or vibrations. **2** the use of ultrasonic waves or vibrations in therapy or diagnostics, e.g. to examine internal bodily structures.

ultraviolet[1] *n* electromagnetic radiation having a wavelength between the violet end of the visible spectrum and X-rays.

ultraviolet[2] *adj* relating to or employing ultraviolet.

ultraviolet light *n* = ULTRAVIOLET[1].

ultra vires *adv and adj* beyond the legal power or authority of a person or body.

ululate *v* to howl or wail, *esp* as an expression of grief. ➤➤ **ululant** *adj,* **ululation** *n.*

umbel *n* a flower cluster typical of plants of the carrot family in which the flower stalks arise from a central point to form a flat or rounded surface of small flowers. ➤➤ **umbellate** *adj.*

umbellifer *n* any of a family of plants, such as the carrot, parsley, fennel, and parsnip, with hollow stems and flower heads made up of umbels. ➤➤ **umbelliferous** *adj.*

umber *n* **1** an earthy substance, greenish brown when raw and dark brown when burned, that is used to colour paint, ink, etc. **2** the dark or yellowish brown colour of burnt umber. ➤➤ **umber** *adj.*

umbilical *adj* relating to or in the region of the navel or the umbilical cord.

umbilical cord *n* a ropelike tube that connects a foetus with the placenta and is detached at the navel after birth.

umbilicus *n* (*pl* **umbilici** *or* **umbilicuses**) **1** *technical* the navel. **2** any of several depressions comparable to an umbilicus, e.g. one at the base of some gastropod shells.

umbra *n* (*pl* **umbras** *or* **umbrae**) **1** a region of total shadow, *esp* in an eclipse. **2** the central dark region of a sunspot. ➤➤ **umbral** *adj.*

umbrage *n* a feeling of pique or resentment.

umbrageous *adj* **1** inclined to take offence easily. **2** *archaic* shadowy or shady.

umbrella *n* **1** a collapsible circular shade for protection against rain, consisting of fabric stretched over hinged ribs radiating from a central rod. **2** something that provides protection or cover. **3** (*used before a noun*) comprising or concerning a broad range of elements or factors.

Umbrian *n* a native or inhabitant of the Italian province of Umbria. ➤➤ **Umbrian** *adj.*

umlaut *n* a mark (¨) placed over a vowel, *esp* to show a change of quality caused e.g. by the influence of a vowel in the following syllable.

umma *or* **ummah** /'oohmə/ *n* the entire community of Muslim believers.

umpire[1] *n* **1** a referee in any of several sports, e.g. cricket and tennis. **2** a person who has the authority to settle a controversy or question between parties.

umpire[2] *v* to act as umpire.

umpteen *adj and n informal* very many; an indefinitely large number. ➤➤ **umpteenth** *adj.*

UN *abbr* United Nations.

un *or* **'un** *pron dialect* one; a person or thing of a specified type.

un-[1] *prefix* forming adjectives, nouns, and adverbs, with the meanings: **1** not; lack of something: *unskilled; unbelief.* **2** opposite of or contrary to something: *ungrateful; unrest.*

Usage note

un- *and* **non-**. Both these prefixes produce negative forms of words. Where they can both be attached to the same root, the resulting *un-* word is generally stronger and judgmental whereas the *non-* word is neutral. A *non-professional* tutor is one who is not qualified; *unprofessional* behaviour contravenes professional ethics.

un-[2] *prefix* forming verbs, with the meanings: **1** the opposite or reversal of the action specified: *unbend; undress.* **2a** deprivation or removal of something: *unfrock; unnerve.* **b** release or removal from something: *untie; unearth; unhorse.*

unabashed *adj* not embarrassed, ashamed, or humbled.

unabated *adj* at full strength or force; undiminished. ⋙ **unabatedly** *adv.*

unable *adj* not able; incapable, unqualified, or powerless.

unabridged *adj* not abridged; complete.

unaccented *adj* **1** without stress or emphasis, e.g. in pronunciation. **2** not marked with an accent.

unacceptable *adj* **1** not satisfactory; not good enough. **2** not tolerable or permissible. ⋙ **unacceptability** *n,* **unacceptably** *adv.*

unaccompanied *adj* **1** alone, *esp* having no companion or escort; not accompanied, *esp* by an adult. **2** without piano or other instrumental accompaniment.

unaccountable *adj* **1** inexplicable; strange. **2** not to be called to account; not responsible. ⋙ **unaccountability** *n,* **unaccountably** *adv.*

unaccounted *adj* (+ for) not explained or taken into account.

unaccustomed *adj* **1** not customary; not usual or common. **2** (+ to) not used to (something). ⋙ **unaccustomedly** *adv.*

unacknowledged *adj* **1** in existence or having taken place but ignored or denied. **2** lacking the appropriate or deserved level of recognition.

unacquainted *adj* **1** (+ with) lacking experience of or familiarity with. **2** never having met.

unadjusted *adj* of information, *esp* statistical data: without any adjustments having been made or taken into account.

unadopted *adj Brit* of a road: not maintained by a local authority.

unadulterated *adj* **1** unmixed, *esp* with anything inferior; pure. **2** complete; utter.

unadventurous *adj* **1** lacking the inclination to do or try new or different things. **2** not offering any challenges. ⋙ **unadventurously** *adv.*

unadvised *adj* not prudent; indiscreet or rash. ⋙ **unadvisedly** *adv.*

unaffected *adj* **1** not influenced or changed by something. **2** free from affectation; genuine. ⋙ **unaffectedly** *adv,* **unaffectedness** *n.*

unaffiliated *adj* of a person or group: not belonging or connected to an organization, *esp* a trade union or political party; independent.

unaffordable *adj* too expensive, *esp* for the average person.

unaided *adj* not requiring any help or done without assistance.

unalienable *adj* = INALIENABLE.

unaligned *adj* **1** not arranged in a straight line or in the correct place relative to each other. **2** = NON-ALIGNED.

unalloyed *adj* **1** not mixed with another metal. **2** of e.g. happiness: complete and perfect.

unalterable *adj* not capable of being altered or changed. ⋙ **unalterableness** *n,* **unalterably** *adv.*

unambiguous *adj* not ambiguous; clear or precise. ⋙ **unambiguously** *adv.*

un-American *adj* **1** not consistent with US customs, principles, or traditions. **2** acting against the interests of the USA, *esp* formerly by sympathizing with Communism. ⋙ **un-Americanism** *n.*

unanimous *adj* **1** being of one mind; all agreeing. **2** having the agreement and consent of all. ⋙ **unanimity** *n,* **unanimously** *adv.*

unannounced *adj* **1** happening without warning; sudden and unexpected. **2** not publicized.

unanswerable *adj* **1** of a question: having no answer. **2** incapable of being argued against; irrefutable. ⋙ **unanswerably** *adv.*

unappealing *adj* not appealing; unattractive or uninviting. ⋙ **unappealingly** *adv.*

unappetizing *or* **unappetising** *adj* not appetizing; insipid or unattractive. ⋙ **unappetizingly** *adv.*

unapproachable *adj* **1** aloof or unfriendly. **2** physically inaccessible. ⋙ **unapproachability** *n,* **unapproachably** *adv.*

unarmed *adj* without weapons; not armed or armoured.

unashamed *adj* without guilt or embarrassment. ⋙ **unashamedly** *adv.*

unasked *adj* **1** not asked or invited. **2** not sought or asked for.

unassailable *adj* **1** not open to doubt or question. **2** not able to be attacked. **3** not able to be challenged or overtaken. ⋙ **unassailability** *n,* **unassailably** *adv.*

unassertive *adj* lacking confidence or forcefulness.

unassisted *adj* not assisted; acting or done without help.

unassuming *adj* not arrogant or presumptuous; modest. ⋙ **unassumingly** *adv,* **unassumingness** *n.*

unattached *adj* **1** not committed or connected, e.g. to a particular task or organization. **2** not involved in a serious or established romantic or sexual relationship. **3** not joined or united.

unattended *adj* **1** not cared for or looked after. **2** not dealt with.

unattractive *adj* not attractive, pleasing, or inviting. ⋙ **unattractively** *adv,* **unattractiveness** *n.*

unauthorized *or* **unauthorised** *adj* without official approval or permission.

unavailable *adj* not available; not capable of being obtained, contacted, etc. ⋙ **unavailability** *n.*

unavailing *adj* futile; useless. ⋙ **unavailingly** *adv.*

unavoidable *adj* not avoidable; inevitable. ⋙ **unavoidability** *n,* **unavoidably** *adv.*

unaware[1] *adj* (*often* + of) not aware; ignorant or lacking knowledge. ⋙ **unawareness** *n.*

unaware[2] *adv* = UNAWARES.

unawares *adv* **1** without noticing or intending. **2** suddenly; unexpectedly.

unbalance[1] *v* **1** to put out of balance. **2** to derange mentally.

unbalance[2] *n* lack of balance; imbalance or instability.

unbalanced *adj* **1** not in equilibrium. **2** mentally disordered or deranged. **3** not giving equal treatment to both sides or aspects; biased or partial.

unbearable *adj* not endurable; intolerable. ⋙ **unbearably** *adv.*

unbeatable *adj* **1** not able to be defeated or surpassed. **2** outstandingly good of its kind. ⋙ **unbeatably** *adv.*

unbeaten *adj* not defeated or surpassed.

unbecoming *adj* **1** not attractive or flattering. **2** improper; unseemly. ⋙ **unbecomingly** *adv,* **unbecomingness** *n.*

unbeknown *adj* (+ to) happening without the knowledge of (somebody).

unbeknownst *adj* = UNBEKNOWN.

unbelief *n* incredulity or scepticism, *esp* in matters of religious faith. ➤➤ **unbeliever** *n,* **unbelieving** *adj.*

unbelievable *adj* **1** too improbable for belief; incredible. **2** extraordinary, *esp* exceptionally good or bad. ➤➤ **unbelievably** *adv.*

unbend *v* (*past tense and past part.* **unbent**) **1** to return to a straight position. **2** to become more relaxed, informal, or outgoing.

unbending *adj* **1** unyielding; inflexible. **2** aloof or unsociable in manner. ➤➤ **unbendingly** *adv,* **unbendingness** *n.*

unbent *v* past tense and past part. of UNBEND.

unbiased *or* **unbiassed** *adj* free from all prejudice and partiality.

unbidden *adj* **1** unasked or uninvited. **2** voluntary or spontaneous.

unbind *v* (*past tense and past part.* **unbound**) **1** to untie or unfasten. **2** to set free.

unblemished *adj* not having or marred by flaws, faults, errors, etc.

unblushing *adj* showing no shame or embarrassment. ➤➤ **unblushingly** *adv.*

unbolt *v* to open or unfasten (e.g. a door) by withdrawing a bolt.

unborn *adj* **1** not yet born. **2** still to appear; future.

unbosom ✱ **unbosom oneself** *formal* to give expression to one's thoughts, feelings, etc.

unbound[1] *adj* **1** not fastened or confined. **2a** not having the leaves fastened together: *an unbound book.* **b** having no binding or case.

unbound[2] *v* past tense and past part. of UNBIND.

unbounded *adj* having no limits or constraints. ➤➤ **unboundedly** *adv,* **unboundedness** *n.*

unbowed *adj* not bowed down, *esp* not subdued.

unbreakable *adj* not capable of being broken.

unbridgeable *adj* **1** of a gap: too wide to be bridged. **2** of a difference in opinions, outlooks, etc: extreme and unlikely to be resolved.

unbridled *adj* unrestrained; uncontrolled.

unbroken *adj* **1** whole; intact. **2** not beaten or surpassed. **3** of a horse: not trained for riding or draught. **4** uninterrupted. ➤➤ **unbrokenly** *adv,* **unbrokenness** *n.*

unbuckle *v* to undo the buckle of (e.g. a belt).

unbundle *v* to divide (something composite) into its constituent parts, *esp* to split up (a conglomerate company) with a view to selling some of the subsidiaries. ➤➤ **unbundler** *n,* **unbundling** *n.*

unburden *v* (**unburdened, unburdening**) **1** to free from a burden. **2** to relieve (oneself, one's conscience, etc) of fears, worries, etc, *esp* by relating them to somebody else.

unbutton *v* **1** to undo the buttons of (a garment). **2** *informal* to become free from constraint, tension, etc; to relax. ➤➤ **unbuttoned** *adj.*

uncalled-for *adj* **1** unnecessary. **2** offered without provocation or justification; gratuitous.

uncanny *adj* (**-ier, -iest**) **1** eerie; mysterious. **2** beyond what is normal or expected. ➤➤ **uncannily** *adv,* **uncanniness** *n.*

uncapped *adj* of a sports player: never selected to play for the national side.

uncared-for *adj* not looked after; neglected.

uncaring *adj* not solicitous, sympathetic, or concerned.

unceasing *adj* never ceasing; continuous or incessant. ➤➤ **unceasingly** *adv.*

unceremonious *adj* **1** not ceremonious; informal. **2** abrupt or rude. ➤➤ **unceremoniously** *adv,* **unceremoniousness** *n.*

uncertain *adj* **1a** not definitely known; undecided or unpredictable. **b** not confident or sure; doubtful. **2** not reliable or trustworthy. **3** variable; changeable. ✱ **in no uncertain terms** forcefully and without ambiguity. ➤➤ **uncertainly** *adv,* **uncertainness** *n,* **uncertainty** *n.*

uncertainty principle *n* a principle in quantum mechanics stating that it is impossible to determine both the momentum and the position of a particle, e.g. a photon, at the same time.

unchangeable *adj* not changing or able to be changed. ➤➤ **unchangeability** *n,* **unchangeableness** *n,* **unchangeably** *adv.*

unchanging *adj* constant; invariable. ➤➤ **unchangingly** *adv.*

uncharacteristic *adj* not typical or distinctive. ➤➤ **uncharacteristically** *adv.*

uncharitable *adj* severe in judging others; harsh or unkind. ➤➤ **uncharitableness** *n,* **uncharitably** *adv.*

uncharted *adj* of an area of land or sea: not recorded or plotted on a map, chart, or plan; *broadly* unknown or unexplored.

unchecked *adj* of something undesirable: allowed to develop without restraint.

unchivalrous *adj* lacking in courtesy or consideration. ➤➤ **unchivalrously** *adv.*

unchristian *adj* **1** contrary to the teachings or spirit of Christianity. **2** uncivilized or pagan. ➤➤ **unchristianly** *adv.*

uncial[1] *adj* written in a style of handwriting formed of somewhat large rounded usu separated letters and used *esp* in Greek and Latin manuscripts. ➤➤ **uncially** *adv.*

uncial[2] *n* **1** an uncial letter or manuscript. **2** the uncial style of handwriting.

unciform *adj* hook-shaped.

uncivil *adj* lacking in courtesy; ill-mannered or impolite. ➤➤ **uncivilly** *adv.*

uncivilized *or* **uncivilised** *adj* **1** of a people: not civilized, *esp* in not having a written language. **2** rude, bad-mannered, or unsophisticated.

unclasp *v* **1** to open the clasp of. **2** to release from a grip.

unclassified *adj* **1** not divided into classes or placed in a class. **2** of information: not subject to a security classification. **3** *Brit* not part of the classified system of motorways, A-roads, and B-roads.

uncle *n* **1** the brother of one's father or mother, or the husband of one's aunt. **2** used by a child as a term of affection for an adult male friend.

unclean *adj* **1** dirty; filthy. **2** morally or spiritually impure. **3a** ritually prohibited as food. **b** ceremonially unfit or defiled. ➤➤ **uncleanness** *n.*

uncleanly *adj* morally or physically unclean. ➤➤ **uncleanliness** *n.*

unclear *adj* not clear, obvious, or easy to understand. ➤➤ **unclearly** *adv,* **unclearness** *n.*

uncleared *adj* **1** of a cheque: with the funds yet to go into the payee's account. **2** of land: under natural vegetation.

Uncle Sam *n* the US nation, people, or government.

Uncle Tom *n chiefly derog* a black American eager to win the approval of white people and willing to cooperate with them.

unclothed *adj* not clothed; naked.

unco[1] *adj chiefly Scot* **1** strange; unknown. **2** extraordinary; remarkable.

unco[2] *adv chiefly Scot* extremely; remarkably.

uncoil *v* to release or become released from a coiled state; to unwind.

uncomfortable *adj* **1** causing discomfort. **2** feeling discomfort; ill at ease. ⋙ **uncomfortableness** *n,* **uncomfortably** *adv.*

uncommercial *adj* **1** not related to commerce. **2** not intended or likely to make a profit.

uncommon *adj* **1** not normally encountered; unusual. **2** remarkable; exceptional. ⋙ **uncommonly** *adv,* **uncommonness** *n.*

uncommunicative *adj* not disposed to talk or impart information; reserved. ⋙ **uncommunicatively** *adv,* **uncommunicativeness** *n.*

uncomplaining *adj* not complaining; patient or stoical. ⋙ **uncomplainingly** *adv.*

uncomplicated *adj* not complex; straightforward.

uncomprehending *adj* having or showing a lack of comprehension or understanding. ⋙ **uncomprehendingly** *adv.*

uncompromising *adj* not making or accepting a compromise; unyielding or inflexible. ⋙ **uncompromisingly** *adv.*

unconcern *n* **1** lack of interest; indifference. **2** freedom from anxiety. ⋙ **unconcerned** *adj,* **unconcernedly** *adv.*

unconditional *adj* absolute; unqualified; without any conditions attached. ⋙ **unconditionally** *adv.*

unconditioned *adj* **1** of behaviour, instinctive reflexes, etc: not dependent on, established by, or subjected to conditioning or learning. **2** = UNCONDITIONAL.

unconfined *adj* **1** without limit. **2** of an emotional response: without restraint.

unconfirmed *adj* not confirmed as true.

uncongenial *adj* **1** not sympathetic, compatible, or suitable. **2** disagreeable; unpleasant.

unconnected *adj* **1** not linked or associated. **2** not connected or joined.

unconquerable *adj* **1** indomitable; unyielding. **2** incapable of being overcome. ⋙ **unconquerably** *adv.*

unconscionable *adj* **1** unscrupulous; unprincipled. **2** excessive; unreasonable. ⋙ **unconscionably** *adv.*

unconscious[1] *adj* **1** not knowing or perceiving. **2a** having lost consciousness. **b** not marked by or resulting from conscious thought, sensation, or feeling. **3** not intentional or deliberate. ⋙ **unconsciously** *adv,* **unconsciousness** *n.*

unconscious[2] *n* the part of the mind that does not ordinarily enter a person's awareness but nevertheless is held to influence behaviour and may be manifested in dreams or slips of the tongue.

unconsidered *adj* **1** disregarded. **2** not carefully thought out.

unconstitutional *adj* not in accordance with the constitution of a nation, organization, etc. ⋙ **unconstitutionality** *n,* **unconstitutionally** *adv.*

uncontrollable *adj* incapable of being controlled. ⋙ **uncontrollably** *adv.*

unconventional *adj* not bound by or conforming with generally accepted standards or practices; different from the norm. ⋙ **unconventionality** *n,* **unconventionally** *adv.*

unconvincing *adj* not convincing; implausible or unimpressive. ⋙ **unconvincingly** *adv.*

uncool *adj informal* not fashionable or sophisticated.

uncoordinated *adj* **1** lacking in coordination, *esp* in bodily movements. **2** *esp* of a joint venture: badly planned or organized.

uncork *v* **1** to draw a cork from (a bottle). **2** to release (e.g. emotions) from a pent-up state.

uncountable *adj* incapable of being counted; too numerous to count. ⋙ **uncountability** *n,* **uncountably** *adv.*

uncountable noun *n* = MASS NOUN.

uncounted *adj* **1** not counted. **2** innumerable.

uncouple *v* to detach or disconnect (e.g. railway wagons).

uncouth *adj* rude, awkward, or uncultivated in speech or behaviour. ⋙ **uncouthly** *adv,* **uncouthness** *n.*

uncover *v* **1** to remove the cover from. **2** to reveal or discover. **3** to take off one's hat as a token of respect.

uncritical *adj* **1** showing no discrimination. **2** showing a lack or improper use of critical standards or procedures. ⋙ **uncritically** *adv.*

uncrowned *adj* **1** not having yet been crowned. **2** having a specified status in fact but not in name.

unction *n* **1** the act or an instance of anointing, *esp* as a rite of consecration. **2** exaggerated or superficial earnestness of language or manner; unctuousness.

unctuous *adj* **1** fatty, oily, or greasy. **2** marked by ingratiating smoothness and false sincerity. ⋙ **unctuously** *adv,* **unctuousness** *n.*

uncultivated *adj* **1** of land: not planted with crops. **2** of a person: not refined or educated.

uncurl *v* to straighten out from a curled or coiled position.

uncut *adj* **1** not cut down or into. **2** not shaped by cutting. **3** of a book, film, etc: not abridged or edited. **4** of alcohol or drugs: undiluted or unadulterated.

undaunted *adj* not discouraged by danger, difficulty, or setbacks, etc. ⋙ **undauntedly** *adv,* **undauntedness** *n.*

undead *adj* of a vampire, etc: having died or been killed but still able to maintain a physical presence.

undecagon *n* a two-dimensional geometrical figure having eleven sides.

undeceive *v* to free from deception, illusion, or error.

undecided *adj* **1** in doubt. **2** without a result. ⋙ **undecidedly** *adv,* **undecidedness** *n.*

undemanding *adj* **1** easy to perform or accomplish. **2** of a person: easy to keep satisfied.

undemocratic *adj* not following democratic practices, principles, or ideals. ⋙ **undemocratically** *adv.*

undemonstrative *adj* not showing one's feelings, *esp* of affection; reserved. ⋙ **undemonstratively** *adv,* **undemonstrativeness** *n.*

undeniable *adj* plainly true; incontestable. ⋙ **undeniably** *adv.*

under[1] *adv* **1** in a position below or beneath something. **2** in a lower rank, number, or quantity. **3** in a condition of subjection, subordination, or unconsciousness. **4** lower on the same or a following page.

under[2] *prep* **1a** below or beneath. **b** covered, protected, or hidden by (something). **c** using (a name) as a pseudonym or alias. **2a** subject to the authority, control, guidance, or instruction of. **b** during the rule or control of. **c** inferior in rank to. **3a** undergoing the action or effect of. **b** bearing (something) as a crop. **4** within the group or designation of: *under this heading*. **5a** less than (a number or quantity). **b** falling short of (a standard or required degree).

under- *comb. form* **1** lying or placed below: *underground*. **2** lower in rank or authority: *undersecretary*. **3** less than usual, proper, or desired: *undernourished*.

underachieve *v* to fail to realize one's full potential, *esp* at school. ►► **underachievement** *n*, **underachiever** *n*.

underact *v* to perform feebly or with restraint.

under-age *adj* **1** being below the legal age. **2** done by somebody below the legal age.

underarm *adj* **1** under or along the underside of the arm. **2** of a throw or hit: made with the hand brought forward and up from below shoulder level. ►► **underarm** *adv*.

underbelly *n* (*pl* **-ies**) **1** the underside of an animal, object, etc. **2** a vulnerable area.

underbid *v* (**underbidding,** *past tense and past part.* **underbid**) **1** to bid less than. **2** in cards, to make a lower bid than the strength of the hand warrants. **3** to bid too low. ►► **underbidder** *n*.

underbite *n* the projection of the teeth of the lower jaw beyond the teeth of the upper jaw.

underbrush *n NAm* undergrowth in a wood or forest.

undercarriage *n* **1** the part of an aircraft's structure that supports it on the ground and assists in takeoff and landing. **2** a supporting framework, e.g. of a motor vehicle.

undercharge *v* to charge too little.

underclass *n* a class of people considered as being below all other social classes, *esp* the very poor.

underclothes *pl n* = UNDERWEAR.

underclothing *n* = UNDERWEAR.

undercoat[1] *n* **1** a coat, e.g. of paint, applied as a base for another coat. **2** a growth of short hair or fur partly concealed by a longer growth.

undercoat[2] *v* to apply an undercoat of paint to (something).

undercover *adj and adv* acting or done in secret; *specif* employed or involved in spying.

undercroft *n* a crypt.

undercurrent *n* **1** a current below the surface or beneath another current. **2** a hidden or underlying opinion, feeling, or tendency.

undercut[1] *v* (**undercutting,** *past tense and past part.* **undercut**) **1** to charge less than (a competitor). **2** to cut or wear away material from the underside of.

undercut[2] *n* **1** the action or result of undercutting. **2** *Brit* the underside of a sirloin of beef. **3** *NAm* a notch cut in a tree before felling to determine the direction in which it will fall.

underdeveloped *adj* **1** not normally or adequately developed. **2** of a country or region: without modern industries or the means of financing them. ►► **underdevelopment** *n*.

underdog *n* **1** a competitor who is expected to lose in a struggle or contest. **2** a victim of injustice, persecution, poverty, etc.

underdone *adj* of food, *esp* meat: not thoroughly cooked.

underdress *v* to dress less formally than is appropriate. ►► **underdressed** *adj*.

underemployed *adj* **1** having less than full-time or adequate employment. **2** employed in work that does not make full use of a person's talents, capabilities, etc. ►► **underemployment** *n*.

underestimate[1] *v* **1** to estimate (something) as being less than the actual size, quantity, etc. **2** to regard (somebody) as less capable, powerful, etc than they actually are. ►► **underestimation** *n*.

underestimate[2] *n* an estimate that is too low.

underexpose *v* to expose (e.g. photographic film) insufficiently. ►► **underexposure** *n*.

underfelt *n* thick felt placed under a carpet for insulation, protection, comfort, etc.

underfoot *adv* **1** under the feet, *esp* against the ground. **2** in the way.

undergarment *n* an item of underwear.

underglaze *n* colour, decorations, etc applied or suitable for applying to pottery before the glaze is put on.

undergo *v* (**undergoes,** *past tense* **underwent,** *past part.* **undergone, undergoing**) **1** to go through or experience. **2** to be subjected to (something unpleasant).

undergrad *n informal* an undergraduate.

undergraduate *n* somebody studying at a college or university for a first degree.

underground[1] *adj* **1** growing, operating, or situated below the ground. **2a** conducted in hiding or in secret. **b** existing, produced, or operating outside the establishment; experimental or avant-garde. ►► **underground** *adv*.

underground[2] *n* **1** *used as sing. or pl* **a** a secret movement or group, *esp* in an occupied country, formed for concerted resistance. **b** a secret conspiratorial organization dedicated to disruption of civil order. **c** an unofficial usu avant-garde group or movement that functions outside the establishment. **2** *Brit* an underground urban railway.

undergrowth *n* vegetation, e.g. saplings, bushes, and ferns, growing on the floor of a wood or forest.

underhand *adj* **1** marked by subterfuge, trickery, and deception; sly. **2** done secretly; clandestine. **3** = UNDERARM (2). ►► **underhand** *adv*.

underhanded *adj* = UNDERHAND. ►► **underhandedly** *adv*.

underinsured *adj* insured for less than the amount needed to cover possible loss or damage. ►► **underinsurance** *n*.

underlaid *v* past tense and past part. of UNDERLAY[1].

underlain *v* past part. of UNDERLIE.

underlay[1] *v* (*past tense and past part.* **underlaid**) to raise or support by laying something underneath.

underlay[2] *n* something designed to be laid under something else, *esp* thick foam, felt, etc laid under a carpet for insulation, protection, etc.

underlie *v* (**underlying,** *past tense* **underlay,** *past part.* **underlain**) **1** to lie or be situated under. **2** to be hidden beneath (e.g. a facade or superficial behaviour). **3** to be the basis, foundation, or cause of (something). ►► **underlying** *adj*.

underline[1] *v* **1** to mark (a word, phrase, or passage) with a line underneath. **2** to emphasize or stress.

underline[2] *n* a line marked underneath a word, phrase, or passage.

underling *n* a subordinate or inferior.

underlip *n* the lower lip.

undermanned *adj* = UNDERSTAFFED.

undermentioned *adj Brit* referred to at a later point in the text.

undermine *v* **1** to excavate the earth beneath (e.g. a fortification). **2** to wear away the base or foundations of (e.g. a rock formation). **3** to subvert, weaken, or destroy gradually or insidiously.

undermost *adj* lowest in relative position.

underneath[1] *prep and adv* **1** directly below. **2** close under, *esp* so as to be hidden. **3** on the lower side.

underneath[2] *n* the bottom part or surface.

undernourished *adj* supplied with less than the minimum amount of the foods essential for sound health and growth. ➤➤ **undernourishment** *n.*

underpaid *v* past tense and past part. of UNDERPAY.

underpants *pl n* an undergarment for men or boys that covers the hips, crotch, and sometimes the upper thighs.

underpart *n* a part lying on the lower side.

underpass *n* a tunnel or passage taking a road or footpath under another road or a railway.

underpay *v* (*past tense and past part.* **underpaid**) **1** to give less than adequate or normal payment to (e.g. a worker). **2** to pay too little for (e.g. a job). ➤➤ **underpayment** *n.*

underpin *v* (**underpinned, underpinning**) **1** to form part of, strengthen, or replace the foundation of (a building or other structure). **2** to support or substantiate. ➤➤ **underpinning** *n.*

underplay *v* **1** to underact. **2** to play down the importance of.

underprice *v* to price (something) too low.

underprivileged *adj* deprived, usu through social or economic conditions, of some of the fundamental rights and opportunities of a civilized society.

underrate *v* to undervalue or underestimate.

underscore[1] *v* = UNDERLINE[1].

underscore[2] *n* = UNDERLINE[2].

undersea *adj* situated, used, or carried on under the sea or under the surface of the sea.

underseal[1] *n* a protective corrosion-proof substance, e.g. bitumen, used *esp* to coat vehicle undersurfaces.

underseal[2] *v* to apply underseal to (something).

undersecretary *n* (*pl* **-ies**) a secretary immediately subordinate to a principal secretary, *esp* a secretary of state.

undersell *v* (*past tense and past part.* **undersold**) **1** to sell at a lower price than. **2a** to make little of the merits of. **b** to publicize in a deliberately low-key manner.

undersexed *adj* lacking or having an unusually low sexual drive or interest.

undershirt *n chiefly NAm* = VEST[1] (1).

undershoot *v* (*past tense and past part.* **undershot**) **1** to shoot short of (a target). **2** of an aircraft: to land short of (a runway).

undershot[1] *adj* of a waterwheel: moved by water passing beneath.

undershot[2] *v* past tense and past part. of UNDERSHOOT.

underside *n* the side or surface lying underneath.

undersigned *n* (**the undersigned**) (*used as sing. or pl*) somebody who signs, or the people who sign, at the end of a document.

undersize *adj* = UNDERSIZED.

undersized *adj* of less than average or normal size.

underskirt *n* an undergarment that hangs loosely from the waist and is worn under a skirt or dress.

undersold *v* past tense and past part. of UNDERSELL.

understaffed *adj* inadequately staffed.

understand *v* (*past tense and past part.* **understood**) **1a** to grasp the meaning of (e.g. words or a speaker). **b** to have a thorough knowledge of or expertise in (a specified subject, etc). **2** to assume, infer, or suppose. **3** to interpret in one of a number of possible ways. **4** to supply mentally (something implied though not expressed). **5** to show a sympathetic or tolerant attitude.

understandable *adj* **1** normal and reasonable, *esp* in a particular situation. **2** capable of being understood. ➤➤ **understandability** *n,* **understandably** *adv.*

understanding[1] *n* **1** a mental grasp; comprehension. **2** the power of comprehending; intelligence. **3a** a friendly or harmonious relationship. **b** an informal mutual agreement. **4** meaning or interpretation. **5** tolerance or sympathy.

understanding[2] *adj* tolerant or sympathetic. ➤➤ **understandingly** *adv.*

understate *v* **1** to state or represent as being less than is the case. **2** to present with restraint, *esp* for greater effect. ➤➤ **understatement** *n.*

understeer *v* of a motor vehicle: to turn less sharply than expected in response to movements of the steering wheel. ➤➤ **understeer** *n.*

understood *v* past tense and past part. of UNDERSTAND.

understudy[1] *v* (**-ies, -ied**) to study another actor's part in order to be able to take it over in an emergency.

understudy[2] *n* (*pl* **-ies**) somebody who is prepared to act another's part or take over another's duties.

undersubscribed *adj* of a course of study, event, etc: having fewer applicants than there are places, tickets, etc on offer.

undertake *v* (*past tense* **undertook,** *past part.* **undertaken**) **1** to take upon oneself as a task or responsibility. **2** to guarantee or promise to do (something).

undertaker *n* somebody whose business is preparing the dead for burial and arranging and managing funerals.

undertaking *n* **1** an enterprise. **2** a pledge or guarantee. **3** the business of an undertaker.

under-the-counter *adj informal esp* of goods: sold or obtained illegally or surreptitiously.

undertone *n* **1** a low or subdued utterance or tone of voice. **2** a quality or feeling underlying an utterance or action. **3** a subdued colour.

undertook *v* past tense of UNDERTAKE.

undertow *n* an undercurrent that flows in a different direction from the surface current, *esp* out to sea.

undervalue *v* (**undervalues, undervalued, undervaluing**) to value, rate, or estimate below the real worth. ➤➤ **undervaluation** *n.*

underwater *adj* situated or used below the surface of the water. ➤➤ **underwater** *adv.*

under way *adv* **1** in or into motion. **2** in progress. **3** of a vessel: moving or beginning to move through the water.

underwear *n* clothing, e.g. knickers, pants, vests, bras, etc, worn under other clothing, *esp* next to the skin.

underweight *adj* weighing less than the normal or requisite weight.

underwent *v* past tense of UNDERGO.

underwhelm *v humorous* to fail to impress.

underwired *adj* of a bra: with a semicircular wire stitched into the underside of each cup for greater uplift.

underwood *n* undergrowth, *esp* small trees and shrubs.

underworld *n* **1** in mythology, the abode of the souls of the dead, regarded as being below the surface of the earth. **2** the world of organized crime.

underwrite *v* (*past tense* **underwrote,** *past part.* **underwritten**) **1** to put one's signature on (an insurance policy) thereby assuming liability in case of specified loss or damage. **2** to guarantee financial support of (an enterprise). **3** to subscribe or agree to (something).

underwriter *n* **1** somebody who underwrites something, *esp* an insurance policy. **2** an employee of an insurance company who rates the acceptability of risks solicited and determines appropriate premiums.

underwritten *v* past part. of UNDERWRITE.

underwrote *v* past tense of UNDERWRITE.

undescended *adj* of a testicle: retained within the abdomen rather than descending into the scrotum at the normal age.

undesirable[1] *adj* unwanted or objectionable. ⋙ **undesirability** *n,* **undesirably** *adv.*

undesirable[2] *n* an undesirable person or thing, *esp* somebody considered socially unacceptable.

undetermined *adj* not resolved or settled.

undeterred *adj* not deterred by setbacks, warnings, etc from pursuing a particular course of action.

undid *v* past tense of UNDO.

undies *pl n informal* underwear, *esp* women's underwear.

undignified *adj* lacking in dignity.

undiminished *adj* not diminished; as great as before.

undisciplined *adj* showing a lack of proper control or self-control.

undisclosed *adj* not revealed or made known.

undisguised *adj* not concealed; frank or open. ⋙ **undisguisedly** *adv.*

undisputed *adj* not questioned or challenged; universally accepted.

undistinguished *adj* lacking in distinction; not exceptional.

undivided *adj* **1** complete; total. **2** not split into separate parts.

undo *v* (*past tense* **undid,** *past part.* **undone**) **1** to open or loosen by releasing a fastening. **2** to reverse or cancel out the effects of. **3** to destroy the standing, reputation, hopes, etc of.

undoing *n* **1** ruin. **2** a cause of ruin or downfall.

undone[1] *v* past part. of UNDO.

undone[2] *adj* **1** not performed or finished. **2** unfastened or untied. **3** ruined or destroyed.

undoubted *adj* not disputed; certain or genuine. ⋙ **undoubtedly** *adv.*

undreamed *or* **undreamt** *adj* (*usu* + of) not conceived of; unimagined.

undress[1] *v* **1** to remove the clothes from (somebody). **2** to take off one's clothes.

undress[2] *n* **1** a state of having little or no clothing on. **2** ordinary clothing or uniform, as opposed to formal or ceremonial dress.

undressed *adj* **1** partially or completely unclothed. **2** not fully processed or finished. **3** of food: served without a dressing.

undrinkable *adj* not safe or pleasant to drink.

undue *adj* excessive; immoderate.

undulant *adj* rising and falling in waves; rolling.

undulant fever *n* the disease brucellosis occurring in human beings.

undulate *v* **1** to rise and fall in waves; to fluctuate. **2** to have a wavy form or appearance. ⋙ **undulating** *adj,* **undulation** *n,* **undulatory** *adj.*

unduly *adv* excessively.

undying *adj* eternal; perpetual.

unearned *adj* not gained by work, service, skill, or merit.

unearned income *n* income derived from investments, rents, etc rather than employment.

unearth *v* **1** to dig up out of the ground. **2** to find or discover, *esp* after searching. **3** to force (*esp* a fox) from a hole, burrow, etc.

unearthly *adj* **1** weird; eerie. **2** *informal* unreasonable; preposterous: *at an unearthly hour.* ⋙ **unearthliness** *n.*

unease *n* a feeling of disquiet or awkwardness.

uneasy *adj* (**-ier, -iest**) **1** marked by lack of *esp* mental ease; uncomfortable or awkward. **2** apprehensive or worried. **3** precarious or unstable. ⋙ **uneasily** *adv,* **uneasiness** *n.*

uneatable *adj* not fit or safe to be eaten; inedible.

uneconomic *adj* not profitable or economically practicable.

uneconomical *adj* wasteful.

uneducated *adj* having or showing a lack of education; ignorant.

unemployable *adj* not acceptable or fitted for any form of employment. ⋙ **unemployability** *n.*

unemployed[1] *adj* **1** not engaged in a job. **2** not being used.

unemployed[2] *pl n* (**the unemployed**) people who are not employed.

unemployment *n* **1** the state of being unemployed. **2** the number or percentage of people out of work in a country, region, etc.

unemployment benefit *n* a sum of money paid, e.g. by the state, at regular intervals to an unemployed person.

unending *adj* never ending; seemingly endless. ⋙ **unendingly** *adv,* **unendingness** *n.*

unenforceable *adj* of a law: incapable of being enforced.

unenterprising *adj* having or showing a lack of enterprise or initiative.

unenthusiastic *adj* not enthusiastic or excited. ⋙ **unenthusiastically** *adv.*

unenviable *adj* not arousing envy; highly undesirable. ⋙ **unenviably** *adv.*

unequal *adj* **1a** not the same in measurement, quantity, or number. **b** not the same for every member of a group, class, or society. **2** badly balanced or matched. **3** (+ to) incapable of meeting the requirements of (e.g. a task). ⋙ **unequally** *adv.*

unequalled (*NAm* **unequaled**) *adj* unparalleled or unrivalled.

unequivocal *adj* clear and unambiguous. ⋙ **unequivocally** *adv,* **unequivocalness** *n.*

unerring *adj* faultless or unfailing. ⋙ **unerringly** *adv,* **unerringness** *n.*

UNESCO *abbr* United Nations Educational, Scientific, and Cultural Organization.

unethical *adj* not conforming to accepted, *esp* professional, standards of conduct or morality. ➤➤ **unethically** *adv.*

uneven *adj* **1a** not level, smooth, or uniform. **b** irregular; inconsistent. **c** varying in quality. **2** badly balanced or matched. ➤➤ **unevenly** *adv,* **unevenness** *n.*

uneventful *adj* without any noteworthy or untoward incidents. ➤➤ **uneventfully** *adv,* **uneventfulness** *n.*

unexampled *adj* having no parallel; unprecedented.

unexceptionable *adj* beyond reproach or criticism; unimpeachable. ➤➤ **unexceptionableness** *n,* **unexceptionably** *adv.*

Usage note

unexceptionable *or* unexceptional? See note at UNEXCEPTIONAL.

unexceptional *adj* commonplace, ordinary, or normal. ➤➤ **unexceptionally** *adv.*

Usage note

unexceptional *or* unexceptionable? These two words are quite close together in meaning and could be confused. *Unexceptional* means 'not outstanding', therefore 'ordinary' or 'rather dull' (*an unexceptional year for wine*). If a thing is *unexceptionable* it causes no offence or controversy: *It was just that one remark – the rest of the speech was totally unexceptionable.* See also note at EXCEPTIONAL.

unexpected *adj* not expected or foreseen. ➤➤ **unexpectedly** *adv,* **unexpectedness** *n.*

unexplained *adj* **1** not explained or made clear. **2** not understandable or accounted for.

unexpurgated *adj* unabridged or uncensored; complete.

unfailing *adj* **1** able to be relied on; constant or sure. **2** continuous. ➤➤ **unfailingly** *adv,* **unfailingness** *n.*

unfair *adj* **1** unjust or unequal. **2** not honest or ethical, *esp* in business dealings. ➤➤ **unfairly** *adv,* **unfairness** *n.*

unfaithful *adj* **1** not adhering to allegiance or duty; disloyal. **2** not faithful to a marriage partner, lover, etc, *esp* in having sexual relations with another person. **3** inaccurate. ➤➤ **unfaithfully** *adv,* **unfaithfulness** *n.*

unfaltering *adj* not wavering or hesitating; firm. ➤➤ **unfalteringly** *adv.*

unfamiliar *adj* **1** not well-known; strange. **2** (+ with) not acquainted with or lacking an understanding of (a subject, etc). ➤➤ **unfamiliarity** *n,* **unfamiliarly** *adv.*

unfancied *adj* of a competitor: considered unlikely to win or attracting few bets.

unfasten *v* **1** to loosen or undo. **2** to untie or detach.

unfathomable *adj* **1** impossible to comprehend. **2** immeasurable. ➤➤ **unfathomableness** *n,* **unfathomably** *adv.*

unfavourable (*NAm* **unfavorable**) *adj* **1** expressing disapproval or lack of support; negative. **2** disadvantageous; adverse. ➤➤ **unfavourably** *adv.*

unfazed *adj informal* not disconcerted or daunted.

unfeeling *adj* **1** not kind or sympathetic; hardhearted. **2** devoid of physical feeling or sensation. ➤➤ **unfeelingly** *adv,* **unfeelingness** *n.*

unfettered *adj* not kept under restraint; uninhibited.

unfinished *adj* **1** not brought to an end or to the desired final state; incomplete. **2** not having been given a finish.

unfit[1] *adj* **1** unsuitable or inappropriate. **2** incapable or incompetent. **3** physically or mentally unsound. ➤➤ **unfitly** *adv,* **unfitness** *n.*

unfit[2] *v* (**unfitted, unfitting**) to make unfit; to disqualify.

unfitting *adj* inappropriate, *esp* to the dignity of a person or occasion.

unfixed *adj* unstable, unsettled, or uncertain.

unflagging *adj* never flagging; tireless. ➤➤ **unflaggingly** *adv.*

unflappable *adj informal* remaining calm and composed; imperturbable. ➤➤ **unflappability** *n,* **unflappably** *adv.*

unflattering *adj* not flattering, *esp* unfavourable. ➤➤ **unflatteringly** *adv.*

unfledged *adj* **1** of a young bird: having not yet developed the feathers necessary for flight. **2** not fully developed; immature.

unflinching *adj* not flinching or shrinking; steadfast. ➤➤ **unflinchingly** *adv.*

unfocused *or* **unfocussed** *adj* **1** lacking direction or a specific aim. **2** not focused or out of focus.

unfold *v* **1** to open the folds of and spread or straighten out. **2** to reveal gradually or be revealed.

unforeseeable *adj* incapable of being foreseen or predicted.

unforeseen *adj* not predicted or expected.

unforgettable *adj* incapable of being forgotten; memorable. ➤➤ **unforgettably** *adv.*

unforgivable *adj* too bad, cruel, etc to be forgiven or excused. ➤➤ **unforgivably** *adv.*

unformed *adj* **1** not shaped. **2** immature or undeveloped.

unfortunate[1] *adj* **1a** unsuccessful or unlucky. **b** accompanied by or resulting in misfortune. **2** unsuitable; inappropriate. ➤➤ **unfortunately** *adv.*

unfortunate[2] *n* an unlucky person.

unfounded *adj* lacking a sound basis; groundless. ➤➤ **unfoundedly** *adv,* **unfoundedness** *n.*

unfreeze *v* (*past tense* **unfroze,** *past part.* **unfrozen**) **1** to thaw or cause to thaw. **2** to free (e.g. prices or assets) from restrictions.

unfrequented *adj* not often visited or travelled over.

unfriendly *adj* (**-ier, -iest**) **1** hostile or unsympathetic. **2** inhospitable or unfavourable. **3** not user-friendly. ➤➤ **unfriendliness** *n.*

unfrock *v* to deprive (*esp* a priest) of the right to exercise the functions of office.

unfroze *v* past tense of UNFREEZE.

unfrozen *v* past part. of UNFREEZE.

unfunded *adj* **1** of a debt: not funded; floating. **2** not provided with funds.

unfurl *v* to open out from a furled state; to unroll.

unfurnished *adj esp* of a rented property: not equipped with furniture.

ungainly *adj* (**-ier, -iest**) **1** lacking in grace or dexterity; clumsy. **2** unwieldy or awkward. ➤➤ **ungainliness** *n.*

ungenerous *adj* **1** petty or uncharitable. **2** showing a lack of generosity; mean. ➤➤ **ungenerously** *adv.*

ungetatable *adj informal* inaccessible; unapproachable.

ungodly *adj* (**-ier, -iest**) **1a** irreligious or impious. **b** wicked or immoral. **2** *informal* unreasonable, inconvenient, or outrageous. ➤➤ **ungodliness** *n.*

ungovernable *adj* not capable of being controlled or restrained. ➤➤ **ungovernably** *adv.*

ungracious *adj* **1** rude; impolite. **2** not pleasing; disagreeable. ⋙ **ungraciously** *adv,* **ungraciousness** *n.*

ungrateful *adj* **1** showing no gratitude. **2** disagreeable; unpleasant. ⋙ **ungratefully** *adv,* **ungratefulness** *n.*

unguarded *adj* **1** showing poor judgment or lack of forethought, *esp* in speech; imprudent or careless. **2** without a guard or screen. ⋙ **unguardedly** *adv,* **unguardedness** *n.*

unguent *n* a soothing or healing salve; an ointment.

ungulate *n* any of the hoofed mammals, e.g. cattle, pigs, horses, and deer.

unhand *v archaic, literary, humorous* to remove one's hands from; to release from one's grasp.

unhappy *adj* (**-ier, -iest**) **1** sad; miserable. **2** not fortunate; unlucky. **3** unsuitable; inappropriate. ⋙ **unhappily** *adv,* **unhappiness** *n.*

unharmed *adj* not damaged or injured.

UNHCR *abbr* United Nations High Commissioner for Refugees.

unhealthy *adj* (**-ier, -iest**) **1a** not in good health. **b** not conducive to good health. **2** unnatural or morbid. ⋙ **unhealthily** *adv,* **unhealthiness** *n.*

unheard *adj* **1** not perceived by the ear. **2** not given a hearing; disregarded.

unheard-of *adj* previously unknown; unprecedented.

unheeded *adj* ignored or disregarded.

unhelpful *adj* not helpful; uncooperative. ⋙ **unhelpfully** *adv.*

unheralded *adj* not previously announced.

unhinge *v* **1** to remove (e.g. a door) from hinges. **2** to disturb the balance of (a person or their mind).

unholy *adj* (**-ier, -iest**) **1** wicked, immoral, or unnatural. **2** *informal* terrible; awful. ⋙ **unholiness** *n.*

unhook *v* **1** to remove from a hook. **2** to unfasten the hooks of.

unhorse *v* to cause to fall from a horse.

unhurried *adj* not hurried; leisurely. ⋙ **unhurriedly** *adv.*

unhurt *adj* not injured or harmed.

unhygienic *adj* not in accordance with the rules of hygiene.

uni *n* (*pl* **unis**) *informal* = UNIVERSITY.

uni- *prefix* one; single: *unicellular; unicorn.*

Uniate *or* **Uniat** *adj* relating to or denoting a Christian Church that adheres to Eastern rites but submits to papal authority.

unicameral *adj* of or having a single legislative chamber. ⋙ **unicamerally** *adv.*

UNICEF *abbr* United Nations Children's Fund (formerly United Nations International Children's Emergency Fund).

unicellular *adj* consisting of a single cell. ⋙ **unicellularity** *n.*

unicorn *n* a mythical animal usu depicted as a white horse with a single straight horn in the middle of the forehead.

unicycle *n* a cycle with a single wheel, used *esp* by acrobats. ⋙ **unicyclist** *n.*

unidentified *adj* not known, recognized, or identified.

unification *n* the process or result of unifying; the state of being unified.

Unification Church *n* the Church of the Moonies (members of a religious sect founded in South Korea; see MOONIE).

uniform[1] *adj* not varying in character, appearance, quantity, etc. ⋙ **uniformity** *n,* **uniformly** *adv,* **uniformness** *n.*

uniform[2] *n* clothing of a distinctive design, colour, etc worn by members of a particular group, e.g. soldiers or pupils of a particular school, and serving as a means of identification.

unify *v* (**-ies, -ied**) to make (a group of people or things) into, or to become, a unit or a coherent whole; to unite. ⋙ **unifiable** *adj,* **unifier** *n.*

unilateral *adj* **1** done or undertaken by only one person or group. **2** of or affecting only one side, e.g. of the body. ⋙ **unilateralism** *n,* **unilaterally** *adv.*

unimaginative *adj* **1** not given to creative thought. **2** not interesting, unusual, or innovative. ⋙ **unimaginatively** *adv.*

unimpeachable *adj* **1** not to be doubted; beyond question. **2** irreproachable; blameless. ⋙ **unimpeachably** *adv.*

unimportant *adj* having little or no importance. ⋙ **unimportance** *n.*

unimproved *adj* **1** not improved for use, e.g. by being cleared or cultivated. **2** not better.

unincorporated *adj* **1** not part of a whole or a corporate body. **2** of a business: privately owned and not legally registered as a company.

uninformed *adj* **1** lacking awareness, knowledge, or understanding of something. **2** of a decision, etc: made without being aware of or understanding all the relevant facts.

uninhabited *adj* having no inhabitants.

uninhibited *adj* acting or speaking spontaneously without constraint or regard for what others might think. ⋙ **uninhibitedly** *adv,* **uninhibitedness** *n.*

uninitiated *adj* lacking special knowledge or experience of something.

uninspiring *adj* not arousing interest or enthusiasm. ⋙ **uninspiringly** *adv.*

unintelligible *adj* not capable of being understood; obscure. ⋙ **unintelligibility** *n,* **unintelligibly** *adv.*

unintentional *adj* not done deliberately; accidental. ⋙ **unintentionally** *adv.*

uninterested *adj* not having the interest aroused or attention engaged; unconcerned. ⋙ **uninterestedly** *adv,* **uninterestedness** *n.*

Usage note

uninterested *or* disinterested? See note at DISINTERESTED.

uninteresting *adj* not engaging the attention; boring. ⋙ **uninterestingly** *adv,* **uninterestingness** *n.*

uninterrupted *adj* **1** not interrupted; continuous. **2** not obstructed. ⋙ **uninterruptedly** *adv.*

uninvited *adj* not having been asked for or invited.

union *n* **1a** the act or an instance of joining two or more things into one. **b** a unified condition. **2** a marriage. **3a** something formed by a combining or coalition of parts or members. **b** an association of independent individuals or groups for some common purpose. **c** an organization run by the students of an educational institution. **d** = TRADE UNION. **4a** (*often* **the Union**) a political unit made up from previously independent units, e.g. England and Scotland in 1707. **b** (**the Union**) the northern states during the American Civil War. **5** a coupling for pipes or pipes and fittings. **6** any of various cloths having the warp and the weft of different fibres.

Union Flag *n* = UNION JACK.

unionise *v* see UNIONIZE.

unionism *n* **1** the principles of trade unions or the adherence to these principles. **2** (**Unionism**) the principles and policies of the Unionist party of N Ireland. ⋙ **unionist** *n.*

unionize *or* **unionise** *v* to join, or cause (a worker or workers) to join, a trade union. ⋙ **unionization** *n.*

Union Jack *n* the national flag of Britain combining the crosses of St George, St Andrew, and St Patrick.

unipolar *adj* having or produced by a single magnetic or electrical pole. ⋙ **unipolarity** *n.*

unique *adj* **1** being the only one; sole. **2a** without a like or equal. **b** (+ to) belonging to or occurring in only one (person, place, etc). ⋙ **uniquely** *adv,* **uniqueness** *n.*

unisex *adj* **1** suitable or designed for either sex. **2** dealing in unisex products or styles.

unisexual *adj* **1** of or restricted to one sex. **2** of an animal or plant: having either male or female reproductive organs but not both. ⋙ **unisexuality** *n,* **unisexually** *adv.*

unison *n* the writing, playing, or singing of parts in a musical passage at the same pitch or one or more octaves apart. ✱ **in unison 1** in perfect agreement or harmony. **2** saying or doing the same thing at the same time. ⋙ **unisonous** *adj.*

unit *n* **1a** a single thing, person, or group that is a constituent of a whole. **b** a part of an organization, e.g. a military establishment, that has a specific function. **c** a piece of apparatus or part of a device serving to perform one particular function. **2** a determinate quantity, e.g. of length, time, heat or value, adopted as a standard of measurement. **3a** the first and lowest natural number; one. **b** the number occupying the position immediately to the left of the decimal point. **4** a group of buildings, a single building, or a distinct part of a building, usu with a specified purpose. ⋙ **unitive** *adj.*

Unitarian *n* a member of a Christian denomination that rejects the doctrine of the Trinity and believes that God is a single being. ⋙ **Unitarian** *adj,* **Unitarianism** *n.*

unitary *adj* **1** of or relating to a unit or units. **2** undivided; whole. ⋙ **unitarily** *adv.*

unitary authority *n* in Britain, a district with a single-tier system of local government.

unit character *n* a genetically determined characteristic that is inherited either as a whole or not at all, *esp* one dependent on the presence or absence of a single gene.

unite *v* **1** to join together to form a single unit. **2** to form, or cause to form, an alliance or association. ⋙ **united** *adj,* **unitive** *adj.*

unit trust *n* an investment company that minimizes the risk to investors by collective purchase of shares in many different enterprises.

unity *n* (*pl* **-ies**) **1** the state of being one or united. **2a** concord; harmony. **b** continuity and agreement, e.g. in aims or interests. **3** singleness of effect or symmetry in a literary or artistic work. **4** a whole made up of related parts. **5** the number one.

universal *adj* **1** including or covering all without limit or exception. **2** present or occurring everywhere or under all conditions. **3** adjustable to meet varied requirements, e.g. of use, shape, or size. ⋙ **universality** *n,* **universally** *adv.*

universalise *v* see UNIVERSALIZE.

universalism *n* **1** (*often* **Universalism**) a theological doctrine that everyone will eventually be saved. **2** the state of being universal. ⋙ **universalist** *n and adj.*

universalize *or* **-ise** *v* to make universal. ⋙ **universalization** *n.*

universal joint *n* a joint uniting two shafts and capable of transmitting rotation from one shaft to the other at an angle.

universe *n* **1** all things that exist; the cosmos. **2** the whole world; everybody. **3** a sphere of activity.

university *n* (*pl* **-ies**) an institution of higher learning that provides facilities for full-time teaching and research and is authorized to grant academic degrees.

unjust *adj* characterized by injustice; unfair. ⋙ **unjustly** *adv,* **unjustness** *n.*

unkempt *adj* **1** not combed; dishevelled. **2** not neat or tidy. ⋙ **unkemptly** *adv,* **unkemptness** *n.*

unkind *adj* lacking in kindness or sympathy; harsh or cruel. ⋙ **unkindly** *adv,* **unkindness** *n.*

unknowable *adj* not knowable, *esp* lying beyond the limits of human experience or understanding.

unknowing *adj* not knowing; unaware. ⋙ **unknowingly** *adv.*

unknown[1] *adj* **1** not known. **2** having an unknown value. **3** not famous or familiar.

unknown[2] *n* **1** somebody who is little known, e.g. to the public. **2** something that requires to be discovered, identified, or clarified.

unknown quantity *n* (*pl* **-ies**) **1** a mathematical quantity whose value is unknown. **2** a person or thing whose behaviour or effect is unpredictable.

Unknown Soldier *n* an unidentified soldier whose body is entombed in a national memorial as a representative of all the members of the armed forces of the same nation who died in a war, *esp* either of the World Wars.

Unknown Warrior *n* = UNKNOWN SOLDIER.

unlace *v* to undo the lacing of (e.g. a shoe).

unlatch *v* to open (e.g. a door) by lifting a latch.

unlawful *adj* **1** against the law or contrary to the rules; illegal. **2** not morally right or conventional. ⋙ **unlawfully** *adv,* **unlawfulness** *n.*

unleaded *adj* **1** *esp* of petrol: not treated or mixed with lead or lead compounds. **2** in printing, not having leads between the lines for spacing.

unlearn *v* (*past tense and past part.* **unlearned** *or* **unlearnt**) **1** to put out of one's knowledge or memory. **2** to discard the habit of.

unlearned *adj* not educated; ignorant. ⋙ **unlearnedly** *adv.*

unlearnt *or* **unlearned** *adj* not gained by study, training, or experience.

unleash *v* to free from a leash; to loose from restraint or control.

unleavened *adj* containing no yeast or other raising agent.

unless *conj* **1** except on the condition that. **2** except when.

unlettered *adj* uneducated or illiterate.

unlicensed *adj* not having a licence, *esp* one permitting the sale of alcoholic drinks.

unlike[1] *prep* **1** different from. **2** not characteristic of. **3** in a different manner from.

unlike[2] *adj* **1** marked by dissimilarity; different. **2** unequal. ⋙ **unlikeness** *n.*

unlikely *adj* (**-ier, -iest**) **1** having a low probability of being or occurring. **2** not believable; incredible. ⋙ **unlikelihood** *n,* **unlikeliness** *n.*

unlimited *adj* **1** lacking any controls or restrictions. **2** boundless; infinite. ➤➤ **unlimitedly** *adv,* **unlimitedness** *n.*

unlined[1] *adj* not marked with lines, creases, wrinkles, etc.

unlined[2] *adj* without a lining.

unlisted *adj* **1** not appearing on a list. **2** *chiefly NAm* = EX-DIRECTORY.

unlit *adj* **1** without any lighting. **2** not lit.

unload *v* **1a** to remove or discharge (e.g. cargo). **b** to take the cargo from (e.g. a lorry or ship). **2** to give vent to (e.g. feelings). **3** to remove the cartridge or projectile from (e.g. a gun) or the film from (a camera). **4a** to get rid of (something unwanted or surplus). **b** to sell (merchandise), *esp* in large quantities. ➤➤ **unloader** *n.*

unlock *v* **1** to unfasten the lock of. **2** to release. **3** to provide a key to (something mysterious).

unlooked-for *adj* not foreseen or expected.

unloose *v* to release from or as if from restraints; to set free.

unloosen *v* = UNLOOSE.

unloved *adj* not loved by anybody.

unlovely *adj* disagreeable; unpleasant. ➤➤ **unloveliness** *n.*

unlucky *adj* (**-ier, -iest**) **1** marked by adversity or failure. **2** likely to bring misfortune. **3** having or meeting with bad luck. ➤➤ **unluckily** *adv,* **unluckiness** *n.*

unmade *adj* **1** of a bed: not put in order ready for sleeping. **2** *Brit* of a road: not having a hard smooth surface.

unmake *v* (*past tense and past part.* **unmade**) to undo or destroy.

unman *v* (**unmanned, unmanning**) *literary, humorous* to deprive (a man) of vigour, courage, resolve, etc.

unmanageable *adj* difficult or impossible to handle or control. ➤➤ **unmanageably** *adv.*

unmanly *adj* **1** lacking in manly virtues; weak or cowardly. **2** effeminate. ➤➤ **unmanliness** *n.*

unmanned *adj* not having or needing a human crew.

unmannerly *adj* discourteous; rude. ➤➤ **unmannerliness** *n.*

unmask *v* **1** to remove a mask or disguise from. **2** to reveal the true character or nature of.

unmatched *adj* not equalled; beyond compare.

unmentionable *adj* not fit to be mentioned; unspeakable. ➤➤ **unmentionableness** *n,* **unmentionably** *adv.*

unmentionables *pl n euphem, humorous* underwear.

unmerciful *adj* **1** showing no mercy. **2** excessive or extreme. ➤➤ **unmercifully** *adv,* **unmercifulness** *n.*

unmindful *adj* (+ of) not taking into account; forgetful of. ➤➤ **unmindfully** *adv,* **unmindfulness** *n.*

unmissable *adj* **1** impossible not to hit or notice. **2** said e.g. of a television programme: too good to miss.

unmistakable *or* **unmistakeable** *adj* not capable of being mistaken or misunderstood; clear or obvious. ➤➤ **unmistakably** *adv.*

unmitigated *adj* **1** not diminished in severity, intensity, etc. **2** out-and-out; downright. ➤➤ **unmitigatedly** *adv.*

unmoved *adj* not affected by emotion. ➤➤ **unmovable** *adj,* **unmoveable** *adj.*

unmurmuring *adj* uncomplaining. ➤➤ **unmurmuringly** *adv.*

unmuzzle *v* **1** to remove a muzzle from (an animal). **2** to restore freedom of expression to.

unnatural *adj* **1** not in accordance with nature or a normal course of events. **2** not in accordance with normal feelings or behaviour. **3** artificial or contrived in manner. **4** *archaic* wicked. ➤➤ **unnaturally** *adv,* **unnaturalness** *n.*

unnecessary *adj* not necessary. ➤➤ **unnecessarily** *adv,* **unnecessariness** *n.*

unnerve *v* to deprive of courage, confidence, etc. ➤➤ **unnerving** *adj,* **unnervingly** *adv.*

unnumbered *adj* **1** innumerable. **2** without an identifying number.

unobserved *adj* not seen or noticed.

unobtainable *adj* impossible to acquire or attain.

unobtrusive *adj* not easily seen or noticed; inconspicuous. ➤➤ **unobtrusively** *adv,* **unobtrusiveness** *n.*

unoccupied *adj* **1** not occupied, *esp* not lived in. **2** not busy.

unofficial *adj* not authorized or official. ➤➤ **unofficially** *adv.*

unorganized *or* **unorganised** *adj* **1** not organized into a coherent or well-ordered whole. **2** not belonging to a trade union.

unorthodox *adj* not conventional in behaviour, beliefs, etc. ➤➤ **unorthodoxly** *adv,* **unorthodoxy** *n.*

unpack *v* **1** to remove the contents of (e.g. a suitcase). **2** to remove from packing or from a container. **3** in computing, to restore (compressed data, files, etc) to the original form. **4** to resolve (something) into its constituent parts, usu for easier analysis. ➤➤ **unpacker** *n.*

unpaid *adj* **1** not paid or not yet paid. **2a** not paying a salary, wage, or fee. **b** not receiving payment.

unpaired *adj* not paired, *esp* not matched or mated.

unpalatable *adj* **1** not pleasing to the taste. **2** unpleasant; disagreeable. ➤➤ **unpalatability** *n,* **unpalatably** *adv.*

unparalleled *adj* having no equal or match; unique.

unpardonable *adj* incapable of being forgiven. ➤➤ **unpardonably** *adv.*

unparliamentary *adj* not in accordance with parliamentary practice.

unpeople *v* to empty (a place) of inhabitants.

unperson *n* (*pl* **unpersons**) a person whose existence is officially denied or unrecognized, usu for political or ideological reasons; a non-person.

unperturbed *adj* not disturbed or concerned. ➤➤ **unperturbedly** *adv.*

unpick *v* **1** to undo (e.g. sewing) by taking out stitches. **2** to take (something, *esp* an argument, theory, etc) apart in order to examine or analyse it.

unpin *v* (**unpinned, unpinning**) to loosen or unfasten by removing a pin or pins.

unplaced *adj* **1** *chiefly Brit* having failed to finish in a leading place in a competition, *esp* a horse race. **2** having no assigned or recognized place.

unpleasant *adj* not pleasant or agreeable; displeasing. ➤➤ **unpleasantly** *adv.*

unpleasantness *n* **1** the quality or state of being unpleasant. **2** an unpleasant situation, experience, etc, *esp* bad feeling between people.

unplug *v* (**unplugged, unplugging**) **1** to disconnect (e.g. an electrical appliance) by removing a plug from a socket. **2** to remove an obstruction from.

unplugged *adj esp* of rock music or musicians: performed or performing on acoustic rather than electric instruments.

unplumbed *adj* **1** not thoroughly explored. **2** of unknown depth. **3** not supplied with plumbing.

unpolled *adj* **1** not having voted at an election. **2** not questioned or canvassed in an opinion poll.

unpopular *adj* **1** viewed or received unfavourably by the general public or a specified group of people. **2** of a person: having few friends. ➤➤ **unpopularity** *n.*

unpractised (*NAm* **unpracticed**) *adj* **1** not skilled or experienced. **2** not done repeatedly to develop proficiency.

unprecedented *adj* having no precedent; novel or unparalleled. ➤➤ **unprecedentedly** *adv.*

unpredictable *adj* not predictable; changeable or erratic. ➤➤ **unpredictability** *n,* **unpredictably** *adv.*

unprejudiced *adj* impartial; fair.

unpremeditated *adj* not resulting from forethought or planning. ➤➤ **unpremeditatedly** *adv.*

unprepared *adj* not ready or made ready. ➤➤ **unpreparedness** *n.*

unprepossessing *adj* not attractive or pleasing.

unpretentious *adj* not seeking to impress others by means of wealth, standing, etc; not affected or ostentatious. ➤➤ **unpretentiously** *adv,* **unpretentiousness** *n.*

unprincipled *adj* without moral principles; unscrupulous. ➤➤ **unprincipledness** *n.*

unprintable *adj* incapable of being printed without causing offence; unfit for publication.

unprofessional *adj* not conforming to the technical or ethical standards of a profession. ➤➤ **unprofessionally** *adv.*

unprofitable *adj* **1** not yielding profit. **2** useless; vain. ➤➤ **unprofitability** *n,* **unprofitably** *adv.*

unpromising *adj* seeming unlikely to prove worthwhile or have a favourable result. ➤➤ **unpromisingly** *adv.*

unpronounceable *adj* very difficult or impossible to pronounce.

unprotected *adj* **1** of sexual intercourse: performed without contraception or protection against the transmission of disease, *esp* without using a condom. **2** not kept or made safe.

unprovoked *adj* done or happening without provocation.

unputdownable *adj chiefly Brit, informal* of a book or story: very interesting or exciting; compulsively readable.

unqualified *adj* **1** not having the necessary qualifications. **2** not modified or restricted by reservations. ➤➤ **unqualifiedly** *adv.*

unquestionable *adj* not able to be doubted or challenged; indisputable. ➤➤ **unquestionability** *n,* **unquestionably** *adv.*

unquestioned *adj* **1** not doubted or challenged; undisputed. **2** accepted without question. **3** not subjected to questioning.

unquestioning *adj* without doubt or hesitation. ➤➤ **unquestioningly** *adv.*

unquiet *adj* **1** agitated; turbulent. **2** physically or mentally restless; uneasy. ➤➤ **unquietly** *adv,* **unquietness** *n.*

unquote *n* used in speech to indicate the end of a direct quotation.

unravel *v* (**unravelled, unravelling,** *NAm* **unraveled, unraveling**) **1** to separate the threads of (something knitted, woven, or tangled), or to become separated. **2** to clear up or solve (something complex or obscure). **3** to begin to come apart, collapse, or fail.

unread *adj* **1** not read. **2** not familiar with or knowledgeable in a specified field.

unreadable *adj* **1** not legible. **2** too difficult, boring, badly composed, etc to read. ➤➤ **unreadability** *n.*

unready *adj* **1** unprepared. **2** slow to act. ➤➤ **unreadiness** *n.*

unreal *adj* **1** lacking in reality, substance, or genuineness; artificial or illusory. **2** *chiefly NAm, informal* excellent; amazing. ➤➤ **unreality** *n,* **unreally** *adv.*

unrealistic *adj* not in accordance with reality, practicality, or good sense. ➤➤ **unrealistically** *adv.*

unreason *n* the absence of reason or sanity; irrationality or madness.

unreasonable *adj* **1a** not governed by or acting according to reason. **b** not based on reason. **2** excessive or immoderate. ➤➤ **unreasonableness** *n,* **unreasonably** *adv.*

unreasoning *adj* not moderated or controlled by reason. ➤➤ **unreasoningly** *adv.*

unregenerate *adj* **1** not repentant or reformed. **2** obstinate; stubborn. ➤➤ **unregeneracy** *n,* **unregenerately** *adv.*

unrelenting *adj* **1** not weakening in determination; hard or stern. **2** not letting up in vigour, pace, etc. ➤➤ **unrelentingly** *adv,* **unrelentingness** *n.*

unreliable *adj* incapable of being relied on; likely to fail. ➤➤ **unreliability** *n,* **unreliably** *adv.*

unremitting *adj* constant; incessant; never lessening or letting up. ➤➤ **unremittingly** *adv,* **unremittingness** *n.*

unremunerative *adj* providing inadequate or no remuneration; unprofitable. ➤➤ **unremuneratively** *adv.*

unrepeatable *adj* **1** incapable of being repeated. **2** too shocking, offensive, rude, etc to be repeated.

unrepresentative *adj* not typical or characteristic, *esp* as a sample or example.

unrequited *adj esp* of love: not returned. ➤➤ **unrequitedly** *adv,* **unrequitedness** *n.*

unreserved *adj* **1** unqualified; without reservation. **2** frank and open in manner. **3** not booked or set aside. ➤➤ **unreservedly** *adv,* **unreservedness** *n.*

unresponsive *adj* not reacting or answering. ➤➤ **unresponsively** *adv,* **unresponsiveness** *n.*

unrest *n* agitation or turmoil, *esp* caused by rebellion or dissatisfaction.

unrestrained *adj* not held in check; uncontrolled. ➤➤ **unrestrainedly** *adv,* **unrestrainedness** *n.*

unrewarding *adj* **1** not yielding a reward. **2** not personally satisfying.

unripe *adj* **1** not ripe; immature. **2** unready; unprepared. ➤➤ **unripeness** *n.*

unrivalled (*NAm* **unrivaled**) *adj* unequalled; unparalleled.

unroll *v* to open out; to uncoil or unwind.

unruffled *adj* **1** poised and serene, *esp* in the face of setbacks or confusion. **2** smooth; calm.

unruly *adj* (**-ier, -iest**) difficult to discipline or manage. ➤➤ **unruliness** *n.*

unsaddle *v* **1** to take the saddle from (a horse). **2** to throw (a rider) from the saddle.

unsafe *adj* **1** not safe to do, use, etc; dangerous. **2** of a legal verdict or conviction: based on false, unreliable, or inadequate evidence. **3** of a sexual activity: exposing the participants to the possibility of contracting a sexually transmitted disease, *esp* through not using a condom.

unsaid[1] *adj* not said, *esp* not spoken aloud.

unsaid[2] *v* past tense and past part. of UNSAY.

unsatisfactory *adj* not acceptable or adequate. ➤➤ **unsatisfactorily** *adv.*

unsaturated *adj* **1** able to form products by chemical addition, *esp* containing double or triple bonds between carbon atoms. **2** of a fat, *esp* vegetable fat: containing a relatively high proportion of fatty acids with double bonds and less likely to result in higher cholesterol levels.

unsavoury (*NAm* **unsavory**) *adj* **1** disagreeable or distasteful, *esp* morally offensive. **2** unpleasant to taste or smell. ➤➤ **unsavourily** *adv,* **unsavouriness** *n.*

unsay *v* (*past tense and past part.* **unsaid**) to retract or withdraw (e.g. a statement, opinion, etc).

unscathed *adj* entirely unharmed or uninjured.

unschooled *adj* **1** untaught; untrained. **2** not artificial; natural.

unscientific *adj* **1** not in accordance with the principles and methods of science. **2** without scientific knowledge. ➤➤ **unscientifically** *adv.*

unscramble *v* **1** to restore (scrambled communication) to intelligible form; to decode. **2** to disentangle or clarify. ➤➤ **unscrambler** *n.*

unscrew *v* **1** to remove the screws from. **2** to loosen or withdraw (a screw, lid, threaded part, etc) by turning.

unscripted *adj* of a speech, play, etc: not following a prepared script.

unscrupulous *adj* without moral scruples; unprincipled. ➤➤ **unscrupulously** *adv,* **unscrupulousness** *n.*

unseal *v* to break or remove the seal of.

unseasonable *adj* **1** untimely; inopportune. **2** not normal for the season of the year. ➤➤ **unseasonableness** *n,* **unseasonably** *adv.*

unseasonal *adj* = UNSEASONABLE (2).

unseat *v* **1** to dislodge from a seat, *esp* on horseback. **2** to remove from a position of power, authority, etc.

unseeded *adj* of a sports player: not seeded; not ranked amongst the best in a tournament.

unseeing *adj* not noticing or perceiving anything.

unseemly *adj* not conforming to established standards of good behaviour or taste. ➤➤ **unseemliness** *n.*

unseen *adj* **1** not observed or perceived. **2** *chiefly Brit* of a passage for translation in an exam: presented to candidates who have not seen it before. ➤➤ **unseen** *n.*

unselfish *adj* not selfish; generous. ➤➤ **unselfishly** *adv,* **unselfishness** *n.*

unsentimental *adj* not affected or influenced by sentiment. ➤➤ **unsentimentally** *adv.*

unserviceable *adj* not fit for use. ➤➤ **unserviceability** *n.*

unsettle *v* **1** to move from a settled state or condition. **2** to perturb or agitate. ➤➤ **unsettlement** *n,* **unsettling** *adj,* **unsettlingly** *adv.*

unsettled *adj* **1a** not calm or tranquil; *esp* anxious or uneasy. **b** variable; changeable. **2** not resolved or worked out; undecided. **3** not inhabited or populated. **4** not paid or discharged. ➤➤ **unsettledness** *n.*

unsex *v* to deprive of sexual power or the typical qualities of their sex.

unshackle *v* to free from shackles or restraints.

unshakable *or* **unshakeable** *adj* incapable of being changed or destroyed; firm and unwavering. ➤➤ **unshakably** *adv.*

unshaven *adj* not having shaved or been shaved.

unsheathe *v* to draw (*esp* a knife or sword) from a sheath or scabbard.

unship *v* (**unshipped, unshipping**) **1** to unload or disembark from a ship. **2** to remove (e.g. an oar or tiller) from position.

unsighted *adj* **1** not having the power of sight. **2** prevented from seeing or from having a clear view.

unsightly *adj* (**-ier, -iest**) not pleasing to the eye; ugly. ➤➤ **unsightliness** *n.*

unsinkable *adj* of a boat or ship: incapable of sinking or being sunk. ➤➤ **unsinkability** *n.*

unskilful (*NAm* **unskillful**) *adj* lacking in skill or proficiency. ➤➤ **unskilfully** *adv,* **unskilfulness** *n.*

unskilled *adj* not having or requiring special skill in any particular branch of work.

unskillful *adj NAm* see UNSKILFUL.

unsling *v* (*past tense and past part.* **unslung**) **1** to remove from being slung. **2** to release (something) from slings.

unsnap *v* (**unsnapped, unsnapping**) to open or free by undoing a catch or fastener, *esp* one that works with a snap.

unsociable *adj* **1** not liking social activity; reserved or solitary. **2** not conducive to sociability. ➤➤ **unsociability** *n,* **unsociableness** *n,* **unsociably** *adv.*

unsocial *adj* **1** = UNSOCIABLE (1). **2** *Brit* of working hours: falling outside the normal working day and preventing participation in social activities. ➤➤ **unsocially** *adv.*

unsolicited *adj* **1** sent or received but not requested or ordered. **2** done or given voluntarily.

unsophisticated *adj* **1** not socially or culturally sophisticated. **2** simple and straightforward; not complex or complicated. ➤➤ **unsophisticatedly** *adv,* **unsophisticatedness** *n,* **unsophistication** *n.*

unsound *adj* **1** not healthy or whole. **2** not firmly made or fixed. **3** not valid or true; fallacious or unreliable. ➤➤ **unsoundly** *adv,* **unsoundness** *n.*

unsparing *adj* **1** not merciful; hard or ruthless. **2** liberal; generous. ➤➤ **unsparingly** *adv,* **unsparingness** *n.*

unspeakable *adj* **1** incapable of being expressed in words. **2** too bad or shocking to be uttered. ➤➤ **unspeakableness** *n,* **unspeakably** *adv.*

unspecified *adj* not named or stated explicitly.

unspoiled *adj* = UNSPOILT.

unspoilt *adj* not spoilt; not changed for the worse, e.g. by modern developments.

unspoken *adj* not expressed in words.

unstable *adj* **1a** apt to move, sway, or fall; not firmly fixed. **b** unsteady or irregular. **2** characterized by or given to sudden changes of mood or an inability to control the emotions. **3** of an atom or chemical element: undergoing spontaneous radioactive decay or decomposition. ➤➤ **unstableness** *n,* **unstably** *adv.*

unsteady *adj* (**-ier, -iest**) **1** not firm or stable; likely to fall. **2** not uniform or even; irregular. ➤➤ **unsteadily** *adv,* **unsteadiness** *n.*

unstick *v* (*past tense and past part.* **unstuck**) to release from being stuck or fixed. ✱ **come unstuck** to go wrong; to be unsuccessful.

unstinting *adj* not sparing or frugal; done or given without restraint.

unstop *v* (**unstopped, unstopping**) **1** to free from an obstruction. **2** to remove a stopper from (e.g. a bottle).

unstoppable *adj* incapable of being stopped, *esp* determined or forceful. ➤➤ **unstoppably** *adv.*

unstressed *adj* **1** not bearing a stress or accent. **2** not subjected to stress.

unstring *v* (*past tense and past part.* **unstrung**) **1** to loosen or remove the strings of (e.g. a violin). **2** to remove (e.g. beads) from a string. **3** to make emotionally upset or mentally disordered.

unstructured *adj* **1** not formally or systematically structured or organized. **2** of a garment: loose-fitting or untailored.

unstrung *v* past tense and past part. of UNSTRING.

unstuck *v* past tense and past part. of UNSTICK.

unstudied *adj* not done or planned for effect; spontaneous or natural.

unsubstantial *adj* lacking substance, firmness, or solidity. ➤➤ **unsubstantiality** *n,* **unsubstantially** *adv.*

unsubstantiated *adj* not verified or established by proof or evidence.

unsuccessful *adj* not meeting with or producing success. ➤➤ **unsuccessfully** *adv,* **unsuccessfulness** *n.*

unsuitable *adj* not suitable or fitting; inappropriate. ➤➤ **unsuitability** *n,* **unsuitably** *adv.*

unsung *adj* not celebrated or praised.

unsure *adj* **1** not certain. **2** lacking self-assurance or confidence. ➤➤ **unsurely** *adv,* **unsureness** *n.*

unsuspected *adj* **1** not imagined to exist or to be possible. **2** not regarded with suspicion. ➤➤ **unsuspectedly** *adv.*

unsuspecting *adj* unaware of something, *esp* something dangerous or undesirable. ➤➤ **unsuspectingly** *adv.*

unswerving *adj* not turning aside; constant.

untangle *v* **1** to free from tangles or entanglement; to unravel. **2** to make less confused or confusing.

untapped *adj* of a resource, etc: not yet drawn on or exploited.

untarnished *adj* **1** not sullied or disgraced. **2** not affected by tarnishing.

untaught *adj* **1** not educated; ignorant. **2** not acquired by teaching; natural or spontaneous.

untenable *adj* **1** of an argument, theory, etc: not able to be defended. **2** of a person's position, standing, etc: no longer able to be maintained. ➤➤ **untenability** *n,* **untenably** *adv.*

untenured *adj* of a college or university teacher or teaching post: not permanent or not yet permanent.

unthinkable *adj* contrary to what is acceptable or probable; out of the question. ➤➤ **unthinkability** *n,* **unthinkably** *adv.*

unthinking *adj* **1** without thinking; heedless or unmindful. **2** lacking concern for others; inconsiderate. ➤➤ **unthinkingly** *adv.*

unthought of *adj* not thought of or imagined.

untidy *adj* (**-ier, -iest**) not neat; slovenly or disorderly. ➤➤ **untidily** *adv,* **untidiness** *n.*

untie *v* (**unties, untied, untying**) **1a** to undo (a knot). **b** to unfasten (something tied). **2** to free from restraint or limitation.

until[1] *prep* **1** up to as late as (a specified time or event). **2** up to as far as (a specified place).

Usage note

until *or* till? See note at TILL[1].

until[2] *conj* up to the time that.

untimely *adj* **1** occurring before the natural or proper time; premature. **2** inopportune; unseasonable. ➤➤ **untimeliness** *n,* **untimely** *adv.*

untitled *adj* **1** e.g. of a book: not having a title. **2** not called by a title.

unto *prep archaic* = TO[1] (indicating destination, relationship, etc).

untold *adj* **1a** incalculable. **b** indescribably great. **2** not told or revealed.

untouchable[1] *adj* **1** not able or permitted to be touched. **2** exempt from criticism or control. **3** unable to be equalled; unparalleled. ➤➤ **untouchability** *n.*

untouchable[2] *n* a member of a large formerly segregated caste who in traditional Hindu belief can defile a member of a higher caste by contact or proximity: compare DALIT, SCHEDULED CASTE.

untouched *adj* **1** not touched or handled. **2** of a subject: not discussed or dealt with. **3** of food or drink: not tasted. **4** in the original state; not altered. **5** not influenced; unaffected.

untoward *adj* **1** not favourable; adverse or unfortunate. **2** unseemly or improper. **3** unexpected or unusual. ➤➤ **untowardly** *adv,* **untowardness** *n.*

untried *adj* **1** not tested or proved by experience. **2** not tried in court.

untrodden *adj* **1** not walked on. **2** unexplored.

untroubled *adj* **1** not troubled; not made uneasy. **2** calm; tranquil.

untrue *adj* **1** false or inaccurate. **2** not faithful; disloyal. **3** not level or exactly aligned. ➤➤ **untruly** *adv.*

untrustworthy *adj* incapable of being trusted; unreliable. ➤➤ **untrustworthiness** *n.*

untruth *n* **1** lack of truthfulness. **2** a lie.

untruthful *adj* not telling the truth; false or lying. ➤➤ **untruthfully** *adv,* **untruthfulness** *n.*

untuck *v* to release (e.g. bedding) from being tucked in or up.

untutored *adj* **1** having no formal learning or education. **2** not produced by instruction; natural.

unusable *adj* not fit or suitable for use.

unused *adj* **1** /un'yoohzd/ **a** not used; fresh or new. **b** not used up. **c** not put to use. **2** /un'yoohst/ (+ to) unaccustomed to (something).

unusual *adj* **1** uncommon; rare. **2** exceptional or remarkable. ➤➤ **unusually** *adv,* **unusualness** *n.*

unutterable *adj* **1** beyond the powers of description; inexpressible. **2** out-and-out; downright. ➤➤ **unutterably** *adv.*

unvarnished *adj* **1** not adorned or glossed; plain. **2** of wood, a surface, etc: not varnished.

unveil *v* **1** to remove a veil or covering from. **2** to make public; to divulge.

unvoiced *adj* **1** not expressed in words; unspoken. **2** of a speech sound, *esp* a consonant: pronounced without vibration of the vocal cords.

unwaged *adj* not in paid employment. ➤➤ **unwaged** *pl n.*

unwanted *adj* not wanted or needed.

unwarrantable *adj* not justifiable; inexcusable. ➤➤ **unwarrantably** *adv.*

unwarranted *adj* not justified; said or done without good reason.

unwary *adj* not alert or cautious; easily fooled or surprised. ➤➤ **unwarily** *adv,* **unwariness** *n.*

unwashed ✱ **the great unwashed** *derog* the common people; the rabble.

unwavering *adj* fixed; steadfast. ➤➤ **unwaveringly** *adv.*

unwearied *adj* not tired or jaded; fresh. ➤➤ **unweariedly** *adv.*

unwelcome *adj* **1** not welcome. **2** not gladly received; unwanted.

unwell *adj* in poor health; ill.

unwholesome *adj* **1** having a harmful effect on physical or mental health or morality. **2** unhealthy, *esp* in appearance.

unwieldy *adj* (**-ier, -iest**) difficult to move or handle; cumbersome. ➤➤ **unwieldily** *adv,* **unwieldiness** *n.*

unwilling *adj* **1** loath; reluctant. **2** done or given reluctantly. ➤➤ **unwillingly** *adv,* **unwillingness** *n.*

unwind *v* (*past tense and past part.* **unwound**) **1** to uncoil or cause to uncoil. **2** to make or become less tense; to relax.

unwise *adj* foolish; imprudent. ➤➤ **unwisdom** *n,* **unwisely** *adv.*

unwitting *adj* **1** not intended; inadvertent. **2** ignorant or unaware. ➤➤ **unwittingly** *adv,* **unwittingness** *n.*

unwonted *adj* **1** uncharacteristic. **2** novel; unaccustomed. ➤➤ **unwontedly** *adv,* **unwontedness** *n.*

unworkable *adj* not practicable or feasible.

unworldly *adj* **1** naive; unsophisticated. **2** not swayed by material considerations, e.g. of wealth or personal gain. **3** not of this world; *specif* spiritual. ➤➤ **unworldliness** *n.*

unworn *adj* **1** not impaired by use; not worn away. **2** never worn; new.

unworthy *adj* (**-ier, -iest**) **1a** lacking in excellence or quality; poor. **b** base; dishonourable. **2a** not deserving. **b** not befitting. ➤➤ **unworthily** *adv,* **unworthiness** *n.*

unwound *v* past tense and past part. of UNWIND.

unwrap *v* (**unwrapped, unwrapping**) to remove the wrapping from.

unwritten *adj* **1** not written down. **2** of a law, rule, etc: established and obeyed on the basis of custom and precedent.

unyielding *adj* **1** lacking in softness or flexibility. **2** stubbornly determined or uncompromising. ➤➤ **unyieldingly** *adv.*

unyoke *v* **1** to release (a draught animal) from a yoke or harness. **2** to set free.

unzip *v* (**unzipped, unzipping**) **1** to undo the zip of (a garment). **2** in computing, to decompress (a zipped file).

up[1] *adv* **1a** at or towards a relatively high level or a plane perceived as higher. **b** above the horizon. **c** in or to a raised or upright position. **d** out of bed. **e** to the top, *esp* so as to be full. **2a** in or towards the north. **b** *chiefly Brit* to or in the capital of a country or a more important place. **c** *chiefly Brit* to or at university. **3a** in or into a relatively more advanced position or status. **b** above a normal or former level. **c** towards a higher number, degree, or rate. **d** ahead of an opponent. **4** in or into existence, prominence, or prevalence: *set up a business.* ✱ **up against 1** touching. **2** faced with; confronting. **up against it** in great difficulties. **up and down 1** to and fro. **2** here and there. **up for 1** being considered for (e.g. election or appointment). **2** *informal* keen or ready (to do something). **3** available. **up to 1** used to indicate an upward limit or boundary. **2** as far as; until. **3a** equal to. **b** good enough for. **4** engaged in (a suspect activity). **5** being the responsibility or choice of: *It's up to you to decide.* **up top** *informal* in the head. **up with** used to express enthusiastic approval or support. **up yours** *Brit, coarse slang* used to express contemptuous defiance and dismissal.

up[2] *adj* **1** moving or directed upwards. **2** going on or taking place, *esp* being the matter. **3** at an end. **4a** well informed. **b** abreast; up-to-date. **5** of a computer system: functioning normally. **6** of a road: being repaired. **7** ahead of an opponent. **8** feeling happy.

up[3] *v* (**upped, upping**) **1** *informal* used with *and* to indicate that the action of the following verb is either surprisingly or abruptly initiated: *He upped and left.* **2** *informal* to increase or raise.

up[4] *prep* **1a** up along, through, towards, into, on, etc. **b** at the top of. **2** *Brit, informal* to: *going up the West End.*

up[5] *n* a period or state of prosperity or success. ✱ **on the up** on an upward trend. **on the up and up** increasingly successful. **ups and downs** alternating rises and falls, *esp* in fortune.

up- *comb. form* **1** upwards: *uphill.* **2** at or to a higher or more advanced position: *upland; upgrade.*

up-and-coming *adj* likely to succeed.

up-and-over *adj* e.g. of a garage door: opening upwards and sliding into a horizontal position above the doorway.

up-and-under *n* a rugby move consisting of a high kick upwards followed by a charge by the forward players to the place where the ball lands.

Upanishad *n* any of a collection of philosophical treatises on the nature of the universe, the deity, and humankind, which form part of Hindu scriptures.

upbeat[1] *n* an unaccented beat in a musical bar, *esp* the last beat of the bar.

upbeat[2] *adj informal* optimistic, cheerful.

upbraid *v* to scold or reproach severely. ➤➤ **upbraider** *n.*

upbringing *n* early training, *esp* a particular way of bringing up a child.

upchuck *v informal* to vomit.

upcoming *adj chiefly NAm* about to happen; forthcoming.

upcountry *adj* **1** characteristic of an inland or outlying region. **2** *chiefly derog* not socially or culturally sophisticated. ➤➤ **upcountry** *adv.*

update[1] *v* to bring up-to-date. ➤➤ **updatable** *adj.*

update[2] *n* **1** an act of updating. **2** something that has been updated.

updraught (*NAm* **updraft**) *n* an upward movement of air or other gas.

upend *v* to cause to stand on end.

up-front[1] *adj* **1** paid or done in advance or at the beginning. **2** *chiefly NAm* uninhibitedly honest; candid.

up-front[2] *adv* in advance or at the beginning.

upgrade[1] *v* **1** to improve the standard, value, performance, etc of. **2** to promote to a job requiring a higher level of skill or greater responsibility. ➤➤ **upgradable** *adj,* **upgradeable** *adj.*

upgrade[2] *n* **1a** the act or an instance of upgrading. **b** an upgraded version, e.g. of computer software. **2** *NAm* an upward gradient or slope.

upheaval *n* **1** a great disturbance or radical change. **2** an upward displacement of something, *esp* part of the earth's crust.

upheave *v* to heave or thrust upwards.

upheld *v* past tense and past part. of UPHOLD.

uphill[1] *adv* upwards on a hill or incline.

uphill[2] *adj* **1** going up; ascending. **2** difficult; laborious.

uphold *v* (*past tense and past part.* **upheld**) **1** to give support to or maintain. **2** to support or defend against opposition or challenge. ➤➤ **upholder** *n.*

upholster *v* to provide (e.g. a chair or sofa) with upholstery. ➤➤ **upholsterer** *n.*

upholstery *n* **1** materials, e.g. fabric, padding, and springs, used to make a soft covering, *esp* for a seat. **2** the art or occupation of upholstering furniture.

upkeep *n* **1** the process of maintaining something in good condition. **2** the cost of such maintenance.

upland *n* (*also in pl*) an area of high land, *esp* when inland.

uplift[1] *v* **1a** to raise or elevate. **b** to cause (a part of the earth's surface) to be raised above adjacent areas. **2** to improve the spiritual, social, moral, or intellectual condition of. ➤➤ **uplifter** *n,* **uplifting** *adj.*

uplift[2] *n* **1a** the act or result of uplifting something. **b** support and lifting for the breasts provided by a bra, etc. **2** a spiritually or morally improving quality or effect.

uplighter *n* a lamp designed to throw its light upwards.

upload[1] *v* to transfer (a program or data) from a smaller to a larger computer.

upload[2] *n* **1** the act or an instance of uploading a program or data. **2** a copy of the program or data that has been uploaded.

up-market[1] *adj* designed to appeal to the more prosperous or higher-status section of a market.

up-market[2] *adv* to or towards the more prosperous or higher-status section of a market.

upmost *adj* = UPPERMOST.

upon *prep chiefly formal* = ON[1].

upper[1] *adj* **1** higher in physical position, rank, or order. **2** (**Upper**) denoting a later division of the specified geological period, system of rocks, etc. ✱ **have/get the upper hand** to have or gain a position of superiority, control, advantage, etc.

upper[2] *n* the parts of a shoe or boot above the sole. ✱ **on one's uppers** at the end of one's resources, *esp* penniless.

upper[3] *n informal* a stimulant drug, *esp* an amphetamine.

upper case *n* capital letters. ➤➤ **upper-case** *adj.*

upper chamber *n* = UPPER HOUSE.

upper class *n* the class occupying the highest position in a society, *esp* the aristocracy. ➤➤ **upper-class** *adj.*

upper crust *pl n* (**the upper crust**) *informal* (*used as sing. or pl*) the highest social class.

uppercut *n* a swinging blow directed upwards with a bent arm.

upper house *n* in a legislature consisting of two houses or chambers, the branch that is usu more restricted in membership, possesses greater traditional prestige, and is often less powerful.

uppermost *adj and adv* in or into the highest or most prominent position.

upper school *n* **1** a secondary school for students aged 14 or upwards. **2** the older students of a secondary school, considered as a separate section of it.

uppish *adj informal* = UPPITY. ➤➤ **uppishly** *adv,* **uppishness** *n.*

uppity *adj informal* **1** putting on airs of superiority; supercilious. **2** excessively self-assertive.

upraise *v* to raise or lift up.

uprate *v* to raise in rank, status, size, power, etc.

upright[1] *adj* **1a** perpendicular; vertical. **b** having the vertical dimension or dimensions greater than the horizontal. **2** characterized by strong moral correctness; honest or honourable. ➤➤ **uprightly** *adv,* **uprightness** *n.*

upright[2] *adv* in an upright position.

upright[3] *n* **1** something that stands upright, *esp* a vertical support. **2** *informal* a piano with a vertical frame and strings.

uprise *v* (*past tense* **uprose,** *past part.* **uprisen**) *archaic, literary* to rise up or to a higher position.

uprising *n* a usu localized rebellion, *esp* against an established government.

upriver *adv and adj* towards or at a point nearer the source of a river.

uproar *n* **1** a noisy commotion or violent disturbance. **2** a noisy or violent protest.

uproarious *adj* **1** characterized by noise and disorder. **2** extremely funny. ➤➤ **uproariously** *adv,* **uproariousness** *n.*

uproot *v* **1** to pull up by the roots. **2** to displace (somebody) from their home, country, or habitual environment. **3** to destroy or eradicate. ➤➤ **uprooter** *n.*

uprose *v* past tense of UPRISE.

uprush *n* an upward rush or flow.

upsadaisy *interj* = UPSYDAISY.

upscale *adj and adv chiefly NAm* = UP-MARKET[1], UP-MARKET[2].

upsell *v* to make an additional sale of a product or service to an existing client or customer.

upset[1] *v* (**upsetting,** *past tense and past part.* **upset**) **1** to knock over; to overturn. **2** to make sad, disappointed, anxious, etc. **3** to throw into disorder; to disrupt. **4** to make physically unwell or somewhat ill. ➤➤ **upsetter** *n,* **upsetting** *adj,* **upsettingly** *adv.*

upset[2] *n* **1** a minor physical disorder. **2** an emotional disturbance. **3** an unexpected defeat, e.g. in politics, a sporting competition, etc.

upset[3] *adj* **1** /up'set/ mentally or emotionally troubled; sad, disappointed, anxious, etc. **2** /'upset/ physically disturbed or disordered.

upshot *n* the final result; the outcome.

upside *n* **1** the favourable or advantageous aspect of something. **2** the upper side or part.

upside down *adv and adj* **1** with the upper and the lower parts reversed; inverted. **2** in or into great disorder or confusion.

upsides *adv Brit, informal* so as to be even or equal with.

upsilon *n* the 20th letter of the Greek alphabet (Υ, υ), equivalent to roman u.

upstage[1] *adv and adj* at or towards the rear of a theatrical stage.

upstage[2] *v* **1** of an actor: to force (another actor) to face away from the audience by moving to or speaking from an upstage position. **2** to steal attention from.

upstair *adj* = UPSTAIRS[2].

upstairs[1] *adv* **1** up the stairs; to or on a higher floor. **2** *informal* to or at a higher position, usu with less responsibility.

upstairs[2] *adj* situated on an upper floor.

upstairs[3] *n* the part of a building above the ground floor.

upstanding *adj* **1** erect; upright. **2** characterized by integrity; honest and respectable. ✱ **be**

upstanding used to ask all present, e.g. in court or at a formal occasion, to rise to their feet.

upstart *n* somebody who has risen suddenly, e.g. from a low position to wealth or power, *esp* somebody who behaves with unwarranted arrogance or self-importance.

upstate[1] *adv and adj* to or in the usu northerly part of a US state that is away from metropolitan areas.

upstate[2] *n* the upstate part of a US state. ➤➤ **upstater** *n.*

upstream *adv and adj* in the direction opposite to the flow of a stream.

upstroke *n* an upward stroke.

upsurge *n* a rapid or sudden rise.

upswept *adj* swept, curved, or brushed upwards.

upswing *n* **1** an upward trend or movement. **2** a marked increase.

upsydaisy *interj* used to express comfort and reassurance to a child after a fall or while being lifted up.

uptake *n* the act or extent of accepting, starting to use, or absorbing something. ✱ **quick/slow on the uptake** *informal* quick or slow to understand or learn.

up-tempo *adj and adv* of a piece of music, *esp* jazz: to be performed at a fast-moving tempo.

upthrust *n* an upward thrust, *esp* an upheaval of part of the earth's surface.

uptight *adj informal* **1** tense or nervous. **2** angry or indignant.

uptime *n* the time during which a piece of equipment, *esp* a computer, is functioning or able to function.

up-to-date *adj* **1** extending up to the present time; including the latest information. **2** abreast of the times; modern. **3** fully informed of the latest developments. ➤➤ **up-to-dateness** *n.*

up-to-the-minute *adj* completely up-to-date.

uptown[1] *adj chiefly NAm* **1** to or in the residential part of a town or city. **2** characteristic of the more affluent neighbourhoods or people of a town or city. ➤➤ **uptown** *adv.*

uptown[2] *n chiefly NAm* the upper part of a town or city, *esp* the residential district. ➤➤ **uptowner** *n.*

upturn[1] *v* to turn up or upside down.

upturn[2] *n* an upward turn, *esp* towards better conditions or higher prices.

UPVC *abbr* unplasticized polyvinyl chloride.

upward[1] *adj* moving or extending upwards; ascending. ➤➤ **upwardly** *adv.*

upward[2] *adv* = UPWARDS.

upwardly mobile *adj* moving, or having the ambition to move, to a higher social status. ➤➤ **upward mobility** *n.*

upwards *adv* **1a** from a lower to a higher place, condition, or level. **b** so as to expose a particular surface: *face upwards.* **2** to an indefinitely greater amount, price, age, rank, etc. ✱ **upwards/upward of** more than; in excess of.

upwind *adv and adj* in the direction from which the wind is blowing.

Ur- *prefix* original; primitive: *Urtext.*

uracil *n* a chemical compound that is one of the four bases whose order in the molecular chain of RNA codes genetic information: compare ADENINE, CYTOSINE, GUANINE, THYMINE.

Uranian *adj* from or relating to the planet Uranus.

uranium *n* a silvery radioactive metallic chemical element used as fuel in nuclear reactors.

urban *adj* of or constituting a city or town.

urban district *n* in Britain in former times, any of various administrative divisions of counties that elected their own councils.

urbane *adj* **1** notably polite or smooth in manner; suave. **2** elegant or sophisticated. ➤➤ **urbanely** *adv.*

urban guerrilla *n* a terrorist who operates in towns and cities.

urbanite *n* a person who lives in a town or city.

urbanity *n* (*pl* **-ies**) **1** the state or quality of being urbane. **2** (*in pl*) urbane acts or conduct; civilities.

urban legend *n* = URBAN MYTH.

urban myth *n* a usu amusing, bizarre, or horrific tale in general circulation that is alleged to be the personal experience of somebody indirectly related to or acquainted with the teller.

urban renewal *n* the planned replacement of substandard urban buildings or redevelopment of dilapidated urban areas.

urchin *n* **1** a mischievous or impudent child, *esp* one who is small and scruffy. **2** = SEA URCHIN.

Urdu *n* the Indic language of the people of Pakistan, closely related to Hindi and also spoken in Bangladesh and parts of India.

-ure *suffix* forming nouns from verbs, denoting: **1** an act or process: *exposure; closure.* **2** an office or function, or the body performing it: *legislature.*

urea *n* a nitrogen-containing chemical compound formed as the final product of protein breakdown and present in the urine of mammals and some other animals.

ureter *n* a duct that carries urine away from a kidney to the bladder or cloaca. ➤➤ **ureteral** *adj,* **ureteric** *adj.*

urethane *or* **urethan** *n* **1** a chemical compound used *esp* as a solvent, an anaesthetic for small animals, and in the treatment of some tumours. **2** = POLYURETHANE.

urethra *n* (*pl* **urethras** *or* **urethrae**) the canal that in most mammals carries urine from the bladder out of the body, and in the male also serves to convey semen. ➤➤ **urethral** *adj.*

urethritis *n* inflammation of the urethra.

urge[1] *v* **1** to strongly encourage or try to persuade. **2** to advocate or demand earnestly or pressingly. **3** to serve as a motive or reason for. **4** to force or impel in a specified direction or to greater speed.

urge[2] *n* a strong impulse or desire.

urgent *adj* **1a** calling for immediate attention; pressing. **b** conveying a sense of urgency. **2** urging insistently; persistent or demanding. ➤➤ **urgency** *n,* **urgently** *adv.*

uric acid *n* a white odourless tasteless chemical compound that is the chief excretory product of birds, most reptiles, and some insects.

urinal *n* **1** a fixture, usu attached to a wall, for men to urinate into. **2** a room, building, etc containing a urinal or urinals.

urinary *adj* **1** of or being the organs concerned with the formation and discharge of urine. **2** of or for urine. **3** excreted as or in urine.

urinate *v* to discharge urine. ➤➤ **urination** *n.*

urine *n* the waste material that is secreted by the kidney in vertebrate animals, contains the end products of protein and nucleic acid breakdown, and forms a usu slightly acid pale yellow to amber liquid in mammals but is semisolid in birds and reptiles.

urinogenital *adj* = GENITOURINARY.

URL *abbr* uniform resource locator: the address of a page on the World Wide Web.

urn *n* **1** an ornamental vase used for storing the ashes of a dead person. **2** a large closed container, usu with a tap at its base, for making and serving large quantities of tea, coffee, etc.

urogenital *adj* = GENITOURINARY.

urology *n* the branch of medicine dealing with the urinary tract. ≫ **urologic** *adj*, **urological** *adj*, **urologist** *n*.

ursine *adj* of or resembling a bear or the bear family.

Ursuline *n* a member of a Roman Catholic teaching order of nuns founded in Brescia, northern Italy, in 1535.

Urtext *n* the original or earliest version of a text.

urticaria *n* an allergic condition marked by raised itchy red or white patches on the skin and caused by a specific factor, e.g. a food or drug. Also called HIVES. ≫ **urticarial** *adj*.

Uruguayan *n* a native or inhabitant of Uruguay in S America. ≫ **Uruguayan** *adj*.

US *abbr* United States.

us *pron* **1** objective case of WE. **2** *chiefly Brit, informal* me.

USA *abbr* United States of America.

usable *or* **useable** *adj* **1** capable of being used. **2** convenient for use. ≫ **usability** *n*.

USAF *abbr* United States Air Force.

usage *n* **1a** established and generally accepted practice or procedure. **b** the way in which words and phrases are actually used in a language. **2** the action, amount, or manner of using.

use[1] /yoohs/ *n* **1a** the action of using or the state of being used. **b** a way of using something. **2a** the right or benefit of using something. **b** the ability or power to use something, e.g. a limb. **3a** a purpose or end. **b** practical worth or application. ✱ **have no use for 1** to have no occasion or need to use. **2** to view with dislike, contempt, or disfavour. **make use of** to use or take advantage of (something).

use[2] /yoohz/ *v* **1** to put into action or service. **2** to employ for a specified purpose. **3a** to expend or consume. **b** to consume or take (e.g. drugs) regularly. **4** to exploit (somebody) as a means to one's own ends. **5** to treat (somebody or something) in a specified manner.

useable *adj* see USABLE.

use-by date *n* a date marked on the packaging of a perishable product by which the product should be used or consumed.

used /yoohzd/ *adj* **1** employed in accomplishing something. **2** that has endured use; *specif* secondhand. **3** /yoohst/ accustomed; habituated. ✱ **used to** used to express a former habitual action or state: *She used to play tennis.*

useful *adj* **1** having a practical worth or applicability. **2** *informal* highly satisfactory in quality; commendable. ≫ **usefully** *adv*, **usefulness** *n*.

useless *adj* **1** having or being of no use. **2** *informal* lacking skill or aptitude; stupid. ≫ **uselessly** *adv*, **uselessness** *n*.

user *n* **1** (*also used in combinations*) somebody who uses something. **2** *informal* a drug addict.

user-friendly *adj* easy to operate or understand. ≫ **user-friendliness** *n*.

use up *v* **1** to consume completely. **2** to deprive wholly of strength or useful properties; to exhaust.

usher[1] *n* **1** somebody who shows people to their seats, e.g. in a theatre or at a wedding. **2** an officer or servant who acts as a doorkeeper, e.g. in a court of law. **3** an officer who walks before a person of rank.

usher[2] *v* **1** to guide or escort to a place. **2** (*usu* + in) to inaugurate or introduce.

usherette *n dated* a woman who shows people to their seats in a theatre or cinema.

USN *abbr* United States Navy.

USS *abbr* United States ship.

USSR *abbr* formerly, Union of Soviet Socialist Republics.

usual[1] *adj* **1** in accordance with custom or habit; normal. **2** commonly or ordinarily used. ✱ **as usual** in the accustomed or habitual way. ≫ **usually** *adv*, **usualness** *n*.

usual[2] *n* **1** (*often* **the usual**) something that is habitually done or that normally happens. **2** (**the/one's usual**) *informal* somebody's usual or preferred drink.

usufruct *n* the legal right of using and enjoying something belonging to another, on condition that the property, etc remains intact and its value is undiminished. ≫ **usufructuary** *n and adj*.

usurer *n* somebody who lends money, *esp* at an exorbitant rate of interest.

usurp *v* **1** to seize and possess by force or without right. **2** to seize authority wrongfully from. ≫ **usurpation** *n*, **usurper** *n*.

usury *n* the lending of money at interest, *esp* at an exorbitant or illegal rate of interest. ≫ **usurious** *adj*, **usuriously** *adv*.

UT *abbr* Utah (US postal abbreviation).

ute *n Aus, NZ, informal* = UTILITY VEHICLE.

utensil *n* a piece of portable equipment, *esp* a tool or container, used in the household.

uteri *n* pl of UTERUS.

uterine *adj* **1** relating to or in the region of the uterus. **2** of two or more offspring: born of the same mother but having different fathers.

uterus *n* (*pl* **uteri**) a thick-walled hollow organ of the female mammal that contains and usu nourishes the young during development before birth; the womb.

utilise *v* see UTILIZE.

utilitarian[1] *n* an advocate of utilitarianism.

utilitarian[2] *adj* **1** designed for practical use rather than beautiful appearance. **2** relating to utilitarianism.

utilitarianism *n* the doctrine that the criterion for right conduct should be the overall value of its consequences; *specif* the theory that the aim of action or social policy should be the greatest happiness of the greatest number.

utility[1] *n* (*pl* **-ies**) **1** fitness for some purpose; ability to be used advantageously. **2** an organization performing a public service, e.g. by providing gas or electricity, and operated privately, by local government, or by the state. **3** in computing, a program or piece of software that carries out a routine task.

utility[2] *adj* **1** serving primarily for utility rather than beauty; utilitarian. **2** designed or adapted for general use. **3** capable of serving as a substitute in various roles or positions.

utility room *n* a room in a house typically with storage space and equipment for carrying out household tasks such as washing.

utility truck *n* = UTILITY VEHICLE.

utility vehicle *n Aus, NZ* a van or truck with an open-topped or fabric-covered rear compartment.

utilize *or* **utilise** *v* to make use of; to turn to practical use or account. ≫ **utilizable** *adj*, **utilization** *n*, **utilizer** *n*.

adj **1** situated at the farthest or most dis- oint. **2** of the greatest or highest degree or ant.

nost[2] *n* the highest point or degree; the extreme limit.

utopia *or* **Utopia** *n* an imagined place or state of perfection, *esp* with regard to laws, government, and social conditions: compare DYSTOPIA.

utopian[1] *or* **Utopian** *adj* **1** impossibly ideal. **2** advocating impractically ideal social and political schemes. ➤➤ **utopianism** *n.*

utopian[2] *or* **Utopian** *n* an advocate of utopian schemes.

utter[1] *adj* absolute; total. ➤➤ **utterly** *adv.*

utter[2] *v* **1a** to emit as a sound. **b** to give *esp* verbal expression to. **2** to circulate (forged or counterfeit money) as if legal or genuine. ➤➤ **utterable** *adj,* **utterer** *n.*

utterance *n* **1** something uttered, *esp* an oral statement. **2** vocal expression; speech.

uttermost *adj and n* = UTMOST[1], UTMOST[2].

U-turn *n* **1** the turning of a vehicle to face the opposite direction without reversing. **2** a total reversal of policy.

UV *abbr* ultraviolet.

UVA *abbr* ultraviolet radiation with a range between 320 and 380 nanometres.

UVB *abbr* ultraviolet radiation with a range between 280 and 320 nanometres.

UVF *abbr* Ulster Volunteer Force.

uvula *n* (*pl* **uvulas** *or* **uvulae**) the fleshy lobe hanging in the middle of the back of the soft palate. ➤➤ **uvular** *adj.*

uxorial *adj formal* relating to or characteristic of a wife.

uxoricide *n* **1** the act or an instance of killing one's own wife. **2** a man who kills his own wife. ➤➤ **uxoricidal** *adj.*

uxorious *adj formal* excessively fond of or submissive to one's wife. ➤➤ **uxoriously** *adv,* **uxoriousness** *n.*

Uzbek *n* **1** (*pl* **Uzbeks** *or* **Uzbek**) a member of an indigenous Turkic people inhabiting Uzbekistan. **2** (*pl* **Uzbeks**) a native or inhabitant of Uzbekistan. **3** the Turkic language of the people of Uzbekistan.

Uzi /'oohzi/ *n* a type of submachine gun made in Israel.

V

V[1] *or* **v** *n* (*pl* **V's** *or* **Vs** *or* **v's**) **1** the 22nd letter of the English alphabet. **2** the Roman numeral for five.

V[2] *abbr* **1** volt. **2** voltage. **3** volume.

V[3] *abbr* the chemical symbol for vanadium.

v *abbr* **1** verb. **2** versus. **3** very. **4** vide.

V-1 *n* a flying bomb used by the Germans in World War II.

V-2 *n* a long-range rocket used by the Germans in World War II.

VA *abbr* **1** *Brit* Order of Victoria and Albert. **2** Virginia (US postal abbreviation).

vac *n Brit, informal* **1** a vacation, *esp* from college or university. **2** = VACUUM CLEANER.

vacancy *n* (*pl* **-ies**) **1a** a place, e.g. a room in a hotel, or property that is not being occupied or used. **b** an unfilled position in a factory, office, etc. **2a** the state of being vacant; emptiness. **b** empty space, or an empty space. **c** emptiness of mind; vacuity; inanity.

vacant *adj* **1** not occupied by an incumbent or officer. **2a** without an occupant. **b** not lived in; empty. **3a** stupid or foolish. **b** expressionless. ➤➤ **vacantly** *adv*, **vacantness** *n*.

vacant possession *n* ownership of property which is available for immediate occupation as the previous owner or tenant has moved out.

vacate *v* **1** to give up the possession or occupancy of (a room, building, etc). **2** to leave a job, position, etc. ➤➤ **vacatable** *adj*.

vacation[1] *n* **1** a scheduled period during which activity, e.g. of a university or the law courts, is suspended. **2** the act or an instance of vacating. **3** *chiefly NAm* a holiday.

vacation[2] *v chiefly NAm* to take or spend a holiday. ➤➤ **vacationer** *n*, **vacationist** *n*.

vaccinate *v* to administer a vaccine to, usu by injection. ➤➤ **vaccination** *n*, **vaccinator** *n*.

vaccine *n* a substance prepared from organisms that cause a disease, administered usu by injection to produce or artificially increase immunity to it. ➤➤ **vaccinal** *adj*.

vaccinia *n* = COWPOX. ➤➤ **vaccinial** *adj*.

vacherin *n* a cake or dessert typically consisting of layers or a shell of meringue sandwiched or filled with whipped cream and often fruit.

vacillate *v* **1** to hesitate or waver in choosing between opinions or courses of action. **2** to fluctuate or oscillate. ➤➤ **vacillatingly** *adv*, **vacillation** *n*, **vacillator** *n*.

vacua *n* pl of VACUUM[1].

vacuole *n* a small cavity or space containing air or fluid in the tissues of an organism or in the protoplasm of an individual cell. ➤➤ **vacuolar** *adj*.

vacuous *adj* **1** stupid; inane. **2** idle; aimless. **3** *archaic* empty. ➤➤ **vacuity** *n*, **vacuously** *adv*, **vacuousness** *n*.

vacuum[1] *n* (*pl* **vacuums** *or* **vacua**) **1a** a space absolutely devoid of matter. **b** a space from which as much air or other substance as possible has been removed, e.g. by an air pump. **c** an air pressure below atmospheric pressure. **2a** a vacant space; a void. **b** a state of isolation from outside influences. **3** *informal* a vacuum cleaner.

vacuum[2] *v informal* to clean using a vacuum cleaner.

vacuum cleaner *n* an electrical appliance for removing dust and dirt, *esp* from carpets or upholstery, by suction.

vacuum flask *n chiefly Brit* a cylindrical container with a vacuum between an inner and an outer wall used to keep material, *esp* liquids, either hot or cold.

vacuum-packed *adj* packed in a wrapping from which most of the air has been removed.

vacuum tube *n* an electronic device that generates and controls a beam of electrons in which there is a vacuum.

vade mecum /ˌvahday 'maykəm, ˌvaydi 'meekəm/ *n* (*pl* **vade mecums**) a book for ready reference; a handbook or manual.

vagabond[1] *n* a wanderer; a tramp.

vagabond[2] *adj* of or characteristic of a wanderer.

vagary *n* (*pl* **-ies**) an erratic, unpredictable, or extravagant motion, action, etc.

vagi *n* pl of VAGUS.

vagina *n* (*pl* **vaginas** *or* **vaginae**) a canal in a female mammal that leads from the uterus to the external orifice of the genital canal. ➤➤ **vaginal** *adj*.

vaginismus *n* a painful spasmodic contraction of the vagina.

vaginitis *n* inflammation of the vagina.

vagrant[1] *n* **1** a person who has no established residence or lawful means of support. **2** *archaic* a wanderer or vagabond.

vagrant[2] *adj* wandering about from place to place, usu with no means of support. ➤➤ **vagrancy** *n*.

vague *adj* **1a** not having a precise meaning. **b** not clearly expressed: *All this amounts to is a few vague* *accusations of impropriety.* **c** not thinking, or expressing one's thoughts, clearly or precisely. **2a** not clearly defined, known, or understood; indistinct: *She has only a vague idea of what happened.* **b** not sharply outlined; hazy. **3** not alert; absentminded. ➤➤ **vaguely** *adv,* **vagueness** *n.*

vagus *n* (*pl* **vagi**) either of a pair of cranial nerves that supply chiefly the heart and viscera. ➤➤ **vagal** *adj.*

vain *adj* **1** having or showing excessive pride in one's appearance, abilities, etc; conceited. **2** unsuccessful; ineffectual: *in a vain attempt to be amusing.* ✱ **in vain** to no end; without success or result. **take somebody's name in vain** to use a name, *esp* the name of God, profanely or without proper respect. ➤➤ **vainly** *adv.*

vainglory *n literary* **1** excessive or ostentatious pride. **2** vanity or boastfulness. ➤➤ **vainglorious** *adj,* **vaingloriously** *adv.*

Vaisya /'viesyə, 'vieshyə/ *or* **Vaishya** /'vieshyə/ *n* a Hindu of an upper caste traditionally following commercial and agricultural occupations: compare BRAHMAN, KSHATRIYA, SUDRA.

valance *or* **valence** *n* **1** a piece of drapery hung as a border, *esp* along the edge of a bed, canopy, or shelf. **2** a pelmet. ➤➤ **valanced** *adj.*

vale *n literary* a valley.

valediction *n formal* **1** an act of bidding farewell. **2** an address or statement of farewell or leave-taking.

valedictorian *n NAm* a student who has attained the highest grades in their class in the final year at a school, and who delivers the farewell address at the commencement ceremony.

valedictory[1] *adj formal* expressing or containing a farewell.

valedictory[2] *n* (*pl* **-ies**) *formal* a valedictory speech.

valence[1] *n NAm* see VALENCY.

valence[2] *n* see VALANCE.

valency (*NAm* **valence**) *n* (*pl* **-ies** *or NAm* **valences**) the degree of combining power of an element or radical as shown by the number of atomic weights of a univalent element, e.g. hydrogen, with which the atomic weight of the element will combine or for which it can be substituted or with which it can be compared.

valentine *n* **1** a sweetheart chosen on St Valentine's Day, 14 February. **2** a greeting card sent or given, often anonymously, *esp* to a sweetheart, on St Valentine's Day.

Word history

St Valentine's Day is the feast day of two saints named Valentine; one martyred in Rome c.270, the other the Bishop of Terni, martyred soon afterwards. The custom of sending cards to one's sweetheart on this day has nothing to do with the saints; it is probably a remnant of the Roman festival Lupercalia, held on 15 February, which included fertility rites, influenced by the belief that birds choose their mates at this time.

valerian *n* **1** any of several species of usu perennial plants, many of which possess medicinal properties. **2** a drug prepared from the roots of valerian, used as a sedative.

valet[1] *n* **1** a man's male servant who performs personal services, or an employee of a hotel, etc who performs similar services for patrons. **2** an employee of a hotel, restaurant, etc who provides valet parking for customers.

valet[2] *v* (**valeted, valeting**) **1** to serve (somebody) as a valet. **2** to clean (a car) as a service.

valeta /və'leetə/ *n* see VELETA.

valet parking *n* a service providing attendants who take a customer's car from the door of a hotel, restaurant, etc, park it, and return it when required.

valetudinarian[1] *n formal* a person of a weak or sickly constitution, *esp* a hypochondriac.

valetudinarian[2] *adj formal* weak; sickly.

Valhalla *or* **Walhalla** /val'halə/ *n* in Norse mythology, a place where the souls of heroes slain in battle were taken to spend eternity in joy and feasting.

valiant *adj* showing valour; courageous. ➤➤ **valiantly** *adv.*

valid *adj* **1a** well-grounded or justifiable; relevant and meaningful. **b** logically sound. **2a** having legal efficacy, *esp* executed according to the proper formalities. **b** (*often* + for) legally acceptable. ➤➤ **validity** *n,* **validly** *adv.*

validate *v* **1** to make legally valid. **2** to corroborate or authenticate. ➤➤ **validation** *n.*

valine *n* an essential amino acid found in most proteins.

Valium *n trademark* a tranquillizer; = DIAZEPAM.

Valkyrie /'valkiri, val'kiəri/ *n* in Norse mythology, any of the maidens, usu twelve in number, who were servants of the god Odin and who chose heroes killed in battle and conducted them to an afterlife of feasting and heroic deeds in Valhalla.

valley *n* (*pl* **-eys**) **1** an elongated depression of the earth's surface, usu between hills or mountains. **2** an area drained by a river and its tributaries.

valor *n NAm* see VALOUR.

valorize *or* **-ise** *v* to enhance, or try to enhance, the price, value, or status of (a commodity) by organized action, *esp* by a government. ➤➤ **valorization** *n.*

valour (*NAm* **valor**) *n* strength of mind or spirit that enables somebody to encounter danger with firmness; personal bravery. ➤➤ **valorous** *adj.*

valuable[1] *adj* **1** having high money value. **2** of great use or worth. ➤➤ **valuably** *adv.*

valuable[2] *n* (*usu in pl*) a personal possession of relatively great monetary value.

valuation *n* **1** the act or an instance of valuing something, *esp* property. **2** the estimated or determined value, *esp* market value, of a thing.

value[1] *n* **1** a fair return or equivalent for something exchanged. **2** the worth in money or commodities of something. **3** relative worth, utility, or importance. **4** (*usu in pl*) a moral principle or standard of behaviour. **5a** a numerical quantity assigned or computed. **b** the magnitude of a physical quantity. **6** the denomination of a note or coin. **7** the relative duration of a musical note.

value[2] *v* (**values, valued, valuing**) **1a** (*often* + at) to estimate the worth of (something) in terms of money. **b** to rate (somebody or something) in terms of usefulness, importance, etc. **2** to consider or rate (something) highly. ➤➤ **valuer** *n.*

value-added tax *n* a tax levied at each stage of the production and distribution of a commodity and passed on to the consumer as a form of purchase tax.

value judgment *n* a judgment attributing a value, e.g. good, evil, or desirable, to a particular action or thing.

valueless *adj* worthless.

valve *n* **1** a structure, *esp* in the heart or a vein, that closes temporarily to obstruct passage of material or permits movement of fluid in one direction only. **2a** any of numerous mechanical devices by which the flow of liquid, gas, or loose material in bulk may be controlled, usu to allow movement in one direction only. **b** a device in a brass musical instrument for varying the tube length in order to change the fundamental tone by a definite interval. **3** either of the two halves of the shell of a bivalve mollusc. ⯮ **valved** *adj.*

valvular *adj* **1a** resembling or functioning as a valve. **b** opening by valves. **2** of a valve, *esp* of the heart.

vamoose *v informal* to depart quickly.

vamp[1] *n informal* a woman who uses her charm to seduce and exploit men. ⯮ **vampish** *adj,* **vampy** *adj.*

vamp[2] *v informal* of a woman: to practise seductive wiles on (a man).

vamp[3] *n* **1** the part of a shoe or boot covering the front of the foot. **2** a simple improvised musical accompaniment.

vamp[4] *v* **1** *informal* (+ up) to rework (something old, e.g. a story or sermon) with new material or in a new way. **2** to play a musical vamp.

vampire *n* **1** a dead person believed to come from the grave at night and suck the blood of sleeping people. **2** a S American bat that feeds on blood and is dangerous to human beings and domestic animals, *esp* as a transmitter of diseases such as rabies. ⯮ **vampiric** *adj,* **vampirism** *n.*

vampire bat *n* = VAMPIRE (2).

van[1] *n* **1** an enclosed motor vehicle used for transport of goods, animals, furniture, etc. **2** *Brit* an enclosed railway goods wagon. **3** *Brit* = CARAVAN (1).

van[2] *n* = VANGUARD.

vanadium *n* a grey metallic chemical element that is hard and malleable, occurs naturally in minerals, and is used *esp* in alloys.

Van Allen belt *n* either of two belts of intense ionizing radiation in the earth's outer atmosphere.

vandal *n* **1** a person who wilfully or ignorantly destroys or defaces property. **2** (**Vandal**) a member of a Germanic people who overran Gaul, Spain, and N Africa in the fourth and fifth cents and in 455 sacked Rome. ⯮ **vandalism** *n.*

vandalize *or* **-ise** *v* to destroy or damage (property), *esp* ignorantly or maliciously.

Vandyke *n* **1** a wide collar with a deeply indented edge. **2** a trim pointed beard.

Vandyke beard *n* = VANDYKE (2).

vane *n* **1** = WEATHER VANE. **2a** a thin flat or curved object that is rotated about an axis by wind or water. **b** a device revolving in a similar manner and moving in water or air. **3** a stabilizing fin or similar part on a projectile, such as any of the feathers fastened to the shaft of an arrow.

vanguard *n* **1** the troops moving at the head of an army. **2** the forefront of an action or movement.

vanilla *n* an extract of a pod of a tropical American climbing orchid, used as a flavouring.

vanillin *n* the chief fragrant component of vanilla.

vanish *v* **1a** to pass quickly from sight; to disappear. **b** to cease to exist. **2** in mathematics, to assume the value zero.

vanishing point *n* a point at which receding parallel lines seem to meet when represented in linear perspective.

vanity *n* (*pl* **-ies**) **1** excessive pride in oneself; conceit. **2** the quality of being vain or futile; worthlessness.

vanity case *n* a small case used by women for carrying toilet articles and cosmetics.

vanity plate *n NAm* a personalized vehicle licence plate.

vanity unit *n* a piece of furniture consisting of a small fitted cupboard with a washbasin set into its upper surface.

vanquish *v literary* **1** to overcome or conquer (somebody or something); to beat. **2** to gain mastery over (an emotion, passion, etc). ⯮ **vanquisher** *n.*

vantage *n* a position giving a strategic advantage or commanding perspective, or the advantage gained from this.

vantage point *n* a place or position that affords one a clear view over an area or a clear perspective on a situation.

Vanuatuan /vanoo'ahtooh·ən/ *n* a native or inhabitant of Vanuatu in the SW Pacific. ⯮ **Vanuatuan** *adj.*

vapid *adj* lacking liveliness, interest, or force; insipid. ⯮ **vapidity** *n,* **vapidly** *adv.*

vapor *n NAm* see VAPOUR.

vaporetto /vapə'retoh/ *n* (*pl* **vaporettos** *or* **vaporetti**) a passenger boat used on the canals of Venice.

vaporise *v* see VAPORIZE.

vaporiser *n* see VAPORIZER.

vaporize *or* **-ise** *v* to convert (liquid) into vapour, e.g. by the application of heat. ⯮ **vaporization** *n.*

vaporizer *or* **vaporiser** *n* **1** = ATOMIZER. **2** a device for converting water or a medicated liquid into a vapour for inhalation.

vapour (*NAm* **vapor**) *n* **1** smoke, fog, etc suspended floating in the air and impairing its transparency. **2** a substance in the gaseous state, *esp* such a substance that is liquid under normal conditions. ⯮ **vaporous** *adj.*

vapour trail *n* a trail of condensed water vapour created in the air by an aircraft flying at high altitude.

vaquero /və'keəroh/ *n* (*pl* **-os**) in the SW USA, a herdsman or cowboy.

variable[1] *adj* **1** able or apt to vary; subject to variation or changes. **2** of behaviour, etc: fickle or inconstant. **3** of a quantity: able to assume any of a range of values. ⯮ **variability** *n,* **variably** *adv.*

variable[2] *n* **1** something that varies or that can be varied. **2a** a quantity that may assume any of a set of values. **b** a symbol representing a variable quantity or entity. **3** = VARIABLE STAR. **4a** a variable wind. **b** (*in pl*) a region where variable winds occur.

variable cost *n* a cost, e.g. for labour or materials, that varies directly with the level of production: compare FIXED COSTS, OVERHEAD[3].

variable star *n* a star with regularly or irregularly varying brightness.

variance *n* **1** the fact, quality, or state of being variable or variant; difference or variation. **2** the fact or state of being in disagreement; dissension or dispute. **3** a discrepancy. **4** in law, an inconsistency, *esp* between two pieces of evidence that are intended to support one another. ✱ **at variance with** not in harmony or agreement with (something).

variant *n* **1** any of two or more people or things displaying usu slight differences. **2** something that shows variation from a type or norm.

variation *n* **1a** the act or an instance of varying. **b** the extent to which or the range in which a thing varies. **c** something showing variation. **2** a varied version of a musical idea. ⯮ **variational** *adj.*

varicella *n technical* = CHICKENPOX.

varicoloured (*NAm* **varicolored**) *adj* having various colours.

varicose *adj* of a vein: abnormally swollen or dilated.

varied *adj* **1** having numerous forms or types; diverse. **2** having a variety of contents or parts. ⋙ **variedly** *adv.*

variegated *adj* marked with patches of different colours. ⋙ **variegation** *n.*

varietal[1] *adj* of a particular variety of animal or plant.

varietal[2] *n* **1** a particular variety of grape. **2** a wine classified and known by the name of the variety of grape it was made from, rather than by its place of origin.

variety *n* (*pl* **-ies**) **1** the state of having different forms or types; diversity. **2** an assortment of different things, *esp* of a particular class. **3a** something differing from others of the same general kind; a sort. **b** any of various groups of plants or animals ranking below a species, sometimes one produced by artificial breeding. **4** theatrical entertainment consisting of separate performances of songs, sketches, acrobatics, etc.

varifocal *adj* of a lens: formed so as to allow focusing on close, middle-distance, and faraway objects.

varifocals *pl n* glasses with varifocal lenses.

variform *adj* varied in form.

variola *n technical* smallpox.

variometer *n* **1** an instrument for measuring magnetic variation. **2** an aeronautical instrument for indicating rate of climb.

variorum *adj* of an edition or text: having notes by different people.

various *adj* **1a** of differing kinds; diverse. **b** dissimilar in nature or form; unlike. **2** more than one; several. ⋙ **variously** *adv,* **variousness** *n.*

varlet *n* **1** *archaic* a base unprincipled person. **2** formerly, a knight's page. **3** formerly, a menial servant.

varmint *n NAm, informal or Brit, dialect* **1** an animal or bird considered a pest. **2** a rascal.

varna *n* any of the four major Hindu castes: see BRAHMAN, KSHATRIYA, VAISYA, SUDRA.

varnish[1] *n* a liquid preparation that forms a hard shiny transparent coating on drying.

varnish[2] *v* to apply varnish to (a floor, fingernails, etc).

vary *v* (**-ies, -ied**) **1** to exhibit or undergo change. **2** (*usu* + from) to deviate. **3** to make a change in. **4** to ensure variety in.

vas /vas, vaz, vahs/ *n* (*pl* **vasa**) an anatomical vessel; a duct.

vasa deferentia /defə'renshi·ə, -shə/ *n* pl of VAS DEFERENS.

vascular *adj* of or being a channel or system of channels conducting blood, sap, etc in a plant or animal. ⋙ **vascularity** *n.*

vascularize *or* **-ise** *v* to become or make vascular.

vascular plant *n* a plant having a specialized system for conducting liquid that includes XYLEM (water-conducting tissue) and PHLOEM (food-conducting tissue).

vas deferens /,vaz 'defərenz, ,vas/ *n* (*pl* **vasa deferentia**) the duct that carries sperm from the testis towards the penis.

vase *n* an ornamental vessel used *esp* for holding flowers.

vasectomy *n* (*pl* **-ies**) surgical cutting out of a section of the vas deferens, usu to induce sterility.

Vaseline *n trademark* petroleum jelly.

vasoactive *adj* affecting, *esp* in relaxing or contracting, the blood vessels.

vasoconstriction *n* narrowing of the diameter of blood vessels. ⋙ **vasoconstrictive** *adj.*

vasodilation *n* widening of the blood vessels, *esp* as a result of nerve action. ⋙ **vasodilatory** *adj.*

vasomotor *adj* of nerves or centres controlling the size of blood vessels.

vasopressor *n* a substance that causes a rise in blood pressure by constricting the blood vessels.

vassal *n* **1** formerly, somebody in a feudal society who vowed homage and loyalty to somebody else as their feudal lord in return for protection and often a source of income, *esp* land. **2** a person, nation, etc in a subservient or subordinate position. ⋙ **vassalage** *n.*

vast *adj* very great in amount, degree, intensity, or *esp* in extent or range. ⋙ **vastly** *adv,* **vastness** *n.*

VAT *n Brit* = VALUE-ADDED TAX.

vat *n* a tub, barrel, or other large vessel, *esp* for holding liquids undergoing chemical change or preparations for dyeing or tanning.

vatic *adj literary* prophetic or oracular.

Vatican *n* (**the Vatican**) the official residence of the pope and the administrative centre of Roman Catholicism.

vatu *n* the basic monetary unit of Vanuatu.

vaudeville *n* a light, often comic, theatrical piece frequently combining pantomime, dialogue, dancing, and song.

vault[1] *n* **1a** an arched structure of masonry, usu forming a ceiling or roof. **b** a room with an arched ceiling that comes down to the floor, *esp* a cellar. **c** an arched or dome-shaped anatomical structure. **2a** an underground passage, room, or storage compartment. **b** a room or compartment for the safekeeping of valuables. **3a** a burial chamber, *esp* beneath a church or in a cemetery. **b** a prefabricated container, usu of metal or concrete, into which a coffin is placed at burial. ⋙ **vaulted** *adj.*

vault[2] *v* to leap over something using the hands or a pole. ⋙ **vaulter** *n.*

vault[3] *n* the act or an instance of vaulting.

vaulting *n* vaults; a vaulted construction.

vaulting horse *n* a padded wooden block without pommels that is used for vaulting in gymnastics.

vaunt *v* to call attention to (something, e.g. one's achievements), proudly and often boastfully. ⋙ **vaunted** *adj,* **vaunting** *adj.*

VC *abbr* Victoria Cross.

V-chip *n* a computer chip that can be installed in a television set and that can be programmed to block material that has been classified as violent or sexually explicit.

VCR *abbr* videocassette recorder.

VD *abbr* venereal disease.

VDU *n* = VISUAL DISPLAY UNIT.

've *contr* have.

veal *n* the flesh of a calf used as food.

vector[1] *n* **1** a quantity, e.g. velocity or force, that has magnitude and direction and that is commonly represented by a directed line segment whose length represents the magnitude and whose orientation in space represents the direction. **2** an organism, e.g. an insect, that transmits a disease-causing agent. **3** a course or compass direction, *esp* of an aircraft. ⋙ **vectorial** *adj.*

vector[2] *v* **1** to change the direction of (the thrust of a jet engine) for steering. **2** to guide (an aircraft, its pilot, or a missile in flight) by means of a vector transmitted by radio.

Veda /'veedə, 'vaydə/ *n* any or all of four canonical collections that comprise the earliest Hindu sacred writings.

Vedanta /və'dahntə, və'dantə/ *n* an orthodox system of Hindu philosophy developing the speculations of the Upanishads on ultimate reality and the liberation of the soul. ⋙ **Vedantic** *adj.*

V-E Day *n* the day on which hostilities in Europe in World War II ended, 8 May 1945, or any anniversary of that day.

Vedic[1] /'veedik, 'vaydik/ *adj* of the Vedas, the language in which they are written, or Hindu history and culture between 1500 BC and 500 BC.

Vedic[2] *n* the form of Sanskrit in which the Vedas are written.

veer[1] *v* **1** to change direction, position, or inclination. **2** of the wind: to shift in a clockwise direction: compare BACK[4] (6).

veer[2] *n* a change in direction, position, or inclination.

veg *n* (*pl* **veg**) *Brit, informal* a vegetable.

vegan *n* a strict vegetarian who avoids food or other products derived from animals.

Vegeburger *n trademark* a veggieburger.

Vegemite *n Aus, trademark* a savoury yeast extract used as a spread.

vegetable *n* **1** a plant, e.g. the cabbage, bean, or potato, grown for an edible part which is usu eaten with the principal course of a meal. **2** *derog* **a** a person with a dull undemanding existence. **b** a person whose physical and *esp* mental capacities are severely impaired by illness or injury.

vegetable oil *n* an oil of plant origin, e.g. olive oil or sunflower oil.

vegetal *adj formal* relating to plants.

vegetarian *n* a person who practises vegetarianism. ⋙ **vegetarian** *adj.*

vegetarianism *n* the theory or practice of living on a diet that excludes the flesh of animals and often other animal products and that is made up of vegetables, fruits, cereals, and nuts.

vegetate *v* to lead a passive monotonous inactive existence.

vegetation *n* plant life, or the total plant cover of an area. ⋙ **vegetational** *adj.*

vegetative *adj* **1a** of or functioning as part of nutrition and growth as contrasted with reproductive functions. **b** of or involving propagation by non-sexual processes or methods. **2** relating to, composed of, or suggesting vegetation. **3** affecting, arising from, or relating to involuntary bodily functions. **4** inactive.

veggie *n informal* a vegetarian. ⋙ **veggie** *adj.*

veggieburger *n* a burger made with vegetable ingredients, e.g. soya beans, rather than meat.

veg out *v* (**vegges, vegged, vegging**) *informal* to spend time idly and inactively; = VEGETATE .

vehement *adj* **1** intensely felt; impassioned. **2** forcibly expressed. ⋙ **vehemence** *n,* **vehemently** *adv.*

vehicle *n* **1** something with wheels and an engine that is used to carry people or goods, e.g. a car, bus, or lorry. **2** a medium through which something is expressed or communicated. **3** a work created to display the talents of a particular performer. **4** any of various usu liquid media acting *esp* as solvents, carriers, or binders for active ingredients, e.g. drugs, or pigments. ⋙ **vehicular** *adj.*

vehicle excise duty *n* a tax paid on road vehicles either yearly or half-yearly.

veil[1] *n* **1** a length of cloth worn by women as a covering for the head and shoulders and often, *esp* in eastern countries, the face. **2a** something that hides or obscures like a veil. **b** a disguise or pretext. **3** the outer covering of a nun's headdress. ✱ **draw a veil over something** to avoid mentioning something unpleasant or undesirable. **take the veil** to become a nun.

veil[2] *v* to cover, provide, or conceal with a veil, or as if with a veil.

veiled *adj* **1** indistinct or muffled. **2** thinly disguised.

vein *n* **1a** any of the tubular converging vessels that carry blood from the capillaries towards the heart: compare ARTERY, CAPILLARY[1]. **b** = BLOOD VESSEL. **2** a distinctive element or quality; a strain. **3** a frame of mind; a mood. **4** a streak or marking suggesting a vein, e.g. in marble. **5a** any of the vascular bundles forming the framework of a leaf. **b** any of the thickened ribs that stiffen the wings of an insect. **6** a deposit of ore, coal, etc, *esp* in a rock fissure. ⋙ **veined** *adj,* **veining** *n,* **veiny** *adj.*

veinous *adj* having prominent veins.

vela *n* pl of VELUM.

velar *adj* **1** of or forming a velum, *esp* the soft palate. **2** of a speech sound: formed with the back of the tongue touching or near the soft palate, e.g. /k/ or /g/.

Velcro *n trademark* a fastening device consisting of two strips of fabric that stick to each other.

veld *or* **veldt** /velt, felt/ *n* grassland, *esp* in southern Africa.

veleta *or* **valeta** /və'leetə/ *n* a ballroom dance of English origin in waltz time.

vellum *n* a fine-grained parchment prepared *esp* for writing on or binding books.

velocimeter *n* a device for measuring velocity.

velocipede *n* **1** an early type of bicycle propelled by the rider's feet in contact with the ground, or a later form propelled by pedalling cranks on the front axle. **2** *NAm* a child's tricycle.

velociraptor *n* a ferocious dinosaur that walked on two legs, using a large curved claw on each foot to attack its prey.

velocity *n* (*pl* **-ies**) **1** speed, *esp* of inanimate things; rapidity. **2** speed in a given direction.

velodrome *n* a stadium or arena for bicycle racing, *esp* in France.

velour *or* **velours** *n* (*pl* **velours**) any of various fabrics with a pile or napped surface resembling velvet.

velouté /və'loohtay/ *n* a basic white sauce made with a roux and chicken, veal, or fish stock.

velum *n* (*pl* **vela**) **1** a curtainlike membrane or anatomical partition. **2** = SOFT PALATE. **3** a swimming organ that is well developed in the later larval stages of certain marine molluscs, e.g. oysters, whelks, or limpets.

velvet *n* **1** any of various clothing or upholstery fabrics of e.g. silk, rayon, or cotton with a short soft dense pile. **2** the soft downy skin that envelops and nourishes the developing antlers of deer.

velveteen *n* a fabric made with a short close pile in imitation of velvet.

velvet glove *n* outward affability concealing ruthless inflexibility: compare IRON HAND.

velvety *adj* soft and smooth like velvet.

vena cava /'kayvə/ *n* (*pl* **venae cavae**) either of the two large veins by which, in humans and other air-breathing vertebrates, the blood is returned to the right atrium of the heart.

venal *adj* open to corrupt influence, *esp* bribery. ⋙ **venality** *n.*

vend *v formal* **1** to sell things; to engage in selling. **2** to sell (goods), *esp* in a small way.

vender *n* see VENDOR.

vendetta *n* **1** a blood feud arising from the murder or injury of a member of one family by a member of another. **2** a prolonged bitter feud.

vending machine *n* a coin-operated machine for selling merchandise.

vendor *or* **vender** *n* **1** a seller. **2** in law, the seller of a house.

veneer[1] *n* **1** a thin layer of wood, plastic, etc of superior appearance, quality, or hardness, used *esp* to give a decorative finish to cheaper material. **2** a superficial or deceptively attractive appearance.

veneer[2] *v* to overlay (a cheap wood, etc) with veneer. ⋙ **veneering** *adj.*

venerable *adj* **1a** commanding respect through age, character, and attainments. **b** impressive by reason of age. **2a** a title for an Anglican archdeacon. **b** a title given to a Roman Catholic who has been accorded the lowest of three degrees of recognition for sainthood.

venerate *v* to regard (somebody or something) with reverence or admiring deference; to honour or respect. ⋙ **veneration** *n,* **venerator** *n.*

venereal *adj* **1** of sexual desire or sexual intercourse. **2** of or affected with venereal disease.

venereal disease *n* a disease transmitted through sexual intercourse, e.g. syphilis or gonorrhoea.

venereology *n* the branch of medicine dealing with venereal diseases. ⋙ **venereologist** *n.*

venery[1] *n archaic* the art, act, or practice of hunting.

venery[2] *n archaic* the pursuit of sexual pleasure.

Venetian *n* a native or inhabitant of Venice. ⋙ **Venetian** *adj.*

venetian blind *n* a window blind made of horizontal slats that may be adjusted so as to vary the amount of light admitted.

Venezuelan *n* a native or inhabitant of Venezuela. ⋙ **Venezuelan** *adj.*

vengeance *n* punishment inflicted on somebody in retaliation for an injury received or offence felt. ✱ **with a vengeance 1** with great force or vehemence. **2** to an extreme or excessive degree.

vengeful *adj* desiring or seeking revenge. ⋙ **vengefully** *adv,* **vengefulness** *n.*

venial *adj* forgivable; pardonable.

venial sin *n* in Christian theology, a sin that does not deprive the soul of divine grace: compare MORTAL SIN.

venison *n* the flesh of a deer used as food.

Venn diagram *n* a graph that uses circles to represent sets and terms of propositions, the logical relations between and operations on the sets and terms being shown by the inclusion, exclusion, or intersection of the shapes.

venom *n* **1** poisonous matter normally secreted by snakes, scorpions, etc and transmitted chiefly by biting or stinging. **2** ill will; malevolence.

venomous *adj* **1a** poisonous. **b** spiteful or malevolent. **2** able to inflict a poisoned wound. ⋙ **venomously** *adv.*

venous *adj* relating to a vein or the veins.

vent[1] *n* **1** an opening for the escape of a gas or liquid or for the relief of pressure, e.g.: **a** the anus, *esp* of the cloaca of a bird or reptile. **b** an outlet of a volcano; = FUMAROLE. **2** a means of escape or release; an outlet. ✱ **give vent to something** to give strong expression to one's feelings, etc.

vent[2] *v* **1** to release (gas, etc) through a vent. **2** (*often* + on) to give vigorous expression to (one's feelings).

vent[3] *n* a slit in a garment; *specif* an opening in the lower part of a seam, e.g. of a jacket.

ventilate *v* **1** to cause fresh air to circulate through (a room, etc). **2** to supply air to (the lungs). **3** to examine (a matter) freely and openly. ⋙ **ventilation** *n.*

ventilator *n* **1** an apparatus or aperture for introducing fresh air or expelling stagnant air. **2** an apparatus for providing artificial respiration for a patient who cannot breathe normally; = RESPIRATOR (2).

ventral *adj* relating to or in the region of the front, lower, or inner surface of something: compare DORSAL. ⋙ **ventrally** *adv.*

ventricle *n* **1** a chamber of the heart that receives blood from a corresponding atrium and from which blood is pumped into the arteries. **2** any of the system of communicating cavities in the brain that are continuous with the central canal of the spinal cord. ⋙ **ventricular** *adj.*

ventriloquism *n* the production of the voice in such a manner that the sound appears to come from a source other than the vocal organs of the speaker and *esp* from a dummy manipulated by the producer of the sound. ⋙ **ventriloquial** *adj,* **ventriloquist** *n,* **ventriloquy** *n.*

venture[1] *v* **1** (*often* + out/forth) to proceed despite danger; to dare to go somewhere or do something. **2** to expose (one's life, etc) to hazard; to risk or gamble. **3** to offer an opinion, etc at the risk of opposition or censure. ⋙ **venturer** *n.*

venture[2] *n* **1** an undertaking involving chance, risk, or danger, e.g. in business. **2** something, e.g. money or property, at risk in a speculative venture.

venture capital *n* capital invested or available to be invested in a new or fresh enterprise. ⋙ **venture capitalist** *n.*

Venture Scout *n* a senior member of the British Scout movement, aged from 16 to 20.

venturesome *adj* ready to take risks; daring.

venturi *n* (*pl* **venturis**) a short tube that is inserted in a wider pipeline and is used for measuring flow rate of a fluid or for providing suction.

venue *n* the place where a gathering or event takes place; a meeting place.

venule *n* a small vein.

Venus flytrap *or* **Venus's-flytrap** *n* an insect-eating plant of the sundew family that has modified leaves consisting of two hinged spiky-edged lobes that snap together to trap insects, which are then digested by the plant.

Venusian *n* a hypothetical native or inhabitant of the planet Venus. ⋙ **Venusian** *adj.*

veracious *adj formal* **1** reliable in testimony; truthful; honest. **2** true or accurate. ⋙ **veracity** *n.*

veranda *or* **verandah** *n* a roofed open gallery or portico attached to the outside of a building.

verb *n* a word that characteristically is the grammatical centre of a predicate and expresses an act, occurrence, or mode of being, e.g. *run, give, be, have.*

verbal[1] *adj* **1** of, involving, or expressed in words. **2** of or formed from a verb. **3** spoken rather than written; oral. **4** verbatim; word-for-word. ⋙ **verbally** *adv.*

verbal[2] *n* **1** a word that combines characteristics of a verb with those of a noun or adjective. **2** *Brit, informal* **a** (*also in pl*) a spoken statement, *esp* one made to the police. **b** (*also in pl*) abuse; rude remarks.

verbalise *v* see VERBALIZE.

verbalism *n* **1** a verbal expression. **2** an excessive emphasis on words as opposed to the ideas or realities they represent.

verbalize *or* **-ise** *v* to express (something) in words. ➤➤ **verbalization** *n.*

verbal noun *n* a noun derived from, and having some of the constructions of, a verb, *esp* a gerund.

verbatim /vuh'baytim, və-/ *adv and adj* in the exact words used; word for word.

verbena *n* a plant or small shrub of the teak family that is often cultivated for its heads or spikes of showy white, pink, red, blue, or purplish flowers.

verbiage *n* wordiness; unnecessary words.

verbose *adj* **1** containing more words than necessary. **2** given to wordiness. ➤➤ **verbosely** *adv,* **verbosity** *n.*

verboten /feə'bohtn, vuh-/ *adj* prohibited, *esp* by authority.

verdant *adj* **1** of plants: green in tint or colour. **2** green with growing plants. ➤➤ **verdancy** *n,* **verdantly** *adv.*

verderer *n* a former English judicial officer of the royal forests.

verdict *n* **1** the decision of a jury on the matter submitted to them. **2** an opinion or judgment.

verdigris *n* a green or bluish deposit formed on copper, brass, or bronze surfaces.

verdure *n* growing vegetation, or its greenness.

verge[1] *n* **1** something that borders, limits, or bounds, e.g. an outer margin of an object or structural part. **2** the brink or threshold of something. **3** *Brit* a surfaced or planted strip of land at the side of a road.

verge[2] ✱ **verge on/upon something** to be close to something: *Their familiarity verged on insolence.*

verger *n* **1** a church official who keeps order during services or serves as an usher or sacristan and caretaker. **2** an attendant who carries a rod or staff, e.g. in front of a bishop.

Vergilian *adj* see VIRGILIAN.

verify *v* (**-ies, -ied**) **1** to ascertain the truth, accuracy, or reality of. **2** to bear out, confirm, or fulfil. **3** to substantiate in law, *esp* formally or on oath. ➤➤ **verifiable** *adj,* **verification** *n,* **verifier** *n.*

verily *adv archaic* **1** certainly. **2** truly.

verisimilitude *n formal* the quality or state of appearing to be true.

verism *n* artistic use of contemporary everyday material in preference to the heroic or legendary.

verismo *n* verism, *esp* in grand opera.

veritable *adj* (*often used to stress the aptness of a metaphor*) being in fact the thing named; not false or imaginary: *She produced a veritable mountain of references.* ➤➤ **veritably** *adv.*

verity *n* (*pl* **-ies**) **1** the quality or state of being true or real. **2** something, e.g. a statement, that is true, *esp* a permanently true value or principle.

vermicelli /vuhmi'cheli/ *pl n* (*used as sing. or pl*) **1** pasta in the form of long thin threads. **2** small thin strands of sugar or chocolate that are used as a decoration, e.g. on iced cakes.

vermicide *n* something, e.g. a drug, that destroys worms, *esp* parasitic worms.

vermicomposting /'vuhmikomposting/ *n* producing compost from household organic waste by means of worms. ➤➤ **vermicompost** *n.*

vermicular *adj* **1** resembling a worm in form or motion. **2** of or caused by worms.

vermiculate *adj* **1** marked with irregular or wavy lines. **2** *archaic* full of worms; worm-eaten.

vermiculated *adj* = VERMICULATE.

vermiculite *n* any of various minerals of hydrous silicates derived from mica that expand on heating to form a lightweight highly water-absorbent material.

vermiform *adj* resembling a worm in shape.

vermifuge *n* something, *esp* a drug, used to destroy or expel parasitic worms.

vermilion *or* **vermillion** *n* **1** mercuric sulphide used as a pigment. **2** the brilliant red colour of this pigment. ➤➤ **vermilion** *adj.*

vermin *n* (*pl* **vermin**) **1** (*in pl*) **a** lice, rats, or other common harmful or objectionable animals. **b** birds and mammals that prey on game. **2** an offensive person. ➤➤ **verminous** *adj.*

vermouth *n* a dry or sweet alcoholic drink that has a white wine base and is flavoured with aromatic herbs.

vernacular[1] *adj* **1a** expressed or written in a language or dialect native to a region or country, rather than a literary, learned, or foreign language. **b** of or being the normal spoken form of a language. **2** of or being the common building style of a period or place.

vernacular[2] *n* **1** the local vernacular language. **2** *informal* the mode of expression of a group or class.

vernal *adj* of or occurring in the spring.

vernal equinox *n* the time in March when the sun crosses the equator and day and night are everywhere of equal length.

vernalize *or* **-ise** *v* to hasten the flowering and fruiting of (plants), *esp* by chilling seeds, bulbs, or seedlings. ➤➤ **vernalization** *n.*

vernier *n* a short, specially graduated scale that slides along another graduated scale allowing fine measurements of parts of graduations to be made.

vernix *n* a waxy protective coating on the skin of a new-born baby.

veronica[1] *n* = SPEEDWELL.

veronica[2] *n* a copy in cloth or metal of the legendary cloth of St Veronica which was said to be imprinted with an image of Christ's face.

verruca *n* (*pl* **verrucas** *or* **verrucae**) a wart or warty skin growth, *esp* on the underside of the foot.

versatile *adj* **1** of a person: turning with ease from one thing to another. **2** embracing or competent in a variety of subjects, fields, or skills. **3** having many uses or applications. ➤➤ **versatility** *n.*

verse *n* **1** one section of a poem, song, or hymn, marked off by a particular set of rhymes or assonances. **2** metrical language or writing distinguished from poetry, e.g. by its lower level of intensity. **3** any of the short divisions into which a chapter of the Bible is traditionally divided.

versed *adj* (+ in) possessing a thorough knowledge of or skill in something.

versicle *n* a short verse or sentence, e.g. one from a psalm, said or sung by a leader in public worship and followed by a response from the congregation.

versify *v* (**-ies, -ied**) **1** to compose verses. **2** to turn into verse. ➤➤ **versification** *n,* **versifier** *n.*

version *n* **1** an account or description of something from a particular point of view, *esp* as contrasted with another account or description. **2** an adaptation of a work of art into another medium. **3** an arrangement of a musical composition. **4** a form or variant of a type or original.

verso *n* (*pl* **-os**) a left-hand page: compare RECTO.

versus *prep* **1** *esp* in sport and other competitive activities: against. **2** in contrast to or as the alternative of.

vert *n* in heraldry, the colour green.

vertebra *n* (*pl* **vertebrae** *or* **vertebras**) any of the bony or cartilaginous segments composing the spinal column. ➤➤ **vertebral** *adj.*

vertebrate[1] *adj* **1** having a spinal column. **2** of the vertebrates.

vertebrate[2] *n* an animal that has a segmented backbone, such as the mammals, birds, reptiles, amphibians, and fishes.

vertex *n* (*pl* **vertices** *or* **vertexes**) **1** the highest point; the summit. **2a** in mathematics, the point opposite to and farthest from the base in a figure. **b** in mathematics, the termination or intersection of lines or curves. **c** in mathematics, a point where a main axis of an ellipse, parabola, or hyperbola intersects the curve. **3** in anatomy, the top of the head.

vertical[1] *adj* perpendicular to the plane of the horizon or to a primary axis. ➤➤ **verticality** *n,* **vertically** *adv.*

vertical[2] *n* **1** verticality. **2** something that is vertical.

vertices *n* pl of VERTEX.

vertiginous *adj* **1** characterized by or suffering from vertigo. **2** causing or tending to cause dizziness. ➤➤ **vertiginously** *adv.*

vertigo *n* a disordered state in which one loses balance and the surroundings seem to whirl dizzily.

vervain *n* a plant that bears heads or spikes of blue, purple, pink, or white flowers.

verve *n* **1** energy or vitality. **2** the spirit and enthusiasm animating artistic work.

vervet monkey *n* a S and E African tree-dwelling monkey with soft dense fur that has a greenish tinge, pale yellow to white underparts, and a black face.

very[1] *adv* **1** to a high degree; exceedingly. **2** used for emphasis: *She makes the very best cakes in town.*

very[2] *adj* **1** actual; genuine: *My father was the very man you met that day.* **2** exact; right: *I have the very thing you need.* **3** being no more than; mere: *The very thought of speaking in public terrified me.*

Very light *n* a white or coloured ball of fire that is fired from a pistol and used as a signal flare.

Very Reverend *n* a title for various ecclesiastical officials, e.g. cathedral deans and canons.

vesica *n* (*pl* **vesicae** *or* **vesicas**) a bladder or bladder-like structure, *esp* the urinary bladder. ➤➤ **vesical** *adj.*

vesicle *n* **1a** a membranous pouch, e.g. a cyst, vacuole, or cell, in a plant or animal, *esp* one filled with fluid or air. **b** a blister. **c** a pocket of embryonic tissue that is the beginning of an organ. **2** a small cavity in a mineral or rock. ➤➤ **vesicular** *adj,* **vesiculation** *n.*

vespers *n* **1** the sixth of the daily religious services making up the Divine Office, said or sung in the late afternoon. **2** a service of evening worship; = EVENSONG.

vessel *n* **1** a hollow utensil, e.g. a jug, cup, or bowl, for holding liquid, etc. **2** a large hollow structure designed to float on and move through water carrying a crew, passengers, or cargo; a ship. **3a** a tube or canal, e.g. an artery, in which a body fluid is contained and conveyed or circulated. **b** a conducting tube in a plant. **4** *esp* in biblical use, a person into whom some quality, e.g. grace, is infused.

vest[1] *n* **1** *Brit* a usu sleeveless undergarment for the upper body. **2** *NAm* = WAISTCOAT.

vest[2] *v* **1** (*usu* + in) to give (property, power, a title, etc) into the possession or discretion of another. **2** (*usu* + with) to give (somebody) a particular authority, right, or property.

vestal[1] *adj* **1** of a vestal virgin. **2** *literary* chaste; virgin.

vestal[2] *n* a priestess of the Roman goddess Vesta, responsible for tending the sacred fire perpetually kept burning on her altar.

vestal virgin *n* = VESTAL[2].

vested interest *n* **1** an interest, e.g. in an existing political or social arrangement, in which the holder has a strong personal commitment, *esp* because of a potential financial benefit. **2** somebody or something having a vested interest in something; *specif* a group enjoying benefits from an existing privilege. **3** an interest carrying a legal right.

vestibule *n* **1** a lobby or chamber between the outer door and the interior of a building. **2** any of various bodily cavities, *esp* when serving as or resembling an entrance to some other cavity or space. ➤➤ **vestibular** *adj.*

vestige *n* **1a** a trace or visible sign left by something that has vanished or been lost. **b** a minute amount. **2** a small or imperfectly formed body part or organ that remains from one more fully developed in an earlier stage of the individual, in a past generation, or in closely related forms. ➤➤ **vestigial** *adj,* **vestigially** *adv.*

vestment *n* **1** *archaic* an outer garment, *esp* a robe of ceremony or office. **2** any of the ceremonial garments and insignia worn by ecclesiastical officiants and assistants as appropriate to their rank and to the rite being celebrated.

vest-pocket *adj NAm* small enough to fit into the waistcoat pocket.

vestry *n* (*pl* **-ies**) a room where vestments are kept and clergy dress, often used as the church office for the clergy; = SACRISTY.

vet[1] *n* = VETERINARY SURGEON.

vet[2] *v* (**vetted, vetting**) *chiefly Brit* to subject (somebody or something) to careful and thorough appraisal.

vetch *n* any of several species of climbing or twining plants of the pea family, some of which are valuable fodder and soil-improving plants.

veteran *n* **1** a person who has had long experience of an occupation, skill, or service, e.g. in the armed forces. **2** *NAm* a former member of the armed forces.

veteran car *n Brit* an old motor car; *specif* one built before 1905.

veterinarian *n NAm* a veterinary surgeon.

veterinary *adj* of the medical care of animals, *esp* domestic animals.

veterinary surgeon *n* a person who is qualified and authorized to treat diseases and injuries of animals.

veto[1] *n* (*pl* **-oes**) **1a** the forbidding or banning of something by somebody in authority. **b** the right to forbid or ban something, e.g. a proposal. **2** a right formally vested in a person or constitutional body to declare decisions made by others to be inoperative.

veto[2] *v* (**vetoes, vetoed, vetoing**) to subject (a proposal, etc) to a veto.

vex *v* to cause irritation, annoyance, or distress to. ➤➤ **vexed** *adj.*

vexation *n* a cause of trouble; an affliction.

vexatious *adj* **1** causing vexation; distressing. **2** of an action in law: brought without sufficient grounds, and simply intended to annoy and harass the defendant.

vexed question *n* a question that has been discussed at length, usu without a satisfactory solution being reached.

VGA *abbr* video graphics array.

VHF *abbr* very high frequency.

VHS *abbr trademark* video home system.

VI *abbr* Virgin Islands.

via *prep* **1** passing through or calling at (a place) on the way. **2** through the medium of; by means of.

viable *adj* **1** capable of working; practicable. **2** of a foetus: born alive and developed enough to be capable of living. **3** of seeds, eggs, etc: capable of growing or developing. ⋙ **viability** *n*, **viably** *adv*.

viaduct *n* a long bridge, *esp* on a series of arches, that carries a road, railway, canal, etc over a deep valley.

Viagra *n trademark* a drug used to treat impotence in men.

vial *n* = PHIAL.

viand *n archaic* an item of food.

viaticum *n* (*pl* **viaticums** *or* **viatica**) the Christian Eucharist given to a person in danger of death.

vibes *pl n informal* **1** (*used as sing. or pl*) = VIBRAPHONE. **2** vibrations (emotional atmosphere; see VIBRATION).

vibrant *adj* **1a** oscillating or pulsating rapidly. **b** pulsating with life, vigour, or activity. **2** sounding as a result of vibration; resonant. ⋙ **vibrancy** *n*, **vibrantly** *adv*.

vibraphone *n* a percussion instrument resembling the xylophone but having metal bars and motor-driven resonators for sustaining its sound and producing a vibrato. ⋙ **vibraphonist** *n*.

vibrate *v* **1a** to move to and fro rapidly. **b** to be in a state of vibration; to quiver. **c** to oscillate. **2** of a sound: to resonate or resound. ⋙ **vibratory** *adj*.

vibration *n* **1** the action, state, or an instance of vibrating or of vibration. **2** *informal* **a** (*usu in pl*) a characteristic aura or spirit felt to emanate from somebody or something and instinctively sensed or experienced. **b** (*usu in pl*) a distinctive, usu emotional, atmosphere capable of being sensed. ⋙ **vibrational** *adj*.

vibrato /vi'brahtoh/ *n* (*pl* **-os**) an effect adding colour and expressiveness to musical tone, by tiny rapid imperceptible variations in pitch.

vibrator *n* a vibrating electrical apparatus used in massage or to provide sexual stimulation.

vibrissa *n* (*pl* **vibrissae**) any of the stiff hairs on a mammal's face, or any of the similar bristles round the beaks of some birds.

viburnum *n* a shrub or tree of the honeysuckle family with white or pink flowers.

vicar *n* **1** a member of the clergy of the Church of England in charge of a parish in which the incumbent was formerly paid a stipend, as opposed to receiving tithes. **2** a member of the clergy of the Anglican or Roman Catholic Churches exercising a broad pastoral responsibility as the representative of a bishop or other high-ranking churchman.

vicarage *n* the house of a vicar.

vicar general *n* (*pl* **vicars general**) an administrative deputy of a Roman Catholic or Anglican bishop or of the head of a religious order.

vicarious *adj* **1** performed or suffered by one person as a substitute for, or to the benefit of, another: *a vicarious sacrifice.* **2** experienced through imaginative participation in the experience of another: *vicarious pleasure.* **3a** serving instead of another. **b** delegated: *vicarious authority.* ⋙ **vicariously** *adv*.

vice[1] *n* **1a** moral depravity or corruption. **b** sexual immorality, *esp* prostitution. **c** a grave moral fault. **2** a habitual and usu minor fault, shortcoming, or character failing.

vice[2] (*NAm* **vise**) *n* any of various tools, usu attached to a workbench, that have two jaws that close by operation of a screw, lever, or cam and hold an object tightly so that it can be worked. ⋙ **vicelike** *adj*.

vice- *comb. form* denoting: person next in rank below or qualified to act in place of; deputy: *vice-president*; *viceroy.*

vice admiral *n* an officer in the Royal Navy and US Navy ranking below an admiral.

vice-chancellor *n* an officer ranking next below a chancellor, *esp* the administrative head of a British university.

vice-president *n* an officer next in rank to a president and usu empowered to serve as president in the president's absence, death, or disability.

viceregal *adj* of a viceroy.

viceroy *n* a male governor of a country or province who rules as the representative of his sovereign. ⋙ **viceroyalty** *n*.

vice squad *n* a police department enforcing laws concerning gambling, pornography, and prostitution.

vice versa /,vies 'vuhsə, ,viesi/ *adv* with the order changed or relations reversed; conversely.

vichyssoise /veeshee'swahz/ *n* a thick soup made of pureed leeks and potatoes, cream, and chicken stock and usu served cold.

vicinal *adj formal* **1** of a limited district; local. **2** adjacent; neighbouring.

vicinity *n* (*pl* **-ies**) a surrounding area or district; a neighbourhood.

vicious *adj* **1a** given to or showing cruelty or violence. **b** showing great ferocity. **2** having the nature or quality of vice; depraved. ⋙ **viciously** *adv*, **viciousness** *n*.

vicious circle *n* a chain of events in which the apparent solution of one difficulty creates a new problem that makes the original difficulty worse.

vicissitude *n* **1** a change or alteration, e.g. in nature or human affairs. **2** (*usu in pl*) an accident of fortune.

victim *n* **1 a** somebody or something that is injured, destroyed, or subjected to oppression or mistreatment. **b** a person who is tricked or cheated; a dupe. **2** a living animal or person offered as a sacrifice in a religious rite. ⋙ **victimless** *adj*.

victimize *or* **-ise** *v* **1** to punish selectively, e.g. by unfair dismissal. **2** to make a victim of (somebody or something). ⋙ **victimization** *n*, **victimizer** *n*.

victimology *n* the study of people who have been victims of criminal acts, e.g. to investigate their role in the commission of the crimes and the psychological effect the crimes have on them.

victor *n* a person, country, etc that defeats an enemy or opponent; a winner.

victoria *n Brit* a large red sweet type of plum.

Victorian *adj* of the reign of Queen Victoria of Great Britain (1837–1901). ⋙ **Victorian** *n*.

Victoriana *pl n* articles, *esp* ornaments, from the Victorian period.

victoria plum *n Brit* = VICTORIA.

Victoria sandwich *n Brit* a sponge cake sandwiched with a layer of jam or cream.

victorious *adj* **1** having won a victory. **2** successful; triumphant. ⋙ **victoriously** *adv*.

victory *n* (*pl* **-ies**) the act or an instance of overcoming an enemy or antagonist.

victualler (*NAm* **victualer**) *n Brit* a person who sells provisions, *esp* alcoholic drink.

vicuña /vi'koohnyə/ *or* **vicuna** /vi'kyoohnə, vi'k-oohnyə/ *n* **1** a wild ruminant mammal of the Andes, related to the domesticated llama and alpaca, that has long fine light-brown to pale-whitish hair. **2** the wool from the fine undercoat of the vicuña, or a fabric made of this.

vid *n informal* a video film.

vide /'viedi/ *v imperative* used to direct a reader to another item: see.

video[1] *n* (*pl* **-os**) **1a** material, e.g. a film or television programme, recorded on videotape, a videodisc, etc. **b** the making or transmission of such material. **c** a videotape or videocassette. **2** a videotape recorder or a machine for playing information recorded on videodisc.

video[2] *adj* **1** of reproduction of a television image, or used in its transmission or reception: compare AUDIO[1]. **2** of a form of magnetic recording for reproduction on a television screen.

video[3] *v* (**videoes, videoed, videoing**) to record (something) on videotape, a videodisc, etc.

videoconference *n* a conference involving people in different places who communicate with each other by electronic means. ⋙ **videoconferencing** *n.*

videodisc *n* a disc on which information is stored in digital form.

video game *n* a game played by manipulating elements of a picture on the screen of a visual display unit.

video jockey *n* a person who introduces videos of music on television.

videophone *n* an electronic device for transmitting both sounds and pictures down a telephone line.

videorecorder *n* = VIDEOTAPE RECORDER.

videotape[1] *n* **1** magnetic tape used for recording visual images. **2** a length of such tape, e.g. a videocassette.

videotape[2] *v* to make a recording of (something that is televised) on magnetic tape.

videotape recorder *n* a tape recorder for recording television pictures on videotape and playing back video recordings.

vie *v* (**vies, vied, vying**) (+ for/with) to strive for superiority; to contend with somebody for something.

Viennese *n* (*pl* **Viennese**) a native or inhabitant of Vienna. ⋙ **Viennese** *adj.*

Vietcong *n* (*pl* **Vietcong**) an adherent of the Vietnamese communist movement supported by N Vietnam and engaged in warfare against the S Vietnamese regime during the Vietnam War.

Vietnamese *n* (*pl* **Vietnamese**) **1** a native or inhabitant of Vietnam. **2** the language of Vietnam. ⋙ **Vietnamese** *adj.*

view[1] *n* **1** a scene or prospect: *There's a lovely view from the balcony.* **2** an aspect: *the rear view of the house.* **3** extent or range of vision; sight: *They tried to keep the ship in view.* **4** a pictorial or photographic representation. **5** a way of regarding something; an opinion. **6a** an intention or object: *He bought a gun with a view to murdering his mother.* **b** a hope. **7** the act or an instance of seeing or examining; inspection. **8** a survey. ✻ **in view of 1** taking the specified feature into consideration: *In view of his age, the police have decided not to prosecute.* **2** able to be seen by or from: *He punched the goalkeeper in full view of the spectators.*

view[2] *v* **1a** to see or watch (somebody or something). **b** (*often* + as) to look on (somebody or something) in a specified way. **2** to look at attentively; to inspect. **3** to survey or examine mentally; to consider. ⋙ **viewable** *adj.*

viewer *n* **1** a person who watches television. **2** an optical device used in viewing.

viewfinder *n* a device on a camera for showing what will be included in the photograph.

viewpoint *n* **1** a standpoint; = POINT OF VIEW. **2** a place from which something, *esp* a panorama or picturesque scene, can be viewed.

vigil *n* **1** the act or a period of keeping awake at times when sleep is customary; a period of wakefulness. **2** a devotional watch formerly kept on the night before a religious festival.

vigilant *adj* alert and watchful, *esp* to avoid trouble or danger. ⋙ **vigilance** *n,* **vigilantly** *adv.*

vigilante /viji'lanti/ *n* a member of a vigilance committee or any similar self-appointed guardian of law and order. ⋙ **vigilantism** *n.*

vigneron /'veenyəronh/ *n* a winegrower.

vignette[1] *n* **1** a picture, e.g. an engraving or photograph, that shades off gradually into the surrounding background. **2a** a short descriptive literary sketch. **b** a brief incident or scene, e.g. in a play or film, *esp* a charming one.

vignette[2] *v* to portray (somebody or something) in a vignette or anything similar.

vigor *n NAm* see VIGOUR.

vigorous *adj* **1** possessing or showing vigour; full of active strength. **2** done with vigour; carried out forcefully and energetically. ⋙ **vigorously** *adv,* **vigorousness** *n.*

vigour (*NAm* **vigor**) *n* **1** active physical or mental strength or force. **2** intensity of action or effect; force. **3** active healthy well-balanced growth, *esp* of plants, or the capacity for this.

Viking *n* a Norse trader and warrior of the eighth to tenth cents.

vile *adj* **1a** morally despicable or abhorrent. **b** physically repulsive; foul. **2** very unpleasant. ⋙ **vilely** *adv,* **vileness** *n.*

vilify *v* (**-ies, -ied**) to utter slanderous or abusive statements against (somebody or something). ⋙ **vilification** *n.*

villa *n* **1** *Brit* a detached or semidetached suburban house, usu having a garden. **2** a country mansion. **3** an ancient Roman mansion and the surrounding agricultural estate.

village *n* **1** a group of houses in the country, larger than a hamlet and smaller than a town. **2** *NAm* a legally constituted municipality smaller than a town. ⋙ **villager** *n.*

villain *n* **1a** a scoundrel or rascal. **b** a criminal. **2** a character in a story or play whose evil actions affect the plot. ⋙ **villainous** *adj,* **villainy** *n.*

villanelle *n* a chiefly French verse form consisting of five three-line stanzas and a four-line stanza using two rhymes, or a poem in this form.

villein *n* **1** formerly, a peasant standing as the slave of a feudal lord. **2** formerly, a free village peasant.

villus *n* (*pl* **villi**) **1** any of the many minute projections from the membrane of the small intestine that provide a large area for the absorption of digested food. **2** any of the branching parts on the surface of the CHORION (outer membrane) of the developing embryo of most mammals that help to form the placenta. ⋙ **villous** *adj.*

vim *n informal* robust energy and enthusiasm.

vinaigrette *n* a sharp sauce of oil and vinegar flavoured with salt, pepper, mustard, herbs, etc and used as a salad dressing.

vinca *n* a periwinkle plant.

vindaloo *n* a very hot Indian curry.

vindicate *v* **1a** to exonerate or absolve. **b** to provide justification for (something, e.g. an opinion). **2** to maintain the existence of; to uphold: *He sought a means to vindicate his honour.* ⋙ **vindication** *n.*

vindictive *adj* **1** disposed to seek revenge; vengeful. **2** intended as revenge. ⋙ **vindictively** *adv,* **vindictiveness** *n.*

vine *n* **1** the climbing plant that bears grapes, or its stem. **2** a plant with a stem that requires support and that climbs by tendrils or twining, or its stem.

vinegar *n* **1** a sour liquid obtained *esp* by acetic fermentation of wine, cider, etc and used as a condiment or preservative. **2** ill humour; peevishness. ⋙ **vinegary** *adj.*

vineyard *n* a plantation of grapevines.

vingt-et-un /,vant ay 'uhn/ *n* = PONTOON[2].

vinho verde /,veenyoh 'verdi/ *n* a light dry wine from northern Portugal.

viniculture *n* = VITICULTURE.

vinification *n* the conversion of a sugar-containing solution, e.g. a fruit juice, into wine by fermentation.

vino /'veenoh/ *n* (*pl* **-os**) *informal* wine.

vin ordinaire /,vanh awdi'neə/ *n* (*pl* **vins ordinaires** /,vanh awdi'neə/) table wine that is undistinguished and sufficiently inexpensive for everyday drinking.

vinous *adj* **1** of wine. **2** made with wine.

vintage[1] *n* **1** a season's yield of grapes or wine from a vineyard. **2a** a wine of a particular type, region, and year and usu of superior quality that is dated and allowed to mature. **b** a collection of contemporaneous and similar people or things; a crop. **3** the act or time of harvesting grapes or making wine. **4** a period of origin or manufacture.

vintage[2] *adj* **1** of a vintage, *esp* being a high-quality wine of one particular year rather than a blend of wines from different years. **2** of enduring interest or quality; classic.

vintage car *n* an old motor car; *specif* one built between 1919 and 1930.

vintner *n* a wine merchant.

vinyl *n* **1** a univalent radical CH_2=CH derived from ethylene by removal of one hydrogen atom. **2** a plastic that is a polymer of a derivative of this radical. **3** *informal* traditional gramophone records, as opposed to CDs, DVDs, or tapes.

viol *n* a bowed stringed musical instrument chiefly of the 16th and 17th cents made in various sizes, usu with six strings and a fretted fingerboard.

viola[1] *n* a stringed musical instrument of the violin family that is intermediate in size and range between the violin and cello and is tuned a fifth below the violin. ⋙ **violist** *n.*

viola[2] *n* a violet, *esp* any of various cultivated violets with flowers resembling but smaller than those of pansies.

viola da gamba /'gambə/ *n* (*pl* **viole da gamba**) a bass member of the viol family having a range like that of the cello.

violate *v* **1** to fail to comply with (a law, etc); to infringe. **2** to do harm to; *specif* to sexually assault or rape. **3** to fail to respect (something sacred); to desecrate. ⋙ **violation** *n,* **violator** *n.*

viole da gamba *n* pl of VIOLA DA GAMBA.

violence *n* **1** exertion of physical force so as to injure or abuse, *esp* unnecessary or unlawful force. **2a** intense or turbulent action or force. **b** vehement feeling or expression, or an instance of such feeling or expression; fervour or forcefulness.

violent *adj* **1a** marked by extreme force or sudden intense activity. **b** of a person: prone to using physical force and causing injury to others. **2** caused by force or violence; not natural: *He died a violent death.* **3** powerfully intense or furious: *a violent denunciation.* ⋙ **violently** *adv.*

violet *n* **1** a plant with often sweet-scented flowers, usu of all one colour. **2** the bluish purple colour at the end of the spectrum next to indigo. ⋙ **violet** *adj.*

violin *n* a bowed stringed musical instrument having a fingerboard with no frets, four strings, and a usual range from G below middle C upwards for more than 4.5 octaves. ⋙ **violinist** *n.*

violoncello /,vie·ələn'cheloh/ *n* (*pl* **-os**) *formal* = CELLO. ⋙ **violoncellist** *n.*

VIP *n* a person of great influence or prestige.

viper *n* **1** the adder, or any of a family of snakes related to it. **2** a malignant or treacherous person. ⋙ **viperish** *adj,* **viperous** *adj.*

viraemia (*NAm* **viremia**) *n* the presence of a particular virus in the blood.

virago *n* (*pl* **-oes** *or* **-os**) a loud overbearing woman; a termagant.

viral *adj* of, relating to, or caused by a virus or viruses.

viral marketing *n* a marketing technique that induces a firm's customers to pass on a marketing message to other potential customers.

viremia *n NAm* see VIRAEMIA.

vireo *n* (*pl* **-os**) a small insect-eating American bird with greenish or greyish upper parts.

Virgilian *or* **Vergilian** *adj* of or relating to the Roman poet Virgil (Publius Vergilius Maro) (d.19 BC).

virgin[1] *n* **1** a person who has not had sexual intercourse. **2** (**the Virgin**) the Virgin Mary. ⋙ **virginity** *n.*

virgin[2] *adj* **1** free of impurity or stain; unsullied. **2** being a virgin. **3** characteristic of or befitting a virgin; modest. **4** untouched or unexploited; *specif* not altered by human activity. **5** initial; maiden. **6** of olive oil: obtained from the first pressing.

virginal[1] *adj* **1** of a virgin or virginity, *esp* pure; chaste. **2** fresh; untouched.

virginal[2] *n* (*also in pl*) a small rectangular harpsichord popular in the 16th and 17th cents.

Virgin Birth *n* (**the Virgin Birth**) the doctrine that Jesus Christ was born of a virgin mother.

Virginia creeper *n* a plant of the grape family that climbs by means of tendrils and has dark berries and leaves that turn red in autumn.

Virgo *n* **1** in astronomy, a constellation (the Virgin) depicted as a young woman. **2** in astrology, the sixth sign of the zodiac, or a person born under this sign. ⋙ **Virgoan** *adj and n.*

viridescent *adj* slightly green, or becoming so. ⋙ **viridescence** *n.*

viridian *n* a chrome oxide pigment having a strong bluish green colour.

virile *adj* **1** having the nature, properties, or qualities typical of, or often thought of as typical of, a man. **2** characteristic of or associated with adult males; masculine. **3** having a great appetite and capacity for intercourse. **4** vigorous; forceful. ⋙ **virility** *n.*

virology *n* a branch of science that deals with viruses. ➤➤ **virological** *adj,* **virologist** *n.*

virtual *adj* **1** being such in essence or effect though not formally recognized or admitted as such. **2a** in computing, relating to a storage capacity that appears greater to the user than the physical amount available as a result of the rapid movement of data between different storage areas. **b** relating to a technique by which a person wearing a special headset, and using articles such as specially equipped gloves or a joystick, has the illusion of being in a computer-simulated environment and is able to interact with it. **c** operating or linked by means of computer links to the Internet. **3** of an image, etc: formed by the apparent rather than the actual convergence of light rays at a point: compare REAL¹. ➤➤ **virtuality** *n.*

virtually *adv* almost entirely; for all practical purposes.

virtual memory *n* = VIRTUAL STORAGE.

virtual reality *n* a computer-simulated environment with which a person can interact almost as if it were part of the real world, or the technique of producing such a simulation.

virtual storage *n* a means of increasing the apparent size of a computer memory by moving data back and forward between the memory and an external storage device such as a floppy disk as required.

virtue *n* **1a** conformity to a standard of right; morality. **b** a particular moral excellence. **2** a beneficial or commendable quality. **3** *archaic* chastity, *esp* in a woman. ✱ **by virtue of** as a result of; because of.

virtuoso /vuhtyooh'ohsoh, -zoh/ *n* (*pl* **virtuosos** *or* **virtuosi**) a person who excels in the technique of an art, *esp* in musical performance. ➤➤ **virtuosic** *adj,* **virtuosity** *n.*

virtuous *adj* **1** having or exhibiting virtue, *esp* morally excellent; righteous. **2** *archaic* said of a woman: chaste. ➤➤ **virtuously** *adv,* **virtuousness** *n.*

virulent *adj* **1a** of a disease: severe and developing rapidly. **b** able to overcome bodily defensive mechanisms. **2** extremely poisonous or venomous. **3** full of malice; malignant. **4** objectionably harsh or strong. ➤➤ **virulence** *n,* **virulently** *adv.*

virus *n* **1a** a minute parasitic entity belonging to a large group that are regarded either as the simplest micro-organisms or as extremely complex molecules, are capable of growth and multiplication only in living cells, and that cause various common diseases in animals and plants. **b** *informal* a disease caused by a virus. **2** a small program or short code that is deliberately and maliciously inserted into a computer program or system to attack the software by destroying data files, erasing disks, etc.

visa *n* an endorsement made on a passport denoting that the bearer may enter, stay in, or leave the country.

visage *n formal or literary* a face or countenance. ➤➤ **visaged** *adj.*

vis-à-vis /ˌvee zah 'vee/ *prep* in relation to.

viscera *n* pl of VISCUS.

visceral *adj* **1** of or located on or among the viscera. **2a** instinctive; unreasoning. **b** deeply or intensely felt. ➤➤ **viscerally** *adv.*

viscid *adj* **1** adhesive; sticky. **2** glutinous; viscous. ➤➤ **viscidity** *n,* **viscidly** *adv.*

viscose *n* **1** a viscous solution made by treating cellulose with caustic alkali solution and carbon disulphide and used in making rayon and cellulose films. **2** viscose rayon.

viscosity *n* (*pl* **-ies**) **1** being viscous. **2** the property of a liquid, gas, or semifluid that enables it to offer resistance to flow, or a measure of the force needed to overcome this.

viscount *n* a member of the peerage in Britain ranking below an earl and above a baron.

viscountess *n* **1** the wife or widow of a viscount. **2** a woman having the same rank as a viscount.

viscous *adj* **1** sticky; glutinous. **2** having or characterized by viscosity, *esp* high viscosity.

viscus *n* (*pl* **viscera**) **1** (*usu in pl*) the heart, liver, intestines, or other internal body organs located *esp* in the great cavity of the trunk. **2** (*in pl*) the intestines.

vise *n NAm* see VICE².

visibility *n* **1** being visible. **2a** the clearness of the atmosphere as revealed by the greatest distance at which prominent objects can be identified visually with the naked eye. **b** this distance. **3** capability of affording an unobstructed view.

visible *adj* **1** (*also* + to) capable of being seen. **2** exposed to view. **3** capable of being perceived; noticeable. **4** of exports, etc: of or being trade in goods rather than services. ➤➤ **visibly** *adv.*

Visigoth *n* a member of the western division of the Goths.

vision *n* **1** the act or power of seeing; sight. **2a** something seen. **b** a lovely or charming sight. **3** the degree of clarity with which something appears on a television screen. **4** something seen in a dream, trance, or ecstasy; *specif* a supernatural appearance that conveys a revelation. **5a** the power of imagination. **b** the manner of perceiving mental images. **6a** discernment; foresight; imagination. **b** (*also in pl*) a mental image of something; a thought or fear.

visionary¹ *adj* **1** showing discernment, foresight, or imagination. **2** able or likely to see visions. **3** of the nature of a vision; illusory. **4** of or characterized by visions or the power of vision.

visionary² *n* (*pl* **-ies**) **1** a person who shows discernment, foresight, or imagination. **2** a person who sees visions; a seer.

visit¹ *v* (**visited, visiting**) **1a** to pay a call on (somebody) for reasons of kindness, friendship, ceremony, or business. **b** to reside with (somebody) temporarily as a guest. **c** to go or come to look at or stay at (a place), e.g. for business or sightseeing. **d** to go or come officially to inspect or oversee (a place). **2a** (*usu passive*) to afflict (something unpleasant) on a person or place: *The city was frequently visited by the plague.* **b** *archaic* (+ on/upon) to inflict punishment on somebody for (something): *He will visit the sins of the fathers upon the children.*

visit² *n* **1** the act or an instance of visiting; a call or stay. **2** an official or professional call; a visitation.

visitant *n* **1** *archaic* = VISITOR (1). **2** a supernatural apparition.

visitation *n* **1a** the act or an instance of visiting, *esp* an official visit, e.g. for inspection. **b** an appearance by a supernatural being, seen or unseen. **2a** a special dispensation of divine favour or wrath. **b** a severe trial; an affliction. **3** (**the Visitation**) the visit of the Virgin Mary to Elizabeth celebrated as a festival in the Christian Church on 2 July (Luke 1:39–56).

visiting card *n Brit* a small card of introduction bearing the name and sometimes the address and profession of the owner.

visiting professor *n* a professor invited to join the academic staff of another institution for a limited time.

visitor *n* **1a** a person who is paying a visit. **b** a person who makes formal visits of inspection. **2** a migratory bird that visits a locality for a short time at regular intervals.

visor *or* **vizor** *n* **1** a movable part of a helmet that covers the face. **2** a flat sunshade attached at the top of a vehicle windscreen. **3** *NAm* a peak on a cap. ⋙ **visored** *adj.*

vista *n* **1** a distant view, *esp* through or along an avenue or opening; a prospect. **2** an extensive mental view, e.g. over a stretch of time or a series of events.

visual[1] *adj* of, used in, or produced by vision. ⋙ **visually** *adv.*

visual[2] *n* (*usu in pl*) a photograph, graph, chart, etc used for illustration, information, advertising, etc.

visual display unit *n chiefly Brit* a device that has a cathode ray tube on which information held in a computer may be displayed or updated.

visualize *or* **-ise** *v* to see or form a mental image of (somebody or something). ⋙ **visualization** *n.*

vital *adj* **1** of the utmost importance; essential. **2** concerned with or necessary to the maintenance of life: *the vital organs.* **3** full of life and vigour; animated. ⋙ **vitally** *adv.*

vital capacity *n* the breathing capacity of the lungs expressed as the maximum volume of air that can be forcibly exhaled.

vital force *n* the creative urge, *esp* for improved and superior evolutionary development, held to be inherent in all living organisms.

vitalise *v* see VITALIZE.

vitalism *n* a doctrine that the functions of a living organism are due to a special life force or principle and are not wholly explicable by the laws of physics and chemistry. ⋙ **vitalist** *n and adj,* **vitalistic** *adj.*

vitality *n* **1** physical or mental liveliness. **2** power of enduring. **3a** the quality that distinguishes the living from the dead or inanimate. **b** capacity to live and develop.

vitalize *or* **-ise** *v* to endow (somebody or something) with vitality; to animate.

vitals *pl n* the vital organs, e.g. the heart, liver, or brain.

vital signs *pl n* the functioning or rate of the heartbeat and breathing, the level of body temperature, and other measurable indicators of body activity and functioning.

vital statistics *pl n* **1** statistics relating to births, deaths, health, etc. **2** *informal* a woman's bust, waist, and hip measurements.

vitamin *n* any of various organic chemical substances naturally present in foods, that are essential in minute quantities in the diet of most animals for the maintenance of health and growth and the proper functioning of life-supporting chemical processes.

vitamin A *n* = RETINOL.

vitamin B *noun* (*pl* **B vitamins**) **1** = VITAMIN B COMPLEX. **2** = VITAMIN B_1. **3** = VITAMIN B_2. **4** = VITAMIN B_6. **5** = VITAMIN B_{12}.

vitamin B_1 *noun* = THIAMINE.

vitamin B_2 *noun* = RIBOFLAVIN.

vitamin B_6 *noun* = PYRIDOXINE.

vitamin B_{12} /ˌbee 'twelv/ *noun* = CYANOCOBALAMIN.

vitamin B complex *noun* a group of water-soluble vitamins that are found in most foods and include biotin, choline, folic acid, nicotinic acid, and pantothenic acid.

vitamin C *noun* = ASCORBIC ACID.

vitamin D *noun* (*pl* **D vitamins**) any of several fat-soluble vitamins chemically related to the steroids and found *esp* in animal products, e.g. fish liver oils, or milk, and that are essential for normal bone and tooth structure, e.g. VITAMIN D_2, VITAMIN D_3.

vitamin D_2 *noun* = CALCIFEROL.

vitamin D_3 *noun* = CHOLECALCIFEROL.

vitamin E *noun* = TOCOPHEROL.

vitamin K *noun* (*pl* **K vitamins**) any of several chemically related naturally occurring or synthetic fat-soluble vitamins essential for the clotting of blood, e.g. VITAMIN K_1, VITAMIN K_2.

vitamin K_1 *noun* = PHYLLOQUINONE.

vitamin K_2 *noun* = MENAQUINONE.

vitelline membrane *n* the membrane that encloses the developing embryo in an egg and that in many invertebrates acts to prevent other spermatozoa from entering.

vitiate *v* **1** to make faulty or defective; to debase. **2** to invalidate (a legal document, etc).

viticulture *n* the science or process of cultivating grapevines; the study of grapes and grapevines. ⋙ **viticultural** *adj,* **viticulturist** *n.*

vitiligo *n* a skin disorder marked by smooth white patches on various parts of the body resulting from the loss of pigment from the skin.

vitreous *adj* **1** of or consisting of glass. **2** resembling glass in colour, composition, brittleness, etc.

vitreous humour *n* the colourless transparent jelly that fills the eyeball behind the lens.

vitrify *v* (**-ies, -ied**) to convert (something) into glass or a glassy substance, e.g. by heat and fusion. ⋙ **vitrification** *n.*

vitrine *n* a glass-sided showcase for delicate articles, works of art, specimens, etc.

vitriol *n* **1** concentrated sulphuric acid. **2** virulent speech, expression, feeling, etc. ⋙ **vitriolic** *adj,* **vitriolically** *adv.*

vittles *pl n archaic* food.

vituperate *v* **1** to subject (somebody or something) to severe or abusive censure; to berate. **2** to use harsh condemnatory language. ⋙ **vituperation** *n,* **vituperative** *adj.*

viva[1] /'veevə/ *interj* used to express goodwill towards or approval of a person or thing.

viva[2] /'vievə/ *n* an examination for an academic degree conducted by word of mouth rather than in writing.

vivace /vi'vahchi/ *adj and adv* of a piece of music: to be performed in a brisk spirited manner.

vivacious *adj* attractively lively in temper or conduct. ⋙ **vivaciously** *adv,* **vivacity** *n.*

vivarium *n* (*pl* **vivaria** *or* **vivariums**) an enclosure for keeping and observing plants or animals indoors.

vivid *adj* **1** of a light or colour: bright, glaring, or intense. **2a** producing a strong or clear impression on the senses. **b** producing strong clear mental pictures; having exciting, realistic, true-to-life, etc descriptions. **c** of the mind: able to create vivid pictures or imaginative stories. ⋙ **vividly** *adv,* **vividness** *n.*

vivify *v* (**-ies, -ied**) **1** to give life, *esp* renewed life to; to animate. **2** to impart vitality or vividness to. ⋙ **vivification** *n.*

viviparous *adj* **1** producing living young rather than eggs from within the body in the manner of nearly all mammals, many reptiles, and a few fishes: compare OVIPAROUS. **2a** of a seed: germinating while still attached to the parent plant. **b** of a plant: having viviparous seeds. **3** of a plant: multiplying by means of shoots, buds, bulbils (small bulbs; see BULBIL), etc rather than seeds. ⋙ **viviparity** *n.*

vivisection *n* **1** operation or physical experimentation on a living animal, usu for scientific investigation. **2** any animal experimentation, e.g. for testing cosmetics, *esp* if causing distress to the subject. ⋙ **vivisectionist** *n,* **vivisector** *n.*

vixen *n* **1** a female fox. **2** a scolding ill-tempered woman. ⋙ **vixenish** *adj.*

viz. *abbr* (Latin) videlicet = namely, used to introduce one or more examples.

vizier *n* a high executive officer of various Muslim countries, *esp* of the former Ottoman Empire.

vizor *n* see VISOR.

V-J Day *n* the day at the end of World War II when Japan surrendered to the Allied forces, 15 August 1945, or any anniversary of that day.

VLF *abbr* very low frequency.

VLSI *abbr* very large-scale integration.

V neck *n* a V-shaped neck on a garment, or a garment with such a neck. ⋙ **V-necked** *adj.*

vocabulary *n* (*pl* **-ies**) **1a** the words employed by a language, group, or individual, or in a field of work or knowledge. **b** a list or collection of terms or codes available for use, e.g. in an indexing system. **2** a list of words, and sometimes phrases, usu arranged alphabetically and defined or translated. **3** a supply of expressive techniques or devices, e.g. of an art form.

vocal[1] *adj* **1** relating to the voice, speech sounds, voiced speech sounds, or vowels. **2** having or exercising the power of producing voice, speech, or sound. **3** given to strident or insistent expression; outspoken. **4** of, composed or arranged for, or sung by the human voice. ⋙ **vocally** *adv.*

vocal[2] *n* **1** (*usu in pl*) a sung part in a piece of music, *esp* popular or jazz music, or the performance of this part. **2** a vocal sound.

vocal cords *pl n* either of a pair of mucous membrane folds in the cavity of the larynx whose free edges vibrate to produce sound.

vocalic *adj* containing, consisting of, or relating to a vowel or vowels.

vocalise[1] *v* see VOCALIZE.

vocalise[2] *n* **1** an exercise for singers, commonly using vowels or special syllables designed to develop vocal beauty or agility. **2** a vocalized melody or passage without words.

vocalist *n* a singer, *esp* with a rock or jazz band or pop group.

vocalize *or* **-ise** *v* **1** to give voice to (thoughts, etc); to utter. **2** to sing (something). **3** to utter (a sound) while vibrating the vocal cords; to voice. ⋙ **vocalization** *n.*

vocation *n* **1** a summons or strong inclination to a particular state or course of action, esp a divine call to the religious life. **2** the work in which a person is regularly employed; a career.

vocational *adj* **1** of or being training in a skill or trade to be pursued as a career. **2** relating to a vocation. ⋙ **vocationally** *adv.*

vocative *adj* denoting a grammatical case expressing the person or thing addressed.

vociferate *v* **1** to cry out about (something); to utter loudly. **2** to clamour or shout. ⋙ **vociferation** *n.*

vociferous *adj* marked by or given to vehement insistent outcry. ⋙ **vociferously** *adv,* **vociferousness** *n.*

vocoder *n* **1** an electronic mechanism that reduces speech signals to low-frequency signals which can be transmitted over a communications system of limited bandwidth. **2** an electronic mechanism that separates speech signals into their component frequencies for transformation by a synthesizer into musical notes that retain the characteristics of speech.

vodka *n* a colourless neutral spirit made by distilling a mash, e.g. of rye or wheat.

voe *n* an inlet or narrow bay of the Orkney or Shetland Islands.

vogue *n* **1** the prevailing, *esp* temporary, fashion. **2** popular acceptance or favour; popularity. ⋙ **voguish** *adj.*

voice[1] *n* **1** sound produced by forcing air from the lungs through the larynx. **2a** musical sound produced by the vocal cords and resonated by the cavities of the head and throat. **b** the power or ability to sing or produce musical tones. **c** the condition of the vocal organs for singing. **d** any of the melodic parts in a vocal or instrumental piece of music. **3** the use of the voice, e.g. in singing or acting. **4a** an instrument or medium of expression: *The party became the voice of the workers.* **b** the expressed wish or opinion: *He claimed to be following the voice of the people.* **5** a willingness to speak, express opinions, etc: *So you've found your voice at last, then.* **6** the ability to speak. **7** in grammar, distinction of form or a particular system of inflections of a verb to indicate the relation of the subject of the verb to the action which the verb expresses.

voice[2] *v* **1** to express (a feeling or opinion) in words. **2** to pronounce (a sound) with vibrations of the vocal cords.

voice box *n* = LARYNX.

voiced *adj* in phonetics, uttered with vocal cord vibration.

voiceless *adj* **1** not having a voice. **2** unexpressed; unspoken. **3** in phonetics, not voiced.

voice mail *n* a system for storing telephone messages in digitalized form so that they can be retrieved at a later time at the user's convenience.

voice-over *n* **1** the voice of an unseen narrator in a film or television programme. **2** the voice of a visible character in a film or television programme indicating their thoughts.

voiceprint *n* a graph of sound frequencies and amplitudes in the voice that is hypothetically distinctive for each person.

void[1] *adj* **1** containing nothing; unoccupied. **2** vain; useless. **3** of no legal effect. **4a** (+ of) devoid: *a nature void of all malice.* **b** having no members or examples.

void[2] *n* **1** empty space; vacuum. **2** an opening or gap.

void[3] *v* **1a** to make empty or vacant; to clear. **b** to remove from a container, etc. **2** to nullify or annul (a contract, transaction, etc). **3** to discharge or emit (urine, excrement, etc). ⋙ **voidable** *adj.*

voila /vwah'lah/ *interj* there you are.

voile *n* a fine soft sheer fabric.

volatile[1] *adj* **1** capable of being readily vaporized at a relatively low temperature. **2a** dangerously unstable; explosive. **b** characterized by rapid change. **3** of a person: frivolously changeable; fickle. **4** of a computer memory: not retaining stored data when the power supply is cut off. ⋙ **volatility** *n.*

volatile[2] *n* a volatile substance.

volatilize *or* **-ise** *v* to evaporate or cause to evaporate as vapour.

vol-au-vent /'vol oh vonh/ *n* a round case of puff pastry filled with meat, vegetables, etc in a thick sauce.

volcanic *adj* **1a** of or produced by a volcano. **b** characterized by volcanoes. **2** explosively violent; volatile. ⋙ **volcanically** *adv.*

volcanic glass *n* natural glass produced by the rapid cooling of molten lava.

volcanicity *n* volcanic power or action.

volcanism *n* = VOLCANICITY.

volcano *n* (*pl* **-oes** *or* **-os**) an outlet in a planet's crust from which molten or hot rock and steam issue, or a hill or mountain surrounding it.

volcanology *or* **vulcanology** *n* a branch of science that deals with volcanoes and volcanic phenomena. ⋙ **volcanologist** *n.*

vole *n* a small plant-eating rodent with a stout body, blunt nose, and short ears.

volition *n* **1** a free choice or decision, or the act of making such a choice or decision. **2** the power of choosing or determining; will. ⋙ **volitional** *adj.*

volley[1] *n* (*pl* **-eys**) **1a** a flight of arrows, bullets, or other missiles. **b** simultaneous discharge of a number of missile weapons. **c** a burst or emission of many things at once or in rapid succession. **2a** a return or succession of returns made by hitting a ball, shuttle, etc before it touches the ground. **b** a kick of the ball in football before it touches the ground.

volley[2] *v* (**-eys, -eyed**) **1** to discharge (something) in a volley, or as if in a volley. **2** to propel (an object, e.g. a ball, that has not yet hit the ground) with an implement or the hand or foot. **3** to say (something) vehemently. ⋙ **volleyer** *n.*

volleyball *n* a game between two teams of usu six players who volley a ball over a high net in the centre of a court using only their hands and arms.

volt *n* the SI unit of electrical potential difference and electromotive force equal to the difference of potential between two points in a conducting wire carrying a constant current of one ampere when the power dissipated between these two points is equal to one watt.

voltage *n* an electric potential difference; electromotive force measured in volts.

voltaic *adj* relating to the production of a direct current of electricity by chemical action, e.g. in a battery; = GALVANIC.

volte-face /ˌvolt ˈfas/ *n* (*pl* **volte-face** *or* **volte-faces**) **1** a sudden reversal of attitude or policy. **2** a turn so as to be facing in the opposite direction.

voltmeter *n* an instrument for measuring in volts the differences of potential between different points of an electrical circuit.

voluble *adj* **1** talking a great deal. **2** spoken at great length. ⋙ **volubility** *n,* **volubly** *adv.*

volume *n* **1a** a book, *esp* one of a set or one forming one part of a large work. **b** a series of printed sheets bound typically in book form. **c** a series of issues of a periodical for a given period of time, *esp* one year. **2a** space occupied as measured in cubic units; cubic capacity. **b** the amount of a substance occupying a particular volume. **3a** an amount. **b** a bulk or large mass. **c** (*also in pl*) a considerable quantity; a great deal. **4** the degree of loudness or the intensity of a sound.

volumetric *adj* of or involving the measurement of volume. ⋙ **volumetrically** *adv.*

voluminous *adj* **1a** having or containing a large volume or quantity; very large. **b** of clothing: very full; having a lot of material. **2a** consisting of or being enough to fill a large volume or several volumes: *her voluminous correspondence.* **b** writing much or at great length. ⋙ **voluminously** *adv.*

voluntarism *n* the principle of relying on voluntary action rather than on compulsion. ⋙ **voluntarist** *n,* **voluntaristic** *adj.*

voluntary[1] *adj* **1** proceeding from free choice or consent; done without compulsion and without payment; spontaneous. **2** acting without compulsion and without payment. **3** intentional: *voluntary manslaughter.* **4** of, subject to, or controlled by the will: *voluntary behaviour.* ⋙ **voluntarily** *adv.*

voluntary[2] *n* (*pl* **-ies**) an organ piece played before or after a religious service.

voluntary-aided *adj* in Britain, denoting a voluntary school that receives part of its funding from the local education authority.

voluntary-controlled *adj* in Britain, denoting a voluntary school that receives all of its funding from the local education authority.

voluntary school *n* in Britain, a school built by an independent, usu religious, body but maintained wholly or largely by a local education authority.

volunteer[1] *n* a person who undertakes a service of their own free will, e.g.: **a** a person who does something without being under any legal or moral obligation to do so. **b** a person who enters into military service voluntarily.

volunteer[2] *v* **1** to offer oneself as a volunteer. **2** to communicate (something) voluntarily. **3a** to offer (help, etc) voluntarily. **b** to say that (somebody else) will be willing to do something.

voluptuary[1] *n* (*pl* **-ies**) a person whose chief interest is luxury and sensual pleasure.

voluptuary[2] *adj* of or providing luxury and sensual pleasure.

voluptuous *adj* **1** causing delight or pleasure to the senses; conducive to, occupied with, or arising from luxury and sensual gratification. **2** sexually attractive, *esp* owing to shapeliness. ⋙ **voluptuously** *adv,* **voluptuousness** *n.*

volute *n* an ornament characteristic of classical architecture that is shaped like a roll of material or a scroll. ⋙ **voluted** *adj.*

vomer *n* a bone of the skull of most vertebrate animals that in human beings forms part of the division between the nostrils.

vomit[1] *v* (**vomited, vomiting**) **1** to disgorge the contents of the stomach through the mouth. **2** to eject violently or abundantly.

vomit[2] *n* vomited matter.

voodoo *n* (*pl* **voodoos**) a set of beliefs and practices, mainly of W African origin, practised chiefly in Haiti and characterized by communication by trance with deities. ⋙ **voodooism** *n,* **voodooist** *n.*

voracious *adj* **1** having a huge appetite; ravenous. **2** excessively eager; insatiable. ⋙ **voraciously** *adv,* **voracity** *n.*

-vore *comb. form* forming nouns, with the meaning: an individual eating or feeding on: *carnivore.*

-vorous *comb. form* forming adjectives, with the meaning: eating; feeding on: *herbivorous.*

vortex *n* (*pl* **vortices** *or* **vortexes**) a mass of whirling water, air, etc that tends to form a cavity or vacuum in the centre of the circle, into which material is drawn, *esp* a whirlpool or whirlwind. ⋙ **vortical** *adj,* **vorticity** *n.*

vortices *n* pl of VORTEX.

vorticism *n* an English art movement active from about 1912 and related to cubism and futurism. ⋙ **vorticist** *n and adj.*

votary *n* (*pl* **-ies**) **1** a staunch admirer, worshipper, or advocate; a devotee. **2** a person, e.g. a monk or nun, who has taken vows to dedicate themselves to religion.

vote[1] *n* **1** the usu formal act or process of expressing one's opinion or will in response to a proposed decision. **2** (*usu* **the vote**) the right to cast a vote, *esp* the right of voting in parliamentary and other elections. **3** a group of voters with some common and identifying characteristics: *the Labour vote.* ✱ **vote of confidence/no confidence** a vote expressing continuing support for, or loss of faith in, a leader or controlling body.

vote² *v* **1** (*often* + for/against) to express one's views by means of a vote, e.g. by raising one's hand or marking a special card or paper. **2** to express an opinion: *People are voting with their feet and looking for new jobs in other companies.* **3a** to choose, endorse, or defeat (somebody) by vote; to cause something to happen to (somebody) by voting for it: *After the financial scandal broke, he was voted out of office.* **b** to authorize or award by vote: *The first thing they did was vote themselves a pay increase.* **4** *informal* to offer as a suggestion; to propose. ➤➤ **voter** *n.*

votive *adj* offered or performed in fulfilment of a vow and often in gratitude or devotion.

vouch *v* **1** (+ for) to give or act as a guarantee for somebody or something. **2** (+ for) to supply supporting evidence or personal assurance for somebody or something. **3** to testify the truth of (something); to substantiate.

voucher *n* **1** a documentary record of a business transaction. **2** *Brit* a ticket that can be exchanged for specific goods or services.

vouchsafe *v* **1** to grant as a special privilege or in a gracious or condescending manner. **2** to condescend or deign (to do something).

vow¹ *n* a solemn and often religiously binding promise or assertion.

vow² *v* to promise something solemnly.

vowel *n* **1** any of a class of speech sounds, e.g. /ee/ or /i/, characterized by lack of closure in the breath channel or lack of audible friction. **2** a letter or character representing such a sound.

vox pop *n informal* **1** = VOX POPULI. **2** an interview with one or more members of the public, e.g. in the street, to determine public opinion.

vox populi *n* the opinion of the general public.

voyage¹ *n* a long journey, *esp* by sea or air.

voyage² *v* to make a voyage. ➤➤ **voyager** *n.*

voyeur /vwah'yuh/ *n* **1** a person who obtains sexual gratification by looking at other people's sexual organs, sexual acts, etc. **2** a prying observer who gets excitement from witnessing other people's suffering or distress. ➤➤ **voyeurism** *n,* **voyeuristic** *adj,* **voyeuristically** *adv.*

VP *abbr* vice-president.

VR *abbr* virtual reality.

VRML *abbr* virtual reality modelling language, used to display three-dimensional data in web pages.

vs. *abbr* versus.

V sign *n* a gesture made by raising the index and middle fingers in a V. With the palm outward it signifies victory; with the palm inward it signifies insult or contempt.

VSO *abbr* Voluntary Service Overseas.

VSOP *abbr* Very Special Old Pale (brandy).

VT *abbr* Vermont (US postal abbreviation).

VTOL *abbr* vertical takeoff and landing.

VTR *abbr* videotape recorder.

vulcanicity *n* = VOLCANICITY.

vulcanise *v* see VULCANIZE.

vulcanism *n* = VOLCANICITY.

vulcanite *n* a hard vulcanized rubber. Also called EBONITE.

vulcanize *or* **-ise** *v* to treat (rubber or similar material) chemically in order to give it elasticity, strength, stability, etc. ➤➤ **vulcanization** *n.*

vulcanology *n* see VOLCANOLOGY.

vulgar *adj* **1a** lacking in cultivation, breeding, or taste; coarse. **b** ostentatious or excessive in expenditure or display; pretentious. **2** lewdly or profanely indecent; obscene. **3** generally used, applied, or accepted. ➤➤ **vulgarity** *n,* **vulgarly** *adv.*

vulgar fraction *n Brit* a fraction in which both the denominator and numerator are explicitly present and are separated by a horizontal or slanted line.

vulgarian *n* a vulgar person, *esp* one who is rich.

vulgarise *v* see VULGARIZE.

vulgarism *n* **1** a word or expression originated or used chiefly by illiterate people. **2** vulgarity.

vulgarize *or* **-ise** *v* **1** to make vulgar, coarse, or less refined. **2** to present or diffuse (information) in a way that can be generally understood by the average person; to popularize. ➤➤ **vulgarization** *n.*

Vulgar Latin *n* the informal Latin of ancient Rome.

vulgate *n* (**the Vulgate**) the Latin version of the Bible authorized and used by the Roman Catholic Church.

vulnerable *adj* **1** capable of being physically or mentally hurt. **2** open to criticism or censure. **3** (*often* + to) open to attack or damage; assailable. ➤➤ **vulnerability** *n,* **vulnerably** *adv.*

vulpine *adj* **1** of or resembling a fox. **2** foxy; crafty.

vulture *n* **1** a large bald-headed bird of prey that is related to the hawks, eagles, and falcons and feeds on carrion. **2** a rapacious or predatory person.

vulva *n* (*pl* **vulvas** *or* **vulvae**) the external parts of the female genital organs, or the opening between them. ➤➤ **vulval** *adj.*

vying *v* present part. of VIE.

W w

W[1] *or* **w** *n* (*pl* **W's** *or* **Ws** *or* **w's**) the 23rd letter of the English alphabet.

W[2] *abbr* **1** watt(s). **2** West. **3** Western. **4** in cricket, wicket(s). **5** won (used in tables of match results).

W[3] *abbr* the chemical symbol for tungsten.

w *abbr* **1** wide. **2** with.

WA *abbr* **1** Washington (US postal abbreviation). **2** Western Australia.

Waaf *n* formerly, a member of the Women's Auxiliary Air Force.

wacky *or* **whacky** *adj* (**-ier, -iest**) *informal* absurdly or amusingly eccentric or irrational; crazy. ➤➤ **wackily** *adv*, **wackiness** *n.*

wad[1] *n* **1** a soft mass of a loose fibrous material used in various ways, e.g. to stop an aperture or pad a garment. **2** a felt, paper, or plastic disc that separates the powder from the shot in a shotgun cartridge. **3** a roll of paper, *esp* paper money. **4** *informal* a large supply of money. **5** *informal* (*also in pl*) a considerable amount.

wad[2] *v* (**wadded, wadding**) **1** to form (material) into a wad or wadding. **2** to stuff, pad, or line with some soft substance.

wadding *n* stuffing or padding in the form of a soft mass or sheet of short loose fibres.

waddle[1] *v* to walk with short steps, swinging the body from side to side.

waddle[2] *n* an awkward clumsy swaying gait.

waddy *n* (*pl* **-ies**) *Aus* a club or stick, *esp* one used as a weapon by Australian Aboriginals.

wade[1] *v* **1** to walk through a medium, e.g. water, that offers more resistance than air. **2** to proceed with difficulty or effort. **3** *informal* (+ in/into) to attack with determination or vigour.

wade[2] *n* the act or an instance of wading.

wader *n* **1** (*usu in pl*) a high waterproof boot used for wading. **2** a long-legged bird, e.g. a sandpiper or snipe, that wades in water in search of food.

wadi *n* (*pl* **wadis**) the bed of a stream in regions of SW Asia and N Africa that is dry except during the rainy season.

wafer *n* **1** a thin crisp biscuit. **2** a round thin piece of unleavened bread used in the Eucharist. **3** an adhesive disc of dried paste used, *esp* formerly, as a seal. **4** a thin disc or ring resembling a wafer and used in various ways, e.g. for a valve or diaphragm. **5** a thin slice of silicon or other material that can be cut into many separate sections for the production of integrated circuits, microprocessors, etc.

waffle[1] *n* a cake of batter that is baked in a waffle iron and has a crisp dimpled surface.

waffle[2] *v chiefly Brit, informal* to talk or write inconsequentially and usu at length. ➤➤ **waffler** *n.*

waffle[3] *n chiefly Brit, informal* empty or pretentious words. ➤➤ **waffly** *adj.*

waffle iron *n* a cooking utensil with two hinged metal parts that shut on each other and impress surface projections on the waffle being cooked.

waft[1] *v* to be conveyed lightly by the impulse of wind or waves, or as if by wind or waves.

waft[2] *n* **1** a slight breeze; a puff. **2** something, e.g. a smell, that is wafted; a whiff.

wag[1] *v* (**wagged, wagging**) to move or move (something) to and fro, *esp* with quick jerky motions.

wag[2] *n* the act or an instance of wagging; a shake.

wag[3] *n informal* a wit or joker.

wage[1] *n* **1** (*usu in pl*) a payment for work or services, *esp* of a manual kind, usu according to contract and on an hourly, daily, weekly, or piecework basis. **2** (*in pl, used as sing. or pl*) recompense or reward: *the wages of sin.* ➤➤ **waged** *adj.*

wage[2] *v* to engage in or carry on (a war, conflict, etc).

wager[1] *n* **1** something, e.g. a sum of money, risked on an uncertain event; a stake. **2** something on which bets are laid; the act or an instance of gambling or betting.

wager[2] *v* **1** (*often* + on) to risk or venture (e.g. a sum of money) on an uncertain final outcome; *specif* to lay as a bet. **2** to state with assurance; to bet.

waggish *adj informal* befitting or characteristic of a wag; humorous. ➤➤ **waggishly** *adv.*

waggle[1] *v* **1** to reel, sway, or move repeatedly from side to side; to wag or wiggle. **2** to cause to move repeatedly one way and the other. ➤➤ **waggly** *adj.*

waggle[2] *n* the act or an instance of waggling.

waggon *n chiefly Brit* see WAGON.

waggoner *n chiefly Brit* see WAGONER.

Wagnerian /vahg'niəri·ən/ *adj* characteristic of the music of Richard Wagner (d.1883), *esp* in being on a grandiose scale or exhibiting dramatic intensity.

wagon *or* **waggon** *n* **1** a usu four-wheeled vehicle for transporting bulky or heavy loads, often having a removable canopy, and drawn orig by animals. **2** *Brit* a railway goods vehicle. **3** *Brit, informal* a lorry.

✱ **on the wagon** *informal* abstaining from alcoholic drink. ➤➤ **wagonload** *n.*

wagoner *or* **waggoner** *n* the driver of a horse-drawn wagon.

wagon-lit /,vagonh 'lee/ *n* (*pl* **wagons-lits**) a sleeping car on a continental train.

wagon train *n* a convoy of wagons, e.g. carrying a group of settlers, travelling overland in N America.

wagtail *n* a bird with a trim slender body and a very long tail that it habitually jerks up and down.

Wahhabi *or* **Wahabi** /wəˈhahbi/ *n* (*pl* **Wahhabis** *or* **Wahabis**) a member of a strict Muslim sect founded in Arabia in the 18th cent. ➤➤ **Wahhabism** *n.*

wah-wah *n* in music, a fluctuating muted effect produced by an electronic device connected to an amplifier and operated by a foot pedal; used with an electric guitar.

waif *n* a stray helpless person or animal, *esp* a homeless child. ➤➤ **waifish** *adj.*

wail[1] *v* **1** to make a sound suggestive of a mournful cry. **2** *literary* to express sorrow by uttering mournful cries; to lament. ➤➤ **wailer** *n.*

wail[2] *n* **1** a usu loud prolonged high-pitched cry expressing grief or pain. **2** a sound suggestive of wailing.

wain *n archaic* a usu large and heavy wagon for farm use.

wainscot[1] *n* a usu panelled wooden lining of an interior wall or lower part of a wall.

wainscot[2] *v* (**wainscoted** *or* **wainscotted, wainscoting** *or* **wainscotting**) to line (a wall or room) with boards or panelling. ➤➤ **wainscoting** *n,* **wainscotting** *n.*

wainwright *n* somebody who makes and repairs wagons.

waist *n* **1** the part of the body between the chest and hips. **2** the part of something corresponding to or resembling the human waist.

waistband *n* a band, e.g. on trousers or a skirt, fitting round the waist.

waistcoat *n Brit* a sleeveless upper garment that fastens down the centre front and usu has a V-neck, *esp* such a garment worn under a jacket as part of a man's suit.

waistline *n* **1** the body circumference at the waist. **2** the part of a garment shaped around the waist.

wait[1] *v* **1** to remain stationary in readiness or expectation. **2** to pause for somebody to catch up. **3** to hold back expectantly. **4** to serve at meals; to act as a waiter. ✱ **wait on/upon** to act as an attendant to.

wait[2] *n* **1** the act or a period of waiting. **2** *Brit, archaic* (*in pl*) a group who serenade for gratuities, *esp* at Christmas. ✱ **in wait** in a hidden position, *esp* in readiness to attack.

waiter *n* somebody who waits at table, e.g. in a restaurant.

waiting list (*NAm* **wait list**) *n* a list of those waiting, e.g. for a vacancy or for something to become available, arranged usu in order of application.

waiting room *n* a room for the use of people who are waiting, e.g. for a train or to see a doctor.

wait list *n NAm* see WAITING LIST.

waitress *n* a girl or woman who waits at tables, e.g. in a restaurant.

waive *v* to refrain from demanding or enforcing (e.g. a right); to relinquish or forgo.

waiver *n* **1** the relinquishing of a right. **2** a document giving proof of this.

Usage note

waiver *or* waver? See note at WAVER.

wake[1] *v* (*past tense* **woke,** *NAm or dialect or archaic* **waked,** *past part.* **woken,** *NAm or dialect or archaic* **waked**) **1** (*often* + up) to stop sleeping, or to rouse (somebody) from sleep. **2a** (+ to) to arouse conscious interest in (something). **b** (+ to) to alert (somebody) to something. **3** (+ up) to pay more attention to what is happening or what one is doing. **4** (+ up to) to realize or become aware of a problem, an unpalatable truth, etc.

wake[2] *n* **1** a watch held over the body of a dead person. **2** festivities after a funeral. **3** (*in pl, used as sing. or pl*) the festivities originally connected with the annual fair or festival of an English parish church and now marked by an annual holiday, typically in the industrial north of England.

wake[3] *n* **1** the track left by a moving body, e.g. a ship, in a fluid, e.g. water. **2** a track or path left behind after something has passed.

wakeful *adj* **1** not sleeping or able to sleep. **2** spent without sleep. ➤➤ **wakefulness** *n.*

waken *v* (*often* + up) = WAKE[1].

Waldenses /wolˈdenseez/ *pl n* a Christian sect arising in S France in the 12th cent. ➤➤ **Waldensian** *adj and n.*

Waldorf salad *n* a salad consisting typically of apples, celery, and walnuts dressed with mayonnaise.

wale *n* **1** any of a series of even ribs in a fabric, e.g. corduroy. **2** any of a number of extra thick and strong planks in the sides of a wooden ship.

Walhalla /valˈhalə/ *n* see VALHALLA.

walk[1] *v* **1** to move along on foot; to advance by steps in such a way that at least one foot is always in contact with the ground. **2** to pass on foot through, along, over, or upon (e.g. a route). **3** to take (an animal) for a walk. **4** to accompany (somebody) on foot; to walk with. ✱ **walk away with** *informal* to steal. **walk it** *informal* to win easily. **walk off with** *informal* to steal. **walk over/all over 1** to treat (somebody) thoughtlessly or with disrespect. **2** to beat (somebody) easily and decisively. ➤➤ **walkable** *adj.*

walk[2] *n* **1** the act or an instance of going on foot, *esp* for exercise or pleasure. **2** a manner of walking. **3** a route for walking. **4** a path specially arranged or surfaced for walking; a footpath. ✱ **walk of life 1** an occupation or calling. **2** a range or sphere of action; a field or province.

walkabout *n* **1** a short period of wandering bush life engaged in by an Australian Aborigine for ceremonial reasons as an occasional interruption of normal life. **2** an informal walk among the crowds by a public figure.

walker *n* **1** somebody who walks. **2** a framework designed to support a baby learning to walk.

walkie-talkie *n* a compact battery-operated radio transmitting and receiving set.

walk-in *adj* large enough for a person to enter and move around in: *a walk-in safe.*

walking stick *n* a stick used as an aid to walking.

Walkman *n* (*pl* **Walkmen** *or* **Walkmans**) *trademark* a small portable cassette player or CD player with earphones.

walk-on *n* **1** a small usu nonspeaking part in a dramatic production. **2** somebody who has such a part.

walkout *n* **1** a strike by workers. **2** the action of leaving a meeting or organization as an expression of protest.

walk out *v* **1** to go on strike. **2** to depart suddenly, often as an expression of protest.

walkover *n* an easily won contest.

walkway *n* a passage, path, or platform for walking.

wall[1] *n* **1** a usu upright and solid structure, *esp* of stone, brick, or concrete, serving to divide, enclose, retain, or support. **2** a structure bounding a garden, park, or estate. **3** any of the upright enclosing structures of a room or house. **4** an upright structure serving to hold back pressure, e.g. of water or sliding earth. **5** in anatomy, a lining or membrane enclosing a cavity or structure. **6** something that acts as a barrier or defence: *a wall of silence.* ✱ **to the wall** *informal* into a hopeless position; out of existence: *During the recession several small firms went to the wall.* **up the wall** into a state of exasperation or unreasoning fury.

wall[2] *v* **1** (*usu* + in) to protect or surround with a wall. **2** (+ off) to separate or shut out by a wall. **3** (+ in/up) to immure (somebody). **4** (+ up) to close (an opening) with a wall. ➤➤ **walling** *n.*

wallaby *n* (*pl* **wallabies** *or* **wallaby**) a small or medium-sized mammal closely related to the kangaroo.

wallah *n Indian or informal* (*usu in combinations*) a person who does a specified type of work or performs a specified duty.

wall bars *pl n* horizontal parallel bars that are attached to a wall and used for gymnastic exercises.

wallet *n* **1** a holder for paper money, usu with compartments for other items, e.g. credit cards. **2** *archaic* a travelling bag.

walleye *n* **1** an eye that turns outwards, showing more than a normal amount of white. **2** an eye with a whitish iris. **3** an eye in which the normally transparent cornea is white and opaque. **4** a N American perch that has opaque eyes. ➤➤ **walleyed** *adj.*

wallflower *n* **1** a hardy plant widely cultivated for its spikelike clusters of typically golden to brown sweet-scented flowers. **2** *informal* a woman who fails to get partners at a dance.

Walloon *n* **1** a member of the French-speaking people of S Belgium and adjacent parts of France: compare FLEMING. **2** the French dialect spoken by the Walloons. ➤➤ **Walloon** *adj.*

wallop[1] *v* (**walloped, walloping**) *informal* **1** to hit (somebody or something) with force. **2** to beat (an opponent) by a wide margin; to trounce.

wallop[2] *n informal* **1** a powerful body blow; a punch. **2** *Brit* beer.

walloping *adj informal* large or whopping.

wallow[1] *v* **1** to roll or lie around lazily or luxuriously. **2** (+ in) to indulge oneself immoderately; to revel. **3** of a ship: to struggle laboriously in or through rough water; to pitch or lurch.

wallow[2] *n* **1** the act or an instance of wallowing. **2** a muddy or dusty area used by animals for wallowing.

wallpaper[1] *n* **1** decorative paper for the walls of a room. **2** something that serves as a bland decorative background. **3** in computing, a decorative background on a monitor.

wallpaper[2] *v* to apply wallpaper to (a room or the walls of a room).

wall-to-wall *adj* **1** of carpeting: covering the whole floor of a room. **2** continuous or uninterrupted.

wally *n* (*pl* **-ies**) *Brit, informal* a silly or useless person.

walnut *n* **1** an edible two-lobed nut with a wrinkled shell. **2** the tree that bears this nut, with richly grained wood used for cabinetmaking and veneers.

Word history

Old English *wealhhnutu* literally 'foreign nut', from *Wealh* Welshman, foreigner + *hnutu* nut. The walnut was introduced to Britain from overseas, prob by the Romans, hence the connection with the Old English word for foreigner.

Walpurgis Night /val'pooəgis/ *n* the eve of May Day on which, according to Germanic legend, witches gather in an annual ceremony.

walrus *n* (*pl* **walruses** *or* **walrus**) either of two large sea mammals of northern seas, related to the seals, and hunted for their tough heavy hide, ivory tusks, and the oil yielded by the blubber.

walrus moustache *n* a thick moustache that droops down at each side.

waltz[1] *n* a ballroom dance in triple time with strong accent on the first beat.

waltz[2] *v* **1** to dance a waltz. **2** to move in a lively or confident manner. **3** to proceed easily or boldly; to breeze.

waltzer *n* **1** somebody who waltzes. **2** a fairground roundabout that moves up and down as well as round and round.

wampum *n* beads of polished shells strung together, formerly used by Native Americans as money and ornaments.

WAN *abbr* wide area network.

wan *adj* (**wanner, wannest**) **1a** suggestive of poor health; pallid. **b** lacking vitality; feeble. **2** of light: dim or faint. ➤➤ **wanly** *adv.*

wand *n* **1** a slender rod used by conjurers and magicians. **2** a slender staff carried as a sign of office. **3** an electronic device used to read bar codes.

wander[1] *v* **1** to go or travel idly or aimlessly. **2** to follow or extend along a winding course; to meander. **3a** to deviate from a course, or as if from a course; to stray. **b** to think or speak incoherently or illogically. ➤➤ **wanderer** *n.*

wander[2] *n* an idle or aimless walk or journey.

Wandering Jew *n* **1** a Jew of medieval legend condemned by Christ to wander over the earth till Christ's second coming. **2** (**wandering Jew**) either of two trailing or creeping plants with showy often white-striped foliage.

wanderlust *n* eager longing for or impulse towards travelling.

wane[1] *v* **1** of the moon: to diminish in apparent size or intensity. **2** of light or colour: to become less brilliant; to dim. **3** to fall gradually from power, prosperity, or influence; to decline.

wane[2] ✱ **on the wane** in a state of decline; waning.

wangle[1] *v* **1** to bring about or get by devious means: *We wangled an invitation to the party.* **2** to adjust or manipulate for personal or fraudulent ends: *She wangled it so that she got an extra day off.* ➤➤ **wangler** *n.*

wangle[2] *n* a devious way of doing or getting something.

wank[1] *v Brit, coarse slang* to masturbate.

wank[2] *n Brit, coarse slang* the act or an instance of masturbating.

wanker *n Brit, coarse slang* a foolish or unpleasant person.

wanna *contr* often used in writing to represent casual or American speech: want to.

wannabe *n informal* a person who wishes to be like something or somebody else.

want[1] *v* **1** to have a desire for. **2** to wish or demand the presence of (somebody). **3** to desire (somebody). **4** to hunt or seek (somebody) in order to apprehend them: *He is wanted for murder.* **5** *chiefly Brit, informal* to require or have need of: *This room wants decorating.* **6** *chiefly Brit, informal* ought: *You want to see a doctor about that toe.* **7** to suffer from the lack of; to need: *Thousands still want food and shelter.* **8** (*usu* + for) to have need; to be lacking in the specified respect: *He never wants for friends.*

want[2] *n* **1** the quality or state of lacking something required or usual; lack. **2** grave and extreme poverty that deprives one of the necessities of life. **3** something wanted; a need or desire.

wanting *adj* **1** not present or in evidence; absent. **2a** not up to the required standard or expectation: *The candidate was tested and found wanting.* **b** lacking in the specified ability or capacity; deficient: *He was wanting in gratitude.*

wanton[1] *adj* **1** sexually unbridled; promiscuous. **2** having no just foundation or provocation; malicious. **3** gratuitously brutal or violent. **4** *literary* luxuriant or lavish. ⋙ **wantonly** *adv,* **wantonness** *n.*

wanton[2] *n archaic* a lewd or lascivious woman.

WAP *abbr* Wireless Application Protocol, technology that allows mobile phone users to send e-mails, get information from the Internet, etc.

wapentake *n* a former subdivision of some English shires, *esp* northern ones, corresponding to a hundred in other shires.

wapiti *n* (*pl* **wapitis** *or* **wapiti**) an American deer similar to the European red deer but larger.

War. *abbr* Warwickshire.

war[1] *n* **1** a state or period of usu open and declared armed hostile conflict between states or nations. **2** a struggle between opposing forces or for a particular end: *a war against disease.*

war[2] *v* (**warred, warring**) to engage in warfare.

waratah *n* an Australasian shrub that has clusters of crimson or scarlet flowers.

warble[1] *v* to sing or sound in a trilling manner or with many turns and variations.

warble[2] *n* **1** a musical trill. **2** a warbled song or tune.

warble[3] *n* a swelling under the hide of cattle, horses, etc caused by the maggot of a warble fly.

warble fly *n* a two-winged fly whose larvae live under the skin of various mammals and cause swellings.

warbler *n* a small active insect-eating bird, many of which are noted singers.

war chest *n* a fund accumulated to finance a war, or one used to finance any campaign.

war crime *n* a crime, e.g. genocide or maltreatment of prisoners, committed during or in connection with war.

war cry *n* **1** a cry used during charging or rallying by a body of fighters in war. **2** a slogan used to rally people to a cause.

ward *n* **1** a division of a hospital, *esp* a large room where a number of patients are accommodated. **2** a division of a city, town, or other area for electoral or administrative purposes. **3** a person under guard, protection, or surveillance, *esp* somebody under the care or control of a legal guardian. **4a** a projecting ridge of metal in a lock casing or keyhole allowing only a key with a corresponding notch to operate. **b** a corresponding notch on a key. **5** the inner court of a castle or fortress. ⋙ **wardship** *n.*

-ward *or* **-wards** *suffix* forming words, with the meanings: **1** facing or tending in the direction specified: *homeward; earthwards.* **2** in the spatial or temporal direction specified: *upward; afterwards.*

war dance *n* a dance performed as preparation for battle or in celebration of victory.

warden *n* **1** somebody who has care or charge of something; a guardian. **2** an official charged with special supervisory duties or with the enforcement of specified laws or regulations. **3** *Brit* any of various college or school officials. **4** *NAm* a prison governor. ⋙ **wardenship** *n.*

warder *n chiefly Brit* a prison guard.

ward off *v* to deflect or avert (somebody or something).

wardress *n* a female prison guard.

wardrobe *n* **1** a large cupboard, *esp* one fitted with shelves and a rail, where clothes are kept. **2a** a collection of clothes, e.g. belonging to one person. **b** a collection of stage costumes and accessories. **3** the department of a royal or noble household entrusted with the care of clothes, jewels, and personal articles.

wardroom *n* the space in a warship allotted to the commissioned officers, except the captain.

-wards *suffix* see -WARD.

ware[1] *n* **1** (*often in combination*) manufactured articles or products of art or craft; goods: *tinware.* **2** (*in pl*) goods for sale. **3** articles of fired clay, *esp* a specified make of pottery or china: *Samian ware.*

ware[2] *v* used chiefly as a command to hunting animals or other hunters: to beware of (something).

warehouse[1] *n* **1** a building or room for the storage of merchandise or commodities. **2** *chiefly Brit* a large retail outlet.

warehouse[2] *v* to deposit, store, or stock (goods) in a warehouse.

warfare *n* **1** hostilities or war. **2** struggle or conflict.

warfarin *n* a synthetic compound that is used in medicine to prevent the blood clotting, e.g. in the treatment of thrombosis, and is also used as a rodent poison.

war game *n* **1** an exercise or simulated battle to test military ability. **2** an enactment of a conflict in miniature using counters or models to represent the combatants.

warhead *n* the section of a missile containing the explosive, chemical, or incendiary charge.

war-horse *n* **1** a powerful horse used in war. **2** *informal* a veteran soldier or public figure.

warlike *adj* **1** fond of war. **2** of or useful in war. **3** threatening war; hostile.

warlock *n* a man practising black magic; a sorcerer.

warlord *n* a supreme military leader.

warm[1] *adj* **1a** having or giving out heat to a moderate or adequate degree. **b** experiencing heat to this degree. **2** serving to maintain or preserve heat, *esp* to a satisfactory degree. **3** feeling or causing sensations of heat brought about by strenuous exertion. **4** marked by enthusiasm; ardent or cordial. **5** affectionate and outgoing in temperament. **6** suggestive of warmth in colour or tone; *specif* of a hue in the range yellow through orange to red. **7** marked by excitement, disagreement, or anger. **8** dangerous or hostile: *The minister got a warm reception from a crowd of angry demonstrators.* **9** newly made; fresh: *a warm scent.* **10** used chiefly in children's games: near to a goal, object, or solution sought. ⋙ **warmly** *adv,* **warmness** *n.*

warm[2] *v* to make or become warm. ✱ **warm to/towards 1** to begin to like (somebody or something). **2** to begin to take interest in (a subject).

warm the cockles of one's heart see COCKLE[1]. ⋙ **warmer** *n.*

warm[3] *n* **1** (**the warm**) a warm place or state. **2** the act or an instance of getting or making warm.

warm-blooded *adj* **1** having a relatively high and constant body temperature more or less independent of the environment: compare COLD-BLOODED. **2** fervent or ardent in spirit.

warmhearted *adj* marked by ready affection, cordiality, or sympathy.

warming pan *n* a usu long-handled flat covered pan, e.g. of brass, filled with hot coals, formerly used to warm a bed.

warmonger *n* somebody who attempts to stir up war.

warmth *n* the quality or state of being warm in temperature or in feeling.

warm up *v* **1** to do gentle exercises before more strenuous physical activity. **2** of an engine or machine: to come to the necessary temperature for comfort or efficient working. **3** to put (an audience) into a receptive mood, e.g. before a comedy show.

warn *v* **1a** to give notice to (somebody) beforehand, *esp* of danger or evil. **b** to give admonishing advice to; to counsel. **c** to notify or inform. **2** (*often* + off/away) to order (somebody) to go or stay away.

warning *n* **1** the act or an instance of warning, or the state of being warned. **2** something that warns or serves to warn. **3** a notice of termination of an agreement, employment, etc. ⋙ **warningly** *adv.*

warp[1] *v* **1** to turn or twist (something) out of shape, *esp* out of flatness or straightness. **2** to falsify or distort. **3** to manoeuvre (a ship) by hauling on a line attached to a fixed object. **4** to become warped.

warp[2] *n* **1** a twist or curve that has developed in something originally flat or straight. **2** a series of yarns extended lengthways in a loom and crossed by the weft. **3a** a rope for warping a ship. **b** a rope used to secure a vessel alongside a quay.

war paint *n* **1** paint put on the body by Native Americans as a sign of going to war. **2** *informal* make-up.

warpath ✱ **on the warpath** pursuing an angry or hostile course; taking or starting to take action in a struggle or conflict.

warplane *n* an armed military aircraft.

warrant[1] *n* **1** a commission or document giving authority, e.g.: **a** a document authorizing somebody to receive money or other consideration. **b** a document authorizing an officer to make an arrest, a search, etc. **c** an official certificate of appointment, e.g. one issued to a warrant officer. **2a** a sanction or authorization. **b** evidence for or a token of authorization. **3** a ground or justification; proof.

warrant[2] *v* **1** to serve as or give adequate ground or reason for: *Nothing could warrant such behaviour; The situation warrants dramatic action.* **2** to give warrant or sanction to (something); to authorize: *The law warrants this procedure.* **3a** to guarantee (e.g. a fact or statement of fact) to be as represented. **b** to guarantee (something), *esp* to guarantee (e.g. goods sold) in respect of the quality or quantity specified. **4** to declare or maintain with certainty; to state as being true. ⋙ **warrantable** *adj.*

warrant officer *n* an officer in the armed forces holding a rank below commissioned officers but above non-commissioned officers.

warranty *n* (*pl* **-ies**) **1** a usu written guarantee of the soundness of a product and of the maker's responsibility for repair or replacement. **2** a collateral undertaking that a fact regarding the subject of a contract is or will be as declared.

warren *n* **1** an area of ground where rabbits breed. **2a** a crowded tenement or district. **b** a maze of narrow passageways or cubbyholes. **c** anything intricate or confused.

warrior *n* a person engaged or experienced in warfare, *esp* tribal or medieval warfare.

warship *n* an armed ship for use in warfare.

wart *n* **1** a lumpy projection on the skin, usu of the hands or feet, caused by a virus. **2** a protuberance, *esp* on a plant, resembling this. ✱ **warts and all** *informal* in an imperfect state; showing any blemishes. ⋙ **warty** *adj.*

warthog *n* an African wild pig with two pairs of rough warty lumps on the face and large protruding tusks.

wartime *n* a period during which a war is in progress.

wary *adj* (**-ier, -iest**) marked by caution and watchful prudence in detecting and escaping danger. ⋙ **warily** *adv,* **wariness** *n.*

was *v* first person and third person sing. past tense of BE.

wasabi /wə'sahbi/ *n* the thick root of a Japanese plant, that is grated or made into a pungent paste and served with sushi or sashimi.

wash[1] *v* **1** to make clean by using water or other liquid and soap or detergent. **2** to send water over or through (something), *esp* to carry off material from the surface or interior. **3** to flow along or dash or overflow against (something): *Waves were washing the shore.* **4** to carry or deposit (something) by or as if by the force of water in motion: *Houses were washed away by the flood.* **5a** to drift along on water. **b** to pour or flow in a stream or current. **6** to wet thoroughly. **7** to cover or daub lightly with an application of a thin liquid, e.g. whitewash or varnish. **8** *informal* (*in negative contexts*) to be convincing: *The story didn't wash with me.* ✱ **wash one's dirty linen in public** *informal* to discuss one's private affairs in public. **wash one's hands of** to disclaim interest in or responsibility for (somebody or something). ⋙ **washable** *adj.*

wash[2] *n* **1** the act or an instance of washing or being washed. **2** articles, *esp* clothes, that have been or are to be washed. **3a** a thin coat of paint, e.g. watercolour. **b** a drawing done mainly in washes of ink or watercolour. **4** a thin liquid used for coating a surface, e.g. a wall. **5** an antiseptic or soothing lotion. **6** loose or eroded surface material of the earth, e.g. rock debris, transported and deposited by running water. **7a** a backwash, e.g. behind a boat. **b** a disturbance in the air produced by the passage of an aircraft. ✱ **come out in the wash 1** *informal* to become known in the course of time. **2** *informal* to reach a satisfactory conclusion.

wash bag *n Brit* a small waterproof bag for toiletries.

washbasin *n* a basin or sink usu connected to a water supply for washing the hands and face.

washboard *n* **1** a board that consists typically of a corrugated rectangular metal surface set into a wooden frame, used for scrubbing clothes when washing. **2** a board like this played as a musical instrument.

washed-out *adj* **1** faded in colour. **2** listless or exhausted.

washed-up *adj informal* no longer successful or useful; finished.

washer *n* **1** somebody or something that washes. **2** a washing machine. **3** a thin flat ring or perforated plate used in various mechanical joints and assemblies.

washer-dryer *n* a combined washing machine and tumble-dryer.

washerwoman *n* (*pl* **washerwomen**) a woman who washes clothes for a living.

washing *n* articles, *esp* clothes, that have been or are to be washed.

washing liquid *n* detergent in liquid form for use in a washing machine.

washing machine *n* a machine for washing clothes and household linen.

washing powder *n* powdered detergent for use in a washing machine.

washing soda *n* a transparent crystalline hydrated sodium carbonate used as a household cleaning agent.

washing-up *n Brit* dishes and utensils to be washed.

washing-up liquid *n* liquid detergent or soap used for washing dirty dishes.

washout *n* **1** *informal* a failure or fiasco. **2** a place where a road, railway line, etc has been washed away by a large amount of water.

wash out *v* to cancel (e.g. an event) because of rain.

washroom *n NAm, euphem* a toilet.

washstand *n* a piece of furniture used, *esp* formerly, to hold a basin, jug, etc needed for washing one's face and hands.

wash up *v* **1** *Brit* to wash the dishes and utensils after a meal. **2** *NAm* to wash one's face and hands.

washy *adj* (**-ier, -iest**) **1** weak or watery. **2** deficient in colour; pallid. **3** lacking in vigour or definite form.

wasn't *contr* was not.

WASP *or* **Wasp** *n* an American of N European stock and of Protestant background, *esp* somebody considered to be a member of the dominant and most privileged class.

wasp *n* a largely flesh-eating slender narrow-waisted insect, many species of which have an extremely painful sting; *esp* a very common social wasp with black and yellow stripes.

waspish *adj* resembling a wasp in behaviour, *esp* snappish. ➤➤ **waspishly** *adv,* **waspishness** *n.*

wassail[1] *n archaic* **1** a liquor made of spiced ale or wine, and served in a large bowl, *esp* formerly, at Christmas and other festive occasions. **2** revelry; carousing.

wassail[2] *v* **1** *archaic* to hold a wassail; to carouse. **2** *Brit, dialect or archaic* to sing carols from house to house at Christmas. ➤➤ **wassailer** *n.*

wast *v* archaic second person sing. past tense of BE.

wastage *n* **1a** loss, decrease, or destruction of something, e.g. by use, decay, or leakage, *esp* wasteful or avoidable loss of something valuable. **b** waste or refuse. **2** reduction or loss in numbers, e.g. of employees or students, usu caused by individuals leaving or retiring voluntarily.

waste[1] *n* **1** the act or an instance of wasting or being wasted. **2** damaged, defective, or superfluous material. **3** human or animal refuse. **4a** a sparsely settled, barren, or devastated region; a desert. **b** uncultivated land. ✱ **go to waste** to be squandered or wasted. **lay waste to** to destroy (something, *esp* a place) completely.

waste[2] *v* **1** to spend or use carelessly or inefficiently; to squander. **2** to fail to use (e.g. an opportunity). **3** to dispose of (something unwanted) as waste. **4** *literary* to lay waste to (a place); to devastate. **5** (*often* + away) to lose weight, strength, substance, or vitality.

waste[3] *adj* **1** discarded as refuse. **2a** uninhabited or desolate. **b** not cultivated or used; not productive.

wasted *adj informal* drunk or affected by illegal drugs.

waste-disposal unit *n* an electrical device that grinds up waste food so that it can be disposed of down a waste pipe.

wasteful *adj* given to or marked by waste; prodigal. ➤➤ **wastefully** *adv,* **wastefulness** *n.*

wasteland *n* **1** an area of barren or uncultivated land. **2** a desolate or barely inhabitable place or area.

waster *n* **1** somebody who spends or consumes extravagantly without thought for the future. **2** *informal* a good-for-nothing; an idler.

wastrel *n* somebody who spends or consumes extravagantly without thought for the future; a waster.

watch[1] *v* **1** to keep one's eyes fixed on (something or somebody). **2** to look at (an event or moving scene). **3** to take an interest in the progress of (something or somebody). **4** to keep (somebody) under surveillance or protective guard. **5** to be careful or cautious about: *You need to watch your speed here.* **6** (+ for) to be attentive or vigilant: *Police surrounded the house, watching for any movement.* ✱ **watch one's step** to proceed with care; to act or talk warily. ➤➤ **watcher** *n.*

watch[2] *n* **1** a small timepiece worn on the wrist or carried in the pocket. **2** the act or an instance of watching. **3** close observation; surveillance. **4** a state of alert and continuous attention; a lookout. **5** a period of keeping guard. **6** a period of time during which a part of a ship's company is on duty while another part rests. **7** somebody who watches; a lookout or watchman. **8** a body of sentinels or watchmen; *specif* those formerly assigned to patrol the streets of a town at night, announce the hours, and act as police. **9** (*usu in pl*) a wakeful interval during the night.

watchable *adj* worth watching.

watchdog *n* **1** a dog kept to guard property. **2** a person or group that guards against inefficiency, undesirable practices, etc.

watchful *adj* **1** carefully observant or attentive. **2** *archaic* wakeful. ➤➤ **watchfully** *adv,* **watchfulness** *n.*

watching brief *n* **1** *Brit* in law, instructions to a barrister to follow a case on behalf of somebody not directly involved. **2** observation of proceedings on behalf of another.

watchman *n* (*pl* **watchmen**) **1** somebody who keeps watch; a guard. **2** a member of a body formerly assigned to patrol the streets at night.

watch night *n* a devotional service lasting until after midnight, *esp* on Christmas Eve or New Year's Eve.

watch out *v* **1** to be vigilant. **2** (*usu in imperative*) to be careful; to take care.

watchtower *n* a tower from which a lookout can keep watch.

watchword *n* **1** a motto that embodies a guiding principle; a slogan. **2** a word or phrase used as a sign of recognition among members of the same group.

water[1] *n* **1a** the colourless odourless liquid that falls from the clouds as rain, forms rivers, lakes, and seas, and is a major constituent of all living matter. **b** one of the four elements of the alchemists, the others being earth, air, and fire. **2** (*in pl*) a stretch of sea under the control of a specified sovereignty. **3** (**the waters**) a natural mineral water. **4** a water supply. **5** the level of water at a specified state of the tide. **6** the surface of the water. **7** a medicinal or cosmetic preparation made with water. **8** a watery liquid, *esp* urine. **9** (*usu in pl*) the amniotic fluid surrounding a foetus in the womb and discharged shortly before birth. **10a** the clarity and lustre of a precious stone, *esp* a diamond. **b** degree of excellence: *She's a pianist of the first water.* ✱ **hold water** to stand up under criticism or analysis. **make/pass water** *euphem* to urinate. **water under the bridge** past events that it is futile to try to alter. ➤➤ **waterless** *adj.*

water[2] *v* **1** to moisten, sprinkle, or soak (e.g. plants or ground) with water. **2** to supply (e.g. a horse) with water to drink. **3** to be a source of water for (an area). **4** to impart a lustrous appearance and wavy pattern to (cloth) by pressing between rollers or plates: *watered silk.* **5** (*often* + down) to dilute by or as if by the addition of water: *The proposals have been watered down.* **6** to form or secrete water or watery matter, e.g. tears or saliva. ➤➤ **waterer** *n.*

water bailiff *n Brit* an official employed to enforce fishing laws.

water bed *n* a bed with a water-filled plastic or rubber mattress.

water biscuit *n* an unsweetened biscuit made with flour and water.

water blister *n* a blister with a clear watery content that does not contain pus or blood.

water boatman *n* an aquatic bug that swims on its back moving its long hind legs like oars.

waterbuck *n* (*pl* **waterbucks** *or* **waterbuck**) a shaggy-haired African antelope found near rivers and lakes.

water buffalo *n* an often domesticated Asiatic buffalo with large horns.

water cannon *n* a device for shooting out a jet of water with great force, e.g. to disperse a crowd.

water chestnut *n* **1** the edible enlarged tuber of a SE Asian sedge, commonly used in Chinese cookery. **2** an aquatic plant with white flowers, floating leaves arranged in a rosette, and edible nutlike fruits. Also called CALTROP.

water clock *n* an instrument designed to measure time by the fall or flow of water.

water closet *n dated* a toilet with a bowl that can be flushed with water.

watercolour (*NAm* **watercolor**) *n* **1** a paint made from pigment mixed with water rather than oil. **2** a picture painted with watercolours. **3** the art of painting with watercolours. ➤➤ **watercolourist** *n.*

watercourse *n* a natural or artificial channel through which water flows or may flow, or the water flowing in such a channel.

watercress *n* a cress that grows in wet places, having peppery-flavoured dark green leaves used in salads.

water-diviner *n Brit* somebody who searches for water using a divining rod; a dowser.

waterfall *n* a vertical or steep descent of the water of a river or stream.

waterfowl *n* (*pl* **waterfowls** *or* **waterfowl**) **1** a bird, *esp* a duck, that frequents water. **2** swimming game birds collectively, as distinguished from upland game birds.

waterfront *n* land or a section of a town fronting or bordering on a body of water.

water hammer *n* the sound of a violent shaking or agitation of a moving liquid or gas, e.g. water or steam, against the sides of a containing pipe or vessel.

water hole *n* a natural hollow in which water collects, used *esp* by animals as a drinking place.

water ice *n* a frozen dessert of water, sugar, and flavouring.

watering can *n* a vessel with a handle and a long spout often fitted with a rose, used for watering plants.

watering hole *n* **1** a pool or water-filled depression where animals come to drink. **2** *informal* a pub, hotel, etc used, *esp* habitually, for convivial drinking.

watering place *n* **1** a place where water may be obtained, *esp* one where animals come to drink. **2** a health or recreational resort featuring mineral springs or bathing, *esp* a spa.

water level *n* **1** the level reached by the surface of a body of water. **2** = WATER TABLE.

water lily *n* an aquatic plant with floating leaves and usu showy colourful flowers.

waterline *n* **1** the level on the hull of a vessel to which the water comes when it is afloat, or a line marking this level. **2** the level that a river or the sea has reached, or a line on a shore or bank marking this level.

waterlogged *adj* filled or soaked with water.

waterloo *n* (*pl* **waterloos**) (*often* **Waterloo**) a decisive defeat.

Word history

named after *Waterloo*, a town in Belgium, scene of Napoleon's defeat by British and Prussian armies in 1815.

water main *n* a major pipe for conveying water.

waterman *n* (*pl* **watermen**) a man who works on or near water, *esp* a boatman whose boat and services are available for hire.

watermark[1] *n* **1** a marking in paper visible when the paper is held up to the light. **2** a mark indicating the height to which water has risen; a waterline.

watermark[2] *v* to mark (paper) with a watermark.

water meadow *n* a meadow that is regularly flooded by a bordering river.

watermelon *n* a large melon with a hard green rind, a sweet watery red pulp, and many seeds.

water mill *n* a mill whose machinery is moved by water.

water moccasin *n* a venomous semiaquatic snake found in marshes and swamps in the southern USA.

water nymph *n* a nymph, e.g. a naiad, associated with a body of water.

water pipe *n* **1** a pipe for conveying water. **2** a large smoking apparatus consisting of a bowl containing tobacco or other material mounted on a vessel of water through which smoke is drawn and cooled before reaching the mouth.

water pistol *n* a toy pistol designed to shoot a jet of liquid.

water polo *n* a game played in water by teams of seven swimmers who try to get an inflated ball into the opposing side's goal.

waterproof[1] *adj* impervious to water, *esp* covered or treated with a material to prevent passage of water.

waterproof[2] *n Brit* a waterproof garment.

waterproof[3] *v* to make waterproof. ➤➤ **waterproofing** *n.*

water rail *n* a Eurasian rail with olive brown upper parts, conspicuous black and white bars on the flanks, and a long red bill.

water rat *n* a rodent that frequents water, *esp* a water vole.

water-repellent *adj* treated with a finish that is resistant but not impervious to penetration by water.

water-resistant *adj* = WATER-REPELLENT.

watershed *n* **1** a dividing ridge between two drainage areas. **2** a crucial turning point. **3** *Brit* the time of day before which material considered unsuitable for children should not be shown on television.

waterside *n* the margin of a body of water.

water ski *n* a board used singly or in pairs for standing on and planing over water while being towed at speed.

water-ski *v* (**water-skis, water-skied** *or* **water-ski'd, water-skiing**) to use water skis. ➤➤ **water-skier** *n*, **water-skiing** *n*.

water-softener *n* a substance or device for softening hard water.

watersplash *n Brit* a stretch of road submerged by water.

waterspout *n* **1** a funnel-shaped column of rotating wind and spray extending from the underside of a cloud down to the surface of a sea, lake, etc. **2** a pipe or orifice from which water is spouted or through which it is carried.

water table *n* the level below which the ground is wholly saturated with water.

watertight *adj* **1** of such tight construction or so closely sealed as to be impermeable to water. **2** of an argument: impossible to disprove; without loopholes.

water torture *n* a form of torture involving the sound or sensation of dripping water.

water tower *n* a tower supporting a raised water tank to provide the necessary steady pressure to distribute water.

water vole *n* a common large vole of W Europe that inhabits river banks and often digs extensive tunnels.

waterway *n* a navigable route or body of water.

waterweed *n* an aquatic plant, e.g. a pondweed, with inconspicuous flowers.

waterwheel *n* **1** a wheel made to rotate by direct action of water, and used *esp* to drive machinery. **2** a wheel for raising water.

water wings *pl n* a pair of usu air-filled floats worn on the arms of somebody learning to swim.

waterworks *n* (*pl* **waterworks**) **1** (*used as sing.*) the reservoirs, buildings, and equipment by which a water supply is obtained and distributed, e.g. to a city. **2** *Brit, euphem or humorous* the urinary system. **3** *informal* the shedding of tears.

watery *adj* **1a** consisting of or filled with water. **b** containing, resembling, or yielding water. **c** of food or drink: containing too much water. **2a** pale or faint. **b** vapid or wishy-washy. ➤➤ **wateriness** *n*.

watt *n* the SI unit of power equal to the expenditure of one joule of energy in one second or to the electrical power required for one amp of current to flow across a potential difference of one volt.

wattage *n* an amount of power expressed in watts, *esp* the amount of electrical power required by an appliance.

watt-hour *n* a unit of work or energy equivalent to the power of one watt operating for one hour.

wattle *n* **1a** a framework of poles interwoven with branches or reeds and used, *esp* formerly, in building. **b** material for such a construction. **2** a fleshy protuberance near or on the head or neck of a bird. **3** an Australian acacia with spikes of brightly coloured flowers.

wattle and daub *n* wattle covered and plastered with clay and used in building construction.

wave[1] *v* **1a** to move the hand or something held in the hand to and fro in greeting, as a signal, etc. **b** to cause (e.g. one's arm or a flag) to move to and fro in this way. **c** to convey (something) by waving: *She waved goodbye*. **d** to direct (somebody) by waving. **2** to brandish or flourish. **3** to flutter or swing loosely to and fro. **4** to sway in the wind. **5** to follow a curving line or take a wavy form; to undulate. **6** to give a curving or undulating shape to (e.g. hair).

wave[2] *n* **1** a moving ridge or swell on the surface of a body of water, e.g. the sea. **2a** a shape or outline that has successive curves. **b** one of the crests of such a form, with or without its adjacent trough. **3** a waviness of the hair. **4** a surge of sensation or emotion. **5** a movement involving large numbers of people in a common activity. **6** a sudden increase or wide occurrence of a phenomenon or activity. **7** an act of waving, *esp* as a signal or greeting. **8** a rolling or undulatory movement. **9** a periodic disturbance or variation of a physical quantity by which energy is transferred progressively from point to point by transient local displacement of the particles of the medium but without its permanent movement. ✱ **make waves 1** *informal* to cause trouble or make a fuss. **2** *informal* to create a considerable, usu good, impression. ➤➤ **waveless** *adj*.

wave band *n* a band of radio frequency waves.

wave equation *n* in mathematics, a differential equation whose solutions describe wave phenomena.

waveform *n* in physics, the graphic representation of the variation of a quantity with respect to some other factor.

wavelength *n* the distance in the line of advance of a wave from any one point to the next point of corresponding phase, e.g. from one peak to the next. ✱ **be on somebody's/the same wavelength** to have the same outlook, views, etc as somebody else.

wavelet *n* a little wave; a ripple.

wave mechanics *pl n* (*used as sing.*) in physics, a theory of matter that gives a mathematical interpretation of the structure of matter based on the concept that elementary particles, e.g. electrons, protons, or neutrons, possess wave properties.

waver *v* **1** to vacillate between choices. **2a** to sway unsteadily to and fro. **b** to quiver or flicker. **c** to hesitate as if about to give way; to falter. ➤➤ **waverer** *n*, **wavery** *adj*.

Usage note

waver *or* **waiver**? These two words are easily confused. To *waver* is a verb meaning 'to be unable to decide', 'to show signs of indecision', or 'to totter': *A week ago she was firmly on our side, but now she's starting to waver. Waiver* is a noun from the verb *to waive* and means 'a statement or document renouncing a right or claim': *We had to sign a waiver giving up our right to compensation in case of injury.*

wave theory *n* in physics, the theory that light and other electromagnetic radiation consists of waves.

wavy *adj* (**-ier, -iest**) **1** having waves. **2** having a wavelike form or outline. ➤➤ **wavily** *adv*, **waviness** *n*.

wax[1] *n* **1** = BEESWAX. **2a** a plant or animal substance that is harder and less greasy than a fat. **b** a solid substance, e.g. paraffin wax, of mineral origin. **c** a pliable or liquid composition used *esp* for sealing, taking impressions, or polishing.

wax[2] *v* **1** to treat or rub (something) with wax, usu for polishing or stiffening. **2** to remove hair from (a part of the body) using melted wax.

wax[3] *v* **1** of the moon: to have an increasing area of the illuminated surface visible. **2** to become, *esp* in speaking or writing: *He waxed lyrical about the book.*

3 *formal or literary* to increase in size, strength, prosperity, etc.

wax[4] *n Brit, informal, dated* a fit of temper.

waxbill *n* an African or Asian bird with a white, pink, or reddish bill of a waxy appearance.

waxcloth *n* = OILCLOTH.

waxed cloth *n* = OILCLOTH.

waxed jacket *n* a waterproof jacket made of waxed fabric.

waxed paper *n* paper coated or impregnated with wax to make it resistant to water and grease, used *esp* as a wrapping for food.

waxen *adj* **1** resembling wax, *esp* in being pliable, smooth, or pallid. **2** made of or covered with wax.

wax paper *n* = WAXED PAPER.

waxwing *n* a Eurasian bird with a pinkish chestnut crest, a short yellow-tipped tail, and red waxlike tips to the secondary wing feathers.

waxwork *n* **1** an effigy in wax, usu of a person. **2** (*in pl, used as sing.*) an exhibition of wax effigies.

waxy *adj* (**-ier, -iest**) **1** resembling wax, *esp* in smooth whiteness or pliability. **2** full of or covered with wax. ⋙ **waxiness** *n.*

way[1] *n* **1** a method of doing something; a means. **2** the manner in which something is done or happens. **3** a characteristic manner of behaving or happening. **4** a feature or respect. **5** a course leading in a direction or towards an objective. **6a** a road or path. **b** an opening for passage: *the way in.* **c** space or room, *esp* for forward movement: *Get out of the way!* **7** the course to be travelled from one place to another; a route. **8** the length of a course; a distance. **9** (*often in combination*) a direction or side: *a one-way street; the other way up.* **10** (*in pl*) used adverbially to denote a specified number of participants: *They split the money four ways.* **11** *informal* the area in which one lives, or the direction of this. **12** a state of affairs; a condition or state. **13** motion or speed of a ship or boat through the water. ✱ **by the way** incidentally. **by way of 1** to be considered as; as a sort of: *by way of light relief.* **2** via. **3** in the form of. **get/have one's own way** to get what one wants. **have a way with** to be good at dealing with (people, animals, etc). **in a way** from one point of view; to some extent. **no way** *informal* under no circumstances. **one way and another** taking everything into consideration; on balance. **one way or the other** somehow; by any possible means. **on the way 1** while moving along a course. **2** coming or approaching. **on the way out** *informal* about to disappear, go out of fashion, be dismissed, etc. **out of the way 1** unusual or remarkable. **2** in or to a secluded or remote place. **3** done or completed. **under way** in progress; started.

way[2] *adv informal* considerably; far. ✱ **way back** long ago.

waybill *n* a document showing the number of passengers or parcels carried on a vehicle and the fares charged.

wayfarer *n literary* a traveller, *esp* on foot. ⋙ **wayfaring** *n.*

wayfaring tree *n* a European and W Asian shrub with white flowers in dense flat-topped clusters and large oval leaves.

waylay *v* (*past tense and past part.* **waylaid**) **1** to ambush and attack. **2** to accost and detain.

waymark *n* a signpost marking out a route, e.g. along a footpath.

waymarker *n* = WAYMARK.

way-out *adj informal* out of the ordinary, *esp* in being daring or experimental.

waypoint *n* a point on a route, e.g. a point at which one's position can be checked or where one can stop or change one's course.

-ways *suffix* forming adverbs, with the meaning: in a stated way, direction, or manner: *sideways.*

ways and means *pl n* methods and resources for accomplishing something.

wayside *n* the side of a road, or land adjacent to a road.

way station *n NAm* an intermediate stopping place.

wayward *adj* **1** following one's own capricious or wanton inclinations; ungovernable. **2** following no clear principle or law; unpredictable. ⋙ **waywardly** *adv,* **waywardness** *n.*

wazzock *n Brit, informal* a fool.

Wb *abbr* weber.

WBA *abbr* World Boxing Association.

WBC *abbr* World Boxing Council.

WC *abbr* **1** *Brit* water closet. **2** West Central (London postcode).

we *pron* **1** I and one or more other people. **2a** used in place of *I* by a sovereign. **b** used in place of *I* by a writer or editor to preserve an impersonal character. **3** used patronizingly in place of *you,* e.g. to children or the sick.

WEA *abbr Brit* Workers' Educational Association.

weak *adj* **1a** deficient in physical vigour; feeble or debilitated. **b** not able to sustain or exert much weight, pressure, or strain. **c** not able to resist external force or withstand attack. **2a** lacking a particular mental or intellectual quality. **b** unable to withstand temptation or persuasion. **3a** unable to function properly. **b** lacking skill or proficiency. **4** without vigour of expression or effect. **5** deficient in strength or flavour; dilute. **6** lacking normal intensity or potency. **7** not having or exerting authority or political power. **8** in grammar, denoting an English verb that forms the past tense and past participle by adding the suffix *-ed* or *-d* or *-t,* or a similar verb in other languages.

weaken *v* to make or become weak or weaker.

weak-kneed *adj* **1** feeling faint and weak. **2** lacking in resolution; easily intimidated.

weakling *n* a weak person or animal.

weakly[1] *adv* in a weak manner.

weakly[2] *adj* (**-ier, -iest**) feeble or sickly. ⋙ **weakliness** *n.*

weakness *n* **1** the quality or state of being weak. **2** a fault or defect. **3** a special desire or fondness, or an object of this.

weal[1] *or* **wheal** *n* a raised mark on the surface of the body; a welt.

weal[2] *n archaic or formal* a sound, healthy, or prosperous state; well-being.

Weald *n* (**the Weald**) an area of open grassland, once wooded, covering parts of Sussex, Kent, and Surrey. ⋙ **Wealden** *adj.*

wealth *n* **1** abundance of money and valuable material possessions. **2** the state of being rich. **3** an abundant supply; a profusion.

wealthy *adj* (**-ier, -iest**) having wealth; rich. ⋙ **wealthily** *adv.*

wean[1] *v* **1** to accustom (a child or other young mammal) to take food other than the mother's milk. **2** (*usu* + off/from) to cause to abandon a state of usu unwholesome dependence or preoccupation. **3** (+ on) to cause to become acquainted with an idea, writer, etc at an early age.

wean[2] /wayn/ *n Scot, N Eng* a small child.

weanling *n* an animal newly weaned.

weapon *n* **1** an instrument of attack or defence, *esp* in combat. **2** a means used to further one's cause in conflict. ➤➤ **weaponless** *adj,* **weaponry** *n.*

wear[1] *v* (*past tense* **wore,** *past part.* **worn**) **1** to have (e.g. a garment) on the body as clothing or adornment. **2** to have or show (a specified expression) on the face. **3a** to damage or diminish by use. **b** to be damaged or diminished by use. **4** to produce (e.g. a hole) gradually by use or friction. **5** *Brit, informal* (*usu in negative contexts*) to find (a claim or proposal) acceptable. **6** to weary or fatigue. **7** to endure use: *The carpet is wearing well.* **8** (*often* + on) of time: to go by slowly or tediously. ✻ **wear the trousers** to have the controlling authority in a household. **wear thin** to become weakened or exhausted. ➤➤ **wearable** *adj,* **wearer** *n.*

wear[2] *n* **1** wearing or being worn. **2** (*often in combinations*) clothing, usu of a specified kind or for a specified occasion: *swimwear.* **3** capacity to withstand use; durability. **4** minor damage or deterioration through use.

wear and tear *n* the normal deterioration or depreciation which something suffers in the course of use.

wear down *v* to weary and overcome by persistence.

wearing *adj* causing fatigue; tiring. ➤➤ **wearingly** *adv.*

wearisome *adj* causing weariness; tiresome.

wear off *v* to lose effectiveness gradually.

wear out *v* **1** to make or become useless by long or excessive wear or use. **2** to tire or exhaust.

weary[1] *adj* (**-ier, -iest**) **1** exhausted or tired. **2** expressing or causing weariness. **3** (+ of) having one's patience, tolerance, or pleasure exhausted. ➤➤ **wearily** *adv,* **weariness** *n.*

weary[2] *v* (**-ies, -ied**) to make or become weary.

weasel[1] *n* (*pl* **weasels** *or* **weasel**) **1** a small slender flesh-eating mammal that is mostly reddish brown and, in northern forms, turns white in winter. **2** *informal* a treacherous person. ➤➤ **weaselly** *adj.*

weasel[2] *v* (**weaselled, weaselling,** *NAm* **weaseled, weaseling**) (*often* + out) to escape from or evade a situation or obligation.

weasel words *pl n* words used to evade a direct or forthright statement.

weather[1] *n* **1** the prevailing atmospheric conditions with regard to heat or cold, wetness or dryness, etc. **2** (*used before a noun*) windward. ✻ **make heavy weather of** *informal* to have unnecessary difficulty in doing or completing. **under the weather** *informal* mildly ill or depressed.

weather[2] *v* **1** to expose or subject to atmospheric conditions. **2** to bear up against and come safely through. **3** to undergo or be resistant to change by weathering.

weather-beaten *adj* **1** worn or damaged by exposure to weather. **2** toughened or tanned by the weather.

weatherboard *n* **1** any of a series of boards fixed horizontally, each overlapping the one below, to form a protective outdoor wall covering that will throw off water. **2** a sloping board fixed to the bottom of a door for excluding rain, snow, etc. ➤➤ **weatherboarding** *n.*

weathercock *n* a weather vane, *esp* one in the figure of a cockerel.

weather eye *n* a constant and shrewd alertness: *Keep a weather eye on the situation.*

weather house *n* a model house containing two figures, one of which emerges in fine weather, the other when it rains.

weathering *n* the action of wind, rain, frost, etc in altering the colour, texture, composition, or form of exposed objects.

weatherman *n* (*pl* **weathermen**) a man, *esp* a meteorologist, who reports and forecasts the weather, usu on the radio or television.

weather station *n* a station for taking, recording, and reporting meteorological observations.

weather strip *n* a strip of material used to exclude rain, snow, and cold air from the joints of a door or window.

weather vane *n* a movable device attached to an elevated structure, e.g. a spire, in order to show the direction of the wind.

weather-wise *adj* **1** skilful in forecasting the weather. **2** skilful in forecasting changes in opinion or feeling.

weatherwoman *n* (*pl* **weatherwomen**) a woman, *esp* a meteorologist, who reports and forecasts the weather, usu on the radio or television.

weatherworn *adj* weather-beaten.

weave[1] *v* (*past tense* **wove,** *past part.* **wove** *or* **woven**) **1a** to form (cloth) by interlacing warp and weft threads. **b** to interlace (e.g. threads) to form cloth. **c** to make (e.g. a basket or wreath) by intertwining. **2** of a spider or an insect: to spin (a web, cocoon, etc). **3** to interlace to form a texture, fabric, or design. **4a** to produce by elaborately combining elements into a coherent whole. **b** (*usu* + in/into) to introduce as an appropriate element.

weave[2] *n* a pattern or method for interlacing the threads of woven fabrics.

weave[3] *v* to move in a winding or zigzag course, *esp* to avoid obstacles.

weaver *n* **1** somebody who weaves, *esp* as an occupation. **2** an African or Asian bird that resembles a finch and constructs elaborate nests of interlaced vegetation.

weaverbird *n* = WEAVER (2).

web *n* **1** the netlike structure spun by most spiders and used as a resting place and a trap for prey. **2** an intricate structure suggestive of something woven; a network. **3** (**the Web**) the World Wide Web. **4** a tissue or membrane of an animal or plant, *esp* that uniting fingers or toes. **5a** a continuous sheet of paper manufactured or undergoing manufacture on a paper machine. **b** a roll of such paper for use in a rotary printing press. **6** a woven fabric, *esp* a length of fabric while on a loom. **7** a snare or entanglement.

webbed *adj* having or denoting toes or fingers joined by a web.

webbing *n* a strong narrow closely woven tape used for straps, upholstery, or harnesses.

webcam /'webkam/ *n* **1** a web page that displays images or videos produced by a digital camera connected to a computer. **2** a camera that produces such images.

webcast *n* a live broadcast on the Internet. ➤➤ **webcasting** *n.*

weber /'vaybə/ *n* the SI unit of magnetic flux.

web offset *n* offset printing by a web press.

web page *n* a hypertext document that can be accessed via the World Wide Web.

web press *n* a press that prints a continuous roll of paper.

web site *n* a group of related web pages giving information about a particular subject.

wed *v* (**wedding,** *past tense and past part.* **wedded** *or* **wed**) **1a** of a minister, priest, etc: to marry (two people). **b** to get married to (somebody). **c** to get married. **2** to unite (two things) as if by marriage.

we'd *contr* **1** we had. **2** we would. **3** we should.

wedded *adj* **1** of marriage; conjugal or connubial. **2** (+ to) strongly emotionally attached to; committed to.

wedding *n* **1** a marriage ceremony, usu with its accompanying festivities. **2** (*usu in combination*) a wedding anniversary or its celebration: *our silver wedding.*

wedding breakfast *n* a celebratory meal that follows a marriage ceremony.

wedding cake *n* a rich iced cake, typically in two or more tiers, served at a wedding reception.

wedding ring *n* a ring, usu of gold, given by one marriage partner to the other during the wedding ceremony and worn thereafter to signify marital status.

wedge[1] *n* **1** a piece of wood, metal, etc tapered to a thin edge and used e.g. for splitting wood or securing heavy objects. **2** something wedge-shaped. **3** a shoe with a wedge-shaped sole raised at the heel and tapering towards the toe. **4** an iron golf club with a broad face angled for maximum loft. **5** something causing a breach or separation: *Financial problems drove a wedge between them.* ✱ **thin end of the wedge** something apparently insignificant that is the forerunner of a more important development.

wedge[2] *v* **1** to secure with or as if with a wedge. **2** (+ in/into) to force into a narrow space.

Wedgwood *n trademark* a type of fine ceramic ware made orig by Josiah Wedgwood (d.1795) and typically decorated with a classical cameo-like design in white relief.

wedlock *n* the state of being married; marriage. ✱ **out of wedlock** *dated* with the natural parents not legally married to each other: *born out of wedlock.*

Wednesday *n* the day of the week following Tuesday.

wee[1] *adj* (**weer, weest**) *chiefly Scot* very small.

wee[2] *n chiefly Brit, informal* urine or an act of passing urine.

wee[3] *v* (**wees, weed, weeing**) *chiefly Brit, informal* to urinate.

weed[1] *n* **1** a wild plant that grows where it is not wanted, *esp* among cultivated plants. **2** *informal* a weak or unattractively thin person. **3** *informal* **a** (**the weed**) tobacco. **b** cannabis.

weed[2] *v* **1** to clear (an area) of weeds. **2** (+ out) to remove (harmful or undesirable people or things). ⪢ **weeder** *n.*

weedkiller *n* a substance used for killing weeds.

weeds *pl n* = WIDOW'S WEEDS.

weedy *adj* (**-ier, -iest**) **1** covered with or consisting of weeds. **2** *informal* weak, thin, and ineffectual. ⪢ **weediness** *n.*

week[1] *n* **1** a period of seven consecutive days. **2** the working days during each seven-day period. **3** a seven-day period beginning with a specified day or containing a specified event.

week[2] *adv chiefly Brit* at a time that is seven days before or after a specified day: *Tuesday week.*

weekday *n* any day of the week except Saturday and Sunday.

weekend[1] *n* Saturday and Sunday.

weekend[2] *v informal* to spend the weekend, e.g. at a place away from home. ⪢ **weekender** *n.*

weekly[1] *adv* **1** every week. **2** once a week. **3** by the week.

weekly[2] *adj* **1** occurring, appearing, or done weekly. **2** calculated by the week.

weekly[3] *n* (*pl* **-ies**) a weekly newspaper or periodical.

weeny *adj* (**-ier, -iest**) *informal* exceptionally small; tiny.

weep[1] *v* (*past tense and past part.* **wept**) **1** to express grief or other emotion by shedding tears. **2** *esp* of a wound: to exude a liquid, pus, etc slowly. ⪢ **weeper** *n.*

weep[2] *n* a period of weeping.

weepie *or* **weepy** *n* (*pl* **-ies**) *informal* a sad or sentimental film, play, or book.

weeping *adj* of a tree or shrub: having slender drooping branches: *a weeping willow.*

weepy[1] *adj* (**-ier, -iest**) *informal* inclined to weep; tearful. ⪢ **weepily** *adv,* **weepiness** *n.*

weepy[2] *n* = WEEPIE.

weevil *n* a small beetle with a long snout bearing jaws at the tip, *esp* one that is harmful to grain, fruit, and plants.

w.e.f. *abbr* with effect from.

weft *n* the thread or yarn that interlaces the warp in a fabric; the crosswise yarn in weaving.

Wehrmacht /'veəmakht/ *n* the German armed forces just before and during World War II.

weigh *v* **1a** to ascertain the heaviness of, *esp* by using scales. **b** to have weight or a specified weight. **2** (*often* + out) to measure (a definite quantity) on scales. **3** (*often* + up) to consider carefully in order to reach a conclusion. **4a** (*often* + down) to make heavy; to weight. **b** (+ down) to oppress with something burdensome. **5** to be considered important; to count. **6** (*often* + on/upon) to press down with or as if with a weight. ✱ **weigh anchor** to pull up an anchor preparatory to sailing. ⪢ **weighable** *adj,* **weigher** *n.*

weighbridge *n* a large scale used for weighing vehicles, usu consisting of a plate level with the surface of a road onto which the vehicles are driven.

weigh in *v* **1** of a jockey, boxer, etc: to be weighed before or after a race or match. **2** *informal* to make a contribution; to join in.

weigh-in *n* (*pl* **weigh-ins**) the act or an instance of officially weighing a jockey, boxer, etc before or after a race or match.

weight[1] *n* **1** the heaviness of a quantity or body; the amount that something weighs. **2** the force with which a body is attracted towards the earth by gravitation and which equals the mass of the body multiplied by the gravitational acceleration. **3a** a system of units of weight or mass. **b** any of the units used in such a system. **c** a piece of metal of known weight for use in weighing articles. **4a** something heavy; a load. **b** a heavy object used to hold or press something down or as a counterbalance. **5** a heavy object lifted as an athletic exercise or contest. **6** the quality of a fabric, e.g. lightness or closeness of weave, that makes it suitable for a particular use. **7** a burden or pressure. **8** excessive fatness. **9** relative importance, authority, or influence.

weight[2] *v* **1** to load, make heavy, or hold down with or as if with a weight. **2** to arrange in such a way as to create a bias.

weighting *n* **1a** an allowance made to compensate for something that has a distorting effect. **b** the amount of such an allowance. **2** *Brit* an additional sum paid on top of wages or salary, *esp* to offset the higher cost of living in a particular area.

weightless *adj* of a body or object in a spacecraft or in space: not apparently acted on by gravity. ⪢ **weightlessly** *adv,* **weightlessness** *n.*

weightlifting *n* a sport that involves competitors lifting progressively heavier barbells or other weights. ⪢ **weightlifter** *n.*

weight training *n* physical training involving the lifting of weights.

weight-watcher *n* somebody who is dieting to lose weight. ⯮ **weight-watching** *n and adj.*

weighty *adj* (**-ier, -iest**) **1** having importance, influence, or consequence; momentous. **2** heavy, *esp* in proportion to bulk. **3** burdensome or onerous. ⯮ **weightily** *adv,* **weightiness** *n.*

Weil's disease /vielz/ *n* a bacterial infection transmitted by rats.

Weimaraner /'viemərahnə/ *n* a gundog of a short-haired breed with a grey coat originating in Germany.

weir *n* **1** a dam in a stream to raise the water level or control its flow. **2** a fence or enclosure set in a waterway for trapping fish.

weird *adj* **1** suggestive of or caused by the supernatural. **2** *informal* very strange or bizarre. ⯮ **weirdly** *adv,* **weirdness** *n.*

weirdo *n* (*pl* **-os**) *informal* somebody who is very strange or eccentric.

weka /'wekə/ *n* a large flightless bird found in New Zealand.

welch *v* see WELSH.

welcome[1] *interj* used to express a greeting to a guest or newcomer on his or her arrival.

welcome[2] *n* a greeting or reception on arrival or first appearance.

welcome[3] *adj* **1** received gladly into one's presence or companionship. **2** received with gladness, *esp* because fulfilling a need. **3** willingly permitted or given the right. ✻ **you're welcome** used as a reply to an expression of thanks.

welcome[4] *v* **1** to greet (somebody) hospitably and with courtesy. **2** to receive or accept (something) with pleasure. ⯮ **welcomer** *n.*

weld[1] *v* **1a** to fuse (metallic parts) together by heating and/or hammering. **b** to unite (plastics) by heating or using a chemical solvent. **c** to repair or produce by or as if by welding. **2** to unite closely or inseparably. ⯮ **welder** *n.*

weld[2] *n* a welded joint.

welfare *n* **1** well-being. **2** aid in the form of money or necessities for those not able to provide for themselves, e.g. through poverty, age, or handicap. **3** = WELFARE WORK. ✻ **on welfare** *chiefly NAm* receiving financial help from the state.

welfare state *n* a social system in which the state assumes responsibility for the individual and social welfare of its citizens, e.g. through the provision of pensions, benefits, health care, etc.

welfare work *n* organized efforts to improve the living conditions of the poor, elderly, etc. ⯮ **welfare worker** *n.*

welkin *n literary* **1** the sky. **2** heaven.

well[1] *adv* (**better, best**) **1a** in a good or proper manner; rightly or satisfactorily. **b** with skill or aptitude. **2** in a kind or friendly manner; favourably. **3** in a prosperous or affluent manner. **4** thoroughly or fully. **5** with good reason. **6** much or considerably. **7** in all likelihood; indeed. **8** *Brit, informal* very. ✻ **well away 1** *informal* making good progress. **2** *informal* drunk. **well out of** lucky to be free from. **well up on** very knowledgeable about.

Usage note

Adjectives such as *well-known, well-mannered,* etc should always be spelt with a hyphen when used before a noun: *a well-known story.* The hyphen is not usually necessary when the adjective is used after a verb: *As is probably well known to most of you…*

well[2] *adj* (**better, best**) **1** satisfactory or pleasing. **2** advisable or desirable. **3** healthy, *esp* cured or recovered. **4** giving cause for thankfulness; fortunate. ⯮ **wellness** *n.*

well[3] *interj* **1** used to express surprise, indignation, or resignation. **2** used to indicate a pause in talking or to introduce a remark.

well[4] *n* **1** a pit, shaft, or hole sunk into the earth to reach a supply of water or a natural deposit, e.g. oil or gas. **2** a vessel, space, or hole made to contain liquid. **3** a source from which something springs. **4** an open space extending vertically through the floors of a structure, e.g. for stairs or a lift.

well[5] *v* **1** of liquid: to rise to the surface and usu flow forth. **2** to rise to the surface like a flood of liquid.

we'll *contr* **1** we will. **2** we shall.

well-advised *adj* acting with or showing wisdom; prudent.

well-appointed *adj* having good and complete facilities, furniture, etc.

well-behaved *adj* showing proper manners or conduct.

well-being *n* the state of being happy, healthy, or prosperous.

well-disposed *adj* having a favourable or sympathetic disposition.

well done *interj* used to express congratulations.

well-done *adj* **1** of food, *esp* meat: cooked thoroughly. **2** completed, performed, or done properly or satisfactorily.

well dressing *n* the custom of decorating village wells with intricate designs or scenes made with flowers, an annual tradition in parts of Britain.

well-endowed *adj informal* of a woman: having large breasts.

well-found *adj* properly equipped.

wellhead *n* **1** the source of a spring or stream. **2** the top of or a structure built over a well.

well-heeled *adj informal* having a great deal of money; wealthy.

well-hung *adj* **1** *informal* of a man: having a large penis or large genitals. **2** of game: having been hung for a relatively long time.

wellie *n* see WELLY.

wellies *pl n informal* wellington boots.

wellington *n* = WELLINGTON BOOT.

wellington boot *n chiefly Brit* a waterproof rubber boot that usu reaches the knee.

Word history

named after Arthur Wellesley, first Duke of *Wellington* d.1852, British general and statesman. Orig denoting a kind of knee-length leather boot worn by Wellington.

well-knit *adj* well constructed, *esp* having a compact usu muscular physique.

well-known *adj* fully or widely known; famous.

well-meaning *adj* having or based on good intentions though often failing.

well-meant *adj* based on good intentions.

well-nigh *adv archaic or literary* almost or nearly.

well-off *adj* **1** prosperous or rich. **2** in a favourable or fortunate situation. **3** well provided: *We're well off for shops.*

well-oiled *adj informal* drunk.

well-preserved *adj* of an older person: retaining a youthful appearance.

well-read *adj* of a person: having read a lot either on a particular subject or on a wide range of subjects.

well-rounded *adj* **1** having a pleasantly curved or rounded shape. **2** having or denoting a background of broad experience or education. **3** agreeably complete and well constructed.

well-spoken *adj* speaking clearly, courteously, and usu with a refined accent.

wellspring *n* **1** a source of continual supply. **2** a spring that is the source of a stream.

well-thumbed *adj* of a book: showing signs of having been read or used many times.

well-to-do *adj* moderately rich; prosperous.

well-tried *adj* thoroughly tested and found reliable.

well-turned *adj* **1** pleasingly formed; shapely. **2** concisely and appropriately expressed.

well-upholstered *adj informal* of a person: plump.

well-wisher *n* somebody who feels or expresses goodwill towards a person, cause, etc.

well-worn *adj* **1** having been much used or worn. **2** of a phrase, joke, idea, etc: made trite by overuse; hackneyed.

welly *or* **wellie** *n Brit, informal* **1** see WELLIES. **2** concentration or power.

Welsh *n* **1** (**the Welsh**) (*used as pl*) the people of Wales. **2** the Celtic language spoken by this people. ➤➤ **Welsh** *adj*, **Welshman** *n*, **Welshness** *n*, **Welshwoman** *n*.

welsh *or* **welch** *v* (*usu* + on) to evade an obligation, *esp* payment of a debt. ➤➤ **welsher** *n*.

Welsh corgi *n* = CORGI.

Welsh dresser *n* a dresser that has open shelves above a flat surface with drawers and small cupboards below.

Welsh rarebit *n* a snack of melted cheese, mixed with seasonings, on toast.

Word history

alteration of *Welsh rabbit*, prob because the earlier term was too obscure or demeaning. *Welsh rabbit* probably comes from the association of Wales with cheese, and the idea of dairy products being a poor substitute for meat.

welt *n* **1** a strip, usu of leather, between a shoe sole and upper through which they are fastened together. **2** a doubled edge, strip, insert, or seam, e.g. on a garment, for ornament or reinforcement. **3** a ridge or lump raised on the body, usu caused by a heavy blow; a weal.

Weltanschauung /'veltahnshow·oong/ *n* (*pl* **Weltanschauungen** /-ən/) a particular conception of the nature and purpose of the world; a philosophy of life.

welter[1] *n* **1** a state of wild disorder; a turmoil. **2** a chaotic mass or jumble.

welter[2] *v* **1a** to writhe or toss. **b** to wallow. **2** to become soaked in something, e.g. blood.

welterweight *n* a weight in boxing and wrestling between lightweight and middleweight.

wen[1] *n* a cyst formed by obstruction of a sebaceous gland and filled with fatty material.

wen[2] *or* **wyn** *n* a letter used in Old English with the value of Modern English *w*.

wench *n archaic or humorous* a young woman; a girl.

wend *v* to proceed on (one's way).

wendy house *n* (*often* **Wendy house**) *chiefly Brit* a small toy house for children to play in.

Wensleydale *n* **1** a crumbly mild-flavoured English cheese. **2** a sheep of a breed with long wool.

went *v* past tense of GO[1].

wept *v* past tense and past part. of WEEP[1].

were *v* second person sing. past, plural past, and past subjunctive of BE.

we're *contr* we are.

weren't *contr* were not.

werewolf /'weəwoolf, 'wiəwoolf/ *n* (*pl* **werewolves**) in folklore, a person who periodically transforms into a wolf or is capable of assuming a wolf's form at will.

wert *v* archaic second person sing. past of BE.

Wesleyanism *n* the system of Methodism taught by John Wesley (d.1791). ➤➤ **Wesleyan** *adj and n*.

west[1] *n* **1** the direction 180° from east that is the general direction of sunset. **2a** regions or countries lying to the west. **b** (*usu* **the West**) the western part of the world, historically and culturally contrasted with the East. ➤➤ **westbound** *adj and adv*.

west[2] *adj and adv* **1** at, towards, or coming from the west. **2** of the wind: blowing from the west. ✱ **west by north/south** in a position or direction between west and west-northwest (or west-southwest).

westerly[1] *adj and adv* **1** in a western position or direction. **2** of a wind: blowing from the west.

westerly[2] *n* (*pl* **-ies**) a wind blowing from the west.

western[1] *adj* **1** in or towards the west; inhabiting the west. **2** (*often* **Western**) of or stemming from the traditions of Europe or N America. ➤➤ **westernmost** *adj*.

western[2] *n* (*often* **Western**) a novel, film, etc dealing with cowboys, frontier life, etc in the western USA, *esp* during the latter half of the 19th cent.

Western Church *n* the Roman Catholic or Protestant branches of Christianity as opposed to the Eastern or Eastern Orthodox Churches.

westernize *or* **-ise** *v* **1** to cause to adopt or be influenced by the culture, economics, politics, etc of N America or Europe. **2** to become westernized. ➤➤ **westernization** *n*.

West Indian *n* a native or inhabitant of the W Indies, or a person descended from W Indians. ➤➤ **West Indian** *adj*.

westing *n* **1** distance due west in longitude from the preceding point of measurement. **2** westerly progress.

west-northwest *n* the direction midway between west and northwest. ➤➤ **west-northwest** *adj and adv*.

west-southwest *n* the direction midway between west and southwest. ➤➤ **west-southwest** *adj and adv*.

westward *adv and adj* towards the west; in a direction going west. ➤➤ **westwards** *adv*.

wet[1] *adj* (**wetter, wettest**) **1** covered or soaked with liquid, e.g. water. **2** of weather: rainy. **3** of paint, cement, etc: not yet dry or set. **4** involving the use or presence of liquid. **5** *Brit, informal* of a person: feeble, ineffectual, or dull. **6** *informal* permitting the sale or consumption of alcoholic drink. ✱ **wet behind the ears** *informal* immature or inexperienced. ➤➤ **wetly** *adv*, **wetness** *n*.

wet[2] *n* **1** moisture or wetness. **2** (**the wet**) rainy weather; rain. **3** *Brit, informal* a feeble, ineffectual, or dull person; a drip. **4** *Brit* a moderate Conservative politician.

wet[3] *v* (**wetting,** *past tense and past part.* **wet** *or* **wetted**) **1** to make wet. **2** to urinate in or on. ✱ **wet one's whistle** *informal* to have a drink, *esp* an alcoholic one.

weta /'waytə/ *n* a large wingless long-horned New Zealand insect resembling a grasshopper.

wet blanket *n informal* a person who spoils other people's fun, e.g. by a lack of enthusiasm.

wet cell *n* a battery cell whose electrolyte is a liquid: compare DRY CELL.

wet dream *n* an erotic dream that results in the involuntary ejaculation of semen.

wet fish *n* fresh uncooked fish, *esp* as opposed to dried, cured, or cooked fish.

wet fly *n* an artificial angling fly designed to be used under water.

wether *n* a male sheep castrated before sexual maturity.

wetland *n* land, e.g. tidal flats or swamps, covered with soil that is more or less permanently saturated.

wetlands *pl n* = WETLAND.

wet look *n* a glossy sheen that suggests surface wetness, e.g. on leather or plastic. ➤➤ **wet-look** *adj.*

wet nurse *n* a woman who cares for and breast-feeds a child or children she did not give birth to.

wet rot *n* **1** a fungus that attacks moist wood and causes it to decay. **2** the resulting state of decay.

wet suit *n* a close-fitting rubber suit that admits water but retains body heat so as to insulate its wearer, e.g. a diver, in cold water: compare DRYSUIT.

we've *contr* we have.

whack[1] *v informal* **1** to strike with a smart or resounding blow. **2** to defeat. **3** to place or insert roughly, casually, or quickly. **4** *chiefly NAm* to murder. ➤➤ **whacker** *n.*

whack[2] *n informal* **1** a smart resounding blow, or the sound of such a blow. **2** *Brit* a portion or share. **3** an attempt or go. ✱ **out of whack** not functioning properly; not working at all. **top/full whack** *chiefly Brit* the maximum amount.

whacked *adj* **1** *chiefly Brit, informal* (*often* + out) completely exhausted. **2** *chiefly NAm, informal* (*often* + out) intoxicated by drugs.

whacking *adj Brit, informal* extremely big; whopping.

whacky *adj* see WACKY.

whale *n* (*pl* **whales** *or* **whale**) an aquatic mammal that superficially resembles a very large fish, having a tail modified as a paddle. ✱ **a whale of a** *informal* an exceptionally good or large example of. **have a whale of a time** to have an exceptionally enjoyable time.

whalebone *n* a horny substance found in two rows of plates attached along the upper jaw of baleen whales and formerly used in strips for stiffening corsets.

whalebone whale *n* = BALEEN WHALE.

whaler *n* a person or ship engaged in whaling.

whaling *n* the occupation of catching and processing whales for oil, food, etc.

wham[1] *n informal* a forceful blow, or the sound made by such a blow.

wham[2] *interj informal* used to express the noise of a forceful blow or impact.

wham[3] *v* (**whammed, whamming**) *informal* to throw or strike with a loud impact.

whammy *n* (*pl* **-ies**) *informal* something that has a bad effect.

whap[1] *v NAm* see WHOP[1].

whap[2] *n NAm* see WHOP[2].

whare /'wori/ *n* **1** a Maori house of traditional design. **2** *NZ* a hut or shack.

wharf *n* (*pl* **wharves** *or* **wharfs**) a structure built along or out from the shore of navigable water so that ships may load and unload.

wharfage *n* **1** the use of a wharf. **2** a charge for this.

wharfie *n Aus, NZ, informal* a docker.

wharfinger /'wawfinjə/ *n* the owner or manager of a commercial wharf.

wharves *n* pl of WHARF.

what[1] *pron* (*pl* **what**) **1** used to ask about the identity, nature, purpose, occupation, etc of something or somebody. **2** used to ask for repetition of something not properly heard or understood. **3** used to express surprise or excitement. **4** used to direct attention to a statement that the speaker is about to make: *Guess what?* **5** that which; the one that. **6** whatever. **7** used in exclamations: how much. ✱ **what about** used to make suggestions. **what for 1** for what purpose or reason; why. **2** *informal* punishment, *esp* by blows or by a sharp reprimand: *She gave him what for.* **what have you** any of various other things that might also be mentioned. **what if 1** what will or would be the result if. **2** what does it matter if. **what it takes** the qualities or resources needed for success or for attainment of a goal. **what not** what have you. **what of it** what does it matter. **what's his/her/its name** used to replace a forgotten name. **what's what** the true state of things. **what with** having as a contributory circumstance or circumstances: *I'm very busy what with all this extra paperwork.*

what[2] *adv* in what respect?; how much?

what[3] *adj* **1a** used with a following noun as an adjective equivalent in meaning to the interrogative pronoun *what*: *What minerals do we export?* **b** how remarkable or striking: *What a suggestion!* **2** the … that; as much or as many … as: *What little I know.*

whatever[1] *pron* **1a** anything or everything that. **b** no matter what. **2** *informal* what in the world?

whatever[2] *adj* **1a** any … that; all … that. **b** no matter what. **2** used after a noun with *any* or with a negative: of any kind at all.

whatnot *n* **1** *informal* other usu related goods, objects, etc. **2** a lightweight open set of shelves for bric-a-brac.

whatsit *n informal* somebody or something that is of unspecified or unknown character, or whose name has been forgotten.

whatsoever *pron and adj* whatever.

wheal *n* see WEAL[1].

wheat *n* a cereal grass cultivated in temperate areas for its grain, which yields a fine white flour.

wheatear *n* a small white-rumped Eurasian bird related to the thrush.

wheaten *adj* made of wheat.

wheat germ *n* the embryo of the wheat kernel separated in milling and used *esp* as a source of vitamins.

wheatmeal *n* brown flour made from wheat with some bran and germ taken out.

wheedle *v* **1** to use soft words or flattery. **2** to influence, persuade, or entice by wheedling. ➤➤ **wheedler** *n.*

wheel[1] *n* **1** a circular disc of hard material, or a circular frame joined to a central hub by spokes, that is attached to and capable of turning on an axle. **2** a wheel that controls the steering of a ship or vehicle. **3** an imaginary turning wheel symbolizing the inconstancy of fortune. **4** a curving or circular movement. **5** a rotation or turn about an axis or centre. **6** (*in pl*) the moving or controlling parts of something compared to a machine: *the wheels of government.* **7** *informal* (*in pl*) a motor vehicle, *esp* a car. ➤➤ **wheelless** *adj.*

wheel[2] *v* **1** to turn or cause to turn as if on an axis; to revolve or rotate. **2** to change or cause to change direction as if revolving on a pivot. **3** to move or extend in a circle or curve. **4a** to push (a wheeled vehicle). **b** to convey or move (somebody or something) on wheels or in a wheeled vehicle. ✱ **wheel and deal** to pursue one's own commercial interests, *esp* in a shrewd or unscrupulous manner.

wheelbarrow *n* a load-carrying device that consists of a shallow box supported at one end by a wheel and at the other by legs or handles.

wheelbase *n* the distance between the front and rear axles of a vehicle.

wheelchair *n* a chair mounted on wheels for somebody unable to walk.

wheel clamp *n* a clamp which is locked onto a wheel of an illegally parked vehicle to immobilize it until a fine is paid. ➤➤ **wheel-clamp** *v.*

wheeler *n* (*in combination*) a vehicle that has the specified number of wheels: *a three-wheeler.*

wheeler and dealer *n* = WHEELER-DEALER.

wheeler-dealer *n* a shrewd operator, *esp* in business or politics. ➤➤ **wheeler-dealing** *n.*

wheelhouse *n* a deckhouse for a vessel's helmsman.

wheelie *n informal* a manoeuvre in which a motorcycle or bicycle is momentarily balanced on its rear wheel.

wheelie bin *or* **wheely bin** *n* a large wheeled dustbin with a hinged lid.

wheelspin *n* the rapid turning of a vehicle's wheels without getting any grip.

wheelwright *n* somebody who makes or repairs wheels, *esp* wooden ones for carts.

wheely bin *n* see WHEELIE BIN.

wheeze[1] *v* **1** to breathe with difficulty, usu with a whistling sound. **2** to make a sound like that of wheezing. ➤➤ **wheezer** *n.*

wheeze[2] *n* **1** a sound of wheezing. **2** *Brit, informal* a cunning trick or a clever scheme. ➤➤ **wheezily** *adv,* **wheeziness** *n,* **wheezy** *adj.*

whelk *n* a large marine snail, *esp* an edible one.

whelp[1] *n* **1** a young dog or similar mammal. **2** a disagreeable or impudent child or youth.

whelp[2] *v* to give birth to (e.g. a puppy).

when[1] *adv* **1** at what time? **2a** at or during which time. **b** and then; whereupon.

when[2] *conj* **1a** at or during the time that. **b** as soon as. **c** whenever. **2** in the event that; if. **3a** considering that. **b** in spite of the fact that; although.

when[3] *pron* what or which time.

whence *adv and conj formal or archaic* **1a** from where?. **b** from which place, source, or cause. **2** to the place from which.

whenever[1] *conj* **1** at every or whatever time. **2** in any circumstance.

whenever[2] *adv informal* when in the world?

whensoever[1] *conj formal* whenever.

whensoever[2] *adv formal* at any time whatever.

where[1] *adv* **1a** at, in, or to what place? **b** at, in, or to what situation, direction, or respect? **2** at, in, or to which place.

where[2] *conj* **1a** at, in, or to the place at which. **b** wherever. **c** in a case, situation, or respect in which. **2** whereas or while.

where[3] *n* what place or point?

whereabouts[1] *adv and conj* in what vicinity.

whereabouts[2] *pl n* (*used as sing. or pl*) the place or general locality where a person or thing is.

whereas *conj* **1** in view of the fact that; since. **2** while on the contrary; although.

whereat *conj* **1** *formal or archaic* at or towards which. **2** in consequence of which; whereupon.

whereby *conj* **1** in accordance with which. **2** *formal* by which means.

wherefore[1] *adv formal* **1** for what reason; why. **2** for that reason; therefore.

wherefore[2] *n* a reason or cause.

wherefrom *conj archaic* from which.

wherein[1] *adv formal* in what; how.

wherein[2] *conj formal* in which; where.

whereof *conj, pronoun, and adv formal* of what, which, or whom.

whereon *adv and conj archaic* on which or what.

wheresoever *conj formal* wherever.

whereto *adv and conj formal or archaic* to which or what; whither.

whereupon *adv and conj* closely following and in consequence of which.

wherever[1] *adv* where in the world?

wherever[2] *conj* at, in, or to every or whatever place.

wherewith *conj formal or archaic* with or by means of which.

wherewithal *n* means or resources; *specif* money.

wherry *n* (*pl* **-ies**) **1** a long light rowing boat used to transport passengers on rivers and about harbours. **2** *Brit* a large light barge, lighter, or fishing boat. ➤➤ **wherryman** *n.*

whet *v* (**whetted, whetting**) **1** to sharpen (a blade) by rubbing on or with something, e.g. a stone. **2** to make keen or more acute; to stimulate.

whether *conj* **1** used to indicate an indirect question involving alternatives. **2** used to indicate a choice between two alternatives. **3** used to indicate indifference between alternatives.

Usage note

whether *and* if. See note at IF[1].

whetstone *n* a stone for sharpening an edge, e.g. of a chisel.

whey *n* the watery part of milk separated from the curd, *esp* in cheese-making.

whey-faced *adj* having a pale face, e.g. from illness, shock, or fear.

which[1] *adj* **1** being what one or ones out of a known or limited group? **2** whichever. **3** used to introduce a non-restrictive relative clause by modifying a noun referring to a preceding word, phrase, or clause: *He may come, in which case I'll ask him.*

which[2] *pron* (*pl* **which**) **1** what one out of a known or specified group? **2** whichever. **3** used to introduce a restrictive or non-restrictive clause, *esp* in reference to an animal, thing, or idea. **4** used in reference to a previous clause: *She can sing, which is an advantage.*

whichever[1] *pron* (*pl* **whichever**) **1** whatever one out of a group. **2** no matter which. **3** *informal* which in the world?

whichever[2] *adj* being whatever one or ones out of a group; no matter which.

whicker *v* to neigh or whinny. ➤➤ **whicker** *n.*

whiff[1] *n* **1** a slight or passing odour. **2** a slight trace. **3** a quick puff or slight gust.

whiff[2] *v* **1** to emit a whiff or whiffs. **2** to inhale, smell, or sniff. **3** *Brit, informal* to smell unpleasant.

whiffle *v* **1** to blow with or emit a light whistling sound. **2** to be undecided; to vacillate. ➤➤ **whiffler** *n.*

Whig *n* **1** a member or supporter of a major British political group of the 18th cent. and early 19th cent. seeking to limit royal authority and increase parliamentary power: compare TORY. **2** an American favouring independence from Britain during the American Revolution. ⋙ **Whiggery** *n,* **Whiggish** *adj,* **Whiggism** *n.*

Word history

short for *Whiggamore*, a member of a largely Presbyterian Scottish group that marched to Edinburgh in 1648 to oppose the court party, prob from Scottish *whig* to drive + *more* MARE[1]. Both *Whig* and *Tory* were introduced as derogatory nicknames for political groups in England during the controversy about the succession to the throne in 1679–80. *Whig* soon lost its derogatory sense and was adopted as the name of one of the two major British political groups until it was superseded by *Liberal* in the mid-19th cent.

while[1] *n* **1** a period of time. **2** the time and effort used; trouble: *It's worth your while.*

while[2] *conj* **1a** during the time that. **b** providing that; as long as. **2a** when on the other hand; whereas. **b** in spite of the fact that; although.

while away *v* to pass (time) in a leisurely, often pleasant, manner.

whilst *conj chiefly Brit* while.

whim *n* a sudden, capricious, or eccentric idea or impulse; a fancy.

whimbrel *n* a small Eurasian curlew.

whimper *v* **1** to make a low plaintive whining sound. **2** to make a petulant complaint or protest. ⋙ **whimper** *n,* **whimperer** *n.*

whimsey *n* see WHIMSY.

whimsical *adj* **1** resulting from or suggesting whimsy; quizzical or playful. **2** full of whims; capricious. ⋙ **whimsicality** *n,* **whimsically** *adv.*

whimsy *or* **whimsey** *n* (*pl* **-ies** *or* **-eys**) **1** an affected or fanciful device, creation, or style, *esp* in writing or art. **2** a whim or caprice.

whin *n* furze.

whinchat *n* a small brown and buff Eurasian songbird.

whine[1] *n* **1** a prolonged high-pitched cry, usu expressive of distress or pain, or a sound resembling such a cry. **2** a querulous or peevish complaint. ⋙ **whiny** *adj.*

whine[2] *v* to utter or make a whine. ⋙ **whiner** *n.*

whinge[1] *v* (**whinges, whingeing, whinged**) *Brit, informal* to complain or moan. ⋙ **whinger** *n.*

whinge[2] *n Brit, informal* a complaint.

whinny *v* (**-ies, -ied**) to utter a gentle neigh or similar sound. ⋙ **whinny** *n.*

whip[1] *v* (**whipped, whipping**) **1** to beat (e.g. eggs or cream) into a froth. **2** to take, pull, or move very quickly and forcefully. **3** to strike (a person or animal) with a whip. **4** to strike (something) as a whiplash does. **5** to thrash about flexibly like a whiplash. **6** to bind or wrap (e.g. a rope or rod) with cord for protection and strength. **7** *informal* to overcome decisively; to defeat. **8** *Brit, informal* to steal. ⋙ **whipper** *n,* **whipping** *n.*

whip[2] *n* **1** an instrument consisting usu of a lash attached to a handle, used for driving animals and for punishment. **2a** somebody appointed by a political party to enforce party discipline and to secure the attendance and votes of party members at important sessions. **b** *Brit* an instruction from such a person to be in attendance for voting. **3** a dessert made by whipping some of the ingredients. **4** a whipping or thrashing motion. **5** a whipper-in. ✱ **the whip hand** the advantage. ⋙ **whiplike** *adj.*

whipcord *n* **1** a thin tough cord made of tightly braided or twisted hemp or catgut. **2** a cotton or worsted cloth with fine diagonal cords or ribs.

whiplash *n* **1** the lash of a whip. **2** injury to the neck resulting from a sudden sharp whipping movement of the neck and head, e.g. in a car collision.

whipper-in *n* (*pl* **whippers-in**) a huntsman's assistant who keeps the hounds from scattering by use of a whip.

whippersnapper *n informal* an insignificant but impudent person, *esp* a child.

whippet *n* a dog of a small slender short-haired breed related to the greyhound.

whipping boy *n* a person who is blamed or punished for the mistakes, incompetence, etc of another person; a scapegoat.

whippoorwill /ˈwipəwil/ *n* a N American nightjar that lives in woodland close to open country and feeds on insects.

whip-round *n Brit, informal* a collection of money made usu for a benevolent purpose.

whipsaw[1] *n* a saw with a long flexible blade.

whipsaw[2] *v* (*past tense* **whipsawed,** *past part.* **whipsawn** *or* **whipsawed**) *NAm* **1** to saw with a whipsaw. **2** *informal* **a** to defeat or victimize in two different ways at once. **b** to subject to two difficult or unwelcome situations simultaneously.

whipstitch *n* a small overcasting stitch.

whip up *v* **1** to stir up or stimulate. **2** to produce in a hurry.

whir[1] *v* see WHIRR[1].

whir[2] *n* see WHIRR[2].

whirl[1] *v* **1** to move along a curving or circling course, *esp* with force or speed. **2** to turn or cause to turn abruptly or rapidly round on an axis; to rotate or wheel. **3** to pass, move, or go quickly. **4** of the head: to become giddy or dizzy; to reel.

whirl[2] *n* **1** a rapid rotating or circling movement. **2a** a confused tumult; a bustle. **b** a confused or disturbed mental state. **3** *informal* an experimental or brief attempt; a try: *I'll give it a whirl.*

whirligig *n* **1** a child's toy, e.g. a top, that whirls. **2** a merry-go-round. **3** a whirligig beetle.

whirligig beetle *n* a small black beetle that lives mostly on the surface of water, moving swiftly about in curves.

whirlpool *n* **1** a circular eddy of rapidly moving water with a central depression into which floating objects may be drawn. **2** a bath equipped with a device to produce whirling currents of hot water.

whirlpool bath *n* = WHIRLPOOL (2).

whirlwind *n* **1** a small rapidly rotating windstorm marked by an inward and upward spiral motion. **2** a confused rush; a whirl. **3** (*used before a noun*) happening with great speed or suddenness: *a whirlwind romance.*

whirr[1] *or* **whir** *v* (**whirred, whirring**) to make or revolve or move with a continuous buzzing or vibrating sound.

whirr[2] *or* **whir** *n* a continuous buzzing or vibratory sound made by something in rapid motion.

whisk[1] *n* **1** a small usu hand-held kitchen utensil used for whisking food. **2** a small bunch of flexible strands, e.g. twigs or feathers, attached to a handle for use as a brush. **3** a quick light brushing or whipping motion.

whisk[2] *v* **1** to mix or fluff up (e.g. egg whites) by beating with a whisk. **2** to convey or remove briskly. **3** to brandish lightly; to flick. **4** to move lightly and swiftly.

whisker *n* **1** a long projecting hair or bristle growing near the mouth of an animal, e.g. a cat. **2** (*in pl*) the hair of a man's beard or moustache. **3** *informal* a hair's breadth. ➤➤ **whiskered** *adj*, **whiskery** *adj.*

whiskey *n* (*pl* **-eys**) whisky produced in Ireland or the USA.

whisky *n* (*pl* **-ies**) a spirit made by distilling rye, corn, wheat, or *esp* barley.

whisper[1] *v* **1** to speak softly with little or no vibration of the vocal cords. **2** to make a hissing or rustling sound like whispered speech. ➤➤ **whisperer** *n.*

whisper[2] *n* **1a** the act or an instance of whispering. **b** a hissing or rustling sound like whispered speech. **2a** a rumour. **b** a hint or trace. ➤➤ **whispery** *adj.*

whispering campaign *n* the systematic dissemination by word of mouth of derogatory rumours or charges, *esp* against a candidate for public office.

whispering gallery *n* a gallery or dome in which sounds carry a long way because of its acoustic properties.

whist *n* a card game scored by winning tricks.

whistle[1] *n* **1** a device in which the forcible passage of air, steam, the breath, etc through a slit produces a loud high-pitched sound. **2** a shrill clear sound produced by whistling or by a whistle. ✱ **blow the whistle on** *informal* to report (a person acting wrongly or a wrong act) to an authority. **clean as a whistle** absolutely clean or perfectly clear or obvious.

whistle[2] *v* **1** to make a sound like a whistle by blowing or drawing air through the puckered lips. **2a** to make a sound like a whistle by rapid movement. **b** to move rapidly with or as if with such a sound. **3** to blow or sound a whistle. ✱ **whistle for** *informal* to demand or request in vain. **whistle in the dark** to pretend to be brave despite being afraid. ➤➤ **whistler** *n.*

whistle-blower *n* *informal* somebody who reveals something secret or informs against another person. ➤➤ **whistle-blowing** *n and adj.*

whistle-stop *n* **1** *NAm* a brief personal appearance, *esp* by a political candidate, during the course of a tour. **2** (*used before a noun*) consisting of brief stops in several places: *a whistle-stop tour.*

Whit *n* Whitsuntide.

whit *n* the smallest part imaginable; a bit: *She was not a whit abashed.*

white[1] *adj* **1** of the colour of new snow or milk, the lightest colour from its reflection of all visible rays of light. **2** free from colour. **3** light or pallid in colour. **4** of wine: made from green grapes, or dark grapes with the skins removed, and having a light yellow or amber colour. **5** *Brit* of coffee or tea: containing milk or cream. **6** (*often* **White**) **a** of or denoting a person having pale skin colour. **b** of, intended for, or consisting of white people. **7** free from moral impurity; innocent. **8** of a wedding: in which the bride wears a white dress as a symbol of purity. **9** snowy: *a white Christmas.* **10** ultraconservative or reactionary in political outlook and action: compare RED[1] (6). **11** of light: containing all the wavelengths in the visible range at approximately equal intensities. ✱ **bleed somebody or something white** to deprive somebody of all their money or use up all the resources of something. ➤➤ **whitely** *adv*, **whiteness** *n*, **whitish** *adj.*

white[2] *n* **1** a white colour. **2** the mass of albumin-containing material surrounding the yolk of an egg. **3** the white part of the ball of the eye. **4a** the light-coloured pieces in a board game (e.g. chess) for two players. **b** the player who uses these pieces. **5** (*also in pl*) white clothing, worn *esp* when playing summer sports. **6** a white animal, e.g. a butterfly or pig. **7** (*often* **White**) a person belonging to a light-skinned people.

white admiral *n* a butterfly that has brown wings with white markings.

white ant *n* a termite.

whitebait *n* the young of a herring or sprat eaten whole.

whitebeam *n* a European tree of the rose family with leaves covered in fine white hairs on the undersurface, white flowers, and scarlet berries.

white belt *n* a white belt worn by a beginner in certain martial arts, *esp* judo and karate.

white blood cell *n* any of the white or colourless blood cells that have nuclei, do not contain haemoglobin, and are primarily concerned with body defence mechanisms and repair; a leucocyte: compare RED BLOOD CELL.

whiteboard *n* a smooth white wipeable surface used in lessons, presentations, etc for writing or drawing on.

white cell *n* = WHITE BLOOD CELL.

white-collar *adj* relating to the class of non-manual employees, *esp* those who work in offices: compare BLUE-COLLAR.

whited sepulchre *n* *literary* a hypocrite.

white dwarf *n* a small whitish star of high surface temperature, low brightness, and high density.

white elephant *n* a possession that is troublesome to maintain or no longer of value to its owner.

Word history

from the story that the kings of Siam made a gift of a white elephant to any courtier they disliked, the cost of maintaining one being ruinous.

white feather *n* a mark or symbol of cowardice.

whitefish *n* (*pl* **whitefishes** *or* **whitefish**) a freshwater food fish related to the salmon and trout.

white fish *n* *Brit* any of various edible marine fish with white flesh, e.g. haddock, cod, etc, *esp* as contrasted with oily fish such as mackerel.

white flag *n* a flag of plain white used to signal a request for a truce or as a token of surrender.

whitefly *n* (*pl* **whiteflies** *or* **whitefly**) a small insect that is a harmful plant pest.

white friar *n* a Carmelite friar.

white gold *n* a pale silvery alloy of gold, *esp* with nickel or palladium.

white goods *pl n* **1** major articles of household equipment, e.g. cookers and refrigerators, that are typically finished in white enamel: compare BROWN GOODS. **2** household linen, e.g. sheets, pillow cases, towels, etc.

whitehead *n* *informal* a small whitish lump in the skin due to blockage of an oil gland duct.

white heat *n* **1** a temperature higher than red heat, at which white light is emitted. **2** *informal* a state of intense mental or physical activity.

white hope *n* (*also* **great white hope**) a person expected to bring fame and glory to his or her group, country, team, etc.

white horses *pl n* waves with crests breaking into white foam.

white-hot *adj* **1** at or radiating white heat. **2** *informal* ardently zealous; fervid.

white knight *n* somebody who comes to the rescue of a person or organization, *esp* by saving a company from an unwelcome takeover.

white-knuckle *adj* causing tension, anxiety, or excitement.

white lie *n* a harmless or unimportant lie, e.g. one that is told to avoid hurting somebody's feelings.

white magic *n* magic used for good purposes, e.g. to cure disease.

white meat *n* light-coloured meat, e.g. poultry breast or veal: compare RED MEAT.

white metal *n* any of several alloys based on tin or sometimes lead.

whiten *v* to make or become white or whiter. ➤➤ **whitener** *n*, **whitening** *n*.

white noise *n* sound or electrical noise that has many continuous frequencies of equal intensity.

whiteout *n* a weather condition in a snowy area in which the horizon cannot be seen and only dark objects are discernible.

white out *v* **1** *esp* of snow: to cause to turn white. **2** to cover (a mistake in writing or typing) with correction fluid. **3** to lose colour vision prior to losing consciousness.

White Paper *n* a British government report containing information about or proposals on a particular issue.

white pudding *n* a sausage made from minced pork meat, oatmeal, and fat: compare BLACK PUDDING.

white rose *n* the emblem of Yorkshire and the House of York.

White Russian *n* **1** a Belorussian. **2** an opponent of the Bolsheviks during the Russian Civil War. ➤➤ **White Russian** *adj*.

white sauce *n* a sauce made with milk, cream, or a chicken, veal, or fish stock.

white slave *n* a woman or girl held unwillingly, *esp* abroad, and forced to be a prostitute. ➤➤ **white slaver** *n*, **white slavery** *n*.

white spirit *n* a flammable liquid distilled from petroleum and used *esp* as a solvent and thinner for paints.

white tie *n* formal evening dress for men; *specif* a tail coat and a white bow tie.

white trash *n NAm, derog* poor white people.

white van man *n informal* a male van driver, *esp* a driver of a white delivery van, who drives in an aggressive manner.

whitewash[1] *n* **1** a liquid mixture, e.g. of lime and water or whiting, size, and water, for whitening outside walls or similar surfaces. **2** a deliberate concealment of a mistake or fault. **3** *informal* an overwhelming defeat.

whitewash[2] *v* **1** to apply whitewash to (e.g. a wall). **2** to gloss over or cover up (e.g. a mistake or fault). **3** *informal* to defeat overwhelmingly in a contest. ➤➤ **whitewashed** *adj*, **whitewasher** *n*.

white water *n* fast-moving choppy water, e.g. in breakers or rapids.

white whale *n* = BELUGA (2).

whitey *n* (*pl* **-eys**) *informal, derog* a white person.

whither *adv and conj formal, archaic, or literary* **1** to or towards what place? **2** to the place at, in, or to which. **3** to which place.

whiting[1] *n* (*pl* **whiting**) a marine food fish related to the cod.

whiting[2] *n* washed and ground chalk used *esp* as a pigment and in paper coating.

whitlow *n* a deep usu pus-producing inflammation of the finger or toe, *esp* round the nail.

Whitsun *n* Whitsuntide.

Whit Sunday *n* a Christian feast commemorating the descent of the Holy Spirit at Pentecost, observed on the seventh Sunday after Easter.

Whitsuntide *n* the week beginning with Whit Sunday.

whittle *v* **1a** to pare or cut off chips from the surface of (wood) with a knife. **b** to shape or form in this way. **2** (+ down/away) to reduce, remove, or destroy gradually.

whiz[1] *v* see WHIZZ[1].

whiz[2] *n* see WHIZZ[2].

whiz-bang *n* see WHIZZ-BANG.

whiz kid *n* see WHIZZ KID.

whizz[1] *or* **whiz** *v* **1** to buzz, whirr, or hiss like a speeding object passing through air. **2** *informal* to move, pass, or go swiftly.

whizz[2] *or* **whiz** *n* **1** a whizzing sound. **2** *informal* a swift movement or passage. **3** (*also* **wiz**) *informal* somebody who is very clever or skilful, *esp* in a specified field. **4** *informal* an act of urinating. **5** *Brit, informal* amphetamines.

whizz-bang *or* **whiz-bang** *n chiefly NAm* a person or thing that is conspicuous for noise, speed, or startling effect.

whizz kid *or* **whiz kid** *n* a person who is unusually clever or successful, *esp* at an early age.

WHO *abbr* World Health Organization.

who *pron* (*pl* **who**) **1** what or which person? **2** used to introduce a restrictive or non-restrictive clause in reference to a person or people.

Usage note

who *or* whom? Grammatically, *who* and *whom* are the subject and object forms respectively of the same word: *Who wrote the letter, and to whom was it addressed? Whom*, however, is being increasingly relegated to very formal use in modern English, except after prepositions.

whoa /'woh·ə, woh/ *interj* used as a command, e.g. to a horse, to stand still.

who'd *contr* **1** who would. **2** who had.

whodunit *or* **whodunnit** *n* a play, film, or story dealing with the detection of crime or criminals.

whoever *pron* **1** whatever person. **2** no matter who. **3** *informal* who in the world?

whole[1] *adj* **1** each or all of; total or entire. **2** having all its proper constituents: *whole milk*. **3** free of defect, damage, or injury; unhurt or intact. **4** used for emphasis: seemingly complete or total: *The whole idea is to help, not hinder.* ➤➤ **wholeness** *n*.

whole[2] *n* **1** a totality lacking no part, member, or element. **2** something constituting a complex unity; a coherent system or organization of parts. ✱ **as a whole** considered all together or in general. **on the whole 1** all things considered. **2** in most instances; typically.

whole[3] *adv* **1** in an undivided piece or state. **2** *informal* to a great extent.

wholefood *or* **wholefoods** *n* food in a simple and natural form that has undergone minimal processing and refining.

wholehearted *adj* earnestly committed or devoted; free from all reserve or hesitation. ➤➤ **wholeheartedly** *adv*.

wholemeal *adj* of bread or flour: produced from ground entire wheat kernels.

whole note *n chiefly NAm* = SEMIBREVE.

whole number *n* a number, e.g. 1, 26, or –8, without fractions; an integer.

wholesale[1] *n* the sale of commodities in large quantities usu for resale by a retailer: compare RETAIL[2].

wholesale[2] *adj* performed on a large scale, *esp* without discrimination.

wholesale[3] *adv* **1** being sold at wholesale. **2** on a large scale.

wholesale[4] *v* to sell (commodities) at wholesale. ⋙ **wholesaler** *n.*

wholesome *adj* promoting health of body or mind. ⋙ **wholesomely** *adv,* **wholesomeness** *n.*

whole-wheat *adj* wholemeal.

wholly *adv* **1** to the full or entire extent; completely. **2** to the exclusion of other things; solely.

whom *pron* used as an interrogative or relative, as the object of a verb or preposition, *esp* a preceding preposition: who.

Usage note

whom *or* who? See note at WHO.

whomever *pron formal* whoever.

whoop[1] /woohp/ *n* **1** a loud yell expressive of eagerness, exuberance, or jubilation. **2** /hoohp/ the crowing intake of breath following a paroxysm in whooping cough.

whoop[2] *v* to utter or make a whoop. ✱ **whoop it up** *informal* to celebrate riotously; to carouse.

whoopee[1] *interj informal* used to express exuberance.

whoopee[2] *n informal* boisterous convivial fun. ✱ **make whoopee 1** *informal* to have great fun; to celebrate noisily. **2** *informal* to have sexual intercourse.

whoopee cushion *n* an inflatable trick cushion that produces the noise of breaking wind when sat on.

whooper swan /'hoohpə/ *n* a large white yellow-billed European swan with a loud ringing call.

whooping cough /'hoohping/ *n* an infectious bacterial disease, *esp* of children, marked by a convulsive spasmodic cough sometimes followed by a crowing intake of breath.

whoops *interj* used to express dismay or an apology, *esp* on making a silly mistake.

whoops-a-daisy *interj* = WHOOPS.

whoosh *or* **woosh** *v* to move quickly with a rushing sound. ⋙ **whoosh** *n,* **whooshing** *adj.*

whop[1] (*NAm* **whap**) *v* (**whopped, whopping**) *informal* **1** to beat or strike. **2** to defeat totally.

whop[2] (*NAm* **whap**) *n informal* a heavy blow; a thump.

whopper *n informal* **1** something unusually large or extreme of its kind. **2** an extravagant or monstrous lie.

whopping *adj informal* extremely big.

whore[1] /haw/ *n* a prostitute or a promiscuous woman. ⋙ **whorish** *adj.*

whore[2] *v* **1** to have sexual intercourse with a prostitute. **2** to work as a prostitute.

whorehouse *n informal* a brothel.

whorl /wuhl, wawl/ *n* **1** an arrangement of similar parts, e.g. leaves, in a circle round a point on an axis, e.g. a stem. **2** something spiral in form or movement; a swirl. **3** a single turn of a spiral, *esp* on a shell. **4** a fingerprint in which the central ridges turn through at least one complete circle. ⋙ **whorled** *adj.*

whortleberry /'wuhtlb(ə)ri, -beri/ *n* (*pl* **-ies**) = BILBERRY.

who's *contr* **1** who is. **2** who has.

Usage note

who's *or* whose? These two words are pronounced the same, but it is important to distinguish between them in writing, especially in questions. *Who's* is the shortened form of *who is* or *who has*: *Who's that? – It's only me; Who's done the washing-up? Whose* is the possessive form of *who*: *Whose is that?* ('Who owns that?'); *Whose turn is it to do the washing-up?*

whose[1] *adj* of whom or which, *esp* as possessor or object of an action.

Usage note

whose *or* who's? See note at WHO'S.

whose[2] *pron* (*pl* **whose**) used without a following noun as a pronoun equivalent in meaning to the adjective *whose.*

whosesoever *adj formal* of whomsoever.

whosoever *pron formal* whoever.

whump[1] *n* a thump or thud.

whump[2] *v* to bang or thump.

whup *v* (**whupped, whupping**) *chiefly NAm, informal* to beat or thrash.

why[1] *adv* for what cause, reason, or purpose? ✱ **why not** used in making a suggestion.

why[2] *conj* **1** the cause, reason, or purpose for which. **2** on which grounds.

why[3] *n* (*pl* **whys**) a reason or cause.

why[4] *interj* used to express mild surprise, approval, disapproval, or impatience.

WI *abbr* **1** West Indies. **2** Wisconsin (US postal abbreviation). **3** *Brit* Women's Institute.

Wicca *n* **1** an ancient religion of the Celtic people. **2** witchcraft. ⋙ **Wiccan** *n and adj.*

wick[1] *n* a cord or strip of material through which a liquid, e.g. paraffin, oil, or melted wax, is drawn by capillary action to the top in a candle, lamp, etc for burning. ✱ **get on somebody's wick** *Brit, informal* to annoy or irritate somebody.

wick[2] *v* to draw by capillary action.

wick[3] *n* used in place names: a village or hamlet.

wicked *adj* **1** morally bad; evil. **2** disposed to mischief; roguish. **3** very unpleasant, vicious, or dangerous. **4** *informal* extremely stylish or skilful; exceptionally good. ⋙ **wickedly** *adv,* **wickedness** *n.*

wicker *n* interlaced twigs, canes, or rods used to make baskets, furniture, etc. ⋙ **wickerwork** *n.*

wicket *n* **1** in cricket, either of the two sets of stumps at which the ball is bowled and which the batsman defends. **2** a small gate or door, *esp* one forming part of or placed near a larger one. **3** *chiefly NAm* an opening like a window, *esp* one through which business is transacted, e.g. at a bank. ✱ **a sticky wicket** *informal* a difficult or awkward situation.

wicketkeeper *n* in cricket, the fielder who is stationed behind the batsman's wicket. ⋙ **wicketkeeping** *n.*

widdershins *or* **withershins** *adv* in a left-handed, wrong, or contrary direction; anticlockwise.

widdle[1] *v informal* to urinate.

widdle[2] *n informal* **1** an act of passing urine. **2** urine.

wide[1] *adj* **1** having great horizontal extent; vast. **2** having a specified width. **3** having great extent between the sides; broad. **4** fully opened. **5** embracing much; comprehensive. **6** extending over a considerable range. **7** distant or deviating from something specified. **8** in cricket, of or denoting a fielding position near a line perpendicular to and equidistant from each wicket. ⋙ **widely** *adv,* **wideness** *n.*

wide[2] *adv* **1** over a great horizontal distance or extent; widely. **2** so as to leave much space or distance between. **3** so as to miss or clear a point by a considerable distance. **4** to the fullest extent; completely or fully.

wide[3] *n* in cricket, a bowled ball that is out of reach of the batsman in the normal position and counts as one run.

-wide *comb. form* forming adjectives, with the meaning: over or throughout the distance, area, or extent specified: *nationwide.*

wide-angle *adj* of a lens: having an angle of view wider than a standard lens.

wide area network *n* a communications system where the various computer terminals are far apart and linked by radio, satellite, etc.

wide-awake *adj* **1** fully awake. **2** alertly watchful, *esp* for advantages or opportunities.

wide ball *n* = WIDE[3].

wide boy *n Brit, informal* a man who is involved in petty crime or who uses unscrupulous methods to earn a living.

wide-eyed *adj* **1** amazed or astonished. **2** marked by uncritical acceptance or admiration; naive.

widen *v* to make or become wider. ⋙ **widener** *n.*

wide-screen *adj* **1** of a format of cinema film: having a projected picture that is substantially wider than the standard one. **2a** of a television broadcast: transmitted in a format that fills the width of a standard television screen, but leaves a gap at the top and bottom of it. **b** of a television set: having a screen that is wider than a standard screen.

widespread *adj* **1** widely extended or spread out. **2** widely diffused or prevalent.

widgeon *n* see WIGEON.

widget *n informal* any small usu mechanical device whose name is unknown or has been forgotten.

widow[1] *n* **1** a woman whose husband has died and who has not remarried. **2** *informal* a woman whose husband spends much time away from her pursuing a specified activity: *a golf widow.*

widow[2] *v* to cause (a woman) to become a widow.

widower *n* a man whose wife has died and who has not remarried.

widowhood *n* the state or period of being a widow.

widow's mite *n* a small gift, *esp* of money, ungrudgingly given by somebody who can little afford it.

widow's peak *n* a point formed by the downward growth of the hairline in the middle of the forehead.

widow's weeds *pl n* black mourning clothes worn by a widow.

width *n* **1a** the measurement taken at right angles to the length. **b** the lesser of two dimensions or the least of three dimensions. **2** largeness of extent or scope.

widthways *adv* in the direction of the width; crosswise.

widthwise *adv* widthways.

wield *v* **1** to handle (a tool or weapon) effectively. **2** to exert or exercise (power or influence). ⋙ **wielder** *n.*

wieldy *adj* (**-ier, -iest**) easy to use or wield.

Wiener schnitzel /'veenə shnitsəl/ *n* a thin breadcrumbed fried veal escalope.

wife *n* (*pl* **wives**) **1** a married woman, *esp* in relation to her husband. **2** *archaic or dialect* a woman. ⋙ **wifehood** *n,* **wifeless** *adj.*

wifely *adj* of or befitting a good wife. ⋙ **wifeliness** *n.*

wife-swapping *n informal* the temporary exchange of sexual partners by two or more married couples.

wig[1] *n* a manufactured covering of natural or synthetic hair for the head.

wig[2] *v* (**wigged, wigging**) *Brit, informal, dated* to chastise or rebuke severely.

wigeon *or* **widgeon** *n* (*pl* **wigeons** *or* **wigeon**) a freshwater dabbling duck, the male of which has a chestnut head.

wigging *n Brit, informal, dated* a severe scolding.

wiggle[1] *v* to move or cause to move with short motions from side to side or up and down. ⋙ **wiggler** *n.*

wiggle[2] *n* **1** a wiggling movement. **2** a wavy line; a squiggle. ⋙ **wiggly** *adj.*

wight *n archaic or dialect* a person, usu of a specified kind.

wigwam *n* a dwelling made from a conical or dome-shaped framework of poles covered with bark, rush mats, or hides, *esp* as used formerly by Native Americans.

wild[1] *adj* **1** living or growing in a state of nature; not tame, domesticated, or cultivated. **2** of land: not inhabited or cultivated. **3** of scenery: desolate. **4** free from restraint or regulation; uncontrolled or unruly. **5** *informal* passionately eager or enthusiastic: *wild about jazz.* **6** *informal* very angry; infuriated. **7** marked by turbulent agitation. **8** going beyond reasonable or conventional bounds; fantastic: *a wild scheme.* **9** uncivilized or barbaric. **10** haphazard. ⋙ **wildly** *adv,* **wildness** *n.*

wild[2] *n* **1** a sparsely inhabited or uncultivated region; a wilderness. **2** (**the wild**) a wild, free, or natural state or existence. **3** (**the wilds**) remote country.

wild[3] *adv* in a wild manner.

wild boar *n* a Eurasian wild pig, having a bristly greyish coat and prominent tusks.

wild card *n* **1** a playing card able to represent any card designated by the holder. **2** a person or team selected to take part in a tournament despite not having qualified to participate through previous performances. **3** an irregular or unpredictable person or thing. **4** in computing, a character that can be used, e.g. in searching, to represent any character or string of characters.

wildcat[1] *n* (*pl* **wildcats** *or* **wildcat**) **1** a cat that resembles but is heavier in build than the domestic cat and is held to be among its ancestors. **2** a savage quick-tempered person. **3** a wildcat oil or gas well.

wildcat[2] *adj* **1** operating, produced, or carried on outside the bounds of standard or legitimate business practices. **2** of or denoting an oil or gas well drilled in territory not known to be productive. **3** of a strike: initiated by a group of workers without formal union approval or in violation of a contract.

wildcat[3] *v* (**wildcatted, wildcatting**) *NAm* to prospect for oil or gas, usu by drilling an experimental well. ⋙ **wildcatter** *n.*

wild cherry *n* = GEAN.

wildebeest /'wildəbeest, 'vil-/ *n* (*pl* **wildebeests** *or* **wildebeest**) = GNU.

wilderness *n* **1** a region or area that is uncultivated and uninhabited by human beings. **2** a confusing multitude or mass. **3** the state of exclusion from office or power. ✻ **a voice in the wilderness** **1** a plea for something, *esp* reform, that is ignored. **2** the person or group making such a plea.

wildfire *n* **1** in former times, an incendiary substance used in warfare. **2** a phosphorescent glow, e.g. will-o'-the-wisp. ✻ **spread like wildfire** to spread very rapidly.

wildfowl *n* (*pl* **wildfowl**) a wild duck, goose, or other game bird, *esp* a waterfowl. ⋙ **wildfowler** *n,* **wildfowling** *n.*

wild-goose chase *n* a hopeless pursuit after something unattainable.

wilding *n* a plant growing uncultivated in the wild, either as a native plant or as a cultivated plant that has run wild.

wildlife *n* the wild animals and plants of a region collectively, *esp* the wild animals.

wildling *n* = WILDING.

wild oat *n* a wild grass that is common in meadows and grows as a weed on arable land.

wild rice *n* a tall aquatic N American grass that yields an edible purplish black grain.

wild silk *n* silk produced by wild silkworms that is coarser and stronger than cultivated silk.

wile *n* (*usu in pl*) a deceitful or beguiling trick or stratagem.

wilful (*NAm* **willful**) *adj* **1** done deliberately; intentional. **2** obstinately and often perversely self-willed. ➤➤ **wilfully** *adv,* **wilfulness** *n.*

will[1] *v* (*third person sing. present tense* **will**, *past tense* **would**) **1** used to express an action or state in the future. **2** used to express intention or determination. **3** used to express willingness or consent. **4** used to express a request or invitation. **5** used to express likelihood or probability. **6** used with emphatic stress to express annoyance. **7** used to express capability. **8** *formal, literary* to wish or desire.

Usage note

will *or* shall? See note at SHALL.

will[2] *n* **1a** a mental power by which one controls one's wishes, choices, intentions, etc or initiates action. **b** an inclination to act in a particular way: *the will to live.* **c** a specified attitude towards others: *ill will.* **2** a desire, wish, intention, or inclination. **3** willpower; self-control. **4** a legal declaration of the manner in which somebody wishes to have their property disposed of after their death. ✱ **at will** as one wishes; as or when it pleases or suits oneself. **with a will** enthusiastically and energetically. **with the best will in the world** no matter how good one's intentions are.

will[3] *v* **1** (+ to) to bequeath (property) to somebody. **2a** to determine deliberately. **b** to decree or ordain. **c** to cause or attempt to cause by exercise of the will. ➤➤ **willer** *n.*

willie *n* see WILLY.

willies *pl n* (**the willies**) *informal* a feeling of nervousness or fear.

willing *adj* **1** inclined or favourably disposed in mind; ready. **2** done or given without reluctance. **3** prompt to act or respond. ➤➤ **willingly** *adv,* **willingness** *n.*

williwaw *n* a sudden strong gust of cold air blowing offshore along a mountainous coast.

will-o'-the-wisp *n* **1** a phosphorescent light sometimes seen at night over marshy ground and often caused by the combustion of gas from decomposed organic matter. **2** an enticing but elusive goal. **3** an unreliable or elusive person.

willow *n* a tree or shrub bearing catkins of flowers with no petals, sometimes grown for its pliant branches used in basketry or for its whitish wood.

willowherb *n* a plant of the evening primrose family, *esp* rosebay willowherb.

willow pattern *n* china tableware decorated with a blue-and-white design of oriental style that usu tells a story.

willowy *adj* **1** full of or shaded by willows. **2** of a person: gracefully tall and slender.

willpower *n* self-control or resoluteness.

willy *or* **willie** *n* (*pl* **-ies**) *Brit, informal* a penis.

willy-nilly *adv* **1** by compulsion; without choice. **2** in a haphazard or random manner.

willy-willy *n* (*pl* **-ies**) *Aus* a whirlwind.

wilt[1] *v* **1** of a plant: to lose freshness and become limp; to droop. **2** of a person: to grow weak, tired, or faint.

wilt[2] *n* a disease of plants marked by wilting.

wilt[3] *v archaic* second person sing. present tense of WILL[1].

Wilts *abbr* Wiltshire.

wily *adj* (**-ier, -iest**) full of wiles; crafty. ➤➤ **wilily** *adv,* **wiliness** *n.*

wimp *n informal* a weak, ineffectual, or cowardly person. ➤➤ **wimpish** *adj,* **wimpishly** *adv,* **wimpy** *adj.*

wimple *n* a cloth covering worn over the head and round the neck and chin by women in the late medieval period and by some nuns.

wimp out *v informal* to withdraw or refuse to take part because of loss or lack of nerve.

win[1] *v* (**winning,** *past tense and past part.* **won**) **1** to gain the victory in a battle, contest, or dispute; to defeat opponents or rivals. **2** to get possession of by personal qualities, good fortune, etc. **3a** to gain (a victory or prize) in or as if in a battle or contest. **b** to defeat opponents or rivals in (a war, competition, etc). **4** (+ over/round) to gain the favour of or persuade somebody. ➤➤ **winnable** *adj.*

win[2] *n* a victory or success, *esp* in a game or sporting contest.

wince *v* to shrink back or grimace involuntarily, e.g. in pain; to flinch. ➤➤ **wince** *n.*

winceyette *n Brit* a lightweight cotton fabric with a nap on one or both sides.

winch[1] *n* **1** a machine or instrument for hoisting or pulling by means of a rope or chain wound round a rotating drum. **2** a crank or handle for giving motion to a machine, e.g. a grindstone.

winch[2] *v* to hoist or pull with a winch. ➤➤ **wincher** *n.*

wind[1] *n* **1** a natural movement of air, *esp* horizontally. **2** breath or the ability to breathe. **3** *Brit* gas generated in the stomach or the intestines. **4** mere talk; idle words. **5** air carrying a scent, e.g. of a hunter or game. **6** musical wind instruments collectively, *esp* as distinguished from string and percussion instruments. ✱ **get/have wind of** to hear a rumour of. **have the wind up** *Brit, informal* to be scared or frightened. **in the wind** about to happen. **put the wind up somebody** *Brit, informal* to scare or frighten somebody. **sail close to the wind 1** to sail as nearly as possible against the main force of the wind. **2** *informal* to come close to a point of danger; to get near the permissible limits. **take the wind out of somebody's sails 1** to frustrate somebody by anticipating or forestalling them. **2** to make somebody less confident or self-important. ➤➤ **windless** *adj.*

wind[2] *v* **1** to make short of breath. **2** *Brit* to help (a baby) to bring up wind after feeding. **3** to detect or follow (an animal) by scent.

wind[3] *v* (*past tense and past part.* **wound**) **1** to have a curving, spiralling, or twisting course. **2** to pass round an object or central core so as to encircle it, *esp* repeatedly. **3** to hoist or haul by means of a rope or chain and a winch or windlass. **4a** to tighten the spring of (a clock, watch, or similar mechanism), e.g. by turning a key, to make it operate. **b** to turn (e.g. a crank or handle) repeatedly. **5** to put into the specified state or position by winding it: *Wind the video back to the beginning.* ➤➤ **winding** *adj.*

wind[4] *n* **1** a coil or turn made by winding. **2** a curve or bend, e.g. in a river.

windbag *n informal* an excessively talkative person.

windbreak *n* something that breaks the force of the wind, e.g. a line of trees, a fence, or a screen.

windburn *n* irritation of the skin caused by the wind. ➤➤ **windburned** *adj*, **windburnt** *adj*.

windcheater *n chiefly Brit* a weatherproof or windproof coat or jacket, *esp* one fitting closely at the neck, waist, and cuffs.

windchill *n* the effect of cold winds, *esp* on living beings.

wind chimes *pl n* an arrangement of small pieces of glass or metal hung loosely so that they tinkle musically in the wind.

wind down *v* **1** *informal* to become gradually more relaxed; to unwind. **2** of a clockwork mechanism: to become slower because of decreasing tension in the spring. **3** to bring to an end gradually.

winder *n* a device for winding something, e.g. a clock.

windfall *n* **1** a fruit blown down by the wind. **2** an unexpected gain or advantage, e.g. a legacy or a large dividend.

windfall tax *n* a tax on a company considered to have made excessive profits.

wind farm *n* an array of wind turbines or windmills for generating electric power.

windflower *n* an anemone, *esp* the wood anemone.

winding *n* **1** a curved or sinuous course, line, or progress. **2** material wound or coiled about an object, e.g. wire around a metal core in an electric motor, or a single turn of the wound material.

winding-sheet *n* a sheet in which a corpse is wrapped for burial.

wind instrument *n* a musical instrument, e.g. a trumpet or clarinet, sounded by air, *esp* by the player's breath.

windjammer *n* in former times, a large fast square-rigged sailing vessel.

windlass[1] *n* **1** a machine for hoisting or hauling, *esp* one consisting of a horizontal drum turned by a crank so that the rope or chain is wound round the drum. **2** a winch used to raise a ship's anchor.

windlass[2] *v* to hoist or haul with a windlass.

wind machine *n* a machine used *esp* in the theatre for producing a gust of wind or the sound of wind.

windmill[1] *n* **1** a mill operated by vanes that are turned by the wind. **2** a similar structure using wind power to generate electricity, pump water, etc.

windmill[2] *v* to move or cause to move like the vanes of a windmill.

window *n* **1** an opening in the wall of a building, side of a vehicle, etc to let in light and air, usu fitted with a frame containing glass. **2** a display area behind the window of a shop. **3** a transparent panel in an envelope, through which the address on the enclosure is visible. **4** in computing, a rectangular area of the display within which a separate file can be displayed. **5** a brief time available for something. **6** something that functions like a window, e.g. in allowing people to see what is normally hidden: *a window on the Western world.* ✱ **go out of the window** *informal* to cease to exist or come to an end. ➤➤ **windowed** *adj*, **windowless** *adj*.

window box *n* a box for growing plants on the outside sill of a window.

window dressing *n* **1** the act or art of arranging a display of merchandise in a shop window. **2** the act or an instance of making something appear more attractive or favourable. ➤➤ **window dresser** *n*.

window pane *n* a panel of transparent material, *esp* glass, forming part of a window.

window seat *n* **1** a seat under a window, *esp* a bay window. **2** a seat beside the window in an aircraft, train, or bus.

window-shop *v* to look at the displays in shop windows without intending to buy anything. ➤➤ **window-shopper** *n*, **window-shopping** *n*.

windowsill *n* the shelf or horizontal member at the bottom of a window opening; the sill of a window.

windpipe *n* = TRACHEA.

windscreen *n Brit* a transparent screen, *esp* of glass, at the front of a motor vehicle.

windscreen wiper *n* a mechanically operated metal arm with a rubber blade for clearing rain from windscreens.

windshield *n NAm* = WINDSCREEN.

wind-sock *n* a cloth cone open at both ends that is mounted on a pole and is used to indicate the direction of the wind, *esp* at an airfield.

windstorm *n* a storm with high winds but little or no rain, snow, etc.

wind-surfing *n* the sport of riding across water on a sailboard. ➤➤ **wind-surfer** *n*.

windswept *adj* **1** swept by strong winds. **2** dishevelled from being exposed to the wind.

wind tunnel *n* a tunnel-like apparatus through which air is blown to determine the effects of wind pressure on or the aerodynamic properties of an object placed inside it.

windup *n* **1** *Brit, informal* an act of teasing or tricking somebody as a joke. **2** a conclusion or finish.

wind up *v* **1a** to bring to a conclusion. **b** to bring (a business) to an end by liquidation. **2** *Brit, informal* to deceive playfully; to tease. **3** to raise to a high level of excitement, tension, etc. **4** *informal* to arrive in a place, situation, or condition at the end of or because of a course of action.

windward[1] *adj and adv* in or facing the direction from which the wind is blowing: compare LEEWARD[1].

windward[2] *n* the side or direction from which the wind is blowing: compare LEEWARD[2].

windy *adj* (**-ier, -iest**) **1a** marked by strong wind. **b** exposed to the wind; windswept. **2** *Brit* suffering from or causing flatulence. **3** *informal* verbose or bombastic. **4** *Brit, informal* frightened or nervous. ➤➤ **windily** *adv*, **windiness** *n*.

wine[1] *n* **1a** an alcoholic drink made from fermented grape juice. **b** an alcoholic drink made from the fermented juice of another plant or fruit. **2** the dark or purplish red colour of red wine.

wine[2] ✱ **wine and dine** to entertain with good food and wine.

wine bar *n* an establishment serving wine and usu food for consumption on the premises.

wine box *n* a carton of wine with a tap for dispensing it.

wine cellar *n* **1** a room for storing wines. **2** a stock of wines.

wineglass *n* a drinking glass for wine, having usu a rounded bowl and mounted on a stem and foot.

winegrower *n* a person who cultivates a vineyard and makes wine.

wine gum *n* a firm jelly-like fruit-flavoured sweet.

winery *n* (*pl* **-ies**) a wine-making establishment.

wineskin *n* a bag that is made from the skin of an animal and is used for holding wine.

wine taster *n* a person who evaluates wine by tasting.

wine tasting *n* an occasion for evaluating wine by tasting, *esp* a promotional event at which wine sellers offer potential customers a chance to sample their products before buying them.

wine vinegar *n* vinegar made from wine.

winey *adj* see WINY.

wing[1] *n* **1** a movable feathered or membranous paired appendage by means of which a bird, bat, or insect flies. **2** either of the horizontal structures projecting from the sides of an aircraft, which provide lift and stability. **3** an appendage or part resembling a wing in shape, function, or position, e.g. a sidepiece at the top of a high-backed armchair. **4** a part of a building projecting from the main or central part. **5** (*used as sing. or pl*) a group or faction holding distinct opinions or policies within an organized body, e.g. a political party. **6** (*in pl*) the area at the sides of a theatre stage out of sight of the audience. **7a** the left or right section of a playing field that is near the sidelines. **b** any of the attacking positions or players in these sections. **8** *Brit* a part of the body of a motor vehicle above the wheels. **9** a membranous, leaflike, or woody growth in a plant, e.g. on a sycamore fruit. **10** a unit of the Royal Air Force higher than a squadron. ✱ **in the wings** in the background; in readiness to act. **on the wing** of a bird: in flight; flying. **spread/stretch one's wings** to venture out into the world; to break away from one's background. **take wing** to fly away. **under one's wing** under one's protection; in one's care. ⋙ **winged** *adj*, **wingless** *adj*.

wing[2] *v* **1a** to wound (a bird) in the wing. **b** to wound (somebody), e.g. with a bullet, without killing them. **2** to make (one's way) by or as if by flying. **3** to go with or as if with wings; to fly. ✱ **wing it** *informal* to perform or speak without rehearsal; to improvise. ⋙ **winged** *adj*.

wingbeat *n* a single complete movement of a wing in flying.

wing case *n* either of the modified front pair of wings in some insects, e.g. beetles, that cover and protect the hind pair of functional wings.

wing chair *n* an upholstered armchair with a high solid back and sidepieces that provide a rest for the head.

wing collar *n* a man's stand-up collar with the upper corners turned down.

wing commander *n* an officer in the Royal Air Force ranking above a squadron leader and below a group captain.

winge[1] *v Aus* = WHINGE[1].

winge[2] *n Aus* = WHINGE[2].

winger *n* a player positioned on the wing in football, hockey, etc.

wing forward *n* = FLANKER (1).

wing mirror *n* a mirror on the outside of a motor vehicle, giving the driver a view of vehicles behind and to either side.

wing nut *n* a nut that has projecting wings or flanges so that it may be turned by finger and thumb.

wingspan *n* the distance from the tip of one of a pair of wings to that of the other.

wingspread *n* = WINGSPAN.

wink[1] *v* **1** to shut one eye briefly as a signal or in teasing. **2** to gleam or flash intermittently; to twinkle. **3** (+ at) to avoid seeing or noting something; to disregard or condone it. ⋙ **winker** *n*.

wink[2] *n* **1** an act of winking. **2** a brief period, *esp* of sleep. **3** an instant: *I'll be there in a wink.* ✱ **tip somebody the wink** *informal* to give somebody a useful piece of information, *esp* covertly.

winkle *n* = PERIWINKLE[2].

winkle out *v chiefly Brit* **1** to displace or extract from a position, *esp* with difficulty. **2** to discover (information) with difficulty.

winkle-picker *n Brit, informal* a shoe with a very pointed toe.

winner *n* **1** somebody or something that wins. **2** *informal* something that is or is expected to be successful.

winning *adj* **1** tending to please or delight; endearing. **2a** that wins or has won. **b** that results in victory. ⋙ **winningly** *adv*.

winning post *n* a post marking the finishing line on a racecourse.

winnings *pl n* money won by success in a game or competition, *esp* in gambling.

winnow *v* **1a** to remove waste matter from (grain) by exposure to a current of air. **b** to remove (waste matter) from grain in this way. **2a** (*often* + out) to separate or select (the most valuable things or people) from a mass or group. **b** (*often* + out) to get rid of (undesirable or unwanted things or people). **3** *literary* of the wind: to blow on; to fan. ⋙ **winnower** *n*.

wino *n* (*pl* **-os**) *informal* an alcoholic, *esp* one who drinks cheap wine.

win out *v* = WIN THROUGH.

winsome *adj* pleasing and engaging. ⋙ **winsomely** *adv*, **winsomeness** *n*.

winter[1] *n* the season between autumn and spring.

winter[2] *adj* of crops: sown in the autumn and harvested the following spring or summer: compare SUMMER[2].

winter[3] *v* **1** to pass or survive the winter. **2** to keep or feed (livestock) during the winter. ⋙ **winterer** *n*.

winter aconite *n* a small Eurasian and African plant of the buttercup family with bright yellow flowers that blooms in early spring.

wintergreen *n* **1** a perennial evergreen plant related to the heathers. **2a** an American evergreen plant of the heather family with white flowers and red berries. **b** an essential oil from this plant, or a similar oil produced synthetically, used medicinally and as a flavouring.

winterize *or* **-ise** *v chiefly NAm* (*usu in passive*) to make ready for or proof against winter weather. ⋙ **winterization** *n*.

winter sport *n* (*usu in pl*) a sport on snow or ice, e.g. skiing or tobogganing.

wintertime *n* the season of winter.

wintery *adj* see WINTRY.

win through *v* to reach a desired or satisfactory end, *esp* after overcoming difficulties.

wintry *or* **wintery** *adj* (**-ier, -iest**) **1** of the weather: characteristic of winter; cold. **2** chilling or cheerless: *a wintry smile.* ⋙ **wintrily** *adv*, **wintriness** *n*.

winy *or* **winey** *adj* (**-ier, -iest**) having the taste, smell, or other qualities of wine.

wipe[1] *v* **1a** to clean or dry by rubbing lightly or quickly, *esp* with or on something soft. **b** to remove (something) by wiping. **2a** to remove as if by rubbing: *Wipe that smile off your face!* **b** to erase (e.g. data or a recording) completely. ✱ **wipe the floor with** *informal* to defeat decisively. ⋙ **wiper** *n*.

wipe[2] *n* **1** an act of wiping. **2** a disposable moist cloth.

wipe out *v informal* **1** to destroy completely; to annihilate. **2** to obliterate or cancel.

wire[1] *n* **1** metal in the form of a flexible thread or slender rod. **2a** a line of wire, usu insulated, for conducting electrical current. **b** a telephone or telegraph wire or system. **c** *informal, dated* a telegram or cablegram. **3** a barrier or fence of barbed wire. ✱ **to the wire** *chiefly NAm, informal* to the last possible moment, *esp* neck and neck until the very end of a contest.

wire[2] *v* **1** to provide or connect with wire or wiring. **2** *chiefly NAm, informal, dated* **a** to send a message to (somebody) by telegraph. **b** to send (money, news, etc) by telegraph. ⪢ **wirer** *n.*

wire brush *n* a brush with short tough wire bristles.

wired *adj* **1** provided with wires, e.g. for electric connections. **2** reinforced or bound with wire. **3** *informal* **a** tense or nervous. **b** intoxicated, *esp* by a drug.

wire grass *n chiefly NAm, Aus* a coarse grass with wiry stems.

wirehaired *adj* of a dog: having stiff wiry hair.

wireless[1] *n chiefly Brit, dated* a radio.

wireless[2] *adj* not having or requiring wires.

wire netting *n* a network of woven or twisted wire used *esp* for fencing.

wire service *n NAm* a news agency that sends out syndicated news copy to subscribers telegraphically or electronically.

wiretapping *n* the act or an instance of tapping a telephone or telegraph wire, e.g. to monitor conversations to obtain information. ⪢ **wiretapper** *n.*

wire wool *n Brit* an abrasive material consisting of fine wire strands woven into a mass and used for scouring.

wireworm *n* the larva of a click beetle that causes damage to plant roots.

wiring *n* a system of carrying electric currents in a device, building, etc.

wiry *adj* (**-ier, -iest**) **1** resembling wire, *esp* in form and flexibility. **2** lean and vigorous; sinewy. ⪢ **wirily** *adv,* **wiriness** *n.*

wisdom *n* **1** good sense; judgment. **2** accumulated learning; knowledge.

wisdom tooth *n* any of the four molar teeth in human beings that are the last to erupt on each side at the back of each jaw.

wise[1] *adj* **1a** characterized by or showing deep understanding, keen discernment, and sound judgment. **b** judicious or prudent. **2** well-informed; knowledgeable. **3** *informal* (+ to) possessing shrewd awareness of something. ✱ **put somebody wise** to inform or enlighten somebody. ⪢ **wisely** *adv.*

wise[2] *n archaic* manner or way.

-wise *comb. form* forming adverbs and adjectives, with the meanings: **1a** in the specified manner: *walking crabwise.* **b** in the specified position or direction: *clockwise.* **2** with regard to or in respect of the specified thing: *Careerwise, it seems like a good move.*

wiseacre *n* a person who claims or pretends to be clever or knowledgeable.

wisecrack[1] *n informal* a flippant remark or witticism.

wisecrack[2] *v informal* to make wisecracks. ⪢ **wisecracker** *n.*

wise guy *n informal* a conceited and self-assertive person, *esp* one who claims to know all about something.

wise up *v informal* to become informed or aware.

wish[1] *v* **1a** to give form to (a wish): *I wish I had more leisure time.* **b** to feel or express a wish for; to want. **c** to request in the form of a wish; to order. **2a** to express the hope that somebody will have or attain (something): *I wish you luck.* **b** to bid (somebody) the specified greeting: *I wished them good night.* ✱ **wish on** to hope that (somebody) will suffer (e.g. an unpleasant situation). ⪢ **wisher** *n.*

wish[2] *n* **1a** an instance of wanting or hoping for something; a desire. **b** an object of desire. **2** a ritual act of wishing. **3a** an expressed will or desire. **b** (*usu in pl*) a conventional greeting.

wishbone *n* a forked bone in front of the breastbone of a bird consisting chiefly of the two clavicles joined at their lower ends.

Word history

from the superstition that when two people pull the bone apart the one getting the longer piece will have a wish granted.

wishful *adj* **1a** expressive of a wish. **b** having a wish; desirous. **2** in accordance with wishes rather than reality: *wishful thinking.* ⪢ **wishfully** *adv,* **wishfulness** *n.*

wish fulfilment *n* the satisfaction of desires, *esp* symbolically through dreams and fantasies.

wishing well *n* a well into which people throw coins in the belief that their wishes will thus be granted.

wishy-washy *adj informal* **1** e.g. of a drink: lacking in strength or flavour. **2** lacking in character or determination; ineffectual. **3** e.g. of a colour: lacking in intensity.

wisp *n* **1a** a thin insubstantial strand, streak, or fragment. **b** something frail, slight, or fleeting. **c** a small thin person. **2** a small handful of hay or straw for grooming an animal. ⪢ **wispy** *adj.*

wist *v* past tense of WIT[2].

wisteria *or* **wistaria** *n* a climbing plant with showy blue, white, purple, or rose flowers.

wistful *adj* **1** full of unfulfilled desire; yearning. **2** musingly sad; pensive. ⪢ **wistfully** *adv,* **wistfulness** *n.*

wit[1] *n* **1a** (*also in pl*) reasoning power; intelligence. **b** (*also in pl*) sanity. **2a** the ability to use words or ideas to create a humorous effect. **b** a talent for making quick clever amusing replies. **c** written or spoken examples of this ability or talent. **d** a person with this ability or talent. **3** *archaic* a person of superior intellect; a thinker. ✱ **be at one's wits' end** to be so harassed or worried that one does not know what to do. **frighten/scare somebody out of their wits** to frighten somebody very much; to terrify them. **have/keep one's wits about one** to be alert. **live by one's wits** to make one's living by clever or cunning methods rather than regular or honest work.

wit[2] *v* (*first and third person sing. present tense* **wot,** *past tense* **wist**) *archaic* to know. ✱ **to wit** that is to say; namely.

witch[1] *n* **1** a woman who is credited with supernatural powers or who practises magic. **2** *informal* an ugly old woman; a hag. ⪢ **witchy** *adj.*

witch[2] *v* **1** to harm by means of witchcraft. **2** to practise witchcraft.

witchcraft *n* the use of sorcery or magic.

witch doctor *n* a professional sorcerer, *esp* in a primitive tribal society, who is credited with healing and other powers.

witch elm *n* see WYCH ELM.

witchery *n* **1** witchcraft or sorcery. **2** an irresistible fascination; charm.

witches'-broom *n* an abnormal tufted growth of small branches on a tree or shrub caused *esp* by fungi or viruses.

witches' sabbath *n* = SABBATH (3).

witchetty *n* (*pl* **-ies**) a large white grub, the larva of an Australian moth, that is eaten *esp* by some Aborigines.

witchetty grub *n* = WITCHETTY.

witch hazel *n* **1** a shrub with yellow flowers borne in late autumn or early spring. **2** a soothing astringent lotion made from the bark and leaves of this shrub.

witch-hunt *n* **1** the searching out and harassment of those with unpopular or unorthodox views, usu on the basis that they pose a threat to others. **2** in former times, a campaign of persecution of those accused of witchcraft.

witching hour *n* the critical or significant time when something is to happen.

with *prep* **1a** used to indicate accompaniment or association. **b** used to indicate reciprocal action or communication. **c** used to express agreement or sympathy. **d** able to follow the reasoning of. **2a** in opposition to; against. **b** so as to be separated or detached from. **3a** in relation to. **b** used to indicate the object of attention, behaviour, or feeling. **c** in respect to. **4a** on the side of (a person or group); for. **b** employed by (a company, institution, etc). **5a** used to indicate the object of a statement of comparison, equality, or harmony. **b** in addition to. **6** by means of; using. **7** used to indicate manner of action. **8a** in possession of; having or bearing. **b** in the possession or care of. **9** in proportion to (something). **10** in the direction of.

withal[1] *adv archaic* **1** together with this; besides. **2** on the other hand; nevertheless.

withal[2] *prep archaic* (*used after its object*) with.

withdraw *v* (*past tense* **withdrew**, *past part.* **withdrawn**) **1a** to draw (something) back, away, or aside; to remove. **b** to remove (money) from a place of deposit, e.g. a bank account. **2** to take (e.g. an offer) back; to retract. **3a** to go back or away; to retire from participation. **b** to leave a place, *esp* to retreat. **4** to become socially or emotionally detached.

withdrawal *n* **1** the act or an instance of withdrawing. **2** the discontinuance of use of a drug, often accompanied by unpleasant side effects.

withdrawn[1] *adj* **1** socially detached and unresponsive; shy. **2** secluded or isolated.

withdrawn[2] *v* past part. of WITHDRAW.

withdrew *v* past tense of WITHDRAW.

withe /with/ *n* a slender flexible branch or twig used for binding things together.

wither *v* **1** to become dry and shrivelled, e.g. from age or disease. **2** to lose vitality, force, or freshness. **3** to cause to wither. **4** to make speechless or incapable of action, *esp* with a scornful look or remark. ▶▶ **withering** *adj*, **witheringly** *adv*.

withers *pl n* the ridge between the shoulder bones of a horse.

withershins *adv* see WIDDERSHINS.

withhold *v* (*past tense and past part.* **withheld**) **1** to refrain from granting or giving. **2** to hold back; to check or restrain. ▶▶ **withholder** *n*.

within[1] *prep* **1** inside. **2** to the inside of; into. **3a** in or into the range of. **b** not beyond the quantity or limitations of. **c** not further than a specified distance. **d** during or before the end of (a period of time).

within[2] *adv* **1** in or into the interior; inside. **2** in one's inner thought, mood, or character.

with-it *or* **with it** *adj informal* **1** *dated* up-to-date; fashionable. **2** (*usu in negative contexts*) mentally quick or alert.

without[1] *prep* **1a** used to indicate the absence or lack of something. **b** used to indicate that something does not happen. **2** *literary* outside.

without[2] *adv* **1** *literary* on or to the exterior; outside. **2** with something lacking or absent: *to go without.*

without[3] *conj dialect* unless.

withstand *v* (*past tense and past part.* **withstood**) **1** to be proof against; to be unharmed by. **2** to resist with determination, *esp* to stand up against it successfully.

withy *n* (*pl* **-ies**) **1** = WITHE. **2** = OSIER.

witless *adj* lacking wit or understanding; foolish. ▶▶ **witlessly** *adv*, **witlessness** *n*.

witness[1] *n* **1** a person who sees or hears an event take place. **2** a person who gives evidence, *esp* in a court of law. **3** a person who watches another sign a document and adds their own signature as an indication of authenticity. **4a** the act of certifying that a fact is true or an event has happened; testimony. **b** something that serves as evidence; proof. **5** public affirmation by word or example of religious faith or conviction.

witness[2] *v* **1** to observe (an event) personally or directly. **2** to be the scene or time of (an event). **3** to act as legal witness of (e.g. the signing of a document). **4** (+ to) to testify to something. **5** to affirm one's religious convictions in public.

witness-box *n* an enclosure in which a witness testifies in court.

witness stand *n NAm* = WITNESS-BOX.

witter *v Brit, informal* to talk in a long-winded rambling fashion, *esp* about inconsequential matters.

witticism *n* a witty remark.

witting *adj* **1** deliberate; intentional. **2** fully aware. ▶▶ **wittingly** *adv*.

witty *adj* (**-ier, -iest**) having or showing wit; cleverly humorous. ▶▶ **wittily** *adv*, **wittiness** *n*.

wives *n* pl of WIFE.

wiz *n* see WHIZZ[2] (3).

wizard[1] *n* **1** somebody skilled in magic, *esp* a man with supernatural powers; a sorcerer. **2** a person who is very clever or skilful, *esp* in a specified field. **3** a computer program providing a step-by-step guide to a particular task. ▶▶ **wizardly** *adj*.

wizard[2] *adj Brit, informal, dated* outstanding or excellent.

wizardry *n* **1** the art or practices of a wizard; sorcery. **2** great cleverness or skill, *esp* in a specified field, or the product of this: *technical wizardry.*

wizen *v* (*usu in passive*) to cause (somebody) to become dry, shrunken, and wrinkled, often as a result of ageing. ▶▶ **wizened** *adj*.

WLTM *abbr* used in personal advertisements: would like to meet.

WNW *abbr* west-northwest.

WO *abbr* Warrant Officer.

wo *interj* = WHOA.

woad *n* **1** a European plant of the mustard family formerly grown for the blue dyestuff obtained from its leaves. **2** the blue dyestuff obtained from this plant.

wobble[1] *v* **1a** to rock unsteadily from side to side. **b** of the voice: to tremble or quaver. **2** to waver or vacillate.

wobble[2] *n* a wobbling movement or sound.

wobble-board *n Aus* a musical instrument consisting of a piece of fibreboard that is flexed repeatedly to produce a low rhythmic sound.

wobbler *n* **1** somebody or something that wobbles. **2** *Brit, informal* = WOBBLY².

wobbly¹ *adj* (**-ier, -iest**) tending to wobble; unsteady. ➤➤ **wobbliness** *n.*

wobbly² ✱ **throw a wobbly** *Brit, informal* to have a fit of temper, irrational behaviour, or great agitation.

wodge *n Brit, informal* a bulky mass or chunk.

woe *n* **1** *literary* great sorrow or suffering caused by misfortune, grief, etc. **2** (*usu in pl*) a trouble or affliction. ✱ **woe betide somebody** somebody will suffer or be punished if they do the specified thing. **woe is me!** an exclamation of distress.

woebegone *adj* expressive of great sorrow or misery.

woeful *adj* **1** feeling or expressing woe. **2** inspiring woe; grievous. ➤➤ **woefully** *adv,* **woefulness** *n.*

wog¹ *n Brit, offensive* a non-white person.

wog² *n Aus, informal* a minor ailment.

woggle *n* a ring, usu of leather, used to secure a Scout's neckerchief at the throat.

wok *n* a large bowl-shaped cooking utensil used *esp* for stir-frying in Chinese cookery.

woke *v* past tense of WAKE¹.

woken *v* past part. of WAKE¹.

wold *n* **1** an upland area of open country. **2** (**the Wolds**) a region of chalk downlands.

wolf¹ *n* (*pl* **wolves** *or* **wolf**) **1** a large predatory flesh-eating mammal of the dog family that hunts in packs. **2** a fiercely rapacious person. **3** *informal* a man who pursues women in an aggressive way. ✱ **cry wolf** to raise a false alarm and risk the possibility that a future real need will not be taken seriously [from the fable of the shepherd boy who repeatedly called for help against a non-existent wolf; when a wolf did attack, nobody believed him]. **keep the wolf from the door** to have enough money to avoid or prevent starvation or want. **wolf in sheep's clothing** a person who hides hostile intentions behind a friendly manner. ➤➤ **wolfish** *adj.*

wolf² *v* (*often* + down) to eat (food) greedily.

Wolf Cub *n chiefly Brit* a former name for CUB SCOUT.

wolfhound *n* a dog of a large breed formerly used in hunting wolves.

wolfram *n* **1** = TUNGSTEN. **2** = WOLFRAMITE.

wolframite *n* a brownish black mineral containing tungsten, iron, and manganese.

wolf spider *n* a spider that lives on the ground and chases its prey.

wolf whistle *n* a distinctive whistle sounded to express sexual admiration, *esp* by a man for a woman. ➤➤ **wolf-whistle** *v.*

wolverine /'woolvəreen/ *n* a flesh-eating mammal of northern forests that is related to the weasel, has blackish fur, and is noted for its strength and ferocity.

wolves *n* pl of WOLF¹.

woman *n* (*pl* **women**) **1a** an adult human female. **b** (*usu used in combinations*) a woman belonging to a usu specified category, e.g. by birth, residence, membership, or occupation: *an Englishwoman.* **2** a female employee or servant. **3** a mistress, girlfriend, or wife. ✱ **woman of the streets** *euphem, dated* a prostitute.

womanhood *n* **1** the condition of being an adult female as distinguished from a child or male. **2** *literary* the women of a country, etc collectively. **3** the distinguishing character or qualities of women.

womanise *v* see WOMANIZE.

womanish *adj derog* unsuitable to a man or to a strong character of either sex; effeminate. ➤➤ **womanishly** *adv,* **womanishness** *n.*

womanize *or* **-ise** *v* of a man: to associate with many women habitually, *esp* for sexual relations. ➤➤ **womanizer** *n.*

womankind *n* female human beings; women as a whole, *esp* as distinguished from men.

womanly *adj* having or showing the good qualities traditionally thought to befit or be typical of a woman, e.g. gentleness or grace. ➤➤ **womanliness** *n.*

womb *n* = UTERUS.

wombat *n* a stocky plant-eating Australian marsupial mammal resembling a small bear.

women *n* pl of WOMAN.

womenfolk *pl n* women in general, *esp* the women of a family or community.

women's lib *n informal* = WOMEN'S LIBERATION.

women's liberation *n* a modern feminist movement stressing the social and psychological emancipation of women as well as the improvement of their civil and legal status.

women's movement *n* a movement working for the improvement of the social and political position of women.

won¹ *v* past tense and past part. of WIN¹.

won² /won/ *n* (*pl* **won**) the basic monetary unit of North and South Korea.

wonder¹ *n* **1** rapt attention, admiration, or astonishment at something unexpected, strange, beautiful, etc. **2** a cause of wonder; a marvel. **3** (*used before a noun*) noted for outstanding success or achievement: *a wonder drug.* ✱ **no/little/small wonder** it is no surprise. **work/do wonders** to have a positive effect.

wonder² *v* **1a** to feel curiosity or doubt; to speculate. **b** to be curious or in doubt about. **2** (*often* + at) to be in a state of wonder; to marvel. ➤➤ **wonderer** *n.*

wonderful *adj* unusually good; admirable or excellent. ➤➤ **wonderfully** *adv,* **wonderfulness** *n.*

wonderland *n* **1** a place that excites wonder. **2** an imaginary place where strange or magical things happen.

wonderment *n* **1** the state of wonder; awe or astonishment. **2** curiosity about something.

wondrous¹ *adj literary* wonderful. ➤➤ **wondrously** *adv,* **wondrousness** *n.*

wondrous² *adv archaic* wonderfully.

wonky *adj* (**-ier, -iest**) *informal* **1** awry or crooked. **2** shaky or unsteady.

wont¹ /wohnt/ *adj archaic* accustomed or used.

wont² *n archaic or humorous* customary practice: *as was his wont.*

wont³ *v* (*past tense and past part.* **wont** *or* **wonted**) *archaic* to make or become accustomed.

won't *contr* will not.

wonted *adj archaic* customary or habitual.

wonton *n* in Chinese cookery, a case of thin dough with a savoury filling that is boiled, steamed, or fried and eaten *esp* in soup.

woo *v* (**woos, wooed, wooing**) **1** to try to win the love of (somebody, *esp* a woman); to court. **2** to try to win the support or favour of (somebody, e.g. a potential customer or voter). ➤➤ **wooer** *n.*

wood[1] *n* **1a** a hard fibrous plant tissue that makes up the greater part of the stems and branches of trees or shrubs. **b** wood suitable or prepared for some use, e.g. burning or building. **2 a** (**the wood**) wooden casks. **b** a golf club with a wooden head. **c** a wooden bowling ball. **3** (*also in pl*) a dense growth of trees, usu smaller than a forest. ❋ **not see the wood for the trees** to fail to have overall understanding of a subject, situation, etc as a result of concentration on details. **out of the wood/woods** (*usu in negative contexts*) escaped from danger or difficulty.

wood[2] *adj* **1** made of wood. **2** (*used before a noun*) suitable for cutting, storing, or carrying wood. **3** (*used before a noun*) living or growing in woods or woodland.

wood alcohol *n* = METHANOL.

wood anemone *n* a common Eurasian anemone that grows in woodland and has white or pinkish flowers.

woodbine *n* **1** = HONEYSUCKLE. **2** *NAm* = VIRGINIA CREEPER.

woodblock *n* a block of wood used to produce a woodcut.

woodchip *n chiefly Brit* a textured wallpaper with small fragments of wood embedded in it.

woodchip paper *n* = WOODCHIP.

woodchuck *n* a thickset N American marmot with reddish brown fur.

woodcock *n* (*pl* **woodcocks** *or* **woodcock**) a long-billed wading bird of wooded regions that is related to the sandpipers.

woodcut *n* a print taken from the surface of a wooden block with a design cut in relief in the direction of the grain: compare WOOD ENGRAVING.

woodcutter *n* **1** a person who cuts down trees or chops wood. **2** a person who makes woodcuts. ⯮ **woodcutting** *n.*

wooded *adj* of land: covered with growing trees.

wooden *adj* **1** made of wood. **2** lacking ease or flexibility; awkwardly stiff. ⯮ **woodenly** *adv,* **woodenness** *n.*

wood engraving *n* **1** a print taken from the surface of a wooden block with a design cut into the end grain: compare WOODCUT. **2** the art of making such prints. ⯮ **wood engraver** *n.*

wooden spoon *n chiefly Brit* a consolation or booby prize.

woodland *n* **1** (*also in pl*) land covered with trees. **2** (*used before a noun*) living or growing in woodland. ⯮ **woodlander** *n.*

woodlouse *n* (*pl* **woodlice**) a small ground-living invertebrate animal with a flattened elliptical body capable of rolling into a ball in defence.

woodpecker *n* a bird with a stiff tail, usu colourful plumage, and a very hard bill used to drill holes in trees to find insects for food or to form nesting cavities.

woodpigeon *n* a large grey-and-white wild pigeon.

wood pulp *n* pulp from wood used in making cellulose derivatives, e.g. paper or rayon.

woodruff *n* a small sweet-scented plant with white flowers used in perfumery and for flavouring drinks.

wood screw *n* a pointed screw that has an external screw thread and a slotted head to receive the blade of a screwdriver.

woodshed *n* a shed for storing wood, *esp* firewood.

woodsman *n* (*pl* **woodsmen**) a man who lives in, frequents, or works in the woods.

wood sorrel *n* a plant of shady places with pink or white flowers and leaves made up of three leaflets.

wood spirit *n* = METHANOL.

woodturning *n* the art of producing wooden articles, e.g. bowls or chair legs, on a lathe. ⯮ **woodturner** *n.*

woodwind *n* **1a** any of a group of orchestral wind instruments including the clarinet, flute, oboe, and bassoon. **b** (*used before a noun*) of or denoting such an instrument or instruments. **2** (*used as sing. or pl*) the woodwind section of an orchestra.

woodwork *n* **1** parts or items made of wood, *esp* wooden interior fittings. **2** *Brit* the craft of constructing things from wood. ⯮ **woodworker** *n,* **woodworking** *n and adj.*

woodworm *n* **1** the larva of a beetle that bores in dead wood. **2** an infestation of such larvae.

woody *adj* (**-ier, -iest**) **1** covered with trees or having many woods. **2a** of or containing wood or wood fibres. **b** of a plant: having woody parts. **3** characteristic of or suggestive of wood. ⯮ **woodiness** *n.*

woodyard *n* a yard where timber is chopped or stored.

woody nightshade *n* a rambling poisonous plant with purple flowers and red berries. Also called BITTERSWEET[2].

woof[1] *n* the low gruff sound characteristic of a dog; a bark.

woof[2] *v* to utter a woof; to bark.

woof[3] /woohf/ *n* = WEFT.

woofer /'woohfə/ *n* a loudspeaker that responds mainly to low frequencies: compare TWEETER.

wool *n* **1** the soft wavy coat of various hairy mammals, *esp* the sheep. **2** yarn made from wool by spinning. **3** articles, *esp* knitted garments or woven fabrics, made of wool. **4** (*usu in combination*) a wiry or fibrous mass, e.g. of steel or glass. ❋ **pull the wool over somebody's eyes** to blind somebody to the true situation; to hoodwink them.

woolgathering *n* indulging in idle daydreaming.

wool grower *n* a person who breeds sheep for their wool.

woollen[1] (*NAm* **woolen**) *adj* **1** made of wool. **2** of or for the manufacture or sale of woollen products.

woollen[2] (*NAm* **woolen**) *n* **1** (*in pl*) woollen garments. **2** a fabric made of wool.

woolly[1] (*NAm* **wooly**) *adj* (**-ier, -iest**) **1a** made of or resembling wool. **b** of an animal or plant: covered with wool or with soft hairs resembling wool. **2a** marked by mental vagueness or confusion. **b** lacking in clearness or sharpness. ⯮ **woolliness** *n.*

woolly[2] (*NAm* **wooly**) *n* (*pl* **-ies**) *chiefly Brit* a woollen jumper or cardigan.

woolly bear *n* a large hairy caterpillar, *esp* the larva of a tiger moth.

woolpack *n* in former times, a bale of wool.

Woolsack *n* in Britain, the official seat of the Lord Chancellor in the House of Lords.

woolshed *n* in Australia and New Zealand, a building or range of buildings in which sheep are sheared and wool is prepared for market.

woomera *n Aus* a wooden rod with a hooked end that is used by Aborigines for throwing a spear.

Woop Woop *n Aus, informal* a remote provincial district or settlement.

woosh *v* see WHOOSH.

woozy *adj* (**-ier, -iest**) *informal* **1** dizzy or slightly nauseous. **2** mentally unclear or hazy. ➤➤ **woozily** *adv,* **wooziness** *n.*

wop *n offensive* an Italian.

Worcester sauce *n* a pungent sauce containing soy sauce, vinegar, and spices.

Worcestershire sauce *n* = WORCESTER SAUCE.

Worcs *abbr* Worcestershire.

word[1] *n* **1** a meaningful unit of language that can stand alone as an utterance and is usu set off by spaces on either side in writing or printing. **2 a** a short remark, statement, or conversation. **b** (*in pl*) talk or discourse. **c** (*in pl*) the text of a vocal musical composition. **3** (*in pl*) an angry utterance or conversation. **4** (**the word**) an order, command, or verbal signal. **5** (**one's word**) a promise. **6** news or information. ✱ **be as good as one's word** to keep a promise. **from the word go** from the beginning. **in a word** in short. **in other words** expressing the same thing in a different and usu more straightforward way. **in so many words** in exactly those terms. **my word!** used to express surprise or astonishment. **of one's word** who can be relied on to keep a promise: *He is a man of his word.* **take somebody at their word** to believe somebody literally. **take somebody's word for it** to believe, without evidence, that what somebody says or writes is true. **take the words out of somebody's mouth** to say the very thing that somebody else was about to say. ➤➤ **wordless** *adj,* **wordlessly** *adv.*

word[2] *v* to express in particular words; to phrase.

word association *n* in psychology, the act of responding to a given word with the first word that comes into one's mind.

word-blindness *n* = DYSLEXIA.

word class *n* a group of grammatically similar linguistic items consisting of words; a part of speech.

word-for-word *adj* e.g. of a report or translation: in or following the exact words; verbatim. ➤➤ **word for word** *adv.*

wording *n* the act or manner of expressing something in words or the words so used.

word of honour *n* a promise pledging one's honour.

word of mouth *n* oral communication.

word-perfect *adj* of an actor or speaker: having memorized something perfectly.

wordplay *n* verbal wit.

word processor *n* a computer or program that stores text for subsequent manipulation, e.g. by deleting, moving, or inserting new material, and that produces printed or typewritten text on paper. ➤➤ **word processing** *n.*

wordy *adj* (**-ier, -iest**) using or containing too many words. ➤➤ **wordily** *adv,* **wordiness** *n.*

wore *v* past tense of WEAR[1].

work[1] *n* **1a** activity in which one exerts physical strength or mental faculties to do or produce something. **b** the activities that provide one's accustomed means of livelihood. **c** a specific task, duty, function, or assignment. **2a** something produced in a specified way or by a specified person, thing, etc: *clever camera work.* **b** (*often used in combinations*) something made from a specified material: *ironwork.* **c** (*usu in pl*) something produced by the exercise of creative talent or effort; an artistic production or creation. **d** something being worked on; a workpiece. **3** a fortified structure. **4** (*in pl, used as sing. or pl; often used in combinations*) a place where industrial activity is carried out; a factory: *the brickworks.* **5** (*in pl*) the working or moving parts of a mechanism. **6a** in physics, the amount of energy that is transferred to a body by a force in producing movement. **b** the transference of energy in this way. **7** (**the works**) **a** *informal* everything possessed, available, or belonging. **b** *informal* subjection to all possible physical violence. **8** (*used before a noun*) used for work. ✱ **have one's work cut out** to have a difficult task. **in the works** *chiefly NAm* in process of preparation, development, or completion. **out of work** without regular employment; unemployed. ➤➤ **workless** *adj.*

work[2] *v* (*past tense and past part.* **worked** *or archaic* **wrought**) **1a** to do work to achieve a result or earn one's living. **b** to cause (a person or animal) to do work. **2** to operate or function. **3** to produce a desired effect; to succeed. **4** to exert an influence or have a tendency. **5a** (+ in) to produce artefacts by shaping or fashioning a specified material. **b** to produce by expending labour; to forge or shape. **c** to make with needlework. **d** to prepare or form into a desired state for use by kneading, hammering, etc. **6a** to get into a specified condition by slow or imperceptible movements: *The knot worked loose.* **b** to be in agitation or restless motion. **7** (+ on) to strive to influence or persuade somebody. **8** to carry on an operation, e.g. farming or mining, in. **9** to finance (something) by working. **10** to operate (something). **11** to bring about (an effect or result). ✱ **work to rule** *chiefly Brit* to obey the rules of one's work precisely and so reduce efficiency, *esp* as a form of industrial action.

workable *adj* **1** capable of being worked. **2** of a plan: practicable or feasible. ➤➤ **workability** *n.*

workaday *adj* **1** prosaic or ordinary. **2** of or suitable for working days.

workaholic *n* a person with an excessive need to work; a compulsive worker.

workbench *n* a bench on which work, *esp* of mechanics or carpenters, is performed.

worked up *adj* emotionally aroused; angry or upset.

worker *n* **1a** a person who works. **b** a member of the working class. **c** a person who works in a specified way: *a slow worker.* **2** any of the usu sterile members of a colony of ants, bees, etc that perform most of the labour and protective duties of the colony.

work ethic *n* = PROTESTANT ETHIC.

work experience *n* a short spell of unpaid employment experience arranged by schools for senior pupils.

workfare *n* a scheme under which certain people receiving state welfare benefits are required to undergo training or do unpaid work on behalf of the community.

workforce *n* **1** (*used as sing. or pl*) the workers employed by a particular company or engaged in a specific activity. **2** (*used as sing. or pl*) the people potentially available for work.

workhorse *n* **1** a willing worker, *esp* for a voluntary cause. **2** a markedly useful or durable vehicle, craft, or machine.

workhouse *n* **1** in Britain in former times, an institution maintained at public expense to house needy people. **2** in the USA, a prison for minor offenders.

work in *v* **1a** to insinuate unobtrusively. **b** to find room for. **2** to cause to penetrate by persistent effort.

working[1] *adj* **1a** that functions or performs work. **b** engaged in paid work. **2** adequate to permit effective work to be done. **3** serving as a basis for further work. **4** during which one works. **5** suitable for or used in work.

working[2] *n* **1** (*usu in pl*) a part of a mine, quarry, or similar excavation. **2** (*usu in pl*) the act or manner of functioning or operating. **3** (*usu in pl*) a record of the steps taken to solve a mathematical problem.

working capital *n* capital actively turned over or available for use in the course of business activity.

working class *n* (*used as sing. or pl*) the class of people who work, *esp* manually, for wages. ➤➤ **working-class** *adj.*

working girl *n euphem* a prostitute.

working party *n* **1** *Brit* a committee set up to investigate and report on a particular problem. **2** a group of prisoners, soldiers, etc assigned to a manual task.

work load *n* the amount of work that somebody has to do.

workman *n* (*pl* **workmen**) **1** a manual worker, *esp* one employed on a casual basis. **2** a person skilled at their trade to the specified degree: *a poor workman.*

workmanlike *adj* skilful or competent.

workmanship *n* **1** the relative art or skill of a workman; craftsmanship. **2** the quality or finish exhibited by a product.

work of art *n* a product of any of the fine arts, *esp* a painting or sculpture of high artistic quality.

work off *v* to dispose of or get rid of (a commitment, emotion, etc) by work or activity.

workout *n* a period of usu vigorous physical exercise.

work out *v* **1a** to determine or solve (a question, problem, etc) by calculation or reasoning. **b** to elaborate (a plan, etc) in detail. **2a** to prove effective or successful. **b** (*often* + at/to) to amount to (a total or calculated figure). **3** to engage in physical exercise.

work over *v informal* to beat (somebody) up.

work permit *n* a document authorizing a foreigner to do paid work in a country.

workpiece *n* something being worked on.

workplace *n* a place, e.g. an office or factory, where paid work is done.

works council *n chiefly Brit* a representative group of employees taking part in talks with their employers.

work sheet *n* **1** a document on which work done and in progress is recorded. **2** a sheet containing problems to be solved or questions to be answered by students.

workshop *n* **1** a room or place in which manufacture or repair work is carried out. **2** a brief intensive session of study, training, or discussion for a relatively small group of people with an emphasis on active participation.

workshy *adj* disliking work; lazy.

workstation *n* a self-contained unit that is equipped with facilities for computing activities, e.g. a VDU and keyboard linked to a computer network in an office.

worktop *n Brit* a flat surface on a kitchen unit that is suitable for working on.

work-to-rule *n chiefly Brit* a form of industrial action designed to reduce output or efficiency by deliberately keeping very rigidly to rules and regulations.

work up *v* **1** to rouse or stir. **2** to produce by mental or physical work. **3** to improve (something), *esp* by mental work. **4** (+ to) to rise gradually in intensity or emotional tone towards something.

world *n* **1** (**the world**) the earth with everybody and everything on it. **2** (**the world**) the course of human affairs. **3** (**the world**) secular affairs as distinguished from religious or spiritual matters. **4a** a division of the inhabitants of the earth distinguished by living together at the same place or at the same time. **b** a distinctive class of people or their sphere of interest. **5** a part or section of the world considered as a separate independent unit. **6** the personal environment of one's life or work. **7** an indefinite or very great number or amount: *a world of difference.* **8** a planet. **9** (*used before a noun*) of the whole world. ✱ **best of both worlds** the advantages of two alternatives, *esp* without their disadvantages. **bring into the world** to deliver or give birth to (a baby). **come into the world** to be born. **in the world** among innumerable possibilities; ever: *What in the world is it?* **out of this world** *informal* of extraordinary excellence; superb. **think the world of** to have great love or admiration for.

world-beater *n* somebody or something that excels all others; a champion.

world-class *adj* of the highest quality in the world.

World Cup *n* an international sporting tournament held at regular intervals, *esp* in football.

world fair *n* an international exhibition featuring exhibits and participants from all over the world.

worldly *adj* (**-ier, -iest**) **1** of or devoted to this world and its pursuits rather than to religion or spiritual affairs. **2** = WORLDLY-WISE. ➤➤ **worldliness** *n.*

worldly-wise *adj* possessing a shrewd understanding of human affairs; sophisticated.

world music *n* a type of popular music that incorporates elements of traditional music from various countries.

world power *n* a nation or state powerful enough to affect the entire world by its influence or actions.

world-shaking *adj* having tremendous importance.

world view *n* = WELTANSCHAUUNG.

world war *n* **1** a war engaged in by most of the principal nations of the world. **2** (**World War**) either of two such wars of the first half of the 20th cent.

world-weary *adj* bored with life and the material pleasures of the world. ➤➤ **world-weariness** *n.*

worldwide[1] *adj* extending throughout or involving the entire world.

worldwide[2] *adv* throughout the entire world.

World Wide Web *n* in computing, a vast information system composed of interconnected sites and files to which individuals have access through the Internet.

worm[1] *n* **1** a relatively small elongated limbless invertebrate animal with a soft body, e.g. an earthworm or a tapeworm. **2** an invertebrate animal resembling a worm, e.g. a silkworm, woodworm, or other insect larva. **3** (*in pl*) infestation with or disease caused by parasitic worms. **4** *informal* a person who is an object of contempt, loathing, or pity; a wretch. **5** a computer program that replicates itself many times in a network, often having a destructive effect. ➤➤ **wormlike** *adj.*

worm[2] *v* **1a** to proceed or cause to proceed windingly or insidiously. **b** to insinuate or introduce (oneself) by devious or subtle means. **c** to make (one's way) insidiously or deviously. **2** (+ out of) to obtain or extract (information) from somebody by artful or persistent questioning. **3** to rid (an animal) of parasitic worms. ➤➤ **wormer** *n.*

wormcast *n* a small heap of earth or sand excreted by a worm on the surface.

worm-eaten *adj* of timber, wooden furniture, etc: eaten or burrowed into by or as if by woodworm.

worm gear *n* a gear consisting of a revolving cylindrical screw and a worm wheel working together.

wormhole *n* **1** a hole or passage burrowed by a worm. **2** in physics, a hypothetical connection between different parts of the space-time continuum.

worm's-eye view *n* a view from a low or humble position.

worm wheel *n* a toothed wheel that engages with the thread of a revolving cylindrical screw in a worm gear.

wormwood *n* **1** a European plant that yields a bitter aromatic oil used in absinthe. Also called ABSINTHE. **2a** something bitter or mortifying. **b** bitterness.

wormy *adj* (**-ier, -iest**) containing, infested with, or damaged by worms. ➤➤ **worminess** *n.*

worn *v* past part. of WEAR[1].

worn-out *adj* **1** exhausted. **2** made useless or destroyed by or as if by wear.

worrisome *adj chiefly NAm* **1** causing distress or worry. **2** inclined to worry or fret. ➤➤ **worrisomely** *adv.*

worry[1] *v* (**-ies, -ied**) **1** to feel or experience concern or anxiety; to fret. **2** to afflict with mental distress or agitation; to make anxious. **3** to bother or disturb (somebody). **4** of an animal, *esp* a dog: to harass (e.g. a sheep or rabbit) by biting, shaking, chasing, etc. **5** to touch or fiddle with repeatedly. ➤➤ **worried** *adj,* **worriedly** *adv,* **worrier** *n,* **worrying** *adj,* **worryingly** *adv.*

worry[2] *n* (*pl* **-ies**) **1** mental distress or agitation resulting from concern; anxiety. **2** a cause of worry; a trouble or difficulty.

worry beads *pl n* a string of beads fingered so as to calm oneself.

worse[1] *adj* **1** of a lower quality. **2** in poorer health. **3** more serious or severe. ✱ **the worse for** harmed by: *He was none the worse for his fall; The carpet was the worse for wear.* **worse off** suffering worse circumstances, *esp* financially.

worse[2] *adv* **1** in a worse manner. **2** to a worse extent or degree.

worse[3] *n* **1** something worse. **2** (**the worse**) what is inferior or less desirable.

worsen *v* to make or become worse.

worship[1] *n* **1** reverence offered to a divine being or supernatural power. **2** a form of religious practice with its set of beliefs and rituals. **3** extravagant admiration for or devotion to an object of esteem. **4** (**Your/His/Her Worship**) *chiefly Brit* used as a title for various officials, e.g. magistrates and mayors.

worship[2] *v* (**worshipped, worshipping,** *NAm* **worshiped, worshiping**) **1** to honour or offer reverence to (a deity). **2** to regard with great or excessive respect, admiration, or devotion. **3** to perform or take part in worship. ➤➤ **worshipper** *n.*

worshipful *adj* **1** rendering worship or veneration. **2** (**Worshipful**) *chiefly Brit* used as a title for various people or groups of rank or distinction.

worst[1] *adj* **1** of the lowest quality. **2** least appropriate or advisable. **3** most severe or serious.

worst[2] *adv* **1** in the worst manner. **2** to the worst extent or degree.

worst[3] *n* (*pl* **worst**) **1** the worst state or part. **2** (**the worst**) what is least desirable. ✱ **at worst/at the worst** under the worst circumstances; seen in the worst light. **do one's worst** to do the utmost harm of which one is capable. **if the worst comes to the worst** if the very worst thing happens.

worst[4] *v* (*usu in passive*) to get the better of; to defeat.

worsted /ˈwoostid/ *n* **1** a smooth compact yarn spun from long wool fibres. **2** a fabric made from worsted yarn, having a firm texture and no nap.

wort[1] *n* (*usu used in combinations*) a herbaceous plant, *esp* one used medicinally in former times: *Saint John's wort.*

wort[2] *n* a dilute solution containing sugars obtained typically from malt by soaking and fermented to form beer.

worth[1] *adj and prep* **1a** equal in value to. **b** having money or property equal to (a sum). **2** deserving of. ✱ **for all one is worth** *informal* with all one's energy or enthusiasm. **worth it** worth the time or effort spent.

worth[2] *n* **1a** value, *esp* financial value. **b** the equivalent of a specified amount or figure: *twenty pounds' worth of petrol.* **2** moral or personal merit, *esp* high merit.

worthless *adj* **1a** lacking worth; valueless. **b** useless. **2** contemptible or despicable. ➤➤ **worthlessly** *adv,* **worthlessness** *n.*

worthwhile *adj* worth the time or effort spent.

worthy[1] *adj* (**-ier, -iest**) **1** good or important enough; deserving. **2a** having moral worth or value. **b** honourable or meritorious. ➤➤ **worthily** *adv,* **worthiness** *n.*

worthy[2] *n* (*pl* **-ies**) *often humorous* a worthy or prominent person.

-worthy *comb. form* forming adjectives, with the meanings: **1** deserving of the specified thing: *praiseworthy.* **2** fit or safe for the specified thing: *seaworthy.*

wot *v* first and third person sing. present tense of WIT[2].

would *v aux* the past tense of WILL[1], used: **1** to introduce a possibility or presumption. **2** after a verb expressing a wish or request. **3** in negative constructions to express doubt. **4** to express a polite request or invitation. **5** in reported speech to express an action or state in the future. **6** to express a preference. **7** to express habitual action in the past. **8** *literary* to express a wish or desire.

Usage note
would *or* should? See note at SHOULD.

would-be *adj often derog* desiring or intended to be.

wouldn't *contr* would not.

wouldst *v* archaic second person sing. past tense of WILL[1].

wound[1] *n* **1** an injury, e.g. from violence, accident, or surgery, that involves tearing, cutting, or breaking of a membrane, *esp* the skin. **2** a mental or emotional hurt or blow.

wound[2] *v* to inflict a wound on. ➤➤ **wounded** *adj,* **wounding** *adj.*

wound[3] *v* past tense and past part. of WIND[1].

wove *v* past tense of WEAVE[1].

woven *v* past part. of WEAVE[1].

wow[1] *interj informal* used to express pleasure, admiration, or surprise.

wow[2] *n informal* a striking success; a hit.

wow[3] *v informal* to excite (e.g. an audience) to enthusiastic admiration or approval.

wow[4] *n* a distortion in reproduced sound that is heard as a slow rise and fall in the pitch of the sound: compare FLUTTER[2] (3).

wowser *n Aus, NZ, informal* **1** an oppressively puritanical person; a killjoy. **2** a teetotaller.

WP *abbr* **1** word processing. **2** word processor.

WPC *abbr Brit* Woman Police Constable.

wpm *abbr* words per minute.

WRAC *abbr* in Britain, formerly, Women's Royal Army Corps.

wrack[1] *v* = RACK[2] (1).

wrack[2] *n* **1** see RACK[4]. **2** see RACK[6].

wrack[3] *n* a brown seaweed, *esp* kelp.

WRAF *abbr* in Britain, formerly, Women's Royal Air Force.

wraith *n* **1** an apparition of a living person in their exact likeness seen shortly before or after death. **2** *literary* an insubstantial replica or shadow. ➤➤ **wraith-like** *adj.*

wrangle[1] *n* an angry or prolonged dispute or quarrel.

wrangle[2] *v* **1** to dispute angrily or peevishly; to bicker. **2** to engage in argument or controversy. **3** *NAm* to herd and care for (livestock, *esp* horses) on the range. ➤➤ **wrangler** *n.*

wrap[1] *v* (**wrapped, wrapping**) **1a** to cover, pack, or enfold in something flexible, e.g. paper or fabric. **b** to fold or wind (something flexible) round somebody or something. **2** to obscure or surround with the specified covering: *wrapped in mist.* **3** in computing, to cause (text) to be automatically carried over to the next line. **4** *informal* to finish filming or recording (something).

wrap[2] *n* **1** an article of clothing that may be wrapped round a person, *esp* a shawl. **2** *chiefly NAm* a wrapping. **3** *informal* the end of a filming or recording session. **4** *informal* a small packet containing an illegal drug. **5** a sandwich filling wrapped in a tortilla, eaten as a cold snack. ✻ **under wraps** secret.

wraparound *adj* of a garment, *esp* a skirt: made to be wrapped round the body with the edges overlapping.

wrapped *adj Aus, informal* extremely pleased; delighted.

wrapper *n* **1** something in which an article is wrapped. **2** *chiefly NAm* a loose dressing gown.

wrapping *n* paper or other material used to wrap an object.

wrap up *v* **1** to bring to a conclusion; to complete or end. **2** (*usu in passive*) to involve completely; to engross. **3** to protect oneself with warm outer garments. **4** *Brit, informal* to stop talking; to shut up.

wrasse *n* (*pl* **wrasses** *or* **wrasse**) a brilliantly coloured marine food fish with spiny fins, thick lips, and strong teeth.

wrath *n* strong vengeful anger or indignation.

wrathful *adj literary* filled with wrath; irate. ➤➤ **wrathfully** *adv,* **wrathfulness** *n.*

wreak *v* **1** to inflict (e.g. revenge). **2** to cause or create (havoc or destruction). ➤➤ **wreaker** *n.*

wreath *n* (*pl* **wreaths**) **1** something, *esp* flowers or leaves, intertwined into a circular shape. **2** a curl, ring, or coil.

wreathe *v* **1** to shape (flowers, leaves, etc) into a wreath. **2** to encircle or coil about. **3** to twist or move in coils. ✻ **wreathed in smiles** with a happy joyful expression.

wreck[1] *n* **1** a shipwreck. **2** wrecking or being wrecked; destruction. **3a** the broken remains of something, e.g. a building or vehicle, wrecked or ruined. **b** a person of broken constitution, health, or spirits.

wreck[2] *v* **1** (*usu in passive*) to cause (a vessel) to sink, break up, or be destroyed. **2** to ruin or destroy by violent action or accident. **3** to bring disaster or ruin to (e.g. plans or a marriage).

wreckage *n* broken parts or material from a wrecked structure.

wrecked *adj informal* drunk or exhausted.

wrecker *n* **1** somebody or something that wrecks something. **2** in former times, a person who wrecked ships for plunder. **3a** *chiefly NAm* a person whose work is the demolition of buildings. **b** *NAm* a person who deals in parts and material salvaged from scrapped motor vehicles.

Wren *n* in Britain, a woman serving in the Women's Royal Naval Service.

wren *n* a very small European bird that has a short erect tail and is noted for its loud song.

wrench[1] *v* **1** to pull or twist violently. **2** to injure (a part of the body) by a violent twisting or straining. **3** to snatch forcibly; to wrest.

wrench[2] *n* **1a** a violent twisting or a sideways pull. **b** a sharp twist or sudden jerk causing a strain to a muscle, ligament, etc. **c** acute emotional distress or something causing this, e.g. a parting. **2** a spanner or similar tool.

wrest *v* **1** to take by violent pulling or twisting. **2** to obtain with difficulty by force or determined labour.

wrestle[1] *v* **1** to contend with an opponent in wrestling. **2** to engage in a violent or determined struggle; to grapple. **3** to push, pull, or manhandle by force. ➤➤ **wrestler** *n.*

wrestle[2] *n* an act of wrestling, *esp* a wrestling bout.

wrestling *n* a sport or contest in which two unarmed people struggle hand to hand according to agreed rules, without hitting each other with closed fists.

wretch *n* **1** a profoundly unhappy or unfortunate person. **2** *informal* a despicable or vile person.

wretched *adj* **1** deeply afflicted or unfortunate. **2** deplorably bad. **3** mean, squalid, or contemptible. **4** used as a general expression of annoyance: *I've lost the wretched key.* ➤➤ **wretchedly** *adv,* **wretchedness** *n.*

wrick *v* = RICK[2]. ➤➤ **wrick** *n.*

wriggle[1] *v* **1** to move to and fro with short writhing motions; to squirm. **2** to move or advance by twisting and turning. **3** (*usu* + out of) to extricate oneself by manoeuvring, equivocation, etc. ➤➤ **wriggler** *n.*

wriggle[2] *n* a wriggling movement. ➤➤ **wriggly** *adj.*

wright *n* (*usu used in combinations*) a person who makes or creates a specified thing: *a shipwright.*

wring[1] *v* (*past tense and past part.* **wrung**) **1** to twist or compress, *esp* so as to extract liquid. **2a** to expel or obtain (liquid) by wringing something. **b** (*often* + from/out of) to exact or extort by coercion or with difficulty. **3a** to twist (an animal's neck), *esp* so as to break it. **b** to clasp and twist together (one's hands) as a sign of anguish. **4** to shake (somebody's hand) vigorously in greeting. **5** to distress or torment.

wring[2] *n* an act of wringing.

wringer *n* = MANGLE[2].

wringing *adj* e.g. of clothes: so wet that liquid is dripping out.

wrinkle[1] *n* **1** a small ridge or crease formed in the skin, in fabric, etc. **2** *informal* a valuable trick or hint for bringing about a result.

wrinkle[2] *v* **1** (*usu in passive*) to contract into wrinkles; to pucker or crease. **2** to become marked with or contracted into wrinkles.

wrinkly[1] *adj* (**-ier, -iest**) having many wrinkles.

wrinkly[2] *n* (*pl* **-ies**) *Brit, derog* an elderly person.

wrist *n* the joint between the hand and the arm.

wristband *n* **1** a band on the sleeve of a garment encircling the wrist. **2** the strap of a wristwatch. **3** a band worn around the wrist, e.g. for identity purposes or to absorb sweat.

wristwatch *n* a watch attached to a strap or bracelet and worn round the wrist.

writ *n* a formal document issued in the name of the sovereign or of a court commanding or forbidding an act specified in it.

write *v* (*past tense* **wrote,** *past part.* **written**) **1a** to form (legible characters, symbols, or words) on a surface, *esp* with a pen, pencil, or similar instrument. **b** to complete or fill in (e.g. a cheque) by writing. **2** to be the author or composer of (a piece of writing, music, etc). **3a** to compose and send (a letter). **b** *chiefly NAm* to communicate with (somebody) in writing. **4** *informal* (*usu in passive*) to make (a quality or condition) evident: *Guilt was written all over his face.* **5** to introduce or transfer (information) into or from a computer memory. ⯮ **writable** *adj.*

write down *v* **1** to record (information) in written form. **2** in accounting, to reduce the book value of (an asset).

write off *v* **1** to concede or deem to be irreparably lost or useless. **2** to cancel the record of (bad debt). **3** to damage (a motor vehicle) beyond repair.

write-off *n* something or somebody written off.

writer *n* **1** a person who writes books, articles, etc as an occupation; an author. **2** a person who has written a particular text or document. **3** a device that writes, e.g. in computing.

writer's cramp *n* a painful spasmodic cramp of the hand or finger muscles brought on by excessive writing.

write up *v* **1a** to write an account of. **b** to put into finished written form. **2** to bring up to date the writing of (a diary, etc).

write-up *n* a written account or review.

writhe *v* **1** to twist in or as if in pain or struggling. **2** to proceed with twists and turns.

writing *n* **1** the act, practice, or occupation of literary composition. **2a** written letters or words, *esp* handwriting. **b** (*usu in pl*) a written composition. ✱ **the writing on the wall** an omen of impending disaster or ruin.

written *v* past part. of WRITE.

WRNS *abbr* in Britain, formerly, Women's Royal Naval Service.

wrong[1] *adj* **1** not according to truth or facts; incorrect. **2** in error; mistaken. **3** against moral standards; evil. **4** not right or proper according to a code, standard, or convention. **5** not satisfactory, e.g. in condition: *There's something wrong with my toe.* **6** being the side of fabric that is not intended to be seen, e.g. on a finished garment. ✱ **get (hold of) the wrong end of the stick** to misunderstand. **on the wrong side of 1** out of favour with. **2** more than the specified age. ⯮ **wrongly** *adv,* **wrongness** *n.*

wrong[2] *adv* **1** without accuracy; incorrectly. **2** without regard for what is right or proper. **3** out of proper working order.

wrong[3] *n* **1** an injurious or unfair act. **2** what is wrong, immoral, or unethical. ✱ **in the wrong 1** mistaken or incorrect. **2** being or appearing to be guilty.

wrong[4] *v* **1** to do wrong to (somebody); to treat unjustly or unfairly. **2** to mistakenly ascribe an unworthy motive to (somebody); to misrepresent. ⯮ **wronger** *n.*

wrongdoer *n* a person who behaves immorally or illegally. ⯮ **wrongdoing** *n.*

wrong-foot *v* **1** *Brit* to make (an opponent) move in the wrong direction, e.g. in tennis or football. **2** to put (somebody) at a disadvantage by a sudden change of approach.

wrongful *adj* wrong, unjust, or unlawful. ⯮ **wrongfully** *adv,* **wrongfulness** *n.*

wrongheaded *adj* stubborn in adherence to wrong opinion or principles; perverse. ⯮ **wrongheadedly** *adv,* **wrongheadedness** *n.*

wrote *v* past tense of WRITE.

wroth *adj archaic* wrathful.

wrought *adj* **1** of metals: beaten into shape by tools. **2** worked or formed by artistry or effort. **3** (+ up) deeply stirred; excited.

wrought iron *n* a tough pure form of iron that is easily worked.

wrung *v* past tense and past part. of WRING[1].

WRVS *abbr* in Britain, Women's Royal Voluntary Service.

wry *adj* (**wryer** *or* **wrier, wryest** *or* **wriest**) **1** ironically or grimly humorous. **2a** bent or twisted, *esp* to one side. **b** contorted into an expression of distaste, disapproval, etc. ⯮ **wryly** *adv,* **wryness** *n.*

wrybill *n* a New Zealand bird related to the plovers that has a beak curved sharply to the right.

wryneck *n* a grey-brown bird that is related to the woodpeckers and can twist its head sideways over its shoulder.

WSW *abbr* west-southwest.

WTO *abbr* World Trade Organization.

wunderkind /'voondəkint/ *n* (*pl* **wunderkinds** *or* **wunderkinder** /-kində/) **1** a child prodigy. **2** a person who succeeds in a competitive field at an early age.

wurst /vooəst, wuhst/ *n* (*usu used in combinations*) a sausage typical of those made in Germany and Austria: *liverwurst.*

wuss /woos/ *n chiefly NAm, Aus, informal* a weak or ineffectual person; a wimp. ⯮ **wussy** *adj.*

WV *abbr* West Virginia (US postal abbreviation).

WWF *abbr* **1** World Wide Fund for Nature. **2** World Wrestling Federation.

WWW *abbr* World Wide Web.

WY *abbr* Wyoming (US postal abbreviation).

wych elm *or* **witch elm** *n* a hardy elm that grows in N Europe and Asia.

wyn *n* see WEN[2].

WYSIWYG /'wiziwig/ *adj* denoting a computer system in which all text and graphics displayed on screen can be reproduced in exactly the same form on printout.

wyvern *n* a mythical and heraldic animal usu represented as a two-legged winged creature with a long tail that resembles a dragon.

X

X *or* **x** *n* (*pl* **X's** *or* **Xs** *or* **x's**) **1** the 24th letter of the English alphabet. **2** the Roman numeral for ten. **3** used to represent the first unknown quantity in an algebraic equation or expression. **4** used to designate the horizontal axis in a plane coordinate system. **5** somebody or something whose identity is unknown or withheld.

xanthine /'zanthien, 'zantheen/ *n* a yellow crystalline compound that occurs in blood and urine and in plant tissue.

X chromosome *n* a sex chromosome that usu occurs paired with another X chromosome in the female sex, and with a dissimilar chromosome in the male sex: compare Y CHROMOSOME.

Xe *abbr* the chemical symbol for xenon.

xebec *or* **zebec** /'zeebek/ *n* a usu three-masted Mediterranean sailing ship with mixed lateen and square rig.

xen- *or* **xeno-** *comb. form* **1** relating to foreigners: *xenophobia*. **2** different, strange, or foreign: *xenolith*.

xenobiotic *adj* denoting or involving a substance, usu a chemical compound, that is foreign to the body or to a particular ecological system.

xenograft *n* a tissue graft carried out between members of different species.

xenolith *n* a fragment of rock embedded in a rock of a different type. ➤➤ **xenolithic** *adj*.

xenon *n* a heavy colourless odourless gaseous element used *esp* in specialized lamps and electronic tubes.

xenophile *n* somebody who is attracted to foreign things, e.g. foreign manners, styles, or people. ➤➤ **xenophilous** *adj*.

xenophobia *n* an intense fear or dislike of foreigners or strangers. ➤➤ **xenophobe** *n*, **xenophobic** *adj*.

xenotransplantation *n* transplantation of cells or organs from one species into a member of another species. ➤➤ **xenotransplant** *n*.

xer- *or* **xero-** *comb. form* dry: *xerophyte*.

xerography *n* a photocopying process in which the action of light on an electrically charged surface produces an image of the original that is developed with a powder and transferred to paper, where it is fixed by heating. ➤➤ **xerographic** *adj*, **xerographically** *adv*.

xerophilous *adj* of a plant or animal: thriving in or adapted to a dry environment. ➤➤ **xerophile** *n*, **xerophily** *n*.

xerophyte *n* a plant, e.g. a cactus, structurally adapted for life and growth with a limited water supply. ➤➤ **xerophytic** *adj*.

Xerox *n trademark* a xerographic copier or copy.

xerox *v* to copy on a Xerox machine.

Xhosa /'khohsə, 'khawsə/ *n* (*pl* **Xhosas** *or* **Xhosa**) **1** a member of a people chiefly inhabiting the Cape Province of South Africa, related to the Zulus. **2** the language spoken by this people. ➤➤ **Xhosa** *adj*.

xi *n* the 14th letter of the Greek alphabet (Ξ, ξ), equivalent to roman x.

XL *abbr* extra large.

Xmas *n informal* Christmas.

XML *abbr* extensible markup language.

X-rated *adj* **1** involving pornography, indecency, or extreme violence. **2** formerly, of a film: suitable only for adults.

X-ray[1] *n* **1** an electromagnetic radiation of extremely short wavelength that has the properties of penetrating various solids and of acting like light to expose photographic films and plates. **2** an examination or photograph made by means of X-rays.

X-ray[2] *v* to examine, treat, or photograph with X-rays.

X-ray astronomy *n* the branch of astronomy concerned with the detection and investigation of objects in outer space by means of the X-rays they emit.

xu /sooh/ *n* (*pl* **xu**) a unit of currency in Vietnam, worth 100th of a dong.

xyl- *or* **xylo-** *comb. form* denoting wood: *xylophone*.

xylem *n* a complex vascular tissue found in higher plants that forms the woody supporting part of their stems and conveys water and nutrients upward from their roots.

xylene *n* a toxic inflammable oily hydrocarbon obtained from wood tar, coal tar, or petroleum.

xylo- *comb. form* see XYL-.

xylography *n* the art of making wood engravings. ➤➤ **xylograph** *n*.

xylophone *n* a percussion instrument that is sounded by striking a series of wooden bars graduated in length with two small wooden hammers. ➤➤ **xylophonist** *n*.

xylose *n* a sugar that occurs *esp* in woody plant tissue and is used in dyes, in tanning, and in foods for diabetics.

Y y

Y[1] *or* **y** *n* (*pl* **Y's** *or* **Ys** *or* **y's**) **1** the 25th letter of the English alphabet. **2** used to represent the second unknown quantity in an algebraic equation or expression. **3** used to designate the vertical axis in a plane coordinate system.

Y[2] *abbr* the chemical symbol for yttrium.

y *abbr* year.

-y[1] *or* **-ey** *suffix* forming adjectives, meaning: **1a** covered with or full of: *dirty.* **b** having the quality of: *waxy.* **2** tending or inclined to: *sleepy.* **3** slightly or rather: *chilly.*

-y[2] *suffix* forming nouns, denoting: **1** a state, condition, or quality: *jealousy.* **2** a group sharing a specified class or state: *soldiery.*

-y[3] *suffix* forming nouns, denoting: an instance of the action specified: *entreaty.*

-y[4] *or* **-ie** *suffix* forming nouns, meaning: **1** somebody or something little or dear: *doggy.* **2** somebody associated with, enthusiastic about, or addicted to something specified: *foodie.*

Y2K *abbr* the year 2000.

yabby *or* **yabbie** *n* (*pl* **-ies**) *Aus* a small Australian freshwater crayfish.

yacht[1] /yot/ *n* a relatively small sailing or powered vessel used for pleasure cruising or racing.

yacht[2] *v* to race or cruise in a yacht. ➤➤ **yachting** *n.*

yack[1] *n informal* see YAK[2].

yack[2] *v* see YAK[3].

yacker *n* see YAKKA.

yah[1] *interj* used to express disgust, defiance, or derision.

yah[2] *interj* used to represent an affected upper-class drawl: yes.

yahoo[1] *n* (*pl* **yahoos**) *informal* an uncouth or rowdy person.

yahoo[2] *interj* used to express wild excitement or delight.

Yahweh *or* **Yahveh** *n* the God of the Hebrews.

yak[1] *n* (*pl* **yaks** *or* **yak**) a large long-haired wild or domesticated ox of Tibet.

yak[2] *or* **yack** *n informal* persistent, voluble, and usu trivial or irritating talk.

yak[3] *or* **yack** *v* (**yakked** *or* **yacked, yakking** *or* **yacking**) *informal* to talk persistently; to chatter.

yakitori *n* a kebab consisting of small pieces of marinated chicken.

yakka *or* **yacker** *n Aus, NZ, informal* work.

yakuza *n* (*pl* **yakuza**) **1** (**the Yakuza**) an organized body of Japanese criminals. **2** a criminal belonging to this organization.

Yale *n trademark* a type of lock that has a revolving barrel which is prevented from turning by a set of pins until the correct key is inserted.

yam *n* **1** an edible starchy tuberous root used as a vegetable and a staple food in tropical areas. **2** *NAm* a moist-fleshed usu orange sweet potato.

yammer *v informal* **1** to talk loudly or volubly; to clamour. **2** to complain or grumble. ➤➤ **yammer** *n,* **yammerer** *n.*

yang *n* in Chinese philosophy, the masculine active principle in nature, expressed in light, heat, dryness, etc, that eternally interacts with its opposite and complementary principle, yin.

Yank *n informal, often derog* an American.

yank *v informal* to pull or extract with a quick vigorous movement. ➤➤ **yank** *n.*

Yankee *n* **1** *informal* an American. **2** *NAm, informal* somebody from New England or the northern USA. **3** *NAm, informal* a Federal soldier in the Civil War. **4** *informal* a combination of bets, e.g. on horse races, covering four selections in different events in all their possible permutations. ➤➤ **Yankee** *adj.*

yap *v* (**yapped, yapping**) **1** to bark in a high-pitched or snappish way. **2** *informal* to talk in a shrill insistent querulous way. ➤➤ **yap** *n,* **yapper** *n,* **yappy** *adj.*

yard[1] *n* **1a** a unit of length equal to three feet (about 0.914m). **b** a unit of volume equal to one cubic yard (about 0.765m^3). **2** a long spar tapered towards the ends to support and spread a sail.

yard[2] *n* **1** *chiefly Brit* **a** a small usu walled and often paved area open to the sky and adjacent to a building. **b** (*used in combinations*) the grounds of a specified building or group of buildings: *a churchyard.* **c** (*usu used in combinations*) an area with its buildings and facilities set aside for a usu specified business or activity: *a timber yard.* **2** *NAm* a garden of a house. **3** a system of tracks for the storage and maintenance of railway vehicles and the making up of trains.

yardage *n* the length, extent, or volume of something as measured in yards.

yardarm *n* either end of the yard of a square-rigged ship.

yardbird *n NAm, slang* **1** a military recruit. **2** a serviceman punished by being confined or assigned to menial tasks. **3** a convict.

Yardie *n* **1** *informal* a member of a West Indian criminal gang originating in Jamaica, *esp* one involved in drug dealing. **2** *Jamaican English* a fellow Jamaican.

yardman *n* (*pl* **yardmen**) **1** a person who works in a timber yard or a railway yard. **2** *NAm* a handyman who does outdoor jobs.

yard of ale *n Brit* the amount of beer, usu about 1 or 2l (2 or 3pt), contained in a slender horn-shaped glass one yard (about 0.9m) tall.

yard sale *n chiefly NAm* a sale of goods, usu household effects, held outdoors at a private house.

yardstick *n* **1** a graduated measuring stick one yard (about 0.9m) long. **2** a standard basis of calculation or judgment; a criterion.

yarmulke *or* **yarmulka** *n* a skullcap worn by *esp* Orthodox and Conservative Jewish males, in the synagogue and the home.

yarn[1] *n* **1** thread, e.g. of wool, cotton, or hemp, prepared and used for weaving, knitting, sewing, and rope-making. **2a** *informal* a narrative of adventures, *esp* a tall tale. **b** *Aus, NZ, informal* a conversation or chat.

yarn[2] *v informal* **1** to tell a yarn. **2** *Aus, NZ* to chat.

yarn-dye *v* to dye (yarn) before weaving or knitting.

yarrow *n* a strong-scented Eurasian plant with dense heads of small usu white flowers.

yashmak *n* a veil worn over the face by Muslim women, so that only the eyes remain exposed.

yatter *v informal* to chatter or prattle. ⋙ **yatter** *n.*

yaw *v* of a ship, aircraft, spacecraft, or projectile: to deviate from a straight course, *esp* by side-to-side movement. ⋙ **yaw** *n.*

yawl *n* a two-masted fore-and-aft rigged sailing vessel with sails set from a mainmast and a mizzenmast that is situated aft of the rudder.

yawn[1] *v* **1** to open the mouth wide and inhale, usu in fatigue or boredom. **2** to be menacingly wide, deep, and open; to gape: *a yawning chasm.* ⋙ **yawner** *n.*

yawn[2] *n* **1** a deep usu involuntary intake of breath through the wide open mouth. **2** *informal* a boring thing or person.

yawp *v* **1** to make a raucous noise; to squawk. **2** *NAm* to clamour or complain. ⋙ **yawp** *n,* **yawper** *n.*

yaws *pl n* (*used as sing. or pl*) an infectious tropical disease marked by ulcerating sores, caused by a bacterium that enters via abrasions in the skin.

Yb *abbr* the chemical symbol for ytterbium.

Y chromosome *n* a sex chromosome that usu occurs paired with a dissimilar chromosome in the male sex and does not occur in the female sex: compare X CHROMOSOME.

yd *abbr* yard.

ye[1] *pron archaic or dialect* the ones being addressed; you.

ye[2] *definite article* used as an archaism: the.

Word history

alteration of Old English þē THE[1]; from the use by early printers of the letter *y* to represent the runic character þ in manuscripts. *Ye* was never pronounced /yee/ until it was revived in modern times as a largely jocular archaism, usually to suggest picturesque quaintness.

yea[1] /yay/ *adv archaic* yes.

yea[2] *n* an affirmation or assent.

yeah *adv informal* yes.

year *n* **1** the period of about 365 solar days required for one revolution of the earth round the sun. **2a** a cycle of 365 or 366 days divided into twelve months beginning with January and ending with December; a calendar year or civil year. **b** a period of time equal to this but beginning at a different time. **3** a period of time, e.g. that in which a school is in session, within a year. **4** (*used as sing. or pl*) the body of students who enter a school, university, etc in one academic year. **5** *informal* (*in pl*) a very long time. **6** (*in pl*) age. ✱ **year in, year out** for an indefinite or seemingly endless number of successive years.

yearbook *n* **1** a book published yearly as a report or summary of statistics or facts. **2** a school publication in the USA, compiled by students in their final year to serve as a record of the year's activities.

yearling *n* **1** an animal one year old or in its second year. **2** a racehorse between 1 January of the year following its birth and the next 1 January. ⋙ **yearling** *adj.*

yearly *adj* **1** done or occurring once every year; annual. **2** reckoned by the year. ⋙ **yearly** *adv.*

yearn *v* to long persistently, wistfully, or sadly. ⋙ **yearner** *n,* **yearning** *noun and adj.*

year-on-year *adj* of figures, etc: compared with corresponding figures, etc from the previous year.

year-round *adj* effective, employed, or operating for the full year; not seasonal.

yeast *n* **1** a minute fungus that is able to ferment sugars and other carbohydrates. **2** a commercial product that is used for the fermentation of alcohol or for raising bread and that contains yeast in a moist or dry medium. **3** a medicinal preparation containing yeast, usu in the form of tablets, used to treat vitamin B deficiency.

yeasty *adj* (**-ier, -iest**) **1** of or resembling yeast. **2** churning with growth and change; turbulent. ⋙ **yeastily** *adv,* **yeastiness** *n.*

yell[1] *v* **1** to utter a sharp loud cry, scream, or shout. **2** to utter in a scream; to shout. ⋙ **yeller** *n.*

yell[2] *n* **1** a sharp loud scream or shout. **2** *NAm* an organized rhythmic chant or shout, *esp* one used to support a sports team.

yellow[1] *adj* **1** of the colour of egg yolk or lemons, between orange and green in the spectrum. **2** *offensive* of people originating from the Far East: having a yellow or light brown complexion or skin. **3** of writing: featuring sensational or scandalous items. **4** *informal* dishonourable or cowardly. ⋙ **yellowish** *adj,* **yellowness** *n.*

yellow[2] *n* a yellow colour. ⋙ **yellowy** *adj.*

yellow[3] *v* to make or become yellow.

yellow-belly *n* (*pl* **-ies**) *informal* a coward. ⋙ **yellow-bellied** *adj.*

yellow card *n* a yellow card held up by a football referee to indicate the taking of a player's name for committing an offence: compare RED CARD. ⋙ **yellow-card** *v.*

yellow fever *n* an often fatal infectious disease of warm regions caused by a virus transmitted by mosquitoes and marked by fever, jaundice, and often bleeding.

yellowfin *n* = YELLOWFIN TUNA.

yellowfin tuna *n* a rather small, widely distributed tuna with yellow-tipped fins and delicate light flesh.

yellow flag *n* **1** a yellow Eurasian iris that grows in damp places. **2** a ship's quarantine flag, usu indicating the presence of disease on board.

yellowhammer *n* a common Eurasian bunting, the male of which is largely yellow with a reddish brown back.

yellow jersey *n* in cycle racing, a yellow jersey awarded to the winner of a particular stage in a race such as the Tour de France, or to the eventual winner.

Yellow Pages *pl n trademark* a telephone directory that lists organizations and services alphabetically within sections classified according to the nature of their business.

yellow peril *n* (**the yellow peril**) *offensive* a danger to Western civilization held to arise from expansion of the power and influence of the peoples of China or SE Asia.

yelp *v* to utter a sharp quick shrill cry or bark. ➤➤ **yelp** *n*, **yelper** *n*.

Yemeni *n* a native or inhabitant of Yemen. ➤➤ **Yemeni** *adj*.

yen[1] *n* (*pl* **yen**) the basic monetary unit of Japan.

yen[2] *n informal* a strong desire or inclination; a longing.

yen[3] *v* (**yenned, yenning**) to yearn.

yeoman *n* (*pl* **yeomen**) **1** formerly, a small farmer who cultivated his own land; *specif* one belonging to a class of English freeholders below the gentry. **2** formerly, a servant or minor official in a royal or noble household. **3** *Brit* a member of the yeomanry. ➤➤ **yeomanly** *adj*.

Yeoman of the Guard *n* a member of a military corps attached to the British Royal Household who serve as ceremonial attendants of the sovereign and as warders of the Tower of London.

yeomanry *n* **1** (*used as sing. or pl*) small landed proprietors considered as a group or class. **2** a British volunteer cavalry force created from yeomen in 1761 as a home defence force and reorganized in 1907 as part of the territorial force.

yerba *n* = MATÉ.

yes[1] *interj* **1** used in answers expressing affirmation, agreement, or willingness; contrasted with no. **2** used to indicate polite interest or attentiveness. **3** used to express great satisfaction or delight.

yes[2] *n* (*pl* **yeses** *or* **yesses**) an affirmative reply or vote.

yeshiva *or* **yeshivah** *n* (*pl* **yeshivas** *or* **yeshivahs** *or* **yeshivoth**) **1** a school for Talmudic study. **2** an Orthodox Jewish rabbinic seminary. **3** a Jewish day school providing secular and religious instruction.

yes-man *n* (*pl* **yes-men**) *informal* somebody who agrees with or supports everything said by a superior; a sycophant.

yesterday[1] *adv* **1** on the day before today. **2** in the recent past.

yesterday[2] *n* **1** the day before today. **2** recent time; time not long past.

yesteryear *n literary* **1** the years of the fairly recent past. **2** last year. ➤➤ **yesteryear** *adv*.

yet[1] *adv* **1a** up to this or that time; so far. **b** only having done so much or got so far; now. **2a** as of now; still. **b** at some future time and despite present appearances. **3a** in addition. **b** used to indicate a still greater degree; even. **4** nevertheless.

yet[2] *conj* but nevertheless.

yeti *n* = ABOMINABLE SNOWMAN.

yettie *n chiefly NAm, informal* a young person making his or her fortune in the Internet-based economy.

yew *n* an evergreen coniferous tree with stiff straight leaves, red fruits, and fine-grained springy wood.

Y-fronts *pl n Brit, trademark* men's closely fitting underpants in which the front seams take the form of an inverted Y.

YHA *abbr Brit* Youth Hostels Association.

yid *n* (*also* **Yid**) *offensive* a Jew.

Yiddish *n* a language closely related to High German containing elements of Hebrew and Slavonic that is spoken by Jews chiefly in or from E Europe. ➤➤ **Yiddish** *adj*.

Yiddisher[1] *adj* **1** Yiddish. **2** Jewish.

Yiddisher[2] *n* **1** a speaker of Yiddish. **2** a Jew.

yield[1] *v* **1a** to bear or bring forth as a natural product. **b** to produce as a result of expended effort. **2** to produce (money or its equivalent) as revenue. **3** (*often* + up) to give up possession of (e.g. a position of advantage or point of superiority); to relinquish. **4a** (*often* + to) to give way to pressure or influence; to submit to urging, persuasion, or temptation. **b** to give way under physical force. **5** to give up and cease resistance or contention; to surrender or submit. ➤➤ **yielder** *n*, **yielding** *adj*.

yield[2] *n* **1** something yielded or produced, or the amount of it. **2** the capacity for yielding produce.

yin *n* in Chinese philosophy, the feminine passive principle in nature, expressed in darkness, cold, wetness, etc, that eternally interacts with its opposite and complementary principle, yang.

yip *v* (**yipped, yipping**) to utter a short sharp cry. ➤➤ **yip** *n*.

yippee *interj* used to express exuberant delight or triumph.

yippie *or* **yippy** *n* (*pl* **-ies**) a politically active hippie, *esp* in the USA in the 1960s.

-yl *suffix* forming nouns, denoting: a chemical radical: *ethyl*.

ylang-ylang *or* **ilang-ilang** /ˌeelang 'eelang/ *n* an essential oil distilled from the fragrant yellow flowers of a Malayan tree and used in perfumery and aromatherapy.

YMCA *abbr* Young Men's Christian Association.

-yne *suffix* forming nouns, denoting: an unsaturated compound containing a triple bond: *alkyne*.

yo *interj informal* used as a greeting or as a way of attracting somebody's attention.

yob *n Brit, slang* a loutish young man, *esp* a hooligan. ➤➤ **yobbery** *n*, **yobbish** *adj*.

yobbo *n* (*pl* **-os** *or* **-oes**) *Brit, slang* = YOB.

yocto- *comb. form* forming words, denoting: one million million million millionth (10^{-24}).

yodel[1] *v* (**yodelled, yodelling,** *NAm* **yodeled, yodeling**) to sing, shout, or call by suddenly changing from a natural voice to a falsetto and back. ➤➤ **yodeller** *n*.

yodel[2] *n* a yodelled song, shout, or cry.

yoga *n* **1** (**Yoga**) a Hindu philosophy teaching the control or suppression of all activity of body, mind, and will so that the self may attain liberation. **2** a system of exercises for attaining bodily or mental control and well-being. ➤➤ **yogic** *adj*.

yoghourt *or* **yoghurt** *n* see YOGURT.

yogi *n* (*pl* **yogis** *or* **yogin**) **1** somebody who practises or is a master of yoga. **2** (**Yogi**) an adherent of Yoga philosophy.

yogurt *or* **yoghurt** *or* **yoghourt** *n* a slightly acid semisolid food made of milk fermented by bacteria.

yoicks *interj* used as a cry of encouragement to foxhounds.

yoke[1] *n* **1** a bar or frame by which two draught animals, e.g. oxen, are joined at the necks for working together. **2** a frame fitted to somebody's shoulders to carry a divided load, e.g. two buckets or baskets. **3** a fitted or shaped piece at the top of a garment from which the rest hangs. **4a** something that is felt to be oppressive or burdensome. **b** a tie or link; *esp* marriage. **5** (*used as sing. or pl*) two animals yoked or worked together.

yoke[2] *v* **1** to put a yoke on (e.g. a pair of oxen). **2** to connect (two things) as if by a yoke; to couple.

yokel *n* a naive or gullible rustic; a country bumpkin.

yolk *n* **1** the usu yellow round mass that forms the inner portion of the egg of a bird or reptile and is surrounded by the white. **2** a mass of protein, lecithin, cholesterol, etc that is stored in an ovum as food for the developing embryo. ➤➤ **yolked** *adj*, **yolky** *adj*.

yolk sac *n* a membranous sac attached to a developing embryo and containing yolk which passes to the intestine through a narrow tubular stalk, providing food for the embryo.

Yom Kippur /,yom ki'pooə, 'kipə/ *n* a Jewish festival observed with fasting and prayer on the tenth day of the Jewish year; the Day of Atonement.

yomp *v Brit, slang* of a soldier: to march or trek over difficult terrain. ➤➤ **yomp** *n*.

yon *adj and adv literary or dialect* = YONDER.

yonder *adj and adv archaic or dialect* over there.

yoni *n* (*pl* **yonis**) a stylized representation of the female genitals used in Hindu temples to symbolize the feminine cosmic principle.

yonks *n Brit, informal* a long time; ages.

yoo-hoo *interj* used to attract attention.

yore ✱ **of yore** *literary* long ago.

yorker *n* in cricket, a ball bowled to bounce on the popping crease and so pass under the bat.

Yorkist *adj* of or supporting the English royal house of York that ruled from 1461 to 1485. ➤➤ **Yorkist** *n*.

Yorks *abbr* Yorkshire.

Yorkshire pudding *n* a savoury baked pudding made from a batter and usu eaten before or with roast beef.

Yorkshire terrier *n* a terrier of a compact toy breed with a long straight silky coat of bluish grey and tan hair.

Yoruba *n* (*pl* **Yorubas** *or* **Yoruba**) **1** a member of an African people of Benin and SW Nigeria. **2** the language of this people. ➤➤ **Yoruba** *adj*.

you *pron* (*pl* **you**) **1** used as subject or object: the person or people being addressed. **2** used as an exclamation with vocatives: *You scoundrel!* **3** a person; one.

you'd *contr* **1** you had. **2** you would.

you'll *contr* **1** you will. **2** you shall.

young[1] *adj* (**younger, youngest**) **1** in the first or an early stage of life, growth, or development. **2** recently come into being or not yet far advanced; new. **3** suitable for or characteristic of young people. ➤➤ **youngish** *adj*.

young[2] *pl n* **1** (*used as pl*) immature offspring, *esp* of an animal. **2** (**the young**) young people; youth.

young blood *n* freshness, vigour, etc brought by new people joining an organization.

young offender *n Brit* a person under the age of 18 who has been convicted of a criminal offence.

youngster *n* a young person or creature.

Young Turk *n* **1** a member of a revolutionary party in Turkey in the early 20th cent. **2** a young person who agitates for radical change.

your *adj* **1a** belonging to or associated with the person or people being addressed. **b** belonging to or associated with an indefinitely indicated person or people in general. **2** used in titles: *Your Majesty*. **3** *informal* used to indicate something or somebody well-known and characteristic: *He's not your typical commuter.*

Usage note

your *or* you're? *Your* is the possessive form of *you* (*It's your turn now; May I borrow your pen?*) and should not be confused with *you're*, which is pronounced the same, but is the shortened form of *you are*: *You're not as young as you were; I hope you're not getting bored.*

you're *contr* you are.

Usage note

you're *or* your? See note at YOUR.

yours *pron* (*pl* **yours**) the one or ones that belong to you or are associated with you. ✱ **of yours** belonging to or associated with you: *friends of yours.*

yourself *pron* (*pl* **yourselves**) **1** used reflexively or for emphasis to refer to the person or people being addressed: *Carry it yourself; Did you hurt yourselves?* **2** = ONESELF.

youth *n* (*pl* **youths**) **1** the time of life when one is young, *esp* adolescence. **2a** a young male adolescent. **b** (*used as sing. or pl*) young people. **3** the quality or state of being youthful.

youth club *n* a local organization providing leisure activities for young people, or the premises where such a club meets.

youthful *adj* **1** relating to or characteristic of youth. **2** not yet mature or old; young. ➤➤ **youthfully** *adv*, **youthfulness** *n*.

youth hostel *n* a lodging providing inexpensive bed and breakfast accommodation, *esp* for young travellers or hikers. ➤➤ **youth-hosteller** *n*, **youth-hostelling** *n*.

you've *contr* you have.

yowl *v* to utter the loud long wail of a cat or dog in pain or distress. ➤➤ **yowl** *n*.

yo-yo[1] *n* (*pl* **yo-yos**) **1** *trademark* a toy consisting of two joined discs that is made to fall and rise when held by a string attached and wound between the discs. **2** *chiefly NAm, informal* a fool.

yo-yo[2] *v* (**yo-yoes** *or* **yo-yos, yo-yoed, yo-yoing**) to fluctuate.

ytterbium *n* a silver-white metallic element that resembles and occurs with yttrium.

yttrium *n* a greyish white metallic element that occurs naturally in various minerals.

yuan /'yooh·ən, yooh'ahn/ *n* (*pl* **yuan**) the basic monetary unit of China.

yucca *n* a treelike plant of the agave family with long often rigid leaves and a large cluster of white flowers.

yuck *or* **yuk** *interj informal* used to express a sense of disgust and revulsion. ➤➤ **yucky** *adj*, **yukky** *adj*.

Yugoslav *n* a native or inhabitant of Yugoslavia. ➤➤ **Yugoslav** *adj*, **Yugoslavian** *n and adj*.

yuk *interj* see YUCK.

Yule *n archaic* Christmas.

yule log *n* **1** a large log formerly put on the hearth on Christmas Eve as the foundation of the fire. **2** a chocolate cake in the shape of a log, traditionally eaten at Christmas.

Yuletide *n archaic* Christmas.

yummy *adj* (**-ier, -iest**) *informal* highly attractive or pleasing, *esp* to the taste; delicious.

Yupik *n* (*pl* **Yupiks** *or* **Yupik**) **1** a member of an Eskimo people of Alaska, the Aleutian Islands, and Siberia. **2** any of the languages of this people. ➤➤ **Yupik** *adj*.

yuppie *or* **yuppy** *n* (*pl* **-ies**) *informal, derog* a young person in a professional job with a high income and a fashionable lifestyle. ➤➤ **yuppiedom** *n.*

yuppie flu *n informal, derog* = CHRONIC FATIGUE SYNDROME.

yuppify *v* (**-ies, -ied**) *informal, derog* to change (e.g. an area) to make it more attractive to yuppies or more in keeping with their lifestyle. ➤➤ **yuppification** *n.*

yuppy *n* see YUPPIE.

yurt *n* a collapsible domed tent of skins or felt used by nomads of Mongolia, Siberia, and Turkey.

YWCA *abbr* Young Women's Christian Association.

Z z

Z *or* **z** *n* (*pl* **Z's** *or* **Zs** *or* **z's**) the 26th letter of the English alphabet.

zabaglione /zabə'lyohni/ *n* a thick creamy dessert made by whipping eggs, sugar, and Marsala wine over hot water.

zaïre /zie'iə, zah'iə/ *n* (*pl* **zaïre**) the basic monetary unit of the Democratic Republic of Congo (formerly Zaire).

Zairean *or* **Zairian** /zie'iəri·ən, zah-/ *n* a native or inhabitant of Zaire, known since 1997 as the Democratic Republic of Congo. ➤➤ **Zairean** *adj.*

Zambian *n* a native or inhabitant of Zambia. ➤➤ **Zambian** *adj.*

zany[1] *adj* (**-ier, -iest**) fantastically or absurdly comical. ➤➤ **zanily** *adv,* **zaniness** *n.*

zany[2] *n* (*pl* **-ies**) **1** a zany person. **2** formerly, an assistant to a clown who mimicked the clown's actions.

zap[1] *interj informal* used to indicate a sudden or instantaneous occurrence.

zap[2] *v* (**zapped, zapping**) *informal* **1** to destroy or kill. **2** to move or cause to move with speed or force. **3** to switch swiftly from channel to channel on a television set by means of a remote control.

zap[3] *n informal* vitality or force; energy.

zapper *n informal* a remote control used to operate a television set or other piece of electronic equipment.

zappy *adj* (**-ier, -iest**) *informal* **1** energetic or dynamic. **2** fast-moving.

zarzuela *n* **1** a traditional Spanish comic opera. **2** a Spanish seafood stew.

zeal *n* eagerness to accomplish something; ardent interest in pursuit of something.

zealot *n* **1** a zealous person; *esp* a fanatical partisan of a religious or political movement. **2** (**Zealot**) a member of a fanatical sect arising in Judea during the first cent. AD who militantly opposed the Roman domination of Palestine. ➤➤ **zealotry** *n.*

zealous *adj* filled with or characterized by zeal. ➤➤ **zealously** *adv,* **zealousness** *n.*

zebec *n* see XEBEC.

zebra *n* (*pl* **zebras** *or* **zebra**) a black and white striped fast-running African mammal related to the horse.

zebra crossing *n Brit* a crossing marked by a series of broad white stripes to indicate that pedestrians have the right of way across a road.

zebu *n* an ox of a domesticated breed with a large fleshy hump over the shoulders, used in Asia as a draught animal.

zed *n chiefly Brit* the letter *z*.

zee *n NAm* = ZED.

zeitgeist /'tsietgiest/ *n* the general intellectual and moral character or cultural climate of an era.

Zen *n* a Japanese sect of Mahayana Buddhism that aims at enlightenment by direct intuition through meditation.

zenana *n* in India and Iran, the women's quarters in a house.

zenith *n* **1** the point of the celestial sphere that is directly opposite the nadir and vertically above the observer. **2** the highest point reached in the heavens by a celestial body. **3** the culminating point or stage. ➤➤ **zenithal** *adj.*

zeolite *n* **1** a hydrous aluminium silicate mineral that can act as an ion-exchanger, e.g. in water softening. **2** a synthetic silicate resembling this. ➤➤ **zeolitic** *adj.*

zephyr *n literary* a gentle breeze, *esp* from the west.

zeppelin *n* (*also* **Zeppelin**) a large rigid cigar-shaped airship of a type built in Germany in the early 20th cent.

zepto- *comb. form* forming words, denoting: one thousand million million millionth (10^{-21}).

zero[1] *n* (*pl* **-os** *or* **-oes**) **1** the arithmetical symbol 0 denoting the absence of all magnitude or quantity; nought. **2** the point from which the graduation of a scale, e.g. of a thermometer, begins. **3** the temperature represented by the zero mark on a thermometer. **4a** nothing; nil. **b** the lowest point or degree. ➤➤ **zero** *adj.*

zero[2] *v* (**zeroes** *or* **zeros, zeroed, zeroing**) **1** to return (a counter) to zero. **2** to adjust the sights of (e.g. a gun).

zero hour *n* the time at which an event, *esp* a military attack, is scheduled to begin.

zero in *v* **1** (+ on) to move near to a target; to close in on it. **2** (+ on) to focus attention on something, e.g. a problem.

zero-rated *adj Brit* exempt from value-added tax.

zero tolerance *n* a policy of total strictness in law enforcement in which not even the most minor offences are overlooked.

zest *n* **1** the outer peel of a citrus fruit used as flavouring. **2** piquancy or spice. **3** keen enjoyment; gusto. ➤➤ **zestful** *adj,* **zesty** *adj.*

zester *n* a small kitchen tool for removing the peel of a citrus fruit in thin strips.

zeta *n* the sixth letter of the Greek alphabet (Z, ζ), equivalent to roman z.

zeugma /ˈzyoohgmə/ *n* the use of a word to modify or govern two or more words, usu in such a manner that it applies to each in a different sense, e.g. in *She opened the door and her heart to him.* ➤➤ **zeugmatic** *adj.*

zidovudine *n* an antiviral drug used in the treatment of Aids.

ziggurat *n* a temple tower of ancient Mesopotamia in the form of a stepped pyramid.

zigzag[1] *n* **1** a line, course, or pattern consisting of a series of alternate sharp turns in opposite directions. **2** a turn that is part of such a course or pattern.

zigzag[2] *adj* forming or going in a zigzag; consisting of zigzags. ➤➤ **zigzag** *adv.*

zigzag[3] *v* (**zigzagged, zigzagging**) to proceed along a zigzag course.

zilch *n chiefly NAm, informal* zero. ➤➤ **zilch** *adj.*

zillion *n* (*pl* **zillions** *or* **zillion**) *informal* (*also in pl*) an indefinitely large number. ➤➤ **zillionth** *adj and n.*

Zimbabwean *n* a native or inhabitant of Zimbabwe. ➤➤ **Zimbabwean** *adj.*

Zimmer *n trademark* an orthopaedic walking frame.

Zimmer frame *n* = ZIMMER.

zinc[1] *n* **1** a bluish white metallic element that occurs abundantly in minerals, and is used *esp* as a protective coating for iron and steel. **2** zinc-coated corrugated iron.

zinc[2] *v* (**zinced** *or* **zincked, zincing** *or* **zincking**) to treat or coat with zinc.

zinc oxide *n* a white solid used *esp* as a pigment and in medicinal and cosmetic preparations.

zine /zeen/ *n informal* **1** a usu noncommercial magazine containing specialized material appealing to a limited number of readers. **2** a fanzine.

Zinfandel *n* a variety of grape used, *esp* in California, in the production of medium-quality red wine, or the wine produced from it.

zing[1] *n informal* **1** energy or vim. **2** a shrill humming noise.

zing[2] *v informal* to move briskly or with a humming sound.

zingy *adj* (**-ier, -iest**) *informal* strikingly exciting or attractive.

zinnia *n* a tropical American plant of the daisy family with large colourful flowers.

Zion *or* **Sion** *n* **1a** the Jewish people; Israel. **b** the Jewish homeland that is symbolic of Judaism or Jewish national aspiration. **2** in Christianity, heaven regarded as the city of God.

Zionism *n* a movement initially for setting up a Jewish homeland in Palestine, now for protecting, developing, and furthering the interests of the state of Israel. ➤➤ **Zionist** *adj and n.*

zip[1] *n* **1** *chiefly Brit* a fastener that joins two edges by means of two flexible spirals or rows of teeth brought together by a sliding clip. **2** *informal* energy or liveliness. **3** a light sharp hissing sound. **4** *NAm, informal* nothing; zero.

zip[2] *v* (**zipped, zipping**) **1** to close or open with a zip. **2** in computing, to compress (a file). **3** *informal* to move with speed and vigour. **4** to travel with a sharp hissing or humming sound.

zip code *n* (*also* **ZIP code**) a number that is used in the postal address of a place in the USA to assist sorting: compare POSTCODE.

zipper *n chiefly NAm* a zip.

zippy *adj* (**-ier, -iest**) *informal* lively or energetic. ➤➤ **zippily** *adv,* **zippiness** *n.*

zip-up *adj chiefly Brit* fastened by means of a zip.

zircon *n* a variously coloured mineral consisting of zirconium silicate and used as a gem when transparent.

zirconium *n* a steel-grey metallic element that is used *esp* in alloys and in heat-resisting ceramic materials.

zit *n chiefly NAm, informal* a pimple on the skin, *esp* of the face.

zither *n* a musical instrument having usu 30 to 40 strings over a shallow horizontal soundboard and played with plectrum and fingers. ➤➤ **zitherist** *n.*

zizz[1] *v Brit, informal* **1** to nap or doze. **2** to make a whizzing sound.

zizz[2] *n Brit, informal* **1** a nap. **2** a whizzing sound.

zloty *n* (*pl* **zlotys** *or* **zloties** *or* **zloty**) the basic monetary unit of Poland.

Zn *abbr* the chemical symbol for zinc.

zo- *or* **zoo-** *comb. form* denoting animals or animal life: *zoology.*

-zoa *comb. form* forming plural nouns, denoting: classes of animals: *protozoa.*

zodiac *n* an imaginary belt in the heavens that encompasses the apparent paths of all the principal planets except Pluto and is divided into twelve constellations or signs for astrological purposes. ➤➤ **zodiacal** *adj.*

zoetrope /ˈzoh·itrohp/ *n* a mechanical toy with pictures on the inside of a drum, which seem to move when viewed through slits as the drum is turned.

-zoic *comb. form* forming adjectives, with the meaning: of or denoting a particular geological era: *Mesozoic.*

zombie *n* **1** a human being capable only of automatic movement who is held, *esp* in Haitian voodooism, to have died and been reanimated. **2** *informal* a person resembling the walking dead; *esp* a shambling automaton.

zonate *adj* marked with or arranged in zones. ➤➤ **zonated** *adj,* **zonation** *n.*

zone[1] *n* **1a** an area distinct from adjoining parts. **b** any of the sections into which an area is divided for a particular purpose. **2** any of five great divisions of the earth's surface with respect to latitude and temperature. **3** an encircling anatomical structure, band of colour, etc. ➤➤ **zonal** *adj.*

zone[2] *v* **1** to arrange in, mark off, or partition into zones. **2** to assign (an area) to a zone.

zone therapy *n* a form of therapy in alternative medicine that involves massaging nerve endings; *esp* reflexology. ➤➤ **zone therapist** *n.*

zonk *v informal* to strike (somebody or something) hard.

zonked *adj* **1** *slang* (*often* + out) highly intoxicated by alcohol or drugs. **2** *informal* completely exhausted.

zonk out *v slang* to lose consciousness or fall asleep, *esp* when intoxicated with drugs or alcohol.

zoo *n* (*pl* **zoos**) a place where a collection of living animals is kept and usu exhibited to the public.

zoo- *comb. form* see ZO-.

zoogeography *n* the branch of zoology dealing with the geographical distribution of animals.

▶▶ **zoogeographer** *n,* **zoogeographic** *adj,* **zoogeographical** *adj,* **zoogeographically** *adv.*

zooid /'zoh·oyd/ *n* an entity that resembles but is not wholly the same as a separate individual organism; *esp* a more or less independent animal produced by fission, proliferation, or other methods that do not directly involve sex. ▶▶ **zooidal** *adj.*

zoology *n* **1** the branch of biology that deals with animals and animal life, usu excluding human beings. **2** the animals found in a particular area or geological era. ▶▶ **zoological** *adj,* **zoologically** *adv,* **zoologist** *n.*

zoom[1] *v* **1a** to move quickly. **b** to move with a loud low hum or buzz. **2** to operate the zoom lens of a camera or microscope.

zoom[2] *n* **1** the action of zooming. **2** a zoom lens.

zoom in *v* (*often* + on) to use a zoom lens to change from long shot to close-up.

zoom lens *n* a lens, e.g. in a camera, in which the image size, and thus the apparent distance of the object, can be varied continuously.

zoomorphic /zoh·ə'mawfik/ *adj* **1** resembling the form of an animal or part of an animal. **2** of a god: having the form or attributes of an animal. ▶▶ **zoomorphism** *n.*

-zoon *comb. form* forming nouns, denoting: an animal: *spermatozoon.*

zoonosis /zoh'onəsis, zoh·ə'nohsis/ *n* (*pl* **zoonoses** /-seez/) any disease, e.g. rabies or anthrax, communicable from lower animals to human beings. ▶▶ **zoonotic** *adj.*

zoophilia /zoh·ə'fili·ə/ *n* sexual attraction to animals; bestiality.

zoophobia /zoh·ə'fohbi·ə/ *n* an abnormal fear or hatred of animals.

zooplankton /zoh·ə'plangktən, -ton/ *n* planktonic animal life.

zoot suit *n* a flamboyant suit worn by men, typically consisting of a thigh-length jacket with wide padded shoulders and trousers tapering to narrow turn-ups.

zorilla *n* a S African animal that is a member of the weasel family and has black and white fur like a skunk.

Zoroastrianism *n* a Persian religion founded in the sixth cent. BC by the prophet Zoroaster and characterized by worship of a supreme god Ahura Mazda. ▶▶ **Zoroastrian** *adj and n.*

Zouave /zooh'ahv, zwahv/ *n* a member of a French infantry unit, orig composed of Algerians, noted for its brilliantly coloured uniform.

zouk /zoohk/ *n* a style of popular music for guitars and synthesizers with a strong beat, originating in the Caribbean.

zounds *interj archaic* used as a mild oath.

Zr *abbr* the chemical symbol for zirconium.

zucchetto /tsooh'ketoh, sooh-, zooh-/ *n* (*pl* **-os**) a skullcap worn by Roman Catholic ecclesiastics, coloured according to the rank of the wearer.

zucchini /zoo'keeni/ *n* (*pl* **zucchinis** *or* **zucchini**) *chiefly NAm* a courgette.

Zulu *n* (*pl* **Zulus** *or* **Zulu**) **1** a member of a Bantu-speaking people living mainly in Kwazulu/Natal province in South Africa. **2** the language spoken by this people. ▶▶ **Zulu** *adj.*

zwieback /'sweebak, 'zweebak/ *n* a usu sweetened rich bread that is baked and then sliced and toasted until dry and crisp.

Zwinglian *adj* of the Swiss Reformation theologian Ulrich Zwingli (d.1531) or his teachings, *esp* the doctrine that Christ's presence in the Eucharist is symbolic. ▶▶ **Zwinglian** *n.*

zydeco *n* a style of dance music originating in southern Louisiana that combines French and Caribbean elements and blues and is usu played by a small group featuring a guitar and accordion.

zygomatic arch *n* the arch of bone that extends along the front or side of the skull beneath the eye socket.

zygomatic bone *n* a bone of the side of the face below the eye that forms part of the zygomatic arch and part of the eye socket; a cheekbone.

zygote *n* **1** a cell formed by the union of two gametes. **2** the developing organism produced from such a cell. ▶▶ **zygotic** *adj.*

zymology *n* the science of fermentation.

zymotic *adj* **1** of, causing, or caused by fermentation. **2** of, denoting, or causing an infectious or contagious disease. ▶▶ **zymotically** *adv.*

zzz *interj* used as a visual representation of sleep or snoring, *esp* in cartoons.

Acknowledgments

Consultant Editor
Robert Allen

Publishing Director
Nigel Wilcockson

Publisher
Martin Toseland

Lexicographers
Stephen Curtis, George Davidson,
Jessica Feinstein, Rosalind Fergusson,
Alice Grandison

Database Editor
Rachael Arthur

Editorial Checking
Fred McDonald

Gazetteer Editor
David Pickering

Proof-readers
Audrey Aitken, Anne Cook,
David Cumming, Stephen Ryan

Designer
Richard Marston

Database Systems
Librios Ltd

Typesetting
Gem Graphics